Official 2012
National Football League
Record
& Fact Book

NATIONAL FOOTBALL LEAGUE
345 Park Avenue, New York, N.Y. 10154 (212) 450-2000. NFL Internet Address: http://www.NFL.com

Copyright © 2012 by the National Football League. All rights reserved. The information in this publication has been compiled for use by the news media to aid in reporting of the games and teams of the National Football League. No part of this book may be reproduced or transmitted in any form or by any means, electronic or mechanical, including photocopying, recording, or by any information storage and retrieval system, without permission in writing from the National Football League.

Printed in the United States of America.

A National Football League Book.

Compiled by the NFL Communications Department and Seymour Siwoff, Elias Sports Bureau.
Statistics by Elias Sports Bureau.

Edited by Jon Zimmer, NFL Communications Department, and Matt Marini. Layout by William Tham.
Cover photo: Super Bowl Most Valuable Player Eli Manning of the Super Bowl XLVI champion New York Giants.
Cover photography by Jamie Squire, Getty Images. Design by NFL Creative.

Time Inc.
HOME ENTERTAINMENT

Time Inc. Home Entertainment
1271 Avenue of the Americas, New York, N.Y. 10020
Manufactured in the United States of America.
First printing, July 2012.
10 9 8 7 6 5 4 3 2 1

TABLE OF CONTENTS

2012 SCHEDULE AND NOTE CALENDAR

All times local. Dates and times subject to change.
Nationally televised games indicated by network in parentheses.

	Sunday, August 5	Hall of Fame Game at Canton, Ohio	
		Arizona _____ vs. New Orleans _____	(NFLN) 8:00

PRESEASON/WEEK 1

Thursday, August 9	Washington_____ at Buffalo_____	7:00
	Baltimore _____ at Atlanta _____	7:30
	New Orleans _____ at New England _____	7:30
	Pittsburgh _____ at Philadelphia _____	7:30
	Green Bay _____ at San Diego_____	(ESPN) 5:00
	Denver _____ at Chicago _____	7:30
Friday, August 10	New York Jets _____ at Cincinnati _____	7:30
	Cleveland _____ at Detroit _____	7:30
	New York Giants _____ at Jacksonville _____	7:30
	Tampa Bay _____ at Miami _____	7:30
	Arizona _____ at Kansas City _____	7:00
	Minnesota _____ at San Francisco _____	6:00
Saturday, August 11	Houston _____ at Carolina _____	7:00
	Tennessee _____ at Seattle _____	7:00
Sunday, August 12	St. Louis _____ at Indianapolis _____	1:30
Monday, August 13	Dallas _____ at Oakland _____	(ESPN) 5:00

PRESEASON/WEEK 2

Thursday, August 16	Cincinnati _____ at Atlanta _____	(FOX) 8:00
	Cleveland _____ at Green Bay _____	7:00
Friday, August 17	Tennessee _____ at Tampa Bay _____	7:30
	Detroit _____ at Baltimore _____	(FOX) 8:00
	Miami _____ at Carolina _____	8:00
	Buffalo _____ at Minnesota _____	7:00
	Oakland _____ at Arizona _____	7:00
Saturday, August 18	New York Giants _____ at New York Jets _____	(NFLN) 7:00
	Washington _____ at Chicago _____	7:00
	San Francisco _____ at Houston _____	7:00
	Jacksonville _____ at New Orleans _____	7:00
	Kansas City _____ at St. Louis _____	7:00
	Seattle _____ at Denver _____	7:00
	Dallas _____ at San Diego _____	6:00
Sunday, August 19	Indianapolis _____ at Pittsburgh _____	(NBC) 8:00
Monday, August 20	Philadelphia _____ at New England _____	(ESPN) 8:00

PRESEASON/WEEK 3

Thursday, August 23	Green Bay _____ at Cincinnati _____	7:00
	Jacksonville _____ at Baltimore _____	7:30
	Arizona _____ at Tennessee ___	(ESPN) 7:00
Friday, August 24	Philadelphia _____ at Cleveland _____	7:30
	Atlanta _____ at Miami _____	7:30
	San Diego _____ at Minnesota ___	7:00
	Chicago _____ at New York Giants ___	(CBS) 8:00
	Seattle _____ at Kansas City _____	7:00
Saturday, August 25	Indianapolis _____ at Washington _____	4:00
	Pittsburgh _____ at Buffalo ___	7:00
	Detroit _____ at Oakland _____	4:00
	New England _____ at Tampa Bay _____	7:30
	St. Louis _____ at Dallas _____	8:00
	Houston _____ at New Orleans _____	(CBS) 7:00
Sunday, August 26	San Francisco _____ at Denver _____	(FOX) 2:00
	Carolina _____ at New York Jets _____	(NBC) 8:00

PRESEASON/WEEK 4

Wednesday, August 29
New England _____ at New York Giants _____	7:30
Tampa Bay _____ at Washington _____	7:30
Miami _____ at Dallas _____	7:30

Thursday, August 30
Atlanta _____ at Jacksonville _____	6:30
New York Jets _____ at Philadelphia _____	6:35
Buffalo _____ at Detroit _____	7:00
Kansas City _____ at Green Bay _____	6:00
Minnesota _____ at Houston _____	6:00
Cincinnati _____ at Indianapolis _____	7:00
New Orleans _____ at Tennessee _____	6:00
Chicago _____ at Cleveland _____	7:30
Carolina _____ at Pittsburgh _____	7:30
Baltimore _____ at St. Louis _____	7:00
Oakland _____ at Seattle _____	7:00
San Diego _____ at San Francisco _____	7:00
Denver _____ at Arizona _____	8:00

KICKOFF 2012

KICKOFF WEEKEND

Wednesday, September 5
Dallas _____ at New York Giants _____	(NBC) 8:30

Sunday, September 9
FOX-TV National Weekend
Indianapolis _____ at Chicago _____	12:00
Philadelphia _____ at Cleveland _____	1:00
St. Louis _____ at Detroit _____	1:00
Miami _____ at Houston _____	12:00
Atlanta _____ at Kansas City _____	12:00
Jacksonville _____ at Minnesota _____	12:00
Washington _____ at New Orleans _____	12:00
Buffalo _____ at New York Jets _____	1:00
New England _____ at Tennessee _____	12:00
Seattle _____ at Arizona _____	1:15
San Francisco _____ at Green Bay _____	3:15
Carolina _____ at Tampa Bay _____	4:15
Pittsburgh _____ at Denver _____	(NBC) 6:20

Monday, September 10
Cincinnati _____ at Baltimore _____	(ESPN) 7:00
San Diego _____ at Oakland _____	(ESPN) 7:15

SECOND WEEK

Thursday, September 13
Chicago _____ at Green Bay _____	(NFLN) 7:20

Sunday, September 16
CBS-TV National Weekend
Kansas City _____ at Buffalo _____	1:00
New Orleans _____ at Carolina _____	1:00
Cleveland _____ at Cincinnati _____	1:00
Minnesota _____ at Indianapolis _____	1:00
Houston _____ at Jacksonville _____	1:00
Oakland _____ at Miami _____	1:00
Arizona _____ at New England _____	1:00
Tampa Bay _____ at New York Giants _____	1:00
Baltimore _____ at Philadelphia _____	1:00
Washington _____ at St. Louis _____	3:05
Dallas _____ at Seattle _____	1:05
New York Jets _____ at Pittsburgh _____	4:15
Tennessee _____ at San Diego _____	1:15
Detroit _____ at San Francisco _____	(NBC) 5:20

Monday, September 17
Denver _____ at Atlanta _____	(ESPN) 8:30

THIRD WEEK

Thursday, September 20
New York Giants _____ at Carolina _____	(NFLN) 8:20

Sunday, September 23
CBS-TV National Weekend
St. Louis _____ at Chicago _____	12:00
Buffalo _____ at Cleveland _____	1:00
Tampa Bay _____ at Dallas _____	12:00
Jacksonville _____ at Indianapolis _____	1:00
New York Jets _____ at Miami _____	1:00
San Francisco _____ at Minnesota _____	12:00
Kansas City _____ at New Orleans _____	12:00
Detroit _____ at Tennessee _____	12:00
Cincinnati _____ at Washington _____	1:00
Philadelphia _____ at Arizona _____	1:05
Atlanta _____ at San Diego _____	1:05
Houston _____ at Denver _____	2:15
Pittsburgh _____ at Oakland _____	1:15
New England _____ at Baltimore _____	(NBC) 8:20

Monday, September 24
Green Bay _____ at Seattle _____	(ESPN) 5:30

FOURTH WEEK
Open Date: Indianapolis, Pittsburgh

Thursday, September 27	Cleveland _____ at Baltimore _____	(NFLN) 8:20
Sunday, September 30	Carolina _____ at Atlanta _____	1:00
FOX-TV National Weekend	New England _____ at Buffalo _____	1:00
	Minnesota _____ at Detroit _____	1:00
	Tennessee _____ at Houston _____	12:00
	San Diego _____ at Kansas City _____	12:00
	San Francisco _____ at New York Jets _____	1:00
	Seattle _____ at St. Louis _____	12:00
	Miami _____ at Arizona _____	1:05
	Cincinnati _____ at Jacksonville _____	4:05
	Oakland _____ at Denver _____	2:05
	New Orleans _____ at Green Bay _____	3:15
	Washington _____ at Tampa Bay _____	4:15
	New York Giants _____ at Philadelphia _____	(NBC) 8:20
Monday, October 1	Chicago _____ at Dallas _____	(ESPN) 7:30

FIFTH WEEK
Open Date: Dallas, Detroit
Oakland, Tampa Bay

Thursday, October 4	Arizona _____ at St. Louis _____	(NFLN) 7:20
Sunday, October 7	Miami _____ at Cincinnati _____	1:00
CBS-TV National Weekend	Green Bay_____ at Indianapolis _____	1:00
	Baltimore _____ at Kansas City _____	12:00
	Tennessee _____ at Minnesota _____	12:00
	Cleveland _____ at New York Giants _____	1:00
	Philadelphia _____ at Pittsburgh _____	1:00
	Atlanta _____ at Washington _____	1:00
	Seattle _____ at Carolina _____	4:05
	Chicago _____ at Jacksonville _____	4:05
	Denver _____ at New England _____	4:15
	Buffalo _____ at San Francisco _____	1:15
	San Diego _____ at New Orleans _____	(NBC) 7:20
Monday, October 8	Houston _____ at New York Jets _____	(ESPN) 8:30

SIXTH WEEK
Open Date: Carolina, Chicago
Jacksonville, New Orleans

Thursday, October 11	Pittsburgh _____ at Tennessee _____	(NFLN) 7:20
Sunday, October 14	Oakland _____ at Atlanta _____	1:00
FOX-TV National Weekend	Dallas _____ at Baltimore _____	1:00
	Cincinnati _____ at Cleveland _____	1:00
	St. Louis _____ at Miami _____	1:00
	Indianapolis _____ at New York Jets _____	1:00
	Detroit _____ at Philadelphia _____	1:00
	Kansas City _____ at Tampa Bay _____	1:00
	Buffalo _____ at Arizona _____	1:05
	New England _____ at Seattle _____	1:05
	New York Giants _____ at San Francisco _____	1:15
	Minnesota _____ at Washington _____	4:15
	Green Bay _____ at Houston _____	(NBC) 7:20
Monday, October 15	Denver _____ at San Diego _____	(ESPN) 5:30

SEVENTH WEEK
Open Date: Atlanta, Denver
Kansas City, Miami
Philadelphia, San Diego

Thursday, October 18	Seattle _____ at San Francisco _____	(NFLN) 5:20
Sunday, October 21	Tennessee _____ at Buffalo _____	1:00
CBS-TV National Weekend	Dallas _____ at Carolina _____	1:00
	Baltimore _____ at Houston _____	12:00
	Cleveland _____ at Indianapolis _____	1:00
	Arizona _____ at Minnesota _____	12:00
	Washington _____ at New York Giants _____	1:00
	Green Bay _____ at St. Louis _____	12:00
	New Orleans _____ at Tampa Bay _____	1:00
	New York Jets _____ at New England _____	4:15
	Jacksonville _____ at Oakland _____	1:15
	Pittsburgh _____ at Cincinnati _____	(NBC) 8:20
Monday, October 22	Detroit _____ at Chicago _____	(ESPN) 7:30

EIGHTH WEEK

INTERNATIONAL SERIES 2012

Open Date: Baltimore, Buffalo
Cincinnati, Houston

Thursday, October 25	Tampa Bay ____ at Minnesota ____	(NFLN) 7:20
Sunday, October 28	Carolina ____ at Chicago ____	12:00
FOX-TV National Weekend	San Diego ____ at Cleveland ____	1:00
	Seattle ____ at Detroit ____	1:00
	Jacksonville ____ at Green Bay ____	12:00
	Miami ____ at New York Jets ____	1:00
	Atlanta ____ at Philadelphia ____	1:00
	Washington ____ at Pittsburgh ____	1:00
	New England ____ at St. Louis (London) ____	6:00
	Indianapolis ____ at Tennessee ____	12:00
	Oakland ____ at Kansas City ____	3:05
	New York Giants ____ at Dallas ____	3:15
	New Orleans ____ at Denver ____	(NBC) 6:20
Monday, October 29	San Francisco ____ at Arizona ____	(ESPN) 5:30

NINTH WEEK
Open Date:
New England, New York Jets,
St. Louis, San Francisco

Thursday, November 1	Kansas City ____ at San Diego ____	(NFLN) 5:20
Sunday, November 4	Denver ____ at Cincinnati ____	1:00
CBS-TV National Weekend	Baltimore ____ at Cleveland ____	1:00
	Arizona ____ at Green Bay ____	12:00
	Buffalo ____ at Houston ____	12:00
	Miami ____ at Indianapolis ____	1:00
	Detroit ____ at Jacksonville ____	1:00
	Chicago ____ at Tennessee ____	12:00
	Carolina ____ at Washington ____	1:00
	Tampa Bay ____ at Oakland ____	1:05
	Minnesota ____ at Seattle ____	1:05
	Pittsburgh ____ at New York Giants ____	4:15
	Dallas ____ at Atlanta ____	(NBC) 8:20
Monday, November 5	Philadelphia ____ at New Orleans ____	(ESPN) 7:30

TENTH WEEK
Open Date:
Arizona, Cleveland,
Green Bay, Washington

Thursday, November 8	Indianapolis ____ at Jacksonville ____	(NFLN) 8:20
Sunday, November 11	Oakland ____ at Baltimore ____	1:00
FOX-TV National Weekend	Denver ____ at Carolina ____	1:00
	New York Giants ____ at Cincinnati ____	1:00
	Tennessee ____ at Miami ____	1:00
	Detroit ____ at Minnesota ____	12:00
	Buffalo ____ at New England ____	1:00
	Atlanta ____ at New Orleans ____	12:00
	San Diego ____ at Tampa Bay ____	1:00
	New York Jets ____ at Seattle ____	1:05
	Dallas ____ at Philadelphia ____	4:15
	St. Louis ____ at San Francisco ____	1:15
	Houston ____ at Chicago ____	(NBC) 7:20
Monday, November 12	Kansas City ____ at Pittsburgh ____	(ESPN) 8:30

ELEVENTH WEEK
Open Date:
Minnesota, New York Giants,
Seattle, Tennessee

Thursday, November 15	Miami ____ at Buffalo ____	(NFLN) 8:20
Sunday, November 18	Arizona ____ at Atlanta ____	1:00
CBS-TV National Weekend	Tampa Bay ____ at Carolina ____	1:00
	Cleveland ____ at Dallas ____	12:00
	Green Bay ____ at Detroit ____	1:00
	Jacksonville ____ at Houston ____	12:00
	Cincinnati ____ at Kansas City ____	12:00
	Indianapolis ____ at New England ____	1:00
	New York Jets ____ at St. Louis ____	12:00
	Philadelphia ____ at Washington ____	1:00
	New Orleans ____ at Oakland ____	1:05
	San Diego ____ at Denver ____	2:15
	Baltimore ____ at Pittsburgh * ____	(NBC) 8:20
Monday, November 19	Chicago ____ at San Francisco ____	(ESPN) 5:30

Sunday Night Games In Weeks 11-16 Subject to Change

2012 SCHEDULE AND NOTE CALENDAR

TWELFTH WEEK

THANKSGIVING 2012

Thursday, November 22	Houston _____ at Detroit _____	(CBS) 12:30
	Washington _____ at Dallas _____	(FOX) 3:15
	New England _____ at New York Jets _____	(NBC) 8:20
Sunday, November 25	Minnesota _____ at Chicago _____	12:00
FOX-TV National Weekend	Oakland _____ at Cincinnati _____	1:00
	Pittsburgh _____ at Cleveland _____	1:00
	Buffalo _____ at Indianapolis _____	1:00
	Tennessee _____ at Jacksonville _____	1:00
	Denver _____ at Kansas City _____	12:00
	Seattle _____ at Miami _____	1:00
	Atlanta _____ at Tampa Bay _____	1:00
	Baltimore _____ at San Diego _____	1:05
	St. Louis _____ at Arizona _____	2:15
	San Francisco _____ at New Orleans _____	3:15
	Green Bay _____ at New York Giants * _____	(NBC) 8:20
Monday, November 26	Carolina _____ at Philadelphia _____	(ESPN) 8:30

Sunday Night Games In Weeks 11-16 Subject to Change

THIRTEENTH WEEK

Thursday, November 29	New Orleans _____ at Atlanta _____	(NFLN) 8:20
Sunday, December 2	Jacksonville _____ at Buffalo _____	1:00
CBS-TV National Weekend	Seattle _____ at Chicago _____	12:00
	Indianapolis _____ at Detroit _____	1:00
	Minnesota _____ at Green Bay _____	12:00
	Carolina _____ at Kansas City _____	12:00
	New England _____ at Miami _____	1:00
	Arizona _____ at New York Jets _____	1:00
	San Francisco _____ at St. Louis _____	12:00
	Houston _____ at Tennessee _____	12:00
	Tampa Bay _____ at Denver _____	2:05
	Pittsburgh _____ at Baltimore _____	4:15
	Cleveland _____ at Oakland _____	1:15
	Cincinnati _____ at San Diego _____	1:15
	Philadelphia _____ at Dallas * _____	(NBC) 7:20
Monday, December 3	New York Giants _____ at Washington _____	(ESPN) 8:30

Sunday Night Games In Weeks 11-16 Subject to Change

FOURTEENTH WEEK

Thursday, December 6	Denver _____ at Oakland _____	(NFLN) 5:20
Sunday, December 9	St. Louis _____ at Buffalo _____	1:00
FOX-TV National Weekend	Atlanta _____ at Carolina _____	1:00
	Dallas _____ at Cincinnati _____	1:00
	Kansas City _____ at Cleveland _____	1:00
	Tennessee _____ at Indianapolis _____	1:00
	New York Jets _____ at Jacksonville _____	1:00
	Chicago _____ at Minnesota _____	12:00
	San Diego _____ at Pittsburgh _____	1:00
	Philadelphia _____ at Tampa Bay _____	1:00
	Baltimore _____ at Washington _____	1:00
	Miami _____ at San Francisco _____	1:05
	New Orleans _____ at New York Giants _____	4:15
	Arizona _____ at Seattle _____	1:15
	Detroit _____ at Green Bay * _____	(NBC) 7:20
Monday, December 10	Houston _____ at New England _____	(ESPN) 8:30

Sunday Night Games In Weeks 11-16 Subject to Change

FIFTEENTH WEEK

Thursday, December 13	Cincinnati _____ at Philadelphia _____	(NFLN) 8:20
Sunday, December 16	New York Giants _____ at Atlanta _____	1:00
CBS-TV National Weekend	Denver _____ at Baltimore _____	1:00
	Green Bay _____ at Chicago _____	12:00
	Washington _____ at Cleveland _____	1:00
	Indianapolis _____ at Houston _____	12:00
	Jacksonville _____ at Miami _____	1:00
	Tampa Bay _____ at New Orleans _____	12:00
	Minnesota _____ at St. Louis _____	12:00
	Detroit _____ at Arizona _____	2:05
	Seattle _____ at Buffalo (Toronto) _____	4:05
	Carolina _____ at San Diego _____	1:05
	Pittsburgh _____ at Dallas _____	3:15
	Kansas City _____ at Oakland _____	1:15
	San Francisco _____ at New England * _____	(NBC) 8:20
Monday, December 17	New York Jets _____ at Tennessee _____	(ESPN) 7:30

Sunday Night Games In Weeks 11-16 Subject to Change

SIXTEENTH WEEK

Saturday, December 22	Atlanta _____ at Detroit _____	(ESPN) 8:30
Sunday, December 23	New York Giants _____ at Baltimore _____	1:00
FOX-TV National Weekend	Oakland _____ at Carolina _____	1:00
	New Orleans _____ at Dallas _____	12:00
	Tennessee _____ at Green Bay _____	12:00
	Minnesota _____ at Houston _____	12:00
	New England _____ at Jacksonville _____	1:00
	Indianapolis _____ at Kansas City _____	12:00
	Buffalo _____ at Miami _____	1:00
	Washington _____ at Philadelphia _____	1:00
	Cincinnati _____ at Pittsburgh _____	1:00
	St. Louis _____ at Tampa Bay _____	1:00
	Cleveland _____ at Denver _____	2:05
	Chicago _____ at Arizona _____	2:15
	San Francisco _____ at Seattle _____	1:15
	San Diego _____ at New York Jets* _____	(NBC) 8:20

Sunday Night Games In Weeks 11-16 Subject to Change

SEVENTEENTH WEEK

Sunday, December 30	Tampa Bay _____ at Atlanta _____	1:00
CBS-TV and FOX-TV National Weekend	New York Jets _____ at Buffalo _____	1:00
	Baltimore _____ at Cincinnati _____	1:00
	Chicago _____ at Detroit _____	1:00
	Houston _____ at Indianapolis _____	1:00
	Green Bay _____ at Minnesota _____	12:00
	Miami _____ at New England _____	1:00
	Carolina _____ at New Orleans _____	12:00
	Philadelphia _____ at New York Giants _____	1:00
	Cleveland _____ at Pittsburgh _____	1:00
	Jacksonville _____ at Tennessee _____	12:00
	Dallas _____ at Washington _____	1:00
	Kansas City _____ at Denver _____	2:15
	Oakland _____ at San Diego _____	1:15
	Arizona _____ at San Francisco _____	1:15
	St. Louis _____ at Seattle _____	1:15

Sunday Night Game In Week 17 TBD

PLAYOFFS

Wild Card Playoff Games
Site Priorities
Two Wild Card teams (division non-champions with best two records) from each conference and the division champions with the third and fourth-best record in each conference will enter the first round of the playoffs. The division champion with the third-best record will play host to the Wild Card team with the second-best record. The division champion with the fourth-best record will play host to the Wild Card team with the best record. There are no restrictions on intra-division games.

Saturday, January 5, 2013 American Football Conference

_____ at _____ (NBC)

National Football Conference

_____ at _____ (NBC)

Sunday, January 6, 2013 American Football Conference

_____ at _____ (CBS)

National Football Conference

_____ at _____ (FOX)

Divisional Playoff Games
Site Priorities
In each conference, the two division champions with the highest won-lost-tied percentage during the regular season will play host to the Wild Card winners. The division champion with the best record in each conference is assured of playing the lowest seeded Wild Card survivor. There are no restrictions on intra-division games.

Saturday, January 12, 2013 American Football Conference

_____ at _____ (CBS)

National Football Conference

_____ at _____ (FOX)

Sunday, January 13, 2013 American Football Conference

_____ at _____ (CBS)

National Football Conference

_____ at _____ (FOX)

Championship Games
Site Priorities for
Championship Games
The home teams will be the surviving playoff winners with the highest seeds. A Wild Card team cannot play host unless two Wild Card teams are in the game, in which case the Wild Card team that was seeded highest in the first round of the playoffs will be the home team.

Sunday, January 20, 2013 American Football Conference

_____ at _____ (CBS)

National Football Conference

_____ at _____ (FOX)

AFC-NFC Pro Bowl

Sunday, January 27, 2013 AFC-NFC Pro Bowl at Aloha Stadium, Honolulu, Hawaii

NFC_____ vs. AFC _____ (NBC)

Super Bowl XLVII

Sunday, February 3, 2013 Super Bowl XLVII at Mercedes-Benz Superdome, New Orleans, Louisiana

_____ vs. _____ (CBS)

2012 NATIONALLY TELEVISED GAMES

All times ET

Wednesday, Sept. 5	Dallas at New York Giants (NBC)	8:30
Sunday, Sept. 9	Pittsburgh at Denver (NBC)	8:20
Monday, Sept. 10	Cincinnati at Baltimore (ESPN)	7:00
	San Diego at Oakland (ESPN)	10:15
Thursday, Sept. 13	Chicago at Green Bay (NFL Network)	8:20
Sunday, Sept. 16	Detroit at San Francisco (NBC)	8:20
Monday, Sept. 17	Denver at Atlanta (ESPN)	8:30
Thursday, Sept. 20	New York Giants at Carolina (NFL Network)	8:20
Sunday, Sept. 23	New England at Baltimore (NBC)	8:20
Monday, Sept. 24	Green Bay at Seattle (ESPN)	8:30
Thursday, Sept. 27	Cleveland at Baltimore (NFL Network)	8:20
Sunday, Sept. 30	New York Giants at Philadelphia (NBC)	8:20
Monday, Oct. 1	Chicago at Dallas (ESPN)	8:30
Thursday, Oct. 4	Arizona at St. Louis (NFL Network)	8:20
Sunday, Oct. 7	San Diego at New Orleans (NBC)	8:20
Monday, Oct. 8	Houston at New York Jets (ESPN)	8:30
Thursday, Oct. 11	Pittsburgh at Tennessee (NFL Network)	8:20
Sunday, Oct. 14	Green Bay at Houston (NBC)	8:20
Monday, Oct. 15	Denver at San Diego (ESPN)	8:30
Thursday, Oct. 18	Seattle at San Francisco (NFL Network)	8:20
Sunday, Oct. 21	Pittsburgh at Cincinnati (NBC)	8:20
Monday, Oct. 22	Detroit at Chicago (ESPN)	8:30
Thursday, Oct. 25	Tampa Bay at Minnesota (NFL Network)	8:20
Sunday, Oct. 28	New Orleans at Denver (NBC)	8:20
Monday, Oct. 29	San Francisco at Arizona (ESPN)	8:30
Thursday, Nov. 1	Kansas City at San Diego (NFL Network)	8:20
Sunday, Nov. 4	Dallas at Atlanta (NBC)	8:20
Monday, Nov. 5	Philadelphia at New Orleans (ESPN)	8:30
Thursday, Nov. 8	Indianapolis at Jacksonville (NFL Network)	8:20
Sunday, Nov. 11	Houston at Chicago (NBC)	8:20
Monday, Nov. 12	Kansas City at Pittsburgh (ESPN)	8:30
Thursday, Nov. 15	Miami at Buffalo (NFL Network)	8:20
Sunday, Nov. 18	Baltimore at Pittsburgh (NBC)*	8:20
Monday, Nov. 19	Chicago at San Francisco (ESPN)	8:30
Thursday, Nov. 22	Houston at Detroit (CBS)	12:30
	Washington at Dallas (FOX)	4:15
	New England at N.Y. Jets (NBC)	8:20
Sunday, Nov. 25	Green Bay at New York Giants (NBC)*	8:20
Monday, Nov. 26	Carolina at Philadelphia (ESPN)	8:30
Thursday, Nov. 29	New Orleans at Atlanta (NFL Network)	8:20
Sunday, Dec. 2	Philadelphia at Dallas (NBC)*	8:20
Monday, Dec. 3	New York Giants at Washington (ESPN)	8:30
Thursday, Dec. 6	Denver at Oakland (NFL Network)	8:20
Sunday, Dec. 9	Detroit at Green Bay (NBC)*	8:20
Monday, Dec. 10	Houston at New England (ESPN)	8:30
Thursday, Dec. 13	Cincinnati at Philadelphia (NFL Network)	8:20
Sunday, Dec. 16	San Francisco at New England (NBC)*	8:20
Monday, Dec. 17	New York Jets at Tennessee (ESPN)	8:30
Saturday, Dec. 22	Atlanta at Detroit (ESPN)	8:30
Sunday, Dec. 23	San Diego at New York Jets (NBC)*	8:20
Sunday, Dec. 30	To be determined (NBC)*	8:20

PLAYOFFS

POSTSEASON GAMES

Saturday, January 5	AFC and NFC Wild Card Playoffs (NBC)
Sunday, January 6	AFC and NFC Wild Card Playoffs (CBS and FOX)
Saturday, January 12	AFC and NFC Divisional Playoffs (CBS and FOX)
Sunday, January 13	AFC and NFC Divisional Playoffs (CBS and FOX)
Sunday, January 20	AFC and NFC Championship Games (CBS and FOX)
Sunday, January 27	AFC-NFC Pro Bowl (NBC)
Sunday, February 3	Super Bowl XLVII in New Orleans (CBS)

*The NFL again will utilize "flexible scheduling" in 2012.

Flexible scheduling moves will be announced at least 12 days before games in Weeks 11-16. In Week 17, the flexible scheduling move will be announced at least six days before the game. Flexible scheduling will ensure quality matchups on Sunday night in those weeks and give "surprise" teams a chance to play their way on to primetime.

2012

Mid-July — Preseason training camps open. Clubs not permitted to open official preseason camp earlier than July 5. Veteran players cannot be required to report earlier than 15 days prior to club's first preseason game.

July 16 — Deadline at 4 P.M., New York time, for any club that designated a Franchise Player to sign such player to a multi-year contract or extension. After this date, the player may sign only a one-year contract with the designating club for the 2012 season, and such contract cannot be extended until after the Club's last regular season game.

July 22 — Signing period ends at 4 P.M., New York time, for Transition Players with outstanding tenders. After this date and through 4 P.M., New York time, on the Tuesday after the 10th regular season weekend, Old Club has exclusive negotiating rights to these players.

July 22# — Signing period ends at 4 P.M., New York time, for Unrestricted Free Agents to whom a June 1 tender was made by Old Club. After this date and through 4 P.M., New York time, on the Tuesday after the 10th regular season weekend, Old Club has exclusive negotiating rights to these players.

#or the first scheduled day of the first NFL training camp, whichever is later.

August 3-5 — Hall of Fame Weekend.

August 5 — Pro Football Hall of Fame Game, Canton, Ohio:
Arizona vs. New Orleans

August 7 — Deadline for players under contract to report to earn a season of free-agency credit.

August 7 — If a Drafted Rookie has not signed with his club by this date, he may not be traded to any other club in 2012.

August 9-13 — First Preseason Weekend.

August 11-15 — Deadline for club to provide written notice to certain unsigned players and the NFLPA of its intent to place them on the Exempt List if they fail to report no later than one day prior to the club's second preseason game. Any player who fails to report prior to the deadline will be ineligible to play or receive compensation for at least three games (preseason or regular season) from the time that he reports.

August 27 — Roster cut-down to maximum of 75 players on Active List by 4 P.M., New York time.

August 28 — All tryouts on this date and for the remainder of the season must be reported to the League office.

August 31 — Roster cut-down to maximum of 53 players on Active/Inactive List by 9 P.M., New York time. Clubs may dress minimum of 43 and maximum of 46 players for each regular-season and postseason game.

August 31 — Simultaneously with the cut-down to 53, clubs that have players in the categories of Active/Physically Unable to Perform or Active/Non-Football Injury or Illness must take one of the following options: Place player on Reserve/Physically Unable to Perform or Reserve/Non-Football Injury or Illness, whichever is applicable; ask waivers; terminate; trade; or continue to count him on Active List.

September 1 — After 12 noon, New York time, clubs may establish a Practice Squad of eight players by signing free agents who do not have an accrued season of free-agency credit or who were on the 46-player Active List for less than nine regular-season games during their only Accrued Season(s). A player cannot participate on the Practice Squad for more than three seasons.

September 5 — All clubs are required to file a personnel (injury) report with their conference information manager by 4:00 P.M., New York time. Reports are to be filed every Wednesday, Thursday and Friday before a regular-season game by 4:00 P.M., New York time (or as soon as possible after the completion of practice). An update must also be reported if there is any change in a player's condition after Friday.

September 5-10 — Regular Season opens.

September 6-11 — Beginning on these dates vested veterans terminated from the Active List or Inactive List (and from Reserve/Injured if the player is placed on Reserve/Injured after the beginning of the regular season) are entitled to receive, after the end of the regular-season schedule, Termination Pay pursuant to the terms of the CBA.

September 25 — Priority on multiple waiver claims is now based on the current season's standing.

October 16 — Beginning the day after the conclusion of the sixth regular-season weekend and continuing through the day after the conclusion of the ninth regular-season weekend, clubs are permitted to begin practicing players on Reserve/Physically Unable to Perform and Reserve/Non-Football Injury or Illness for a period not to exceed 21 days. Players may be activated during the 21-day practice period or until 4 P.M., New York time, on the day after the conclusion of the 21-day period.

October 16 — All trading ends at 4 P.M., New York time.

October 17 — Players with at least four previous pension-credited seasons are subject to the waiver system for the remainder of the regular season and postseason.

November 13	Signing period ends at 4 P.M., New York time, for Franchise Players who are eligible to receive Offer Sheets.
November 13	Deadline for clubs to sign by 4 P.M., New York time, their unsigned Franchise and Transition Players, including Franchise Players who were eligible to receive Offer Sheets until this date. If still unsigned after this date, such players are prohibited from playing in NFL in 2012.
November 13	Deadline for clubs to sign by 4 P.M., New York time, their Unrestricted Free Agents to whom June 1 tender was made. If still unsigned after this date, such players are prohibited from playing in NFL in 2012.
November 13	Deadline for clubs to sign by 4 P.M., New York time, their Restricted Free Agents to whom June 1 tender was made. If such players remain unsigned, they are prohibited from playing in NFL in 2012.
November 13	Deadline for clubs to sign Drafted players by 4 P.M., New York time. If such players remain unsigned, they are prohibited from playing in NFL in 2012.
November 30	Deadline for reinstatement of players in Reserve List categories of Retired, Did Not Report, and Exclusive Rights, and of players who were placed on Reserve/Left Squad in a previous season.
December 28	Deadline for waiver requests in 2012, except for "special waiver requests," which have a 10-day claiming period, with termination or assignment delayed until after the Super Bowl.
December 31	Clubs may begin signing free-agent players for the 2013 season.

2013

January 5-6	Wild Card Playoff Games.
January 12-13	Divisional Playoff Games.
January 20	AFC and NFC Championship Games.
January 27	AFC-NFC Pro Bowl.
February 3	Super Bowl XLVII, Mercedes-Benz Superdome, New Orleans, Louisiana.

2014

February 2*	Super Bowl XLVIII, MetLife Stadium, New York-New Jersey.

2015

February 1*	Super Bowl XLIX, University of Phoenix Stadium, Glendale, Arizona.

Tentative date

The NFL is online to provide fans and media quick and easy access to all the latest professional football information.

NFL.COM—(http://NFL.com)

NFL.com, the league's year-round home page on the Internet, enters its 16th season in cyberspace. The site provides NFL information during the regular season, postseason, and offseason, including::

NEWS/STATS: Up-to-the-minute NFL news and analysis, plus game previews, injury reports, and player and team stats.

GAMEDAY COVERAGE: Live game coverage with instant highlights, play-by-play, scores, and statistics, including graphical drive charts and comprehensive scoreboard that reloads automatically with the latest information.

VIDEO HIGHLIGHTS: The site showcases instant game highlights, NFL Films video highlights of the previous week's games as well as upcoming matchups. Video also supports feature stories and team highlight clips from every game last season. In addition, exclusive NFL Network programming is featured as well as original video content.

SUBSCRIPTION PRODUCTS: Three premium video products, NFL Preseason Live, NFL Game Rewind & NFL Game Pass, that enable fans in the United States and around the world to watch games online, on demand and in HD with DVR controls.

NFL MOBILE PRODUCTS: A suite of mobile products including the premium product "NFL Mobile only from Verizon" that delivers live NFL Network *Thursday Night Football*, NBC's *Sunday Night Football*, ESPN's *Monday Night Football* and NFL RedZone to fans on the go.

NFL.COM/ESPANOL POWERED BY UNIVISION.COM— (http://NFL.COM/ESPANOL)

The official Spanish-language site of the NFL provides in depth information on teams and players, and offers highlights of every NFL game in Spanish. The site includes Hispanic player diaries, live radio broadcasts, up-to-date stats, fantasy football, and more.

NFLHEALTHANDSAFETY.COM—(http://nflhealthandsafety.com)

The site outlines the ways the NFL is addressing player health and safety issues. It houses information on the partnerships, programs and initiatives the NFL supports to protect the health of current and former NFL players and to promote safe play and healthy lifestyles at all levels of football and other sports. The site provides information to promote health and safety at all playing levels, including partnerships with USA Football and the Centers for Disease Control and Prevention. To view the evolution of playing rules as they pertain to health and safety, visit www.nfl.com/evolution.

NFLFLAG.COM—(http://nflflag.com)

NFLFLAG.com focuses on the NFL FLAG Program, which is also part of NFL PLAY 60. Boys and girls ages 5-17 nationwide have the opportunity to display their skills in a non-contact environment by playing against their peers in five-on-five flag football games. Our website is a resource for league organizers, coaches, parents and youth organizations who want to start or find a local NFL FLAG league in their area as well as promote a positive experience for their youth participants.

NFLRUSH.COM—(http://www.NFLRUSH.com)

NFLRUSH.com, which is targeted to kids 6-15, is the official kids' website of the National Football League, offering unique customizable content, games, fantasy football for kids, contests, videos, fun daily features on NFL players and information on the NFL's Youth Football programs. NFLRUSH.com also features fun and interactive fitness information as part of the NFL PLAY 60 campaign, which encourages kids to be active for 60 minutes a day. The NFLRUSH ZONE, a role playing game on NFLRUSH.com, is an immersive virtual world where kids are able to create avatars, join their favorite team, play games, chat, watch the NFL RUSH ZONE animated series and compete with friends in safe and fun environment.

USAFOOTBALL.COM—(http://usafootball.com)

USA Football is an independent, non-profit organization which is leading the growth and development of youth, high school and international amateur football. USA Football helps youth and amateur football organizations keep the sport fun, safe, and accessible by offering resources focused on coaching education, league enhancement, officiating development and health and safety awareness. The organization also serves as the designated United States representatives to the International Federation of American Football. Based Indianapolis, USA Football was endowed by the NFL and NFLPA in 2002.

NFL.COM/COMMUNITY—(http://www.nfl.com/community)

This site is dedicated to the community service initiatives of the National Football League and the 32 member clubs. It provides news, history and informative links relating to the NFL's three primary service themes: reversing childhood obesity trends (NFL PLAY 60), the global fight against breast cancer (A Crucial Catch), and honoring the Veterans and men and women of the US Armed Forces (Salute to Service). The NFL also takes pride in recognizing the philanthropic efforts of its players, coaches and staff through the annual presentations of the Walter Payton NFL Man of the Year, Salute to Service, and NFL Teacher of the Year awards.

PROFOOTBALLHOF.COM—(http://profootballhof.com)

Profootballhof.com is the official site of the Pro Football Hall of Fame in Canton, Ohio. In addition to a complete visitor's guide to the Hall, the site features bios, stories and Q & A's with Hall of Fame inductees, a detailed archive of football history, and information on appearances by members of the Hall.

OFFICIAL NFL TEAM SITES

In addition to a dedicated area on NFL.com, all 32 teams have their own Websites, which have separate URLs, and are linked from NFL.com.

Arizona Cardinals (www.azcardinals.com)
Atlanta Falcons (www.atlantafalcons.com)
Baltimore Ravens (www.baltimoreravens.com)
Buffalo Bills (www.buffalobills.com)
Carolina Panthers (www.panthers.com)
Chicago Bears (www.chicagobears.com)
Cincinnati Bengals (www.bengals.com)
Cleveland Browns (www.clevelandbrowns.com)
Dallas Cowboys (www.dallascowboys.com)
Denver Broncos (www.denverbroncos.com)
Detroit Lions (www.detroitlions.com)
Green Bay Packers (www.packers.com)
Houston Texans (www.houstontexans.com)
Indianapolis Colts (www.colts.com)
Jacksonville Jaguars (www.jaguars.com)
Kansas City Chiefs (www.kcchiefs.com)
Miami Dolphins (www.miamidolphins.com)
Minnesota Vikings (www.vikings.com)
New England Patriots (www.patriots.com)
New Orleans Saints (www.neworleanssaints.com)
New York Giants (www.giants.com)
New York Jets (www.newyorkjets.com)
Oakland Raiders (www.raiders.com)
Philadelphia Eagles (www.philadelphiaeagles.com)
Pittsburgh Steelers (www.steelers.com)
St. Louis Rams (www.stlouisrams.com)
San Diego Chargers (www.chargers.com)
San Francisco 49ers (www.sf49ers.com)
Seattle Seahawks (www.seahawks.com)
Tampa Bay Buccaneers (www.buccaneers.com)
Tennessee Titans (www.titansonline.com)
Washington Redskins (www.redskins.com)

NFL Network provides fans with a network to call their own. Seven days a week, 24 hours a day, 365 days a year, fans turn to NFL Network to receive information and insight straight from the field, team headquarters, league offices and everywhere the NFL is making news.

NFL Network gives fans unprecedented year-round inside access to all NFL events, including the Super Bowl, Playoffs, regular season, preseason, Pro Bowl, Pro Football Hall of Fame induction weekend, NFL Draft, Scouting Combine, Senior Bowl, league meetings, minicamps and training camps.

In addition, NFL Network is the only place on television for fans to view NFL games outside their initial live airings. From original broadcast versions of past Super Bowls, in-week replays of current games, original network telecasts of classic NFL regular season and postseason games, to every preseason game, and an expanded 13-game regular season *Thursday Night Football* schedule beginning Week 2. NFL Network is truly the year-round destination for football fans. NFL Network is available on cable, telcos and satellite television through your local service provider, as well as on NFL Mobile only on Verizon. If your provider doesn't currently offer NFL Network, please call (866) NFL-NETWORK.

KEY PROGRAMMING

EXCLUSIVE LIVE PRIMETIME GAMES
NFL Network's expanded 13-game, regular-season Thursday Night primetime schedule kicks off in high definition on September 13. Each game, at 8:00 PM ET, will be preceded by a two-hour pregame show and followed by a live post-game show.

NFL TOTAL ACCESS
NFL Network's signature show is the football show of record. *NFL Total Access* is uniquely structured to see the game through the participants' eyes, airing at 7:00 PM ET Monday through Saturday.

Covering all 32 teams, *NFL Total Access* features interviews with players, coaches and other key league personnel. Using "Team Cams" at every facility, *NFL Total Access* has the ability to go live to any NFL team headquarters at any time.

FIRST ON THE FIELD
Debuting this fall, *First on the Field* kicks off at 7:00 AM ET each Sunday and takes the first look at the day's NFL action. The new program is the first live show to originate from NFL Films in Mt. Laurel, New Jersey.

NFL GAMEDAY MORNING
NFL GameDay Morning is the first NFL pregame show on the air Sundays at 9:00 AM ET during the regular season and playoffs, providing fans with the earliest news and notes as well as live reports from around the league.

NFL GAMEDAY SCOREBOARD
After Sunday's early games conclude, *NFL GameDay Scoreboard* takes viewers around the league for post-game press conferences and game highlights. *NFL GameDay Scoreboard* airs at 4:00 PM ET on Sundays and continues through the Sunday afternoon games.

NFL GAMEDAY HIGHLIGHTS
Following the late afternoon games, analysts Deion Sanders and Steve Mariucci join host Rich Eisen to analyze the events of the day on *NFL GameDay Highlights*. Includes highlights from all completed games, commentary, on-field interviews and postgame press conferences.

NFL GAMEDAY FINAL
After each Sunday's final game, the 90-minute *NFL GameDay Final* delivers comprehensive coverage of the day's action. Host Fran Charles is joined by Steve Mariucci, Deion Sanders and Michael Irvin. *NFL GameDay Final* kicks off at 11:30 PM ET and features highlights, post-game press conferences, on-field interviews, analysis and more in wrapping up each NFL Sunday.

NFL REPLAY
NFL games will be re-aired with the original television announcers and cameras. This offering features the most exciting games each week in an abbreviated format (eliminating halftime and other non-critical elements). Enhancements to each broadcast include additional camera angles, sideline sound and post-game interviews.

PLAYBOOK
NFL Network uses the "all 22" game film watched each week by coaches and players to present football's ultimate chalkboard show. *Playbook*, produced at NFL Films, offers 60-minute strategy sessions with NFL Network analysts, who focus on each week's key matchups and discuss technique and game planning with coaches and players.

THE TOP 100: PLAYERS OF 2012
The Top 100 is the annual series which sparks wide debate each offseason on NFL Network. Current players vote for their peers to compile a list of the top 100 playmakers today. Counting down from 100 to 1, 10 players are featured in each episode.

AMERICA'S GAME
The Sports Emmy-winning original series continues its profiles of Super Bowl champions with the 2011 New York Giants.

A FOOTBALL LIFE
The Emmy-nominated *A Football Life* biography series returns for a second season on NFL Network. The NFL Films-produced series features 13 one-hour episodes offering a look inside the untold stories of NFL icons.

NFL's TOP 10
Putting a fresh twist on the countdown genre, *NFL's Top 10* is a fast-paced series that provides an irreverent look at some of the most intriguing subjects in the NFL, creating and debating a top ten list for each category. Each 60-minute episode counts down from No. 10 to the top ranking in each category.

SOUND FX
The sounds of the game that only NFL Films can capture – with exclusive on-field and sideline microphone access – will be featured on the Emmy award-winning *Sound FX*.

PRESEASON GAMES
NFL Network is the only place on television where fans can view all 65 NFL preseason games in high-definition, including 11 LIVE national preseason telecasts.

Log on to www.NFL.com/NFLnetwork for more information on NFL Network.

SCHEDULING FORMULA

The NFL expanded to 32 teams in 2002 with the addition of the Houston Texans. In addition, the NFL realigned for the first time since 1970—into eight divisions of four teams each—and the scheduling formula that was introduced guarantees for the first time that all teams play each other on a regular, rotating basis. Although the number of teams has increased to 32, the number of playoff teams remains the same at 12.

Under the NFL scheduling formula, every team within a division plays 16 games as follows:

- Home and away against its three division opponents (6 games).
- The four teams from another division within its conference on a rotating three-year cycle (4 games).
- The four teams from a division in the other conference on a rotating four-year cycle (4 games).
- Two intraconference games based on the prior year's standings (2 games). These games will match a first-place team against the first-place teams in the two same-conference divisions the team is not scheduled to play that season. The second-place, third-place, and fourth-place teams in a conference will be matched in the same way each year.

The schedule format takes each team through a cycle of games—home and away—against every other team in the league. From 2002-2009, every team played every other team at least twice—once home and once away. After the 2008 season, a decision was made to continue with the same rotation in 2010 and beyond.

In determining how to begin the divisional rotation in 2002, the displacement of teams from their old divisions in the new alignment was taken into account. Preference was given to scheduling games with former division rivals and other regional opponents for clubs realigned from otherwise intact divisions.

FUTURE SCHEDULING ROTATION

		2012	2013
AFC EAST	Intraconference	AFCS	AFCN
	Interconference	NFCW	NFCS
AFC NORTH	Intraconference	AFCW	AFCE
	Interconference	NFCE	NFCN
AFC SOUTH	Intraconference	AFCE	AFCW
	Interconference	NFCN	NFCW
AFC WEST	Intraconference	AFCN	AFCS
	Interconference	NFCS	NFCE
NFC EAST	Intraconference	NFCS	NFCN
	Interconference	AFCN	AFCW
NFC NORTH	Intraconference	NFCW	NFCE
	Interconference	AFCS	AFCN
NFC SOUTH	Intraconference	NFCE	NFCW
	Interconference	AFCW	AFCE
NFC WEST	Intraconference	NFCN	NFCS
	Interconference	AFCE	AFCS

AFC EAST NON-DIVISIONAL OPPONENTS 2012

	BUFFALO		MIAMI		NEW ENGLAND		N.Y. JETS	
	Home	Away	Home	Away	Home	Away	Home	Away
Intraconference by Division	JAX	HOU	JAX	HOU	HOU	JAX	HOU	JAX
	TENN	IND	TENN	IND	IND	TENN	IND	TENN
Interconference by Division	STL	ARIZ	STL	ARIZ	ARIZ	STL	ARIZ	STL
	SEA	SF	SEA	SF	SF	SEA	SF	SEA
Intraconference by Position	AFCW	AFCN	AFCW	AFCN	AFCW	AFCN	AFCW	AFCN

AFC EAST NON-DIVISIONAL OPPONENTS 2013

	BUFFALO		MIAMI		NEW ENGLAND		N.Y. JETS	
	Home	Away	Home	Away	Home	Away	Home	Away
Intraconference by Division	BALT	CLE	BALT	CLE	CLE	BALT	CLE	BALT
	CIN	PITT	CIN	PITT	PITT	CIN	PITT	CIN
Interconference by Division	ATL	NO	ATL	NO	NO	ATL	NO	ATL
	CAR	TB	CAR	TB	TB	CAR	TB	CAR
Intraconference by Position	AFCW	AFCS	AFCW	AFCS	AFCW	AFCS	AFCW	AFCS

AFC NORTH NON-DIVISIONAL OPPONENTS 2012

	BALTIMORE		CINCINNATI		CLEVELAND		PITTSBURGH	
	Home	Away	Home	Away	Home	Away	Home	Away
Intraconference by Division	DEN	KC	DEN	KC	KC	DEN	KC	DEN
	OAK	SD	OAK	SD	SD	OAK	SD	OAK
Interconference by Division	DALL	PHIL	DALL	PHIL	PHIL	DALL	PHIL	DALL
	NYG	WASH	NYG	WASH	WASH	NYG	WASH	NYG
Intraconference by Position	AFCE	AFCS	AFCE	AFCS	AFCE	AFCS	AFCE	AFCS

AFC NORTH NON-DIVISIONAL OPPONENTS 2013

	BALTIMORE		CINCINNATI		CLEVELAND		PITTSBURGH	
	Home	Away	Home	Away	Home	Away	Home	Away
Intraconference by Division	NE	BUFF	NE	BUFF	BUFF	NE	BUFF	NE
	NYJ	MIA	NYJ	MIA	MIA	NYJ	MIA	NYJ
Interconference by Division	GB	CHI	GB	CHI	CHI	GB	CHI	GB
	MINN	DET	MINN	DET	DET	MINN	DET	MINN
Intraconference by Position	AFCS	AFCW	AFCS	AFCW	AFCS	AFCW	AFCS	AFCW

SCHEDULING FORMULA

AFC SOUTH NON-DIVISIONAL OPPONENTS 2012

	HOUSTON		INDIANAPOLIS		JACKSONVILLE		TENNESSEE	
	Home	Away	Home	Away	Home	Away	Home	Away
Intraconference by Division	BUFF	NE	BUFF	NE	NE	BUFF	NE	BUFF
	MIA	NYJ	MIA	NYJ	NYJ	MIA	NYJ	MIA
Interconference by Division	GB	CHI	GB	CHI	CHI	GB	CHI	GB
	MINN	DET	MINN	DET	DET	MINN	DET	MINN
Intraconference by Position	AFCN	AFCW	AFCN	AFCW	AFCN	AFCW	AFCN	AFCW

AFC SOUTH NON-DIVISIONAL OPPONENTS 2013

	HOUSTON		INDIANAPOLIS		JACKSONVILLE		TENNESSEE	
	Home	Away	Home	Away	Home	Away	Home	Away
Intraconference by Division	DEN	KC	DEN	KC	KC	DEN	KC	DEN
	OAK	SD	OAK	SD	SD	OAK	SD	OAK
Interconference by Division	STL	ARIZ	STL	ARIZ	ARIZ	STL	ARIZ	STL
	SEA	SF	SEA	SF	SF	SEA	SF	SEA
Intraconference by Position	AFCE	AFCN	AFCE	AFCN	AFCE	AFCN	AFCE	AFCN

AFC WEST NON-DIVISIONAL OPPONENTS 2012

	DENVER		KANSAS CITY		OAKLAND		SAN DIEGO	
	Home	Away	Home	Away	Home	Away	Home	Away
Intraconference by Division	CLE	BALT	BALT	CLE	CLE	BALT	BALT	CLE
	PITT	CIN	CIN	PITT	PITT	CIN	CIN	PITT
Interconference by Division	NO	ATL	ATL	NO	NO	ATL	ATL	NO
	TB	CAR	CAR	TB	TB	CAR	CAR	TB
Intraconference by Position	AFCS	AFCE	AFCS	AFCE	AFCS	AFCE	AFCS	AFCE

AFC WEST NON-DIVISIONAL OPPONENTS 2013

	DENVER		KANSAS CITY		OAKLAND		SAN DIEGO	
	Home	Away	Home	Away	Home	Away	Home	Away
Intraconference by Division	JAX	HOU	HOU	JAX	JAX	HOU	HOU	JAX
	TENN	IND	IND	TENN	TENN	IND	IND	TENN
Interconference by Division	PHIL	DALL	DALL	PHIL	PHIL	DALL	DALL	PHIL
	WASH	NYG	NYG	WASH	WASH	NYG	NYG	WASH
Intraconference by Position	AFCN	AFCE	AFCN	AFCE	AFCN	AFCE	AFCN	AFCE

NFC EAST NON-DIVISIONAL OPPONENTS 2012

	DALLAS Home	DALLAS Away	N.Y. GIANTS Home	N.Y. GIANTS Away	PHILADELPHIA Home	PHILADELPHIA Away	WASHINGTON Home	WASHINGTON Away
Intraconference by Division	NO	ATL	NO	ATL	ATL	NO	ATL	NO
	TB	CAR	TB	CAR	CAR	TB	CAR	TB
Interconference by Division	CLE	BALT	CLE	BALT	BALT	CLE	BALT	CLE
	PITT	CIN	PITT	CIN	CIN	PITT	CIN	PITT
Intraconference by Position	NFCN	NFCW	NFCN	NFCW	NFCN	NFCW	NFCN	NFCW

NFC EAST NON-DIVISIONAL OPPONENTS 2013

	DALLAS Home	DALLAS Away	N.Y. GIANTS Home	N.Y. GIANTS Away	PHILADELPHIA Home	PHILADELPHIA Away	WASHINGTON Home	WASHINGTON Away
Intraconference by Division	GB	CHI	GB	CHI	CHI	GB	CHI	GB
	MINN	DET	MINN	DET	DET	MINN	DET	MINN
Interconference by Division	DEN	KC	DEN	KC	KC	DEN	KC	DEN
	OAK	SD	OAK	SD	SD	OAK	SD	OAK
Intraconference by Position	NFCW	NFCS	NFCW	NFCS	NFCW	NFCS	NFCW	NFCS

NFC NORTH NON-DIVISIONAL OPPONENTS 2012

	CHICAGO Home	CHICAGO Away	DETROIT Home	DETROIT Away	GREEN BAY Home	GREEN BAY Away	MINNESOTA Home	MINNESOTA Away
Intraconference by Division	STL	ARIZ	STL	ARIZ	ARIZ	STL	ARIZ	STL
	SEA	SF	SEA	SF	SF	SEA	SF	SEA
Interconference by Division	HOU	JAX	HOU	JAX	JAX	HOU	JAX	HOU
	IND	TENN	IND	TENN	TENN	IND	TENN	IND
Intraconference by Position	NFCS	NFCE	NFCS	NFCE	NFCS	NFCE	NFCS	NFCE

NFC NORTH NON-DIVISIONAL OPPONENTS 2013

	CHICAGO Home	CHICAGO Away	DETROIT Home	DETROIT Away	GREEN BAY Home	GREEN BAY Away	MINNESOTA Home	MINNESOTA Away
Intraconference by Division	DALL	PHIL	DALL	PHIL	PHIL	DALL	PHIL	DALL
	NYG	WASH	NYG	WASH	WASH	NYG	WASH	NYG
Interconference by Division	BALT	CLE	BALT	CLE	CLE	BALT	CLE	BALT
	CIN	PITT	CIN	PITT	PITT	CIN	PITT	CIN
Intraconference by Position	NFCS	NFCW	NFCS	NFCW	NFCS	NFCW	NFCS	NFCW

NFC SOUTH NON-DIVISIONAL OPPONENTS 2012

	ATLANTA		CAROLINA		NEW ORLEANS		TAMPA BAY	
	Home	Away	Home	Away	Home	Away	Home	Away
Intraconference by Division	DALL	PHIL	DALL	PHIL	PHIL	DALL	PHIL	DALL
	NYG	WASH	NYG	WASH	WASH	NYG	WASH	NYG
Interconference by Division	DEN	KC	DEN	KC	KC	DEN	KC	DEN
	OAK	SD	OAK	SD	SD	OAK	SD	OAK
Intraconference by Position	NFCW	NFCN	NFCW	NFCN	NFCW	NFCN	NFCW	NFCN

NFC SOUTH NON-DIVISIONAL OPPONENTS 2013

	ATLANTA		CAROLINA		NEW ORLEANS		TAMPA BAY	
	Home	Away	Home	Away	Home	Away	Home	Away
Intraconference by Division	STL	ARIZ	STL	ARIZ	ARIZ	STL	ARIZ	STL
	SEA	SF	SEA	SF	SF	SEA	SF	SEA
Interconference by Division	NE	BUFF	NE	BUFF	BUFF	NE	BUFF	NE
	NYJ	MIA	NYJ	MIA	MIA	NYJ	MIA	NYJ
Intraconference by Position	NFCE	NFCN	NFCE	NFCN	NFCE	NFCN	NFCE	NFCN

NFC WEST NON-DIVISIONAL OPPONENTS 2012

	ARIZONA		ST. LOUIS		SAN FRANCISCO		SEATTLE	
	Home	Away	Home	Away	Home	Away	Home	Away
Intraconference by Division	CHI	GB	GB	CHI	CHI	GB	GB	CHI
	DET	MINN	MINN	DET	DET	MINN	MINN	DET
Interconference by Division	BUFF	NE	NE	BUFF	BUFF	NE	NE	BUFF
	MIA	NYJ	NYJ	MIA	MIA	NYJ	NYJ	MIA
Intraconference by Position	NFCE	NFCS	NFCE	NFCS	NFCE	NFCS	NFCN	NFCS

NFC WEST NON-DIVISIONAL OPPONENTS 2013

	ARIZONA		ST. LOUIS		SAN FRANCISCO		SEATTLE	
	Home	Away	Home	Away	Home	Away	Home	Away
Intraconference by Division	ATL	NO	NO	ATL	ATL	NO	NO	ATL
	CAR	TB	TB	CAR	CAR	TB	TB	CAR
Interconference by Division	HOU	JAX	JAX	HOU	HOU	JAX	JAX	HOU
	IND	TENN	TENN	IND	IND	TENN	TENN	IND
Intraconference by Position	NFCN	NFCE	NFCN	NFCE	NFCN	NFCE	NFCN	NFCE

TOP ACTIVE PASSERS
1,000 or more attempts

		Yrs.	Att.	Comp.	Pct. Comp.	Yards	TD	Pct. TD	Had Int.	Pct. Int.	Ratings Pts.
1.	Aaron Rodgers	7	2,113	1,381	65.4	17,366	132	6.2	38	1.8	104.1
2.	Tony Romo	8	2,592	1,672	64.5	20,834	149	5.7	72	2.8	96.9
3.	Tom Brady	12	5,321	3,397	63.8	39,979	300	5.6	115	2.2	96.4
4.	Philip Rivers	8	3,037	1,930	63.5	24,285	163	5.4	78	2.6	95.5
5.	Peyton Manning	14	7,210	4,682	64.9	54,828	399	5.5	198	2.7	94.9
6.	Drew Brees	11	5,479	3,613	65.9	40,742	281	5.1	146	2.7	94.0
7.	Matt Schaub	8	2,279	1,466	64.3	17,936	98	4.3	58	2.5	92.2
8.	Ben Roethlisberger	8	3,313	2,090	63.1	26,579	165	5.0	100	3.0	92.1
9.	Matt Ryan	4	2,022	1,232	60.9	14,238	95	4.7	46	2.3	88.4
10.	Jeff Garcia	11	3,676	2,264	61.6	25,537	161	4.4	83	2.3	87.5
11.	Carson Palmer	8	3,545	2,223	62.7	25,447	167	4.7	116	3.3	86.3
12.	Joe Flacco	4	1,958	1,190	60.8	13,816	80	4.1	46	2.3	86.0
13.	David Garrard	9	2,281	1,406	61.6	16,003	89	3.9	54	2.4	85.8
14.	Donovan McNabb	13	5,374	3,170	59.0	37,276	234	4.4	117	2.2	85.6
15.	Matthew Stafford	3	1,136	679	59.8	7,840	60	5.3	37	3.3	84.7
16.	Jay Cutler	6	2,521	1,541	61.1	18,283	117	4.6	86	3.4	84.5
17.	Mark Brunell	18	4,640	2,761	59.5	32,072	184	4.0	108	2.3	84.0
18.	Jason Campbell	6	2,131	1,296	60.8	14,417	74	3.5	50	2.3	82.8
19.	Matt Cassel	7	1,767	1,042	59.0	11,699	76	4.3	45	2.5	82.5
20.	Matt Hasselbeck	13	4,797	2,891	60.3	33,150	194	4.0	142	3.0	82.2
21.	Eli Manning	8	3,921	2,291	58.4	27,579	185	4.7	129	3.3	82.1
22.	Jake Delhomme	11	2,932	1,741	59.4	20,975	126	4.3	101	3.4	81.3
23.	Michael Vick	9	2,538	1,422	56.0	17,912	111	4.4	72	2.8	80.9
24.	Byron Leftwich	8	1,552	905	58.3	10,260	58	3.7	41	2.6	79.7
25.	Kyle Orton	6	2,204	1,284	58.3	14,532	80	3.6	57	2.6	79.4

TOP ACTIVE SCORERS
(number in parentheses represents 2-point conversions scored)

		Yrs.	TD	FG	PAT	TP
1.	Jason Hanson	20	0	463	627	2,016
2.	John Kasay	21	0	461	587	1,970
3.	Adam Vinatieri	16	0	387	589(1)	1,752
4.	Ryan Longwell	15	0	361	604	1,687
5.	Olindo Mare	15	0	350	480	1,530
6.	David Akers	14	0	338	477	1,491
7.	Sebastian Janikowski	12	0	293	392	1,271
8.	Jay Feely	11	1	274	382	1,210
9.	Neil Rackers	12	0	264	372	1,164
10.	Phil Dawson	13	1	276	321	1,155
11.	Rian Lindell	12	0	262	362	1,148
12.	LaDainian Tomlinson	11	162	0	0	972
13.	Shayne Graham	11	0	214	323	965
14.	Josh Brown	9	0	220	302	962
15.	Randy Moss	13	154	0	0(4)	932
16.	Matt Bryant	10	0	200	280	880
17.	Nate Kaeding	8	0	173	343	862
18.	Rob Bironas	7	0	189	239	806
	Robbie Gould	7	0	187	245	806
20.	Lawrence Tynes	8	0	157	311	782
21.	Josh Scobee	8	0	167	254	755
22.	Stephen Gostkowski	6	0	141	289	712
23.	Mason Crosby	5	0	131	256	649
24.	Billy Cundiff	8	0	132	200	596
25.	Tony Gonzalez	15	95	0	0(3)	576

TOP ACTIVE SCORERS (TOUCHDOWNS)

		Yrs.	Rush	Rec.	Ret.	Tot.
1.	LaDainian Tomlinson	11	145	17	0	162
2.	Randy Moss	13	0	153	1	154
3.	Tony Gonzalez	15	0	95	0	95
4.	Antonio Gates	9	0	76	0	76
5.	Maurice Jones-Drew	6	62	10	2	74
6.	Larry Fitzgerald	8	0	73	0	73
	Reggie Wayne	11	0	73	0	73
8.	Thomas Jones	12	68	3	0	71
9.	Chad Ochocinco	11	0	67	0	67
	Adrian Peterson	5	64	3	0	67
	Steve Smith	11	2	59	6	67
12.	Willis McGahee	8	59	5	0	64
13.	Plaxico Burress	11	0	63	0	63
14.	Donald Driver	13	1	59	0	60
	Brandon Jacobs	7	56	4	0	60
	Steven Jackson	8	52	8	0	60
17.	Santana Moss	11	0	56	3	59
	Marion Barber	7	53	6	0	59
19.	Michael Turner	8	56	0	0	56
20.	Anquan Boldin	9	1	54	0	55
21.	Frank Gore	7	43	9	0	52
	Andre Johnson	9	0	52	0	52
23.	Calvin Johnson	5	1	49	0	50
24.	Greg Jennings	6	0	49	0	49
25.	Marques Colston	6	0	48	0	48
	Joseph Addai	6	39	9	0	48

TOP ACTIVE RUSHERS

	Yrs.	Att.	Yards	TD
1. LaDainian Tomlinson	11	3,174	13,684	145
2. Thomas Jones	12	2,678	10,591	68
3. Steven Jackson	8	2,138	9,093	52
4. Frank Gore	7	1,653	7,625	43
5. Willis McGahee	8	1,790	7,366	59
6. Maurice Jones-Drew	6	1,484	6,854	62
7. Adrian Peterson	5	1,406	6,752	64
8. Michael Turner	8	1,417	6,538	56
9. Cedric Benson	7	1,529	5,769	31
10. Chris Johnson	4	1,187	5,645	38
11. Michael Vick	9	729	5,219	33
12. DeAngelo Williams	6	996	5,047	38
13. Ronnie Brown	7	1,170	4,951	37
14. Brandon Jacobs	7	1,078	4,849	56
15. Marion Barber	7	1,156	4,780	53
16. Chester Taylor	10	1,160	4,740	26
17. Marshawn Lynch	5	1,137	4,542	35
18. Joseph Addai	6	1,095	4,453	39
19. Ray Rice	4	959	4,377	24
20. Matt Forte	4	1,014	4,233	21
21. Cadillac Williams	7	1,055	4,038	21
22. Ryan Grant	5	924	4,016	25
23. Fred Jackson	5	817	3,794	16
24. Maurice Morris	10	867	3,648	13
25. Kevin Faulk	13	864	3,607	16

TOP ACTIVE SCRIMMAGE YARDS LEADERS

	Yrs.	Rush	Rec	Total	TD
1. LaDainian Tomlinson	11	13,684	4,772	18,456	162
2. Randy Moss	13	159	14,858	15,017	154
3. Tony Gonzalez	15	14	13,338	13,352	95
4. Thomas Jones	12	10,591	2,023	12,614	71
5. Steven Jackson	12	9,093	3,003	12,096	60
6. Reggie Wayne	11	0	11,708	11,708	73
7. Chad Ochocinco	11	175	11,059	11,234	67
8. Steve Smith	11	360	10,278	10,638	67
9. Donald Driver	13	217	10,060	10,277	60
10. Frank Gore	7	7,625	2,397	10,022	52
11. Andre Johnson	9	54	9,656	9,710	52
12. Larry Fitzgerald	8	55	9,615	9,670	73
13. Anquan Boldin	9	211	9,244	9,455	55
14. Santana Moss	11	248	9,142	9,390	59
15. Maurice Jones-Drew	6	6,854	2,473	9,327	74
16. Willis McGahee	8	7,366	1,098	8,464	64
17. Plaxico Burress	10	7	8,457	8,450	63
18. Adrian Peterson	5	6,752	1,309	8,061	67
19. Jason Witten	9	0	7,909	7,909	41
20. Antonio Gates	9	0	7,783	7,783	76
21. Roddy White	7	19	7,374	7,393	45
22. T.J. Houshmandzadeh	11	142	7,237	7,379	45
23. Wes Welker	8	131	7,226	7,357	33
24. Kevin Faulk	13	3,607	3,701	7,308	33
25. Chris Johnson	4	5,645	1,426	7,071	42

TOP ACTIVE PASS RECEIVERS

	Yrs.	No.	Yards	TD
1. Tony Gonzalez	15	1,149	13,338	95
2. Randy Moss	13	954	14,858	153
3. Reggie Wayne	11	862	11,708	73
4. Chad Ochocinco	11	766	11,059	67
5. Donald Driver	13	735	10,060	59
6. Anquan Boldin	9	707	9,244	54
7. Andre Johnson	9	706	9,656	52
8. Steve Smith	11	699	10,278	59
9. Jason Witten	9	696	7,909	41
10. Larry Fitzgerald	8	693	9,615	73
11. Wes Welker	8	650	7,226	32
12. Santana Moss	11	639	9,142	56
13. T.J. Houshmandzadeh	11	627	7,237	44
14. LaDainian Tomlinson	11	624	4,772	17
15. Antonio Gates	9	593	7,783	76
16. Plaxico Burress	10	550	8,457	63
17. Jeremy Shockey	10	547	6,143	37
18. Roddy White	7	530	7,374	45
19. Deion Branch	10	502	6,499	39
20. Brandon Marshall	6	494	6,247	34
21. Todd Heap	11	491	5,775	42
22. Marques Colston	6	449	6,240	48
23. Jabar Gaffney	10	443	5,622	24
24. Kellen Winslow	7	437	4,836	23
25. Kevin Faulk	13	431	3,701	15

TOP ACTIVE INTERCEPTORS

	Yrs.	No.	Yards	TD
1. Ed Reed	10	57	1,463	6
2. Charles Woodson	14	54	896	11
3. Champ Bailey	13	50	446	4
4. Asante Samuel	9	45	617	5
5. Ronde Barber	15	43	763	7
6. Brian Dawkins	16	37	513	2
7. Nate Clements	11	35	487	5
DeAngelo Hall	8	35	727	3
9. Terence Newman	9	32	345	3
10. Ray Lewis	16	31	503	3
11. Deon Grant	11	30	267	0
Rashean Mathis	9	30	512	3
Charles Tillman	9	30	535	5
14. Troy Polamalu	9	29	361	2
15. Chris Gamble	8	27	326	2
16. Adrian Wilson	11	26	510	2
17. Oshiomogho Atogwe	7	25	382	1
18. Antoine Winfield	13	24	222	2
19. Sheldon Brown	10	23	399	3
20. Antonio Cromartie	6	22	407	2
21. Nick Collins	7	21	507	4
Al Harris	14	21	407	3
Marcus Trufant	9	21	370	2
Brian Urlacher	12	21	278	1
25. Phillip Buchanon	10	20	432	5
Leon Hall	5	20	184	1
Chris Hope	10	20	367	1
Tramon Williams	5	20	373	1

TOP ACTIVE PUNT RETURNERS
40 or more punt returns

	Yrs.	No.	Yards	Avg.	TD
1. Patrick Peterson	1	44	699	15.9	4
2. Devin Hester	6	206	2,654	12.9	12
3. Julian Edelman	3	55	680	12.4	2
4. Roscoe Parrish	7	135	1,622	12.0	3
5. Eddie Royal	4	81	967	11.9	2
6. Santana Moss	11	112	1,268	11.3	3
7. Danny Amendola	3	72	812	11.3	0
8. Marc Mariani	2	73	819	11.2	2
9. Ted Ginn	5	98	1,099	11.2	3
10. Domenik Hixon	5	51	561	11.0	1
11. Josh Cribbs	7	157	1,697	10.8	3
12. Eric Weems	5	77	815	10.6	1
13. DeSean Jackson	4	116	1,226	10.6	4
14. Brandon Tate	3	52	547	10.5	1
15. Davone Bess	4	111	1,166	10.5	0
16. Leon Washington	6	127	1,312	10.3	0
17. Javier Arenas	2	71	732	10.3	0
18. Brandon Banks	2	74	759	10.3	0
19. Jacoby Jones	5	179	1,820	10.2	3
20. Wes Welker	8	216	2,174	10.1	0
21. Jim Leonhard	7	82	820	10.0	0
22. Quan Cosby	3	97	968	10.0	0
23. Adam Jones	5	91	907	10.0	4
24. Nate Clements	11	82	816	10.0	2
25. Captain Munnerlyn	3	61	605	9.9	0

TOP ACTIVE PUNTERS
50 or more punts

	Yrs.	No.	Avg.	LG
1. Shane Lechler	12	933	47.6	80
2. Britton Colquitt	7	187	46.1	66
3. Thomas Morstead	3	161	45.8	64
4. Andy Lee	8	723	45.7	82
5. Brandon Fields	5	377	45.7	71
6. Donnie Jones	8	648	45.3	80
7. Mat McBriar	8	494	45.3	75
8. Jon Ryan	6	483	45.0	77
9. Zoltan Mesko	2	115	44.8	65
10. Mike Scifres	9	492	44.8	71
11. Tim Masthay	2	126	44.6	71
12. Pat McAfee	3	217	44.5	66
13. Dustin Colquitt	7	574	44.4	81
14. Chris Kluwe	7	551	44.4	70
15. Brett Hartmann	1	58	44.4	69
16. Brett Kern	4	273	44.4	68
17. Ben Graham	7	462	44.2	69
18. Sam Koch	6	475	44.2	74
19. Brian Moorman	11	847	43.9	84
20. Daniel Sepulveda	4	221	43.7	66
21. Steve Weatherford	6	445	43.4	66
22. Kevin Huber	3	248	43.3	72
23. Jeremy Kapinos	5	140	43.2	59
24. Dave Zastudil	9	668	43.0	67
25. Adam Podlesh	5	318	42.9	76

TOP ACTIVE KICKOFF RETURNERS
40 or more kickoff returns

	Yrs.	No.	Yards	Avg.	TD
1. Johnny Knox	3	55	1,506	27.4	1
2. Danieal Manning	6	114	3,067	26.9	1
3. Percy Harvin	3	98	2,609	26.6	4
4. Terrence McGee	9	207	5,450	26.3	5
5. Stefan Logan	3	143	3,746	26.2	1
6. Quintin Demps	4	63	1,638	26.0	1
Maurice Jones-Drew	6	79	2,054	26.0	2
8. Leodis McKelvin	4	73	1,897	26.0	1
9. Antonio Brown	2	44	1,134	25.8	1
10. Josh Cribbs	7	344	8,837	25.7	8
11. Eric Weems	5	113	2,896	25.6	1
12. Leon Washington	6	217	5,531	25.5	7
13. Jerious Norwood	6	145	3,695	25.5	0
14. Darren Sproles	6	298	7,558	25.4	2
15. Jacoby Ford	2	64	1,621	25.3	4
16. Brad Smith	6	89	2,250	25.3	3
17. LaRod Stephens-Howling	3	145	3,662	25.3	3
18. Michael Turner	8	44	1,111	25.3	0
19. Micheal Spurlock	5	73	1,830	25.1	2
20. Adam Jones	5	77	1,925	25.0	0
21. Courtney Roby	6	121	3,007	24.9	1
22. Brandon Tate	3	87	2,161	24.8	2
23. Marc Mariani	2	92	2,278	24.8	1
24. Deji Karim	2	77	1,900	24.7	0
25. Josh Wilson	5	100	2,467	24.7	1

TOP ACTIVE QUARTERBACK SACKERS

	Yrs.	No.
1. John Abraham	12	112.0
2. Jared Allen	8	105.0
3. Dwight Freeney	10	102.5
4. Julius Peppers	10	100.0
5. DeMarcus Ware	7	99.5
6. Joey Porter	13	98.0
7. Robert Mathis	9	83.5
8. Terrell Suggs	9	82.5
9. Andre Carter	11	76.0
10. Shaun Ellis	12	73.5
11. Justin Smith	11	72.5
12. Osi Umenyiora	8	69.0
13. Trent Cole	7	68.0
14. James Hall	12	63.0
15. Vonnie Holliday	14	62.5
16. Will Smith	8	61.5
17. Shaun Phillips	8	60.0
18. James Harrison	9	58.0
Aaron Kampman	10	58.0
20. Richard Seymour	11	54.5
Kyle Vanden Bosch	10	54.5
Kevin Williams	9	54.5
23. Tamba Hali	12	53.5
24. Mario Williams	6	53.0
25. Elvis Dumervil	5	52.5

The **New York Giants** need five regular-season victories to become the third team in NFL history with 650 regular-season victories. The Giants (645-531-33) would join Chicago (712-520-42) and Green Bay (679-525-36) as the only teams to accomplish the feat.

The **Pittsburgh Steelers** need nine victories to become the first AFC team to reach 600 total victories. Pittsburgh's all-time record is 591-538-21.

The **Arizona Cardinals** need four regular-season victories to reach 500 regular-season victories. Arizona's all-time regular season record is 496-689-39.

The **San Diego Chargers** need eight regular-season victories to reach 400 total regular-season victories. San Diego's all-time regular-season record is 392-385-11.

The **Chargers** need to score a touchdown in their next game to join Cleveland (166 games from 1957-1969) as the only teams in NFL history to score a touchdown in 150 consecutive games. San Diego has scored a touchdown in each of its past 149 games.

Bill Belichick, New England, needs 14 victories to surpass Chuck Knox (193), Dan Reeves (201) and Marty Schottenheimer (205) for sixth place all-time in career victories. In 17 seasons, Belichick has 192 career victories.

Mike Shanahan, Washington, needs 10 victories to surpass Bud Grant (168), Paul Brown (170), Joe Gibbs (171) and Mike Holmgren (174) for 11th place all-time in career victories. In 18 seasons, Shanahan has 165 career victories.

Jeff Fisher, St. Louis, needs three victories to become the 20th coach in NFL history to win 150 games. In 17 seasons, Fisher has 147 career victories.

Peyton Manning, Denver, needs 4,000 passing yards to become the first player in NFL history with 12 4,000-yard seasons. Manning is the only quarterback to accomplish the feat in 11 seasons.

Manning needs 22 touchdown passes to surpass Dan Marino (420) for second place all-time. In 14 seasons, Manning has thrown 399 touchdown passes.

Manning needs 286 pass completions to surpass Dan Marino (4,967) for second place all-time. In 14 seasons, Manning has 4,682 completions.

Manning has 22 games with four or more touchdown passes and needs two such games to surpass Brett Favre (23) for the most games with four touchdown passes in NFL history.

Manning has passed for 300 yards in a game 63 times in his career, tied with Dan Marino for the most all-time. Manning needs one 300-yard passing game to attain sole possession of first place (see Brees note).

Manning has led the league in touchdown passes three times in his career and can tie Len Dawson, Brett Favre, Johnny Unitas and Steve Young (4) for the most seasons leading the league in touchdown passes (see Brady and Brees notes).

Drew Brees, New Orleans, needs to throw a touchdown pass in each of his next five games to surpass Johnny Unitas (47) for the most consecutive games with a touchdown pass in NFL history. Brees has thrown a touchdown pass in each of his past 43 games.

Brees can extend his NFL-record streak of consecutive games with 300 passing yards. He has passed for 300 yards in each of his past seven games, the longest streak in NFL history.

Brees needs four touchdown passes in each of his next three games to surpass Dan Marino and Peyton Manning (5) for the most consecutive games with four touchdown passes in NFL history. Brees has passed for at least four touchdowns in each of his past three games.

Brees needs 4,000 passing yards to join Peyton Manning (11) as the only players in NFL history with at least seven 4,000-yard passing seasons. In 11 seasons, Brees has six 4,000-yard passing seasons, which is currently tied with Brett Favre and Dan

Marino for the second most all-time.

Brees needs to pass for 300 yards in seven games to surpass Brett Favre (62), Peyton Manning (63) and Dan Marino (63) for the most 300-yard passing games in NFL history (see Manning note). In 11 seasons, Brees has 57 300-yard passing games.

Brees has led the league in touchdown passes three times in his career and can tie Len Dawson, Brett Favre, Johnny Unitas and Steve Young (4) for the most seasons leading the league in touchdown passes (see Brady and Manning notes).

Breeds needs 20 touchdown passes to surpass Johnny Unitas (290), Warren Moon (291), Tom Brady (300) and John Elway (300) for fifth place all-time (see Brady note). In 11 seasons, Brees has 281 touchdown passes.

Brees needs 387 completions to become the fifth player in history with 4,000 career completions. In 11 seasons, Brees has 3,613 completions.

Brees needs 3,870 passing yards to surpass Kerry Collins (40,922), Dan Fouts (43,040) and Drew Bledsoe (44,611) for eighth place all-time (see Brady note). In 11 seasons, Brees has 40,742 passing yards.

Tom Brady, New England, has led the league in touchdown passes three times in his career and can tie Len Dawson, Brett Favre, Johnny Unitas and Steve Young (4) for the most seasons leading the league in touchdown passes (see Brees and Manning notes).

Brady has 300 career touchdown passes, tied with John Elway for the fifth most all-time. He needs one touchdown pass to earn sole possession of fifth place (see Brees note).

Brady needs 4,000 passing yards to join Drew Brees (6), Brett Favre (6), Dan Marino (6) and Peyton Manning (11) as the only players in NFL history with at least five 4,000-yard passing seasons (see Rivers note). In 12 seasons, Brady has four 4,000-yard passing seasons.

Brady needs 4,633 passing yards to surpass Drew Brees (40,742), Kerry Collins (40,922), Dan Fouts (43,040) and Drew Bledsoe (44,611) for eighth place all-time (see Brees note). In 12 seasons, Brady has 39,979 passing yards.

Philip Rivers, San Diego, has led the league in average yards per pass three times in his career and can join Steve Young (5) and Sid Luckman (7) as the only players in NFL history to do so in at least four seasons.

Rivers needs 4,000 passing yards to join Drew Brees (6), Brett Favre (6), Dan Marino (6) and Peyton Manning (11) as the only players in NFL history with at least five 4,000-yard passing seasons (see Brady note). In eight seasons, Rivers has four 4,000-yard passing seasons.

LaDainian Tomlinson needs five rushing touchdowns to become the second player with 150 rushing touchdowns. Tomlinson has scored 145 rushing touchdowns and would join Emmitt Smith (164) as the only players to accomplish the feat.

Tomlinson needs eight touchdowns to join Jerry Rice (208) and Emmitt Smith (175) as the only players with 170 touchdowns. In 11 seasons, Tomlinson has scored 162 touchdowns.

Tomlinson needs 418 rushing yards to surpass Curtis Martin (14,101) for fourth place all-time. In 11 seasons, Tomlinson has rushed for 13,684 yards.

Tomlinson needs 699 scrimmage yards to surpass Marshall Faulk (19,154) for fourth place all-time. In 11 seasons, Tomlinson has 18,456 scrimmage yards.

Steven Jackson, St. Louis, needs 1,000 rushing yards to join LaDainian Tomlinson (8), Thurman Thomas (8), Curtis Martin (10), Barry Sanders (10) and Emmitt Smith (11) as the only players in NFL history to rush for 1,000 yards in eight consecutive seasons. Jackson has rushed for 1,000 yards in each of the past seven seasons.

Ray Rice, Baltimore, can join Marshall Faulk (4) as the only players in NFL history to record at least 1,000 rushing yards and

700 receiving yards in three different seasons. In four seasons, Rice has accomplished the feat twice.

Tony Gonzalez, Atlanta, needs 51 receptions to join Jerry Rice (1,549) as the only players in NFL history with 1,200 career catches. In 15 seasons, Gonzalez has 1,149 receptions – the most ever by a tight end.

Gonzalez needs 50 receptions to join Jerry Rice (17) as the only players in NFL history with 15 50-reception seasons. Gonzalez is the only player in NFL history with 14 consecutive 50-reception seasons.

Gonzalez needs six touchdown catches to surpass Don Hutson (99), Steve Largent (100) and Tim Brown (100) for sixth place all-time. In 15 seasons, Gonzalez has 95 touchdown catches – the most ever by a tight end.

Gonzalez needs 667 receiving yards to surpass Torry Holt (13,382), Henry Ellard (13,777), Cris Carter (13,899) and James Lofton (14,004) for seventh place all-time. In 15 seasons, Gonzalez has 13,338 receiving yards – the most ever by a tight end.

Randy Moss, San Francisco, needs seven receiving touchdowns to become the second player in NFL history with 160 touchdown catches. Moss can join Jerry Rice (197) as the only players in NFL history with 160 receiving touchdowns. In 13 seasons, Moss has 153 touchdown receptions.

Moss needs six touchdowns to become the fourth player with 160 touchdowns. Moss would join Jerry Rice (208), Emmitt Smith (175) and LaDainian Tomlinson (162) as the only players to accomplish the feat. In 13 seasons, Moss has scored 154 touchdowns.

Moss needs 351 receiving yards to surpass Tim Brown (14,934) and Isaac Bruce (15,208) for third place all-time. In 13 seasons, Moss has 14,858 receiving yards.

Moss needs 46 receptions to become the ninth player in NFL history with 1,000 receptions. In 13 seasons, Moss has 954 receptions.

Moss has recorded 1,000 receiving yards in a season 10 times in his 13-year NFL career. Moss can join Jerry Rice (14) as the only players in NFL history with 11 seasons with 1,000 receiving yards.

Wes Welker, New England, needs 100 receptions to become the first player in NFL history with five 100-catch seasons. Welker, Marvin Harrison and Jerry Rice are the only players with four 100-reception seasons.

Welker has led the league in receptions three times and can join Lionel Taylor (5) and Don Hutson (8) as the only players to lead the league in receptions at least four times.

Welker needs three games with 10 receptions and 100 receiving yards to become the NFL's all-time career leader. Welker has 13 games with at least 10 catches and 100 receiving yards in his career and can surpass Andre Johnson (14), Marvin Harrison (14) and Jerry Rice (15) for the most such games in NFL history (see Johnson note).

Andre Johnson, Houston, needs 1,500 receiving yards to join Marvin Harrison (3) and Jerry Rice (4) as the only players with three 1,500-yard seasons.

Johnson needs two games with 10 receptions and 100 receiving yards to become the NFL's all-time career leader. Johnson has 14 games with at least 10 catches and 100 receiving yards in his career and can surpass Marvin Harrison (14) and Jerry Rice (15) for the most such games in NFL history (see Welker note).

Johnson needs 100 receptions to become the fourth player in NFL history with four 100-catch seasons. Johnson can join Marvin Harrison, Jerry Rice and Wes Welker as the only players with four 100-reception seasons (see Marshall and Wayne notes).

Brandon Marshall, Chicago, needs 100 receptions to become the fourth player in NFL history with four 100-catch seasons.

Marshall can join Marvin Harrison, Jerry Rice and Wes Welker as the only players with four 100-reception seasons (see Johnson and Wayne notes).

Reggie Wayne, Indianapolis, needs 100 receptions to become the fourth player in NFL history with four 100-catch seasons. Wayne can join Marvin Harrison, Jerry Rice and Wes Welker as the only players with four 100-reception seasons (see Johnson and Marshall notes).

Rob Gronkowski, New England, can become the first tight end in NFL history to score 10 touchdowns in three consecutive seasons. Gronkowski and Antonio Gates are the only tight ends to accomplish the feat in back-to-back seasons.

Ray Lewis, Baltimore, needs 28 interception-return yards to surpass Derrick Brooks (530) for the most interception-return yards all-time by a linebacker. In 16 seasons, Lewis has 503 interception-return yards.

Ed Reed, Baltimore, needs 21 interception-return yards to surpass Rod Woodson (1,483) for the most all-time. In 10 seasons, Reed has 1,463 interception-return yards.

Reed is tied with Everson Walls (3) for the most seasons leading the league in interceptions and can become the first player in NFL history to lead the league in INTs four times.

Reed needs seven interceptions to surpass Everson Walls (57), Johnny Robinson (57), Eugene Robinson (57), Bobby Boyd (57), Mel Blount (57), Emmitt Thomas (58), Dick LeBeau (62), Dave Brown (62), Darren Sharper (63) and Ronnie Lott (63) to move into sixth place all-time. In 10 seasons, Reed has 57 interceptions.

Charles Woodson, Green Bay, needs two interception-return touchdowns to surpass Darren Sharper (11) and Rod Woodson (12) for the most all-time. In 14 seasons, Woodson has 11 interception-return touchdowns.

Jared Allen, Minnesota, has led the league in sacks twice in his career and can become the first player to lead the league three times since the sack became an official statistic in 1982 (see Ware note).

Allen, who led the league in sacks in 2011, can join Mark Gastineau and Reggie White as the only players to lead the NFL in sacks in back-to-back years since 1982.

DeMarcus Ware, Dallas, has led the league in sacks twice in his career and can become the first player to lead the league three times since the sack became an official statistic in 1982 (see Allen note).

Devin Hester, Chicago, needs two return touchdowns to surpass Deion Sanders (19) for the most all-time. In six seasons, Hester has 18 return touchdowns (12 punt return, five kickoff return, one missed field goal return).

Joshua Cribbs, Cleveland, needs two kickoff-return touchdowns to become the first player in history with 10 kickoff return TDs (see Washington note). In seven seasons, Cribbs is the all-time leader with eight kickoff-return touchdowns.

Cribbs needs 1,864 total return yards to surpass Desmond Howard (10,854) and Dante Hall (12,397) for fifth place all-time. In seven seasons, Cribbs has 10,534 total return yards.

Leon Washington, Seattle, needs two kickoff-return touchdowns to surpass Joshua Cribbs (8) for the most all-time (see Cribbs note). In six seasons, Washington has seven kickoff return TDs.

Jason Hanson, Detroit, needs 47 points to surpass John Carney (2,062) for third place all-time (see Kasay note). In 20 seasons, Hanson has 2,016 points.

John Kasay, New Orleans, needs 93 points to surpass Jason Elam (1,983), George Blanda (2,002), Matt Stover (2,004), Jason Hanson (2,016) and John Carney (2,062) for third place all-time (see Hanson note). In 20 seasons, Kasay has 1,970 points.

ACTIVE COACHES' CAREER RECORDS (Order Based on Career Victories)
Start of 2012 Season

Coach	Team(s)	Yrs.	Regular Season Won	Lost	Tied	Pct.	Postseason Won	Lost	Pct.	Career Won	Lost	Tied	Pct.
Bill Belichick	Cleveland Browns, New England Patriots	17	175	97	0	.643	17	7	.708	192	104	0	.649
Mike Shanahan	Los Angeles Raiders, Denver Broncos, Washington Redskins	18	157	119	0	.569	8	5	.615	165	124	0	.571
Tom Coughlin	Jacksonville Jaguars, New York Giants	16	142	114	0	.555	12	7	.632	154	121	0	.560
Jeff Fisher	Houston/Tennessee Oilers, Tennessee Titans, St. Louis Rams	17	142	120	0	.542	5	6	.455	147	126	0	.538
Andy Reid	Philadelphia Eagles	13	126	81	1	.608	10	9	.526	136	90	1	.601
Norv Turner	Washington Redskins, Oakland Raiders, San Diego Chargers	14	107	113	1	.486	4	4	.500	111	117	1	.487
John Fox	Carolina Panthers, Denver Broncos	10	81	79	0	.506	6	4	.600	87	83	0	.512
Lovie Smith	Chicago Bears	8	71	57	0	.555	3	3	.500	74	60	0	.552
Marvin Lewis	Cincinnati Bengals	9	69	74	1	.483	0	3	.000	69	77	1	.473
Mike McCarthy	Green Bay Packers	6	63	33	0	.656	5	3	.625	68	36	0	.654
Sean Payton	New Orleans Saints	6	62	34	0	.646	5	3	.625	67	37	0	.644
Mike Tomlin	Pittsburgh Steelers	5	55	25	0	.688	5	3	.625	60	28	0	.682
John Harbaugh	Baltimore Ravens	4	44	20	0	.688	5	4	.556	49	24	0	.671
Pete Carroll	New York Jets, New England Patriots, Seattle Seahawks	6	47	49	0	.490	2	3	.400	49	52	0	.485
Gary Kubiak	Houston Texans	6	47	49	0	.490	1	1	.500	48	50	0	.490
Ken Whisenhunt	Arizona Cardinals	5	40	40	0	.500	4	2	.667	44	42	0	.512
Mike Smith	Atlanta Falcons	4	43	21	0	.672	0	3	.000	43	24	0	.642
Rex Ryan	New York Jets	3	28	20	0	.583	4	2	.667	32	22	0	.593
Chan Gailey	Dallas Cowboys, Buffalo Bills	4	28	36	0	.438	0	2	.000	28	38	0	.424
Romeo Crennel	Cleveland Browns, Kansas City Chiefs	5	26	41	0	.388	0	0	---	26	41	0	.388
Jim Schwartz	Detroit Lions	3	18	30	0	.375	0	1	.000	18	31	0	.367
Jim Harbaugh	San Francisco 49ers	1	13	3	0	.813	1	1	.500	14	4	0	.778
Mike Mularkey	Buffalo Bills, Jacksonville Jaguars	2	14	18	0	.438	0	0	---	14	18	0	.438
Jason Garrett	Dallas Cowboys	2	13	11	0	.542	0	0	---	13	11	0	.542
Mike Munchak	Tennessee Titans	1	9	7	0	.563	0	0	---	9	7	0	.563
Ron Rivera	Carolina Panthers	1	6	10	0	.375	0	0	---	6	10	0	.375
Leslie Frazier	Minnesota Vikings	2	6	16	0	.273	0	0	---	6	16	0	.273
Pat Shurmur	Cleveland Browns	1	4	12	0	.250	0	0	---	4	12	0	.250
Dennis Allen	Oakland Raiders	0	0	0	0	---	0	0	---	0	0	0	---
Chuck Pagano	Indianapolis Colts	0	0	0	0	---	0	0	---	0	0	0	---
Joe Philbin	Miami Dolphins	0	0	0	0	---	0	0	---	0	0	0	---
Greg Schiano	Tampa Bay Buccaneers	0	0	0	0	---	0	0	---	0	0	0	---

COACHES WITH 100 CAREER VICTORIES (Order Based on Career Victories)
Start of 2012 Season

Coach	Team(s)	Yrs.	Won	Lost	Tied	Pct.	Won	Lost	Pct.	Won	Lost	Tied	Pct.
			Regular Season				**Postseason**			**Career**			
1. Don Shula	Baltimore Colts, Miami Dolphins	33	328	156	6	.677	19	17	.528	347	173	6	.666
2. George Halas	Chicago Bears	40	318	148	31	.682	6	3	.667	324	151	31	.682
3. Tom Landry	Dallas Cowboys	29	250	162	6	.607	20	16	.556	270	178	6	.603
4. Earl (Curly) Lambeau	Green Bay Packers, Chicago Cardinals, Washington Redskins	33	226	132	22	.631	3	2	.600	229	134	22	.631
5. Chuck Noll	Pittsburgh Steelers	23	193	148	1	.566	16	8	.667	209	156	1	.572
6. Marty Schottenheimer	Cleveland Browns, Kansas City Chiefs, Washington Redskins, San Diego Chargers	21	200	126	1	.613	5	13	.278	205	139	1	.596
7. Dan Reeves	Denver Broncos, New York Giants, Atlanta Falcons	23	190	165	2	.535	11	9	.550	201	174	2	.536
8. Chuck Knox	Los Angeles Rams, Buffalo Bills, Seattle Seahawks	22	186	147	1	.558	7	11	.389	193	158	1	.550
9. **Bill Belichick**	Cleveland Browns, New England Patriots	17	175	97	0	.643	17	7	.708	192	104	0	.649
10. Bill Parcells	New York Giants, New England Patriots, New York Jets, Dallas Cowboys	19	172	130	1	.569	11	8	.579	183	138	1	.570
11. Mike Holmgren	Green Bay Packers, Seattle Seahawks	17	161	111	0	.592	13	11	.542	174	122	0	.588
12. Joe Gibbs	Washington Redskins	16	154	94	0	.621	17	7	.708	171	101	0	.629
13. Paul Brown	Cleveland Browns, Cincinnati Bengals	21	166	100	6	.624	4	8	.333	170	108	6	.612
14. Bud Grant	Minnesota Vikings	18	158	96	5	.621	10	12	.455	168	108	5	.608
15. **Mike Shanahan**	Los Angeles Raiders, Denver Broncos, Washington Redskins	18	157	119	0	.569	8	5	.615	165	124	0	.571
16. Bill Cowher	Pittsburgh Steelers	15	149	90	1	.623	12	9	.571	161	99	1	.619
17. Marv Levy	Kansas City Chiefs, Buffalo Bills	17	143	112	0	.561	11	8	.579	154	120	0	.562
Tom Coughlin	Jacksonville Jaguars, New York Giants	16	142	114	0	.555	12	7	.632	154	121	0	.560
19. Steve Owen	New York Giants	23	151	100	17	.602	2	8	.200	153	108	17	.586
20. Tony Dungy	Tampa Bay Buccaneers, Indianapolis Colts	13	139	69	0	.668	9	10	.474	148	79	0	.652
21. **Jeff Fisher**	Houston/Tennessee Oilers, Tennessee Titans, St. Louis Rams	17	142	120	0	.542	5	6	.455	147	126	0	.539
22. **Andy Reid**	Philadelphia Eagles	13	126	81	1	.608	10	9	.526	136	90	1	.601
Hank Stram	Kansas City Chiefs, New Orleans Saints	17	131	97	10	.574	5	3	.625	136	100	10	.576
24. Weeb Ewbank	Baltimore Colts, New York Jets	20	130	129	7	.502	4	1	.800	134	130	7	.508
25. Mike Ditka	Chicago Bears, New Orleans Saints	14	121	95	0	.560	6	6	.500	127	101	0	.557
26. Dick Vermeil	Philadelphia Eagles, St. Louis Rams, Kansas City Chiefs	15	120	109	0	.524	6	5	.545	126	114	0	.525
27. Jim Mora	New Orleans Saints, Indianapolis Colts	15	125	106	0	.541	0	6	.000	125	112	0	.527
28. George Seifert	San Francisco 49ers, Carolina Panthers	11	114	62	0	.648	10	5	.667	124	67	0	.649
29. Sid Gillman	Los Angeles Rams, Los Angeles-San Diego Chargers, Houston Oilers	18	122	99	7	.552	1	5	.167	123	104	7	.542
30. George Allen	Los Angeles Rams, Washington Redskins	12	116	47	5	.712	2	7	.222	118	54	5	.686
31. Dennis Green	Minnesota Vikings, Arizona Cardinals	13	113	94	0	.546	4	8	.333	117	102	0	.534
32. Don Coryell	St. Louis Cardinals, San Diego Chargers	14	111	83	1	.572	3	6	.333	114	89	1	.561
33. John Madden	Oakland Raiders	10	103	32	7	.759	9	7	.563	112	39	7	.739
34. **Norv Turner**	Washington Redskins, Oakland Raiders, San Diego Chargers	14	107	113	1	.486	4	4	.500	111	117	1	.487
35. Ray (Buddy) Parker	Chicago Cardinals, Detroit Lions, Pittsburgh Steelers	15	104	75	9	.581	3	1	.750	107	76	9	.585
36. Vince Lombardi	Green Bay Packers, Washington Redskins	10	96	34	6	.739	9	1	.900	105	35	6	.750
Tom Flores	Oakland-Los Angeles Raiders, Seattle Seahawks	12	97	87	0	.527	8	3	.727	105	90	0	.538
38. Bill Walsh	San Francisco 49ers	10	92	59	1	.609	10	4	.714	102	63	1	.617
39. Jon Gruden	Oakland Raiders, Tampa Bay Buccaneers	11	95	81	0	.540	5	4	.556	100	85	0	.541

Active coaches in bold.
From 1920-71, tie games were not included in winning percentage.

DRAFT LIST FOR 2012

77th Annual NFL Draft, April 26-28, 2012
+Denotes Compensatory Selection
#Denotes Underclassman Selection

ARIZONA CARDINALS
1. Michael Floyd—13, WR, Notre Dame
3. Jamell Fleming—80, DB, Oklahoma
4.# Bobby Massie—112, T, Mississippi
5. Senio Kelemete—151, G, Washington
6. Justin Bethel—177, DB, Presbyterian, from WASHINGTON
   Ryan Lindley—185, QB, San Diego State
7. Nate Potter—221, T, Boise State

ATLANTA FALCONS
2.# Peter Konz—55, G, Wisconsin
3. Lamar Holmes—91, T, Southern Mississippi,
        from BALTIMORE
5. Bradie Ewing—157, RB, Wisconsin
   Jonathan Massaquoi—164, DE, Troy, from BALTIMORE
6. Charles Mitchell—192, DB, Mississippi State
7.+ Travian Robinson—249, NT, South Carolina

BALTIMORE RAVENS
2. Courtney Upshaw—35, LB, Alabama, from MINNESOTA
   Kelechi Osemele—60, T, Iowa State
3.# Bernard Pierce—84, RB, Temple, from ATLANTA
4. Gino Gradkowski—98, G, Delaware, from MINNESOTA
   + Christian Thompson—130, DB, South Carolina State
5.+ Asa Jackson—169, DB, Cal Poly
6.# Tommy Streeter—198, WR, Miami
7. DeAngelo Tyson—236, DE, Georgia

BUFFALO BILLS
1.# Stephon Gilmore—10, DB, South Carolina
2. Cordy Glenn—41, T, Georgia
3. T.J. Graham—69, WR, North Carolina State,
        from WASHINGTON
4. Nigel Bradham—105, LB, Florida State
   Ron Brooks—124, DB, Louisiana State, from BALTIMORE
5. Zebrie Sanders—144, T, Florida State
   Tank Carder—147, LB, Texas Christian, from SEATTLE
6. Mark Asper—178, G, Oregon
7.+ John Potter—251, K, Western Michigan

CAROLINA PANTHERS
1.# Luke Kuechly—9, LB, Boston College
2. Amini Silatolu—40, G, Midwestern State
4. Frank Alexander—103, DE, Oklahoma,
        from MIAMI through SAN FRANCISCO
   Joe Adams—104, WR, Arkansas
5. Josh Norman—143, DB, Coastal Carolina
6.+ Brad Nortman—207, P, Wisconsin
7. D.J. Campbell—216, DB, California

CHICAGO BEARS
1. Shea McClellin—19, DE, Boise State
2.# Alshon Jeffery—45, WR, South Carolina,
        from DALLAS through ST. LOUIS
3. Brandon Hardin—79, DB, Oregon State
4. Evan Rodriguez—111, TE, Temple
6. Isaiah Frey—184, DB, Nevada
7. Greg McCoy—220, DB, Texas Christian

CINCINNATI BENGALS
1.# Dre Kirkpatrick—17, DB, Alabama, from OAKLAND
   Kevin Zeitler—27, G, Wisconsin,
        from NEW ORLEANS through NEW ENGLAND
2. Devon Still—53, DT, Penn State
3.# Mohamed Sanu—83, WR, Rutgers
   Brandon Thompson—93, DT, Clemson,
        from NEW ENGLAND
4.# Orson Charles—116, TE, Georgia
5. Shaun Prater—156, DB, Iowa
   Marvin Jones—166, WR, California, from NEW ENGLAND
   George Iloka—167, DB, Boise State,
        from NEW YORK GIANTS
6. Dan Herron—191, RB, Ohio State

CLEVELAND BROWNS
1.# Trent Richardson—3, RB, Alabama, from MINNESOTA
   Brandon Weeden—22, QB, Oklahoma State, from ATLANTA
2. Mitchell Schwartz—37, T, California
3. John Hughes—87, DT, Cincinnati, from DENVER
4. Travis Benjamin—100, WR, Miami
   James-Michael Johnson—120, LB, Nevada, from DENVER
5. Ryan Miller—160, T, Colorado
6.+ Emmanuel Acho—204, LB, Texas
   + Billy Winn—205, DT, Boise State
7.+ Trevin Wade—245, DB, Arizona
   + Brad Smelley—247, RB, Alabama

DALLAS COWBOYS
1.# Morris Claiborne—6, DB, Louisiana State,
        from WASHINGTON through ST. LOUIS
3. Tyrone Crawford—81, DE, Boise State
4. Kyle Wilber—113, DE, Wake Forest
   + Matt Johnson—135, DB, Eastern Washington
5. Danny Coale—152, WR, Virginia Tech
6. James Hanna—186, TE, Oklahoma
7. Caleb McSurdy—222, LB, Montana

DENVER BRONCOS
2. Derek Wolfe—36, DT, Cincinnati, from TAMPA BAY
   # Brock Osweiler—57, QB, Arizona State
3.# Ronnie Hillman—67, RB, San Diego State,
        from CLEVELAND
4. Omar Bolden—101, DB, Arizona State,
        from JACKSONVILLE through TAMPA BAY
   Philip Blake—108, C, Baylor, from NEW YORK JETS
5. Malik Jackson—137, DE, Tennessee, from ST. LOUIS
6. Danny Trevathan—188, LB, Kentucky,
        from NEW YORK JETS

DETROIT LIONS
1.# Riley Reiff—23, T, Iowa
2. Ryan Broyles—54, WR, Oklahoma
3. Dwight Bentley—85, DB, Louisiana-Lafayette
4.# Ronnell Lewis—125, DE, Oklahoma, from SAN FRANCISCO
5. Tahir Whitehead—138, LB, Temple, from MINNESOTA
   Chris Greenwood—148, DB, Albion, from OAKLAND
6. Jonte Green—196, DB, New Mexico State,
        from NEW ORLEANS through MIAMI
        and SAN FRANCISCO
7. Travis Lewis—223, LB, Oklahoma,
        from PHILADELPHIA through NEW ENGLAND
        and MINNESOTA

GREEN BAY PACKERS
1.# Nick Perry—28, LB, Southern California
2.# Jerel Worthy—51, DE, Michigan State,
      from ARIZONA through PHILADELPHIA
    Casey Hayward—62, DB, Vanderbilt, from NEW ENGLAND
4.+ Mike Daniels—132, DE, Iowa
  + Jerron McMillian—133, DB, Maine
5.# Terrell Manning—163, LB, North Carolina State,
      reacquired through NEW ENGLAND
7.+ Andrew Datko—241, T, Florida State
  + B.J. Coleman—243, QB, Tennessee-Chattanooga

HOUSTON TEXANS
1.# Whitney Mercilus—26, LB, Illinois
3. DeVier Posey—68, WR, Ohio State, from TAMPA BAY
    Brandon Brooks—76, G, Miami (OH), from PHILADELPHIA
4. Ben Jones—99, C, Georgia,
      from TAMPA BAY through PHILADELPHIA
    Keshawn Martin—121, WR, Michigan State
    Jared Crick—126, DE, Nebraska,
      from NEW ENGLAND through DENVER
      and TAMPA BAY
5. Randy Bullock—161, K, Texas A&M
6. Nick Mondek—195, T, Purdue

INDIANAPOLIS COLTS
1.# Andrew Luck—1, QB, Stanford
2. Coby Fleener—34, TE, Stanford
3.# Dwayne Allen—64, TE, Clemson
    T.Y. Hilton—92, WR, Florida International,
      from SAN FRANCISCO
5. Josh Chapman—136, DT, Alabama
  + Vick Ballard—170, RB, Mississippi State
6.+ LaVon Brazill—206, WR, Ohio
7. Justin Anderson—208, G, Georgia
    Tim Fugger—214, LB, Vanderbilt,
      from JACKSONVILLE through NEW YORK JETS
  + Chandler Harnish—253, QB, Northern Illinois

JACKSONVILLE JAGUARS
1.# Justin Blackmon—5, WR, Oklahoma State,
      from TAMPA BAY
2. Andre Branch—38, DE, Clemson
3. Bryan Anger—70, P, California
5. Brandon Marshall—142, LB, Nevada
6. Mike Harris—176, DB, Florida State
7. Jeris Pendleton—228, DT, Ashland, from CINCINNATI

KANSAS CITY CHIEFS
1.# Dontari Poe—11, NT, Memphis
2. Jeff Allen—44, T, Illinois
3. Donald Stephenson—74, T, Oklahoma
4. Devon Wylie—107, WR, Fresno State
5. DeQuan Menzie—146, DB, Alabama
6. Cyrus Gray—182, RB, Texas A&M
7. Jerome Long—218, DT, San Diego State
    Junior Hemingway—238, WR, Michigan,
      from NEW ENGLAND

MIAMI DOLPHINS
1. Ryan Tannehill—8, QB, Texas A&M
2.# Jonathan Martin—42, T, Stanford
3.# Olivier Vernon—72, DE, Miami
    Michael Egnew—78, TE, Missouri, from SAN DIEGO
4.# Lamar Miller—97, RB, Miami,
      from INDIANAPOLIS through SAN FRANCISCO
5. Josh Kaddu—155, LB, Oregon, from TENNESSEE
6. B.J. Cunningham—183, WR, Michigan State,
      from SAN DIEGO
7. Kheeston Randall—215, DT, Texas
    Rishard Matthews—227, WR, Nevada, from TENNESSEE

MINNESOTA VIKINGS
1.# Matt Kalil—4, T, Southern California, from CLEVELAND
    Harrison Smith—29, DB, Notre Dame, from BALTIMORE
3.# Josh Robinson—66, DB, Central Florida
4. Jarius Wright—118, WR, Arkansas,
      from ATLANTA through CLEVELAND
  + Rhett Ellison—128, TE, Southern California
  + Greg Childs—134, WR, Arkansas
5. Robert Blanton—139, DB, Notre Dame, from CLEVELAND
6. Blair Walsh—175, K, Georgia, from CLEVELAND
7. Audie Cole—210, LB, North Carolina State
    Trevor Guyton—219, DT, California,
      from SEATTLE through DETROIT

NEW ENGLAND PATRIOTS
1.# Chandler Jones—21, DE, Syracuse, from CINCINNATI
  # Dont'a Hightower—25, LB, Alabama, from DENVER
2. Tavon Wilson—48, DB, Illinois, from OAKLAND
3. Jake Bequette—90, DE, Arkansas, from GREEN BAY
6. Nate Ebner—197, DB, Ohio State, from GREEN BAY
7. Alfonzo Dennard—224, DB, Nebraska,
      from NEW YORK JETS through GREEN BAY
    Jeremy Ebert—235, WR, Northwestern, from GREEN BAY

NEW ORLEANS SAINTS
3. Akiem Hicks—89, DT, Regina (Canada)
4. Nick Toon—122, WR, Wisconsin
5. Corey White—162, DB, Samford
6. Andrew Tiller—179, G, Syracuse, from MIAMI
7. Marcel Jones—234, T, Nebraska

NEW YORK GIANTS
1.# David Wilson—32, RB, Virginia Tech
2.# Rueben Randle—63, WR, Louisiana State
3.# Jayron Hosley—94, DB, Virginia Tech
4. Adrien Robinson—127, TE, Cincinnati
  + Brandon Mosley—131, T, Auburn
6. Matt McCants—201, T, Alabama-Birmingham
7. Markus Kuhn—239, DT, North Carolina State

DRAFT LIST FOR 2012

NEW YORK JETS
1. Quinton Coples—16, DE, North Carolina
2. #Stephen Hill—43, WR, Georgia Tech, from SEATTLE
3. Demario Davis—77, LB, Arkansas State
6. Josh Bush—187, DB, Wake Forest,
   from PHILADELPHIA through INDIANAPOLIS
   + Terrance Ganaway—202, RB, Baylor
   + Robert Griffin—203, G, Baylor
7. +Antonio Allen—242, DB, South Carolina
   + Jordan White—244, WR, Western Michigan

OAKLAND RAIDERS
3. Choice Exercised in 2011 Supplemental Draft
   for Terrelle Pryor, QB, Ohio State
   + Tony Bergstrom—95, G, Utah
4. +Miles Burris—129, LB, San Diego State
5. Jack Crawford—158, DE, Penn State, from DETROIT
   + Juron Criner—168, WR, Arizona
6. Christo Bilukidi—189, DT, Georgia State
7. Nathan Stupar—230, LB, Penn State, from DETROIT

PHILADELPHIA EAGLES
1. #Fletcher Cox—12, DT, Mississippi State, from SEATTLE
2. Mychal Kendricks—46, LB, California
   Vinny Curry—59, DE, Marshall, from GREEN BAY
3. Nick Foles—88, QB, Arizona, from HOUSTON
4. Brandon Boykin—123, DB, Georgia, from GREEN BAY
5. Dennis Kelly—153, T, Purdue
6. Marvin McNutt—194, WR, Iowa, from DENVER
   # Brandon Washington—200, G, Miami, from NEW ENGLAND
7. #Bryce Brown—229, RB, Kansas State

PITTSBURGH STEELERS
1. #David DeCastro—24, G, Stanford
2. Mike Adams—56, T, Ohio State
3. Sean Spence—86, LB, Miami
4. Alameda Ta'amu—109, DT, Washington,
   from OAKLAND through WASHINGTON
5. Chris Rainey—159, RB, Florida
7. Toney Clemons—231, WR, Colorado
   + David Paulson—240, TE, Oregon
   + Terrence Frederick—246, DB, Texas A&M
   + Kelvin Beachum—248, T, Southern Methodist

ST. LOUIS RAMS
1. #Michael Brockers—14, DT, Louisiana State
2. Brian Quick—33, WR, Appalachian State
   Janoris Jenkins—39, DB, North Alabama,
   from WASHINGTON
   Isaiah Pead—50, RB, Cincinnati, from CHICAGO
3. Trumaine Johnson—65, DB, Montana
4. #Chris Givens—96, WR, Wake Forest
5. Rokevious Watkins—150, G, South Carolina,
   from CHICAGO
6. Greg Zuerlein—171, K, Missouri Western
7. Aaron Brown—209, LB, Hawai'i
   + Daryl Richardson—252, RB, Abilene Christian

SAN DIEGO CHARGERS
1. Melvin Ingram—18, LB, South Carolina
2. Kendall Reyes—49, DE, Connecticut
3. Brandon Taylor—73, DB, Louisiana State
   from CAROLINA through CHICAGO and MIAMI
4. Ladarius Green—110, TE, Louisiana-Lafayette
5. Johnnie Troutman—149, G, Penn State
7. David Molk—226, C, Michigan
#+Edwin Baker—250, RB, Michigan State

SAN FRANCISCO 49ERS
1. A.J. Jenkins—39, WR, Illinois
2. #LaMichael James—61, RB, Oregon
4. Joe Looney—117, G, Wake Forest, from DETROIT
5. Darius Fleming—165, LB, Notre Dame
6. Trenton Robinson—180, DB, Michigan State,
   from CAROLINA
   Jason Slowey—199, T, Western Oregon
7. Cam Johnson—237, LB, Virginia

SEATTLE SEAHAWKS
1. Bruce Irvin—15, DE, West Virginia, from PHILADELPHIA
2. Bobby Wagner—47, LB, Utah State, from NEW YORK JETS
3. Russell Wilson—75, QB, Wisconsin
4. Robert Turbin—106, RB, Utah State
   Jaye Howard—114, DT, Florida, from PHILADELPHIA
5. Korey Toomer—154, LB, Idaho, from NEW YORK JETS
6. Jeremy Lane—172, DB, Northwestern State (LA),
   from INDIANAPOLIS through PHILADELPHIA
   Winston Guy—181, DB, Kentucky
7. J.R. Sweezy—225, T, North Carolina State, from OAKLAND
   Greg Scruggs—232, DE, Louisville,
   from DENVER through NEW YORK JETS

TAMPA BAY BUCCANEERS
1. Mark Barron—7, DB, Alabama, from JACKSONVILLE
   Doug Martin—31, RB, Boise State,
   from NEW ENGLAND through DENVER
2. Lavonte David—58, LB, Nebraska
5. Najee Goode—140, LB, West Virginia
6. Keith Tandy—174, DB, West Virginia
7. Michael Smith—212, RB, Utah State
   Drake Dunsmore—233, TE, Northwestern, from HOUSTON

TENNESSEE TITANS
1. Kendall Wright—20, WR, Baylor
2. Zach Brown—52, LB, North Carolina
3. Mike Martin—82, DT, Michigan
4. Coty Sensabaugh—115, DB, Clemson
5. Taylor Thompson—145, TE, Southern Methodist,
   from MIAMI
6. Markelle Martin—190, DB, Oklahoma State
7. Scott Solomon—211, DE, Rice,
   from CLEVELAND through MINNESOTA

WASHINGTON REDSKINS
1. #Robert Griffin III—2, QB, Baylor, from ST. LOUIS
3. Josh LeRibeus—71, G, Southern Methodist, from BUFFALO
4. Kirk Cousins—102, QB, Michigan State
   Keenan Robinson—119, LB, Texas, from PITTSBURGH
5. Adam Gettis—141, G, Iowa
6. Alfred Morris—173, RB, Florida Atlantic, from MINNESOTA
   Tom Compton—193, T, South Dakota, from PITTSBURGH
7. Richard Crawford—213, DB, Southern Methodist
   Jordan Bernstine—217, DB, Iowa, from BUFFALO

NUMBER OF PLAYERS DRAFTED— 2012

BY POSITION:

Defensive Backs	50
Linebackers	33
Wide Receivers	33
Tackles	24
Defensive Ends	22
Running Backs	21
Defensive Tackles	18
Guards	18
Tight Ends	12
Quarterbacks	11
Kicker	4
Centers	3
Nose Tackles	2
Punters	2

BY COLLEGE:

Alabama	8
Georgia	7
Oklahoma	7
Boise State	6
California	6
Iowa	6
Miami	6
Michigan State	6
South Carolina	6
Wisconsin	6
Baylor	5
Louisiana State	5
North Carolina State	5
Arkansas	4
Cincinnati	4
Clemson	4
Florida State	4
Illinois	4
Nebraska	4
Nevada	4
Notre Dame	4
Ohio State	4
Oregon	4
Penn State	4
San Diego State	4
Southern Methodist	4
Stanford	4
Texas A&M	4
Wake Forest	4
Arizona	3
Michigan	3
Mississippi State	3
Oklahoma State	3
Southern California	3
Temple	3
Texas	3
Utah State	3
Virginia Tech	3
West Virginia	3
Arizona State	2
Colorado	2
Florida	2
Kentucky	2
Louisiana-Lafayette	2
Montana	2
North Carolina	2
Northwestern	2
Purdue	2
Syracuse	2
Texas Christian	2
Vanderbilt	2
Washington	2
Western Michigan	2
Abilene Christian	1
Alabama-Birmingham	1
Albion	1
Appalachian State	1
Arkansas State	1
Ashland	1
Auburn	1
Boston College	1
Cal Poly	1
Central Florida	1
Coastal Carolina	1
Connecticut	1
Delaware	1
Eastern Washington	1
Florida Atlantic	1
Florida International	1
Fresno State	1
Georgia State	1
Georgia Tech	1
Hawai'i	1
Idaho	1
Iowa State	1
Kansas State	1
Louisville	1
Maine	1
Marshall	1
Memphis	1
Miami (Ohio)	1
Midwestern State	1
Mississippi	1
Missouri	1
Missouri Western	1
New Mexico State	1
North Alabama	1
Northern Illinois	1
Northwestern State (LA)	1
Ohio	1
Oregon State	1
Presbyterian	1
Regina (Canada)	1
Rice	1
Rutgers	1
Samford	1
South Carolina State	1
South Dakota	1
Southern Mississippi	1
Tennessee	1
Tennessee-Chattanooga	1
Troy	1
Utah	1
Virginia	1
Western Oregon	1

BY CONFERENCE:

Southeastern	42
Big Ten	41
Atlantic Coast	31
Pacific 12	28
Big 12	25
Big East	12
Mountain West	12
Western Athletic	11
Conference USA	10
Mid-American	8
Sun Belt	6
Independent	5
Big Sky	3
Southern	3
Big South	2
Colonial Athletic	2
Great West Football	2
Lone Star	2
Canada West Universities Athletic	1
Great Lakes Intercollegiate Athletic	1
Great Northwest Athletic	1
Gulf South	1
Michigan Intercollegiate Athletic	1
Mid-America Intercollegiate Athletic	1
Mid-Eastern Athletic	1
Southland	1

UNDERCLASSMEN IN THE DRAFT

Year	D1-FBS	Drafted	In Top 10
1990	28	18	5
1991	23	19	1
1992	30	21	5
1993	34	24	5
1994	31	25	6
1995	33	22	2
1996	24	16	4
1997	34	25	6
1998	32	19	3
1999	31	22	5
2000	26	20	4
2001	35	27	5
2002	38	26	2
2003	47	32	5
2004	43	35	5
2005	51	37	4
2006	52	33	6
2007	40	29	5
2008	53	39	4
2009	46	41	5
2010	53	46	5
2011	56	43	8
2012	65	44	8

The NFL uses a system of Referee Replay Review to aid officiating. The following procedures will be used:

Reviews by Referee: All Replay Reviews will be conducted by the Referee on a field-level monitor after consultation with the other covering official(s), prior to review. A decision will be reversed only when the Referee has indisputable visual evidence available to him that warrants the change.

Coaches' Challenge: In each game, a team will be permitted two challenges that will initiate Instant Replay reviews except for plays when the on-field ruling is a score for either team, an interception, a fumble or backward pass that is recovered by an opponent or goes out of bounds through an opponent's end zone, or a muffed scrimmage kick recovered by the kicking team. A team is also prohibited from challenging any ruling after the two-minute warning of each half, and throughout any overtime period. Each challenge will require the use of a team time out. If a challenge is upheld, the time out will be restored to the challenging team. If both challenges are upheld, a third challenge will be awarded to the challenging team. No challenges will be recognized from a team that has exhausted its time outs.

Replay Official's Request for Review: After all scoring plays, interceptions, fumbles and backward passes that are recovered by an opponent or go out of bounds through an opponent's end zone, muffed scrimmage kicks recovered by the kicking team, and after the two-minute warning of each half throughout any overtime period, any Replay Review will be initiated by a Replay Official from a Replay Booth comparable to the location of the coaches' booth or Press Box. There is no limit to the number of Replay Reviews that may be initiated by the Replay Official. His ability to initiate a review will be unrelated to the number of time outs that either team has remaining, and no time out will be charged for any review initiated by the Replay Official.

Time Limit: Each review will be a maximum of 60 seconds in length, timed from when the Referee begins his review of the replay at the field-level monitor.

Reviewable Plays: The Replay System will cover the following play situations only:

A. Plays governed by Sideline, Goal Line, End Zone, and End Line:
   1. Scoring plays, including a runner breaking the plane of the goal line.
   2. Pass complete/incomplete/intercepted at sideline, goal line, end zone, and end line.
   3. Runner/receiver in or out of bounds.
   4. Recovery of loose ball in or out of bounds.

B. Passing Plays:
   1. Pass ruled complete/incomplete/intercepted in the field of play.
   2. Touching of a forward pass by an ineligible receiver.
   3. Touching of a forward pass by a defensive player.
   4. Quarterback (Passer) forward pass or fumble.
   5. Illegal forward pass beyond the line of scrimmage.
   6. Illegal forward pass after change of possession.
   7. Forward or backward pass thrown from behind the line of scrimmage.

C. Other Reviewable Plays:
   1. Runner not ruled down by defensive contact.
   2. Runner ruled down by defensive contact when the recovery of a fumble by an opponent or a teammate occurs in the action that happens following the fumble.
   3. Runner ruled out of bounds when the recovery of a fumble by an opponent or a teammate occurs in the action that happens following the fumble.
   4. Ruling of incomplete pass when the recovery of a passer's fumble, or the recovery of a backward pass, by an opponent or a teammate occurs in the action following the fumble and backward pass.
   5. Ruling of a loose ball out of bounds when it is recovered in the field of play by an opponent or a teammate in the action after the ball hits the ground.

Note 1: If the ruling of down by contact or incomplete pass is changed, the ball belongs to the recovering player at the spot of the recovery of the fumble, and any advance is nullified. If the ball goes out of bounds in an end zone, the result of the play will be either a touchback or a safety.

Note 2: If the Referee does not have indisputable visual evidence as to which player recovered the loose ball, the ruling on the field will stand.

Note 3: This does not apply to complete/incomplete passes, or the ruling of forward progress.
   6. Forward progress with respect to a first down.
   7. Touching of a kick.
   8. A field goal or Try attempt that crosses below or above the crossbar, inside or outside the uprights when it is lower than the top of the uprights, or touches anything.
   9. Number of players on the field at the snap.
   10. Illegal forward handoff.
   11. A loose ball in play striking a video board, guide wire, sky cam, or any other object.

Non-reviewable plays include, but are not limited to:
1. Status of the clock.
2. Proper down.
3. Penalty administration.
4. Runner ruled down by defensive contact (not involving fumbles).
5. Forward progress not relating to first down or goal line.
6. Recovery of a loose ball that does not involve a boundary line or the end zone.
7. Field goal or try attempts that cross above either upright without touching anything.
8. Inadvertent whistle.

INSTANT REPLAY HISTORY

From 1986-1991, a limited system of Instant Replay was used on a year-by-year basis. Replay also was experimented with during the 1996 and 1998 preseasons. For the 1999 season, the NFL introduced a system of Referee Replay Review to aid officiating. That system was extended on a one-year basis for the 2000 season and then approved for the next three years through 2003. The system was extended on a five-year basis in March 2004 and was later installed permanently in March 2007.

Following are the results of the different systems:

REGULAR SEASON, 1986-1991

Year	Games	Plays Closely Reviewed	Reversals
1986	224	374	38
1987	210	490	57
1988	224	537	53
1989	224	492	65
1990	224	504	73
1991	224	570	90
TOTAL	1,330	2,967	376

PRESEASON, 1996, 1998

Year	Games	Challenges	Reversals
1996	10	13	3
1998	10	10	3
TOTAL	20	23	6

REGULAR SEASON, 1999-2011

Year	Games	Total Replay Reviews	Challenges	Reversals
1999	248	195	133	57
2000	248	247	179	84
2001	248	258	191	89
2002	256	294	208	94
2003	256	255	184	66
2004	256	283	233	88
2005	256	295	223	92
2006	256	311	237	107
2007	256	327	250	122
2008	256	315	229	117
2009	256	328	228	126
2010	256	361	252	133
2011	256	390	209	172
TOTAL	3,304	3,859	2,756	1,347

TIE-BREAKING PROCEDURES

The following procedures will be used to break standings ties for postseason playoffs and to determine regular-season schedules. Note: Tie games count as one-half win and one-half loss for both clubs.

TO BREAK A TIE WITHIN A DIVISION

If, at the end of the regular season, two or more clubs in the same division finish with the best won-lost-tied percentage, the following steps will be taken until a champion is determined:

TWO CLUBS

1. Head-to-head (best won-lost-tied percentage in games between the clubs.)

2. Best won-lost-tied percentage in games played within the division.

3. Best won-lost-tied percentage in common games.

4. Best won-lost-tied percentage in games played within the conference.

5. Strength of victory in all games.

6. Strength of schedule in all games.

7. Best combined ranking among conference teams in points scored and points allowed in all games.

8. Best combined ranking among all teams in points scored and points allowed in all games.

9. Best net points in common games.

10. Best net points in all games.

11. Best net touchdowns in all games.

12. Coin toss.

THREE OR MORE CLUBS

(Note: If two clubs remain tied after one or more clubs are eliminated during any step, tie-breaker re-starts at Step One of two-club format. If three clubs remain tied after a fourth club is eliminated during any step, tie-breaker re-starts at Step One of three-club format.)

1. Head-to-head (best won-lost-tied percentage in games among the clubs.)

2. Best won-lost-tied percentage in games played within the division.

3. Best won-lost-tied percentage in common games.

4. Best won-lost-tied percentage in games played within the conference.

5. Strength of victory in all games.

6. Strength of schedule in all games.

7. Best combined ranking among conference teams in points scored and points allowed in all games.

8. Best combined ranking among all teams in points scored and points allowed in all games.

9. Best net points in common games.

10. Best net points in all games.

11. Best net touchdowns in all games.

12. Coin toss.

TO BREAK A TIE FOR THE WILD-CARD TEAM

If necessary to break ties to determine the two Wild Card clubs from each conference, the following steps will be taken:

A. If all the tied clubs are from the same division, apply division tie-breaker.

B. If the tied clubs are from different divisions, apply the following steps:

TWO CLUBS

1. Head-to-head, if applicable.

2. Best won-lost-tied percentage in the games played within the conference.

3. Best won-lost-tied percentage in common games, minimum of four.

4. Strength of victory in all games.

5. Strength of schedule in all games.

6. Best combined ranking among conference teams in points scored and points allowed in all games.

7. Best combined ranking among all teams in points scored and points allowed in all games.

8. Best net points in conference games.

9. Best net points in all games.

10. Best net touchdowns in all games.

11. Coin toss.

THREE OR MORE CLUBS

(Note: If two clubs remain tied after one or more clubs are eliminated during any step, tie-breaker re-starts at Step One of two-club format. If three clubs remain tied after a fourth club is eliminated during any step, tie-breaker re-starts at Step Two of three-club format.)

1. Apply division tie-breaker to eliminate all but highest ranked club in each division prior to proceeding to step two. The original seeding within a division upon application of the division tie-breaker remains the same for all subsequent applications of the procedure that are necessary to identify the two Wild Card participants.

2. Head-to-head sweep (apply only if one has defeated each of the others or one club has lost to each of the others.)

3. Best won-lost-tied percentage in games played within the conference.

4. Best won-lost-tied percentage in common games, minimum of four.

5. Strength of victory in all games.

6. Strength of schedule in all games.

7. Best combined ranking among conference teams in points scored and points allowed in all games.

8. Best combined ranking among all teams in points scored and points allowed in all games.

9. Best net points in conference games.

10. Best net points in all games.

11. Best net touchdowns in all games.

12. Coin toss.

When the first Wild Card Team has been identified, the procedure is repeated to name the second Wild Card (i.e., eliminate all but the highest ranked club in each division prior to proceeding to step two). In situations where three teams from the same division are involved in the procedure, the original seeding of the teams remains the same for subsequent applications of the tie-breaker if the top-ranked team in that division qualifies for a Wild Card berth.

OTHER TIE-BREAKING PROCEDURES

1. Only one club advances to the playoffs in any tie-breaking step. Remaining tied clubs revert to the first step of the applicable division or Wild Card tie-breakers. As an example, if two clubs remain tied in any tie-breaker step after all other clubs have been eliminated, the procedure reverts to Step 1 of the two-club format to determine the winner. When one club wins the tie-breaker, all other clubs revert to Step 1 of the applicable two-club or three-club format.

2. In comparing records against common opponents among tied teams, the best won-lost-tied percentage is the deciding factor since teams may have played an unequal number of games.

3. To determine home-field priority among division-titlists, apply Wild Card tie-breakers.

4. To determine home-field priority for Wild Card qualifiers, apply division tie-breakers (if teams are from the same division) or Wild Card tie-breakers (if teams are from different divisions).

5. To determine the best combined ranking among conference teams in points scored and points allowed, add a team's position in the two categories, and the lowest score wins. For example, if Team A is first in points scored and second in points allowed, its combined ranking is "3." If Team B is third in points scored and first in points allowed, its combined ranking is "4." Team A then wins the tiebreaker. If two teams are tied for a position, both teams are awarded the ranking as if they held it solely. For example, if Team A and Team B are tied for first in points scored, each team is assigned a ranking of "1" in that category, and if Team C is third, its ranking will still be "3."

TIE-BREAKING PROCEDURE FOR SELECTION MEETING

1. Clubs not participating in the playoffs shall select in the first through 20th positions in reverse standings order.

2. The Super Bowl winner is last and Super Bowl loser is next-to-last.

3. The losers of the Conference Championship games shall select 29th and 30th based on won-lost-tied percentage.

4. The losers of the Divisional playoff games shall select 25th through 28th based on won-lost-tied percentage.

5. The losers of the Wild Card games shall select 21st through 24th based on won-lost-tied percentage.

If ties exist in any grouping except (2) above, such ties shall be broken by strength-of-schedule. If any ties cannot be broken by strength-of-schedule, the divisional or conference tie-breakers, if applicable, shall be applied. Any ties that still exist shall be broken by a coin flip.

WAIVERS

The waiver system is a procedure by which player contracts or NFL rights to players are made available by a club to other clubs in the League. During the procedure, the 31 other clubs either file claims to obtain the players or waive the opportunity to do so—thus the term "waiver." Claiming clubs are assigned players on a priority based on the inverse of won-and-lost standing. The claiming period is 24 hours from the first business day after the Super Bowl through the conclusion of the regular season. If a player passes through waivers unclaimed, he becomes a free agent. All waivers are no recall and no withdrawal. Under the Collective Bargaining Agreement, from the beginning of the waiver system each year through the trading deadline, any veteran who has acquired four years of pension credit is not subject to the waiver system if the club desires to release him. After the trading deadline, such players are subject to the waiver system.

ACTIVE/INACTIVE LIST

The Active/Inactive List is the principal status for players participating for a club. It consists of all players under contract who are eligible for preseason, regular-season, and postseason games. Teams are permitted to open training camp with no more than 90 players under contract and thereafter must meet two mandatory roster reductions prior to the season opener. Teams will be permitted an Active List of 46 players and an Inactive List of seven players for each regular-season and postseason game. Teams also are permitted to establish Practice Squads of up to eight players who are eligible to participate in practice, but these players remain free agents and are eligible to sign with any other team in the league.

August 27	Roster reduction to 75 players
August 31	Roster reduction to 53 players
September 1	Teams establish a Practice Squad of up to eight players

In addition to the squad limits described above, the overall roster limit of 90 players remains in effect throughout the regular season and postseason. The overall limit is applicable to players on a team's Active, Inactive, and certain Exempt Lists, players on the Practice Squad, and players on the Reserve List as Injured, Physically Unable to Perform, Non-Football Illness/Injury, and Suspended by Club.

RESERVE LIST

The Reserve List is a status for players who, for reasons of injury, retirement, military service, or other circumstances, are not immediately available for participation with a club. Players on Reserve/Injured are not eligible to practice or return to the Active/Inactive List in the same season that they are placed on Reserve. Players in the category of Reserve/Retired, Reserve/Did Not Report, Reserve/Exclusive Rights, and players who were placed in the category of Reserve/Left Squad in a previous season may not be reinstated during the period from 30 days before the end of the regular season through the postseason.

ANNUAL ACTIVE PLAYER LIMITS

NFL

Year(s)	Limit
2011-12	46
1991-2010	45**
1985-90	45
1983-84	49
1982	45†-49
1978-81	45
1975-77	43
1974	47
1964-73	40
1963	37
1961-62	36
1960	38
1959	36
1957-58	35
1951-56	33
1949-50	32
1948	35
1947	35*-34
1945-46	33
1943-44	28
1940-42	33
1938-39	30
1936-37	25
1935	24
1930-34	20
1926-29	18
1925	16

** 45 plus a third quarterback
† 45 for first two games
* 35 for first three games

AFL

Year(s)	Limit
1966-69	40
1965	38
1964	34
1962-63	33
1960-61	35

NFL FREE AGENCY MOVEMENT

The following chart details veteran free agents who signed with new teams:

	Unrestricted	Restricted	Transition	Franchise	TOTALS
1993	108	8	4	1	121
1994	121	7	4	0	132
1995	171	6	2	0	179
1996	100	4	2	0	106
1997	86	2	2	0	90
1998	112	4	1	2	119
1999	115	2	1	0	118
2000	107	4	0	0	111
2001	93	4	0	0	97
2002	130	1	0	0	131
2003	111	5	1	0	117
2004	124	1	1	0	126
2005	104	3	0	0	107
2006	149	4	1	0	154
2007	126	4	0	0	130
2008	132	3	0	0	135
2009	128	0	0	0	128
2010	51	1	0	0	52
2011	163	0	0	0	163

The AFC

American Football Conference
North Division
Team Colors: Black, Purple, and Metallic
Gold
1 Winning Drive
Owings Mills, Maryland 21117
Telephone: (410) 701-4000

2012 SCHEDULE
PRESEASON
Aug. 9   at Atlanta............................7:30
Aug. 17 **Detroit** 8:00
Aug. 23 **Jacksonville**.......................7:30
Aug. 30 at St. Louis.........................8:00

REGULAR SEASON
Sep. 10 **Cincinnati** (Mon)...............7:00
Sep. 16 at Philadelphia....................1:00
Sep. 23 **New England** 8:20
Sep. 27 **Cleveland** (Thurs) 8:20
Oct. 7   at Kansas City 1:00
Oct. 14 **Dallas** 1:00
Oct. 21 at Houston 1:00
Oct. 28 BYE
Nov. 4   at Cleveland 1:00
Nov. 11 **Oakland** 1:00
Nov. 18 at Pittsburgh...................*8:20
Nov. 25 at San Diego 4:05
Dec. 2   **Pittsburgh**.........................4:15
Dec. 9   at Washington 1:00
Dec. 16 **Denver**..............................1:00
Dec. 23 **New York Giants**...............1:00
Dec. 30 at Cincinnati 1:00
*All times ET; Sunday night games in
Weeks 11-16 subject to change*

Stadium: M&T Bank Stadium
            (opened in 1998)
          • **Capacity:** 71,008
            1101 Russell Street
            Baltimore, Maryland 21230
Playing Surface: Sportexe Momentum
Training Camp: 1 Winning Drive
            Owings Mills, MD 21117

M&T BANK STADIUM

CLUB OFFICIALS
Owner: Steve Bisciotti
President: Dick Cass
Executive Vice President/General
  Manager: Ozzie Newsome
Senior Vice President/Public and
  Community Relations: Kevin Byrne
Vice President of Football Administration:
  Pat Moriarty
Assistant General Manager:
  Eric DeCosta
Vice President and Chief Financial
  Officer: Jeff Goering
Vice President, Regional Partnerships
  and Sales: Ed Burchell
Vice President, Marketing:
  Gabrielle Dow
Vice President, Operations: Bob Eller
Vice President, Information Technology:
  Bill Jankowski
Vice President, Ticket Sales and
  Operations: Baker Koppelman
Vice President, National Partnerships and
  Sales: Kevin Rochlitz
Vice President, Broadcasting:
  Larry Rosen
Vice President, Stadium Operations:
  Roy Sommerhof
Vice President of Digital Media:
  Michelle Andres
Director of College Scouting: Joe Hortiz
Director of Pro Personnel:
  Vincent Newsome
Senior Personnel Assistant:
  George Kokinis
Assistant Director of Pro Personnel:
  Chad Alexander
Senior Advisor of Player Development:
  O.J. Brigance
Director of Media Relations:
  Chad Steele
Director of Player Development:
  Harry Swayne
National Scout: Joe Douglas
Scouts: Mark Azevedo, David Blackburn,
  Jack Glowik, Milt Hendrickson,
  Andrew Weidl, Lonnie Young
Equipment Manager: William Sheridan
Head Athletic Trainer: Mark Smith
Director of Football Video Operations:
  Jon Dubé
Assistant Director of Football Video
  Operations: Mark Bienvenu
Senior Director, Fields & Grounds/Head
  Groundskeeper: Don Follett
Director of Premium Services/Suites:
  Theresa Abato
Controller: Jim Coller
Director, Broadcasting Administration:
  Don DiRaddo
Director, Information Technology:
  Nick Fusee
Director, Human Resources:
  Elizabeth Jackson
Director, Security: Darren Sanders

COACHING HISTORY
(150-122-1)
Records include postseason games
1996-98   Ted Marchibroda........16-31-1
1999-2007 Brian Billick................85-67-0
2008-2011 John Harbaugh 49-24-0

PAID ATTENDANCE
Home 557,307   Away 487,726
Total 1,045,033
Single-game home record,
  71,547 (1/15/12)
Single-season home record, 557,792
  (2008)

2012 DRAFT CHOICES
Round	Name	Pos.	College
2	Courtney Upshaw	LB	Alabama
	Kelechi Osemele	G/T	Iowa St.
3	Bernard Pierce	RB	Temple
4	Gino Gradkowski	G/C	Delaware
	Christian Thompson	S	South Carolina St.
5	Asa Jackson	CB/RS	Cal Poly
6	Tommy Streeter	WR	Miami
7	DeAngelo Tyson	DE	Georgia

BALTIMORE RAVENS

2011 TEAM RECORD

PRESEASON (3-1)

Date	Result	Opponent
8/11	L 6-13	at Philadelphia
8/19	W 31-13	Kansas City
8/25	W 34-31	Washington
9/1	W 21-7	at Atlanta

REGULAR SEASON (12-4)

Date	Result	Opponent
9/11	W 35-7	Pittsburgh
9/18	L 13-26	at Tennessee
9/25	W 37-7	at St. Louis
10/2	W 34-17	New York Jets
10/16	W 29-14	Houston
10/24	L 7-12	at Jacksonville
10/30	W 30-27	Arizona
11/6	W 23-20	at Pittsburgh
11/13	L 17-22	at Seattle
11/20	W 31-24	Cincinnati
11/24	W 16-6	San Francisco
12/4	W 24-10	at Cleveland
12/11	W 24-10	Indianapolis
12/18	L 14-34	at San Diego
12/24	W 20-14	Cleveland
1/1	W 24-16	at Cincinnati

POSTSEASON (1-1)

Date	Result	Opponent
1/15	W 20-13	Houston
1/22	L 20-23	at New England

SCORE BY PERIODS

Ravens	95	110	78	95	0	—	378
Opponents	43	86	71	66	0	—	266

2011 TEAM STATISTICS

	Ravens	Opp.
Total First Downs	312	269
Rushing	98	79
Passing	181	166
Penalty	33	24
3rd Down: Made/Att	97/229	71/221
3rd Down Pct.	42.4	32.1
4th Down: Made/Att	4/7	10/21
4th Down Pct.	57.1	47.6
Possession Avg.	30:35	29:25
Total Net Yards	5419	4622
Avg. Per Game	338.7	288.9
Total Plays	1036	1002
Avg. Per Play	5.2	4.6
Net Yards Rushing	1996	1482
Avg. Per Game	124.8	92.6
Total Rushes	459	419
Net Yards Passing	3423	3140
Avg. Per Game	213.9	196.3
Sacked/Yards Lost	33/206	48/290
Gross Yards	3629	3430
Att./Completions	544/314	535/288
Completion Pct.	57.7	53.8
Had Intercepted	12	15
Punts/Average	73/46.5	86/43.6
Net Punting Avg.	73/38.6	86/38.4
Penalties/Yards	92/742	103/1032
Fumbles/Ball Lost	24/12	27/11
Touchdowns	41	26
Rushing	15	10
Passing	21	11
Returns	5	5

2011 INDIVIDUAL STATISTICS

PASSING

	Att.	Comp.	Yds.	Pct.	TD	Int.	Tkld.	Rate
Flacco	542	312	3610	57.6	20	12	31/203	80.9
Rice	1	1	1	100.0	1	0	0/0	118.8
Taylor	1	1	18	100.0	0	0	2/3	118.8
Ravens	544	314	3629	57.7	21	12	33/206	81.7
Opponents	535	288	3430	53.8	11	15	48/290	68.8

SCORING

	TD R	TD P	TD Rt	PAT	FG	Saf	PTS
Cundiff	0	0	0	38/38	28/37	0	122
Rice	12	3	0	0/0	0/0	0	90
T. Smith	0	7	0	0/0	0/0	0	42
Dickson	0	5	0	0/0	0/0	0	30
Graham	0	0	0	2/2	2/2	0	8
Boldin	0	3	0	0/0	0/0	0	18
Pitta	0	3	0	0/0	0/0	0	18
Webb	0	0	2	0/0	0/0	0	12
R. Williams	2	0	0	0/0	0/0	0	12
Flacco	1	0	0	0/0	0/0	0	6
Johnson	0	0	1	0/0	0/0	0	6
McClain	0	0	1	0/0	0/0	0	6
Ngata	0	0	1	0/0	0/0	0	6
Koch	0	0	0	0/0	0/0	0	2
Ravens	15	21	5	40/40	30/39	0	378
Opponents	10	11	5	26/26	28/31	0	266

2-Pt Conversions: Koch
Ravens 1-1, Opponents 0-0

RUSHING

	No.	Yds	Avg	LG	TD
Rice	291	1364	4.7	70t	12
R. Williams	108	444	4.1	28	2
Flacco	39	88	2.3	33	1
T. Smith	4	39	9.8	16	0
Leach	12	35	2.9	6	0
D. Reed	1	16	16.0	16	0
Allen	3	8	2.7	3	0
Taylor	1	2	2.0	2	0
Ravens	459	1996	4.3	70t	15
Opponents	419	1482	3.5	25t	10

RECEIVING

	No.	Yds	Avg	LG	TD
Rice	76	704	9.3	52	3
Boldin	57	887	15.6	56	3
Dickson	54	528	9.8	25	5
T. Smith	50	841	16.8	74t	7
Pitta	40	405	10.1	39	3
Leach	15	69	4.6	11	0
R. Williams	13	83	6.4	18	0
Evans	4	74	18.5	32	0
L. Williams	4	46	11.5	15	0
Flacco	1	-8	-8.0	-8	0
Ravens	314	3629	11.6	74t	21
Opponents	288	3430	11.9	66	11

INTERCEPTIONS

	No.	Yds	Avg	LG	TD
Webb	5	81	16.2	73t	1
E. Reed	3	25	8.3	16	0
J. Smith	2	48	24.0	32	0
Suggs	2	9	4.5	9	0
McClain	1	8	8.0	8	0
Lewis	1	4	4.0	4	0
Pollard	1	0	0.0	0	0
Ravens	15	175	11.7	73t	1
Opponents	12	159	13.3	45	1

PUNTING

	No.	Yds.	Avg.	In 20	LG
Koch	73	3393	46.5	21	63
Ravens	73	3393	46.5	21	63
Opponents	86	3746	43.6	25	65

PUNT RETURNS

	Ret	FC	Yds	Avg	LG	TD
Webb	30	20	301	10.0	68t	1
E. Reed	3	5	29	9.7	16	0
Carr	2	2	15	7.5	8	0
L. Williams	1	0	0	0.0	0	0
Ravens	36	27	345	9.6	68t	1
Opponents	33	11	392	11.9	84t	2

KICKOFF RETURNS

	No.	Yds	Avg	LG	TD
D. Reed	18	534	29.7	77	0
Zbikowski	9	209	23.2	30	0
L. Williams	5	109	21.8	37	0
Leach	2	29	14.5	15	0
McCann	2	53	26.5	27	0
Webb	2	59	29.5	37	0
Carr	1	20	20.0	20	0
E. Jones	1	0	0.0	0	0
Nakamura	1	8	8.0	8	0
T. Smith	1	24	24.0	24	0
Mattison	0	2	—	2	0
Ravens	42	1047	24.9	77	0
Opponents	36	1050	29.2	107t	1

FIELD GOALS

	1-19	20-29	30-39	40-49	50+
Cundiff	1/1	9/9	10/12	7/9	1/6
Graham	0/0	0/0	0/0	2/2	0/0
Ravens	1/1	9/9	10/12	9/11	1/6
Opponents	0/0	8/8	9/12	7/7	4/4

SACKS

	No.
Suggs	14.0
McPhee	6.0
Kruger	5.5
Ngata	5.0
Redding	4.5
Johnson	2.5
Lewis	2.0
Pollard	2.0
Ayanbadejo	1.5
Carr	1.0
McClain	1.0
E. Reed	1.0
Webb	1.0
Zbikowski	1.0
Ravens	48.0
Opponents	33.0

RECORD HOLDERS
INDIVIDUAL RECORDS—CAREER

Category	Name	Performance
Rushing (Yds.)	Jamal Lewis, 2000-06	7,801
Passing (Yds.)	Joe Flacco, 2008-2011	13,816
Passing (TDs)	Joe Flacco, 2008-2011	80
Receiving (No.)	Derrick Mason, 2005-2010	471
Receiving (Yds.)	Derrick Mason, 2005-2010	5,777
Interceptions	Ed Reed, 2002-2011	57
Punting (Avg.)	Sam Koch, 2006-2011	44.2
Punt Return (Avg.)	Jermaine Lewis, 1996-2001	11.8
Kickoff Return (Avg.)	Corey Harris, 1998-2001	24.0
Field Goals	Matt Stover, 1996-2008	354
Touchdowns (Tot.)	Jamal Lewis, 2000-06	47
Points	Matt Stover, 1996-2008	1,464
*Sacks	Terrell Suggs, 2003-2011	82.5

INDIVIDUAL RECORDS—SINGLE SEASON

Category	Name	Performance
Rushing (Yds.)	Jamal Lewis, 2003	2,066
Passing (Yds.)	Vinny Testaverde, 1996	4,177
Passing (TDs)	Vinny Testaverde, 1996	33
Receiving (No.)	Derrick Mason, 2007	103
Receiving (Yds.)	Michael Jackson, 1996	1,201
Interceptions	Ed Reed, 2004, 2008	9
Punting (Avg.)	Sam Koch, 2011	46.5
Punt Return (Avg.)	Jermaine Lewis, 2000	16.1
Kickoff Return (Avg.)	David Reed, 2010	29.3
Field Goals	Matt Stover, 2000	35
Touchdowns (Tot.)	Ray Rice, 2011	15
Points	Matt Stover, 2000	135
*Sacks	Peter Boulware, 2001	15.0

INDIVIDUAL RECORDS—SINGLE GAME

Category	Name	Performance
Rushing (Yds.)	Jamal Lewis, 9-14-03	295
Passing (Yds.)	Vinny Testaverde, 10-27-96	429
Passing (TDs)	Tony Banks, 9-10-00	5
Receiving (No.)	Priest Holmes, 10-11-98	13
Receiving (Yds.)	Qadry Ismail, 12-12-99	268
Interceptions	Many times	2
	Last time by Ed Reed, 9-11-11	
Field Goals	Matt Stover, 9-21-97, 12-26-99, 10-28-00, 10-14-07	5
	Billy Cundiff, 11-22-09, 10-16-11	5
Touchdowns (Tot.)	Marcus Robinson, 11-23-03	4
Points	Marcus Robinson, 11-23-03	24
*Sacks	Michael McCrary, 11-8-98	4.0
	Peter Boulware, 1-7-02	4.0

*Sacks became an official statistic in 1982.

2012 VETERAN ROSTER

No.	Name	Pos.	Ht.	Wt.	Birthdate	NFL Exp.	College	Hometown	How Acq.	'11 Games/ Starts
35	Allen, Anthony	RB	6-1	230	8/6/88	2	Georgia Tech	Tampa, Fla.	D7-'11	5/0
51	Ayanbadejo, Brendon	LB	6-1	225	9/6/76	10	UCLA	Santa Cruz, Calif.	UFA(Chi)-'08	16/0
77	Birk, Matt	C	6-4	310	7/23/76	15	Harvard	St. Paul, Minn.	UFA(Minn)-'09	16/16
81	Boldin, Anquan	WR	6-1	223	10/3/80	10	Florida State	Pahokee, Fla.	T(Ariz)-'10	14/14
23	Brown, Chykie	CB	5-11	190	12/26/86	2	Texas	Houston, Texas	D5a-'11	7/0
62	Cody, Terrence	NT	6-4	349	6/28/88	3	Alabama	Fort Myers, Fla.	D2b-'10	16/16
37	Considine, Sean	S	6-0	212	12/17/82	8	Iowa	Byron, Ill.	FA-'12	12/0*
26	Cook, Emanuel	S	5-10	202	1/20/88	3	South Carolina	Riviera Beach, Fla.	FA-'11	5/0
46	Cox, Morgan	LS	6-4	241	4/26/86	3	Tennessee	Collierville, Tenn.	FA-'10	16/0
7	Cundiff, Billy	K	6-1	212	2/30/80	8	Drake	Harlan, Iowa	FA-'09	15/0
84	Dickson, Ed	TE	6-4	255	7/25/87	3	Oregon	Bellflower, Calif.	D3-'10	16/16
17	Doss, Tandon	WR	6-2	205	9/22/89	2	Indiana	Indianapolis, Ind.	D4-'11	6/0
59	Ellerbe, Dannell	ILB	6-1	240	11/29/85	4	Georgia	Hamlet, N.C.	FA-'09	9/3
5	Flacco, Joe	QB	6-6	245	1/16/85	5	Delaware	Audubon, N.J.	D1-'08	16/16
54	Glenn, Cody	ILB	6-2	240	10/6/86	3	Nebraska	Rusk, Texas	FA-'12	0*
36	Gorrer, Danny	DB	6-0	185	6/1/86	3	Texas A&M	Port Arthur, Texas	FA-'10	11/0
24	Graham, Corey	CB	6-0	196	7/25/85	6	New Hampshire	Buffalo, N.Y.	FA-'12	16/0*
65	#Gurode, Andre	C	6-4	318	3/6/79	11	Colorado	Houston, Texas	FA-'11	13/5
70	Harewood, Ramon	T	6-6	340	2/3/87	3	Morehouse	St. Michael, Barbados	D6-'10	0*
97	Jones, Arthur	DE	6-3	313	6/3/86	3	Syracuse	Endicott, N.Y.	D5b-'10	14/1
56	#Jones, Edgar	OLB	6-3	262	12/1/84	6	Southeast Missouri St.	Rayville, La.	FA-'11	9/0
12	Jones, Jacoby	WR/RS	6-2	212	7/11/84	6	Lane	New Orleans, La.	FA-'12	16/10*
96	Kemoeatu, Maake	NT	6-5	345	1/10/79	10	Utah	Tonga	FA-'12	0*
94	Kindle, Sergio	OLB	6-3	250	9/20/87	2	Texas	Dallas, Texas	D2a-'10	2/0
4	Koch, Sam	P	6-1	220	8/13/82	7	Nebraska	Seward, Neb.	D6a-'06	16/0
99	Kruger, Paul	OLB	6-4	265	2/15/86	4	Utah	Orem, Utah	D2-'09	16/0
44	Leach, Vonta	FB	6-0	260	11/6/81	9	East Carolina	Rowland, N.C.	UFA(Hou)-'11	16/16
52	Lewis, Ray	ILB	6-1	250	5/15/75	17	Miami	Lakeland, Fla.	D1b-'96	12/12
58	McAdoo, Michael	OLB	6-7	245	7/9/90	2	North Carolina	Antioch, Tenn.	FA-'11	0*
98	McBean, Ryan	DT	6-5	305	4/23/84	5	Oklahoma State	Euless, Texas	FA-'12	16/3*
53	McClain, Jameel	ILB	6-1	245	7/25/85	5	Syracuse	Philadelphia, Pa.	FA-'08	16/16
50	McClellan, Albert	LB	6-2	255	6/4/86	2	Marshall	Lakeland, Fla.	FA-'10	16/1
78	McKinnie, Bryant	T	6-8	360	9/23/79	11	Miami	Woodbury, N.J.	FA-'11	16/16
90	McPhee, Pernell	DE	6-3	280	12/17/88	2	Mississippi State	Pahokee, Fla.	D5b-'11	16/0
92	Ngata, Haloti	DT	6-4	330	1/21/84	7	Oregon	Salt Lake City, Utah	D1-'06	16/16
74	Oher, Michael	T	6-4	315	5/28/86	4	Mississippi	Memphis, Tenn.	D1-'09	16/16
8	Painter, Curtis	QB	6-4	230	6/24/85	4	Purdue	Vincennes, Ind.	FA-'12	9/8*
88	Pitta, Dennis	TE	6-4	245	6/29/85	3	Brigham Young	Moorpark, Calif.	D4-'10	16/2
31	Pollard, Bernard	S	6-1	224	12/23/84	7	Purdue	Fort Wayne, Ind.	UFA(Hou)-'11	16/13
16	Reed, David	WR/RS	6-0	190	3/22/87	3	Utah	New Britain, Conn.	D5a-'10	11/0
20	Reed, Ed	S	5-11	200	9/11/78	11	Miami	St. Rose, La.	D1-'02	16/16
76	Reid, Jah	T	6-7	335	7/21/88	2	Central Florida	Haines City, Fla.	D3-'11	16/0
27f	Ray Rice	RB	5-8	212	1/22/87	5	Rutgers	New Rochelle, N.Y.	D2-'08	16/16
22	Smith, Jimmy	CB	6-2	210	7/26/88	2	Colorado	Colton, Calif.	D1-'11	12/3
82	Smith, Torrey	WR	6-0	205	1/26/89	2	Maryland	Falmouth, Va.	D2-'11	16/14
55	Suggs, Terrell	OLB	6-3	260	10/11/82	10	Arizona State	Chandler, Ariz.	D1a-'03	16/16
2	Taylor, Tyrod	QB	6-1	215	8/3/89	2	Virginia Tech	Hampton, Va.	D6-'11	3/0
21	Webb, Lardarius	CB/RS	5-10	182	10/12/85	4	Nicholls State	Opelika, Ala.	D3-'09	16/15
29	Williams, Cary	CB	6-1	190	12/23/84	4	Washburn	Hollywood, Fla.	FA-'09	16/16
47	Williams, Chavis	OLB	6-3	240	7/10/89	2	Alabama	Dora, Ala.	FA-'11	5/0
15	Williams, LaQuan	WR	6-0	200	6/27/88	2	Maryland	Baltimore, Md.	FA-'11	12/0
87	#Wilson, Kris	TE	6-2	245	8/22/81	9	Pittsburgh	Lancaster, Pa.	FA-'11	15/0
73	Yanda, Marshal	G/T	6-3	315	9/15/84	6	Iowa	Anamosa, Iowa	D3b-'07	16/16

* Considine played 4 games with Carolina and 8 games with Arizona in '11; Glenn last active with Indianapolis in '10; Graham played 16 games with Chicago; Harewood missed '11 season because of injury; J. Jones played 16 games with Houston; Kemoeatu last active with Washington in '10; McAdoo missed '11 season because of injury; McBean played 16 games with Denver; Painter played 9 games with Indianapolis.

#Unrestricted free agent; subject to developments.

f- Unsigned franchise player; subject to developments.

Players lost through free agency (6): G Ben Grubbs (NO; 10); LB Jarret Johnson (SD; 16); DT Brandon McKinney (Ind; 12); S Haruki Nakamura (Car; 15); DE Cory Redding (Ind; 15); S Tom Zbikowski (Ind; 14).

Also played with Ravens in '11–LB Prescott Burgess (3 games), CB Chris Carr (9), WR Lee Evans (9), CB Domonique Foxworth (2), K Shayne Graham (1), T Mark LeVoir (3), G/C Bryan Mattison (8), CB/RS Bryan McCann (3), RB Ricky Williams (16).

FIRST-YEAR ROSTER

Name	Pos.	Ht.	Wt.	Birthdate	College	Hometown	How Acq.
Balasavage, Matt	TE	6-4	256	2/15/89	Temple	Lancaster, Pa.	FA
Barbieri, Howard (1)	G	6-5	300	11/7/87	Rutgers	Leonardo, N.J.	FA
Berry, Damien (1)	RB	5-10	211	10/21/88	Miami	Belle Glade, Fla.	FA-'11
Boren, Justin (1)	G/C	6-2	325	4/28/88	Ohio State	Pickerington, Ohio	FA-'11
Bradley, Rodney (1)	WR	5-11	191	9/10/88	Hawaii	Dallas, Texas	FA-'11
Brantley, John	QB	6-3	218	3/3/89	Florida	Ocala, Fla.	FA
Brown, Omar	S	5-11	195	6/6/88	Marshall	Moncks Corner, S.C.	FA
Bynes, Josh (1)	LB	6-1	240	8/24/89	Auburn	Lauderdale Lakes, Fla.	FA-'11
Carr, Nigel	LB	6-2	232	1/22/90	Alabama State	Jacksonville, Fla.	FA
Cornell, Jack	G/T	6-6	315	6/4/89	Illinois	Quincy, Ill.	FA
Drew, Davon (1)	TE	6-4	260	12/9/85	East Carolina	New Bern, N.C.	D5b-'09
Figgins, Bruce	TE	6-4	272	12/7/88	Georgia	Columbus, Ga.	FA
Goda, Devin	WR	6-2	225	5/5/89	Slippery Rock	Pittsburgh, Pa.	FA
Gradkowski, Gino	G/C	6-3	300	11/5/88	Delaware	Pittsburgh, Pa.	D4a
Graham, Dorian	WR	5-9	188	9/20/89	Syracuse	Fort Lauderdale, Fla.	FA
Hall, Bryan (1)	DT	6-0	295	9/12/88	Arkansas State	Paducah, Ky.	FA-'11
Henigan, Elliott	DT/DE	6-4	280	5/10/90	Alabama-Birmingham	Atlanta, Ga.	FA
Jackson, Asa	CB/RS	5-10	190	12/2/89	Cal Poly	Sacramento, Calif.	D5
Jean-Baptiste, Nicolas	NT	6-1	329	3/8/89	Baylor	Houston, Texas	FA
Kitchen, Ishmaa'ily	NT	6-1	334	8/24/88	Kent State	Youngstown, Ohio	FA
Lawrence, Addison	OL	6-4	300	1/14/89	Mississippi State	Senatobia, Miss.	FA
Livas, Phillip (1)	WR/RS	5-8	175	4/24/89	Louisiana Tech	Houma, La.	FA-'11
Maybin, Jordan	CB	5-11	180	10/31/88	Northwestern	Northfield Center, Ohio	FA
McClain, Antoine	G	6-5	329	12/6/89	Clemson	Anniston, Ala.	FA
Moore, Terrence	DE	6-3	290	1/31/89	Nebraska	New Orleans, La.	FA
Newton, Cecil (1)	C	6-2	315	3/20/86	Tennessee State	Atlanta, Ga.	FA-'11
Osemele, Kelechi	G/T	6-5	333	6/24/89	Iowa State	Houston, Texas	D2b
Pendergrass, Brandon	RB	5-9	200	1/21/89	Wake Forest	Royal Palm Beach, Fla.	FA
Pierce, Bernard	RB	6-0	218	5/10/90	Temple	Glen Mills, Pa.	D3
Quarles, Cyhl	S	6-3	210	4/6/89	Wake Forest	Norcross, Ga.	FA
Rainey, Bobby	RB	5-8	205	10/16/87	Western Kentucky	Griffin, Ga.	FA
Scales, Patrick (1)	LS	6-4	228	2/11/88	Utah State	Louisville, Ky.	FA
Stewart, Chester	QB	6-3	214	1/26/89	Temple	Hanover, Md.	FA
Streeter, Tommy	WR	6-5	220	10/7/89	Miami	Miami, Fla.	D6
Thompson, Christian	S	6-0	211	6/14/90	South Carolina State	North Lauderdale, Fla.	D4b
Thompson, Deonte	WR	6-0	200	2/14/89	Florida	Belle Glades, Fla.	FA
Tyson, DeAngelo	DE	6-2	315	4/12/89	Georgia	Statesboro, Ga.	D7
Upshaw, Courtney	OLB	6-2	272	12/13/89	Alabama	Eufaula, Ala.	D2a
Williams, Patrick (1)	WR	6-1	204	1/13/86	Colorado	DeSoto, Texas	FA-'11

The term NFL Rookie is defined as a player who is in his first season of professional football and has not been on the roster of another professional football team for any regular-season or postseason games. A Rookie is designated by an "R" on NFL rosters. Players who have been active in another professional football league or players who have NFL experience, including either preseason training camp or being on an Active List or Inactive List, or on Reserve/Injured or Reserve/Physically Unable to Perform for fewer than six regular-season games, are termed NFL First-Year Players. An NFL First-Year Player is designated by a "1" on NFL rosters. Thereafter, a player is credited with an additional year of experience for each season in which he accumulates six games on the Active List or Inactive List, or on Reserve/Injured or Reserve/Physically Unable to Perform.

Log on to www.baltimoreravens.com for an up-to-date roster.

COACHING STAFF

Head Coach,
John Harbaugh

Pro Career: John Harbaugh was hired as the third head coach in Baltimore Ravens history on January 19, 2008. In each of his four seasons (2008-2011), the Ravens have earned a playoff berth, with Baltimore becoming the only NFL team to reach the postseason every year during that span. Impressively, Harbaugh is also the only head coach in NFL history (since 1970 merger) to win a playoff game in each of his first four years. All four teams that defeated the Ravens eventually represented the AFC in the Super Bowl (2008 Pittsburgh, 2009 Indianapolis, 2010 Pittsburgh, and 2011 New England). In 2011, Baltimore won the AFC North by producing its second-straight 12-4 record, also going undefeated at home for the first time in team history. In 2008, his initial campaign with the team, Baltimore set an NFL record that season for most total wins (13) by a team with both a rookie head coach and a rookie starting quarterback (Joe Flacco). Harbaugh spent his first 10 NFL seasons (1998-2007) with the Philadelphia Eagles. He was the team's secondary coach in 2007, after nine seasons as its special teams coordinator. Following the 2001 campaign, he was voted the NFL's Special Teams Coach of the Year by his coaching peers. Harbaugh was also named *The Dallas Morning News* Special Teams Coach of the Year that season. Career record: 49-24.

Background: Played defensive back at Miami (Ohio) from 1980-83, earned degree in political science. Coached collegiately at Western Michigan (1984-86), Pittsburgh (1987), Morehead State (1988), Cincinnati (1989-1996), and Indiana (1997).

Personal: Born in Perrysburg, Ohio on September 23, 1962, Harbaugh and his wife, Ingrid, have a daughter, Alison. He is the son of longtime college coach Jack Harbaugh, and his brother, Jim, the current 49ers head coach, played for the Ravens in 1998. John's brother-in-law, Tom Crean, Indiana University's basketball coach, is married to his sister, Joani.

ASSISTANT COACHES

Teryl Austin, secondary; born March 3, 1965, Sharon, Pa. Defensive back Pittsburgh 1984-87. Pro defensive back Montreal Machine (WLAF) 1991. College coach: Penn State 1991-94, Wake Forest 1993-95, Syracuse 1996-98, Michigan 1999-2002, Florida 2010. Pro coach: Seattle Seahawks 2003-06, Arizona Cardinals 2007-09, joined Ravens in 2011.

Clarence Brooks, defensive line; born May 20, 1951, New York, N.Y. Guard Massachusetts 1970-73. No pro playing experience. College coach: Massachusetts

1976-1980, Syracuse 1981-89, Arizona 1990-92. Pro coach: Chicago Bears 1993-98, Cleveland Browns 1999, Miami Dolphins 2000-04, joined Ravens in 2005.

Jason Brooks, offensive quality control; born Jan. 19, 1978, Amherst, Mass. Attended Middle Tennessee State 2005-06. College coach: Middle Tennessee State 2006, Massachusetts 2007, Norwich 2008. Pro coach: Miami Dolphins 2007, joined Ravens in 2009.

Jim Caldwell, quarterbacks; born January 16, 1955, Beloit, Wisc. Defensive back Iowa 1973-76. No pro playing experience. College coach: Iowa 1997, Southern Illinois 1978-1980, Northwestern 1981, Colorado 1982-84, Louisville 1985, Penn State 1986-1992, Wake Forest 1993-2000 (head coach). Pro coach: Tampa Bay Buccaneers 2001, Indianapolis Colts 2002-2011 (head coach 2008-2011), joined Ravens in 2012.

Cam Cameron, offensive coordinator; born February 6, 1961, Chapel Hill, N.C. Quarterback Indiana 1980-83. No pro playing experience. College coach: Michigan 1984-1993, Indiana 1997-2001 (head coach). Pro coach: Washington Redskins 1994-96, San Diego Chargers 2002-06, Miami Dolphins 2007 (head coach), joined Ravens in 2008.

Wade Harman, tight ends; born October 1, 1963, Corydon, Iowa. Linebacker Drake 1985, Utah State 1986. No pro playing experience. College coach: Utah State 1987-1991, Pacific 1992-95, Morningside 1996. Pro coach: Minnesota Vikings 1997-98, joined Ravens in 1999.

Chris Hewitt, asst. special teams; born July 22, 1974, Kingston, Jamaica. Defensive back Cincinnati 1993-96. Pro defensive back New Orleans Saints 1997-99. College coach: Notre Dame 2003, Rutgers 2004-2011. Pro coach: Joined Ravens in 2012.

Jim Hostler, wide receivers; born November 11, 1966, Pittsburgh, Pa. Defensive back Indiana (Pa.) 1986-89. No pro playing experience. College coach: Indiana (Pa.) 1990-92, 1994-99, Juniata (Pa.) 1993. Pro coach: Kansas City Chiefs 2000, New Orleans Saints 2001-02, New York Jets 2003-04, San Francisco 49ers 2005-07, joined Ravens in 2008.

Don Martindale, inside linebackers; born May 19, 1963, Dayton, Ohio. Linebacker Defiance College 1981-84. College coach: Defiance 1986-87, Notre Dame 1994-95, Cincinnati 1996-98, Western Illinois 1999, Western Kentucky 2001-03. Pro coach: Oakland Raiders 2004-08, Denver Broncos 2009-2010, joined Ravens in 2012.

Andy Moeller, offensive line; June 15, 1964, Grand Rapids, Mich. Linebacker Michigan 1983-86. No pro playing experience. College coach: Indiana 1987, Army 1988-1993, Missouri 1994-99, Michigan 2000-07. Pro coach: Joined Ravens in 2008.

Ted Monachino, linebackers; born October 15, 1966, Council Bluffs, Iowa. Defensive lineman Missouri 1988-1990. No pro playing experience. College coach: Texas Christian 1996-97, James Madison 1998, Southwest Missouri State 1999, Boise State 2000, Arizona State 2001-05. Pro coach: Jacksonville Jaguars 2006-09, joined Ravens in 2010.

Wilbert Montgomery, running backs; born September 16, 1954, Greenville, Miss. Running back Abilene Christian 1973-76. Pro running back Philadelphia Eagles 1977-1984, Detroit Lions 1985. Pro Coach: St. Louis Rams 1997-2005, Detroit Lions 2006-07, joined Ravens in 2008.

Dean Pees, defensive coordinator; born September 4, 1949, Dunkirk, Ohio. Attended Bowling Green State. No college or pro playing experience. College coach: Findlay 1979-1982, Miami (Ohio) 1983-86, Naval Academy 1987-89, Toledo 1990-93, Notre Dame 1994, Michigan State 1995-97, Kent State 1998-2003. Pro coach: New England Patriots 2004-09, joined Ravens in 2010.

Bob Rogucki, strength and conditioning; born September 27, 1953, Clarksburg, W.Va. No college or pro playing experience. College coach: Penn State 1981, Weber State 1982, Army 1983-89. Pro coach: Arizona Cardinals 1990-2003, Jacksonville Jaguars 2004, Philadelphia Eagles 2006-07, joined Ravens in 2008.

Jerry Rosburg, special teams coordinator/asst. head coach; born November 24, 1955, Fairmont, Minn. Linebacker North Dakota State 1974-77. No pro playing experience. College coach: Northern Michigan 1981-86, Western Michigan 1987-1991, Cincinnati 1992-95, Minnesota 1996, Boston College 1997-98, Notre Dame 1999-2000. Pro coach: Cleveland Browns 2001-06, Atlanta Falcons 2007, joined Ravens in 2008.

Craig Ver Steeg, offensive assistant/quarterbacks; born September 11, 1960, Inglewood, Calif. No college or pro playing experience. College coach: Southern California 1984-85, Utah 1986-89, Cincinnati 1990-93, Harvard 1994-95, Illinois 1998-2000, Utah 2001-02, Rutgers 2003-07. Pro coach: Chicago Bears 1996-97, joined Ravens in 2008.

Todd Washington, asst. offensive line; born July 19, 1976, Nassawadox, Va. Guard/center Virginia Tech 1993-97. Pro guard/center Tampa Bay 1998-2002, Houston 2003-05. College coach: San Diego 2007-09. Pro coach: Hartford Colonials (UFL) 2010, joined Ravens in 2011.

Matt Weiss, defensive assistant; born March 1, 1983, New Haven, Conn. Punter Vanderbilt 2001-02. No pro playing experience. College coach: Stanford 2008. Pro coach: Joined Ravens in 2009.

American Football Conference
East Division
Team Colors: Royal, Red, White and
Navy
One Bills Drive
Orchard Park, New York 14127-2296
Telephone: (716) 648-1800

2012 SCHEDULE
PRESEASON
Aug. 9	**Washington**	7:00
Aug. 17	at Minnesota	8:00
Aug. 25	**Pittsburgh**	7:00
Aug. 30	at Detroit	7:00

REGULAR SEASON
Sep. 9	at New York Jets	1:00
Sep. 16	**Kansas City**	1:00
Sep. 23	at Cleveland	1:00
Sep. 30	**New England**	1:00
Oct. 7	at San Francisco	4:15
Oct. 14	at Arizona	4:05
Oct. 21	**Tennessee**	1:00
Oct. 28	BYE	
Nov. 4	at Houston	1:00
Nov. 11	at New England	1:00
Nov. 15	**Miami** (Thurs)	8:20
Nov. 25	at Indianapolis	1:00
Dec. 2	**Jacksonville**	1:00
Dec. 9	**St. Louis**	1:00
Dec. 16	**Seattle** (Toronto)	4:05
Dec. 23	at Miami	1:00
Dec. 30	**New York Jets**	1:00

* All times ET

Stadium: Ralph Wilson Stadium
(opened in 1973)
•**Capacity:** 73,967
One Bills Drive
Orchard Park, New York
14127-2296
Playing Surface: A-Turf Titan
Training Camp: St. John Fisher College
Rochester, N.Y. 14618

RALPH WILSON STADIUM

CLUB OFFICIALS
Owner and President:
Ralph C. Wilson, Jr.
Chief Financial Officer:
Jeffrey C. Littmann
Chief Executive Officer: Russ Brandon
Executive Vice President/
General Manager: Buddy Nix
Executive Vice President of Strategic
Planning: Mary Owen
Senior Vice President of
Communications: Scott Berchtold
Senior Vice President of Marketing and
Broadcasting: Marc Honan
Senior Vice President of Government
Relations and External Affairs:
Bill Munson
Senior Vice President of Football
Administration: Jim Overdorf
Senior Vice President of Business
Development: Bruce Popko
Senior Vice President of Business
Operations: Dave Wheat
Vice President of Community Relations:
Gretchen Geitter
Vice President of Information
Technology: Dan Evans
Vice President Event Operations and
Guest Experience: Andy Major
Consultant: Christy Wilson Hofmann
Assistant General Manager/Director of
Player Personnel: Doug Whaley
Director of Pro Personnel: Tom Gibbons
Director of College Scouting: Chuck Cook
Director of Security: Chris Clark
Director of Stadium Operations: Perry Dix
Director of Merchandise: Tim Kehoe
Director of Player Programs:
Paul Lancaster
Controller: Frank Wojnicki
Equipment Manager: Dave Hojnowski
Director of Equipment Operations:
Jeff Mazurek
Assistant Equipment Managers:
Randy Ribbeck, Spencer Haws
Head Athletic Trainer: Bud Carpenter
Athletic Trainers: Chris Fischetti,
Shone Gipson, Greg McMillen
Video Director: Greg Estes
Video System Analyst: Wes Burnard
Video Assistant: Dexter Carlo
Coordinator of College Scouting:
Doug Majeski
Scouts: Brian Fisher, Brad Forsyth,
Matt Hand, Shawn Heilen,
CJ Leak (BLESTO), Darrell Moody,
Tom Roth, (emeritus) David G. Smith,
(emeritus) David W. Smith,
Theo Young

COACHING HISTORY
(378-431-8)
Records include postseason games
1960-61	Buster Ramsey	11-16-1
1962-65	Lou Saban	38-18-3
1966-68	Joe Collier*	13-17-1
1968	Harvey Johnson	1-10-1
1969-1970	John Rauch	7-20-1
1971	Harvey Johnson	1-13-0
1972-76	Lou Saban**	32-29-1
1976-77	Jim Ringo	3-20-0
1978-1982	Chuck Knox	38-38-0
1983-85	Kay Stephenson***	10-26-0
1985-86	Hank Bullough****	4-17-0
1986-1997	Marv Levy	123-78-0
1998-2000	Wade Phillips	29-21-0
2001-03	Gregg Williams	17-31-0
2004-05	Mike Mularkey	14-18-0
2006-09	Dick Jauron#	24-33-0
2009	Perry Fewell	3-4-0
2010-11	Chan Gailey	10-22-0

*Released after two games in 1968
**Resigned after five games in 1976
***Released after four games in 1985
****Released after nine games in 1986
#Released after nine games in 2009

PAID ATTENDANCE
Home 474,563   Away 519,553
Total 994,116
Single-game home record,
80,368 (10/4/92)
Single-season home record,
635,889 (1991)

2012 DRAFT CHOICES
Round	Name	Pos.	College
1	Stephon Gilmore	DB	South Carolina
2	Cordy Glenn	T	Georgia
3	T.J. Graham	WR	North Carolina St.
4	Nigel Bradham	LB	Florida St.
	Ron Brooks	DB	Louisiana St.
5	Zebrie Sanders	T	Florida St.
	Tank Carder	LB	Texas Christian
6	Mark Asper	G	Oregon
7	John Potter	K	Western Michigan

2011 TEAM RECORD
PRESEASON (1-3)

Date	Result		Opponent
8/13	L	3-10	at Chicago
8/20	L	34-21	at Denver
8/27	W	35-32	Jacksonville (OT)
9/1	L	6-16	Detroit

REGULAR SEASON (6-10)

Date	Result		Opponent
9/11	W	41-7	at Kansas City
9/18	W	38-35	Oakland
9/25	W	34-31	New England
10/2	L	20-23	at Cincinnati
10/9	W	31-24	Philadelphia
10/16	L	24-27	at New York Giants
10/30	W	23-0	Washington
11/6	L	11-27	New York Jets
11/13	L	7-44	at Dallas
11/20	L	8-35	at Miami
11/27	L	24-28	at New York Jets
12/4	L	17-23	Tennessee
12/11	L	10-37	at San Diego
12/18	L	23-30	Miami
12/24	W	40-14	Denver
1/1	L	21-49	at New England
(OT) Overtime			

SCORE BY PERIODS

Bills	87	96	78	111	0	—	372
Opponents	76	140	109	109	0	—	434

2011 TEAM STATISTICS

	Bills	Opp.
Total First Downs	313	340
Rushing	100	120
Passing	180	196
Penalty	33	24
3rd Down: Made/Att	62/191	75/189
3rd Down Pct.	32.5	39.7
4th Down: Made/Att	9/22	9/13
4th Down Pct.	40.9	69.2
Possession Avg.	30:11	29:49
Total Net Yards	5624	5938
Avg. Per Game	351.5	371.1
Total Plays	992	1003
Avg. Per Play	5.7	5.9
Net Yards Rushing	1921	2224
Avg. Per Game	120.1	139.0
Total Rushes	391	467
Net Yards Passing	3703	3714
Avg. Per Game	231.4	232.1
Sacked/Yards Lost	23/154	29/210
Gross Yards	3857	3924
Att./Completions	578/356	507/321
Completion Pct.	61.6	63.3
Had Intercepted	25	20
Punts/Average	73/47.6	68/44.7
Net Punting Avg.	73/38.1	68/38.7
Penalties/Yards	86/743	85/871
Fumbles/Ball Lost	16/5	21/11
Touchdowns	43	53
Rushing	12	19
Passing	24	30
Returns	7	4

2011 INDIVIDUAL STATISTICS

PASSING	Att.	Comp.	Yds.	Pct.	TD	Int.	Tkld.	Rate
Fitzpatrick	569	353	3832	62.0	24	23	22/148	79.1
Thigpen	8	3	25	37.5	0	1	0/0	6.8
B. Smith	1	0	0	0.0	0	1	0/0	0.0
Bills	578	356	3857	61.6	24	25	23/154	77.0
Opponents	507	321	3924	63.3	30	20	29/210	90.4

SCORING	TD R	TD P	TD Rt	PAT	FG	Saf	PTS
Lindell	0	0	0	25/25	13/15	0	64
Rayner	0	0	0	13/13	10/15	0	43
St. Johnson	0	7	0	0/0	0/0	0	42
Chandler	0	6	0	0/0	0/0	0	36
Jackson	6	0	0	0/0	0/0	0	36
Spiller	4	2	0	0/0	0/0	0	36
Nelson	0	5	0	0/0	0/0	0	30
Scott	0	0	2	0/0	0/0	0	12
B. Smith	1	1	0	0/0	0/0	0	12
Barnett	0	0	1	0/0	0/0	0	6
Byrd	0	0	1	0/0	0/0	0	6
Choice	1	0	0	0/0	0/0	0	6
Florence	0	0	1	0/0	0/0	0	6
Hagan	0	1	0	0/0	0/0	0	6
Sp. Johnson	0	0	1	0/0	0/0	0	6
Jones	0	1	0	0/0	0/0	0	6
McKelvin	0	0	1	0/0	0/0	0	6
Roosevelt	0	1	0	0/0	0/0	0	6
Coutu	0	0	0	3/3	0/1	0	3
Fitzpatrick	0	0	0	0/0	0/0	0	2
Sheppard	0	0	0	0/0	0/0	1	2
Bills	12	24	7	41/41	23/31	1	372
Opponents	19	30	4	51/52	21/25	0	434

2-Pt Conversions: Fitzpatrick
Bills 1-2, Opponents 1-1

RUSHING	No.	Yds	Avg	LG	TD
Jackson	170	934	5.5	80t	6
Spiller	107	561	5.2	38	4
Fitzpatrick	56	215	3.8	18	0
B. Smith	20	87	4.4	18	1
Choice	23	70	3.0	12	1
J. White	12	38	3.2	13	0
Thigpen	1	8	8.0	8	0
Wilson	1	6	6.0	6	0
Jones	1	2	2.0	2	0
Bills	391	1921	4.9	80t	12
Opponents	467	2224	4.8	76t	19

RECEIVING	No.	Yds	Avg	LG	TD
St. Johnson	76	1004	13.2	55	7
Nelson	61	658	10.8	35	5
Jackson	39	442	11.3	49	0
Spiller	39	269	6.9	19	2
Chandler	38	389	10.2	31	6
B. Smith	23	240	10.4	36t	1
Jones	23	231	10.0	48	1
Roosevelt	16	257	16.1	60t	1
Hagan	13	138	10.6	29	1
Choice	7	51	7.3	15	0
R. Martin	7	82	11.7	28	0
Caussin	5	41	8.2	13	0
L. Smith	4	11	2.8	6	0
Brock	2	27	13.5	21	0
Parrish	1	16	16.0	16	0
McIntyre	1	4	4.0	4	0
J. White	1	-3	-3.0	-3	0
Bills	356	3857	10.8	60t	24
Opponents	321	3924	12.2	65t	30

INTERCEPTIONS	No.	Yds	Avg	LG	TD
Wilson	4	26	6.5	12	0
Byrd	3	88	29.3	37t	1
Barnett	3	80	26.7	33	1
Florence	3	64	21.3	30	1
Scott	2	43	21.5	43t	1
McKelvin	1	21	21.0	21	0
Justin Rogers	1	15	15.0	15	0
Corner	1	4	4.0	4	0
Searcy	1	0	0.0	0	0
A. Williams	1	0	0.0	0	0
Sp. Johnson	0	0	—	—	0
Bills	20	341	17.1	43t	4
Opponents	25	327	13.1	43t	3

PUNTING	No.	Yds.	Avg.	In 20	LG
Moorman	72	3472	48.2	20	66
Bills	73	3472	47.6	20	66
Opponents	68	3039	44.7	27	64

PUNT RETURNS	Ret	FC	Yds	Avg	LG	TD
Spiller	13	8	127	9.8	45	0
McKelvin	8	11	156	19.5	80t	1
Parrish	5	2	46	9.2	28	0
Bills	26	21	329	12.7	80t	1
Opponents	43	8	494	11.5	26	0

KICKOFF RETURNS	No.	Yds	Avg	LG	TD
B. Smith	15	282	18.8	28	0
Rogers	13	373	28.7	54	0
Spiller	6	143	23.8	35	0
McKelvin	2	43	21.5	22	0
Caussin	1	12	12.0	12	0
Bills	37	853	23.1	54	0
Opponents	56	1144	20.4	59	0

FIELD GOALS	1-19	20-29	30-39	40-49	50+
Lindell	0/0	6/6	2/3	5/6	0/0
Rayner	0/0	5/6	3/4	0/1	2/4
Coutu	0/0	0/0	0/0	0/1	0/0
Bills	0/0	11/12	5/7	5/8	2/4
Opponents	0/0	9/9	4/4	7/9	1/3

SACKS	No.
Dareus	5.5
Kelsay	5.0
Barnett	3.0
Edwards	2.5
Moats	2.5
Heard	2.0
Sp. Johnson	2.0
Byrd	1.0
Carrington	1.0
Merriman	1.0
Morrison	1.0
Scott	1.0
(group)	1.0
Batten	0.5
Bills	29.0
Opponents	23.0

RECORD HOLDERS
INDIVIDUAL RECORDS—CAREER

Category	Name	Performance
Rushing (Yds.)	Thurman Thomas, 1988-1999	11,938
Passing (Yds.)	Jim Kelly, 1986-1996	35,467
Passing (TDs)	Jim Kelly, 1986-1996	237
Receiving (No.)	Andre Reed, 1985-1999	941
Receiving (Yds.)	Andre Reed, 1985-1999	13,095
Interceptions	George (Butch) Byrd, 1964-1970	40
Punting (Avg.)	Brian Moorman, 2001-2011	43.9
Punt Return (Avg.)	Roscoe Parrish, 2005-2011	12.0
Kickoff Return (Avg.)	O.J. Simpson, 1969-1977	30.0
Field Goals	Steve Christie, 1992-2000	234
Touchdowns (Tot.)	Andre Reed, 1985-1999	87
	Thurman Thomas, 1988-1999	87
Points	Steve Christie, 1992-2000	1,011
*Sacks	Bruce Smith, 1985-1999	**171.0

INDIVIDUAL RECORDS—SINGLE SEASON

Category	Name	Performance
Rushing (Yds.)	O.J. Simpson, 1973	2,003
Passing (Yds.)	Drew Bledsoe, 2002	4,359
Passing (TDs)	Jim Kelly, 1991	33
Receiving (No.)	Eric Moulds, 2002	100
Receiving (Yds.)	Eric Moulds, 1998	1,368
Interceptions	Billy Atkins, 1961	10
	Tom Janik, 1967	10
Punting (Avg.)	Brian Moorman, 2011	48.2
Punt Return (Avg.)	Roscoe Parrish, 2007	16.3
Kickoff Return (Avg.)	Terrence McGee, 2005	30.24
Field Goals	Steve Christie, 1998	33
Touchdowns (Tot.)	O.J. Simpson, 1975	23
Points	Steve Christie, 1998	140
*Sacks	Bruce Smith, 1990	19.0

INDIVIDUAL RECORDS—SINGLE GAME

Category	Name	Performance
Rushing (Yds.)	O.J. Simpson, 11-25-76	273
Passing (Yds.)	Drew Bledsoe, 9-15-02	463
Passing (TDs)	Jim Kelly, 9-8-91	6
Receiving (No.)	Andre Reed, 11-20-94	15
Receiving (Yds.)	Lee Evans, 11-19-06	265
Interceptions	Many times	3
	Last time by Nate Clements, 10-20-02	
Field Goals	Steve Christie, 10-20-96	6
Touchdowns (Tot.)	Cookie Gilchrist, 12-8-63	5
Points	Cookie Gilchrist, 12-8-63	30
*Sacks	Cornelius Bennett, 12-27-87	4.0
	Bruce Smith, 12-9-90, 9-18-94	4.0

*Sacks became an official statistic in 1982.
**NFL Record

2012 VETERAN ROSTER

No.	Name	Pos.	Ht.	Wt.	Birthdate	NFL Exp.	College	Hometown	How Acq.	'11 Games/ Starts
93	Anderson, Mark	DE	6-4	255	5/26/83	7	Alabama	Tulsa, Okla.	UFA(NE)-'12	16/1*
50	Barnett, Nick	OLB	6-2	228	5/27/81	10	Oregon State	Barstow, Calif.	FA-'11	16/16
57	Batten, Danny	DE	6-4	250	12/8/87	2	South Dakota State	Gilbert, Ariz.	D6B-'10	16/4
74	Brown, Colin	C	6-7	326	8/29/85	2	Missouri	Braymer, Mo.	FA-'10	11/1
31	Byrd, Jairus	FS	5-10	203	10/7/86	4	Oregon	Clayton, Mo.	D2a-'09	16/14
92	Carrington, Alex	DT	6-5	301	6/19/87	3	Arkansas State	Tupelo, Miss.	D3-'10	16/6
83	Caussin, Mike	TE	6-5	243	2/26/87	2	James Madison	Springfield, Va.	FA-'10	6/2
84	Chandler, Scott	TE	6-7	260	7/23/85	3	Iowa	Bedford, Texas	FA-'10	14/9
30	Choice, Tashard	RB	5-10	210	11/20/84	5	Georgia Tech	Hampton, Ga.	FA-'11	13/1*
17	Clowney, David	WR	6-0	188	7/8/85	3	Virginia Tech	Delray Beach, Fla.	FA-'12	0*
27	#Corner, Reggie	CB	5-9	180	11/17/83	5	Akron	Canton, Ohio	FA-'11	11/1
99	Dareus, Marcell	DT	6-3	331	3/13/90	2	Alabama	Huffman, Ala.	D1-'11	16/15
54	#Davis, Andra	LB	6-1	252	12/23/78	11	Florida	Live, Oak, Fla.	FA-'11	16/3
97	Dotson, Lionel	DE	6-4	286	2/11/85	3	Arizona	Houston, Texas	FA-'11	5/0
81	Easley, Marcus	WR	6-2	207	11/2/87	2	Connecticut	Stratford, Conn.	D4-'10	0*
98	Edwards, Dwan	DE	6-3	302	5/16/81	8	Oregon State	Columbus, Mont.	FA-'10	16/13
14	Fitzpatrick, Ryan	QB	6-2	225	11/24/82	7	Harvard	Gilbert, Ariz.	FA-'09	16/16
29	Florence, Drayton	CB	6-0	195	12/19/80	10	Tuskegee	Ocala, Fla.	FA-'09	16/16
73	Gilbert, Jarron	DT	6-5	289	9/30/86	2	San Jose State	Chino, Calif.	FA-'11	0*
80	Hagan, Derek	WR	6-2	210	9/21/84	7	Arizona State	Northridge, Calif.	FA-'11	10/3*
75	Hairston, Chris	LT	6-6	330	4/26/89	2	Clemson	Winston-Salem, N.C.	D4b-'11	13/7
72	Heard, Kellen	DT	6-6	339	10/17/85	2	Memphis	Wharton, Texas	FA-'10	15/2
22	Jackson, Fred	RB	6-1	216	2/20/81	6	Coe College	Fort Worth, Texas	FA-'06	10/10
91	Johnson, Spencer	DE	6-3	304	12/12/81	9	Auburn	Silas, Ala.	FA-'08	16/11
13	Johnson, Stevie	WR	6-2	207	7/22/86	5	Kentucky	San Francisco, Calif.	D7b-'08	16/16
19	Jones, Donald	WR	6-0	208	12/17/87	3	Youngstown State	Plainfield, N.J.	UFA-'10	8/7
90	Kelsay, Chris	LB	6-4	263	10/31/79	10	Nebraska	Auburn, Neb.	D2-'03	12/12
67	Levitre, Andy	LG	6-2	305	5/15/86	4	Oregon State	Los Gatos, Calif.	D2b-'09	16/16
9	Lindell, Rian	K	6-3	227	1/20/77	13	Washington St.	Vancouver, Wash.	FA-'03	8/0
82	Martin, Ruvell	WR	6-4	214	8/10/82	7	Saginaw Valley State	Muskegon, Mich.	FA-'11	14/0
24	McGee, Terrence	CB	5-9	205	10/14/80	10	Northwestern State	Athens, Texas	D4a-'03	6/6
38	McIntyre, Corey	FB	6-0	245	1/25/79	8	West Virginia	Indiantown, Fla.	FA-'08	16/1
28	McKelvin, Leodis	CB	5-10	185	9/1/85	5	Troy	Waycross, Ga.	D1-'08	16/6
59	McKillop, Scott	ILB	6-2	243	3/4/86	2	Pittsburgh	Export, Pa.	FA-'12	0*
56	Merriman, Shawne	DE	6-4	261	5/15/84	7	Maryland	Washington, D.C.	FA-'10	5/5
52	Moats, Arthur	OLB	6-2	250	3/14/88	3	James Madison	Portsmouth, Va.	D6a-'10	14/0
94	Moore, Kyle	DE	6-6	263	10/25/86	4	Southern California	Kathleen, Ga.	FA-'11	4/0
8	Moorman, Brian	P	6-0	174	2/5/76	12	Pittsburg State	Sedgwick, Kan.	FA-'01	16/0
58	Morrison, Kirk	OLB	6-2	245	2/19/82	8	San Diego State	Oakland, Calif.	FA-'11	13/0
86	Nelson, David	WR	6-5	214	11/7/86	3	Florida	Wichita Falls, Texas	FA-'10	16/13
89	Onobun, Fendi	TE	6-6	260	11/17/86	2	Houston	Houston, Texas	FA-'11	1/0*
79	Pears, Erik	T	6-8	316	6/25/82	8	Colorado State	Price, Utah	FA-'10	16/16
3	#Rayner, Dave	K	6-2	213	10/26/82	6	Michigan State	Oxford, Miss.	FA-'11	8/0*
76	Rinehart, Chad	G	6-5	307	5/4/85	4	Northern Iowa	Boone, Iowa	FA-'10	4/3
26	Rogers, Justin	CB	5-11	181	1/16/88	2	Richmond	Baton Rouge, La.	D7a-'11	13/1
18	Roosevelt, Naaman	WR	6-0	189	12/24/87	3	Buffalo	Buffalo, N.Y.	FA-'10	10/0
65	Sanborn, Garrison	LS	6-1	240	7/31/85	4	Florida State	Tampa, Fla.	FA-'09	16/0
43	Scott, Bryan	SS	6-1	220	4/13/81	10	Penn State	Doylestown, Pa.	FA-'07	16/7
25	Searcy, Da'Norris	SS	5-11	216	11/16/88	2	North Carolina	Decatur, Ga.	D4a-'11	16/3
55	Sheppard, Kelvin	ILB	6-2	244	1/2/88	2	Louisiana State	Stone Mountain, Ga.	D3-'11	16/9
16	Smith, Brad	QB/WR	6-2	213	12/12/83	7	Missouri	Youngstown, Ohio	FA-'11	15/5
85	Smith, Lee	TE	6-6	265	11/21/87	2	Marshall	Powell, Tenn.	FA-'11	10/3
21	Spiller, C.J.	RB	5-11	200	8/5/87	3	Clemson	Lake Butler, Fla.	D1-'10	16/11
4	Thigpen, Tyler	QB	6-1	218	4/14/84	4	Coastal Carolina	Winnsboro, S.C.	FA-'11	3/0
53	#Torbor, Reggie	LB	6-2	254	1/25/81	8	Auburn	Baton Rouge, La.	FA-'10	0*
96	Troup, Torell	NT	6-3	327	6/23/88	3	Central Florida	Conyers, Ga.	D2-'10	6/0
60	Urbik, Kraig	G	6-5	324	9/23/85	2	Wisconsin	Hudson, Wisc.	FA-'10	13/13
51	White, Chris	OLB	6-3	238	1/15/89	2	Mississippi State	Vancleave, Miss.	D6-'11	7/0
20	White, Johnny	RB	5-10	202	2/3/88	2	North Carolina	Asheville, N.C.	D5-'11	12/0
23	Williams, Aaron	CB	6-0	199	4/23/90	2	Texas	Round Rock, Texas	D2-'11	9/6
95	Williams, Kyle	NT	6-1	303	6/10/83	7	Louisiana State	Ruston, La.	D5a-'06	5/5
	Williams, Mario	DE	6-6	292	1/31/85	7	North Carolina State	Richlands, N.C.	UFA(Hou)-'12	5/5*
37	Wilson, George	FS	6-0	214	3/14/81	7	Arkansas	Paducah, Ky.	FA-'04	13/13
70	Wood, Eric	RG	6-4	310	3/18/86	4	Louisville	Cincinnati, Ohio	D1b-'09	9/9
71	Young, Sam	RT	6-8	316	6/24/87	3	Notre Dame	Coral Springs, Fla.	FA-'11	4/0
10	Young, Vince	QB	6-5	232	5/18/83	7	Texas	Houston, Texas	UFA(Phil)-'12	6/3*

* Anderson played 16 games with New England in '11; Choice played 6 games with Dallas, 1 with Washington, and 6 with Buffalo; Clowney last active with Carolina in '10; Easley missed '11 season because of injury; Gilbert inactive for 3 games; McKillop missed '10 season with San Francisco because of injury; Onobun played 1 game with Jacksonville; Rayner played 1 game with Oakland and 7 games with Buffalo; Torbor missed '11 season because of injury; M. Williams played 5 games with Houston; V. Young played 6 games with Philadelphia.

\#   Unrestricted Free Agent; subject to developments

Players lost through free agency (2): T Demetress Bell (Phil; 7 games), WR Roscoe Parrish (SD; 2).

Also played with Bills in '11—LB Antonio Coleman (3 games), K Brandon Coutu (1), TE David Martin (3).

FIRST-YEAR ROSTER

Name	Pos.	Ht.	Wt.	Birthdate	College	Hometown	How Acq.
Aiken, Kamar (1)	WR	6-2	213	5/30/89	Central Florida	Hollywood, Fla.	FA-'11
Asper, Mark	OL	6-7	325	11/8/85	Oregon	Idaho Falls, Idaho	D6
Bradham, Nigel	LB	6-1	241	9/4/89	Florida State	Crawfordville, Fla.	D4a
Brock, Kevin (1)	TE	6-5	249	4/9/86	Rutgers	Parsippany, N.J.	FA-'11
Brooks, Ron	CB	6-0	177	10/16/88	Louisiana State	Irving, Texas	D4b
Carder, Tank	LB	6-3	237	1/18/89	Texas Christian	Sweeny, Texas	D5b
Carmon, James	OL	6-7	320	2/21/89	Mississippi State	Baltimore, Md.	FA
Dickerson, Dorin	TE/FB	6-2	227	3/31/88	Pittsburgh	Imperial, Pa.	FA
Douglas, Chris	RB	5-9	213	6/11/89	Missouri State	Lawrenceville, Ga.	FA
Eddins, Robert (1)	DE	6-3	246	10/11/88	Ball State	Detroit, Mich.	FA-'11
Gilmore, Stephon	CB	6-0	193	10/19/90	South Carolina	Rock Hill, S.C.	D1
Glenn, Cordy	OL	6-5	348	9/18/89	Georgia	Riverdale, Ga.	D2
Graham, TJ	WR	6-0	180	7/27/89	North Carolina State	Raleigh, N.C.	D3
Hill, Cris	CB	5-11	180	8/29/89	Virginia Tech	Richmond, Va.	FA
Howell, Delano	SS	5-11	198	11/17/89	Stanford	Newhall, Calif.	FA
Jasper, Michael (1)	OL	6-4	375	10/8/86	Bethel	Mt. Juliet, Tenn.	D7b-'11
Madsen, Paul	OL	6-4	309	2/12/86	Colorado State	Provo, Utah	FA
Nesbitt, Josh (1)	FS	6-1	213	4/15/88	Georgia Tech	Greensboro, Ga.	FA-'11
Potter, John	K	6-2	209	1/24/90	Western Michigan	Grand Haven, Mich.	D7
Powell, Shawn	P	6-4	235	11/29/88	Florida State	Rome, Ga.	FA
Ross, Jay (1)	DT	6-3	319	10/3/87	East Carolina	Wilmington, NC	FA-'11
Saenz, Nick	S	6-1	190	2/23/90	Houston	Pearland, Texas	FA
Sanders, Zebrie	OT	6-5	308	12/4/89	Florida State	Dayton, Ohio	D5a
Snow, David	OL	6-4	305	11/9/89	Texas	Gilmer, Texas	FA
Sukay, Nick	DB	6-1	219	3/9/89	Penn State	Mt. Pleasant, Pa.	FA
Vermiglio, Jake (1)	G	6-5	339	11/20/87	North Carolina State	Rochester, MI	FA-'11
Williams, Garrick	LB	6-2	232	10/26/89	Texas A&M	Desoto, Texas	FA
Williams, Keith (1)	G	6-5	330	4/8/88	Nebraska	Florissant, MO	FA-'11

The term NFL Rookie is defined as a player who is in his first season of professional football and has not been on the roster of another professional football team for any regular-season or postseason games. A Rookie is designated by an "R" on NFL rosters. Players who have been active in another professional football league or players who have NFL experience, including either preseason training camp or being on an Active List or Inactive List, or on Reserve/Injured or Reserve/Physically Unable to Perform for fewer than six regular-season games, are termed NFL First-Year Players. An NFL First-Year Player is designated by a "1" on NFL rosters. Thereafter, a player is credited with an additional year of experience for each season in which he accumulates six games on the Active List or Inactive List, or on Reserve/Injured or Reserve/Physically Unable to Perform.

Log on to www.buffalobills.com for an up-to-date roster.

COACHING STAFF

Head Coach,
Chan Gailey

Pro Career: Gailey was named Buffalo's fifteenth head coach on January 19, 2010. Gailey has over three decades of coaching experience, including head coaching experience in college, World League and the NFL. Gailey served as head coach of the Dallas Cowboys from 1998-1999, leading the Cowboys to playoff berths in each season and compiling an 18-14 regular season record. Gailey also has four stints as offensive coordinator in the NFL with Denver (1989-1990), Pittsburgh (1996-1997), Miami (2000-2001) and Kansas City (2008). With the Cowboys, in 1998, Gailey became the first coach in NFC East history to lead his team to a perfect 8-0 record in division play. Spent nine of his previous fifteen NFL seasons as either a head coach or offensive coordinator. In those nine seasons, his teams made the playoffs seven times and had a 1,000-yard rusher in seven different years. In total, he has made playoff appearances in 11 of his 15 seasons in NFL coaching. His résumé also boasts four Super Bowl berths, including one with Pittsburgh (XXX) and three with Denver (XXI, XXII and XXIV). Served as the head coach at Georgia Tech from 2002-2007, becoming the first coach in school history to lead the Yellow Jackets to bowl appearance in his first six seasons. Began his NFL career as an assistant with the Broncos from 1985-1990 under head coach Dan Reeves, where he worked with John Elway. As the team's offensive coordinator/wide receivers coach in 1989, Denver advanced to Super Bowl XXIV. Career record: 28-38.

Background: Gailey was a three-year letter-winner at quarterback for Florida. He coached collegiately at Florida (1974-75), Troy State (1976-78), Air Force (1979-1982). Gailey was an all-state quarterback at Americus High School in Americus, Ga.

Personal: Born January 5, 1952, Gainesville, Ga. He and his wife, Laurie, have two sons, Tate and Andrew, and five grandchildren.

ASSISTANT COACHES

Bob Bicknell, wide receivers; born November, 13, 1969, Holliston, Mass. Tight end Boston College 1988-1991. No pro playing experience. College coach: Boston University 1993-97, Temple 2006. Pro coach: Frankfurt Galaxy (NFLE) 1998-99, Berlin Thunder 2000-03 (NFLE), Cologne Centurions (NFLE) 2004-05, Kansas City Chiefs 2007-09, joined Bills in 2010.

George Catavolos, defensive backs; born May 8, 1945, Chicago, Ill. Defensive back Purdue 1964-67. No pro playing experience. College coach: Purdue 1967-68, 1971-76, Middle Tennessee State 1969, Louisville 1970, Kentucky 1977-1981, Tennessee 1982-83. Pro coach: Indianapolis Colts 1984-1994, 1998- 2001, Carolina Panthers 1995-97, Washington Redskins 2002-03, Detroit Lions 2004-05, joined Bills in 2006.

Eric Ciano, co-head strength and conditioning; born August 8, 1973, Waltham, Mass. Offensive line Springfield (Mass.) College 1993-97. No pro playing experience. College coach: Tennessee 1997-99, Louisiana Tech 2000-02, Tennessee 2002-04, Georgia Tech 2005-09. Pro coach: Joined Bills in 2010.

Joe D'Alessandris, offensive line; born April, 29, 1954, Aliquippa, Pa. Guard Western Carolina 1972-76. No pro playing experience. College coach: Western Carolina 1977-78, Livingston 1979-1983, Memphis 1984-85, Tennessee-Chattanooga 1986-89, Samford 1993, Texas A&M 1994, Pittsburgh 1996, Duke 1997-2001, Georgia Tech 2002-07. Pro coach: Ottawa Rough Riders (CFL) 1990, Birmingham Fire (WLAF) 1991-92, Memphis (AFL) 1995, Kansas City Chiefs 2008-09, joined Bills in 2010.

Andrew Dees, offensive line; born December 1, 1969, Babylon, N.Y. Offensive line/tight end Syracuse 1988-1991. Pro offensive line Cincinnati Bengals 1992, Seattle Seahawks 1993. College coach: Wagner 1997, Stony Brook 1998-2000, Buffalo 2001-05, Temple 2006-2010, Massachusetts 2011. Pro coach: Joined Bills in 2012.

Bruce DeHaven, special teams coordinator; born September 6, 1948, Trousdale, Kan. Attended Southwestern (Kan.) College. No college or pro playing experience. College coach: Kansas 1979-1981, New Mexico State 1982. Pro coach: New Jersey Generals (USFL) 1983, Pittsburgh Maulers (USFL) 1984, Orlando Renegades (USFL) 1985, Buffalo Bills 1987-1999, San Francisco 49ers 2000-02, Dallas Cowboys 2003-06, Seattle Seahawks 2007-09, rejoined Bills in 2010.

John Gamble, co-head strength and conditioning; born June 26, 1957, Richmond, Va. Linebacker Hampton 1975-78. No pro playing experience. College coach: Virginia 1982-1993. Pro coach: Miami Dolphins 1994-2005, joined Bills in 2010.

William Inge, asst. defensive line; born December 17, 1973, Kirkwood, Mo. Defensive end Iowa 1993-96. Pro defensive end Tennessee Titans 1997. College coach: Iowa 1998-2000, Northern Iowa 2001-04, Colorado 2005, San Diego State 2006-07, Cincinnati 2008-09, Buffalo 2010-11. Pro coach: Joined Bills in 2012.

Stan Kwan, asst. special teams; born November 2, 1967, Phoenix, Ariz. Attended South Mountain (Ariz.) C.C., San Diego State. No college or pro playing experience. Pro coach: San Diego Chargers 1991-96, Detroit Lions 1997-2000, Arizona Cardinals 2001-03, Detroit Lions 2004-09, joined Bills in 2010.

David Lee, quarterbacks; born July 2, 1953, Cape Girardeau, Mo. Quarterback Vanderbilt 1971-74. No pro playing experience. College coach: Tennessee-Martin 1975-1976, Vanderbilt 1977, Mississippi 1978-1982, 2011, New Mexico 1983, Arkansas 1984-88, 2001-02, 2007, Texas-El Paso 1989-1993 (head coach), Rice

1994-2000. Pro coach: Dallas Cowboys 2003-06, Miami Dolphins 2008-2010, joined Bills in 2012.

Pete Metzelaars, tight ends; born May 24, 1960, Three Rivers, Mich. Tight end Wabash College 1978-1981. Pro tight end Seattle Seahawks 1982-84, Buffalo Bills 1985-1994, Carolina Panthers 1995, Detroit Lions 1996-97. College coach: Wingate 2003. Pro coach: Barcelona Dragons (NFLE) 2003, Indianapolis Colts 2004-2011, joined Bills in 2012.

Curtis Modkins, offensive coordinator/running backs; born November 15, 1970, Marlin, Texas. Running back Texas Christian 1989-1992. No pro playing experience. College coach: Texas Christian 1995-97, New Mexico 1998-2001, Georgia Tech 2002-07. Pro coach: Kansas City Chiefs 2008, Arizona Cardinals 2009, joined Bills in 2010.

Kevin Patullo, offensive quality control; born July 14, 1981, Hillsborough, N.J. Quarterback/wide receiver South Florida 1999-2001. College coach: South Florida 2002-03, Arizona 2004-06. Pro coach: Kansas City Chiefs 2007-2008, joined Bills in 2010.

Bob Sanders, linebackers; born December 5, 1953, Jacksonville, N.C. Linebacker Davidson College 1973-75. No pro playing experience. College coach: Georgia Tech 1978, East Carolina 1980-82, Richmond 1983-84, Duke 1985-89, Florida 1990-2000. Pro coach: Miami Dolphins 2001-04, Green Bay Packers 2005-08, joined Bills in 2009.

Giff Smith, defensive line; born October 23, 1968, Atlanta, Ga. Defensive end Georgia Southern 1986-1990. No pro playing experience. Attended College coach: Arkansas 1991-93, Georgia 1994-1995, Georgia Southern 1996-98, Tulane 1999-2003, Georgia Tech 2004-09. Pro coach: Joined Bills in 2010.

Eric Thatcher, defensive quality control; born December 5, 1984, Cincinnati, Ohio. Defensive back Pittsburgh 2005-08. No pro playing experience. College coach: St. Vincent College 2009, Pittsburgh 2010, Mercyhurst 2011. Pro coach: Joined Bills in 2012.

Dave Wannstedt, asst. head coach/defensive coordinator; born May 21, 1952, Baldwin, Pa. Tackle Pittsburgh 1970-73. No pro playing experience. College coach: Pittsburgh 1975-78, 2005-2010 (head coach 2005-2010), Oklahoma State 1979-1982, Southern California 1983-85, Miami 1986-88. Pro coach: Dallas Cowboys 1989-1992, Chicago Bears 1993-98 (head coach), Miami Dolphins 1999-2004 (head coach 2000-04), joined Bills in 2011.

Adrian White, defensive quality control; born April 6, 1964, Orange Park, Fla. Defensive back Southern Illinois 1983, Florida 1985-86. Pro defensive back: N.Y. Giants 1987-1991, Green Bay Packers 1992, New England Patriots 1993. Pro coach: Rhein Fire (NFLE) 2001-07, joined Bills in 2008.

American Football Conference
North Division
Team Colors: Black, Orange, and White
One Paul Brown Stadium
Cincinnati, Ohio 45202-3492
Telephone: (513) 621-3550
Ticket Office (513) 621-TDTD (8383)

2012 SCHEDULE
PRESEASON
Aug. 10 **New York Jets** 7:30
Aug. 16 at Atlanta..........................8:00
Aug. 23 **Green Bay**.........................7:00
Aug. 30 at Indianapolis...................7:00

REGULAR SEASON
Sep. 10 at Baltimore (Mon) 7:00
Sep. 16 **Cleveland** 1:00
Sep. 23 at Washington 1:00
Sep. 30 at Jacksonville...................4:05
Oct. 7 **Miami**...............................1:00
Oct. 14 at Cleveland 1:00
Oct. 21 **Pittsburgh**.......................8:20
Oct. 28 BYE
Nov. 4 **Denver**..............................1:00
Nov. 11 **New York Giants**...............1:00
Nov. 18 at Kansas City 1:00
Nov. 25 **Oakland** 1:00
Dec. 2 at San Diego 4:15
Dec. 9 **Dallas**...............................1:00
Dec. 13 at Philadelphia (Thurs)........8:20
Dec. 23 at Pittsburgh......................1:00
Dec. 30 **Baltimore**.........................1:00
All times ET

Stadium: Paul Brown Stadium
(opened in 2000)
•**Capacity:** 65,515
One Paul Brown Stadium
Cincinnati, Ohio 45202-3492
Playing Surface: Synthetic
Training Camp: Paul Brown Stadium
Cincinnati, Ohio 45202

PAUL BROWN STADIUM

CLUB OFFICIALS
President: Mike Brown
Senior Vice President: Pete Brown
Executive Vice President: Katie Blackburn
Vice President: Paul Brown
Vice President: John Sawyer
Vice President: Troy Blackburn
Business Manager: Bill Connelly
Chief Financial Officer: Bill Scanlon
Director of Business Development:
  Bob Bedinghaus
Managing Director of Paul Brown
  Stadium: Eric Brown
Directors of Technology: Michael Kayes,
  Jo Ann Ralstin
Bengals.com Editor: Geoff Hobson
Director of Security: Rusty Guy
Director of Sales and Public Affairs:
  Jeff Berding
Director of Corporate Sales, Marketing
  and Broadcasting: Brian Sells
Ticket Manager: Tim Kelly
Director of Player Relations: Eric Ball
Director of Player Personnel: Duke Tobin
Public Relations Director: Jack Brennan
Athletic Trainer: Paul Sparling
Equipment Manager: Jeff Brickner
Video Director: Travis Brammer

COACHING HISTORY
(300-389-2)
Records include postseason games
1968-1975 Paul Brown..................55-59-1
1976-78   Bill Johnson* 18-15-0
1978-79   Homer Rice 8-19-0
1980-83   Forrest Gregg 34-27-0
1984-1991 Sam Wyche................64-68-0
1992-96   Dave Shula**..............19-52-0
1996-2000 Bruce Coslet*** 21-39-0
2000-02   Dick LeBeau 12-33-0
2003-2011 Marvin Lewis..............69-77-1
  * Resigned after five games in 1978
 ** Released after seven games in 1996
*** Resigned after three games in 2000

PAID ATTENDANCE
Home 370,333   Away 502,539
Total 872,872
Single-game home record,
  66,188 (10/28/07)
Single-season home record, 516,154
  (2006)

2012 DRAFT CHOICES
Round	Name	Pos.	College
1	Dre Kirkpatrick	DB	Alabama
	Kevin Zeitler	G	Wisconsin
2	Devon Still	DT	Penn St.
3	Mohamed Sanu	WR	Rutgers
	Brandon Thompson	DT	Clemson
4	Orson Charles	TE	Georgia
5	Shaun Prater	DB	Iowa
	Marvin Jones	WR	California
	George Iloka	DB	Boise St.
6	Dan Herron	RB	Ohio St.

2011 TEAM RECORD

PRESEASON (1-3)

Date	Result		Opponent
8/12	L	3-34	at Detroit
8/21	L	7-27	at New York Jets
8/25	W	24-13	Carolina
9/1	L	13-17	Indianapolis

REGULAR SEASON (9-7)

Date	Result		Opponent
9/11	W	27-17	at Cleveland
9/18	L	22-24	at Denver
9/25	L	8-13	San Francisco
10/2	W	23-20	Buffalo
10/9	W	30-20	at Jacksonville
10/16	W	27-17	Indianapolis
10/30	W	34-12	at Seattle
11/6	W	24-17	at Tennessee
11/13	L	17-24	Pittsburgh
11/20	L	24-31	at Baltimore
11/27	W	23-20	Cleveland
12/4	L	7-35	at Pittsburgh
12/11	L	19-20	Houston
12/18	W	20-13	at St. Louis
12/24	W	23-16	Arizona
1/1	L	16-24	Baltimore

POSTSEASON (0-1)

1/7	L	10-31	at Houston

SCORE BY PERIODS

Bengals	83	59	86	116	0	—	344
Opponents	51	132	50	90	0	—	323

2011 TEAM STATISTICS

	Bengals	Opp.
Total First Downs	285	284
Rushing	93	94
Passing	160	170
Penalty	32	20
3rd Down: Made/Att	80/219	78/220
3rd Down Pct.	36.5	35.5
4th Down: Made/Att	4/10	4/11
4th Down Pct.	40.0	36.4
Possession Avg.	30:19	29:41
Total Net Yards	5118	5060
Avg. Per Game	319.9	316.3
Total Plays	1015	1009
Avg. Per Play	5.0	5.0
Net Yards Rushing	1778	1675
Avg. Per Game	111.1	104.7
Total Rushes	455	425
Net Yards Passing	3340	3385
Avg. Per Game	208.8	211.6
Sacked/Yards Lost	25/167	45/277
Gross Yards	3507	3662
Att./Completions	535/308	539/319
Completion Pct.	57.6	59.2
Had Intercepted	14	10
Punts/Average	91/44.2	98/46.6
Net Punting Avg.	91/39.2	98/38.9
Penalties/Yards	99/874	101/878
Fumbles/Ball Lost	17/8	26/12
Touchdowns	35	37
Rushing	10	14
Passing	21	21
Returns	4	2

2011 INDIVIDUAL STATISTICS

PASSING

	Att.	Comp.	Yds.	Pct.	TD	Int.	Tkld.	Rate
Dalton	516	300	3398	58.1	20	13	24/160	80.4
Gradkowski	18	8	109	44.4	1	1	1/7	59.7
Scott	1	0	0	0.0	0	0		39.6
Bengals	535	308	3507	57.6	21	14	25/167	79.6
Opponents	539	319	3662	59.2	21	10	45/277	85.0

SCORING

	TD R	TD P	TD Rt	PAT	FG	Saf	PTS
Nugent	0	0	0	33/34	33/38	0	132
Green	0	7	0	0/0	0/0	0	42
Benson	6	0	0	0/0	0/0	0	36
Gresham	0	6	0	0/0	0/0	0	36
Simpson	0	4	0	0/0	0/0	0	24
Caldwell	0	3	0	0/0	0/0	0	18
Scott	3	0	0	0/0	0/0	0	18
Atkins	0	0	1	0/0	0/0	0	6
Cochart	0	1	0	0/0	0/0	0	6
Dalton	1	0	0	0/0	0/0	0	6
Dunlap	0	0	1	0/0	0/0	0	6
Nelson	0	0	1	0/0	0/0	0	6
Tate	0	0	1	0/0	0/0	0	6
Bengals	10	21	4	33/34	33/38	1	344
Opponents	14	21	2	35/35	22/27	0	323

2-Pt Conversions: Bengals 0-1, Opponents 0-2

RUSHING

	No.	Yds	Avg	LG	TD
Benson	273	1067	3.9	42	6
Scott	112	380	3.4	25t	3
Dalton	37	152	4.1	17	1
Leonard	17	85	5.0	14	0
Green	5	53	10.6	22	0
Hawkins	5	25	5.0	8	0
Peerman	3	15	5.0	11	0
Gradkowski	3	1	0.3	1	0
Bengals	455	1778	3.9	42	10
Opponents	425	1675	3.9	70t	14

RECEIVING

	No.	Yds	Avg	LG	TD
Green	65	1057	16.3	58	7
Gresham	56	596	10.6	31	6
Simpson	50	725	14.5	84	4
Caldwell	37	317	8.6	49t	3
Hawkins	23	263	11.4	26	0
Leonard	22	210	9.5	37	0
Benson	15	82	5.5	11	0
Scott	13	38	2.9	14	0
Lee	11	115	10.5	26	0
Cochart	5	44	8.8	25	1
Whalen	4	27	6.8	13	0
Shipley	4	14	3.5	5	0
Pressley	3	19	6.3	9	0
Bengals	308	3507	11.4	84	21
Opponents	319	3662	11.5	74t	21

INTERCEPTIONS

	No.	Yds	Avg	LG	TD
Nelson	4	115	28.8	75t	1
Hall	2	15	7.5	15	0
Clements	2	5	2.5	7	0
Maualuga	1	2	2.0	2	0
Mich. Johnson	1	0	0.0	0	0
Bengals	10	137	13.7	75t	1
Opponents	14	159	11.4	43t	1

PUNTING

	No.	Yds.	Avg.	In 20	LG
Huber	91	4023	44.2	24	71
Bengals	91	4023	44.2	24	71
Opponents	98	4562	46.6	23	65

PUNT RETURNS

	Ret	FC	Yds	Avg	LG	TD
Tate	51	17	543	10.6	56t	1
Jones	2	0	67	33.5	63	0
Clements	0	1	0	—	—	0
Bengals	53	18	610	11.5	63	1
Opponents	38	26	273	7.2	60t	1

KICKOFF RETURNS

	No.	Yds	Avg	LG	TD
Tate	42	998	23.8	45	0
Clements	1	4	4.0	4	0
Peerman	1	10	10.0	10	0
Scott	1	26	26.0	26	0
Jones	0	-12	—	-12	0
Bengals	45	1026	22.8	45	0
Opponents	44	916	20.8	51	0

FIELD GOALS

	1-19	20-29	30-39	40-49	50+
Nugent	0/0	14/14	5/8	14/16	0/0
Bengals	0/0	14/14	5/8	14/16	0/0
Opponents	1/1	8/8	4/4	7/9	2/5

SACKS

	No.
Atkins	7.5
Fanene	6.5
Mich. Johnson	6.0
Dunlap	4.5
Rucker	4.0
Crocker	3.5
Geathers	2.5
Peko	2.5
Nelson	2.0
Lawson	1.5
Clements	1.0
Howard	1.0
Jennings	1.0
Sims	1.0
Skuta	0.5
Bengals	45.0
Opponents	25.0

RECORD HOLDERS
INDIVIDUAL RECORDS—CAREER

Category	Name	Performance
Rushing (Yds.)	Corey Dillon, 1997-2003	8,061
Passing (Yds.)	Ken Anderson, 1971-1986	32,838
Passing (TDs)	Ken Anderson, 1971-1986	197
Receiving (No.)	Chad Ochocinco, 2001-2010	751
Receiving (Yds.)	Chad Ochocinco, 2001-2010	10,783
Interceptions	Ken Riley, 1969-1983	65
Punting (Avg.)	Dave Lewis, 1970-73	43.8
Punt Return (Avg.)	Brandon Tate, 2011	10.6
Kickoff Return (Avg.)	Lemar Parrish, 1970-77	24.7
Field Goals	Jim Breech, 1980-1992	225
Touchdowns (Tot.)	Pete Johnson, 1977-1983	70
Points	Jim Breech, 1980-1992	1,151
*Sacks	Eddie Edwards, 1977-1988	47.5

INDIVIDUAL RECORDS—SINGLE SEASON

Category	Name	Performance
Rushing (Yds.)	Rudi Johnson, 2005	1,458
Passing (Yds.)	Carson Palmer, 2007	4,131
Passing (TDs)	Carson Palmer, 2005	32
Receiving (No.)	T.J. Houshmandzadeh, 2007	112
Receiving (Yds.)	Chad Ochocinco, 2007	1,440
Interceptions	Delta O'Neal, 2005	10
Punting (Avg.)	Dave Lewis, 1970	46.2
Punt Return (Avg.)	Lemar Parrish, 1974	18.8
Kickoff Return (Avg.)	Tremain Mack, 1999	27.1
Field Goals	Mike Nugent, 2011	33
Touchdowns (Tot.)	Carl Pickens, 1995	17
Points	Mike Nugent, 2011	132
*Sacks	Eddie Edwards, 1983	13.0

INDIVIDUAL RECORDS—SINGLE GAME

Category	Name	Performance
Rushing (Yds.)	Corey Dillon, 10-22-00	278
Passing (Yds.)	Boomer Esiason, 10-7-90	490
Passing (TDs)	Carson Palmer, 9-16-07	6
Receiving (No.)	Carl Pickens, 10-11-98	13
Receiving (Yds.)	Chad Ochocinco, 11-12-06	260
Interceptions	Many times	3
	Last time by Leon Hall, 12-21-08	
Field Goals	Shayne Graham, 11-11-07	7
Touchdowns (Tot.)	Larry Kinnebrew, 10-28-84	4
	Corey Dillon, 12-4-97	4
Points	Larry Kinnebrew, 10-28-84	24
	Corey Dillon, 12-4-97	24
*Sacks	Antwan Odom, 9-20-09	5.0

*Sacks became an official statistic in 1982.

2012 VETERAN ROSTER

No.	Name	Pos.	Ht.	Wt.	Birthdate	NFL Exp.	College	Hometown	How Acq.	'11 Games/ Starts
25	Allen, Jason	CB	6-1	200	7/5/83	6	Tennessee	Muscle Shoals, Ala.	UFA(Hou)-'12	16/4*
92	Anderson, Jamaal	DE	6-6	289	2/6/86	6	Arkansas	Little Rock, Ark.	UFA(Ind)-'12	15/1*
97	Atkins, Geno	DT	6-1	300	3/28/88	3	Georgia	Pembroke Pines, Fla.	D4a-'10	16/16
32	#Benson, Cedric	HB	5-11	227	12/28/82	8	Texas	Midland, Texas.	FA-'08	15/15
22	Clements, Nate	CB	6-0	200	12/12/79	12	Ohio State	Shaker Heights, Ohio	FA-'11	15/15
81	Cochart, Colin	TE	6-4	254	7/7/87	2	South Dakota State	Kewaunee, Wisc.	FA-'11	10/3
73	Collins, Anthony	T	6-5	315	11/2/85	5	Kansas	Beaumont, Texas	D4-'08	7/2
64	Cook, Kyle	C	6-3	316	7/25/83	5	Michigan State	Macomb, Mich.	FA-'07	16/16
14	Dalton, Andy	QB	6-2	220	10/29/87	2	Texas Christian	Katy, Texas	D2-'11	16/16
96	Dunlap, Carlos	DE	6-6	289	2/28/89	3	Florida	North Charleston, S.C.	D2-'10	12/1
91	Geathers, Robert	DE	6-3	280	8/11/83	9	Georgia	Georgetown, S.C.	D4b-'04	14/13
21	Ghee, Brandon	CB	6-0	193	6/6/87	3	Wake Forest	Fayetteville, N.C.	D3b-'10	7/0
7	Gradkowski, Bruce	QB	6-1	220	1/27/83	7	Toledo	Pittsburgh, Pa.	UFA(Oak)-'11	2/0
18	Green, A.J.	WR	6-4	207	7/31/88	2	Georgia	Summerville, S.C.	D1-'11	15/15
42	Green-Ellis, BenJarvus	HB	5-11	224	7/2/85	5	Mississippi	New Orleans, La.	UFA(NE)-'12	16/6*
84	Gresham, Jermaine	TE	6-5	260	6/16/88	3	Oklahoma	Ardmore, Okla.	D1-'10	14/13
29	Hall, Leon	CB	5-11	195	12/9/84	6	Michigan	Vista, Calif.	D1-'07	9/9
46	Harris, Clark	LS	6-5	252	7/10/84	4	Rutgers	Manahawkin, N.J.	FA-'09	16/0
95	Harvey, Derrick	DE	6-5	268	11/9/86	5	Florida	Greenbelt, Md.	UFA(Den)-'12	5/0*
16	Hawkins, Andrew	WR	5-7	175	3/10/86	2	Toledo	Johnstown, Pa.	W(StL)-'11	13/0
98	Hayden, Nick	DT	6-4	292	2/4/86	3	Wisconsin	Hartland, Wisc.	FA-'11	2/0
53	Howard, Thomas	LB	6-3	240	7/14/83	7	Texas-El Paso	Lubbock, Texas	UFA(Oak)-'11	16/15
10	Huber, Kevin	P	6-1	208	7/16/85	4	Cincinnati	Cincinnati, Ohio	D5-'09	16/0
60	Hudson, Otis	G	6-5	311	7/19/86	2	Eastern Illinois	Barrington, Ill.	D5-'10	0*
60	#Jennings, Kelly	CB	5-11	180	11/30/82	7	Miami	Live Oak, Fla..	T(Sea)-'11	13/1
59	#Johnson, Brandon	LB	6-5	245	4/5/83	7	Louisville	Birmingham, Ala.	FA-'08	16/1
93	Johnson, Michael	DE	6-7	267	2/7/87	4	Georgia Tech	Selma, Ala.	D3a-'09	16/5
24	Jones, Adam	CB	5-10	185	9/30/83	6	West Virginia	Atlanta, Ga.	FA-'10	8/7
99	Lawson, Manny	LB	6-5	240	7/3/84	7	North Carolina State	Goldsboro, N.C.	UFA(SF)-'11	16/15
86	Lee, Donald	TE	6-4	248	8/31/80	10	Mississippi State	Maben, Miss.	FA-'11	9/4
40	Leonard, Brian	HB	6-1	225	2/3/84	6	Rutgers	Gouverneur, N.Y.	T(StL)-'09	13/0
58	Maualuga, Rey	LB	6-2	260	1/20/87	4	Southern California	Eureka, Calif.	D2-'09	13/13
26	Mays, Taylor	S	6-3	230	2/7/88	3	Southern California	Seattle, Wash.	T(SF)-'11	10/0
45	Miles, Jeromy	S	6-2	210	7/20/87	3	Massachusetts	Sicklerville, N.J.	FA-'10	16/0
52	Moch, Dontay	LB	6-2	241	7/19/88	2	Nevada	Phoenix, Ariz.	D3-'11	0*
56	Muckelroy, Roddrick	LB	6-2	245	10/27/86	3	Texas	Hallsville, Texas	D4b-'10	0*
20	Nelson, Reggie	S	5-11	206	9/21/83	6	Florida	Melbourne, Fla.	T(Jax)-'10	16/16
23	Newman, Terence	CB	5-10	192	9/4/78	10	Kansas State	Salina, Kan.	FA-'12	14/14*
2	Nugent, Mike	K	5-10	183	3/2/82	8	Ohio State	Centerville, Ohio	FA-'10	16/0
30	Peerman, Cedric	HB	5-10	211	10/10/86	3	Virginia	Gladys, Va.	W(Det)-'10	15/0
94	Peko, Domata	DT	6-3	322	11/27/84	7	Michigan State	Pago Pago, American Samoa	D4'06	16/16
36	Pressley, Chris	FB	5-11	256	8/8/86	4	Wisconsin	Woodbury, N.J.	FA-'10	15/10
57	Rey, Vincent	LB	6-2	247	9/6/87	2	Duke	Far Rockaway, N.Y.	FA-'10	16/0
5	Robinson, Zac	QB	6-3	218	9/29/86	2	Oklahoma State	Littleton, Colo.	FA-'11	0*
74	Roland, Dennis	T	6-9	322	3/10/83	5	Georgia	Bolivar, Mo.	FA-'08	16/3
31	Sands, Robert	S	6-4	209	11/3/89	2	West Virginia	Carol City, Fla.	D5-'11	1/0
28	#Scaife, Bo	TE	6-3	249	1/6/81	8	Texas	Denver, Colo.	UFA(Tenn)-'11	0*
28	Scott, Bernard	HB	5-10	198	2/10/84	4	Abilene Christian	Vernon, Texas	D6b-'09	16/1
11	Shipley, Jordan	WR	6-0	188	12/23/85	3	Texas	Burnet, Texas	D3a-'10	2/0
90	Sims, Pat	DT	6-2	330	11/29/85	5	Auburn	Fort Lauderdale, Fla.	D3a-'08	11/1
51	Skuta, Dan	LB	6-2	248	4/21/86	4	Grand Valley State	Flint, Mich.	FA-'09	16/3
71	Smith, Andre	T	6-4	335	1/25/87	4	Alabama	Birmingham, Ala.	D1-'09	14/14
19	Tate, Brandon	WR	6-1	195	10/5/87	4	North Carolina	Burlington, N.C.	W(NE)-'11	16/0
88	Whalen, Ryan	WR	6-1	202	7/26/89	2	Stanford	Alamo, Calif.	D6-'11	4/0
70	Wharton, Travelle	G	6-4	312	5/19/81	9	South Carolina	Fountain Inn, S.C.	FA-'12	16/16*
77	Whitworth, Andrew	OT	6-7	335	12/12/81	7	Louisiana State	West Monroe, La.	D2-'06	16/16
63	#Williams, Bobbie	G	6-4	340	9/25/76	13	Arkansas	Jefferson, Texas	UFA(Phil)-'04	9/9
27	#Wilson, Gibril	S	6-0	206	11/12/81	9	Tennessee	San Jose, Calif.	FA-'10	16/1

* Allen played 16 games with Houston in '11; Anderson played 15 games with Indianapolis; Green-Ellis played 16 games with New England; Harvey played 5 games with Denver; Hudson inactive for 7 games; Moch inactive for 16 games; Muckelroy missed '11 season because of injury; Newman played 14 games with Dallas; Robinson last active with Seattle and Detroit in '10; Scaife missed '11 season because of injury; Wharton played 16 games with Carolina.

Unrestricted free agent; subject to developments.

Traded—LB Keith Rivers (0 games in '11) to New York Giants, QB Carson Palmer (0) to Oakland.

Players lost through free agency (6): WR Andre Caldwell (Den; 13 games), DE Jonathan Fanene (NE; 16), G Nate Livings (Dall; 16), G Mike McGlynn (Ind; 7), DE Frostee Rucker (Cle; 16), WR Jerome Simpson (Minn; 16).

Also played with Bengals in '11—S Chris Crocker (16 games), S Rico Murray (1), S Morgan Trent (6).

FIRST-YEAR ROSTER

Name	Pos.	Ht.	Wt.	Birthdate	College	Hometown	How Acq.
Binns, Armon (1)	WR	6-3	210	9/8/89	Cincinnati	Pasadena, Calif.	FA-'11
Burfict, Vontaze	LB	6-1	248	9/24/90	Arizona State	Corona, Calif.	FA
Charles, Orson	TE	6-3	250	1/27/91	Georgia	Tampa, Fla.	D4
Davis, Bryce	LS	6-3	250	6/16/89	Central Oklahoma	Duncan, Okla.	FA
Develin, James (1)	FB	6-3	251	7/23/88	Brown	Gilbertsville, Pa.	FA-'10
Dye, Tony	S	5-10	200	2/11/90	UCLA	Corona, Calif.	FA
Evans, DeQuin (1)	DE	6-2	250	5/17/87	Kentucky	Long Beach, Calif.	FA-'11
Hansen, Tyler	QB	6-1	218	12/6/89	Colorado	Murrieta, Calif.	FA
Hazelton, Vidal (1)	WR	6-2	218	1/29/88	Cincinnati	Staten Island, N.Y.	FA-'11
Herron, Daniel	HB	5-10	215	3/21/89	Ohio State	Warren, Ohio	D6
Hilton, Justin	WR	6-2	190	12/8/88	Indiana State	Kissimmee, Fla.	FA
Hunter, Grant	LB	6-2	245	5/30/88	Butler	Liberty Township, Ohio	FA
Iloka, George	S	6-4	225	6/20/90	Boise State	Houston, Texas	D5c
Johnson, Micah (1)	LB	6-2	258	6/22/88	Kentucky	Woodbridge, Va.	FA-'11
Joiner, Brandon	LB	6-3	225	4/27/89	Arkansas State	Killeen, Texas	FA
Jones, Marvin	WR	6-2	200	3/12/90	California	Fontana, Calif.	D5b
Kirkpatrick, Dre	CB	6-2	186	10/26/89	Alabama	Gadsden, Ala.	D1a
Meatoga, Vaughn	DT	6-1	294	8/19/89	Hawaii	Kalaheo, Hawaii	W(Wash)
Moore, Kashif	WR	5-9	180	11/21/88	Connecticut	Burlington, N.J.	FA
O'Donnell, Matthew (1)	T	6-9	328	3/26/89	Queen's (Canada)	Kingston, Ontario, Canada	FA-'11
Prater, Shaun	CB	5-10	190	10/27/89	Iowa	Omaha, Neb.	D5a
Robinson, Trevor	G/C	6-5	310	5/16/90	Notre Dame	Elkhorn, Neb.	FA
Rogers, Taveon	WR	5-11	188	8/17/90	New Mexico State	Lancaster, Calif.	FA
Sanu, Mohamed	WR	6-2	210	8/22/89	Rutgers	South Brunswick, N.J.	D3a
Stewart, Rodney	HB	5-7	180	1/3/90	Colorado	Westerville, Ohio	FA
Still, Devon	DT	6-5	305	7/11/89	Penn State	Wilmington, Del.	D2
Thompson, Brandon	DT	6-2	315	10/19/89	Clemson	Thomasville, Ga.	D3b
Weber, Thomas (1)	K	6-0	204	9/27/87	Arizona State	Downey, Calif.	FA-'11
Zeitler, Kevin	G	6-4	315	3/8/90	Wisconsin	Waukesha, Wisc.	D1b

The term NFL Rookie is defined as a player who is in his first season of professional football and has not been on the roster of another professional football team for any regular-season or postseason games. A Rookie is designated by an "R" on NFL rosters. Players who have been active in another professional football league or players who have NFL experience, including either preseason training camp or being on an Active List or Inactive List, or on Reserve/Injured or Reserve/Physically Unable to Perform for fewer than six regular-season games, are termed NFL First-Year Players. An NFL First-Year Player is designated by a "1" on NFL rosters. Thereafter, a player is credited with an additional year of experience for each season in which he accumulates six games on the Active List or Inactive List, or on Reserve/Injured or Reserve/Physically Unable to Perform.

Log on to www.bengals.com for an up-to-date roster.

CINCINNATI BENGALS

COACHING STAFF
Head Coach,
Marvin Lewis
Pro Career: Marvin Lewis is in his 10th season as Bengals head coach, having posted the longest tenure and most wins (69) of any head coach in franchise history. His Bengals are among only 10 NFL teams to make the playoffs in two or more of the last three seasons, and they were one of the NFL's surprise success stories last season. The youngest squad in the AFC based on opening-day rosters, they developed new stars and finished with a 9-7 record, earning a Wild Card playoff berth. Lewis led the Bengals to AFC North Division championships in 2005 and 2009, and he was the consensus choice as NFL Coach of the Year in 2009, when the Bengals swept all six division games. In 2011, the offense featured rookie standouts in QB Andy Dalton and WR A.J. Green, and won five games featuring fourth-quarter comebacks. Dalton and Green became the first rookie QB-WR duo from the same team to play in the Pro Bowl. Lewis was named the ninth head coach in Bengals history on January 14, 2003. In 2002, Lewis was Washington Redskins defensive coordinator and assistant head coach. He spent six seasons (1996-2001) as defensive coordinator with the Baltimore Ravens, a tenure that included a Super Bowl victory in the 2000 season. In 2000, Lewis' defense set the NFL record for fewest points allowed in a 16-game campaign (165), and the unit has been widely considered as one of the best NFL defenses of all time. Prior to Baltimore, Lewis spent four seasons (1992-95) with the Pittsburgh Steelers as linebackers coach. Career record: 69-77-1.
Background: Earned All-Big Sky Conference honors as a linebacker at Idaho State (1978-1980), and saw action at quarterback and free safety. Received his bachelor's degree in physical education and Master's degree in athletic administration. Inducted into Idaho State's Hall of Fame in 2001. Began his coaching career at Idaho State (1981-84), winning an NCAA Division I-AA championship in 1981. Was also the linebackers coach at Long Beach State (1985-86), New Mexico (1987-89), and Pittsburgh (1990-91).
Personal: Born September 23, 1958, McDonald, Pa. Lewis and his wife, Peggy, have two children—Whitney and Marcus.

ASSISTANT COACHES
Paul Alexander, asst. head coach/offensive line; born February 12, 1960, Rochester, N.Y. Tackle Cortland State 1979-1981. No pro playing experience. College coach: Penn State 1982-84, Michigan 1985-86, Central Michigan 1987-1991. Pro coach: New York Jets 1992-93, joined Bengals in 1994.
Jim Anderson, running backs; born March 27, 1948, Harrisburg, Pa.

Linebacker/defensive end California Western 1967-69. No pro playing experience. College coach: California Western 1970-71, Scottsdale (Ariz.) C.C. 1973, Nevada-Las Vegas 1974-75, Southern Methodist 1976-1980, Stanford 1981-83. Pro coach: Joined Bengals in 1984.
Mark Carrier, defensive backs; born April 28, 1968, Lake Charles, La. Defensive back Southern California 1987-89. Pro defensive back Chicago Bears 1990-96, Detroit Lions 1997-99, Washington Redskins 2000. College coach: Arizona State 2004-05. Pro coach: Baltimore Ravens 2006-09, New York Jets 2010-11, joined Bengals in 2012.
Kyle Caskey, offensive quality control/asst. offensive line; born Dec. 7, 1978, Daingerfield, Texas. Tight end Texas A&M 1997-98. No pro playing experience. College coach: Louisiana-Monroe 2004-05, Indiana State 2006-08, Mississippi 2009. Pro coach: Joined Bengals in 2010.
Brayden Coombs, offensive assistant; born Oct. 24, 1986, Cincinnati, Ohio. Wide receiver-defensive back Miami (Ohio) 2005-09. No pro playing experience. Pro coach: Joined Bengals in 2012.
Jeff Friday, asst. strength and conditioning; born Oct. 11, 1966, Milwaukee, Wisc. Attended Wisconsin-Milwaukee. No college or pro playing experience. College coach: Illinois State 1990-91, Northwestern 1992-95. Pro coach: Minnesota Vikings 1996-98, Baltimore Ravens 1999-2007, joined Bengals in 2010.
Jay Gruden, offensive coordinator; born March 4, 1967, Tiffin, Ohio. Quarterback Louisville 1985-88. Pro quarterback Barcelona Dragons (WLAF) 1990, Sacramento Surge (WLAF) 1990, Tampa Bay Storm (AFL) 1991-96, Orlando Predators (AFL) 2002-03. Pro coach: Nashville Katz (AFL) 1997, Orlando Predators (AFL) 1998-2001 (head coach) and 2004-08 (head coach), Tampa Bay Buccaneers 2002-08, Florida Tuskers (UFL) 2009-10 (head coach 2010), joined Bengals in 2011.
Paul Guenther, linebackers; born Nov. 22, 1971, Richboro, Pa. Linebacker Ursinus College 1990-93. No pro playing experience. College coach: Western Maryland 1994-95, Ursinus College 1996, 1997-2001 (head coach 1997-2001), Jacksonville 1997. Pro coach: Washington Redskins 2002-03, joined Bengals in 2005.
Jay Hayes, defensive line; born March 3, 1960, South Fayette, Pa. Defensive end Idaho 1978-1981. Pro defensive end/linebacker Michigan Panthers (USFL) 1984, Memphis Showboats (USFL) 1985. College coach: Notre Dame 1988-1991, California 1992-94, Wisconsin 1995-98. Pro coach: Pittsburgh Steelers 1999-2001, Minnesota Vikings 2002, joined Bengals in 2003.
Jonathan Hayes, tight ends; born Aug.

11, 1962, South Fayette, Pa. Linebacker/tight end Iowa 1981-84. Pro tight end Kansas City Chiefs 1985-1993, Pittsburgh Steelers 1994-96. College coach: Oklahoma 1999-2002. Pro coach: Joined Bengals in 2003.
Hue Jackson, asst. special teams/asst. defensive backs; born Oct. 22, 1965, Los Angeles, Calif. Quarterback Pacific 1985-86. No pro playing experience. College coach: Pacific 1987-89, Cal State-Fullerton 1990-91, Arizona State 1992-95, California 1996, Southern California 1997-2000. Pro coach: London Monarchs (WFL) 1991, Washington Redskins 2001-03, Cincinnati Bengals 2004-06, Atlanta Falcons 2007, Baltimore Ravens 2008-09, Oakland Raiders 2010-11 (head coach 2011), re-joined Bengals in 2012.
David Lippincott, defensive quality control/asst. linebackers; born July 6, 1977, Cincinnati, Ohio. Attended Dayton. No college or pro playing experience. College coach: Bluffton 2000-02, Minnesota 2003-04, Richmond 2005-07. Pro coach: Joined Bengals in 2011.
Chip Morton, strength and conditioning; born November 27, 1962, Hamden, Conn. Attended North Carolina. No college or pro playing experience. College coach: Ohio State 1985-86, Penn State 1987-1991. Pro coach: San Diego Chargers 1992-94, Carolina Panthers 1995-98, Baltimore Ravens 1999-2001, Washington Redskins 2002, joined Bengals in 2003.
Darrin Simmons, special teams; born April 9, 1973, Elkhart, Kan. Punter Kansas 1993-95. No pro playing experience. College coach: Kansas 1996, Minnesota 1997. Pro coach: Baltimore Ravens 1998, Carolina Panthers 1999-2002, joined Bengals in 2003.
James Urban, wide receivers; born Dec. 1, 1973, Mechanicsburg, Pa. Wide receiver Washington and Lee 1993-96. No pro playing experience. College coach: Clarion 1997-98, Pennsylvania 1999-2003: Pro coach: Philadelphia Eagles 2004-10, joined Bengals in 2011.
Ken Zampese, quarterbacks; born July 19, 1967, Santa Maria, Calif. Wide receiver San Diego 1985-88. No pro playing experience. College coach: San Diego 1989, Southern California 1990-91, Northern Arizona 1992-95, Miami (Ohio) 1996-97. Pro coach: Philadelphia Eagles 1998, Green Bay Packers 1999, St. Louis Rams 2000-02, joined Bengals in 2003.
Mike Zimmer, defensive coordinator; born June 5, 1956, Peoria, Ill. Quarterback/linebacker Illinois State 1974-76. No pro playing experience. College coach: Missouri 1979-1980, Weber State 1981-88, Washington State 1989-1993. Pro coach: Dallas Cowboys 1994-2006, Atlanta Falcons 2007, joined Bengals in 2008.

American Football Conference
North Division
Team Colors: Brown, Orange, and White
76 Lou Groza Blvd.
Berea, Ohio 44017
Telephone: (440) 891-5000

2012 SCHEDULE
PRESEASON
Aug. 10	at Detroit	7:30
Aug. 16	at Green Bay	8:00
Aug. 24	**Philadelphia**	7:30
Aug. 30	**Chicago**	7:30

REGULAR SEASON
Sep. 9	**Philadelphia**	1:00
Sep. 16	at Cincinnati	1:00
Sep. 23	**Buffalo**	1:00
Sep. 27	at Baltimore (Thurs)	8:20
Oct. 7	at New York Giants	1:00
Oct. 14	**Cincinnati**	1:00
Oct. 21	at Indianapolis	1:00
Oct. 28	**San Diego**	1:00
Nov. 4	**Baltimore**	1:00
Nov. 11	BYE	
Nov. 18	at Dallas	1:00
Nov. 25	**Pittsburgh**	1:00
Dec. 2	at Oakland	4:15
Dec. 9	**Kansas City**	1:00
Dec. 16	**Washington**	1:00
Dec. 23	at Denver	4:05
Dec. 30	at Pittsburgh	1:00

All times ET
Stadium: Cleveland Browns Stadium
(opened in 1999)
 •**Capacity:** 73,300
 100 Alfred Lerner Way
 Cleveland, Ohio 44114
Playing Surface: Grass
Headquarters/Training Camp:
 76 Lou Groza Boulevard
 Berea, Ohio 44017

CLEVELAND BROWNS STADIUM

CLUB OFFICIALS
Owner: Randolph D. Lerner
President: Mike Holmgren
General Manager: Tom Heckert
Head Coach: Pat Shurmur
Executive Vice President, Business
 Operations: Bryan Wiedmeier
Senior Advisor to the President:
 Gil Haskell
General Counsel & Special Counsel to
 the President: Fred Nance
Senior Vice President, Finance &
 Administration: David A. Jenkins
Senior Vice President, Security:
 Lew Merletti
Senior Vice President, Business
 Development: Jim Ross
Vice President, Tickets Sales & Service:
 Chris Gallagher
Vice President, Media Relations:
 Neal Gulkis
Vice President, Community Outreach:
 Renee Harvey
Vice President, Security: Carl Meyer
Vice President, Corporate Sales &
 Services: John Penhollow
Vice President, Marketing: Brett Reynolds
Vice President, Football Operations:
 Mark Schiefelbein
Vice President, Football Administration:
 Matt Thomas
Director, Stadium Operations:
 Todd Argust
Director, Content & Production:
 Reagan Berube
Director, Video: Chad Bogard
Director, Information Technology:
 Brandon Covert
Director, Operations: Phil Dangerfield
Director, Club Level Sales: Jason England
Director, Season & Group Ticket Sales:
 Eric Lapointe
Director, Corporate Sales: Paul Mocho
Director, Creative Services:
 George Muller
Director, Administration: Mike Nikolaus
Director, Client Services: Nicole Peters
Controller: Laurie Rice
Director, Legal Affairs: Megan Rogers
Director, Finance: Gregory Rush
Director, Player Personnel: Jon Sandusky
Director, Ticket Operations: John Schulze
Director, Player Engagement: Aaron Shea
Director, College Scouting: John Spytek
Director, Community Outreach:
 Jenner Tekancic
Director, Guest Relations:
 Lauren Voorhies
Head Athletic Trainer: Joe Sheehan
Head Equipment Manager: Brad Melland
Head Groundskeeper: Chris Powell
Senior Editor: Vic Carucci

COACHING HISTORY
(453-426-10)
Records include postseason games
1950-1962	Paul Brown	115-49-5
1963-1970	Blanton Collier	79-38-2
1971-74	Nick Skorich	30-26-2
1975-77	Forrest Gregg*	18-23-0
1977	Dick Modzelewski	0-1-0
1978-1984	Sam Rutigliano**	47-52-0
1984-88	Marty Schottenheimer	46-31-0
1989-1990	Bud Carson***	12-14-1
1990	Jim Shofner	1-6-0
1991-95	Bill Belichick	37-45-0
1999-2000	Chris Palmer	5-27-0
2001-04	Butch Davis****	24-36-0
2004	Terry Robiskie	1-4-0
2005-08	Romeo Crennel	24-40-0
2009-2010	Eric Mangini	10-22-0
2011	Pat Shurmur	4-12-0

*Resigned after 13 games in 1977
**Released after eight games in 1984
***Released after nine games in 1990
****Resigned after 11 games in 2004

PAID ATTENDANCE
Home 526,997   Away 486,462
Total 1,013,459
Single-game home record,
 85,073 (9/21/70)
Single-season home record, 620,496
 (1980)

2012 DRAFT CHOICES
Round	Name	Pos.	College
1	Trent Richardson	RB	Alabama
	Brandon Weeden	QB	Oklahoma St.
2	Mitchell Schwartz	T	California
3	John Hughes	DT	Cincinnati
4	Travis Benjamin	WR	Miami
	James-Michael Johnson	LB	Nevada
5	Ryan Miller	T	Colorado
6	Emmanuel Acho	LB	Texas
	Billy Winn	DT	Boise St.
7	Trevin Wade	DB	Arizona
	Brad Smelley	RB	Alabama

CLEVELAND BROWNS

2011 TEAM RECORD
PRESEASON (1-3)

Date	Result	Opponent
8/13	W 27-17	Green Bay
8/19	L 28-30	Detroit
8/25	L 14-24	at Philadelphia
9/1	L 14-24	at Chicago

REGULAR SEASON (4-12)

Date	Result	Opponent
9/11	L 17-27	Cincinnati
9/18	W 27-19	at Indianapolis
9/25	W 17-16	Miami
10/2	L 13-31	Tennessee
10/16	L 17-24	at Oakland
10/23	W 6-3	Seattle
10/30	L 10-20	at San Francisco
11/6	L 12-30	at Houston
11/13	L 12-13	St. Louis
11/20	W 14-10	Jacksonville
11/27	L 20-23	at Cincinnati
12/4	L 10-24	Baltimore
12/8	L 3-14	at Pittsburgh
12/18	L 17-20	at Arizona (OT)
12/24	L 14-20	at Baltimore
1/1	L 9-13	Pittsburgh

(OT) Overtime

SCORE BY PERIODS

Browns	26	83	35	74	0	—	218
Opponents	82	94	62	66	3	—	307

2011 TEAM STATISTICS

	Browns	Opp.
Total First Downs	278	301
Rushing	77	124
Passing	173	149
Penalty	28	28
3rd Down: Made/Att	92/238	95/230
3rd Down Pct.	38.7	41.3
4th Down: Made/Att	10/18	6/14
4th Down Pct.	55.6	42.9
Possession Avg.	29:07	30:53
Total Net Yards	4621	5318
Avg. Per Game	288.8	332.4
Total Plays	1024	1035
Avg. Per Play	4.5	5.1
Net Yards Rushing	1531	2359
Avg. Per Game	95.7	147.4
Total Rushes	415	534
Net Yards Passing	3090	2959
Avg. Per Game	193.1	184.9
Sacked/Yards Lost	39/210	32/199
Gross Yards	3300	3158
Att./Completions	570/320	469/265
Completion Pct.	56.1	56.5
Had Intercepted	13	9
Punts/Average	89/40.1	76/46.1
Net Punting Avg.	89/36.3	76/37.9
Penalties/Yards	95/847	90/726
Fumbles/Ball Lost	22/6	20/11
Touchdowns	21	31
Rushing	4	12
Passing	16	16
Returns	1	3

2011 INDIVIDUAL STATISTICS

PASSING

	Att.	Comp.	Yds.	Pct.	TD	Int.	Tkld.	Rate
McCoy	463	265	2733	57.2	14	11	32/173	74.6
Wallace	107	55	567	51.4	2	2	6/30	65.4
Cribbs	0	0	0	—	0	0	1/7	—
Browns	570	320	3300	56.1	14	13	39/210	72.8
Opponents	469	265	3158	56.5	16	9	32/199	80.6

SCORING

	TD R	TD P	TD Rt	PAT	FG	Saf	PTS
Dawson	0	0	0	20/20	24/29	0	92
Cribbs	0	4	1	0/0	0/0	0	30
Moore	0	4	0	0/0	0/0	0	24
Hillis	3	0	0	0/0	0/0	0	18
Little	0	2	0	0/0	0/0	0	12
Massaquoi	0	2	0	0/0	0/0	0	12
Watson	0	2	0	0/0	0/0	0	12
Norwood	0	1	0	0/0	0/0	0	6
Ogbonnaya	1	0	0	0/0	0/0	0	6
Al. Smith	0	1	0	0/0	0/0	0	6
Browns	4	16	1	20/20	24/29	0	218
Opponents	12	16	3	31/31	30/34	0	307

2-Pt Conversions: Browns 0-1, Opponents 0-0

RUSHING

	No.	Yds	Avg	LG	TD
Hillis	161	587	3.6	24t	3
Ogbonnaya	73	334	4.6	40	1
Hardesty	88	266	3.0	19	0
McCoy	61	212	3.5	20	0
Wallace	7	70	10.0	27	0
Cribbs	7	25	3.6	15	0
Little	3	15	5.0	13	0
Clayton	8	12	1.5	4	0
Marecic	4	8	2.0	3	0
Ar. Smith	3	2	0.7	6	0
Browns	415	1531	3.7	40	4
Opponents	534	2359	4.4	67	12

RECEIVING

	No.	Yds	Avg	LG	TD
Little	61	709	11.6	76t	2
Cribbs	41	518	12.6	45t	4
Watson	37	410	11.1	34t	2
Moore	34	324	9.5	33	4
Massaquoi	31	384	12.4	56	2
Norwood	23	268	11.7	51	1
Ogbonnaya	23	165	7.2	19	0
Hillis	22	130	5.9	52	0
Al. Smith	14	131	9.4	20	1
Hardesty	14	122	8.7	27	0
Cameron	6	33	5.5	15	0
Marecic	5	31	6.2	11	0
C. Mitchell	3	31	10.3	19	0
Robiskie	3	25	8.3	14	0
Wallace	1	21	21.0	21	0
Clayton	1	3	3.0	3	0
McCoy	1	-5	-5.0	-5	0
Browns	320	3300	10.3	76t	16
Opponents	265	3158	11.9	80t	16

INTERCEPTIONS

	No.	Yds	Avg	LG	TD
Adams	3	33	11.0	29	0
S. Brown	2	0	0.0	0	0
Young	1	28	28.0	28	0
D. Jackson	1	24	24.0	24	0
Skrine	1	5	5.0	5	0
Fujita	1	3	3.0	3	0
Browns	9	93	10.3	29	0
Opponents	13	241	18.5	97t	1

PUNTING

	No.	Yds.	Avg.	In 20	LG
Maynard	81	3282	40.5	32	63
McGee	8	288	36.0	0	48
Browns	89	3570	40.1	32	63
Opponents	76	3505	46.1	19	67

PUNT RETURNS

	Ret	FC	Yds	Avg	LG	TD
Cribbs	34	8	388	11.4	84t	1
Norwood	4	1	35	8.8	14	0
Browns	38	9	423	11.1	84t	1
Opponents	26	28	303	11.7	68t	0

KICKOFF RETURNS

	No.	Yds	Avg	LG	TD
Cribbs	39	974	25.0	63	0
Marecic	4	46	11.5	13	0
Skrine	3	72	24.0	32	0
Adams	2	42	21.0	30	0
Browns	48	1134	23.6	63	0
Opponents	46	1055	22.9	101t	1

FIELD GOALS

	1-19	20-29	30-39	40-49	50+
Dawson	0/0	7/9	3/4	7/8	7/8
Browns	0/0	7/9	3/4	7/8	7/8
Opponents	1/1	14/14	6/7	7/9	2/3

SACKS

	No.
Sheard	8.5
Rubin	5.0
Taylor	4.0
Gocong	3.5
D. Jackson	3.5
J. Mitchell	1.5
T. Brown	1.0
Haden	1.0
Paxson	1.0
Ward	1.0
(group)	1.0
Benard	0.5
Schaefering	0.5
Browns	32.0
Opponents	39.0

RECORD HOLDERS
INDIVIDUAL RECORDS—CAREER

Category	Name	Performance
Rushing (Yds.)	Jim Brown, 1957-1965	12,312
Passing (Yds.)	Brian Sipe, 1974-1983	23,713
Passing (TDs)	Brian Sipe, 1974-1983	154
Receiving (No.)	Ozzie Newsome, 1978-1990	662
Receiving (Yds.)	Ozzie Newsome, 1978-1990	7,980
Interceptions	Thom Darden, 1972-74, 1976-1981	45
Punting (Avg.)	Dave Zastudil, 2006-2010	44.1
Punt Return (Avg.)	Greg Pruitt, 1973-1981	11.8
Kickoff Return (Avg.)	Greg Pruitt, 1973-1981	26.3
Field Goals	Phil Dawson, 1999-2011	276
Touchdowns (Tot.)	Jim Brown, 1957-1965	126
Points	Lou Groza, 1950-59, 1961-67	1,349
*Sacks	Clay Matthews, 1978-1993	62.0

INDIVIDUAL RECORDS—SINGLE SEASON

Category	Name	Performance
Rushing (Yds.)	Jim Brown, 1963	1,863
Passing (Yds.)	Brian Sipe, 1980	4,132
Passing (TDs)	Brian Sipe, 1980	30
Receiving (No.)	Ozzie Newsome, 1983	89
	Ozzie Newsome, 1984	89
	Kellen Winslow, 2006	89
Receiving (Yds.)	Braylon Edwards, 2007	1,289
Interceptions	Thom Darden, 1978	10
	Anthony Henry, 2001	10
Punting (Avg.)	Gary Collins, 1965	46.7
Punt Return (Avg.)	Leroy Kelly, 1965	15.6
Kickoff Return (Avg.)	Billy Lefear, 1975	31.7
Field Goals	Phil Dawson, 2008	30
Touchdowns (Tot.)	Jim Brown, 1965	21
Points	Jim Brown, 1965	126
*Sacks	Reggie Camp, 1984	14.0

INDIVIDUAL RECORDS—SINGLE GAME

Category	Name	Performance
Rushing (Yds.)	Jerome Harrison, 12-20-09	286
Passing (TDs)	Frank Ryan, 12-12-64	5
	Bill Nelsen, 11-2-69	5
	Brian Sipe, 10-7-79	5
	Kelly Holcomb, 11-28-04	5
	Derek Anderson, 9-16-07	5
Receiving (No.)	Ozzie Newsome, 10-14-84	14
Receiving (Yds.)	Ozzie Newsome, 10-14-84	191
Interceptions	Many times	3
	Last time by Anthony Henry, 11-18-01	
Field Goals	Phil Dawson, 11-5-06	6
Touchdowns (Tot.)	Dub Jones, 11-25-51	**6
Points	Dub Jones, 11-25-51	36
*Sacks	Andra Davis, 11-9-03	4.0

*Sacks became an official statistic in 1982.
**NFL Record

2012 VETERAN ROSTER

No.	Name	Pos.	Ht.	Wt.	Birthdate	NFL Exp.	College	Hometown	How Acq.	'11 Games/ Starts
58	Benard, Marcus	DL	6-2	256	7/26/85	4	Jackson State	Adrian, Mich.	FA-'09	4/0
24	Brown, Sheldon	DB	5-10	200	3/19/79	11	South Carolina	Fort Lawn, S.C.	T(Phil)-'10	16/16
84	Cameron, Jordan	TE	6-5	245	8/7/88	2	Southern California	Newbury Park, Calif.	D4a-'11	2/8
72	Cousins, Oniel	OL	6-4	315	6/29/84	5	Texas-El Paso	Fullerton, Calif.	W(Balt)-'11	4/1
16	Cribbs, Joshua	WR	6-1	215	6/9/83	8	Kent State	Washington, D.C.	FA-'05	16/7
62	Daniels, Stanley	OL	6-4	320	11/30/84	2	Washington	San Diego, Calif.	FA-'12	0*
4	Dawson, Phil	K	5-11	200	1/23/75	14	Texas	Dallas, Texas	FA-'99	16/0
31	Dockery, James	DB	6-1	185	11/9/88	2	Oregon State	La Quinta, Calif.	FA-'11	12/0
94	English, Auston	DL	6-3	250	3/10/87	2	Oklahoma	Canadian, Texas	FA-'11	7/0
99	Fujita, Scott	LB	6-5	250	4/28/79	11	California	Ventura, Calif.	UFA(NO)-'10	10/10
51	Gocong, Chris	LB	6-2	263	11/16/83	7	Cal Poly-San Luis Obispo	Santa Barbara, Calif.	T(Phil)-'10	16/16
77	Greco, John	OL	6-4	315	3/24/85	5	Toledo	Youngstown, Ohio	T(StL)-'11	15/0
87	Gronkowski, Dan	TE	6-5	255	1/21/85	3	Maryland	Williamsville, N.Y.	Fa-'11	7/1*
23	Haden, Joe	DB	5-11	190	4/14/89	3	Florida	Fort Washington, Md.	D1-'10	15/15
27	Hagg, Eric	DB	6-1	205	9/15/89	2	Nebraska	Peoria, Ariz.	D7-'11	10/0
20	Hardesty, Montario	RB	6-0	225	2/1/87	3	Tennessee	New Bern, N.C.	D2b-'10	10/4
2	Hodges, Reggie	P	6-0	220	1/26/82	6	Ball State	Champaign, Ill.	FA-'09	0*
29	Jackson, Brandon	RB	5-10	216	10/2/85	6	Nebraska	Horn Lake, Miss.	UFA(GB)-'11	0*
52	Jackson, D'Qwell	LB	6-0	240	9/26/83	7	Maryland	Largo, Fla.	D2-'06	16/16
66	Lauvao, Shawn	OL	6-3	315	10/26/87	3	Arizona State	Honolulu, Hawaii	D3b-'10	15/15
9	Lewis, Thaddeus	QB	6-2	200	11/19/87	2	Duke	Opa-Locka, Fla.	W(StL)-'11	0*
15	Little, Greg	WR	6-2	220	5/30/89	2	North Carolina	Durham, N.C.	D2b-'11	16/12
55	Mack, Alex	OL	6-4	311	11/19/85	4	California	Santa Barbara, Calif.	D1-'09	16/16
56	Maiava, Kaluka	LB	6-0	229	12/27/86	4	Southern California	Wailuku, Hawaii	D4-'09	16/6
48	Marecic, Owen	FB	6-0	245	10/4/88	2	Stanford	Portland, Ore.	D4b-'11	14/4
11	Massaquoi, Mohamed	WR	6-2	207	11/24/86	4	Georgia	Charlotte, N.C.	D2b-'09	14/3
#11	Maynard, Brad	P	6-1	188	2/9/74	15	Ball State	Tipton, Ind.	FA-'11	15/0
12	McCoy, Colt	QB	6-1	215	9/5/86	3	Texas	Tuscola, Texas	D3a-'10	13/13
18	Mitchell, Carlton	WR	6-3	215	4/6/88	3	South Florida	Gainesville, Fla.	D6a-'10	11/0
89	Moore, Evan	TE	6-6	250	1/3/85	4	Stanford	Brea, Calif.	FA-'09	16/4
10	Norwood, Jordan	WR	5-11	180	9/29/86	2	Penn State	State College, Pa.	FA-'10	14/4
25	Ogbonnaya, Chris	RB	6-0	225	5/5/86	3	Texas	Houston, Texas	FA-'11	13/4*
95	Parker, Juqua	DL	6-2	250	5/15/78	12	Oklahoma State	Houston, Texas	UFA(Phil)-'12	12/0*
21	Patterson, Dimitri	DB	5-10	200	6/18/83	6	Tuskegee	Orlando, Fla.	UFA(Phil)-'11	14/1
69	Paxson, Scott	DL	6-4	290	2/3/83	3	Penn State	Philadelphia, Pa.	FA-'11	16/0
62	Pinkston, Jason	OL	6-4	305	9/5/87	2	Pittsburgh	Pittsburgh, Pa.	D5b-'11	16/16
71	Rubin, Ahtyba	DL	6-2	330	7/25/86	5	Iowa State	Pensacola, Fla.	D6a-'08	16/16
92	Rucker, Frostee	DL	6-3	280	9/14/83	7	Southern California	Tustin, Calif.	UFA(Cin)-'12	16/11*
91	Schaefering, Brian	DL	6-4	295	8/20/83	3	Lindenwood	St. Louis, Mo.	FA-'09	16/0
97	Sheard, Jabaal	DL	6-2	265	5/10/89	2	Pittsburgh	Hollywood, Hills, Fla.	D2a-'11	16/16
22	Skrine, Buster	DB	5-9	185	4/26/89	2	Chattanooga	Woodstock, Ga.	D5a-'11	16/0
81	Smith, Alex	TE	6-4	258	5/22/82	8	Stanford	Denver, Colo.	FA-'10	14/4
90	Spears, Quinton	LB	6-4	234	5/11/88	2	Prairie View A&M	Montgomery, Texas	W(Mia)-'11	13/0
96	Stephens, Emmanuel	DL	6-3	255	2/17/87	2	Mississippi	Houston, Texas	W(Atl)-'11	11/3
98	Taylor, Phil	DL	6-3	335	4/7/88	2	Baylor	Clinton, Md.	D1-'11	16/16
73	Thomas, Joe	OL	6-6	312	12/4/84	6	Wisconsin	Brookfield, Wisc.	D1a-'07	16/16
67	Tripp, Kiante	DL	6-6	276	10/7/87	2	Georgia	Atlanta, Ga.	FA-'11	3/0
41	Ventrone, Ray	DB	5-10	200	10/21/82	7	Villanova	Pittsburgh, Pa.	FA-'09	15/0
6	Wallace, Seneca	QB	5-11	200	8/6/80	10	Iowa State	Sacramento, Calif.	T(Sea)-'10	Jun-08
43	Ward, T.J.	DB	5-10	200	12/12/86	3	Oregon	San Francisco, Calif.	D2a-'10	Aug-08
82	Watson, Benjamin	TE	6-3	255	12/18/80	9	Georgia	Rock Hill, S.C.	UFA(NE)-'10	13/11
44	Williams, Eddie	FB	6-1	242	8/22/87	2	Idaho	San Mateo, Calif.	FA-'11	6/0*
28	Young, Usama	DB	6-0	200	5/8/85	6	Kent State	Largo, Md.	UFA(NO)-'11	16/7
57	Yount, Christian	LS	6-1	256	7/8/88	2	UCLA	Coto de Caza, Calif.	FA-'11	12/0*

Daniels last active with Denver in '10; Gronkowski played 5 games with New England and 2 with Cleveland in '11; Hodges missed '11 season because of injury; B. Jackson missed '11 season because of injury; Lewis inactive for 13 games; Ogbonnaya played 2 games with Houston and 11 with Cleveland; Parker played 12 games with Philadelphia; Rucker played 16 games with Cincinnati; Williams played 3 games with Seattle and 3 games with Cleveland; Yount played 7 games with Tampa Bay and 5 with Cleveland.

\#   Unrestricted Free Agent, subject to developments.

Retired—Billy Yates, 9-year center, 0 games in '11.

Players lost through free agency (3): DB Mike Adams (Den; 16 games), RB Peyton Hillis (KC; 10), OL Steve Vallos (Phil; 1).

Also played with Browns in '11—LB Titus Browns (10 games), RB Thomas Clayton (3), OL Artis Hicks (9), P Richmond McGee (1), DL Jayme Mitchell (14), OL Tony Pashos (12), LS Ryan Pontbriand (11), WR Brian Robiskie (6), RB Armond Smith (3), Brian Smith (2).

FIRST-YEAR ROSTER

Name	Pos.	Ht.	Wt.	Birthdate	College	Hometown	How Acq.
Acho, Emmanuel	LB	6-1	240	11/10/90	Texas	Dallas, Texas	D6a
Alford, Dominic (1)	OL	6-3	320	2/22/88	Minnesota	Cleveland, Ohio	FA-'11
Allen, Mike	DB	6-0	180	8/26/88	James Madison	Powhatan, Va.	FA
Anderson, Jake	OL	6-5	305	1/17/89	Akron	Erie, Pa.	FA
Bademosi, Johnson	DB	6-0	200	7/23/90	Stanford	Silver Springs, Md.	FA
Benjamin, Travis	WR	5-10	175	12/29/89	Miami	Belle Glade, Fla.	D4a
Cleveland, Matt	OL	6-3	295	8/15/89	Idaho	Kent, Wash.	FA
Cooper, Josh	WR	5-10	190	1/8/89	Oklahoma State	Mustang, Okla.	FA
Davis, Emanuel	DB	5-10	195	8/9/88	East Carolina	Manteo, N.C.	FA
Dickson, JoJo (1)	LB	6-1	245	7/13/89	Idaho	Wailuku, Hawaii	FA
Fort, L.J.	LB	6-0	230	1/3/90	Northern Iowa	Waynesville, Mo.	FA
Gerhart, Garth	OL	6-1	305	10/21/88	Arizona State	Norco, Calif.	FA
Gipson, Tashaun	DB	5-11	205	8/7/90	Wyoming	Dallas, Texas	FA
Green, William	DL	6-3	250	4/28/90	Florida	Hoover, Ala.	FA
Hughes, John	DL	6-2	320	4/27/88	Cincinnati	Gahanna, Ohio	D3
Jacobs, Benjamin (1)	LB	6-4	243	4/17/88	Fresno State	Las Vegas, Nev.	FA-'11
Johnson, James-Michael	LB	6-1	240	8/20/89	Nevada	Las Vegas, Nev.	D4b
Lanning, Spencer (1)	P	5-11	200	5/21/88	South Carolina	Rock Hill, S.C.	FA
Miller, Ryan	OL	6-7	320	7/6/89	Colorado	Littleton, Colo.	D5
Reed, Antwuan	DB	5-10	190	11/29/89	Pittsburgh	Johnstown, Pa.	FA
Reed, Bert	WR	5-10	180	6/1/88	Florida State	Panama City, Fla.	FA
Richardson, Trent	RB	5-9	230	7/10/90	Alabama	Pensacola, Fla.	D1a
Robertson, Craig (1)	LB	6-1	229	2/11/88	North Texas	Stafford, Texas	FA-'11
Saffold, Jermaine	WR	6-0	200	3/5/89	Missouri State	Grandview, Mo.	FA
Sanford, Brian (1)	DL	6-2	280	9/12/87	Temple	Hartford, Conn.	FA-'10
Schwartz, Mitchell	OL	6-5	320	6/8/89	California	Pacific Palisades, Calif.	D2
Shaw, Jarrod (1)	OL	6-3	316	1/7/88	Tennessee	Lafayette, La.	FA-'11
Shugarts, Jeff	OL	6-6	305	10/26/89	Ohio State	Klein, Texas	FA
Sims, David (1)	DB	5-9	204	10/20/86	Iowa State	Gainesville, Fla.	FA-'11
Smelley, Brad	FB	6-2	235	4/20/89	Alabama	Tuscaloosa, Ala.	D7b
Spencer, Owen (1)	WR	6-3	185	11/2/87	North Carolina State	Leland, N.C.	FA-'11
Thomas, Adonis	RB	5-9	185	2/25/89	Toledo	Newark, N.J.	FA
Wade, Trevin	DB	5-10	190	8/1/89	Arizona	Austin, Texas	D7a
Weeden, Brandon	QB	6-3	220	10/14/83	Oklahoma State	Edmond, Okla.	D1b
Windsor, Rod (1)	WR	6-2	205	4/24/85	Western New Mexico	Bessemer, Ala.	FA-'11
Winn, Billy	DL	6-4	295	4/15/89	Boise State	Las Vegas, Nev.	D6b
Wolfert, Jeff (1)	K	6-2	185	10/22/85	Missouri	Overland Park, Kansas	FA

The term NFL Rookie is defined as a player who is in his first season of professional football and has not been on the roster of another professional football team for any regular-season or postseason games. A Rookie is designated by an "R" on NFL rosters. Players who have been active in another professional football league or players who have NFL experience, including either preseason training camp or being on an Active List or Inactive List, or on Reserve/Injured or Reserve/Physically Unable to Perform for fewer than six regular-season games, are termed NFL First-Year Players. An NFL First-Year Player is designated by a "1" on NFL rosters. Thereafter, a player is credited with an additional year of experience for each season in which he accumulates six games on the Active List or Inactive List, or on Reserve/Injured or Reserve/Physically Unable to Perform.

Log on to www.clevelandbrowns.com for an up-to-date roster.

CLEVELAND BROWNS

COACHING STAFF

Head Coach,
Pat Shurmur

Pro Career: Pat Shurmur was named the 13th full-time head coach in Browns history on January 13, 2011. In his first season at the helm, Shurmur led the Browns to a 4-12 mark. In 12 seasons as an NFL assistant, he has been a part of teams that have qualified for the playoffs seven times, won five division crowns, and appeared in one Super Bowl. Spent the 2009-2010 seasons as St. Louis' offensive coordinator, where he helped shape quarterback Sam Bradford. Spent 10 seasons with the Philadelphia Eagles (1999-2008), the first three seasons as the tight ends coach and last seven as the quarterbacks coach. Coached collegiately at Michigan State (1988-1997) and Stanford (1998). Career record: 4-12.

Background: Shurmur earned All-Big Ten conference honors and All-America honorable mention as a center for Michigan State in 1987. Was the school's first graduate student football player, with a master's degree in financial administration.

Personal: Born April 14, 1965, Dearborn, Mich. He and his wife, Jennifer, have four children, daughters Allyson, Erica and Claire, and a son, Kyle. His uncle, the late Fritz Shurmur, coached in the NFL for 24 years and was the Green Bay Packers' defensive coordinator from 1994-98.

ASSISTANT COACHES

Chris Beake, offensive assistant; born September 10, 1972, Kansas City, Mo. Quarterback Air Force 1991-92. No pro playing experience. College coach: Air Force 1994. Pro coach: San Francisco 49ers 1999-2003, Atlanta Falcons 2004-06, Seattle Seahawks 2008-09, San Francisco 49ers 2010, joined Browns in 2011.

Dwaine Board, defensive line; born November 29, 1956, Rocky Mount, Va. Defensive lineman North Carolina A&T 1974-77. Pro defensive lineman San Francisco 49ers 1979-1987, New Orleans Saints 1988. Pro coach: San Francisco 49ers 1990-2002, Seattle Seahawks 2003-08, Oakland Raiders 2009, joined Browns in 2011.

Gary Brown, running backs; born July 1, 1969, Williamsport, Pa. Running back Penn State 1987-1990. Pro running back Houston Oilers 1991-95, San Diego Chargers 1997, New York Giants 1998- 99. College coach: Lycoming 2003-05, Susquehanna 2006-07, Rutgers 2008. Pro coach: Joined Browns in 2009.

Chuck Bullough, defensive assistant; born March 3, 1968, East Lansing, Mich. Linebacker Michigan State 1988-1991. Pro linebacker: Miami Dolphins 1993-95. College coach: Michigan State 1997-98, Lake Forest 2004, Western Michigan 2005, UCLA 2006-2010. Pro coach: Chicago Bears 1999-2003, joined Browns in 2011.

Brad Childress, offensive coordinator; born June 27, 1956, Aurora, Ill. Quarterback/wide receiver Eastern Illinois 1975. No pro playing experience. College coach: Illinois 1978-1984,

Northern Arizona 1986-89, Utah 1990, Wisconsin 1991-98. Pro coach: Indianapolis Colts 1985, Philadelphia Eagles 1999-2005, Minnesota Vikings 2006-2010 (head coach), joined Browns in 2012.

Nolan Cromwell, senior assistant-offense; born January 30, 1955, Smith Center, Kan. Defensive back/quarterback Kansas 1973-76. Pro safety Los Angeles Rams 1977-1987. College coach: Texas A&M 2008-09. Pro coach: Los Angeles/St. Louis Rams 1991, 2010-11, Green Bay Packers 1992-98, Seattle Seahawks 1999-2007, joined Browns in 2012.

Bill Davis, linebackers; born November 5, 1965, Youngstown, Ohio. Quarterback Cincinnati 1984-88. College coach: Michigan State 1990-91. Pro coach: Pittsburgh Steelers 1992-94, Carolina Panthers 1995-98, Cleveland Browns 1999, Green Bay Packers 2000, Atlanta Falcons 2001-03, New York Giants 2004, San Francisco 49ers 2005-06, Arizona Cardinals 2007-10, re-joined Browns in 2011.

Steve Hagen, tight ends; born September 15, 1961, Forest City, Iowa. Wide receiver Cal Lutheran 1979-1982. No pro playing experience. College coach: Illinois 1984, Kansas 1985-86, Northern Arizona 1987-88, Notre Dame 1989-1990, Kent State 1991, Nevada 1992-93, Nevada-Las Vegas 1994-95, Wartburg 1996, San Jose State 1997-98, California 1999- 2000, Fresno State 2006, North Carolina 2007-08. Pro coach: Cleveland Browns 2001-04, re-joined Browns in 2009.

Tim Hauck, defensive backs; born December 20, 1966, Butte, Mont. Defensive back Pacific 1985, Montana 1986-89. Pro safety New England Patriots 1990, Green Bay Packers 1991-94, Denver Broncos 1995-96, Seattle Seahawks 1997, Indianapolis Colts 1998, Philadelphia Eagles 1999-2001, San Francisco 2002. College coach: Montana 2004-07, UCLA 2008. Pro coach: Tennessee Titans 2009-2010, joined Browns in 2012.

Dick Jauron, defensive coordinator; born October 7, 1950. Running back Yale, 1970-72. Pro safety Detroit Lions 1973-77, Cincinnati Bengals 1978-1980. Pro coach: Buffalo Bills 1985, Green Bay Packers 1986-1994, Jacksonville Jaguars 1995-98, Chicago Bears 1999-2003 (head coach), Detroit Lions 2004-05 (head coach 2005), Buffalo Bills 2006-09 (head coach), Philadelphia Eagles 2010, joined Browns in 2011.

Kent Johnston, strength and conditioning; born February 21, 1966, Mexia, Texas. Defensive back Stephen F. Austin 1974- 77. No pro playing experience. College coach: Northwestern Louisiana 1981, Alabama 1985-86, 2004-05. Pro coach: Tampa Bay Buccaneers 1987-1991, Green Bay Packers 1992-98, Seattle Seahawks 1999-2003, joined Browns in 2010.

Rick Lyle, asst. strength and conditioning; born February 26, 1971, Monroe, La. Defensive lineman Missouri 1989-1993. Pro defensive lineman Cleveland Browns 1994-95, Baltimore Ravens 1996, New York Jets 1997-2001, New England Patriots 2002-03. Pro coach: New York Jets 2006-08, joined Browns

in 2009.

Shawn Mennenga, special teams assistant; born January 8, 1971, Melbourne, Iowa. Defensive back Missouri 1992. No pro playing experience. College coach: Southwest Baptist 1994-96, Western Kentucky 1997, Hutchinson (Kan.) C.C. 1998-2000, Culver-Stockton 2001-04 (head coach 2002-04), Fort Hays State 2005-08, South Dakota State 2009-10. Pro coach: Joined Browns in 2011.

Ray Rhodes, senior assistant-defense; born October 20, 1950, Mexia, Texas. Running back Texas Christian 1969-1970, wide receiver/defensive back/kick returner Tulsa 1972-73. Pro wide receiver/defensive back New York Giants 1974-79, San Francisco 49ers 1980. Pro coach: San Francisco 49ers 1981-1991, 1994, Arizona Cardinals 1992-93, 1999 (head coach 1999), Philadelphia Eagles 1995-98 (head coach), Washington Redskins 2000, Denver Broncos 2001-02, Seattle Seahawks 2003-07, Houston Texans 2008-10, joined Browns in 2011.

Luke Steckel, assistant to the head coach; born April 28, 1985, Brentwood, Tenn. Linebacker Princeton 2003-06. No pro playing experience. Pro coach: Joined Browns in 2009.

Chris Tabor, special teams coordinator; born March 4, 1971, St. Joseph, Mo. Quarterback Benedictine College 1989-1992. No pro playing experience. College coach: Hutchinson (Kan.) C.C. 1994, Central Methodist College 1995-96, Missouri 1997-2000, Culver-Stockton College 2001 (head coach), Utah State 2002-05, Western Michigan 2006-07. Pro coach: Chicago Bears 2008-10, joined Browns in 2011.

George Warhop, offensive line; born September 19, 1961, Riverside, Calif. Guard/center Mt. San Jacinto (Calif.) J.C. 1979-1980, Cincinnati 1981-82. No pro playing experience. College coach: Cincinnati 1983, Kansas 1984-86, Vanderbilt 1987-89, New Mexico 1990, Southern Methodist 1993, Boston College 1994-95. Pro coach: London Monarchs (World League) 1991-92, St. Louis Rams 1996-97, Arizona Cardinals 1998-2002, Dallas Cowboys 2003-04, San Francisco 49ers 2005-08, joined Browns in 2009.

Mark Whipple, quarterbacks; born April 1, 1957; Tarrytown, N.Y. Quarterback Brown 1976-78. No pro playing experience. College coach: St. Lawrence 1980, Union 1981-82, Brown 1983, New Hampshire 1986-87, New Haven 1988-1993 (head coach), Brown 1994-97 (head coach), Massachusetts 1998-2003 (head coach), Miami 2009-10. Pro coach: Arizona Wranglers (USFL) 1984, Pittsburgh Steelers 2004-06, Philadelphia Eagles 2007, joined Browns in 2011.

Mike Wilson, wide receivers; born December 19, 1958; Los Angeles, Calif. Wide receiver Washington State 1978-80. Pro wide receiver San Francisco 49ers 1981-90. College coach: Stanford 1992-94, Southern California 1997-99. Pro coach: Oakland Raiders 1995-96, Arizona Cardinals 2004-06, Las Vegas Locomotives (UFL) 2009-10, joined Browns in 2011.

**American Football Conference
West Division
Team Colors:** Orange, Broncos Navy
Blue, and White
**13655 Broncos Parkway
Englewood, Colorado 80112
Telephone:** (303) 649-9000

2012 SCHEDULE
PRESEASON
Aug. 9	at Chicago	6:30
Aug. 18	**Seattle**	7:00
Aug. 26	**San Francisco**	2:00
Aug. 30	at Arizona	9:00

REGULAR SEASON
Sep. 9	**Pittsburgh**	6:20
Sep. 17	at Atlanta (Mon)	6:30
Sep. 23	**Houston**	2:15
Sep. 30	**Oakland**	2:05
Oct. 7	at New England	2:15
Oct. 15	at San Diego (Mon)	6:30
Oct. 21	BYE	
Oct. 28	**New Orleans**	6:20
Nov. 4	at Cincinnati	11:00a
Nov. 11	at Carolina	11:00a
Nov. 18	**San Diego**	2:15
Nov. 25	at Kansas City	11:00a
Dec. 2	**Tampa Bay**	2:05
Dec. 6	at Oakland (Thurs)	6:20
Dec. 16	at Baltimore	11:00a
Dec. 23	**Cleveland**	2:05
Dec. 30	**Kansas City**	2:15

All times MT

Stadium: Sports Authority Field at Mile
High (opened in 2001)
•**Capacity:** 76,125
1701 Bryant Street
Denver, Colorado 80204
Playing Surface: DD Grassmaster
Training Camp: 13655 Broncos Parkway
Englewood, Colorado
80112

SPORTS AUTHORITY FIELD AT MILE HIGH

CLUB OFFICIALS
Owner and CEO: Pat Bowlen
President: Joe Ellis
Executive VP of Football Operations:
John Elway
Head Coach: John Fox
FOOTBALL STAFF
Director of Player Personnel: Matt Russell
Director of Pro Personnel: Keith Kidd
Director of Football Administration:
Mike Sullivan
Head Athletic Trainer: Steve Antonopulos
BUSINESS STAFF
General Counsel/Executive Vice
President: Rich Slivka
Vice President of Corporate
Communications: Jim Saccomano
Vice President of Community
Development: Cindy Kellogg
Executive Director of Media Relations:
Patrick Smyth
Executive Director of Ticket Operations
and Administration: Kirk Dyer
STADIUM MANAGEMENT COMPANY
Senior Vice President of Business
Development: Mac Freeman

COACHING HISTORY
(424-388-10)
Records include postseason games
1960-61	Frank Filchock	7-20-1
1962-64	Jack Faulkner*	9-22-1
1964-66	Mac Speedie**	6-19-1
1966	Ray Malavasi	4-8-0
1967-1971	Lou Saban***	20-42-3
1971	Jerry Smith	2-3-0
1972-76	John Ralston	34-33-3
1977-1980	Robert (Red) Miller	42-25-0
1981-1992	Dan Reeves	117-79-1
1993-94	Wade Phillips	16-17-0
1995-2008	Mike Shanahan	146-91-0
2009-2010	Josh McDaniels****	11-17-0
2010	Eric Studesville	1-3-0
2011	John Fox	9-9-0

*Released after four games in 1964
**Resigned after two games in 1966
***Resigned after nine games in 1971
****Released after 12 games in 2010

PAID ATTENDANCE
Home 590,615   Away 491,405
Total 1,082,020
Single-game home record,
76,716 (11/9/09)
Single-season home record, 597,984
(2007)

2012 DRAFT CHOICES
Round	Name	Pos.	College
2	Derek Wolfe	DT	Cincinnati
	Brock Osweiler	QB	Arizona St.
3	Ronnie Hillman	RB	San Diego St.
4	Omar Bolden	DB	Arizona St.
	Philip Blake	C	Baylor
5	Malik Jackson	DE	Tennessee
6	Danny Trevathan	LB	Kentucky

2011 TEAM RECORD
PRESEASON (2-2)

Date	Result	Opponent
8/11	L 23-24	at Dallas
8/20	W 24-10	Buffalo
8/27	W 23-20	Seattle
9/1	L 7-26	at Arizona

REGULAR SEASON (8-8)

Date	Result	Opponent
9/12	L 20-23	Oakland
9/18	W 24-22	Cincinnati
9/25	L 14-17	at Tennessee
10/2	L 23-49	at Green Bay
10/9	L 24-29	San Diego
10/23	W 18-15	at Miami (OT)
10/30	L 10-45	Detroit
11/6	W 38-24	at Oakland
11/13	W 17-10	at Kansas City
11/17	W 17-13	New York Jets
11/27	W 16-13	at San Diego (OT)
12/4	W 35-32	at Minnesota
12/11	W 13-10	Chicago (OT)
12/18	L 23-41	New England
12/24	L 14-40	at Buffalo
1/1	L 3-7	Kansas City

(OT) Overtime

POSTSEASON (1-1)

1/8	W 29-23	Pittsburgh (OT)
1/14	L 10-45	at New England

SCORE BY PERIODS

Broncos	74	33	75	118	9	—	309
Opponents	52	154	91	93	0	—	390

2011 TEAM STATISTICS

	Broncos	Opp.
Total First Downs	286	315
Rushing	129	101
Passing	130	182
Penalty	27	32
3rd Down: Made/Att	66/214	73/218
3rd Down Pct.	30.8	33.5
4th Down: Made/Att	3/13	3/9
4th Down Pct.	23.1	33.3
Possession Avg.	28:51	31:09
Total Net Yards	5066	5725
Avg. Per Game	316.6	357.8
Total Plays	1017	1063
Avg. Per Play	5.0	5.4
Net Yards Rushing	2632	2021
Avg. Per Game	164.5	126.3
Total Rushes	546	488
Net Yards Passing	2434	3704
Avg. Per Game	152.1	231.5
Sacked/Yards Lost	42/274	41/283
Gross Yards	2708	3987
Att./Completions	429/217	534/333
Completion Pct.	50.6	62.4
Had Intercepted	13	9
Punts/Average	101/47.4	92/47.3
Net Punting Avg.	101/40.2	92/38.2
Penalties/Yards	101/842	99/845
Fumbles/Ball Lost	30/17	19/9
Touchdowns	36	42
Rushing	11	11
Passing	20	24
Returns	5	7

2011 INDIVIDUAL STATISTICS

PASSING

PASSING	Att.	Comp.	Yds.	Pct.	TD	Int.	Tkld.	Rate
Tebow	271	126	1729	46.5	12	6	33/225	72.9
K. Orton	155	91	979	58.7	8	7	9/49	75.7
Colquitt	1	0	0	0.0	0	0	0/0	39.6
Decker	1	0	0	0.0	0	0	0/0	39.6
D. Thomas	1	0	0	0.0	0	0	0/0	39.6
Broncos	429	217	2708	50.6	20	13	42/274	73.5
Opponents	534	333	3987	62.4	24	9	41/283	93.1

SCORING

SCORING	TD R	TD P	TD Rt	PAT	FG	Saf	PTS
Prater	0	0	0	30/30	19/25	0	87
Decker	0	8	1	0/0	0/0	0	54
Tebow	6	0	0	0/0	0/0	0	40
McGahee	4	1	0	0/0	0/0	0	32
D. Thomas	0	4	0	0/0	0/0	0	24
Fells	0	3	0	0/0	0/0	0	18
Ball	1	1	0	0/0	0/0	0	12
Royal	0	1	1	0/0	0/0	0	12
Goodman	0	0	1	0/0	0/0	0	6
Haggan	0	0	1	0/0	0/0	0	6
Moreno	0	1	0	0/0	0/0	0	6
Vaughn	0	0	1	0/0	0/0	0	6
Willis	0	1	0	0/0	0/0	0	6
Broncos	11	20	5	30/30	19/25	0	309
Opponents	11	24	7	40/40	32/39	1	390

2-Pt Conversions: Tebow 2, McGahee
Broncos 3-6, Opponents 0-2

RUSHING

RUSHING	No.	Yds	Avg	LG	TD
McGahee	249	1199	4.8	60t	4
Tebow	122	660	5.4	32	6
Ball	96	402	4.2	34	1
Moreno	37	179	4.8	24	0
J. Johnson	14	77	5.5	25	0
Royal	7	48	6.9	11	0
Larsen	14	44	3.1	6	0
K. Orton	5	17	3.4	13	0
D. Thomas	1	5	5.0	5	0
Decker	1	1	1.0	1	0
Broncos	546	2632	4.8	60t	11
Opponents	488	2021	4.1	47	11

RECEIVING

RECEIVING	No.	Yds	Avg	LG	TD
Decker	44	612	13.9	56t	8
D. Thomas	32	551	17.2	47	4
Lloyd	19	283	14.9	44	0
Fells	19	256	13.5	32	3
Royal	19	155	8.2	26t	1
Willis	18	267	14.8	42	1
Ball	16	148	9.3	34	1
McGahee	12	51	4.3	12	1
Moreno	11	101	9.2	28t	1
Larsen	9	76	8.4	16	0
Rosario	7	117	16.7	32	0
J. Johnson	7	62	8.9	17	0
Green	3	24	8.0	9	0
J. Thomas	1	5	5.0	5	0
Broncos	217	2708	12.5	56t	20
Opponents	333	3987	12.0	84	24

INTERCEPTIONS

INTERCEPTIONS	No.	Yds	Avg	LG	TD
Goodman	2	46	23.0	26t	1
Bailey	2	0	0.0	0	0
Vaughn	1	55	55.0	55t	1
Moore	1	18	18.0	18	0
Haggan	1	16	16.0	16t	1
C. Harris	1	15	15.0	15	0
Wilhite	1	2	2.0	2	0
Broncos	9	152	16.9	55t	3
Opponents	13	276	21.2	100t	3

PUNTING

PUNTING	No.	Yds.	Avg.	In 20	LG
Colquitt	101	4783	47.4	33	66
Broncos	101	4783	47.4	33	66
Opponents	92	4350	47.3	30	77

PUNT RETURNS

PUNT RETURNS	Ret	FC	Yds	Avg	LG	TD
Cosby	27	9	269	10.0	30	0
Royal	12	9	194	16.2	85t	1
Decker	6	1	133	22.2	90t	1
Goodman	1	0	0	0.0	0	0
Willis	1	0	0	0.0	0	0
Broncos	47	19	596	12.7	90t	2
Opponents	51	27	585	11.5	80t	1

KICKOFF RETURNS

KICKOFF RETURNS	No.	Yds	Avg	LG	TD
Cosby TM	17	457	26.9	63	0
Willis	8	163	20.4	29	0
Vaughn	7	210	30.0	67	0
Royal	3	47	15.7	20	0
Decker	2	50	25.0	34	0
Ball	1	9	9.0	9	0
Fells	1	20	20.0	20	0
Broncos	39	956	24.5	67	0
Opponents	20	491	24.6	40	0

FIELD GOALS

FIELD GOALS	1-19	20-29	30-39	40-49	50+
Prater	0/0	5/6	8/8	3/7	3/4
Broncos	0/0	5/6	8/8	3/7	3/4
Opponents	0/0	12/12	9/10	6/9	5/8

SACKS

SACKS	No.
Miller	11.5
Dumervil	9.5
Williams	5.0
McBean	4.0
Ayers	3.0
Dawkins	3.0
Wilhite	2.0
Q. Carter	1.0
Hunter	1.0
(group)	1.0
Broncos	41.0
Opponents	42.0

RECORD HOLDERS
INDIVIDUAL RECORDS—CAREER

Category	Name	Performance
Rushing (Yds.)	Terrell Davis, 1995-2002	7,607
Passing (Yds.)	John Elway, 1983-1998	51,475
Passing (TDs)	John Elway, 1983-1998	300
Receiving (No.)	Rod Smith, 1995-2007	849
Receiving (Yds.)	Rod Smith, 1995-2007	11,389
Interceptions	Steve Foley, 1976-1986	44
Punting (Avg.)	Jim Fraser, 1962-64	45.2
Punt Return (Avg.)	Darrien Gordon, 1997-98	12.5
Kickoff Return (Avg.)	Abner Haynes, 1965-66	26.3
Field Goals	Jason Elam, 1993-2007	395
Touchdowns (Tot.)	Rod Smith, 1995-2007	71
Points	Jason Elam, 1993-2007	1,786
*Sacks	Simon Fletcher, 1985-1995	97.5

INDIVIDUAL RECORDS—SINGLE SEASON

Category	Name	Performance
Rushing (Yds.)	Terrell Davis, 1998	2,008
Passing (Yds.)	Jay Cutler, 2008	4,526
Passing (TDs)	John Elway, 1997	27
	Jake Plummer, 2004	27
Receiving (No.)	Rod Smith, 2001	113
Receiving (Yds.)	Rod Smith, 2000	1,602
Interceptions	Goose Gonsoulin, 1960	11
Punting (Avg.)	Britton Colquitt, 2011	47.4
Punt Return (Avg.)	Floyd Little, 1967	16.9
Kickoff Return (Avg.)	Bill Thompson, 1969	28.5
Field Goals	Jason Elam, 1995, 2001	31
Touchdowns (Tot.)	Terrell Davis, 1998	23
Points	Terrell Davis, 1998	138
*Sacks	Elvis Dumervil, 2009	17.0

INDIVIDUAL RECORDS—SINGLE GAME

Category	Name	Performance
Rushing (Yds.)	Mike Anderson, 12-3-00	251
Passing (Yds.)	Jake Plummer, 10-31-04	499
Passing (TDs)	Frank Tripucka, 10-28-62	5
	John Elway, 11-18-84	5
	Gus Frerotte, 11-19-00	5
Receiving (No.)	Brandon Marshall, 12-13-09	**21
Receiving (Yds.)	Shannon Sharpe, 10-20-02	214
Interceptions	Goose Gonsoulin, 9-18-60	**4
	Willie Brown, 11-15-64	**4
	Deltha O'Neal, 10-7-01	**4
Field Goals	Gene Mingo, 10-6-63	5
	Rich Karlis, 11-20-83	5
	Jason Elam, 9-3-95, 10-13-02	5
Touchdowns (Tot.)	Clinton Portis, 12-7-03	5
Points	Clinton Portis, 12-7-03	30
*Sacks	Karl Mecklenburg, 9-15-85, 12-1-85	4.0
	Simon Fletcher, 11-4-90	4.0
	Elvis Dumervil, 9-20-09	4.0

*Sacks became an official statistic in 1982.
**NFL Record

DENVER BRONCOS

2012 VETERAN ROSTER

No.	Name	Pos.	Ht.	Wt.	Birthdate	NFL Exp.	College	Hometown	How Acq.	'11 Games/ Starts
20	Adams, Mike	S	5-11	200	3/24/81	9	Delaware	Wayne, N.J.	UFA(Cle)-'12	16/16*
91	Ayers, Robert	DE	6-3	274	9/6/85	4	Tennessee	Bennettsville, S.C.	D1b-'09	16/13
24	Bailey, Champ	CB	6-0	192	6/22/78	14	Georgia	Folkston, Ga.	T(Wash)-'04	13/13
35	Ball, Lance	RB	5-9	215	6/2/85	4	Maryland	Teaneck, N.J.	FA-'10	16/0
97	Bannan, Justin	DT	6-3	312	4/18/79	11	Colorado	Fair Oaks, Calif.	FA-'12	15/14*
68	Beadles, Zane	G	6-4	305	11/19/86	3	Utah	Sandy, Utah	D2-'10	16/16
30	Bruton, David	S	6-2	217	7/23/87	4	Notre Dame	Miamisburg, Ohio	D4a-'09	15/1
36	Bush, Rafael	S	5-11	200	5/12/87	3	South Carolina State	Williston, S.C.	FA-'11	6/0
17	Caldwell, Andre	WR	6-0	190	4/15/85	5	Florida	Tampa, Fla.	UFA(Cin)-'12	13/2*
28	Carter, Quinton	S	6-1	200	7/20/88	2	Oklahoma	Las Vegas, Nev.	D4a-'11	16/10
32	Carter, Tony	CB	5-9	175	5/24/86	4	Florida State	Jacksonville, Fla.	FA-'11	3/0
78	Clady, Ryan	T	6-6	315	9/6/86	5	Boise State	Rialto, Calif.	D1-'08	16/16
75	Clark, Chris	T	6-5	305	10/1/85	3	Southern Mississippi	New Orleans, La.	W(Minn)-'10	16/6
4	Colquitt, Britton	P	6-3	205	3/20/85	4	Tennessee	Knoxville, Tenn.	FA-'09	16/0
71	Davis, C.J.	G	6-2	308	2/2/87	3	Pittsburgh	Imperial, Pa.	FA-'12	0*
87	Decker, Eric	WR	6-3	218	3/15/87	3	Minnesota	Cold Spring, Minn.	D3b-'10	16/13
81	Dreessen, Joel	TE	6-4	245	7/26/82	7	Colorado State	Fort Morgan, Colo.	UFA(Hou)-'12	16/10*
92	Dumervil, Elvis	DE	5-11	260	1/19/84	7	Louisville	Miami, Fla.	D4b-'06	14/14
74	Franklin, Orlando	T	6-7	330	12/16/87	2	Miami	Delray Beach, Fla.	D2b-'11	16/16
85	Green, Virgil	TE	6-5	252	8/3/88	2	Nevada	Tulare, Calif.	D7a-'11	15/3
16	Hanie, Caleb	QB	6-2	222	9/11/85	5	Colorado State	Forney, Texas	UFA(Chi)-'12	6/4*
25	Harris, Chris	CB	5-10	190	6/18/89	2	Kansas	Bixby, Okla.	FA-'11	16/4
72	Harris, Ryan	T	6-5	300	3/11/85	6	Notre Dame	Minneapolis, Minn.	FA-'12	0*
83	Hill, Jason	WR	6-0	202	2/20/85	6	Washington State	San Francisco, Calif.	FA-'12	10/10*
76	Hills, Tony	T	6-5	304	11/4/84	5	Texas	Houston, Texas	FA-'11	0*
90	Hunter, Jason	DE	6-4	271	8/28/83	7	Appalachian State	Fayetteville, N.C.	FA-'10	16/2
56	Irving, Nate	MLB	6-1	240	7/12/88	2	North Carolina State	Wallace, N.C.	D3-'11	16/0
93	Jarmon, Jeremy	DT	6-3	286	11/20/87	4	Kentucky	Germantown, Tenn.	FA-'12	0*
37	Johnson, Jeremiah	RB	5-9	200	2/15/87	3	Oregon	Los Angeles, Calif.	FA-'10	8/0
73	Kuper, Chris	G	6-4	303	12/19/82	7	North Dakota	Anchorage, Alaska	D5-'06	16/16
18	Manning, Peyton	QB	6-5	230	3/24/76	15	Tennessee	New Orleans, La.	FA-'12	0*
51	Mays, Joe	MLB	5-11	250	7/6/85	5	North Dakota State	Chicago, Ill.	T(Phil)-'10	16/12
23	McGahee, Willis	RB	6-0	235	10/20/81	10	Miami	Miami, Fla.	FA-'11	15/14
58	Miller, Von	SLB	6-3	237	3/26/89	2	Texas A&M	DeSoto, Texas	D1-'11	15/15
53	Mohamed, Mike	SLB	6-3	245	3/11/88	2	California	Brawley, Calif.	D6-'11	2/0
26	Moore, Rahim	S	6-1	196	2/11/90	2	UCLA	Loa Angeles, Calif.	D2a-'11	15/7
27	Moreno, Knowshon	RB	5-11	200	7/16/87	4	Georgia	Middletown, N.J.	D1a-'09	7/2
54	Obiozor, Cyril	DE	6-4	249	9/26/86	4	Texas A&M	Pearland, Texas	FA-'12	0*
66	Paxton, Lonie	LS	6-2	270	3/13/78	13	Sacramento State	Corona, Calif.	UFA(NE)-'09	16/0
21	Porter, Tracy	CB	5-11	186	8/11/86	5	Indiana	Port Allen, La.	UFA(NO)-'12	14/11*
5 f-	Prater, Matt	K	5-10	195	8/10/84	6	Central Florida	Estero, Fla.	PS(Mia)-'07	16/0
65	Ramirez, Manny	G	6-3	313	2/13/83	6	Texas Tech	Houston, Texas	FA-'11	2/0
29	Robinson, Ramzee	CB	5-10	190	2/20/84	5	Alabama	Huntsville, Ala.	FA-'12	0*
14	Stokley, Brandon	WR	6-0	194	6/23/76	14	Southwestern Louisiana	Lafayette, La.	FA-'12	2/0*
84	Tamme, Jacob	TE	6-3	236	3/15/85	5	Kentucky	Danville, Ky.	UFA(Ind)-'12	16/5*
88	Thomas, Demaryius	WR	6-3	229	12/25/87	3	Georgia Tech	Montrose, Ga.	D1a-'10	11/5
80	Thomas, Julius	TE	6-5	255	6/27/88	2	Portland State	Stockton, Calif.	D4b-'11	5/1
22	Thompson, Syd'Quan	CB	5-9	191	2/7/87	3	California	Sacramento, Calif.	D7a-'10	0*
96	Unrein, Mitch	DT	6-4	291	3/25/87	3	Wyoming	Eaton, Colo.	FA-'10	14/0
41	Vaughn, Cassius	CB	5-11	195	11/3/87	3	Mississippi	Memphis, Tenn.	FA-'10	9/3
99	Vickerson, Kevin	DT	6-5	290	1/8/83	7	Michigan State	Detroit, Mich.	FA-'10	5/4
50	Walton, J.D.	C	6-3	305	3/24/87	3	Baylor	Allen, Texas	D3a-'10	16/16
94	Warren, Ty	DT	6-5	300	2/6/81	10	Texas A&M	Bryan, Texas	FA-'11	0*
55	Williams, D.J.	WLB	6-1	242	7/20/82	9	Miami	Concord, Calif.	D1-'04	13/13
12	Willis, Matthew	WR	6-0	190	4/13/84	5	UCLA	Anaheim, Calif.	FA-'08	16/0
52	Woodyard, Wesley	WLB	6-0	229	7/21/86	5	Kentucky	LaGrange, Ga.	FA-'08	15/7

* Adams played 16 games with Cleveland in '11; Bannan played 15 games with St. Louis; Caldwell played 13 games with Cincinnati; Davis last active with Carolina in '10; Dreessen played 16 games with Houston; Hanie played 6 games with Chicago; R. Harris last active with Denver in '10; Hill played 10 games with Jacksonville; Hills inactive for 15 games, didn't play in 1 game; Jarmon last active with Washington in '10; Manning inactive for 16 games with Indianapolis; Obiozor last active with Arizona in '10; Porter played 14 games with New Orleans; Robinson last active with Cleveland in '09; Tamme played 16 games with Indianapolis; Thompson missed '11 season because of injury; Warren missed '11 season because of injury.

Traded—QB Tim Tebow (15 games in '11) to New York Jets, WR Brandon Lloyd (4) to St. Louis.

f-   Unsigned franchise player; subject to developments.

Players lost through free agency (9): DT Broderick Bunkley (NO; 16 games), S Brian Dawkins (Phil; 14), TE Daniel Fells (NE; 16), DE Derrick Harvey (Cin; 5), FB Spencer Larsen (NE; 16), QB Brady Quinn (KC; 0), TE Dante Rosario (SD; 14), WR Eddie Royal (SD; 13), DB Jonathan Wilhite (Chi; 15).

Also played with Broncos in '11—KR Quan Cosby (10 games), LB Mario Haggan (16), G Russ Hochstein (16), DE Ryan McBean (16), S Kyle McCarthy (4), QB Kyle Orton (5), DT Marcus Thomas (12).

FIRST-YEAR ROSTER

Name	Pos.	Ht.	Wt.	Birthdate	College	Hometown	How Acq.
Beal, Jeremy (1)	DE	6-3	276	12/2/87	Oklahoma	Carrollton, Texas	D7b-'11
Blake, Philip	G/C	6-3	320	11/27/85	Baylor	Lennoxville, Que., Canada	D4b
Blatnick, Jamie	DE	6-3	265	6/24/89	Oklahoma State	Celina, Texas	FA
Bolden, Omar	CB	5-10	195	12/20/88	Arizona State	Ontario, Calif.	D4a
Brewer, Aaron	LS	6-5	225	7/5/90	San Diego State	Fullerton, Calif.	FA
Coffey, Elliot	LB	6-0	235	12/3/89	Baylor	Sugar Land, Texas	FA
Dell, Mark (1)	WR	6-2	195	5/28/89	Michigan State	Farmington Hills, Mich.	FA-'11
Fannin, Mario (1)	RB	5-11	224	12/4/87	Auburn	Hampton, Ga.	FA-'11
Franklin, Jerry	LB	6-1	245	1/10/88	Arkansas	Marion, Ark.	FA
Garland, Ben (1)	DE	6-5	275	4/6/88	Air Force	Grand Junction, Colo.	FA-'10
Goodwin, D'Andre (1)	WR	5-11	188	12/26/87	Washington	Lancaster, Calif.	FA-'11
Grant, Adam (1)	T	6-6	320	5/2/86	Arizona	Puyallup, Wash.	FA-'11
Grisham, Tyler (1)	WR	5-11	180	6/11/87	Clemson	Hoover, Ala.	FA
Hillman, Ronnie	RB	5-10	190	9/14/91	San Diego State	La Habra, Calif.	D3
Ihenacho, Duke	S	6-1	205	6/16/89	San Jose State	San Mateo, Calif.	FA
Ingram, Cornelius	TE	6-4	250	6/10/85	Florida	Hawthorne, Fla.	FA-'11
Jackson, Malik	DE	6-5	270	1/11/90	Tennessee	Van Nuys, Calif.	D5
Johnson, Steven	LB	6-1	237	3/28/88	Kansas	Wallingford, Pa.	FA
Judie, Coryell	CB	5-11	190	10/14/87	Texas A&M	Marlin, Texas	FA
Miller, Anthony	TE	6-4	260	1/22/90	California	San Jose, Calif.	FA
Moore, Joshua (1)	CB	5-11	184	8/20/88	Kansas State	Pompano Beach, Fla.	FA
Omon, Xavier (1)	RB	5-11	227	2/15/85	Northwest Missouri State	Beatrice, Neb.	FA-'11
Orton, Greg (1)	WR	6-3	199	12/17/86	Purdue	Dayton, Ohio	FA-'11
Osweiler, Brock	QB	6-8	240	11/22/90	Arizona State	Kalispell, Mont.	D2b
Page, Eric	WR	5-10	180	9/23/91	Toledo	Springfield, Ohio	FA
Remmers, Mike	T	6-5	303	4/11/89	Oregon State	Portland, Ore.	FA
Robinson, Gerell	WR	6-4	222	10/13/89	Arizona State	Chandler, Ariz.	FA
Siliga, Sealver (1)	DT	6-2	307	4/26/90	Utah	West Jordan, Utah	FA-'11
Sylvester, Austin (1)	FB	6-1	248	4/15/88	Washington	Reno, Nev.	FA-'11
Trevathan, Danny	LB	6-1	232	3/24/90	Kentucky	Leesburg, Fla.	D6
Tribue, Wayne	G	6-3	329	4/30/90	Temple	York, Pa.	FA
Weber, Adam (1)	QB	6-3	210	8/3/87	Minnesota	Arden Hills, Minn.	FA-'11
Wolfe, Derek	DT	6-5	300	2/24/90	Cincinnati	Lisbon, Ohio	D2a
Wuebbels, Austin	G	6-4	295	10/27/88	Missouri	Troy, Ill.	FA

The term NFL Rookie is defined as a player who is in his first season of professional football and has not been on the roster of another professional football team for any regular-season or postseason games. A Rookie is designated by an "R" on NFL rosters. Players who have been active in another professional football league or players who have NFL experience, including either preseason training camp or being on an Active List or Inactive List, or on Reserve/Injured or Reserve/Physically Unable to Perform for fewer than six regular-season games, are termed NFL First-Year Players. An NFL First-Year Player is designated by a "1" on NFL rosters. Thereafter, a player is credited with an additional year of experience for each season in which he accumulates six games on the Active List or Inactive List, or on Reserve/Injured or Reserve/Physically Unable to Perform.

Log on to www.denverbroncos.com for an up-to-date roster.

COACHING STAFF
Head Coach,
John Fox
Pro Career: John Fox was named the 14th head coach in Denver Broncos history on January 13, 2011. He joined the Broncos after spending the previous nine seasons (2002-2010) as the head coach of the Carolina Panthers. In 23 NFL seasons, he has appeared in two Super Bowls and three conference championship games as a head coach or coordinator. During that span, he has coached 27 players to a total of 49 Pro Bowl selections. He compiled a 73-71 (.507) regular-season record with the Panthers that included two 11-win campaigns, two NFC South Division titles and three playoff appearances. Carolina went 5-3 in the postseason under Fox, appearing in two NFC Championship Games and one Super Bowl (XXXVIII in 2003). Has registered four postseason road victories. Prior to coaching the Panthers, Fox was the defensive coordinator for the N.Y. Giants (1997-2001). In 2000, Fox helped the Giants reach Super Bowl XXXV, including posting the first shutout in a conference title game since 1986. Before joining the Giants, was a consultant for the Rams (1996), defensive coordinator for the Raiders (1994-95), defensive backs coach for the Chargers (1992-93) and Steelers (1989-1991), and secondary coach for the USFL's Los Angeles Express (1985). Career record: 87-83.
Background: Defensive back at San Diego State (1976-77). Coached at San Diego State (1978), U.S. International (1979) Boise State (1980), Long Beach State (1981), Utah (1982), Kansas (1983), Iowa State (1984), and Pittsburgh (1986-88). Received bachelor's degree in physical education and earned a teaching credential from San Diego State.
Personal: Born February 8, 1955, in Virginia Beach, Va. He and his wife, Robin, have four children—Mathew, Mark, Cody, and Halle.

ASSISTANT COACHES
Clancy Barone, tight ends; born July 26, 1963, San Andreas, Calif. Offensive lineman Cal State-Sacramento 1981-82, Nevada 1985-86. No pro playing experience. College coach: American River (Calif.) J.C. 1987-89, Cal State-Sacramento 1990-92, Texas A&M 1993, Eastern Illinois 1994-96, Wyoming 1997-99, Houston 2000-02, Texas State 2003. Pro coach: Atlanta Falcons 2004-06, San Diego Chargers 2007-08, joined Broncos in 2009.
Keith Burns, asst. special teams; born May 16, 1972, Greeleyville, S.C. Linebacker Oklahoma State 1991-94. Pro linebacker Denver Broncos 1994-98, 2000-03, 2005-06, Chicago Bears 1999, Tampa Bay Buccaneers 2004. Pro coach: Joined Broncos in 2007.

Brian Callahan, quality control-offense; born June 10, 1984, Champaign, Ill. Quarterback UCLA 2002-06. No pro playing experience. College coach: UCLA 2006-07. Pro coach: Joined Broncos in 2010.
Jack Del Rio, defensive coordinator; born April 4, 1963, Castro Valley, Calif. Linebacker Southern California 1981-84. Pro linebacker New Orleans Saints 1985-86, Kansas City Chiefs 1987-88, Dallas Cowboys 1989-1991, Minnesota Vikings 1992-95. Pro coach: New Orleans Saints 1997-98, Baltimore Ravens 1999-2001, Carolina Panthers 2002, Jacksonville Jaguars 2003-2011 (head coach), joined Broncos in 2012.
Mike Eubanks, asst. strength and conditioning; born December 31, 1980, Kansas City, Kan. Defensive back Wisconsin-Eau Claire. No pro playing experience. Pro coach: Jacksonville 2009-2011, joined Broncos in 2012.
Sam Garnes, asst. secondary; born July 12, 1974, Bronx, N.Y. Safety Cincinnati 1992-96. Pro safety N.Y. Giants 1997-2001, N.Y. Jets 2002-03. Pro coach: Cologne Centurions (NFL Europe) 2006, Las Vegas Locomotives (UFL) 2009, Carolina Panthers 2010, joined Broncos in 2011.
Adam Gase, quarterbacks; born March 29, 1978, Ypsilanti, Mich. Attended Michigan State. No college or pro playing experience. College coach: Louisiana State 2000-02. Pro coach: Detroit Lions 2003-07, San Francisco 49ers 2008, joined Broncos in 2009.
Jason George, asst. strength and conditioning; born October 3, 1968, Winnipeg, Manitoba, Canada. Safety Manitoba 1991-92. No pro playing experience. College coach: Kansas 1997-98, Fordham 1998-2008. Pro coach: Jacksonville 2009-2011, joined Broncos in 2012.
Anthony Lomando, asst. strength and conditioning; born October 4, 1982, Katy, Tex. Cal Poly State University-San Louis Obispo. No college or pro playing experience. Pro coach: Jacksonville 2009-2011; joined Broncos in 2012.
Dave Magazu, offensive line; born June 10, 1957, Taunton, Mass. Defensive tackle Springfield College 1976-79. No pro playing experience. College coach: Ithaca 1980, Western Michigan 1981, Eastern Michigan 1982, Michigan 1983, Northern Illinois 1984, Ball State 1985-86, Navy 1987-89, Indiana State 1990-91, Colorado State 1992-94, Kentucky 1995-96, Memphis 1997-98, Boston College 1999-2002. Pro coach: Carolina Panthers 2003-10, joined Broncos in 2011.
Mike McCoy, offensive coordinator; born April 1, 1972, San Francisco, Calif. Quarterback Long Beach State 1990-91, Utah 1992-94. Pro quarterback Amsterdam Admirals (NFLE) 1997, Calgary Stampeders (CFL) 1999. Pro

coach: Carolina Panthers 1999-2008, joined Broncos in 2009.
Ron Milus, secondary; born November, 25, 1963, Tacoma, Wash. Cornerback Washington 1982-85. College coach: Washington 1991-98, Texas A&M 1999. Pro coach: Denver Broncos 2000-02, Arizona Cardinals 2003, New York Giants 2004-05, St. Louis Rams 2006-08, Carolina Panthers 2009-2010, re-joined Broncos in 2011.
Luke Richesson, strength and conditioning; born April 29, 1974, Kansas City, Mo. Defensive back Kansas 1992-96. No pro playing experience. College coach: Wyoming 1998, Arizona State 1999-2000. Pro coach: Jacksonville 2009-2011, joined Broncos in 2012.
Jay Rodgers, defensive line; born August 29, 1976, St. Paul, Minn. Quarterback Indiana 1996-98, Missouri State 1999. No pro playing experience. College coach: Missouri State 2004, Stephen F. Austin 2005-06, Iowa State 2007-08. Pro coach: Joined Broncos in 2009.
Jeff Rodgers, special teams coordinator; born January 12, 1978, St. Paul, Minn. Linebacker North Texas 1996-99. College coach: Arizona 2001-02, Kansas State 2008. Pro coach: San Francisco 49ers 2003-07, Carolina Panthers 2009-2010, joined Broncos in 2011.
Richard Smith, linebackers; born October 17, 1955, Los Angeles, Calif. Offensive lineman Rio Hondo (Calif.) J.C. 1975-76, Fresno State 1977-78. College coach: Rio Hondo (Calif.) J.C. 1979-1980, Cal State-Fullerton 1981-83, California 1984-86, Arizona 1987. Pro coach: Houston Oilers 1988-1992, Denver Broncos 1993-96, San Francisco 49ers 1997-2002, Detroit Lions 2003-04, Miami Dolphins 2005, Houston Texans 2006-08, Carolina Panthers 2009-2010, re-joined Broncos 2011.
Eric Studesville, running backs; born May 29, 1967, Madison, Wisc. Defensive back Wisconsin-Whitewater 1985-88. No pro playing experience. College coach: Wingate 1994, Kent State 1995-96. Pro coach: Chicago Bears 1997-2000, New York Giants 2001-03, Buffalo Bills 2004-2009, joined Broncos in 2010 (interim head coach, four games in 2010).
Tyke Tolbert, wide receivers; born September 15, 1967, Conroe, Texas. Wide receiver Louisiana State 1988-1990. No pro playing experience. College coach: Louisiana State 1994, Ohio 1995, Northeast Louisiana 1995-97, Auburn 1998, Louisiana-Lafayette 1999-2001, Florida 2002. Pro coach: Arizona Cardinals 2003, Buffalo Bills 2004-09, Carolina Panthers 2010, joined Broncos in 2011.

American Football Conference
South Division
Team Colors: Deep Steel Blue, Battle
    Red, and Liberty White
Two Reliant Park
Houston, Texas 77054
Telephone: (832) 667-2000

2012 SCHEDULE
PRESEASON
Aug. 11 at Carolina..........................6:00
Aug. 18 **San Francisco** 7:00
Aug. 25 at New Orleans..................7:00
Aug. 30 **Minnesota** 6:00

REGULAR SEASON
Sep. 9   **Miami**.............................12:00
Sep. 16 at Jacksonville..................12:00
Sep. 23 at Denver...........................3:15
Sep. 30 **Tennessee** 12:00
Oct. 8   at New York Jets (Mon) 7:30
Oct. 14 **Green Bay**........................7:20
Oct. 21 **Baltimore**........................12:00
Oct. 28 BYE
Nov. 4   **Buffalo**............................12:00
Nov. 11 at Chicago.........................7:20
Nov. 18 **Jacksonville**....................12:00
Nov. 22 at Detroit (Thurs) 11:30a
Dec. 2   at Tennessee....................12:00
Dec. 10 at New England (Mon).......7:30
Dec. 16 **Indianapolis**...................12:00
Dec. 23 **Minnesota** 12:00
Dec. 30 at Indianapolis.................12:00
All times CT

Stadium: Reliant Stadium
    (opened in 2002)
    •**Capacity:** 71,054
    Houston, Texas 77054
Playing Surface: Grass
Training Camp: Methodist Training
    Center

RELIANT STADIUM

CLUB OFFICIALS
Chairman and CEO: Robert C. McNair
Vice Chairman: Philip J. Burguiéres
Vice Chairman and COO: D. Cal McNair
General Manager/Executive Vice
    President: Rick Smith
President: Jamey Rootes
Senior Vice President, Treasurer and
    CFO: Scott Schwinger
Executive Vice President, General
    Counsel and CAO: Suzie Thomas
Vice President and Controller:
    Marilan Logan
Vice President, Football Administration:
    Chris Olsen
Vice President of Security: Ryan Reichert
Sr. Vice President, Ticketing and Event
    Management: John Schriever
Vice President, Finance: Greg Watson
Director of Football Operations:
    Doug West
Director of Player Development:
    Sean Washington
Director of College Scouting:
    Mike Maccagnan
Director of Pro Personnel: Brian Gardner
Associate Director of Pro Scouting:
    Bobby Grier
Pro Scout: Kevin Murphy, Larry Wright
National College Scouts: Ed Lambert,
    Dale Strahm
College Scouts: Jon Carr,
    Ryan Cavanaugh, Mike Martin,
    Bob Merritt, Nathan Trott
Director of Sports Medicine/Head Athletic
    Trainer: Geoff Kaplan
Coordinator of Rehabilitation/Assistant
    Athletic Trainer: Roland Ramirez
Assistant Athletic Trainer:
    A.J. Van Valkenburgh
Director of Equipment Services:
    Jay Brunetti
Equipment Services Assistants:
    Mike Parson, Christian Snell
Director of Video Operations: Joe Malota
Assistant Director of Video Operations:
    Tim Brog
Video Operations Asst. Gresham Oliver
Sr. Director of Communications:
    Kevin Cooper
Sr. Director of Corporate Development:
    Greg Grissom
Sr. Director of Accounting and Risk
    Management: Jan Kelly
Associate General Counsel/Sr. Director:
    Greg Kondritz
Sr. Director of Human Resources:
    Glenda Morrison
Sr. Director of Event Operations and
    Guest Services: Diane Crossey
Director of Marketing: Jennifer Davenport
Director of Integrated Media:
    Nick Schenck
Sr. Director of Information Technology:
    Jeff Schmitz
Sr. Director of Treasury: Jon Southern
Director of Premium Seating:
    Brian Varnadoe
Director of Ticket and Event Sales:
    Derek Beeman
Director of Accounting:
    Tamala Croasmun

COACHING HISTORY
(66-96-0)

2002-05	Dom Capers		18-46-0
2006-2011	Gary Kubiak		48-50-0

PAID ATTENDANCE
Home 559,308   Away 451,843
Total 1,011,151
Single-game home record,
    71,725 (1/7/12)
Single-season home record,
    559,308 (2011)

2012 DRAFT CHOICES

Round	Name	Pos.	College
1	Whitney Mercilus	LB	Illinois
3	DeVier Posey	WR	Ohio St.
	Brandon Brooks	G	Miami (OH)
4	Ben Jones	C	Georgia
	Keshawn Martin	WR	Michigan St.
	Jared Crick	DE	Nebraska
5	Randy Bullock	K	Texas A&M
6	Nick Mondek	T	Purdue

2011 TEAM RECORD
PRESEASON (3-1)
Date	Result	Opponent
8/15	W 20-16	New York Jets
8/20	W 27-14	New Orleans
8/27	W 30-7	at San Francisco
9/1	L 0-28	at Minnesota

REGULAR SEASON (10-6)
Date	Result	Opponent
9/11	W 34-7	Indianapolis
9/18	W 23-13	at Miami
9/25	L 33-40	at New Orleans
10/2	W 17-10	Pittsburgh
10/9	L 20-25	Oakland
10/16	L 14-29	at Baltimore
10/23	W 41-7	at Tennessee
10/30	W 24-14	Jacksonville
11/6	W 30-12	Cleveland
11/13	W 37-9	at Tampa Bay
11/27	W 20-13	at Jacksonville
12/4	W 17-10	Atlanta
12/11	W 20-19	at Cincinnati
12/18	L 13-28	Carolina
12/22	L 16-19	at Indianapolis
1/1	L 22-23	Tennessee

POSTSEASON (1-1)
Date	Result	Opponent
1/7	W 31-10	Cincinnati
1/15	L 13-20	at Baltimore

SCORE BY PERIODS
Texans	110	107	63	101	0	— 381
Opponents	39	78	56	105	0	— 278

2011 TEAM STATISTICS
	Texans	Opp.
Total First Downs	321	270
Rushing	131	73
Passing	176	166
Penalty	14	31
3rd Down: Made/Att	93/224	76/212
3rd Down Pct.	41.5	35.8
4th Down: Made/Att	3/11	6/13
4th Down Pct.	27.3	46.2
Possession Avg.	32:41	27:20
Total Net Yards	5954	4571
Avg. Per Game	372.1	285.7
Total Plays	1046	960
Avg. Per Play	5.7	4.8
Net Yards Rushing	2448	1536
Avg. Per Game	153.0	96.0
Total Rushes	546	378
Net Yards Passing	3506	3035
Avg. Per Game	219.1	189.7
Sacked/Yards Lost	33/190	44/287
Gross Yards	3696	3322
Att./Completions	467/288	538/279
Completion Pct.	61.7	51.9
Had Intercepted	9	17
Punts/Average	74/44.0	83/46.9
Net Punting Avg.	74/37.7	83/39.6
Penalties/Yards	99/852	88/686
Fumbles/Ball Lost	20/11	18/10
Touchdowns	41	27
Rushing	18	8
Passing	20	18
Returns	3	1

2011 INDIVIDUAL STATISTICS
PASSING
	Att.	Comp.	Yds.	Pct.	TD	Int.	Tkld.	Rate
Schaub	292	178	2479	61.0	15	6	16/98	96.8
Yates	134	82	949	61.2	3	3	15/74	80.7
Delhomme	28	18	211	64.3	1	0	2/18	99.0
Leinart	13	10	57	76.9	1	0	0/0	110.1
Texans	467	288	3696	61.7	20	9	33/190	92.7
Opponents	538	279	3322	51.9	18	17	44/287	69.0

SCORING
	TD R	TD P	TD Rt	PAT	FG	Saf	PTS
Rackers	0	0	0	39/40	32/38	0	135
Foster	10	2	0	0/0	0/0	0	72
Dreessen	0	6	0	0/0	0/0	0	36
Tate	4	0	0	0/0	0/0	0	24
Daniels	0	3	0	0/0	0/0	0	18
Jones	0	2	1	0/0	0/0	0	18
Walter	0	3	0	0/0	0/0	0	18
A. Johnson	0	2	0	0/0	0/0	0	12
Schaub	2	0	0	0/0	0/0	0	12
Ward	2	0	0	0/0	0/0	0	12
Casey	0	1	0	0/0	0/0	0	6
B. Johnson	0	1	0	0/0	0/0	0	6
McCain	0	0	1	0/0	0/0	0	6
W. Smith	0	0	1	0/0	0/0	0	6
Texans	18	20	3	39/40	32/38	0	381
Opponents	8	18	1	22/22	30/36	0	278

2-Pt Conversions: Texans 0-1, Opponents 2-5

RUSHING
	No.	Yds	Avg	LG	TD
Foster	278	1224	4.4	43	10
Tate	175	942	5.4	56	4
Ward	45	154	3.4	15	2
Yates	14	57	4.1	17	0
Slaton	7	20	2.9	13	0
Jones	4	17	4.3	15	0
Casey	1	11	11.0	11	0
Schaub	15	9	0.6	3	2
A. Johnson	1	8	8.0	8	0
Ogbonnaya	3	6	2.0	4	0
B. Johnson	1	1	1.0	1	0
Vickers	1	0	0.0	0	0
Leinart	1	-1	-1.0	-1	0
Texans	546	2448	4.5	56	18
Opponents	378	1536	4.1	42	8

RECEIVING
	No.	Yds	Avg	LG	TD
Daniels	54	677	12.5	34	3
Foster	53	617	11.6	78t	2
Walter	39	474	12.2	41	3
A. Johnson	33	492	14.9	50	2
Jones	31	512	16.5	80t	2
Dreessen	28	353	12.6	56t	6
Casey	18	260	14.4	62	1
Tate	13	98	7.5	14	0
B. Johnson	6	90	15.0	40	1
Mason	6	55	9.2	16	0
Vickers	4	29	7.3	17	0
Graham	1	24	24.0	24	0
Anderson	1	9	9.0	9	0
Slaton	1	6	6.0	6	0
Texans	288	3696	12.8	80t	20
Opponents	279	3322	11.9	56	18

INTERCEPTIONS
	No.	Yds	Avg	LG	TD
Joseph	4	40	10.0	29	0
Allen	4	34	8.5	34	0
McCain	2	48	24.0	38t	1
Demps	2	47	23.5	42	0
Manning	2	22	11.0	22	0
Cushing	2	5	2.5	5	0
Jackson	1	0	0.0	0	0
Texans	17	196	11.5	42	1
Opponents	9	132	14.7	27	0

PUNTING
	No.	Yds.	Avg.	In 20	LG
Hartmann	58	2573	44.4	15	69
Turk	16	683	42.7	4	55
Texans	74	3256	44.0	19	69
Opponents	83	3896	46.9	25	70

PUNT RETURNS
	Ret	FC	Yds	Avg	LG	TD
Jones	49	7	518	10.6	79t	1
Holliday	1	3	0	0.0	0	0
Keo	1	1	11	11.0	11	0
Texans	51	11	529	10.4	79t	1
Opponents	32	20	307	9.6	33	0

KICKOFF RETURNS
	No.	Yds	Avg	LG	TD
Manning	13	356	27.4	46	0
McManis	10	205	20.5	45	0
Demps	5	169	33.8	50	0
Casey	1	0	0.0	0	0
Dreessen	0	0	—	—	0
Texans	29	730	25.2	50	0
Opponents	46	1030	22.4	63	0

FIELD GOALS
	1-19	20-29	30-39	40-49	50+
Rackers	0/0	14/14	10/11	4/8	4/5
Texans	0/0	14/14	10/11	4/8	4/5
Opponents	1/1	7/8	7/10	9/10	6/7

SACKS
	No.
Barwin	11.5
A. Smith	6.5
Reed	6.0
Watt	5.5
M. Williams	5.0
Cushing	4.0
Jamison	2.0
Cody	1.0
Mitchell	1.0
Braman	0.5
Nading	0.5
Nolan	0.5
Texans	44.0
Opponents	33.0

RECORD HOLDERS
INDIVIDUAL RECORDS—CAREER

Category	Name	Performance
Rushing (Yds.)	Domanick Williams, 2003-06	3,195
Passing (Yds.)	Matt Schaub, 2007-2011	16,903
Passing (TDs)	Matt Schaub, 2007-2011	92
Receiving (No.)	Andre Johnson, 2003-2011	706
Receiving (Yds.)	Andre Johnson, 2003-2011	9,656
Interceptions	Dunta Robinson, 2004-09	13
Punting (Avg.)	Matt Turk, 2007-2011	42.3
Punt Return (Avg.)	Jacoby Jones, 2007-2011	10.2
Kickoff Return (Avg.)	André Davis, 2007-09	25.4
Field Goals	Kris Brown, 2002-09	172
Touchdowns (Tot.)	Andre Johnson, 2003-2011	52
Points	Kris Brown, 2002-09	767
*Sacks	Mario Williams, 2006-2011	53.0

INDIVIDUAL RECORDS—SINGLE SEASON

Category	Name	Performance
Rushing (Yds.)	Arian Foster, 2010	1,616
Passing (Yds.)	Matt Schaub, 2009	4,770
Passing (TDs)	Matt Schaub, 2009	29
Receiving (No.)	Andre Johnson, 2008	115
Receiving (Yds.)	Andre Johnson, 2008	1,575
Interceptions	Marcus Coleman, 2003	7
Punting (Avg.)	Brett Hartmann, 2011	44.4
Punt Return (Avg.)	Jacoby Jones, 2008	12.1
Kickoff Return (Avg.)	André Davis, 2007	30.3
Field Goals	Neil Rackers, 2011	32
Touchdowns (Tot.)	Arian Foster, 2010	18
Points	Neil Rackers, 2011	135
*Sacks	Mario Williams, 2007	14.0

INDIVIDUAL RECORDS—SINGLE GAME

Category	Name	Performance
Rushing (Yds.)	Arian Foster, 9-12-10	231
Passing (Yds.)	Matt Schaub, 9-19-10	497
Passing (TDs)	Sage Rosenfels, 10-21-07	4
	Matt Schaub, 9-20-09, 10-18-09	4
Receiving (No.)	Andre Johnson, 10-10-04, 11-27-05, 9-19-10	12
	Kevin Walter, 10-14-07	12
Receiving (Yds.)	Andre Johnson, 12-14-08	207
Interceptions	Glover Quin, 10-28-10	3
Field Goals	Kris Brown, 9-7-03, 12-4-05, 10-7-07	5
Touchdowns (Tot.)	Ryan Moats, 11-1-09	3
	Arian Foster, 9-12-10, 10-23-11	3
Points	Ryan Moats, 11-1-09	18
	Arian Foster, 9-12-10, 10-23-11	18
*Sacks	Connor Barwin, 11-27-11	4.0

*Sacks became an official statistic in 1982.

2012 VETERAN ROSTER

No.	Name	Pos.	Ht.	Wt.	Birthdate	NFL Exp.	College	Hometown	How Acq.	'11 Games/ Starts
54	Alexander, Mister	ILB	6-3	242	6/2/88	2	Florida State	Aldine, Texas	FA-'11	8/0
61	Austin, Thomas	G	6-4	303	11/14/86	2	Clemson	Camden, S.C.	W(NE)-'11	3/0
34	#Barber, Dominique	SS	6-0	210	8/2/86	5	Minnesota	Wayzata, Minn.	D6-'08	6/0
98	Barwin, Connor	OLB	6-4	264	10/15/86	4	Cincinnati	Detroit, Mich.	D2-'09	16/16
12	Beck, John	QB	6-2	215	8/21/81	6	Brigham Young	Hayward, Calif.	FA-'12	4/3*
50	Braman, Bryan	OLB	6-5	246	5/4/87	2	West Texas A&M	Spokane, Wash.	FA-'11	16/0
76	Brown, Duane	T	6-4	320	8/30/85	5	Virginia Tech	Richmond, Va.	D1-'08	16/16
93	#Bulman, Tim	DE	6-4	281	10/31/82	6	Boston College	Dorchester, Mass.	FA-'06	10/0
78	Butler, Rashad	T	6-4	317	2/10/83	7	Miami	West Palm Beach, Fla.	W(Car)-'07	2/0
62	Caldwell, Antoine	G	6-3	311	4/19/86	4	Alabama	Montgomery, Ala.	D3-'09	5/3
36	Carmichael, Roc	CB	5-10	184	9/9/88	2	Virginia Tech	Clinton, Md.	D4-'11	0*
86	Casey, James	FB	6-3	243	9/22/84	4	Rice	Azle, Texas	D5-'09	14/7
95	Cody, Shaun	NT	6-4	301	1/22/83	8	Southern California	Hacienda Heights, Calif.	UFA(Det)-'09	16/16
56	Cushing, Brian	ILB	6-3	248	1/24/87	4	Southern California	Park Ridge, N.J.	D1-'09	16/16
81	Daniels, Owen	TE	6-3	247	11/9/82	7	Wisconsin	Naperville, Ill.	D4-'06	15/15
17	#Delhomme, Jake	QB	6-2	215	1/10/75	13	Louisiana-Lafayette	Breaux Bridge, La.	FA-'11	1/0
27	Demps, Quintin	FS	5-11	206	6/29/85	5	Texas-El Paso	San Antonio, Texas	FA-'10	9/0
52	Dobbins, Tim	ILB	6-1	245	12/10/82	7	Iowa State	Nashville, Tenn.	FA-'11	15/0
23	Foster, Arian	RB	6-1	229	8/24/86	4	Tennessee	San Diego, Calif.	FA-'09	13/13
7	#Garcia, Jeff	QB	6-1	205	2/24/70	12	San Jose State	Gilroy, Calif.	FA-'11	0*
66	Gardner, Andrew	T	6-6	308	4/4/86	3	Georgia Tech	Tyrone, Ga.	FA-'11	1/0
88	Graham, Garrett	TE	6-3	240	8/4/1986	3	Wisconsin	Brick, N.J.	D4b-'10	7/0
26	Harris, Brandon	CB	5-10	195	1/24/90	2	Miami	Miami, Fla.	D2b-'11	7/0
2	Hartmann, Brett	P	6-2	227	8/17/87	2	Central Michigan	Menomonee Falls, Wisc.	FA-'11	12/0
16	Holliday, Trindon	WR	5-5	170	4/27/86	2	Louisiana State	Zachary, La.	D6b-'10	1/0
19	Iglesias, Juaquin	WR	6-0	205	8/22/87	2	Oklahoma	Killeen, Texas	FA-'11	0*
25	Jackson, Kareem	CB	5-10	188	4/10/88	3	Alabama	Macon, Ga.	D1-'10	15/13
53	James, Bradie	ILB	6-2	246	1/17/81	10	Louisiana State	Monroe, La.	UFA(Dall)-'12	16/13*
96	Jamison, Tim	DE	6-3	285	2/26/86	4	Michigan	Harvey, Ill.	FA-'09	16/0
18	Jean, Lestar	WR	6-3	205	2/5/88	2	Florida Atlantic	Miami, Fla.	FA-'11	0*
80	Johnson, Andre	WR	6-3	226	7/11/81	10	Miami	Miami, Fla.	D1-'03	7/7
89	#Johnson, Bryant	WR	6-3	212	3/7/81	10	Penn State	Baltimore, Md.	FA-'11	16/0
5	Jones, Donnie	P	6-2	220	7/5/80	9	Louisiana State	Baton Rouge, La.	UFA(StL)-'12	16/0*
24	Joseph, Johnathan	CB	5-11	191	4/16/84	7	South Carolina	Rock Hill, S.C.	UFA(Cin)-'11	15/15
31	Keo, Shiloh	FS	5-11	212	12/17/87	2	Idaho	Everett, Wash.	D5-'11	10/0
38	Manning, Danieal	FS	5-11	209	8/9/82	7	Abilene Christian	Corsicana, Texas	UFA(Chi)-'11	13/13
21	McCain, Brice	CB	5-9	180	12/10/86	4	Utah	Terrell, Texas	D6-'09	16/0
22	McManis, Sherrick	CB	6-1	193	12/19/87	3	Northwestern	Peoria, Ill.	D5-'10	10/0
92	Mitchell, Earl	NT	6-3	289	9/25/87	3	Arizona	Galena Park, Texas	D3-'10	16/0
55	Myers, Chris	C	6-4	289	9/15/81	8	Miami	Miami, Fla.	T(Den)-'08	16/16
57	Nading, Jesse	OLB	6-5	261	7/3/1985	4	Colorado State	Highlands Ranch, Colo.	FA-'08	11/0
75	Newton, Derek	T	6-6	307	11/16/87	2	Arkansas State	Utica, Miss.	D7a-'11	14/0
33	Nolan, Troy	FS	6-2	202	9/7/86	4	Arizona State	Woodland Hills, Calif.	D7-'09	14/3
29	Quin, Glover	SS	6-0	209	1/15/86	4	New Mexico	Summit, Miss.	D4a-'09	16/16
58	Reed, Brooks	OLB	6-3	250	2/28/87	2	Arizona	Tucson, Ariz.	D2a-'11	16/11
8	Schaub, Matt	QB	6-5	241	6/25/81	9	Virginia	West Chester, Pa.	T(Atl)-'07	10/10
51	Sharpton, Darryl	ILB	5-11	230	1/1/1988	3	Miami	Coral Gables, Fla.	D4a-'10	8/0
94	Smith, Antonio	DE	6-4	280	10/21/81	9	Oklahoma State	Oklahoma City, Okla.	UFA(Ariz)-'09	16/16
71	Smith, Shelley	G	6-4	297	5/21/87	3	Colorado State	Phoenix, Ariz.	D6a-'10	0*
74	Smith, Wade	G	6-4	310	4/26/81	9	Memphis	Dallas, Texas	UFA(KC)-'10	16/16
64	#Studdard, Kasey	G	6-3	306	7/1/84	6	Texas	Lone Tree, Colo.	D6-'07	0*
44	Tate, Ben	RB	5-11	214	8/21/88	3	Auburn	Salisbury, Md.	D2-'10	15/2
1	#Turk, Matt	P	6-5	251	6/6/68	16	Wisconsin-Whitewater	Greenfield, Wisc.	FA-'07	4/0
70	Wallace, Cody	C	6-4	300	11/26/84	3	Texas A&M	Cuero, Texas	FA-'11	0*
83	Walter, Kevin	WR	6-3	217	8/4/81	10	Eastern Michigan	Vernon Hills, Ill.	RFA(Cin)-'06	15/14
32	#Ward, Derrick	RB	5-11	240	8/30/80	9	Ottawa (Kansas)	Moreno Valley, Calif.	FA-'10	12/1
99	Watt, J.J.	DE	6-4	288	3/22/89	2	Wisconsin	Pewaukee, Wisc.	D1-'11	16/16
46	Weeks, Jon	LS	5-10	242	2/17/86	3	Baylor	Bethpage, N.Y.	FA-'11	16/0
40	Williams, Javarris	RB	5-10	223	4/8/86	3	Tennessee State	Richmond, Texas	FA-'11	0*
13	Yates, T.J.	QB	6-4	220	5/28/87	2	North Carolina	Marietta, Ga.	D5b-'11	6/5

* Beck played 4 games with Washington in '11; Carmichael missed '11 season because of injury; Garcia inactive for 4 games; Iglesias last active with Chicago in '09; James played 16 games with Dallas; Jean missed '11 season because of injury; Jones played 16 games with St. Louis; S. Smith missed '11 season because of injury; Studdard missed '11 season because of injury; Wallace last active with San Francisco in '09; Williams last active with Kansas City in '09.

\# Unrestricted free agent; subject to developments.

Traded—LB DeMeco Ryans (16 games in '11) to Philadelphia.

Players lost through free agency (5): CB Jason Allen (Cin; 16 games in '11), G Mike Brisiel (Oak; 13), TE Joel Dreessen (Den; 16), K Neil Rackers (Wash; 16), LB Mario Williams (Buff; 5).

Also played with Texans in '11—WR David Anderson (2 games), WR Jacoby Jones (16), QB Matt Leinart (2), WR Derrick Mason (7), RB Chris Ogbonnaya (2), RB Steve Slaton (3), FB Lawrence Vickers (14), T Eric Winston (16).

FIRST-YEAR ROSTER

Name	Pos.	Ht.	Wt.	Birthdate	College	Hometown	How Acq.
Brock, Logan	TE	6-3	244	10/5/88	Texas Christian	Copperas Cove, Texas	FA
Brooks, Brandon	G	6-5	346	8/19/89	Miami (Ohio)	Milwaukee, Wisc.	D3b
Bryant, D.J.	OLB	6-3	248	3/3/89	James Madison	Baltimore, Md.	FA
Bullock, Randy	K	5-9	208	12/16/89	Texas A&M	Klein, Texas	D5
Crick, Jared	DE	6-4	276	8/21/89	Nebraska	Cozad, Neb.	D4c
Fangupo, Hebron	NT	6-0	324	7/19/85	Brigham Young	Santa Ana, Calif.	FA
Ford, Jason	FB	5-10	251	12/1/89	Illinois	Belleville, Ill.	FA
Grimes, Jonathan	RB	5-10	207	12/21/89	William & Mary	Willingboro, N.J.	FA
Harris, Ra'Shon (1)	NT	6-5	300	8/26/86	Oregon	Pensacola, Fla.	FA-'11
Hunter, David	NT	6-2	306	9/19/89	Houston	Houston, Texas	FA
Jackson, Jerrell	WR	6-0	192	2/6/90	Missouri	Houston, Texas	FA
Johnson, Delano	OLB	6-4	266	1/13/88	Bowie State	Baltimore, Md.	FA
Jones, Ben	C	6-3	303	7/2/89	Georgia	Centreville, Ala.	D4a
Jones, Dwight	WR	6-3	230	1/1/89	North Carolina	Burlington, N.C.	FA
Keenum, Case	QB	6-1	206	2/12/88	Houston	Abilene, Texas	FA
Loiseau, Shawn	ILB	6-0	236	10/10/89	Merrimack	Shrewsbury, Mass.	FA
Louis, Mario	WR	6-0	190	9/11/88	Grambling State	New Orleans, La.	FA
Maehl, Jeff (1)	WR	6-0	178	3/16/89	Oregon	Paradise, Calif.	FA-'11
Marrow, Desmond	FS	6-2	208	12/28/87	Toledo	Youngstown, Ohio	FA
Martin, Keshawn	WR	5-11	194	3/15/90	Michigan State	Inkster, Mich.	D4b
Meggett, Davin	RB	5-8	211	3/22/90	Maryland	Clinton, Md.	FA
Menkin, Nathan	TE	6-4	296	10/4/88	Mary Hardin-Baylor	Lago Vista, Texas	FA
Mercilus, Whitney	OLB	6-4	254	7/21/90	Illinois	Akron, Ohio	D1
Mondek, Nick	T	6-5	304	11/3/88	Purdue	Naperville, Ill.	D6
Moore, Rennie	DE	6-3	271	11/29/88	Clemson	St. Marys, Ga.	FA
Pleasant, Eddie	SS	5-10	213	12/17/88	Oregon	Compton, Calif.	FA
Posey, DeVier	WR	6-1	208	3/15/90	Ohio State	Cincinnati, Ohio	D3a
Robertson, Tracy	TE	6-4	285	9/26/89	Baylor	Houston, Texas	FA
Smith, Derrell (1)	LB	6-2	232	6/23/88	Syracuse	Philadelphia, Pa.	FA-'11
Supernaw, Phillip	TE	6-5	246	1/30/90	Ouachita Baptist	Katy, Texas	FA
White, Cody	G	6-3	303	7/1/88	Illinois State	Columbus, Ohio	FA
Williams, Greg	ILB	6-1	239	12/6/88	Pittsburgh	Naples, Fla.	FA
Williams, Torri (1)	FS	6-2	210	8/29/86	Purdue	Cedar Park, Texas	FA-'11

The term NFL Rookie is defined as a player who is in his first season of professional football and has not been on the roster of another professional football team for any regular-season or postseason games. A Rookie is designated by an "R" on NFL rosters. Players who have been active in another professional football league or players who have NFL experience, including either preseason training camp or being on an Active List or Inactive List, or on Reserve/Injured or Reserve/Physically Unable to Perform for fewer than six regular-season games, are termed NFL First-Year Players. An NFL First-Year Player is designated by a "1" on NFL rosters. Thereafter, a player is credited with an additional year of experience for each season in which he accumulates six games on the Active List or Inactive List, or on Reserve/Injured or Reserve/Physically Unable to Perform.

Log on to www.houstontexans.com for an up-to-date roster.

COACHING STAFF
Head Coach,
Gary Kubiak

Pro Career: Gary Kubiak is in his seventh season as head coach of the Houston Texans and is the winningest coach in franchise history. In 2011, the Texans finished with a franchise-best 10-6 record, won their first division title, advanced to the playoffs for the first time and won their first ever playoff game. Kubiak has led the Texans to the four best seasons in franchise history, including 2011, going 8-8 in 2007 and 2008 before producing the first winning season in team history in 2009 at 9-7. His tenure has produced the top five scoring, total offense and passing season marks in franchise history from 2007-2011. The top two rushing seasons in franchise history have come on Kubiak's watch as well, including a franchise-record 153.0 yards per game in 2011, which ranked second in the NFL. Four of the Texans' top five defensive seasons have come under Kubiak, including in 2011 with the third-largest defensive turnaround in NFL history. The 2011 Texans gave up 285.7 yards per game to finish second in the NFL after giving up 376.9 yards per game and finishing 30th in 2010. The Texans are the only team in the NFL to produce a rushing, receiving and passing yardage champion since Kubiak became head coach. Kubiak guided the Texans to a 9-7 record in 2009, highlighted by a season-ending four-game win streak to capture the franchise's first winning season, missing the playoffs on a tie-breaker. Prior to joining the Texans, Kubiak spent 20 of the previous 23 year in Denver, including 11 years (1995-2005) as Denver's offensive coordinator, helping guide the Broncos to back-to-back World Championships in Super Bowls XXXII and XXXIII. Kubiak tutored Hall of Fame QB John Elway from 1995-98 and RB Terrell Davis was named NFL Most Valuable Player in 1998. Kubiak began his coaching career as Texas A&M's running backs coach (1992-93). Kubiak was the San Francisco 49ers quarterbacks coach in 1994, winning Super Bowl XXIX in his only season. Kubiak is a veteran of six Super Bowls—three as a player and three as a coach. Career record: 48-50.

Background: Kubiak starred at quarterback for Texas A&M (1979-1982), earning all-Southwest Conference honors as a senior. He played for the Broncos (1983-1991) as John Elway's backup. Kubiak played in 119 career games, tossed 14 touchdowns, and was a part of three teams that reached the Super Bowl.

Personal: Born August 15, 1961 in Houston, Texas. He and his wife, Rhonda, have three sons—Klint, Klay, and Klein.

ASSISTANT COACHES
John Benton, offensive line; born December 13, 1963, Los Angeles, Calif. Offensive lineman Colorado State 1986-1990. No pro playing experience. College coach: California University (Pa.) 1990-94, Colorado State 1996-2003. Pro coach: St. Louis Rams 2004-05, joined Texans in 2006.

Perry Carter, asst. defensive backs; born August 15, 1971, McComb, Miss. Defensive back Southern Mississippi 1989-1993. Pro defensive back Arizona Cardinals 1994, Kansas City Chiefs 1995, Oakland Raiders 1996-98, Edmonton Eskimos (CFL) 2000-01, Montreal Alouettes (CFL) 2002, British Columbia Lions (CFL) 2003-04. College coach: Texas A&M-Commerce 2004. Pro coach: Hamburg Sea Devils (NFLEL) 2006, joined Texans in 2006.

Rick Dennison, offensive coordinator; born June 22, 1958, Kalispell, Mont. Tight end Colorado State 1976-79. Pro linebacker Denver Broncos 1982-1990. Pro coach: Denver Broncos 1995-2009, joined Texans in 2010.

Karl Dorrell, quarterbacks; born December 18, 1968, Alameda, Calif. Wide receiver UCLA 1982-86. No pro playing experience. College coach: UCLA 1988, 2003-07 (head coach 2003-07), Central Florida 1989, Northern Arizona 1990-91, Colorado 1992-93, 1995-98, Arizona State 1994, Washington 1999. Pro coach: Denver Broncos 2000-02, Miami Dolphins 2008-2011, joined Texans in 2012.

Dan Hammerschmidt, offensive assistant; born May 20, 1964, Pomona, Calif. Safety Colorado State 1982-85. No pro playing experience. College coach: Colorado State 1986, 1996-2007, 2010-11, Texas Christian 1987, Duke 1988-1994, Virginia Military Institute 1995, Rice 2008, Wyoming 2009. Pro coach: Joined Texans in 2012.

Chick Harris, running backs; born September 21, 1945, Durham, N.C. Running back Northern Arizona 1966-69. No pro playing experience. College coach: Colorado State 1970-71, Long Beach State 1972-73, Washington 1975-1980. Pro coach: Detroit Wheels (WFL) 1974, Buffalo Bills 1981-82, Seattle Seahawks 1983-1991, Los Angeles Rams 1992-94, Carolina Panthers 1995-2001, joined Texans in 2002.

Reggie Herring, linebackers; born July 3, 1959, Myrtle Beach, S.C. Linebacker Florida State 1978-1980. No pro playing experience. College coach: Oklahoma State 1981-85, Auburn 1986-1991, Texas Christian 1992-93, Clemson 1994-2001, North Carolina State 2004, Arkansas 2005-07 (interim head coach 2007). Pro coach: Houston Texans 2002-03, Dallas Cowboys 2008-2010, re-joined Texans in 2011.

Vance Joseph, defensive backs; born September 20, 1972, Marrero, La. Defensive back Colorado 1990-94. Pro defensive back New York Jets 1995, Indianapolis Colts 1996. College coach: Colorado 1999-2001, 2002-03, Wyoming 2002, Bowling Green State 2004. Pro coach: San Francisco 49ers 2005-2010, joined Texans in 2011.

Bobby King, asst. linebackers; born June 29, 1978, Louisville, Ky. Defensive line Texas El-Paso 1998-2000. No pro playing experience.

College coach: Texas El-Paso 2002-03, West Texas A&M 2005, 2008-09, Baylor 2006-07. Pro coach: Dallas Cowboys 2010, joined Texans in 2011.

Larry Kirksey, wide receivers; born January 6, 1951, Harlan, Ky. Wide receiver Eastern Kentucky 1970-73. No pro playing experience. College coach: Miami (Ohio) 1974-76, Kentucky 1977-1981, Kansas 1982, Kentucky State 1983 (head coach), Florida 1984-88, Pittsburgh 1989, Alabama 1990-93, Texas A&M 2000, Middle Tennessee State 2006. Pro coach: San Francisco 49ers 1994-99, Detroit Lions 2001-02, Jacksonville Jaguars 2003, Denver Broncos 2004, joined Texans in 2007.

Bill Kollar, asst. head coach/defensive line; born November 27, 1952, Warren, Ohio. Defensive end Montana State 1971-73. Pro defensive end Cincinnati Bengals 1974-76, Tampa Bay Buccaneers 1977-1981. College coach: Illinois 1985-87, Purdue 1988-89. Pro coach: Tampa Bay Buccaneers 1984, Atlanta Falcons 1990-2000, St. Louis Rams 2001-05, Buffalo Bills 2006-08, joined Texans in 2009.

Marc Lubick, asst. wide receivers; born November 13, 1977, Bozeman, Mont. Defensive back Montana State 1996-99. No pro playing experience. College coach: Colorado State 2000-02, 2005-09. Pro coach: St. Louis Rams 2003-04 (scout), joined Texans in 2010.

Joe Marciano, special teams coordinator; born February 10, 1954, Dunmore, Pa. Quarterback Temple 1972-75. No pro playing experience. College coach: East Stroudsburg State 1977, Rhode Island 1978-79, Villanova 1980, Penn State 1981, Temple 1982. Pro coach: Philadelphia/Baltimore Stars (USFL) 1983-85, New Orleans Saints 1986-1995, Tampa Bay Buccaneers 1996-2001, joined Texans in 2002.

Brian Pariani, tight ends; born July 2, 1965, San Francisco, Calif. No college or pro playing experience. College coach: UCLA 1989, Syracuse 2005. Pro coach: San Francisco 49ers 1991-94, Denver Broncos 1994-2004, joined Texans in 2006.

Wade Phillips, defensive coordinator; born June 21, 1947, Orange, Texas. Linebacker Houston 1966-68. No pro playing experience. College coach: Houston 1969, Oklahoma State 1973-74, Kansas 1975. Pro coach: Houston Oilers 1976-1980, New Orleans Saints 1981-85 (interim head coach for four games 1985), Philadelphia Eagles 1986-88, Denver Broncos 1989-1994 (head coach 1993-94), Buffalo Bills 1995-2000 (head coach 1998-2000), Atlanta Falcons 2002-03 (interim head coach for three games in 2003), San Diego Chargers 2004-06, Dallas Cowboys 2007-10 (head coach), joined Texans in 2011.

Jim Ryan, asst. offensive line; born May 18, 1957, Bellmawr, N.J. Linebacker William & Mary 1974-78. Linebacker Denver Broncos 1979-1988. Pro coach: Denver Broncos 2005-08, Omaha Nighthawks (UFL) 2010, joined Texans in 2011.

**American Football Conference
South Division
Team Colors:** Royal Blue and White
**P.O. Box 535000
Indianapolis, Indiana 46253
Telephone:** (317) 297-2658

2012 SCHEDULE
PRESEASON
Aug. 12	**St. Louis**	1:30
Aug. 19	at Pittsburgh	8:00
Aug. 25	at Washington	4:00
Aug. 30	**Cincinnati**	7:00

REGULAR SEASON
Sep. 9	at Chicago	1:00
Sep. 16	**Minnesota**	1:00
Sep. 23	**Jacksonville**	1:00
Sep. 30	BYE	
Oct. 7	**Green Bay**	1:00
Oct. 14	at New York Jets	1:00
Oct. 21	**Cleveland**	1:00
Oct. 28	at Tennessee	1:00
Nov. 4	**Miami**	1:00
Nov. 8	at Jacksonville (Thurs)	8:20
Nov. 18	at New England	1:00
Nov. 25	**Buffalo**	1:00
Dec. 2	at Detroit	1:00
Dec. 9	**Tennessee**	1:00
Dec. 16	at Houston	1:00
Dec. 23	at Kansas City	1:00
Dec. 30	**Houston**	1:00

*All times ET

Stadium: Lucas Oil Stadium (opened in
2008) •**Capacity:** 63,000
500 South Capitol Avenue
Indianapolis, Indiana 46225
Playing Surface: FieldTurf
Training Camp: Anderson University
1100 East Fifth Street
Anderson, IN 46012

LUCAS OIL STADIUM

CLUB OFFICIALS
Owner and CEO: James Irsay
Vice Chairman/Owner:
Carlie Irsay-Gordon
Vice Chairman/Owner: Casey Irsay Foyt
Vice Chairman/Owner: Kalen Irsay
General Manager: Ryan Grigson
Head Coach: Chuck Pagano
Chief Operating Officer: Pete Ward
Senior Vice President of Sponsorship
Sales: Jay Souers
Vice President-Finance: Kurt Humphrey
Vice President-Ticket Operations/Guest
Services: Larry Hall
Senior Director of Communications:
Avis Roper
Vice President of Sponsorship Sales:
Matt Godbout
Vice President of Premium Seating and
Ticket Sales: Greg Hylton
Vice President and General Counsel:
Dan Emerson
Vice President of Football Operations:
Tom Telesco
Director of Football Administration:
Mike Bluem
Associate Director of Pro Personnel:
Kevin Rogers
Equipment Manager: Jon Scott
Video Director: Erik Kunttu
Head Athletic Trainer: Dave Hammer
Director of Rehabilitation: Erin Barill
Assistant Equipment Managers:
Mike Mays, Sean Sullivan,
Brian Seabrooks
Assistant Trainers: Dave Walston,
Kyle Davis
Assistant Video Director: John Starliper

COACHING HISTORY
**Baltimore 1953-1983
(472-430-7)**
Records include postseason games
1953	Keith Molesworth	3-9-0
1954-1962	Weeb Ewbank	61-52-1
1963-69	Don Shula	73-26-4
1970-72	Don McCafferty*	26-11-1
1972	John Sandusky	4-5-0
1973-74	Howard Schnellenberger**	4-13-0
1974	Joe Thomas	2-9-0
1975-79	Ted Marchibroda	41-36-0
1980-81	Mike McCormack	9-23-0
1982-84	Frank Kush***	11-28-1
1984	Hal Hunter	0-1-0
1985-86	Rod Dowhower****	5-24-0
1986-1991	Ron Meyer#	36-36-0
1991	Rick Venturi	1-10-0
1992-95	Ted Marchibroda	32-35-0
1996-97	Lindy Infante	12-21-0
1998-2001	Jim Mora	32-34-0
2002-08	Tony Dungy	92-33-0
2009-2011	Jim Caldwell	28-24-0

*Released after five games in 1972
**Released after three games in 1974
***Resigned after 15 games in 1984
****Released after 13 games in 1986
#Released after five games in 1991

PAID ATTENDANCE
Home 503,534   Away 496,973
Total 1,000,507
Single-game home record,
67,650 (1/24/10)
Single-season home record,
520,687 (2010)

2012 DRAFT CHOICES
Round	Name	Pos.	College
1	Andrew Luck	QB	Stanford
2	Coby Fleener	TE	Stanford
3	Dwayne Allen	TE	Clemson
	T.Y. Hilton	WR	Florida International
5	Josh Chapman	DT	Alabama
	Vick Ballard	RB	Mississippi St.
6	LaVon Brazill	WR	Ohio
7	Justin Anderson	G	Georgia
	Tim Fugger	LB	Vanderbilt
	Chandler Harnish	QB	Northern Illinois

2011 TEAM RECORD
PRESEASON (1-3)

Date	Result		Opponent
8/13	L	10-33	at St. Louis
8/19	L	3-16	Washington
8/26	L	21-24	Green Bay
9/1	W	17-13	at Cincinnati

REGULAR SEASON (2-14)

Date	Result		Opponent
9/11	L	7-34	at Houston
9/18	L	19-27	Cleveland
9/25	L	20-23	Pittsburgh
10/3	L	17-24	at Tampa Bay
10/9	L	24-28	Kansas City
10/16	L	17-27	at Cincinnati
10/23	L	7-62	at New Orleans
10/30	L	10-27	at Tennessee
11/6	L	7-31	Atlanta
11/13	L	3-17	Jacksonville
11/27	L	19-27	Carolina
12/4	L	24-31	at New England
12/11	L	10-24	at Baltimore
12/18	W	27-13	Tennessee
12/22	W	19-16	Houston
1/1	L	13-19	at Jacksonville

SCORE BY PERIODS

Colts	19	89	36	99	0 —	243
Opponents	108	129	92	101	0 —	430

2011 TEAM STATISTICS

	Colts	Opp.
Total First Downs	258	343
Rushing	69	136
Passing	170	193
Penalty	19	14
3rd Down: Made/Att	74/214	98/216
3rd Down Pct.	34.6	45.4
4th Down: Made/Att	4/11	3/6
4th Down Pct.	36.4	50.0
Possession Avg.	26:13	33:47
Total Net Yards	4589	5935
Avg. Per Game	286.8	370.9
Total Plays	951	1062
Avg. Per Play	4.8	5.6
Net Yards Rushing	1594	2303
Avg. Per Game	99.6	143.9
Total Rushes	382	540
Net Yards Passing	2995	3632
Avg. Per Game	187.2	227.0
Sacked/Yards Lost	35/228	29/192
Gross Yards	3223	3824
Att./Completions	534/302	493/351
Completion Pct.	56.6	71.2
Had Intercepted	14	8
Punts/Average	89/46.0	74/43.6
Net Punting Avg.	89/39.2	74/40.3
Penalties/Yards	76/549	84/804
Fumbles/Ball Lost	24/15	15/9
Touchdowns	25	49
Rushing	8	19
Passing	14	25
Returns	3	5

2011 INDIVIDUAL STATISTICS

PASSING	Att.	Comp.	Yds.	Pct.	TD	Int.	Tkld.	Rate
Painter	243	132	1541	54.3	6	9	16/104	66.6
Orlovsky	193	122	1201	63.2	6	4	14/84	82.4
Collins	98	48	481	49.0	2	1	5/40	65.9
Colts	534	302	3223	56.6	14	14	35/228	72.2
Opponents	493	351	3824	71.2	25	8	29/192	103.9

SCORING	TD R	TD P	TD Rt	PAT	FG	Saf	PTS
Vinatieri	0	0	0	24/24	23/27	0	93
Garcon	0	6	0	0/0	0/0	0	36
D. Brown	5	0	0	0/0	0/0	0	30
Wayne	0	4	0	0/0	0/0	0	24
Carter	2	0	0	0/0	0/0	0	12
Clark	0	2	0	0/0	0/0	0	12
Addai	1	0	0	0/0	0/0	0	6
Anderson	0	0	1	0/0	0/0	0	6
Collie	0	1	0	0/0	0/0	0	6
Lacey	0	0	1	0/0	0/0	0	6
Powers	0	0	1	0/0	0/0	0	6
Tamme	0	1	0	0/0	0/0	0	6
Colts	8	14	3	24/24	23/27	0	243
Opponents	19	25	5	49/49	29/34	0	430

2-Pt Conversions: Colts 0-1, Opponents 0-0

RUSHING	No.	Yds	Avg	LG	TD
D. Brown	134	645	4.8	80t	5
Addai	118	433	3.7	16	1
Carter	101	377	3.7	42	2
Painter	17	107	6.3	24	0
Garcon	4	28	7.0	18	0
Orlovsky	6	5	0.8	7	0
Collins	2	-1	-.5	0	0
Colts	382	1594	4.2	80t	8
Opponents	540	2303	4.3	56	19

RECEIVING	No.	Yds	Avg	LG	TD
Wayne	75	960	12.8	56t	4
Garcon	70	947	13.5	87t	6
Collie	54	514	9.5	27	1
Clark	34	352	10.4	21	2
Tamme	19	177	9.3	29	1
D. Brown	16	86	5.4	17	0
Addai	15	93	6.2	12	0
Eldridge	9	45	5.0	8	0
Carter	5	18	3.6	7	0
Felton	2	16	8.0	9	0
Hill	2	10	5.0	5	0
Mahaffey	1	5	5.0	5	0
Colts	302	3223	10.7	87t	14
Opponents	351	3824	10.9	81t	25

INTERCEPTIONS	No.	Yds	Avg	LG	TD
Lefeged	2	25	12.5	25	0
Powers	2	19	9.5	13	1
Lacey	1	32	32.0	32t	1
Brackett	1	27	27.0	27	0
Bullitt	1	15	15.0	15	0
Angerer	1	0	0.0	0	0
Colts	8	118	14.8	32t	2
Opponents	14	119	8.5	42t	1

PUNTING	No.	Yds.	Avg.	In 20	LG
McAfee	88	4098	46.6	21	64
Colts	89	4098	46.0	21	64
Opponents	74	3230	43.6	26	60

PUNT RETURNS	Ret	FC	Yds	Avg	LG	TD
Garcon	16	8	44	2.8	20	0
Lefeged	9	4	42	4.7	21	0
White	7	10	22	3.1	13	0
Powers	0	1	0	—	—	0
Colts	32	23	108	3.4	21	0
Opponents	48	18	550	11.5	79t	1

KICKOFF RETURNS	No.	Yds	Avg	LG	TD
Lefeged	31	578	18.6	51	0
Colts	31	578	18.6	51	0
Opponents	19	584	30.7	76	0

FIELD GOALS	1-19	20-29	30-39	40-49	50+
Vinatieri	0/0	8/8	9/10	9/10	0/0
Colts	0/0	8/8	9/10	9/10	0/0
Opponents	0/0	9/9	10/10	7/9	5/8

SACKS	No.
Mathis	9.5
Freeney	8.5
Anderson	3.0
Brayton	2.0
Moala	2.0
Angerer	1.0
Hughes	1.0
Mathews	1.0
Wheeler	1.0
Colts	29.0
Opponents	35.0

RECORD HOLDERS
INDIVIDUAL RECORDS—CAREER

Category	Name	Performance
Rushing (Yds.)	Edgerrin James, 1999-2005	9,226
Passing (Yds.)	Peyton Manning, 1998-2010	54,828
Passing (TDs)	Peyton Manning, 1998-2010	399
Receiving (No.)	Marvin Harrison, 1996-2008	1,102
Receiving (Yds.)	Marvin Harrison, 1996-2008	14,580
Interceptions	Bob Boyd, 1960-68	57
Punting (Avg.)	Chris Gardocki, 1995-98	44.8
Punt Return (Avg.)	Ron Gardin, 1970-71	13.5
Kickoff Return (Avg.)	Jim Duncan, 1969-1971	32.6
Field Goals	Mike Vanderjagt, 1998-2005	217
Touchdowns (Tot.)	Marvin Harrison, 1996-2008	128
Points	Mike Vanderjagt, 1998-2005	995
*Sacks	Dwight Freeney, 2002-2011	102.5

INDIVIDUAL RECORDS—SINGLE SEASON

Category	Name	Performance
Rushing (Yds.)	Edgerrin James, 2000	1,709
Passing (Yds.)	Peyton Manning, 2010	4,700
Passing (TDs)	Peyton Manning, 2004	49
Receiving (No.)	Marvin Harrison, 2002	**143
Receiving (Yds.)	Marvin Harrison, 2002	1,722
Interceptions	Tom Keane, 1953	11
Punting (Avg.)	Pat McAfee, 2011	46.6
Punt Return (Avg.)	T.J. Rushing, 2007	13.1
Kickoff Return (Avg.)	Jim Duncan, 1970	35.4
Field Goals	Mike Vanderjagt, 2003	37
Touchdowns (Tot.)	Lenny Moore, 1964	20
Points	Mike Vanderjagt, 2003	157
*Sacks	Dwight Freeney, 2004	16.0

INDIVIDUAL RECORDS—SINGLE GAME

Category	Name	Performance
Rushing (Yds.)	Edgerrin James, 10-15-00	219
Passing (Yds.)	Peyton Manning, 10-31-04	472
Passing (TDs)	Peyton Manning, 9-28-03, 11-25-04	6
Receiving (No.)	Reggie Wayne, 10-3-10	15
Receiving (Yds.)	Raymond Berry, 11-10-57	224
Interceptions	Many times Last time by Mike Prior, 12-20-92	3
Field Goals	Many times Last time by Mike Vanderjagt, 12-7-03	5
Touchdowns (Tot.)	Many times Last time by Joseph Addai, 11-26-06	4
Points	Many times Last time by Joseph Addai, 11-26-06	24
*Sacks	Johnie Cooks, 11-25-84	4.5

*Sacks became an official statistic in 1982.
**NFL Record

2012 VETERAN ROSTER

No.	Name	Pos.	Ht.	Wt.	Birthdate	NFL Exp.	College	Hometown	How Acq.	'11 Games/ Starts
97	Addison, Mario	OLB	6-3	257	9/6/87	2	Troy	Birmingham, Ala.	W(Chi)-'11	3/0
51	Angerer, Pat	ILB	6-0	236	1/31/87	3	Iowa	Bettendorf, Iowa	D2-'10	16/16
11	Avery, Donnie	WR	5-11	200	6/12/84	5	Houston	Houston, Texas	UFA(Tenn)-'12	8/0*
#Bentley, Kevin		ILB	6-0	247	12/29/79	11	Northwestern	Northridge, Calif.	W(Jax)-'11	3/0
41	Bethea, Antoine	S	5-11	196	7/27/84	7	Howard	Newport News, Va.	D6-'06	16/16
#Brackett, Gary		LB	5-11	235	5/23/80	10	Rutgers	Glassboro, N.J.	FA-'03	1/1
#Brayton, Tyler		DE	6-6	280	11/20/79	9	Colorado	Pasco, Was.	UFA(Car)-'11	16/1
31	Brown, Donald	RB	5-10	210	4/11/87	4	Connecticut	Atlantic Highlands, N.J.	D1-'09	16/2
#Bullitt, Melvin		S	6-1	201	11/13/84	6	Texas A&M	Bryan, Texas	FA-'07	2/2
30	Caldwell, David	S	5-11	212	5/19/87	2	William & Mary	Montclair, N.J.	FA-'11	16/13
34	Carter, Delone	RB	5-9	238	6/22/87	2	Syracuse	Copley, Ohio	D4-'11	16/3
74	Castonzo, Anthony	T	6-7	315	8/9/88	2	Boston College	Hawthorn Woods, Ill.	D1-'11	12/12
#Clark, Dallas		TE	6-3	252	6/12/79	10	Iowa	Livermore, Iowa	D1-'03	11/10
17	Collie, Austin	WR	6-0	204	11/11/85	4	Brigham Young	El Dorado Hills, Calif.	D4-'09	16/5
#Collins, Kerry		QB	6-5	247	12/30/72	18	Penn State	Lebanon, Pa.	FA-'11	3/3
53	Conner, Kavell	ILB	6-0	243	2/23/87	3	Clemson	Richmond, Va.	D7-'10	16/15
14	Cosby, Quan	WR	5-9	195	12/23/82	4	Texas	Waco, Texas	W(Den)-'11	10/0*
52	Edds, A.J.	ILB	6-4	185	9/18/87	3	Iowa	Greenwood, Ind.	FA-'11	9/0
81	Eldridge, Brody	TE	6-5	265	3/31/87	2	Oklahoma	La Cygne, Kan.	D5-'10	13/8
#Felton, Jerome		FB	6-0	246	7/3/86	5	Furman	Duren, West Germany	FA-'11	5/2
#Foster, Eric		DT	6-2	265	4/5/85	4	Rutgers	Homestead, Fla.	FA-'08	4/3
93	Freeney, Dwight	OLB	6-1	268	2/19/80	11	Syracuse	Hartford, Conn.	D1-'02	16/15
49	Gronkowski, Chris	FB	6-2	242	12/26/86	3	Arizona	Amherst, N.Y.	W(Dall)-'11	7/0
#Hill, Anthony		TE	6-6	278	1/2/85	2	North Carolina State	Houston, Texas	FA-'11	7/2
26	Hines, Jermale	S	6-1	222	11/11/87	2	Ohio State	Cleveland, Ohio	FA-'11	5/0
92	Hughes, Jerry	OLB	6-2	254	8/13/88	3	Texas Christian	Sugar Land, Texas	D1-'10	12/1
71	Ijalana, Ben	G	6-4	337	8/6/89	2	Villanova	Hainesport, N.J.	D2-'11	4/0
99	Johnson, Antonio	NT	6-3	310	12/8/84	6	Mississippi State	Leland, Miss.	FA-'08	16/12
23	Johnson, Terrence	CB	5-9	195	7/5/86	2	California (Pa)	Braddock, Pa.	FA-'11	10/2
69	t- Justice, Winston	T	6-6	317	9/14/84	7	Southern California	Long Beach, Calif.	T(Phil)-'12	6/1*
37	King, Brandon	CB	5-10	185	1/28/87	2	Purdue	Warner Robins, Ga.	FA-'11	4/0
35	Lefeged, Joe	S	6-0	205	6/2/88	2	Rutgers	Germantown, Md.	FA-'11	16/1
72	Linkenbach, Jeff	T	6-6	323	6/9/87	3	Cincinnati	Sandusky, Ohio	FA-'10	16/16
47	Mahaffey, Ryan	FB	6-1	251	11/28/87	2	Northern Iowa	Des Moines, Iowa	FA-'11	6/0
91	Mathews, Ricardo	DT	6-3	310	7/30/87	3	Cincinnati	Jacksonville, Fla.	D7-'10	12/0
98	Mathis, Robert	OLB	6-2	245	2/26/81	10	Alabama A&M	Atlanta, Ga.	D5-'03	16/15
1	McAfee, Pat	P	6-1	220	5/2/87	4	West Virginia	Plum, Pa.	D7-'09	16/0
75	McGlynn, Mike	G/C	6-4	327	3/8/85	5	Pittsburgh	Austintown, Ohio	UFA(Cin)-'11	7/4*
96	McKinney, Brandon	NT	6-2	345	8/24/83	7	Michigan State	Dayton, Ohio	UFA(Balt)-'12	12/0*
95	Moala, Fili	DE	6-4	310	6/23/85	4	Southern California	Buena Park, Calif.	D2-'09	14/14
94	Nevis, Drake	DT	6-1	310	5/8/89	2	Louisiana State	Harvey, La.	D3-'11	5/0
38	Newton, Mike	S	5-10	207	11/11/87	2	Buffalo	Pasadena, Md.	FA-'12	0*
73	Olsen, Seth	G	6-5	305	11/17/85	3	Iowa	Omaha, Neb.	W(Minn)-'11	6/1
25	Powers, Jerraud	CB	5-10	187	7/19/87	4	Auburn	Decatur, Ala.	D3-'09	12/12
90	Redding, Cory	DE	6-4	315	11/15/80	10	Texas	Houston, Texas	UFA(Balt)-'12	15/11*
76	Reitz, Joe	G	6-7	322	8/24/85	2	Western Michigan	Indianapolis, Ind.	FA-'10	11/9
#Richard, Jamey		G	6-5	295	10/9/84	5	Buffalo	Weston, Conn.	FA-'11	9/0
36	Rucker, Chris	CB	6-1	209	10/12/88	2	Michigan State	Warren, Ohio	D6-'11	15/4
66	Satele, Samson	C	6-3	299	11/29/84	6	Hawaii	Kailua, Hawaii	UFA(Oak)-'12	15/15*
#Sims, Ernie		OLB	6-0	230	12/31/84	7	Florida State	Tallahassee, Fla.	UFA(Phil)-'11	13/4
43	Smith, Andre	TE	6-5	267	9/26/88	2	Virginia Tech	Germantown, Md.	W(Chi)-'12	0*
48	Snow, Justin	LS	6-3	245	12/21/76	13	Baylor	Abilene, Texas	FA-'00	16/0
5	t- Stanton, Drew	QB	6-3	243	5/7/84	5	Michigan State	Okemos, Mich.	T(NYJ)-'12	0*
67	Tepper, Mike	T	6-6	354	12/11/85	2	California	Cypress, Calif.	FA-'11	6/4
21	Thomas, Kevin	CB	6-0	192	9/20/86	3	Southern California	Oxnard, Calif.	D3-'10	9/5
4	Vinatieri, Adam	K	6-0	206	12/28/72	17	South Dakota State	Rapid City, S.D.	UFA(NE)-'06	16/0
87	Wayne, Reggie	WR	6-0	198	11/17/78	12	Miami	New Orleans, La.	D1-'01	16/16
#White, Blair		WR	6-2	205	2/20/87	2	Michigan State	Saginaw, Mich.	FA-'10	7/0
28	Zbikowski, Tom	S	5-11	200	5/22/85	5	Notre Dame	Park Ridge, Ill.	UFA(Balt)-'12	14/4*

* Avery played 8 games with Tennessee in '11; Cosby played 10 games with Denver and inactive for 1 game with Indianapolis; Justice played 6 games with Philadelphia; McGlynn played 7 games with Cincinnati; McKinney played 12 games with Baltimore; Newton last active with Indianapolis in '10; Redding played 15 games with Baltimore; Satele played 15 games with Oakland; Smith inactive for 8 games with Chicago; Stanton inactive for 16 games with Detroit; Zbikowski played 14 games with Baltimore.

t- Colts traded for Justice (Phil) and Stanton (NYJ).

Players lost through free agency (10): DE Jamaal Anderson (Cin; 15 games), FB Jerome Felton (Minn; 5), WR Pierre Garcon (Wash; 16), WR Anthony Gonzalez (NE; 8), T Quinn Ojinnaka (StL; 9), QB Dan Orlovsky (TB; 8), G Mike Pollak (Car; 15), C Jeff Saturday (GB; 16), TE Justin Tamme (Den; 16), LB Philip Wheeler (Oak; 13).

Also played with Colts in '11—RB Joseph Addai (12 games), DB Stevie Brown (8 games), G Ryan Diem (11), LB Zac Diles (4), RB Darren Evans (2), CB Jacob Lacey (16), TE Mike McNeill (4), LB Adrian Moten (10), DT Daniel Muir (4), QB Curtis Painter (9), T Michael Toudouze (2), DB Morgan Trent (1), LB Nate Triplett (3), DB Justin Tryon (3).

FIRST-YEAR ROSTER

Name	Pos.	Ht.	Wt.	Birthdate	College	Hometown	How Acq.
Aiono, James	DE	6-3	305	1/23/89	Utah	West Valley, Utah	FA
Allen, Dwayne	TE	6-3	255	2/24/90	Clemson	Fayetteville, N.C.	D3
Anderson, Justin	G	6-5	342	4/15/88	Georgia	Ocilla, Ga.	D7
Anunoby, Chigbo	DT	6-4	324	1/4/89	Morehouse	Jefferson City, Mo.	FA
Baker, Steven	T	6-8	310	11/24/88	East Carolina	Rocky Mount, N.C.	FA
Ballard, Vick	RB	5-10	217	7/16/90	Mississippi State	Pascagoula, Miss.	D5
Brazill, LaVon	WR	5-11	191	3/15/89	Ohio	Lantana, Fla.	D6
Chapman, Josh	NT	6-0	316	6/10/89	Alabama	Hoover, Ala.	D5
Chism, Cameron	CB	5-10	190	12/25/90	Maryland	Washington, D.C.	FA
Eagan, Kevin	OLB	6-4	276	3/16/90	Endicott	West Hartford, Conn.	FA
Evans, Darren (1)	RB	6-0	232	11/9/88	Virginia Tech	Indianapolis, Ind.	FA-'11
Fayson, Jarred (1)	WR	6-0	213	10/3/87	Illinois	Tampa, Fla.	FA-'11
Fenelus, Antonio	CB	5-9	190	1/19/90	Wisconsin	Boca Raton, Fla.	FA
Fleener, Coby	TE	6-5	252	9/20/88	Stanford	Lemont, Ill.	D2
Foster, Jason	G	6-5	305	10/21/88	Rhode Island	East Pittsford, Vt.	FA
Freeman, Jerrell	ILB	6-0	234	5/1/86	Mary Hardin-Baylor	Waco, Texas	FA
Fugger, Tim	OLB	6-4	250	7/1/89	Vanderbilt	Oak Brook, Ill.	D7
Galippo, Chris	ILB	6-2	250	4/12/89	Southern California	Corona, Calif.	FA
Harnish, Chandler	QB	6-2	220	7/28/88	Northern Illinois	Bluffton, Ind.	D7
Harvey, Mario	ILB	6-0	264	8/10/87	Marshall	Chatham, Va.	FA
Hickman, Justin	OLB	6-2	258	7/20/85	UCLA	El Paso, Texas	FA
Hicks, Hayworth	G	6-3	336	10/3/88	Iowa State	Palmdale, Calif.	FA
Hilton, T.Y.	WR	5-9	183	11/14/89	Florida International	Miami, Fla.	D3
Jackson, Buddy	CB	6-1	180	3/3/89	Pittsburgh	Plantation, Fla.	FA
Jones, Dominique	TE	6-3	255	8/15/87	Shepherd	San Diego, Calif.	FA
Kirkpatrick, Jake	C	6-3	296	7/7/87	Texas Christian	Tyler, Texas	FA
Luck, Andrew	QB	6-4	234	9/12/89	Stanford	Houston, Texas	D1
Lutrus, Scott (1)	ILB	6-3	247	4/23/88	Connecticut	Brookfield, Calif.	FA-'11
Merletti, Matt	S	5-11	205	7/18/88	North Carolina	Cleveland, Ohio	FA
Miller, Kyle	TE	6-5	260	4/18/88	Mount Union	Elida, Ohio	FA
Murphy, Matt (1)	G	6-4	307	7/27/89	Nevada-Las Vegas	Lake Forest, Calif.	FA-'11
Ogbu, Ollie (1)	DT	6-1	305	5/18/87	Penn State	Staten Island, N.Y.	FA-'11
Overton, Matt	LS	6-1	254	7/6/85	Western Washington	Tracy, Calif.	FA
Peguese, Brandon	OLB	6-1	239	10/29/87	Hampton	Greensboro, N.C.	FA
Pellerin, Micah	S	6-1	195	11/23/88	Hampton	New Orleans, La.	FA
Ross, Jeremy (1)	WR	5-11	222	3/6/88	California	Sacramento, Calif.	FA-'11
Sambrano, Jabin	WR	5-11	175	3/12/90	Montana	Temecula, Calif.	FA
Shipley, A.Q.	C	6-1	309	5/22/86	Penn State	Beaver County, Pa.	FA
Stahovich, Brian	P	6-0	190	4/14/90	San Diego State	Solana Beach, Calif.	FA
Thomas, Latarrius	S	6-1	210	3/22/88	Eastern Michigan	New Smyrna Beach, Fla.	FA
Vittatoe, Trevor	QB	6-2	230	1/4/88	Texas-El Paso	Bedford, Texas	FA
Whalen, Griff	WR	6-1	185	3/1/90	Stanford	Sylvania, Ohio	FA

The term NFL Rookie is defined as a player who is in his first season of professional football and has not been on the roster of another professional football team for any regular-season or postseason games. A Rookie is designated by an "R" on NFL rosters. Players who have been active in another professional football league or players who have NFL experience, including either preseason training camp or being on an Active List or Inactive List, or on Reserve/Injured or Reserve/Physically Unable to Perform for fewer than six regular-season games, are termed NFL First-Year Players. An NFL First-Year Player is designated by a "1" on NFL rosters. Thereafter, a player is credited with an additional year of experience for each season in which he accumulates six games on the Active List or Inactive List, or on Reserve/Injured or Reserve/Physically Unable to Perform.

Log on to www.colts.com for an up-to-date roster.

COACHING STAFF

Head Coach,
Chuck Pagano

Pro Career: Chuck Pagano was named head coach of the Colts on January 26, 2012, after spending four seasons with the Baltimore Ravens (2008-2011), including last season as the defensive coordinator. Under his direction the Ravens defense ranked third in the NFL in total defense (288.9 ypg), second against the run (92.6 ypg) and fourth against the pass (196.3 ypg), and helped the team finish first in the AFC North with a record of 12-4. Prior to 2011, Pagano coached Baltimore's secondary for three seasons. The Ravens finished as the third-best scoring defense in each of those campaigns as well as giving up a league-low 16.1 points per game and 80 touchdowns (tied with Pittsburgh for best in the NFL). During that span, Baltimore ranked second in the NFL for most interceptions at home (38) and home yards given up per game (272.9). In his first season in Baltimore (2008), the Ravens led the NFL with 26 interceptions, including Ed Reed's league-leading nine picks. Pagano also served as the defensive backs coach of the Oakland Raiders (2005-06) and the secondary coach of the Cleveland Browns (2001-04). Career record: 0-0.

Background: Pagano was a safety at Wyoming from 1980-83. No pro playing experience. He was a college coach at Southern California 1984-85, Miami 1986, Boise State 1987-88, East Carolina 1989, Nevada-Las Vegas 1990-91, East Carolina 1992-94, Miami 1995-2000, North Carolina 2007.

Personal: Born in Boulder, Colo. on October 2, 1960. He and his wife, Tina, have three daughters: Tara, Taylor and Tori. His brother, John, is the defensive coordinator of the San Diego Chargers.

ASSISTANT COACHES

Roy Anderson, safeties; born October 5, 1979, Tallahassee, Fla. Quarterback Howard 1997-2001. No pro playing experience. Pro coach: Baltimore Ravens 2009-2011, joined Colts in 2012.

Bruce Arians, offensive coordinator; born October 3, 1952, Paterson, N.J. Quarterback Virginia Tech 1970-74. No Pro playing experience. College coach: Virginia Tech 1975-77, Mississippi State 1978-1980, Alabama 1981-82, Temple 1983-88 (head coach), Mississippi State 1993-95, Alabama 1997. Pro coach: Kansas City Chiefs 1989-1992, New Orleans Saints 1996, Indianapolis Colts 1998-2000, Cleveland Browns 2001-03, Pittsburgh Steelers 2004-2011, re-joined Colts in 2012.

Brant Boyer, asst. special teams; born June 27, 1971, Ogden, Utah. Linebacker Arizona 1992-94. Pro linebacker Miami Dolphins 1994, Jacksonville Jaguars 1995-2000, Cleveland Browns 2001-03.

Pro coach: Joined Colts in 2012.

Clyde Christensen, quarterbacks; born January 28, 1956, Covina, Calif. Quarterback Fresno City College 1975, North Carolina 1976-78. No pro playing experience. College coach: Mississippi 1979, East Tennessee State 1980-82, Temple 1983-85, East Carolina 1986-88, Holy Cross 1989-1990, South Carolina 1991, Maryland 1992-93, Clemson 1994-95. Pro coach: Tampa Bay Buccaneers 1996-2001, joined Colts in 2002.

Gary Emanuel, defensive line; born October 30, 1958, New London, Conn. Offensive lineman Westchester (N.Y.) C.C. 1976-78, Plymouth State 1979-1980. No pro playing experience. College coach: Plymouth State 1981-84, West Chester 1985-86, Massachusetts 1986-88, Dartmouth 1988-1990, Syracuse 1991-93, Washington State 1994-96, Purdue 1997-2004, San Jose State 2007, Rutgers 2008-09, Purdue 2010-11. Pro coach: San Francisco 49ers 2005-06, joined Colts in 2012.

Jeff FitzGerald, linebackers; born April 18, 1960, Burbank, Calif. Linebacker Oregon State 1980. No pro playing experience. College coach: Cincinnati 1985, Alabama 1986-89, San Diego State 1994-97. Pro coach: Tampa Bay Buccaneers 1990-93, Washington Redskins 1998-99, Arizona Cardinals 2000-03, Baltimore Ravens 2004-07, Cincinnati Bengals 2008-2011, joined Colts in 2012.

Joe Gilbert, asst. offensive line; born January 22, 1965, Horseheads, N.Y. Offensive lineman Hamilton University 1984-87. No pro playing experience. College coach: Albany 1987-88, Pennsylvania 1989-1990, Northeastern 1991-93, Maine 1994-99, Mansfield 2000 (head coach), Toledo 2001-03, Central Florida 2004-06, Toledo 2007, Houston 2008, Illinois 2009-2011. Pro coach: Joined Colts in 2012.

Mike Gillhamer, secondary; born February 20, 1956, Oakland, Calif. Defensive back Carroll College 1972, Wenatchee (Wash.) J.C. 1973, Humboldt State 1974-75. No pro playing experience. College coach: College of the Sequoias 1979-1983, Weber State 1984, Utah 1985-1989, San Jose State 1990-93, Nevada 1994-95, Oregon 2001-02, Louisville 2003, Illinois 2011. Pro coach: New York Giants 1997-2000, Carolina Panthers 2004-2010, joined Colts in 2012.

Frank Giufre, offensive quality control; born April 5, 1977, Canastota, N.Y. Offensive lineman Syracuse 1995-99. No pro playing experience. College coach: Miami 2001-03, Sacred Heart 2004-06, Maine 2007-2011. Pro coach: Joined Colts in 2012.

Harold Goodwin, offensive line; born November 14, 1973, Columbia, S.C. Offensive lineman Michigan 1992-94. No pro playing experience. College coach: Michigan 1995-97, Eastern Michigan

1998-99, Central Michigan 2000-03. Pro coach: Chicago Bears 2004-06, Pittsburgh Steelers 2007-2011, joined Colts in 2012.

Richard Howell, asst. strength & conditioning; born February 19, 1972, Bladenboro, N.C. Quarterback Davidson 1990-93. No pro playing experience. College coach: Davidson 1994-98, North Carolina 1998-99. Pro coach: Barcelona Dragons (NFLE) 1999, joined Colts in 2000.

Marwan Maalouf, special teams coordinator; born November 26, 1976, Beirut, Lebanon. Guard Baldwin-Wallace 1997-99. No pro playing experience. College coach: Baldwin-Wallace 2000, Fordham 2001, Rutgers 2002-03. Pro coach: Cleveland Browns 2004-06, Baltimore Ravens 2008-2011, joined Colts in 2012.

Greg Manusky, defensive coordinator; born August 12, 1966, Wilkes-Barre, Pa. Linebacker Colgate 1983-87. Pro linebacker Washington Redskins 1988-1990, Minnesota Vikings 1991-93, Kansas City Chiefs 1994-99. Pro coach: Washington Redskins 2001, San Diego Chargers 2002-06, San Francisco 49ers 2007-2010, San Diego Chargers 2011, joined Colts in 2012.

Roger Marandino, strength & conditioning; born February 19, 1971, Elmer, N.J. No college or pro playing experience. College coach: Connecticut 1993-95, Brown 1995-2011. Pro coach: Philadelphia Eagles 2011, joined Colts in 2012.

Alfredo Roberts, tight ends; born March 17, 1965, Fort Lauderdale, Fla. Tight end Miami 1983-87. Pro tight end Kansas City Chiefs 1988-1990, Dallas Cowboys 1991-93. College coach: Florida Atlantic 1999-2002. Pro coach: Jacksonville Jaguars 2003-06, Cleveland Browns 2007-08, Tampa Bay Buccaneers 2009-2011, joined Colts in 2012.

David Walker, running backs; born December 4, 1969, Rochester, N.Y. Running back Syracuse 1989-1992. No pro playing experience. College coach: Syracuse 1995-2004, Pittsburgh 2005-2010. Pro coach: Joined Colts in 2011.

Brad White, defensive quality control; born August 13, 1982, Concord, Mass. Linebacker Georgia 2000, Wake Forest 2002-04. No pro playing experience. College coach: Wake Forest 2007-08, Murray State 2009, Air Force 2010-11. Pro coach: Joined Colts in 2012.

Charlie Williams, wide receivers; born January 31, 1958, Torrance, Calif. Defensive back Colorado State 1978-79. No pro playing experience. College coach: Long Beach City College 1984, New Mexico 1986-87, TCU 1988-1991, Minnesota 1992, Miami 1993-95, South Carolina 2003, Arizona 2004-06, North Carolina 2007-2011. Pro coach: Tampa Bay Buccaneers 1996-2001, joined Colts in 2012.

American Football Conference
South Division
Team Colors: Teal, Black, and Gold
EverBank Field
One EverBank Field Drive
Jacksonville, Florida 32202
Telephone: (904) 633-6000

2012 SCHEDULE
PRESEASON
Aug. 10 **New York Giants**...............7:30
Aug. 18 at New Orleans..................8:00
Aug. 23 at Baltimore.....................7:30
Aug. 30 **Atlanta**...............................6:30

REGULAR SEASON
Sep. 9 at Minnesota 1:00
Sep. 16 **Houston** 1:00
Sep. 23 at Indianapolis 1:00
Sep. 30 **Cincinnati** 4:05
Oct. 7 **Chicago** 4:05
Oct. 14 BYE
Oct. 21 at Oakland.........................4:15
Oct. 28 at Green Bay 1:00
Nov. 4 **Detroit** 1:00
Nov. 8 **Indianapolis** (Thurs) 8:20
Nov. 18 at Houston 1:00
Nov. 25 **Tennessee** 1:00
Dec. 2 at Buffalo 1:00
Dec. 9 **New York Jets** 1:00
Dec. 16 at Miami...........................1:00
Dec. 23 **New England** 1:00
Dec. 30 at Tennessee 1:00
All times ET
Stadium: EverBank Field
 (opened in 1995)
 •**Capacity:** 67,246
 One EverBank Field Drive
 Jacksonville, Florida 32202
Playing Surface: Grass
Training Camp: EverBank Field
 One EverBank Field Drive
 Jacksonville, Florida 32202

EVERBANK FIELD

CLUB OFFICIALS
Owner: Shahid Khan
President: Mark Lamping
Chief Financial Officer: Bill Prescott
Senior Vice President, Communications:
 Dan Edwards
Senior Vice President, Sales:
 Macky Weaver
Senior Vice President, Fan Experience:
 Hussain Naqi
Senior Vice President, Partnerships:
 Scott Massey
General Counsel: Sashi Brown
President, Jaguars Foundation:
 Peter Racine
Vice President, Information Technology:
 Bruce Swindell
Director, Ticket Operations: Tim Bishko
Director, Team Security: Skip Richardson
Director, Football Administration:
 Tim Walsh
Director, Public Relations: Ryan Robinson
Director, Game & Event Operations:
 Kurt Wisenbaugh
Director, Facility Operations & Guest
 Services: Nicola Drake

General Manager: Gene Smith
Director, Player Personnel:
 Terry McDonough
Director, Pro Personnel: Louis Clark
Director, College Personnel: Andy Dengler
Assistant Director, College Personnel:
 Tim Mingey
College Scouts: Jason DesJarlais,
 Marty Miller, Chris Prescott,
 Brian Simmons
Pro Scout: Chris Driggers
BLESTO Scout: David Allen
Executive Assistant, Player Personnel:
 Dana DesJarlais
Scouting Assistant, Player Personnel:
 Jarrod Highberger
Administrative Assistant, Player
 Personnel: Asil Mulbah

Head Athletic Trainer: Michael Ryan
Video Director: Mike Perkins
Equipment Manager: George Pellicer

Communications Coordinator:
 J.P. Shadrick
Community Relations Coordinator:
 Renzo Sheppard
Executive Assistant to SVP,
 Communications: Katie Vaughn

COACHING HISTORY
(143-140-0)
Records include postseason games
1995-2002 Tom Coughlin 72-64-0
2003-2011 Jack Del Rio* 69-73-0
2011 Mel Tucker.................2-3-0
 *Released after 11 games in 2011

PAID ATTENDANCE
Home 422,700   Away 531,602
Total 954,302
Single-game home record,
 74,143 (12/28/98)
Single-season home record,
 561,472 (1998)

2012 DRAFT CHOICES

Round	Name	Pos.	College
1	Justin Blackmon	WR	Oklahoma St.
2	Andre Branch	DE	Clemson
3	Bryan Anger	P	California
5	Brandon Marshall	LB	Nevada
6	Mike Harris	DB	Florida St.
7	Jeris Pendleton	DT	Ashland

JACKSONVILLE JAGUARS

2011 TEAM RECORD
PRESEASON (1-3)

Date	Result		Opponent
8/13	L	12-47	at New England
8/21	W	15-13	Atlanta
8/28	L	32-35	at Buffalo (OT)
9/2	L	17-24	St. Louis

REGULAR SEASON (5-11)

Date	Result		Opponent
9/11	W	16-14	Tennessee
9/18	L	3-32	at New York Jets
9/25	L	10-16	at Carolina
10/2	L	10-23	New Orleans
10/9	L	20-30	Cincinnati
10/16	L	13-17	at Pittsburgh
10/24	W	12-7	Baltimore
10/30	L	14-24	at Houston
11/13	W	17-3	at Indianapolis
11/20	L	10-14	at Cleveland
11/27	L	13-20	Houston
12/5	L	14-38	San Diego
12/11	W	41-14	Tampa Bay
12/15	L	14-41	at Atlanta
12/24	L	17-23	at Tennessee
1/1	W	19-13	Indianapolis

(OT) Overtime

SCORE BY PERIODS

Jaguars	44	100	33	66	0	—	243
Opponents	83	103	64	79	0	—	329

2011 TEAM STATISTICS

	Jaguars	Opp.
Total First Downs	251	268
Rushing	103	73
Passing	122	175
Penalty	26	20
3rd Down: Made/Att	81/241	79/218
3rd Down Pct.	33.6	36.2
4th Down: Made/Att	6/17	4/9
4th Down Pct.	35.3	44.4
Possession Avg.	30:02	29:58
Total Net Yards	4149	5008
Avg. Per Game	259.3	313.0
Total Plays	1002	979
Avg. Per Play	4.1	5.1
Net Yards Rushing	1970	1667
Avg. Per Game	123.1	104.2
Total Rushes	489	435
Net Yards Passing	2179	3341
Avg. Per Game	136.2	208.8
Sacked/Yards Lost	44/331	31/213
Gross Yards	2510	3554
Att./Completions	469/240	513/326
Completion Pct.	51.2	63.5
Had Intercepted	15	17
Punts/Average	99/41.9	89/43.3
Net Punting Avg.	99/36.5	89/39.4
Penalties/Yards	77/680	105/895
Fumbles/Ball Lost	27/8	21/11
Touchdowns	25	37
Rushing	9	14
Passing	12	21
Returns	4	2

2011 INDIVIDUAL STATISTICS

PASSING

PASSING	Att.	Comp.	Yds.	Pct.	TD	Int.	Tkld.	Rate
Gabbert	413	210	2214	50.8	12	11	40/293	65.4
McCown	56	30	296	53.6	0	4	4/38	39.0
Jaguars	469	240	2510	51.2	12	15	44/331	62.2
Opponents	513	326	3554	63.5	21	17	31/213	83.7

SCORING

SCORING	TD R	TD P	TD Rt	PAT	FG	Saf	PTS
Scobee	0	0	0	24/24	23/25	0	93
Jones-Drew	8	3	0	0/0	0/0	0	66
Hill	0	3	0	0/0	0/0	0	18
West	0	2	0	0/0	0/0	0	12
Cloherty	0	0	1	0/0	0/0	0	6
Collins	0	0	1	0/0	0/0	0	6
Dillard	0	1	0	0/0	0/0	0	6
G. Jones	1	0	0	0/0	0/0	0	6
Miller	0	1	0	0/0	0/0	0	6
Potter	0	0	1	0/0	0/0	0	6
Shorts	0	1	0	0/0	0/0	0	6
Thomas	0	1	0	0/0	0/0	0	6
Youboty	0	0	1	0/0	0/0	0	6
Jaguars	9	12	4	24/24	23/25	0	243
Opponents	14	21	2	35/36	22/29	2	329

2-Pt Conversions: Jaguars 0-1, Opponents 1-1

RUSHING

RUSHING	No.	Yds	Avg	LG	TD
Jones-Drew	343	1606	4.7	56	8
Karim	63	130	2.1	14	0
Gabbert	48	98	2.0	12	0
D. Harris	9	42	4.7	24	0
Owens	10	39	3.9	9	0
McCown	7	23	3.3	9	0
Bolen	2	14	7.0	10	0
Thomas	3	11	3.7	12	0
G. Jones	2	7	3.5	6	1
N. Harris	1	0	0.0	0	0
Turk	1	0	0.0	0	0
Jaguars	489	1970	4.0	56	9
Opponents	435	1667	3.8	68	14

RECEIVING

RECEIVING	No.	Yds	Avg	LG	TD
Thomas	44	415	9.4	47	1
Jones-Drew	43	374	8.7	48	3
Lewis	39	460	11.8	62	0
Dillard	29	292	10.1	25	1
Hill	25	367	14.7	74t	3
Karim	14	120	8.6	20	0
West	13	163	12.5	23t	2
Potter	5	50	10.0	22	0
Osgood	5	42	8.4	19	0
Cloherty	4	57	14.3	21	0
Miller	4	42	10.5	14t	1
G. Jones	4	19	4.8	10	0
Price	2	39	19.5	21	0
Shorts	2	30	15.0	25	1
Bolen	2	6	3.0	4	0
Owens	2	2	1.0	6	0
Whimper	1	17	17.0	17	0
Sims-Walker	1	11	11.0	11	0
D. Harris	1	4	4.0	4	0
Jaguars	240	2510	10.5	74t	12
Opponents	326	3554	10.9	80t	21

PUNTING

PUNTING	No.	Yds.	Avg.	In 20	LG
N. Harris	72	3075	42.7	13	55
Turk	27	1072	39.7	7	65
Jaguars	99	4147	41.9	20	65
Opponents	89	3852	43.3	25	71

INTERCEPTIONS

INTERCEPTIONS	No.	Yds	Avg	LG	TD
Landry	2	28	14.0	28	0
Lowery	2	26	13.0	30	0
Trent	2	17	8.5	22	0
Coleman	2	5	2.5	8	0
Posluszny	2	2	1.0	2	0
Rutland	1	37	37.0	25	0
Da. Smith	1	25	25.0	25	0
Middleton	1	11	11.0	11	0
Mincey	1	5	5.0	5	0
Allen	1	3	3.0	3	0
Mathis	1	1	1.0	1	0
Youboty	1	0	0.0	0	0
Jaguars	17	160	9.4	30	0
Opponents	15	177	11.8	37	0

PUNT RETURNS

PUNT RETURNS	Ret	FC	Yds	Avg	LG	TD
Thomas	19	5	88	4.6	28	0
Shorts	12	6	50	4.2	27	0
Dillard	3	6	10	3.3	5	0
Mathis	0	2	0	—	—	0
Jaguars	34	19	148	4.4	28	0
Opponents	48	17	333	6.9	42	0

KICKOFF RETURNS

KICKOFF RETURNS	No.	Yds	Avg	LG	TD
Karim	27	652	24.1	37	0
D. Harris	14	308	22.0	35	0
Shorts	4	82	20.5	23	0
Owens	1	13	13.0	13	0
Potter	1	0	0.0	0	0
Jaguars	47	1055	22.4	37	0
Opponents	26	632	24.3	46	0

FIELD GOALS

FIELD GOALS	1-19	20-29	30-39	40-49	50+
Scobee	1/1	5/5	5/5	7/8	5/6
Jaguars	1/1	5/5	5/5	7/8	5/6
Opponents	0/0	5/5	10/11	4/6	3/7

SACKS

SACKS	No.
Mincey	8.0
Roth	3.5
Da. Smith	3.5
Alualu	2.5
Chick	2.5
Coleman	2.0
Posluszny	2.0
Douzable	1.0
Lane	1.0
Lowery	1.0
Mosley	1.0
Session	1.0
Allen	0.5
Collins	0.5
Landry	0.5
Selvie	0.5
Jaguars	31.0
Opponents	44.0

RECORD HOLDERS
INDIVIDUAL RECORDS—CAREER

Category	Name	Performance
Rushing (Yds.)	Fred Taylor, 1998-2008	11,271
Passing (Yds.)	Mark Brunell, 1995-2003	25,698
Passing (TDs)	Mark Brunell, 1995-2003	144
Receiving (No.)	Jimmy Smith, 1995-2005	862
Receiving (Yds.)	Jimmy Smith, 1995-2005	12,287
Interceptions	Rashean Mathis, 2003-2011	30
Punting (Avg.)	Bryan Barker, 1995-2000	43.5
Punt Return (Avg.)	Bobby Shaw, 2002	12.4
Kickoff Return (Avg.)	Maurice Jones-Drew, 2006-2011	26.0
Field Goals	Mike Hollis, 1995-2001	175
Touchdowns (Tot.)	Maurice Jones-Drew, 2006-2011	74
Points	Mike Hollis, 1995-2001	764
*Sacks	Tony Brackens, 1996-2003	55.0

INDIVIDUAL RECORDS—SINGLE SEASON

Category	Name	Performance
Rushing (Yds.)	Maurice Jones-Drew, 2011	1,606
Passing (Yds.)	Mark Brunell, 1996	4,367
Passing (TDs)	David Garrard, 2010	23
Receiving (No.)	Jimmy Smith, 1999	116
Receiving (Yds.)	Jimmy Smith, 1999	1,636
Interceptions	Rashean Mathis, 2006	8
Punting (Avg.)	Bryan Barker, 1998	45.0
Punt Return (Avg.)	Reggie Barlow, 1998	12.9
Kickoff Return (Avg.)	Maurice Jones-Drew, 2006	27.7
Field Goals	Mike Hollis, 1997, 1999	31
Touchdowns (Tot.)	Fred Taylor, 1998	17
Points	Mike Hollis, 1997	134
*Sacks	Tony Brackens, 1999	12.0

INDIVIDUAL RECORDS—SINGLE GAME

Category	Name	Performance
Rushing (Yds.)	Fred Taylor, 11-19-00	234
Passing (Yds.)	Mark Brunell, 9-22-96	432
Passing (TDs)	Mark Brunell, 11-29-98	4
	Quinn Gray, 12-30-07	4
	David Garrard, 10-31-10	4
Receiving (No.)	Keenan McCardell, 10-20-96	16
Receiving (Yds.)	Jimmy Smith, 9-10-00	291
Interceptions	Many times	2
	Last time by Rashean Mathis, 11-5-06	
Field Goals	Mike Hollis, 12-1-96, 11-30-97, 9-10-00	5
	Josh Scobee, 11-25-07, 10-10-10	5
Touchdowns (Tot.)	James Stewart, 10-12-97	5
Points	James Stewart, 10-12-97	30
*Sacks	Kelvin Pritchett, 10-5-97	3.0
	John Henderson, 10-6-02	3.0
	Paul Spicer, 9-25-05	3.0

Sacks became an official statistic in 1982.

2012 VETERAN ROSTER

No.	Name	Pos.	Ht.	Wt.	Birthdate	NFL Exp.	College	Hometown	How Acq.	'11 Games/ Starts
50	Allen, Russell	LB	6-3	234	5/5/86	4	San Diego State	Oceanside, Calif.	FA-'09	16/6
93	Alualu, Tyson	DT	6-3	304	5/12/87	3	California	Honolulu, Hawaii	D1-'10	16/16
44	Bolen, Brock	FB/RB	6-0	233	3/24/85	4	Louisville	Germantown, Ohio	FA-'09	13/0
56	Bosworth, Kyle	LB	6-1	236	11/21/86	3	UCLA	Plano, Texas	FA-'10	9/0
78	Bradfield, Cameron	T	6-4	302	9/14/87	2	Grand Valley State	Grand Rapids, Mich.	FA-'11	10/2
73	Britton, Eben	OL	6-6	310	10/14/87	4	Arizona	Brooklyn, N.Y.	D2-'09	4/3
48	Cain, Jeremy	LS	6-1	245	3/24/80	7	Massachusetts	Fort Lauderdale, Fla.	W(Wash)-'09	16/0
97	Chick, John	DE	6-3	248	11/20/82	2	Utah State	Gillette, Wyo.	FA-'11	11/0
83	Cloherty, Colin	TE	6-2	245	9/16/87	2	Brown	Bethesda, Md.	FA-'11	4/1
2	Coutu, Brandon	K	5-11	194	9/29/84	2	Georgia	Lawrenceville, Ga.	FA-'12	1/0*
21	Cox, Derek	CB	6-1	190	9/22/86	4	William & Mary	Greenville, N.C.	D3b-'09	6/5
62	Estes, John	C	6-2	302	3/25/87	3	Hawaii	Stockton, Calif.	FA-'10	2/0
83	Evans, Lee	WR	5-10	197	3/11/81	9	Wisconsin	Bedford, Ohio	FA-'12	9/2*
11	Gabbert, Blaine	QB	6-5	233	10/15/89	2	Missouri	Ballwin, Mo.	D1-'11	15/14
36	Greene, Courtney	S	6-0	212	11/23/86	4	Rutgers	New Rochelle, N.Y.	FA-'09	7/2
40	Harris, DuJuan	RB	5-7	197	9/3/88	2	Troy	Brooksville, Fla.	FA-'11	5/0
41	Heath, T.J.	CB	6-0	179	9/11/87	2	Jacksonville State	Alexandria, Ala.	FA-'11	5/0
7	Henne, Chad	QB	6-3	230	7/2/85	4	Michigan	Wyomissing, Pa.	UFA(Mia)-'12	4/4*
95	Irvin, Corvey	DT	6-3	302	5/3/85	2	Georgia	Augusta, Ga.	FA-'11	4/0
6	Issac, Rod	DB	5-11	196	2/20/89	2	Middle Tennessee State	Miami, Fla.	D5-'11	3/0
23	Jennings, Rashad	RB	6-1	228	3/26/85	4	Liberty	Forest, Va.	D7a-'09	0*
33	Jones, Greg	FB	6-1	254	5/9/81	9	Florida State	Beaufort, S.C.	D2b-'04	16/9
32	Jones-Drew, Maurice	RB	5-7	208	3/23/85	7	UCLA	Antioch, Calif.	D2-'06	16/16
74	Kampman, Aaron	DE	6-4	260	11/30/79	11	Iowa	Kesley, Iowa	UFA(GB)-'10	3/0
96	Knighton, Terrance	DT	6-3	336	7/4/86	4	Temple	Hartford, Conn.	D3a-'09	13/13
26	Landry, Dawan	S	6-0	210	12/30/82	7	Georgia Tech	Boutte, La.	UFA(Balt)-'11	16/16
92	Lane, Austen	DE	6-6	274	11/9/87	3	Murray State	Iola, Wisc.	D5b-'10	6/1
89	Lewis, Marcedes	TE	6-6	275	5/19/84	7	UCLA	Long Beach, Calif.	D1-'06	15/15
25	Lowery, Dwight	DB	5-11	198	1/23/86	5	San Jose State	Santa Cruz, Calif.	T(NYJ)-'11	13/11
27	Mathis, Rashean	CB	6-1	193	8/27/80	10	Bethune-Cookman	Jacksonville, Fla.	D2-'03	9/9
63	Meester, Brad	C	6-3	302	3/23/77	13	Northern Iowa	Parkersburg, Iowa	D2-'00	16/16
29	Middleton, William	CB	5-11	194	7/28/86	4	Furman	Marist, Ga.	ps(Atl)-'09	11/6
86	Miller, Zach	TE	6-4	245	10/4/84	4	Nebraska-Omaha	Weston, Neb.	D6-'09	4/0
94	Mincey, Jeremy	DL	6-3	270	12/14/83	5	Florida	Statesboro, Ga.	FA-'10	16/16
75	Monroe, Eugene	T	6-5	308	4/18/87	4	Virginia	Plainfield, N.J.	D1-'09	15/14
58	Morgan, Aaron	DE	6-4	238	12/30/88	3	Louisiana-Monroe	Amite, La.	FA-'10	0*
99	Mosley, C.J.	DL	6-3	305	8/6/83	8	Missouri	Fort Knox, Ky.	FA-'10	15/3
39	Murphy, Richard	RB	6-1	208	9/18/86	1	Louisiana State	Rayville, La.	FA-'11	0*
77	Nwaneri, Uche	G/C	6-3	318	3/20/84	6	Purdue	Garland, Texas	D5a-'07	16/16
24	Owens, Montell	RB	5-10	225	5/4/84	7	Maine	Wilmington, Del.	FA-'06	13/0
5	Palmer, Jordan	QB	6-5	229	5/30/84	4	Texas-El Paso	Mission Viejo, Calif.	FA-'12	0*
34	Parmele, Jalen	RB	5-11	222	12/30/85	3	Toledo	Midland, Mich.	FA-'12	0*
51	Posluszny, Paul	LB	6-1	238	10/10/84	6	Penn State	Aliquippa, Pa.	UFA(Buff)-'11	16/16
88	Potter, Zach	TE	6-7	280	5/4/86	3	Nebraska	Omaha, Neb.	FA-'09	15/7
15	Price, Taylor	WR	6-0	205	10/8/87	3	Ohio	Hilliard, Ohio	W(NE)-'11	2/0
42	Prosinski, Chris	S	6-1	201	4/28/87	2	Wyoming	Buffalo, Wyo.	D4b-'11	13/1
65	Rackley, Will	G/C	6-3	309	10/11/89	2	Lehigh	Riverdale, Ga.	D3-'11	15/14
81	Robinson, Laurent	WR	6-2	194	5/20/85	6	Illinois State	Rockledge, Fla.	UFA(Dall)-'12	14/4*
70	Robinson, William	T	6-5	297	12/20/84	3	San Diego State	Pomona, Calif.	W(NO)-'11	0*
18	Robiskie, Brian	WR	6-3	209	12/3/87	4	Ohio State	Cleveland, Ohio	W(Cle)-'11	0*
20	Ross, Aaron	DB	6-0	197	9/15/82	6	Texas	Tyler, Texas	UFA(NYG)-'12	16/15*
22	Rutland, Kevin	CB	6-0	188	4/2/88	2	Missouri	Houston, Texas	FA-'11	14/4
10 f-	Scobee, Josh	K	6-1	210	6/23/82	9	Louisiana Tech	Longview, Texas	D5a-'04	16/0
91	Selvie, George	DE	6-4	251	3/6/87	3	South Florida	Pensacola, Fla.	FA-'11	7/0
55	Session, Clint	LB	6-0	235	9/22/84	6	Pittsburgh	Pompano Beach, Fla.	UFA(Ind)-'11	9/6
84	Shorts III, Cecil	WR/RS	6-0	193	12/22/87	2	Mount Union	Cleveland, Ohio	D4a-'11	10/0
95	Smith, D'Anthony	DT	6-2	298	6/9/88	3	Louisiana State	Pickering, La.	D3-'10	0*
52	Smith, Daryl	LB	6-2	249	3/14/82	9	Georgia Tech	Albany, Ga.	D2a-'04	16/16
67	Spitz, Jason	G/C	6-3	305	12/19/82	7	Louisville	Jacksonville, Fla.	UFA(GB)-'11	10/0
45	Tahi, Naufahu	FB	6-0	251	10/3/81	6	Brigham Young	Fontana, Calif.	FA-'12	0*
80	Thomas, Mike	WR	5-8	198	6/4/87	4	Arizona	DeSoto, Texas	D4-'09	15/13
37	Trent, Morgan	CB	6-1	193	12/14/85	4	Michigan	San Diego, CA	FA-'11	5/2
17	West, Chastin	WR	6-1	214	5/1/87	2	Fresno State	Moorpark, Calif.	FA-'11	12/1
68	Whimper, Guy	T	6-5	302	5/21/83	7	East Carolina	Havelock, N.C.	FA-'10	15/15
31	Youboty, Ashton	CB	5-11	189	7/7/84	7	Ohio State	Houston, Texas	FA-'11	6/5

* Coutu played 1 game with Buffalo in '11; Evans played 9 games with Baltimore; Henne played 4 games with Miami; Jennings missed '11 season because of injury; Morgan missed '11 season because of injury; Murphy missed '11 season because of injury; Palmer last active with Cincinnati in '10; Parmele last active with Baltimore in '10; L. Robinson played 14 games with Dallas; W. Robinson inactive for 1 game; Robiskie missed of '11 season because of injury; Ross played 16 games with New York Giants; D'Anthony Smith missed '11 season because of injury; Tahi last active with Minnesota in '10.

f- Unsigned franchise player; subject to developments.

Players lost through free agency (0): None.

Also played with Jaguars in '11—LB Kevin Bentley (1 game), DB C.C. Brown (2), DB Drew Coleman (16), DT Nate Collins (12), WR Jarett Dillard (14), DE Leger Douzable (16), LB Stephen Franklin (5), P Nick Harris (11), WR Jason Hill (10), CB David Jones (5), RB Deji Karim (12), LB Jammie Kirlew (1), S Darcel McBath (1), CB Trumaine McBride (1), QB Luke McCown (4), WR Jamar Newsome (2), TE Fendi Onobun (1), S Akwasi Owusu-Ansah (4), WR Kassim Osgood (12), DE Matt Roth (9), TE Martin Rucker (1), WR Mike Sims-Walker (2), P Matt Turk (5).

FIRST-YEAR ROSTER

Name	Pos.	Ht.	Wt.	Birthdate	College	Hometown	How Acq.
Adams, Kendrick	DE	6-5	244	12/3/88	Louisiana State	Enterprise, Ala.	FA
Anger, Bryan	P	6-3	208	10/6/88	California	Camarillo, Calif.	D3
Baldridge, Daniel (1)	T	6-8	311	10/21/85	Marshall	Opelousas, La.	FA-'10
Barbiasz, Lee	T	6-7	310	7/3/88	Northern Colorado	Milford, N.H.	FA
Blackmon, Justin	WR	6-1	215	1/9/90	Oklahoma State	Ardmore, Okla.	D1
Blake, Antwon	CB	5-9	198	8/8/90	Texas-El Paso	Houston, Texas	FA
Branch, Andre	DE	6-4	258	7/14/89	Clemson	Richmond, Va.	D2
Brewster, Mike	C	6-4	314	7/27/89	Ohio State	Orlando, Fla.	FA
Brown, Jeremiah	S	6-0	204	2/13/90	Wagner	Brooklyn, N.Y.	FA
Brown, Mike	WR	5-10	205	2/9/89	Liberty	Charlottesville, Va.	FA
Davis, Ryan	DE	6-2	261	2/24/89	Bethune-Cookman	Tampa, Fla.	FA
Dennard, Antonio	CB	5-11	185	12/20/89	Langston	Chicago, Ill.	FA
Elliott, Kevin	WR	6-3	213	12/21/88	Florida A&M	Orlando, Fla.	FA
Forcier, Chris	WR	6-3	213	10/24/88	Furman	San Diego, Calif.	FA
Hall Jr., D.J.	G	6-1	319	12/24/88	Texas State	Palestine, Texas	FA
Harris, Mike	CB	5-10	184	1/5/89	Florida State	Miami, Fla.	D6
Jones, Joshua	LB	6-1	234	12/19/88	Elon	Tampa, Fla.	FA
Marshall, Brandon	LB	6-2	243	9/10/89	Nevada	North Las Vegas, Nev.	D5
Nowak, Drew	DT	6-3	292	3/7/90	Western Michigan	Green Bay, Wisc.	FA
Pendleton, Jeris	DT	6-2	328	11/7/83	Ashland	Chicago, Ill.	D7
Ray, Odrick (1)	DE	6-4	273	5/24/89	Tulsa	Athens, Texas	FA
Richard, Donovan	LB	6-0	215	8/16/89	South Carolina State	Georgetown, S.C.	FA
Schaffer, J.K.	LB	6-0	232	6/10/90	Cincinnati	Cincinnati, Ohio	FA
Stanford, Julian	LB	6-1	229	9/2/90	Wagner	Bloomfield, Conn.	FA
Veldman, Matt	TE	6-7	256	8/12/88	North Dakota State	Becker, Minn.	FA

The term NFL Rookie is defined as a player who is in his first season of professional football and has not been on the roster of another professional football team for any regular-season or postseason games. A Rookie is designated by an "R" on NFL rosters. Players who have been active in another professional football league or players who have NFL experience, including either preseason training camp or being on an Active List or Inactive List, or on Reserve/Injured or Reserve/Physically Unable to Perform for fewer than six regular-season games, are termed NFL First-Year Players. An NFL First-Year Player is designated by a "1" on NFL rosters. Thereafter, a player is credited with an additional year of experience for each season in which he accumulates six games on the Active List or Inactive List, or on Reserve/Injured or Reserve/Physically Unable to Perform.

Log on to www.jaguars.com for an up-to-date roster.

COACHING STAFF
Head Coach,
Mike Mularkey
Pro Career: Mike Mularkey was named head coach of the Jaguars on January 11, 2012. He is the fourth head coach in Jaguars history. A veteran of 27 years in the NFL, played nine seasons in the league and has been coaching the past 18. Began coaching career at Concordia College in 1993 before entering NFL as quality control coach and then tight ends coach for the Tampa Bay Buccaneers (1994-95). Spent next eight seasons with Pittsburgh Steelers as tight ends coach (1996-2000) and offensive coordinator (2001-03). Posted a record of 14-18 in two seasons as Buffalo Bills' head coach, including a 9-7 mark in 2004. Coached two seasons for the Miami Dolphins (2006-07). Was Atlanta Falcons' offensive coordinator (2008-2011), with three playoff appearances. Named 2010 Coordinator of the Year by *The Sporting News*. Career record: 14-18.
Background: Three-year letterman as tight end at Florida (1979-1982). Drafted in the ninth round by the San Francisco 49ers in 1983 and played nine seasons as a tight end for the Minnesota Vikings (1983-88) and Pittsburgh Steelers (1989-1991). Had career totals of 102 catches, 1,222 yards, nine touchdowns.
Personal: Born November 19, 1961 in Ft. Lauderdale, Fla. Played quarterback at Northeast High in Ft. Lauderdale. He and his wife Betsy, have two sons, Patrick and Shane. Patrick is a strength assistant for the Jaguars.

ASSISTANT COACHES
Craig Aukerman, asst. special teams; born November 22, 1976, McComb, Ohio. Defensive back/wide receiver Findlay 1995-98. No pro playing experience. College coach: Findlay 2000, Miami (Ohio) 2001-02, 2005-08, Western Kentucky 2003-04, Kent State 2009. Pro coach: Denver Broncos 2010, joined Jaguars in 2011.
Brandon Blaney, defensive assistant; born November 3, 1975, Joplin, Mo. Attended Youngstown State. No college or pro playing experience. College coach: Youngstown State 1995-98, Oklahoma 1999-2000, Ohio State 2001, Kansas 2002-09. Pro coach: Joined Jaguars in 2011.
John Bonamego, special teams coordinator; born August 14, 1963, Waynesboro, Pa. Wide receiver/quarterback Central Michigan 1985-86. No pro playing experience. College coach: Maine 1988-1991, Lehigh 1992, Army 1993-98. Pro coach: Jacksonville Jaguars 1999-2002, Green Bay Packers 2003-05, New Orleans Saints 2006-07, 2011, Miami Dolphins 2008-10, re-joined Jaguars in 2012.
Bob Bratkowski, offensive coordinator; born December 2, 1955, San Angelo, Texas. Wide receiver Washington State 1975-77. No pro playing experience. College coach: Missouri 1978-1980, Weber State 1981-85, Wyoming 1986, Washington State 1987-88, Miami 1989-1991. Pro coach: Seattle Seahawks 1992-98, Pittsburgh Steelers 1999-2000, Cincinnati Bengals 2001-2010, Atlanta

Falcons 2011, joined Jaguars in 2012.
Sylvester Croom, running backs; born September 25, 1954, Tuscaloosa, Ala. Linebacker/tight end/center Alabama 1971-74. Pro center New Orleans Saints 1975. College coach: Alabama 1976-1986, Mississippi State 2004-08 (head coach). Pro coach: Tampa Bay Buccaneers 1987-1990, Indianapolis Colts 1991, San Diego Chargers 1992-96, Detroit Lions 1997-2000, Green Bay Packers 2001-03, St. Louis Rams 2009-2011, joined Jaguars in 2012.
Joe Cullen, defensive line; born December 15, 1967, Quincy, Mass. Nose guard Massachusetts 1986-89. No pro playing experience. College coach: Massachusetts 1990-91, Richmond 1992-98, 2000, Louisiana State 1999, Memphis 2001, Indiana 2002-04, Illinois 2005, Idaho State 2009. Pro coach: Detroit Lions 2006-08, joined Jaguars in 2010.
Mark Duffner, linebackers; born July 19, 1953, Annandale, Va. Defensive lineman William & Mary 1972-74. No pro playing experience. College coach: Ohio State 1975-76, Cincinnati 1977-1980, Holy Cross 1981-1991 (head coach 1986-1991), Maryland 1992-1996 (head coach). Pro coach: Cincinnati Bengals 1997-2002, Green Bay Packers 2003-2005, joined Jaguars in 2006.
Andy Heck, offensive line; born January 1, 1967, Fargo, N.D. Tackle Notre Dame 1985-88. Pro tackle Seattle Seahawks 1989-1993, Chicago Bears 1994-98, Washington Redskins 1999-2000. College coach: Virginia 2001-03. Pro coach: Joined Jaguars in 2003.
Josh Hingst, asst. strength and conditioning; born December 29, 1978, Fremont, Neb. Attended Nebraska. No college or pro playing experience. College coach: Florida State 2002-07, Nebraska 2009-2011. Pro coach: Atlanta Falcons 2008, joined Jaguars in 2012.
Bobby Johnson, offensive line; born February 28, 1963, Akron, Ohio. Offensive lineman Miami (Ohio) 1992-94. No pro playing experience. College coach: Akron 1995-98, Miami (Ohio) 1999-2004, Indiana 2005-09. Pro coach: Buffalo Bills 2010-11, joined Jaguars in 2012.
Marlon McCree, asst. secondary; born March 17, 1977, Orlando, Fla. Safety/linebacker Kentucky 1997-2000. Pro safety Jacksonville Jaguars 2001-03, Houston Texans 2003-04, Carolina Panthers 2005, San Diego Chargers 2006-07, Denver Broncos 2008. Pro coach: Joined Jaguars in 2012.
Patrick Mularkey, strength assistant; born February 15, 1986, Eden Prairie, Minn. Attended Clemson. No college or pro playing experience. Pro coach: Joined Jaguars in 2012.
Tom Myslinski, strength and conditioning; born December 7, 1968, Rome, N.Y. Guard Tennessee 1988-1991. Pro guard Washington Redskins 1992, Buffalo Bills 1993, Chicago Bears 1993-94, Jacksonville Jaguars 1995, Pittsburgh Steelers 1996-97, 2000, Indianapolis Colts 1998, Dallas Cowboys 1999. College coach: Robert Morris 2005-06, Memphis 2010, North Carolina 2011. Pro coach: Cleveland Browns 2003-04, 2007-09, joined Jaguars in 2012.
Tony Oden, secondary; born June 30, 1973,

Cleveland, Ohio. Linebacker Baldwin-Wallace College 1991-95. No pro playing experience. College coach: Millersville (Pa.) 1996, Boston College 1997, Army 1998-99, East Carolina 2000-02, Eastern Michigan 2003. Pro coach: Houston Texans 2004-05, New Orleans Saints 2006-2011, joined Jaguars in 2012.
Greg Olson, asst. head coach/quarterbacks; born March 1, 1963, Richland, Wash. Quarterback Spokane Falls (Wash.) J.C. 1981-82. No pro playing experience. College coach: Washington State 1987-89, Central Washington 1990-93, Idaho 1994-96, Purdue 1997-2000, 2002. Pro coach: San Francisco 49ers 2001, Chicago Bears 2003, Detroit Lions 2004-05, St. Louis Rams 2006-07, Tampa Bay Buccaneers 2008-2011, joined Jaguars in 2012.
Jake Peetz, offensive assistant; born April 5, 1983, O'Neill, Neb. Defensive back Nebraska 2003-05. No pro playing experience. College coach: Santa Barbara (Calif.) C.C. 2006, UCLA 2007. Pro coach: Joined Jaguars in 2012.
Ron Prince, asst. offensive line; born September 18, 1969, Omaha, Neb. Offensive lineman Dodge City (Kan.) C.C. 1988-89, Appalachian State 1990-91. No pro playing experience. College coach: Dodge City (Kan.) C.C. 1992, Alabama A&M 1993, South Carolina State 1994, James Madison 1995-97, Cornell 1998-2000, Virginia 2001-05, 2009, Kansas State 2006-08 (head coach). Pro coach: Indianapolis Colts 2010-11, joined Jaguars in 2012.
Cedric Scott, strength assistant; born October 19, 1977, Gulfport, Miss. Defensive end Southern Mississippi 1997-2000. Pro defensive end New York Giants 2001, Cleveland Browns 2002. College coach: Southern Mississippi 2009-2011. Pro coach: Joined Jaguars in 2012.
Charlie Skalaski, asst. to head coach/ offensive assistant; born October 16, 1956, Miami, Fla. Defensive back Florida 1974-77. No pro playing experience. College coach: Liberty 2003-11. Pro coach: Joined Jaguars in 2012.
Paul Spicer, asst. defensive line; born August 18, 1975, Indianapolis. Linebacker College of DuPage 1994-95, defensive end Saginaw Valley State 1996-97. Pro defensive end Detroit Lions 1999, Jacksonville Jaguars 2000-08, New Orleans Saints 2009. Pro coach: Joined Jaguars in 2011.
Jerry Sullivan, wide receivers; born July 13, 1944, Miami, Fla. Quarterback Florida State 1963-64. No pro playing experience. College coach: Kansas State 1971-72, Texas Tech 1973-75, South Carolina 1976-1982, Indiana 1983, Louisiana State 1984-1990, Ohio State 1991. Pro coach: San Diego Chargers 1992-96, Detroit Lions 1997-2000, Arizona Cardinals 2001-03, Miami Dolphins 2004, San Francisco 49ers 2005-2010, joined Jaguars in 2012.
Mel Tucker, asst. head coach/defensive coordinator; born January 4, 1972, Cleveland, Ohio. Defensive back Wisconsin 1992-95. No pro playing experience. College coach: Michigan State 1997-98, Miami (Ohio) 1999, Louisiana State 2000, Ohio State 2001-04. Pro coach: Cleveland Browns 2005-08, joined Jaguars in 2009 (interim head coach 2011).

American Football Conference
West Division
Team Colors: Red, Gold, and White
One Arrowhead Drive
Kansas City, Missouri 64129
Telephone: (816) 920-9300

2012 SCHEDULE
PRESEASON
Aug. 10 **Arizona** 7:00
Aug. 18 at St. Louis..........................7:00
Aug. 24 **Seattle**................................7:00
Aug. 30 at Green Bay 6:00

REGULAR SEASON
Sep. 9 **Atlanta** 12:00
Sep. 16 at Buffalo 12:00
Sep. 23 at New Orleans.................12:00
Sep. 30 **San Diego**.........................12:00
Oct. 7 **Baltimore**........................12:00
Oct. 14 at Tampa Bay 12:00
Oct. 21 BYE
Oct. 28 **Oakland** 3:05
Nov. 1 at San Diego (Thurs) 7:20
Nov. 12 at Pittsburgh (Mon) 7:30
Nov. 18 **Cincinnati** 12:00
Nov. 25 **Denver**...........................12:00
Dec. 2 **Carolina**..........................12:00
Dec. 9 at Cleveland 12:00
Dec. 16 at Oakland 3:15
Dec. 23 **Indianapolis**....................12:00
Dec. 30 at Denver...........................3:15
All times CT

Stadium: Arrowhead Stadium
(opened in 1972,
fully renovated in 2010)
• **Capacity:** 76,416
One Arrowhead Drive
Kansas City, Missouri 64129
Playing Surface: Grass
Training Camp: Missouri Western St. Univ.
St. Joseph, MO 64507

ARROWHEAD STADIUM

CLUB OFFICIALS
Chairman & CEO: Clark Hunt
General Manager: Scott Pioli
President: Mark Donovan
Assistant General Manager: Joel Collier
Senior Vice President of Business
Operations: Bill Chapin
Chief Financial Officer: Dan Crumb
Director of Pro Personnel: Ray Farmer
Director of Football Administration:
Trip MacCracken
Director of Player Development:
Katie Douglass
Vice President of Communications:
Ted Crews
Vice President of Media and Marketing:
Rob Alberino
Vice President of Human Resources and
Administration: Kirsten Krug
Vice President of Stadium Operations:
David Young
Director of Security: Jason Stone
Director of Facilities: Brandon Hamilton
Director of Special Events: Gary Spani
Director of Information Technology:
Bob Stirton
Equipment Manager: Allen Wright
Assistant Equipment Managers:
Chris Shropshire, Kyle Crumbaugh,
Jimmy White
Head Athletic Trainer: David Price
Assistant Athletic Trainers: David Glover,
Jimmy Ntelekos, Nick Potter
Director of Video Operations: Pat Brazil
Assistant Director of Video Operations:
Ken Radino
Video Assistant: Josh Schmidt

COACHING HISTORY
Dallas Texans 1960-62
(410-388-12)
Records include postseason games
1960-1974 Hank Stram 129-79-10
1975-77   Paul Wiggin* 11-24-0
1977   Tom Bettis 1-6-0
1978-1982 Marv Levy 31-42-0
1983-86   John Mackovic 30-35-0
1987-88   Frank Gansz...................8-22-1
1989-1998 Marty Schottenheimer...104-65-1
1999-2000 Gunther Cunningham 16-16-0
2001-05   Dick Vermeil..................44-37-0
2006-08   Herm Edwards.............15-34-0
2009-2011 Todd Haley** 19-26-0
2011   Romeo Crennel................2-1-0
*Released after seven games in 1977
**Released after 13 games in 2011

PAID ATTENDANCE
Home 557,037   Away 514,201
Total 1,071,238
Single-game home record,
*82,893 (10/2/00)
Single-season home record,
629,569 (1999)
*Arrowhead Stadium attendance: 78,502
Kauffman Stadium attendance: 4,391

2012 DRAFT CHOICES

Round	Name	Pos.	College
1	Dontari Poe	DT	Memphis
2	Jeff Allen	OL	Illinois
3	Donald Stephenson	OL	Oklahoma
4	Devon Wylie	WR	Fresno St.
5	DeQuan Menzie	DB	Alabama
6	Cyrus Gray	RB	Texas A&M
7	Jerome Long	DT	San Diego St.
	Junior Hemingway	WR	Michigan

2011 TEAM RECORD
PRESEASON (0-4)

Date	Result		Opponent
8/12	L	0-25	Tampa Bay
8/19	L	13-31	at Baltimore
8/26	L	10-14	St. Louis
9/1	L	19-20	at Green Bay

REGULAR SEASON (7-9)

Date	Result		Opponent
9/11	L	7-41	Buffalo
9/18	L	3-48	at Detroit
9/25	L	17-20	at San Diego
10/2	W	22-17	Minnesota
10/9	W	28-24	at Indianapolis
10/23	W	28-0	at Oakland
10/31	W	23-20	San Diego (OT)
11/6	L	3-31	Miami
11/13	L	10-17	Denver
11/21	L	3-34	at New England
11/27	L	9-13	Pittsburgh
12/4	W	10-3	at Chicago
12/11	L	10-37	at New York Jets
12/18	W	19-14	Green Bay
12/24	L	13-16	Oakland (OT)
1/1	W	7-3	at Denver

(OT) Overtime

SCORE BY PERIODS

Chiefs	58	40	43	68	3 —	212
Opponents	59	106	95	75	3 —	338

2011 TEAM STATISTICS

	Chiefs	Opp.
Total First Downs	277	291
Rushing	89	96
Passing	163	169
Penalty	25	26
3rd Down: Made/Att	81/225	72/210
3rd Down Pct.	36.0	34.3
4th Down: Made/Att	7/17	7/16
4th Down Pct.	41.2	43.8
Possession Avg.	29:10	30:50
Total Net Yards	4973	5333
Avg. Per Game	310.8	333.3
Total Plays	1021	991
Avg. Per Play	4.9	5.4
Net Yards Rushing	1893	2112
Avg. Per Game	118.3	132.0
Total Rushes	487	508
Net Yards Passing	3080	3221
Avg. Per Game	192.5	201.3
Sacked/Yards Lost	34/208	29/186
Gross Yards	3288	3407
Att./Completions	500/299	454/257
Completion Pct.	59.8	56.6
Had Intercepted	18	20
Punts/Average	89/45.9	83/47.6
Net Punting Avg.	89/40.1	83/39.7
Penalties/Yards	110/916	108/834
Fumbles/Ball Lost	17/10	18/6
Touchdowns	20	38
Rushing	5	14
Passing	13	23
Returns	2	1

2011 INDIVIDUAL STATISTICS

PASSING

	Att.	Comp.	Yds.	Pct.	TD	Int.	Tkld.	Rate
Cassel	269	160	1713	59.5	10	9	22/120	76.6
Palko	134	80	796	59.7	2	7	11/83	59.8
Orton	97	59	779	60.8	1	2	1/5	81.1
Chiefs	500	299	3288	59.8	13	18	34/208	73.0
Opponents	454	257	3407	56.6	23	20	29/186	79.1

SCORING

	TD R	TD P	TD Rt	PAT	FG	Saf	PTS
Succop	0	0	0	20/20	24/30	0	92
Bowe	0	5	0	0/0	0/0	0	30
Battle	2	0	0	0/0	0/0	0	12
Breaston	0	2	0	0/0	0/0	0	12
McClain	1	1	0	0/0	0/0	0	12
McCluster	1	1	0	0/0	0/0	0	12
Arenas	1	0	0	0/0	0/0	0	6
Baldwin	0	1	0	0/0	0/0	0	6
Charles	1	0	0	0/0	0/0	0	6
Flowers	0	0	1	0/0	0/0	0	6
K. Lewis	0	0	1	0/0	0/0	0	6
Pope	0	1	0	0/0	0/0	0	6
Urban	0	1	0	0/0	0/0	0	6
Chiefs	5	13	2	20/20	24/30	0	212
Opponents	14	23	1	37/37	23/28	1	338

2-Pt Conversions: Chiefs 0-0, Opponents 1-1

RUSHING

	No.	Yds	Avg	LG	TD
Battle	149	597	4.0	34	2
McCluster	114	516	4.5	32	1
Jones	153	478	3.1	26	0
Cassel	25	99	4.0	11	0
Charles	12	83	6.9	24	0
McClain	15	51	3.4	12	1
Breaston	1	25	25.0	25	0
Palko	5	15	3.0	12	0
Arenas	3	12	4.0	7t	1
Bowe	1	12	12.0	12	0
Urban	1	7	7.0	7	0
Horne	1	5	5.0	5	0
Colquitt	1	-3	-3.0	-3	0
Orton	6	-4	-0.7	2	0
Chiefs	487	1893	3.9	34	5
Opponents	508	2112	4.2	35	14

RECEIVING

	No.	Yds	Avg	LG	TD
Bowe	81	1159	14.3	52t	5
Breaston	61	785	12.9	43	2
McCluster	46	328	7.1	49	1
Pope	24	247	10.3	39	1
Baldwin	21	254	12.1	39t	1
McClain	14	82	5.9	14	1
Colbert	9	89	9.9	19	0
Battle	9	68	7.6	24	0
Copper	8	114	14.3	43	0
O'Connell	7	52	7.4	15	0
Jones	5	43	8.6	27	0
Charles	5	9	1.8	9	1
Urban	4	35	8.8	24t	1
Becht	3	26	8.7	16	0
Maneri	1	1	1.0	1	0
Cassel	1	-4	-4.0	-4	0
Chiefs	299	3288	11.0	52t	13
Opponents	257	3407	13.3	67t	23

INTERCEPTIONS

	No.	Yds	Avg	LG	TD
Flowers	4	95	23.8	58t	1
Carr	4	17	4.3	14	0
K. Lewis	3	119	39.7	59t	1
McGraw	3	4	1.3	4	0
Daniels	2	25	12.5	25	0
Johnson	2	18	9.0	17	0
Arenas	2	5	2.5	5	0
Chiefs	20	283	14.2	59t	2
Opponents	18	247	13.7	62	0

PUNTING

	No.	Yds.	Avg.	In 20	LG
Colquitt	89	4084	45.9	27	68
Chiefs	89	4084	45.9	27	68
Opponents	83	3951	47.6	32	76

PUNT RETURNS

	Ret	FC	Yds	Avg	LG	TD
Arenas	32	7	410	12.8	37	0
McCluster	6	3	65	10.8	22	0
Brown	1	0	0	0.0	0	0
Piscitelli	1	0	0	0.0	0	0
Chiefs	40	10	475	11.9	37	0
Opponents	36	26	411	11.4	72t	1

KICKOFF RETURNS

	No.	Yds	Avg	LG	TD
McCluster	25	557	22.3	35	0
Arenas	17	362	21.3	35	0
Horne	2	44	22.0	24	0
Bailey	1	4	4.0	4	0
Copper	1	12	12.0	12	0
Chiefs	46	979	21.3	35	0
Opponents	25	605	24.2	91	0

FIELD GOALS

	1-19	20-29	30-39	40-49	50+
Succop	1/1	7/7	6/7	7/12	3/3
Chiefs	1/1	7/7	6/7	7/12	3/3
Opponents	1/1	6/6	8/8	6/8	2/5

SACKS

	No.
Hali	12.0
Houston	5.5
Gilberry	2.5
Gordon	2.0
Johnson	2.0
Arenas	1.0
Bailey	1.0
Gregg	1.0
Jackson	1.0
McGraw	1.0
Chiefs	29.0
Opponents	34.0

RECORD HOLDERS
INDIVIDUAL RECORDS—CAREER

Category	Name	Performance
Rushing (Yds.)	Priest Holmes, 2001-07	6,070
Passing (Yds.)	Len Dawson, 1962-1975	28,507
Passing (TDs)	Len Dawson, 1962-1975	237
Receiving (No.)	Tony Gonzalez, 1997-2008	916
Receiving (Yds.)	Tony Gonzalez, 1997-2008	10,940
Interceptions	Emmitt Thomas, 1966-1978	58
Punting (Avg.)	Dustin Colquitt, 2005-2011	44.4
Punt Return (Avg.)	Noland Smith, 1967-69	11.1
Kickoff Return (Avg.)	Noland Smith, 1967-69	26.8
Field Goals	Nick Lowery, 1980-1993	329
Touchdowns (Tot.)	Priest Holmes, 2001-07	83
Points	Nick Lowery, 1980-1993	1,466
*Sacks	Derrick Thomas, 1989-1999	126.5

INDIVIDUAL RECORDS—SINGLE SEASON

Category	Name	Performance
Rushing (Yds.)	Larry Johnson, 2006	1,789
Passing (Yds.)	Trent Green, 2004	4,591
Passing (TDs)	Len Dawson, 1964	30
Receiving (No.)	Tony Gonzalez, 2004	102
Receiving (Yds.)	Derrick Alexander, 2000	1,391
Interceptions	Emmitt Thomas, 1974	12
Punting (Avg.)	Dustin Colquitt, 2011	45.9
Punt Return (Avg.)	Dante Hall, 2003	16.3
Kickoff Return (Avg.)	Dave Grayson, 1962	29.7
Field Goals	Nick Lowery, 1990	34
Touchdowns (Tot.)	Priest Holmes, 2003	27
Points	Priest Holmes, 2003	162
*Sacks	Derrick Thomas, 1990	20.0

INDIVIDUAL RECORDS—SINGLE GAME

Category	Name	Performance
Rushing (Yds.)	Jamaal Charles, 1-3-10	259
Passing (Yds.)	Elvis Grbac, 11-5-00	504
Passing (TDs)	Len Dawson, 11-1-64	6
Receiving (No.)	Tony Gonzalez, 1-2-05	14
Receiving (Yds.)	Stephone Paige, 12-22-85	309
Interceptions	Bobby Ply, 12-16-62	**4
	Bobby Hunt, 10-4-64	**4
	Deron Cherry, 9-29-85	**4
Field Goals	Many times	5
	Last time by Ryan Succop, 10-2-11	
Touchdowns (Tot.)	Abner Haynes, 11-26-61	5
Points	Abner Haynes, 11-26-61	30
*Sacks	Derrick Thomas, 11-11-90	**7.0

*Sacks became an official statistic in 1982.
**NFL Record

2012 VETERAN ROSTER

No.	Name	Pos.	Ht.	Wt.	Birthdate	NFL Exp.	College	Hometown	How Acq.	'11 Games/ Starts
76	Albert, Branden	T	6-5	316	11/4/84	5	Virginia	Glen Burnie, Md.	D1b-'08	16/16
21	Arenas, Javier	CB	5-9	197	10/28/87	3	Alabama	Tampa, Fla.	D2b-'10	15/1
73	Asamoah, Jon	G	6-4	305	7/21/88	3	Illinois	Park Forest, Ill.	D3a-'10	16/16
97	Bailey, Allen	DL	6-3	288	3/25/89	2	Miami	Sapelo Island, Ga.	D3b-'11	16/0
90	Bair, Brandon	DL	6-7	272	11/24/84	2	Oregon	St. Anthony, Idaho	FA-'11	0*
89	Baldwin, Jonathan	WR	6-4	230	8/10/89	2	Pittsburgh	Aliquippa, Pa.	D1-'11	11/3
59	Belcher, Jovan	LB	6-2	228	7/24/87	4	Maine	West Babylon, N.Y.	FA-'09	16/16
29	Berry, Eric	S	6-0	211	12/29/88	3	Tennessee	Fairburn, Ga.	D1-'10	1/1
80	Boss, Kevin	TE	6-6	255	1/11/84	6	Western Oregon	Philomath, Ore.	FA-'12	14/11*
82 f-	Bowe, Dwayne	WR	6-2	221	9/21/84	6	Louisiana State	Miami, Fla.	D1-'07	16/14
15	Breaston, Steve	WR	6-0	189	8/20/83	6	Michigan	North Braddock, Pa.	UFA(Ariz)-'11	16/13
30	Brown, Jalil	DB	6-1	204	10/14/87	2	Colorado	Phoenix, Ariz.	D4-'11	14/0
7	Cassel, Matt	QB	6-4	230	5/17/82	8	Southern California	Chatsworth, Calif.	T(NE)-'09	9/9
25	Charles, Jamaal	RB	5-11	199	12/27/86	5	Texas	Port Arthur, Texas	D3a-'08	2/1
2	Colquitt, Dustin	P	6-3	210	5/6/82	8	Tennessee	Knoxville, Tenn.	D3-'05	16/0
10	Copper, Terrance	WR	6-0	207	3/12/82	9	East Carolina	Washington, N.C.	UFA(KC)-'11	16/2
34	Daniels, Travis	DB	6-1	195	9/8/82	8	Louisiana State	Hollywood, Fla.	FA-'12	16/0
72	Dorsey, Glenn	DE	6-1	297	8/1/85	5	Louisiana State	Gonzales, La.	D1a-'08	15/15
24	Flowers, Brandon	CB	5-9	187	2/18/86	5	Virginia Tech	Delray Beach, Fla.	D2-'08	16/16
43	Gafford, Thomas	LS	6-2	250	1/29/83	5	Houston	Friendswood, Texas	FA-'09	16/0
99	Gordon, Amon	DL	6-2	305	10/13/81	6	Stanford	San Diego, Calif.	UFA(Sea)-'11	16/2
93	Greenwood, Cory	LB	6-2	235	6/5/85	3	Concordia	Kingston, Ont., Canada	FA-'10	16/0
91	Hali, Tamba	LB	6-3	275	11/3/83	7	Penn State	Teaneck, N.J.	D1-'06	16/16
40	Hillis, Peyton	RB	6-2	250	1/21/86	5	Arkansas	Conway, Ark.	UFA(Cle)-'12	10/9*
11	Horne, Jeremy	WR	6-2	193	10/25/86	2	Massachusetts	Albany, N.Y.	FA-'11	9/0
50	Houston, Justin	LB	6-3	258	1/12/89	2	Georgia	Statesboro, Ga.	D3a-'11	16/10
61	Hudson, Rodney	OL	6-2	299	7/12/89	2	Florida State	Mobile, Ala.	D2-'11	16/1
94	Jackson, Tyson	DE	6-4	296	6/6/86	4	Louisiana State	Edgard, La.	D1-'09	16/14
56	Johnson, Derrick	LB	6-3	242	11/22/82	8	Texas	Waco, Texas	D1-'05	16/16
23	Lewis, Kendrick	S	6-0	198	6/16/88	3	Mississippi	New Orleans, La.	D5a-'10	16/16
65	Lilja, Ryan	G	6-2	290	10/15/81	9	Kansas State	Shawnee Mission, Kan.	FA-'10	15/15
87	Maneri, Steve	TE	6-6	290	3/20/88	2	Temple	Saddle Brook, N.J.	W(NE)-'11	6/1
41	McCarthy, Kyle	DB	6-1	210	9/30/86	3	Notre Dame	Youngstown, Ohio	FA-'12	4/0*
22	McCluster, Dexter	RB	5-8	170	8/25/88	3	Mississippi	Largo, Fla.	D2a-'10	16/4
51	Miller, Gabe	LB	6-3	257	12/5/87	2	Oregon State	Lake Oswego, Ore.	D5b-'11	0*
81	Moeaki, Tony	TE	6-3	252	6/8/87	3	Iowa	Wheaton, Ill.	D3b-'10	0*
85	O'Connell, Jake	TE	6-3	250	11/6/85	4	Miami (Ohio)	Naples, Fla.	D7b-'09	8/4
77	Pitoitua, Ropati	DE	6-8	315	4/6/85	4	Washington State	Lakewood, Wash.	FA-'12	14/0*
95	Powe, Jerrell	DL	6-2	331	3/15/87	2	Mississippi	Waynesboro, Miss.	D6-'11	1/0
9	Quinn, Brady	QB	6-3	235	10/27/84	6	Notre Dame	Columbus, Ohio	UFA(Den)-'12	0*
35	Reeves, Jacques	DB	5-11	188	10/8/82	7	Purdue	Lancaster, Texas	FA-'12	0*
26	Routt, Stanford	CB	6-1	195	7/26/83	8	Houston	Pflugerville, Texas	FA-'12	16/15*
83	Rucker, Martin	TE	6-5	251	5/4/85	2	Missouri	St. Joseph, Mo.	FA-'12	2/0*
55	Sheffield, Cameron	LB	6-2	257	2/12/88	3	Troy	Portal, Ga.	D5b-'10	16/1
52	Siler, Brandon	LB	6-2	239	12/5/85	6	Florida	Orlando, Fla.	UFA(SD)-'11	0*
12	Stanzi, Ricky	QB	6-4	228	9/3/87	2	Iowa	Mentor, Ohio	D5a-'11	0*
96	Studebaker, Andy	LB	6-3	248	9/16/85	5	Wheaton (Ill.)	Eureka, Ill.	FA-'08	16/5
6	Succop, Ryan	K	6-2	218	9/19/86	4	South Carolina	Hickory, N.C.	D7c-'09	16/0
98	Toribio, Anthony	DL	6-1	315	3/1/85	2	Carson-Newman	Miami, Fla.	FA-'12	0*
27	Washington, Donald	S	6-1	197	7/28/86	4	Ohio State	Indianapolis, Ind.	D4-'09	12/3
66	Williams, Leon	LB	6-3	248	7/30/83	5	Miami	Brooklyn, N.Y.	FA-'12	0*
74	Winston, Eric	T	6-7	302	11/17/83	7	Miami	Midland, Texas	FA-'12	16/16*

* Bair inactive for 16 games; Boss played 14 games with Oakland in '11; Hillis played 10 games with Cleveland; McCarthy played 4 games with Denver; Miller missed '11 season because of injury; Moeaki missed '11 season because of injury; O'Callaghan missed '11 season because of injury; Pitoitua played 14 games with the New York Jets; Quinn did not play in 14 games, inactive for 2 games with Denver; Reeves last active with Houston '11; Routt played 16 games with Oakland; Rucker played 1 game with Dallas and 1 game with Jacksonville; Siler missed '11 season because of injury; Stanzi did not play in 10 games, inactive for 6 games; Toribio last active with Kansas City in '10; Williams last active with Dallas in '10; Winston played 16 games with Houston.

f- Unsigned franchise player; subject to developments.

Players lost through free agency (4): CB Brandon Carr (Dall; 16), FB Le'Ron McClain (SD; 16), QB Kyle Orton (Dall; 4), TE Leonard Pope (Pitt; 16).

Also played with Chiefs in '11—RB Jackie Battle (15 games), TE Anthony Becht (9), WR Keary Colbert (7), T Jared Gaither (10), DE Wallace Gilberry (16), DL Kelly Gregg (16), RB Thomas Jones (16), S Reshard Langford (11), S Jon McGraw (10), QB Tyler Palko (6), S Sabby Piscitelli (16), T Barry Richardson (16), WR Jerheme Urban (6), C Casey Wiegmann (16), LB Demorrio Williams (12).

FIRST-YEAR ROSTER

Name	Pos.	Ht.	Wt.	Birthdate	College	Hometown	How Acq.
Allen, Jeff	OL	6-4	306	1/8/90	Illinois	Chicago, Ill.	D2
Baker, Mikail (1)	DB	6-0	205	6/19/87	Baylor	Dallas, Texas	FA
Bannon, Shane (1)	FB	6-3	245	4/20/89	Yale	Southbury, Conn.	FA
Bellamy, Josh	WR	6-0	206	5/18/89	Louisville	St. Petersburg, Fla.	FA
Biere, Tim	TE	6-4	260	9/10/89	Kansas	Omaha, Neb.	FA
Bruggeman, Rob (1)	OL	6-4	286	3/21/86	Iowa	Washington, Iowa	FA
Campbell, Caleb (1)	LB	6-2	237	6/19/86	Army	Perryton, Texas	FA
Cheadle, Justin	OL	6-2	290	3/11/89	California	Bakersfield, Calif.	FA
Draughn, Shaun (1)	RB	6-0	205	12/7/87	North Carolina	Tarboro, N.C.	FA-'11
Eachus, Nate	RB	5-10	212	6/15/90	Colgate	Drums, Pa.	FA
Ellis, Dominique	DB	5-11	195	8/25/89	South Carolina State	Union City, Ga.	FA
Fanor, Jean	DB	6-1	200	6/17/89	Bethune-Cookman	Miami, Fla.	FA
Fenner, Chandler	DB	6-1	189	7/6/90	Holy Cross	Virginia Beach, Va.	FA
Gentry, Taylor	FB	6-2	250	8/22/89	North Carolina State	Raleigh, N.C.	FA
Gray, Cyrus	RB	5-10	206	11/18/89	Texas A&M	DeSoto, Texas	D6
Harris, Darryl (1)	G	6-4	300	1/14/85	Mississippi	Clarksdale, Miss.	FA
Hartman, Tysyn	DB	6-3	206	8/9/89	Kansas State	Wichita, Kan.	FA
Hemingway, Junior	WR	6-1	225	12/27/88	Michigan	Conway, S.C.	D7b
Heyman, Dexter	LB	6-3	238	10/16/89	Louisville	Louisville, Ky.	FA
Holland, Cam	OL	6-2	320	3/26/89	North Carolina	Pittsburgh, Pa.	FA
Johnson, Ethan	DE	6-4	300	12/18/89	Notre Dame	Portland, Ore.	FA
Kinnie, Brandon	WR	6-3	220	12/27/88	Nebraska	Kansas City, Mo.	FA
Long, Jerome	DL	6-5	285	4/9/90	San Diego State	Los Osos, Calif.	D7a
Markshausen, Zeke (1)	WR	5-11	185	1/26/87	Northwestern	Poplar Grove, Ill.	FA
Menzie, DeQuan	DB	5-11	202	1/11/90	Alabama	Columbus, Ga.	D5
Mims, David (1)	OL	6-8	335	5/18/88	Virginia Union	Charlotte, N.C.	FA-'11
Newsome, Jamar (1)	WR	6-1	201	11/5/87	Central Florida	Boca Ciega, Fla.	FA
Parks, Terrance	DB	6-2	218	4/14/90	Florida State	Fairburn, Ga.	FA
Patterson, Lucas (1)	OL	6-4	295	9/19/87	Texas A&M	Kingsville, Texas	FA
Poe, Dontari	DT	6-3	346	8/18/90	Memphis	Memphis, Tenn.	D1
Ranglin, Rich (1)	OL	6-3	315	9/27/85	Central Connecticut State	Younkers, N.Y.	FA
Stephenson, Donald	OL	6-6	312	9/30/88	Oklahoma	Blue Springs, Mo.	D3
Szymanski, Matt	K	6-1	196	8/13/88	Southern Methodist	College Station, Texas	FA
Thorpe, Neiko	DB	6-2	185	2/11/90	Auburn	Tucker, Ga.	FA
Wylie, Devon	WR	5-9	187	9/2/88	Fresno State	Roseville, Calif.	D4

The term NFL Rookie is defined as a player who is in his first season of professional football and has not been on the roster of another professional football team for any regular-season or postseason games. A Rookie is designated by an "R" on NFL rosters. Players who have been active in another professional football league or players who have NFL experience, including either preseason training camp or being on an Active List or Inactive List, or on Reserve/Injured or Reserve/Physically Unable to Perform for fewer than six regular-season games, are termed NFL First-Year Players. An NFL First-Year Player is designated by a "1" on NFL rosters. Thereafter, a player is credited with an additional year of experience for each season in which he accumulates six games on the Active List or Inactive List, or on Reserve/Injured or Reserve/Physically Unable to Perform.

Log on to www.kcchiefs.com for an up-to-date roster.

COACHING STAFF

Head Coach,
Romeo Crennel

Pro Career: Romeo Crennel was named the 12th head coach in Kansas City Chiefs history on January 9, 2012. He is entering his 31st season in the National Football League and his fifth season as an NFL head coach in 2012. Crennel originally joined the Chiefs in January 2010 as the club's defensive coordinator. He took over head coach responsibilities on December 12, 2011 after the first 13 games of the season. He led the Chiefs to a 2-1 record in the final three games in 2011. Crennel has coached in six Super Bowls and has been a member of five teams that have claimed Super Bowl wins. Prior to joining the Chiefs in 2010, Crennel served a four-year stint as head coach of the Cleveland Browns (2005-08). Before leading the Browns, Crennel spent four seasons as the defensive coordinator for the New England Patriots (2001-04). During that four-year span, the Patriots won three Super Bowls (XXXVI, XXXVIII and XXXIX) and he was named the NFL's Assistant Coach of the Year in 2003. He also served as defensive coordinator/defensive line coach in Cleveland (2000), defensive line coach with the New York Jets (1997-99) and defensive line coach in New England (1993-96), earning a berth in Super Bowl XXXI with that squad. Crennel's initial NFL coaching experience came with the New York Giants from 1981-1992. During that 12-year span, he was part of New York's victories in Super Bowls XXI and XXV. He also made collegiate coaching stops at Georgia Tech (1980), Mississippi (1978-79) and Texas Tech (1975-77). He began his coaching career at his alma mater, Western Kentucky (1970-74). Career record: 26-41.

Background: Crennel earned both B.A. and M.E. degrees from Western Kentucky in 1970 and 1971, respectively, and was a four-year starter from 1966-69.

Personal: Born on June 18, 1947 in Lynchburg, Va. Romeo and his wife, Rosemary, have three children and eight grandchildren.

ASSISTANT COACHES

Jack Bicknell, Jr., offensive line; born February 7, 1963, North Plainfield, N.J. Center Boston College 1981-85. No pro playing experience. College coach: Boston College 1985-87, 2007-08, New Hampshire 1987-1996, Louisiana Tech 1997-2006 (head coach 1999-2006). Pro coach: New York Giants 2009-2011, joined Chiefs in 2012.

Maurice Carthon, asst. head coach; born April 24, 1961, Chicago, Ill. Running back Arkansas State 1979-1982. Pro running back New Jersey Generals (USFL) 1983-85, New York Giants 1985-1991, Indianapolis Colts 1992. Pro coach: New England Patriots 1994-96, New York Jets 1997-2000, Detroit Lions 2001-02, Dallas Cowboys 2003-04, Cleveland Browns 2005-06, Arizona Cardinals 2007-08, joined Chiefs in 2009.

Mike Clark, strength and conditioning; born August 22, 1954, Wichita, Kan. Center Ottawa 1973-76. No pro playing experience. College coach: Kansas 1977-78, 1982, Wyoming 1981, Oregon 1983-87, Southern California 1988-89, Texas A&M 1990-2003. Pro coach: Seattle Seahawks 2004-09, joined Chiefs in 2010.

Jim Bob Cooter, offensive quality control; born July 3, 1984, Huntsville, Ala. Quarterback Tennessee 2002-06. No pro playing experience. College coach: Tennessee 2007-08. Pro coach: Indianapolis Colts 2009-2011, joined Chiefs in 2012.

Brian Daboll, offensive coordinator; born April 14, 1975, Welland, Ontario, Canada. Safety Rochester 1995-97. No pro playing experience. College coach: William & Mary 1997, Michigan State 1998-99. Pro coach: New England Patriots 2000-06, New York Jets 2007-08, Cleveland Browns 2009-2010, Miami Dolphins 2011, joined Chiefs in 2012.

Gary Gibbs, linebackers; born August 13, 1952, Beaumont, Texas. Linebacker Oklahoma 1972-74. No pro playing experience. College coach: Oklahoma 1975-1994 (head coach 1989-1994), Georgia 2000, Louisiana State 2001. Pro coach: Dallas Cowboys 2002-04, New Orleans Saints 2006-08, joined Chiefs in 2009.

Tom McMahon, special teams; born July 12, 1969, Helena, Mont. Cornerback Carroll College 1988-1992. No pro playing experience. College coach: Carroll College 1992, 1994, Utah State 1995-2005, Louisville 2006. Pro coach: Atlanta Falcons 2007-08, St. Louis Rams 2009-2011, joined Chiefs in 2012.

Bernie Parmalee, tight ends; born September 16, 1967, Jersey City, N.J. Running back Ball State 1988-1991. Pro running back Miami Dolphins 1992-98, New York Jets 1999-2000. College coach: Notre Dame 2005-09. Pro coach: Miami Dolphins 2002-04, joined Chiefs in 2010.

Anthony Pleasant, defensive line; born January 27, 1968, Century, Fla. Defensive end Tennessee State 1987-89. Pro defensive end Cleveland Browns 1990-95, Baltimore Ravens 1996, Atlanta Falcons 1997, New York Jets 1998-99, San Francisco 49ers 2000, New England Patriots 2001-03. Pro coach: Joined Chiefs in 2010.

Brent Salazar, asst. strength and conditioning; born May 22, 1980, Denver, Colo. Attended New Mexico. No college or pro playing experience. College coach: New Mexico 2002-03, Nevada-Las Vegas 2004, Pacific 2006. Pro coach: Joined Chiefs in 2007.

Nick Sirianni, wide receivers; born June 15, 1981, Jamestown, N.Y. Wide receiver Mount Union 2000-03. No pro playing experience. College coach: Mount Union 2004-05, Indiana (Pa.) 2006-08. Pro coach: Joined Chiefs in 2009.

Otis Smith, defensive quality control; born October 22, 1965, New Orleans, La. Defensive back Taft (Calif.) Junior College 1986-87, Missouri 1988-89. Pro defensive back Philadelphia Eagles 1991-94, New York Jets 1995-96, 1997-99, New England Patriots 1996, 2000-02, Detroit Lions 2003. Pro coach: Philadelphia Eagles 2008, joined Chiefs in 2010.

Steven Smith, asst. offensive line; born December 18, 1976, Chicago, Ill. Fullback Southern Illinois 1995-98. No pro playing experience. College coach: Delta State 2007-08, Albany State 2009-2010, Tennessee State 2011. Pro coach: Joined Chiefs in 2012.

Derius Swinton, special teams quality control; born April 26, 1985, Newport News, Va. Safety Hampton 2003-06. No pro playing experience. College coach: Tennessee 2007-08. Pro coach: St. Louis Rams 2009-2011, joined Chiefs in 2012

Emmitt Thomas, defensive backs; born June 3, 1943, Angleton, Texas. Quarterback/wide receiver Bishop (Texas) College 1963-65. Pro defensive back Kansas City Chiefs 1966-1978. Inducted into Pro Football Hall of Fame 2008. College coach: Central Missouri State 1979-1980. Pro coach: St. Louis Cardinals 1981-85, Washington Redskins 1986-1994, Philadelphia Eagles 1995-98, Green Bay Packers 1999, Minnesota Vikings 2000-01, Atlanta Falcons 2002-09 (interim head coach 2007), re-joined Chiefs in 2010.

Adam Zimmer, defensive assistant/asst. linebackers; born January 13, 1984, Ogden, Utah. Defensive back Trinity (Texas) 2002-05. No pro playing experience. Pro coach: New Orleans Saints 2006-09, joined Chiefs in 2010.

Jim Zorn, quarterbacks; born May 10, 1953, Whittier, Calif. Quarterback Cal Poly Pomona 1973-74. Pro quarterback Seattle Seahawks 1976-1984, Green Bay Packers 1985, Winnipeg Blue Bombers (CFL) 1986, Tampa Bay Buccaneers 1987. College coach: Boise State 1989-1991, Utah State 1992-94, Minnesota 1995-96. Pro coach: Seattle Seahawks 1997, 2001-07, Detroit Lions 1998-2000, Washington Redskins 2008-09 (head coach), Baltimore Ravens 2010, joined Chiefs in 2011.

American Football Conference
East Division
Team Colors: Aqua, Coral, Blue, and White
7500 S.W. 30th Street
Davie, Florida 33314
Telephone: (954) 452-7000

2012 SCHEDULE
PRESEASON
Aug. 10	**Tampa Bay**	7:30
Aug. 17	at Carolina	8:00
Aug. 24	**Atlanta**	7:30
Aug. 29	at Dallas	8:30

REGULAR SEASON
Sep. 9	at Houston	1:00
Sep. 16	**Oakland**	4:15
Sep. 23	**New York Jets**	1:00
Sep. 30	at Arizona	4:05
Oct. 7	at Cincinnati	1:00
Oct. 14	**St. Louis**	1:00
Oct. 21	BYE	
Oct. 28	at New York Jets	1:00
Nov. 4	at Indianapolis	1:00
Nov. 11	**Tennessee**	1:00
Nov. 15	at Buffalo (Thurs)	8:20
Nov. 25	**Seattle**	1:00
Dec. 2	**New England**	1:00
Dec. 9	at San Francisco	4:05
Dec. 16	**Jacksonville**	1:00
Dec. 23	**Buffalo**	1:00
Dec. 30	at New England	1:00

All times ET

Stadium: Sun Life Stadium
(opened in 1987)
•**Capacity:** 75,192
2269 Dan Marino Blvd.
Miami Gardens, Florida 33056
Playing Surface: Grass (PAT)
Training Camp: Nova Southeastern Univ.
7500 S.W. 30th Street
Davie, Florida 33314

SUN LIFE STADIUM

CLUB OFFICIALS
Chairman of the Board/Managing General
Partner: Stephen M. Ross
Chief Executive Officer: Mike Dee
General Manager: Jeff Ireland
Chief Revenue Officer: Jim Rushton
Senior Vice President of Football
Operations: Dawn Aponte
Senior Vice President-Operations:
Bill Galante
Senior Vice President-Media Relations:
Harvey Greene
Senior Vice President-Chief Technology
Officer: Tery Howard
Senior Vice President, Chief Marketing
Officer: Claudia Lezcano
Vice President/Special Advisor:
Nat Moore
Director of Player Personnel:
Brian Gaine
Director of College Scouting: Chris Grier
Assistant Director of Pro Scouting:
Chris Shea
Head Athletic Trainer: Kevin O'Neill
Equipment Manager: Joe Cimino
Video Director: Bob Hack
Director of Player Development:
Kaleb Thornhill
Senior Director of Internet and
Publications: Scott Stone
Director of Media Relations:
Jason Jenkins
Director of Communications: Fitz Ollison
Senior Director of Programming and
Production: Jeff Griffith
Senior Director of Cheerleaders and
Entertainment: Dorie Grogan
Cheerleader Coordinator: Emily Snow
Director of Records and Archives:
Kristin Hingston
Senior Director of Community Relations:
Ilona Wolpin
Director of Youth Programs: Twan Russell
Director of Security: Stuart Weinstein

COACHING HISTORY
(420-320-4)
Records include postseason games
1966-69	George Wilson	15-39-2
1970-1995	Don Shula	274-147-2
1996-99	Jimmy Johnson	38-31-0
2000-04	Dave Wannstedt*	43-33-0
2004	Jim Bates	3-4-0
2005-06	Nick Saban	15-17-0
2007	Cam Cameron	1-15-0
2008-2011	Tony Sparano**	29-33-0
2011	Todd Bowles	2-1-0

*Resigned after nine games in 2004
**Released after 13 games in 2011

PAID ATTENDANCE
Home 482,698   Away 551,572
Total 1,034,270
Single-game home record,
75,283 (10/27/96)
Single-season home record, 592,161
(1999)

2012 DRAFT CHOICES
Round	Name	Pos.	College
1	Ryan Tannehill	QB	Texas A&M
2	Jonathan Martin	T	Stanford
3	Olivier Vernon	DE	Miami
	Michael Egnew	TE	Missouri
4	Lamar Miller	RB	Miami
5	Josh Kaddu	LB	Oregon
6	B.J. Cunningham	WR	Michigan St.
7	Kheeston Randall	DT	Texas
	Rishard Matthews	WR	Nevada

MIAMI DOLPHINS

2011 TEAM RECORD
PRESEASON (3-1)

Date	Result	Opponent
8/12	W 28-23	at Atlanta
8/19	W 20-10	Carolina
8/26	L 13-17	at Tampa Bay
9/1	W 17-3	Dallas

REGULAR SEASON (6-10)

Date	Result	Opponent
9/12	L 24-38	New England
9/18	L 13-23	Houston
9/25	L 16-17	at Cleveland
10/2	L 16-26	at San Diego
10/17	L 6-24	at New York Jets
10/23	L 15-18	Denver (OT)
10/30	L 17-20	at New York Giants
11/6	W 31-3	at Kansas City
11/13	W 20-9	Washington
11/20	W 35-8	Buffalo
11/24	L 19-20	at Dallas
12/4	W 34-14	Oakland
12/11	L 10-26	Philadelphia
12/18	W 30-23	at Buffalo
12/24	L 24-27	at New England
1/1	W 19-17	New York Jets

(OT) Overtime

SCORE BY PERIODS

Dolphins	84	86	91	68	0 —	329
Opponents	53	87	50	120	3 —	313

2011 TEAM STATISTICS

	Dolphins	Opp.
Total First Downs	287	310
Rushing	89	88
Passing	166	198
Penalty	32	24
3rd Down: Made/Att	69/207	74/219
3rd Down Pct.	33.3	33.8
4th Down: Made/Att	6/16	7/14
4th Down Pct.	37.5	50.0
Possession Avg.	30:23	29:37
Total Net Yards	5078	5522
Avg. Per Game	317.4	345.1
Total Plays	990	1043
Avg. Per Play	5.1	5.3
Net Yards Rushing	1987	1530
Avg. Per Game	124.2	95.6
Total Rushes	469	412
Net Yards Passing	3091	3992
Avg. Per Game	193.2	249.5
Sacked/Yards Lost	52/334	41/241
Gross Yards	3425	4233
Att./Completions	469/280	590/350
Completion Pct.	59.7	59.3
Had Intercepted	13	16
Punts/Average	78/48.8	95/45.4
Net Punting Avg.	78/41.1	95/38.6
Penalties/Yards	85/779	112/975
Fumbles/Ball Lost	28/12	17/3
Touchdowns	33	33
Rushing	11	8
Passing	20	24
Returns	2	1

2011 INDIVIDUAL STATISTICS

PASSING

PASSING	Att.	Comp.	Yds.	Pct.	TD	Int.	Tkld.	Rate
Mat. Moore	347	210	2497	60.5	16	9	36/229	87.1
Henne	112	64	868	57.1	4	4	11/67	79.0
Losman	10	6	60	60.0	0	0	5/38	77.1
Dolphins	469	280	3425	59.7	20	13	52/334	84.9
Opponents	590	350	4233	59.3	24	16	41/241	83.7

SCORING

SCORING	TD R	TD P	TD Rt	PAT	FG	Saf	PTS
Carpenter	0	0	0	26/26	29/34	0	113
Bush	6	1	0	0/0	0/0	0	42
Marshall	0	6	0	0/0	0/0	0	36
Fasano	0	5	0	0/0	0/0	0	30
Bess	0	3	0	0/0	0/0	0	18
Clay	0	3	0	0/0	0/0	0	18
Graham	0	0	0	6/6	4/5	0	18
Hilliard	1	0	1	0/0	0/0	0	12
Mat. Moore	2	0	0	0/0	0/0	0	12
Burnett	0	0	1	0/0	0/0	0	6
Hartline	0	1	0	0/0	0/0	0	6
Henne	1	0	0	0/0	0/0	0	6
Slaton	1	0	0	0/0	0/0	0	6
Thomas	0	1	0	0/0	0/0	0	6
Dolphins	11	20	2	32/32	33/39	0	329
Opponents	8	24	1	31/31	26/33	2	313

2-Pt Conversions: Team 0-1, Opponents 1-2

RUSHING

RUSHING	No.	Yds	Avg	LG	TD
Bush	216	1086	5.0	76t	6
Thomas	165	581	3.5	28	0
Henne	15	112	7.5	20	1
Mat. Moore	32	65	2.0	16	2
Slaton	17	64	3.8	28	1
Hilliard	16	41	2.6	4	1
Marshall	1	13	13.0	13	0
Bess	2	9	4.5	5	0
Hartline	1	9	9.0	9	0
Gates	1	4	4.0	4	0
L. Johnson	1	2	2.0	2	0
Losman	2	1	0.5	1	0
Dolphins	469	1987	4.2	76t	11
Opponents	412	1530	3.7	24t	8

RECEIVING

RECEIVING	No.	Yds	Avg	LG	TD
Marshall	81	1214	15.0	65t	6
Bess	51	537	10.5	41	3
Bush	43	296	6.9	34	1
Hartline	35	549	15.7	41	1
Fasano	32	451	14.1	35t	5
Clay	16	233	14.6	46	3
Thomas	12	72	6.0	12	1
Hilliard	5	49	9.8	18	0
Gates	2	19	9.5	11	0
Slaton	2	-3	-1.5	-1	0
Mastrud	1	8	8.0	8	0
Dolphins	280	3425	12.2	65t	20
Opponents	350	4233	12.1	99t	24

INTERCEPTIONS

INTERCEPTIONS	No.	Yds	Avg	LG	TD
Davis	4	60	15.0	28	0
Starks	2	21	10.5	18	0
Smith	2	7	3.5	7	0
Mitchell	1	55	55.0	55	0
Odrick	1	39	39.0	39	0
Burnett	1	34	34.0	34t	1
Bell	1	20	20.0	20	0
Dansby	1	14	14.0	14	0
Wilson	1	5	5.0	5	0
R. Jones	1	1	1.0	1	0
Carroll	1	0	0.0	0	0
Dolphins	16	256	16.0	55	1
Opponents	13	224	17.2	100t	1

PUNTING

PUNTING	No.	Yds.	Avg.	In 20	LG
Fields	78	3810	48.8	32	70
Dolphins	78	3810	48.8	32	70
Opponents	95	4313	45.4	28	69

PUNT RETURNS

PUNT RETURNS	Ret	FC	Yds	Avg	LG	TD
Bess	37	24	442	11.9	25	0
Bush	6	0	52	8.7	16	0
Gates	3	0	32	10.7	17	0
Dolphins	46	24	526	11.4	25	0
Opponents	47	10	463	9.9	45	0

KICKOFF RETURNS

KICKOFF RETURNS	No.	Yds	Avg	LG	TD
Gates	34	843	24.8	77	0
Slaton	3	85	28.3	42	0
Bess	1	0	0.0	0	0
Hilliard	1	14	14.0	14	0
Dolphins	39	942	24.2	77	0
Opponents	41	937	22.9	54	0

FIELD GOALS

FIELD GOALS	1-19	20-29	30-39	40-49	50+
Carpenter	0/0	10/11	6/7	11/12	2/4
Graham	0/0	4/4	0/0	0/1	0/0
Dolphins	0/0	14/15	6/7	11/13	2/4
Opponents	0/0	11/12	7/7	6/10	2/4

SACKS

SACKS	No.
Wake	8.5
Taylor	7.0
Odrick	6.0
Starks	4.5
Burnett	2.5
McDaniel	2.5
Bell	2.0
Dansby	2.0
R. Jones	2.0
Culver	1.0
Davis	1.0
Misi	1.0
Mitchell	1.0
Dolphins	41.0
Opponents	52.0

RECORD HOLDERS
INDIVIDUAL RECORDS—CAREER

Category	Name	Performance
Rushing (Yds.)	Larry Csonka, 1968-1974, 1979	6,737
Passing (Yds.)	Dan Marino, 1983-1999	61,361
Passing (TDs)	Dan Marino, 1983-1999	420
Receiving (No.)	Mark Clayton, 1983-1992	550
Receiving (Yds.)	Mark Duper, 1982-1992	8,869
Interceptions	Jake Scott, 1970-75	35
Punting (Avg.)	Brandon Fields, 2007-2011	45.7
Punt Return (Avg.)	Jeff Ogden, 2000-01	13.7
Kickoff Return (Avg.)	Mercury Morris, 1969-1975	26.5
Field Goals	Olindo Mare, 1997-2006	245
Touchdowns (Tot.)	Mark Clayton, 1983-1992	82
Points	Olindo Mare, 1997-2006	1,048
*Sacks	Jason Taylor, 1997-2007, 2009, 2011	131.0

INDIVIDUAL RECORDS—SINGLE SEASON

Category	Name	Performance
Rushing (Yds.)	Ricky Williams, 2002	1,853
Passing (Yds.)	Dan Marino, 1984	5,084
Passing (TDs)	Dan Marino, 1984	48
Receiving (No.)	O.J. McDuffie, 1998	90
Receiving (Yds.)	Mark Clayton, 1984	1,389
Interceptions	Dick Westmoreland, 1967	10
Punting (Avg.)	Brandon Fields, 2011	48.8
Punt Return (Avg.)	Jeff Ogden, 2000	17.0
Kickoff Return (Avg.)	Duriel Harris, 1976	32.9
Field Goals	Olindo Mare, 1999	39
Touchdowns (Tot.)	Mark Clayton, 1984	18
Points	Olindo Mare, 1999	144
*Sacks	Jason Taylor, 2002	18.5

INDIVIDUAL RECORDS—SINGLE GAME

Category	Name	Performance
Rushing (Yds.)	Ricky Williams, 12-1-02	228
Passing (Yds.)	Dan Marino, 10-23-88	521
Passing (TDs)	Bob Griese, 11-24-77	6
	Dan Marino, 9-21-86	6
Receiving (No.)	Chris Chambers, 12-4-05	15
Receiving (Yds.)	Chris Chambers, 12-4-05	238
Interceptions	Dick Anderson, 12-3-73	**4
Field Goals	Olindo Mare, 10-17-99	6
Touchdowns (Tot.)	Paul Warfield, 12-15-73	4
	Mark Ingram, 11-27-94	4
	Ronnie Brown, 9-21-08	4
Points	Paul Warfield, 12-15-73	24
	Mark Ingram, 11-27-94	24
	Ronnie Brown, 9-21-08	24
*Sacks	Doug Betters, 9-4-83	4.0
	E.J. Junior, 10-6-91	4.0
	Joey Porter, 9-21-08	4.0

*Sacks became an official statistic in 1982.
**NFL Record

2012 VETERAN ROSTER

No.	Name	Pos.	Ht.	Wt.	Birthdate	NFL Exp.	College	Hometown	How Acq.	'11 Games/ Starts
90	Baker, Ryan	DE	6-5	295	11/25/84	4	Purdue	Indianapolis, Ind.	FA-'09	2/0
61	Barker, Will	T	6-7	325	7/3/87	3	Virginia	Bryn Mawr, Pa.	FA-'11	0*
15	Bess, Davone	WR	5-10	190	9/13/85	5	Hawaii	Oakland, Calif.	FA-'08	16/4
56	Burnett, Kevin	LB	6-3	240	12/24/82	8	Tennessee	Inglewood, Calif.	UFA(SD)-'11	16/16
22	Bush, Reggie	RB	6-0	203	3/2/85	7	Southern California	San Diego, Calif.	T(NO)-'11	15/15
5	Carpenter, Dan	K	6-2	225	11/25/85	5	Montana	Helena, Mont.	FA-'08	14/0
28	Carroll, Nolan	CB	6-1	202	1/18/87	3	Maryland	Green Grove Spring, Fla.	D5a-'10	15/3
42	Clay, Charles	FB/TE	6-3	239	2/13/89	2	Tulsa	Little Rock, Ark.	D6-'11	14/9
30	Clemons, Chris	FS	6-1	210	9/15/85	4	Clemson	Arcadia, Fla.	D5b-'09	14/0
62	Cook, Ryan	G/C	6-6	328	5/8/83	7	New Mexico	Albuquerque, N.M.	FA-'11	7/0
29	Culver, Tyrone	S	6-1	210	7/6/83	7	Fresno State	Palmdale, Calif.	FA-'08	16/4
58	Dansby, Karlos	LB	6-4	250	11/3/81	9	Auburn	Birmingham, Ala.	UFA(Ariz)-'10	16/16
21	Davis, Vontae	CB	5-11	203	5/27/88	4	Illinois	Washington, D.C.	D1-'09	12/12
92	Denney, John	LS	6-5	255	12/13/78	8	Brigham Young	Thornton, Colo.	FA-'05	16/0
7	Devlin, Pat	QB	6-3	225	4/12/88	2	Delaware	Exton, Pa.	FA, '11	0*
80	Fasano, Anthony	TE	6-4	255	4/20/84	7	Notre Dame	Verona, N.J.	T(Dall)-'08	15/15
69	Feinga, Ray	G	6-4	337	5/8/86	3	Brigham Young	West Valley City, Utah	FA-'10	0*
2	Fields, Brandon	P	6-5	245	5/21/84	6	Michigan State	Toledo, Ohio	D7b-'07	16/0
75	Garner, Nate	T	6-7	325	1/18/85	5	Arkansas	Roland, Ark.	W(NYJ)-'08	16/1
9	Garrard, David	QB	6-1	235	2/14/78	9	East Carolina	Durham, N.C.	FA-'12	0*
10	Gates, Clyde	WR	5-11	197	6/13/86	2	Abilene Christian	Vernon, Texas	D4-'11	15/0
59	Guyton, Gary	LB	6-3	245	11/14/85	5	Georgia Tech	Hinesville, Ga.	UFA(NE)-'12	13/6*
82	Hartline, Brian	WR	6-2	199	11/22/86	4	Ohio State	North Canton, Ohio	D4-'09	16/10
73	Hicks, Artis	T	6-4	325	11/28/78	10	Memphis	Jackson, Tenn.	UFA(Cle)-'12	9/3*
68	Incognito, Richie	G	6-3	324	7/5/83	8	Nebraska	Englewood, N.J.	UFA(Buff)-'10	15/15
74	Jerry, John	G	6-5	328	6/14/86	3	Mississippi	Batesville, Miss.	D3-'10	13/3
26	Johnson, Tyrell	S	6-0	207	11/15/82	5	Arkansas State	Rison, Ark.	UFA(Minn)-'12	11/3*
20	Jones, Reshad	S	6-1	214	2/25/88	3	Georgia	Atlanta, Ga.	D5b-'10	15/12
36	Lawrence, Quinten	DB	6-0	184	9/21/84	2	McNeese State	Carencro, La.	FA-'12	0*
77	Long, Jake	T	6-7	317	5/9/85	5	Michigan	Lapeer, Mich.	D1-'08	14/14
31	Marshall, Richard	DB	5-11	198	12/12/84	6	Fresno State	Los Angeles, Calif.	UFA(Ariz)-'12	16/9*
88	Mastrud, Jeron	TE	6-6	253	12/17/87	3	Kansas State	Beaverton, Ore.	FA-'10	14/3
78	McDaniel, Tony	DT	6-7	305	1/20/85	7	Tennessee	Columbia, S.C.	T(Jax)-'09	12/1
55	Misi, Koa	LB	6-3	251	1/17/87	3	Utah	Santa Rosa, Calif.	D2-'10	12/9
14	Moore, Marlon	WR	6-0	190	9/3/87	3	Fresno State	Sacramento, Calif.	FA-'10	6/0
8	Moore, Matt	QB	6-3	203	8/9/84	6	Oregon State	Newhall, Calif.	UFA(Car)-'11	13/12
76	Murtha, Lydon	T	6-7	315	11/13/85	4	Nebraska	Hutchinson, Minn.	FA-'09	0*
19	Naanee, Legedu	WR	6-2	220	9/16/83	6	Boise State	Portland, Ore.	UFA(Car)-'12	15/10*
98	Odrick, Jared	DE	6-5	304	12/31/87	3	Penn State	Lebanon County, Pa.	D1-'10	16/7
51	Pouncey, Mike	C	6-5	303	7/24/89	2	Florida	Lakeland, Fla.	D1-'11	16/16
11	Pruitt, Julius	WR	6-2	206	12/30/85	3	Ouachita Baptist	Newport, Ark.	FA-'11	9/0
23	Slaton, Steve	RB	5-9	199	1/4/86	5	West Virginia	Levittown, Pa.	W(Hou)-'11	6/0*
24	Smith, Sean	CB	6-3	214	7/14/87	4	Utah	Pasadena, Calif.	D2b-'09	16/16
96	Soliai, Paul	DT	6-4	355	12/30/83	6	Utah	Pago Pago, American Samoa	D4-'07	16/12
53	Spitler, Austin	LB	6-2	243	10/26/86	3	Ohio State	Bellbrook, Ohio	D7b-'10	16/0
94	Starks, Randy	DE	6-3	305	12/14/83	9	Maryland	Waldorf, Md.	UFA(Tenn)-'08	16/15
33	Thomas, Daniel	RB	6-1	228	10/29/87	2	Kansas State	Hilliard, Fla.	D2-'11	13/2
93	Trusnik, Jason	LB	6-4	250	6/6/84	6	Ohio Northern	Macedonia, Ohio	UFA(Cle)-'11	16/0
25	Wade, Jonathan	DB	5-11	200	3/27/84	5	Tennessee	Shreveport, La.	FA-'12	2/0
91	Wake, Cameron	LB	6-3	250	1/30/82	4	Penn State	Hyattsville, Md.	FA, '09	16/14
18	Wallace, Roberto	WR	6-4	225	5/10/86	3	San Diego State	Oceanside, Calif.	FA, '10	2/0
52	Westerman, Jamaal	LB	6-3	255	2/21/85	4	Rutgers	Brampton, Ont., Canada	FA-'12	16/3*
27	Wilson, Jimmy	CB	5-11	185	7/30/86	2	Montana	San Diego, Calif.	D7b, '11	15/1
89	Yeatman, Will	TE	6-6	268	4/10/88	2	Maryland	Naples, Italy	W(NE)-'11	3/2

* Barker inactive for 12 games in '11; Devlin inactive for 2 games; Feinga inactive for 5 games; Garrard last active with Jacksonville in '10; Guyton played 13 games with New England in '11; Hicks played 9 games with Cleveland; Johnson played 11 games with Minnesota; Lawrence inactive 2 games in '10 with Kansas City; Marshall played 16 games with Arizona; Murtha missed '11 season because of injury; Naanee played 15 games with Carolina; Slaton played 3 games with Houston and 3 games with Miami; Westerman played 16 games with New York Jets.

Retired—Jason Taylor, 15-year defensive end, 16 games in '11.

Traded—WR Brandon Marshall (16 games in '11) to Chicago.

Players lost through free agency (5): CB Will Allen (NE; 14 games), T Marc Colombo (Dall; 16), QB Chad Henne (Jax; 4), DE Kendall Langford (StL; 16), LB Marvin Mitchell (Minn; 16).

Also played with Dolphins in '11—DE Ikaika Alama-Francis (5 games), DB Gerald Alexander (2), S Yeremiah Bell (16), G Vernon Carey (15), K Shayne Graham (2), FB Lex Hilliard (16), RB Larry Johnson (1), DB Nate Jones (2), QB J.P. Losman (2), DT Phillip Merling (10), DT Igor Olshansky (8).

FIRST-YEAR ROSTER

Name	Pos.	Ht.	Wt.	Birthdate	College	Hometown	How Acq.
Aaitui, Isaako	NT	6-4	315	1/25/87	Nevada-Las Vegas	Pago Pago, American Samoa	FA
Agnew, Vincent	CB	5-10	192	12/28/87	Central Michigan	Grand Rapids, Mich.	FA
Alecxih, Chas	DT	6-3	296	2/10/89	Pittsburgh	Lancaster, Pa.	FA
Brown, Les	TE	6-4	238	6/29/87	Westminster	Salt Lake City, Utah	FA
Brown, Marcus (1)	CB	6-1	195	1/27/87	Arkansas State	Marianna, Ark.	FA
Brown, Terence	C	6-3	303	2/19/86	Brigham Young	Summerville, S.C.	FA
Collins, Cameron	LB	6-2	241	9/29/89	Oregon State	Santa Monica, Calif.	FA
Cunningham, B.J.	WR	6-2	215	5/29/89	Michigan State	Westerville, Ohio	D6
Dennis, Derek	G	6-3	315	7/16/88	Temple	Peekskill, N.Y.	FA
Egnew, Michael	TE	6-5	251	11/1/89	Missouri	Plainview, Texas	D3b
Freeny, Jonathan	LB	6-2	242	6/15/89	Rutgers	Margate, Fla.	FA
Fuller, Jeff	WR	6-4	223	4/20/90	Texas A&M	McKinney, Texas	FA
Gray, Jonas	RB	5-9	223	6/27/90	Notre Dame	Pontiac, Mich.	FA
Hogan, Chris	WR	6-1	220	10/24/88	Monmouth	Ramapo , N.J.	FA
Hughes, Trenton	DB	5-10	195	3/5/89	Maryland	Virginia Beach, Va.	FA
Kaddu, Josh	LB	6-3	239	3/12/90	Oregon	Vacaville, Calif.	D5
Lyons, Shelly	LB	6-1	238	1/19/90	Arizona State	Corona, Calif.	FA
Martin, Jonathan	T	6-5	304	8/19/89	Stanford	North Hollywood, Calif.	D2
Matthews, Rishard	WR	6-0	217	10/12/89	Nevada	Santa Ana, Calif.	D7b
McCray, Kelcie	S	6-1	202	9/21/88	Arkansas State	Columbus, Ga.	FA
McDonald, Andrew	T	6-6	316	9/8/88	Indiana	Indianapolis, Ind	FA
Medlin, Richard (1)	RB	5-11	200	3/4/87	Fayetteville State	Raleigh, N.C.	FA-'11
Messam, Jerome	RB	6-4	248	4/2/85	Graceland	Toronto, Ont., Canada	FA
Miller, Lamar	RB	5-10	212	4/25/91	Miami	Miami, Fla.	D4
Moye, Derek	WR	6-4	209	8/12/88	Penn State	Rochester, Pa.	FA
Randall, Kheeston	DT	6-5	307	5/7/89	Texas	Beaumont, Texas	D7a
Root, Jarrell	DE	6-3	270	5/14/88	Boise State	Boise, Idaho	FA
Russell, Anderson (1)	DB	6-0	205	5/30/87	Ohio State	Atlanta, Ga.	FA
Samuda, Josh	G	6-3	310	12/23/88	Massachusetts	Hollywood, Fla.	FA
Scott, Kevyn	DB	5-10	204	11/10/88	Syracuse	Tamarac, Fla.	FA
Shelby, Derrick	DE	6-2	266	3/4/89	Utah	Houston, Texas	FA
Smith, Jacquies	DE	6-2	253	3/18/90	Missouri	Dallas, Texas	FA
Tannehill, Ryan	QB	6-4	221	7/27/88	Texas A&M	Big Spring, Texas	D1
Thigpen, Marcus	RB	5-9	193	5/15/86	Indiana	Detroit, Mich.	FA
Vernon, Olivier	DE	6-2	261	10/7/90	Miami	Miami, Fla.	D3a
Waldron, Dustin	T	6-5	305	5/24/90	Portland State	Pleasant Hill, Ore.	FA

The term NFL Rookie is defined as a player who is in his first season of professional football and has not been on the roster of another professional football team for any regular-season or postseason games. A Rookie is designated by an "R" on NFL rosters. Players who have been active in another professional football league or players who have NFL experience, including either preseason training camp or being on an Active List or Inactive List, or on Reserve/Injured or Reserve/Physically Unable to Perform for fewer than six regular-season games, are termed NFL First-Year Players. An NFL First-Year Player is designated by a "1" on NFL rosters. Thereafter, a player is credited with an additional year of experience for each season in which he accumulates six games on the Active List or Inactive List, or on Reserve/Injured or Reserve/Physically Unable to Perform.

Log on to www.miamidolphins.com for an up-to-date roster.

COACHING STAFF
Head Coach,
Joe Philbin
Pro Career: Became the ninth coach in Dolphins history on January 20, 2012. Philbin joins Miami after serving as the offensive coordinator with the Green Bay Packers since 2007. Ever since Philbin took over, his offense ranked in the top 10 in points scored and total yards every season. In four seasons at the helm of the Packers' prolific offense, the team scored 1,703 points and committed just 83 turnovers. The turnovers ranked the Packers first in the NFC and second only to New England in the NFL during the four-year span. Philbin joined the Packers in 2003 as an assistant offensive line coach. He served as the tight ends/assistant offensive line coach from 2004-05 and offensive line coach in 2006. Career record: 0-0.
Background: Philbin played one year at Washington & Jefferson, where he earned his degree in sociology. He has coached collegiately at Tulane (1984-85), Worcester Polytechnic Institute (1986-87), Allegheny (1990-93), Ohio (1994), Northeastern (1995-96), Harvard (1997-98) and Iowa (1999-2002).
Personal: Born July 2, 1961 in Springfield, Mass. He and his wife Diane have six children Matthew, John, Kevin, Tim, Colleen and a deceased son, Michael.

ASSISTANT COACHES
Blue Adams, asst. defensive backs; born October 15, 1979, Miami, Fla. Defensive back Cincinnati 1998-2003. Pro defensive back New York Giants/Jacksonville Jaguars 2003, Rhein Fire 2004, Tampa Bay Buccaneers 2005-06, Cincinnati Bengals 2007. College coach: Purdue 2010, Northern Iowa 2011. Pro coach: Joined Dolphins in 2012.
Lou Anarumo, defensive backs; born August 18, 1966, Staten Island, N.Y. Attended Wagner. No college or pro playing experience. College coach: U.S. Merchant Marine Academy 1989-1990, 1992-94, Wagner 1990, Syracuse 1990-91, Harvard 1995-2000, Marshall 2001-03, Purdue 2004-2011. Pro coach: Joined Dolphins in 2012.
Charlie Bullen, defensive assistant; born September 28, 1984, Palatine, Ill. Attended Iowa. No college or pro playing experience. College coach: Iowa 2007-2011. Pro coach: Joined Dolphins in 2012.
Dan Campbell, tight ends; born April 13, 1976, Clifton, Texas. Tight end Texas A&M 1994-98. Pro tight end New York Giants 1999-2002, Dallas Cowboys 2003-05, Detroit Lions 2006-08, New Orleans Saints 2009. Pro coach: Joined Dolphins in 2010.
David Corrao, defensive quality control; born June 11, 1974, Mission Viejo, Calif.

Running back San Diego 1992. No pro playing experience. College coach: Syracuse 2000-03, Northeastern 2004, Mississippi 2005-07. Pro coach: Joined Dolphins in 2008.
Kevin Coyle, defensive coordinator: born January 14, 1956, Staten Island, N.Y. Defensive back Massachusetts 1975-77. No pro playing experience. College coach: Cincinnati 1978-79, Arkansas 1980, U.S. Merchant Marine Academy 1981, Holy Cross 1982-1990, Syracuse 1991-93, Maryland 1994-96, Fresno State 1997-2000. Pro coach: Cincinnati Bengals 2001-2010. Pro coach: Joined Dolphins in 2012.
George Edwards, linebackers: born January 16, 1967, Siler City, N.C. Linebacker Duke 1985-89. No pro playing experience. College coach: Florida 1990-91, Appalachian State 1992-95, Duke 1996, Georgia 1997. Pro coach: Dallas Cowboys 1998-2001, Washington Redskins 2002-03, Cleveland Browns 2004, Miami Dolphins 2005-09, Buffalo Bills 2010-11, re-joined Dolphins in 2012.
Dave Fipp, asst. special teams; born August 8, 1974, Albuquerque, N.M. Safety Arizona 1994-97. No pro playing experience. College coach: Holy Cross 1998-99, Arizona 2000, Cal Poly 2001-03, Nevada 2004, San Jose State 2005-07. Pro coach: San Francisco 49ers 2008-2010, joined Dolphins in 2011.
Ben Johnson, offensive asst., born May 11, 1986, Charleston, S.C. Quarterback North Carolina 2004-08. No pro playing experience. College coach: Boston College 2010-11. Pro coach: Joined Dolphins in 2012.
Darren Krein, head strength & conditioning; born July 7, 1971, Aurora, Colo. Linebacker/defensive end Miami 1989-1993. Pro linebacker San Diego Chargers 1994, Barcelona Dragons (NFLE) 1996. Pro coach: Seattle Seahawks 1997-98, 2002-09, joined Dolphins in 2011.
Phil McGeoghan, asst. wide receivers, July 8, 1979 in Springfield, Mass. Wide receiver Maine 1998-2000. Pro wide receiver Denver 2001. College coach: Maine 2007, Naval Academy Prep 2008, South Florida 2009-2011. Pro coach: Joined Dolphins in 2012.
Chris Mosley, asst. offensive line, born December 5, 1977, Jacksonville, Fla. Running back Southeast Missouri State 1997-98, Washington & Jefferson 1999-2000. College coach: Washington & Jefferson 2004, Akron 2005, Villanova 2006, Boston College 2007, Princeton 2008, St. Aslem 2011 Pro coach: Tampa Bay Buccaneers 2009-10, joined Dolphins in 2012.
Jeff Nixon, special teams quality control; born October 16, 1974, Rochester, Pa. Running back West Virginia 1993-94, Penn State 1996. No pro playing experience. College coach: Penn State 1997, Princeton 1998, Shippensburg 1999-

2002, Tennessee-Chattanooga 2003-05, Temple 2006. Pro coach: Philadelphia Eagles 2007-2010, joined Dolphins in 2011.
Ken O'Keefe, wide receivers; born August 18, 1953, Milford, Conn. No pro playing experience. College coach: New Haven 1976-77, Allegheny 1986-1997, Fordham 1998, Iowa 1999-2011. Pro coach: Joined Dolphins in 2012.
Dave Puloka, asst. strength and conditioning; born January 12, 1979, Arlington, Mass. Linebacker Holy Cross 1997-2000. No pro playing experience. College coach: Stevens Institute of Technology 2005, Virginia 2006. Pro coach: Atlanta Falcons 2007, joined Dolphins in 2008.
Darren Rizzi, special teams coordinator; born July 21, 1970, Hillsdale, N.J. Tight end Rhode Island 1988-1991. College coach: Rhode Island 1992, Colgate 1993, New Haven 1993-97, Northeastern 1998, New Haven 1999-2001 (head coach), Rutgers 2002-07, Rhode Island 2008 (head coach). Pro coach: Joined Dolphins in 2009.
Kacy Rodgers, defensive line; born June 24, 1969, Humboldt, Tenn. Linebacker/defensive end Tennessee 1988-1991. Pro linebacker Shreveport Pirates (CFL) 1994. College coach: Tennessee-Martin 1994-97, Louisiana-Monroe 1998, Middle Tennessee State 1999-2001, Arkansas 2002. Pro coach: Dallas Cowboys 2003-07, joined Dolphins in 2008.
Mike Sherman, offensive coordinator; born December 19, 1954, Norwood, Mass. Defensive end/offensive tackle Central Connecticut State 1974-77. No pro playing experience. College coach: Pittsburgh 1981-82, Tulane 1983-84, Holy Cross 1985-88, Texas A&M 1989-1993, 95-97, 2008-2011 (head coach 2008-2011), UCLA 1994. Pro coach: Green Bay Packers 2000-05 (head coach 2002-05), Houston Texans 2006-07, joined Dolphins in 2012.
Zac Taylor, asst. quarterbacks; born May 10, 1983, Norman Okla. Quarterback Nebraska 2005-06. Pro quarterback Tampa Bay Buccaneers 2007. College coach: Texas A&M 2011. Pro coach: Joined Dolphins in 2012.
Jim Turner, offensive line; born January 15, 1965, Boston, Mass. Fullback 1983-86. No pro playing experience. College coach: Northeastern 1994-98, Louisiana Tech 1999, Harvard 2000-02, Temple 2003-05, Delaware 2005-06, Texas A&M 2008-2011. Pro coach: Joined Dolphins in 2012.

**American Football Conference
East Division
Team Colors:** Blue, Red, Silver, and White
**Gillette Stadium
One Patriot Place
Foxborough, Massachusetts 02035
Telephone:** (508) 543-8200

2012 SCHEDULE
PRESEASON
Aug. 9	**New Orleans**	7:30
Aug. 20	**Philadelphia**	8:00
Aug. 25	at Tampa Bay	7:30
Aug. 29	at New York Giants	7:30

REGULAR SEASON
Sep. 9	at Tennessee	1:00
Sep. 16	**Arizona**	1:00
Sep. 23	at Baltimore	8:20
Sep. 30	at Buffalo	1:00
Oct. 7	**Denver**	4:15
Oct. 14	at Seattle	4:05
Oct. 21	**New York Jets**	4:15
Oct. 28	at St. Louis (London)	1:00
Nov. 4	BYE	
Nov. 11	**Buffalo**	1:00
Nov. 18	**Indianapolis**	1:00
Nov. 22	at New York Jets (Thurs)	8:20
Dec. 2	at Miami	1:00
Dec. 10	**Houston** (Mon)	8:30
Dec. 16	**San Francisco**	*8:20
Dec. 23	at Jacksonville	1:00
Dec. 30	**Miami**	1:00

*All times ET; Sunday night games in
Weeks 11-16 subject to change*
Stadium: Gillette Stadium
(opened in 2002)
• **Capacity:** 68,756
One Patriot Place
Foxborough, Massachusetts 02035
Playing Surface: FieldTurf
Training Camp: Gillette Stadium
Foxborough, MA 02035

GILLETTE STADIUM

CLUB OFFICIALS
Chairman & CEO: Robert K. Kraft
President: Jonathan A. Kraft
President of New England Patriots
 Charitable Foundation: Josh Kraft
Director of Player Development:
 Kevin Anderson
Vice President of Human Resources:
 Robin Boudreau
Chief Operating Officer of TeamOps
 Security: Mark Briggs
Equipment Manager: Don Brocher
Director of Player Personnel:
 Nick Caserio
Vice President of Information
 Technology: Pat Curley
Video Director: Jimmy Dee
Senior Vice President of Marketing and
 Brand Development: Jennifer Ferron
Vice President of Customer Marketing
 and Strategy: Jessica Gelman
Vice President of the Kraft Group:
 Robyn Glaser
Vice President of Media and Community
 Relations: Stacey James
Publisher and Vice President of Content:
 Fred Kirsch
Vice President of Corporate Sales:
 Murray Kohl
Director of Research: Richard Miller
Vice President of Stadium Business
 Development and External Affairs:
 Dan Murphy
Director of Football / Head Coach
 Administration: Berj Najarian
Senior Vice President of Finance,
 Administration and Operation:
 James Nolan
Vice President of Corporate
 Relationships: David Pearlstein
Senior Football Advisor: Floyd Reese
Senior Executive Producer of Broadcast
 Production: Matt Smith
Director of Cheerleaders: Tracy Sormanti
Executive Director of Community Affairs:
 Andre Tippett
Senior Director of Marketing Services
 and Operations: Gail Titus
Head Athletic Trainer: Jim Whalen
Vice President of Food and Beverage:
 David Wheeler
Vice President of Finance: Jim Wilson

COACHING HISTORY
**Boston 1960-1970
(437-381-9)**
Records include postseason games
1960-61	Lou Saban*	7-12-0
1961-68	Mike Holovak	53-47-9
1969-1970	Clive Rush**	5-16-0
1970-72	John Mazur***	9-21-0
1972	Phil Bengtson	1-4-0
1973-78	Chuck Fairbanks****	46-41-0
1978	Hank Bullough-Ron Erhardt#	0-1-0
1979-1981	Ron Erhardt	21-27-0
1982-84	Ron Meyer##	18-16-0
1984-89	Raymond Berry	51-41-0
1990	Rod Rust	1-15-0
1991-92	Dick MacPherson	8-24-0
1993-96	Bill Parcells	34-34-0
1997-99	Pete Carroll	28-23-0
2000-2011	Bill Belichick	155-59-0

*Released after five games in 1961
**Released after seven games in 1970
***Resigned after nine games in 1972
****Suspended for final regular-season game in 1978
#Co-coaches
##Released after eight games in 1984

PAID ATTENDANCE
Home 542,216   Away 552,239
Total 1,094,455
Single-game home record,
 71,768 (11/30/08)
Single-season home record,
 579,182 (2007)

2012 DRAFT CHOICES
Round	Name	Pos.	College
1	Chandler Jones	DE	Syracuse
	Dont'a Hightower	LB	Alabama
2	Tavon Wilson	DB	Illinois
3	Jake Bequette	DE	Arkansas
6	Nate Ebner	DB	Ohio St.
7	Alfonzo Dennard	DB	Nebraska
	Jeremy Ebert	WR	Northwestern

2011 TEAM RECORD
PRESEASON (2-2)

Date	Result	Opponent
8/11	W 47-12	Jacksonville
8/18	W 31-14	at Tampa Bay
8/27	L 10-34	at Detroit
9/1	L 17-18	New York Giants

REGULAR SEASON (13-3)

Date	Result	Opponent
9/12	W 38-24	at Miami
9/18	W 35-21	San Diego
9/25	L 31-34	at Buffalo
10/2	W 31-19	at Oakland
10/9	W 30-21	New York Jets
10/16	W 20-16	Dallas
10/30	L 17-25	at Pittsburgh
11/6	L 20-24	New York Giants
11/13	W 37-16	at New York Jets
11/21	W 34-3	Kansas City
11/27	W 38-20	at Philadelphia
12/4	W 31-24	Indianapolis
12/11	W 34-27	at Washington
12/18	W 41-23	at Denver
12/24	W 27-24	Miami
1/1	W 49-21	Buffalo

POSTSEASON (2-1)

Date	Result	Opponent
1/14	W 45-10	Denver
1/22	W 23-20	Baltimore
2/5	L 17-21	vs. New York Giants at Indianapolis

SCORE BY PERIODS

Patriots	82	148	141	142	0 —	513
Opponents	87	83	50	122	0 —	342

2011 TEAM STATISTICS

	Patriots	Opp.
Total First Downs	399	370
Rushing	107	101
Passing	262	245
Penalty	30	24
3rd Down: Made/Att	89/194	87/202
3rd Down Pct.	45.9	43.1
4th Down: Made/Att	7/11	8/19
4th Down Pct.	63.6	42.1
Possession Avg.	28:47	31:13
Total Net Yards	6848	6577
Avg. Per Game	428.0	411.1
Total Plays	1082	1064
Avg. Per Play	6.3	6.2
Net Yards Rushing	1764	1874
Avg. Per Game	110.3	117.1
Total Rushes	438	405
Net Yards Passing	5084	4703
Avg. Per Game	317.8	293.9
Sacked/Yards Lost	32/173	40/274
Gross Yards	5257	4977
Att./Completions	612/402	619/386
Completion Pct.	65.7	62.4
Had Intercepted	12	23
Punts/Average	57/46.5	67/45.5
Net Punting Avg.	57/41.5	67/39.1
Penalties/Yards	87/815	115/907
Fumbles/Ball Lost	13/5	21/11
Touchdowns	61	40
Rushing	18	13
Passing	39	26
Returns	4	1

2011 INDIVIDUAL STATISTICS

PASSING

	Att.	Comp.	Yds.	Pct.	TD	Int.	Tkld.	Rate
Brady	611	401	5235	65.6	39	12	32/173	105.6
Hoyer	1	1	22	100.0	0	0	0/0	118.8
Patriots	612	402	5257	65.7	39	12	32/173	105.7
Opponents	619	386	4977	62.4	26	23	40/274	86.1

SCORING

	TD R	TD P	TD Rt	PAT	FG	Saf	PTS
Gostkowski	0	0	0	59/59	28/33	0	143
R. Gronkowski	1	17	0	0/0	0/0	0	108
Green-Ellis	11	0	0	0/0	0/0	0	66
Welker	0	9	0	0/0	0/0	0	54
Hernandez	0	7	0	0/0	0/0	0	42
Branch	0	5	0	0/0	0/0	0	30
Brady	3	0	0	0/0	0/0	0	18
Woodhead	1	0	0	0/0	0/0	0	10
Edelman	0	0	1	0/0	0/0	0	6
S. Moore	0	0	1	0/0	0/0	0	6
Ninkovich	0	0	1	0/0	0/0	0	6
Ochocinco	0	1	0	0/0	0/0	0	6
Ridley	1	0	0	0/0	0/0	0	6
Vereen	1	0	0	0/0	0/0	0	6
Wilfork	0	0	1	0/0	0/0	0	6
Patriots	18	39	4	59/59	28/33	0	513
Opponents	13	26	1	38/38	20/23	2	342

2-Pt Conversions: Woodhead 2
Patriots 2-2, Opponents 0-2

RUSHING

	No.	Yds	Avg	LG	TD
Green-Ellis	181	667	3.7	18	11
Ridley	87	441	5.1	33t	1
Woodhead	77	351	4.6	12	1
Brady	43	109	2.5	13	3
Faulk	17	57	3.4	9	0
Vereen	15	57	3.8	19	1
Hernandez	5	45	9.0	19	0
Welker	4	30	7.5	19	0
Edelman	4	8	2.0	6	0
R. Gronkowski	1	2	2.0	2t	1
Hoyer	4	-3	-.8	0	0
Patriots	438	1764	4.0	33t	18
Opponents	405	1874	4.6	41	13

RECEIVING

	No.	Yds	Avg	LG	TD
Welker	122	1569	12.9	99t	9
R. Gronkowski	90	1327	14.7	52t	17
Hernandez	79	910	11.5	46	7
Branch	51	702	13.8	63	5
Woodhead	18	157	8.7	16	0
Ochocinco	15	276	18.4	53	1
Green-Ellis	9	159	17.7	53	0
Faulk	7	34	4.9	18	0
Edelman	4	34	8.5	11	0
Underwood	3	30	10.0	13	0
Ridley	3	13	4.3	8	0
Slater	1	46	46.0	46	0
Patriots	402	5257	13.1	99t	39
Opponents	386	4977	12.9	58	26

PUNTING

	No.	Yds.	Avg.	In 20	LG
Mesko	57	2648	46.5	24	65
Patriots	57	2648	46.5	24	65
Opponents	67	3051	45.5	26	64

INTERCEPTIONS

	No.	Yds	Avg	LG	TD
Arrington	7	92	13.1	28	0
Wilfork	2	47	23.5	28	0
Molden	2	40	20.0	27	0
McCourty	2	38	19.0	38	0
Ninkovich	2	30	15.0	18	1
S. Moore	2	26	13.0	21t	1
Mayo	2	4	2.0	2	0
Guyton	1	17	17.0	17	0
Brown	1	2	2.0	2	0
Adams	1	0	0.0	0	0
Chung	1	0	0.0	0	0
Patriots	23	296	12.9	38	2
Opponents	12	186	15.5	42	1

PUNT RETURNS

	Ret	FC	Yds	Avg	LG	TD
Edelman	28	7	296	10.6	72t	1
Welker	8	6	82	10.3	25	0
Faulk	2	0	11	5.5	7	0
Patriots	38	13	389	10.2	72t	1
Opponents	26	18	220	8.5	26	0

KICKOFF RETURNS

	No.	Yds	Avg	LG	TD
Woodhead	20	437	21.9	37	0
Edelman	12	284	23.7	37	0
Ridley	7	152	21.7	32	0
Slater	4	68	17.0	22	0
R. Gronkowski	1	11	11.0	11	0
McCourty	1	24	24.0	24	0
Ninkovich	1	10	10.0	10	0
Patriots	46	986	21.4	37	0
Opponents	60	1294	21.6	88	0

FIELD GOALS

	1-19	20-29	30-39	40-49	50+
Gostkowski	1/1	12/13	5/6	9/11	1/2
Patriots	1/1	12/13	5/6	9/11	1/2
Opponents	0/0	14/15	2/2	4/6	0/0

SACKS

	No.
Anderson	10.0
A. Carter	10.0
Ninkovich	6.5
Wilfork	3.5
Love	3.0
Deaderick	2.0
Chung	1.0
Ellis	1.0
Mayo	1.0
Warren	1.0
Pryor	0.5
Wright	0.5
Patriots	40.0
Opponents	32.0

RECORD HOLDERS
INDIVIDUAL RECORDS—CAREER

Category	Name	Performance
Rushing (Yds.)	Sam Cunningham, 1973-79, 1981-82	5,453
Passing (Yds.)	Tom Brady, 2000-2011	39,979
Passing (TDs)	Tom Brady, 2000-2011	300
Receiving (No.)	Troy Brown, 1993-2007	557
Receiving (Yds.)	Stanley Morgan, 1977-1989	10,352
Interceptions	Raymond Clayborn, 1977-1989	36
	Ty Law, 1995-2004	36
Punting (Avg.)	Zoltan Mesko, 2010-2011	44.8
Punt Return (Avg.)	Julian Edelman, 2009-2011	12.4
Kickoff Return (Avg.)	Ellis Hobbs, 2005-08	27.7
Field Goals	Adam Vinatieri, 1996-2005	263
Touchdowns (Tot.)	Stanley Morgan, 1977-1989	68
Points	Adam Vinatieri, 1996-2005	1,158
*Sacks	Andre Tippett, 1982-1993	100.0

INDIVIDUAL RECORDS—SINGLE SEASON

Category	Name	Performance
Rushing (Yds.)	Corey Dillon, 2004	1,635
Passing (Yds.)	Tom Brady, 2011	5,235
Passing (TDs)	Tom Brady, 2007	**50
Receiving (No.)	Wes Welker, 2009	123
Receiving (Yds.)	Wes Welker, 2011	1,569
Interceptions	Ron Hall, 1964	11
Punting (Avg.)	Zoltan Mesko, 2011	46.5
Punt Return (Avg.)	Julian Edelman, 2010	15.3
Kickoff Return (Avg.)	Raymond Clayborn, 1977	31.0
Field Goals	Stephen Gostkowski, 2008	36
Touchdowns (Tot.)	Randy Moss, 2007	23
Points	Gino Cappelletti, 1964	155
*Sacks	Andre Tippett, 1984	18.5

INDIVIDUAL RECORDS—SINGLE GAME

Category	Name	Performance
Rushing (Yds.)	Tony Collins, 9-18-83	212
Passing (Yds.)	Tom Brady, 9-12-11	517
Passing (TDs)	Tom Brady, 10-21-07, 10-18-09	6
Receiving (No.)	Troy Brown, 9-22-02	16
	Wes Welker, 9-25-11	16
Receiving (Yds.)	Wes Welker, 9-25-11	217
Interceptions	Many times	3
	Last time by Leigh Bodden 11-22-09	
Field Goals	Gino Cappelletti, 10-4-64	6
Touchdowns (Tot.)	Randy Moss, 11-18-07	4
Points	Gino Cappelletti, 12-18-65	28
*Sacks	Andre Carter, 11-13-11	4.0

*Sacks became an official statistic in 1982.
**NFL Record

2012 VETERAN ROSTER

No.	Name	Pos.	Ht.	Wt.	Birthdate	NFL Exp.	College	Hometown	How Acq.	'11 Games/ Starts
	Addai, Joseph	RB	5-11	214	5/3/83	7	Louisiana State	Houston, Texas	FA-'12	12/11*
48	Aiken, Danny	LS	6-4	252	8/28/88	2	Virginia	Roanoke, Va.	W(Buff)-'11	16/0
26	Allen, Will	CB	5-10	195	8/5/78	11	Syracuse	Syracuse, N.Y.	UFA(Mia)-'12	15/6*
24	Arrington, Kyle	CB	5-10	196	8/12/86	4	Hofstra	Accokeek, Md.	FA-'09	16/14
30	Barrett, Josh	S	6-2	225	11/22/84	5	Arizona State	Reno, Nev.	W(Den)-'10	5/4
97	Brace, Ron	DL	6-3	330	12/18/86	4	Boston College	Worcester, Mass.	D2b-'09	7/0
12	Brady, Tom	QB	6-4	225	8/3/77	13	Michigan	San Mateo, Calif.	D6b-'00	16/16
84	Branch, Deion	WR	5-9	195	7/18/79	11	Louisville	Albany, Ga.	T(Sea)-'10	15/15
31	Brown, Sergio	S	6-2	210	5/22/88	3	Notre Dame	Maywood, Ill.	FA-'10	15/3
61	Cannon, Marcus	OL	6-5	358	5/6/88	2	Texas Christian	Odessa, Texas	D5a-'11	7/0
59	Carpenter, Bobby	LB	6-2	249	8/1/83	7	Ohio State	Lancaster, Ohio	UFA(Det)-'12	16/3*
93	#Carter, Andre	DE	6-4	255	5/12/79	12	California	San Jose, Calif.	FA-'11	14/14
25	Chung, Patrick	S	5-11	212	8/19/87	4	Oregon	Rancho Cucamonga, Calif.	D2a-'09	8/8
23	Cole, Marquice	CB	5-10	192	11/13/83	4	Northwestern	Hazel Crest, Ill.	FA-'12	14/0*
63	Connolly, Dan	OL	6-4	313	9/2/82	7	Southeast Missouri St.	St. Louis, Mo.	FA-'08	13/11
96	Cunningham, Jermaine	LB	6-3	260	4/24/88	3	Florida	Stone Mountain, Ga.	D2b-'10	9/0
71	Deaderick, Brandon	DL	6-4	305	8/19/87	3	Alabama	Elizabethtown, Ky.	D7b-'10	10/5
21	Dowling, Ras-I	CB	6-1	198	5/9/88	2	Virginia	Chesapeake, Va.	D2a-'11	2/2
11	Edelman, Julian	WR	5-10	198	5/22/86	4	Kent State	Redwood City, Calif.	D7a-'09	13/0
94	#Ellis, Shaun	DE	6-5	290	6/24/77	13	Tennessee	Anderson, S.C.	UFA(NYJ)-'11	14/10
98	Fanene, Jonathan	DE	6-4	285	3/19/82	8	Utah	Pago Pago, Amer. Samoa	UFA(Cin)-'12	16/2*
33	#Faulk, Kevin	RB	5-8	202	6/5/76	14	Louisiana State	Carencro, La.	D2-'99	7/3
86	Fells, Daniel	TE	6-4	252	9/23/83	6	UC Davis	Fullerton, Calif.	UFA(Den)-'12	16/15*
42	Fiammetta, Tony	FB	6-0	242	8/22/86	4	Syracuse	Walkersville, Md.	FA-'12	10/6*
52	Fletcher, Dane	LB	6-2	244	9/14/86	3	Montana State	Bozeman, Mont.	FA-'10	10/5
10	Gaffney, Jabar	WR	6-2	200	12/1/80	11	Florida	Jacksonville, Fla.	FA-'12	16/15*
72	Gallery, Robert	OL	6-7	325	7/26/80	9	Iowa	Winthrop, Iowa	FA-'12	12/12*
16	Gonzalez, Anthony	WR	6-0	193	9/18/84	6	Ohio State	Cleveland, Ohio	UFA(Ind)-'12	8/0*
3	Gostkowski, Stephen	K	6-1	215	1/28/84	7	Memphis	Madison, Miss.	D4b-'06	16/0
28	Gregory, Steve	S	5-11	195	1/8/83	7	Syracuse	Staten Island, N.Y.	UFA(SD)-'12	15/13*
87	Gronkowski, Rob	TE	6-6	265	5/14/89	3	Arizona State	Pittsburgh, Pa.	D2a-'10	16/16
94	Harrison, Marcus	DL	6-3	316	7/10/84	4	Arkansas	Little Rock, Ark.	FA-'11	0*
81	Hernandez, Aaron	TE	6-1	245	11/6/89	3	Florida	Bristol, Conn.	D4-'10	14/12
69	Hix, Kyle	OL	6-7	325	9/23/88	2	Texas	Aledo, Texas	FA-'11	0*
8	Hoyer, Brian	QB	6-2	215	10/13/85	4	Michigan State	North Olmsted, Ohio	FA-'09	3/0
44	#Ihedigbo, James	S	6-1	215	12/3/83	6	Massachusetts	Northampton, Mass.	UFA(NYJ)-'11	16/12
23	#Jones, Nate	DB	5-10	185	6/15/82	9	Rutgers	Scotch Plains, N.J.	FA-'11	7/1*
68	Kopa, Matt	OL	6-6	303	2/25/87	2	Stanford	Elk Grove, Calif.	FA-'11	0*
67	Koppen, Dan	C	6-2	296	9/12/79	10	Boston College	Whitehall, Pa.	D5-'03	1/1
90	Koutouvides, Niko	LB	6-2	238	3/25/81	9	Purdue	New Britain, Conn.	FA-'11	8/1
46	Larsen, Spencer	FB	6-2	243	3/4/84	5	Arizona	Gilbert, Ariz.	UFA(Den)-'12	16/6*
88	Lloyd, Brandon	WR	6-0	188	7/5/81	10	Illinois	Blue Springs, Mo.	UFA(StL)-'12	15/14*
74	Love, Kyle	DL	6-1	310	11/18/86	3	Mississippi State	Fairburn, Ga.	FA-'10	16/13
15	Mallett, Ryan	QB	6-6	238	6/5/88	2	Arkansas	Texarkana, Texas	D3b-'11	0*
70	Mankins, Logan	G	6-4	310	3/10/82	8	Fresno State	Catheys Valley, Calif.	D1-'05	15/15
51	Mayo, Jerod	LB	6-1	245	2/23/86	5	Tennessee	Hampton, Va.	D1-'08	14/13
32	McCourty, Devin	CB	5-10	193	8/13/87	3	Rutgers	Montvale, N.J.	D1-'10	14/14
65	McDonald, Nick	OL	6-4	316	6/27/87	3	Grand Valley State	Sterling Heights, Mich.	FA-'11	4/2
14	Mesko, Zoltan	P	6-5	231	3/16/86	3	Michigan	Twinsburg, Ohio	D5-'10	16/0
29	Moore, Sterling	DB	5-10	205	2/3/90	2	Southern Methodist	Antioch, Calif.	FA-'11	6/3
50	Ninkovich, Rob	LB	6-2	255	2/1/84	7	Purdue	Blue Island, Ill.	FA-'09	16/16
85	Ochocinco, Chad	WR	6-1	192	1/9/78	12	Oregon State	Miami, Fla.	T(Cin)-'11	15/3
91	Pryor, Myron	DL	6-1	310	6/13/86	4	Kentucky	Louisville, Ky.	D6b-'09	2/0
22	Ridley, Stevan	RB	5-11	225	1/27/89	2	Louisiana State	Natchez, Miss.	D3a-'11	16/2
99	Scott, Trevor	LB	6-5	255	8/30/84	5	Buffalo	Potsdam, N.Y.	UFA(Oak)-'12	16/0*
18	Slater, Matthew	WR	6-0	200	9/9/85	5	UCLA	Anaheim, Calif.	D5-'08	16/3
77	Solder, Nate	T	6-8	319	4/12/88	2	Colorado	Buena Vista, Colo.	D1-'11	16/13
55	Spikes, Brandon	LB	6-2	250	9/3/87	3	Florida	Shelby, N.C.	D2c-'10	8/6
19	Stallworth, Donte'	WR	6-0	220	11/10/80	10	Tennessee	Sacramento, Calif.	UFA(Wash)-'12	11/0*
53	Tarpinian, Jeff	LB	6-3	238	10/16/87	2	Iowa	Omaha, Neb.	FA-'11	7/1
64	Thomas, Donald	OL	6-4	310	9/25/85	5	Connecticut	New Haven, Conn.	FA-'11	10/1
35	Ventrone, Ross	DB	5-8	190	9/27/86	2	Villanova	Pittsburgh, Pa.	FA-'10	8/0
34	Vereen, Shane	RB	5-9	205	5/9/89	2	California	Valencia, Calif.	D2b-'11	5/0
76	Vollmer, Sebastian	OL	6-8	315	7/10/84	4	Houston	Kaarst, Germany	D2d-'09	6/5
92	Warren, Gerard	DL	6-4	325	7/25/78	12	Florida	Lake Butler, Fla.	FA-'10	12/0
54	Waters, Brian	G	6-3	320	2/18/77	13	North Texas	Waxahachie, Texas	FA-'11	16/16
83	Welker, Wes	WR	5-9	185	5/1/81	9	Texas Tech	Oklahoma City, Okla.	T(Mia)-'07	16/15

2012 VETERAN ROSTER CONTINUED

No.	Name	Pos.	Ht.	Wt.	Birthdate	NFL Exp.	College	Hometown	How Acq.	'11 Games/ Starts
62	Wendell, Ryan	OL	6-2	290	3/4/86	4	Fresno State	Diamond Bar, Calif.	FA-'08	14/3
58	White, Tracy	LB	6-0	230	4/14/81	10	Howard	St. Stephen, S.C.	T(Phil)-'10	15/1
75	Wilfork, Vince	NT	6-2	325	11/4/81	9	Miami	Boynton Beach, Fla.	D1a-'04	16/16
41	Williams, Malcolm	DB	5-11	200	11/22/87	2	Texas Christian	Grand Prairie, Texas	D7-'11	2/0
39	Woodhead, Danny	RB	5-8	195	1/25/85	5	Chadron State	North Platte, Neb.	FA-'10	15/3

*   Addai played 12 games with Indianapolis in '11; Allen played 15 games with Miami; Carpenter played 16 games with Detroit; Cole played 14 games with New York Jets; Fanene played 16 games with Cincinnati; Fells played 16 games with Denver; Fiammetta played 10 games with Dallas; Gaffney played 16 games with Washington; Gallery played 12 games with Seattle; Gonzalez played 8 games with Indianapolis; Gregory played 15 games with San Diego; Harrison last active with Chicago in '10; Hix missed '11 season because of injury; Jones played 2 games with Miami and 5 games with New England; Kopa last active with Miami in '10; Larsen played 16 games with Denver; Lloyd played 4 games with Denver and 11 games with St. Louis; Mallett did not play in 1 game and inactive for 15 games; Scott played 16 games with Oakland; Stallworth played 11 games with Washington.

\#   Unrestricted free agent; subject to developments.

Retired—T Matt Light, 11-year veteran, 15 games in '11.

Players lost through free agency (4): DL Mark Anderson (Buff; 16 games), RB BenJarvus Green-Ellis (Cin; 15), LB Gary Guyton (Mia; 16), CB Antwaun Molden (NYG; 16).

Also played with Patriots in '11—DB Phillip Adams (6 games), CB Leigh Bodden (5), DL Landon Cohen (1), LB A.J. Edds (2), TE Dan Gronkowski (5), DL Albert Haynesworth (6), DL Eric Moore (2), FB Lousaka Polite (1), WR Taylor Price (3), WR Tiquan Underwood (6), OL Thomas Welch (3), DE Mike Wright (1).

FIRST-YEAR ROSTER

Name	Pos.	Ht.	Wt.	Birthdate	College	Hometown	How Acq.
Bequette, Jake	DE	6-4	264	2/21/89	Arkansas	Little Rock, Ark.	D3
Bolden, Brandon	RB	5-11	215	1/26/90	Mississippi	Baton Rouge, La.	FA
Carter, Markell (1)	LB	6-4	248	12/21/89	Central Arkansas	Bartlesville, Okla.	D6-'11
Davis, Britt (1)	WR	6-3	205	4/23/86	Northern Illinois	Broadview, Ill.	FA-'11
Dennard, Alfonzo	DB	5-10	205	9/9/89	Nebraska	Rochelle, Ga.	D7a
Ebert, Jeremy	WR	6-0	195	4/6/89	Northwestern	Hilliard, Ohio	D7b
Ebner, Nate	DB	6-0	205	12/14/88	Ohio State	Dublin, Ohio	D6
Forston, Marcus	DL	6-3	300	9/28/89	Miami	Miami, Fla.	FA
Francis, Justin	DE	6-4	275	2/8/89	Rutgers	Opa-Locke, Fla.	FA
Herman, Brad	TE	6-5	255	12/29/89	Iowa	Metamora, Ill.	FA
Hightower, Dont'a	LB	6-3	262	3/12/90	Alabama	Lewisburg, Tenn.	D1b
Jones, Chandler	DE	6-5	265	2/27/90	Syracuse	Endicott, N.Y.	D1a
Kettani, Eric (1)	RB	5-11	235	3/26/87	Navy	Kirtland, Ohio	FA
Koepplin, Chris (1)	K	6-3	210	10/11/85	Massachusetts	Manhasset, N.Y.	FA
Lavarias, Aaron (1)	DE	6-3	248	4/27/88	Idaho	Woodinville, Wash.	FA-'11
Rivera, Mike (1)	LB	6-2	252	1/10/86	Kansas	Shawnee Mission, Kan.	FA-'11
Roark, Matt	WR	6-5	214	10/20/89	Kentucky	Acworth, Ga.	FA
Silvestro, Alex (1)	DE	6-3	287	11/15/88	Rutgers	Gibbstown, N.J.	FA-'11
Warren, Jeremiah	OL	6-4	329	9/20/87	South Florida	Panama City, Fla.	FA
White, Shun (1)	WR	5-8	195	12/9/85	Navy	Memphis, Tenn.	FA-'09
Wilson, Tavon	DB	6-0	205	3/19/90	Illinois	Washington, D.C.	D2
Zusevics, Markus	T	6-5	300	4/25/89	Iowa	Arlington Heights, Ill.	FA

The term NFL Rookie is defined as a player who is in his first season of professional football and has not been on the roster of another professional football team for any regular-season or postseason games. A Rookie is designated by an "R" on NFL rosters. Players who have been active in another professional football league or players who have NFL experience, including either preseason training camp or being on an Active List or Inactive List, or on Reserve/Injured or Reserve/Physically Unable to Perform for fewer than six regular-season games, are termed NFL First-Year Players. An NFL First-Year Player is designated by a "1" on NFL rosters. Thereafter, a player is credited with an additional year of experience for each season in which he accumulates six games on the Active List or Inactive List, or on Reserve/Injured or Reserve/Physically Unable to Perform.

Log on to www.patriots.com for an up-to-date roster.

COACHING STAFF

Head Coach,
Bill Belichick

Pro Career: Bill Belichick is in his 38th season as an NFL coach and is the only head coach in NFL history to win three Super Bowl titles in a four-year span. He has won more regular-season games (123) and more games overall (136) during a 10-year stretch (2002-2011) than any other head coach in NFL history over any decade. Belichick leads all active head coaches and is currently ranked 9th on the NFL's all-time list with 192 total victories. Hired by Chairman and CEO Robert Kraft on January 27, 2000, Belichick is in his 13th season as New England's head coach. Through 12 seasons, Belichick has delivered three Super Bowl championships, five conference titles, nine division crowns and 16 playoff victories, while posting an overall record of 155-59. Belichick directed the Patriots to victories in Super Bowls XXXVI (2001), XXXVIII (2003) and XXXIX (2004), and in 2007 he became the first NFL head coach to guide his team to a 16-0 regular season. Only one coach (Pittsburgh's Chuck Noll, 4) has won more Super Bowls than Belichick, and his three Super Bowl titles tie Washington's Joe Gibbs and San Francisco's Bill Walsh for second place on the NFL's all-time list. Belichick has led the Patriots to a winning record in each of the last 11 seasons. The only other NFL coach to have 10 consecutive winning seasons with one team since the 1970 merger was Tom Landry, who led the Dallas Cowboys to 16 consecutive winning seasons (1970-1985). In 2011, Belichick guided the Patriots to a 13-3 record and his fifth AFC Conference Championship. Belichick is the only head coach in NFL history to win at least 13 regular-season games in five separate seasons. Belichick's Patriots teams own the all-time NFL records for consecutive victories, including the postseason (21 from 2003-04) and consecutive playoff victories (10 from 2001-05). Belichick's 17 postseason wins are tied with Joe Gibbs for third all-time, behind Tom Landry (20) and Don Shula (19). Over a 100-game span from 2003-08, he directed the Patriots to an 82-18 record – the best record for any 100-game span in NFL history. Belichick (.649) has the third highest winning percentage among coaches with at least 150 wins, trailing only Hall of Famers George Halas (.682) and Don Shula (.666). Belichick's recent accomplishments are the latest triumphs in a career during which he has helped produce five Super Bowl titles, eight conference championships and 16 division titles since entering the NFL in 1975. He won his first two Super Bowls as the defensive coordinator for the New York Giants in 1986 and 1990 before claiming three Super Bowl championships with the Patriots. George Seifert is the only other man to have won multiple Super Bowls both as a head coach and as an assistant coach. Belichick launched his coaching career in 1975 with the Baltimore Colts and continued as an assistant coach with Detroit (1976-77), Denver (1978) and the New York Giants (1979-1990). Belichick was named head coach of the Cleveland Browns in 1991, becoming the youngest head coach in the NFL at age 38. By 1994, Belichick brought the Browns back to the playoffs, finishing 11-5 and advancing to the second round of the playoffs, while allowing a league-low 204 total points. In 1996, Belichick joined New England and was a key contributor to the Patriots first division title in 10 years en route to the Patriots' appearance in Super Bowl XXXI. Belichick then spent three seasons with the New York Jets from 1997 to 1999, helping New York improve from a 1-15 season in 1996 to an appearance in the AFC Championship Game in 1998. Career record: 192-104.

Background: Belichick was a center/tight end at Wesleyan 1971-74.

Personal: Born April 16, 1952, Nashville, Tenn.

ASSISTANT COACHES

Josh Boyer, cornerbacks; born January 21, 1977, Heath, Ohio. Wide receiver/defensive back Muskingum College 1996-99. No pro playing experience. College coach: King's College (Pa.) 2000, Dayton 2001, Kent State 2002-03, Bryant University 2004, South Dakota School of Mines and Technology 2005. Pro coach: Joined Patriots in 2006.

Moses Cabrera, asst. strength and conditioning; born August 20, 1978, Deming, N.M. Oral Roberts 1996-2000. No pro playing experience. College coach: Fresno State 2004-09, Colorado 2010. Pro coach: Joined Patriots in 2010.

Ivan Fears, running backs; born November 15, 1954, Portsmouth, Va. Running back William & Mary 1973-75. No pro playing experience. College coach: William & Mary 1977-79, Syracuse 1980-1990. Pro coach: New England Patriots 1991-92, Chicago Bears 1993-98, re-joined Patriots in 1999.

Brian Flores, safeties; born February 24, 1981, Brooklyn, N.Y. Linebacker Boston College 1999-2003. No pro playing experience. Pro coach: Joined Patriots in 2008.

George Godsey, tight ends; born January 1, 1979, Tampa, Fla. Quarterback Georgia Tech 1998-2001. Pro quarterback Tampa Bay Storm (AFL) 2003. College coach: Central Florida 2004-2010. Pro coach: Joined Patriots in 2011.

Patrick Graham, defensive line; born January 24, 1979, Des Plaines, Ill. Defensive line Yale 1997-2001. College coach: Wagner College 2002-03, Richmond 2004-06, Notre Dame 2007-08. Pro coach: Joined Patriots in 2009.

Pepper Johnson, linebackers; born July 29, 1964, Detroit, Mich. Linebacker Ohio State 1982-85. Pro linebacker New York Giants 1986-1992, Cleveland Browns 1993-95, Detroit Lions 1996, New York Jets 1997-98. Pro coach: Joined Patriots in 2001.

Joe Judge, special teams assistant; born December 31, 1981, Philadelphia, Pa. Running back Mississippi State 2000-04. No pro playing experience. College coach: 2005-07 Mississippi State, Birmingham-Southern 2008, Alabama 2009-11. Pro coach: Joined Patriots in 2011.

Josh McDaniels, offensive coordinator/quarterbacks; born April 22, 1976, Canton, Ohio. No pro playing experience. College coach: Michigan State 1999-2000. Pro coach: New England Patriots 2001-2008, Denver Broncos, 2009-2010 (head coach), St. Louis Rams 2011, re-joined Patriots in 2012.

Harold Nash, strength and conditioning; born May 5, 1970, New Orleans, La. Defensive back Louisiana-Lafayette 1988-1993. Pro defensive back Shreveport Pirates (CFL) 1994-95, Montreal Alouettes (CFL) 1996-99, Winnipeg Blue Bombers (CFL) 1999-2003, Edmonton Eskimos (CFL) 2004. Pro coach: Joined Patriots in 2005.

Scott O'Brien, special teams; born June 25, 1957, Superior, Wisc. Linebacker Wisconsin-Superior 1975-78. No pro playing experience. College coach: Wisconsin-Superior 1980-82, Nevada-Las Vegas 1983-85, Rice 1986, Pittsburgh 1987-1990. Pro coach: Cleveland Browns 1991-95, Baltimore Ravens 1996-98, Carolina Panthers 1999-2004, Miami Dolphins 2005-06, Denver Broncos 2007-08, joined Patriots in 2009.

Chad O'Shea, receivers; born December 18, 1972, Houston, Texas. Quarterback Marshall 1991-93, Houston 1994-95. No pro playing experience. College coach: Houston 1996-99, Southern Mississippi 2000-02. Pro coach: Kansas City Chiefs 2003-05, Minnesota Vikings 2006-08, joined Patriots in 2009.

Matt Patricia, defensive coordinator; born September 13, 1974, Sherrill, N.Y. Center-guard Rensselaer 1992-96. No pro playing experience. College coach: Rensselaer 1996, Amherst 1999-2000, Syracuse 2001-03. Pro coach: Joined Patriots in 2004.

Dante Scarnecchia, asst. head coach/offensive line; born February 15, 1948, Los Angeles, Calif. Center/guard California Western 1968-1970. No pro playing experience. College coach: California Western 1970-72, Iowa State 1973-74, Southern Methodist 1975-76, Pacific 1977-78, Northern Arizona 1979, Southern Methodist 1980-81. Pro coach: New England Patriots 1982-88, Indianapolis Colts 1989-1990, re-joined Patriots in 1991.

**American Football Conference
East Division**
Team Colors: Green and White
1 Jets Drive
Florham Park, New Jersey 07932
Telephone (973) 549-4800

2012 SCHEDULE
PRESEASON
Aug. 10 at Cincinnati 7:30
Aug. 18 **New York Giants** 7:00
Aug. 26 **Carolina** 8:00
Aug. 30 at Philadelphia 6:35

REGULAR SEASON
Sep. 9 **Buffalo** 1:00
Sep. 16 at Pittsburgh 4:15
Sep. 23 at Miami 1:00
Sep. 30 **San Francisco** 1:00
Oct. 8 **Houston** (Mon) 8:30
Oct. 14 **Indianapolis** 1:00
Oct. 21 at New England 4:15
Oct. 28 **Miami** 1:00
Nov. 4 BYE
Nov. 11 at Seattle 4:05
Nov. 18 at St. Louis 1:00
Nov. 22 **New England** (Thurs) 8:20
Dec. 2 **Arizona** 1:00
Dec. 9 at Jacksonville 1:00
Dec. 17 at Tennessee (Mon) 8:30
Dec. 23 **San Diego** *8:20
Dec. 30 at Buffalo 1:00
*All times ET; Sunday night games in
  Weeks 11-16 subject to change
Stadium: MetLife Stadium
        (opened in 2010)
        •**Capacity:** 82,500
        East Rutherford, New Jersey
        07073
Playing Surface: FieldTurf
Training Camp: SUNY Cortland
        Cortland, New York 13045

METLIFE STADIUM

CLUB OFFICIALS
Chairman and CEO:
  Robert Wood Johnson IV
Team President: Neil Glat
Executive V.P./ General Manager:
  Mike Tannenbaum
Assistant G.M.: Scott Cohen
S.V.P., Programming and Media
  Production: Bob Parente
S.V.P., Corporate Sales: Marc Riccio
S.V.P., Consumer Sales and Services:
  Rob Sullivan
Chief Financial Officer: Brian Friedman
Senior Counsel, Business and Legal
  Affairs: Hymie Elhai
V.P., IT: Tom Murphy
V.P., Security: Steve Yarnell
Senior Personnel Executive:
  Terry Bradway
Assistant Director, Player Personnel:
  JoJo Wooden
Director, Pro Personnel: Brendan Prophett
Pro Scout: Cole Hufnagel
Assistant Director, College Scouting:
  Michael Davis
Coordinator, College Scouting:
  Dan Zbojovsky
Personnel Scouts: Jeff Bauer,
  Matt Bazirgan, Joe Bommarito,
  Jay Mandolesi, Brock Sunderland
Assistant, Pro Personnel: Greg Nejmeh
Assistant, Player Personnel:
  Kathryn Smith
Director, Football Administration:
  Ari Nissim
Manager, Football Administration:
  Jacqueline Davidson
Senior Director, Athletic Training:
  John Mellody
Assistant Athletic Trainers: Josh Koch,
  Dave Zuffelato
Senior Director, Marketing and Business
  Development: Bob Brennfleck
Senior Director, New Business
  Development: Jeff Fernandez
Senior Director, Multimedia & Production:
  Rich Gentile
Senior Director, Football Operations:
  Clay Hampton
Senior Director, Ticket Operations:
  Jeff Hecker
Senior Director, Corporate Partnerships:
  Jennifer Linn
Senior Director, Facilities Security:
  Robert Mastroddi
Senior Director, Events & Game
  Operations: Brian Mulligan
Senior Director, Merchandise and
  Concessions: Chris Pierce
Senior Director, Media Relations:
  Bruce Speight
Director, Equipment: Gus Granneman
Manager, Equipment: Vito Contento
Assistant Manager, Equipment:
  Jim Gallione
Assistant, Equipment: Brendan Burger
Director, Community Relations:
  Jesse Linder
Director, Player Development: David Szott
Director, Video: Tim Tubito

COACHING HISTORY
**New York Titans 1960-62
(371-434-8)**
Records include postseason games
1960-61   Sammy Baugh 14-14-0
1962   Clyde (Bulldog) Turner 5-9-0
1963-1973 Weeb Ewbank 73-78-6
1974-75   Charley Winner* 9-14-0
1975   Ken Shipp 1-4-0
1976   Lou Holtz** 3-10-0
1976   Mike Holovak 0-1-0
1977-1982 Walt Michaels 41-49-1
1983-89   Joe Walton 54-59-1
1990-93   Bruce Coslet...............26-39-0
1994   Pete Carroll 6-10-0
1995-96   Rich Kotite 4-28-0
1997-99   Bill Parcells 30-20-0
2000   Al Groh 9-7-0
2001-05   Herman Edwards 41-44-0
2006-08   Eric Mangini 23-26-0
2009-2011 Rex Ryan 32-22-0
  *Released after nine games in 1975
  **Resigned after 13 games in 1976

PAID ATTENDANCE
Home 607,086   Away 542,637
Total 1,149,723
Single-game home record,
  79,572 (11/19/06)
Single-season home record,
  628,773 (2002)

2012 DRAFT CHOICES
Round	Name	Pos.	College
1	Quinton Coples	DE	North Carolina
2	Stephen Hill	WR	Georgia Tech
3	Demario Davis	LB	Arkansas St.
6	Josh Bush	DB	Wake Forest
	Terrance Ganaway	RB	Baylor
	Robert Griffin	G	Baylor
7	Antonio Allen	DB	South Carolina
	Jordan White	WR	Western Michigan

NEW YORK JETS

2011 TEAM RECORD

PRESEASON (2-2)

Date	Result	Opponent
8/15	L 16-20	at Houston
8/21	W 27-7	Cincinnati
8/27	W 17-3	at New York Giants
9/1	L 14-24	Philadelphia

REGULAR SEASON (8-8)

Date	Result	Opponent
9/11	W 27-24	Dallas
9/18	W 32-3	Jacksonville
9/25	L 24-34	at Oakland
10/2	L 17-34	at Baltimore
10/9	L 21-30	at New England
10/17	W 24-6	Miami
10/23	W 27-21	San Diego
11/6	W 27-11	at Buffalo
11/13	L 16-37	New England
11/17	L 13-17	at Denver
11/27	W 28-24	Buffalo
12/4	W 34-19	at Washington
12/11	W 37-10	Kansas City
12/18	L 19-45	at Philadelphia
12/24	L 14-29	New York Giants
1/1	L 17-19	at Miami

SCORE BY PERIODS

Jets	61	123	75	118	0	—	377
Opponents	94	90	79	100	0	—	363

2011 TEAM STATISTICS

	Jets	Opp.
Total First Downs	301	272
Rushing	92	83
Passing	173	167
Penalty	36	22
3rd Down: Made/Att	74/213	69/211
3rd Down Pct.	34.7	32.7
4th Down: Made/Att	4/11	1/10
4th Down Pct.	36.4	10.0
Possession Avg.	30:49	29:11
Total Net Yards	4989	4993
Avg. Per Game	311.8	312.1
Total Plays	1030	993
Avg. Per Play	4.8	5.0
Net Yards Rushing	1692	1777
Avg. Per Game	105.8	111.1
Total Rushes	443	451
Net Yards Passing	3297	3216
Avg. Per Game	206.1	201.0
Sacked/Yards Lost	40/245	35/198
Gross Yards	3542	3414
Att./Completions	547/310	507/275
Completion Pct.	56.7	54.2
Had Intercepted	18	19
Punts/Average	92/42.7	92/45.0
Net Punting Avg.	92/38.8	92/38.2
Penalties/Yards	102/849	110/966
Fumbles/Ball Lost	25/16	25/12
Touchdowns	45	39
Rushing	14	17
Passing	26	15
Returns	5	7

2011 INDIVIDUAL STATISTICS

PASSING

	Att.	Comp.	Yds.	Pct.	TD	Int.	Tkld.	Rate
Sanchez	543	308	3474	56.7	26	18	39/243	78.2
Brunell	3	1	27	33.3	0	0	0/0	67.4
Kerley	1	1	41	100.0	0	0	0/0	118.8
Tomlinson	0	0	0	—	0	0	1/2	—
Jets	547	310	3542	56.7	26	18	40/245	78.4
Opponents	507	275	3414	54.2	15	19	35/198	69.6

SCORING

	TD R	TD P	TD Rt	PAT	FG	Saf	PTS
Folk	0	0	0	44/44	19/25	0	101
Burress	0	8	0	0/0	0/0	0	48
Holmes	0	8	0	0/0	0/0	0	48
Greene	6	0	0	0/0	0/0	0	36
Sanchez	6	0	0	0/0	0/0	0	36
Keller	0	5	0	0/0	0/0	0	30
Tomlinson	1	2	0	0/0	0/0	0	18
Baker	0	1	0	0/0	0/0	0	6
Conner	1	0	0	0/0	0/0	0	6
Harris	0	0	1	0/0	0/0	0	6
Kerley	0	1	0	0/0	0/0	0	6
J. McKnight	0	0	1	0/0	0/0	0	6
Revis	0	0	1	0/0	0/0	0	6
Slauson	0	0	1	0/0	0/0	0	6
Trufant	0	0	1	0/0	0/0	0	6
P. Turner	0	1	0	0/0	0/0	0	6
Pouha	0	0	0	0/0	0/0	1	2
Wilkerson	0	0	0	0/0	0/0	1	2
Jets	14	26	5	44/44	19/25	2	377
Opponents	17	15	7	38/38	29/30	1	363

2-Pt Conversions: Team 0-1, Opponents 1-1

RUSHING

	No.	Yds	Avg	LG	TD
Greene	253	1054	4.2	31	6
Tomlinson	75	280	3.7	20	1
J. McKnight	43	134	3.1	11	0
Sanchez	37	103	2.8	25	6
Conner	13	44	3.4	13	1
Kerley	5	28	5.6	16	0
Holmes	3	27	9.0	23	0
Powell	13	21	1.6	6	0
Cromartie	1	1	1.0	1	0
Jets	443	1692	3.8	31	14
Opponents	451	1777	3.9	70t	17

RECEIVING

	No.	Yds	Avg	LG	TD
Keller	65	815	12.5	41	5
Holmes	51	654	12.8	38t	8
Burress	45	612	13.6	30	8
Tomlinson	42	449	10.7	74	2
Greene	30	211	7.0	36	0
Kerley	29	314	10.8	38	1
J. McKnight	13	139	10.7	27	0
Mason	13	115	8.8	30	0
P. Turner	8	96	12.0	25	1
Mulligan	5	58	11.6	41	0
Baker	3	27	9.0	17	1
Cumberland	2	35	17.5	33	0
Conner	2	9	4.5	9	0
Powell	1	7	7.0	7	0
Slauson	1	1	1.0	1	0
Jets	310	3542	11.4	74	26
Opponents	275	3414	12.4	99t	15

PUNTING

	No.	Yds.	Avg.	In 20	LG
Conley	92	3926	42.7	32	63
Jets	92	3926	42.7	32	63
Opponents	92	4141	45.0	34	67

INTERCEPTIONS

	No.	Yds	Avg	LG	TD
Revis	4	184	46.0	100t	1
Cromartie	4	105	26.3	42	0
Harris	4	55	13.8	35t	1
K. Wilson	2	13	6.5	10	0
Mauga	1	11	11.0	11	0
Pace	1	8	8.0	8	0
Smith	1	2	2.0	2	0
Leonhard	1	0	0.0	0	0
Pool	1	0	0.0	0	0
Jets	19	378	19.9	100t	2
Opponents	18	382	21.2	73t	3

PUNT RETURNS

	Ret	FC	Yds	Avg	LG	TD
Kerley	29	16	317	10.9	53	0
Leonhard	9	5	83	9.2	15	0
J. McKnight	5	0	26	5.2	12	0
Cromartie	1	0	0	0.0	0	0
Jets	44	21	426	9.7	53	0
Opponents	32	31	241	7.5	25	0

KICKOFF RETURNS

	No.	Yds	Avg	LG	TD
J. McKnight	34	1073	31.6	107t	1
Cromartie	17	417	24.5	46	0
Baker	3	60	20.0	29	0
Conner	2	29	14.5	18	0
Kerley	1	15	15.0	15	0
McIntyre	1	0	0.0	0	0
Mulligan	1	20	20.0	20	0
Revis	1	3	3.0	3	0
P. Turner	1	-1	-1.0	-1	0
K. Wilson	1	17	17.0	17	0
Jets	62	1633	26.3	107t	1
Opponents	61	1291	21.2	67	0

FIELD GOALS

	1-19	20-29	30-39	40-49	50+
Folk	0/0	5/6	6/6	5/7	3/6
Jets	0/0	5/6	6/6	5/7	3/6
Opponents	0/0	9/9	7/7	7/7	6/7

SACKS

	No.
Maybin	6.0
Harris	5.0
Pace	4.5
Scott	4.5
Westerman	3.5
Wilkerson	3.0
Smith	2.5
Dixon	1.5
DeVito	1.0
Pitoitua	1.0
Pouha	1.0
Strickland	1.0
Pool	0.5
Jets	35.0
Opponents	40.0

RECORD HOLDERS
INDIVIDUAL RECORDS—CAREER

Category	Name	Performance
Rushing (Yds.)	Curtis Martin, 1998-2005	10,302
Passing (Yds.)	Joe Namath, 1965-1976	27,057
Passing (TDs)	Joe Namath, 1965-1976	170
Receiving (No.)	Don Maynard, 1960-1972	627
Receiving (Yds.)	Don Maynard, 1960-1972	11,732
Interceptions	Bill Baird, 1963-69	34
Punting (Avg.)	Ben Graham, 2005-08	43.7
Punt Return (Avg.)	Dick Christy, 1961-63	16.2
Kickoff Return (Avg.)	Joe McKnight, 2010-11	30.6
Field Goals	Pat Leahy, 1974-1991	304
Touchdowns (Tot.)	Don Maynard, 1960-1972	88
Points	Pat Leahy, 1974-1991	1,470
*Sacks	Mark Gastineau, 1979-1988	74.0

INDIVIDUAL RECORDS—SINGLE SEASON

Category	Name	Performance
Rushing (Yds.)	Curtis Martin, 2004	1,697
Passing (Yds.)	Joe Namath, 1967	4,007
Passing (TDs)	Vinny Testaverde, 1998	29
Receiving (No.)	Al Toon, 1988	93
Receiving (Yds.)	Don Maynard, 1967	1,434
Interceptions	Dainard Paulson, 1964	12
Punting (Avg.)	Curley Johnson, 1965	45.3
Punt Return (Avg.)	Dick Christy, 1961	21.3
Kickoff Return (Avg.)	Joe McKnight, 2011	31.6
Field Goals	Jim Turner, 1968	34
Touchdowns (Tot.)	Thomas Jones, 2008	15
Points	Jim Turner, 1968	145
*Sacks	Mark Gastineau, 1984	22.0

INDIVIDUAL RECORDS—SINGLE GAME

Category	Name	Performance
Rushing (Yds.)	Thomas Jones, 10-18-09	210
Passing (Yds.)	Joe Namath, 9-24-72	496
Passing (TDs)	Joe Namath, 9-24-72	6
	Brett Favre, 9-28-08	6
Receiving (No.)	Clark Gaines, 9-21-80	17
Receiving (Yds.)	Don Maynard, 11-17-68	228
Interceptions	Many times	3
	Last time by Ty Law, 1-1-06	
Field Goals	Jim Turner, 11-3-68	6
	Bobby Howfield, 12-3-72	6
Touchdowns (Tot.)	Wesley Walker, 9-21-86	4
Points	Wesley Walker, 9-21-86	24
*Sacks	Mark Gastineau, 11-6-83, 9-2-84	4.0
	John Abraham, 11-4-01	4.0

*Sacks became an official statistic in 1982.

2012 VETERAN ROSTER

No.	Name	Pos.	Ht.	Wt.	Birthdate	NFL Exp.	College	Hometown	How Acq.	'11 Games/ Starts
45	Baker, Josh	FB/TE	6-3	244	12/25/86	2	Northwest Missouri State	Chesapeake, Va.	FA-'11	11/0
54	Bellore, Nick	LB	6-1	250	5/12/89	2	Central Michigan	Whitefish Bay, Wisc.	FA-'11	16/0
3	Brown, Josh	K	6-0	202	4/29/79	10	Nebraska	Foyil, Okla.	FA-12	16/0*
8	#Brunell, Mark	QB	6-1	215	9/17/70	20	Washington	Santa Maria, Calif.	FA-'10	16/0
17	#Burress, Plaxico	WR	6-5	232	8/12/77	11	Michigan State	Virginia Beach, Va.	FA-'11	16/13
4	Conley, T.J.	P	6-3	220	8/29/85	2	Idaho	Walla Walla, Wash.	FA-'11	16/0
38	Conner, John	FB	5-11	245	6/8/87	3	Kentucky	West Chester, Ohio	D5-'10	16/8
31	Cromartie, Antonio	CB	6-2	210	4/15/84	7	Florida State	Tallahassee, Fla.	T(SD)-'10	16/16
86	Cumberland, Jeff	TE	6-4	260	5/2/87	3	Illinois	Columbus, Ohio	FA-'10	3/0
70	DeVito, Mike	DE	6-3	305	6/10/84	6	Maine	Wellfleet, Mass.	FA-'07	12/11
94	Dixon, Marcus	DT	6-4	295	9/16/84	3	Hampton	Rome, Ga.	W(Dall)-'10	16/3
62	Ducasse, Vladimir	OL	6-5	325	10/15/87	3	Massachusetts	Stamford, Conn.	D2-'10	16/1
93	Ellis, Kenrick	DT	6-4	346	12/10/87	2	Hampton	Greenacres, Fla.	D3-'11	5/2
83	Epps, Dedrick	TE	6-3	250	6/19/88	2	Miami	Richmond, Va.	FA-'11	0*
60	Ferguson, D'Brickashaw	T	6-6	310	12/10/83	7	Virginia	Freeport, N.Y.	D1a-'06	16/16
2	Folk, Nick	K	6-1	222	11/05/84	6	Arizona	Hollywood, Calif.	FA-'10	16/0
23	Greene, Shonn	RB	5-11	226	8/21/85	4	Iowa	Sicklerville, N.J.	D3-'09	16/15
52	Harris, David	LB	6-2	250	1/21/84	6	Michigan	Grand Rapids, Mich.	D2-'07	16/16
10	Holmes, Santonio	WR	5-11	192	3/3/84	7	Ohio State	Belle Glade, Fla.	T(Pitt)-'10	16/16
77	Howard, Austin	T	6-7	333	3/22/87	3	Northern Iowa	Davenport, Iowa	FA-'11	0*
78	Hunter, Wayne	T	6-5	318	7/2/81	9	Hawaii	Honolulu, Hawaii	FA-'07	16/16
89	Jackson, Dexter	WR	5-9	182	8/5/86	2	Appalachian State	Dunwoody, Ga.	FA-'11	0*
81	Keller, Dustin	TE	6-2	250	9/25/84	5	Purdue	Lafayette, Ind.	D1b-'08	16/12
11	Kerley, Jeremy	WR	5-9	188	11/8/88	2	Texas Christian	Hutto, Texas	D5-'11	14/1
66	Kroul, Matt	OL	6-3	300	2/25/86	2	Iowa	Mount Vernon, Iowa	FA-'09	0*
30	Landry, LaRon	S	6-0	220	10/14/84	6	Louisiana State	Metairie, La.	UFA(Wash)-'12	8/8*
26	Lankster, Ellis	CB	5-9	190	6/3/87	3	West Virginia	Whistler, Ala.	FA-'11	7/0
36	#Leonhard, Jim	S	5-8	188	10/27/82	8	Wisconsin	Ladysmith, Wisc.	UFA(Balt)-'09	13/13
74	Mangold, Nick	C	6-4	307	1/13/84	7	Ohio State	Centerville, Ohio	D1b-'06	14/14
53	Mauga, Josh	LB	6-1	245	6/20/87	3	Nevada	Fallon, Nev.	FA-'09	16/1
51	Maybin, Aaron	LB	6-4	240	4/6/88	4	Penn State	Ellicott City, Md.	FA-'11	13/0
14	McElroy, Greg	QB	6-2	225	5/10/88	2	Alabama	Southlake, Texas	D7a-'11	0*
50	McIntyre, Garrett	LB	6-3	255	11/26/84	2	Fresno State	South Lake Tahoe, Calif.	FA-'11	13/3
25	McKnight, Joe	RB	5-11	205	4/16/88	3	Southern California	River Ridge, La.	D4-'10	15/0
65	Moore, Brandon	G	6-3	305	6/3/80	10	Illinois	Gary, Ind.	FA-'03	16/16
7	#O'Connell, Kevin	QB	6-5	225	5/25/85	5	San Diego State	Carlsbad, Calif.	W(Mia)-'11	0*
97	Pace, Calvin	LB	6-4	265	10/28/80	10	Wake Forest	Douglasville, Ga.	UFA(Ariz)-'08	16/16
91	Pouha, Sione	DT	6-3	325	2/3/79	8	Utah	Salt Lake City, Utah	D3-'05	16/15
29	Powell, Bilal	RB	5-10	204	10/27/88	2	Louisville	Lakeland, Fla.	D4-'11	2/0
46	Purdum, Tanner	LS	6-3	270	8/15/84	3	Baker	Enid, Okla.	FA-'10	16/0
24	Revis, Darrelle	CB	5-11	198	7/14/85	6	Pittsburgh	Aliquippa, Pa.	D1-'07	16/16
98	Richardson, Jay	DE	6-6	280	1/27/84	5	Ohio State	Dublin, Ohio	FA-'12	0*
6	Sanchez, Mark	QB	6-2	225	11/11/86	4	Southern California	Mission Viejo, Calif.	D1-'09	16/16
92	Sapp, Ricky	LB	6-4	252	11/14/86	2	Clemson	Bamberg, S.C.	FA-'11	0*
85	Schilens, Chaz	WR	6-4	225	11/7/85	5	San Diego State	Mesa, Ariz.	UFA(Oak)-'12	15/5*
72	Schlauderaff, Caleb	G	6-4	302	11/7/87	2	Utah	Shelton, Wash.	T(GB)-'11	6/1
57	Scott, Bart	LB	6-2	242	8/18/80	11	Southern Illinois	Detroit, Mich.	UFA(Balt)-'09	16/15
68	Slauson, Matt	G	6-5	315	2/18/86	4	Nebraska	Colorado Springs, Colo.	D6-'09	16/16
22	Smith, DeAngelo	S	5-11	200	7/17/86	2	Cincinnati	Columbus, Ohio	FA-'12	0*
33	Smith, Eric	S	6-1	207	3/17/83	7	Michigan State	Groveport, Ohio	D3b-'06	16/14
30	#Strickland, Donald	CB	5-10	185	11/24/80	9	Colorado	Redwood City, Calif.	FA-'11	15/1
15	t- Tebow, Tim	QB	6-3	236	8/14/87	3	Florida	Jacksonville, Fla.	T(Den)-'12	16/11*
95	Tevaseu, Martin	DT	6-2	325	10/7/87	2	Nevada - Las Vegas	Oakland, Calif.	FA-'10	5/0
58	Thomas, Bryan	LB	6-4	265	6/7/79	11	Alabama-Birmingham	Birmingham, Ala.	D1-'02	4/3
21	#Tomlinson, LaDainian	RB	5-10	215	6/23/79	12	Texas Christian	Rosebud, Texas	FA-'10	14/1
35	Trufant, Isaiah	CB	5-8	170	12/9/82	2	Eastern Washington	Tacoma, Wash.	FA-'11	13/0
88	Turner, Patrick	5-10	6-5	220	5/19/87	4	Southern California	Nashville, Tenn.	W(Mia)-'10	15/1
96	Wilkerson, Muhammad	DL	6-4	315	10/29/89	2	Temple	Linden, N.J.	D1-'11	16/16
20	Wilson, Kyle	CB	5-10	190	5/30/87	3	Boise State	Piscataway, N.J.	D1-'10	16/6
37	Wilson, Tracy	S	6-2	203	2/27/89	2	Northern Illinois	Harvey, Ill.	FA-'11	5/0

* Brown played 16 games with St. Louis in '11; Epps last active with Miami in '10; Howard inactive for 6 games; Jackson last active with Tampa Bay in '08; Kroul last active with New York Jets in '10; Landry played 8 games with Washington; McElroy missed '11 season because of injury; O'Connell inactive for 16 games; Payne inactive for 6 games; Richardson last active for Seattle in '10; Sapp inactive for 1 game; Schilens played 15 games with Oakland; D. Smith last active with Detroit in '09; Tebow played 16 games with Denver.

\#   Unrestricted free agent; subject to developments.

t-   Jets traded for Tim Tebow (Den).

Traded—QB Drew Stanton (0 games with Detroit in '11) to IND.

Players lost through free agency (2): S Brodney Pool (Dall; 14 games), OL Rob Turner (StL; 0).

Also played with Jets in '11—S Gerald Alexander (1 game), C Colin Baxter (3), CB Marquice Cole (14), S Emanuel Cook (8), WR Derrick Mason (5), TE Matt Mulligan (16), DE Ropati Pitoitua (14), WR Eron Riley (1), LB Jamaal Westerman (16).

FIRST-YEAR ROSTER

Name	Pos.	Ht.	Wt.	Birthdate	College	Hometown	How Acq.
Adams, Royce (1)	DB	6-0	190	5/3/88	Purdue	Cleveland, Ohio	FA
Allen, Antonio	S	6-1	210	9/23/88	South Carolina	Ocala, Fla.	D7a
Baltz, Travis (1)	P	6-3	210	11/18/88	Maryland	Whitehouse, Ohio	FA
Berning, Matthias (1)	LB	6-0	236	9/22/86	Central Michigan	Duisburg, Germany	FA
Bush, Josh	S	5-11	205	3/5/89	Wake Forest	Lexington, N.C.	D6a
Chard, Derek (1)	LS	6-3	237	6/23/88	Connecticut	Burlington, Conn.	FA
Coples, Quinton	DE	6-6	290	6/22/90	North Carolina	Kinston, N.C.	D1
Cullen, John	OL	6-5	300	5/16/90	Utah	La Mirada, Calif.	FA
Davis, Demario	LB	6-2	239	1/11/89	Arkansas State	Brandon, Miss.	D3
Dowtin, Marcus	LB	6-2	226	1/22/89	North Alabama	Upper Marlboro, Md.	FA
Fletcher, Donnie	CB	6-1	195	5/23/90	Boston College	Cleveland, Ohio	FA
Ganaway, DaMarcus (1)	WR	6-2	185	4/7/87	Kentucky Wesleyan	Indianapolis, Ind.	FA
Ganaway, Terrance	RB	6-0	239	10/7/88	Baylor	DeKalb, Texas	D6b
Griffin, John (1)	RB	5-11	208	12/17/88	Massachusetts	Westminster, Mass.	FA
Griffin, Robert	G	6-6	330	11/22/89	Baylor	Euless, Texas	D6c
Harrison, Damon	DL	6-4	350	11/29/88	William Penn	Lake Charles, La.	FA
Hill, Stephen	WR	6-4	215	4/25/91	Georgia Tech	Lithonia, Ga.	D2
Jones, Eddie (1)	LB	6-3	260	1/11/88	Texas	Kilgore, Texas	FA
Kinne, G.J.	QB	6-2	234	12/1/88	Tulsa	Gilmer, Texas	FA
Koloto, Fred	OL	6-3	297	5/9/89	San Jose State	Palo Alto, Calif.	FA
Landolt, Dennis (1)	T	6-4	306	10/15/86	Penn State	Burlington, N.J.	FA
Linthicum, Brian	TE	6-5	245	11/28/87	Michigan State	St. Louis, Mo.	FA
Lynn, D'Anton	DB	6-1	208	10/24/89	Penn State	Celina, Texas	FA
McKnight, Scotty (1)	WR	5-11	185	2/11/88	Colorado	Coto de Caza, Calif.	D7b-'11
Pollard, Royce	WR	6-1	175	6/3/89	Hawai'i	San Diego, Calif.	FA
Posey, Julian (1)	CB	5-11	187	7/17/88	Ohio	Cincinnati, Ohio	FA
Riley, Eron (1)	WR	6-3	207	8/5/87	Duke	Savannah, Ga.	FA
Robinson, Donovan	LB	6-3	250	1/19/89	Jackson State	Milwaukee, Wisc.	FA
Roy, Brett	LB	6-4	270	3/19/89	Nevada	Yucalpa, Calif.	FA
Simms, Matt	QB	6-3	210	9/27/88	Tennessee	Franklin Lakes, N.J.	FA
Smith, Hayden	TE	6-6	255	4/10/85	Metropolitan State - Denver	Penrith, Australia	FA
Steed, Ryan	CB	5-11	185	7/21/90	Furman	Mt. Pleasant, S.C.	FA
White, Jordan	WR	6-0	215	6/4/88	Western Michigan	Cleveland, Ohio	D7b

The term NFL Rookie is defined as a player who is in his first season of professional football and has not been on the roster of another professional football team for any regular-season or postseason games. A Rookie is designated by an "R" on NFL rosters. Players who have been active in another professional football league or players who have NFL experience, including either preseason training camp or being on an Active List or Inactive List, or on Reserve/Injured or Reserve/Physically Unable to Perform for fewer than six regular-season games, are termed NFL First-Year Players. An NFL First-Year Player is designated by a "1" on NFL rosters. Thereafter, a player is credited with an additional year of experience for each season in which he accumulates six games on the Active List or Inactive List, or on Reserve/Injured or Reserve/Physically Unable to Perform.

Log on to www.newyorkjets.com for an up-to-date roster.

COACHING STAFF

Head Coach,
Rex Ryan

Pro Career: Named the 15th full-time head coach of the New York Jets on January 19, 2009. Since becoming head coach, has overseen the team's best three-year defensive run, with his teams finishing first (2009), third (2010) and fifth (2011) in total defense and averaging 285.3 yards allowed per game. In 2011, team ended the season with an 8-8 record as the defense finished fifth in total defense, while the offense led the league in red zone efficiency. In 2010, directed team to 11-5 record and became second coach in NFL history to guide team to the conference championship game in his first two seasons after inheriting a team that did not reach the playoffs the year prior to him becoming head coach. The defense ranked third in the league in total yards and rushing yards allowed. In 2009, led team to 9-7 record and AFC Championship Game with offense that ranked first in the NFL in rushing and defense that finished first in total defense, points allowed and passing defense. Ryan spent 10 seasons with the Baltimore Ravens. From 1999-2008, the Ravens ranked first in the NFL for fewest points allowed, fewest rushing yards allowed, most takeaways, most interceptions and most interceptions returned for touchdowns. Ravens allowed fewest points in NFL history for 16-game season (165) in 2000 en route to winning Super Bowl XXXV. Began NFL career with Arizona under his father, Buddy Ryan, as coach for defensive line (1994) and linebackers (1995). Career record: 32-22.
Background: Coached at Eastern Kentucky (1987-88), New Mexico Highlands (1989), Morehead State (1990-93), Cincinnati (1996-97) and Oklahoma (1998). Played defensive end at Southwestern Oklahoma State with his twin brother, Rob, who is currently the Dallas defensive coordinator. Earned his Bachelor's and Master's Degree in Physical Education at Eastern Kentucky.
Personal: Born December 13, 1963, Ardmore, Okla. Ryan and his wife Michelle have two sons, Payton and Seth.

ASSISTANT COACHES

Matt Cavanaugh, quarterbacks; born October 27, 1956, Youngstown, Ohio. Quarterback Pittsburgh 1974-77. Pro quarterback New England Patriots 1978-1982, San Francisco 49ers 1983-85, Philadelphia Eagles 1986-89, New York Giants 1990-91. College coach: Pittsburgh 1991-93, 2005-08. Pro coach: Arizona Cardinals 1994-95, San Francisco 49ers 1996, Chicago Bears 1997-98, Baltimore Ravens 1999-2004, joined Jets in 2009.
Dave DeGuglielmo, offensive line; born July 15, 1968, Cambridge, Mass. Offensive line Boston University 1987-

1990. No pro playing experience. College coach: Boston College 1991-92, Boston University 1993-96, Connecticut 1997-98, South Carolina 1999-2003. Pro coach: New York Giants 2004-08, Miami Dolphins 2009-2011, joined Jets in 2012.
Mike Devlin, tight ends/asst. offensive line; born November 16, 1969, Blacksburg, Va. Offensive line Iowa 1989-1992. Pro offensive lineman Buffalo Bills 1993-95, Arizona Cardinals 1996-99. College coach: Toledo 2004-05. Pro coach: Arizona Cardinals 2000-03, joined Jets in 2006.
Karl Dunbar, defensive line; born May 18, 1967, Plaisance, La. Defensive lineman Louisiana State 1986-89. Pro defensive lineman Pittsburgh Steelers 1990, New Orleans Saints 1992-93, Arizona Cardinals 1994-95. College coaching: Nicholls State 1998-99, Louisiana State 2000-01, Oklahoma State 2022-03. Pro coach: Chicago Bears 2004, Minnesota Vikings 2006-2011, joined Jets in 2012.
Justus Galac, asst. strength and conditioning; born August 15, 1980, Cattaraugus, N.Y. Nose tackle SUNY Brockport 1998-2001. No pro playing experience. College coach: SUNY Brockport 2002, Dickenson College 2003-04, Villanova 2005-11. Pro coach: Joined Jets in 2012.
Bill Hughan, head strength and conditioning; born February 8, 1975, Oxford, Conn. Attended Springfield College. No college or pro playing experience. College coach: Yale 1997-98, Columbia 1999-2000, Missouri 2001-03. Pro coach: Oakland Raiders 2004-07, Atlanta Falcons 2008-10, joined Jets in 2011.
Ben Kotwica, asst. special teams; born December 8, 1974, Tinley Park, Ill. Linebacker Army 1995-97. No pro playing experience. Pro coach: Joined Jets in 2007.
Sanjay Lal, wide receivers; born July 23, 1969, London, England. Wide receiver UCLA 1989, Washington 1990-92. Pro receiver St. Louis Rams 1998, Scottish Claymores (NFLE) 1999. College coach: Los Medanos (Calif.) College 2003, St. Mary's College 2004, California 2005-06. Pro coach: Oakland Raiders 2007-2011, joined Jets in 2012.
Anthony Lynn, running backs; born December 21, 1968, McKinney, Texas. Running back Texas Tech 1987-1991. Pro running back Denver Broncos 1993, 1997-99, San Francisco 49ers 1995-96. Pro coach: Denver Broncos 2000-02, Jacksonville Jaguars 2003-04, Dallas Cowboys 2005-06, Cleveland Browns 2007-08, joined Jets in 2009.
Jim O'Neil, asst. defensive backs; born Oct. 26, 1978, Philadelphia, Pa. Defensive end Towson 1997-2000. No pro playing experience. College coach: SUNY Albany 2001, Pennsylvania 2002, Northwestern 2003-04, Towson 2005, Eastern Michigan 2006-08. Pro coach: Joined Jets in 2009.
Mike Pettine, defensive coordinator; born September 25, 1966, Doylestown, Pa.

Safety Virginia 1984-87. No pro playing experience. College coach: Pittsburgh 1993-94. Pro coach: Baltimore Ravens 2003-08, joined Jets in 2009.
Paul Ricci, asst. strength and conditioning; born November 15, 1969, Washington Township, N.J. Offensive lineman Penn State 1988-89. No pro playing experience. College coach: Maryland 2008-2010, Texas Tech 2011. Pro coach: Arizona Cardinals 1996-97, Baltimore Ravens 1999-2007, joined Jets in 2012.
Brian Smith, quality control/defense; born July 15, 1979, Wilmington, Del. Defensive back Massachusetts 1997-2000. No pro playing experience. College coach: Massachusetts 2004-2006. Pro coach: Joined Jets in 2007.
Mike Smith, outside linebackers; born September 2, 1981, Lubbock, Texas. Linebacker Texas Tech 2000-24. Pro linebacker Baltimore Ravens 2005-07. College coach: Hawai'i 2009. Pro coach: Joined Jets in 2010.
Tony Sparano, offensive coordinator; born October 7, 1961, West Haven, Ct. Center New Haven 1978-1982. No pro playing experience. College coach: New Haven 1984-87, Boston University 1988-93, New Haven 1994-98 (head coach). Pro coach: Cleveland Browns 1999-2000, Washington Redskins 2001, Jacksonville Jaguars 2002, Dallas Cowboys 2003-2007, Miami Dolphins 2008-11 (head coach), joined Jets in 2012.
Bob Sutton, asst. head coach/linebackers; born January 28, 1951, Ypsilanti, Mich. Attended Eastern Michigan. No college or pro playing experience. College coach: Michigan 1972-73, Syracuse 1974, Western Michigan 1975-76, 1980-81, Illinois 1977-79, North Carolina State 1982, Army 1983-1999 (head coach 1991-99). Pro coach: Joined Jets in 2000.
Lance Taylor, asst. tight ends/quality control; born July 17, 1981, Mobile, Ala. Wide receiver Alabama 2000-2003. No pro playing experience. College coach: Alabama 2008, Appalachian State 2009. Pro coach: Joined Jets in 2010.
Dennis Thurman, defensive backs; born April 13, 1956, Los Angeles, Calif. Defensive back Southern California 1974-77. Pro defensive back Dallas Cowboys 1978-1985, St. Louis Cardinals 1986, Phoenix Cardinals 1988-89. College coach: Southern California 1993-2000. Pro coach: Ohio Glory (WLAF) 1992, Baltimore Ravens 2002-07, joined Jets in 2009.
Mike Westhoff, special teams coordinator; born January 19, 1948, Pittsburgh, Pa. Linebacker Wyoming 1965, center/linebacker Wichita State 1967-69. No pro playing experience. College coach: Indiana 1974-75, Dayton 1976, Indiana State 1977, Northwestern 1978-1980, Texas Christian 1981. Pro coach: Baltimore Colts 1982-83, Indianapolis Colts 1984, Arizona Outlaws (USFL) 1985, Miami Dolphins 1986-2000, joined Jets in 2001.

American Football Conference
West Division
Team Colors: Silver and Black
1220 Harbor Bay Parkway
Alameda, California 94502
Telephone: (510) 864-5000

2012 SCHEDULE
PRESEASON
Aug. 13 **Dallas**.................................5:00
Aug. 17 at Arizona 7:00
Aug. 25 **Detroit**................................4:00
Aug. 30 at Seattle............................7:00

REGULAR SEASON
Sep. 10 **San Diego** (Mon) 7:15
Sep. 16 at Miami........................10:00a
Sep. 23 **Pittsburgh** 1:15
Sep. 30 at Denver 1:05
Oct. 7   BYE
Oct. 14 at Atlanta.......................10:00a
Oct. 21 **Jacksonville** 1:15
Oct. 28 at Kansas City....................1:05
Nov. 4 **Tampa Bay** 1:05
Nov. 11 at Baltimore...................10:00a
Nov. 18 **New Orleans** 1:05
Nov. 25 at Cincinnati 10:00a
Dec. 2 **Cleveland** 1:15
Dec. 6 **Denver** (Thurs) 5:20
Dec. 16 **Kansas City**.......................1:15
Dec. 23 at Carolina 10:00a
Dec. 30 at San Diego 1:15
All times PT

Stadium: Oakland-Alameda County Coliseum
         (opened in 1966)
         •**Capacity:** 63,132
         7000 Coliseum Way
         Oakland, CA 94621-1917
Playing Surface: Grass
Training Camp: Napa Valley Marriott
              Napa, California 94558

OAKLAND-ALAMEDA COUNTY COLISEUM

CLUB OFFICIALS
Owner: Mark Davis
General Manager: Reggie McKenzie
Chief Executive: Amy Trask
Director – Football Administration:
    Tom Delaney
Player Personnel: Joey Clinkscales
Director – College Scouting:
    Shaun Herock
College Scouting Coordinator:
    Teddy Atlas
Pro Scouts: Von Hutchins, Larry Marmie,
    Dane Vandernat
College Scouts: Calvin Branch, Zack
    Crockett, Brad Kaplan, Mickey Marvin,
    David McCloughan, Raleigh McKenzie,
    Trey Scott
Head Athletic Trainer: H. Rod Martin
Team Orthopedist: Dr. Warren King
Equipment Manager: Bob Romanski
Video Director: Dave Nash
Assistant to Head Coach: Tom Jones
Director – Media Relations: Zak Gilbert
Director – Player Engagement:
    Lamonte Winston
Football Operations: Pete Caracciolo
Legal: Jeff Birren, Dan Ventrelle
Finance: Marc Badain, Tom Blanda
Tickets, Suites & Premium Seats:
    Mark Shearer
Community Relations: Scott Fink
Youth Initiatives: Rosie Bone
Sponsorships: Robert Kinnard
Director – Public Affairs: Mike Taylor
Internet: Jerry Knaak
Broadcasting: Vittorio DeBartolo
Technology: Matthew Pasco

COACHING HISTORY
Oakland 1960-1981
Los Angeles 1982-1994
(451-369-11)
Records include postseason games

1960-61	Eddie Erdelatz*	6-10-0
1961-62	Marty Feldman**	2-15-0
1962	Red Conkright	1-8-0
1963-65	Al Davis	23-16-3
1966-68	John Rauch	35-10-1
1969-1978	John Madden	112-39-7
1979-1987	Tom Flores	91-56-0
1988-89	Mike Shanahan***	8-12-0
1989-1994	Art Shell	56-41-0
1995-96	Mike White	15-17-0
1997	Joe Bugel	4-12-0
1998-2001	Jon Gruden	40-28-0
2002-03	Bill Callahan	17-18-0
2004-05	Norv Turner	9-23-0
2006	Art Shell	2-14-0
2007-08	Lane Kiffin****	5-15-0
2008-2010	Tom Cable	17-27-0
2011	Hue Jackson	8-8-0

   * Released after two games in 1961
  ** Released after five games in 1962
 *** Released after four games in 1989
**** Released after four games in 2008

PAID ATTENDANCE
Home 453,851   Away 535,312
Total 989,163
Single-game home record,
   62,660 (11/3/02)
Single-season home record,
   471,151 (2002)

2012 DRAFT CHOICES
Round	Name	Pos.	College
3	Tony Bergstrom	G	Utah
4	Miles Burris	LB	San Diego St.
5	Jack Crawford	DE	Penn St.
	Juron Criner	WR	Arizona
6	Christo Bilukidi	DT	Georgia St.
7	Nathan Stupar	LB	Penn St.

2011 TEAM RECORD
PRESEASON (0-4)

Date	Result		Opponent
8/11	L	18-24	Arizona
8/20	L	3-17	at San Francisco
8/28	L	20-40	New Orleans
9/2	L	3-20	at Seattle

REGULAR SEASON (8-8)

Date	Result		Opponent
9/12	W	23-20	at Denver
9/18	L	35-38	at Buffalo
9/25	W	34-24	New York Jets
10/2	L	19-31	New England
10/09	W	25-20	at Houston
10/16	W	24-17	Cleveland
10/23	L	0-28	Kansas City
11/6	L	24-38	Denver
11/10	W	24-17	at San Diego
11/20	W	27-21	at Minnesota
11/27	W	25-20	Chicago
12/4	L	14-34	at Miami
12/11	L	16-46	at Green Bay
12/18	L	27-28	Detroit
12/24	L	16-13	at Kansas City (OT)
1/1	L	26-38	San Diego

(OT) Overtime

SCORE BY PERIODS

Raiders	56	137	66	97	3	—	359
Opponents	92	92	115	134	0	—	433

2011 TEAM STATISTICS

	Raiders	Opp.
Total First Downs	328	369
Rushing	110	105
Passing	186	206
Penalty	32	58
3rd Down: Made/Att	71/199	92/219
3rd Down Pct.	35.7	42.0
4th Down: Made/Att	7/13	4/14
4th Down Pct.	53.8	28.6
Possession Avg.	29:51	30:09
Total Net Yards	6072	6201
Avg. Per Game	379.5	387.6
Total Plays	1015	1070
Avg. Per Play	6.0	5.8
Net Yards Rushing	2110	2178
Avg. Per Game	131.9	136.1
Total Rushes	466	430
Net Yards Passing	3962	4023
Avg. Per Game	247.6	251.4
Sacked/Yards Lost	25/157	39/239
Gross Yards	4119	4262
Att./Completions	524/315	601/324
Completion Pct.	60.1	53.9
Had Intercepted	23	18
Punts/Average	78/50.8	68/46.5
Net Punting Avg.	78/40.9	68/40.8
Penalties/Yards	163/1358	120/982
Fumbles/Ball Lost	16/7	13/8
Touchdowns	38	53
Rushing	16	15
Passing	20	31
Returns	2	7

2011 INDIVIDUAL STATISTICS

PASSING

	Att.	Comp.	Yds.	Pct.	TD	Int.	Tkld.	Rate
Palmer	328	199	2753	60.7	13	16	17/119	80.5
J. Campbell	165	100	1170	60.6	6	4	5/19	84.2
Boller	28	15	161	53.6	0	3	3/19	31.1
Lechler	3	1	35	33.3	1	0	0/0	118.1
Raiders	524	315	4119	60.1	20	23	25/157	79.4
Opponents	601	324	4262	53.9	31	18	39/239	81.3

SCORING

	TD R	TD P	TD Rt	PAT	FG	Saf	PTS
Janikowski	0	0	0	36/36	31/35	0	129
Bush	7	1	0	0/0	0/0	0	48
D. Moore	1	5	0	0/0	0/0	0	36
McFadden	4	1	0	0/0	0/0	0	30
Heyward-Bey	0	4	0	0/0	0/0	0	24
Boss	0	3	0	0/0	0/0	0	18
J. Campbell	2	0	0	0/0	0/0	0	12
Ford	0	1	1	0/0	0/0	0	12
Reece	0	2	0	0/0	0/0	0	12
Schilens	0	2	0	0/0	0/0	0	12
Curry	0	0	1	0/0	0/0	0	6
Houshmandzadeh	0	1	0	0/0	0/0	0	6
Murphy	1	0	0	0/0	0/0	0	6
Palmer	1	0	0	0/0	0/0	0	6
McClain	0	0	0	0/0	0/0	1	2
Raiders	16	20	2	36/36	31/35	1	359
Opponents	15	31	7	52/52	21/29	0	433

2-Pt Conversions: Raiders 0-2, Opponents 0-0

RUSHING

	No.	Yds	Avg	LG	TD
Bush	256	977	3.8	44	7
McFadden	113	614	5.4	70t	4
Reece	17	112	6.6	26	0
T. Jones	16	73	4.6	14	0
Murphy	6	69	11.5	27	1
D. Moore	5	61	12.2	25	1
J. Campbell	18	60	3.3	17	2
Cartwright	4	45	11.3	35	0
Boller	9	38	4.2	20	0
Ford	4	31	7.8	30	0
Palmer	16	20	1.3	10	1
Tonga	1	12	12.0	12	0
Ausberry	1	-2	-2.0	-2	0
Raiders	466	2110	4.5	70t	16
Opponents	430	2178	5.1	60t	15

RECEIVING

	No.	Yds	Avg	LG	TD
Heyward-Bey	64	975	15.2	58	4
Bush	37	418	11.3	55	1
D. Moore	33	618	18.7	78	5
Boss	28	368	13.1	35t	3
Reece	27	301	11.1	47	2
Schilens	23	271	11.8	30	2
Ford	19	279	14.7	41	1
McFadden	19	154	8.1	26	1
Myers	16	151	9.4	24	0
Murphy	15	241	16.1	47	0
Houshmandzadeh	11	146	13.3	40t	1
Hagan	11	114	10.4	25	0
Cartwright	4	24	6.0	9	0
Tonga	3	18	6.0	11	0
T. Jones	2	25	12.5	30	0
Ausberry	2	14	7.0	10	0
Gordon	1	2	2.0	2	0
Raiders	315	4119	13.1	78	20
Opponents	324	4262	13.2	81	31

INTERCEPTIONS

	No.	Yds	Avg	LG	TD
Giordano	5	130	26.0	62	0
Routt	4	7	1.8	3	0
Huff	2	24	12.0	24	0
Wimbley	1	73	73.0	73	0
Houston	1	15	15.0	15	0
Van Dyke	1	2	2.0	2	0
Kelly	1	1	1.0	1	0
Branch	1	0	0.0	0	0
Mitchell	1	0	0.0	0	0
Ndukwe	1	0	0.0	0	0
Raiders	18	252	14.0	73	0
Opponents	23	234	10.2	59t	3

PUNTING

	No.	Yds.	Avg.	In 20	LG
Lechler	78	3960	50.8	27	80
Raiders	78	3960	50.8	27	80
Opponents	68	3161	46.5	22	71

PUNT RETURNS

	Ret	FC	Yds	Avg	LG	TD
D. Moore	25	7	216	8.6	34	0
McCann	3	1	29	9.7	17	0
N. Miller	2	0	19	9.5	12	0
Blackstock	1	0	0	0.0	0	0
Houshmandzadeh	1	0	0	0.0	0	0
Raiders	32	9	264	8.3	34	0
Opponents	44	8	593	13.5	90t	2

KICKOFF RETURNS

	No.	Yds	Avg	LG	TD
McCann	13	361	27.8	91	0
Ford	11	341	31.0	101t	1
T. Jones	8	165	20.6	46	0
N. Miller	4	61	15.3	18	0
Cartwright	3	15	5.0	14	0
Branch	2	31	15.5	16	0
D. Moore	2	37	18.5	20	0
Raiders	43	1011	23.5	101t	1
Opponents	47	1210	25.7	105t	1

FIELD GOALS

	1-19	20-29	30-39	40-49	50+
Janikowski	1/1	8/8	5/5	10/11	7/10
Raiders	1/1	8/8	5/5	10/11	7/10
Opponents	0/0	6/6	5/6	6/12	4/5

SACKS

	No.
Kelly	7.5
Wimbley	7.0
Seymour	6.0
Bryant	5.0
McClain	5.0
Moss	1.5
Branch	1.0
Giordano	1.0
Houston	1.0
Mitchell	1.0
Shaughnessy	1.0
Sheppard	1.0
(group)	1.0
Raiders	39.0
Opponents	25.0

RECORD HOLDERS
INDIVIDUAL RECORDS—CAREER

Category	Name	Performance
Rushing (Yds.)	Marcus Allen, 1982-1992	8,545
Passing (Yds.)	Ken Stabler, 1970-79	19,078
Passing (TDs)	Ken Stabler, 1970-79	150
Receiving (No.)	Tim Brown, 1988-2003	1,070
Receiving (Yds.)	Tim Brown, 1988-2003	14,734
Interceptions	Willie Brown, 1967-1978	39
	Lester Hayes, 1977-1986	39
Punting (Avg.)	Shane Lechler, 2000-2011	**47.6
Punt Return (Avg.)	Claude Gibson, 1963-65	12.6
Kickoff Return (Avg.)	Jack Larscheid, 1960-61	28.4
Field Goals	Sebastian Janikowski, 2000-2011	293
Touchdowns (Tot.)	Tim Brown, 1988-2003	104
Points	Sebastian Janikowski, 2000-2011	1,271
*Sacks	Greg Townsend, 1983-1993, 1997	107.5

INDIVIDUAL RECORDS—SINGLE SEASON

Category	Name	Performance
Rushing (Yds.)	Marcus Allen, 1985	1,759
Passing (Yds.)	Rich Gannon, 2002	4,689
Passing (TDs)	Daryle Lamonica, 1969	34
Receiving (No.)	Tim Brown 1997	104
Receiving (Yds.)	Tim Brown, 1997	1,408
Interceptions	Lester Hayes, 1980	13
Punting (Avg.)	Shane Lechler, 2009	51.1
Punt Return (Avg.)	Claude Gibson, 1964	14.4
Kickoff Return (Avg.)	Harold Hart, 1975	30.5
Field Goals	Jeff Jaeger, 1993	35
Touchdowns (Tot.)	Marcus Allen, 1984	18
Points	Sebastian Janikowski, 2010	142
*Sacks	Derrick Burgess, 2005	16.0

INDIVIDUAL RECORDS—SINGLE GAME

Category	Name	Performance
Rushing (Yds.)	Napoleon Kaufman, 10-19-97	227
Passing (Yds.)	Cotton Davidson, 10-25-64	427
Passing (TDs)	Tom Flores, 12-22-63	6
	Daryle Lamonica, 10-19-69	6
Receiving (No.)	Tim Brown, 12-21-97	14
Receiving (Yds.)	Art Powell, 12-22-63	247
Interceptions	Many times	3
	Last time by Rod Woodson, 9-29-02	
Field Goals	Sebastian Janikowski, 11-27-11	6
Touchdowns (Tot.)	Art Powell, 12-22-63	4
	Marcus Allen, 9-24-84	4
	Harvey Williams, 11-16-97	4
	Darren McFadden, 10-24-10	4
Points	Art Powell, 12-22-63	24
	Marcus Allen, 9-24-84	24
	Harvey Williams, 11-16-97	24
	Darren McFadden, 10-24-10	24
*Sacks	Howie Long, 10-2-83	5.0

*Sacks became an official statistic in 1982.
**NFL Record

2012 VETERAN ROSTER

No.	Name	Pos.	Ht.	Wt.	Birthdate	NFL Exp.	College	Hometown	How Acq.	'11 Games/ Starts
86	Ausberry, David	TE	6-4	245	9/25/87	2	Southern California	Lemoore, Calif.	D7-'11	12/0
72	Barksdale, Joe	T	6-4	325	1/1/88	2	Louisiana State	Detroit, Mich.	D3-'11	16/0
69	Barnes, Khalif	T	6-5	325	4/21/82	8	Washington	Spring Valley, Calif.	UFA(Jax)-'09	16/16
21	Bartell, Ron	CB	6-1	210	2/22/82	8	Howard	Detroit, Mich.	FA-'12	1/1*
	#Blackstock, Darryl	LB	6-3	245	5/30/83	6	Virginia	Newport News, Va.	FA-'11	16/1
	#Boller, Kyle	QB	6-3	220	6/17/81	10	California	Newhall, Calif.	UFA(StL)-'10	2/1
	#Boyd, Jerome	S	6-2	225	5/26/86	3	Oregon	Los Angeles, Calif.	FA-'09	14/1
33	Branch, Tyvon	S	6-0	205	12/11/86	5	Connecticut	Cicero, N.Y.	D4-'08	16/16
65	Brisiel, Mike	G	6-5	300	3/14/83	7	Colorado State	Fayetteville, Ark.	UFA(Hou)-'12	13/13*
95	Brodine, Mason	DE	6-7	255	2/18/88	2	Nebraska-Kearney	Elm Creek, Neb.	FA-'11	2/0
90	Bryant, Desmond	DT	6-5	290	12/15/85	4	Harvard	Elizabethtown, N.C.	FA-'09	16/11
14	Calhoun, Duke	WR	6-2	200	9/1/87	2	Memphis	Memphis, Tenn.	FA-'12	0*
66	Carlisle, Cooper	G	6-5	295	8/11/77	13	Florida	McComb, Miss.	UFA(Den)-'07	16/16
35	Chekwa, Chimdi	CB	6-0	190	9/7/88	2	Ohio State	Clermont, Fla.	D4-'11	4/1
59	Condo, Jon	LS/LB	6-3	250	8/26/81	7	Maryland	Philipsburg, Pa.	FA-'06	16/0
51	t- Curry, Aaron	LB	6-2	255	4/6/86	4	Wake Forest	Fayetteville, N.C.	T(Sea)-'11	16/9*
75	Davis, Hall	DE	6-6	262	3/2/87	2	Louisiana-Lafayette	Baton Rouge, La.	FA-'12	0*
12	Ford, Jacoby	WR	5-9	185	7/27/87	3	Clemson	Royal Palm Beach, Fla.	D4-'10	8/3
27	Giordano, Matt	S	5-11	210	10/16/82	8	California	Clovis, Calif.	FA-'11	16/8
50	Goethel, Travis	LB	6-2	240	7/27/87	2	Arizona State	Vista, Calif.	D6-'10	0*
25	t- Goodson, Mike	RB	6-0	210	5/23/87	4	Texas A&M	Spring, Texas	T(Car)-'12	4/0*
82	Gordon, Richard	TE	6-4	265	6/7/87	2	Miami	Miami, Fla.	D6-'11	14/1
	#Groves, Quentin	LB	6-3	265	7/5/85	5	Auburn	Greenville, Miss.	T(Jax)-'10	16/3
60	Haslam, Kevin	T	6-5	304	11/8/86	2	Rutgers	Mahwah, N.J.	FA-'12	0*
	#Heyer, Stephon	T	6-6	330	1/16/84	6	Maryland	Lawrenceville, Ga.	FA-'11	12/2
85	Heyward-Bey, Darrius	WR	6-2	210	2/26/87	4	Maryland	Owings Mills, Md.	D1-'09	15/14
	#Houshmandzadeh, T.J.	WR	6-2	200	9/26/77	12	Oregon State	Barstow, Calif.	FA-'11	9/0
99	Houston, Lamarr	DE	6-3	305	6/24/87	3	Texas	Colorado Springs, Colo.	D2-'10	16/14
24	Huff, Michael	S	6-1	205	3/6/83	7	Texas	Irving, Texas	D1-'06	12/11
11	Janikowski, Sebastian	K	6-2	250	3/2/78	13	Florida State	Daytona Beach, Fla.	D1-'00	16/0
22	Jones, Taiwan	RB	6-0	195	7/26/88	2	Eastern Washington	Antioch, Calif.	D4-'11	10/0
93	Kelly, Tommy	DT	6-6	300	12/27/80	9	Mississippi State	Jackson, Miss.	FA-'04	16/16
9	Lechler, Shane	P	6-2	225	8/7/76	13	Texas A&M	Sealy, Texas	D5-'00	16/0
26	Lee, Pat	CB	6-0	195	2/20/84	5	Auburn	Miami, Fla.	UFA(GB)-'12	16/0*
7	Leinart, Matt	QB	6-5	227	5/11/83	7	Southern California	Santa Ana, Calif.	FA-'12	2/1*
29	McCann, Bryan	CB	5-10	185	9/29/87	3	Southern Methodist	Oklahoma City, Okla.	FA-'11	7/0
55	McClain, Rolando	LB	6-3	255	7/14/89	3	Alabama	Decatur, Ala.	D1-'10	15/14
20	McFadden, Darren	RB	6-2	210	8/27/87	5	Arkansas	North Little Rock, Ark.	D1-'08	7/7
46	Miller, Lonyae	RB	6-0	230	4/29/88	2	Fresno State	Fontana, Calif.	FA-'11	0*
34	Mitchell, Mike	S	6-1	205	6/10/87	4	Ohio	Ft. Thomas, Ky.	D2-'09	13/2
17	Moore, Denarius	WR	6-0	195	12/9/88	2	Tennessee	Tatum, Texas	D5-'11	13/10
	#Moss, Jarvis	DE	6-7	260	8/3/84	6	Florida	Denton, Texas	W(Den)-'10	14/1
18	Murphy, Louis	WR	6-2	200	5/11/87	4	Florida	St. Petersburg, Fla.	D4-'09	11/1
83	Myers, Brandon	TE	6-4	250	9/4/85	4	Iowa	Prairie City, Iowa	D6-'09	16/7
3	t- Palmer, Carson	QB	6-5	235	12/27/79	10	Southern California	Rancho Santa Margarita, Calif.	T(Cin)-'11	10/9
6	Pryor, Terrelle	QB	6-6	230	6/20/89	2	Ohio State	Jeanette, Pa.	SD3-'11	1/0
45	Reece, Marcel	FB	6-3	240	6/23/85	4	Washington	Hesperia, Calif.	FA-'08	12/6
44	Schmitt, Owen	FB	6-2	245	2/13/85	5	West Virginia	Fairfax, Va.	FA-'12	16/5*
92	Seymour, Richard	DT	6-6	310	10/6/79	12	Georgia	Gadsden, S.C.	T(NE)-'09	16/15
77	Shaughnessy, Matt	DE	6-5	270	9/23/86	4	Wisconsin	Norwich, Conn.	D3-'09	3/3
	#Sheppard, Lito	CB	5-10	195	4/8/81	11	Florida	Jacksonville, Fla.	FA-'11	9/7
36	Spencer, Shawntae	CB	6-1	190	2/22/82	9	Pittsburgh	Pittsburgh, Pa.	FA-'12	9/0*
39	Taylor, Curtis	S	6-2	210	7/13/85	3	Louisiana State	Franklinton, La.	FA-'12	0*
58	Tollefson, Dave	DE	6-4	266	7/10/82	6	Northwest Missouri	Concord, Calif.	UFA(NYG)-'12	16/2*
41	Tonga, Manase	FB	5-11	245	2/28/84	2	Brigham Young	San Mateo, Calif.	FA-'11	11/3
28	Underwood, Brandon	CB	6-1	190	6/24/86	3	Cincinnati	Hamilton, Ohio	FA-'12	0*
23	Van Dyke, DeMarcus	CB	6-1	180	1/17/89	2	Miami	Miami, Fla.	D3-'11	14/4
68	Veldheer, Jared	T	6-8	315	6/14/87	3	Hillsdale	Grand Rapids, Mich.	D3-'10	16/16
73	Wang, Ed	OL	6-5	321	3/12/87	2	Virginia Tech	Ashburn, Va.	FA-'12	0*
52	Wheeler, Phillip	LB	6-2	240	12/12/84	5	Georgia Tech	Columbus, Ga.	UFA(Ind)-'12	13/11*
61	Wisniewski, Stefen	G/C	6-3	315	3/22/89	2	Penn State	Pittsburgh, Pa.	D2-'11	16/16

* Bartell played 1 game with St. Louis in '11; Brisiel played 13 games with Houston; Calhoun last active with New York Giants in '10; Curry played 5 games with Seattle and 11 with Oakland; Davis last active with Tennessee in '10; Goethel missed '11 season because of injury; Goodson played 4 games with Carolina; Haslam last active with Jacksonville in '10; Lee played 16 games with Green Bay; Leinart played 2 games with Houston; Miller last active with Dallas in '10; Schmitt played 16 games with Philadelphia; Spencer played 9 games with San Francisco; Taylor last active with San Francisco in '10; Tollefson played 16 games with New York Giants; Underwood last active with Green Bay in '10; Wang last active with Buffalo in '10; Wheeler played 13 games with Indianapolis.

t— Raiders traded for Curry (Sea), Goodson (Car) and Palmer (Cin).

\# Unrestricted free agent; subject to developments.

Traded—G/T Bruce Campbell (4 games in '11) to Carolina.

Players lost through free agency (6): RB Michael Bush (Chi; 16 games), QB Jason Campbell (Chi; 6), RB Rock Cartwright (SF; 15), C Samson Satele (Ind; 15), WR Chaz Schilens (NYJ; 15), DE Trevor Scott (NE; 16).

Also played with Raiders in '11—TE Kevin Boss (14 games), LB Ricky Brown (3), LB Bruce Davis II (4), WR Derek Hagan (6), DT John Henderson (13), CB Chris Johnson (4), WR Nick Miller (2), S Chinedum Ndukwe (2), CB Ron Parker (3), CB Joe Porter (6), K Dave Rayner (1), CB Stanford Routt (6), LB Kamerion Wimbley (16).

FIRST-YEAR ROSTER

Name	Pos.	Ht.	Wt.	Birthdate	College	Hometown	How Acq.
Bergstrom, Tony	OL	6-5	313	8/8/86	Utah	Salt Lake City, Utah	D3
Bilukidi, Christo	DT	6-5	311	12/13/89	Georgia State	Ottawa, Ont., Canada	D6
Black, Conroy	CB	6-0	182	10/31/88	Utah	Miramar, Fla.	FA
Burnett, Kaelin	LB	6-0	234	9/6/89	Nevada	Bellflower, Calif.	FA
Burris, Miles	LB	6-2	236	6/27/88	San Diego State	Granite Bay, Calif.	D4
Carmona, Eddy	P/K	5-10	203	9/4/88	Harding	Conway, Ark.	FA
Carrier, Derek	WR	6-0	238	7/25/90	Beloit	Edgerton, Wisc.	FA
Carswell, Brandon	WR	6-1	201	5/22/89	Southern California	Milpitas, Calif.	FA
Crawford, Jack	DE	6-5	274	9/7/88	Penn State	Longport, N.J.	D5
Criner, Juron	WR	6-3	221	12/12/89	Arizona	Las Vegas, Nev.	D5
Cumbie, Jamie (1)	DT	6-7	291	2/18/88	Clemson	Morris, Ill.	FA-'11
Dorsey, Wayne	DE	6-6	272	10/9/90	Mississippi	Baltimore, Md.	FA
Efaw, Kyle	TE	6-4	247	3/13/88	Boise State	Boise, Idaho	FA
Hamilton, Dominique	DT	6-5	313	1/18/89	Missouri	El Paso, Texas	FA
Henry, Aaron	S	6-0	208	11/28/88	Wisconsin	Immokalee, Fla.	FA
Hurd, Zach (1)	T	6-7	316	9/30/88	Connecticut	Waterford, Conn.	FA-'11
Ihenacho, Carl (1)	LB	6-2	255	5/28/88	San Jose State	Gardena, Calif.	FA-'11
Ivey, Travis (1)	DT	6-4	341	12/22/86	Maryland	Marlboro, Md.	FA
Jackson, Rashawn (1)	FB	6-1	239	1/15/87	Virginia	Jersey City, N.J.	FA
King, Marquette	P	6-0	192	10/26/88	Fort Valley State	Rutland, Ga.	FA
Knapp, Dan	T	6-5	304	9/1/88	Arizona State	Reno, Nev.	FA
Kurn, Mario	LB	6-2	238	7/3/90	San Diego	Encinitas, Calif.	FA
Lambert, Terrail (1)	CB	5-11	190	12/1/85	Notre Dame	Ventura, Calif.	FA--'11
Lewis, LeQuan (1)	CB	5-11	187	12/17/89	Arizona State	Norwalk, Calif.	FA
Mayo, Thomas	WR	6-1	205	2/13/90	California (Pa.)	Reston, Va.	FA
McGee, Eddie (1)	WR	6-3	210	1/23/88	Illinois	Washington D.C.	FA-'11
Miller, Colin (1)	C	6-3	300	11/22/87	Central Michigan	Centreville, Va.	FA
Nix, Lucas	G	6-5	317	9/28/89	Pittsburgh	Jefferson Hills, Pa.	FA
Parsons, Alex (1)	G	6-4	316	9/14/87	Southern California	Irvine, Calif.	FA-'10
Powell, Chaz	S	6-0	207	1/1/88	Penn State	New Freedom, Pa.	FA
Robinson, TréShawn	FB	5-11	246	12/2/90	Idaho	Upland, Calif.	FA
Session, Travionte	WR	6-2	191	7/18/89	Nevada	Long Beach, Calif.	FA
Streater, Rod	WR	6-2	193	2/9/88	Temple	Burlington, N.J.	FA
Stupar, Nathan	LB	6-2	238	3/14/88	Penn State	State College, Pa.	D7

The term NFL Rookie is defined as a player who is in his first season of professional football and has not been on the roster of another professional football team for any regular-season or postseason games. A Rookie is designated by an "R" on NFL rosters. Players who have been active in another professional football league or players who have NFL experience, including either preseason training camp or being on an Active List or Inactive List, or on Reserve/Injured or Reserve/Physically Unable to Perform for fewer than six regular-season games, are termed NFL First-Year Players. An NFL First-Year Player is designated by a "1" on NFL rosters. Thereafter, a player is credited with an additional year of experience for each season in which he accumulates six games on the Active List or Inactive List, or on Reserve/Injured or Reserve/Physically Unable to Perform.

Log on to www.raiders.com for an up-to-date roster.

COACHING STAFF

Head Coach,
Dennis Allen

Pro Career: Allen becomes the 18th head coach in the 52-year history of the Oakland Raiders. At age 39, Allen is the youngest current head coach in the NFL. Allen has 16 years of coaching experience, including 10 as an NFL assistant. He was on the coaching staff of teams that captured the division title four times—Denver, 2011; New Orleans, 2009, 2006; Atlanta, 2004—and qualified for the postseason in two other seasons—2010 and 2002. Allen was the NFL's second-youngest defensive coordinator at the time of his hiring by the Denver Broncos in 2011. He coordinated a defense that helped the Broncos win the AFC West and advance to the AFC Divisional round with a wild card victory. The Broncos improved 12 spots over the previous year in overall defensive ranking (from 32nd to 20th) and bettered their points allowed eight spots (from 32nd to 24th). From 2006-2010, Allen was an assistant coach for five seasons with New Orleans, first as assistant defensive line coach for two season, then as Saints defensive backs coach. Tutored a secondary that played a key role in helping the Saints to their first Super Bowl victory (XLIV). His unit accounted for an NFL-high six interception returns for touchdowns and totaled 22 picks en route to their championship. First NFL coaching position was as a defensive assistant for Atlanta (2002-05). Career record: 0-0.

Background: Allen played at Texas A&M, where he was a four-year letterman as a safety. Coached with the Aggies (1996-99) and Tulsa (2000-01). Was signed by Buffalo as an undrafted college free agent and spent training camp with the Bills (1996). Father played as a linebacker for the Atlanta Falcons from 1968-1972.

Personal: Born September 22, 1972, in Atlanta, Ga. Allen and his wife, Alisson, have a son, Garrison, and a daughter, Layla.

ASSISTANT COACHES

Keith Burns, asst. special teams; born September 26, 1960, Hurst, Texas. Safety Arkansas 1980-82. College coach: Arkansas 1984, Pacific 1985-88, Rice 1989-1992, Southern California 1993-97, Arkansas 1998-99, Tulsa 2000-02, San Jose State 2004-09, Kansas State 2010, Mississippi 2011. Pro coach: Joined Raiders in 2012.

John DeFilippo, quarterbacks; born April 12, 1978, Youngstown, Ohio. Quarterback James Madison 1996-1999. College coach: Fordham 2000, Notre Dame 2001-02, Columbia 2003-04, San Jose State 2010-11. Pro coach: New York Giants 2005-06, Oakland Raiders 2007-08, New York Jets 2009, re-joined Raiders in 2012.

Ted Gilmore, wide receivers; born March

21, 1967, Wichita, Kan. Receiver Butler County (Kan.) Community College 1986-87, Wyoming 1988-89. No pro playing experience. College coach: Wyoming 1994-98, Kansas 1999, Houston 2000, Purdue 2001-02, Colorado 2003-04, Nebraska 2005-10, Southern California 2011. Pro coach: Joined Raiders in 2012.

John Grieco, asst. strength and conditioning; born October 7, 1972, Greensburg, Pa. No pro playing experience. College coach: Florida 1995-2003, East Carolina 2004-05, Nevada-Las Vegas 2006-09, Louisiana-Monroe 2010-11. Pro coach: Joined Raiders in 2012.

Justin Griffith, quality control-offense; born July 21, 1980, Magee, Miss. Running back Mississippi State 1999-2002. Pro running back Atlanta Falcons 2003-06, Oakland Raiders 2007-08, Seattle Seahawks 2009. Pro coach: Seattle Seahawks 2011, joined Raiders in 2012.

Steve Hoffman, special teams coordinator; born September 8, 1958, Camden, N.J. Quarterback/wide receiver/running back/kicker/punter Dickinson College 1976-79. Pro punter Washington Federals (USFL) 1983. College coach: Miami 1985-88. Pro coach: Dallas Cowboys 1989-2004, Atlanta Falcons 2006, Miami Dolphins 2007-08, Kansas City Chiefs 2009-2011, joined Raiders in 2012.

Johnny Holland, linebackers; born March 11, 1965, Bellville, Texas. Inside linebacker Texas A&M 1983-86. Pro linebacker Green Bay Packers 1987-1993. Pro coach: Green Bay Packers 1995-99, Seattle Seahawks 2000-02, Detroit Lions 2003-05, Houston Texans 2006-2010, joined Raiders in 2012.

Mark Hutson, tight ends; born August 29, 1966, Fort Smith, Ark. Offensive line Oklahoma 1984-87. No pro playing experience. College coach: Oklahoma 1990-92, Murray State 1993-97, Boise State 1997, Arkansas 1998-99, Tulsa 2000-02, Eastern Illinois 2003-2006 (interim head coach 2006), Tulane 2007-2011 (interim head coach 2011). Pro coach: Joined Raiders in 2012.

Greg Knapp, offensive coordinator; born March 5, 1963, Seal Beach, Calif. Quarterback Sacramento State 1982-85. No pro playing experience. College coach: Sacramento State 1986-1994. Pro coach: San Francisco 49ers 1995-2003, Atlanta Falcons 2004-06, Oakland Raiders 2007-08, Seattle Seahawks 2009, Houston Texans 2010-11, re-joined Raiders in 2012.

Clayton Lopez, defensive backs; born May 26, 1970, Los Angeles, Calif. Defensive back Nevada 1991-94. No pro playing experience. College coach: Nevada 1995-98, Seattle Seahawks 1999-2003, Oakland Raiders 2004-05, Detroit Lions 2006-08, St. Louis Rams 2009-2011, re-joined Raiders in 2012.

Johnnie Lynn, defensive backs; born December 19, 1956, Los Angeles, Calif. Defensive back UCLA 1975-78.

Cornerback New York Jets 1979-1986. College coach: Arizona 1987-1993. Pro coach: Tampa Bay Buccaneers 1994-95, San Francisco 49ers 1996, New York Giants 1997-2003, Baltimore Ravens 2004-05, San Francisco 49ers 2006-2010, Philadelphia Eagles 2011, joined Raiders in 2012.

Al Miller, strength and conditioning; born August 29, 1947, El Dorado, Ark. No pro playing experience. College coach: Mississippi State 1980, Northeast Louisiana 1981, Alabama 1982-85. Pro coach: Denver Broncos 1985-1992, New York Giants 1993-96, Atlanta Falcons 1997-2005, joined Raiders in 2012.

Frank Pollack, offensive line; born November 5, 1967, Camp Springs, Md. Offensive tackle/offensive guard Northern Arizona 1985-89. Pro offensive tackle, offensive guard San Francisco 49ers 1990-97. College coach: Northern Arizona 2005-06. Pro coach: Houston Texans 2007-2011, joined Raiders in 2012.

Eric Sanders, quality control-defense; born August 2, 1983, Poughkeepsie, N.Y. No pro playing experience. College coach: UC Davis 2006, 2008-09, Utah State 2007. Pro coach: Joined Raiders in 2010.

Al Saunders, senior offensive assistant; born February 1, 1947, London, England. Defensive back San Jose State 1966-68. No pro playing experience. College coach: Southern California 1970-71, Missouri 1972, Utah State 1973-75, California 1976-1981, Tennessee 1982. Pro coach: San Diego Chargers 1983-88 (head coach 1986-88), Kansas City Chiefs 1989-1998, St. Louis Rams 1999-2000, Kansas City Chiefs 2001-05, Washington Redskins 2006-07, St. Louis Rams 2008, Baltimore Ravens, 2009-2010, joined Raiders in 2011.

Kelly Skipper, running backs; born July 25, 1967, Brawley, Calif. Running back Fresno State 1985-88. No pro playing experience. College coach: Fresno State 1989-1997, UCLA 1998-2002, Washington State 2003-06. Pro coach: Joined Raiders in 2007.

Jason Tarver, defensive coordinator; born August 28, 1974, Palo Alto, Calif. No pro playing experience. College coach: UCLA 1998-2000, Stanford 2011. Pro coach: San Francisco 49ers 2001-2010, joined Raiders in 2012.

Terrell Williams, defensive line; born June 19, 1974, Los Angeles, Calif. Nose guard East Carolina 1995-96. No pro playing experience. College coach: Fort Scott Community College 1998, North Carolina A&T 1999-2001, Youngstown State 2002-2003, Akron 2004-2005, Purdue 2006-2009, Texas A&M 2010-11. Pro coach: Joined Raiders in 2012.

Steve Wisniewski, asst. offensive line, born April 7, 1967, Rutland, Vt. Offensive lineman Penn State 1985-88. Pro offensive lineman Los Angeles/Oakland Raiders 1989-2001. College coach: Stanford 2010. Pro coach: Joined Raiders in 2011.

American Football Conference
North Division
Team Colors: Black and Gold
3400 South Water Street
Pittsburgh, Pennsylvania 15203
Telephone: (412) 432-7800

2012 SCHEDULE
PRESEASON
Aug. 9	at Philadelphia	7:30
Aug. 19	**Indianapolis**	8:00
Aug. 25	at Buffalo	7:00
Aug. 30	**Carolina**	7:30

REGULAR SEASON
Sep. 9	at Denver	8:20
Sep. 16	**New York Jets**	4:15
Sep. 23	at Oakland	4:15
Sep. 30	BYE	
Oct. 7	**Philadelphia**	1:00
Oct. 11	at Tennessee (Thurs)	8:20
Oct. 21	at Cincinnati	8:20
Oct. 28	**Washington**	1:00
Nov. 4	at New York Giants	4:15
Nov. 12	**Kansas City** (Mon)	8:30
Nov. 18	**Baltimore**	*8:20
Nov. 25	at Cleveland	1:00
Dec. 2	at Baltimore	4:15
Dec. 9	**San Diego**	1:00
Dec. 16	at Dallas	4:15
Dec. 23	**Cincinnati**	1:00
Dec. 30	**Cleveland**	1:00

All times ET; Sunday night games in Weeks 11-16 subject to change
Stadium: Heinz Field (opened in 2001)
• **Capacity:** 65,500
100 Art Rooney Avenue
Pittsburgh, Pennsylvania 15212
Playing Surface: Natural Grass
Training Camp: St. Vincent College
Latrobe, PA 15650

HEINZ FIELD

CLUB OFFICIALS
Chairman Emeritus: Daniel M. Rooney
President: Arthur J. Rooney II
Vice President: John R. McGinley
Vice President: Arthur J. Rooney Jr.
Administration Advisor: Charles H. Noll
Director of Planning & Development:
Mark Hart
Director of Finance: Bob Tyler
Director of Business & Administration:
Omar Khan
General Manager: Kevin Colbert
College Scouting Coordinator:
Ron Hughes
Pro Scouting Coordinator: Brandon Hunt
Head Athletic Trainer: John Norwig
Director of Marketing: Tony Quatrini
Communications Coordinator:
Burt Lauten
Director of Stadium Management:
Jim Sacco
Video Coordinator: Bob McCartney
Human Relations/Office Coordinator:
Geraldine Glenn
Ticket Manager: Ben Lentz

COACHING HISTORY
Pittsburgh Pirates 1933-39
(591-538-21)
Records include postseason games
1933	Forrest (Jap) Douds	3-6-2
1934	Luby DiMelio	2-10-0
1935-36	Joe Bach	10-14-0
1937-39	Johnny (Blood) McNally*	6-19-0
1939-1940	Walt Kiesling	3-13-3
1941	Bert Bell**	0-2-0
	Aldo (Buff) Donelli***	0-5-0
1941-44	Walt Kiesling****	13-20-2
1945	Jim Leonard	2-8-0
1946-47	Jock Sutherland	13-10-1
1948-1951	Johnny Michelosen	20-26-2
1952-53	Joe Bach	11-13-0
1954-56	Walt Kiesling	14-22-0
1957-1964	Raymond (Buddy) Parker	51-47-6
1965	Mike Nixon	2-12-0
1966-68	Bill Austin	11-28-3
1969-1991	Chuck Noll	209-156-1
1992-2006	Bill Cowher	161-99-1
2007-2011	Mike Tomlin	60-28-0

*Released after three games in 1939
**Resigned after two games in 1941
***Released after five games in 1941
****Co-coach with Earle (Greasy) Neale in Philadelphia-Pittsburgh merger in 1943 and with Phil Handler in Chicago Cardinals-Pittsburgh merger in 1944

PAID ATTENDANCE
Home 512,636   Away 531,338
Total 1,043,974
Single-game home record,
66,662 (1/23/11)
Single-season home record,
517,599 (2009)

2012 DRAFT CHOICES
Round	Name	Pos.	College
1	David DeCastro	G	Stanford
2	Mike Adams	T	Ohio St.
3	Sean Spence	LB	Miami
4	Alameda Ta'amu	DT	Washington
5	Chris Rainey	RB	Florida
7	Toney Clemons	WR	Colorado
	David Paulson	TE	Oregon
	Terrence Frederick	DB	Texas A&M
	Kelvin Beachum	T	Southern Methodist

PITTSBURGH STEELERS

2011 TEAM RECORD

PRESEASON (3-1)

Date	Result	Opponent
8/12	L 7-16	at Washington
8/18	W 24-14	Philadelphia
8/27	W 34-16	Atlanta
9/1	W 33-17	at Carolina

REGULAR SEASON (12-4)

Date	Result	Opponent
9/11	L 7-35	at Baltimore
9/18	W 24-0	Seattle
9/25	W 23-20	at Indianapolis
10/2	L 10-17	at Houston
10/9	W 38-17	Tennessee
10/16	W 17-13	Jacksonville
10/23	W 32-20	at Arizona
10/30	W 25-17	New England
11/6	L 20-23	Baltimore
11/13	W 24-17	at Cincinnati
11/27	W 13-9	at Kansas City
12/4	W 35-7	Cincinnati
12/8	W 14-3	Cleveland
12/19	L 3-20	at San Francisco
12/24	W 27-0	St. Louis
1/1	W 13-9	at Cleveland

POSTSEASON (0-1)

Date	Result	Opponent
1/8	L 23-29	at Denver (OT)
(OT) Overtime		

SCORE BY PERIODS

Steelers	69	121	63	72	0 —	325
Opponents	43	71	56	57	0 —	227

2011 TEAM STATISTICS

	Steelers	Opp.
Total First Downs	341	264
Rushing	96	82
Passing	221	156
Penalty	24	26
3rd Down: Made/Att	90/196	86/221
3rd Down Pct.	45.9	38.9
4th Down: Made/Att	3/8	8/13
4th Down Pct.	37.5	61.5
Possession Avg.	32:33	27:27
Total Net Yards	5957	4348
Avg. Per Game	372.3	271.8
Total Plays	1015	964
Avg. Per Play	5.9	4.5
Net Yards Rushing	1903	1597
Avg. Per Game	118.9	99.8
Total Rushes	434	399
Net Yards Passing	4054	2751
Avg. Per Game	253.4	171.9
Sacked/Yards Lost	42/279	35/230
Gross Yards	4333	2981
Att./Completions	539/341	530/289
Completion Pct.	63.3	54.5
Had Intercepted	15	11
Punts/Average	60/44.7	87/43.6
Net Punting Avg.	60/38.6	87/38.9
Penalties/Yards	101/854	96/777
Fumbles/Ball Lost	16/13	13/4
Touchdowns	36	23
Rushing	13	7
Passing	21	15
Returns	2	1

2011 INDIVIDUAL STATISTICS

PASSING

PASSING	Att.	Comp.	Yds.	Pct.	TD	Int.	Tkld.	Rate
Roethlisberger	513	324	4077	63.2	21	14	40/269	90.1
C. Batch	24	15	208	62.5	0	1	2/10	72.9
Sanders	1	1	15	100.0	0	0	0/0	118.8
Sepulveda	1	1	33	100.0	0	0	0/0	118.8
Steelers	539	341	4333	63.3	21	15	42/279	89.7
Opponents	530	289	2981	54.5	15	11	35/230	71.7

SCORING

SCORING	TD R	TD P	TD Rt	PAT	FG	Saf	PTS
Suisham	0	0	0	36/36	23/31	0	105
Mendenhall	9	0	0	0/0	0/0	0	54
Wallace	0	8	0	0/0	0/0	0	48
A. Brown	0	2	1	0/0	0/0	0	18
Redman	3	0	0	0/0	0/0	0	18
Cotchery	0	2	0	0/0	0/0	0	12
Miller	0	2	0	0/0	0/0	0	12
Sanders	0	2	0	0/0	0/0	0	12
Ward	0	2	0	0/0	0/0	0	12
Clay	1	0	0	0/0	0/0	0	6
Johnson	0	1	0	0/0	0/0	0	6
Moore	0	1	0	0/0	0/0	0	6
Polamalu	0	0	1	0/0	0/0	0	6
Saunders	0	1	0	0/0	0/0	0	6
Steelers	13	21	2	36/36	23/31	2	325
Opponents	7	15	1	21/21	22/27	0	227

2-Pt Conversions: Team 0-0, Opponents 1-2

RUSHING

RUSHING	No.	Yds	Avg	LG	TD
Mendenhall	228	928	4.1	68	9
Redman	110	479	4.4	27	3
Moore	22	157	7.1	21	0
Dwyer	16	123	7.7	76	0
Roethlisberger	31	70	2.3	11	0
Wallace	5	57	11.4	21	0
A. Brown	7	41	5.9	10	0
Clay	10	41	4.1	10t	1
Miller	1	6	6.0	6	0
Cotchery	1	3	3.0	3	0
C. Batch	3	-2	-.7	0	0
Steelers	434	1903	4.4	76	13
Opponents	399	1597	4.0	42t	7

RECEIVING

RECEIVING	No.	Yds	Avg	LG	TD
Wallace	72	1193	16.6	95t	8
A. Brown	69	1108	16.1	79t	2
Miller	51	631	12.4	39	2
Ward	46	381	8.3	31	2
Sanders	22	288	13.1	32	2
Mendenhall	18	154	8.6	35	0
Redman	18	78	4.3	12	0
Cotchery	16	237	14.8	36	2
Johnson	12	91	7.6	25	1
Moore	11	104	9.5	24	1
Saunders	4	29	7.3	14	1
Mundy	1	33	33.0	33	0
Dwyer	1	6	6.0	6	0
Steelers	341	4333	12.7	95t	21
Opponents	289	2981	10.3	73t	15

INTERCEPTIONS

INTERCEPTIONS	No.	Yds	Avg	LG	TD
Polamalu	2	33	16.5	33	0
Taylor	2	29	14.5	29	0
Gay	2	12	6.0	12	0
Clark	1	10	10.0	10	0
Lewis	1	9	9.0	9	0
Mundy	1	5	5.0	5	0
Woodley	1	1	1.0	1	0
Timmons	1	0	0.0	0	0
Steelers	11	99	9.0	33	0
Opponents	15	201	13.4	31	0

PUNTING

PUNTING	No.	Yds.	Avg.	In 20	LG
Kapinos	34	1530	45.0	10	59
Sepulveda	25	1153	46.1	8	66
Steelers	60	2683	44.7	18	66
Opponents	87	3789	43.6	30	63

PUNT RETURNS

PUNT RETURNS	Ret	FC	Yds	Avg	LG	TD
A. Brown	30	26	325	10.8	60t	1
Sanders	3	0	22	7.3	10	0
Steelers	33	26	347	10.5	60t	1
Opponents	29	13	245	8.4	20	0

KICKOFF RETURNS

KICKOFF RETURNS	No.	Yds	Avg	LG	TD
A. Brown	27	737	27.3	52	0
Sanders	5	93	18.6	25	0
Cotchery	1	19	19.0	19	0
Moore	1	10	10.0	10	0
Redman	1	18	18.0	18	0
Steelers	35	877	25.1	52	0
Opponents	43	1018	23.7	45	0

FIELD GOALS

FIELD GOALS	1-19	20-29	30-39	40-49	50+
Suisham	2/2	8/8	6/8	6/11	1/2
Steelers	2/2	8/8	6/8	6/11	1/2
Opponents	1/1	8/8	2/4	10/12	1/2

SACKS

SACKS	No.
Harrison	9.0
Woodley	9.0
Keisel	3.0
Worlids	3.0
Farrior	2.0
Timmons	2.0
Foote	1.5
Hood	1.5
Clark	1.0
Heyward	1.0
McLendon	1.0
Polamalu	1.0
Steelers	35.0
Opponents	42.0

RECORD HOLDERS
INDIVIDUAL RECORDS—CAREER

Category	Name	Performance
Rushing (Yds.)	Franco Harris, 1972-1983	11,950
Passing (Yds.)	Terry Bradshaw, 1970-1983	27,989
Passing (TDs)	Terry Bradshaw, 1970-1983	212
Receiving (No.)	Hines Ward, 1998-2011	1,000
Receiving (Yds.)	Hines Ward, 1998-2011	12,083
Interceptions	Mel Blount, 1970-1983	57
Punting (Avg.)	Bobby Joe Green, 1960-61	45.7
Punt Return (Avg.)	Bobby Gage, 1949-1950	14.9
Kickoff Return (Avg.)	Lynn Chandnois, 1950-56	29.6
Field Goals	Gary Anderson, 1982-1994	309
Touchdowns (Tot.)	Franco Harris, 1972-1983	100
Points	Gary Anderson, 1982-1994	1,343
*Sacks	Jason Gildon, 1994-2003	77.0

INDIVIDUAL RECORDS—SINGLE SEASON

Category	Name	Performance
Rushing (Yds.)	Barry Foster, 1992	1,690
Passing (Yds.)	Ben Roethlisberger, 2009	4,328
Passing (TDs)	Ben Roethlisberger, 2007	32
Receiving (No.)	Hines Ward, 2002	112
Receiving (Yds.)	Yancey Thigpen, 1997	1,398
Interceptions	Mel Blount, 1975	11
Punting (Avg.)	Bobby Joe Green, 1961	47.0
Punt Return (Avg.)	Bobby Gage, 1949	16.0
Kickoff Return (Avg.)	Lynn Chandnois, 1952	35.2
Field Goals	Norm Johnson, 1995	34
Touchdowns (Tot.)	Willie Parker, 2006	16
Points	Norm Johnson, 1995	141
*Sacks	James Harrison, 2008	16.0

INDIVIDUAL RECORDS—SINGLE GAME

Category	Name	Performance
Rushing (Yds.)	Willie Parker, 12-7-06	223
Passing (Yds.)	Ben Roethlisberger, 12-20-09	503
Passing (TDs)	Terry Bradshaw, 11-15-81	5
	Mark Malone, 9-8-85	5
	Ben Roethlisberger, 11-5-07, 10-9-11	5
Receiving (No.)	Courtney Hawkins, 11-1-98	14
Receiving (Yds.)	Plaxico Burress, 11-10-02	253
Interceptions	Jack Butler, 12-13-53	**4
Field Goals	Gary Anderson, 10-23-88	6
	Jeff Reed, 12-1-02	6
Touchdowns (Tot.)	Ray Mathews, 10-17-54	4
	Roy Jefferson, 11-3-68	4
Points	Ray Mathews, 10-17-54	24
	Roy Jefferson, 11-3-68	24
*Sacks	Chad Brown, 10-13-96	4.5

*Sacks became an official statistic in 1982.
**NFL Record

PITTSBURGH STEELERS

2012 VETERAN ROSTER

No.	Name	Pos.	Ht.	Wt.	Birthdate	NFL Exp.	College	Hometown	How Acq.	'11 Games/ Starts
28	Allen, Cortez	CB	6-1	196	10/29/88	2	The Citadel	Ocala, Fla.	D4-'11	15/0
26	Allen, Will	S	6-1	200	6/17/82	9	Ohio State	Dayton, Ohio	FA-'10	16/0
20	Batch, Baron	RB	5-10	210	12/21/87	2	Texas Tech	Midland, Texas	D7-'11	0*
16	Batch, Charlie	QB	6-2	216	12/5/74	15	Eastern Michigan	Homestead, Pa.	FA-'02	4/1
84	Brown, Antonio	WR	5-10	186	7/10/88	3	Central Michigan	Miami, Fla.	D6b-'10	16/3
31	Brown, Curtis	CB	6-0	185	9/24/88	2	Texas	Longview, Texas	D3-'11	12/0
54	Carter, Chris	LB	6-1	248	4/6/89	2	Fresno State	Fontana, Calif.	D5-'11	8/0
25	Clark, Ryan	S	5-11	205	10/12/79	11	Louisiana State	Marrero, La.	UFA(Wash)-'06	16/3
74	Colon, Willie	T	6-3	315	4/9/83	7	Hofstra	Bronx, N.Y.	D4a-'06	1/1
89	Cotchery, Jerricho	WR	6-1	200	6/16/82	9	North Carolina State	Birmingham, Ala.	FA-'11	13/0
27	Dwyer, Jonathan	RB	5-11	229	7/26/89	3	Georgia Tech	Marietta, Ga.	D6a-'10	7/0
79	Essex, Trai	G	6-5	324	12/5/82	8	Northwestern	Fort Wayne, Ind.	D3-'05	16/3
50	Foote, Larry	LB	6-1	239	6/12/80	11	Michigan	Detroit, Mich.	FA-'10	15/5
73	Foster, Ramon	G	6-6	325	1/7/86	4	Tennessee	Henning, Tenn.	FA-'09	15/14
77	Gilbert, Marcus	T	6-6	330	2/15/88	2	Florida	Fort Lauderdale, Fla.	D2-'11	14/13
98	Hampton, Casey	NT	6-1	325	9/3/77	12	Texas	Galveston, Texas	D1-'01	13/12
92	Harrison, James	LB	6-0	242	5/4/78	9	Kent State	Akron, Ohio	FA-'04	11/11
97	Heyward, Cameron	DE	6-5	288	5/6/89	2	Ohio State	Pittsburgh, Pa.	D1-'11	16/0
96	Hood, Ziggy	DE	6-3	300	2/16/87	4	Missouri	Amarillo, Texas	D1-'09	16/14
57	Ivy, Mortty	LB	6-1	239	4/26/86	2	West Virginia	Monroeville, Pa.	FA-'11	6/0
85	Johnson, David	TE	6-2	260	8/26/87	4	Arkansas State	Pine Bluff, Ark.	D7b-'09	16/16
13	Kapinos, Jeremy	P	6-1	233	8/23/84	5	Penn State	West Point, N.Y.	FA-'11	8/0
99	Keisel, Brett	DE	6-5	285	9/19/78	11	Brigham Young	Greybull, Wyo.	D7b-'02	14/14
4	Leftwich, Byron	QB	6-5	250	1/14/80	10	Marshall	Washington, D.C.	FA-'11	0*
64	Legursky, Doug	C/G	6-1	315	6/9/86	4	Marshall	Frankfort, Germany	FA-'08	10/10
23	Lewis, Keenan	CB	6-0	208	5/17/86	4	Oregon State	New Orleans, La.	D3c-'09	16/1
39	McFadden, Walter	CB	5-10	180	1/21/87	2	Auburn	Pompano Beach, Fla.	FA-'12	0*
90	McLendon, Steve	NT	6-4	280	1/3/86	3	Troy	Ozark, Ala.	FA-'09	14/1
34	Mendenhall, Rashard	RB	5-10	225	6/19/87	4	Illinois	Skokie, Ill.	D1-'08	15/15
83	Miller, Heath	TE	6-5	256	10/22/82	8	Virginia	Swords Creek, Va.	D1-'05	16/16
29	Mundy, Ryan	S	6-1	209	2/11/85	4	West Virginia	Pittsburgh, Pa.	D6b-'08	16/0
43	Polamalu, Troy	S	5-10	207	4/19/81	10	Southern California	Santa Ana, Calif.	D1-'03	16/16
45	Pope, Leonard	TE	6-8	264	9/10/83	7	Georgia	Americus, Ga.	UFA(KC)-'12	16/10*
53	Pouncey, Maurkice	C	6-4	304	7/24/89	3	Florida	Lakeland, Fla.	D1-'10	14/14
33	Redman, Isaac	RB	6-0	230	11/10/84	3	Bowie State	Paulsboro, N.J.	FA-'09	16/1
7	Roethlisberger, Ben	QB	6-5	241	3/2/82	9	Miami (Ohio)	Cory Rawson, Ohio	D1-'04	15/15
88	Sanders, Emmanuel	WR	5-11	180	3/17/87	3	Southern Methodist	Bellville, Texas	D3-'10	11/0
82	Saunders, Weslye	TE	6-5	270	1/16/89	2	South Carolina	Durham, N.C.	FA-'11	16/6
71	Scott, Chris	T	6-4	319	8/4/87	2	Tennessee	Riverdale, Ga.	FA-'11	2/0
72	Scott, Jonathan	T	6-6	318	1/10/83	6	Texas	Dallas, Texas	FA-'10	12/5
10	Smith, Troy	QB	6-0	217	7/20/84	5	Ohio State	Cleveland, Ohio	FA-'12	0*
6	Suisham, Shaun	K	6-0	200	12/29/81	8	Bowling Green	Wallaceburg, Ont. Canada	FA-'10	16/0
55	Sylvester, Stevenson	LB	6-2	231	7/18/88	3	Utah	Las Vegas, Nev.	D5c-'10	15/1
24	Taylor, Ike	CB	6-2	195	5/5/80	10	Louisiana-Lafayette	Gretna, La.	D4-'03	16/16
94	Timmons, Lawrence	LB	6-1	234	5/14/86	6	Florida State	Florence, S.C.	D1-'07	16/16
17 +	Wallace, Mike	WR	6-0	199	8/1/86	4	Mississippi	New Orleans, La.	D3b-'09	16/14
60	Warren, Greg	LS	6-3	252	10/18/81	8	North Carolina	Goldsboro, N.C.	FA-'05	16/0
67	Weston, Kade	DT	6-5	315	11/29/83	2	Georgia	Red Bank, N.J.	FA-'12	0*
15	Williams, Derrick	WR	5-11	197	7/6/86	3	Penn State	Washington, D.C.	FA-'12	0*
56	Woodley, LaMarr	LB	6-2	265	11/3/84	6	Michigan	Saginaw, Mich.	D2-'07	10/10
65	Woods, Al	DE	6-4	307	3/25/87	3	Louisiana State	Jennings, La.	FA-'11	2/0*
93	Worilds, Jason	LB	6-2	262	3/3/88	3	Virginia Tech	Carteret, N.J.	D2-'10	12/7

* Batch missed '11 season because of injury; Leftwich missed '11 season because of injury; McFadden last active with Oakland in '10; Pope played 16 games with Kansas City; Smith last active with San Francisco in '10; Weston missed the '10 season with New England because of injury; Williams last active with Detroit in '10; Woods played 2 games with Seattle.

+ Restricted free agent; subject to developments.

Retired—Hines Ward, 14-year wide receiver, 15 games in '11.

Players lost through free agency (1): CB William Gay (Ariz; 16 games).

Also played with Steelers in '11—WR Arnaz Battle (10 games), LB James Farrior (16), NT Chris Hoke (6), G Chris Kemoeatu (13), CB Bryant McFadden (13), Jamon Meredith (4), RB Mewelde Moore (12), P Daniel Sepulveda (8), DE Aaron Smith (4), T Max Starks (12).

FIRST-YEAR ROSTER

Name	Pos.	Ht.	Wt.	Birthdate	College	Hometown	How Acq.
Adams, Mike	T	6-7	323	3/10/90	Ohio State	Farrell, Pa.	D2
Beachum, Kelvin	G	6-3	303	6/8/89	Southern Methodist	Mexia, Texas	D7d
Beiler, Tyler (1)	WR	6-0	190	11/14/88	Bridgewater College (VA)	Ronks, Pa.	FA
Blanc, Mike (1)	DT	6-3	286	4/13/87	Auburn	Pompano Beach, Fla.	FA
Bryant, Corbin (1)	DE	6-4	297	1/4/88	Northwestern	Chicago, Ill.	FA-'11
Butler, Drew	P	6-1	204	5/10/89	Georgia	Duluth, Ga.	FA
Carter, Terry	CB	5-10	184	4/28/88	Louisiana Tech	West Monroe, La.	FA
Clay, John (1)	RB	6-1	248	1/4/88	Wisconsin	Racine, Wisc.	FA-"11
Clemons, Toney	WR	6-2	210	10/11/88	Colorado	Pittsburgh, Pa.	D7a
Cromartie-Smith, Damon (1)	S	6-2	210	2/19/87	Texas-El Paso	Riverside, Calif.	FA-'11
DeCastro, David	G	6-5	316	1/11/90	Stanford	Bellevue, Wash.	D1
Dixon, Connor	WR	6-5	222	9/10/87	Duquesne	South Park, Pa.	FA
Frederick, Terrence	CB	5-10	187	2/10/90	Texas A&M	Katy, Texas	D7c
Gilreath, David (1)	WR	5-10	169	12/11/88	Wisconsin	New Hope, Minn.	FA
Golden, Robert	S	5-11	202	9/13/90	Arizona	Fresno, Calif.	FA
Hicks, Brandon (1)	LB	6-2	228	3/22/89	Florida	Jacksonville, Fla.	FA
Hrapmann, Daniel	K	5-9	164	4/21/89	Southern Mississippi	New Orleans, La.	FA
Igbinosun, Ikponmwosa	DE	6-4	288	9/10/90	Southern Connecticut State	Elizabeth, N.J.	FA
Johnson, Jerrod (1)	QB	6-5	251	7/27/88	Texas A&M	Houston, Texas	FA
Johnson, Will (1)	FB	6-2	238	11/14/89	West Virginia	Dayton, Ohio	FA
Jolly, Kyle (1)	T	6-6	300	7/22/87	North Carolina	Powhatan, Va.	FA-'11
Lee, Ryan	C/G	6-3	308	10/16/88	Furman	Carrollton, Ga.	FA
Lindsey, Brandon	LB	6-2	254	1/10/89	Pittsburgh	Aliquippa, Pa.	FA
Lyons, Wes	TE	6-9	250	9/12/88	West Virginia	North Braddock, Pa.	FA
Malecki, John (1)	OG	6-2	298	5/26/88	Pittsburgh	Murrysville, Pa.	FA-'11
Maze, Marquis	WR	5-8	186	3/2/89	Alabama	Birmingham, Ala.	FA
McCoy, Jamie (1)	TE	6-3	240	7/21/87	Texas A&M	Midland, Texas	FA-'11
McFadden, Marshall (1)	LB	6-1	233	8/4/86	South Carolina State	Lamar, S.C.	FA
Paulson, David	TE	6-4	246	2/22/89	Oregon	Auburn, Wash.	D7b
Rainey, Chris	RB	5-9	180	3/2/88	Florida	Lakeland, Fla.	D5
Robinson, Adrian	LB	6-1	250	11/21/89	Temple	Harrisburg, Pa.	FA
Rolle, Myron (1)	S	6-2	215	10/30/86	Florida State	Houston, Texas	FA
Spence, Sean	LB	5-11	231	6/7/90	Miami	Miami, Fla.	D3
Stewart, Juamorris (1)	WR	6-2	198	12/6/86	Southern	Baton Rouge, La.	FA
Stoller, Jake	DE	6-3	284	12/2/89	Yale	Shaker Heights, Ohio	FA
Ta'amu, Alameda	NT	6-3	348	8/23/90	Washington	Kent, Wash.	D4
Turner, Trevis (1)	T	6-7	333	5/2/87	Abilene Christian	DeSoto, Texas	FA-'11
Young, Jimmy (1)	WR	6-0	204	1/25/87	Texas Christian	Monroe, La.	FA

The term NFL Rookie is defined as a player who is in his first season of professional football and has not been on the roster of another professional football team for any regular-season or postseason games. A Rookie is designated by an "R" on NFL rosters. Players who have been active in another professional football league or players who have NFL experience, including either preseason training camp or being on an Active List or Inactive List, or on Reserve/Injured or Reserve/Physically Unable to Perform for fewer than six regular-season games, are termed NFL First-Year Players. An NFL First-Year Player is designated by a "1" on NFL rosters. Thereafter, a player is credited with an additional year of experience for each season in which he accumulates six games on the Active List or Inactive List, or on Reserve/Injured or Reserve/Physically Unable to Perform.

Log on to www.steelers.com for an up-to-date roster.

PITTSBURGH STEELERS

COACHING STAFF

Head Coach,
Mike Tomlin

Pro Career: Named the sixteenth head coach in Steelers history when he replaced Bill Cowher on January 22, 2007. Became the youngest coach (36 years, 323 days) in NFL history to win a Super Bowl when the Steelers defeated the Arizona Cardinals, 27-23, in Super Bowl XLIII on February 1, 2009. Tomlin has reached the playoffs four times in his first five seasons and he is the only coach in Steelers' history to win division titles each of his first two seasons. In 2010 Tomlin's club won its third division title in in a four-year span. In 2008, Tomlin directed the Steelers to a 12-4 record, winning his second-consecutive AFC North title. That season culminated with a Super Bowl triumph, making Tomlin one of only seven coaches in league history to win a Super Bowl within his first two seasons as an NFL head coach. In his first season, Tomlin guided the Steelers to a 10-6 record and their first AFC North title since 2004. Tomlin was the Minnesota Vikings defensive coordinator in 2006 after spending the previous five seasons (2001-05) as defensive backs coach for the Tampa Bay Buccaneers. Tomlin coached one of the top defensive backfields in the NFL for the Buccaneers, culminating with its performance in Super Bowl XXXVII. The secondary recorded four interceptions, returning two for touchdowns to help Tampa Bay capture the franchise's first Super Bowl title. Tomlin served two seasons as the defensive backs coach at the University of Cincinnati (1999-2000) before going to Tampa Bay. Prior to joining the Cincinnati staff, Tomlin had a short stint on the coaching staff at Tennessee-Martin and then spent two seasons at Arkansas State. He spent the 1996 season as a graduate assistant at Memphis. Tomlin began his coaching career in 1995 as wide receivers coach at Virginia Military Institute. Career record: 60-28.

Background: Was a three-year starter at wide receiver at William & Mary (1990-94) and finished his career with 101 receptions for 2,046 yards and a school-record 20 touchdown receptions. A first-team All-Yankee Conference selection in 1994, he established a school record with a 20.2 yards per catch average. Tomlin was a teammate of current Viking Pro Bowl safety Darren Sharper at William and Mary. Graduated in 1994 with a degree in sociology.

Personal: Born in Hampton, Va., on March 15, 1972. He and his wife, Kiya, have two sons, Dino and Mason, and a daughter Harlyn Quinn.

ASSISTANT COACHES

Keith Butler, linebackers; born May 16, 1956, Anniston, Ala. Linebacker Memphis 1974-77. Pro linebacker Seattle Seahawks 1978-1987. College coach: Memphis 1990-97, Arkansas State 1998. Pro coach: Cleveland Browns 1999-2002, joined Steelers in 2003.

James Daniel, tight ends; born January 17, 1953, Wetumpka, Ala. Guard Alabama State 1970-73. No pro playing experience. College coach: Auburn 1981-1992. Pro coach: New York Giants 1993-96, Atlanta Falcons 1997-2003, joined Steelers in 2004.

Al Everest, special teams; born August 22, 1950, Santa Barbara, Calif. Safety Southern Methodist 1970-71. No pro playing experience. College coach: Southern Methodist 1972, North Texas 1973-74, Cameron University 1974-75. Pro coach: Arizona Cardinals 1996-99, New Orleans Saints 2000-05, San Francisco 49ers 2007-09, joined Steelers in 2010.

Randy Fichtner, quarterbacks; born November 7, 1963, Cleveland, Ohio. Defensive back Purdue 1982-85. No pro playing experience. College coach: Michigan 1986-87, Southern California 1988, Nevada-Las Vegas 1989, Memphis 1990-93, Purdue 1994-96, Arkansas State 1997-2000, Memphis 2001-06. Pro coach: Joined Steelers in 2007.

Todd Haley, offensive coordinator; February 28, 1967, Atlanta, Ga. No college or pro playing experience. Pro coach: New York Jets 1997-2000, Chicago Bears 2001-03, Dallas Cowboys 2004-06, Arizona Cardinals 2007-08, Kansas City Chiefs 2009-2011, joined Steelers in 2012.

Amos Jones, asst. special teams; born December 31, 1959, Tallahassee, Fla.. Safety/running back Alabama 1978-1980. No pro playing experience. College coach: Alabama 1981-82, Temple 1983-88, Alabama 1990-91, Pittsburgh 1992, Tulane 1995-96, Cincinnati 1999-2002, James Madison 2003, Mississippi State 2004-06. Pro coach: British Columbia (CFL) 1997, joined Steelers in 2007.

Sean Kugler, offensive line; born August 9, 1966, Lockport, N.Y. Offensive line Texas-El Paso 1985-89. No pro playing experience. College coach: Texas-El Paso 1993-2000, Boise State 2006. Pro coach: Detroit Lions 2001-05, Buffalo Bills 2007-09, joined Steelers in 2010.

Carnell Lake, defensive backs; born July 15, 1967, Salt Lake City, Utah. Outside linebacker UCLA 1985-1988. Pro defensive back Pittsburgh Steelers 1989-1998, Jacksonville Jaguars 1999-2000, Baltimore Ravens 2001. College coach: UCLA 2009. Pro coach: Joined Steelers in 2011.

Dick LeBeau, defensive coordinator; born September 9, 1937, London, Ohio. Defensive back Ohio State 1955-58. Pro cornerback Detroit Lions 1959-1972. Pro coach: Philadelphia Eagles 1973-75, Green Bay Packers 1976-79, Cincinnati Bengals 1980-1991, 1997-2002 (head coach 2000-02), Pittsburgh Steelers 1992-96, Buffalo Bills 2003, re-joined Steelers in 2004.

John Mitchell, asst. head coach/ defensive line; born October 14, 1951, Mobile, Ala. Defensive end Eastern Arizona J.C. 1969-1970, Alabama 1971-72. No pro playing experience. College coach: Alabama 1973-76, Arkansas 1977-1982, Temple 1986, Louisiana State 1987-1990. Pro coach: Birmingham Stallions (USFL) 1983-85, Cleveland Browns 1991-93, joined Steelers in 1994.

Scottie Montgomery, wide receivers; born May 26, 1978, Shelby, N.C. Wide receiver Duke 1996-99. Pro wide receiver Carolina Panthers 2000, Denver Broncos 2000-02, Oakland Raiders 2003, Georgia Force (AFL) 2005. College coach: Duke 2006-09. Pro coach: Joined Steelers in 2010.

Kirby Wilson, running backs; born August 24, 1961, Los Angeles, Calif. Running back/wide receiver Pasadena (Calif.) C.C. 1979-1980, Illinois 1981-82. Pro cornerback Winnipeg Blue Bombers (CFL) 1983, Toronto Argonauts (CFL) 1984. College coach: Pasadena (Calif.) C.C. 1985, L.A. Southwest (Calif.) J.C. 1989-1990, Southern Illinois 1991-92, Wyoming 1993-94, Iowa State 1995-96, Southern California 2001. Pro coach: New England Patriots 1997-99, Washington Redskins 2000, Tampa Bay Buccaneers 2002-03, Arizona Cardinals 2004-06, joined Steelers in 2007.

American Football Conference
West Division
Team Colors: Navy Blue, Powder Blue,
White, and Gold
P.O. Box 609609
San Diego, California 92160-9609
Telephone: (858) 874-4500

2012 SCHEDULE
PRESEASON
Aug. 9   **Green Bay**...........................5:00
Aug. 18 **Dallas**................................6:00
Aug. 24 at Minnesota 5:00
Aug. 30 at San Francisco................7:00

REGULAR SEASON
Sep. 10 at Oakland (Mon)................7:15
Sep. 16 **Tennessee** 1:15
Sep. 23 **Atlanta**..............................1:05
Sep. 30 at Kansas City 10:00a
Oct. 7   at New Orleans..................5:20
Oct. 15 **Denver** (Mon) 5:30
Oct. 21 BYE
Oct. 28 at Cleveland..................10:00a
Nov. 1   **Kansas City** (Thurs)..........5:20
Nov. 11 at Tampa Bay 10:00a
Nov. 18 at Denver...........................1:15
Nov. 25 **Baltimore**..........................1:05
Dec. 2   **Cincinnati** 1:15
Dec. 9   at Pittsburgh..................10:00a
Dec. 16 **Carolina**...........................1:05
Dec. 23 at New York Jets *5:20
Dec. 30 **Oakland** 1:15
*All times PT; Sunday night games in
Weeks 11-16 subject to change

Stadium: Qualcomm Stadium
(opened in 1967)
• **Capacity:** 70,000 (app.)
9449 Friars Road
San Diego, California 92108
Playing Surface: Grass
Training Camp: Chargers Park
4020 Murphy Canyon Rd.
San Diego, CA 92123

QUALCOMM STADIUM

CLUB OFFICIALS
Owner: Alex G. Spanos
Chairman of the Board-President:
Dean A. Spanos
Executive Vice President:
Michael A. Spanos
Executive Vice President-Chief Executive
Officer: A.G. Spanos
Executive Vice President-General
Manager: A.J. Smith
Executive Vice President of Football
Operations-Assistant General
Manager: Ed McGuire
Executive Vice President-Chief Financial
Officer: Jeanne M. Bonk
Senior Vice President-Chief Marketing
Officer: Ken Derrett
Director of Player Personnel:
Jimmy Raye
Director of College Scouting:
John Spanos
Director of Pro Scouting:
Dennis Abraham
Senior Executive: Randy Mueller
Head Athletic Trainer: James Collins
Director of Video Operations:
Brian Duddy
Equipment Manager: Bob Wick
Director of Player Development:
Arthur Hightower
Vice President of Marketing Partnerships:
Dennis O'Leary
Senior Director of Ticket Sales and
Service: Todd Poulsen
Senior Director Premium Seat Sales:
Rod Emmons
Director of Business Operations:
John Hinek
Director of Public Relations: Bill Johnston
Director of Public Affairs &
Corporate/Community Relations:
Kimberley Layton
Director of Security: Dick Lewis
Director of Stadium/Game Operations &
Events: Sean O'Connor
Controller: Marsha Wells
Director of Ticket Operations:
Michael L. Dougherty

COACHING HISTORY
Los Angeles 1960
(402-401-11)
Records include postseason games
1960-69 Sid Gillman* 83-51-6
1969-1970 Charlie Waller 9-7-3
1971   Sid Gillman** 4-6-0
1971-73 Harland Svare*** 7-17-2
1973   Ron Waller.....................1-5-0
1974-78 Tommy Prothro**** ...21-39-0
1978-1986 Don Coryell# 72-60-0
1986-88 Al Saunders 17-22-0
1989-1991 Dan Henning............16-32-0
1992-96 Bobby Ross...............50-36-0
1997-98 Kevin Gilbride...............6-16-0
1998   June Jones 3-7-0
1999-2001 Mike Riley.................14-34-0
2002-06 Marty Schottenheimer.47-35-0
2007-2011 Norv Turner 52-34-0
    *Retired after nine games in 1969
    **Resigned after 10 games in 1971
   ***Resigned after eight games in 1973
  ****Resigned after four games in 1978
     #Resigned after eight games in 1986
   ##Released after six games in 1998

PAID ATTENDANCE
Home 523,262   Away 520,177
Total 1,043,439
Single-game home record,
69,288 (11/7/99)
Single-season home record,
547,937 (2005)

2012 DRAFT CHOICES
Round	Name	Pos.	College
1	Melvin Ingram	LB	South Carolina
2	Kendall Reyes	DE	Connecticut
3	Brandon Taylor	DB	Louisiana St.
4	Ladarius Green	TE	Louisiana-Lafayette
5	Johnnie Troutman	G	Penn St.
7	David Molk	C	Michigan
	Edwin Baker	RB	Michigan St.

2011 TEAM RECORD
PRESEASON (2-2)

Date	Result	Opponent
8/11	L 17-24	Seattle
8/20	W 20-7	at Dallas
8/27	W 34-31	at Arizona
9/1	L 17-20	at San Francisco

REGULAR SEASON (8-8)

Date	Result	Opponent
9/11	W 24-17	Minnesota
9/18	L 21-35	at New England
9/25	W 20-17	Kansas City
10/2	W 26-16	Miami
10/9	W 29-24	at Denver
10/23	L 21-27	at New York Jets
10/31	L 20-23	at Kansas City (OT)
11/6	L 38-45	Green Bay
11/10	L 17-24	Oakland
11/20	L 20-31	at Chicago
11/27	L 13-16	Denver (OT)
12/5	W 38-14	at Jacksonville
12/11	W 37-10	Buffalo
12/18	W 34-14	Baltimore
12/24	L 10-38	at Detroit
1/1	W 38-26	at Oakland

(OT) Overtime

SCORE BY PERIODS

Chargers	81	124	116	85	0	—	406
Opponents	89	118	67	97	6	—	377

2011 TEAM STATISTICS

	Chargers	Opp.
Total First Downs	359	311
Rushing	97	102
Passing	234	186
Penalty	28	23
3rd Down: Made/Att	103/211	96/195
3rd Down Pct.	48.8	49.2
4th Down: Made/Att	4/11	1/9
4th Down Pct.	36.4	11.1
Possession Avg.	31:39	28:21
Total Net Yards	6290	5546
Avg. Per Game	393.1	346.6
Total Plays	1048	958
Avg. Per Play	6.0	5.8
Net Yards Rushing	1864	1955
Avg. Per Game	116.5	122.2
Total Rushes	436	448
Net Yards Passing	4426	3591
Avg. Per Game	276.6	224.4
Sacked/Yards Lost	30/198	32/187
Gross Yards	4624	3778
Att./Completions	582/366	478/299
Completion Pct.	62.9	62.6
Had Intercepted	20	17
Punts/Average	47/47.5	60/47.0
Net Punting Avg.	47/39.7	60/41.0
Penalties/Yards	91/753	92/760
Fumbles/Ball Lost	20/8	11/4
Touchdowns	46	43
Rushing	16	8
Passing	27	29
Returns	3	6

2011 INDIVIDUAL STATISTICS

PASSING	Att.	Comp.	Yds.	Pct.	TD	Int.	Tkld.	Rate
Rivers	582	366	4624	62.9	27	20	30/198	88.7
Chargers	582	366	4624	62.9	27	20	30/198	88.7
Opponents	478	299	3778	62.6	29	17	32/187	92.5

SCORING	TD R	TD P	TD Rt	PAT	FG	Saf	PTS
Novak	0	0	0	41/42	27/34	0	122
Tolbert	8	2	0	0/0	0/0	0	60
Jackson	0	9	0	0/0	0/0	0	54
Gates	0	7	0	0/0	0/0	0	42
Mathews	6	0	0	0/0	0/0	0	36
Floyd	0	5	0	0/0	0/0	0	30
V. Brown	0	2	0	0/0	0/0	0	12
Brinkley	1	0	0	0/0	0/0	0	8
Butler	0	0	1	0/0	0/0	0	6
Crayton	0	1	0	0/0	0/0	0	6
Goodman	0	0	1	0/0	0/0	0	6
Gregory	0	0	1	0/0	0/0	0	6
Hester	0	1	0	0/0	0/0	0	6
Rivers	1	0	0	0/0	0/0	0	6
Scifres	0	0	0	3/3	1/1	0	6
Chargers	16	27	3	44/45	28/35	0	406
Opponents	8	29	6	40/40	25/28	0	377

2-Pt Conversions: Brinkley
Chargers 1-1, Opponents 2-3

RUSHING	No.	Yds	Avg	LG	TD
Mathews	222	1091	4.9	39	6
Tolbert	121	490	4.0	40	8
Brinkley	30	101	3.4	12	1
Hester	28	90	3.2	16	0
Jackson	3	51	17.0	41	0
Rivers	26	36	1.4	15	1
Weddle	1	10	10.0	10	0
Volek	5	-5	-1.0	-1	0
Chargers	436	1864	4.3	41	16
Opponents	448	1955	4.4	46	8

RECEIVING	No.	Yds	Avg	LG	TD
Gates	64	778	12.2	38t	7
Jackson	60	1106	18.4	58	9
Tolbert	54	433	8.0	27	2
Mathews	50	455	9.1	42	0
Floyd	43	856	19.9	52t	5
McMichael	30	271	9.0	30	0
Crayton	23	248	10.8	26t	1
V. Brown	19	329	17.3	31	2
Hester	12	48	4.0	11	1
Brinkley	7	41	5.9	20	0
Walters	3	27	9.0	13	0
Sperry	1	32	32.0	32	0
Chargers	366	4624	12.6	58	27
Opponents	299	3778	12.6	78	29

INTERCEPTIONS	No.	Yds	Avg	LG	TD
Weddle	7	89	12.7	26	0
Cason	2	69	34.5	64	0
Gilchrist	2	22	11.0	21	0
Phillips	2	0	0.0	0	0
Spikes	1	45	45.0	45	0
Gregory	1	26	26.0	26t	1
Oliver	1	7	7.0	7	0
Butler	1	2	2.0	2	0
Chargers	17	260	15.3	64	1
Opponents	20	522	26.1	76	4

PUNTING	No.	Yds.	Avg.	In 20	LG
Scifres	47	2234	47.5	17	71
Chargers	47	2234	47.5	17	71
Opponents	60	2822	47.0	18	68

PUNT RETURNS	Ret	FC	Yds	Avg	LG	TD
Crayton	22	9	202	9.2	31	0
Walters	8	3	45	5.6	13	0
Cason	1	0	17	17.0	17	0
Chargers	31	12	264	8.5	31	0
Opponents	25	12	329	13.2	37	0

KICKOFF RETURNS	No.	Yds	Avg	LG	TD
Goodman	34	936	27.5	105t	1
Gilchrist	3	46	15.3	20	0
Hester	3	71	23.7	24	0
Brinkley	2	34	17.0	22	0
Sperry	1	13	13.0	13	0
Chargers	43	1100	25.6	105t	1
Opponents	57	1451	25.5	103t	1

FIELD GOALS	1-19	20-29	30-39	40-49	50+
Novak	0/0	11/11	4/5	8/11	4/7
Scifres	0/0	0/0	0/0	1/1	0/0
Chargers	0/0	11/11	4/5	9/12	4/7
Opponents	0/0	4/4	11/13	7/7	3/4

SACKS	No.
Barnes	11.0
Thomas	4.0
Phillips	3.5
Harris	3.0
Garay	2.5
Butler	2.0
English	2.0
LaBoy	1.0
Liuget	1.0
Martin	1.0
Spikes	1.0
Chargers	32.0
Opponents	30.0

RECORD HOLDERS
INDIVIDUAL RECORDS—CAREER

Category	Name	Performance
Rushing (Yds.)	LaDainian Tomlinson, 2001-09	12,490
Passing (Yds.)	Dan Fouts, 1973-1987	43,040
Passing (TDs)	Dan Fouts, 1973-1987	254
Receiving (No.)	Antonio Gates, 2003-2011	593
Receiving (Yds.)	Lance Alworth, 1962-1970	9,584
Interceptions	Gill Byrd, 1983-1992	42
Punting (Avg.)	Mike Scifres, 2003-2011	44.8
Punt Return (Avg.)	Darrien Gordon, 1993-96	13.7
Kickoff Return (Avg.)	Leslie (Speedy) Duncan, 1964-1970	25.3
Field Goals	John Carney, 1990-2000	261
Touchdowns (Tot.)	LaDainian Tomlinson, 2001-09	153
Points	John Carney, 1990-2000	1,076
*Sacks	Leslie O'Neal, 1986-1995	105.5

INDIVIDUAL RECORDS—SINGLE SEASON

Category	Name	Performance
Rushing (Yds.)	LaDainian Tomlinson, 2006	1,815
Passing (Yds.)	Dan Fouts, 1981	4,802
Passing (TDs)	Philip Rivers, 2008	34
Receiving (No.)	LaDainian Tomlinson, 2003	100
Receiving (Yds.)	Lance Alworth, 1965	1,602
Interceptions	Antonio Cromartie, 2007	10
Punting (Avg.)	Mike Scifres, 2010	46.7
Punt Return (Avg.)	Leslie (Speedy) Duncan, 1965	15.5
Kickoff Return (Avg.)	Keith Lincoln, 1962	28.4
Field Goals	John Carney, 1994	34
Touchdowns (Tot.)	LaDainian Tomlinson, 2006	**31
Points	LaDainian Tomlinson, 2006	**186
*Sacks	Leslie O'Neal, 1992	17.0
	Shawne Merriman, 2006	17.0

INDIVIDUAL RECORDS—SINGLE GAME

Category	Name	Performance
Rushing (Yds.)	LaDainian Tomlinson, 12-28-03	243
Passing (Yds.)	Philip Rivers, 9-26-10	455
Passing (TDs)	Dan Fouts, 11-22-81	6
Receiving (No.)	Kellen Winslow, 10-7-84	15
Receiving (Yds.)	Wes Chandler, 12-20-82	260
Interceptions	Many times	3
	Last time by Antonio Cromartie, 11-11-07	
Field Goals	John Carney, 9-5-93, 9-18-93	6
	Greg Davis, 10-5-97	6
Touchdowns (Tot.)	Kellen Winslow, 11-22-81	5
Points	Kellen Winslow, 11-22-81	30
*Sacks	Leslie O'Neal, 11-16-86	5.0

*Sacks became an official statistic in 1982.
**NFL Record

2012 VETERAN ROSTER

No.	Name	Pos.	Ht.	Wt.	Birthdate	NFL Exp.	College	Hometown	How Acq.	'11 Games/ Starts
98	Barnes, Antwan	OLB	6-1	251	10/19/84	6	Florida International	Miami, Fla.	FA-'10	16/5
64	Baxter, Colin	C	6-3	310	7/31/87	2	Arizona	Rolling Hills, Calif.	FA-'11	8/2*
27	Bigby, Atari	SS	5-11	215	9/19/81	7	Central Florida	Miami, Fla.	UFA(Sea)-'12	15/2*
97	Bird, Bront	ILB	6-4	250	3/17/89	2	Texas Tech	Odessa, Texas	FA-'11	9/0
36	Brinkley, Curtis	RB	5-9	208	9/20/85	3	Syracuse	Philadelphia, Pa.	FA-'09	10/1
86	Brown, Vincent	WR	5-11	184	1/25/89	2	San Diego State	Rancho Cucamonga, Calif.	D3a-'11	14/4
56	Butler, Donald	ILB	6-1	248	10/17/88	3	Washington	Sacramento, Calif.	D3-'10	16/16
20	Cason, Antoine	CB	6-1	195	7/9/86	5	Arizona	Long Beach, Calif.	D1-'08	16/14
93	Castillo, Luis	DE	6-3	290	8/4/83	8	Northwestern	Garfield, N.J.	D1b-'05	1//1
74	Cesaire, Jacques	DE	6-2	295	8/30/80	10	So. Connecticut St.	Gardner, Mass.	FA-'03	12/2
66	Clary, Jeromey	T	6-6	320	11/5/83	6	Kansas State	Mansfield, Texas	D6a-'06	16/16
62	Dombrowski, Brandyn	G	6-5	323	4/3/85	4	San Diego State	Henderson, Nev.	FA-'08	15/2
52	English, Larry	OLB	6-2	255	1/22/86	4	Northern Illinois	Aurora, Ill.	D1-'09	5/0
80	Floyd, Malcom	WR	6-5	225	9/8/81	7	Wyoming	Sacramento, Calif.	FA-'04	12/9
59	Gachkar, Andrew	ILB	6-3	228	11/4/88	2	Missouri	Overland Park, Kan.	D7-'11	16/0
78	Gaither, Jared	T	6-9	340	3/18/86	6	Maryland	Greenbelt, Md.	W(KC)-'11	15/5*
53	Gamble, Darryl	OLB	6-2	255	11/17/87	2	Georgia	Bainbridge, Ga.	FA-'11	5/0
71	Garay, Antonio	DT	6-4	320	11/30/79	6	Boston College	Rahway, N.J.	FA-'09	16/13
85	Gates, Antonio	TE	6-4	260	6/18/80	10	Kent State	Detroit, Mich.	FA-'03	13/13
38	Gilchrist, Marcus	CB	5-10	193	12/8/88	2	Clemson	High Point, N.C.	D2A-'11	14/4
15	Goodman, Richard	WR/KR	6-0	192	4/23/87	2	Florida State	Ft. Lauderdale, Fla.	FA-'10	16/0
69	Green, Tyronne	G/T	6-2	316	4/6/86	4	Auburn	Pensacola, Fla.	D4b-'09	13/8
67	Hadnot, Rex	C/G	6-2	310	1/28/82	9	Houston	Lufkin, Texas	FA-'12	16/16*
61	Hardwick, Nick	C	6-4	305	9/2/81	9	Purdue	Indianapolis, Ind.	D3b-'04	16/16
75	Henderson, Mario	T	6-7	340	10/29/84	5	Florida State	Lehigh Acres, Fla.	FA-'12	0*
22	Hester, Jacob	FB	5-11	235	5/8/85	5	Louisiana State	Shreveport, La.	D3-'08	16/3
23	Jammer, Quentin	CB	6-0	204	6/19/79	11	Texas	Angleton, Texas	D1-'02	15/15
96	Johnson, Jarret	OLB	6-3	260	8/14/81	10	Alabama	Chiefland, Fla.	UFA(Balt)-'12	16/16*
10	Kaeding, Nate	K	6-0	187	3/26/82	9	Iowa	Iowa City, Iowa	D3a-'04	1/0
94	Liuget, Corey	DE	6-2	300	3/18/90	2	Illinois	Miami, Fla.	D1-'11	15/13
92	Martin, Vaughn	DE/DT	6-4	308	4/18/86	4	Western Ontario	London, Ont., Canada	D4a-'09	16/15
24	Mathews, Ryan	RB	6-0	218	10/10/87	3	Fresno State	Bakersfield, Calif.	D1-'10	14/14
33	McClain, Le'Ron	FB	6-0	260	12/27/84	6	Alabama	Northport, Ala.	UFA(KC)-'12	16/9*
81	McMichael, Randy	TE	6-3	248	6/28/79	11	Georgia	Fort Valley, Ga.	FA-'10	16/14
12	Meachem, Robert	WR	6-2	215	9/28/84	6	Tennessee	Tulsa, Okla.	UFA(NO)-'12	16/8*
57	Mouton, Jonas	ILB	6-2	240	3/17/88	2	Michigan	Los Angeles, Calif.	D2b-'11	0*
9	Novak, Nick	K	6-0	198	8/21/81	5	Maryland	Charlottesville, Va.	FA-'11	16/0
13	Parrish, Roscoe	WR/KR	5-9	175	7/16/82	8	Miami	Miami, Fla.	UFA(Buff)-'12	2/2*
95	Phillips, Shaun	OLB	6-3	250	5/13/81	9	Purdue	Willingboro, N.J.	D4-'04	12/12
41	Polk, Nick	S	5-11	218	10/6/86	2	Indiana	Milwaukee, Wisc.	FA-'11	0*
17	Rivers, Philip	QB	6-5	228	12/8/81	9	North Carolina State	Athens, Ala.	T(NYG)-'04	16/16
88	Rosario, Dante	TE	6-4	250	10/25/84	6	Oregon	Dayton, Ore.	UFA(Den)-'12	14/3*
11	Royal, Eddie	WR/KR	5-10	185	5/21/86	5	Virginia Tech	Chantilly, Va.	UFA(Den)-'12	12/8*
70	Schilling, Stephen	T	6-5	308	7/21/88	2	Michigan	Bellevue, Wash.	D6b-'11	9/2
5	Scifres, Mike	P	6-2	221	10/8/80	10	Western Illinois	Destrehan, La.	D5-'03	16/0
82	Sperry, Kory	TE	6-5	265	4/10/85	4	Colorado State	Vineland, Colo.	FA-'10	16/4
51	Spikes, Takeo	ILB	6-2	242	12/17/76	15	Auburn	Sandersville, Ga.	UFA(SF)-'11	16/16
87	Spurlock, Micheal	WR/KR	5-11	210	1/31/83	5	Mississippi	Gentry, Miss.	UFA(TB)-'12	12/0*
25	Stuckey, Darrell	S	5-11	208	6/16/87	3	Kansas	Kansas City, Kan.	D4-'10	14/0
76	Thomas, Cam	DT	6-4	335	12/12/86	3	North Carolina	Robbins, N.C.	D5a-'10	16/2
65	Vasquez, Louis	G	6-5	335	4/11/87	4	Texas Tech	Corsicana, Texas	D3-'09	14/14
32	Weddle, Eric	FS	5-11	200	1/4/85	6	Utah	Alta Loma, Calif.	D2-'07	16/16
6	Whitehurst, Charlie	QB	6-5	228	8/6/82	7	Clemson	Alpharetta, Ga.	UFA(Sea)-'12	3/2*
58	Williams, Demorrio	OLB	6-1	235	7/6/80	9	Nebraska	Beckville, Texas	FA-'12	12/0*
47	Windt, Mike	LS	6-1	252	5/29/86	3	Cincinnati	Cincinnati, Ohio	FA-'10	16/0
29	Wright, Shareece	CB	5-11	182	4/8/87	2	Southern California	Colton, Calif.	D3b-'11	7/0

* Baxter played in 3 games for New York Jets and 5 games with San Diego in '11; Bigby played 15 games with Seattle; Gaither played 10 games with Kansas City and 5 with San Diego; Hadnot played 16 games with Arizona; Henderson last active with Oakland in '10; Johnson played 16 games with Baltimore; McClain played 16 games with Kansas City; Meachem played 16 games with New Orleans; Mouton missed '11 season because of injury; Parrish played 2 games with Buffalo; Polk missed '11 season because of injury; Rosario played 14 games with Denver; Royal played 12 games with Denver; Spurlock played 12 games with Tampa Bay; Whitehurst played 3 games with Seattle; Williams played 12 games with Kansas City.

Retired—Kris Dielman, 9-year guard, 6 games in '11.

Players lost through free agency (3): S Steve Gregory (NE; 15 games), WR Vincent Jackson (TB; 16), RB Mike Tolbert (Car; 15).

Also played with Chargers in '11—DE Everette Brown (3 games), LB Stephen Cooper (5), WR Patrick Crayton (14), LB Na'il Diggs (13), DT Tommie Harris (13), CB Dante Hughes (16), LB Travis LaBoy (14), T Marcus McNeill (9), G Tony Moll (3), G Scott Mruczkowski (10), G-T Ike Ndukwe (2), DE/DT Ogemdi Nwagbuo (4), S Paul Oliver (13), QB Billy Volek (2), S C.J. Wallace (1), WR Bryan Walters (4).

FIRST-YEAR ROSTER

Name	Pos.	Ht.	Wt.	Birthdate	College	Hometown	How Acq.
Baker, Edwin	RB	5-8	200	6/1/91	Michigan State	Highland Park, Mich.	D7b
Barnes, Jason	WR	6-3	210	5/31/89	South Carolina	Charlotte, N.C.	FA
Bell, Cordell	T	6-3	320	8/9/90	Minnesota State-Mankato	Melvindale, Mich.	FA
Brown, Eddie	DT	6-0	320	3/13/90	Texas A&M	Waller, Texas	FA
Brown, Garrett (1)	DT	6-2	300	9/20/88	Minnesota	Fairfield, Conn.	FA
Bryant, Charlie (1)	G/T	6-6	320	9/11/87	Memphis	Collierville, Tenn.	FA-'11
Cattouse, Sean	FS	6-2	210	10/4/88	California	Chicago, Ill.	FA
Cox, Paul	WR	6-4	205	7/9/89	Mississippi Valley State	Patterson, La.	FA
Elmore, Ricky (1)	OLB	6-5	255	2/1/88	Arizona	Simi Valley, Calif.	FA
Embree, Taylor	WR	6-3	210	10/3/88	UCLA	Overland Park, Kan.	FA
Gatson, Greg	CB	5-11	165	3/24/89	Arkansas	Memphis, Tenn.	FA
Green, Ladarius	TE	6-6	240	5/29/90	Louisiana-Lafayette	Pensacola, Fla.	D4
Guess, Nick	LS	6-2	250	10/7/88	Tennessee	Knoxville, Tenn.	FA
Harrell, Logan	DE	6-2	280	9/25/89	Fresno State	Santa Margarita, Calif.	FA
Harris, Mike	T	6-5	310	12/5/88	UCLA	Duarte, Calif.	FA
Hayes, Michael	RB	5-8	200	6/18/90	Houston	East Bernard, Texas	FA
Hobbs, Arthur	CB	5-10	190	11/18/89	Nebraska-Kearney	Spring Valley, Calif.	FA
Ingram, Melvin	OLB	6-2	265	4/26/89	South Carolina	Rockingham, N.C.	D1
Lee, Jarrett	QB	6-1	210	6/2/89	Louisiana State	Brenham, Texas	FA
Linam, Josh	ILB	6-2	240	10/21/88	Central Florida	Tavares, Fla.	FA
Marah, Mohamed	FB	6-0	240	8/15/88	San Jose State	San Jose, Calif.	FA
Molk, David	C	6-1	300	12/15/88	Michigan	Lemont, Ill.	D7a
Payne, Phillip	WR	6-3	210	2/6/90	Nevada-Las Vegas	Las Vegas, Nev.	FA
Presley, DeAndre	CB	5-10	185	1/10/90	Appalachian State	Tampa, Fla.	FA
Reyes, Kendall	DE	6-4	300	9/26/89	Connecticut	Nashua, N.H.	D2
Scafe, Damik (1)	DE	6-2	300	4/26/88	Boston College	Windsor, Conn.	FA-'11
Taylor, Brad (1)	TE	6-3	240	11/11/87	Baylor	Madisonville, Texas	FA-'11
Taylor, Brandon	SS	5-11	210	1/29/90	Louisiana State	Franklinton, La.	D3
Troutman, Johnnie	G	6-4	330	11/11/87	Penn State	Brown Mills, N.J.	D5
Willie, Michael	WR	6-2	220	6/17/90	Arizona State	Long Beach, Calif.	FA

The term NFL Rookie is defined as a player who is in his first season of professional football and has not been on the roster of another professional football team for any regular-season or postseason games. A Rookie is designated by an "R" on NFL rosters. Players who have been active in another professional football league or players who have NFL experience, including either preseason training camp or being on an Active List or Inactive List, or on Reserve/Injured or Reserve/Physically Unable to Perform for fewer than six regular-season games, are termed NFL First-Year Players. An NFL First-Year Player is designated by a "1" on NFL rosters. Thereafter, a player is credited with an additional year of experience for each season in which he accumulates six games on the Active List or Inactive List, or on Reserve/Physically Unable to Perform.

Log on to www.chargers.com for an up-to-date roster.

SAN DIEGO CHARGERS

COACHING STAFF
Head Coach,
Norv Turner
Pro Career: A veteran coach of 27 NFL seasons, Turner became the 14th head coach in team history on February 19, 2007. Entering 2012, Turner has the top overall winning percentage (52-34, .605) in team history. In his first three seasons, Turner led the Chargers to three-straight AFC West titles. In the postseason, he led the Chargers to the 2007 AFC Championship Game and the 2008 and 2009 Divisional Playoffs. Turner's 27 years of coaching experience include 14 as a head coach—seven for the Washington Redskins (1994-2000), two with the Oakland Raiders (2004-05), and five with the Chargers (2007-2011). In 1999, he led the Redskins to a division title. He spent 13 seasons as an NFL assistant coach, including seven as an offensive coordinator with the Cowboys (1991-93), Chargers (2001), Dolphins (2002-03), and 49ers (2006). Turner began his NFL coaching career as an assistant with the Rams (1985-1990). Turner made his coaching mark during his three seasons in Dallas as the Cowboys won back-to-back Super Bowls (XXVII and XXVIII) following the 1992 and 1993 seasons. Career record: 111-117-1.
Background: Turner played quarterback at Oregon, spending two seasons behind former Charger and NFL Hall of Fame quarterback Dan Fouts. Turner coached at Oregon (1975) and Southern California (1976-1984). During his nine-year tenure at USC, the Trojans played in four Rose Bowls, winning all four. One of those was a win over Michigan after the 1978 season that capped a 12-1 season and gave USC the National Championship.
Personal: Born in LeJeune, N.C., May 17, 1952. Turner and his wife, Nancy, have three children—Scott, Stephanie, and Drew.

ASSISTANT COACHES
Joe Barry, linebackers; born July 5, 1970, Murphysboro, Ill. Linebacker Michigan 1989-1990, Southern California 1991-93. No pro playing experience. College coach: Southern California 1995, 2010-11, Northern Arizona 1996-98, Nevada-Las Vegas 1999. Pro coach: San Francisco 49ers 2004, Tampa Bay Buccaneers 2001-06, 2009, Detroit Lions 2007-08, joined Chargers in 2012.
Rich Bisaccia, asst. head coach/special teams; born June 3, 1960, Yonkers, N.Y. Defensive back Yankton College 1979-1982. Pro defensive back Philadelphia Stars (USFL) 1983. College coach: Wayne State College 1983-87, South Carolina 1988-1993, Clemson 1994-98, Mississippi 1999-2001. Pro coach: Tampa Bay Buccaneers 2002-2010, joined Chargers in 2011.
Cris Dishman, asst. secondary; born August 13, 1965, Louisville, Ky.

Cornerback Purdue 1984-87. Pro cornerback Houston Oilers 1988-1996, Washington Redskins 1997-98, Kansas City Chiefs 1999, Minnesota Vikings 2000. College coach: Menlo College 2006-08. Pro coach: Joined Chargers in 2009.
Steve Fairchild, senior offensive assistant-special assignments; born June 21, 1958, Decatur, Ill. Quarterback Mesa (Ariz.) C.C. 1976-77, Colorado State 1978-1980. No pro playing experience. College coach: Mesa (Ariz.) C.C. 1982-83, Ferris State 1984-85, San Diego State 1986, 1990-92, New Mexico 1987-89, Colorado State 1993-2000, 2008-2011. Pro coach: Buffalo Bills 2001-02, 2006-07, St. Louis Rams 2003-05, joined Chargers in 2012.
Hal Hunter, offensive coordinator/offensive line; born July 8, 1959, Canonsburg, Pa. Linebacker Northwestern 1978. College coach: William & Mary 1982, Pittsburgh 1983-84, Columbia 1985, Indiana (Pa.) 1986, Akron 1987-1990, Vanderbilt 1991-94, Louisiana State 1995-99, Indiana 2000-01, North Carolina 2002-05. Pro coach: Joined Chargers in 2006.
Jeff Hurd, strength and conditioning; born April 24, 1958, Pomona, Calif. No college or pro playing experience. College coach: Fort Hays State 1984, Delta State 1985-86, Clemson 1986-87, Western Michigan 1987-1992, Tulsa 1994. Pro coach: Jacksonville Jaguars 1995-97, Kansas City Chiefs 1998-2006, joined Chargers in 2007.
Don Johnson, defensive line; born November 3, 1954, Newark, N.J. Linebacker Jersey City State 1973-76. College coach: Jersey City State 1984-85. Riverside (Calif.) C.C. 1987-1990, Cal State-Fullerton 1991-92, Nevada 1995-98, UCLA 1999-2004. Pro coach: Chicago Bears 2005-06, Oakland Raiders 2007-08, joined Chargers in 2009.
Charlie Joiner, receivers; born October 14, 1947, Many, La. Wide receiver Grambling State 1965-68. Pro defensive back/wide receiver Houston Oilers 1969-1972, Cincinnati Bengals 1972-75, San Diego Chargers 1976-1986. Inducted into Pro Football Hall of Fame 1996. Pro coach: San Diego Chargers 1987-1991, Buffalo Bills 1992-2000, Kansas City Chiefs 2001-07, re-joined Chargers in 2008.
Ron Meeks, secondary; born August 27, 1954, Jacksonville, Fla. Defensive back Arkansas State 1972-76. Pro defensive back Hamilton Tiger-Cats (CFL) 1977-79, Ottawa Rough Riders (CFL) 1979, Toronto Argonauts (CFL) 1980-81. College coach: Arkansas State 1984-85, Miami 1986-87, New Mexico State 1988, Fresno State 1989-1990. Pro coach: Dallas Cowboys 1991, Cincinnati Bengals 1992-96, Atlanta Falcons 1997-99, Washington Redskins 2000, St. Louis Rams 2001, Indianapolis Colts 2002-08, Carolina Panthers 2009-2011, joined Chargers in 2012.
Jason Michael, tight ends; born October 15, 1978, Portsmouth, Ohio. Quarterback

Western Kentucky 1999-2002. No pro playing experience. College coach: Tennessee 2003-04, 2008. Pro coach: Oakland Raiders 2005, New York Jets 2006-07, San Francisco 49ers 2009-2010, joined Chargers in 2011.
John Pagano, defensive coordinator; born March 30, 1967, Boulder, Colo. Linebacker Mesa State College 1985-88. No pro playing experience. College coach: Mesa State College 1989, Nevada-Las Vegas 1990-91, Louisiana Tech 1994, Mississippi 1995. Pro coach: New Orleans Saints 1996-97, Indianapolis Colts 1998-2001, joined Chargers in 2002.
Carlos Polk, special teams assistant; born February 22, 1977, Memphis, Tenn. Linebacker Nebraska 1996-2000. Pro linebacker San Diego Chargers 2001-07, Dallas Cowboys 2008. College coach: Grossmont (Calif.) J.C. 2009. Pro coach: Joined Chargers in 2010.
John Ramsdell, quarterbacks; born August 16, 1954, Lafayette, Ind. Running back Springfield (Mass.) College 1972-75. No pro playing experience. College coach: San Francisco State 1976-77, Long Beach State 1978, Pacific 1979-1982, Oregon 1983-1994. Pro coach: St. Louis Rams 1995-2005, joined Chargers in 2006.
Vernon Stephens, asst. strength and conditioning; born November 30, 1974, Jacksonville, Fla. No college or pro playing experience. College coach: North Florida 1999-2002, Colorado 2003-06. Pro coach: Jacksonville Jaguars 2002-03, joined Chargers in 2007.
Byron Storer, special teams assistant; born May 1, 1984, Modesto, Calif. Fullback California 2002-06. Pro fullback Tampa Bay Buccaneers 2007-09. Pro coach: Tampa Bay Buccaneers 2009-2011, joined Chargers in 2012.
Mike Sullivan, offensive line; born December 22, 1967, Chicago, Ill. Offensive lineman Miami 1986-90. Pro offensive lineman Dallas Cowboys 1991, Tampa Bay Buccaneers 1992-95. College coach: Miami 2000, Western Michigan 2005-06. Pro coach: Cleveland Browns 2001-04, 2007-08, joined Chargers in 2009.
Greg Williams, asst. linebackers; born March 12, 1976, Chicago, Ill. Wide receiver/defensive back North Carolina 1994-97. Pro defensive back Amsterdam Admirals (NFL Europe) 1999-2000, San Francisco Demons (XFL) 2001, Indiana Firebirds (AFL) 2001-03, Chicago Rush (AFL) 2004. College coach: Arizona State 2003, College of DuPage 2004-05, Arkansas Tech 2006-07, Pittsburgh 2008. Pro coach: Joined Chargers in 2009.
Ollie Wilson, running backs; born March 3, 1951, Worcester, Mass. Wide receiver Springfield 1971-73. No pro playing experience. College coach: Springfield 1975, Northeastern 1976-1982, California 1983-1990. Pro coach: Atlanta Falcons 1991-96, 2002-07, San Diego Chargers 1997-2001, re-joined Chargers in 2008.

American Football Conference
South Division
Team Colors: Navy, Titans Blue, Red, Silver
460 Great Circle Road
Nashville, Tennessee 37228
Telephone: (615) 565-4000

2012 SCHEDULE
PRESEASON
Aug. 11 at Seattle.............................9:00
Aug. 17 at Tampa Bay 6:30
Aug. 23 **Arizona** 7:00
Aug. 30 **New Orleans**......................6:00

REGULAR SEASON
Sep. 9 **New England** 12:00
Sep. 16 at San Diego 3:15
Sep. 23 **Detroit** 12:00
Sep. 30 at Houston 12:00
Oct. 7 at Minnesota 12:00
Oct. 11 **Pittsburgh** (Thurs) 7:20
Oct. 21 at Buffalo 12:00
Oct. 28 **Indianapolis**.....................12:00
Nov. 4 **Chicago** 12:00
Nov. 11 at Miami............................12:00
Nov. 18 BYE
Nov. 25 at Jacksonville...................12:00
Dec. 2 **Houston** 12:00
Dec. 9 at Indianapolis 12:00
Dec. 17 **New York Jets** (Mon) 7:30
Dec. 23 at Green Bay 12:00
Dec. 30 **Jacksonville**....................12:00
*All times CT

Stadium: LP Field (opened in 1999)
•**Capacity:** 69,143
One Titans Way
Nashville, Tennessee 37213
Playing Surface: Natural Grass
Training Camp: Baptist Sports Park
460 Great Circle Road
Nashville, TN 37228

LP FIELD

CLUB OFFICIALS
Founder/Owner/Chairman of the Board/CEO/ President:
K.S. "Bud" Adams, Jr.
Senior Executive Vice President/COO:
Mike Reinfeldt
Executive V.P. of Administration/Facilities:
Don MacLachlan
Executive V.P./General Manager:
Ruston Webster
Senior Vice President/Asst. General Counsel: Elza Bullock
Vice President/Community Relations:
Bob Hyde
Vice President/CFO: Jenneen Kaufman
Vice President/Marketing:
Ralph Ockenfels
Vice President/Business Operations and Sales: Stuart Spears
Vice President/Player Personnel:
Lake Dawson
Vice President/Football Administration:
Vincent Marino
Head Coach: Mike Munchak
Director of Player Development:
Tina Tuggle
Equipment Manager: Paul Noska
Asst. Equipment Manager: Joey Barranco
Video Director: Anthony Pastrana
Asst. Video Director: Craig Patterson
Head Athletic Trainer: Brad Brown
Asst. Athletic Trainers: Don Moseley, Casey Carter
National Supervisor of College Scouting:
C.O. Brocato
Scouting Coordinator: Blake Beddingfield
College Scouts: Ray Biggs, Johnny Meads, Phil Neri, Cole Proctor, Jon Salge, Richard Shelton, Marvin Sunderland, Brandon Taylor
Pro Personnel Assistants: Trey Koziol, Dale Thompson
Operations Manager: Brent Akers
Marketing Manager: Brad McClanahan
Director of Broadcasting: Mike Keith
Director of Information Systems:
Russ Hudson
Asst. Dir. of Information Systems:
Craig Pelat
Director of Internet Operations/Publications: Gary Glenn
Internet Coordinator: Jeff Harding
Community Relations Coordinator:
Jerry Blessing
Asst. General Counsel: Blu Whipple
Director of Security: Steve Berk
Director of Cheerleading: Stacie Kinder
Mascot Coordinator: Pete Nelson
Director of Media Relations:
Robbie Bohren
Asst. Director of Media Relations:
Dwight Spradlin
Media Relations Assistant: Jared Puffer
Senior Director of Ticketing:
Marty Collins
Asst. Dir. Of Ticket Operations:
Tim Zenner
Asst. Ticket Manager: Josh Ward
Ticketing/Hospitality Club Member Manager: Anthony Hall
Director of Suite Sales and Services:
Bill Wainwright
General Manager of LP Field:
Walter Overton
Head Groundskeeper: Terry Porch

COACHING HISTORY
Houston 1960-1996
(400-415-6)
Records include postseason games
1960-61	Lou Rymkus*	12-7-1
1961	Wally Lemm	10-0-0
1962-63	Frank (Pop) Ivy	17-12-0
1964	Sammy Baugh	4-10-0
1965	Hugh Taylor	4-10-0
1966-1970	Wally Lemm	28-40-4
1971	Ed Hughes	4-9-1
1972-73	Bill Peterson**	1-18-0
1973-74	Sid Gillman	8-15-0
1975-1980	O.A. (Bum) Phillips	59-38-0
1981-83	Ed Biles***	8-23-0
1983	Chuck Studley	2-8-0
1984-85	Hugh Campbell****	8-22-0
1985-89	Jerry Glanville	35-35-0
1990-94	Jack Pardee#	44-35-0
1994-2010	Jeff Fisher	147-126-0
2011	Mike Munchak	9-7-0

*Released after five games in 1961
**Released after five games in 1973
***Resigned after six games in 1983
****Released after 14 games in 1985
#Released after 10 games in 1994

PAID ATTENDANCE
Home 514,648   Away 505,840
Total 1,020,488
Single-game home record,
69,149, many times (last: 12/18/05)
Single-season home record,
553,192 (2005)

2012 DRAFT CHOICES
Round	Name	Pos.	College
1	Kendall Wright	WR	Baylor
2	Zach Brown	LB	North Carolina
3	Mike Martin	DT	Michigan
4	Coty Sensabaugh	DB	Clemson
5	Taylor Thompson	TE	Southern Methodist
6	Markelle Martin	DB	Oklahoma St.
7	Scott Solomon	DE	Rice

2011 TEAM RECORD
PRESEASON (3-1)

Date	Result	Opponent
8/13	W 14-3	Minnesota
8/20	L 16-17	at St. Louis
8/27	W 14-13	Chicago
9/1	W 32-9	New Orleans

REGULAR SEASON (9-7)

Date	Result	Opponent
9/11	L 14-16	at Jacksonville
9/18	W 26-13	Baltimore
9/25	W 17-14	Denver
10/2	W 31-13	at Cleveland
10/9	L 17-38	at Pittsburgh
10/23	L 7-41	Houston
10/30	W 27-10	Indianapolis
11/6	L 17-24	Cincinnati
11/13	W 30-3	at Carolina
11/20	L 17-23	at Atlanta
11/27	W 23-17	Tampa Bay
12/4	W 23-17	at Buffalo
12/11	L 17-22	New Orleans
12/18	L 13-27	at Indianapolis
12/24	W 23-17	Jacksonville
1/1	W 23-22	at Houston

SCORE BY PERIODS

Titans	57	110	67	91	0 —	325
Opponents	64	79	74	100	0 —	317

2011 TEAM STATISTICS

	Titans	Opp.
Total First Downs	281	324
Rushing	71	111
Passing	185	187
Penalty	25	26
3rd Down: Made/Att	80/218	96/236
3rd Down Pct.	36.7	40.7
4th Down: Made/Att	10/14	8/20
4th Down Pct.	71.4	40.0
Possession Avg.	27:52	32:08
Total Net Yards	5361	5682
Avg. Per Game	335.1	355.1
Total Plays	984	1080
Avg. Per Play	5.4	5.3
Net Yards Rushing	1438	2053
Avg. Per Game	89.9	128.3
Total Rushes	376	461
Net Yards Passing	3923	3629
Avg. Per Game	245.2	226.8
Sacked/Yards Lost	24/190	28/180
Gross Yards	4113	3809
Att./Completions	584/353	591/369
Completion Pct.	60.4	62.4
Had Intercepted	14	11
Punts/Average	86/43.6	83/43.7
Net Punting Avg.	86/39.4	83/36.4
Penalties/Yards	104/960	99/812
Fumbles/Ball Lost	17/8	20/12
Touchdowns	34	34
Rushing	8	10
Passing	22	21
Returns	4	3

2011 INDIVIDUAL STATISTICS

PASSING

	Att.	Comp.	Yds.	Pct.	TD	Int.	Tkld.	Rate
Hasselbeck	518	319	3571	61.6	18	14	19/153	82.4
Locker	66	34	542	51.5	4	0	5/37	99.4
Titans	584	353	4113	60.4	22	14	24/190	84.4
Opponents	591	369	3809	62.4	21	11	28/180	85.1

SCORING

	TD R	TD P	TD Rt	PAT	FG	Saf	PTS
Bironas	0	0	0	34/34	29/32	0	121
Washington	1	7	0	0/0	0/0	0	48
Williams	0	5	0	0/0	0/0	0	30
C. Johnson	4	0	0	0/0	0/0	0	24
Britt	0	3	0	0/0	0/0	0	18
Cook	0	3	0	0/0	0/0	0	18
Avery	0	1	0	0/0	0/0	0	6
Babineaux	0	0	1	0/0	0/0	0	6
Campbell	0	0	1	0/0	0/0	0	6
D. Graham	0	1	0	0/0	0/0	0	6
Harper	1	0	0	0/0	0/0	0	6
L. Hawkins	0	1	0	0/0	0/0	0	6
Locker	1	0	0	0/0	0/0	0	6
Mariani	0	0	1	0/0	0/0	0	6
McCourty	0	0	1	0/0	0/0	0	6
Ringer	1	0	0	0/0	0/0	0	6
Stevens	0	1	0	0/0	0/0	0	6
Titans	8	22	4	34/34	29/32	0	325
Opponents	10	21	3	32/32	27/28	0	317

2-Pt Conversions: Titans 0-0, Opponents 0-2

RUSHING

	No.	Yds	Avg	LG	TD
C. Johnson	262	1047	4.0	48t	4
Ringer	59	185	3.1	25	1
Locker	8	56	7.0	17	1
Hasselbeck	20	52	2.6	21	0
Harper	17	44	2.6	12	1
Hall	6	24	4.0	12	0
Kern	1	21	21.0	21	0
Washington	2	5	2.5	3t	1
Mariani	1	4	4.0	4	0
Titans	376	1438	3.8	48t	8
Opponents	461	2053	4.5	80t	10

RECEIVING

	No.	Yds	Avg	LG	TD
Washington	74	1023	13.8	57	7
C. Johnson	57	418	7.3	34	0
Cook	49	759	15.5	80t	3
L. Hawkins	47	470	10.0	32	1
Williams	45	592	13.2	54	5
Ringer	28	187	6.7	18	0
Britt	17	289	17.0	80t	3
Stevens	9	166	18.4	58	1
Hall	9	46	5.1	10	0
Mariani	5	24	4.8	6	0
Harper	4	32	8.0	21	0
Avery	3	45	15.0	23	1
Q. Johnson	3	30	10.0	13	0
D. Graham	2	25	12.5	21	1
Amano	1	7	7.0	7	0
Titans	353	4113	11.7	80t	22
Opponents	369	3809	10.3	78t	21

INTERCEPTIONS

	No.	Yds	Avg	LG	TD
McCourty	2	52	26.0	30	0
Griffin	2	0	0.0	0	0
Babineaux	1	97	97.0	97t	1
Finnegan	1	8	8.0	8	0
Hope	1	7	7.0	7	0
Witherspoon	1	7	7.0	7	0
Ruud	1	4	4.0	4	0
Verner	1	4	4.0	4	0
McCarthy	1	0	0.0	0	0
Titans	11	179	16.3	97t	1
Opponents	14	167	11.9	38t	3

PUNTING

	No.	Yds.	Avg.	In 20	LG
Kern	86	3747	43.6	31	64
Titans	86	3747	43.6	31	64
Opponents	83	3628	43.7	22	65

PUNT RETURNS

	Ret	FC	Yds	Avg	LG	TD
Mariani	46	18	490	10.7	79t	1
Campbell	1	0	0	0.0	0	0
Titans	47	18	490	10.4	79t	1
Opponents	36	23	221	6.1	30	0

KICKOFF RETURNS

	No.	Yds	Avg	LG	TD
Mariani	32	748	23.4	49	0
Campbell	0	84	—	84t	1
Titans	32	832	26.0	100t	1
Opponents	30	680	22.7	77	0

FIELD GOALS

	1-19	20-29	30-39	40-49	50+
Bironas	0/0	5/5	9/10	9/10	6/7
Titans	0/0	5/5	9/10	9/10	6/7
Opponents	2/2	11/11	5/5	7/7	2/3

SACKS

	No.
Klug	7.0
Ball	4.0
Jones	3.0
Casey	2.5
Morgan	2.5
Ayers	2.0
Witherspoon	2.0
Hayes	1.5
Finnegan	1.0
McCourty	1.0
S. Smith	1.0
Marks	0.5
Titans	28.0
Opponents	24.0

RECORD HOLDERS
INDIVIDUAL RECORDS—CAREER
Category Name Performance

Category	Name	Performance
Rushing (Yds.)	Eddie George, 1996-2003	10,009
Passing (Yds.)	Warren Moon, 1984-1993	33,685
Passing (TDs)	Warren Moon, 1984-1993	196
Receiving (No.)	Ernest Givins, 1986-1994	542
Receiving (Yds.)	Ernest Givins, 1986-1994	7,935
Interceptions	Jim Norton, 1960-68	45
Punting (Avg.)	Greg Montgomery, 1988-1993	43.6
Punt Return (Avg.)	Billy Johnson, 1974-1980	13.2
Kickoff Return (Avg.)	Bobby Jancik, 1962-67	26.5
Field Goals	Al Del Greco, 1991-2000	246
Touchdowns (Tot.)	Eddie George, 1996-2003	74
Points	Al Del Greco, 1991-2000	1,060
*Sacks	Ray Childress, 1985-1995	75.5

INDIVIDUAL RECORDS—SINGLE SEASON
Category Name Performance

Category	Name	Performance
Rushing (Yds.)	Chris Johnson, 2009	2,006
Passing (Yds.)	Warren Moon, 1991	4,690
Passing (TDs)	George Blanda, 1961	36
Receiving (No.)	Charley Hennigan, 1964	101
Receiving (Yds.)	Charley Hennigan, 1961	1,746
Interceptions	Fred Glick, 1963	12
	Mike Reinfeldt, 1979	12
Punting (Avg.)	Craig Hentrich, 1998	47.2
Punt Return (Avg.)	Billy Johnson, 1977	15.4
Kickoff Return (Avg.)	Ken Hall, 1960	31.3
Field Goals	Al Del Greco, 1998	36
Touchdowns (Tot.)	Earl Campbell, 1979	19
Points	Al Del Greco, 1998	136
*Sacks	William Fuller, 1991	15.0

INDIVIDUAL RECORDS—SINGLE GAME
Category Name Performance

Category	Name	Performance
Rushing (Yds.)	Chris Johnson, 11-1-09	228
Passing (Yds.)	Warren Moon, 12-16-90	527
Passing (TDs)	George Blanda, 11-19-61	**7
Receiving (No.)	Charley Hennigan, 10-13-61	13
	Haywood Jeffires, 10-13-91	13
	Drew Bennett, 12-19-04	13
Receiving (Yds.)	Charley Hennigan, 10-13-61	272
Interceptions	Many times	3
	Last time by Keith Bulluck, 9-24-07	
Field Goals	Rob Bironas, 10-21-07	**8
Touchdowns (Tot.)	Billy Cannon, 12-10-61	5
Points	Billy Cannon, 12-10-61	30
*Sacks	William Fuller, 11-28-93	4.0

*Sacks became an official statistic in 1982.
**NFL Record

2012 VETERAN ROSTER

No.	Name	Pos.	Ht.	Wt.	Birthdate	NFL Exp.	College	Hometown	How Acq.	'11 Games/ Starts
38	Afalava, Al	S	5-11	212	1/20/87	3	Oregon State	Laie, Hawaii	FA-'12	0*
54	Amano, Eugene	G/C	6-3	300	3/1/82	9	Southeast Missouri State	San Diego, Calif.	D7-'04	16/16
58	#Amato, Ken	LB/LS	6-2	240	5/18/77	10	Montana State	Miami, Fla.	FA-'03	16/0
56	Ayers, Akeem	LB	6-3	254	7/10/89	2	UCLA	Los Angeles, Calif.	D2-'11	16/16
26	Babineaux, Jordan	S	6-0	210	8/31/82	9	Southern Arkansas	Port Arthur, Texas	UFA(Sea)-'11	16/14
57	Bailey, Patrick	LB	6-4	235	11/19/85	5	Duke	Elmendorf, Texas	W(Pitt)-'10	15/0
98	Ball, Dave	DE	6-5	255	1/4/81	8	UCLA	Dixon, Calif.	FA-'08	14/8
2	Bironas, Rob	K	6-0	210	1/29/78	8	Ga. Southern/Auburn	Louisville, Ky.	FA-'05	16/0
18	Britt, Kenny	WR	6-3	215	9/19/88	4	Rutgers	Bayonne, N.J.	D1-'09	3/3
37	Campbell, Tommie	DB	6-3	205	9/19/87	2	California (Pa.)	Aliquippa, Pa.	D7b-'11	15/0
99	Casey, Jurrell	DT	6-1	300	12/5/89	2	Southern California	Long Beach, Calif.	D3-'11	16/15
69	Clayton, Zach	DT	6-2	299	1/1/88	2	Auburn	Opelika, Ala.	D7a-'11	3/0
89	Cook, Jared	TE	6-5	248	4/7/87	4	South Carolina	Suwanee, Ga.	D3a-'09	16/5
75	Dawson, Keyunta	DE	6-3	254	9/13/85	5	Texas Tech	Shreveport, La.	FA-'12	2/0*
49	Diles, Zac	LB	6-2	245	6/11/85	6	Kansas State	Abilene, Texas	FA-'12	11/0*
72	Divens, Lamar	DT	6-3	343	11/12/85	2	Tennessee State	Fayetteville, Tenn.	FA-'12	0*
78	Douzable, Leger	DE	6-4	284	5/31/86	4	Central Florida	Tampa, Fla.	FA-'12	16/6*
77	Durand, Ryan	G	6-5	301	11/17/85	2	Syracuse	Walpole, N.H.	D7a-'09	0*
86	Graham, Daniel	TE	6-3	257	11/16/78	11	Colorado	Torrance, Calif.	UFA(Den)-'11	16/7
33	f- Griffin, Michael	S	6-0	203	1/4/85	6	Texas	Austin, Texas	D1-'07	16/16
45	#Hall, Ahmard	FB	5-11	241	11/13/79	7	Texas	Angleton, Texas	FA-'06	12/7
23	Harper, Jamie	RB	5-11	233	9/11/89	2	Clemson	Jacksonville, Fla.	D4b-'11	13/0
64	Harris, Leroy	G/C	6-3	303	6/6/84	6	North Carolina State	Raleigh, N.C.	D4a-'07	16/16
8	Hasselbeck, Matt	QB	6-4	225	9/25/75	14	Boston College	Westwood, Mass.	UFA(Sea)-'11	16/16
35	Hawkins, Chris	CB	6-1	184	4/12/86	2	Louisiana State	Baton Rouge, La.	FA-'10	9/0
87	Hawkins, Lavelle	WR	5-11	194	7/12/86	5	California	Stockton, Calif.	D4b-'08	16/2
24	#Hope, Chris	S	6-0	204	9/29/80	11	Florida State	Rock Hill, S.C.	UFA(Pitt)-'06	10/2
73	Hutchinson, Steve	G	6-5	313	11/1/77	12	Michigan	Fort Lauderdale, Fla.	FA-'12	14/14*
47	Ingram, Jake	LB/LS	6-3	240	10/23/85	3	Hawaii	Albuquerque, N.M.	FA-'12	0*
28	Johnson, Chris	RB	5-11	191	9/23/85	5	East Carolina	Orlando, Fla.	D1-'08	16/16
44	Johnson, Quinn	FB	6-1	263	9/30/86	4	Louisiana State	New Orleans, La.	T(GB)-'11	4/1
32	Johnson, Robert	S	6-2	206	2/13/87	2	Utah	Los Angeles, Calif.	D5-'10	3/0
6	Kern, Brett	P	6-2	217	2/17/86	5	Toledo	Grand Island, N.Y.	W(Den)-'09	16/0
97	Klug, Karl	DL	6-3	275	3/31/88	2	Iowa	Caledonia, Minn.	D5-'11	16/1
70	Kropog, Troy	T/G	6-6	308	7/31/86	3	Tulane	Metairie, La.	D4b-'09	0*
10	Locker, Jake	QB	6-3	234	6/15/88	2	Washington	Ferndale, Wash.	D1-'11	5/0
83	Mariani, Marc	WR	6-1	190	5/2/87	3	Montana	Havre, Mont.	D7a-'10	16/0
94	Marks, Sen'Derrick	DT	6-2	294	2/23/87	4	Auburn	Mobile, Ala.	D2-'09	16/9
60	Matthews, Kevin	C	6-3	302	2/4/87	2	Texas A&M	Houston, Texas	FA-'10	0*
52	McCarthy, Colin	LB	6-1	238	5/30/88	2	Miami	Tampa, Fla.	D4a-'11	13/7
30	McCourty, Jason	CB	6-0	188	8/13/87	4	Rutgers	Nyack, N.Y.	D6a-'09	15/15
51	McRath, Gerald	LB	6-3	228	6/16/86	4	Southern Mississippi	Powder Springs, Ga.	D4a-'09	12/0
91	Morgan, Derrick	DE	6-3	278	1/6/89	3	Georgia Tech	Coatesville, Pa.	D1-'10	15/10
29	Mouton, Ryan	CB	5-9	184	9/23/86	4	Hawaii	Houston, Texas	D3b-'09	0*
15	Murdock, O.J.	WR	5-11	200	2/15/87	2	Fort Hays State	Tampa, Fla.	FA-'11	0*
66	Otto, Mike	T	6-5	310	7/24/83	5	Purdue	Kokomo, Ind.	D7-'07	15/1
39	Reynaud, Darius	RB	5-9	201	12/29/84	4	West Virginia	Boutte, La.	FA-'12	0*
21	Ringer, Javon	RB	5-9	207	2/2/87	4	Michigan State	Dayton, Ohio	D5-'09	12/0
71	Roos, Michael	T	6-7	320	10/5/82	8	Eastern Washington	Vancouver, Wash.	D2-'05	16/16
73	#Scott, Jake	G	6-5	292	4/16/81	9	Idaho	Lewiston, Idaho	UFA(Ind)-'08	16/16
59	Shaw, Tim	LB	6-1	236	3/27/84	5	Penn State	Livonia, Mich.	W(Chi)-'10	16/0
96	Sheppard, Malcolm	DL	6-2	289	2/13/88	3	Arkansas	Bainbridge, Ga.	FA-'10	13/1
25	#Smith, Anthony	S	6-0	200	9/20/83	7	Syracuse	Hubbard, Ohio	UFA(GB)-'11	13/0
11	Smith, Rusty	QB	6-5	226	1/28/87	3	Florida Atlantic	Jacksonville, Fla.	D6a-'10	0*
93	Smith, Shaun	DT	6-2	325	8/19/81	9	South Carolina	Brooklyn, N.Y.	UFA(KC)-'11	15/6
88	Stevens, Craig	TE	6-3	268	9/1/84	5	California	San Pedro, Calif.	D3-'08	15/11
76	Stewart, David	T	6-7	315	8/28/82	8	Mississippi State	Moulton, Ala.	D4b-'05	15/15
68	Stingily, Byron	T	6-5	313	9/9/88	2	Louisville	Country Club Hills, Ill.	D6-'11	0*
61	Velasco, Fernando	C/G	6-4	312	2/22/85	3	Georgia	Wrens, Ga.	FA-'08	16/0
20	Verner, Alterraun	CB	5-10	187	12/13/88	3	UCLA	Carson, Calif.	D4-'10	16/3
85	Washington, Nate	WR	6-1	177	8/28/83	8	Tiffin	Toledo, Ohio	UFA(Pitt)-'09	16/15
22	Wheatley, Terrence	CB	5-9	185	5/5/85	3	Colorado	Walnut Creek, Calif.	FA-'11	0*
17	Williams, Damian	WR	6-1	199	5/26/88	3	Southern California	Springdale, Ark.	D3a-'10	15/13
95	Wimbley, Kamerion	DE	6-4	255	10/13/83	7	Florida State	Wichita, Kansas	FA-'12	16/16*
92	Witherspoon, Will	LB	6-1	240	8/19/80	11	Georgia	Panama City, Fla.	FA-'10	16/14

* Afalava last active with Indianapolis in '10; Dawson played 2 games with Detroit in '11; Diles played 7 games with Tampa Bay and 4 games with Indianapolis; Divens last active with Baltimore in '10; Douzable played 16 games with Jacksonville; Durand spent 16 weeks on the practice squad; Hutchinson played 14 games with Minnesota; Ingram last active with New Orleans in '10; Kropog spent 16 weeks on the practice squad; Matthews inactive for 15 games and did not play in 1 game; Mouton missed '11 season because of injury; Murdock missed '11 season because of injury; Reynaud last active with New York Giants in '10; R. Smith inactive for 15 games and did not play in 1 game in '11; Stingily inactive for 15 games and did not play in 1 game in '11; Wheatley last active with Jacksonville in '10; Wimbley played 16 games with Oakland.

\# Unrestricted free agent; subject to developments.

f- Unsigned franchise player; subject to developments.

Players lost through free agency (5): WR Donnie Avery (Ind; 8 games in '11), CB Cortland Finnegan (StL; 16), DE William Hayes (StL; 10), DE Jason Jones (Sea, 14), LB Barrett Ruud (Sea, 9).

FIRST-YEAR ROSTER

Name	Pos.	Ht.	Wt.	Birthdate	College	Hometown	How Acq.
Aguilar, Devin	WR	5-11	200	10/22/88	Washington	Denver, Colo.	FA
Barden, Brandon	TE	6-4	251	3/15/89	Vanderbilt	Lincolnton, Ga.	FA
Batson, Will	P/K	6-3	194	9/8/86	North Alabama	Killen, Ala.	FA
Bias, George	G/T	6-2	312	12/3/89	Stephen F. Austin	Houston, Texas	FA
Brinkley, Beau	LS/TE	6-3	226	1/25/90	Missouri	Kearney, Mo.	FA
Brown, Zach	LB	6-1	242	10/23/89	North Carolina	Columbia, Md.	D2
Burden, Chandler	G	6-4	315	11/17/89	Kentucky	Blue Ash, Ohio	FA
Deadder, Chase	WR	6-4	224	11/20/88	Sacramento State	Modesto, Calif.	FA
Donaldson, Herb (1)	RB	5-11	221	12/13/85	Western Illinois	St. Louis, Mo.	FA-'10
Egboh, Pannel (1)	DE	6-6	287	3/23/86	Stanford	Mesquite, Texas	FA-'10
Evans, LaQuinton	WR	6-1	203	7/12/90	Southern	Mansfield, La.	FA
Graham, Cameron (1)	TE	6-3	244	2/6/89	Louisville	Inglewood, Calif.	FA-'11
Harris, DaJohn	DT	6-3	306	1/24/89	Southern California	Inglewood, Calif.	FA
Kirkendoll, James (1)	WR	5-10	175	8/14/89	Texas	Round Rock, Texas	FA-'11
Malast, Kevin (1)	LB	6-2	235	6/6/86	Rutgers	Manchester, N.J.	FA-'11
Martin, Markelle	S	6-0	207	6/20/90	Oklahoma State	Wichita Falls, Texas	D6
Martin, Mike	DT	6-1	306	9/1/90	Michigan	Detroit, Mich.	D3
Mooney, Collin	FB	5-10	247	4/3/86	Army	Katy, Texas	FA
Preston, Michael (1)	WR	6-5	206	6/1/89	Heidelberg	Maple Heights, Ohio	FA-'11
Scott, Christian	S	5-11	220	1/9/89	Texas	Dallas, Texas	FA
Sensabaugh, Coty	CB	5-11	189	11/15/88	Clemson	Kingsport, Tenn.	D4
Solomon, Scott	DE	6-3	262	11/5/88	Rice	San Antonio, Texas	D7
Stephens, Nick	QB	6-3	230	5/19/87	Tarleton State	Flower Mound, Texas	FA
Thompson, Taylor	TE	6-6	259	10/19/89	Southern Methodist	Prosper, Texas	D5
Vlachos, William	C	6-0	321	5/26/88	Alabama	Birmingham, Ala.	FA
Watkins, Alex	LB	6-2	237	9/17/89	Alabama	Brownsville, Tenn.	FA
Whiting, Darryl	RB	6-3	226	4/7/89	Fordham	East Elmhurst, N.Y.	FA
Wilburn, Gary	CB	5-11	195	2/2/89	Connecticut	Washington, Ga.	FA
Woods, D.J.	WR	5-11	180	11/29/89	Cincinnati	Strongsville, Ohio	FA
Wright, Kendall	WR	5-10	196	11/12/89	Baylor	Pittsburg, Texas	D1

The term NFL Rookie is defined as a player who is in his first season of professional football and has not been on the roster of another professional football team for any regular-season or postseason games. A Rookie is designated by an "R" on NFL rosters. Players who have been active in another professional football league or players who have NFL experience, including either preseason training camp or being on an Active List or Inactive List, or on Reserve/Injured or Reserve/Physically Unable to Perform for fewer than six regular-season games, are termed NFL First-Year Players. An NFL First-Year Player is designated by a "1" on NFL rosters. Thereafter, a player is credited with an additional year of experience for each season in which he accumulates six games on the Active List or Inactive List, or on Reserve/Injured or Reserve/Physically Unable to Perform.

Log on to www.titansonline.com for an up-to-date roster.

TENNESSEE TITANS

COACHING STAFF
Head Coach,
Mike Munchak
Pro Career: Munchak became the 16th head coach in franchise history on Feb. 7, 2011, after spending the previous 29 seasons with the team as a player and coach. In leading the Titans to a 9-7 record in 2011, he became the sixth Titans/Oilers head coach to reach nine wins in his first season. After his playing career, Munchak spent three seasons as an offensive assistant/quality control coach (1994-96). In 1997, he became the offensive line coach and held that position for 14 years. Four of his offensive linemen totaled 10 Pro Bowl invitations, and his offensive lines paved the way for five different running backs to total 11 1,000-yard rushing seasons. His offensive line allowed the second fewest sacks (28.3 sacks per season) in the NFL since he assumed control of the group in 1997. During a 12-year playing career as a guard for the Houston Oilers (1982-1993), Munchak started 156 games (seventh in franchise history) and earned nine Pro Bowl invitations. He was selected to the NFL's "All-Decade" team for the 1980s. In 1996, his No. 63 jersey was retired by the club, and in 2001, he became the fifth franchise player to be inducted into the Pro Football Hall of Fame. Career record: 9-7.
Background: Played at Penn State (1979-81) for Joe Paterno. Graduated with a degree in business administration. The Oilers made him the eighth overall pick and the first offensive lineman selected in the 1982 NFL Draft.
Personal: Born March 5, 1960, in Scranton, Pa. Munchak and his wife, Marci, have two daughters, Alexandra and Julie.

ASSISTANT COACHES
Steve Brown, asst. secondary; born March 20, 1960, Sacramento, Calif. Defensive back Oregon 1978-1982. Pro cornerback Houston Oilers 1983-1990. College coach: Kentucky 2003-2011. Pro coach: St. Louis Rams 1995-2000, joined Titans in 2012.
Frank Bush, linebackers; born January 10, 1963, Athens, Ga. Linebacker North Carolina State 1981-84. Pro linebacker Houston Oilers 1985-86. Pro coach: Houston Oilers 1987-1991 (scout), 1992-94, Denver Broncos 1995-2003, Arizona Cardinals 2004-06, Houston Texans 2007-2010, joined Titans in 2011.
Jonathan Gannon, defensive assistant/quality control; born Jan. 4, 1983, Cleveland. Safety Louisville 2001-02. No pro playing experience. College coach: Louisville 2006. Pro coach: Atlanta Falcons 2007, St. Louis Rams 2009-2011 (scout), joined Titans in 2012.
Jerry Gray, defensive coordinator; born December 16, 1962, Lubbock, Texas. Safety Texas 1981-84. Pro defensive back

Los Angeles Rams 1985-1991, Houston Oilers 1992, Tampa Bay Buccaneers 1993. College coach: Southern Methodist 1995-96. Pro coach: Tennessee Titans 1997-2000, Buffalo Bills 2001-05, Washington Redskins 2006- 09, Seattle Seahawks 2010, joined Titans in 2011.
Nate Kaczor, asst. offensive line; born April 8, 1967, Scott City, Kan. Center Utah State 1987-89. No pro playing experience. College coach: Utah State 1991-99, Nebraska- Kearney 2000-03, Idaho 2004-05, Louisiana-Monroe 2006-07. Pro coach: Jacksonville Jaguars 2008-2011, joined Titans in 2012.
Dowell Loggains, quarterbacks/passing game; born October 1, 1980, Newport, Ark. Quarterback Arkansas 2000-04. No pro playing experience. Pro coach: Dallas Cowboys 2005, joined Titans in 2006.
Alan Lowry, special teams; born November 21, 1950, Miami, Okla. Defensive back/ quarterback Texas 1970-72. No pro playing experience. College coach: Virginia Tech 1974, Wyoming 1975, Texas 1977-1981. Pro coach: Dallas Cowboys 1982-1990, Tampa Bay Buccaneers 1991, San Francisco 49ers 1992-95, joined Titans/Oilers in 1996.
Bruce Matthews, offensive line; born August 8, 1961, Raleigh, N.C. Offensive lineman Southern California, 1979-1982. Pro offensive lineman Houston Oilers/Tennessee Titans 1983-2001. Inducted into Pro Football Hall of Fame in 2007. Pro coach: Houston Texans 2009-2010, joined Titans in 2011.
Brett Maxie, secondary; born January 13, 1962, Dallas, Texas. Safety Texas Southern 1982-84. Pro safety New Orleans Saints 1985-1993, Atlanta Falcons 1994, Carolina Panthers 1995-96, San Francisco 49ers 1997. Pro coach: Carolina Panthers 1998, San Francisco 49ers 1999-2003, Miami Dolphins 2007, Dallas Cowboys 2008-2011, joined Titans in 2012.
Keith Millard, defensive assistant/pass rush specialist; born March 18, 1962, Pleasanton, Calif. Defensive lineman Washington State 1980-84. Pro defensive lineman Jacksonville Bulls (USFL) 1985, Minnesota Vikings 1985- 1991, Seattle Seahawks 1992, Green Bay Packers 1992, Philadelphia Eagles 1993. College coach: Fort Lewis 1996, Menlo College 1997-2000. Pro coach: San Francisco Demons (XFL), Denver Broncos 2002-04, Oakland Raiders 2005-08, Tampa Bay Buccaneers 2011, joined Titans in 2012.
Chris Palmer, offensive coordinator; born September 23, 1949, Brewster, N.Y. Quarterback Southern Connecticut State 1968-1971. No pro playing experience. College coach: Connecticut 1972-74, Lehigh 1975, Colgate 1976-1982, New Haven 1986-87 (head coach), Boston 1988-89 (head coach). Pro coach: Montreal Concordes (CFL) 1983, New Jersey Generals (USFL) 1984-85,

Houston Oilers 1990-92, New England Patriots 1993-96, Jacksonville Jaguars 1997-98, Cleveland Browns 1999-2000 (head coach), Houston Texans 2001-05, Dallas Cowboys 2006, New York Giants 2007-09, Hartford Colonials (UFL, head coach) 2010, joined Titans in 2011.
Chet Parlavecchio, special teams assistant; born February 14, 1960, Irvington, N.J. Linebacker Penn State 1978-1981. Pro linebacker Green Bay Packers 1982-83, St. Louis Cardinals 1983. College coach: Temple 1992-93. Pro coach: Joined Titans in 2011.
Dave Ragone, wide receivers; born October 3, 1979, Middleburg Heights, Ohio. Quarterback Louisville 1999-2002. Pro quarterback Houston Texans 2003-05. Pro coach: Hartford Colonels (UFL) 2010, joined Titans in 2011.
Tracy Rocker, defensive line; born April 9, 1966, Atlanta. Defensive tackle Auburn 1984-88. Pro defensive tackle Washington Redskins 1989-1990, Orlando Thunder (WFL) 1991. College coach: West Alabama 1994-96, Troy 1997-2001, Cincinnati 2002, Arkansas 2003-07, Ole Miss 2008, Auburn 2009-2010. Pro coach: Joined Titans in 2011.
Jim Skipper, running backs; born January 23, 1949, Breaux Bridge, La. Defensive back Whittier College 1971-72. No pro playing experience. College coach: Cal Poly- Pomona 1974-76, San Jose State 1977-78, Pacific 1979, Oregon 1980-82. Pro coach: Philadelphia/Baltimore Stars (USFL) 1983- 85, New Orleans Saints 1986-1995, Arizona Cardinals 1996, New York Giants 1997- 2000, San Francisco Demons (XFL) 2001 (head coach), Carolina Panthers 2002-2010, joined Titans in 2011.
Arthur Smith, offensive assistant/quality control; born May 27, 1982, Memphis, Tenn. Offensive lineman North Carolina 2001-05.No pro playing experience. College coach: North Carolina 2006. Pro coach: Washington Redskins 2007-08, joined Titans in 2011.
Steve Watterson, asst. head coach/ strength & conditioning; born November 27, 1956, Newport, R.I. Attended Rhode Island. No college or pro playing experience. Pro coach: Philadelphia Eagles 1984-85, joined Titans/Oilers in 1986.
John Zernhelt, tight ends, born January 4, 1954, Pottsville, Pa. Offensive lineman Maryland 1974-77. No pro playing experience. College coach: Ferrum 1977-1980, Marshall 1981, East Carolina 1982-86, Maryland 1987-1991, Rice 1992-93, Duke 1994-95, South Carolina 1996-98, James Madison 1999-2002, The Citadel 2003-04 (head coach 2004). Pro coach: New York Jets 2005, joined Titans in 2006.

The NFC

National Football Conference
West Division
Team Colors: Cardinal Red, Black, and
White
8701 S. Hardy Drive
Tempe, Arizona 85284
Telephone: (602) 379-0101

2012 SCHEDULE
PRESEASON
Aug. 5   vs. New Orleans (Canton)...5:00
Aug. 10 at Kansas City 5:00
Aug. 17 **Oakland** 7:00
Aug. 23 at Tennessee 5:00
Aug. 30 **Denver**..............................8:00

REGULAR SEASON
Sep. 9   **Seattle** 1:15
Sep. 16 at New England 10:00a
Sep. 23 **Philadelphia** 1:05
Sep. 30 **Miami** 1:05
Oct. 4   at St. Louis (Thurs) 5:20
Oct. 14 **Buffalo** 1:05
Oct. 21 at Minnesota..................10:00a
Oct. 29 **San Francisco** (Mon) 5:30
Nov. 4   at Green Bay..................11:00a
Nov. 11 BYE
Nov. 18 at Atlanta 11:00a
Nov. 25 **St. Louis** 2:15
Dec. 2   at New York Jets.............11:00a
Dec. 9   at Seattle............................2:15
Dec. 16 **Detroit** 2:05
Dec. 23 **Chicago** 2:15
Dec. 30 at San Francisco.................2:15
All times MDT/PST
Stadium: University of Phoenix Stadium
(opened in 2006)
• **Capacity:** 65,000
1 Cardinals Drive
Glendale, Arizona 85305
Playing Surface: Grass
Training Camp: Northern Arizona University
Flagstaff, Arizona 86011

UNIVERSITY OF PHOENIX STADIUM

CLUB OFFICIALS
Owner: William V. Bidwill
President: Michael Bidwill
General Manager: Rod Graves
Executive Vice President/Chief Operating
Officer: Ron Minegar
Vice President, Player Personnel:
Steve Keim
Chief Financial Officer: Greg Lee
General Counsel: David Koeninger
Vice President, Media Relations:
Mark Dalton
Vice President, Marketing: Lisa Manning
Vice President, Business Development:
Steve Ryan
Vice President, Information Technology:
Mark Feller
Vice President, Security: Rick Knight
Vice President, Stadium Operations:
John Drum
Senior Director, Player Programs:
Anthony Edwards
Senior Director, Broadcasting/Executive
Producer: Tim DeLaney
Senior Director, Community Relations:
Luis Zendejas
Senior Director, Ticketing: Steve Bomar
Senior Director, Ticket Sales:
Ron Campbell
Director, Player Personnel: Jason Licht
Director, Football Administration:
Reggie Terry
Director, Premium Seat & Guest
Services: Cari Mass
Director, Business Development:
Mike Iaquinta
Director, Corporate Partnership Service &
Activation: Scott Coleman
Director, Cheerleading: Heather Karberg
Website Manager: Darren Urban
Video Director: Rob Brakel
Head Athletic Trainer: Tom Reed
Assistant Athletic Trainers:
Jim Shearer, Jeff Herndon,
Chad Cook
Equipment Manager: Mark Ahlemeier
Assistant Equipment Manager:
Steve Christensen

COACHING HISTORY
Chicago 1920-1959, St. Louis 1960-1987
(502-706-39)
Records include postseason games
1920-22   John (Paddy) Driscoll 17-8-4
1923-24   Arnold Horween.................13-8-1
1925-26   Norman Barry.....................16-8-2
1927   Guy Chamberlin 3-7-1
1928   Fred Gillies.........................1-5-0
1929   Dewey Scanlon....................6-6-1
1930   Ernie Nevers.......................5-6-2
1931   LeRoy Andrews* 0-1-0
1931   Ernie Nevers 5-3-0
1932   Jack Chevigny 2-6-2
1933-34   Paul Schissler.....................6-15-1
1935-38   Milan Creighton 16-26-4
1939   Ernie Nevers 1-10-0
1940-42   Jimmy Conzelman 8-22-3
1943-45   Phil Handler** 1-29-0
1946-48   Jimmy Conzelman 27-10-0
1949   Phil Handler-Buddy Parker***.2-4-0
1949   Raymond (Buddy) Parker......4-1-1
1950-51   Earl (Curly) Lambeau****....7-15-0
1951   Phil Handler-Cecil Isbell# 1-1-0
1952   Joe Kuharich 4-8-0
1953-54   Joe Stydahar 3-20-1
1955-57   Ray Richards 14-21-1
1958-1961 Frank (Pop) Ivy##.............15-31-2
1961   Chuck Drulis-Ray Prochaska-
Ray Willsey### 2-0-0
1962-65   Wally Lemm 27-26-3
1966-1970 Charley Winner 35-30-5
1971-72   Bob Hollway 8-18-2
1973-77   Don Coryell 42-29-1
1978-79   Bud Wilkinson####..........9-20-0
1979   Larry Wilson.......................2-1-0
1980-85   Jim Hanifan 39-50-1
1986-89   Gene Stallings@................23-34-1
1989   Hank Kuhlmann 0-5-0
1990-93   Joe Bugel 20-44-0
1994-95   Buddy Ryan 12-20-0
1996-2000 Vince Tobin@@ 29-44-0
2000-03   Dave McGinnis 17-40-0
2004-06   Dennis Green 16-32-0
2007-2011 Ken Whisenhunt...............44-42-0

    * Resigned after one game in 1931
   ** Co-coach with Walt Kiesling in Chicago
Cardinals-Pittsburgh merger in 1944
  *** Co-coaches for first six games in 1949
**** Resigned after 10 games in 1951
    # Co-coaches
   ## Resigned after 12 games in 1961
 ### Co-coaches
Released after 13 games in 1979
   @ Released after 11 games in 1989
  @@ Released after seven games in 2000

PAID ATTENDANCE
Home 446,005   Away 485,055
Total 931,060
Single-game home record, 73,025*
(9/19/93)
Single-season home record, 516,646 (2007)
*Team also had attendance of 103,467 for regular-
season home game at Azteca Stadium, Mexico City,
Mexico

2012 DRAFT CHOICES
Round	Name	Pos.	College
1	Michael Floyd	WR	Notre Dame
3	Jamell Fleming	DB	Oklahoma
4	Bobby Massie	T	Mississippi
5	Senio Kelemete	G	Washington
6	Justin Bethel	DB	Presbyterian
	Ryan Lindley	QB	San Diego St.
7	Nate Potter	T	Boise St.

ARIZONA CARDINALS

2011 TEAM RECORD
PRESEASON (2-2)

Date	Result	Opponent
8/11	W 24-18	at Oakland
8/19	L 20-28	at Green Bay
8/27	L 31-34	San Diego
9/1	W 26-7	Washington

REGULAR SEASON (8-8)

9/11	W 28-21	Carolina
9/18	L 21-22	at Washington
9/25	L 10-13	at Seattle
10/2	L 27-31	New York Giants
10/9	L 10-34	at Minnesota
10/23	L 20-32	Pittsburgh
10/30	L 27-30	at Baltimore
11/6	W 19-13	St. Louis (OT)
11/13	W 21-17	at Philadelphia
11/20	L 7-23	at San Francisco
11/27	W 23-20	at St. Louis
12/4	W 19-13	Dallas (OT)
12/11	W 21-19	San Francisco
12/18	W 20-17	Cleveland (OT)
12/24	L 16-23	at Cincinnati
1/1	W 23-20	Seattle (OT)

(OT) Overtime

SCORE BY PERIODS

Cardinals	36	68	79	111	18 —	312
Opponents	81	107	85	75	0 —	348

2011 TEAM STATISTICS

	Cardinals	Opp.
Total First Downs	286	333
Rushing	83	118
Passing	175	174
Penalty	28	41
3rd Down: Made/Att	66/205	71/226
3rd Down Pct.	32.2	31.4
4th Down: Made/Att	9/15	4/8
4th Down Pct.	60.0	50.0
Possession Avg.	28:11	31:49
Total Net Yards	5192	5682
Avg. Per Game	324.5	355.1
Total Plays	993	1095
Avg. Per Play	5.2	5.2
Net Yards Rushing	1625	1986
Avg. Per Game	101.6	124.1
Total Rushes	389	475
Net Yards Passing	3567	3696
Avg. Per Game	222.9	231.0
Sacked/Yards Lost	54/387	42/304
Gross Yards	3954	4000
Att./Completions	550/307	578/340
Completion Pct.	55.8	58.8
Had Intercepted	23	10
Punts/Average	92/45.0	92/44.4
Net Punting Avg.	92/37.3	92/36.2
Penalties/Yards	106/1004	122/950
Fumbles/Ball Lost	24/9	15/9
Touchdowns	37	34
Rushing	12	15
Passing	21	17
Returns	4	2

2011 INDIVIDUAL STATISTICS

PASSING

	Att.	Comp.	Yds.	Pct.	TD	Int.	Tkld.	Rate
J. Skelton	275	151	1913	54.9	11	14	23/162	68.9
Kolb	253	146	1955	57.7	9	8	30/219	81.1
Bartel	22	10	86	45.5	1	1	1/6	52.5
Cardinals	550	307	3954	55.8	21	23	54/387	73.9
Opponents	578	340	4000	58.8	17	10	42/304	82.5

SCORING

	TD R	TD P	TD Rt	PAT	FG	Saf	PTS
Feely	0	0	0	33/33	19/24	0	90
Wells	10	0	0	0/0	0/0	0	60
Fitzgerald	0	8	0	0/0	0/0	0	48
Doucet	0	5	0	0/0	0/0	0	30
Peterson	0	0	4	0/0	0/0	0	24
King	0	3	0	0/0	0/0	0	18
Roberts	0	2	0	0/0	0/0	0	12
Stephens-Howling	0	2	0	0/0	0/0	0	12
Heap	0	1	0	0/0	0/0	0	6
Smith	1	0	0	0/0	0/0	0	6
Taylor	1	0	0	0/0	0/0	0	6
Cardinals	12	21	4	33/33	19/24	0	312
Opponents	15	17	2	33/33	35/48	3	348

2-Pt Conversions: Cardinals 0-2, Opponents 0-1

RUSHING

	No.	Yds	Avg	LG	TD
Wells	245	1047	4.3	71	10
Stephens-Howling	43	167	3.9	39	0
J. Skelton	28	128	4.6	14	0
Smith	30	102	3.4	12	1
Taylor	20	77	3.9	34	1
Kolb	17	65	3.8	17	0
Roberts	3	27	9.0	12	0
Bartel	1	9	9.0	9	0
Sherman	1	3	3.0	3	0
Peterson	1	0	0.0	0	0
Cardinals	389	1625	4.2	71	12
Opponents	475	1986	4.2	48t	15

RECEIVING

	No.	Yds	Avg	LG	TD
Fitzgerald	80	1411	17.6	73t	8
Doucet	54	689	12.8	70t	5
Roberts	51	586	11.5	45	2
King	27	271	10.0	48t	3
Heap	24	283	11.8	28	1
Taylor	14	91	6.5	17	0
Stephens-Howling	13	234	18.0	73t	2
Housler	12	133	11.1	21	0
Wells	10	52	5.2	10	0
Sherman	8	72	9.0	19	0
Stuckey	4	39	9.8	12	0
Sampson	3	36	12.0	15	0
Smith	3	21	7.0	13	0
Dray	2	25	12.5	20	0
Maui'a	1	12	12.0	12	0
Peterson	1	-1	-1.0	-1	0
Cardinals	307	3954	12.9	73t	21
Opponents	340	4000	11.8	95t	17

INTERCEPTIONS

	No.	Yds	Avg	LG	TD
Marshall	3	83	27.7	49	0
Washington	2	16	8.0	16	0
Peterson	2	1	0.5	1	0
Wilson	1	17	17.0	17	0
Campbell	1	0	0.0	0	0
Jefferson	1	0	0.0	0	0
Cardinals	10	117	11.7	49	0
Opponents	23	296	12.9	52	1

PUNTING

	No.	Yds.	Avg.	In 20	LG
Zastudil	87	3929	45.2	24	66
Graham	5	212	42.4	2	55
Cardinals	92	4141	45.0	26	66
Opponents	92	4087	44.4	39	66

PUNT RETURNS

	Ret	FC	Yds	Avg	LG	TD
Peterson	44	22	699	15.9	99t	4
Roberts	2	0	-3	-1.5	-1	0
Cardinals	46	22	696	15.1	99t	4
Opponents	50	20	610	12.2	88t	1

KICKOFF RETURNS

	No.	Yds	Avg	LG	TD
Stephens-Howling	36	857	23.8	37	0
Jefferson	14	356	25.4	51	0
Roberts	2	33	16.5	21	0
Cardinals	52	1246	24.0	51	0
Opponents	52	1300	25.0	69	0

FIELD GOALS

	1-19	20-29	30-39	40-49	50+
Feely	0/0	9/9	4/6	5/7	1/2
Cardinals	0/0	9/9	4/6	5/7	1/2
Opponents	0/0	12/13	9/12	11/17	3/6

SACKS

	No.
Campbell	8.0
Acho	7.0
Washington	5.0
Schofield	4.5
Dockett	3.5
Haggans	3.0
Lenon	3.0
Marshall	2.0
Rhodes	2.0
Carter	1.0
Eason	1.0
Peterson	1.0
Porter	1.0
Cardinals	42.0
Opponents	54.0

RECORD HOLDERS
INDIVIDUAL RECORDS—CAREER

Category	Name	Performance
Rushing (Yds.)	Ottis Anderson, 1979-1986	7,999
Passing (Yds.)	Jim Hart, 1966-1983	34,639
Passing (TDs)	Jim Hart, 1966-1983	209
Receiving (No.)	Larry Fitzgerald, 2004-2011	693
Receiving (Yds.)	Larry Fitzgerald, 2004-2011	9,615
Interceptions	Larry Wilson, 1960-1972	52
Punting (Avg.)	Jerry Norton, 1959-1961	44.9
Punt Return (Avg.)	Charley Trippi, 1947-1955	13.7
Kickoff Return (Avg.)	Ollie Matson, 1952, 1954-58	28.5
Field Goals	Jim Bakken, 1962-1978	282
Touchdowns (Tot.)	Larry Fitzgerald, 2004-2011	73
Points	Jim Bakken, 1962-1978	1,380
*Sacks	Freddie Joe Nunn, 1985-1993	66.5

INDIVIDUAL RECORDS—SINGLE SEASON

Category	Name	Performance
Rushing (Yds.)	Ottis Anderson, 1979	1,605
Passing (Yds.)	Neil Lomax, 1984	4,614
Passing (TDs)	Kurt Warner, 2008	30
Receiving (No.)	Larry Fitzgerald, 2005	103
Receiving (Yds.)	David Boston, 2001	1,598
Interceptions	Bob Nussbaumer, 1949	12
Punting (Avg.)	Ben Graham, 2009	47.0
Punt Return (Avg.)	John (Red) Cochran, 1949	20.9
Kickoff Return (Avg.)	Ollie Matson, 1958	35.5
Field Goals	Neil Rackers, 2005	**40
Touchdowns (Tot.)	John David Crow, 1962	17
Points	Neil Rackers, 2005	140
*Sacks	Simeon Rice, 1999	16.5

INDIVIDUAL RECORDS—SINGLE GAME

Category	Name	Performance
Rushing (Yds.)	Beanie Wells, 11-27-11	228
Passing (Yds.)	Boomer Esiason, 11-10-96 (OT)	522
Passing (TDs)	Jim Hardy, 10-2-50	6
	Charley Johnson, 9-26-65, 11-2-69	6
Receiving (No.)	Sonny Randle, 11-4-62	16
Receiving (Yds.)	Sonny Randle, 11-4-62	256
Interceptions	Bob Nussbaumer, 11-13-49	**4
	Jerry Norton, 11-20-60	**4
	Kwamie Lassiter, 12-27-98	**4
Field Goals	Jim Bakken, 9-24-67	7
Touchdowns (Tot.)	Ernie Nevers, 11-28-29	**6
Points	Ernie Nevers, 11-28-29	**40
*Sacks	Curtis Greer, 12-18-83	4.5

*Sacks became an official statistic in 1982.
**NFL Record

2012 VETERAN ROSTER

No.	Name	Pos.	Ht.	Wt.	Birthdate	NFL Exp.	College	Hometown	How Acq.	'11 Games/ Starts
94	Acho, Sam	LB	6-3	257	9/6/88	2	Texas	Dallas, Texas	D4-'11	16/10
27	Adams, Michael	CB	5-8	181	6/17/85	6	Louisiana-Lafayette	Dallas, Texas	FA-'07	15/1
2	Bartel, Richard	QB	6-4	230	2/3/83	4	Tarleton State	Grapevine, Texas	FA-'10	2/0
74	Batiste, D'Anthony	T	6-4	314	3/29/82	7	Louisiana-Lafayette	Marksville, La.	FA-'10	3/0
55	Bradley, Stewart	LB	6-4	258	11/1/83	6	Nebraska	Salt Lake City, Utah	UFA(Phil)-'11	16/1
73	Bridges, Jeremy	T	6-5	318	4/19/80	10	Southern Mississippi	South Pike, Miss.	FA-'09	16/5
75	Brown, Levi	T	6-6	324	3/16/84	6	Penn State	Norfolk, Va.	D1-'07	16/16
22	Butler, Crezdon	CB	6-0	191	5/26/87	3	Clemson	Asheville, N.C.	W(Pitt)-'11	1/0
93	Campbell, Calais	DE	6-8	300	9/1/86	5	Miami	Aurora, Colo.	D2-'08	16/16
79	Carter, David	DT	6-5	300	12/10/87	2	UCLA	Fontana, Calif.	D6b-'11	16/0
69	Cohen, Landon	DE	6-3	300	8/3/86	4	Ohio	Spartanburg, S.C.	FA-'12	1/0
57	Coleman, Antonio	LB	6-1	254	9/1/86	3	Auburn	Mobile, Ala.	FA-'12	3/0*
71	Colledge, Daryn	G	6-4	308	2/11/82	7	Boise State	North Pole, Alaska	UFA(GB)-'11	16/16
90	Dockett, Darnell	DT	6-4	290	5/27/81	9	Florida State	Burtonsville, Md.	D3-'04	16/16
85	Doucet, Early	WR	6-0	212	10/28/85	5	Louisiana State	St. Martinville, La.	D3-'08	16/6
81	Dray, Jim	TE	6-5	255	12/31/86	3	Stanford	Paramus, N.J.	D7-'10	10/0
98	Eason, Nick	DT	6-3	305	5/29/80	10	Clemson	Lyons, Ga.	UFA(Pitt)-'11	16/6
3	Feely, Jay	K	6-0	208	5/23/76	12	Michigan	Tampa, Fla.	UFA(NYJ)-'10	16/0
11	Fitzgerald, Larry	WR	6-3	218	8/31/83	9	Pittsburgh	Minneapolis, Minn.	D1-'04	16/16
23	Gay, William	CB	5-10	190	1/1/85	6	Louisville	Tallahassee, Fla.	UFA(Pitt)-'12	16/15*
30	Green, Marshay	CB	5-10	175	1/14/86	3	Mississippi	Bastrop, La.	FA-'10	1/0
86	Heap, Todd	TE	6-5	252	3/16/80	12	Arizona State	Mesa, Ariz.	FA-'11	10/4
84	Housler, Rob	TE	6-5	250	3/17/88	2	Florida Atlantic	Converse, Texas	D3-'11	12/2
45	James, Javarris	RB	6-0	208	9/18/87	2	Miami	Immokalee, Fla.	FA-'12	0*
20	Jefferson, A.J.	CB	6-1	190	4/4/88	3	Fresno State	Bakersfield, Calif.	FA-'10	16/7
83	Johnson, Jaymar	WR	6-0	183	7/10/84	3	Jackson State	Gary, Ind.	FA-'11	1/0
49	Johnson, Rashad	S	5-11	204	1/2/86	4	Alabama	Sulligent, Ala.	D3-'09	16/9
87	King, Jeff	TE	6-3	260	2/19/83	7	Virginia Tech	Pulaski, Va.	UFA(Car)-'11	16/10
4	Kolb, Kevin	QB	6-3	218	8/24/84	6	Houston	Stephenville, Texas	T(Phil)-'11	9/9
82	Leach, Mike	LS	6-2	235	10/18/76	13	William & Mary	Jefferson Township, N.J.	FA-'09	16/0
51	Lenon, Paris	LB	6-2	240	11/26/77	11	Richmond	Lynchburg, Va.	UFA(StL)-'10	16/16
32	Lindsey, Korey	CB	5-10	194	2/3/89	2	Southern Illinois	Baton Rouge, La.	W(Cin)-'11	0*
21	Peterson, Patrick	CB	6-1	219	7/11/90	2	Louisiana State	Pompano Beach, Fla.	D1-'11	16/16
25	Rhodes, Kerry	FS	6-3	212	8/2/82	8	Louisville	Bessemer, Ala.	T(NYJ)-'10	7/7
12	Roberts, Andre	WR	5-11	195	1/9/88	3	The Citadel	Columbia, S.C.	D3-'10	16/16
10	Sampson, DeMarco	WR	6-2	204	12/19/86	2	San Diego State	Chula Vista, Calif.	D7-'11	11/0
39	Sanders, James	S	5-10	210	11/11/83	8	Fresno State	Porterville, Calif.	UFA(Atl)-'12	15/6*
50	Schofield, O'Brien	LB	6-3	242	4/3/87	3	Wisconsin	Great Lakes, Ill.	D4-'10	16/0
63	Sendlein, Lyle	C	6-3	308	3/16/84	6	Texas	Scottsdale, Ariz.	FA-'07	16/16
35	Sherman, Anthony	FB	5-10	242	12/11/88	2	Connecticut	North Attleboro, Mass.	D5-'11	15/7
19	Skelton, John	QB	6-6	244	3/17/88	3	Fordham	El Paso, Texas	D5-'10	8/7
46	Smith, Alfonso	RB	6-1	208	1/23/87	3	Kentucky	Louisville, Ky.	FA-'10	15/0
68	Snyder, Adam	G	6-6	325	1/30/82	8	Oregon	Fullerton, Calif.	UFA(SF)-'12	16/13*
36	Stephens-Howling, LaRod	RB	5-7	185	4/26/87	4	Pittsburgh	Johnstown, Pa.	D7a-'09	14/1
96	Talley, Ronald	DE	6-3	286	2/21/86	4	Delaware	Detroit, Mich.	FA-'11	6/0
28	Toler, Greg	CB	6-0	192	1/2/85	4	Saint Paul's (Va.)	Washington, D.C.	D4-'09	0*
56	Walker, Reggie	LB	6-0	244	12/15/86	4	Kansas State	Sacramento, Calif.	FA-'09	16/0
58	Washington, Daryl	LB	6-2	230	10/9/86	3	Texas Christian	Irving, Texas	D2-'10	15/14
26	Wells, Beanie	RB	6-2	229	8/7/88	4	Ohio State	Akron, Ohio	D1-'09	14/14
59	Williams, Brandon	LB	6-3	250	6/21/88	3	Texas Tech	Fort Worth, Texas	FA-'11	0*
92	Williams, Dan	DT	6-3	327	6/1/87	3	Tennessee	Memphis, Tenn.	D1-'10	10/10
34	Williams, Ryan	RB	5-9	207	4/9/90	2	Virginia Tech	Manassas, Va.	D2-'11	0*
18	Williams, Stephen	WR	6-5	208	6/29/86	3	Toledo	Houston, Texas	FA-'10	2/0
24	Wilson, Adrian	SS	6-3	230	10/12/79	12	North Carolina State	High Point, N.C.	D3-'01	16/16
9	Zastudil, Dave	P	6-3	220	10/26/78	11	Ohio	Bay Village, Ohio	FA-'11	15/0

* Coleman played 3 games with Buffalo in '11; Gay played 16 games with Pittsburgh; James last active with Indianapolis in '10; Lindsey did not play in 1 game, inactive for 3 games; Sanders played 15 games with San Francisco; Snyder played 16 games with San Francisco; Toler missed '11 season because of injury; B. Williams inactive for 2 games; R. Williams missed '11 season because of injury.

Players lost through free agency (3): DB Sean Considine (Balt; 8), G Deuce Lutui (Sea; 15), CB Richard Marshall (Mia; 16).

Also played with Cardinals in '11—S Hamza Abdullah (16 games), P Ben Graham (1), CB Marshay Green (1), G Rex Hadnot (16), LB Clark Haggans (16), DE Vonnie Holliday (16), T Brandon Keith (13), FB Reagan Mai'a (3), LB Joey Porter (6), WR Chansi Stuckey (9), RB Chester Taylor (12).

FIRST-YEAR ROSTER

Name	Pos.	Ht.	Wt.	Birthdate	College	Hometown	How Acq.
Arukwe, Stanley	WR	6-0	184	4/5/89	Troy	Tracy, Calif.	FA
Bartholomew, Ryan (1)	C	6-1	310	3/21/88	Syracuse	Mitchellville, Md.	FA-'11
Bethel, Justin	S	6-0	200	6/17/90	Presbyterian	Blythewood, S.C.	D6a
Binns, Broderick	LB	6-2	261	7/23/89	Iowa	St. Paul, Minn.	FA
Byrd, LaRon	WR	6-4	220	8/18/89	Miami	Hahnville, La.	FA
Clayson, Braeden	G	6-6	300	11/10/89	Idaho State	Burley, Idaho	FA
Crank, Jared	FB	6-2	238	1/17/89	Purdue	Richardson, Texas	FA
DeChristopher, Blake	G	6-5	311	9/8/88	Virginia Tech	Midlothian, Va.	FA
Elder, Eddie	S	5-10	185	2/14/89	Arizona State	Sacramento, Calif.	FA
Fleming, Jamell	CB	5-11	206	5/5/89	Oklahoma	Arlington, Texas	D3
Floyd, Michael	WR	6-2	220	11/27/89	Notre Dame	St. Paul, Minn.	D1
Gideon, Blake	S	6-1	205	7/25/89	Texas	Leander, Texas	FA
Gray, Tre	WR	5-10	175	9/1/89	Richmond	Cuero, Texas	FA
Kelemete, Senio	G	6-3	300	5/10/90	Washington	Seattle, Wash.	D5
Lindley, Ryan	QB	6-3	232	6/22/89	San Diego State	Alpine, Calif.	D6b
Lumpkin, Ricky (1)	DT	6-4	306	9/7/88	Kentucky	Clarksville, Tenn.	FA-'11
Massie, Bobby	T	6-6	316	8/1/89	Mississippi	Lynchburg, Va.	D4
McGraw, Marcus	LB	6-0	228	10/5/89	Houston	Arlington, Texas	FA
Nash, Zack	LB	6-4	260	9/23/89	Sacramento State	Vacaville, Calif.	FA
Nixon, James	CB	6-1	190	2/2/88	California (Pa.)	New Haven, Conn.	FA
Obi, Conrad	DE	6-3	290	12/21/88	Colorado	Grayson, Ga.	FA
Parker, Colin	LB	6-1	223	5/6/89	Arizona State	Chandler, Ariz.	FA
Parker, Larry	CB	5-11	176	1/17/89	San Diego State	San Diego, Calif.	FA
Potter, Nate	T	6-5	295	5/16/88	Boise State	Boise, Idaho	D7
Powell, William (1)	RB	5-9	207	3/9/88	Kansas State	Duncanville, Texas	FA-'11
Schmitt, Ricky (1)	K/P	6-3	217	8/17/85	Shepherd	Virginia Beach, Va.	FA
Skelton, Steve (1)	TE	6-5	250	8/6/89	Fordham	El Paso, Texas	FA-'11
Stewart, Chris (1)	G	6-4	325	9/12/87	Notre Dame	Spring, Texas	FA
Sturdivant, Quan (1)	LB	6-1	241	12/5/88	North Carolina	Oakboro, N.C.	D6a-'11
Vassallo, Paul	LB	6-3	247	12/16/89	Arizona	Reno, Nev.	FA
Webb, Martell (1)	TE	6-3	276	11/10/89	Michigan	Pontiac, Mich.	FA
Wedige, Scott	C	6-4	310	11/20/88	Northern Illinois	Elkhorn, Wisc.	FA
Williams, Isaiah (1)	WR	6-3	200	1/30/87	Maryland	Montclair, N.J.	FA
Wilson, Marc	WR	5-11	190	6/16/89	St. Anselm	Farmington, Conn.	FA
Young, D.J. (1)	T	6-5	298	1/26/88	Michigan State	Lansing, Mich.	FA-'11

The term NFL Rookie is defined as a player who is in his first season of professional football and has not been on the roster of another professional football team for any regular-season or postseason games. A Rookie is designated by an "R" on NFL rosters. Players who have been active in another professional football league or players who have NFL experience, including either preseason training camp or being on an Active List or Inactive List, or on Reserve/Injured or Reserve/Physically Unable to Perform for fewer than six regular-season games, are termed NFL First-Year Players. An NFL First-Year Player is designated by a "1" on NFL rosters. Thereafter, a player is credited with an additional year of experience for each season in which he accumulates six games on the Active List or Inactive List, or on Reserve/Injured or Reserve/Physically Unable to Perform.

Log on to www.azcardinals.com for an up-to-date roster.

COACHING STAFF
Head Coach,
Ken Whisenhunt

Pro Career: Became an NFL head coach for the first time when hired by Arizona on January 14, 2007. In five seasons he has posted 44 victories, the most of any head coach in franchise history. The Cardinals have posted a record of .500 or better in four of his five seasons. He has led Arizona to a 7-2 overtime record including an NFL record of 4-0 mark in home overtime games in 2011. His 4-2 career postseason record is among the league leaders in winning percentage. Led the Cardinals to NFC West titles in 2008 and 2009, the team's first back-to-back division crowns since 1974-75. Arizona's 8-8 mark in his first season of 2007 was the team's best record since going 9-7 in 1998. The 2008 season brought the franchise's first postseason appearance since 1998, first division crown since 1975, and first home playoff game since 1947. It ended with the team's first-ever conference title and Super Bowl appearance. Arizona's 12 total wins in 2008 were the most in team history. In 2009, led Cards to 10 regular season wins for first time since 1976 and posted 6 road victories, the franchise's most since 1963. Prior to joining the Cardinals, Whisenhunt spent the previous six seasons as an assistant with the Pittsburgh Steelers, the first three as tight ends coach and the last three as offensive coordinator. Whisenhunt became offensive coordinator in 2004, the same year the team drafted quarterback Ben Roethlisberger, who went on to set an NFL record with wins in his first 13 career starts en route to Offensive Rookie of the Year honors. The next season he became the youngest quarterback in NFL history to win a Super Bowl and finished third in the league in passer rating (98.6). In Whisenhunt's first year as coordinator, the Steelers rushing attack improved from thirty-first to second. His second year ended with an NFL title after the Steelers offense averaged 26.8 points per game in the playoffs. He joined the Steelers in January of 2001 as tight ends coach. Whisenhunt previously coached at the pro level with the New York Jets (tight ends, 2000), Cleveland Browns (special teams, 1999) and Baltimore Ravens (tight ends, 1997-98). He began his coaching career in the collegiate ranks with Vanderbilt for two seasons (1995-96). Whisenhunt was selected in the 12th round of the 1985 NFL Draft by the Atlanta Falcons out of Georgia Tech. He went on to play nine NFL seasons with the Falcons (1985-88), Washington Redskins (1989-1990), and New York Jets (1991-93). In 74 career games (37 starts), he caught 62 passes for 601 yards and 6 touchdowns. Career record: 44-42.

Background: After going to Georgia Tech as a walk-on, he played four seasons as a tight end/H-back. He finished his Yellow Jackets' career ranked second on the receiving yardage list (1,264 yards) and fourth in receptions (82). As a senior in 1984, he was a consensus All-ACC and honorable mention All-America selection when he averaged 19.1 yards-per-catch.

Personal: Born February 28, 1962 in Atlanta, Ga. Whisenhunt earned a degree in civil engineering from Georgia Tech. Ken and his wife, Alice, have two children—Kenneth, Jr. and Mary Ashley.

ASSISTANT COACHES

Ron Aiken, defensive line; born August 18, 1955, Moncks Corner, S.C. Guard/center North Carolina A&T 1973-76. No pro playing experience. College coach: Bethany College 1979-1981, Tarkio College 1982-84, Rensselaer Polytechnic Institute 1985, Langston 1986-89, New Mexico 1990-94, Vanderbilt 1995-96, Texas 1997, San Diego State 1998, Iowa 1999-2006. Pro coach: Joined Cardinals in 2007.

Pete Alosi, asst. strength and conditioning; born July 31, 1982, Massapequa, N.Y. Linebacker Salisbury University 2000-02. No pro playing experience. Pro coach: Joined Cardinals in 2010.

Louie Cioffi, defensive backs; born September 21, 1973, Greenlawn, N.Y. Attended SUNY-Stony Brook. No college or pro playing experience. College coach: C.W. Post 1995-96. Pro coach: New York Jets 1993-94, Cincinnati Bengals 1997-2010, joined Cardinals in 2011.

Chad Grimm, offensive quality control; born May 18, 1985, Fairfax, Va. Linebacker Virginia Tech 2003-06. No pro playing experience. Pro coach: Joined Cardinals in 2009.

Russ Grimm, asst. head coach/offensive line; born May 2, 1959, Scottdale, Pa. Center Pittsburgh 1977-1980. Pro guard Washington Redskins 1981-1991. Inducted into Pro Football Hall of Fame in 2010. Pro coach: Washington Redskins 1992-2000, Pittsburgh Steelers 2001-06, joined Cardinals in 2007.

Ray Horton, defensive coordinator; born April 12, 1960, Tacoma, Wash. Cornerback Washington 1979-1982. Pro cornerback Cincinnati Bengals 1983-88, Dallas Cowboys 1989-1992. Pro coach: Washington Redskins 1994-96, Cincinnati Bengals 1997-2001, Detroit Lions 2002-03, Pittsburgh Steelers 2004-2010, joined Cardinals in 2011.

Freddie Kitchens, tight ends; born November 29, 1974, Gadsden, Ala. Quarterback Alabama 1994-97. No pro playing experience. College coach: Glenville State College 1999, Louisiana State 2000, North Texas 2001-03, Mississippi State 2004-05. Pro coach: Dallas Cowboys 2006, joined Cardinals in 2007.

John Lott, strength and conditioning; born May 9, 1964, Denton, Texas. Offensive lineman North Texas 1983-86. Pro offensive lineman Pittsburgh Steelers 1987.

College coach: North Texas 1989-1990, Houston 1991-96. Pro coach: New York Jets 1997-2004, Cleveland Browns 2005-06, joined Cardinals in 2007.

John McNulty, quarterbacks; born May 29, 1968, Scranton, Pa. Safety Penn State 1988-1990. No pro playing experience. College coach: Michigan 1991-94, Connecticut 1995-97, Rutgers 2004-08. Pro coach: Jacksonville Jaguars 1998-2002, Dallas Cowboys 2003, joined Cardinals in 2009.

Mike Miller, offensive coordinator; born April 9, 1970, Plum Borough, Pa. Attended Clarion. No college or pro playing experience. College coach: Robert Morris 1997-98, 2006. Pro coach: Pittsburgh Steelers 1999-2003, Buffalo Bills 2004-05, Berlin Thunder (NFLE) 2006, joined Cardinals in 2007.

Matt Raich, linebackers; born August 16, 1970, Monaca, Pa. Middle linebacker Westminster College 1989-1992. No pro playing experience. College coach: Westminster 1993-94, Robert Morris 1996-98, 2000-02, Glenville State 1999. Pro coach: Pittsburgh Steelers 2004-06, joined Cardinals in 2007.

Frank Reich, wide receivers; born December 4, 1961, Freeport, N.Y. Quarterback Maryland 1981-84. Pro quarterback Buffalo Bills 1985-1994, Carolina Panthers 1995, New York Jets 1996, Detroit Lions 1997-98. Pro coach: Indianapolis Colts 2008-2011, joined Cardinals in 2012.

Tommie Robinson, running backs; born April 4, 1963, Columbus, Ga. Safety Troy State 1982-85. No pro playing experience. College coach: Arkansas 1991, Utah State 1992-93, TCU 1994-97, Nevada-Las Vegas 1998, Oklahoma State 2001, Georgia Tech 2002-05, Memphis 2006, Miami 2007-09. Pro coach: Dallas Cowboys 1998-2000, joined Cardinals in 2010.

Ryan Slowik, outside linebackers; born Dec. 27, 1980, Chicago, Ill. Safety Wisconsin-Oshkosh 2002-03. No pro playing experience. College coach: Wisconsin-Oshkosh 2004. Pro coach: Denver Broncos 2005-08, joined Cardinals in 2009.

Kevin Spencer, special teams; born November 2, 1953, Queens, N.Y. Outside linebacker Springfield College 1971. No pro playing experience. College coach: SUNY-Cortland 1975-76, Cornell 1979-1980, Ithaca 1981-86, Wesleyan 1987-1991. Pro coach: Cleveland Browns 1991-94, Oakland Raiders 1995-97, Indianapolis Colts 1998-2001, Pittsburgh Steelers 2002-06, joined Cardinals in 2007.

Deshea Townsend, asst. defensive backs; born September 8, 1975, Batesville, Miss. Cornerback Alabama 1994-97. Pro cornerback Pittsburgh Steelers 1998-2009, Indianapolis Colts 2010. Pro coach: Joined Cardinals in 2011.

National Football Conference
South Division
Team Colors: Black, Red, Silver, and White
4400 Falcon Parkway
Flowery Branch, Georgia 30542
Telephone: (770) 965-3115

2012 SCHEDULE
PRESEASON
Aug. 12	**Baltimore**	7:30
Aug. 19	**Cincinnati**	8:00
Aug. 27	at Miami	7:30
Sep. 1	at Jacksonville	7:30

REGULAR SEASON
Sep. 9	at Kansas City	1:00
Sep. 17	**Denver** (Mon)	8:30
Sep. 23	at San Diego	4:05
Sep. 30	**Carolina**	1:00
Oct. 7	at Washington	1:00
Oct. 14	**Oakland**	1:00
Oct. 21	BYE	
Oct. 28	at Philadelphia	1:00
Nov. 4	**Dallas**	8:20
Nov. 11	at New Orleans	1:00
Nov. 18	**Arizona**	1:00
Nov. 25	at Tampa Bay	1:00
Nov. 29	**New Orleans** (Thurs)	8:20
Dec. 9	at Carolina	1:00
Dec. 16	**New York Giants**	1:00
Dec. 22	at Detroit (Sat)	8:30
Dec. 30	**Tampa Bay**	1:00

All times ET

Stadium: Georgia Dome
　　　　(opened in 1992)
　　　　•**Capacity:** 71,228
　　　　One Georgia Dome Drive
　　　　Atlanta, Georgia 30313
Playing Surface: FieldTurf
Training Camp: Atlanta Falcons
　　　　　　4400 Falcon Parkway
　　　　　　Flowery Branch, GA 30542

GEORGIA DOME

CLUB OFFICIALS
Owner & CEO: Arthur M. Blank
President: Rich McKay
General Manager: Thomas Dimitroff
Head Coach: Mike Smith
Director of Human Resources:
　Karen Walters
Senior Vice President & CFO:
　Greg Beadles
Controller: Rob Geoffroy
Vice President of Football
　Communications: Reggie Roberts
Vice President of Information
　Technology: Danny Branch
Chief Marketing Officer: Jim Smith
Vice President of Sponsorship Sales:
　Tim Zulawski
Senior Director of Media Relations:
　Frank Kleha
Senior Director of Player Development:
　Kevin Winston
Director of Logistics and Facilities:
　Spencer Treadwell
Director of Ticket Operations:
　Mike Gilsenan
Director of Community Relations:
　Kendyl Baugh Moss
Director of Event Marketing: Roddy White
Director of Football Administration:
　Nick Polk
Director of Player Personnel: Les Snead
Director of Player Personnel:
　David Caldwell
Director of Pro Personnel: DeJuan Polk
Associate Director of Player Personnel:
　Lionel Vital
Eastern Regional Scout: Marvin Allen
Western Regional Scout: Mark Olson
Area Scouts: Shepley Heard,
　Anthony Robinson, Mike Ross,
　Steve Sabo, Chris Polian
Pro Scout: Bob Kronenberg
Scouting Assistant: Mike Potts
Head Athletic Trainer: Marty Lauzon
Assistant Athletic Trainer: Danny Long
Video Director: Mike Crews
Video Assistant: Phil Tieman
Equipment Manager: Brian Boigner
Director of New Media: Dan Levak
Football Communications Coordinator:
　Brian Cearns
Football Communications Coordinator:
　Matt Haley

COACHING HISTORY
(305-410-6)
Records include postseason games
1966-68	Norb Hecker*	4-26-1
1968-1974	Norm Van Brocklin**	37-49-3
1974-76	Marion Campbell***	6-19-0
1976	Pat Peppler	3-6-0
1977-1982	Leeman Bennett	47-44-0
1983-86	Dan Henning	22-41-1
1987-89	Marion Campbell****	11-32-0
1989	Jim Hanifan	0-4-0
1990-93	Jerry Glanville	28-38-0
1994-96	June Jones	19-30-0
1997-2003	Dan Reeves#	52-61-1
2003	Wade Phillips	2-1-0
2004-06	Jim Mora	27-23-0
2007	Bobby Petrino##	3-10-0
2007	Emmitt Thomas	1-2-0
2008-2011	Mike Smith	43-24-0

*Released after three games in 1968
**Released after eight games in 1974
***Released after five games in 1976
****Retired after 12 games in 1989
#Released after 13 games in 2003
##Resigned after 13 games in 2007

PAID ATTENDANCE
Home 535,161　　　　Away 504,911
Total 1,040,072
Single-game home record,
　71,151 (10/22/06)
Single-season home record,
　553,979 (1992)

2012 DRAFT CHOICES
Round	Name	Pos.	College
2	Peter Konz	G	Wisconsin
3	Lamar Holmes	T	Southern Mississippi
5	Bradie Ewing	RB	Wisconsin
	Jonathan Massaquoi	DE	Troy
6	Charles Mitchell	DB	Mississippi St.
7	Travian Robertson	NT	South Carolina

2011 TEAM RECORD

PRESEASON (0-4)

Date	Result	Opponent
8/12	L 23-28	Miami
8/19	L 13-15	at Jacksonville
8/27	L 16-34	at Pittsburgh
9/1	L 7-21	Baltimore

REGULAR SEASON (10-6)

Date	Result	Opponent
9/11	L 12-30	at Chicago
9/18	W 35-31	Philadelphia
9/25	L 13-16	at Tampa Bay
10/2	W 30-28	at Seattle
10/9	L 14-25	Green Bay
10/16	W 31-17	Carolina
10/23	W 23-16	at Detroit
11/6	W 31-7	at Indianapolis
11/13	L 23-26	New Orleans (OT)
11/20	W 23-17	Tennessee
11/27	W 24-14	Minnesota
12/4	L 10-17	at Houston
12/11	W 31-23	at Carolina
12/15	W 41-14	Jacksonville
12/26	L 16-45	at New Orleans
1/1	W 45-24	Tampa Bay
(OT) Overtime		

POSTSEASON (0-1)

1/8	L 2-24	at New York Giants

SCORE BY PERIODS

Falcons	120	115	74	93	0	—	402
Opponents	39	110	127	71	3	—	350

2011 TEAM STATISTICS

	Falcons	Opp.
Total First Downs	349	292
Rushing	100	87
Passing	215	186
Penalty	34	19
3rd Down: Made/Att	99/224	93/211
3rd Down Pct.	44.2	44.1
4th Down: Made/Att	4/13	6/11
4th Down Pct.	30.8	54.5
Possession Avg.	32:05	27:55
Total Net Yards	6026	5338
Avg. Per Game	376.6	333.6
Total Plays	1073	965
Avg. Per Play	5.6	5.5
Net Yards Rushing	1834	1552
Avg. Per Game	114.6	97.0
Total Rushes	453	372
Net Yards Passing	4192	3786
Avg. Per Game	262.0	236.6
Sacked/Yards Lost	26/173	33/231
Gross Yards	4365	4017
Att./Completions	594/365	560/340
Completion Pct.	61.4	60.7
Had Intercepted	13	19
Punts/Average	71/42.1	75/46.1
Net Punting Avg.	71/38.9	75/40.6
Penalties/Yards	93/769	101/843
Fumbles/Ball Lost	12/8	19/10
Touchdowns	46	40
Rushing	14	10
Passing	29	25
Returns	3	5

2011 INDIVIDUAL STATISTICS

PASSING

	Att.	Comp.	Yds.	Pct.	TD	Int.	Tkld.	Rate
Ryan	566	347	4177	61.3	29	12	26/173	92.2
Redman	28	18	188	64.3	0	1	0/0	68.8
Falcons	594	365	4365	61.4	29	13	26/173	91.1
Opponents	560	340	4017	60.7	25	19	33/231	83.3

SCORING

	TD R	TD P	TD Rt	PAT	FG	Saf	PTS
Bryant	0	0	0	45/45	27/29	0	126
Turner	11	0	0	0/0	0/0	0	66
Jones	0	8	0	0/0	0/0	0	48
White	0	8	0	0/0	0/0	0	48
Gonzalez	0	7	0	0/0	0/0	0	42
Mughelli	0	2	0	0/0	0/0	0	12
Rodgers	1	1	0	0/0	0/0	0	12
Ryan	2	0	0	0/0	0/0	0	12
Biermann	0	0	1	0/0	0/0	0	6
Douglas	0	1	0	0/0	0/0	0	6
Lofton	0	0	1	0/0	0/0	0	6
Palmer	0	1	0	0/0	0/0	0	6
Peters	0	0	1	0/0	0/0	0	6
Snelling	0	1	0	0/0	0/0	0	6
Falcons	14	29	3	45/45	27/29	0	402
Opponents	10	25	5	37/37	23/28	1	350

2-Pt Conversions: Falcons 0-1, Opponents 1-3

RUSHING

	No.	Yds	Avg	LG	TD
Turner	301	1340	4.5	81t	11
Rodgers	57	205	3.6	13	1
Snelling	44	151	3.4	18	0
Ryan	37	84	2.3	12	2
Jones	6	56	9.3	19	0
Douglas	1	3	3.0	3	0
Mughelli	2	1	0.5	1	0
Redman	5	-6	-1.2	-1	0
Falcons	453	1834	4.0	81t	14
Opponents	372	1552	4.2	74t	10

RECEIVING

	No.	Yds	Avg	LG	TD
White	100	1296	13.0	43	8
Gonzalez	80	875	10.9	30	7
Jones	54	959	17.8	80t	8
Douglas	39	498	12.8	49	1
Snelling	26	179	6.9	21t	1
Rodgers	21	188	9.0	31t	1
Turner	17	168	9.9	32	0
Weems	11	90	8.2	18	0
Palmer	10	72	7.2	11	1
Mughelli	4	25	6.3	19	2
Cox	2	8	4.0	8	0
Kelly	1	7	7.0	7	0
Falcons	365	4365	12.0	80t	29
Opponents	340	4017	11.8	70t	25

INTERCEPTIONS

	No.	Yds	Avg	LG	TD
DeCoud	4	77	19.3	49	0
Moore	2	56	28.0	29	0
Lofton	2	30	15.0	26t	1
Robinson	2	28	14.0	14	0
Hayden	2	3	1.5	2	0
Franks	2	0	0.0	0	0
Biermann	1	50	50.0	50t	1
Grimes	1	29	29.0	29	0
Walls	1	23	23.0	23	0
Peterson	1	4	4.0	4	0
Peters	1	1	1.0	1	0
Falcons	19	301	15.8	50t	2
Opponents	13	178	13.7	40t	2

PUNTING

	No.	Yds.	Avg.	In 20	LG
Bosher	70	2990	42.7	27	59
Falcons	71	2990	42.1	27	59
Opponents	75	3460	46.1	19	66

PUNT RETURNS

	Ret	FC	Yds	Avg	LG	TD
Weems	32	19	315	9.8	42	0
Franks	1	0	0	0.0	0	0
Falcons	33	19	315	9.5	42	0
Opponents	31	24	150	4.8	33	0

KICKOFF RETURNS

	No.	Yds	Avg	LG	TD
Weems	24	563	23.5	37	0
Falcons	24	563	23.5	37	0
Opponents	60	1487	24.8	104	0

FIELD GOALS

	1-19	20-29	30-39	40-49	50+
Bryant	2/2	9/9	9/9	5/7	2/2
Falcons	2/2	9/9	9/9	5/7	2/2
Opponents	0/0	8/8	4/5	9/10	2/5

SACKS

	No.
Abraham	9.5
Sidbury	4.0
Weatherspoon	4.0
Edwards	3.5
Peters	3.0
Biermann	2.5
Walker	2.0
Babineaux	1.0
Lofton	1.0
Owens	1.0
(group)	1.0
Moore	0.5
Falcons	33.0
Opponents	26.0

RECORD HOLDERS
INDIVIDUAL RECORDS—CAREER

Category	Name	Performance
Rushing (Yds.)	Gerald Riggs, 1982-88	6,631
Passing (Yds.)	Steve Bartkowski, 1975-1985	23,470
Passing (TDs)	Steve Bartkowski, 1975-1985	154
Receiving (No.)	Terance Mathis, 1994-2001	573
Receiving (Yds.)	Roddy White, 2005-2011	7,374
Interceptions	Rolland Lawrence, 1973-1980	39
Punting (Avg.)	Rick Donnelly, 1985-89	42.6
Punt Return (Avg.)	Darrien Gordon, 2001	14.1
Kickoff Return (Avg.)	Darrick Vaughn, 2000-01	25.7
Field Goals	Morten Andersen, 1995-2000, 2006-07	184
Touchdowns (Tot.)	Terance Mathis, 1994-2001	57
Points	Morten Andersen, 1995-2000, 2006-07	806
Sacks*	Chuck Smith, 1992-99	58.5

INDIVIDUAL RECORDS—SINGLE SEASON

Category	Name	Performance
Rushing (Yds.)	Jamal Anderson, 1998	1,846
Passing (Yds.)	Matt Ryan, 2011	4,177
Passing (TDs)	Steve Bartkowski, 1980	31
Receiving (No.)	Roddy White, 2010	115
Receiving (Yds.)	Roddy White, 2010	1,389
Interceptions	Scott Case, 1988	10
Punting (Avg.)	Billy Lothridge, 1968	44.3
Punt Return (Avg.)	Darrien Gordon, 2001	14.1
Kickoff Return (Avg.)	Darrick Vaughn, 2000	27.7
Field Goals	Jay Feely, 2002	32
Touchdowns (Tot.)	Michael Turner, 2008	17
Points	Jay Feely, 2002	138
Sacks*	John Abraham, 2008	16.5

INDIVIDUAL RECORDS—SINGLE GAME

Category	Name	Performance
Rushing (Yds.)	Michael Turner, 9-7-08	220
Passing (Yds.)	Chris Chandler, 12-23-01	431
Passing (TDs)	Wade Wilson, 12-13-92	5
Receiving (No.)	William Andrews, 11-15-81	15
Receiving (Yds.)	Roddy White, 10-11-09	210
Interceptions	Many times	2
	Last time by Brent Grimes, 12-20-09	
Field Goals	Norm Johnson, 11-13-94	6
Touchdowns (Tot.)	T.J. Duckett, 12-12-04	4
	Michael Turner, 11-23-08	4
Points	T.J. Duckett, 12-12-04	24
	Michael Turner, 11-23-08	24
Sacks*	Chuck Smith, 10-12-97	5.0

Sacks became an official statistic in 1982.

ATLANTA FALCONS

2012 VETERAN ROSTER

No.	Name	Pos.	Ht.	Wt.	Birthdate	NFL Exp.	College	Hometown	How Acq.	'11 Games/ Starts
55	Abraham, John	DE	6-4	263	5/6/78	13	South Carolina	Timmonsville, S.C.	T(NYJ)-'06	15/15
59	Adkins, Spencer	LB	5-11	236	5/16/87	4	Miami	Naples, Fla.	D6-'09	10/1
95	Babineaux, Jonathan	DT	6-2	300	10/12/81	8	Iowa	Port Arthur, Texas	D2-'05	13/13
72	Baker, Sam	T	6-5	301	5/30/85	5	Southern California	Tustin, Calif.	D1b-'08	12/6
71	Biermann, Kroy	DE	6-3	255	9/12/85	5	Montana	Hardin, Mont.	D5b-'08	16/1
63	Blalock, Justin	G	6-4	326	12/20/83	6	Texas	Dallas, Texas	D2a-'07	16/16
5	Bosher, Matt	K/P	6-0	208	10/18/87	1	Miami	Jupiter, Fla.	D6-'10	16/0
3	Bryant, Matt	K	5-9	203	5/29/75	11	Baylor	Orange, Texas	FA-'09	16/16
77	Clabo, Tyson	T	6-6	329	10/17/81	8	Wake Forest	Knoxville, Tenn.	FA-'11	16/16
42	Cox, Mike	FB	6-0	252	7/11/85	5	Georgia Tech	Lewisberry, Pa.	FA-'11	9/5
28	DeCoud, Thomas	S	6-2	192	3/19/85	5	California	Vallejo, Calif.	D3c-'08	16/15
52	Dent, Akeem	LB	6-1	239	9/27/87	2	Georgia	Atlanta, Ga.	D3-'11	16/0
83	Douglas, Harry	WR	6-0	183	9/16/84	4	Louisville	Jonesboro, Ga.	D3b-'08	16/4
93	Edwards, Ray	DE	6-5	268	1/1/85	7	Purdue	Cincinnati, Ohio	FA-'11	16/16
24	Franks, Dominique	CB	6-0	197	10/8/87	3	Oklahoma	Tulsa, Okla.	D5a-'10	14/4
88	Gonzalez, Tony	TE	6-5	247	2/27/76	16	California	Torrance, Calif.	T(KC)-'09	16/16
20	Grimes, Brent	CB	5-10	183	7/19/83	5	Shippensburg	Philadelphia, Pa.	FA-'07	12/12
61	Hawley, Joe	C	6-3	302	10/22/88	3	Nevada-Las Vegas	Yorba Linda, Calif.	D4-'10	16/12
50	James, Robert	LB	5-11	224	12/26/83	3	Arizona State	Glendale, Ariz.	FA-'10	1/0
94	Jerry, Peria	DT	6-2	295	8/23/84	4	Mississippi	Batesville, Miss.	D1-'09	16/4
79	Johnson, Mike	G	6-6	304	4/2/87	2	Alabama	Pensacola, Fla.	D3b-'10	2/0
11	Jones, Julio	WR	6-3	220	2/3/89	2	Alabama	Foley, Ala.	D1-'11	13/13
65	Manuwai, Vince	G	6-2	333	7/12/80	9	Hawaii	Honolulu, Hawaii	FA-'12	0*
98	Matthews, Cliff	DE	6-4	268	8/5/89	2	South Carolina	Cheraw, S.C.	D7b-'11	0*
27	McClain, Robert	CB	5-9	195	7/22/88	3	Connecticut	Philadelphia, Pa.	FA-'12	0*
62	McClure, Todd	C	6-1	296	2/16/77	14	Louisiana State	Baton Rouge, La.	D7a-'99	13/13
80	Meier, Kerry	WR	6-3	220	11/12/86	3	Kansas	Pittsburg, Kan.	D5b-'10	12/0
25	Moore, William	S	6-0	221	5/18/85	3	Missouri	Hayti, Mo.	D2-'09	12/11
34	Mughelli, Ovie	FB	6-1	250	6/10/80	10	Wake Forest	Boston, Mass.	UFA(Balt)-'07	7/5
54	Nicholas, Stephen	LB	6-3	236	5/1/83	6	South Florida	Jacksonville, Fla.	D4a-'07	10/8
21	Owens, Christopher	CB	5-9	180	12/1/86	4	San Jose State	Los Angeles, Calif.	D3-'09	14/2
81	Palmer, Michael	TE	6-5	252	1/18/88	3	Clemson	Stone Mountain, Ga.	FA-'10	16/2
91	Peters, Corey	DT	6-3	305	6/8/88	3	Kentucky	Louisville, Ky.	D3a-'10	15/15
97	Powell, Carlton	DT	6-3	312	8/14/85	2	Virginia Tech	Chesapeake, Va.	FA-'11	3/0
8	Redman, Chris	QB	6-3	225	7/7/77	10	Louisville	Louisville, Ky.	FA-'07	5/0
75	Reynolds, Garrett	G	6-7	310	7/1/87	4	North Carolina	Knoxville, Tenn.	D5b-'09	16/7
23	Robinson, Dunta	CB	5-10	183	4/11/82	9	South Carolina	Athens, Ga.	FA-'10	16/16
32	Rodgers, Jacquizz	RB	5-6	196	2/6/90	2	Oregon State	Richmond, Texas	D5-'11	16/0
2	Ryan, Matt	QB	6-4	217	5/17/85	5	Boston College	Exton, Pa.	D1a-'08	16/16
22 t-	Samuel, Asante	CB	5-10	185	1/6/81	10	Central Florida	Lauderdale Lakes, Fla.	T(Phil)-'12	14/14*
39	Schillinger, Shann	S	6-0	200	5/22/86	3	Montana	Baker, Mont.	D6-'10	16/0
90	Sidbury, Lawrence	DE	6-3	261	2/6/86	4	Richmond	Cheltenham, Md.	D4-'09	16/0
35	Smith, Antone	RB	5-9	192	9/17/85	3	Florida State	Pahokee, Fla.	FA-'09	12/0
44	Snelling, Jason	RB	5-11	234	12/29/83	6	Virginia	Chester, Va.	D7-'07	15/0
74	Svitek, Will	T	6-6	308	1/8/82	7	Stanford	Prague, Czech Republic	FA-'09	16/10
51	Tatupu, Lofa	LB	6-0	250	11/15/82	7	Southern California	Wrentham, Mass.	FA-'12	0*
33	Turner, Michael	RB	5-10	247	2/13/82	9	Northern Illinois	Waukegan, Ill.	UFA(SD)-'08	16/15
99	Walker, Vance	DT	6-2	304	4/26/87	4	Georgia Tech	Fort Mill, S.C.	D7-'09	16/0
29	Walls, Darrin	CB	6-0	190	6/20/88	2	Notre Dame	Pittsburgh, Pa.	FA-'11	5/0
56	Weatherspoon, Sean	LB	6-2	244	12/29/87	3	Missouri	Jasper, Texas	D1-'10	16/16
84	White, Roddy	WR	6-0	211	11/2/81	8	Alabama-Birmingham	James Island, S.C.	D1-'05	16/16
4	Wilson, John Parker	QB	6-2	215	10/17/85	4	Alabama	Hoover, Ala.	FA-'09	0*
82	Zelenka, Joe	LS	6-3	266	3/9/76	14	Wake Forest	Cleveland, Ohio	FA-'09	16/0

* Manuwai last active with Jacksonville in '10; Matthews inactive for 16 games; McClain inactive 2 games with Jacksonville; Samuel played 14 games with Philadelphia; Tatupu last active with Seattle in '10; Wilson inactive for 5 games.

t- Falcons traded for Samuel (Phil).

Players lost through free agency (4): DB Kelvin Hayden (Chi; 8), LB Curtis Lofton (NO; 16), DB James Sanders (Ariz; 15), WR Eric Weems (Chi; 16).

Also played with Falcons in '11—C Rob Bruggeman (1 game), T Kirk Chambers (3), TE Reggie Kelly (16), LB Mike Peterson (15), C Brett Romberg (2).

FIRST-YEAR ROSTER

Name	Pos.	Ht.	Wt.	Birthdate	College	Hometown	How Acq.
Adams, Corey	LS	6-4	251	7/26/89	Kansas State	Monument, Colo.	FA
Branson, Marquez (1)	TE	6-3	247	2/14/87	Central Arkansas	Starkville, Miss.	FA-'10
Brown, Lamark	TE	6-3	220	7/5/89	Minnesota-Mankato	St. Louis, Mo.	FA
Calvin, Michael	WR	6-3	215	6/7/89	California	San Lorenzo, Calif.	FA
Cone, Kevin (1)	WR	6-2	216	3/20/88	Georgia Tech	Stone Mountain, Ga.	FA-'11
Council, Rico	LB	6-1	255	12/6/88	Tennessee State	Chattanooga, Tenn.	FA
Davis, Dominique	QB	6-3	210	7/17/89	East Carolina	Lakeland, Fla.	FA
Davis, Drew (1)	WR	6-1	205	1/4/89	Oregon	Denver, Colo.	FA-'11
Donahue, Tyler	T	6-6	298	4/26/88	Bowling Green	Naperville, Ill.	FA
Ewing, Bradie	FB	5-11	243	12/26/89	Wisconsin	Richland Center, Wisc.	D5a
Farquharson, Harcourt	CB	5-10	190	9/23/86	Clark Atlanta	Miami, Fla.	FA
Faulcon, Chad	S	6-0	190	12/21/89	Montclair State	Cranford, N.J.	FA
Folk, Erik	K	5-11	185	1/26/89	Washington	Woodland Hills, Calif.	FA
Frey, Robbie	RB	6-0	203	3/8/89	Kutztown	Lehighton, Pa.	FA
Gallarda, Tommy (1)	TE	6-5	262	5/8/88	Boise State	Brea, Calif.	FA-'11
Gruder, Max	LB	6-2	230	3/15/89	Pittsburgh	Charlotte, N.C.	FA
Hansen, Matt (1)	LB	6-1	230	9/10/89	Rhode Island	Providence, R.I.	FA-'11
Harris, Bryce	T	6-6	300	1/16/89	Fresno State	Tulare, Calif.	FA
Harris, Josh	LS	6-1	224	4/27/89	Auburn	Carrollton, Ga.	FA
Harris, Jerrell	LB	6-3	242	7/8/89	Alabama	Gadsden, Ala.	FA
Holmes, Lamar	T	6-6	333	7/8/89	Southern Mississippi	Gastonia, N.C.	D3
Horn, Tyler	C	6-4	305	3/1/89	Miami	Memphis, Tenn.	FA
Jackson, Andrew (1)	G	6-5	299	10/18/88	Fresno State	Grass Valley, Calif.	D7a-'11
Jackson, Marcus	WR	6-1	195	5/20/89	Lamar	Tyler, Texas	FA
Kibble, Ray	DT	6-4	305	1/22/90	Kansas State	Houston, Texas	FA
Konz, Peter	G	6-5	317	6/9/89	Wisconsin	Neenah, Wisc.	D2
Manley, Phillipkeith	G	6-5	309	5/7/90	Toledo	Hamilton, Ohio	FA
Mark, Lampford	RB	6-1	200	10/3/89	Nevada	Fresno, Calif.	FA
Markett, Marty	CB	5-10	162	11/7/89	South Carolina	York, S.C.	FA
Massaquoi, Jonathan	DE	6-2	264	5/18/88	Troy	Lawrenceville, Ga.	D5b
Meisner, Lee	FB	6-0	245	3/16/90	Colorado-Pueblo	Sterling, Colo.	FA
Melton, Tyler	WR	6-0	206	3/16/90	Georgia Tech	Houston, Texas	FA
Mitchell, Charles	S	5-11	205	9/13/89	Mississippi State	Clarksdale, Miss.	D6
Nissley, Adam	TE	6-6	267	5/6/88	Central Florida	Cumming, Ga.	FA
Nzegwu, Louis	DE	6-4	255	5/15/89	Wisconsin	Platteville, Wisc.	FA
Pearcy, Cody	WR	5-11	160	10/4/89	Huntingdon	Phenix City, Ala.	FA
Raymond, Jerome	DE	6-4	245	7/30/90	Morehead State	Lawrenceville, Ga.	FA
Regis, Micanor	DT	6-3	305	11/3/89	Miami	Pahokee, Fla.	FA
Robertson, Travian	DT	6-4	304	12/9/88	South Carolina	Laurinburg, N.C.	D7
Rodgers, James	WR	5-7	188	12/20/88	Oregon State	Richmond, Texas	FA
Rowan, Taylor	K	6-0	190	1/12/87	Western Illinois	Melbourne, Fla.	FA
Schiller, Pat	LB	6-2	235	11/12/88	Northern Illinois	Geneva, Ill.	FA
Stafford, Kenny	WR	6-4	204	6/20/90	Toledo	Columbus, Ohio	FA
Thompson, Peyton	CB	5-11	180	9/26/90	San Jose State	Granite Bay, Calif.	FA
Tuimaunei, Suaesi (1)	S	6-1	205	2/11/88	Oregon State	Laie, Hawaii	FA-'11
White, Aron	TE	6-4	239	10/8/88	Georgia	Columbia, Mo.	FA
Zimmerman, Dawson	P	6-2	205	11/15/89	Clemson	Lawrenceville, Ga.	FA

The term NFL Rookie is defined as a player who is in his first season of professional football and has not been on the roster of another professional football team for any regular-season or postseason games. A Rookie is designated by an "R" on NFL rosters. Players who have been active in another professional football league or players who have NFL experience, including either preseason training camp or being on an Active List or Inactive List, or on Reserve/Injured or Reserve/Physically Unable to Perform for fewer than six regular-season games, are termed NFL First-Year Players. An NFL First-Year Player is designated by a "1" on NFL rosters. Thereafter, a player is credited with an additional year of experience for each season in which he accumulates six games on the Active List or Inactive List, or on Reserve/Injured or Reserve/Physically Unable to Perform.

Log on to www.atlantafalcons.com for an up-to-date roster.

ATLANTA FALCONS

COACHING STAFF
Head Coach,
Mike Smith

Pro Career: Mike Smith was named the 14th head coach in Atlanta Falcons franchise history on January 23, 2008. In three seasons with the team, he has compiled a 33-15 record, third-best mark among all NFL head coaches, two playoff appearances and three straight winning seasons for the first time in franchise history. His .688 winning percentage is the best in team history over a three-year period. Smith's 33 wins are easily the most victories by a Falcons head coach in his first three years on the job. His team boasts a 20-4 home record and .833 winning percentage since 2008, the second-best mark in the NFL. Smith's club posted the NFC's top record at 13-3 in 2010, the number one seed in the conference and was the second-most wins in a season in team annals. Smith's charges also captured the NFC South title last season for only the fourth Division crown in franchise history (and first since 2004) and the eight consecutive victories in 2010 was the second longest streak ever. Under Smith's direction last year, the Falcons were the only team to rank in the top 5 in both scoring offense and scoring defense. In 2008, Smith guided the Falcons to an 11-5 record, marking a seven-win turnaround from the previous season. For his efforts, he was named the Associated Press and *Sporting News* NFL Coach of the Year. From 2003-07, Smith served as the defensive coordinator for the Jacksonville Jaguars following a four-year stint with the Baltimore Ravens from 1999-2002, which included the team's 2000 Super Bowl season. Prior to the NFL, Smith coached at San Diego State (1982-85), Morehead State (1986), and Tennessee Tech (1987-1998). Career record: 43-24.

Background: Played linebacker for the CFL's Winnipeg Blue Bombers (1982). He played at East Tennessee (1977-1981) and named defensive MVP twice at his position. Led team with 186 tackles as a senior.

Personal: Born November 30, 1959 in Chicago, Ill. Native of Daytona Beach, Florida. He and his wife Julie have one daughter, Logan.

ASSISTANT COACHES

Keith Armstrong, special teams coordinator; born December 15, 1963, Levittown, Pa. Running back Temple 1983-86. No pro playing experience. College coach: Temple 1987, Miami 1988, Akron 1989, Oklahoma State 1990-92, Notre Dame 1993. Pro coach: Atlanta Falcons 1994-96, Chicago Bears 1997-2000, Miami Dolphins 2001-2007, re-joined Falcons 2008.

Jonas Beauchemin, strength and conditioning assistant; born October 11, 1984, Burlington, Vt. Attended Keene State. No college or pro playing experience. Pro coach: Joined Falcons in 2009.

Gerald Brown, running backs; born

September 4, 1959, Sweetwater, Tenn. Attended Memphis State. No college or pro playing experience. College coach: Tennessee Tech 1991-2000, Indiana 2002-07. Pro coach: Joined Falcons in 2008.

Mark Collins, defensive assistant; born August 30, 1975, Sault Ste. Marie, Mich. Defensive end/outside linebacker East Tennessee State 1995-98. No pro playing experience. College coach: East Tennessee State 1999-2002, Michigan 2003-04, Elon, 2005, Georgia Southern, 2006, Georgia 2007, Louisiana-Monroe 2009. Pro coach: Joined Falcons in 2010.

Paul Dunn, offensive line; born July 7, 1960, Philadelphia, Pa. Offensive lineman Pittsburgh 1978-1982. No pro playing experience. College coach: Pittsburgh 1983, 2005-07, Penn State 1984-85, Edinboro 1986-88, Rutgers 1989, Maine 1990-93, Cincinnati 1994-95, Vanderbilt 1996-97, Kansas State 1998-2002, Kentucky 2003-04. Pro coach: Joined Falcons in 2008.

Jeff Fish, director of athletic performance; born June 6, 1966, Ithaca, N.Y. Wide receiver Western Carolina 1985-88. No pro playing experience. College coach: Western Michigan 1989, Clemson 1991-92, Kent State 1993-94, Tulsa 1995-97, Missouri 2001-03. Pro coach: Tampa Bay Buccaneers 1997, Kansas City Chiefs 1998-2000, Oakland Raiders 2004-07, joined Falcons in 2008.

Ray Hamilton, defensive line; born January 20, 1951, Omaha, Neb. Nose tackle Oklahoma 1969-1972. Pro defensive lineman New England Patriots 1973-1981. College coach: Tennessee 1992. Pro coach: New England Patriots 1985-89, Tampa Bay Buccaneers 1991, Los Angeles Raiders 1993-94, New York Jets 1994-96, 2000, New England Patriots 1997-99, Cleveland Browns 2001-02, Jacksonville Jaguars 2003-07, joined Falcons in 2008.

Pat Hill, offensive line; born December 17, 1951, Los Angeles, Calif. Center UC Riverside 1970-1973. No pro playing experience. College coach: Los Angeles Valley College 1974-76, Utah 1977-1980, Nevada-Las Vegas 1981-82, Fresno State 1984-89, 1997-2011 (head coach 1997-2011), Arizona 1990-91. Pro coach: Calgary Stampeders (CFL) 1983, Cleveland Browns 1992-95, Baltimore Ravens 1996, joined Falcons in 2012.

Dirk Koetter, offensive coordinator; born February 5, 1959, Pocatello, Idaho. Quarterback Idaho State 1978-1981. No pro playing experience. College coach: San Francisco State 1985, Texas El-Paso 1986-88, Missouri 1989-1993, Boston College 1994-95, Oregon 1996-97, Boise State 1998-2000 (head coach), Arizona State 2001-06 (head coach). Pro coach: Jacksonville Jaguars 2007-2011, joined Falcons in 2012.

Tim Lewis, secondary; born December 18, 1961, Quakertown, Pa. Cornerback Pittsburgh 1979-1982. Pro cornerback Green Bay Packers 1983-86. Pro coach:

Pittsburgh Steelers 1995-2003, New York Giants 2004-06, Carolina Panthers 2007-08, Seattle Seahawks 2009, joined Falcons in 2010.

Mike Nolan, defensive coordinator; born March 7, 1965, Haverhill, Mass. Safety Oregon 1978-1980. No pro playing experience. College coach: Oregon 1981, Stanford 1982-83, Rice 1984-85, Louisiana State 1986. Pro coach: Denver Broncos 1987-1992, 2009, New York Giants 1993-96, Washington Redskins 1997-99, New York Jets 2000, Baltimore Ravens 2001-04, San Francisco 49ers 2005-08 (head coach), Miami Dolphins 2010-11, joined Falcons in 2012.

Glenn Pires, linebackers; born September 13, 1958, New Bedford, Mass. Offensive lineman Springfield College 1976-79. No pro playing experience. College coach: Dartmouth 1985-88, Syracuse 1989-1994, Michigan State 1995. Pro coach: Arizona Cardinals 1996-2000, Detroit Lions 2001-02, Miami Dolphins 2003-07, joined Falcons in 2008.

Alvin Reynolds, defensive backs; born June 24, 1959, Pineville, La. Safety Indiana State 1978-1981. No pro playing experience. College coach: Indiana State 1982-1992. Pro coach: Denver Broncos 1993-95, Baltimore Ravens 1996-98, Carolina Panthers 1999-2002, Jacksonville Jaguars 2003-07, joined Falcons in 2008.

Terry Robiskie, wide receivers; born November 12, 1954, New Orleans, La. Running back Louisiana State 1973-76. Pro running back Oakland Raiders 1977-79, Miami Dolphins 1980-81. Pro coach: Los Angeles Raiders 1982-1993, Washington Redskins 1994-2000 (interim head coach 2000), Cleveland Browns 2001-06 (interim head coach 2004), Miami Dolphins 2007, joined Falcons in 2008.

Chris Scelfo, tight ends; born September 30, 1963, New Iberia, La. Center Northeast Louisiana 1981-84. No pro playing experience. College coach: Northeast Louisiana 1986-87, Oklahoma 1988-89, Marshall 1990-95, Georgia 1996-98, Tulane 1998-2006. Pro coach: Joined Falcons in 2008.

Eric Sutulovich, asst. special teams; born February 28, 1974, Kansas City, Kan. Tight end Louisiana Tech 1993-95. No pro playing experience. College coach: Louisiana Tech 1997-99, Pittsburgh 2000, Kansas 2006. Pro coach: Houston Texans 2002-05, Detroit Lions 2008, joined Falcons in 2009.

Glenn Thomas, quarterbacks; born September 22, 1977, Eastland, Texas. Attended Texas Tech. No college or pro playing experience. College coach: Texas Tech 1998-2001, Midwestern State 2001-07. Pro coach: Joined Falcons in 2008.

Andrew Weidinger, offensive assistant; born July 10, 1982, Phoenix, Ariz. Attended Arizona. No college or pro playing experience. Pro coach: Joined Falcons in 2008.

National Football Conference
South Division
Team Colors: Black, Panther Blue, and
Silver
800 South Mint Street
Charlotte, North Carolina 28202-1502
Telephone: (704) 358-7000

2012 SCHEDULE
PRESEASON
Aug. 11 **Houston** 7:00
Aug. 17 **Miami** 8:00
Aug. 26 at New York Jets 8:00
Aug. 30 at Pittsburgh.......................7:30

REGULAR SEASON
Sep. 9 at Tampa Bay 4:15
Sep. 16 **New Orleans** 1:00
Sep. 20 **New York Giants** (Thurs)....8:20
Sep. 30 at Atlanta............................1:00
Oct. 7 **Seattle** 4:05
Oct. 14 BYE
Oct. 21 **Dallas** 1:00
Oct. 28 at Chicago...........................1:00
Nov. 4 at Washington 1:00
Nov. 11 **Denver**..............................1:00
Nov. 18 **Tampa Bay**........................1:00
Nov. 26 at Philadelphia (Mon)..........8:30
Dec. 2 at Kansas City 1:00
Dec. 9 **Atlanta**..............................1:00
Dec. 16 at San Diego 4:05
Dec. 23 **Oakland** 1:00
Dec. 30 at New Orleans...................1:00
All times ET
Stadium: Bank of America Stadium
(opened in 1996)
• **Capacity:** 73,504
Charlotte, North Carolina
28202-1502
Playing Surface: Grass
Training Camp: Wofford College
Spartanburg,
South Carolina 29303

BANK OF AMERICA STADIUM

CLUB OFFICIALS
Owner/Founder: Jerry Richardson
President, Panthers Football LLC:
Danny Morrison
General Manager: Marty Hurney
General Counsel: Richard Thigpen
Chief Financial Officer: Dave Olsen
Controller: Mike Dudan
Director of Human Resources:
Jackie Jeffries
Director of Pro Scouting: Mark Koncz
Director of College Scouting:
Don Gregory
College Scouts: Matt Allen, Jeff Beathard,
Ryan Cowden, Khary Darlington,
Robert Haines, Jeff Morrow,
John Peterson, Mike Szabo
Director of Communications:
Charlie Dayton
Assistant Director of Communications:
Steven Drummond
Director of Ticket Operations:
Phil Youtsey
Director of Community Relations and
Cheerleader/Mascot Programs:
Riley Fields
Director of Sponsor Sales and Services:
John Berger
Director of Broadcast Administration:
Henry Thomas
Executive Producer-Television:
Greg Brannon
Executive Producer-Radio: David Langton
Director of Team Administration:
Rob Rogers
Director of Team Operations:
Brandon Beane
Video Director: Mark Hobbs
Assistant Video Director: Jeff Mueller
Head Trainer: Ryan Vermillion
Assistant Trainer: Mark Shermansky
Equipment Manager: Jackie Miles
Assistant Equipment Manager: Don Toner
Director of Security: Gene Brown
Stadium Operations Manager: Scott Paul
Director of Entertainment and
Panthervision: Kyle Ritchie
Facility Manager: Matthew Getz
Head Groundskeeper: Tom Vaughan

COACHING HISTORY
(131-151-0)
Records include postseason games
1995-98   Dom Capers 31-35-0
1999-2001 George Seifert 16-32-0
2002-2010 John Fox....................78-74-0
2011   Ron Rivera..................6-10-0

PAID ATTENDANCE
Home 559,907   Away 487,129
Total 1,047,036
Single-game home record,
76,136 (12/10/95)
Single-season home record, 579,192
(2006)

2012 DRAFT CHOICES
Round	Name	Pos.	College
1	Luke Kuechly	LB	Boston College
2	Amini Silatolu	G	Midwestern St.
4	Frank Alexander	DE	Oklahoma
	Joe Adams	WR	Arkansas
5	Josh Norman	DB	Coastal Carolina
6	Brad Nortman	P	Wisconsin
7	D.J. Campbell	DB	California

CAROLINA PANTHERS

2011 TEAM RECORD

PRESEASON (1-3)

Date	Result	Opponent
8/13	W 20-10	New York Giants
8/19	L 10-20	at Miami
8/25	L 13-24	at Cincinnati
9/1	L 17-33	Pittsburgh

REGULAR SEASON (6-10)

Date	Result	Opponent
9/11	L 21-28	at Arizona
9/18	L 23-30	Green Bay
9/25	W 16-10	Jacksonville
10/2	L 29-34	at Chicago
10/9	L 27-30	New Orleans
10/16	L 17-31	at Atlanta
10/23	W 33-20	Washington
10/30	L 21-24	Minnesota
11/13	L 3-30	Tennessee
11/20	L 35-49	at Detroit
11/27	W 27-19	at Indianapolis
12/4	W 38-19	at Tampa Bay
12/11	L 23-31	Atlanta
12/18	W 28-13	at Houston
12/24	W 48-16	Tampa Bay
1/1	L 17-45	at New Orleans

SCORE BY PERIODS

Panthers	92	148	83	83	0 —	406
Opponents	79	117	90	143	0 —	429

2011 TEAM STATISTICS

	Panthers	Opp.
Total First Downs	345	329
Rushing	139	110
Passing	175	191
Penalty	31	28
3rd Down: Made/Att	75/185	83/194
3rd Down Pct.	40.5	42.8
4th Down: Made/Att	6/10	4/12
4th Down Pct.	60.0	33.3
Possession Avg.	30:16	29:44
Total Net Yards	6237	6042
Avg. Per Game	389.8	377.6
Total Plays	999	972
Avg. Per Play	6.2	6.2
Net Yards Rushing	2408	2093
Avg. Per Game	150.5	130.8
Total Rushes	445	451
Net Yards Passing	3829	3949
Avg. Per Game	239.3	246.8
Sacked/Yards Lost	35/260	31/170
Gross Yards	4089	4119
Att./Completions	519/312	490/318
Completion Pct.	60.1	64.9
Had Intercepted	17	14
Punts/Average	66/42.7	52/43.2
Net Punting Avg.	66/34.1	52/37.9
Penalties/Yards	113/1013	98/901
Fumbles/Ball Lost	13/6	20/10
Touchdowns	48	50
Rushing	26	18
Passing	21	28
Returns	1	4

2011 INDIVIDUAL STATISTICS

PASSING

	Att.	Comp.	Yds.	Pct.	TD	Int.	Tkld.	Rate
Newton	517	310	4051	60.0	21	17	35/260	84.5
A. Edwards	1	1	11	100.0	0	0	0/0	112.5
Naanee	1	1	27	100.0	0	0	0/0	118.8
Panthers	519	312	4089	60.1	21	17	35/260	84.8
Opponents	490	318	4119	64.9	28	14	31/170	98.3

SCORING

	TD R	TD P	TD Rt	PAT	FG	Saf	PTS
Mare	0	0	0	44/45	22/28	0	110
Newton	14	0	0	0/0	0/0	0	84
S. Smith	0	7	0	0/0	0/0	0	44
D. Williams	7	0	0	0/0	0/0	0	42
Olsen	0	5	0	0/0	0/0	0	32
Stewart	4	1	0	0/0	0/0	0	30
Shockey	0	4	0	0/0	0/0	0	24
LaFell	0	3	0	0/0	0/0	0	18
Brockel	1	0	0	0/0	0/0	0	6
Naanee	0	1	0	0/0	0/0	0	6
Pilares	0	0	1	0/0	0/0	0	6
Applewhite	0	0	0	0/0	0/0	1	2
Hardy	0	0	0	0/0	0/0	1	2
Panthers	26	21	1	44/45	22/28	2	406
Opponents	18	28	4	48/48	27/31	0	429

2-Pt Conversions: Olsen, S. Smith
Panthers 2-3, Opponents 0-2

RUSHING

	No.	Yds	Avg	LG	TD
D. Williams	155	836	5.4	74t	7
Stewart	142	761	5.4	32	4
Newton	126	706	5.6	49t	14
S. Smith	6	56	9.3	23	0
Vaughan	7	24	3.4	9	0
Brockel	3	12	4.0	7t	1
Felton	3	10	3.3	4	0
A. Edwards	1	5	5.0	5	0
D. Anderson	2	-2	-1.0	-1	0
Panthers	445	2408	5.4	74t	26
Opponents	451	2093	4.6	46	18

RECEIVING

	No.	Yds	Avg	LG	TD
S. Smith	79	1394	17.6	77t	7
Stewart	47	413	8.8	26	1
Olsen	45	540	12.0	44t	5
Naanee	44	467	10.6	28	1
Shockey	37	455	12.3	29	4
LaFell	36	613	17.0	91t	3
D. Williams	16	135	8.4	32	0
Brockel	3	13	4.3	5	0
Felton	2	24	12.0	17	0
Newton	1	27	27.0	27	0
Ajirotutu	1	4	4.0	4	0
Goodson	1	4	4.0	4	0
Panthers	312	4089	13.1	91t	21
Opponents	318	4119	13.0	84t	28

INTERCEPTIONS

	No.	Yds	Avg	LG	TD
Gamble	3	43	14.3	24	0
Martin	3	16	5.3	15	0
Godfrey	2	30	15.0	21	0
J. Anderson	2	5	2.5	5	0
Stanford	1	53	53.0	53	0
Senn	1	21	21.0	21	0
Nelson	1	20	20.0	20	0
Keiser	1	9	9.0	9	0
Panthers	14	197	14.1	53	0
Opponents	17	229	13.5	49	1

PUNTING

	No.	Yds.	Avg.	In 20	LG
Baker	66	2819	42.7	19	56
Panthers	66	2819	42.7	19	56
Opponents	52	2248	43.2	15	64

PUNT RETURNS

	Ret	FC	Yds	Avg	LG	TD
A. Edwards	32	9	176	5.5	17	0
Panthers	32	9	176	5.5	17	0
Opponents	35	15	466	13.3	89t	3

KICKOFF RETURNS

	No.	Yds	Avg	LG	TD
Pilares	23	590	25.7	101t	1
Goodson	11	250	22.7	31	0
A. Edwards	3	35	11.7	17	0
Pugh	2	51	25.5	28	0
Brockel	0	0	—	—	0
Panthers	39	926	23.7	101t	1
Opponents	30	811	27.0	78	0

FIELD GOALS

	1-19	20-29	30-39	40-49	50+
Mare	1/1	7/7	6/9	8/9	0/2
Panthers	1/1	7/7	6/9	8/9	0/2
Opponents	1/1	5/5	10/11	9/12	2/2

SACKS

	No.
Johnson	9.0
Hardy	4.0
Keiser	4.0
Neblett	2.5
Shirley	2.5
Applewhite	2.0
Munnerlyn	2.0
J. Anderson	1.5
Gaither	1.0
Godfrey	1.0
McClain	1.0
Kearse	0.5
Panthers	31.0
Opponents	35.0

RECORD HOLDERS
INDIVIDUAL RECORDS—CAREER

Category	Name	Performance
Rushing (Yds.)	DeAngelo Williams, 2006-2011	5,047
Passing (Yds.)	Jake Delhomme, 2003-09	19,258
Passing (TDs)	Jake Delhomme, 2003-09	120
Receiving (No.)	Steve Smith, 2001-2011	699
Receiving (Yds.)	Steve Smith, 2001-2011	10,278
Interceptions	Chris Gamble, 2004-2011	27
Punting (Avg.)	Todd Sauerbrun, 2001-04	45.5
Punt Return (Avg.)	Winslow Oliver, 1996-98	10.7
Kickoff Return (Avg.)	Michael Bates, 1996-2000	25.7
Field Goals	John Kasay, 1995-2010	351
Touchdowns (Tot.)	Steve Smith, 2001-2011	67
Points	John Kasay, 1995-2010	1,482
*Sacks	Julius Peppers, 2002-09	81.0

INDIVIDUAL RECORDS—SINGLE SEASON

Category	Name	Performance
Rushing (Yds.)	DeAngelo Williams, 2008	1,515
Passing (Yds.)	Steve Beuerlein, 1999	4,436
Passing (TDs)	Steve Beuerlein, 1999	36
Receiving (No.)	Steve Smith, 2005	103
Receiving (Yds.)	Steve Smith, 2005	1,563
Interceptions	Doug Evans, 2001	8
Punting (Avg.)	Todd Sauerbrun, 2001	47.5
Punt Return (Avg.)	Winslow Oliver, 1996	11.5
Kickoff Return (Avg.)	Michael Bates, 1996	30.2
Field Goals	John Kasay, 1996	37
Touchdowns (Tot.)	DeAngelo Williams, 2008	20
Points	John Kasay, 1996	145
*Sacks	Kevin Greene, 1998	15.0

INDIVIDUAL RECORDS—SINGLE GAME

Category	Name	Performance
Rushing (Yds.)	DeAngelo Williams, 12-8-08	186
Passing (Yds.)	Chris Weinke, 12-10-06	423
Passing (TDs)	Steve Beuerlein, 1-2-00	5
Receiving (No.)	Steve Smith, 11-20-05	14
Receiving (Yds.)	Steve Smith, 10-30-05	201
Interceptions	Deon Grant, 9-22-02	3
Field Goals	John Kasay, 12-5-04	6
Touchdowns (Tot.)	DeAngelo Williams, 11-30-08, 12-21-08	4
Points	DeAngelo Williams, 11-30-08, 12-21-08	24
*Sacks	Many times	3.0
	Julius Peppers, 11-9-08	

*Sacks became an official statistic in 1982.

CAROLINA PANTHERS

2012 VETERAN ROSTER

No.	Name	Pos.	Ht.	Wt.	Birthdate	NFL Exp.	College	Hometown	How Acq.	'11 Games/ Starts
86	Adams, Darvin	WR	6-2	194	1/5/90	2	Auburn	Kennesaw, Ga.	FA-'11	2/0
19	Ajirotutu, Seyi	WR	6-3	211	6/12/87	3	Fresno State	El Dorado Hills, Calif.	W(SD)-'11	14/0
66	Allen, Roger	G	6-3	323	2/10/86	3	Missouri Western	Raytown, Mo.	FA-'11	0*
3	Anderson, Derek	QB	6-6	235	6/15/83	8	Oregon State	Scappoose, Ore.	FA-'11	2/0
50	Anderson, James	LB	6-2	235	9/26/83	7	Virginia Tech	Chesapeake, Va.	D3a-'06	16/16
93	Applewhite, Antwan	DE	6-3	258	12/31/85	5	San Diego State	Harbor City, Calif.	FA-'11	12/1
82	Barnidge, Gary	TE	6-5	247	9/22/85	5	Louisville	Middleburg, Fla.	D5-'08	0*
52	Beason, Jon	LB	6-0	237	1/14/85	6	Miami	Miami, Fla.	D1-'07	1/1
77	Bell, Byron	T	6-5	339	1/17/89	2	New Mexico	Greenville, Texas	FA-'11	16/12
47	Brockel, Richie	TE/FB	6-1	251	7/24/86	2	Boise State	Phoenix, Ariz.	FA-'11	11/2
27	Butler, Darius	CB	5-10	190	3/18/86	4	Connecticut	Fort Lauderdale, Fla.	W(NE)-'11	13/6
73	t- Campbell, Bruce	T	6-6	315	5/25/88	3	Maryland	Hamden, Conn.	T(Oak)-'12	4/0*
2	Clausen, Jimmy	QB	6-2	222	9/21/87	3	Notre Dame	Westlake Village, Calif.	D2-'11	13/10
58	Davis, Thomas	LB	6-0	240	3/22/83	8	Georgia	Shellman, Ga.	D1-'05	2/2
46	Dillard, Phillip	LB	6-2	252	12/10/86	2	Nebraska	Jenks, Okla.	FA-'11	0*
14	Edwards, Armanti	WR	5-11	182	3/8/88	3	Appalachian State	Greenwood, S.C.	D3b-'11	16/0
96	Edwards, Ron	DT	6-3	315	7/12/79	12	Texas A&M	Houston, Texas	UFA(KC)-'11	0*
94	Fua, Sione	DT	6-2	308	6/15/88	2	Stanford	Encino, Calif.	D3b-'11	11/11
59	#Gaither, Omar	LB	6-2	235	3/18/84	7	Tennessee	Charlotte, N.C.	UFA(Phil)-'11	10/4
20	Gamble, Chris	CB	6-1	200	3/11/83	9	Ohio State	Sunrise, Fla.	D1-'04	15/15
12	Gettis, David	WR	6-3	216	8/27/87	3	Baylor	Los Angeles, Calif.	D6b-'11	0*
30	Godfrey, Charles	S	5-11	205	11/15/85	5	Iowa	Baytown, Texas	D3a-'08	14/14
25	#Gordon, Cletis	CB	6-1	212	4/23/83	6	Jackson State	Amite, La.	FA-'11	0*
69	Gross, Jordan	T	6-4	305	7/20/80	10	Utah	Fruitland, Idaho	D1-'03	15/15
63	Hangartner, Geoff	C/G	6-5	301	4/22/82	8	Texas A&M	New Braunfels, Texas	FA-'11	16/16
76	Hardy, Greg	DE	6-4	277	7/28/88	3	Mississippi	Millington, Tenn.	D6a-'11	16/16
84	Hartsock, Ben	TE	6-4	270	7/5/80	9	Ohio State	Chillicothe, Ohio	FA-'11	15/2
21	Hogan, Brandon	CB	5-10	192	4/1/88	2	West Virginia	Manassas, Va.	D4-'11	3/0
44	Jansen, J.J.	LS	6-2	256	1/20/86	5	Notre Dame	Phoenix, Ariz.	T(GB)-'09	16/0
95	Johnson, Charles	DE	6-2	275	7/10/86	6	Georgia	Hawkinsville, Ga.	D3-'07	15/15
67	Kalil, Ryan	C	6-2	295	3/29/85	6	Southern California	Corona, Calif.	D2b-'07	16/16
99	Kearse, Frank	DT	6-3	325	10/28/88	2	Alabama A&M	Savannah, Ga.	FA-'11	6/4
98	Keiser, Thomas	DE	6-3	261	3/28/89	2	Stanford	Wexford, Pa.	FA-'11	8/0
11	LaFell, Brandon	WR	6-2	211	11/4/86	3	Louisiana State	Houston, Texas	D3a-'11	16/6
10	Mare, Olindo	K	5-11	192	6/6/73	16	Syracuse	Cooper City, Fla.	UFA(Sea)-'11	16/0
23	Martin, Sherrod	S	6-1	198	10/12/84	4	Troy	Griffin, Ga.	D2b-'09	16/16
97	McClain, Terrell	DT	6-2	291	7/20/88	2	South Florida	Pensacola, Fla.	D3a-'11	12/12
41	Munnerlyn, Captain	CB	5-8	186	4/10/88	4	South Carolina	Mobile, Ala.	D7-'09	14/14
43	Nakamura, Haruki	S	5-10	200	4/18/86	5	Cincinnati	Lakewood, Ohio	UFA(Balt)-'12	15/0*
68	Neblett, Andre	DT	6-0	295	6/7/88	3	Temple	Rahway, N.J.	FA-'11	12/4
1	Newton, Cam	QB	6-5	248	5/11/89	2	Auburn	College Park, Ga.	D1-'11	16/16
92	Norwood, Eric	DE	6-1	241	5/24/88	3	South Carolina	Kennesaw, Ga.	D4-'11	13/0
78	Nwagbuo, Ogemdi	DT	6-4	312	12/24/85	4	Michigan State	Spring Valley, Calif.	FA-'11	8/1
88	Olsen, Greg	TE	6-5	255	3/11/85	6	Miami	Wayne, N.J.	T(Chi)-'11	16/13
56	Onatolu, Kenny	LB	6-2	225	10/8/82	4	Nebraska-Omaha	Papillion, Neb.	UFA(Minn)-'12	16/1*
79	Otah, Jeff	T	6-6	330	6/17/86	5	Pittsburgh	New Castle, Del.	D1b-'08	4/4
53	Phillips, Jason	LB	6-1	242	2/14/86	4	Texas Christian	Waller, Texas	W(Balt)-'11	4/0
81	Pilares, Kealoha	WR	5-10	201	2/20/88	2	Hawaii	Wahiawa, Hawaii	D5-'11	12/0
74	Pollak, Mike	G	6-3	301	2/15/86	5	Arizona State	Tempe, Ariz.	UFA(Ind)-'12	15/8*
29	Pugh, Jordan	S	5-11	196	1/29/88	3	Texas A&M	Plano, Texas	D6c-'11	12/1
57	Senn, Jordan	LB	5-11	224	6/11/84	5	Portland State	Beaverton, Ore.	FA-'09	16/7
71	Shirley, Jason	DT	6-5	345	9/30/85	2	Fresno State	Fontana, Calif.	FA-'11	4/0
80	#Shockey, Jeremy	TE	6-5	251	8/18/80	11	Miami	Ada, Okla.	FA-'11	15/13
31	Smith, Reggie	S	6-1	200	9/3/86	5	Oklahoma	Edmond, Okla.	UFA(SF)-'12	16/0*
89	Smith, Steve	WR	5-9	185	5/12/79	12	Utah	Los Angeles, Calif.	D3-'01	16/16
25	Stanford, R.J.	CB	5-10	183	5/6/88	2	Utah	Chino, Calif.	D7a-'11	12/0
28	Stewart, Jonathan	RB	5-10	235	3/21/87	5	Oregon	Lacey, Wash.	D1a-'08	16/3
22	Thomas, Josh	CB	5-10	191	5/3/89	2	Buffalo	Cedar Hills, Texas	W(Dall)-'11	9/0
35	Tolbert, Mike	FB	5-9	243	11/23/85	5	Coastal Carolina	Douglasville, Ga.	UFA(SD)-'12	15/1*
55	Tucker, Jyles	DE	6-3	258	9/18/83	5	Wake Forest	Morristown, N.J.	FA-'12	0*
32	Vaughan, Josh	RB	6-0	232	12/3/86	2	Richmond	Richmond, Va.	FA-'11	7/0
34	Williams, DeAngelo	RB	5-9	217	4/25/83	7	Memphis	Wynne, Ark.	D1-'06	16/14
65	Williams, Garry	T	6-3	296	8/20/86	4	Kentucky	Louisville, Ky.	FA-'09	0*
54	Williams, Jason	LB	6-1	244	4/23/86	4	Western Illinois	Chicago, Ill.	W(Dall)-'10	14/2
64	Williams, Zack	C	6-3	309	12/27/88	2	Washington State	Pasadena, Calif.	D6b-'11	0*
91	Wilson, Kion	LB	6-0	240	10/24/86	3	South Florida	Jacksonville, Fla.	FA-'11	5/0
75	Ziemba, Lee	T	6-6	318	3/29/89	2	Auburn	Rogers, Ark.	D7-'11	6/0

* Allen last active with St. Louis in '09; Barnidge missed '11 season because of injury; Campbell played 4 games with Oakland; Dillard last active with New York Giants in '10; R. Edwards missed '11 season because of injury; Gettis missed '11 season because of injury; Gordon missed '11 season because of injury; Nakamura played 15 games with Baltimore; Onatolu played 16 games with Minnesota; Pollak played 15 games with Indianapolis; R. Smith played 16 games with San Francisco; Tolbert played 15 games with San Diego; Tucker last active with San Diego in '10; G. Williams missed '11 season because of injury; Z. Williams missed '11 season because of injury.

\# Unrestricted free agent; subject to developments.

t- Panthers traded for Campbell (Oak).

Traded—RB Mike Goodson (4 games in '11) to Oakland.

Players lost through free agency (3): OL Mackenzy Bernadeau (Dall; 15 games in '11), LB Dan Connor (Dall; 15), WR Legedu Naanee (Mia; 15).

Also played with Panthers in '11—P Jason Baker (16 games), S Sean Considine (4), FB Jerome Felton (9), DT Ron Fields (6), RB Mike Goodson (4), S Jermale Hines (5), DT DeMario Pressley (1), DE George Selvie (4), Reggie Wells (5), Travelle Wharton (16), LB Thomas Williams (7).

FIRST-YEAR ROSTER

Name	Pos.	Ht.	Wt.	Birthdate	College	Hometown	How Acq.
Adams, Joe	WR	5-11	179	11/22/89	Arkansas	Little Rock, Ark.	D4b
Alexander, Frank	DE	6-4	271	12/17/89	Oklahoma	Baton Rouge, La.	D4a
Bersin, Brenton	WR	6-3	205	5/9/90	Wofford	Charlotte, N.C.	FA
Blackwell, Will	G	6-4	290	1/24/89	Louisiana State	West Monroe, La.	FA
Browning, Bryant (1)	G	6-4	313	6/26/88	Ohio State	Cleveland, Ohio	W(StL)-'11
Byers, Jeff (1)	C	6-4	301	9/7/85	Southern California	Loveland, Colo.	FA-'11
Campbell, D.J.	S	6-0	200	7/24/89	California	North Las Vegas, Nev.	D7
Chandler, Nate	DT	6-4	292	6/1/89	UCLA	San Diego, Calif.	FA
Green, Jared	WR	6-1	191	4/1/89	Southern	Vienna, Va.	FA
Kemp, Wes	WR	6-4	220	9/18/89	Missouri	St. Louis, Mo.	FA
Kuechly, Luke	LB	6-2	242	8/20/91	Boston College	Cincinnati, Ohio	D1
Lloyd, Tarren	TE	6-7	258	1/25/89	Utah State	Bountiful, Utah	FA
Manno, Chris (1)	WR	6-1	196	8/28/85	Hofstra	Ronkonkoma, N.Y.	FA
Medlock, Justin (1)	K	5-11	201	10/23/83	UCLA	Freemont, Calif.	FA
McCarty, Princeton	RB	5-8	192	7/3/88	Idaho	Bakersfield, Calif.	FA
Nelson, Jonathan (1)	S	5-11	195	5/6/88	Oklahoma	Arlington, Texas	FA-'11
Norman, Josh	CB	6-0	190	12/15/87	Coastal Carolina	Greenwood, S.C.	D5
Nortman, Brad	P	6-2	209	9/12/89	Wisconsin	Brookfield, Wisc.	D6
Poole, Tauren	RB	510	215	10/19/89	Tennessee	Toccoa, Ga.	FA
Reynolds, Matt	T	6-6	305	5/31/86	Brigham Young	Provo, Utah	FA
Rowells, Lyndon	RB	5-10	200	3/18/88	Humboldt State	Largo, Fla.	FA
Silatolu, Amini	G	6-3	311	9/16/88	Midwestern State	Tracy, Calif.	D2
Smith, Greg (1)	TE	6-4	245	1/13/88	Texas	Montgomery, Texas	FA-'11
Sullivan, Reggie (1)	CB	6-2	210	2/24/85	Johnson C. Smith	Miami, Fla.	FA-'11
Van Bergen, Ryan	DE	6-6	288	3/18/89	Michigan	Whitehall, Mich.	FA
Wallace, Rico	WR	6-3	210	5/25/90	Shenandoah	Hanover, Md.	FA

The term NFL Rookie is defined as a player who is in his first season of professional football and has not been on the roster of another professional football team for any regular-season or postseason games. A Rookie is designated by an "R" on NFL rosters. Players who have been active in another professional football league or players who have NFL experience, including either preseason training camp or being on an Active List or Inactive List, or on Reserve/Injured or Reserve/Physically Unable to Perform for fewer than six regular-season games, are termed NFL First-Year Players. An NFL First-Year Player is designated by a "1" on NFL rosters. Thereafter, a player is credited with an additional year of experience for each season in which he accumulates six games on the Active List or Inactive List, or on Reserve/Injured or Reserve/Physically Unable to Perform.

Log on to www.panthers.com for an up-to-date roster.

CAROLINA PANTHERS

COACHING STAFF
Head Coach,
Ron Rivera
Pro Career: Became the fourth coach in Carolina Panthers history on January 11, 2011. In his first season at the helm, the Panthers won four more games than in 2010 on the strength of a prolific offense which improved from last in the NFL in 2010 to seventh in 2011. Before joining the Panthers, Rivera worked with the San Diego Chargers from 2007-2010, coaching inside linebackers before taking over as defensive coordinator midway through the 2008 season. In 2010, San Diego led the NFL with an average of 271.6 total yards allowed per game and gave up a league-low 177.8 passing yards per game. In 2009, the team ranked 16th in total defense and 11th against the pass. From 2004-06, Rivera oversaw the Chicago Bears defense, guiding the unit to two top-five finishes in the league. In 2006, the Bears defense led the NFL with 44 takeaways and finished fifth in total defense and third in scoring defense, helping propel Chicago to an appearance in Super Bowl XLI. In 2005, Rivera's defensive unit ranked second in the NFL in total defense and first in scoring defense. The Bears went 43 consecutive quarters without allowing more than seven points – the longest streak in the NFL since 1969. Prior to serving as defensive coordinator with the Bears, Rivera was linebackers coach for the Eagles (1999-2003) and defensive quality control coach for the Bears (1997-98). He is just the third Latino head coach in NFL history, joining Tom Flores with the Oakland Raiders (1979-1987) and Seattle Seahawks (1992-94) and Tom Fears with the New Orleans Saints (1967-1970). A second-round draft choice in 1984 by Chicago, Rivera played nine seasons with the Bears. Primarily an outside linebacker, he was a member of the Super Bowl XX championship team in 1985. Career record: 6-10.
Background: Linebacker at California (1980-83).
Personal: Born January 7, 1962 in Fort Ord, Calif. He and his wife, Stephanie, have two children—Christopher and Courtney.

ASSISTANT COACHES
Warren Belin, linebackers; born October 20, 1967, Marshville, N.C. Linebacker Wake Forest 1987-1990. No pro playing experience. College coach: Cornell 1991, 1993-94, East Tennessee State 1992, William & Mary 1995-96, Southern Methodist 1997-2001, Vanderbilt 2002-09, Georgia 2010. Pro coach: Joined Panthers in 2011.
Ray Brown, asst. offensive line; born December 12, 1962, Marion, Ark. Offensive lineman/tight end Arkansas State 1983-85. Pro offensive lineman St. Louis/Phoenix Cardinals 1986-88, Washington Redskins 1989-1995, 2004-

05, San Francisco 49ers 1996-2001, Detroit Lions 2002-03. Pro coach: Washington Redskins 2006, Buffalo Bills 2008-09, San Francisco 49ers 2010, joined Panthers in 2011.
Rod Chudzinski, offensive coordinator; born May 12, 1968, Toledo, Ohio. Tight end Miami 1986-1990. No pro playing experience. College coach: Miami 1994-2003. Pro coach: Cleveland Browns 2004, 2007-08, San Diego Chargers 2005-06, 2009-2010, joined Panthers in 2011.
Fred Graves, wide receivers; born March 2, 1950, Los Angeles, Calif. Halfback/split end Utah 1969-1971. No pro playing experience. College coach: Northeast Missouri State 1975-76, Western Illinois 1977-78, New Mexico State 1979-1981, Utah 1982-2000. Pro coach: Buffalo Bills 2001-03, Cleveland Browns 2004, Detroit Lions 2005, Tennessee Titans 2007-2010, joined Panthers in 2011.
Pete Hoener, tight ends; born June 14, 1954, Peoria, Ill. Tight end/defensive end Bradley 1969-1970. No pro playing experience. College coach: Missouri 1975-76, Illinois State 1977, Indiana State 1978-1984, Illinois 1987-88, Purdue 1989-1991, Texas Christian 1992-97, Iowa State 1998-99, Texas A&M 2000. Pro coach: St. Louis/Arizona Cardinals 1985-86, 2001-03, Chicago Bears 2004, San Francisco 49ers 2005-2010, joined Panthers in 2011.
Joe Kenn, strength and conditioning; born October 13, 1966, Far Rockaway, N.Y. Guard Wake Forest 1987-88. No pro playing experience. College coach: Wake Forest 1991 (winter/spring), Boise State 1991-98, Utah 1999-2000, Arizona State 2001-07, Louisville 2008-09. Pro coach: Joined Panthers in 2011.
John Matsko, offensive line; born February 2, 1951, Cleveland, Ohio. Fullback Kent State 1970-72. No pro playing experience. College coach: Miami (Ohio) 1974-75, 1977, North Carolina 1978-1984, Navy 1985, Arizona 1986, Southern California 1987-1991. Pro coach: Phoenix Cardinals 1992-93, New Orleans Saints 1994-96, New York Giants 1997-98, St. Louis Rams 1999-2005, Kansas City Chiefs 2006-07, Baltimore Ravens 2008-2010, joined Panthers in 2011.
Sean McDermott, defensive coordinator; born March 21, 1974, Omaha, Neb. Safety William & Mary 1994-97. No pro playing experience. College coach: William & Mary 1998. Pro coach: Philadelphia Eagles 1999-2010, joined Panthers in 2011.
Sam Mills III, defensive quality control/asst. defensive line; born May 20, 1978, Long Branch, N.J. Defensive back Montclair State 1997-1999. No pro playing experience. Pro coach: Joined Panthers in 2005.
Brian Murphy, special teams coordinator; born July 17, 1969, Elmwood Park, Ill. Defensive lineman Lehigh 1988-1991. No pro playing experience. College coach:

Benedictine 1992, Wisconsin 1994-96, 2002-05, Baylor 1997, San Diego 1998, Lehigh 1999. Pro coach: Minnesota Vikings 2006-2010, joined Panthers in 2011.
Ricky Proehl, offensive consultant; born March 7, 1968, Bronx, N.Y. Wide receiver Wake Forest 1986-89. Pro wide receiver Phoenix/Arizona Cardinals 1990-94, Seattle Seahawks 1995-96, Chicago Bears 1997, St. Louis Rams 1998-2002, Carolina Panthers 2003-05, Indianapolis Colts 2006. Pro coach: Joined Panthers in 2011.
Richard Rogers, asst. special teams; born October 28, 1961, St. Louis, Mo. Linebacker California 1980-83. No pro playing experience. College coach: Diablo Valley (Calif.) C.C. 1989-94, San Jose State, 1995-1996, Portland State 1997-2000, New Mexico State 2001-2004, Holy Cross 2005-2011. Pro coach: Joined Panthers in 2012.
John Settle, running backs; born June 2, 1965, Reidsville, N.C. Running back Appalachian State 1983-86. Pro running back Atlanta Falcons 1987-1990, Washington Redskins 1991-92. College coach: Appalachian State 1994, Fresno State 1998-2005, Wisconsin 2006-2010. Pro coach: Cleveland Browns/Baltimore Ravens 1995-97, joined Panthers in 2011.
Mike Shula, quarterbacks; born June 3, 1965, Baltimore, Md. Quarterback Alabama 1984-86. Pro quarterback Tampa Bay Buccaneers 1987. College coach: Alabama 2003-06 (head coach). Pro coach: Tampa Bay Buccaneers 1988-1990, 1996-99, Miami Dolphins 1991-92, 2000-02, Chicago Bears 1993-95, Jacksonville Jaguars 2007-2010, joined Panthers in 2011.
Scott Turner, offensive quality control; born August 7, 1982, Englewood, Calif. Quarterback Nevada-Las Vegas 2002-04. No pro playing experience. College coach: Oregon State 2005, Pittsburgh 2008-2010. Pro coach: Joined Panthers in 2011.
Eric Washington, defensive line; born October 29, 1969, Shreveport, La. Tight end Grambling State 1989-1990. No pro playing experience. College coach: Texas A&M 1997, Ohio 2001-03, Northwestern 2004-07. Pro coach: Chicago Bears 2008-2010, joined Panthers in 2011.
Steve Wilks, secondary/passing defense coordinator; born August 8, 1969, Charlotte, N.C. Defensive back Appalachian State 1987-1991. No pro playing experience. College coach: Johnson C. Smith 1995-96, Savannah State 1997-1999, Illinois State 2000, Appalachian State 2001, East Tennessee State 2002, Bowling Green State 2003, Notre Dame 2004, Washington 2005. Pro coach: Chicago Bears 2006-2008, San Diego Chargers 2009-2011, joined Panthers in 2012.

National Football Conference
North Division
Team Colors: Navy Blue, Orange, and
White
Halas Hall at Conway Park
1920 Football Drive
Lake Forest, Illinois 60045
Telephone: (847) 295-6600

2012 SCHEDULE
PRESEASON
Aug. 9	**Denver**	7:30
Aug. 18	**Washington**	7:00
Aug. 24	at New York Giants	7:00
Aug. 30	at Cleveland	6:30

REGULAR SEASON
Sep. 9	**Indianapolis**	12:00
Sep. 13	at Green Bay (Thurs)	7:20
Sep. 23	**St. Louis**	12:00
Oct. 1	at Dallas (Mon)	7:30
Oct. 7	at Jacksonville	3:05
Oct. 14	BYE	
Oct. 22	**Detroit** (Mon)	7:30
Oct. 28	**Carolina**	12:00
Nov. 4	at Tennessee	12:00
Nov. 11	**Houston**	7:20
Nov. 19	at San Francisco (Mon)	7:30
Nov. 25	**Minnesota**	12:00
Dec. 2	**Seattle**	12:00
Dec. 9	at Minnesota	12:00
Dec. 16	**Green Bay**	12:00
Dec. 23	at Arizona	3:15
Dec. 30	at Detroit	12:00

*All times CT
Stadium: Soldier Field
(opened in 1924)
•**Capacity:** 61,500
1410 S. Museum Campus Dr.
Chicago, Illinois 60605
Playing Surface: Natural Grass
Training Camp: Olivet-Nazarene Univ.
Bourbonnais, Illinois
60901

SOLDIER FIELD

CLUB OFFICIALS
Chairman of the Board:
George H. McCaskey
Secretary: Virginia H. McCaskey
President and CEO: Ted Phillips
General Manager: Phil Emery
Senior Director of Special Projects:
Pat McCaskey
Senior Director of Business Development
& Alumni Relations: Brian McCaskey
Vice President of Business
Administration: John Bostrom
Vice President of Sales & Marketing:
Chris Hibbs
Vice President of Communications:
Scott Hagel
Vice President of Football Administration
and General Counsel: Cliff Stein
Chief Financial Officer & Treasurer:
Karen Murphy
Senior Director of Ticket Operations:
Lee Twarling
Director of Player Development:
Isaiah Harris
Director of Video Services:
Dave Hendrickson
Assistant Video Director: Dean Pope
College Video Coordinator: Dan Tuohy
Video Assistant: Jack Dowling
Head Athletic Trainer: Chris Hanks
Assistant Head Athletic Trainer/Director
of Rehabilitation: Bobby Slater
Head Equipment Manager: Tony Medlin
Assistant Equipment Managers:
Carl Piekarski, John Perkins,
Joseph Shaw
Scouts: Chris Ballard, Marty Barrett,
Rex Hogan, Ted Monago,
Mark Sadowski, Jeff Shiver
Assistant Director of Pro Personnel:
Kevin Turks
Pro Scout: James Kirkland
Director of Community Relations:
Caroline Guip Schrenker
Director of Broadcasting & Scoreboard
Operations: Greg Miller
Media Services Manager: Jim Christman
Media Relations Coordinator: Mike Corbo

COACHING HISTORY
Decatur Staleys 1920,
Chicago Staleys 1921
(729-538-42)
Records include postseason games
1920-29	George Halas	84-31-19
1930-32	Ralph Jones	24-10-7
1933-1942	George Halas*	88-24-4
1942-45	Hunk Anderson- Luke Johnsos**	24-12-2
1946-1955	George Halas	76-43-2
1956-57	John (Paddy) Driscoll	14-10-1
1958-1967	George Halas	76-53-6
1968-1971	Jim Dooley	20-36-0
1972-74	Abe Gibron	11-30-1
1975-77	Jack Pardee	20-23-0
1978-1981	Neill Armstrong	30-35-0
1982-1992	Mike Ditka	112-68-0
1993-98	Dave Wannstedt	41-57-0
1999-2003	Dick Jauron	35-46-0
2004-2011	Lovie Smith	74-60-0

*Retired after five games to enter U.S. Navy
**Co-coaches

PAID ATTENDANCE
Home 482,179	Away 541,118

Total 1,023,297
Single-game home record,
66,900 (9/5/93)
Single-season home record, 527,769
(1999)

2012 DRAFT CHOICES
Round	Name	Pos.	College
1	Shea McClellin	DE	Boise St.
2	Alshon Jeffery	WR	South Carolina
3	Brandon Hardin	DB	Oregon St.
4	Evan Rodriguez	TE	Temple
6	Isaiah Frey	DB	Nevada
7	Greg McCoy	DB	Texas Christian

2011 TEAM RECORD

PRESEASON (2-2)

Date	Result	Opponent
8/14	W 10-3	Buffalo
8/22	L 13-41	at New York Giants
8/27	L 13-14	at Tennessee
9/1	W 24-14	Cleveland

REGULAR SEASON (8-8)

Date	Result	Opponent
9/11	W 30-12	Atlanta
9/18	L 13-30	at New Orleans
9/25	L 17-27	Green Bay
10/2	W 34-29	Carolina
10/10	L 13-24	at Detroit
10/16	W 39-10	Minnesota
10/23	W 24-18	at Tampa Bay
11/7	W 30-24	at Philadelphia
11/13	W 37-13	Detroit
11/20	W 31-20	San Diego
11/27	L 20-25	at Oakland
12/4	L 3-10	Kansas City
12/11	L 10-13	at Denver (OT)
12/18	L 14-38	Seattle
12/25	L 21-35	at Green Bay
1/1	W 17-13	at Minnesota

(OT) Overtime

SCORE BY PERIODS

Bears	77	128	82	66	0 —	353
Opponents	51	99	95	93	3 —	341

2011 TEAM STATISTICS

	Bears	Opp.
Total First Downs	271	291
Rushing	97	75
Passing	153	199
Penalty	21	17
3rd Down: Made/Att	66/203	80/229
3rd Down Pct.	32.5	34.9
4th Down: Made/Att	2/8	7/17
4th Down Pct.	25.0	41.2
Possession Avg.	30:13	29:47
Total Net Yards	5026	5607
Avg. Per Game	314.1	350.4
Total Plays	978	1048
Avg. Per Play	5.1	5.4
Net Yards Rushing	2015	1542
Avg. Per Game	125.9	96.4
Total Rushes	456	384
Net Yards Passing	3011	4065
Avg. Per Game	188.2	254.1
Sacked/Yards Lost	49/335	33/208
Gross Yards	3346	4273
Att./Completions	473/268	631/383
Completion Pct.	56.7	60.7
Had Intercepted	20	20
Punts/Average	89/43.9	85/42.7
Net Punting Avg.	89/40.4	85/36.7
Penalties/Yards	104/800	98/719
Fumbles/Ball Lost	26/9	23/11
Touchdowns	38	36
Rushing	10	10
Passing	18	22
Returns	10	4

2011 INDIVIDUAL STATISTICS

PASSING

	Att.	Comp.	Yds.	Pct.	TD	Int.	Tkld.	Rate
Cutler	314	182	2319	58.0	13	7	23/159	85.7
Hanie	102	51	613	50.0	3	9	19/133	41.8
McCown	55	35	414	63.6	2	4	7/43	68.3
Forte	1	0	0	0.0	0	0	0/0	39.6
Podlesh	1	0	0	0.0	0	0	0/0	39.6
Bears	473	268	3346	56.7	18	20	49/335	73.8
Opponents	631	383	4273	60.7	22	20	33/208	79.3

SCORING

	TD R	TD P	TD Rt	PAT	FG	Saf	PTS
Gould	0	0	0	37/37	28/32	0	121
Barber	6	0	0	0/0	0/0	0	36
K. Davis	0	5	0	0/0	0/0	0	30
Forté	3	1	0	0/0	0/0	0	24
Hester	0	1	3	0/0	0/0	0	24
Sanzenbacher	0	3	0	0/0	0/0	0	18
Knox	0	2	0	0/0	0/0	0	12
Spaeth	0	2	0	0/0	0/0	0	12
Tillman	0	0	2	0/0	0/0	0	12
R. Williams	0	2	0	0/0	0/0	0	12
Bell	0	1	0	0/0	0/0	0	6
Bennett	0	1	0	0/0	0/0	0	6
Cutler	1	0	0	0/0	0/0	0	6
Idonije	0	0	1	0/0	0/0	0	6
D. Moore	0	0	1	0/0	0/0	0	6
Urlacher	0	0	1	0/0	0/0	0	6
E. Williams	0	0	1	0/0	0/0	0	6
Wright	0	0	1	0/0	0/0	0	6
McCown	0	0	0	0/0	0/0	0	2
Paea	0	0	0	0/0	0/0	1	2
Bears	10	18	10	37/37	28/32	1	353
Opponents	10	22	4	33/33	30/36	1	341

2-Pt Conversions: McCown

Bears 1-1, Opponents 0-3

RUSHING

	No.	Yds	Avg	LG	TD
Forté	203	997	4.9	46	3
Barber	114	422	3.7	29	6
Bell	79	337	4.3	26	0
Hanie	13	98	7.5	24	0
McCown	12	68	5.7	28	0
Cutler	18	55	3.1	12	1
Allen	15	48	3.2	13	0
Sanzenbacher	1	-4	-4.0	-4	0
Hester	1	-6	-6.0	-6	0
Bears	456	2015	4.4	46	10
Opponents	384	1542	4.0	88t	10

RECEIVING

	No.	Yds	Avg	LG	TD
Forté	52	490	9.4	56t	1
Knox	37	727	19.6	81	2
R. Williams	37	507	13.7	25t	2
Sanzenbacher	27	276	10.2	22	3
Hester	26	369	14.2	53	1
Bennett	24	381	15.9	49	1
Bell	19	133	7.0	25t	1
K. Davis	18	206	11.4	32t	5
Hurd	8	109	13.6	28	0
Clutts	8	48	6.0	10	0
Spaeth	7	50	7.1	13	2
Barber	5	50	10.0	16	0
Bears	268	3346	12.5	81	18
Opponents	383	4273	11.2	79t	22

INTERCEPTIONS

	No.	Yds	Avg	LG	TD
D. Moore	4	31	7.8	20t	1
Tillman	3	66	22.0	44t	2
Wright	3	60	20.0	36	1
Graham	3	11	3.7	10	0
Urlacher	3	7	2.3	8	0
Jennings	2	2	1.0	1	0
Briggs	1	0	0.0	0	0
Conte	1	0	0.0	0	0
Bears	20	177	8.9	44t	4
Opponents	20	380	19.0	73	3

PUNTING

	No.	Yds.	Avg.	In 20	LG
Podlesh	89	3903	43.9	21	70
Bears	89	3903	43.9	21	70
Opponents	85	3628	42.7	27	80

PUNT RETURNS

	Ret	FC	Yds	Avg	LG	TD
Hester	28	15	454	16.2	82t	2
Bennett	1	1	7	7.0	7	0
Knox	1	0	9	9.0	9	0
Bears	30	16	470	15.7	82t	2
Opponents	41	27	223	5.4	36	0

KICKOFF RETURNS

	No.	Yds	Avg	LG	TD
Hester	33	723	21.9	98t	1
Knox	15	397	26.5	56	0
Bell	2	45	22.5	25	0
Spaeth	2	14	7.0	7	0
Ky. Adams	1	0	0.0	0	0
Allen	1	17	17.0	17	0
Bennett	1	9	9.0	9	0
Clutts	1	9	9.0	9	0
Hurd	1	24	24.0	24	0
Bears	57	1238	21.7	98t	1
Opponents	35	855	24.4	44	0

FIELD GOALS

	1-19	20-29	30-39	40-49	50+
Gould	0/0	10/10	6/6	6/10	6/6
Bears	0/0	10/10	6/6	6/10	6/6
Opponents	1/1	9/10	10/12	7/8	3/5

SACKS

	No.
Peppers	11.0
Melton	7.0
Idonije	5.0
Okoye	4.0
Paea	2.0
C. Davis	1.0
Steltz	1.0
Tillman	1.0
(group)	1.0
Bears	33.0
Opponents	49.0

RECORD HOLDERS
INDIVIDUAL RECORDS—CAREER

Category	Name	Performance
Rushing (Yds.)	Walter Payton, 1975-1987	16,726
Passing (Yds.)	Sid Luckman, 1939-1950	14,686
Passing (TDs)	Sid Luckman, 1939-1950	137
Receiving (No.)	Walter Payton, 1975-1987	492
Receiving (Yds.)	Johnny Morris, 1958-1967	5,059
Interceptions	Gary Fencik, 1976-1987	38
Punting (Avg.)	George Gulyanics, 1947-1952	44.5
Punt Return (Avg.)	Devin Hester, 2006-2011	**12.9
Kickoff Return (Avg.)	Gale Sayers, 1965-1971	**30.6
Field Goals	Kevin Butler, 1985-1995	243
Touchdowns (Tot.)	Walter Payton, 1975-1987	125
Points	Kevin Butler, 1985-1995	1,116
*Sacks	Richard Dent, 1983-1993, 1995	124.5

INDIVIDUAL RECORDS—SINGLE SEASON

Category	Name	Performance
Rushing (Yds.)	Walter Payton, 1977	1,852
Passing (Yds.)	Erik Kramer, 1995	3,838
Passing (TDs)	Erik Kramer, 1995	29
Receiving (No.)	Marty Booker, 2001	100
Receiving (Yds.)	Marcus Robinson, 1999	1,400
Interceptions	Mark Carrier, 1990	10
Punting (Avg.)	Bobby Joe Green, 1963	46.5
Punt Return (Avg.)	Devin Hester, 2010	17.1
Kickoff Return (Avg.)	Gale Sayers, 1967	37.7
Field Goals	Robbie Gould, 2006	32
Touchdowns (Tot.)	Gale Sayers, 1965	22
Points	Kevin Butler, 1985	144
*Sacks	Richard Dent, 1984	17.5

INDIVIDUAL RECORDS—SINGLE GAME

Category	Name	Performance
Rushing (Yds.)	Walter Payton, 11-20-77	275
Passing (Yds.)	Johnny Lujack, 12-11-49	468
Passing (TDs)	Sid Luckman, 11-14-43	**7
Receiving (No.)	Jim Keane, 10-23-49	14
Receiving (Yds.)	Harlon Hill, 10-31-54	214
Interceptions	Many times	3
	Last time by Mark Carrier, 12-9-90	
Field Goals	Roger LeClerc, 12-3-61	5
	Mac Percival, 10-20-68	5
Touchdowns (Tot.)	Gale Sayers, 12-12-65	**6
Points	Gale Sayers, 12-12-65	36
*Sacks	Richard Dent, 11-4-84, 12-27-87	4.5

Sacks became an official statistic in 1982.
**NFL Record*

2012 VETERAN ROSTER

No.	Name	Pos.	Ht.	Wt.	Birthdate	NFL Exp.	College	Hometown	How Acq.	'11 Games/ Starts
86	Adams, Kyle	TE	6-4	255	1/19/88	2	Purdue	Austin, Texas	FA-'11	9/0
32	Bell, Kahlil	RB	5-11	219	12/10/86	4	UCLA	San Anselmo, Calif.	FA-'09	13/3
80	Bennett, Earl	WR	6-0	206	3/23/87	5	Vanderbilt	Birmingham, Ala.	D3a-'08	11/4
55	Briggs, Lance	LB	6-1	244	11/12/80	10	Arizona	Sacramento, Calif.	D3-'03	16/16
29	Bush, Michael	RB	6-1	245	6/16/84	6	Louisville	Louisville, Ky.	UFA(Oak)-'12	16/9*
2	Campbell, Jason	QB	6-5	230	12/31/81	8	Auburn	Taylorsville, Miss.	UFA(Oak)-'12	6/6*
72	Carimi, Gabe	T	6-7	316	6/13/88	2	Wisconsin	Cottage Grove, Wisc.	D1-'11	2/2
44	Clutts, Tyler	FB	6-2	260	11/9/84	2	Fresno State	Clovis, Calif.	FA-'11	16/8
47	Conte, Chris	S	6-2	203	2/23/89	2	California	Los Angeles, Calif.	D3-'11	14/9
57	Costanzo, Blake	LB	6-1	235	4/14/84	6	Lafayette	Franklin Lakes, N.J.	UFA(SF)-'12	16/0*
6	Cutler, Jay	QB	6-3	220	4/29/83	7	Vanderbilt	Santa Claus, Ind.	T(Den)-'09	10/10
94	Davis, Chauncey	DE	6-2	271	1/27/83	8	Florida State	Bartow, Fla.	FA-'11	6/0
87	Davis, Kellen	TE	6-7	267	10/11/85	5	Michigan State	Adrian, Mich.	D5b-'08	16/15
58	DeCicco, Dom	LB	6-4	230	9/11/88	2	Pittsburgh	Jefferson Hills, Pa.	FA-'11	16/0
10	Enderle, Nathan	QB	6-4	240	1/12/88	2	Idaho	North Platte, Neb.	D5-'11	0*
22	f- Forté, Matt	RB	6-2	218	12/10/85	5	Tulane	Slidell, La.	D2-'08	12/12
63	Garza, Roberto	G/C	6-2	310	3/26/79	12	Texas A&M-Kingsville	Rio Hondo, Texas	UFA(Atl)-'05	16/16
93	Gibson, Thaddeus	DE	6-2	243	10/21/87	2	Ohio State	Euclid, Ohio	FA-'11	2/0
9	Gould, Robbie	K	6-0	185	12/30/81	8	Penn State	Lock Haven, Pa.	FA-'05	16/0
24	Hayden, Kelvin	CB	6-0	195	7/23/83	8	Illinois	Chicago, Ill.	UFA(Atl)-'12	8/1*
91	Hayes, Geno	LB	6-1	226	8/10/87	5	Florida State	Greenville, Fla.	UFA(TB)-'12	16/13*
64	Henry, Ricky	G	6-4	310	7/27/87	2	Nebraska	Omaha, Neb.	FA-'11	1/0
23	Hester, Devin	WR	5-11	190	11/4/82	7	Miami	Riviera Beach, Fla.	D2b-'06	16/8
71	Idonije, Israel	DL	6-6	275	11/17/80	9	Manitoba	Lagos, Nigeria	FA-'03	16/16
26	Jennings, Tim	CB	5-8	185	12/24/83	7	Georgia	Orangeburg, S.C.	UFA(Ind)-'10	16/15
13	Knox, Johnny	WR	6-0	185	11/3/86	4	Abilene Christian	Houston, Texas	D5a-'09	14/11
60	Louis, Lance	G	6-3	320	4/24/85	4	San Diego State	New Orleans, La.	D7a-'09	14/13
65	Mannelly, Patrick	LS	6-5	265	4/18/75	15	Duke	Atlanta, Ga.	D6b-'98	10/0
15	t- Marshall, Brandon	WR	6-4	230	3/23/84	7	Central Florida	Pittsburgh, Pa.	T(Mia)-'12	16/16*
45	# Massey, Chris	LS	6-0	245	8/21/79	10	Marshall	Chesapeake, W. Va.	FA-'11	6/0
70	McCargo, John	DT	6-2	307	8/19/83	7	North Carolina State	Charlotte Court House, Va.	FA-'12	4/0*
12	McCown, Josh	QB	6-4	213	7/4/79	10	Sam Houston State	Jacksonville, Texas	FA-'11	3/2
69	Melton, Henry	DL	6-3	295	10/11/86	4	Texas	Grapevine, Texas	D4a-'09	15/15
30	Moore, D.J.	CB	5-9	180	3/22/87	4	Vanderbilt	Spartanburg, S.C.	D4b-'09	13/1
92	Paea, Stephen	DT	6-1	300	5/11/88	2	Oregon State	Los Altos, Calif.	D2-'11	11/0
90	Peppers, Julius	DE	6-7	287	1/18/80	11	North Carolina	Bailey, N.C.	UFA(Car)-'10	16/16
8	Podlesh, Adam	P	5-11	200	8/11/83	6	Maryland	Pittsford, N.Y.	UFA(Jax)-'11	16/0
68	Pressley, DeMario	DT	6-3	301	11/3/85	4	North Carolina State	Greensboro, N.C.	FA-'12	1/0*
62	Rachal, Chilo	G	6-5	323	3/15/86	5	Southern California	Compton, Calif.	UFA(SF)-'12	16/3*
53	Roach, Nick	LB	6-1	234	6/16/85	6	Northwestern	Milwaukee, Wisc.	FA-'07	16/15
18	Sanzenbacher, Dane	WR	5-11	180	10/13/88	2	Ohio State	Toledo, Ohio	FA-'11	16/1
89	Spaeth, Matt	TE	6-7	260	11/24/83	6	Minnesota	Albertville, Minn.	UFA(Pitt)-'11	15/8
67	Spencer, Chris	G/C	6-3	309	3/28/82	8	Mississippi	Madison, Miss.	UFA(Sea)-'11	15/14
20	Steltz, Craig	S	6-1	210	5/7/86	5	Louisiana State	Metairie, La.	D4-'08	16/5
11	Thomas, Devin	WR	6-2	221	11/15/86	5	Michigan State	Ann Arbor, Mich.	UFA(NYG)-'12	16/0*
97	Thomas, J.T.	LB	6-1	236	8/15/88	2	West Virginia	Ft. Lauderdale, Fla.	D6-'11	0*
33	Tillman, Charles	CB	6-2	198	2/23/81	10	Louisiana-Lafayette	Copperas Cove, Texas	D2-'03	16/16
75	Toeaina, Matt	DT	6-2	308	10/9/84	5	Oregon	Utulei, American Samoa	FA-'07	12/12
59	Trahan, Patrick	LB	6-2	236	11/7/86	2	Mississippi	New Orleans, La.	FA-'11	5/0
45	Unga, Harvey	RB	6-0	237	1/18/87	2	Brigham Young	Provo, Utah	S7-'10	0*
54	Urlacher, Brian	LB	6-4	258	5/25/78	13	New Mexico	Lovington, N.M.	D1-'00	16/16
49	Venable, Winston	S	5-11	210	3/31/87	2	Boise State	San Rafael, Calif.	FA-'11	12/0
37	Walters, Anthony	S	6-1	207	9/19/88	2	Delaware	Philadelphia, Pa.	FA-'11	4/0
73	Webb, J'Marcus	T	6-7	333	8/8/88	3	West Texas A&M	Mesquite, Texas	D7-'10	16/16
14	Weems, Eric	WR/KR	5-9	195	7/4/85	6	Bethune-Cookman	Dayton Beach, Fla.	UFA(Atl)-'12	16/2*
27	Wilhite, Jonathan	CB	5-11	185	2/23/84	5	Auburn	Monroe, La.	UFA(Den)-'12	15/2*
74	Williams, Chris	G/T	6-6	320	8/26/85	5	Vanderbilt	Glynn, La.	D1-'08	9/9
70	Williams, Edwin	G/C	6-3	315	12/10/86	3	Maryland	Washington, D.C.	FA-'10	15/7
52	Williams, Jabara	LB	6-2	238	7/6/89	2	Stephen F. Austin	Nacogdoches, Texas	FA-'11	5/0
11	# Williams, Roy	WR	6-3	215	12/20/81	9	Texas	Odessa, Texas	FA-'11	15/9
98	Wootton, Corey	DE	6-6	270	6/22/87	3	Northwestern	Rutherford, N.J.	D4-'10	7/0
21	Wright, Major	S	5-11	204	7/1/88	3	Florida	Miramar, Fla.	D3-'10	12/11
76	Wrotto, Mansfield	G	6-3	310	10/12/84	5	Georgia Tech	Snellville, Ga.	FA-'11	0*

* Bush played 16 games with Oakland in '11; Campbell played 6 games with Oakland; Costanzo played 16 games with San Francisco; Enderle inactive 12 games and did not play in 4 games; Hayden played 8 games with Atlanta; Hayes played 16 games with Tampa Bay; Marshall played 16 games with Miami; McCargo played 4 games with Tampa Bay; Pressley played 1 game with Carolina; Rachal played 16 games with San Francisco; D. Thomas played 16 games with New York Giants; J. Thomas missed '11 season because of injury; Unga missed '11 season after leaving team; Weems played 16 games with Atlanta; Wilhite played 15 games with Denver; Wrotto inactive for 1 game.

\# Unrestricted free agent; subject to developments.

f- Unsigned franchise player; subject to developments.

t- Traded for Marshall (Mia).

Retired—Marion Barber, 7-year running back, 11 games in '11.

Players lost through free agency (5): CB Zackary Bowman (Minn; 16 games in '11), CB Corey Graham (Balt; 16), QB Caleb Hanie (Den; 6), S Brandon Meriweather (Wash; 11), DT Amobi Okoye (TB; 16).

Also played with Bears in '11—DT Anthony Adams (11 games), DE Mario Addison (3), S Chris Harris (3), WR Sam Hurd (12), LB Brian Iwuh (11), WR Max Komar (2), T Frank Omiyale (16), DE Nick Reed (7).

FIRST-YEAR ROSTER

Name	Pos.	Ht.	Wt.	Birthdate	College	Hometown	How Acq.
Alexander, Alvester	RB	5-10	206	10/17/90	Wyoming	Houston, Texas	FA
Allen, Armando (1)	RB	5-10	190	4/30/89	Notre Dame	Opa Locka, Fla.	FA-'11
Anderson, Joe	WR	6-1	196	11/21/88	Texas Southern	Texarkana, Ark.	FA
Blanchard, Matt	QB	6-3	225	3/21/89	Wisconsin-Whitewater	Lake Zurich, Ill.	FA
Brown, James	G/T	6-4	306	11/30/88	Troy	Magnolia, Miss.	FA
Cameron, Ronnie	DT	6-2	304	8/15/89	Old Dominion	Westbury, N.Y.	FA
Cole, Adrien	LB	5-11	235	2/1/90	Louisiana Tech	Mobile, Ala.	FA
Coston, Trevor	S	5-10	199	10/12/89	Maine	Greenlawn, N.Y.	FA
Crump, Terriun	WR	6-2	223	7/23/89	Western Illinois	Country Club Hills, Ill.	FA
Frey, Isaiah	CB	6-0	190	4/6/90	Nevada	Olivehurst, Calif.	D6
Golden, Brittan	WR	5-11	186	7/20/88	West Texas A&M	Denver City, Texas	FA
Greene, A.J.	T	6-5	298	9/25/89	Auburn	Madison, Tenn.	FA
Hardin, Brandon	S	6-3	217	10/30/89	Oregon State	Kealakekua, Hawaii	D3
Hendrickson, Tyler	T	6-8	313	2/24/89	Concordia (Minn)	St. Paul, Minn.	FA
Jeffery, Alshon	WR	6-3	216	2/14/90	South Carolina	St. Matthews, S.C.	D2
Jones, Jeremy	S	5-10	197	7/18/89	Wayne State	Grand Rapids, Mich.	FA
McClellin, Shea	DE	6-3	260	8/1/89	Boise State	Caldwell, Idaho	D1
McCoy, Greg	CB	5-10	178	9/8/88	Texas Christian	Dallas, Texas	D7
Miller, Jordan (1)	DT	6-2	315	2/1/88	Southern	Upper Marlboro, Md.	FA-'11
Ozougwu, Cheta (1)	DE	6-2	255	11/18/88	Rice	Houston, Texas	FA
Pieschel, Nick	G	6-6	309	12/7/88	Central Florida	Fort Lauderdale, Fla.	FA
Quigley, Ryan	P	6-3	188	1/26/90	Boston College	Little River, S.C.	FA
Rodriguez, Evan	TE	6-2	239	9/21/88	Temple	North Bergen, N.J.	D4
Ross, Draylen (1)	TE	6-4	271	3/21/88	North Texas	Fort Worth, Texas	FA-'11
Summers, Chris	WR	6-5	213	7/10/89	Liberty	Jacksonville, Fla.	FA
Teggart, David	K	6-1	203	10/23/88	Connecticut	Northborough, Mass.	FA
Thornton, Ronnie	LB	6-2	244	7/10/89	Southern Mississippi	Miami, Fla.	FA
Venson, Brandon	TE	6-3	245	2/17/88	Illinois State	Glendale Heights, Ill.	FA
Warren, Donovan (1)	CB	5-11	193	1/31/89	Michigan	Long Beach, Calif.	FA

The term NFL Rookie is defined as a player who is in his first season of professional football and has not been on the roster of another professional football team for any regular-season or postseason games. A Rookie is designated by an "R" on NFL rosters. Players who have been active in another professional football league or players who have NFL experience, including either preseason training camp or being on an Active List or Inactive List, or on Reserve/Injured or Reserve/Physically Unable to Perform for fewer than six regular-season games, are termed NFL First-Year Players. An NFL First-Year Player is designated by a "1" on NFL rosters. Thereafter, a player is credited with an additional year of experience for each season in which he accumulates six games on the Active List or Inactive List, or on Reserve/Injured or Reserve/Physically Unable to Perform.

Log on to www.chicagobears.com for an up-to-date roster.

COACHING STAFF

Head Coach,
Lovie Smith

Pro Career: Named the thirteenth head coach in Chicago Bears history on January 15, 2004. Smith enters his ninth season as the head coach of the Chicago Bears. Smith has led the Bears to three division titles, two NFC Championship game appearances and the 2006 NFC crown. His 74 overall wins (71-57 regular season; 3-3 postseason) are third most in franchise history, trailing only Hall of Famers George Halas and Mike Ditka. Smith has led the Bears to three 11-win seasons during his tenure, including a career-high 13 wins in 2006 when he led Chicago to home-field advantage in the NFC Playoffs and the team's first NFC Championship since its Super Bowl season of 1985. A year earlier, Smith earned the 2005 AP NFL Coach of the Year Award after turning a 1-3 start to the season into 11 victories, the most by a second-year coach in club annals, and the second seed in the NFC Playoffs. Fueled by an eight-game win streak, Smith led a worst-to-first revival in the NFC North division as the Bears six-win improvement from the previous season was tied for the biggest in the NFL in 2005. Since Smith's arrival, the Bears lead the NFL with 266 take-aways. Smith came to Chicago from St. Louis (2001-03), where he served as defensive coordinator. In 2001 he helped the Rams return to the Super Bowl after missing the playoffs the previous season. Smith previously coached the linebackers for the Tampa Bay Buccaneers (1996-2000). Career record: 74-60.

Background: Played at Tulsa (1976-79), where he was a linebacker before moving to strong safety and earning two-time All-America and three-time All-Missouri Conference defensive back honors. Began his coaching career at his hometown high school (Big Sandy, Texas) in 1980 before moving to Cascia Hall Prep in Tulsa the following year. Two years later Smith began coaching collegiately at Tulsa (1983-86), Wisconsin (1987), Arizona State (1988-1991), Kentucky (1992), Tennessee (1993-94), and Ohio State (1995).

Personal: Born May 8, 1958, Gladewater, Texas. Lovie and his wife MaryAnne have three sons—Mikal, Matthew and Miles and twin grandsons—Malachi and Noah.

ASSISTANT COACHES

Jim Arthur, strength and conditioning assistant; born July 12, 1978, Cheshire, Conn. Attended Springfield (Mass.) College. No college or pro playing experience. College coach: Springfield (Mass.) College 2000, Louisiana Tech 2001, Boston College 2002. Pro coach: Joined Bears in 2005.

Bob Babich, linebackers; born February 20, 1961, Aliquippa, Pa. Linebacker Mesa (Colo.) C.C. 1979-1980, Tulsa 1981-82. No pro playing experience. College coach: Tulsa 1984-87, 1990, Wisconsin 1988-89, Bowling Green 1991, East Carolina 1992-93, Pittsburgh 1994-96, North Dakota State 1997-2002 (head coach). Pro coach: St. Louis Rams 2003, joined Bears in 2004.

Jeremy Bates, quarterbacks; August 27, 1976, Manhattan, Kan. Quarterback Tennessee 1995, Rice 1997- 99. No pro playing experience. College coach: Southern California 2009. Pro coach: Tampa Bay Buccaneers 2002-04, New York Jets 2005, Denver Broncos 2006-08, Seattle Seahawks 2010, joined Bears in 2012.

Gill Byrd, asst. defensive backs/safeties; born February 20, 1961, San Francisco, Calif. Cornerback San Jose State 1979-1982. Pro cornerback San Diego Chargers 1983-1992. Pro coach: St. Louis Rams 2003-05, joined Bears in 2006.

Mike DeBord, tight ends; born February 7, 1956, Muncie, Ind. Offensive line Manchester College 1974-77. No pro playing experience. College coach: Franklin 1982-83, Fort Hays State 1984-86, Eastern Illinois 1987-88, Ball State 1989, Colorado State 1990-91, Northwestern 1992, Michigan 1992-99, 2004-07, Central Michigan 2000-03 (head coach). Pro coach: Seattle Seahawks 2008-09, joined Bears in 2010.

Darryl Drake, wide receivers; born December 11, 1956, Louisville, Ky. Wide receiver Western Kentucky 1975-78. Pro wide receiver Washington Redskins 1979, Ottawa Rough Riders (CFL) 1981, Cincinnati Bengals 1983. College coach: Western Kentucky 1983-1991, Georgia 1992-96, Baylor 1997, Texas 1998-2003. Pro coach: Joined Bears in 2004.

Andrew Hayes-Stoker, offensive assistant/wide receivers; born January 9, 1979, Arlington, Texas. Running back Texas Christian 1999-2001. No pro playing experience. Pro coach: Joined Bears in 2010.

Jon Hoke, defensive backs; born January 24, 1957, Kettering, Ohio. Defensive back Ball State 1976-79. Pro defensive back Chicago Bears 1980. College coach: Bowling Green 1983-86, San Diego State 1987-88, Kent State 1989-1993, Missouri 1994-98, Florida 1999-2001. Pro coach: Houston Texans 2002-08, joined Bears in 2009.

Tim Holt, offensive line; born November 29, 1973, Dighton, Mass. Offensive line Southern Connecticut State 1991-94. No pro playing experience. College coach: Southern Connecticut State 1995-96, 2004-07, Lehigh 1997-98, Cornell 1999-2000, American International 2001-03, Stonehill 2008. Pro coach: Tampa Bay Buccaneers 2009-2011, joined Bears in 2012.

Rusty Jones, strength and conditioning coordinator; born August 14, 1953, Berwick, Maine. Attended Springfield (Mass.) College. No college or pro playing experience. College coach: Springfield (Mass.) College 1979-1982. Pro coach: Buffalo Bills 1985-2004, joined Bears in 2005.

Rod Marinelli, defensive coordinator/asst. head coach; born July 13, 1949, Rosemead, Calif. Offensive/defensive tackle Utah 1968, offensive tackle California Lutheran 1970-72. No pro playing experience. College coach: Utah State 1976, California 1983-1991, Arizona State 1992-94, Southern California 1995. Pro coach: Tampa Bay Buccaneers 1996-2005, Detroit Lions 2006-08 (head coach), joined Bears in 2009.

Kevin O'Dea, asst. special teams; born June 9, 1960, Williamsport, Pa. Wide receiver/defensive back Lock Haven 1984-85. No pro playing experience. College coach: Lock Haven 1986, Cornell 1987, Virginia 1988-1990, Penn State 1991-93. Pro coach: San Diego Chargers 1994-95, Tampa Bay Buccaneers 1996-2001, Detroit Lions 2002-03, Arizona Cardinals 2004-05, Chicago Bears 2006-07, New York Jets 2008-09, joined Bears in 2011.

Mike Phair, defensive line; born November 8, 1969, Mesa, Ariz. Linebacker Mesa (Ariz.) C.C. 1988-89, Arizona State 1990-91. No pro playing experience. College coach: Arizona State 1999-2000, Tiffin University 2001. Pro coach: Seattle Seahawks 2008-2010, joined Bears in 2011.

Mikal Smith, defensive quality control; born November 16, 1976, Dallas. Safety Arizona 1995-97. No pro playing experience. College coach: Trinity International 2006-07. Pro coach: Joined Bears in 2010.

Tim Spencer, running backs; born December 10, 1960, Martin Ferry, Ohio. Running back Ohio State 1979-1982. Pro running back Chicago Blitz (USFL) 1983, Arizona Wranglers (USFL) 1984, Memphis Showboats (USFL) 1985, San Diego Chargers 1985-1990. College coach: Ohio State 1994-2003. Pro coach: Joined Bears in 2004.

Mike Tice, offensive coordinator; born February 2, 1959, Bay Shore, N.Y. Quarterback Maryland 1977-1980. Pro tight end Seattle Seahawks 1981-88, 1990-91, Washington Redskins 1989, Minnesota Vikings 1992-93, 1995. Pro coach: Minnesota Vikings 1996-2005 (head coach 2001-05), Jacksonville Jaguars 2006-09, joined Bears in 2010.

Dave Toub, special teams coordinator; born June 1, 1962, Ossining, N.Y. Offensive lineman Springfield College 1980-81, Texas-El Paso 1983-84. No pro playing experience. College coach: Texas El-Paso 1987-89, Missouri 1989-2000. Pro coach: Philadelphia Eagles 2001-03, joined Bears in 2004.

**National Football Conference
East Division
Team Colors:** Royal Blue, Metallic Silver
Blue, and White
**Cowboys Center, One Cowboys Parkway
Irving, Texas 75063
Telephone:** (972) 556-9900

2012 SCHEDULE
PRESEASON
Aug. 13 at Oakland 7:00
Aug. 18 at San Diego 8:00
Aug. 25 **St. Louis** 7:00
Aug. 29 **Miami** 7:30

REGULAR SEASON
Sep. 5   at New York Giants (Wed)...7:30
Sep. 16 at Seattle 3:05
Sep. 23 **Tampa Bay**......................12:00
Oct. 1   **Chicago** (Mon)...................7:30
Oct. 7   BYE
Oct. 14 at Baltimore.....................12:00
Oct. 21 at Carolina.......................12:00
Oct. 28 **New York Giants** 3:15
Nov. 4   at Atlanta...........................7:20
Nov. 11 at Philadelphia...................3:15
Nov. 18 **Cleveland** 12:00
Nov. 22 **Washington** (Thurs) 3:15
Dec. 2   **Philadelphia** *7:20
Dec. 9   at Cincinnati 12:00
Dec. 16 **Pittsburgh**........................3:15
Dec. 23 **New Orleans**...................12:00
Dec. 30 at Washington 12:00
*All times CT; Sunday night games in
Weeks 11-16 subject to change
Stadium: Cowboys Stadium (opened in 2009)
 •**Capacity:** 80,000 (expandable to
100,000 for special events)
One Legends Way
Arlington, Texas 76011
Playing Surface: Sportfield Softtop
Training Camp: Marriott Residence Inn
Oxnard, California 93030

COWBOYS STADIUM

CLUB OFFICIALS
Owner/President/General Manager:
Jerry Jones
Chief Operating Officer/Executive Vice
President/Director of Player Personnel:
Stephen Jones
Executive Vice President/VP of Brand
Management/President Charity
Foundation: Charlotte Anderson
Executive Vice President/Chief Sales and
Marketing Officer: Jerry Jones Jr.
CFO: David Frey
Senior Vice President, Sales and
Marketing: Greg McElroy
Senior Vice President and General
Counsel: Alec Scheiner
Vice President Public Relations/
Communications: Rich Dalrymple
Director of Corporate Communications:
Brett Daniels
Director of Community Relations and
Alumni Affairs: Emily Robbins
Director of College and Pro Scouting:
Tom Ciskowski
Director of Player Development:
Bryan Wansley
Director of Information Technology:
John Winborn
Director of Broadcasting: Scott Purcel
Internet Director: Derek Eagleton
Director of Ticket Operations:
Ann Bihari
Head Athletic Trainer: Jim Maurer
Equipment Manager: Mike McCord
Video Director: Robert Blackwell
Cheerleader Director: Kelli Finglass

COACHING HISTORY
(481-357-6)
Records include postseason games
1960-1988 Tom Landry 270-178-6
1989-1993 Jimmy Johnson 51-37-0
1994-97   Barry Switzer 45-26-0
1998-99   Chan Gailey 18-16-0
2000-02   Dave Campo 15-33-0
2003-06   Bill Parcells 34-32-0
2007-2010 Wade Phillips* 35-24-0
2010-11   Jason Garrett 13-11-0
*Released after eight games in 2010

PAID ATTENDANCE
Home 592,045   Away 555,846
Total 1,147,891
Single-game home record,
105,121 (9/20/09)
Single-season home record,
629,749 (2009)

2012 DRAFT CHOICES

Round	Name	Pos.	College
1	Morris Claiborne	DB	Louisiana St.
3	Tyrone Crawford	DE	Boise St.
4	Kyle Wilber	LB	Wake Forest
	Matt Johnson	DB	Eastern Washington
5	Danny Coale	WR	Virginia Tech
6	James Hanna	TE	Oklahoma
7	Caleb McSurdy	LB	Montana

DALLAS COWBOYS

2011 TEAM RECORD
PRESEASON (2-2)

Date	Result	Opponent
8/11	W 24-23	Denver
8/20	L 7-20	San Diego
8/27	W 23-17	at Minnesota
9/1	L 3-17	at Miami

REGULAR SEASON (8-8)

Date	Result	Opponent
9/11	L 24-27	at New York Jets
9/18	W 27-24	at San Francisco (OT)
9/26	W 18-16	Washington
10/2	L 30-34	Detroit
10/16	L 16-20	at New England
10/23	W 34-7	St. Louis
10/30	L 7-34	at Philadelphia
11/6	W 23-13	Seattle
11/13	W 44-7	Buffalo
11/20	W 27-24	at Washington (OT)
11/24	W 20-19	Miami
12/4	L 13-19	at Arizona (OT)
12/11	L 34-37	New York Giants
12/17	W 31-15	at Tampa Bay
12/24	L 7-20	Philadelphia
1/1	L 14-31	at New York Giants

(OT) Overtime

SCORE BY PERIODS

Cowboys	72	110	62	119	6	—	369
Opponents	51	112	75	103	6	—	347

2011 TEAM STATISTICS

	Cowboys	Opp.
Total First Downs	327	305
Rushing	91	78
Passing	219	199
Penalty	17	28
3rd Down: Made/Att	78/198	81/204
3rd Down Pct.	39.4	39.7
4th Down: Made/Att	5/10	4/11
4th Down Pct.	50.0	36.4
Possession Avg.	30:55	29:05
Total Net Yards	6008	5491
Avg. Per Game	375.5	343.2
Total Plays	1017	972
Avg. Per Play	5.9	5.6
Net Yards Rushing	1807	1585
Avg. Per Game	112.9	99.1
Total Rushes	408	385
Net Yards Passing	4201	3906
Avg. Per Game	262.6	244.1
Sacked/Yards Lost	39/252	42/243
Gross Yards	4453	4149
Att./Completions	570/376	545/336
Completion Pct.	66.0	61.7
Had Intercepted	12	15
Punts/Average	71/42.9	72/47.5
Net Punting Avg.	71/36.7	72/41.8
Penalties/Yards	114/816	85/650
Fumbles/Ball Lost	24/9	20/10
Touchdowns	39	38
Rushing	5	10
Passing	33	24
Returns	1	4

2011 INDIVIDUAL STATISTICS

PASSING

	Att.	Comp.	Yds.	Pct.	TD	Int.	Tkld.	Rate
Romo	522	346	4184	66.3	31	10	36/227	102.5
McGee	38	24	182	63.2	1	0	3/25	83.4
Kitna	10	6	87	60.0	1	2	0/0	82.1
Cowboys	570	376	4453	66.0	33	12	39/252	100.1
Opponents	545	336	4149	61.7	24	15	42/243	88.4

SCORING

	TD R	TD P	TD Rt	PAT	FG	Saf	PTS
Bailey	0	0	0	39/39	32/37	0	135
Robinson	0	11	0	0/0	0/0	0	66
Bryant	0	9	0	0/0	0/0	0	54
Austin	0	7	0	0/0	0/0	0	42
Witten	0	5	0	0/0	0/0	0	30
Murray	2	0	0	0/0	0/0	0	12
F. Jones	1	0	0	0/0	0/0	0	6
Newman	0	0	1	0/0	0/0	0	6
Phillips	0	1	0	0/0	0/0	0	6
Romo	1	0	0	0/0	0/0	0	6
Tanner	1	0	0	0/0	0/0	0	6
Cowboys	5	33	1	39/39	32/37	0	369
Opponents	10	24	4	35/35	26/33	1	347

2-Pt Conversions: Team 0-0, Opponents 2-2

RUSHING

	No.	Yds	Avg	LG	TD
Murray	164	897	5.5	91t	2
F. Jones	127	575	4.5	40	1
Morris	28	98	3.5	15	0
Tanner	22	76	3.5	17	1
Choice	28	75	2.7	14	0
Romo	22	46	2.1	17	1
McGee	4	28	7.0	12	0
Bryant	1	5	5.0	5	0
Fiammetta	4	4	1.0	3	0
Austin	2	3	1.5	5	0
Ogletree	2	3	1.5	7	0
Washington	1	-1	-1.0	-1	0
Kitna	3	-2	-.7	0	0
Cowboys	408	1807	4.4	91t	5
Opponents	385	1585	4.1	40	10

RECEIVING

	No.	Yds	Avg	LG	TD
Witten	79	942	11.9	64	5
Bryant	63	928	14.7	50t	9
Robinson	54	858	15.9	74	11
Austin	43	579	13.5	53t	7
F. Jones	33	221	6.7	27	0
Murray	26	183	7.0	18	0
Bennett	17	144	8.5	15	0
Ogletree	15	164	10.9	33	0
Phillips	15	101	6.7	12t	1
Choice	11	71	6.5	18	0
Holley	7	169	24.1	77	0
Morris	5	13	2.6	9	0
Fiammetta	3	39	13.0	15	0
Tanner	2	19	9.5	11	0
Washington	2	13	6.5	15	0
Chapas	1	9	9.0	9	0
Cowboys	376	4453	11.8	77	33
Opponents	336	4149	12.3	74t	24

INTERCEPTIONS

	No.	Yds	Avg	LG	TD
Lee	4	87	21.8	37	0
Newman	4	80	20.0	43t	1
Sensabaugh	2	11	5.5	11	0
Hatcher	1	16	16.0	16	0
Ball	1	15	15.0	15	0
Walker	1	5	5.0	5	0
Jenkins	1	3	3.0	3	0
Scandrick	1	0	0.0	0	0
Cowboys	15	217	14.5	43t	1
Opponents	12	158	13.2	56t	2

PUNTING

	No.	Yds.	Avg.	In 20	LG
McBriar	58	2542	43.8	21	68
C. Jones	10	426	42.6	4	54
Bailey	2	79	39.5	0	41
Cowboys	71	3047	42.9	25	68
Opponents	72	3420	47.5	21	70

PUNT RETURNS

	Ret	FC	Yds	Avg	LG	TD
Bryant	15	5	103	6.9	20	0
Harris	15	6	80	5.3	14	0
Owusu-Ansah	6	3	47	7.8	21	0
McCann	2	0	13	6.5	16	0
Ogletree	2	0	35	17.5	25	0
Holley	1	0	15	15.0	15	0
Cowboys	41	14	293	7.1	25	0
Opponents	30	17	278	9.3	55	0

KICKOFF RETURNS

	No.	Yds	Avg	LG	TD
Harris	8	231	28.9	51	0
F. Jones	7	186	26.6	69	0
Ogletree	6	114	19.0	25	0
Bryant	3	55	18.3	26	0
Owusu-Ansah	3	56	18.7	23	0
Murray	2	36	18.0	22	0
Phillips	2	26	13.0	16	0
Lissemore	1	38	38.0	38	0
McCann	1	26	26.0	26	0
Cowboys	33	768	23.3	69	0
Opponents	52	1114	21.4	43	0

FIELD GOALS

	1-19	20-29	30-39	40-49	50+
Bailey	1/1	8/9	11/11	10/12	2/4
Cowboys	1/1	8/9	11/11	10/12	2/4
Opponents	0/0	12/12	4/5	5/9	5/7

SACKS

	No.
Ware	19.5
Spencer	6.0
Hatcher	4.5
V. Butler	3.0
Lissemore	2.0
Ratliff	2.0
Scandrick	2.0
Coleman	1.0
McCray	1.0
Spears	1.0
Cowboys	42.0
Opponents	39.0

RECORD HOLDERS
INDIVIDUAL RECORDS—CAREER

Category	Name	Performance
Rushing (Yds.)	Emmitt Smith, 1990-2002	**17,162
Passing (Yds.)	Troy Aikman, 1989-2000	32,942
Passing (TDs)	Troy Aikman, 1989-2000	165
Receiving (No.)	Michael Irvin, 1988-1999	750
Receiving (Yds.)	Michael Irvin, 1988-1999	11,904
Interceptions	Mel Renfro, 1964-1977	52
Punting (Avg.)	Mat McBriar, 2004-2011	45.3
Punt Return (Avg.)	Deion Sanders, 1995-99	13.3
Kickoff Return (Avg.)	Mel Renfro, 1964-1977	26.4
Field Goals	Rafael Septien, 1978-1986	162
Touchdowns (Tot.)	Emmitt Smith, 1990-2002	164
Points	Emmitt Smith, 1990-2002	986
*Sacks	DeMarcus Ware, 2005-2011	99.5

INDIVIDUAL RECORDS—SINGLE SEASON

Category	Name	Performance
Rushing (Yds.)	Emmitt Smith, 1995	1,773
Passing (Yds.)	Tony Romo, 2009	4,483
Passing (TDs)	Tony Romo, 2007	36
Receiving (No.)	Michael Irvin, 1995	111
Receiving (Yds.)	Michael Irvin, 1995	1,603
Interceptions	Everson Walls, 1981	11
Punting (Avg.)	Mat McBriar, 2006	48.2
Punt Return (Avg.)	Bob Hayes, 1968	20.8
Kickoff Return (Avg.)	Mel Renfro, 1965	30.0
Field Goals	Richie Cunningham, 1997	34
Touchdowns (Tot.)	Emmitt Smith, 1995	25
Points	Emmitt Smith, 1995	150
*Sacks	DeMarcus Ware, 2008	20.0

INDIVIDUAL RECORDS—SINGLE GAME

Category	Name	Performance
Rushing (Yds.)	DeMarco Murray, 10-23-11	253
Passing (Yds.)	Don Meredith, 11-10-63	460
Passing (TDs)	Many times	5
	Last time by Tony Romo, 11-23-06	
Receiving (No.)	Jason Witten, 12-9-07	15
Receiving (Yds.)	Miles Austin, 10-11-09	250
Interceptions	Many times	3
	Last time by Terence Newman, 12-14-03	
Field Goals	Chris Boniol, 11-18-96	7
	Billy Cundiff, 9-15-03	7
Touchdowns (Tot.)	Many times	4
	Last time by Terrell Owens, 11-18-07	
Points	Many times	24
	Last time by Terrell Owens, 11-18-07	
*Sacks	Jim Jeffcoat, 11-10-85	5.0

*Sacks became an official statistic in 1982.
**NFL Record

2012 VETERAN ROSTER

No.	Name	Pos.	Ht.	Wt.	Birthdate	NFL Exp.	College	Hometown	How Acq.	'11 Games/ Starts
55	Albright, Alex	LB	6-5	256	1/29/88	2	Boston College	Cincinnati, Ohio	FA-'11	16/0
59	Atkins, Baraka	DE	6-4	271	8/28/84	4	Miami	Sarasota, Fla.	FA-'12	0*
19	Austin, Miles	WR	6-2	215	6/30/84	7	Monmouth	Garfield, N.J.	FA-'06	10/10
5	Bailey, Dan	K	6-0	188	1/26/88	2	Oklahoma State	Mustang, Okla.	FA-'11	16/0
73	Bernadeau, Mackenzy	G	6-4	308	1/3/86	5	Bentley	Waltham, Ma.	UFA(Car)-'12	15/1*
92	Brent, Josh	NT	6-2	320	1/30/88	3	Illinois	Bloomington, Ill.	S7-'10	11/0
88	Bryant, Dez	WR	6-2	225	11/4/88	3	Oklahoma State	Lufkin, Texas	D1-'10	15/13
57	Butler, Victor	LB	6-2	249	7/29/87	4	Oregon State	Rialto, Calif.	D4b-'09	16/0
11	Carpenter, Rudy	QB	6-2	212	4/15/86	3	Arizona State	Mt. Morris, Mich.	W(TB)-'12	1/0*
39	Carr, Brandon	CB	6-0	207	5/19/86	5	Grand Valley State	Flint, Mich.	UFA(KC)-'12	16/16*
54	Carter, Bruce	LB	6-3	246	2/19/88	2	North Carolina	Havelock, N.C.	D2-'11	10/0
42	Church, Barry	S	6-2	220	2/11/88	3	Toledo	Pittsburgh, Pa.	FA-'10	13/1
99	Coleman, Kenyon	DE	6-5	306	4/10/79	11	UCLA	Alta Loma, Calif.	UFA(Cle)-'11	16/15
52	Connor, Dan	LB	6-2	231	11/2/85	5	Penn State	Wallingford, Pa.	UFA(Car)-'12	15/11*
67	Costa, Phil	C	6-3	314	7/11/87	3	Maryland	Moorestown, N.J.	FA-'10	16/16
68	Free, Doug	T	6-6	323	1/6/84	6	Northern Illinois	Manitowoc, Wisc.	D4b-'07	16/16
96	Geathers, Clifton	DE	6-7	320	12/11/87	2	South Carolina	Georgetown, S.C.	W(Sea)-'10	5/0
17	Harris, Dwayne	WR	5-10	208	9/16/87	2	East Carolina	Stone Mountain, Ga.	D6-'11	7/0
97	Hatcher, Jason	DE	6-6	302	7/13/82	7	Grambling State	Jena, La.	D3b-'06	13/10
21	Jenkins, Mike	CB	5-10	202	3/22/85	5	South Florida	Bradenton, Fla.	D1b-'08	12/12
28	Jones, Felix	RB	5-10	217	5/8/87	5	Arkansas	Tulsa, Okla.	D1a-'08	12/8
60	Kowalski, Kevin	C/G	6-4	301	1/2/89	2	Toledo	Macedonia, Ohio	FA-'11	11/0
91	Ladouceur, Louis-Philippe	LS	6-5	260	3/13/81	8	California	Pointe-Claire, Quebec	FA-'05	16/0
50	Lee, Sean	LB	6-2	245	7/22/86	3	Penn State	Pittsburgh, Pa.	D2-'10	15/15
95	Lissemore, Sean	DE	6-4	306	9/11/87	3	William & Mary	Durmont, N.J.	D7-'10	16/0
71	Livings, Nate	G	6-5	332	3/16/82	5	Louisiana State	Lake Charles, La.	UFA(Cin)-'12	16/16*
40	McCray, Danny	S	6-1	222	3/10/88	3	Louisiana State	Houston, Texas	FA-'10	14/0
7	McGee, Stephen	QB	6-3	229	9/27/85	4	Texas A&M	Burnet, Texas	D4a-'09	1/0
29	Murray, DeMarco	RB	6-0	227	2/12/88	2	Oklahoma	Las Vegas, Nev.	D3-'11	13/7
61	Nagy, Bill	G	6-3	303	10/26/87	2	Wisconsin	Hudson, Ohio	D7b-'11	4/4
85	Ogletree, Kevin	WR	6-1	190	8/5/87	4	Virginia	Queens, N.Y.	FA-'09	14/1
18	Orton, Kyle	QB	6-4	225	11/14/82	8	Purdue	Altoona, Iowa	UFA(KC)-'12	9/8*
27	Owusu-Ansah, Akwasi	S	6-0	210	4/10/88	3	Indiana (PA)	Columbus, Ohio	W(Jac)-'12	7/2*
78	Parnell, Jermey	T	6-6	305	7/20/86	3	Mississippi	Blytheville, Ark.	FA-'10	3/0
89	Phillips, John	TE	6-5	261	6/11/87	4	Virginia	Warm Springs, Va.	D6b-'09	16/7
23	Pool, Brodney	S	6-2	210	5/24/84	8	Oklahoma	Houston, Texas	UFA(NYJ)-'12	14/6*
90	Ratliff, Jay	NT	6-4	287	8/29/81	8	Auburn	Valdosta, Ga.	D7-'05	16/16
9	Romo, Tony	QB	6-2	228	4/21/80	10	Eastern Illinois	Burlington, Wisc.	FA-'03	16/16
32	Scandrick, Orlando	CB	5-10	191	2/10/87	5	Boise State	Los Alamitos, Calif.	D5-'08	13/7
43	Sensabaugh, Gerald	S	6-1	208	6/13/83	8	North Carolina	Kingsport, Tenn.	UFA(Jax)-'09	16/16
77	Smith, Tyron	T	6-5	311	12/12/90	2	Southern California	Moreno Valley, Calif.	D1-'11	16/16
98	Spears, Marcus	DE	6-4	315	3/8/83	8	Louisiana State	Baton Rouge, La.	D1b-'05	16/5
93	Spencer, Anthony	LB	6-3	257	1/23/84	6	Purdue	Fort Wayne, Ind.	D1-'07	16/15
34	Tanner, Phillip	RB	6-0	218	8/8/88	2	Middle Tennessee State	Dallas, Texas	FA-'11	9/0
47	Vickers, Lawrence	FB	6-0	250	5/8/83	7	Colorado	Houston, Texas	FA-'12	14/1*
94	Ware, DeMarcus	LB	6-4	260	7/31/82	8	Troy	Auburn, Ala.	D1a-'05	16/16
27	Wilson, C.J.	CB	6-1	195	4/2/85	4	Baylor	Terrell, Texas	FA-'11	0*
82	Witten, Jason	TE	6-6	265	5/6/82	10	Tennessee	Elizabethton, Tenn.	D3-'03	16/16

* Atkins last active with Seattle in '08; Bernadeau played 15 games with Carolina in '11; Carpenter played in 1 game with Tampa Bay; Carr played 16 games with Kansas City; Connor played 15 games with Carolina; Livings played 16 games with Cincinnati; Orton played 5 games with Denver and 4 games with Kansas City; Owusu-Ansah played four games with Jacksonville in '11; Pool played 14 games with New York Jets; Vickers played 14 games with Houston; Wilson last active with Carolina in '10.

Players lost through free agency (3): TE Martellus Bennett (NYG; 14 games), LB Bradie James (Hou; 16), WR Laurent Robinson (Jax; 14).

Also played with Cowboys in '11—CB Alan Ball (16 games), LB Keith Brooking (16), K David Buehler (4), RB Tashard Choice (6), G Derrick Dockery (9), S Abram Elam (16), FB Tony Fiammetta (10), G Montrae Holland (10), WR Jesse Holley (16), QB Jon Kitna (3), G Kyle Kosier (16), P Mat McBriar (14), CB Bryan McCann (2), RB Sammy Morris (3), CB Terence Newman (14), S Akwasi Owusu-Ansah (3), TE Martin Rucker (1), CB Frank Walker (14), RB Chauncey Washington (2).

FIRST-YEAR ROSTER

Name	Pos.	Ht.	Wt.	Birthdate	College	Hometown	How Acq.
Adams, Jeff	T	6-6	308	9/6/89	Columbia	Western Springs, Ill.	FA
Adcock, Levy	T	6-5	320	11/12/88	Oklahoma State	Claremore, Okla.	FA
Arkin, David (1)	G	6-5	310	10/7/87	Missouri State	Wichita, Kan.	D4-'11
Bass, Ben	DE	6-4	288	10/12/89	Texas A&M	Plano, Texas	FA
Beasley, Cole	WR	5-8	174	4/26/89	Southern Methodist	Little Elm, Texas	FA
Benford, Tim	WR	5-11	205	9/7/89	Tennessee Tech	Chattanooga, Tenn.	FA
Bryan, George	TE	6-5	258	5/11/89	North Carolina State	Castle Hayne, N.C.	FA
Butler, Mario (1)	CB	6-1	191	10/19/84	Georgia Tech	Jacksonville, Fla.	FA-'11
Callaway, Robert (1)	DT	6-5	312	2/14/88	Saginaw Valley State	Mt. Morris, Mich.	FA-'11
Chapas, Shaun (1)	FB	6-2	249	5/2/88	Georgia	St. Augustine, Fla.	D7a-'11
Claiborne, Morris	CB	5-11	188	2/7/90	Louisiana State	Shreveport, La.	D1
Coale, Danny	WR	5-11	201	6/27/88	Virginia Tech	Lexington, Va.	FA
Crawford, Tyrone	DE	6-4	282	11/22/89	Boise State	Windsor, Ontario, Canada	FA
Dever, Taylor	T	6-5	298	5/6/89	Notre Dame	Nevada City, Calif.	FA
Dunbar, Lance	RB	5-8	197	1/25/90	North Texas	Haltom City, Texas	FA
Greenhouse, Isaiah (1)	LB	6-2	239	7/15/87	Northwestern State	Marksville, La.	FA
Gunn, Harland	G	6-2	319	8/30/89	Miami	Omaha, Neb.	FA
Hakim, Saalim	WR	5-11	191	2/1/90	Tarleton State	Atlanta, Ga.	FA
Hamilton, Adrian	LB	6-2	248	11/29/87	Prairie View A&M	Dallas, Texas	FA
Hanna, James	TE	6-4	252	7/14/89	Oklahoma	Flower Mound, Texas	D6
Holmes, Andre (1)	WR	6-5	208	6/16/88	Hillsdale	Elk Grove, Ill.	FA-'11
Hughlett, Charley	LS	6-4	258	5/16/90	Central Florida	Tampa, Fla.	FA
Johnson, Matt	S	6-1	211	7/22/89	Eastern Washington	Olympia, Wash.	D4b
Jones, Chris (1)	P	6-0	200	7/21/89	Carson Newman	Rome, Ga.	FA-'11
Kemp, Donavon	WR	6-1	191	12/29/88	Texas-El Paso	DeSoto, Texas	FA
Leary, Ronald	G	6-3	315	4/29/89	Memphis	Baton Rouge, La.	FA
Lemon, Orie (1)	LB	6-1	251	9/9/87	Oklahoma State	Houston, Texas	FA-'11
Madison, Isaac	CB	5-10	180	4/30/89	Arkansas	Dallas, Texas	FA
McSurdy, Caleb	LB	6-1	246	2/24/90	Montana	Boise, Idaho	D7
Novikoff, Tyrone	T	6-7	316	5/25/88	Idaho	Curlew, Wash.	FA
Olawale, Jamize	FB	6-0	235	4/17/89	North Texas	Long Beach, Calif.	FA
Radway, Raymond (1)	WR	6-3	198	7/5/87	Abilene Christian	McKinney, Texas	FA-'11
Rogers, Jake	P	6-3	195	5/24/87	Cincinnati	Warsaw, Indiana	W(TB)
Scott, Darrell	RB	6-0	233	4/16/89	South Florida	Ventura, Calif.	FA
Silva, Mana (1)	S	6-1	220	8/17/88	Hawaii	Hilo, Hawaii	FA-'11
Smith, Lionel	CB	5-11	192	8/18/87	Texas A&M	Houston, Texas	FA
Szczerba, Andrew	TE	6-6	262	7/16/88	Penn State	Wilmington, Del.	FA
Taplin-Ross, Justin (1)	S	6-3	214	3/26/89	Utah	Murrieta, Calif.	FA
Whiteside, Aston	LB	6-2	260	5/19/89	Abilene Christian	Vernon, Texas	FA
Whitley, Eddie	S	6-0	191	10/26/89	Virginia Tech	Charlotte, N.C.	FA
Wilber, Kyle	LB	6-4	242	4/26/89	Wake Forest	Apopka, Fla.	D4a
Williams, Teddy (1)	CB	6-3	205	7/3/88	Texas, San Antonio	Tyler, Texas	FA-'10

The term NFL Rookie is defined as a player who is in his first season of professional football and has not been on the roster of another professional football team for any regular-season or postseason games. A Rookie is designated by an "R" on NFL rosters. Players who have been active in another professional football league or players who have NFL experience, including either preseason training camp or being on an Active List or Inactive List, or on Reserve/Injured or Reserve/Physically Unable to Perform for fewer than six regular-season games, are termed NFL First-Year Players. An NFL First-Year Player is designated by a "1" on NFL rosters. Thereafter, a player is credited with an additional year of experience for each season in which he accumulates six games on the Active List or Inactive List, or on Reserve/Injured or Reserve/Physically Unable to Perform.

Log on to www.dallascowboys.com for an up-to-date roster.

COACHING STAFF

Head Coach,
Jason Garrett
Pro Career: Named the eighth head coach in Dallas Cowboys history on January 5, 2011 and became the first former Cowboys player to become the team's head coach. Named the club's interim head coach at the midpoint of the 2010 season and went on to guide a Dallas team that had started the season with a 1-7 record to a 5-3 mark down the stretch. Since the 2007 season Garrett had been the Cowboys offensive coordinator, and in 2008, he was assigned the additional duties of being the club's assistant head coach. Under Garrett, the Dallas offense finished among the NFL's top-10 three times: 2010 (10th), 2009 (2nd), and 2007 (2nd). From 2007 to 2009 the cumulative numbers for total net yards (17,753), gross yards (12,761) and passing yards (12,181) represented the best totals over a three-year span in the history of the organization. En route to winning the 2009 NFC Eastern Division title, Dallas established club records for total offensive yards (6,390), net passing yards (4,287) and pass completions (347). Dallas won the NFC East in 2007 with a team-record tying 13 victories and finished second in the NFL in scoring. Garrett was named *Pro Football Weekly's* NFL's Assistant Coach of the Year in March of 2008. Career record: 13-11.
Background: Played quarterback at Princeton (1987-88) and was named the Ivy League's Player of the Year and honorable mention All American as a senior. Played professionally in World League and Canadian Football League (both 1991) before joining Dallas (1992-99), Giants (2000-03), Buccaneers (2004) and Dolphins (also 2004). Key reserve on three Super Bowl teams with the Cowboys and one with the Giants. Began his coaching career as quarterbacks coach with Dolphins for Nick Saban.
Personal: Born March 28, 1966, in Abington, Pa. He and his wife Brill reside in Dallas.

ASSISTANT COACHES

Brian Baker, defensive line; born June 20, 1962, Baltimore, Md. Linebacker Maryland 1981-83. No pro playing experience. College coach: Maryland 1984-85, Army 1986, Georgia Tech 1987-1995. Pro coach: San Diego Chargers 1996, Detroit Lions 1997-2000, Minnesota Vikings 2001-05, St. Louis Rams 2006-2008, Carolina Panthers 2009-2010, joined Cowboys in 2011.
Joe Baker, asst. secondary coach; born June 29, 1969, Glen Ridge, N.J. Wide receiver Princeton 1987-1990. No pro playing experience. College coach: East Stroudsburg 1991, Samford 1993, Wisconsin 1999. Pro coach: Birmingham Fire (WFL) 1992, Jacksonville

1995-98, New Orleans Saints 2000-04, Green Bay Packers 2005, St. Louis Rams 2006, Denver Broncos 2007-08, Tampa Bay Buccaneers 2009-2011, joined Cowboys in 2012.
Ben Bloom, defensive quality control/linebackers; born October 17, 1982, Wellesley, Mass. Offensive line Tufts 2001-04. No pro playing experience. College coach: Tufts 2005-07, Harvard 2008. Pro coach: Cleveland Browns 2010, joined Cowboys in 2011.
Chris Boniol, asst. special teams/kickers; born December 9, 1971, Alexandria, La. Kicker Louisiana Tech 1990-93. Pro kicker Dallas Cowboys 1994-96, Philadelphia Eagles 1997-98, Chicago Bears 1999. Pro coach: Joined Cowboys in 2010.
Dave Borgonzi, offensive/defensive assistant; born November 19, 1982, Everett, Mass. Linebacker Amherst College 2001-04. No pro playing experience. College coach: Syracuse 2006-07, Harvard 2008-10. Pro coach: Joined Cowboys in 2011.
Bill Callahan, offensive coordinator/offensive line; born July 31, 1956, Chicago, Ill. Quarterback Benedictine 1975-77. No pro playing experience. College coach: Illinois 1980-86, Northern Arizona 1987-88, Southern Illinois 1989, Wisconsin 1990-94, Nebraska 2004-07 (head coach). Pro coach: Philadelphia Eagles 1995-97, Oakland Raiders 1998-2003 (head coach 2002-03), New York Jets 2008-2011, joined Cowboys in 2012.
Joe DeCamillis, special teams coordinator; born June 29, 1965, Arvada, Colo. Attended Wyoming. No college or pro playing experience. Pro coach: Denver Broncos 1988-1992, New York Giants 1993-96, Atlanta Falcons 1997-2006, Jacksonville Jaguars 2007-08, joined Cowboys in 2009.
Matt Eberflus, linebackers; born May 17, 1970, Toledo, Ohio. Linebacker Toledo 1988-1991. No pro playing experience. College coach: Toledo 1992-2000, Missouri 2001-08. Pro coach: Cleveland Browns 2009-2010, joined Cowboys in 2011.
John Garrett, passing game coordinator/tight ends; born March 2, 1965, Danville, Pa. Wide receiver Columbia 1983-85, Princeton 1986-87. Pro wide receiver Cincinnati Bengals 1989, Buffalo Bills 1991, San Antonio Riders (World League) 1991. College coach: Virginia 2004-06. Pro coach: Cincinnati Bengals 1995-98, 2001-02, Arizona Cardinals 1999-2000, joined Cowboys in 2007.
Jerome Henderson, secondary; born August 8, 1969, Portsmouth, Va. Defensive back Clemson 1987-1990. Pro cornerback New England Patriots 1991-93, 1996, Buffalo Bills 1993-94, Philadelphia Eagles 1995, New York Jets 1997-98. Pro coach: New York Jets 2007-08, Cleveland Browns 2009-2011, joined Cowboys in 2012.
Leon Lett, defensive assistant/defensive line; born October 12, 1968, Mobile, Ala.

Defensive tackle Hinds (Miss.) C.C. 1987-88, Emporia State 1989-1990. Pro defensive tackle Dallas Cowboys 1991-2000, Denver Broncos 2001. College coach: Louisiana-Monroe 2009-2010. Pro coach: Joined Cowboys in 2011.
Keith O'Quinn, offensive quality control/wide receivers; born July 28, 1973, Pensacola, Fla. Safety North Texas 1991-96. No pro playing experience. College coach: Hardin-Simmons 2000-02, Abilene Christian 2003-04. Pro coach: Joined Cowboys in 2010.
Skip Peete, running backs; born January 30, 1963, Mesa, Ariz. Wide receiver Arizona 1981-82, Kansas 1984-85. Pro wide receiver New York Jets 1987. College coach: Pittsburgh 1988-1992, Michigan State 1993-94, Rutgers 1995, UCLA 1996-97. Pro coach: Oakland Raiders 1998-2006, joined Cowboys in 2007.
Wes Phillips, asst. offensive line; born February 17, 1979, Houston, Texas. Quarterback Texas-El Paso 1997-2001. Pro quarterback San Diego Riptide (AFL2) 2002-03. College coach: Texas-El Paso 2003, West Texas A&M 2004-05, Baylor 2006. Pro coach: Joined Cowboys in 2007.
Jimmy Robinson, asst. head coach/wide receivers; born January 3, 1953, Atlanta, Ga. Wide receiver Georgia Tech 1972-74. Pro wide receiver N.Y. Giants 1976-79, San Francisco 49ers 1980, Denver Broncos 1981. College coach: Georgia Tech 1987-89. Pro coach: Memphis Showboats (USFL) 1984-85, Atlanta Falcons 1990-93, Indianapolis Colts 1994-97, New York Giants 1998-2003, New Orleans Saints 2004-05, Green Bay Packers 2006-2010, joined Cowboys in 2011.
Rob Ryan, defensive coordinator; born December 13, 1962, Ardmore, Okla. Linebacker Oklahoma State 1984. Southwestern Oklahoma State 1985-86. No pro playing experience. College coach: Western Kentucky 1987, Ohio State 1988, Tennessee State 1989-1993, Hutchinson (Kan.) C.C. 1996, Oklahoma State 1997-99. Pro coach: Arizona Cardinals 1994-95, New England Patriots 2000-03, Oakland Raiders 2004-08, Cleveland Browns 2009-2010, joined Cowboys in 2011.
Wade Wilson, quarterbacks; born February 1, 1959, Commerce, Texas. Quarterback East Texas State 1977-1980. Pro quarterback Minnesota Vikings 1981-1991, Atlanta Falcons 1992, New Orleans Saints 1993-94, Dallas Cowboys 1995-97, Oakland Raiders 1998-99. Pro coach: Dallas Cowboys 2000-02, Chicago Bears 2004-06, re-joined Cowboys in 2007.
Mike Woicik, strength and conditioning; born September 26, 1956, Baltimore. Attended Boston College. No college or pro playing experience. College coach: Springfield College 1978-1980, Syracuse 1980-89. Pro coach: Dallas Cowboys 1990-96, New Orleans Saints 1997-99, New England Patriots 2000-10, re-joined Cowboys in 2011.

National Football Conference
North Division
Team Colors: Honolulu Blue and Silver
222 Republic Drive
Allen Park, Michigan 48101
Telephone: (313) 216-4000

2012 SCHEDULE
PRESEASON
Aug. 10 **Cleveland** 7:30
Aug. 17 at Baltimore........................8:00
Aug. 25 at Oakland..........................7:00
Aug. 30 **Buffalo**...............................7:00

REGULAR SEASON
Sep. 9   **St. Louis** 1:00
Sep. 16 at San Francisco.................8:20
Sep. 23 at Tennessee 1:00
Sep. 30 **Minnesota** 1:00
Oct. 7   BYE
Oct. 14 at Philadelphia....................1:00
Oct. 22 at Chicago (Mon) 8:30
Oct. 28 **Seattle**...............................1:00
Nov. 4   at Jacksonville....................1:00
Nov. 11 at Minnesota 1:00
Nov. 18 **Green Bay**.........................1:00
Nov. 22 **Houston** (Thurs)...............12:30
Dec. 2   **Indianapolis**......................1:00
Dec. 9   at Green Bay *8:20
Dec. 16 at Arizona............................4:05
Dec. 22 **Atlanta** (Sat) 8:30
Dec. 30 **Chicago** 1:00
*All times ET; Sunday night games in
   Weeks 11-16 subject to change*

Stadium: Ford Field (opened in 2002)
   •**Capacity:** 64,500
   2000 Brush Street
   Detroit, Michigan 48226
Playing Surface: FieldTurf
Training Camp: 222 Republic Drive
   Allen Park, Michigan
   48101

FORD FIELD

CLUB OFFICIALS
Chairman and Owner: William Clay Ford
Vice Chairman: William Clay Ford, Jr.
President: Tom Lewand
Executive Vice President of Football
   Operations and General Manager:
   Martin Mayhew
Senior Vice President of
   Communications: Bill Keenist
Senior Vice President & CFO: Luis Perez
Corporate Secretary: David Hempstead
Senior Personnel Executive: James Harris
Vice President of Pro Personnel:
   Sheldon White
Vice President of Football Operations:
   Cedric Saunders
Director of College Scouting:
   Scott McEwen
Player Personnel: Cary Conklin,
   Chad Henry, Joe Kelleher,
   Rob Lohman, Miller McCalmon,
   Silas McKinnie, Lance Newmark,
   Charlie Sanders, Dave Sears,
   Dave Uyrus
Senior Director of Community Affairs:
   Robert Wooley
Director of Media Relations:
   Matt Barnhart
Director of Broadcasting and Production:
   Bryan Bender
Director of Ticket Operations:
   Mark Graham
Coordinator of Athletic Medicine/Athletic
   Trainer: Dean Kleinschmidt
Athletic Trainer: Al Bellamy
Equipment Manager: Tim O'Neill
Video Director: Robert Yanagi

COACHING HISTORY
Portsmouth Spartans 1930-33
(513-610-32)
Records include postseason games

1930	Hal (Tubby) Griffen	5-6-3
1931-36	George (Potsy) Clark	...49-20-6
1937-38	Earl (Dutch) Clark	14-8-0
1939	Elmer (Gus) Henderson	...6-5-0
1940	George (Potsy) Clark	5-5-1
1941-42	Bill Edwards*	4-9-1
1942	John Karcis	0-8-0
1943-47	Charles (Gus) Dorais	...20-31-2
1948-1950	Alvin (Bo) McMillin	12-24-0
1951-56	Raymond (Buddy) Parker	..50-24-2
1957-1964	George Wilson	55-45-6
1965-66	Harry Gilmer	10-16-2
1967-1972	Joe Schmidt	43-35-7
1973	Don McCafferty	6-7-1
1974-76	Rick Forzano**	15-17-0
1976-77	Tommy Hudspeth	11-13-0
1978-1984	Monte Clark	43-63-1
1985-88	Darryl Rogers***	18-40-0
1988-1996	Wayne Fontes	67-71-0
1997-2000	Bobby Ross****	27-32-0
2000	Gary Moeller	4-3-0
2001-02	Marty Mornhinweg	5-27-0
2003-05	Steve Mariucci#	15-28-0
2005	Dick Jauron	1-4-0
2006-08	Rod Marinelli	10-38-0
2009-2011	Jim Schwartz	18-31-0

   *Released after three games in 1942
   **Resigned after four games in 1976
   ***Released after 11 games in 1988
   ****Resigned after nine games in 2000
   # Released after 11 games in 2005

PAID ATTENDANCE
Home 498,983   Away 509,713
Total 1,008,696
Single-game home record,
   80,444 (12/20/81)
Single-season home record, 644,904
   (1980)

2012 DRAFT CHOICES

Round	Name	Pos.	College
1	Riley Reiff	T	Iowa
2	Ryan Broyles	WR	Oklahoma
3	Dwight Bentley	DB	Louisiana-Lafayette
4	Ronnell Lewis	DE	Oklahoma
5	Tahir Whitehead	LB	Temple
	Chris Greenwood	DB	Albion
6	Jonte Green	DB	New Mexico St.
7	Travis Lewis	LB	Oklahoma

2011 TEAM RECORD
PRESEASON (4-0)

Date	Result	Opponent
8/12	W 34-3	Cincinnati
8/19	W 30-28	at Cleveland
8/27	W 34-10	New England
9/1	W 16-6	at Buffalo

REGULAR SEASON (10-6)

Date	Result	Opponent
9/11	W 27-20	at Tampa Bay
9/18	W 48-3	Kansas City
9/25	W 26-23	at Minnesota (OT)
10/2	W 34-30	at Dallas
10/10	W 24-13	Chicago
10/16	L 19-25	San Francisco
10/23	L 16-23	Atlanta
10/30	W 45-10	at Denver
11/13	L 13-37	at Chicago
11/20	W 49-35	Carolina
11/24	L 15-27	Green Bay
12/4	L 17-31	at New Orleans
12/11	W 34-28	Minnesota
12/18	W 28-27	at Oakland
12/24	W 38-10	San Diego
1/1	L 41-45	at Green Bay

(OT) Overtime

POSTSEASON (0-1)

1/7	L 28-45	at New Orleans

SCORE BY PERIODS

Lions	80	125	125	141	3	—	474
Opponents	86	145	74	82	0	—	387

2011 TEAM STATISTICS

	Lions	Opp.
Total First Downs	349	325
Rushing	71	91
Passing	244	195
Penalty	34	39
3rd Down: Made/Att	76/212	67/205
3rd Down Pct.	35.8	32.7
4th Down: Made/Att	8/14	8/19
4th Down Pct.	57.1	42.1
Possession Avg.	30:06	29:54
Total Net Yards	6337	5881
Avg. Per Game	396.1	367.6
Total Plays	1058	1055
Avg. Per Play	6.0	5.6
Net Yards Rushing	1523	2050
Avg. Per Game	95.2	128.1
Total Rushes	356	410
Net Yards Passing	4814	3831
Avg. Per Game	300.9	239.4
Sacked/Yards Lost	36/257	41/271
Gross Yards	5071	4102
Att./Completions	666/423	604/376
Completion Pct.	63.5	62.3
Had Intercepted	16	21
Punts/Average	82/43.6	78/45.3
Net Punting Avg.	82/36.0	78/40.1
Penalties/Yards	128/1075	119/982
Fumbles/Ball Lost	20/7	25/13
Touchdowns	57	42
Rushing	9	10
Passing	41	26
Returns	7	6

2011 INDIVIDUAL STATISTICS

PASSING

	Att.	Comp.	Yds.	Pct.	TD	Int.	Tkld.	Rate
Stafford	663	421	5038	63.5	41	16	36/257	97.2
Sh. Hill	3	2	33	66.7	0	0	0/0	103.5
Lions	666	423	5071	63.5	41	16	36/257	97.2
Opponents	604	376	4102	62.3	26	21	41/271	82.1

SCORING

	TD R	TD P	TD Rt	PAT	FG	Saf	PTS
Hanson	0	0	0	54/54	24/29	0	126
Johnson	0	16	0	0/0	0/0	0	96
K. Smith	4	3	0	0/0	0/0	0	42
Scheffler	0	6	0	0/0	0/0	0	38
T. Young	0	6	0	0/0	0/0	0	38
Pettigrew	0	5	0	0/0	0/0	0	30
Best	2	1	0	0/0	0/0	0	18
Burleson	0	3	0	0/0	0/0	0	18
Avril	0	0	2	0/0	0/0	0	12
Houston	0	0	2	0/0	0/0	0	12
Morris	1	1	0	0/0	0/0	0	12
K. Williams	2	0	0	0/0	0/0	0	12
Carpenter	0	0	1	0/0	0/0	0	6
A. Smith	0	0	1	0/0	0/0	0	6
Tulloch	0	0	1	0/0	0/0	0	6
Lions	9	41	7	54/54	24/29	1	474
Opponents	10	26	6	41/41	30/34	1	387

2-Pt Conversions: Scheffler, T. Young
Lions 2 -3, Opponents 1-1

RUSHING

	No.	Yds	Avg	LG	TD
Best	84	390	4.6	88t	2
K. Smith	72	356	4.9	43	4
Morris	80	316	4.0	31	1
K. Williams	58	195	3.4	18	2
Burleson	11	85	7.7	20	0
Stafford	22	78	3.5	22	0
Harrison	14	41	2.9	9	0
Logan	9	32	3.6	16	0
T. Young	2	15	7.5	11	0
Johnson	1	11	11.0	11	0
Scheffler	1	5	5.0	5	0
A. Brown	1	0	0.0	0	0
Sh. Hill	1	-1	-1.0	-1	0
Lions	356	1523	4.3	88t	9
Opponents	410	2050	5.0	65t	10

RECEIVING

	No.	Yds	Avg	LG	TD
Johnson	96	1681	17.5	73t	16
Pettigrew	83	777	9.4	27	5
Burleson	73	757	10.4	47	3
T. Young	48	607	12.6	57t	6
Best	27	287	10.6	60	1
Scheffler	26	347	13.3	36t	6
Morris	26	230	8.8	16	1
K. Smith	22	179	8.1	28t	3
K. Williams	8	62	7.8	12	0
Heller	6	42	7.0	12	0
R. Davis	4	63	15.8	22	0
Logan	1	19	19.0	19	0
A. Brown	1	9	9.0	9	0
Stovall	1	8	8.0	8	0
Harrison	1	3	3.0	3	0
Lions	423	5071	12.0	73t	41
Opponents	376	4102	10.9	80t	26

INTERCEPTIONS

	No.	Yds	Avg	LG	TD
Houston	5	225	45.0	100t	2
Wright	4	49	12.3	22	0
A. Smith	3	64	21.3	30t	1
Spievey	3	47	15.7	30	0
Tulloch	2	9	4.5	9	0
Carpenter	1	34	34.0	34t	1
C. Harris	1	19	19.0	19	0
Levy	1	7	7.0	7	0
Avril	1	4	4.0	4t	1
Lions	21	458	21.8	100t	5
Opponents	16	140	8.8	44t	3

PUNTING

	No.	Yds.	Avg.	In 20	LG
Donahue	49	2093	42.7	13	60
Graham	28	1235	44.1	10	58
Malone	5	245	49.0	0	62
Lions	82	3573	43.6	23	62
Opponents	78	3530	45.3	25	70

PUNT RETURNS

	Ret	FC	Yds	Avg	LG	TD
Logan	37	28	301	8.1	28	0
McDonald	1	0	0	0.0	0	0
Lions	38	28	301	7.9	28	0
Opponents	36	13	484	13.4	82t	1

KICKOFF RETURNS

	No.	Yds	Avg	LG	TD
Logan	33	832	25.2	42	0
R. Davis	2	34	17.0	18	0
Fluellen	1	6	6.0	6	0
Morris	1	15	15.0	15	0
Lions	37	887	24.0	42	0
Opponents	49	1255	25.6	101t	1

FIELD GOALS

	1-19	20-29	30-39	40-49	50+
Hanson	0/0	9/9	8/9	2/4	5/7
Lions	0/0	9/9	8/9	2/4	5/7
Opponents	0/0	5/5	13/13	9/12	3/4

SACKS

	No.
Avril	11.0
Vanden Bosch	8.0
Jackson	4.5
Suh	4.0
Tulloch	3.0
W. Young	3.0
C. Williams	2.0
Sa. Hill	1.5
Durant	1.0
Fairley	1.0
Levy	1.0
Spievey	1.0
Lions	41.0
Opponents	36.0

RECORD HOLDERS
INDIVIDUAL RECORDS—CAREER

Category	Name	Performance
Rushing (Yds.)	Barry Sanders, 1989-1998	15,269
Passing (Yds.)	Bobby Layne, 1950-58	15,710
Passing (TDs)	Bobby Layne, 1950-58	118
Receiving (No.)	Herman Moore, 1991-2001	670
Receiving (Yds.)	Herman Moore, 1991-2001	9,174
Interceptions	Dick LeBeau, 1959-1972	62
Punting (Avg.)	Yale Lary, 1952-53, 1956-1964	44.3
Punt Return (Avg.)	Jack Christiansen, 1951-58	12.8
Kickoff Return (Avg.)	Pat Studstill, 1961-67	25.7
Field Goals	Jason Hanson, 1992-2011	463
Touchdowns (Tot.)	Barry Sanders, 1989-1998	109
Points	Jason Hanson, 1992-2011	2,016
*Sacks	Robert Porcher, 1992-2003	95.5

INDIVIDUAL RECORDS—SINGLE SEASON

Category	Name	Performance
Rushing (Yds.)	Barry Sanders, 1997	2,053
Passing (Yds.)	Matthew Stafford, 2011	5,038
Passing (TDs)	Matthew Stafford, 2011	41
Receiving (No.)	Herman Moore, 1995	123
Receiving (Yds.)	Herman Moore, 1995	1,686
Interceptions	Don Doll, 1950	12
	Jack Christiansen, 1953	12
Punting (Avg.)	Yale Lary, 1963	48.9
Punt Return (Avg.)	Pat Studstill, 1962	15.8
Kickoff Return (Avg.)	Mel Gray, 1994	28.4
Field Goals	Jason Hanson, 1993	34
Touchdowns (Tot.)	Barry Sanders, 1991	17
Points	Jason Hanson, 1995	132
*Sacks	Robert Porcher, 1999	15.0

INDIVIDUAL RECORDS—SINGLE GAME

Category	Name	Performance
Rushing (Yds.)	Barry Sanders, 11-13-94	237
Passing (Yds.)	Matthew Stafford, 1-1-12	520
Passing (TDs)	Gary Danielson, 12-9-78	5
	Matthew Stafford, 11-9-09, 11-20-11, 1-1-12	5
Receiving (No.)	Herman Moore, 12-4-95	14
Receiving (Yds.)	Cloyce Box, 12-3-50	302
Interceptions	Don Doll, 10-23-49	**4
Field Goals	Garo Yepremian, 11-13-66	6
	Jason Hanson, 10-17-99	6
Touchdowns (Tot.)	Dutch Clark, 10-22-34	4
	Cloyce Box, 12-3-50	4
	Barry Sanders, 11-24-91	4
Points	Dutch Clark, 10-22-34	24
	Cloyce Box, 12-3-50	24
	Barry Sanders, 11-24-91	24
*Sacks	Bill Gay, 9-4-83	5.5

*Sacks became an official statistic in 1982.
**NFL Record

2012 VETERAN ROSTER

No.	Name	Pos.	Ht.	Wt.	Birthdate	NFL Exp.	College	Hometown	How Acq.	'11 Games/ Starts
92	f-Avril, Cliff	DE	6-3	260	4/8/86	5	Purdue	Green Cove Springs, Fla.	D3c-'08	16/16
76	Backus, Jeff	T	6-5	305	9/21/77	12	Michigan	Norcross, Ga.	D1-'01	16/16
35	Bell, Joique	RB	5-11	220	8/4/86	2	Wayne State	Benton Harbor, Mich.	FA-'11	0*
32	Berry, Aaron	CB	5-11	180	6/25/88	3	Pittsburgh	Harrisburg, Pa.	FA-'10	11/3
44	Best, Jahvid	RB	5-10	199	1/30/89	3	California	Richmond, Calif.	D1b-'10	6/6
95	Brown, Everette	DE	6-1	256	8/7/87	3	Florida State	Stantonsburg, N.C.	FA-'12	3/0*
13	Burleson, Nate	WR	6-0	198	8/19/81	10	Nevada	Seattle, Wash.	UFA(Sea)-'10	16/11
31	Carey, Don	CB	5-11	192	2/14/87	4	Norfolk State	Norfolk, Va.	FA-'11	5/0
77	Cherilus, Gosder	T	6-7	325	6/28/84	5	Boston College	Somerville, Mass.	D1-'08	16/15
24	Coleman, Erik	S	5-10	207	5/6/82	9	Washington State	Spokane, Wash.	FA-'11	4/0
72	Culbreath, Johnny	T	6-5	322	1/27/88	2	South Carolina State	Monroe, Ga.	D7-'11	0*
26	Delmas, Louis	S	5-11	202	4/12/87	4	Western Michigan	North Miami Beach, Fla.	D2-'09	11/11
6	Donahue, Ryan	P	6-3	190	3/17/88	2	Iowa	Evergreen Park, Ill.	FA-'11	8/0
52	Durant, Justin	LB	6-1	240	9/20/85	6	Hampton	Florence, S.C.	UFA(Jax)-'11	13/12
98	Fairley, Nick	DT	6-4	298	1/23/88	2	Auburn	Mobile, Ala.	D1-'11	10/0
96	Fluellen, Andre	DT	6-2	302	3/7/85	5	Florida State	Cartersville, Ga.	D3b-'08	13/0
70	Fox, Jason	T	6-6	314	5/2/88	3	Miami	Fort Worth, Texas	D4-'10	0*
65	Gandy, Dylan	G	6-3	295	3/8/82	7	Texas Tech	Harlingen, Texas	FA-'09	16/0
2	Graham, Ben	P	6-5	236	11/2/73	8	Deakin (Australia)	Geelong, Victoria, Australia	FA-'11	7/0
4	Hanson, Jason	K	6-0	190	6/17/70	21	Washington State	Spokane, Wash.	D2b-'92	16/0
36	Harrison, Jerome	RB	5-9	205	2/26/83	7	Washington State	Kalamazoo, Mich.	UFA(Phil)-'11	4/0
89	Heller, Will	TE	6-6	275	2/28/81	10	Georgia Tech	Dunwoody, Ga.	UFA(Sea)-'09	16/6
91	Hill, Sammie	DT	6-4	329	11/8/86	4	Stillman	West Blocton, Ala.	D(4)-'09	16/3
14	Hill, Shaun	QB	6-3	220	1/9/80	11	Maryland	Parsons, Kan.	T(SF)-'10	2/0
78	Hilliard, Corey	T	6-6	300	4/26/85	4	Oklahoma State	New Orleans, La.	FA-'09	16/1
57	Hogue, Doug	LB	6-2	226	2/1/89	2	Syracuse	Yonkers, N.Y.	D(5)-'11	13/0
23	Houston, Chris	CB	5-11	178	10/18/84	6	Arkansas	Austin, Texas	T(Atl)-'10	14/13
86	Hughes, Nate	WR	6-2	195	1/18/85	3	Alcorn State	Starkville, Miss	FA-'11	0*
94	Jackson, Lawrence	DE	6-4	271	8/30/85	5	Southern California	Inglewood, Calif.	T(Sea)-'10	11/0
81	Johnson, Calvin	WR	6-5	236	9/29/85	6	Georgia Tech	Tyrone, Ga.	D1-'07	16/16
21	Lacey, Jacob	CB	5-10	177	5/28/87	4	Oklahoma State	Garland, Texas	FA-'12	15/10*
25	Leshoure, Mikel	RB	6-0	233	1/25/88	2	Illinois	Champaign, Ill.	D2b-'11	0*
54	Levy, DeAndre	LB	6-2	238	3/26/87	4	Wisconsin	Milwaukee, Wisc.	D3a-'09	16/16
11	Logan, Stefan	WR	5-6	180	6/2/81	4	South Dakota	Miami, Fla.	W(Pitt)-'10	16/1
80	Long, Lance	WR	5-11	186	5/4/86	2	Mississippi State	Shelby Township, Mich.	FA-'12	0*
63	McClendon, Jacques	G	6-3	324	12/10/87	2	Tennessee	Cleveland, Tenn.	FA-'11	0*
48	Muhlbach, Don	LS	6-4	265	8/17/81	9	Texas A&M	Lufkin, Texas	FA-'04	16/0
49	Norris, Slade	LB	6-2	232	10/25/85	4	Oregon State	Portland, Ore.	FA-'11	0*
58	Palmer, Ashlee	LB	6-1	236	4/7/86	4	Mississippi	Compton, Calif.	W(Buff)-'10	16/0
66	Peterman, Stephen	G	6-4	323	1/11/82	8	Louisiana State	Waveland, Miss.	FA-'06	16/16
87	Pettigrew, Brandon	TE	6-5	265	2/23/85	4	Oklahoma State	Tyler, Texas	D(1b)-'09	16/16
51	Raiola, Dominic	C	6-1	295	12/30/78	12	Nebraska	Honolulu, Hawaii	D(2a)-'01	16/16
85	Scheffler, Tony	TE	6-5	255	2/15/83	7	Western Michigan	Chelsea, Mich.	T(Den)-'10	15/5
67	Sims, Rob	G	6-3	312	12/6/83	7	Ohio State	Macedonia, Ohio	T(Sea)-'10	16/16
27	Smith, Alphonso	CB	5-9	190	10/20/85	4	Wake Forest	Pahokee, Fla.	T(Den)-'10	11/1
30	Smith, Kevin	RB	6-1	217	12/7/86	4	Central Florida	Miami, Fla.	FA-'11	7/4
42	Spievey, Amari	CB	5-11	195	4/15/88	3	Iowa	Middleton, Conn.	D3-'10	15/15
9	Stafford, Matthew	QB	6-3	232	2/7/88	4	Georgia	Highland Park, Texas	D1a-'09	16/16
90	Suh, Ndamukong	DT	6-4	307	1/6/87	3	Nebraska	Portland, Ore.	D1a-'10	14/14
55	Tulloch, Stephen	LB	5-11	240	1/1/85	7	North Carolina State	Miami, Fla.	UFA(Tenn)-'11	16/16
93	Vanden Bosch, Kyle	DE	6-4	278	11/17/78	12	Nebraska	Larchwood, Iowa	UFA(Tenn)-'10	16/16
29	Wendling, John	S	6-1	222	6/4/83	6	Wyoming	Rock Springs, Wyo.	FA-'10	16/1
99	Williams, Corey	DT	6-4	320	8/17/80	9	Arkansas State	Camden, Ark.	T(Cle)-'10	15/15
34	Williams, Keiland	RB	5-11	230	8/14/86	3	Louisiana State	Lafayette, La.	W(Wash)-'11	15/0
16	Young, Titus	WR	5-11	174	8/21/89	2	Boise State	Los Angeles, Calif.	D2a-'11	16/9
79	Young, Willie	DE	6-4	251	9/19/85	3	North Carolina State	Palm Beach Gardens, Fla.	D7a-'10	14/0

* Bell inactive for 1 game; E. Brown played 3 games with San Diego in '11; Culbreath missed '11 season because of injury; Fox missed '11 season because of injury; Hughes last active with Jacksonville in '09; Lacey played 15 games with Indianapolis; Leshoure missed '11 season because of injury; Long last active with Kansas City in '09; McClendon inactive for 4 games; Norris last active with Jacksonville in '10.

f- Unsigned franchise player; subject to developments.

Players lost through free agency (3): LB Bobby Carpenter (NE; 16 games), QB Drew Stanton (NYJ; 0), CB Eric Wright (TB; 16).

Also played with Lions in '11—RB Eldra Buckley (2 games), WR Rashied Davis (11), DE Keyunta Dawson (2), LB Isaiah Ekejiuba (3), S Vincent Fuller (1), S Chris Harris (8), DT Jovan Haye (1), CB Anthony Madison (5), P Robert Malone (1), CB Brandon McDonald (13), RB Maurice Morris (16), WR Maurice Stovall (15).

FIRST-YEAR ROSTER

Name	Pos.	Ht.	Wt.	Birthdate	College	Hometown	How Acq.
Austin, Rodney	G	6-4	311	12/4/88	Elon	Charlotte, N.C.	FA
Barham, Quinn	T	6-3	304	8/8/89	Penn State	Durham, N.C.	FA
Bentley, Dwight	CB	5-10	176	5/16/89	Louisiana-Lafayette	Pahokee, Fla.	D3
Boyle, Pat	G	6-5	301	5/30/90	Temple	Towson, Md.	FA
Broyles, Ryan	WR	5-10	188	4/9/88	Oklahoma	Norman, Okla.	D2
Bryant, James	FB	6-3	257	12/18/85	Louisville	Reading, Pa.	FA
Burrell, Troy	WR	5-10	182	7/12/89	Wayne State	Port Huron, Mich.	FA
Chinasa, Ugo (1)	DE	6-5	252	7/30/88	Oklahoma State	Richardson, Texas	FA '11
Cosgrove, Michael	DT	6-4	300	5/29/89	Idaho	Las Vegas, Nev.	FA
Dimke, Derek	K	6-0	180	4/16/90	Illinois	Rockford, Ill.	FA
Edwards, Patrick	WR	5-9	175	10/25/88	Houston	Hearne, Texas	FA
Gerberry, Dan (1)	C	6-3	302	11/10/85	Ball State	Austintown, Ohio	FA-'09
Gottlieb, Alex	TE	6-4	255	7/4/90	William & Mary	Delray Beach, Fla.	FA
Green, Jonte	CB	6-0	184	7/19/89	New Mexico State	St. Petersburg, Fla.	D6
Green, Stephfon	RB	5-10	193	5/28/89	Penn State	Bronx, N.Y.	FA
Greenwood, Chris	CB	6-1	193	7/10/89	Albion College	Detroit, Mich.	D5b
Harris, Marcus (1)	WR	6-1	185	3/1/89	Murray State	St. Louis, Mo.	FA-'11
Karstetter, Jared	WR	6-4	213	9/20/89	Washington State	Spokane, Wash.	FA
Lawrence, Alonzo	S	6-2	215	10/15/89	Gulf Coast (Miss.) C.C.	Lucedale, Miss.	FA
Lewis, Ronnell	DE	6-2	253	9/17/90	Oklahoma	Dewar, Okla.	D4
Lewis, Travis	LB	6-2	222	1/15/88	Oklahoma	San Antonio, Texas	D7
McClam, Edmon	DE	6-6	280	2/17/89	Old Dominion	Coward, S.C.	FA
Messina, Carmen	LB	6-2	236	9/8/88	New Mexico	Addison, Ill.	FA
Miles, Wallace	WR	6-0	191	8/1/89	North Carolina A&T	Atlanta, Ga.	FA
Moore, Kellen	QB	6-0	197	7/12/89	Boise State	Prosser, Wash.	FA
Oram, J.C.	G	6-4	300	7/18/89	Weber State	Marriott-Slaterville, Utah	FA
Overbay, Nathan (1)	TE	6-5	270	1/4/87	Eastern Washington	Lakewood, Wash.	FA-'11
Proctor, Sam	S	6-0	220	9/4/88	Oklahoma	Pearland, Texas	FA
Reiff, Riley	T	6-6	313	12/1/88	Iowa	Parkston, S.D.	D1
Silva, Ricardo (1)	S	6-3	225	5/9/88	Hampton	Baltimore, Md.	FA-'11
Sneed, Ronnie	LB	6-2	241	6/26/89	Kentucky	Tallahassee, Fla.	FA
Toliver, Terrence (1)	WR	6-5	204	5/7/88	Louisiana State	Hempstead, Texas	FA-'11
Weaver, Ross (1)	DB	6-1	203	1/9/87	Michigan State	Southfield, Mich.	FA-'11
Wells, Austin	TE	6-3	255	3/28/89	Northern Iowa	Norfolk, Neb.	FA
Whitehead, Tahir	LB	6-2	228	4/2/90	Temple	Newark, N.J.	D5a

The term NFL Rookie is defined as a player who is in his first season of professional football and has not been on the roster of another professional football team for any regular-season or postseason games. A Rookie is designated by an "R" on NFL rosters. Players who have been active in another professional football league or players who have NFL experience, including either preseason training camp or being on an Active List or Inactive List, or on Reserve/Injured or Reserve/Physically Unable to Perform for fewer than six regular-season games, are termed NFL First-Year Players. An NFL First-Year Player is designated by a "1" on NFL rosters. Thereafter, a player is credited with an additional year of experience for each season in which he accumulates six games on the Active List or Inactive List, or on Reserve/Injured or Reserve/Physically Unable to Perform.

Log on to www.detroitlions.com for an up-to-date roster.

COACHING STAFF

**Head Coach,
Jim Schwartz**

Pro Career: Named Lions' twenty-fifth head coach on January 16, 2009. Schwartz enters his fourth season in Detroit after helping the team to their first playoff appearance since 1999. He came to Detroit following 10 seasons with the Tennessee Titans, including the past eight as defensive coordinator. As the Titans' defensive coordinator since 2001, Schwartz's defensive unit held firm in two major defensive categories that factored significantly in the team's overall success; rushing defense and third-down conversion. From 2001-08, Tennessee ranked fifth in rushing yards allowed per game (103.5) and sixth in third-down conversion percentage (36.1). Before joining the Titans in 1999, he spent three years (1996-98) as a defensive assistant/quality control coach with the Baltimore Ravens. During his tenure in Baltimore, he also coached the team's outside linebackers. After the Cleveland Browns moved to Baltimore following the 1995 season, Schwartz made the transition from player personnel to coaching. From 1993-95, he worked in the Browns' player personnel department, serving as both a college and pro scout. Career record: 18-31.

Background: Schwartz worked on the college level for four years before moving onto the NFL. He began his coaching career as a graduate assistant coach at the University of Maryland, tutoring the Terrapins' linebackers in 1989 and then served as graduate assistant at the University of Minnesota (1990). He became a position coach in the secondary at North Carolina Central (1991) before moving to Colgate (1992) as linebackers coach. Played collegiately at Georgetown University where he lettered four years at linebacker. In 1988 he earned numerous honors that include Division III CoSIDA/GTE Academic All-America, All-America and team captain.

Personal: Born June 2, 1966, in Baltimore, Md. He and his wife, Kathy, have twins Christian and Allison along with a younger daughter Maria. He earned a degree in economics at Georgetown as well as Distinguished Economics Graduate honors.

ASSISTANT COACHES

Jason Arapoff, director of physical development; born July 8, 1965, Weymouth, Mass. Defensive back Springfield College 1985-88. No pro playing experience. Pro coach: Washington Redskins 1992-2000, joined Lions in 2001.

Bradford Banta, asst. linebackers; born December 14, 1979, Baton Rouge, La. Tight end Southern California 1990-93, Pro tight end/long snapper Indianapolis Colts 1993-99, New York Jets 2000, Detroit Lions 2001-03, Buffalo Bills 2004. College coach: Tennessee-Chattanooga 2007. Pro coach: Joined Lions in 2008.

Matt Burke, linebackers; born March 25, 1976, Hudson, Mass. Safety Dartmouth 1994-97. No pro playing experience. College coach: Boston College 2000-02, Harvard 2003. Pro coach: Tennessee Titans 2006-08, joined Lions in 2009.

Danny Crossman, special teams; born January 17, 1967, El Paso, Texas. Defensive back Kansas 1985, Pittsburgh 1987-89. Pro defensive back Washington Redskins 1990, Detroit Lions 1991-92. College coach: U.S. Coast Guard Academy 1993, Western Kentucky 1994-96, Central Florida 1997-98, Georgia Tech 1999-2001, Michigan State 2002. Pro coach: Carolina Panthers 2003-09, joined Lions in 2010.

Gunther Cunningham, defensive coordinator; born June 19, 1946, Munich, Germany. Linebacker/placekicker Oregon 1966-68. No pro playing experience. College coach: Oregon 1969-1971, Arkansas 1972, Stanford 1973-76, California 1977-1980. Pro coach: Hamilton Tiger-Cats (CFL) 1981, Baltimore/Indianapolis Colts 1982-84, San Diego Chargers 1985-1990, L.A. Raiders 1991-94, Kansas City Chiefs 1995-2000, 2004-08 (head coach 1999-2000), Tennessee Titans 2001-03, joined Lions in 2009.

Todd Downing, asst. quarterbacks; born July 22, 1980, Eden Prairie, Minn. Attended Minnesota. No college or pro playing experience. Pro coach: Minnesota Vikings 2003-05, St. Louis Rams 2006-08, joined Lions in 2009.

Sam Gash, running backs; born March 7, 1969, Henderson, N.C. Fullback Penn State 1987-1991. Pro fullback New England Patriots 1992-97, Buffalo Bills 1998-99, 2003, Baltimore Ravens 2000-02. Pro coach: New York Jets 2005-06, joined Lions in 2007.

Shawn Jefferson, wide receivers; born February 22, 1969, Jacksonville, Fla. Wide receiver Central Florida 1988-1990. Pro wide receiver San Diego Chargers 1991-95, New England Patriots 1996-99, Atlanta Falcons 2000-02, Detroit Lions 2003. Pro coach: Joined Lions in 2005.

Kris Kocurek, defensive line; born November 15, 1978, Rockdale, Texas. Defensive tackle Texas Tech 1997-2000. Pro defensive tackle Seattle Seahawks 2001, Tennessee Titans 2002. College coach: Texas Tech 2003, Texas A&M-Kingsville 2004-05, Texas A&M-Commerce 2006, West Texas A&M 2007, Stephen F. Austin State 2008. Pro coach: Joined Lions in 2009.

Tim Lappano, tight ends: born October 14, 1956, Spokane, Wash. Running back Idaho 1978-1981. No pro playing experience. College coach: Idaho 1982-85, Wyoming 1986, Washington State 1987-1991, California 1992-95, Wyoming 1996, Purdue 1997, Oregon State 2000-02, Washington 2005-08. Pro coach: Seattle Seahawks 1998, San Francisco 49ers 2003-04, joined Lions in 2009.

Scott Linehan, offensive coordinator; born September 17, 1963, Sunnyside, Wash. Quarterback Idaho 1982-86. No pro playing experience. College coach: Idaho 1989-1990, 1992-93, Nevada-Las Vegas 1991, Washington 1994-98, Louisville 1999-2001. Pro coach: Minnesota Vikings 2002-04, Miami Dolphins 2005, St Louis Rams 2006-08 (head coach), joined Lions in 2009.

Ted Rath, strength and conditioning assistant: born November 22, 1983, Monroe, Mich. Linebacker Toledo 2003-06. No pro playing experience. College coach: Toledo 2007-09. Pro coach: Joined Lions in 2009.

Marcus Robertson, defensive assistant/secondary; born October 2, 1969, Pasadena, Calif. Defensive back Iowa State 1987-1990. Pro safety Houston Oilers/Tennessee Titans 1991-2000, Seattle Seahawks 2001-02. College coach: Tennessee Titans 2007-2011, joined Lions in 2012.

Tim Walton, secondary/third down package; born March 11, 1971, Grenada, Miss. Defensive back Ohio State 1990-94. No pro playing experience. College coach: Bowling Green 1995-99, Memphis 2000-01, 2008, Syracuse 2002, Louisiana State 2003, Miami 2004-07. Pro coach: Joined Lions in 2009.

George Yarno, offensive line; born August 12, 1957, Spokane, Wash. Offensive line Washington State 1975-78. Pro offensive line Tampa Bay Buccaneers 1979-1983, 1985-87, Denver Gold (USFL) 1984-85, Atlanta Falcons 1988, Houston Oilers 1989, Green Bay Packers 1990. College coach: Louisiana State 2001-02, Washington State 2003-07. Pro coach: Tampa Bay Buccaneers 2008, joined Lions in 2009.

National Football Conference
North Division
Team Colors: Dark Green, Gold, and White
Lambeau Field Atrium
1265 Lombardi Avenue
Green Bay, Wisconsin 54304
Telephone: (920) 569-7500

2012 SCHEDULE
PRESEASON
Aug. 9 at San Diego 7:00
Aug. 16 Cleveland 7:00
Aug. 23 at Cincinnati 6:00
Aug. 30 Kansas City 6:00

REGULAR SEASON
Sep. 9 San Francisco 3:15
Sep. 13 Chicago (Thurs) 7:20
Sep. 24 at Seattle (Mon) 7:30
Sep. 30 New Orleans.....................3:15
Oct. 7 at Indianapolis 12:00
Oct. 14 at Houston 7:20
Oct. 21 at St. Louis 12:00
Oct. 28 Jacksonville....................12:00
Nov. 4 Arizona 12:00
Nov. 11 BYE
Nov. 18 at Detroit.........................12:00
Nov. 25 at New York Giants *7:20
Dec. 2 Minnesota 12:00
Dec. 9 Detroit *7:20
Dec. 16 at Chicago.......................12:00
Dec. 23 Tennessee 12:00
Dec. 30 at Minnesota 12:00
*All times CT; Sunday night games in
  Weeks 11-16 subject to change
Stadium: Lambeau Field (opened in 1957)
  •Capacity: 73,094
  1265 Lombardi Avenue
  Green Bay, Wisconsin 54304
Playing Surface: DD GrassMaster
Training Camp: St. Norbert College
  De Pere, Wisconsin 54115

LAMBEAU FIELD

CLUB OFFICIALS
President and Chief Executive Officer:
  Mark Murphy
Executive Vice President/General
  Manager/Director of Football
  Operations: Ted Thompson
Vice President of Football Administration/
  Player Finance: Russ Ball
Vice President of Finance: Paul Baniel
Vice President of Sales and Marketing:
  Tim Connolly
Director - Football Operations:
  John Dorsey
Director of Pro Personnel: Eliot Wolf
Director of College Scouting:
  Brian Gutekunst
Director of Player Development:
  Rob Davis
Director of Research and Development:
  Mike Eayrs
Director of Public Relations:
  Jason Wahlers
Director of Public Affairs:
  Aaron Popkey
Assistant Director of Public Relations:
  Sarah Quick
Communications Manager: Tom Fanning
Public Relations Coordinator:
  Jonathan Butnick
Director of Ticket Operations:
  Mark Wagner
Director of Marketing and Corporate
  Sales: Craig Benzel
Director of Guest and Stadium
  Experience: Jennifer Ark
Director of Human Resources:
  Nicole Ledvina
Director of Retail Operations:
  Kate Hogan
Director of Information Technology:
  Wayne Wichlacz
Director of Facility Operations:
  Ted Eisenreich
Director of Security/Risk Management:
  Doug Collins
Manager of Community Outreach &
  Player/Alumni Relations:
  Cathy Dworak
Director of Packers Media Group:
  Joan Malcheski
Senior Personnel Executive:
  Alonzo Highsmith
West Regional Scout: Sam Seale
Assistant Director of Pro Personnel:
  Tim Terry
Area Scouts: Lee Gissendaner,
  Jon-Eric Sullivan,
  John Wojciechowski,
  Richmond Williams
Pro Scouts: Chad Brinker, Glenn Cook
College Scout: Michael Owen
College Scouting Coordinator: Danny
  Mock
Coaching Administrator: Jason Simmons
Strength and Conditioning Assistants:
  Thadeus Jackson, Zac Woodfin
Football Administration Coordinator:
  Matt Klein
Video Director: Bob Eckberg
Head Athletic Trainer: Pepper Burruss
Equipment Manager: Gordon (Red) Batty

COACHING HISTORY
(708-542-36)
Records include postseason games

Years	Coach	Record
1921-1949	Earl (Curly) Lambeau	.212-106-21
1950-53	Gene Ronzani*	14-31-1
1953	Hugh Devore-	
	Ray (Scooter) McLean**	0-2-0
1954-57	Lisle Blackbourn	17-31-0
1958	Ray (Scooter) McLean	1-10-1
1959-1967	Vince Lombardi	98-30-4
1968-1970	Phil Bengtson	20-21-1
1971-74	Dan Devine	25-28-4
1975-1983	Bart Starr	53-77-3
1984-87	Forrest Gregg	25-37-1
1988-1991	Lindy Infante	24-40-0
1992-98	Mike Holmgren	84-42-0
1999	Ray Rhodes	8-8-0
2000-05	Mike Sherman	59-43-0
2006-2011	Mike McCarthy	68-36-0

*Resigned after 10 games in 1953
**Co-coaches

PAID ATTENDANCE
Home 564,100   Away 548,488
Total 1,112,588
Single-game home record,
  71,213 (11/1/09)
Single-season home record,
  566,418 (2007)

2012 DRAFT CHOICES

Round	Name	Pos.	College
1	Nick Perry	LB	Southern California
2	Jerel Worthy	DE	Michigan St.
	Casey Hayward	CB	Vanderbilt
4	Mike Daniels	DT	Iowa
	Jerron McMillian	S	Maine
5	Terrell Manning	LB	North Carolina St.
7	Andrew Datko	T	Florida St.
	B.J. Coleman	QB	Tennessee-Chattanooga

2011 TEAM RECORD
PRESEASON (3-1)

Date	Result	Opponent
8/13	L 17-27	at Cleveland
8/19	W 28-20	Arizona
8/26	W 24-21	at Indianapolis
9/1	W 20-19	Kansas City

REGULAR SEASON (15-1)

Date	Result	Opponent
9/8	W 42-34	New Orleans
9/18	W 30-23	at Carolina
9/25	W 27-17	at Chicago
10/2	W 49-23	Denver
10/9	W 25-14	at Atlanta
10/16	W 24-3	St. Louis
10/23	W 33-27	at Minnesota
11/6	W 45-38	at San Diego
11/14	W 45-7	Minnesota
11/20	W 35-26	Tampa Bay
11/24	W 27-15	at Detroit
12/4	W 38-35	at New York Giants
12/11	W 46-16	Oakland
12/18	L 14-19	at Kansas City
12/25	W 35-21	Chicago
1/1	W 45-41	Detroit

POSTSEASON (0-1)

Date	Result	Opponent
1/15	L 20-37	New York Giants

SCORE BY PERIODS

Packers	132	154	150	124	0 —	560
Opponents	66	97	66	130	0 —	359

2011 TEAM STATISTICS

	Packers	Opp.
Total First Downs	353	358
Rushing	89	96
Passing	230	246
Penalty	34	16
3rd Down: Made/Att	91/189	83/195
3rd Down Pct.	48.1	42.6
4th Down: Made/Att	4/8	4/16
4th Down Pct.	50.0	25.0
Possession Avg.	30:29	29:31
Total Net Yards	6482	6585
Avg. Per Game	405.1	411.6
Total Plays	988	1049
Avg. Per Play	6.6	6.3
Net Yards Rushing	1558	1789
Avg. Per Game	97.4	111.8
Total Rushes	395	383
Net Yards Passing	4924	4796
Avg. Per Game	307.8	299.8
Sacked/Yards Lost	41/237	29/192
Gross Yards	5161	4988
Att./Completions	552/376	637/390
Completion Pct.	68.1	61.2
Had Intercepted	8	31
Punts/Average	55/45.6	58/43.0
Net Punting Avg.	55/38.6	58/37.2
Penalties/Yards	76/591	122/948
Fumbles/Ball Lost	15/6	19/7
Touchdowns	70	41
Rushing	12	10
Passing	51	29
Returns	7	2

2011 INDIVIDUAL STATISTICS

PASSING

PASSING	Att.	Comp.	Yds.	Pct.	TD	Int.	Tkld.	Rate
Rodgers	502	343	4643	68.3	45	6	36/219	122.5
Flynn	49	33	518	67.3	6	2	5/18	124.8
Cobb	1	0	0	0.0	0	0	0/0	39.6
Packers	552	376	5161	68.1	51	8	41/237	122.6
Opponents	637	390	4988	61.2	29	31	29/192	80.6

SCORING

SCORING	TD R	TD P	TD Rt	PAT	FG	Saf	PTS
Crosby	0	0	0	68/69	24/28	0	140
Nelson	0	15	0	0/0	0/0	0	90
G. Jennings	0	9	0	0/0	0/0	0	54
Finley	0	8	0	0/0	0/0	0	48
Ja. Jones	0	7	0	0/0	0/0	0	42
Driver	0	6	0	0/0	0/0	0	36
Kuhn	4	2	0	0/0	0/0	0	36
Cobb	0	1	2	0/0	0/0	0	18
Grant	2	1	0	0/0	0/0	0	18
Rodgers	3	0	0	0/0	0/0	0	18
Crabtree	0	1	0	0/0	0/0	0	6
Flynn	1	0	0	0/0	0/0	0	6
Matthews	0	0	1	0/0	0/0	0	6
Peprah	0	0	1	0/0	0/0	0	6
Raji	1	0	0	0/0	0/0	0	6
Starks	1	0	0	0/0	0/0	0	6
R. Taylor	0	1	0	0/0	0/0	0	6
Walden	0	0	1	0/0	0/0	0	6
T. Williams	0	0	1	0/0	0/0	0	6
Woodson	0	0	1	0/0	0/0	0	6
Packers	12	51	7	68/69	24/28	0	560
Opponents	10	29	2	35/35	22/27	2	359

2-Pt Conversions: Packers 0-1, Opponents 4-6

RUSHING

RUSHING	No.	Yds	Avg	LG	TD
Starks	133	578	4.3	40	1
Grant	134	559	4.2	47t	2
Rodgers	60	257	4.3	25	3
Kuhn	30	78	2.6	12	4
Saine	18	69	3.8	10	0
A. Green	3	11	3.7	8	0
Masthay	1	6	6.0	6	0
Cobb	2	5	2.5	4	0
Raji	1	1	1.0	1t	1
Flynn	13	-6	-.5	3t	1
Packers	395	1558	3.9	47t	12
Opponents	383	1789	4.7	54t	10

RECEIVING

RECEIVING	No.	Yds	Avg	LG	TD
Nelson	68	1263	18.6	93t	15
G. Jennings	67	949	14.2	79t	9
Finley	55	767	13.9	41	8
Ja. Jones	38	635	16.7	70t	7
Driver	37	445	12.0	35t	6
Starks	29	216	7.4	17	0
Cobb	25	375	15.0	61	1
Grant	19	268	14.1	80t	1
Kuhn	15	77	5.1	11	2
Saine	10	69	6.9	22	0
Crabtree	6	38	6.3	15	1
Quarless	3	36	12.0	21	0
D. Williams	2	13	6.5	7	0
A. Green	1	6	6.0	6	0
R. Taylor	1	4	4.0	4t	1
Packers	376	5161	13.7	93t	51
Opponents	390	4988	12.8	72	29

INTERCEPTIONS

INTERCEPTIONS	No.	Yds	Avg	LG	TD
Woodson	7	63	9.0	30t	1
Peprah	5	147	29.4	76	1
T. Williams	4	92	23.0	43t	1
Shields	4	68	17.0	60	0
Matthews	3	47	15.7	38t	1
Burnett	3	0	0	0	0
Bush	2	39	19.5	35	0
Francois	2	1	0.5	1	0
Smith	1	11	11.0	11	0
Packers	31	468	15.1	76	4
Opponents	8	63	7.9	30	0

PUNTING

PUNTING	No.	Yds.	Avg.	In 20	LG
Masthay	55	2506	45.6	23	71
Packers	55	2506	45.6	23	71
Opponents	58	2492	43.0	18	71

PUNT RETURNS

PUNT RETURNS	Ret	FC	Yds	Avg	LG	TD
Cobb	26	18	295	11.3	80t	1
Bush	1	0	0	0.0	0	0
Nelson	0	1	0	—	—	0
Packers	27	19	295	10.9	80t	1
Opponents	24	10	305	12.7	72t	1

KICKOFF RETURNS

KICKOFF RETURNS	No.	Yds	Avg	LG	TD
Cobb	34	941	27.7	108t	1
Driver	2	5	2.5	5	0
Saine	2	40	20.0	20	0
Crabtree	1	11	11.0	11	0
Lee	1	-1	-1.0	-1	0
Woodson	1	9	9.0	9	0
Packers	41	1005	24.5	108t	1
Opponents	59	1378	23.4	57	0

FIELD GOALS

FIELD GOALS	1-19	20-29	30-39	40-49	50+
Crosby	1/1	4/5	14/14	3/5	2/3
Packers	1/1	4/5	14/14	3/5	2/3
Opponents	1/1	6/6	10/11	2/5	3/4

SACKS

SACKS	No.
Matthews	6.0
Bishop	5.0
Raji	3.0
Walden	3.0
Wynn	3.0
Woodson	2.0
Bush	1.5
Hawk	1.5
Burnett	1.0
B. Jones	1.0
So'oto	1.0
Zombo	1.0
Packers	29.0
Opponents	41.0

RECORD HOLDERS
INDIVIDUAL RECORDS—CAREER

Category	Name	Performance
Rushing (Yds.)	Ahman Green, 2000-06, 2009	8,322
Passing (Yds.)	Brett Favre, 1992-2007	**61,655
Passing (TDs)	Brett Favre, 1992-2007	**442
Receiving (No.)	Donald Driver, 1999-2011	735
Receiving (Yds.)	Donald Driver, 1999-2011	10,060
Interceptions	Bobby Dillon, 1952-59	52
Punting (Avg.)	Craig Hentrich, 1994-97	42.8
Punt Return (Avg.)	Desmond Howard, 1996, 1999	13.8
Kickoff Return (Avg.)	Travis Williams, 1967-1970	26.7
Field Goals	Ryan Longwell, 1997-2005	226
Touchdowns (Tot.)	Don Hutson, 1935-1945	105
Points	Ryan Longwell, 1997-2005	1,054
*Sacks	Kabeer Gbaja-Biamila, 2000-08	74.5

INDIVIDUAL RECORDS—SINGLE SEASON

Category	Name	Performance
Rushing (Yds.)	Ahman Green, 2003	1,883
Passing (Yds.)	Aaron Rodgers, 2011	4,643
Passing (TDs)	Aaron Rodgers, 2011	45
Receiving (No.)	Sterling Sharpe, 1993	112
Receiving (Yds.)	Robert Brooks, 1995	1,497
Interceptions	Irv Comp, 1943	10
Punting (Avg.)	Tim Masthay, 2011	45.6
Punt Return (Avg.)	Billy Grimes, 1950	19.1
Kickoff Return (Avg.)	Travis Williams, 1967	**41.1
Field Goals	Chester Marcol, 1972	33
	Ryan Longwell, 2000	33
Touchdowns (Tot.)	Ahman Green, 2003	20
Points	Paul Hornung, 1960	176
*Sacks	Tim Harris, 1989	19.5

INDIVIDUAL RECORDS—SINGLE GAME

Category	Name	Performance
Rushing (Yds.)	Ahman Green, 12-28-03	218
Passing (Yds.)	Matt Flynn, 1-1-12	480
Passing (TDs)	Matt Flynn, 1-1-12	6
Receiving (No.)	Don Hutson, 11-22-42	14
Receiving (Yds.)	Billy Howton, 10-21-56	257
Interceptions	Bobby Dillon, 11-26-53	**4
	Willie Buchanon, 9-24-78	**4
Field Goals	Chris Jacke, 11-11-90, 10-14-96	5
	Ryan Longwell, 9-24-00	5
Touchdowns (Tot.)	Paul Hornung, 12-12-65	5
Points	Paul Hornung, 10-8-61	33
*Sacks	Vonnie Holliday, 12-22-02	5.0

*Sacks became an official statistic in 1982.
**NFL Record

2012 VETERAN ROSTER

No.	Name	Pos.	Ht.	Wt.	Birthdate	NFL Exp.	College	Hometown	How Acq.	'11 Games/ Starts
55	Bishop, Desmond	LB	6-2	238	7/24/84	6	California	Fairfield, Calif.	D6b-'07	13/13
75	Bulaga, Bryan	T	6-5	314	3/21/89	3	Iowa	Woodstock, Ill.	D1-'10	12/12
42	Burnett, Morgan	S	6-1	209	1/13/89	3	Georgia Tech	College Park, Ga.	D3-'10	16/16
24	Bush, Jarrett	CB	6-0	200	5/21/84	7	Utah State	Vacaville, Calif.	W(Car)-'06	16/2
18	Cobb, Randall	WR	5-10	192	8/22/90	2	Kentucky	Alcoa, Tenn.	D2-'11	15/0
83	Crabtree, Tom	TE	6-4	245	11/4/85	3	Miami (Ohio)	Carroll, Ohio	FA-'09	16/9
2	Crosby, Mason	K	6-1	207	9/3/84	6	Colorado	Georgetown, Texas	D6c-'07	16/0
62	Dietrich-Smith, Evan	C/G	6-2	308	7/19/86	3	Idaho State	Salinas, Calif.	FA-'11	16/3
73	Dominguez, Ray	G	6-4	334	7/12/88	2	Arkansas	Bainbridge, Ga.	FA-'11	0*
80	Driver, Donald	WR	6-0	194	2/2/75	14	Alcorn State	Houston, Texas	D7b-'99	16/15
88	Finley, Jermichael	TE	6-5	247	3/26/87	5	Texas	Diboll, Texas	D3-'08	16/13
49	Francois, Robert	LB	6-2	255	5/14/85	3	Boston College	Byfield, Mass.	FA-'09	11/2
61	Goode, Brett	LS	6-1	255	11/2/84	5	Arkansas	Fort Smith, Ark.	FA-'08	16/0
25	# Grant, Ryan	RB	6-1	222	12/9/82	6	Notre Dame	Ramsey, N.J.	T(NYG)-'07	15/14
20	Green, Alex	RB	6-0	225	6/23/88	2	Hawaii	Portland, Ore.	D3-'11	4/0
95	# Green, Howard	DT	6-2	340	1/12/79	8	Louisiana State	Donaldsonville, La.	W(NYJ)-'10	16/5
91	Guy, Lawrence	DE	6-4	304	3/17/90	2	Arizona State	Las Vegas, Nev.	D7b-'11	0*
95	Hargrove, Anthony	DE	6-3	282	7/20/83	8	Georgia Tech	Port Charlotte, Fla.	UFA(Sea)-'12	15/0*
50	Hawk, A.J.	LB	6-1	247	1/6/84	7	Ohio State	Centerville, Ohio	D1-'06	14/14
31	House, Davon	CB	6-0	195	7/10/89	2	New Mexico State	Palmdale, Calif.	D4-'11	2/0
85	Jennings, Greg	WR	5-11	198	9/21/83	7	Western Michigan	Kalamazoo, Mich.	D2b-'06	13/13
43	Jennings, M.D.	S	6-0	187	7/25/88	2	Arkansas State	Calhoun City, Miss.	FA-'11	15/0
59	Jones, Brad	LB	6-3	242	4/1/86	4	Colorado	East Lansing, Mich.	D7-'09	15/1
89	Jones, James	WR	6-1	208	3/31/84	6	San Jose State	San Jose, Calif.	D3a-'07	16/0
30	Kuhn, John	FB	6-0	250	9/9/82	7	Shippensburg	York, Pa.	W(Pitt)-'07	16/3
70	Lang, T.J.	G	6-4	318	9/20/87	4	Eastern Michigan	Birmingham, Mich.	D4-'09	16/16
57	Lattimore, Jamari	LB	6-2	230	10/6/88	2	Middle Tennessee State	Hialeah, Fla.	FA-'11	9/0
8	Masthay, Tim	P	6-1	200	3/16/87	3	Kentucky	Murray, Ky.	FA-'10	16/0
52	Matthews, Clay	LB	6-3	255	5/14/86	4	Southern California	Agoura Hills, Calif.	D1b-'09	15/15
77	Muir, Daniel	DT	6-2	312	9/12/83	5	Kent State	Riverdale, Md.	FA-'12	4/2*
96	Neal, Mike	DE	6-3	294	6/26/87	3	Purdue	Merrillville, Ind.	D2-'10	7/0
87	Nelson, Jordy	WR	6-3	217	5/31/85	5	Kansas State	Riley, Kan.	D2a-'08	16/9
74	Newhouse, Marshall	T	6-4	319	9/29/88	3	Texas Christian	Dallas, Texas	D5b-'10	16/13
26	Peprah, Charlie	S	5-11	203	2/24/83	7	Alabama	Plano, Texas	FA-'10	16/14
79	Pickett, Ryan	DT	6-2	340	10/8/79	12	Ohio State	Zephyrhills, Fla.	UFA(StL)-'06	14/14
81	Quarless, Andrew	TE	6-4	252	10/6/88	3	Penn State	Uniondale, N.Y.	D5a-'10	10/2
90	Raji, B.J.	DT	6-2	337	7/11/86	4	Boston College	Washington Township, N.J.	D1a-'09	16/15
12	Rodgers, Aaron	QB	6-2	225	12/2/83	8	California	Chico, Calif.	D1-'05	15/15
33	Saine, Brandon	RB	5-11	220	12/14/88	2	Ohio State	Piqua, Ohio	FA-'11	5/0
63	Saturday, Jeff	C	6-2	295	6/18/75	14	North Carolina	Decatur, Ga.	UFA(Ind)-'12	16/16*
78	Sherrod, Derek	T	6-5	321	4/23/89	2	Mississippi State	Caledonia, Miss.	D1-'11	5/0
37	Shields, Sam	CB	5-11	184	12/8/87	3	Miami	Sarasota, Fla.	FA-'10	15/7
71	Sitton, Josh	G	6-3	318	6/16/86	5	Central Florida	Pensacola, Fla.	D4b-'08	14/14
51	Smith, D.J.	LB	5-11	239	2/24/89	2	Appalachian State	Charlotte, N.C.	D6b-'11	16/3
16	Smithson, Shaky	WR	5-11	202	8/23/87	2	Utah	Baltimore, Md.	FA-'11	0*
97	So'oto, Vic	LB	6-3	263	8/19/87	2	Brigham Young	Carlsbad, Calif.	FA-'11	7/0
44	Starks, James	RB	6-2	218	2/25/86	3	Buffalo	Niagara Falls, N.Y.	D6-'10	13/2
72	Taylor, Herb	T	6-4	305	9/22/84	3	Texas Christian	Houston, Texas	FA-'11	0*
82	Taylor, Ryan	TE	6-3	254	11/16/87	2	North Carolina	Winston-Salem, N.C.	D7a-'11	15/0
93	Walden, Erik	LB	6-2	250	8/21/85	5	Middle Tennessee State	Dublin, Ga.	FA-'10	16/15
84	Williams, D.J.	TE	6-2	245	9/10/88	2	Arkansas	Little Rock, Ark.	D5-'11	13/0
38	Williams, Tramon	CB	5-11	191	3/16/83	6	Louisiana Tech	Napoleonville, La.	FA-'06	15/15
98	Wilson, C.J.	DE	6-3	290	3/30/87	3	East Carolina	Pinetown, N.C.	D7-'10	16/2
21	Woodson, Charles	CB	6-1	202	10/7/76	15	Michigan	Fremont, Ohio	UFA(Oak)-'06	15/15
94	Wynn, Jarius	DE	6-3	285	8/29/86	4	Georgia	Lincolnton, Ga.	D6a-'09	16/4
58	Zombo, Frank	LB	6-3	254	3/5/87	3	Central Michigan	Sterling Heights, Mich.	FA-'10	5/1

* Dominguez did not play in 5 games and inactive for 5 games; Guy missed '11 season because of injury; Hargrove played 15 games with Seattle in '11; Muir played 4 games with Indianapolis; Saturday played 16 games with Indianapolis; Smithson missed '11 season because of injury; H. Taylor did not play in 2 games.

\#   Unrestricted free agent; subject to developments.

Players lost through free agency (3): QB Matt Flynn (Sea; 4 games), CB Pat Lee (Oak; 16), C Scott Wells (StL; 16).

Also played with Packers in '11—T Chad Clifton (6 games), S Nick Collins (2).

FIRST-YEAR ROSTER

Name	Pos.	Ht.	Wt.	Birthdate	College	Hometown	How Acq.
Allard, Shea	T	6-5	305	8/27/89	Delaware	Wareham, Mass.	FA
Barclay, Don	G	6-4	305	4/18/89	West Virginia	Germantown, Md.	FA
Bennett, Du'ane	RB	5-9	213	6/11/89	Minnesota	O'Fallon, Ill.	FA
Borel, Diondre (1)	WR	6-0	199	12/12/88	Utah State	Oakley, Calif.	FA-'11
Boykin, Jarrett	WR	6-2	218	11/4/89	Virginia Tech	Matthews, N.C.	FA
Brooks, Jaymes	G	6-2	300	7/31/89	Virginia Tech	Newport News, Va.	FA
Coleman, B.J.	QB	6-3	231	9/16/88	Tennessee-Chattanooga	Chattanooga, Tenn.	D7b
Cook, Grant	G	6-4	318	3/17/89	Arkansas	Jonesboro, Ark.	FA
Cooper, Nic	FB	5-10	249	4/9/89	Winston-Salem State	Clinton, N.C.	FA
Daniels, Mike	DT	6-0	291	5/5/89	Iowa	Blackwood, N.J.	D4a
Datko, Andrew	T	6-6	315	8/15/90	Florida State	Fort Lauderdale, Fla.	D7a
Draheim, Tommie	C	6-4	309	12/23/88	San Diego State	Lakeside, Calif.	FA
Ford, Cameron	TE	6-3	245	12/16/88	Wake Forest	Anderson, S.C.	FA
Genus, Sampson (1)	C	6-0	315	5/2/88	South Florida	Lake City, Fla.	FA-'11
Gilleylen, Curenski	WR	5-11	213	3/15/89	Nebraska	Leander, Texas	FA
Gurley, Tori (1)	WR	6-4	216	11/22/87	South Carolina	Rock Hill, S.C.	FA-'11
Harrell, Graham (1)	QB	6-2	215	5/22/85	Texas Tech	Ennis, Texas	FA-'10
Hayward, Casey	CB	5-11	192	9/9/89	Vanderbilt	Perry, Ga.	D2b
Hill, Nick (1)	QB	6-3	215	4/5/85	Southern Illinois	Duquoin, Ill.	FA
Hoese, Jon (1)	FB	6-2	238	7/4/89	Minnesota	Glencoe, Minn.	FA-'11
Jones, Johnny (1)	DL	6-4	310	10/19/88	Marshall	Clewiston, Fla.	FA-'11
Lair, Eric	TE	6-2	238	3/10/90	Minnesota	Houston, Texas	FA
Levine, Anthony (1)	S	5-11	199	3/27/87	Tennessee State	Winston-Salem, N.C.	FA-'10
Manning, Terrell	LB	6-2	237	4/16/90	North Carolina State	Laurinburg, N.C.	D5
McCabe, Mike	T	6-5	313	1/19/89	Holy Cross	Watertown, Conn.	FA
McMillian, Jerron	S	5-11	203	4/2/89	Maine	Hillside, N.J.	D4b
Merrill, Otis	CB	5-11	188	6/6/88	Illinois State	Cleveland, Ohio	FA
Moses, Dezman	LB	6-2	249	1/4/89	Tulane	Willingboro, N.J.	FA
Moss, Dale	WR	6-3	213	9/24/88	South Dakota State	Brandon, S.D.	FA
Perry, Nick	LB	6-3	265	4/12/90	Southern California	Detroit, Mich.	D1
Richardson, Sean	S	6-2	216	1/21/90	Vanderbilt	Linden, Ala.	FA
Rivers, Marcus	WR	6-3	218	8/2/89	Buffalo	Lackawanna, N.Y.	FA
Ross, Brandian (1)	CB	6-0	191	9/28/89	Youngstown State	Richmond, Va.	FA-'11
Turner, Dion	CB	5-11	194	5/23/89	Southern Utah	Oakland, Calif.	FA
Tyler, Marc	RB	5-11	226	9/27/88	Southern California	Westlake Village, Calif.	D2a
Worthy, Jerel	DE	6-2	308	4/28/90	Michigan State	Huber Heights, Ohio	D2a

The term NFL Rookie is defined as a player who is in his first season of professional football and has not been on the roster of another professional football team for any regular-season or postseason games. A Rookie is designated by an "R" on NFL rosters. Players who have been active in another professional football league or players who have NFL experience, including either preseason training camp or being on an Active List or Inactive List, or on Reserve/Injured or Reserve/Physically Unable to Perform for fewer than six regular-season games, are termed NFL First-Year Players. An NFL First-Year Player is designated by a "1" on NFL rosters. Thereafter, a player is credited with an additional year of experience for each season in which he accumulates six games on the Active List or Inactive List, or on Reserve/Injured or Reserve/Physically Unable to Perform.

Log on to www.packers.com for an up-to-date roster.

COACHING STAFF
Head Coach,
Mike McCarthy

Pro Career: Named the fourteenth head coach in team history January 12, 2006. Joined Vince Lombardi and Mike Holmgren as the only coaches to guide the Packers to a Super Bowl title with a win over Pittsburgh in Super Bowl XLV. Joined Pittsburgh's Bill Cowher (2005) as the only Super Bowl-winning coaches to lead their respective teams to three road wins as the No. 6 seed in the postseason en route to a world title. Has led the Packers to playoff appearances in four of his six seasons at the helm, and the team's four postseason berths over the past five seasons are the most by an NFC team. His .654 winning percentage (including playoffs) ranks No. 3 among active NFL coaches (min. 50 games) entering 2012. Including the post-season, Green Bay's 40 wins since 2009 rank second in the NFL behind only New Orleans (41). In 2011, guided the team to a franchise-record 15 wins as well as team marks for points (560), touchdowns (70), total net yards (6,482), net passing yards (4,924), passing TDs (51) and fewest give-aways (14) on the way to the NFC North title and the top seed in the conference for the first time since 1996. The offense has ranked in the top 10 in total yards each of his six seasons as head coach, one of only two teams in the league (New Orleans) to accomplish that feat over that span. Named Motorola Coach of the Year, matched a then-franchise record with 13 wins, and won NFC North Division title in 2007. Became the first coach since Lombardi to lead Packers to a championship game in his second season. Had returned to Green Bay after serving as the team's quarterbacks coach in 1999. Was then a highly successful offensive coordinator for the New Orleans Saints (2000-04). The list of quarterbacks he has coached includes Joe Montana, Elvis Grbac, Rich Gannon, Brett Favre, Matt Flynn, Aaron Rodgers, Matt Hasselbeck, Aaron Brooks, Jake Delhomme, Marc Bulger, Steve Bono, and Jeff Blake—a collection that has combined for 37 career Pro Bowl selections and 10 Super Bowl starts. Career record: 68-36.

Background: Graduated with business administration degree from Baker University. Was an all-conference tight end (1985-86), helping the school to a NAIA Division II runner-up finish as a senior captain. Coached collegiately at Fort Hays State (1987-88) and Pittsburgh (1989-1992), before moving to the NFL with the Chiefs (1993-98), Packers (1999), Saints (2000-04) and 49ers (2005).

Personal: Born November 10, 1963, in Pittsburgh, Pa. Family includes wife Jessica and children Alexandra, Jack, George, Gabrielle and Isabella.

ASSISTANT COACHES
Edgar Bennett, wide receivers; born February 15, 1969, Jacksonville, Fla. Running back Florida State 1987, 1989-1991. Pro running back Green Bay Packers 1992-96, Chicago Bears 1998-99. Pro coach: Joined Packers in 2001.

James Campen, offensive line; born June 11, 1964, Sacramento, Calif. Center Sacramento City (Calif.) J.C. 1982-83, Tulane 1984-85. Pro center New Orleans Saints 1987-88, Green Bay Packers 1989-1993. Pro coach: Joined Packers in 2004.

Dom Capers, defensive coordinator; born August 7, 1950, Cambridge, Ohio. Defensive back Mount Union 1968-1971. No pro playing experience. College coach: Kent State 1972-74, Hawaii 1975-76, San Jose State 1977, California 1978-79, Tennessee 1980-81, Ohio State 1982-83. Pro coach: Philadelphia/Baltimore Stars (USFL) 1984-85, New Orleans Saints 1986-1991, Pittsburgh Steelers 1992-94, Carolina Panthers 1995-98 (head coach), Jacksonville Jaguars 1999-2000, Houston Texans 2001-05 (head coach), Miami Dolphins 2006-07, New England Patriots 2008, joined Packers in 2009.

Tom Clements, offensive coordinator; born June 18, 1953, McKees Rocks, Pa. Quarterback Notre Dame 1972-74. Pro quarterback Ottawa Rough Riders (CFL) 1975-78, Hamilton Tiger-Cats (CFL) 1979, 1981-82, Kansas City Chiefs 1980, Winnipeg Blue Bombers (CFL) 1983-87. College coach: Notre Dame 1992-95. Pro coach: New Orleans Saints 1997-99, Kansas City Chiefs 2000, Pittsburgh Steelers 2001-03, Buffalo Bills 2004-05, joined Packers in 2006.

Jerry Fontenot, tight ends; born November 21, 1966, Lafayette, La. Guard Texas A&M 1985-88. Pro center Chicago Bears 1989-1996, New Orleans Saints 1997-2003, Cincinnati Bengals 2004. Pro coach: Joined Packers in 2006.

Kevin Greene, outside linebackers; born July 31, 1962, Schenectady, N.Y. Linebacker Auburn 1980-85. Pro linebacker Los Angeles Rams 1985-1992, Pittsburgh Steelers 1993-95, Carolina Panthers 1996, San Francisco 49ers 1997, Carolina Panthers 1998-99. Pro coach: Joined Packers in 2009.

Joel Hilgenberg, asst. offensive line; born July 10, 1962, Iowa City, Iowa. Center Iowa 1980-83. Pro center/guard New Orleans Saints 1984-1993. Pro coach: Joined Packers in 2011.

Mark Lovat, strength & conditioning coordinator; born Oct. 9, 1969, Pocatello, Idaho. Attended Butler. No college or pro playing experience. Pro coach: Joined Packers in 1999.

Ben McAdoo, quarterbacks; born July 7, 1977, Homer City, Pa. Attended Indiana University (Pa.). No college or pro playing experience. College coach: Michigan State 2001, Fairfield 2002, Pittsburgh 2003, Akron 2004, Stanford 2005. Pro coach: New Orleans Saints 2004, San Francisco 49ers 2005, joined Packers in 2006.

Scott McCurley, defensive quality control; born August 1, 1980, New Castle, Pa. Linebacker Pittsburgh 1998-2002. No pro playing experience. College coach: Pittsburgh 2003-05. Pro coach: Joined Packers in 2006.

Chad Morton, special teams assistant; born April 4, 1977, Torrance, Calif. Running back Southern California 1995-99. Pro running back New Orleans Saints 2000, N.Y. Jets 2001-02, Washington Redskins 2003-04, New York Giants 2005-06. Pro coach: Joined Packers in 2009.

Winston Moss, asst. head coach/inside linebackers; born December 24, 1965, Miami, Fla. Linebacker Miami 1983-86. Pro linebacker Tampa Bay Buccaneers 1987-1990, Los Angeles Raiders 1991-94, Seattle Seahawks 1995-97. Pro coach: Seattle Seahawks 1998, New Orleans Saints 2000-05, joined Packers in 2006.

Darren Perry, secondary-safeties; born December 29, 1968, Norfolk, Va. Safety Penn State 1989-1991. Pro safety Pittsburgh Steelers 1992-98, San Diego Chargers 1999, New Orleans Saints 2000. Pro coach: Cincinnati Bengals 2002, Pittsburgh Steelers 2003-06, Oakland Raiders 2007-08, joined Packers in 2009.

John Rushing, offensive assistant/special teams; born February 26, 1972, Merced, Calif. Defensive back Washington State 1991-94. No pro playing experience. College coach: Willamette (Ore.) 1996-97, Boise State 1998-99, Montana State 2000-02, Utah State 2003-08. Pro coach: Joined Packers in 2009.

Shawn Slocum, special teams coordinator; born February 21, 1965, Bryan, Texas. Linebacker Texas A&M 1983-84. No pro playing experience. College coach: Texas A&M 1989, 1991-97, 2000-02, Pittsburgh 1990, Southern California 1998-99, Mississippi 2005. Pro coach: Joined Packers in 2006.

Mike Trgovac, defensive line; born February 27, 1959, Youngstown, Ohio. Defensive lineman Michigan 1977-1980. No pro playing experience. College coach: Michigan 1984-85, Ball State 1986-88, Navy 1989, Colorado State 1990-91, Notre Dame 1992-94. Pro coach: Philadelphia Eagles 1995-98, Green Bay Packers 1999, Washington Redskins 2000-01, Carolina Panthers 2002-08, re-joined Packers in 2009.

Alex Van Pelt, running backs; born May 1, 1970, Pittsburgh, Pa. Quarterback Pittsburgh 1989-1992. Pro quarterback Buffalo Bills 1995-2003. College coach: Buffalo 2005. Pro coach: Frankfurt Galaxy (NFLE) 2005, Buffalo Bills 2006-09, Tampa Bay Buccaneers 2010-11, joined Packers in 2012.

Joe Whitt Jr., secondary-cornerbacks; born July 19, 1978, Auburn, Ala. Wide receiver Auburn 1997-99. No pro playing experience. College coach: Auburn 2000-01, The Citadel 2002, Louisville 2003-06. Pro coach: Atlanta Falcons 2007, joined Packers in 2008.

National Football Conference
North Division
Team Colors: Purple, Gold, and White
9520 Viking Drive
Eden Prairie, Minnesota 55344
Telephone: (952) 828-6500

2012 SCHEDULE
PRESEASON
Aug. 10   at San Francisco................8:00
Aug. 17   **Buffalo**.............................7:00
Aug. 24   **San Diego**.......................7:00
Aug. 30   at Houston 6:00

REGULAR SEASON
Sep. 9   **Jacksonville**...................12:00
Sep. 16   at Indianapolis 12:00
Sep. 23   **San Francisco**...............12:00
Sep. 30   at Detroit 12:00
Oct. 7   **Tennessee** 12:00
Oct. 14   at Washington 3:15
Oct. 21   **Arizona** 12:00
Oct. 25   **Tampa Bay** (Thurs) 7:20
Nov. 4   at Seattle 3:05
Nov. 11   **Detroit** 12:00
Nov. 18   BYE
Nov. 25   at Chicago.......................12:00
Dec. 2   at Green Bay 12:00
Dec. 9   **Chicago** 12:00
Dec. 16   at St. Louis......................12:00
Dec. 23   at Houston 12:00
Dec. 30   **Green Bay**......................12:00
All times CT
Stadium: Mall of America Field at
          Hubert H. Humphrey Metrodome
          (opened in 1982)
          •**Capacity:** 63,731
          425 Chicago Avenue
          Minneapolis, Minnesota 55415
Playing Surface: Sportexe Momentum
Training Camp: Minnesota State-Mankato
          Mankato, Minnesota
          56001

MALL OF AMERICA FIELD AT HUBERT H. HUMPHREY METRODOME

CLUB OFFICIALS
Owner/Chairman: Zygi Wilf
Owner/President: Mark Wilf
Owner/Vice Chairman: Leonard Wilf
Ownership Partners: Reggie Fowler,
   Alan Landis, David Mandelbaum
Vice President of Public Affairs/Stadium
   Development: Lester Bagley
Vice President of Football Operations:
   Rob Brzezinski
Vice President of Sales and Marketing:
   Steve LaCroix
Vice President of Finance: Steve Poppen
General Manager: Rick Spielman
Vice President of Operations and Legal
   Counsel: Kevin Warren
Director of College Scouting:
   Scott Studwell
Director of Public Relations: Bob Hagan
Director of Community Relations:
   Brad Madson
Director of Operations/Team Travel:
   Luther Hippe
Director of Operations & Facilities:
   Chad Lundeen
Director of Ticketing and Hospitality:
   Phil Huebner
Director of Video: Bob Marcus
Executive Director of Player
   Development/Legal: Les Pico
Director of Security: Kim Klawiter
Head Athletic Trainer: Eric Sugarman
Equipment Manager: Dennis Ryan
Director of Marketing & Business
   Development: Dannon Hulskotter
Director of Corporate Sales: Mike Slates

COACHING HISTORY
(435-375-9)
Records include postseason games
1961-66   Norm Van Brocklin 29-51-4
1967-1983   Bud Grant 161-99-5
1984   Les Steckel 3-13-0
1985   Bud Grant 7-9-0
1986-1991   Jerry Burns...............55-46-0
1992-2001   Dennis Green* 101-70-0
2001-05   Mike Tice 33-34-0
2006-2010   Brad Childress** 40-37-0
2010-11   Leslie Frazier...............6-16-0
   *Resigned after 15 games in 2001
   **Released after 10 games in 2010

PAID ATTENDANCE
Home 485,529   Away 540,372
Total 1,025,901
Single-game home record,
   64,482 (11/2/03)
Single-season home record,
   510,741 (1998)

2012 DRAFT CHOICES
Round	Name	Pos.	College
1	Matt Kalil	T	Southern California
	Harrison Smith	DB	Notre Dame
3	Josh Robinson	DB	Central Florida
4	Jarius Wright	WR	Arkansas
	Rhett Ellison	TE	Southern California
	Greg Childs	WR	Arkansas
5	Robert Blanton	DB	Notre Dame
6	Blair Walsh	K	Georgia
7	Audie Cole	LB	North Carolina St.
	Trevor Guyton	DT	California

2011 TEAM RECORD
PRESEASON (2-2)

Date	Result		Opponent
8/13	L	3-14	at Tennessee
8/20	W	20-7	at Seattle
8/27	L	17-23	Dallas
9/1	W	28-0	Houston

REGULAR SEASON (3-13)

Date	Result		Opponent
9/11	L	17-24	at San Diego
9/18	L	20-24	Tampa Bay
9/25	L	23-26	Detroit (OT)
10/2	L	17-22	at Kansas City
10/9	W	34-10	Arizona
10/16	L	10-39	at Chicago
10/23	L	27-33	Green Bay
10/30	W	24-21	at Carolina
11/14	L	7-45	at Green Bay
11/20	L	21-27	Oakland
11/27	L	14-24	at Atlanta
12/4	L	32-35	Denver
12/11	L	28-34	at Detroit
12/18	L	20-42	New Orleans
12/24	W	33-26	at Washington
1/1	L	13-17	Chicago
(OT) Overtime			

SCORE BY PERIODS

Vikings	104	91	61	84	0 —	340
Opponents	92	121	132	101	3 —	449

2011 TEAM STATISTICS

	Vikings	Opp.
Total First Downs	297	332
Rushing	118	92
Passing	159	213
Penalty	20	27
3rd Down: Made/Att	83/216	92/208
3rd Down Pct.	38.4	44.2
4th Down: Made/Att	7/18	5/9
4th Down Pct.	38.9	55.6
Possession Avg.	28:39	31:21
Total Net Yards	5275	5731
Avg. Per Game	329.7	358.2
Total Plays	1007	1027
Avg. Per Play	5.2	5.6
Net Yards Rushing	2318	1712
Avg. Per Game	144.9	107.0
Total Rushes	448	439
Net Yards Passing	2957	4019
Avg. Per Game	184.8	251.2
Sacked/Yards Lost	49/298	50/342
Gross Yards	3255	4361
Att./Completions	510/286	538/367
Completion Pct.	56.1	68.2
Had Intercepted	17	8
Punts/Average	77/45.7	67/47.1
Net Punting Avg.	77/38.0	67/41.1
Penalties/Yards	109/908	97/834
Fumbles/Ball Lost	20/9	26/15
Touchdowns	39	50
Rushing	18	10
Passing	20	34
Returns	1	6

2011 INDIVIDUAL STATISTICS

Passing	Att.	Comp.	Yds.	Pct.	TD	Int.	Tkld.	Rate
Ponder	291	158	1853	54.3	13	13	30/164	70.1
McNabb	156	94	1026	60.3	4	2	16/113	82.9
Webb	63	34	376	54.0	3	2	3/21	74.6
Vikings	510	286	3255	56.1	20	17	49/298	74.6
Opponents	538	367	4361	68.2	34	8	50/342	107.6

SCORING	TD R	TD P	TD Rt	PAT	FG	Saf	PTS
Longwell	0	0	0	38/39	22/28	0	104
Peterson	12	1	0	0/0	0/0	0	78
Harvin	2	6	1	0/0	0/0	0	54
Gerhart	1	3	0	0/0	0/0	0	24
Jenkins	0	3	0	0/0	0/0	0	18
Rudolph	0	3	0	0/0	0/0	0	18
Shiancoe	0	3	0	0/0	0/0	0	18
Webb	2	0	0	0/0	0/0	0	12
Aromashodu	0	1	0	0/0	0/0	0	6
McNabb	1	0	0	0/0	0/0	0	6
J. Allen	0	0	0	0/0	0/0	1	2
Vikings	18	20	1	38/39	22/28	1	340
Opponents	10	34	6	49/49	32/35	1	449

2-Pt Conversions: Vikings 0-0, Opponents 1-1

RUSHING	No.	Yds	Avg	LG	TD
Peterson	208	970	4.7	54	12
Gerhart	109	531	4.9	67	1
Harvin	52	345	6.6	39	2
Ponder	28	219	7.8	28	0
Webb	22	154	7.0	65t	2
McNabb	14	59	4.2	23	1
Booker	13	52	4.0	25	0
Kluwe	2	-12	-6.0	0	0
Vikings	448	2318	5.2	67	18
Opponents	439	1712	3.9	28	10

RECEIVING	No.	Yds	Avg	LG	TD
Harvin	87	967	11.1	52t	6
Jenkins	38	466	12.3	72	3
Shiancoe	36	409	11.4	37	3
Aromashodu	26	468	18.0	60	1
Rudolph	26	249	9.6	41	3
Gerhart	23	190	8.3	42	3
Peterson	18	139	7.7	22	1
Camarillo	9	121	13.4	23	0
Booker	8	82	10.3	15	0
Berrian	7	91	13.0	30	0
S. Burton	2	38	19.0	21	0
D'Imperio	2	7	3.5	6	0
Arceneaux	1	10	10.0	10	0
Webb	1	9	9.0	9	0
Reisner	1	5	5.0	5	0
Kleinsasser	1	4	4.0	4	0
Vikings	286	3255	11.4	72	20
Opponents	367	4361	11.9	79t	34

INTERCEPTIONS	No.	Yds	Avg	LG	TD
Sanford	2	69	34.5	52	0
Abdullah	1	32	32.0	32	0
Raymond	1	31	31.0	31	0
J. Allen	1	14	14.0	14	0
A. Allen	1	3	3.0	3	0
Winfield	1	3	3.0	3	0
Griffin	1	0	0.0	0	0
Vikings	8	152	19.0	52	0
Opponents	17	213	12.5	42	3

PUNTING	No.	Yds.	Avg.	In 20	LG
Kluwe	77	3517	45.7	22	60
Vikings	77	3517	45.7	22	60
Opponents	67	3153	47.1	22	65

PUNT RETURNS	Ret	FC	Yds	Avg	LG	TD
Sherels	33	20	277	8.4	53	0
Vikings	33	20	277	8.4	53	0
Opponents	43	19	532	12.4	80t	1

KICKOFF RETURNS	No.	Yds	Avg	LG	TD
Booker	19	450	23.7	68	0
Harvin	16	520	32.5	104	1
Sherels	16	445	27.8	78	0
D'Imperio	1	6	6.0	6	0
Griffen	1	7	7.0	7	0
Vikings	53	1428	26.9	104	1
Opponents	57	1403	24.6	98t	1

FIELD GOALS	1-19	20-29	30-39	40-49	50+
Longwell	0/0	7/7	7/8	6/10	2/3
Vikings	0/0	7/7	7/8	6/10	2/3
Opponents	0/0	14/14	5/6	6/7	7/8

SACKS	No.
J. Allen	22.0
Robison	8.0
Williams	5.0
Griffen	4.0
Greenway	2.0
E.J. Henderson	2.0
Ayodele	1.5
Er. Henderson	1.5
Abdullah	1.0
Sherels	1.0
Winfield	1.0
(group)	1.0
Vikings	50.0
Opponents	49.0

RECORD HOLDERS
INDIVIDUAL RECORDS—CAREER

Category	Name	Performance
Rushing (Yds.)	Robert Smith, 1993-2000	6,818
Passing (Yds.)	Fran Tarkenton, 1961-66, 1972-78	33,098
Passing (TDs)	Fran Tarkenton, 1961-66, 1972-78	239
Receiving (No.)	Cris Carter, 1990-2001	1,004
Receiving (Yds.)	Cris Carter, 1990-2001	12,383
Interceptions	Paul Krause, 1968-1979	53
Punting (Avg.)	Chris Kluwe, 2005-2011	44.4
Punt Return (Avg.)	Mewelde Moore, 2004-07	10.4
Kickoff Return (Avg.)	Percy Harvin, 2009-2011	26.6
Field Goals	Fred Cox, 1963-1977	282
Touchdowns (Tot.)	Cris Carter, 1990-2001	110
Points	Fred Cox, 1963-1977	1,365
*Sacks	John Randle, 1990-2000	114.0

INDIVIDUAL RECORDS—SINGLE SEASON

Category	Name	Performance
Rushing (Yds.)	Adrian Peterson, 2008	1,760
Passing (Yds.)	Daunte Culpepper, 2004	4,717
Passing (TDs)	Daunte Culpepper, 2004	39
Receiving (No.)	Cris Carter, 1994, 1995	122
Receiving (Yds.)	Randy Moss, 2003	1,632
Interceptions	Paul Krause, 1975	10
Punting (Avg.)	Chris Kluwe, 2008	47.6
Punt Return (Avg.)	David Palmer, 1995	13.2
Kickoff Return (Avg.)	Aundrae Allison, 2007	28.7
Field Goals	Gary Anderson, 1998	35
Touchdowns (Tot.)	Chuck Foreman, 1975	22
Points	Gary Anderson, 1998	164
*Sacks	Jared Allen, 2011	22.0

INDIVIDUAL RECORDS—SINGLE GAME

Category	Name	Performance
Rushing (Yds.)	Adrian Peterson, 11-4-07	**296
Passing (Yds.)	Tommy Kramer, 11-2-86	490
Passing (TDs)	Joe Kapp, 9-28-69	**7
Receiving (No.)	Rickey Young, 12-16-79	15
Receiving (Yds.)	Sammy White, 11-7-76	210
Interceptions	Many Times	3
	Last time by Darren Sharper, 11-13-05	
Field Goals	Rich Karlis, 11-5-89	7
Touchdowns (Tot.)	Chuck Foreman, 12-20-75	4
	Ahmad Rashad, 9-2-79	4
Points	Chuck Foreman, 12-20-75	24
	Ahmad Rashad, 9-2-79	24
*Sacks	Randy Holloway, 9-16-84	5.0

*Sacks became an official statistic in 1982.
**NFL Record

2012 VETERAN ROSTER

No.	Name	Pos.	Ht.	Wt.	Birthdate	NFL Exp.	College	Hometown	How Acq.	'11 Games/ Starts
21	Allen, Asher	CB	5-9	194	1/22/88	4	Georgia	Tucker, Ga.	D3-'09	13/9
69	Allen, Jared	DE	6-6	270	4/3/82	9	Idaho State	Los Gatos, Calif.	T(KC)-'08	16/16
16	Arceneaux, Emmanuel	WR	6-2	215	9/17/87	2	Alcorn State	Alexandria, La.	FA-'11	3/0
19	Aromashodu, Devin	WR	6-2	201	5/23/84	4	Auburn	Miami, Fla.	UFA(Chi)-'11	16/6
99	Ballard, Christian	DT	6-4	283	1/3/89	2	Iowa	Lawrence, Kan.	D4-'11	16/2
61	Berger, Joe	C	6-5	305	5/25/82	7	Michigan Tech	Newaygo, Mich.	FA-'11	13/7
24	Bowman, Zackary	DB	6-1	195	11/18/84	4	Nebraska	Anchorage, Alaska	UFA(Chi)-'12	16/1
54	Brinkley, Jasper	LB	6-1	252	7/12/85	3	South Carolina	Thomson, Ga.	D5-'09	0*
79	Brown, Pat	T	6-5	310	12/25/86	3	Central Florida	St. Charles, Ill.	FA-'10	15/0
36	Burton, Brandon	CB	5-11	190	7/31/89	2	Utah	Houston, Texas	D5-'11	10/1
86	Burton, Stephen	WR	6-1	224	12/11/89	2	West Texas A&M	Lakewood, Calif.	D7b-'11	3/0
89	Carlson, John	TE	6-5	248	5/12/84	4	Notre Dame	Litchfield, Minn.	UFA(Sea)-'12	0*
25	Carr, Chris	CB	5-10	181	4/30/83	8	Boise State	Reno, Nev.	FA-'12	9/1*
20	Cook, Chris	CB	6-2	212	2/15/87	3	Virginia	Lynchburg, Va.	D2a-'10	6/3
51	Dean, Larry	LB	6-0	226	8/7/88	2	Valdosta State	Tifton, Ga.	FA-'11	16/0
72	DeGeare, Chris	G	6-4	335	2/17/87	2	Wake Forest	Kernersville, N.C.	D5a-'10	0*
44	D'Imperio, Ryan	FB	6-3	240	8/15/87	2	Rutgers	Sewell, N.J.	D7b-'10	12/1
90	Evans, Fred	DT	6-4	305	11/6/83	6	Texas St.-San Marcos	Morgan Park, Ill.	FA-'07	16/0
42	Felton, Jerome	RB	6-0	248	7/3/86	5	Furman	Madisonville, Tenn	UFA(Ind)-'12	14/3*
37	Frampton, Eric	S	5-11	205	2/6/84	6	Washington State	San Jose, Calif.	W(Det)-'07	16/0
63	Fusco, Brandon	C	6-4	306	7/26/88	2	Slippery Rock	Cranberry Township, Pa.	D6c-'11	3/0
32	Gerhart, Toby	RB	6-0	231	3/28/87	3	Stanford	Norco, Calif.	D2b-'10	16/5
52	Greenway, Chad	LB	6-2	242	1/12/83	6	Iowa	Mt. Vernon, S.D.	D1-'06	16/16
97	Griffen, Everson	DE	6-3	273	12/22/87	3	Southern California	Avondale, Ariz.	D4-'10	16/0
98	Guion, Letroy	DT	6-4	303	6/21/87	5	Florida State	Starke, Fla.	D5b-'08	16/3
12	Harvin, Percy	WR	5-11	184	5/28/88	4	Florida	Virginia Beach, Va.	D1-'09	16/14
50	Henderson, Erin	LB	6-3	244	7/1/86	4	Maryland	Aberdeen, Md.	FA-'08	15/11
	Hilliard, Lex	RB	5-11	235	7/30/84	4	Montana	Kalispell, Mont.	FA-'12	16/4*
84	Jenkins, Michael	WR	6-4	214	6/18/82	9	Ohio State	Tampa, Fla.	UFA(Atl)-'11	11/7
74	Johnson, Charlie	T	6-4	305	5/2/84	7	Oklahoma State	Sherman, Texas	UFA(Ind)-'11	16/16
5	Kluwe, Chris	P	6-4	215	12/24/81	8	UCLA	Los Alamitos, Calif.	W(Sea)-'05	16/0
71	Loadholt, Phil	T	6-8	343	1/21/86	4	Oklahoma	Fountain, Colo.	D2-'09	16/16
46	Loeffler, Cullen	LS	6-5	241	1/27/81	9	Texas	Ingram, Texas	FA-'04	11/0
8	Longwell, Ryan	K	6-0	200	8/16/74	16	California	Bend, Ore.	UFA(GB)-'06	16/0
58	McKenzie, Tyrone	LB	6-2	245	12/11/85	2	South Florida	Riverview, Fla.	FA-'11	0*
55	Mitchell, Marvin	LB	6-3	246	10/21/84	6	Tennessee	Norfolk, Va.	UFA(Mia)-'12	16/0*
28	Peterson, Adrian	RB	6-1	217	3/21/85	6	Oklahoma	Palestine, Texas	D1-'07	12/12
7	Ponder, Christian	QB	6-2	229	2/25/88	2	Florida State	Colleyville, Texas	D1-'11	11/10
30	Raymond, Mistral	S	6-1	194	9/7/87	2	South Florida	Palmetto, Fla.	D6b-'11	10/5
83	Reisner, Allen	TE	6-3	255	9/29/88	2	Iowa	Cedar Rapids, Iowa	FA-'11	6/0
96	Robison, Brian	DE	6-3	259	4/27/83	6	Texas	Splendora, Texas	D4-'07	16/16
18	Rosenfels, Sage	QB	6-4	225	3/6/78	12	Iowa State	Maquoketa, Iowa	W(Mia)-'11	0*
82	Rudolph, Kyle	TE	6-6	258	11/9/89	2	Notre Dame	Cincinnati, Ohio	D2-'11	15/8
33	Sanford, Jamarca	S	5-10	200	8/27/85	4	Mississippi	Batesville, Miss.	D7-'09	15/15
76	Schwartz, Geoff	T	6-6	340	7/11/86	3	Oregon	Pacific Palisades, Calif.	FA-'12	0*
34	Sendejo, Andrew	S	6-1	200	9/9/87	2	Rice	Spring Branch, Texas	FA-'11	3/0
35	Sherels, Marcus	CB	5-10	175	9/30/87	2	Minnesota	Rochester, Minn.	FA-'10	16/3
86	Shuler, Mickey	TE	6-4	247	10/9/86	2	Penn State	Enola, Pa.	FA-'11	0*
	Simpson, Jerome	WR	6-2	189	2/4/86	5	Coastal Carolina	Reidsville, N.C.	UFA(Cin)-'12	16/14*
65	Sullivan, John	C	6-4	301	8/8/85	5	Notre Dame	Old Greenwich, Conn.	D6a-'08	15/15
	Walters, Bryan	WR	6-0	190	11/4/87	2	Cornell	Kirkland, Wash.	FA-'12	4/0*
14	Webb, Joe	QB	6-4	220	11/14/86	3	Alabama-Birmingham	Birmingham, Ala.	D6-'10	10/1
93	Williams, Kevin	DT	6-5	311	8/16/80	10	Oklahoma State	Fordyce, Ark.	D1-'03	14/14
26	Winfield, Antoine	CB	5-9	180	6/24/77	14	Ohio State	Akron, Ohio	UFA(Buff)-'04	5/5

* Bowman appeared in 16 games with Chicago in '11; Brinkley missed '11 season because of injury; Carlson missed '11 season with Seattle because of injury; Carr played 9 games with Baltimore; DeGeare spent '11 on the Minnesota practice squad, last active in '10 with Minnesota; Felton played 9 games with Carolina and 5 games with Indianapolis; Hilliard played 16 games with Miami; McKenzie spent the '11 season on the Minnesota practice squad, last active with Tampa Bay in '10; Mitchell played 16 games with Miami; Rosenfels did not play in 2 games with Miami and 5 games with Minnesota in '11; Schwartz missed '11 season because to injury; Shuler last active with Minnesota in '10; Simpson played 16 games with Cincinnati; Walters played 4 games with San Diego.

Players lost through free agency (4): DT Remi Ayodele (NO; 16 games), CB Cedric Griffin (Wash; 16), S Tyrell Johnson (Mia; 11), LB Kenny Onatolu (Car; 16).

Also played with Vikings in '11—S Husain Abdullah (9 games), LB Xavier Adibi (4), DE Adrian Awasom, WR Bernard Berrian (5), RB Lorenzo Booker (15), LB E.J. Henderson (16), LS Matt Katula (5), TE Jimmy Kleinsasser (16), QB Donovan McNabb (6), DB Jarrad Page (5), CB Benny Sapp (5), TE Visanthe Shiancoe (16).

FIRST-YEAR ROSTER

Name	Pos.	Ht.	Wt.	Birthdate	College	Hometown	How Acq.
Adams, Kris (1)	WR	6-4	194	9/4/87	Texas-El Paso	Ft. Worth, Texas	FA-'11
Asiata, Matt (1)	FB	6-0	234	7/24/87	Utah	Santa Ana, Calif.	FA-'11
Baker, Chase	DT	6-2	300	5/21/88	Boise State	Rocklin, Calif.	FA
Bethel-Thompson, McLeod (1)	QB	6-3	230	7/3/88	Sacramento State	San Francisco, Calif.	FA
Blanton, Robert	S	6-1	200	9/7/89	Notre Dame	Matthews, N.C.	D5
Childs, Greg	WR	6-3	217	3/10/90	Arkansas	Warren, Ark.	D4c
Cole, Audie	LB	6-5	239	6/1/89	North Carolina State	Monroe, Mich.	D7a
Coleman, Derrick	RB	6-0	233	10/18/90	UCLA	Fullerton, Calif.	FA
Cyrille, Kevin	DE	6-3	281	3/16/88	Florida Atlantic	Miami, Fla.	FA
Elimimian, Solomon (1)	LB	6-0	230	10/21/86	Hawaii	Los Angeles, Calif.	FA
Ellison, Rhett	FB	6-5	250	10/3/88	Southern California	Portola Valley, Calif.	D4b
Felder, Bobby	CB	5-11	200	9/23/90	Nicholls State	McComb, Miss.	FA
Guyton, Trevor	DT	6-3	280	1/9/90	California	Woodinville, Wash.	D7b
Jones, Reggie (1)	DB	6-0	195	3/15/86	Portland State	Kent, Wash.	FA-'11
Jorden, Kamar	WR	6-3	205	5/17/89	Bowling Green	Lansdowne, Pa.	FA
Kalil, Matt	T	6-7	308	7/6/89	Southern California	Corona, Calif.	D1a
Latimore, Eric	DE	6-5	280	2/16/87	Penn State	Middletown, Del.	FA
Love, DeMarcus (1)	T	6-4	315	3/7/88	Arkansas	Lancaster, Texas	D6a-'11
Nielsen, Tyler	LB	6-3	238	6/1/88	Iowa	Humboldt, Iowa	FA
Owusu, Ernest	DE	6-4	275	5/26/88	California	Princeton, N.J.	FA
Paredes, Corey	LB	5-10	230	8/23/89	Hawaii	Sacramento, Calif.	FA
Pasztor, Austin	G	6-7	308	11/26/90	Virginia	Fork Union, Va.	FA
Powell, Tydreke	DT	6-3	325	6/14/88	North Carolina	Ahoskie, N.C.	FA
Reed, D'Aundre (1)	DE	6-4	260	1/1/88	Arizona	Moreno Valley, Calif.	D7a-'11
Resonno, Terrell	DT	6-3	305	8/6/88	Missouri	Jefferson City, Mo.	FA
Robinson, Josh	CB	5-10	199	1/8/91	Central Florida	Sunrise, Fla.	D3
Saulsberry, Quentin	C	6-3	305	10/14/88	Mississippi State	Independence, Miss.	FA
Smith, Harrison	S	6-2	214	2/2/89	Notre Dame	Knoxville, Tenn.	D1b
Taylor, Kerry (1)	WR	6-0	200	2/20/89	Arizona State	Chandler, Ariz.	FA-'11
Taylor, Nicholas	DB	5-9	175	3/27/88	Florida International	Miami, Fla.	FA
Todman, Jordan (1)	RB	5-10	198	2/24/90	Connecticut	Dartmouth, Mass.	FA(SD-PS)-'11
Valdez, Jose (1)	T	6-5	310	12/13/86	Arkansas	St. Francis, Wisc.	FA
Walsh, Blair	K	5-10	192	1/8/90	Georgia	Boca Raton, Fla.	D6
Weems, Darrion	T	6-5	320	9/4/88	Oregon	Woodland Hills, Calif.	FA
Whitlock, C.C.	CB	5-9	184	4/1/89	South Carolina	Chester, S.C.	FA
Wright, Jarius	WR	5-10	180	11/25/89	Arkansas	Warren, Ark.	D4a

The term NFL Rookie is defined as a player who is in his first season of professional football and has not been on the roster of another professional football team for any regular-season or postseason games. A Rookie is designated by an "R" on NFL rosters. Players who have been active in another professional football league or players who have NFL experience, including either preseason training camp or being on an Active List or Inactive List, or on Reserve/Injured or Reserve/Physically Unable to Perform for fewer than six regular-season games, are termed NFL First-Year Players. An NFL First-Year Player is designated by a "1" on NFL rosters. Thereafter, a player is credited with an additional year of experience for each season in which he accumulates six games on the Active List or Inactive List, or on Reserve/Injured or Reserve/Physically Unable to Perform.

Log on to www.vikings.com for an up-to-date roster.

MINNESOTA VIKINGS

COACHING STAFF
Head Coach,
Leslie Frazier

Pro Career: Named the eighth head coach in Vikings' history on January 3, 2011 after serving as the club's interim head coach for the final six games of the 2010 season. The 2011 campaign was Frazier's first full season as a head coach and the Vikings finished at 3-13. In Frazier's first game as interim head coach he snapped a nine-game road losing streak by defeating the Washington Redskins. The Vikings finished the season 3-3, picking up two road victories, despite having to move two home games off-site after the Metrodome roof collapsed due to a major Twin Cities snow storm. Before coming head coach of the Vikings, Frazier led one of the NFL's top defenses from 2007-2010 in Minnesota. From 2008-2010, Frazier's defensive units ranked in the top 10 in total defense, a feat that hasn't been accomplished in Minnesota since 1992-94. Frazier enjoyed back-to-back NFC North division titles in 2008 and 2009 where his defense was first and second in the NFL against the run, respectively, and ranked first in rush defense in 2007, as well. Frazier won Super Bowl as a player (starting cornerback with 1985 Bears in Super Bowl XX) and coach (Super Bowl XLI as a defensive backs coach with Indianapolis). In his 13 seasons as an NFL coach, and 11 years of collegiate experience prior to that, Frazier has suffered a losing season only three times. He has coached on seven playoff teams in his 13 NFL seasons and been a part of six division championships. Career record: 6-16.

Background: Coached at Trinity (1988-1996) and Illinois (1997-98). Coached professionally with the Eagles (1999-2002), Bengals (2003-04), and Colts (2005-06) before joining the Vikings as their assistant head coach/defensive coordinator in 2007. Played defensive back collegially at Alcorn State (1977-1980) and professionally with the Bears (1981-86).

Personal: Born April 3, 1959 in Columbus, Miss. He and wife Gayle have three children: Kieron, Chantel and Corey, who plays defensive back at Rice. Frazier earned degree in business administration.

ASSISTANT COACHES

Brendan Daly, defensive line; born September 10, 1975, Springfield, Ill. Tight end Drake 1993-96. No pro playing experience. College coach: Drake 1998, Villanova 1999, 2005, Maryland 2000, Oklahoma State 2001-03, Illinois State 2004. Pro coach: Minnesota Vikings 2006-08, St. Louis Rams 2009-2011, joined Vikings in 2012.

Jeff Davidson, offensive line; born October 3, 1967, Akron, Ohio. Offensive line Ohio State 1986-89. Pro offensive lineman Denver Broncos 1990-92, New Orleans Saints 1994. Pro coach: New Orleans Saints 1995-96, New England Patriots 1997-2004, Cleveland Browns 2005-06, Carolina Panthers 2007-10, joined Vikings in 2011.

Ryan Ficken, asst. wide receivers; born

February 20, 1980, Aurora, Colo. Wide receiver Arizona State 1998-99. No pro playing experience. College coach: UCLA 2004-06. Pro coach: Joined Vikings in 2007.

Jeff Imamura, defensive assistant/linebackers; born May 22, 1974, Lubbock, Texas. Attended Texas Christian. No college or pro playing experience. College coach: Texas Christian 1997-99, Northern Arizona 2000-02, Saginaw Valley State 2003. Pro coach: Joined Vikings in 2006.

Craig Johnson, quarterbacks; born March 3, 1960, Rome, N.Y. Quarterback Wyoming 1979-1982. No pro playing experience. College coach: Wyoming 1983, Arkansas 1984, Army 1985, Rutgers 1986-88, Virginia Military Institute 1989-1991, Northwestern 1992-96, Maryland 1997-99. Pro coach: Tennessee Titans 2000-10, joined Vikings in 2011.

Jimmie Johnson, tight ends; born October 6, 1966, Augusta, Ga. Tight end Howard 1985-88. Pro tight end Washington Redskins 1989-1991, Detroit Lions 1992-93, Kansas City Chiefs 1994, Philadelphia Eagles 1995-98. College coach: South Carolina State 2001, Shaw 2002-03, Texas Southern 2004-05. Pro coach: Joined Vikings in 2006.

Tom Kanavy, strength and conditioning; born April 8, 1970, Archibald, Pa. Attended Penn State. No college or pro playing experience. College coach: Miami 1993, Penn State 1993-95. Pro coach: Philadelphia Eagles 1995-2005, joined Vikings in 2006.

Bill Musgrave, offensive coordinator; born November 11, 1967, Grand Junction, Colo. Quarterback Oregon 1987-1990. Pro quarterback San Francisco 49ers 1991-94, Denver Broncos 1995-96. College coach: Virginia 2001-02. Pro coach: Oakland Raiders 1997, Philadelphia Eagles 1998, Carolina Panthers 1999-2000, Jacksonville Jaguars 2003-04, Washington Redskins 2005, Atlanta Falcons 2006-2010, joined Vikings in 2011.

Fred Pagac, linebackers; born April 26, 1952, Richeyville, Pa. Tight end Ohio State 1971-73. Pro tight end Chicago Bears 1974, Tampa Bay Buccaneers 1976. College coach: Ohio State 1978-2000. Pro coach: Oakland Raiders 2001-03, Kansas City Chiefs 2004-05, joined Vikings in 2006.

Mike Priefer, special teams coordinator; born August 21, 1966, Cleveland, Ohio. Quarterback/wide receiver Navy 1985-88. No pro playing experience. College coach: Navy 1994-96, Youngstown State 1997-98, Virginia Military Institute 1999, Northern Illinois 2000-01. Pro coach: Jacksonville Jaguars 2002, N.Y. Giants 2003-05, Kansas City Chiefs 2006-08, Denver Broncos 2009-10, joined Vikings in 2011.

Diron Reynolds, asst. defensive line; born February 23, 1971, Aiken, S.C. Linebacker Wake Forest 1990-93. No pro playing experience. College coach: Wake Forest 1997-2000, Indiana 2001. Pro coach: Indianapolis Colts 2002-06, Miami Dolphins 2007, joined Vikings in 2009.

James Saxon, running backs; born March 23, 1966, Beaufort, S.C. Running back American River (Calif.) C.C. 1984-85, San Jose State 1986-

87. Pro running back Kansas City Chiefs 1988-1991, Miami Dolphins 1992-94, Philadelphia Eagles 1995. College coach: Rutgers 1997-98, Menlo 1999. Pro coach: Buffalo Bills 2000, Kansas City Chiefs 2001-07, Miami Dolphins 2008-10, joined Vikings in 2011.

Ryan Silverfield, asst. offensive line; born August 4, 1980, Jacksonville, Fla. Attended Hampden-Sydney. No college or pro playing experience. College coach: Hampden-Sydney 2000-03, Jacksonville 2005, Central Florida 2006-07. Pro coach: Joined Vikings in 2008.

Mike Singletary, special asst. to head coach/linebackers; born October 9, 1958, Houston, Texas. Linebacker Baylor 1977-1980. Pro linebacker Chicago Bears 1981-1992. Pro coach: Baltimore Ravens 2003-04, San Francisco 49ers 2005-2010 (head coach 2008-2010), joined Vikings in 2011.

Kevin Stefanski, asst. quarterbacks; born May 8, 1982, Philadelphia, Pa. Safety Pennsylvania 2000-04. No pro playing experience. College coach: Pennsylvania 2005. Pro coach: Joined Vikings in 2006.

George Stewart, wide receivers; born December 29, 1958, Little Rock, Ark. Guard Arkansas 1977-1980. No pro playing experience. College coach: Minnesota 1984-85, Notre Dame 1986-88. Pro coach: Pittsburgh Steelers 1989-1991, Tampa Bay Buccaneers 1992-95, San Francisco 49ers 1996-2002, Atlanta Falcons 2003-06, joined Vikings in 2007.

Martin Streight, asst. strength and conditioning; born June 20, 1969, Trenton, N.J. Attended Indiana (Penn.). No college or pro playing experience. College coach: Penn State 1994, Princeton 1995-96. Pro coach: Philadelphia Eagles 1995-96, Arizona Cardinals 1997-2003, Scottish Claymores (NFLE) 2003, Berlin Thunder (NFLE) 2004-05, joined Vikings in 2006.

Cameron Turner, asst. to head coach; born July 29, 1987, Huntington Beach, Calif. Quarterback/wide receiver The Citadel 2007-09. No pro playing experience. College coach: The Citadel 2010. Pro coach: Joined Vikings in 2011.

Chris White, asst. special teams; born June 29, 1967, Haverhill, Mass. Quarterback Colby College 1986-89. No pro playing experience. College coach: Syracuse 1990-92, 2000-08, Arkansas State 1992-93, Holy Cross 1993-94, Nevada-Las Vegas 1996-98, Cal Poly-San Luis Obispo 1999. Pro coach: Joined Vikings in 2009.

Alan Williams, defensive coordinator; born November 4, 1969, Norfolk, Va. Running back William & Mary 1988-1991. No pro playing experience. College coach: William & Mary 1996-2000. Pro coach: Tampa Bay Buccaneers 2001, Indianapolis Colts 2002-2011, joined Vikings in 2012.

Joe Woods, defensive backs; born June 25, 1970, Natrona Heights, Pa. Safety Illinois State 1988-1991. College coach: Muskingum 1992, Eastern Michigan 1993, Northwestern (La.) State 1994, Grand Valley State 1994-96, Kent State 1997, Hofstra 1998-2000, Western Michigan 2001-03. Pro coach: Tampa Bay Buccaneers 2004-05, joined Vikings in 2006.

National Football Conference
South Division
Team Colors: Old Gold, Black, and White
5800 Airline Drive
Metairie, Louisiana 70003
Telephone: (504) 733-0255

2012 SCHEDULE
PRESEASON
Aug. 5	vs. Arizona (Canton)	7:00
Aug. 9	at New England	6:30
Aug. 18	**Jacksonville**	7:00
Aug. 25	**Houston**	7:00
Aug. 30	at Tennessee	6:00

REGULAR SEASON
Sep. 9	**Washington**	12:00
Sep. 16	at Carolina	12:00
Sep. 23	**Kansas City**	12:00
Sep. 30	at Green Bay	3:15
Oct. 7	**San Diego**	7:20
Oct. 14	BYE	
Oct. 21	at Tampa Bay	12:00
Oct. 28	at Denver	7:20
Nov. 5	**Philadelphia** (Mon)	7:30
Nov. 11	**Atlanta**	12:00
Nov. 18	at Oakland	3:05
Nov. 25	**San Francisco**	3:15
Nov. 29	at Atlanta (Thurs)	7:20
Dec. 9	at New York Giants	3:15
Dec. 16	**Tampa Bay**	12:00
Dec. 23	at Dallas	12:00
Dec. 30	**Carolina**	12:00

*All times CT
Stadium: Mercedes-Benz Superdome
(opened in 1975)
• **Capacity:** 73,000
1500 Poydras Street
New Orleans, Louisiana 70112
Playing Surface: UBU Speed Series-S5-M
Training Camp: New Orleans Saints
Metairie, Louisiana 70003

MERCEDES-BENZ SUPERDOME

CLUB OFFICIALS
Owner/President: Tom Benson
Owner/Executive Vice President:
Rita Benson LeBlanc
Executive Vice President/General
Manager: Mickey Loomis
Executive Vice President/Chief Financial
Officer: Dennis Lauscha
Vice President of Communications:
Greg Bensel
Vice President of Marketing and
Business Development: Ben Hales
Vice President/General Counsel:
Vicky Neumeyer
Vice President of Ticket and Suite Sales:
Mike Stanfield
Director of Football Administration:
Khai Harley
Director of Operations: James Nagaoka
Pro Scouting Director: Ryan Pace
Pro Scouts: Terry Fontenot, Ryan Powell
Director of College Scouting:
Rick Reiprish
Assistant Director of College Scouting:
Brian Adams
College Scouting Coordinator:
Jason Mitchell
Area Scouts: Mike Baugh,
Dwaune Jones, Josh Lucas,
Jim Monos, Terry Wooden
Combine Scout: Ryan Hollern
Salary Cap Analyst/Player Personnel:
Joseph Laine
Scouting Assistants: Matt Manocherian,
Joey Vitt
Equipment Manager: Dan Simmons
Assistant Equipment Managers:
Glennon (Silky) Powell,
John Baumgartner
Head Athletic Trainer: Scottie B. Patton
Assistant Athletic Trainers:
Duane Brooks, Kevin Mangum
Video Director: Dave Desposito
Video Assistants: Joe Alley, Paul Zimmer,
Ryan Murphy
Director of Player Development:
Fred McAfee
Director of Security: Danny Lawless
Senior Director of Communications:
Doug Miller
Communications Manager:
Justin Macione
Director of Photography:
Michael C. Hebert
Information Technology/Network
Manager: Jeff Huffman
Facilities Manager: Terry Ashburn
Administrative Director: Jay Romig

COACHING HISTORY
(305-394-5)
Records include postseason games
1967-70	Tom Fears*	13-34-2
1970-72	J.D. Roberts	7-25-3
1973-75	John North**	11-23-0
1975	Ernie Hefferle	1-7-0
1976-77	Hank Stram	7-21-0
1978-80	Dick Nolan***	15-29-0
1980	Dick Stanfel	1-3-0
1981-85	O.A. (Bum) Phillips****	27-42-0
1985	Wade Phillips	1-3-0
1986-96	Jim Mora#	93-78-0
1996	Rick Venturi	1-7-0
1997-99	Mike Ditka	15-33-0
2000-05	Jim Haslett	46-52-0
2006-2011	Sean Payton	67-37-0

*Released after seven games in 1970
**Released after six games in 1975
***Released after 12 games in 1980
****Resigned after 12 games in 1985
#Resigned after eight games in 1996

PAID ATTENDANCE
Home 560,941   Away 499,298
Total 1,060,239
Single-game home record,
73,085 (12/26/11)
Single-season home record,
573,876 (2008)

2012 DRAFT CHOICES
Round	Name	Pos.	College
3	Akiem Hicks	DT	Regina (Canada)
4	Nick Toon	WR	Wisconsin
5	Corey White	CB	Samford
6	Andrew Tiller	G	Syracuse
7	Marcel Jones	T	Nebraska

NEW ORLEANS SAINTS

2011 TEAM RECORD

PRESEASON (2-2)

Date	Result	Opponent
8/12	W 24-3	San Francisco
8/20	L 14-27	at Houston
8/28	W 40-20	at Oakland
9/1	L 9-32	Tennessee

REGULAR SEASON (13-3)

Date	Result	Opponent
9/8	L 34-42	at Green Bay
9/18	W 30-13	Chicago
9/25	W 40-33	Houston
10/2	W 23-10	at Jacksonville
10/9	W 30-27	at Carolina
10/16	L 20-26	at Tampa Bay
10/23	W 62-7	Indianapolis
10/30	L 21-31	at St. Louis
11/6	W 27-16	Tampa Bay
11/13	W 26-23	at Atlanta (OT)
11/28	W 49-24	New York Giants
12/4	W 31-17	Detroit
12/11	W 22-17	at Tennessee
12/18	W 42-20	at Minnesota
12/26	W 45-16	Atlanta
1/1	W 45-17	Carolina

POSTSEASON (1-1)

Date	Result	Opponent
1/7	W 45-28	Detroit
1/14	L 32-36	at San Francisco

(OT) Overtime

SCORE BY PERIODS

Saints	99	166	126	153	3	—	547
Opponents	70	113	67	89	0	—	339

2011 TEAM STATISTICS

	Saints	Opp.
Total First Downs	416	326
Rushing	116	92
Passing	280	196
Penalty	20	38
3rd Down: Made/Att	118/208	67/202
3rd Down Pct.	56.7	33.2
4th Down: Made/Att	3/10	6/22
4th Down Pct.	30.0	27.3
Possession Avg.	31:46	28:14
Total Net Yards	7474	5895
Avg. Per Game	467.1	368.4
Total Plays	1117	1010
Avg. Per Play	6.7	5.8
Net Yards Rushing	2127	1738
Avg. Per Game	132.9	108.6
Total Rushes	431	351
Net Yards Passing	5347	4157
Avg. Per Game	334.2	259.8
Sacked/Yards Lost	24/158	33/256
Gross Yards	5505	4413
Att./Completions	662/472	626/362
Completion Pct.	71.3	57.8
Had Intercepted	14	9
Punts/Average	47/47.3	71/44.3
Net Punting Avg.	47/43.1	71/38.5
Penalties/Yards	99/851	109/912
Fumbles/Ball Lost	6/5	20/7
Touchdowns	66	37
Rushing	16	11
Passing	46	24
Returns	4	2

2011 INDIVIDUAL STATISTICS

PASSING

	Att.	Comp.	Yds.	Pct.	TD	Int.	Tkld.	Rate
Brees	657	468	5476	71.2	46	14	24/158	110.6
Daniel	5	4	29	80.0	0	0	0/0	90.8
Saints	662	472	5505	71.3	46	14	24/158	110.5
Opponents	626	362	4413	57.8	24	9	33/256	86.4

SCORING

	TD R	TD P	TD Rt	PAT	FG	Saf	PTS
Kasay	0	0	0	63/63	28/34	0	147
Graham	0	11	0	0/0	0/0	0	66
Sproles	2	7	1	0/0	0/0	0	60
Moore	0	8	0	0/0	0/0	0	52
Colston	0	8	0	0/0	0/0	0	48
Meachem	0	6	0	0/0	0/0	0	36
P. Thomas	5	1	0	0/0	0/0	0	36
Ingram	5	0	0	0/0	0/0	0	30
Collins	2	2	0	0/0	0/0	0	24
Henderson	0	2	0	0/0	0/0	0	12
Brees	1	0	0	0/0	0/0	0	6
Gilmore	0	1	0	0/0	0/0	0	6
Ivory	1	0	0	0/0	0/0	0	6
Jenkins	0	0	1	0/0	0/0	0	6
Torrence	0	0	1	0/0	0/0	0	6
Vilma	0	0	1	0/0	0/0	0	6
Saints	16	46	4	63/63	28/34	0	547
Opponents	11	24	2	36/37	27/32	0	339

2-Pt Conversions: Moore 2
Saints 2-3, Opponents 0-0

RUSHING

	No.	Yds	Avg	LG	TD
Sproles	87	603	6.9	36	2
P. Thomas	110	562	5.1	33	5
Ingram	122	474	3.9	35t	5
Ivory	79	374	4.7	35t	1
Brees	21	86	4.1	20	1
Meachem	4	18	4.5	8	0
Henderson	1	9	9.0	9	0
Collins	4	4	1.0	2	2
Daniel	3	-3	-1.0	-1	0
Saints	431	2127	4.9	36	16
Opponents	351	1738	5.0	69t	11

RECEIVING

	No.	Yds	Avg	LG	TD
Graham	99	1310	13.2	59	11
Sproles	86	710	8.3	39	7
Colston	80	1143	14.3	50	8
Moore	52	627	12.1	47t	8
P. Thomas	50	425	8.5	57	1
Meachem	40	620	15.5	67t	6
Henderson	32	503	15.7	79t	2
Collins	11	50	4.5	14	2
Ingram	11	46	4.2	9	0
D. Thomas	5	16	3.2	8	0
Gilmore	3	20	6.7	9	1
Arrington	2	31	15.5	17	0
Higgins	1	4	4.0	4	0
Saints	472	5505	11.7	79t	46
Opponents	362	4413	12.2	72t	24

INTERCEPTIONS

	No.	Yds	Avg	LG	TD
P. Robinson	4	31	7.8	25	0
Torrence	1	42	42.0	42t	1
Shanle	1	12	12.0	12	0
Greer	1	2	2.0	2	0
Herring	1	0	0.0	0	0
Porter	1	-7	-7.0	-7	0
Saints	9	80	8.9	42t	1
Opponents	14	162	11.6	53	1

PUNTING

	No.	Yds.	Avg.	In 20	LG
Morstead	46	2224	48.3	13	64
Saints	47	2224	47.3	13	64
Opponents	71	3146	44.3	24	59

PUNT RETURNS

	Ret	FC	Yds	Avg	LG	TD
Sproles	29	19	294	10.1	72t	1
Saints	29	19	294	10.1	72t	1
Opponents	19	10	118	6.2	14	0

KICKOFF RETURNS

	No.	Yds	Avg	LG	TD
Sproles	40	1089	27.2	92	0
Collins	1	7	7.0	7	0
P. Thomas	1	15	15.0	15	0
Graham	0	0	—	0	0
Saints	42	1111	26.5	92	0
Opponents	36	927	25.8	108t	1

FIELD GOALS

	1-19	20-29	30-39	40-49	50+
Kasay	0/0	11/11	10/10	5/8	2/5
Saints	0/0	11/11	10/10	5/8	2/5
Opponents	0/0	6/6	9/9	11/13	1/4

SACKS

	No.
Harper	7.5
Smith	6.5
Galette	4.5
Casillas	3.0
McBride	2.0
Charleston	1.0
Dunbar	1.0
Humber	1.0
Jenkins	1.0
Johnson	1.0
Jordan	1.0
Shanle	1.0
Torrence	1.0
Wilson	1.0
Ellis	0.5
Saints	33.0
Opponents	24.0

RECORD HOLDERS
INDIVIDUAL RECORDS—CAREER

Category	Name	Performance
Rushing (Yds.)	Deuce McAllister, 2001-09	6,096
Passing (Yds.)	Drew Brees, 2006-2011	28,394
Passing (TDs)	Drew Brees, 2006-2011	201
Receiving (No.)	Eric Martin, 1985-1993	532
Receiving (Yds.)	Eric Martin, 1985-1993	7,854
Interceptions	Dave Waymer, 1980-89	37
Punting (Avg.)	Thomas Morstead, 2009-2011	45.8
Punt Return (Avg.)	Mel Gray, 1986-88	13.4
Kickoff Return (Avg.)	Walt Roberts, 1967	26.3
Field Goals	Morten Andersen, 1982-1994	302
Touchdowns (Tot.)	Deuce McAllister, 2001-09	55
Points	Morten Andersen, 1982-1994	1,318
*Sacks	Rickey Jackson, 1981-1993	115.0

INDIVIDUAL RECORDS—SINGLE SEASON

Category	Name	Performance
Rushing (Yds.)	George Rogers, 1981	1,674
Passing (Yds.)	Drew Brees, 2011	**5,476
Passing (TDs)	Drew Brees, 2011	46
Receiving (No.)	Jimmy Graham, 2011	99
Receiving (Yds.)	Joe Horn, 2004	1,399
Interceptions	Dave Whitsell, 1967	10
Punting (Avg.)	Thomas Morstead, 2011	48.3
Punt Return (Avg.)	Mel Gray, 1987	14.7
Kickoff Return (Avg.)	John Gilliam, 1967	30.1
Field Goals	Morten Andersen, 1985	31
	John Carney, 2002	31
Touchdowns (Tot.)	Dalton Hilliard, 1989	18
Points	John Kasay, 2011	147
*Sacks	Pat Swilling, 1991	17.0
	La'Roi Glover, 2000	17.0

INDIVIDUAL RECORDS—SINGLE GAME

Category	Name	Performance
Rushing (Yds.)	George Rogers, 9-4-83	206
Passing (Yds.)	Drew Brees, 11-19-06	510
Passing (TDs)	Billy Kilmer, 11-2-69	6
	Drew Brees, 9-13-09	6
Receiving (No.)	Tony Galbreath, 9-10-78	14
Receiving (Yds.)	Wes Chandler, 9-2-79	205
Interceptions	Tommy Myers, 9-3-78	3
	Dave Waymer, 10-6-85	3
	Reggie Sutton, 10-18-87	3
	Gene Atkins, 12-22-91	3
	Sammy Knight, 9-9-01	3
Field Goals	Many times	5
	Last time by John Carney, 9-26-04	
Touchdowns (Tot.)	Joe Horn, 12-14-03	4
	Reggie Bush, 12-3-06	4
Points	Joe Horn, 12-14-03	24
	Reggie Bush, 12-3-06	24
*Sacks	Many times	4.0
	Last time by Wayne Martin, 9-21-97	

*Sacks became an official statistic in 1982.
**NFL Record

2012 VETERAN ROSTER

No.	Name	Pos.	Ht.	Wt.	Birthdate	NFL Exp.	College	Hometown	How Acq.	'11 Games/ Starts
42	Abdul-Quddus, Isa	S	6-1	220	8/3/89	2	Fordham	Union, N.J.	FA-'11	16/1
40	Amaya, Jonathon	S	6-2	205	11/25/88	3	Nevada	Diamond Bar, Calif.	T(Mia)-'11	16/0
87	Arrington, Adrian	WR	6-3	192	11/7/85	3	Michigan	Cedar Rapids, Iowa	D7-'08	3/0
92	Ayodele, Remi	DT	6-2	318	4/22/83	6	Oklahoma	Grand Prairie, Texas	UFA(Minn)-'12	16/13*
9	e-Brees, Drew	QB	6-0	209	1/15/79	12	Purdue	Austin, Texas	UFA(SD)-'06	16/16
71	Brown, Charles	T	6-5	297	4/10/87	3	Southern California	Chino Hills, Calif.	D2-'10	8/5
77	Bunkley, Brodrick	DT	6-2	306	11/23/83	7	Florida State	Tampa, Fla.	UFA(Den)-'12	16/13*
74	Bushrod, Jermon	T	6-5	315	8/19/84	6	Towson	King George, Va.	D4b-'07	16/16
52	Casillas, Jonathan	LB	6-1	227	6/3/87	4	Wisconsin	New Brunswick, N.J.	FA-'09	12/4
56	Chamberlain, Chris	LB	6-1	238	9/30/85	5	Tulsa	Bethany, Okla.	UFA(StL)-'12	16/13*
45	Collins, Jed	FB	6-1	255	3/3/86	2	Washington State	Mission Viejo, Calif.	FA-'10	16/11
12	Colston, Marques	WR	6-4	225	6/5/83	7	Hofstra	Harrisburg, Pa.	D7b-'06	14/7
10	Daniel, Chase	QB	6-0	225	10/7/86	4	Missouri	Southlake, Texas	FA-'09	16/0
60	de la Puente, Brian	G	6-3	306	5/13/85	3	California	San Clemente, Calif.	FA-'10	16/12
47	Drescher, Justin	LS	6-1	235	1/1/88	3	Colorado	Southlake, Texas	FA-'10	16/0
98	Ellis, Sedrick	DT	6-1	307	7/9/85	5	Southern California	Chino, Calif.	D1-'08	15/15
73	Evans, Jahri	G	6-4	318	8/22/83	7	Bloomsburg	Philadelphia, Pa.	D4-'06	16/16
93	Galette, Junior	DE	6-2	258	3/27/88	3	Stillman	Montvale, N.J.	FA-'10	16/1
80	Graham, Jimmy	TE	6-7	265	11/24/86	3	Miami	Goldsboro, N.C.	D3-'10	16/11
33	Greer, Jabari	CB	5-11	180	2/11/82	9	Tennessee	Jackson, Tenn.	UFA(Buff)-'09	16/16
66	Grubbs, Ben	G	6-3	310	3/10/84	6	Auburn	Eclectic, Ala.	UFA(Balt)-'12	10/10*
35	Hall, Korey	FB	6-0	236	8/5/83	6	Boise State	Glenns Ferry, Idaho	UFA(GB)-'11	13/0
41	Harper, Roman	S	6-1	200	12/11/82	7	Alabama	Prattville, Ala.	D2-'06	16/16
5	Hartley, Garrett	K	5-8	195	5/16/86	5	Oklahoma	Southlake, Texas	FA-'08	0*
57	Hawthorne, David	LB	6-0	246	5/14/85	5	Texas Christian	Corsicana, Texas	UFA(Sea)-'12	15/14*
19	Henderson, Devery	WR	5-11	200	3/26/82	9	Louisiana State	Opelousas, La.	D2a-'04	16/13
54	Herring, Will	LB	6-3	241	8/28/83	6	Auburn	Opelika, Ala.	UFA(Sea)-'11	11/2
81	Higgins, Michael	TE	6-5	242	12/7/87	2	Nebraska-Omaha	Beatrice, Neb.	FA-'11	2/0
28	Ingram, Mark	RB	5-9	215	12/21/89	2	Alabama	Flint, Mich.	D1b-'11	10/4
29	Ivory, Chris	RB	6-0	222	3/22/88	3	Tiffin	Longview, Texas	FA-'10	6/2
27	Jenkins, Malcolm	S	6-0	204	12/20/87	4	Ohio State	Piscataway, N.J.	D1-'09	15/15
49	Johnson, Marquis	CB	5-11	203	5/18/88	2	Alabama	Sarasota, Fla.	FA-'12	3/0*
96	Johnson, Tom	DT	6-3	288	8/30/84	2	Southern Mississippi	Moss Point, Miss.	FA-'11	13/0
94	Jordan, Cameron	DE	6-4	287	7/10/89	2	California	Chandler, Ariz.	D1a-'11	16/15
2	Kasay, John	K	5-10	210	10/27/69	22	Georgia	Athens, Ga.	FA-'11	16/0
50	Lofton, Curtis	LB	6-0	241	6/2/86	5	Oklahoma	Kingfisher, Okla.	UFA(Atl)-'12	16/16*
90	McBride, Turk	DE	6-2	278	5/30/85	6	Tennessee	Camden, N.J.	UFA(Det)-'11	8/2
16	Moore, Lance	WR	5-9	190	8/31/83	7	Toledo	Westerville, Ohio	FA-'07	14/7
13	Morgan, Joseph	WR	6-1	184	3/23/88	2	Walsh	Canton, Ohio	FA-'11	0*
6	Morstead, Thomas	P	6-4	235	3/7/86	4	Southern Methodist	Pearland, Texas	D5-'09	16/0
69	Olsen, Eric	G	6-3	305	6/16/88	2	Notre Dame	Staten Island, N.Y.	FA-'11	0*
32	Patrick, Johnny	CB	5-11	191	8/17/88	2	Louisville	DeLand, Fla.	D3b-'11	9/0
21	Robinson, Patrick	CB	5-11	191	9/7/87	3	Florida State	Miami, Fla.	D1-'10	15/7
15	Roby, Courtney	WR	6-0	189	1/10/83	7	Indiana	Indianapolis, Ind.	FA-'09	16/0
58	Shanle, Scott	LB	6-2	245	11/23/79	10	Nebraska	St. Edward, Neb.	T(Dall)-'06	16/14
91	Smith, Will	DE	6-3	282	7/4/81	9	Ohio State	Utica, N.Y.	D1-'04	14/14
43	Sproles, Darren	RB	5-6	190	6/20/83	8	Kansas State	Olathe, Kan.	UFA(SD)-'11	16/4
64	Strief, Zach	T	6-7	320	9/22/83	7	Northwestern	Milford, Ohio	D7a-'06	11/11
36	Taylor, Chris	RB	6-0	224	11/7/83	4	Indiana	Memphis, Tenn.	FA-'10	0*
65	Tennant, Matt	C/G	6-4	300	3/19/87	3	Boston College	Cincinnati, Ohio	D5-'10	12/0
85	Thomas, David	TE	6-3	248	7/5/83	7	Texas	Plainview, Texas	T(NE)-'09	5/2
23	Thomas, Pierre	RB	5-11	215	12/18/84	6	Illinois	Lynwood, Ill.	FA-'07	16/7
72	Tupou, Fenuki	T	6-5	323	5/2/85	2	Oregon	Sacramento, Calif.	FA-'11	0*
51	Vilma, Jonathan	LB	6-1	230	4/16/82	9	Miami	Coral Gables, Fla.	T(NYJ)-'08	11/11
95	Wilson, Martez	LB	6-4	252	9/21/88	2	Illinois	Chicago, Ill.	D3a-'11	13/1

* Ayodele played 16 games with Minnesota in '11; Bunkley played 16 games with Denver; Chamberlain played 16 games with St. Louis; Grubbs played 10 games with Baltimore; Hartley missed '11 season because of injury; Hawthorne played 15 games with Seattle; M. Johnson played 3 games with St. Louis; Lofton played 16 games with Atlanta; Morgan missed '11 season because of injury; Olsen inactive for 2 postseason games; Taylor missed '09 season with New England because of injury; Tupou missed '09 season with Philadelphia because of injury.

e-Exclusive rights franchise player; subject to developments.

Players lost through free agency (6): LB Jo-Lonn Dunbar (StL; 16), WR Robert Meachem (SD; 10), G Carl Nicks (TB; 16), CB Tracy Porter (Den; 14), DT Shaun Rogers (NYG; 16), CB Leigh Torrence (Wash; 13).

Also played with Saints in '11—DE Jeff Charleston (10 games), DT Aubrayo Franklin (16), TE John Gilmore (14), LB Ramon Humber (13), C Olin Kreutz (4), Pat McQuistan (10).

FIRST-YEAR ROSTER

Name	Pos.	Ht.	Wt.	Birthdate	College	Hometown	How Acq.
Anderson, Kadarron	LB	6-1	234	6/6/89	Furman	Greenwood, S.C.	FA
Beyah, Malcolm	WR	5-11	192	10/23/89	Middle Tennessee State	Chamblee, Ga.	FA
Broughton, Braylon	DE	6-6	272	12/25/87	Texas Christian	Dallas, Texas	FA
Bussey, Nate (1)	LB	6-2	220	2/20/89	Illinois	Washington, D.C.	FA-'11
Butler, Ezra (1)	LB	6-2	248	11/20/84	Nevada	Calabasas, Calif.	FA-'11
Byrne, Jake	TE	6-4	260	1/24/90	Wisconsin	Rogers, Ark.	FA
Cadet, Travaris	RB	6-1	210	2/1/89	Appalachian State	Miami, Fla.	FA
Canfield, Sean (1)	QB	6-4	223	11/12/86	Oregon State	Carlsbad, Calif.	FA-'11
Davis, A.J.	CB	6-0	183	7/6/89	Jacksonville State	Pinson, Ala.	FA
Eckerson, Hutch (1)	T	6-6	310	2/19/88	South Carolina	Lumberton, N.C.	FA
Folkerts, Brian	C	6-4	310	1/30/90	Washburn	Florissant, Mo.	FA
Givens, Chris	WR	6-2	203	1/28/89	Miami (Ohio)	Chillicothe, Ohio	FA
Gumbs, Jose	S	5-10	210	4/20/88	Monmouth	Queens, N.Y.	FA
Hardy, Kevin	WR	6-0	186	4/27/90	Citadel	Ocala, Fla.	FA
Hicks, Akiem	DT	6-5	324	11/16/89	Regina	Fair Oaks, Calif.	D3
Hixson, Nick	CB	6-0	189	1/15/89	Hillsdale	Remus, Mich.	FA
Jones, Marcel	T	6-7	320	9/4/88	Nebraska	Phoenix, Ariz.	D7
King, Mitch (1)	DT	6-2	280	5/5/86	Iowa	Burlington, Iowa	FA-'11
McIlwain, Kamaal (1)	CB	5-10	175	3/9/88	Newberry	Van Wyck, S.C.	FA-'11
Miller, Swanson (1)	DT	6-4	310	3/24/88	Oklahoma State	Alachua, Fla.	FA-'11
Nelson, Jerico	S	5-10	216	9/19/89	Arkansas	Destrehan, La.	FA
Pannell, DeOn'tae	G	6-5	323	3/19/90	Penn State	Southfield, Mich.	FA
Parks, Cord (1)	CB	5-11	182	11/12/86	Northeastern	Atlanta, Ga.	FA-'11
Romeus, Greg (1)	DE	6-5	267	4/29/88	Pittsburgh	Coral Springs, Fla.	D7a-'11
Scott, Laron	RS	5-9	179	7/12/87	Georgia Southern	Warner Robins, Ga.	FA
Simmons, Aderious	T	6-7	310	2/22/87	Arizona State	Marrero, La.	FA
Tanner, Andy (1)	WR	6-0	183	5/16/88	Midwestern State	Rockwall, Texas	FA-'11
Tevis, Aaron	LB	6-3	234	12/4/88	Boise State	Oro Valley, Ariz.	FA
Thomas, Johnny	S	5-11	205	10/24/89	Oklahoma State	Texas City, Texas	FA
Tiller, Andrew	G	6-5	326	3/13/89	Syracuse	Central Islip, N.Y.	D6
Toon, Nick	WR	6-4	218	11/4/88	Wisconsin	Middleton, Wisc.	D4
Walker, Tyrunn	DL	6-3	294	3/18/90	Tulsa	New Iberia, La.	FA
White, Corey	CB	6-1	205	5/9/90	Samford	Dunwoody, Ga.	D5

The term NFL Rookie is defined as a player who is in his first season of professional football and has not been on the roster of another professional football team for any regular-season or postseason games. A Rookie is designated by an "R" on NFL rosters. Players who have been active in another professional football league or players who have NFL experience, including either preseason training camp or being on an Active List or Inactive List, or on Reserve/Injured or Reserve/Physically Unable to Perform for fewer than six regular-season games, are termed NFL First-Year Players. An NFL First-Year Player is designated by a "1" on NFL rosters. Thereafter, a player is credited with an additional year of experience for each season in which he accumulates six games on the Active List or Inactive List, or on Reserve/Injured or Reserve/Physically Unable to Perform.

Log on to www.neworleanssaints.com for an up-to-date roster.

COACHING STAFF

Head Coach,
Sean Payton

Pro Career: Named the fourteenth head coach in Saints history on Jan. 18, 2006 and has led the team to four playoff appearances, three NFC South titles, two NFC Championship appearances and the Super Bowl XLIV title. Earned unanimous NFL Coach of the Year honors in his first season in 2006 and received the same honors from some outlets in 2009. Considered one of the NFL's brightest offensive minds, the Saints have ranked among the league's top ten offenses each season since his arrival, including finishing first in the NFL with a league record 7,474 yards in 2011, 2009, 2008 and 2006. With Dallas Cowboys (2003-05), served as the assistant head coach/passing game coordinator in 2005 after spending his first two seasons as assistant head coach/quarterbacks. Coached four years with the New York Giants (1999-2002), the last three seasons as offensive coordinator, and was quarterbacks coach for the Philadelphia Eagles (1997-98). Career record: 67-37.

Background: Earned a degree in communications at Eastern Illinois, where he departed with a school-record 10,665 passing yards, then the third-highest total in NCAA Division I-AA history. A three-time All-American, Payton had brief playing stops with Chicago of the Arena League, the CFL's Ottawa Rough Riders and the Chicago Bears in 1987. Payton coached collegiately at San Diego State (1988-89, 1992-93), Indiana State (1990-91), and Miami (Ohio) in 1994-95.

Personal: Born Dec. 29, 1963 in San Mateo, Calif. and raised in Naperville, Ill., Payton and his wife, Beth, have a daughter, Meghan, and a son, Connor.

ASSISTANT COACHES

Charles Byrd, asst. strength and conditioning; born June 24, 1981, Oxford, Ohio. Defensive back Morehead State 2001-04. Pro defensive back Las Vegas Gladiators (AFL) 2006. College coach: Miami (Ohio) 2006-07. Pro coach: Joined Saints in 2008.

Pete Carmichael, offensive coordinator; born October 6, 1971, Framingham, Mass. Attended Boston College. No college or pro playing experience. College coach: New Hampshire 1994, Louisiana Tech 1995-99. Pro coach: Cleveland Browns 2000, Washington Redskins 2001, San Diego Chargers 2002-05, joined Saints in 2006.

Andre Curtis, asst. secondary; born December 8, 1976, Beaverdam, Va. Linebacker Virginia Military Institute 1996-99. No pro playing experience. College coach: Virginia Military Institute 2000-03, Georgia Southern 2004-05. Pro coach: New York Giants 2006-08, St. Louis Rams 2009-2011, joined Saints in 2012.

Dan Dalrymple, head strength and conditioning; born Aug. 26, 1965, Cleveland, Ohio. Offensive lineman Miami (Ohio)

1983-86. No pro playing experience. College coach: Miami (Ohio) 1987-2005. Pro coach: Joined Saints in 2006.

Henry Ellard, wide receivers; born July 21, 1961, Fresno, Calif. Wide receiver Fresno State 1979-1982. Pro wide receiver/punt returner Los Angeles Rams 1983-1993, Washington Redskins 1994-98, New England Patriots 1998. College coach: Fresno State 2000. Pro coach: St. Louis Rams 2001-08, New York Jets 2009-2011, joined Saints in 2012.

Ken Flajole, secondary; born October 5, 1954, Seattle, Wash. Linebacker Wenatchee Valley (Wash.) C.C. 1972-73, Pacific Lutheran 1974-75. No pro playing experience. College coach: Pacific Lutheran 1977-78, Washington 1979, Montana 1980-85, Texas El-Paso 1986-88, Missouri 1989-1993, Richmond 1994, Hawaii 1995, Nevada 1996-97. Pro coach: Green Bay Packers 1998, Seattle Seahawks 1999-2002, Carolina Panthers 2003-08, St. Louis Rams 2009-2011, joined Saints in 2012.

Bret Ingalls, running backs; born Aug. 19, 1960, San Jose, Calif. Running back Wichita State 1979-1981. No pro playing experience. College coach: Idaho 1982-88, San Diego State 1989-1993, Eastern Michigan 1994, Louisville 1995-96, Northern Iowa 1997-99, Idaho 2000-03, Indiana State 2004, Miami (Ohio) 2005, Northwestern 2006-08. Pro coach: Joined Saints in 2009.

Bill Johnson, defensive line; born June 23, 1955, Monroe, La. Defensive lineman Northwestern (La.) State 1976-79. No pro playing experience. College coach: Northwestern (La.) State 1980-84, McNeese State 1985-86, Miami 1987, Louisiana Tech 1988-89, Arkansas 1990-91, 2000, Texas A&M 1992-99. Pro coach: Atlanta Falcons 2001-06, Denver Broncos 2007-08, joined Saints in 2009.

Travis Jones, asst. defensive line; born June 6, 1972, Milledgeville, Ga. Linebacker Georgia 1991-94. Pro linebacker Baltimore Stallions (CFL) 1995. College coach: Georgia 1997, Appalachian State 1998-2000, Kansas 2001-02, Louisiana State 2003-04. Pro coach: Miami Dolphins 2005-07, joined Saints in 2008.

Aaron Kromer, offensive line/running game; born April 30, 1967, Sandusky, Ohio. Offensive tackle Miami (Ohio) 1986-89. No pro playing experience. College coach: Miami (Ohio) 1990-98, Northwestern 1999-2000. Pro coach: Oakland Raiders 2001-04, Tampa Bay Buccaneers 2005-07, joined Saints in 2008.

Joe Lombardi, quarterbacks; born June 6, 1971, Seattle, Wash. Tight end Air Force 1992-94. No pro playing experience. College coach: Dayton 1996-98, Virginia Military Institute 1999, Bucknell 2000, Mercyhurst 2002-05. Pro coach: New York/New Jersey Hitmen (XFL) 2001, Atlanta Falcons 2006, joined Saints in 2007.

Mike Mallory, asst. special teams; born Nov. 16, 1962, Bowling Green, Ohio.

Linebacker Michigan 1982-85. No pro playing experience. College coach: Indiana 1986-87, Kent State 1989-1990, Eastern Illinois 1991-92, Rhode Island 1993-95, Northern Illinois 1996-99, Maryland 2000, Illinois 2001-05, Kansas 2006, Louisville 2007. Pro coach: Joined Saints in 2008.

Terry Malone, tight ends; born February 26, 1960, Buffalo, N.Y. Tight end Holy Cross 1978-1982. No pro playing experience. College coach: Arizona 1983-84, Holy Cross 1985, Bowling Green 1986-1995, Boston College 1996, Michigan 1997-2005. Pro coach: Joined Saints in 2006.

Greg McMahon, special teams coordinator; born Jan. 2, 1960, Rantoul, Ill. Defensive back Eastern Illinois 1978-1981. No pro playing experience. College coach: Eastern Illinois 1982, Minnesota 1983-84, North Alabama 1985-87, Southern Illinois 1988, Valdosta State 1989, Nevada Las-Vegas 1990-91, Illinois 1992-2004, East Carolina 2005. Pro coach: Joined Saints in 2006.

Carter Sheridan, offensive assistant/wide receivers; born Nov. 20, 1977, New Orleans, La. Defensive back Florida A&M 1996-98. No pro playing experience. Pro coach: Joined Saints in 2006.

Frank Smith, offensive assistant/offensive line; born February 21, 1981, Milwaukee, Wisc. Offensive lineman Miami (Ohio) 1999-2003. No pro playing experience. College coach: Miami (Ohio) 2004-05, Butler 2006-09. Pro coach: Joined Saints in 2010.

Steve Spagnuolo, defensive coordinator; born December 21, 1959, Whitinsville, Mass. Wide receiver Springfield (Mass.) College 1978-1981. No pro playing experience. College coach: Massachusetts 1982-83, Lafayette 1984-86, Connecticut 1987-1991, Maine 1993-94, Rutgers 1994-95, Bowling Green 1996-97. Pro coach: Barcelona Dragons (WLAF) 1992, Frankfurt Galaxy (NFL Europe) 1998, Philadelphia Eagles 1999-2006, New York Giants 2007-08, St. Louis Rams 2009-2011 (head coach), joined Saints in 2012.

Marcus Ungaro, defensive assistant; born October 9, 1984, Seattle. Defensive back Southwestern College 2004-05. No pro playing experience. Pro coach: Joined Saints in 2010.

Joe Vitt, asst. head coach/linebackers; born August 23, 1954, Syracuse, N.Y. Linebacker Towson State 1974-78. No pro playing experience. Pro coach: Baltimore Colts 1979-1981, Seattle Seahawks 1982-1991, Los Angeles Rams 1992-94, Philadelphia Eagles 1995-98, Green Bay Packers 1999, Kansas City Chiefs 2000-03, St. Louis Rams 2004-05 (head coach, final 11 games of 2005), joined Saints in 2006.

Brian Young, defensive assistant/linebackers; born July 8, 1977, Lawton, Okla. Defensive tackle Texas El-Paso 1996-99. Pro defensive tackle St. Louis Rams 2000-03, New Orleans Saints 2004-08. Pro coach: Joined Saints in 2009.

**National Football Conference
East Division
Team Colors:** Blue, Red, and White
**Timex Performance Center
1925 Giants Drive
East Rutherford, New Jersey 07073
Telephone:** (201) 935-8111

2012 SCHEDULE
PRESEASON
Aug. 10 at Jacksonville....................7:30
Aug. 18 at New York Jets 7:00
Aug. 24 **Chicago** 8:00
Aug. 29 **New England** 7:30

REGULAR SEASON
Sep. 5 **Dallas** (Wed).....................8:30
Sep. 16 **Tampa Bay**......................1:00
Sep. 20 at Carolina (Thurs) 8:20
Sep. 30 at Philadelphia...................8:20
Oct. 7 **Cleveland** 1:00
Oct. 14 at San Francisco.................4:15
Oct. 21 **Washington** 1:00
Oct. 28 at Dallas............................4:15
Nov. 4 **Pittsburgh**.......................4:15
Nov. 11 at Cincinnati 1:00
Nov. 18 BYE
Nov. 25 **Green Bay**......................*8:20
Dec. 3 at Washington (Mon).........8:30
Dec. 9 **New Orleans**....................4:15
Dec. 16 at Atlanta...........................1:00
Dec. 23 at Baltimore.......................1:00
Dec. 30 **Philadelphia** 1:00
*All times ET; Sunday night games in
Weeks 11-16 subject to change*
Stadium: MetLife Stadium
(opened in 2010)
•**Capacity:** 82,500
East Rutherford, New Jersey 07073
Playing Surface: FieldTurf
Training Camp: University at Albany
1400 Washington Avenue
Albany, New York 12222

METLIFE STADIUM

CLUB OFFICIALS
President/CEO: John K. Mara
Chairman/EVP: Steve Tisch
Treasurer: Jonathan Tisch
Senior Vice President-General Manager:
Jerry Reese
Senior Vice President and Chief
Marketing Officer: Michael Stevens
Senior Vice President and General
Counsel: William J. Heller, Esq.
Senior Vice President, Player Personnel:
Chris Mara
Senior Vice President, Medical Services:
Ronnie Barnes
Senior Vice President and Chief Financial
Officer: Christine Procops
Senior Vice President, Corporate
Partnerships: John Maguire
Senior Vice President, Communications:
Pat Hanlon
Vice President, Communications:
Peter John-Baptiste
Vice President of Community Relations:
Frank Mara
Vice President of Marketing:
Rusty Hawley
Vice President of Media and
Partnerships: Dan Lynch
Vice President, Giants Entertainment:
Don Sperling
Vice President, Business Development:
Doug Smoyer
Vice President of Finance:
Steven Hamrahi
Assistant General Manager:
Kevin Abrams
Director of Pro Player Personnel:
Dave Gettleman
Assistant Director of Pro Player
Personnel: Ken Sternfeld
Director of College Scouting: Marc Ross
Director of Player Development:
Charles Way
Pro Scouts: Patrick Hanscomb,
Matthew Shauger
College Scouts: Joe Collins,
Jeremiah Davis, Jerry Shay,
Steve Verderosa, Jeremy Breit,
Steve Devine, Donnie Etheridge,
Ryan Jones, Steve Malin, Chris Pettit,
Chris Watts
Director of Ticketing: John Gorman
Director of Administration: Jim Phelan
Director of Community Relations:
Allison Stangeby
Director of Creative Services:
Doug Murphy
Communications Manager:
DeAndré Phillips
Head Athletic Trainer: Ronnie Barnes
Assistant Head Athletic Trainer:
Steve Kennelly
Coordinator or Rehabilitation:
Byron Hansen
Physical Therapist/Assistant Athletic
Trainer: Leigh Weiss
Equipment/Locker Room Manager:
Ed Wagner, Jr.
Equipment Director: Joseph Skiba
Assistant Equipment Managers:
Ed Skiba, Tim Slaman
Video Director: Dave Maltese
Assistant Video Directors:
Carmen Pizzano, Ed Triggs,
Steve Venditti
Assistant Director of Community
Relations: Jen Conley
Directors of Information Technology:
Julie Glisky, Justin Warren
Director of Client Services:
Ethan Medley

COACHING HISTORY
(669-555-33)
Records include postseason games
1925	Bob Folwell	8-4-0
1926	Joe Alexander	8-4-1
1927-28	Earl Potteiger	15-8-3
1929-1930	LeRoy Andrews*	24-5-1
1930	Benny Friedman-Steve Owen	2-0-0
1931-1953	Steve Owen	153-108-17
1954-1960	Jim Lee Howell	55-29-4
1961-68	Allie Sherman	57-54-4
1969-1973	Alex Webster	29-40-1
1974-76	Bill Arnsparger**	7-28-0
1976-78	John McVay	14-23-0
1979-1982	Ray Perkins	24-35-0
1983-1990	Bill Parcells	85-52-1
1991-92	Ray Handley	14-18-0
1993-96	Dan Reeves	32-34-0
1997-2003	Jim Fassel	60-56-1
2004-2011	Tom Coughlin	82-57-0

*Released after 15 games in 1930
**Released after seven games in 1976

PAID ATTENDANCE
Home 625,509   Away 560,538
Total 1,186,047
Single-game home record,
81,077 (1/1/12)
Single-season home record,
629,874 (2004)

2012 DRAFT CHOICES
Round	Name	Pos.	College
1	David Wilson	RB	Virginia Tech
2	Rueben Randle	WR	Louisiana St.
3	Jayron Hosley	DB	Virginia Tech
4	Adrien Robinson	TE	Cincinnati
	Brandon Mosley	T	Auburn
6	Matt McCants	T	Alabama-Birmingham
7	Markus Kuhn	DT	North Carolina St.

NEW YORK GIANTS

2011 TEAM RECORD

PRESEASON (2-2)

Date	Result	Opponent
8/14	L 10-20	at Carolina
8/22	W 41-13	Chicago
8/27	L 3-17	New York Jets
9/1	W 18-17	at New England

REGULAR SEASON (9-7)

Date	Result	Opponent
9/11	L 14-28	at Washington
9/19	W 28-16	St. Louis
9/25	W 29-16	at Philadelphia
10/2	W 31-27	at Arizona
10/9	L 25-36	Seattle
10/16	W 27-24	Buffalo
10/30	W 20-17	Miami
11/6	W 24-20	at New England
11/13	L 20-27	at San Francisco
11/20	L 10-17	Philadelphia
11/28	L 24-49	at New Orleans
12/4	L 35-38	Green Bay
12/11	W 37-34	at Dallas
12/18	L 10-23	Washington
12/24	W 29-14	at New York Jets
1/1	W 31-14	Dallas

POSTSEASON (4-0)

1/8	W 20-13	Atlanta
1/15	W 37-20	at Green Bay
1/22	W 20-17	at San Francisco (OT)
2/5	W 21-17	vs. New England at Indianapolis

(OT) Overtime

SCORE BY PERIODS

Giants	70	108	59	157	0 —	394
Opponents	71	115	79	135	0 —	400

2011 TEAM STATISTICS

	Giants	Opp.
Total First Downs	331	338
Rushing	84	103
Passing	216	210
Penalty	31	25
3rd Down: Made/Att	77/206	84/220
3rd Down Pct.	37.4	38.2
4th Down: Made/Att	4/13	10/18
4th Down Pct.	30.8	55.6
Possession Avg.	29:30	30:30
Total Net Yards	6161	6022
Avg. Per Game	385.1	376.4
Total Plays	1028	1072
Avg. Per Play	6.0	5.6
Net Yards Rushing	1427	1940
Avg. Per Game	89.2	121.3
Total Rushes	411	435
Net Yards Passing	4734	4082
Avg. Per Game	295.9	255.1
Sacked/Yards Lost	28/199	48/335
Gross Yards	4933	4417
Att./Completions	589/359	589/361
Completion Pct.	61.0	61.3
Had Intercepted	16	20
Punts/Average	82/45.7	75/44.3
Net Punting Avg.	82/39.2	75/40.7
Penalties/Yards	94/795	110/933
Fumbles/Ball Lost	18/8	21/11
Touchdowns	47	46
Rushing	17	15
Passing	29	28
Returns	1	3

2011 INDIVIDUAL STATISTICS

PASSING	Att.	Comp.	Yds.	Pct.	TD	Int.	Tkld.	Rate
Manning	589	359	4933	61.0	29	16	28/199	92.9
Giants	589	359	4933	61.0	29	16	28/199	92.9
Opponents	589	361	4417	61.3	28	20	48/335	86.1

SCORING	TD R	TD P	TD Rt	PAT	FG	Saf	PTS
Tynes	0	0	0	43/43	19/24	0	100
Bradshaw	9	2	0	0/0	0/0	0	68
Cruz	0	9	0	0/0	0/0	0	54
Jacobs	7	1	0	0/0	0/0	0	50
Nicks	0	7	0	0/0	0/0	0	42
Ballard	0	4	0	0/0	0/0	0	24
Manningham	0	4	0	0/0	0/0	0	24
Beckum	0	1	0	0/0	0/0	0	6
Boley	0	0	1	0/0	0/0	0	6
Hixon	0	1	0	0/0	0/0	0	6
Manning	1	0	0	0/0	0/0	0	6
Ware	0	0	0	0/0	0/0	0	4
Canty	0	0	0	0/0	0/0	1	2
Pierre-Paul	0	0	0	0/0	0/0	1	2
Giants	17	29	1	43/43	19/24	2	394
Opponents	15	28	3	45/45	25/31	1	400

2-Pt Conversions: Ware 2, Bradshaw, Jacobs
Giants 4-4, Opponents 1-1

RUSHING	No.	Yds	Avg	LG	TD
Bradshaw	171	659	3.9	37	9
Jacobs	152	571	3.8	28	7
Ware	46	163	3.5	17	0
Scott	5	16	3.2	8	0
Manning	35	15	0.4	12	1
Cruz	1	3	3.0	3	0
Weatherford	1	0	0.0	0	0
Giants	411	1427	3.5	37	17
Opponents	435	1940	4.5	80t	15

RECEIVING	No.	Yds	Avg	LG	TD
Cruz	82	1536	18.7	99t	9
Nicks	76	1192	15.7	68	7
Manningham	39	523	13.4	47t	4
Ballard	38	604	15.9	41	4
Bradshaw	34	267	7.9	26	2
Ware	27	170	6.3	22	0
Jacobs	15	128	8.5	40t	1
Pascoe	12	136	11.3	22	0
Hynoski	12	83	6.9	14	0
Barden	9	94	10.4	26	0
Beckum	5	93	18.6	67t	1
Hixon	4	50	12.5	22t	1
D. Thomas	3	37	12.3	14	0
Scott	2	13	6.5	9	0
Stokley	1	7	7.0	7	0
Giants	359	4933	13.7	99t	29
Opponents	361	4417	12.2	74	28

INTERCEPTIONS	No.	Yds	Avg	LG	TD
Webster	6	71	11.8	25	0
Phillips	4	50	12.5	31	0
Ross	4	19	4.8	19	0
Rolle	2	-1	-.5	0	0
Blackburn	1	9	9.0	9	0
Kiwanuka	1	9	9.0	9	0
Amukamara	1	0	0.0	0	0
Grant	1	0	0.0	0	0
Giants	20	157	7.9	31	0
Opponents	16	291	18.2	94t	3

PUNTING	No.	Yds.	Avg.	In 20	LG
Weatherford	82	3745	45.7	25	62
Giants	82	3745	45.7	25	62
Opponents	75	3321	44.3	28	64

PUNT RETURNS	Ret	FC	Yds	Avg	LG	TD
Ross	14	13	99	7.1	18	0
Blackmon	6	2	25	4.2	16	0
Cruz	3	2	12	4.0	11	0
Hixon	3	3	31	10.3	18	0
Rolle	2	0	4	2.0	3	0
Jernigan	0	1	0	—	—	0
Giants	28	21	171	6.1	18	0
Opponents	41	15	407	9.9	51	0

KICKOFF RETURNS	No.	Yds	Avg	LG	TD
D. Thomas	25	607	24.3	40	0
Scott	14	341	24.4	38	0
Jernigan	8	186	23.3	31	0
Blackmon	2	43	21.5	32	0
Ware	2	17	8.5	17	0
Hynoski	1	15	15.0	15	0
Giants	52	1209	23.3	40	0
Opponents	46	1053	22.9	42	0

FIELD GOALS	1-19	20-29	30-39	40-49	50+
Tynes	0/0	12/12	3/4	3/5	1/3
Giants	0/0	12/12	3/4	3/5	1/3
Opponents	0/0	9/10	7/8	7/10	2/3

SACKS	No.
Pierre-Paul	16.5
Umenyiora	9.0
Tollefson	5.0
Tuck	5.0
Canty	4.0
Kiwanuka	3.5
Joseph	2.0
Boley	1.0
Grant	1.0
J. Williams	1.0
Giants	48.0
Opponents	28.0

RECORD HOLDERS
INDIVIDUAL RECORDS—CAREER

Category	Name	Performance
Rushing (Yds.)	Tiki Barber, 1997-2006	10,449
Passing (Yds.)	Phil Simms, 1979-1993	33,462
Passing (TDs)	Phil Simms, 1979-1993	199
Receiving (No.)	Amani Toomer, 1996-2008	668
Receiving (Yds.)	Amani Toomer, 1996-2008	9,497
Interceptions	Emlen Tunnell, 1948-1958	74
Punting (Avg.)	Don Chandler, 1956-1964	43.8
Punt Return (Avg.)	Ward Cuff, 1941-45	12.1
Kickoff Return (Avg.)	Rocky Thompson, 1971-73	27.2
Field Goals	Pete Gogolak, 1966-1974	126
Touchdowns (Tot.)	Frank Gifford, 1952-1964	78
Points	Pete Gogolak, 1966-1974	646
*Sacks	Michael Strahan, 1993-2007	141.5

INDIVIDUAL RECORDS—SINGLE SEASON

Category	Name	Performance
Rushing (Yds.)	Tiki Barber, 2005	1,860
Passing (Yds.)	Eli Manning, 2011	4,933
Passing (TDs)	Y.A. Tittle, 1963	36
Receiving (No.)	Steve Smith, 2009	107
Receiving (Yds.)	Victor Cruz, 2011	1,536
Interceptions	Otto Schnellbacher, 1951	11
	Jim Patton, 1958	11
Punting (Avg.)	Don Chandler, 1959	46.6
Punt Return (Avg.)	Merle Hapes, 1942	15.5
Kickoff Return (Avg.)	John Salscheider, 1949	31.6
Field Goals	Ali Haji-Sheikh, 1983	35
	Jay Feely, 2005	35
	John Carney, 2008	35
Touchdowns (Tot.)	Joe Morris, 1985	21
Points	Jay Feely, 2005	148
*Sacks	Michael Strahan, 2001	**22.5

INDIVIDUAL RECORDS—SINGLE GAME

Category	Name	Performance
Rushing (Yds.)	Tiki Barber, 12-30-06	234
Passing (Yds.)	Phil Simms, 10-13-85	513
Passing (TDs)	Y.A. Tittle, 10-28-62	**7
Receiving (No.)	Tiki Barber, 1-2-00	13
Receiving (Yds.)	Del Shofner, 10-28-62	269
Interceptions	Many times	3
	Last time by Terry Kinard, 9-20-87	
Field Goals	Joe Danelo, 10-18-81	6
Touchdowns (Tot.)	Ron Johnson, 10-2-72	4
	Earnest Gray, 9-7-80	4
	Rodney Hampton, 9-24-95	4
Points	Ron Johnson, 10-2-72	24
	Earnest Gray, 9-7-80	24
	Rodney Hampton, 9-24-95	24
*Sacks	Osi Umenyiora, 9-30-07	6.0

*Sacks became an official statistic in 1982.
**NFL Record

2012 VETERAN ROSTER

No.	Name	Pos.	Ht.	Wt.	Birthdate	NFL Exp.	College	Hometown	How Acq.	'11 Games/ Starts
20	Amukamara, Prince	CB	6-0	207	6/6/89	2	Nebraska	Glendale, Ariz.	D1-'11	7/9
78	# Andrews, Stacy	T	6-6	318	6/2/81	9	Mississippi	Camden, Ark.	UFA(Sea)-'11	9/3
64	Baas, David	C	6-4	312	9/28/81	8	Michigan	Sarasota, Fla.	UFA(SF)-'11	11/11
85	Ballard, Jake	TE	6-6	275	12/21/87	3	Ohio State	Springboro, Ohio	FA-'10	14/12
13	Barden, Ramses	WR	6-6	224	1/1/86	4	Cal Poly	La Canada Flintridge, Calif.	D3-'09	8/0
65	Beatty, Will	T	6-6	319	3/2/85	4	Connecticut	York, Pa.	D2-'09	10/10
47	Beckum, Travis	TE	6-3	234	1/24/87	4	Wisconsin	Milwaukee, Wisc.	D3-'09	13/3
89	Bennett, Martellus	TE	6-6	265	1/10/87	5	Texas A&M	Katy, Texas	UFA(Dall)-'12	14/7*
95	# Bernard, Rocky	DT	6-3	301	4/19/79	11	Texas A&M	Sterling, Texas	FA-'11	16/1
93	Blackburn, Chase	LB	6-4	242	6/10/83	8	Akron	Bellefontaine, Ohio	FA-'11	4/3
36	# Blackmon, Will	CB	6-0	206	10/27/84	6	Boston College	Providence, R.I.	FA-'11	6/0
59	Boley, Michael	LB	6-3	230	8/24/82	8	Southern Miss	Elkmont, Ala.	UFA(Atl)-'09	14/13
77	Boothe, Kevin	G	6-5	320	7/5/83	7	Cornell	Fort Lauderdale, Fla.	W(Oak)-'07	16/9
44	Bradshaw, Ahmad	RB	5-10	214	3/19/86	6	Marshall	Bluefield, Va.	D7b-'07	12/9
73	Brewer, James	T	6-6	330	12/23/87	2	Indiana	Indianapolis, Ind.	D4-'11	0*
35	Brown, Andre	RB	6-0	227	12/15/86	4	North Carolina State	Greenville, S.C.	FA-'11	0*
27	Brown, Steve	DB	5-11	221	7/17/87	2	Michigan	Columbus, Ind.	FA-'12	8/0*
99	Canty, Chris	DT	6-7	317	11/10/82	8	Virginia	Charlotte, N.C.	UFA(Dall)-'09	16/16
8	Carr, David	QB	6-3	212	7/21/79	11	Fresno State	Stockdale, Calif.	FA-'11	0*
83	# Clayton, Michael	WR	6-3	202	10/13/82	9	Louisiana State	Baton Rouge, La.	FA-'11	5/3
37	Coe, Michael	CB	6-0	187	12/17/83	5	Alabama State	Memphis, Tenn.	FA-'10	10/0
80	Cruz, Victor	WR	6-0	204	11/11/86	3	Massachusetts	Paterson, N.J.	FA-'10	16/7
51	DeOssie, Zak	LS	6-4	249	5/24/84	6	Brown	No. Andover, Mass.	D4-'07	16/0
66	Diehl, David	G	6-5	304	9/15/80	10	Illinois	Oak Lawn, Ill.	D5-'03	16/16
34	# Grant, Deon	S	6-2	215	3/14/79	13	Tennessee	Augusta, Ga.	FA-'10	16/9
58	Herzlich, Mark	LB	6-4	246	9/1/87	2	Boston College	Wayne, Pa	FA-'11	11/2
87	Hixon, Domenik	WR	6-2	197	10/8/84	7	Akron	Columbus, Ohio	W(Den)-'07	2/0
41	Horton, Chris	S	6-1	215	12/29/84	5	UCLA	New Orleans, La.	FA-'12	0*
45	Hynoski, Henry	FB	6-1	266	12/30/88	2	Pittsburgh	Elysburg, Pa.	FA-'11	11/4
12	Jernigan, Jerrel	WR	5-8	189	6/14/89	2	Troy	Eufaula, Ala.	D3-'11	8/3
25	Johnson, Bruce	CB	5-11	182	12/18/87	4	Miami	Live Oak, Fla.	FA-'09	0*
53	Jones, Greg	LB	6-0	248	10/5/84	2	Michigan State	Cincinnati, Ohio	D6-'11	16/5
97	Joseph, Linval	DT	6-4	323	10/10/88	3	East Carolina	Gainesville, Fla.	D2-'10	16/15
73	# Kennedy, Jimmy	DT	6-4	302	11/15/79	10	Penn State	Yonkers, N.Y.	FA-'11	6/0
94	Kiwanuka, Mathias	LB	6-5	267	3/8/83	7	Boston College	Indianapolis, Ind.	D1-'06	16/15
75	Locklear, Sean	T	6-4	310	5/29/81	9	North Carolina State	Lumberton, N.C.	UFA(Wash)-'12	9/4*
10	Manning, Eli	QB	6-4	218	1/3/81	9	Mississippi	New Orleans, La.	T(SD)-'04	16/16
22	# Martin, Derrick	DB	5-10	198	5/16/85	6	Wyoming	Denver, Colo.	FA-'11	14/0
67	# McKenzie, Kareem	T	6-6	330	5/24/79	11	Penn State	Willingboro, N.J.	UFA(NYJ)-'05	20/20
22	Molden, Antwaun	CB	6-1	199	1/23/85	5	Eastern Kentucky	Cleveland, Ohio	UFA(NE)-'12	16/2*
88	Nicks, Hakeem	WR	6-1	208	1/14/88	4	North Carolina	Charlotte, N.C.	D1-'09	15/15
86	Pascoe, Bear	TE	6-5	283	2/23/86	4	Fresno State	Porterville, Calif.	FA-'09	16/11
49	Paysinger, Spencer	LB	6-2	236	6/28/88	2	Oregon	Los Angeles, Calif.	FA-'11	16/2
62	Petrus, Mitch	G	6-3	315	5/11/87	3	Arkansas	Carlisle, Ark.	D5-'10	6/3
21	Phillips, Kenny	S	6-2	217	11/24/86	5	Miami	Miami, Fla.	D1-'08	15/15
90	Pierre-Paul, Jason	DE	6-5	278	1/1/89	3	South Florida	Deerfield Beach, Fla.	D1-'10	16/12
83	Purvis, Ryan	TE	6-4	261	5/8/86	3	Boston College	Allentown, Pa.	FA-'11	0*
55	t- Rivers, Keith	LB	6-2	235	5/5/86	4	Southern California	Lake Mary, Fla.	T(Cin)-'12	0*
95	Rogers, Shaun	DT	6-4	350	3/12/79	12	Texas	LaPorte, Texas	UFA(NO)-'12	16/4*
26	Rolle, Antrel	S	6-0	206	12/16/82	7	Miami	Homestead, Fla.	FA-'10	16/16
39	Sash, Tyler	S	6-0	215	5/27/88	2	Iowa	Oskaloosa, Iowa	D6-'11	16/0
33	Scott, Da'Rel	RB	5-11	210	5/26/88	2	Maryland	Conshohocken, Pa.	D7-'11	11/0
52	Sintim, Clint	LB	6-3	246	2/21/86	4	Virginia	Woodbridge, Va.	D2-'09	0*
76	Snee, Chris	G	6-3	305	1/18/82	9	Boston College	Montrose, Pa.	D2-'04	15/15
18	Stanback, Isaiah	WR	6-2	228	8/16/84	4	Washington	Seattle, Wash.	FA-'11	0*
24	Thomas, Terrell	CB	6-0	191	1/8/85	5	Southern California	Alto Loma, Calif.	D2-'08	0*
69	Trattou, Justin	DE	6-4	255	3/28/88	2	Florida	Ramsey, N.J.	FA-'11	6/2
30	Tryon, Justin	CB	5-9	180	5/29/84	5	Arizona State	Woodland Hills, Calif.	FA-'11	3/0
91	Tuck, Justin	DE	6-5	268	3/29/83	8	Notre Dame	Kellyton, Ala.	D3-'05	12/11
9	Tynes, Lawrence	PK	6-1	194	5/3/78	9	Troy	Milton, Fla.	T(KC)-'07	16/0
70	# Ugoh, Tony	T	6-5	304	11/17/83	5	Arkansas	Houston, Texas	FA-'11	3/1
72	Umenyiora, Osi	DE	6-3	255	11/16/81	10	Troy	Auburn, Ala.	D2-'03	9/7
28	Ware, D.J.	RB	6-0	225	2/18/85	6	Georgia	Rockmart, Ga.	FA-'07	16/1
5	Weatherford, Steve	P	6-2	211	12/17/82	8	Illinois	Terre Haute, Ind.	FA-'11	16/0
23	Webster, Corey	CB	6-0	200	3/2/82	8	Louisiana State	Vacherie, La.	D2-'05	16/16
61	White, Chris	C	6-2	303	2/28/83	8	Southern Mississippi	Winona, Miss.	FA-'12	0*

2012 VETERAN ROSTER CONTINUED

No.	Name	Pos.	Ht.	Wt.	Birthdate	NFL Exp.	College	Hometown	How Acq.	'11 Games/ Starts
57	Williams, Jacquian	LB	6-3	224	7/20/88	2	South Florida	Apopka, Fla.	D6-'11	16/2
29	Witherspoon, Brian	CB	5-10	180	6/5/85	4	Stillman	Butler, Ala.	FA-'10	0*

* Bennett played 14 games with Dallas in '11; Brewer did not play in 2 games, inactive for 14 games; A. Brown last active with Carolina, Indianapolis, and Denver in '10; S. Brown played 8 games with Indianapolis; Carr did not play in 16 games; Horton last active with Washington in '10; Johnson missed '11 season because of injury; Locklear played 9 games with Washington; Molden played 16 games with New England; Purvis last active with Tampa Bay in '10; Rivers last active with Cincinnati in '10; Rogers played 16 games with New Orleans; Sintim missed '11 season because of injury; Stanback last active with New England in '09; T. Thomas missed '11 season because of injury; White last active with Seattle in '10; Witherspoon missed '11 season because of injury.

t- Giants traded for Rivers (Cin).

Unrestricted free agent; subject to developments.

Players lost through free agency (5): LB Jonathan Goff (Wash; 0 games), WR Mario Manningham (SF; 12), CB Aaron Ross (Jax; 16), WR Devin Thomas (Chi; 16), DE Dave Tollefson (Oak; 16).

Also played with the Giants in '11—C Jim Cordle (9 games), RB Brandon Jacobs (14), WR Brandon Stokley (2), Brian Williams (4).

FIRST-YEAR ROSTER

Name	Pos.	Ht.	Wt.	Birthdate	College	Hometown	How Acq.
Bing, Brandon (1)	CB	5-9	175	8/8/89	Rutgers	Wyncote, Pa.	FA-'11
Capers, Selvish (1)	OL	6-5	315	11/13/86	West Virginia	Kenner, La.	FA-'11
DePalma, Dan (1)	WR	5-11	192	7/21/89	West Chester (Pa.)	Verona, N.J.	FA-'11
Donnell, Larry	TE	6-6	269	11/1/88	Grambling	Ozark, Ala.	FA
Hendricks, Dwayne (1)	DT	6-3	305	3/17/86	Miami	Millville, N.J.	FA-'11
Hopkins, Christian (1)	TE	6-5	277	2/26/85	Toledo	Chicago, Ill.	FA-'11
Hosley, Jayron	CB	5-10	178	9/18/90	Virginia Tech	Delray Beach, Fla.	D3
Kuhn, Markus	DT	6-4	299	5/5/86	North Carolina State	Weinheim, Germany	D7
Marshall, Craig (1)	DE	6-4	280	2/10/88	South Florida	Fort Walton Beach, Fla.	FA-'11
McCants, Matt	T	6-5	309	8/18/89	Alabama-Birmingham	Mobile, Ala.	D6
Mosley, Brandon	T	6-5	318	12/21/88	Auburn	Jefferson, Ga.	D4
Perrilloux, Ryan	QB	6-3	204	1/1/87	Jacksonville State	Reserve, La.	FA
Randle, Rueben	WR	6-2	208	5/7/91	Louisiana State	Bastrop, La	D2
Reinders, Joel	T	6-8	317	10/2/87	Waterloo (Canada)	Oakville, Ontario, Canada	FA
Robinson, Adrien	TE	6-4	264	9/23/88	Cincinnati	Indianapolis, Ind.	D4
Tracy, Adrian (1)	LB	6-2	245	4/6/87	William & Mary	Sterling, Va.	D6-'10
Wilson, David	RB	5-9	205	6/15/91	Virginia Tech	Danville, Va.	D1

The term NFL Rookie is defined as a player who is in his first season of professional football and has not been on the roster of another professional football team for any regular-season or postseason games. A Rookie is designated by an "R" on NFL rosters. Players who have been active in another professional football league or players who have NFL experience, including either preseason training camp or being on an Active List or Inactive List, or on Reserve/Injured or Reserve/Physically Unable to Perform for fewer than six regular-season games, are termed NFL First-Year Players. An NFL First-Year Player is designated by a "1" on NFL rosters. Thereafter, a player is credited with an additional year of experience for each season in which he accumulates six games on the Active List or Inactive List, or on Reserve/Injured or Reserve/Physically Unable to Perform.

Log on to www.giants.com for an up-to-date roster.

NEW YORK GIANTS

COACHING STAFF

Head Coach,
Tom Coughlin
Pro Career: Was named the sixteenth head coach in Giants history on January 6, 2004. This season marks Coughlin's ninth with the Giants and seventeenth as an NFL head coach. In 2011, Coughlin helmed the Giants to their second championship in four seasons with a 21-17 win against the New England Patriots in Super Bowl XLVI. He also guided the team to a 9-7 record, en route to winning an NFC East crown. In 2010, the Giants posted a record of 10-6. The Giants finished the 2009 season with an 8-8 record. In the 2008 season the Giants finished with a 12-4 record, which won the NFC East division. Coughlin directed the Giants 17-14 win over the New England Patriots in Super Bowl XLII on February 3, 2008, the third championship in the team's history. Coached the Giants to an 11-5 record, the NFC East title and the playoffs in 2005-06, his second and third seasons with the team. Coughlin previously spent eight years (1995-2002) with the Jacksonville Jaguars. Under Coughlin, the Jaguars had the most victories of any NFL expansion team in its first seven seasons. They were also the only expansion team in NFL history to advance to the playoffs five times in their first five seasons. Coughlin's team went 9-7 in 1996 and an NFL-best 14-2 in 1999, both times reaching the AFC Championship Game. Coughlin previously coached the Philadelphia Eagles (1984-85), Green Bay Packers (1986-87), and Giants (1988-1990). He was a member of the Giants' Super Bowl XXV champion coaching staff. Career record: 154-121.
Background: Served as head coach at Boston College (1991-93), and coached at Syracuse (1969, 1974-1980), Rochester Institute of Technology 1970-73 (head coach), and Boston College (1981-83). Played wingback for Syracuse (1965-67).
Personal: Born August 31, 1946, Waterloo, N.Y. and his wife Judy have two daughters, Keli and Katie; two son-in-laws named Chris; two sons, Brian and Tim; two daughters-in-law, Andrea (Tim's wife) and Susie (Brian's wife); and 10 grandchildren, Emma Rose, Dylan, Shea, Cooper, Caroline, Marin, Wesley, Brennon, Clara, and Walker.

ASSISTANT COACHES

Perry Fewell, defensive coordinator; born September 7, 1962, Gastonia, N.C. Defensive back Lenoir-Rhyne 1981-84. No pro playing experience. College coach: North Carolina 1985-86, Army 1987, 1992-94, Kent State 1988-1991, Vanderbilt 1995-97. Pro coach: Jacksonville Jaguars 1998-2002, St. Louis Rams 2003-04, Chicago Bears 2005, Buffalo Bills 2006-09, joined Giants in 2010.
Pat Flaherty, offensive line; born April 27, 1956, Hanover, Pa. Center East Stroudsburg 1974-77. No pro playing experience.

College coach: East Stroudsburg 1980-81, Penn State 1982-83, Rutgers 1984-1991, East Carolina 1992, Wake Forest 1993-98, Iowa 1999. Pro coach: Washington Redskins 2000, Chicago Bears 2001-03, joined Giants in 2004.
Kevin Gilbride, offensive coordinator; born August 27, 1951, New Haven, Conn. Quarterback/tight end Southern Connecticut State 1971-73. No pro playing experience. College coach: Idaho State 1974-75, Tufts 1976-77, American International 1978-79, Southern Connecticut State 1980-84, East Carolina 1987-88. Pro coach: Ottawa Rough Riders (CFL) 1985-86, Houston Oilers 1989-1994, Jacksonville Jaguars 1995-96, San Diego Chargers 1997-98 (head coach), Pittsburgh Steelers 1999-2000, Buffalo Bills 2002-2003, joined Giants in 2004.
Kevin M. Gilbride, wide receivers; born December 14, 1979, Jacksonville, Fla. Quarterback Hawaii 2000. No pro playing experience. College coach: Syracuse 2004-05, Georgetown 2006, Temple 2007-09. Pro coach: Joined Giants in 2010.
Peter Giunta, secondary/corners; born August 11, 1956, Salem, Mass. Running back/defensive back Northeastern 1974-77. No pro playing experience. College coach: Penn State 1981-83, Brown 1984-87, Lehigh 1988-1990. Pro coach: Philadelphia Eagles 1991-94, N.Y. Jets 1995-96, St. Louis Rams 1997-2000, Kansas City Chiefs 2001-2005, joined Giants in 2006.
Jim Hermann, linebackers; born December 8, 1960, Hollywood, Calif. Linebacker Michigan 1979-1982. No pro playing experience. College coach: Michigan 1983, 1986-2005. Pro coach: New York Jets 2006-2008, joined Giants in 2009.
Al Holcomb, defensive quality control; born October 22, 1970, Queens, N.Y. Attended West Virginia. No college or pro playing experience. College coach: Temple 1995-96, Colby College 1997, Bloomsburg 1998-2003, Kutztown 2004-05, Lafayette 2006-08. Pro coach: Joined Giants in 2009.
Jerald Ingram, running backs; born December 24, 1960, Dayton, Ohio. Fullback Michigan 1979-1983. College coach: Michigan 1984, Ball State 1985-1990, Boston College 1991-93. Pro coach: Jacksonville Jaguars 1994-2002, joined Giants in 2004.
Larry Izzo, asst. special teams; born September 26, 1974, Fort Belvoir, Va. Linebacker Rice 1992-95. Pro linebacker/special teamer Miami Dolphins 1996-2000, New England Patriots 2001-08, New York Jets 2009. Pro coach: Joined Giants in 2011.
David Merritt Sr., secondary/safeties; born September 8, 1971, Raleigh, N.C. Linebacker North Carolina State 1989-1992. Pro linebacker Miami Dolphins 1993, Arizona Cardinals 1993-96, Rhein

Fire (NFLE) 1997. College coach: Chattanooga 1997, Virginia Military Institute 1998-2000. Pro coach: New York Jets 2001-2003, joined Giants in 2004.
Robert Nunn, defensive line; born June 10, 1965, Apache, Okla. Linebacker Oklahoma State 1984-87. No pro playing experience. College coach: Northeastern Oklahoma 1988, Tennessee 1989-1990, Georgia Military 1991-99. Pro coach: Miami Dolphins 2000-02, 2004, Washington Redskins 2003, Green Bay Packers 2005-08, Tampa Bay Buccaneers 2009, joined Giants in 2010.
Jerry Palmieri, strength and conditioning; born October 30, 1958, Englewood, N.J. Attended Montclair State. No college or pro playing experience. College coach: North Carolina 1982-83, Oklahoma State 1984-86, Kansas State 1987-1992, Boston College 1993-94. Pro coach: Jacksonville Jaguars 1995-2002, New Orleans Saints 2003, joined Giants in 2004.
Marcus Paul, asst. strength and conditioning; born April 1, 1966, Orlando, Fla. Safety Syracuse 1984-88. Pro safety Chicago Bears 1989-1993, Tampa Bay Buccaneers 1993. Pro coach: New Orleans Saints 1998-99, New England Patriots 2000-04, New York Jets 2005-2006, joined Giants in 2007.
Michael Pope, tight ends; born March 15, 1942, Monroe, N.C. Quarterback Lenoir-Rhyne 1962-64. No pro playing experience. College coach: Florida State 1970-74, Texas Tech 1975-77, Mississippi 1978-1982. Pro coach: New York Giants 1983-1991, Cincinnati Bengals 1992-93, New England Patriots 1994-96, Washington Redskins 1997-99, re-joined Giants in 2000.
Tom Quinn, special teams coordinator; born January 27, 1968, Pasadena, Calif. Linebacker Arizona 1986-1990. No pro playing experience. College coach: Davidson College 1991, James Madison 1992-94, Boston 1995, Holy Cross 1996-98, San Jose State 1999-2001, Stanford 2002-05. Pro coach: Joined Giants in 2006.
Matt Rhule, asst. offensive line; born January 31, 1975, State College, Pa. Linebacker Penn State 1994-97. No pro playing experience. College coach: Penn State 1998, Albright College 1998, Buffalo 1999-2000, UCLA 2001, Western Carolina 2002-05, Temple 2006-2011. Pro coach: Joined Giants in 2012.
Sean Ryan, quarterbacks; born May 1, 1972, Glenn Falls, N.Y. Defensive back Hamilton College 1994. No pro playing experience. College coach: Albany 1998-99, Colgate 2000, Boston College 2001-02, Columbia 2003-04, Harvard 2006. Pro coach: Joined Giants in 2007.
Lunda Wells, offensive assistant; born February 10, 1983, Baker, Ala. Offensive line Southern 2003-07. No pro playing experience. College coach: Louisiana State 2008-2011. Pro coach: Joined Giants in 2012.

**National Football Conference
East Division**
Team Colors: Midnight Green, Silver, Black, and White
NovaCare Complex
One NovaCare Way
Philadelphia, Pennsylvania 19145
Telephone: (215) 463-2500

2012 SCHEDULE
PRESEASON
Aug. 9   **Pittsburgh**..........................7:30
Aug. 20   at New England 8:00
Aug. 24   at Cleveland 7:30
Aug. 30   **New York Jets** 6:35

REGULAR SEASON
Sep. 9   at Cleveland 1:00
Sep. 16   **Baltimore**..........................1:00
Sep. 23   at Arizona............................4:05
Sep. 30   **New York Giants**...............8:20
Oct. 7   at Pittsburgh........................1:00
Oct. 14   **Detroit** 1:00
Oct. 21   BYE
Oct. 28   **Atlanta**..............................1:00
Nov. 5   at New Orleans (Mon) 8:30
Nov. 11   **Dallas**................................4:15
Nov. 18   at Washington 1:00
Nov. 26   **Carolina** (Mon) 8:30
Dec. 2   at Dallas........................ *8:20
Dec. 9   at Tampa Bay 1:00
Dec. 13   **Cincinnati** (Thurs).............8:20
Dec. 23   **Washington** 1:00
Dec. 30   at New York Giants 1:00
All times ET; Sunday night games in Weeks 11-16 subject to change
Stadium: Lincoln Financial Field
    (opened in 2003)
    •**Capacity:** 69,144
    One Lincoln Financial Field Way
    Philadelphia, Pennsylvania 19148
Playing Surface: Natural Grass
Training Camp: Lehigh University
    Bethlehem, PA 18015

LINCOLN FINANCIAL FIELD

CLUB OFFICIALS
Chairman/Chief Executive Officer:
    Jeffrey Lurie
President: Joe Banner
Head Coach/Executive Vice President of
    Football Operations: Andy Reid
General Manager: Howie Roseman
Chief Operating Officer: Don Smolenski
Senior Vice President/Business:
    Ari Roitman
Executive Director of Eagles Youth
    Partnership: Sarah Martinez-Helfman
Director of Pro Personnel: Louis Riddick
Director of Football Media Relations:
    Derek Boyko
Senior Vice President/Chief Marketing
    Officer: Tim McDermott
Director of Human Resources:
    Kristie Pappal
Manager of Community Relations:
    Julie Hirshey
Director of Events: Leonard Bonacci
Director of Ticket Operations:
    Laini Delawter
Director of Ticket Client Relations:
    Leo Carlin
Director of Merchandise:
    Brendan McQuillen
Director of Team Security: Dom DiSandro
Head Athletic Trainer: Rick Burkholder
Asst. Athletic Trainers: Chris Peduzzi,
    Joe O'Pella
Video Director: Mike Dougherty
Head Equipment Manager:
    Greg Delimitros

COACHING HISTORY
(536-569-26)
Records include postseason games
Year	Coach	Record
1933-35	Lud Wray	9-21-1
1936-1940	Bert Bell	10-44-2
1941-1950	Earle (Greasy) Neale*	66-44-5
1951	Alvin (Bo) McMillin**	2-0-0
1951	Wayne Millner	2-8-0
1952-55	Jim Trimble	25-20-3
1956-57	Hugh Devore	7-16-1
1958-1960	Lawrence (Buck) Shaw	20-16-1
1961-63	Nick Skorich	15-24-3
1964-68	Joe Kuharich	28-41-1
1969-1971	Jerry Williams***	7-22-2
1971-72	Ed Khayat	8-15-2
1973-75	Mike McCormack	16-25-1
1976-1982	Dick Vermeil	57-51-0
1983-85	Marion Campbell****	17-29-1
1985	Fred Bruney	1-0-0
1986-1990	Buddy Ryan	43-38-1
1991-94	Rich Kotite	37-29-0
1995-98	Ray Rhodes	30-36-1
1999-2011	Andy Reid	136-90-1

*Co-coach with Walt Kiesling in Philadelphia-Pittsburgh merger in 1943
**Retired after two games in 1951
***Released after three games in 1971
****Released after 15 games in 1985

PAID ATTENDANCE
Home 533,944   Away 553,253
Total 1,087,197
Single-game home record,
    72,111 (11/1/81)
Single-season home record,
    557,325 (1980)

2012 DRAFT CHOICES
Round	Name	Pos.	College
1	Fletcher Cox	DT	Mississippi St.
2	Mychal Kendricks	LB	California
	Vinny Curry	DE	Marshall
3	Nick Foles	QB	Arizona
4	Brandon Boykin	DB	Georgia
5	Dennis Kelly	T	Purdue
6	Marvin McNutt	WR	Iowa
	Brandon Washington	G	Miami
7	Bryce Brown	RB	Kansas St.

PHILADELPHIA EAGLES

2011 TEAM RECORD

PRESEASON (3-1)

Date	Result	Opponent
8/11	W 13-6	Baltimore
8/18	L 14-24	at Pittsburgh
8/25	W 24-14	Cleveland
9/1	W 24-14	at New York Jets

REGULAR SEASON (8-8)

Date	Result	Opponent
9/11	W 31-13	at St. Louis
9/18	L 31-35	at Atlanta
9/25	L 16-29	New York Giants
10/2	L 23-24	San Francisco
10/9	L 24-31	at Buffalo
10/16	W 20-13	at Washington
10/30	W 34-7	Dallas
11/7	L 24-30	Chicago
11/13	L 17-21	Arizona
11/20	W 17-10	at New York Giants
11/27	L 20-38	New England
12/1	L 14-31	at Seattle
12/11	W 26-10	at Miami
12/18	W 45-19	N.Y. Jets
12/24	W 20-7	at Dallas
1/1	W 34-10	Washington

SCORE BY PERIODS

Eagles	76	165	74	81	0	—	396
Opponents	63	90	64	111	0	—	328

2011 TEAM STATISTICS

	Eagles	Opp.
Total First Downs	356	289
Rushing	134	84
Passing	197	173
Penalty	25	32
3rd Down: Made/Att	85/205	75/211
3rd Down Pct.	41.5	35.5
4th Down: Made/Att	7/15	7/17
4th Down Pct.	46.7	41.2
Possession Avg.	31:23	28:37
Total Net Yards	6386	5198
Avg. Per Game	399.1	324.9
Total Plays	1036	982
Avg. Per Play	6.2	5.3
Net Yards Rushing	2276	1801
Avg. Per Game	142.3	112.6
Total Rushes	450	414
Net Yards Passing	4110	3397
Avg. Per Game	256.9	212.3
Sacked/Yards Lost	32/166	50/316
Gross Yards	4276	3713
Att./Completions	554/330	518/301
Completion Pct.	59.6	58.1
Had Intercepted	25	15
Punts/Average	67/42.2	85/43.2
Net Punting Avg.	67/36.9	85/39.3
Penalties/Yards	107/853	97/813
Fumbles/Ball Lost	23/13	18/9
Touchdowns	46	40
Rushing	20	11
Passing	22	27
Returns	4	2

2011 INDIVIDUAL STATISTICS

PASSING

	Att.	Comp.	Yds.	Pct.	TD	Int.	Tkld.	Rate
Vick	423	253	3303	59.8	18	14	23/126	84.9
Young	114	66	866	57.9	4	9	8/34	60.8
Kafka	16	11	107	68.8	0	2	1/6	47.7
Henry	1	0	0	0.0	0	0	0/0	39.6
Eagles	554	330	4276	59.6	22	25	32/166	78.3
Opponents	518	301	3713	58.1	27	15	50/316	85.7

SCORING

	TD R	TD P	TD Rt	PAT	FG	Saf	PTS
McCoy	17	3	0	0/0	0/0	0	120
Henery	0	0	0	46/46	24/27	0	118
Celek	0	5	0	0/0	0/0	0	30
Maclin	0	5	0	0/0	0/0	0	30
D. Jackson	0	4	0	0/0	0/0	0	24
Parker	0	0	2	0/0	0/0	0	12
Avant	0	1	0	0/0	0/0	0	6
Brown	1	0	0	0/0	0/0	0	6
Cooper	0	1	0	0/0	0/0	0	6
Hall	0	1	0	0/0	0/0	0	6
Harbor	0	1	0	0/0	0/0	0	6
Lewis	1	0	0	0/0	0/0	0	6
Rolle	0	0	1	0/0	0/0	0	6
Samuel	0	0	1	0/0	0/0	0	6
Smith	0	1	0	0/0	0/0	0	6
Vick	1	0	0	0/0	0/0	0	6
Hunt	0	0	0	0/0	0/0	1	2
Eagles	20	22	4	46/46	24/27	1	396
Opponents	11	27	2	38/38	16/24	0	328

2-Pt Conversions: Eagles 0-0, Opponents 1-2

RUSHING

	No.	Yds	Avg	LG	TD
McCoy	273	1309	4.8	60	17
Vick	76	589	7.8	53	1
Brown	42	136	3.2	15	1
Lewis	23	102	4.4	20	1
Young	18	79	4.4	13	0
D. Jackson	7	41	5.9	18	0
Hall	3	13	4.3	7	0
Schmitt	4	6	1.5	4	0
Maclin	1	1	1.0	1	0
Kafka	3	0	0.0	2	0
Eagles	450	2276	5.1	60	20
Opponents	414	1801	4.4	61	11

RECEIVING

	No.	Yds	Avg	LG	TD
Maclin	63	859	13.6	59	5
Celek	62	811	13.1	73	5
D. Jackson	58	961	16.6	62t	4
Avant	52	679	13.1	35	1
McCoy	48	315	6.6	26	3
Cooper	16	315	19.7	58	1
Harbor	13	163	12.5	27	1
Smith	11	124	11.3	20	1
Schmitt	3	32	10.7	13	0
Hall	3	20	6.7	16	1
Lewis	1	-3	-3.0	-3	0
Eagles	330	4276	13.0	73	22
Opponents	301	3713	12.3	74t	27

PUNTING

	No.	Yds.	Avg.	In 20	LG
Henry	66	2830	42.9	19	60
Eagles	67	2830	42.2	19	60
Opponents	85	3673	43.2	29	68

PUNT RETURNS

	Ret	FC	Yds	Avg	LG	TD
D. Jackson	17	12	114	6.7	51	0
Hall	7	12	76	10.9	30	0
Maclin	4	3	29	7.3	11	0
Marsh	1	0	-5	-5.0	0	0
Smith	1	1	0	0.0	0	0
Rodgers-Cromartie	0	0	-2	—	-2	0
Eagles	30	28	212	7.1	51	0
Opponents	31	16	176	5.7	25	0

INTERCEPTIONS

	No.	Yds	Avg	LG	TD
Coleman	4	60	15.0	35	0
Samuel	3	53	17.7	20t	1
Chaney	3	25	8.3	14	0
Asomugha	3	10	3.3	6	0
Allen	2	44	22.0	31	0
Eagles	15	192	12.8	35	1
Opponents	25	368	14.7	77t	2

KICKOFF RETURNS

	No.	Yds	Avg	LG	TD
Lewis	31	669	21.6	33	0
Brown	2	28	14.0	25	0
Hall	2	43	21.5	24	0
Rodgers-Cromartie	2	52	26.0	29	0
Cooper	1	16	16.0	16	0
D. Jackson	1	7	7.0	7	0
Eagles	39	815	20.9	33	0
Opponents	51	1178	23.1	51	0

FIELD GOALS

	1-19	20-29	30-39	40-49	50+
Henery	0/0	10/10	9/11	4/4	1/2
Eagles	0/0	10/10	9/11	4/4	1/2
Opponents	0/0	7/7	3/6	4/8	2/3

SACKS

	No.
Babin	18.0
Cole	11.0
Jenkins	5.5
Patterson	2.5
Tapp	2.5
Hunt	2.0
Landri	2.0
Parker	1.5
Chaney	1.0
Laws	1.0
Matthews	1.0
Rodgers-Cromartie	1.0
Rolle	1.0
Eagles	50.0
Opponents	32.0

RECORD HOLDERS
INDIVIDUAL RECORDS—CAREER

Category	Name	Performance
Rushing (Yds.)	Wilbert Montgomery, 1977-1984	6,538
Passing (Yds.)	Donovan McNabb, 1999-2009	32,873
Passing (TDs)	Donovan McNabb, 1999-2009	216
Receiving (No.)	Harold Carmichael, 1971-1983	589
Receiving (Yds.)	Harold Carmichael, 1971-1983	8,978
Interceptions	Bill Bradley, 1969-1976	34
	Eric Allen, 1988-1994	34
	Brian Dawkins, 1996-2008	34
Punting (Avg.)	Joe Muha, 1946-1950	42.9
Punt Return (Avg.)	Ernie Steele, 1942-48	16.8
Kickoff Return (Avg.)	Steve Van Buren, 1944-1951	26.7
Field Goals	David Akers, 1999-2010	294
Touchdowns (Tot.)	Harold Carmichael, 1971-1983	79
Points	David Akers, 1999-2010	1,323
*Sacks	Reggie White, 1985-1992	124.0

INDIVIDUAL RECORDS—SINGLE SEASON

Category	Name	Performance
Rushing (Yds.)	Wilbert Montgomery, 1979	1,512
Passing (Yds.)	Donovan McNabb, 2008	3,916
Passing (TDs)	Sonny Jurgensen, 1961	32
Receiving (No.)	Brian Westbrook, 2007	90
Receiving (Yds.)	Mike Quick, 1983	1,409
Interceptions	Bill Bradley, 1971	11
Punting (Avg.)	Joe Muha, 1948	47.2
Punt Return (Avg.)	Steve Van Buren, 1944	15.3
Kickoff Return (Avg.)	Al Nelson, 1972	29.1
Field Goals	David Akers, 2008	33
Touchdowns (Tot.)	LeSean McCoy, 2011	20
Points	David Akers, 2008	144
*Sacks	Reggie White, 1987	21.0

INDIVIDUAL RECORDS—SINGLE GAME

Category	Name	Performance
Rushing (Yds.)	Steve Van Buren, 11-27-49	205
Passing (Yds.)	Donovan McNabb, 12-5-04	464
Passing (TDs)	Adrian Burk, 10-17-54	**7
Receiving (No.)	Don Looney, 12-1-40	14
	Brian Westbrook, 11-4-07	14
Receiving (Yds.)	Tommy McDonald, 12-10-60	237
Interceptions	Russ Craft, 9-24-50	**4
Field Goals	Tom Dempsey, 11-12-72	6
Touchdowns (Tot.)	Many times	4
	Last time by Brian Westbrook, 11-27-08	
Points	Bobby Walston, 10-17-54	25
*Sacks	Clyde Simmons, 9-15-91	4.5
	Hugh Douglas, 10-18-98	4.5

*Sacks became an official statistic in 1982.
**NFL Record

PHILADELPHIA EAGLES

2012 VETERAN ROSTER

No.	Name	Pos.	Ht.	Wt.	Birthdate	NFL Exp.	College	Hometown	How Acq.	'11 Games/ Starts
29	Allen, Nate	S	6-1	210	11/30/87	3	South Florida	Cape Coral, Fla.	D2-'10	15/12
30	Anderson, Colt	S	5-10	194	10/25/85	3	Montana	Butte, Mont.	UFA(Minn)-'10	12/0
24	Asomugha, Nnamdi	CB	6-2	210	7/6/81	10	California	Los Angeles, Calif.	UFA(Oak)-'11	16/15
81	Avant, Jason	WR	6-0	212	4/20/83	7	Michigan	Chicago, Ill.	D4b-'06	16/7
93	Babin, Jason	DE	6-3	267	5/24/80	9	Western Michigan	Paw Paw, Mich.	UFA(Tenn)-'11	16/16
77	Bell, Demetress	T	6-5	311	5/3/84	5	Northwestern State	Summerfield, La.	UFA(Buff)-'12	7/6*
87	Celek, Brent	TE	6-4	255	1/25/85	6	Cincinnati	Cincinnati, Ohio	D5b-'07	16/16
51	Chaney, Jamar	LB	6-0	242	10/11/86	3	Mississippi State	St. Lucie, Fla.	D7a-'10	16/16
57	Clayton, Keenan	LB	6-1	229	6/19/87	3	Oklahoma	Sulphur Springs, Texas	D4b-'10	14/0
58	Cole, Trent	DE	6-3	270	10/5/82	8	Cincinnati	Xenia, Ohio	D5a-'05	14/14
42	Coleman, Kurt	S	5-11	195	7/1/88	3	Ohio State	Clayton, Ohio	D7c-'10	15/13
14	Cooper, Riley	WR	6-3	222	9/9/87	3	Florida	Clearwater, Fla.	D5b-'10	16/3
90	Dixon, Antonio	DT	6-3	322	7/17/85	4	Miami	Miami, Fla.	W(Wash)-'09	4/0
46	Dorenbos, Jon	LS	6-0	250	7/21/80	10	Texas-El Paso	Garden Grove, Calif.	FA-'06	16/0
65	Dunlap, King	T	6-9	330	9/14/85	5	Auburn	Brentwood, Tenn.	D7-'08	12/2
11	Edwards, Trent	QB	6-4	230	10/30/83	5	Stanford	Los Gatos, Calif.	FA-'12	0*
53	Fokou, Moise	LB	6-1	236	8/28/85	4	Maryland	Potomac, Md.	D7b-'09	11/7
64	Gibson, Mike	G/C	6-4	305	11/18/85	4	California	Napa, Calif.	FA-'12	3/0*
19	Gilyard, Mardy	WR	5-11	194	12/2/86	2	Cincinnati	Bunnell, Fla.	FA-'12	0*
54	Graham, Brandon	DE	6-2	268	4/3/88	3	Michigan	Detroit, Mich.	D1-'10	3/0
16	Hall, Chad	WR	5-8	187	5/23/86	3	Air Force	Atlanta, Ga.	FA-'10	7/0
21	Hanson, Joselio	CB	5-9	185	8/13/81	8	Texas Tech	Playa del Rey, Calif.	FA-'06	16/1
82	Harbor, Clay	TE	6-3	252	7/2/87	3	Missouri State	Dwight, Ill.	D4d-'10	16/3
6	Henery, Alex	K/P	6-1	177	8/18/87	2	Nebraska	Omaha, Neb.	D4b-'11	16/0
8	Henry, Chas	P	6-3	219	1/16/89	2	Florida	Dallas, Ga.	FA-'11	16/0
79	Herremans, Todd	G/T	6-6	321	10/13/82	8	Saginaw Valley State	Ravenna, Mich.	D4b-'05	16/16
27	Hughes, Brandon	CB	5-11	188	5/23/86	4	Oregon State	Bloomington, Ill.	UFA(NYG)-'10	13/1
76	Hunt, Phillip	DE	6-0	248	1/10/86	2	Houston	Fort Worth, Texas	FA-'11	9/0
10	Jackson, DeSean	WR	5-10	175	12/1/86	5	California	Long Beach, Calif.	D2b-'08	15/15
26	Jarrett, Jaiquawn	S	6-0	196	9/21/89	2	Temple	Brooklyn, N.Y.	D2-'11	12/2
97	Jenkins, Cullen	DT	6-2	305	1/20/81	9	Central Michigan	Belleville, Mich.	UFA(GB)-'11	16/16
33	Johnson, D.J.	CB	6-1	191	11/7/85	3	Jackson State	LaMarque, Texas	FA-'11	0*
56	Jordan, Akeem	LB	6-1	230	8/17/86	6	James Madison	Harrisonburg, Va.	FA-'07	15/7
3	Kafka, Mike	QB	6-3	225	7/25/87	3	Northwestern	Chicago, Ill.	D4c-'10	4/0
62	Kelce, Jason	C	6-3	282	11/5/87	2	Cincinnati	Cleveland, Ohio	D6a-'11	16/16
94	Landri, Derek	DT	6-2	290	9/21/83	6	Notre Dame	Concord, Calif.	UFA(Car)-'11	12/0
28	Lewis, Dion	RB	5-8	195	9/27/90	2	Pittsburgh	Blairstown, N.J.	D5a-'11	15/0
35	Lindley, Trevard	CB	6-0	183	2/2/86	2	Kentucky	Hiram, Ga.	D4a-'10	0*
18	Maclin, Jeremy	WR	6-0	198	5/11/88	4	Missouri	Kirkwood, Mo.	D1-'09	13/13
31	Marsh, Curtis	CB	6-1	197	3/1/88	2	Utah State	Simi Valley, Calif.	D3-'11	7/0
69	Mathis, Evan	G	6-5	302	11/1/81	8	Alabama	Homewood, Ala.	UFA(Cin)-'11	15/15
50	Matthews, Casey	LB	6-1	232	1/16/89	2	Oregon	Westlake Village, Calif.	D4a-'11	16/3
25	McCoy, LeSean	RB	5-11	208	7/12/88	4	Pittsburgh	Harrisburg, Pa.	D2-'09	15/15
49	Nelson, Tom	S	5-11	200	12/4/86	3	Illinois State	Arlington Heights, Ill.	FA-'11	4/0
98	Patterson, Mike	DT	6-1	300	9/1/83	8	Southern California	Los Alamitos, Calif.	D1-'05	15/15
71	Peters, Jason	T	6-4	340	1/22/82	9	Arkansas	Queen City, Texas	T(Buff)-'09	14/14
23	Rodgers-Cromartie, Dominique	CB	6-2	182	4/7/86	5	Tennessee State	Bradenton, Fla.	T-Arz-'11	13/3
52	Rolle, Brian	LB	5-10	227	11/20/88	2	Ohio State	Immokalee, Fla.	D6b-'11	16/13
59	t- Ryans, DeMeco	LB	6-1	247	7/28/84	7	Alabama	Bessemer, Ala.	T(Hou)-'12	16/16*
55	Tapp, Darryl	DE	6-1	270	9/13/84	7	Virginia Tech	Chesapeake, Va.	T(Sea)-'10	12/2
68	Vallos, Steve	C/G	6-3	310	12/28/83	5	Wake Forest	Youngstown, Ohio	UFA(Cle)-'12	1/0*
73	Vandervelde, Julian	G	6-2	300	10/7/87	2	Iowa	Davenport, Iowa	D5b-'11	1/0
7	Vick, Michael	QB	6-0	215	6/26/80	11	Virginia Tech	Newport News, Va.	FA-'09	13/13
63	Watkins, Danny	G	6-3	310	11/6/84	2	Baylor	Kelowna, B.C., Canada	D1-'11	12/12

* - Bell played 7 games with Buffalo in '11; Edwards last active with Jacksonville in '10; Gibson played 3 games with Seattle; Gilyard last active with St. Louis in '10; Johnson last active with the New York Jets in '10; Lindley last active with Philadelphia in '10 Ryans played 16 games with Houston; Vallos played 1 game with Cleveland.

t - Eagles traded for Ryans (Hou).

Retired—Brian Dawkins, 16-year safety, 14 games with Denver in '11.

Traded—T Winston Justice (6 games in '11) to Indianapolis.

Players lost through free agency (3): DE Juqua Parker (Cle; 12 games), DT Trevor Laws (StL; 14), WR Steve Smith (StL; 9).

Also played with Eagles in '11—DE Victor Abiamiri (0 games), RB Ronnie Brown (16), Kyle DeVan (5), C Jamaal Jackson (16), S Jarrad Page (6), CB Asante Samuel (14), FB Owen Schmitt (16), QB Vince Young (6).

FIRST-YEAR ROSTER

Name	Pos.	Ht.	Wt.	Birthdate	College	Hometown	How Acq.
Akpla, Elvis	WR	6-1	190	1/6/89	Montana State	Portland, Ore.	FA
Boykin, Brandon	CB	5-9	182	7/13/90	Georgia	Fayetteville, Ga.	D4
Brackett, Brett (1)	TE	6-5	246	12/13/87	Penn State	Lawrence, N.J.	FA-'11
Brown, Bryce	RB	6-0	223	5/14/91	Kansas State	Wichita, Kan.	D7
Camilli, Matt	LS	6-4	245	2/15/89	Texas-El Paso	Las Cruces, N.M.	FA
Cooper, Graig (1)	RB	5-10	205	7/12/87	Miami	Milford, N.Y.	FA-'11
Cox, Fletcher	DT	6-4	298	12/13/90	Mississippi State	Yazoo City, Miss.	D1
Curry, Vinny	DE	6-3	266	6/30/88	Marshall	Neptune, N.J.	D2b
Foles, Nick	QB	6-6	243	1/20/89	Arizona	Austin, Texas	D3
Ford, Chase	TE	6-6	245	7/19/90	Miami	Corrigan, Texas	FA
Fountain, Maurice (1)	DE	6-4	275	9/22/82	Clemson	Camden, S.C.	FA-'11
Hamler, Jamel (1)	WR	6-2	195	12/7/88	Fresno State	San Leandro, Calif.	FA-'11
Harris, Cliff	CB	5-11	180	12/12/90	Oregon	Fresno, Calif.	FA
Havili, Stanley (1)	FB	6-0	230	11/14/87	Southern California	Salt Lake City, Utah	D7b-'11
Igwenagu, Emil	FB	6-2	245	3/27/89	Massachusetts	Boylston, Mass.	FA
Jacobson, McKay	WR	5-11	199	10/7/87	Brigham Young	Southlake, Texas	FA
Johnson, Damaris	WR	5-8	170	11/22/89	Tulsa	Destrehan, La.	FA
Johnson, Ron (1)	WR	5-10	185	8/3/88	Southern California	Muskegon, Mich.	FA-'11
Jones, D.J. (1)	T	6-5	310	5/8/88	Nebraska	Stuart, Va.	W(Balt)
Kelly, Dennis	T	6-8	321	1/16/90	Purdue	Chicago Heights, Ill.	D5
Kendricks, Mychal	LB	5-11	239	9/28/90	California	Fresno, Calif.	D2a
Lloyd, Greg (1)	LB	6-1	247	2/10/89	Connecticut	Clermont, Fla.	D7a-'11
McNutt, Marvin	WR	6-2	216	7/4/89	Iowa	St. Louis, Mo.	D6a
Pflugrad, Aaron	WR	5-10	182	9/24/88	Arizona State	Eugene, Ore.	FA
Polk, Chris	RB	5-11	222	12/16/89	Washington	Redlands, Calif.	FA
Reynolds, Dallas (1)	G/C	6-4	320	4/23/84	Brigham Young	Provo, Utah	FA-'09
Simmons, Monte (1)	LB	6-3	226	1/29/89	Kent State	Pittsburgh, Pa.	FA
Stewart, Jeremy	FB	6-1	218	2/17/89	Stanford	Baton Rouge, La.	FA
Taylor, Zane (1)	C	6-2	309	4/23/88	Utah	Moab, Utah	FA-'11
Thomas, Phillip	S	5-11	198	11/15/90	Syracuse	Miami, Fla.	FA
Thornton, Cedric (1)	DT	6-4	309	6/21/88	Southern Arkansas	Star City, Ark.	FA-'11
Tydlacka, Ryan	P	6-1	190	1/27/89	Kentucky	Louisville, Ky.	FA
Washington, Brandon	G	6-2	320	8/13/88	Miami	Miami, Fla.	D6b
Williams, Darnell	WR	6-2	195	2/22/89	Louisiana College	Orlando, Fla.	FA

The term NFL Rookie is defined as a player who is in his first season of professional football and has not been on the roster of another professional football team for any regular-season or postseason games. A Rookie is designated by an "R" on NFL rosters. Players who have been active in another professional football league or players who have NFL experience, including either preseason training camp or being on an Active List or Inactive List, or on Reserve/Injured or Reserve/Physically Unable to Perform for fewer than six regular-season games, are termed NFL First-Year Players. An NFL First-Year Player is designated by a "1" on NFL rosters. Thereafter, a player is credited with an additional year of experience for each season in which he accumulates six games on the Active List or Inactive List, or on Reserve/Injured or Reserve/Physically Unable to Perform.

Log on to www.philadelphiaeagles.com for an up-to-date roster.

COACHING STAFF

**Head Coach/Executive Vice President of Football Operations,
Andy Reid**

Pro Career: Reid has earned NFL Coach of the Year honors three times, compiled the best win total (136), winning percentage (.601) and playoff victory total (10) in team history. He has captured six division titles and five trips to the NFC Championship Game. Since he was hired in 1999, only New England (8) has earned more divisional playoff round appearances (7) than Philadelphia. Reid is one of 11 coaches in NFL history to win 60% or more of 200-plus games. In his 20-year NFL coaching career, Reid's teams have made the playoffs 15 times (19-14 record). He has coached in the Super Bowl three times, the NFC Championship game nine times, and the Pro Bowl five times. Reid became the 20th head coach in franchise history on January 11, 1999, and was promoted to head coach/executive vice president of football operations in 2001. He was named NFL Coach of the Year in 2000 and 2002. He joined the Eagles after a seven-year stint as an assistant coach with Green Bay (1992-98) under Mike Holmgren. With Green Bay, Reid helped the Packers earn a Super Bowl XXXI victory over New England. Career record: 136-90-1.

Background: Coached at Brigham Young (1982), San Francisco State (1983-85), Northern Arizona (1986), Texas-El Paso (1987-88), and Missouri (1989-1991). Reid first met Holmgren, who was a member of BYU's coaching staff, when Reid was an offensive tackle and guard on three Cougar Holiday Bowl teams. Reid graduated with a bachelor's degree in physical education. He also received a master's degree in professional leadership in physical education and athletics.

Personal: Born in Los Angeles, Calif. on March 19, 1958, Reid and his wife Tammy have five children—Garrett, Britt, Crosby, Drew Ann, and Spencer.

ASSISTANT COACHES

Bobby April, special teams coordinator; born April 15, 1963, New Orleans, La. Linebacker/defensive end Nicholls State 1972-75. No pro playing experience. College coach: Southern Mississippi 1978, Tulane 1979, Arizona 1980-86, Southern California 1987-1990. Pro coach: Atlanta Falcons 1991-93, Pittsburgh Steelers 1994-95, New Orleans Saints 1996-99, St. Louis Rams 2001-02, Buffalo Bills 2004-09, joined Eagles in 2010.

Bobby April III, defensive quality control; born August 15, 1981, Tucson, Ariz. Attended Louisiana-Lafayette. No college or pro playing experience. College coach: Tulane 2005-06, Portland State 2007-09, Nicholls State 2010. Pro coach: Joined Eagles in 2011.

Todd Bowles, secondary; born November 18, 1963, Elizabeth, N.J. Defensive back Temple 1982-85. Pro defensive back Washington Redskins 1986-1990, 1992-93, San Francisco 49ers 1991. College coach: Morehouse College 1997, Grambling State 1998-99. Pro coach: New York Jets 2000, Cleveland Browns 2001-04, Dallas Cowboys 2005-07, Miami Dolphins 2008-2011 (interim head coach 2011), joined Eagles in 2012.

Mike Caldwell, linebackers; born August 31, 1971, Oak Ridge, Tenn. Linebacker Middle Tennessee State 1989-1992. Pro linebacker Cleveland Browns 1993-95, Baltimore Ravens 1996, Arizona Cardinals 1997, Philadelphia Eagles 1998-2001, Chicago Bears 2002, Carolina Panthers 2003. Pro coach: Joined Eagles in 2008.

Juan Castillo, defensive coordinator; born October 8, 1959, Port Isabel, Texas. Linebacker Texas A&I (now Texas A&M-Kingsville) 1978-1980. Pro linebacker San Antonio Gunslingers (USFL) 1984-85. College coach: Texas A&I/Texas A&M-Kingsville 1982-85, 1990-94. Pro coach: Joined Eagles in 1995.

David Culley, wide receivers; born September 17, 1955, Sparta, Tenn. Quarterback Vanderbilt 1973-77. No pro playing experience. College coach: Austin Peay 1978, Vanderbilt 1979-1981, Middle Tennessee State 1982, Tennessee-Chattanooga 1983, Western Kentucky 1984, Southwestern Louisiana 1985-88, Texas-El Paso 1989-1990, Texas A&M 1991-93. Pro coach: Tampa Bay Buccaneers 1994-95, Pittsburgh Steelers 1996-1998, joined Eagles in 1999.

Tom Melvin, tight ends; born October 1, 1961, Redwood City, Calif. Offensive lineman San Francisco State 1982-83. No pro playing experience. College coach: San Francisco State 1984-85, Northern Arizona 1986-87, California-Santa Barbara 1988-1990, Occidental College 1991-98. Pro coach: Joined Eagles in 1999.

Marty Mornhinweg, asst. head coach/offensive coordinator; born March 29, 1962, Edmond, Okla. Quarterback Montana 1981-84. Pro quarterback Denver Dynamite (AFL) 1987. College coach: Montana 1985, Texas-El Paso 1986-87, Northern Arizona 1988, 1994, Southeast Missouri State 1989-1990, Missouri 1991-93. Pro coach: Green Bay Packers 1995-96, San Francisco 49ers 1997-2000, Detroit Lions 2001-02 (head coach), joined Eagles in 2003.

Howard Mudd, offensive line; born February 10, 1942, Midland, Mich. Guard Hillsdale (Mich.) College 1960-63. Pro offensive lineman San Francisco 49ers 1964-69, Chicago Bears 1969-1971. College coach: California 1972-73. Pro coach: San Diego Chargers 1974-76, San Francisco 49ers 1977, Seattle Seahawks 1978-1982, 1993-97, Cleveland Browns 1983-88, Kansas City Chiefs 1989-1992,

Indianapolis Colts 1998-2009, joined Eagles in 2011.

Matt Nagy, offensive quality control; born April 24, 1978, Plainfield, N.J. Quarterback Delaware 1996-2000. Pro quarterback New York Dragons (AFL) 2002, Carolina Cobras (AFL) 2004, Georgia Force (AFL) 2005-06, Columbus Destroyers (AFL) 2007-08. Pro coach: Joined Eagles in 2011.

Doug Pederson, quarterbacks; born January 31, 1968, Bellingham, Wash. Quarterback Louisiana-Monroe 1987-1990. Pro experience: Miami Dolphins 1993-95, Green Bay Packers 1995-98, 2001-04, Philadelphia Eagles 1999, Cleveland Browns 2000. Pro coach: Joined Eagles in 2009.

Barry Rubin, strength and conditioning; born June 25, 1957, Monroe, La. Running back/punter Louisiana State 1976-77, tight end/punter Northwestern (La.) State 1978-1980. No pro playing experience. College coach: Northeast Louisiana 1981-83, 1987-1990, 1994, Louisiana State 1984-85. Pro coach: Green Bay Packers 1995-2005, joined Eagles in 2008.

Duce Staley, special teams quality control; born February 27, 1975, Tampa, Fla. Running back South Carolina 1995-96. Pro running back Philadelphia Eagles 1997-2003, Pittsburgh Steelers 2004-06. Pro coach: Joined Eagles in 2011.

Jim Washburn, defensive line; born December 2, 1949, Shelby, N.C. Offensive lineman Gardner-Webb 1969-1973. No pro playing experience. College coach: Southern Methodist 1976, Lees McRae (N.C.) J.C. 1977-78, Livingston 1979, New Mexico 1980-82, South Carolina 1983-88, Purdue 1989, Arkansas 1994-97, Houston 1998. Pro coach: London Monarchs (WLAF) 1991, Charlotte Rage (AFL) 1993, Tennessee Titans 1999-2010, joined Eagles in 2011.

Ted Williams, running backs; born November 17, 1943, Lyons, Texas. Attended Cal Poly-Pomona. No college or pro playing experience. College coach: UCLA 1980-89, Washington State 1991-93, Arizona 1994. Pro coach: Joined Eagles in 1995.

Michael Zordich, secondary/safeties; born October 12, 1963, Youngstown, Ohio. Safety Penn State 1982-85. Pro safety New York Jets 1987-88, Phoenix Cardinals 1989-1993, Philadelphia Eagles 1994-98. Pro coach: Joined Eagles in 2009.

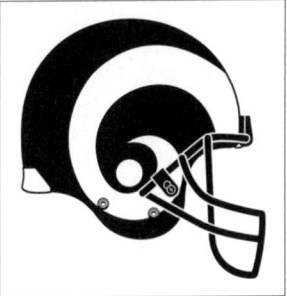

National Football Conference
West Division
Team Colors: New Century Gold, Millennium Blue, and White
One Rams Way
St. Louis, Missouri 63045
Telephone: (314) 982-7267

2012 SCHEDULE
PRESEASON
Aug. 12 at Indianapolis 12:30
Aug. 18 **Kansas City** 7:00
Aug. 25 at Dallas...........................7:00
Aug. 30 **Baltimore**...........................7:00

REGULAR SEASON
Sep. 9 at Detroit 12:00
Sep. 16 **Washington** 3:05
Sep. 23 at Chicago.......................12:00
Sep. 30 **Seattle**...........................12:00
Oct. 4 **Arizona** (Thurs).................7:20
Oct. 14 at Miami..........................12:00
Oct. 21 **Green Bay**.....................12:00
Oct. 28 **New England** (London) 12:00
Nov. 4 BYE
Nov. 11 at San Francisco................3:15
Nov. 18 **New York Jets** 12:00
Nov. 25 at Arizona.........................3:15
Dec. 2 **San Francisco** 12:00
Dec. 9 at Buffalo........................12:00
Dec. 16 **Minnesota** 12:00
Dec. 23 at Tampa Bay 12:00
Dec. 30 at Seattle..........................3:15
All times CT
Stadium: Edward Jones Dome
(opened in 1995)
•**Capacity:** 66,000
901 N. Broadway
St. Louis, Missouri 63101
Playing Surface: FieldTurf
Training Camp: Russell Training Center
1 Rams Way
St. Louis, Missouri 63045

CLUB OFFICIALS
Owner/Chairman: Stan Kroenke
Executive Vice President of Football
Operations/Chief Operating Officer:
Kevin Demoff
General Manager: Les Snead
Treasurer: Jeff Brewer
Vice President of Finance:
Michael T. Naughton
General Counsel: Todd Davis
Executive Vice President/Chief Revenue
Officer: Bob Reif
Vice President of Broadcasting and
Creative: Scott Brooks
Vice President of Corporate
Communications and Civic Affairs:
Molly Higgins
Vice President of Marketing and Brand
Strategy: Brian Killingsworth
Vice President/Executive Services,
Special Projects: Mike Moyneur
Vice President of Sales: Mike O'Keefe
Senior Director of Communications:
Artis Twyman
Director of Ticket Sales and Premium
Seating: Jake Bye
Director of Video Operations:
Larry Clerico
Director of Information Technology:
Bill Consoli
Director of Special Events: Keely Fimbres
Director of Player Engagement:
La'Roi Glover
Director of Internet Services and
Business Development: Keith Harris
Director of Player Personnel:
Lawrence McCutcheon
Director of College Scouting:
John Mancini
Director of Security: Steve Miller
Director of Scouting Administration:
Debbie Pollom
Director of Partnership Development and
Administration: Susan Slemmer
Director of Operations: Bruce Warwick
Director of Corporate Sales:
Chad Watson
Director of Ticket Operations:
Kanyon West
Head Trainer: Reggie Scott
Assistant Trainers: Byron Cunningham,
James Lomax, Tyler Williams
Equipment Manager: Jim Lake
Assistant Equipment Managers:
Matt Taylor, John Welby, Ben Bloomer
Scouts: Ray Agnew, Evan Ardoin,
Drew Casani, Luke Driscoll,
Brian Heimerdinger, Brad Holmes,
Steve Kazor
Scouting Assistants: Brian Shields,
Will Rodriguez

COACHING HISTORY
Cleveland 1937-1945,
Los Angeles 1946-1994
(532-530-20)
Records include postseason games
1937-38	Hugo Bezdek*	1-13-0
1938	Art Lewis	4-4-0
1939-1942	Earl (Dutch) Clark	16-26-2
1944	Aldo (Buff) Donelli	4-6-0
1945-46	Adam Walsh	16-5-1
1947	Bob Snyder	6-6-0
1948-49	Clark Shaughnessy	14-8-3
1950-52	Joe Stydahar**	19-9-0
1952-54	Hamp Pool	23-11-2
1955-59	Sid Gillman	28-32-1
1960-62	Bob Waterfield***	9-24-1
1962-65	Harland Svare	14-31-3
1966-1970	George Allen	49-19-4
1971-72	Tommy Prothro	14-12-2
1973-77	Chuck Knox	57-20-1
1978-1982	Ray Malavasi	43-36-0
1983-1991	John Robinson	79-74-0
1992-94	Chuck Knox	15-33-0
1995-96	Rich Brooks	13-19-0
1997-99	Dick Vermeil	25-26-0
2000-05	Mike Martz****	56-36-0
2005	Joe Vitt	4-7-0
2006-08	Scott Linehan#	11-25-0
2008	Jim Haslett	2-10-0
2009-2011	Steve Spagnuolo	10-38-0

* Released after three games in 1938
** Resigned after one game in 1952
*** Resigned after eight games in 1962
**** Took medical leave after five games in 2005
\# Released after four games in 2008

PAID ATTENDANCE
Home 429,875   Away 532,030
Total 961,905
Single-game home record,
66,273 (12/10/00)
Single-season home record,
520,926 (1999)

2012 DRAFT CHOICES
Round	Name	Pos.	College
1	Michael Brockers	DT	Louisiana St.
2	Brian Quick	WR	Appalachian St.
	Janoris Jenkins	DB	North Alabama
	Isaiah Pead	RB	Cincinnati
3	Trumaine Johnson	DB	Montana
4	Chris Givens	WR	Wake Forest
5	Rokevious Watkins	G	South Carolina
6	Greg Zuerlein	K	Missouri Western
7	Aaron Brown	LB	Hawaii
	Daryl Richardson	RB	Abilene Christian

EDWARD JONES DOME

ST. LOUIS RAMS

2011 TEAM RECORD
PRESEASON (4-0)

Date	Result	Opponent
8/13	W 33-10	Indianapolis
8/20	W 17-16	Tennessee
8/26	W 14-10	at Kansas City
9/1	W 24-17	at Jacksonville

REGULAR SEASON (2-14)

Date	Result	Opponent
9/11	L 13-31	Philadelphia
9/19	L 16-28	at New York Giants
9/25	L 7-37	Baltimore
10/2	L 10-17	Washington
10/16	L 3-24	at Green Bay
10/23	L 7-34	at Dallas
10/30	W 31-21	New Orleans
11/6	L 13-19	at Arizona (OT)
11/13	W 13-12	at Cleveland
11/20	L 7-24	Seattle
11/27	L 20-23	Arizona
12/4	L 0-26	at San Francisco
12/12	L 13-30	at Seattle
12/18	L 13-20	Cincinnati
12/24	L 0-27	at Pittsburgh
1/1	L 27-34	San Francisco
(OT) Overtime		

SCORE BY PERIODS

Rams	37	58	37	61	0 —	193
Opponents	94	103	100	104	6 —	407

2011 TEAM STATISTICS

	Rams	Opp.
Total First Downs	267	313
Rushing	79	122
Passing	159	166
Penalty	29	25
3rd Down: Made/Att	64/228	83/216
3rd Down Pct.	28.1	38.4
4th Down: Made/Att	8/23	5/8
4th Down Pct.	34.8	62.5
Possession Avg.	28:07	31:53
Total Net Yards	4537	5734
Avg. Per Game	283.6	358.4
Total Plays	1013	1033
Avg. Per Play	4.5	5.6
Net Yards Rushing	1667	2433
Avg. Per Game	104.2	152.1
Total Rushes	409	510
Net Yards Passing	2870	3301
Avg. Per Game	179.4	206.3
Sacked/Yards Lost	55/388	39/261
Gross Yards	3258	3562
Att./Completions	549/292	484/293
Completion Pct.	53.2	60.5
Had Intercepted	10	12
Punts/Average	106/43.9	81/44.9
Net Punting Avg.	106/37.0	81/39.2
Penalties/Yards	112/899	111/951
Fumbles/Ball Lost	27/13	24/6
Touchdowns	18	45
Rushing	7	17
Passing	9	21
Returns	2	7

2011 INDIVIDUAL STATISTICS

PASSING

	Att.	Comp.	Yds.	Pct.	TD	Int.	Tkld.	Rate
Bradford	357	191	2164	53.5	6	6	36/248	70.5
Feeley	97	53	548	54.6	1	2	10/72	66.0
Clemens	91	48	546	52.7	2	1	9/68	73.8
Brandstater	2	0	0	0.0	0	0	0/0	39.6
Lloyd	1	0	0	0.0	0	0	0/0	39.6
Norwood	1	0	0	0.0	0	1	0/0	0.0
Rams	549	292	3258	53.2	9	10	55/388	69.0
Opponents	484	293	3562	60.5	21	12	39/261	87.3

SCORING

	TD R	TD P	TD Rt	PAT	FG	Saf	PTS
Jo. Brown	0	0	0	18/18	21/28	0	81
S. Jackson	5	1	0	0/0	0/0	0	36
Lloyd	0	5	0	0/0	0/0	0	30
Alexander	0	2	0	0/0	0/0	0	12
Clemens	1	0	0	0/0	0/0	0	6
B. Gibson	0	1	0	0/0	0/0	0	6
N. Miller	0	0	1	0/0	0/0	0	6
Stewart	0	0	1	0/0	0/0	0	6
C. Williams	1	0	0	0/0	0/0	0	6
Hall	0	0	0	0/0	0/0	1	2
Rams	7	9	2	18/18	21/28	2	193
Opponents	17	21	7	44/44	31/37	0	407

2-Pt Conversions: Rams 0-0, Opponents 0-0

RUSHING

	No.	Yds	Avg	LG	TD
S. Jackson	260	1145	4.4	47t	5
C. Williams	87	361	4.1	23	1
Norwood	24	61	2.5	10	0
Clemens	6	37	6.2	18t	1
Bradford	18	26	1.4	17	0
B. Gibson	2	16	8.0	11	0
B. Miller	5	14	2.8	12	0
D. Jones	1	9	9.0	9	0
Salas	1	8	8.0	8	0
Feeley	3	4	1.3	6	0
Pettis	1	-6	-6.0	-6	0
Kendricks	1	-8	-8.0	-8	0
Rams	409	1667	4.1	47t	7
Opponents	510	2433	4.8	91t	17

RECEIVING

	No.	Yds	Avg	LG	TD
Lloyd	51	683	13.4	37	5
S. Jackson	42	333	7.9	50	1
B. Gibson	36	431	12.0	34t	1
Kendricks	28	352	12.6	45	0
Salas	27	264	9.8	21	0
Pettis	27	256	9.5	35	0
Alexander	26	431	16.6	68	2
C. Williams	14	93	6.6	16	0
Sims-Walker	11	139	12.6	33	0
Bajema	9	71	7.9	19	0
Hoomanawanui	7	83	11.9	27	0
Amendola	5	45	9.0	18	0
B. Miller	3	41	13.7	20	0
Clayton	3	26	8.7	12	0
Spach	2	2	1.0	3	0
N. Miller	1	8	8.0	8	0
Rams	292	3258	11.2	68	9
Opponents	293	3562	12.2	93t	21

INTERCEPTIONS

	No.	Yds	Avg	LG	TD
Gordy	3	37	12.3	30	0
Laurinaitis	2	15	7.5	15	0
Mikell	2	11	5.5	11	0
King	1	51	51.0	51	0
Hood	1	27	27.0	27	0
Stewart	1	27	27.0	27t	1
Chamberlain	1	4	4.0	4	0
C. Dahl	1	-3	-3.0	-3	0
Rams	12	169	14.1	51	1
Opponents	10	40	4.0	13	0

PUNTING

	No.	Yds.	Avg.	In 20	LG
D. Jones	105	4652	44.3	29	65
Rams	106	4652	43.9	29	65
Opponents	81	3636	44.9	29	71

PUNT RETURNS

	Ret	FC	Yds	Avg	LG	TD
Pettis	15	10	139	9.3	39	0
N. Miller	8	10	128	16.0	88t	1
Salas	2	3	29	14.5	29	0
Amendola	1	0	0	0.0	0	0
Porter	1	1	1	1.0	1	0
Clayton	0	1	0	—	—	0
Rams	27	25	297	11.0	88t	1
Opponents	45	28	552	12.3	99t	2

KICKOFF RETURNS

	No.	Yds	Avg	LG	TD
Porter	25	554	22.2	32	0
Norwood	24	611	25.5	47	0
Pettis	3	62	20.7	24	0
N. Miller	2	43	21.5	23	0
Sims	1	10	10.0	10	0
Rams	55	1280	23.3	47	0
Opponents	36	902	25.1	54	0

FIELD GOALS

	1-19	20-29	30-39	40-49	50+
Jo. Brown	0/0	7/7	6/7	8/12	0/2
Rams	0/0	7/7	6/7	8/12	0/2
Opponents	2/2	9/10	12/13	7/9	1/3

SACKS

	No.
Long	13.0
Hall	6.0
Quinn	5.0
G. Gibson	3.0
Laurinaitis	3.0
Stewart	3.0
Chamberlain	2.0
Ah You	1.0
King	1.0
Mikell	1.0
Robbins	1.0
Rams	39.0
Opponents	55.0

RECORD HOLDERS
INDIVIDUAL RECORDS—CAREER

Category	Name	Performance
Rushing (Yds.)	Steven Jackson, 2004-2011	9,093
Passing (Yds.)	Jim Everett, 1986-1993	23,758
Passing (TDs)	Roman Gabriel, 1962-1972	154
Receiving (No.)	Isaac Bruce, 1994-2007	942
Receiving (Yds.)	Isaac Bruce, 1994-2007	14,109
Interceptions	Ed Meador, 1959-1970	46
Punting (Avg.)	Danny Villanueva, 1960-64	44.3
Punt Return (Avg.)	Az-Zahir Hakim, 1998-2001	11.4
Kickoff Return (Avg.)	Ron Brown, 1984-89, 1991	26.3
Field Goals	Jeff Wilkins, 1997-2007	265
Touchdowns (Tot.)	Marshall Faulk, 1999-2005	85
Points	Jeff Wilkins, 1997-2007	1,223
*Sacks	Leonard Little, 1998-2008	81.0

INDIVIDUAL RECORDS—SINGLE SEASON

Category	Name	Performance
Rushing (Yds.)	Eric Dickerson, 1984	**2,105
Passing (Yds.)	Kurt Warner, 2001	4,830
Passing (TDs)	Kurt Warner, 1999	41
Receiving (No.)	Isaac Bruce, 1995	119
Receiving (Yds.)	Isaac Bruce, 1995	1,781
Interceptions	Dick (Night Train) Lane, 1952	**14
Punting (Avg.)	Donnie Jones, 2008	50.0
Punt Return (Avg.)	Woodley Lewis, 1952	18.5
Kickoff Return (Avg.)	Verda (Vitamin T) Smith, 1950	33.7
Field Goals	Jeff Wilkins, 2003	39
Touchdowns (Tot.)	Marshall Faulk, 2000	26
Points	Jeff Wilkins, 2003	163
*Sacks	Kevin Carter, 1999	17.0

INDIVIDUAL RECORDS—SINGLE GAME

Category	Name	Performance
Rushing (Yds.)	Willie Ellison, 12-5-71	247
Passing (Yds.)	Norm Van Brocklin, 9-28-51	**554
Passing (TDs)	Many times	5
	Last time by Kurt Warner, 10-10-99	
Receiving (No.)	Tom Fears, 12-3-50	18
Receiving (Yds.)	Willie Anderson, 11-26-89	**336
Interceptions	Many times	3
	Last time by Keith Lyle, 12-15-96	
Field Goals	Bob Waterfield, 12-9-51	5
	Jeff Wilkins, 10-1-00	5
Touchdowns (Tot.)	Many times	4
	Last time by Marshall Faulk, 10-20-02	
Points	Many times	24
	Last time by Marshall Faulk, 10-20-02	
*Sacks	Gary Jeter, 9-18-88	5.0

*Sacks became an official statistic in 1982.
**NFL Record

2012 VETERAN ROSTER

No.	Name	Pos.	Ht.	Wt.	Birthdate	NFL Exp.	College	Hometown	How Acq.	'11 Games/ Starts
99	#Ah You, C.J.	DE	6-4	265	7/7/82	3	Oklahoma	Highland, Utah	FA-'07	9/2
84	Alexander, Danario	WR	6-5	217	8/7/88	3	Missouri	Marlin, Texas	FA'10	10/4
16	Amendola, Danny	WR	5-11	188	11/2/85	3	Texas Tech	The Woodlands, Texas	FA-'09	1/1
47	#Bajema, Billy	TE	6-4	259	10/31/82	7	Oklahoma State	Oklahoma City, Okla.	UFA(SF)-'09	16/11
8	Bradford, Sam	QB	6-4	224	11/8/87	3	Oklahoma	Oklahoma City, Okla.	D1-'10	10/10
5	Brandstater, Tom	QB	6-5	222	10/21/84	2	Fresno State	Turlock, Calif.	FA-'11	1/0
37	#Butler, James	S	6-3	218	9/7/82	7	Georgia Tech	Bainbridge, Ga.	UFA(NYG)-'09	16/0
89	#Clayton, Mark	WR	5-10	190	7/2/82	7	Oklahoma	Arlington, Texas	T(Balt)-'10	2/1
10	Clemens, Kellen	QB	6-2	220	6/6/83	7	Oregon	Burns, Ore.	W(Hou)-'11	3/3
52	Cole, Justin	LB	6-3	242	11/22/87	3	San Jose State	Chino Hills, Calif.	FA-'11	4/0
93	Cudjo, Jermelle	DT	6-2	311	9/28/86	3	Central Oklahoma	Lawton, Okla.	FA-'10	0*
43	Dahl, Craig	S	6-1	212	6/17/85	5	North Dakota State	Mankato, Minn.	FA-'09	16/5
62	Dahl, Harvey	G	6-5	308	6/24/81	6	Nevada-Reno	Fallon, Nev.	UFA(Atl)-'11	16/16
58	Dunbar, Jo-Lonn	LB	6-0	226	3/13/85	5	Boston College	Syracuse, N.Y.	UFA(NO)-'12	16/14*
4	#Feeley, A.J.	QB	6-3	216	5/16/77	11	Oregon	Caldwell, Idaho	UFA(Car)-'10	5/3
31	Finnegan, Cortland	CB	5-10	188	2/2/84	7	Samford	Milton, Fla.	UFA(Tenn)-'12	16/16*
32	Fletcher, Bradley	CB	6-0	200	6/25/86	4	Iowa	Youngstown, Ohio	D3-'09	4/4
11	Gibson, Brandon	WR	6-0	205	8/13/87	4	Washington State	Puyallup, Wash.	T(Phil)-'09	15/9
73	#Goldberg, Adam	G	6-7	305	8/12/80	8	Wyoming	Edina, Minn.	T(Minn)-'06	16/8
38	Gordy, Josh	CB	5-11	195	2/9/1987	2	Central Michigan	Warthan, Ga.	FA-'11	14/9
31	#Harris, Al	CB	6-1	194	12/7/74	14	Texas A&M-Kingsville	Pompano Beach, Fla.	UFA(Mia)-'11	9/5
95	Hayes, William	DE	6-3	272	5/2/85	5	Winston-Salem State	High Point, N.C.	UFA(Tenn)-'12	10/1*
26	#Hood, Rod	CB	5-11	201	10/3/81	9	Auburn	Columbus, Ga.	FA-'11	9/4
86	Hoomanawanui, Michael	TE	6-4	263	7/4/88	3	Illinois	Bloomington, Ill.	D5a-'10	8/7
70	Hughes, Kevin	G/T	6-4	300	8/6/88	2	Southeast Louisiana	New Orleans, La.	FA-'11	3/0
56	Hull, Josh	LB	6-3	245	5/21/87	2	Penn State	Millheim, Pa.	D7c-'10	11/0
39	Jackson, Steven	RB	6-2	240	7/22/83	9	Oregon State	Las Vegas, Nev.	D1-'04	15/15
88	Kendricks, Lance	TE	6-3	247	1/30/88	2	Wisconsin	Milwaukee, Wisc.	D2-'11	15/10
21	#King, Justin	CB	5-11	197	5/11/87	4	Penn State	Pittsburgh, Pa.	D4a-'08	12/12
98	Langford, Kendall	DT	6-6	295	1/27/86	5	Hampton	Petersburg, Va.	UFA(Mia)-'12	16/12*
55	Laurinaitis, James	LB	6-2	250	12/3/86	4	Ohio State	Plymouth, Minn.	D2-'09	16/16
99	Laws, Trevor	DT	6-1	304	6/14/85	5	Notre Dame	Dayton, Ohio	UFA(Phil)-'12	14/1*
59	#Leber, Ben	LB	6-3	245	12/7/78	10	Kansas State	Vermillion, S.D.	FA-'11	7/3
79	#LeVoir, Mark	T	6-7	310	7/29/82	5	Notre Dame	Minneapolis, Minn.	FA-'11	7/3
91	Long, Chris	DE	6-3	270	3/28/85	5	Virginia	Charlottesville, Va.	D1-'08	16/16
67	Mattison, Bryan	G	6-3	310	5/15/84	3	Iowa	Mishawaka, Ind.	W(Balt)-'11	5/4
81	McNeill, Mike	TE	6-4	235	3/7/88	2	Nebraska	St. Louis, Mo.	FA-'11	0*
44	McQuaide, Jake	LS	6-2	247	12/7/87	2	Ohio State	Cincinnati, Ohio	FA-'11	16/0
27	Mikell, Quintin	S	5-10	204	9/16/80	10	Boise State	Eugene, Ore.	UFA(Phil)-'11	16/16
49	Miller, Brit	FB	6-1	253	9/15/86	4	Illinois	Decatur, Ill.	FA-'10	12/2
67	#Miller, Drew	C	6-5	303	7/6/85	3	Florida	Paducah, Ky.	FA-'09	1/0
82	Mulligan, Matthew	TE	6-4	265	1/18/85	4	Maine	Bangor, Maine	FA-'12	16/9*
23	Murphy, Jerome	CB	6-0	200	1/13/87	2	South Florida	Elizabeth, N.J.	D3-10	0*
34	#Norwood, Jerious	RB	5-11	205	7/29/83	6	Mississippi State	Jackson, Miss.	UFA(Atl)-'11	9/0
69	Ojinnaka, Quinn	G	6-5	306	4/23/84	7	Syracuse	Seabrook, Md.	UFA(Ind)-'12	9/3*
18	Pettis, Austin	WR	6-3	207	5/6/88	2	Boise State	Orange, Calif.	D3-'11	12/3
51	#Poppinga, Brady	LB	6-3	252	9/21/79	7	Brigham Young	Evanston, Wyo.	UFA(GB)-'11	15/12
94	Quinn, Robert	DE	6-4	264	5/18/90	2	North Carolina	Ladson, S.C.	D1-'11	15/1
76	Saffold, Rodger	T	6-5	314	6/6/88	3	Indiana	Bedford, Ohio	D2-'10	9/9
87	Salas, Greg	WR	6-1	209	8/25/88	2	Hawaii	Chino, Calif.	D4-'11	6/1
97	Scott, Darell	DT	6-3	317	3/15/86	4	Clemson	Columbia, S.C.	D4-'11	13/0
92	Sims, Eugene	DE	6-6	265	3/18/86	3	West Texas A&M	Mt. Olive, Miss.	D6b-'10	16/0
10	#Sims-Walker, Mike	WR	6-2	212	11/21/84	5	Central Florida	Orlando, Fla.	FA-'11	4/3
77	Smith, Jason	T	6-5	308	4/30/86	4	Baylor	Dallas, Texas	D1-'09	6/6
12	Smith, Steve	WR	5-11	195	5/6/85	6	Southern California	Woodland Hills, Calif.	UFA(Phil)-'12	9/1*
20	Stewart, Darian	S	5-11	214	8/4/88	3	South Carolina	Huntsville, Ala.	FA-'10	15/10
59	Turner, Robert	OL	6-4	308	8/20/84	4	New Mexico	Austin, Texas	UFA(NYJ)-'12	16/0*
63	Wells, Scott	C	6-2	300	1/7/81	9	Tennessee	Brentwood, Tenn.	UFA(GB)-'12	16/16*
33	#Williams, Cadillac	RB	5-11	218	4/21/1982	6	Auburn	Gadsden, Ala.	UFA(TB)-'11	12/1
52	Williams, Jabara	LB	6-2	238	7/6/1989	2	Stephen F. Austin	Garrison, Texas	D7b-'11	2/0
64	#Wragge, Tony	C/G	6-4	310	8/14/1979	7	New Mexico State	Creighton, N.M.	FA-'11	14/8

* Dunbar played 16 with New Orleans in '11; Finnegan played 16 games with Tennessee; Hayes played 10 games with Tennessee; Langford played 16 games with Miami; Laws played 14 games with Miami; McNeill inactive for 2 games; Mulligan played 16 games with New York Jets; Murphy missed '11 season because of injury; Ojinnaka played 9 games with Indianapolis; S. Smith played 9 games with Philadelphia; Turner played 16 games with New York Jets; Wells played 16 games with Green Bay.

Unrestricted free agent; subject to developments.

Players lost through free agency (6): G Jacob Bell (Cin; 12 games), LB Chris Chamberlain (NO; 16), DT Gary Gibson (TB; 16), P Donnie Jones (Hou; 16), LB Bryan Kehl (Wash; 14), WR Brandon Lloyd (NE; 15).

Also played with Rams in '11—DT Justin Bannan (15 games), CB Ron Bartell (1), C Jason Brown (14), K Josh Brown (16), WR Dominique Curry (16), DE James Hall (15), CB Brian Jackson (1), CB Marquis Johnson (3), WR Nick Miller (6), CB Nate Ness (4), LB David Nixon (8), RB Quinn Porter (12), DT Fred Robbins (15), CB Chris Smith (3), TE Stephen Spach (10), T Thomas Welch (4).

FIRST-YEAR ROSTER

Name	Pos.	Ht.	Wt.	Birthdate	College	Hometown	How Acq.
Anderson, Todd	RB	6-1	267	9/15/88	Michigan State	Napoleon, Mich.	FA
Banks, Cornell (1)	DT	6-2	310	1/3/86	Fresno State	San Jose, Calif.	FA-'11
Barnes, Tim (1)	C	6-4	300	5/14/88	Missouri	Longwood, Mo.	FA-'11
Brockers, Michael	DT	6-6	322	12/21/90	Louisiana State	Houston, Texas	D1
Brown, Aaron	LB	6-0	237	9/24/88	Hawaii	Puyallup, Wash.	D7a
Brown, Sammy	LB	6-2	242	4/17/90	Houston	Hattiesburg, Miss.	FA
Burney, Kendric (1)	CB	5-9	190	2/14/88	North Carolina	Jacksonville, N.C.	FA-'11
Caldwell, Jeremy	CB	5-9	183	6/16/88	Eastern Kentucky	Chattanooga, Tenn.	FA
Childers, Jamie	TE	6-5	230	6/26/88	Coastal Carolina	Mt. Pleasant, S.C.	FA
Choice, Derrick	LB	6-1	220	12/4/89	Stephen F. Austin	Tyler, Texas	FA
Conrath, Matthew	DT	6-7	290	8/11/89	Virginia	Oak Lawn, Ill.	FA
Cosby, Demarco (1)	TE	6-3	241	7/2/88	Central Missouri	Kansas City, Mo.	FA-'11
Daniels, Matthew	DB	6-1	211	9/27/89	Duke	Fayetteville, Ga.	FA
Davis, Austin	QB	6-2	221	6/2/89	Southern Mississippi	Meridian, Miss.	FA
Givens, Chris	WR	6-0	198	12/6/89	Wake Forest	Wylie, Texas	D4
Guidugli, Ben (1)	TE	6-1	248	10/22/87	Cincinnati	Ft. Thomas, Ky.	FA-'11
Harkey, Cory	TE	6-4	260	6/17/90	UCLA	Chino Hills, Calif.	FA
Hay, Michael	G	6-4	307	9/19/89	Syracuse	College Point, N.Y.	FA
Hebert, T-Bob	C	6-3	300	2/9/89	Louisiana State	Norcross, Ga.	FA
Hekker, John	P	6-5	227	2/8/90	Oregon State	Bothell, Wash.	FA
Henderson, John (1)	DT	6-1	303	2/10/88	Southern Mississippi	Oakland City, Calif.	FA-'11
Hoffman-Ellis, Alex	LB	6-0	232	8/14/89	Washington State	Los Angeles, Calif.	FA
Jarrett, Jamaar	DE	6-5	265	3/28/90	Arizona State	San Marcos, Calif.	FA
Jenkins, Janoris	CB	5-10	193	10/29/88	North Alabama	Pahokee, Fla.	D2b
Johnson, Nick	WR	5-11	187	8/16/89	Henderson State	Santa Cruz, Calif.	FA
Johnson, Trumaine	CB	6-2	204	1/1/90	Montana	Stockton, Calif.	D3
Keller, Noah	LB	6-1	245	12/5/88	Ohio	Kearney, Neb.	FA
Lindholm, Garrett (1)	K	5-9	190	8/10/88	Tarleton State	Pflugerville, Texas	FA
Long, Joe	T	6-5	304	7/27/89	Wayne State	Lapeer, Mich.	FA
Malone, Tom (1)	P	6-0	205	3/29/84	Southern California	Lake Elsinore, Calif.	FA
McKee, Ryan (1)	T	6-6	308	11/4/86	Southern Mississippi	Daphne, Ala.	W(NYJ)-'09
McLeod, Rodney	S	5-11	183	6/23/90	Virginia	Oxon Hill, Md.	FA
Middleton, Calvin	RB	5-11	220	5/19/90	Jacksonville State	Acworth, Ga.	FA
Pead, Isaiah	RB	5-11	200	12/14/89	Cincinnati	Columbus, Ohio	D2c
Peterson, Deangelo	TE	6-4	243	1/11/89	Louisiana State	New Orleans, La.	FA
Pointer, Quinton	DB	5-9	195	4/16/88	Nevada-Las Vegas	Fort Myers, Fla.	FA
Quick, Brian	WR	6-3	220	6/5/89	Appalachian State	Columbia, S.C.	D2a
Reynolds, Chase (1)	RB	6-0	200	10/22/87	Montana	Drummond, Mont.	FA-'11
Richardson, Daryl	RB	5-10	196	4/12/90	Abilene Christian	Jacksonville, Fla.	D7b
Schwieger, Nicholas	RB	5-10	210	1/30/90	Dartmouth	Norton, Mass.	FA
Smith, Scott	DE	6-7	261	6/6/88	Texas Tech	Kailua, Hawaii	FA
Tripucka, Travis	LS	6-1	240	5/3/89	Massachusetts	Boonton Township, N.J.	FA
Watkins, Rokevious	G	6-3	338	2/24/89	South Carolina	Fairburn, Ga.	D5
Zuerlein, Greg	K	6-0	187	12/27/87	Missouri Western	Lincoln, Neb.	D6

The term NFL Rookie is defined as a player who is in his first season of professional football and has not been on the roster of another professional football team for any regular-season or postseason games. A Rookie is designated by an "R" on NFL rosters. Players who have been active in another professional football league or players who have NFL experience, including either preseason training camp or being on an Active List or Inactive List, or on Reserve/Injured or Reserve/Physically Unable to Perform for fewer than six regular-season games, are termed NFL First-Year Players. An NFL First-Year Player is designated by a "1" on NFL rosters. Thereafter, a player is credited with an additional year of experience for each season in which he accumulates six games on the Active List or Inactive List, or on Reserve/Injured or Reserve/Physically Unable to Perform.

Log on to www.stlouisrams.com for an up-to-date roster.

COACHING STAFF
Head Coach,
Jeff Fisher

Pro Career: Named the twenty-sixth head coach in franchise history on January 17, 2012. Fisher ranks 21st on the NFL's career wins list (147) and fourth among active coaches. Spent 16 full seasons as head coach of the Tennessee Titans, 11 as executive vice president. Guided the Titans to six playoff appearances, three division titles, two AFC Championship games (1999, 2002) and one Super Bowl appearance (XXXIV). Joined the Oilers'/Titans' coaching staff in 1994. He was elevated to head coach in November 1994, replacing Jack Pardee, for the season's final six games. Previously coached with Philadelphia Eagles (defensive backs, 1986-88), Los Angeles Rams (youngest defensive coordinator in NFL, 1989-1991), and San Francisco 49ers (defensive backs, 1992-93). Played with Chicago Bears (1981-85) as a defensive back and return specialist. Earned a Super Bowl ring following Chicago's Super Bowl XX victory (1985), despite spending the year on injured reserve with an ankle injury that prematurely ended his playing career. Fisher began his post-playing career that season by assisting Buddy Ryan as the Bears' "unofficial" coach. Career record: 147-126.
Background: Played defensive back at Southern California.
Personal: Born February 25, 1958 in Woodland Hills, California. Has three children: sons Brandon (age 24) and Trent (age 19), and daughter Tara (age 22).

ASSISTANT COACHES

Adam Bailey, asst. strength coach; born March 30, 1976, Lindale, Texas. No college or pro playing experience. College coach: Texas 1996-97, Louisville 1998-99, Auburn 2000-01, Missouri 2002-03. Pro coach: New Orleans Saints 2004-09, joined Rams in 2010.

Rob Boras, tight ends; born Sept. 30, 1970, Glen Ellyn, Ill. Center De Pauw 1988-1991. No pro playing experience. College coach: DePauw 1992-93, Texas 1994-97, Benedictine 1998 (head coach), Nevada-Las Vegas 1999-2003. Pro coach: Chicago Bears 2004-09, Jacksonville Jaguars 2010-11, joined Rams in 2012.

Paul Boudreau, offensive line; born Dec. 30, 1949, Arlington, Mass. Guard Boston College 1970-73. No pro playing experience. Pro coach: New Orleans Saints 1987-1993, Detroit Lions 1994-96, New England Patriots 1997-98, Miami Dolphins 1999-2000, Carolina Panthers 2001-02, Jacksonville Jaguars 2003-05, St. Louis Rams 2006-07, Atlanta Falcons 2008-2011, re-joined Rams in 2012.

Paul F. Boudreau, asst. special teams; born June 2, 1975, Boston, Mass. No college or pro playing experience. College coach: Northeastern 1997-98, Cincinnati 1998-99, Brown 2000-06, Central Connecticut State 2007-08, Massachusetts Maritime 2010, Widener 2011. Pro coach: Joined Rams in 2012.

Joe Bowden, asst. linebackers; born February 25, 1970, Dallas, Texas. Linebacker Oklahoma 1988-1991. Pro linebacker Houston Oilers/Tennessee Titans 1992-99, Dallas Cowboys 2000. College coach: Central Oklahoma 2006-08. Pro coach: Joined Rams in 2012.

Chuck Cecil, secondary; born Nov. 8, 1964, Red Bluff, Calif. Defensive back Arizona 1983-87. Pro safety Green Bay Packers 1988-1992, Phoenix Cardinals 1993, Houston Oilers 1995. Pro coach: Tennessee Titans 2001-2010, joined Rams in 2012.

Frank Cignetti, quarterbacks; born October 4, 1965, Pittsburgh, Pa. Safety Indiana Univ. (Pa.) 1985-88. No pro playing experience. College coach: Pittsburgh 1989, Indiana Univ. (Pa.) 1990-98, Fresno State 2002-05, North Carolina 2006, California 2008, Pittsburgh 2009-2010, Rutgers 2011. Pro coach: Kansas City Chiefs 1999, New Orleans Saints 2000-01, San Francisco 49ers 2007, joined Rams in 2012.

Andy Dickerson, asst. offensive line; born January 29, 1982, Wilmington, Del. Offensive lineman Tufts 1999-2002. No pro playing experience. College coach: Tufts 2003. Pro coach: New York Jets 2006-08, 2011, Cleveland Browns 2009-2010, joined Rams in 2012.

John Fassel, special teams coordinator; born January 10, 1974, Anaheim, Calif. Wide receiver/quarterback Pacific 1994-95, Weber State 1996-98. No pro playing experience. College coach: Bucknell 1999, 2001, Idaho State 2000, New Mexico Highlands 2002-03. Pro coach: Amsterdam Admirals (NFLE) 2000, Baltimore Ravens 2005-07, Oakland Raiders 2008-2011, joined Rams in 2012.

Brandon Fisher, asst. secondary; born June 16, 1987, Franklin, Tenn. Safety/linebacker Montana 2007-09. No pro playing experience. Pro coach: Detroit Lions 2011, joined Rams in 2012.

Rock Gullickson, strength; born April 11, 1955, Moorhead, Minn. Guard Moorhead State 1973-76. No pro playing experience. College coach: Moorhead State 1978, Maryville State (N.D.) 1979-1980, South Dakota State 1981, Montana State 1982-89, Rutgers 1990-92, Texas 1993-97, Louisville 1998-99. Pro coach: New Orleans Saints 2000-05, Green Bay Packers 2006-08, joined Rams in 2009.

Dave McGinnis, asst. head coach; born August 7, 1951, Independence, Kan. Defensive back Texas Christian 1970-73. No pro playing experience. College coach: Texas Christian 1973-74, 1982, Missouri 1975-77, Indiana State 1978, 1980-81, Kansas State 1983-85. Pro coach: Chicago Bears 1986-1995, Arizona Cardinals 1996-2003 (head coach 2000-03), Tennessee Titans 2004-2011, joined Rams in 2012.

Brian Schottenheimer, offensive coordinator; born October 16, 1973, Denver, Colo. Quarterback Kansas 1992, Florida 1993-96. No pro playing experience. College coach: Syracuse 1999, Southern California 2000. Pro coach: St. Louis Rams 1997, Kansas City Chiefs 1998, Washington Redskins 2001, San Diego Chargers 2002-05, New York Jets 2006-2011, joined Rams in 2012.

Ray Sherman, wide receivers; born Nov. 27, 1951, Berkeley, Calif. Wide receiver/defensive back Fresno State 1971-72. No pro playing experience. College coach: San Jose State 1974, California 1975, 1981, Michigan State 1976-77, Wake Forest 1978-1980, Purdue 1982-85, Georgia 1986-87. Pro coach: Houston Oilers 1988-89, Atlanta Falcons 1990, San Francisco 49ers 1991-93, New York Jets 1994, Minnesota Vikings 1995-97, 1999, Pittsburgh Steelers 1998, Green Bay Packers 2000-04, Tennessee Titans 2005-06, Dallas Cowboys 2007-2010, joined Rams in 2012.

Clyde Simmons, asst. defensive line; born August 4, 1964, Lanes, S.C. Defensive end Western Carolina 1982-85. Pro defensive end Philadelphia Eagles 1986-1993, Arizona Cardinals 1994-95, Jacksonville Jaguars 1996-97, Cincinnati Bengals 1998, Chicago Bears 1999-2000. Pro coach: New York Jets 2010, joined Rams in 2012.

Ben Sirmans, running backs; born October 17, 1970, East Orange, N.J. Running back Maine 1990-93. No pro playing experience. College coach: Maine 1996-99, Kent State 2000-04, Michigan State 2005-06, Boston College 2007-2011. Pro coach: Joined Rams in 2012.

Andy Sugarman, offensive quality control; born May 23, 1972, Lafayette, Calif. No college or pro playing experience. College coach: California 1991-97. Pro coach: San Francisco 49ers 1998-2002, Detroit Lions 2003-05, Atlanta Falcons 2007, joined Rams in 2009.

Mike Waufle, defensive line; born June 27, 1954, Hornell, N.Y. U.S. Marines 1972-75. Defensive lineman Bakersfield (Calif.) J.C. 1975-76, Utah State 1977-78. No pro playing experience. College coach: Alfred 1979, Utah State 1980-84, Fresno State 1985-88, UCLA 1989, Oregon State 1990-91, California 1992-97. Pro coach: Oakland Raiders 1998-2003, 2010-11, New York Giants 2004-09, joined Rams in 2012.

Blake Williams, linebackers; born Dec. 30, 1984, Independence, Mo. Defensive back Princeton 2003-07. No pro playing experience. Pro coach: Washington Redskins 2006-07, Jacksonville Jaguars 2008, New Orleans Saints 2009-2011, joined Rams in 2012.

Dennard Wilson, defensive quality control; born March 31, 1982, Upper Marlboro, Md. Safety Maryland 2000-03. Pro safety Washington Redskins 2004. College coach: Maryland 2007-08. Pro coach: Joined Rams in 2012.

**National Football Conference
West Division**
Team Colors: 49ers Gold and 49ers Red
4949 Centennial Boulevard
Santa Clara, California 95054
Telephone: (408) 562-4949

2012 SCHEDULE
PRESEASON
Aug. 10 **Minnesota**............................6:00
Aug. 18 at Houston............................5:00
Aug. 26 at Denver...............................1:00
Aug. 30 **San Diego**...........................7:00

REGULAR SEASON
Sep. 9   at Green Bay 1:15
Sep. 16 **Detroit**...............................5:20
Sep. 23 at Minnesota..................10:00a
Sep. 30 at New York Jets............10:00a
Oct. 7   **Buffalo** 1:15
Oct. 14 **New York Giants**...............1:15
Oct. 18 **Seattle** (Thurs)..................5:20
Oct. 29 at Arizona (Mon) 5:30
Nov. 4   BYE
Nov. 11 **St. Louis** 1:15
Nov. 19 **Chicago** (Mon)..................5:30
Nov. 25 at New Orleans...................1:15
Dec. 2   at St. Louis....................10:00a
Dec. 9   **Miami** 1:05
Dec. 16 at New England *5:20
Dec. 23 at Seattle.............................1:15
Dec. 30 **Arizona** 1:15
*All times PT; Sunday night games in
Weeks 11-16 subject to change*
Stadium: Candlestick Park
(opened in 1960)
 •**Capacity:** 69,732
San Francisco, California 94124
Playing Surface: Natural Grass
Training Camp: Marie P. DeBartolo
 Sports Centre
 4949 Centennial Boulevard
 Santa Clara, CA 95054

CANDLESTICK PARK

CLUB OFFICIALS
OWNERSHIP
Co-Chairman/Owner:
 Denise DeBartolo York
Co-Chairman/Owner: John York
Chief Executive Officer: Jed York
President & Limited Partner: Gideon Yu
Limited Partner: Mark Wan
MANAGEMENT
General Manager: Trent Baalke
Chief Operating Officer: Paraag Marathe
Chief Financial Officer: Larry MacNeil
Chief Sales Officer: John Vidalin
Chief Technology Officer: Kunal Malik
Executive Vice President: Patty Inglis
Vice President of Ticketing & Suites:
 Jamie Brandt
Vice President of Corporate Sales:
 Ethan Casson
Vice President of Stadium Operations &
 Security: Jim Mercurio
Vice President of Strategic Planning:
 Josh Proctor
Vice President of Football Affairs:
 Keena Turner
Director of Legal Affairs: Hannah Gordon
Director of Player Personnel:
 Tom Gamble
Director of College Scouting: Joel Patten
Director of Public Relations: Bob Lange
Director of Corporate Communications:
 Steve Weakland
Director of Football Operations and
 Sports Medicine: Jeff Ferguson
Equipment Manager: Steve Urbaniak
Video Operations Manager: Mike Bracken
Director of Football Administration:
 Brian Hampton
Director of Broadcasting & Corporate
 Sales: Bob Sargent
Director of Marketing: Ali Towle
Director of Stadium Operations:
 Larry Minasian
Director of Engineering Operations:
 Pat Rogan
Director of Finance: Scott Sabatino
Controller: Debye Whelchel
Director of Security: Dan Cory
Senior Director, Technology:
 Dan Williams
Director of Alumni Relations:
 Guy McIntrye
Senior Manager of Ticket Office:
 Lynn Carrozzi
Senior Human Resources Manager:
 Amy Fleming
Director of Community Relations/49ers
 Foundation: Joanne Pasternack
Director of Facilities: Bill Howell

COACHING HISTORY
(503-418-13)
Records include postseason games
1950-54   Lawrence (Buck) Shaw..33-25-2
1955   Norman (Red) Strader 4-8-0
1956-58   Frankie Albert...............19-17-1
1959-1963 Howard (Red) Hickey* .27-27-1
1963-67   Jack Christiansen 26-38-3
1968-1975 Dick Nolan...................56-56-5
1976   Monte Clark.....................8-6-0
1977   Ken Meyer........................5-9-0
1978   Pete McCulley** 1-8-0
1978   Fred O'Connor 1-6-0
1979-1988 Bill Walsh 102-63-1
1989-1996 George Seifert 108-35-0
1997-2002 Steve Mariucci.............60-43-0
2003-04   Dennis Erickson 9-23-0
2005-08   Mike Nolan***..............18-37-0
2008-2010 Mike Singletary****.....19-22-0
2010   Jim Tomsula......................1-0-0
2011   Jim Harbaugh.................14-4-0
     * Resigned after three games in 1963
    ** Released after nine games in 1978
   *** Released after seven games in 2008
  **** Released after 15 games in 2010

PAID ATTENDANCE
Home 526,341   Away 487,507
Total 1,013,848
Single-game home record,
 69,732 (1/22/12)
Single-season home record,
 544,228 (1999)

2012 DRAFT CHOICES

Round	Name	Pos.	College
1	A.J. Jenkins	WR	Illinois
2	LaMichael James	RB	Oregon
4	Joe Looney	G	Wake Forest
5	Darius Fleming	LB	Notre Dame
6	Trenton Robinson	S	Michigan St.
	Jason Slowey	OL	Western Oregon
7	Cam Johnson	LB	Virginia

SAN FRANCISCO 49ERS

2011 TEAM RECORD
PRESEASON (2-2)

Date	Result	Opponent
8/12	L 3-24	at New Orleans
8/20	W 17-3	Oakland
8/27	L 7-30	Houston
9/1	W 20-17	at San Diego

REGULAR SEASON (13-3)

Date	Result	Opponent
9/11	W 33-17	Seattle
9/18	L 24-27	Dallas (OT)
9/25	W 13-8	at Cincinnati
10/2	W 24-23	at Philadelphia
10/9	W 48-3	Tampa Bay
10/16	W 25-19	at Detroit
10/30	W 20-10	Cleveland
11/6	W 19-11	at Washington
11/13	W 27-20	New York Giants
11/20	W 23-7	Arizona
11/24	L 6-16	at Baltimore
12/4	W 26-0	St. Louis
12/11	L 19-21	at Arizona
12/19	W 20-3	Pittsburgh
12/24	W 19-17	at Seattle
1/1	W 34-27	at St. Louis

POSTSEASON (1-1)

1/14	W 36-32	New Orleans
1/22	L 17-20	New York Giants (OT)

(OT) Overtime

SCORE BY PERIODS

49ers	45	125	101	109	0 —	380
Opponents	43	42	40	101	3 —	229

2011 TEAM STATISTICS

	49ers	Opp.
Total First Downs	282	267
Rushing	101	53
Passing	150	190
Penalty	31	24
3rd Down: Made/Att	65/221	76/216
3rd Down Pct.	29.4	35.2
4th Down: Made/Att	9/14	7/17
4th Down Pct.	64.3	41.2
Possession Avg.	32:02	27:58
Total Net Yards	4974	4931
Avg. Per Game	310.9	308.2
Total Plays	993	974
Avg. Per Play	5.0	5.1
Net Yards Rushing	2044	1236
Avg. Per Game	127.8	77.3
Total Rushes	498	353
Net Yards Passing	2930	3695
Avg. Per Game	183.1	230.9
Sacked/Yards Lost	44/263	42/283
Gross Yards	3193	3978
Att./Completions	451/277	579/333
Completion Pct.	61.4	57.5
Had Intercepted	5	23
Punts/Average	79/50.3	87/45.0
Net Punting Avg.	79/44.0	87/37.1
Penalties/Yards	113/1014	98/867
Fumbles/Ball Lost	14/5	31/15
Touchdowns	35	23
Rushing	14	3
Passing	18	20
Returns	3	0

2011 INDIVIDUAL STATISTICS

PASSING

PASSING	Att.	Comp.	Yds.	Pct.	TD	Int.	Tkld.	Rate
Ale. Smith	445	273	3144	61.3	17	5	44/263	90.7
Kaepernick	5	3	35	60.0	0	0	0/0	81.3
Akers	1	1	14	100.0	1	0	0/0	158.3
49ers	451	277	3193	61.4	18	5	44/263	91.4
Opponents	579	333	3978	57.5	20	23	42/283	73.6

SCORING

SCORING	TD R	TD P	TD Rt	PAT	FG	Saf	PTS
Akers	0	0	0	34/34	44/52	0	166
Gore	8	0	0	0/0	0/0	0	48
V. Davis	0	6	0	0/0	0/0	0	36
Crabtree	0	4	0	0/0	0/0	0	26
Walker	0	3	0	0/0	0/0	0	18
K. Williams	0	3	0	0/0	0/0	0	18
Dixon	2	0	0	0/0	0/0	0	12
Ginn	0	0	2	0/0	0/0	0	12
Hunter	2	0	0	0/0	0/0	0	12
Ale. Smith	2	0	0	0/0	0/0	0	12
Miller	0	1	0	0/0	0/0	0	6
Morgan	0	1	0	0/0	0/0	0	6
Rogers	0	0	1	0/0	0/0	0	6
Ald. Smith	0	0	0	0/0	0/0	1	2
49ers	14	18	3	34/34	44/52	1	380
Opponents	3	20	0	21/21	22/27	1	229

2-Pt Conversions: Crabtree

49ers 1-1, Opponents 1-2

RUSHING

RUSHING	No.	Yds	Avg	LG	TD
Gore	282	1211	4.3	55	8
Hunter	112	473	4.2	44	2
Ale. Smith	52	179	3.4	14	2
Dixon	29	87	3.0	9	2
Ginn	8	68	8.5	24	0
K. Williams	2	32	16.0	25	0
Miller	4	8	2.0	3	0
Crabtree	1	6	6.0	6	0
Walker	3	5	1.7	14	0
Kaepernick	2	-2	-1.0	-1	0
V. Davis	2	-5	-2.5	-2	0
Lee	1	-18	-18.0	-18	0
49ers	498	2044	4.1	55	14
Opponents	353	1236	3.5	34	3

RECEIVING

RECEIVING	No.	Yds	Avg	LG	TD
Crabtree	72	874	12.1	52t	4
V. Davis	67	792	11.8	44	6
K. Williams	20	241	12.1	56t	3
Ginn	19	220	11.6	26	0
Walker	19	198	10.4	29t	3
Gore	17	114	6.7	13	0
Hunter	16	195	12.2	44	0
Morgan	15	220	14.7	30t	1
Edwards	15	181	12.1	24	0
Miller	11	83	7.5	30t	1
Swain	2	15	7.5	9	0
Peelle	1	19	19.0	19	0
Sopoaga	1	18	18.0	18	0
Staley	1	17	17.0	17	0
Dixon	1	6	6.0	6	0
49ers	277	3193	11.5	56t	18
Opponents	333	3978	11.9	77	20

INTERCEPTIONS

INTERCEPTIONS	No.	Yds	Avg	LG	TD
Rogers	6	106	17.7	31t	1
Goldson	6	53	8.8	21	0
Brown	4	15	3.8	11	0
Whitner	2	48	24.0	48	0
Brock	2	18	9.0	18	0
Culliver	1	23	23.0	23	0
R. Smith	1	11	11.0	11	0
Willis	1	10	10.0	10	0
49ers	23	284	12.3	48	1
Opponents	5	51	10.2	30	0

PUNTING

PUNTING	No.	Yds.	Avg.	In 20	LG
Lee	78	3970	50.9	28	68
49ers	79	3970	50.3	28	68
Opponents	87	3911	45.0	21	77

PUNT RETURNS

PUNT RETURNS	Ret	FC	Yds	Avg	LG	TD
Ginn	38	18	466	12.3	55t	1
R. Smith	4	1	37	9.3	14	0
K. Williams	2	4	41	20.5	36	0
49ers	44	23	544	12.4	55t	1
Opponents	39	17	315	8.1	24	0

KICKOFF RETURNS

KICKOFF RETURNS	No.	Yds	Avg	LG	TD
Ginn	29	800	27.6	102t	1
Hunter	6	156	26.0	43	0
K. Williams	4	104	26.0	33	0
49ers	39	1060	27.2	102t	1
Opponents	46	1061	23.1	39	0

FIELD GOALS

FIELD GOALS	1-19	20-29	30-39	40-49	50+
Akers	2/2	16/16	13/14	6/11	7/9
49ers	2/2	16/16	13/14	6/11	7/9
Opponents	2/2	8/9	6/8	3/4	3/4

SACKS

SACKS	No.
Ald. Smith	14.0
J. Smith	7.5
Brooks	7.0
McDonald	5.5
Bowman	2.0
Grant	2.0
Haralson	2.0
Willis	2.0
49ers	42.0
Opponents	44.0

RECORD HOLDERS
INDIVIDUAL RECORDS—CAREER

Category	Name	Performance
Rushing (Yds.)	Frank Gore, 2005-2011	7,625
Passing (Yds.)	Joe Montana, 1979-1992	35,124
Passing (TDs)	Joe Montana, 1979-1992	244
Receiving (No.)	Jerry Rice, 1985-2000	1,281
Receiving (Yds.)	Jerry Rice, 1985-2000	19,247
Interceptions	Ronnie Lott, 1981-1990	51
Punting (Avg.)	Andy Lee, 2004-2011	45.7
Punt Return (Avg.)	Dana McLemore, 1982-87	10.8
Kickoff Return (Avg.)	Abe Woodson, 1958-1964	29.4
Field Goals	Ray Wersching, 1977-1987	190
Touchdowns (Tot.)	Jerry Rice, 1985-2000	187
Points	Jerry Rice, 1985-2000	1,130
*Sacks	Bryant Young, 1994-2007	89.5

INDIVIDUAL RECORDS—SINGLE SEASON

Category	Name	Performance
Rushing (Yds.)	Frank Gore, 2006	1,695
Passing (Yds.)	Jeff Garcia, 2000	4,278
Passing (TDs)	Steve Young, 1998	36
Receiving (No.)	Jerry Rice, 1995	122
Receiving (Yds.)	Jerry Rice, 1995	**1,848
Interceptions	Dave Baker, 1960	10
	Ronnie Lott, 1986	10
Punting (Avg.)	Andy Lee, 2011	50.9
Punt Return (Avg.)	Jimmy Williams, 2002	16.8
Kickoff Return (Avg.)	Joe Arenas, 1953	34.4
Field Goals	David Akers, 2011	44
Touchdowns (Tot.)	Jerry Rice, 1987	23
Points	David Akers, 2011	166
*Sacks	Fred Dean, 1983	17.5

INDIVIDUAL RECORDS—SINGLE GAME

Category	Name	Performance
Rushing (Yds.)	Frank Gore, 11-19-06	212
Passing (Yds.)	Joe Montana, 10-14-90	476
Passing (TDs)	Joe Montana, 10-14-90	6
Receiving (No.)	Terrell Owens, 12-17-00	20
Receiving (Yds.)	Jerry Rice, 12-18-95	289
Interceptions	Dave Baker, 12-4-60	**4
Field Goals	Ray Wersching, 10-16-83	6
	Jeff Wilkins, 9-29-96	6
Touchdowns (Tot.)	Jerry Rice, 10-14-90	5
Points	Jerry Rice, 10-14-90	30
*Sacks	Fred Dean, 11-13-83	6.0

*Sacks became an official statistic in 1982.
**NFL Record

2012 VETERAN ROSTER

No.	Name	Pos.	Ht.	Wt.	Birthdate	NFL Exp.	College	Hometown	How Acq.	'11 Games/ Starts
2	Akers, David	K	5-10	200	12/9/74	14	Louisville	Lexington, Ky.	FA-'11	16/0
75	Boone, Alex	T	6-8	300	5/4/87	3	Ohio State	Cleveland, Ohio	FA-'09	16/0
53	Bowman, NaVorro	LB	6-0	242	5/28/88	3	Penn State	Forestville, Md.	D3-'10	16/16
26	Brock, Tramaine	CB	5-10	197	8/20/88	3	Belhaven	Long Beach, Miss.	FA-'10	11/0
55	Brooks, Ahmad	LB	6-3	259	3/14/84	7	Virginia	Woodbridge, Va.	W(Cin)-'08	16/16
25	Brown, Tarell	CB	5-10	193	1/6/85	6	Texas	Mesquite, Texas	D5-'07	16/16
82	Byham, Nate	TE	6-4	264	6/27/88	3	Pittsburgh	Franklin, Pa.	D6b-'10	0*
28	Cartwright, Rock	RB	5-8	215	12/3/79	11	Kansas State	Conroe, Texas	FA-'12	15/0*
20	Cox, Perrish	CB	6-0	190	1/7/87	2	Oklahoma State	Waco, Texas	FA-'12	0*
15	Crabtree, Michael	WR	6-1	214	9/14/87	4	Texas Tech	Dallas, Texas	D1-'09	15/14
29	Culliver, Chris	CB	6-0	199	8/17/88	2	South Carolina	Garner, N.C.	D3-'11	16/0
76	Davis, Anthony	T	6-5	323	10/11/89	3	Rutgers	Piscataway, N.J.	D1a-'10	16/16
85	Davis, Vernon	TE	6-3	250	1/31/84	7	Maryland	Washington, D.C.	D1a-'06	16/16
24	Dixon, Anthony	RB	6-1	233	9/24/87	3	Mississippi State	Terry, Miss.	D6a-'10	16/0
96	Dobbs, Demarcus	DT	6-6	275	11/30/87	2	Georgia	Savannah, Ga.	FA-'11	12/0
19	Ginn Jr., Ted	WR	5-11	180	4/12/85	6	Ohio State	Cleveland, Ohio	T(Mia)-'10	14/3
38	Goldson, Dashon	S	6-2	200	9/18/84	6	Washington	Carson, Calif.	D4b-'07	14/14
56	Gooden, Tavares	LB	6-1	242	10/7/84	5	Miami	Ft. Lauderdale, Fla.	FA-'11	16/0
59	Goodwin, Jonathan	C	6-3	318	12/2/78	11	Michigan	Columbia, S.C.	FA-'11	16/16
21	Gore, Frank	RB	5-9	217	5/14/83	8	Miami	Coral Gables, Fla.	D3a-'05	16/15
54	Grant, Larry	LB	6-1	251	2/16/85	4	Ohio State	Santa Rosa, Calif.	FA-'11	16/3
98	Haralson, Parys	LB	6-0	255	1/24/84	7	Tennessee	Madison, Miss.	D5-'06	16/16
13	Hastings, Joe	WR	6-0	185	5/5/87	2	Washburn	Wichita, Kan.	FA-'11	1/0
41	Holcomb, Curtis	CB	5-10	190	9/3/88	2	Florida A&M	Miami, Fla.	D7c-'11	0*
32	Hunter, Kendall	RB	5-7	199	9/16/88	2	Oklahoma State	Tyler, Texas	D4-'11	16/1
77	Iupati, Mike	G	6-5	331	5/12/87	3	Idaho	Anaheim, Calif.	D1b-'10	16/16
45	Jacobs, Brandon	RB	6-4	264	7/6/82	8	Southern Illinois	Napoleonville, La.	FA-'12	14/6*
95	Jean Francois, Ricky	DT	6-3	295	11/23/86	4	Louisiana State	Miami Gardens, Fla.	D7b-'09	16/2
86	Jennings, Brian	TE/LS	6-5	242	10/14/76	13	Arizona State	Mesa, Ariz.	D7b-'00	16/0
1	Johnson, Josh	QB	6-3	205	5/15/86	4	San Diego	Oakland, Calif.	FA-'12	9/1*
43	Jones, Colin	S	6-0	208	10/27/87	2	Texas Christian	Bridgeport, Texas	D6b-'11	16/0
7	Kaepernick, Colin	QB	6-4	230	11/3/87	2	Nevada	Turlock, Calif.	D2-'11	3/0
67	Kilgore, Daniel	G	6-3	308	12/18/87	2	Appalachian State	Kingsport, Tenn.	D5-'11	1/0
4	Lee, Andy	P	6-2	180	8/11/82	9	Pittsburgh	Westminster, S.C.	D6a-'04	16/0
14	Manningham, Mario	WR	6-0	185	5/25/86	5	Michigan	Warren, Ohio	FA-'12	12/10*
91	McDonald, Ray	DT	6-3	290	9/2/84	6	Florida	Belle Glade, Fla.	D3b-'07	15/15
49	Miller, Bruce	FB	6-2	248	8/6/87	2	Central Florida	Woodstock, Ga.	D7a-'11	15/8
84	Moss, Randy	WR	6-4	210	2/13/77	14	Marshall	Rand, W. Va.	FA-'12	0*
78	Person, Mike	G	6-4	299	6/17/88	2	Montana State	Glendive, Mont.	D7b-'11	0*
64	Pontbriand, Ryan	LS	6-2	255	10/1/79	10	Rice	Houston, Texas	FA-'12	11/0*
22	Rogers, Carlos	CB	6-0	192	7/2/81	8	Auburn	Augusta, Ga.	FA-'11	16/16
99	Smith, Aldon	LB	6-4	258	9/25/89	2	Missouri	Raytown, Mo.	D1-'11	16/0
11	Smith, Alex	QB	6-4	217	5/7/84	8	Utah	La Mesa, Calif.	D1-'05	16/16
94	Smith, Justin	DT	6-4	285	9/30/79	12	Missouri	Jefferson City, Mo.	UFA-'08	16/16
90	Sopoaga, Isaac	DT	6-2	330	9/4/81	9	Hawaii	Pago Pago, American Samoa	D4a-'04	15/15
27	Spillman, C.J.	S	6-0	199	5/6/86	4	Marshall	Louisville, Ky.	W(SD)-'10	16/0
74	Staley, Joe	T	6-5	315	8/30/84	6	Central Michigan	Rockford, Mich.	D1b-'07	16/16
18	Swain, Brett	WR	6-0	200	6/21/85	4	San Diego State	Asheville, N.C.	FA-'11	5/1
3	Tolzien, Scott	QB	6-3	208	9/4/87	2	Wisconsin	Rolling Meadows, Ill.	W(SD)-'11	0*
92	Tukuafu, Will	DT	6-4	293	1/3/84	2	Oregon	Salt Lake City, Utah	FA-'10	4/0
46	Walker, Delanie	TE	6-0	242	8/12/84	7	Central Missouri	Pomona, Calif.	D6a-'06	15/7
31	Whitner, Donte	S	5-10	208	7/24/85	7	Ohio State	Cleveland, Ohio	FA-'11	15/15
93	Williams, Ian	NT	6-1	305	8/31/89	2	Notre Dame	Altamonte Springs, Fla.	FA-'11	1/0
10	Williams, Kyle	WR	5-10	186	7/19/88	3	Arizona State	Scottsdale, Ariz.	D6c-'10	13/1
52	Willis, Patrick	LB	6-1	240	1/25/85	6	Mississippi	Bruceton, Tenn.	D1a-'07	13/13

* Byham missed '11 season because of injury; Cartwright played 15 games with Oakland in '11; Cox last active with Denver in '10; Holcomb missed '11 season because of injury; Jacobs played 14 games with New York Giants; Johnson played 9 games with Tampa Bay; Manningham played 12 games with New York Giants; Matthews spent 10 games on San Francisco practice squad; Moss last active with Tennessee in '10; Person inactive for all 16 games; Pontbriand played 11 games with Cleveland; Tolzien inactive third quarterback for all 16 games.

Players lost through free agency (6): LB Blake Costanzo (Chi; 16 games), WR Joshua Morgan (Wash; 5), G Chilo Rachal (Chi; 16), S Reggie Smith (Car; 16), G Adam Snyder (Ariz; 16), S Madieu Williams (Wash; 15).

Also played with 49ers in '11—WR Braylon Edwards (10 games), FB Moran Norris (5), TE Justin Peelle (14), CB Shawntae Spencer (9).

FIRST-YEAR ROSTER

Name	Pos.	Ht.	Wt.	Birthdate	College	Hometown	How Acq.
Bakhtiari, Eric (1)	LB	6-3	250	12/2/84	San Diego	Burlingame, Calif.	FA
Beeler, Chase (1)	C	6-3	285	12/28/87	Stanford	Jenks, Okla.	FA-'11
Bell, Cameron	FB	6-2	252	9/8/88	Northern Illinois	Columbia, S.C.	FA
Brown, Kourtnei	LB	6-6	255	4/17/88	Clemson	Charlotte, N.C.	FA
Butrym, Patrick	DT	6-4	285	6/13/88	Wisconsin	New Berlin, Wisc.	FA
Celek, Garrett	TE	6-5	252	5/29/88	Michigan State	Cincinnati, Ohio	FA
Chisolm, Garrett (1)	G	6-6	299	4/2/88	South Carolina	Charleston, S.C.	FA
Fleming, Darius	LB	6-2	255	7/19/89	Notre Dame	Chicago, Ill.	D5
Gonzales, David	OL	6-6	286	10/20/90	Washington State	Fresno, Calif.	FA
Hall, Derek (1)	T	6-5	307	11/23/87	Stanford	Overland Park, Kan.	FA-'11
Hampton, Jewel	RB	5-9	210	12/23/89	Southern Illinois	Indianapolis, Ind.	FA
Hannula, Ben (1)	DB	6-2	206	10/13/85	San Diego	Tacoma, Wash.	FA
Holland, Joe	LB	6-1	229	8/20/88	Purdue	Indianapolis, Ind.	FA
James, LaMichael	RB	5-9	195	10/22/89	Oregon	Texarkana, Texas	D2
Jenkins, A.J.	WR	6-0	192	9/30/89	Illinois	Jacksonville, Fla.	D1
Jerod-Eddie, Tony	DT	6-5	301	3/29/90	Texas A&M	DeSoto, Texas	FA
Johnson, Cam	LB	6-3	268	5/24/90	Virginia	Greenbelt, Md.	D7
LeGree, Mark (1)	S	6-0	210	7/8/89	Appalachian State	Columbus, Ga.	FA
Looney, Joe	G	6-3	309	8/31/90	Wake Forest	Lake Worth, Fla.	D4
Masifilo, Matt	DT	6-3	280	10/1/89	Stanford	Ewa Beach, Hawaii	FA
Mosley, Anthony	CB	6-0	178	8/31/89	Kentucky	Cleveland, Ohio	FA
Murphy, Kevin	T	6-7	295	2/16/90	Harvard	San Clemente, Calif.	FA
Nelms, Cory (1)	CB	6-0	195	2/27/87	Miami	Neptune, N.J.	FA-'11
Nelson, Kyle (1)	WR	6-3	240	10/3/86	New Mexico State	Waco, Texas	FA
Netter, Al	G	6-6	310	7/21/89	Northwestern	Rohnert Park, Calif.	FA
Owusu, Chris	WR	6-2	200	1/6/90	Stanford	Westlake Village, Calif.	FA
Palmer, Nathan	WR	5-11	195	4/14/89	Northern Illinois	Elkhart, Ind.	FA
Purvis, Deante	CB	5-11	195	11/4/89	Nevada-Las Vegas	Richmond, Calif.	FA
Reuland, Konrad (1)	TE	6-4	260	4/4/87	Stanford	Mission Viejo, Calif.	FA-'11
Robinson, Trenton	S	5-9	193	2/16/90	Michigan State	Bay City, Mich.	D6a
Slowey, Jason	OL	6-4	305	1/27/89	Western Oregon	Medford, Ore.	D6b
Tavecchio, Giorgio	K	5-10	178	7/16/90	California	Milan, Italy	FA
Thomas, Michael	S	5-11	182	3/17/89	Stanford	Houston, Texas	FA
Tyms, Brian	WR	6-3	210	2/21/89	Florida A&M	Fort Lauderdale, Fla.	FA
Wiggins, Kenny (1)	T	6-6	314	8/8/88	Fresno State	Elk Grove, Calif.	FA
Wilhoite, Michael (1)	LB	6-0	240	12/7/86	Washburn	Topeka, Kan.	FA-'11

The term NFL Rookie is defined as a player who is in his first season of professional football and has not been on the roster of another professional football team for any regular-season or postseason games. A Rookie is designated by an "R" on NFL rosters. Players who have been active in another professional football league or players who have NFL experience, including either preseason training camp or being on an Active List or Inactive List, or on Reserve/Injured or Reserve/Physically Unable to Perform for fewer than six regular-season games, are termed NFL First-Year Players. An NFL First-Year Player is designated by a "1" on NFL rosters. Thereafter, a player is credited with an additional year of experience for each season in which he accumulates six games on the Active List or Inactive List, or on Reserve/Injured or Reserve/Physically Unable to Perform.

Log on to www.sf49ers.com for an up-to-date roster.

COACHING STAFF
Head Coach,
Jim Harbaugh

Pro Career: Named the seventeenth head coach in 49ers history on Jan. 7, 2011. In 2011, Harbaugh led the 49ers to a 13-3 regular season record, its best since 1997, and a NFC West title, its first since 2002. The consensus NFL Coach of the Year also led his squad to its first appearance in the NFC Championship Game since 1998. Harbaugh's 13-3 record made him just the 4th rookie head coach in NFL history to take a team with a losing record the previous year, to 13 wins. Harbaugh was previously the head coach at Stanford (2007-2010), where he led the Cardinal to its first BCS game appearance and victory in the Orange Bowl, in 2010. He was head coach at the University of San Diego (2004-06). Harbaugh started in the NFL as an offensive assistant with the Oakland Raiders (2002-03). His first coaching job came from his father, Jack Harbaugh, at Western Kentucky as a volunteer assistant coach. Played 15 years with the Bears (1987 first-round pick), Colts, Ravens, Chargers and Panthers. He appeared in one Pro Bowl and was placed in the Colts' Ring of Honor in 2005. Career record: 14-14.

Background: Harbaugh earned first team All-America and Big Ten Player of the Year honors as a senior at Michigan, finishing third in the Heisman Trophy balloting.

Personal: Born December 23, 1963, Toledo, Ohio. He and his wife, Sarah, have two daughters, Addison and Katherine. He also has three children, Jay, James Jr. and Grace.

ASSISTANT COACHES

Michael Christianson, offensive assistant & coordinator of football technology; born April 7, 1965, Boise, Idaho. Western Oregon. No pro playing experience. College coach: Western Oregon 1992-94, Lewis & Clark College 1995, Portland State 1995-99, Montana State 2000-01, Nebraska 2004-05, San Diego 2006. Pro coach: Tampa Bay Buccaneers 2002, joined 49ers in 2011.

Geep Chryst, quarterbacks; born June 25, 1962, Madison, Wisc. Linebacker Princeton 1981-84. Pro linebacker Orlando Thunder (World League) 1992. College coach: Wisconsin-Platteville 1987, Wisconsin 1988, Wyoming 1989-1990. Pro coach: Orlando Thunder (World League) 1991, Chicago Bears 1991-95, Arizona Cardinals 1996-98, San Diego Chargers 1999-2000, Arizona Cardinals 2001-03, Carolina Panthers 2006-2010, joined 49ers in 2011.

Reggie Davis, tight ends; born September 3, 1976, Long Beach, Calif. Linebacker/tight end Washington 1994-98. Pro tight end San Diego Chargers 1999-2000. College coach: San Diego State 2004, UNLV 2005-07, Oregon State 2008-2010. Pro coach: Joined 49ers in 2011.

Ed Donatell, secondary; born February 4, 1957, Akron, Ohio. Defensive back Glenville (W. Va.) State 1975-78. No pro playing experience. College coach: Kent State 1979-1980, Washington 1981-82, 2008, Pacific 1983-85, Idaho 1986-88, Cal State Fullerton 1989. Pro coach: New York Jets 1990-94, Denver Broncos 1995-99, Green Bay Packers 2000-03, Atlanta Falcons 2004-06, New York Jets 2007, Denver Broncos 2009-2010, joined 49ers in 2011.

Tim Drevno, offensive line; born April 20, 1969, Torrance, Calif. Offensive lineman El Camino (Calif.) J.C. 1987-88, Cal State Fullerton 1989-1991. No pro playing experience. College coach: Cal State Fullerton 1991-92, Montana State 1993-97, UNLV 1998, San Jose State 1999, Idaho 2000-02, San Diego 2003-06, Stanford 2007-2010. Pro coach: Joined 49ers in 2011.

Ejiro Evero, offensive assistant; born January 6, 1981, Colchester, England. Safety California-Davis 2000-03. No pro playing experience. College coach: California-Davis 2005-06, Redlands 2010. Pro coach: Tampa Bay Buccaneers 2007-09, joined 49ers in 2011.

Vic Fangio, defensive coordinator; born August 22, 1958, Dunmore, Pa. Attended East Stroudsburg State. No pro playing experience. College coach: North Carolina 1983, Stanford 2010. Pro coach: Philadelphia/Baltimore Stars (USFL) 1984-85, New Orleans Saints 1986-1994, Carolina Panthers 1995-98, Indianapolis Colts 1999-2001, Houston Texans 2002-05, Baltimore Ravens 2006-09, joined 49ers in 2011.

Peter Hansen, defensive assistant/quality control; born May 30, 1979, Palo Alto, Calif. Tight end/quarterback Arizona 1997-2001. Pro player Cannes Iron Mask (France) 2003. College coach: Stanford 2008-2010. Pro coach: Joined 49ers in 2011.

Greg Jackson, asst. secondary; born August 20, 1966, Hialeah, Fla. College safety Louisiana State 1985-88. Pro safety New York Giants 1989-1993, Philadelphia Eagles 1994-95, New Orleans Saints 1996, San Diego Chargers 1997-2000. College coach: Idaho 2003, Louisiana-Monroe 2004-2006, Tulane 2007-09, Wisconsin 2010. Pro coach: Joined 49ers in 2011.

Jim Leavitt, linebackers; born December 5, 1956, Harlingen, Texas. No college or pro playing experience. College coach: Missouri 1978-79, Dubuque 1980-81, Morning Side 1983-87, Iowa 1988-89, Kansas State 1990-95, South Florida 1995-2009. Pro Coach: Joined 49ers in 2011.

John Morton, wide receivers; born Sept. 24, 1969, Rochester Hills, Mich. Wide receiver Western Michigan 1991-92. Pro wide receiver Toronto Argonauts (CFL) 1995-96, Frankfurt Galaxy (World League) 1997. College coach: San Diego 2005, Southern California 2007-2010. Pro coach: Oakland Raiders 2002-04, New Orleans Saints 2006, joined 49ers in 2011.

Tom Rathman, running backs; born October 7, 1962, Grand Island, Neb. Running back Nebraska 1983-85. Pro running back San Francisco 49ers 1986-1993, Los Angeles Raiders 1994. College coach: Menlo College 1996. Pro coach: San Francisco 1997-2002, Detroit Lions 2003-05, Oakland Raiders 2007-08, re-joined 49ers in 2009.

Greg Roman, offensive coordinator; born August 19, 1972, Atlantic City, N.J. Defensive line/linebacker John Carroll 1990-94. No pro playing experience. College coach: Stanford 2009-2010. Pro coach: Carolina Panthers 1995-2001, Houston Texans 2002-05, Baltimore Ravens 2006-07, joined 49ers in 2011.

Brad Seely, special teams coordinator/asst. head coach; born September 6, 1956, Vinton, Iowa. Offensive lineman South Dakota State 1974-77. No pro playing experience. College coach: South Dakota State 1978, Colorado State 1980, Southern Methodist 1981, North Carolina State 1982, Pacific 1983, Oklahoma State 1984-88. Pro coach: Indianapolis Colts 1989-1993, New York Jets 1994, Carolina Panthers 1995-98, New England Patriots 1999-2008, Cleveland Browns 2009-2010, joined 49ers in 2011.

Tracy Smith, special teams assistant; born February 23, 1982, Beaumont, Texas. No college or pro playing experience. College coach: Utah State 2006-08. Pro coach: Cleveland Browns 2009-10, Seattle Seahawks 2011, joined 49ers in 2012.

Mike Solari, offensive line, born January 16, 1955, Daly City, Calif. Offensive lineman San Diego State 1972-75. No pro playing experience. College coach: Mira Costa (Calif.) J.C. 1978, U.S. International 1979, Boise State 1980, Cincinnati 1981-82, Kansas 1983-85, Pittsburgh 1986, Alabama 1990-91. Pro coach: Dallas Cowboys 1987-88, Phoenix Cardinals 1989, San Francisco 49ers 1992-1996, Kansas City Chiefs 1997-2007, Seattle Seahawks 2008-09, rejoined 49ers in 2010.

Kevin Tolbert, asst. strength and conditioning; born September 11, 1958, St. Albans, N.Y. Fullback Naval Academy 1978-1980. No pro playing experience. College coach: Miami 1998-2000, Michigan 2001-07, Stanford 2009-2010. Pro coach: Philadelphia Eagles 1996-97, Detroit Lions 2008, joined 49ers in 2011.

Jim Tomsula, defensive line; born April 14, 1967, Homestead, Pa. Middle Tennessee State 1985-86, Catawba College 1987-1990. No pro playing experience. College coach: Charleston Southern 1997. Pro coach: London Monarchs (NFLE) 1998, Scottish Claymores (NFLE) 1999-2003, Berlin Thunder (NFLE) 2004-05, Rhein Fire (NFLE) 2006 (head coach), joined 49ers in 2007 (interim head coach, one game, 2010).

Mark Uyeyama, head strength and conditioning; born December 2, 1975, Vancouver, B.C. Nose Guard Butte (Mont.) C.C. 1994-95, Northern State 1996-97. No pro playing experience. College coach: Arizona State 2001-03, Utah State 2004-07. Pro coach: Joined 49ers in 2008.

National Football Conference
West Division
Team Colors: Action Green, College Navy, Wolf Grey
Virginia Mason Athletic Center
12 Seahawks Way
Renton, Washington 98056
Telephone: (425) 203-8000

2012 SCHEDULE
PRESEASON
Aug. 11 **Tennessee** 7:00
Aug. 18 at Denver.............................6:00
Aug. 24 at Kansas City 5:00
Aug. 30 **Oakland** 7:00

REGULAR SEASON
Sep. 9   at Arizona..........................1:15
Sep. 16 **Dallas** 1:05
Sep. 24 **Green Bay** (Mon) 5:30
Sep. 30 at St. Louis....................10:00a
Oct. 7   at Carolina.........................1:05
Oct. 14 **New England** 1:05
Oct. 18 at San Francisco (Thurs) 5:20
Oct. 28 at Detroit 10:00a
Nov. 4   **Minnesota** 1:05
Nov. 11 **New York Jets** 1:05
Nov. 18 BYE
Nov. 25 at Miami 10:00a
Dec. 2   at Chicago 10:00a
Dec. 9   **Arizona** 1:15
Dec. 16 at Buffalo (Toronto) 1:05
Dec. 23 **San Francisco** 1:15
Dec. 30 **St. Louis** 1:15
All times PT
Stadium: CenturyLink Field
(opened in 2002)
• **Capacity:** 67,000
Playing Surface: FieldTurf
Training Camp: VMAC
Renton, WA 98056

CENTURYLINK FIELD

CLUB OFFICIALS
Chairman: Paul Allen
President: Peter McLoughlin
Executive Vice President of Football
Operations & Head Coach: Pete Carroll
General Manager: John Schneider
CFO & VP/Finance: Karen Beckman
VP/Ticket and Retail Sales & Service:
Chuck Arnold
VP/Community Outreach: Mike Flood
VP/Football Administration: John Idzik
VP/Corporate Partnerships: Ron Jenkins
VP/General Counsel: Lance Lopes
VP/Communications & Broadcasting:
Dave Pearson
Sr. Personnel Executive:
Scot McCloughan
Director of Corp. Hospitality, Suite Sales
& Service: Amy Sprangers
Director of Pro Personnel: Tag Ribary
Director of Communications:
Lane Gammel
Director of Community Outreach:
Sandy Gregory
Gameday Presentation: Rick Crawford
Video Director Football: Brad Campbell
Head Athletic Trainer: Sam Ramsden
Equipment Manager: Erik Kennedy
Team Travel: Jeremy Young

COACHING HISTORY
(277-306-0)
Records include postseason games
1976-1982 Jack Patera* 35-59-0
1982 Mike McCormack 4-3-0
1983-1991 Chuck Knox 83-67-0
1992-94 Tom Flores...................14-34-0
1995-98 Dennis Erickson...........31-33-0
1999-2008 Mike Holmgren 90-80-0
2009 Jim Mora......................5-11-0
2010-11 Pete Carroll.................15-19-0
*Released after two games in 1982

PAID ATTENDANCE
Home 515,559   Away 510,547
Total 1,026,106
Single-game home record,
68,681 (12/16/00)
Single-season home record,
533,657 (2007)

2012 DRAFT CHOICES
Round	Name	Pos.	College
1	Bruce Irvin	DE	West Virginia
2	Bobby Wagner	LB	Utah St.
3	Russell Wilson	QB	Wisconsin
4	Robert Turbin	RB	Utah St.
	Jaye Howard	DT	Florida
5	Korey Toomer	LB	Idaho
6	Jeremy Lane	DB	Northwestern St. (LA)
	Winston Guy	DB	Kentucky
7	J.R. Sweezy	G	North Carolina St.
	Greg Scruggs	DE	Louisville

SEATTLE SEAHAWKS

2011 TEAM RECORD
PRESEASON (2-2)
Date	Result	Opponent
8/11	W 24-17	at San Diego
8/20	L 7-20	Minnesota
8/27	L 20-23	at Denver
9/2	W 20-3	Oakland

REGULAR SEASON (7-9)
Date	Result	Opponent
9/11	L 17-33	at San Francisco
9/18	L 0-24	at Pittsburgh
9/25	W 13-10	Arizona
10/2	L 28-30	Atlanta
10/9	W 36-25	at New York Giants
10/23	L 3-6	at Cleveland
10/30	L 12-34	Cincinnati
11/6	L 13-23	at Dallas
11/13	W 22-17	Baltimore
11/20	W 24-7	at St. Louis
11/27	L 17-23	Washington
12/1	W 31-14	Philadelphia
12/12	W 30-13	St. Louis
12/18	W 38-14	at Chicago
12/24	L 17-19	San Francisco
1/1	L 20-23	at Arizona (OT)

(OT) Overtime

SCORE BY PERIODS
Seahawks	61	58	90	112	0	—	321
Opponents	62	103	40	107	3	—	315

2011 TEAM STATISTICS
	Seahawks	Opp.
Total First Downs	265	310
Rushing	89	96
Passing	153	174
Penalty	23	40
3rd Down: Made/Att	77/228	77/221
3rd Down Pct.	33.8	34.8
4th Down: Made/Att	7/15	7/11
4th Down Pct.	46.7	63.6
Possession Avg.	28:07	31:53
Total Net Yards	4861	5315
Avg. Per Game	303.8	332.2
Total Plays	1003	1049
Avg. Per Play	4.8	5.1
Net Yards Rushing	1756	1797
Avg. Per Game	109.8	112.3
Total Rushes	444	473
Net Yards Passing	3105	3518
Avg. Per Game	194.1	219.9
Sacked/Yards Lost	50/339	33/232
Gross Yards	3444	3750
Att./Completions	509/299	543/324
Completion Pct.	58.7	59.7
Had Intercepted	14	22
Punts/Average	95/46.6	81/44.6
Net Punting Avg.	95/39.3	81/37.7
Penalties/Yards	138/1047	96/907
Fumbles/Ball Lost	22/9	18/9
Touchdowns	35	33
Rushing	15	10
Passing	15	18
Returns	5	5

2011 INDIVIDUAL STATISTICS
PASSING
	Att.	Comp.	Yds.	Pct.	TD	Int.	Tkld.	Rate
Jackson	450	271	3091	60.2	14	13	42/293	79.2
Whitehurst	56	27	298	48.2	1	1	8/46	62.9
Lynch	2	0	0	0.0	0	0	0/0	39.6
Rice	1	1	55	100.0	0	0	0/0	118.8
Seahawks	509	299	3444	58.7	15	14	50/339	77.6
Opponents	543	324	3750	59.7	18	22	33/232	74.8

SCORING
	TD R	TD P	TD Rt	PAT	FG	Saf	PTS
Hauschka	0	0	0	34/34	25/30	0	109
Lynch	12	1	0	0/0	0/0	0	78
Baldwin	0	4	0	0/0	0/0	0	24
Tate	0	3	0	0/0	0/0	0	18
Browner	0	0	2	0/0	0/0	0	12
Obomanu	0	2	0	0/0	0/0	0	12
Rice	0	2	0	0/0	0/0	0	12
Robinson	0	1	1	0/0	0/0	0	12
Bryant	0	0	1	0/0	0/0	0	6
Forsett	1	0	0	0/0	0/0	0	6
Hawthorne	0	0	1	0/0	0/0	0	6
Jackson	1	0	0	0/0	0/0	0	6
Lockette	0	1	0	0/0	0/0	0	6
Washington	1	0	0	0/0	0/0	0	6
M. Williams	0	1	0	0/0	0/0	0	6
Hargrove	0	0	0	0/0	0/0	1	2
Seahawks	15	15	5	34/34	25/30	1	321
Opponents	10	18	5	31/32	28/37	0	315

2-Pt Conversions:
Seahawks 0-1, Opponents 1-1

RUSHING
	No.	Yds	Avg	LG	TD
Lynch	285	1204	4.2	47	12
Washington	53	248	4.7	48t	1
Forsett	46	145	3.2	22t	1
Jackson	40	108	2.7	13	1
Tate	5	14	2.8	14	0
Obomanu	1	13	13.0	13	0
Whitehurst	4	13	3.3	7	0
Robinson	4	7	1.8	3	0
Rice	2	3	1.5	3	0
E. Williams	2	2	1.0	1	0
Morrah	1	1	1.0	1	0
Baldwin	1	-2	-2.0	-2	0
Seahawks	444	1756	4.0	48t	15
Opponents	473	1797	3.8	39	10

RECEIVING
	No.	Yds	Avg	LG	TD
Baldwin	51	788	15.5	55t	4
Obomanu	37	436	11.8	55	2
Tate	35	382	10.9	33	3
Rice	32	484	15.1	52t	2
Lynch	28	212	7.6	26	1
Miller	25	233	9.3	28	0
Forsett	23	128	5.6	18	0
M. Williams	18	236	13.1	55	1
A. McCoy	13	146	11.2	31	0
Washington	10	48	4.8	9	0
Robinson	9	74	8.2	19	1
Morrah	6	74	12.3	21	0
Butler	6	51	8.5	15	0
Durham	3	30	10.0	12	0
Lockette	2	105	52.5	61t	1
E. Williams	1	17	17.0	17	0
Seahawks	299	3444	11.5	61t	15
Opponents	324	3750	11.6	68t	18

INTERCEPTIONS
	No.	Yds	Avg	LG	TD
Browner	6	220	36.7	94t	2
Sherman	4	45	11.3	33	0
Chancellor	4	27	6.8	9	0
Hawthorne	3	111	37.0	77t	1
Bryant	2	25	12.5	20t	1
Thomas	2	19	9.5	11	0
Trufant	1	15	15.0	15	0
Seahawks	22	462	21.0	94t	4
Opponents	14	187	13.4	75t	1

PUNTING
	No.	Yds.	Avg.	In 20	LG
Ryan	95	4431	46.6	34	77
Seahawks	95	4431	46.6	34	77
Opponents	81	3616	44.6	18	66

PUNT RETURNS
	Ret	FC	Yds	Avg	LG	TD
Washington	41	16	464	11.3	37	0
Tate	1	0	0	0.0	0	0
Seahawks	42	16	464	11.0	37	0
Opponents	47	20	541	11.5	63	2

KICKOFF RETURNS
	No.	Yds	Avg	LG	TD
Washington	43	1084	25.2	54	0
Baldwin	1	37	37.0	37	0
Byrd	1	10	10.0	10	0
Forsett	1	11	11.0	11	0
Seahawks	46	1142	24.8	54	0
Opponents	48	1249	26.0	102t	1

FIELD GOALS
	1-19	20-29	30-39	40-49	50+
Hauschka	2/2	5/6	9/10	7/8	2/4
Seahawks	2/2	5/6	9/10	7/8	2/4
Opponents	1/1	10/12	4/4	9/12	4/8

SACKS
	No.
Clemons	11.0
Hill	4.0
Branch	3.0
Brock	3.0
Hargrove	3.0
Hawthorne	2.0
Wright	2.0
Bigby	1.0
Bryant	1.0
Chancellor	1.0
Smith	1.0
Cox	0.5
Lewis	0.5
Seahawks	33.0
Opponents	50.0

RECORD HOLDERS
INDIVIDUAL RECORDS—CAREER

Category	Name	Performance
Rushing (Yds.)	Shaun Alexander, 2000-07	9,429
Passing (Yds.)	Matt Hasselbeck, 2001-2010	29,434
Passing (TDs)	Dave Krieg, 1980-1991	195
Receiving (No.)	Steve Largent, 1976-1989	819
Receiving (Yds.)	Steve Largent, 1976-1989	13,089
Interceptions	Dave Brown, 1976-1986	50
Punting (Avg.)	Jon Ryan, 2008-2011	45.0
Punt Return (Avg.)	Charlie Rogers, 1999-2001	12.7
Kickoff Return (Avg.)	Josh Wilson, 2007-09	25.8
Field Goals	Norm Johnson, 1982-1990	159
Touchdowns (Tot.)	Shaun Alexander, 2000-07	112
Points	Norm Johnson, 1982-1990	810
*Sacks	Jacob Green, 1980-1991	97.5

INDIVIDUAL RECORDS—SINGLE SEASON

Category	Name	Performance
Rushing (Yds.)	Shaun Alexander, 2005	1,880
Passing (Yds.)	Matt Hasselbeck, 2007	3,966
Passing (TDs)	Dave Krieg, 1984	32
Receiving (No.)	Bobby Engram, 2007	94
Receiving (Yds.)	Steve Largent, 1985	1,287
Interceptions	John Harris, 1981	10
	Kenny Easley, 1984	10
Punting (Avg.)	Jon Ryan, 2011	46.6
Punt Return (Avg.)	Charlie Rogers, 1999	14.5
Kickoff Return (Avg.)	Steve Broussard, 1998	26.9
Field Goals	Todd Peterson, 1999	34
Touchdowns (Tot.)	Shaun Alexander, 2005	28
Points	Shaun Alexander, 2005	168
*Sacks	Michael Sinclair, 1998	16.5

INDIVIDUAL RECORDS—SINGLE GAME

Category	Name	Performance
Rushing (Yds.)	Shaun Alexander, 11-11-01	266
Passing (Yds.)	Matt Hasselbeck, 12-29-02	449
Passing (TDs)	Dave Krieg, 12-2-84, 9-15-85, 11-28-88	5
	Warren Moon, 10-26-97	5
	Matt Hasselbeck, 11-23-03, 9-24-06	5
Receiving (No.)	Steve Largent, 10-18-87	15
Receiving (Yds.)	Steve Largent, 10-18-87	261
Interceptions	Kenny Easley, 9-3-84	3
	Eugene Robinson, 12-6-92	3
	Darryl Williams, 9-21-97	3
	Lofa Tatupu, 12-2-07	3
	Marcus Trufant, 12-9-07	3
Field Goals	Norm Johnson, 9-20-87, 12-18-88	5
	Olindo Mare, 10-24-10, 11-14-10	5
	Todd Peterson, 9-26-99	5
	Steven Hauschka, 11-13-11	5
Touchdowns (Tot.)	Shaun Alexander, 9-29-02	5
Points	Shaun Alexander, 9-29-02	30
*Sacks	Many times	4.0
	Last time by Darryl Tapp, 10-21-07	

Sacks became an official statistic in 1982.

2012 VETERAN ROSTER

No.	Name	Pos.	Ht.	Wt.	Birthdate	NFL Exp.	College	Hometown	How Acq.	'11 Games/ Starts
35	Adams, Phillip	CB	5-11	192	7/20/88	3	South Carolina State	Rock Hill, S.C.	FA-'11	7/0*
89	Baldwin, Doug	WR	5-10	189	9/21/88	2	Stanford	Gulf Breeze, Fla.	FA-'11	16/1
78	Barbre, Allen	T	6-4	305	6/22/84	6	Missouri Southern	Neosho, Mo.	FA-'10	4/0
44	Bradford, Allen	LB	5-11	235	8/31/88	2	Southern California	San Bernardino, Calif.	W(TB)-'11	1/0*
99	Branch, Alan	DT	6-6	325	12/29/84	6	Michigan	Rio Rancho, N.M.	UFA(Ariz)-'11	15/15
39	Browner, Brandon	CB	6-4	221	8/2/84	2	Oregon State	Sylmar, Calif.	FA-'11	16/16
79	Bryant, Red	DE	6-4	323	4/18/84	5	Texas A&M	Jasper, Texas	D4-'08	16/16
11	Butler, Deon	WR	5-10	182	1/4/86	4	Penn State	Woodbridge, Va.	D3-'09	5/0
75	Carpenter, James	T	6-5	321	3/22/89	2	Alabama	Augusta, Ga.	D1-'11	9/9
31	Chancellor, Kam	SS	6-3	232	4/3/88	3	Virginia Tech	Norfolk, Va.	D5-'10	15/15
91	Clemons, Chris	DE	6-3	254	10/30/81	9	Georgia	Griffin, Ga.	T(Phil)-'10	16/16
58	Davis, Dexter	DE	6-1	244	11/10/86	3	Arizona State	Phoenix, Ariz.	D7a-'10	1/0
16	Durham, Kris	WR	6-6	216	3/17/88	2	Georgia	Calhoun, Ga.	D4b-'11	3/0
66	Fanaika, Paul	G	6-5	327	4/9/86	4	Arizona State	San Mateo, Calif.	PS(Cle)-'10	3/0
55	Farwell, Heath	LB	6-0	235	12/31/81	8	San Diego State	Fontana, Calif.	FA-'11	11/0
15	Flynn, Matt	QB	6-2	225	6/20/85	5	Louisiana State	Tyler, Texas	UFA(GB)-'12	5/1*
37	Francies, Coye	CB	6-0	185	11/15/86	4	San Jose State	Bakersfield, Calif.	FA-'11	0*
68	Giacomini, Breno	T	6-7	318	9/27/85	5	Louisville	Cambridge, Mass.	PS(GB)-'10	15/8
49	Gresham, Clint	LS	6-3	240	8/24/86	3	Texas Christian	Corpus Christi, Texas	FA-'10	16/0
4	Hauschka, Steven	K	6-4	210	6/29/85	5	North Carolina State	Needham, Mass.	W(Den)-'11	16/0
56	Hill, Leroy	LB	6-1	238	9/14/82	8	Clemson	Haddock, Ga.	D3(b)-'05	16/16
7	Jackson, Tarvaris	QB	6-2	225	4/21/83	7	Alabama State	Montgomery, Ala.	UFA(Minn)-'11	15/14
61	Jeanpierre, Lemuel	G/C	6-3	301	5/19/87	3	South Carolina	Orlando, Fla.	FA-'11	16/5
32	Johnson, Jeron	SS	5-10	212	6/12/88	2	Boise State	Compton, Calif.	FA-'11	7/0
90	Jones, Jason	DE	6-5	276	5/23/86	5	Eastern Michigan	Detroit, Mich.	UFA(Tenn)-'12	14/13*
46	Konz, Jameson	LB	6-3	234	7/2/86	3	Kent State	Uniontown, Ohio	D7-'10	1/0
93	Levingston, Pep	DT	6-4	292	11/16/87	2	Louisiana State	Ruston, La.	D7-'11	4/0
34	Lewis, Roy	CB	5-10	190	5/19/85	5	Washington	Los Angeles, Calif.	FA-'09	10/1
83	Lockette, Ricardo	WR	6-2	211	5/21/86	2	Fort Valley State	Albany, Ga.	FA-'11	2/0
20	Lumpkin, Kregg	RB	5-11	228	5/15/84	4	Georgia	Albany, Ga.	FA-'12	16/0*
72	Lutui, Deuce	G	6-4	338	5/5/83	7	Southern California	Mesa, Ariz.	UFA(Ariz)-'12	15/0*
24	Lynch, Marshawn	RB	5-11	215	4/22/86	6	California	Oakland, Calif.	T(Buff)-'10	15/15
42	Maragos, Chris	CB	5-10	200	1/6/87	3	Wisconsin	Racine, Wis.	FA-'11	11/0
14	Martin, Charly	WR	6-1	212	3/20/84	3	West Texas A&M	Walla Walla, Wash.	FA-'12	0*
41	Maxwell, Byron	CB	6-1	207	2/23/88	2	Clemson	Charleston, S.C.	D6-'11	9/0
85	McCoy, Anthony	TE	6-5	259	12/28/87	3	Southern California	Fresno, Calif.	D6-'10	16/9
52	McCoy, Matt	LB	6-0	232	10/14/82	8	San Diego State	Tustin, Calif.	UFA(TB)-'10	4/1
69	McDonald, Clinton	DT	6-2	297	1/6/87	4	Memphis	Jacksonville, Ark.	T(Cin)-'11	15/1
67	McQuistan, Paul	T	6-6	315	4/30/83	7	Weber State	San Diego, Calif.	FA-'11	16/10
92	Mebane, Brandon	DT	6-1	311	1/15/85	6	California	Los Angeles, Calif.	D3-'07	16/16
86	Miller, Zach	TE	6-5	255	12/11/85	6	Arizona State	Phoenix, Ariz.	UFA(Oak)-'11	15/15
74	Moffitt, John	G	6-4	319	10/28/86	2	Wisconsin	Guilford, Conn.	D3-'11	9/9
48	Morgan, Mike	LB	6-3	226	1/16/88	2	Southern California	Dallas, Texas	FA-'11	5/0
88	Morrah, Cameron	TE	6-3	251	3/18/87	4	California	Claremont, Calif.	D7c-'09	9/3
59	Moten, Adrian	LB	6-2	230	4/22/88	2	Maryland	Brandywine, Md.	W(Ind)-'11	12/0
82	Nalbone, John	TE	6-4	255	5/14/86	4	Monmouth	Trenton, N.J.	FA-'11	0*
87	Obomanu, Ben	WR	6-1	204	10/30/83	7	Auburn	Selma, Ala.	D7b-'06	16/7
76	Okung, Russell	T	6-5	310	10/7/87	3	Oklahoma State	Houston, Texas	D1a-'10	12/12
65	Omiyale, Frank	T/G	6-4	315	1/23/82	8	Tennessee Tech	Nashville, Tenn.	FA-'12	16/3*
36	Parker, Ron	CB	6-0	206	8/17/87	2	Newberry College	St. Helena Island, S.C.	FA-'11	5/0
2	Portis, Josh	QB	6-3	211	7/14/87	2	California Univ. (Pa.)	Woodland Hills, Calif.	FA-'11	0*
18	Rice, Sidney	WR	6-4	202	9/1/86	6	South Carolina	Gaffney, S.C.	UFA(Minn)-'11	9/9
26	Robinson, Michael	FB	6-1	240	2/6/83	7	Penn State	Richmond, Va.	FA-'10	14/5
57	Ruud, Barrett	LB	6-2	241	5/20/83	8	Nebraska	Lincoln, Neb.	UFA(Tenn)-'12	9/9*
9	Ryan, Jon	P	6-0	217	11/26/81	7	Regina	Regina, Saskatchewan	FA-'08	16/0
25	Sherman, Richard	CB	6-3	195	3/30/88	2	Stanford	Compton, Calif.	D5a-'11	16/10
53	Smith, Malcolm	LB	6-0	226	7/5/89	2	Southern California	Northridge, Calif.	D7b-'11	12/0
30	Sutton, Tyrell	RB	5-8	213	12/19/86	3	Northwestern	Akron, Ohio	FA-'12	0*
81	Tate, Golden	WR	5-10	202	8/2/88	3	Notre Dame	Hendersonville, Tenn.	D2-'10	16/5
29	Thomas, Earl	FS	5-10	202	5/7/89	3	Texas	Orange, Texas	D1b-'10	16/16
28	Thurmond, Walter	CB	5-11	190	8/12/87	3	Oregon	West Covina, Calif.	D4a-'10	6/3
23	Trufant, Marcus	CB	5-11	199	12/25/80	10	Washington State	Tacoma, Wash.	D1-'03	4/4
60	Unger, Max	C	6-5	305	4/14/86	4	Oregon	Kailua-Kona, Hawaii	D2-'09	15/15
33	Washington, Leon	RB	5-8	203	8/29/82	7	Florida State	Jacksonville, Fla.	T(NYJ)-'10	16/1
17	Williams, Mike	WR	6-5	235	1/4/84	6	Southern California	Tampa, Fla.	FA-'10	12/10
50	Wright, K.J.	LB	6-4	246	7/23/89	2	Mississippi State	Olive Branch, Miss.	D4a-'11	16/12

* Adams played 6 games with New England and 1 game with Seattle in '11; Bradford played 1 game with Tampa Bay; Flynn played 5 games with Green Bay; Francies last active with Cleveland in '10; Jones played 14 games with Tennessee; Lumpkin played 16 games with Tampa Bay; Lutui played 15 games with Arizona; Martin last active with Carolina in '10; Nalbone last active with Miami in '10; Omiyale played 16 games with Chicago; Portis inactive for 15 games and did not play in 1 game; Ruud played 9 games with Tennessee; Sutton last active with Carolina in '10.

Traded—Linebacker Aaron Curry (5 games in '11) to Oakland.

Players lost through free agency (4): S Atari Bigby (SD; 15 games), TE John Carlson (Minn; 0), DE Anthony Hargrove (GB; 15), QB Charlie Whitehurst (SD; 3).

Also played with Seahawks in '11—DE Raheem Brock (16 games), TE Dominique Byrd (1), CB Kennard Cox (12), RB Justin Forsett (16), G Robert Gallery (12), G Mike Gibson (3), LB David Hawthorne (15), Jarriel King (1), T Tyler Polumbus (5), David Vobora (6), Eddie Williams (3), Al Woods (2).

FIRST-YEAR ROSTER

Name	Pos.	Ht.	Wt.	Birthdate	College	Hometown	How Acq.
Allen, Pierre (1)	DE	6-4	273	11/18/87	Nebraska	Denver, Colo.	FA-'11
Baptiste, Tressor	LB	6-0	230	9/13/88	Texas A&M-Kingsville	Staten Island, N.Y.	FA
Bates, Phil	WR	6-1	220	9/20/89	Ohio University	Omaha, Neb.	FA
Durham, London	CB	6-0	180	12/8/88	McNeese State	Beaumont, Texas	FA
Graves, John (1)	DE	6-3	286	6/25/87	Virginia Tech	Richmond, Va.	FA-'11
Guy, Winston	SS	6-1	218	4/23/90	Kentucky	Lexington, Ky.	D6b
Hoffman, Jesse	DB	6-0	196	1/18/88	Eastern Washington	Seattle, Wash.	FA
Howard, Jaye	DT	6-3	301	12/20/88	Florida	Apopka, Fla.	D4b
Irvin, Bruce	DE	6-3	245	11/1/87	West Virginia	Atlanta, Ga.	D1
Johnson, Rishaw	G	6-3	313	2/23/89	California (Pa.)	Hammond, La.	FA
Kearse, Jermaine	WR	6-1	209	2/6/90	Washington	Lakewood, Wash.	FA
Lane, Jeremy	CB	6-0	190	7/14/90	Northwestern State (La.)	Tyler, Texas	D6a
Law, Cordarro	DE	6-1	254	10/15/88	Southern Mississippi	Whitfield, Ala.	FA
McGrath, Sean	TE	6-5	247	12/3/87	Henderson State (Ark.)	Chicago, Ill.	FA
Opperud, Jon	T	6-7	305	2/13/90	Montana	Portland, Ore.	FA
Scruggs, Greg	DE	6-3	284	8/17/90	Louisville	Cincinnati, Ohio	D7b
Shead, DeShawn	DB	6-1	220	6/28/88	Portland State	Palmdale, Calif.	FA
Sweezy, J.R.	G	6-5	298	4/8/89	North Carolina State	Mooresville, N.C.	D7a
Taua, Vai (1)	RB	5-10	211	10/11/88	Nevada	Fountain Valley, Calif.	FA-'11
Taylor, Adrian	DT	6-3	311	6/21/88	Oklahoma	Mansfield, Texas	FA
Taylor, Monte	DE	6-4	265	2/10/89	Cincinnati	Los Angeles, Calif.	FA
Toomer, Korey	LB	6-2	234	12/9/88	Idaho	Las Vegas, Nev.	D5
Tuinei, Lavasier	WR	6-4	220	9/29/90	Oregon	Arcadia, Ind.	FA
Turbin, Robert	RB	5-10	222	12/2/89	Utah State	Fremont, Calif.	D4a
Wagner, Bobby	LB	6-0	241	6/27/90	Utah State	Ontario, Calif.	D2
Wiggs, Carson	K	6-1	222	2/20/90	Purdue	Grand Prairie, Texas	FA
Wilson, Russell	QB	5-11	206	11/29/88	Wisconsin	Richmond, Va.	D3

The term NFL Rookie is defined as a player who is in his first season of professional football and has not been on the roster of another professional football team for any regular-season or postseason games. A Rookie is designated by an "R" on NFL rosters. Players who have been active in another professional football league or players who have NFL experience, including either preseason training camp or being on an Active List or Inactive List, or on Reserve/Injured or Reserve/Physically Unable to Perform for fewer than six regular-season games, are termed NFL First-Year Players. An NFL First-Year Player is designated by a "1" on NFL rosters. Thereafter, a player is credited with an additional year of experience for each season in which he accumulates six games on the Active List or Inactive List, or on Reserve/Injured or Reserve/Physically Unable to Perform.

Log on to www.seahawks.com for an up-to-date roster.

SEATTLE SEAHAWKS

COACHING STAFF

Head Coach,
Pete Carroll
Pro Career: Named as Seattle's eighth head coach on January 11, 2010. Began his NFL career as defensive backs coach for the Buffalo Bills (1984) and Minnesota Vikings (1985-89), before becoming the N.Y. Jets defensive coordinator (1990-93) and head coach (1994). He spent two years as the San Francisco 49ers defensive coordinator (1995-96) before leading the New England Patriots to a 27-21 record and two playoff appearances as head coach (1997-99). He returned to the NFL after spending nine years (2001-09) as head coach at USC, where he won seven consecutive Pac-10 titles (2002-08), two national championships and led the Trojans to a 97-19 record. Career record: 49-52.
Background: Two-time All-Pacific Coast Conference safety at Pacific (1971-72). Earned degree in business administration (1973) and secondary teaching credential and master's degree in physical education (1976) from Pacific. College coach: Pacific 1974-76, 1983, Arkansas 1977, Iowa State 1978, Ohio State 1979, North Carolina State 1980-82, USC 2001-09.
Personal: Born September 15, 1951 in San Francisco, Calif. He and his wife, Glena, have three children: Brennan, Nate, Jaime, and one grandson: Dillon.

ASSISTANT COACHES

Darrell Bevell, offensive coordinator; born January 6, 1970, Yuma, Ariz. Quarterback Northern Arizona 1989, Wisconsin 1992-95. No pro playing experience. College coach: Westmar 1996, Iowa State 1997, Connecticut 1998-99. Pro coach: Green Bay Packers 2000-05, Minnesota Vikings 2006-2010, joined Seahawks in 2011.
Casey (Gus) Bradley, defensive coordinator; born July 5, 1966, Zumbrota, Minn. Safety/punter North Dakota State 1984-88. No pro playing experience. College coach: North Dakota State 1990-91, 1996-2005, Fort Lewis College 1992-96. Pro coach: Tampa Bay Buccaneers 2006-2008, joined Seahawks in 2009.
Kippy Brown, wide receivers; born March 6, 1955, Sweetwater, Tenn. Quarterback Memphis State 1974-77. No pro playing experience. College coach: Memphis State 1978-1980, Louisville 1982, Tennessee 1983-89, 1993-94, 2009. Pro coach: New York Jets 1990-92, Tampa Bay Buccaneers 1995, Miami Dolphins 1996-99, Green Bay Packers 2000, Houston Texans 2002-05, Detroit Lions 2006-08, joined Seahawks in 2010.
Tom Cable, asst. head coach/offensive line; born November 26, 1964, Merced, Calif. Offensive lineman Idaho 1982-86. Pro lineman Indianapolis Colts 1987. College coach: Idaho 1987-88, San Diego State 1989, Cal State-Fullerton 1990, UNLV 1991, California 1992-97, Idaho 2000-03, UCLA 2004-05. Pro coach: Atlanta Falcons

2006, Oakland Raiders 2007-10 (head coach 2008-2010), joined Seahawks in 2011.
Dave Canales, quality control/offense; born May 7, 1981, Carson, Calif. Wide receiver Azusa Pacific 2000-03. No pro playing experience. College coach: El Camino (Calif.) J.C. 2006-08, Southern California 2009. Pro coach: Joined Seahawks in 2010.
Chris Carlisle, head strength & conditioning; born August 7, 1962, Mason City, Iowa. Offensive lineman North Iowa Area Community College 1980-81, Chadron (Neb.) State College 1982-83. No pro playing experience. College coach: Arkansas 1992-93, Trinity Valley (Texas) C.C. 1997, Tennessee 1998-2000, Southern California 2001-09. Pro coach: Joined Seahawks in 2010.
Nate Carroll, defensive assistant; born March 24, 1987, Edina, Minn. Attended Southern California. No college or pro playing experience. Pro coach: Joined Seahawks in 2010.
Keith Carter, quality control/offense; born July 2, 1982, Downingtown, Pa. Tight end UCLA 2001-04. No pro playing experience. College coach: Wagner College 2006, Redlands 2007-08, University of San Diego 2009-2011. Pro coach: Joined Seahawks in 2011.
Mondray Gee, asst. strength & conditioning; born June 15, 1976, Detroit, Mich. Attended Michigan State. No college or pro playing experience. College coach: Michigan State 2000-01. Pro coach: Detroit Lions 2001-07, Green Bay Packers 2008-09, joined Seahawks in 2010.
Marquand Manuel, asst. special teams; born July 11, 1979, Miami, Fla. Safety Florida 1998-2001. Pro safety Cincinnati Bengals 2002-03, Seattle Seahawks 2004-05, Green Bay Packers 2006, Carolina Panthers 2007, Denver Broncos 2008, Detroit Lions 2009. Pro coach: Joined Seahawks in 2011.
Pat McPherson, tight ends; born April 15, 1969, Santa Clara, Calif. Linebacker Santa Clara 1991-92. No pro playing experience. Pro coach: San Francisco 49ers 1996, Denver Broncos 1998-2008, joined Seahawks in 2010.
Ken Norton, Jr., linebackers; born September 29, 1966, Lincoln, Ill. Linebacker UCLA 1984-87. Pro linebacker Dallas Cowboys 1988-1993, San Francisco 49ers 1994-2000. College coach: Southern California 2004-09. Pro coach: Joined Seahawks in 2010.
Kris Richard, defensive backs/cornerbacks; born October 28, 1978, Carson, Calif. Defensive back Southern California 1998-2001. Pro defensive back Seattle Seahawks 2002-04, San Francisco 49ers 2005. College coach: Southern California 2008-09. Pro coach: Joined Seahawks in 2010.
Pat Ruel, asst. offensive line; born December 5, 1950, Coral Gables, Fla.

Offensive lineman Miami 1971-72. No pro playing experience. College coach: Miami 1974-76, Arkansas 1977, Washington State 1978-1981, Texas A&M 1982-84, Northern Illinois 1985-87, Kansas 1988-1996, Michigan State 1998-99, USC 2005-09. Pro coach: Detroit Lions 2000, Green Bay Packers 2001-02, Buffalo Bills 2003, New York Giants 2004, joined Seahawks in 2010.
Robert Saleh, quality control/defense; born January 31, 1979, Dearborn, Mich. Tight end Northern Michigan 1997-2000. No pro playing experience. College coach: Michigan State 2002-03, Central Michigan 2004. Pro coach: Houston Texans 2005-2010, joined Seahawks in 2011.
Brian Schneider, special teams coordinator; born May 16, 1971, San Diego, Calif. Linebacker Colorado State 1989-1993. No pro playing experience. College coach: Colorado State 1994-2002, UCLA 2003-05, Iowa State 2006, Air Force 2007, Southern California 2009. Pro coach: Oakland Raiders 2007-08, joined Seahawks in 2010.
Rocky Seto, asst. defensive backs/safeties; born March 12, 1976, Arcadia, Calif. Linebacker Southern California 1997-98. No pro playing experience. College coach: Southern California 1999-2009. Pro coach: Joined Seahawks in 2010.
Carl Smith, quarterbacks; born April 26, 1948, Wasco, Calif. Quarterback Bakersfield 1966-67, defensive back Cal Poly-San Luis Obispo 1969-1970. No pro playing experience. College coach: Cal Poly-San Luis Obispo 1971, Colorado 1972-73, Southwestern Louisiana 1974-78, Lamar 1979-1981, North Carolina State 1982, Southern California 2004. Pro coach: Philadelphia/Baltimore Stars 1983-85, New Orleans Saints 1986-1996, New England Patriots 1997-99, Cleveland Browns 2001-03, 2009-2010, Jacksonville Jaguars 2005-06, joined Seahawks in 2011.
Sherman Smith, running backs; born November 1, 1954, Youngstown, Ohio. Quarterback Miami (Ohio) 1972-75. Pro running back Seattle Seahawks 1976-1982, San Diego Chargers 1983-84. College coach: Miami (Ohio) 1990-91, Illinois 1992-94. Pro coach: Houston Oilers/Tennessee Titans 1995-2007, Washington Redskins 2008-09, joined Seahawks in 2010.
Todd Wash, defensive line; born July 19, 1968, Miles City, Mont. Linebacker North Dakota State 1988-1991. No pro playing experience. College coach: Fort Lewis College 1996-99, Nebraska-Kearney 2000-01, North Dakota State 2002-03, 2005-06, Missouri Southern State 2004. Pro coach: Tampa Bay Buccaneers 2006-2010, joined Seahawks in 2011.
Jamie Yanchar, asst. strength & conditioning, born December 29, 1963, Cleveland, Ohio. Attended Louisville. No college or pro playing experience. College coach: Southern California 1990-2009. Pro coach: Joined Seahawks in 2010.

**National Football Conference
South Division
Team Colors:** Buccaneer Red, Pewter,
Black, and Orange
**One Buccaneer Place
Tampa, Florida 33607
Telephone:** (813) 870-2700

2012 SCHEDULE
PRESEASON
Aug. 10 at Miami 7:30
Aug. 17 **Tennessee** 7:30
Aug. 25 **New England** 7:30
Aug. 29 at Washington 7:30

REGULAR SEASON
Sep. 9   **Carolina**............................4:15
Sep. 16 at New York Giants 1:00
Sep. 23 at Dallas 1:00
Sep. 30 **Washington** 4:15
Oct. 7   BYE
Oct. 14 **Kansas City** 1:00
Oct. 21 **New Orleans**.......................1:00
Oct. 25 at Minnesota (Thurs) 8:20
Nov. 4   at Oakland 4:05
Nov. 11 **San Diego**..........................1:00
Nov. 18 at Carolina.........................1:00
Nov. 25 **Atlanta**..............................1:00
Dec. 2   at Denver 4:05
Dec. 9   **Philadelphia** 1:00
Dec. 16 at New Orleans...................1:00
Dec. 23 **St. Louis** 1:00
Dec. 30 at Atlanta...........................1:00
All times ET

Stadium: Raymond James Stadium
(opened in 1998)
 • **Capacity:** 65,908
Tampa, Florida 33607
Playing Surface: Grass
Training Camp: One Buccaneer Place
Tampa, Florida 33607

RAYMOND JAMES STADIUM

CLUB OFFICIALS
Owner/President: Malcolm Glazer
Co-Chairman: Bryan Glazer
Co-Chairman: Joel Glazer
Co-Chairman: Edward Glazer
General Manager: Mark Dominik
Vice President of Business
  Administration: Brian Ford
Director of Player Personnel:
  Dennis Hickey
Director of Player Engagement:
  Terry Cousin
Director of Football Operations:
  Kevin MacConnell
Director of Team Security: Henry Duran
Special Assistant to the Head Coach:
  Butch Davis
Coordinator of Pro Scouting:
  Shelton Quarles
Coordinator of Football Administration:
  Mike Greenberg
Pro Personnel Assistant: Rob McCartney
National Scout: Jim Abrams
College Scouts: Andre Forde,
  Brian Hudspeth, Byron Kiefer,
  Tony Kinkela, Jared Kirksey, Bill Rees,
  Justin Sheridan, Seth Turner,
  Mike Yowarsky
Combine Scout: Tony Hardie
Chief Financial Officer: Joe Fada
Chief Legal Officer: Steve Johnston
Chief Marketing Officer: Jason Dial
Chief Partnership Officer: Jim Pyne
Director of Communications:
  Jonathan Grella
Director of Community Relations:
  Miray Holmes
Director of Corporate Security and
  Facilities: Andres Trescastro
Director of Creative Services:
  Clark Moss
Director of Group Sales: Amy Saxon
Director of Guest/Member Relations:
  Barbara Stevens
Director of Sales: Ben Milsom
Director of Special Events and Game
  Operations: TBD
Director of Sports Medicine and
  Performance: Todd Toriscelli
Director of Rehabilitation:
  Shannon Merrick
Team Sports Dietitian : Kevin Luhrs
Head Equipment Manager: James Sorenson
Asst. Equipment Manager: Mike Myrick
Video Director: Dave Levy
Asst. Video Director: Chris Bryan
Broadcast Operations Manager:
  Jeff Ryan
Cheerleading Manager: Catherine Boyd
Human Resources Manager:
  Raeni Ware
Player Benefits and Alumni Program
  Manager: Jill Hobbs
IT Manager: Ed Johnston
Public Relations Manager:
  Michael Pehanich
Purchasing Manager: Brian Mathiews
Special Events and Game Day Manager:
  Jim Mackes
Team Operations Manager: Tim Jarocki
Senior Ticket Operations Manager: Chris
  Roberts
Ticket Operations Manager: Amy Weber
Video Production Manager: Ed Bottger
Website Manager: Scott Smith

COACHING HISTORY
(228-350-1)
Records include postseason games
1976-1984 John McKay 45-91-1
1985-86   Leeman Bennett 4-28-0
1987-1990 Ray Perkins* 19-41-0
1990-91   Richard Williamson 4-15-0
1992-95   Sam Wyche 23-41-0
1996-2001 Tony Dungy 56-46-0
2002-08   Jon Gruden 60-57-0
2009-2011 Raheem Morris 17-31-0
*Released after 13 games in 1990

PAID ATTENDANCE
Home 420,483   Away 511,773
Total 932,256
Single-game home record,
  73,523 (12/7/97)
Single-season home record,
  545,980 (1979)

2012 DRAFT CHOICES
Round	Name	Pos.	College
1	Mark Barron	DB	Alabama
	Doug Martin	RB	Boise St.
2	Lavonte David	LB	Nebraska
5	Najee Goode	LB	West Virginia
6	Keith Tandy	DB	West Virginia
7	Michael Smith	RB	Utah St.
	Drake Dunsmore	TE	Northwestern

TAMPA BAY BUCCANEERS

2011 TEAM RECORD
PRESEASON (2-2)

Date	Result	Opponent
8/12	W 25-0	at Kansas City
8/18	L 14-31	New England
8/26	W 17-13	Miami
9/1	L 24-29	at Washington

REGULAR SEASON (4-12)

Date	Result	Opponent
9/11	L 20-27	Detroit
9/18	W 24-20	at Minnesota
9/25	W 16-13	Atlanta
10/3	W 24-17	Indianapolis
10/9	L 3-48	at San Francisco
10/16	W 26-20	New Orleans
10/23	L 18-24	Chicago
11/6	L 16-27	at New Orleans
11/13	L 9-37	Houston
11/20	L 26-35	at Green Bay
11/27	L 17-23	at Tennessee
12/4	L 19-38	Carolina
12/11	L 14-41	at Jacksonville
12/17	L 15-31	Dallas
12/24	L 16-48	at Carolina
1/1	L 24-45	at Atlanta

SCORE BY PERIODS

Buccaneers	34	96	65	92	0 —	287
Opponents	126	178	86	104	0 —	494

2011 TEAM STATISTICS

	Buccaneers	Opp.
Total First Downs	277	356
Rushing	74	135
Passing	180	188
Penalty	23	33
3rd Down: Made/Att	76/206	73/185
3rd Down Pct.	36.9	39.5
4th Down: Made/Att	8/21	9/13
4th Down Pct.	38.1	69.2
Possession Avg.	29:04	30:56
Total Net Yards	5108	6311
Avg. Per Game	319.3	394.4
Total Plays	966	1002
Avg. Per Play	5.3	6.3
Net Yards Rushing	1458	2497
Avg. Per Game	91.1	156.1
Total Rushes	346	498
Net Yards Passing	3650	3814
Avg. Per Game	228.1	238.4
Sacked/Yards Lost	32/188	23/148
Gross Yards	3838	3962
Att./Completions	588/365	481/301
Completion Pct.	62.1	62.6
Had Intercepted	24	14
Punts/Average	67/45.1	58/43.4
Net Punting Avg.	67/40.3	58/37.7
Penalties/Yards	123/1007	95/786
Fumbles/Ball Lost	30/16	21/10
Touchdowns	30	61
Rushing	9	26
Passing	17	30
Returns	4	5

2011 INDIVIDUAL STATISTICS

PASSING

	Att.	Comp.	Yds.	Pct.	TD	Int.	Tkld.	Rate
Freeman	551	346	3592	62.8	16	22	29/164	74.6
J. Johnson	36	19	246	52.8	1	2	3/24	60.6
Spurlock	1	0	0	0.0	0	0	0/0	39.6
Buccaneers	588	365	3838	62.1	17	24	32/188	73.6
Opponents	481	301	3962	62.6	30	14	23/148	97.2

SCORING

	TD R	TD P	TD Rt	PAT	FG	Saf	PTS
Barth	0	0	0	23/23	26/28	0	101
Briscoe	0	6	0	0/0	0/0	0	36
Blount	5	0	0	0/0	0/0	0	30
Freeman	4	0	0	0/0	0/0	0	24
Benn	0	3	0	0/0	0/0	0	18
Parker	0	3	0	0/0	0/0	0	18
Williams	0	3	0	0/0	0/0	0	18
Winslow	0	2	0	0/0	0/0	0	16
Talib	0	0	2	0/0	0/0	0	12
Mack	0	0	1	0/0	0/0	0	6
Watson	0	0	1	0/0	0/0	0	6
Barber	0	0	0	0/0	0/0	1	2
Buccaneers	9	17	4	23/23	26/28	1	287
Opponents	26	30	5	59/60	23/29	0	494

2-Pt Conversions: Winslow 2
Buccaneers 2-7, Opponents 0-1

RUSHING

	No.	Yds	Avg	LG	TD
Blount	184	781	4.2	54t	5
Freeman	55	238	4.3	25	4
Graham	37	206	5.6	34	0
Lumpkin	31	105	3.4	19	0
J. Johnson	11	67	6.1	14	0
Madu	15	55	3.7	15	0
Bradford	5	13	2.6	4	0
Williams	1	3	3.0	3	0
Parker	1	-3	-3.0	-3	0
Benn	6	-7	-1.2	9	0
Buccaneers	346	1458	4.2	54t	9
Opponents	498	2497	5.0	81t	26

RECEIVING

	No.	Yds	Avg	LG	TD
Winslow	75	763	10.2	37	2
Williams	65	771	11.9	42	3
Lumpkin	41	291	7.1	16	0
Parker	40	554	13.9	51	3
Briscoe	35	387	11.1	46	6
Benn	30	441	14.7	65t	3
Graham	26	163	6.3	19	0
Blount	15	148	9.9	35	0
Stocker	12	92	7.7	24	0
Madu	10	72	7.2	15	0
Lorig	6	53	8.8	22	0
Stroughter	4	52	13.0	29	0
Pianalto	4	40	10.0	15	0
Spurlock	2	13	6.5	7	0
Penn	0	2	—	2	0
Freeman	0	-4	—	-4	0
Buccaneers	365	3838	10.5	65t	17
Opponents	301	3962	13.2	91t	30

INTERCEPTIONS

	No.	Yds	Avg	LG	TD
Barber	3	12	4.0	12	0
Jackson	2	59	29.5	43	0
Talib	2	55	27.5	28t	2
Mack	2	47	23.5	40t	1
Lynch	1	14	14.0	14	0
Hayes	1	8	8.0	8	0
Biggers	1	0	0.0	0	0
Q. Black	1	0	0.0	0	0
Foster	1	0	0.0	0	0
Buccaneers	14	195	13.9	43	3
Opponents	24	266	11.1	32	2

PUNTING

	No.	Yds.	Avg.	In 20	LG
Koenen	67	3023	45.1	24	65
Buccaneers	67	3023	45.1	24	65
Opponents	58	2518	43.4	17	63

PUNT RETURNS

	Ret	FC	Yds	Avg	LG	TD
Parker	23	13	210	9.1	34	0
Spurlock	6	1	21	3.5	15	0
Buccaneers	29	14	231	8.0	34	0
Opponents	36	14	266	7.4	55	0

KICKOFF RETURNS

	No.	Yds	Avg	LG	TD
Parker	20	439	22.0	45	0
Stroughter	20	540	27.0	78	0
Spurlock	2	33	16.5	21	0
Briscoe	1	12	12.0	12	0
Crowder	1	0	0.0	0	0
Madu	1	0	0.0	0	0
Pianalto	1	0	0.0	0	0
Buccaneers	46	1024	22.3	78	0
Opponents	25	570	22.8	100t	1

FIELD GOALS

	1-19	20-29	30-39	40-49	50+
Barth	0/0	5/5	6/6	13/14	2/3
Buccaneers	0/0	5/5	6/6	13/14	2/3
Opponents	1/1	12/13	7/8	2/6	1/1

SACKS

	No.
Clayborn	7.5
Bennett	4.0
Price	3.0
Foster	2.0
Bowers	1.5
Barber	1.0
Jones	1.0
McCoy	1.0
Watson	1.0
(group)	1.0
Buccaneers	23.0
Opponents	32.0

RECORD HOLDERS
INDIVIDUAL RECORDS—CAREER

Category	Name	Performance
Rushing (Yds.)	James Wilder, 1981-89	5,957
Passing (Yds.)	Vinny Testaverde, 1987-1992	14,820
Passing (TDs)	Vinny Testaverde, 1987-1992	77
Receiving (No.)	James Wilder, 1981-89	430
Receiving (Yds.)	Mark Carrier, 1987-1992	5,018
Interceptions	Ronde Barber, 1997-2011	43
Punting (Avg.)	Josh Bidwell, 2004-08	44.0
Punt Return (Avg.)	Clifton Smith, 2008	14.1
Kickoff Return (Avg.)	Aaron Stecker, 2000-03	23.8
Field Goals	Martín Gramatica, 1999-2004	137
Touchdowns (Tot.)	Mike Alstott, 1996-2006	71
Points	Martín Gramatica, 1999-2004	592
*Sacks	Warren Sapp, 1995-2003	77.0

INDIVIDUAL RECORDS—SINGLE SEASON

Category	Name	Performance
Rushing (Yds.)	James Wilder, 1984	1,544
Passing (Yds.)	Brad Johnson, 2003	3,811
Passing (TDs)	Brad Johnson, 2003	26
Receiving (No.)	Keyshawn Johnson, 2001	106
Receiving (Yds.)	Mark Carrier, 1989	1,422
Interceptions	Ronde Barber, 2001	10
Punting (Avg.)	Josh Bidwell, 2005	45.6
Punt Return (Avg.)	Karl Williams, 1996	21.1
Kickoff Return (Avg.)	Sammie Stroughter, 2009	29.5
Field Goals	Martín Gramatica, 2002	32
	Matt Bryant, 2008	32
Touchdowns (Tot.)	James Wilder, 1984	13
Points	Matt Bryant, 2008	131
*Sacks	Warren Sapp, 2000	16.5

INDIVIDUAL RECORDS—SINGLE GAME

Category	Name	Performance
Rushing (Yds.)	James Wilder, 11-6-83	219
Passing (Yds.)	Doug Williams, 11-16-80	486
Passing (TDs)	Steve DeBerg, 9-13-87	5
	Brad Johnson, 11-3-02	5
	Josh Freeman, 12-26-10	5
Receiving (No.)	James Wilder, 9-15-85	13
	Earnest Graham, 10-21-07	13
Receiving (Yds.)	Mark Carrier, 12-6-87	212
Interceptions	Ronde Barber, 12-23-01, 12-4-05	3
	Aqib Talib, 9-21-08	3
Field Goals	Martín Gramatica, 12-29-02	5
Touchdowns (Tot.)	Jimmie Giles, 10-20-85	4
Points	Jimmie Giles, 10-20-85	24
*Sacks	Marcus Jones, 10-19-00	4.0
	Simeon Rice, 10-12-03	4.0

*Sacks became an official statistic in 1982.

TAMPA BAY BUCCANEERS

2012 VETERAN ROSTER

No.	Name	Pos.	Ht.	Wt.	Birthdate	NFL Exp.	College	Hometown	How Acq.	'11 Games/ Starts
36	Asante, Larry	S	6-0	210	3/7/88	2	Nebraska	Alexandria, Va.	FA-'10	10/0
20	Barber, Ronde	CB	5-10	184	4/7/75	16	Virginia	Roanoke, Va.	D3b-'97	16/16
10	#Barth, Connor	K	5-11	193	4/11/86	5	North Carolina	Wilmington, N.C.	FA-'09	16/0
17	Benn, Arrelious	WR	6-2	220	9/8/88	3	Illinois	Washington, D.C.	D2b-'10	14/14
71	Bennett, Michael	DL	6-4	274	11/13/85	4	Texas A&M	Alief, Texas	W(Sea)-'09	14/10
31	Biggers, E.J.	CB	6-0	180	6/13/87	4	Western Michigan	North Miami Beach, Fla.	D7a-'09	16/6
58	Black, Quincy	LB	6-2	240	2/28/84	6	New Mexico	Chicago, Ill.	D3-'07	14/12
27	Blount, LeGarrette	RB	6-0	247	12/5/86	3	Oregon	Perry, Fla.	W(Tenn)-'10	14/14
91	Bowers, Da'Quan	DE	6-4	277	2/23/90	2	Clemson	Bamberg, S.C.	D2-'11	16/6
89	Briscoe, Dezmon	WR	6-2	210	8/31/89	2	Kansas	Dallas, Texas	FA-'10	16/2
94	Clayborn, Adrian	DE	6-3	287	7/6/88	2	Iowa	St. Louis, Mo.	D1-'11	16/16
46	Coffman, Chase	TE	6-6	250	11/11/86	3	Missouri	Peculiar, Mo.	FA-'12	0*
45	Curran, Rennie	LB	5-11	230	11/10/88	2	Georgia	Snellville, Ga.	FA-'12	0*
51	Cutrera, Jacob	LB	6-3	238	5/18/88	3	Louisiana State	Lafayette, La.	FA-'11	8/0
69	Dotson, Demar	T	6-9	315	10/11/85	4	Southern Miss	Alexandria, La.	FA-'09	13/2
48	Economos, Andrew	LS	6-1	250	6/24/82	7	Georgia Tech	Atlanta, Ga.	FA-'06	9/0
59	Foster, Mason	LB	6-1	241	3/1/89	2	Washington	Seaside, Calif.	D3-'11	16/15
5	Freeman, Josh	QB	6-6	248	1/13/88	4	Kansas State	Kansas City, Mo.	D1-'09	15/15
26	Gaitor, Anthony	CB	5-10	178	10/9/88	2	Florida International	Miami, Fla.	D7a-'11	8/0
95	Gibson, Gary	DT	6-3	312	5/5/82	6	Rutgers	Lafayette, N.Y.	UFA(StL)-'12	16/1*
	#Graham, Earnest	RB	5-9	225	1/15/80	9	Florida	Ft. Myers, Fla.	FA-'03	7/2
35	Grimm, Cody	S	5-11	210	2/26/87	3	Virginia Tech	Fairfax, Va.	D7a-'10	3/3
73	Hardman, Derek	T	6-6	300	9/13/86	3	Eastern Kentucky	Spencer, W. Va.	FA-'10	3/0
	#Haye, Jovan	DT	6-2	280	6/21/82	8	Vanderbilt	Fort Lauderdale, Fla.	FA-'11	2/0*
57	Hayward, Adam	LB	6-1	240	6/23/84	6	Portland State	Westminster, Calif.	D6-'07	16/2
30	Holland, Devin	S	6-0	205	10/18/88	2	McNeese State	Baton Rouge, La.	FA-'11	4/0
83	Jackson, Vincent	WR	6-5	230	1/14/83	8	Northern Colorado	Colorado Springs, Colo.	UFA(SD)-'12	16/16*
97	Johnson, George	DE	6-4	265	12/11/87	2	Rutgers	Glassboro, N.J.	FA-'10	4/0
	#Jones, Sean	S	6-1	220	3/2/82	9	Georgia	Atlanta, Ga.	UFA(Phil)-'12	16/16
75	Joseph, Davin	G	6-3	313	11/22/83	7	Oklahoma	Hallandale, Fla.	D1-'06	16/16
9	Koenen, Michael	P	5-11	198	7/13/82	8	Western Washington	Ferndale, Wash.	UFA(Atl)-'11	16/0
62	Larsen, Ted	C/G	6-2	305	6/13/87	3	North Carolina State	Palm Beach, Fla.	W(NE)-'10	16/3
23	Lewis, Myron	CB	6-2	203	11/24/87	3	Vanderbilt	Pompano Beach, Fla.	D3-'10	10/0
44	Lorig, Erik	FB/TE	6-4	275	11/17/86	3	Stanford	Palos Verdes, Calif.	D7c-'10	16/7
	#Lynch, Corey	S	6-0	206	5/7/85	5	Appalachian State	Ft. Myers, Fla.	FA-'09	16/3
	#Mack, Elbert	CB	5-10	175	7/14/86	5	Troy	Wichita, Kan.	FA-'08	16/1
32	Madu, Mossis	RB	6-0	197	11/4/87	2	Oklahoma	Norman, Okla.	FA-'11	9/0
93	McCoy, Gerald	DT	6-4	295	2/25/88	3	Oklahoma	Oklahoma City, Okla.	D1-'10	6/6
79	Meredith, Jamon	T	6-5	312	5/11/86	4	South Carolina	Simpsonville, S.C.	FA-'12	4/0*
90	Miller, Roy	DT	6-2	310	7/9/87	4	Texas	Killeen, Texas	D3-'09	16/3
77	Nicks, Carl	G	6-5	343	5/14/85	5	Nebraska	Salinas, Calif.	UFA(NO)-'12	16/16*
98	Okam, Frank	DT	6-5	350	10/16/85	5	Texas	Dallas, Texas	FA-'10	9/3
96	Okoye, Amobi	DT	6-2	292	6/10/87	6	Louisville	Huntsville, Ala.	UFA(Chi)-'12	16/1*
6	Orlovsky, Dan	QB	6-5	230	8/18/83	7	Connecticut	Shelton, Conn.	UFA(Ind)-12	8/5*
87	Parker, Preston	WR	6-0	200	2/13/87	3	North Alabama	Delray Beach, Fla.	FA-'10	16/0
70	Penn, Donald	T	6-5	305	4/27/83	7	Utah State	Playa Del Rey, Calif.	FA-'06	16/16
80	Pianalto, Zack	TE	6-4	250	5/27/89	2	North Carolina	Springdale, Alaska	W(Buff)-'11	13/0
92	Price, Brian	DT	6-1	303	4/10/89	3	UCLA	Los Angeles, Calif.	D2a-'10	15/15
7	Ratliff, Brett	QB	6-4	224	8/8/85	3	Utah	Chico, Calif.	FA-'11	0*
28	Roberson, Derrick	CB	5-10	182	3/12/85	2	Rutgers	Ft. Lauderdale, Fla.	FA-'12	0*
88	Stocker, Luke	TE	6-5	253	7/17/88	2	Tennessee	Berea, Ky.	D4-'11	14/9
18	Strougther, Sammie	WR	5-10	189	1/3/86	4	Oregon State	Sacramento, Calif.	D7b-'09	6/0
25	Talib, Aqib	CB	6-1	205	2/13/86	5	Kansas	Richardson, Texas	D1-'08	13/13
67	Taylor, Hilee	DE	6-2	250	7/18/86	4	North Carolina	Laurinburg, N.C.	FA-'12	0*
50	Te'o-Nesheim, Daniel	DE	6-3	263	6/12/87	3	Washington	Kameula, Hawaii	FA-'11	1/0
65	Trueblood, Jeremy	T	6-8	320	5/10/83	7	Boston College	Indianapolis, Ind.	D2-'06	15/15
11	Underwood, Tiquan	WR	6-1	183	2/17/87	4	Rutgers	Lawrenceville, N.J.	FA-'12	6/0*
56	Watson, Dekoda	LB	6-2	240	3/3/88	3	Florida State	Aiken, S.C.	D7b-'10	14/2
19	Williams, Mike	WR	6-2	212	5/18/87	3	Syracuse	Buffalo, N.Y.	D4-'10	16/15
78	Wilson, E.J.	DT	6-3	289	10/28/87	3	North Carolina	Lawrenceville, Va.	FA-'10	0*
82	Winslow, Kellen	TE	6-4	240	7/21/83	9	Miami	San Diego, Calif.	T(Cle)-'09	16/15
21	Wright, Eric	CB	5-10	190	7/24/85	6	Nevada-Las Vegas	San Francisco, Calif.	UFA(Det)-'12	16/16*
76	Zuttah, Jeremy	C	6-4	308	6/1/86	5	Rutgers	Edison, N.J.	D3-'08	15/14

* Coffman last active with Cincinnati in '10; Curran last active with Tennessee in '10; Gibson played 16 games with St. Louis in '11; Haye played 1 game with Detroit; Jackson played 16 games with San Diego; Meredith played 4 games with Pittsburgh; Nicks played 16 games with New Orleans; Okoye played 16 games with Chicago; Orlovsky played 8 games with Indianapolis; Ratliff last active with Cleveland in '10; Roberson last active with Cleveland in '10; Taylor last active with Carolina in '10; Underwood played 6 games with New England; Wilson missed '11 season because of injury; Wright played 16 games with Detroit.

\# Unrestricted free agent; subject to developments.

Players lost through free agency (4): LB Geno Hayes (Chi; 16 games in '11), QB Josh Johnson (SF; 9); T James Lee (Wash; 3), WR Micheal Spurlock (SD; 12).

Also played with Buccaneers in '11—RB Allen Bradford (1 game), QB Rudy Carpenter (1), DE Tim Crowder (10), LB Zac Diles (7), C Jeff Faine (15), DT Albert Haynesworth (7), S Tanard Jackson (10), RB Kregg Lumpkin (16), DT John McCargo (4), DE Nick Reed (3), LS Christian Yount (7).

FIRST-YEAR ROSTER

Name	Pos.	Ht.	Wt.	Birthdate	College	Hometown	How Acq.
Anderson, Quintin	DE	6-5	280	2/10/89	Wagner	Rochester, N.Y.	FA
Baker, Sean	S	6-1	209	11/6/88	Ball State	Canfield, Ohio	FA
Barron, Mark	S	6-2	213	10/27/89	Alabama	Mobile, Ala.	D1a
Black, Ahmad (1)	S	5-9	184	12/12/89	Florida	Lakeland, Fla.	D5-'11
Curtis, De'Anthony	RB	5-9	211	5/8/90	Arkansas	Camden, Ark.	FA
David, Lavonte	LB	6-1	233	1/23/90	Nebraska	Miami, Fla.	D2
Dunsmore, Drake	TE	6-3	235	11/4/88	Northwestern	Lenexa, Kan.	D7b
Forbath, Kai (1)	K	5-11	197	9/2/87	UCLA	Sherman Oaks, Calif.	W(Dall)
Franklin, Collin (1)	TE	6-5	252	7/20/88	Iowa State	Simi Valley, Calif.	W(NYJ)-'11
Gant, Ed (1)	WR	6-3	200	1/24/87	North Alabama	Cape Coral, Fla.	FA-'10
Goode, Najee	LB	6-0	244	6/4/89	West Virginia	Cleveland, Ohio	D5
Guthrie, Eric	P	6-6	245	2/10/89	Iowa	Nevada, Iowa	FA
Hardrick, Jermarcus	T	6-7	320	5/30/90	Nebraska	Batesville, Miss.	FA
Hughes, Robert (1)	RB	5-11	235	6/21/89	Notre Dame	Chicago, Ill.	FA
Ingersoll, Mike (1)	T	6-5	300	1/9/88	North Carolina	Matthews, N.C.	FA-'11
Johnson, Cody	FB	5-11	252	3/16/89	Texas	Waller, Texas	FA
Johnson, Leonard	CB	5-10	202	3/30/90	Iowa State	Clearwater, Fla.	FA
Leak, Antonio	LB	6-2	248	7/26/87	Henderson State	Forrest City, Ark.	FA
LeGrand, Eric	DT			9/4/90	Rutgers	Colonia, N.J.	FA
Martin, Doug	RB	5-9	223	1/13/89	Boise State	Oakland, Calif.	D1b
Nix, Jordan	DT	6-3	295	10/17/88	North Carolina	Lawton, Okla.	FA
Noble, Danny	TE	6-5	248	3/30/89	Toledo	Elyria, Ohio	FA
Petrus, Moe	C	6-2	302	2/22/86	Connecticut	St. Laurent, Que., Canada	FA
Shoemaker, Tyler	WR	6-1	213	9/14/88	Boise State	Meridian, Idaho	FA
Smith, Michael	RB	5-9	205	8/9/88	Utah State	Tucson, Ariz.	D7a
Sowell, Bradley	T	6-7	320	6/6/89	Mississippi	Hernando, Miss.	FA
Tandy, Keith	CB	5-10	199	2/12/89	West Virginia	Hopkinsville, Ky.	D6
Thomas, Tramain	S	6-0	204	3/17/90	Arkansas	Winnie, Texas	FA
Urban, Tyler	TE	6-5	251	9/30/89	West Virginia	North Huntington, Pa.	FA
VanDerMeulen, Mike	T	6-7	304	8/16/89	Toledo	Marshall, Mich.	FA
Wade, Myles	DT	6-1	300	8/30/89	Portland State	Portland, Ore.	FA
Wynn, Desmond	T	6-6	303	8/31/88	Rutgers	Wilmington, Del.	FA

The term NFL Rookie is defined as a player who is in his first season of professional football and has not been on the roster of another professional football team for any regular-season or postseason games. A Rookie is designated by an "R" on NFL rosters. Players who have been active in another professional football league or players who have NFL experience, including either preseason training camp or being on an Active List or Inactive List, or on Reserve/Injured or Reserve/Physically Unable to Perform for fewer than six regular-season games, are termed NFL First-Year Players. An NFL First-Year Player is designated by a "1" on NFL rosters. Thereafter, a player is credited with an additional year of experience for each season in which he accumulates six games on the Active List or Inactive List, or on Reserve/Injured or Reserve/Physically Unable to Perform.

Log on to www.buccaneers.com for an up-to-date roster.

TAMPA BAY BUCCANEERS

COACHING STAFF
Head Coach,
Greg Schiano
Pro Career: Named the ninth head coach in franchise history on January 27, 2012, Greg Schiano enters his first season at the helm of the Tampa Bay Buccaneers. This will mark the fourth season of NFL coaching experience for Schiano, who was with the Chicago Bears as a defensive assistant (1996) and defensive backfield coach (1997-98). He was a college football coach for 21 seasons, including the last 12 years as the head coach for Rutgers. Under his leadership, Rutgers–which had advanced to a postseason bowl just once in the previous 135 years–qualified for six bowls and won five from 2005-2011. Career record: 0-0.
Background: Played linebacker at Bucknell (1986-88). Coached at Ramapo High School (NJ) in 1988 before serving a season at Rutgers (1989 graduate assistant) followed by six seasons at Penn State (1990 graduate assistant and 1991-95 defensive backfield). After three years with the Bears, Schiano spent two seasons at Miami (FL) as (1998-99 defensive coordinator) before becoming the Rutgers head coach (2000-2011).
Personal: Born on June 1, 1966 in Wyckoff, N.J. He and his wife, Christy, have four children: Joey, John, Matt, and Katie.

ASSISTANT COACHES
Brian Angelichio, tight ends; born December 27, 1972, Ilion, N.Y. Linebacker St. Lawrence 1991-95. No pro playing experience. College coach: SUNY-Brockport 1995, Ithaca 1996-2005, Pittsburgh 2006-2010, Rutgers 2011. Pro coach: Joined Buccaneers in 2012.
Bob Bostad, offensive line; born September 7, 1966, Pardeeville, Wisc. Linebacker UW-Stevens Point 1986-89. No pro playing experience. College coach: UW-Stevens Point 1990-91, Minnesota 1992-94, Cal State-Northridge 1995-96, San Jose State 1997-98, New Mexico 1999-2005, Wisconsin 2006-2011. Pro coach: Joined Buccaneers in 2012.
Jay Butler, head strength and conditioning; born September 10, 1969, Hillsborough, N.J. Offensive tackle Bucknell 1988-1991. No pro playing experience. College coach: East Carolina 1992-95, Dartmouth 1996-2000, Rutgers 2001-2011. Pro coach: Joined Buccaneers in 2012.
Earnest Byner, running backs; born September 15, 1962, Milledgeville, Ga. Running back East Carolina 1980-1993. Pro running back Cleveland Browns 1984-88, 1994-95, Washington Redskins 1989-1993, Baltimore Ravens 1996-97. Pro coach: Washington Redskins 2004-07, Tennessee Titans 2008-09, Jacksonville Jaguars 2010-11, joined Buccaneers in 2012.
Ron Cooper, defensive backs; born February 11, 1962, Huntsville, Ala. Linebacker Jacksonville State 1979-1982. No pro playing experience. College coach: Appalachian State 1983, Minnesota 1984, Austin Peay 1985-86, Murray State 1987-88, East Carolina 1989, Nevada-Las Vegas 1990, Notre Dame 1991-92, Eastern Michigan 1993-94, Louisville 1995-97, Alabama A&M 1998-2001, Wisconsin 2002, Mississippi State 2003, South Carolina 2004-08, Louisiana State 2009-11. Pro coach: Joined Buccaneers in 2012.
Bryan Cox, defensive front seven; born February 17, 1968, East St. Louis, Ill. Linebacker Western Illinois 1987-1990. Pro linebacker Miami Dolphins 1991-95, Chicago Bears 1996-97, New York Jets 1998-2000, New England Patriots 2001, New Orleans Saints 2002. Pro coach: New York Jets 2006-08, Cleveland Browns 2009-2010, Miami Dolphins 2011, joined Buccaneers in 2012.
P.J. Fleck, wide receivers; born November 29, 1980, Sugar Grove, Ill. Wide receiver Northern Illinois 1999-2003. Pro wide receiver San Francisco 49ers 2004-05. College coach: Ohio State 2006, Northern Illinois 2007-09, Rutgers 2010-11. Pro coach: Joined Buccaneers in 2012.
Bob Fraser, linebackers; born January 18, 1963, Pittsburgh, Pa. Defensive lineman Allegheny 1981-84. No pro playing experience. College coach: Allegheny 1985-86, 1989-1991, 1997-2005, Rutgers 1987-88, 2006-2011, Holy Cross 1992-95, Northeastern 1996. Pro coach: Joined Buccaneers in 2012.
Phil Galiano, asst. special teams; born September 8, 1977, Norristown, Pa. Safety Shippensburg 1997-99. No pro playing experience. College coach: Dickinson 2000, New Haven 2001, Villanova 2002, Rutgers 2003-06, 2010-11, Florida International 2007-09. Pro coach: Joined Buccaneers in 2012.
Jeff Hafley, asst. defensive backs; born April 4, 1979, Montvale, N.J. Wide receiver Siena 1997-2000. No pro playing experience. College coach: Worcester Polytechnic 2001, Albany 2002-05, Pittsburgh 2006-2010, Rutgers 2011. Pro coach: Joined Buccaneers in 2012.
Bob Ligashesky, special teams coordinator; born June 2, 1962, Pittsburgh, Pa. Defensive back Indiana (Pa.) 1982-84. No pro playing experience. Pro coach: Jacksonville Jaguars 2004, St. Louis Rams 2005-06, Pittsburgh Steelers 2007-09, Denver Broncos 2010, Oakland Raiders 2011, joined Buccaneers in 2012.
Steve Loney, asst. offensive line; born April 26, 1952, Marshalltown, Iowa. Offensive lineman Iowa State 1970-73. No pro playing experience. College coach: Iowa State 1974, 1995-97, 2000-01, Missouri Western State 1975-76, Morehead State 1979-1983, The Citadel 1984-86, Colorado State 1989-1992, Connecticut 1994, Minnesota 1998-99, Drake 2007. Pro coach: Phoenix Cardinals 1993, Minnesota Vikings 2002-2005, Arizona Cardinals 2006, St. Louis Rams 2008-2011, joined Buccaneers in 2012.
Tem Lukabu, defensive assistant; born August 6, 1981, Avenel, N.J. Linebacker Colgate 2002-04. No pro playing experience. College coach: Rhode Island 2008-09, Rutgers 2010-11. Pro coach: Joined Buccaneers in 2012.
Ben McDaniels, offensive assistant; born June 6, 1980, Barberton, Ohio. Quarterback Kent State 1999-2001. No pro playing experience. College coach: Minnesota 2004-05. Pro coach: Denver Broncos 2009-2010, joined Buccaneers 2012.
Randy Melvin, defensive line; born April 3, 1959, Aurora, Ill. Defensive line Eastern Illinois 1978-1981. No pro playing experience. College coach: Eastern Illinois 1988-1994, Wyoming 1995-96, Purdue 1997-99, Rutgers 2002-04, 2010, Temple 2009. Pro coach: New England Patriots 2000-01, Cleveland Browns 2005-08, British Columbia Lions (CFL) 2011, joined Buccaneers in 2012.
Jimmy Raye, senior offensive assistant; born March 26, 1946, Fayetteville, N.C. Quarterback Michigan State 1965-67. Pro quarterback Philadelphia Eagles 1969. College coach: Michigan State 1971-75, Wyoming 1976. Pro coach: San Francisco 49ers 1977, 2009-2010, Detroit Lions 1978-79, Atlanta Falcons 1980-82, 1987-89, Los Angeles Rams 1983-84, 1991, Tampa Bay Buccaneers 1985-86, New England Patriots 1990, Kansas City Chiefs 1992-2000, Washington Redskins 2001, New York Jets 2002-03, 2006-08, Oakland Raiders 2004-05, re-joined Buccaneers in 2012.
Bill Sheridan, defensive coordinator; born January 27, 1959, Detroit, Mich. Linebacker Grand Valley State 1977-1981. No pro playing experience. College coach: Michigan 1985-86, 2002-04, Maine 1987-88, Cincinnati 1989-1991, Army 1992-97, Michigan State 1998-2000. Pro coach: New York Giants 2005-09, Miami Dolphins 2010-11, joined Buccaneers in 2012.
Mike Sullivan, offensive coordinator; born January 28, 1967, Santa Maria, Calif. Defensive back Army 1986-89. No pro playing experience. College coach: Humboldt State 1993-94, Army 1995-96, 1999-2000, Youngstown State 1997-98, Ohio 2001. Pro coach: Jacksonville Jaguars 2002-03, New York Giants 2004-2011, joined Buccaneers in 2012.
Ron Turner, quarterbacks; born December 5, 1953, Martinez, Calif. Wide receiver Pacific 1975-76. No pro playing experience. College coach: Pacific 1977, Arizona 1978-1980, Northwestern 1981-82, Pittsburgh 1983-84, Southern California 1985-87, Texas A&M 1988, Stanford 1989-1991, San Jose State 1992, Illinois 1997-2004, 2005-09. Pro coach: Chicago Bears 1993-96, 2005-09, Indianapolis Colts 2010-11, joined Buccaneers in 2012.
Joe Vaughn, asst. strength and conditioning; born November 14, 1982, Del City, Okla. Center Northeastern Oklahoma 2001-02, Kansas 2003-04. No pro playing experience. College coach: Kansas 2006, 2007-2011, Oklahoma 2007. Pro coach: Joined Buccaneers in 2012.

National Football Conference
East Division
Team Colors: Burgundy and Gold
Redskins Park
21300 Redskins Park Drive
Ashburn, Virginia 20147
Telephone: (703) 726-7000

2012 SCHEDULE
PRESEASON

Aug. 9	at Buffalo	7:00
Aug. 18	at Chicago	8:00
Aug. 25	**Indianapolis**	4:00
Aug. 29	**Tampa Bay**	7:30

REGULAR SEASON

Sep. 9	at New Orleans	1:00
Sep. 16	at St. Louis	4:05
Sep. 23	**Cincinnati**	1:00
Sep. 30	at Tampa Bay	4:15
Oct. 7	**Atlanta**	1:00
Oct. 14	**Minnesota**	4:15
Oct. 21	at New York Giants	1:00
Oct. 28	at Pittsburgh	1:00
Nov. 4	**Carolina**	1:00
Nov. 11	BYE	
Nov. 18	**Philadelphia**	1:00
Nov. 22	at Dallas (Thurs)	4:15
Dec. 3	**New York Giants** (Mon)	8:30
Dec. 9	**Baltimore**	1:00
Dec. 16	at Cleveland	1:00
Dec. 23	at Philadelphia	1:00
Dec. 30	**Dallas**	1:00

All times ET

Stadium: FedExField (opened in 1997)
  •**Capacity:** 85,000
  1600 FedEx Way
  Landover, Maryland 20785
Playing Surface: Natural Grass
Training Camp: Redskins Park
  Ashburn, Virginia 20147

FEDEXFIELD

CLUB OFFICIALS
Owner: Daniel M. Snyder
Executive Vice President/General
  Manager: Bruce Allen
Executive Vice President/Head Coach:
  Mike Shanahan
Chief Financial Officer: Nico Foris
Chief Marketing Officer: Mitch Gershman
Senior Vice President, Communications:
  Tony Wyllie
Senior Vice President, Stadium
  Operations: Lon Rosenberg
Executive Director, Washington Redskins
  Charitable Foundation: Brian Gaines
Director of Player Personnel:
  Scott Campbell
Director of Pro Personnel:
  Morocco Brown
Pro Scouts: Richard Mann II, Alex Santos
College Scouts: Tim Gribble, Kyle Smith,
  Cole Spencer, David Whittington,
  Jim Zeches
Vice President, Football Administration:
  Eric Schaffer
Director of Football Operations:
  Paul Kelly
Director of Player Development:
  Phillip Daniels
Video Director: Mike Bracken
Video Department: Zachary Kennedy,
  Mike Adams
Head Athletic Trainer: Larry Hess
Assistant Athletic Trainers: Elliott Jermyn,
  Eli Bisnett-Cobb, Kyle Blackman
Equipment Manager: Brad Berlin
Assistant Equipment Manager:
  Anders Beutel

COACHING HISTORY
Boston 1932-36
(575-544-27)
Records include postseason games

1932	Lud Wray	4-4-2
1933-34	William (Lone Star) Dietz	11-11-2
1935	Eddie Casey	2-8-1
1936-1942	Ray Flaherty	56-23-3
1943	Arthur (Dutch) Bergman	7-4-1
1944-45	Dudley DeGroot	14-6-1
1946-48	Glen (Turk) Edwards	16-18-1
1949	John Whelchel*	3-3-1
1949-1951	Herman Ball**	4-16-0
1951	Dick Todd	5-4-0
1952-53	Earl (Curly) Lambeau	10-13-1
1954-58	Joe Kuharich	26-32-2
1959-1960	Mike Nixon	4-18-2
1961-65	Bill McPeak	21-46-3
1966-68	Otto Graham	17-22-3
1969	Vince Lombardi	7-5-2
1970	Bill Austin	6-8-0
1971-77	George Allen	69-35-1
1978-1980	Jack Pardee	24-24-0
1981-1992	Joe Gibbs	140-65-0
1993	Richie Petitbon	4-12-0
1994-2000	Norv Turner***	50-60-1
2000	Terry Robiskie	1-2-0
2001	Marty Schottenheimer	8-8-0
2002-03	Steve Spurrier	12-20-0
2004-07	Joe Gibbs	31-36-0
2008-09	Jim Zorn	12-20-0
2010-11	Mike Shanahan	11-21-0

*Released after seven games in 1949
**Released after three games in 1951
***Released after 13 games in 2000

PAID ATTENDANCE
Home 587,354   Away 513,709
Total 1,101,063
Single-game home record,
  90,910 (12/30/07)
Single-season home record,
  * 711,471 (2007)
NFL Record

2012 DRAFT CHOICES

Round	Name	Pos.	College
1	Robert Griffin	QB	Baylor
3	Josh LeRibeus	G	Southern Methodist
4	Kirk Cousins	QB	Michigan St.
	Keenan Robinson	LB	Texas
5	Adam Gettis	G	Iowa
6	Alfred Morris	RB	Florida Atlantic
	Tom Compton	T	South Dakota
7	Richard Crawford	DB	Southern Methodist
	Jordan Bernstine	DB	Iowa

WASHINGTON REDSKINS

2011 TEAM RECORD
PRESEASON (3-1)
Date	Result		Opponent
8/12	W	16-7	Pittsburgh
8/19	W	16-3	at Indianapolis
8/25	L	31-34	at Baltimore
9/1	W	29-24	Tampa Bay

REGULAR SEASON (5-11)
Date	Result		Opponent
9/11	W	28-14	New York Giants
9/18	W	22-21	Arizona
9/26	L	16-18	at Dallas
10/2	W	17-10	at St. Louis
10/16	L	13-20	Philadelphia
10/23	L	20-33	at Carolina
10/30	L	0-23	at Buffalo
11/6	L	11-19	San Francisco
11/13	L	9-20	at Miami
11/20	L	24-27	Dallas (OT)
11/27	W	23-17	at Seattle
12/4	L	19-34	New York Jets
12/11	L	27-34	New England
12/18	W	23-10	at New York Giants
12/24	L	26-33	Minnesota
1/1	L	10-34	at Philadelphia
(OT) Overtime			

SCORE BY PERIODS
Redskins	43	103	60	82	0	—	288
Opponents	75	90	73	126	3	—	367

2011 TEAM STATISTICS
	Redskins	Opp.
Total First Downs	312	295
Rushing	79	95
Passing	204	180
Penalty	29	20
3rd Down: Made/Att	81/219	77/206
3rd Down Pct.	37.0	37.4
4th Down: Made/Att	4/13	4/10
4th Down Pct.	30.8	40.0
Possession Avg.	30:06	29:54
Total Net Yards	5387	5437
Avg. Per Game	336.7	339.8
Total Plays	1032	988
Avg. Per Play	5.2	5.5
Net Yards Rushing	1614	1884
Avg. Per Game	100.9	117.8
Total Rushes	400	438
Net Yards Passing	3773	3553
Avg. Per Game	235.8	222.1
Sacked/Yards Lost	41/285	41/251
Gross Yards	4058	3804
Att./Completions	591/346	509/308
Completion Pct.	58.5	60.5
Had Intercepted	24	13
Punts/Average	66/43.1	70/45.3
Net Punting Avg.	66/39.0	70/37.8
Penalties/Yards	91/897	123/1006
Fumbles/Ball Lost	25/11	26/8
Touchdowns	28	38
Rushing	8	15
Passing	19	22
Returns	1	1

2011 INDIVIDUAL STATISTICS
PASSING
	Att.	Comp.	Yds.	Pct.	TD	Int.	Tkld.	Rate
Grossman	458	265	3151	57.9	16	20	25/201	72.4
Beck	132	80	858	60.6	2	4	16/84	72.1
Banks	1	1	49	100.0	1	0	0/0	158.3
Redskins	591	346	4058	58.5	19	24	41/285	73.3
Opponents	509	308	3804	60.5	22	13	41/251	87.4

SCORING
	TD R	TD P	TD Rt	PAT	FG	Saf	PTS
Gano	0	0	0	25/26	31/41	0	118
Gaffney	0	5	0	0/0	0/0	0	30
Moss	0	4	0	0/0	0/0	0	24
F. Davis	0	3	0	0/0	0/0	0	18
Helu	2	1	0	0/0	0/0	0	18
Armstrong	0	2	0	0/0	0/0	0	12
Beck	2	0	0	0/0	0/0	0	12
Hightower	1	1	0	0/0	0/0	0	12
Stallworth	0	2	0	0/0	0/0	0	12
Anderson	0	1	0	0/0	0/0	0	6
Grossman	1	0	0	0/0	0/0	0	6
Kerrigan	0	0	1	0/0	0/0	0	6
Torain	1	0	0	0/0	0/0	0	6
Young	1	0	0	0/0	0/0	0	6
Hankerson	0	0	0	0/0	0/0	0	2
Redskins	8	19	1	25/26	31/41	0	288
Opponents	15	22	1	37/38	34/41	0	367

2-Pt Conversions: Hankerson
Redskins 1-2, Opponents 0-0

RUSHING
	No.	Yds	Avg	LG	TD
Helu	151	640	4.2	28t	2
Royster	56	328	5.9	28	0
Hightower	84	321	3.8	22	1
Torain	59	200	3.4	39	1
Beck	10	43	4.3	12	2
Young	6	33	5.5	12	1
Armstrong	2	19	9.5	14	0
Grossman	20	11	0.6	6	1
Choice	6	7	1.2	9	0
Paul	1	7	7.0	7	0
Cooley	2	3	1.5	3	0
Banks	1	1	1.0	1	0
Stallworth	2	1	0.5	2	0
Redskins	400	1614	4.0	39	8
Opponents	438	1884	4.3	67	15

RECEIVING
	No.	Yds	Avg	LG	TD
Gaffney	68	947	13.9	45	5
F. Davis	59	796	13.5	42	3
Helu	49	379	7.7	47t	1
Moss	46	584	12.7	49t	4
Stallworth	22	309	14.0	51	2
Young	15	146	9.7	27	0
Hankerson	13	163	12.5	23	0
Austin	12	137	11.4	32	0
Paulsen	11	138	12.5	24	0
Hightower	10	78	7.8	19	1
Royster	9	68	7.6	16	0
Cooley	8	65	8.1	17	0
Armstrong	7	103	14.7	50t	2
Anderson	6	70	11.7	23	1
Torain	6	23	3.8	7	0
Paul	2	25	12.5	14	0
Sellers	1	15	15.0	15	0
Banks	1	10	10.0	10	0
Choice	1	2	2.0	2	0
Redskins	346	4058	11.7	51	19
Opponents	308	3804	12.4	73t	22

INTERCEPTIONS
	No.	Yds	Avg	LG	TD
Hall	3	46	15.3	26	0
Atogwe	3	42	14.0	26	0
Barnes	2	30	15.0	30	0
Fletcher	2	0	0.0	0	0
Wilson	2	0	0.0	0	0
Kerrigan	1	9	9.0	9t	1
Redskins	13	127	9.8	30	1
Opponents	24	353	14.7	51	0

PUNTING
	No.	Yds.	Avg.	In 20	LG
Rocca	66	2842	43.1	28	63
Redskins	66	2842	43.1	28	63
Opponents	70	3172	45.3	20	67

PUNT RETURNS
	Ret	FC	Yds	Avg	LG	TD
Banks	36	9	328	9.1	55	0
Paul	1	0	0	0.0	0	0
Redskins	37	9	328	8.9	55	0
Opponents	32	21	250	7.8	30	0

KICKOFF RETURNS
	No.	Yds	Avg	LG	TD
Banks	51	1174	23.0	47	0
Paulsen	2	7	3.5	7	0
Armstrong	1	28	28.0	28	0
Paul	1	15	15.0	15	0
Sellers	1	15	15.0	15	0
Redskins	56	1239	22.1	47	0
Opponents	36	749	20.8	51	0

FIELD GOALS
	1-19	20-29	30-39	40-49	50+
Gano	0/0	14/15	5/9	8/11	4/6
Redskins	0/0	14/15	5/9	8/11	4/6
Opponents	0/0	12/12	9/10	11/16	2/3

SACKS
	No.
Orakpo	9.0
Kerrigan	7.5
Bowen	6.0
Carriker	5.5
Cofield	3.0
Neild	2.0
Fletcher	1.5
Golston	1.5
Landry	1.5
McIntosh	1.0
Riley	1.0
(group)	1.0
Atogwe	0.5
Redskins	41.0
Opponents	41.0

RECORD HOLDERS
INDIVIDUAL RECORDS—CAREER

Category	Name	Performance
Rushing (Yds.)	John Riggins, 1976-79, 1981-85	7,472
Passing (Yds.)	Joe Theismann, 1974-1985	25,206
Passing (TDs)	Sammy Baugh, 1937-1952	187
Receiving (No.)	Art Monk, 1980-1993	888
Receiving (Yds.)	Art Monk, 1980-1993	12,026
Interceptions	Darrell Green, 1983-2001	54
Punting (Avg.)	Sammy Baugh, 1937-1952	45.1
Punt Return (Avg.)	Johnny Williams, 1952-53	12.8
Kickoff Return (Avg.)	Bobby Mitchell, 1962-68	28.5
Field Goals	Mark Moseley, 1974-1986	263
Touchdowns (Tot.)	Charley Taylor, 1964-1977	90
Points	Mark Moseley, 1974-1986	1,206
*Sacks	Dexter Manley, 1981-89	91.0

INDIVIDUAL RECORDS—SINGLE SEASON

Category	Name	Performance
Rushing (Yds.)	Clinton Portis, 2005	1,516
Passing (Yds.)	Jay Schroeder, 1986	4,109
Passing (TDs)	Sonny Jurgensen, 1967	31
Receiving (No.)	Art Monk, 1984	106
Receiving (Yds.)	Santana Moss, 2005	1,483
Interceptions	Dan Sandifer, 1948	13
Punting (Avg.)	Sammy Baugh, 1940	**51.4
Punt Return (Avg.)	Johnny Williams, 1952	15.3
Kickoff Return (Avg.)	Mike Nelms, 1981	29.7
Field Goals	Mark Moseley, 1983	33
Touchdowns (Tot.)	John Riggins, 1983	24
Points	Mark Moseley, 1983	161
*Sacks	Dexter Manley, 1986	18.5

INDIVIDUAL RECORDS—SINGLE GAME

Category	Name	Performance
Rushing (Yds.)	Gerald Riggs, 9-17-89	221
Passing (Yds.)	Brad Johnson, 12-26-99	471
Passing (TDs)	Sammy Baugh, 10-31-43, 11-23-47	6
	Mark Rypien, 11-10-91	6
Receiving (No.)	Roy Helu, 11-6-11	14
Receiving (Yds.)	Anthony Allen, 10-4-87	255
Interceptions	Sammy Baugh, 11-14-43	**4
	Dan Sandifer, 10-31-48	**4
	DeAngelo Hall, 10-24-10	**4
Field Goals	Many times	5
	Last time by Shaun Suisham, 11-4-07	
Touchdowns (Tot.)	Dick James, 12-17-61	4
	Larry Brown, 12-16-73	4
Points	Dick James, 12-17-61	24
	Larry Brown, 12-16-73	24
*Sacks	Dexter Manley, 10-2-88	4.0
	Ken Harvey, 11-23-97	4.0
	Phillip Daniels, 12-18-05	4.0
	Brian Orakpo, 12-13-09	4.0

*Sacks became an official statistic in 1982.
**NFL Record

2012 VETERAN ROSTER

No.	Name	Pos.	Ht.	Wt.	Birthdate	NFL Exp.	College	Hometown	How Acq.	'11 Games/ Starts
97	Alexander, Lorenzo	LB	6-1	275	5/31/83	6	California	Berkeley, Calif.	FA-'07	16/0
#	Anderson, David	WR	5-10	193	7/28/83	7	Colorado State	Thousand Oaks, Calif.	FA-'11	6/0*
13	Armstrong, Anthony	WR	5-11	185	3/29/83	3	West Texas A&M	Carrollton, Texas	FA-'09	14/2
18	Austin, Terrence	WR	5-11	175	8/25/88	3	UCLA	Long Beach, Calif.	D7-'10	13/0
93	Balmer, Kentwan	DE	6-5	315	10/15/86	5	North Carolina	Ashoskie, N.C.	FA-'11	3/0
16	Banks, Brandon	WR	5-7	155	12/21/87	3	Kansas State	Garner, N.C.	FA-'10	16/0
22	Barnes, Kevin	CB	6-1	190	9/15/86	4	Maryland	Glen Burnie, Md.	D3-'09	14/0
72	Bowen, Stephen	DL	6-5	306	3/28/84	7	Hofstra	Dix, N.Y.	UFA(Dall)-'11	16/16
77	Brown, Jammal	T	6-6	313	3/30/81	8	Oklahoma	Waxahachie, Texas	T(NO)-'10	12/12
#	Buchanon, Phillip	DB	5-11	190	9/19/80	11	Miami	Ft. Myers, Fla.	FA-'10	1/0
94	Carriker, Adam	DL	6-6	315	5/6/84	6	Nebraska	Kennewick, Wash.	T(StL)-'10	16/16
66	Chester, Chris	OL	6-3	315	1/12/83	7	Oklahoma	Tustin, Calif.	UFA(Balt)-'11	16/16
96	Cofield, Barry	DL	6-4	306	3/19/84	7	Northwestern	Cleveland Heights, Ohio	UFA(NYG)-'11	16/16
58	Cook, Erik	OL	6-6	320	7/5/87	2	New Mexico	Albuquerque, N.M.	D7-'10	7/2
47	Cooley, Chris	TE	6-3	255	7/11/82	9	Utah State	Logan, Utah	D3-'04	5/5
83	Davis, Fred	TE	6-4	258	1/15/86	5	Southern California	Toledo, Ohio	D2-'08	12/12
37	Doughty, Reed	S	6-1	210	11/4/82	7	Northern Colorado	Johnstown, Colo.	D6-'06	16/11
59	Fletcher, London	LB	5-10	245	5/19/75	15	John Carroll	Cleveland, Ohio	UFA(Buff)-'07	16/16
#	Fox, Keyaron	LB	6-3	235	1/24/82	9	Georgia Tech	Atlanta, Ga.	FA-'11	13/0
4	Gano, Graham	K	6-2	200	4/9/87	3	Florida State	Cantonment, Fla.	FA-'09	16/0
88	Garçon, Pierre	WR	6-0	210	8/8/86	5	Mount Union	Greenacres, Fla.	UFA(Ind)-'12	16/16*
54	Goff, Jonathan	LB	6-2	241	12/12/85	5	Vanderbilt	Danvers, Mass.	UFA(NYG)-'12	0*
64	Golston, Kedric	DL	6-4	310	5/30/83	7	Georgia	Tyrone, Ga.	D6-'06	9/0
24	Gomes, DeJon	FS	6-0	208	11/17/89	2	Nebraska	Union City, Calif.	D5-'11	15/5
20	Griffin, Cedric	CB	6-0	203	11/11/82	7	Texas	San Antonio, Texas	UFA(Minn)-'12	16/14*
8	Grossman, Rex	QB	6-1	225	8/23/80	10	Florida	Bloomington, Ind.	UFA(Hous)-'10	13/13
23	Hall, DeAngelo	CB	5-10	195	11/19/83	9	Virginia Tech	Chesapeake, Va.	FA-'08	16/16
85	Hankerson, Leonard	WR	6-2	205	1/30/89	2	Miami	Fort Lauderdale, Fla.	D3-'11	4/2
29	Helu, Roy	RB	5-11	216	12/7/88	2	Nebraska	Danville, Calif.	D4-'11	15/5
25	Hightower, Tim	RB	6-0	222	5/23/86	5	Richmond	Alexandria, Va.	T(Ariz)-'11	5/5
79	Hurt, Maurice	G	6-3	320	11/8/87	2	Florida	Milledgeville, Ga.	D7-'11	8/8
50	Jackson, Rob	LB	6-4	255	11/3/85	4	Kansas State	West Haven, Conn.	D7-'08	16/0
34	Jackson, Tanard	S	6-0	200	7/21/85	5	Syracuse	Potomac, Md.	FA-'12	10/10*
99	Jenkins, Jarvis	DE	6-4	304	4/24/88	2	Clemson	Central, S.C.	D2-'11	0*
53	Kehl, Bryan	LB	6-2	244	6/16/84	5	Brigham Young	Cottonwood Heights, Utah	UFA(StL)-'12	14/1*
91	Kerrigan, Ryan	LB	6-4	263	8/16/88	2	Purdue	Muncie, Ind.	D1-'11	16/16
75	Lee, James	T	6-4	305	8/17/85	5	South Carolina State	Belle Glade, Fla.	UFA(TB)-'12	3/1*
78	Lichtensteiger, Kory	G/C	6-2	292	3/22/85	4	Bowling Green	Convoy, Ohio	FA-'10	5/5
#	McIntosh, Rocky	LB	6-2	242	11/15/82	7	Miami	Gaffney, S.C.	D2-'06	15/8
31	Meriweather, Brandon	S	5-11	200	1/14/84	6	Miami	Apopka, Fla.	UFA(Chi)-'12	11/4*
63	Montgomery, Will	OL	6-3	310	2/13/83	7	Virginia Tech	Clifton, Va.	FA-'08	16/16
15	Morgan, Joshua	WR	6-1	215	6/20/85	5	Virginia Tech	Washington, D.C.	UFA(SF)-'12	5/5*
89	Moss, Santana	WR	5-10	205	6/1/79	12	Miami	Carol City, Fla.	T(NYJ)-'05	12/12
95	Neild, Chris	NT	6-2	313	12/1/87	2	West Virginia	Stroudsburg, Pa.	D7-'11	16/0
98	Orakpo, Brian	LB	6-4	260	7/31/86	4	Texas	Houston, Texas	D1-'09	16/16
84	Paul, Niles	TE	6-1	235	8/9/89	2	Nebraska	Omaha, Neb.	D5-'11	13/2
82	Paulsen, Logan	TE	6-5	268	2/26/87	3	UCLA	West Hills, Calif.	FA-'10	16/6
74	Polumbus, Tyler	T	6-8	300	4/10/85	4	Colorado	Englewood, Colo.	FA-'11	5/4
80	Quinn, Richard	TE	6-4	258	9/6/86	3	North Carolina	Maple Heights, Ohio	FA-'11	1/0
1	Rackers, Neil	K	6-1	202	8/16/76	13	Illinois	St. Louis, Mo.	UFA(Hou)-'12	16/0*
56	Riley, Perry	LB	6-0	242	5/3/88	3	Louisiana State	Stone Mountain, Ga.	D4-'10	16/8
6	Rocca, Sav	P	6-5	265	11/20/73	6	Lakeside	Reservoir, Australia	UFA(Phil)-'11	16/0
35	Royster, Evan	RB	6-0	213	11/26/87	2	Penn State	Chantilly, Va.	D6-'11	6/2
76	Scott, Darrion	DL	6-3	310	10/25/81	6	Ohio State	Charleston, W.Va.	FA-'10	7/0
69	Smith, Willie	OL	6-6	290	11/13/86	2	East Carolina	Smithfield, N.C.	FA-'11	4/3
57	Sundberg, Nick	LS	6-0	250	7/29/87	3	California	Phoenix, Ariz.	FA-'10	16/0
32	Thompson, Brandyn	CB	5-10	177	10/30/89	2	Boise State	Elk Grove, Calif.	D7-'11	6/0
30	Torrence, Leigh	CB	5-11	179	1/4/82	7	Stanford	Atlanta, Ga.	UFA(NO)-'11	13/0*
55	White, Markus	LB	6-4	262	11/25/87	2	Florida State	West Palm Beach, Fla.	D7-'11	2/0
41	Williams, Madieu	S	6-1	203	10/18/81	9	Maryland	Lanham, Md.	UFA(SF)-'12	15/3*
71	Williams, Trent	T	6-5	318	7/19/88	3	Oklahoma	Longview, Texas	D1-'10	10/10
51	Wilson, Chris	LB	6-4	247	7/10/82	5	Northwood	Flint, Mich.	FA-'12	0*
26	Wilson, Josh	CB	5-9	192	3/11/85	6	Maryland	Upper Marlboro, Md.	UFA(Balt)-'11	16/16
36	Young, Darrel	FB	5-11	246	4/8/87	3	Villanova	Amityville, N.Y.	FA-'10	13/8

* Anderson played 2 games with Houston and 4 games with Washington in '11; Garçon played 16 games with Indianapolis; Goff missed '11 season with New York Giants because of injury; Griffin played 16 games with Minnesota; T. Jackson played 10 games with Tampa Bay; Kehl played 14 games with St. Louis; Lee played 3 games with Tampa Bay; Meriweather played 11 games with Chicago; Morgan played 5 games with San Francisco; Rackers played 16 games with Houston; Torrence played 13 games with New Orleans; M. Williams played 15 games with San Francisco; Wilson last active with Washington in '10.

\# Unrestricted free agent; subject to developments.

Players lost through free agency (3): S LaRon Landry (NYJ; 8 games in '11), T Sean Locklear (NYG; 9), WR Donté Stallworth (NE; 11).

Also played with Redskins in '11—S Oshiomogho Atogwe (13 games), QB John Beck (4), TE Dominique Byrd (2), RB Tashard Choice (1), WR Jabar Gaffney (16), FB/TE Mike Sellers (12), RB Ryan Torain (8), DB Byron Westbrook (15).

FIRST-YEAR ROSTER

Name	Pos.	Ht.	Wt.	Birthdate	College	Hometown	How Acq.
Baker, Chris (1)	DL	6-2	329	10/8/87	Hampton	Windsor, Conn.	FA-'11
Bellamy, Travon (1)	DB	5-11	205	1/11/88	Illinois	Greenbelt, Md.	FA-'11
Bernstine, Jordan	S	5-11	205	5/31/89	Iowa	Des Moines, Iowa	D7b
Compton, Tom	T	6-5	314	5/10/89	South Dakota	Rosemount, Minn.	D6b
Cousins, Kirk	QB	6-3	214	8/19/88	Michigan State	Holland, Mich.	D4a
Crawford, Richard	CB	5-11	191	8/1/90	Southern Methodist	Oceanside, Calif.	D7a
Crompton, Jonathan (1)	QB	6-3	222	7/25/87	Tennessee	Waynesville, N.C.	FA-'11
Davis, Tristan (1)	RB	5-10	212	5/5/86	Auburn	East Point, Ga.	FA-'11
Gettis, Adam	G	6-2	293	12/9/88	Iowa	Frankfort, Ill.	D5
Griffin III, Robert	QB	6-2	223	2/12/90	Baylor	Copperas Cove, Texas	D1
LeRibeus, Josh	G	6-2	312	7/2/89	Southern Methodist	Richardson, Texas	D3
McCaskill, Nevin (1)	OL	6-3	309	12/29/83	Hampton	Tallahassee, Fla.	FA
Morris, Alfred	RB	5-10	219	12/12/88	Florida Atlantic	Pensacola, Fla.	D6a
Robinson, Aldrick (1)	WR	5-10	178	11/24/88	Southern Methodist	Waxahachie, Texas	D6-'11
Robinson, Keenan	LB	6-3	242	7/7/89	Texas	Plano, Texas	D4b
Worthington, Doug (1)	DE	6-5	292	8/10/87	Ohio State	Athol Springs, N.Y.	W(TB)-'11

The term NFL Rookie is defined as a player who is in his first season of professional football and has not been on the roster of another professional football team for any regular-season or postseason games. A Rookie is designated by an "R" on NFL rosters. Players who have been active in another professional football league or players who have NFL experience, including either preseason training camp or being on an Active List or Inactive List, or on Reserve/Injured or Reserve/Physically Unable to Perform for fewer than six regular-season games, are termed NFL First-Year Players. An NFL First-Year Player is designated by a "1" on NFL rosters. Thereafter, a player is credited with an additional year of experience for each season in which he accumulates six games on the Active List or Inactive List, or on Reserve/Injured or Reserve/Physically Unable to Perform.

Log on to www.redskins.com for an up-to-date roster.

COACHING STAFF

Head Coach,
Mike Shanahan

Pro Career: Became the 28th coach in franchise history when he replaced Jim Zorn on January 6, 2010. Mike Shanahan joined the Redskins after spending 14 seasons as head coach of the Denver Broncos (1995-2008). Shanahan led the Broncos to back-to-back Super Bowl championships in 1997 and 1998, becoming just the fifth head coach to accomplish that feat, and is the only coach to win seven consecutive postseason games in a two-year period. During his NFL career, Shanahan has been a part of teams that have played in nine conference championship games and six Super Bowls. In 31 seasons as a pro and college coach, Shanahan's teams have participated in postseason or bowl games 22 times. Under Shanahan's guidance, Denver set then-NFL records by posting the most victories in both a two-year (33, 1997-98) and three-year (46, 1996-98) span. In 17 years (14 with Denver and three as offensive coordinator with the San Francisco 49ers), Shanahan's offenses finished number one in the NFL four times, second three times and third twice. Shanahan was an assistant with Denver (1984-87, 1989-1991) and San Francisco (1992-94). Returned to Denver as quarterbacks coach on October 6, 1989, after posting 8-12 record as the Los Angeles Raiders' head coach. Career record: 165-124.

Background: Shanahan coached at Oklahoma (1975-76), Northern Arizona (1977), Eastern Illinois (1978), Minnesota (1979), and Florida (1980-83).

Personal: Born in Oak Park, Illinois, on August 24, 1952. He was a wishbone quarterback/defensive back at Eastern Illinois. Mike and his wife, Peggy, have two children—Kyle and Krystal.

ASSISTANT COACHES

Jacob Burney, defensive line; born January 24, 1959, Chattanooga, Tenn. Defensive tackle Tennessee-Chattanooga 1977-1980. No pro playing experience. College coach: New Mexico 1983-86, Tulsa 1987, Mississippi State 1988, Wisconsin 1989, UCLA 1990-92, Tennessee 1993. Pro coach: Cleveland Browns/Baltimore Ravens 1994-98, Carolina Panthers 1999-2001, Denver Broncos 2002-08, joined Redskins in 2010.

Chad Englehart, asst. strength and conditioning; born June 5, 1981, New Orleans, La. Attended Southeastern Louisiana. No college or pro playing experience. College coach: New Orleans 2006. Pro coach: Florida Tuskers (UFL) 2009, joined Redskins in 2010.

Richmond Flowers, coaching assistant; born May 4, 1978, Birmingham, Ala. Wide receiver Duke 1996, 1998-99,

Tennessee-Chattanooga 2000. Pro wide receiver Dallas Cowboys 2001, Washington Redskins 2002. Pro coach: joined Redskins in 2010.

Chris Foerster, offensive line; born October 12, 1961, Milwaukee, Wisc. Center Colorado State 1979-1982. No pro playing experience. College coach: Colorado State 1983-87, Stanford 1988-1991, Minnesota 1992. Pro coach: Minnesota Vikings 1993-95, Tampa Bay Buccaneers 1996-2001, Indianapolis Colts 2002-03, Miami Dolphins 2004, Baltimore Ravens 2005-07, San Francisco 49ers 2008-09, joined Redskins in 2010.

Jim Haslett, defensive coordinator; born December 9, 1955, Pittsburgh, Pa. Defensive end Indiana (Pa.) 1975-78. Pro linebacker Buffalo Bills 1979-1986, N.Y. Jets 1987. College coach: Buffalo 1988-1990. Pro coach: Sacramento Surge (NFLE) 1991-92, Los Angeles Raiders 1993-94, New Orleans Saints 1995-96, Pittsburgh Steelers 1997-99, New Orleans Saints 2000-05 (head coach), St. Louis Rams 2006-08 (head coach 2008), Florida Tuskers (UFL head coach 2009), joined Redskins in 2010.

Richard Hightower, special teams assistant; born September 15, 1980, Houston, Texas. Wide receiver/defensive back Texas 1998-2002. No pro playing experience. College coach: Minnesota 2009. Pro coach: Houston Texans 2006-08, joined Redskins in 2010.

Ike Hilliard, wide receivers; born April 5, 1976, Patterson, La. Wide receiver Florida 1994-96. Pro wide receiver New York Giants 1997-2004, Tampa Bay Buccaneers 2005-08. Pro coach: Florida Tuskers (UFL) 2009-2010, Miami Dolphins 2011, joined Redskins in 2012.

Matt LaFleur, quarterbacks; born November 3, 1979, Mt. Pleasant, Mich. Quarterback/wide receiver Western Michigan 1998-99, Saginaw Valley State 2000-02. Pro quarterback Omaha Beef (NIFL) 2002, Billings Outlaws (NIFL) 2002. College coach: Saginaw Valley State 2003, Central Michigan 2004-05, Northern Michigan 2006, Ashland 2007. Pro coach: Houston Texans 2008-09, joined Redskins in 2010.

Mike McDaniel, offensive assistant; born March 6, 1983, Greeley, Colo. Wide receiver Yale 2001-04. No pro playing experience. Pro coach: Houston Texans 2006-08, California Redwoods (UFL) 2009, Sacramento Mountain Lions (UFL) 2010, joined Redskins in 2011.

Sean McVay, tight ends; born January 24, 1986, Marietta, Ga. Wide receiver Miami (Ohio) 2004-07. No pro playing experience. Pro coach: Tampa Bay Buccaneers 2008, Florida Tuskers (UFL) 2009, joined Redskins in 2010.

Chris Morgan, asst. offensive line; born September 24 1976, Killeen, Texas. Offensive lineman Colorado 1996-99. No

pro playing experience. College coach: Idaho 2003. Pro coach: Oakland Raiders 2009-2010, joined Redskins in 2011.

Raheem Morris, defensive backs; born September 3, 1976, Irvington, N.J. Safety Hofstra 1994-97. No pro playing experience. College coach: Hofstra 1998, 2000-01, Cornell 1999, Kansas State 2006. Pro coach: Tampa Bay Buccaneers 2002-05, 2007-2011 (head coach 2009-2011), joined Redskins in 2012.

Kyle Shanahan, offensive coordinator; born December 14, 1979, Minneapolis,. Minn. Wide receiver Duke 1998-99, Texas 2000-02. No pro playing experience. College coach: UCLA 2003. Pro coach: Tampa Bay Buccaneers 2004-05, Houston Texans 2006-09, joined Redskins in 2010.

Bob Slowik, linebackers; born May 16, 1954, Pittsburgh, Pa. Defensive back Delaware 1973-76. No pro playing experience. College coach: Delaware 1978, Florida 1979-1982, Drake 1983, Rutgers 1984-89, East Carolina 1990-91. Pro coach: Dallas Cowboys 1992, Chicago Bears 1993-98, Cleveland Browns 1999, Green Bay Packers 2000-04, Denver Broncos 2005-2008, joined Redskins 2010.

Bobby Slowik, defensive assistant; born June 7, 1987, Princeton, N.J. Wide receiver Michigan Tech 2005-09. No pro playing experience. Pro coach: Joined Redskins in 2011.

Danny Smith, special teams; born September 7, 1953, Pittsburgh, Pa. Defensive back Edinboro State 1972-75. No pro playing experience. College coach: Edinboro State 1976, Clemson 1979, William & Mary 1980-83, Citadel 1984-86, Georgia Tech 1987-1994. Pro coach: Philadelphia Eagles 1995-98, Detroit Lions 1999-2000, Buffalo Bills 2001-03, joined Redskins in 2004.

Bobby Turner, asst. head coach/running backs; born May 6, 1949, East Chicago, Ind. Defensive back Indiana State 1968-1971. No pro playing experience. College coach: Indiana State 1975-1982, Fresno State 1983-88, Ohio State 1989-1990, Purdue 1991-94. Pro coach: Denver Broncos 1995-2009, joined Redskins in 2010.

Ray Wright, strength and conditioning; born December 30, 1971, Fort Worth, Texas. Running back/wide receiver Duke 1990-95. No pro playing experience. College coach: Cornell 2000, Maryland 2001. Pro coach: Houston Texans 2002-09, joined Washington in 2010.

2011 Season in Review

2011 TRADES (since May 1)

Wide receiver **Jabar Gaffney** from Denver to Washington for defensive tackle **Jeremy Jarmon**. (7/27)

Quarterback **Donovan McNabb** from Washington to Minnesota for an unannounced future selection. (7/28)

Running back **Reggie Bush** and an unannounced future selection from New Orleans to Miami for defensive back **Jonathon Amaya** and an unannounced future selection. (7/28)

Tight end **Greg Olsen** from Chicago to Carolina for an unannounced future selection. (7/29)

Quarterback **Kevin Kolb** from Philadelphia to Arizona for defensive back **Dominique Rodgers-Cromartie** and an unannounced future selection. (7/29)

Nose tackle **Albert Haynesworth** from Washington to New England for an unannounced future selection. (7/29)

Wide receiver **Chad Ochocinco** from Cincinnati to New England for an unannounced future selection. (7/29)

Defensive tackle **Brodrick Bunkley** from Philadelphia to Cleveland for an unannounced selection. (7/31) (On August 1, 2011, Bunkley reverted to the Eagles and the selection choice reverted to the Browns pursuant to the terms of the trade agreement.)

Guard **John Greco** from St. Louis to Cleveland for an unannounced selection. (7/31)

Running back **Tim Hightower** from Arizona to Washington for defensive tackle **Vonnie Holliday** and an unannounced selection. (8/1)

Linebacker **Brodrick Bunkley** from Philadelphia to Denver for an unannounced selection. (8/2)

Wide receiver **Lee Evans** from Buffalo to Baltimore for an unannounced selection. (8/12)

Defensive back **Taylor Mays** from San Francisco to Cincinnati for an unannounced future selection. (8/23)

Defensive back **Kelly Jennings** from Seattle to Cincinnati for defensive tackle **Clinton McDonald**. (8/29)

Running back **Quinn Johnson** from Green Bay to Tennessee for an unannounced selection. (9/3)

Defensive back **Dwight Lowery** from New York Jets to Jacksonville for an unannounced future selection. (9/3)

Guard **Caleb Schlauderaff** from Green Bay to the New York Jets for an unannounced future selection. (9/3)

Wide receiver **Derrick Mason** from the New York Jets to Houston for an unannounced future selection. (10/12)

Linebacker **Aaron Curry** from Seattle to Oakland for an unannounced future selection. (10/14)

Wide receiver **Brandon Lloyd** from Denver to St. Louis for an unannounced future selection. (10/17)

Quarterback **Carson Palmer** from Cincinnati to Oakland for an unannounced future selection. (10/18)

Running back **Ronnie Brown** from Philadelphia to Detroit for running back **Jerome Harrison** and an unannounced future selection. (10/18) (On October 20, 2011, Brown reverted to the Eagles and Harrison and the selection choice reverted to the Lions pursuant to the terms of the trade agreement.)

* Draft choice number is listed if club later traded the pick.

2012 TRADES

Wide receiver **Brandon Marshall** from Miami to Chicago for Dolphins' 2012 third-round selection (#73) and an unannounced future selection. (3/14)

St. Louis trades Rams' 2012 first-round selection (QB **Robert Griffin III**) to Washington for Redskins' 2012 first-round selection (#6), 2012 second-round selection (DB **Janoris Jenkins**), and an unannounced future selection. (3/14)

Tackle **Winston Justice** and Eagles' 2012 sixth-round selection (#187) from Philadelphia to Indianapolis for the Colts' 2012 sixth-round selection (#172). (3/14)

Linebacker **DeMeco Ryans** and Texans' 2012 third-round selection (QB **Nick Foles**) from Houston to Philadelphia for the Eagles' 2012 third-round selection (G **Brandon Brooks**) and the Buccaneers' 2012 fourth-round selection (C **Ben Jones**). (3/21)

Quarterback **Tim Tebow** and Broncos' 2012 seventh-round selection (#232) from Denver to the New York Jets for the Jets' 2012 fourth-round selection (C **Philip Blake**) and 2012 sixth-round selection (LB **Danny Trevathan**). (3/26)

Quarterback **Drew Stanton** and the Jaguars' 2012 seventh-round selection (LB **Tim Fugger**) from the New York Jets to Indianapolis for Eagles' 2012 sixth-round selection (DB **Josh Bush**). (3/26)

Running back **Mike Goodson** from Carolina to Oakland for tackle **Bruce Campbell**. (3/30)

Linebacker **Keith Rivers** from Cincinnati to the New York Giants for Giants'

2012 fifth-round selection (DB **George Iloka**). (4/12)

Cornerback Asante Samuel from Philadelphia to Atlanta for Falcons' 2012 seventh-round selection (RB **Bryce Brown**). (4/26)

Minnesota trades Vikings' 2012 first-round selection (RB **Trent Richardson**) from Minnesota to Cleveland for Browns' 2012 first-round selection (T **Matt Kalil**), Falcons' 2012 first-round selection (WR **Jarius Wright**), Browns' 2012 fifth-round selection (DB **Robert Blanton**), and Browns' seventh-round selection (#211). (4/26)

Jacksonville trades Jaguars' 2012 first-round selection (DB **Mark Barron**) and the Jaguars' 2012 fourth-round selection (#101) from Jacksonville to Tampa Bay for Buccaneers' 2012 first-round selection (WR **Justin Blackmon**). (4/26)

Dallas trades Cowboys' 2012 first-round selection (DT **Michael Brockers**) and 2012 second-round selection (#45) from Dallas to St. Louis for Redskins' 2012 first-round selection (DB **Morris Claiborne**). (4/26)

Philadelphia trades Eagles' 2012 first-round selection (DE **Bruce Irvin**), 2012 fourth-round selection (DT **Jaye Howard**), 2012 Colts' sixth-round selection (DB **Jeremy Lane**) from Philadelphia to Seattle for Seahawks' 2012 first-round selection (DT **Fletcher Cox**). (4/26)

Cincinnati trades Bengals' 2012 first-round selection (DE **Chandler Jones**) from Cincinnati to New England for Saints' 2012 first-round selection (G **Kevin Zeitler**) and 2012 third-round selection (DT **Brandon Thompson**). (4/26)

Denver trades Broncos' 2012 first-round selection (LB **Dont'a Hightower**) from Denver to New England for Patriots' 2012 first-round selection (#31) and Patriots' 2012 fourth-round selection (#126). (4/26)

Baltimore trades Ravens' 2012 first-round selection (DB **Harrison Smith**) from Baltimore to Minnesota for Vikings' 2012 second-round selection (LB **Courtney Upshaw**) and Vikings' 2012 fourth-round selection (G **Gino Gradkowski**). (4/26)

Denver trades Patriots' 2012 first-round selection (RB **Doug Martin**) and Patriots' 2012 fourth-round selection (#126) from Denver to Tampa Bay for Buccaneers' 2012 second-round selection (DT **Derek Wolfe**) and Jaguars'

2012 fourth-round selection (DB **Omar Bolden**). (4/26)

Seattle trades Seahawks' 2012 second-round selection (WR **Stephen Hill**) from Seattle to the New York Jets for Jets' 2012 second-round selection (LB **Bobby Wagner**), the Jets' 2012 fifth-round selection (LB **Korey Toomer**), and Broncos' 2012 seventh-round selection (DE **Greg Scruggs**). (4/27)

St. Louis trades Cowboys' 2012 second-round selection (WR **Alshon Jeffery**) from St. Louis to Chicago for Bears' 2012 second-round selection (RB **Isaiah Pead**) and Bears' 2012 fifth-round selection (G **Rokevious Watkins**). (4/27)

Philadelphia trades Cardinals' 2012 second-round selection (DE **Jerel Worthy**) from Philadelphia to Green Bay for Packers' 2012 second-round selection (DE **Vinny Curry**) and Packers' 2012 fourth-round selection (DB **Brandon Boykin**). (4/27)

Houston trades Texans' 2012 second-round selection (LB **Lavonte David**) and Texans' 2012 seventh-round selection (TE **Drake Dunsmore**) from Houston to Tampa Bay for Buccaneers' 2012 third-round selection (WR **DeVier Posey**) and Patriots' 2012 fourth-round selection (DE **Jared Crick**). (4/27)

New England trades Patriots' 2012 second-round selection (DB **Casey Hayward**) from New England to Green Bay for Packers' 2012 third-round selection (DE **Jake Bequette**) and Packers' 2012 fifth-round selection (#163). (4/27)

Cleveland trades Browns' 2012 third-round selection (#71) from Cleveland to Denver for Broncos' 2012 third-round selection (DT **John Hughes**) and Broncos' 2012 fourth-round selection (LB **James-Michael Johnson**). (4/27)

Washington trades Redskins' 2012 third-round selection (WR **T.J. Graham**) from Washington to Buffalo for Bills' 2012 third-round selection (G **Josh LeRibeus**) and Patriots' 2012 seventh-round selection (DB **Jordan Bernstine**). (4/27)

Miami trades Panthers' 2012 third-round selection (DB **Brandon Taylor**) from Miami to San Diego for Chargers' 2012 third-round selection (TE **Michael Egnew**) and Chargers' 2012 sixth-round selection (WR **B.J. Cunningham**). (4/27)

Atlanta trades Falcons' 2012 third-round selection (RB **Bernard Pierce**) from Atlanta to Baltimore for Ravens' 2012 third-round selection (T **Lamar Holmes**) and Ravens' 2012 fifth-round selection (DE **Jonathan Massaquoi**). (4/27)

San Francisco trades 49ers' 2012 third-round selection (WR **T.Y. Hilton**) from San Francisco to Indianapolis for Colts' 2012 fourth-round selection (#97) and Colts' 2013 fifth-round selection. (4/27)

San Francisco trades Colts' 2012 fourth-round selection (RB **Lamar Miller**) from San Francisco to Miami for Dolphins' 2012 fourth-round selection (#103), the Saints' 2012 sixth-round selection (#196) and Dolphins' 2013 sixth-round selection. (4/28)

San Francisco trades Dolphins' 2012 fourth-round selection (DE **Frank Alexander**) from San Francisco to Carolina for Panthers' 2012 sixth-round selection (DB **Trenton Robinson**) and Panthers' 2013 third-round selection. (4/28)

Washington trades Raiders' 2012 fourth-round selection (DT **Alameda Ta'amu**) from Washington to Pittsburgh for Steelers' 2012 fourth-round selection (LB **Keenan Robinson**) and Steelers' 2012 sixth-round selection (T **Tom Compton**). (4/28)

Detroit trades Lions' 2012 fourth-round selection (G **Joe Looney**) from Detroit to San Francisco for 49ers' 2012 fourth-round selection (DE **Ronnell Lewis**) and Saints' 2012 sixth-round selection (DB **Jonte Green**). (4/28)

Detroit trades Seahawks' 2012 seventh-round selection (#219) and the Lions' 2013 fourth-round selection from Detroit to Minnesota for Vikings' 2012 fifth-round selection (LB **Tahir Whitehead**) and Eagles' 2012 seventh-round selection (LB **Travis Lewis**). (4/28)

Miami trades Dolphins' 2012 fifth-round selection (TE **Taylor Thompson**) from Miami to Tennessee for Titans' 2012 fifth-round selection (LB **Josh Kaddu**) and Titans' 2012 seventh-round selection (WR **Rishard Matthews**). (4/28)

Oakland trades Raiders' 2012 fifth-round selection (#148) from Oakland to Detroit for Lions' 2012 fifth-round selection (DE **Jack Crawford**) and Lions' 2012 seventh-round selection (LB **Nathan Stupar**). (4/28)

New England trades Packers' 2012 fifth-round selection (LB **Terrell Manning**) from New England to Green Bay for Packers' 2012 sixth-round selection (DB **Nate Ebner**), the Jets' 2012 seventh-round selection (DB **Alfonzo Dennard**) and Packers' 2012 seventh-round selection (WR **Jeremy Ebert**). (4/28)

Minnesota trades Browns' 2012 seventh-round selection (DE **Scott Solomon**) from Minnesota to Tennessee for Titans' 2013 sixth-round selection. (4/28)

* Draft choice number is listed if club later traded the pick.

PRESEASON STANDINGS
AMERICAN FOOTBALL CONFERENCE
East Division

	W	L	T	Pct.	Pts.	OP
Miami	3	1	0	.750	78	53
New England	2	2	0	.500	105	78
New York Jets	2	2	0	.500	74	54
Buffalo	1	3	0	.250	54	82

North Division

	W	L	T	Pct.	Pts.	OP
Baltimore	3	1	0	.750	92	64
Pittsburgh	3	1	0	.750	98	63
Cincinnati	1	3	0	.250	47	91
Cleveland	1	3	0	.250	83	95

South Division

	W	L	T	Pct.	Pts.	OP
Houston	3	1	0	.750	77	65
Tennessee	3	1	0	.750	76	42
Indianapolis	1	3	0	.250	51	86
Jacksonville	1	3	0	.250	76	119

West Division

	W	L	T	Pct.	Pts.	OP
Denver	2	2	0	.500	77	80
San Diego	2	2	0	.500	88	82
Kansas City	0	4	0	.000	42	90
Oakland	0	4	0	.000	44	101

AFC PRESEASON RECORDS—TEAM BY TEAM

East Division

BUFFALO (1-3)

3	at Chicago	10
10	at Denver	24
35	Jacksonville (OT)	32
6	Detroit	16
54		82

MIAMI (3-1)

28	at Atlanta	23
20	Carolina	10
13	at Tampa Bay	17
17	Dallas	3
78		53

NEW ENGLAND (2-2)

47	Jacksonville	12
31	at Tampa Bay	14
10	at Detroit	34
17	New York Giants	18
105		78

NEW YORK JETS (2-2)

16	at Houston	20
27	Cincinnati	7
17	at New York Giants	3
14	Philadelphia	24
74		54

North Division

BALTIMORE (3-1)

6	at Philadelphia	13
31	Kansas City	13
34	Washington	31
21	at Atlanta	7
92		64

CINCINNATI (1-3)

3	at Detroit	34
7	at New York Jets	27
24	Carolina	13
13	Indianapolis	17
47		91

CLEVELAND (1-3)

27	Green Bay	17
28	Detroit	30
14	at Philadelphia	24
14	at Chicago	24
83		95

PITTSBURGH (3-1)

7	at Washington	16
24	Philadelphia	14
34	Atlanta	16
33	at Carolina	17
98		63

South Division

HOUSTON (3-1)

20	New York Jets	16
27	New Orleans	14
30	at San Francisco	7
0	at Minnesota	28
77		65

INDIANAPOLIS (1-3)

10	at St. Louis	33
3	Washington	16
21	Green Bay	24
17	at Cincinnati	13
51		86

JACKSONVILLE (1-3)

12	at New England	47
15	Atlanta	13
32	at Buffalo (OT)	35
17	St. Louis	24
76		119

TENNESSEE (3-1)

14	Minnesota	3
16	at St. Louis	17
14	Chicago	13
32	New Orleans	9
76		42

West Division

DENVER (2-2)

23	at Dallas	24
24	Buffalo	10
23	Seattle	20
7	at Arizona	26
77		80

KANSAS CITY (0-4)

0	Tampa Bay	25
13	at Baltimore	31
10	St. Louis	14
19	at Green Bay	20
42		90

OAKLAND (0-4)

18	Arizona	24
3	at San Francisco	17
20	New Orleans	40
3	at Seattle	20
44		101

SAN DIEGO (2-2)

17	Seattle	24
20	at Dallas	7
34	at Arizona	31
17	San Francisco	20
88		82

NFC PRESEASON RECORDS—TEAM BY TEAM

East Division
DALLAS (2-2)

24	Denver	23
7	San Diego	20
23	at Minnesota	17
3	at Miami	17
57		**77**

NEW YORK GIANTS (2-2)

10	at Carolina	20
41	Chicago	13
3	New York Jets	17
18	at New England	17
72		**67**

PHILADELPHIA (3-1)

13	Baltimore	6
14	at Pittsburgh	24
24	Cleveland	14
24	at New York Jets	14
75		**58**

WASHINGTON (3-1)

16	Pittsburgh	7
16	at Indianapolis	3
31	at Baltimore	34
29	Tampa Bay	24
92		**68**

North Division
CHICAGO (2-2)

10	Buffalo	3
13	at New York Giants	41
13	at Tennessee	14
24	Cleveland	14
60		**72**

DETROIT (4-0)

34	Cincinnati	3
30	at Cleveland	28
34	New England	10
16	at Buffalo	6
114		**47**

GREEN BAY (3-1)

17	at Cleveland	27
28	Arizona	20
24	at Indianapolis	21
20	Kansas City	19
89		**87**

MINNESOTA (2-2)

3	at Tennessee	14
20	at Seattle	7
17	Dallas	23
28	Houston	0
68		**44**

South Division
ATLANTA (0-4)

23	Miami	28
13	at Jacksonville	15
16	at Pittsburgh	34
7	Baltimore	21
59		**98**

CAROLINA (1-3)

20	New York Giants	10
10	at Miami	20
13	at Cincinnati	24
17	Pittsburgh	33
60		**87**

NEW ORLEANS (2-2)

24	San Francisco	3
14	at Houston	27
40	at Oakland	20
9	Tennessee	32
87		**82**

TAMPA BAY (2-2)

25	at Kansas City	0
14	New England	31
17	Miami	13
24	at Washington	29
80		**73**

West Division
ARIZONA (2-2)

24	at Oakland	18
20	at Green Bay	28
31	San Diego	34
26	Denver	7
101		**87**

ST. LOUIS (4-0)

33	Indianapolis	10
17	Tennessee	16
14	at Kansas City	10
24	at Jacksonville	17
88		**53**

SAN FRANCISCO (2-2)

3	at New Orleans	24
17	Oakland	3
7	Houston	30
20	at San Diego	17
47		**74**

SEATTLE (2-2)

24	at San Diego	17
7	Minnesota	20
20	at Denver	23
20	Oakland	3
71		**63**

PRESEASON STANDINGS
NATIONAL FOOTBALL CONFERENCE
East Division

	W	L	T	Pct.	Pts.	OP
Philadelphia	3	1	0	.750	75	58
Washington	3	1	0	.750	92	68
Dallas	2	2	0	.500	57	77
New York Giants	2	2	0	.500	72	67

North Division

	W	L	T	Pct.	Pts.	OP
Detroit	4	0	0	1.000	114	47
Green Bay	3	1	0	.750	89	87
Chicago	2	2	0	.500	60	72
Minnesota	2	2	0	.500	68	44

South Division

	W	L	T	Pct.	Pts.	OP
New Orleans	2	2	0	.500	87	82
Tampa Bay	2	2	0	.500	80	73
Carolina	1	3	0	.250	60	87
Atlanta	0	4	0	.000	59	98

West Division

	W	L	T	Pct.	Pts.	OP
St. Louis	4	0	0	1.000	88	53
Arizona	2	2	0	.500	101	87
San Francisco	2	2	0	.500	47	74
Seattle	2	2	0	.500	71	63

AMERICAN FOOTBALL CONFERENCE

BALTIMORE RAVENS (12-4)
35	Pittsburgh	7
13	at Tennessee	26
37	at St. Louis	7
34	New York Jets	17
29	Houston	14
7	at Jacksonville	12
30	Arizona	27
23	at Pittsburgh	20
17	at Seattle	22
31	Cincinnati	24
16	San Francisco	6
24	at Cleveland	10
24	Indianapolis	10
14	at San Diego	34
20	Cleveland	14
24	at Cincinnati	16
378		**266**

BUFFALO BILLS (6-10)
41	at Kansas City	7
38	Oakland	35
34	New England	31
20	at Cincinnati	23
31	Philadelphia	24
24	at New York Giants	27
23	Washington	0
11	New York Jets	27
7	at Dallas	44
8	at Miami	35
24	at New York Jets	28
17	Tennessee	23
10	at San Diego	37
23	Miami	30
40	Denver	14
21	at New England	49
372		**434**

CINCINNATI BENGALS (9-7)
27	at Cleveland	17
22	at Denver	24
8	San Francisco	13
23	Buffalo	20
30	at Jacksonville	20
27	Indianapolis	17
34	at Seattle	12
24	at Tennessee	17
17	Pittsburgh	24
24	at Baltimore	31
23	Cleveland	20
7	at Pittsburgh	35
19	Houston	20
20	at St. Louis	13
23	Arizona	16
16	Baltimore	24
344		**323**

CLEVELAND BROWNS (4-12)
17	Cincinnati	27
27	at Indianapolis	19
17	Miami	16
13	Tennessee	31
17	at Oakland	24
6	Seattle	3
10	at San Francisco	20
12	at Houston	30
12	St. Louis	13
14	Jacksonville	10
20	at Cincinnati	23
10	Baltimore	24
3	at Pittsburgh	14
17	at Arizona (OT)	20
14	at Baltimore	20
9	Pittsburgh	13
218		**307**

DENVER BRONCOS (8-8)
20	Oakland	23
24	Cincinnati	22
14	at Tennessee	17
23	at Green Bay	49
24	San Diego	29
18	at Miami (OT)	15
10	Detroit	45
38	at Oakland	24
17	at Kansas City	10
17	New York Jets	13
16	at San Diego (OT)	13
35	at Minnesota	32
13	Chicago (OT)	10
23	New England	41
14	at Buffalo	40
3	Kansas City	7
309		**390**

HOUSTON TEXANS (10-6)
34	Indianapolis	7
23	at Miami	13
33	at New Orleans	40
17	Pittsburgh	10
20	Oakland	25
14	at Baltimore	29
41	at Tennessee	7
24	Jacksonville	14
30	Cleveland	12
37	at Tampa Bay	9
20	at Jacksonville	13
17	Atlanta	10
20	at Cincinnati	19
13	Carolina	28
16	at Indianapolis	19
22	Tennessee	23
381		**278**

INDIANAPOLIS COLTS (2-14)
7	at Houston	34
19	Cleveland	27
20	Pittsburgh	23
17	at Tampa Bay	24
24	Kansas City	28
17	at Cincinnati	27
7	at New Orleans	62
10	at Tennessee	27
7	Atlanta	31
3	Jacksonville	17
19	Carolina	27
24	at New England	31
10	at Baltimore	24
27	Tennessee	13
19	Houston	16
13	at Jacksonville	19
243		**430**

JACKSONVILLE JAGUARS (5-11)
16	Tennessee	14
3	at New York Jets	32
10	at Carolina	16
10	New Orleans	23
20	Cincinnati	30
13	at Pittsburgh	17
12	Baltimore	7
14	at Houston	24
17	at Indianapolis	3
10	at Cleveland	14
13	Houston	20
14	San Diego	38
41	Tampa Bay	14
14	at Atlanta	41
17	at Tennessee	23
19	Indianapolis	13
243		**329**

KANSAS CITY CHIEFS (7-9)
7	Buffalo	41
3	at Detroit	48
17	at San Diego	20
22	Minnesota	17
28	at Indianapolis	24
28	at Oakland	0
23	San Diego (OT)	20
3	Miami	31
10	Denver	17
3	at New England	34
9	Pittsburgh	13
10	at Chicago	3
10	at New York Jets	37
19	Green Bay	14
13	Oakland (OT)	16
7	at Denver	3
212		**338**

MIAMI DOLPHINS (6-10)
24	New England	38
13	Houston	23
16	at Cleveland	17
16	at San Diego	26
6	at New York Jets	24
15	Denver (OT)	18
17	at New York Giants	20
31	at Kansas City	3
20	Washington	9
35	Buffalo	8
19	at Dallas	20
34	Oakland	14
10	Philadelphia	26
30	at Buffalo	23
24	at New England	27
19	New York Jets	17
329		**313**

NEW ENGLAND PATRIOTS (13-3)
38	at Miami	24
35	San Diego	21
31	at Buffalo	34
31	at Oakland	19
30	New York Jets	21
20	Dallas	16
17	at Pittsburgh	25
20	New York Giants	24
37	at New York Jets	16
34	Kansas City	3
38	at Philadelphia	20
31	Indianapolis	24
34	at Washington	27
41	at Denver	23
27	Miami	24
49	Buffalo	21
513		**342**

NEW YORK JETS (8-8)
27	Dallas	24
32	Jacksonville	3
24	at Oakland	34
17	at Baltimore	34
21	at New England	30
24	Miami	6
27	San Diego	21
27	at Buffalo	11
16	New England	37
13	at Denver	17
28	Buffalo	24
34	at Washington	19
37	Kansas City	10
19	at Philadelphia	45
14	New York Giants	29
17	at Miami	19
377		**363**

OAKLAND RAIDERS (8-8)
23	at Denver	20
35	at Buffalo	38
34	New York Jets	24
19	New England	31
25	at Houston	20
24	Cleveland	17
0	Kansas City	28
24	Denver	38
24	at San Diego	17
27	at Minnesota	21
25	Chicago	20
14	at Miami	34
16	at Green Bay	46
27	Detroit	28
16	at Kansas City (OT)	13
26	San Diego	38
359		**433**

PITTSBURGH STEELERS (12-4)
7	at Baltimore	35
24	Seattle	0
23	at Indianapolis	20
10	at Houston	17
38	Tennessee	17
17	Jacksonville	13
32	at Arizona	20
25	New England	17
20	Baltimore	23
24	at Cincinnati	17
13	at Kansas City	9
35	Cincinnati	7
14	Cleveland	3
3	at San Francisco	20
27	St. Louis	0
13	at Cleveland	9
325		**227**

SAN DIEGO CHARGERS (8-8)
24	Minnesota	17
21	at New England	35
20	Kansas City	17
26	Miami	16
29	at Denver	24
21	at New York Jets	27
20	at Kansas City (OT)	23
38	Green Bay	45
17	Oakland	24
20	at Chicago	31
13	Denver (OT)	16
38	at Jacksonville	14
37	Buffalo	10
34	Baltimore	14
10	at Detroit	38
38	at Oakland	26
406		**377**

TENNESSEE TITANS (9-7)
14	at Jacksonville	16
26	Baltimore	13
17	Denver	14
31	at Cleveland	13
17	at Pittsburgh	38
7	Houston	41
27	Indianapolis	10
17	Cincinnati	24
30	at Carolina	3
17	at Atlanta	23
23	Tampa Bay	17
23	at Buffalo	17
17	New Orleans	22
13	at Indianapolis	27
23	Jacksonville	17
23	at Houston	22
325		**317**

NATIONAL FOOTBALL CONFERENCE

ARIZONA CARDINALS (8-8)
28	Carolina	21
21	at Washington	22
10	at Seattle	13
27	New York Giants	31
10	at Minnesota	34
20	Pittsburgh	32
27	at Baltimore	30
19	St. Louis (OT)	13
21	at Philadelphia	17
7	at San Francisco	23
23	at St. Louis	20
19	Dallas (OT)	13
21	San Francisco	19
20	Cleveland (OT)	17
16	at Cincinnati	23
23	Seattle (OT)	20
312		**348**

DALLAS COWBOYS (8-8)
24	at New York Jets	27
27	at San Francisco (OT)	24
18	Washington	16
30	Detroit	34
16	at New England	20
34	St. Louis	7
7	at Philadelphia	34
23	Seattle	13
44	Buffalo	7
27	at Washington (OT)	24
20	Miami	19
13	at Arizona (OT)	19
34	New York Giants	37
31	at Tampa Bay	15
7	Philadelphia	20
14	at New York Giants	31
369		**347**

NEW ORLEANS SAINTS (13-3)
34	at Green Bay	42
30	Chicago	13
40	Houston	33
23	at Jacksonville	10
30	at Carolina	27
20	at Tampa Bay	26
62	Indianapolis	7
21	at St. Louis	31
27	Tampa Bay	16
26	at Atlanta (OT)	23
49	New York Giants	24
31	Detroit	17
22	at Tennessee	17
42	at Minnesota	20
45	Atlanta	16
45	Carolina	17
547		**339**

SAN FRANCISCO 49ERS (13-3)
33	Seattle	17
24	Dallas (OT)	27
13	at Cincinnati	8
24	at Philadelphia	23
48	Tampa Bay	3
25	at Detroit	19
20	Cleveland	10
19	at Washington	11
27	New York Giants	20
23	Arizona	7
6	at Baltimore	16
26	St. Louis	0
19	at Arizona	21
20	Pittsburgh	3
19	at Seattle	17
34	at St. Louis	27
380		**229**

ATLANTA FALCONS (10-6)
12	at Chicago	30
35	Philadelphia	31
13	at Tampa Bay	16
30	at Seattle	28
14	Green Bay	25
31	Carolina	17
23	at Detroit	16
31	at Indianapolis	7
23	New Orleans (OT)	26
23	Tennessee	17
24	Minnesota	14
10	at Houston	17
31	at Carolina	23
41	Jacksonville	14
16	at New Orleans	45
45	Tampa Bay	24
402		**350**

DETROIT LIONS (10-6)
27	at Tampa Bay	20
48	Kansas City	3
26	at Minnesota (OT)	23
34	at Dallas	30
24	Chicago	13
19	San Francisco	25
16	Atlanta	23
45	at Denver	10
13	at Chicago	37
49	Carolina	35
15	Green Bay	27
17	at New Orleans	31
34	Minnesota	28
28	at Oakland	27
38	San Diego	10
41	at Green Bay	45
474		**387**

NEW YORK GIANTS (9-7)
14	at Washington	28
28	St. Louis	16
29	at Philadelphia	16
31	at Arizona	27
25	Seattle	36
27	Buffalo	24
20	Miami	17
24	at New England	20
20	at San Francisco	27
10	Philadelphia	17
24	at New Orleans	49
35	Green Bay	38
37	at Dallas	34
10	Washington	23
29	at New York Jets	14
31	Dallas	14
394		**400**

SEATTLE SEAHAWKS (7-9)
17	at San Francisco	33
0	at Pittsburgh	24
13	Arizona	10
28	Atlanta	30
36	at New York Giants	25
3	at Cleveland	6
12	Cincinnati	34
13	at Dallas	23
22	Baltimore	17
24	at St. Louis	7
17	Washington	23
31	Philadelphia	14
30	St. Louis	13
38	at Chicago	14
17	San Francisco	19
20	at Arizona (OT)	23
321		**315**

CAROLINA PANTHERS (6-10)
21	at Arizona	28
23	Green Bay	30
16	Jacksonville	10
29	at Chicago	34
27	New Orleans	30
17	at Atlanta	31
33	Washington	20
21	Minnesota	24
3	Tennessee	30
35	at Detroit	49
27	at Indianapolis	19
38	at Tampa Bay	19
23	Atlanta	31
28	at Houston	13
48	Tampa Bay	16
17	at New Orleans	45
406		**429**

GREEN BAY PACKERS (15-1)
42	New Orleans	34
30	at Carolina	23
27	at Chicago	17
49	Denver	23
25	at Atlanta	14
24	St. Louis	3
33	at Minnesota	27
45	at San Diego	38
45	Minnesota	7
35	Tampa Bay	26
27	at Detroit	15
38	at New York Giants	35
46	Oakland	16
14	at Kansas City	19
35	Chicago	21
45	Detroit	41
560		**359**

PHILADELPHIA EAGLES (8-8)
31	at St. Louis	13
31	at Atlanta	35
16	New York Giants	29
23	San Francisco	24
24	at Buffalo	31
20	at Washington	13
34	Dallas	7
24	Chicago	30
17	Arizona	21
17	at New York Giants	10
20	New England	38
14	at Seattle	31
26	at Miami	10
45	New York Jets	19
20	at Dallas	7
34	Washington	10
396		**328**

TAMPA BAY BUCCANEERS (4-12)
20	Detroit	27
24	at Minnesota	20
16	Atlanta	13
24	Indianapolis	17
3	at San Francisco	48
26	New Orleans	20
18	Chicago	24
16	at New Orleans	27
9	Houston	37
26	at Green Bay	35
17	at Tennessee	23
19	Carolina	38
14	at Jacksonville	41
15	Dallas	31
16	at Carolina	48
24	at Atlanta	45
287		**494**

CHICAGO BEARS (8-8)
30	Atlanta	12
13	at New Orleans	30
17	Green Bay	27
34	Carolina	29
13	at Detroit	24
39	Minnesota	10
24	at Tampa Bay	18
30	at Philadelphia	24
37	Detroit	13
31	San Diego	20
20	at Oakland	25
3	Kansas City	10
10	at Denver (OT)	13
14	Seattle	38
21	at Green Bay	35
17	at Minnesota	13
353		**341**

MINNESOTA VIKINGS (3-13)
17	at San Diego	24
20	Tampa Bay	24
23	Detroit (OT)	26
17	at Kansas City	22
34	Arizona	10
10	at Chicago	39
27	Green Bay	33
24	at Carolina	21
7	at Green Bay	45
21	Oakland	27
14	at Atlanta	24
32	Denver	35
28	at Detroit	34
20	New Orleans	42
33	at Washington	26
13	Chicago	17
340		**449**

ST. LOUIS RAMS (2-14)
13	Philadelphia	31
16	at New York Giants	28
7	Baltimore	37
10	Washington	17
3	at Green Bay	24
7	at Dallas	34
31	New Orleans	21
13	at Arizona (OT)	19
13	at Cleveland	12
7	Seattle	24
20	Arizona	23
0	at San Francisco	26
13	at Seattle	30
13	Cincinnati	20
0	at Pittsburgh	27
27	San Francisco	34
193		**407**

WASHINGTON REDSKINS (5-11)
28	New York Giants	14
22	Arizona	21
16	at Dallas	18
17	at St. Louis	10
13	Philadelphia	20
20	at Carolina	33
0	at Buffalo	23
11	San Francisco	19
9	at Miami	20
24	Dallas (OT)	27
23	at Seattle	17
19	New York Jets	34
27	New England	34
23	at New York Giants	10
26	Minnesota	33
10	at Philadelphia	34
288		**367**

FINAL STANDINGS

AMERICAN FOOTBALL CONFERENCE

East Division	W	L	T	Pct.	Pts.	OP
* New England	13	3	0	.813	513	342
New York Jets	8	8	0	.500	377	363
Miami	6	10	0	.375	329	313
Buffalo	6	10	0	.375	372	434
North Division	**W**	**L**	**T**	**Pct.**	**Pts.**	**OP**
* Baltimore	12	4	0	.750	378	266
# Pittsburgh	12	4	0	.750	325	227
# Cincinnati	9	7	0	.563	344	323
Cleveland	4	12	0	.250	218	307
South Division	**W**	**L**	**T**	**Pct.**	**Pts.**	**OP**
* Houston	10	6	0	.625	381	278
Tennessee	9	7	0	.563	325	317
Jacksonville	5	11	0	.313	243	329
Indianapolis	2	14	0	.125	243	430
West Division	**W**	**L**	**T**	**Pct.**	**Pts.**	**OP**
* Denver	8	8	0	.500	309	390
San Diego	8	8	0	.500	406	377
Oakland	8	8	0	.500	359	433
Kansas City	7	9	0	.438	212	338

NATIONAL FOOTBALL CONFERENCE

East Division	W	L	T	Pct.	Pts.	OP
* New York Giants	9	7	0	.563	394	400
Philadelphia	8	8	0	.500	396	328
Dallas	8	8	0	.500	369	347
Washington	5	11	0	.313	288	367
North Division	**W**	**L**	**T**	**Pct.**	**Pts.**	**OP**
* Green Bay	15	1	0	.938	560	359
# Detroit	10	6	0	.625	474	387
Chicago	8	8	0	.500	353	341
Minnesota	3	13	0	.188	340	449
South Division	**W**	**L**	**T**	**Pct.**	**Pts.**	**OP**
* New Orleans	13	3	0	.813	547	339
# Atlanta	10	6	0	.625	402	350
Carolina	6	10	0	.375	406	429
Tampa Bay	4	12	0	.250	287	494
West Division	**W**	**L**	**T**	**Pct.**	**Pts.**	**OP**
* San Francisco	13	3	0	.813	380	229
Arizona	8	8	0	.500	312	348
Seattle	7	9	0	.438	321	315
St. Louis	2	14	0	.125	193	407

* *Division champion*
\# *Wild Card team*

Miami finished ahead of Buffalo based on head-to-head sweep. Baltimore finished ahead of Pittsburgh based on head-to-head sweep. Denver finished ahead of San Diego and Oakland based on best record in common games (Denver 5-5; Oakland 4-6; San Diego 4-6). San Diego finished ahead of Oakland based on better conference record (7-5 to 6-6). Cincinnati finished ahead of Tennessee based on head-to-head victory. Philadelphia finished ahead of Dallas based on head-to-head sweep. Atlanta finished ahead of Detroit based on head-to-head victory. San Francisco finished ahead of New Orleans based on head-to-head victory.

WILD CARD PLAYOFFS

AFC
HOUSTON 31, Cincinnati 10
DENVER 29, Pittsburgh 23 (OT)
NFC
NEW ORLEANS 45, Detroit 28
NEW YORK GIANTS 24, Atlanta 2

DIVISIONAL PLAYOFFS

AFC
NEW ENGLAND 45, Denver 10
BALTIMORE 20, Houston 13
NFC
SAN FRANCISCO 36, New Orleans 32
New York Giants 37, GREEN BAY 20

CHAMPIONSHIP GAMES

AFC
NEW ENGLAND 23, Baltimore 20
NFC
New York Giants 20, SAN FRANCISCO 17 (OT)

AFC-NFC PRO BOWL

AFC 59, NFC 41
at Aloha Stadium, Honolulu, Hawaii

SUPER BOWL XLVI

New York Giants (NFC) 21, New England (AFC) 17
at Lucas Oil Stadium, Indianapolis, Indiana

Home teams in playoff games are indicated in CAPS.

FIRST WEEK STANDINGS

American Football Conference

East Division	W	L	T	Pct.	Pts.	OP
Buffalo	1	0	0	1.000	41	7
New England	1	0	0	1.000	38	24
New York Jets	1	0	0	1.000	27	24
Miami	0	1	0	.000	24	38
North Division	**W**	**L**	**T**	**Pct.**	**Pts.**	**OP**
Baltimore	1	0	0	1.000	35	7
Cincinnati	1	0	0	1.000	27	17
Cleveland	0	1	0	.000	17	27
Pittsburgh	0	1	0	.000	7	35
South Division	**W**	**L**	**T**	**Pct.**	**Pts.**	**OP**
Houston	1	0	0	1.000	34	7
Jacksonville	1	0	0	1.000	16	14
Indianapolis	0	1	0	.000	7	34
Tennessee	0	1	0	.000	14	16
West Division	**W**	**L**	**T**	**Pct.**	**Pts.**	**OP**
Oakland	1	0	0	1.000	23	20
San Diego	1	0	0	1.000	24	17
Denver	0	1	0	.000	20	23
Kansas City	0	1	0	.000	7	41

National Football Conference

East Division	W	L	T	Pct.	Pts.	OP
Philadelphia	1	0	0	1.000	31	13
Washington	1	0	0	1.000	28	14
Dallas	0	1	0	.000	24	27
New York Giants	0	1	0	.000	14	28
North Division	**W**	**L**	**T**	**Pct.**	**Pts.**	**OP**
Chicago	1	0	0	1.000	30	12
Detroit	1	0	0	1.000	27	20
Green Bay	1	0	0	1.000	42	34
Minnesota	0	1	0	.000	17	24
South Division	**W**	**L**	**T**	**Pct.**	**Pts.**	**OP**
Atlanta	0	1	0	.000	12	30
Carolina	0	1	0	.000	21	28
New Orleans	0	1	0	.000	34	42
Tampa Bay	0	1	0	.000	20	27
West Division	**W**	**L**	**T**	**Pct.**	**Pts.**	**OP**
Arizona	1	0	0	1.000	28	21
San Francisco	1	0	0	1.000	33	17
St. Louis	0	1	0	.000	13	31
Seattle	0	1	0	.000	17	33

SECOND WEEK STANDINGS

American Football Conference

East Division	W	L	T	Pct.	Pts.	OP
Buffalo	2	0	0	1.000	79	42
New England	2	0	0	1.000	73	45
New York Jets	2	0	0	1.000	59	27
Miami	0	2	0	.000	37	61
North Division	**W**	**L**	**T**	**Pct.**	**Pts.**	**OP**
Baltimore	1	1	0	.500	48	33
Cincinnati	1	1	0	.500	49	41
Cleveland	1	1	0	.500	44	46
Pittsburgh	1	1	0	.500	31	35
South Division	**W**	**L**	**T**	**Pct.**	**Pts.**	**OP**
Houston	2	0	0	1.000	57	20
Jacksonville	1	1	0	.500	19	46
Tennessee	1	1	0	.500	40	29
Indianapolis	0	2	0	.000	26	61
West Division	**W**	**L**	**T**	**Pct.**	**Pts.**	**OP**
Denver	1	1	0	.500	44	45
Oakland	1	1	0	.500	58	58
San Diego	1	1	0	.500	45	52
Kansas City	0	2	0	.000	10	89

National Football Conference

East Division	W	L	T	Pct.	Pts.	OP
Washington	2	0	0	1.000	50	35
Dallas	1	1	0	.500	51	51
New York Giants	1	1	0	.500	42	44
Philadelphia	1	1	0	.500	62	48
North Division	**W**	**L**	**T**	**Pct.**	**Pts.**	**OP**
Detroit	2	0	0	1.000	75	23
Green Bay	2	0	0	1.000	72	57
Chicago	1	1	0	.500	43	48
Minnesota	0	2	0	.000	37	48
South Division	**W**	**L**	**T**	**Pct.**	**Pts.**	**OP**
Atlanta	1	1	0	.500	47	61
New Orleans	1	1	0	.500	64	55
Tampa Bay	1	1	0	.500	44	47
Carolina	0	2	0	.000	44	58
West Division	**W**	**L**	**T**	**Pct.**	**Pts.**	**OP**
Arizona	1	1	0	.500	49	43
San Francisco	1	1	0	.500	57	44
St. Louis	0	2	0	.000	29	59
Seattle	0	2	0	.000	17	57

THIRD WEEK STANDINGS

American Football Conference

East Division	W	L	T	Pct.	Pts.	OP
Buffalo	3	0	0	1.000	113	73
New England	2	1	0	.667	104	79
New York Jets	2	1	0	.667	83	61
Miami	0	3	0	.000	53	78
North Division	**W**	**L**	**T**	**Pct.**	**Pts.**	**OP**
Baltimore	2	1	0	.667	85	40
Cleveland	2	1	0	.667	61	62
Pittsburgh	2	1	0	.667	54	55
Cincinnati	1	2	0	.333	57	54
South Division	**W**	**L**	**T**	**Pct.**	**Pts.**	**OP**
Houston	2	1	0	.667	90	60
Tennessee	2	1	0	.667	57	43
Jacksonville	1	2	0	.333	29	62
Indianapolis	0	3	0	.000	46	84
West Division	**W**	**L**	**T**	**Pct.**	**Pts.**	**OP**
Oakland	2	1	0	.667	92	82
San Diego	2	1	0	.667	65	69
Denver	1	2	0	.333	58	62
Kansas City	0	3	0	.000	27	109

National Football Conference

East Division	W	L	T	Pct.	Pts.	OP
Dallas	2	1	0	.667	69	67
New York Giants	2	1	0	.667	71	60
Washington	2	1	0	.667	66	53
Philadelphia	1	2	0	.333	78	77
North Division	**W**	**L**	**T**	**Pct.**	**Pts.**	**OP**
Detroit	3	0	0	1.000	101	46
Green Bay	3	0	0	1.000	99	74
Chicago	1	2	0	.333	60	69
Minnesota	0	3	0	.000	60	74
South Division	**W**	**L**	**T**	**Pct.**	**Pts.**	**OP**
New Orleans	2	1	0	.667	104	88
Tampa Bay	2	1	0	.667	60	60
Atlanta	1	2	0	.333	60	77
Carolina	1	2	0	.333	60	68
West Division	**W**	**L**	**T**	**Pct.**	**Pts.**	**OP**
San Francisco	2	1	0	.667	70	52
Arizona	1	2	0	.333	59	56
Seattle	1	2	0	.333	30	67
St. Louis	0	3	0	.000	36	96

WEEK 1 RESULTS

Thursday, September 8
GREEN BAY 42, New Orleans 34

Sunday, September 11
BALTIMORE 35, Pittsburgh 7
CHICAGO 30, Atlanta 12
Cincinnati 27, CLEVELAND 17
HOUSTON 34, Indianapolis 7
JACKSONVILLE 16, Tennessee 14
Buffalo 41, KANSAS CITY 7
Philadelphia 31, ST. LOUIS 13
Detroit 27, TAMPA BAY 20
ARIZONA 28, Carolina 21
SAN DIEGO 24, Minnesota 17
SAN FRANCISCO 33, Seattle 17
WASHINGTON 28, New York Giants 14
NEW YORK JETS 27, Dallas 24

Monday, September 12
New England 38, MIAMI 24
Oakland 23, DENVER 20

In the 2011 Week By Week section, home teams are indicated by ALL CAPS.

For game recaps, box scores, and video highlights, please visit www.NFL.com/scores.

WEEK 2 RESULTS

Sunday, September 18
BUFFALO 38, Oakland 35
Green Bay 30, CAROLINA 23
DETROIT 48, Kansas City 3
Cleveland 27, INDIANAPOLIS 19
Tampa Bay 24, MINNESOTA 20
NEW ORLEANS 30, Chicago 13
NEW YORK JETS 32, Jacksonville 3
PITTSBURGH 24, Seattle 0
TENNESSEE 26, Baltimore 13
WASHINGTON 22, Arizona 21
Dallas 27, SAN FRANCISCO 24 (OT)
DENVER 24, Cincinnati 22
Houston 23, MIAMI 13
NEW ENGLAND 35, San Diego 21
ATLANTA 35, Philadelphia 31

Monday, September 19
NEW YORK GIANTS 28, St. Louis 16

WEEK 3 RESULTS

Sunday, September 25
BUFFALO 34, New England 31
CAROLINA 16, Jacksonville 10
San Francisco 13, CINCINNATI 8
CLEVELAND 17, Miami 16
Detroit 26, MINNESOTA 23 (OT)
NEW ORLEANS 40, Houston 33
New York Giants 29, PHILADELPHIA 16
TENNESSEE 17, Denver 14
OAKLAND 34, New York Jets 24
Baltimore 37, ST. LOUIS 7
SAN DIEGO 20, Kansas City 17
Green Bay 27, CHICAGO 17
SEATTLE 13, Arizona 10
TAMPA BAY 16, Atlanta 13
Pittsburgh 23, INDIANAPOLIS 20

Monday, September 26
DALLAS 18, Washington 16

FOURTH WEEK STANDINGS
American Football Conference

East Division	W	L	T	Pct.	Pts.	OP
Buffalo	3	1	0	.750	133	96
New England	3	1	0	.750	135	98
New York Jets	2	2	0	.500	100	95
Miami	0	4	0	.000	69	104

North Division	W	L	T	Pct.	Pts.	OP
Baltimore	3	1	0	.750	119	57
Cincinnati	2	2	0	.500	80	74
Cleveland	2	2	0	.500	74	93
Pittsburgh	2	2	0	.500	64	72

South Division	W	L	T	Pct.	Pts.	OP
Houston	3	1	0	.750	107	70
Tennessee	3	1	0	.750	88	56
Jacksonville	1	3	0	.250	39	85
Indianapolis	0	4	0	.000	63	108

West Division	W	L	T	Pct.	Pts.	OP
San Diego	3	1	0	.750	91	85
Oakland	2	2	0	.500	111	113
Denver	1	3	0	.250	81	111
Kansas City	1	3	0	.250	49	126

National Football Conference

East Division	W	L	T	Pct.	Pts.	OP
New York Giants	3	1	0	.750	102	87
Washington	3	1	0	.750	83	63
Dallas	2	2	0	.500	99	101
Philadelphia	1	3	0	.250	101	101

North Division	W	L	T	Pct.	Pts.	OP
Detroit	4	0	0	1.000	135	76
Green Bay	4	0	0	1.000	148	97
Chicago	2	2	0	.500	94	98
Minnesota	0	4	0	.000	77	96

South Division	W	L	T	Pct.	Pts.	OP
New Orleans	3	1	0	.750	127	98
Tampa Bay	3	1	0	.750	84	77
Atlanta	2	2	0	.500	90	105
Carolina	1	3	0	.250	89	102

West Division	W	L	T	Pct.	Pts.	OP
San Francisco	3	1	0	.750	94	75
Arizona	1	3	0	.250	86	87
Seattle	1	3	0	.250	58	97
St. Louis	0	4	0	.000	46	113

WEEK 4 RESULTS
Sunday, October 2

CHICAGO 34, Carolina 29
CINCINNATI 23, Buffalo 20
Tennessee 31, CLEVELAND 13
Detroit 34, DALLAS 30
HOUSTON 17, Pittsburgh 10
New Orleans 23, JACKSONVILLE 10
KANSAS CITY 22, Minnesota 17
San Francisco 24, PHILADELPHIA 23
Washington 17, ST. LOUIS 10
New York Giants 31, ARIZONA 27
Atlanta 30, SEATTLE 28
GREEN BAY 49, Denver 23
New England 31, OAKLAND 19
SAN DIEGO 26, Miami 16
BALTIMORE 34, New York Jets 17

Monday, October 3

TAMPA BAY 24, Indianapolis 17

FIFTH WEEK STANDINGS
American Football Conference

East Division	W	L	T	Pct.	Pts.	OP
Buffalo	4	1	0	.800	164	120
New England	4	1	0	.800	165	119
New York Jets	2	3	0	.400	121	125
Miami	0	4	0	.000	69	104

North Division	W	L	T	Pct.	Pts.	OP
Baltimore	3	1	0	.750	119	57
Cincinnati	3	2	0	.600	110	94
Pittsburgh	3	2	0	.600	102	89
Cleveland	2	2	0	.500	74	93

South Division	W	L	T	Pct.	Pts.	OP
Houston	3	2	0	.600	127	95
Tennessee	3	2	0	.600	105	94
Jacksonville	1	4	0	.200	59	115
Indianapolis	0	5	0	.000	87	136

West Division	W	L	T	Pct.	Pts.	OP
San Diego	4	1	0	.800	120	109
Oakland	2	2	0	.600	136	133
Kansas City	2	3	0	.400	77	150
Denver	1	4	0	.200	105	140

National Football Conference

East Division	W	L	T	Pct.	Pts.	OP
Washington	3	1	0	.750	83	63
New York Giants	3	2	0	.600	127	123
Dallas	2	2	0	.500	99	101
Philadelphia	1	4	0	.200	125	132

North Division	W	L	T	Pct.	Pts.	OP
Detroit	5	0	0	1.000	159	89
Green Bay	5	0	0	1.000	173	111
Chicago	2	3	0	.400	107	122
Minnesota	1	4	0	.200	111	106

South Division	W	L	T	Pct.	Pts.	OP
New Orleans	4	1	0	.800	157	125
Tampa Bay	3	2	0	.600	87	125
Atlanta	2	3	0	.400	104	130
Carolina	1	4	0	.200	116	132

West Division	W	L	T	Pct.	Pts.	OP
San Francisco	4	1	0	.800	142	78
Seattle	2	3	0	.400	94	122
Arizona	1	4	0	.200	96	121
St. Louis	0	4	0	.000	46	113

WEEK 5 RESULTS
Sunday, October 9

BUFFALO 31, Philadelphia 24
New Orleans 30, CAROLINA 27
Oakland 25, HOUSTON 20
Kansas City 28, INDIANAPOLIS 24
Cincinnati 30, JACKSONVILLE 20
MINNESOTA 34, Arizona 10
Seattle 36, NEW YORK GIANTS 25
PITTSBURGH 38, Tennessee 17
SAN FRANCISCO 48, Tampa Bay 3
San Diego 29, DENVER 24
NEW ENGLAND 30, New York Jets 21
Green Bay 25, ATLANTA 14

Monday, October 10

DETROIT 24, Chicago 13

Byes: Baltimore, Cleveland, Dallas, Miami, St. Louis, Washington

SIXTH WEEK STANDINGS
American Football Conference

East Division	W	L	T	Pct.	Pts.	OP
New England	5	1	0	.833	185	135
Buffalo	4	2	0	.667	188	147
New York Jets	3	3	0	.500	145	131
Miami	0	5	0	.000	75	128

North Division	W	L	T	Pct.	Pts.	OP
Baltimore	4	1	0	.800	148	71
Cincinnati	4	2	0	.667	137	111
Pittsburgh	4	2	0	.667	119	102
Cleveland	2	3	0	.400	91	117

South Division	W	L	T	Pct.	Pts.	OP
Tennessee	3	2	0	.600	105	94
Houston	3	3	0	.500	141	124
Jacksonville	1	5	0	.167	72	132
Indianapolis	0	6	0	.000	104	163

West Division	W	L	T	Pct.	Pts.	OP
San Diego	4	1	0	.800	120	109
Oakland	4	2	0	.667	160	150
Kansas City	2	3	0	.400	77	150
Denver	1	4	0	.200	105	140

National Football Conference

East Division	W	L	T	Pct.	Pts.	OP
New York Giants	4	2	0	.667	154	147
Washington	3	2	0	.600	96	83
Dallas	2	3	0	.400	115	121
Philadelphia	2	4	0	.333	145	145

North Division	W	L	T	Pct.	Pts.	OP
Green Bay	6	0	0	1.000	197	114
Detroit	5	1	0	.833	178	114
Chicago	3	3	0	.500	146	132
Minnesota	1	5	0	.167	121	145

South Division	W	L	T	Pct.	Pts.	OP
New Orleans	4	2	0	.667	177	151
Tampa Bay	4	2	0	.667	113	145
Atlanta	3	3	0	.500	135	147
Carolina	1	5	0	.167	133	163

West Division	W	L	T	Pct.	Pts.	OP
San Francisco	5	1	0	.833	167	97
Seattle	2	3	0	.400	94	122
Arizona	1	4	0	.200	96	121
St. Louis	0	5	0	.000	49	137

WEEK 6 RESULTS
Sunday, October 16

ATLANTA 31, Carolina 17
CINCINNATI 27, Indianapolis 17
San Francisco 25, DETROIT 19
GREEN BAY 24, St. Louis 3
NEW YORK GIANTS 27, Buffalo 24
PITTSBURGH 17, Jacksonville 13
Philadelphia 20, WASHINGTON 13
BALTIMORE 29, Houston 14
OAKLAND 24, Cleveland 17
NEW ENGLAND 20, Dallas 16
TAMPA BAY 26, New Orleans 20
CHICAGO 39, Minnesota 10

Monday, October 17

NEW YORK JETS 24, Miami 6

Byes: Arizona, Denver, Kansas City, San Diego, Seattle, Tennessee

SEVENTH WEEK STANDINGS
American Football Conference

East Division	W	L	T	Pct.	Pts.	OP
New England	5	1	0	.833	185	135
Buffalo	4	2	0	.667	188	147
New York Jets	4	3	0	.571	172	152
Miami	0	6	0	.000	90	146

North Division	W	L	T	Pct.	Pts.	OP
Pittsburgh	5	2	0	.714	151	122
Baltimore	4	2	0	.667	155	83
Cincinnati	4	2	0	.667	137	111
Cleveland	3	3	0	.500	97	120

South Division	W	L	T	Pct.	Pts.	OP
Houston	4	3	0	.571	182	131
Tennessee	3	3	0	.500	112	135
Jacksonville	2	5	0	.286	84	139
Indianapolis	0	7	0	.000	111	225

West Division	W	L	T	Pct.	Pts.	OP
San Diego	4	2	0	.667	141	136
Oakland	4	3	0	.571	160	178
Kansas City	3	3	0	.500	105	150
Denver	2	4	0	.333	123	155

National Football Conference

East Division	W	L	T	Pct.	Pts.	OP
New York Giants	4	2	0	.667	154	147
Dallas	3	3	0	.500	149	128
Washington	3	3	0	.500	116	116
Philadelphia	2	4	0	.333	145	145

North Division	W	L	T	Pct.	Pts.	OP
Green Bay	7	0	0	1.000	230	141
Detroit	5	2	0	.714	194	137
Chicago	4	3	0	.571	170	150
Minnesota	1	6	0	.143	148	178

South Division	W	L	T	Pct.	Pts.	OP
New Orleans	5	2	0	.714	239	158
Atlanta	4	3	0	.571	158	163
Tampa Bay	4	3	0	.571	131	169
Carolina	2	5	0	.286	166	183

West Division	W	L	T	Pct.	Pts.	OP
San Francisco	5	1	0	.833	167	97
Seattle	2	4	0	.333	97	128
Arizona	1	5	0	.167	116	153
St. Louis	0	6	0	.000	56	171

WEEK 7 RESULTS
Sunday, October 23
CAROLINA 33, Washington 20
CLEVELAND 6, Seattle 3
Atlanta 23, DETROIT 16
Denver 18, MIAMI 15 (OT)
NEW YORK JETS 27, San Diego 21
Chicago 24, TAMPA BAY 18
   (London)
Houston 41, TENNESSEE 7
Pittsburgh 32, ARIZONA 20
Kansas City 28, OAKLAND 0
DALLAS 34, St. Louis 7
Green Bay 33, MINNESOTA 27
NEW ORLEANS 62, Indianapolis 7

Monday, October 24
JACKSONVILLE 12, Baltimore 7

Byes: Buffalo, Cincinnati,
   New England, New York Giants,
   Philadelphia, San Francisco

EIGHTH WEEK STANDINGS
American Football Conference

East Division	W	L	T	Pct.	Pts.	OP
Buffalo	5	2	0	.714	211	147
New England	5	2	0	.714	202	160
New York Jets	4	3	0	.571	172	152
Miami	0	7	0	.000	107	166

North Division	W	L	T	Pct.	Pts.	OP
Pittsburgh	6	2	0	.750	176	139
Baltimore	5	2	0	.714	185	110
Cincinnati	5	2	0	.714	171	123
Cleveland	3	4	0	.429	107	140

South Division	W	L	T	Pct.	Pts.	OP
Houston	5	3	0	.625	206	145
Tennessee	4	3	0	.571	139	145
Jacksonville	2	6	0	.250	98	163
Indianapolis	0	8	0	.000	121	252

West Division	W	L	T	Pct.	Pts.	OP
Kansas City	4	3	0	.571	128	170
Oakland	4	3	0	.571	160	178
San Diego	4	3	0	.571	161	159
Denver	2	5	0	.286	133	200

National Football Conference

East Division	W	L	T	Pct.	Pts.	OP
New York Giants	5	2	0	.714	174	164
Dallas	3	4	0	.429	156	162
Philadelphia	3	4	0	.429	179	152
Washington	3	4	0	.429	116	139

North Division	W	L	T	Pct.	Pts.	OP
Green Bay	7	0	0	1.000	230	141
Detroit	6	2	0	.750	239	147
Chicago	4	3	0	.571	170	150
Minnesota	2	6	0	.250	172	199

South Division	W	L	T	Pct.	Pts.	OP
New Orleans	5	3	0	.625	260	189
Atlanta	4	3	0	.571	158	163
Tampa Bay	4	3	0	.571	131	169
Carolina	2	6	0	.250	187	207

West Division	W	L	T	Pct.	Pts.	OP
San Francisco	6	1	0	.857	187	107
Seattle	2	5	0	.286	109	162
Arizona	1	6	0	.143	143	183
St. Louis	1	6	0	.143	87	192

WEEK 8 RESULTS
Sunday, October 30
BALTIMORE 30, Arizona 27
Minnesota 24, CAROLINA 21
HOUSTON 24, Jacksonville 14
NEW YORK GIANTS 20, Miami 17
ST. LOUIS 31, New Orleans 21
TENNESSEE 27, Indianapolis 10
BUFFALO 23, Washington 0
   (Toronto)
Detroit 45, DENVER 10
PITTSBURGH 25, New England 17
SAN FRANCISCO 20, Cleveland 10
Cincinnati 34, SEATTLE 12
PHILADELPHIA 34, Dallas 7

Monday, October 31
KANSAS CITY 23, San Diego 20 (OT)

Byes: Atlanta, Chicago, Green Bay,
   New York Jets, Oakland, Tampa Bay

NINTH WEEK STANDINGS
American Football Conference

East Division	W	L	T	Pct.	Pts.	OP
Buffalo	5	3	0	.625	222	174
New England	5	3	0	.625	222	184
New York Jets	5	3	0	.625	199	163
Miami	1	7	0	.125	138	169

North Division	W	L	T	Pct.	Pts.	OP
Baltimore	6	2	0	.750	208	130
Cincinnati	6	2	0	.750	195	140
Pittsburgh	6	3	0	.667	196	162
Cleveland	3	5	0	.375	119	170

South Division	W	L	T	Pct.	Pts.	OP
Houston	6	3	0	.667	236	157
Tennessee	4	4	0	.500	156	169
Jacksonville	2	6	0	.250	98	163
Indianapolis	0	9	0	.000	128	283

West Division	W	L	T	Pct.	Pts.	OP
Kansas City	4	4	0	.500	131	201
Oakland	4	4	0	.500	184	216
San Diego	4	4	0	.500	199	204
Denver	3	5	0	.375	171	224

National Football Conference

East Division	W	L	T	Pct.	Pts.	OP
New York Giants	6	2	0	.750	198	184
Dallas	4	4	0	.500	179	175
Philadelphia	3	5	0	.375	203	182
Washington	3	5	0	.375	127	158

North Division	W	L	T	Pct.	Pts.	OP
Green Bay	8	0	0	1.000	275	179
Detroit	6	2	0	.750	239	147
Chicago	5	3	0	.625	200	174
Minnesota	2	6	0	.250	172	199

South Division	W	L	T	Pct.	Pts.	OP
New Orleans	6	3	0	.667	287	205
Atlanta	5	3	0	.625	189	170
Tampa Bay	4	4	0	.500	147	196
Carolina	2	6	0	.250	187	207

West Division	W	L	T	Pct.	Pts.	OP
San Francisco	7	1	0	.875	206	118
Arizona	2	6	0	.250	162	196
Seattle	2	6	0	.250	122	185
St. Louis	1	7	0	.125	100	211

WEEK 9 RESULTS
Sunday, November 6
New York Jets 27, BUFFALO 11
DALLAS 23, Seattle 13
HOUSTON 30, Cleveland 12
Atlanta 31, INDIANAPOLIS 7
Miami 31, KANSAS CITY 3
NEW ORLEANS 27, Tampa Bay 16
San Francisco 19, WASHINGTON 11
Denver 38, OAKLAND 24
Cincinnati 24, TENNESSEE 17
ARIZONA 19, St. Louis 13 (OT)
New York Giants 24, NEW ENGLAND 20
Green Bay 45, SAN DIEGO 38
Baltimore 23, PITTSBURGH 20

Monday, November 7
Chicago 30, PHILADELPHIA 24

Byes: Carolina, Detroit,
   Jacksonville, Minnesota

TENTH WEEK STANDINGS
American Football Conference

East Division	W	L	T	Pct.	Pts.	OP
New England	6	3	0	.667	259	200
Buffalo	5	4	0	.556	229	218
New York Jets	5	4	0	.556	215	200
Miami	2	7	0	.222	158	178
North Division	**W**	**L**	**T**	**Pct.**	**Pts.**	**OP**
Pittsburgh	7	3	0	.700	220	179
Baltimore	6	3	0	.667	225	152
Cincinnati	6	3	0	.667	212	164
Cleveland	3	6	0	.333	131	183
South Division	**W**	**L**	**T**	**Pct.**	**Pts.**	**OP**
Houston	7	3	0	.700	273	166
Tennessee	5	4	0	.556	186	172
Jacksonville	3	6	0	.333	115	166
Indianapolis	0	10	0	.000	131	300
West Division	**W**	**L**	**T**	**Pct.**	**Pts.**	**OP**
Oakland	5	4	0	.556	208	233
Denver	4	5	0	.444	188	234
Kansas City	4	5	0	.444	141	218
San Diego	4	5	0	.444	216	228

National Football Conference

East Division	W	L	T	Pct.	Pts.	OP
New York Giants	6	3	0	.667	218	211
Dallas	5	4	0	.556	223	182
Philadelphia	3	6	0	.333	220	203
Washington	3	6	0	.333	136	178
North Division	**W**	**L**	**T**	**Pct.**	**Pts.**	**OP**
Green Bay	9	0	0	1.000	320	186
Chicago	6	3	0	.667	237	187
Detroit	6	3	0	.667	252	184
Minnesota	2	7	0	.222	179	244
South Division	**W**	**L**	**T**	**Pct.**	**Pts.**	**OP**
New Orleans	7	3	0	.700	313	228
Atlanta	5	4	0	.556	212	196
Tampa Bay	4	5	0	.444	156	233
Carolina	2	7	0	.222	190	237
West Division	**W**	**L**	**T**	**Pct.**	**Pts.**	**OP**
San Francisco	8	1	0	.889	233	138
Arizona	3	6	0	.333	182	213
Seattle	3	6	0	.333	144	202
St. Louis	2	7	0	.222	113	223

ELEVENTH WEEK STANDINGS
American Football Conference

East Division	W	L	T	Pct.	Pts.	OP
New England	7	3	0	.700	293	203
Buffalo	5	5	0	.500	237	253
New York Jets	5	5	0	.500	228	217
Miami	3	7	0	.300	193	186
North Division	**W**	**L**	**T**	**Pct.**	**Pts.**	**OP**
Baltimore	7	3	0	.700	256	176
Pittsburgh	7	3	0	.700	220	179
Cincinnati	6	4	0	.600	236	195
Cleveland	4	6	0	.400	145	193
South Division	**W**	**L**	**T**	**Pct.**	**Pts.**	**OP**
Houston	7	3	0	.700	273	166
Tennessee	5	5	0	.500	203	195
Jacksonville	3	7	0	.300	125	180
Indianapolis	0	10	0	.000	131	300
West Division	**W**	**L**	**T**	**Pct.**	**Pts.**	**OP**
Oakland	6	4	0	.600	235	254
Denver	5	5	0	.500	205	247
Kansas City	4	6	0	.400	144	252
San Diego	4	6	0	.400	236	259

National Football Conference

East Division	W	L	T	Pct.	Pts.	OP
Dallas	6	4	0	.600	250	206
New York Giants	6	4	0	.600	228	228
Philadelphia	4	6	0	.400	237	213
Washington	3	7	0	.300	160	205
North Division	**W**	**L**	**T**	**Pct.**	**Pts.**	**OP**
Green Bay	10	0	0	1.000	355	212
Chicago	7	3	0	.700	268	207
Detroit	7	3	0	.700	301	219
Minnesota	2	8	0	.200	200	271
South Division	**W**	**L**	**T**	**Pct.**	**Pts.**	**OP**
New Orleans	7	3	0	.700	313	228
Atlanta	6	4	0	.600	235	213
Tampa Bay	4	6	0	.400	182	268
Carolina	2	8	0	.200	225	286
West Division	**W**	**L**	**T**	**Pct.**	**Pts.**	**OP**
San Francisco	9	1	0	.900	256	145
Seattle	4	6	0	.400	168	209
Arizona	3	7	0	.300	190	236
St. Louis	2	8	0	.200	120	247

TWELFTH WEEK STANDINGS
American Football Conference

East Division	W	L	T	Pct.	Pts.	OP
New England	8	3	0	.727	331	223
New York Jets	6	5	0	.545	256	241
Buffalo	5	6	0	.455	261	281
Miami	3	8	0	.273	212	206
North Division	**W**	**L**	**T**	**Pct.**	**Pts.**	**OP**
Baltimore	8	3	0	.727	272	182
Pittsburgh	8	3	0	.727	233	188
Cincinnati	7	4	0	.636	259	215
Cleveland	4	7	0	.364	165	216
South Division	**W**	**L**	**T**	**Pct.**	**Pts.**	**OP**
Houston	8	3	0	.727	293	179
Tennessee	6	5	0	.545	226	212
Jacksonville	3	8	0	.273	138	200
Indianapolis	0	11	0	.000	150	327
West Division	**W**	**L**	**T**	**Pct.**	**Pts.**	**OP**
Oakland	7	4	0	.636	260	274
Denver	6	5	0	.545	221	260
Kansas City	4	7	0	.364	153	265
San Diego	4	7	0	.364	249	275

National Football Conference

East Division	W	L	T	Pct.	Pts.	OP
Dallas	7	4	0	.636	270	225
New York Giants	6	5	0	.545	252	277
Philadelphia	4	7	0	.364	257	251
Washington	4	7	0	.364	183	222
North Division	**W**	**L**	**T**	**Pct.**	**Pts.**	**OP**
Green Bay	11	0	0	1.000	382	227
Chicago	7	4	0	.636	288	232
Detroit	7	4	0	.636	316	246
Minnesota	2	9	0	.182	214	295
South Division	**W**	**L**	**T**	**Pct.**	**Pts.**	**OP**
New Orleans	8	3	0	.727	362	252
Atlanta	7	4	0	.636	259	227
Tampa Bay	4	7	0	.364	199	291
Carolina	3	8	0	.273	252	305
West Division	**W**	**L**	**T**	**Pct.**	**Pts.**	**OP**
San Francisco	9	2	0	.818	262	161
Arizona	4	7	0	.364	213	256
Seattle	4	7	0	.364	185	232
St. Louis	2	9	0	.182	140	270

WEEK 10 RESULTS
Thursday, November 10
Oakland 24, SAN DIEGO 17

Sunday, November 13
New Orleans 26, ATLANTA 23 (OT)
Tennessee 30, CAROLINA 3
Pittsburgh 24, CINCINNATI 17
St. Louis 13, CLEVELAND 12
DALLAS 44, Buffalo 7
Jacksonville 17, INDIANAPOLIS 3
Denver 17, KANSAS CITY 10
MIAMI 20, Washington 9
Arizona 21, PHILADELPHIA 17
Houston 37, TAMPA BAY 9
SEATTLE 22, Baltimore 17
SAN FRANCISCO 27, New York Giants 20
CHICAGO 37, Detroit 13
New England 37, NEW YORK JETS 16

Monday, November 14
GREEN BAY 45, Minnesota 7

WEEK 11 RESULTS
Thursday, November 17
DENVER 17, New York Jets 13

Sunday, November 20
BALTIMORE 31, Cincinnati 24
CLEVELAND 14, Jacksonville 10
DETROIT 49, Carolina 35
GREEN BAY 35, Tampa Bay 26
MIAMI 35, Buffalo 8
Oakland 27, MINNESOTA 21
Dallas 27, WASHINGTON 24 (OT)
Seattle 24, ST. LOUIS 7
SAN FRANCISCO 23, Arizona 7
CHICAGO 31, San Diego 20
ATLANTA 23, Tennessee 17
Philadelphia 17, NEW YORK GIANTS 10

Monday, November 21
NEW ENGLAND 34, Kansas City 3

Byes: Houston, Indianapolis,
New Orleans, Pittsburgh

WEEK 12 RESULTS
Thursday, November 24
Green Bay 27, DETROIT 15
DALLAS 20, Miami 19
BALTIMORE 16, San Francisco 6

Sunday, November 27
ATLANTA 24, Minnesota 14
CINCINNATI 23, Cleveland 20
Carolina 27, INDIANAPOLIS 19
Houston 20, JACKSONVILLE 13
NEW YORK JETS 28, Buffalo 24
Arizona 23, ST. LOUIS 20
TENNESSEE 23, Tampa Bay 17
OAKLAND 25, Chicago 20
Washington 23, SEATTLE 17
New England 38, PHILADELPHIA 20
Denver 16, SAN DIEGO 13 (OT)
Pittsburgh 13, KANSAS CITY 9

Monday, November 28
NEW ORLEANS 49, New York Giants 24

THIRTEENTH WEEK STANDINGS
American Football Conference

East Division	W	L	T	Pct.	Pts.	OP
New England	9	3	0	.750	362	247
New York Jets	7	5	0	.583	290	260
Buffalo	5	7	0	.417	278	304
Miami	4	8	0	.333	246	220
North Division	W	L	T	Pct.	Pts.	OP
Baltimore	9	3	0	.750	296	192
Pittsburgh	9	3	0	.750	268	195
Cincinnati	7	5	0	.583	266	250
Cleveland	4	8	0	.333	175	240
South Division	W	L	T	Pct.	Pts.	OP
Houston	9	3	0	.750	310	189
Tennessee	7	5	0	.583	249	229
Jacksonville	3	9	0	.250	152	238
Indianapolis	0	12	0	.000	174	358
West Division	W	L	T	Pct.	Pts.	OP
Denver	7	5	0	.583	274	308
Oakland	7	5	0	.583	256	292
Kansas City	5	7	0	.417	163	268
San Diego	5	7	0	.417	287	289

National Football Conference

East Division	W	L	T	Pct.	Pts.	OP
Dallas	7	5	0	.583	283	244
New York Giants	6	6	0	.500	287	315
Philadelphia	4	8	0	.333	271	282
Washington	4	8	0	.333	202	256
North Division	W	L	T	Pct.	Pts.	OP
Green Bay*	12	0	0	1.000	420	262
Chicago	7	5	0	.583	291	242
Detroit	7	5	0	.583	333	277
Minnesota	2	10	0	.167	246	330
South Division	W	L	T	Pct.	Pts.	OP
New Orleans	9	3	0	.750	393	269
Atlanta	7	5	0	.583	269	244
Carolina	4	8	0	.333	290	324
Tampa Bay	4	8	0	.333	218	329
West Division	W	L	T	Pct.	Pts.	OP
San Francisco*	10	2	0	.833	288	161
Arizona	5	7	0	.417	232	269
Seattle	5	7	0	.417	216	246
St. Louis	2	10	0	.167	140	296

*Clinched division title

WEEK 13 RESULTS
Thursday, December 1
SEATTLE 31, Philadelphia 14

Sunday, December 4
Tennessee 23, BUFFALO 17
Kansas City 10, CHICAGO 3
HOUSTON 17, Atlanta 10
MIAMI 34, Oakland 14
Carolina 38, TAMPA BAY 19
New York Jets 34, WASHINGTON 19
Denver 35, MINNESOTA 32
NEW ENGLAND 31, Indianapolis 24
PITTSBURGH 35, Cincinnati 7
Baltimore 24, CLEVELAND 10
ARIZONA 19, Dallas 13 (OT)
Green Bay 38, NEW YORK GIANTS 35
SAN FRANCISCO 26, St. Louis 0
NEW ORLEANS 31, Detroit 17

Monday, December 5
San Diego 38, JACKSONVILLE 14

FOURTEENTH WEEK STANDINGS
American Football Conference

East Division	W	L	T	Pct.	Pts.	OP
New England	10	3	0	.769	396	274
New York Jets	8	5	0	.615	327	270
Buffalo	5	8	0	.385	288	341
Miami	4	9	0	.308	256	246
North Division	W	L	T	Pct.	Pts.	OP
Baltimore	10	3	0	.769	320	202
Pittsburgh	10	3	0	.769	282	198
Cincinnati	7	6	0	.538	285	270
Cleveland	4	9	0	.308	178	254
South Division	W	L	T	Pct.	Pts.	OP
Houston*	10	3	0	.769	330	208
Tennessee	7	6	0	.538	266	251
Jacksonville	4	9	0	.308	193	252
Indianapolis	0	13	0	.000	184	382
West Division	W	L	T	Pct.	Pts.	OP
Denver	8	5	0	.615	269	302
Oakland	7	6	0	.538	290	354
San Diego	6	7	0	.462	324	299
Kansas City	5	8	0	.385	173	305

National Football Conference

East Division	W	L	T	Pct.	Pts.	OP
Dallas	7	6	0	.538	317	281
New York Giants	7	6	0	.538	324	349
Philadelphia	5	8	0	.385	297	292
Washington	4	9	0	.308	229	290
North Division	W	L	T	Pct.	Pts.	OP
Green Bay*	13	0	0	1.000	466	278
Detroit	8	5	0	.615	367	305
Chicago	7	6	0	.538	301	255
Minnesota	2	11	0	.154	274	364
South Division	W	L	T	Pct.	Pts.	OP
New Orleans#	10	3	0	.769	415	286
Atlanta	8	5	0	.615	300	267
Carolina	4	9	0	.308	313	355
Tampa Bay	4	9	0	.308	232	370
West Division	W	L	T	Pct.	Pts.	OP
San Francisco*	10	3	0	.769	307	182
Arizona	6	7	0	.462	253	288
Seattle	6	7	0	.462	246	259
St. Louis	2	11	0	.154	153	326

*Clinched division title
#Clinched playoff berth

WEEK 14 RESULTS
Thursday, December 8
PITTSBURGH 14, Cleveland 3

Sunday, December 11
BALTIMORE 24, Indianapolis 10
Atlanta 31, CAROLINA 23
Houston 20, CINCINNATI 19
DETROIT 34, Minnesota 28
JACKSONVILLE 41, Tampa Bay 14
Philadelphia 26, MIAMI 10
NEW YORK JETS 37, Kansas City 10
New Orleans 22, TENNESSEE 17
New England 34, WASHINGTON 27
ARIZONA 21, San Francisco 19
DENVER 13, Chicago 10 (OT)
SAN DIEGO 37, Buffalo 10
GREEN BAY 46, Oakland 16
New York Giants 37, DALLAS 34

Monday, December 12
SEATTLE 30, St. Louis 13

FIFTEENTH WEEK STANDINGS
American Football Conference

East Division	W	L	T	Pct.	Pts.	OP
New England*	11	3	0	.786	437	297
New York Jets	8	6	0	.571	346	315
Buffalo	5	9	0	.357	311	371
Miami	5	9	0	.357	286	269
North Division	W	L	T	Pct.	Pts.	OP
Baltimore#	10	4	0	.714	334	236
Pittsburgh#	10	4	0	.714	285	218
Cincinnati	8	6	0	.571	305	283
Cleveland	4	10	0	.286	195	274
South Division	W	L	T	Pct.	Pts.	OP
Houston*	10	4	0	.714	343	236
Tennessee	7	7	0	.500	279	278
Jacksonville	4	10	0	.286	207	293
Indianapolis	1	13	0	.071	211	395
West Division	W	L	T	Pct.	Pts.	OP
Denver	8	6	0	.571	292	343
Oakland	7	7	0	.500	317	382
San Diego	7	7	0	.500	358	313
Kansas City	6	8	0	.429	192	319

National Football Conference

East Division	W	L	T	Pct.	Pts.	OP
Dallas	8	6	0	.571	348	296
New York Giants	7	7	0	.500	334	372
Philadelphia	6	8	0	.429	342	311
Washington	5	9	0	.357	252	300
North Division	W	L	T	Pct.	Pts.	OP
Green Bay*	13	1	0	.929	480	297
Detroit	9	5	0	.643	395	332
Chicago	7	7	0	.500	315	293
Minnesota	2	12	0	.143	294	406
South Division	W	L	T	Pct.	Pts.	OP
New Orleans#	11	3	0	.786	457	306
Atlanta	9	5	0	.643	341	281
Carolina	5	9	0	.357	341	368
Tampa Bay	4	10	0	.286	247	401
West Division	W	L	T	Pct.	Pts.	OP
San Francisco*	11	3	0	.786	327	185
Arizona	7	7	0	.500	273	305
Seattle	7	7	0	.500	284	273
St. Louis	2	12	0	.143	166	346

*Clinched division title
#Clinched playoff berth

WEEK 15 RESULTS
Thursday, December 15
ATLANTA 41, Jacksonville 14

Saturday, December 17
Dallas 31, TAMPA BAY 15

Sunday, December 18
Miami 30, BUFFALO 23
Seattle 38, CHICAGO 14
Carolina 28, HOUSTON 13
INDIANAPOLIS 27, Tennessee 13
KANSAS CITY 19, Green Bay 14
New Orleans 42, MINNESOTA 20
Washington 23, NEW YORK GIANTS 10
Cincinnati 20, ST. LOUIS 13
Detroit 28, OAKLAND 27
ARIZONA 20, Cleveland 17 (OT)
New England 41, DENVER 23
PHILADELPHIA 45, New York Jets 19
SAN DIEGO 34, Baltimore 14

Monday, December 19
SAN FRANCISCO 20, Pittsburgh 3

SIXTEENTH WEEK STANDINGS
American Football Conference

East Division	W	L	T	Pct.	Pts.	OP
New England*	12	3	0	.800	464	321
New York Jets	8	7	0	.533	360	344
Buffalo	6	9	0	.400	351	385
Miami	5	10	0	.333	310	296
North Division	**W**	**L**	**T**	**Pct.**	**Pts.**	**OP**
Baltimore#	11	4	0	.733	354	250
Pittsburgh#	11	4	0	.733	312	218
Cincinnati	9	6	0	.600	328	299
Cleveland	4	11	0	.267	209	294
South Division	**W**	**L**	**T**	**Pct.**	**Pts.**	**OP**
Houston*	10	5	0	.667	359	255
Tennessee	8	7	0	.533	302	295
Jacksonville	4	11	0	.267	224	316
Indianapolis	2	13	0	.133	230	411
West Division	**W**	**L**	**T**	**Pct.**	**Pts.**	**OP**
Denver	8	7	0	.533	306	383
Oakland	8	7	0	.533	333	395
San Diego	7	8	0	.467	368	351
Kansas City	6	9	0	.400	205	335

National Football Conference

East Division	W	L	T	Pct.	Pts.	OP
Dallas	8	7	0	.533	355	316
New York Giants	8	7	0	.533	363	386
Philadelphia	7	8	0	.467	362	318
Washington	5	10	0	.333	278	333
North Division	**W**	**L**	**T**	**Pct.**	**Pts.**	**OP**
Green Bay*	14	1	0	.933	515	318
Detroit#	10	5	0	.667	433	342
Chicago	7	8	0	.467	336	328
Minnesota	3	12	0	.200	327	432
South Division	**W**	**L**	**T**	**Pct.**	**Pts.**	**OP**
New Orleans*	12	3	0	.800	502	322
Atlanta#	9	6	0	.600	357	326
Carolina	6	9	0	.400	389	384
Tampa Bay	4	11	0	.267	263	449
West Division	**W**	**L**	**T**	**Pct.**	**Pts.**	**OP**
San Francisco*	12	3	0	.800	346	202
Arizona	7	8	0	.467	289	328
Seattle	7	8	0	.467	301	292
St. Louis	2	13	0	.133	166	373

*Clinched division title
#Clinched playoff berth

WEEK 16 RESULTS
Thursday, December 22
INDIANAPOLIS 19, Houston 16

Saturday, December 24
BALTIMORE 20, Cleveland 14
BUFFALO 40, Denver 14
CAROLINA 48, Tampa Bay 16
CINCINNATI 23, Arizona 16
Oakland 16, KANSAS CITY 13 (OT)
NEW ENGLAND 27, Miami 16
New York Giants 29, NEW YORK JETS 14
PITTSBURGH 27, St. Louis 0
TENNESSEE 23, Jacksonville 17
Minnesota 33, WASHINGTON 26
DETROIT 38, San Diego 10
Philadelphia 20, DALLAS 7
San Francisco 19, SEATTLE 17

Sunday, December 25
GREEN BAY 35, Chicago 21

Monday, December 26
NEW ORLEANS 45, Atlanta 16

SEVENTEENTH WEEK STANDINGS
American Football Conference

East Division	W	L	T	Pct.	Pts.	OP
New England*	13	3	0	.813	513	342
New York Jets	8	8	0	.500	377	363
Miami	6	10	0	.375	329	313
Buffalo	6	10	0	.375	372	434
North Division	**W**	**L**	**T**	**Pct.**	**Pts.**	**OP**
Baltimore*	12	4	0	.750	378	266
Pittsburgh#	12	4	0	.750	325	227
Cincinnati#	9	7	0	.563	344	323
Cleveland	4	12	0	.250	218	307
South Division	**W**	**L**	**T**	**Pct.**	**Pts.**	**OP**
Houston*	10	6	0	.625	381	278
Tennessee	9	7	0	.563	325	317
Jacksonville	5	11	0	.313	243	329
Indianapolis	2	14	0	.125	243	430
West Division	**W**	**L**	**T**	**Pct.**	**Pts.**	**OP**
Denver*	8	8	0	.500	309	390
San Diego	8	8	0	.500	406	377
Oakland	8	8	0	.500	359	433
Kansas City	7	9	0	.438	212	338

National Football Conference

East Division	W	L	T	Pct.	Pts.	OP
New York Giants*	9	7	0	.563	394	400
Philadelphia	8	8	0	.500	396	328
Dallas	8	8	0	.500	369	347
Washington	5	11	0	.313	288	367
North Division	**W**	**L**	**T**	**Pct.**	**Pts.**	**OP**
Green Bay*	15	1	0	.938	560	359
Detroit#	10	6	0	.625	474	387
Chicago	8	8	0	.500	353	341
Minnesota	3	13	0	.188	340	449
South Division	**W**	**L**	**T**	**Pct.**	**Pts.**	**OP**
New Orleans*	13	3	0	.813	547	339
Atlanta#	10	6	0	.625	402	350
Carolina	6	10	0	.375	406	429
Tampa Bay	4	12	0	.250	287	494
West Division	**W**	**L**	**T**	**Pct.**	**Pts.**	**OP**
San Francisco*	13	3	0	.813	380	229
Arizona	8	8	0	.500	312	348
Seattle	7	9	0	.438	321	315
St. Louis	2	14	0	.125	193	407

*Clinched division title
#Clinched wild-card berth

WEEK 17 RESULTS
Sunday, January 1, 2012
GREEN BAY 45, Detroit 41
Tennessee 23, HOUSTON 22
JACKSONVILLE 19, Indianapolis 13
MIAMI 19, New York Jets 17
Chicago 17, MINNESOTA 13
NEW ENGLAND 49, Buffalo 21
PHILADELPHIA 34, Washington 10
San Francisco 34, ST. LOUIS 27
NEW ORLEANS 45, Carolina 17
ARIZONA 23, Seattle 20 (OT)
ATLANTA 45, Tampa Bay 24
Baltimore 24, CINCINNATI 16
Pittsburgh 13, CLEVELAND 9
Kansas City 7, DENVER 3
San Diego 38, OAKLAND 26
NEW YORK GIANTS 31, Dallas 14

2011 NFL PAID ATTENDANCE BREAKDOWN

Games	Attendance	Average
NFL Preseason Total		
64	3,568,186	55,753
NFL Regular-Season Total		
256	16,562,706	64,698
NFL Postseason Total		
12	828,457	69,038
NFL All Games		
332	20,959,349	63,131

1.1-MILLION CLUB
During the 2011 season, five teams drew more than 1.1 million paid attendance home and away during the regular season. The New York Giants led the NFL in regular-season paid attendance (1,186,047). The Giants also led the league in home paid attendance (625,509).

Team	Total Paid Home Attendance	Total Paid Visiting Attendance	Total Paid Cumulative Attendance
New York Giants	625,509	560,538	1,186,047
New York Jets	607,086	542,637	1,149,723
Dallas	592,045	555,846	1,147,891
Green Bay	564,100	548,488	1,112,588
Washington	587,354	513,709	1,101,063

For complete year-by-year attendance records, see pages 533-534.

2011 AFC PLAYERS OF THE WEEK

	Offense	Defense	Special Teams
Week 1	QB Tom Brady, New England	LB Terrell Suggs, Baltimore	K Sebastian Janikowski, Oakland
Week 2	QB Tom Brady, New England	CB Antonio Cromartie, N.Y. Jets	KR-WR Joshua Cribbs, Cleveland
Week 3	RB Darren McFadden, Oakland	LB Ray Lewis, Baltimore	K Rian Lindell, Buffalo
Week 4	RB Arian Foster, Houston	LB Jarret Johnson, Baltimore	K Ryan Succop, Kansas City
Week 5	QB Ben Roethlisberger, Pittsburgh	S George Wilson, Buffalo	K Sebastian Janikowski, Oakland
Week 6	RB Rashard Mendenhall, Pittsburgh	CB Darrelle Revis, New York Jets	KR-WR Jacoby Ford, Oakland
Week 7	RB Arian Foster, Houston	CB Brandon Flowers, Kansas City	K Josh Scobee, Jacksonville
Week 8	QB Ben Roethlisberger, Pittsburgh	LB Derrick Johnson, Kansas City	KR-WR Brandon Tate, Cincinnati
Week 9	QB Matt Moore, Miami	LB David Harris, N.Y. Jets	PR-WR Eddie Royal, Denver
Week 10	RB Michael Bush, Oakland	DE Andre Carter, New England	PR-WR Marc Mariani, Tennessee
Week 11	WR Torrey Smith, Baltimore	LB Von Miller, Denver	PR-WR Julian Edelman, New England
Week 12	RB Chris Johnson, Tennessee	LB Terrell Suggs, Baltimore	K Sebastian Janikowski, Oakland
Week 13	RB Ray Rice, Baltimore	LB Colin McCarthy, Tennessee	PR-WR Antonio Brown, Pittsburgh
Week 14	TE Rob Gronkowski, New England	LB Terrell Suggs, Baltimore	K Matt Prater, Denver
Week 15	RB Reggie Bush, Miami	LB Antwan Barnes, San Diego	K Ryan Succop, Kansas City
Week 16	QB Tom Brady, New England	DE Robert Mathis, Indianapolis	DT Richard Seymour, Oakland
Week 17	RB Ray Rice, Baltimore	S Troy Polamalu, Pittsburgh	KR-WR Richard Goodman, San Diego

2011 AFC PLAYERS OF THE MONTH

	Offense	Defense	Special Teams
September	QB Ryan Fitzpatrick, Buffalo	LB D'Qwell Jackson, Cleveland	K Sebastian Janikowski, Oakland
October	RB Arian Foster, Houston	LB LaMarr Woodley, Pittsburgh	KR-RB Joe McKnight, N.Y. Jets
November	QB Tom Brady, New England	LB Connor Barwin, Houston	K Sebastian Janikowski, Oakland
December	QB Tom Brady, New England	LB Terrell Suggs, Baltimore	K Matt Prater, Denver

2011 NFC PLAYERS OF THE WEEK

	Offense	Defense	Special Teams
Week 1	QB Aaron Rodgers, Green Bay	LB Brian Urlacher, Chicago	KR-PR Ted Ginn Jr., San Francisco
Week 2	QB Tony Romo, Dallas	S Roman Harper, New Orleans	K Jason Hanson, Detroit
Week 3	QB Eli Manning, N.Y. Giants	CB Ronde Barber, Tampa Bay	K Dan Bailey, Dallas
Week 4	QB Aaron Rodgers, Green Bay	LB Brian Orakpo, Washington	PR-KR Devin Hester, Chicago
Week 5	RB Adrian Peterson, Minnesota	LB Patrick Willis, San Francisco	K Mason Crosby, Green Bay
Week 6	RB Ahmad Bradshaw, N.Y. Giants	S Kurt Coleman, Philadelphia	KR-PR-WR Devin Hester, Chicago
Week 7	QB Drew Brees, New Orleans	LB Lance Briggs, Chicago	K Mason Crosby, Green Bay
Week 8	RB LeSean McCoy, Philadelphia	DE Cliff Avril, Detroit	DE Robert Quinn, St. Louis
Week 9	QB Aaron Rodgers, Green Bay	LB Mathias Kiwanuka, N.Y. Giants	PR-CB Patrick Peterson, Arizona
Week 10	WR Larry Fitzgerald, Arizona	S Roman Harper, New Orleans	PR Devin Hester, Chicago
Week 11	RB Kevin Smith, Detroit	DE Chris Clemons, Seattle	KR Kealoha Pilares, Carolina
Week 12	QB Drew Brees, New Orleans	CB DeAngelo Hall, Washington	PR-CB Patrick Peterson, Arizona
Week 13	QB Cam Newton, Carolina	LB David Hawthorne, Seattle	P Tim Masthay, Green Bay
Week 14	QB Matt Ryan, Atlanta	DE Jason Pierre-Paul, N.Y. Giants	ST-WR Doug Baldwin, Seattle
Week 15	WR Calvin Johnson, Detroit	DE John Abraham, Atlanta	P Andy Lee, San Francisco
Week 16	QB Drew Brees, New Orleans	DE Jason Pierre-Paul, N.Y. Giants	K David Akers, San Francisco
Week 17	QB Matt Flynn, Green Bay	LB Curtis Lofton, Atlanta	K David Akers, San Francisco

2011 NFC PLAYERS OF THE MONTH

	Offense	Defense	Special Teams
September	QB Aaron Rodgers, Green Bay	LB Sean Lee, Dallas	K Jason Hanson, Detroit
October	QB Aaron Rodgers, Green Bay	DE Jared Allen, Minnesota	PR-KR Devin Hester, Chicago
November	QB Aaron Rodgers, Green Bay	DE Julius Peppers, Chicago	PR-CB Patrick Peterson, Arizona
December	QB Drew Brees, New Orleans	DE Jason Pierre-Paul, N.Y. Giants	K David Akers, San Francisco

2011 NFL ROOKIES OF THE MONTH

	Offense (College)		Defense (College)	
September	QB	Cam Newton, Carolina (Auburn)	LB	Ryan Kerrigan, Washington (Purdue)
October	QB	Andy Dalton, Cincinnati (TCU)	LB	Aldon Smith, San Francisco (Missouri)
November	RB	DeMarco Murray, Dallas (Oklahoma)	LB	Von Miller, Denver (Texas A&M)
Dec./Jan.	WR	Julio Jones, Atlanta (Alabama)	LB	Aldon Smith, San Francisco (Missouri)

2011 PRO FOOTBALL AWARDS

ASSOCIATED PRESS
Most Valuable Player	Aaron Rodgers
Offensive Player of the Year	Drew Brees
Defensive Player of the Year	Terrell Suggs
Offensive Rookie of the Year	Cam Newton
Defensive Rookie of the Year	Von Miller
Coach of the Year	Jim Harbaugh
Comeback Player of the Year	Matthew Stafford

THE SPORTING NEWS
Offensive Player of the Year	Aaron Rodgers
Defensive Player of the Year	Jared Allen
Rookie of the Year	Cam Newton
Coach of the Year	Jim Harbaugh
Coordinator of the Year	Wade Phillips
Executive of the Year	Ted Thompson

PRO FOOTBALL WEEKLY/PFWA
Most Valuable Player	Aaron Rodgers
Defensive Player of the Year	Terrell Suggs
Offensive Rookie of the Year	Cam Newton
Defensive Rookie of the Year	Aldon Smith
Comeback Player of the Year	Matthew Stafford
Most Improved	Victor Cruz
Golden Toe	David Akers
	Andy Lee
Coach of the Year	Jim Harbaugh
Assistant Coach of the Year	Wade Phillips
Executive of the Year	Trent Baalke

SPORTS ILLUSTRATED
Most Valuable Player	Aaron Rodgers
Offensive Rookie of the Year	Cam Newton
Defensive Rookie of the Year	Von Miller
Coach of the Year	Jim Harbaugh

MAXWELL CLUB PLAYER OF THE YEAR
Bert Bell Trophy	Aaron Rodgers

MAXWELL CLUB COACH OF THE YEAR
Earle "Greasy" Neale Trophy	Mike McCarthy

WALTER PAYTON/ NFL MAN OF THE YEAR
Man of the Year	Matt Birk
Man of the Year Finalist	Philip Rivers
Man of the Year Finalist	Charles Tillman

SUPER BOWL XLVI MOST VALUABLE PLAYER
Pete Rozelle Trophy	Eli Manning

AFC-NFC 2012 PRO BOWL MOST VALUABLE PLAYER
Pro Bowl MVP	Brandon Marshall

FEDEX AIR & GROUND NFL PLAYERS OF THE YEAR
FedEx Air NFL Player of the Year	Drew Brees
FedEx Ground NFL Player of the Year	LeSean McCoy

PEPSI ROOKIE OF THE YEAR
Rookie of the Year	Cam Newton

GMC NEVER SAY NEVER MOMENT OF THE YEAR
Moment of the Year Award	Tim Tebow

MADDEN MOST VALUABLE PROTECTORS AWARD PRESENTED BY PRILOSEC OTC
New Orleans Saints Offensive Line

2011 ALL-PRO TEAMS

2011 PFW/PFWA ALL-PRO TEAM
Selected by *Pro Football Weekly* and the Professional Football Writers of America

Offense:
Aaron Rodgers, Green Bay	Quarterback
Maurice Jones-Drew, Jacksonville	Running Back
LeSean McCoy, Philadelphia	Running Back
Rob Gronkowski, New England	Tight End
Calvin Johnson, Detroit	Wide Receiver
Wes Welker, New England	Wide Receiver
Jason Peters, Philadelphia	Tackle
Joe Thomas, Cleveland	Tackle
Carl Nicks, New Orleans	Guard
Jahri Evans, New Orleans	Guard
Maurkice Pouncey, Pittsburgh	Center

Defense:
Jared Allen, Minnesota	End
Jason Pierre-Paul, N.Y. Giants	End
Haloti Ngata, Baltimore	Tackle
Justin Smith, San Francisco	Tackle
Terrell Suggs, Baltimore	Outside Linebacker
DeMarcus Ware, Dallas	Outside Linebacker
Patrick Willis, San Francisco	Inside Linebacker
Charles Woodson, Green Bay	Cornerback
Darrelle Revis, N.Y. Jets	Cornerback
Troy Polamalu, Pittsburgh	Safety
Eric Weddle, San Diego	Safety

Special Teams:
David Akers, San Francisco	Kicker
Andy Lee, San Francisco	Punter
Joe McKnight, N.Y. Jets	Kick Returner
Patrick Peterson, Arizona	Punt Returner
Matthew Slater, New England	Special Teams Player

2011 ASSOCIATED PRESS ALL-PRO TEAM
Selected by the Associated Press

Offense:
Aaron Rodgers, Green Bay	Quarterback
Maurice Jones-Drew, Jacksonville	Running Back
LeSean McCoy, Philadelphia	Running Back
Vonta Leach, Baltimore	Fullback
Rob Gronkowski, New England	Tight End
Calvin Johnson, Detroit	Wide Receiver
Wes Welker, New England	Wide Receiver
Jason Peters, Philadelphia	Tackle
Joe Thomas, Cleveland	Tackle
Carl Nicks, New Orleans	Guard
Jahri Evans, New Orleans	Guard
Maurkice Pouncey, Pittsburgh	Center

Defense:
Jared Allen, Minnesota	End
Jason Pierre-Paul, N.Y. Giants	End
Haloti Ngata, Baltimore	Tackle
Justin Smith, San Francisco	Tackle
Terrell Suggs, Baltimore	Outside Linebacker
DeMarcus Ware, Dallas	Outside Linebacker
Patrick Willis, San Francisco	Inside Linebacker
NaVorro Bowman, San Francisco	Inside Linebacker
Derrick Johnson, Kansas City	Inside Linebacker
Charles Woodson, Green Bay	Cornerback
Darrelle Revis, N.Y. Jets	Cornerback
Troy Polamalu, Pittsburgh	Safety
Eric Weddle, San Diego	Safety

Special Teams:
David Akers, San Francisco	Kicker
Andy Lee, San Francisco	Punter
Patrick Peterson, Arizona	Kick Returner

2011 ALL-NFL TEAM

Selected by the Associated Press, *Pro Football Weekly,* and the Professional Football Writers of America

Offense:

Aaron Rodgers, Green Bay (PFW, AP)	Quarterback
Maurice Jones-Drew, Jacksonville (PFW, AP)	Running Back
LeSean McCoy, Philadelphia (PFW, AP)	Running Back
Vonta Leach, Baltimore (AP)	Fullback
Rob Gronkowski, New England (PFW, AP)	Tight End
Calvin Johnson, Detroit (PFW, AP)	Wide Receiver
Wes Welker, New England (PFW, AP)	Wide Receiver
Jason Peters, Philadelphia (PFW, AP)	Tackle
Joe Thomas, Cleveland (PFW, AP)	Tackle
Carl Nicks, New Orleans (PFW, AP)	Guard
Jahri Evans, New Orleans (PFW, AP)	Guard
Maurkice Pouncey, Pittsburgh (PFW, AP)	Center

Defense:

Jared Allen, Minnesota (PFW, AP)	End
Jason Pierre-Paul, N.Y. Giants (PFW, AP)	End
Haloti Ngata, Baltimore (PFW, AP)	Tackle
Justin Smith, San Francisco (PFW, AP)	Tackle
Terrell Suggs, Baltimore (PFW, AP)	Outside Linebacker
DeMarcus Ware, Dallas (PFW, AP)	Outside Linebacker
Patrick Willis, San Francisco (PFW, AP)	Inside Linebacker
NaVorro Bowman, San Francisco (AP)	Inside Linebacker
Derrick Johnson, Kansas City (AP)	Inside Linebacker
Charles Woodson, Green Bay (PFW, AP)	Cornerback
Darrelle Revis, N.Y. Jets (PFW, AP)	Cornerback
Troy Polamalu, Pittsburgh (PFW, AP)	Safety
Eric Weddle, San Diego (PFW, AP)	Safety

Special Teams:

David Akers, San Francisco (PFW, AP)	Kicker
Andy Lee, San Francisco (PFW, AP)	Punter
Joe McKnight, N.Y. Jets (PFW)	Kick Returner
Patrick Peterson, Arizona (PFW, AP)	Punt Returner
Matthew Slater, New England (PFW)	Special Teams Player

2011 PFW/PFWA ALL-ROOKIE TEAM

Selected by *Pro Football Weekly* and the Professional Football Writers of America

Offense:

Cam Newton, Carolina	Quarterback
DeMarco Murray, Dallas	Running Back
Roy Helu, Washington	Running Back
Kyle Rudolph, Minnesota	Tight End
A.J. Green, Cincinnati	Wide Receiver
Julio Jones, Atlanta	Wide Receiver
Tyron Smith, Dallas	Tackle
Nate Solder, New England	Tackle
Danny Watkins, Philadelphia	Guard
Stefen Wisniewski, Oakland	Guard
Mike Pouncey, Miami	Center

Defense:

J.J. Watt, Houston	Defensive Lineman
Jabaal Sheard, Cleveland	Defensive Lineman
Marcell Dareus, Buffalo	Defensive Lineman
Phil Taylor, Cleveland	Defensive Lineman
Aldon Smith, San Francisco	Outside Linebacker
Von Miller, Denver	Outside Linebacker
Ryan Kerrigan, Washington	Middle Linebacker
Patrick Peterson, Arizona	Cornerback
Richard Sherman, Seattle	Cornerback
Chris Conte, Chicago	Safety
Chris Harris, Denver	Safety

Special Teams:

Dan Bailey, Dallas	Kicker
Matt Bosher, Atlanta	Punter
Patrick Peterson, Arizona	Punt Returner
Randall Cobb, Green Bay	Kick Returner
Akeem Dent, Atlanta	Special Teams Player

TEN BEST RUSHING PERFORMANCES, 2011

	Att.	Yards	TD
1. DeMarco Murray	25	253	1
Dallas vs. St. Louis, Oct. 23			
2. Beanie Wells	27	228	1
Arizona vs. St. Louis, Nov. 27			
3. Matt Forté	25	205	1
Chicago vs. Carolina, Oct. 2			
4. Ray Rice	29	204	1
Baltimore vs. Cleveland, Dec. 4			
5. Reggie Bush	25	203	1
Miami vs. Buffalo, Dec. 18			
6. Ray Rice	24	191	2
Baltimore vs. Cincinnati, Jan. 1			
7. Chris Johnson	23	190	0
Tennessee vs. Tampa Bay, Nov. 27			
8. LeSean McCoy	30	185	2
Philadelphia vs. Dallas, Oct. 30			
9. Adrian Peterson	24	175	1
Minnesota vs. Green Bay, Oct. 23			
10. Michael Turner	17	172	2
Atlanta vs. Tampa Bay, Jan. 1			

There were 131 100-yard rushing performances in 2011.

MOST 100-YARD RUSHING PERFORMANCES, 2011

Player, Team	100-Yd. Games
Arian Foster, Houston	7
Willis McGahee, Denver	7
Fred Jackson, Buffalo	6
Maurice Jones-Drew, Jacksonville	6
Marshawn Lynch, Seattle	6
LeSean McCoy, Philadelphia	6
Ray Rice, Baltimore	6
Michael Turner, Atlanta	6
Reggie Bush, Miami	5
Frank Gore, San Francisco	5
Matt Forté, Chicago	4
Steven Jackson, St. Louis	4
Chris Johnson, Tennessee	4
Ryan Mathews, San Diego	4
Ben Tate, Houston	4
Cedric Benson, Cincinnati	3
LeGarrette Blount, Tampa Bay	3
Roy Helu, Washington	3
Felix Jones, Dallas	3
DeMarco Murray, Dallas	3
Adrian Peterson, Minnesota	3
Michael Bush, Oakland	2
Shonn Greene, New York Jets	2
Darren McFadden, Oakland	2
Rashard Mendenhall, Pittsburgh	2
Evan Royster, Washington	2
Chris Wells, Arizona	2
21 players tied with	1

TEN BEST PASSING PERFORMANCES, 2011

	Att.	Comp.	Yds.	TD
1. Matthew Stafford	36	59	520	5
Detroit vs. Green Bay, Jan. 1				
2. Tom Brady	32	48	517	4
New England vs. Miami, Sept. 12				
3. Matt Flynn	31	44	480	6
Green Bay vs. Detroit, Jan. 1				
4. Cam Newton	28	46	432	1
Carolina vs. Green Bay, Sept. 18				
5. Tom Brady	31	40	423	3
New England vs. San Diego, Sept. 18				
6. Cam Newton	24	37	422	2
Carolina vs. Arizona, Sept. 11				
7. Eli Manning	24	39	420	3
New York Giants vs. Seattle, Oct. 9				
8. Drew Brees	32	49	419	3
New Orleans vs. Green Bay, Sept. 8				
9. Carson Palmer	28	43	417	2
Oakland vs. San Diego, Jan. 1				
10. Michael Vick	30	46	416	2
Philadelphia vs. San Francisco, Oct. 2				

There were 121 300-yard passing performances in 2011.

MOST 300-YARD PASSING PERFORMANCES, 2011

Player, Team	300-Yd. Games
Drew Brees, New Orleans	13
Tom Brady, New England	11
Eli Manning, New York Giants	8
Aaron Rodgers, Green Bay	8
Matthew Stafford, Detroit	8
Philip Rivers, San Diego	6
Matt Ryan, Atlanta	6
Ben Roethlisberger, Pittsburgh	5
Tony Romo, Dallas	5
Joe Flacco, Baltimore	4
Carson Palmer, Oakland	4
Ryan Fitzpatrick, Buffalo	3
Matt Hasselbeck, Tennessee	3
Cam Newton, Carolina	3
Mark Sanchez, New York Jets	3
Michael Vick, Philadelphia	3
Sam Bradford, St. Louis	2
Jason Campbell, Oakland	2
Jay Cutler, Chicago	2
Andy Dalton, Cincinnati	2
Josh Freeman, Tampa Bay	2
Rex Grossman, Washington	2
Tarvaris Jackson, Seattle	2
Kyle Orton, Denver/Kansas City	2
Matt Schaub, Houston	2
John Skelton, Arizona	2
8 players tied with	1

TEN BEST RECEIVING PERFORMANCES, 2011

	No.	Yards	TD
1. Calvin Johnson	11	244	1
Detroit vs. Green Bay, Jan. 1			
2. Wes Welker	16	217	2
New England vs. Buffalo, Sept. 25			
3. Calvin Johnson	9	214	2
Detroit vs. Oakland, Dec. 18			
4. Steve Smith	8	181	0
Carolina vs. Chicago, Oct. 2			
5. Victor Cruz	6	178	1
New York Giants vs. Dallas, Jan. 1			
Steve Smith	8	178	2
Carolina vs. Arizona, Sept. 11			
7. Vincent Jackson	10	172	2
San Diego vs. New England, Sept. 18			
8. DeSean Jackson	6	171	0
Philadelphia vs. San Francisco, Oct. 2			
Jeremy Maclin	13	171	2
Philadelphia vs. Atlanta, Sept. 18			
10. Jared Cook	8	169	1
Tennessee vs. Jacksonville, Dec. 24			

There were 192 100-yard receiving performances in 2011.

MOST 100-YARD RECEIVING PERFORMANCES, 2011

Player, Team	100-Yd. Games
Calvin Johnson, Detroit	8
Wes Welker, New England	8
Victor Cruz, New York Giants	7
Larry Fitzgerald, Arizona	6
Steve Smith, Carolina	6
Rob Gronkowski, New England	5
Julio Jones, Atlanta	5
Brandon Marshall, Miami	5
Jordy Nelson, Green Bay	5
Roddy White, Atlanta	5
Marques Colston, New Orleans	4
Malcom Floyd, San Diego	4
Jimmy Graham, New Orleans	4
A.J. Green, Cincinnati	4
Vincent Jackson, San Diego	4
Mike Wallace, Pittsburgh	4
Dwayne Bowe, Kansas City	3
Antonio Brown, Pittsburgh	3
Arian Foster, Houston	3
Pierre Garcon, Indianapolis	3
Aaron Hernandez, New England	3
Darrius Heyward-Bey, Oakland	3
Greg Jennings, Green Bay	3
Jeremy Maclin, Philadelphia	3
Denarius Moore, Oakland	3
Hakeem Nicks, New York Giants	3
Laurent Robinson, Dallas	3
Jerome Simpson, Cincinnati	3
Reggie Wayne, Indianapolis	3
Jason Avant, Philadelphia	2
Anquan Boldin, Baltimore	2
Deion Branch, New England	2
Kenny Britt, Tennessee	2
Jared Cook, Tennessee	2
Vernon Davis, San Francisco	2
Percy Harvin, Minnesota	2
Devery Henderson, New Orleans	2
DeSean Jackson, Philadelphia	2
Brandon Lloyd, St. Louis/Denver	2
Brandon Pettigrew, Detroit	2
Sidney Rice, Seattle	2
Torrey Smith, Baltimore	2
Demaryius Thomas, Denver	2

Player, Team	100-Yd. Games
Nate Washington, Tennessee	2
Jason Witten, Dallas	2
37 players tied with	1

TOP QUARTERBACK SACK PERFORMANCES, 2011

	No.
1. DeMarcus Ware	4.0
Dallas vs. Philadelphia, Oct. 30	
Kamerion Wimbley	4.0
Oakland vs. San Diego, Oct. 10	
Andre Carter	4.0
New England vs. New York Jets, Nov. 13	
Connor Barwin	4.0
Houston vs. Jacksonville, Oct. 27	
Antwan Barnes	4.0
San Diego vs. Baltimore, Dec. 18	
6. John Abraham	3.5
Atlanta vs. Jacksonville, Dec. 15	
Jared Allen	3.5
Minnesota vs. Chicago, Jan. 1	
8. Terrell Suggs	3.0
Baltimore vs. Pittsburgh, Sept. 11	
Jared Allen	3.0
Minnesota vs. Detroit, Sept. 25	
Jason Babin	3.0
Philadelphia vs. San Francisco, Oct. 2	
Chris Long	3.0
St. Louis vs. New Orleans, Oct. 30	
James Harrison	3.0
Pittsburgh vs. Baltimore, Nov. 6	
Chris Clemons	3.0
Seattle vs. St. Louis, Nov. 20	
Terrell Suggs	3.0
Baltimore vs. San Francisco, Nov. 24	
Justin Houston	3.0
Kansas City vs. Chicago, Dec. 4	
James Harrison	3.0
Pittsburgh vs. Cincinnati, Dec. 4	
Terrell Suggs	3.0
Baltimore vs. Indianapolis, Dec. 11	
Jared Allen	3.0
Minnesota vs. Detroit, Dec. 11	
Jason Babin	3.0
Philadelphia vs. Miami, Dec. 11	
Trent Cole	3.0
Philadelphia vs. Miami, Dec. 11	
Tamba Hali	3.0
Kansas City vs. Green Bay, Dec. 18	
Jason Babin	3.0
Philadelphia vs. New York Jets, Dec. 18	
Chris Kelsay	3.0
Buffalo vs. Denver, Dec. 24	

There were 23 3.0-plus sack performances in 2011.

MOST 3.0-PLUS SACK PERFORMANCES, 2011

Player, Team	3.0-Sack Games
Jared Allen, Minnesota	3
Jason Babin, Philadelphia	3
Terrell Suggs, Baltimore	3
James Harrison, Pittsburgh	2
12 players tied with	1

For week-by-week listings of top performances from 1970 to the present, please visit www.NFL.com/stats/topperformers.

AMERICAN FOOTBALL CONFERENCE OFFENSE

	Balt.	Buff.	Cin.	Cle.	Den.	Hou.	Ind.	Jax.	KC	Mia.	NE	NYJ	Oak.	Pitt.	SD	Tenn.
First Downs	312	313	285	278	286	321	258	251	277	287	399	301	328	341	359	281
Rushing	98	100	93	77	129	131	69	103	89	89	107	92	110	96	97	71
Passing	181	180	160	173	130	176	170	122	163	166	262	173	186	221	234	185
Penalty	33	33	32	28	27	14	19	26	25	32	30	36	32	24	28	25
Rushes	459	391	455	415	546	546	382	489	487	469	438	443	466	434	436	376
Net Yds. Gained	1996	1921	1778	1531	2632	2448	1594	1970	1893	1987	1764	1692	2110	1903	1864	1438
Avg. Gain	4.3	4.9	3.9	3.7	4.8	4.5	4.2	4.0	3.9	4.2	4.0	3.8	4.5	4.4	4.3	3.8
Avg. Yds. per Game	124.8	120.1	111.1	95.7	164.5	153.0	99.6	123.1	118.3	124.2	110.3	105.8	131.9	118.9	116.5	89.9
Passes Attempted	544	578	535	570	429	467	534	469	500	469	612	547	524	539	582	584
Completed	314	356	308	320	217	288	302	240	299	280	402	310	315	341	366	353
% Completed	57.7	61.6	57.6	56.1	50.6	61.7	56.6	51.2	59.8	59.7	65.7	56.7	60.1	63.3	62.9	60.4
Total Yds. Gained	3629	3857	3507	3300	2708	3696	3223	2510	3288	3425	5257	3542	4119	4333	4624	4113
Times Sacked	33	23	25	39	42	33	35	44	34	52	32	40	25	42	30	24
Yds. Lost	206	154	167	210	274	190	228	331	208	334	173	245	157	279	198	190
Net Yds. Gained	3423	3703	3340	3090	2434	3506	2995	2179	3080	3091	5084	3297	3962	4054	4426	3923
Avg. Yds. per Game	213.9	231.4	208.8	193.1	152.1	219.1	187.2	136.2	192.5	193.2	317.8	206.1	247.6	253.4	276.6	245.2
Net Yds. per Pass Play	5.93	6.16	5.96	5.07	5.17	7.01	5.26	4.25	5.77	5.93	7.89	5.62	7.22	6.98	7.23	6.45
Yds. Gained per Comp.	11.56	10.83	11.39	10.31	12.48	12.83	10.67	10.46	11.00	12.23	13.08	11.43	13.08	12.71	12.63	11.65
Combined Net Yds. Gained	5419	5624	5118	4621	5066	5954	4589	4149	4973	5078	6848	4989	6072	5957	6290	5361
% Total Yds. Rushing	36.8	34.2	34.7	33.1	52.0	41.1	34.7	47.5	38.1	39.1	25.8	33.9	34.7	31.9	29.6	26.8
% Total Yds. Passing	63.2	65.8	65.3	66.9	48.0	58.9	65.3	52.5	61.9	60.9	74.2	66.1	65.3	68.1	70.4	73.2
Avg. Yds. per Game	338.7	351.5	319.9	288.8	316.6	372.1	286.8	259.3	310.8	317.4	428.0	311.8	379.5	372.3	393.1	335.1
Ball Control Plays	1036	992	1015	1024	1017	1046	951	1002	1021	990	1082	1030	1015	1015	1048	984
Avg. Yds. per Play	5.2	5.7	5.0	4.5	5.0	5.7	4.8	4.1	4.9	5.1	6.3	4.8	6.0	5.9	6.0	5.4
Avg. Time of Poss.	30:35	30:11	30:19	29:07	28:51	32:41	26:13	30:02	29:10	30:23	28:47	30:49	29:51	32:33	31:39	27:52
Third Down Efficiency	42.4	32.5	36.5	38.7	30.8	41.5	34.6	33.6	36.0	33.3	45.9	34.7	35.7	45.9	48.8	36.7
Had Intercepted	12	25	14	13	13	9	14	15	18	13	12	18	23	15	20	14
Yds. Opp Returned	159	327	159	241	276	132	119	177	247	224	186	382	234	201	522	167
Ret. by Opp. for TD	1	3	1	1	3	0	1	0	0	1	1	3	3	0	4	3
Punts	73	73	91	89	101	74	89	99	89	78	57	92	78	60	47	86
Yds. Punted	3393	3472	4023	3570	4783	3256	4098	4147	4084	3810	2648	3926	3960	2683	2234	3747
Avg. Yds. per Punt	46.5	47.6	44.2	40.1	47.4	44.0	46.0	41.9	45.9	48.8	46.5	42.7	50.8	44.7	47.5	43.6
Punt Returns	36	26	53	38	47	51	32	34	40	46	38	44	32	33	31	47
Yds. Returned	345	329	610	423	596	529	108	148	475	526	389	426	264	347	264	490
Avg. Yds. per Return	9.6	12.7	11.5	11.1	12.7	10.4	3.4	4.4	11.9	11.4	10.2	9.7	8.3	10.5	8.5	10.4
Returned for TD	1	1	1	1	2	1	0	0	0	0	1	0	0	1	0	1
Kickoff Returns	42	37	45	48	39	29	31	47	46	39	46	62	43	35	43	32
Yds. Returned	1047	853	1026	1134	956	730	578	1055	979	942	986	1633	1011	877	1100	832
Avg. Yds. per Return	24.9	23.1	22.8	23.6	24.5	25.2	18.6	22.4	21.3	24.2	21.4	26.3	23.5	25.1	25.6	26.0
Returned for TD	0	0	0	0	0	0	0	0	0	0	0	1	1	0	1	1
Fumbles	24	16	17	22	30	20	24	27	17	28	13	25	16	16	20	17
Lost	12	5	8	6	17	11	15	8	10	12	5	16	7	13	8	8
Out of Bounds	0	1	2	2	2	0	0	2	0	2	2	2	0	0	2	1
Own Rec. for TD	0	0	0	0	0	1	0	0	0	0	0	1	0	0	0	0
Opp. Rec. by	11	11	12	11	9	10	9	11	6	3	11	12	8	4	4	12
Opp. Rec. for TD	3	2	2	0	0	0	1	3	0	0	1	0	1	1	1	0
Penalties	92	86	99	95	101	99	76	77	110	85	87	102	163	101	91	104
Yds. Penalized	742	743	874	847	842	852	549	680	916	779	815	849	1358	854	753	960
Total Points Scored	378	372	344	218	309	381	243	243	212	329	513	377	359	325	406	325
Total TDs	41	43	35	21	36	41	25	25	20	33	61	45	38	36	46	34
TDs Rushing	15	12	10	4	11	18	8	9	5	11	18	14	16	13	16	8
TDs Passing	21	24	21	16	20	20	14	12	13	20	39	26	20	21	27	22
TDs on Ret. and Rec.	5	7	4	1	5	3	3	4	2	2	4	5	2	2	3	4
Extra Point Kicks	40	41	33	20	30	39	24	24	20	32	59	44	36	36	44	34
Extra Point Kicks Att.	40	41	34	20	30	40	24	24	20	32	59	44	36	36	44	34
2Pt Conversions	1	1	0	0	3	0	0	0	0	0	2	0	0	0	1	0
2Pt Conversions Att.	1	2	1	1	6	1	1	1	0	1	2	1	2	0	1	0
Safeties	0	1	1	0	0	0	0	0	0	0	0	3	1	2	0	0
Field Goals Made	30	23	33	24	19	32	23	23	24	33	28	19	31	23	28	29
Field Goals Attempted	39	31	38	29	25	38	27	25	30	39	33	25	35	31	35	32
% Successful	76.9	74.2	86.8	82.8	76.0	84.2	85.2	92.0	80.0	84.6	84.8	76.0	88.6	74.2	80.0	90.6

AMERICAN FOOTBALL CONFERENCE DEFENSE

	Balt.	Buff.	Cin.	Cle.	Den.	Hou.	Ind.	Jax.	KC	Mia.	NE	NYJ	Oak.	Pitt.	SD	Tenn.
First Downs	269	340	284	301	315	270	343	268	291	310	370	272	369	264	311	324
Rushing	79	120	94	124	101	73	136	73	96	88	101	83	105	82	102	111
Passing	166	196	170	149	182	166	193	175	169	198	245	167	206	156	186	187
Penalty	24	24	20	28	32	31	14	20	26	24	24	22	58	26	23	26
Rushes	419	467	425	534	488	378	540	435	508	412	405	451	430	399	448	461
Net Yds. Gained	1482	2224	1675	2359	2021	1536	2303	1667	2112	1530	1874	1777	2178	1597	1955	2053
Avg. Gain	3.5	4.8	3.9	4.4	4.1	4.1	4.3	3.8	4.2	3.7	4.6	3.9	5.1	4.0	4.4	4.5
Avg. Yds. per Game	92.6	139.0	104.7	147.4	126.3	96.0	143.9	104.2	132.0	95.6	117.1	111.1	136.1	99.8	122.2	128.3
Passes Attempted	535	507	539	469	534	538	493	513	454	590	619	507	601	530	478	591
Completed	288	321	319	265	333	279	351	326	257	350	386	275	324	289	299	369
% Completed	53.8	63.3	59.2	56.5	62.4	51.9	71.2	63.5	56.6	59.3	62.4	54.2	53.9	54.5	62.6	62.4
Total Yds. Gained	3430	3924	3662	3158	3987	3322	3824	3554	3407	4233	4977	3414	4262	2981	3778	3809
Times Sacked	48	29	45	32	41	44	29	31	29	41	40	35	39	35	32	28
Yds. Lost	290	210	277	199	283	287	192	213	186	241	274	198	239	230	187	180
Net Yds. Gained	3140	3714	3385	2959	3704	3035	3632	3341	3221	3992	4703	3216	4023	2751	3591	3629
Avg. per Game	196.3	232.1	211.6	184.9	231.5	189.7	227.0	208.8	201.3	249.5	293.9	201.0	251.4	171.9	224.4	226.8
Net Yds. per Pass Play	5.39	6.93	5.80	5.91	6.44	5.21	6.96	6.14	6.67	6.33	7.14	5.93	6.29	4.87	7.04	5.86
Yds. Gained per Comp.	11.91	12.22	11.48	11.92	11.97	11.91	10.89	10.90	13.26	12.09	12.89	12.41	13.15	10.31	12.64	10.32
Combined Net																
Yds. Gained	4622	5938	5060	5318	5725	4571	5935	5008	5333	5522	6577	4993	6201	4348	5546	5682
% Total Yds. Rushing	32.1	37.5	33.1	44.4	35.3	33.6	38.8	33.3	39.6	27.7	28.5	35.6	35.1	36.7	35.3	36.1
% Total Yds. Passing	67.9	62.5	66.9	55.6	64.7	66.4	61.2	66.7	60.4	72.3	71.5	64.4	64.9	63.3	64.7	63.9
Avg. Yds. per Game	288.9	371.1	316.3	332.4	357.8	285.7	370.9	313.0	333.3	345.1	411.1	312.1	387.6	271.8	346.6	355.1
Ball Control Plays	1002	1003	1009	1035	1063	960	1062	979	991	1043	1064	993	1070	964	958	1080
Avg. Yds. per Play	4.6	5.9	5.0	5.1	5.4	4.8	5.6	5.1	5.4	5.3	6.2	5.0	5.8	4.5	5.8	5.3
Avg. Time of Poss.	29:25	29:49	29:41	30:53	31:09	27:20	33:47	29:58	30:50	29:37	31:13	29:11	30:09	27:27	28:21	32:08
Third Down Efficiency	32.1	39.7	35.5	41.3	33.5	35.8	45.4	36.2	34.3	33.8	43.1	32.7	42.0	38.9	49.2	40.7
Intercepted By	15	20	10	9	9	17	8	17	20	16	23	19	18	11	17	11
Yds. Returned By	175	341	137	93	152	196	118	160	283	256	296	378	252	99	260	179
Returned for TD	1	4	1	0	3	1	2	0	2	1	2	2	0	0	1	1
Punts	86	68	98	76	92	83	74	89	83	95	67	92	68	87	60	83
Yds. Punted	3746	3039	4562	3505	4350	3896	3230	3852	3951	4313	3051	4141	3161	3789	2822	3628
Avg. Yds. per Punt	43.6	44.7	46.6	46.1	47.3	46.9	43.6	43.3	47.6	45.4	45.5	45.0	46.5	43.6	47.0	43.7
Punt Returns	33	43	38	26	51	32	48	48	36	47	26	32	44	29	25	36
Yds. Returned	392	494	273	303	585	307	550	333	411	463	220	241	593	245	329	221
Avg. Yds. per Return	11.9	11.5	7.2	11.7	11.5	9.6	11.5	6.9	11.4	9.9	8.5	7.5	13.5	8.4	13.2	6.1
Returned for TD	2	0	1	1	1	0	1	0	1	0	0	0	2	0	0	0
Kickoff Returns	36	56	44	46	20	46	19	26	25	41	60	61	47	43	57	30
Yds. Returned	1050	1144	916	1055	491	1030	584	632	605	937	1294	1291	1210	1018	1451	680
Avg. Yds. per Return	29.2	20.4	20.8	22.9	24.6	22.4	30.7	24.3	24.2	22.9	21.6	21.2	25.7	23.7	25.5	22.7
Returned for TD	1	0	0	1	0	0	0	0	0	0	0	0	1	0	1	0
Fumbles	27	21	26	20	19	18	15	21	18	17	21	25	13	13	11	20
Lost	11	11	12	11	9	10	9	11	6	3	11	12	8	4	4	12
Out of Bounds	3	2	1	2	0	0	0	1	0	0	0	4	1	3	1	0
Own Rec. for TD	1	0	0	0	1	0	0	0	0	0	0	0	0	0	0	0
Opp. Rec. by	12	5	8	6	17	11	15	8	10	12	5	16	7	13	8	8
Opp. Rec. for TD	0	0	0	0	2	1	2	2	0	0	0	4	1	1	1	0
Penalties	103	85	101	90	99	88	84	105	108	112	115	110	120	96	92	99
Yds. Penalized	1032	871	878	726	845	686	804	895	834	975	907	966	982	777	760	812
Total Points Scored	266	434	323	307	390	278	430	329	338	313	342	363	433	227	377	317
Total TDs	26	53	37	31	42	27	49	37	38	33	40	39	53	23	43	34
TDs Rushing	10	19	14	12	11	8	19	14	14	8	13	17	15	7	8	10
TDs Passing	11	30	21	16	24	18	25	21	23	24	26	15	31	15	29	21
TDs on Ret. and Rec.	5	4	2	3	7	1	5	2	1	1	1	7	7	1	6	3
Extra Point Kicks	26	51	35	31	40	22	49	35	37	31	38	38	52	21	40	32
Extra Point Kicks Att.	26	52	35	31	40	22	49	36	37	31	38	38	53	21	40	32
2Pt Conversions	0	1	0	0	0	2	0	1	1	1	0	0	0	1	2	0
2Pt Conversions Att.	0	1	2	0	2	5	0	1	1	2	2	1	0	2	3	2
Safeties	0	0	0	0	1	0	0	2	1	2	2	1	0	0	0	0
Field Goals Made	28	21	22	30	32	30	29	22	23	26	20	29	21	22	25	27
Field Goals Attempted	31	25	27	34	39	36	34	29	28	33	23	30	29	27	28	28
% Successful	90.3	84.0	81.5	88.2	82.1	83.3	85.3	75.9	82.1	78.8	87.0	96.7	72.4	81.5	89.3	96.4

NATIONAL FOOTBALL CONFERENCE OFFENSE

	Ariz.	Atl.	Car.	Chi.	Dall.	Det.	GB	Minn.	NO	NYG	Phil.	StL	SF	Sea.	TB	Wash.
First Downs	286	349	345	271	327	349	353	297	416	331	356	267	282	265	277	312
Rushing	83	100	139	97	91	71	89	118	116	84	134	79	101	89	74	79
Passing	175	215	175	153	219	244	230	159	280	216	197	159	150	153	180	204
Penalty	28	34	31	21	17	34	34	20	20	31	25	29	31	23	23	29
Rushes	389	453	445	456	408	356	395	448	431	411	450	409	498	444	346	400
Net Yds. Gained	1625	1834	2408	2015	1807	1523	1558	2318	2127	1427	2276	1667	2044	1756	1458	1614
Avg. Gain	4.2	4.0	5.4	4.4	4.4	4.3	3.9	5.2	4.9	3.5	5.1	4.1	4.1	4.0	4.2	4.0
Avg. Yds. per Game	101.6	114.6	150.5	125.9	112.9	95.2	97.4	144.9	132.9	89.2	142.3	104.2	127.8	109.8	91.1	100.9
Passes Attempted	550	594	519	473	570	666	552	510	662	589	554	549	451	509	588	591
Completed	307	365	312	268	376	423	376	286	472	359	330	292	277	299	365	346
% Completed	55.8	61.4	60.1	56.7	66.0	63.5	68.1	56.1	71.3	61.0	59.6	53.2	61.4	58.7	62.1	58.5
Total Yds. Gained	3954	4365	4089	3346	4453	5071	5161	3255	5505	4933	4276	3258	3193	3444	3838	4058
Times Sacked	54	26	35	49	39	36	41	49	24	28	32	55	44	50	32	41
Yds. Lost	387	173	260	335	252	257	237	298	158	199	166	388	263	339	188	285
Net Yds. Gained	3567	4192	3829	3011	4201	4814	4924	2957	5347	4734	4110	2870	2930	3105	3650	3773
Avg. Yds. per Game	222.9	262.0	239.3	188.2	262.6	300.9	307.8	184.8	334.2	295.9	256.9	179.4	183.1	194.1	228.1	235.8
Net Yds. per Pass Play	5.91	6.76	6.91	5.77	6.90	6.86	8.30	5.29	7.79	7.67	7.01	4.75	5.92	5.55	5.89	5.97
Yds. Gained per Comp.	12.88	11.96	13.11	12.49	11.84	11.99	13.73	11.38	11.66	13.74	12.96	11.16	11.53	11.52	10.52	11.73
Combined Net Yds. Gained	5192	6026	6237	5026	6008	6337	6482	5275	7474	6161	6386	4537	4974	4861	5108	5387
% Total Yds. Rushing	31.3	30.4	38.6	40.1	30.1	24.0	24.0	43.9	28.5	23.2	35.6	36.7	41.1	36.1	28.5	30.0
% Total Yds. Passing	68.7	69.6	61.4	59.9	69.9	76.0	76.0	56.1	71.5	76.8	64.4	63.3	58.9	63.9	71.5	70.0
Avg. Yds. per Game	324.5	376.6	389.8	314.1	375.5	396.1	405.1	329.7	467.1	385.1	399.1	283.6	310.9	303.8	319.3	336.7
Ball Control Plays	993	1073	999	978	1017	1058	988	1007	1117	1028	1036	1013	993	1003	966	1032
Avg. Yds. per Play	5.2	5.6	6.2	5.1	5.9	6.0	6.6	5.2	6.7	6.0	6.2	4.5	5.0	4.8	5.3	5.2
Avg. Time of Poss.	28:11	32:05	30:16	30:13	30:55	30:06	30:29	28:39	31:46	29:30	31:23	28:07	32:02	28:07	29:04	30:06
Third Down Efficiency	32.2	44.2	40.5	32.5	39.4	35.8	48.1	38.4	56.7	37.4	41.5	28.1	29.4	33.8	36.9	37.0
Had Intercepted	23	13	17	20	12	16	8	17	14	16	25	10	5	14	24	24
Yds. Opp Returned	296	178	229	380	158	140	63	213	162	291	368	40	51	187	266	353
Ret. by Opp. for TD	1	2	1	3	2	3	0	3	1	3	2	0	0	1	2	0
Punts	92	71	66	89	71	82	55	77	47	82	67	106	79	95	67	66
Yds. Punted	4141	2990	2819	3903	3047	3573	2506	3517	2224	3745	2830	4652	3970	4431	3023	2842
Avg. Yds. per Punt	45.0	42.1	42.7	43.9	42.9	43.6	45.6	45.7	47.3	45.7	42.2	43.9	50.3	46.6	45.1	43.1
Punt Returns	46	33	32	30	41	38	27	33	29	28	30	27	44	42	29	37
Yds. Returned	696	315	176	470	293	301	295	277	294	171	212	297	544	464	231	328
Avg. Yds. per Return	15.1	9.5	5.5	15.7	7.1	7.9	10.9	8.4	10.1	6.1	7.1	11.0	12.4	11.0	8.0	8.9
Returned for TD	4	0	0	2	0	0	1	0	1	0	0	1	1	0	0	0
Kickoff Returns	52	24	39	57	33	37	41	53	42	52	39	55	39	46	46	56
Yds. Returned	1246	563	926	1238	768	887	1005	1428	1111	1209	815	1280	1060	1142	1024	1239
Avg. Yds. per Return	24.0	23.5	23.7	21.7	23.3	24.0	24.5	26.9	26.5	23.3	20.9	23.3	27.2	24.8	22.3	22.1
Returned for TD	0	0	1	1	0	0	1	1	0	0	0	0	1	0	0	0
Fumbles	24	12	13	26	24	20	15	20	6	18	23	27	14	22	30	25
Lost	9	8	6	9	9	7	6	9	5	8	13	13	5	9	16	11
Out of Bounds	1	2	2	4	1	2	2	3	1	0	2	2	2	1	2	1
Own Rec. for TD	0	0	0	1	0	0	0	0	0	0	0	0	0	0	0	0
Opp. Rec. by	9	10	10	11	9	13	7	15	7	11	9	6	15	9	10	8
Opp. Rec. for TD	0	1	0	2	0	2	1	0	2	1	3	0	0	0	1	0
Penalties	106	93	113	104	114	128	76	109	99	94	107	112	113	138	123	91
Yds. Penalized	1004	769	1013	800	816	1075	591	908	851	795	853	899	1014	1047	1007	897
Total Points Scored	312	402	406	353	369	474	560	340	547	394	396	193	380	321	287	288
Total TDs	37	46	48	38	39	57	70	39	66	47	46	18	35	35	30	28
TDs Rushing	12	14	26	10	5	9	12	18	16	17	20	7	14	15	9	8
TDs Passing	21	29	21	18	33	41	51	20	46	29	22	9	18	15	17	19
TDs on Ret. and Rec.	4	3	1	10	1	7	7	1	4	1	4	2	3	5	4	1
Extra Point Kicks	33	45	44	37	39	54	68	38	63	43	46	18	34	34	23	25
Extra Point Kicks Att.	33	45	45	37	39	54	69	39	63	43	46	18	34	34	23	26
2Pt Conversions	0	0	2	0	0	0	0	0	2	4	0	0	1	0	2	1
2Pt Conversions Att.	2	1	3	1	0	3	1	0	3	4	0	2	1	1	7	2
Safeties	0	0	2	1	0	1	0	1	0	2	1	2	1	1	1	0
Field Goals Made	19	27	22	28	32	24	24	22	28	19	24	21	44	25	26	31
Field Goals Attempted	24	29	28	32	37	29	28	28	34	24	27	28	52	30	28	41
% Successful	79.2	93.1	78.6	87.5	86.5	82.8	85.7	78.6	82.4	79.2	88.9	75.0	84.6	83.3	92.9	75.6

NATIONAL FOOTBALL CONFERENCE DEFENSE

	Ariz.	Atl.	Car.	Chi.	Dall.	Det.	GB	Minn.	NO	NYG	Phil.	StL	SF	Sea.	TB	Wash.
First Downs	333	292	329	291	305	325	358	332	326	338	289	313	267	310	356	295
Rushing	118	87	110	75	78	91	96	92	92	103	84	122	53	96	135	95
Passing	174	186	191	199	199	195	246	213	196	210	173	166	190	174	188	180
Penalty	41	19	28	17	28	39	16	27	38	25	32	25	24	40	33	20
Rushes	475	372	451	384	385	410	383	439	351	435	414	510	353	473	498	438
Net Yds. Gained	1986	1552	2093	1542	1585	2050	1789	1712	1738	1940	1801	2433	1236	1797	2497	1884
Avg. Gain	4.2	4.2	4.6	4.0	4.1	5.0	4.7	3.9	5.0	4.5	4.4	4.8	3.5	3.8	5.0	4.3
Avg. Yds. per Game	124.1	97.0	130.8	96.4	99.1	128.1	111.8	107.0	108.6	121.3	112.6	152.1	77.3	112.3	156.1	117.8
Passes Attempted	578	560	490	631	545	604	637	538	626	589	518	484	579	543	481	509
Completed	340	340	318	383	336	376	390	367	362	361	301	293	333	324	301	308
% Completed	58.8	60.7	64.9	60.7	61.7	62.3	61.2	68.2	57.8	61.3	58.1	60.5	57.5	59.7	62.6	60.5
Total Yds. Gained	4000	4017	4119	4273	4149	4102	4988	4361	4413	4417	3713	3562	3978	3750	3962	3804
Times Sacked	42	33	31	33	42	41	29	50	33	48	50	39	42	33	23	41
Yds. Lost	304	231	170	208	243	271	192	342	256	335	316	261	283	232	148	251
Net Yds. Gained	3696	3786	3949	4065	3906	3831	4796	4019	4157	4082	3397	3301	3695	3518	3814	3553
Avg. Yds. per Game	231.0	236.6	246.8	254.1	244.1	239.4	299.8	251.2	259.8	255.1	212.3	206.3	230.9	219.9	238.4	222.1
Net Yds. per Pass Play	5.96	6.38	7.58	6.12	6.65	5.94	7.20	6.84	6.31	6.41	5.98	6.31	5.95	6.11	7.57	6.46
Yds. Gained per Comp.	11.76	11.81	12.95	11.16	12.35	10.91	12.79	11.88	12.19	12.24	12.34	12.16	11.95	11.57	13.16	12.35
Combined Net Yds. Gained	5682	5338	6042	5607	5491	5881	6585	5731	5895	6022	5198	5734	4931	5315	6311	5437
% Total Yds. Rushing	35.0	29.1	34.6	27.5	28.9	34.9	27.2	29.9	29.5	32.2	34.6	42.4	25.1	33.8	39.6	34.7
% Total Yds. Passing	65.0	70.9	65.4	72.5	71.1	65.1	72.8	70.1	70.5	67.8	65.4	57.6	74.9	66.2	60.4	65.3
Avg. Yds. per Game	355.1	333.6	377.6	350.4	343.2	367.6	411.6	358.2	368.4	376.4	324.9	358.4	308.2	332.2	394.4	339.8
Ball Control Plays	1095	965	972	1048	972	1055	1049	1027	1010	1072	982	1033	974	1049	1002	988
Avg. Yds. per Play	5.2	5.5	6.2	5.4	5.6	5.6	6.3	5.6	5.8	5.6	5.3	5.6	5.1	5.1	6.3	5.5
Avg. Time of Poss.	31:49	27:55	29:44	29:47	29:05	29:54	29:31	31:21	28:14	30:30	28:37	31:53	27:58	31:53	30:56	29:54
Third Down Efficiency	31.4	44.1	42.8	34.9	39.7	32.7	42.6	44.2	33.2	38.2	35.5	38.4	35.2	34.8	39.5	37.4
Intercepted By	10	19	14	20	15	21	31	8	9	20	15	12	23	22	14	13
Yds. Returned By	117	301	197	177	217	458	468	152	80	157	192	169	284	462	195	127
Returned for TD	0	2	0	4	1	5	4	0	1	0	1	1	1	4	3	1
Punts	92	75	52	85	72	78	58	67	71	75	85	81	87	81	58	70
Yds. Punted	4087	3460	2248	3628	3420	3530	2492	3153	3146	3321	3673	3636	3911	3616	2518	3172
Avg. Yds. per Punt	44.4	46.1	43.2	42.7	47.5	45.3	43.0	47.1	44.3	44.3	43.2	44.9	45.0	44.6	43.4	45.3
Punt Returns	50	31	35	41	30	36	24	43	19	41	31	45	39	47	36	32
Yds. Returned	610	150	466	223	278	484	305	532	118	407	176	552	315	541	266	250
Avg. Yds. per Return	12.2	4.8	13.3	5.4	9.3	13.4	12.7	12.4	6.2	9.9	5.7	12.3	8.1	11.5	7.4	7.8
Returned for TD	1	0	3	0	0	1	1	1	0	0	0	2	0	2	0	0
Kickoff Returns	52	60	30	35	52	49	59	57	36	46	51	36	46	48	25	36
Yds. Returned	1300	1487	811	855	1114	1255	1378	1403	927	1053	1178	902	1061	1249	570	749
Avg. Yds. per Return	25.0	24.8	27.0	24.4	21.4	25.6	23.4	24.6	25.8	22.9	23.1	25.1	23.1	26.0	22.8	20.8
Returned for TD	0	0	0	0	0	1	0	1	1	0	0	0	0	1	1	0
Fumbles	15	19	20	23	20	25	19	26	20	21	18	24	31	18	21	26
Lost	9	10	10	11	10	13	7	15	7	11	9	6	15	9	10	8
Out of Bounds	0	4	1	2	2	1	4	4	4	1	0	0	0	0	3	2
Own Rec. for TD	0	0	0	0	0	0	1	0	0	0	0	0	0	0	0	0
Opp. Rec. by	9	8	6	9	9	7	6	9	5	8	12	13	5	9	16	11
Opp. Rec. for TD	0	2	0	1	1	1	0	1	0	0	0	4	0	1	2	1
Penalties	122	101	98	98	85	119	122	97	109	110	97	111	98	96	95	123
Yds. Penalized	950	843	901	719	650	982	948	834	912	933	813	951	867	907	786	1006
Total Points Scored	348	350	429	341	347	387	359	449	339	400	328	407	229	315	494	367
Total TDs	34	40	50	36	38	42	41	50	37	46	40	45	23	33	61	38
TDs Rushing	15	10	18	10	10	10	10	10	11	15	11	17	3	10	26	15
TDs Passing	17	25	28	22	24	26	29	34	24	28	27	21	20	18	30	22
TDs on Ret. and Rec.	2	5	4	4	4	6	2	6	2	3	2	7	0	5	5	1
Extra Point Kicks	33	37	48	33	35	41	35	49	36	45	38	44	21	31	59	37
Extra Point Kicks Att.	33	37	48	33	35	41	35	49	37	45	38	44	21	32	60	38
2Pt Conversions	0	1	0	0	2	1	4	1	0	1	1	0	1	1	0	0
2Pt Conversions Att.	1	3	2	3	2	1	6	1	0	1	2	0	2	1	1	0
Safeties	3	1	0	1	1	1	2	1	0	1	0	0	1	0	0	0
Field Goals Made	35	23	27	30	26	30	22	32	27	25	16	31	22	28	23	34
Field Goals Attempted	48	28	31	36	33	34	27	35	32	31	24	37	27	37	29	41
% Successful	72.9	82.1	87.1	83.3	78.8	88.2	81.5	91.4	84.4	80.6	66.7	83.8	81.5	75.7	79.3	82.9

AFC, NFC, AND NFL SUMMARY

	AFC Offense Total	AFC Offense Average	AFC Defense Total	AFC Defense Average	NFC Offense Total	NFC Offense Average	NFC Defense Total	NFC Defense Average	NFL Total	NFL Average
First Downs	4877	304.8	4901	306.3	5083	317.7	5059	316.2	9960	311.3
Rushing	1551	96.9	1568	98.0	1544	96.5	1527	95.4	3095	96.7
Passing	2882	180.1	2911	181.9	3109	194.3	3080	192.5	5991	187.2
Penalty	444	27.8	422	26.4	430	26.9	452	28.3	874	27.3
Rushes	7232	452.0	7200	450.0	6739	421.2	6771	423.2	13971	436.6
Net Yds. Gained	30521	1907.6	30343	1896.4	29457	1841.1	29635	1852.2	59978	1874.3
Avg. Gain	—	4.2	—	4.2	—	4.4	—	4.4	—	4.3
Avg. Yds. per Game	—	119.2	—	118.5	—	115.1	—	115.8	—	117.1
Passes Attempted	8483	530.2	8498	531.1	8927	557.9	8912	557.0	17410	544.1
Completed	5011	313.2	5031	314.4	5453	340.8	5433	339.6	10464	327.0
% Completed	—	59.1	—	59.2	—	61.1	—	61.0	—	60.1
Total Yds. Gained	59131	3695.7	59722	3732.6	66199	4137.4	65608	4100.5	125330	3916.6
Times Sacked	553	34.6	578	36.1	635	39.7	610	38.1	1188	37.1
Yds. Lost	3544	221.5	3686	230.4	4185	261.6	4043	252.7	7729	241.5
Net Yds. Gained	55587	3474.2	56036	3502.3	62014	3875.9	61565	3847.8	117601	3675.0
Avg. Yds. per Game	—	217.1	—	218.9	—	242.2	—	240.5	—	229.7
Net Yds. per Pass Play	—	6.15	—	6.17	—	6.49	—	6.47	—	6.32
Yds. Gained per Comp.	—	11.80	—	11.87	—	12.14	—	12.08	—	11.98
Combined Net										
Yds. Gained	86108	5381.8	86379	5398.7	91471	5716.9	91200	5700.0	177579	5549.3
% Total Yds. Rushing	—	35.4	—	35.1	—	32.2	—	32.5	—	33.8
% Total Yds. Passing	—	64.6	—	64.9	—	67.8	—	67.5	—	66.2
Avg. Yds. per Game	—	336.4	—	337.4	—	357.3	—	356.3	—	346.8
Ball Control Plays	16268	1016.8	16276	1017.3	16301	1018.8	16293	1018.3	32569	1017.8
Avg. Yds. per Play	—	5.3	—	5.3	—	5.6	—	5.6	—	5.5
Third Down Efficiency	—	37.9	—	38.3	—	38.1	—	37.7	—	38.0
Interceptions	248	15.5	240	15.0	258	16.1	266	16.6	506	15.8
Yds. Returned	3753	234.6	3375	210.9	3375	210.9	3753	234.6	7128	222.8
Returned for TD	25	1.6	21	1.3	24	1.5	28	1.8	49	1.5
Punts	1276	79.8	1301	81.3	1212	75.8	1187	74.2	2488	77.8
Yds. Punted	57834	3614.6	59036	3689.8	54213	3388.3	53011	3313.2	112047	3501.5
Avg. Yds. per Punt	—	45.3	—	45.4	—	44.7	—	44.7	—	45.0
Punt Returns	628	39.3	594	37.1	546	34.1	580	36.3	1174	36.7
Yds. Returned	6269	391.8	5960	372.5	5364	335.3	5673	354.6	11633	363.5
Avg. Yds. per Return	—	10.0	—	10.0	—	9.8	—	9.8	—	9.9
Returned for TD	10	0.6	9	0.6	10	0.6	11	0.7	20	0.6
Kickoff Returns	664	41.5	657	41.1	711	44.4	718	44.9	1375	43.0
Yds. Returned	15739	983.7	15388	961.8	16941	1058.8	17292	1080.8	32680	1021.3
Avg. Yds. per Return	—	23.7	—	23.4	—	23.8	—	24.1	—	23.8
Returned for TD	4	0.3	4	0.3	5	0.3	5	0.3	9	0.3
Fumbles	332	20.8	305	19.1	319	19.9	346	21.6	651	20.3
Lost	161	10.1	144	9.0	143	8.9	160	10.0	304	9.5
Out of Bounds	18	1.1	18	1.1	28	1.8	28	1.8	46	1.4
Own Rec. for TD	2	0.1	2	0.1	1	0.1	1	0.1	3	0.1
Opp. Rec.	144	9.0	161	10.1	159	9.9	142	8.9	303	9.5
Opp. Rec. for TD	15	0.9	14	0.9	13	0.8	14	0.9	28	0.9
Penalties	1568	98.0	1607	100.4	1720	107.5	1681	105.1	3288	102.8
Yds. Penalized	13413	838.3	13750	859.4	14339	896.2	14002	875.1	27752	867.3
Total Points Scored	5334	333.4	5467	341.7	6022	376.4	5889	368.1	11356	354.9
Total TDs	580	36.3	605	37.8	679	42.4	654	40.9	1259	39.3
TDs Rushing	188	11.8	199	12.4	212	13.3	201	12.6	400	12.5
TDs Passing	336	21.0	350	21.9	409	25.6	395	24.7	745	23.3
TDs on Ret. and Rec.	56	3.5	56	3.5	58	3.6	58	3.6	114	3.6
Extra Point Kicks	556	34.8	578	36.1	644	40.3	622	38.9	1200	37.5
Extra Point Kicks Att.	559	34.9	581	36.3	648	40.5	626	39.1	1207	37.7
2Pt Conversions	8	0.5	10	0.6	15	0.9	13	0.8	23	0.7
2Pt Conversions Att.	21	1.3	24	1.5	29	1.8	26	1.6	50	1.6
Safeties	8	0.5	9	0.6	13	0.8	12	0.8	21	0.7
Field Goals Made	422	26.4	407	25.4	416	26.0	431	26.9	838	26.2
Field Goals Attempted	512	32.0	481	30.1	499	31.2	530	33.1	1011	31.6
% Successful	—	82.4	—	84.6	—	83.4	—	81.3	—	82.9

CLUB LEADERS

	Offense	Defense
First Downs	New Orleans 416	Pittsburgh 264
Rushing	Carolina 139	San Francisco 53
Passing	New Orleans 280	Cleveland 149
Penalty	N.Y. Jets 36	Indianapolis 14
Rushes	Denver & Houston 546	New Orleans 351
Net Yds. Gained	Denver 2632	San Francisco 1236
Avg. Gain	Carolina 5.4	San Francisco 3.5
Passes Attempted	Detroit 666	Kansas City 454
Completed	New Orleans 472	Kansas City 257
% Completed	New Orleans 71.3	Houston 51.9
Total Yds. Gained	New Orleans 5505	Pittsburgh 2981
Times Sacked	Buffalo 23	Minnesota & Philadelphia 50
Yds. Lost	Buffalo 154	Minnesota 342
Net Yds. Gained	New Orleans 5347	Pittsburgh 2751
Net Yds. per Pass Play	Green Bay 8.3	Pittsburgh 4.9
Yds. Gained per Comp.	N.Y. Giants 13.7	Pittsburgh 10.3
Combined Net Yds. Gained	New Orleans 7474	Pittsburgh 4348
% Total Yds. Rushing	Denver 52.0	San Francisco 25.1
% Total Yds. Passing	N.Y. Giants 76.8	Cleveland 55.6
Ball Control Plays	New Orleans 1117	San Diego 958
Avg. Yds. per Play	New Orleans 6.7	Pittsburgh 4.5
Avg. Time of Poss.	Houston 32:40	—
Third Down Efficiency	New Orleans 56.7	Arizona 31.4
Interceptions	—	Green Bay 31
Yds. Returned	—	Green Bay 468
Returned for TD	—	Detroit 5
Punts	St. Louis 106	—
Yds. Punted	Denver 4783	—
Avg. Yds. per Punt	Oakland 50.8	—
Punt Returns	Cincinnati 53	New Orleans 19
Yds. Returned	Arizona 696	New Orleans 118
Avg. Yds. per Return	Chicago 15.7	Atlanta 4.8
Returned for TD	Arizona 4	—
Kickoff Returns	N.Y. Jets 62	Indianapolis 19
Yds. Returned	N.Y. Jets 1633	Denver 491
Avg. Yds. per Return	San Francisco 27.2	Buffalo 20.4
Returned for TD	Carolina & Chicago & Green Bay & Minnesota & N.Y. Jets & Oakland & San Diego & San Francisco & Tennessee 1	—
Total Points Scored	Green Bay 560	Pittsburgh 227
Total TDs	Green Bay 70	Pittsburgh & San Francisco 23
TDs Rushing	Carolina 26	San Francisco 3
TDs Passing	Green Bay 51	Baltimore 11
TDs on Ret. and Rec.	Chicago 10	San Francisco 0
Extra Point Kicks	Green Bay 68	Pittsburgh & San Francisco 21
2-Point Conversions	N.Y. Giants 4	—
Safeties	N.Y. Jets 3	—
Field Goals Made	San Francisco 44	Philadelphia 16
Field Goals Attempted	San Francisco 52	New England 23
% Successful	Atlanta 93.1	Philadelphia 66.7

NFL CLUB RANKINGS BY YARDS

	Offense			Defense		
	Total	Rush	Pass	Total	Rush	Pass
Arizona	19	24	17	18T	21	17
Atlanta	10	17	8	12	6	20
Baltimore	15	10	19	3	2	4
Buffalo	14	13	15	26	28	19
Carolina	7	3	13	28	25	24
Chicago	24	9	26	17	5	28
Cincinnati	20	19	20	7	10	9
Cleveland	29	28	24	10	30	2
Dallas	11	18	7	14	7	23
Denver	23	*1	31	20	22	18
Detroit	5	29	4	23	23	22
Green Bay	3	27	3	32	14	32
Houston	13	2	18	2	4	3
Indianapolis	30	26	27	25	29	15
Jacksonville	32	12	32	6	9	8
Kansas City	27	15	25	11	26	6
Miami	22	11	23	15	3	25
Minnesota	18	4	28	21	11	26
New England	2	20	2	31	17	31
New Orleans	*1	6	*1	24	12	30
New York Giants	8	32	5	27	19	29
New York Jets	25	22	21	5	13	5
Oakland	9	7	11	29	27	27
Philadelphia	4	5	9	8	16	10
Pittsburgh	12	14	10	*1	8	*1
St. Louis	31	23	30	22	31	7
San Diego	6	16	6	16	20	13
San Francisco	26	8	29	4	*1	16
Seattle	28	21	22	9	15	11
Tampa Bay	21	30	16	30	32	21
Tennessee	17	31	12	18T	24	14
Washington	16	25	14	13	18	12

T = Tied for position   * = League Leader

AFC TAKEAWAYS/GIVEAWAYS

	Takeaways			Giveaways			Net
	Int	Fum	Total	Int	Fum	Total	Diff.
New England	23	11	34	12	5	17	+17
Houston	17	10	27	9	11	20	+7
Jacksonville	17	11	28	15	8	23	+5
Baltimore	15	11	26	12	12	24	+2
Buffalo	20	11	31	25	5	30	+1
Cleveland	9	11	20	13	6	19	+1
Tennessee	11	12	23	14	8	22	+1
Cincinnati	10	12	22	14	8	22	0
Kansas City	20	6	26	18	10	28	-2
N.Y. Jets	19	12	31	18	16	34	-3
Oakland	18	8	26	23	7	30	-4
Miami	16	3	19	13	12	25	-6
San Diego	17	4	21	20	8	28	-7
Denver	9	9	18	13	17	30	-12
Indianapolis	8	9	17	14	15	29	-12
Pittsburgh	11	4	15	15	13	28	-13
Totals	240	144	384	248	161	409	-25

NFC TAKEAWAYS/GIVEAWAYS

	Takeaways			Giveaways			Net
	Int	Fum	Total	Int	Fum	Total	Diff.
San Francisco	23	15	38	5	5	10	+28
Green Bay	31	7	38	8	6	14	+24
Detroit	21	13	34	16	7	23	+11
Atlanta	19	10	29	13	8	21	+8
Seattle	22	9	31	14	9	23	+8
N.Y. Giants	20	11	31	16	8	24	+7
Dallas	15	10	25	12	9	21	+4
Chicago	20	11	31	20	9	29	+2
Carolina	14	10	24	17	6	23	+1
Minnesota	8	15	23	17	9	26	-3
New Orleans	9	7	16	14	5	19	-3
St. Louis	12	6	18	10	13	23	-5
Arizona	10	9	19	23	9	32	-13
Philadelphia	15	9	24	25	13	38	-14
Washington	13	8	21	24	11	35	-14
Tampa Bay	14	10	24	24	16	40	-16
Totals	266	160	426	258	143	401	+25

SCORING
POINTS
NFC:	166	David Akers, San Francisco
AFC:	143	Stephen Gostkowski, New England

TOUCHDOWNS
NFC:	20	LeSean McCoy, Philadelphia
AFC:	18	Rob Gronkowski, New England

EXTRA POINT KICKS
NFC:	68	Mason Crosby, Green Bay
AFC:	59	Stephen Gostkowski, New England

TWO-POINT EXTRA POINT PLAYS
AFC:	2	Tim Tebow, Denver
	2	Danny Woodhead, New England
NFC:	2	Lance Moore, New Orleans
	2	D.J. Ware, N.Y. Giants
	2	Kellen Winslow, Tampa Bay

FIELD GOALS
NFC:	44	David Akers, San Francisco
AFC:	33	Mike Nugent, Cincinnati

FIELD GOAL ATTEMPTS
NFC:	52	David Akers, San Francisco
AFC:	38	Mike Nugent, Cincinnati
	38	Neil Rackers, Houston

LONGEST FIELD GOAL
AFC:	63	Sebastian Janikowski, Oakland at Denver, September 12
NFC:	59	Graham Gano, Washington vs. San Francisco, November 6

MOST POINTS, GAME
AFC:	24	Maurice Jones-Drew, Jacksonville vs. Tampa Bay, December 11 (4 TD)
NFC:	18	Miles Austin, Dallas at San Francisco, September 18 (3 TD) - (OT)
	18	Jermichael Finley, Green Bay at Chicago, September 25 (3 TD)
	18	* Dan Bailey, Dallas vs. Washington, September 26 (6-6 FG)
	18	Beanie Wells, Arizona vs. N.Y. Giants, October 2 (3 TD)
	18	Adrian Peterson, Minnesota vs. Arizona, October 9 (3 TD)
	18	Ahmad Bradshaw, N.Y. Giants vs. Buffalo, October 16 (3 TD)
	18	Kevin Smith, Detroit vs. Carolina, November 20 (3 TD)
	18	* Cam Newton, Carolina at Tampa Bay, December 4 (3 TD)
	18	LeSean McCoy, Philadelphia vs. N.Y. Jets, December 18 (3 TD)
	18	Jordy Nelson, Green Bay vs. Detroit, January 1 (3 TD)

TEAM LEADERS, POINTS
AFC: BALTIMORE, 122, Billy Cundiff; BUFFALO, 64, Rian Lindell; CINCINNATI, 132, Mike Nugent; CLEVELAND, 92, Phil Dawson; DENVER, 87, Matt Prater; HOUSTON, 135, Neil Rackers; INDIANAPOLIS, 93, Adam Vinatieri; JACKSONVILLE, 93, Josh Scobee; KANSAS CITY, 92, Ryan Succop; MIAMI, 113, Dan Carpenter; NEW ENGLAND, 143, Stephen Gostkowski; N.Y. JETS, 101, Nick Folk; OAKLAND, 129, Sebastian Janikowski; PITTSBURGH, 105, Shaun Suisham; SAN DIEGO, 122, Nick Novak; TENNESSEE, 121, Rob Bironas

NFC: ARIZONA, 90, Jay Feely; ATLANTA, 126, Matt Bryant; CAROLINA, 110, Olindo Mare; CHICAGO, 121, Robbie Gould; DALLAS, 135, *Dan Bailey; DETROIT, 126, Jason Hanson; GREEN BAY, 140, Mason Crosby; MINNESOTA, 104, Ryan Longwell; NEW ORLEANS, 147, John Kasay; N.Y. GIANTS, 100, Lawrence Tynes; PHILADELPHIA, 120, LeSean McCoy; ST. LOUIS, 81, Josh Brown; SAN FRANCISCO, 166, David Akers; SEATTLE, 109, Steven Hauschka; TAMPA BAY, 101, Connor Barth; WASHINGTON, 118, Graham Gano

TEAM CHAMPION
NFC:	560	Green Bay
AFC:	513	New England

NFL TOP TEN SCORERS—KICKERS
	XP	XPA	FG	FGA	PTS
Akers, David, S.F.	34	34	44	52	166
Kasay, John, N.O.	63	63	28	34	147
Gostkowski, Stephen, N.E.	59	59	28	33	143
Crosby, Mason, G.B.	68	69	24	28	140
* Bailey, Dan, Dal.	39	39	32	37	135
Rackers, Neil, Hou.	39	40	32	38	135
Nugent, Mike, Cin.	33	34	33	38	132
Janikowski, Sebastian, Oak.	36	36	31	35	129
Bryant, Matt, Atl.	45	45	27	29	126
Hanson, Jason, Det.	54	54	24	29	126

NFL TOP TEN SCORERS—NONKICKERS
	TD	TDR	TDP	TDM	2-PT.	PTS
McCoy, LeSean, Phi.	20	17	3	0	0	120
Gronkowski, Rob, N.E.	18	1	17	0	0	108
Johnson, Calvin, Det.	16	0	16	0	0	96
Nelson, Jordy, G.B.	15	0	15	0	0	90
Rice, Ray, Bal.	15	12	3	0	0	90
* Newton, Cam, Car.	14	14	0	0	0	84
Lynch, Marshawn, Sea.	13	12	1	0	0	78
Peterson, Adrian, Min.	13	12	1	0	0	78
Foster, Arian, Hou.	12	10	2	0	0	72
Bradshaw, Ahmad, NY-G	11	9	2	0	1	68

AFC—INDIVIDUAL SCORERS
KICKERS
	XP	XPA	FG	FGA	PTS
Gostkowski, Stephen, N.E.	59	59	28	33	143
Rackers, Neil, Hou.	39	40	32	38	135
Nugent, Mike, Cin.	33	34	33	38	132
Janikowski, Sebastian, Oak.	36	36	31	35	129
Cundiff, Billy, Bal.	38	38	28	37	122
Novak, Nick, S.D.	41	42	27	34	122
Bironas, Rob, Ten.	34	34	29	32	121
Carpenter, Dan, Mia.	26	26	29	34	113
Suisham, Shaun, Pit.	36	36	23	31	105
Folk, Nick, NYJ	44	44	19	25	101
Scobee, Josh, Jac.	24	24	23	25	93
Vinatieri, Adam, Ind.	24	24	23	27	93
Dawson, Phil, Cle.	20	20	24	29	92
Succop, Ryan, K.C.	20	20	24	30	92
Prater, Matt, Den.	30	30	19	25	87
Lindell, Rian, Buf.	25	25	13	15	64
Rayner, Dave, Buf.	13	13	10	15	43
Graham, Shayne, Mia.-Bal.	8	8	6	7	26
Scifres, Mike, S.D.	3	3	1	1	6
Coutu, Brandon, Buf.	3	3	0	1	3

Player that was a rookie in 2011

NONKICKERS

Player	TD	TDR	TDP	TDM	2-PT.	PTS
Gronkowski, Rob, N.E.	18	1	17	0	0	108
Rice, Ray, Bal.	15	12	3	0	0	90
Foster, Arian, Hou.	12	10	2	0	0	72
Green-Ellis, BenJarvus, N.E.	11	11	0	0	0	66
Jones-Drew, Maurice, Jac.	11	8	3	0	0	66
Tolbert, Mike, S.D.	10	8	2	0	0	60
Decker, Eric, Den.	9	0	8	1	0	54
Jackson, Vincent, S.D.	9	0	9	0	0	54
Mendenhall, Rashard, Pit.	9	9	0	0	0	54
Welker, Wes, N.E.	9	0	9	0	0	54
Burress, Plaxico, NYJ	8	0	8	0	0	48
Bush, Michael, Oak.	8	7	1	0	0	48
Holmes, Santonio, NYJ	8	0	8	0	0	48
Wallace, Mike, Pit.	8	0	8	0	0	48
Washington, Nate, Ten.	8	1	7	0	0	48
Bush, Reggie, Mia.	7	6	1	0	0	42
Gates, Antonio, S.D.	7	0	7	0	0	42
* Green, A.J., Cin.	7	0	7	0	0	42
Hernandez, Aaron, N.E.	7	0	7	0	0	42
Johnson, Steve, Buf.	7	0	7	0	0	42
* Smith, Torrey, Bal.	7	0	7	0	0	42
Tebow, Tim, Den.	6	6	0	0	2	40
Benson, Cedric, Cin.	6	6	0	0	0	36
Chandler, Scott, Buf.	6	0	6	0	0	36
Dreessen, Joel, Hou.	6	0	6	0	0	36
Garcon, Pierre, Ind.	6	0	6	0	0	36
Greene, Shonn, NYJ	6	6	0	0	0	36
Gresham, Jermaine, Cin.	6	0	6	0	0	36
Jackson, Fred, Buf.	6	6	0	0	0	36
Marshall, Brandon, Mia.	6	0	6	0	0	36
Mathews, Ryan, S.D.	6	6	0	0	0	36
* Moore, Denarius, Oak.	6	1	5	0	0	36
Sanchez, Mark, NYJ	6	6	0	0	0	36
Spiller, C.J., Buf.	6	4	2	0	0	36
McGahee, Willis, Den.	5	4	1	0	1	32
Bowe, Dwayne, K.C.	5	0	5	0	0	30
Branch, Deion, N.E.	5	0	5	0	0	30
Brown, Donald, Ind.	5	5	0	0	0	30
Cribbs, Josh, Cle.	5	0	4	1	0	30
Dickson, Ed, Bal.	5	0	5	0	0	30
Fasano, Anthony, Mia.	5	0	5	0	0	30
Floyd, Malcom, S.D.	5	0	5	0	0	30
Keller, Dustin, NYJ	5	0	5	0	0	30
McFadden, Darren, Oak.	5	4	1	0	0	30
Nelson, David, Buf.	5	0	5	0	0	30
Williams, Damian, Ten.	5	0	5	0	0	30
Heyward-Bey, Darrius, Oak.	4	0	4	0	0	24
Johnson, Chris, Ten.	4	4	0	0	0	24
Moore, Evan, Cle.	4	0	4	0	0	24
Simpson, Jerome, Cin.	4	0	4	0	0	24
Tate, Ben, Hou.	4	4	0	0	0	24
Thomas, Demaryius, Den.	4	0	4	0	0	24
Wayne, Reggie, Ind.	4	0	4	0	0	24
Bess, Davone, Mia.	3	0	3	0	0	18
Boldin, Anquan, Bal.	3	0	3	0	0	18
Boss, Kevin, Oak.	3	0	3	0	0	18
Brady, Tom, N.E.	3	3	0	0	0	18
Britt, Kenny, Ten.	3	0	3	0	0	18
Brown, Antonio, Pit.	3	0	2	1	0	18
Caldwell, Andre, Cin.	3	0	3	0	0	18
* Clay, Charles, Mia.	3	0	3	0	0	18
Cook, Jared, Ten.	3	0	3	0	0	18
Daniels, Owen, Hou.	3	0	3	0	0	18
Fells, Daniel, Den.	3	0	3	0	0	18
Hill, Jason, Jac.	3	0	3	0	0	18
Hillis, Peyton, Cle.	3	3	0	0	0	18
Jones, Jacoby, Hou.	3	0	2	1	0	18
Pitta, Dennis, Bal.	3	0	3	0	0	18
Redman, Isaac, Pit.	3	3	0	0	0	18
Scott, Bernard, Cin.	3	3	0	0	0	18
Tomlinson, LaDainian, NYJ	3	1	2	0	0	18
Walter, Kevin, Hou.	3	0	3	0	0	18
Ball, Lance, Den.	2	1	1	0	0	12
Battle, Jackie, K.C.	2	2	0	0	0	12
Breaston, Steve, K.C.	2	0	2	0	0	12
* Brown, Vincent, S.D.	2	0	2	0	0	12
Campbell, Jason, Oak.	2	2	0	0	0	12
* Carter, Delone, Ind.	2	2	0	0	0	12
Clark, Dallas, Ind.	2	0	2	0	0	12
Cotchery, Jerricho, Pit.	2	0	2	0	0	12
Ford, Jacoby, Oak.	2	0	1	1	0	12
Hilliard, Lex, Mia.	2	1	0	1	0	12
Johnson, Andre, Hou.	2	0	2	0	0	12
* Little, Greg, Cle.	2	0	2	0	0	12
Massaquoi, Mohamed, Cle.	2	0	2	0	0	12
McClain, Le'Ron, K.C.	2	1	1	0	0	12
McCluster, Dexter, K.C.	2	1	1	0	0	12
Miller, Heath, Pit.	2	0	2	0	0	12
Moore, Matt, Mia.	2	2	0	0	0	12
Reece, Marcel, Oak.	2	0	2	0	0	12
Royal, Eddie, Den.	2	0	1	1	0	12
Sanders, Emmanuel, Pit.	2	0	2	0	0	12
Schaub, Matt, Hou.	2	2	0	0	0	12
Schilens, Chaz, Oak.	2	0	2	0	0	12
Scott, Bryan, Buf.	2	0	0	2	0	12
Smith, Brad, Buf.	2	1	1	0	0	12
Ward, Derrick, Hou.	2	2	0	0	0	12
Ward, Hines, Pit.	2	0	2	0	0	12
Watson, Benjamin, Cle.	2	0	2	0	0	12
Webb, Lardarius, Bal.	2	0	0	2	0	12
West, Chastin, Jac.	2	0	2	0	0	12
Williams, Ricky, Bal.	2	2	0	0	0	12
Woodhead, Danny, N.E.	1	1	0	0	2	10
Brinkley, Curtis, S.D.	1	1	0	0	1	8
Addai, Joseph, Ind.	1	1	0	0	0	6
Anderson, Jamaal, Ind.	1	0	0	1	0	6
Arenas, Javier, K.C.	1	1	0	0	0	6
Atkins, Geno, Cin.	1	0	0	1	0	6
Avery, Donnie, Ten.	1	0	1	0	0	6
Babineaux, Jordan, Ten.	1	0	0	1	0	6
* Baker, Josh, NYJ	1	0	1	0	0	6
* Baldwin, Jon, K.C.	1	0	1	0	0	6
Barnett, Nick, Buf.	1	0	0	1	0	6
Burnett, Kevin, Mia.	1	0	0	1	0	6
Butler, Donald, S.D.	1	0	0	1	0	6
Byrd, Jairus, Buf.	1	0	0	1	0	6
* Campbell, Tommie, Ten.	1	0	0	1	0	6
Casey, James, Hou.	1	0	1	0	0	6
Charles, Jamaal, K.C.	1	0	1	0	0	6
Choice, Tashard, Buf.	1	1	0	0	0	6
* Clay, John, Pit.	1	1	0	0	0	6
Cloherty, Colin, Jac.	1	0	0	1	0	6
* Cochart, Colin, Cin.	1	0	1	0	0	6
Collie, Austin, Ind.	1	0	1	0	0	6
Collins, Nate, Jac.	1	0	0	1	0	6
Conner, John, NYJ	1	1	0	0	0	6
Crayton, Patrick, S.D.	1	0	1	0	0	6
Curry, Aaron, Oak.	1	0	0	1	0	6
* Dalton, Andy, Cin.	1	1	0	0	0	6
Dillard, Jarett, Jac.	1	0	1	0	0	6
Dunlap, Carlos, Cin.	1	0	0	1	0	6
Edelman, Julian, N.E.	1	0	0	1	0	6
Flacco, Joe, Bal.	1	1	0	0	0	6
Florence, Drayton, Buf.	1	0	0	1	0	6
Flowers, Brandon, K.C.	1	0	0	1	0	6
Goodman, André, Hou.	1	0	0	1	0	6
Goodman, Richard, S.D.	1	0	0	1	0	6
Graham, Daniel, Ten.	1	0	1	0	0	6
Gregory, Steve, S.D.	1	0	0	1	0	6
Hagan, Derek, Oak.-Buf.	1	0	1	0	0	6
Haggan, Mario, Den.	1	0	0	1	0	6
* Harper, Jamie, Ten.	1	1	0	0	0	6

	TD	TDR	TDP	TDM	2-PT	PTS
Harris, David, NYJ	1	0	0	1	0	6
Hartline, Brian, Mia.	1	0	1	0	0	6
Hawkins, Lavelle, Ten.	1	0	1	0	0	6
Henne, Chad, Mia.	1	1	0	0	0	6
Hester, Jacob, S.D.	1	0	1	0	0	6
Houshmandzadeh, T.J., Oak.	1	0	1	0	0	6
Johnson, Bryant, Hou.	1	0	1	0	0	6
Johnson, David, Pit.	1	0	1	0	0	6
Johnson, Jarret, Bal.	1	0	0	1	0	6
Johnson, Spencer, Buf.	1	0	0	1	0	6
Jones, Donald, Buf.	1	0	1	0	0	6
Jones, Greg, Jac.	1	1	0	0	0	6
* Kerley, Jeremy, NYJ	1	0	1	0	0	6
Lacey, Jacob, Ind.	1	0	0	1	0	6
Lewis, Kendrick, K.C.	1	0	0	1	0	6
* Locker, Jake, Ten.	1	1	0	0	0	6
Mariani, Marc, Ten.	1	0	0	1	0	6
McCain, Brice, Hou.	1	0	0	1	0	6
McClain, Jameel, Bal.	1	0	0	1	0	6
McCourty, Jason, Ten.	1	0	0	1	0	6
McKelvin, Leodis, Buf.	1	0	0	1	0	6
McKnight, Joe, NYJ	1	0	0	1	0	6
Miller, Zach, Jac.	1	0	1	0	0	6
Moore, Mewelde, Pit.	1	0	1	0	0	6
* Moore, Sterling, N.E.	1	0	0	1	0	6
Moreno, Knowshon, Den.	1	0	1	0	0	6
Murphy, Louis, Oak.	1	1	0	0	0	6
Nelson, Reggie, Cin.	1	0	0	1	0	6
Ngata, Haloti, Bal.	1	0	0	1	0	6
Ninkovich, Rob, N.E.	1	0	0	1	0	6
Norwood, Jordan, Cle.	1	0	1	0	0	6
Ochocinco, Chad, N.E.	1	0	1	0	0	6
Ogbonnaya, Chris, Cle.	1	1	0	0	0	6
Palmer, Carson, Oak.	1	1	0	0	0	6
Polamalu, Troy, Pit.	1	0	0	1	0	6
Pope, Leonard, K.C.	1	0	1	0	0	6
Potter, Zach, Jac.	1	0	1	0	0	6
Powers, Jerraud, Ind.	1	0	0	1	0	6
Revis, Darrelle, NYJ	1	0	0	1	0	6
* Ridley, Stevan, N.E.	1	1	0	0	0	6
Ringer, Javon, Ten.	1	1	0	0	0	6
Rivers, Philip, S.D.	1	1	0	0	0	6
Roosevelt, Naaman, Buf.	1	0	1	0	0	6
* Saunders, Weslye, Pit.	1	0	1	0	0	6
* Shorts, Cecil, Jac.	1	0	1	0	0	6
Slaton, Steve, Mia.	1	1	0	0	0	6
Slauson, Matt, NYJ	1	0	0	1	0	6
Smith, Alex, Cle.	1	0	1	0	0	6
Smith, Wade, Hou.	1	0	0	1	0	6
Stevens, Craig, Ten.	1	0	1	0	0	6
Tamme, Jacob, Ind.	1	0	1	0	0	6
Tate, Brandon, Cin.	1	0	0	1	0	6
* Thomas, Daniel, Mia.	1	0	1	0	0	6
Thomas, Mike, Jac.	1	0	1	0	0	6
Trufant, Isaiah, NYJ	1	0	0	1	0	6
Turner, Patrick, NYJ	1	0	1	0	0	6
Urban, Jerheme, K.C.	1	0	1	0	0	6
Vaughn, Cassius, Den.	1	0	0	1	0	6
* Vereen, Shane, N.E.	1	1	0	0	0	6
Wilfork, Vince, N.E.	1	0	0	1	0	6
Willis, Matt, Den.	1	0	1	0	0	6
Youboty, Ashton, Jac.	1	0	0	1	0	6
Fitzpatrick, Ryan, Buf.	0	0	0	0	1	2
Koch, Sam, Bal.	0	0	0	0	1	2
McClain, Rolando, Oak.	0	0	0	0	0	^2
Pouha, Sione, NYJ	0	0	0	0	0	^2
* Sheppard, Kelvin, Buf.	0	0	0	0	0	^2
* Wilkerson, Muhammad, NYJ	0	0	0	0	0	^2

^ *Safety*
Team safety credited to Cincinnati, N.Y. Jets, Pittsburgh (2)

NFC—INDIVIDUAL SCORERS

KICKERS

	XP	XPA	FG	FGA	PTS
Akers, David, S.F.	34	34	44	52	166
Kasay, John, N.O.	63	63	28	34	147
Crosby, Mason, G.B.	68	69	24	28	140
* Bailey, Dan, Dal.	39	39	32	37	135
Bryant, Matt, Atl.	45	45	27	29	126
Hanson, Jason, Det.	54	54	24	29	126
Gould, Robbie, Chi.	37	37	28	32	121
Gano, Graham, Was.	25	26	31	41	118
* Henery, Alex, Phi.	46	46	24	27	118
Mare, Olindo, Car.	44	45	22	28	110
Hauschka, Steven, Sea.	34	34	25	30	109
Longwell, Ryan, Min.	38	39	22	28	104
Barth, Connor, T.B.	23	23	26	28	101
Tynes, Lawrence, NY-G	43	43	19	24	100
Feely, Jay, Ariz	33	33	19	24	90
Brown, Josh, St.L	18	18	21	28	81

NONKICKERS

	TD	TDR	TDP	TDM	X2G	PTS
McCoy, LeSean, Phi.	20	17	3	0	0	120
Johnson, Calvin, Det.	16	0	16	0	0	96
Nelson, Jordy, G.B.	15	0	15	0	0	90
* Newton, Cam, Car.	14	14	0	0	0	84
Lynch, Marshawn, Sea.	13	12	1	0	0	78
Peterson, Adrian, Min.	13	12	1	0	0	78
Bradshaw, Ahmad, NY-G	11	9	2	0	1	68
Graham, Jimmy, N.O.	11	0	11	0	0	66
Robinson, Laurent, Dal.	11	0	11	0	0	66
Turner, Michael, Atl.	11	11	0	0	0	66
Sproles, Darren, N.O.	10	2	7	1	0	60
Wells, Beanie, Ariz	10	10	0	0	0	60
Bryant, Dez, Dal.	9	0	9	0	0	54
Cruz, Victor, NY-G	9	0	9	0	0	54
Harvin, Percy, Min.	9	2	6	1	0	54
Jennings, Greg, G.B.	9	0	9	0	0	54
Moore, Lance, N.O.	8	0	8	0	2	52
Jacobs, Brandon, NY-G	8	7	1	0	1	50
Colston, Marques, N.O.	8	0	8	0	0	48
Finley, Jermichael, G.B.	8	0	8	0	0	48
Fitzgerald, Larry, Ariz	8	0	8	0	0	48
Gore, Frank, S.F.	8	8	0	0	0	48
* Jones, Julio, Atl.	8	0	8	0	0	48
White, Roddy, Atl.	8	0	8	0	0	48
Smith, Steve, Car.	7	0	7	0	1	44
Austin, Miles, Dal.	7	0	7	0	0	42
Gonzalez, Tony, Atl.	7	0	7	0	0	42
Jones, James, G.B.	7	0	7	0	0	42
Nicks, Hakeem, NY-G	7	0	7	0	0	42
Smith, Kevin, Det.	7	4	3	0	0	42
Williams, DeAngelo, Car.	7	7	0	0	0	42
Scheffler, Tony, Det.	6	0	6	0	1	38
* Young, Titus, Det.	6	0	6	0	1	38
Barber, Marion, Chi.	6	6	0	0	0	36
Briscoe, Dezmon, T.B.	6	0	6	0	0	36
Davis, Vernon, S.F.	6	0	6	0	0	36
Driver, Donald, G.B.	6	0	6	0	0	36
Jackson, Steven, St.L	6	5	1	0	0	36
Kuhn, John, G.B.	6	4	2	0	0	36
Meachem, Robert, N.O.	6	0	6	0	0	36
Thomas, Pierre, N.O.	6	5	1	0	0	36
Olsen, Greg, Car.	5	0	5	0	1	32
Blount, LeGarrette, T.B.	5	5	0	0	0	30
Celek, Brent, Phi.	5	0	5	0	0	30
Davis, Kellen, Chi.	5	0	5	0	0	30
Doucet, Early, Ariz	5	0	5	0	0	30
Gaffney, Jabar, Was.	5	0	5	0	0	30
* Ingram, Mark, N.O.	5	5	0	0	0	30
Lloyd, Brandon, St.L	5	0	5	0	0	30
Maclin, Jeremy, Phi.	5	0	5	0	0	30

	TD	TDR	TDP	TDM	2-PT.	PTS		TD	TDR	TDP	TDM	2-PT.	PTS
Pettigrew, Brandon, Det.	5	0	5	0	0	30	Bell, Kahlil, Chi.	1	0	1	0	0	6
Stewart, Jonathan, Car.	5	4	1	0	0	30	Bennett, Earl, Chi.	1	0	1	0	0	6
Witten, Jason, Dal.	5	0	5	0	0	30	Biermann, Kroy, Atl.	1	0	0	1	0	6
Crabtree, Michael, S.F.	4	0	4	0	1	26	Boley, Michael, NY-G	1	0	0	1	0	6
* Baldwin, Doug, Sea.	4	0	4	0	0	24	Brees, Drew, N.O.	1	1	0	0	0	6
Ballard, Jake, NY-G	4	0	4	0	0	24	Brockel, Richie, Car.	1	1	0	0	0	6
Collins, Jed, N.O.	4	2	2	0	0	24	Brown, Ronnie, Phi.	1	1	0	0	0	6
Forté, Matt, Chi.	4	3	1	0	0	24	Bryant, Red, Sea.	1	0	0	1	0	6
Freeman, Josh, T.B.	4	4	0	0	0	24	Carpenter, Bobby, Det.	1	0	0	1	0	6
Gerhart, Toby, Min.	4	1	3	0	0	24	Clemens, Kellen, St.L	1	1	0	0	0	6
Hester, Devin, Chi.	4	0	1	3	0	24	Cooper, Riley, Phi.	1	0	1	0	0	6
Jackson, DeSean, Phi.	4	0	4	0	0	24	Crabtree, Tom, G.B.	1	0	1	0	0	6
Manningham, Mario, NY-G	4	0	4	0	0	24	Cutler, Jay, Chi.	1	1	0	0	0	6
Moss, Santana, Was.	4	0	4	0	0	24	Douglas, Harry, Atl.	1	0	1	0	0	6
* Peterson, Patrick, Ariz	4	0	0	4	0	24	Flynn, Matt, G.B.	1	1	0	0	0	6
Shockey, Jeremy, Car.	4	0	4	0	0	24	Forsett, Justin, Sea.	1	1	0	0	0	6
Benn, Arrelious, T.B.	3	0	3	0	0	18	Gibson, Brandon, St.L	1	0	1	0	0	6
Best, Jahvid, Det.	3	2	1	0	0	18	Gilmore, John, N.O.	1	0	1	0	0	6
Burleson, Nate, Det.	3	0	3	0	0	18	Grossman, Rex, Was.	1	1	0	0	0	6
* Cobb, Randall, G.B.	3	0	1	2	0	18	Hall, Chad, Phi.	1	0	1	0	0	6
Davis, Fred, Was.	3	0	3	0	0	18	Harbor, Clay, Phi.	1	0	1	0	0	6
Grant, Ryan, G.B.	3	2	1	0	0	18	Hawthorne, David, Sea.	1	0	0	1	0	6
* Helu, Roy, Was.	3	2	1	0	0	18	Heap, Todd, Ariz	1	0	1	0	0	6
Jenkins, Michael, Min.	3	0	3	0	0	18	Hixon, Domenik, NY-G	1	0	1	0	0	6
King, Jeff, Ariz	3	0	3	0	0	18	Idonije, Israel, Chi.	1	0	0	1	0	6
LaFell, Brandon, Car.	3	0	3	0	0	18	Ivory, Chris, N.O.	1	1	0	0	0	6
Parker, Preston, T.B.	3	0	3	0	0	18	Jackson, Tarvaris, Sea.	1	1	0	0	0	6
Rodgers, Aaron, G.B.	3	3	0	0	0	18	Jenkins, Malcolm, N.O.	1	0	0	1	0	6
* Rudolph, Kyle, Min.	3	0	3	0	0	18	Jones, Felix, Dal.	1	1	0	0	0	6
* Sanzenbacher, Dane, Chi.	3	0	3	0	0	18	* Kerrigan, Ryan, Was.	1	0	0	1	0	6
Shiancoe, Visanthe, Min.	3	0	3	0	0	18	* Lewis, Dion, Phi.	1	1	0	0	0	6
Tate, Golden, Sea.	3	0	3	0	0	18	* Lockette, Ricardo, Sea.	1	0	1	0	0	6
Walker, Delanie, S.F.	3	0	3	0	0	18	Lofton, Curtis, Atl.	1	0	0	1	0	6
Williams, Kyle, S.F.	3	0	3	0	0	18	Mack, Elbert, T.B.	1	0	0	1	0	6
Williams, Mike, T.B.	3	0	3	0	0	18	Manning, Eli, NY-G	1	1	0	0	0	6
Winslow, Kellen, T.B.	2	0	2	0	2	16	Matthews, Clay, G.B.	1	0	0	1	0	6
Alexander, Danario, St.L	2	0	2	0	0	12	McNabb, Donovan, Min.	1	1	0	0	0	6
Armstrong, Anthony, Was.	2	0	2	0	0	12	* Miller, Bruce, S.F.	1	0	1	0	0	6
Avril, Cliff, Det.	2	0	0	2	0	12	Miller, Nick, St.L	1	0	0	1	0	6
Beck, John, Was.	2	2	0	0	0	12	Moore, D.J., Chi.	1	0	0	1	0	6
Browner, Brandon, Sea.	2	0	0	2	0	12	Morgan, Josh, S.F.	1	0	1	0	0	6
Dixon, Anthony, S.F.	2	2	0	0	0	12	Naanee, Legedu, Car.	1	0	1	0	0	6
Ginn, Ted, S.F.	2	0	0	2	0	12	Newman, Terence, Dal.	1	0	0	1	0	6
Henderson, Devery, N.O.	2	0	2	0	0	12	Palmer, Michael, Atl.	1	0	1	0	0	6
Hightower, Tim, Was.	2	1	1	0	0	12	Peprah, Charlie, G.B.	1	0	0	1	0	6
Houston, Chris, Det.	2	0	0	2	0	12	Peters, Corey, Atl.	1	0	0	1	0	6
* Hunter, Kendall, S.F.	2	2	0	0	0	12	Phillips, John, Dal.	1	0	1	0	0	6
Knox, Johnny, Chi.	2	0	2	0	0	12	* Pilares, Kealoha, Car.	1	0	1	0	0	6
Morris, Maurice, Det.	2	1	1	0	0	12	Raji, B.J., G.B.	1	1	0	0	0	6
Mughelli, Ovie, Atl.	2	0	2	0	0	12	Rogers, Carlos, S.F.	1	0	0	1	0	6
* Murray, DeMarco, Dal.	2	2	0	0	0	12	* Rolle, Brian, Phi.	1	0	0	1	0	6
Obomanu, Ben, Sea.	2	0	2	0	0	12	Romo, Tony, Dal.	1	1	0	0	0	6
Parker, Juqua, Phi.	2	0	0	2	0	12	Samuel, Asante, Phi.	1	0	0	1	0	6
Rice, Sidney, Sea.	2	0	2	0	0	12	Smith, Alfonso, Ariz	1	1	0	0	0	6
Roberts, Andre, Ariz	2	0	2	0	0	12	Smith, Alphonso, Det.	1	0	0	1	0	6
Robinson, Michael, Sea.	2	0	1	1	0	12	Smith, Steve, Phi.	1	0	1	0	0	6
* Rodgers, Jacquizz, Atl.	2	1	1	0	0	12	Snelling, Jason, Atl.	1	0	1	0	0	6
Ryan, Matt, Atl.	2	2	0	0	0	12	Starks, James, G.B.	1	1	0	0	0	6
Smith, Alex, S.F.	2	2	0	0	0	12	Stewart, Darian, St.L	1	0	0	1	0	6
Spaeth, Matt, Chi.	2	0	2	0	0	12	* Tanner, Phillip, Dal.	1	1	0	0	0	6
Stallworth, Donte', Was.	2	0	2	0	0	12	Taylor, Chester, Ariz	1	1	0	0	0	6
Stephens-Howling, LaRod, Ariz	2	0	2	0	0	12	* Taylor, Ryan, G.B.	1	0	1	0	0	6
Talib, Aqib, T.B.	2	0	0	2	0	12	Torain, Ryan, Was.	1	1	0	0	0	6
Tillman, Charles, Chi.	2	0	0	2	0	12	Torrence, Leigh, N.O.	1	0	0	1	0	6
Webb, Joe, Min.	2	2	0	0	0	12	Tulloch, Stephen, Det.	1	0	0	1	0	6
Williams, Keiland, Det.	2	0	2	0	0	12	Urlacher, Brian, Chi.	1	0	0	1	0	6
Williams, Roy, Chi.	2	0	2	0	0	12	Vick, Michael, Phi.	1	1	0	0	0	6
Anderson, David, Was.	1	0	1	0	0	6	Vilma, Jonathan, N.O.	1	0	0	1	0	6
Aromashodu, Devin, Min.	1	0	1	0	0	6	Walden, Erik, G.B.	1	0	0	1	0	6
Avant, Jason, Phi.	1	0	1	0	0	6	Washington, Leon, Sea.	1	1	0	0	0	6
Beckum, Travis, NY-G	1	0	1	0	0	6	Watson, Dekoda, T.B.	1	0	0	1	0	6

	TD	TDR	TDP	TDM	2-PT.	PTS
Williams, Cadillac, St.L	1	1	0	0	0	6
Williams, Edwin, Chi.	1	0	0	1	0	6
Williams, Mike, Sea.	1	0	1	0	0	6
Williams, Tramon, G.B.	1	0	0	1	0	6
Woodson, Charles, G.B.	1	0	0	1	0	6
Wright, Major, Chi.	1	0	0	1	0	6
Young, Darrel, Was.	1	1	0	0	0	6
Ware, D.J., NY-G	0	0	0	0	2	4
Allen, Jared, Min.	0	0	0	0	0	^2
Applewhite, Antwan, Car.	0	0	0	0	0	^2
Barber, Ronde, T.B.	0	0	0	0	0	^2
Canty, Chris, NY-G	0	0	0	0	0	^2
Hall, James, St.L	0	0	0	0	0	^2
* Hankerson, Leonard, Was.	0	0	0	0	1	2
Hardy, Greg, Car.	0	0	0	0	0	^2
Hargrove, Anthony, Sea.	0	0	0	0	0	^2

	TD	TDR	TDP	TDM	2-PT.	PTS
Hunt, Phillip, Phi.	0	0	0	0	0	^2
McCown, Josh, Chi.	0	0	0	0	1	2
* Paea, Stephen, Chi.	0	0	0	0	0	^2
Pierre-Paul, Jason, NY-G	0	0	0	0	0	^2
* Smith, Aldon, S.F.	0	0	0	0	0	^2

^ Safety
Team safety credited to Detroit and St. Louis

AMERICAN FOOTBALL CONFERENCE—SCORING

	TD	TDR	TDP	TDM	XKG	XKAtt	X2G	X2Att	FG	FGA	SAF	POINTS
New England	61	18	39	4	59	59	2	2	28	33	0	513
San Diego	46	16	27	3	44	45	1	1	28	35	0	406
Houston	41	18	20	3	39	40	0	1	32	38	0	381
Baltimore	41	15	21	5	40	40	1	1	30	39	0	378
N.Y. Jets	45	14	26	5	44	44	0	1	19	25	3	377
Buffalo	43	12	24	7	41	41	1	2	23	31	1	372
Oakland	38	16	20	2	36	36	0	2	31	35	1	359
Cincinnati	35	10	21	4	33	34	0	1	33	38	1	344
Miami	33	11	20	2	32	32	0	1	33	39	0	329
Pittsburgh	36	13	21	2	36	36	0	0	23	31	2	325
Tennessee	34	8	22	4	34	34	0	1	29	32	0	325
Denver	36	11	20	5	30	30	3	6	19	25	0	309
Indianapolis	25	8	14	3	24	24	0	1	23	27	0	243
Jacksonville	25	9	12	4	24	24	0	1	23	25	0	243
Cleveland	21	4	16	1	20	20	0	1	24	29	0	218
Kansas City	20	5	13	2	20	20	0	0	24	30	0	212
AFC Total	580	188	336	56	556	559	8	21	422	512	8	5334
AFC Average	36.3	11.8	21.0	3.5	34.8	34.9	0.5	1.3	26.4	32.0	0.5	333.4

NATIONAL FOOTBALL CONFERENCE—SCORING

	TD	TDR	TDP	TDM	XKG	XKAtt	X2G	X2Att	FG	FGA	SAF	POINTS
Green Bay	70	12	51	7	68	69	0	1	24	28	0	560
New Orleans	66	16	46	4	63	63	2	3	28	34	0	547
Detroit	57	9	41	7	54	54	2	3	24	29	1	474
Carolina	48	26	21	1	44	45	2	3	22	28	2	406
Atlanta	46	14	29	3	45	45	0	1	27	29	0	402
Philadelphia	46	20	22	4	46	46	0	0	24	27	1	396
N.Y. Giants	47	17	29	1	43	43	4	4	19	24	2	394
San Francisco	35	14	18	3	34	34	1	1	44	52	1	380
Dallas	39	5	33	1	39	39	0	0	32	37	0	369
Chicago	38	10	18	10	37	37	1	1	28	32	1	353
Minnesota	39	18	20	1	38	39	0	0	22	28	1	340
Seattle	35	15	15	5	34	34	0	1	25	30	1	321
Arizona	37	12	21	4	33	33	0	2	19	24	0	312
Washington	28	8	19	1	25	26	1	2	31	41	0	288
Tampa Bay	30	9	17	4	23	23	2	7	26	28	1	287
St. Louis	18	7	9	2	18	18	0	0	21	28	2	193
NFC Total	679	212	409	58	644	648	15	29	416	499	13	6022
NFC Average	42.4	13.3	25.6	3.6	40.3	40.5	0.9	1.8	26.0	31.2	0.8	376.4
NFL Total	1259	400	745	114	1200	1207	23	50	838	1011	21	11356
NFL Average	39.3	12.5	23.3	3.6	37.5	37.7	0.7	1.6	26.2	31.6	0.7	354.9

FIELD GOALS

FIELD GOAL PERCENTAGE
NFC: .931 Matt Bryant, Atlanta
AFC: .920 Josh Scobee, Jacksonville

FIELD GOALS
NFC: 44 David Akers, San Francisco
AFC: 33 Mike Nugent, Cincinnati

FIELD GOAL ATTEMPTS
NFC: 52 David Akers, San Francisco
AFC: 38 Mike Nugent, Cincinnati
38 Neil Rackers, Houston

FIELD GOALS, GAME
AFC: 6 Sebastian Janikowski, Oakland vs. Chicago, November 27 (6 attempts)
NFC: 6 * Dan Bailey, Dallas vs. Washington, September 26 (6 attempts)

LONGEST FIELD GOAL
AFC: 63 Sebastian Janikowski, Oakland at Denver, September 12
NFC: 59 Graham Gano, Washington vs. San Francisco, November 6

AVERAGE YARDS MADE
AFC: 39.9 Rob Bironas, Tennessee
NFC: 39.1 Connor Barth, Tampa Bay

AMERICAN FOOTBALL CONFERENCE—FIELD GOALS

	FG	FGA	Pct	Long
Jacksonville	23	25	.920	55
Tennessee	29	32	.906	53
Oakland	31	35	.886	63
Cincinnati	33	38	.868	49
Indianapolis	23	27	.852	53
New England	28	33	.848	50
Miami	33	39	.846	58
Houston	32	38	.842	54
Cleveland	24	29	.828	54
Kansas City	24	30	.800	54
San Diego	28	35	.800	53
Baltimore	30	39	.769	51
Denver	19	25	.760	59
N.Y. Jets	19	25	.760	51
Buffalo	23	31	.742	56
Pittsburgh	23	31	.742	51
AFC Total	422	512	—	63
AFC Average	26.4	32.0	.824	—

NATIONAL FOOTBALL CONFERENCE—FIELD GOALS

	FG	FGA	Pct	Long
Atlanta	27	29	.931	51
Tampa Bay	26	28	.929	55
Philadelphia	24	27	.889	51
Chicago	28	32	.875	57
Dallas	32	37	.865	51
Green Bay	24	28	.857	58
San Francisco	44	52	.846	55
Seattle	25	30	.833	52
Detroit	24	29	.828	51
New Orleans	28	34	.824	53
Arizona	19	24	.792	51
N.Y. Giants	19	24	.792	50
Carolina	22	28	.786	45
Minnesota	22	28	.786	53
Washington	31	41	.756	59
St. Louis	21	28	.750	49
NFC Total	416	499	—	59
NFC Average	26.0	31.2	.834	—
League Total	838	1011	—	63
League Average	26.2	31.6	.829	—

AFC—INDIVIDUAL FIELD GOALS

	1-19 Yards	20-29 Yards	30-39 Yards	40-49 Yards	50 or Longer	Totals	Avg Yds Att	Avg Yds Made	Avg Yds Miss	Long
Scobee, Josh, Jac.	1-1 1.000	5-5 1.000	5-5 1.000	7-8 .875	5-6 .833	23-25 .920	39.5	38.6	50.0	55
Bironas, Rob, Ten.	0-0 —	5-5 1.000	9-10 .900	9-10 .900	6-7 .857	29-32 .906	40.6	39.9	47.3	53
Janikowski, Sebastian, Oak.	1-1 1.000	8-8 1.000	5-5 1.000	10-11 .909	7-10 .700	31-35 .886	41.6	39.6	57.3	63
Nugent, Mike, Cin.	0-0 —	14-14 1.000	5-8 .625	14-16 .875	0-0 —	33-38 .868	34.7	34.0	39.0	49
Carpenter, Dan, Mia.	0-0 —	10-11 .909	6-7 .857	11-12 .917	2-4 .500	29-34 .853	36.4	35.4	42.2	58
Vinatieri, Adam, Ind.	0-0 —	7-7 1.000	6-7 .857	8-10 .800	2-3 .667	23-27 .852	36.9	35.8	43.5	53
Gostkowski, Stephen, N.E.	1-1 1.000	12-13 .923	5-6 .833	9-11 .818	1-2 .500	28-33 .848	34.3	33.0	41.4	50
Rackers, Neil, Hou.	0-0 —	14-14 1.000	10-11 .909	4-8 .500	4-5 .800	32-38 .842	35.5	33.6	45.7	54
Dawson, Phil, Cle.	0-0 —	7-9 .778	3-4 .750	7-8 .875	7-8 .875	24-29 .828	38.7	38.9	37.4	54
Succop, Ryan, K.C.	1-1 1.000	7-7 1.000	6-7 .857	7-12 .583	3-3 1.000	24-30 .800	36.9	34.8	45.5	54
Novak, Nick, S.D.	0-0 —	11-11 1.000	4-5 .800	8-11 .727	4-7 .571	27-34 .794	38.9	36.5	47.9	53
Folk, Nick, NYJ	0-0 —	5-6 .833	6-6 1.000	5-7 .714	3-6 .500	19-25 .760	39.0	37.0	45.2	51
Prater, Matt, Den.	0-0 —	5-6 .833	8-8 1.000	3-7 .429	3-4 .750	19-25 .760	38.7	37.3	43.3	59
Cundiff, Billy, Bal.	1-1 1.000	9-9 1.000	10-12 .833	7-9 .778	1-6 .167	28-37 .757	36.7	34.0	45.2	51
Suisham, Shaun, Pit.	2-2 1.000	8-8 1.000	6-8 .750	6-11 .545	1-2 .500	23-31 .742	35.5	33.0	42.5	51
(Nonqualifiers)										
Lindell, Rian, Buf.	0-0 —	6-6 1.000	2-3 .667	5-6 .833	0-0 —	13-15 .867	35.4	34.5	41.5	49
Rayner, Dave, Buf.	0-0 —	5-6 .833	3-4 .750	0-1 .000	2-4 .500	10-15 .667	36.7	34.4	41.4	56
Graham, Shayne, Mia.-Bal.	0-0 —	4-4 1.000	0-0 —	2-3 .667	0-0 —	6-7 .857	34.6	32.5	47.0	48
Coutu, Brandon, Buf.	0-0 —	0-0 —	0-0 —	0-1 .000	0-0 —	0-1 .000	45.0	—	45.0	0
Scifres, Mike, S.D.	0-0 —	0-0 —	0-0 —	1-1 1.000	0-0 —	1-1 1.000	40.0	40.0	—	40
AFC Totals	7-7 1.000	142-149 .953	99-116 .853	123-163 .755	51-77 .662	422-512 .824	37.4	35.9	44.3	63
NFL Totals	16-16 1.000	285-296 .963	225-259 .869	222-300 .740	90-140 .643	838-1011 .829	36.9	35.4	44.4	63

Leader based on overall percentage, minimum 16 field goals

NFC—INDIVIDUAL FIELD GOALS

	1-19 Yards	20-29 Yards	30-39 Yards	40-49 Yards	50 or Longer	Totals	Avg Yds Att	Avg Yds Made	Avg Yds Miss	Long
Bryant, Matt, Atl.	2-2 1.000	9-9 1.000	9-9 1.000	5-7 .714	2-2 1.000	27-29 .931	33.3	32.5	43.5	51
Barth, Connor, T.B.	0-0 —	5-5 1.000	6-6 1.000	13-14 .929	2-3 .667	26-28 .929	39.9	39.1	50.5	55
* Henery, Alex, Phi.	0-0 —	10-10 1.000	9-11 .818	4-4 1.000	1-2 .500	24-27 .889	33.4	32.0	45.0	51
Gould, Robbie, Chi.	0-0 —	10-10 1.000	6-6 1.000	6-10 .600	6-6 1.000	28-32 .875	37.3	36.5	43.5	57
* Bailey, Dan, Dal.	1-1 1.000	8-9 .889	11-11 1.000	10-12 .833	2-4 .500	32-37 .865	36.4	35.2	44.4	51
Crosby, Mason, G.B.	1-1 1.000	4-5 .800	14-14 1.000	3-5 .600	2-3 .667	24-28 .857	36.6	35.5	43.3	58
Akers, David, S.F.	2-2 1.000	16-16 1.000	13-14 .929	6-11 .545	7-9 .778	44-52 .846	36.7	35.1	45.5	55
Hauschka, Steven, Sea.	2-2 1.000	5-6 .833	9-10 .900	7-8 .875	2-4 .500	25-30 .833	36.7	35.4	43.0	52
Hanson, Jason, Det.	0-0 —	9-9 1.000	8-9 .889	2-4 .500	5-7 .714	24-29 .828	36.9	34.8	47.0	51
Kasay, John, N.O.	0-0 —	11-11 1.000	10-10 1.000	5-8 .625	2-5 .400	28-34 .824	36.6	34.3	47.3	53
Feely, Jay, Ariz	0-0 —	9-9 1.000	4-6 .667	5-7 .714	1-2 .500	19-24 .792	35.8	34.0	42.8	51
Tynes, Lawrence, NY-G	0-0 —	12-12 1.000	3-4 .750	3-5 .600	1-3 .333	19-24 .792	33.9	30.6	46.6	50
Longwell, Ryan, Min.	0-0 —	7-7 1.000	7-8 .875	6-10 .600	2-3 .667	22-28 .786	38.1	36.0	45.8	53
Mare, Olindo, Car.	1-1 1.000	7-7 1.000	6-9 .667	8-9 .889	0-2 .000	22-28 .786	35.0	33.2	41.3	45
Gano, Graham, Was.	0-0 —	14-15 .933	5-9 .556	8-11 .727	4-6 .667	31-41 .756	36.8	35.4	41.3	59
Brown, Josh, St.L	0-0 —	7-7 1.000	6-7 .857	8-12 .667	0-2 .000	21-28 .750	38.6	36.4	45.1	49
NFC Totals	9-9 1.000	143-147 .973	126-143 .881	99-137 .723	39-63 .619	416-499 .834	36.4	34.8	44.4	59
NFL Totals	16-16 1.000	285-296 .963	225-259 .869	222-300 .740	90-140 .643	838-1011 .829	36.9	35.4	44.4	63

Leader based on overall percentage, minimum 16 field goals
* *Player that was a rookie in 2011*

RUSHING

YARDS
AFC:	1606	Maurice Jones-Drew, Jacksonville
NFC:	1340	Michael Turner, Atlanta

YARDS, GAME
NFC:	253	* DeMarco Murray, Dallas vs. St. Louis, October 23 (25 attempts, 1 TD)
AFC:	204	Ray Rice, Baltimore at Cleveland, December 4 (29 attempts, 1 TD)

LONGEST
NFC:	91	* DeMarco Murray, Dallas vs. St. Louis, October 23 - TD
AFC:	80	Fred Jackson, Buffalo at N.Y. Giants, October 16 - TD
	80	Donald Brown, Indianapolis vs. Tennessee, December 18 - TD

ATTEMPTS
AFC:	343	Maurice Jones-Drew, Jacksonville
NFC:	301	Michael Turner, Atlanta

ATTEMPTS, GAME
AFC:	33	Montario Hardesty, Cleveland vs. Seattle, October 23 (0 TD)
	33	Arian Foster, Houston vs. Jacksonville, October 30 (112 yards, 1 TD)
NFC:	32	Marshawn Lynch, Seattle vs. Baltimore, November 13 (109 yards, 1 TD)

YARDS PER ATTEMPT
NFC:	5.6*	Cam Newton, Carolina
AFC:	5.5	Fred Jackson, Buffalo

TOUCHDOWNS
NFC:	17	LeSean McCoy, Philadelphia
AFC:	12	Ray Rice, Baltimore

TEAM LEADERS, YARDS

AFC: BALTIMORE, 1,364, Ray Rice; BUFFALO, 934, Fred Jackson; CINCINNATI, 1067, Cedric Benson; CLEVELAND, 587, Peyton Hillis; DENVER, 1199, Willis McGahee; HOUSTON, 1224, Arian Foster; INDIANAPOLIS, 645, Donald Brown; JACK-SONVILLE, 1606, Maurice Jones-Drew; KANSAS CITY, 597, Jackie Battle; MIAMI, 1086, Reggie Bush; NEW ENGLAND, 667, BenJarvus Green-Ellis; N.Y. JETS, 1054, Shonn Greene; OAKLAND, 977, Michael Bush; PITTSBURGH, 928, Rashard Mendenhall; SAN DIEGO, 1091, Ryan Mathews; TENNESSEE, 1047, Chris Johnson

NFC: ARIZONA, 1047, Beanie Wells; ATLANTA, 1340, Michael Turner; CAROLINA, 836, DeAngelo Williams; CHICAGO, 997, Matt Forté; DALLAS, 897, *DeMarco Murray; DETROIT, 390, Jahvid Best; GREEN BAY, 578, James Starks; MINNESOTA, 970, Adrian Peterson; NEW ORLEANS, 603, Darren Sproles; N.Y. GIANTS, 659, Ahmad Bradshaw; PHILADELPHIA, 1309, LeSean McCoy; ST. LOUIS, 1145, Steven Jackson; SAN FRANCISCO, 1211, Frank Gore; SEATTLE, 1204, Marshawn Lynch; TAMPA BAY, 781, LeGarrette Blount; WASHINGTON, 640, *Roy Helu

TEAM CHAMPION
AFC:	2632	Denver
NFC:	2408	Carolina

Player that was a rookie in 2011

NFL TOP TEN RUSHERS

	Att	Yards	Avg	Long	TD
Jones-Drew, Maurice, Jac.	343	1606	4.7	56	8
Rice, Ray, Bal.	291	1364	4.7	70t	12
Turner, Michael, Atl.	301	1340	4.5	81t	11
McCoy, LeSean, Phi.	273	1309	4.8	60	17
Foster, Arian, Hou.	278	1224	4.4	43	10
Gore, Frank, S.F.	282	1211	4.3	55	8
Lynch, Marshawn, Sea.	285	1204	4.2	47	12
McGahee, Willis, Den.	249	1199	4.8	60t	4
Jackson, Steven, St.L	260	1145	4.4	47t	5
Mathews, Ryan, S.D.	222	1091	4.9	39	6

AFC—INDIVIDUAL RUSHERS

	Att	Yards	Avg	Long	TD
Jones-Drew, Maurice, Jac.	343	1606	4.7	56	8
Rice, Ray, Bal.	291	1364	4.7	70t	12
Foster, Arian, Hou.	278	1224	4.4	43	10
McGahee, Willis, Den.	249	1199	4.8	60t	4
Mathews, Ryan, S.D.	222	1091	4.9	39	6
Bush, Reggie, Mia.	216	1086	5.0	76t	6
Benson, Cedric, Cin.	273	1067	3.9	42	6
Greene, Shonn, NYJ	253	1054	4.2	31	6
Johnson, Chris, Ten.	262	1047	4.0	48t	4
Bush, Michael, Oak.	256	977	3.8	44	7
Tate, Ben, Hou.	175	942	5.4	56	4
Jackson, Fred, Buf.	170	934	5.5	80t	6
Mendenhall, Rashard, Pit.	228	928	4.1	68	9
Green-Ellis, BenJarvus, N.E.	181	667	3.7	18	11
Tebow, Tim, Den.	122	660	5.4	32	6
Brown, Donald, Ind.	134	645	4.8	80t	5
McFadden, Darren, Oak.	113	614	5.4	70t	4
Battle, Jackie, K.C.	149	597	4.0	34	2
Hillis, Peyton, Cle.	161	587	3.6	24t	3
* Thomas, Daniel, Mia.	165	581	3.5	28	0
Spiller, C.J., Buf.	107	561	5.2	38	4
McCluster, Dexter, K.C.	114	516	4.5	32	1
Tolbert, Mike, S.D.	121	490	4.0	40	8
Redman, Isaac, Pit.	110	479	4.4	27	3
Jones, Thomas, K.C.	153	478	3.1	26	0
Williams, Ricky, Bal.	108	444	4.1	28	2
* Ridley, Stevan, N.E.	87	441	5.1	33t	1
Addai, Joseph, Ind.	118	433	3.7	16	1
Ball, Lance, Den.	96	402	4.2	34	1
Scott, Bernard, Cin.	112	380	3.4	25t	3
* Carter, Delone, Ind.	101	377	3.7	42	2
Woodhead, Danny, N.E.	77	351	4.6	12	1
Ogbonnaya, Chris, Hou.-Cle.	76	340	4.5	40	1
Tomlinson, LaDainian, NYJ	75	280	3.7	20	1
Hardesty, Montario, Cle.	88	266	3.0	19	0
Fitzpatrick, Ryan, Buf.	56	215	3.8	18	0
McCoy, Colt, Cle.	61	212	3.5	20	0
Ringer, Javon, Ten.	59	185	3.1	25	1
Moreno, Knowshon, Den.	37	179	4.8	24	0
Moore, Mewelde, Pit.	22	157	7.1	21	0
Ward, Derrick, Hou.	45	154	3.4	15	2
Choice, Tashard, Dal.-Was.-Buf.	57	152	2.7	14	1
* Dalton, Andy, Cin.	37	152	4.1	17	1
McKnight, Joe, NYJ	43	134	3.1	11	0
Karim, Deji, Jac.	63	130	2.1	14	0
Dwyer, Jonathan, Pit.	16	123	7.7	76	0
Henne, Chad, Mia.	15	112	7.5	20	1
Reece, Marcel, Oak.	17	112	6.6	26	0
Brady, Tom, N.E.	43	109	2.5	13	3
Painter, Curtis, Ind.	17	107	6.3	24	0
Sanchez, Mark, NYJ	37	103	2.8	25	6
Brinkley, Curtis, S.D.	30	101	3.4	12	1
Cassel, Matt, K.C.	25	99	4.0	11	0
* Gabbert, Blaine, Jac.	48	98	2.0	12	0

	Att	Yards	Avg	Long	TD
Hester, Jacob, S.D.	28	90	3.2	16	0
Flacco, Joe, Bal.	39	88	2.3	33	1
Smith, Brad, Buf.	20	87	4.4	18	1
Leonard, Brian, Cin.	17	85	5.0	14	0
Slaton, Steve, Hou.-Mia.	24	84	3.5	28	1
Charles, Jamaal, K.C.	12	83	6.9	24	0
Johnson, Jeremiah, Den.	14	77	5.5	25	0
* Jones, Taiwan, Oak.	16	73	4.6	14	0
Roethlisberger, Ben, Pit.	31	70	2.3	11	0
Wallace, Seneca, Cle.	7	70	10.0	27	0
Murphy, Louis, Oak.	6	69	11.5	27	1
Moore, Matt, Mia.	32	65	2.0	16	2
* Moore, Denarius, Oak.	5	61	12.2	25	1
Campbell, Jason, Oak.	18	60	3.3	17	2
Faulk, Kevin, N.E.	17	57	3.4	9	0
* Vereen, Shane, N.E.	15	57	3.8	19	1
Wallace, Mike, Pit.	5	57	11.4	21	0
* Yates, T.J., Hou.	14	57	4.1	17	0
* Locker, Jake, Ten.	8	56	7.0	17	1
* Green, A.J., Cin.	5	53	10.6	22	0
Hasselbeck, Matt, Ten.	20	52	2.6	21	0
Jackson, Vincent, S.D.	3	51	17.0	41	0
McClain, Le'Ron, K.C.	15	51	3.4	12	1
Royal, Eddie, Den.	7	48	6.9	11	0
Cartwright, Rock, Oak.	4	45	11.3	35	0
Hernandez, Aaron, N.E.	5	45	9.0	19	0
Conner, John, NYJ	13	44	3.4	13	1
* Harper, Jamie, Ten.	17	44	2.6	12	1
Larsen, Spencer, Den.	14	44	3.1	6	0
* Harris, DuJuan, Jac.	9	42	4.7	24	0
Brown, Antonio, Pit.	7	41	5.9	10	0
* Clay, John, Pit.	10	41	4.1	10t	1
Hilliard, Lex, Mia.	16	41	2.6	4	1
Owens, Montell, Jac.	10	39	3.9	9	0
* Smith, Torrey, Bal.	4	39	9.8	16	0
Boller, Kyle, Oak.	9	38	4.2	20	0
* White, Johnny, Buf.	12	38	3.2	13	0
Rivers, Philip, S.D.	26	36	1.4	15	1
Leach, Vonta, Bal.	12	35	2.9	6	0
Ford, Jacoby, Oak.	4	31	7.8	30	0
Welker, Wes, N.E.	4	30	7.5	19	0
Garcon, Pierre, Ind.	4	28	7.0	18	0
* Kerley, Jeremy, NYJ	5	28	5.6	16	0
Holmes, Santonio, NYJ	3	27	9.0	23	0
Breaston, Steve, K.C.	1	25	25.0	25	0
Cribbs, Josh, Cle.	7	25	3.6	15	0
Hawkins, Andrew, Cin.	5	25	5.0	8	0
Hall, Ahmard, Ten.	6	24	4.0	12	0
McCown, Luke, Jac.	7	23	3.3	9	0
Kern, Brett, Ten.	1	21	21.0	21	0
* Powell, Bilal, NYJ	13	21	1.6	6	0
Palmer, Carson, Oak.	16	20	1.3	10	1
Jones, Jacoby, Hou.	4	17	4.3	15	0
Reed, David, Bal.	1	16	16.0	16	0
* Little, Greg, Cle.	3	15	5.0	13	0
Palko, Tyler, K.C.	5	15	3.0	12	0
Peerman, Cedric, Cin.	3	15	5.0	11	0
Bolen, Brock, Jac.	2	14	7.0	10	0
Marshall, Brandon, Mia.	1	13	13.0	13	0
Orton, Kyle, Den.-K.C.	11	13	1.2	13	0
Arenas, Javier, K.C.	3	12	4.0	7t	1
Bowe, Dwayne, K.C.	1	12	12.0	12	0
Clayton, Thomas, Cle.	8	12	1.5	4	0
Tonga, Manase, Oak.	1	12	12.0	12	0
Casey, James, Hou.	1	11	11.0	11	0
Thomas, Mike, Jac.	3	11	3.7	12	0
Weddle, Eric, S.D.	1	10	10.0	10	0
Bess, Davone, Mia.	2	9	4.5	5	0
Hartline, Brian, Mia.	1	9	9.0	9	0
Schaub, Matt, Hou.	15	9	0.6	3	2
* Allen, Anthony, Bal.	3	8	2.7	3	0
Edelman, Julian, N.E.	4	8	2.0	6	0
Johnson, Andre, Hou.	1	8	8.0	8	0
* Marecic, Owen, Cle.	4	8	2.0	3	0
Thigpen, Tyler, Buf.	1	8	8.0	8	0
Jones, Greg, Jac.	2	7	3.5	6	1
Urban, Jerheme, K.C.	1	7	7.0	7	0
Miller, Heath, Pit.	1	6	6.0	6	0
Wilson, George, Buf.	1	6	6.0	6	0
Horne, Jeremy, K.C.	1	5	5.0	5	0
Orlovsky, Dan, Ind.	6	5	0.8	7	0
Thomas, Demaryius, Den.	1	5	5.0	5	0
Washington, Nate, Ten.	2	5	2.5	3t	1
* Gates, Clyde, Mia.	1	4	4.0	4	0
Mariani, Marc, Ten.	1	4	4.0	4	0
Cotchery, Jerricho, Pit.	1	3	3.0	3	0
Gronkowski, Rob, N.E.	1	2	2.0	2t	1
Johnson, Larry, Mia.	1	2	2.0	2	0
Jones, Donald, Buf.	1	2	2.0	2	0
* Smith, Armond, Cle.	3	2	0.7	6	0
* Taylor, Tyrod, Bal.	1	2	2.0	2	0
Cromartie, Antonio, NYJ	1	1	1.0	1	0
Decker, Eric, Den.	1	1	1.0	1	0
Gradkowski, Bruce, Cin.	3	1	0.3	1	0
Johnson, Bryant, Hou.	1	1	1.0	1	0
Losman, J.P., Mia.	2	1	0.5	1	0
Harris, Nick, Jac.	1	0	0.0	0	0
Turk, Matt, Jac.	1	0	0.0	0	0
Vickers, Lawrence, Hou.	1	0	0.0	0	0
Collins, Kerry, Ind.	2	-1	-0.5	0	0
Leinart, Matt, Hou.	1	-1	-1.0	-1	0
* Ausberry, David, Oak.	1	-2	-2.0	-2	0
Batch, Charlie, Pit.	3	-2	-0.7	0	0
Colquitt, Dustin, K.C.	1	-3	-3.0	-3	0
Hoyer, Brian, N.E.	4	-3	-0.8	0	0
Volek, Billy, S.D.	5	-5	-1.0	-1	0

t = Touchdown
Leader based on most yards gained
* Player that was a rookie in 2011

NFC—INDIVIDUAL RUSHERS

	Att	Yards	Avg	Long	TD
Turner, Michael, Atl.	301	1340	4.5	81t	11
McCoy, LeSean, Phi.	273	1309	4.8	60	17
Gore, Frank, S.F.	282	1211	4.3	55	8
Lynch, Marshawn, Sea.	285	1204	4.2	47	12
Jackson, Steven, St.L	260	1145	4.4	47t	5
Wells, Beanie, Ariz	245	1047	4.3	71	10
Forté, Matt, Chi.	203	997	4.9	46	3
Peterson, Adrian, Min.	208	970	4.7	54	12
* Murray, DeMarco, Dal.	164	897	5.5	91t	2
Williams, DeAngelo, Car.	155	836	5.4	74t	7
Blount, LeGarrette, T.B.	184	781	4.2	54t	5
Stewart, Jonathan, Car.	142	761	5.4	32	4
* Newton, Cam, Car.	126	706	5.6	49t	14
Bradshaw, Ahmad, NY-G	171	659	3.9	37	9
* Helu, Roy, Was.	151	640	4.2	28t	2
Sproles, Darren, N.O.	87	603	6.9	36	2
Vick, Michael, Phi.	76	589	7.8	53	1
Starks, James, G.B.	133	578	4.3	40	1
Jones, Felix, Dal.	127	575	4.5	40	1
Jacobs, Brandon, NY-G	152	571	3.8	28	7
Thomas, Pierre, N.O.	110	562	5.1	33	5
Grant, Ryan, G.B.	134	559	4.2	47t	2
Gerhart, Toby, Min.	109	531	4.9	67	1

	Att	Yards	Avg	Long	TD
* Ingram, Mark, N.O.	122	474	3.9	35t	5
* Hunter, Kendall, S.F.	112	473	4.2	44	2
Barber, Marion, Chi.	114	422	3.7	29	6
Best, Jahvid, Det.	84	390	4.6	88t	2
Ivory, Chris, N.O.	79	374	4.7	35t	1
Williams, Cadillac, St.L	87	361	4.1	23	1
Smith, Kevin, Det.	72	356	4.9	43	4
Harvin, Percy, Min.	52	345	6.6	39	2
Bell, Kahlil, Chi.	79	337	4.3	26	0
* Royster, Evan, Was.	56	328	5.9	28	0
Hightower, Tim, Was.	84	321	3.8	22	1
Morris, Maurice, Det.	80	316	4.0	31	1
Rodgers, Aaron, G.B.	60	257	4.3	25	3
Washington, Leon, Sea.	53	248	4.7	48t	1
Freeman, Josh, T.B.	55	238	4.3	25	4
* Ponder, Christian, Min.	28	219	7.8	28	0
Graham, Earnest, T.B.	37	206	5.6	34	0
* Rodgers, Jacquizz, Atl.	57	205	3.6	13	1
Torain, Ryan, Was.	59	200	3.4	39	1
Williams, Keiland, Det.	58	195	3.4	18	2
Smith, Alex, S.F.	52	179	3.4	14	2
Stephens-Howling, LaRod, Ariz	43	167	3.9	39	0
Ware, D.J., NY-G	46	163	3.5	17	0
Webb, Joe, Min.	22	154	7.0	65t	2
Snelling, Jason, Atl.	44	151	3.4	18	0
Forsett, Justin, Sea.	46	145	3.2	22t	1
Brown, Ronnie, Phi.	42	136	3.2	15	1
Skelton, John, Ariz	28	128	4.6	14	0
Jackson, Tarvaris, Sea.	40	108	2.7	13	1
Lumpkin, Kregg, T.B.	31	105	3.4	19	0
* Lewis, Dion, Phi.	23	102	4.4	20	1
Smith, Alfonso, Ariz	30	102	3.4	12	1
Hanie, Caleb, Chi.	13	98	7.5	24	0
Morris, Sammy, Dal.	28	98	3.5	15	0
Dixon, Anthony, S.F.	29	87	3.0	9	2
Brees, Drew, N.O.	21	86	4.1	20	1
Burleson, Nate, Det.	11	85	7.7	20	0
Ryan, Matt, Atl.	37	84	2.3	12	2
Young, Vince, Phi.	18	79	4.4	13	0
Kuhn, John, G.B.	30	78	2.6	12	4
Stafford, Matthew, Det.	22	78	3.5	22	0
Taylor, Chester, Ariz	20	77	3.9	34	1
* Tanner, Phillip, Dal.	22	76	3.5	17	1
* Saine, Brandon, G.B.	18	69	3.8	10	0
Ginn, Ted, S.F.	8	68	8.5	24	0
McCown, Josh, Chi.	12	68	5.7	28	0
Johnson, Josh, T.B.	11	67	6.1	14	0
Kolb, Kevin, Ariz	17	65	3.8	17	0
Norwood, Jerious, St.L	24	61	2.5	10	0
McNabb, Donovan, Min.	14	59	4.2	23	1
* Jones, Julio, Atl.	6	56	9.3	19	0
Smith, Steve, Car.	6	56	9.3	23	0
Cutler, Jay, Chi.	18	55	3.1	12	1
* Madu, Mossis, T.B.	15	55	3.7	15	0
Booker, Lorenzo, Min.	13	52	4.0	25	0
* Allen, Armando, Chi.	15	48	3.2	13	0
Romo, Tony, Dal.	22	46	2.1	17	1
Beck, John, Was.	10	43	4.3	12	2
Harrison, Jerome, Det.	14	41	2.9	9	0
Jackson, DeSean, Phi.	7	41	5.9	18	0
Clemens, Kellen, St.L	6	37	6.2	18t	1
Young, Darrel, Was.	6	33	5.5	12	1
Logan, Stefan, Det.	9	32	3.6	16	0
Williams, Kyle, S.F.	2	32	16.0	25	0
McGee, Stephen, Dal.	4	28	7.0	12	0
Roberts, Andre, Ariz	3	27	9.0	12	0
Bradford, Sam, St.L	18	26	1.4	17	0
Vaughan, Josh, Car.	7	24	3.4	9	0
Armstrong, Anthony, Was.	2	19	9.5	14	0
Meachem, Robert, N.O.	4	18	4.5	8	0
Gibson, Brandon, St.L	2	16	8.0	11	0
* Scott, Da'Rel, NY-G	5	16	3.2	8	0
Manning, Eli, NY-G	35	15	0.4	12	1
* Young, Titus, Det.	2	15	7.5	11	0
Miller, Brit, St.L	5	14	2.8	12	0
Tate, Golden, Sea.	5	14	2.8	14	0
* Bradford, Allen, T.B.	5	13	2.6	4	0
Hall, Chad, Phi.	3	13	4.3	7	0
Obomanu, Ben, Sea.	1	13	13.0	13	0
Whitehurst, Charlie, Sea.	4	13	3.3	7	0
Brockel, Richie, Car.	3	12	4.0	7t	0
* Green, Alex, G.B.	3	11	3.7	8	0
Grossman, Rex, Was.	20	11	0.6	6	1
Johnson, Calvin, Det.	1	11	11.0	11	0
Felton, Jerome, Car.	3	10	3.3	4	0
Bartel, Richard, Ariz	1	9	9.0	9	0
Henderson, Devery, N.O.	1	9	9.0	9	0
Jones, Donnie, St.L	1	9	9.0	9	0
* Miller, Bruce, S.F.	4	8	2.0	3	0
* Salas, Greg, St.L	1	8	8.0	8	0
* Paul, Niles, Was.	1	7	7.0	7	0
Robinson, Michael, Sea.	4	7	1.8	3	0
Crabtree, Michael, S.F.	1	6	6.0	6	0
Masthay, Tim, G.B.	1	6	6.0	6	0
Schmitt, Owen, Phi.	4	6	1.5	4	0
Bryant, Dez, Dal.	1	5	5.0	5	0
* Cobb, Randall, G.B.	2	5	2.5	4	0
Edwards, Armanti, Car.	1	5	5.0	5	0
Scheffler, Tony, Det.	1	5	5.0	5	0
Walker, Delanie, S.F.	3	5	1.7	14	0
Collins, Jed, N.O.	4	4	1.0	2	2
Feeley, A.J., St.L	3	4	1.3	6	0
Fiammetta, Tony, Dal.	4	4	1.0	3	0
Austin, Miles, Dal.	2	3	1.5	5	0
Cooley, Chris, Was.	2	3	1.5	3	0
Cruz, Victor, NY-G	1	3	3.0	3	0
Douglas, Harry, Atl.	1	3	3.0	3	0
Ogletree, Kevin, Dal.	2	3	1.5	7	0
Rice, Sidney, Sea.	2	3	1.5	3	0
* Sherman, Anthony, Ariz	1	3	3.0	3	0
Williams, Mike, T.B.	1	3	3.0	3	0
Williams, Eddie, Sea.	2	2	1.0	1	0
Banks, Brandon, Was.	1	1	1.0	1	0
Maclin, Jeremy, Phi.	1	1	1.0	1	0
Morrah, Cameron, Sea.	1	1	1.0	1	0
Mughelli, Ovie, Atl.	2	1	0.5	1	0
Raji, B.J., G.B.	1	1	1.0	1t	1
Stallworth, Donte', Was.	2	1	0.5	2	0
Brown, Aaron, Det.	1	0	0.0	0	0
Kafka, Mike, Phi.	3	0	0.0	2	0
* Peterson, Patrick, Ariz	1	0	0.0	0	0
Weatherford, Steve, NY-G	1	0	0.0	0	0
Hill, Shaun, Det.	1	-1	-1.0	-1	0
Washington, Chauncey, Dal.	1	-1	-1.0	-1	0
Anderson, Derek, Car.	2	-2	-1.0	-1	0
* Baldwin, Doug, Sea.	1	-2	-2.0	-2	0
* Kaepernick, Colin, S.F.	2	-2	-1.0	-1	0
Kitna, Jon, Dal.	3	-2	-0.7	0	0
Daniel, Chase, N.O.	3	-3	-1.0	-1	0
Parker, Preston, T.B.	1	-3	-3.0	-3	0
* Sanzenbacher, Dane, Chi.	1	-4	-4.0	-4	0
Davis, Vernon, S.F.	2	-5	-2.5	-2	0
Flynn, Matt, G.B.	13	-6	-0.5	3t	1
Hester, Devin, Chi.	1	-6	-6.0	-6	0

	Att	Yards	Avg	Long	TD
* Pettis, Austin, St.L	1	-6	-6.0	-6	0
Redman, Chris, Atl.	5	-6	-1.2	-1	0
Benn, Arrelious, T.B.	6	-7	-1.2	9	0
* Kendricks, Lance, St.L	1	-8	-8.0	-8	0
Kluwe, Chris, Min.	2	-12	-6.0	0	0
Lee, Andy, S.F.	1	-18	-18.0	-18	0

t = Touchdown
Leader based on most yards gained
* Player that was a rookie in 2011

AMERICAN FOOTBALL CONFERENCE—RUSHING

	Att	Yards	Avg	Long	TD
Denver	546	2632	4.8	60t	11
Houston	546	2448	4.5	56	18
Oakland	466	2110	4.5	70t	16
Baltimore	459	1996	4.3	70t	15
Miami	469	1987	4.2	76t	11
Jacksonville	489	1970	4.0	56	9
Buffalo	391	1921	4.9	80t	12
Pittsburgh	434	1903	4.4	76	13
Kansas City	487	1893	3.9	34	5
San Diego	436	1864	4.3	41	16
Cincinnati	455	1778	3.9	42	10
New England	438	1764	4.0	33t	18
N.Y. Jets	443	1692	3.8	31	14
Indianapolis	382	1594	4.2	80t	8
Cleveland	415	1531	3.7	40	4
Tennessee	376	1438	3.8	48t	8
AFC Total	7232	30521	4.2	80t	188
AFC Average	452.0	1907.6	4.2	—	11.8

NATIONAL FOOTBALL CONFERENCE—RUSHING

	Att	Yards	Avg	Long	TD
Carolina	445	2408	5.4	74t	26
Minnesota	448	2318	5.2	67	18
Philadelphia	450	2276	5.1	60	20
New Orleans	431	2127	4.9	36	16
San Francisco	498	2044	4.1	55	14
Chicago	456	2015	4.4	46	10
Atlanta	453	1834	4.0	81t	14
Dallas	408	1807	4.4	91t	5
Seattle	444	1756	4.0	48t	15
St. Louis	409	1667	4.1	47t	7
Arizona	389	1625	4.2	71	12
Washington	400	1614	4.0	39	8
Green Bay	395	1558	3.9	47t	12
Detroit	356	1523	4.3	88t	9
Tampa Bay	346	1458	4.2	54t	9
N.Y. Giants	411	1427	3.5	37	17
NFC Total	6739	29457	4.4	91t	212
NFC Average	421.2	1841.1	4.4	—	13.3
League Total	13971	59978	—	91t	400
League Average	436.6	1874.3	4.3	—	12.5

PASSING

HIGHEST RATING
NFC: 122.5   Aaron Rodgers, Green Bay
AFC: 105.6   Tom Brady, New England

COMPLETION PERCENTAGE
NFC: 71.2   Drew Brees, New Orleans
AFC: 65.6   Tom Brady, New England

ATTEMPTS
NFC: 663   Matthew Stafford, Detroit
AFC: 611   Tom Brady, New England

COMPLETIONS
NFC: 468   Drew Brees, New Orleans
AFC: 401   Tom Brady, New England

YARDS
NFC: 5476   Drew Brees, New Orleans
AFC: 5235   Tom Brady, New England

YARDS, GAME
NFC: 520   Matthew Stafford, Detroit at Green Bay, January 1 (36-59, 5 TD)
AFC: 517   Tom Brady, New England at Miami, September 12 (32-48, 4 TD)

LONGEST
AFC: 99   Tom Brady (to Wes Welker), New England at Miami, September 12 - TD
NFC: 99   Eli Manning (to Victor Cruz), N.Y. Giants at N.Y. Jets, December 24 - TD

YARDS PER ATTEMPT
NFC: 9.25   Aaron Rodgers, Green Bay
AFC: 8.57   Tom Brady, New England

TOUCHDOWN PASSES
NFC: 46   Drew Brees, New Orleans
AFC: 39   Tom Brady, New England

TOUCHDOWN PASSES, GAME
NFC: 6   Matt Flynn, Green Bay vs. Detroit, January 1 (31-44, 480 yards)
AFC: 5   Ben Roethlisberger, Pittsburgh vs. Tennessee, October 9 (24-34, 228 yards)

LOWEST INTERCEPTION PERCENTAGE
NFC: 1.1   Alex Smith, San Francisco
AFC: 2.0   Tom Brady, New England

TEAM CHAMPION (MOST NET YARDS)
NFC: 5347   New Orleans
AFC: 5084   New England

NFL TOP TEN PASSERS

	Att	Comp	Pct Comp	Yds	Avg Gain	TD	Pct TD	Long	Int	Pct Int	Sack	Yds Lost	Rating Points
Rodgers, Aaron, G.B.	502	343	68.3	4643	9.25	45	9.0	93t	6	1.2	36	219	122.5
Brees, Drew, N.O.	657	468	71.2	5476	8.33	46	7.0	79t	14	2.1	24	158	110.6
Brady, Tom, N.E.	611	401	65.6	5235	8.57	39	6.4	99t	12	2.0	32	173	105.6
Romo, Tony, Dal.	522	346	66.3	4184	8.02	31	5.9	77	10	1.9	36	227	102.5
Stafford, Matthew, Det.	663	421	63.5	5038	7.60	41	6.2	73t	16	2.4	36	257	97.2
Schaub, Matt, Hou.	292	178	61.0	2479	8.49	15	5.1	80t	6	2.1	16	98	96.8
Manning, Eli, NY-G	589	359	61.0	4933	8.38	29	4.9	99t	16	2.7	28	199	92.9
Ryan, Matt, Atl.	566	347	61.3	4177	7.38	29	5.1	80t	12	2.1	26	173	92.2
Smith, Alex, S.F.	445	273	61.3	3144	7.07	17	3.8	56t	5	1.1	44	263	90.7
Roethlisberger, Ben, Pit.	513	324	63.2	4077	7.95	21	4.1	95t	14	2.7	40	269	90.1

AMERICAN FOOTBALL CONFERENCE—PASSING

	Att	Comp	Pct Comp	Gross Yards	Sacked	Yds Lost	Net Yards	Yds/ Att	Yards/ Comp	TD	Pct TD	Long	Int	Pct Int
New England	612	402	65.7	5257	32	173	5084	8.59	13.08	39	6.37	99t	12	2.0
San Diego	582	366	62.9	4624	30	198	4426	7.95	12.63	27	4.64	58	20	3.4
Pittsburgh	539	341	63.3	4333	42	279	4054	8.04	12.71	21	3.90	95t	15	2.8
Oakland	524	315	60.1	4119	25	157	3962	7.86	13.08	20	3.82	78	23	4.4
Tennessee	584	353	60.4	4113	24	190	3923	7.04	11.65	22	3.77	80t	14	2.4
Buffalo	578	356	61.6	3857	23	154	3703	6.67	10.83	24	4.15	60t	25	4.3
Houston	467	288	61.7	3696	33	190	3506	7.91	12.83	20	4.28	80t	9	1.9
Baltimore	544	314	57.7	3629	33	206	3423	6.67	11.56	21	3.86	74t	12	2.2
N.Y. Jets	547	310	56.7	3542	40	245	3297	6.48	11.43	26	4.75	74	18	3.3
Cincinnati	535	308	57.6	3507	25	167	3340	6.56	11.39	21	3.93	84	14	2.6
Miami	469	280	59.7	3425	52	334	3091	7.30	12.23	20	4.26	65t	13	2.8
Cleveland	570	320	56.1	3300	39	210	3090	5.79	10.31	16	2.81	76t	13	2.3
Kansas City	500	299	59.8	3288	34	208	3080	6.58	11.00	13	2.60	52t	13	3.6
Indianapolis	534	302	56.6	3223	35	228	2995	6.04	10.67	14	2.62	87t	14	2.6
Denver	429	217	50.6	2708	42	274	2434	6.31	12.48	20	4.66	56t	13	3.0
Jacksonville	469	240	51.2	2510	44	331	2179	5.35	10.46	12	2.56	74t	15	3.2
AFC Total	8483	5011	—	59131	553	3544	55587	—	—	336	—	99t	248	—
AFC Average	530.2	313.2	59.1	3695.7	34.6	221.5	3474.2	6.97	11.80	21.0	4.0	—	15.5	2.9

NATIONAL FOOTBALL CONFERENCE—PASSING

	Att	Comp	Pct Comp	Gross Yards	Sacked	Yds Lost	Net Yards	Yds/ Att	Yards/ Comp	TD	Pct TD	Long	Int	Pct Int
New Orleans	662	472	71.3	5505	24	158	5347	8.32	11.66	46	6.95	79t	14	2.1
Green Bay	552	376	68.1	5161	41	237	4924	9.35	13.73	51	9.24	93t	8	1.4
Detroit	666	423	63.5	5071	36	257	4814	7.61	11.99	41	6.16	73t	16	2.4
N.Y. Giants	589	359	61.0	4933	28	199	4734	8.38	13.74	29	4.92	99t	16	2.7
Dallas	570	376	66.0	4453	39	252	4201	7.81	11.84	33	5.79	77	12	2.1
Atlanta	594	365	61.4	4365	26	173	4192	7.35	11.96	29	4.88	80t	13	2.2
Philadelphia	554	330	59.6	4276	32	166	4110	7.72	12.96	22	3.97	73	25	4.5
Carolina	519	312	60.1	4089	35	260	3829	7.88	13.11	21	4.05	91t	17	3.3
Washington	591	346	58.5	4058	41	285	3773	6.87	11.73	19	3.21	51	24	4.1
Arizona	550	307	55.8	3954	54	387	3567	7.19	12.88	21	3.82	73t	23	4.2
Tampa Bay	588	365	62.1	3838	32	188	3650	6.53	10.52	17	2.89	65t	24	4.1
Seattle	509	299	58.7	3444	50	339	3105	6.77	11.52	15	2.95	61t	14	2.8
Chicago	473	268	56.7	3346	49	335	3011	7.07	12.49	18	3.81	81	20	4.2
St. Louis	549	292	53.2	3258	55	388	2870	5.93	11.16	9	1.64	68	10	1.8
Minnesota	510	286	56.1	3255	49	298	2957	6.38	11.38	20	3.92	72	17	3.3
San Francisco	451	277	61.4	3193	44	263	2930	7.08	11.53	18	3.99	56t	5	1.1
NFC Total	8927	5453	—	66199	635	4185	62014	—	—	409	—	99t	258	—
NFC Average	557.9	340.8	61.1	4137.4	39.7	261.6	3875.9	7.42	12.14	25.6	4.6	—	16.1	2.9
League Total	17410	10464	—	125330	1188	7729	117601	—	—	745	—	99t	506	—
League Average	544.1	327.0	60.1	3916.6	37.1	241.5	3675.0	7.20	11.98	23.3	4.3	—	15.8	2.9

AFC—INDIVIDUAL PASSERS

	Att	Comp	Pct Comp	Yds	Avg Gain	TD	Pct TD	Long	Int	Pct Int	Sack	Yds Lost	Rating Points
Brady, Tom, N.E.	611	401	65.6	5235	8.57	39	6.4	99t	12	2.0	32	173	105.6
Schaub, Matt, Hou.	292	178	61.0	2479	8.49	15	5.1	80t	6	2.1	16	98	96.8
Roethlisberger, Ben, Pit.	513	324	63.2	4077	7.95	21	4.1	95t	14	2.7	40	269	90.1
Rivers, Philip, S.D.	582	366	62.9	4624	7.95	27	4.6	58	20	3.4	30	198	88.7
Moore, Matt, Mia.	347	210	60.5	2497	7.20	16	4.6	65t	9	2.6	36	229	87.1
Hasselbeck, Matt, Ten.	518	319	61.6	3571	6.89	18	3.5	80t	14	2.7	19	153	82.4
Flacco, Joe, Bal.	542	312	57.6	3610	6.66	20	3.7	74t	12	2.2	31	203	80.9
Palmer, Carson, Oak.	328	199	60.7	2753	8.39	13	4.0	78	16	4.9	17	119	80.5
* Dalton, Andy, Cin.	516	300	58.1	3398	6.59	20	3.9	84	13	2.5	24	160	80.4
Fitzpatrick, Ryan, Buf.	569	353	62.0	3832	6.73	24	4.2	60t	23	4.0	22	148	79.1
Sanchez, Mark, NYJ	543	308	56.7	3474	6.40	26	4.8	74	18	3.3	39	243	78.2
Orton, Kyle, Den.-K.C.	252	150	59.5	1758	6.98	9	3.6	52t	9	3.6	10	54	77.8
Cassel, Matt, K.C.	269	160	59.5	1713	6.37	10	3.7	52t	9	3.3	22	120	76.6
McCoy, Colt, Cle.	463	265	57.2	2733	5.90	14	3.0	56	11	2.4	32	173	74.6
Tebow, Tim, Den.	271	126	46.5	1729	6.38	12	4.4	56t	6	2.2	33	225	72.9
Painter, Curtis, Ind.	243	132	54.3	1541	6.34	6	2.5	87t	9	3.7	16	104	66.6
* Gabbert, Blaine, Jac.	413	210	50.8	2214	5.36	12	2.9	74t	11	2.7	40	293	65.4
(Nonqualifiers)													
Leinart, Matt, Hou.	13	10	76.9	57	4.38	1	7.7	20t	0	0.0	0	0	110.1
* Locker, Jake, Ten.	66	34	51.5	542	8.21	4	6.1	54	0	0.0	5	37	99.4
Delhomme, Jake, Hou.	28	18	64.3	211	7.54	1	3.6	40	0	0.0	2	18	99.0
Campbell, Jason, Oak.	165	100	60.6	1170	7.09	6	3.6	58	4	2.4	5	19	84.2
Orlovsky, Dan, Ind.	193	122	63.2	1201	6.22	6	3.1	40	4	2.1	14	84	82.4
* Yates, T.J., Hou.	134	82	61.2	949	7.08	3	2.2	50	3	2.2	15	74	80.7
Henne, Chad, Mia.	112	64	57.1	868	7.75	4	3.6	41	4	3.6	11	67	79.0
Losman, J.P., Mia.	10	6	60.0	60	6.00	0	0.0	25	0	0.0	5	38	77.1
Batch, Charlie, Pit.	24	15	62.5	208	8.67	0	0.0	46	1	4.2	2	10	72.9
Collins, Kerry, Ind.	98	48	49.0	481	4.91	2	2.0	36	1	1.0	5	40	65.9
Wallace, Seneca, Cle.	107	55	51.4	567	5.30	2	1.9	76t	2	1.9	6	30	65.4
Palko, Tyler, K.C.	134	80	59.7	796	5.94	2	1.5	38t	7	5.2	11	83	59.8
Gradkowski, Bruce, Cin.	18	8	44.4	109	6.06	1	5.6	41t	1	5.6	1	7	59.7
McCown, Luke, Jac.	56	30	53.6	296	5.29	0	0.0	26	4	7.1	4	38	39.0
Boller, Kyle, Oak.	28	15	53.6	161	5.75	0	0.0	27	3	10.7	3	19	31.1
(Fewer than 10 attempts)													
Brunell, Mark, NYJ	3	1	33.3	27	9.00	0	0.0	27	0	0.0	0	0	67.4
Colquitt, Britton, Den.	1	0	0.0	0	0.00	0	0.0	—	0	0.0	0	0	39.6
Cribbs, Josh, Cle.	0	0	—	0	—	0	—	—	0	—	1	7	-1.0
Decker, Eric, Den.	1	0	0.0	0	0.00	0	0.0	—	0	0.0	0	0	39.6
Hoyer, Brian, N.E.	1	1	100.0	22	22.00	0	0.0	22	0	0.0	0	0	118.8
* Kerley, Jeremy, NYJ	1	1	100.0	41	41.00	0	0.0	41	0	0.0	0	0	118.8
Lechler, Shane, Oak.	3	1	33.3	35	11.67	1	33.3	35t	0	0.0	0	0	118.1
Rice, Ray, Bal.	1	1	100.0	1	1.00	1	100.0	1t	0	0.0	0	0	118.8
Sanders, Emmanuel, Pit.	1	1	100.0	15	15.00	0	0.0	15	0	0.0	0	0	118.8
Scott, Bernard, Cin.	1	0	0.0	0	0.00	0	0.0	—	0	0.0	0	0	39.6
Sepulveda, Daniel, Pit.	1	1	100.0	33	33.00	0	0.0	33	0	0.0	0	0	118.8
Smith, Brad, Buf.	1	0	0.0	0	0.00	0	0.0	—	1	100.0	1	6	0.0
* Taylor, Tyrod, Bal.	1	1	100.0	18	18.00	0	0.0	18	0	0.0	2	3	118.8
Thigpen, Tyler, Buf.	8	3	37.5	25	3.13	0	0.0	13	1	12.5	0	0	6.8
Thomas, Demaryius, Den.	1	0	0.0	0	0.00	0	0.0	—	0	0.0	0	0	39.6
Tomlinson, LaDainian, NYJ	0	0	—	0	—	0	—	—	0	—	1	2	—

t = Touchdown
Leader based on rating points, minimum 224 attempts
* Player that was a rookie in 2011

NFC—INDIVIDUAL PASSERS

	Att	Comp	Pct Comp	Yds	Avg Gain	TD	Pct TD	Long	Int	Pct Int	Sack	Yds Lost	Rating Points
Rodgers, Aaron, G.B.	502	343	68.3	4643	9.25	45	9.0	93t	6	1.2	36	219	122.5
Brees, Drew, N.O.	657	468	71.2	5476	8.33	46	7.0	79t	14	2.1	24	158	110.6
Romo, Tony, Dal.	522	346	66.3	4184	8.02	31	5.9	77	10	1.9	36	227	102.5
Stafford, Matthew, Det.	663	421	63.5	5038	7.60	41	6.2	73t	16	2.4	36	257	97.2
Manning, Eli, NY-G	589	359	61.0	4933	8.38	29	4.9	99t	16	2.7	28	199	92.9
Ryan, Matt, Atl.	566	347	61.3	4177	7.38	29	5.1	80t	12	2.1	26	173	92.2
Smith, Alex, S.F.	445	273	61.3	3144	7.07	17	3.8	56t	5	1.1	44	263	90.7
Cutler, Jay, Chi.	314	182	58.0	2319	7.39	13	4.1	56t	7	2.2	23	159	85.7
Vick, Michael, Phi.	423	253	59.8	3303	7.81	18	4.3	73	14	3.3	23	126	84.9
* Newton, Cam, Car.	517	310	60.0	4051	7.84	21	4.1	91t	17	3.3	35	260	84.5
Kolb, Kevin, Ariz	253	146	57.7	1955	7.73	9	3.6	73t	8	3.2	30	219	81.1
Jackson, Tarvaris, Sea.	450	271	60.2	3091	6.87	14	3.1	61t	13	2.9	42	293	79.2
Freeman, Josh, T.B.	551	346	62.8	3592	6.52	16	2.9	65t	22	4.0	29	164	74.6
Grossman, Rex, Was.	458	265	57.9	3151	6.88	16	3.5	51	20	4.4	25	201	72.4
Bradford, Sam, St.L	357	191	53.5	2164	6.06	6	1.7	68	6	1.7	36	248	70.5
* Ponder, Christian, Min.	291	158	54.3	1853	6.37	13	4.5	72	13	4.5	30	164	70.1
Skelton, John, Ariz	275	151	54.9	1913	6.96	11	4.0	60t	14	5.1	23	162	68.9
(Nonqualifiers)													
Flynn, Matt, G.B.	49	33	67.3	518	10.57	6	12.2	80t	2	4.1	5	18	124.8
McGee, Stephen, Dal.	38	24	63.2	182	4.79	1	2.6	19	0	0.0	3	25	83.4
McNabb, Donovan, Min.	156	94	60.3	1026	6.58	4	2.6	60	2	1.3	16	113	82.9
Kitna, Jon, Dal.	10	6	60.0	87	8.70	1	10.0	33	2	20.0	0	0	82.1
Webb, Joe, Min.	63	34	54.0	376	5.97	3	4.8	36	2	3.2	3	21	74.6
Clemens, Kellen, St.L	91	48	52.7	546	6.00	2	2.2	36t	1	1.1	9	68	73.8
Beck, John, Was.	132	80	60.6	858	6.50	2	1.5	32	4	3.0	16	84	72.1
Redman, Chris, Atl.	28	18	64.3	188	6.71	0	0.0	22	1	3.6	0	0	68.8
McCown, Josh, Chi.	55	35	63.6	414	7.53	2	3.6	49	4	7.3	7	43	68.3
Feeley, A.J., St.L	97	53	54.6	548	5.65	1	1.0	34	2	2.1	10	72	66.0
Whitehurst, Charlie, Sea.	56	27	48.2	298	5.32	1	1.8	38	1	1.8	8	46	62.9
Young, Vince, Phi.	114	66	57.9	866	7.60	4	3.5	58	9	7.9	8	34	60.8
Johnson, Josh, T.B.	36	19	52.8	246	6.83	1	2.8	42	2	5.6	3	24	60.6
Bartel, Richard, Ariz	22	10	45.5	86	3.91	1	4.5	23t	1	4.5	1	6	52.5
Kafka, Mike, Phi.	16	11	68.8	107	6.69	0	0.0	43	2	12.5	1	6	47.7
Hanie, Caleb, Chi.	102	51	50.0	613	6.01	3	2.9	81	9	8.8	19	133	41.8
(Fewer than 10 attempts)													
Akers, David, S.F.	1	1	100.0	14	14.00	1	100.0	14t	0	0.0	0	0	158.3
Banks, Brandon, Was.	1	1	100.0	49	49.00	1	100.0	49t	0	0.0	0	0	158.3
Brandstater, Tom, St.L	2	0	0.0	0	0.00	0	0.0	—	0	0.0	0	0	39.6
* Cobb, Randall, G.B.	1	0	0.0	0	0.00	0	0.0	—	0	0.0	0	0	39.6
Daniel, Chase, N.O.	5	4	80.0	29	5.80	0	0.0	14	0	0.0	0	0	90.8
Edwards, Armanti, Car.	1	1	100.0	11	11.00	0	0.0	11	0	0.0	0	0	112.5
Forté, Matt, Chi.	1	0	0.0	0	0.00	0	0.0	—	0	0.0	0	0	39.6
* Henry, Chas, Phi.	1	0	0.0	0	0.00	0	0.0	—	0	0.0	0	0	39.6
Hill, Shaun, Det.	3	2	66.7	33	11.00	0	0.0	28	0	0.0	0	0	103.5
* Kaepernick, Colin, S.F.	5	3	60.0	35	7.00	0	0.0	19	0	0.0	0	0	81.3
Lloyd, Brandon, St.L	1	0	0.0	0	0.00	0	0.0	—	0	0.0	0	0	39.6
Lynch, Marshawn, Sea.	2	0	0.0	0	0.00	0	0.0	—	0	0.0	0	0	39.6
Naanee, Legedu, Car.	1	1	100.0	27	27.00	0	0.0	27	0	0.0	0	0	118.8
Norwood, Jerious, St.L	1	0	0.0	0	0.00	0	0.0	—	1	100.0	0	0	0.0
Podlesh, Adam, Chi.	1	0	0.0	0	0.00	0	0.0	—	0	0.0	0	0	39.6
Rice, Sidney, Sea.	1	1	100.0	55	55.00	0	0.0	55	0	0.0	0	0	118.8
Spurlock, Micheal, T.B.	1	0	0.0	0	0.00	0	0.0	—	0	0.0	0	0	39.6

t = Touchdown
Leader based on rating points, minimum 224 attempts
* Player that was a rookie in 2011

PASS RECEIVING

RECEPTIONS

AFC: 122 Wes Welker, New England
NFC: 100 Roddy White, Atlanta

RECEPTIONS, GAME

AFC: 16 Wes Welker, New England at Buffalo,
September 25 (217 yards, 2 TD)
NFC: 14 * Roy Helu, Washington vs. San Francisco,
November 6 (105 yards, 0 TD)

YARDS

NFC: 1681 Calvin Johnson, Detroit
AFC: 1569 Wes Welker, New England

YARDS, GAME

NFC: 244 Calvin Johnson, Detroit at Green Bay,
January 1 (11 receptions, 1 TD)
AFC: 217 Wes Welker, New England at Buffalo,
September 25 (16 receptions, 2 TD)

LONGEST

AFC: 99 Wes Welker (from Tom Brady), New England at
Miami, September 12 - TD
NFC: 99 Victor Cruz (from Eli Manning), N.Y. Giants at
N.Y. Jets, December 24 - TD

YARDS PER RECEPTION

AFC: 19.9 Malcom Floyd, San Diego
NFC: 19.6 Johnny Knox, Chicago

TOUCHDOWNS

AFC: 17 Rob Gronkowski, New England
NFC: 16 Calvin Johnson, Detroit

TEAM LEADERS, RECEPTIONS

AFC: BALTIMORE, 76, Ray Rice; BUFFALO, 76, Steve Johnson; CINCINNATI, 65, *A.J. Green; CLEVELAND, 61, *Greg Little; DENVER, 44, Eric Decker; HOUSTON, 54, Owen Daniels; INDIANAPOLIS, 75, Reggie Wayne; JACKSONVILLE, 44, Mike Thomas; KANSAS CITY, 81, Dwayne Bowe; MIAMI, 81, Brandon Marshall; NEW ENGLAND, 122, Wes Welker; N.Y. JETS, 65, Dustin Keller; OAKLAND, 64, Darrius Heyward-Bey; PITTSBURGH, 72, Mike Wallace; SAN DIEGO, 64, Antonio Gates; TENNESSEE, 74, Nate Washington

NFC: ARIZONA, 80, Larry Fitzgerald; ATLANTA, 100, Roddy White; CAROLINA, 79, Steve Smith; CHICAGO, 52, Matt Forté; DALLAS, 79, Jason Witten; DETROIT, 96, Calvin Johnson; GREEN BAY, 68, Jordy Nelson; MINNESOTA, 87, Percy Harvin; NEW ORLEANS, 99, Jimmy Graham; N.Y. GIANTS, 82, Victor Cruz; PHILADELPHIA, 63, Jeremy Maclin; ST. LOUIS, 51, Brandon Lloyd; SAN FRANCISCO, 72, Michael Crabtree; SEATTLE, 51, *Doug Baldwin; TAMPA BAY, 75, Kellen Winslow; WASHINGTON, 68, Jabar Gaffney

NFL TOP TEN PASS RECEIVERS

	No	Yards	Avg	Long	TD
Welker, Wes, N.E.	122	1569	12.9	99t	9
White, Roddy, Atl.	100	1296	13.0	43	8
Graham, Jimmy, N.O.	99	1310	13.2	59	11
Johnson, Calvin, Det.	96	1681	17.5	73t	16
Gronkowski, Rob, N.E.	90	1327	14.7	52t	17
Harvin, Percy, Min.	87	967	11.1	52t	6
Sproles, Darren, N.O.	86	710	8.3	39	7
Pettigrew, Brandon, Det.	83	777	9.4	27	5

	No	Yards	Avg	Long	TD
Cruz, Victor, NY-G	82	1536	18.7	99t	9
Bowe, Dwayne, K.C.	81	1159	14.3	52t	5
Marshall, Brandon, Mia.	81	1214	15.0	65t	6

NFL TOP TEN RECEIVERS BY YARDS

	Yards	No	Avg	Long	TD
Johnson, Calvin, Det.	1681	96	17.5	73t	16
Welker, Wes, N.E.	1569	122	12.9	99t	9
Cruz, Victor, NY-G	1536	82	18.7	99t	9
Fitzgerald, Larry, Ariz	1411	80	17.6	73t	8
Smith, Steve, Car.	1394	79	17.6	77t	7
Gronkowski, Rob, N.E.	1327	90	14.7	52t	17
Graham, Jimmy, N.O.	1310	99	13.2	59	11
White, Roddy, Atl.	1296	100	13.0	43	8
Nelson, Jordy, G.B.	1263	68	18.6	93t	15
Marshall, Brandon, Mia.	1214	81	15.0	65t	6

AFC—INDIVIDUAL RECEIVERS

	No	Yards	Avg	Long	TD
Welker, Wes, N.E.	122	1569	12.9	99t	9
Gronkowski, Rob, N.E.	90	1327	14.7	52t	17
Marshall, Brandon, Mia.	81	1214	15.0	65t	6
Bowe, Dwayne, K.C.	81	1159	14.3	52t	5
Hernandez, Aaron, N.E.	79	910	11.5	46	7
Johnson, Steve, Buf.	76	1004	13.2	55	7
Rice, Ray, Bal.	76	704	9.3	52	3
Wayne, Reggie, Ind.	75	960	12.8	56t	4
Washington, Nate, Ten.	74	1023	13.8	57	7
Wallace, Mike, Pit.	72	1193	16.6	95t	8
Garcon, Pierre, Ind.	70	947	13.5	87t	6
Brown, Antonio, Pit.	69	1108	16.1	79t	2
* Green, A.J., Cin.	65	1057	16.3	58	7
Keller, Dustin, NYJ	65	815	12.5	41	5
Heyward-Bey, Darrius, Oak.	64	975	15.2	58	4
Gates, Antonio, S.D.	64	778	12.2	38t	7
Breaston, Steve, K.C.	61	785	12.9	43	2
* Little, Greg, Cle.	61	709	11.6	76t	2
Nelson, David, Buf.	61	658	10.8	35	5
Jackson, Vincent, S.D.	60	1106	18.4	58	9
Boldin, Anquan, Bal.	57	887	15.6	56	3
Johnson, Chris, Ten.	57	418	7.3	34	0
Gresham, Jermaine, Cin.	56	596	10.6	31	6
Daniels, Owen, Hou.	54	677	12.5	34	3
Dickson, Ed, Bal.	54	528	9.8	25	5
Collie, Austin, Ind.	54	514	9.5	27	1
Tolbert, Mike, S.D.	54	433	8.0	27	2
Foster, Arian, Hou.	53	617	11.6	78t	2
Branch, Deion, N.E.	51	702	13.8	63	5
Holmes, Santonio, NYJ	51	654	12.8	38t	8
Miller, Heath, Pit.	51	631	12.4	39	2
Bess, Davone, Mia.	51	537	10.5	41	3
* Smith, Torrey, Bal.	50	841	16.8	74t	7
Simpson, Jerome, Cin.	50	725	14.5	84	4
Mathews, Ryan, S.D.	50	455	9.1	42	0
Cook, Jared, Ten.	49	759	15.5	80t	3
Hawkins, Lavelle, Ten.	47	470	10.0	32	1
Ward, Hines, Pit.	46	381	8.3	31	2
McCluster, Dexter, K.C.	46	328	7.1	49	1
Burress, Plaxico, NYJ	45	612	13.6	30	8
Williams, Damian, Ten.	45	592	13.2	54	5
Decker, Eric, Den.	44	612	13.9	56t	8
Thomas, Mike, Jac.	44	415	9.4	47	1
Floyd, Malcom, S.D.	43	856	19.9	52t	5
Jones-Drew, Maurice, Jac.	43	374	8.7	48	3
Bush, Reggie, Mia.	43	296	6.9	34	1
Tomlinson, LaDainian, NYJ	42	449	10.7	74	2
Cribbs, Josh, Cle.	41	518	12.6	45t	4
Pitta, Dennis, Bal.	40	405	10.1	39	3
Walter, Kevin, Hou.	39	474	12.2	41	3

274

	No	Yards	Avg	Long	TD
Lewis, Marcedes, Jac.	39	460	11.8	62	0
Jackson, Fred, Buf.	39	442	11.3	49	0
Spiller, C.J., Buf.	39	269	6.9	19	2
Chandler, Scott, Buf.	38	389	10.2	31	6
Bush, Michael, Oak.	37	418	11.3	55	1
Watson, Benjamin, Cle.	37	410	11.1	34t	2
Caldwell, Andre, Cin.	37	317	8.6	49t	3
Hartline, Brian, Mia.	35	549	15.7	41	1
Clark, Dallas, Ind.	34	352	10.4	21	2
Moore, Evan, Cle.	34	324	9.5	33	4
* Moore, Denarius, Oak.	33	618	18.7	78	5
Johnson, Andre, Hou.	33	492	14.9	50	2
Thomas, Demaryius, Den.	32	551	17.2	47	4
Fasano, Anthony, Mia.	32	451	14.1	35t	5
Jones, Jacoby, Hou.	31	512	16.5	80t	2
Massaquoi, Mohamed, Cle.	31	384	12.4	56	2
McMichael, Randy, S.D.	30	271	9.0	30	0
Greene, Shonn, NYJ	30	211	7.0	36	0
* Kerley, Jeremy, NYJ	29	314	10.8	38	1
Dillard, Jarett, Jac.	29	292	10.1	25	1
Boss, Kevin, Oak.	28	368	13.1	35t	3
Dreessen, Joel, Hou.	28	353	12.6	56t	6
Ringer, Javon, Ten.	28	187	6.7	18	0
Reece, Marcel, Oak.	27	301	11.1	47	2
Hill, Jason, Jac.	25	367	14.7	74t	3
Hagan, Derek, Buf.	24	252	10.5	29	1
Pope, Leonard, K.C.	24	247	10.3	39	1
Schilens, Chaz, Oak.	23	271	11.8	30	2
Norwood, Jordan, Cle.	23	268	11.7	51	1
Hawkins, Andrew, Cin.	23	263	11.4	26	0
Crayton, Patrick, S.D.	23	248	10.8	26t	1
Smith, Brad, Buf.	23	240	10.4	36t	1
Jones, Donald, Buf.	23	231	10.0	48	1
Ogbonnaya, Chris, Cle.	23	165	7.2	19	0
Sanders, Emmanuel, Pit.	22	288	13.1	32	2
Leonard, Brian, Cin.	22	210	9.5	37	0
Hillis, Peyton, Cle.	22	130	5.9	52	0
* Baldwin, Jon, K.C.	21	254	12.1	39t	1
* Brown, Vincent, S.D.	19	329	17.3	41	2
Ford, Jacoby, Oak.	19	279	14.7	41	1
Fells, Daniel, Den.	19	256	13.5	32	3
Tamme, Jacob, Ind.	19	177	9.3	29	1
Mason, Derrick, NYJ-Hou.	19	170	8.9	30	0
Royal, Eddie, Den.	19	155	8.2	26t	1
McFadden, Darren, Oak.	19	154	8.1	26	1
Choice, Tashard, Dal.-Was.-Buf.	19	124	6.5	18	0
Willis, Matt, Den.	18	267	14.8	42	1
Casey, James, Hou.	18	260	14.4	62	1
Woodhead, Danny, N.E.	18	157	8.7	16	0
Mendenhall, Rashard, Pit.	18	154	8.6	35	0
Redman, Isaac, Pit.	18	78	4.3	12	0
Britt, Kenny, Ten.	17	289	17.0	80t	3
Roosevelt, Naaman, Buf.	16	257	16.1	60t	1
Cotchery, Jerricho, Pit.	16	237	14.8	36	2
* Clay, Charles, Mia.	16	233	14.6	46	3
Myers, Brandon, Oak.	16	151	9.4	24	0
Ball, Lance, Den.	16	148	9.3	34	1
Brown, Donald, Ind.	16	86	5.4	17	0
Ochocinco, Chad, N.E.	15	276	18.4	53	1
Murphy, Louis, Oak.	15	241	16.1	47	0
Addai, Joseph, Ind.	15	93	6.2	12	0
Benson, Cedric, Cin.	15	82	5.5	11	0
Leach, Vonta, Bal.	15	69	4.6	11	0
Smith, Alex, Cle.	14	131	9.4	20	1
Hardesty, Montario, Cle.	14	122	8.7	27	0
Karim, Deji, Jac.	14	120	8.6	20	0
McClain, Le'Ron, K.C.	14	82	5.9	14	1
West, Chastin, Jac.	13	163	12.5	23t	2
McKnight, Joe, NYJ	13	139	10.7	27	0
Tate, Ben, Hou.	13	98	7.5	14	0
Williams, Ricky, Bal.	13	83	6.4	18	0
Scott, Bernard, Cin.	13	38	2.9	14	0
Sims-Walker, Mike, St.L-Jac.	12	150	12.5	33	0
Johnson, David, Pit.	12	91	7.6	25	1
* Thomas, Daniel, Mia.	12	72	6.0	12	1
McGahee, Willis, Den.	12	51	4.3	12	1
Hester, Jacob, S.D.	12	48	4.0	11	1
Houshmandzadeh, T.J., Oak.	11	146	13.3	40t	1
Lee, Donald, Cin.	11	115	10.5	26	0
Moore, Mewelde, Pit.	11	104	9.5	24	1
Moreno, Knowshon, Den.	11	101	9.2	28t	1
Stevens, Craig, Ten.	9	166	18.4	58	1
Green-Ellis, BenJarvus, N.E.	9	159	17.7	53	0
Colbert, Keary, K.C.	9	89	9.9	19	0
Larsen, Spencer, Den.	9	76	8.4	16	0
Battle, Jackie, K.C.	9	68	7.6	24	0
Hall, Ahmard, Ten.	9	46	5.1	10	0
Eldridge, Brody, Ind.	9	45	5.0	8	0
Copper, Terrance, K.C.	8	114	14.3	43	0
Turner, Patrick, NYJ	8	96	12.0	25	1
Rosario, Dante, Den.	7	117	16.7	32	0
Martin, Ruvell, Den.	7	82	11.7	28	0
Johnson, Jeremiah, Den.	7	62	8.9	17	0
O'Connell, Jake, K.C.	7	52	7.4	15	0
Brinkley, Curtis, S.D.	7	41	5.9	20	0
Faulk, Kevin, N.E.	7	34	4.9	18	0
Johnson, Bryant, Hou.	6	90	15.0	40	1
* Cameron, Jordan, Cle.	6	33	5.5	15	0
Mulligan, Matthew, NYJ	5	58	11.6	41	0
Potter, Zach, Jac.	5	50	10.0	22	0
Hilliard, Lex, Mia.	5	49	9.8	18	0
* Cochart, Colin, Cin.	5	44	8.8	25	1
Jones, Thomas, K.C.	5	43	8.6	27	0
Osgood, Kassim, Jac.	5	42	8.4	19	0
Caussin, Mike, Buf.	5	41	8.2	13	0
* Marecic, Owen, Cle.	5	31	6.2	11	0
Mariani, Marc, Ten.	5	24	4.8	6	0
* Carter, Delone, Ind.	5	18	3.6	7	0
Charles, Jamaal, K.C.	5	9	1.8	9	1
Evans, Lee, Bal.	4	74	18.5	32	0
Cloherty, Colin, Jac.	4	57	14.3	21	0
* Williams, LaQuan, Bal.	4	46	11.5	15	0
Miller, Zach, Jac.	4	42	10.5	14t	1
Felton, Jerome, Car.-Ind.	4	40	10.0	17	0
Urban, Jerheme, K.C.	4	35	8.8	24t	1
Edelman, Julian, N.E.	4	34	8.5	11	0
* Harper, Jamie, Ten.	4	32	8.0	21	0
* Saunders, Weslye, Pit.	4	29	7.3	14	1
Vickers, Lawrence, Hou.	4	29	7.3	17	0
* Whalen, Ryan, Cin.	4	27	6.8	13	0
Cartwright, Rock, Oak.	4	24	6.0	9	0
Jones, Greg, Jac.	4	19	4.8	10	0
Shipley, Jordan, Cin.	4	14	3.5	5	0
* Smith, Lee, Buf.	4	11	2.8	6	0
Avery, Donnie, Ten.	3	45	15.0	23	1
Mitchell, Carlton, Cle.	3	31	10.3	19	0
Johnson, Quinn, Ten.	3	30	10.0	13	0
Underwood, Tiquan, N.E.	3	30	10.0	13	0
* Baker, Josh, NYJ	3	27	9.0	17	1
Walters, Bryan, S.D.	3	27	9.0	13	0
Becht, Anthony, K.C.	3	26	8.7	16	0
Robiskie, Brian, Cle.	3	25	8.3	14	0
* Green, Virgil, Den.	3	24	8.0	9	0
Pressley, Chris, Cin.	3	19	6.3	9	0
Tonga, Manase, Oak.	3	18	6.0	11	0
* Ridley, Stevan, N.E.	3	13	4.3	8	0
Slaton, Steve, Hou.-Mia.	3	3	1.0	6	0
Price, Taylor, Jac.	2	39	19.5	21	0

2011 INDIVIDUAL STATISTICS—PASS RECEIVING

	No	Yards	Avg	Long	TD
Cumberland, Jeff, NYJ	2	35	17.5	33	0
* Shorts, Cecil, Jac.	2	30	15.0	25	1
Brock, Kevin, Buf.	2	27	13.5	21	0
Graham, Daniel, Ten.	2	25	12.5	21	1
* Jones, Taiwan, Oak.	2	25	12.5	30	0
* Gates, Clyde, Mia.	2	19	9.5	11	0
* Ausberry, David, Oak.	2	14	7.0	10	0
Hill, Anthony, Ind.	2	10	5.0	5	0
Conner, John, NYJ	2	9	4.5	9	0
Bolen, Brock, Jac.	2	6	3.0	4	0
Owens, Montell, Jac.	2	2	1.0	6	0
Slater, Matthew, N.E.	1	46	46.0	46	0
Mundy, Ryan, Pit.	1	33	33.0	33	0
Sperry, Kory, S.D.	1	32	32.0	32	0
Graham, Garrett, Hou.	1	24	24.0	24	0
Wallace, Seneca, Cle.	1	21	21.0	21	0
Whimper, Guy, Jac.	1	17	17.0	17	0
Parrish, Roscoe, Buf.	1	16	16.0	16	0
Mastrud, Jeron, Mia.	1	8	8.0	8	0
Amano, Eugene, Ten.	1	7	7.0	7	0
* Powell, Bilal, NYJ	1	7	7.0	7	0
Dwyer, Jonathan, Pit.	1	6	6.0	6	0
* Mahaffey, Ryan, Ind.	1	5	5.0	5	0
* Thomas, Julius, Den.	1	5	5.0	5	0
* Harris, DuJuan, Jac.	1	4	4.0	4	0
McIntyre, Corey, Buf.	1	4	4.0	4	0
Clayton, Thomas, Cle.	1	3	3.0	3	0
* Gordon, Richard, Oak.	1	2	2.0	2	0
Maneri, Steve, K.C.	1	1	1.0	1	0
Slauson, Matt, NYJ	1	1	1.0	1	0
* White, Johnny, Buf.	1	-3	-3.0	-3	0
Cassel, Matt, K.C.	1	-4	-4.0	-4	0
McCoy, Colt, Cle.	1	-5	-5.0	-5	0
Flacco, Joe, Bal.	1	-8	-8.0	-8	0

*t = Touchdown; * Player that was a rookie in 2011
Leader based on receptions*

NFC—INDIVIDUAL RECEIVERS

	No	Yards	Avg	Long	TD
White, Roddy, Atl.	100	1296	13.0	43	8
Graham, Jimmy, N.O.	99	1310	13.2	59	11
Johnson, Calvin, Det.	96	1681	17.5	73t	16
Harvin, Percy, Min.	87	967	11.1	52t	6
Sproles, Darren, N.O.	86	710	8.3	39	7
Pettigrew, Brandon, Det.	83	777	9.4	27	5
Cruz, Victor, NY-G	82	1536	18.7	99t	9
Fitzgerald, Larry, Ariz	80	1411	17.6	73t	8
Colston, Marques, N.O.	80	1143	14.3	50	8
Gonzalez, Tony, Atl.	80	875	10.9	30	7
Smith, Steve, Car.	79	1394	17.6	77t	7
Witten, Jason, Dal.	79	942	11.9	64	5
Nicks, Hakeem, NY-G	76	1192	15.7	68	7
Winslow, Kellen, T.B.	75	763	10.2	37	2
Burleson, Nate, Det.	73	757	10.4	47	3
Crabtree, Michael, S.F.	72	874	12.1	52t	4
Lloyd, Brandon, Den.-St.L	70	966	13.8	44	5
Nelson, Jordy, G.B.	68	1263	18.6	93t	15
Gaffney, Jabar, Was.	68	947	13.9	45	5
Jennings, Greg, G.B.	67	949	14.2	79t	9
Davis, Vernon, S.F.	67	792	11.8	44	6
Williams, Mike, T.B.	65	771	11.9	42	3
Bryant, Dez, Dal.	63	928	14.7	50t	9
Maclin, Jeremy, Phi.	63	859	13.6	59	5
Celek, Brent, Phi.	62	811	13.1	73	5
Davis, Fred, Was.	59	796	13.5	42	3
Jackson, DeSean, Phi.	58	961	16.6	62t	4
Finley, Jermichael, G.B.	55	767	13.9	41	8
* Jones, Julio, Atl.	54	959	17.8	80t	8
Robinson, Laurent, Dal.	54	858	15.9	74	11
Doucet, Early, Ariz	54	689	12.8	70t	5
Avant, Jason, Phi.	52	679	13.1	35	1
Moore, Lance, N.O.	52	627	12.1	47t	8
Forté, Matt, Chi.	52	490	9.4	56t	1
* Baldwin, Doug, Sea.	51	788	15.5	55t	4
Roberts, Andre, Ariz	51	586	11.5	45	2
Thomas, Pierre, N.O.	50	425	8.5	57	1
* Helu, Roy, Was.	49	379	7.7	47t	1
* Young, Titus, Det.	48	607	12.6	57t	6
McCoy, LeSean, Phi.	48	315	6.6	26	3
Stewart, Jonathan, Car.	47	413	8.8	26	1
Moss, Santana, Was.	46	584	12.7	49t	4
Olsen, Greg, Car.	45	540	12.0	44t	5
Naanee, Legedu, Car.	44	467	10.6	28	1
Austin, Miles, Dal.	43	579	13.5	53t	7
Jackson, Steven, St.L	42	333	7.9	50	1
Lumpkin, Kregg, T.B.	41	291	7.1	16	0
Meachem, Robert, N.O.	40	620	15.5	67t	6
Parker, Preston, T.B.	40	554	13.9	51	3
Manningham, Mario, NY-G	39	523	13.4	47t	4
Douglas, Harry, Atl.	39	498	12.8	49	1
Jones, James, G.B.	38	635	16.7	70t	7
Ballard, Jake, NY-G	38	604	15.9	41	4
Jenkins, Michael, Min.	38	466	12.3	72	3
Knox, Johnny, Chi.	37	727	19.6	81	2
Williams, Roy, Chi.	37	507	13.7	25t	2
Shockey, Jeremy, Car.	37	455	12.3	29	4
Driver, Donald, G.B.	37	445	12.0	35t	6
Obomanu, Ben, Sea.	37	436	11.8	55	2
LaFell, Brandon, Car.	36	613	17.0	91t	3
Gibson, Brandon, St.L	36	431	12.0	34t	1
Shiancoe, Visanthe, Min.	36	409	11.4	37	3
Briscoe, Dezmon, T.B.	35	387	11.1	46	6
Tate, Golden, Sea.	35	382	10.9	33	3
Bradshaw, Ahmad, NY-G	34	267	7.9	26	2
Jones, Felix, Dal.	33	221	6.7	27	0
Henderson, Devery, N.O.	32	503	15.7	79t	2
Rice, Sidney, Sea.	32	484	15.1	52t	2
Benn, Arrelious, T.B.	30	441	14.7	65t	3
Starks, James, G.B.	29	216	7.4	17	0
* Kendricks, Lance, St.L	28	352	12.6	45	0
Lynch, Marshawn, Sea.	28	212	7.6	26	1
Best, Jahvid, Det.	27	287	10.6	60	1
* Sanzenbacher, Dane, Chi.	27	276	10.2	22	3
King, Jeff, Ariz	27	271	10.0	48t	3
* Salas, Greg, St.L	27	264	9.8	21	0
* Pettis, Austin, St.L	27	256	9.5	35	0
Ware, D.J., NY-G	27	170	6.3	22	0
Aromashodu, Devin, Min.	26	468	18.0	60	1
Alexander, Danario, St.L	26	431	16.6	68	2
Hester, Devin, Chi.	26	369	14.2	53	1
Scheffler, Tony, Det.	26	347	13.3	36t	6
* Rudolph, Kyle, Min.	26	249	9.6	41	3
Morris, Maurice, Det.	26	230	8.8	16	1
* Murray, DeMarco, Dal.	26	183	7.0	18	0
Snelling, Jason, Atl.	26	179	6.9	21t	1
Graham, Earnest, T.B.	26	163	6.3	19	0
* Cobb, Randall, G.B.	25	375	15.0	61	1
Miller, Zach, Sea.	25	233	9.3	28	0
Bennett, Earl, Chi.	24	381	15.9	49	1
Heap, Todd, Ariz	24	283	11.8	28	1
Gerhart, Toby, Min.	23	190	8.3	42	3
Forsett, Justin, Sea.	23	128	5.6	18	0
Stallworth, Donte', Was.	22	309	14.0	51	2
Smith, Kevin, Det.	22	179	8.1	28t	3
* Rodgers, Jacquizz, Atl.	21	188	9.0	31t	1
Williams, Kyle, S.F.	20	241	12.1	56t	3
Grant, Ryan, G.B.	19	268	14.1	80t	1

	No	Yards	Avg	Long	TD		No	Yards	Avg	Long	TD
Ginn, Ted, S.F.	19	220	11.6	26	0	Thomas, David, N.O.	5	16	3.2	8	0
Walker, Delanie, S.F.	19	198	10.4	29t	3	Morris, Sammy, Dal.	5	13	2.6	9	0
Bell, Kahlil, Chi.	19	133	7.0	25t	1	Davis, Rashied, Det.	4	63	15.8	22	0
Williams, Mike, Sea.	18	236	13.1	55	1	Stroughter, Sammie, T.B.	4	52	13.0	29	0
Davis, Kellen, Chi.	18	206	11.4	32t	5	Hixon, Domenik, NY-G	4	50	12.5	22t	1
Peterson, Adrian, Min.	18	139	7.7	22	1	* Pianalto, Zack, T.B.	4	40	10.0	15	0
Turner, Michael, Atl.	17	168	9.9	32	0	Stuckey, Chansi, Ariz	4	39	9.8	12	0
Bennett, Martellus, Dal.	17	144	8.5	15	0	Mughelli, Ovie, Atl.	4	25	6.3	19	2
Gore, Frank, S.F.	17	114	6.7	13	0	Miller, Brit, St.L	3	41	13.7	20	0
Cooper, Riley, Phi.	16	315	19.7	58	1	Fiammetta, Tony, Dal.	3	39	13.0	15	0
* Hunter, Kendall, S.F.	16	195	12.2	44	0	Thomas, Devin, NY-G	3	37	12.3	14	0
Williams, DeAngelo, Car.	16	135	8.4	32	0	Quarless, Andrew, G.B.	3	36	12.0	21	0
Morgan, Josh, S.F.	15	220	14.7	30t	1	* Sampson, DeMarco, Ariz	3	36	12.0	15	0
Edwards, Braylon, S.F.	15	181	12.1	24	0	Schmitt, Owen, Phi.	3	32	10.7	13	0
Ogletree, Kevin, Dal.	15	164	10.9	33	0	* Durham, Kris, Sea.	3	30	10.0	12	0
Blount, LeGarrette, T.B.	15	148	9.9	35	0	Clayton, Mark, St.L	3	26	8.7	12	0
Young, Darrel, Was.	15	146	9.7	27	0	Smith, Alfonso, Ariz	3	21	7.0	13	0
Jacobs, Brandon, NY-G	15	128	8.5	40t	1	Gilmore, John, N.O.	3	20	6.7	9	1
Phillips, John, Dal.	15	101	6.7	12t	1	Hall, Chad, Phi.	3	20	6.7	16	1
Kuhn, John, G.B.	15	77	5.1	11	2	Brockel, Richie, Car.	3	13	4.3	5	0
Williams, Cadillac, St.L	14	93	6.6	16	0	* Lockette, Ricardo, Sea.	2	105	52.5	61t	1
Taylor, Chester, Ariz	14	91	6.5	17	0	* Burton, Stephen, Min.	2	38	19.0	21	0
Stephens-Howling, LaRod, Ariz	13	234	18.0	73t	2	Arrington, Adrian, N.O.	2	31	15.5	17	0
* Hankerson, Leonard, Was.	13	163	12.5	23	0	Dray, Jim, Ariz	2	25	12.5	20	0
Harbor, Clay, Phi.	13	163	12.5	27	1	* Paul, Niles, Was.	2	25	12.5	14	0
McCoy, Anthony, Sea.	13	146	11.2	31	0	* Tanner, Phillip, Dal.	2	19	9.5	11	0
Austin, Terrence, Was.	12	137	11.4	32	0	Swain, Brett, S.F.	2	15	7.5	9	0
Pascoe, Bear, NY-G	12	136	11.3	22	0	* Scott, Da'Rel, NY-G	2	13	6.5	9	0
* Housler, Rob, Ariz	12	133	11.1	21	0	Spurlock, Micheal, T.B.	2	13	6.5	7	0
* Stocker, Luke, T.B.	12	92	7.7	24	0	Washington, Chauncey, Dal.	2	13	6.5	15	0
* Hynoski, Henry, NY-G	12	83	6.9	14	0	* Williams, D.J., G.B.	2	13	6.5	7	0
Paulsen, Logan, Was.	11	138	12.5	24	0	Cox, Mike, Atl.	2	8	4.0	8	0
Smith, Steve, Phi.	11	124	11.3	20	1	D'Imperio, Ryan, Min.	2	7	3.5	6	0
Weems, Eric, Atl.	11	90	8.2	18	0	Spach, Stephen, St.L	2	2	1.0	3	0
* Miller, Bruce, S.F.	11	83	7.5	30t	1	* Newton, Cam, Car.	1	27	27.0	27	0
Collins, Jed, N.O.	11	50	4.5	14	2	Logan, Stefan, Det.	1	19	19.0	19	0
* Ingram, Mark, N.O.	11	46	4.2	9	0	Peelle, Justin, S.F.	1	19	19.0	19	0
Hightower, Tim, Was.	10	78	7.8	19	1	Sopoaga, Isaac, S.F.	1	18	18.0	18	0
* Madu, Mossis, T.B.	10	72	7.2	15	0	Staley, Joe, S.F.	1	17	17.0	17	0
Palmer, Michael, Atl.	10	72	7.2	11	1	Williams, Eddie, Sea.	1	17	17.0	17	0
* Saine, Brandon, G.B.	10	69	6.9	22	0	Sellers, Mike, Was.	1	15	15.0	15	0
Wells, Beanie, Ariz	10	52	5.2	10	0	Maui'a, Reagan, Ariz	1	12	12.0	12	0
Washington, Leon, Sea.	10	48	4.8	9	0	* Arceneaux, Emmanuel, Min.	1	10	10.0	10	0
Camarillo, Greg, Min.	9	121	13.4	23	0	Banks, Brandon, Was.	1	10	10.0	10	0
Barden, Ramses, NY-G	9	94	10.4	26	0	Brown, Aaron, Det.	1	9	9.0	9	0
Robinson, Michael, Sea.	9	74	8.2	19	1	* Chapas, Shaun, Dal.	1	9	9.0	9	0
Bajema, Billy, St.L	9	71	7.9	19	0	Webb, Joe, Min.	1	9	9.0	9	0
* Royster, Evan, Was.	9	68	7.6	16	0	Miller, Nick, St.L	1	8	8.0	8	0
Hurd, Sam, Chi.	8	109	13.6	28	0	Stovall, Maurice, Det.	1	8	8.0	8	0
Booker, Lorenzo, Min.	8	82	10.3	15	0	Kelly, Reggie, Atl.	1	7	7.0	7	0
* Sherman, Anthony, Ariz	8	72	9.0	19	0	Stokley, Brandon, NY-G	1	7	7.0	7	0
Cooley, Chris, Was.	8	65	8.1	17	0	Dixon, Anthony, S.F.	1	6	6.0	6	0
Williams, Keiland, Det.	8	62	7.8	12	0	* Green, Alex, G.B.	1	6	6.0	6	0
Clutts, Tyler, Chi.	8	48	6.0	10	0	* Reisner, Allen, Min.	1	5	5.0	5	0
Holley, Jesse, Dal.	7	169	24.1	77	0	Ajirotutu, Seyi, Car.	1	4	4.0	4	0
Armstrong, Anthony, Was.	7	103	14.7	50t	2	Goodson, Mike, Car.	1	4	4.0	4	0
Berrian, Bernard, Min.	7	91	13.0	30	0	* Higgins, Mike, N.O.	1	4	4.0	4	0
Hoomanawanui, Michael, St.L	7	83	11.9	27	0	Kleinsasser, Jimmy, Min.	1	4	4.0	4	0
Anderson, David, Hou.-Was.	7	79	11.3	23	1	* Taylor, Ryan, G.B.	1	4	4.0	4t	1
Spaeth, Matt, Chi.	7	50	7.1	13	2	Harrison, Jerome, Det.	1	3	3.0	3	0
Morrah, Cameron, Sea.	6	74	12.3	21	0	* Peterson, Patrick, Ariz	1	-1	-1.0	-1	0
Lorig, Erik, T.B.	6	53	8.8	22	0	* Lewis, Dion, Phi.	1	-3	-3.0	-3	0
Butler, Deon, Sea.	6	51	8.5	15	0	Penn, Donald, T.B.	0	2	—	2	0
Heller, Will, Det.	6	42	7.0	12	0	Freeman, Josh, T.B.	0	-4	—	-4	0
Crabtree, Tom, G.B.	6	38	6.3	15	1						
Torain, Ryan, Was.	6	23	3.8	7	0						
Beckum, Travis, NY-G	5	93	18.6	67t	1	*t = Touchdown; * Player that was a rookie in 2011*					
Barber, Marion, Chi.	5	50	10.0	16	0	*Leader based on receptions*					
Amendola, Danny, St.L	5	45	9.0	18	0						

INTERCEPTIONS

INTERCEPTIONS

AFC:	7	Kyle Arrington, New England
	7	Eric Weddle, San Diego
NFC:	7	Charles Woodson, Green Bay

INTERCEPTIONS, GAME

NFC:	3	Kurt Coleman, Philadelphia at Washington, October 16 (25 yards, 0 TD)
AFC:	2	Ed Reed, Baltimore vs. Pittsburgh, September 11 (25 yards, 0 TD)
	2	Antonio Cromartie, N.Y. Jets vs. Jacksonville, September 18 (63 yards, 0 TD)
	2	Kyle Arrington, New England at Buffalo, September 25 (25 yards, 0 TD)
	2	Nick Barnett, Buffalo vs. Philadelphia, October 9 (47 yards, 1 TD)
	2	Darrelle Revis, N.Y. Jets vs. Miami, October 17 (100 yards, 1 TD)
	2	Brandon Flowers, Kansas City at Oakland, October 23 (52 yards, 1 TD)
	2	Eric Weddle, San Diego at Kansas City, October 31 (18 yards, 0 TD) - (OT)
	2	Champ Bailey, Denver at Oakland, November 6 (0 yards, 0 TD)
	2	Rob Ninkovich, New England at N.Y. Jets, November 13 (30 yards, 1 TD)
	2	Kyle Arrington, New England vs. Kansas City, November 21 (44 yards, 0 TD)
	2	Vontae Davis, Miami at Buffalo, December 18 (7 yards, 0 TD)
	2	Randy Starks, Miami vs. N.Y. Jets, January 1 (21 yards, 0 TD)
	2	* Sterling Moore, New England vs. Buffalo, January 1 (26 yards, 1 TD)

YARDS

| NFC: | 225 | Chris Houston, Detroit |
| AFC: | 184 | Darrelle Revis, N.Y. Jets |

LONGEST

| AFC: | 100 | Darrelle Revis, N.Y. Jets vs. Miami, October 17 - TD |
| NFC: | 100 | Chris Houston, Detroit at Denver, October 30 - TD |

TOUCHDOWNS

NFC:	2	Brandon Browner, Seattle
	2	Chris Houston, Detroit
	2	Aqib Talib, Tampa Bay
	2	Charles Tillman, Chicago
AFC:	1	Jordan Babineaux, Tennessee
	1	Nick Barnett, Buffalo
	1	Kevin Burnett, Miami
	1	Jairus Byrd, Buffalo
	1	Drayton Florence, Buffalo
	1	Brandon Flowers, Kansas City
	1	André Goodman, Denver
	1	Steve Gregory, San Diego
	1	Mario Haggan, Denver
	1	David Harris, N.Y. Jets
	1	Jacob Lacey, Indianapolis
	1	Kendrick Lewis, Kansas City
	1	Brice McCain, Houston
	1	* Sterling Moore, Oakland-New England
	1	Reggie Nelson, Cincinnati
	1	Rob Ninkovich, New England
	1	Jerraud Powers, Indianapolis
	1	Darrelle Revis, N.Y. Jets
	1	Bryan Scott, Buffalo

| | 1 | Cassius Vaughn, Denver |
| | 1 | Lardarius Webb, Baltimore |

TEAM LEADERS, INTERCEPTIONS

AFC: BALTIMORE, 5, Lardarius Webb; BUFFALO, 4, George Wilson; CINCINNATI, 4, Reggie Nelson; CLEVELAND, 3, Mike Adams; DENVER, 2, Champ Bailey, André Goodman; HOUSTON, 4, Jason Allen, Johnathan Joseph; INDIANAPOLIS, 2, *Joe Lefeged, Jerraud Powers; JACKSONVILLE, 2, Drew Coleman, Dawan Landry, Dwight Lowery, Paul Posluszny, Morgan Trent; KANSAS CITY, 4, Brandon Carr, Brandon Flowers; MIAMI, 4, Vontae Davis; NEW ENGLAND, 7, Kyle Arrington; N.Y. JETS, 4, Antonio Cromartie, David Harris, Darrelle Revis; OAKLAND, 5, Matt Giordano; PITTSBURGH, 2, William Gay, Troy Polamalu, Ike Taylor; SAN DIEGO, 7, Eric Weddle; TENNESSEE, 2, Michael Griffin, Jason McCourty

NFC: ARIZONA, 3, Richard Marshall; ATLANTA, 4, Thomas DeCoud; CAROLINA, 3, Chris Gamble, Sherrod Martin; CHICAGO, 4, D.J. Moore; DALLAS, 4, Sean Lee, Terence Newman; DETROIT, 5, Chris Houston; GREEN BAY, 7, Charles Woodson; MINNESOTA, 2, Jamarca Sanford; NEW ORLEANS, 4, Patrick Robinson; N.Y. GIANTS, 6, Corey Webster; PHILADELPHIA, 4, Kurt Coleman; ST. LOUIS, 3, Josh Gordy; SAN FRANCISCO, 6, Dashon Goldson, Carlos Rogers; SEATTLE, 6, Brandon Browner; TAMPA BAY, 3, Ronde Barber; WASHINGTON, 3, Oshiomogho Atogwe, DeAngelo Hall

TEAM CHAMPION

| NFC: | 31 | Green Bay |
| AFC: | 23 | New England |

NFL TOP TEN INTERCEPTORS

	No	Yards	Avg	Long	TD
Arrington, Kyle, N.E.	7	92	13.1	28	0
Weddle, Eric, S.D.	7	89	12.7	26	0
Woodson, Charles, G.B.	7	63	9.0	30t	1
Browner, Brandon, Sea.	6	220	36.7	94t	2
Goldson, Dashon, S.F.	6	53	8.8	21	0
Rogers, Carlos, S.F.	6	106	17.7	31t	1
Webster, Corey, NY-G	6	71	11.8	25	0
Giordano, Matt, Oak.	5	130	26.0	62	0
Houston, Chris, Det.	5	225	45.0	100t	2
Peprah, Charlie, G.B.	5	147	29.4	76	1
Webb, Lardarius, Bal.	5	81	16.2	73t	1

AFC—INDIVIDUAL INTERCEPTORS

	No	Yards	Avg	Long	TD
Arrington, Kyle, N.E.	7	92	13.1	28	0
Weddle, Eric, S.D.	7	89	12.7	26	0
Giordano, Matt, Oak.	5	130	26.0	62	0
Webb, Lardarius, Bal.	5	81	16.2	73t	1
Revis, Darrelle, NYJ	4	184	46.0	100t	1
Nelson, Reggie, Cin.	4	115	28.8	75t	1
Cromartie, Antonio, NYJ	4	105	26.3	42	0
Flowers, Brandon, K.C.	4	95	23.8	58t	1
Davis, Vontae, Mia.	4	60	15.0	28	0
Harris, David, NYJ	4	55	13.8	35t	1
Joseph, Johnathan, Hou.	4	40	10.0	29	0
Allen, Jason, Hou.	4	34	8.5	34	0
Wilson, George, Buf.	4	26	6.5	12	0
Carr, Brandon, K.C.	4	17	4.3	14	0
Routt, Stanford, Oak.	4	7	1.8	3	0
Lewis, Kendrick, K.C.	3	119	39.7	59t	1
Byrd, Jairus, Buf.	3	88	29.3	37t	1
Barnett, Nick, Buf.	3	80	26.7	33	1

	No	Yards	Avg	Long	TD
Florence, Drayton, Buf.	3	64	21.3	30	1
Adams, Mike, Cle.	3	33	11.0	29	0
Reed, Ed, Bal.	3	25	8.3	16	0
McGraw, Jon, K.C.	3	4	1.3	4	0
Cason, Antoine, S.D.	2	69	34.5	64	0
McCourty, Jason, Ten.	2	52	26.0	30	0
McCain, Brice, Hou.	2	48	24.0	38t	1
* Smith, Jimmy, Bal.	2	48	24.0	32	0
Demps, Quintin, Hou.	2	47	23.5	42	0
Wilfork, Vince, N.E.	2	47	23.5	28	0
Goodman, André, Den.	2	46	23.0	26t	1
Scott, Bryan, Buf.	2	43	21.5	43t	1
Molden, Antwaun, N.E.	2	40	20.0	27	0
McCourty, Devin, N.E.	2	38	19.0	38	0
Polamalu, Troy, Pit.	2	33	16.5	33	0
Ninkovich, Rob, N.E.	2	30	15.0	18	1
Taylor, Ike, Pit.	2	29	14.5	29	0
Landry, Dawan, Jac.	2	28	14.0	28	0
Lowery, Dwight, Jac.	2	26	13.0	30	0
* Moore, Sterling, N.E.	2	26	13.0	21t	1
Daniels, Travis, K.C.	2	25	12.5	25	0
* Lefeged, Joe, Ind.	2	25	12.5	25	0
Huff, Michael, Oak.	2	24	12.0	24	0
* Gilchrist, Marcus, S.D.	2	22	11.0	21	0
Manning, Danieal, Hou.	2	22	11.0	22	0
Starks, Randy, Mia.	2	21	10.5	18	0
Powers, Jerraud, Ind.	2	19	9.5	13	1
Johnson, Derrick, K.C.	2	18	9.0	17	0
Trent, Morgan, Jac.	2	17	8.5	22	0
Hall, Leon, Cin.	2	15	7.5	15	0
Wilson, Kyle, NYJ	2	13	6.5	10	0
Gay, William, Pit.	2	12	6.0	12	0
Suggs, Terrell, Bal.	2	9	4.5	9	0
Smith, Sean, Mia.	2	7	3.5	7	0
Arenas, Javier, K.C.	2	5	2.5	5	0
Clements, Nate, Cin.	2	5	2.5	7	0
Coleman, Drew, Jac.	2	5	2.5	8	0
Cushing, Brian, Hou.	2	5	2.5	5	0
Mayo, Jerod, N.E.	2	4	2.0	2	0
Posluszny, Paul, Jac.	2	2	1.0	2	0
Bailey, Champ, Den.	2	0	0.0	0	0
Brown, Sheldon, Cle.	2	0	0.0	0	0
Griffin, Michael, Ten.	2	0	0.0	0	0
Phillips, Shaun, S.D.	2	0	0.0	0	0
Babineaux, Jordan, Ten.	1	97	97.0	97t	1
Wimbley, Kamerion, Oak.	1	73	73.0	73	0
Mitchell, Marvin, Mia.	1	55	55.0	55	0
Vaughn, Cassius, Den.	1	55	55.0	55t	0
Spikes, Takeo, S.D.	1	45	45.0	45	0
Odrick, Jared, Mia.	1	39	39.0	39	0
* Rutland, Kevin, Jac.	1	37	37.0	25	0
Burnett, Kevin, Mia.	1	34	34.0	34t	1
Lacey, Jacob, Ind.	1	32	32.0	32t	1
Young, Usama, Cle.	1	28	28.0	28	0
Brackett, Gary, Ind.	1	27	27.0	27	0
Gregory, Steve, S.D.	1	26	26.0	26t	1
Smith, Daryl, Jac.	1	25	25.0	25	0
Jackson, D'Qwell, Cle.	1	24	24.0	24	0
McKelvin, Leodis, Buf.	1	21	21.0	21	0
Bell, Yeremiah, Mia.	1	20	20.0	20	0
* Moore, Rahim, Den.	1	18	18.0	18	0
Guyton, Gary, N.E.	1	17	17.0	17	0
Haggan, Mario, Den.	1	16	16.0	16t	1
Bullitt, Melvin, Ind.	1	15	15.0	15	0
* Harris, Chris, Den.	1	15	15.0	15	0
Houston, Lamarr, Oak.	1	15	15.0	15	0
* Rogers, Justin, Buf.	1	15	15.0	15	0
Dansby, Karlos, Mia.	1	14	14.0	14	0
Mauga, Josh, NYJ	1	11	11.0	11	0
Middleton, William, Jac.	1	11	11.0	11	0
Clark, Ryan, Pit.	1	10	10.0	10	0
Lewis, Keenan, Pit.	1	9	9.0	9	0
Finnegan, Cortland, Ten.	1	8	8.0	8	0
McClain, Jameel, Bal.	1	8	8.0	8	0
Pace, Calvin, NYJ	1	8	8.0	8	0
Hope, Chris, Ten.	1	7	7.0	7	0
Oliver, Paul, S.D.	1	7	7.0	7	0
Witherspoon, Will, Ten.	1	7	7.0	7	0
Mincey, Jeremy, Jac.	1	5	5.0	5	0
Mundy, Ryan, Pit.	1	5	5.0	5	0
* Skrine, Buster, Cle.	1	5	5.0	5	0
* Wilson, Jimmy, Mia.	1	5	5.0	5	0
Corner, Reggie, Buf.	1	4	4.0	4	0
Lewis, Ray, Bal.	1	4	4.0	4	0
Ruud, Barrett, Ten.	1	4	4.0	4	0
Verner, Alterraun, Ten.	1	4	4.0	4	0
Allen, Russell, Jac.	1	3	3.0	3	0
Fujita, Scott, Cle.	1	3	3.0	3	0
Brown, Sergio, N.E.	1	2	2.0	2	0
Butler, Donald, S.D.	1	2	2.0	2	0
Maualuga, Rey, Cin.	1	2	2.0	2	0
Smith, Eric, NYJ	1	2	2.0	2	0
* Van Dyke, DeMarcus, Oak.	1	2	2.0	2	0
Wilhite, Jonathan, Den.	1	2	2.0	2	0
Jones, Reshad, Mia.	1	1	1.0	1	0
Kelly, Tommy, Oak.	1	1	1.0	1	0
Mathis, Rashean, Jac.	1	1	1.0	1	0
Woodley, LaMarr, Pit.	1	1	1.0	1	0
Adams, Phillip, N.E.	1	0	0.0	0	0
Angerer, Pat, Ind.	1	0	0.0	0	0
Branch, Tyvon, Oak.	1	0	0.0	0	0
Carroll, Nolan, Mia.	1	0	0.0	0	0
Chung, Patrick, N.E.	1	0	0.0	0	0
Jackson, Kareem, Hou.	1	0	0.0	0	0
Johnson, Michael, Cin.	1	0	0.0	0	0
Leonhard, Jim, NYJ	1	0	0.0	0	0
* McCarthy, Colin, Ten.	1	0	0.0	0	0
Mitchell, Mike, Oak.	1	0	0.0	0	0
Ndukwe, Chinedum, Oak.	1	0	0.0	0	0
Pollard, Bernard, Bal.	1	0	0.0	0	0
Pool, Brodney, NYJ	1	0	0.0	0	0
* Searcy, Da'Norris, Buf.	1	0	0.0	0	0
Timmons, Lawrence, Pit.	1	0	0.0	0	0
* Williams, Aaron, Buf.	1	0	0.0	0	0
Youboty, Ashton, Jac.	1	0	0.0	0	0

t = Touchdown; *Player that was a rookie in 2011
Leader based on interceptions

NFC—INDIVIDUAL INTERCEPTORS

	No	Yards	Avg	Long	TD
Woodson, Charles, G.B.	7	63	9.0	30t	1
Browner, Brandon, Sea.	6	220	36.7	94t	2
Rogers, Carlos, S.F.	6	106	17.7	31t	1
Webster, Corey, NY-G	6	71	11.8	25	0
Goldson, Dashon, S.F.	6	53	8.8	21	0
Houston, Chris, Det.	5	225	45.0	100t	2
Peprah, Charlie, G.B.	5	147	29.4	76	1
Williams, Tramon, G.B.	4	92	23.0	43t	1
Lee, Sean, Dal.	4	87	21.8	37	0
Newman, Terence, Dal.	4	80	20.0	43t	1
DeCoud, Thomas, Atl.	4	77	19.3	49	0
Shields, Sam, G.B.	4	68	17.0	60	0
Coleman, Kurt, Phi.	4	60	15.0	35	0
Phillips, Kenny, NY-G	4	50	12.5	31	0
Wright, Eric, Det.	4	49	12.3	22	0
* Sherman, Richard, Sea.	4	45	11.3	33	0
Moore, D.J., Chi.	4	31	7.8	20t	1

	No	Yards	Avg	Long	TD
Robinson, Patrick, N.O.	4	31	7.8	25	0
Chancellor, Kam, Sea.	4	27	6.8	9	0
Ross, Aaron, NY-G	4	19	4.8	19	0
Brown, Tarell, S.F.	4	15	3.8	11	0
Hawthorne, David, Sea.	3	111	37.0	77t	1
Marshall, Richard, Ariz	3	83	27.7	49	0
Tillman, Charles, Chi.	3	66	22.0	44t	2
Smith, Alphonso, Det.	3	64	21.3	30t	1
Wright, Major, Chi.	3	60	20.0	36	1
Samuel, Asante, Phi.	3	53	17.7	20t	1
Matthews, Clay, G.B.	3	47	15.7	38t	1
Spievey, Amari, Det.	3	47	15.7	30	0
Hall, DeAngelo, Was.	3	46	15.3	26	0
Gamble, Chris, Car.	3	43	14.3	24	0
Atogwe, Oshiomogho, Was.	3	42	14.0	26	0
Gordy, Josh, St.L	3	37	12.3	30	0
Chaney, Jamar, Phi.	3	25	8.3	14	0
Martin, Sherrod, Car.	3	16	5.3	15	0
Barber, Ronde, T.B.	3	12	4.0	12	0
Graham, Corey, Chi.	3	11	3.7	10	0
Asomugha, Nnamdi, Phi.	3	10	3.3	6	0
Urlacher, Brian, Chi.	3	7	2.3	8	0
Burnett, Morgan, G.B.	3	0	0.0	0	0
Sanford, Jamarca, Min.	2	69	34.5	52	0
Jackson, Tanard, T.B.	2	59	29.5	43	0
Moore, William, Atl.	2	56	28.0	29	0
Talib, Aqib, T.B.	2	55	27.5	28t	2
Whitner, Donte, S.F.	2	48	24.0	48	0
Mack, Elbert, T.B.	2	47	23.5	40t	1
Allen, Nate, Phi.	2	44	22.0	31	0
Bush, Jarrett, G.B.	2	39	19.5	35	0
Barnes, Kevin, Was.	2	30	15.0	30	0
Godfrey, Charles, Car.	2	30	15.0	21	0
Lofton, Curtis, Atl.	2	30	15.0	26t	1
Robinson, Dunta, Atl.	2	28	14.0	14	0
Bryant, Red, Sea.	2	25	12.5	20t	1
Thomas, Earl, Sea.	2	19	9.5	11	0
Brock, Tramaine, S.F.	2	18	9.0	18	0
Washington, Daryl, Ariz	2	16	8.0	16	0
Laurinaitis, James, St.L	2	15	7.5	15	0
Mikell, Quintin, St.L	2	11	5.5	11	0
Sensabaugh, Gerald, Dal.	2	11	5.5	11	0
Tulloch, Stephen, Det.	2	9	4.5	9	0
Anderson, James, Car.	2	5	2.5	5	0
Hayden, Kelvin, Atl.	2	3	1.5	2	0
Jennings, Tim, Chi.	2	2	1.0	1	0
Francois, Rob, G.B.	2	1	0.5	1	0
* Peterson, Patrick, Ariz	2	1	0.5	1	0
Fletcher, London, Was.	2	0	0.0	0	0
Franks, Dominique, Atl.	2	0	0.0	0	0
Wilson, Josh, Was.	2	0	0.0	0	0
Rolle, Antrel, NY-G	2	-1	-0.5	0	0
Stanford, R.J., Car.	1	53	53.0	53	0
King, Justin, St.L	1	51	51.0	51	0
Biermann, Kroy, Atl.	1	50	50.0	50t	1
Torrence, Leigh, N.O.	1	42	42.0	42t	1
Carpenter, Bobby, Det.	1	34	34.0	34t	1
Abdullah, Husain, Min.	1	32	32.0	32	0
* Raymond, Mistral, Min.	1	31	31.0	31	0
Grimes, Brent, Atl.	1	29	29.0	29	0
Hood, Roderick, St.L	1	27	27.0	27	0
Stewart, Darian, St.L	1	27	27.0	27t	1
* Culliver, Chris, S.F.	1	23	23.0	23	0
* Walls, Darrin, Atl.	1	23	23.0	23	0
Senn, Jordan, Car.	1	21	21.0	21	0
* Nelson, Jonathan, Car.	1	20	20.0	20	0
Harris, Chris, Det.	1	19	19.0	19	0
Wilson, Adrian, Ariz	1	17	17.0	17	0
Hatcher, Jason, Dal.	1	16	16.0	16	0

	No	Yards	Avg	Long	TD
Ball, Alan, Dal.	1	15	15.0	15	0
Trufant, Marcus, Sea.	1	15	15.0	15	0
Allen, Jared, Min.	1	14	14.0	14	0
Lynch, Corey, T.B.	1	14	14.0	14	0
Shanle, Scott, N.O.	1	12	12.0	12	0
* Smith, D.J., G.B.	1	11	11.0	11	0
Smith, Reggie, S.F.	1	11	11.0	11	0
Willis, Patrick, S.F.	1	10	10.0	10	0
Blackburn, Chase, NY-G	1	9	9.0	9	0
* Keiser, Thomas, Car.	1	9	9.0	9	0
* Kerrigan, Ryan, Was.	1	9	9.0	9t	1
Kiwanuka, Mathias, NY-G	1	9	9.0	9	0
Hayes, Geno, T.B.	1	8	8.0	8	0
Levy, DeAndre, Det.	1	7	7.0	7	0
Walker, Frank, Dal.	1	5	5.0	5	0
Avril, Cliff, Det.	1	4	4.0	4t	1
Chamberlain, Chris, St.L	1	4	4.0	4	0
Peterson, Mike, Atl.	1	4	4.0	4	0
Allen, Asher, Min.	1	3	3.0	3	0
Jenkins, Mike, Dal.	1	3	3.0	3	0
Winfield, Antoine, Min.	1	3	3.0	3	0
Greer, Jabari, N.O.	1	2	2.0	2	0
Peters, Corey, Atl.	1	1	1.0	1	0
* Amukamara, Prince, NY-G	1	0	0.0	0	0
Biggers, E.J., T.B.	1	0	0.0	0	0
Black, Quincy, T.B.	1	0	0.0	0	0
Briggs, Lance, Chi.	1	0	0.0	0	0
Campbell, Calais, Ariz	1	0	0.0	0	0
* Conte, Chris, Chi.	1	0	0.0	0	0
* Foster, Mason, T.B.	1	0	0.0	0	0
Grant, Deon, NY-G	1	0	0.0	0	0
Griffin, Cedric, Min.	1	0	0.0	0	0
Herring, Will, N.O.	1	0	0.0	0	0
Jefferson, A.J., Ariz	1	0	0.0	0	0
Scandrick, Orlando, Dal.	1	0	0.0	0	0
Dahl, Craig, St.L	1	-3	-3.0	-3	0
Porter, Tracy, N.O.	1	-7	-7.0	-7	0

t = Touchdown; Leader based on interceptions
* Player that was a rookie in 2011

AMERICAN FOOTBALL CONFERENCE—INTERCEPTIONS

	No	Yards	Avg	Long	TD
New England	23	296	12.9	38	2
Buffalo	20	341	17.1	43t	4
Kansas City	20	283	14.2	59t	2
N.Y. Jets	19	378	19.9	100t	2
Oakland	18	252	14.0	73	0
Houston	17	196	11.5	42	1
Jacksonville	17	160	9.4	30	0
San Diego	17	260	15.3	64	1
Miami	16	256	16.0	55	1
Baltimore	15	175	11.7	73t	1
Pittsburgh	11	99	9.0	33	0
Tennessee	11	179	16.3	97t	1
Cincinnati	10	137	13.7	75t	1
Cleveland	9	93	10.3	29	0
Denver	9	152	16.9	55t	3
Indianapolis	8	118	14.8	32t	2
AFC Total	240	3375	14.1	100t	21
AFC Average	15.0	210.9	14.1	—	1.3

NATIONAL FOOTBALL CONFERENCE—INTERCEPTIONS

	No	Yards	Avg	Long	TD
Green Bay	31	468	15.1	76	4
San Francisco	23	284	12.3	48	1
Seattle	22	462	21.0	94t	4
Detroit	21	458	21.8	100t	5
Chicago	20	177	8.9	44t	4
N.Y. Giants	20	157	7.9	31	0
Atlanta	19	301	15.8	50t	2
Dallas	15	217	14.5	43t	1
Philadelphia	15	192	12.8	35	1
Carolina	14	197	14.1	53	0
Tampa Bay	14	195	13.9	43	3
Washington	13	127	9.8	30	1
St. Louis	12	169	14.1	51	1
Arizona	10	117	11.7	49	0
New Orleans	9	80	8.9	42t	1
Minnesota	8	152	19.0	52	0
NFC Total	266	3753	14.1	100t	28
NFC Average	16.6	234.6	14.1	—	1.8
League Total	506	7128	—	100t	49
League Average	15.8	222.8	14.1	—	1.5

KICKOFF RETURNS

YARDS PER RETURN
AFC: 31.6 Joe McKnight, N.Y. Jets
NFC: 27.7* Randall Cobb, Green Bay

YARDS
NFC: 1174 Brandon Banks, Washington
AFC: 1073 Joe McKnight, N.Y. Jets

YARDS, GAME
AFC: 215 Richard Goodman, San Diego at Oakland, January 1 (6 returns, 1 TD)
NFC: 176 Ted Ginn, San Francisco vs. Seattle, September 11 (4 returns, 1 TD)

LONGEST
NFC: 108 * Randall Cobb, Green Bay vs. New Orleans, September 8 - TD
AFC: 107 Joe McKnight, N.Y. Jets at Baltimore, October 2 - TD

RETURNS
NFC: 51 Brandon Banks, Washington
AFC: 42 Brandon Tate, Cincinnati

RETURNS, GAME
AFC: 7 Matt Willis, Denver at Buffalo, December 24 (138 yards, 0 TD)
NFC: 6 Sammie Stroughter, Tampa Bay at Green Bay, November 20 (152 yards, 0 TD)
6 Brandon Banks, Washington vs. N.Y. Jets, December 4 (136 yards, 0 TD)
6 Brandon Banks, Washington vs. New England, December 11 (117 yards, 0 TD)
6 Jerious Norwood, St. Louis at Seattle, December 12 (170 yards, 0 TD)

TOUCHDOWNS
AFC: 1 * Tommie Campbell, Tennessee
1 Jacoby Ford, Oakland
1 Richard Goodman, San Diego
1 Joe McKnight, N.Y. Jets
NFC: 1 * Randall Cobb, Green Bay
1 Ted Ginn, San Francisco
1 Percy Harvin, Minnesota
1 Devin Hester, Chicago
1 * Kealoha Pilares, Carolina

TEAM CHAMPION
NFC: 27.2 San Francisco
AFC: 26.3 N.Y. Jets

NFL TOP TEN KICKOFF RETURNERS

	No	Yards	Avg	Long	TD
McKnight, Joe, NYJ	34	1073	31.6	107t	1
* Cobb, Randall, G.B.	34	941	27.7	108t	1
Ginn, Ted, S.F.	29	800	27.6	102t	1
Goodman, Richard, S.D.	34	936	27.5	105t	1
Brown, Antonio, Pit.	27	737	27.3	52	0
Sproles, Darren, N.O.	40	1089	27.2	92	0
Stroughter, Sammie, T.B.	20	540	27.0	78	0
* Pilares, Kealoha, Car.	23	590	25.7	101t	1
Norwood, Jerious, St.L	24	611	25.5	47	0
Logan, Stefan, Det.	33	832	25.2	42	0

AFC—INDIVIDUAL KICKOFF RETURNERS

	No	Yards	Avg	Long	TD
McKnight, Joe, NYJ	34	1073	31.6	107t	1
Goodman, Richard, S.D.	34	936	27.5	105t	1
Brown, Antonio, Pit.	27	737	27.3	52	0
Cribbs, Josh, Cle.	39	974	25.0	63	0
* Gates, Clyde, Mia.	34	843	24.8	77	0
Karim, Deji, Jac.	27	652	24.1	37	0
Tate, Brandon, Cin.	42	998	23.8	45	0
Mariani, Marc, Ten.	32	748	23.4	49	0
McCluster, Dexter, K.C.	25	557	22.3	35	0
Woodhead, Danny, N.E.	20	437	21.9	37	0
* Lefeged, Joe, Ind.	31	578	18.6	51	0
(Nonqualifiers)					
Reed, David, Bal.	18	534	29.7	77	0
Cosby, Quan, Den.	17	457	26.9	63	0
Cromartie, Antonio, NYJ	17	417	24.5	46	0
Arenas, Javier, K.C.	17	362	21.3	35	0
McCann, Bryan, Dal.-Bal.-Oak.	16	440	27.5	91	0
Smith, Brad, Buf.	15	282	18.8	28	0
* Harris, DuJuan, Jac.	14	308	22.0	35	0
* Rogers, Justin, Buf.	13	373	28.7	54	0
Manning, Danieal, Hou.	13	356	27.4	46	0
Edelman, Julian, N.E.	12	284	23.7	37	0
Ford, Jacoby, Oak.	11	341	31.0	101t	1
McManis, Sherrick, Hou.	10	205	20.5	45	0
Zbikowski, Tom, Bal.	9	209	23.2	30	0
* Jones, Taiwan, Oak.	8	165	20.6	46	0
Willis, Matt, Den.	8	163	20.4	29	0
Vaughn, Cassius, Den.	7	210	30.0	67	0
* Ridley, Stevan, N.E.	7	152	21.7	32	0
Spiller, C.J., Buf.	6	143	23.8	35	0
Demps, Quintin, Hou.	5	169	33.8	50	0
* Williams, LaQuan, Bal.	5	109	21.8	37	0
Sanders, Emmanuel, Pit.	5	93	18.6	25	0
* Shorts, Cecil, Jac.	4	82	20.5	23	0
Slater, Matthew, N.E.	4	68	17.0	22	0
* Marecic, Owen, Cle.	4	46	11.5	13	0
Slaton, Steve, Mia.	3	85	28.3	42	0
* Skrine, Buster, Cle.	3	72	24.0	32	0
Hester, Jacob, S.D.	3	71	23.7	24	0
* Baker, Josh, NYJ	3	60	20.0	29	0
Royal, Eddie, Den.	3	47	15.7	20	0
* Gilchrist, Marcus, S.D.	3	46	15.3	20	0
Cartwright, Rock, Oak.	3	15	5.0	14	0
Webb, Lardarius, Bal.	2	59	29.5	37	0
Decker, Eric, Den.	2	50	25.0	34	0
Horne, Jeremy, K.C.	2	44	22.0	24	0
McKelvin, Leodis, Buf.	2	43	21.5	22	0
Adams, Mike, Cle.	2	42	21.0	30	0
* Moore, Denarius, Oak.	2	37	18.5	20	0
Brinkley, Curtis, S.D.	2	34	17.0	22	0
Branch, Tyvon, Oak.	2	31	15.5	16	0
Conner, John, NYJ	2	29	14.5	18	0
Leach, Vonta, Bal.	2	29	14.5	15	0
Scott, Bernard, Cin.	1	26	26.0	26	0
McCourty, Devin, N.E.	1	24	24.0	24	0
* Smith, Torrey, Bal.	1	24	24.0	24	0
Carr, Chris, Bal.	1	20	20.0	20	0
Fells, Daniel, Den.	1	20	20.0	20	0
Mulligan, Matthew, NYJ	1	20	20.0	20	0
Cotchery, Jerricho, Pit.	1	19	19.0	19	0
Redman, Isaac, Pit.	1	18	18.0	18	0
Wilson, Kyle, NYJ	1	17	17.0	17	0
* Kerley, Jeremy, NYJ	1	15	15.0	15	0
Hilliard, Lex, Mia.	1	14	14.0	14	0
Owens, Montell, Jac.	1	13	13.0	13	0
Sperry, Kory, S.D.	1	13	13.0	13	0
Caussin, Mike, Buf.	1	12	12.0	12	0

	No	Yards	Avg	Long	TD
Copper, Terrance, K.C.	1	12	12.0	12	0
Gronkowski, Rob, N.E.	1	11	11.0	11	0
Moore, Mewelde, Pit.	1	10	10.0	10	0
Ninkovich, Rob, N.E.	1	10	10.0	10	0
Peerman, Cedric, Cin.	1	10	10.0	10	0
Ball, Lance, Den.	1	9	9.0	9	0
Nakamura, Haruki, Bal.	1	8	8.0	8	0
* Bailey, Allen, K.C.	1	4	4.0	4	0
Clements, Nate, Cin.	1	4	4.0	4	0
Revis, Darrelle, NYJ	1	3	3.0	3	0
Bess, Davone, Mia.	1	0	0.0	0	0
Casey, James, Hou.	1	0	0.0	0	0
Jones, Edgar, Bal.	1	0	0.0	0	0
McIntyre, Garrett, NYJ	1	0	0.0	0	0
Potter, Zach, Jac.	1	0	0.0	0	0
Turner, Patrick, NYJ	1	-1	-1.0	-1	0
* Campbell, Tommie, Ten.	0	84	—	84t	1
Mattison, Bryan, Bal.	0	2	—	2	0
Jones, Adam, Cin.	0	-12	—	-12	0

t = Touchdown; f = Fair Catch
Leader based on average return, minimum 20 returns
* Player that was a rookie in 2011

NFC—INDIVIDUAL KICKOFF RETURNERS

	No	Yards	Avg	Long	TD
* Cobb, Randall, G.B.	34	941	27.7	108t	1
Ginn, Ted, S.F.	29	800	27.6	102t	1
Sproles, Darren, N.O.	40	1089	27.2	92	0
Stroughter, Sammie, T.B.	20	540	27.0	78	0
* Pilares, Kealoha, Car.	23	590	25.7	101t	1
Norwood, Jerious, St.L	24	611	25.5	47	0
Logan, Stefan, Det.	33	832	25.2	42	0
Washington, Leon, Sea.	43	1084	25.2	54	0
Thomas, Devin, NY-G	25	607	24.3	40	0
Stephens-Howling, LaRod, Ariz	36	857	23.8	37	0
Weems, Eric, Atl.	24	563	23.5	37	0
Banks, Brandon, Was.	51	1174	23.0	47	0
Porter, Quinn, St.L	25	554	22.2	32	0
Parker, Preston, T.B.	20	439	22.0	45	0
Hester, Devin, Chi.	33	723	21.9	98t	1
* Lewis, Dion, Phi.	31	669	21.6	33	0
(Nonqualifiers)					
Booker, Lorenzo, Min.	19	450	23.7	68	0
Harvin, Percy, Min.	16	520	32.5	104	1
Sherels, Marcus, Min.	16	445	27.8	78	0
Knox, Johnny, Chi.	15	397	26.5	56	0
Jefferson, A.J., Ariz	14	356	25.4	51	0
* Scott, Da'Rel, NY-G	14	341	24.4	38	0
Goodson, Mike, Car.	11	250	22.7	31	0
* Harris, Dwayne, Dal.	8	231	28.9	51	0
* Jernigan, Jerrel, NY-G	8	186	23.3	31	0
Jones, Felix, Dal.	7	186	26.6	69	0
* Hunter, Kendall, S.F.	6	156	26.0	43	0
Ogletree, Kevin, Dal.	6	114	19.0	25	0
Miller, Nick, Oak.-St.L	6	104	17.3	23	0
Williams, Kyle, S.F.	4	104	26.0	33	0
* Pettis, Austin, St.L	3	62	20.7	24	0
Owusu-Ansah, Akwasi, Dal.	3	56	18.7	23	0
Bryant, Dez, Dal.	3	55	18.3	26	0
Edwards, Armanti, Car.	3	35	11.7	17	0
Rodgers-Cromartie, Dominique, Phi.	2	52	26.0	29	0
Pugh, Jordan, Car.	2	51	25.5	28	0
Bell, Kahlil, Chi.	2	45	22.5	25	0
Blackmon, Will, NY-G	2	43	21.5	32	0
Hall, Chad, Phi.	2	43	21.5	24	0
* Saine, Brandon, G.B.	2	40	20.0	20	0

	No	Yards	Avg	Long	TD
* Murray, DeMarco, Dal.	2	36	18.0	22	0
Davis, Rashied, Det.	2	34	17.0	18	0
Roberts, Andre, Ariz	2	33	16.5	21	0
Spurlock, Micheal, T.B.	2	33	16.5	21	0
Brown, Ronnie, Phi.	2	28	14.0	25	0
Phillips, John, Dal.	2	26	13.0	16	0
Ware, D.J., NY-G	2	17	8.5	17	0
Spaeth, Matt, Chi.	2	14	7.0	7	0
Paulsen, Logan, Was.	2	7	3.5	7	0
Driver, Donald, G.B.	2	5	2.5	5	0
Lissemore, Sean, Dal.	1	38	38.0	38	0
* Baldwin, Doug, Sea.	1	37	37.0	37	0
Armstrong, Anthony, Was.	1	28	28.0	28	0
Hurd, Sam, Chi.	1	24	24.0	24	0
* Allen, Armando, Chi.	1	17	17.0	17	0
Cooper, Riley, Phi.	1	16	16.0	16	0
* Hynoski, Henry, NY-G	1	15	15.0	15	0
Morris, Maurice, Det.	1	15	15.0	15	0
* Paul, Niles, Was.	1	15	15.0	15	0
Sellers, Mike, Was.	1	15	15.0	15	0
Thomas, Pierre, N.O.	1	15	15.0	15	0
Briscoe, Dezmon, T.B.	1	12	12.0	12	0
Crabtree, Tom, G.B.	1	11	11.0	11	0
Forsett, Justin, Sea.	1	11	11.0	11	0
Byrd, Dominique, Sea.	1	10	10.0	10	0
Sims, Eugene, St.L	1	10	10.0	10	0
Bennett, Earl, Chi.	1	9	9.0	9	0
Clutts, Tyler, Chi.	1	9	9.0	9	0
Woodson, Charles, G.B.	1	9	9.0	9	0
Collins, Jed, N.O.	1	7	7.0	7	0
Griffen, Everson, Min.	1	7	7.0	7	0
Jackson, DeSean, Phi.	1	7	7.0	7	0
D'Imperio, Ryan, Min.	1	6	6.0	6	0
Fluellen, Andre, Det.	1	6	6.0	6	0
* Adams, Kyle, Chi.	1	0	0.0	0	0
Crowder, Tim, T.B.	1	0	0.0	0	0
* Madu, Mossis, T.B.	1	0	0.0	0	0
* Pianalto, Zack, T.B.	1	0	0.0	0	0
Lee, Pat, G.B.	1	-1	-1.0	-1	0
Brockel, Richie, Car.	f0	0	—	—	0

t = Touchdown; f = Fair Catch
Leader based on average return, minimum 20 returns
* *Player that was a rookie in 2011*

AMERICAN FOOTBALL CONFERENCE—KICKOFF RETURNS

	No	Yards	Avg	Long	TD
N.Y. Jets	62	1633	26.3	107t	1
Tennessee	32	832	26.0	100t	1
San Diego	43	1100	25.6	105t	1
Houston	29	730	25.2	50	0
Pittsburgh	35	877	25.1	52	0
Baltimore	42	1047	24.9	77	0
Denver	39	956	24.5	67	0
Miami	39	942	24.2	77	0
Cleveland	48	1134	23.6	63	0
Oakland	43	1011	23.5	101t	1
Buffalo	37	853	23.1	54	0
Cincinnati	45	1026	22.8	45	0
Jacksonville	47	1055	22.4	37	0
New England	46	986	21.4	37	0
Kansas City	46	979	21.3	35	0
Indianapolis	31	578	18.6	51	0
AFC Total	664	15739	23.7	107t	4
AFC Average	41.5	983.7	23.7	—	0.3

NATIONAL FOOTBALL CONFERENCE—KICKOFF RETURNS

	No	Yards	Avg	Long	TD
San Francisco	39	1060	27.2	102t	1
Minnesota	53	1428	26.9	104	1
New Orleans	42	1111	26.5	92	0
Seattle	46	1142	24.8	54	0
Green Bay	41	1005	24.5	108t	1
Detroit	37	887	24.0	42	0
Arizona	52	1246	24.0	51	0
Carolina	39	926	23.7	101t	1
Atlanta	24	563	23.5	37	0
Dallas	33	768	23.3	69	0
St. Louis	55	1280	23.3	47	0
N.Y. Giants	52	1209	23.3	40	0
Tampa Bay	46	1024	22.3	78	0
Washington	56	1239	22.1	47	0
Chicago	57	1238	21.7	98t	1
Philadelphia	39	815	20.9	33	0
NFC Total	711	16941	23.8	108t	5
NFC Average	44.4	1058.8	23.8	—	0.3
League Total	1375	32680	—	108t	9
League Average	43.0	1021.3	23.8	—	0.3

AVERAGE YARDS PER PUNT
NFC: 50.9 Andy Lee, San Francisco
AFC: 50.8 Shane Lechler, Oakland

NET AVERAGE YARDS PER PUNT
NFC: 44.0 Andy Lee, San Francisco
AFC: 41.5 Zoltan Mesko, New England

LONGEST
AFC: 80 Shane Lechler, Oakland vs. Chicago,
   November 27
NFC: 77 Jon Ryan, Seattle at San Francisco,
   September 11

PUNTS
NFC: 105 Donnie Jones, St. Louis
AFC: 101 Britton Colquitt, Denver

PUNTS, GAME
AFC: 11 Dustin Colquitt, Kansas City at Chicago,
   December 4 (447 yards)
NFC: 11 Adam Podlesh, Chicago at Denver,
   December 11 (526 yards) - (OT)

TEAM CHAMPION
AFC: 50.8 Oakland
NFC: 50.3 San Francisco

AMERICAN FOOTBALL CONFERENCE—PUNTING

	Total Punts	Yards	Long	Avg	TB	Blk	Opp Ret	Return Yards	In 20	Net Avg
Oakland	78	3960	80	50.8	9	0	44	593	27	40.9
Miami	78	3810	70	48.8	7	0	47	463	32	41.1
Buffalo	73	3472	66	47.6	10	1	43	494	20	38.1
San Diego	47	2234	71	47.5	2	0	25	329	17	39.7
Denver	101	4783	66	47.4	7	0	51	585	33	40.2
Baltimore	73	3393	63	46.5	9	0	33	392	21	38.6
New England	57	2648	65	46.5	3	0	26	220	24	41.5
Indianapolis	89	4098	64	46.0	3	1	48	550	21	39.2
Kansas City	89	4084	68	45.9	5	0	36	411	27	40.1
Pittsburgh	60	2683	66	44.7	6	1	29	245	18	38.6
Cincinnati	91	4023	71	44.2	9	0	38	273	24	39.2
Houston	74	3256	69	44.0	8	0	32	307	19	37.7
Tennessee	86	3747	64	43.6	7	0	36	221	31	39.4
N.Y. Jets	92	3926	63	42.7	6	0	32	241	32	38.8
Jacksonville	99	4147	65	41.9	10	0	48	333	20	36.5
Cleveland	89	3570	63	40.1	2	0	26	303	32	36.3
AFC Total	1276	57834	80	—	103	3	594	5960	398	—
AFC Average	79.8	3614.6	--	45.3	6.4	0.2	37.1	372.5	24.9	39.0

NATIONAL FOOTBALL CONFERENCE—PUNTING

	Total Punts	Yards	Long	Avg	TB	Blk	Opp Ret	Return Yards	In 20	Net Avg
San Francisco	79	3970	68	50.3	9	1	39	315	28	44.0
New Orleans	47	2224	64	47.3	4	1	19	118	13	43.1
Seattle	95	4431	77	46.6	8	0	47	541	34	39.3
Minnesota	77	3517	60	45.7	3	0	43	532	22	38.0
N.Y. Giants	82	3745	62	45.7	6	0	41	407	25	39.2
Green Bay	55	2506	71	45.6	4	0	24	305	23	38.6
Tampa Bay	67	3023	65	45.1	3	0	36	266	24	40.3
Arizona	92	4141	66	45.0	5	0	50	610	26	37.3
St. Louis	106	4652	65	43.9	9	1	45	552	29	37.0
Chicago	89	3903	70	43.9	4	0	41	223	21	40.4
Detroit	82	3573	62	43.6	7	0	36	484	23	36.0
Washington	66	2842	63	43.1	1	0	32	250	28	39.0
Dallas	71	3047	68	42.9	8	1	30	278	25	36.7
Carolina	66	2819	56	42.7	5	0	35	466	19	34.1
Philadelphia	67	2830	60	42.2	9	1	31	176	19	36.9
Atlanta	71	2990	59	42.1	4	1	31	150	27	38.9
NFC Total	1212	54213	77	—	89	6	580	5673	386	—
NFC Average	75.8	3388.3	--	44.7	5.6	0.4	36.3	354.6	24.1	38.6
NFL Total	2488	112047	80	—	192	9	1174	11633	784	—
NFL Average	77.8	3501.5	--	45.0	6.0	0.3	36.7	363.5	24.5	38.8

NFL TOP TEN PUNTERS

	No	Yards	Long	Avg	Total Punts	TB	Blk	Opp Ret	Return Yards	In 20	Net Avg
Lee, Andy, S.F.	78	3970	68	50.9	79	9	1	39	315	28	44.0
Lechler, Shane, Oak.	78	3960	80	50.8	78	9	0	44	593	27	40.9
Fields, Brandon, Mia.	78	3810	70	48.8	78	7	0	47	463	32	41.1
Morstead, Thomas, N.O.	46	2224	64	48.3	47	4	1	19	118	13	43.1
Moorman, Brian, Buf.	72	3472	66	48.2	73	10	1	43	494	20	38.1
Scifres, Mike, S.D.	47	2234	71	47.5	47	2	0	25	329	17	39.7
Colquitt, Britton, Den.	101	4783	66	47.4	101	7	0	51	585	33	40.2
Ryan, Jon, Sea.	95	4431	77	46.6	95	8	0	47	541	34	39.3
McAfee, Pat, Ind.	88	4098	64	46.6	89	3	1	48	550	21	39.2
Koch, Sam, Bal.	73	3393	63	46.5	73	9	0	33	392	21	38.6

AFC—INDIVIDUAL PUNTERS

	No	Yards	Long	Avg	Total Punts	TB	Blk	Opp Ret	Return Yards	In 20	Net Avg
Lechler, Shane, Oak.	78	3960	80	50.8	78	9	0	44	593	27	40.9
Fields, Brandon, Mia.	78	3810	70	48.8	78	7	0	47	463	32	41.1
Moorman, Brian, Buf.	72	3472	66	48.2	73	10	1	43	494	20	38.1
Scifres, Mike, S.D.	47	2234	71	47.5	47	2	0	25	329	17	39.7
Colquitt, Britton, Den.	101	4783	66	47.4	101	7	0	51	585	33	40.2
McAfee, Pat, Ind.	88	4098	64	46.6	89	3	1	48	550	21	39.2
Koch, Sam, Bal.	73	3393	63	46.5	73	9	0	33	392	21	38.6
Mesko, Zoltan, N.E.	57	2648	65	46.5	57	3	0	26	220	24	41.5
Colquitt, Dustin, K.C.	89	4084	68	45.9	89	5	0	36	411	27	40.1
* Hartmann, Brett, Hou.	58	2573	69	44.4	58	7	0	26	243	15	37.8
Huber, Kevin, Cin.	91	4023	71	44.2	91	9	0	38	273	24	39.2
Kern, Brett, Ten.	86	3747	64	43.6	86	7	0	36	221	31	39.4
Harris, Nick, Jac.	72	3075	55	42.7	72	5	0	39	246	13	37.9
Conley, T.J., NYJ	92	3926	63	42.7	92	6	0	32	241	32	38.8
Turk, Matt, Jac.-Hou.	43	1755	65	40.8	43	6	0	15	151	11	34.5
Maynard, Brad, Cle.	81	3282	63	40.5	81	1	0	25	288	32	36.7
(Nonqualifiers)											
Kapinos, Jeremy, Pit.	34	1530	59	45.0	34	1	0	21	208	10	38.3
Sepulveda, Daniel, Pit.	25	1153	66	46.1	26	5	1	8	37	8	39.1
McGee, Richmond, Cle.	8	288	48	36.0	8	1	0	1	15	0	31.6

Leader based on average, minimum 40 punts

NFC—INDIVIDUAL PUNTERS

	No	Yards	Long	Avg	Total Punts	TB	Blk	Opp Ret	Return Yards	In 20	Net Avg
Lee, Andy, S.F.	78	3970	68	50.9	79	9	1	39	315	28	44.0
Morstead, Thomas, N.O.	46	2224	64	48.3	47	4	1	19	118	13	43.1
Ryan, Jon, Sea.	95	4431	77	46.6	95	8	0	47	541	34	39.3
Kluwe, Chris, Min.	77	3517	60	45.7	77	3	0	43	532	22	38.0
Weatherford, Steve, NY-G	82	3745	62	45.7	82	6	0	41	407	25	39.2
Masthay, Tim, G.B.	55	2506	71	45.6	55	4	0	24	305	23	38.6
Zastudil, Dave, Ariz	87	3929	66	45.2	87	5	0	48	565	24	37.5
Koenen, Michael, T.B.	67	3023	65	45.1	67	3	0	36	266	24	40.3
Jones, Donnie, St.L	105	4652	65	44.3	106	9	1	45	552	29	37.0
Podlesh, Adam, Chi.	89	3903	70	43.9	89	4	0	41	223	21	40.4
McBriar, Mat, Dal.	58	2542	68	43.8	59	7	1	26	272	21	36.1
Rocca, Sav, Was.	66	2842	63	43.1	66	1	0	32	250	28	39.0
* Henry, Chas, Phi.	66	2830	60	42.9	67	9	1	31	176	19	36.9
* Bosher, Matt, Atl.	70	2990	59	42.7	71	4	1	31	150	27	38.9
* Donahue, Ryan, Det.	49	2093	60	42.7	49	4	0	22	270	13	35.6
Baker, Jason, Car.	66	2819	56	42.7	66	5	0	35	466	19	34.1
(Nonqualifiers)											
Graham, Ben, Ariz-Det.	33	1447	58	43.8	33	3	0	13	137	12	37.9
* Jones, Chris, Dal.	10	426	54	42.6	10	1	0	3	1	4	40.5
Malone, Robert, Det.	5	245	62	49.0	5	0	0	3	122	0	24.6
* Bailey, Dan, Dal.	2	79	41	39.5	2	0	0	1	5	0	37.0

Leader based on average, minimum 40 punts
* Player that was a rookie in 2011

PUNT RETURNS

YARDS PER RETURN
NFC:	16.2	Devin Hester, Chicago
AFC:	12.8	Javier Arenas, Kansas City

YARDS
NFC:	699	* Patrick Peterson, Arizona
AFC:	543	Brandon Tate, Cincinnati

YARDS, GAME
AFC:	135	Leodis McKelvin, Buffalo vs. Denver, December 24 (3 returns, 1 TD)
NFC:	127	* Patrick Peterson, Arizona vs. St. Louis, November 6 (4 returns, 1 TD) - (OT)

LONGEST
NFC:	99	* Patrick Peterson, Arizona vs. St. Louis, November 6 - TD - (OT)
AFC:	90	Eric Decker, Denver vs. Oakland, September 12 - TD

RETURNS
AFC:	51	Brandon Tate, Cincinnati
NFC:	44	* Patrick Peterson, Arizona

RETURNS, GAME
AFC:	8	Quan Cosby, Denver vs. Chicago, December 11 (73 yards, 0 TD) - (OT)
NFC:	7	Leon Washington, Seattle at St. Louis, November 20 (74 yards, 0 TD)

FAIR CATCHES
NFC:	28	Stefan Logan, Detroit
AFC:	26	Antonio Brown, Pittsburgh

TOUCHDOWNS
NFC:	4	* Patrick Peterson, Arizona
AFC:	1	Antonio Brown, Pittsburgh
	1	Josh Cribbs, Cleveland
	1	Eric Decker, Denver
	1	Julian Edelman, New England
	1	Jacoby Jones, Houston
	1	Marc Mariani, Tennessee
	1	Leodis McKelvin, Buffalo
	1	Eddie Royal, Denver
	1	Brandon Tate, Cincinnati
	1	Lardarius Webb, Baltimore

TEAM CHAMPION
NFC:	15.7	Chicago
AFC:	12.7	Denver

NFL TOP TEN PUNT RETURNERS
	No	FC	Yards	Avg	Long	TD
Hester, Devin, Chi.	28	15	454	16.2	82t	2
* Peterson, Patrick, Ariz	44	22	699	15.9	99t	4
Arenas, Javier, K.C.	32	7	410	12.8	37	0
Ginn, Ted, S.F.	38	18	466	12.3	55t	1
Bess, Davone, Mia.	37	24	442	11.9	25	0
Cribbs, Josh, Cle.	34	8	388	11.4	84t	1
* Cobb, Randall, G.B.	26	18	295	11.3	80t	1
Washington, Leon, Sea.	41	16	464	11.3	37	0
* Kerley, Jeremy, NYJ	29	16	317	10.9	53	0
Brown, Antonio, Pit.	30	26	325	10.8	60t	1

AFC—INDIVIDUAL PUNT RETURNERS
	No	FC	Yards	Avg	Long	TD
Arenas, Javier, K.C.	32	7	410	12.8	37	0
Bess, Davone, Mia.	37	24	442	11.9	25	0
Cribbs, Josh, Cle.	34	8	388	11.4	84t	1
* Kerley, Jeremy, NYJ	29	16	317	10.9	53	0
Brown, Antonio, Pit.	30	26	325	10.8	60t	1
Mariani, Marc, Ten.	46	18	490	10.7	79t	1
Tate, Brandon, Cin.	51	17	543	10.6	56t	1
Jones, Jacoby, Hou.	49	7	518	10.6	79t	1
Edelman, Julian, N.E.	28	7	296	10.6	72t	1
Webb, Lardarius, Bal.	30	20	301	10.0	68t	1
Cosby, Quan, Den.	27	9	269	10.0	30	0
Crayton, Patrick, S.D.	22	9	202	9.2	31	0
* Moore, Denarius, Oak.	25	7	216	8.6	34	0
(Nonqualifiers)						
Thomas, Mike, Jac.	19	5	88	4.6	28	0
Garcon, Pierre, Ind.	16	8	44	2.8	20	0
Spiller, C.J., Buf.	13	8	127	9.8	45	0
Royal, Eddie, Den.	12	9	194	16.2	85t	1
* Shorts, Cecil, Jac.	12	6	50	4.2	27	0
Leonhard, Jim, NYJ	9	5	83	9.2	15	0
* Lefeged, Joe, Ind.	9	4	42	4.7	21	0
McKelvin, Leodis, Buf.	8	11	156	19.5	80t	1
Welker, Wes, N.E.	8	6	82	10.3	25	0
Walters, Bryan, S.D.	8	3	45	5.6	13	0
White, Blair, Ind.	7	10	22	3.1	13	0
Decker, Eric, Den.	6	1	133	22.2	90t	1
McCluster, Dexter, K.C.	6	3	65	10.8	22	0
Bush, Reggie, Mia.	6	0	52	8.7	16	0
Parrish, Roscoe, Buf.	5	2	46	9.2	28	0
McCann, Bryan, Dal.-Oak.	5	1	42	8.4	17	0
McKnight, Joe, NYJ	5	0	26	5.2	12	0
Norwood, Jordan, Cle.	4	1	35	8.8	14	0
* Gates, Clyde, Mia.	3	0	32	10.7	17	0
Reed, Ed, Bal.	3	5	29	9.7	16	0
Sanders, Emmanuel, Pit.	3	0	22	7.3	10	0
Dillard, Jarett, Jac.	3	6	10	3.3	5	0
Jones, Adam, Cin.	2	0	67	33.5	63	0
Carr, Chris, Bal.	2	2	15	7.5	8	0
Faulk, Kevin, N.E.	2	0	11	5.5	7	0
Cason, Antoine, S.D.	1	0	17	17.0	17	0
* Keo, Shiloh, Hou.	1	1	11	11.0	11	0
Blackstock, Darryl, Oak.	1	0	0	0.0	0	0
* Brown, Jalil, K.C.	1	0	0	0.0	0	0
* Campbell, Tommie, Ten.	1	0	0	0.0	0	0
Cromartie, Antonio, NYJ	1	0	0	0.0	0	0
Goodman, André, Den.	1	0	0	0.0	0	0
Holliday, Trindon, Hou.	1	3	0	0.0	0	0
Houshmandzadeh, T.J., Oak.	1	1	0	0.0	0	0
Piscitelli, Sabby, K.C.	1	0	0	0.0	0	0
* Williams, LaQuan, Bal.	1	0	0	0.0	0	0
Willis, Matt, Den.	1	0	0	0.0	0	0
Clements, Nate, Cin.	0	1	0	—	—	0
Mathis, Rashean, Jac.	0	2	0	—	—	0
Powers, Jerraud, Ind.	0	1	0	—	—	0

t = Touchdown
Leader based on average return, minimum 20 returns
* Player that was a rookie in 2011

NFC—INDIVIDUAL PUNT RETURNERS

	No	FC	Yards	Avg	Long	TD
Hester, Devin, Chi.	28	15	454	16.2	82t	2
* Peterson, Patrick, Ariz	44	22	699	15.9	99t	4
Ginn, Ted, S.F.	38	18	466	12.3	55t	1
* Cobb, Randall, G.B.	26	18	295	11.3	80t	1
Washington, Leon, Sea.	41	16	464	11.3	37	0
Sproles, Darren, N.O.	29	19	294	10.1	72t	1
Weems, Eric, Atl.	32	19	315	9.8	42	0
Parker, Preston, T.B.	23	13	210	9.1	34	0
Banks, Brandon, Was.	36	9	328	9.1	55	0
Sherels, Marcus, Min.	33	20	277	8.4	53	0
Logan, Stefan, Det.	37	28	301	8.1	28	0
Edwards, Armanti, Car.	32	9	176	5.5	17	0
(Nonqualifiers)						
Jackson, DeSean, Phi.	17	12	114	6.7	51	0
* Pettis, Austin, St.L	15	10	139	9.3	39	0
Bryant, Dez, Dal.	15	5	103	6.9	20	0
* Harris, Dwayne, Dal.	15	6	80	5.3	14	0
Ross, Aaron, NY-G	14	13	99	7.1	18	0
Miller, Nick, Oak.-St.L	10	10	147	14.7	88t	0
Hall, Chad, Phi.	7	12	76	10.9	30	0
Owusu-Ansah, Akwasi, Dal.	6	3	47	7.8	21	0
Blackmon, Will, NY-G	6	2	25	4.2	16	0
Spurlock, Micheal, T.B.	6	1	21	3.5	15	0
Smith, Reggie, S.F.	4	1	37	9.3	14	0
Maclin, Jeremy, Phi.	4	3	29	7.3	11	0
Hixon, Domenik, NY-G	3	3	31	10.3	18	0
Cruz, Victor, NY-G	3	2	12	4.0	11	0
Williams, Kyle, S.F.	2	4	41	20.5	36	0
Ogletree, Kevin, Dal.	2	0	35	17.5	25	0
* Salas, Greg, St.L	2	3	29	14.5	29	0
Rolle, Antrel, NY-G	2	0	4	2.0	3	0
Roberts, Andre, Ariz	2	0	-3	-1.5	-1	0
Holley, Jesse, Dal.	1	0	15	15.0	15	0
Knox, Johnny, Chi.	1	0	9	9.0	9	0
Bennett, Earl, Chi.	1	1	7	7.0	7	0
Porter, Quinn, St.L	1	1	1	1.0	1	0
Amendola, Danny, St.L	1	0	0	0.0	0	0
Bush, Jarrett, G.B.	1	0	0	0.0	0	0
Franks, Dominique, Atl.	1	0	0	0.0	0	0
McDonald, Brandon, Det.	1	0	0	0.0	0	0
* Paul, Niles, Was.	1	0	0	0.0	0	0
Smith, Steve, Phi.	1	1	0	0.0	0	0
Tate, Golden, Sea.	1	0	0	0.0	0	0
* Marsh, Curtis, Phi.	1	0	-5	-5.0	0	0
Clayton, Mark, St.L	0	1	0	—	—	0
* Jernigan, Jerrel, NY-G	0	1	0	—	—	0
Nelson, Jordy, G.B.	0	1	0	—	—	0
Rodgers-Cromartie, Dominique, Phi.	0	0	-2	—	-2	0

t = Touchdown
Leader based on average return, minimum 20 returns
* Player that was a rookie in 2011

AMERICAN FOOTBALL CONFERENCE—PUNT RETURNS

	No	FC	Yards	Avg	Long	TD
Denver	47	19	596	12.7	90t	2
Buffalo	26	21	329	12.7	80t	1
Kansas City	40	10	475	11.9	37	0
Cincinnati	53	18	610	11.5	63	1
Miami	46	24	526	11.4	25	0
Cleveland	38	9	423	11.1	84t	1
Pittsburgh	33	26	347	10.5	60t	1
Tennessee	47	18	490	10.4	79t	1
Houston	51	11	529	10.4	79t	1
New England	38	13	389	10.2	72t	1
N.Y. Jets	44	21	426	9.7	53	0
Baltimore	36	27	345	9.6	68t	1
San Diego	31	12	264	8.5	31	0
Oakland	32	9	264	8.3	34	0
Jacksonville	34	19	148	4.4	28	0
Indianapolis	32	23	108	3.4	21	0
AFC Total	628	280	6269	10.0	90t	10
AFC Average	39.3	17.5	391.8	10.0	—	0.6

NATIONAL FOOTBALL CONFERENCE—PUNT RETURNS

	No	FC	Yards	Avg	Long	TD
Chicago	30	16	470	15.7	82t	2
Arizona	46	22	696	15.1	99t	4
San Francisco	44	23	544	12.4	55t	1
Seattle	42	16	464	11.0	37	0
St. Louis	27	25	297	11.0	88t	1
Green Bay	27	19	295	10.9	80t	1
New Orleans	29	19	294	10.1	72t	1
Atlanta	33	19	315	9.5	42	0
Washington	37	9	328	8.9	55	0
Minnesota	33	20	277	8.4	53	0
Tampa Bay	29	14	231	8.0	34	0
Detroit	38	28	301	7.9	28	0
Dallas	41	14	293	7.1	25	0
Philadelphia	30	28	212	7.1	51	0
N.Y. Giants	28	21	171	6.1	18	0
Carolina	32	9	176	5.5	17	0
NFC Total	546	302	5364	9.8	99t	10
NFC Average	34.1	18.9	335.3	9.8	—	0.6
League Total	1174	582	11633	—	99t	20
League Average	36.7	18.2	363.5	9.9	—	0.6

SACKS

MOST SACKS
NFC: 22.0 Jared Allen, Minnesota
AFC: 14.0 Terrell Suggs, Baltimore

MOST SACKS, GAME
AFC: 4.0 Kamerion Wimbley, Oakland at San Diego, November 10
4.0 Andre Carter, New England at N.Y. Jets, November 13
4.0 Connor Barwin, Houston at Jacksonville, November 27
4.0 Antwan Barnes, San Diego vs. Baltimore, December 18
NFC: 4.0 DeMarcus Ware, Dallas at Philadelphia, October 30

TEAM LEADERS, SACKS
AFC: BALTIMORE, 14, Terrell Suggs; BUFFALO, 5.5, *Marcell Dareus; CINCINNATI, 7.5, Geno Atkins; CLEVELAND, 8.5, *Jabaal Sheard; DENVER, 11.5, *Von Miller; HOUSTON, 11.5, Connor Barwin; INDIANAPOLIS, 9.5, Robert Mathis; JACKSONVILLE, 8, Jeremy Mincey; KANSAS CITY, 12, Tamba Hali; MIAMI, 8.5, Cameron Wake; NEW ENGLAND, 10, Mark Anderson, Andre Carter; N.Y. JETS, 6, Aaron Maybin; OAKLAND, 7.5, Tommy Kelly; PITTSBURGH, 9, James Harrison, LaMarr Woodley; SAN DIEGO, 11, Antwan Barnes; TENNESSEE, 7, *Karl Klug

NFC: ARIZONA, 8, Calais Campbell; ATLANTA, 9.5, John Abraham; CAROLINA, 9, Charles Johnson; CHICAGO, 11, Julius Peppers; DALLAS, 19.5, DeMarcus Ware; DETROIT, 11, Cliff Avril; GREEN BAY, 6, Clay Matthews; MINNESOTA, 22, Jared Allen; NEW ORLEANS, 7.5, Roman Harper; N.Y. GIANTS, 16.5, Jason Pierre-Paul; PHILADELPHIA, 18, Jason Babin; ST. LOUIS, 13, Chris Long; SAN FRANCISCO, 14, *Aldon Smith; SEATTLE, 11, Chris Clemons; TAMPA BAY, 7.5, *Adrian Clayborn; WASHINGTON, 9, Brian Orakpo

TEAM CHAMPION
NFC: 50.0 Minnesota
50.0 Philadelphia

NFL TOP TEN LEADERS—SACKS

	Sacks
Allen, Jared, Min.	22.0
Ware, DeMarcus, Dal.	19.5
Babin, Jason, Phi.	18.0
Pierre-Paul, Jason, NY-G	16.5
* Smith, Aldon, S.F.	14.0
Suggs, Terrell, Bal.	14.0
Long, Chris, St.L	13.0
Hali, Tamba, K.C.	12.0
Barwin, Connor, Hou.	11.5
* Miller, Von, Den.	11.5

AMERICAN FOOTBALL CONFERENCE—SACKS

	Sacks	Yards
Baltimore	48	290
Cincinnati	45	277
Houston	44	287
Denver	41	283
Miami	41	241
New England	40	274
Oakland	39	239
N.Y. Jets	35	198
Pittsburgh	35	230
Cleveland	32	199
San Diego	32	187
Jacksonville	31	213
Buffalo	29	210
Indianapolis	29	192
Kansas City	29	186
Tennessee	28	180
AFC Total	578	3686
AFC Average	36.1	230.4

NATIONAL FOOTBALL CONFERENCE—SACKS

	Sacks	Yards
Minnesota	50	342
Philadelphia	50	316
N.Y. Giants	48	335
Arizona	42	304
Dallas	42	243
San Francisco	42	283
Detroit	41	271
Washington	41	251
St. Louis	39	261
Atlanta	33	231
Chicago	33	208
New Orleans	33	256
Seattle	33	232
Carolina	31	170
Green Bay	29	192
Tampa Bay	23	148
NFC Total	610	4043
NFC Average	38.1	252.7
League Total	1188	7729
League Average	37.1	241.5

AFC—INDIVIDUAL SACKS

	Sacks
Suggs, Terrell, Bal.	14.0
Hali, Tamba, K.C.	12.0
Barwin, Connor, Hou.	11.5
* Miller, Von, Den.	11.5
Barnes, Antwan, S.D.	11.0
Anderson, Mark, N.E.	10.0
Carter, Andre, N.E.	10.0
Dumervil, Elvis, Den.	9.5
Mathis, Robert, Ind.	9.5
Harrison, James, Pit.	9.0
Woodley, LaMarr, Pit.	9.0
Freeney, Dwight, Ind.	8.5
* Sheard, Jabaal, Cle.	8.5
Wake, Cameron, Mia.	8.5
Mincey, Jeremy, Jac.	8.0
Atkins, Geno, Cin.	7.5
Kelly, Tommy, Oak.	7.5
* Klug, Karl, Ten.	7.0
Taylor, Jason, Mia.	7.0
Wimbley, Kamerion, Oak.	7.0
Fanene, Jonathan, Cin.	6.5
Ninkovich, Rob, N.E.	6.5
Smith, Antonio, Hou.	6.5
Johnson, Michael, Cin.	6.0
Maybin, Aaron, NYJ	6.0
* McPhee, Pernell, Bal.	6.0
Odrick, Jared, Mia.	6.0
* Reed, Brooks, Hou.	6.0
Seymour, Richard, Oak.	6.0
* Dareus, Marcell, Buf.	5.5
* Houston, Justin, K.C.	5.5
Kruger, Paul, Bal.	5.5
* Watt, J.J., Hou.	5.5
Bryant, Desmond, Oak.	5.0
Harris, David, NYJ	5.0
Kelsay, Chris, Buf.	5.0
McClain, Rolando, Oak.	5.0
Ngata, Haloti, Bal.	5.0
Rubin, Ahtyba, Cle.	5.0
Williams, D.J., Den.	5.0
Williams, Mario, Hou.	5.0
Dunlap, Carlos, Cin.	4.5
Pace, Calvin, NYJ	4.5
Redding, Cory, Bal.	4.5
Scott, Bart, NYJ	4.5
Starks, Randy, Mia.	4.5
Ball, Dave, Ten.	4.0
Cushing, Brian, Hou.	4.0
McBean, Ryan, Den.	4.0
Rucker, Frostee, Cin.	4.0
* Taylor, Phillip, Cle.	4.0
Thomas, Cam, S.D.	4.0
Crocker, Chris, Cin.	3.5
Gocong, Chris, Cle.	3.5
Jackson, D'Qwell, Cle.	3.5
Phillips, Shaun, S.D.	3.5
Roth, Matt, Jac.	3.5
Smith, Daryl, Jac.	3.5
Westerman, Jamaal, NYJ	3.5
Wilfork, Vince, N.E.	3.5
Anderson, Jamaal, Ind.	3.0
Ayers, Robert, Den.	3.0
Barnett, Nick, Buf.	3.0
Dawkins, Brian, Den.	3.0
Harris, Tommie, S.D.	3.0
Jones, Jason, Ten.	3.0
Keisel, Brett, Pit.	3.0
Love, Kyle, N.E.	3.0

	Sacks		Sacks	NFC—INDIVIDUAL SACKS	
					Sacks
* Wilkerson, Muhammad, NYJ	3.0	* Heyward, Cameron, Pit.	1.0	Allen, Jared, Min.	22.0
Worilds, Jason, Pit.	3.0	Houston, Lamarr, Oak.	1.0	Ware, DeMarcus, Dal.	19.5
Alualu, Tyson, Jac.	2.5	Howard, Thomas, Cin.	1.0	Babin, Jason, Phi.	18.0
Burnett, Kevin, Mia.	2.5	Hughes, Jerry, Ind.	1.0	Pierre-Paul, Jason, NY-G	16.5
* Casey, Jurrell, Ten.	2.5	Hunter, Jason, Den.	1.0	* Smith, Aldon, S.F.	14.0
Chick, John, Jac.	2.5	Jackson, Tyson, K.C.	1.0	Long, Chris, St.L	13.0
Edwards, Dwan, Buf.	2.5	Jennings, Kelly, Cin.	1.0	Avril, Cliff, Det.	11.0
Garay, Antonio, S.D.	2.5	LaBoy, Travis, S.D.	1.0	Clemons, Chris, Sea.	11.0
Geathers, Robert, Cin.	2.5	Lane, Austen, Jac.	1.0	Cole, Trent, Phi.	11.0
Gilberry, Wallace, K.C.	2.5	* Liuget, Corey, S.D.	1.0	Peppers, Julius, Chi.	11.0
Johnson, Jarret, Bal.	2.5	Lowery, Dwight, Jac.	1.0	Abraham, John, Atl.	9.5
McDaniel, Tony, Mia.	2.5	Martin, Vaughn, S.D.	1.0	Johnson, Charles, Car.	9.0
Moats, Arthur, Buf.	2.5	Mathews, Ricardo, Ind.	1.0	Orakpo, Brian, Was.	9.0
Morgan, Derrick, Ten.	2.5	Mayo, Jerod, N.E.	1.0	Umenyiora, Osi, NY-G	9.0
Peko, Domata, Cin.	2.5	McClain, Jameel, Bal.	1.0	Campbell, Calais, Ariz	8.0
Smith, Eric, NYJ	2.5	McCourty, Jason, Ten.	1.0	Robison, Brian, Min.	8.0
* Ayers, Akeem, Ten.	2.0	McGraw, Jon, K.C.	1.0	Vanden Bosch, Kyle, Det.	8.0
Bell, Yeremiah, Mia.	2.0	McLendon, Steve, Pit.	1.0	* Clayborn, Adrian, T.B.	7.5
Brayton, Tyler, Ind.	2.0	Merriman, Shawne, Buf.	1.0	Harper, Roman, N.O.	7.5
Butler, Donald, S.D.	2.0	Misi, Koa, Mia.	1.0	* Kerrigan, Ryan, Was.	7.5
Coleman, Drew, Jac.	2.0	Mitchell, Earl, Hou.	1.0	Smith, Justin, S.F.	7.5
Dansby, Karlos, Mia.	2.0	Mitchell, Marvin, Mia.	1.0	* Acho, Sam, Ariz	7.0
Deaderick, Brandon, N.E.	2.0	Mitchell, Mike, Oak.	1.0	Brooks, Ahmad, S.F.	7.0
English, Larry, S.D.	2.0	Morrison, Kirk, Buf.	1.0	Melton, Henry, Chi.	7.0
Farrior, James, Pit.	2.0	Mosley, C.J., Jac.	1.0	Smith, Will, N.O.	6.5
Gordon, Amon, K.C.	2.0	Paxson, Scott, Cle.	1.0	Bowen, Stephen, Was.	6.0
Heard, Kellen, Buf.	2.0	Pitoitua, Ropati, NYJ	1.0	Hall, James, St.L	6.0
Jamison, Tim, Hou.	2.0	Polamalu, Troy, Pit.	1.0	Matthews, Clay, G.B.	6.0
Johnson, Derrick, K.C.	2.0	Pouha, Sione, NYJ	1.0	Spencer, Anthony, Dal.	6.0
Johnson, Spencer, Buf.	2.0	Reed, Ed, Bal.	1.0	Carriker, Adam, Was.	5.5
Jones, Reshad, Mia.	2.0	Scott, Bryan, Buf.	1.0	Jenkins, Cullen, Phi.	5.5
Lewis, Ray, Bal.	2.0	Session, Clint, Jac.	1.0	McDonald, Ray, S.F.	5.5
Moala, Fili, Ind.	2.0	Shaughnessy, Matt, Oak.	1.0	Bishop, Desmond, G.B.	5.0
Nelson, Reggie, Cin.	2.0	Sheppard, Lito, Oak.	1.0	Idonije, Israel, Chi.	5.0
Pollard, Bernard, Bal.	2.0	Sims, Pat, Cin.	1.0	* Quinn, Robert, St.L	5.0
Posluszny, Paul, Jac.	2.0	Smith, Shaun, Ten.	1.0	Tollefson, Dave, NY-G	5.0
Timmons, Lawrence, Pit.	2.0	Spikes, Takeo, S.D.	1.0	Tuck, Justin, NY-G	5.0
Wilhite, Jonathan, Den.	2.0	Strickland, Donald, NYJ	1.0	Washington, Daryl, Ariz	5.0
Witherspoon, Will, Ten.	2.0	Ward, T.J., Cle.	1.0	Williams, Kevin, Min.	5.0
Ayanbadejo, Brendon, Bal.	1.5	Warren, Gerard, N.E.	1.0	Galette, Junior, N.O.	4.5
Dixon, Marcus, NYJ	1.5	Webb, Lardarius, Bal.	1.0	Hatcher, Jason, Dal.	4.5
Foote, Larry, Pit.	1.5	Wheeler, Philip, Ind.	1.0	Jackson, Lawrence, Det.	4.5
Hayes, William, Ten.	1.5	Zbikowski, Tom, Bal.	1.0	Schofield, O'Brien, Ariz	4.5
Hood, Ziggy, Pit.	1.5	Allen, Russell, Jac.	0.5	Bennett, Michael, T.B.	4.0
Lawson, Manny, Cin.	1.5	Batten, Danny, Buf.	0.5	Canty, Chris, NY-G	4.0
Mitchell, Jayme, Cle.	1.5	Benard, Marcus, Cle.	0.5	Griffen, Everson, Min.	4.0
Moss, Jarvis, Oak.	1.5	* Braman, Bryan, Hou.	0.5	Hardy, Greg, Car.	4.0
Angerer, Pat, Ind.	1.0	Collins, Nate, Jac.	0.5	Hill, Leroy, Sea.	4.0
Arenas, Javier, K.C.	1.0	Landry, Dawan, Jac.	0.5	* Keiser, Thomas, Car.	4.0
* Bailey, Allen, K.C.	1.0	Marks, Sen'Derrick, Ten.	0.5	Okoye, Amobi, Chi.	4.0
Branch, Tyvon, Oak.	1.0	Nading, Jesse, Hou.	0.5	Sidbury, Lawrence, Atl.	4.0
Brown, Titus, Cle.	1.0	Nolan, Troy, Hou.	0.5	Suh, Ndamukong, Det.	4.0
Byrd, Jairus, Buf.	1.0	Pool, Brodney, NYJ	0.5	Weatherspoon, Sean, Atl.	4.0
Carr, Chris, Bal.	1.0	Pryor, Myron, N.E.	0.5	Dockett, Darnell, Ariz	3.5
Carrington, Alex, Buf.	1.0	Schaefering, Brian, Cle.	0.5	Edwards, Ray, Atl.	3.5
* Carter, Quinton, Den.	1.0	Selvie, George, Jac.	0.5	Kiwanuka, Mathias, NY-G	3.5
Chung, Patrick, N.E.	1.0	Skuta, Dan, Cin.	0.5	Branch, Alan, Sea.	3.0
Clark, Ryan, Pit.	1.0	Wright, Mike, N.E.	0.5	Brock, Raheem, Sea.	3.0
Clements, Nate, Cin.	1.0			Butler, Victor, Dal.	3.0
Cody, Shaun, Hou.	1.0	* Player that was a rookie in 2011		Casillas, Jonathan, N.O.	3.0
Culver, Tyrone, Mia.	1.0			Cofield, Barry, Was.	3.0
Davis, Vontae, Mia.	1.0			Gibson, Gary, St.L	3.0
DeVito, Mike, NYJ	1.0			Haggans, Clark, Ariz	3.0
Douzable, Leger, Jac.	1.0			Hargrove, Anthony, Sea.	3.0
Ellis, Shaun, N.E.	1.0			Laurinaitis, James, St.L	3.0
Finnegan, Cortland, Ten.	1.0			Lenon, Paris, Ariz	3.0
Giordano, Matt, Oak.	1.0			Peters, Corey, Atl.	3.0
Gregg, Kelly, K.C.	1.0			Price, Brian, T.B.	3.0
Haden, Joe, Cle.	1.0				

	Sacks		Sacks
Raji, B.J., G.B.	3.0	Humber, Ramon, N.O.	1.0
Stewart, Darian, St.L	3.0	Jenkins, Malcolm, N.O.	1.0
Tulloch, Stephen, Det.	3.0	Johnson, Tom, N.O.	1.0
Walden, Erik, G.B.	3.0	Jones, Brad, G.B.	1.0
Wynn, Jarius, G.B.	3.0	Jones, Sean, T.B.	1.0
Young, Willie, Det.	3.0	* Jordan, Cameron, N.O.	1.0
Biermann, Kroy, Atl.	2.5	King, Justin, St.L	1.0
Neblett, Andre, Car.	2.5	Laws, Trevor, Phi.	1.0
Patterson, Mike, Phi.	2.5	Levy, DeAndre, Det.	1.0
Shirley, Jason, Car.	2.5	Lofton, Curtis, Atl.	1.0
Tapp, Darryl, Phi.	2.5	* Matthews, Casey, Phi.	1.0
Applewhite, Antwan, Car.	2.0	* McClain, Terrell, Car.	1.0
Bowman, NaVorro, S.F.	2.0	McCoy, Gerald, T.B.	1.0
Chamberlain, Chris, St.L	2.0	McCray, Danny, Dal.	1.0
* Foster, Mason, T.B.	2.0	McIntosh, Rocky, Was.	1.0
Grant, Larry, S.F.	2.0	Mikell, Quintin, St.L	1.0
Greenway, Chad, Min.	2.0	Owens, Chris, Atl.	1.0
Haralson, Parys, S.F.	2.0	* Peterson, Patrick, Ariz	1.0
Hawthorne, David, Sea.	2.0	Porter, Joey, Ariz	1.0
Henderson, E.J., Min.	2.0	Riley, Perry, Was.	1.0
Hunt, Phillip, Phi.	2.0	Robbins, Fred, St.L	1.0
Joseph, Linval, NY-G	2.0	Rodgers-Cromartie, Domin, Phi.	1.0
Landri, Derek, Phi.	2.0	* Rolle, Brian, Phi.	1.0
Lissemore, Sean, Dal.	2.0	Shanle, Scott, N.O.	1.0
Marshall, Richard, Ariz	2.0	Sherels, Marcus, Min.	1.0
McBride, Turk, N.O.	2.0	* Smith, Malcolm, Sea.	1.0
Munnerlyn, Captain, Car.	2.0	* So'oto, Vic, G.B.	1.0
* Neild, Chris, Was.	2.0	Spears, Marcus, Dal.	1.0
* Paea, Stephen, Chi.	2.0	Spievey, Amari, Det.	1.0
Ratliff, Jay, Dal.	2.0	Steltz, Craig, Chi.	1.0
Rhodes, Kerry, Ariz	2.0	Tillman, Charles, Chi.	1.0
Scandrick, Orlando, Dal.	2.0	Torrence, Leigh, N.O.	1.0
Walker, Vance, Atl.	2.0	Watson, Dekoda, T.B.	1.0
Williams, Corey, Det.	2.0	* Williams, Jacquian, NY-G	1.0
Willis, Patrick, S.F.	2.0	* Wilson, Martez, N.O.	1.0
Woodson, Charles, G.B.	2.0	Winfield, Antoine, Min.	1.0
* Wright, K.J., Sea.	2.0	Zombo, Frank, G.B.	1.0
Anderson, James, Car.	1.5	Atogwe, Oshiomogho, Was.	0.5
Ayodele, Remi, Min.	1.5	Cox, Kennard, Sea.	0.5
* Bowers, Da'Quan, T.B.	1.5	Ellis, Sedrick, N.O.	0.5
Bush, Jarrett, G.B.	1.5	* Kearse, Frank, Car.	0.5
Fletcher, London, Was.	1.5	Lewis, Roy, Sea.	0.5
Golston, Kedric, Was.	1.5	Moore, William, Atl.	0.5
Hawk, A.J., G.B.	1.5		
Henderson, Erin, Min.	1.5	* Player that was a rookie in 2011	
Hill, Sammie Lee, Det.	1.5		
Landry, LaRon, Was.	1.5		
Parker, Juqua, Phi.	1.5		
Abdullah, Husain, Min.	1.0		
Ah You, C.J., St.L	1.0		
Babineaux, Jonathan, Atl.	1.0		
Barber, Ronde, T.B.	1.0		
Bigby, Atari, Sea.	1.0		
Boley, Michael, NY-G	1.0		
Bryant, Red, Sea.	1.0		
Burnett, Morgan, G.B.	1.0		
* Carter, David, Ariz	1.0		
Chancellor, Kam, Sea.	1.0		
Chaney, Jamar, Phi.	1.0		
Charleston, Jeff, N.O.	1.0		
Coleman, Kenyon, Dal.	1.0		
Davis, Chauncey, Chi.	1.0		
Dunbar, Jo-Lonn, N.O.	1.0		
Durant, Justin, Det.	1.0		
Eason, Nick, Ariz	1.0		
* Fairley, Nick, Det.	1.0		
Gaither, Omar, Car.	1.0		
Godfrey, Charles, Car.	1.0		
Grant, Deon, NY-G	1.0		

FUMBLES

MOST FUMBLES
AFC:	14 *	Blaine Gabbert, Jacksonville
	14	Matt Moore, Miami
NFC:	10	Sam Bradford, St. Louis
	10	Michael Vick, Philadelphia

MOST FUMBLES, GAME
AFC:	4	Mark Sanchez, N.Y. Jets at Baltimore, October 2
	4	Colt McCoy, Cleveland at San Francisco, October 30
NFC:	3	Tarvaris Jackson, Seattle at San Francisco, September 11
	3	Michael Vick, Philadelphia at Atlanta, September 18
	3	Michael Vick, Philadelphia vs. N.Y. Giants, September 25
	3	Phil Costa, Dallas vs. Washington, September 26

OWN FUMBLES RECOVERED
NFC:	6	Tony Romo, Dallas
AFC:	5	Colt McCoy, Cleveland

OWN FUMBLES RECOVERED, GAME
NFC:	4	Tony Romo, Dallas vs. Washington, September 26 (0 yards, 0 TD)
AFC:	3	Colt McCoy, Cleveland at San Francisco, October 30 (0 yards, 0 TD)

OPPONENTS' FUMBLES RECOVERED
NFC:	4	Jared Allen, Minnesota
AFC:	3	D'Qwell Jackson, Cleveland
	3	Robert Mathis, Indianapolis
	3	Haloti Ngata, Baltimore
	3	Rob Ninkovich, New England

OPPONENTS' FUMBLES RECOVERED, GAME
AFC:	2	Haloti Ngata, Baltimore vs. Pittsburgh, September 11 (0 yards, 0 TD)
	2 *	Colin McCarthy, Tennessee at Buffalo, December 4 (0 yards, 0 TD)
	2	Ellis Lankster, N.Y. Jets at Philadelphia, December 18 (0 yards, 0 TD)
NFC:	2	Kerry Rhodes, Arizona at Cincinnati, December 24 (1 yard, 0 TD)

YARDS
NFC:	103	Juqua Parker, Philadelphia
AFC:	47	Jamaal Anderson, Indianapolis

LONGEST
NFC:	65	Michael Boley, N.Y. Giants vs. St. Louis, September 19 - TD
AFC:	47	Jamaal Anderson, Indianapolis vs. Pittsburgh, September 25 - TD

AFC—TOUCHDOWNS ON FUMBLE RECOVERIES
Anderson, Jamaal, Ind.	1
Atkins, Geno, Cin.	1
Butler, Donald, S.D.	1
Cloherty, Colin, Jac.	1
Collins, Nate, Jac.	1
Curry, Aaron, Oak.	1
Dunlap, Carlos, Cin.	1
Johnson, Jarret, Bal.	1
Johnson, Spencer, Buf.	1
McClain, Jameel, Bal.	1
Ngata, Haloti, Bal.	1

Polamalu, Troy, Pit.	1
Scott, Bryan, Buf.	1
Slauson, Matt, NYJ	1
Smith, Wade, Hou.	1
Wilfork, Vince, N.E.	1
Youboty, Ashton, Jac.	1

NFC—TOUCHDOWNS ON FUMBLE RECOVERIES
Parker, Juqua, Phi.	2
Avril, Cliff, Det.	1
Boley, Michael, NY-G	1
Idonije, Israel, Chi.	1
Jenkins, Malcolm, N.O.	1
Peters, Corey, Atl.	1
* Rolle, Brian, Phi.	1
Tulloch, Stephen, Det.	1
Urlacher, Brian, Chi.	1
Vilma, Jonathan, N.O.	1
Walden, Erik, G.B.	1
Watson, Dekoda, T.B.	1
Williams, Edwin, Chi.	1

AFC FUMBLES—INDIVIDUAL
	Fum	Own Rec	Opp Rec	Yards	Tot Rec
Adams, Mike, Cle.	0	0	1	0	1
Addai, Joseph, Ind.	1	1	0	0	1
Alualu, Tyson, Jac.	0	0	1	7	1
Amato, Ken, Ten.	1	0	0	0	0
Anderson, Jamaal, Ind.	0	0	1	47	1
Anderson, Mark, N.E.	0	0	1	0	1
Angerer, Pat, Ind.	0	0	1	10	1
Arenas, Javier, K.C.	1	0	1	0	1
Arrington, Kyle, N.E.	0	0	1	0	1
Asamoah, Jon, K.C.	0	1	0	-2	1
Atkins, Geno, Cin.	1	0	2	19	2
* Ausberry, David, Oak.	0	1	0	0	1
Ayanbadejo, Brendon, Bal.	0	2	0	0	2
* Ayers, Akeem, Ten.	0	0	1	0	1
Ayers, Robert, Den.	0	0	1	0	1
Babineaux, Jordan, Ten.	0	0	1	0	1
* Bailey, Allen, K.C.	0	0	1	0	1
Ball, Dave, Ten.	0	0	1	0	1
Ball, Lance, Den.	2	0	0	0	0
Batten, Danny, Buf.	0	0	1	0	1
Bell, Yeremiah, Mia.	0	0	1	0	1
Benson, Cedric, Cin.	5	2	0	0	2
Bess, Davone, Mia.	5	3	0	0	3
Bethea, Antoine, Ind.	0	0	1	0	1
Boller, Kyle, Oak.	3	2	0	-6	2
Bowe, Dwayne, K.C.	1	2	0	0	2
Brady, Tom, N.E.	6	3	0	-8	3
* Braman, Bryan, Hou.	0	0	1	0	1
Branch, Tyvon, Oak.	0	0	1	0	1
Britt, Kenny, Ten.	1	0	0	0	0
Brown, Colin, Buf.	1	0	0	-9	0
* Brown, Jalil, K.C.	1	1	0	0	1
Brown, Sheldon, Cle.	0	0	1	0	1
Bush, Michael, Oak.	1	0	0	0	0
Bush, Reggie, Mia.	4	3	0	0	3
Butler, Donald, S.D.	0	0	1	37	1
Byrd, Jairus, Buf.	0	0	1	0	1
Cain, Jeremy, Jac.	1	0	0	-39	0
Campbell, Jason, Oak.	3	1	0	0	1
* Campbell, Tommie, Ten.	1	0	0	0	0
Carey, Vernon, Mia.	0	1	0	0	1
* Carter, Delone, Ind.	3	0	0	0	0
* Casey, Jurrell, Ten.	0	0	1	0	1
Cassel, Matt, K.C.	5	0	0	-3	0
Chandler, Scott, Buf.	1	1	0	0	1
Charles, Jamaal, K.C.	1	0	0	0	0

	Fum	Own Rec	Opp Rec	Yards	Tot Rec
Choice, Tashard, Dal.-Buf.	3	1	0	-1	1
Clark, Dallas, Ind.	1	0	0	0	0
Clements, Nate, Cin.	1	0	2	0	2
Cloherty, Colin, Jac.	0	0	1	8	1
Cody, Shaun, Hou.	0	0	1	0	1
Colbert, Keary, K.C.	1	0	0	0	0
Cole, Marquice, NYJ	0	0	1	0	1
Collins, Kerry, Ind.	4	0	0	0	0
Collins, Nate, Jac.	0	0	1	0	1
Colquitt, Dustin, K.C.	1	0	0	0	0
Conner, Kavell, Ind.	0	0	1	0	1
Cook, Jared, Ten.	2	0	0	0	0
Cosby, Quan, Den.	2	1	0	0	1
Crayton, Patrick, S.D.	2	1	0	0	1
Cribbs, Josh, Cle.	3	2	0	0	2
Cromartie, Antonio, NYJ	2	0	0	0	0
Culver, Tyrone, Mia.	0	0	1	0	1
Curry, Aaron, Oak.	0	0	2	6	2
* Dalton, Andy, Cin.	4	0	0	0	0
* Dareus, Marcell, Buf.	0	0	1	0	1
Decker, Eric, Den.	1	0	0	0	0
Delhomme, Jake, Hou.	1	0	0	0	0
Dillard, Jarett, Jac.	1	1	0	-8	1
Dixon, Marcus, NYJ	0	0	1	0	1
Dombrowski, Brandyn, S.D.	0	1	0	0	1
Dumervil, Elvis, Den.	0	0	1	0	1
Dunlap, Carlos, Cin.	0	0	1	35	1
Edelman, Julian, N.E.	3	2	0	0	2
Essex, Trai, Pit.	0	1	0	0	1
Fanene, Jonathan, Cin.	0	0	2	0	2
Fasano, Anthony, Mia.	0	1	0	0	1
Fells, Daniel, Den.	2	0	0	0	0
Ferguson, D'Brickashaw, NYJ	0	1	0	0	1
Finnegan, Cortland, Ten.	0	0	1	0	1
Fitzpatrick, Ryan, Buf.	7	4	0	0	4
Flacco, Joe, Bal.	11	4	0	-7	4
Fletcher, Dane, N.E.	0	0	1	1	1
Florence, Drayton, Buf.	0	0	1	0	1
Ford, Jacoby, Oak.	3	0	0	0	0
Foster, Arian, Hou.	5	2	0	0	2
* Franklin, Orlando, Den.	0	1	0	0	1
* Gabbert, Blaine, Jac.	14	3	0	-39	3
Gaither, Jared, S.D.	0	1	0	0	1
Garcon, Pierre, Ind.	2	1	0	0	1
Gay, William, Pit.	0	0	1	2	1
* Gilchrist, Marcus, S.D.	0	1	0	40	1
Gocong, Chris, Cle.	0	0	1	0	1
Goodman, André, Den.	1	1	1	0	2
* Green, A.J., Cin.	1	1	0	0	1
Greene, Shonn, NYJ	1	1	0	0	1
Gresham, Jermaine, Cin.	1	0	0	0	0
Haden, Joe, Cle.	0	0	1	0	1
* Hagg, Eric, Cle.	0	0	1	0	1
Hall, Ahmard, Ten.	1	0	0	0	0
Hall, Leon, Cin.	0	0	1	10	1
Hardesty, Montario, Cle.	1	0	0	0	0
Hardwick, Nick, S.D.	0	1	0	0	1
* Harper, Jamie, Ten.	1	1	0	0	1
* Harris, Chris, Den.	0	1	0	0	1
Harris, Nick, Jac.	0	1	0	0	1
Harvey, Derrick, Den.	0	0	1	0	1
Hasselbeck, Matt, Ten.	4	1	0	0	1
Hawkins, Andrew, Cin.	0	1	0	0	1
Hawkins, Lavelle, Ten.	1	0	0	0	0
Henne, Chad, Mia.	1	0	0	-4	0
Hernandez, Aaron, N.E.	1	0	0	0	0
Hester, Jacob, S.D.	2	0	0	0	0
Heyward-Bey, Darrius, Oak.	1	0	0	0	0
Hillis, Peyton, Cle.	2	0	0	0	0
Holmes, Santonio, NYJ	2	0	0	0	0
Hope, Chris, Ten.	0	0	2	0	2
* Houston, Justin, K.C.	0	0	1	0	1
Houston, Lamarr, Oak.	0	0	2	0	2
Hughes, Dante, S.D.	0	0	1	0	1
Hunter, Jason, Den.	0	0	1	18	1
Incognito, Richie, Mia.	0	1	0	0	1
Jackson, D'Qwell, Cle.	0	0	3	1	3
Jackson, Fred, Buf.	2	0	0	0	0
Jamison, Tim, Hou.	0	0	1	0	1
Jammer, Quentin, S.D.	0	0	1	0	1
Johnson, Chris, Ten.	3	1	0	0	1
Johnson, Derrick, K.C.	0	0	1	0	1
Johnson, Jarret, Bal.	0	0	1	26	1
Johnson, Michael, Cin.	0	0	1	0	1
Johnson, Spencer, Buf.	0	0	1	17	1
* Jones, Taiwan, Oak.	0	1	1	0	2
Jones-Drew, Maurice, Jac.	6	3	0	-16	3
Karim, Deji, Jac.	1	0	0	0	0
Keisel, Brett, Pit.	0	0	1	0	1
Keller, Dustin, NYJ	1	0	0	0	0
Kelly, Tommy, Oak.	0	0	1	0	1
* Kerley, Jeremy, NYJ	3	1	0	0	1
Kern, Brett, Ten.	0	1	0	0	1
Knighton, Terrance, Jac.	0	0	0	7	0
Koutouvides, Niko, N.E.	0	0	1	0	1
Kruger, Paul, Bal.	0	0	2	0	2
Kuper, Chris, Den.	0	1	0	0	1
Lacey, Jacob, Ind.	0	0	1	4	1
Landry, Dawan, Jac.	0	0	1	0	1
Lankster, Ellis, NYJ	0	0	2	0	2
Leach, Vonta, Bal.	0	1	0	0	1
* Lefeged, Joe, Ind.	1	0	0	0	0
Leonhard, Jim, NYJ	0	0	1	3	1
Levitre, Andy, Buf.	1	0	0	-6	0
Lewis, Kendrick, K.C.	0	0	1	0	1
Lewis, Marcedes, Jac.	0	2	0	0	2
Linkenbach, Jeffrey, Ind.	0	2	0	0	2
* Liuget, Corey, S.D.	0	0	1	0	1
Lloyd, Brandon, Den.	1	1	0	0	1
Losman, J.P., Mia.	1	1	0	0	1
Love, Kyle, N.E.	0	0	1	0	1
Lowery, Dwight, Jac.	0	0	1	23	1
Mack, Alex, Cle.	0	1	0	0	1
Mangold, Nick, NYJ	1	0	0	-22	0
Manning, Danieal, Hou.	1	0	0	0	0
* Marecic, Owen, Cle.	1	1	0	0	1
Mariani, Marc, Ten.	1	1	0	0	1
Marshall, Brandon, Mia.	1	0	0	0	0
Mathews, Ryan, S.D.	5	1	0	0	1
Mathis, Rashean, Jac.	0	0	1	0	1
Mathis, Robert, Ind.	0	0	3	0	3
Maualuga, Rey, Cin.	0	0	1	0	1
* McCarthy, Colin, Ten.	0	0	2	0	2
McClain, Jameel, Bal.	0	0	2	6	2
McCluster, Dexter, K.C.	4	0	0	0	0
McCourty, Jason, Ten.	0	0	1	0	1
McCown, Luke, Jac.	2	0	0	0	0
McCoy, Colt, Cle.	11	5	0	-9	5
McFadden, Darren, Oak.	1	2	0	0	2
McGahee, Willis, Den.	4	1	0	0	1
McGraw, Jon, K.C.	1	0	0	0	0
McIntyre, Garrett, NYJ	1	0	0	0	0
McKelvin, Leodis, Buf.	1	1	2	0	3
McKinnie, Bryant, Bal.	0	1	0	0	1
McKnight, Joe, NYJ	3	1	0	0	1
McManis, Sherrick, Hou.	1	0	0	0	0
McMichael, Randy, S.D.	0	1	0	0	1
* McPhee, Pernell, Bal.	0	0	1	0	1
Meester, Brad, Jac.	0	1	0	0	1
Mendenhall, Rashard, Pit.	1	0	0	0	0

	Fum	Own Rec	Opp Rec	Yards	Tot Rec
Miller, Heath, Pit.	1	0	0	0	0
Mincey, Jeremy, Jac.	0	0	1	0	1
Mitchell, Earl, Hou.	0	2	0	0	2
Mitchell, Jayme, Cle.	0	0	1	2	1
Moats, Arthur, Buf.	0	0	1	0	1
Molden, Antwaun, N.E.	0	1	0	0	1
Monroe, Eugene, Jac.	0	2	0	0	2
* Moore, Denarius, Oak.	1	0	0	0	0
Moore, Matt, Mia.	14	3	0	-24	3
Moore, Mewelde, Pit.	2	0	0	0	0
* Moore, Rahim, Den.	0	0	1	0	1
Moreno, Knowshon, Den.	1	0	0	0	0
* Moten, Adrian, Ind.	0	1	0	0	1
Mulligan, Matthew, NYJ	0	1	0	0	1
Nading, Jesse, Hou.	0	0	1	0	1
Ngata, Haloti, Bal.	0	0	3	28	3
Ninkovich, Rob, N.E.	0	0	3	0	3
Norwood, Jordan, Cle.	1	1	0	0	1
Nwaneri, Uche, Jac.	0	2	0	0	2
O'Connell, Jake, K.C.	0	1	0	0	1
Ogbonnaya, Chris, Cle.	2	0	0	0	0
Orlovsky, Dan, Ind.	7	1	0	0	1
Orton, Kyle, Den.	2	0	0	0	0
Pace, Calvin, NYJ	0	0	1	0	1
Painter, Curtis, Ind.	5	1	0	-17	1
Palko, Tyler, K.C.	1	0	0	-1	0
Palmer, Carson, Oak.	2	1	0	-1	1
Paxson, Scott, Cle.	0	0	1	0	1
Pears, Erik, Buf.	0	1	0	0	1
Peko, Domata, Cin.	0	0	1	0	1
Polamalu, Troy, Pit.	0	0	1	16	1
Pollard, Bernard, Bal.	0	0	1	0	1
Pool, Brodney, NYJ	0	0	1	33	1
Pouha, Sione, NYJ	0	0	2	0	2
* Pouncey, Mike, Mia.	0	1	0	0	1
* Powell, Bilal, NYJ	1	0	0	0	0
* Prosinski, Chris, Jac.	0	1	0	0	1
Quin, Glover, Hou.	0	0	1	0	1
Redding, Cory, Bal.	0	0	1	0	1
Redman, Isaac, Pit.	2	0	0	0	0
Reece, Marcel, Oak.	1	1	0	0	1
* Reed, Brooks, Hou.	0	0	2	0	2
Reed, David, Bal.	3	0	0	0	0
Reitz, Joe, Ind.	0	1	0	0	1
Rice, Ray, Bal.	2	0	0	0	0
* Ridley, Stevan, N.E.	1	0	0	0	0
Rinehart, Chad, Buf.	0	1	0	0	1
Ringer, Javon, Ten.	1	1	0	0	1
Rivers, Philip, S.D.	9	3	0	-1	3
Roethlisberger, Ben, Pit.	8	2	0	-10	2
Roth, Matt, Jac.	0	0	1	5	1
* Rucker, Chris, Ind.	0	0	1	-1	1
Sanchez, Mark, NYJ	10	1	0	-18	1
Sanders, Emmanuel, Pit.	0	0	1	0	1
Saturday, Jeff, Ind.	0	1	0	0	1
Schaub, Matt, Hou.	3	1	0	-13	1
Scott, Bart, NYJ	0	0	1	9	1
Scott, Bryan, Buf.	0	0	1	0	1
Scott, Jake, Ten.	0	2	0	0	2
Selvie, George, Jac.	0	0	1	0	1
Session, Clint, Jac.	0	0	0	10	0
* Sheard, Jabaal, Cle.	0	0	1	5	1
* Sheppard, Kelvin, Buf.	0	0	1	0	1
Shipley, Jordan, Cin.	1	0	0	0	0
Simpson, Jerome, Cin.	0	1	0	0	1
Slater, Matthew, N.E.	1	0	0	0	0
Slauson, Matt, NYJ	0	1	0	1	1
Smith, Andre, Cin.	0	1	0	0	1
Smith, Alex, Cle.	0	1	0	0	1
Smith, Eric, NYJ	0	0	1	0	1
* Smith, Jimmy, Bal.	1	0	0	0	0
* Smith, Torrey, Bal.	1	0	0	0	0
Smith, Wade, Hou.	0	2	0	0	2
Spiller, C.J., Buf.	2	1	0	0	1
Spitler, Austin, Mia.	0	0	1	0	1
Studebaker, Andy, K.C.	0	0	1	-1	1
Tate, Ben, Hou.	4	0	0	0	0
Tate, Brandon, Cin.	3	1	0	0	1
Tebow, Tim, Den.	13	3	0	-4	3
* Thomas, Daniel, Mia.	2	0	0	0	0
Thomas, Joe, Cle.	0	3	0	0	3
Thomas, Mike, Jac.	1	0	0	0	0
Tolbert, Mike, S.D.	2	0	0	0	0
Trent, Morgan, Jac.	0	0	1	0	1
Turk, Matt, Jac.	1	1	0	-11	1
* Van Dyke, DeMarcus, Oak.	0	0	1	0	1
Vaughn, Cassius, Den.	0	0	1	0	1
Wallace, Mike, Pit.	1	0	0	0	0
Wallace, Seneca, Cle.	1	0	0	0	0
Walter, Kevin, Hou.	0	1	0	0	1
Ward, Hines, Pit.	1	0	0	0	0
Warren, Gerard, N.E.	0	0	1	0	1
* Watt, J.J., Hou.	0	0	2	2	2
Webb, Lardarius, Bal.	2	2	0	0	2
Welker, Wes, N.E.	1	0	0	0	0
Westerman, Jamaal, NYJ	0	0	1	0	1
Wiegmann, Casey, K.C.	0	2	0	0	2
Wilfork, Vince, N.E.	0	0	2	0	2
Williams, D.J., Den.	0	0	1	0	1
* Williams, LaQuan, Bal.	2	1	0	0	1
Williams, Ricky, Bal.	2	0	0	0	0
Willis, Matt, Den.	1	1	0	0	2
Wilson, George, Buf.	0	0	1	0	1
Wilson, Kyle, Cin.	0	0	1	0	1
Winston, Eric, Hou.	0	0	1	0	1
Witherspoon, Will, Ten.	0	0	2	2	2
Yanda, Marshal, Bal.	0	1	0	0	1
* Yates, T.J., Hou.	5	1	0	-5	1
Youboty, Ashton, Jac.	0	0	1	38	1

Yards includes aborted plays, own recoveries and opponents' recoveries.
* *Player that was a rookie in 2011*

NFC FUMBLES—INDIVIDUAL

	Fum	Own Rec	Opp Rec	Yards	Tot Rec
Abraham, John, Atl.	0	0	1	0	1
* Acho, Sam, Ariz	0	0	1	1	1
Allen, Jared, Min.	0	0	4	6	4
Amendola, Danny, St.L	1	1	0	0	1
* Amukamara, Prince, NY-G	0	1	0	0	1
Anderson, James, Car.	0	0	3	0	3
Aromashodu, Devin, Min.	1	1	0	5	1
Austin, Miles, Dal.	1	0	0	0	0
Austin, Terrence, Was.	1	0	0	0	0
Avant, Jason, Phi.	2	0	0	0	0
Avril, Cliff, Det.	0	0	3	24	3
Backus, Jeff, Det.	0	1	0	0	1
Ball, Alan, Dal.	0	1	0	0	1
Banks, Brandon, Was.	7	5	0	0	5
Barber, Marion, Chi.	1	0	0	0	0
Barber, Ronde, T.B.	0	0	1	0	1
Beck, John, Was.	3	2	0	0	2
Bell, Kahlil, Chi.	3	0	0	0	0
Bennett, Earl, Chi.	1	0	0	0	0
Bennett, Michael, T.B.	0	0	2	0	2
Bernard, Rocky, NY-G	0	0	1	0	1
Best, Jahvid, Det.	0	1	0	0	1

2010 INDIVIDUAL STATISTICS—FUMBLES

	Fum	Own Rec	Opp Rec	Yards	Tot Rec		Fum	Own Rec	Opp Rec	Yards	Tot Rec
Bigby, Atari, Sea.	0	0	1	0	1	Guion, Letroy, Min.	0	0	1	0	1
* Black, Ahmad, T.B.	0	0	1	0	1	Haggans, Clark, Ariz	0	0	1	0	1
Blackmon, Will, NY-G	1	0	0	0	0	Hanie, Caleb, Chi.	1	1	0	0	1
Blount, LeGarrette, T.B.	5	0	0	0	0	Hanson, Joselio, Phi.	0	1	1	4	2
Boley, Michael, NY-G	0	0	3	78	3	Harper, Roman, N.O.	0	0	1	0	1
Booker, Lorenzo, Min.	3	0	0	0	0	Harris, Al, St.L	0	0	1	3	1
Boothe, Kevin, NY-G	1	1	0	-8	1	Hartsock, Ben, Car.	0	1	0	0	1
Bowen, Stephen, Was.	0	0	1	-1	1	Harvin, Percy, Min.	2	0	0	0	0
* Bowers, Da'Quan, T.B.	0	0	1	0	1	Hawthorne, David, Sea.	0	0	1	9	1
Bowman, NaVorro, S.F.	0	0	3	0	3	* Helu, Roy, Was.	2	1	0	0	1
Bowman, Zack, Chi.	0	0	1	0	1	Henderson, Devery, N.O.	1	0	0	0	0
Bradford, Sam, St.L	10	2	0	-26	2	Herremans, Todd, Phi.	0	1	0	0	1
Bradshaw, Ahmad, NY-G	1	0	0	0	0	Herrera, Anthony, Min.	0	1	0	0	1
Brees, Drew, N.O.	1	0	0	-15	0	Hester, Devin, Chi.	5	4	0	0	4
Brown, Jason, St.L	0	1	0	0	1	Hightower, Tim, Was.	0	1	0	0	1
Brown, Levi, Ariz	0	1	0	0	1	Hill, Sammie Lee, Det.	0	0	1	0	1
Brown, Ronnie, Phi.	1	0	0	0	0	Hoomanawanui, Michael, St.L	0	1	0	0	1
Bryant, Dez, Dal.	3	1	0	0	1	* Housler, Rob, Ariz	1	0	0	0	0
Bulaga, Bryan, G.B.	0	1	0	0	1	Hurd, Sam, Chi.	1	0	1	2	1
Burleson, Nate, Det.	1	1	0	3	1	Idonije, Israel, Chi.	0	0	2	0	2
Burnett, Morgan, G.B.	0	0	2	25	2	* Ingram, Mark, N.O.	1	0	0	0	0
Campbell, Calais, Ariz	0	0	1	0	1	Jackson, DeSean, Phi.	1	0	0	0	0
Chancellor, Kam, Sea.	0	0	1	0	1	Jackson, Lawrence, Det.	0	0	1	0	1
Clemens, Kellen, St.L	2	1	0	0	1	Jackson, Steven, St.L	2	2	0	0	2
Clutts, Tyler, Chi.	1	0	0	0	0	Jackson, Tanard, T.B.	0	0	1	13	1
* Cobb, Randall, G.B.	3	0	0	0	0	Jackson, Tarvaris, Sea.	9	4	0	-8	4
Cofield, Barry, Was.	0	0	1	3	1	Jacobs, Brandon, NY-G	3	2	0	0	2
Colledge, Daryn, Ariz	0	1	0	0	1	James, Bradie, Dal.	0	0	1	0	1
Colston, Marques, N.O.	1	0	0	0	0	Jefferson, A.J., Ariz	0	1	0	17	1
Considine, Sean, Car.	0	0	1	0	1	Jenkins, Cullen, Phi.	0	0	1	3	1
Costa, Phil, Dal.	4	0	0	-11	0	Jenkins, Malcolm, N.O.	0	0	1	30	1
Cox, Mike, Atl.	1	0	0	0	0	Jenkins, Michael, Min.	2	0	0	0	0
Crosby, Mason, G.B.	0	0	1	2	1	Jennings, Tim, Chi.	0	0	1	0	1
Cruz, Victor, NY-G	1	1	0	0	1	Johnson, Calvin, Det.	1	0	0	0	0
Curry, Dominique, St.L	0	1	0	0	1	Johnson, Josh, T.B.	1	0	0	0	0
Cutler, Jay, Chi.	7	4	0	-8	4	Johnson, Rashad, Ariz	0	0	1	0	1
Davis, Fred, Was.	1	0	0	0	0	* Jones, Colin, S.F.	0	1	0	0	1
Davis, Thomas, Car.	0	0	1	0	1	Jones, Felix, Dal.	5	1	0	0	1
Davis, Vernon, S.F.	3	0	0	0	0	* Jones, Greg, NY-G	0	1	0	0	1
Delmas, Louis, Det.	0	0	1	0	1	Jones, James, G.B.	1	0	0	0	0
Diehl, David, NY-G	0	1	0	0	1	* Jones, Julio, Atl.	1	0	0	0	0
D'Imperio, Ryan, Min.	0	0	2	0	2	Jones, Sean, T.B.	0	0	2	0	2
Dockett, Darnell, Ariz	0	0	2	0	2	* Jordan, Cameron, N.O.	0	0	1	0	1
Doucet, Early, Ariz	1	0	0	0	0	Keith, Brandon, Ariz	0	1	0	0	1
Doughty, Reed, Was.	0	0	1	0	1	* Kelce, Jason, Phi.	1	0	0	0	0
Edwards, Ray, Atl.	0	0	2	64	2	* Kendricks, Lance, St.L	1	0	0	0	0
Elam, Abram, Dal.	0	0	1	1	1	Kiwanuka, Mathias, NY-G	0	0	1	0	1
Faine, Jeff, T.B.	1	0	0	-7	0	Kluwe, Chris, Min.	1	0	0	-6	0
Feeley, A.J., St.L	3	0	0	0	0	Knox, Johnny, Chi.	1	0	0	0	0
Flynn, Matt, G.B.	1	0	0	0	0	Kolb, Kevin, Ariz	8	0	0	-8	0
Forté, Matt, Chi.	2	0	0	0	0	Kosier, Kyle, Dal.	0	1	0	0	1
* Foster, Mason, T.B.	0	0	1	0	1	Landri, Derek, Phi.	0	0	1	5	1
Franks, Dominique, Atl.	1	0	0	0	0	Landry, LaRon, Was.	0	0	1	3	1
Free, Doug, Dal.	0	1	0	0	1	Lang, T.J., G.B.	0	1	0	0	1
Freeman, Josh, T.B.	9	2	0	-13	2	Laurinaitis, James, St.L	0	0	1	0	1
Gaffney, Jabar, Was.	1	0	0	0	0	Leber, Ben, St.L	0	0	1	0	1
Gandy, Dylan, Det.	0	1	0	0	1	Lee, Sean, Dal.	0	0	2	0	2
Garza, Roberto, Chi.	1	0	0	0	0	Lenon, Paris, Ariz	0	0	1	0	1
Gerhart, Toby, Min.	1	1	1	0	2	* Lewis, Dion, Phi.	1	0	0	0	0
Ginn, Ted, S.F.	0	1	0	0	1	Lewis, Roy, Sea.	0	1	1	7	2
Goldson, Dashon, S.F.	0	0	1	0	1	Loadholt, Phil, Min.	0	1	0	0	1
Gordy, Josh, St.L	0	1	0	0	1	Lofton, Curtis, Atl.	0	0	1	0	1
Gore, Frank, S.F.	2	0	0	0	0	Logan, Stefan, Det.	6	4	0	0	4
Graham, Earnest, T.B.	1	3	0	-2	3	Longwell, Ryan, Min.	0	1	0	0	1
Graham, Jimmy, N.O.	1	0	0	0	0	Lorig, Erik, T.B.	0	1	0	0	1
Grant, Deon, NY-G	0	0	1	1	1	Lynch, Marshawn, Sea.	3	2	0	0	2
Grant, Ryan, G.B.	1	0	0	0	0	Maclin, Jeremy, Phi.	1	0	0	0	0
Greenway, Chad, Min.	0	0	1	0	1	* Madu, Mossis, T.B.	0	1	0	0	1
Griffen, Everson, Min.	0	0	1	9	1	Manning, Eli, NY-G	8	3	0	-3	3
Grossman, Rex, Was.	8	2	0	-9	2	* Marsh, Curtis, Phi.	2	0	0	0	0

	Fum	Own Rec	Opp Rec	Yards	Tot Rec
Masthay, Tim, G.B.	2	1	0	0	1
Mattison, Bryan, St.L	0	1	0	0	1
* Maxwell, Byron, Sea.	0	1	0	1	1
* McClain, Terrell, Car.	0	0	1	0	1
McCown, Josh, Chi.	2	2	0	0	2
McCoy, Anthony, Sea.	0	1	0	0	1
McCoy, LeSean, Phi.	1	0	0	0	0
McDonald, Brandon, Det.	1	0	0	0	0
McDonald, Clinton, Sea.	1	0	1	2	1
McDonald, Ray, S.F.	0	0	1	0	1
McNabb, Donovan, Min.	2	0	0	0	0
McQuistan, Paul, Sea.	0	1	0	0	1
Mikell, Quintin, St.L	0	0	1	14	1
* Miller, Bruce, S.F.	1	0	0	0	0
Montgomery, Will, Was.	1	0	0	-8	0
Morris, Maurice, Det.	1	0	0	0	0
Munnerlyn, Captain, Car.	0	0	1	0	1
* Murray, DeMarco, Dal.	1	2	0	0	2
Neblett, Andre, Car.	0	0	2	0	1
Newhouse, Marshall, G.B.	1	1	0	0	1
Newman, Terence, Dal.	0	0	1	7	1
* Newton, Cam, Car.	5	3	0	-4	3
Nicholas, Stephen, Atl.	0	0	1	2	1
Obomanu, Ben, Sea.	0	0	1	0	1
Ogletree, Kevin, Dal.	1	0	0	0	0
Olsen, Greg, Car.	1	0	0	0	0
Orakpo, Brian, Was.	0	0	1	0	1
Parker, Juqua, Phi.	0	0	2	103	2
Parker, Preston, T.B.	8	4	0	-8	4
Patterson, Mike, Phi.	0	0	2	0	2
* Paysinger, Spencer, NY-G	0	0	1	0	1
Peppers, Julius, Chi.	0	0	2	0	2
Peters, Corey, Atl.	0	0	1	13	1
Peters, Jason, Phi.	0	1	0	7	1
Peterson, Adrian, Min.	1	3	0	0	3
* Peterson, Patrick, Ariz	4	2	0	-1	2
* Pettis, Austin, St.L	2	0	0	0	0
* Pilares, Kealoha, Car.	1	1	0	0	1
* Ponder, Christian, Min.	6	0	0	-9	0
Poppinga, Brady, St.L	0	0	2	0	2
Porter, Quinn, St.L	1	1	0	0	1
Porter, Tracy, N.O.	0	0	1	0	1
Raji, B.J., G.B.	0	0	1	1	1
Ratliff, Jay, Dal.	0	0	1	0	1
* Raymond, Mistral, Min.	0	0	1	26	1
Rhodes, Kerry, Ariz	0	0	2	1	2
Rice, Sidney, Sea.	1	0	0	0	0
Riley, Perry, Was.	0	0	2	3	2
Roberts, Andre, Ariz	1	2	0	0	2
Robinson, Michael, Sea.	1	0	0	0	0
Robison, Brian, Min.	0	0	2	0	2
Rodgers, Aaron, G.B.	4	2	0	0	2
* Rodgers, Jacquizz, Atl.	1	0	0	0	0
* Rolle, Brian, Phi.	0	0	1	22	1
Romo, Tony, Dal.	6	6	0	-3	6
Ross, Aaron, NY-G	2	0	0	0	0
Ryan, Matt, Atl.	5	2	0	0	2
* Salas, Greg, St.L	3	0	0	0	0
Samuel, Asante, Phi.	0	0	1	0	1
Sanders, James, Atl.	0	0	1	25	1
Sanford, Jamarca, Min.	0	0	2	3	2
Scheffler, Tony, Det.	1	0	1	0	1
* Scott, Da'Rel, NY-G	1	0	0	0	0
Sendlein, Lyle, Ariz	0	2	0	0	2
Sensabaugh, Gerald, Dal.	0	0	2	0	2
Shockey, Jeremy, Car.	2	0	0	0	0
Sims, Rob, Det.	0	1	0	0	1
Skelton, John, Ariz	4	2	0	-10	2
* Smith, Aldon, S.F.	0	0	1	0	1
Smith, Alex, S.F.	7	4	0	0	4
Smith, Alphonso, Det.	0	0	1	0	1
Smith, Justin, S.F.	0	0	1	0	1
Smith, Kevin, Det.	1	0	0	0	0
Smith, Reggie, S.F.	1	0	0	0	0
Smith, Steve, Phi.	1	0	0	0	0
Smith, Steve, Car.	3	0	0	0	0
Snelling, Jason, Atl.	0	0	1	0	1
Sopoaga, Isaac, S.F.	0	0	1	0	1
Spaeth, Matt, Chi.	0	1	0	0	1
Spievey, Amari, Det.	0	0	1	0	1
Stafford, Matthew, Det.	5	1	0	-4	1
Starks, James, G.B.	2	1	0	0	1
Stewart, Jonathan, Car.	1	0	0	0	0
Stroughter, Sammie, T.B.	1	0	0	0	0
Stuckey, Chansi, Ariz	1	0	0	0	0
Tate, Golden, Sea.	1	0	0	0	0
Taylor, Chester, Ariz	0	1	0	0	1
Thomas, Earl, Sea.	0	0	2	0	2
* Thomas, Josh, Car.	0	0	1	0	1
Thomas, Pierre, N.O.	1	0	0	0	0
* Thompson, Brandyn, Was.	0	1	0	0	1
Tillman, Charles, Chi.	0	0	2	4	2
Tollefson, Dave, NY-G	0	0	1	0	1
Torain, Ryan, Was.	1	1	0	0	1
Tukuafu, Will, S.F.	0	0	1	12	1
Tulloch, Stephen, Det.	0	0	3	4	3
Turner, Michael, Atl.	3	0	0	0	0
Unger, Max, Sea.	2	0	0	-14	0
Urlacher, Brian, Chi.	0	0	2	29	2
Vanden Bosch, Kyle, Det.	0	0	1	0	1
Vick, Michael, Phi.	10	4	0	-2	4
Vilma, Jonathan, N.O.	0	0	3	0	3
Walden, Erik, G.B.	0	0	1	5	1
Walker, Delanie, S.F.	0	1	1	0	2
Walker, Vance, Atl.	0	0	1	0	1
Ware, DeMarcus, Dal.	0	0	1	0	1
Washington, Leon, Sea.	2	1	0	0	1
Watson, Dekoda, T.B.	0	0	1	7	1
Weatherspoon, Sean, Atl.	0	0	1	0	1
Webb, Joe, Min.	1	0	0	0	0
Wells, Beanie, Ariz	4	1	0	0	1
Whitehurst, Charlie, Sea.	2	1	0	0	1
Whitner, Donte, S.F.	0	0	3	3	3
Williams, Cadillac, St.L	1	0	0	0	0
Williams, Edwin, Chi.	0	1	0	0	1
* Williams, Jacquian, NY-G	0	0	3	0	3
Williams, Keiland, Det.	2	0	0	0	0
Williams, Mike, T.B.	2	0	0	0	0
Williams, Tramon, G.B.	0	0	1	0	1
Willis, Patrick, S.F.	0	0	2	0	2
Wilson, Josh, Was.	0	0	1	4	1
Winslow, Kellen, T.B.	2	0	0	-4	0
Witten, Jason, Dal.	1	1	0	0	1
Woodson, Charles, G.B.	0	0	1	-1	1
Wragge, Tony, St.L	1	0	0	-8	0
* Wright, K.J., Sea.	0	0	1	30	1
* Young, Titus, Det.	1	1	0	0	1
Young, Vince, Phi.	2	2	0	0	2
Zuttah, Jeremy, T.B.	0	1	0	0	1

Yards includes aborted plays, own recoveries and opponents' recoveries.

* Player that was a rookie in 2011

AMERICAN FOOTBALL CONFERENCE—FUMBLES

	Fum	Own Rec	Fum OB	TD	Opp Rec	TD	Fum Yards	Tot Rec
New England	13	6	2	0	11	1	-7	17
Buffalo	16	10	1	0	11	2	1	21
Oakland	16	9	0	0	8	1	-1	17
Pittsburgh	16	3	0	0	4	1	8	7
Cincinnati	17	7	2	0	12	2	64	19
Kansas City	17	7	0	0	6	0	-7	13
Tennessee	17	8	1	0	12	0	2	20
Houston	20	9	0	1	10	0	-16	19
San Diego	20	10	2	0	4	1	76	14
Cleveland	22	14	2	0	11	0	-1	25
Baltimore	24	12	0	0	11	3	53	23
Indianapolis	24	9	0	0	9	1	43	18
N.Y. Jets	25	7	2	1	12	0	6	19
Jacksonville	27	17	2	0	11	3	-15	28
Miami	28	14	2	0	3	0	-28	17
Denver	30	11	2	0	9	0	14	20
AFC Total	332	153	18	2	144	15	192	297
AFC Average	20.8	9.6	1.1	0.1	9.0	0.9	12.0	18.6

NATIONAL FOOTBALL CONFERENCE—FUMBLES

	Fum	Own Rec	Fum OB	TD	Opp Rec	TD	Fum Yards	Tot Rec
New Orleans	6	0	1	0	7	2	15	7
Atlanta	12	2	2	0	10	1	104	12
Carolina	13	5	2	0	10	0	-4	15
San Francisco	14	7	2	0	15	0	15	22
Green Bay	15	7	2	0	7	1	32	14
N.Y. Giants	18	10	0	0	11	1	68	21
Detroit	20	11	2	0	13	2	27	24
Minnesota	20	8	3	0	15	0	34	23
Seattle	22	12	1	0	9	0	27	21
Philadelphia	23	9	2	0	9	3	142	18
Arizona	24	14	1	0	9	0	0	23
Dallas	24	14	1	0	9	0	-6	23
Washington	25	13	1	0	8	0	-5	21
Chicago	26	13	4	1	11	2	27	24
St. Louis	27	12	2	0	6	0	-17	18
Tampa Bay	30	12	2	0	10	1	-14	22
NFC Total	319	149	28	1	159	13	445	308
NFC Average	19.9	9.3	1.8	0.1	9.9	0.8	27.8	19.3
NFL Total	651	302	46	3	303	28	637	605
NFL Average	20.3	9.4	1.4	0.1	9.5	0.9	19.9	18.9

Inside the Numbers

GREATEST COMEBACKS IN NFL HISTORY
(Most Points Overcome To Win Game)

REGULAR SEASON GAMES

FROM 28 POINTS BEHIND TO WIN:
December 7, 1980, at San Francisco

New Orleans	14	21	0	0	0	— 35
San Francisco	0	7	14	14	3	— 38

- NO — Harris 33 pass from Manning (Ricardo kick)
- NO — Childs 21 pass from Manning (Ricardo kick)
- NO — Holmes 1 run (Ricardo kick)
- SF — Solomon 57 punt return (Wersching kick)
- NO — Holmes 1 run (Ricardo kick)
- NO — Harris 41 pass from Manning (Ricardo kick)
- SF — Montana 1 run (Wersching kick)
- SF — Clark 71 pass from Montana (Wersching kick)
- SF — Solomon 14 pass from Montana (Wersching kick)
- SF — Elliott 7 run (Wersching kick)
- SF — FG Wersching 36

FROM 26 POINTS BEHIND TO WIN:
September 21, 1997, at Buffalo

Indianapolis	14	12	0	9	— 35
Buffalo	0	10	6	21	— 37

- Ind — Bailey 10 pass from Harbaugh (Blanchard kick)
- Ind — Faulk 10 run (Blanchard kick)
- Ind — FG Blanchard 39
- Ind — FG Blanchard 36
- Ind — FG Blanchard 49
- Ind — FG Blanchard 22
- Buff — Johnson 16 pass from Collins (Christie kick)
- Buff — FG Christie 27
- Buff — A. Smith 15 run (2-pt attempt failed)
- Ind — FG Blanchard 25
- Buff — Early 4 pass from Collins (Christie kick)
- Buff — A. Smith 1 run (Christie kick)
- Buff — A. Smith 54 run (Christie kick)
- Ind — Harrison 2 pass from Justin (2-pt attempt failed)

FROM 25 POINTS BEHIND TO WIN:
November 8, 1987, at St. Louis

Tampa Bay	7	7	14	0	— 28
St. Louis	0	3	0	28	— 31

- TB — Carrier 5 pass from DeBerg (Igwebuike kick)
- TB — Carter 3 pass from DeBerg (Igwebuike kick)
- StL — FG Gallery 31
- TB — Smith 34 pass from DeBerg (Igwebuike kick)
- TB — Smith 3 run (Igwebuike kick)
- StL — Awalt 4 pass from Lomax (Gallery kick)
- StL — Noga 23 fumble recovery (Gallery kick)
- StL — J. Smith 11 pass from Lomax (Gallery kick)
- StL — J. Smith 17 pass from Lomax (Gallery kick)

FROM 24 POINTS BEHIND TO WIN:
October 27, 1946, at Washington

Philadelphia	0	0	14	14	— 28
Washington	10	14	0	0	— 24

- Wash — Rosato 2 run (Poillon kick)
- Wash — FG Poillon 28
- Wash — Rosato 4 run (Poillon kick)
- Wash — Lapka recovered fumble in end zone (Poillon kick)
- Phil — Steele 1 run (Lio kick)
- Phil — Pritchard 45 pass from Thompson (Lio kick)
- Phil — Steinke 7 pass from Thompson (Lio kick)
- Phil — Ferrante 30 pass from Thompson (Lio kick)

FROM 24 POINTS BEHIND TO WIN:
October 20, 1957, at Detroit

Baltimore	7	14	6	0	— 27
Detroit	0	3	7	21	— 31

- Balt — Mutscheller 15 pass from Unitas (Rechichar kick)
- Det — FG Martin 47
- Balt — Moore 72 pass from Unitas (Rechichar kick)
- Balt — Mutscheller 52 pass from Unitas (Rechichar kick)
- Balt — Moore 4 pass from Unitas (kick failed)
- Det — Junker 14 pass from Rote (Layne kick)
- Det — Cassady 26 pass from Layne (Layne kick)
- Det — Johnson 1 run (Layne kick)
- Det — Cassady 29 pass from Layne (Layne kick)

FROM 24 POINTS BEHIND TO WIN:
October 25, 1959, at Minneapolis

Philadelphia	0	0	21	7	— 28
Chicago Cardinals	7	10	7	0	— 24

- Cardinals — Crow 10 pass from Roach (Conrad kick)
- Cardinals — J. Hill 77 blocked field goal return (Conrad kick)
- Cardinals — FG Conrad 15
- Cardinals — Lane 37 interception return (Conrad kick)
- Phil — Barnes 1 run (Walston kick)
- Phil — McDonald 29 pass from Van Brocklin (Walston kick)
- Phil — Barnes 2 run (Walston kick)
- Phil — McDonald 22 pass from Van Brocklin (Walston kick)

FROM 24 POINTS BEHIND TO WIN:
October 23, 1960, at Denver

Boston	10	7	7	0	— 24
Denver	0	0	14	17	— 31

- Bos — FG Cappelletti 12
- Bos — Colclough 10 pass from Songin (Cappelletti kick)
- Bos — Wells 6 pass from Songin (Cappelletti kick)
- Bos — Miller 47 pass from Songin (Cappelletti kick)
- Den — Carmichael 21 pass from Tripucka (Mingo kick)
- Den — Jessup 19 pass from Tripucka (Mingo kick)
- Den — Carmichael 35 lateral from Taylor, pass from Tripucka (Mingo kick)
- Den — Taylor 8 pass from Tripucka (Mingo kick)
- Den — FG Mingo 9

FROM 24 POINTS BEHIND TO WIN:
December 15, 1974, at Miami

New England	21	3	0	3	— 27
Miami	0	17	7	10	— 34

- NE — Hannah recovered fumble in end zone (J. Smith kick)
- NE — Sanders 23 interception return (J. Smith kick)
- NE — Herron 4 pass from Plunkett (J. Smith kick)
- NE — FG J. Smith 35
- Mia — Nottingham 1 run (Yepremian kick)
- Mia — Baker 37 pass from Morrall (Yepremian kick)
- Mia — FG Yepremian 28
- Mia — Baker 46 pass from Morrall (Yepremian kick)
- NE — FG J. Smith 34
- Mia — Nottingham 2 run (Yepremian kick)
- Mia — FG Yepremian 40

FROM 24 POINTS BEHIND TO WIN:
December 4, 1977, at Minnesota

San Francisco	0	10	14	3	— 27
Minnesota	0	0	7	21	— 28

- SF — Delvin Williams 2 run (Wersching kick)
- SF — FG Wersching 31
- SF — Dave Williams 80 kickoff return (Wersching kick)
- SF — Delvin Williams 5 run (Wersching kick)
- Minn — McClanahan 15 pass from Lee (Cox kick)
- Minn — Rashad 8 pass from Kramer (Cox kick)
- Minn — Tucker 9 pass from Kramer (Cox kick)
- SF — FG Wersching 31
- Minn — S. White 69 pass from Kramer (Cox kick)

FROM 24 POINTS BEHIND TO WIN:
September 23, 1979, at Denver

Seattle	10	10	14	0	— 34
Denver	0	10	21	6	— 37

- Sea — FG Herrera 28
- Sea — Doornink 5 run (Herrera kick)
- Den — FG Turner 27
- Sea — Doornink 5 run (Herrera kick)
- Den — Armstrong 2 run (Turner kick)
- Sea — FG Herrera 22
- Sea — McCullum 13 pass from Zorn (Herrera kick)
- Sea — Smith 1 run (Herrera kick)
- Den — Studdard 2 pass from Morton (Turner kick)
- Den — Moses 11 pass from Morton (Turner kick)
- Den — Upchurch 35 pass from Morton (Turner kick)
- Den — Lytle 1 run (kick failed)

FROM 24 POINTS BEHIND TO WIN:
September 23, 1979, at Cincinnati

Houston	0	10	17	0	3	— 30
Cincinnati	14	10	0	3	0	— 27

- Cin — Johnson 1 run (Bahr kick)
- Cin — Alexander 2 run (Bahr kick)
- Cin — Johnson 1 run (Bahr kick)
- Cin — FG Bahr 52
- Hou — Burrough 35 pass from Pastorini (Fritsch kick)
- Hou — FG Fritsch 33

Hou — Campbell 8 run
(Fritsch kick)
Hou — Caster 22 pass from Pastorini
(Fritsch kick)
Hou — FG Fritsch 47
Cin — FG Bahr 55
Hou — FG Fritsch 29

FROM 24 POINTS BEHIND TO WIN:
November 22, 1982, at Los Angeles
San Diego   10 14 0 0 — 24
L.A. Raiders   0 7 14 7 — 28
SD — FG Benirschke 19
SD — Scales 29 pass from Fouts
(Benirschke kick)
SD — Muncie 2 run
(Benirschke kick)
SD — Muncie 1 run
(Benirschke kick)
Raiders — Christensen 1 pass from
Plunkett (Bahr kick)
Raiders — Allen 3 run (Bahr kick)
Raiders — Allen 6 run (Bahr kick)
Raiders — Hawkins 1 run (Bahr kick)

FROM 24 POINTS BEHIND TO WIN:
September 26, 1988, at Denver
L.A. Raiders   0 0 14 13 3 — 30
Denver   7 17 0 3 0 — 27
Den — Dorsett 1 run (Karlis kick)
Den — Dorsett 1 run (Karlis kick)
Den — Sewell 7 pass from Elway
(Karlis kick)
Den — FG Karlis 39
Raiders — Smith 40 pass from
Schroeder (Bahr kick)
Raiders — Smith 42 pass from
Schroeder (Bahr kick)
Raiders — FG Bahr 28
Raiders — Allen 4 run (Bahr kick)
Den — FG Karlis 25
Raiders — FG Bahr 44
Raiders — FG Bahr 35

FROM 24 POINTS BEHIND TO WIN:
December 6, 1992, at Tampa
L.A. Rams   0 3 21 7 — 31
Tampa Bay   6 21 0 0 — 27
TB — FG Murray 34
TB — FG Murray 47
TB — Armstrong 81 pass from
Testaverde (Murray kick)
TB — Jones 26 fumble recovery
(Murray kick)
Rams — FG Zendejas 18
TB — Carrier 10 pass from
Testaverde (Murray kick)
Rams — Anderson 40 pass from
Everett (Zendejas kick)
Rams — Chadwick 27 pass from
Everett (Zendejas kick)
Rams — Lang 1 run (Zendejas kick)
Rams — Carter 8 pass from Everett
(Zendejas kick)

FROM 24 POINTS BEHIND TO WIN:
October 2, 2011, at Dallas
Detroit   0 3 14 17 — 34
Dallas   7 13 10 0 — 30
Dall — Bryant 25 pass from Romo
(Bailey kick)
Dall — Bryant 6 pass from Romo
(Bailey kick)
Dall — FG Bailey 41
Det — FG Hanson 33
Dall — FG Bailey 35
Dall — Witten 1 pass from Romo
(Bailey kick)

Det — Carpenter 34 interception
return (Hanson kick)
Det — Houston 56 interception
return (Hanson kick)
Dall — FG Bailey 23
Det — Johnson 23 pass from
Stafford (Hanson kick)
Det — FG Hanson 51
Det — Johnson 2 pass from Stafford
(Hanson kick)

POSTSEASON GAMES

FROM 32 POINTS BEHIND TO WIN:
AFC First-Round Playoff Game
January 3, 1993, at Buffalo
Houston   7 21 7 3 0 — 38
Buffalo   3 0 28 7 3 — 41
Hou — Jeffires 3 pass from Moon
(Del Greco kick)
Buff — FG Christie 36
Hou — Slaughter 7 pass from Moon
(Del Greco kick)
Hou — Duncan 26 pass from Moon
(Del Greco kick)
Hou — Jeffires 27 pass from Moon
(Del Greco kick)
Hou — McDowell 58 interception
return (Del Greco kick)
Buff — Davis 1 run (Christie kick)
Buff — Beebe 38 pass from Reich
(Christie kick)
Buff — Reed 26 pass from Reich
(Christie kick)
Buff — Reed 18 pass from Reich
(Christie kick)
Buff — Reed 17 pass from Reich
(Christie kick)
Hou — FG Del Greco 26
Buff — FG Christie 32

FROM 24 POINTS BEHIND TO WIN:
NFC First-Round Playoff Game
January 5, 2003, at San Francisco
N.Y. Giants   7 21 10 0 — 38
San Francisco   7 7 8 17 — 39
SF — Owens 76 pass from Garcia
(Chandler kick)
NYG — Toomer 12 pass from Collins
(Bryant kick)
NYG — Shockey 2 pass from Collins
(Bryant kick)
SF — Barlow 1 run (Chandler kick)
NYG — Toomer 8 pass from Collins
(Bryant kick)
NYG — Toomer 24 pass from Collins
(Bryant kick)
NYG — Barber 6 run (Bryant kick)
NYG — FG Bryant 21
SF — Owens 26 pass from Garcia
(Owens from Garcia)
SF — Garcia 14 run
(Owens from Garcia)
SF — Garcia 14 run
(Owens from Garcia)
SF — FG Chandler 25
SF — Streets 13 pass from Garcia
(2-pt attempt failed)

FROM 20 POINTS BEHIND TO WIN:
Western Conference Playoff Game
December 22, 1957, at San Francisco
Detroit   0 7 14 10 — 31
San Francisco   14 10 3 0 — 27
SF — Owens 34 pass from Tittle
(Soltau kick)
SF — McElhenny 47 pass from
Tittle (Soltau kick)

Det — Junker 4 pass from Rote
(Martin kick)
SF — Wilson 12 pass from Tittle
(Soltau kick)
SF — FG Soltau 25
SF — FG Soltau 10
Det — Tracy 2 run (Martin kick)
Det — Tracy 58 run (Martin kick)
Det — Gedman 3 run (Martin kick)
Det — FG Martin 14

FROM 18 POINTS BEHIND TO WIN:
NFC Divisional Playoff Game
December 23, 1972, at San Francisco
Dallas   3 10 0 17 — 30
San Francisco   7 14 7 0 — 28
SF — Washington 97 kickoff return
(Gossett kick)
Dall — FG Fritsch 37
SF — Schreiber 1 run
(Gossett kick)
SF — Schreiber 1 run
(Gossett kick)
Dall — FG Fritsch 45
Dall — Alworth 28 pass from Morton
(Fritsch kick)
SF — Schreiber 1 run
(Gossett kick)
Dall — FG Fritsch 27
Dall — Parks 20 pass from Staubach
(Fritsch kick)
Dall — Sellers 10 pass from
Staubach (Fritsch kick)

FROM 18 POINTS BEHIND TO WIN:
AFC Divisional Playoff Game
January 4, 1986, at Miami
Cleveland   7 7 7 0 — 21
Miami   3 0 14 7 — 24
Mia — FG Reveiz 51
Cle — Newsome 16 pass from
Kosar (Bahr kick)
Cle — Byner 21 run (Bahr kick)
Cle — Byner 66 run (Bahr kick)
Mia — Moore 6 pass from Marino
(Reveiz kick)
Mia — Davenport 31 run
(Reveiz kick)
Mia — Davenport 1 run
(Reveiz kick)

FROM 18 POINTS BEHIND TO WIN:
AFC Divisional Playoff Game
January 21, 2007, at Indianapolis
New England   7 14 7 6 — 34
Indianapolis   3 3 15 17 — 38
NE — Mankins 0 fumble recovery
(Gostkowski kick)
Ind — FG Vinatieri 42
NE — Dillon 7 run (Gostkowski
kick)
NE — Samuel 39 interception return
(Gostkowski kick)
Ind — FG Vinatieri 26
Ind — Manning 1 run (Vinatieri kick)
Ind — Klecko 1 pass from Manning
(Harrison from Manning)
NE — Gaffney 6 pass from Brady
(Gostkowski kick)
Ind — Saturday 0 fumble recovery
(Vinatieri kick)
NE — FG Gostkowski 28
Ind — FG Vinatieri 36
NE — FG Gostkowski 43
Ind — Addai 3 run (Vinatieri kick)

RECORDS FOR NFL TEAMS FOR MOST POINTS IN A GAME (REGULAR SEASON ONLY)

Note: When the record has been achieved more than once, only the most recent game is shown; summaries are listed in alphabetical order by conference. Bold face indicates team holding record.

BALTIMORE RAVENS
December 13, 2009, at Baltimore

Detroit	0	3	0	0 —	3
Baltimore	3	17	21	7 —	48

TD: Balt—Willis McGahee 2, Derrick Mason, Le'Ron McClain, Ray Rice, Troy Smith. TD Passes: Balt—Joe Flacco. FG: Balt—Billy Cundiff 2; Det—Jason Hanson.

BUFFALO BILLS
September 18, 1966, at Buffalo

Miami	3	7	0	14 —	24
Buffalo	21	27	3	7 —	58

TD: Buff—Bobby Burnett 2, Butch Byrd 2, Jack Spikes 2, Bobby Crockett, Jack Kemp; Mia—Dave Kocourek, Bo Roberson, John Roderick. TD Passes: Buff—Jack Kemp, Daryle Lamonica; Mia—George Wilson 3. FG: Buff—Booth Lusteg; Mia—Gene Mingo.

CINCINNATI BENGALS
December 17, 1989, at Cincinnati

Houston	0	0	0	7 —	7
Cincinnati	21	10	21	9 —	61

TD: Cin—Eddie Brown 2, Eric Ball, James Brooks, Ira Hillary, Rodney Holman, Tim McGee, Craig Taylor; Hou—Lorenzo White. TD Passes: Cin—Boomer Esiason 4, Erik Wilhelm. FG: Cin—Jim Breech 2.

CLEVELAND BROWNS
November 7, 1954, at Cleveland

Washington	0	3	0	0 —	3
Cleveland	13	14	21	14 —	62

TD: Cle—Darrell Brewster 2, Mo Bassett, Ken Gorgal, Otto Graham, Dub Jones, Dante Lavelli, Curley Morrison. TD Passes: Cle—George Ratterman 3, Otto Graham. FG: Cle—Lou Groza 2; Wash—Vic Janowicz.

DENVER BRONCOS
October 6, 1963, at Denver

San Diego	13	7	0	14 —	34
Denver	3	14	9	24 —	50

TD: Den—Lionel Taylor 2, Goose Gonsoulin, Gene Prebola, Donnie Stone; SD—Keith Lincoln 2, Lance Alworth, Paul Lowe, Jacque MacKinnon. TD Passes: Den—John McCormick 3; SD—Tobin Rote 3, John Hadl 2. FG: Den—Gene Mingo 5.

HOUSTON TEXANS
December 30, 2007 at Houston

Jacksonville	7	7	7	7 —	28
Houston	0	21	14	7 —	42

TD: Jax—Earnest Wilford 2, Matt Jones, Reggie Williams; Hou—Andre Davis 2, Ron Dayne 2, Owen Daniels, Darius Walker. TD Passes: Jax—Quinn Gray 4; Hou—Sage Rosenfels.

INDIANAPOLIS COLTS
December 12, 1976, at Baltimore

Buffalo	3	3	7	7 —	20
Baltimore Colts	7	13	28	10 —	58

TD: Balt—Roger Carr, Raymond Chester, Glenn Doughty, Roosevelt Leaks, Derrel Luce, Lydell Mitchell, Howard Stevens; Buff—Bob Chandler, O.J. Simpson. TD Passes: Balt—Bert Jones 3; Buff—Gary Marangi. FG: Balt—Toni Linhart 3; Buff—George Jakowenko 2.

JACKSONVILLE JAGUARS
December 23, 2007, at Jacksonville

Oakland	0	3	0	8 —	11
Jacksonville	14	14	7	14 —	49

TD: Oak—Zach Miller; Jax—Richard Angulo, David Garrard, Greg Jones, Matt Jones, Maurice Jones-Drew, Fred Taylor, Reggie Williams. TD Passes: Oak—JaMarcus Russell; Jax—David Garrard 2, Quinn Gray 2. FG: Oak—Sebastian Janikowski.

KANSAS CITY CHIEFS
September 7, 1963, at Denver

Kansas City	14	14	21	10 —	59
Denver	0	7	0	0 —	7

TD: KC—Chris Burford 2, Frank Jackson 2, Dave Grayson, Abner Haynes, Sherrill Headrick, Curtis McClinton; Den—Lionel Taylor. TD Passes: KC—Len Dawson 4, Curtis McClinton; Den—Mickey Slaughter. FG: KC—Tommy Brooker.

MIAMI DOLPHINS
November 24, 1977, at St. Louis

Miami	14	14	20	7 —	55
St. Louis Cardinals	7	0	0	7 —	14

TD: Mia—Nat Moore 3, Gary Davis, Duriel Harris, Leroy Harris, Benny Malone, Andre Tillman; StL—Ike Harris, Terry Metcalf. TD Passes: Mia—Bob Griese 6; StL—Jim Hart.

NEW ENGLAND PATRIOTS
October 18, 2009, at New England

Tennessee	0	0	0	0 —	0
New England	10	35	14	0 —	59

TD: NE—Randy Moss 3, Wes Welker 2, Kevin Faulk, Brian Hoyer, Laurence Maroney. TD Passes: NE—Tom Brady 6. FG: NE—Stephen Gostkowski.

NEW YORK JETS
November 17, 1985, at New York

Tampa Bay	14	7	7	0 —	28
New York Jets	17	24	14	7 —	62

TD: NYJ—Mickey Shuler 3, Johnny Hector 2, Tony Paige, Al Toon, Wesley Walker; TB—James Wilder 2, Kevin House, Calvin Magee. TD Passes: NYJ—Ken O'Brien 5; TB—Steve DeBerg 2. FG: NYJ—Pat Leahy 2.

OAKLAND RAIDERS
October 24, 2010, at Denver

Oakland	24	14	21	0 —	59
Denver	0	7	7	0 —	14

TD: Oak—Darren McFadden 4, Michael Bush, Chris Johnson, Zach Miller, Marcel Reese; Den—Knowshon Moreno 2. TD Passes: Oak—Jason Campbell 2; Den—Kyle Orton 2. FG: Oak—Sebastian Janikowski.

PITTSBURGH STEELERS
November 30, 1952, at Pittsburgh

New York Giants	0	0	7	0 —	7
Pittsburgh	14	14	7	28 —	63

TD: Pitt—Lynn Chandnois 2, Dick Hensley 2, Jack Butler, George Hays, Ray Mathews, Ed Modzelewski, Elbie Nickel; NYG—Bill Stribling. TD Passes: Pitt—Jim Finks 4, Gary Kerkorian; NYG—Tom Landry.

SAN DIEGO CHARGERS
December 22, 1963, at San Diego

Denver	7	10	3	0 —	20
San Diego	10	16	10	22 —	58

TD: SD—Paul Lowe 2, Chuck Allen, Bobby Jackson, Dave Kocourek, Keith Lincoln, Jacque MacKinnon; Den—Billy Joe, Donnie Stone. TD Passes: SD—John Hadl, Tobin Rote; Den—Don Breaux. FG: SD—George Blair 3; Den—Gene Mingo 2.

TENNESSEE TITANS
December 9, 1990, at Houston

Cleveland	0	7	7	0 —	14
Houston Oilers	14	31	7	6 —	58

TD: Hou—Lorenzo White 4, Ernest Givins, Leonard Harris, Tony Jones, Terry Kinard; Cle—Eric Metcalf 2. TD Passes: Hou—Warren Moon 2, Cody Carlson; Cle—Bernie Kosar. FG: Hou—Teddy Garcia.

ARIZONA CARDINALS
November 13, 1949, at New York

Chicago Cardinals	7	31	14	13	— 65
New York Bulldogs	7	0	6	7	— 20

TD: Chi—Red Cochran 2, Pat Harder 2, Bill Dewell, Mel Kutner, Bob Ravensburg, Vic Schwall, Charlie Trippi; NY—Joe Golding, Frank Muehlheuser, Johnny Rauch. TD Passes: Chi—Paul Christman 3, Jim Hardy 3; NY—Bobby Layne. FG: Chi—Pat Harder.

ATLANTA FALCONS
September 16, 1973, at New Orleans

Atlanta	0	24	21	17	— 62
New Orleans	0	0	7	0	— 7

TD: Atl—Ken Burrow 2, Eddie Ray 2, Wes Chesson, Tom Hayes, Art Malone, Joe Profit; NO—Bill Butler. TD Passes: Atl—Dick Shiner 3, Bob Lee; NO—Archie Manning. FG: Atl—Nick Mike-Mayer 2.

CAROLINA PANTHERS
December 8, 2002, at Carolina

Cincinnati	7	10	14	0	— 31
Carolina	9	7	21	15	— 52

TD: Car—Steve Smith 3, Dee Brown, Muhsin Muhammad, Al Wallace, Wesley Walls; Cin—Peter Warrick 2, Jon Kitna, Takeo Spikes. TD Passes: Car—Rodney Peete 3; Cin—Jon Kitna 2. FG: Cin—Neil Rackers.

CHICAGO BEARS
December 7, 1980, at Chicago

Green Bay	0	7	0	0	— 7
Chicago	0	28	13	20	— 61

TD: Chi—Walter Payton 3, Brian Baschnagel, Robin Earl, Roland Harper, Willie McClendon, Len Walterscheid, Rickey Watts; GB—James Lofton. TD Passes: Chi—Vince Evans 3; GB—Lynn Dickey.

DALLAS COWBOYS
October 12, 1980, at Dallas

San Francisco	0	7	0	7	— 14
Dallas	14	24	14	7	— 59

TD: Dall—Drew Pearson 3, Ron Springs 2, Tony Dorsett, Billy Joe DuPree, Robert Newhouse; SF—Dwight Clark 2. TD Passes: Dall—Danny White 4; SF—Steve DeBerg 2. FG: Dall—Rafael Septien.

DETROIT LIONS
November 27, 1997, at Detroit

Chicago	14	6	0	0	— 20
Detroit	3	14	17	21	— 55

TD: Det—Herman Moore, Johnnie Morton, Ron Rivers, Barry Sanders 3, Tracy Scroggins; Chi—Raymont Harris, Ricky Proehl. TD Passes: Det—Scott Mitchell 2; Chi—Erik Kramer. FG: Det—Jason Hanson 2; Chi—Jeff Jaeger 2.

GREEN BAY PACKERS
October 7, 1945, at Milwaukee

Detroit	0	7	7	7	— 21
Green Bay	0	41	9	7	— 57

TD: GB—Don Hutson 4, Charley Brock, Irv Comp, Ted Fritsch, Clyde Goodnight; Det—Chuck Fenenbock, John Greene, Bob Westfall. TD Passes: GB—Tex McKay 4, Lou Brock, Irv Comp; Det—Dave Ryan.

MINNESOTA VIKINGS
October 18, 1970, at Minnesota

Dallas	3	3	0	7	— 13
Minnesota	14	20	17	3	— 54

TD: Minn—Clint Jones 2, Ed Sharockman 2, John Beasley, Dave Osborn; Dall—Calvin Hill. TD Pass: Minn—Gary Cuozzo. FG: Minn—Fred Cox 4; Dall—Mike Clark 2.

NEW ORLEANS SAINTS
October 23, 2011, at New Orleans

Indianapolis	0	7	0	0	— 7
New Orleans	21	13	14	14	— 62

TD: NO—Marques Colston 2, Jimmy Graham 2, Darren Sproles 2, Jed Collins, Leigh Torrence; IND—Delone Carter. TD Passes: NO—Drew Brees 5. FG: NO—John Kasay 2.

NEW YORK GIANTS
November 26, 1972, at New York

Philadelphia	3	7	0	0	— 10
New York Giants	14	24	10	14	— 62

TD: NYG—Don Herrmann 2, Ron Johnson 2, Bob Tucker 2, Randy Johnson; Phil—Harold Jackson. TD Passes: NYG—Norm Snead 3, Randy Johnson 2; Phil—John Reaves. FG: NYG—Pete Gogolak 2; Phil—Tom Dempsey.

PHILADELPHIA EAGLES
November 6, 1934, at Philadelphia

Cincinnati Reds	0	0	0	0	— 0
Philadelphia	26	6	12	20	— 64

TD: Phil—Joe Carter 3, Swede Hanson 3, Marvin Ellstrom, Roger Kirkman, Ed Matesic, Ed Storm. TD Passes: Phil—Ed Matesic 2, Albert Weiner 2, Marvin Ellstrom.

ST. LOUIS RAMS
October 22, 1950, at Los Angeles

Baltimore	13	0	7	7	— 27
Los Angeles Rams	21	14	14	21	— 70

TD: LA—Bob Boyd 2, Vitamin T. Smith 2, Tom Fears, Elroy (Crazylegs) Hirsch, Dick Hoerner, Ralph Pasquariello, Dan Towler, Bob Waterfield; Balt—Chet Mutryn 2, Adrian Burk, Billy Stone. TD Passes: LA—Norm Van Brocklin 2, Bob Waterfield 2, Glenn Davis; Balt—Adrian Burk 3.

SAN FRANCISCO 49ERS
October 18, 1992, at San Francisco

Atlanta	7	3	0	7	— 17
San Francisco	21	21	14	0	— 56

TD: SF—Jerry Rice 3, Ricky Watters 3, Brent Jones, Tom Rathman; Atl—Michael Haynes, Jason Phillips. TD Passes: SF—Steve Young 3; Atl—Chris Miller, Wade Wilson. FG: Atl—Norm Johnson.

SEATTLE SEAHAWKS
October 30, 1977, at Seattle

Buffalo	3	0	7	7	— 17
Seattle	14	28	7	7	— 56

TD: Sea—Steve Largent 2, Duke Fergerson, Al Hunter, David Sims, Sherman Smith, Don Testerman, Jim Zorn; Buff—Joe Ferguson, John Kimbrough. TD Passes: Sea—Jim Zorn 4; Buff—Joe Ferguson. FG: Buff—Carson Long.

TAMPA BAY BUCCANEERS
December 23, 2001, at Tampa Bay

New Orleans	0	0	7	14	— 21
Tampa Bay	17	13	3	15	— 48

TD: TB—Mike Alstott, Ronde Barber, Warrick Dunn, Dave Moore, Karl Williams; NO—Joe Horn 2, Eddie Williams. TD Passes: TB—Brad Johnson 3; NO—Aaron Brooks 3. FG: TB—Martin Gramatica 4.

WASHINGTON REDSKINS
November 27, 1966, at Washington

New York Giants	0	14	14	13	— 41
Washington	13	21	14	24	— 72

TD: Wash—A.D. Whitfield 3, Brig Owens 2, Charley Taylor 2, Rickie Harris, Joe Don Looney, Bobby Mitchell; NYG—Allen Jacobs, Homer Jones, Dan Lewis, Joe Morrison, Aaron Thomas, Gary Wood. TD Passes: Wash—Sonny Jurgensen 3; NYG—Gary Wood 2, Tom Kennedy. FG: Wash—Charlie Gogolak.

RECORDS OF NFL TEAMS SINCE 1970 AFL-NFL MERGER

AFC	W	L	T	Pct.	Division Titles	Playoff Berths	Postseason Record	Super Bowl Record
Pittsburgh	396	250	2	.613	20	26	33-20	6-2
Miami	385	261	2	.596	13	22	20-20	2-3
Denver	367	275	6	.571	11	18	18-16	2-4
Baltimore***	140	115	1	.549	3	8	10-7	1-0
Oakland	349	293	6	.543	12	18	22-15	3-1
New England	351	297	0	.542	13	18	22-15	3-4
Jacksonville**	138	134	0	.507	2	6	5-6	0-0
Indianapolis	320	326	2	.495	13	19	15-17	2-1
Kansas City	315	326	7	.491	6	12	3-12	0-0
Tennessee	316	330	2	.489	5	16	12-16	0-1
San Diego	306	337	5	.476	10	12	9-12	0-1
Buffalo	299	337	2	.463	7	13	12-13	0-4
New York Jets	290	356	2	.449	2	12	10-12	0-0
Cincinnati	288	359	1	.445	7	10	5-10	0-2
Cleveland+	262	335	3	.439	6	11	4-11	0-0
Houston****	65	95	0	.406	1	1	1-1	0-0

NFC	W	L	T	Pct.	Division Titles	Playoff Berths	Postseason Record	Super Bowl Record
Dallas	381	267	0	.588	17	26	32-21	5-3
San Francisco	364	281	3	.564	18	22	26-17	5-0
Minnesota	364	282	3	.563	16	24	17-24	0-3
Washington	348	298	2	.539	6	16	20-13	3-2
Green Bay	335	305	8	.523	9	16	17-14	2-1
Philadelphia	333	307	8	.520	8	19	15-19	0-2
Chicago	325	322	1	.502	10	14	10-13	1-1
St. Louis	322	322	4	.500	11	19	16-18	1-2
New York Giants	321	324	3	.498	8	15	20-11	4-1
Seattle*	269	295	0	.477	7	11	8-11	0-1
Carolina**	125	147	0	.460	3	4	6-4	0-1
Atlanta	287	356	5	.447	4	11	6-11	0-1
New Orleans	287	357	4	.446	5	9	6-8	1-0
Arizona	264	378	6	.412	4	6	5-6	0-1
Detroit	264	380	4	.410	3	10	1-10	0-0
Tampa Bay*	222	341	1	.395	6	10	6-9	1-0

*Entered NFL in 1976.
**Entered NFL in 1995.
***Entered NFL in 1996.
****Entered NFL in 2002.
+Did not play, 1996-98.
Oakland totals include L.A. Raiders, 1982-1994.
Tennessee totals include Houston, 1970-1996.
Indianapolis totals include Baltimore, 1970-1983.
St. Louis totals include L.A. Rams, 1970-1994.
Arizona totals include St. Louis, 1970-1987, and Phoenix, 1988-1993.
Tie games before 1972 are not calculated in won-lost percentage.

HOME RECORDS OF NFL TEAMS SINCE 1970 AFL-NFL MERGER

AFC	W	L	T	Pct.
Pittsburgh	234	89	1	.724
Baltimore***	88	39	1	.691
Denver	221	100	4	.687
Miami	218	104	1	.676
New England	201	123	0	.620
Jacksonville**	83	53	0	.610
Oakland	192	130	2	.596
Kansas City	190	130	3	.593
Tennessee	180	143	1	.557
San Diego	176	145	2	.548
Cincinnati	176	147	1	.545
Buffalo	176	148	1	.543
Indianapolis	171	151	2	.531
Cleveland+	146	151	2	.492
Houston****	39	41	0	.488
New York Jets	156	166	1	.485

NFC	W	L	T	Pct.
Dallas	217	107	0	.670
Minnesota	215	109	1	.663
Green Bay	200	119	5	.625
San Francisco	200	122	2	.621
Washington	196	125	2	.610
Chicago	192	131	1	.594
Seattle*	162	121	0	.572
Philadelphia	183	139	3	.568
St. Louis	178	144	2	.553
New York Giants	174	150	1	.537
Atlanta	172	152	1	.531
Detroit	171	152	1	.529
Carolina**	69	67	0	.507
Arizona	159	161	3	.497
Tampa Bay*	136	145	1	.484
New Orleans	153	170	1	.474

*Entered NFL in 1976.
**Entered NFL in 1995.
***Entered NFL in 1996.
****Entered NFL in 2002.
+Did not play, 1996-98.
Oakland totals include L.A. Raiders, 1982-1994.
Tennessee totals include Houston, 1970-1996.
Indianapolis totals include Baltimore, 1970-1983.
St. Louis totals include L.A. Rams, 1970-1994.
Arizona totals include St. Louis, 1970-1987, and Phoenix, 1988-1993.
Tie games before 1972 are not calculated in won-lost percentage.

ROAD RECORDS OF NFL TEAMS SINCE 1970 AFL-NFL MERGER

AFC	W	L	T	Pct.
Miami	167	157	1	.515
Pittsburgh	162	161	1	.502
Oakland	157	163	4	.491
New England	150	174	0	.463
Indianapolis	149	175	0	.460
Denver	146	175	2	.455
Tennessee	136	187	1	.421
New York Jets	134	190	1	.414
Baltimore***	52	76	0	.406
San Diego	130	192	3	.404
Jacksonville**	55	81	0	.404
Kansas City	125	196	4	.390
Cleveland+	116	184	1	.387
Buffalo	123	199	1	.382
Cincinnati	112	212	0	.346
Houston****	26	54	0	.325

NFC	W	L	T	Pct.
San Francisco	164	159	1	.508
Dallas	164	160	0	.506
Philadelphia	150	168	5	.472
Washington	152	173	0	.468
Minnesota	149	173	1	.463
New York Giants	147	174	2	.458
St. Louis	144	178	2	.448
Green Bay	135	186	3	.421
New Orleans	134	187	3	.418
Carolina**	56	80	0	.412
Chicago	133	191	0	.410
Seattle*	107	174	0	.381
Atlanta	115	204	4	.361
Arizona	105	217	3	.327
Tampa Bay*	86	196	0	.305
Detroit	93	228	3	.291

*Entered NFL in 1976.
**Entered NFL in 1995.
***Entered NFL in 1996.
****Entered NFL in 2002.
+Did not play, 1996-98.
Oakland totals include L.A. Raiders, 1982-1994.
Tennessee totals include Houston, 1970-1996.
Indianapolis totals include Baltimore, 1970-1983.
St. Louis totals include L.A. Rams, 1970-1994.
Arizona totals include St. Louis, 1970-1987, and Phoenix, 1988-1993.
Tie games before 1972 are not calculated in won-lost percentage.

RECORDS OF TEAMS ON KICKOFF WEEKEND

AFC	W	L	T	Pct.	Longest W Strk.	Longest L Strk.	Current Streak
Jacksonville	11	6	0	.647	6	3	W-2
Denver	32	19	1	.627	4	4	L-2
San Diego	30	22	0	.577	6	6	W-1
Pittsburgh	40	33	4	.548	8	3	L-1
New England	28	24	0	.538	8	3	W-8
Miami	24	21	1	.533	11	5	L-1
Kansas City	27	25	0	.519	7	4	L-1
Tennessee	27	25	0	.519	4	3	L-1
Indianapolis	34	33	1	.507	8	8	L-2
Baltimore	8	8	0	.500	4	4	W-4
Houston	5	5	0	.500	2	3	W-2
Oakland	25	27	0	.481	5	8	W-1
Cleveland	27	32	0	.458	5	7	L-7
Cincinnati	20	24	0	.455	4	4	W-1
New York Jets	23	29	0	.442	3	5	W-1
Buffalo	21	31	0	.404	6	5	W-1

NFC	W	L	T	Pct.	Longest W Strk.	Longest L Strk.	Current Streak
Dallas	34	17	1	.667	17	5	L-2
Chicago	52	35	5	.598	9	6	W-2
New York Giants	49	33	5	.598	4	3	L-1
Green Bay	52	36	3	.591	5	6	W-5
Minnesota	28	22	1	.560	5	3	L-2
Detroit	43	37	2	.538	10	4	W-1
San Francisco	32	29	1	.525	5	3	W-1
Atlanta	24	22	0	.522	5	3	L-2
St. Louis	38	36	0	.514	5	6	L-5
Washington	39	37	4	.513	6	5	W-2
Arizona	37	52	2	.416	6	7	W-2
Philadelphia	32	45	1	.416	5	9	W-1
Tampa Bay	14	22	0	.389	3	5	L-1
Seattle	13	23	0	.361	3	8	L-1
New Orleans	16	29	0	.356	3	6	L-1
Carolina	6	11	0	.353	3	4	L-3

Kansas City totals include Dallas Texans, 1960-62.
Oakland totals include L.A. Raiders, 1982-1994.
San Diego totals include L.A. Chargers, 1960.
Indianapolis totals include Baltimore, 1953-1983.
Tennessee total include Houston, 1960-1996.
New England totals include Boston, 1960-1970.
St. Louis totals include Cleveland, 1937-1942 and 1944-45, and L.A. Rams, 1946-1994.
Detroit totals include Portsmouth, 1930-33.
Arizona totals include Chi. Cardinals, 1920-1959, St. Louis, 1960-1987, and Phoenix, 1988-1993.
Chicago totals include Decatur, 1920.
Washington totals include Boston Braves, 1932 and Boston Redskins, 1933-36.
NOTE: All tied games occurred prior to 1972, when calculation of ties in percentage as half-win.

RECORDS OF NFL TEAMS, 2002-2011

AFC	W	L	T	Pct.	Division Titles	Playoff Berths	Postseason Record	Super Bowl Record
New England	123	37	0	.769	8	8	13-6	2-2
Indianapolis	111	49	0	.694	7	9	9-8	1-1
Pittsburgh	105	54	1	.659	5	7	11-5	2-1
San Diego	96	64	0	.600	5	5	3-5	0-0
Baltimore	94	66	0	.588	3	6	5-6	0-0
Denver	86	74	0	.538	2	4	2-4	0-0
Tennessee	86	74	0	.538	2	4	2-4	0-0
New York Jets	80	80	0	.500	1	5	6-5	0-0
Jacksonville	76	84	0	.475	0	2	1-2	0-0
Kansas City	74	86	0	.463	2	3	0-3	0-0
Cincinnati	71	88	1	.447	2	3	0-3	0-0
Miami	70	90	0	.438	1	1	0-1	0-0
Buffalo	65	95	0	.406	0	0	0-0	0-0
Houston	65	95	0	.406	1	1	1-1	0-0
Cleveland	56	104	0	.350	0	1	0-1	0-0
Oakland	56	104	0	.350	1	1	2-1	0-1

NFC	W	L	T	Pct.	Division Titles	Playoff Berths	Postseason Record	Super Bowl Record
Philadelphia	99	60	1	.622	5	7	7-7	0-1
Green Bay	99	61	0	.619	5	7	6-6	1-0
New Orleans	90	70	0	.563	3	4	5-3	1-0
New York Giants	88	72	0	.550	3	6	8-4	2-0
Atlanta	87	72	1	.547	2	5	2-5	0-0
Dallas	86	74	0	.538	2	4	1-4	0-0
Chicago	82	78	0	.513	3	3	3-3	0-1
Seattle	81	79	0	.506	5	6	5-6	0-1
Carolina	79	81	0	.494	2	3	5-3	0-1
Minnesota	77	83	0	.481	2	3	2-3	0-0
Tampa Bay	74	86	0	.463	3	3	3-2	1-0
San Francisco	69	91	0	.431	2	2	2-2	0-0
Arizona	65	95	0	.406	2	2	4-2	0-1
Washington	65	95	0	.406	0	2	1-2	0-0
St. Louis	56	104	0	.350	1	2	1-2	0-0
Detroit	47	113	0	.294	0	1	0-1	0-0

HOME RECORDS, 2002-2011

AFC	W - L - T	Pct.
New England	67-13-0	.838
Baltimore	61-19-0	.763
Indianapolis	59-21-0	.738
Pittsburgh	58-21-1	.731
San Diego	55-25-0	.688
Denver	48-32-0	.600
Tennessee	47-33-0	.588
Jacksonville	46-34-0	.575
New York Jets	46-34-0	.575
Kansas City	45-35-0	.563
Cincinnati	41-38-1	.519
Buffalo	39-41-0	.488
Houston	39-41-0	.488
Miami	38-42-0	.475
Cleveland	31-49-0	.388
Oakland	31-49-0	.388

NFC	W - L - T	Pct.
Green Bay	55-25-0	.688
Seattle	51-29-0	.638
Atlanta	50-30-0	.625
Philadelphia	50-30-0	.625
Chicago	49-31-0	.613
Dallas	48-32-0	.600
Minnesota	48-32-0	.600
New Orleans	45-35-0	.563
Arizona	44-36-0	.550
San Francisco	44-36-0	.550
Carolina	42-38-0	.525
New York Giants	42-38-0	.525
Tampa Bay	42-38-0	.525
Washington	36-44-0	.450
St. Louis	35-45-0	.438
Detroit	32-48-0	.400

ROAD RECORDS, 2002-2011

AFC	W-L-T	Pct.
New England	56-24-0	.700
Indianapolis	52-28-0	.650
Pittsburgh	47-33-0	.588
San Diego	41-39-0	.513
Tennessee	39-41-0	.488
Denver	38-42-0	.475
New York Jets	34-46-0	.425
Baltimore	33-47-0	.413
Miami	32-48-0	.400
Cincinnati	30-50-0	.375
Jacksonville	30-50-0	.375
Kansas City	29-51-0	.363
Buffalo	26-54-0	.325
Houston	26-54-0	.325
Cleveland	25-55-0	.313
Oakland	25-55-0	.313

NFC	W-L-T	Pct.
Philadelphia	49-30-1	.619
New York Giants	46-34-0	.575
New Orleans	45-35-0	.563
Green Bay	44-36-0	.550
Dallas	38-42-0	.475
Atlanta	37-42-1	.469
Carolina	37-43-0	.463
Chicago	33-47-0	.413
Tampa Bay	32-48-0	.400
Seattle	30-50-0	.375
Minnesota	29-51-0	.363
Washington	29-51-0	.363
San Francisco	25-55-0	.313
Arizona	21-59-0	.263
St. Louis	21-59-0	.263
Detroit	15-65-0	.188

RECORDS BY MONTHS, 2002-2011

AFC	Sept. W-L-T	Oct. W-L-T	Nov. W-L-T	Dec. W-L-T	Total W-L-T	Pct.
New England	22-9-0	32-9-0	29-12-0	40-7-0	123-37-0	.769
Indianapolis	24-8-0	24-13-0	31-12-0	32-16-0	111-49-0	.694
Pittsburgh	20-13-0	25-13-0	25-15-1	35-13-0	105-54-1	.659
San Diego	16-17-0	22-18-0	23-16-0	35-13-0	96-64-0	.600
Baltimore	19-12-0	20-18-0	26-18-0	29-18-0	94-66-0	.588
Denver	23-11-0	21-19-0	21-17-0	21-27-0	86-74-0	.538
Tennessee	16-17-0	21-19-0	22-16-0	27-22-0	86-74-0	.538
New York Jets	16-17-0	17-21-0	23-17-0	24-25-0	80-80-0	.500
Jacksonville	16-16-0	18-22-0	21-18-0	21-28-0	76-84-0	.475
Kansas City	14-19-0	24-15-0	15-25-0	21-27-0	74-86-0	.463
Cincinnati	14-19-0	15-24-0	21-19-1	21-26-0	71-88-1	.447
Miami	11-21-0	13-25-0	23-19-0	23-25-0	70-90-0	.438
Buffalo	15-18-0	17-23-0	14-25-0	19-29-0	65-95-0	.406
Houston	11-21-0	19-20-0	14-26-0	21-28-0	65-95-0	.406
Oakland	14-18-0	13-27-0	14-26-0	15-33-0	56-104-0	.350
Cleveland	10-24-0	17-21-0	13-27-0	16-32-0	56-104-0	.350

December totals include January.

NFC	Sept. W-L-T	Oct. W-L-T	Nov. W-L-T	Dec. W-L-T	Total W-L-T	Pct.
Philadelphia	19-14-0	23-14-0	24-17-1	33-15-0	99-60-1	.622
Green Bay	20-14-0	23-14-0	24-18-0	32-15-0	99-61-0	.619
New Orleans	19-14-0	23-19-0	23-14-0	25-23-0	90-70-0	.563
New York Giants	20-12-0	28-11-0	17-24-0	23-25-0	88-72-0	.550
Atlanta	17-16-0	22-15-0	24-17-1	24-24-0	87-72-1	.547
Dallas	21-11-0	18-22-0	29-13-0	18-28-0	86-74-0	.538
Chicago	16-17-0	19-18-0	24-18-0	23-25-0	82-78-0	.513
Seattle	20-12-0	14-23-0	22-21-0	25-23-0	81-79-0	.506
Carolina	15-17-0	19-22-0	16-23-0	29-19-0	79-81-0	.494
Minnesota	15-19-0	19-18-0	22-19-0	21-27-0	77-83-0	.481
Tampa Bay	18-15-0	19-21-0	19-20-0	18-30-0	74-86-0	.463
San Francisco	13-20-0	15-24-0	17-23-0	24-24-0	69-91-0	.431
Arizona	12-22-0	14-22-0	16-26-0	23-25-0	65-95-0	.406
Washington	17-14-0	16-25-0	12-29-0	20-27-0	65-95-0	.406
St. Louis	8-26-0	18-21-0	15-24-0	15-33-0	56-104-0	.350
Detroit	12-20-0	13-25-0	9-34-0	13-34-0	47-113-0	.294

December totals include January.

TAKEAWAYS/GIVEAWAYS, 2002-2011

AFC	Takeaways			Giveaways			
	Int.	Fum.	Total	Int.	Fum.	Total	Net.Diff.
New England	198	114	312	118	93	211	+101
Indianapolis	148	129	277	135	86	221	+ 56
Kansas City	163	115	278	143	92	235	+ 43
Baltimore	208	106	314	140	139	279	+ 35
San Diego	171	98	269	138	96	234	+ 35
Jacksonville	162	90	252	124	108	232	+ 20
Tennessee	173	108	281	146	116	262	+ 19
Cincinnati	169	118	287	168	102	270	+ 17
New York Jets	159	113	272	161	94	255	+ 17
Pittsburgh	162	116	278	156	107	263	+ 15
Denver	123	114	237	154	111	265	- 28
Miami	154	106	260	171	117	288	- 28
Buffalo	161	107	268	173	126	299	- 31
Houston	131	99	230	152	114	266	- 36
Cleveland	158	96	254	192	118	310	- 56
Oakland	139	97	236	172	126	298	- 62

NFC	Takeaways			Giveaways			
	Int.	Fum.	Total	Int.	Fum.	Total	Net.Diff.
Green Bay	212	100	312	161	103	264	+ 48
Atlanta	168	123	291	142	103	245	+ 46
Philadelphia	170	122	292	144	121	265	+ 27
Carolina	175	131	306	173	116	289	+ 17
Tampa Bay	185	109	294	162	120	282	+ 12
Seattle	162	114	276	163	108	271	+ 5
San Francisco	161	110	271	153	122	275	- 4
New York Giants	150	131	281	167	119	286	- 5
Chicago	181	133	314	194	126	320	- 6
Minnesota	161	119	280	165	125	290	- 10
New Orleans	140	121	261	160	124	284	- 23
Detroit	135	143	278	207	95	302	- 24
Dallas	151	110	261	177	111	288	- 27
Washington	136	93	229	150	130	280	- 51
St. Louis	136	127	263	197	126	323	- 60
Arizona	155	119	274	199	137	336	- 62

BEST TAKEAWAY/GIVEAWAY DIFFERENTIAL, SEASON
+43   Washington, 1983
+28   New England, 2010
      San Francisco, 2011
+26   Kansas City, 1990

HIGH AND LOW SINGLE-GAME YARDAGE TOTALS, 2002-2011
Most Total Yards, Game
645   Pittsburgh vs. Atlanta, Nov. 10, 2002 (OT)
622   New England at Miami, Sept. 12, 2011
619   New England vs. Tennessee, Oct. 18, 2009
617   New Orleans vs. Carolina, Jan. 1, 2012
605   Minnesota at New Orleans, Oct. 17, 2004
Fewest Total Yards, Game
26   Cleveland at Buffalo, Dec. 12, 2004
47   Houston at Pittsburgh, Dec. 8, 2002
67   Kansas City at San Diego, Dec. 12, 2010
72   Cincinnati at New York Jets, Jan. 3, 2010
77   Oakland vs. Atlanta, Nov. 2, 2008
Most Yards Rushing, Game
378   Minnesota vs. San Diego, Nov. 4, 2007
375   Jacksonville vs. Indianapolis, Dec. 10, 2006
351   Cleveland at Kansas City, Dec. 20, 2009
343   Baltimore at Cleveland, Sept. 14, 2003
332   Tennessee at Kansas City, Oct. 19, 2008
Fewest Yards Rushing, Game
-18   Detroit at Arizona, Nov. 11, 2007
-3   Detroit vs. Minnesota, Dec. 10, 2006
1   Dallas at Washington, Dec. 30, 2007
4   Seattle at Minnesota, Nov. 22, 2009
5   New England at Pittsburgh, Oct. 31, 2004

Most Yards Passing, Game
516   New England at Miami, Sept. 12, 2011
504   New Orleans vs. Cincinnati, Nov. 19, 2006
502   Detroit at Green Bay, Jan. 1, 2012
499   Denver vs. Atlanta, Oct. 31, 2004
472   Indianapolis at Kansas City, Oct. 31, 2004
472   Pittsburgh vs. Green Bay, Dec. 20, 2009
472   Denver vs. Indianapolis, Sept. 26, 2010
Fewest Yards Passing, Game
-7   Tennessee at New England, Oct. 18, 2009
-5   Houston at Oakland, Dec. 3, 2006
-3   Cleveland at Buffalo, Dec. 12, 2004
0   Oakland at San Diego, Dec. 28, 2003
    Cincinnati at New York Jets, Jan. 3, 2010

NFL INDIVIDUAL LEADERS, 2002-2011

Points		**Passing Yards**	
David Akers	1,242	Drew Brees	40,521
Jay Feely	1,095	Peyton Manning	38,410
Ryan Longwell	1,091	Tom Brady	37,130
Adam Vinatieri	1,064	Brett Favre	33,211
Sebastian Janikowski	1,048	Matt Hasselbeck	30,982

Touchdowns		**TD Passes**	
LaDainian Tomlinson	152	Peyton Manning	288
Randy Moss	100	Tom Brady	282
Terrell Owens	96	Drew Brees	280
Shaun Alexander	94	Brett Favre	221
Clinton Portis	80	Two tied	185

Field Goals		**Receptions**	
David Akers	280	Reggie Wayne	835
Sebastian Janikowski	248	Tony Gonzalez	815
Jay Feely	245	Hines Ward	782
Neil Rackers	235	Derrick Mason	760
Phil Dawson	232	Chad Ochocinco	738

Rushes		**Reception Yards**	
LaDainian Tomlinson	2,835	Reggie Wayne	11,363
Thomas Jones	2,454	Chad Ochocinco	10,730
Jamal Lewis	2,233	Steve Smith	10,124
Clinton Portis	2,230	Terrell Owens	9,764
Steven Jackson	2,138	Andre Johnson	9,656

Rushing Yards		**Receiving TDs**	
LaDainian Tomlinson	12,448	Randy Moss	100
Clinton Portis	9,923	Terrell Owens	94
Thomas Jones	9,838	Antonio Gates	76
Jamal Lewis	9,243	Larry Fitzgerald	73
Steven Jackson	9,093	Reggie Wayne	73

Rushing TDs		**Interceptions**	
LaDainian Tomlinson	135	Ed Reed	57
Shaun Alexander	84	Asante Samuel	45
Clinton Portis	75	Darren Sharper	43
Priest Holmes	68	Charles Woodson	43
Adrian Peterson	64	Champ Bailey	37

Pass Attempts		**Sacks**	
Drew Brees	5,452	Jared Allen	105.0
Peyton Manning	4,984	Dwight Freeney	102.5
Tom Brady	4,905	Julius Peppers	100.0
Brett Favre	4,728	Jason Taylor	100.0
Matt Hasselbeck	4,447	DeMarcus Ware	99.5

Completions	
Drew Brees	3,598
Peyton Manning	3,325
Tom Brady	3,132
Brett Favre	2,989
Matt Hasselbeck	2,702

NFL GAMES IN WHICH A TEAM HAS SCORED 60 OR MORE POINTS

(Home team in capitals)

Regular Season

WASHINGTON 72, New York Giants 41 ....November 27, 1966
LOS ANGELES RAMS 70, Baltimore 27 ....October 22, 1950
Chicago Cardinals 65, NEW YORK BULLDOGS 20.......................November 13, 1949
LOS ANGELES RAMS 65, Detroit 24 ....October 29, 1950
PHILADELPHIA 64, Cincinnati 0 ....November 6, 1934
CHICAGO CARDINALS 63, New York Giants 35 ....October 17, 1948
PITTSBURGH 63, New York Giants 7 ....November 30, 1952
AKRON 62, Oorang 0...October 29, 1922
CLEVELAND 62, New York Giants 14 ....December 6, 1953
CLEVELAND 62, Washington 3 ....November 7, 1954
NEW YORK GIANTS 62, Philadelphia 10.................................November 26, 1972
Atlanta 62, NEW ORLEANS 7 ....September 16, 1973
NEW YORK JETS 62, Tampa Bay 28 ....November 17, 1985
NEW ORLEANS 62, Indianapolis 7.......................................October 23, 2011
CHICAGO 61, San Francisco 20 ....December 12, 1965
Cincinnati 61, HOUSTON 17...December 17, 1972
CHICAGO 61, Green Bay 7 ....December 7, 1980
CINCINNATI 61, Houston 7 ....December 17, 1989
ROCK ISLAND 60, Evansville 0 ....October 15, 1922
CHICAGO CARDINALS 60, Rochester 0 ....October 7, 1923

Postseason

Chicago Bears 73, WASHINGTON 0 ....December 8, 1940
JACKSONVILLE 62, Miami 7 ....January 15, 2000

YOUNGEST AND OLDEST PLAYERS IN NFL IN 2011

10 Youngest Players

Player	Birthdate	Games	Starts	Position
Tyron Smith, Dallas	12/12/90	16	16	T
Dion Lewis, Philadelphia	9/27/90	15	0	RB
Randall Cobb, Green Bay	8/22/90	15	0	WR
Patrick Peterson, Arizona	7/11/90	16	16	CB
Robert Quinn, St. Louis	5/18/90	15	1	DE
Aaron Williams, Buffalo	4/23/90	9	6	CB
Corey Liuget, San Diego	3/18/90	15	13	DE
Da'Quan Bowers, Tampa Bay	2/23/90	16	6	DE
Rahim Moore, Denver	2/11/90	15	7	FS
Jacquizz Rodgers, Atlanta	2/6/90	16	0	RB

10 Oldest Players

Player	Birthdate	Games	Starts	Position
Matt Turk, Jacksonville-Houston	6/16/68	9	0	P
John Kasay, New Orleans	10/27/69	16	0	K
Jason Hanson, Detroit	6/17/70	16	0	K
Mark Brunell, New York Jets	9/17/70	16	0	QB
Jon Kitna, Dallas	9/21/72	3	0	QB
Adam Vinatieri, Indianapolis	12/28/72	16	0	K
Kerry Collins, Indianapolis	12/30/72	3	3	QB
Olindo Mare, Carolina	6/6/73	16	0	K
Casey Wiegmann, Kansas City	7/20/73	16	16	C
Brian Dawkins, Denver	10/13/73	14	12	SS

YOUNGEST AND OLDEST REGULAR STARTERS BY POSITION IN 2011

Minimum: 8 Games Started

	Youngest		Oldest	
QB	10/15/89	Blaine Gabbert, Jax.	9/25/75	Matt Hasselbeck, Tenn.
RB	2/13/89	Charles Clay, Mia.	8/19/78	Thomas Jones, K.C.
WR	8/21/89	Titus Young, Det.	2/2/75	Donald Driver, G.B.
TE	11/9/89	Kyle Rudolph, Minn.	2/27/76	Tony Gonzalez, Atl.
T	12/12/90	Tyron Smith, Dall.	9/21/77	Jeff Backus, Det.
G	10/11/89	Will Rackley, Jax.	9/25/76	Bobbie Williams, Cin.
C	7/24/89	Maurkice Pouncey, Pitt.	7/20/73	Casey Wiegmann, K.C.
		Mike Pouncey, Mia.		
DE	3/18/90	Corey Liuget, S.D.	2/4/77	James Hall, St.L.
DT	12/5/89	Jurrell Casey, Tenn.	11/1/76	Kelly Gregg, K.C.
LB	7/23/89	K.J. Wright, Sea.	1/6/75	James Farrior, Pitt.
CB	7/11/90	Patrick Peterson, Ariz.	4/7/75	Ronde Barber, T.B.
S	5/7/89	Earl Thomas, Sea.	10/13/73	Brian Dawkins, Den.

OLDEST INDIVIDUAL SINGLE-SEASON OR SINGLE-GAME RECORDS IN NFL RECORD & FACT BOOK

Most Points, Game—40, Ernie Nevers, Chi. Cardinals vs. Chi. Bears, Nov. 28, 1929 (6-td, 4-pat)

Most Touchdowns Rushing, Game—6, Ernie Nevers, Chi. Cardinals vs. Chi. Bears, Nov. 28, 1929

Highest Rushing Average Gain, Season (Qualifiers)—8.44, Beattie Feathers, Chi. Bears, 1934 (119-1,004)

Highest Punting Average, Season (Qualifiers)—51.40, Sammy Baugh, Washington, 1940 (35-1,799)

Highest Punting Average, Rookie, Season (Qualifiers)—45.92, Frank Sinkwich, Detroit, 1943 (12-551)

Highest Punting Average, Game (minimum: 4 punts)—61.75, Bob Cifers, Detroit vs. Chi. Bears, Nov. 24, 1946 (4-247)

Highest Average Gain, Pass Receptions, Season (minimum: 24 receptions)—32.58, Don Currivan, Boston, 1947 (24-782)

Highest Average Gain, Passing, Game (minimum: 20 passes)—18.58, Sammy Baugh, Washington vs. Boston, Oct. 31, 1948 (24-446)

Most Touchdowns, Fumble Recoveries, Game—2, Fred (Dippy) Evans, Chi. Bears vs. Washington, Nov. 28, 1948

Most Yards Gained, Intercepted Passes, Rookie, Season—301, Don Doll, Detroit, 1949

Most Passes Had Intercepted, Game—8, Jim Hardy, Chi. Cardinals vs. Philadelphia, Sept. 24, 1950

Highest Kickoff Return Average, Game (minimum: 3 returns)—73.50, Wally Triplett, Detroit vs. Los Angeles, Oct. 29, 1950 (4-294)

Highest Punt Return Average, Season (Qualifiers)—23.00, Herb Rich, Baltimore, 1950 (12-276)

Highest Punt Return Average, Rookie, Season (Qualifiers)—23.00, Herb Rich, Baltimore, 1950 (12-276)

Most Yards Passing, Game—554, Norm Van Brocklin, Los Angeles vs. New York Yanks, Sept. 28, 1951

Most Touchdowns, Punt Returns, Rookie, Season—4, Jack Christiansen, Detroit, 1951

Most Interceptions By, Season—14, Dick (Night Train) Lane, Los Angeles, 1952

Most Interceptions By, Rookie, Season—14, Dick (Night Train) Lane, Los Angeles, 1952

Highest Average Gain, Passing, Season (Qualifiers)—11.17, Tommy O'Connell, Cleveland, 1957 (110-1,229)

Most Yards Gained, Pass Receptions, Rookie, Season—1,473, Bill Groman, Houston, 1960

NFL INDIVIDUAL LEADERS OVER RECENT SEASONS

Last 2 Seasons		Last 3 Seasons		Last 4 Seasons	
Points					
309	David Akers	448	David Akers	592	David Akers
271	Sebastian Janikowski	381	Mason Crosby	508	Mason Crosby
259	Neil Rackers	366	Sebastian Janikowski	476	Rob Bironas
254	Matt Bryant	349	Rob Bironas	472	Stephen Gostkowski
252	Mason Crosby	344	Neil Rackers	466	John Kasay
Touchdowns					
30	Arian Foster	44	Adrian Peterson	54	Adrian Peterson
29	LeSean McCoy	34	Maurice Jones-Drew	50	Michael Turner
28	Rob Gronkowski	33	Four tied	48	Maurice Jones-Drew
28	Calvin Johnson			45	Calvin Johnson
26	Adrian Peterson			42	Chris Johnson
Field Goals					
76	David Akers	108	David Akers	141	David Akers
64	Sebastian Janikowski	90	Sebastian Janikowski	114	Sebastian Janikowski
59	Dan Carpenter	84	Dan Carpenter	109	Rob Bironas
59	Neil Rackers	80	Rob Bironas	105	Dan Carpenter
55	Two tied	77	Robbie Gould	104	Josh Brown
Rushes					
642	Maurice Jones-Drew	954	Maurice Jones-Drew	1,189	Michael Turner
635	Michael Turner	936	Chris Johnson	1,187	Chris Johnson
605	Arian Foster	914	Steven Jackson	1,168	Adrian Peterson
598	Ray Rice	895	Cedric Benson	1,067	Steven Jackson
594	Cedric Benson	852	Ray Rice	1,151	Maurice Jones-Drew
Rushing Yards					
2,930	Maurice Jones-Drew	4,417	Chris Johnson	5,645	Chris Johnson
2,840	Arian Foster	4,321	Maurice Jones-Drew	5,411	Adrian Peterson
2,711	Michael Turner	3,923	Ray Rice	5,281	Michael Turner
2,584	Ray Rice	3,802	Steven Jackson	5,145	Maurice Jones-Drew
2,411	Chris Johnson	3,651	Adrian Peterson	4,844	Steven Jackson
Rushing Touchdowns					
26	Arian Foster	42	Adrian Peterson	52	Adrian Peterson
24	BenJarvus Green-Ellis	33	Michael Turner	50	Michael Turner
24	LeSean McCoy	29	Arian Foster	40	Maurice Jones-Drew
24	Adrian Peterson	29	Chris Johnson	38	Chris Johnson
23	Michael Turner	29	Rashard Mendenhall	36	Brandon Jacobs
Passes					
1,315	Drew Brees	1,829	Drew Brees	2,464	Drew Brees
1,137	Matt Ryan	1,668	Tom Brady	2,116	Eli Manning
1,128	Eli Manning	1,637	Eli Manning	2,087	Philip Rivers
1,123	Philip Rivers	1,609	Philip Rivers	2,054	Aaron Rodgers
1,103	Tom Brady	1,588	Matt Ryan	2,022	Matt Ryan
Completions					
916	Drew Brees	1,279	Drew Brees	1,692	Drew Brees
725	Tom Brady	1,096	Tom Brady	1,352	Philip Rivers
723	Philip Rivers	1,040	Philip Rivers	1,346	Aaron Rodgers
704	Matt Ryan	1,015	Eli Manning	1,304	Eli Manning
698	Eli Manning	1,005	Aaron Rodgers	1,232	Matt Ryan
Passing Yards					
10,096	Drew Brees	14,484	Drew Brees	19,553	Drew Brees
9,334	Philip Rivers	13,588	Philip Rivers	17,597	Philip Rivers
9,135	Tom Brady	13,533	Tom Brady	17,037	Aaron Rodgers
8,935	Eli Manning	12,999	Aaron Rodgers	16,194	Eli Manning
8,565	Aaron Rodgers	12,956	Eli Manning	14,906	Ben Roethlisberger

Last 2 Seasons	Last 3 Seasons	Last 4 Seasons
Touchdown Passes		
79 Drew Brees	113 Drew Brees	147 Drew Brees
75 Tom Brady	103 Tom Brady	131 Aaron Rodgers
73 Aaron Rodgers	103 Aaron Rodgers	119 Philip Rivers
60 Eli Manning	87 Eli Manning	108 Eli Manning
57 Two tied	85 Philip Rivers	103 Tom Brady
Receptions		
215 Roddy White	331 Wes Welker	442 Wes Welker
208 Wes Welker	300 Roddy White	388 Roddy White
186 Reggie Wayne	286 Reggie Wayne	372 Brandon Marshall
173 Calvin Johnson	268 Brandon Marshall	368 Reggie Wayne
173 Jason Witten	267 Two tied	363 Larry Fitzgerald
Receiving Yards		
2,801 Calvin Johnson	3,838 Roddy White	5,220 Roddy White
2,685 Roddy White	3,785 Calvin Johnson	5,116 Calvin Johnson
2,548 Larry Fitzgerald	3,765 Wes Welker	5,071 Larry Fitzgerald
2,450 Mike Wallace	3,640 Larry Fitzgerald	4,930 Wes Welker
2,417 Wes Welker	3,579 Reggie Wayne	4,852 Andre Johnson
Receiving Touchdowns		
28 Calvin Johnson	33 Calvin Johnson	45 Calvin Johnson
27 Rob Gronkowski	29 Roddy White	39 Larry Fitzgerald
21 Greg Jennings	27 Larry Fitzgerald	36 Roddy White
20 Dwayne Bowe	27 Rob Gronkowski	34 Greg Jennings
18 Three tied	26 Vernon Davis	33 Antonio Gates
Interceptions		
11 Ed Reed	19 Asante Samuel	25 Charles Woodson
10 Jason Allen	18 Charles Woodson	23 Ed Reed
10 Asante Samuel	14 Ed Reed	23 Asante Samuel
10 Corey Webster	14 Tramon Williams	19 Troy Polamalu
10 Tramon Williams	13 Four players tied	19 Tramon Williams
Sacks		
35.0 DeMarcus Ware	47.5 Jared Allen	66.0 DeMarcus Ware
33.0 Jared Allen	46.0 DeMarcus Ware	62.0 Jared Allen
30.5 Jason Babin	35.0 Tamba Hali	45.5 James Harrison
26.5 Tamba Hali	33.5 Trent Cole	44.5 John Abraham
25.0 Terrell Suggs	33.0 Jason Babin	44.0 Two tied

NFL TEAM LEADERS OVER RECENT SEASONS

Highest Won-Lost Percentage		
.844 New England	.771 New England	.750 New England
.781 Green Bay	.771 New Orleans	.703 New Orleans
.750 Baltimore	.750 Green Bay	.703 Pittsburgh
.750 New Orleans	.688 Baltimore	.688 Baltimore
.750 Pittsburgh	.688 Pittsburgh	.672 Atlanta
Most Points		
1,031 New England	1,458 New England	1,904 New Orleans
948 Green Bay	1,441 New Orleans	1,868 New England
931 New Orleans	1,409 Green Bay	1,828 Green Bay
847 San Diego	1,301 San Diego	1,740 San Diego
836 Detroit	1,264 Philadelphia	1,680 Philadelphia
Most Total Yards		
13,434 New Orleans	19,895 New Orleans	26,466 New Orleans
12,668 New England	19,025 New England	24,872 New England
12,619 San Diego	18,380 San Diego	24,382 Houston
12,616 Philadelphia	18,342 Philadelphia	23,964 San Diego
12,246 New York Giants	18,277 Green Bay	23,950 Philadelphia

Last 2 Seasons		Last 3 Seasons		Last 4 Seasons	
Most Rushing Yards					
4,604	Oakland	6,822	New York Jets	9,189	Carolina
4,600	Philadelphia	6,752	Carolina	8,826	New York Jets
4,520	Kansas City	6,449	Kansas City	8,516	Minnesota
4,490	Houston	6,394	Jacksonville	8,403	Baltimore
4,365	Jacksonville	6,305	Oakland	8,292	Oakland
Most Passing Yards					
9,788	New Orleans	14,143	New Orleans	19,120	New Orleans
9,048	Green Bay	13,367	New England	17,141	San Diego
8,945	San Diego	13,283	San Diego	17,041	Green Bay
8,931	New England	13,228	Green Bay	16,936	New England
8,624	Detroit	12,638	New York Giants	16,571	Houston
Fewest Turnovers					
27	New England	49	New England	70	New England
33	San Francisco	52	Green Bay	73	Green Bay
36	Green Bay	57	San Francisco	84	Atlanta
38	Atlanta	63	Atlanta	87	Baltimore
38	Houston	66	Two tied	92	San Francisco
Fewest Points Allowed					
459	Pittsburgh	783	Pittsburgh	1,006	Pittsburgh
536	Baltimore	797	Baltimore	1,041	Baltimore
575	San Francisco	856	San Francisco	1,237	San Francisco
599	Green Bay	896	Green Bay	1,249	New England
627	Chicago	903	New York Jets	1,259	New York Jets
Fewest Total Yards Allowed					
8,777	Pittsburgh	13,662	Pittsburgh	17,457	Pittsburgh
9,657	New York Jets	13,694	New York Jets	18,709	Baltimore
9,724	Baltimore	14,532	Baltimore	18,964	New York Jets
9,891	San Diego	15,123	San Diego	19,959	Philadelphia
10,175	San Francisco	15,194	Cincinnati	20,300	Minnesota
Fewest Rushing Yards Allowed					
2,601	Pittsburgh	4,039	Pittsburgh	5,323	Pittsburgh
2,783	San Francisco	4,335	San Francisco	5,779	Baltimore
2,983	Chicago	4,477	Baltimore	5,971	Minnesota
2,985	Baltimore	4,741	Minnesota	6,044	San Francisco
3,131	Miami	4,767	Dallas	6,327	New York Jets
Fewest Passing Yards Allowed					
6,176	Pittsburgh	8,885	New York Jets	12,134	Pittsburgh
6,426	New York Jets	9,623	Pittsburgh	12,637	New York Jets
6,436	San Diego	9,734	Buffalo	12,930	Baltimore
6,490	Cleveland	9,784	San Diego	13,005	Buffalo
6,739	Baltimore	10,055	Baltimore	13,241	Philadelphia
Most Opponents' Turnovers					
72	New England	110	Green Bay	138	Green Bay
70	Green Bay	100	New England	126	Chicago
70	New York Giants	96	Philadelphia	125	Philadelphia
66	Chicago	94	Chicago	122	New England
63	Detroit	94	New York Giants	122	New York Jets

RETIRED UNIFORM NUMBERS IN NFL

AFC

Baltimore	None	
Buffalo	Jim Kelly	12
Cincinnati	Bob Johnson	54
Cleveland	Otto Graham	14
	Jim Brown	32
	Ernie Davis	45
	Don Fleming	46
	Lou Groza	76
Denver	John Elway	7
	Floyd Little	44
Houston	None	
Indianapolis	Peyton Manning	18
	Johnny Unitas	19
	Buddy Young	22
	Lenny Moore	24
	Art Donovan	70
	Jim Parker	77
	Raymond Berry	82
	Gino Marchetti	89
Jacksonville	None	
Kansas City	Jan Stenerud	3
	Len Dawson	16
	Emmitt Thomas	18
	Abner Haynes	28
	Stone Johnson	33
	Mack Lee Hill	36
	Derrick Thomas	58
	Willie Lanier	63
	Bobby Bell	78
	Buck Buchanan	86
Miami	Bob Griese	12
	Dan Marino	13
	Larry Csonka	39
New England	Gino Cappelletti	20
	Mike Haynes	40
	Steve Nelson	57
	John Hannah	73
	Bruce Armstrong	78
	Jim Lee Hunt	79
	Bob Dee	89
New York Jets	Joe Namath	12
	Don Maynard	13
	Joe Klecko	73
Oakland	None	
Pittsburgh	Ernie Stautner	70
San Diego	Dan Fouts	14
	Lance Alworth	19
Tennessee	Warren Moon	1
	Earl Campbell	34
	Jim Norton	43
	Mike Munchak	63
	Elvin Bethea	65
	Bruce Matthews	74

NFC

Arizona	Larry Wilson	8
	Pat Tillman	40
	Stan Mauldin	77
	J.V. Cain	88
	Marshall Goldberg	99
Atlanta	Steve Bartkowski	10
	William Andrews	31
	Jeff Van Note	57
	Tommy Nobis	60
Carolina	Sam Mills	51
Chicago	Bronko Nagurski	3
	George McAfee	5
	George Halas	7
	Willie Galimore	28
	Walter Payton	34
	Gale Sayers	40
	Brian Piccolo	41
	Sid Luckman	42
	Dick Butkus	51
	Bill Hewitt	56
	Bill George	61
	Bulldog Turner	66
	Red Grange	77
Dallas	None	
Detroit	Dutch Clark	7
	Bobby Layne	22
	Doak Walker	37
	Joe Schmidt	56
	Chuck Hughes	85
Green Bay	Tony Canadeo	3
	Don Hutson	14
	Bart Starr	15
	Ray Nitschke	66
	Reggie White	92
Minnesota	Fran Tarkenton	10
	Mick Tingelhoff	53
	Jim Marshall	70
	Korey Stringer	77
	Cris Carter	80
	Alan Page	88
New Orleans	Jim Taylor	31
	Doug Atkins	81
New York Giants	Ray Flaherty	1
	Tuffy Leemans	4
	Mel Hein	7
	Phil Simms	11
	Y.A. Tittle	14
	Frank Gifford	16
	Al Blozis	32
	Joe Morrison	40
	Charlie Conerly	42
	Ken Strong	50
	Lawrence Taylor	56
Philadelphia	Steve Van Buren	15
	Tom Brookshier	40
	Pete Retzlaff	44
	Chuck Bednarik	60
	Al Wistert	70
	Reggie White	92
	Jerome Brown	99
St. Louis	Bob Waterfield	7
	Marshall Faulk	28
	Eric Dickerson	29
	Merlin Olsen	74
	Deacon Jones	75
	Jackie Slater	78
	Isaac Bruce	80
	Jack Youngblood	85
San Francisco	Steve Young	8
	John Brodie	12
	Joe Montana	16
	Joe Perry	34
	Jimmy Johnson	37
	Hugh McElhenny	39
	Ronnie Lott	42
	Charlie Krueger	70
	Leo Nomellini	73
	Bob St. Clair	79
	Jerry Rice	80
	Dwight Clark	87
Seattle	"Fans/the twelfth man"	12
	Walter Jones	71
	Steve Largent	80
Tampa Bay	Lee Roy Selmon	63
Washington	Sammy Baugh	33

INSIDE THE NUMBERS

The NFL rates its passers for statistical purposes against a fixed performance standard based on statistical achievements of all qualified pro passers since 1960. The current system replaced one that rated passers in relation to their position in a total group based on various criteria. The current system, which was adopted in 1973, removes inequities that existed in the former method and, at the same time, provides a means of comparing passing performances from one season to the next.

It is important to remember that the system is used to rate passers, not quarterbacks. Statistics do not reflect leadership, play-calling, and other intangible factors that go into making a successful professional quarterback. Four categories are used as a basis for compiling a rating:

—Percentage of completions per attempt
—Average yards gained per attempt
—Percentage of touchdown passes per attempt
—Percentage of interceptions per attempt

The average standard is 1.000. The bottom is .000. To earn a 2.000 rating, a passer must perform at exceptional levels, i.e., 70 percent in completions, 10 percent in touchdowns, 1.5 percent in interceptions, and 11 yards average gain per pass attempt. The maximum a passer can receive in any category is 2.375.

For example, to gain a 2.375 in completion percentage, a passer would have to complete 77.5 percent of his passes. The NFL record is 70.55 by Ken Anderson (Cincinnati, 1982). To earn a 2.375 in percentage of touchdowns, a passer would have to achieve a percentage of 11.9. The record is 13.9 by Sid Luckman (Chicago, 1943). To gain 2.375 in percentage of interceptions, a passer would have to go the entire season without an interception. The 2.375 figure in average yards is 12.50, compared with the NFL record of 11.17 by Tommy O'Connell (Cleveland, 1957).

In order to make the rating more understandable, the point rating is then converted into a scale of 100, with 158.3 being the highest rating a passer can achieve. In cases where statistical performance has been superior, it is possible for a passer to sur-

pass a 100 rating. For example, take Aaron Rodgers' record-setting season in 2011 when he completed 343 of 502 passes for 4,643 yards, 45 touchdowns, and 6 interceptions. The four calculations would be:

—Percentage of Completions—343 of 502 is 68.33 percent. Subtract 30 from the completion percentage (38.33) and multiply the result by 0.05. The result is a point rating of 1.916.
Note: If the result is less than zero (Comp. Pct. less than 30.0), award zero points. If the results are greater than 2.375 (Comp. Pct. greater than 77.5), award 2.375.

—Average Yards Gained Per Attempt—4,643 yards divided by 502 attempts is 9.25. Subtract three yards from yards-per-attempt (6.25) and multiply the result by 0.25. The result is 1.562.
Note: If the result is less than zero (yards per attempt less than 3.0), award zero points. If the result is greater than 2.375 (yards per attempt greater than 12.5), award 2.375 points.

—Percentage of Touchdown Passes—45 touchdowns in 502 attempts is 8.96 percent. Multiply the touchdown percentage by 0.2. The result is 1.793.
Note: If the result is greater than 2.375 (touchdown percentage greater than 11.875), award 2.375.

—Percentage of Interceptions—Six interceptions in 502 attempts is 1.20 percent. Multiply the interception percentage by 0.25 (0.299) and subtract the number from 2.375. The result is 2.076.
Note: If the result is less than zero (interception percentage greater than 9.5), award zero points.

The sum of the four steps is (1.916 + 1.562 + 1.793 + 2.076) 7.348. The sum is then divided by six (1.225) and multiplied by 100. In this case, the result is 122.5. This same formula can be used to determine a passer rating for any player who attempts at least one pass.

The following is a list of the Top 25 single-season passer ratings among qualifying players:

TOP 25 NFL SINGLE-SEASON PASSER RATINGS (QUALIFYING PLAYERS)

Player, Team	Season	Rating	Att.	Comp.	Pct.	Yds.	Yds. Avg.	TD	TD Pct.	Int.	Int. Pct.
Aaron Rodgers, Green Bay	2011	*122.5	502	343	68.3	4,643	9.25	45	9.0	6	1.2
Peyton Manning, Indianapolis	2004	121.1	497	336	67.6	4,557	9.17	49	9.9	10	2.0
Tom Brady, New England	2007	117.2	578	398	68.9	4,806	8.31	*50	8.7	8	1.4
Steve Young, San Francisco	1994	112.8	461	324	70.2	3,969	8.61	35	7.6	10	2.2
Joe Montana, San Francisco	1989	112.4	386	271	70.2	3,521	9.12	26	6.7	8	2.1
Tom Brady, New England	2010	111.0	492	324	65.9	3,900	7.93	36	7.3	4	0.8
Daunte Culpepper, Minnesota	2004	110.9	548	379	69.2	4,717	8.61	39	7.1	11	2.0
Drew Brees, New Orleans	2011	110.6	657	468	*71.2	*5,476	8.33	46	7.0	14	2.1
Milt Plum, Cleveland	1960	110.4	250	151	60.4	2,297	9.19	21	8.4	5	2.0
Sammy Baugh, Washington	1945	109.9	182	128	70.3	1,669	9.17	11	6.0	4	2.2
Drew Brees, New Orleans	2009	109.6	514	363	70.6	4,388	8.54	34	6.6	11	2.1
Kurt Warner, St. Louis	1999	109.2	499	325	65.1	4,353	8.72	41	8.2	13	2.6
Dan Marino, Miami	1984	108.9	564	362	64.2	5,084	9.01	48	8.5	17	3.0
Sid Luckman, Chicago Bears	1943	107.5	202	110	54.5	2,194	10.86	28	13.9	12	5.9
Brett Favre, Minnesota	2009	107.2	531	363	68.4	4,202	7.91	30	5.6	7	1.3
Steve Young, San Francisco	1992	107.0	402	268	66.7	3,465	8.62	25	6.2	7	1.7
Randall Cunningham, Minnesota	1998	106.0	425	259	60.9	3,704	8.72	34	8.0	10	2.4
Tom Brady, New England	2011	105.6	611	401	65.6	5,235	8.57	39	6.4	12	2.0
Philip Rivers, San Diego	2008	105.5	478	312	65.3	4,009	8.39	34	7.1	11	2.3
Bart Starr, Green Bay	1966	105.0	251	156	62.2	2,257	8.99	14	5.6	3	1.2
Drew Brees, San Diego	2004	104.8	400	262	65.5	3,159	7.90	27	6.8	7	1.8
Roger Staubach, Dallas	1971	104.8	211	126	59.7	1,882	8.92	15	7.1	4	1.9
Y.A. Tittle, New York Giants	1963	104.8	367	221	60.2	3,145	8.57	36	9.8	14	3.8
Donovan McNabb, Philadelphia	2004	104.7	469	300	64.0	3,875	8.06	31	6.6	8	1.7
Steve Young, San Francisco	1997	104.7	356	241	67.7	3,029	8.51	19	5.3	6	1.7

*NFL Record

HIGHEST NFL POSTSEASON PASSER RATINGS (MINIMUM: 150 ATTEMPTS)

Player	Games	Att.	Cmp.	Pct.	Yards	Avg. Gain	TD	Int.	Rating
Aaron Rodgers	7	220	144	65.5	1,781	8.10	15	4	105.5
Bart Starr	10	213	130	61.0	1,753	8.23	15	3	104.8
Drew Brees	9	391	262	67.0	2,980	7.62	22	4	104.2
Kurt Warner	13	462	307	66.5	3,952	8.55	31	14	102.8
Joe Montana	23	734	460	62.7	5,772	7.86	45	21	95.6
Mark Sanchez	6	157	95	60.5	1,155	7.36	9	3	94.3
Ken Anderson	6	166	110	66.3	1,321	7.96	9	6	93.5
Joe Theismann	10	211	128	60.7	1,782	8.45	11	7	91.4
Eli Manning	11	356	219	61.5	2,516	7.07	17	8	89.3
Peyton Manning	19	718	453	63.1	5,389	7.51	29	19	88.4

HIGHEST NFL POSTSEASON PASSER RATINGS, ACTIVE PLAYERS (MINIMUM: 150 ATTEMPTS)

Player	Games	Att.	Cmp.	Pct.	Yards	Avg. Gain	TD	Int.	Rating
Aaron Rodgers	7	220	144	65.5	1,781	8.10	15	4	105.5
Drew Brees	9	391	262	67.0	2,980	7.62	22	4	104.2
Mark Sanchez	6	157	95	60.5	1,155	7.36	9	3	94.3
Eli Manning	11	356	219	61.5	2,516	7.07	17	8	89.3
Peyton Manning	19	718	453	63.1	5,389	7.51	29	19	88.4
Tom Brady	22	793	499	62.9	5,285	6.66	38	20	87.8
Matt Hasselbeck	11	406	237	58.4	2,741	6.75	18	9	84.4
Ben Roethlisberger	14	409	248	60.6	3,150	7.70	20	17	83.7
Jake Delhomme	8	226	130	57.5	1,847	8.17	12	10	83.3
Donovan McNabb	16	577	341	59.1	3,752	6.50	24	17	80.0

ALL-TIME RANKINGS OF PLAYERS IN FOUR CATEGORIES THAT DETERMINE NFL PASSER RATING

Minimum: 1,500 Attempts

COMPLETION PERCENTAGE	Pct.	Att.	Comp.
Chad Pennington	66.05	2,471	1,632
Drew Brees	65.94	5,479	3,613
Kurt Warner	65.50	4,070	2,666
Aaron Rodgers	65.36	2,113	1,381
Peyton Manning	64.94	7,210	4,682
Tony Romo	64.51	2,592	1,672
Matt Schaub	64.33	2,279	1,466
Steve Young	64.28	4,149	2,667
Tom Brady	63.84	5,321	3,397
Philip Rivers	63.55	3,037	1,930

TOUCHDOWN PERCENTAGE	Pct.	Att.	TD
Sid Luckman	7.86	1,744	137
Frank Ryan	6.99	2,133	149
Len Dawson	6.39	3,741	239
Daryle Lamonica	6.31	2,601	164
Aaron Rodgers	6.25	2,113	132
Sammy Baugh	6.24	2,995	187
Charlie Conerly	6.11	2,833	173
Bob Waterfield	6.00	1,617	97
Earl Morrall	5.99	2,689	161
Sonny Jurgensen	5.98	4,262	255

AVERAGE YARDS PER PASS	Avg.	Att.	Yards
Otto Graham	8.63	1,565	13,499
Sid Luckman	8.42	1,744	14,686
Aaron Rodgers	8.22	2,113	17,366
Norm Van Brocklin	8.16	2,895	23,611
Tony Romo	8.04	2,592	20,834
Ben Roethlisberger	8.02	3,313	26,579
Philip Rivers	8.00	3,037	24,285
Steve Young	7.98	4,149	33,124
Kurt Warner	7.95	4,070	32,344
Matt Schaub	7.87	2,279	17,936

INTERCEPTION PERCENTAGE	Pct.	Att.	Int.
Aaron Rodgers	1.80	2,113	38
Neil O'Donnell	2.11	3,229	68
Tom Brady	2.16	5,321	115
Donovan McNabb	2.18	5,374	117
Jeff Garcia	2.26	3,676	83
Matt Ryan	2.27	2,022	46
Mark Brunell	2.33	4,640	108
Jason Campbell	2.35	2,131	50
Joe Flacco	2.35	1,958	46
David Garrard	2.37	2,281	54

STARTING RECORDS OF ACTIVE NFL QUARTERBACKS

Minimum: 10 starts

	W - L - T	Pct.
Tom Brady	124-35-0	.780
Ben Roethlisberger	80-33-0	.708
Matt Ryan	43-19-0	.694
Joe Flacco	44-20-0	.688
Peyton Manning	141-67-0	.678
Aaron Rodgers	41-21-0	.661
Philip Rivers	63-33-0	.656
John Skelton	7- 4-0	.636
Vince Young	31-19-0	.620
Donovan McNabb	98-62-1	.612
Tony Romo	47-30-0	.610
Drew Brees	92-61-0	.601
Michael Vick	53-37-1	.588
Jake Delhomme	56-40-0	.583
Eli Manning	69-50-0	.580
Mark Sanchez	27-20-0	.574
Tim Tebow	8- 6-0	.571
Andy Dalton	9- 7-0	.563
Rex Grossman	25-22-0	.532
Matt Hasselbeck	78-69-0	.531
Jay Cutler	41-37-0	.526
Matt Moore	13-12-0	.520
Matt Cassel	28-26-0	.519
Mark Brunell	78-73-0	.517
David Garrard	39-37-0	.513
Kyle Orton	35-34-0	.507
Jeff Garcia	58-58-0	.500
Shaun Hill	13-13-0	.500
Tarvaris Jackson	17-17-0	.500
Sage Rosenfels	6- 6-0	.500
Byron Leftwich	24-25-0	.490
Matt Schaub	32-34-0	.485
Alex Smith	32-34-0	.485
Carson Palmer	50-56-0	.472
Charlie Batch	24-29-0	.453
Kerry Collins	81-99-0	.450
Matthew Stafford	13-16-0	.448
A.J. Feeley	8-10-0	.444
Matt Leinart	8-10-0	.444
Jason Campbell	31-39-0	.443
Kyle Boller	20-27-0	.426
Josh Freeman	17-23-0	.425
Trent Edwards	14-19-0	.424
Chad Henne	13-18-0	.419
Derek Anderson	18-25-0	.419
Josh McCown	13-20-0	.394
Kevin Kolb	6-10-0	.375
Cam Newton	6-10-0	.375
Ryan Fitzpatrick	18-33-1	.356
Kellen Clemens	4- 8-0	.333
Chris Redman	4- 8-0	.333
Sam Bradford	8-18-0	.308
J.P. Losman	10-23-0	.303
Bruce Gradkowski	6-14-0	.300
Billy Volek	3- 7-0	.300
David Carr	23-56-0	.291
Blaine Gabbert	4-10-0	.286
Colt McCoy	6-15-0	.286
Seneca Wallace	6-15-0	.286
Brady Quinn	3- 9-0	.250
Christian Ponder	2- 8-0	.200
Dan Orlovsky	2-10-0	.167
Jimmy Clausen	1- 9-0	.100
Tyler Thigpen	1-11-0	.083

MOST GAME-WINNING DRIVES IN FOURTH QUARTER OR OVERTIME SINCE 1970

47	Dan Marino, Miami, 1983-1999
45	Peyton Manning, Indianapolis, 1998-2010
43	Brett Favre, Atlanta, 1991; Green Bay, 1992-2007; New York Jets, 2008; Minnesota, 2009-2010
40	John Elway, Denver, 1983-1998

35	Warren Moon, Houston, 1984-1993; Minnesota, 1994-96; Seattle, 1997-98; Kansas City, 1999-2000

TEAMS THAT FINISHED IN FIRST PLACE IN THEIR DIVISION THE SEASON AFTER FINISHING IN LAST PLACE

Season	Team	Record	Prior Season
1967	Houston	9-4-1	*3-11-0
1968	Minnesota	8-6-0	3-8-3
1970	Cincinnati	8-6-0	4-9-1
1970	San Francisco	10-3-1	4-8-2
1972	Green Bay	10-4-0	4-8-2
1975	Baltimore	10-4-0	2-12-0
1979	Tampa Bay	10-6-0	5-11-0
1981	Cincinnati	12-4-0	6-10-0
1981	Tampa Bay	9-7-0	*5-10-1
1987	Indianapolis	9-6-0	3-13-0
1988	Cincinnati	12-4-0	4-11-0
1990	Cincinnati	9-7-0	8-8-0
1991	Denver	12-4-0	5-11-0
1992	San Diego	11-5-0	4-12-0
1993	Detroit	10-6-0	*5-11-0
1996	Carolina	12-4-0	*7-9-0
1996	Denver	13-3-0	*8-8-0
1997	New York Giants	10-5-1	6-10-0
1999	Indianapolis	13-3-0	3-13-0
1999	St. Louis	13-3-0	*4-12-0
2000	New Orleans	10-6-0	3-13-0
2001	Chicago	13-3-0	5-11-0
2001	New England	11-5-0	5-11-0
2003	Carolina	11-5-0	7-9-0
2003	Kansas City	13-3-0	*8-8-0
2004	Atlanta	11-5-0	5-11-0
2004	San Diego	12-4-0	*4-12-0
2005	Chicago	11-5-0	5-11-0
2005	New York Giants	11-5-0	*6-10-0
2005	Tampa Bay	11-5-0	5-11-0
2006	Baltimore	13-3-0	*6-10-0
2006	New Orleans	10-6-0	3-13-0
2006	Philadelphia	10-6-0	6-10-0
2007	Tampa Bay	9-7-0	4-12-0
2008	Miami	11-5-0	1-15-0
2009	New Orleans	13-3-0	8-8-0
2010	Kansas City	10-6-0	4-12-0
2011	Denver	8-8-0	4-12-0
2011	Houston	10-6-0	*6-10-0

*tied for last place

LONGEST WINNING STREAKS SINCE 1970

23	Indianapolis, 2008-09	(9 in 2008; 14 in 2009)
21	New England, 2006-08	(3 in 2006, 16 in 2007, 2 in 2008)
18	New England, 2003-04	(12 in 2003, 6 in 2004)
16	Miami, 1971-73	(1 in 1971, 14 in 1972, 1 in 1973)
16	Miami, 1983-84	(5 in 1983, 11 in 1984)
16	Pittsburgh, 2004-05	(14 in 2004, 2 in 2005)
15	San Francisco, 1989-90	(5 in 1989, 10 in 1990)
15	Green Bay, 2010-11	(2 in 2010, 13 in 2011)
14	Oakland, 1976-77	(10 in 1976, 4 in 1977)
14	Denver, 1997-98	(1 in 1997, 13 in 1998)
13	Minnesota, 1974-75	(3 in 1974, 10 in 1975)
13	Chicago, 1984-85	(1 in 1984, 12 in 1985)
13	New York Giants, 1989-90	(3 in 1989, 10 in 1990)
13	Indianapolis, 2005	
13	Tennessee, 2007-08	(3 in 2007, 10 in 2008)
13	New Orleans, 2009	
12	Washington, 1990-91	(1 in 1990, 11 in 1991)
11	Pittsburgh, 1975	
11	Baltimore, 1975-76	(9 in 1975, 2 in 1976)
11	Chicago, 1986-87	(7 in 1986, 4 in 1987)
11	Houston, 1993	
11	San Francisco, 1997	
11	Jacksonville, 1999	
11	Indianapolis, 1999	
11	Seattle, 2005	
11	San Diego, 2006-07	(10 in 2006, 1 in 2007)
11	San Diego, 2009	

NFL PLAYOFF APPEARANCES BY SEASONS

Team	Number of Seasons in Playoffs
New York Giants	31
Dallas	30
Green Bay	27
Pittsburgh	27
St. Louis	27
Minnesota	26
Chicago	25
Cleveland	24
Indianapolis	24
Philadelphia	23
San Francisco	23
Miami	22
Washington	22
Oakland	21
Tennessee	21
New England	19
Denver	18
Buffalo	17
San Diego	17
Kansas City	16
Detroit	15
New York Jets	14
Atlanta	11
Seattle	11
Cincinnati	10
Tampa Bay	10
New Orleans	9
Arizona	8
Baltimore	8
Jacksonville	6
Carolina	4
Houston	1

TEAMS IN SUPER BOWL CONTENTION (1978-2011)

	With 3 Weeks to Play	With 2 Weeks to Play	With 1 Week to Play
1978	20	17	12
1979	19	15	13
1980	20	14	12
1981	21	20	16
1982	*27	25	*22
1983	24	19	15
1984	18	14	13
1985	21	18	13
1986	19	17	14
1987	19	19	15
1988	21	18	15
1989	21	18	17
1990	23	20	15
1991	20	18	13
1992	20	16	14
1993	20	18	16
1994	25	22	15
1995	*27	21	18
1996	23	21	13
1997	22	18	14
1998	22	19	14
1999	23	20	16
2000	19	17	16
2001	23	16	13
2002	21	21	19
2003	22	17	14
2004	*27	*26	17
2005	18	17	14
2006	25	24	20
2007	23	16	15
2008	22	19	18
2009	24	19	17
2010	23	20	16
2011	22	22	17

RECORD OF TEAMS ON THE ROAD (1970-2011)

Year	W	L	T	Pct
1970	72	101	9	.420
1971	74	100	8	.429
1972	87	90	5	.492
1973	66	109	7	.382
1974	82	99	1	.453
1975	81	101	0	.445
1976	83	112	1	.426
1977	83	113	0	.423
1978	93	130	1	.417
1979	92	132	0	.411
1980	101	122	1	.453
1981	84	139	1	.377
1982	57	68	1	.456
1983	104	119	1	.467
1984	94	129	1	.422
1985	80	144	0	.357
1986	104	118	2	.469
1987	95	114	1	.455
1988	92	131	1	.413
1989	95	128	1	.426
1990	93	131	0	.415
1991	92	132	0	.411
1992	88	136	0	.393
1993	101	123	0	.451
1994	96	128	0	.429
1995	96	144	0	.400
1996	91	149	0	.379
1997	93	145	2	.392
1998	89	151	0	.371
1999	100	148	0	.403
2000	110	138	0	.444
2001	112	136	0	.452
2002	107	148	1	.420
2003	99	157	0	.387
2004	111	145	0	.434
2005	105	151	0	.410
2006	120	136	0	.469
2007	109	147	0	.426
2008	109	146	1	.428
2009	110	146	0	.430
2010	113	143	0	.441
2011	111	145	0	.434

GAMES DECIDED BY 7 POINTS OR FEWER AND 3 POINTS OR FEWER (1970-2011)

	Games Decided by 7 Points or Fewer	Games Decided by 3 Points or Fewer
1970	59 of 182 (32.4%)	34 of 182 (18.7%)
1971	76 of 182 (41.8%)	35 of 182 (19.2%)
1972	71 of 182 (39.0%)	38 of 182 (20.9%)
1973	60 of 182 (32.9%)	28 of 182 (15.4%)
1974	91 of 182 (50.0%)	37 of 182 (20.3%)
1975	62 of 182 (34.1%)	35 of 182 (19.2%)
1976	73 of 196 (37.2%)	38 of 196 (19.4%)
1977	85 of 196 (43.4%)	36 of 196 (18.4%)
1978	108 of 224 (48.2%)	49 of 224 (21.9%)
1979	104 of 224 (46.4%)	51 of 224 (22.8%)
1980	108 of 224 (48.2%)	58 of 224 (25.9%)
1981	91 of 224 (40.6%)	60 of 224 (26.8%)
1982	61 of 126 (48.4%)	33 of 126 (26.2%)
1983	106 of 224 (47.3%)	54 of 224 (24.1%)
1984	95 of 224 (42.4%)	58 of 224 (25.9%)
1985	87 of 224 (38.8%)	38 of 224 (17.0%)
1986	106 of 224 (47.3%)	48 of 224 (21.4%)
1987	99 of 210 (47.1%)	40 of 210 (19.0%)
1988	113 of 224 (50.4%)	62 of 224 (27.7%)
1989	107 of 224 (47.8%)	55 of 224 (24.6%)
1990	97 of 224 (43.3%)	54 of 224 (24.1%)
1991	112 of 224 (50.0%)	57 of 224 (25.4%)
1992	88 of 224 (39.3%)	48 of 224 (21.4%)
1993	*105 of 224 (46.9%)	53 of 224 (23.7%)
1994	115 of 224 (51.3%)	60 of 224 (26.8%)

	Games Decided by 7 Points or Fewer	Games Decided by 3 Points or Fewer
1995	115 of 240 (47.9%)	61 of 240 (25.4%)
1996	109 of 240 (45.4%)	47 of 240 (19.6%)
1997	111 of 240 (46.3%)	67 of 240 (27.9%)
1998	113 of 240 (47.1%)	50 of 240 (20.8%)
1999	115 of 248 (46.4%)	**64 of 248 (25.8%)
2000	109 of 248 (44.0%)	61 of 248 (24.6%)
2001	121 of 248 (48.8%)	62 of 248 (25.0%)
2002	126 of 256 (49.2%)	63 of 256 (24.6%)
2003	124 of 256 (48.4%)	60 of 256 (23.4%)
2004	116 of 256 (45.3%)	61 of 256 (23.8%)
2005	114 of 256 (44.5%)	60 of 256 (23.4%)
2006	117 of 256 (45.7%)	61 of 256 (23.8%)
2007	110 of 256 (43.0%)	55 of 256 (21.5%)
2008	115 of 256 (44.9%)	50 of 256 (19.5%)
2009	110 of 256 (43.0%)	54 of 256 (21.1%)
2010	121 of 256 (47.3%)	65 of 256 (25.4%)
2011	125 of 256 (48.8%)	50 of 256 (19.5%)

*Week record: Dec. 11-13, 1993 (Week 15), 12 of 14 games (86%) decided by 7 points or fewer.

**Week record: Oct. 10-11, 1999 (Week 5), 10 of 14 games (71%) decided by 3 points or fewer.

GAMES DECIDED BY 8 PTS. OR FEWER (1994-2011)

1994	121 of 224 (54.0%)	2005	123 of 256 (48.0%)
1995	123 of 240 (51.3%)	2006	126 of 256 (49.2%)
1996	115 of 240 (47.9%)	2007	120 of 256 (46.9%)
1997	120 of 240 (50.0%)	2008	118 of 256 (46.1%)
1998	120 of 240 (50.0%)	2009	120 of 256 (46.9%)
1999	124 of 248 (50.0%)	2010	131 of 256 (51.2%)
2000	119 of 248 (48.0%)	2011	132 of 256 (51.6%)
2001	*128 of 248 (51.6%)	*Week record: Oct. 14-15,	
2002	137 of 256 (53.5%)	2001 (Week 5), 12 of 14	
2003	132 of 256 (51.6%)	games (86%) decided by 8	
2004	121 of 256 (47.3%)	points or fewer	

TWO-POINT CONVERSION RESULTS (1994-2011)

1994	59 of 116 (50.9%)	2003	29 of 66 (43.9%)
1995	40 of 104 (38.5%)	2004	37 of 76 (48.7%)
1996	44 of 92 (47.8%)	2005	27 of 53 (50.9%)
1997	47 of 109 (43.1%)	2006	21 of 41 (51.2%)
1998	41 of 105 (39.1%)	2007	30 of 61 (49.2%)
1999	31 of 84 (36.9%)	2008	28 of 68 (41.2%)
2000	35 of 85 (41.2%)	2009	24 of 60 (40.0%)
2001	40 of 90 (44.4%)	2010	26 of 53 (49.1%)
2002	47 of 98 (48.0%)	2011	23 of 50 (46.0%)

RECORDS AFTER BYE WEEKS (1990-2011)

AFC		NFC	
Baltimore	11-5	Arizona	10-13
Buffalo	15-8	Atlanta	13-10
Cincinnati	6-16-1	Carolina	8-9
Cleveland	7-11	Chicago	15-8
Denver	17-6	Dallas	16-7
Houston	3-7	Detroit	10-13
Indianapolis	13-10	Green Bay	14-9
Jacksonville	9-8	Minnesota	17-6
Kansas City	13-10	New Orleans	11-12
Miami	13-10	New York Giants	8-15
New England	13-10	Philadelphia	19-4
New York Jets	12-11	San Francisco	10-13
Oakland	9-14	Seattle	6-17
Pittsburgh	14-9	St. Louis	11-12
San Diego	11-11	Tampa Bay	10-13
Tennessee	13-10	Washington	11-12

2011 RECORDS OF TEAMS IN CLOSE GAMES

AFC	Overall Record	Decided by 8 Pts. or Fewer	Decided By 3 Pts. or Fewer
Baltimore	12-4	5-2	2-0
Buffalo	6-10	3-5	2-2
Cincinnati	9-7	5-6	2-2
Cleveland	4-12	4-6	2-3
Denver	8-8	7-4	5-2
Houston	10-6	4-4	1-2
Indianapolis	2-14	1-7	1-1
Jacksonville	5-11	3-5	1-0
Kansas City	7-9	6-4	1-2
Miami	6-10	2-5	1-5
New England	13-3	4-3	1-1
New York Jets	8-8	3-2	1-1
Oakland	8-8	7-2	2-2
Pittsburgh	12-4	6-2	1-1
San Diego	8-8	3-5	1-2
Tennessee	9-7	5-4	2-1

NFC	Overall Record	Decided by 8 Pts. or Fewer	Decided By 3 Pts. or Fewer
Arizona	8-8	8-5	4-3
Atlanta	10-6	5-3	1-2
Carolina	6-10	2-6	0-2
Chicago	8-8	4-3	0-1
Dallas	8-8	4-5	4-2
Detroit	10-6	5-3	2-0
Green Bay	15-1	6-1	1-0
Minnesota	3-13	2-9	1-2
New Orleans	13-3	4-2	2-0
New York Giants	9-7	5-3	3-1
Philadelphia	8-8	2-5	0-1
San Francisco	13-3	7-2	2-2
Seattle	7-9	2-5	1-4
St. Louis	2-14	1-5	1-1
Tampa Bay	4-12	4-3	1-0
Washington	5-11	3-6	1-2

SUPER BOWL CHAMPIONS THAT DID NOT MAKE PLAYOFFS THE FOLLOWING YEAR

Pittsburgh—Super Bowl XLIII champions did not make playoffs in 2009 season.

Pittsburgh—Super Bowl XL champions did not make playoffs in 2006 season.

Tampa Bay—Super Bowl XXXVII champions did not make playoffs in 2003 season.

New England—Super Bowl XXXVI champions did not make playoffs in the 2002 season.

Denver—Super Bowl XXXIII champions did not make playoffs in the 1999 season.

New York Giants—Super Bowl XXV champions did not make playoffs in the 1991 season.

Washington—Super Bowl XXII champions did not make playoffs in the 1988 season.

New York Giants—Super Bowl XXI champions did not make playoffs in the 1987 season.

San Francisco—Super Bowl XVI champions did not make playoffs in the 1982 season.

Oakland—Super Bowl XV champions did not make playoffs in the 1981 season.

Pittsburgh—Super Bowl XIV champions did not make playoffs in the 1980 season.

Kansas City—Super Bowl IV champions did not make playoffs in the 1970 season.

Green Bay—Super Bowl II champions did not make playoffs in the 1968 season.

NON-DIVISION WINNERS THAT PLAYED IN SUPER BOWL

2010	Green Bay Packers ....Super Bowl XLV (Defeated Pittsburgh, 31-25)	
2007	New York Giants ....Super Bowl XLII (Defeated New England, 17-14)	
2005	Pittsburgh Steelers ....Super Bowl XL (Defeated Seattle, 21-10)	
2000	Baltimore Ravens ....Super Bowl XXXV (Defeated New York Giants, 34-7)	
1999	Tennessee Titans ....Super Bowl XXXIV (Lost to St. Louis, 23-16)	
1997	Denver Broncos.................................Super Bowl XXXII (Defeated Green Bay, 31-24)	
1992	Buffalo Bills ....Super Bowl XXVII (Lost to Dallas, 52-17)	

1985	New England Patriots	Super Bowl XX
	(Lost to Chicago, 46-10)	
1980	Oakland Raiders	Super Bowl XV
	(Defeated Philadelphia, 27-10)	
1975	Dallas Cowboys	Super Bowl X
	(Lost to Pittsburgh, 21-17)	
1969	Kansas City Chiefs	Super Bowl IV
	(Defeated Minnesota, 23-7)	

TEAMS AT OR UNDER .500 IN POSTSEASON PLAY

2011	Denver Broncos	8-8
2010	Seattle Seahawks	7-9
2008	San Diego Chargers	8-8
2006	New York Giants	8-8
2004	Minnesota Vikings	8-8
2004	St. Louis Rams	8-8
1999	Dallas Cowboys	8-8
1999	Detroit Lions	8-8
1991	New York Jets	8-8
1990	New Orleans Saints	8-8
1985	Cleveland Browns	8-8
1982	Cleveland Browns	4-5
1982	Detroit Lions	4-5
1969	Houston Oilers	6-6-2

TEAMS TO BEAT OPPOSING TEAM THREE TIMES IN A SEASON SINCE 1970

Year	Team	Opponent
2009	Dallas Cowboys	Philadelphia Eagles
2008	Pittsburgh Steelers	Baltimore Ravens
2004	St. Louis Rams	Seattle Seahawks
2002	Pittsburgh Steelers	Cleveland Browns
2000	New York Giants	Philadelphia Eagles
1999	Tennessee Titans	Jacksonville Jaguars
1997	Green Bay Packers	Tampa Bay Buccaneers
1997	New England Patriots	Miami Dolphins
1994	Pittsburgh Steelers	Cleveland Browns
1993	Los Angeles Raiders	Denver Broncos
1991	Kansas City Chiefs	Los Angeles Raiders
1986	New York Giants	Washington Redskins
1982	Miami Dolphins	New York Jets

COLDEST NFL GAMES ON RECORD

-13 degrees (-48 degree wind chill)—December 31, 1967, Lambeau Field, Green Bay, Wisconsin, NFL Championship (Green Bay 21, Dallas 17)

-9 degrees (-59 degree wind chill)—January 10, 1982, Riverfront Stadium, Cincinnati, Ohio, AFC Championship (Cincinnati 27, San Diego 7)

-1 degrees (-23 degree wind chill)—January 20, 2008, Lambeau Field, Green Bay, Wisconsin, NFC Championship (New York Giants 23, Green Bay 20 in OT)

TEAM LEADERS

Offense	Most Scored	Fewest Scored
1st Quarter	132 Green Bay	19 Indianapolis
2nd Quarter	166 New Orleans	33 Denver
3rd Quarter	150 Green Bay	33 Jacksonville
4th Quarter	157 New York Giants	61 St. Louis
Defense	**Most Scored**	**Fewest Scored**
1st Quarter	39 Hou. & Atl.	126 Tampa Bay
2nd Quarter	42 San Francisco	178 Tampa Bay
3rd Quarter	40 S.F. & Sea.	132 Minnesota
4th Quarter	57 Pittsburgh	143 Carolina

2011 NFL SCORE BY QUARTERS

AFC Offense	1	2	3	4	OT	PTS
New England	82	148	141	142	0	513
San Diego	81	124	116	85	0	406
Houston	110	107	63	101	0	381
Baltimore	95	110	78	95	0	378
New York Jets	61	123	75	118	0	377
Buffalo	87	96	78	111	0	372
Oakland	56	137	66	97	3	359
Cincinnati	83	59	86	116	0	344
Miami	84	86	91	68	0	329
Pittsburgh	69	121	63	72	0	325
Tennessee	57	110	67	91	0	325
Denver	74	33	75	118	9	309
Indianapolis	19	89	36	99	0	243
Jacksonville	44	100	33	66	0	243
Cleveland	26	83	35	74	0	218
Kansas City	58	40	43	68	3	212

NFC Offense	1	2	3	4	OT	PTS
Green Bay	132	154	150	124	0	560
New Orleans	99	166	126	153	3	547
Detroit	80	125	125	141	3	474
Carolina	92	148	83	83	0	406
Atlanta	120	115	74	93	0	402
Philadelphia	76	165	74	81	0	396
New York Giants	70	108	59	157	0	394
San Francisco	45	125	101	109	0	380
Dallas	72	110	62	119	6	369
Chicago	77	128	82	66	0	353
Minnesota	104	91	61	84	0	340
Seattle	61	58	90	112	0	321
Arizona	36	68	79	111	18	312
Washington	43	103	60	82	0	288
Tampa Bay	34	96	65	92	0	287
St. Louis	37	58	37	61	0	193

AFC Defense	1	2	3	4	OT	PTS
Pittsburgh	43	71	56	57	0	227
Baltimore	43	86	71	66	0	266
Houston	39	78	56	105	0	278
Cleveland	82	94	62	66	3	307
Miami	53	87	50	120	3	313
Tennessee	64	79	74	100	0	317
Cincinnati	51	132	50	90	0	323
Jacksonville	83	103	64	79	0	329
Kansas City	59	106	95	75	3	338
New England	87	83	50	122	0	342
New York Jets	94	90	79	100	0	363
San Diego	89	118	67	97	6	377
Denver	52	154	91	93	0	390
Indianapolis	108	129	92	101	0	430
Oakland	92	92	115	134	0	433
Buffalo	76	140	109	109	0	434

NFC Defense	1	2	3	4	OT	PTS
San Francisco	43	42	40	101	3	229
Seattle	62	103	40	107	3	315
Philadelphia	63	90	64	111	0	328
New Orleans	70	113	67	89	0	339
Chicago	51	99	95	93	3	341
Dallas	51	112	75	103	6	347
Arizona	81	107	85	75	0	348
Atlanta	39	110	127	71	3	350
Green Bay	66	97	66	130	0	359
Washington	75	90	73	126	3	367
Detroit	86	145	74	82	0	387
New York Giants	71	115	79	135	0	400
St. Louis	94	103	100	104	6	407
Carolina	79	117	90	143	0	429
Minnesota	92	121	132	101	3	449
Tampa Bay	126	178	86	104	0	494
NFL TOTALS	**2,399**	**3,583**	**2,585**	**3,358**	**54**	**11,979**

2012 TOP 100 TELEVISION MARKETS
(NFL TEAM MARKETS IN BOLD)

RANK	MARKET	TV HOUSEHOLDS	% of U.S.
1	**New York**	**7,387,810**	**6.444**
2	Los Angeles	5,569,780	4.858
3	**Chicago**	**3,493,480**	**3.047**
4	**Philadelphia**	**2,993,370**	**2.611**
5	**Dallas-Ft. Worth**	**2,571,310**	**2.243**
6	**San Francisco-Oak-San Jose**	**2,506,510**	**2.186**
7	**Boston (Manchester)**	**2,379,690**	**2.076**
8	**Washington, DC (Hagrstwn)**	**2,360,180**	**2.059**
9	**Atlanta**	**2,292,640**	**2.000**
10	**Houston**	**2,185,260**	**1.906**
11	**Detroit**	**1,842,650**	**1.607**
12	**Seattle-Tacoma**	**1,811,420**	**1.580**
13	**Phoenix (Prescott)**	**1,811,330**	**1.580**
14	**Tampa-St. Pete (Sarasota)**	**1,788,240**	**1.560**
15	**Minneapolis-St. Paul**	**1,721,940**	**1.502**
16	**Miami-Ft. Lauderdale**	**1,583,800**	**1.381**
17	**Denver**	**1,548,570**	**1.351**
18	**Cleveland-Akron (Canton)**	**1,514,170**	**1.321**
19	Orlando-Daytona Bch-Melbrn	1,465,460	1.278
20	Sacramnto-Stkton-Modesto	1,388,510	1.211
21	**St. Louis**	**1,253,920**	**1.094**
22	Portland, OR	1,190,010	1.038
23	**Pittsburgh**	**1,171,490**	**1.022**
24	Raleigh-Durham (Fayetvlle)	1,143,420	0.997
25	**Charlotte**	**1,140,900**	**0.995**
26	**Indianapolis**	**1,109,970**	**0.968**
27	**Baltimore**	**1,097,310**	**0.957**
28	**San Diego**	**1,077,600**	**0.940**
29	**Nashville**	**1,024,560**	**0.894**
30	Hartford & New Haven	1,006,280	0.878
31	**Kansas City**	**939,740**	**0.820**
32	Columbus, OH	932,680	0.814
33	Salt Lake City	927,540	0.809
34	Milwaukee	907,660	0.792
35	**Cincinnati**	**896,090**	**0.782**
36	San Antonio	880,690	0.768
37	Greenvll-Spart-Ashevll-And	860,930	0.751
38	West Palm Beach-Ft. Pierce	788,020	0.687
39	Birmingham (Ann and Tusc)	738,790	0.644
40	Las Vegas	737,300	0.643
41	Harrisburg-Lncstr-Leb-York	729,440	0.636
42	Grand Rapids-Kalmzoo-B.Crk	722,150	0.630
43	Norfolk-Portsmth-Newpt Nws	718,750	0.627
44	Oklahoma City	712,630	0.622
45	Albuquerque-Santa Fe	710,050	0.619
46	Greensboro-H.Point-W.Salem	691,200	0.603
47	Austin	686,830	0.599
48	Louisville	674,050	0.588
49	Memphis	669,940	0.584
50	**Jacksonville**	**669,840**	**0.584**

2012 TOP 100 TELEVISION MARKETS
(NFL TEAM MARKETS IN BOLD)

RANK	MARKET	TV HOUSEHOLDS	% of U.S.
51	**Buffalo**	**645,190**	**0.563**
52	**New Orleans**	**643,660**	**0.561**
53	Providence-New Bedford	620,010	0.541
54	Wilkes Barre-Scranton-Hztn	590,740	0.515
55	Fresno-Visalia	574,800	0.501
56	Little Rock-Pine Bluff	571,630	0.499
57	Richmond-Petersburg	559,390	0.488
58	Albany-Schenectady-Troy	551,120	0.481
59	Tulsa	529,100	0.461
60	Mobile-Pensacola (Ft Walt)	527,930	0.460
61	Knoxville	527,790	0.460
62	Ft. Myers-Naples	504,240	0.440
63	Dayton	493,600	0.431
64	Lexington	488,850	0.426
65	Charleston-Huntington	465,030	0.406
66	Roanoke-Lynchburg	455,860	0.398
67	Wichita-Hutchinson Plus	454,590	0.397
68	Flint-Saginaw-Bay City	451,880	0.394
69	**Green Bay-Appleton**	**445,760**	**0.389**
70	Tucson (Sierra Vista)	442,020	0.386
71	Honolulu	434,730	0.379
72	Des Moines-Ames	431,300	0.376
73	Spokane	426,690	0.372
74	Toledo	426,280	0.372
75	Springfield, MO	423,010	0.369
76	Omaha	415,510	0.362
77	Columbia, SC	404,830	0.353
78	Portland-Auburn	401,370	0.350
79	Rochester, NY	398,790	0.348
80	Huntsville-Decatur (Flor)	394,010	0.344
81	Paducah-Cape Girard-Harsbg	393,330	0.343
82	Champaign&Sprngfld-Decatur	386,160	0.337
83	Shreveport	386,150	0.337
84	Syracuse	386,090	0.337
85	Madison	378,290	0.330
86	Chattanooga	366,790	0.320
87	Harlingen-Wslco-Brnsvl-McA	361,820	0.316
88	Waco-Temple-Bryan	353,190	0.308
89	Cedar Rapids-Wtrlo-IWC&Dub	344,150	0.300
90	Colorado Springs-Pueblo	343,160	0.299
91	El Paso (Las Cruces)	336,570	0.294
92	Savannah	335,080	0.292
93	Jackson, MS	334,530	0.292
94	Baton Rouge	333,010	0.290
95	Burlington-Plattsburgh	323,750	0.282
96	Tri-Cities, TN-VA	323,640	0.282
97	South Bend-Elkhart	322,090	0.281
98	Charleston, SC	311,260	0.271
99	Greenville-N.Bern-Washngtn	307,610	0.268
100	Davenport-R.Island-Moline	307,050	0.268
	TOTAL NFL MARKETS	**53,908,400**	**47.020**
	TOTAL TOP 100 MARKETS	**98,659,390**	**86.053**
	TOTAL MARKETS	**114,649,310**	**100.00**

ALL-TIME REGULAR-SEASON RECORDS OF CURRENT NFL TEAMS

AFC
BALTIMORE RAVENS

	All Games			Home Games			Road Games		
Season	W	L	T	W	L	T	W	L	T
1996	4	12		4	4		0	8	
1997	6	9	1	3	4	1	3	5	
1998	6	10		4	4		2	6	
1999	8	8		4	4		4	4	
2000	12	4		6	2		6	2	
2001	10	6		6	2		4	4	
2002	7	9		4	4		3	5	
2003	10	6		7	1		3	5	
2004	9	7		6	2		3	5	
2005	6	10		6	2		0	8	
2006	13	3		7	1		6	2	
2007	5	11		4	4		1	7	
2008	11	5		6	2		5	3	
2009	9	7		6	2		3	5	
2010	12	4		7	1		5	3	
2011	12	4		8	0		4	4	
	140	115	1	88	39	1	52	76	

BUFFALO BILLS

	All Games			Home Games			Road Games		
Season	W	L	T	W	L	T	W	L	T
1960	5	8	1	3	4		2	4	1
1961	6	8		2	5		4	3	
1962	7	6	1	3	3	1	4	3	
1963	7	6	1	4	2	1	3	4	
1964	12	2		6	1		6	1	
1965	10	3	1	5	2		5	1	1
1966	9	4	1	4	2	1	5	2	
1967	4	10		2	5		2	5	
1968	1	12	1	1	6		0	6	1
1969	4	10		4	3		0	7	
1970	3	10	1	1	6		2	4	1
1971	1	13		1	6		0	7	
1972	4	9	1	2	4	1	2	5	
1973	9	5		5	2		4	3	
1974	9	5		5	2		4	3	
1975	8	6		3	4		5	2	
1976	2	12		1	6		1	6	
1977	3	11		1	6		2	5	
1978	5	11		4	4		1	7	
1979	7	9		3	5		4	4	
1980	11	5		6	2		5	3	
1981	10	6		7	1		3	5	
1982	4	5		4	1		0	4	
1983	8	8		3	5		5	3	
1984	2	14		2	6		0	8	
1985	2	14		2	6		0	8	
1986	4	12		3	5		1	7	
1987	7	8		4	4		3	4	
1988	12	4		8	0		4	4	
1989	9	7		6	2		3	5	
1990	13	3		8	0		5	3	
1991	13	3		7	1		6	2	
1992	11	5		6	2		5	3	
1993	12	4		6	2		6	2	
1994	7	9		4	4		3	5	
1995	10	6		6	2		4	4	
1996	10	6		7	1		3	5	
1997	6	10		4	4		2	6	
1998	10	6		6	2		4	4	
1999	11	5		6	2		5	3	
2000	8	8		5	3		3	5	
2001	3	13		1	7		2	6	
2002	8	8		5	3		3	5	
2003	6	10		4	4		2	6	
2004	9	7		5	3		4	4	
2005	5	11		4	4		1	7	
2006	7	9		4	4		3	5	
2007	7	9		4	4		3	5	
2008	7	9		3	5		4	4	
2009	6	10		3	5		3	5	
2010	4	12		2	6		2	6	
2011	6	10		5	3		1	7	
	364	416	8	210	181	4	154	235	4

CINCINNATI BENGALS

	All Games			Home Games			Road Games		
Season	W	L	T	W	L	T	W	L	T
1968	3	11		2	5		1	6	
1969	4	9	1	4	3		0	6	1
1970	8	6		5	2		3	4	
1971	4	10		3	4		1	6	
1972	8	6		4	3		4	3	
1973	10	4		7	0		3	4	
1974	7	7		4	3		3	4	
1975	11	3		6	1		5	2	
1976	10	4		6	1		4	3	
1977	8	6		5	2		3	4	
1978	4	12		3	5		1	7	
1979	4	12		4	4		0	8	
1980	6	10		3	5		3	5	
1981	12	4		6	2		6	2	
1982	7	2		4	0		3	2	
1983	7	9		4	4		3	5	
1984	8	8		5	3		3	5	
1985	7	9		5	3		2	6	
1986	10	6		6	2		4	4	
1987	4	11		1	7		3	4	
1988	12	4		8	0		4	4	
1989	8	8		5	3		3	5	
1990	9	7		5	3		4	4	
1991	3	13		3	5		0	8	
1992	5	11		3	5		2	6	
1993	3	13		3	5		0	8	
1994	3	13		2	6		1	7	
1995	7	9		3	5		4	4	
1996	8	8		6	2		2	6	
1997	7	9		6	2		1	7	
1998	3	13		1	7		2	6	
1999	4	12		2	6		2	6	
2000	4	12		3	5		1	7	
2001	6	10		4	4		2	6	
2002	2	14		1	7		1	7	
2003	8	8		5	3		3	5	
2004	8	8		5	3		3	5	
2005	11	5		5	3		6	2	
2006	8	8		4	4		4	4	
2007	7	9		5	3		2	6	
2008	4	11	1	3	4	1	1	7	
2009	10	6		6	2		4	4	
2010	4	12		3	5		1	7	
2011	9	7		4	4		5	3	
	295	379	2	182	155	1	113	224	1

CLEVELAND BROWNS*

	All Games			Home Games			Road Games		
Season	W	L	T	W	L	T	W	L	T
1950	10	2		5	1		5	1	
1951	11	1		6	0		5	1	
1952	8	4		4	2		4	2	
1953	11	1		6	0		5	1	
1954	9	3		5	1		4	2	

Season	All Games W	L	T	Home Games W	L	T	Road Games W	L	T
1955	9	2	1	5	1		4	1	1
1956	5	7		1	5		4	2	
1957	9	2	1	6	0		3	2	1
1958	9	3		4	2		5	1	
1959	7	5		3	3		4	2	
1960	8	3	1	4	2		4	1	1
1961	8	5	1	4	3		4	2	1
1962	7	6	1	4	2	1	3	4	
1963	10	4		5	2		5	2	
1964	10	3	1	5	1	1	5	2	
1965	11	3		5	2		6	1	
1966	9	5		5	2		4	3	
1967	9	5		6	1		3	4	
1968	10	4		5	2		5	2	
1969	10	3	1	5	1	1	5	2	
1970	7	7		4	3		3	4	
1971	9	5		4	3		5	2	
1972	10	4		4	3		6	1	
1973	7	5	2	5	1	1	2	4	1
1974	4	10		3	4		1	6	
1975	3	11		3	4		0	7	
1976	9	5		6	1		3	4	
1977	6	8		2	5		4	3	
1978	8	8		5	3		3	5	
1979	9	7		5	3		4	4	
1980	11	5		6	2		5	3	
1981	5	11		3	5		2	6	
1982	4	5		2	2		2	3	
1983	9	7		6	2		3	5	
1984	5	11		2	6		3	5	
1985	8	8		5	3		3	5	
1986	12	4		6	2		6	2	
1987	10	5		5	2		5	3	
1988	10	6		6	2		4	4	
1989	9	6	1	5	2	1	4	4	
1990	3	13		2	6		1	7	
1991	6	10		3	5		3	5	
1992	7	9		4	4		3	5	
1993	7	9		4	4		3	5	
1994	11	5		6	2		5	3	
1995	5	11		3	5		2	6	
1999	2	14		0	8		2	6	
2000	3	13		2	6		1	7	
2001	7	9		4	4		3	5	
2002	9	7		3	5		6	2	
2003	5	11		2	6		3	5	
2004	4	12		3	5		1	7	
2005	6	10		4	4		2	6	
2006	4	12		2	6		2	6	
2007	10	6		7	1		3	5	
2008	4	12		1	7		3	5	
2009	5	11		3	5		2	6	
2010	5	11		3	5		2	6	
2011	4	12		3	5		1	7	
	442	406	10	239	184	5	203	222	5

*Did not play from 1996-98.

Season	All Games W	L	T	Home Games W	L	T	Road Games W	L	T
1968	5	9		3	4		2	5	
1969	5	8	1	4	2	1	1	6	
1970	5	8	1	3	3	1	2	5	
1971	4	9	1	2	4	1	2	5	
1972	5	9		3	4		2	5	
1973	7	5	2	3	3	1	4	2	1
1974	7	6	1	3	3	1	4	3	
1975	6	8		5	2		1	6	
1976	9	5		6	1		3	4	
1977	12	2		6	1		6	1	
1978	10	6		6	2		4	4	
1979	10	6		6	2		4	4	
1980	8	8		4	4		4	4	
1981	10	6		8	0		2	6	
1982	2	7		1	4		1	3	
1983	9	7		6	2		3	5	
1984	13	3		7	1		6	2	
1985	11	5		6	2		5	3	
1986	11	5		7	1		4	4	
1987	10	4	1	7	1		3	3	1
1988	8	8		6	2		2	6	
1989	11	5		6	2		5	3	
1990	5	11		4	4		1	7	
1991	12	4		7	1		5	3	
1992	8	8		7	1		1	7	
1993	9	7		5	3		4	4	
1994	7	9		4	4		3	5	
1995	8	8		6	2		2	6	
1996	13	3		8	0		5	3	
1997	12	4		8	0		4	4	
1998	14	2		8	0		6	2	
1999	6	10		3	5		3	5	
2000	11	5		6	2		5	3	
2001	8	8		6	2		2	6	
2002	9	7		5	3		4	4	
2003	10	6		6	2		4	4	
2004	10	6		6	2		4	4	
2005	13	3		8	0		5	3	
2006	9	7		4	4		5	3	
2007	7	9		5	3		2	6	
2008	8	8		4	4		4	4	
2009	8	8		4	4		4	4	
2010	4	12		3	5		1	7	
2011	8	8		3	5		5	3	
	406	372	10	245	143	7	161	229	3

HOUSTON TEXANS

Season	All Games W	L	T	Home Games W	L	T	Road Games W	L	T
2002	4	12		2	6		2	6	
2003	5	11		3	5		2	6	
2004	7	9		3	5		4	4	
2005	2	14		2	6		0	8	
2006	6	10		4	4		2	6	
2007	8	8		6	2		2	6	
2008	8	8		6	2		2	6	
2009	9	7		4	4		5	3	
2010	6	10		4	4		2	6	
2011	10	6		5	3		5	3	
	65	95		39	41		26	54	

DENVER BRONCOS

Season	All Games W	L	T	Home Games W	L	T	Road Games W	L	T
1960	4	9	1	2	4	1	2	5	
1961	3	11		2	5		1	6	
1962	7	7		3	4		4	3	
1963	2	11	1	2	5		0	6	1
1964	2	11	1	2	4	1	0	7	
1965	4	10		2	5		2	5	
1966	4	10		3	4		1	6	
1967	3	11		1	6		2	5	

INDIANAPOLIS COLTS*

Season	All Games W	L	T	Home Games W	L	T	Road Games W	L	T
1953	3	9		2	4		1	5	
1954	3	9		2	4		1	5	
1955	5	6	1	4	1	1	1	5	
1956	5	7		4	2		1	5	

Season	All Games W	L	T	Home Games W	L	T	Road Games W	L	T
1957	7	5		4	2		3	3	
1958	9	3		6	0		3	3	
1959	9	3		4	2		5	1	
1960	6	6		4	2		2	4	
1961	8	6		5	2		3	4	
1962	7	7		3	4		4	3	
1963	8	6		4	3		4	3	
1964	12	2		7	1		5	1	
1965	10	3	1	5	2		5	1	1
1966	9	5		5	2		4	3	
1967	11	1	2	6	0	1	5	1	1
1968	13	1		6	1		7	0	
1969	8	5	1	4	2	1	4	3	
1970	11	2	1	5	1	1	6	1	
1971	10	4		5	2		5	2	
1972	5	9		2	5		3	4	
1973	4	10		3	4		1	6	
1974	2	12		0	7		2	5	
1975	10	4		5	2		5	2	
1976	11	3		6	1		5	2	
1977	10	4		6	1		4	3	
1978	5	11		2	6		3	5	
1979	5	11		3	5		2	6	
1980	7	9		2	6		5	3	
1981	2	14		1	7		1	7	
1982	0	8	1	0	3	1	0	5	
1983	7	9		3	5		4	4	
1984	4	12		2	6		2	6	
1985	5	11		4	4		1	7	
1986	3	13		1	7		2	6	
1987	9	6		4	4		5	2	
1988	9	7		6	2		3	5	
1989	8	8		6	2		2	6	
1990	7	9		3	5		4	4	
1991	1	15		0	8		1	7	
1992	9	7		4	4		5	3	
1993	4	12		2	6		2	6	
1994	8	8		5	3		3	5	
1995	9	7		5	3		4	4	
1996	9	7		6	2		3	5	
1997	3	13		2	6		1	7	
1998	3	13		3	5		0	8	
1999	13	3		7	1		6	2	
2000	10	6		6	2		4	4	
2001	6	10		3	5		3	5	
2002	10	6		5	3		5	3	
2003	12	4		5	3		7	1	
2004	12	4		7	1		5	3	
2005	14	2		7	1		7	1	
2006	12	4		8	0		4	4	
2007	13	3		6	2		7	1	
2008	12	4		6	2		6	2	
2009	14	2		7	1		7	1	
2010	10	6		6	2		4	4	
2011	2	14		2	6		0	8	
	453	410	7	246	185	5	207	225	2

includes Baltimore Colts (1953-1983).

JACKSONVILLE JAGUARS

Season	All Games W	L	T	Home Games W	L	T	Road Games W	L	T
1995	4	12		2	6		2	6	
1996	9	7		7	1		2	6	
1997	11	5		7	1		4	4	
1998	11	5		7	1		4	4	
1999	14	2		7	1		7	1	
2000	7	9		4	4		3	5	
2001	6	10		3	5		3	5	
2002	6	10		3	5		3	5	
2003	5	11		5	3		0	8	
2004	9	7		4	4		5	3	
2005	12	4		6	2		6	2	
2006	8	8		6	2		2	6	
2007	11	5		6	2		5	3	
2008	5	11		2	6		3	5	
2009	7	9		5	3		2	6	
2010	8	8		5	3		3	5	
2011	5	11		4	4		1	7	
	138	134		83	53		55	81	

KANSAS CITY CHIEFS*

Season	All Games W	L	T	Home Games W	L	T	Road Games W	L	T
1960	8	6		5	2		3	4	
1961	6	8		4	3		2	5	
1962	11	3		6	1		5	2	
1963	5	7	2	4	3		1	4	2
1964	7	7		4	3		3	4	
1965	7	5	2	5	2		2	3	2
1966	11	2	1	4	2	1	7	0	
1967	9	5		4	3		5	2	
1968	12	2		6	1		6	1	
1969	11	3		6	1		5	2	
1970	7	5	2	4	1	2	3	4	
1971	10	3	1	7	0		3	3	1
1972	8	6		3	4		5	2	
1973	7	5	2	5	1	1	2	4	1
1974	5	9		1	6		4	3	
1975	5	9		3	4		2	5	
1976	5	9		1	6		4	3	
1977	2	12		1	6		1	6	
1978	4	12		3	5		1	7	
1979	7	9		3	5		4	4	
1980	8	8		3	5		5	3	
1981	9	7		5	3		4	4	
1982	3	6		2	2		1	4	
1983	6	10		5	3		1	7	
1984	8	8		5	3		3	5	
1985	6	10		5	3		1	7	
1986	10	6		6	2		4	4	
1987	4	11		3	4		1	7	
1988	4	11	1	4	4		0	7	1
1989	8	7	1	5	3		3	4	1
1990	11	5		6	2		5	3	
1991	10	6		6	2		4	4	
1992	10	6		7	1		3	5	
1993	11	5		7	1		4	4	
1994	9	7		5	3		4	4	
1995	13	3		8	0		5	3	
1996	9	7		5	3		4	4	
1997	13	3		8	0		5	3	
1998	7	9		5	3		2	6	
1999	9	7		6	2		3	5	
2000	7	9		5	3		2	6	
2001	6	10		3	5		3	5	
2002	8	8		6	2		2	6	
2003	13	3		8	0		5	3	
2004	7	9		4	4		3	5	
2005	10	6		7	1		3	5	
2006	9	7		6	2		3	5	
2007	4	12		2	6		2	6	
2008	2	14		1	7		1	7	
2009	4	12		1	7		3	5	
2010	10	6		7	1		3	5	
2011	7	9		3	5		4	4	
	402	374	12	238	151	4	164	223	8

includes Dallas Texans (1960-62).

MIAMI DOLPHINS

Season	All Games W	L	T	Home Games W	L	T	Road Games W	L	T
1966	3	11		2	5		1	6	
1967	4	10		4	3		0	7	
1968	5	8	1	1	5	1	4	3	
1969	3	10	1	2	4	1	1	6	
1970	10	4		6	1		4	3	
1971	10	3	1	6	1		4	2	1
1972	14	0		7	0		7	0	
1973	12	2		7	0		5	2	
1974	11	3		7	0		4	3	
1975	10	4		5	2		5	2	
1976	6	8		3	4		3	4	
1977	10	4		6	1		4	3	
1978	11	5		7	1		4	4	
1979	10	6		6	2		4	4	
1980	8	8		5	3		3	5	
1981	11	4	1	6	1	1	5	3	
1982	7	2		4	0		3	2	
1983	12	4		7	1		5	3	
1984	14	2		7	1		7	1	
1985	12	4		8	0		4	4	
1986	8	8		4	4		4	4	
1987	8	7		4	3		4	4	
1988	6	10		4	4		2	6	
1989	8	8		4	4		4	4	
1990	12	4		7	1		5	3	
1991	8	8		5	3		3	5	
1992	11	5		6	2		5	3	
1993	9	7		4	4		5	3	
1994	10	6		6	2		4	4	
1995	9	7		5	3		4	4	
1996	8	8		4	4		4	4	
1997	9	7		6	2		3	5	
1998	10	6		7	1		3	5	
1999	9	7		5	3		4	4	
2000	11	5		5	3		6	2	
2001	11	5		7	1		4	4	
2002	9	7		7	1		2	6	
2003	10	6		4	4		6	2	
2004	4	12		3	5		1	7	
2005	9	7		5	3		4	4	
2006	6	10		4	4		2	6	
2007	1	15		1	7		0	8	
2008	11	5		5	3		6	2	
2009	7	9		4	4		3	5	
2010	7	9		1	7		6	2	
2011	6	10		4	4		2	6	
	400	300	4	227	121	3	173	179	1

NEW ENGLAND PATRIOTS*

Season	All Games W	L	T	Home Games W	L	T	Road Games W	L	T
1960	5	9		3	4		2	5	
1961	9	4	1	4	2	1	5	2	
1962	9	4	1	6	1		3	3	1
1963	7	6	1	5	1	1	2	5	
1964	10	3	1	4	2	1	6	1	
1965	4	8	2	1	4	2	3	4	
1966	8	4	2	4	2	1	4	2	1
1967	3	10	1	2	4		1	6	1
1968	4	10		2	5		2	5	
1969	4	10		2	5		2	5	
1970	2	12		1	6		1	6	
1971	6	8		5	2		1	6	
1972	3	11		2	5		1	6	
1973	5	9		3	4		2	5	
1974	7	7		3	4		4	3	
1975	3	11		2	5		1	6	
1976	11	3		6	1		5	2	
1977	9	5		6	1		3	4	
1978	11	5		5	3		6	2	
1979	9	7		6	2		3	5	
1980	10	6		6	2		4	4	
1981	2	14		2	6		0	8	
1982	5	4		3	1		2	3	
1983	8	8		5	3		3	5	
1984	9	7		5	3		4	4	
1985	11	5		7	1		4	4	
1986	11	5		4	4		7	1	
1987	8	7		5	3		3	4	
1988	9	7		7	1		2	6	
1989	5	11		3	5		2	6	
1990	1	15		0	8		1	7	
1991	6	10		4	4		2	6	
1992	2	14		1	7		1	7	
1993	5	11		3	5		2	6	
1994	10	6		5	3		5	3	
1995	6	10		3	5		3	5	
1996	11	5		6	2		5	3	
1997	10	6		6	2		4	4	
1998	9	7		6	2		3	5	
1999	8	8		5	3		3	5	
2000	5	11		3	5		2	6	
2001	11	5		6	2		5	3	
2002	9	7		5	3		4	4	
2003	14	2		8	0		6	2	
2004	14	2		8	0		6	2	
2005	10	6		5	3		5	3	
2006	12	4		5	3		7	1	
2007	16	0		8	0		8	0	
2008	11	5		5	3		6	2	
2009	10	6		8	0		2	6	
2010	14	2		8	0		6	2	
2011	13	3		7	1		6	2	
	414	365	9	234	153	6	180	212	3

*includes Boston Patriots (1960-1970).

NEW YORK JETS*

Season	All Games W	L	T	Home Games W	L	T	Road Games W	L	T
1960	7	7		3	4		4	3	
1961	7	7		5	2		2	5	
1962	5	9		2	5		3	4	
1963	5	8	1	4	2	1	1	6	
1964	5	8	1	5	1	1	0	7	
1965	5	8	1	3	3	1	2	5	
1966	6	6	2	4	3		2	3	2
1967	8	5	1	4	2	1	4	3	
1968	11	3		6	1		5	2	
1969	10	4		5	2		5	2	
1970	4	10		2	5		2	5	
1971	6	8		4	3		2	5	
1972	7	7		4	3		3	4	
1973	4	10		2	4		2	6	
1974	7	7		3	4		4	3	
1975	3	11		1	6		2	5	
1976	3	11		2	5		1	6	
1977	3	11		1	6		2	5	
1978	8	8		4	4		4	4	
1979	8	8		6	2		2	6	
1980	4	12		2	6		2	6	
1981	10	5	1	6	2		4	3	1
1982	6	3		3	1		3	2	
1983	7	9		2	6		5	3	
1984	7	9		3	5		4	4	
1985	11	5		7	1		4	4	

INSIDE THE NUMBERS

Season	All Games W	L	T	Home Games W	L	T	Road Games W	L	T
1986	10	6		5	3		5	3	
1987	6	9		4	4		2	5	
1988	8	7	1	5	2	1	3	5	
1989	4	12		1	7		3	5	
1990	6	10		3	5		3	5	
1991	8	8		4	4		4	4	
1992	4	12		3	5		1	7	
1993	8	8		3	5		5	3	
1994	6	10		4	4		2	6	
1995	3	13		2	6		1	7	
1996	1	15		0	8		1	7	
1997	9	7		5	3		4	4	
1998	12	4		7	1		5	3	
1999	8	8		4	4		4	4	
2000	9	7		5	3		4	4	
2001	10	6		3	5		7	1	
2002	9	7		5	3		4	4	
2003	6	10		4	4		2	6	
2004	10	6		6	2		4	4	
2005	4	12		4	4		0	8	
2006	10	6		4	4		6	2	
2007	4	12		3	5		1	7	
2008	9	7		5	3		4	4	
2009	9	7		4	4		5	3	
2010	11	5		5	3		6	2	
2011	8	8		6	2		2	6	
	359	421	8	197	191	5	162	230	3

*includes New York Titans (1960-62).

OAKLAND RAIDERS*

Season	All Games W	L	T	Home Games W	L	T	Road Games W	L	T
1960	6	8		3	4		3	4	
1961	2	12		1	6		1	6	
1962	1	13		1	6		0	7	
1963	10	4		6	1		4	3	
1964	5	7	2	5	2		0	5	2
1965	8	5	1	5	2		3	3	1
1966	8	5	1	3	3	1	5	2	
1967	13	1		7	0		6	1	
1968	12	2		6	1		6	1	
1969	12	1	1	7	0		5	1	1
1970	8	4	2	6	1		2	3	2
1971	8	4	2	5	1	1	3	3	1
1972	10	3	1	5	1	1	5	2	
1973	9	4	1	5	2		4	2	1
1974	12	2		6	1		6	1	
1975	11	3		6	1		5	2	
1976	13	1		7	0		6	1	
1977	11	3		6	1		5	2	
1978	9	7		4	4		5	3	
1979	9	7		6	2		3	5	
1980	11	5		6	2		5	3	
1981	7	9		4	4		3	5	
1982	8	1		4	0		4	1	
1983	12	4		6	2		6	2	
1984	11	5		6	2		5	3	
1985	12	4		7	1		5	3	
1986	8	8		3	5		5	3	
1987	5	10		3	5		2	5	
1988	7	9		3	5		4	4	
1989	8	8		7	1		1	7	
1990	12	4		6	2		6	2	
1991	9	7		5	3		4	4	
1992	7	9		5	3		2	6	
1993	10	6		5	3		5	3	
1994	9	7		4	4		5	3	
1995	8	8		4	4		4	4	
1996	7	9		4	4		3	5	
1997	4	12		2	6		2	6	
1998	8	8		4	4		4	4	
1999	8	8		5	3		3	5	
2000	12	4		7	1		5	3	
2001	10	6		5	3		5	3	
2002	11	5		6	2		5	3	
2003	4	12		4	4		0	8	
2004	5	11		3	5		2	6	
2005	4	12		2	6		2	6	
2006	2	14		2	6		0	8	
2007	4	12		2	6		2	6	
2008	5	11		4	4		1	7	
2009	5	11		2	6		3	5	
2010	8	8		5	3		3	5	
2011	8	8		3	5		5	3	
	426	351	11	238	153	3	188	198	8

*includes Los Angeles Raiders (1982-1994).

PITTSBURGH STEELERS*

Season	All Games W	L	T	Home Games W	L	T	Road Games W	L	T
1933	3	6	2	2	3		1	3	2
1934	2	10		1	5		1	5	
1935	4	8		2	5		2	3	
1936	6	6		4	1		2	5	
1937	4	7		2	4		2	3	
1938	2	9		0	5		2	4	
1939	1	9	1	1	4		0	5	1
1940	2	7	2	1	2	2	1	5	
1941	1	9	1	1	4		0	5	1
1942	7	4		3	2		4	2	
1945	2	8		1	4		1	4	
1946	5	5	1	4	1		1	4	1
1947	8	4		5	1		3	3	
1948	4	8		4	2		0	6	
1949	6	5	1	3	2	1	3	3	
1950	6	6		2	4		4	2	
1951	4	7	1	1	4	1	3	3	
1952	5	7		2	4		3	3	
1953	6	6		3	3		3	3	
1954	5	7		4	2		1	5	
1955	4	8		3	2		1	6	
1956	5	7		3	3		2	4	
1957	6	6		4	2		2	4	
1958	7	4	1	5	1		2	3	1
1959	6	5	1	3	2	1	3	3	
1960	5	6	1	4	2		1	4	1
1961	6	8		4	3		2	5	
1962	9	5		4	3		5	2	
1963	7	4	3	5	0	2	2	4	1
1964	5	9		2	5		3	4	
1965	2	12		1	6		1	6	
1966	5	8	1	3	3	1	2	5	
1967	4	9	1	1	6		3	3	1
1968	2	11	1	1	6		1	5	1
1969	1	13		1	6		0	7	
1970	5	9		4	3		1	6	
1971	6	8		5	2		1	6	
1972	11	3		7	0		4	3	
1973	10	4		7	1		3	3	
1974	10	3	1	5	2		5	1	1
1975	12	2		6	1		6	1	
1976	10	4		6	1		4	3	
1977	9	5		6	1		3	4	
1978	14	2		7	1		7	1	
1979	12	4		8	0		4	4	
1980	9	7		6	2		3	5	

Season	All Games W	L	T	Home Games W	L	T	Road Games W	L	T
1981	8	8		5	3		3	5	
1982	6	3		4	0		2	3	
1983	10	6		4	4		6	2	
1984	9	7		6	2		3	5	
1985	7	9		5	3		2	6	
1986	6	10		4	4		2	6	
1987	8	7		4	3		4	4	
1988	5	11		4	4		1	7	
1989	9	7		4	4		5	3	
1990	9	7		6	2		3	5	
1991	7	9		5	3		2	6	
1992	11	5		7	1		4	4	
1993	9	7		6	2		3	5	
1994	12	4		7	1		5	3	
1995	11	5		6	2		5	3	
1996	10	6		7	1		3	5	
1997	11	5		7	1		4	4	
1998	7	9		5	3		2	6	
1999	6	10		2	6		4	4	
2000	9	7		4	4		5	3	
2001	13	3		7	1		6	2	
2002	10	5	1	5	2	1	5	3	
2003	6	10		4	4		2	6	
2004	15	1		8	0		7	1	
2005	11	5		5	3		6	2	
2006	8	8		5	3		3	5	
2007	10	6		7	1		3	5	
2008	12	4		6	2		6	2	
2009	9	7		6	2		3	5	
2010	12	4		5	3		7	1	
2011	12	4		7	1		5	3	
	553	503	20	324	201	9	229	302	11

*includes Pittsburgh Pirates (1933-39).

SAN DIEGO CHARGERS*

Season	All Games W	L	T	Home Games W	L	T	Road Games W	L	T
1960	10	4		5	2		5	2	
1961	12	2		6	1		6	1	
1962	4	10		3	4		1	6	
1963	11	3		6	1		5	2	
1964	8	5	1	4	3		4	2	1
1965	9	2	3	4	1	2	5	1	1
1966	7	6	1	5	2		2	4	1
1967	8	5	1	5	2	1	3	3	
1968	9	5		4	3		5	2	
1969	8	6		5	2		3	4	
1970	5	6	3	2	3	2	3	3	1
1971	6	8		6	1		0	7	
1972	4	9	1	2	5		2	4	1
1973	2	11	1	2	5		0	6	1
1974	5	9		3	4		2	5	
1975	2	12		1	6		1	6	
1976	6	8		3	4		3	4	
1977	7	7		3	4		4	3	
1978	9	7		5	3		4	4	
1979	12	4		7	1		5	3	
1980	11	5		6	2		5	3	
1981	10	6		5	3		5	3	
1982	6	3		3	1		3	2	
1983	6	10		4	4		2	6	
1984	7	9		4	4		3	5	
1985	8	8		6	2		2	6	
1986	4	12		2	6		2	6	
1987	8	7		4	3		4	4	
1988	6	10		3	5		3	5	
1989	6	10		4	4		2	6	
1990	6	10		3	5		3	5	

Season	All Games W	L	T	Home Games W	L	T	Road Games W	L	T
1991	4	12		3	5		1	7	
1992	11	5		6	2		5	3	
1993	8	8		4	4		4	4	
1994	11	5		5	3		6	2	
1995	9	7		5	3		4	4	
1996	8	8		5	3		3	5	
1997	4	12		2	6		2	6	
1998	5	11		4	4		1	7	
1999	8	8		4	4		4	4	
2000	1	15		1	7		0	8	
2001	5	11		4	4		1	7	
2002	8	8		5	3		3	5	
2003	4	12		2	6		2	6	
2004	12	4		7	1		5	3	
2005	9	7		4	4		5	3	
2006	14	2		8	0		6	2	
2007	11	5		7	1		4	4	
2008	8	8		5	3		3	5	
2009	13	3		6	2		7	1	
2010	9	7		6	2		3	5	
2011	8	8		5	3		3	5	
	392	385	11	223	166	5	169	219	6

*includes Los Angeles Chargers (1960).

TENNESSEE TITANS*

Season	All Games W	L	T	Home Games W	L	T	Road Games W	L	T
1960	10	4		6	1		4	3	
1961	10	3	1	6	1		4	2	1
1962	11	3		6	1		5	2	
1963	6	8		4	3		2	5	
1964	4	10		3	4		1	6	
1965	4	10		3	4		1	6	
1966	3	11		3	4		0	7	
1967	9	4	1	5	2		4	2	1
1968	7	7		3	4		4	3	
1969	6	6	2	4	2	1	2	4	1
1970	3	10	1	1	6		2	4	1
1971	4	9	1	3	3	1	1	6	
1972	1	13		1	6		0	7	
1973	1	13		0	7		1	6	
1974	7	7		3	4		4	3	
1975	10	4		5	2		5	2	
1976	5	9		3	4		2	5	
1977	8	6		5	2		3	4	
1978	10	6		5	3		5	3	
1979	11	5		6	2		5	3	
1980	11	5		6	2		5	3	
1981	7	9		5	3		2	6	
1982	1	8		1	4		0	4	
1983	2	14		2	6		0	8	
1984	3	13		2	6		1	7	
1985	5	11		4	4		1	7	
1986	5	11		4	4		1	7	
1987	9	6		5	2		4	4	
1988	10	6		7	1		3	5	
1989	9	7		6	2		3	5	
1990	9	7		6	2		3	5	
1991	11	5		7	1		4	4	
1992	10	6		5	3		5	3	
1993	12	4		7	1		5	3	
1994	2	14		2	6		0	8	
1995	7	9		3	5		4	4	
1996	8	8		2	6		6	2	
1997	8	8		6	2		2	6	
1998	8	8		3	5		5	3	
1999	13	3		8	0		5	3	
2000	13	3		7	1		6	2	

Season	W	L	T	W	L	T	W	L	T
2001	7	9		3	5		4	4	
2002	11	5		6	2		5	3	
2003	12	4		7	1		5	3	
2004	5	11		2	6		3	5	
2005	4	12		3	5		1	7	
2006	8	8		4	4		4	4	
2007	10	6		5	3		5	3	
2008	13	3		7	1		6	2	
2009	8	8		5	3		3	5	
2010	6	10		3	5		3	5	
2011	9	7		5	3		4	4	
	386	396	6	223	169	2	163	227	4

*includes Houston (1960-1996) and Tennessee Oilers (1997-98)

NFC
ARIZONA CARDINALS*

	All Games			Home Games			Road Games		
Season	W	L	T	W	L	T	W	L	T
1920	6	2	2	5	1	1	1	1	1
1921	3	3	2	3	3	1	0	0	1
1922	8	3		8	3		0	0	
1923	8	4		8	3		0	1	
1924	5	4	1	5	3	1	0	1	
1925	11	2	1	11	2		0	0	1
1926	5	6	1	3	3		2	3	1
1927	3	7	1	2	3	1	1	4	
1928	1	5		1	1		0	4	
1929	6	6	1	3	2		3	4	1
1930	5	6	2	3	2		2	4	2
1931	5	4		3	0		2	4	
1932	2	6	2	1	2	1	1	4	1
1933	1	9	1	0	4	1	1	5	
1934	5	6		2	2		3	4	
1935	6	4	2	2	2		4	2	2
1936	3	8	1	3	1	1	0	7	
1937	5	5	1	1	3		4	2	1
1938	2	9		1	4		1	5	
1939	1	10		0	4		1	6	
1940	2	7	2	2	1	1	0	6	1
1941	3	7	1	0	3	1	3	4	
1942	3	8		2	2		1	6	
1943	0	10		0	3		0	7	
1945	1	9		0	3		1	6	
1946	6	5		2	2		4	3	
1947	9	3		5	0		4	3	
1948	11	1		5	1		6	0	
1949	6	5	1	2	3	1	4	2	
1950	5	7		3	3		2	4	
1951	3	9		1	5		2	4	
1952	4	8		2	4		2	4	
1953	1	10	1	0	5	1	1	5	
1954	2	10		2	4		0	6	
1955	4	7	1	3	2	1	1	5	
1956	7	5		4	2		3	3	
1957	3	9		0	6		3	3	
1958	2	9	1	1	4	1	1	5	
1959	2	10		2	4		0	6	
1960	6	5	1	3	2	1	3	3	
1961	7	7		3	4		4	3	
1962	4	9	1	2	4	1	2	5	
1963	9	5		3	4		6	1	
1964	9	3	2	4	1	1	5	2	1
1965	5	9		2	5		3	4	
1966	8	5	1	5	1	1	3	4	
1967	6	7	1	3	3	1	3	4	
1968	9	4	1	4	2	1	5	2	
1969	4	9	1	3	4		1	5	1
1970	8	5	1	6	1		2	4	1
1971	4	9	1	1	5	1	3	4	
1972	4	9	1	2	5		2	4	1

	All Games			Home Games			Road Games		
Season	W	L	T	W	L	T	W	L	T
1973	4	9	1	2	4	1	2	5	
1974	10	4		5	2		5	2	
1975	11	3		6	1		5	2	
1976	10	4		6	1		4	3	
1977	7	7		4	3		3	4	
1978	6	10		3	5		3	5	
1979	5	11		3	5		2	6	
1980	5	11		2	6		3	5	
1981	7	9		5	3		2	6	
1982	5	4		1	3		4	1	
1983	8	7	1	4	3	1	4	4	
1984	9	7		5	3		4	4	
1985	5	11		4	4		1	7	
1986	4	11	1	3	5		1	6	1
1987	7	8		4	3		3	5	
1988	7	9		4	4		3	5	
1989	5	11		2	6		3	5	
1990	5	11		3	5		2	6	
1991	4	12		2	6		2	6	
1992	4	12		3	5		1	7	
1993	7	9		4	4		3	5	
1994	8	8		5	3		3	5	
1995	4	12		3	5		1	7	
1996	7	9		5	3		2	6	
1997	4	12		3	5		1	7	
1998	9	7		5	3		4	4	
1999	6	10		4	4		2	6	
2000	3	13		3	5		0	8	
2001	7	9		3	5		4	4	
2002	5	11		3	5		2	6	
2003	4	12		4	4		0	8	
2004	6	10		5	3		1	7	
2005	5	11		3	5		2	6	
2006	5	11		3	5		2	6	
2007	8	8		6	2		2	6	
2008	9	7		6	2		3	5	
2009	10	6		4	4		6	2	
2010	5	11		4	4		1	7	
2011	8	8		6	2		2	6	
	496	689	39	292	296	22	204	393	17

*includes Chicago Cardinals (1920-1959), St. Louis Cardinals (1960-1987), and Phoenix Cardinals (1988-1993).

ATLANTA FALCONS

	All Games			Home Games			Road Games		
Season	W	L	T	W	L	T	W	L	T
1966	3	11		1	6		2	5	
1967	1	12	1	1	5	1	0	7	
1968	2	12		1	6		1	6	
1969	6	8		4	3		2	5	
1970	4	8	2	3	4		1	4	2
1971	7	6	1	4	3		3	3	1
1972	7	7		4	3		3	4	
1973	9	5		4	3		5	2	
1974	3	11		2	5		1	6	
1975	4	10		3	4		1	6	
1976	4	10		3	4		1	6	
1977	7	7		4	3		3	4	
1978	9	7		7	1		2	6	
1979	6	10		3	5		3	5	
1980	12	4		6	2		6	2	
1981	7	9		4	4		3	5	
1982	5	4		2	3		3	1	
1983	7	9		4	4		3	5	
1984	4	12		2	6		2	6	
1985	4	12		3	5		1	7	
1986	7	8	1	2	5	1	5	3	
1987	3	12		2	6		1	6	

Season	All Games W	L	T	Home Games W	L	T	Road Games W	L	T
1988	5	11		2	6		3	5	
1989	3	13		3	5		0	8	
1990	5	11		5	3		0	8	
1991	10	6		6	2		4	4	
1992	6	10		5	3		1	7	
1993	6	10		4	4		2	6	
1994	7	9		5	3		2	6	
1995	9	7		7	1		2	6	
1996	3	13		2	6		1	7	
1997	7	9		3	5		4	4	
1998	14	2		8	0		6	2	
1999	5	11		4	4		1	7	
2000	4	12		3	5		1	7	
2001	7	9		3	5		4	4	
2002	9	6	1	5	3		4	3	1
2003	5	11		2	6		3	5	
2004	11	5		7	1		4	4	
2005	8	8		4	4		4	4	
2006	7	9		3	5		4	4	
2007	4	12		3	5		1	7	
2008	11	5		7	1		4	4	
2009	9	7		6	2		3	5	
2010	13	3		7	1		6	2	
2011	10	6		6	2		4	4	
	299	399	6	179	172	2	120	227	4

CAROLINA PANTHERS

Season	All Games W	L	T	Home Games W	L	T	Road Games W	L	T
1995	7	9		5	3		2	6	
1996	12	4		8	0		4	4	
1997	7	9		2	6		5	3	
1998	4	12		2	6		2	6	
1999	8	8		5	3		3	5	
2000	7	9		5	3		2	6	
2001	1	15		0	8		1	7	
2002	7	9		4	4		3	5	
2003	11	5		6	2		5	3	
2004	7	9		3	5		4	4	
2005	11	5		5	3		6	2	
2006	8	8		4	4		4	4	
2007	7	9		2	6		5	3	
2008	12	4		8	0		4	4	
2009	8	8		5	3		3	5	
2010	2	14		2	6		0	8	
2011	6	10		3	5		3	5	
	125	147		69	67		56	80	

CHICAGO BEARS*

Season	All Games W	L	T	Home Games W	L	T	Road Games W	L	T
1920	10	1	2	6	0	1	4	1	1
1921	9	1	1	9	1	1	0	0	
1922	9	3		7	1		2	2	
1923	9	2	1	7	1	1	2	1	
1924	6	1	4	5	0	3	1	1	1
1925	9	5	3	7	1	1	2	4	2
1926	12	1	3	10	0	2	2	1	1
1927	9	3	2	7	1	1	2	2	1
1928	7	5	1	6	3		1	2	1
1929	4	9	2	1	5	2	3	4	
1930	9	4	1	5	2	1	4	2	
1931	8	5		6	3		2	2	
1932	7	1	6	6	1	1	1	0	5
1933	10	2	1	6	0		4	2	1
1934	13	0		5	0		8	0	
1935	6	4	2	1	2	2	5	2	
1936	9	3		3	1		6	2	

Season	All Games W	L	T	Home Games W	L	T	Road Games W	L	T
1937	9	1	1	4	1		5	0	1
1938	6	5		2	3		4	2	
1939	8	3		4	1		4	2	
1940	8	3		5	0		3	3	
1941	10	1		5	1		5	0	
1942	11	0		6	0		5	0	
1943	8	1	1	5	0		3	1	1
1944	6	3	1	4	0	1	2	3	
1945	3	7		2	3		1	4	
1946	8	2	1	4	1	1	4	1	
1947	8	4		4	2		4	2	
1948	10	2		5	1		5	1	
1949	9	3		5	1		4	2	
1950	9	3		6	0		3	3	
1951	7	5		3	3		4	2	
1952	5	7		3	3		2	4	
1953	3	8	1	1	4	1	2	4	
1954	8	4		4	2		4	2	
1955	8	4		5	1		3	3	
1956	9	2	1	6	0		3	2	1
1957	5	7		2	4		3	3	
1958	8	4		5	1		3	3	
1959	8	4		4	2		4	2	
1960	5	6	1	4	2		1	4	1
1961	8	6		5	2		3	4	
1962	9	5		4	3		5	2	
1963	11	1	2	6	0	1	5	1	1
1964	5	9		2	5		3	4	
1965	9	5		5	2		4	3	
1966	5	7	2	4	1	2	1	6	
1967	7	6	1	3	3	1	4	3	
1968	7	7		2	5		5	2	
1969	1	13		1	6		0	7	
1970	6	8		3	4		3	4	
1971	6	8		4	3		2	5	
1972	4	9	1	1	5	1	3	4	
1973	3	11		1	6		2	5	
1974	4	10		4	3		0	7	
1975	4	10		3	4		1	6	
1976	7	7		4	3		3	4	
1977	9	5		5	2		4	3	
1978	7	9		4	4		3	5	
1979	10	6		6	2		4	4	
1980	7	9		5	3		2	6	
1981	6	10		4	4		2	6	
1982	3	6		2	2		1	4	
1983	8	8		5	3		3	5	
1984	10	6		6	2		4	4	
1985	15	1		8	0		7	1	
1986	14	2		7	1		7	1	
1987	11	4		6	2		5	2	
1988	12	4		7	1		5	3	
1989	6	10		4	4		2	6	
1990	11	5		7	1		4	4	
1991	11	5		6	2		5	3	
1992	5	11		4	4		1	7	
1993	7	9		3	5		4	4	
1994	9	7		5	3		4	4	
1995	9	7		5	3		4	4	
1996	7	9		6	2		1	7	
1997	4	12		2	6		2	6	
1998	4	12		3	5		1	7	
1999	6	10		3	5		3	5	
2000	5	11		3	5		2	6	
2001	13	3		7	1		6	2	
2002	4	12		3	5		1	7	
2003	7	9		6	2		1	7	
2004	5	11		2	6		3	5	

Season	All Games W	L	T	Home Games W	L	T	Road Games W	L	T
2005	11	5		7	1		4	4	
2006	13	3		6	2		7	1	
2007	7	9		4	4		3	5	
2008	9	7		6	2		3	5	
2009	7	9		5	3		2	6	
2010	11	5		5	3		6	2	
2011	8	8		5	3		3	5	
	712	520	42	419	216	24	293	304	18

includes Decatur Staleys (1920) and Chicago Staleys (1921).

DALLAS COWBOYS

Season	All Games W	L	T	Home Games W	L	T	Road Games W	L	T
1960	0	11	1	0	6		0	5	1
1961	4	9	1	2	4	1	2	5	
1962	5	8	1	2	4	1	3	4	
1963	4	10		3	4		1	6	
1964	5	8	1	2	4	1	3	4	
1965	7	7		5	2		2	5	
1966	10	3	1	6	1		4	2	1
1967	9	5		5	2		4	3	
1968	12	2		5	2		7	0	
1969	11	2	1	6	0	1	5	2	
1970	10	4		6	1		4	3	
1971	11	3		6	1		5	2	
1972	10	4		5	2		5	2	
1973	10	4		6	1		4	3	
1974	8	6		5	2		3	4	
1975	10	4		5	2		5	2	
1976	11	3		6	1		5	2	
1977	12	2		6	1		6	1	
1978	12	4		7	1		5	3	
1979	11	5		6	2		5	3	
1980	12	4		8	0		4	4	
1981	12	4		8	0		4	4	
1982	6	3		3	2		3	1	
1983	12	4		6	2		6	2	
1984	9	7		5	3		4	4	
1985	10	6		7	1		3	5	
1986	7	9		3	5		4	4	
1987	7	8		3	4		4	4	
1988	3	13		1	7		2	6	
1989	1	15		0	8		1	7	
1990	7	9		5	3		2	6	
1991	11	5		6	2		5	3	
1992	13	3		7	1		6	2	
1993	12	4		6	2		6	2	
1994	12	4		6	2		6	2	
1995	12	4		6	2		6	2	
1996	10	6		6	2		4	4	
1997	6	10		5	3		1	7	
1998	10	6		6	2		4	4	
1999	8	8		7	1		1	7	
2000	5	11		3	5		2	6	
2001	5	11		4	4		1	7	
2002	5	11		4	4		1	7	
2003	10	6		6	2		4	4	
2004	6	10		4	4		2	6	
2005	9	7		5	3		4	4	
2006	9	7		4	4		5	3	
2007	13	3		6	2		7	1	
2008	9	7		6	2		3	5	
2009	11	5		6	2		5	3	
2010	6	10		2	6		4	4	
2011	8	8		5	3		3	5	
	448	332	6	253	136	4	195	196	2

DETROIT LIONS*

Season	All Games W	L	T	Home Games W	L	T	Road Games W	L	T
1930	5	6	3	5	1	2	0	5	1
1931	11	3		8	0		3	3	
1932	6	2	4	3	0	2	3	2	2
1933	6	5		4	1		2	4	
1934	10	3		6	2		4	1	
1935	7	3	2	5	0	1	2	3	1
1936	8	4		5	1		3	3	
1937	7	4		4	2		3	2	
1938	7	4		4	3		3	1	
1939	6	5		4	2		2	3	
1940	5	5	1	3	3		2	2	1
1941	4	6	1	3	2		1	4	1
1942	0	11		0	7		0	4	
1943	3	6	1	2	2	1	1	4	
1944	6	3	1	4	2		2	1	1
1945	7	3		4	1		3	2	
1946	1	10		1	5		0	5	
1947	3	9		2	4		1	5	
1948	2	10		2	4		0	6	
1949	4	8		2	4		2	4	
1950	6	6		4	2		2	4	
1951	7	4	1	3	3	1	4	1	
1952	9	3		6	1		3	2	
1953	10	2		5	1		5	1	
1954	9	2	1	5	0	1	4	2	
1955	3	9		3	4		0	5	
1956	9	3		5	1		4	2	
1957	8	4		5	1		3	3	
1958	4	7	1	2	4		2	3	1
1959	3	8	1	2	4		1	4	1
1960	7	5		5	1		2	4	
1961	8	5	1	2	5		6	0	1
1962	11	3		7	0		4	3	
1963	5	8	1	3	3	1	2	5	
1964	7	5	2	3	3	1	4	2	1
1965	6	7	1	2	4	1	4	3	
1966	4	9	1	3	4		1	5	1
1967	5	7	2	3	4		2	3	2
1968	4	8	2	1	4	2	3	4	
1969	9	4	1	5	2		4	2	1
1970	10	4		6	1		4	3	
1971	7	6	1	3	4		4	2	1
1972	8	5	1	5	2		3	3	1
1973	6	7	1	4	3		2	4	1
1974	7	7		5	2		2	5	
1975	7	7		4	3		3	4	
1976	6	8		5	2		1	6	
1977	6	8		5	2		1	6	
1978	7	9		5	3		2	6	
1979	2	14		2	6		0	8	
1980	9	7		6	2		3	5	
1981	8	8		7	1		1	7	
1982	4	5		2	3		2	2	
1983	9	7		6	2		3	5	
1984	4	11	1	2	5	1	2	6	
1985	7	9		6	2		1	7	
1986	5	11		1	7		4	4	
1987	4	11		1	6		3	5	
1988	4	12		2	6		2	6	
1989	7	9		4	4		3	5	
1990	6	10		3	5		3	5	
1991	12	4		8	0		4	4	
1992	5	11		3	5		2	6	
1993	10	6		5	3		5	3	
1994	9	7		6	2		3	5	
1995	10	6		7	1		3	5	
1996	5	11		4	4		1	7	

Season	All Games W	L	T	Home Games W	L	T	Road Games W	L	T
1997	9	7		6	2		3	5	
1998	5	11		4	4		1	7	
1999	8	8		6	2		2	6	
2000	9	7		4	4		5	3	
2001	2	14		2	6		0	8	
2002	3	13		3	5		0	8	
2003	5	11		5	3		0	8	
2004	6	10		3	5		3	5	
2005	5	11		3	5		2	6	
2006	3	13		2	6		1	7	
2007	7	9		5	3		2	6	
2008	0	16		0	8		0	8	
2009	2	14		2	6		0	8	
2010	6	10		4	4		2	6	
2011	10	6		5	3		5	3	
	506	599	32	316	249	14	190	350	18

*includes Portsmouth Spartans (1930-33).

GREEN BAY PACKERS

Season	All Games W	L	T	Home Games W	L	T	Road Games W	L	T
1921	3	2	1	2	1		1	1	1
1922	4	3	3	4	1	1	0	2	2
1923	7	2	1	4	2	1	3	0	
1924	7	4		5	0		2	4	
1925	8	5		6	0		2	5	
1926	7	3	3	4	1	2	3	2	1
1927	7	2	1	6	1		1	1	1
1928	6	4	3	2	2	2	4	2	1
1929	12	0	1	5	0		7	0	1
1930	10	3	1	6	0		4	3	1
1931	12	2		8	0		4	2	
1932	10	3	1	5	0	1	5	3	
1933	5	7	1	3	2	1	2	5	
1934	7	6		4	2		3	4	
1935	8	4		5	2		3	2	
1936	10	1	1	5	1		5	0	1
1937	7	4		3	2		4	2	
1938	8	3		4	2		4	1	
1939	9	2		4	1		5	1	
1940	6	4	1	4	2		2	2	1
1941	10	1		4	1		6	0	
1942	8	2	1	4	1		4	1	1
1943	7	2	1	2	1	1	5	1	
1944	8	2		5	0		3	2	
1945	6	4		4	1		2	3	
1946	6	5		2	3		4	2	
1947	6	5	1	4	2		2	3	1
1948	3	9		2	4		1	5	
1949	2	10		1	5		1	5	
1950	3	9		3	3		0	6	
1951	3	9		2	4		1	5	
1952	6	6		3	3		3	3	
1953	2	9	1	1	5		1	4	1
1954	4	8		2	4		2	4	
1955	6	6		5	1		1	5	
1956	4	8		2	4		2	4	
1957	3	9		1	5		2	4	
1958	1	10	1	1	4	1	0	6	
1959	7	5		4	2		3	3	
1960	8	4		4	2		4	2	
1961	11	3		6	1		5	2	
1962	13	1		7	0		6	1	
1963	11	2	1	6	1		5	1	1
1964	8	5	1	4	3		4	2	1
1965	10	3	1	6	1		4	2	1
1966	12	2		6	1		6	1	
1967	9	4	1	4	2	1	5	2	

Season	All Games W	L	T	Home Games W	L	T	Road Games W	L	T
1968	6	7	1	2	5		4	2	1
1969	8	6		5	2		3	4	
1970	6	8		4	3		2	5	
1971	4	8	2	3	3	1	1	5	1
1972	10	4		4	3		6	1	
1973	5	7	2	3	2	2	2	5	
1974	6	8		4	3		2	5	
1975	4	10		3	4		1	6	
1976	5	9		4	3		1	6	
1977	4	10		2	5		2	5	
1978	8	7	1	5	2	1	3	5	
1979	5	11		4	4		1	7	
1980	5	10	1	4	4		1	6	1
1981	8	8		4	4		4	4	
1982	5	3	1	3	1		2	2	1
1983	8	8		5	3		3	5	
1984	8	8		5	3		3	5	
1985	8	8		5	3		3	5	
1986	4	12		1	7		3	5	
1987	5	9	1	2	5	1	3	4	
1988	4	12		2	6		2	6	
1989	10	6		6	2		4	4	
1990	6	10		3	5		3	5	
1991	4	12		2	6		2	6	
1992	9	7		6	2		3	5	
1993	9	7		6	2		3	5	
1994	9	7		7	1		2	6	
1995	11	5		7	1		4	4	
1996	13	3		8	0		5	3	
1997	13	3		8	0		5	3	
1998	11	5		7	1		4	4	
1999	8	8		5	3		3	5	
2000	9	7		6	2		3	5	
2001	12	4		7	1		5	3	
2002	12	4		8	0		4	4	
2003	10	6		5	3		5	3	
2004	10	6		4	4		6	2	
2005	4	12		3	5		1	7	
2006	8	8		3	5		5	3	
2007	13	3		7	1		6	2	
2008	6	10		4	4		2	6	
2009	11	5		6	2		5	3	
2010	10	6		7	1		3	5	
2011	15	1		8	0		7	1	
	679	525	36	391	212	16	288	313	20

MINNESOTA VIKINGS

Season	All Games W	L	T	Home Games W	L	T	Road Games W	L	T
1961	3	11		3	4		0	7	
1962	2	11	1	1	5	1	1	6	
1963	5	8	1	3	4		2	4	1
1964	8	5	1	4	3		4	2	1
1965	7	7		2	5		5	2	
1966	4	9	1	2	5		2	4	1
1967	3	8	3	1	4	2	2	4	1
1968	8	6		4	3		4	3	
1969	12	2		7	0		5	2	
1970	12	2		7	0		5	2	
1971	11	3		5	2		6	1	
1972	7	7		3	4		4	3	
1973	12	2		7	0		5	2	
1974	10	4		4	3		6	1	
1975	12	2		7	0		5	2	
1976	11	2	1	6	0	1	5	2	
1977	9	5		5	2		4	3	
1978	8	7	1	5	3		3	4	1
1979	7	9		5	3		2	6	

Season	All Games W	L	T	Home Games W	L	T	Road Games W	L	T
1980	9	7		5	3		4	4	
1981	7	9		5	3		2	6	
1982	5	4		4	1		1	3	
1983	8	8		3	5		5	3	
1984	3	13		2	6		1	7	
1985	7	9		4	4		3	5	
1986	9	7		5	3		4	4	
1987	8	7		5	3		3	4	
1988	11	5		7	1		4	4	
1989	10	6		8	0		2	6	
1990	6	10		4	4		2	6	
1991	8	8		4	4		4	4	
1992	11	5		5	3		6	2	
1993	9	7		4	4		5	3	
1994	10	6		6	2		4	4	
1995	8	8		6	2		2	6	
1996	9	7		5	3		4	4	
1997	9	7		5	3		4	4	
1998	15	1		8	0		7	1	
1999	10	6		6	2		4	4	
2000	11	5		7	1		4	4	
2001	5	11		5	3		0	8	
2002	6	10		4	4		2	6	
2003	9	7		6	2		3	5	
2004	8	8		5	3		3	5	
2005	9	7		6	2		3	5	
2006	6	10		3	5		3	5	
2007	8	8		5	3		3	5	
2008	10	6		6	2		4	4	
2009	12	4		8	0		4	4	
2010	6	10		4	4		2	6	
2011	3	13		1	7		2	6	
	416	349	9	242	142	4	174	207	5

NEW ORLEANS SAINTS

Season	All Games W	L	T	Home Games W	L	T	Road Games W	L	T
1967	3	11		2	5		1	6	
1968	4	9	1	3	4		1	5	1
1969	5	9		3	4		2	5	
1970	2	11	1	2	5		0	6	1
1971	4	8	2	2	4	1	2	4	1
1972	2	11	1	2	5		0	6	1
1973	5	9		5	2		0	7	
1974	5	9		4	3		1	6	
1975	2	12		2	5		0	7	
1976	4	10		2	5		2	5	
1977	3	11		2	5		1	6	
1978	7	9		3	5		4	4	
1979	8	8		3	5		5	3	
1980	1	15		0	8		1	7	
1981	4	12		2	6		2	6	
1982	4	5		2	3		2	2	
1983	8	8		5	3		3	5	
1984	7	9		3	5		4	4	
1985	5	11		3	5		2	6	
1986	7	9		4	4		3	5	
1987	12	3		6	1		6	2	
1988	10	6		5	3		5	3	
1989	9	7		5	3		4	4	
1990	8	8		5	3		3	5	
1991	11	5		6	2		5	3	
1992	12	4		6	2		6	2	
1993	8	8		4	4		4	4	
1994	7	9		3	5		4	4	
1995	7	9		4	4		3	5	
1996	3	13		2	6		1	7	
1997	6	10		3	5		3	5	

Season	All Games W	L	T	Home Games W	L	T	Road Games W	L	T
1998	6	10		4	4		2	6	
1999	3	13		3	5		0	8	
2000	10	6		3	5		7	1	
2001	7	9		3	5		4	4	
2002	9	7		4	4		5	3	
2003	8	8		5	3		3	5	
2004	8	8		3	5		5	3	
2005	3	13		1	7		2	6	
2006	10	6		4	4		6	2	
2007	7	9		3	5		4	4	
2008	8	8		6	2		2	6	
2009	13	3		6	2		7	1	
2010	11	5		5	3		6	2	
2011	13	3		8	0		5	3	
	299	386	5	161	183	1	138	203	4

NEW YORK GIANTS

Season	All Games W	L	T	Home Games W	L	T	Road Games W	L	T
1925	8	4		7	2		1	2	
1926	8	4	1	5	2	1	3	2	
1927	11	1	1	7	1		4	0	1
1928	4	7	2	1	2	2	3	5	
1929	13	1	1	7	1		6	0	1
1930	13	4		6	2		7	2	
1931	7	6	1	4	2	1	3	4	
1932	4	6	2	3	2	1	1	4	1
1933	11	3		7	0		4	3	
1934	8	5		5	1		3	4	
1935	9	3		4	2		5	1	
1936	5	6	1	3	3	1	2	3	
1937	6	3	2	4	2	1	2	1	1
1938	8	2	1	6	1		2	1	1
1939	9	1	1	6	0		3	1	1
1940	6	4	1	4	3		2	1	1
1941	8	3		5	2		3	1	
1942	5	5	1	3	2	1	2	3	
1943	6	3	1	4	2		2	1	1
1944	8	1	1	5	1		3	0	1
1945	3	6	1	2	4		1	2	1
1946	7	3	1	5	1	1	2	2	
1947	2	8	2	2	3	1	0	5	1
1948	4	8		2	4		2	4	
1949	6	6		2	4		4	2	
1950	10	2		5	1		5	1	
1951	9	2	1	5	1		4	1	1
1952	7	5		2	4		5	1	
1953	3	9		2	4		1	5	
1954	7	5		4	2		3	3	
1955	6	5	1	4	1	1	2	4	
1956	8	3	1	4	1	1	4	2	
1957	7	5		3	3		4	2	
1958	9	3		5	1		4	2	
1959	10	2		5	1		5	1	
1960	6	4	2	1	3	2	5	1	
1961	10	3	1	4	2	1	6	1	
1962	12	2		6	1		6	1	
1963	11	3		5	2		6	1	
1964	2	10	2	2	5		0	5	2
1965	7	7		3	4		4	3	
1966	1	12	1	1	6		0	6	1
1967	7	7		5	2		2	5	
1968	7	7		3	4		4	3	
1969	6	8		5	2		1	6	
1970	9	5		5	2		4	3	
1971	4	10		1	6		3	4	
1972	8	6		4	3		4	3	
1973	2	11	1	2	4	1	0	7	

Season	All Games W	L	T	Home Games W	L	T	Road Games W	L	T
1974	2	12		0	7		2	5	
1975	5	9		2	5		3	4	
1976	3	11		3	4		0	7	
1977	5	9		3	4		2	5	
1978	6	10		5	3		1	7	
1979	6	10		4	4		2	6	
1980	4	12		2	6		2	6	
1981	9	7		4	4		5	3	
1982	4	5		2	3		2	2	
1983	3	12	1	1	7		2	5	1
1984	9	7		6	2		3	5	
1985	10	6		6	2		4	4	
1986	14	2		8	0		6	2	
1987	6	9		5	3		1	6	
1988	10	6		5	3		5	3	
1989	12	4		7	1		5	3	
1990	13	3		7	1		6	2	
1991	8	8		5	3		3	5	
1992	6	10		4	4		2	6	
1993	11	5		6	2		5	3	
1994	9	7		4	4		5	3	
1995	5	11		3	5		2	6	
1996	6	10		3	5		3	5	
1997	10	5	1	6	2		4	3	1
1998	8	8		5	3		3	5	
1999	7	9		4	4		3	5	
2000	12	4		5	3		7	1	
2001	7	9		5	3		2	6	
2002	10	6		5	3		5	3	
2003	4	12		1	7		3	5	
2004	6	10		3	5		3	5	
2005	11	5		7	1		4	4	
2006	8	8		3	5		5	3	
2007	10	6		3	5		7	1	
2008	12	4		7	1		5	3	
2009	8	8		4	4		4	4	
2010	10	6		5	3		5	3	
2011	9	7		4	4		5	3	
	645	531	33	357	249	16	288	282	17

PHILADELPHIA EAGLES

Season	All Games W	L	T	Home Games W	L	T	Road Games W	L	T
1933	3	5	1	2	3	1	1	2	
1934	4	7		2	4		2	3	
1935	2	9		0	5		2	4	
1936	1	11		1	6		0	5	
1937	2	8	1	0	5	1	2	3	
1938	5	6		2	3		3	3	
1939	1	9	1	1	3	1	0	6	
1940	1	10		1	4		0	6	
1941	2	8	1	1	4	1	1	4	
1942	2	9		0	5		2	4	
1944	7	1	2	3	1	2	4	0	
1945	7	3		6	0		1	3	
1946	6	5		3	2		3	3	
1947	8	4		6	1		2	3	
1948	9	2	1	6	0		3	2	1
1949	11	1		6	0		5	1	
1950	6	6		2	4		4	2	
1951	4	8		1	5		3	3	
1952	7	5		4	2		3	3	
1953	7	4	1	5	0	1	2	4	
1954	7	4	1	5	1		2	3	1
1955	4	7	1	4	2		0	5	1
1956	3	8	1	2	3	1	1	5	
1957	4	8		3	3		1	5	
1958	2	9	1	2	4		0	5	1

Season	All Games W	L	T	Home Games W	L	T	Road Games W	L	T
1959	7	5		5	1		2	4	
1960	10	2		5	1		5	1	
1961	10	4		5	2		5	2	
1962	3	10	1	2	5		1	5	1
1963	2	10	2	1	5	1	1	5	1
1964	6	8		3	4		3	4	
1965	5	9		2	5		3	4	
1966	9	5		5	2		4	3	
1967	6	7	1	5	2		1	5	1
1968	2	12		1	6		1	6	
1969	4	9	1	2	5		2	4	1
1970	3	10	1	3	3	1	0	7	
1971	6	7	1	3	4		3	3	1
1972	2	11	1	0	6	1	2	5	
1973	5	8	1	4	3		1	5	1
1974	7	7		5	2		2	5	
1975	4	10		2	5		2	5	
1976	4	10		2	5		2	5	
1977	5	9		4	3		1	6	
1978	9	7		5	3		4	4	
1979	11	5		5	3		6	2	
1980	12	4		7	1		5	3	
1981	10	6		6	2		4	4	
1982	3	6		1	4		2	2	
1983	5	11		1	7		4	4	
1984	6	9	1	5	3		1	6	1
1985	7	9		4	4		3	5	
1986	5	10	1	2	5	1	3	5	
1987	7	8		4	4		3	4	
1988	10	6		5	3		5	3	
1989	11	5		6	2		5	3	
1990	10	6		6	2		4	4	
1991	10	6		4	4		6	2	
1992	11	5		8	0		3	5	
1993	8	8		3	5		5	3	
1994	7	9		5	3		2	6	
1995	10	6		6	2		4	4	
1996	10	6		5	3		5	3	
1997	6	9	1	6	2		0	7	1
1998	3	13		3	5		0	8	
1999	5	11		4	4		1	7	
2000	11	5		5	3		6	2	
2001	11	5		4	4		7	1	
2002	12	4		7	1		5	3	
2003	12	4		5	3		7	1	
2004	13	3		7	1		6	2	
2005	6	10		4	4		2	6	
2006	10	6		5	3		5	3	
2007	8	8		3	5		5	3	
2008	9	6	1	6	2		3	4	1
2009	11	5		6	2		5	3	
2010	10	6		4	4		6	2	
2011	8	8		3	5		5	3	
	512	545	25	287	247	12	225	298	13

ST. LOUIS RAMS*

Season	All Games W	L	T	Home Games W	L	T	Road Games W	L	T
1937	1	10		0	5		1	5	
1938	4	7		2	2		2	5	
1939	5	5	1	3	2	1	2	3	
1940	4	6	1	3	1	1	1	5	
1941	2	9		1	4		1	5	
1942	5	6		3	2		2	4	
1944	4	6		1	2		3	4	
1945	9	1		4	0		5	1	
1946	6	4	1	3	2		3	2	1
1947	6	6		3	3		3	3	

INSIDE THE NUMBERS

Season	All Games W	L	T	Home Games W	L	T	Road Games W	L	T
1948	6	5	1	3	2	1	3	3	
1949	8	2	2	5	1		3	1	2
1950	9	3		5	1		4	2	
1951	8	4		5	2		3	2	
1952	9	3		5	1		4	2	
1953	8	3	1	5	1		3	2	1
1954	6	5	1	3	2	1	3	3	
1955	8	3	1	5	1		3	2	1
1956	4	8		4	2		0	6	
1957	6	6		5	1		1	5	
1958	8	4		4	2		4	2	
1959	2	10		0	6		2	4	
1960	4	7	1	2	3	1	2	4	
1961	4	10		4	3		0	7	
1962	1	12	1	0	7		1	5	1
1963	5	9		3	4		2	5	
1964	5	7	2	3	2	2	2	5	
1965	4	10		3	4		1	6	
1966	8	6		5	2		3	4	
1967	11	1	2	5	1	1	6	0	1
1968	10	3	1	5	2		5	1	1
1969	11	3		5	2		6	1	
1970	9	4	1	3	3	1	6	1	
1971	8	5	1	4	2	1	4	3	
1972	6	7	1	4	3		2	4	1
1973	12	2		7	0		5	2	
1974	10	4		6	1		4	3	
1975	12	2		6	1		6	1	
1976	10	3	1	5	2		5	1	1
1977	10	4		7	0		3	4	
1978	12	4		6	2		6	2	
1979	9	7		4	4		5	3	
1980	11	5		6	2		5	3	
1981	6	10		4	4		2	6	
1982	2	7		1	4		1	3	
1983	9	7		5	3		4	4	
1984	10	6		5	3		5	3	
1985	11	5		6	2		5	3	
1986	10	6		6	2		4	4	
1987	6	9		3	4		3	5	
1988	10	6		4	4		6	2	
1989	11	5		6	2		5	3	
1990	5	11		2	6		3	5	
1991	3	13		2	6		1	7	
1992	6	10		4	4		2	6	
1993	5	11		3	5		2	6	
1994	4	12		3	5		1	7	
1995	7	9		4	4		3	5	
1996	6	10		4	4		2	6	
1997	5	11		2	6		3	5	
1998	4	12		2	6		2	6	
1999	13	3		8	0		5	3	
2000	10	6		5	3		5	3	
2001	14	2		6	2		8	0	
2002	7	9		6	2		1	7	
2003	12	4		8	0		4	4	
2004	8	8		6	2		2	6	
2005	6	10		3	5		3	5	
2006	8	8		4	4		4	4	
2007	3	13		1	7		2	6	
2008	2	14		1	7		1	7	
2009	1	15		0	8		1	7	
2010	7	9		5	3		2	6	
2011	2	14		1	7		1	7	
	513	506	20	285	219	10	228	287	10

*includes Cleveland Rams (1937-1942, 1944-45) and Los Angeles Rams (1946-1994).

SAN FRANCISCO 49ERS

Season	All Games W	L	T	Home Games W	L	T	Road Games W	L	T
1950	3	9		3	3		0	6	
1951	7	4	1	5	1		2	3	1
1952	7	5		3	3		4	2	
1953	9	3		5	1		4	2	
1954	7	4	1	4	2		3	2	1
1955	4	8		2	4		2	4	
1956	5	6	1	3	3		2	3	1
1957	8	4		5	1		3	3	
1958	6	6		4	2		2	4	
1959	7	5		4	2		3	3	
1960	7	5		3	3		4	2	
1961	7	6	1	5	1	1	2	5	
1962	6	8		1	6		5	2	
1963	2	12		2	5		0	7	
1964	4	10		3	4		1	6	
1965	7	6	1	4	2	1	3	4	
1966	6	6	2	4	2	1	2	4	1
1967	7	7		3	4		4	3	
1968	7	6	1	3	3	1	4	3	
1969	4	8	2	3	3	1	1	5	1
1970	10	3	1	5	1	1	5	2	
1971	9	5		4	3		5	2	
1972	8	5	1	4	2	1	4	3	
1973	5	9		3	4		2	5	
1974	6	8		3	4		3	4	
1975	5	9		2	5		3	4	
1976	8	6		4	3		4	3	
1977	5	9		3	4		2	5	
1978	2	14		2	6		0	8	
1979	2	14		2	6		0	8	
1980	6	10		4	4		2	6	
1981	13	3		7	1		6	2	
1982	3	6		0	5		3	1	
1983	10	6		4	4		6	2	
1984	15	1		7	1		8	0	
1985	10	6		5	3		5	3	
1986	10	5	1	6	2		4	3	1
1987	13	2		6	1		7	1	
1988	10	6		4	4		6	2	
1989	14	2		6	2		8	0	
1990	14	2		6	2		8	0	
1991	10	6		7	1		3	5	
1992	14	2		7	1		7	1	
1993	10	6		6	2		4	4	
1994	13	3		7	1		6	2	
1995	11	5		6	2		5	3	
1996	12	4		6	2		6	2	
1997	13	3		8	0		5	3	
1998	12	4		8	0		4	4	
1999	4	12		3	5		1	7	
2000	6	10		4	4		2	6	
2001	12	4		7	1		5	3	
2002	10	6		5	3		5	3	
2003	7	9		6	2		1	7	
2004	2	14		1	7		1	7	
2005	4	12		3	5		1	7	
2006	7	9		4	4		3	5	
2007	5	11		3	5		2	6	
2008	7	9		4	4		3	5	
2009	8	8		6	2		2	6	
2010	6	10		5	3		1	7	
2011	13	3		7	1		6	2	
	484	409	13	269	177	7	215	232	6

SEATTLE SEAHAWKS

Season	All Games W	L	T	Home Games W	L	T	Road Games W	L	T
1976	2	12		1	6		1	6	
1977	5	9		3	4		2	5	
1978	9	7		5	3		4	4	
1979	9	7		5	3		4	4	
1980	4	12		0	8		4	4	
1981	6	10		5	3		1	7	
1982	4	5		3	2		1	3	
1983	9	7		5	3		4	4	
1984	12	4		7	1		5	3	
1985	8	8		5	3		3	5	
1986	10	6		7	1		3	5	
1987	9	6		6	2		3	4	
1988	9	7		5	3		4	4	
1989	7	9		3	5		4	4	
1990	9	7		5	3		4	4	
1991	7	9		5	3		2	6	
1992	2	14		1	7		1	7	
1993	6	10		4	4		2	6	
1994	6	10		3	5		3	5	
1995	8	8		5	3		3	5	
1996	7	9		4	4		3	5	
1997	8	8		4	4		4	4	
1998	8	8		6	2		2	6	
1999	9	7		5	3		4	4	
2000	6	10		3	5		3	5	
2001	9	7		6	2		3	5	
2002	7	9		3	5		4	4	
2003	10	6		8	0		2	6	
2004	9	7		5	3		4	4	
2005	13	3		8	0		5	3	
2006	9	7		5	3		4	4	
2007	10	6		7	1		3	5	
2008	4	12		2	6		2	6	
2009	5	11		4	4		1	7	
2010	7	9		5	3		2	6	
2011	7	9		4	4		3	5	
	269	295		162	121		107	174	

Season	All Games W	L	T	Home Games W	L	T	Road Games W	L	T
2002	12	4		6	2		6	2	
2003	7	9		3	5		4	4	
2004	5	11		4	4		1	7	
2005	11	5		6	2		5	3	
2006	4	12		3	5		1	7	
2007	9	7		6	2		3	5	
2008	9	7		6	2		3	5	
2009	3	13		1	7		2	6	
2010	10	6		4	4		6	2	
2011	4	12		3	5		1	7	
	222	341	1	136	145	1	86	196	

TAMPA BAY BUCCANEERS

Season	All Games W	L	T	Home Games W	L	T	Road Games W	L	T
1976	0	14		0	7		0	7	
1977	2	12		1	6		1	6	
1978	5	11		3	5		2	6	
1979	10	6		5	3		5	3	
1980	5	10	1	2	5	1	3	5	
1981	9	7		6	2		3	5	
1982	5	4		4	1		1	3	
1983	2	14		1	7		1	7	
1984	6	10		6	2		0	8	
1985	2	14		2	6		0	8	
1986	2	14		1	7		1	7	
1987	4	11		2	5		2	6	
1988	5	11		3	5		2	6	
1989	5	11		2	6		3	5	
1990	6	10		4	4		2	6	
1991	3	13		3	5		0	8	
1992	5	11		3	5		2	6	
1993	5	11		3	5		2	6	
1994	6	10		4	4		2	6	
1995	7	9		5	3		2	6	
1996	6	10		5	3		1	7	
1997	10	6		5	3		5	3	
1998	8	8		6	2		2	6	
1999	11	5		7	1		4	4	
2000	10	6		6	2		4	4	
2001	9	7		5	3		4	4	

WASHINGTON REDSKINS*

Season	All Games W	L	T	Home Games W	L	T	Road Games W	L	T
1932	4	4	2	2	3	1	2	1	1
1933	5	5	2	4	2		1	3	2
1934	6	6		4	3		2	3	
1935	2	8	1	2	5		0	3	1
1936	7	5		4	3		3	2	
1937	8	3		4	2		4	1	
1938	6	3	2	3	1	1	3	2	1
1939	8	2	1	5	0	1	3	2	
1940	9	2		6	0		3	2	
1941	6	5		4	2		2	3	
1942	10	1		5	1		5	0	
1943	6	3	1	4	2		2	1	1
1944	6	3	1	4	2		2	1	1
1945	8	2		6	0		2	2	
1946	5	5	1	3	2	1	2	3	
1947	4	8		4	2		0	6	
1948	7	5		4	2		3	3	
1949	4	7	1	3	3		1	4	1
1950	3	9		1	5		2	4	
1951	5	7		2	4		3	3	
1952	4	8		1	5		3	3	
1953	6	5	1	3	3		3	2	1
1954	3	9		3	3		0	6	
1955	8	4		3	3		5	1	
1956	6	6		4	2		2	4	
1957	5	6	1	2	3	1	3	3	
1958	4	7	1	3	2	1	1	5	
1959	3	9		2	4		1	5	
1960	1	9	2	1	4	1	0	5	1
1961	1	12	1	1	6		0	6	1
1962	5	7	2	3	4		2	3	2
1963	3	11		1	6		2	5	
1964	6	8		4	3		2	5	
1965	6	8		3	4		3	4	
1966	7	7		4	3		3	4	
1967	5	6	3	2	4	1	3	2	2
1968	5	9		3	4		2	5	
1969	7	5	2	4	2	1	3	3	1
1970	6	8		4	3		2	5	
1971	9	4	1	4	2	1	5	2	
1972	11	3		6	1		5	2	
1973	10	4		7	0		3	4	
1974	10	4		6	1		4	3	
1975	8	6		5	2		3	4	
1976	10	4		5	2		5	2	
1977	9	5		5	2		4	3	
1978	8	8		5	3		3	5	
1979	10	6		6	2		4	4	
1980	6	10		4	4		2	6	
1981	8	8		5	3		3	5	
1982	8	1		3	1		5	0	
1983	14	2		7	1		7	1	
1984	11	5		7	1		4	4	

Season	All Games W	L	T	Home Games W	L	T	Road Games W	L	T
1985	10	6		5	3		5	3	
1986	12	4		7	1		5	3	
1987	11	4		6	1		5	3	
1988	7	9		4	4		3	5	
1989	10	6		4	4		6	2	
1990	10	6		7	1		3	5	
1991	14	2		7	1		7	1	
1992	9	7		6	2		3	5	
1993	4	12		3	5		1	7	
1994	3	13		0	8		3	5	
1995	6	10		4	4		2	6	
1996	9	7		5	3		4	4	
1997	8	7	1	5	2	1	3	5	
1998	6	10		4	4		2	6	
1999	10	6		6	2		4	4	
2000	8	8		4	4		4	4	
2001	8	8		4	4		4	4	
2002	7	9		5	3		2	6	
2003	5	11		3	5		2	6	
2004	6	10		3	5		3	5	
2005	10	6		6	2		4	4	
2006	5	11		3	5		2	6	
2007	9	7		5	3		4	4	
2008	8	8		4	4		4	4	
2009	4	12		3	5		1	7	
2010	6	10		2	6		4	4	
2011	5	11		2	6		3	5	
	552	527	27	317	234	11	235	293	16

*includes Boston Braves (1932) and Boston Redskins (1933-36).

ALL-TIME REGULAR-SEASON RECORDS OF NFL TEAMS

AFC	W	L	T	Pct.
Miami	400	300	4	.571
Baltimore	140	115	1	.549
Oakland	426	351	11	.548
New England	414	365	9	.531
Indianapolis	453	410	7	.525
Pittsburgh	553	503	20	.524
Denver	406	372	10	.522
Cleveland	442	406	10	.521
Kansas City	402	374	12	.518
Jacksonville	138	134	0	.507
San Diego	392	385	11	.504
Tennessee	386	396	6	.494
Buffalo	364	416	8	.467
N.Y. Jets	359	421	8	.460
Cincinnati	295	379	2	.438
Houston	65	95	0	.406

NFC	W	L	T	Pct.
Chicago	712	520	42	.578
Dallas	448	332	6	.574
Green Bay	679	525	36	.564
N.Y. Giants	645	531	33	.548
Minnesota	416	349	9	.544
San Francisco	484	409	13	.542
Washington	552	527	27	.512
St. Louis	513	506	20	.503
Philadelphia	512	545	25	.484
Seattle	269	295	0	.477
Carolina	125	147	0	.460
Detroit	506	599	32	.458
New Orleans	299	386	5	.437
Atlanta	299	399	6	.429
Arizona	496	689	39	.419
Tampa Bay	222	341	1	.395

From 1920-1971, tie games were not included in win percentage.

History

The Professional Football Hall of Fame is located in Canton, Ohio, site of the organizational meeting on September 17, 1920, from which the National Football League evolved. The NFL recognized Canton as the Hall of Fame site on April 27, 1961. Canton area individuals, foundations, and companies donated almost $400,000 in cash and services to provide funds for the construction of the original two-building complex, which was dedicated on September 7, 1963. Four expansions have occurred (1971, 1978, 1995, and the current "Future 50" Expansion & Renovation Project) over the years that have resulted in the museum growing from its original 19,000 square feet to today's 117,000-square foot facility.

The Hall of Fame's current expansion & renovation project is the largest in the museum's nearly 50-year history. The two-year, $27 million project was coined the "Future 50" because it will be completed in time for the Hall of Fame's 50th Anniversary in 2013 and will put the foundation in place from the next 50 years of success.

The Hall has renovated four of its six major exhibition galleries in recent years. The *Lamar Hunt Super Bowl Gallery*, featuring the Super Bowl Theater, opened in summer 2009. The *Moments, Memories & Mementos Gallery* and *Pro Football Today Gallery* were opened—one in 2008 preceded by a brand new *Hall of Fame Gallery*, home to enshrinees bronze busts, in 2003. Other highlights of the Hall include an extensive archive and information center and a large museum store. Throughout the years, the Pro Football Hall of Fame has become an extremely popular tourist attraction. The Hall of Fame will welcome its nine millionth visitor during the summer of 2012.

New members of the Pro Football Hall of Fame are elected annually by a 44-member Selection Committee, made up of media representatives from every league city, eleven at-large representatives, and a representative of the Pro Football Writers of America.

Between four and seven new members are elected each year. An affirmative vote of approximately 80 percent is needed for election.

Any fan may nominate any eligible player or contributor simply by writing to the Pro Football Hall of Fame. Players and coaches must have last played or coached at least five years before he is eligible. Contributors (administrators, owners, *et al.*) may be elected while they are still active.

The charter class of 17 enshrinees was elected in 1963 and the honor roll now stands at 273 (158 living as of May 1, 2012) with the election of a six-man class in 2012. That class consists of Jack Butler, Dermontti Dawson, Chris Doleman, Cortez Kennedy, Curtis Martin, and Willie Roaf.

ROSTER OF MEMBERS

HERB ADDERLEY
Cornerback. 6-0, 205. Born in Philadelphia, Pennsylvania, June 8, 1939. Michigan State. Inducted in 1980. 1961-69 Green Bay Packers, 1970-72 Dallas Cowboys. **Highlights:** 48 interceptions, 7 touchdowns. Played in four Super Bowls, five Pro Bowls.

TROY AIKMAN
Quarterback. 6-4, 219. Born in West Covina, California, November 21, 1966. Oklahoma, UCLA. Inducted in 2006. 1989-2000 Dallas Cowboys. **Highlights:** His 90 wins in 1990s make him winningest quarterback of any decade. Led Cowboys to three Super Bowl wins. Passed for 32,942 yards, 165 touchdowns. Named to six Pro Bowls.

GEORGE ALLEN
Coach. Born in Detroit, Michigan, April 29, 1918. Died December 31, 1990. Alma College, Eastern Michigan, Marquette, Michigan. Inducted in 2002. 1966-1970 Los Angeles Rams, 1971-77 Washington Redskins. **Highlights:** 118-54-5 overall record. Never suffered a losing season, and ranked tenth in coaching victories at time of retirement.

MARCUS ALLEN
Running back. 6-2, 210. Born in San Diego, California, March 26, 1960. Southern California. Inducted in 2003. 1982-1992 Los Angeles Raiders, 1993-1997 Kansas City Chiefs. **Highlights:** First player in NFL history to tally 10,000 rushing yards and 5,000 receiving yards. MVP, Super Bowl XVIII.

LANCE ALWORTH
Wide receiver. 6-0, 184. Born in Houston, Texas, August 3, 1940. Arkansas. Inducted in 1978. 1962-1970 San Diego Chargers, 1971-72 Dallas Cowboys. **Highlights:** 542 receptions for 10,266 yards, 85 touchdowns. All-AFL seven times, seven All-Star games.

DOUG ATKINS
Defensive end. 6-8, 275. Born in Humboldt, Tennessee, May 8, 1930. Tennessee. Inducted in 1982. 1953-54 Cleveland Browns, 1955-1966 Chicago Bears, 1967-69 New Orleans Saints. **Highlights:** Eight Pro Bowls, All-NFL four times. Played for 17 years, 205 games.

MORRIS (RED) BADGRO
End. 6-0, 190. Born in Orillia, Washington, December 1, 1902. Died July 13, 1998. Southern California. Inducted in 1981. 1927-28 New York Yankees, 1930-35 New York Giants, 1936 Brooklyn Dodgers. **Highlights:** First- or second-team All-NFL four times. Scored first touchdown in NFL Championship Game series.

LEM BARNEY
Cornerback. 6-0, 190. Born in Gulfport, Mississippi, September 8, 1945. Jackson State. Inducted in 1992. 1967-1977 Detroit Lions. **Highlights:** 56 interceptions for 1,077 yards, 11 touchdowns (7 defensive, 4 special teams). Seven Pro Bowls, All-NFL/NFC four times.

CLIFF BATTLES
Halfback. 6-1, 195. Born in Akron, Ohio, May 1, 1910. Died April 28, 1981. West Virginia Wesleyan. Inducted in 1968. 1932 Boston Braves, 1933-36 Boston Redskins, 1937 Washington Redskins. **Highlights:** NFL rushing champion 1932, 1937. First to gain more than 200 yards in a game, 1933.

SAMMY BAUGH
Quarterback. 6-2, 180. Born in Temple, Texas, March 17, 1914. Died December 17, 2008. Texas Christian. Inducted in 1963. 1937-1952 Washington Redskins. **Highlights:** Charter enshrinee. Six-time NFL passing leader. NFL passing, punting, interception champ, 1943.

CHUCK BEDNARIK
Center-linebacker. 6-3, 230. Born in Bethlehem, Pennsylvania, May 1, 1925. Pennsylvania. Inducted in 1967. 1949-1962 Philadelphia Eagles. **Highlights:** Eight Pro Bowls. Missed three games in 14 years. Named NFL all-time center, 1969.

BERT BELL
Team owner. Commissioner. Born in Philadelphia, Pennsylvania, February 25, 1895. Died October 11, 1959. Pennsylvania. Inducted in 1963. 1933-1940 Philadelphia Eagles, 1941-42 Pittsburgh Steelers, 1943 Phil-Pitt, 1944 Card-Pitt, 1945-46 Pittsburgh Steelers. Commissioner, 1946-1959. **Highlights:** Charter enshrinee. Built NFL image as commissioner, 1946-1959. Set up long-term television policies.

BOBBY BELL
Linebacker. 6-4, 225. Born in Shelby, North Carolina, June 17, 1940. Minnesota. Inducted in 1983. 1963-1974 Kansas City Chiefs. **Highlights:** 26 interceptions. All-AFL/AFC eight times. Nine career touchdowns, 1 on onside kick return.

RAYMOND BERRY
End. 6-2, 187. Born in Corpus Christi, Texas, February 27, 1933. Southern Methodist. Inducted in 1973. 1955-1967 Baltimore Colts. **Highlights:** 631 receptions for 9,275 yards, 68 touchdowns. Set NFL title game mark with 12 catches for 178 yards, 1958.

ELVIN BETHEA
Defensive end. 6-2, 260. Born in Trenton, New Jersey, March 1, 1946. North Carolina A&T. Inducted in 2003. 1968-1983 Houston Oilers. **Highlights:** Led team in sacks six times. Elected to eight Pro Bowls. Played for 16 years, 210 games.

CHARLES W. BIDWILL SR.
Team owner. Born in Chicago, Illinois, September 16, 1895. Died April 19, 1947. Loyola of Chicago. Inducted in 1967. 1933-1943 Chicago Cardinals, 1944 Card-Pitt, 1945-47 Chicago Cardinals. **Highlights:** Guiding light for NFL during depression years. Built famous "Dream Backfield."

FRED BILETNIKOFF
Wide receiver. 6-1, 190. Born in Erie, Pennsylvania, February 23, 1943. Florida State. Inducted in 1988. 1965-1978 Oakland Raiders. **Highlights:** 589 receptions for 8,974 yards, 76 touchdowns. 40 catches 10 straight years. MVP, Super Bowl XI.

GEORGE BLANDA
Quarterback-kicker. 6-2, 215. Born in Youngwood, Pennsylvania, September 17, 1927. Died September 27, 2010. Kentucky. Inducted in 1981. 1949-1958 Chicago Bears, 1950 Baltimore Colts, 1960-66 Houston Oilers, 1967-1975 Oakland Raiders. **Highlights:** 2,002 career points. 26-season, 340-game career longest in NFL history at retirement.

MEL BLOUNT
Cornerback. 6-3, 205. Born in Vidalia, Georgia, April 10, 1948. Southern University. Inducted in 1989. 1970-1983 Pittsburgh Steelers. **Highlights:** 57 interceptions for 736 yards. NFL defensive MVP, 1975. Played in five Pro Bowls.

TERRY BRADSHAW
Quarterback. 6-3, 210. Born in Shreveport, Louisiana, September 2, 1948. Louisiana Tech. Inducted in 1989. 1970-1983 Pittsburgh Steelers. **Highlights:** 27,989 yards passing, 212 touchdowns. MVP in Super Bowls XIII, XIV.

BOB (BOOMER) BROWN
Tackle. 6-4, 280. Born in Cleveland, Ohio, December 8, 1941. Nebraska. Inducted in 2004. 1964-68 Philadelphia Eagles, 1969-1970 Los Angeles Rams, 1971-73 Oakland Raiders. **Highlights:** All-NFL seven of 10 seasons, six Pro Bowls. Named to 1960s All-Decade Team.

JIM BROWN
Fullback. 6-2, 228. Born in St. Simons, Georgia, February 17, 1936. Syracuse. Inducted in 1971. 1957-1965 Cleveland Browns. **Highlights:** 12,312 yards rushing, 756 points. Led NFL rushers eight years. Nine consecutive Pro Bowls.

PAUL BROWN
Coach. Born in Norwalk, Ohio, September 7, 1908. Died August 5, 1991. Miami (Ohio). Inducted in 1967. 1946-49 Cleveland Browns (AAFC), 1950-1962 Cleveland Browns. **Highlights:** Built Cleveland dynasty with 167-53-8 record, four AAFC titles, three NFL crowns. Returned to coaching with Cincinnati Bengals after induction, 1968-1975.

ROOSEVELT BROWN
Tackle. 6-3, 255. Born in Charlottesville, Virginia, October 20, 1932. Died June 9, 2004. Morgan State. Inducted in 1975. 1953-1965 New York Giants. **Highlights:** All-NFL eight consecutive years, nine Pro Bowls. NFL's lineman of year, 1956.

WILLIE BROWN
Cornerback. 6-1, 210. Born in Yazoo City, Mississippi, December 2, 1940. Grambling. Inducted in 1984. 1963-66 Denver Broncos, 1967-1978 Oakland Raiders. **Highlights:** 54 interceptions for 472 yards. Scored on 75-yard interception in Super Bowl XI.

BUCK BUCHANAN
Defensive tackle. 6-7, 274. Born in Gainesville, Alabama, September 10, 1940. Died July 16, 1992. Grambling. Inducted in 1990. 1963-1975 Kansas City Chiefs. **Highlights:** Led Chiefs defensive efforts in Super Bowl I, IV. Did not miss a game in 13 years.

NICK BUONICONTI
Linebacker. 5-11, 220. Born in Springfield, Massachusetts, December 15, 1940. Notre Dame. Inducted in 2001. 1962-68 Boston Patriots, 1969-1974, 1976 Miami Dolphins. **Highlights:** All-AFL/AFC eight times. Named to AFL's All-Time Team.

DICK BUTKUS
Linebacker. 6-3, 245. Born in Chicago, Illinois, December 9, 1942. Illinois. Inducted in 1979. 1965-1973 Chicago Bears. **Highlights:** All-NFL six years, eight consecutive Pro Bowls. 27 fumble recoveries.

JACK BUTLER
Cornerback. 6-1, 200. Born in Pittsburgh, Pennsylvania, November 12, 1927. St. Bonaventure. Inducted in 2012. 1951-59 Pittsburgh Steelers. **Highlights:** Retired as NFL's second all-time leading interceptor with 52 career picks returned for 827 yards, 4 TDs. Named to four Pro Bowls and selected to the NFL's All-Decade Team of 1950s.

EARL CAMPBELL
Running back. 5-11, 233. Born in Tyler, Texas, March 29, 1955. Texas. Inducted in 1991. 1978-1984 Houston Oilers, 1984-85 New Orleans Saints. **Highlights:** 9,407 yards rushing, 74 touchdowns. 1,934 yards rushing in 1980, including four games with at least 200 yards.

TONY CANADEO
Halfback. 5-11, 195. Born in Chicago, Illinois, May 5, 1919. Died November 29, 2003. Gonzaga. Inducted in 1974. 1941-44, 1946-1952 Green Bay Packers. **Highlights:** Two-way player. Third player to rush for 1,000 yards in single season, 1949.

JOE CARR
NFL president. Born in Columbus, Ohio, October 23, 1879. Died May 20, 1939. Did not attend college. Inducted in 1963. President, 1921-1939 National Football League. **Highlights:** Charter enshrinee. NFL co-organizer, 1920. Introduced standard player contract.

HARRY CARSON
Linebacker. 6-2, 237. Born in Florence, South Carolina, November 26, 1953. South Carolina State. Inducted in 2006. 1976-1988 New York Giants. **Highlights:** 11 career interceptions. Named to nine Pro Bowls. Named first- or second-team All-NFL six times.

DAVE CASPER
Tight end. 6-4, 240. Born in Bemidji, Minnesota, February 2, 1952. Notre Dame. Inducted in 2002. 1974-1980 Oakland Raiders, 1980-83 Houston Oilers, 1983 Minnesota Vikings, 1984 Los Angeles Raiders. **Highlights:** 378 receptions for 5,216 yards, 52 touchdowns. Five consecutive Pro Bowls.

GUY CHAMBERLIN
End. Coach. 6-2, 196. Born in Blue Springs, Nebraska, January 16, 1894. Died April 4, 1967. Nebraska. Inducted in 1965. 1919 Canton Bulldogs, 1920-21 Decatur Staleys/Chicago Staleys, player-coach 1922-23 Canton Bulldogs, 1924 Cleveland Bulldogs, 1925-26 Frankford Yellowjackets, 1927-28 Chicago Cardinals. **Highlights:** Player-coach of four NFL championship teams. Six-year coaching record of 58-16-7.

JACK CHRISTIANSEN
Safety. 6-1, 185. Born in Sublette, Kansas, December 20, 1928. Died June 29, 1986. Colorado State. Inducted in 1970. 1951-58 Detroit Lions. **Highlights:** 46 interceptions. NFL interception leader, 1953, 1957. Eight punt returns for touchdowns.

EARL (DUTCH) CLARK
Quarterback. 6-0, 185. Born in Fowler, Colorado, October 11, 1906. Died August 5, 1978. Colorado College. Inducted in 1963. 1931-32 Portsmouth Spartans, 1934-38 Detroit Lions. **Highlights:** Charter enshrinee. NFL scoring champion three years. Led Lions to 1935 NFL title.

GEORGE CONNOR
Tackle-linebacker. 6-3, 240. Born in Chicago, Illinois, January 21, 1925. Died March 31, 2003. Holy Cross, Notre Dame. Inducted in 1975. 1948-1955 Chicago Bears. **Highlights:** All-NFL at three positions—T, DT, LB. All-NFL five years. Played in first four Pro Bowls.

JIMMY CONZELMAN
Quarterback. Coach. Team owner. 6-0, 180. Born in St. Louis, Missouri, March 6, 1898. Died July 31, 1970. Washington of St. Louis. Inducted in 1964. 1920 Decatur Staleys, 1921-22 Rock Island Independents, 1922-24 Milwaukee Badgers; owner-coach 1925-26 Detroit Panthers; player-coach 1927-29, coach 1930 Providence Steam Roller; coach 1940-42, 1946-48 Chicago Cardinals. **Highlights:** Player-coach of four NFL teams in 1920s. Coached Cardinals to 1947 NFL crown.

LOU CREEKMUR
Tackle-guard. 6-4, 255. Born in Hopelawn, New Jersey. January 22, 1927. Died July 5, 2009. William & Mary. Inducted in 1996. 1950-59 Detroit Lions. **Highlights:** All-NFL six times, twice at guard and four times at tackle. Selected to eight Pro Bowls and played on three NFL championship teams.

LARRY CSONKA
Running back. 6-3, 235. Born in Stow, Ohio, December 25, 1946. Syracuse. Inducted in 1987. 1968-1974, 1979 Miami Dolphins, 1976-78 New York Giants. **Highlights:** 8,081 yards rushing, 68 touchdowns. MVP Super Bowl VIII. Only 21 fumbles in 1,891 carries and 106 receptions.

AL DAVIS
Coach-Commissioner-Owner. Born in Brockton, Massachusetts, July 4, 1929. Died October 8, 2011. Wittenberg, Syracuse. Inducted in 1992. 1963-1981, 1995-2011 Oakland Raiders, 1982-1994 Los Angeles Raiders, 1966 American Football League. **Highlights:** Only person to serve in pros as personnel assistant, scout, assistant coach, head coach, general manager, commissioner, team owner/CEO.

WILLIE DAVIS
Defensive end. 6-3, 245. Born in Lisbon, Louisiana, July 24, 1934. Grambling. Inducted in 1981. 1958-59 Cleveland Browns, 1960-69 Green Bay Packers. **Highlights:** All-NFL five seasons, five Pro Bowls. Did not miss game in 12-year career.

DERMONTTI DAWSON
Center. 6-2, 288. Born in Lexington, Kentucky, June 17, 1965. Kentucky. Inducted in 2012. 1988-2000 Pittsburgh Steelers. **Highlights:** Played in 170 straight games. Named first-team All-Pro six consecutive seasons and voted to seven straight Pro Bowls. Is member of the NFL's All-Decade Team of the 1990s.

LEN DAWSON
Quarterback. 6-0, 190. Born in Alliance, Ohio, June 20, 1935. Purdue. Inducted in 1987. 1957-59 Pittsburgh Steelers, 1960-61 Cleveland Browns, 1962 Dallas Texans, 1963-1975 Kansas City Chiefs. **Highlights:** 28,711 yards passing, 239 touchdowns. Four AFL passing crowns. MVP, Super Bowl IV.

FRED DEAN
Defensive end. 6-3, 230. Born in Arcadia, Louisiana, February 24, 1952. Louisiana Tech. Inducted in 2008. 1975-1981 San Diego Chargers, 1981-85 San Francisco 49ers. **Highlights:** Had career-high 17.5 sacks in 1983. Played on two Super Bowl championship teams with 49ers (Super Bowls XVI, XIX).

JOE DeLAMIELLEURE
Guard. 6-3, 254. Born in Detroit, Michigan, March 16, 1951. Michigan State. Inducted in 2003. 1973-1979, 1985 Buffalo Bills, 1980-1984 Cleveland Browns. **Highlights:** Selected All-Pro and All-AFC six consecutive times, 1975-1980. Named to six Pro Bowls. Played 13 years, 185 games.

RICHARD DENT
Defensive end. 6-5, 265. Born in Atlanta, Georgia, December 13, 1960. Tennessee State. Inducted in 2011. 1983-1993, 1995 Chicago Bears, 1994 San Francisco 49ers, 1996 Indianapolis Colts, 1997 Philadelphia Eagles. **Highlights:** Named MVP of Super Bowl XX. Had double-digit sack totals 10 times. Recorded 137.5 career sacks, third most at time of retirement. Named first- or second-team All-NFL four times, voted to four Pro Bowls.

ERIC DICKERSON
Running back. 6-3, 220. Born in Sealy, Texas, September 2, 1960. Southern Methodist. Inducted in 1999. 1983-87 Los Angeles Rams, 1987-1991 Indianapolis Colts, 1992 Los Angeles Raiders, 1993 Atlanta Falcons. **Highlights:** Rushed for 13,259 career yards, including an NFL record 2,105 yards in 1984. All-Pro five times, six Pro Bowls.

DAN DIERDORF
Tackle. 6-3, 290. Born in Canton, Ohio, June 29, 1949. Michigan. Inducted in 1996. 1971-1983 St. Louis Cardinals. **Highlights:** All-Pro five times, played in six Pro Bowls, named NFL's best blocker three times.

MIKE DITKA
Tight end. 6-3, 225. Born in Carnegie, Pennsylvania, October 18, 1939. Pittsburgh. Inducted in 1988. 1961-66 Chicago Bears, 1967-68 Philadelphia Eagles, 1969-1972 Dallas Cowboys. **Highlights:** 427 receptions for 5,812 yards, 43 touchdowns. First tight end selected to Hall of Fame. Five consecutive Pro Bowls.

CHRIS DOLEMAN
Defensive end-linebacker. 6-5, 270. Born in Indianapolis, Indiana, October 16, 1961. Pittsburgh. Inducted in 2012. 1985-1993, 1999 Minnesota Vikings, 1994-95 Atlanta Falcons, 1996-98 San Francisco 49ers. **Highlights:** Career sack total of 150.5 was fourth best all-time at retirement. Recorded 10 or more sacks in a season eight times. Led NFL with 21 sacks, 1989, one short of season record at time. Voted to eight Pro Bowls.

ART DONOVAN
Defensive tackle. 6-3, 265. Born in Bronx, New York, June 5, 1925. Boston College. Inducted in 1968. 1950 Baltimore Colts, 1951 New York Yanks, 1952 Dallas Texans, 1953-1961 Baltimore Colts. **Highlights:** Five Pro Bowls. Vital part of Baltimore's climb to powerhouse status in 1950s.

TONY DORSETT
Running back. 5-11, 184. Born in Rochester, Pennsylvania, April 7, 1954. Pittsburgh. Inducted in 1994. 1977-1987 Dallas Cowboys, 1988 Denver Broncos. **Highlights:** 12,739 yards rushing, 398 receptions, 91 touchdowns. Ran record 99 yards for touchdown vs. Minnesota, January, 1983.

JOHN (PADDY) DRISCOLL
Quarterback. 5-11, 160. Born in Evanston, Illinois, January 11, 1895. Died June 29, 1968. Northwestern. Inducted in 1965. 1919 Hammond Pros, 1920 Decatur Staleys, 1920-25 Chicago Cardinals, 1926-29 Chicago Bears. **Highlights:** All-NFL seven times. Dropkicked record 4 field goals in one game, 1925.

BILL DUDLEY
Halfback. 5-10, 182. Born in Bluefield, Virginia, December 24, 1921. Died February 4, 2010. Virginia. Inducted in 1966. 1942, 1945-46 Pittsburgh Steelers, 1947-49 Detroit Lions, 1950-51, 1953 Washington Redskins. **Highlights:** Won NFL rushing, interception, punt return titles, 1946. All-NFL 1942, 1946, and 1947.

ALBERT GLEN (TURK) EDWARDS
Tackle. 6-2, 260. Born in Mold, Washington, September 28, 1907. Died January 12, 1973. Washington State. Inducted in 1969. 1932 Boston Braves, 1933-36 Boston Redskins, 1937-1940 Washington Redskins. **Highlights:** All-NFL 1932-34, 1936, 1937. Steamrolling blocker, smothering tackler.

CARL ELLER
Defensive end. 6-6, 247. Born in Winston-Salem, North Carolina, January 25, 1942. Minnesota. Inducted in 2004. 1964-1978 Minnesota Vikings, 1979 Seattle Seahawks. **Highlights:** Fixture on Vikings' "Purple People Eaters" defensive line, All-Pro five time, elected to six Pro Bowls.

JOHN ELWAY
Quarterback. 6-3, 215. Born in Port Angeles, Washington, June 28, 1960. Stanford. Inducted in 2004. 1983-1998 Denver Broncos. **Highlights:** Passed for 51,475 yards, 300 touchdowns. Named to nine Pro Bowls. NFL MVP, 1987; MVP, Super Bowl XXXIII.

WEEB EWBANK
Coach. Born in Richmond, Indiana, May 6, 1907. Died November 17, 1998. Miami (Ohio). Inducted in 1978. 1954-1962 Baltimore Colts, 1963-1973 New York Jets. **Highlights:** Only coach to win championships in both NFL, AFL. Led both Colts (1958 and 1959) and Jets (1968) to championships.

MARSHALL FAULK
Running back. 5-10, 208. Born in New Orleans, Louisiana, February 26, 1973. San Diego State. Inducted in 2011. 1994-98 Indianapolis Colts, 1999-2005 St. Louis Rams. **Highlights:** Became second player to eclipse 1,000 yards in rushing and receiving same season when he set then-record for yards from scrimmage, 1999. NFL's MVP in 2000. Rushed for 1,000 yards in seven of first eight seasons.

TOM FEARS
End. 6-2, 215. Born in Guadalajara, Mexico, December 3, 1922. Died January 4, 2000. Santa Clara, UCLA. Inducted in 1970. 1948-1956 Los Angeles Rams. **Highlights:** 400 receptions for 5,397 yards, 38 touchdowns. Led NFL receivers first three seasons. Had then-record 18 receptions in single game.

JIM FINKS
Administrator. Born in St. Louis, Missouri, August 31, 1927. Died May 8, 1994. Tulsa. Inducted 1995. 1964-1973 Minnesota Vikings, 1974-1982 Chicago Bears, 1986-1993 New Orleans Saints. **Highlights:** Developed Vikings, Bears, Saints—all teams with losing records—into winners.

RAY FLAHERTY
Coach. Born in Spokane, Washington, September 1, 1903. Died July 19, 1994. Gonzaga. Inducted in 1976. 1936-1942 Boston/Washington Redskins, 1946-48 New York Yankees (AAFC), 1949 Chicago Hornets (AAFC). **Highlights:** 82-41-5 coaching record. Introduced screen pass in 1937 title game and platoon system.

LEN FORD
Defensive end. 6-4, 260. Born in Washington, D.C., February 18, 1926. Died March 14, 1972. Morgan State, Michigan. Inducted in 1976. 1948-49 Los Angeles Dons (AAFC), 1950-57 Cleveland Browns, 1958 Green Bay Packers. **Highlights:** All-NFL five times, four Pro Bowls. Recovered 20 opponents' fumbles.

DAN FORTMANN
Guard. 6-0, 210. Born in Pearl River, New York, April 11, 1916. Died May 23, 1995. Colgate. Inducted in 1965. 1936-1943 Chicago Bears. **Highlights:** At 20, became youngest starter in NFL. First- or second-team All-NFL every season of career.

DAN FOUTS
Quarterback. 6-3, 210. Born in San Francisco, California, June 10, 1951. Oregon. Inducted in 1993. 1973-1987 San Diego Chargers. **Highlights:** 43,040 passing yards, 254 touchdowns. Six Pro Bowls, NFL MVP, 1982.

BENNY FRIEDMAN
Quarterback. 5-10, 183. Born in Cleveland, Ohio, March 18, 1905. Died November 23, 1982. Michigan. Inducted in 2005. 1927 Cleveland Bulldogs, 1928 Detroit Wolverines, 1929-1931 New York Giants, 1932-34 Brooklyn Dodgers. **Highlights:** NFL's first great passer. Set league mark for touchdowns with 20 in 1929. Led NFL in touchdown passes each of his first four seasons.

FRANK GATSKI
Center. 6-3, 240. Born in Farmington, West Virginia, March 18, 1919. Marshall, Auburn. Died November 22, 2005. Inducted in 1985. 1946-49 Cleveland Browns (AAFC), 1950-56 Cleveland Browns, 1957 Detroit Lions. **Highlights:** Never missed game in high school, college, or pro football. Played 11 championship games, winning eight.

BILL GEORGE
Linebacker. 6-2, 230. Born in Waynesburg, Pennsylvania, October 27, 1929. Died September 30, 1982. Wake Forest. Inducted in 1974. 1952-1965 Chicago Bears, 1966 Los Angeles Rams. **Highlights:** All-NFL eight years, eight consecutive Pro Bowls. 14 years of service, longest of any Bears player.

JOE GIBBS
Coach. Born in Mocksville, North Carolina, November 25, 1940. Cerritos (Calif.) J.C., San Diego State. Inducted in 1996. 1981-1992 Washington Redskins. **Highlights:** 124-60-0 record in regular season, 16-5 in postseason, including four Super Bowl appearances—winning three. Won 10 or more games eight times.

FRANK GIFFORD
Halfback. 6-1, 195. Born in Santa Monica, California, August 16, 1930. Southern California. Inducted in 1977. 1952-1960, 1962-64 New York Giants. **Highlights:** Starred on both offense and defense. Named to eight Pro Bowls, 1956 NFL player of the year.

SID GILLMAN
Coach. Born in Minneapolis, Minnesota, October 26, 1911. Died January 3, 2003. Ohio State. Inducted in 1983. 1955-59 Los Angeles Rams, 1960-69, 1971 Los Angeles/San Diego Chargers, 1973-74 Houston Oilers. **Highlights:** 123-104-7 coaching record. First to win division titles in both NFL, AFL.

OTTO GRAHAM
Quarterback. 6-1, 195. Born in Waukegan, Illinois, December 6, 1921. Died December 17, 2003. Northwestern. Inducted in 1965. 1946-49 Cleveland Browns (AAFC), 1950-55 Cleveland Browns. **Highlights:** 23,584 passing yards, 174 touchdowns. Guided Browns to 10 division or league crowns in 10 years.

HAROLD (RED) GRANGE
Halfback. 6-0, 185. Born in Forksville, Pennsylvania, June 13, 1903. Died January 28, 1991. Illinois. Inducted in 1963. 1925, 1929-1934 Chicago Bears, 1926 New York Yankees (AFL), 1927 New York Yankees. **Highlights:** Charter enshrinee. Nicknamed "Galloping Ghost." Name produced first huge pro football crowds.

BUD GRANT
Coach. Born in Superior, Wisconsin, May 20, 1927. Minnesota. Inducted in 1994. 1967-1983, 1985 Minnesota Vikings. **Highlights:** 168-108-5 coaching record. Led Vikings to 11 division championships, four Super Bowls.

DARRELL GREEN
Cornerback. . 5-8, 176. Born in Houston, Texas, February 15, 1960. Texas A&I. Inducted in 2008. 1983-2002 Washington Redskins. **Highlights:** 54 interceptions, 621 yards, 6 TDs. Played 20 seasons. Recorded interception in NFL record 19 straight seasons. Selected to seven Pro Bowls.

JOE GREENE
Defensive tackle. 6-4, 260. Born in Temple, Texas, September 24, 1946. North Texas State. Inducted in 1987. 1969-1981 Pittsburgh Steelers. **Highlights:** NFL defensive player of the year, 1972, 1974. Four-time Super Bowl champion, 10 Pro Bowls.

FORREST GREGG
Tackle. 6-4, 250. Born in Birthright, Texas, October 18, 1933. Southern Methodist. Inducted in 1977. 1956, 1958-1970 Green Bay Packers, 1971 Dallas Cowboys. **Highlights:** Played 188 consecutive games. Nine Pro Bowls. Played on six NFL championship teams, three Super Bowl winners.

BOB GRIESE
Quarterback. 6-1, 190. Born in Evansville, Indiana, February 3, 1945. Purdue. Inducted in 1990. 1967-1980 Miami Dolphins. **Highlights:** 25,092 passing yards, 192 touchdowns. Led Miami to three AFC titles, Super Bowl VII, VIII wins.

RUSS GRIMM
Guard. 6-3, 273. Born in Scottdale, Pennsylvania, May 2, 1959. Pittsburgh. Inducted in 2010. 1981-1991 Washington Redskins. **Highlights:** Member of famed "Hogs" offensive line, All-NFL four times, four Pro Bowls. Member of All-Decade Team 1980s.

LOU GROZA
Tackle-kicker. 6-3, 250. Born in Martins Ferry, Ohio, January 25, 1924. Died November 29, 2000. Ohio State. Inducted in 1974. 1946-49 Cleveland Browns (AAFC), 1950-59, 1961-67 Cleveland Browns. **Highlights:** 1,608 points in 21 years. Nine Pro Bowls, All-NFL six years. NFL player of the year, 1954.

JOE GUYON
Halfback. 6-1, 180. Born on White Earth Indian Reservation, Minnesota, November 26, 1892. Died November 27, 1971. Carlisle, Georgia Tech. Inducted in 1966. 1919-1920 Canton Bulldogs, 1921 Cleveland Indians, 1922-23 Oorang Indians, 1924 Rock Island Independents, 1924-25 Kansas City Cowboys, 1927 New York Giants. **Highlights:** Touchdown pass gave Giants victory over Bears to win 1927 championship.

GEORGE HALAS
End. Coach. Team owner. Born in Chicago, Illinois, February 2, 1895. Died October 31, 1983. Illinois. Inducted in 1963. Player-coach 1920 Decatur Staleys, 1921 Chicago Staleys, 1922-29 Chicago Bears; coach 1933-1942, 1946-1955, 1958-1967 Chicago Bears. **Highlights:** Charter enshrinee. 324 coaching wins. Only person associated with NFL throughout first 50 years. Coached Bears 40 seasons, won six NFL titles.

JACK HAM
Linebacker. 6-1, 225. Born in Johnstown, Pennsylvania, December 23, 1948. Penn State. Inducted in 1988. 1971-1982 Pittsburgh Steelers. **Highlights:** Won four Super Bowls, 21 opponents' fumbles recovered, 32 interceptions. Eight consecutive Pro Bowls.

DAN HAMPTON
Defensive tackle-defensive end. 6-5, 264. Born in Oklahoma City, Oklahoma, September 19, 1957. Arkansas. Inducted in 2002. 1979-1990 Chicago Bears. **Highlights:** A versatile player, he earned all-pro honors at both defensive tackle and defensive end. Named to four Pro Bowls.

CHRIS HANBURGER
Linebacker. 6-2, 218. Born in Fort Bragg, North Carolina, August 13, 1941. North Carolina. Inducted in 2011. 1965-1978 Washington Redskins. **Highlights:** Leader of dominant Redskins defenses. Named first-team All-NFL four times in five-season span. Voted to nine Pro Bowls. Three fumble recoveries for TDs tied for NFL record at time of his retirement.

JOHN HANNAH
Guard. 6-3, 265. Born in Canton, Georgia, April 4, 1951. Alabama. Inducted in 1991. 1973-1985 New England Patriots. **Highlights:** Renowned as premier guard of era. All-Pro 10 years, nine Pro Bowls.

FRANCO HARRIS
Running back. 6-2, 225. Born in Fort Dix, New Jersey, March 7, 1950. Penn State. Inducted in 1990. 1972-1983 Pittsburgh Steelers, 1984 Seattle Seahawks. **Highlights:** 12,120 rushing yards, 100 total touchdowns. 1,556 rushing yards in 19 postseason games. MVP in Super Bowl IX.

BOB HAYES
Wide receiver. 5-11, 185. Born in Jacksonville, Florida, December 20, 1942. Died September 18, 2002. Florida A&M. Inducted in 2009. 1965-1974 Dallas Cowboys, 1975 San Francisco 49ers. **Highlights:** Olympic gold medalist with world class speed led Cowboys in receiving three times. 371 receptions for 7,414 yards, 71 TDs. Three Pro Bowls.

MIKE HAYNES
Cornerback. 6-2, 195. Born in Denison, Texas, July 1, 1953. Arizona State. Inducted in 1997. 1976-1982 New England Patriots, 1983-89 Los Angeles Raiders. **Highlights:** Defensive rookie of the year. Selected to nine Pro Bowls and intercepted 46 passes, plus one pick in Super Bowl XVIII.

ED HEALEY
Tackle. 6-3, 220. Born in Indian Orchard, Massachusetts, December 28, 1894. Died December 9, 1978. Dartmouth. Inducted in 1964. 1920-22 Rock Island Independents, 1922-27 Chicago Bears. **Highlights:** Two-way star. Perennial all-pro with Bears.

MEL HEIN
Center. 6-2, 225. Born in Redding, California, August 22, 1909. Died January 31, 1992. Washington State. Inducted in 1963. 1931-1945 New York Giants. **Highlights:** Charter enshrinee. 60-minute regular for 15 years. All-NFL eight consecutive years.

TED HENDRICKS
Linebacker. 6-7, 235. Born in Guatemala City, Guatemala, November 1, 1947. Miami. Inducted in 1990. 1969-1973 Baltimore Colts, 1974 Green Bay Packers, 1975-1981 Oakland Raiders, 1982-83 Los Angeles Raiders. **Highlights:** 25 blocked field goals, extra points, and punts, 26 interceptions. Played in 215 consecutive games.

WILBUR (PETE) HENRY
Tackle. 6-0, 250. Born in Mansfield, Ohio, October 31, 1897. Died February 7, 1952. Washington & Jefferson. Inducted in 1963. 1920-23, 1925-26 Canton Bulldogs, 1927 New York Giants, 1927-28 Pottsville Maroons. **Highlights:** Charter enshrinee. Largest player of his time at 250 pounds. Bulwark of Canton's championship lines.

ARNIE HERBER
Quarterback. 6-0, 200. Born in Green Bay, Wisconsin, April 2, 1910. Died October 14, 1969. Wisconsin, Regis College. Inducted in 1966. 1930-1940 Green Bay Packers, 1944-45 New York Giants. **Highlights:** NFL passing leader 1932, 1934, 1936. Came out of retirement to lead 1944 Giants to NFL Eastern crown.

BILL HEWITT
End. 5-11, 191. Born in Bay City, Michigan, October 8, 1909. Died January 14, 1947. Michigan. Inducted in 1971. 1932-36 Chicago Bears, 1937-39 Philadelphia Eagles, 1943 Phil.-Pitt. **Highlights:** First to be named all-NFL with two teams—1933, 1934, 1936 Bears; 1937 Eagles.

GENE HICKERSON
Guard. 6-3, 248. Born in Trenton, Tennessee, February 15, 1935. Died October 20, 2008. Mississippi. Inducted in 2007. 1958-1973 Cleveland Browns. **Highlights:** Blocked for three Hall of Fame running backs. Voted to six straight Pro Bowls. Named to NFL's All-Decade Team of the 1960s.

CLARKE HINKLE
Fullback. 5-11, 201. Born in Toronto, Ohio, April 10, 1909. Died November 9, 1988. Bucknell. Inducted in 1964. 1932-1941 Green Bay Packers. **Highlights:** 3,860 yards rushing, 379 points. Fullback on offense, linebacker on defense.

ELROY (CRAZYLEGS) HIRSCH
Halfback-end. 6-2, 190. Born in Wausau, Wisconsin, June 17, 1923. Died January 28, 2004. Wisconsin, Michigan. Inducted in 1968. 1946-48 Chicago Rockets (AAFC), 1949-1957 Los Angeles Rams. **Highlights:** 387 receptions for 7,029 yards, 60 touchdowns. Key part of Rams' revolutionary "three end" offense, 1949.

PAUL HORNUNG
Halfback. 6-2, 220. Born in Louisville, Kentucky, December 23, 1935. Notre Dame. Inducted in 1986. 1957-1962, 1964-66 Green Bay Packers. **Highlights:** 760 points. Led NFL scorers three years, including record 176 points, 1960. Record 19 points scored in 1961 NFL title game.

KEN HOUSTON
Safety. 6-3, 198. Born in Lufkin, Texas, November 12, 1944. Prairie View A&M. Inducted in 1986. 1967-1972 Houston Oilers, 1973-1980 Washington Redskins. **Highlights:** 49 interceptions, 898 yards, 9 touchdowns. NFL's premier strong safety of 1970s. 12 Pro Bowls.

ROBERT (CAL) HUBBARD
Tackle. 6-5, 250. Born in Keytesville, Missouri, October 31, 1900. Died October 17, 1977. Centenary, Geneva. Inducted in 1963. 1927-28, 1936 New York Giants, 1929-1933, 1935 Green Bay Packers, 1936 Pittsburgh Pirates. **Highlights:** Charter enshrinee. Most feared lineman of his time. All-NFL six years, 1927-29, 1931-33.

SAM HUFF
Linebacker. 6-1, 230. Born in Morgantown, West Virginia, October 4, 1934. West Virginia. Inducted in 1982. 1956-1963 New York Giants, 1964-67, 1969 Washington Redskins. **Highlights:** 30 interceptions. Played in six NFL title games, five Pro Bowls. Redskins player-coach, 1969.

LAMAR HUNT
Team owner. Born in El Dorado, Arkansas, August 2, 1932. Died December 13, 2006. Southern Methodist. Inducted in 1972. 1960-2006 Dallas Texans/Kansas City Chiefs. **Highlights:** Driving force behind organization of AFL. Spearheaded merger negotiations with NFL, 1966.

DON HUTSON
End. 6-1, 180. Born in Pine Bluff, Arkansas, January 31, 1913. Died June 26, 1997. Alabama. Inducted in 1963. 1935-1945 Green Bay Packers. **Highlights:** Charter enshrinee. 488 receptions for 7,991 yards, 99 touchdowns. NFL receiving champion eight years. NFL MVP, 1941, 1942.

MICHAEL IRVIN
Wide receiver. 6-2, 207. Born in Ft. Lauderdale, Florida, March 5, 1966. Miami. Inducted in 2007. 1988-1999 Dallas Cowboys. **Highlights:** 750 career receptions for 11,904 yards, 65 touchdowns. Had NFL record eleven 100-yard receiving games, 1995.

RICKEY JACKSON
Linebacker. 6-2, 243. Born in Pahokee, Florida, March 20, 1958. Pittsburgh. Inducted in 2010. 1981-1993 New Orleans Saints, 1994-95 San Francisco 49ers. **Highlights:** Recorded double-digit sacks in six seasons. Six Pro Bowls, named All-Pro four times. Finished career as defensive end with 49ers.

JIMMY JOHNSON
Cornerback. 6-2, 187. Born in Dallas, Texas, March 31, 1938. UCLA. Inducted in 1994. 1961-1976 San Francisco 49ers. **Highlights:** 47 interceptions for 615 yards. Five Pro Bowls. Opposing passers avoided throwing in his area.

JOHN HENRY JOHNSON
Fullback. 6-2, 225. Born in Waterproof, Louisiana, November 24, 1929. Died June 3, 2011. St. Mary's, Arizona State. Inducted in 1987. 1954-56 San Francisco 49ers, 1957-59 Detroit Lions, 1960-65 Pittsburgh Steelers, 1966 Houston Oilers. **Highlights:** 6,803 yards rushing, 55 total touchdowns. Member of San Francisco's "Million-Dollar" backfield.

CHARLIE JOINER
Wide receiver. 5-11, 180. Born in Many, Louisiana, October 14, 1947. Grambling. Inducted in 1996. 1969-1972 Houston Oilers, 1972-75 Cincinnati Bengals, 1976-1986 San Diego Chargers. **Highlights:** 750 receptions for 12,146 yards and 65 touchdowns. Played 18 seasons, 239 games, most ever for wide receiver at time of retirement.

DAVID (DEACON) JONES
Defensive end. 6-5, 260. Born in Eatonville, Florida, December 9, 1938. South Carolina State, Mississippi Vocational. Inducted in 1980. 1961-1971 Los Angeles Rams, 1972-73 San Diego Chargers, 1974 Washington Redskins. **Highlights:** Specialized in quarterback "sacks," a term he invented. Unanimous all-league five consecutive years.

STAN JONES
Guard-defensive tackle. 6-1, 250. Born in Altoona, Pennsylvania, November 24, 1931. Died May 21, 2010. Maryland. Inducted in 1991. 1954-1965 Chicago Bears, 1966 Washington Redskins. **Highlights:** Seven consecutive Pro Bowls. First to rely on weightlifting for football preparation.

HENRY JORDAN
Defensive tackle, 6-3, 240. Born in Emporia, Virginia, January 26, 1935. Died February 21, 1977. Virginia. Inducted in 1995. 1957-58 Cleveland Browns, 1959-1969 Green Bay Packers. **Highlights:** Fixture at DT during Packers' dynasty. Played in four Pro Bowls, seven NFL title games, Super Bowls I, II.

SONNY JURGENSEN
Quarterback. 6-0, 203. Born in Wilmington, North Carolina, August 23, 1934. Duke. Inducted in 1983. 1957-1963 Philadelphia Eagles, 1964-1974 Washington Redskins. **Highlights:** 32,224 yards passing, 255 touchdowns, 82.63 passer rating. Surpassed 3,000 yards passing in five seasons.

JIM KELLY
Quarterback. 6-3, 225. Born in Pittsburgh, Pennsylvania, February 14, 1960. Miami. Inducted in 2002. 1986-1996 Buffalo Bills. **Highlights:** Passed for more than 3,000 yards eight times. Mastered the no-huddle offense that propelled Bills to four consecutive Super Bowls.

LEROY KELLY
Running back. 6-0, 205. Born in Philadelphia, Pennsylvania, May 20, 1942. Morgan State. Inducted in 1994. 1964-1973 Cleveland Browns. **Highlights:** 7,274 yards rushing, 90 total touchdowns, 1,000-yard rusher first three years as starter. Punt return champion, 1965.

CORTEZ KENNEDY
Defensive tackle. 6-3, 298. Born in Osceola, Arkansas, August 23, 1968. Northwest Mississippi Community College, Miami. Inducted in 2012. 1990-2000 Seattle Seahawks. **Highlights:** NFL Defensive Player of the Year, 1992. Voted to eight Pro Bowls and selected first-team All-Pro three times. Named to the NFL's All-Decade Team of the 1990s.

WALT KIESLING
Guard. Coach. 6-2, 245. Born in St. Paul, Minnesota, March 27, 1903. Died March 2, 1962. St. Thomas (Minnesota). Inducted in 1966. 1926-27 Duluth Eskimos, 1928 Pottsville Maroons, 1929-1933 Chicago Cardinals, 1934 Chicago Bears, 1935-36 Green Bay Packers, 1937-38 Pittsburgh Pirates; coach, 1939 Pittsburgh Pirates, 1940-42 Pittsburgh Steelers; co-coach, 1943 Phil-Pitt, 1944 Card-Pitt; coach, 1954-56 Pittsburgh Steelers. **Highlights:** 34-year career as pro player, assistant coach, head coach. Led Steelers to first winning season, 1942.

FRANK (BRUISER) KINARD
Tackle. 6-1, 210. Born in Pelahatchie, Mississippi, October 23, 1914. Died September 7, 1985. Mississippi. Inducted in 1971. 1938-1943 Brooklyn Dodgers, 1944 Brooklyn Tigers, 1946-47 New York Yankees (AAFC). **Highlights:** First man to earn both All-NFL, All-AAFC honors. Out because of injury only once.

PAUL KRAUSE
Safety. 6-3, 200. Born in Flint, Michigan, February 19, 1942. Iowa. Inducted in 1998. 1964-67 Washington Redskins, 1968-1979 Minnesota Vikings. **Highlights:** NFL all-time leader with 81 interceptions. Played in eight Pro Bowls. Starting safety in four Super Bowls.

EARL (CURLY) LAMBEAU
Coach. Born in Green Bay, Wisconsin, April 9, 1898. Died June 1, 1965. Notre Dame. Inducted in 1963. 1919-1949 Green Bay Packers, 1950-51 Chicago Cardinals, 1952-53 Washington Redskins. **Highlights:** Charter enshrinee. 229-134-22 coaching record with six NFL championships. Founded pre-NFL Packers, 1919.

JACK LAMBERT
Linebacker. 6-4, 220. Born in Mantua, Ohio, July 8, 1952. Kent State. Inducted in 1990. 1974-1984 Pittsburgh Steelers. **Highlights:** Leader of 'Steel Curtain.' NFL defensive player of year in 1976, nine Pro Bowls.

TOM LANDRY
Coach. Born in Mission, Texas, September 11, 1924. Died February 12, 2000. Texas. Inducted in 1990. 1960-1988 Dallas Cowboys. **Highlights:** 270-178-6 coaching record. 20 consecutive winning seasons. Innovator on offense and defense.

DICK (NIGHT TRAIN) LANE
Cornerback. 6-2, 210. Born in Austin, Texas, April 16, 1928. Died January 29, 2002. Scottsbluff Junior College. Inducted in 1974. 1952-53 Los Angeles Rams, 1954-59 Chicago Cardinals, 1960-65 Detroit Lions. **Highlights:** 68 interceptions for 1,207 yards, 5 touchdowns. Record 14 interceptions as rookie. Seven Pro Bowls.

JIM LANGER
Center. 6-2, 255. Born in Little Falls, Minnesota, May 16, 1948. South Dakota State. Inducted in 1987. 1970-79 Miami Dolphins, 1980-81 Minnesota Vikings. **Highlights:** Played every offensive down in Dolphins' perfect 1972 season. Six Pro Bowls.

WILLIE LANIER
Linebacker. 6-1, 245. Born in Clover, Virginia, August 21, 1945. Morgan State. Inducted in 1986. 1967-1977 Kansas City Chiefs. **Highlights:** 27 interceptions. Defensive star in Super Bowl IV upset. Nicknamed 'Contact' for ferocious tackling.

STEVE LARGENT
Wide receiver. 5-11, 191. Born in Tulsa, Oklahoma, September 28, 1954. Tulsa. Inducted in 1995. 1976-1989 Seattle Seahawks. **Highlights:** 819 receptions for 13,089 yards, 100 touchdowns. Receptions in 177 consecutive games.

YALE LARY
Safety. 5-11, 189. Born in Fort Worth, Texas, November 24, 1930. Texas A&M. Inducted in 1979. 1952-53, 1956-1964 Detroit Lions. **Highlights:** 50 interceptions. Three NFL punting crowns, three touchdowns on punt returns. Nine Pro Bowls.

DANTE LAVELLI
End. 6-0, 199. Born in Hudson, Ohio, February 23, 1923. Died January 20, 2009. Ohio State. Inducted in 1975. 1946-49 Cleveland Browns (AAFC), 1950-56 Cleveland Browns. **Highlights:** 386 receptions for 6,488 yards, 62 touchdowns. 24 catches in six NFL title games.

BOBBY LAYNE
Quarterback. 6-2, 190. Born in Santa Anna, Texas, December 19, 1926. Died December 1, 1986. Texas. Inducted in 1967. 1948 Chicago Bears, 1949 New York Bulldogs, 1950-58 Detroit Lions, 1958-1962 Pittsburgh Steelers. **Highlights:** 26,768 yards passing, 196 touchdowns, 2,451 yards rushing. Late touchdown pass won 1953 NFL title game.

DICK LeBEAU
Cornerback. 6-1, 185. Born in London, Ohio, September 9, 1937. Ohio State. Inducted in 2010. 1959-1972 Detroit Lions. **Highlights:** Recorded 62 career interceptions for 762 yards, 3 TDs, ranked third all-time in interceptions at retirement. Voted to three Pro Bowls.

ALPHONSE (TUFFY) LEEMANS
Fullback. 6-0, 200. Born in Superior, Wisconsin, November 12, 1912. Died January 19, 1979. Oregon, George Washington. Inducted in 1978. 1936-1943 New York Giants. **Highlights:** 3,132 yards rushing, 2,318 yards passing, 422 yards receiving. Led NFL rushers as rookie, 1936.

MARV LEVY
Coach. Born in Chicago, Illinois, August 3, 1925. Wyoming, Coe College, Harvard. Inducted in 2001. 1978-1982 Kansas City Chiefs, 1986-1997 Buffalo Bills. **Highlights:** Led Bills to unprecedented four consecutive Super Bowls. Had 154-120 record. Coaching victories ranked 10th when retired.

BOB LILLY
Defensive tackle. 6-5, 260. Born in Olney, Texas, July 26, 1939. Texas Christian. Inducted in 1980. 1961-1974 Dallas Cowboys. **Highlights:** Eleven Pro Bowls. Played 196 consecutive games. Foundation of great Dallas defensive units.

FLOYD LITTLE
Running back. 5-10, 196. Born in New Haven, Connecticut, July 4, 1942. Syracuse. Inducted in 2010. 1967-1975 Denver Broncos. **Highlights:** Broncos' first 1,000-yard rusher, won NFL rushing title in 1971. Amassed more than 12,000 career all-purpose yards, 54 TDs, five AFL All-Star Games/Pro Bowls.

LARRY LITTLE
Guard. 6-1, 265. Born in Groveland, Georgia, November 2, 1945. Bethune-Cookman. Inducted in 1993. 1967-68 San Diego Chargers, 1969-1980 Miami Dolphins. **Highlights:** Five Pro Bowls, started in three Super Bowls. Epitome of powerful Dolphins rushing game of 1970s.

JAMES LOFTON
Wide receiver. 6-3, 192. Born in Fort Ord, California, July 5, 1956. Stanford. Inducted in 2003. 1978-1986 Green Bay Packers, 1987-88 Los Angeles Raiders, 1989-1992 Buffalo Bills, 1993 Los Angeles Rams, 1993 Philadelphia Eagles. **Highlights:** Played 16 seasons, 233 games. Caught 764 passes for 75 touchdowns and a then-record 14,004 yards. All-Pro four times, eight Pro Bowls.

VINCE LOMBARDI
Coach. Born in Brooklyn, New York, June 11, 1913. Died September 3, 1970. Fordham. Inducted in 1971. 1959-1967 Green Bay Packers, 1969 Washington Redskins. **Highlights:** 105-35-6 coaching record in 10 years, including five NFL titles and victories in Super Bowls I and II.

HOWIE LONG
Defensive end. 6-5, 268. Born in Somerville, Massachusetts, January 6, 1960. Villanova. Inducted in 2000. 1981-1993 Oakland/Los Angeles Raiders. **Highlights:** All-Pro 1983, 1984, 1985. Named All-AFC four times, 1983-1986. Eight Pro Bowls.

RONNIE LOTT
Cornerback-safety. 6-0, 203. Born in Albuquerque, New Mexico, May 8, 1959. Southern California. Inducted in 2000. 1981-1990 San Francisco 49ers, 1991-92 Los Angeles Raiders, 1993-94 New York Jets. **Highlights:** Ten Pro Bowls, 63 career interceptions, and was named to the NFL's 75th Anniversary Team.

SID LUCKMAN
Quarterback. 6-0, 195. Born in Brooklyn, New York, November 21, 1916. Died July 5, 1998. Columbia. Inducted in 1965. 1939-1950 Chicago Bears. **Highlights:** 137 touchdown passes. All-NFL five times. League MVP in 1943.

WILLIAM ROY (LINK) LYMAN
Tackle. 6-2, 252. Born in Table Rock, Nebraska, November 30, 1898. Died December 28, 1972. Nebraska. Inducted in 1964. 1922-23, 1925 Canton Bulldogs, 1924 Cleveland Bulldogs, 1925 Frankford Yellowjackets, 1926-28, 1930-31, 1933-34 Chicago Bears. **Highlights:** Played for four NFL champions. In 16 seasons of college and pro football, played on one losing team.

TOM MACK
Guard. 6-3, 250. Born in Cleveland, Ohio, November 1, 1943. Michigan. Inducted in 1999. 1966-1978 Los Angeles Rams. **Highlights:** Never missed a game in entire 184-game career. Elected to 11 Pro Bowls.

JOHN MACKEY
Tight end. 6-2, 224. Born in New York, New York, September 24, 1941. Died July 6, 2011. Syracuse. Inducted in 1992. 1963-1971 Baltimore Colts, 1972 San Diego Chargers. **Highlights:** 331 receptions for 5,236 yards, 38 touchdowns. Second tight end to enter Hall of Fame.

JOHN MADDEN
Coach. Born in Austin, Minnesota, April 10, 1936. San Mateo Junior College, California Polytechnic College at San Luis Obispo. Inducted in 2006. 1969-1978 Oakland Raiders. **Highlights:** Became one of youngest coaches in history when hired at age 32. 112-39-7 overall record. Owns best regular season winning percentage among coaches with 100 wins.

TIM MARA
Founder-Team Owner. Born in New York, New York, July 29, 1887. Died February 16, 1959. Did not attend college. Inducted in 1963. 1925-1959 New York Giants. **Highlights:** Charter enshrinee. Founder of New York Giants. Built team into powerhouse winning four NFL titles, 10 division titles.

WELLINGTON MARA
Team owner. Born in New York, New York, August 14, 1916. Died October 25, 2005. Fordham. Inducted in 1997. 1937-2005 New York Giants. **Highlights:** Lifetime contributor to NFL and New York Giants. Worked as Giants' ballboy, secretary, vice-president, president and co-CEO. NFC president 1984-present.

GINO MARCHETTI
Defensive end. 6-4, 245. Born in Smithers, West Virginia, January 2, 1927. San Francisco. Inducted in 1972. 1952 Dallas Texans, 1953-1964, 1966 Baltimore Colts. **Highlights:** Named top defensive end of NFL's first 50 years. 10 consecutive Pro Bowls. All-NFL seven times.

DAN MARINO
Quarterback. 6-4, 218. Born in Pittsburgh, Pennsylvania, September 15, 1961. Pittsburgh. Inducted in 2005. 1983-1999 Miami Dolphins. **Highlights:** Held NFL records for career passing yardage (61,361), completions (4,967), attempts (8,358), and touchdowns (420). Voted to nine Pro Bowls.

GEORGE PRESTON MARSHALL
Team owner. Born in Grafton, West Virginia, October 11, 1896. Died August 9, 1969. Randolph-Macon. Inducted in 1963. 1932 Boston Braves, 1933-36 Boston Redskins, 1937-1969 Washington Redskins. **Highlights:** Charter enshrinee. Sponsored progressive rules changes. Organized first team band, pioneered halftime shows.

CURTIS MARTIN
Running back. 5-11, 207. Born in Pittsburgh, Pennsylvania, May 1, 1973. Pittsburgh. Inducted in 2012. 1995-97 New England Patriots, 1998-2005 New York Jets. **Highlights:** Second player in NFL history to start career with 10 straight 1,000-yard rushing seasons. Retired as fourth-leading rusher of all-time with 14,101 yards. Racked up 17,421 combined net yards and 100 career TDs (90 rushing, 10 receiving). NFL rushing title, 2004.

OLLIE MATSON
Halfback. 6-2, 220. Born in Trinity, Texas, May 1, 1930. Died February 19, 2011. San Francisco. Inducted in 1972. 1952, 1954-58 Chicago Cardinals, 1959-1962 Los Angeles Rams, 1963 Detroit Lions, 1964-66 Philadelphia Eagles. **Highlights:** Nine touchdowns on kickoff, punt returns. Traded for nine players in 1959.

BRUCE MATTHEWS
Guard-tackle-center. 6-5, 289. Born in Raleigh, North Carolina, August 8, 1961. Southern California. Inducted in 2007. 1983-2001 Houston Oilers/Tennessee Oilers/Titans. **Highlights:** Played in 296 games, most ever by positional player at time of his retirement. Named to a record-tying 14 straight Pro Bowls. All-Pro nine times, All-AFC 12 times.

DON MAYNARD
Wide receiver. 6-1, 185. Born in Crosbyton, Texas, January 25, 1935. Texas Western. Inducted in 1987. 1958 New York Giants, 1960-62 New York Titans, 1963-1972 New York Jets, 1973 St. Louis Cardinals. **Highlights:** 633 receptions for 11,834 yards, 88 touchdowns. At least 50 catches and 1,000 yards in five different seasons.

PRO FOOTBALL HALL OF FAME

GEORGE McAFEE
Halfback. 6-0, 177. Born in Corbin, Kentucky, March 13, 1918. Died March 4, 2009. Duke. Inducted in 1966. 1940-41, 1945-1950 Chicago Bears. **Highlights:** Two-way star. 25 interceptions, 234 points. Career punt-return average of 12.78 yards per return.

MIKE McCORMACK
Tackle. 6-4, 250. Born in Chicago, Illinois, June 21, 1930. Kansas. Inducted in 1984. 1951 New York Yanks, 1954-1962 Cleveland Browns. **Highlights:** Excelled as offensive right tackle for eight years. Six Pro Bowls.

RANDALL McDANIEL
Guard. 6-3, 276. Born in Phoenix, Arizona, December 19, 1964. Arizona State. Inducted in 2009. 1988-1999 Minnesota Vikings, 2000-01 Tampa Bay Buccaneers. **Highlights:** 12 Pro Bowls, All-Pro nine straight times. Blocked for six different 1,000-yard rushers, five 3,000-yard passers.

TOMMY McDONALD
Wide receiver. 5-9, 175. Born in Roy, New Mexico, July 26, 1934. Oklahoma. Inducted in 1998. 1957-1963 Philadelphia Eagles, 1964 Dallas Cowboys, 1965-66 Los Angeles Rams, 1967 Atlanta Falcons, 1968 Cleveland Browns. **Highlights:** Recorded 495 receptions for 8,410 yards, 84 touchdowns.

HUGH McELHENNY
Halfback. 6-1, 198. Born in Los Angeles, California, December 31, 1928. Washington. Inducted in 1970. 1952-1960 San Francisco 49ers, 1961-62 Minnesota Vikings, 1963 New York Giants, 1964 Detroit Lions. **Highlights:** 5,281 rushing yards, 360 points. Totaled 11,369 yards rushing, receiving, and returning kicks.

JOHNNY (BLOOD) McNALLY
Halfback. 6-0, 185. Born in New Richmond, Wisconsin, November 27, 1903. Died November 28, 1985. Notre Dame, St. John's (Minnesota). Inducted in 1963. 1925-26 Milwaukee Badgers, 1926-27 Duluth Eskimos, 1928 Pottsville Maroons, 1929-1933, 1935-36 Green Bay Packers, 1934 Pittsburgh Pirates; player-coach, 1937-38 Pittsburgh Pirates. **Highlights:** Charter enshrinee. 49 touchdowns, 297 points in 14 seasons with five teams.

MIKE MICHALSKE
Guard. 6-0, 209. Born in Cleveland, Ohio, April 24, 1903. Died October 26, 1983. Penn State. Inducted in 1964. 1926 New York Yankees (AFL), 1927-28 New York Yankees, 1929-1935, 1937 Green Bay Packers. **Highlights:** Anchored Packers' championship lines, 1929-1931. First guard enshrined in Canton.

WAYNE MILLNER
End. 6-0, 191. Born in Roxbury, Massachusetts, January 31, 1913. Died November 19, 1976. Notre Dame. Inducted in 1968. 1936 Boston Redskins, 1937-1941, 1945 Washington Redskins. **Highlights:** Redskins' all-time leader with 124 catches when retired. 55- and 78-yard touchdown receptions in 1937 NFL Championship Game.

BOBBY MITCHELL
Running back-wide receiver. 6-0, 195. Born in Hot Springs, Arkansas, June 6, 1935. Illinois. Inducted in 1983. 1958-1961 Cleveland Browns, 1962-68 Washington Redskins. **Highlights:** 91 touchdowns, including 8 on kickoff and punt returns. 14,078 combined yards.

RON MIX
Tackle. 6-4, 255. Born in Los Angeles, California, March 10, 1938. Southern California. Inducted in 1979. 1960 Los Angeles Chargers, 1961-69 San Diego Chargers, 1971 Oakland Raiders. **Highlights:** All-AFL nine times. Only two holding penalties in 10 years with the Chargers.

ART MONK
Wide receiver. 6-3, 210. Born in White Plains, New York, December 5, 1957. Syracuse. Inducted in 2008. 1980-1993 Washington Redskins, 1994 New York Jets, 1995 Philadelphia Eagles. **Highlights:** 940 receptions, 12,721 yards, 68 TDs. Set then-single season record, 106 catches, 1984. Had 50 or more catches in a season nine times.

JOE MONTANA
Quarterback. 6-2, 200. Born in New Eagle, Pennsylvania, June, 11, 1956. Notre Dame. Inducted in 2000. 1979-1990, 1992 San Francisco 49ers, 1993-94 Kansas City Chiefs. **Highlights:** MVP in Super Bowl's XVI, XIX, and XXIV. Eight Pro Bowls and All-NFL three times.

WARREN MOON
Quarterback. 6-3, 212. Born in Los Angeles, California, November 18, 1956. West Los Angeles Junior College, Washington. Inducted in 2006. 1984-1993 Houston Oilers, 1994-1996 Minnesota Vikings, 1997-1998 Seattle Seahawks, 1999-2000 Kansas City Chiefs. **Highlights:** Passed for 49,325 yards and 291 touchdowns in 17 NFL seasons. Elected to nine Pro Bowls including eight straight. Threw for 3,000 yards in nine seasons.

LENNY MOORE
Flanker-running back. 6-1, 198. Born in Reading, Pennsylvania, November 25, 1933. Penn State. Inducted in 1975. 1956-1967 Baltimore Colts. **Highlights:** From 1963-65, scored touchdowns in record 18 consecutive games. 113 career touchdowns, 12,451 combined net yards.

MARION MOTLEY
Fullback. 6-1, 238. Born in Leesburg, Georgia, June 5, 1920. Died June 27, 1999. South Carolina State, Nevada. Inducted in 1968. 1946-49 Cleveland Browns (AAFC), 1950-53 Cleveland Browns, 1955 Pittsburgh Steelers. **Highlights:** AAFC's all-time rushing champion. Led league in rushing in first NFL season.

MIKE MUNCHAK
Guard. 6-3, 281. Born in Scranton, Pennsylvania, March 5, 1960. Penn State. Inducted in 2001. 1982-1993 Houston Oilers. **Highlights:** Devastating blocker, All-AFC seven times, elected to nine Pro Bowls.

ANTHONY MUÑOZ
Tackle. 6-6, 278. Born in Ontario, California, August 19, 1958. Southern California. Inducted in 1998. 1980-1992 Cincinnati Bengals. **Highlights:** All-Pro choice 11 consecutive years, 1981-1991. Selected to 11 straight Pro Bowls.

GEORGE MUSSO
Guard-tackle. 6-2, 270. Born in Collinsville, Illinois. April 8, 1910. Died September 5, 2000. Millikin. Inducted in 1982. 1933-1944 Chicago Bears. **Highlights:** First player to achieve All-NFL status at two positions—tackle in 1935 and guard in 1937.

BRONKO NAGURSKI
Fullback. 6-2, 225. Born in Rainy River, Ontario, Canada, November 3, 1908. Died January 7, 1990. Minnesota. Inducted in 1963. 1930-37, 1943 Chicago Bears. **Highlights:** Charter enshrinee. 2,778 rushing yards in nine seasons. All-NFL five times.

JOE NAMATH
Quarterback. 6-2, 200. Born in Beaver Falls, Pennsylvania, May 31, 1943. Alabama. Inducted in 1985. 1965-1976 New York Jets, 1977 Los Angeles Rams. **Highlights:** First quarterback to pass for more than 4,000 yards in season, 1967. Guaranteed victory over Colts in Super Bowl III.

EARLE (GREASY) NEALE
Coach. Born in Parkersburg, West Virginia, November 5, 1891. Died November 2, 1973. West Virginia Wesleyan. Inducted in 1969. 1941-42, 1944-1950 Philadelphia Eagles; co-coach, 1943 Phil-Pitt. **Highlights:** Turned Eagles into winners with three consecutive division crowns, NFL championships in 1948 and 1949.

ERNIE NEVERS
Fullback. 6-1, 205. Born in Willow River, Minnesota, June 11, 1903. Died May 3, 1976. Stanford. Inducted in 1963. 1926-27 Duluth Eskimos, 1929-1931 Chicago Cardinals. **Highlights:** Charter enshrinee. Holds NFL's longest-standing record, 40 points in one game in 1929.

OZZIE NEWSOME
Tight end. 6-2, 232. Born in Muscle Shoals, Alabama, March 16, 1956. Alabama. Inducted in 1999. 1978-1990 Cleveland Browns. **Highlights:** Finished career as all-time leader among tight ends with 662 receptions for 7,980 yards.

RAY NITSCHKE
Linebacker. 6-3, 235. Born in Elmwood Park, Illinois, December 29, 1936. Died March 8, 1998. Illinois. Inducted in 1978. 1958-1972 Green Bay Packers. **Highlights:** MVP of 1962 title game. Named NFL's all-time linebacker in 1969.

CHUCK NOLL
Coach. Born in Cleveland, Ohio, January 5, 1932. Dayton. Inducted in 1993. 1969-1991 Pittsburgh Steelers. **Highlights:** Coached for 23 years. Only coach to win four Super Bowl titles (IX, X, XIII, XIV).

LEO NOMELLINI
Defensive tackle. 6-3, 264. Born in Lucca, Italy, June 19, 1924. Died October 17, 2000. Minnesota. Inducted in 1969. 1950-1963 San Francisco 49ers. **Highlights:** Played every 49ers game for 14 seasons. 10 Pro Bowls.

MERLIN OLSEN
Defensive tackle. 6-5, 270. Born in Logan, Utah, September 15, 1940. Died March 11, 2010. Utah State. Inducted in 1982. 1962-1976 Los Angeles Rams. **Highlights:** Member of the Fearsome "Foursome. Named" to 14 consecutive Pro Bowls, Rams' all-time team.

JIM OTTO
Center. 6-2, 255. Born in Wausau, Wisconsin, January 5, 1938. Miami. Inducted in 1980. 1960-1974 Oakland Raiders. **Highlights:** Named AFL's all-time center. Played in 210 games, 12 AFL All-Star Games or Pro Bowls, six AFL/AFC title games.

STEVE OWEN
Tackle. Coach. 6-2, 235. Born in Cleo Springs, Oklahoma, April 21, 1898. Died May 17, 1964. Phillips. Inducted in 1966. 1924-25 Kansas City Cowboys, 1925 Cleveland Bulldogs, 1926-1931, 1933 New York Giants; coach, 1930-1953 New York Giants. **Highlights:** Both player and coach. Coached Giants to record of 155-108-17, eight divisional titles, two NFL championships.

ALAN PAGE
Defensive tackle. 6-4, 225. Born in Canton, Ohio, August 7, 1945. Notre Dame. Inducted in 1988. 1967-1978 Minnesota Vikings, 1978-1981 Chicago Bears. **Highlights:** Dominating defensive tackle played in 238 consecutive games, four Super Bowls. Won league MVP honors in 1971.

CLARENCE (ACE) PARKER
Quarterback. 5-11, 168. Born in Portsmouth, Virginia, May 17, 1912. Duke. Inducted in 1972. 1937-1941 Brooklyn Dodgers, 1945 Boston Yanks, 1946 New York Yankees (AAFC). **Highlights:** Two-way threat. Two-time All-NFL performer, league MVP in 1940.

JIM PARKER
Guard-tackle. 6-3, 273. Born in Macon, Georgia, April 3, 1934. Died July 18, 2005. Ohio State. Inducted in 1973. 1957-1967 Baltimore Colts. **Highlights:** First full-time offensive lineman elected to Hall of Fame. All-NFL eight consecutive years, eight Pro Bowls.

WALTER PAYTON
Running back. 5-10, 202. Born in Columbia, Mississippi, July 25, 1954. Died November 1, 1999. Jackson State. Inducted in 1993. 1975-1987 Chicago Bears. **Highlights:** NFL's all-time leading rusher with 16,726 yards and combined net yardage with 21,803 at time of retirement.

JOE PERRY
Fullback. 6-0, 200. Born in Stevens, Arkansas, January 22, 1927. Died April 25, 2011. Compton Junior College. Inducted in 1969. 1948-49 San Francisco 49ers (AAFC), 1950-1960, 1963 San Francisco 49ers, 1961-62 Baltimore Colts. **Highlights:** First player in NFL history to gain 1,000 yards two consecutive seasons. 12,532 combined yards.

PETE PIHOS
End. 6-1, 210. Born in Orlando, Florida, October 22, 1923. Died August 16, 2011. Indiana. Inducted in 1970. 1947-1955 Philadelphia Eagles. **Highlights:** Three-time NFL receiving champion. Caught winning touchdown in 1949 NFL Championship Game.

FRITZ POLLARD
Halfback-Coach. 5-9, 165. Born in Chicago, Illinois, January 27, 1894. Died May 11, 1986. Brown. Inducted in 2005. 1919-1921, 1925-26 Akron Pros/Indians, 1922 Milwaukee Badgers, 1923, 1925 Hammond Pros, 1925 Providence Steam Roller. **Highlights:** True pioneer as one of two African American players in the NFL in 1920 and helped lead Akron to league title that season. In 1921, became the league's first black head coach.

JOHN RANDLE
Defensive tackle. 6-1, 278. Born in Hearne, Texas, December 12, 1967. Trinity Valley Community College; Texas A&I. Inducted in 2010. 1990-2000 Minnesota Vikings, 2001-03 Seattle Seahawks. **Highlights:** Undrafted free agent rookie, record eight straight seasons with 10 or more sacks, had 137.5 career sacks. Voted to seven Pro Bowls, named All-Pro/NFC six consecutive years, All-AFC once.

HUGH (SHORTY) RAY
Supervisor of officials 1938-1952. Born in Highland Park, Illinois, September 21, 1884. Died September 16, 1956. Illinois. Inducted in 1966. **Highlights:** Supervisor of Officials, 1938-1952. Streamlined rules to improve game tempo, player safety.

DAN REEVES
Team owner. Born in New York, New York, June 30, 1912. Died April 15, 1971. Georgetown. Inducted in 1967. 1941-45 Cleveland Rams, 1946-1971 Los Angeles Rams. **Highlights:** Moved Rams to Los Angeles in 1946 and opened up West Coast to pro football. First postwar owner to sign African-American player.

MEL RENFRO
Cornerback-safety. 6-0, 192. Born in Houston, Texas, December 30, 1941. Oregon. Inducted in 1996. 1964-1977 Dallas Cowboys. **Highlights:** 52 interceptions for 626 yards and 3 touchdowns. Also added 842 yards on punt returns, 2,246 yards on kickoff returns. Elected to Pro Bowl first 10 seasons.

JERRY RICE
Wide receiver. 6-2, 200. Born in Starksville, Mississippi, October 13, 1962. Mississippi Valley State. Inducted in 2010. 1985-2000 San Francisco 49ers, 2001-04 Oakland Raiders, 2004 Seattle Seahawks. **Highlights:** NFL's all-time reception leader with 1,549 catches for 22,895 yards, 208 total touchdowns. Had 14 seasons with 1,000 yards receiving; 23,546 combined net yards. All-Pro 11 times, Super Bowl XXIII MVP.

LES RICHTER
Linebacker. 6-3, 238. Born in Fresno, California, October 6, 1930. Died June 12, 2010. California. Inducted in 2011. 1954-1962 Los Angeles Rams. **Highlights:** Second overall pick in 1952 by New York Yanks. Rights traded to Rams in exchange for 11 players. Rugged, fierce competitor. Voted to eight straight Pro Bowls. Recorded 16 career interceptions, also handled Rams' placekicking duties early in career.

JOHN RIGGINS
Running back. 6-2, 240. Born in Seneca, Kansas, August 4, 1949. Kansas. Inducted in 1992. 1971-75 New York Jets, 1976-79, 1981-85 Washington Redskins. **Highlights:** 11,352 rushing yards, 116 total touchdowns. MVP of Super Bowl XVII with 166 rushing yards including game-winning 43-yard touchdown.

JIM RINGO
Center. 6-2, 230. Born in Orange, New Jersey, November 21, 1931. Died November 19, 2007. Syracuse. Inducted in 1981. 1953-1963 Green Bay Packers, 1964-67 Philadelphia Eagles. **Highlights:** Ten-time Pro Bowl selection, seven-time All-NFL selection. Started in then-record 182 consecutive games.

WILLIE ROAF
Tackle. 6-5, 300. Born in Pine Bluff, Arkansas, April 18, 1970. Louisiana Tech. Inducted in 2012. 1993-2001 New Orleans Saints, 2002-05 Kansas City Chiefs. **Highlights:** Voted to 11 Pro Bowls, named first-team All-Pro seven times. Member of both the NFL's All-Decade Team of the 1990s and 2000s.

ANDY ROBUSTELLI
Defensive end. 6-0, 230. Born in Stamford, Connecticut, December 6, 1925. Died May 31, 2011. Arnold College. Inducted in 1971. 1951-55 Los Angeles Rams, 1956-1964 New York Giants. **Highlights:** Anchored defense in eight championship games. Named NFL's top player in 1962.

ART ROONEY
Founder-Team Owner. Born in Coulterville, Pennsylvania, January 27, 1901. Died August 25, 1988. Georgetown, Duquesne. Inducted in 1964. 1933-39 Pittsburgh Pirates, 1940-42, 1945-1988 Pittsburgh Steelers, 1943 Phil-Pitt, 1944 Card-Pitt. **Highlights:** Founded Pittsburgh Pirates in 1933 and renamed them Steelers in 1940. Team won four Super Bowls in 1970s.

DAN ROONEY
Administrator-Team Owner. Born in Pittsburgh, Pennsylvania, July, 20, 1932. Duquesne. Inducted in 2000. 1955-present Pittsburgh Steelers. **Highlights:** Has been on the board of directors for the NFL Trust Fund, NFL Films, and Scheduling Committee. Played a key role in the labor agreement reached in 1993 between the NFL owners and players.

PETE ROZELLE
Commissioner. Born in South Gate, California, March 1, 1926. Died December 6, 1996. Compton Junior College, San Francisco. Inducted in 1985. Commissioner, 1960-1989. **Highlights:** Negotiated first league-wide television contract in 1962. Generally recognized as premiere commissioner in all of sports. Credited with making NFL the nation's most popular sport.

BOB ST. CLAIR
Tackle. 6-9, 265. Born in San Francisco, California, February 18, 1931. San Francisco, Tulsa. Inducted in 1990. 1953-1963 San Francisco 49ers. **Highlights:** Exceptional offensive lineman. Also played goal-line defense and had 10 blocked field goals, 1956.

ED SABOL
Founder-President-Chairman. Born in Atlantic City, New Jersey, September 11, 1916. Ohio State. Inducted in 2011. 1964-1995 NFL Films. **Highlights:** Bid and received rights to film 1962 NFL Championship Game. Two years later, founded NFL Films. During his tenure, NFL Films won 52 Emmys. Vision and innovations changed the way in which sports were presented.

BARRY SANDERS
Running back. 5-8, 203. Born in Wichita, Kansas, July 16, 1968. Oklahoma State. Inducted in 2004. 1989-1998 Detroit Lions. **Highlights:** 15,269 rushing yards, 99 touchdowns. Rushed for 1,000 yards in each of 10 seasons. NFL co-MVP, 1997. Selected to 10 Pro Bowls.

CHARLIE SANDERS
Tight end. 6-4, 230. Born in Richlands, North Carolina, August 25, 1946. Minnesota. Inducted in 2007. 1968-1977 Detroit Lions. **Highlights:** 336 career receptions for 4,817 yards and 31 touchdowns. Selected to seven Pro Bowls. Named to the NFL's All-Decade Team of 1970s.

DEION SANDERS
Cornerback-Kick returner-Punt returner. 6-1, 195. Born in Fort Myers, Florida, August 9, 1967. Florida State. Inducted in 2011. 1989-1993 Atlanta Falcons, 1994 San Francisco 49ers, 1995-99 Dallas Cowboys, 2000 Washington Redskins, 2004-05 Baltimore Ravens. **Highlights:** First-team All-NFL nine times. Voted to the NFL's All-Decade Team of the 1990s at both cornerback and punt returner. 53 career interceptions. Career touchdowns include six on punt returns, three on kickoff returns, nine on interceptions, one fumble recovery, and three receiving.

GALE SAYERS
Running back. 6-0, 200. Born in Wichita, Kansas, May 30, 1943. Kansas. Inducted in 1977. 1965-1971 Chicago Bears. **Highlights:** Broke into league by scoring rookie-record 22 touchdowns. Led league in rushing in 1966, 1969. MVP of three Pro Bowls.

JOE SCHMIDT
Linebacker. 6-0, 222. Born in Pittsburgh, Pennsylvania, January 18, 1932. Pittsburgh. Inducted in 1973. 1953-1965 Detroit Lions. **Highlights:** 24 interceptions. Lions' team captain for nine years. Mastered middle linebacker position that evolved in 1950s.

TEX SCHRAMM
Team president-general manager. Born in San Gabriel, California, June 2, 1920. Died July 15, 2003. Texas. Inducted in 1991. 1947-1956 Los Angeles Rams. 1960-1989 Dallas Cowboys. **Highlights:** Played prominent role in AFL-NFL merger. Chairman of Competition Committee from 1966-1988.

LEE ROY SELMON
Defensive end. 6-3, 250. Born in Eufaula, Oklahoma, October 20, 1954. Died September 4, 2011. Oklahoma. Inducted in 1995. 1976-1984 Tampa Bay Buccaneers. **Highlights:** 78½ sacks, 380 quarterback pressures, forced 28 fumbles. Six consecutive Pro Bowl selections.

SHANNON SHARPE
Tight end. 6-2, 230. Born in Chicago, Illinois, June 26, 1968. Savannah State. Inducted in 2011. 1990-99, 2002-03 Denver Broncos, 2000-01 Baltimore Ravens. **Highlights:** Retired as the NFL's all-time leader among tight ends for catches (815), receiving yards (10,060) and TD receptions (62). Selected as first- or second-team All-Pro five times, named to eight Pro Bowls. Played on three Super Bowl championship teams in four seasons.

BILLY SHAW
Guard. 6-2, 258. Born in Natchez, Mississippi, December 15, 1938. Georgia Tech. Inducted in 1999. 1961-69 Buffalo Bills. **Highlights:** First player who played entire career in AFL to be elected to Hall of Fame. Named to AFL's all-time team.

ART SHELL
Tackle. 6-5, 285. Born in Charleston, South Carolina, November 26, 1946. Maryland State-Eastern Shore. Inducted in 1989. 1968-82 Oakland/Los Angeles Raiders. **Highlights:** Cornerstone of Raiders' offensive line in 1970s. 207 regular-season games, 23 postseason games, eight Pro Bowls.

DON SHULA
Coach. Born in Grand River, Ohio, January 4, 1930. John Carroll. Inducted in 1997. 1963-69 Baltimore Colts, 1970-1995 Miami Dolphins. **Highlights:** Won more games (347) than any coach in NFL history. Won two Super Bowl titles, including Super Bowl VII when Dolphins recorded NFL's only perfect season (17-0).

O.J. SIMPSON
Running back. 6-1, 212. Born in San Francisco, California, July 9, 1947. City College (San Francisco), Southern California. Inducted in 1985. 1969-1977 Buffalo Bills, 1978-79 San Francisco 49ers. **Highlights:** In 1973, became first player to rush for 2,000 yards in season. Finished career with four rushing titles, 11,236 yards.

MIKE SINGLETARY
Linebacker. 6-0, 230. Born in Houston, Texas, October 9, 1958. Baylor. Inducted in 1998. 1981-1992 Chicago Bears. **Highlights:** All-Pro choice eight times and All-NFC nine consecutive seasons. Selected to 10 Pro Bowls.

JACKIE SLATER
Tackle. 6-4, 277. Born in Jackson, Mississippi, May 27, 1954. Jackson State. Inducted in 2001. 1976-1995 Los Angeles/St. Louis Rams. **Highlights:** Played 20 seasons, 259 games. Blocked for seven different 1,000-yard rushers. Seven Pro Bowls.

BRUCE SMITH
Defensive end. 6-4, 280. Born in Norfolk, Virginia, June 18, 1963. Virginia Tech. Inducted in 2009. 1985-1999 Buffalo Bills, 2000-03 Washington Redskins. **Highlights:** NFL's all-time leader in sacks with 200. Named All-Pro nine times, 11 Pro Bowls. Selected to NFL's All-Decade Team of 1980s and 1990s.

EMMITT SMITH
Running back. 5-9, 207. Born in Pensacola, Florida, May 15, 1969. Florida. Inducted in 2010. 1990-2002 Dallas Cowboys, 2003-04 Arizona Cardinals. **Highlights:** Won four rushing titles in five years, recorded record 11 straight 1,000-yard seasons. NFL's all-time leading rusher with 18,355 yards, 164 rushing TDs. Won NFL MVP and Super Bowl XXVIII MVP in 1993.

JACKIE SMITH
Tight end. 6-4, 232. Born in Columbia, Mississippi, February 23, 1940. Northwestern State (Louisiana). Inducted in 1994. 1963-1977 St. Louis Cardinals, 1978 Dallas Cowboys. **Highlights:** 480 receptions for 7,918 yards, 40 touchdowns. Third tight end to be elected to Hall of Fame.

JOHN STALLWORTH
Wide receiver. 6-2, 191. Born in Tuscaloosa, Alabama, July 15, 1952. Alabama A&M. Inducted in 2002. 1974-1987 Pittsburgh Steelers. **Highlights:** 537 receptions for 8,723 yards, 63 touchdowns. Scored go-ahead touchdown in Super Bowl XIV on 73-yard reception.

BART STARR
Quarterback. 6-1, 200. Born in Montgomery, Alabama, January 9, 1934. Alabama. Inducted in 1977. 1956-1971 Green Bay Packers. **Highlights:** Quarterbacked Packers to six division titles, five NFL titles, and first two Super Bowls in which he was MVP.

ROGER STAUBACH
Quarterback. 6-3, 202. Born in Cincinnati, Ohio, February 5, 1942. New Mexico Military Institute, Navy. Inducted in 1985. 1969-1979 Dallas Cowboys. **Highlights:** Led Cowboys to four NFC titles and victories in Super Bowls VI, XII. When retired, 83.4 career passer rating was best of all time.

ERNIE STAUTNER
Defensive tackle. 6-2, 235. Born in Prinzing-by-Cham, Bavaria, April 20, 1925. Died February 16, 2006. Boston College. Inducted in 1969. 1950-1963 Pittsburgh Steelers. **Highlights:** Played in nine Pro Bowls and won the best lineman award in 1957. Recorded 3 safeties.

JAN STENERUD
Kicker. 6-2, 190. Born in Fetsund, Norway, November 26, 1942. Montana State. Inducted in 1991. 1967-1979 Kansas City Chiefs, 1980-83 Green Bay Packers, 1984-85 Minnesota Vikings. **Highlights:** 1,699 points on 580 extra points, 373 field goals. First pure placekicker to enter Hall of Fame.

DWIGHT STEPHENSON
Center. 6-2, 255. Born in Murfreesboro, North Carolina, November 20, 1957. Alabama. Inducted in 1998. 1980-87 Miami Dolphins. **Highlights:** Recognized as premier center of his time. All-Pro, All-AFC five straight years. Selected to five Pro Bowls.

HANK STRAM
Coach. Born in Chicago, Illinois, January 3, 1923. Died July 4, 2005. Purdue. Inducted in 2003. 1960-1974 Dallas Texans/Kansas City Chiefs, 1976-1977 New Orleans Saints. **Highlights:** Overall record of 136-100-10. Recorded most wins in AFL history. Guided teams to titles in 1962, 1966, and 1969. Led Chiefs to AFL win in Super Bowl IV.

KEN STRONG
Halfback. 5-11, 210. Born in West Haven, Connecticut, April 21, 1906. Died October 5, 1979. New York University. Inducted in 1967. 1929-1932 Staten Island Stapletons, 1933-35, 1939, 1944-47 New York Giants, 1936-37 New York Yanks (AFL). **Highlights:** Scored 17 points to lead Giants to victory in 1934 'Sneakers' game, led NFL with 64 points, 1933.

JOE STYDAHAR
Tackle. 6-4, 230. Born in Kaylor, Pennsylvania, March 17, 1912. Died March 23, 1977. West Virginia. Inducted in 1967. 1936-1942, 1945-46 Chicago Bears. **Highlights:** One of stalwarts of Bears' 'Monsters of the Midway.' Played on five divisional, three NFL championship teams.

LYNN SWANN
Wide receiver. 5-11, 180. Born in Alcoa, Tennessee, March 7, 1952. Southern California. Inducted in 2001. 1974-1982 Pittsburgh Steelers. **Highlights:** All-AFC three times. Selected to three Pro Bowls. MVP, Super Bowl X.

FRAN TARKENTON
Quarterback. 6-0, 185. Born in Richmond, Virginia, February 3, 1940. Georgia. Inducted in 1986. 1961-66, 1972-78 Minnesota Vikings, 1967-1971 New York Giants. **Highlights:** At retirement, held NFL records for attempts (6,467), completions (3,686), yards (47,003), and touchdowns (342). Four touchdown passes in first NFL game.

CHARLEY TAYLOR
Running back-wide receiver. 6-3, 210. Born in Grand Prairie, Texas, September 28, 1941. Arizona State. Inducted in 1984. 1964-1975, 1977 Washington Redskins. **Highlights:** Won rookie of year honors as running back. Switched to wide receiver and won receiving titles in 1966, 1967.

JIM TAYLOR
Fullback. 6-0, 216. Born in Baton Rouge, Louisiana, September 20, 1935. Hinds Junior College; Louisiana State. Inducted in 1976. 1958-1966 Green Bay Packers, 1967 New Orleans Saints. **Highlights:** 8,597 rushing yards, 558 points. In 1962, led league in rushing and scoring with 19 touchdowns.

LAWRENCE TAYLOR
Linebacker. 6-3, 237. Born in Williamsburg, Virginia, February 4, 1959. North Carolina. Inducted in 1999. 1981-1993 New York Giants. **Highlights:** Redefined the position of outside linebacker. All-Pro nine times, 10 Pro Bowls. NFL MVP in 1986.

DERRICK THOMAS
Linebacker. 6-3, 243. Born in Miami, Florida, January 1, 1967. Died February 8, 2000. Alabama. Inducted in 2009. 1989-1999 Kansas City Chiefs. **Highlights:** Set NFL record with 7 sacks in one game. Recorded most sacks in NFL during 1990s. Nine Pro Bowls. Named to NFL's All-Decade Team of 1990s.

EMMITT THOMAS
Cornerback. 6-2, 192. Born in Angleton, Texas, June 3, 1943. Bishop. Inducted in 2008. 1966-1978 Kansas City Chiefs. **Highlights:** Undrafted free agent. 58 interceptions, 937 yards, 5 TDs. Ranked fifth all-time in interceptions at retirement. Interception leader —AFL, 1969 and NFL, 1974.

THURMAN THOMAS
Running back. 5-10, 198. Born in Houston, Texas, May 16, 1966. Oklahoma State. Inducted in 2007. 1988-1999 Buffalo Bills, 2000 Miami Dolphins. **Highlights:** Amassed 16,532 total yards including 12,074 yards rushing. Scored 88 touchdowns. Only player in history to lead league in yards from scrimmage four straight seasons.

JIM THORPE
Halfback. 6-1, 190. Born in Prague, Oklahoma, May 28, 1888. Died March 28, 1953. Carlisle. Inducted in 1963. 1915-17, 1919-1920, 1926 Canton Bulldogs, 1921 Cleveland Indians, 1922-23 Oorang Indians, 1924 Rock Island Independents, 1925 New York Giants, 1928 Chicago Cardinals. **Highlights:** Charter enshrinee. First president of American Professional Football Association, 1920. Played for 12 seasons.

ANDRE TIPPETT
Linebacker. 6-3, 240. Born in Birmingham, Alabama, December 27, 1959. Iowa; Ellsworth (IA) Jr. College. Inducted in 2008. 1982-1988, 1990-93 New England Patriots. **Highlights:** Recorded 100 career sacks including personal best 18.5 sacks, 1984. Named to five straight Pro Bowls, 1985-89.

Y.A. TITTLE
Quarterback. 6-0, 200. Born in Marshall, Texas, October 24, 1926. Louisiana State. Inducted in 1971. 1948-49 Baltimore Colts (AAFC), 1950 Baltimore Colts, 1951-1960 San Francisco 49ers, 1961-64 New York Giants. **Highlights:** 33,070 yards, 242 touchdowns. 33 touchdown passes in 1962 and 36 in 1963. Two-time league MVP.

GEORGE TRAFTON
Center. 6-2, 235. Born in Chicago, Illinois, December 6, 1896. Died September 5, 1971. Notre Dame. Inducted in 1964. 1920-1932 Decatur Staleys/Chicago Staleys/Chicago Bears. **Highlights:** First center to snap with one hand. Named top NFL center of 1920s.

CHARLEY TRIPPI
Halfback-quarterback. 6-0, 185. Born in Pittston, Pennsylvania, December 14, 1922. Georgia. Inducted in 1968. 1947-1955 Chicago Cardinals. **Highlights:** One of football's most versatile performers. Played halfback five years, quarterback for two, defense for two.

EMLEN TUNNELL
Safety. 6-1, 200. Born in Bryn Mawr, Pennsylvania, March 29, 1925. Died July 22, 1975. Toledo, Iowa. Inducted in 1967. 1948-1958 New York Giants, 1959-1961 Green Bay Packers. **Highlights:** 79 interceptions. Gained more yards on kickoff, punt, and interception returns (924) in 1952 than that season's NFL rushing leader.

CLYDE (BULLDOG) TURNER
Center. 6-2, 235. Born in Plains, Texas, March 10, 1919. Died October 30, 1998. Hardin-Simmons. Inducted in 1966. 1940-1952 Chicago Bears. **Highlights:** Anchored defense for four NFL championship teams, including 4 interceptions in five title games.

JOHNNY UNITAS
Quarterback. 6-1, 195. Born in Pittsburgh, Pennsylvania, May 7, 1933. Died September 11, 2002. Louisville. Inducted in 1979. 1956-1972 Baltimore Colts, 1973 San Diego Chargers. **Highlights:** 40,239 passing yards, 290 touchdowns. Led Colts to two NFL championships. Passed for at least one touchdown in 47 consecutive games.

GENE UPSHAW
Guard. 6-5, 255. Born in Robstown, Texas, August 15, 1945. Died August 20, 2008. Texas A & I. Inducted in 1987. 1967-1981 Oakland Raiders. **Highlights:** Premier guard of his era played in 10 AFL/AFC Championship Games, three Super Bowls, seven Pro Bowls.

NORM VAN BROCKLIN
Quarterback. 6-1, 190. Born in Eagle Butte, South Dakota, March 15, 1926. Died May 2, 1983. Oregon. Inducted in 1971. 1949-1957 Los Angeles Rams, 1958-1960 Philadelphia Eagles. **Highlights:** NFL-record 554 yards passing in 1951 season opener. Guided Eagles to NFL crown as league's Most Outstanding Player in 1960.

STEVE VAN BUREN
Halfback. 6-1, 200. Born in La Ceiba, Honduras, December 28, 1920. Louisiana State. Inducted in 1965. 1944-1951 Philadelphia Eagles. **Highlights:** Four-time rushing champion. Won 1944 punt-return title and 1945 kickoff-return champion.

DOAK WALKER
Halfback. 5-11, 173. Born in Dallas, Texas, January 1, 1927. Died September 27, 1998. Southern Methodist. Inducted in 1986. 1950-55 Detroit Lions. **Highlights:** 534 points. Won two NFL scoring titles. Had winning 67-yard scoring run in 1952 title game.

BILL WALSH
Coach. Born in Los Angeles, California, November 30, 1931. Died July 30, 2007. San Jose State. Inducted in 1993. 1979-1988 San Francisco 49ers. **Highlights:** 102-63-1 coaching record. Guided 49ers to three Super Bowl titles (XVI, XIX, XXIII) in 10 years.

PAUL WARFIELD
Wide receiver. 6-0, 188. Born in Warren, Ohio, November 28, 1942. Ohio State. Inducted in 1983. 1964-69, 1976-77 Cleveland Browns, 1970-74 Miami Dolphins. **Highlights:** 8,565 yards receiving, 85 touchdowns. Eight-time Pro Bowl player. Key to both Cleveland and Miami offenses.

BOB WATERFIELD
Quarterback. 6-2, 200. Born in Elmira, New York, July 26, 1920. Died March 25, 1983. UCLA. Inducted in 1965. 1945 Cleveland Rams, 1946-1952 Los Angeles Rams. **Highlights:** NFL MVP as rookie in 1945 and led Rams to NFL title. Grabbed 20 interceptions in limited defensive duties.

MIKE WEBSTER
Center. 6-2, 260. Born in Tomahawk, Wisconsin, March 18, 1952. Died September 24, 2002. Inducted in 1997. 1974-1988 Pittsburgh Steelers, 1989-1990 Kansas City Chiefs. **Highlights:** Played in 245 games, nine Pro Bowls, and won four Super Bowls during 17-year career.

ROGER WEHRLI
Cornerback. 6-0, 190. Born in New Point, Missouri, November 26, 1947. Missouri. Inducted in 2007. 1969-1982 St. Louis Cardinals. **Highlights:** 40 career interceptions. Named to the NFL's All-Decade Team of 1970s. All-Pro five times, selected to seven Pro Bowls.

ARNIE WEINMEISTER
Defensive tackle. 6-4, 235. Born in Rhein, Saskatchewan, Canada, March 23, 1923. Died June 29, 2000. Washington. Inducted in 1984. 1948-49 New York Yankees (AAFC), 1950-53 New York Giants. **Highlights:** Dominant defensive tackle of his time. Four-time All-NFL selection, four Pro Bowls.

RANDY WHITE
Defensive tackle. 6-4, 265. Born in Pittsburgh, Pennsylvania, January 15, 1953. Maryland. Inducted in 1994. 1975-1988 Dallas Cowboys. **Highlights:** Missed only one game in 14 seasons. Co-MVP of Super Bowl XII. Nine-time Pro Bowl selection.

REGGIE WHITE
Defensive end. 6-5, 291. Born in Chattanooga, Tennessee, December 19, 1961. Died December 26, 2004. Tennessee. Inducted in 2006. 1985-1992 Philadelphia Eagles, 1993-1998 Green Bay Packers, 2000 Carolina Panthers. **Highlights:** Retired as all-time sack leader with 198. Named All-Pro 13 of 15 seasons including 10 as first-team selection. Named to 13 straight Pro Bowls.

DAVE WILCOX
Linebacker. 6-3, 241. Born in Ontario, Oregon, September, 29, 1942. Boise State, Oregon. Inducted in 2000. 1964-1974 San Francisco 49ers. **Highlights:** Seven Pro Bowls, All-NFL five times. Missed only one game because of injury.

BILL WILLIS
Guard. 6-2, 215. Born in Columbus, Ohio, October 5, 1921. Died November 27, 2007. Ohio State. Inducted in 1977. 1946-1953 Cleveland Browns (AAFC/NFL). **Highlights:** Two-way player who excelled on defense. Four-time All-NFL player, played in three Pro Bowls.

LARRY WILSON
Safety. 6-0, 190. Born in Rigby, Idaho, March 24, 1938. Utah. Inducted in 1978. 1960-1972 St. Louis Cardinals. **Highlights:** 52 interceptions. Had interception in seven consecutive games in 1966. Made "safety blitz" famous.

RALPH WILSON, JR.
Owner-founder. Born in Columbus, Ohio, October 17, 1918. Virginia. Michigan. Inducted in 2009. 1960-present Buffalo Bills. **Highlights:** Founded team. Bills teams captured back-to-back AFL titles in mid-1960s. Unprecedented four straight Super Bowl appearances.

KELLEN WINSLOW
Tight end. 6-5, 250. Born in St. Louis, Missouri, November 5, 1957. Missouri. Inducted in 1995. 1979-1987 San Diego Chargers **Highlights:** 541 receptions for 6,741 yards, 45 touchdowns. 13 catches, blocked field goal in 1981 playoff win over Miami.

ALEX WOJCIECHOWICZ
Center. 6-0, 235. Born in South River, New Jersey, August 12, 1915. Died July 13, 1992. Fordham. Inducted in 1968. 1938-1946 Detroit Lions, 1946-1950 Philadelphia Eagles. **Highlights:** One of league's first iron men. Played both ways for eight years with Lions.

WILLIE WOOD
Safety. 5-10, 190. Born in Washington, D.C., December 23, 1936. Southern California. Inducted in 1989. 1960-1971 Green Bay Packers. **Highlights:** 48 interceptions. Competed in six NFL Championship Games and Super Bowls I and II.

ROD WOODSON
Cornerback-safety. 6-0, 200. Born in Fort Wayne, Indiana, March 10, 1965. Purdue. Inducted in 2009. 1987-1996 Pittsburgh Steelers, 1997 San Francisco 49ers, 1998-2001 Baltimore Ravens, 2002-03 Oakland Raiders. **Highlights:** 71 interceptions returned for 1,483 yards and NFL record 12 TDs. Named NFL Defensive Player of Year, 1993. Member of NFL's 75th Anniversary Team. 11 Pro Bowls.

RAYFIELD WRIGHT
Tackle. 6-6, 255. Born in Griffin, Georgia, August 23, 1945. Fort Valley State. Inducted in 2006. 1967-1979 Dallas Cowboys. **Highlights:** Named first- or second-team All-Pro and voted to Pro Bowl six straight seasons, 1971-76. Played in six NFC championship games and five Super Bowls. Named to NFL's All-Decade Team of 1970s.

RON YARY
Tackle. 6-5, 255. Born in Chicago, Illinois, July 16, 1946. Cerritos (Calif.) J.C., Southern California. Inducted in 2001. 1968-1981 Minnesota Vikings, 1982 Los Angeles Rams. **Highlights:** All-Pro six consecutive seasons, All-NFC eight consecutive years. Named to seven Pro Bowls. Started in four Super Bowls and five NFL/NFC Championship Games.

STEVE YOUNG
Quarterback. 6-2, 205. Born in Salt Lake City, Utah, October 11, 1961. Brigham Young. Inducted in 2005. 1985-86 Tampa Bay Buccaneers, 1987-1999 San Francisco 49ers. **Highlights:** Led the NFL in passing a record-tying six times. Passed for more than 33,000 yards and 232 touchdowns in career. MVP of Super Bowl XXIX. Elected to seven Pro Bowls.

JACK YOUNGBLOOD
Defensive end. 6-4, 247. Born in Jacksonville, Florida, January 26, 1950. Florida. Inducted in 2001. 1971-1984 Los Angeles Rams. **Highlights:** Played in club-record 201 consecutive games. Played in five NFC Championship Games, one Super Bowl. Named All-Pro five times, All-NFC seven times. Elected to seven consecutive Pro Bowls. Lions.

GARY ZIMMERMAN
Tackle. 6-6, 294. Born in Fullerton, California, December 13, 1961. Oregon. Inducted in 2008. 1986-1992 Minnesota Vikings, 1993-97 Denver Broncos. **Highlights:** Named to seven Pro Bowls. One of handful of players to be named to two NFL All-Decade Teams, 1980s and 1990s.

ENSHRINEES BY YEAR OF INDUCTION

*Deceased
(Date of enshrinement in parentheses)

1963 CHARTER CLASS
(September 7, 1963)
Sammy Baugh*
Bert Bell*
Joe Carr*
Earl (Dutch) Clark*
Harold (Red) Grange*
George Halas*
Mel Hein*
Wilbur (Pete) Henry*
Robert (Cal) Hubbard*
Don Hutson*
Earl (Curly) Lambeau*
Tim Mara*
George Preston Marshall*
John (Blood) McNally*
Bronko Nagurski*
Ernie Nevers*
Jim Thorpe*

CLASS OF 1964
(September 6, 1964)
Jimmy Conzelman*
Ed Healey*
Clarke Hinkle*
William Roy (Link) Lyman*
Mike Michalske*
Art Rooney*
George Trafton*

CLASS OF 1965
(September 12, 1965)
Guy Chamberlin*
John (Paddy) Driscoll*
Dan Fortmann*
Otto Graham*
Sid Luckman*
Steve Van Buren*
Bob Waterfield*

CLASS OF 1966
(September 17, 1966)
Bill Dudley*
Joe Guyon*
Arnie Herber*
Walt Kiesling*
George McAfee*
Steve Owen*
Hugh (Shorty) Ray*
Clyde (Bulldog) Turner*

CLASS OF 1967
(August 5, 1967)
Chuck Bednarik
Charles W. Bidwill Sr.*
Paul Brown*
Bobby Layne*
Dan Reeves*
Ken Strong*
Joe Stydahar*
Emlen Tunnell*

CLASS OF 1968
(August 3, 1968)
Cliff Battles*
Art Donovan
Elroy (Crazylegs) Hirsch*
Wayne Millner*
Marion Motley*
Charley Trippi
Alex Wojciechowicz*

CLASS OF 1969
(September 13, 1969)
Albert Glen (Turk) Edwards*
Earle (Greasy) Neale*
Leo Nomellini*
Joe Perry*
Ernie Stautner*

CLASS OF 1970
(August 8, 1970)
Jack Christiansen*
Tom Fears*
Hugh McElhenny
Pete Pihos*

CLASS OF 1971
(July 31, 1971)
Jim Brown
Bill Hewitt*
Frank (Bruiser) Kinard*
Vince Lombardi*
Andy Robustelli*
Y. A. Tittle
Norm Van Brocklin*

CLASS OF 1972
(July 29, 1972)
Lamar Hunt*
Gino Marchetti
Ollie Matson*
Clarence (Ace) Parker

CLASS OF 1973
(July 28, 1973)
Raymond Berry
Jim Parker*
Joe Schmidt

CLASS OF 1974
(July 27, 1974)
Tony Canadeo*
Bill George*
Lou Groza*
Dick (Night Train) Lane*

CLASS OF 1975
(August 2, 1975)
Roosevelt Brown*
George Connor*
Dante Lavelli*
Lenny Moore

CLASS OF 1976
(July 24, 1976)
Ray Flaherty*
Len Ford*
Jim Taylor

CLASS OF 1977
(July 30, 1977)
Frank Gifford
Forrest Gregg
Gale Sayers
Bart Starr
Bill Willis*

CLASS OF 1978
(July 29, 1978)
Lance Alworth
Weeb Ewbank*
Alphonse (Tuffy) Leemans*
Ray Nitschke*
Larry Wilson

CLASS OF 1979
(July 28, 1979)
Dick Butkus
Yale Lary
Ron Mix
Johnny Unitas*

CLASS OF 1980
(August 2, 1980)
Herb Adderley
David (Deacon) Jones
Bob Lilly
Jim Otto

CLASS OF 1981
(August 1, 1981)
Morris (Red) Badgro*
George Blanda*
Willie Davis
Jim Ringo*

CLASS OF 1982
(August 7, 1982)
Doug Atkins
Sam Huff
George Musso*
Merlin Olsen*

CLASS OF 1983
(July 30, 1983)
Bobby Bell
Sid Gillman*
Sonny Jurgensen
Bobby Mitchell
Paul Warfield

CLASS OF 1984
(July 28, 1984)
Willie Brown
Mike McCormack
Charley Taylor
Arnie Weinmeister*

CLASS OF 1985
(August 3, 1985)
Frank Gatski*
Joe Namath
Pete Rozelle*
O. J. Simpson
Roger Staubach

CLASS OF 1986
(August 2, 1986)
Paul Hornung
Ken Houston
Willie Lanier
Fran Tarkenton
Doak Walker*

CLASS OF 1987
(August 8, 1987)
Larry Csonka
Len Dawson
Joe Greene
John Henry Johnson*
Jim Langer
Don Maynard
Gene Upshaw*

CLASS OF 1988
(July 30, 1988)
Fred Biletnikoff
Mike Ditka
Jack Ham
Alan Page

CLASS OF 1989
(August 5, 1989)
Mel Blount
Terry Bradshaw
Art Shell
Willie Wood

CLASS OF 1990
(August 4, 1990)
Buck Buchanan*
Bob Griese
Franco Harris
Ted Hendricks
Jack Lambert
Tom Landry*
Bob St. Clair

CLASS OF 1991
(July 27, 1991)
Earl Campbell
John Hannah
Stan Jones*
Tex Schramm*
Jan Stenerud

CLASS OF 1992
(August 1, 1992)
Lem Barney
Al Davis*
John Mackey*
John Riggins

CLASS OF 1993
(July 31, 1993)
Dan Fouts
Larry Little
Chuck Noll
Walter Payton*
Bill Walsh*

CLASS OF 1994
(July 30, 1994)
Tony Dorsett
Bud Grant
Jimmy Johnson
Leroy Kelly
Jackie Smith
Randy White

CLASS OF 1995
(July 29, 1995)
Jim Finks*
Henry Jordan*
Steve Largent
Lee Roy Selmon*
Kellen Winslow

CLASS OF 1996
(July 27, 1996)
Lou Creekmur*
Dan Dierdorf
Joe Gibbs
Charlie Joiner
Mel Renfro

CLASS OF 1997
(July 26, 1997)
Mike Haynes
Wellington Mara*
Don Shula
Mike Webster*

CLASS OF 1998
(August 1, 1998)
Paul Krause
Tommy McDonald
Anthony Muñoz
Mike Singletary
Dwight Stephenson

CLASS OF 1999
(August 7, 1999)
Eric Dickerson
Tom Mack
Ozzie Newsome
Billy Shaw
Lawrence Taylor

CLASS OF 2000
(July 29, 2000)
Howie Long
Ronnie Lott
Joe Montana
Dan Rooney
Dave Wilcox

CLASS OF 2001
(August 4, 2001)
Nick Buoniconti
Marv Levy
Mike Munchak
Jackie Slater
Lynn Swann
Ron Yary
Jack Youngblood

CLASS OF 2002
(August 3, 2002)
George Allen*
Dave Casper
Dan Hampton
Jim Kelly
John Stallworth

CLASS OF 2003
(August 3, 2003)
Marcus Allen
Elvin Bethea
Joe DeLamielleure
James Lofton
Hank Stram*

CLASS OF 2004
(August 8, 2004)
Bob (Boomer) Brown
Carl Eller
John Elway
Barry Sanders

CLASS OF 2005
(August 7, 2005)
Benny Friedman*
Dan Marino
Fritz Pollard*
Steve Young

CLASS OF 2006
(August 6, 2006)
Troy Aikman
Harry Carson
John Madden
Warren Moon
Reggie White*
Rayfield Wright

CLASS OF 2007
(August 4, 2007)
Gene Hickerson*
Michael Irvin
Bruce Matthews
Charlie Sanders
Thurman Thomas
Roger Wehrli

CLASS OF 2008
(August 2, 2008)
Fred Dean
Darrell Green
Art Monk
Emmitt Thomas
Andre Tippett
Gary Zimmerman

CLASS OF 2009
(August 8, 2009)
Bob Hayes*
Randall McDaniel
Bruce Smith
Derrick Thomas*
Ralph Wilson, Jr.
Rod Woodson

CLASS OF 2010
(August 7, 2010)
Russ Grimm
Rickey Jackson
Dick LeBeau
Floyd Little
John Randle
Jerry Rice
Emmitt Smith

CLASS OF 2011
(August 6, 2011)
Richard Dent
Marshall Faulk
Chris Hanburger
Les Richter*
Ed Sabol
Deion Sanders
Shannon Sharpe

CLASS OF 2012
(August 4, 2012)
Jack Butler
Dermontti Dawson
Chris Doleman
Cortez Kennedy
Curtis Martin
Willie Roaf

HALL OF FAME GAMES

PRO FOOTBALL HALL OF FAME GAME (48)

Date	Winner	Loser	Attendance
August 11, 1962	New York Giants 21 (tie)	St. Louis Cardinals 21 (tie)	14,000
September 8, 1963	Pittsburgh Steelers 16	Cleveland Browns 7	18,462
September 6, 1964	Baltimore Colts 48	Pittsburgh Steelers 17	11,479
September 12, 1965	Washington Redskins 20	Detroit Lions 3	14,416
1966	No game was played		
August 5, 1967	Philadelphia Eagles 28	Cleveland Browns 13	17,304
August 3, 1968	Chicago Bears 30	Dallas Cowboys 24	14,578
September 13, 1969	Green Bay Packers 38	Atlanta Falcons 24	17,411
August 8, 1970	New Orleans Saints 14	Minnesota Vikings 13	17,932
July 31, 1971	Los Angeles Rams (NFC) 17	Houston Oilers (AFC) 6	19,384
July 29, 1972	Kansas City Chiefs (AFC) 23	New York Giants (NFC) 17	19,304
July 28, 1973	San Francisco 49ers (NFC) 20	New England Patriots (AFC) 7	19,685
July 27, 1974	St. Louis Cardinals (NFC) 21	Buffalo Bills (AFC) 13	17,286
August 2, 1975	Washington Redskins (NFC) 17	Cincinnati Bengals (AFC) 9	19,360
July 24, 1976	Denver Broncos (AFC) 10	Detroit Lions (NFC) 7	17,639
July 30, 1977	Chicago Bears (NFC) 20	New York Jets (AFC) 6	19,057
July 29, 1978	Philadelphia Eagles (NFC) 17	Miami Dolphins (AFC) 3	19,255
July 28, 1979	Oakland Raiders (AFC) 20	Dallas Cowboys (NFC) 13	20,648
August 2, 1980*	San Diego Chargers (AFC) 0	Green Bay Packers (NFC) 0	19,972
August 1, 1981	Cleveland Browns (AFC) 24	Atlanta Falcons (NFC) 10	23,921
August 7, 1982	Minnesota Vikings (NFC) 30	Baltimore Colts (AFC) 14	23,379
July 30, 1983	Pittsburgh Steelers (AFC) 27	New Orleans Saints (NFC) 14	23,909
July 28, 1984	Seattle Seahawks (AFC) 38	Tampa Bay Buccaneers (NFC) 0	22,250
August 3, 1985	New York Giants (NFC) 21	Houston Oilers (AFC) 20	23,940
August 2, 1986	New England Patriots (AFC) 21	St. Louis Cardinals (NFC) 16	22,739
August 8, 1987	San Francisco 49ers (NFC) 20	Kansas City Chiefs (AFC) 7	23,826
July 30, 1988	Cincinnati Bengals (AFC) 14	Los Angeles Rams (NFC) 7	23,801
August 5, 1989	Washington Redskins (NFC) 31	Buffalo Bills (AFC) 6	23,948
August 4, 1990	Chicago Bears (NFC) 13	Cleveland Browns (AFC) 0	23,952
July 27, 1991	Detroit Lions (NFC) 14	Denver Broncos (AFC) 3	23,815
August 1, 1992	New York Jets (AFC) 41	Philadelphia Eagles (NFC) 14	23,853
July 31, 1993	Los Angeles Raiders (AFC) 19	Green Bay Packers (NFC) 3	23,863
July 30, 1994	Atlanta Falcons (NFC) 21	San Diego Chargers (AFC) 17	23,185
July 29, 1995	Carolina Panthers (NFC) 20	Jacksonville Jaguars (AFC) 14	24,625
July 27, 1996	Indianapolis Colts (AFC) 10	New Orleans Saints (NFC) 3	23,376
July 26, 1997	Minnesota Vikings (NFC) 28	Seattle Seahawks (AFC) 26	23,846
August 1, 1998	Tampa Bay Buccaneers (NFC) 30	Pittsburgh Steelers (AFC) 6	23,875
August 9, 1999	Cleveland Browns (AFC) 20	Dallas Cowboys (NFC) 17 (OT)	25,156
July 31, 2000	New England Patriots (AFC) 20	San Francisco 49ers (NFC) 0	22,840
August 6, 2001	St. Louis Rams (NFC) 17	Miami Dolphins (AFC) 10	22,736
August 5, 2002	New York Giants (NFC) 34	Houston Texans (AFC) 17	22,461
August 4, 2003**	Kansas City Chiefs (AFC) 9	Green Bay Packers (NFC) 0	22,385
August 9, 2004	Washington Redskins (NFC) 20	Denver Broncos (AFC) 17	22,177
August 8, 2005	Chicago Bears (NFC) 27	Miami Dolphins (AFC) 24	22,292
August 6, 2006	Oakland Raiders (AFC) 16	Philadelphia Eagles (NFC) 10	22,200
August 5, 2007	Pittsburgh Steelers (AFC) 20	New Orleans Saints (NFC) 7	22,302
August 3, 2008	Washington Redskins (NFC) 30	Indianapolis Colts (AFC) 16	22,216
August 9, 2009	Tennessee Titans (AFC) 21	Buffalo Bills (AFC) 18	22,153
August 8, 2010	Dallas Cowboys (NFC) 16	Cincinnati Bengals (AFC) 7	22,364
2011	No game was played		

*Game called with 5:29 remaining in the fourth quarter because of severe thunder and lightning.
**Game called with 5:49 remaining in the third quarter because of lightning and torrential rain.

1869

Rutgers and Princeton played a college soccer football game, the first ever, November 6. The game used modified London Football Association rules. During the next seven years, rugby gained favor with the major eastern schools over soccer, and modern football began to develop from rugby.

1876

At the Massasoit convention, the first rules for American football were written. Walter Camp, who would become known as the father of American football, first became involved with the game.

1892

In an era in which football was a major attraction of local athletic clubs, an intense competition between two Pittsburgh-area clubs, the Allegheny Athletic Association (AAA) and the Pittsburgh Athletic Club (PAC), led to the making of the first professional football player. Former Yale All-America guard William (Pudge) Heffelfinger was paid $500 by the AAA to play in a game against the PAC, becoming the first person to be paid to play football, November 12. The AAA won the game 4-0 when Heffelfinger picked up a PAC fumble and ran 35 yards for a touchdown.

1893

The Pittsburgh Athletic Club signed one of its players, probably halfback Grant Dibert, to the first known pro football contract, which covered all of the PAC's games for the year.

1895

John Brallier became the first football player to openly turn pro, accepting $10 and expenses to play for the Latrobe YMCA against the Jeannette Athletic Club.

1896

The Allegheny Athletic Association team fielded the first completely professional team for its abbreviated two-game season.

1897

The Latrobe Athletic Association football team went entirely professional, becoming the first team to play a full season with only professionals.

1898

A touchdown was changed from four points to five.

Chris O'Brien formed a neighborhood team, which played under the name the Morgan Athletic Club, on the south side of Chicago. The team later became known as the Normals, then the Racine (for a street in Chicago) Cardinals, the Chicago Cardinals, the St. Louis Cardinals, the Phoenix Cardinals, and, in 1994, the Arizona Cardinals. The team remains the oldest continuing operation in pro football.

1900

William C. Temple took over the team payments for the Duquesne Country and Athletic Club, becoming the first known individual club owner.

1902

Baseball's Philadelphia Athletics, managed by Connie Mack, and the Philadelphia Phillies formed professional football teams, joining the Pittsburgh Stars in the first attempt at a pro football league, named the National Football League. The Athletics won the first night football game ever played, 39-0 over Kanaweola AC at Elmira, New York, November 21.

All three teams claimed the pro championship for the year, but the league president, Dave Berry, named the Stars the champions. Pitcher Rube Waddell was with the Athletics, and pitcher Christy Mathewson a fullback for Pittsburgh.

The first World Series of pro football, actually a five-team tournament, was played among a team made up of players from both the Athletics and the Phillies, but simply named New York; the New York Knickerbockers; the Syracuse AC; the Warlow AC; and the Orange (New Jersey) AC at New York's original Madison Square Garden. New York and Syracuse played the first indoor football game before 3,000, December 28. Syracuse, with Glen (Pop) Warner at guard, won 6-0 and went on to win the tournament.

1903

The Franklin (Pa.) Athletic Club won the second and last World Series of pro football over the Oreos AC of Asbury Park, New Jersey; the Watertown Red and Blacks; and the Orange AC.

Pro football was popularized in Ohio when the Massillon Tigers, a strong amateur team, hired four Pittsburgh pros to play in the season-ending game against Akron. At the same time, pro football declined in the Pittsburgh area, and the emphasis on the pro game moved west from Pennsylvania to Ohio.

1904

A field goal was changed from five points to four.

Ohio had at least seven pro teams, with Massillon winning the Ohio Independent Championship, that is, the pro title. Talk surfaced about forming a state-wide league to end spiraling salaries brought about by constant bidding for players and to write universal rules for the game. The feeble attempt to start the league failed.

Halfback Charles Follis signed a contract with the Shelby (Ohio) AC, making him the first known black pro football player.

1905

The Canton AC, later to become known as the Bulldogs, became a professional team. Massillon again won the Ohio League championship.

1906

The forward pass was legalized. The first authenticated pass completion in a pro game came on October 25, when George (Peggy) Parratt of Massillon threw a completion to Dan (Bullet) Riley in a victory over a combined Benwood-Moundsville team.

Arch-rivals Canton and Massillon, the two best pro teams in America, played twice, with Canton winning the first game but Massillon winning the second and the Ohio League championship. A betting scandal and the financial disaster wrought upon the two clubs by paying huge salaries caused a temporary decline in interest in pro football in the two cities and, somewhat, throughout Ohio.

1909

A field goal dropped from four points to three.

1912

A touchdown was increased from five points to six.

Jack Cusack revived a strong pro team in Canton.

1913

Jim Thorpe, a former football and track star at the Carlisle Indian School (Pa.) and a double gold medal winner at the 1912 Olympics in Stockholm, played for the Pine Village Pros in Indiana.

1915

Massillon again fielded a major team, reviving the old rivalry with Canton. Cusack signed Thorpe to play for Canton for $250 a game.

1916

With Thorpe and former Carlisle teammate Pete Calac starring, Canton went 9-0-1, won the Ohio League championship, and was acclaimed the pro football champion.

1917

Despite an upset by Massillon, Canton again won the Ohio League championship.

1919

Canton again won the Ohio League championship, despite the team having been turned over from Cusack to Ralph Hay. Thorpe and Calac were joined in the backfield by Joe Guyon.

Earl (Curly) Lambeau and George Calhoun organized the Green Bay Packers. Lambeau's employer at the Indian Packing Company provided $500 for equipment and allowed the team to use the company field for practices. The Packers went 10-1.

1920

Pro football was in a state of confusion due to three major problems: dramatically rising salaries; players continually jumping from one team to another following the highest offer; and the use of college players still enrolled in school. A league in which all the members would follow the same rules seemed the answer. An organizational meeting, at which the Akron Pros, Canton Bulldogs, Cleveland Indians, and Dayton Triangles were represented, was held at the Jordan and Hupmobile auto showroom in Canton, Ohio, August 20. This meeting resulted in the formation of the American Professional Football Conference.

A second organizational meeting was held in Canton, September 17. The teams were from four states—Akron, Canton, Cleveland, and Dayton from Ohio; the Hammond Pros and Muncie Flyers from Indiana; the Rochester Jeffersons from New York; and the Rock Island Independents, Decatur Staleys, and Racine Cardinals from Illinois. The name of the league was changed to the American Professional Football Association. Hoping to capitalize on his fame, the members elected Thorpe president; Stanley Cofall of Cleveland was elected vice president. A membership fee of $100 per team was charged to give an appearance of respectability, but no team ever paid it. Scheduling was left up to the teams, and there were wide variations, both in the overall number of games played and in the number played against APFA member teams.

Four other teams—the Buffalo All-Americans, Chicago Tigers, Columbus Panhandles, and Detroit Heralds—joined the league sometime during the year. On September 26, the first game featuring an APFA team was played at Rock Island's Douglas Park. A crowd of 800 watched the Independents defeat the St. Paul Ideals 48-0. A week later, October 3, the first game matching two APFA teams was held. At Triangle Park, Dayton defeated Columbus 14-0, with Lou Partlow of Dayton scoring the first touchdown in a game between Association teams. The same day, Rock Island defeated Muncie 45-0.

By the beginning of December, most of the teams in the APFA had abandoned their hopes for a championship, and some of them, including the Chicago Tigers and the Detroit Heralds, had finished their seasons, disbanded, and

had their franchises canceled by the Association. Four teams—Akron, Buffalo, Canton, and Decatur—still had championship aspirations, but a series of late-season games among them left Akron as the only undefeated team in the Association. At one of these games, Akron sold tackle Bob Nash to Buffalo for $300 and five percent of the gate receipts—the first APFA player deal.

1921

At the league meeting in Akron, April 30, the championship of the 1920 season was awarded to the Akron Pros. The APFA was reorganized, with Joe Carr of the Columbus Panhandles named president and Carl Storck of Dayton secretary-treasurer. Carr moved the Association's headquarters to Columbus, drafted a league constitution and by-laws, gave teams territorial rights, restricted player movements, developed membership criteria for the franchises, and issued standings for the first time, so that the APFA would have a clear champion.

The Association's membership increased to 22 teams, including the Green Bay Packers, who were awarded to John Clair of the Acme Packing Company.

Thorpe moved from Canton to the Cleveland Indians, but he was hurt early in the season and played very little.

A.E. Staley turned the Decatur Staleys over to player-coach George Halas, who moved the team to Cubs Park in Chicago. Staley paid Halas $5,000 to keep the name Staleys for one more year. Halas made halfback Ed (Dutch) Sternaman his partner.

Player-coach Fritz Pollard of the Akron Pros became the first black head coach.

The Staleys claimed the APFA championship with a 9-1-1 record, as did Buffalo at 9-1-2. Carr ruled in favor of the Staleys, giving Halas his first championship.

1922

After admitting the use of players who had college eligibility remaining during the 1921 season, Clair and the Green Bay management withdrew from the APFA, January 28. Curly Lambeau promised to obey league rules and then used $50 of his own money to buy back the franchise. Bad weather and low attendance plagued the Packers, and Lambeau went broke, but local merchants arranged a $2,500 loan for the club. A public nonprofit corporation was set up to operate the team, with Lambeau as head coach and manager.

The American Professional Football Association changed its name to the National Football League, June 24. The Chicago Staleys became the Chicago Bears.

The NFL fielded 18 teams, including the new Oorang Indians of Marion, Ohio, an all-Indian team featuring Thorpe, Joe Guyon, and Pete Calac, and sponsored by the Oorang dog kennels.

Canton, led by player-coach Guy Chamberlin and tackles Link Lyman and Wilbur (Pete) Henry, emerged as the league's first true powerhouse, going 10-0-2.

1923

For the first time, all of the franchises considered to be part of the NFL fielded teams. Thorpe played his second and final season for the Oorang Indians. Against the Bears, Thorpe fumbled, and Halas picked up the ball and returned it 98 yards for a touchdown, a record that would last until 1972.

Canton had its second consecutive undefeated season, going 11-0-1 for the NFL title.

1924

The league had 18 franchises, including new ones in Kansas City, Kenosha, and Frankford, a section of Philadelphia. League champion Canton, successful on the field but not at the box office, was purchased by the owner of the Cleveland franchise, who kept the Canton franchise inactive, while using the best players for his Cleveland team, which he renamed the Bulldogs. Cleveland won the title with a 7-1-1 record.

1925

Five new franchises were admitted to the NFL—the New York Giants, who were award-

ed to Tim Mara and Billy Gibson for $500; the Detroit Panthers, featuring Jimmy Conzelman as owner, coach, and tailback; the Providence Steam Roller; a new Canton Bulldogs team; and the Pottsville Maroons, who had been perhaps the most successful independent pro team. The NFL established its first player limit, at 16 players.

Late in the season, the NFL made its greatest coup in gaining national recognition. Shortly after the University of Illinois season ended in November, All-America halfback Harold (Red) Grange signed a contract to play with the Chicago Bears. On Thanksgiving Day, a crowd of 36,000—the largest in pro football history—watched Grange and the Bears play the Chicago Cardinals to a scoreless tie at Wrigley Field. At the beginning of December, the Bears left on a barnstorming tour that saw them play eight games in 12 days, in St. Louis, Philadelphia, New York City, Washington, Boston, Pittsburgh, Detroit, and Chicago. A crowd of 73,000 watched the game against the Giants at the Polo Grounds, helping assure the future of the troubled NFL franchise in New York. The Bears then played nine more games in the South and West, including a game in Los Angeles, in which 75,000 fans watched them defeat the Los Angeles Tigers in the Los Angeles Memorial Coliseum.

Pottsville and the Chicago Cardinals were the top contenders for the league title, with Pottsville winning a late-season meeting 21-7. Pottsville scheduled a game against a team of former Notre Dame players for Shibe Park in Philadelphia. Frankford lodged a protest not only because the game was in Frankford's protected territory, but because it was being played the same day as a Yellow Jackets home game. Carr gave three different notices forbidding Pottsville to play the game, but Pottsville played anyway, December 12. That day, Carr fined the club, suspended it from all rights and privileges (including the right to play for the NFL championship), and returned its franchise to the league. The Cardinals, who ended the season with the best record in the league, were named the 1925 champions.

1926

Grange's manager, C.C. Pyle, told the Bears that Grange wouldn't play for them unless he was paid a five-figure salary and given one-third ownership of the team. The Bears refused. Pyle leased Yankee Stadium in New York City, then petitioned for an NFL franchise. After he was refused, he started the first American Football League. It lasted one season and included Grange's New York Yankees and eight other teams. The AFL champion Philadelphia Quakers played a December game against the New York Giants, seventh in the NFL, and the Giants won 31-0. At the end of the season, the AFL folded.

Halas pushed through a rule that prohibited any team from signing a player whose college class had not graduated.

The NFL grew to 22 teams, including the Duluth Eskimos, who signed All-America fullback Ernie Nevers of Stanford, giving the league a gate attraction to rival Grange. The 15-member Eskimos, dubbed the Iron Men of the North, played 29 exhibition and league games, 28 on the road, and Nevers played in all but 29 minutes of them.

Frankford edged the Bears for the championship, despite Halas having obtained John (Paddy) Driscoll from the Cardinals. On December 4, the Yellow Jackets scored in the final two minutes to defeat the Bears 7-6 and move ahead of them in the standings.

1927

At a special meeting in Cleveland, April 23, Carr decided to secure the NFL's future by eliminating the financially weaker teams and consolidating the quality players onto a limited number of more successful teams. The new-look NFL dropped to 12 teams, and the center of gravity of the league left the Midwest, where the NFL had started, and began to emerge in the large cities of the East. One of the new teams was Grange's New

York Yankees, but Grange suffered a knee injury and the Yankees finished in the middle of the pack. The NFL championship was won by the cross-town rival New York Giants, who posted 10 shutouts in 13 games.

1928

Grange and Nevers both retired from pro football, and Duluth disbanded, as the NFL was reduced to only 10 teams. The Providence Steam Roller of Jimmy Conzelman and Pearce Johnson won the championship, playing in the Cycledrome, a 10,000-seat oval that had been built for bicycle races.

1929

Chris O'Brien sold the Chicago Cardinals to David Jones, July 27.

The NFL added a fourth official, the field judge, July 28.

Grange and Nevers returned to the NFL. Nevers scored six rushing touchdowns and four extra points as the Cardinals beat Grange's Bears 40-6, November 28. The 40 points set a record that remains the NFL's oldest.

Providence became the first NFL team to host a game at night under floodlights, against the Cardinals, November 6.

The Packers added back Johnny Blood (McNally), tackle Cal Hubbard, and guard Mike Michalske, and won their first NFL championship, edging the Giants, who featured quarterback Benny Friedman.

1930

Dayton, the last of the NFL's original franchises, was purchased by William B. Dwyer and John C. Depler, moved to Brooklyn, and renamed the Dodgers. The Portsmouth, Ohio, Spartans entered the league.

The Packers edged the Giants for the title, but the most improved team was the Bears. Halas retired as a player and replaced himself as coach of the Bears with Ralph Jones, who refined the T-formation by introducing wide ends and a halfback in motion. Jones also introduced rookie All-America fullback-tackle Bronko Nagurski.

The Giants defeated a team of former Notre Dame players coached by Knute Rockne 22-0 before 55,000 at the Polo Grounds, December 14. The proceeds went to the New York Unemployment Fund to help those suffering because of the Great Depression, and the easy victory helped give the NFL credibility with the press and the public.

1931

The NFL decreased to 10 teams, and halfway through the season the Frankford franchise folded. Carr fined the Bears, Packers, and Portsmouth $1,000 each for using players whose college classes had not graduated.

The Packers won an unprecedented third consecutive title, beating out the Spartans, who were led by rookie backs Earl (Dutch) Clark and Glenn Presnell.

1932

George Preston Marshall, Vincent Bendix, Jay O'Brien, and M. Dorland Doyle were awarded a franchise for Boston, July 9. Despite the presence of two rookies—halfback Cliff Battles and tackle Glen (Turk) Edwards—the new team, named the Braves, lost money and Marshall was left as the sole owner at the end of the year.

NFL membership dropped to eight teams, the lowest in history. Official statistics were kept for the first time. The Bears and the Spartans finished the season in the first-ever tie for first place. After the season finale, the league office arranged for an additional regular-season game to determine the league champion. The game was moved indoors to Chicago Stadium because of bitter cold and heavy snow. The arena allowed only an 80-yard field that came right to the walls. The goal posts were moved from the end lines to the goal lines and, for safety, inbounds lines or hashmarks where the ball would be put in play were drawn 10 yards from the walls that butted against the sidelines. The Bears won 9-0, December 18, scoring the winning touchdown on a two-yard pass from Nagurski to Grange. The Spartans claimed Nagurski's pass was thrown

from less than five yards behind the line of scrimmage, violating the existing passing rule, but the play stood.

1933

The NFL, which long had followed the rules of college football, made a number of significant changes from the college game for the first time and began to develop rules serving its needs and the style of play it preferred. The innovations from the 1932 championship game—inbounds line or hashmarks and goal posts on the goal lines—were adopted. Also the forward pass was legalized from anywhere behind the line of scrimmage, February 25.

Marshall and Halas pushed through a proposal that divided the NFL into two divisions, with the winners to meet in an annual championship game, July 8.

Three new franchises joined the league—the Pittsburgh Pirates of Art Rooney, the Philadelphia Eagles of Bert Bell and Lud Wray, and the Cincinnati Reds. The Staten Island Stapletons suspended operations for a year, but never returned to the league.

Halas bought out Sternaman, became sole owner of the Bears, and reinstated himself as head coach. Marshall changed the name of the Boston Braves to the Redskins. David Jones sold the Chicago Cardinals to Charles W. Bidwill.

In the first NFL Championship Game scheduled before the season, the Western Division champion Bears defeated the Eastern Division champion Giants 23-21 at Wrigley Field, December 17.

1934

G.A. (Dick) Richards purchased the Portsmouth Spartans, moved them to Detroit, and renamed them the Lions.

Professional football gained new prestige when the Bears were matched against the best college football players in the first Chicago College All-Star Game, August 31. The game ended in a scoreless tie before 79,432 at Soldier Field.

The Cincinnati Reds lost their first eight games, then were suspended from the league for defaulting on payments. The St. Louis Gunners, an independent team, joined the NFL by buying the Cincinnati franchise and went 1-2 the last three weeks.

Rookie Beattie Feathers of the Bears became the NFL's first 1,000-yard rusher, gaining 1,004 on 101 carries. The Thanksgiving Day game between the Bears and the Lions became the first NFL game broadcast nationally, with Graham McNamee announcer for NBC radio.

In the championship game, on an extremely cold and icy day at the Polo Grounds, the Giants trailed the Bears 13-3 in the third quarter before changing to basketball shoes for better footing. The Giants won 30-13 in what has come to be known as the Sneakers Game, December 9.

The player waiver rule was adopted, December 10.

1935
The NFL adopted Bert Bell's proposal to hold an annual draft of college players, to begin in 1936, with teams selecting in an inverse order of finish, May 19. The inbounds line or hashmarks were moved nearer the center of the field, 15 yards from the sidelines.

All-America end Don Hutson of Alabama joined Green Bay. The Lions defeated the Giants 26-7 in the NFL Championship Game, December 15.

1936
There were no franchise transactions for the first year since the formation of the NFL. It also was the first year in which all member teams played the same number of games.

The Eagles made University of Chicago halfback and Heisman Trophy winner Jay Berwanger the first player ever selected in the NFL draft, February 8. The Eagles traded his rights to the Bears, but Berwanger never played pro football. The first player selected to actually sign was the number-two pick, Riley Smith of Alabama, who was selected by Boston.

A rival league was formed, and it became the second to call itself the American Football League. The Boston Shamrocks were its champions.

Because of poor atten-

dance, Marshall, the owner of the host team, moved the Championship Game from Boston to the Polo Grounds in New York. Green Bay defeated the Redskins 21-6, December 13.

1937
Homer Marshman was granted a Cleveland franchise, named the Rams, February 12. Marshall moved the Redskins to Washington, D.C., February 13. The Redskins signed TCU All-America tailback Sammy Baugh, who led them to a 28-21 victory over the Bears in the NFL Championship Game, December 12.

The Los Angeles Bulldogs had an 8-0 record to win the AFL title, but then the 2-year-old league folded.

1938
At the suggestion of Halas, Hugh (Shorty) Ray became a technical advisor on rules and officiating to the NFL. A new rule called for a 15-yard penalty for roughing the passer.

Rookie Byron (Whizzer) White of the Pittsburgh Pirates led the NFL in rushing. The Giants defeated the Packers 23-17 for the NFL title, December 11.

Marshall, *Los Angeles Times* sports editor Bill Henry, and promoter Tom Gallery established the Pro Bowl game between the NFL champion and a team of pro all-stars.

1939
The New York Giants defeated the Pro All-Stars 13-10 in the first Pro Bowl, at Wrigley Field, Los Angeles, January 15.

Carr, NFL president since 1921, died in Columbus, May 20. Carl Storck was named acting president, May 25.

An NFL game was televised for the first time when NBC broadcast the Brooklyn Dodgers-Philadelphia Eagles game from Ebbets Field to the approximately 1,000 sets then in New York, October 22.

Green Bay defeated New York 27-0 in the NFL Championship Game, December 10 at Milwaukee. NFL attendance exceeded 1 million in a season for the first time, reaching 1,071,200.

1940
A six-team rival league, the third to call itself the American Football League, was formed, and the Columbus Bullies won its championship.

Halas' Bears, with additional coaching by Clark Shaughnessy of Stanford, defeated the Redskins 73-0 in the NFL Championship Game, December 8. The game, which was the most decisive victory in NFL history, popularized the Bears' T-formation with a man-in-motion. It was the first championship carried on network radio, broadcast by Red Barber to 120 stations of the Mutual Broadcasting System, which paid $2,500 for the rights.

Art Rooney sold the Pittsburgh franchise to Alexis Thompson, December 9, then bought part interest in the Philadelphia Eagles.

Bell and Rooney traded the Eagles to Thompson for the Pirates, then re-named their new team the Steelers.

1941
Elmer Layden was named the first Commissioner of the NFL, March 1; Storck, the acting president, resigned, April 5. NFL headquarters were moved to Chicago.

Homer Marshman sold the Rams to Daniel F. Reeves and Fred Levy, Jr.

The league by-laws were revised to provide for playoffs in case there were ties in division races, and sudden-death overtimes in case a playoff game was tied after four quarters. An official *NFL Record Manual* was published for the first time.

Columbus again won the championship of the AFL, but the two-year-old league then folded.

The Bears and the Packers finished in a tie for the Western Division championship, setting up the first divisional playoff game in league history. The Bears won 33-14, then defeated the Giants 37-9 for the NFL championship, December 21.

1942
Players departing for service in World War II depleted the rosters of NFL teams. Halas left the Bears in midseason to join the Navy, and Luke John-

sos and Heartley (Hunk) Anderson served as co-coaches as the Bears went 11-0 in the regular season. The Redskins defeated the Bears 14-6 in the NFL Championship Game, December 13.

1943
The Cleveland Rams, with co-owners Reeves and Levy in the service, were granted permission to suspend operations for one season, April 6. Levy transferred his stock in the team to Reeves, April 16.

The NFL adopted free substitution, April 7. The league also made the wearing of helmets mandatory and approved a 10-game schedule for all teams.

Philadelphia and Pittsburgh were granted permission to merge for one season, June 19. The team, known as Phil-Pitt (and called the Steagles by fans), divided home games between the two cities, and Earle (Greasy) Neale of Philadelphia and Walt Kiesling of Pittsburgh served as co-coaches. The merger automatically dissolved the last day of the season, December 5.

Ted Collins was granted a franchise for Boston, to become active in 1944.

Sammy Baugh led the league in passing, punting, and interceptions. He led the Redskins to a tie with the Giants for the Eastern Division title, and then to a 28-0 victory in a divisional playoff game. The Bears beat the Redskins 41-21 in the NFL Championship Game, December 26.

1944
Collins, who had wanted a franchise in Yankee Stadium in New York, named his new team in Boston the Yanks. Cleveland resumed operations. The Brooklyn Dodgers changed their name to the Tigers.

Coaching from the bench was legalized, April 20.

The Cardinals and the Steelers were granted permission to merge for one year under the name Card-Pitt, April 21. Phil Handler of the Cardinals and Walt Kiesling of the Steelers served as co-coaches. The merger automatically dissolved the last day of the season, December 3.

In the NFL Championship Game, Green Bay defeated the New York Giants 14-7, December 17.

1945

The inbounds lines or hashmarks were moved from 15 yards away from the sidelines to nearer the center of the field—20 yards from the sidelines.

Brooklyn and Boston merged into a team that played home games in both cities and was known simply as The Yanks. The team was coached by former Boston head coach Herb Kopf. In December, the Brooklyn franchise withdrew from the NFL to join the new All-America Football Conference; all the players on its active and reserve lists were assigned to The Yanks, who once again became the Boston Yanks.

Halas rejoined the Bears late in the season after service with the U.S. Navy. Although Halas took over much of the coaching duties, Anderson and Johnsos remained the coaches of record throughout the season.

Steve Van Buren of Philadelphia led the NFL in rushing, kickoff returns, and scoring.

After the Japanese surrendered ending World War II, a count showed that the NFL service roster, limited to men who had played in league games, totaled 638, 21 of whom had died in action.

Rookie quarterback Bob Waterfield led Cleveland to a 15-14 victory over Washington in the NFL Championship Game, December 16.

1946

The contract of Commissioner Layden was not renewed, and Bert Bell, the co-owner of the Steelers, replaced him, January 11. Bell moved the league headquarters from Chicago to the Philadelphia suburb of Bala-Cynwyd.

Free substitution was withdrawn and substitutions were limited to no more than three men at a time. Forward passes were made automatically incomplete upon striking the goal posts, January 11.

The NFL took on a truly national appearance for the first time when Reeves was granted permission by the league to move his NFL champion Rams to Los Angeles.

Halfback Kenny Washington (March 21) and end Woody Strode (May 7) signed with the Los Angeles Rams to become the first African-Americans to play in the NFL in the modern era. Guard Bill Willis (August 6) and running back Marion Motley (August 9) joined the AAFC with the Cleveland Browns.

The rival All-America Football Conference began play with eight teams. The Cleveland Browns, coached by Paul Brown, won the AAFC's first championship, defeating the New York Yankees 14-9.

Bill Dudley of the Steelers led the NFL in rushing, interceptions, and punt returns, and won the league's most valuable player award.

Backs Frank Filchock and Merle Hapes of the Giants were questioned about an attempt by a New York man to fix the championship game with the Bears. Bell suspended Hapes but allowed Filchock to play; he played well, but Chicago won 24-14, December 15.

1947

The NFL added a fifth official, the back judge.

A bonus choice was made for the first time in the NFL draft. One team each year would select the special choice before the first round began. The Chicago Bears won a lottery and the rights to the first choice and drafted back Bob Fenimore of Oklahoma A&M.

The Cleveland Browns again won the AAFC title, defeating the New York Yankees 14-3.

Charles Bidwill, Sr., owner of the Cardinals, died April 19, but his wife and sons retained ownership of the team. On December 28, the Cardinals won the NFL Championship Game 28-21 over the Philadelphia Eagles, who had beaten Pittsburgh 21-0 in a playoff.

1948

Plastic helmets were prohibited. A flexible artificial tee was permitted at the kickoff. Officials other than the referee were equipped with whistles, not horns, January 14.

Fred Mandel sold the Detroit Lions to a syndicate headed by D. Lyle Fife, January 15.

Halfback Fred Gehrke of the Los Angeles Rams painted horns on the Rams' helmets, the first modern helmet emblems in pro football.

The Cleveland Browns won their third straight championship in the AAFC, going 14-0 and then defeating the Buffalo Bills 49-7.

In a blizzard, the Eagles defeated the Cardinals 7-0 in the NFL Championship Game, December 19.

1949

Alexis Thompson sold the champion Eagles to a syndicate headed by James P. Clark, January 15. The Boston Yanks became the New York Bulldogs, sharing the Polo Grounds with the Giants.

Free substitution was adopted for one year, January 20.

The NFL had two 1,000-yard rushers in the same season for the first time—Steve Van Buren of Philadelphia and Tony Canadeo of Green Bay.

The AAFC played its season with a one-division, seven-team format. On December 9, Bell announced a merger agreement in which three AAFC franchises—Cleveland, San Francisco, and Baltimore—would join the NFL in 1950. The Browns won their fourth consecutive AAFC title, defeating the 49ers 21-7, December 11.

In a heavy rain, the Eagles defeated the Rams 14-0 in the NFL Championship Game, December 18.

1950

Unlimited free substitution was restored, opening the way for the era of two platoons and specialization in pro football, January 20.

Curly Lambeau, founder of the franchise and Green Bay's head coach since 1921, resigned under fire, February 1.

The name National Football League was restored after about three months as the National-American Football League. The American and National conferences were created to replace the Eastern and Western divisions, March 3.

The New York Bulldogs became the Yanks and divided the players of the former AAFC Yankees with the Giants. A special allocation draft was held in which the 13 teams drafted the remaining AAFC players, with special consideration for Baltimore, which received 15 choices compared to 10 for other teams.

The Los Angeles Rams became the first NFL team to have all of its games—both home and away—televised. The Washington Redskins followed the Rams in arranging to televise their games; other teams made deals to put selected games on television.

In the first game of the season, former AAFC champion Cleveland defeated NFL champion Philadelphia 35-10. For the first time, deadlocks occurred in both conferences and playoffs were necessary. The Browns defeated the Giants in the American and the Rams defeated the Bears in the National. Cleveland defeated Los Angeles 30-28 in the NFL Championship Game, December 24.

1951

The Pro Bowl game, dormant since 1942, was revived under a new format matching the all-stars of each conference at the Los Angeles Memorial Coliseum. The American Conference defeated the National Conference 28-27, January 14.

Abraham Watner returned the Baltimore franchise and its player contracts back to the NFL for $50,000. Baltimore's former players were made available for drafting at the same time as college players, January 18.

A rule was passed that no tackle, guard, or center would be eligible to catch a forward pass, January 18.

The Rams reversed their television policy and televised only road games.

The NFL Championship Game was televised coast-to-coast for the first time, December 23. The DuMont Network paid $75,000 for the rights to the game, in which the Rams defeated the Browns 24-17.

1952

Ted Collins sold the New York Yanks' franchise back to the NFL, January 19. A new franchise was awarded to a group in Dallas after it purchased the assets of the Yanks, January 24. The new Texans went 1-11, with the owners turning the franchise back to the league in midseason. For the last five games of the season, the commissioner's office operated the Texans as a road team, using Hershey, Pennsylvania, as a home base. At the end of the season the franchise was canceled, the last time an NFL team failed.

The Pittsburgh Steelers abandoned the Single-Wing for the T-formation, the last pro team to do so.

The Detroit Lions won their first NFL championship in 17 years, defeating the Browns 17-7 in the title game, December 28.

1953
A Baltimore group headed by Carroll Rosenbloom was granted a franchise and was awarded the holdings of the defunct Dallas organization, January 23. The team, named the Colts, put together the largest trade in league history, acquiring 10 players from Cleveland in exchange for five.

The names of the American and National conferences were changed to the Eastern and Western conferences, January 24.

Jim Thorpe died, March 28.

Mickey McBride, founder of the Cleveland Browns, sold the franchise to a syndicate headed by Dave R. Jones, June 10.

The NFL policy of blacking out home games was upheld by Judge Allan K. Grim of the U.S. District Court in Philadelphia, November 12.

The Lions again defeated the Browns in the NFL Championship Game, winning 17-16, December 27.

1954
The Canadian Football League began a series of raids on NFL teams, signing quarterback Eddie LeBaron and defensive end Gene Brito of Washington and defensive tackle Arnie Weinmeister of the Giants, among others.

Fullback Joe Perry of the 49ers became the first player in league history to gain 1,000 yards rushing in consecutive seasons.

Cleveland defeated Detroit 56-10 in the NFL Championship Game, December 26.

1955
The sudden-death overtime rule was used for the first time in a preseason game between the Rams and Giants at Portland, Oregon, August 28. The Rams won 23-17 three minutes into overtime.

A rule change declared the ball dead immediately if the ball carrier touched the ground with any part of his body except his hands or feet while in the grasp of an opponent.

The Baltimore Colts made an 80-cent phone call to Johnny Unitas and signed him as a free agent. Another quarterback, Otto Graham, played his last game as the Browns defeated the Rams 38-14 in the NFL Championship Game, December 26. Graham had quarterbacked the Browns to 10 championship-game appearances in 10 years.

NBC replaced DuMont as the network for the title game, paying a rights fee of $100,000.

1956
The NFL Players Association was founded.

Grabbing an opponent's facemask (other than the ball carrier) was made illegal. Using radio receivers to communicate with players on the field was prohibited. A natural leather ball with white end stripes replaced the white ball with black stripes for night games.

The Giants moved from the Polo Grounds to Yankee Stadium.

Halas retired as coach of the Bears, and was replaced by Paddy Driscoll.

CBS became the first network to broadcast some NFL regular-season games to selected television markets across the nation.

The Giants routed the Bears 47-7 in the NFL Championship Game, December 30.

1957
Pete Rozelle was named general manager of the Rams. Anthony J. Morabito, founder and co-owner of the 49ers, died of a heart attack during a game against the Bears at Kezar Stadium, October 28.

An NFL-record crowd of 102,368 saw the 49ers-Rams game at the Los Angeles Memorial Coliseum, November 10.

The Lions came from 20 points down to post a 31-27 playoff victory over the 49ers, December 22. Detroit defeated Cleveland 59-14 in the NFL Championship Game, December 29.

1958
The bonus selection in the draft was eliminated, January 29. The last selection was quarterback King Hill of Rice by the Chicago Cardinals.

Halas reinstated himself as coach of the Bears.

Jim Brown of Cleveland gained an NFL-record 1,527 yards rushing. In a divisional playoff game, the Giants held Brown to eight yards and defeated Cleveland 10-0.

Baltimore, coached by Weeb Ewbank, defeated the Giants 23-17 in the first sudden-death overtime in an NFL Championship Game, December 28. The game ended when Colts fullback Alan Ameche scored on a one-yard touchdown run after 8:15 of overtime.

1959
Vince Lombardi was named head coach of the Green Bay Packers, January 28. Tim Mara, the co-founder of the Giants, died, February 17.

Lamar Hunt of Dallas announced his intentions to form a second pro football league. The first meeting was held in Chicago, August 14, and consisted of Hunt representing Dallas; Bob Howsam, Denver; K.S. (Bud) Adams, Houston; Barron Hilton, Los Angeles; Max Winter and Bill Boyer, Minneapolis; and Harry Wismer, New York City. They made plans to begin play in 1960.

The new league was named the American Football League, August 22. Buffalo, owned by Ralph Wilson, became the seventh franchise, October 28. Boston, owned by William H. Sullivan, became the eighth team, November 22. The first AFL draft, lasting 33 rounds, was held, November 22. Joe Foss was named AFL Commissioner, November 30. An additional draft of 20 rounds

was held by the AFL, December 2.

NFL Commissioner Bert Bell died of a heart attack suffered at Franklin Field, Philadelphia, during the last two minutes of a game between the Eagles and the Steelers, October 11. Treasurer Austin Gunsel was named president in the office of the commissioner, October 14.

The Colts again defeated the Giants in the NFL Championship Game, 31-16, December 27.

1960
Pete Rozelle was elected NFL Commissioner as a compromise choice on the twenty-third ballot, January 26. Rozelle moved the league offices to New York City.

Hunt was elected AFL president for 1960, January 26. Minneapolis withdrew from the AFL, January 27, and the same ownership was given an NFL franchise for Minnesota (to start in 1961), January 28. Dallas received an NFL franchise for 1960, January 28. Oakland received an AFL franchise, January 30.

The AFL adopted the two-point option on points after touchdown, January 28. A no-tampering verbal pact, relative to players' contracts, was agreed to between the NFL and AFL, February 9.

The NFL owners voted to allow the transfer of the Chicago Cardinals to St. Louis, March 13.

The AFL signed a five-year television contract with ABC, June 9.

The Boston Patriots defeated the Buffalo Bills 28-7 before 16,000 at Buffalo in the first AFL preseason game, July 30. The Denver Broncos defeated the Patriots 13-10 before 21,597 at Boston in the first AFL regular-season game, September 9.

Philadelphia defeated Green Bay 17-13 in the NFL Championship Game, December 26.

1961
The Houston Oilers defeated the Los Angeles Chargers 24-16 before 32,183 in the first AFL Championship Game, January 1.

Detroit defeated Cleveland 17-16 in the first Playoff Bowl, or Bert Bell Benefit Bowl, between second-place teams in each conference in Miami, January 7.

End Willard Dewveall of the Bears played out his option and joined the Oilers, becoming the first player to play out his contract and jump from the NFL to the AFL, January 14.

Ed McGah, Wayne Valley, and Robert Osborne bought out their partners in the ownership of the Raiders, January 17. The Chargers were transferred to San Diego, February 10. Dave R. Jones sold the Browns to a group headed by Arthur B. Modell, March 22. The Howsam brothers sold the Broncos to a group headed by Calvin Kunz and Gerry Phipps, May 26.

NBC was awarded a two-year contract for radio and television rights to the NFL Championship Game for $615,000 annually, $300,000 of which was to go directly into the NFL Player Benefit Plan, April 5.

Canton, Ohio, where the league that became the NFL was formed in 1920, was chosen as the site of the Pro Football Hall of Fame, April 27.

A bill legalizing single-network television contracts by professional sports leagues was introduced in Congress by Representative Emanuel Celler. It passed the House and Senate and was signed into law by President John F. Kennedy, September 30.

Houston defeated San Diego 10-3 for the AFL championship, December 24. Green Bay won its first NFL championship since 1944, defeating the New York Giants 37-0, December 31.

1962
The Western Division defeated the Eastern Division 47-27 in the first AFL All-Star Game, played before 20,973 in San Diego, January 7.

Both leagues prohibited grabbing any player's facemask. The AFL voted to make the scoreboard clock the official timer of the game.

The NFL entered into a single-network agreement with CBS for telecasting all regular-season games for $4.65 million annually, January 10.

Judge Roszel Thompson of the U.S. District Court in Baltimore ruled against the AFL in

its antitrust suit against the NFL, May 21. The AFL had charged the NFL with monopoly and conspiracy in areas of expansion, television, and player signings. The case lasted two and a half years, the trial two months.

McGah and Valley acquired controlling interest in the Raiders, May 24. The AFL assumed financial responsibility for the New York Titans, November 8. With Commissioner Rozelle as referee, Daniel F. Reeves regained the ownership of the Rams, outbidding his partners in sealed-envelope bidding for the team, November 27.

The Dallas Texans defeated the Oilers 20-17 for the AFL championship at Houston after 17 minutes, 54 seconds of overtime on a 25-yard field goal by Tommy Brooker. The game lasted a then record 77 minutes, 54 seconds, December 23.

Judge Edward Weinfeld of the U.S. District Court in New York City upheld the legality of the NFL's television blackout within a 75-mile radius of home games and denied an injunction that would have forced the championship game between the Giants and the Packers to be televised in the New York City area, December 28. The Packers beat the Giants 16-7 for the NFL title, December 30.

1963
Don Shula, who went on to become the winningest head coach in NFL history, replaced Weeb Ewbank as head coach of the Colts, January 8.

Paul Brown, head coach of the Browns since their inception, was fired on January 9 and replaced the following day by Blanton Collier.

The Dallas Texans transferred to Kansas City, becoming the Chiefs, February 8. The New York Titans were sold to a five-man syndicate headed by David (Sonny) Werblin, March 28. Weeb Ewbank became the Titans' new head coach and the team's name was changed to the Jets, April 15. They began play in the Polo Grounds.

NFL Properties, Inc., was founded to serve as the licensing arm of the NFL.

Rozelle indefinitely sus-

pended Green Bay halfback Paul Hornung and Detroit defensive tackle Alex Karras for placing bets on their own teams and on other NFL games; he also fined five other Detroit players $2,000 each for betting on one game in which they did not participate, and the Detroit Lions Football Company $2,000 on each of two counts for failure to report information promptly and for lack of sideline supervision, April 17.

The AFL allowed the Jets and Raiders to select players from other franchises in hopes of giving the league more competitive balance, May 11.

NBC was awarded exclusive network broadcasting rights for the 1963 NFL Championship Game for $926,000, May 23.

The Pro Football Hall of Fame was dedicated at Canton, Ohio, September 7.

The U.S. Fourth Circuit Court of Appeals reaffirmed the lower court's finding for the NFL in the $10-million suit brought by the AFL, ending three and a half years of litigation, November 21.

Jim Brown of Cleveland rushed for an NFL single-season record 1,863 yards.

Boston defeated Buffalo 26-8 in the first divisional playoff game in AFL history, December 28.

The Bears defeated the Giants 14-10 in the NFL Championship Game, a record sixth and last title for Halas in his thirty-sixth season as the Bears' coach, December 29.

1964
The Chargers defeated the Patriots 51-10 in the AFL Championship Game, January 5.

William Clay Ford, the Lions' president since 1961, purchased the team, January 10. A group representing the late James P. Clark sold the Eagles to a group headed by Jerry Wolman, January 21. Carroll Rosenbloom, the majority owner of the Colts since 1953, acquired complete ownership of the team, January 23.

The AFL signed a five-year, $36-million television contract with NBC to begin with the 1965 season, January 29.

Hornung and Karras were reinstated by Rozelle, March

16.

CBS submitted the winning bid of $14.1 million per year for the NFL regular-season television rights for 1964 and 1965, January 24. CBS acquired the rights to the championship games for 1964 and 1965 for $1.8 million per game, April 17.

Pete Gogolak of Cornell signed a contract with Buffalo, becoming the first soccer-style kicker in pro football.

Buffalo defeated San Diego 20-7 in the AFL Championship Game, December 26. Cleveland defeated Baltimore 27-0 in the NFL Championship Game, December 27.

1965
The NFL teams pledged not to sign college seniors until completion of all their games, including bowl games, and empowered the Commissioner to discipline the clubs up to as much as the loss of an entire draft list for a violation of the pledge, February 15.

The NFL added a sixth official, the line judge, February 19. The color of the officials' penalty flags was changed from white to bright gold, April 5.

Commissioner Rozelle negotiated an agreement on behalf of the NFL clubs to purchase Ed Sabol's Blair Motion Pictures, which was renamed NFL Films, April.

Atlanta was awarded an NFL franchise for 1966, with Rankin Smith, Sr., as owner, June 30. Miami was awarded an AFL franchise for 1966, with Joe Robbie and Danny Thomas as owners, August 16.

Field Judge Burl Toler became the first black official in NFL history, September 19.

According to a Harris survey, sports fans chose professional football (41 percent) as their favorite sport, overtaking baseball (38 percent) for the first time, October.

Green Bay defeated Baltimore 13-10 in sudden-death overtime in a Western Conference playoff game. Don Chandler kicked a 25-yard field goal for the Packers after 13 minutes, 39 seconds of overtime, December 26. The Packers then defeated the Browns 23-12 in the NFL Championship Game, January 2.

In the AFL Championship Game, the Bills defeated the

Chargers, 23-0, December 26.

CBS acquired the rights to the NFL regular-season games in 1966 and 1967, with an option for 1968, for $18.8 million per year, December 29.

1966

The AFL-NFL war reached its peak, as the leagues spent a combined $7 million to sign their 1966 draft choices. The NFL signed 75 percent of its 232 draftees, the AFL 46 percent of its 181. Of the 111 common draft choices, 79 signed with the NFL, 28 with the AFL, and 4 went unsigned.

Buddy Young became the first African-American to work in the league office when Commissioner Rozelle named him director of player relations, February 1.

The rights to the 1966 and 1967 NFL Championship Games were sold to CBS for $2 million per game, February 14.

Foss resigned as AFL Commissioner, April 7. Al Davis, the head coach and general manager of the Raiders, was named to replace him, April 8.

Goal posts offset from the goal line, painted bright yellow, and with uprights 20 feet above the cross-bar were made standard in the NFL, May 16.

A series of secret meetings regarding a possible AFL-NFL merger were held in the spring between Hunt of Kansas City and Tex Schramm of Dallas. Rozelle announced the merger, June 8. Under the agreement, the two leagues would combine to form an expanded league with 24 teams, to be increased to 26 in 1968 and to 28 by 1970 or soon thereafter. All existing franchises would be retained, and no franchises would be transferred outside their metropolitan areas. While maintaining separate schedules through 1969, the leagues agreed to play an annual AFL-NFL World Championship Game beginning in January, 1967, and to hold a combined draft, also beginning in 1967. Preseason games would be held between teams of each league starting in 1967. Official regular-season play would start in 1970 when the two leagues would officially merge to form one league with two conferences.

Rozelle was named Commissioner of the expanded league setup.

Davis rejoined the Raiders, and Milt Woodard was named president of the AFL, July 25.

The St. Louis Cardinals moved into newly constructed Busch Memorial Stadium.

Barron Hilton sold the Chargers to a group headed by Eugene Klein and Sam Schulman, August 25.

Congress approved the AFL-NFL merger, passing legislation exempting the agreement itself from antitrust action, October 21.

New Orleans was awarded an NFL franchise to begin play in 1967, November 1. John Mecom, Jr., of Houston was designated majority stockholder and president of the franchise, December 15.

The NFL was realigned for the 1967-69 seasons into the Capitol and Century Divisions in the Eastern Conference and the Central and Coastal Divisions in the Western Conference, December 2. New Orleans and the New York Giants agreed to switch divisions in 1968 and to return to the 1967 alignment in 1969.

The rights to the Super Bowl for four years were sold to CBS and NBC for $9.5 million, December 13.

1967

Green Bay earned the right to represent the NFL in the first AFL-NFL World Championship Game by defeating Dallas 34-27, January 1. The same day, Kansas City defeated Buffalo 31-7 to represent the AFL. The Packers defeated the Chiefs 35-10 before 61,946 fans at the Los Angeles Memorial Coliseum in the first game between AFL and NFL teams, January 15. The winning players' share for the Packers was $15,000 each, and the losing players' share for the Chiefs was $7,500 each. The game was televised by both CBS and NBC.

The "sling-shot" goal post and a six-foot-wide border around the field were made standard in the NFL, February 22.

Baltimore made Bubba Smith, a Michigan State defensive lineman, the first choice in the first combined AFL-NFL draft, March 14.

The AFL awarded a franchise to begin play in 1968 to Cincinnati, May 23. A group with Paul Brown as part owner, general manager, and head coach, was awarded the Cincinnati franchise, September 27.

Arthur B. Modell, the president of the Cleveland Browns, was elected president of the NFL, May 28.

Defensive back Emlen Tunnell of the New York Giants became the first black player to enter the Pro Football Hall of Fame, August 5.

An AFL team defeated an NFL team for the first time, when Denver beat Detroit 13-7 in a preseason game, August 5.

Green Bay defeated Dallas 21-17 for the NFL championship on a last-minute 1-yard quarterback sneak by Bart Starr in 13-below-zero temperature at Green Bay, December 31. The same day, Oakland defeated Houston 40-7 for the AFL championship.

1968

Green Bay defeated Oakland 33-14 in Super Bowl II at Miami, January 14. The game had the first $3-million gate in pro football history.

Vince Lombardi resigned as head coach of the Packers, but remained as general manager, January 28.

Werblin sold his shares in the Jets to his partners Don Lillis, Leon Hess, Townsend Martin, and Phil Iselin, May 21. Lillis assumed the presidency of the club, but then died July 23. Iselin was appointed president, August 6.

Halas retired for the fourth and last time as head coach of the Bears, May 27.

The Oilers left Rice Stadium for the Astrodome and became the first NFL team to play its home games in a domed stadium.

The movie Heidi became a footnote in sports history when NBC didn't show the last 50 seconds of the Jets-Raiders game in order to permit the children's special to begin on time. The Raiders scored two touchdowns in the last 42 seconds to win 43-32, November 17.

Ewbank became the first coach to win titles in both the NFL and AFL when his Jets

defeated the Raiders 27-23 for the AFL championship, December 29. The same day, Baltimore defeated Cleveland 34-0.

1969

The AFL established a playoff format for the 1969 season, with the winner in one division playing the runner-up in the other, January 11.

An AFL team won the Super Bowl for the first time, as the Jets defeated the Colts 16-7 at Miami, January 12 in Super Bowl III. The title Super Bowl was recognized by the NFL for the first time.

Vince Lombardi became part owner, executive vice-president, and head coach of the Washington Redskins, February 7.

Wolman sold the Eagles to Leonard Tose, May 1.

Baltimore, Cleveland, and Pittsburgh agreed to join the AFL teams to form the 13-team American Football Conference of the NFL in 1970, May 10. The NFL also agreed on a playoff format that would include one "wild-card" team per conference—the second-place team with the best record.

The NFL announced a three-year agreement with ABC to televise Monday Night Football. The new series makes the NFL the first league with a regular series of national telecasts in prime time, May 26.

George Preston Marshall, president emeritus of the Redskins, died at 72, August 9.

The NFL marked its fiftieth year by the wearing of a special patch by each of the 16 teams.

1970

Kansas City defeated Minnesota 23-7 in Super Bowl IV at New Orleans, January 11. The gross receipts of approximately $3.8 million were the largest ever for a one-day sports event.

A special league meeting was held to determine the divisional realignment of the National Football Conference. With no consensus, Rozelle ordered the five most viable plans be written down on sheets of paper. Rozelle's assistant, Thelma Elkjer, picked the winning one out of a vase at random, January 17.

Four-year television contracts, under which CBS would televise all NFC games and NBC all AFC games (except Monday night games) and the two would divide televising the Super Bowl and AFC-NFC Pro Bowl games, were announced, January 26.

Art Modell resigned as president of the NFL, March 12. Milt Woodard resigned as president of the AFL, March 13. Lamar Hunt was elected president of the AFC and George Halas was elected president of the NFC, March 19.

The merged 26-team league adopted rules changes putting names on the backs of players' jerseys, making a point after touchdown worth only one point, and making the scoreboard clock the official timing device of the game, March 18.

The Players Negotiating Committee and the NFL Players Association announced a four-year agreement guaranteeing approximately $4,535,000 annually to player pension and insurance benefits, August 3. The owners also agreed to contribute $250,000 annually to improve or implement items such as disability payments, widows' benefits, maternity benefits, and dental benefits. The agreement also provided for increased preseason game and per diem payments, averaging approximately $2.6 million annually.

The Pittsburgh Steelers moved into Three Rivers Stadium. The Cincinnati Bengals moved to Riverfront Stadium.

Vince Lombardi died of cancer at 57, September 3.

The Super Bowl trophy was renamed the Vince Lombardi trophy, September 10.

Tom Dempsey of New Orleans kicked a game-winning NFL-record 63-yard field goal against Detroit, November 8.

1971

Baltimore defeated Dallas 16-13 on Jim O'Brien's 32-yard field goal with five seconds to go in Super Bowl V at Miami, January 17.

The NFC defeated the AFC 27-6 in the first AFC-NFC Pro Bowl at Los Angeles, January 24.

The Boston Patriots changed their name to the New England Patriots, March 25. Their new stadium, Schaefer Stadium, was dedicated in a 20-14 preseason victory over the Giants.

The Philadelphia Eagles left Franklin Field and played their games at the new Veterans Stadium.

The San Francisco 49ers left Kezar Stadium and moved their games to Candlestick Park.

Daniel F. Reeves, the president and general manager of the Rams, died at 58, April 15.

The Dallas Cowboys moved from the Cotton Bowl into their new home, Texas Stadium, October 24.

Miami defeated Kansas City 27-24 in sudden-death overtime in an AFC Divisional Playoff Game, December 25. Garo Yepremian kicked a 37-yard field goal for the Dolphins after 22 minutes, 40 seconds of overtime, as the game lasted 82 minutes, 40 seconds overall, making it the longest game in history.

1972

Dallas defeated Miami 24-3 in Super Bowl VI at New Orleans, January 16.

The inbounds lines or hashmarks were moved nearer the center of the field, 23 yards, 1 foot, 9 inches from the sidelines, March 23. The method of determining won-lost percentage in standings changed. Tie games, previously not counted in the standings, were made equal to a half-game won and a half-game lost, May 24.

Robert Irsay purchased the Los Angeles Rams and transferred ownership of the club to Carroll Rosenbloom in exchange for the Baltimore Colts, July 13.

William V. Bidwill purchased the stock of his brother Charles (Stormy) Bidwill to become the sole owner of the St. Louis Cardinals, September 2.

The National District Attorneys Association endorsed the position of professional leagues in opposing proposed legalization of gambling on professional team sports, September 28.

Franco Harris' "Immaculate Reception" gave the Steelers their first postseason win ever, 13-7 over the Raiders, December 23.

1973

Rozelle announced that all Super Bowl VII tickets were sold and that the game would be telecast in Los Angeles, the site of the game, on an experimental basis, January 3.

Miami defeated Washington 14-7 in Super Bowl VII at Los Angeles, completing a 17-0 season, the first perfect-record regular-season and postseason mark in NFL history, January 14.

The AFC defeated the NFC 33-28 in the Pro Bowl in Dallas, the first time since 1942 that the game was played outside Los Angeles, January 21.

A jersey numbering system was adopted, April 5: 1-19 for quarterbacks and specialists, 20-49 for running backs and defensive backs, 50-59 for centers and linebackers, 60-79 for defensive linemen and interior offensive linemen other than centers, and 80-89 for wide receivers and tight ends. Players who had been in the NFL in 1972 could continue to use old numbers.

NFL Charities, a nonprofit organization, was created to derive an income from monies generated from NFL Properties' licensing of NFL trademarks and team names, June 26. NFL Charities was set up to support education and charitable activities and to supply economic support to persons formerly associated with professional football who were no longer able to support themselves.

Congress adopted experimental legislation (for three years) requiring any NFL game that had been declared a sellout 72 hours prior to kickoff to be made available for local televising, September 14. The legislation provided for an annual review to be made by the Federal Communications Commission.

The Buffalo Bills moved their home games from War Memorial Stadium to Rich Stadium in nearby Orchard Park. The Giants tied the Eagles 23-23 in the final game in Yankee Stadium, September 23. The Giants played the rest of their home games at the Yale Bowl in New Haven, Connecti-

cut.

A rival league, the World Football League, was formed and was reported in operation, October 2. It had plans to start play in 1974.

O.J. Simpson of Buffalo became the first player to rush for more than 2,000 yards in a season, gaining 2,003.

1974

Miami defeated Minnesota 24-7 in Super Bowl VIII at Houston, the second consecutive Super Bowl championship for the Dolphins, January 13.

Rozelle was given a 10-year contract effective January 1, 1973, February 27.

Tampa Bay was awarded the twenty-seventh franchise to begin operation in 1976, April 24.

Sweeping rules changes were adopted to add action and tempo to games: one sudden-death overtime period was added for preseason and regular-season games; the goal posts were moved from the goal line to the end lines; kickoffs were moved from the 40- to the 35-yard line; after missed field goals from beyond the 20, the ball was to be returned to the line of scrimmage; restrictions were placed on members of the punting team to open up return possibilities; roll-blocking and cutting of wide receivers was eliminated; the extent of downfield contact a defender could have with an eligible receiver was restricted; the penalties for offensive holding, illegal use of the hands, and tripping were reduced from 15 to 10 yards; wide receivers blocking back toward the ball within three yards of the line of scrimmage were prevented from blocking below the waist, April 25.

Seattle was awarded the twenty-eighth NFL franchise to begin play in 1976, June 4. Lloyd W. Nordstrom, president of the Seattle Seahawks, and Hugh Culverhouse, president of the Tampa Bay Buccaneers, signed franchise agreements, December 5.

The Birmingham Americans defeated the Florida Blazers 22-21 in the WFL World Bowl, winning the league championship, December 5.

1975

Pittsburgh defeated Minnesota 16-6 in Super Bowl IX at New Orleans, the Steelers' first championship since entering the NFL in 1933, January 12.

The Memphis Southmen of the WFL signed Larry Csonka, Jim Kiick, and Paul Warfield of Miami, March 31.

The divisional winners with the highest won-loss percentage were made the home team for the divisional play-offs, and the surviving winners with the highest percentage made home teams for championship games. Previously, the home sites were pre-determined by division on a rotating basis, June 26.

Referees were equipped with wireless microphones for all preseason, regular-season, and playoff games.

The Lions moved to the new Pontiac Silverdome. The Giants played their home games in Shea Stadium. The Saints moved into the Louisiana Superdome.

The World Football League folded, October 22.

1976

Pittsburgh defeated Dallas 21-17 in Super Bowl X in Miami. The Steelers joined Green Bay and Miami as the only teams to win two Super Bowls; the Cowboys became the first wild-card team to play in the Super Bowl, January 18.

Lloyd Nordstrom, the president of the Seahawks, died at 66, January 20. His brother Elmer succeeded him as majority representative of the team.

The owners adopted the use of two 30-second clocks for all games, visible to both players and fans to note the official time between the ready-for-play signal and snap of the ball, March 16.

A veteran player allocation was held to stock the Seattle and Tampa Bay franchises with 39 players each, March 30-31. In the college draft, Seattle and Tampa Bay each received eight extra choices, April 8-9.

The Giants moved into new Giants Stadium in East Rutherford, New Jersey.

The Steelers defeated the College All-Stars in a storm-shortened Chicago College All-Star Game, the last of the series, July 23. St. Louis defeated San Diego 20-10 in a preseason game before 38,000 in Korakuen Stadium, Tokyo, in the first NFL game outside of North America, August 16.

1977

Oakland defeated Minnesota 32-14 in Super Bowl XI at Pasadena, January 9. The paid attendance was a pro record 103,438.

The NFL Players Association and the NFL Management Council ratified a collective bargaining agreement extending until 1982, covering five football seasons while continuing the pension plan—including years 1974, 1975, and 1976—with contributions totaling more than $55 million. The total cost of the agreement was estimated at $107 million. The agreement called for a college draft at least through 1986; contained a no-strike, no-suit clause; established a 43-man active player limit; reduced pension vesting to four years; provided for increases in minimum salaries and preseason and postseason pay; improved insurance, medical, and dental benefits; modified previous practices in player movement and control; and reaffirmed the NFL Commissioner's disciplinary authority. Additionally, the agreement called for the NFL member clubs to make payments totaling $16 million the next 10 years to settle various legal disputes, February 25.

The San Francisco 49ers were sold to Edward J. DeBartolo, Jr., March 28.

A 16-game regular season, 4-game preseason was adopted to begin in 1978, March 29. A second wild-card team was adopted for the playoffs beginning in 1978, with the wild-card teams to play each other and the winners advancing to a round of eight postseason series.

The Seahawks were permanently aligned in the AFC Western Division and the Buccaneers in the NFC Central Division, March 31.

Rules changes were adopted to open up the passing game and to cut down on injuries. Defenders were permitted to make contact with eligible receivers only once; the head slap was outlawed; offensive linemen were prohibited from thrusting their hands to an opponent's neck, face, or head; and wide receivers were prohibited from clipping, even in the legal clipping zone.

Rozelle negotiated contracts with the three television networks to televise all NFL regular-season and postseason games, plus selected preseason games, for four years beginning with the 1978 season. ABC was awarded yearly rights to 16 Monday night games, four primetime games, the AFC-NFC Pro Bowl, and the Hall of Fame games. CBS received the rights to all NFC regular-season and postseason games (except those in the ABC package) and to Super Bowls XIV and XVI. NBC received the rights to all AFC regular-season and postseason games (except those in the ABC package) and to Super Bowls XIII and XV. Industry sources considered it the largest single television package ever negotiated, October 12.

1978

Dallas defeated Denver 27-10 in Super Bowl XII, held indoors for the first time, at the Louisiana Superdome in New Orleans, January 15. Dallas' victory was the first for the NFC in six years.

According to a Louis Harris Sports Survey, 70 percent of the nation's sports fans said they followed football, compared to 54 percent who followed baseball. Football increased its lead as the country's favorite, 26 percent to 16 percent for baseball, January 19.

A seventh official, the side judge, was added to the officiating crew, March 14.

The NFL continued a trend toward opening up the game. Rules changes permitted a defender to maintain contact with a receiver within five yards of the line of scrimmage, but restricted contact beyond that point. The pass-blocking rule was interpreted to permit the extending of arms and open hands, March 17.

A study on the use of instant replay as an officiating aid was made during seven nationally televised preseason games.

The NFL played for the first time in Mexico City, with the Saints defeating the Eagles 14-7 in a preseason game, August 5.

Bolstered by the expansion of the regular-season schedule from 14 to 16 weeks, NFL paid attendance exceeded 12 million (12,771,800) for the first time. The per-game average of 57,017 was the third-highest in league history and the most since 1973.

1979

Pittsburgh defeated Dallas 35-31 in Super Bowl XIII at Miami to become the first team ever to win three Super Bowls, January 21.

NFL rules changes emphasized additional player safety. The changes prohibited players on the receiving team from blocking below the waist during kickoffs, punts, and field-goal attempts; prohibited the wearing of torn or altered equipment and exposed pads that could be hazardous; extended the zone in which there could be no crackback blocks; and instructed officials to quickly whistle a play dead when a quarterback was clearly in the grasp of a tackler, March 16.

Carroll Rosenbloom, the president of the Rams, drowned at 72, April 2. His widow, Georgia, assumed control of the club.

1980

Pittsburgh defeated the Los Angeles Rams 31-19 in Super Bowl XIV at Pasadena to become the first team to win four Super Bowls, January 20.

The AFC-NFC Pro Bowl, won 37-27 by the NFC, was played before 48,060 fans at Aloha Stadium in Honolulu, Hawaii. It was the first time in the 30-year history of the Pro Bowl that the game was played in a non-NFL city.

Rules changes placed greater restrictions on contact in the area of the head, neck, and face. Under the heading of "personal foul," players were prohibited from directly striking, swinging, or clubbing on the head, neck, or face. Starting in 1980, a penalty could be called for such contact whether or not the initial contact was made below the neck area.

CBS, with a record bid of $12 million, won the national radio rights to 26 NFL regular-season games, including Monday Night Football, and all 10 postseason games for the 1980-83 seasons.

The Los Angeles Rams moved their home games to Anaheim Stadium in nearby Orange County, California.

The Oakland Raiders joined the Los Angeles Coliseum Commission's antitrust suit against the NFL. The suit contended the league violated antitrust laws in declining to approve a proposed move by the Raiders from Oakland to Los Angeles.

The NFL Draft is televised for the first time by ESPN, April 29.

Television ratings in 1980 were the second-best in NFL history, trailing only the combined ratings of the 1976 season. All three networks posted gains, and NBC's 15.0 rating was its best ever. CBS and ABC had their best ratings since 1977, with 15.3 and 20.8 ratings, respectively. CBS Radio reported a record audience of 7 million for Monday night and special games.

1981

Oakland defeated Philadelphia 27-10 in Super Bowl XV at the Louisiana Superdome in New Orleans, to become the first wild-card team to win a Super Bowl, January 25.

Edgar F. Kaiser, Jr., purchased the Denver Broncos from Gerald and Allan Phipps, February 26.

The owners adopted a disaster plan for re-stocking a team should the club be involved in a fatal accident, March 20.

A CBS-New York Times poll showed that 48 percent of sports fans preferred football to 31 percent for baseball.

The NFL teams hosted 167 representatives from 44 predominantly black colleges during training camps for a total of 289 days. The program was adopted for renewal during each training camp period.

ABC and CBS set all-time rating highs. ABC finished with a 21.7 rating and CBS with a 17.5 rating. NBC was down slightly to 13.9.

1982

San Francisco defeated Cincinnati 26-21 in Super Bowl XVI at the Pontiac Silverdome, in the first Super Bowl held in the North, January 24. The CBS telecast achieved the highest rating of any televised sports event ever, 49.1 with a 73.0 share.

The NFL signed a five-year contract with the three television networks (ABC, CBS, and NBC) to televise all NFL regular-season and postseason games starting with the 1982 season.

A jury ruled against the NFL in the antitrust trial brought by the Los Angeles Coliseum Commission and the Oakland Raiders, May 7. The verdict cleared the way for the Raiders to move to Los Angeles, where they defeated Green Bay 24-3 in their first preseason game, August 29.

The 1982 season was reduced from a 16-game schedule to nine as the result of a 57-day players' strike. The strike was called by the NFLPA at midnight on Monday, September 20, following the Green Bay at New York Giants game. Play resumed November 21-22 following ratification of the Collective Bargaining Agreement by NFL owners, November 17 in New York.

Under the Collective Bargaining Agreement, which was to run through the 1986 season, the NFL draft was extended through 1992 and the veteran free-agent system was left basically unchanged. A minimum salary schedule for years of experience was established; training camp and postseason pay were increased; players' medical, insurance, and retirement benefits were increased; and a severance-pay system was introduced to aid in career transition, a first in professional sports.

Despite the players' strike, the average paid attendance in 1982 was 58,472, the fifth-highest in league history.

1983

Because of the shortened season, the NFL adopted a format of 16 teams competing in a Super Bowl Tournament for the 1982 playoffs. The NFC's number-one seed, Washing-

ton, defeated the AFC's number-two seed, Miami, 27-17 in Super Bowl XVII at the Rose Bowl in Pasadena, January 30.

Super Bowl XVII was the second-highest rated live television program of all time, giving the NFL a sweep of the top 10 live programs in television history.

George Halas, the owner of the Bears and the last surviving member of the NFL's second organizational meeting, died at 88, October 31.

1984

The Los Angeles Raiders defeated Washington 38-9 in Super Bowl XVIII at Tampa Stadium, January 22.

An 11-man group headed by H.R. (Bum) Bright purchased the Dallas Cowboys from Clint Murchison, Jr., March 20. Club president Tex Schramm was designated as managing general partner.

Wellington Mara was named president of the NFC, March 20.

Patrick Bowlen purchased a majority interest in the Denver Broncos from Edgar Kaiser, Jr., March 21.

The Colts relocated to Indianapolis, March 28. Their new home became the Hoosier Dome.

The New York Jets moved their home games to Giants Stadium in East Rutherford, New Jersey.

Alex G. Spanos purchased a majority interest in the San Diego Chargers from Eugene V. Klein, August 28.

Houston defeated Pittsburgh 23-20 to mark the one-hundredth overtime game in regular-season play since overtime was adopted in 1974, December 2.

On the field, many all-time records were set: Dan Marino of Miami passed for 5,084 yards and 48 touchdowns; Eric Dickerson of the Los Angeles Rams rushed for 2,105 yards; Art Monk of Washington caught 106 passes; and Walter Payton of Chicago broke Jim Brown's career rushing mark, finishing the season with 13,309 yards.

According to a CBS Sports/New York Times survey, 53 percent of the nation's sports fans said they most enjoyed watching football,

compared to 18 percent for baseball, December 2-4.

1985

San Francisco defeated Miami 38-16 in Super Bowl XIX at Stanford Stadium in Stanford, California, January 20. President Ronald Reagan, who took his second oath of office before tossing the coin for the game, was one of 115,936,000 viewers. Super Bowl XIX had a direct economic impact of $113.5 million on the San Francisco Bay area.

NBC Radio and the NFL entered into a two-year agreement granting NBC the radio rights to a 37-game package in each of the 1985-86 seasons, March 6. The package included 27 regular-season games and 10 postseason games.

Norman Braman, in partnership with Edward Leibowitz, bought the Philadelphia Eagles from Leonard Tose, April 29.

A group headed by Tom Benson, Jr., was approved to purchase the New Orleans Saints from John W. Mecom, Jr., June 3.

The NFL owners adopted a resolution calling for a series of overseas preseason games, beginning in 1986, with one game to be played in England/Europe and/or one game in Japan each year. The game would be a fifth preseason game for the clubs involved and all arrangements and selection of the clubs would be under the control of the Commissioner, May 23.

The league-wide conversion to videotape from movie film for coaching study was approved.

A Louis Harris poll in December revealed that pro football remained the sport most followed by Americans. Fifty-nine percent of those surveyed followed pro football, compared with 54 percent who followed baseball.

The Chicago-Miami Monday game had the highest rating, 29.6, and share, 46.0, of any primetime game in NFL history, December 2. The game was viewed in more than 25 million homes.

The NFL showed a ratings increase on all three networks for the season, gaining 4 percent on NBC, 10 on CBS, and

16 on ABC.

1986

Chicago defeated New England 46-10 in Super Bowl XX at the Louisiana Superdome, January 26. The Patriots had earned the right to play the Bears by becoming the first wild-card team to win three consecutive games on the road. The NBC telecast replaced the final episode of *M*A*S*H* as the most-viewed television program in history, with an audience of 127 million viewers, according to A.C. Nielsen figures. In addition to drawing a 48.3 rating and a 70 percent share in the United States, Super Bowl XX was televised to 59 foreign countries and beamed via satellite to the QE II.

The owners adopted limited use of instant replay as an officiating aid, prohibited players from wearing or otherwise displaying equipment, apparel, or other items that carry commercial names, names of organizations, or personal messages of any type, March 11.

After an 11-week trial, a jury in U.S. District Court in New York awarded the United States Football League one dollar in its $1.7 billion antitrust suit against the NFL. The jury rejected all of the USFL's television-related claims, which were the self-proclaimed heart of the USFL's case. The jury deliberated five days, July 29.

Chicago defeated Dallas 17-6 at Wembley Stadium in London in the first American Bowl. The game drew a sellout crowd of 82,699 and the NBC national telecast in this country produced a 12.4 rating and 36 percent share, making it the highest daytime preseason television audience ever with 10.65-million viewers, August 3.

ABC's *NFL Monday Night Football*, in its seventeenth season, became the longest-running primetime series in the history of the network.

1987

The New York Giants defeated Denver 39-20 in Super Bowl XXI and captured their first NFL title since 1956. The game, played in Pasadena's Rose Bowl, drew a sellout crowd of 101,063, January 25.

New three-year TV contracts with ABC, CBS, and NBC were announced for 1987-89 at the NFL annual meeting in Maui, Hawaii, March 15. Commissioner Rozelle and Broadcast Committee Chairman Art Modell also announced a three-year contract with ESPN to televise 13 primetime games each season. The ESPN contract was the first with a cable network. However, NFL games on ESPN also were scheduled for regular television in the city of the visiting team and in the home city if the game was sold out 72 hours in advance.

A special payment program was adopted to benefit nearly 1,000 former NFL players who participated in the League before the current Bert Bell NFL Pension Plan was created and made retroactive to the 1959 season. Players covered by the new program spent at least five years in the League and played all or part of their career prior to 1959. Each vested player would receive $60 per month for each year of service in the League for life.

NFL and CBS Radio jointly announced agreement granting CBS the radio rights to a 40-game package in each of the next three NFL seasons, 1987-89, April 7.

Over 400 former NFL players from the pre-1959 era received first payments from NFL owners, July 1.

The NFL's debut on ESPN produced the two highest-rated and most-watched sports programs in basic cable history. The Chicago at Miami game on August 16 drew an 8.9 rating in 3.81 million homes. Those records fell two weeks later when the Los Angeles Raiders at Dallas game achieved a 10.2 cable rating in 4.36 million homes.

The 1987 season was reduced from a 16-game season to 15 as the result of a 24-day players' strike. The strike was called by the NFLPA on Tuesday, September 22, following the New England at New York Jets game. Games scheduled for the third weekend were canceled but the games of weeks four, five, and six were played with replace-ment teams. Striking players returned for the seventh week of the season, October 25.

In a three-team deal involving 10 players and/or draft choices, the Los Angeles Rams traded running back Eric Dickerson to the Indianapolis Colts for six draft choices and two players. Buffalo obtained the rights to linebacker Cornelius Bennett from Indianapolis, sending Greg Bell and three draft choices to the Rams. The Colts added Owen Gill and three draft choices of their own to complete the deal with the Rams, October 31.

The Chicago at Minnesota game became the highest-rated and most-watched sports program in basic cable history when it drew a 14.4 cable rating in 6.5 million homes, December 6.

1988

Washington defeated Denver 42-10 in Super Bowl XXII to earn its second victory this decade in the NFL Championship Game. The game, played for the first time in San Diego Jack Murphy Stadium, drew a sellout crowd of 73,302. Doug Williams, the game's MVP, became the first African-American quarterback to play in a Super Bowl, January 31.

In a unanimous 3-0 decision, the 2nd Circuit Court of Appeals in New York upheld the verdict of the jury that in July, 1986, had awarded the United States Football League one dollar in its $1.7 billion antitrust suit against the NFL. In a 91-page opinion, Judge Ralph K. Winter said the USFL sought through court decree the success it failed to gain among football fans, March 10.

By a 23-5 margin, owners voted to continue the instant replay system for the third consecutive season with the Instant Replay Official to be assigned to a regular seven-man, on-the-field crew. At the NFL annual meeting in Phoenix, Arizona, a 45-second clock was also approved to replace the 30-second clock. For a normal sequence of plays, the interval between plays was changed to 45 seconds from the time the ball is signaled dead until it is snapped on the succeeding play.

NFL owners approved the transfer of the Cardinals' franchise from St. Louis to Phoenix; approved two supplemental drafts each year—one prior to training camp and one prior to the regular season; and voted to initiate an annual series of games in Japan/Asia as early as the 1989 preseason, March 14-18.

The NFL Annual Selection Meeting returned to a separate two-day format and for the first time originated on a Sunday. ESPN drew a 3.6 rating during their seven-hour coverage of the draft, which was viewed in 1.6 million homes, April 24-25.

Art Rooney, founder and owner of the Steelers, died at 87, August 25.

Johnny Grier became the first African-American referee in NFL history, September 4.

Commissioner Rozelle announced that two teams would play a preseason game as part of the American Bowl series on August 6, 1989, in the Korakuen Tokyo Dome in Japan, December 16.

1989

San Francisco defeated Cincinnati 20-16 in Super Bowl XXIII. The game, played for the first time at Joe Robbie Stadium in Miami, was attended by a sellout crowd of 75,129, January 22.

Commissioner Rozelle announced his retirement, pending the naming of a successor, March 22 at the NFL annual meeting in Palm Desert, California.

Following the announcement, AFC president Lamar Hunt and NFC president Wellington Mara announced the formation of a six-man search committee composed of Art Modell, Robert Parins, Dan Rooney, and Ralph Wilson. Hunt and Mara served as co-chairmen.

By a 24-4 margin, owners voted to continue the instant replay system for the fourth straight season. A strengthened policy regarding anabolic steroids and masking agents was announced by Commissioner Rozelle. NFL clubs called for strong disciplinary measures in cases of feigned injuries and adopted a joint proposal by the Long-Range Planning and Finance committees regarding player personnel rules, March 19-23.

Two hundred twenty-nine unconditional free agents signed with new teams under management's Plan B system, April 1.

Jerry Jones purchased a majority interest in the Dallas Cowboys from H.R. (Bum) Bright, April 18.

Tex Schramm was named president of the new World League of American Football to work with a six-man committee of Dan Rooney, chairman; Norman Braman, Lamar Hunt, Victor Kiam, Mike Lynn, and Bill Walsh, April 18.

NFL and CBS Radio jointly announced agreement extending CBS's radio rights to an annual 40-game package through the 1994 season, April 18.

As of opening day, September 10, of the 229 Plan B free agents, 111 were active and 23 others were on teams' reserve lists. Ninety-two others were waived and three retired.

Art Shell was named head coach of the Los Angeles Raiders making him the NFL's first black head coach since Fritz Pollard coached the Akron Pros in 1921, October 3.

The site of the New England Patriots at San Francisco 49ers game scheduled for Candlestick Park on October 22 was switched to Stanford Stadium in the aftermath of the Bay Area Earthquake of October 17. The change was announced on October 19.

Paul Tagliabue became the seventh chief executive of the NFL on October 26 when he was chosen to succeed Commissioner Pete Rozelle on the sixth ballot of a three-day meeting in Cleveland, Ohio.

In all, 12 ballots were required to select Tagliabue. Two were conducted at a meeting in Chicago on July 6, and four at a meeting in Dallas on October 10-11. On the twelfth ballot, with Seattle absent, Tagliabue received more than the 19 affirmative votes required for election from among the 27 clubs present.

The transfer from Commis-

sioner Rozelle to Commissioner Tagliabue took place at 12:01 A.M. on Sunday, November 5.

NFL Charities donated $1 million through United Way to benefit Bay Area earthquake victims, November 6.

1990

San Francisco defeated Denver 55-10 in Super Bowl XXIV at the Louisiana Superdome, January 28. San Francisco joined Pittsburgh as the NFL's only teams to win four Super Bowls.

The NFL announced revisions in its 1990 draft eligibility rules. College juniors became eligible but must renounce their collegiate football eligibility before applying for the NFL Draft, February 16.

Commissioner Tagliabue announced NFL teams will play their 16-game schedule over 17 weeks in 1990-92 and 16 games over 18 weeks in 1993, February 27.

The NFL revised its playoff format to include two additional wild-card teams (one per conference), which raised the total to six wild-card teams.

Commissioner Tagliabue and Broadcast Committee Chairman Art Modell announced a four-year contract with Turner Broadcasting to televise nine Sunday-night games.

New four-year TV agreements were ratified for 1990-93 for ABC, CBS, NBC, ESPN, and TNT at the NFL annual meeting in Orlando, Florida, March 12. The contracts totaled $3.6 billion, the largest in TV history.

The NFL announced plans to expand its American Bowl series of preseason games. In addition to games in London and Tokyo, American Bowl games were scheduled for Berlin, Germany, and Montreal, Canada, in 1990.

For the fifth straight year, NFL owners voted to continue a limited system of Instant Replay. Beginning in 1990, the replay official will have a two-minute time limit to make a decision. The vote was 21-7, March 12.

Commissioner Tagliabue announced the formation of a Committee on Expansion and Realignment, March 13. He also named a Player Advisory

Council, comprised of 12 former NFL players, March 14.

One-hundred eighty-four Plan B unconditional free agents signed with new teams, April 2.

Commissioner Tagliabue appointed Dr. John Lombardo as the League's Drug Advisor for Anabolic Steroids, April 25 and named Dr. Lawrence Brown as the League's Advisor for Drugs of Abuse, May 17.

NFL International Week was celebrated with four preseason games in seven days in Tokyo, London, Berlin, and Montreal. More than 200,000 fans on three continents attended the four games, August 4-11.

Commissioner Tagliabue announced the NFL Teacher of the Month program in which the League furnishes grants and scholarships in recognition of teachers who provided a positive influence upon NFL players in elementary and secondary schools, September 20.

For the first time since 1957, every NFL club won at least one of its first four games, October 1.

The Super Bowl Most Valuable Player trophy was renamed the Pete Rozelle trophy, October 8.

1991

The New York Giants defeated Buffalo 20-19 in Super Bowl XXV to capture their second title in five years. The game was played before a sellout crowd of 73,813 at Tampa Stadium and became the first Super Bowl decided by one point, January 26.

New York businessman Robert Tisch purchased a 50 percent interest in the New York Giants from Mrs. Helen Mara Nugent and her children, Tim Mara and Maura Mara Concannon, February 2.

NFL clubs voted to continue a limited system of Instant Replay for the sixth consecutive year. The vote was 21-7, March 19.

The NFL launched the World League of American Football, the first sports league to operate on a weekly basis on two separate continents, March 23.

NFL Charities presented a $250,000 donation to the

United Service Organization. The donation was the second largest single grant ever by NFL Charities, April 5.

Commissioner Tagliabue named Harold Henderson as Executive Vice President for Labor Relations and Chairman of the NFL Management Council Executive Committee, April 8.

NFL clubs approved a recommendation by the Expansion and Realignment Committee to add two teams for the 1994 season, resulting in six divisions of five teams each, May 22.

"NFL International Week" featured six 1990 playoff teams playing nationally televised games in London, Berlin, and Tokyo on July 28 and August 3-4. The games drew more than 150,000 fans.

Paul Brown, founder of the Cleveland Browns and Cincinnati Bengals, died at age 82, August 5.

NFL clubs approved a resolution establishing an international division. A three-year financial plan for the World League was approved by NFL clubs at a meeting in Dallas, October 23.

1992

The NFL agreed to provide a minimum of $2.5 million in financial support to the NFL Alumni Association and assistance to NFL Alumni-related programs. The agreement included contributions from NFL Charities to the Pre-59ers and Dire Need Programs for former players, January 25.

The Washington Redskins defeated the Buffalo Bills 37-24 in Super Bowl XXVI to capture their third world championship in 10 years, January 26. The game was played before a sellout crowd of 63,130 at the Hubert H. Humphrey Metrodome in Minneapolis.

The use in officiating of a limited system of Instant Replay was not approved. The vote was 17-11 in favor of approval (21 votes were required). Instant Replay had been used for six consecutive years (1986-1991), March 18.

St. Louis businessman James Orthwein purchased controlling interest in the New England Patriots from Victor

Kiam, May 11.

In a Harris Poll taken during the NFL offseason, professional football again was declared the nation's most popular sport. Professional football finished atop similar surveys conducted by Harris in 1985 and 1989, May 23.

NFL clubs accepted the report of the Expansion Committee at a league meeting in Pasadena. The report names five cities as finalists for the two expansion teams—Baltimore, Charlotte, Jacksonville, Memphis, and St. Louis, May 19.

At a league meeting in Dallas, NFL clubs approved a proposal by the World League Board of Directors to restructure the World League and place future emphasis on its international success, September 17.

The Professional and Amateur Sports Protection Act made it unlawful for a government entity to operate a lottery or other betting scheme based on pro or collegiate games. Four states that already had such betting were grandfathered, October 6.

NFL teams played their 16-game regular-season schedule over 18 weeks for the only time in league history.

1993
The NFL and lawyers for the players announced a settlement of various lawsuits and an agreement on the terms of a seven-year deal that included a new player system to be in place through the 1999 season, January 6.

Commissioner Tagliabue announced the establishment of the "NFL World Partnership Program" to develop amateur football internationally through a series of clinics conducted by former NFL players and coaches, January 14.

As part of Super Bowl XXVII, the NFL announced the creation of the first NFL Youth Education Town, a facility located in south central Los Angeles for inner city youth, January 25.

The Dallas Cowboys defeated the Buffalo Bills 52-17 in Super Bowl XXVII to capture their first NFL title since 1978. The game was played before a crowd of 98,374 at the Rose Bowl in

Pasadena, California, January 31.

The NFL and the NFL Players Association officially signed a 7-year Collective Bargaining Agreement in Washington, D.C., which guarantees more than $1 billion in pension, health, and post-career benefits for current and retired players—the most extensive benefits plan in pro sports. It was the NFL's first CBA since the 1982 agreement expired in 1987, June 29.

NFL Enterprises, a newly formed division of the NFL responsible for NFL Films, home video, and special domestic and international television programming was announced, August 19.

NFL announced plans to allow fans, for the first time ever, to join players and coaches in selecting the annual AFC and NFC Pro Bowl teams, October 12.

NFL clubs unanimously awarded the league's twenty-ninth franchise to the Carolina Panthers and owner Jerry Richardson at a meeting in Chicago, October 26.

At the same meeting in Chicago, NFL clubs approved a plan to form a European league with joint venture partners, October 27.

Don Shula became the winningest coach in NFL history when Miami beat Philadelphia to give Shula his 325th victory, one more than George Halas, November 14.

NFL clubs awarded the league's thirtieth franchise to the Jacksonville Jaguars and owner Wayne Weaver at a meeting in Chicago, November 30.

The NFL announced new 4-year television agreements with NBC, ABC, ESPN, TNT, and NFL newcomer FOX, which took over the NFC package from CBS, December 18.

The NFL completed its new TV agreements by announcing that NBC would retain the rights to the AFC package, December 20.

1994
The Dallas Cowboys defeated the Buffalo Bills 30-13 in Super Bowl XXVIII to become the fifth team to win back-to-back Super Bowl titles, January 30.

NFL clubs unanimously approved the transfer of the New England Patriots from James Orthwein to Robert Kraft at a meeting in Orlando, February 22.

In a move to increase offensive production, NFL clubs at the league's annual meeting in Orlando adopted a package of changes, including modifications in line play, chucking rules, and the roughing-the-passer rule, plus the adoption of the two-point conversion and moving the spot of the kickoff back to the 30-yard line, March 22.

NFL clubs approved transfer of the majority interest in the Miami Dolphins from the Robbie family to H. Wayne Huizenga, March 23.

The NFL and FOX announced the formation of a joint venture to create a six-team World League to begin play in Europe in April, 1995, March 23.

The Carolina Panthers earned the right to select first in the 1995 NFL draft by winning a coin toss with the Jacksonville Jaguars. The Jaguars received the second selection in the 1995 draft, April 24.

NFL clubs approved the transfer of the Philadelphia Eagles from Norman Braman to Jeffrey Lurie, May 6.

The NFL launched "NFL Sunday Ticket," a new season subscription service for satellite television dish owners, June 1.

An all-time NFL record crowd of 112,376 attended the American Bowl game between Dallas and Houston in Mexico City. It concluded the biggest American Bowl series in NFL history with four games attracting a record 256,666 fans, August 15.

The NFL reached agreement on a new seven-year contract with its game officials, September 22.

The NFL Management Council and the NFL Players Association announced an agreement on the formulation and implementation of the most comprehensive drug and alcohol policy in sports, October 28.

At an NFL meeting in Chicago, Commissioner Tagliabue slotted the two new expansion teams into the AFC Central (Jacksonville Jaguars) and

NFC West (Carolina Panthers) for the 1995 season only. He also appointed a special committee on realignment to make recommendations on the 1996 season and beyond, November 2.

1995
The San Francisco 49ers became the first team to win five Super Bowls when they defeated the San Diego Chargers 49-26 in Super Bowl XXIX at Joe Robbie Stadium in Miami, January 29.

Carolina and Jacksonville stocked their expansion rosters with a total of 66 players from other NFL teams in a veteran player allocation draft in New York, February 16.

CBS Radio and the NFL agreed to a new four-year contract for an annual 53-game package of games, continuing a relationship that spanned 15 of the past 17 years, February 22.

NFL clubs approved the transfer of the Tampa Bay Buccaneers from the estate of the late Hugh Culverhouse to South Florida businessman Malcolm Glazer, March 13.

After a two-year hiatus, the World League of American Football returned to action with six teams in Europe, April 8.

The NFL became the first major sports league to establish a site on the Internet system of on-line computer communication, April 10.

The transfer of the Rams from Los Angeles to St. Louis was approved by a vote of the NFL clubs at a meeting in Dallas, April 12.

ABC's *NFL Monday Night Football* finished the 1994-95 television season as the fifth highest-rated show out of 146 with a 17.8 average rating, the highest finish in the 25-year history of the series, April 18.

The Frankfurt Galaxy defeated the Amsterdam Admirals 26-22 to win the 1995 World Bowl before a crowd of 23,847 in Amsterdam's Olympic Stadium, June 23.

The transfer of the Raiders from Los Angeles to Oakland was approved by a vote of the NFL clubs at a meeting in Chicago, July 22.

Jacksonville Municipal Stadium opened in Jacksonville, Florida before a sold-out crowd of more than 70,000 as the St. Louis Rams defeated the Jacksonville Jaguars 27-10 in their first preseason game, August 18.

NFL Charities and 50 NFL players donated $1 million to the United Negro College Fund in honor of the fiftieth anniversary of the UNCF and the integration of the modern NFL, September 15.

The Trans World Dome opened in St. Louis with a sold-out crowd of 65,598 as the Rams defeated the Carolina Panthers 28-17, November 12.

On the field, many significant records and milestones were achieved: Miami's Dan Marino surpassed Pro Football Hall of Famer Fran Tarkenton in four major passing categories—attempts, completions, yards, and touchdowns—to become the NFL's all-time career leader. San Francisco's Jerry Rice became the all-time reception and receiving-yardage leader.

1996
The Dallas Cowboys won their third Super Bowl title in four years when they defeated the Pittsburgh Steelers 27-17 in Super Bowl XXX at Sun Devil Stadium in Tempe, Arizona, January 28.

An agreement between the NFL and the city of Cleveland regarding the Cleveland Browns' relocation was approved by a vote of the NFL clubs, February 9. According to the agreement, the city of Cleveland retained the Browns' heritage and records, including the name, logo, colors, history, playing records, trophies, and memorabilia, and committed to building a new 72,000-seat stadium for a reactivated Browns' franchise to begin play there no later than 1999. Art Modell received approval to move his franchise to Baltimore and rename it.

The transfer of the Oilers from Houston to Nashville for the 1998 season was approved by a vote of the NFL clubs at a meeting in Atlanta, April 30.

The Scottish Claymores defeated the Frankfurt Galaxy 32-27 to win the 1996 World Bowl in front of 38,982 at Murrayfield Stadium in Edinburgh, Scotland, June 23.

The NFL returned to Balti-

more when the new Baltimore Ravens defeated the Philadelphia Eagles 17-9 in a preseason game before a crowd of 63,804 at Memorial Stadium, August 3.

Ericsson Stadium opened in Charlotte, North Carolina with a crowd of 65,350 as the Carolina Panthers defeated Chicago Bears 30-12 in a preseason game, August 3.

Former NFL Commissioner Pete Rozelle died at his home in Rancho Santa Fe, California. Rozelle, regarded as the premiere commissioner in sports history, led the NFL for 29 years, from 1960-1989, December 6.

1997
Indianapolis Colts owner Robert Irsay died from complications related to a stroke he suffered in 1995. Irsay acquired the club in 1972 when he traded his Los Angeles Rams to Carrol Rosenbloom for the Colts. He later moved the Colts from Baltimore to Indianapolis in 1984, January 14.

The Green Bay Packers won their first NFL title in 29 years by defeating the New England Patriots 35-21 in Super Bowl XXXI at the Louisiana Superdome in New Orleans, January 26.

The rules governing cross-ownership were modified, permitting NFL club owners to also own teams in other sports in their home market or markets without NFL teams. The vote was 24-5 (one abstention) in favor of approval, March 11.

Washington Redskins owner Jack Kent Cooke died at his home in Washington, D.C. Cooke became majority owner in 1974 and the Redskins won three Super Bowls under his leadership, April 6.

The Barcelona Dragons defeated the Rhein Fire 38-24 to win the 1997 World Bowl in front of 31,100 fans at Estadi Olimpic de Montjuic in Barcelona, Spain, June 22.

NFL clubs approved the transfer of the Seattle Seahawks from Ken Behring to Paul Allen, August 19.

Jack Kent Cooke Stadium opened in Raljon, Maryland with a crowd of 78,270 as the Washington Redskins defeated the Arizona Cardinals 19-13 in overtime, September 14.

The 10,000th regular-season game in NFL history was played when the Seattle Seahawks defeated the Tennessee Oilers 16-13 at the Kingdome in Seattle, October 5.

Atlanta Falcons owner Rankin Smith died of heart failure three days prior to his seventy-third birthday. Smith was the founder of the Falcons and was instrumental in bringing Super Bowls XXVIII and XXXIV to Atlanta, October 26.

1998
The NFL reached agreement on record eight-year television contracts with four networks. ABC (*NFL Monday Night Football*) and FOX (NFC) retained their previous rights, CBS took over the AFC package from NBC, and ESPN won the right to broadcast the entire Sunday night cable package, January 13.

The World League was renamed the NFL Europe League, January 22.

The Denver Broncos won their first Super Bowl by defeating the defending champion Green Bay Packers 31-24 in Super Bowl XXXII at Qualcomm Stadium in San Diego, January 25.

The NFL clubs approved an extension of the Collective Bargaining Agreement through 2003. The extended CBA also created a $100 million fund for youth football, March 22.

The NFL clubs unanimously approved an expansion team for Cleveland to fulfill the commitment to return the Browns to the field in 1999, March 23.

The Rhein Fire defeated the Frankfurt Galaxy 34-10 to win the 1998 World Bowl in front of 47,846 fans in Frankfurt's Waldstadion—the biggest crowd to witness a World Bowl since 1991, June 14.

NFL clubs approved the transfer of the Minnesota Vikings from a 10-man ownership group to Red McCombs, July 28.

The NFL Stadium at Camden Yards opened in Baltimore, Maryland before a crowd of 65,938 as the Baltimore Ravens defeated the Chicago Bears 19-14 in a preseason game, August 8.

Raymond James Stadium opened in Tampa, Florida before a crowd of 62,410 as the Tampa Bay Buccaneers

defeated the Chicago Bears 27-15, September 20.

Tennessee Oilers owner Bud Adams announced the team will change its name to the Tennessee Titans following the 1998 season. The NFL announced that the name Oilers will be retired—a first in league history, November 14.

1999
The Denver Broncos won their second consecutive Super Bowl title by defeating the NFC champion Atlanta Falcons 34-19 in Super Bowl XXXIII at Pro Player Stadium in Miami, January 31.

Jim Pyne, a center allocated by the Detroit Lions, was the first selection of the Cleveland Browns in the 1999 NFL Expansion Draft. The Browns eventually selected 37 players, February 9.

CBS Radio/Westwood One agreed to a 3-year extension of their exclusive national radio rights to NFL games, March 11.

By a vote of 28-3, the owners adopted an instant replay system as an officiating aid for the 1999 season, March 17.

New York Jets owner Leon Hess died from complications of a blood disease. Hess had been involved in the ownership of the Jets since 1963 and was sole owner of the club since 1984, May 9.

A group led by Washington area businessman Daniel Snyder is approved by NFL clubs as the new owner of the Washington Redskins at a league meeting in Atlanta, May 25.

The Frankfurt Galaxy became the first team in NFL Europe League history to win a second World Bowl by defeating the Barcelona Dragons 38-24 at Rheinstadion, in Düsseldorf, Germany, June 27.

The Cleveland Browns returned to the field for the first time since 1995 and defeated the Dallas Cowboys 20-17 in overtime in the annual Hall of Fame Game at Canton, Ohio, August 9.

Cleveland Browns Stadium opened in Cleveland, Ohio before a crowd of 71,398 as the Minnesota Vikings defeated the Browns in a preseason game, 24-17, August 21.

Adelphia Coliseum opened

in Nashville, Tennessee before a crowd of 65,729 with the Tennessee Titans defeating the Atlanta Falcons 17-3 in a preseason game, August 26.

Houston, Texas and owner Robert McNair were awarded the NFL's thirty-second franchise in a vote of the NFL clubs at a league meeting in Atlanta. The team will begin play in 2002. The NFL clubs also voted to realign into eight divisions of four teams each for the 2002 season, October 6.

Walter Payton, the NFL's all-time leading rusher, died of liver cancer at the age of 45, November 1. The NFL Man of the Year Award, the only NFL award that recognizes a player for his community service activities as well as his excellence on the field, was renamed in his honor shortly after his passing.

Former NFL Commissioner Pete Rozelle, who guided a still-developing league to its position today as America's most popular sport, was named by The Sporting News as the most powerful person in sports in the 20th Century, December 15.

2000

New York businessman Robert Wood Johnson IV was approved by NFL clubs as the new owner of the New York Jets at a league meeting, January 18.

The St. Louis Rams won their first Super Bowl by defeating the AFC champion Tennessee Titans 23-16 in Super Bowl XXXIV at the Georgia Dome in Atlanta, January 30.

For the first time in league history, paid attendance topped 16 million for the regular season and more than 65,000 per game, an increase of 1,300 per game over 1998. Paid attendance for all NFL games increased in 1999 for the third year in a row and was the highest ever in the 80-year history of the league. It marked the first time in league history that the 20-million paid attendance mark was reached for all games in a season, March 27.

The Rhein Fire won their second World Bowl in three years, defeating the Scottish Claymores 13-10 to win World

Bowl 2000 in front of 35,680 at Frankfurt's Waldstadion, June 25.

More than 100 of the 136 living members of the Pro Football Hall of Fame gathered to celebrate Pro Football's Greatest Reunion in Canton, Ohio, July 28-31.

Paul Brown Stadium opened in Cincinnati, Ohio with a crowd of 56,180 as the Cincinnati Bengals defeated the Chicago Bears 24-20 in a preseason game, August 19.

Minnesota's Gary Anderson converted a 21-yard field goal against Buffalo to pass George Blanda as the NFL's all-time scoring leader with 2,004 points, October 22.

2001

NFL clubs approved additional league-wide revenue sharing at a special league meeting in Dallas. The teams agreed to pool the visiting team share of gate receipts for all preseason and regular-season games and divide the pool equally starting in 2002, January 17.

The Baltimore Ravens won their first Super Bowl by defeating the NFC champion New York Giants 34-7 in Super Bowl XXXV at Raymond James Stadium in Tampa Bay, January 28.

The Sports Business Daily named NFL Commissioner Paul Tagliabue the 2000 Sports Industrialist of the Year, February 28.

NFL owners unanimously approved a realignment plan for the league starting in 2002. With the addition of the Houston Texans, the league's 32 teams will be divided into eight four-team divisions. Seven clubs change divisions, and the Seattle Seahawks change conferences, moving from the AFC to the NFC. A new scheduling format ensures that every team meets every other team in the league at least once every four years, May 22.

The Berlin Thunder won their first World Bowl, defeating the Barcelona Dragons 24-17 to win World Bowl IX in front of 32,116 at Amsterdam ArenA, June 30.

Heinz Field opened in Pittsburgh, Pennsylvania before a crowd of 57,829 with the Pittsburgh Steelers defeating the Detroit Lions 20-7 in a pre-

season game; and INVESCO Field at Mile High opened in Denver, Colorado before a crowd of 74,063 with the Denver Broncos defeating the New Orleans Saints 31-24 in a preseason game, August 25.

President George W. Bush became the first United States President to be involved in an NFL regular-season pregame coin toss as he helped kick off the 2001 season from the White House. Via satellite, President Bush tossed the coin for the 10 regular-season games that started at 1:00 P.M. ET, September 9.

In the wake of the September 11 terrorist attacks, Commissioner Paul Tagliabue postponed the games scheduled for September 16-17, September 13.

The league's 16-game regular season was retained when the postponed Week 2 games were rescheduled for the weekend of January 6-7, September 18.

The NFL and its game officials agreed to a new six-year Collective Bargaining Agreement, ending a two-week lockout of the regular officials, who returned to work on September 23, September 19.

The NFL announced that the league's prohibition of anabolic steroids and related substances had been strengthened to include supplements containing ephedrine and other high-risk supplements, September 27.

The NFL announced that the Super Bowl would be rescheduled from January 27 to February 3 in order to retain the full playoff format for the 2001 season. It will be the first Super Bowl played in February, October 3.

President Bush designated Super Bowl XXXVI as a "National Special Security Event," allowing all security for the game to be coordinated by the Secret Service, November 26.

2002

The NFL and the NFL Players Association agreed to a fourth extension of the 1993 Collective Bargaining Agreement through 2007, January 7.

In an AFC Wild Card matchup, the Oakland Raiders defeated the New York Jets 38-24 in the NFL's first-ever

primetime playoff game, January 12.

In a special meeting in New Orleans, NFL owners voted unanimously to approve the purchase of the Atlanta Falcons to Home Depot co-founder Arthur Blank, February 2.

The New England Patriots won their first Super Bowl by defeating the NFC champion St. Louis Rams 20-17 in Super Bowl XXXVI at the Louisiana Superdome in New Orleans. The game marked the first time in Super Bowl history that the winning points came on the final play, a 48-yard field goal by Patriots kicker Adam Vinatieri, February 3.

Tony Boselli, a five-time Pro Bowl tackle allocated by the Jacksonville Jaguars, was the first selection of the Houston Texans in the 2002 NFL Expansion Draft. The Texans selected 19 players, February 18.

The NFL and Westwood One/CBS Radio Sports announced the renewal of a multiyear agreement for Westwood One/CBS Radio Sports to continue as the exclusive network radio home of the NFL, April 9.

NFL Europe kicked off its tenth season with a record 254 players allocated by NFL clubs, April 13-14.

The Berlin Thunder became the first team to win consecutive World Bowls, defeating the Rhein Fire 26-20 to win World Bowl X in front of 53,109 fans at Rheinstadion, June 22.

Seahawks Stadium opened in Seattle, Washington with an attendance of 52,902 fans as the Indianapolis Colts defeated the Seattle Seahawks 28-10 in a preseason game, August 10.

Gillette Stadium opened in Foxboro, Massachusetts with a crowd of 68,436 fans as the New England Patriots defeated the Philadelphia Eagles 16-15 in a preseason game, August 17.

Reliant Stadium opened in Houston, Texas with 69,432 fans in attendance, the largest non-Super Bowl crowd to ever watch an NFL game in Houston as the Miami Dolphins defeated the Houston Texans 24-3 in a preseason game, August 24.

For the first time, the NFL

season kicked off on a Thursday night in prime time as the San Francisco 49ers defeated the New York Giants 16-13 at Giants Stadium. The game was preceded by "NFL Kickoff Live From Times Square," presented by New York City and the NFL, a football and music festival honoring the resilient spirit of New York and America, September 5.

Week 1 of the 2002 season produced the highest-scoring and most competitive Kickoff Weekend in NFL history. The 16 games averaged 49.3 points per game. A total of 788 points and 89 touchdowns were scored, the most in league history for an opening weekend. Eleven of the 16 games were decided by one score (eight points or less), a Kickoff Weekend record, September 5-9.

Oakland Raiders wide receiver Jerry Rice became the all-time leader in yards from scrimmage, surpassing Pro Football Hall of Fame running back Walter Payton (21,281 yards), September 29.

Cleveland Browns owner Al Lerner, the NFL Finance Committee Chairman and Chairman and CEO of MBNA Corporation, died at the age of 69, October 23.

Dallas Cowboys running back Emmitt Smith became the NFL's all-time rushing leader, surpassing Pro Football Hall of Fame running back Walter Payton (16,726 yards), October 27.

The NFL and NFLPA announced the creation of USA Football, the first national advocacy organization representing all levels of amateur football, December 5.

NFL clubs implemented an expanded program to promote diversity in their coaching and front office ranks based upon recommendations of the NFL Committee on Workplace Diversity, December 19. The committee, appointed by Commissioner Tagliabue on October 31, comprised 10 owners and team executives with Pittsburgh Steelers owner Dan Rooney serving as chairman.

The 2002 season concluded with 25 overtime games, the most in NFL history, December 30.

2003

The Tampa Bay Buccaneers won their first Super Bowl by defeating the AFC champion Oakland Raiders 48-21 in Super Bowl XXXVII at Qualcomm Stadium in San Diego, January 26.

Chicago Bears chairman emeritus Edward W. McCaskey died at the age of 83, April 8.

The Frankfurt Galaxy became the first team to win three World Bowls, defeating the Rhein Fire 35-16 to win World Bowl XI in front of 28,138 fans at Hampden Park, June 14.

Tex Schramm, the legendary team president and general manager of the Dallas Cowboys and a member of the Pro Football Hall of Fame, died at the age of 83, July 15.

Lincoln Financial Field opened in Philadelphia, Pennsylvania with an attendance of 66,279 fans as the New England Patriots defeated the Philadelphia Eagles 24-12 in a preseason game, August 22.

A renovated Lambeau Field opened in Green Bay, Wisconsin with a crowd of 69,831 fans as the Carolina Panthers defeated the Green Bay Packers 20-7 in a preseason game, August 23.

A renovated Soldier Field opened in Chicago, Illinois with an attendance of 61,500 fans as the Green Bay Packers defeated the Chicago Bears 38-23 in a regular season game on ABC's *NFL Monday Night Football*, September 29.

NFL Network, the first 24-hour, year-round television channel dedicated to the NFL and the sport of football, launched on DirecTV, November 4.

2004

The New England Patriots won their second Super Bowl in three years by defeating the NFC champion Carolina Panthers 32-29 in Super Bowl XXXVIII at Reliant Stadium in Houston, February 1.

By a vote of 29-3, NFL owners extended the instant replay system for another five seasons through 2008, March 30.

Steve Bisciotti took over as the controlling owner of the Baltimore Ravens, succeeding Art Modell, who operated the

franchise for 43 years, April 8.

Former Arizona Cardinals safety Pat Tillman was killed in a firefight while on combat patrol with the U.S. Army Rangers in Afghanistan, April 22.

A federal appeals court formally ruled in favor of the NFL's draft eligibility rule in Maurice Clarett's lawsuit, citing federal labor policy in permitting the NFL and the Players Association to set rules for when players can enter the league, May 24.

The Berlin Thunder defeated the Frankfurt Galaxy 30-24 to win World Bowl XII in front of 35,413 fans at Arena Auf-Schalke, June 12.

The New England Patriots defeated the New York Jets 13-7 for their NFL-record 18th consecutive regular-season victory, October 24.

The NFL reached an agreement on six-year contract extensions with two of its network television partners—CBS and FOX—to run through the 2011 season, November 8.

The NFL and DirecTV announced a five-year extension on the NFL Sunday Ticket subscription television package to run through the 2010 season, November 8.

NFL Europe named the Hamburg Sea Devils as the league's newest team, November 24.

2005

Indianapolis Colts quarterback Peyton Manning set the NFL single-season record with 49 touchdown passes, January 2.

The New England Patriots became the second team in NFL history to win three Super Bowls in four seasons by defeating the Philadelphia Eagles 24-21 in Super Bowl XXXIX at ALLTEL Stadium in Jacksonville, February 6.

The Pat Tillman USO Center opened in Afghanistan. The NFL donated $250,000 to the USO to honor the memory of the former Arizona Cardinals player who died in Afghanistan while serving in the U.S. Army, April 1.

The NFL reached long-term agreements for its Sunday and Monday primetime TV packages. NBC returned to the NFL by acquiring the Sunday night

package for six years (2006-2011). ESPN agreed on an eight-year deal to televise *Monday Night Football* from 2006-2013, April 18.

The NFL strengthened its steroids program by adopting the Olympic testosterone testing standard, tripling the number of times a player can be randomly tested during the offseason from two to six, adding substances to the list of banned substances, and putting new language in the policy to allow for testing of designer drugs and other substances that may have evaded detection, April 27.

NFL owners voted unanimously to approve the sale of the Minnesota Vikings to real-estate developer Zygi Wilf, May 25.

The Amsterdam Admirals defeated the Berlin Thunder 27-21 to win World Bowl XIII in front of 35,134 fans at LTU Arena in Düsseldorf, Germany, June 11.

The NFL designated September 18-19 as "Hurricane Relief Weekend," which concluded with a telethon in conjunction with a Monday Night Football doubleheader on ABC and ESPN. The New York Giants-New Orleans Saints game, originally scheduled for the Louisiana Superdome, was moved to Giants Stadium following Hurricane Katrina. In total, the NFL, its owners, teams, players, and fans contributed $21 million to aid the Hurricane Katrina rebuilding effort, September 19.

An NFL record 103,467 fans attended the Arizona Cardinals' 31-14 victory over the San Francisco 49ers at Mexico City's Azteca Stadium, the first-ever regular-season NFL game played outside the United States, October 2.

Wellington Mara, the New York Giants' president and co-chief executive officer, died at the age of 89, October 25.

Preston Robert Tisch, the Giants' chairman and co-chief executive officer, died at the age of 79, November 15.

2006

The NFL announced that NFL Network would begin airing a "Road To The Playoffs" package of eight primetime regular season NFL games starting in 2006, January 28.

The Pittsburgh Steelers won their fifth Super Bowl, defeating the Seattle Seahawks 21-10 in Super Bowl XL at Ford Field in Detroit, Michigan, February 5.

The NFL clubs approved an extension of the Collective Bargaining Agreement through 2012, March 8.

Commissioner Tagliabue announced his decision to retire by the end of July. The NFL enjoyed an era of unrivaled prosperity in the Tagliabue Era, including labor peace throughout his 17-year tenure, March 20.

NFL clubs unanimously decided to return the name of the official game ball to "The Duke" in honor of the late New York Giants owner Wellington Mara, March 27.

The Amsterdam Admirals defeated the Berlin Thunder 22-7 to win World Bowl XIV in front of 36,286 fans at LTU Arena in Düsseldorf, Germany, May 27.

Roger Goodell became the eighth chief executive of the NFL on August 8 when he was chosen to succeed Paul Tagliabue as commissioner by a unanimous vote of the clubs at a three-day meeting in Chicago, Illinois. The transfer from Commissioner Tagliabue to Commissioner Goodell took place at 6:00 A.M. on Friday, September 1.

Cardinals Stadium opened in Glendale, Arizona with a crowd of 63,400 fans on August 12 as the Arizona Cardinals defeated the Pittsburgh Steelers 21-13 in a preseason game. The facility was later renamed University of Phoenix Stadium on September 26.

President George W. Bush signed into law HR 4954, which included the Internet Gambling Prohibition and Enforcement Act. The bill prohibits online gamblers from using credit cards, checks and electronic fund transfers to place and settle bets, strengthening enforcement of federal and state gambling laws that had been evaded by overseas gambling operations using the Internet, October 13.

NFL owners approved a resolution to stage a limited number of international regular-season games—up to two per season—beginning in 2007 and continuing through 2011, October 24.

The NFL Network broadcast its first-ever regular-season game as the Kansas City Chiefs defeated the Denver Broncos 19-10 at Arrowhead Stadium on Thanksgiving night, November 23.

San Diego Chargers running back LaDainian Tomlinson set the NFL single-season record for touchdowns with 29 on December 10. He finished the season with 31 touchdowns and also set a single-season record for points with 186.

Lamar Hunt, founder of the Kansas City Chiefs and the American Football League, died at the age of 74, December 13.

2007

The Indianapolis Colts won their second Super Bowl, defeating the Chicago Bears 29-17 in Super Bowl XLI at Dolphin Stadium in South Florida, February 4. Both teams were coached by African-Americans: Tony Dungy of the Colts and Lovie Smith of the Bears.

NFL clubs approved additional league-wide revenue sharing at a league meeting in Phoenix, Arizona. The teams agreed to redistribute up to $430 million over a four-year span, retroactive to 2006, March 26.

The NFL announced changes to its long-standing personal conduct policy and programs for players, coaches, and other team and league employees. The modifications focus on expanded educational and support programs in addition to increased levels of discipline for violations of the policy, April 10.

The NFL, NFL Players Association, NFL Retired Players Association, NFL Alumni Association, NFL Charities and Pro Football Hall of Fame formed the first-ever Alliance to coordinate medical support services for former players, May 22.

The Hamburg Sea Devils defeated the Frankfurt Galaxy 37-28 to win World Bowl XV in front of 48,125 fans at Commerzbank-Arena in Frankfurt, Germany, June 23.

The NFL announced it will focus its international business strategy on reaching the widest possible global audience, including the staging of international regular-season games, and discontinued NFL Europa after 15 seasons of operation, June 29.

NFL owners unanimously approved $10 million in additional Alliance funding for retired players to help pay for joint replacement surgeries and other medical assistance, supplementing the initial $7 million committed in July by Alliance members, October 24.

The New York Giants defeated the Miami Dolphins 13-10 at London's in front of 81,176 fans at Wembley Stadium in the first regular-season game played outside of North America, October 28.

On the field in the 2007 season, many significant records and milestones were achieved: Green Bay quarterback Brett Favre surpassed Pro Football Hall of Famer Dan Marino in both passing categories—touchdowns and yards—to become the NFL's all-time career leader. Patriots quarterback Tom Brady set the single-season record with 50 touchdown passes, including 23 to wide receiver Randy Moss—also a record. New England, which became the first team ever to finish 16-0 in the regular season, scored a record 589 points.

2008

The NFL, United States Olympic Committee, United States Anti-Doping Agency and MLB announced a partnership to form a clean competition anti-doping research collaborative, January 10.

Georgia Frontiere, majority owner of the St. Louis Rams, died at the age of 80, January 18.

The NFL announced it will stage a regular-season game in the United Kingdom during each of the next three seasons, beginning with the New Orleans Saints hosting the San Diego Chargers on October 26, 2008 at London's Wembley Stadium, February 1.

The New York Giants scored with 35 seconds remaining to win their third Super Bowl, defeating the New England Patriots 17-14 in Super Bowl XLII at University of Phoenix Stadium in Glendale, Arizona, February 3.

The NFL set an all-time paid attendance record in 2007 for the sixth consecutive season. Attendance for all 2007 games was 22,256,502, an increase of 56,790 over the previous mark. The Washington Redskins set an all-time NFL regular-season home paid attendance record of 711,471 for eight games, breaking their own record of 708,852 in 2006.

NFL clubs voted unanimously to exercise their option to shorten by two years the current Collective Bargaining Agreement, which now will run through the 2010 season and 2011 NFL Draft, May 20.

Lucas Oil Stadium opened in Indianapolis, Indiana with a crowd of 65,333 as the Buffalo Bills defeated the Indianapolis Colts by a score of 20-7 in a preseason game, August 24.

The NFL established a new fan code of conduct to help support a positive fan environment at all NFL stadiums, August 5.

NFLPA Executive Director and Pro Football Hall of Famer Gene Upshaw died at the age of 63, August 20.

For the first time, an NFL game was broadcast on NBC and also streamed live in its entirety to fans on the Internet via NFL.com and NBCSports.com as the Giants beat the Redskins 16-7 in the 2009 NFL Kickoff game, September 4.

Owners approved a restructured ownership plan for the Pittsburgh Steelers that will keep the team under the control of chairman Dan Rooney and team president Art Rooney II, December 17.

The NFL announced that the 2010 Pro Bowl will be played a week prior to Super Bowl XLIV on Sunday, January 31, 2010. Both games will be played in South Florida, December 30.

In the 256 regular-season games of 2008, 44.1 points per game were scored—the highest average since 1970.

2009

Stephen M. Ross purchased an additional 45 percent of the Miami Dolphins from Wayne Huizenga and became the team's managing partner. Coupled with his April 1, 2008 purchase of 50 percent of the franchise, the stadium, and the excess developable land, Ross now owns 95 percent of the Dolphins and the stadium while Huizenga retains a five percent share of both and remains a 50 percent partner in that land, January 20.

The NFL re-named its minority coaching internship program the Bill Walsh NFL Minority Coaching Fellowship, honoring the Pro Football Hall of Fame coach who conceived of the program, January 29.

The Pittsburgh Steelers scored a touchdown with 42 seconds remaining to claim their NFL-record sixth Super Bowl title, defeating the Arizona Cardinals 27-23 in Super Bowl XLIII at Raymond James Stadium in Tampa Bay, February 1.

The NFL and Westwood One announced a new two-year agreement for Westwood One to continue as the exclusive network radio partner of the NFL, March 12.

The NFLPA selected Washington-based attorney DeMaurice Smith as its new executive director, March 16.

The NFL and DIRECTV announced an agreement to extend DIRECTV's rights to carry NFL Sunday Ticket through the 2014 season, March 23.

The NFL reached an agreement on two-year contract extensions with two of its network television partners – CBS and FOX – to run through the 2013 season, May 19.

The NFL extended by two years its broadcast partnership with NBC to televise the Sunday night package through the 2013 season, August 19.

Cowboys Stadium opened in Arlington, Texas with a crowd of 75,720 as the Dallas Cowboys defeated the Tennessee Titans by a score of 30-10 in a preseason game, August 21.

The NFL announced games that were blacked out in home team markets during the 2009 season would be shown on NFL.com in their entirety on a delayed basis, September 10.

The NFL launched a new "Red Zone Channel," offering fans crucial live action cut-ins of all Sunday afternoon games, September 13.

Pro Football Hall of Fame head coach and broadcaster John Madden was appointed special advisor to Commissioner Goodell, September 10.

NFL appointed former head coach Tony Dungy to lead a new NFL Player Advisory Forum and serve as a special advisor to Commissioner Goodell, November 19.

Commissioner Goodell notified NFL teams of new and expanded guidelines on return-to-play for any player who sustains a concussion, December 2.

2010

For the first time, the Pro Bowl was played in the Super Bowl city the week before the Super Bowl, as the AFC All-Stars beat the NFC All-Stars 41-34 in the 2010 Pro Bowl at Sun Life Stadium in South Florida. The game drew 70,697 fans – the highest attendance for a Pro Bowl since 1959, January 31.

The New Orleans Saints won their first Super Bowl title, defeating the Indianapolis Colts 31-17 in Super Bowl XLIV at Sun Life Stadium in South Florida, February 7.

Dr. Hunt Batjer of Northwestern University Feinberg School of Medicine and Dr. Richard G. Ellenbogen of the University of Washington School of Medicine were named the new co-chairs of the NFL Head, Neck and Spine Medical Committee, March 16.

NFL owners voted to amend postseason overtime rules to a modified sudden death format, guaranteeing at least one possession for each club if the receiving team fails to score a touchdown on its first overtime possession, March 23.

The NFL and NFL Alumni Association announced a new neurological care program for retired players, one of a series of NFL initiatives addressing the quality of life of retired players, March 24.

NFL rules changes emphasized additional player safety. Protection for defenseless players was standardized and expanded, protecting a player who has just completed a catch from blows to the head or neck by an opponent who launches. Additional protection was also given to longsnappers. Play will now stop if a ball carrier's helmet is removed, March 24.

The NFL Draft debuted a new three-day format, with the first two days broadcast in primetime. A record combined total of 45.4 million viewers tuned in to watch the 75th NFL Draft on NFL Network, ESPN and ESPN2, April 22-24.

New Meadowlands Stadium opened in East Rutherford, New Jersey as the New York Giants defeat the New York Jets by a score of 31-16 in a preseason game, August 16.

Stan Kroenke purchased an additional 60 percent of the St. Louis Rams from the Rosenbloom family and became the team's sole owner and chairman, August 25.

A renovated Arrowhead Stadium opened in Kansas City, Missouri as the Philadelphia Eagles defeated the Kansas City Chiefs 20-17 in a preseason game, August 27.

A poster created by the NFL and the Centers for Disease Control and Prevention (CDC) to help educate young athletes on concussions was released to the public. The poster, similar to one on display in NFL locker rooms, stresses the importance of recognizing a concussion, taking time to recover, and not returning to play too soon, October 11.

The NFL, NFL Alumni and Gay Culverhouse Players' Outreach Program announced a partnership to expand services for retired NFL players. The outreach program identifies retired players in need, ensuring they receive comprehensive medical evaluations and assistance in applying for the expanded benefits and services created in recent years by the NFL, October 12.

Commissioner Roger Goodell notified NFL teams that more significant discipline, including suspensions, would be imposed on players that strike an opponent in the head or neck area in violation of the rules, October 20.

The NFL and Westwood One Radio announced the renewal of a multi-year agreement for Westwood One to continue as the exclusive network radio home of the NFL, December 22.

2011

The NFL appointed Pro Football Hall of Famers Ronnie Lott and John Madden as co-chairs of a new Player Safety Advisory Panel. The panel provides recommendations on a variety of safety-related football matters, while taking a long-term view towards making the game safer at every level of the sport, January 4.

The Green Bay Packers won their fourth Super Bowl title, defeating the Pittsburgh Steelers 31-25 in Super Bowl XLV at Cowboys Stadium in North Texas. The game was viewed by 162.9 million people, making it the most-watched program in U.S. television history, February 6.

The NFL Head, Neck and Spine Committee announced a new standardized sideline concussion assessment protocol for team medical personnel. The new protocol includes a symptom checklist, limited neurologic examination and balance assessment, February 25.

On the steps of the Pro Football Hall of Fame in Canton, Ohio, Commissioner Goodell & NFLPA Executive Director DeMaurice Smith formally announced a comprehensive settlement of litigation and signed a new 10-year Collective Bargaining Agreement, August 4. The agreement included additional funding for player alumni of $1 billion, including a $620 million "Legacy Fund" to increase benefits for pre-1993 retirees.

A record 107.4 million fans tuned into Kickoff Weekend games on CBS, ESPN, FOX and NBC, September 8, 11-12.

The NFL announced an eight-year extension of its contract with ESPN for the broadcast rights to Monday Night Football through the 2021 season, September 8.

NFL teams, players and fans remembered the courage and resilience that followed the events of September 11, 2001 with special tributes in each stadium and on television during all games on Sunday, September 11.

Al Davis, the Oakland Raiders' owner and Pro Football Hall of Famer, died at the age of 82, October 8.

NFL owners approved a resolution to continue playing regular-season games in the United Kingdom through the 2016 season, October 11.

The NFL reached an agreement on nine-year contract

extensions of its Sunday broadcast television packages with CBS, FOX and NBC to run through the 2022 season, December 14. The agreements also enabled the NFL to expand its Thursday night package of games on NFL Network, which increased from eight to 13 games for the 2012 season.

NFL clubs unanimously approved the majority ownership transfer of the Jacksonville Jaguars from Wayne Weaver to businessman Shahid Khan at a meeting in Dallas, December 14.

On the field, many all-time records were set: 11,356 points were scored, the most of any season in NFL history; New Orleans' Drew Brees passed for 5,476 yards; and Green Bay's Aaron Rodgers led the league with a 122.5 passer rating.

2012

NFL clubs extended Commissioner Goodell's contract through March 31, 2019, January 25.

The New York Giants won their fourth Super Bowl title, defeating the New England Patriots 21-17 in Super Bowl XLVI at Lucas Oil Stadium in Indianapolis, February 6.

NFL COMMISSIONERS AND PRESIDENTS*

1920....Jim Thorpe, President
1921-39 ...Joe Carr, President
1939-41.Carl Storck, President
1941-46 ....Elmer Layden, Commissioner
1946-1959 ....Bert Bell, Commissioner
1960-1989 ....Pete Rozelle, Commissioner
1989-2006 .....Paul Tagliabue, Commissioner
2006-present ..Roger Goodell, Commissioner

*NFL treasurer Austin Gunsel served as president in the office of the commissioner following the death of Bert Bell (Oct. 11, 1959) until the election of Pete Rozelle (Jan. 26, 1960).

2011

AMERICAN CONFERENCE

East Division

	W	L	T	Pct.	Pts.	OP
New England#	13	3	0	.813	513	342
New York Jets	8	8	0	.500	377	363
Miami	6	10	0	.375	329	313
Buffalo	6	10	0	.375	372	434

North Division

	W	L	T	Pct.	Pts.	OP
Baltimore	12	4	0	.750	378	266
Pittsburgh*	12	4	0	.750	325	227
Cincinnati*	9	7	0	.563	344	323
Cleveland	4	12	0	.250	218	307

South Division

	W	L	T	Pct.	Pts.	OP
Houston	10	6	0	.625	381	278
Tennessee	9	7	0	.563	325	317
Jacksonville	5	11	0	.313	243	329
Indianapolis	2	14	0	.125	243	430

West Division

	W	L	T	Pct.	Pts.	OP
Denver	8	8	0	.500	309	390
San Diego	8	8	0	.500	406	377
Oakland	8	8	0	.500	359	433
Kansas City	7	9	0	.438	212	338

NATIONAL CONFERENCE

East Division

	W	L	T	Pct.	Pts.	OP
New York Giants	9	7	0	.563	394	400
Philadelphia	8	8	0	.500	396	328
Dallas	8	8	0	.500	369	347
Washington	5	11	0	.313	288	367

North Division

	W	L	T	Pct.	Pts.	OP
Green Bay#	15	1	0	.938	560	359
Detroit*	10	6	0	.625	474	387
Chicago	8	8	0	.500	353	341
Minnesota	3	13	0	.188	340	449

South Division

	W	L	T	Pct.	Pts.	OP
New Orleans	13	3	0	.813	547	339
Atlanta*	10	6	0	.625	402	350
Carolina	6	10	0	.375	406	429
Tampa Bay	4	12	0	.250	287	494

West Division

	W	L	T	Pct.	Pts.	OP
San Francisco	13	3	0	.813	380	229
Arizona	8	8	0	.500	312	348
Seattle	7	9	0	.438	321	315
St. Louis	2	14	0	.125	193	407

*Wild Card qualifier for playoffs; #Top playoff seed in conference
Miami finished ahead of Buffalo based on head-to-head sweep.
   Baltimore finished ahead of Pittsburgh based on head-to-head
   sweep. Denver finished ahead of San Diego and Oakland based
   on best record in common games (Denver 5-5; Oakland 4-6; San
   Diego 4-6). San Diego finished ahead of Oakland based on better
   conference record (7-5 to 6-6). Cincinnati finished ahead of
   Tennessee based on head-to-head victory. Philadelphia finished
   ahead of Dallas based on head-to-head sweep. Atlanta finished
   ahead of Detroit based on head-to-head victory. San Francisco
   finished ahead of New Orleans based on head-to-head victory.
Wild Card Playoff Games: HOUSTON 31, Cincinnati 10;
   DENVER 29, Pittsburgh 23 (OT)
Divisional Playoff Games: NEW ENGLAND 45, Denver 10;
   BALTIMORE 20, Houston 13
AFC Championship Game: NEW ENGLAND 23, Baltimore 20
Wild Card Playoff Games: NEW ORLEANS 45, Detroit 28;
   NEW YORK GIANTS 24, Atlanta 2
Divisional Playoff Games: SAN FRANCISCO 36, New Orleans 32;
   New York Giants 37, GREEN BAY 20
NFC Championship Game: New York Giants 20, SAN FRANCISCO 17 (OT)
Super Bowl XLVI: New York Giants (NFC) 21, New England (AFC) 17
   at Lucas Oil Stadium, Indianapolis

*In Past Standings section, home teams in playoff games are
indicated by capital letters.*

Playoff Seeds

AFC
1. **New England**
2. Baltimore
3. Houston
4. Denver
5. Pittsburgh
6. Cincinnati

NFC
1. Green Bay
2. San Francisco
3. New Orleans
4. **New York Giants**
5. Atlanta
6. Detroit

2010

AMERICAN CONFERENCE

East Division

	W	L	T	Pct.	Pts.	OP
New England#	14	2	0	.875	518	313
New York Jets*	11	5	0	.688	367	304
Miami	7	9	0	.438	273	333
Buffalo	4	12	0	.250	283	425

North Division

	W	L	T	Pct.	Pts.	OP
Pittsburgh	12	4	0	.750	375	232
Baltimore*	12	4	0	.750	357	270
Cleveland	5	11	0	.313	271	332
Cincinnati	4	12	0	.250	322	395

South Division

	W	L	T	Pct.	Pts.	OP
Indianapolis	10	6	0	.625	435	388
Jacksonville	8	8	0	.500	353	419
Houston	6	10	0	.375	390	427
Tennessee	6	10	0	.375	356	339

West Division

	W	L	T	Pct.	Pts.	OP
Kansas City	10	6	0	.625	366	326
San Diego	9	7	0	.563	441	322
Oakland	8	8	0	.500	410	371
Denver	4	12	0	.250	344	471

NATIONAL CONFERENCE

East Division

	W	L	T	Pct.	Pts.	OP
Philadelphia	10	6	0	.625	439	377
New York Giants	10	6	0	.625	394	347
Dallas	6	10	0	.375	394	436
Washington	6	10	0	.375	302	377

North Division

	W	L	T	Pct.	Pts.	OP
Chicago	11	5	0	.688	334	286
Green Bay*	10	6	0	.625	388	240
Detroit	6	10	0	.375	362	369
Minnesota	6	10	0	.375	281	348

South Division

	W	L	T	Pct.	Pts.	OP
Atlanta#	13	3	0	.813	414	288
New Orleans*	11	5	0	.688	384	307
Tampa Bay	10	6	0	.625	341	318
Carolina	2	14	0	.125	196	408

West Division

	W	L	T	Pct.	Pts.	OP
Seattle	7	9	0	.438	310	407
St. Louis	7	9	0	.438	289	328
San Francisco	6	10	0	.375	305	346
Arizona	5	11	0	.313	289	434

*Wild Card qualifier for playoffs; #Top playoff seed in conference
Pittsburgh finished ahead of Baltimore based on better division
   record (5-1 to 4-2). Indianapolis finished ahead of Kansas City
   based on head-to-head victory. Houston finished ahead of
   Tennessee based on better division record (3-3 to 2-4).
   Philadelphia finished ahead of the Giants based on head-to-head
   sweep. Dallas finished ahead of Washington based on better
   division record (3-3 to 2-4). Green Bay finished ahead of the
   Giants and Tampa Bay based on best strength of victory
   (Green Bay .475; Giants .400; Tampa Bay .344). Detroit finished
   ahead of Minnesota based on better division record (2-4 to 1-5).
   Seattle finished ahead of St. Louis based on better division record
   (4-2 to 3-3).
Wild Card Playoff Games: N.Y. Jets 17, INDIANAPOLIS 16;
   Baltimore 30, KANSAS CITY 7
Divisional Playoff Games: PITTSBURGH 31, Baltimore 24;
   N.Y. Jets 28, NEW ENGLAND 21
AFC Championship Game: PITTSBURGH 24, N.Y. Jets 19
Wild Card Playoff Games: SEATTLE 41, New Orleans 36;
   Green Bay 21, PHILADELPHIA 16
Divisional Playoff Games: Green Bay 48, ATLANTA 21;
   CHICAGO 35, Seattle 24
NFC Championship Game: Green Bay 21, CHICAGO 14
Super Bowl XLV: Green Bay (NFC) 31, Pittsburgh (AFC) 25
   at Cowboys Stadium, North Texas

Playoff Seeds

AFC
1. New England
2. **Pittsburgh**
3. Indianapolis
4. Kansas City
5. Baltimore
6. N.Y. Jets

NFC
1. Atlanta
2. Chicago
3. Philadelphia
4. Seattle
5. New Orleans
6. **Green Bay**

2009

AMERICAN CONFERENCE

East Division

	W	L	T	Pct.	Pts.	OP
New England	10	6	0	.625	427	285
New York Jets*	9	7	0	.563	348	236
Miami	7	9	0	.438	360	390
Buffalo	6	10	0	.375	258	326

North Division

	W	L	T	Pct.	Pts.	OP
Cincinnati	10	6	0	.625	305	291
Baltimore*	9	7	0	.563	391	261
Pittsburgh	9	7	0	.563	368	324
Cleveland	5	11	0	.313	245	375

South Division

	W	L	T	Pct.	Pts.	OP
Indianapolis#	14	2	0	.875	416	307
Houston	9	7	0	.563	388	333
Tennessee	8	8	0	.500	354	402
Jacksonville	7	9	0	.438	290	380

West Division

	W	L	T	Pct.	Pts.	OP
San Diego	13	3	0	.813	454	320
Denver	8	8	0	.500	326	324
Oakland	5	11	0	.313	197	379
Kansas City	4	12	0	.250	294	424

NATIONAL CONFERENCE

East Division

	W	L	T	Pct.	Pts.	OP
Dallas	11	5	0	.688	361	250
Philadelphia*	11	5	0	.688	429	337
New York Giants	8	8	0	.500	402	427
Washington	4	12	0	.250	266	336

North Division

	W	L	T	Pct.	Pts.	OP
Minnesota	12	4	0	.750	470	312
Green Bay*	11	5	0	.688	461	297
Chicago	7	9	0	.438	327	375
Detroit	2	14	0	.125	262	494

South Division

	W	L	T	Pct.	Pts.	OP
New Orleans#	13	3	0	.813	510	341
Atlanta	9	7	0	.563	363	325
Carolina	8	8	0	.500	315	308
Tampa Bay	3	13	0	.188	244	400

West Division

	W	L	T	Pct.	Pts.	OP
Arizona	10	6	0	.625	375	325
San Francisco	8	8	0	.500	330	281
Seattle	5	11	0	.313	280	390
St. Louis	1	15	0	.063	175	436

*Wild Card qualifier for playoffs; #Top playoff seed in conference
New England finished ahead of Cincinnati based on better strength of victory (.450 to Bengals' .438). Baltimore finished ahead of Pittsburgh based on better division record (3-3 to Steelers' 2-4). New York Jets finished ahead of Baltimore for first Wild Card based on better record vs. common opponents (4-1 to Ravens' 1-4) and ahead of Houston based on better conference record (7-5 to Texans' 6-6). Baltimore was second Wild Card based on better conference record than Houston (7-5 to Texans' 6-6). Dallas finished ahead of Philadelphia based on head-to-head sweep (2-0). Green Bay was first Wild Card ahead of Philadelphia based on better record vs. common opponents (4-1 to Eagles' 3-2).
Wild Card Playoff: New York Jets 24, CINCINNATI 14; Baltimore 33, NEW ENGLAND 14
Divisional Playoff: INDIANAPOLIS 20, Baltimore 3; New York Jets 17, SAN DIEGO 14
AFC Championship: INDIANAPOLIS 30, New York Jets 17
Wild Card Playoff: DALLAS 34, Philadelphia 14; ARIZONA 51, Green Bay 45 (OT)
Divisional Playoff Games: NEW ORLEANS 45, Arizona 14; MINNESOTA 34, Dallas 3
NFC Championship Game: NEW ORLEANS 31, Minnesota 28 (OT)
Super Bowl XLIV: New Orleans (NFC) 31, Indianapolis (AFC) 17 at Sun Life Stadium, South Florida

Playoff Seeds

AFC	NFC
1. Indianapolis	**1. New Orleans**
2. San Diego	2. Minnesota
3. New England	3. Dallas
4. Cincinnati	4. Arizona
5. New York Jets	5. Green Bay
6. Baltimore	6. Philadelphia

2008

AMERICAN CONFERENCE

East Division

	W	L	T	Pct.	Pts.	OP
Miami	11	5	0	.688	345	317
New England	11	5	0	.688	410	309
New York Jets	9	7	0	.563	405	356
Buffalo	7	9	0	.438	336	342

North Division

	W	L	T	Pct.	Pts.	OP
Pittsburgh	12	4	0	.750	347	223
Baltimore*	11	5	0	.688	385	244
Cincinnati	4	11	1	.281	204	364
Cleveland	4	12	0	.250	232	350

South Division

	W	L	T	Pct.	Pts.	OP
Tennessee#	13	3	0	.813	375	234
Indianapolis*	12	4	0	.750	377	298
Houston	8	8	0	.500	366	394
Jacksonville	5	11	0	.313	302	367

West Division

	W	L	T	Pct.	Pts.	OP
San Diego	8	8	0	.500	439	347
Denver	8	8	0	.500	370	448
Oakland	5	11	0	.313	263	388
Kansas City	2	14	0	.125	291	440

NATIONAL CONFERENCE

East Division

	W	L	T	Pct.	Pts.	OP
New York Giants#	12	4	0	.750	427	294
Philadelphia*	9	6	1	.594	416	289
Dallas	9	7	0	.563	362	365
Washington	8	8	0	.500	265	296

North Division

	W	L	T	Pct.	Pts.	OP
Minnesota	10	6	0	.625	379	333
Chicago	9	7	0	.563	375	350
Green Bay	6	10	0	.375	419	380
Detroit	0	16	0	.000	268	517

South Division

	W	L	T	Pct.	Pts.	OP
Carolina	12	4	0	.750	414	329
Atlanta*	11	5	0	.688	391	325
Tampa Bay	9	7	0	.563	361	323
New Orleans	8	8	0	.500	463	393

West Division

	W	L	T	Pct.	Pts.	OP
Arizona	9	7	0	.563	427	426
San Francisco	7	9	0	.438	339	381
Seattle	4	12	0	.250	294	392
St. Louis	2	14	0	.125	232	465

*Wild Card qualifier for playoffs; #Top playoff seed in conference
Miami finished ahead of New England based on better conference record (8-4 to Patriots' 7-5). Baltimore was second Wild Card ahead of New England based on better conference record (8-4 to Patriots' 7-5). San Diego finished ahead of Denver based on better division record (5-1 to Broncos' 3-3). N.Y. Giants finished ahead of Carolina based on head-to-head victory.
Wild Card Playoff: SAN DIEGO 23, Indianapolis 17; Baltimore 27, MIAMI 9
Divisional Playoff: Baltimore 13, TENNESSEE 10; PITTSBURGH 35, San Diego 24
AFC Championship: PITTSBURGH 23, Baltimore 14
Wild Card Playoff: ARIZONA 30, Atlanta 24; Philadelphia 26, MINNESOTA 14
Divisional Playoff: Arizona 33, CAROLINA 13; Philadelphia 23, N.Y. GIANTS 11
NFC Championship: ARIZONA 32, Philadelphia 25
Super Bowl XLIII: Pittsburgh (AFC) 27, Arizona (NFC) 23 at Raymond James Stadium, Tampa, Florida

Playoff Seeds

AFC	NFC
1. Tennessee	1. N.Y. Giants
2. Pittsburgh	2. Carolina
3. Miami	3. Minnesota
4. San Diego	**4. Arizona**
5. Indianapolis	5. Atlanta
6. Baltimore	6. Philadelphia

2007

AMERICAN CONFERENCE

East Division

	W	L	T	Pct.	Pts.	OP
New England#	16	0	0	1.000	589	274
Buffalo	7	9	0	.438	252	354
New York Jets	4	12	0	.250	268	355
Miami	1	15	0	.063	267	437

North Division

	W	L	T	Pct.	Pts.	OP
Pittsburgh	10	6	0	.625	393	269
Cleveland	10	6	0	.625	402	382
Cincinnati	7	9	0	.438	380	385
Baltimore	5	11	0	.313	275	384

South Division

	W	L	T	Pct.	Pts.	OP
Indianapolis	13	3	0	.813	450	262
Jacksonville*	11	5	0	.688	411	304
Tennessee*	10	6	0	.625	301	297
Houston	8	8	0	.500	379	384

West Division

	W	L	T	Pct.	Pts.	OP
San Diego	11	5	0	.688	412	284
Denver	7	9	0	.438	320	409
Kansas City	4	12	0	.250	226	335
Oakland	4	12	0	.250	283	398

NATIONAL CONFERENCE

East Division

	W	L	T	Pct.	Pts.	OP
Dallas#	13	3	0	.813	455	325
New York Giants*	10	6	0	.625	373	351
Washington*	9	7	0	.563	334	310
Philadelphia	8	8	0	.500	336	300

North Division

	W	L	T	Pct.	Pts.	OP
Green Bay	13	3	0	.813	435	291
Minnesota	8	8	0	.500	365	311
Detroit	7	9	0	.438	346	444
Chicago	7	9	0	.438	334	348

South Division

	W	L	T	Pct.	Pts.	OP
Tampa Bay	9	7	0	.563	334	270
Carolina	7	9	0	.438	267	347
New Orleans	7	9	0	.438	379	388
Atlanta	4	12	0	.250	259	414

West Division

	W	L	T	Pct.	Pts.	OP
Seattle	10	6	0	.625	393	291
Arizona	8	8	0	.500	404	399
San Francisco	5	11	0	.313	219	364
St. Louis	3	13	0	.188	263	438

*Wild Card qualifier for playoffs; #Top playoff seed in conference
Pittsburgh finished ahead of Cleveland based on head-to-head sweep (2-0). Tennessee finished ahead of Cleveland based on better record vs. common opponents (4-1 to Browns' 3-2). Kansas City finished ahead of Oakland based on better record vs. common opponents (2-10 to Raiders' 1-11). Dallas finished ahead of Green Bay based on head-to-head victory. Detroit finished ahead of Chicago based on head-to-head sweep (2-0). Carolina finished ahead of New Orleans based on better conference record (7-5 to Saints' 6-6).
Wild Card Playoff: Jacksonville 31, PITTSBURGH 29; SAN DIEGO 17, Tennessee 6
Divisional Playoff: NEW ENGLAND 31, Jacksonville 20; San Diego 28, INDIANAPOLIS 24
AFC Championship: NEW ENGLAND 21, San Diego 12
Wild Card Playoff: SEATTLE 35, Washington 14; N.Y. Giants 24, TAMPA BAY 14
Divisional Playoff: GREEN BAY 42, Seattle 20; N.Y. Giants 21, DALLAS 17
NFC Championship: N.Y. Giants 23, GREEN BAY 20 (OT)
Super Bowl XLII: N.Y. Giants (NFC) 17, New England (AFC) 14 at University of Phoenix Stadium, Glendale, Arizona

Playoff Seeds

AFC	NFC
1. New England	1. Dallas
2. Indianapolis	2. Green Bay
3. San Diego	3. Seattle
4. Pittsburgh	4. Tampa Bay
5. Jacksonville	**5. N.Y. Giants**
6. Tennessee	6. Washington

2006

AMERICAN CONFERENCE

East Division

	W	L	T	Pct.	Pts.	OP
New England	12	4	0	.750	385	237
New York Jets*	10	6	0	.625	316	295
Buffalo	7	9	0	.438	300	311
Miami	6	10	0	.375	260	283

North Division

	W	L	T	Pct.	Pts.	OP
Baltimore	13	3	0	.813	353	201
Cincinnati	8	8	0	.500	373	331
Pittsburgh	8	8	0	.500	353	315
Cleveland	4	12	0	.250	238	356

South Division

	W	L	T	Pct.	Pts.	OP
Indianapolis	12	4	0	.750	427	360
Tennessee	8	8	0	.500	324	400
Jacksonville	8	8	0	.500	371	274
Houston	6	10	0	.375	267	366

West Division

	W	L	T	Pct.	Pts.	OP
San Diego#	14	2	0	.875	492	303
Kansas City*	9	7	0	.563	331	315
Denver	9	7	0	.563	319	305
Oakland	2	14	0	.125	168	332

NATIONAL CONFERENCE

East Division

	W	L	T	Pct.	Pts.	OP
Philadelphia	10	6	0	.625	398	328
Dallas*	9	7	0	.563	425	350
New York Giants*	8	8	0	.500	355	362
Washington	5	11	0	.313	307	376

North Division

	W	L	T	Pct.	Pts.	OP
Chicago#	13	3	0	.813	427	255
Green Bay	8	8	0	.500	301	366
Minnesota	6	10	0	.375	282	327
Detroit	3	13	0	.188	305	398

South Division

	W	L	T	Pct.	Pts.	OP
New Orleans	10	6	0	.625	413	322
Carolina	8	8	0	.500	270	305
Atlanta	7	9	0	.438	292	328
Tampa Bay	4	12	0	.250	211	353

West Division

	W	L	T	Pct.	Pts.	OP
Seattle	9	7	0	.563	335	341
St. Louis	8	8	0	.500	367	381
San Francisco	7	9	0	.438	298	412
Arizona	5	11	0	.313	314	389

*Wild Card qualifier for playoffs; #Top playoff seed in conference
Indianapolis finished ahead of New England based on head-to-head victory. Cincinnati finished ahead of Pittsburgh based on better division record (4-2 to Steelers' 3-3). Tennessee finished ahead of Jacksonville based on better division record (4-2 to Jaguars' 2-4). Kansas City finished ahead of Denver based on better division record (4-2 to Broncos' 3-3). New Orleans finished ahead of Philadelphia based on head-to-head victory. N.Y. Giants finished ahead of Carolina and St. Louis based on better conference record (Giants' 7-5 to Panthers' 6-6 and Rams' 6-6) and ahead of Green Bay based on strength of victory (.422 to Packers' .383).
Wild Card Playoff: INDIANAPOLIS 23, Kansas City 8; NEW ENGLAND 37, N.Y. Jets 16
Divisional Playoff: Indianapolis 15, BALTIMORE 6; New England 24, SAN DIEGO 21
AFC Championship: INDIANAPOLIS 38, New England 34
Wild Card Playoff: SEATTLE 21, Dallas 20; PHILADELPHIA 23, N.Y. Giants 20
Divisional Playoff: NEW ORLEANS 27, Philadelphia 24; CHICAGO 27, Seattle 24 (OT)
NFC Championship: CHICAGO 39, New Orleans 14
Super Bowl XLI: Indianapolis (AFC) 29, Chicago (NFC) 17 at Dolphin Stadium, Miami, Florida

Playoff Seeds

AFC	NFC
1. San Diego	**1. Chicago**
2. Baltimore	2. New Orleans
3. Indianapolis	3. Philadelphia
4. New England	4. Seattle
5. N.Y. Jets	5. Dallas
6. Kansas City	6. N.Y. Giants

2005

AMERICAN CONFERENCE

East Division

	W	L	T	Pct.	Pts.	OP
New England	10	6	0	.625	379	338
Miami	9	7	0	.563	318	317
Buffalo	5	11	0	.313	271	367
N.Y. Jets	4	12	0	.250	240	355

North Division

	W	L	T	Pct.	Pts.	OP
Cincinnati	11	5	0	.688	421	350
Pittsburgh*	11	5	0	.688	389	258
Baltimore	6	10	0	.375	265	299
Cleveland	6	10	0	.375	232	301

South Division

	W	L	T	Pct.	Pts.	OP
Indianapolis#	14	2	0	.875	439	247
Jacksonville*	12	4	0	.750	361	269
Tennessee	4	12	0	.250	299	421
Houston	2	14	0	.125	260	431

West Division

	W	L	T	Pct.	Pts.	OP
Denver	13	3	0	.813	395	258
Kansas City	10	6	0	.625	403	325
San Diego	9	7	0	.563	418	312
Oakland	4	12	0	.250	290	383

NATIONAL CONFERENCE

East Division

	W	L	T	Pct.	Pts.	OP
N.Y. Giants	11	5	0	.688	422	314
Washington*	10	6	0	.625	359	293
Dallas	9	7	0	.563	325	308
Philadelphia	6	10	0	.375	310	388

North Division

	W	L	T	Pct.	Pts.	OP
Chicago	11	5	0	.688	260	202
Minnesota	9	7	0	.563	306	344
Detroit	5	11	0	.313	254	345
Green Bay	4	12	0	.250	298	344

South Division

	W	L	T	Pct.	Pts.	OP
Tampa Bay	11	5	0	.688	300	274
Carolina*	11	5	0	.688	391	259
Atlanta	8	8	0	.500	351	341
New Orleans	3	13	0	.188	235	398

West Division

	W	L	T	Pct.	Pts.	OP
Seattle#	13	3	0	.813	452	271
St. Louis	6	10	0	.375	363	429
Arizona	5	11	0	.313	311	387
San Francisco	4	12	0	.250	239	428

*Wild Card qualifier for playoffs; #Top playoff seed in conference
Cincinnati finished ahead of Pittsburgh based on better division record (5-1 to Steelers' 4-2). Baltimore finished ahead of Cleveland based on better division record (2-4 to Browns' 1-5). Tampa Bay finished ahead of Carolina based on better division record (5-1 to Panthers' 4-2). Chicago finished ahead of Tampa Bay, and Tampa Bay finished ahead of the N.Y. Giants, based on better record (Bears' 10-2 to Buccaneers' 9-3 to Giants' 8-4).
Wild Card playoff: NEW ENGLAND 28, Jacksonville 3; Pittsburgh 31, CINCINNATI 17
Divisional playoff: DENVER 27, New England 13; Pittsburgh 21, INDIANAPOLIS 18
AFC Championship: Pittsburgh 34, DENVER 17
Wild Card playoffs: Washington 17, TAMPA BAY 10; Carolina 23, NEW YORK GIANTS 0
Divisional playoff: SEATTLE 20, Washington 10; Carolina 29, CHICAGO 21
NFC Championship: SEATTLE 34, Carolina 14
Super Bowl XL: Pittsburgh (AFC) 21, Seattle (NFC) 10 at Ford Field, Detroit, Michigan

Playoff Seeds

AFC	NFC
1. Indianapolis	**1. Seattle**
2. Denver	2. Chicago
3. Cincinnati	3. Tampa Bay
4. New England	4. New York Giants
5. Jacksonville	5. Carolina
6. Pittsburgh	6. Washington

2004

AMERICAN CONFERENCE

East Division

	W	L	T	Pct.	Pts.	OP
New England	14	2	0	.875	437	260
N.Y. Jets*	10	6	0	.625	333	261
Buffalo	9	7	0	.563	395	284
Miami	4	12	0	.250	275	354

North Division

	W	L	T	Pct.	Pts.	OP
Pittsburgh#	15	1	0	.938	372	251
Baltimore	9	7	0	.563	317	268
Cincinnati	8	8	0	.500	374	372
Cleveland	4	12	0	.250	276	390

South Division

	W	L	T	Pct.	Pts.	OP
Indianapolis	12	4	0	.750	522	351
Jacksonville	9	7	0	.563	261	280
Houston	7	9	0	.438	309	339
Tennessee	5	11	0	.313	344	439

West Division

	W	L	T	Pct.	Pts.	OP
San Diego	12	4	0	.750	446	313
Denver*	10	6	0	.625	381	304
Kansas City	7	9	0	.438	483	435
Oakland	5	11	0	.313	320	442

NATIONAL CONFERENCE

East Division

	W	L	T	Pct.	Pts.	OP
Philadelphia#	13	3	0	.813	386	260
N.Y. Giants	6	10	0	.375	303	347
Dallas	6	10	0	.375	293	405
Washington	6	10	0	.375	240	265

North Division

	W	L	T	Pct.	Pts.	OP
Green Bay	10	6	0	.625	424	380
Minnesota*	8	8	0	.500	405	395
Detroit	6	10	0	.375	296	350
Chicago	5	11	0	.313	231	331

South Division

	W	L	T	Pct.	Pts.	OP
Atlanta	11	5	0	.688	340	337
New Orleans	8	8	0	.500	348	405
Carolina	7	9	0	.438	355	339
Tampa Bay	5	11	0	.313	301	304

West Division

	W	L	T	Pct.	Pts.	OP
Seattle	9	7	0	.563	371	373
St. Louis*	8	8	0	.500	319	392
Arizona	6	10	0	.375	284	322
San Francisco	2	14	0	.125	259	452

*Wild Card qualifier for playoffs; #Top playoff seed in conference
Indianapolis finished ahead of San Diego based on head-to-head victory. N.Y. Jets finished ahead of Denver based on better record vs. common opponents (5-0 to Broncos' 3-2). St. Louis finished ahead of New Orleans and Minnesota based on best conference record (7-5 to Saints' 6-6 to Vikings' 5-7), and Minnesota finished ahead of New Orleans based on head-to-head victory. N.Y. Giants finished ahead of Dallas and Washington based on better head-to-head record (3-1 to Cowboys' 2-2 to Redskins' 1-3), and Dallas finished ahead of Washington based on head-to-head sweep (2-0).
Wild Card playoffs: N.Y. Jets 20, SAN DIEGO 17 (OT); INDIANAPOLIS 49, Denver 24
Divisional playoffs: PITTSBURGH 20, N.Y. Jets 17 (OT); NEW ENGLAND 20, Indianapolis 3
AFC Championship: New England 41, PITTSBURGH 27
Wild Card playoffs: St. Louis 27, SEATTLE 20; Minnesota 31, GREEN BAY 17
Divisional playoffs: ATLANTA 47, St. Louis 17; PHILADELPHIA 27, Minnesota 14
NFC Championship: PHILADELPHIA 27, Atlanta 10
Super Bowl XXXIX: New England (AFC) 24, Philadelphia (NFC) 21 at Alltel Stadium, Jacksonville, Florida

Playoff Seeds

AFC	NFC
1. Pittsburgh	**1. Philadelphia**
2. New England	2. Atlanta
3. Indianapolis	3. Green Bay
4. San Diego	4. Seattle
5. N.Y. Jets	5. St. Louis
6. Denver	6. Minnesota

2003

AMERICAN CONFERENCE

East Division

	W	L	T	Pct.	Pts.	OP
New England#	14	2	0	.875	348	238
Miami	10	6	0	.625	311	261
Buffalo	6	10	0	.375	243	279
N.Y. Jets	6	10	0	.375	283	299

North Division

	W	L	T	Pct.	Pts.	OP
Baltimore	10	6	0	.625	391	281
Cincinnati	8	8	0	.500	346	384
Pittsburgh	6	10	0	.375	300	327
Cleveland	5	11	0	.313	254	322

South Division

	W	L	T	Pct.	Pts.	OP
Indianapolis	12	4	0	.750	447	336
Tennessee*	12	4	0	.750	435	324
Jacksonville	5	11	0	.313	276	331
Houston	5	11	0	.313	255	380

West Division

	W	L	T	Pct.	Pts.	OP
Kansas City	13	3	0	.813	484	332
Denver*	10	6	0	.625	381	301
Oakland	4	12	0	.250	270	379
San Diego	4	12	0	.250	313	441

NATIONAL CONFERENCE

East Division

	W	L	T	Pct.	Pts.	OP
Philadelphia#	12	4	0	.750	374	287
Dallas*	10	6	0	.625	289	260
Washington	5	11	0	.313	287	372
N.Y. Giants	4	12	0	.250	243	387

North Division

	W	L	T	Pct.	Pts.	OP
Green Bay	10	6	0	.625	442	307
Minnesota	9	7	0	.563	416	353
Chicago	7	9	0	.438	283	346
Detroit	5	11	0	.313	270	379

South Division

	W	L	T	Pct.	Pts.	OP
Carolina	11	5	0	.688	325	304
New Orleans	8	8	0	.500	340	326
Tampa Bay	7	9	0	.438	301	264
Atlanta	5	11	0	.313	299	422

West Division

	W	L	T	Pct.	Pts.	OP
St. Louis	12	4	0	.750	447	328
Seattle*	10	6	0	.625	404	327
San Francisco	7	9	0	.438	384	337
Arizona	4	12	0	.250	225	452

Wild Card qualifier for playoffs; #Top playoff seed in conference
Buffalo finished ahead of N.Y. Jets based on better division record (2-4 to Jets' 1-5). Indianapolis finished ahead of Tennessee based on head-to-head sweep (2-0). Jacksonville finished ahead of Houston based on better division record (2-4 to Texans' 1-5). Denver finished ahead of Miami based on better conference record (9-3 to Dolphins' 7-5). Oakland finished ahead of San Diego based on better conference record (3-9 to Chargers' 2-10). Philadelphia finished ahead of St. Louis based on better conference record (9-3 to Rams' 8-4). Seattle finished ahead of Dallas based on better strength of victory (65-95 to Cowboys' 62-98).

Wild Card playoffs: Tennessee 20, BALTIMORE 17; INDIANAPOLIS 41, Denver 10
Divisional playoffs: NEW ENGLAND 17, Tennessee 14; Indianapolis 38, KANSAS CITY 31
AFC Championship: NEW ENGLAND 24, Indianapolis 14
Wild Card playoffs: CAROLINA 29, Dallas 10; GREEN BAY 33, Seattle 27 (OT)
Divisional playoffs: Carolina 29, ST. LOUIS 23 (2OT); PHILADELPHIA 20, Green Bay 17 (OT)
NFC Championship: Carolina 14, PHILADELPHIA 3
Super Bowl XXXVIII: New England (AFC) 32, Carolina (NFC) 29 at Reliant Stadium, Houston, Texas

Playoff Seeds

AFC	NFC
1. New England	1. Philadelphia
2. Kansas City	2. St. Louis
3. Indianapolis	**3. Carolina**
4. Baltimore	4. Green Bay
5. Tennessee	5. Seattle
6. Denver	6. Dallas

2002

AMERICAN CONFERENCE

East Division

	W	L	T	Pct.	Pts.	OP
N.Y. Jets	9	7	0	.563	359	336
New England	9	7	0	.563	381	346
Miami	9	7	0	.563	378	301
Buffalo	8	8	0	.500	379	397

North Division

	W	L	T	Pct.	Pts.	OP
Pittsburgh	10	5	1	.656	390	345
Cleveland*	9	7	0	.563	344	320
Baltimore	7	9	0	.438	316	354
Cincinnati	2	14	0	.125	279	456

South Division

	W	L	T	Pct.	Pts.	OP
Tennessee	11	5	0	.688	367	324
Indianapolis*	10	6	0	.625	349	313
Jacksonville	6	10	0	.375	328	315
Houston	4	12	0	.250	213	356

West Division

	W	L	T	Pct.	Pts.	OP
Oakland#	11	5	0	.688	450	304
Denver	9	7	0	.563	392	344
San Diego	8	8	0	.500	333	367
Kansas City	8	8	0	.500	467	399

NATIONAL CONFERENCE

East Division

	W	L	T	Pct.	Pts.	OP
Philadelphia#	12	4	0	.750	415	241
N.Y. Giants*	10	6	0	.625	320	279
Washington	7	9	0	.438	307	365
Dallas	5	11	0	.313	217	329

North Division

	W	L	T	Pct.	Pts.	OP
Green Bay	12	4	0	.750	398	328
Minnesota	6	10	0	.375	390	442
Chicago	4	12	0	.250	281	379
Detroit	3	13	0	.188	306	451

South Division

	W	L	T	Pct.	Pts.	OP
Tampa Bay	12	4	0	.750	346	196
Atlanta*	9	6	1	.594	402	314
New Orleans	9	7	0	.563	432	388
Carolina	7	9	0	.438	258	302

West Division

	W	L	T	Pct.	Pts.	OP
San Francisco	10	6	0	.625	367	351
St. Louis	7	9	0	.438	316	369
Seattle	7	9	0	.438	355	369
Arizona	5	11	0	.313	262	417

Wild Card qualifier for playoffs; #Top playoff seed in conference
New York Jets finished ahead of New England based on better record in common games (8-4 to Patriots' 7-5) and Miami based on better division record (4-2 to Dolphins' 2-4). New England finished ahead of Miami based on better division record (4-2 to Dolphins' 2-4). Cleveland finished ahead of Denver and New England based on better conference record (7-5 to Broncos' 5-7 and Patriots' 6-6). Oakland finished ahead of Tennessee based on better head-to-head record (1-0). San Diego finished ahead of Kansas City based on better division record (3-3 to Chiefs' 2-4). Philadelphia finished ahead of Green Bay and Tampa Bay based on better conference record (11-1 to Packers' 9-3 and Buccaneers' 9-3). Tampa Bay finished ahead of Green Bay based on better head-to-head record (1-0). St. Louis finished ahead of Seattle based on better division record (4-2 to Seahawks' 2-4).

Wild Card playoffs: N.Y. JETS 41, Indianapolis 0; PITTSBURGH 36, Cleveland 33
Divisional playoffs: TENNESSEE 34, Pittsburgh 31 (OT); OAKLAND 30, N.Y. Jets 10
AFC Championship: OAKLAND 41, Tennessee 24
Wild Card playoffs: Atlanta 27, GREEN BAY 7; SAN FRANCISCO 39, N.Y. Giants 38
Divisional playoffs: PHILADELPHIA 20, Atlanta 6; TAMPA BAY 31, San Francisco 6
NFC Championship: Tampa Bay 27, PHILADELPHIA 10
Super Bowl XXXVII: Tampa Bay (NFC) 48, Oakland (AFC) 21 at Qualcomm Stadium, San Diego, California

Playoff Seeds

AFC	NFC
1. Oakland	1. Philadelphia
2. Tennessee	**2. Tampa Bay**
3. Pittsburgh	3. Green Bay
4. N.Y. Jets	4. San Francisco
5. Indianapolis	5. N.Y. Giants
6. Cleveland	6. Atlanta

2001

AMERICAN CONFERENCE

Eastern Division

	W	L	T	Pct.	Pts.	OP
New England	11	5	0	.688	371	272
Miami*	11	5	0	.688	344	290
N.Y. Jets*	10	6	0	.625	308	295
Indianapolis	6	10	0	.375	413	486
Buffalo	3	13	0	.188	265	420

Central Division

	W	L	T	Pct.	Pts.	OP
Pittsburgh#	13	3	0	.813	352	212
Baltimore*	10	6	0	.625	303	265
Cleveland	7	9	0	.438	285	319
Tennessee	7	9	0	.438	336	388
Jacksonville	6	10	0	.375	294	286
Cincinnati	6	10	0	.375	226	309

Western Division

	W	L	T	Pct.	Pts.	OP
Oakland	10	6	0	.625	399	327
Seattle	9	7	0	.563	301	324
Denver	8	8	0	.500	340	339
Kansas City	6	10	0	.375	320	344
San Diego	5	11	0	.313	332	321

NATIONAL CONFERENCE

Eastern Division

	W	L	T	Pct.	Pts.	OP
Philadelphia	11	5	0	.688	343	208
Washington	8	8	0	.500	256	303
N.Y. Giants	7	9	0	.438	294	321
Arizona	7	9	0	.438	295	343
Dallas	5	11	0	.313	246	338

Central Division

	W	L	T	Pct.	Pts.	OP
Chicago	13	3	0	.813	338	203
Green Bay*	12	4	0	.750	390	266
Tampa Bay*	9	7	0	.563	324	280
Minnesota	5	11	0	.313	290	390
Detroit	2	14	0	.125	270	424

Western Division

	W	L	T	Pct.	Pts.	OP
St. Louis#	14	2	0	.875	503	273
San Francisco*	12	4	0	.750	409	282
New Orleans	7	9	0	.438	333	409
Atlanta	7	9	0	.438	291	377
Carolina	1	15	0	.063	253	410

*Wild Card qualifier for playoffs; #Top playoff seed in conference
New England finished ahead of Miami based on better division record (6-2 to Dolphins' 5-3). Baltimore was second Wild Card ahead of N.Y. Jets based on better record against common opponents (3-2 to Jets' 2-2). Cleveland finished ahead of Tennessee based on better division record (5-5 to Titans' 3-7). Jacksonville finished ahead of Cincinnati based on head-to-head record (2-0). N.Y. Giants finished ahead of Arizona based on head-to-head record (2-0). Green Bay was first Wild Card ahead of San Francisco based on better conference record (9-3 to 49ers' 8-4). New Orleans finished ahead of Atlanta based on better division record (4-4 to Falcons' 3-5).
Wild Card playoffs: OAKLAND 38, N.Y. Jets 24;
BALTIMORE 20, MIAMI 3
Divisional playoffs: NEW ENGLAND 16, Oakland 13 (OT);
PITTSBURGH 27, Baltimore 10
AFC Championship: New England 24, PITTSBURGH 17
Wild Card playoffs: PHILADELPHIA 31, Tampa Bay 9;
GREEN BAY 25, San Francisco 15
Divisional playoffs: Philadelphia 33, CHICAGO 19;
ST. LOUIS 45, Green Bay 17
NFC Championship: ST. LOUIS 29, Philadelphia 24
Super Bowl XXXVI: New England (AFC) 20, St. Louis (NFC) 17
at Louisiana Superdome, New Orleans, Louisiana

Playoff Seeds

AFC	NFC
1. Pittsburgh	1. St. Louis
2. New England	2. Chicago
3. Oakland	3. Philadelphia
4. Miami	4. Green Bay
5. Baltimore	5. San Francisco
6. N.Y. Jets	6. Tampa Bay

2000

AMERICAN CONFERENCE

Eastern Division

	W	L	T	Pct.	Pts.	OP
Miami	11	5	0	.688	323	226
Indianapolis*	10	6	0	.625	429	326
N.Y. Jets	9	7	0	.563	321	321
Buffalo	8	8	0	.500	315	350
New England	5	11	0	.313	276	338

Central Division

	W	L	T	Pct.	Pts.	OP
Tennessee#	13	3	0	.813	346	191
Baltimore*	12	4	0	.750	333	165
Pittsburgh	9	7	0	.563	321	255
Jacksonville	7	9	0	.438	367	327
Cincinnati	4	12	0	.250	185	359
Cleveland	3	13	0	.188	161	419

Western Division

	W	L	T	Pct.	Pts.	OP
Oakland	12	4	0	.750	479	299
Denver*	11	5	0	.688	485	369
Kansas City	7	9	0	.438	355	354
Seattle	6	10	0	.375	320	405
San Diego	1	15	0	.063	269	440

NATIONAL CONFERENCE

Eastern Division

	W	L	T	Pct.	Pts.	OP
N.Y. Giants#	12	4	0	.750	328	246
Philadelphia*	11	5	0	.688	351	245
Washington	8	8	0	.500	281	269
Dallas	5	11	0	.313	294	361
Arizona	3	13	0	.188	210	443

Central Division

	W	L	T	Pct.	Pts.	OP
Minnesota	11	5	0	.688	397	371
Tampa Bay*	10	6	0	.625	388	269
Green Bay	9	7	0	.563	353	323
Detroit	9	7	0	.563	307	307
Chicago	5	11	0	.313	216	355

Western Division

	W	L	T	Pct.	Pts.	OP
New Orleans	10	6	0	.625	354	305
St. Louis*	10	6	0	.625	540	471
Carolina	7	9	0	.438	310	310
San Francisco	6	10	0	.375	388	422
Atlanta	4	12	0	.250	252	413

*Wild Card qualifier for playoffs; #Top playoff seed in conference
Green Bay finished ahead of Detroit based on better division record (5-3 to Lions' 3-5). New Orleans finished ahead of St. Louis based on better division record (7-1 to Rams' 5-3). Tampa Bay was second Wild Card based on head-to-head victory over St. Louis (1-0).
Wild Card playoffs: MIAMI 23, Indianapolis 17 (OT);
BALTIMORE 21, Denver 3
Divisional playoffs: OAKLAND 27, Miami 0;
Baltimore 24, TENNESSEE 10
AFC Championship: Baltimore 16, OAKLAND 3
Wild Card playoffs: NEW ORLEANS 31, St. Louis 28;
PHILADELPHIA 21, Tampa Bay 3
Divisional playoffs: MINNESOTA 34, New Orleans 16;
N.Y. GIANTS 20, Philadelphia 10
NFC Championship: N.Y. GIANTS 41, Minnesota 0
Super Bowl XXXV: Baltimore (AFC) 34, N.Y. Giants (NFC) 7
at Raymond James Stadium, Tampa, Florida

Playoff Seeds

AFC	NFC
1. Tennessee	1. N.Y. Giants
2. Oakland	2. Minnesota
3. Miami	3. New Orleans
4. Baltimore	4. Philadelphia
5. Denver	5. Tampa Bay
6. Indianapolis	6. St. Louis

1999

AMERICAN CONFERENCE

Eastern Division

	W	L	T	Pct.	Pts.	OP
Indianapolis	13	3	0	.813	423	333
Buffalo*	11	5	0	.688	320	229
Miami*	9	7	0	.563	326	336
N.Y. Jets	8	8	0	.500	308	309
New England	8	8	0	.500	299	284

Central Division

	W	L	T	Pct.	Pts.	OP
Jacksonville#	14	2	0	.875	396	217
Tennessee*	13	3	0	.813	392	324
Baltimore	8	8	0	.500	324	277
Pittsburgh	6	10	0	.375	317	320
Cincinnati	4	12	0	.250	283	460
Cleveland	2	14	0	.125	217	437

Western Division

	W	L	T	Pct.	Pts.	OP
Seattle	9	7	0	.563	338	298
Kansas City	9	7	0	.563	390	322
San Diego	8	8	0	.500	269	316
Oakland	8	8	0	.500	390	329
Denver	6	10	0	.375	314	318

NATIONAL CONFERENCE

Eastern Division

	W	L	T	Pct.	Pts.	OP
Washington	10	6	0	.625	443	377
Dallas*	8	8	0	.500	352	276
N.Y. Giants	7	9	0	.438	299	358
Arizona	6	10	0	.375	245	382
Philadelphia	5	11	0	.313	272	357

Central Division

	W	L	T	Pct.	Pts.	OP
Tampa Bay	11	5	0	.688	270	235
Minnesota*	10	6	0	.625	399	335
Detroit*	8	8	0	.500	322	323
Green Bay	8	8	0	.500	357	341
Chicago	6	10	0	.375	272	341

Western Division

	W	L	T	Pct.	Pts.	OP
St. Louis#	13	3	0	.813	526	242
Carolina	8	8	0	.500	421	381
Atlanta	5	11	0	.313	285	380
San Francisco	4	12	0	.250	295	453
New Orleans	3	13	0	.188	260	434

*Wild Card qualifier for playoffs; #Top playoff seed in conference
Miami was third Wild Card ahead of Kansas City based on better
record against common opponents (6-1 to Chiefs' 5-3). N.Y. Jets
finished ahead of New England based on better division record
(4-4 to Patriots' 2-6). Seattle finished ahead of Kansas City based
on head-to-head sweep (2-0). San Diego finished ahead of
Oakland based on better division record (5-3 to Raiders' 3-5).
Dallas was second Wild Card based on better record against
common opponents (4-2 to Lions' 3-3) and better conference
record than Carolina (7-5 to Panthers' 6-6). Detroit was third Wild
Card based on better conference record than Green Bay
(7-5 to Packers' 6-6) and head-to-head victory over Carolina.
Wild Card playoffs: TENNESSEE 22, Buffalo 16;
  Miami 20, SEATTLE 17
Divisional playoffs: JACKSONVILLE 62, Miami 7;
  Tennessee 19, INDIANAPOLIS 16
AFC Championship: Tennessee 33, JACKSONVILLE 14
Wild Card playoffs: WASHINGTON 27, Detroit 13;
  MINNESOTA 27, Dallas 10
Divisional playoffs: TAMPA BAY 14, Washington 13;
  ST. LOUIS 49, Minnesota 37
NFC Championship: ST. LOUIS 11, Tampa Bay 6
Super Bowl XXXIV: St. Louis (NFC) 23, Tennessee (AFC) 16
  at Georgia Dome, Atlanta, Georgia

Playoff Seeds

AFC	NFC
1. Jacksonville	1. St. Louis
2. Indianapolis	2. Tampa Bay
3. Seattle	3. Washington
4. Tennessee	4. Minnesota
5. Buffalo	5. Dallas
6. Miami	6. Detroit

1998

AMERICAN CONFERENCE

Eastern Division

	W	L	T	Pct.	Pts.	OP
N.Y. Jets	12	4	0	.750	416	266
Miami*	10	6	0	.625	321	265
Buffalo*	10	6	0	.625	400	333
New England*	9	7	0	.563	337	329
Indianapolis	3	13	0	.188	310	444

Central Division

	W	L	T	Pct.	Pts.	OP
Jacksonville	11	5	0	.688	392	338
Tennessee	8	8	0	.500	330	320
Pittsburgh	7	9	0	.438	263	303
Baltimore	6	10	0	.375	269	335
Cincinnati	3	13	0	.188	268	452

Western Division

	W	L	T	Pct.	Pts.	OP
Denver#	14	2	0	.875	501	309
Oakland	8	8	0	.500	288	356
Seattle	8	8	0	.500	372	310
Kansas City	7	9	0	.438	327	363
San Diego	5	11	0	.313	241	342

NATIONAL CONFERENCE

Eastern Division

	W	L	T	Pct.	Pts.	OP
Dallas	10	6	0	.625	381	275
Arizona*	9	7	0	.563	325	378
N.Y. Giants	8	8	0	.500	287	309
Washington	6	10	0	.375	319	421
Philadelphia	3	13	0	.188	161	344

Central Division

	W	L	T	Pct.	Pts.	OP
Minnesota#	15	1	0	.938	556	296
Green Bay*	11	5	0	.688	408	319
Tampa Bay	8	8	0	.500	314	295
Detroit	5	11	0	.313	306	378
Chicago	4	12	0	.250	276	368

Western Division

	W	L	T	Pct.	Pts.	OP
Atlanta	14	2	0	.875	442	289
San Francisco*	12	4	0	.750	479	328
New Orleans	6	10	0	.375	305	359
Carolina	4	12	0	.250	336	413
St. Louis	4	12	0	.250	285	378

*Wild Card qualifier for playoffs; #Top playoff seed in conference
Miami finished ahead of Buffalo based on better net division points
(6 to Bills' 0). Oakland finished ahead of Seattle based on head-
to-head sweep (2-0). Carolina finished ahead of St. Louis based
on head-to-head sweep (2-0).
Wild Card playoffs: MIAMI 24, Buffalo 17;
  JACKSONVILLE 25, New England 10
Divisional playoffs: DENVER 38, Miami 3;
  N.Y. JETS 34, Jacksonville 24
AFC Championship: DENVER 23, N.Y. Jets 10
Wild Card playoffs: Arizona 20, DALLAS 7;
  SAN FRANCISCO 30, Green Bay 27
Divisional playoffs: ATLANTA 20, San Francisco 18;
  MINNESOTA 41, Arizona 21
NFC Championship: Atlanta 30, MINNESOTA 27 (OT)
Super Bowl XXXIII: Denver (AFC) 34, Atlanta (NFC) 19,
  at Pro Player Stadium, Miami, Florida

Playoff Seeds

AFC	NFC
1. Denver	1. Minnesota
2. N.Y. Jets	2. Atlanta
3. Jacksonville	3. Dallas
4. Miami	4. San Francisco
5. Buffalo	5. Green Bay
6. New England	6. Arizona

1997

AMERICAN CONFERENCE

Eastern Division

	W	L	T	Pct.	Pts.	OP
New England	10	6	0	.625	369	289
Miami*	9	7	0	.563	339	327
N.Y. Jets	9	7	0	.563	348	287
Buffalo	6	10	0	.375	255	367
Indianapolis	3	13	0	.188	313	401

Central Division

	W	L	T	Pct.	Pts.	OP
Pittsburgh	11	5	0	.688	372	307
Jacksonville*	11	5	0	.688	394	318
Tennessee	8	8	0	.500	333	310
Cincinnati	7	9	0	.438	355	405
Baltimore	6	9	1	.406	326	345

Western Division

	W	L	T	Pct.	Pts.	OP
Kansas City*	13	3	0	.813	375	232
Denver*	12	4	0	.750	472	287
Seattle	8	8	0	.500	365	362
Oakland	4	12	0	.250	324	419
San Diego	4	12	0	.250	266	425

NATIONAL CONFERENCE

Eastern Division

	W	L	T	Pct.	Pts.	OP
N.Y. Giants	10	5	1	.656	307	265
Washington	8	7	1	.531	327	289
Philadelphia	6	9	1	.406	317	372
Dallas	6	10	0	.375	304	314
Arizona	4	12	0	.250	283	379

Central Division

	W	L	T	Pct.	Pts.	OP
Green Bay	13	3	0	.813	422	282
Tampa Bay*	10	6	0	.625	299	263
Detroit*	9	7	0	.563	379	306
Minnesota*	9	7	0	.563	354	359
Chicago	4	12	0	.250	263	421

Western Division

	W	L	T	Pct.	Pts.	OP
San Francisco#	13	3	0	.813	375	265
Carolina	7	9	0	.438	265	314
Atlanta	7	9	0	.438	320	361
New Orleans	6	10	0	.375	237	327
St. Louis	5	11	0	.313	299	359

*Wild Card qualifier for playoffs; #Top playoff seed in conference
Miami finished ahead of N.Y. Jets based on head-to-head sweep
(2-0). Pittsburgh finished ahead of Jacksonville based on better
net division points (78 to Jaguars' 23). Oakland finished ahead of
San Diego based on better division record (2-6 to Chargers' 1-7).
San Francisco was top playoff seed based on better conference
record than Green Bay (11-1 to Packers' 10-2). Detroit finished
ahead of Minnesota based on head-to-head sweep (2-0).
Carolina finished ahead of Atlanta based on head-to-head sweep
(2-0).
Wild Card playoffs: DENVER 42, Jacksonville 17;
     NEW ENGLAND 17, Miami 3
Divisional playoffs: PITTSBURGH 7, New England 6;
     Denver 14, KANSAS CITY 10
AFC Championship: Denver 24, PITTSBURGH 21
Wild Card playoffs: Minnesota 23, N.Y. GIANTS 22;
     TAMPA BAY 20, Detroit 10
Divisional playoffs: SAN FRANCISCO 38, Minnesota 22;
     GREEN BAY 21, Tampa Bay 7
NFC Championship: Green Bay 23, SAN FRANCISCO 10
Super Bowl XXXII: Denver (AFC) 31, Green Bay (NFC) 24,
     at Qualcomm Stadium, San Diego, California

Playoff Seeds

AFC	NFC
1. Kansas City	1. San Francisco
2. Pittsburgh	**2. Green Bay**
3. New England	3. N.Y. Giants
4. Denver	4. Tampa Bay
5. Jacksonville	5. Detroit
6. Miami	6. Minnesota

1996

AMERICAN CONFERENCE

Eastern Division

	W	L	T	Pct.	Pts.	OP
New England	11	5	0	.688	418	313
Buffalo*	10	6	0	.625	319	266
Indianapolis*	9	7	0	.563	317	334
Miami	8	8	0	.500	339	325
N.Y. Jets	1	15	0	.063	279	454

Central Division

	W	L	T	Pct.	Pts.	OP
Pittsburgh	10	6	0	.625	344	257
Jacksonville*	9	7	0	.563	325	335
Cincinnati	8	8	0	.500	372	369
Houston	8	8	0	.500	345	319
Baltimore	4	12	0	.250	371	441

Western Division

	W	L	T	Pct.	Pts.	OP
Denver#	13	3	0	.813	391	275
Kansas City	9	7	0	.563	297	300
San Diego	8	8	0	.500	310	376
Oakland	7	9	0	.438	340	293
Seattle	7	9	0	.438	317	376

NATIONAL CONFERENCE

Eastern Division

	W	L	T	Pct.	Pts.	OP
Dallas	10	6	0	.625	286	250
Philadelphia*	10	6	0	.625	363	341
Washington	9	7	0	.563	364	312
Arizona	7	9	0	.438	300	397
N.Y. Giants	6	10	0	.375	242	297

Central Division

	W	L	T	Pct.	Pts.	OP
Green Bay#	13	3	0	.813	456	210
Minnesota*	9	7	0	.563	298	315
Chicago	7	9	0	.438	283	305
Tampa Bay	6	10	0	.375	221	293
Detroit	5	11	0	.313	302	368

Western Division

	W	L	T	Pct.	Pts.	OP
Carolina	12	4	0	.750	367	218
San Francisco*	12	4	0	.750	398	257
St. Louis	6	10	0	.375	303	409
Atlanta	3	13	0	.188	309	461
New Orleans	3	13	0	.188	229	339

*Wild Card qualifier for playoffs; #Top playoff seed in conference
Jacksonville was second Wild Card ahead of Indianapolis and
Kansas City based on better conference record (7-5 to Colts' 6-6
and Chiefs' 5-7). Indianapolis was third Wild Card based on
head-to-head victory over Kansas City (1-0). Cincinnati finished
ahead of Houston based on better net division points (19 to
Oilers' 11). Oakland finished ahead of Seattle based on better
division record (3-5 to Seahawks' 2-6). Dallas finished ahead of
Philadelphia based on better record against common opponents
(7-4 to Eagles' 6-5). Minnesota was third Wild Card based on
better conference record than Washington (8-4 to Redskins'
6-6). Carolina finished ahead of San Francisco based on head-to-
head sweep (2-0). Atlanta finished ahead of New Orleans based
on head-to-head sweep (2-0).
Wild Card playoffs: Jacksonville 30, BUFFALO 27;
     PITTSBURGH 42, Indianapolis 14
Divisional playoffs: Jacksonville 30, DENVER 27;
     NEW ENGLAND 28, Pittsburgh 3
AFC Championship: NEW ENGLAND 20, Jacksonville 6
Wild Card playoffs: DALLAS 40, Minnesota 15;
     SAN FRANCISCO 14, Philadelphia 0
Divisional playoffs: GREEN BAY 35, San Francisco 14;
     CAROLINA 26, Dallas 17
NFC Championship: GREEN BAY 30, Carolina 13
Super Bowl XXXI: Green Bay (NFC) 35, New England (AFC) 21,
     at Louisiana Superdome, New Orleans, Louisiana

Playoff Seeds

AFC	NFC
1. Denver	**1. Green Bay**
2. New England	2. Carolina
3. Pittsburgh	3. Dallas
4. Buffalo	4. San Francisco
5. Jacksonville	5. Philadelphia
6. Indianapolis	6. Minnesota

1995

AMERICAN CONFERENCE

Eastern Division

	W	L	T	Pct.	Pts.	OP
Buffalo	10	6	0	.625	350	335
Indianapolis*	9	7	0	.563	331	316
Miami*	9	7	0	.563	398	332
New England	6	10	0	.375	294	377
N.Y. Jets	3	13	0	.188	233	384

Central Division

	W	L	T	Pct.	Pts.	OP
Pittsburgh	11	5	0	.688	407	327
Cincinnati	7	9	0	.438	349	374
Houston	7	9	0	.438	348	324
Cleveland	5	11	0	.313	289	356
Jacksonville	4	12	0	.250	275	404

Western Division

	W	L	T	Pct.	Pts.	OP
Kansas City#	13	3	0	.813	358	241
San Diego*	9	7	0	.563	321	323
Seattle	8	8	0	.500	363	366
Denver	8	8	0	.500	388	345
Oakland	8	8	0	.500	348	332

NATIONAL CONFERENCE

Eastern Division

	W	L	T	Pct.	Pts.	OP
Dallas#	12	4	0	.750	435	291
Philadelphia*	10	6	0	.625	318	338
Washington	6	10	0	.375	326	359
N.Y. Giants	5	11	0	.313	290	340
Arizona	4	12	0	.250	275	422

Central Division

	W	L	T	Pct.	Pts.	OP
Green Bay	11	5	0	.688	404	314
Detroit*	10	6	0	.625	436	336
Chicago	9	7	0	.563	392	360
Minnesota	8	8	0	.500	412	385
Tampa Bay	7	9	0	.438	238	335

Western Division

	W	L	T	Pct.	Pts.	OP
San Francisco	11	5	0	.688	457	258
Atlanta*	9	7	0	.563	362	349
St. Louis	7	9	0	.438	309	418
Carolina	7	9	0	.438	289	325
New Orleans	7	9	0	.438	319	348

*Wild Card qualifier for playoffs; #Top playoff seed in conference
Indianapolis finished ahead of Miami based on head-to-head sweep (2-0). San Diego was first Wild Card based on head-to-head victory over Indianapolis (1-0). Cincinnati finished ahead of Houston based on better division record (4-4 to Oilers' 3-5). Seattle finished ahead of Denver and Oakland based on best head-to-head record (3-1 to Broncos' 2-2 and Raiders' 1-3). Denver finished ahead of Oakland based on head-to-head sweep (2-0). Philadelphia was first Wild Card ahead of Detroit based on better conference record (9-3 to Lions' 7-5). San Francisco was second playoff seed ahead of Green Bay based on better conference record (8-4 to Packers' 7-5). Atlanta was third Wild Card ahead of Chicago based on better record against common opponents (4-2 to Bears' 3-3). St. Louis finished ahead of Carolina and New Orleans based on best head-to-head record (3-1 to Panthers' 1-3 and Saints' 2-2). Carolina finished ahead of New Orleans based on better conference record (4-8 to 3-9).
Wild Card playoffs: BUFFALO 37, Miami 22;
  Indianapolis 35, SAN DIEGO 20
Divisional playoffs: PITTSBURGH 40, Buffalo 21;
  Indianapolis 10, KANSAS CITY 7
AFC Championship: PITTSBURGH 20, Indianapolis 16
Wild Card playoffs: PHILADELPHIA 58, Detroit 37;
  GREEN BAY 37, Atlanta 20
Divisional playoffs: Green Bay 27, SAN FRANCISCO 17;
  DALLAS 30, Philadelphia 11
NFC Championship: DALLAS 38, Green Bay 27
Super Bowl XXX: Dallas (NFC) 27, Pittsburgh (AFC) 17,
  at Sun Devil Stadium, Tempe, Arizona

Playoff Seeds

AFC	NFC
1. Kansas City	1. Dallas
2. Pittsburgh	2. San Francisco
3. Buffalo	3. Green Bay
4. San Diego	4. Philadelphia
5. Indianapolis	5. Detroit
6. Miami	6. Atlanta

1994

AMERICAN CONFERENCE

Eastern Division

	W	L	T	Pct.	Pts.	OP
Miami	10	6	0	.625	389	327
New England	10	6	0	.625	351	312
Indianapolis	8	8	0	.500	307	320
Buffalo	7	9	0	.438	340	356
N.Y. Jets	6	10	0	.375	264	320

Central Division

	W	L	T	Pct.	Pts.	OP
Pittsburgh#	12	4	0	.750	316	234
Cleveland*	11	5	0	.688	340	204
Cincinnati	3	13	0	.188	276	406
Houston	2	14	0	.125	226	352

Western Division

	W	L	T	Pct.	Pts.	OP
San Diego	11	5	0	.688	381	306
Kansas City*	9	7	0	.563	319	298
L.A. Raiders	9	7	0	.563	303	327
Denver	7	9	0	.438	347	396
Seattle	6	10	0	.375	287	323

NATIONAL CONFERENCE

Eastern Division

	W	L	T	Pct.	Pts.	OP
Dallas	12	4	0	.750	414	248
N.Y. Giants	9	7	0	.563	279	305
Arizona	8	8	0	.500	235	267
Philadelphia	7	9	0	.438	308	308
Washington	3	13	0	.188	320	412

Central Division

	W	L	T	Pct.	Pts.	OP
Minnesota	10	6	0	.625	356	314
Green Bay*	9	7	0	.563	382	287
Detroit*	9	7	0	.563	357	342
Chicago*	9	7	0	.563	271	307
Tampa Bay	6	10	0	.375	251	351

Western Division

	W	L	T	Pct.	Pts.	OP
San Francisco#	13	3	0	.813	505	296
New Orleans	7	9	0	.438	348	407
Atlanta	7	9	0	.438	317	385
L.A. Rams	4	12	0	.250	286	365

*Wild Card qualifier for playoffs; #Top playoff seed in conference
Miami finished ahead of New England based on head-to-head sweep (2-0). Kansas City finished ahead of L.A. Raiders based on head-to-head sweep (2-0). Green Bay was first Wild Card based on best head-to-head record (3-1) vs. Detroit (2-2) and Chicago (1-3) and better conference record (8-4) than N.Y. Giants (6-6). Detroit was second Wild Card based on better division record (4-4) than Chicago (3-5) and head-to-head victory over N.Y. Giants (1-0). Chicago was third Wild Card based on better record against common opponents (4-4) than N.Y. Giants (3-5). New Orleans finished ahead of Atlanta based on head-to-head sweep (2-0).
Wild Card playoffs: MIAMI 27, Kansas City 17;
  CLEVELAND 20, New England 13
Divisional playoffs: PITTSBURGH 29, Cleveland 9;
  SAN DIEGO 22, Miami 21
AFC Championship: San Diego 17, PITTSBURGH 13
Wild Card playoffs: GREEN BAY 16, Detroit 12;
  Chicago 35, MINNESOTA 18
Divisional playoffs: SAN FRANCISCO 44, Chicago 15;
  DALLAS 35, Green Bay 9
NFC Championship: SAN FRANCISCO 38, Dallas 28
Super Bowl XXIX: San Francisco (NFC) 49, San Diego (AFC) 26,
  at Joe Robbie Stadium, Miami, Florida

Playoff Seeds

AFC	NFC
1. Pittsburgh	1. San Francisco
2. San Diego	2. Dallas
3. Miami	3. Minnesota
4. Cleveland	4. Green Bay
5. New England	5. Detroit
6. Kansas City	6. Chicago

1993

AMERICAN CONFERENCE
Eastern Division

	W	L	T	Pct.	Pts.	OP
Buffalo#	12	4	0	.750	329	242
Miami	9	7	0	.563	349	351
N.Y. Jets	8	8	0	.500	270	247
New England	5	11	0	.313	238	286
Indianapolis	4	12	0	.250	189	378

Central Division

	W	L	T	Pct.	Pts.	OP
Houston	12	4	0	.750	368	238
Pittsburgh*	9	7	0	.563	308	281
Cleveland	7	9	0	.438	304	307
Cincinnati	3	13	0	.188	187	319

Western Division

	W	L	T	Pct.	Pts.	OP
Kansas City	11	5	0	.688	328	291
L.A. Raiders	10	6	0	.625	306	326
Denver*	9	7	0	.563	373	284
San Diego	8	8	0	.500	322	290
Seattle	6	10	0	.375	280	314

NATIONAL CONFERENCE
Eastern Division

	W	L	T	Pct.	Pts.	OP
Dallas#	12	4	0	.750	376	229
N.Y. Giants*	11	5	0	.688	288	205
Philadelphia	8	8	0	.500	293	315
Phoenix	7	9	0	.438	326	269
Washington	4	12	0	.250	230	345

Central Division

	W	L	T	Pct.	Pts.	OP
Detroit	10	6	0	.625	298	292
Minnesota*	9	7	0	.563	277	290
Green Bay*	9	7	0	.563	340	282
Chicago	7	9	0	.438	234	230
Tampa Bay	5	11	0	.313	237	376

Western Division

	W	L	T	Pct.	Pts.	OP
San Francisco	10	6	0	.625	473	295
New Orleans	8	8	0	.500	317	343
Atlanta	6	10	0	.375	316	385
L.A. Rams	5	11	0	.313	221	367

Wild Card qualifier for playoffs; #Top playoff seed in conference
Buffalo was top playoff seed based on head-to-head victory over
    Houston (1-0). Denver was second Wild Card ahead of Pittsburgh
    and Miami based on better conference record (8-4 to Steelers'
    7-5 to Dolphins' 6-6). Pittsburgh was third Wild Card ahead of
    Miami based on head-to-head victory. San Francisco was second
    playoff seed based on head-to-head victory over Detroit (1-0).
    Minnesota finished ahead of Green Bay based on head-to-head
    sweep (2-0).
Wild Card playoffs: KANSAS CITY 27, Pittsburgh 24 (OT);
    L.A. RAIDERS 42, Denver 24
Divisional playoffs: BUFFALO 29, L.A. Raiders 23;
    Kansas City 28, HOUSTON 20
AFC Championship: BUFFALO 30, Kansas City 13
Wild Card playoffs: Green Bay 28, DETROIT 24;
    N.Y. GIANTS 17, Minnesota 10
Divisional playoffs: SAN FRANCISCO 44, N.Y. Giants 3;
    DALLAS 27, Green Bay 17
NFC Championship: DALLAS 38, San Francisco 21
Super Bowl XXVIII: Dallas (NFC) 30, Buffalo (AFC) 13,
    at Georgia Dome, Atlanta, Georgia

Playoff Seeds

AFC	NFC
1. Buffalo	1. Dallas
2. Houston	2. San Francisco
3. Kansas City	3. Detroit
4. L.A. Raiders	4. N.Y. Giants
5. Denver	5. Minnesota
6. Pittsburgh	6. Green Bay

1992

AMERICAN CONFERENCE
Eastern Division

	W	L	T	Pct.	Pts.	OP
Miami	11	5	0	.688	340	281
Buffalo*	11	5	0	.688	381	283
Indianapolis	9	7	0	.563	216	302
N.Y. Jets	4	12	0	.250	220	315
New England	2	14	0	.125	205	363

Central Division

	W	L	T	Pct.	Pts.	OP
Pittsburgh#	11	5	0	.688	299	225
Houston*	10	6	0	.625	352	258
Cleveland	7	9	0	.438	272	275
Cincinnati	5	11	0	.313	274	364

Western Division

	W	L	T	Pct.	Pts.	OP
San Diego	11	5	0	.688	335	241
Kansas City*	10	6	0	.625	348	282
Denver	8	8	0	.500	262	329
L.A. Raiders	7	9	0	.438	249	281
Seattle	2	14	0	.125	140	312

NATIONAL CONFERENCE
Eastern Division

	W	L	T	Pct.	Pts.	OP
Dallas	13	3	0	.813	409	243
Philadelphia*	11	5	0	.688	354	245
Washington*	9	7	0	.563	300	255
N.Y. Giants	6	10	0	.375	306	367
Phoenix	4	12	0	.250	243	332

Central Division

	W	L	T	Pct.	Pts.	OP
Minnesota	11	5	0	.688	374	249
Green Bay	9	7	0	.563	276	296
Tampa Bay	5	11	0	.313	267	365
Chicago	5	11	0	.313	295	361
Detroit	5	11	0	.313	273	332

Western Division

	W	L	T	Pct.	Pts.	OP
San Francisco#	14	2	0	.875	431	236
New Orleans*	12	4	0	.750	330	202
Atlanta	6	10	0	.375	327	414
L.A. Rams	6	10	0	.375	313	383

Wild Card qualifier for playoffs; #Top playoff seed in conference
Pittsburgh was top playoff seed, and Miami was second playoff seed
    ahead of San Diego, based on conference record (10-2 to Dol-
    phins' 9-3 to Chargers' 9-5). Miami finished ahead of Buffalo
    based on better conference record (9-3 to Bills' 7-5). Houston
    was second Wild Card based on head-to-head victory over
    Kansas City (1-0). Washington was third Wild Card based on
    better conference record than Green Bay (7-5 to Packers' 6-6).
    Tampa Bay finished ahead of Chicago and Chicago finished ahead
    of Detroit based on better conference record (5-9 to Bears' 4-8
    and Lions' 3-9). Atlanta finished ahead of L.A. Rams based on
    better record against common opponents (5-7 to Rams' 4-8).
Wild Card playoffs: SAN DIEGO 17, Kansas City 0;
    BUFFALO 41, Houston 38 (OT)
Divisional playoffs: Buffalo 24, PITTSBURGH 3;
    MIAMI 31, San Diego 0
AFC Championship: Buffalo 29, MIAMI 10
Wild Card playoffs: Washington 24, MINNESOTA 7;
    Philadelphia 36, NEW ORLEANS 20
Divisional playoffs: SAN FRANCISCO 20, Washington 13;
    DALLAS 34, Philadelphia 10
NFC Championship: Dallas 30, SAN FRANCISCO 20
Super Bowl XXVII: Dallas (NFC) 52, Buffalo (AFC) 17,
    at Rose Bowl, Pasadena, California

Playoff Seeds

AFC	NFC
1. Pittsburgh	1. San Francisco
2. Miami	2. Dallas
3. San Diego	3. Minnesota
4. Buffalo	4. New Orleans
5. Houston	5. Philadelphia
6. Kansas City	6. Washington

1991

AMERICAN CONFERENCE

Eastern Division

	W	L	T	Pct.	Pts.	OP
Buffalo#	13	3	0	.813	458	318
N.Y. Jets*	8	8	0	.500	314	293
Miami	8	8	0	.500	343	349
New England	6	10	0	.375	211	305
Indianapolis	1	15	0	.063	143	381

Central Division

	W	L	T	Pct.	Pts.	OP
Houston	11	5	0	.688	386	251
Pittsburgh	7	9	0	.438	292	344
Cleveland	6	10	0	.375	293	298
Cincinnati	3	13	0	.188	263	435

Western Division

	W	L	T	Pct.	Pts.	OP
Denver	12	4	0	.750	304	235
Kansas City*	10	6	0	.625	322	252
L.A. Raiders*	9	7	0	.563	298	297
Seattle	7	9	0	.438	276	261
San Diego	4	12	0	.250	274	342

NATIONAL CONFERENCE

Eastern Division

	W	L	T	Pct.	Pts.	OP
Washington#	14	2	0	.875	485	224
Dallas*	11	5	0	.688	342	310
Philadelphia	10	6	0	.625	285	244
N.Y. Giants	8	8	0	.500	281	297
Phoenix	4	12	0	.250	196	344

Central Division

	W	L	T	Pct.	Pts.	OP
Detroit	12	4	0	.750	339	295
Chicago*	11	5	0	.688	299	269
Minnesota	8	8	0	.500	301	306
Green Bay	4	12	0	.250	273	313
Tampa Bay	3	13	0	.188	199	365

Western Division

	W	L	T	Pct.	Pts.	OP
New Orleans	11	5	0	.688	341	211
Atlanta*	10	6	0	.625	361	338
San Francisco	10	6	0	.625	393	239
L.A. Rams	3	13	0	.188	234	390

*Wild Card qualifier for playoffs; #Top playoff seed in conference
N.Y. Jets finished ahead of Miami based on head-to-head sweep (2-0). Chicago was first Wild Card based on better conference record than Dallas (9-3 to Cowboys' 8-4). Atlanta finished ahead of San Francisco based on head-to-head sweep (2-0), and was third Wild Card ahead of Philadelphia based on better conference record (7-5 to Eagles' 6-6).

Wild Card playoffs: KANSAS CITY 10, L.A. Raiders 6; HOUSTON 17, N.Y. Jets 10
Divisional playoffs: DENVER 26, Houston 24; BUFFALO 37, Kansas City 14
AFC Championship: BUFFALO 10, Denver 7
Wild Card playoffs: Atlanta 27, NEW ORLEANS 20; Dallas 17, CHICAGO 13
Divisional playoffs: WASHINGTON 24, Atlanta 7; DETROIT 38, Dallas 6
NFC Championship: WASHINGTON 41, Detroit 10
Super Bowl XXVI: Washington (NFC) 37, Buffalo (AFC) 24, at Hubert H. Humphrey Metrodome, Minneapolis, Minnesota

Playoff Seeds

AFC	NFC
1. Buffalo	1. Washington
2. Denver	2. Detroit
3. Houston	3. New Orleans
4. Kansas City	4. Chicago
5. L.A. Raiders	5. Dallas
6. N.Y. Jets	6. Atlanta

1990

AMERICAN CONFERENCE

Eastern Division

	W	L	T	Pct.	Pts.	OP
Buffalo#	13	3	0	.813	428	263
Miami*	12	4	0	.750	336	242
Indianapolis	7	9	0	.438	281	353
N.Y. Jets	6	10	0	.375	295	345
New England	1	15	0	.063	181	446

Central Division

	W	L	T	Pct.	Pts.	OP
Cincinnati	9	7	0	.563	360	352
Houston*	9	7	0	.563	405	307
Pittsburgh	9	7	0	.563	292	240
Cleveland	3	13	0	.188	228	462

Western Division

	W	L	T	Pct.	Pts.	OP
L.A. Raiders	12	4	0	.750	337	268
Kansas City*	11	5	0	.688	369	257
Seattle	9	7	0	.563	306	286
San Diego	6	10	0	.375	315	281
Denver	5	11	0	.313	331	374

NATIONAL CONFERENCE

Eastern Division

	W	L	T	Pct.	Pts.	OP
N.Y. Giants	13	3	0	.813	335	211
Philadelphia*	10	6	0	.625	396	299
Washington*	10	6	0	.625	381	301
Dallas	7	9	0	.438	244	308
Phoenix	5	11	0	.313	268	396

Central Division

	W	L	T	Pct.	Pts.	OP
Chicago	11	5	0	.688	348	280
Tampa Bay	6	10	0	.375	264	367
Detroit	6	10	0	.375	373	413
Green Bay	6	10	0	.375	271	347
Minnesota	6	10	0	.375	351	326

Western Division

	W	L	T	Pct.	Pts.	OP
San Francisco#	14	2	0	.875	353	239
New Orleans*	8	8	0	.500	274	275
L.A. Rams	5	11	0	.313	345	412
Atlanta	5	11	0	.313	348	365

*Wild Card qualifier for playoffs; #Top playoff seed in conference
Cincinnati finished ahead of Houston and Pittsburgh based on best head-to-head record (3-1 to Oilers' 2-2 to Steelers' 1-3). Houston was Wild Card based on better conference record (8-4) than Seattle (7-5) and Pittsburgh (6-6). Philadelphia finished ahead of Washington based on better division record (5-3 to Redskins' 4-4). Tampa Bay was second in NFC Central based on best head-to-head record (5-1) against Detroit (2-4), Green Bay (3-3), and Minnesota (2-4). Detroit finished third based on best net division points (minus 8) against Green Bay (minus 40). Green Bay finished ahead of Minnesota based on better conference record (5-7 to Vikings' 4-8). The L.A. Rams finished ahead of Atlanta based on net points in division (plus 1 to Falcons' minus 31).

Wild Card playoffs: MIAMI 17, Kansas City 16; CINCINNATI 41, Houston 14
Divisional playoffs: BUFFALO 44, Miami 34; L.A. RAIDERS 20, Cincinnati 10
AFC Championship: BUFFALO 51, L.A. Raiders 3
Wild Card playoffs: Washington 20, PHILADELPHIA 6; CHICAGO 16, New Orleans 6
Divisional playoffs: SAN FRANCISCO 28, Washington 10; N.Y. GIANTS 31, Chicago 3
NFC Championship: N.Y. Giants 15, SAN FRANCISCO 13
Super Bowl XXV: N.Y. Giants (NFC) 20, Buffalo (AFC) 19, at Tampa Stadium, Tampa, Florida

Playoff Seeds

AFC	NFC
1. Buffalo	1. San Francisco
2. L.A. Raiders	2. N.Y. Giants
3. Cincinnati	3. Chicago
4. Miami	4. Philadelphia
5. Kansas City	5. Washington
6. Houston	6. New Orleans

1989

AMERICAN CONFERENCE
Eastern Division

	W	L	T	Pct.	Pts.	OP
Buffalo	9	7	0	.563	409	317
Indianapolis	8	8	0	.500	298	301
Miami	8	8	0	.500	331	379
New England	5	11	0	.313	297	391
N.Y. Jets	4	12	0	.250	253	411

Central Division

	W	L	T	Pct.	Pts.	OP
Cleveland	9	6	1	.594	334	254
Houston*	9	7	0	.563	365	412
Pittsburgh*	9	7	0	.563	265	326
Cincinnati	8	8	0	.500	404	285

Western Division

	W	L	T	Pct.	Pts.	OP
Denver#	11	5	0	.688	362	226
Kansas City	8	7	1	.531	318	286
L.A. Raiders	8	8	0	.500	315	297
Seattle	7	9	0	.438	241	327
San Diego	6	10	0	.375	266	290

NATIONAL CONFERENCE
Eastern Division

	W	L	T	Pct.	Pts.	OP
N.Y. Giants	12	4	0	.750	348	252
Philadelphia*	11	5	0	.688	342	274
Washington	10	6	0	.625	386	308
Phoenix	5	11	0	.313	258	377
Dallas	1	15	0	.063	204	393

Central Division

	W	L	T	Pct.	Pts.	OP
Minnesota	10	6	0	.625	351	275
Green Bay	10	6	0	.625	362	356
Detroit	7	9	0	.438	312	364
Chicago	6	10	0	.375	358	377
Tampa Bay	5	11	0	.313	320	419

Western Division

	W	L	T	Pct.	Pts.	OP
San Francisco#	14	2	0	.875	442	253
L.A. Rams*	11	5	0	.688	426	344
New Orleans	9	7	0	.563	386	301
Atlanta	3	13	0	.188	279	437

*Wild Card qualifier for playoffs; #Top playoff seed in conference
Indianapolis finished ahead of Miami based on better conference record (7-5 vs. Dolphins' 6-8). Houston finished ahead of Pittsburgh based on head-to-head sweep (2-0). The L.A. Rams did not play San Francisco in the divisional playoffs because, from 1970-1989, two teams from the same division could not meet prior to the conference championship game. Philadelphia was first Wild Card ahead of L.A. Rams based on better record against common opponents (7-3 to Rams' 5-4). Minnesota finished ahead of Green Bay based on better division record (6-2 vs. Packers' 5-3).
Wild Card playoff: Pittsburgh 26, HOUSTON 23 (OT)
Divisional playoffs: CLEVELAND 34, Buffalo 30;
   DENVER 24, Pittsburgh 23
AFC Championship: DENVER 37, Cleveland 21
Wild Card playoff: L.A. Rams 21, PHILADELPHIA 7
Divisional playoffs: L.A. Rams 19, N.Y. GIANTS 13 (OT);
   SAN FRANCISCO 41, Minnesota 13
NFC Championship: SAN FRANCISCO 30, L.A. Rams 3
Super Bowl XXIV: San Francisco (NFC) 55, Denver (AFC) 10, at Louisiana Superdome, New Orleans, Louisiana

1988

AMERICAN CONFERENCE
Eastern Division

	W	L	T	Pct.	Pts.	OP
Buffalo	12	4	0	.750	329	237
Indianapolis	9	7	0	.563	354	315
New England	9	7	0	.563	250	284
N.Y. Jets	8	7	1	.531	372	354
Miami	6	10	0	.375	319	380

Central Division

	W	L	T	Pct.	Pts.	OP
Cincinnati#	12	4	0	.750	448	329
Cleveland*	10	6	0	.625	304	288
Houston*	10	6	0	.625	424	365
Pittsburgh	5	11	0	.313	336	421

Western Division

	W	L	T	Pct.	Pts.	OP
Seattle	9	7	0	.563	339	329
Denver	8	8	0	.500	327	352
L.A. Raiders	7	9	0	.438	325	369
San Diego	6	10	0	.375	231	332
Kansas City	4	11	1	.281	254	320

NATIONAL CONFERENCE
Eastern Division

	W	L	T	Pct.	Pts.	OP
Philadelphia	10	6	0	.625	379	319
N.Y. Giants	10	6	0	.625	359	304
Washington	7	9	0	.438	345	387
Phoenix	7	9	0	.438	344	398
Dallas	3	13	0	.188	265	381

Central Division

	W	L	T	Pct.	Pts.	OP
Chicago#	12	4	0	.750	312	215
Minnesota*	11	5	0	.688	406	233
Tampa Bay	5	11	0	.313	261	350
Detroit	4	12	0	.250	220	313
Green Bay	4	12	0	.250	240	315

Western Division

	W	L	T	Pct.	Pts.	OP
San Francisco	10	6	0	.625	369	294
L.A. Rams*	10	6	0	.625	407	293
New Orleans	10	6	0	.625	312	283
Atlanta	5	11	0	.313	244	315

*Wild Card qualifier for playoffs; #Top playoff seed in conference
Cincinnati was top playoff seed ahead of Buffalo based on head-to-head victory (1-0). Indianapolis finished ahead of New England based on better record against common opponents (7-5 to Patriots' 6-6). Cleveland finished ahead of Houston based on better division record (4-2 to Oilers' 3-3). Houston did not play Cincinnati, and Minnesota did not play Chicago in the divisional playoffs because, from 1970-1989, two teams from the same division could not meet prior to the conference championship game. Philadelphia finished first in NFC East based on head-to-head sweep of N.Y. Giants (2-0). Washington finished third in NFC East based on better division record (4-4) than Phoenix (3-5). Detroit finished fourth in NFC Central based on head-to-head sweep of Green Bay (2-0). San Francisco finished first in NFC West based on better head-to-head record (3-1) against L.A. Rams (2-2) and New Orleans (1-3). San Francisco finished with second playoff seed ahead of Philadelphia based on better record against common opponents (5-3 to Eagles' 5-4). L.A. Rams finished second in NFC West based on better division record (4-2) than New Orleans (3-3) and earned Wild-Card position based on better conference record (8-4) than N.Y. Giants (9-5) and New Orleans (6-6).
Wild Card playoff: Houston 24, CLEVELAND 23
Divisional playoffs: CINCINNATI 21, Seattle 13;
   BUFFALO 17, Houston 10
AFC Championship: CINCINNATI 21, Buffalo 10
Wild Card playoff: MINNESOTA 28, L.A. Rams 17
Divisional playoffs: CHICAGO 20, Philadelphia 12;
   SAN FRANCISCO 34, Minnesota 9
NFC Championship: San Francisco 28, CHICAGO 3
Super Bowl XXIII: San Francisco (NFC) 20, Cincinnati (AFC) 16, at Joe Robbie Stadium, Miami, Florida

1987

AMERICAN CONFERENCE

Eastern Division

	W	L	T	Pct.	Pts.	OP
Indianapolis	9	6	0	.600	300	238
New England	8	7	0	.533	320	293
Miami	8	7	0	.533	362	335
Buffalo	7	8	0	.467	270	305
N.Y. Jets	6	9	0	.400	334	360

Central Division

	W	L	T	Pct.	Pts.	OP
Cleveland	10	5	0	.667	390	239
Houston*	9	6	0	.600	345	349
Pittsburgh	8	7	0	.533	285	299
Cincinnati	4	11	0	.267	285	370

Western Division

	W	L	T	Pct.	Pts.	OP
Denver#	10	4	1	.700	379	288
Seattle*	9	6	0	.600	371	314
San Diego	8	7	0	.533	253	317
L.A. Raiders	5	10	0	.333	301	289
Kansas City	4	11	0	.267	273	388

NATIONAL CONFERENCE

Eastern Division

	W	L	T	Pct.	Pts.	OP
Washington	11	4	0	.733	379	285
Dallas	7	8	0	.467	340	348
St. Louis	7	8	0	.467	362	368
Philadelphia	7	8	0	.467	337	380
N.Y. Giants	6	9	0	.400	280	312

Central Division

	W	L	T	Pct.	Pts.	OP
Chicago	11	4	0	.733	356	282
Minnesota*	8	7	0	.533	336	335
Green Bay	5	9	1	.367	255	300
Tampa Bay	4	11	0	.267	286	360
Detroit	4	11	0	.267	269	384

Western Division

	W	L	T	Pct.	Pts.	OP
San Francisco#	13	2	0	.867	459	253
New Orleans*	12	3	0	.800	422	283
L.A. Rams	6	9	0	.400	317	361
Atlanta	3	12	0	.200	205	436

*Wild Card qualifier for playoffs; #Top playoff seed in conference
New England finished ahead of Miami based on head-to-head sweep (2-0). Houston was first Wild Card ahead of Seattle based on better conference record (7-4 to Seahawks' 5-6). Chicago was second playoff seed ahead of Washington based on better conference record (9-2 to Redskins' 9-3). Dallas finished ahead of St. Louis and Philadelphia based on better division record (4-4 to Cardinals' 3-5 and Eagles' 3-5). St. Louis finished ahead of Philadelphia based on better conference record (7-7 to Eagles' 4-7). Tampa Bay finished ahead of Detroit based on better division record (3-4 to Lions' 2-5).
Wild Card playoff: HOUSTON 23, Seattle 20 (OT)
Divisional playoffs: CLEVELAND 38, Indianapolis 21; DENVER 34, Houston 10
AFC Championship: DENVER 38, Cleveland 33
Wild Card playoff: Minnesota 44, NEW ORLEANS 10
Divisional playoffs: Minnesota 36, SAN FRANCISCO 24; Washington 21, CHICAGO 17
NFC Championship: WASHINGTON 17, Minnesota 10
Super Bowl XXII: Washington (NFC) 42, Denver (AFC) 10, at San Diego Jack Murphy Stadium, San Diego, California
Note: 1987 regular season was reduced from 16 to 15 games for each team due to players' strike.

1986

AMERICAN CONFERENCE

Eastern Division

	W	L	T	Pct.	Pts.	OP
New England	11	5	0	.688	412	307
N.Y. Jets*	10	6	0	.625	364	386
Miami	8	8	0	.500	430	405
Buffalo	4	12	0	.250	287	348
Indianapolis	3	13	0	.188	229	400

Central Division

	W	L	T	Pct.	Pts.	OP
Cleveland#	12	4	0	.750	391	310
Cincinnati	10	6	0	.625	409	394
Pittsburgh	6	10	0	.375	307	336
Houston	5	11	0	.313	274	329

Western Division

	W	L	T	Pct.	Pts.	OP
Denver	11	5	0	.688	378	327
Kansas City*	10	6	0	.625	358	326
Seattle	10	6	0	.625	366	293
L.A. Raiders	8	8	0	.500	323	346
San Diego	4	12	0	.250	335	396

NATIONAL CONFERENCE

Eastern Division

	W	L	T	Pct.	Pts.	OP
N.Y. Giants#	14	2	0	.875	371	236
Washington*	12	4	0	.750	368	296
Dallas	7	9	0	.438	346	337
Philadelphia	5	10	1	.344	256	312
St. Louis	4	11	1	.281	218	351

Central Division

	W	L	T	Pct.	Pts.	OP
Chicago	14	2	0	.875	352	187
Minnesota	9	7	0	.563	398	273
Detroit	5	11	0	.313	277	326
Green Bay	4	12	0	.250	254	418
Tampa Bay	2	14	0	.125	239	473

Western Division

	W	L	T	Pct.	Pts.	OP
San Francisco	10	5	1	.656	374	247
L.A. Rams*	10	6	0	.625	309	267
Atlanta	7	8	1	.469	280	280
New Orleans	7	9	0	.438	288	287

*Wild Card qualifier for playoffs; #Top playoff seed in conference
Denver was second playoff seed ahead of New England based on head-to-head victory (1-0). N.Y. Jets were first Wild Card based on better conference record (8-4) than Kansas City (9-5), Seattle (7-5), and Cincinnati (7-5). Kansas City was second Wild Card based on better conference record (9-5) than Seattle (7-5) and Cincinnati (7-5). N.Y. Giants were top playoff seed based on better conference record than Chicago (11-1 to Bears' 10-2). Washington did not play the N.Y. Giants in the divisional playoffs because, from 1970-1989, two teams from the same division could not meet prior to the conference championship game.
Wild Card playoff: N.Y. JETS 35, Kansas City 15
Divisional playoffs: CLEVELAND 23, N.Y. Jets 20 (OT); DENVER 22, New England 17
AFC Championship: Denver 23, CLEVELAND 20 (OT)
Wild Card playoff: WASHINGTON 19, L.A. Rams 7
Divisional playoffs: Washington 27, CHICAGO 13
N.Y. GIANTS 49, San Francisco 3
NFC Championship: N.Y. GIANTS 17, Washington 0
Super Bowl XXI: N.Y. Giants (NFC) 39, Denver (AFC) 20, at Rose Bowl, Pasadena, California

1985

AMERICAN CONFERENCE

Eastern Division

	W	L	T	Pct.	Pts.	OP
Miami	12	4	0	.750	428	320
N.Y. Jets*	11	5	0	.688	393	264
New England*	11	5	0	.688	362	290
Indianapolis	5	11	0	.313	320	386
Buffalo	2	14	0	.125	200	381

Central Division

	W	L	T	Pct.	Pts.	OP
Cleveland	8	8	0	.500	287	294
Cincinnati	7	9	0	.438	441	437
Pittsburgh	7	9	0	.438	379	355
Houston	5	11	0	.313	284	412

Western Division

	W	L	T	Pct.	Pts.	OP
L.A. Raiders#	12	4	0	.750	354	308
Denver	11	5	0	.688	380	329
Seattle	8	8	0	.500	349	303
San Diego	8	8	0	.500	467	435
Kansas City	6	10	0	.375	317	360

NATIONAL CONFERENCE

Eastern Division

	W	L	T	Pct.	Pts.	OP
Dallas	10	6	0	.625	357	333
N.Y. Giants*	10	6	0	.625	399	283
Washington	10	6	0	.625	297	312
Philadelphia	7	9	0	.438	286	310
St. Louis	5	11	0	.313	278	414

Central Division

	W	L	T	Pct.	Pts.	OP
Chicago#	15	1	0	.938	456	198
Green Bay	8	8	0	.500	337	355
Minnesota	7	9	0	.438	346	359
Detroit	7	9	0	.438	307	366
Tampa Bay	2	14	0	.125	294	448

Western Division

	W	L	T	Pct.	Pts.	OP
L.A. Rams	11	5	0	.688	340	277
San Francisco*	10	6	0	.625	411	263
New Orleans	5	11	0	.313	294	401
Atlanta	4	12	0	.250	282	452

*Wild Card qualifier for playoffs; #Top playoff seed in conference
L.A. Raiders were top playoff seed ahead of Miami based on better record against common opponents (5-1 to 4-2). N.Y. Jets were first Wild Card based on better conference record (9-3) than New England (8-4) and Denver (8-4). New England was second Wild Card ahead of Denver based on better record against common opponents (4-2 to Broncos' 3-3). Cincinnati finished ahead of Pittsburgh based on head-to-head sweep (2-0). Seattle finished ahead of San Diego based on head-to-head sweep (2-0). Dallas finished ahead of N.Y. Giants and Washington based on better head-to-head record (4-0 to Giants' 1-3 and Redskins' 1-3). N.Y. Giants were first Wild Card based on better conference record (8-4) than San Francisco (7-5) and Washington (6-6). San Francisco was second Wild Card based on head-to-head victory over Washington (1-0). Minnesota finished ahead of Detroit based on better division record (3-5 to Lions' 2-6).
Wild Card playoff: New England 26, N.Y. JETS 14
Divisional playoffs: MIAMI 24, Cleveland 21;
New England 27, L.A. RAIDERS 20
AFC Championship: New England 31, MIAMI 14
Wild Card playoff: N.Y. GIANTS 17, San Francisco 3
Divisional playoffs: L.A. RAMS 20, Dallas 0;
CHICAGO 21, N.Y. Giants 0
NFC Championship: CHICAGO 24, L.A. Rams 0
Super Bowl XX: Chicago (NFC) 46, New England (AFC) 10,
at Louisiana Superdome, New Orleans, Louisiana

1984

AMERICAN CONFERENCE

Eastern Division

	W	L	T	Pct.	Pts.	OP
Miami#	14	2	0	.875	513	298
New England	9	7	0	.563	362	352
N.Y. Jets	7	9	0	.438	332	364
Indianapolis	4	12	0	.250	239	414
Buffalo	2	14	0	.125	250	454

Central Division

	W	L	T	Pct.	Pts.	OP
Pittsburgh	9	7	0	.563	387	310
Cincinnati	8	8	0	.500	339	339
Cleveland	5	11	0	.313	250	297
Houston	3	13	0	.188	240	437

Western Division

	W	L	T	Pct.	Pts.	OP
Denver	13	3	0	.813	353	241
Seattle*	12	4	0	.750	418	282
L.A. Raiders*	11	5	0	.688	368	278
Kansas City	8	8	0	.500	314	324
San Diego	7	9	0	.438	394	413

NATIONAL CONFERENCE

Eastern Division

	W	L	T	Pct.	Pts.	OP
Washington	11	5	0	.688	426	310
N.Y. Giants*	9	7	0	.563	299	301
St. Louis	9	7	0	.563	423	345
Dallas	9	7	0	.563	308	308
Philadelphia	6	9	1	.406	278	320

Central Division

	W	L	T	Pct.	Pts.	OP
Chicago	10	6	0	.625	325	248
Green Bay	8	8	0	.500	390	309
Tampa Bay	6	10	0	.375	335	380
Detroit	4	11	1	.281	283	408
Minnesota	3	13	0	.188	276	484

Western Division

	W	L	T	Pct.	Pts.	OP
San Francisco#	15	1	0	.938	475	227
L.A. Rams*	10	6	0	.625	346	316
New Orleans	7	9	0	.438	298	361
Atlanta	4	12	0	.250	281	382

*Wild Card qualifier for playoffs; #Top playoff seed in conference
N.Y. Giants finished ahead of St. Louis and Dallas based on best head-to-head record (3-1 to Cardinals' 2-2 and Cowboys' 1-3). St. Louis finished ahead of Dallas based on better division record (5-3 to Cowboys' 3-5).
Wild Card playoff: SEATTLE 13, L.A. Raiders 7
Divisional playoffs: MIAMI 31, Seattle 10;
Pittsburgh 24, DENVER 17
AFC Championship: MIAMI 45, Pittsburgh 28
Wild Card playoff: N.Y. Giants 16, L.A. RAMS 13
Divisional playoffs: SAN FRANCISCO 21, N.Y. Giants 10;
Chicago 23, WASHINGTON 19
NFC Championship: SAN FRANCISCO 23, Chicago 0
Super Bowl XIX: San Francisco (NFC) 38, Miami (AFC) 16,
at Stanford Stadium, Stanford, California

1983

AMERICAN CONFERENCE

Eastern Division

	W	L	T	Pct.	Pts.	OP
Miami	12	4	0	.750	389	250
New England	8	8	0	.500	274	289
Buffalo	8	8	0	.500	283	351
Baltimore	7	9	0	.438	264	354
N.Y. Jets	7	9	0	.438	313	331

Central Division

	W	L	T	Pct.	Pts.	OP
Pittsburgh	10	6	0	.625	355	303
Cleveland	9	7	0	.563	356	342
Cincinnati	7	9	0	.438	346	302
Houston	2	14	0	.125	288	460

Western Division

	W	L	T	Pct.	Pts.	OP
L.A. Raiders#	12	4	0	.750	442	338
Seattle*	9	7	0	.563	403	397
Denver*	9	7	0	.563	302	327
San Diego	6	10	0	.375	358	462
Kansas City	6	10	0	.375	386	367

NATIONAL CONFERENCE

Eastern Division

	W	L	T	Pct.	Pts.	OP
Washington#	14	2	0	.875	541	332
Dallas*	12	4	0	.750	479	360
St. Louis	8	7	1	.531	374	428
Philadelphia	5	11	0	.313	233	322
N.Y. Giants	3	12	1	.219	267	347

Central Division

	W	L	T	Pct.	Pts.	OP
Detroit	9	7	0	.563	347	286
Green Bay	8	8	0	.500	429	439
Chicago	8	8	0	.500	311	301
Minnesota	8	8	0	.500	316	348
Tampa Bay	2	14	0	.125	241	380

Western Division

	W	L	T	Pct.	Pts.	OP
San Francisco	10	6	0	.625	432	293
L.A. Rams*	9	7	0	.563	361	344
New Orleans	8	8	0	.500	319	337
Atlanta	7	9	0	.438	370	389

*Wild Card qualifier for playoffs; #Top playoff seed in conference
L.A. Raiders were top playoff seed ahead of Miami based on head-to-head victory (1-0). Seattle was first Wild Card ahead of Denver based on better division record (5-3 to Broncos' 3-5) after Cleveland was eliminated from three-way tie based on losing head-to-head to both Seattle and Denver. Seattle did not play the L.A. Raiders in the divisional playoffs because, from 1970-1989, two teams from the same division could not meet prior to the conference championship game. New England finished ahead of Buffalo based on head-to-head sweep (2-0). Baltimore finished ahead of N.Y. Jets based on better conference record (5-9 to Jets' 4-8). San Diego finished ahead of Kansas City based on head-to-head sweep (2-0). Green Bay finished ahead of Chicago based on better record against common opponents (4-4 to Bears' 3-5) after Minnesota was eliminated from three-way tie based on conference record (Chicago 7-7 and Green Bay 6-6 to Vikings' 4-8).
Wild Card playoff: SEATTLE 31, Denver 7
Divisional playoffs: Seattle 27, MIAMI 20;
  L.A. RAIDERS 38, Pittsburgh 10
AFC Championship: L.A. RAIDERS 30, Seattle 14
Wild Card playoff: L.A. Rams 24, DALLAS 17
Divisional playoffs: SAN FRANCISCO 24, Detroit 23;
  WASHINGTON 51, L.A. Rams 7
NFC Championship: WASHINGTON 24, San Francisco 21
Super Bowl XVIII: L.A. Raiders (AFC) 38, Washington (NFC) 9,
  at Tampa Stadium, Tampa, Florida

1982

AMERICAN CONFERENCE

	W	L	T	Pct.	Pts.	OP
L.A. Raiders#	8	1	0	.889	260	200
Miami	7	2	0	.778	198	131
Cincinnati	7	2	0	.778	232	177
Pittsburgh	6	3	0	.667	204	146
San Diego	6	3	0	.667	288	221
N.Y. Jets	6	3	0	.667	245	166
New England	5	4	0	.556	143	157
Cleveland	4	5	0	.444	140	182
Buffalo	4	5	0	.444	150	154
Seattle	4	5	0	.444	127	147
Kansas City	3	6	0	.333	176	184
Denver	2	7	0	.222	148	226
Houston	1	8	0	.111	136	245
Baltimore	0	8	1	.056	113	236

NATIONAL CONFERENCE

	W	L	T	Pct.	Pts.	OP
Washington#	8	1	0	.889	190	128
Dallas	6	3	0	.667	226	145
Green Bay	5	3	1	.611	226	169
Minnesota	5	4	0	.556	187	198
Atlanta	5	4	0	.556	183	199
St. Louis	5	4	0	.556	135	170
Tampa Bay	5	4	0	.556	158	178
Detroit	4	5	0	.444	181	176
New Orleans	4	5	0	.444	129	160
N.Y. Giants	4	5	0	.444	164	160
San Francisco	3	6	0	.333	209	206
Chicago	3	6	0	.333	141	174
Philadelphia	3	6	0	.333	191	195
L.A. Rams	2	7	0	.222	200	250

As the result of a 57-day players' strike, the 1982 NFL regular season schedule was reduced from 16 weeks to 9. At the conclusion of the regular season, the NFL conducted a 16-team postseason Super Bowl Tournament. Eight teams from each conference were seeded 1-8 based on their records during the season.
#Top playoff seed in conference
Miami finished ahead of Cincinnati based on better conference record (6-1 to Bengals' 6-2). Pittsburgh finished ahead of San Diego based on better record against common opponents (3-1 to Chargers' 2-1) after N.Y. Jets were eliminated from three-way tie based on conference record (Pittsburgh and San Diego 5-3 to Jets' 2-3). Cleveland finished ahead of Buffalo and Seattle based on better conference record (4-3 to Bills' 3-3 to Seahawks' 3-5). Buffalo finished ahead of Seattle based on better conference record (3-3 to Seahawks' 3-5). Minnesota (4-1), Atlanta (4-3), St. Louis (5-4), Tampa Bay (3-3) seeds were determined by best won-lost record in conference games. Detroit finished ahead of New Orleans and the N.Y. Giants based on best conference record (4-4 to Saints' 3-5 to Giants' 3-5). New Orleans finished ahead of N.Y. Giants based on better record against common opponents (1-3 to Giants' 0-4). San Francisco finished ahead of Chicago, and Chicago finished ahead of Philadelphia, based on conference record (49ers' 2-3 to Bears' 2-5 to Eagles' 1-5).
First round playoff: MIAMI 28, New England 13;
  L.A. RAIDERS 27, Cleveland 10;
  N.Y. Jets 44, CINCINNATI 17;
  San Diego 31, PITTSBURGH 28
Second round playoff: N.Y. Jets 17, L.A. RAIDERS 14;
  MIAMI 34, San Diego 13
AFC Championship: MIAMI 14, N.Y. Jets 0
First round playoff: WASHINGTON 31, Detroit 7;
  GREEN BAY 41, St. Louis 16;
  MINNESOTA 30, Atlanta 24;
  DALLAS 30, Tampa Bay 17
Second round playoff: WASHINGTON 21, Minnesota 7;
  DALLAS 37, Green Bay 26
NFC Championship: WASHINGTON 31, Dallas 17
Super Bowl XVII: Washington (NFC) 27, Miami (AFC) 17,
  at Rose Bowl, Pasadena, California

1981

AMERICAN CONFERENCE

Eastern Division

	W	L	T	Pct.	Pts.	OP
Miami	11	4	1	.719	345	275
N.Y. Jets*	10	5	1	.656	355	287
Buffalo*	10	6	0	.625	311	276
Baltimore	2	14	0	.125	259	533
New England	2	14	0	.125	322	370

Central Division

	W	L	T	Pct.	Pts.	OP
Cincinnati#	12	4	0	.750	421	304
Pittsburgh	8	8	0	.500	356	297
Houston	7	9	0	.438	281	355
Cleveland	5	11	0	.313	276	375

Western Division

	W	L	T	Pct.	Pts.	OP
San Diego	10	6	0	.625	478	390
Denver	10	6	0	.625	321	289
Kansas City	9	7	0	.563	343	290
Oakland	7	9	0	.438	273	343
Seattle	6	10	0	.375	322	388

NATIONAL CONFERENCE

Eastern Division

	W	L	T	Pct.	Pts.	OP
Dallas	12	4	0	.750	367	277
Philadelphia*	10	6	0	.625	368	221
N.Y. Giants*	9	7	0	.563	295	257
Washington	8	8	0	.500	347	349
St. Louis	7	9	0	.438	315	408

Central Division

	W	L	T	Pct.	Pts.	OP
Tampa Bay	9	7	0	.563	315	268
Detroit	8	8	0	.500	397	322
Green Bay	8	8	0	.500	324	361
Minnesota	7	9	0	.438	325	369
Chicago	6	10	0	.375	253	324

Western Division

	W	L	T	Pct.	Pts.	OP
San Francisco#	13	3	0	.813	357	250
Atlanta	7	9	0	.438	426	355
Los Angeles	6	10	0	.375	303	351
New Orleans	4	12	0	.250	207	378

*Wild Card qualifier for playoffs; #Top playoff seed in conference
Baltimore finished ahead of New England based on head-to-head sweep (2-0). San Diego finished ahead of Denver based on better division record (6-2 to Broncos' 5-3). Buffalo was second Wild Card based on head-to-head victory over Denver (1-0). Detroit finished ahead of Green Bay based on better record against common opponents (4-4 to Packers' 3-5).
Wild Card playoff: Buffalo 31, N.Y. JETS 27
Divisional playoffs: San Diego 41, MIAMI 38 (OT);
    CINCINNATI 28, Buffalo 21
AFC Championship: CINCINNATI 27, San Diego 7
Wild Card playoff: N.Y. Giants 27, PHILADELPHIA 21
Divisional playoffs: DALLAS 38, Tampa Bay 0;
    SAN FRANCISCO 38, N.Y. Giants 24
NFC Championship: SAN FRANCISCO 28, Dallas 27
Super Bowl XVI: San Francisco (NFC) 26, Cincinnati (AFC) 21,
    at Silverdome, Pontiac, Michigan

1980

AMERICAN CONFERENCE

Eastern Division

	W	L	T	Pct.	Pts.	OP
Buffalo	11	5	0	.688	320	260
New England	10	6	0	.625	441	325
Miami	8	8	0	.500	266	305
Baltimore	7	9	0	.438	355	387
N.Y. Jets	4	12	0	.250	302	395

Central Division

	W	L	T	Pct.	Pts.	OP
Cleveland	11	5	0	.688	357	310
Houston*	11	5	0	.688	295	251
Pittsburgh	9	7	0	.563	352	313
Cincinnati	6	10	0	.375	244	312

Western Division

	W	L	T	Pct.	Pts.	OP
San Diego#	11	5	0	.688	418	327
Oakland*	11	5	0	.688	364	306
Kansas City	8	8	0	.500	319	336
Denver	8	8	0	.500	310	323
Seattle	4	12	0	.250	291	408

NATIONAL CONFERENCE

Eastern Division

	W	L	T	Pct.	Pts.	OP
Philadelphia	12	4	0	.750	384	222
Dallas*	12	4	0	.750	454	311
Washington	6	10	0	.375	261	293
St. Louis	5	11	0	.313	299	350
N.Y. Giants	4	12	0	.250	249	425

Central Division

	W	L	T	Pct.	Pts.	OP
Minnesota	9	7	0	.563	317	308
Detroit	9	7	0	.563	334	272
Chicago	7	9	0	.438	304	264
Tampa Bay	5	10	1	.344	271	341
Green Bay	5	10	1	.344	231	371

Western Division

	W	L	T	Pct.	Pts.	OP
Atlanta#	12	4	0	.750	405	272
Los Angeles*	11	5	0	.688	424	289
San Francisco	6	10	0	.375	320	415
New Orleans	1	15	0	.063	291	487

*Wild Card qualifier for playoffs; #Top playoff seed in conference
San Diego was top playoff seed based on better conference record than Cleveland and Buffalo (9-3 to Browns' 8-4 and Bills' 8-4). Cleveland was second playoff seed based on better record against common opponents (5-2 to Bills' 5-3). Cleveland finished ahead of Houston based on better conference record (8-4 to Oilers' 7-5). Oakland was first Wild Card based on better conference record than Houston (9-3 to Oilers' 7-5). San Diego finished ahead of Oakland based on better net points in division games (plus 60 net points to Raiders' plus 37). Oakland did not play San Diego in the divisional playoffs because, from 1970-1989, two teams from the same division could not meet prior to the conference championship game. Kansas City finished ahead of Denver based on head-to-head sweep (2-0). Atlanta was top playoff seed based on head-to-head victory over Philadelphia (1-0). Philadelphia finished ahead of Dallas based on better net points in division games (plus 84 net points to Cowboys' plus 50). Minnesota finished ahead of Detroit based on better conference record (8-4 to Lions' 9-5). Tampa Bay finished ahead of Green Bay based on better head-to-head record (1-0-1 to Packers' 0-1-1).
Wild Card playoff: OAKLAND 27, Houston 7
Divisional playoffs: SAN DIEGO 20, Buffalo 14;
    Oakland 14, CLEVELAND 12
AFC Championship: Oakland 34, SAN DIEGO 27
Wild Card playoff: DALLAS 34, Los Angeles 13
Divisional playoffs: PHILADELPHIA 31, Minnesota 16;
    Dallas 30, ATLANTA 27
NFC Championship: PHILADELPHIA 20, Dallas 7
Super Bowl XV: Oakland (AFC) 27, Philadelphia (NFC) 10,
    at Louisiana Superdome, New Orleans, Louisiana

1979

AMERICAN CONFERENCE

Eastern Division

	W	L	T	Pct.	Pts.	OP
Miami	10	6	0	.625	341	257
New England	9	7	0	.563	411	326
N.Y. Jets	8	8	0	.500	337	383
Buffalo	7	9	0	.438	268	279
Baltimore	5	11	0	.313	271	351

Central Division

	W	L	T	Pct.	Pts.	OP
Pittsburgh	12	4	0	.750	416	262
Houston*	11	5	0	.688	362	331
Cleveland	9	7	0	.563	359	352
Cincinnati	4	12	0	.250	337	421

Western Division

	W	L	T	Pct.	Pts.	OP
San Diego#	12	4	0	.750	411	246
Denver*	10	6	0	.625	289	262
Seattle	9	7	0	.563	378	372
Oakland	9	7	0	.563	365	337
Kansas City	7	9	0	.438	238	262

NATIONAL CONFERENCE

Eastern Division

	W	L	T	Pct.	Pts.	OP
Dallas#	11	5	0	.688	371	313
Philadelphia*	11	5	0	.688	339	282
Washington	10	6	0	.625	348	295
N.Y. Giants	6	10	0	.375	237	323
St. Louis	5	11	0	.313	307	358

Central Division

	W	L	T	Pct.	Pts.	OP
Tampa Bay	10	6	0	.625	273	237
Chicago*	10	6	0	.625	306	249
Minnesota	7	9	0	.438	259	337
Green Bay	5	11	0	.313	246	316
Detroit	2	14	0	.125	219	365

Western Division

	W	L	T	Pct.	Pts.	OP
Los Angeles	9	7	0	.563	323	309
New Orleans	8	8	0	.500	370	360
Atlanta	6	10	0	.375	300	388
San Francisco	2	14	0	.125	308	416

*Wild Card qualifier for playoffs; #Top playoff seed in conference
San Diego was top playoff seed based on head-to-head victory over Pittsburgh (1-0). Seattle finished ahead of Oakland based on head-to-head sweep (2-0). Dallas finished ahead of Philadelphia based on better conference record (10-2 to Eagles' 9-3). Philadelphia did not play Dallas in the divisional playoffs because, from 1970-1989, two teams from the same division could not meet prior to the conference championship game. Tampa Bay finished ahead of Chicago based on a better division record (6-2 to Bears' 5-3). Chicago was second Wild Card ahead of Washington based on better net points in all games (57 to Redskins' 53).
Wild Card playoff: HOUSTON 13, Denver 7
Divisional playoffs: Houston 17, SAN DIEGO 14;
PITTSBURGH 34, Miami 14
AFC Championship: PITTSBURGH 27, Houston 13
Wild Card playoff: PHILADELPHIA 27, Chicago 17
Divisional playoffs: TAMPA BAY 24, Philadelphia 17;
Los Angeles 21, DALLAS 19
NFC Championship: Los Angeles 9, TAMPA BAY 0
Super Bowl XIV: Pittsburgh (AFC) 31, Los Angeles (NFC) 19,
at Rose Bowl, Pasadena, California

1978

AMERICAN CONFERENCE

Eastern Division

	W	L	T	Pct.	Pts.	OP
New England	11	5	0	.688	358	286
Miami*	11	5	0	.688	372	254
N.Y. Jets	8	8	0	.500	359	364
Buffalo	5	11	0	.313	302	354
Baltimore	5	11	0	.313	239	421

Central Division

	W	L	T	Pct.	Pts.	OP
Pittsburgh#	14	2	0	.875	356	195
Houston*	10	6	0	.625	283	298
Cleveland	8	8	0	.500	334	356
Cincinnati	4	12	0	.250	252	284

Western Division

	W	L	T	Pct.	Pts.	OP
Denver	10	6	0	.625	282	198
Oakland	9	7	0	.563	311	283
Seattle	9	7	0	.563	345	358
San Diego	9	7	0	.563	355	309
Kansas City	4	12	0	.250	243	327

NATIONAL CONFERENCE

Eastern Division

	W	L	T	Pct.	Pts.	OP
Dallas	12	4	0	.750	384	208
Philadelphia*	9	7	0	.563	270	250
Washington	8	8	0	.500	273	283
St. Louis	6	10	0	.375	248	296
N.Y. Giants	6	10	0	.375	264	298

Central Division

	W	L	T	Pct.	Pts.	OP
Minnesota	8	7	1	.531	294	306
Green Bay	8	7	1	.531	249	269
Detroit	7	9	0	.438	290	300
Chicago	7	9	0	.438	253	274
Tampa Bay	5	11	0	.313	241	259

Western Division

	W	L	T	Pct.	Pts.	OP
Los Angeles#	12	4	0	.750	316	245
Atlanta*	9	7	0	.563	240	290
New Orleans	7	9	0	.438	281	298
San Francisco	2	14	0	.125	219	350

*Wild Card qualifier for playoffs; #Top playoff seed in conference
New England finished ahead of Miami based on better division record (6-2 to Dolphins' 5-3). Buffalo finished ahead of Baltimore based on head-to-head sweep (2-0). Oakland finished ahead of Seattle and San Diego based on better record against common opponents (6-2 to Seahawks' 5-3 and Chargers' 4-4). Atlanta was first Wild Card ahead of Philadelphia based on better record against common opponents (5-2 to Eagles' 5-3). Houston did not play Pittsburgh, and Atlanta did not play Los Angeles in the divisional playoffs because, from 1970-1989, two teams from the same division could not meet prior to the conference championship game. Los Angeles was top playoff seed based on head-to-head victory over Dallas (1-0). St. Louis finished ahead of N.Y. Giants based on better division record (3-5 to Giants' 2-6). Minnesota finished ahead of Green Bay based on head-to-head record (1-0-1). Detroit finished ahead of Chicago based on better division record (4-4 to Bears' 3-5).
Wild Card playoff: Houston 17, MIAMI 9
Divisional playoffs: Houston 31, NEW ENGLAND 14;
PITTSBURGH 33, Denver 10
AFC Championship: PITTSBURGH 34, Houston 5
Wild Card playoff: ATLANTA 14, Philadelphia 13
Divisional playoffs: DALLAS 27, Atlanta 20;
LOS ANGELES 34, Minnesota 10
NFC Championship: Dallas 28, LOS ANGELES 0
Super Bowl XIII: Pittsburgh (AFC) 35, Dallas (NFC) 31,
at Orange Bowl, Miami, Florida

1977

AMERICAN CONFERENCE
Eastern Division

	W	L	T	Pct.	Pts.	OP
Baltimore	10	4	0	.714	295	221
Miami	10	4	0	.714	313	197
New England	9	5	0	.643	278	217
N.Y. Jets	3	11	0	.214	191	300
Buffalo	3	11	0	.214	160	313

Central Division

	W	L	T	Pct.	Pts.	OP
Pittsburgh	9	5	0	.643	283	243
Houston	8	6	0	.571	299	230
Cincinnati	8	6	0	.571	238	235
Cleveland	6	8	0	.429	269	267

Western Division

	W	L	T	Pct.	Pts.	OP
Denver#	12	2	0	.857	274	148
Oakland*	11	3	0	.786	351	230
San Diego	7	7	0	.500	222	205
Seattle	5	9	0	.357	282	373
Kansas City	2	12	0	.143	225	349

NATIONAL CONFERENCE
Eastern Division

	W	L	T	Pct.	Pts.	OP
Dallas#	12	2	0	.857	345	212
Washington	9	5	0	.643	196	189
St. Louis	7	7	0	.500	272	287
Philadelphia	5	9	0	.357	220	207
N.Y. Giants	5	9	0	.357	181	265

Central Division

	W	L	T	Pct.	Pts.	OP
Minnesota	9	5	0	.643	231	227
Chicago*	9	5	0	.643	255	253
Detroit	6	8	0	.429	183	252
Green Bay	4	10	0	.286	134	219
Tampa Bay	2	12	0	.143	103	223

Western Division

	W	L	T	Pct.	Pts.	OP
Los Angeles	10	4	0	.714	302	146
Atlanta	7	7	0	.500	179	129
San Francisco	5	9	0	.357	220	260
New Orleans	3	11	0	.214	232	336

*Wild Card qualifier for playoffs; #Top playoff seed in conference
Baltimore finished ahead of Miami based on better conference record (9-3 to Dolphins' 8-4). N.Y. Jets finished ahead of Buffalo based on better point-differential in head-to-head competition (1 point). Houston finished ahead of Cincinnati based on better point-differential in head-to-head competition (2 points). Oakland did not play Denver in the divisional playoffs because, from 1970-1989, two teams from the same division could not meet prior to the conference championship game. Minnesota finished ahead of Chicago based on better point-differential in head-to-head competition (3 points). Chicago won Wild Card ahead of Washington based on better net points in conference games (48 to Redskins' 4). Philadelphia finished ahead of N.Y. Giants based on head-to-head sweep (2-0).
Divisional playoffs: DENVER 34, Pittsburgh 21; Oakland 37, BALTIMORE 31 (OT)
AFC Championship: DENVER 20, Oakland 17
Divisional playoffs: DALLAS 37, Chicago 7; Minnesota 14, LOS ANGELES 7
NFC Championship: DALLAS 23, Minnesota 6
Super Bowl XII: Dallas (NFC) 27, Denver (AFC) 10, at Louisiana Superdome, New Orleans, Louisiana

1976

AMERICAN CONFERENCE
Eastern Division

	W	L	T	Pct.	Pts.	OP
Baltimore	11	3	0	.786	417	246
New England*	11	3	0	.786	376	236
Miami	6	8	0	.429	263	264
N.Y. Jets	3	11	0	.214	169	383
Buffalo	2	12	0	.143	245	363

Central Division

	W	L	T	Pct.	Pts.	OP
Pittsburgh	10	4	0	.714	342	138
Cincinnati	10	4	0	.714	335	210
Cleveland	9	5	0	.643	267	287
Houston	5	9	0	.357	222	273

Western Division

	W	L	T	Pct.	Pts.	OP
Oakland#	13	1	0	.929	350	237
Denver	9	5	0	.643	315	206
San Diego	6	8	0	.429	248	285
Kansas City	5	9	0	.357	290	376
Tampa Bay	0	14	0	.000	125	412

NATIONAL CONFERENCE
Eastern Division

	W	L	T	Pct.	Pts.	OP
Dallas	11	3	0	.786	296	194
Washington*	10	4	0	.714	291	217
St. Louis	10	4	0	.714	309	267
Philadelphia	4	10	0	.286	165	286
N.Y. Giants	3	11	0	.214	170	250

Central Division

	W	L	T	Pct.	Pts.	OP
Minnesota#	11	2	1	.821	305	176
Chicago	7	7	0	.500	253	216
Detroit	6	8	0	.429	262	220
Green Bay	5	9	0	.357	218	299

Western Division

	W	L	T	Pct.	Pts.	OP
Los Angeles	10	3	1	.750	351	190
San Francisco	8	6	0	.571	270	190
New Orleans	4	10	0	.286	253	346
Atlanta	4	10	0	.286	172	312
Seattle	2	12	0	.143	229	429

*Wild Card qualifier for playoffs; #Top playoff seed in conference
Baltimore finished ahead of New England based on better division record (7-1 to Patriots' 6-2). Pittsburgh finished ahead of Cincinnati based on head-to-head sweep (2-0). Washington finished ahead of St. Louis based on head-to-head sweep (2-0). New Orleans finished ahead of Atlanta based on better point-differential in head-to-head competition (27 points).
Divisional playoffs: OAKLAND 24, New England 21; Pittsburgh 40, BALTIMORE 14
AFC Championship: OAKLAND 24, Pittsburgh 7
Divisional playoffs: MINNESOTA 35, Washington 20; Los Angeles 14, DALLAS 12
NFC Championship: MINNESOTA 24, Los Angeles 13
Super Bowl XI: Oakland (AFC) 32, Minnesota (NFC) 14, at Rose Bowl, Pasadena, California

1975

AMERICAN CONFERENCE

Eastern Division

	W	L	T	Pct.	Pts.	OP
Baltimore	10	4	0	.714	395	269
Miami	10	4	0	.714	357	222
Buffalo	8	6	0	.571	420	355
N.Y. Jets	3	11	0	.214	258	433
New England	3	11	0	.214	258	358

Central Division

	W	L	T	Pct.	Pts.	OP
Pittsburgh#	12	2	0	.857	373	162
Cincinnati*	11	3	0	.786	340	246
Houston	10	4	0	.714	293	226
Cleveland	3	11	0	.214	218	372

Western Division

	W	L	T	Pct.	Pts.	OP
Oakland	11	3	0	.786	375	255
Denver	6	8	0	.429	254	307
Kansas City	5	9	0	.357	282	341
San Diego	2	12	0	.143	189	345

NATIONAL CONFERENCE

Eastern Division

	W	L	T	Pct.	Pts.	OP
St. Louis	11	3	0	.786	356	276
Dallas*	10	4	0	.714	350	268
Washington	8	6	0	.571	325	276
N.Y. Giants	5	9	0	.357	216	306
Philadelphia	4	10	0	.286	225	302

Central Division

	W	L	T	Pct.	Pts.	OP
Minnesota#	12	2	0	.857	377	180
Detroit	7	7	0	.500	245	262
Chicago	4	10	0	.286	191	379
Green Bay	4	10	0	.286	226	285

Western Division

	W	L	T	Pct.	Pts.	OP
Los Angeles	12	2	0	.857	312	135
San Francisco	5	9	0	.357	255	286
Atlanta	4	10	0	.286	240	289
New Orleans	2	12	0	.143	165	360

Wild Card qualifier for playoffs; #Top playoff seed in conference
Baltimore finished ahead of Miami based on head-to-head sweep (2-0). Cincinnati did not play Pittsburgh in the divisional playoffs because, from 1970-1989, two teams from the same division could not meet prior to the conference championship game. N.Y. Jets finished ahead of New England based on head-to-head sweep (2-0). Minnesota was top playoff seed based on better Point Rating system than Los Angeles (3 to 6). Chicago finished ahead of Green Bay based on better division record (2-4 to Bears' 1-5).

Divisional playoffs: PITTSBURGH 28, Baltimore 10;
   OAKLAND 31, Cincinnati 28
AFC Championship: PITTSBURGH 16, Oakland 10
Divisional playoffs: LOS ANGELES 35, St. Louis 23;
   Dallas 17, MINNESOTA 14
NFC Championship: Dallas 37, LOS ANGELES 7
Super Bowl X: Pittsburgh (AFC) 21, Dallas (NFC) 17,
   at Orange Bowl, Miami, Florida

1974

AMERICAN CONFERENCE

Eastern Division

	W	L	T	Pct.	Pts.	OP
Miami	11	3	0	.786	327	216
Buffalo*	9	5	0	.643	264	244
N.Y. Jets	7	7	0	.500	279	300
New England	7	7	0	.500	348	289
Baltimore	2	12	0	.143	190	329

Central Division

	W	L	T	Pct.	Pts.	OP
Pittsburgh	10	3	1	.750	305	189
Houston	7	7	0	.500	236	282
Cincinnati	7	7	0	.500	283	259
Cleveland	4	10	0	.286	251	344

Western Division

	W	L	T	Pct.	Pts.	OP
Oakland	12	2	0	.857	355	228
Denver	7	6	1	.536	302	294
Kansas City	5	9	0	.357	233	293
San Diego	5	9	0	.357	212	285

NATIONAL CONFERENCE

Eastern Division

	W	L	T	Pct.	Pts.	OP
St. Louis	10	4	0	.714	285	218
Washington*	10	4	0	.714	320	196
Dallas	8	6	0	.571	297	235
Philadelphia	7	7	0	.500	242	217
N.Y. Giants	2	12	0	.143	195	299

Central Division

	W	L	T	Pct.	Pts.	OP
Minnesota	10	4	0	.714	310	195
Detroit	7	7	0	.500	256	270
Green Bay	6	8	0	.429	210	206
Chicago	4	10	0	.286	152	279

Western Division

	W	L	T	Pct.	Pts.	OP
Los Angeles	10	4	0	.714	263	181
San Francisco	6	8	0	.429	226	236
New Orleans	5	9	0	.357	166	263
Atlanta	3	11	0	.214	111	271

Wild Card qualifier for playoffs
N.Y. Jets finished ahead of New England based on better conference record (5-6 to Patriots' 4-7). Houston finished ahead of Cincinnati based on head-to-head sweep (2-0). Kansas City finished ahead of San Diego based on better point-differential in head-to-head competition (3 points). St. Louis finished ahead of Washington based on head-to-head sweep (2-0).

Divisional playoffs: OAKLAND 28, Miami 26;
   PITTSBURGH 32, Buffalo 14
AFC Championship: Pittsburgh 24, OAKLAND 13
Divisional playoffs: MINNESOTA 30, St. Louis 14;
   LOS ANGELES 19, Washington 10
NFC Championship: MINNESOTA 14, Los Angeles 10
Super Bowl IX: Pittsburgh (AFC) 16, Minnesota (NFC) 6,
   at Tulane Stadium, New Orleans, Louisiana

From 1933-1974, sites for league/conference championship games alternated by division.

1973

AMERICAN CONFERENCE

Eastern Division

	W	L	T	Pct.	Pts.	OP
Miami	12	2	0	.857	343	150
Buffalo	9	5	0	.643	259	230
New England	5	9	0	.357	258	300
N.Y. Jets	4	10	0	.286	240	306
Baltimore	4	10	0	.286	226	341

Central Division

	W	L	T	Pct.	Pts.	OP
Cincinnati	10	4	0	.714	286	231
Pittsburgh*	10	4	0	.714	347	210
Cleveland	7	5	2	.571	234	255
Houston	1	13	0	.071	199	447

Western Division

	W	L	T	Pct.	Pts.	OP
Oakland	9	4	1	.679	292	175
Kansas City	7	5	2	.571	231	192
Denver	7	5	2	.571	354	296
San Diego	2	11	1	.179	188	386

NATIONAL CONFERENCE

Eastern Division

	W	L	T	Pct.	Pts.	OP
Dallas	10	4	0	.714	382	203
Washington*	10	4	0	.714	325	198
Philadelphia	5	8	1	.393	310	393
St. Louis	4	9	1	.321	286	365
N.Y. Giants	2	11	1	.179	226	362

Central Division

	W	L	T	Pct.	Pts.	OP
Minnesota	12	2	0	.857	296	168
Detroit	6	7	1	.464	271	247
Green Bay	5	7	2	.429	202	259
Chicago	3	11	0	.214	195	334

Western Division

	W	L	T	Pct.	Pts.	OP
Los Angeles	12	2	0	.857	388	178
Atlanta	9	5	0	.643	318	224
San Francisco	5	9	0	.357	262	319
New Orleans	5	9	0	.357	163	312

Wild Card qualifier for playoffs

Cincinnati finished ahead of Pittsburgh based on better conference record (8-3 to Steelers' 7-4). N.Y. Jets finished ahead of Baltimore based on head-to-head sweep (2-0). Kansas City finished ahead of Denver based on better division record (4-2 to Broncos' 3-2-1). Dallas finished ahead of Washington based on better point differential in head-to-head games (13 points). San Francisco finished ahead of New Orleans based on better division record (2-4 to Saints' 1-5).

Divisional playoffs: OAKLAND 33, Pittsburgh 14;
MIAMI 34, Cincinnati 16

AFC Championship: MIAMI 27, Oakland 10

Divisional playoffs: MINNESOTA 27, Washington 20;
DALLAS 27, Los Angeles 16

NFC Championship: Minnesota 27, DALLAS 10

Super Bowl VIII: Miami (AFC) 24, Minnesota (NFC) 7,
at Rice Stadium, Houston, Texas

1972

AMERICAN CONFERENCE

Eastern Division

	W	L	T	Pct.	Pts.	OP
Miami	14	0	0	1.000	385	171
N.Y. Jets	7	7	0	.500	367	324
Baltimore	5	9	0	.357	235	252
Buffalo	4	9	1	.321	257	377
New England	3	11	0	.214	192	446

Central Division

	W	L	T	Pct.	Pts.	OP
Pittsburgh	11	3	0	.786	343	175
Cleveland*	10	4	0	.714	268	249
Cincinnati	8	6	0	.571	299	229
Houston	1	13	0	.071	164	380

Western Division

	W	L	T	Pct.	Pts.	OP
Oakland	10	3	1	.750	365	248
Kansas City	8	6	0	.571	287	254
Denver	5	9	0	.357	325	350
San Diego	4	9	1	.321	264	344

NATIONAL CONFERENCE

Eastern Division

	W	L	T	Pct.	Pts.	OP
Washington	11	3	0	.786	336	218
Dallas*	10	4	0	.714	319	240
N.Y. Giants	8	6	0	.571	331	247
St. Louis	4	9	1	.321	193	303
Philadelphia	2	11	1	.179	145	352

Central Division

	W	L	T	Pct.	Pts.	OP
Green Bay	10	4	0	.714	304	226
Detroit	8	5	1	.607	339	290
Minnesota	7	7	0	.500	301	252
Chicago	4	9	1	.321	225	275

Western Division

	W	L	T	Pct.	Pts.	OP
San Francisco	8	5	1	.607	353	249
Atlanta	7	7	0	.500	269	274
Los Angeles	6	7	1	.464	291	286
New Orleans	2	11	1	.179	215	361

Wild Card qualifier for playoffs

Dallas did not play Washington in the divisional playoffs because, from 1970-1989, two teams from the same division could not meet prior to the conference championship game.

Divisional playoffs: PITTSBURGH 13, Oakland 7;
MIAMI 20, Cleveland 14

AFC Championship: Miami 21, PITTSBURGH 17

Divisional playoffs: Dallas 30, SAN FRANCISCO 28;
WASHINGTON 16, Green Bay 3

NFC Championship: WASHINGTON 26, Dallas 3

Super Bowl VII: Miami (AFC) 14, Washington (NFC) 7,
at Memorial Coliseum, Los Angeles, California

1971

AMERICAN CONFERENCE

Eastern Division

	W	L	T	Pct.	Pts.	OP
Miami	10	3	1	.769	315	174
Baltimore*	10	4	0	.714	313	140
New England	6	8	0	.429	238	325
N.Y. Jets	6	8	0	.429	212	299
Buffalo	1	13	0	.071	184	394

Central Division

	W	L	T	Pct.	Pts.	OP
Cleveland	9	5	0	.643	285	273
Pittsburgh	6	8	0	.429	246	292
Houston	4	9	1	.308	251	330
Cincinnati	4	10	0	.286	284	265

Western Division

	W	L	T	Pct.	Pts.	OP
Kansas City	10	3	1	.769	302	208
Oakland	8	4	2	.667	344	278
San Diego	6	8	0	.429	311	341
Denver	4	9	1	.308	203	275

NATIONAL CONFERENCE

Eastern Division

	W	L	T	Pct.	Pts.	OP
Dallas	11	3	0	.786	406	222
Washington*	9	4	1	.692	276	190
Philadelphia	6	7	1	.462	221	302
St. Louis	4	9	1	.308	231	279
N.Y. Giants	4	10	0	.286	228	362

Central Division

	W	L	T	Pct.	Pts.	OP
Minnesota	11	3	0	.786	245	139
Detroit	7	6	1	.538	341	286
Chicago	6	8	0	.429	185	276
Green Bay	4	8	2	.333	274	298

Western Division

	W	L	T	Pct.	Pts.	OP
San Francisco	9	5	0	.643	300	216
Los Angeles	8	5	1	.615	313	260
Atlanta	7	6	1	.538	274	277
New Orleans	4	8	2	.333	266	347

Wild Card qualifier for playoffs
New England finished ahead of N.Y. Jets based on better point-differential in head-to-head competition (13 points).
Divisional playoffs: Miami 27, KANSAS CITY 24 (OT);
  Baltimore 20, CLEVELAND 3
AFC Championship: MIAMI 21, Baltimore 0
Divisional playoffs: Dallas 20, MINNESOTA 12;
  SAN FRANCISCO 24, Washington 20
NFC Championship: DALLAS 14, San Francisco 3
Super Bowl VI: Dallas (NFC) 24, Miami (AFC) 3,
  at Tulane Stadium, New Orleans, Louisiana

From 1920-1971, tie games were not included in winning percentage.

1970

AMERICAN CONFERENCE

Eastern Division

	W	L	T	Pct.	Pts.	OP
Baltimore	11	2	1	.846	321	234
Miami*	10	4	0	.714	297	228
N.Y. Jets	4	10	0	.286	255	286
Buffalo	3	10	1	.231	204	337
Boston Patriots	2	12	0	.143	149	361

Central Division

	W	L	T	Pct.	Pts.	OP
Cincinnati	8	6	0	.571	312	255
Cleveland	7	7	0	.500	286	265
Pittsburgh	5	9	0	.357	210	272
Houston	3	10	1	.231	217	352

Western Division

	W	L	T	Pct.	Pts.	OP
Oakland	8	4	2	.667	300	293
Kansas City	7	5	2	.583	272	244
San Diego	5	6	3	.455	282	278
Denver	5	8	1	.385	253	264

NATIONAL CONFERENCE

Eastern Division

	W	L	T	Pct.	Pts.	OP
Dallas	10	4	0	.714	299	221
N.Y. Giants	9	5	0	.643	301	270
St. Louis	8	5	1	.615	325	228
Washington	6	8	0	.429	297	314
Philadelphia	3	10	1	.231	241	332

Central Division

	W	L	T	Pct.	Pts.	OP
Minnesota	12	2	0	.857	335	143
Detroit*	10	4	0	.714	347	202
Green Bay	6	8	0	.429	196	293
Chicago	6	8	0	.429	256	261

Western Division

	W	L	T	Pct.	Pts.	OP
San Francisco	10	3	1	.769	352	267
Los Angeles	9	4	1	.692	325	202
Atlanta	4	8	2	.333	206	261
New Orleans	2	11	1	.154	172	347

Wild Card qualifier for playoffs
Miami did not play Baltimore, and Detroit did not play Minnesota, in the divisional playoffs because, from 1970-1989, two teams from the same division could not meet prior to the conference championship game. Green Bay finished ahead of Chicago based on better division record (2-4 to Bears' 1-5).
Divisional playoffs: BALTIMORE 17, Cincinnati 0;
  OAKLAND 21, Miami 14
AFC Championship: BALTIMORE 27, Oakland 17
Divisional playoffs: DALLAS 5, Detroit 0;
  San Francisco 17, MINNESOTA 14
NFC Championship: Dallas 17, SAN FRANCISCO 10
Super Bowl V: Baltimore (AFC) 16, Dallas (NFC) 13,
  at Orange Bowl, Miami, Florida

1969 NFL

EASTERN CONFERENCE
Capitol Division

	W	L	T	Pct.	Pts.	OP
Dallas	11	2	1	.846	369	223
Washington	7	5	2	.583	307	319
New Orleans	5	9	0	.357	311	393
Philadelphia	4	9	1	.308	279	377

Century Division

	W	L	T	Pct.	Pts.	OP
Cleveland	10	3	1	.769	351	300
N.Y. Giants	6	8	0	.429	264	298
St. Louis	4	9	1	.308	314	389
Pittsburgh	1	13	0	.071	218	404

WESTERN CONFERENCE
Coastal Division

	W	L	T	Pct.	Pts.	OP
Los Angeles	11	3	0	.786	320	243
Baltimore	8	5	1	.615	279	268
Atlanta	6	8	0	.429	276	268
San Francisco	4	8	2	.333	277	319

Central Division

	W	L	T	Pct.	Pts.	OP
Minnesota	12	2	0	.857	379	133
Detroit	9	4	1	.692	259	188
Green Bay	8	6	0	.571	269	221
Chicago	1	13	0	.071	210	339

Conference championships: Cleveland 38, DALLAS 14; MINNESOTA 23, Los Angeles 20
NFL championship: MINNESOTA 27, Cleveland 7
Super Bowl IV: Kansas City (AFL) 23, Minnesota (NFL) 7, at Tulane Stadium, New Orleans, Louisiana

1969 AFL

EASTERN DIVISION

	W	L	T	Pct.	Pts.	OP
N.Y. Jets	10	4	0	.714	353	269
Houston	6	6	2	.500	278	279
Boston Patriots	4	10	0	.286	266	316
Buffalo	4	10	0	.286	230	359
Miami	3	10	1	.231	233	332

WESTERN DIVISION

	W	L	T	Pct.	Pts.	OP
Oakland	12	1	1	.923	377	242
Kansas City	11	3	0	.786	359	177
San Diego	8	6	0	.571	288	276
Denver	5	8	1	.385	297	344
Cincinnati	4	9	1	.308	280	367

Divisional playoffs: Kansas City 13, N.Y. JETS 6; OAKLAND 56, Houston 7
AFL championship: Kansas City 17, OAKLAND 7

1968 NFL

EASTERN CONFERENCE
Capitol Division

	W	L	T	Pct.	Pts.	OP
Dallas	12	2	0	.857	431	186
N.Y. Giants	7	7	0	.500	294	325
Washington	5	9	0	.357	249	358
Philadelphia	2	12	0	.143	202	351

Century Division

	W	L	T	Pct.	Pts.	OP
Cleveland	10	4	0	.714	394	273
St. Louis	9	4	1	.692	325	289
New Orleans	4	9	1	.308	246	327
Pittsburgh	2	11	1	.154	244	397

WESTERN CONFERENCE
Coastal Division

	W	L	T	Pct.	Pts.	OP
Baltimore	13	1	0	.929	402	144
Los Angeles	10	3	1	.769	312	200
San Francisco	7	6	1	.538	303	310
Atlanta	2	12	0	.143	170	389

Central Division

	W	L	T	Pct.	Pts.	OP
Minnesota	8	6	0	.571	282	242
Chicago	7	7	0	.500	250	333
Green Bay	6	7	1	.462	281	227
Detroit	4	8	2	.333	207	241

Conference championships: CLEVELAND 31, Dallas 20; BALTIMORE 24, Minnesota 14
NFL championship: Baltimore 34, CLEVELAND 0
Super Bowl III: N.Y. Jets (AFL) 16, Baltimore (NFL) 7, at Orange Bowl, Miami, Florida

1968 AFL

EASTERN DIVISION

	W	L	T	Pct.	Pts.	OP
N.Y. Jets	11	3	0	.786	419	280
Houston	7	7	0	.500	303	248
Miami	5	8	1	.385	276	355
Boston Patriots	4	10	0	.286	229	406
Buffalo	1	12	1	.077	199	367

WESTERN DIVISION

	W	L	T	Pct.	Pts.	OP
Oakland	12	2	0	.857	453	233
Kansas City	12	2	0	.857	371	170
San Diego	9	5	0	.643	382	310
Denver	5	9	0	.357	255	404
Cincinnati	3	11	0	.214	215	329

Western Division playoff: OAKLAND 41, Kansas City 6
AFL championship: N.Y. JETS 27, Oakland 23

1967 NFL

EASTERN CONFERENCE
Capitol Division

	W	L	T	Pct.	Pts.	OP
Dallas	9	5	0	.643	342	268
Philadelphia	6	7	1	.462	351	409
Washington	5	6	3	.455	347	353
New Orleans	3	11	0	.214	233	379

Century Division

	W	L	T	Pct.	Pts.	OP
Cleveland	9	5	0	.643	334	297
N.Y. Giants	7	7	0	.500	369	379
St. Louis	6	7	1	.462	333	356
Pittsburgh	4	9	1	.308	281	320

WESTERN CONFERENCE
Coastal Division

	W	L	T	Pct.	Pts.	OP
Los Angeles	11	1	2	.917	398	196
Baltimore	11	1	2	.917	394	198
San Francisco	7	7	0	.500	273	337
Atlanta	1	12	1	.077	175	422

Central Division

	W	L	T	Pct.	Pts.	OP
Green Bay	9	4	1	.692	332	209
Chicago	7	6	1	.538	239	218
Detroit	5	7	2	.417	260	259
Minnesota	3	8	3	.273	233	294

Los Angeles finished ahead of Baltimore based on better point differential in head-to-head games (net 24 points).
Conference championships: DALLAS 52, Cleveland 14; GREEN BAY 28, Los Angeles 7
NFL championship: GREEN BAY 21, Dallas 17
Super Bowl II: Green Bay (NFL) 33, Oakland (AFL) 14, at Orange Bowl, Miami, Florida

1967 AFL

EASTERN DIVISION

	W	L	T	Pct.	Pts.	OP
Houston	9	4	1	.692	258	199
N.Y. Jets	8	5	1	.615	371	329
Buffalo	4	10	0	.286	237	285
Miami	4	10	0	.286	219	407
Boston Patriots	3	10	1	.231	280	389

WESTERN DIVISION

	W	L	T	Pct.	Pts.	OP
Oakland	13	1	0	.929	468	233
Kansas City	9	5	0	.643	408	254
San Diego	8	5	1	.615	360	352
Denver	3	11	0	.214	256	409

AFL championship: OAKLAND 40, Houston 7

1966 NFL

EASTERN CONFERENCE

	W	L	T	Pct.	Pts.	OP
Dallas	10	3	1	.769	445	239
Cleveland	9	5	0	.643	403	259
Philadelphia	9	5	0	.643	326	340
St. Louis	8	5	1	.615	264	265
Washington	7	7	0	.500	351	355
Pittsburgh	5	8	1	.385	316	347
Atlanta	3	11	0	.214	204	437
N.Y. Giants	1	12	1	.077	263	501

WESTERN CONFERENCE

	W	L	T	Pct.	Pts.	OP
Green Bay	12	2	0	.857	335	163
Baltimore	9	5	0	.643	314	226
Los Angeles	8	6	0	.571	289	212
San Francisco	6	6	2	.500	320	325
Chicago	5	7	2	.417	234	272
Detroit	4	9	1	.308	206	317
Minnesota	4	9	1	.308	292	304

NFL championship: Green Bay 34, DALLAS 27
Super Bowl I: Green Bay (NFL) 35, Kansas City (AFL) 10, at Memorial Coliseum, Los Angeles, California

1966 AFL

EASTERN DIVISION

	W	L	T	Pct.	Pts.	OP
Buffalo	9	4	1	.692	358	255
Boston Patriots	8	4	2	.677	315	283
N.Y. Jets	6	6	2	.500	322	312
Houston	3	11	0	.214	335	396
Miami	3	11	0	.214	213	362

WESTERN DIVISION

	W	L	T	Pct.	Pts.	OP
Kansas City	11	2	1	.846	448	276
Oakland	8	5	1	.615	315	288
San Diego	7	6	1	.538	335	284
Denver	4	10	0	.286	196	381

AFL championship: Kansas City 31, BUFFALO 7

1965 NFL

EASTERN CONFERENCE	W	L	T	Pct.	Pts.	OP	WESTERN CONFERENCE	W	L	T	Pct.	Pts.	OP
Cleveland	11	3	0	.786	363	325	Green Bay	10	3	1	.769	316	224
Dallas	7	7	0	.500	325	280	Baltimore	10	3	1	.769	389	284
N.Y. Giants	7	7	0	.500	270	338	Chicago	9	5	0	.643	409	275
Washington	6	8	0	.429	257	301	San Francisco	7	6	1	.538	421	402
Philadelphia	5	9	0	.357	363	359	Minnesota	7	7	0	.500	383	403
St. Louis	5	9	0	.357	296	309	Detroit	6	7	1	.462	257	295
Pittsburgh	2	12	0	.143	202	397	Los Angeles	4	10	0	.286	269	328

Western Conference playoff: GREEN BAY 13, Baltimore 10 (OT)
NFL championship: GREEN BAY 23, Cleveland 12

1965 AFL

EASTERN DIVISION	W	L	T	Pct.	Pts.	OP	WESTERN DIVISION	W	L	T	Pct.	Pts.	OP
Buffalo	10	3	1	.769	313	226	San Diego	9	2	3	.818	340	227
N.Y. Jets	5	8	1	.385	285	303	Oakland	8	5	1	.615	298	239
Boston Patriots	4	8	2	.333	244	302	Kansas City	7	5	2	.583	322	285
Houston	4	10	0	.286	298	429	Denver	4	10	0	.286	303	392

AFL championship: Buffalo 23, SAN DIEGO 0

1964 NFL

EASTERN CONFERENCE	W	L	T	Pct.	Pts.	OP	WESTERN CONFERENCE	W	L	T	Pct.	Pts.	OP
Cleveland	10	3	1	.769	415	293	Baltimore	12	2	0	.857	428	225
St. Louis	9	3	2	.750	357	331	Green Bay	8	5	1	.615	342	245
Philadelphia	6	8	0	.429	312	313	Minnesota	8	5	1	.615	355	296
Washington	6	8	0	.429	307	305	Detroit	7	5	2	.583	280	260
Dallas	5	8	1	.385	250	289	Los Angeles	5	7	2	.417	283	339
Pittsburgh	5	9	0	.357	253	315	Chicago	5	9	0	.357	260	379
N.Y. Giants	2	10	2	.167	241	399	San Francisco	4	10	0	.286	236	330

NFL championship: CLEVELAND 27, Baltimore 0

1964 AFL

EASTERN DIVISION	W	L	T	Pct.	Pts.	OP	WESTERN DIVISION	W	L	T	Pct.	Pts.	OP
Buffalo	12	2	0	.857	400	242	San Diego	8	5	1	.615	341	300
Boston Patriots	10	3	1	.769	365	297	Kansas City	7	7	0	.500	366	306
N.Y. Jets	5	8	1	.385	278	315	Oakland	5	7	2	.417	303	350
Houston	4	10	0	.286	310	355	Denver	2	11	1	.154	240	438

AFL championship: BUFFALO 20, San Diego 7

1963 NFL

EASTERN CONFERENCE	W	L	T	Pct.	Pts.	OP	WESTERN CONFERENCE	W	L	T	Pct.	Pts.	OP
N.Y. Giants	11	3	0	.786	448	280	Chicago	11	1	2	.917	301	144
Cleveland	10	4	0	.714	343	262	Green Bay	11	2	1	.846	369	206
St. Louis	9	5	0	.643	341	283	Baltimore	8	6	0	.571	316	285
Pittsburgh	7	4	3	.636	321	295	Detroit	5	8	1	.385	326	265
Dallas	4	10	0	.286	305	378	Minnesota	5	8	1	.385	309	390
Washington	3	11	0	.214	279	398	Los Angeles	5	9	0	.357	210	350
Philadelphia	2	10	2	.167	242	381	San Francisco	2	12	0	.143	198	391

NFL championship: CHICAGO 14, N.Y. Giants 10

1963 AFL

EASTERN DIVISION	W	L	T	Pct.	Pts.	OP	WESTERN DIVISION	W	L	T	Pct.	Pts.	OP
Boston Patriots	7	6	1	.538	327	257	San Diego	11	3	0	.786	399	255
Buffalo	7	6	1	.538	304	291	Oakland	10	4	0	.714	363	282
Houston	6	8	0	.429	302	372	Kansas City	5	7	2	.417	347	263
N.Y. Jets	5	8	1	.385	249	399	Denver	2	11	1	.154	301	473

Eastern Division playoff: Boston 26, BUFFALO 8
AFL championship: SAN DIEGO 51, Boston 10

1962 NFL

EASTERN CONFERENCE	W	L	T	Pct.	Pts.	OP	WESTERN CONFERENCE	W	L	T	Pct.	Pts.	OP
N.Y. Giants	12	2	0	.857	398	283	Green Bay	13	1	0	.929	415	148
Pittsburgh	9	5	0	.643	312	363	Detroit	11	3	0	.786	315	177
Cleveland	7	6	1	.538	291	257	Chicago	9	5	0	.643	321	287
Washington	5	7	2	.417	305	376	Baltimore	7	7	0	.500	293	288
Dallas Cowboys	5	8	1	.385	398	402	San Francisco	6	8	0	.429	282	331
St. Louis	4	9	1	.308	287	361	Minnesota	2	11	1	.154	254	410
Philadelphia	3	10	1	.231	282	356	Los Angeles	1	12	1	.077	220	334

NFL championship: Green Bay 16, N.Y. GIANTS 7

1962 AFL

EASTERN DIVISION	W	L	T	Pct.	Pts.	OP	WESTERN DIVISION	W	L	T	Pct.	Pts.	OP
Houston	11	3	0	.786	387	270	Dallas Texans	11	3	0	.786	389	233
Boston Patriots	9	4	1	.692	346	295	Denver	7	7	0	.500	353	334
Buffalo	7	6	1	.538	309	272	San Diego	4	10	0	.286	314	392
N.Y. Titans	5	9	0	.357	278	423	Oakland	1	13	0	.071	213	370

AFL championship: Dallas Texans 20, HOUSTON 17 (OT)

1961 NFL

EASTERN CONFERENCE	W	L	T	Pct.	Pts.	OP	WESTERN CONFERENCE	W	L	T	Pct.	Pts.	OP
N.Y. Giants	10	3	1	.769	368	220	Green Bay	11	3	0	.786	391	223
Philadelphia	10	4	0	.714	361	297	Detroit	8	5	1	.615	270	258
Cleveland	8	5	1	.615	319	270	Baltimore	8	6	0	.571	302	307
St. Louis	7	7	0	.500	279	267	Chicago	8	6	0	.571	326	302
Pittsburgh	6	8	0	.429	295	287	San Francisco	7	6	1	.538	346	272
Dallas Cowboys	4	9	1	.308	236	380	Los Angeles	4	10	0	.286	263	333
Washington	1	12	1	.077	174	392	Minnesota	3	11	0	.214	285	407

NFL championship: GREEN BAY 37, N.Y. Giants 0

1961 AFL

EASTERN DIVISION	W	L	T	Pct.	Pts.	OP	WESTERN DIVISION	W	L	T	Pct.	Pts.	OP
Houston	10	3	1	.769	513	242	San Diego	12	2	0	.857	396	219
Boston Patriots	9	4	1	.692	413	313	Dallas Texans	6	8	0	.429	334	343
N.Y. Titans	7	7	0	.500	301	390	Denver	3	11	0	.214	251	432
Buffalo	6	8	0	.429	294	342	Oakland	2	12	0	.143	237	458

AFL championship: Houston 10, SAN DIEGO 3

1960 NFL

EASTERN CONFERENCE	W	L	T	Pct.	Pts.	OP	WESTERN CONFERENCE	W	L	T	Pct.	Pts.	OP
Philadelphia	10	2	0	.833	321	246	Green Bay	8	4	0	.667	332	209
Cleveland	8	3	1	.727	362	217	Detroit	7	5	0	.583	239	212
N.Y. Giants	6	4	2	.600	271	261	San Francisco	7	5	0	.583	208	205
St. Louis	6	5	1	.545	288	230	Baltimore	6	6	0	.500	288	234
Pittsburgh	5	6	1	.455	240	275	Chicago	5	6	1	.455	194	299
Washington	1	9	2	.100	178	309	L.A. Rams	4	7	1	.364	265	297
							Dallas Cowboys	0	11	1	.000	177	369

NFL championship: PHILADELPHIA 17, Green Bay 13

1960 AFL

EASTERN CONFERENCE	W	L	T	Pct.	Pts.	OP	WESTERN CONFERENCE	W	L	T	Pct.	Pts.	OP
Houston	10	4	0	.714	379	285	L.A. Chargers	10	4	0	.714	373	336
N.Y. Titans	7	7	0	.500	382	399	Dallas Texans	8	6	0	.571	362	253
Buffalo	5	8	1	.385	296	303	Oakland	6	8	0	.429	319	388
Boston Patriots	5	9	0	.357	286	349	Denver	4	9	1	.308	309	393

AFL championship: HOUSTON 24, L.A. Chargers 16

1959

EASTERN CONFERENCE	W	L	T	Pct.	Pts.	OP	WESTERN CONFERENCE	W	L	T	Pct.	Pts.	OP
N.Y. Giants	10	2	0	.833	284	170	Baltimore	9	3	0	.750	374	251
Cleveland	7	5	0	.583	270	214	Chi. Bears	8	4	0	.667	252	196
Philadelphia	7	5	0	.583	268	278	Green Bay	7	5	0	.583	248	246
Pittsburgh	6	5	1	.545	257	216	San Francisco	7	5	0	.583	255	237
Washington	3	9	0	.250	185	350	Detroit	3	8	1	.273	203	275
Chi. Cardinals	2	10	0	.167	234	324	Los Angeles	2	10	0	.167	242	315

NFL championship: BALTIMORE 31, N.Y. Giants 16

1958

EASTERN CONFERENCE	W	L	T	Pct.	Pts.	OP	WESTERN CONFERENCE	W	L	T	Pct.	Pts.	OP
N.Y. Giants	9	3	0	.750	246	183	Baltimore	9	3	0	.750	381	203
Cleveland	9	3	0	.750	302	217	Chi. Bears	8	4	0	.667	298	230
Pittsburgh	7	4	1	.636	261	230	Los Angeles	8	4	0	.667	344	278
Washington	4	7	1	.364	214	268	San Francisco	6	6	0	.500	257	324
Chi. Cardinals	2	9	1	.182	261	356	Detroit	4	7	1	.364	261	276
Philadelphia	2	9	1	.182	235	306	Green Bay	1	10	1	.091	193	382

Eastern Conference playoff: N.Y. GIANTS 10, Cleveland 0
NFL championship: Baltimore 23, N.Y. GIANTS 17 (OT)

1957

EASTERN CONFERENCE	W	L	T	Pct.	Pts.	OP	WESTERN CONFERENCE	W	L	T	Pct.	Pts.	OP
Cleveland	9	2	1	.818	269	172	Detroit	8	4	0	.667	251	231
N.Y. Giants	7	5	0	.583	254	211	San Francisco	8	4	0	.667	260	264
Pittsburgh	6	6	0	.500	161	178	Baltimore	7	5	0	.583	303	235
Washington	5	6	1	.455	251	230	Los Angeles	6	6	0	.500	307	278
Philadelphia	4	8	0	.333	173	230	Chi. Bears	5	7	0	.417	203	211
Chi. Cardinals	3	9	0	.250	200	299	Green Bay	3	9	0	.250	218	311

Western Conference playoff: Detroit 31, SAN FRANCISCO 27
NFL championship: DETROIT 59, Cleveland 14

1956

EASTERN CONFERENCE	W	L	T	Pct.	Pts.	OP	WESTERN CONFERENCE	W	L	T	Pct.	Pts.	OP
N.Y. Giants	8	3	1	.727	264	197	Chi. Bears	9	2	1	.818	363	246
Chi. Cardinals	7	5	0	.583	240	182	Detroit	9	3	0	.750	300	188
Washington	6	6	0	.500	183	225	San Francisco	5	6	1	.455	233	284
Cleveland	5	7	0	.417	167	177	Baltimore	5	7	0	.417	270	322
Pittsburgh	5	7	0	.417	217	250	Green Bay	4	8	0	.333	264	342
Philadelphia	3	8	1	.273	143	215	Los Angeles	4	8	0	.333	291	307

NFL championship: N.Y. GIANTS 47, Chi. Bears 7

1955

EASTERN CONFERENCE	W	L	T	Pct.	Pts.	OP	WESTERN CONFERENCE	W	L	T	Pct.	Pts.	OP
Cleveland	9	2	1	.818	349	218	Los Angeles	8	3	1	.727	260	231
Washington	8	4	0	.667	246	222	Chi. Bears	8	4	0	.667	294	251
N.Y. Giants	6	5	1	.545	267	223	Green Bay	6	6	0	.500	258	276
Chi. Cardinals	4	7	1	.364	224	252	Baltimore	5	6	1	.455	214	239
Philadelphia	4	7	1	.364	248	231	San Francisco	4	8	0	.333	216	298
Pittsburgh	4	8	0	.333	195	285	Detroit	3	9	0	.250	230	275

NFL championship: Cleveland 38, LOS ANGELES 14

1954

EASTERN CONFERENCE	W	L	T	Pct.	Pts.	OP	WESTERN CONFERENCE	W	L	T	Pct.	Pts.	OP
Cleveland	9	3	0	.750	336	162	Detroit	9	2	1	.818	337	189
Philadelphia	7	4	1	.636	284	230	Chi. Bears	8	4	0	.667	301	279
N.Y. Giants	7	5	0	.583	293	184	San Francisco	7	4	1	.636	313	251
Pittsburgh	5	7	0	.417	219	263	Los Angeles	6	5	1	.545	314	285
Washington	3	9	0	.250	207	432	Green Bay	4	8	0	.333	234	251
Chi. Cardinals	2	10	0	.167	183	347	Baltimore	3	9	0	.250	131	279

NFL championship: CLEVELAND 56, Detroit 10

1953

EASTERN CONFERENCE	W	L	T	Pct.	Pts.	OP	WESTERN CONFERENCE	W	L	T	Pct.	Pts.	OP
Cleveland	11	1	0	.917	348	162	Detroit	10	2	0	.833	271	205
Philadelphia	7	4	1	.636	352	215	San Francisco	9	3	0	.750	372	237
Washington	6	5	1	.545	208	215	Los Angeles	8	3	1	.727	366	236
Pittsburgh	6	6	0	.500	211	263	Chi. Bears	3	8	1	.273	218	262
N.Y. Giants	3	9	0	.250	179	277	Baltimore	3	9	0	.250	182	350
Chi. Cardinals	1	10	1	.091	190	337	Green Bay	2	9	1	.182	200	338

NFL championship: DETROIT 17, Cleveland 16

1952

AMERICAN CONFERENCE	W	L	T	Pct.	Pts.	OP	NATIONAL CONFERENCE	W	L	T	Pct.	Pts.	OP
Cleveland	8	4	0	.667	310	213	Detroit	9	3	0	.750	344	192
N.Y. Giants	7	5	0	.583	234	231	Los Angeles	9	3	0	.750	349	234
Philadelphia	7	5	0	.583	252	271	San Francisco	7	5	0	.583	285	221
Pittsburgh	5	7	0	.417	300	273	Green Bay	6	6	0	.500	295	312
Chi. Cardinals	4	8	0	.333	172	221	Chi. Bears	5	7	0	.417	245	326
Washington	4	8	0	.333	240	287	Dallas Texans	1	11	0	.083	182	427

National Conference playoff: DETROIT 31, Los Angeles 21
NFL championship: Detroit 17, CLEVELAND 7

1951

AMERICAN CONFERENCE	W	L	T	Pct.	Pts.	OP	NATIONAL CONFERENCE	W	L	T	Pct.	Pts.	OP
Cleveland	11	1	0	.917	331	152	Los Angeles	8	4	0	.667	392	261
N.Y. Giants	9	2	1	.818	254	161	Detroit	7	4	1	.636	336	259
Washington	5	7	0	.417	183	296	San Francisco	7	4	1	.636	255	205
Pittsburgh	4	7	1	.364	183	235	Chi. Bears	7	5	0	.583	286	282
Philadelphia	4	8	0	.333	234	264	Green Bay	3	9	0	.250	254	375
Chi. Cardinals	3	9	0	.250	210	287	N.Y. Yanks	1	9	2	.100	241	382

NFL championship: LOS ANGELES 24, Cleveland 17

1950

AMERICAN CONFERENCE	W	L	T	Pct.	Pts.	OP	NATIONAL CONFERENCE	W	L	T	Pct.	Pts.	OP
Cleveland	10	2	0	.833	310	144	Los Angeles	9	3	0	.750	466	309
N.Y. Giants	10	2	0	.833	268	150	Chi. Bears	9	3	0	.750	279	207
Philadelphia	6	6	0	.500	254	141	N.Y. Yanks	7	5	0	.583	366	367
Pittsburgh	6	6	0	.500	180	195	Detroit	6	6	0	.500	321	285
Chi. Cardinals	5	7	0	.417	233	287	Green Bay	3	9	0	.250	244	406
Washington	3	9	0	.250	232	326	San Francisco	3	9	0	.250	213	300
							Baltimore	1	11	0	.083	213	462

American Conference playoff: CLEVELAND 8, N.Y. Giants 3
National Conference playoff: LOS ANGELES 24, Chi. Bears 14
NFL championship: CLEVELAND 30, Los Angeles 28

1949

EASTERN DIVISION	W	L	T	Pct.	Pts.	OP	WESTERN DIVISION	W	L	T	Pct.	Pts.	OP
Philadelphia	11	1	0	.917	364	134	Los Angeles	8	2	2	.800	360	239
Pittsburgh	6	5	1	.545	224	214	Chi. Bears	9	3	0	.750	332	218
N.Y. Giants	6	6	0	.500	287	298	Chi. Cardinals	6	5	1	.545	360	301
Washington	4	7	1	.364	268	339	Detroit	4	8	0	.333	237	259
N.Y. Bulldogs	1	10	1	.091	153	368	Green Bay	2	10	0	.167	114	329

NFL championship: Philadelphia 14, LOS ANGELES 0

1948

EASTERN DIVISION	W	L	T	Pct.	Pts.	OP	WESTERN DIVISION	W	L	T	Pct.	Pts.	OP
Philadelphia	9	2	1	.818	376	156	Chi. Cardinals	11	1	0	.917	395	226
Washington	7	5	0	.583	291	287	Chi. Bears	10	2	0	.833	375	151
N.Y. Giants	4	8	0	.333	297	388	Los Angeles	6	5	1	.545	327	269
Pittsburgh	4	8	0	.333	200	243	Green Bay	3	9	0	.250	154	290
Boston	3	9	0	.250	174	372	Detroit	2	10	0	.167	200	407

NFL championship: PHILADELPHIA 7, Chi. Cardinals 0

1947

EASTERN DIVISION	W	L	T	Pct.	Pts.	OP	WESTERN DIVISION	W	L	T	Pct.	Pts.	OP
Philadelphia	8	4	0	.667	308	242	Chi. Cardinals	9	3	0	.750	306	231
Pittsburgh	8	4	0	.667	240	259	Chi. Bears	8	4	0	.667	363	241
Boston	4	7	1	.364	168	256	Green Bay	6	5	1	.545	274	210
Washington	4	8	0	.333	295	367	Los Angeles	6	6	0	.500	259	214
N.Y. Giants	2	8	2	.200	190	309	Detroit	3	9	0	.250	231	305

Eastern Division playoff: Philadelphia 21, PITTSBURGH 0
NFL championship: CHI. CARDINALS 28, Philadelphia 21

1946

EASTERN DIVISION	W	L	T	Pct.	Pts.	OP	WESTERN DIVISION	W	L	T	Pct.	Pts.	OP
N.Y. Giants	7	3	1	.700	236	162	Chi. Bears	8	2	1	.800	289	193
Philadelphia	6	5	0	.545	231	220	Los Angeles	6	4	1	.600	277	257
Washington	5	5	1	.500	171	191	Green Bay	6	5	0	.545	148	158
Pittsburgh	5	5	1	.500	136	117	Chi. Cardinals	6	5	0	.545	260	198
Boston	2	8	1	.200	189	273	Detroit	1	10	0	.091	142	310

NFL championship: Chi. Bears 24, N.Y. GIANTS 14

1945

EASTERN DIVISION	W	L	T	Pct.	Pts.	OP	WESTERN DIVISION	W	L	T	Pct.	Pts.	OP
Washington	8	2	0	.800	209	121	Cleveland	9	1	0	.900	244	136
Philadelphia	7	3	0	.700	272	133	Detroit	7	3	0	.700	195	194
N.Y. Giants	3	6	1	.333	179	198	Green Bay	6	4	0	.600	258	173
Boston	3	6	1	.333	123	211	Chi. Bears	3	7	0	.300	192	235
Pittsburgh	2	8	0	.200	79	220	Chi. Cardinals	1	9	0	.100	98	228

NFL championship: CLEVELAND 15, Washington 14

1944

EASTERN DIVISION	W	L	T	Pct.	Pts.	OP	WESTERN DIVISION	W	L	T	Pct.	Pts.	OP
N.Y. Giants	8	1	1	.889	206	75	Green Bay	8	2	0	.800	238	141
Philadelphia	7	1	2	.875	267	131	Chi. Bears	6	3	1	.667	258	172
Washington	6	3	1	.667	169	180	Detroit	6	3	1	.667	216	151
Boston	2	8	0	.200	82	233	Cleveland	4	6	0	.400	188	224
Brooklyn	0	10	0	.000	69	166	Card-Pitt	0	10	0	.000	108	328

NFL championship: Green Bay 14, N.Y. GIANTS 7

1943

EASTERN DIVISION	W	L	T	Pct.	Pts.	OP	WESTERN DIVISION	W	L	T	Pct.	Pts.	OP
Washington	6	3	1	.667	229	137	Chi. Bears	8	1	1	.889	303	157
N.Y. Giants	6	3	1	.667	197	170	Green Bay	7	2	1	.778	264	172
Phil-Pitt	5	4	1	.556	225	230	Detroit	3	6	1	.333	178	218
Brooklyn	2	8	0	.200	65	234	Chi. Cardinals	0	10	0	.000	95	238

Eastern Division playoff: Washington 28, N.Y. GIANTS 0
NFL championship: CHI. BEARS 41, Washington 21

1942

EASTERN DIVISION	W	L	T	Pct.	Pts.	OP	WESTERN DIVISION	W	L	T	Pct.	Pts.	OP
Washington	10	1	0	.909	227	102	Chi. Bears	11	0	0	1.000	376	84
Pittsburgh	7	4	0	.636	167	119	Green Bay	8	2	1	.800	300	215
N.Y. Giants	5	5	1	.500	155	139	Cleveland	5	6	0	.455	150	207
Brooklyn	3	8	0	.273	100	168	Chi. Cardinals	3	8	0	.273	98	209
Philadelphia	2	9	0	.182	134	239	Detroit	0	11	0	.000	38	263

NFL championship: WASHINGTON 14, Chi. Bears 6

1941

EASTERN DIVISION	W	L	T	Pct.	Pts.	OP	WESTERN DIVISION	W	L	T	Pct.	Pts.	OP
N.Y. Giants	8	3	0	.727	238	114	Chi. Bears	10	1	0	.909	396	147
Brooklyn	7	4	0	.636	158	127	Green Bay	10	1	0	.909	258	120
Washington	6	5	0	.545	176	174	Detroit	4	6	1	.400	121	195
Philadelphia	2	8	1	.200	119	218	Chi. Cardinals	3	7	1	.300	127	197
Pittsburgh	1	9	1	.100	103	276	Cleveland	2	9	0	.182	116	244

Western Division playoff: CHI. BEARS 33, Green Bay 14
NFL championship: CHI. BEARS 37, N.Y. Giants 9

1940

EASTERN DIVISION	W	L	T	Pct.	Pts.	OP	WESTERN DIVISION	W	L	T	Pct.	Pts.	OP
Washington	9	2	0	.818	245	142	Chi. Bears	8	3	0	.727	238	152
Brooklyn	8	3	0	.727	186	120	Green Bay	6	4	1	.600	238	155
N.Y. Giants	6	4	1	.600	131	133	Detroit	5	5	1	.500	138	153
Pittsburgh	2	7	2	.222	60	178	Cleveland	4	6	1	.400	171	191
Philadelphia	1	10	0	.091	111	211	Chi. Cardinals	2	7	2	.222	139	222

NFL championship: Chi. Bears 73, WASHINGTON 0

1939

EASTERN DIVISION	W	L	T	Pct.	Pts.	OP	WESTERN DIVISION	W	L	T	Pct.	Pts.	OP
N.Y. Giants	9	1	1	.900	168	85	Green Bay	9	2	0	.818	233	153
Washington	8	2	1	.800	242	94	Chi. Bears	8	3	0	.727	298	157
Brooklyn	4	6	1	.400	108	219	Detroit	6	5	0	.545	145	150
Philadelphia	1	9	1	.100	105	200	Cleveland	5	5	1	.500	195	164
Pittsburgh	1	9	1	.100	114	216	Chi. Cardinals	1	10	0	.091	84	254

NFL championship: GREEN BAY 27, N.Y. Giants 0

1938

EASTERN DIVISION	W	L	T	Pct.	Pts.	OP	WESTERN DIVISION	W	L	T	Pct.	Pts.	OP
N.Y. Giants	8	2	1	.800	194	79	Green Bay	8	3	0	.727	223	118
Washington	6	3	2	.667	148	154	Detroit	7	4	0	.636	119	108
Brooklyn	4	4	3	.500	131	161	Chi. Bears	6	5	0	.545	194	148
Philadelphia	5	6	0	.455	154	164	Cleveland	4	7	0	.364	131	215
Pittsburgh	2	9	0	.182	79	169	Chi. Cardinals	2	9	0	.182	111	168

NFL championship: N.Y. GIANTS 23, Green Bay 17

1937

EASTERN DIVISION	W	L	T	Pct.	Pts.	OP	WESTERN DIVISION	W	L	T	Pct.	Pts.	OP
Washington	8	3	0	.727	195	120	Chi. Bears	9	1	1	.900	201	100
N.Y. Giants	6	3	2	.667	128	109	Green Bay	7	4	0	.636	220	122
Pittsburgh	4	7	0	.364	122	145	Detroit	7	4	0	.636	180	105
Brooklyn	3	7	1	.300	82	174	Chi. Cardinals	5	5	1	.500	135	165
Philadelphia	2	8	1	.200	86	177	Cleveland	1	10	0	.091	75	207

NFL championship: Washington 28, CHI. BEARS 21

1936

EASTERN DIVISION	W	L	T	Pct.	Pts.	OP	WESTERN DIVISION	W	L	T	Pct.	Pts.	OP
Boston	7	5	0	.583	149	110	Green Bay	10	1	1	.909	248	118
Pittsburgh	6	6	0	.500	98	187	Chi. Bears	9	3	0	.750	222	94
N.Y. Giants	5	6	1	.455	115	163	Detroit	8	4	0	.667	235	102
Brooklyn	3	8	1	.273	92	161	Chi. Cardinals	3	8	1	.273	74	143
Philadelphia	1	11	0	.083	51	206							

NFL championship: Green Bay 21, Boston 6, at Polo Grounds, N.Y.

1935

EASTERN DIVISION	W	L	T	Pct.	Pts.	OP	WESTERN DIVISION	W	L	T	Pct.	Pts.	OP
N.Y. Giants	9	3	0	.750	180	96	Detroit	7	3	2	.700	191	111
Brooklyn	5	6	1	.455	90	141	Green Bay	8	4	0	.667	181	96
Pittsburgh	4	8	0	.333	100	209	Chi. Bears	6	4	2	.600	192	106
Boston	2	8	1	.200	65	123	Chi. Cardinals	6	4	2	.600	99	97
Philadelphia	2	9	0	.182	60	179							

NFL championship: DETROIT 26, N.Y. Giants 7
One game between Boston and Philadelphia was canceled.

1934

EASTERN DIVISION	W	L	T	Pct.	Pts.	OP	WESTERN DIVISION	W	L	T	Pct.	Pts.	OP
N.Y. Giants	8	5	0	.615	147	107	Chi. Bears	13	0	0	1.000	286	86
Boston	6	6	0	.500	107	94	Detroit	10	3	0	.769	238	59
Brooklyn	4	7	0	.364	61	153	Green Bay	7	6	0	.538	156	112
Philadelphia	4	7	0	.364	127	85	Chi. Cardinals	5	6	0	.455	80	84
Pittsburgh	2	10	0	.167	51	206	St. Louis	1	2	0	.333	27	61
							Cincinnati	0	8	0	.000	10	243

NFL championship: N.Y. GIANTS 30, Chi. Bears 13

1933

EASTERN DIVISION	W	L	T	Pct.	Pts.	OP	WESTERN DIVISION	W	L	T	Pct.	Pts.	OP
N.Y. Giants	11	3	0	.786	244	101	Chi. Bears	10	2	1	.833	133	82
Brooklyn	5	4	1	.556	93	54	Portsmouth	6	5	0	.545	128	87
Boston	5	5	2	.500	103	97	Green Bay	5	7	1	.417	170	107
Philadelphia	3	5	1	.375	77	158	Cincinnati	3	6	1	.333	38	110
Pittsburgh	3	6	2	.333	67	208	Chi. Cardinals	1	9	1	.100	52	101

NFL championship: CHI. BEARS 23, N.Y. Giants 21

1932

	W	L	T	Pct.
Chicago Bears	7	1	6	.875
Green Bay Packers	10	3	1	.769
Portsmouth Spartans	6	2	4	.750
Boston Braves	4	4	2	.500
New York Giants	4	6	2	.400
Brooklyn Dodgers	3	9	0	.250
Chicago Cardinals	2	6	2	.250
Staten Island Stapletons	2	7	3	.222

Chicago Bears and Portsmouth finished regularly scheduled games tied for first place. Bears won playoff game, which counted in standings, 9-0.

1931

	W	L	T	Pct.
Green Bay Packers	12	2	0	.857
Portsmouth Spartans	11	3	0	.786
Chicago Bears	8	5	0	.615
Chicago Cardinals	5	4	0	.556
New York Giants	7	6	1	.538
Providence Steam Roller	4	4	3	.500
Staten Island Stapletons	4	6	1	.400
Cleveland Indians	2	8	0	.200
Brooklyn Dodgers	2	12	0	.143
Frankford Yellow Jackets	1	6	1	.143

1930

	W	L	T	Pct.
Green Bay Packers	10	3	1	.769
New York Giants	13	4	0	.765
Chicago Bears	9	4	1	.692
Brooklyn Dodgers	7	4	1	.636
Providence Steam Roller	6	4	1	.600
Staten Island Stapletons	5	5	2	.500
Chicago Cardinals	5	6	2	.455
Portsmouth Spartans	5	6	3	.455
Frankford Yellow Jackets	4	13	1	.222
Minneapolis Red Jackets	1	7	1	.125
Newark Tornadoes	1	10	1	.091

1929

	W	L	T	Pct.
Green Bay Packers	12	0	1	1.000
New York Giants	13	1	1	.929
Frankford Yellow Jackets	10	4	5	.714
Chicago Cardinals	6	6	1	.500
Boston Bulldogs	4	4	0	.500
Staten Island Stapletons	3	4	3	.429
Providence Steam Roller	4	6	2	.400
Orange Tornadoes	3	5	4	.375
Chicago Bears	4	9	2	.308
Buffalo Bisons	1	7	1	.125
Minneapolis Red Jackets	1	9	0	.100
Dayton Triangles	0	6	0	.000

1928

	W	L	T	Pct.
Providence Steam Roller	8	1	2	.889
Frankford Yellow Jackets	11	3	2	.786
Detroit Wolverines	7	2	1	.778
Green Bay Packers	6	4	3	.600
Chicago Bears	7	5	1	.583
New York Giants	4	7	2	.364
New York Yankees	4	8	1	.333
Pottsville Maroons	2	8	0	.200
Chicago Cardinals	1	5	0	.167
Dayton Triangles	0	7	0	.000

1927

	W	L	T	Pct.
New York Giants	11	1	1	.917
Green Bay Packers	7	2	1	.778
Chicago Bears	9	3	2	.750
Cleveland Bulldogs	8	4	1	.667
Providence Steam Roller	8	5	1	.615
New York Yankees	7	8	1	.467
Frankford Yellow Jackets	6	9	3	.400
Pottsville Maroons	5	8	0	.385
Chicago Cardinals	3	7	1	.300
Dayton Triangles	1	6	1	.143
Duluth Eskimos	1	8	0	.111
Buffalo Bisons	0	5	0	.000

1926

	W	L	T	Pct.
Frankford Yellow Jackets	14	1	2	.933
Chicago Bears	12	1	3	.923
Pottsville Maroons	10	2	2	.833
Kansas City Cowboys	8	3	0	.727
Green Bay Packers	7	3	3	.700
Los Angeles Buccaneers	6	3	1	.667
New York Giants	8	4	1	.667
Duluth Eskimos	6	5	3	.545
Buffalo Rangers	4	4	2	.500
Chicago Cardinals	5	6	1	.455
Providence Steam Roller	5	7	1	.417
Detroit Panthers	4	6	2	.400
Hartford Blues	3	7	0	.300
Brooklyn Lions	3	8	0	.273
Milwaukee Badgers	2	7	0	.222
Akron Indians	1	4	3	.200
Dayton Triangles	1	4	1	.200
Racine Tornadoes	1	4	0	.200
Columbus Tigers	1	6	0	.143
Canton Bulldogs	1	9	3	.100
Hammond Pros	0	4	0	.000
Louisville Colonels	0	4	0	.000

1925

	W	L	T	Pct.
Chicago Cardinals	11	2	1	.846
Pottsville Maroons	10	2	0	.833
Detroit Panthers	8	2	2	.800
New York Giants	8	4	0	.667
Akron Indians	4	2	2	.667
Frankford Yellow Jackets	13	7	0	.650
Chicago Bears	9	5	3	.643
Rock Island Independents	5	3	3	.625
Green Bay Packers	8	5	0	.615
Providence Steam Roller	6	5	1	.545
Canton Bulldogs	4	4	0	.500
Cleveland Bulldogs	5	8	1	.385
Kansas City Cowboys	2	5	1	.286
Hammond Pros	1	4	0	.200
Buffalo Bisons	1	6	2	.143
Duluth Kelleys	0	3	0	.000
Rochester Jeffersons	0	6	1	.000
Milwaukee Badgers	0	6	0	.000
Dayton Triangles	0	7	1	.000
Columbus Tigers	0	9	0	.000

1924

	W	L	T	Pct.
Cleveland Bulldogs	7	1	1	.875
Chicago Bears	6	1	4	.857
Frankford Yellow Jackets	11	2	1	.846
Duluth Kelleys	5	1	0	.833
Rock Island Independents	5	2	2	.714
Green Bay Packers	7	4	0	.636
Racine Legion	4	3	3	.571
Chicago Cardinals	5	4	1	.556
Buffalo Bisons	6	5	0	.545
Columbus Tigers	4	4	0	.500
Hammond Pros	2	2	1	.500
Milwaukee Badgers	5	8	0	.385
Akron Indians	2	6	0	.250
Dayton Triangles	2	6	0	.250
Kansas City Blues	2	7	0	.222
Kenosha Maroons	0	4	1	.000
Minneapolis Marines	0	6	0	.000
Rochester Jeffersons	0	7	0	.000

1923

	W	L	T	Pct.
Canton Bulldogs	11	0	1	1.000
Chicago Bears	9	2	1	.818
Green Bay Packers	7	2	1	.778
Milwaukee Badgers	7	2	3	.778
Cleveland Indians	3	1	3	.750
Chicago Cardinals	8	4	0	.667
Duluth Kelleys	4	3	0	.571
Buffalo All-Americans	5	4	3	.556
Columbus Tigers	5	4	1	.556
Racine Legion	4	4	2	.500
Toledo Maroons	3	3	2	.500
Rock Island Independents	2	3	3	.400
Minneapolis Marines	2	5	2	.286
St. Louis All-Stars	1	4	2	.200
Hammond Pros	1	5	1	.167
Dayton Triangles	1	6	1	.143
Akron Indians	1	6	0	.143
Oorang Indians	1	10	0	.091
Louisville Brecks	0	3	0	.000
Rochester Jeffersons	0	4	0	.000

1922

	W	L	T	Pct.
Canton Bulldogs	10	0	2	1.000
Chicago Bears	9	3	0	.750
Chicago Cardinals	8	3	0	.727
Toledo Maroons	5	2	2	.714
Rock Island Independents	4	2	1	.667
Racine Legion	6	4	1	.600
Dayton Triangles	4	3	1	.571
Green Bay Packers	4	3	3	.571
Buffalo All-Americans	5	4	1	.556
Akron Pros	3	5	2	.375
Milwaukee Badgers	2	4	3	.333
Oorang Indians	3	6	0	.333
Minneapolis Marines	1	3	0	.250
Louisville Brecks	1	3	0	.250
Evansville Crimson Giants	0	3	0	.000
Rochester Jeffersons	0	4	1	.000
Hammond Pros	0	5	1	.000
Columbus Panhandles	0	8	0	.000

1921

	W	L	T	Pct.
Chicago Staleys	9	1	1	.900
Buffalo All-Americans	9	1	2	.900
Akron Pros	8	3	1	.727
Canton Bulldogs	5	2	3	.714
Rock Island Independents	4	2	1	.667
Evansville Crimson Giants	3	2	0	.600
Green Bay Packers	3	2	1	.600
Dayton Triangles	4	4	1	.500
Chicago Cardinals	3	3	2	.500
Rochester Jeffersons	2	3	0	.400
Cleveland Indians	3	5	0	.375
Washington Senators	1	2	0	.333
Cincinnati Celts	1	3	0	.250
Hammond Pros	1	3	1	.250
Minneapolis Marines	1	3	0	.250
Detroit Tigers	1	5	1	.167
Columbus Panhandles	1	8	0	.111
Tonawanda Kardex	0	1	0	.000
Muncie Flyers	0	2	0	.000
Louisville Brecks	0	2	0	.000
New York Giants	0	2	0	.000

1920*

	W	L	T	Pct.
Akron Pros	8	0	3	1.000
Decatur Staleys	10	1	2	.909
Buffalo All-Americans	9	1	1	.900
Chicago Cardinals	6	2	2	.750
Rock Island Independents	6	2	2	.750
Dayton Triangles	5	2	2	.714
Rochester Jeffersons	6	3	2	.667
Canton Bulldogs	7	4	2	.636
Detroit Heralds	2	3	3	.400
Cleveland Tigers	2	4	2	.333
Chicago Tigers	2	5	1	.286
Hammond Pros	2	5	0	.286
Columbus Panhandles	2	6	2	.250
Muncie Flyers	0	1	0	.000

No official standings were maintained for the 1920 season, and the championship was awarded to the Akron Pros in a League meeting on April 30, 1921. Clubs played schedules that included games against nonleague opponents.

NFL OPENING KICKOFF GAMES (10)
(Home Team in capitals)

Date	Sites*	Teams
Sept. 5, 2002	Giants Stadium (East Rutherford, New Jersey) Times Square (New York, New York)	San Francisco 16, N.Y. GIANTS 13
Sept. 4, 2003	FedExField (Landover, Maryland) National Mall (Washington, D.C.)	WASHINGTON 16, N.Y. Jets 13
Sept. 9, 2004	Gillette Stadium (Foxboro, Massachusetts) Metropolitan Park (Jacksonville, Florida)	NEW ENGLAND 27, Indianapolis 24
Sept. 8, 2005	Gillette Stadium (Foxboro, Massachusetts) Detroit, Michigan Los Angeles Coliseum (Los Angeles, California)	NEW ENGLAND 30, Oakland 20
Sept. 7, 2006	Heinz Field (Pittsburgh, Pennsylvania) Miami, Florida	PITTSBURGH 28, Miami 17
Sept. 6, 2007	RCA Dome (Indianapolis, Indianapolis)	INDIANAPOLIS 41, New Orleans 10
Sept. 4, 2008	Giants Stadium (East Rutherford, New Jersey) Columbus Circle (New York, New York)	N.Y. GIANTS 16, Washington 7
Sept. 10, 2009	Heinz Field (Pittsburgh, Pennsylvania) Point State Park (Pittsburgh, Pennsylvania)	PITTSBURGH 13, Tennessee 10 (OT)
Sept. 9, 2010	Louisiana Superdome (New Orleans, Louisiana) Jackson Square (New Orleans, Louisiana)	NEW ORLEANS 14, Minnesota 9
Sept. 8, 2011	Lambeau Field (Green Bay, Wisconsin)	GREEN BAY 42, New Orleans 34

The first site listed each year designates location of Thursday Night NFL Kickoff Weekend game; subsequent locations indicate site(s) of NFL Kickoff Weekend concert.

RS=REGULAR SEASON
PS=POSTSEASON
*ARIZONA vs. ATLANTA
RS: Cardinals lead series, 14-11
PS: Cardinals lead series, 1-0
1966—Falcons, 16-10 (Atl)
1968—Cardinals, 17-12 (StL)
1971—Cardinals, 26-9 (Atl)
1973—Cardinals, 32-10 (Atl)
1975—Cardinals, 23-20 (StL)
1978—Cardinals, 42-21 (StL)
1980—Falcons, 33-27 (StL) OT
1981—Falcons, 41-20 (Atl)
1982—Cardinals, 23-20 (Atl)
1986—Falcons, 33-13 (Atl)
1987—Cardinals, 34-21 (Atl)
1989—Cardinals, 34-20 (P)
1990—Cardinals, 24-13 (Atl)
1991—Cardinals, 16-10 (P)
1992—Falcons, 20-17 (Atl)
1993—Cardinals, 27-10 (Atl)
1994—Falcons, 10-6 (Atl)
1995—Cardinals, 40-37 (Ariz) OT
1997—Cardinals, 29-26 (Ariz)
1999—Falcons, 37-14 (Atl)
2001—Falcons, 34-14 (Ariz)
2004—Falcons, 6-3 (Atl)
2006—Falcons, 32-10 (Atl)
2007—Cardinals, 30-27 (Ariz) OT
2008—**Cardinals, 30-24 (Ariz)
2010—Falcons, 41-7 (Atl)
(RS Pts.—Falcons 559, Cardinals 538)
(PS Pts.—Cardinals 30, Falcons 24)
**Franchise known as Phoenix prior to
1994 and in St. Louis prior to 1988
**NFC First-Round Playoff*
*ARIZONA vs. BALTIMORE
RS: Ravens lead series, 4-1
1997—Cardinals, 16-13 (B)
2000—Ravens, 13-7 (A)
2003—Ravens, 26-18 (A)
2007—Ravens, 26-23 (B)
2011—Ravens, 30-27 (B)
(RS Pts.—Ravens 108, Cardinals 91)
*ARIZONA vs. BUFFALO
RS: Bills lead series, 5-4
1971—Cardinals, 28-23 (B)
1975—Bills, 32-14 (StL)
1981—Cardinals, 24-0 (StL)
1984—Cardinals, 37-7 (StL)
1986—Bills, 17-10 (B)
1990—Bills, 45-14 (B)
1999—Bills, 31-21 (A)
2004—Bills, 38-14 (B)
2008—Cardinals, 41-17 (A)
(RS Pts.—Bills 210, Cardinals 203)
**Franchise known as Phoenix prior to
1994 and in St. Louis prior to 1988*
ARIZONA vs. CAROLINA
RS: Panthers lead series, 8-3
PS: Cardinals lead series, 1-0
1995—Panthers, 27-7 (C)
2001—Cardinals, 30-7 (C)
2002—Cardinals, 16-13 (C)
2003—Panthers, 20-17 (A)
2004—Panthers, 35-10 (C)
2005—Panthers, 24-20 (A)
2007—Panthers, 25-10 (A)
2008—Panthers, 27-23 (C)
        *Cardinals, 33-13 (C)
2009—Panthers, 34-21 (A)
2010—Panthers, 19-12 (C)

2011—Cardinals, 28-21 (A)
(RS Pts.—Panthers 252, Cardinals 194)
(PS Pts.—Cardinals 33, Panthers 13)
*NFC Divisional Playoff
*ARIZONA vs. **CHICAGO
RS: Bears lead series, 55-27-6
(NP denotes Normal Park;
Wr denotes Wrigley Field;
Co denotes Comiskey Park;
So denotes Soldier Field;
all Chicago)
1920—Cardinals, 7-6 (NP)
        Staleys, 10-0 (Wr)
1921—Tie, 0-0 (Wr)
1922—Cardinals, 6-0 (Co)
        Cardinals, 9-0 (Co)
1923—Bears, 3-0 (Wr)
1924—Bears, 6-0 (Wr)
        Bears, 21-0 (Co)
1925—Cardinals, 9-0 (Co)
        Tie, 0-0 (Wr)
1926—Bears, 16-0 (Wr)
        Bears, 10-0 (So)
        Tie, 0-0 (Wr)
1927—Bears, 9-0 (NP)
        Cardinals, 3-0 (Wr)
1928—Bears, 15-0 (NP)
        Bears, 34-0 (Wr)
1929—Tie, 0-0 (Wr)
        Cardinals, 40-6 (Co)
1930—Bears, 32-6 (Co)
        Bears, 6-0 (Wr)
1931—Bears, 26-13 (Wr)
        Bears, 18-7 (Wr)
1932—Tie, 0-0 (Wr)
        Bears, 34-0 (Wr)
1933—Bears, 12-9 (Wr)
        Bears, 22-6 (Wr)
1934—Bears, 20-0 (Wr)
        Bears, 17-6 (Wr)
1935—Tie, 7-7 (Wr)
        Bears, 13-0 (Wr)
1936—Bears, 7-3 (Wr)
        Cardinals, 14-7 (Wr)
1937—Bears, 16-7 (Wr)
        Bears, 42-28 (Wr)
1938—Bears, 16-13 (So)
        Bears, 34-28 (Wr)
1939—Bears, 44-7 (Wr)
        Bears, 48-7 (Co)
1940—Cardinals, 21-7 (Co)
        Bears, 31-23 (Wr)
1941—Bears, 53-7 (Wr)
        Bears, 34-24 (Co)
1942—Bears, 41-14 (Wr)
        Bears, 21-7 (Co)
1943—Bears, 20-0 (Wr)
        Bears, 35-24 (Co)
1945—Cardinals, 16-7 (Wr)
        Bears, 28-20 (Co)
1946—Bears, 34-17 (Co)
        Cardinals, 35-28 (Wr)
1947—Cardinals, 31-7 (Co)
        Cardinals, 30-21 (Wr)
1948—Bears, 28-17 (Co)
        Cardinals, 24-21 (Wr)
1949—Bears, 17-7 (Co)
        Bears, 52-21 (Wr)
1950—Bears, 27-6 (Wr)
        Cardinals, 20-10 (Co)
1951—Cardinals, 28-14 (Co)
        Cardinals, 24-14 (Wr)

1952—Cardinals, 21-10 (Co)
        Bears, 10-7 (Wr)
1953—Cardinals, 24-17 (Wr)
1954—Bears, 29-7 (Co)
1955—Cardinals, 53-14 (Co)
1956—Bears, 10-3 (Wr)
1957—Bears, 14-6 (Co)
1958—Bears, 30-14 (Wr)
1959—Bears, 31-7 (So)
1965—Bears, 34-13 (Wr)
1966—Cardinals, 24-17 (StL)
1967—Bears, 30-3 (Wr)
1969—Cardinals, 20-17 (StL)
1972—Bears, 27-10 (StL)
1975—Cardinals, 34-20 (So)
1977—Cardinals, 16-13 (StL)
1978—Bears, 17-10 (So)
1979—Bears, 42-6 (So)
1982—Cardinals, 10-7 (So)
1984—Cardinals, 38-21 (StL)
1990—Bears, 31-21 (P)
1994—Bears, 19-16 (A) OT
1998—Cardinals, 20-7 (A)
2001—Bears, 20-13 (C)
2003—Bears, 28-3 (C)
2006—Bears, 24-23 (A)
2009—Cardinals, 41-21 (C)
(RS Pts.—Bears 1,667, Cardinals 1,114)
**Franchise known as Phoenix prior to
1994, in St. Louis prior to 1988, and in
Chicago prior to 1960
**Franchise in Decatur prior to 1921 and
known as Staleys prior to 1922*
*ARIZONA vs. CINCINNATI
RS: Bengals lead series, 6-4
1973—Bengals, 42-24 (C)
1979—Bengals, 34-28 (C)
1985—Cardinals, 41-27 (StL)
1988—Bengals, 21-14 (C)
1994—Cardinals, 28-7 (A)
1997—Bengals, 24-21 (C)
2000—Bengals, 24-13 (C)
2003—Cardinals, 17-14 (A)
2007—Cardinals, 35-27 (C)
2011—Bengals, 23-16 (C)
(RS Pts.—Bengals 243, Cardinals 237)
**Franchise known as Phoenix prior to
1994 and in St. Louis prior to 1988*
*ARIZONA vs. CLEVELAND
RS: Browns lead series, 33-13-3
1950—Browns, 34-24 (Cle)
        Browns, 10-7 (Chi)
1951—Browns, 34-17 (Chi)
        Browns, 49-28 (Cle)
1952—Browns, 28-13 (Chi)
        Browns, 10-0 (Cle)
1953—Browns, 27-7 (Chi)
        Browns, 27-16 (Cle)
1954—Browns, 31-7 (Cle)
        Browns, 35-3 (Chi)
1955—Browns, 26-20 (Chi)
        Browns, 35-24 (Cle)
1956—Cardinals, 9-7 (Chi)
        Cardinals, 24-7 (Cle)
1957—Browns, 17-7 (Chi)
        Browns, 31-0 (Cle)
1958—Browns, 35-28 (Chi)
        Browns, 38-24 (Chi)
1959—Browns, 34-7 (Chi)
        Browns, 17-7 (Cle)
1960—Browns, 28-27 (Cle)
        Tie, 17-17 (StL)

1961—Browns, 20-17 (Cle)
Browns, 21-10 (StL)
1962—Browns, 34-7 (StL)
Browns, 38-14 (Cle)
1963—Cardinals, 20-14 (Cle)
Browns, 24-10 (StL)
1964—Tie, 33-33 (Cle)
Cardinals, 28-19 (StL)
1965—Cardinals, 49-13 (Cle)
Browns, 27-24 (StL)
1966—Cardinals, 34-28 (Cle)
Browns, 38-10 (StL)
1967—Browns, 20-16 (Cle)
Browns, 20-16 (StL)
1968—Cardinals, 27-21 (Cle)
Cardinals, 27-16 (StL)
1969—Tie, 21-21 (Cle)
Browns, 27-21 (StL)
1974—Cardinals, 29-7 (StL)
1979—Browns, 38-20 (StL)
1985—Cardinals, 27-24 (Cle) OT
1988—Browns, 29-21 (P)
1994—Browns, 32-0 (Cle)
2000—Cardinals, 29-21 (A)
2003—Browns, 44-6 (Cle)
2007—Cardinals, 27-21 (A)
2011—Cardinals, 20-17 (A) OT
(RS Pts.—Browns 1,244, Cardinals 879)
*Franchise known as Phoenix prior to
1994, in St. Louis prior to 1988,
and in Chicago prior to 1960
ARIZONA vs. DALLAS
RS: Cowboys lead series, 55-30-1
PS: Cardinals lead series, 1-0
1960—Cardinals, 12-10 (StL)
1961—Cardinals, 31-17 (D)
Cardinals, 31-13 (StL)
1962—Cardinals, 28-24 (D)
Cardinals, 52-20 (StL)
1963—Cardinals, 34-7 (D)
Cowboys, 28-24 (StL)
1964—Cardinals, 16-6 (D)
Cowboys, 31-13 (StL)
1965—Cardinals, 20-13 (StL)
Cowboys, 27-13 (D)
1966—Tie, 10-10 (StL)
Cowboys, 31-17 (D)
1967—Cardinals, 46-21 (D)
1968—Cowboys, 27-10 (StL)
1969—Cowboys, 24-3 (D)
1970—Cardinals, 20-7 (StL)
Cardinals, 38-0 (D)
1971—Cowboys, 16-13 (StL)
Cowboys, 31-12 (D)
1972—Cowboys, 33-24 (D)
Cowboys, 27-6 (StL)
1973—Cowboys, 45-10 (D)
Cowboys, 30-3 (StL)
1974—Cardinals, 31-28 (StL)
Cowboys, 17-14 (D)
1975—Cowboys, 37-31 (D) OT
Cardinals, 31-17 (StL)
1976—Cardinals, 21-17 (StL)
Cowboys, 19-14 (D)
1977—Cowboys, 30-24 (StL)
Cardinals, 24-17 (D)
1978—Cowboys, 21-12 (D)
Cowboys, 24-21 (StL) OT
1979—Cowboys, 22-21 (StL)
Cowboys, 22-13 (D)
1980—Cowboys, 27-24 (StL)
Cowboys, 31-21 (D)

1981—Cowboys, 30-17 (D)
Cardinals, 20-17 (StL)
1982—Cowboys, 24-7 (StL)
1983—Cowboys, 34-17 (StL)
Cowboys, 35-17 (D)
1984—Cardinals, 31-20 (D)
Cowboys, 24-17 (StL)
1985—Cardinals, 21-10 (StL)
Cowboys, 35-17 (D)
1986—Cowboys, 31-7 (StL)
Cowboys, 37-6 (D)
1987—Cardinals, 24-13 (StL)
Cowboys, 21-16 (D)
1988—Cowboys, 17-14 (P)
Cardinals, 16-10 (D)
1989—Cardinals, 19-10 (D)
Cardinals, 24-20 (P)
1990—Cardinals, 20-3 (P)
Cowboys, 41-10 (D)
1991—Cowboys, 17-9 (P)
Cowboys, 27-7 (D)
1992—Cowboys, 31-20 (D)
Cowboys, 16-10 (P)
1993—Cowboys, 17-10 (P)
Cowboys, 20-15 (D)
1994—Cowboys, 38-3 (D)
Cowboys, 28-21 (A)
1995—Cowboys, 34-20 (D)
Cowboys, 37-13 (A)
1996—Cowboys, 17-3 (D)
Cowboys, 10-6 (A)
1997—Cardinals, 25-22 (A) OT
Cowboys, 24-6 (D)
1998—Cowboys, 38-10 (D)
Cowboys, 35-28 (A)
**Cardinals, 20-7 (D)
1999—Cowboys, 35-7 (D)
Cardinals, 13-9 (A)
2000—Cardinals, 32-31 (A)
Cowboys, 48-7 (D)
2001—Cowboys, 17-3 (D)
Cardinals, 17-10 (A)
2002—Cardinals, 9-6 (A) OT
2003—Cowboys, 24-7 (D)
2005—Cowboys, 34-13 (D)
2006—Cowboys, 27-10 (A)
2008—Cardinals, 30-24 (A) OT
2010—Cardinals, 27-26 (A)
2011—Cardinals, 19-13 (A) OT
(RS Pts.—Cowboys 1,999, Cardinals 1,483)
(PS Pts.—Cardinals 20, Cowboys 7)
*Franchise known as Phoenix prior to
1994 and in St. Louis prior to 1988
**NFC First-Round Playoff
ARIZONA vs. DENVER
RS: Broncos lead series, 7-1-1
1973—Tie, 17-17 (StL)
1977—Broncos, 7-0 (D)
1989—Broncos, 37-0 (P)
1991—Broncos, 24-19 (D)
1995—Broncos, 38-6 (D)
2001—Broncos, 38-17 (A)
2002—Broncos, 37-7 (D)
2006—Broncos, 37-20 (A)
2010—Cardinals, 43-13 (A)
(RS Pts.—Broncos 248, Cardinals 129)
*Franchise known as Phoenix prior to
1994 and in St. Louis prior to 1988
ARIZONA vs. **DETROIT
RS: Lions lead series, 31-24-5
1930—Tie, 0-0 (Port)
Cardinals, 23-0 (C)

1931—Spartans, 13-3 (Port)
Cardinals, 20-19 (C)
1932—Tie, 7-7 (Port)
1933—Spartans, 7-6 (Port)
1934—Lions, 6-0 (D)
Lions, 17-13 (C)
1935—Tie, 10-10 (D)
Lions, 7-6 (C)
1936—Lions, 39-0 (D)
Lions, 14-7 (C)
1937—Lions, 16-7 (C)
Lions, 16-7 (D)
1938—Lions, 10-0 (D)
Lions, 7-3 (C)
1939—Lions, 21-3 (D)
Lions, 17-3 (C)
1940—Tie, 0-0 (Buffalo)
Lions, 43-14 (C)
1941—Tie, 14-14 (C)
Lions, 21-3 (D)
1942—Cardinals, 13-0 (C)
Cardinals, 7-0 (D)
1943—Lions, 35-17 (D)
Lions, 7-0 (Buffalo)
1945—Lions, 10-0 (Milwaukee)
Lions, 26-0 (D)
1946—Cardinals, 34-14 (C)
Cardinals, 36-14 (D)
1947—Cardinals, 45-21 (C)
Cardinals, 17-7 (D)
1948—Cardinals, 56-20 (C)
Cardinals, 28-14 (D)
1949—Lions, 24-7 (C)
Cardinals, 42-19 (D)
1959—Lions, 45-21 (D)
1961—Lions, 45-14 (StL)
1967—Lions, 38-28 (StL)
1969—Lions, 20-0 (D)
1970—Lions, 16-3 (D)
1973—Lions, 20-16 (StL)
1975—Cardinals, 24-13 (D)
1978—Cardinals, 21-14 (StL)
1980—Lions, 20-7 (D)
Cardinals, 24-23 (StL)
1989—Cardinals, 16-13 (D)
1993—Lions, 26-20 (D)
Lions, 21-14 (Phx)
1995—Cardinals, 20-17 (D)
1998—Cardinals, 17-15 (D)
1999—Cardinals, 23-19 (A)
2001—Cardinals, 45-38 (A)
2002—Cardinals, 23-20 (A) OT
2003—Lions, 42-24 (D)
2004—Lions, 26-12 (D)
2005—Lions, 29-21 (D)
2006—Cardinals, 17-10 (A)
2007—Cardinals, 31-21 (A)
2009—Cardinals, 31-24 (D)
(RS Pts.—Lions 1,093, Cardinals 943)
*Franchise known as Phoenix prior to
1994, in St. Louis prior to 1988,
and in Chicago prior to 1960
**Franchise in Portsmouth prior to 1934
and known as the Spartans
ARIZONA vs. GREEN BAY
RS: Packers lead series, 43-22-4
PS: Series tied, 1-1
1921—Tie, 3-3 (C)
1922—Cardinals, 16-3 (C)
1924—Cardinals, 3-0 (C)
1925—Cardinals, 9-6 (C)
1926—Cardinals, 13-7 (GB)

Packers, 3-0 (C)
1927—Packers, 13-0 (GB)
Tie, 6-6 (C)
1928—Packers, 20-0 (GB)
1929—Packers, 9-2 (GB)
Packers, 7-6 (C)
Packers, 12-0 (C)
1930—Packers, 14-0 (GB)
Cardinals, 13-6 (C)
1931—Packers, 26-7 (GB)
Cardinals, 21-13 (C)
1932—Packers, 15-7 (GB)
Packers, 19-9 (C)
1933—Packers, 14-6 (C)
1934—Packers, 15-0 (GB)
Cardinals, 9-0 (Mil)
Cardinals, 6-0 (C)
1935—Cardinals, 7-6 (GB)
Cardinals, 3-0 (Mil)
Cardinals, 9-7 (C)
1936—Packers, 10-7 (GB)
Packers, 24-0 (Mil)
Tie, 0-0 (C)
1937—Cardinals, 14-7 (GB)
Packers, 34-13 (Mil)
1938—Packers, 28-7 (Mil)
Packers, 24-22 (Buffalo)
1939—Packers, 14-10 (GB)
Packers, 27-20 (Mil)
1940—Packers, 31-6 (Mil)
Packers, 28-7 (C)
1941—Packers, 14-13 (Mil)
Packers, 17-9 (GB)
1942—Packers, 17-13 (C)
Packers, 55-24 (GB)
1943—Packers, 28-7 (C)
Packers, 35-14 (Mil)
1945—Packers, 33-14 (GB)
1946—Packers, 19-7 (C)
Cardinals, 24-6 (GB)
1947—Cardinals, 14-10 (GB)
Cardinals, 21-20 (C)
1948—Cardinals, 17-7 (Mil)
Cardinals, 42-7 (C)
1949—Cardinals, 39-17 (Mil)
Cardinals, 41-21 (C)
1955—Packers, 31-14 (GB)
1956—Packers, 24-21 (C)
1962—Packers, 17-0 (Mil)
1963—Packers, 30-7 (StL)
1967—Packers, 31-23 (StL)
1969—Packers, 45-28 (GB)
1971—Tie, 16-16 (StL)
1973—Packers, 25-21 (GB)
1976—Cardinals, 29-0 (StL)
1982—**Packers, 41-16 (GB)
1984—Packers, 24-23 (GB)
1985—Cardinals, 43-28 (StL)
1988—Packers, 26-17 (P)
1990—Packers, 24-21 (P)
1999—Packers, 49-24 (GB)
2000—Packers, 29-3 (A)
2003—Cardinals, 20-13 (A)
2006—Packers, 31-14 (GB)
2009—Packers, 33-7 (A)
**Cardinals, 51-45 (A) OT
(RS Pts.—Packers 1,233, Cardinals 891)
(PS Pts.—Packers 86, Cardinals 67)
*Franchise known as Phoenix prior to
1994, in St. Louis prior to 1988,
and in Chicago prior to 1960
**NFC First-Round Playoff

ARIZONA vs. HOUSTON
RS: Series tied, 1-1
2005—Texans, 30-19 (H)
2009—Cardinals, 28-21 (A)
(RS Pts.—Texans 51, Cardinals 47)
*ARIZONA vs. **INDIANAPOLIS
RS: Colts lead series, 8-6
1961—Colts, 16-0 (B)
1964—Colts, 47-27 (B)
1968—Colts, 27-0 (B)
1972—Cardinals, 10-3 (B)
1976—Cardinals, 24-17 (StL)
1978—Colts, 30-17 (StL)
1980—Cardinals, 17-10 (B)
1981—Cardinals, 35-24 (B)
1984—Cardinals, 34-33 (I)
1990—Cardinals, 20-17 (P)
1992—Colts, 16-13 (I)
1996—Colts, 20-13 (I)
2005—Colts, 17-13 (I)
2009—Colts, 31-10 (A)
(RS Pts.—Colts 308, Cardinals 233)
*Franchise known as Phoenix prior to
1994 and in St. Louis prior to 1988
**Franchise in Baltimore prior to 1984
ARIZONA vs. JACKSONVILLE
RS: Jaguars lead series, 2-1
2000—Jaguars, 44-10 (J)
2005—Jaguars, 24-17 (A)
2009—Cardinals, 31-17 (J)
(RS Pts.—Jaguars 85, Cardinals 58)
*ARIZONA vs. KANSAS CITY
RS: Chiefs lead series, 8-2-1
1970—Tie, 6-6 (KC)
1974—Chiefs, 17-13 (StL)
1980—Chiefs, 21-13 (StL)
1983—Chiefs, 38-14 (KC)
1986—Cardinals, 23-14 (StL)
1995—Chiefs, 24-3 (A)
1998—Chiefs, 34-24 (KC)
2001—Cardinals, 24-16 (A)
2002—Chiefs, 49-0 (KC)
2006—Chiefs, 23-20 (A)
2010—Chiefs, 31-13 (KC)
(RS Pts.—Chiefs 273, Cardinals 153)
*Franchise known as Phoenix prior to
1994 and in St. Louis prior to 1988
*ARIZONA vs. MIAMI
RS: Dolphins lead series, 8-2
1972—Dolphins, 31-10 (M)
1977—Dolphins, 55-14 (StL)
1978—Dolphins, 24-10 (M)
1981—Dolphins, 20-7 (StL)
1984—Dolphins, 36-28 (StL)
1990—Dolphins, 23-3 (M)
1996—Dolphins, 38-10 (A)
1999—Dolphins, 19-16 (M)
2004—Cardinals, 24-23 (M)
2008—Cardinals, 31-10 (A)
(RS Pts.—Dolphins 279, Cardinals 153)
*Franchise known as Phoenix prior to
1994 and in St. Louis prior to 1988
*ARIZONA vs. MINNESOTA
RS: Vikings lead series, 12-10
PS: Vikings lead series, 2-0
1963—Cardinals, 56-14 (M)
1967—Cardinals, 34-24 (M)
1969—Vikings, 27-10 (StL)
1972—Cardinals, 19-17 (M)
1974—Vikings, 28-24 (StL)
**Vikings, 30-14 (M)
1977—Cardinals, 27-7 (M)

1979—Cardinals, 37-7 (StL)
1981—Cardinals, 30-17 (StL)
1983—Cardinals, 41-31 (StL)
1991—Vikings, 34-7 (M)
Vikings, 28-0 (P)
1994—Cardinals, 17-7 (A)
1995—Vikings, 30-24 (A) OT
1996—Vikings, 41-17 (M)
1997—Vikings, 20-19 (A)
1998—**Vikings, 41-21 (M)
2000—Vikings, 31-14 (M)
2003—Cardinals, 18-17 (A)
2006—Vikings, 31-26 (M)
2008—Vikings, 35-14 (A)
2009—Cardinals, 30-17 (A)
2010—Vikings, 27-24 (M) OT
2011—Vikings, 34-10 (M)
(RS Pts.—Vikings 524, Cardinals 498)
(PS Pts.—Vikings 71, Cardinals 35)
*Franchise known as Phoenix prior to
1994 and in St. Louis prior to 1988
**NFC Divisional Playoff
*ARIZONA vs. **NEW ENGLAND
RS: Series tied, 6-6
1970—Cardinals, 31-0 (StL)
1975—Cardinals, 24-17 (StL)
1978—Patriots, 16-6 (StL)
1981—Cardinals, 27-20 (NE)
1984—Cardinals, 33-10 (NE)
1990—Cardinals, 34-14 (P)
1991—Cardinals, 24-10 (P)
1993—Patriots, 23-21 (P)
1996—Patriots, 31-0 (NE)
1999—Patriots, 27-3 (A)
2004—Patriots, 23-12 (A)
2008—Patriots, 47-7 (NE)
(RS Pts.—Patriots 238, Cardinals 222)
*Franchise known as Phoenix prior to
1994 and in St. Louis prior to 1988
**Franchise in Boston prior to 1971
*ARIZONA vs. NEW ORLEANS
RS: Cardinals lead series, 14-12
PS: Saints lead series, 1-0
1967—Cardinals, 31-20 (StL)
1968—Cardinals, 21-20 (NO)
Cardinals, 31-17 (StL)
1969—Saints, 51-42 (StL)
1970—Cardinals, 24-17 (StL)
1974—Saints, 14-0 (NO)
1977—Cardinals, 49-31 (StL)
1980—Cardinals, 40-7 (NO)
1981—Cardinals, 30-3 (StL)
1982—Cardinals, 21-7 (NO)
1983—Saints, 28-17 (NO)
1984—Saints, 34-24 (NO)
1985—Cardinals, 28-16 (StL)
1986—Saints, 16-7 (StL)
1987—Cardinals, 24-19 (StL)
1990—Saints, 28-7 (NO)
1991—Saints, 27-3 (P)
1992—Saints, 30-21 (P)
1993—Saints, 20-17 (P)
1996—Cardinals, 28-14 (NO)
1997—Cardinals, 27-10 (NO)
1998—Cardinals, 19-17 (A)
2000—Saints, 21-10 (A)
2004—Cardinals, 34-10 (A)
2007—Saints, 31-24 (NO)
2009—**Saints, 45-14 (NO)
2010—Cardinals, 30-20 (A)
(RS Pts.—Cardinals 592, Saints 545)
(PS Pts.—Saints 45, Cardinals 14)

*Franchise known as Phoenix prior to 1994 and in St. Louis prior to 1988
**NFC Divisional Playoff

*ARIZONA vs. N.Y. GIANTS
RS: Giants lead series, 80-42-2
1926—Giants, 20-0 (NY)
1927—Giants, 28-7 (NY)
1929—Giants, 24-21 (NY)
1930—Giants, 25-12 (NY)
    Giants, 13-7 (C)
1935—Cardinals, 14-13 (NY)
1936—Giants, 14-6 (NY)
1938—Giants, 6-0 (NY)
1939—Giants, 17-7 (NY)
1941—Cardinals, 10-7 (NY)
1942—Giants, 21-7 (NY)
1943—Giants, 24-13 (NY)
1946—Giants, 28-24 (NY)
1947—Giants, 35-31 (NY)
1948—Cardinals, 63-35 (NY)
1949—Giants, 41-38 (C)
1950—Cardinals, 17-3 (C)
    Giants, 51-21 (NY)
1951—Giants, 28-17 (NY)
    Giants, 10-0 (C)
1952—Cardinals, 24-23 (NY)
    Giants, 28-6 (C)
1953—Giants, 21-7 (NY)
    Giants, 23-20 (C)
1954—Giants, 41-10 (C)
    Giants, 31-17 (NY)
1955—Cardinals, 28-17 (C)
    Giants, 10-0 (NY)
1956—Cardinals, 35-27 (C)
    Giants, 23-10 (NY)
1957—Giants, 27-14 (NY)
    Giants, 28-21 (C)
1958—Giants, 37-7 (Buffalo)
    Cardinals, 23-6 (NY)
1959—Giants, 9-3 (NY)
    Giants, 30-20 (Minn)
1960—Giants, 35-14 (StL)
    Cardinals, 20-13 (NY)
1961—Cardinals, 21-10 (NY)
    Giants, 24-9 (StL)
1962—Giants, 31-14 (StL)
    Giants, 31-28 (NY)
1963—Giants, 38-21 (StL)
    Cardinals, 24-17 (NY)
1964—Giants, 34-17 (NY)
    Tie, 10-10 (StL)
1965—Giants, 14-10 (NY)
    Giants, 28-15 (StL)
1966—Cardinals, 24-19 (StL)
    Cardinals, 20-17 (NY)
1967—Giants, 37-20 (StL)
    Giants, 37-14 (NY)
1968—Cardinals, 28-21 (NY)
1969—Cardinals, 42-17 (StL)
    Giants, 49-6 (NY)
1970—Giants, 35-17 (NY)
    Giants, 34-17 (StL)
1971—Giants, 21-20 (StL)
    Cardinals, 24-7 (NY)
1972—Giants, 27-21 (NY)
    Giants, 13-7 (StL)
1973—Cardinals, 35-27 (StL)
    Giants, 24-13 (New Haven)
1974—Cardinals, 23-21 (New Haven)
    Cardinals, 26-14 (StL)
1975—Cardinals, 26-14 (StL)
    Cardinals, 20-13 (NY)

1976—Cardinals, 27-21 (StL)
    Cardinals, 17-14 (NY)
1977—Cardinals, 28-0 (StL)
    Giants, 27-7 (NY)
1978—Cardinals, 20-10 (StL)
    Giants, 17-0 (NY)
1979—Cardinals, 27-14 (NY)
    Cardinals, 29-20 (StL)
1980—Giants, 41-35 (StL)
    Cardinals, 23-7 (NY)
1981—Giants, 34-14 (NY)
    Giants, 20-10 (StL)
1982—Cardinals, 24-21 (StL)
1983—Tie, 20-20 (StL) OT
    Cardinals, 10-6 (NY)
1984—Giants, 16-10 (NY)
    Cardinals, 31-21 (StL)
1985—Giants, 27-17 (NY)
    Giants, 34-3 (StL)
1986—Giants, 13-6 (StL)
    Giants, 27-7 (NY)
1987—Giants, 30-7 (NY)
    Cardinals, 27-24 (StL)
1988—Cardinals, 24-17 (P)
    Giants, 44-7 (NY)
1989—Giants, 35-7 (NY)
    Giants, 20-13 (P)
1990—Giants, 20-19 (NY)
    Giants, 24-21 (P)
1991—Giants, 20-9 (NY)
    Giants, 21-14 (P)
1992—Giants, 31-21 (NY)
    Cardinals, 19-0 (P)
1993—Giants, 19-17 (NY)
    Cardinals, 17-6 (P)
1994—Giants, 20-17 (A)
    Cardinals, 10-9 (NY)
1995—Giants, 27-21 (NY) OT
    Giants, 10-6 (A)
1996—Giants, 16-8 (NY)
    Cardinals, 31-23 (A)
1997—Giants, 27-13 (A)
    Giants, 19-10 (NY)
1998—Giants, 34-7 (NY)
    Giants, 23-19 (A)
1999—Cardinals, 14-3 (A)
    Cardinals, 34-24 (NY)
2000—Giants, 21-16 (NY)
    Giants, 31-7 (A)
2001—Giants, 17-10 (A)
    Giants, 17-13 (NY)
2002—Cardinals, 21-7 (A)
2004—Cardinals, 17-14 (A)
2005—Giants, 42-19 (NY)
2008—Giants, 37-29 (A)
2009—Cardinals, 24-17 (NY)
2011—Giants, 31-27 (A)
(RS Pts.—Giants 2,746, Cardinals 2,126)
*Franchise known as Phoenix prior to 1994, in St. Louis prior to 1988, and in Chicago prior to 1960

*ARIZONA vs. N.Y. JETS
RS: Jets lead series, 5-2
1971—Cardinals, 17-10 (StL)
1975—Cardinals, 37-6 (NY)
1978—Jets, 23-10 (NY)
1996—Jets, 31-21 (A)
1999—Jets, 12-7 (NY)
2004—Jets, 13-3 (A)
2008—Jets, 56-35 (NY)
(RS Pts.—Jets 151, Cardinals 130)
*Franchise known as Phoenix prior to

1994 and in St. Louis prior to 1988
*ARIZONA vs. **OAKLAND
RS: Raiders lead series, 5-3
1973—Raiders, 17-10 (StL)
1983—Cardinals, 34-24 (LA)
1989—Raiders, 16-14 (LA)
1998—Raiders, 23-20 (A)
2001—Cardinals, 34-31 (O) OT
2002—Raiders, 41-20 (A)
2006—Raiders, 22-9 (O)
2010—Cardinals, 24-23 (A)
(RS Pts.— Raiders 197, Cardinals 165)
*Franchise known as Phoenix prior to 1994 and in St. Louis prior to 1988
**Franchise in Los Angeles from 1982-1994

*ARIZONA vs. PHILADELPHIA
RS: Cardinals lead series, 54-53-5
PS: Cardinals lead series, 2-1
1935—Cardinals, 12-3 (C)
1936—Cardinals, 13-0 (C)
1937—Tie, 6-6 (P)
1938—Eagles, 7-0 (Erie, Pa.)
1941—Eagles, 21-14 (P)
1945—Eagles, 21-6 (P)
1947—Cardinals, 45-21 (P)
    **Cardinals, 28-21 (C)
1948—Cardinals, 21-14 (C)
    **Eagles, 7-0 (C)
1949—Eagles, 28-3 (P)
1950—Eagles, 45-7 (C)
    Cardinals, 14-10 (P)
1951—Eagles, 17-14 (C)
1952—Eagles, 10-7 (P)
    Cardinals, 28-22 (C)
1953—Eagles, 56-17 (C)
    Eagles, 38-0 (P)
1954—Eagles, 35-16 (C)
    Eagles, 30-14 (P)
1955—Tie, 24-24 (C)
    Eagles, 27-3 (P)
1956—Cardinals, 20-6 (P)
    Cardinals, 28-17 (C)
1957—Eagles, 38-21 (C)
    Cardinals, 31-27 (P)
1958—Tie, 21-21 (C)
    Eagles, 49-21 (P)
1959—Eagles, 28-24 (Minn)
    Eagles, 27-17 (P)
1960—Eagles, 31-27 (P)
    Eagles, 20-6 (StL)
1961—Cardinals, 30-27 (P)
    Eagles, 20-7 (StL)
1962—Cardinals, 27-21 (P)
    Cardinals, 45-35 (StL)
1963—Cardinals, 28-24 (P)
    Cardinals, 38-14 (StL)
1964—Cardinals, 38-13 (P)
    Cardinals, 36-34 (StL)
1965—Eagles, 34-27 (P)
    Eagles, 28-24 (StL)
1966—Cardinals, 16-13 (StL)
    Cardinals, 41-10 (P)
1967—Cardinals, 48-14 (StL)
1968—Cardinals, 45-17 (P)
1969—Eagles, 34-30 (StL)
1970—Cardinals, 35-20 (P)
    Cardinals, 23-14 (StL)
1971—Eagles, 37-20 (StL)
    Eagles, 19-7 (P)
1972—Tie, 6-6 (P)
    Cardinals, 24-23 (StL)

1973—Cardinals, 34-23 (P)
    Eagles, 27-24 (StL)
1974—Cardinals, 7-3 (StL)
    Cardinals, 13-3 (P)
1975—Cardinals, 31-20 (StL)
    Cardinals, 24-23 (P)
1976—Cardinals, 33-14 (StL)
    Cardinals, 17-14 (P)
1977—Cardinals, 21-17 (P)
    Cardinals, 21-16 (StL)
1978—Cardinals, 16-10 (P)
    Eagles, 14-10 (StL)
1979—Eagles, 24-20 (StL)
    Eagles, 16-13 (P)
1980—Cardinals, 24-14 (StL)
    Eagles, 17-3 (P)
1981—Eagles, 52-10 (StL)
    Eagles, 38-0 (P)
1982—Cardinals, 23-20 (P)
1983—Cardinals, 14-11 (P)
    Cardinals, 31-7 (StL)
1984—Cardinals, 34-14 (P)
    Cardinals, 17-16 (StL)
1985—Eagles, 30-7 (P)
    Eagles, 24-14 (StL)
1986—Cardinals, 13-10 (StL)
    Tie, 10-10 (P) OT
1987—Eagles, 28-23 (StL)
    Cardinals, 31-19 (P)
1988—Eagles, 31-21 (P)
    Eagles, 23-17 (Phx)
1989—Eagles, 17-5 (Phx)
    Eagles, 31-14 (P)
1990—Cardinals, 23-21 (P)
    Eagles, 23-21 (Phx)
1991—Cardinals, 26-10 (P)
    Eagles, 34-14 (Phx)
1992—Eagles, 31-14 (Phx)
    Eagles, 7-3 (P)
1993—Eagles, 23-17 (P)
    Cardinals, 16-3 (Phx)
1994—Eagles, 17-7 (P)
    Cardinals, 12-6 (A)
1995—Eagles, 31-19 (A)
    Eagles, 21-20 (P)
1996—Cardinals, 36-30 (A)
    Eagles, 29-19 (P)
1997—Eagles, 13-10 (P) OT
    Cardinals, 31-21 (A)
1998—Eagles, 17-3 (A)
    Cardinals, 20-17 (P) OT
1999—Cardinals, 25-24 (P)
    Cardinals, 21-17 (A)
2000—Eagles, 33-14 (A)
    Eagles, 34-9 (P)
2001—Cardinals, 21-20 (P)
    Eagles, 21-7 (A)
2002—Eagles, 38-14 (P)
2005—Cardinals, 27-21 (A)
2008—Eagles, 48-20 (P)
    ***Cardinals, 32-25 (A)
2011—Cardinals, 21-17 (P)
(RS Pts.—Eagles 2,405, Cardinals 2,174)
(PS Pts.—Cardinals 60, Eagles 53)
*Franchise known as Phoenix prior to
1994, in St. Louis prior to 1988,
and in Chicago prior to 1960
**NFL Championship
***NFC Championship
*ARIZONA vs. **PITTSBURGH
RS: Steelers lead series, 32-23-3
PS: Steelers lead series, 1-0

1933—Pirates, 14-13 (P)
1935—Pirates, 17-13 (P)
1936—Cardinals, 14-6 (C)
1937—Cardinals, 13-7 (P)
1939—Cardinals, 10-0 (P)
1940—Tie, 7-7 (P)
1942—Steelers, 19-3 (P)
1945—Steelers, 23-0 (P)
1946—Steelers, 14-7 (P)
1948—Cardinals, 24-7 (P)
1950—Steelers, 28-17 (C)
    Steelers, 28-7 (P)
1951—Steelers, 28-14 (C)
    Steelers, 17-14 (P)
1952—Steelers, 34-28 (P)
    Steelers, 17-14 (P)
1953—Steelers, 31-28 (P)
    Steelers, 21-17 (C)
1954—Cardinals, 17-14 (C)
    Steelers, 20-17 (P)
1955—Steelers, 14-7 (P)
    Cardinals, 27-13 (C)
1956—Steelers, 14-7 (P)
    Cardinals, 38-27 (C)
1957—Steelers, 29-20 (P)
    Steelers, 27-2 (C)
1958—Steelers, 27-20 (C)
    Steelers, 38-21 (P)
1959—Cardinals, 45-24 (C)
    Steelers, 35-20 (P)
1960—Steelers, 27-14 (P)
    Cardinals, 38-7 (StL)
1961—Steelers, 30-27 (P)
    Cardinals, 20-0 (StL)
1962—Steelers, 26-17 (StL)
    Steelers, 19-7 (P)
1963—Steelers, 23-10 (P)
    Cardinals, 24-23 (StL)
1964—Cardinals, 34-30 (StL)
    Cardinals, 21-20 (P)
1965—Cardinals, 20-7 (P)
    Cardinals, 21-17 (StL)
1966—Steelers, 30-9 (P)
    Cardinals, 6-3 (StL)
1967—Cardinals, 28-14 (P)
    Tie, 14-14 (StL)
1968—Tie, 28-28 (StL)
    Cardinals, 20-10 (P)
1969—Cardinals, 27-14 (P)
    Cardinals, 47-10 (StL)
1972—Steelers, 25-19 (StL)
1979—Steelers, 24-21 (StL)
1985—Steelers, 23-10 (P)
1988—Cardinals, 31-14 (Phx)
1994—Cardinals, 20-17 (A) OT
1997—Steelers, 26-20 (A) OT
2003—Steelers, 28-15 (P)
2007—Cardinals, 21-14 (A)
2008—***Steelers, 27-23 (Tampa Bay)
2011—Steelers, 32-20 (A)
(RS Pts.—Steelers 1,138, Cardinals 1,079)
(PS Pts.—Steelers 27, Cardinals 23)
*Franchise known as Phoenix prior to
1994, in St. Louis prior to 1988,
and in Chicago prior to 1960
**Steelers known as Pirates prior to 1940
***Super Bowl XLIII
*ARIZONA vs. **ST. LOUIS
RS: Cardinals lead series, 33-31-2
PS: Rams lead series, 1-0
1937—Cardinals, 6-0 (Cle)
    Cardinals, 13-7 (Chi)
1938—Cardinals, 7-6 (Cle)

    Cardinals, 31-17 (Chi)
1939—Rams, 24-0 (Chi)
    Rams, 14-0 (Cle)
1940—Rams, 26-14 (Cle)
    Cardinals, 17-7 (Chi)
1941—Rams, 10-6 (Cle)
    Cardinals, 7-0 (Chi)
1942—Cardinals, 7-0 (Buffalo)
    Rams, 7-3 (Cle)
1945—Rams, 21-0 (Cle)
    Rams, 35-21 (Chi)
1946—Cardinals, 34-10 (Chi)
    Rams, 17-14 (LA)
1947—Rams, 27-7 (LA)
    Cardinals, 17-10 (Chi)
1948—Cardinals, 27-22 (LA)
    Cardinals, 27-24 (Chi)
1949—Tie, 28-28 (Chi)
    Cardinals, 31-27 (LA)
1951—Rams, 45-21 (LA)
1953—Tie, 24-24 (Chi)
1954—Rams, 28-17 (LA)
1958—Rams, 20-14 (Chi)
1960—Cardinals, 43-21 (LA)
1965—Rams, 27-3 (StL)
1968—Rams, 24-13 (StL)
1970—Rams, 34-13 (LA)
1972—Cardinals, 24-14 (StL)
1975—***Rams, 35-23 (LA)
1976—Cardinals, 30-28 (LA)
1979—Rams, 21-0 (LA)
1980—Cardinals, 21-13 (StL)
1984—Rams, 16-13 (StL)
1985—Rams, 46-14 (LA)
1986—Rams, 16-10 (StL)
1987—Rams, 27-24 (StL)
1988—Cardinals, 41-27 (LA)
1989—Rams, 37-14 (LA)
1991—Cardinals, 24-14 (LA)
1992—Cardinals, 20-14 (LA)
1993—Cardinals, 38-10 (P)
1994—Rams, 14-12 (LA)
1996—Cardinals, 31-28 (A) OT
1998—Cardinals, 20-17 (StL)
2002—Rams, 27-14 (A)
    Rams, 30-28 (StL)
2003—Rams, 37-13 (StL)
    Rams, 30-27 (A) OT
2004—Rams, 17-10 (StL)
    Cardinals, 31-7 (A)
2005—Rams, 17-12 (A)
    Cardinals, 38-28 (StL)
2006—Rams, 16-14 (A)
    Cardinals, 34-20 (StL)
2007—Cardinals, 34-31 (StL)
    Cardinals, 48-19 (A)
2008—Cardinals, 34-13 (StL)
    Cardinals, 34-10 (A)
2009—Cardinals, 21-13 (StL)
    Cardinals, 31-10 (A)
2010—Cardinals, 17-13 (StL)
    Rams, 19-6 (A)
2011—Cardinals, 19-13 (A) OT
    Cardinals, 23-20 (StL)
(RS Pts.—Rams 1,302, Cardinals 1,281)
(PS Pts.—Rams 35, Cardinals 23)
*Franchise known as Phoenix prior to
1994, in St. Louis prior to 1988,
and in Chicago prior to 1960
**Franchise in Los Angeles prior to 1995
and in Cleveland prior to 1946
***NFC Divisional Playoff

*ARIZONA vs. SAN DIEGO
RS: Chargers lead series, 9-3
1971—Chargers, 20-17 (SD)
1976—Chargers, 43-24 (SD)
1983—Cardinals, 44-14 (StL)
1987—Chargers, 28-24 (SD)
1989—Chargers, 24-13 (P)
1992—Chargers, 27-21 (P)
1995—Chargers, 28-25 (SD)
1998—Cardinals, 16-13 (A)
2001—Cardinals, 20-17 (SD)
2002—Chargers, 23-15 (A)
2006—Chargers, 27-20 (SD)
2010—Chargers, 41-10 (SD)
(RS Pts.—Chargers 305, Cardinals 249)
Franchise known as Phoenix prior to 1994, in St. Louis prior to 1988,
*ARIZONA vs. SAN FRANCISCO
RS: 49ers lead series, 24-17
1951—Cardinals, 27-21 (SF)
1957—Cardinals, 20-10 (SF)
1962—49ers, 24-17 (StL)
1964—Cardinals, 23-13 (SF)
1968—49ers, 35-17 (SF)
1971—49ers, 26-14 (StL)
1974—Cardinals, 34-9 (SF)
1976—Cardinals, 23-20 (StL) OT
1978—Cardinals, 16-10 (SF)
1979—Cardinals, 13-10 (StL)
1980—49ers, 24-21 (SF) OT
1982—49ers, 31-20 (StL)
1983—49ers, 42-27 (SF)
1986—49ers, 43-17 (SF)
1987—49ers, 34-28 (SF)
1988—49ers, 24-23 (P)
1991—49ers, 14-10 (SF)
1992—Cardinals, 24-14 (P)
1993—49ers, 28-14 (SF)
1999—49ers, 24-10 (A)
2000—49ers, 27-20 (SF)
2002—49ers, 38-28 (SF)
    49ers, 17-14 (A)
2003—Cardinals, 16-13 (A) OT
    49ers, 50-14 (SF)
2004—49ers, 31-28 (SF) OT
    49ers, 31-28 (A) OT
2005—Cardinals, 31-14 (Mex. City)
    Cardinals, 17-10 (SF)
2006—Cardinals, 34-27 (A)
    Cardinals, 26-20 (SF)
2007—49ers, 20-17 (SF)
    49ers, 37-31 (A) OT
2008—Cardinals, 23-13 (SF)
    Cardinals, 29-24 (A)
2009—49ers, 20-16 (A)
    49ers, 24-9 (SF)
2010—49ers, 27-6 (A)
    49ers, 38-7 (SF)
2011—49ers, 23-7 (SF)
    Cardinals, 21-19 (A)
(RS Pts.—49ers 978, Cardinals 821)
Franchise known as Phoenix prior to 1994, in St. Louis prior to 1988, and in Chicago prior to 1960
*ARIZONA vs. SEATTLE
RS: Cardinals lead series, 14-12
1976—Cardinals, 30-24 (S)
1983—Cardinals, 33-28 (StL)
1989—Cardinals, 34-24 (S)
1993—Cardinals, 30-27 (S) OT
1995—Cardinals, 20-14 (A) OT
1998—Seahawks, 33-14 (S)

2002—Cardinals, 24-13 (S)
    Seahawks, 27-6 (A)
2003—Seahawks, 38-0 (A)
    Seahawks, 28-10 (S)
2004—Cardinals, 25-17 (A)
    Seahawks, 24-21 (S)
2005—Seahawks, 37-12 (S)
    Seahawks, 33-19 (A)
2006—Seahawks, 21-10 (S)
    Cardinals, 27-21 (A)
2007—Cardinals, 23-20 (A)
    Seahawks, 42-21 (S)
2008—Cardinals, 26-20 (S)
    Cardinals, 34-21 (A)
2009—Cardinals, 27-3 (S)
    Cardinals, 31-20 (A)
2010—Seahawks, 22-10 (S)
    Seahawks, 36-18 (A)
2011—Seahawks, 13-10 (S)
    Cardinals, 23-20 (A) OT
(RS Pts.—Seahawks 626, Cardinals 538)
Franchise known as Phoenix prior to 1994 and in St. Louis prior to 1988
*ARIZONA vs. TAMPA BAY
RS: Buccaneers lead series, 9-8
1977—Buccaneers, 17-7 (TB)
1981—Buccaneers, 20-10 (TB)
1983—Cardinals, 34-27 (TB)
1985—Buccaneers, 16-0 (TB)
1986—Cardinals, 30-19 (TB)
    Cardinals, 21-17 (StL)
1987—Cardinals, 31-28 (StL)
    Cardinals, 31-14 (TB)
1988—Cardinals, 30-24 (TB)
1989—Buccaneers, 14-13 (P)
1992—Buccaneers, 23-7 (TB)
    Buccaneers, 7-3 (P)
1996—Cardinals, 13-9 (A)
1997—Buccaneers, 19-18 (TB)
2004—Cardinals, 12-7 (A)
2007—Buccaneers, 17-10 (TB)
2010—Buccaneers, 38-35 (A)
(RS Pts.—Buccaneers 316, Cardinals 305)
Franchise known as Phoenix prior to 1994 and in St. Louis prior to 1988
*ARIZONA vs. **TENNESSEE
RS: Cardinals lead series, 5-4
1970—Cardinals, 44-0 (StL)
1974—Cardinals, 31-27 (H)
1979—Cardinals, 24-17 (H)
1985—Oilers, 20-10 (StL)
1988—Oilers, 38-20 (H)
1994—Cardinals, 30-12 (H)
1997—Oilers, 41-14 (A)
2005—Cardinals, 20-10 (A)
2009—Titans, 20-17 (T)
(RS Pts.—Cardinals 210, Titans 185)
Franchise known as Phoenix prior to 1994 and in St. Louis prior to 1988
**Franchise in Houston prior to 1997; known as Oilers prior to 1999
*ARIZONA vs. **WASHINGTON
RS: Redskins lead series, 74-44-2
1932—Cardinals, 9-0 (B)
    Braves, 8-6 (C)
1933—Redskins, 10-0 (C)
    Tie, 0-0 (B)
1934—Redskins, 9-0 (B)
1935—Cardinals, 6-0 (B)
1936—Redskins, 13-10 (B)
1937—Cardinals, 21-14 (W)
1939—Redskins, 28-7 (W)

1940—Redskins, 28-21 (W)
1942—Redskins, 28-0 (W)
1943—Redskins, 13-7 (W)
1945—Redskins, 24-21 (W)
1947—Redskins, 45-21 (W)
1949—Cardinals, 38-7 (C)
1950—Cardinals, 38-28 (W)
1951—Redskins, 7-3 (C)
    Redskins, 20-17 (W)
1952—Redskins, 23-7 (C)
    Cardinals, 17-6 (W)
1953—Redskins, 24-13 (C)
    Redskins, 28-17 (W)
1954—Cardinals, 38-16 (C)
    Redskins, 37-20 (W)
1955—Cardinals, 24-10 (W)
    Redskins, 31-0 (C)
1956—Cardinals, 31-3 (W)
    Redskins, 17-14 (C)
1957—Redskins, 37-14 (C)
    Cardinals, 44-14 (W)
1958—Cardinals, 37-10 (C)
    Redskins, 45-31 (W)
1959—Cardinals, 49-21 (C)
    Redskins, 23-14 (W)
1960—Cardinals, 44-7 (StL)
    Cardinals, 26-14 (W)
1961—Cardinals, 24-0 (W)
    Cardinals, 38-24 (StL)
1962—Redskins, 24-14 (W)
    Tie, 17-17 (StL)
1963—Cardinals, 21-7 (W)
    Cardinals, 24-20 (StL)
1964—Cardinals, 23-17 (W)
    Cardinals, 38-24 (StL)
1965—Cardinals, 37-16 (W)
    Redskins, 24-20 (StL)
1966—Cardinals, 23-7 (StL)
    Redskins, 26-20 (W)
1967—Cardinals, 27-21 (W)
1968—Cardinals, 41-14 (StL)
1969—Redskins, 33-17 (W)
1970—Cardinals, 27-17 (StL)
    Redskins, 28-27 (W)
1971—Redskins, 24-17 (StL)
    Redskins, 20-0 (W)
1972—Redskins, 24-10 (W)
    Redskins, 33-3 (StL)
1973—Cardinals, 34-27 (StL)
    Redskins, 31-13 (W)
1974—Cardinals, 17-10 (W)
    Cardinals, 23-20 (StL)
1975—Redskins, 27-17 (W)
    Cardinals, 20-17 (StL) OT
1976—Redskins, 20-10 (W)
    Redskins, 16-10 (StL)
1977—Redskins, 24-14 (W)
    Redskins, 26-20 (StL)
1978—Redskins, 28-10 (StL)
    Cardinals, 27-17 (W)
1979—Redskins, 17-7 (StL)
    Redskins, 30-28 (W)
1980—Cardinals, 23-0 (W)
    Redskins, 31-7 (StL)
1981—Cardinals, 40-30 (StL)
    Redskins, 42-21 (W)
1982—Redskins, 12-7 (StL)
    Redskins, 28-0 (W)
1983—Redskins, 38-14 (StL)
    Redskins, 45-7 (W)
1984—Cardinals, 26-24 (StL)
    Redskins, 29-27 (W)

1985—Redskins, 27-10 (W)
    Redskins, 27-16 (StL)
1986—Redskins, 28-21 (W)
    Redskins, 20-17 (StL)
1987—Redskins, 28-21 (W)
    Redskins, 34-17 (StL)
1988—Cardinals, 30-21 (P)
    Redskins, 33-17 (W)
1989—Redskins, 30-28 (W)
    Redskins, 29-10 (P)
1990—Redskins, 31-0 (W)
    Redskins, 38-10 (P)
1991—Redskins, 34-0 (W)
    Redskins, 20-14 (P)
1992—Cardinals, 27-24 (P)
    Redskins, 41-3 (W)
1993—Cardinals, 17-10 (W)
    Cardinals, 36-6 (P)
1994—Cardinals, 19-16 (W) OT
    Cardinals, 17-15 (A)
1995—Redskins, 27-7 (W)
    Cardinals, 24-20 (A)
1996—Cardinals, 37-34 (W) OT
    Cardinals, 27-26 (A)
1997—Redskins, 19-13 (W) OT
    Redskins, 38-28 (A)
1998—Cardinals, 29-27 (A)
    Cardinals, 45-42 (W)
1999—Redskins, 24-10 (A)
    Redskins, 28-3 (W)
2000—Cardinals, 16-15 (A)
    Redskins, 20-3 (W)
2001—Redskins, 20-10 (A)
    Redskins, 20-17 (W)
2002—Redskins, 31-23 (W)
2005—Redskins, 17-13 (A)
2007—Redskins, 21-19 (W)
2008—Redskins, 24-17 (W)
2011—Redskins, 22-21 (W)
(RS Pts.—Redskins 2,667, Cardinals 2,224)
*Franchise known as Phoenix prior to
1994, in St. Louis prior to 1988,
and in Chicago prior to 1960
**Franchise in Boston prior to 1937 and
known as Braves prior to 1933

ATLANTA vs. ARIZONA
RS: Cardinals lead series, 14-11
PS: Cardinals lead series, 1-0;
See Arizona vs. Atlanta
ATLANTA vs. BALTIMORE
RS: Series tied, 2-2
1999—Ravens, 19-13 (A) OT
2002—Falcons, 20-17 (A)
2006—Ravens, 24-10 (B)
2010—Falcons, 26-21 (A)
(RS Pts.—Ravens 81, Falcons 69)
ATLANTA vs. BUFFALO
RS: Falcons lead series, 6-4
1973—Bills, 17-6 (A)
1977—Bills, 3-0 (B)
1980—Falcons, 30-14 (B)
1983—Falcons, 31-14 (A)
1989—Falcons, 30-28 (A)
1992—Bills, 41-14 (B)
1995—Bills, 23-17 (B)
2001—Falcons, 33-30 (A)
2005—Falcons, 24-16 (B)
2009—Falcons, 31-3 (A)
(RS Pts.—Falcons 216, Bills 189)
ATLANTA vs. CAROLINA
RS: Falcons lead series, 22-12

1995—Falcons, 23-20 (A) OT
    Panthers, 21-17 (C)
1996—Panthers, 29-6 (C)
    Falcons, 20-17 (A)
1997—Panthers, 9-6 (A)
    Panthers, 21-12 (C)
1998—Falcons, 19-14 (C)
    Falcons, 51-23 (A)
1999—Falcons, 27-20 (A)
    Panthers, 34-28 (C)
2000—Falcons, 15-10 (C)
    Falcons, 13-12 (A)
2001—Falcons, 24-16 (A)
    Falcons, 10-7 (C)
2002—Falcons, 30-0 (A)
    Falcons, 41-0 (C)
2003—Panthers, 23-3 (C)
    Falcons, 20-14 (A) OT
2004—Falcons, 27-10 (C)
    Falcons, 34-31 (A) OT
2005—Panthers, 24-6 (C)
    Panthers, 44-11 (A)
2006—Falcons, 20-6 (C)
    Panthers, 10-3 (A)
2007—Panthers, 27-20 (A)
    Falcons, 20-13 (C)
2008—Falcons, 24-9 (C)
    Falcons, 45-28 (A)
2009—Falcons, 28-20 (A)
    Panthers, 28-19 (C)
2010—Falcons, 31-10 (C)
    Falcons, 31-10 (A)
2011—Falcons, 31-17 (A)
    Falcons, 31-23 (C)
(RS Pts.—Falcons 731, Panthers 615)
ATLANTA vs. CHICAGO
RS: Bears lead series, 13-12
1966—Bears, 23-6 (C)
1967—Bears, 23-14 (A)
1968—Falcons, 16-13 (C)
1969—Falcons, 48-31 (A)
1970—Bears, 23-14 (A)
1972—Falcons, 37-21 (C)
1973—Falcons, 46-6 (A)
1974—Falcons, 13-10 (A)
1976—Falcons, 10-0 (C)
1977—Falcons, 16-10 (C)
1978—Bears, 13-7 (C)
1980—Falcons, 28-17 (A)
1983—Falcons, 20-17 (C)
1985—Bears, 36-0 (C)
1986—Falcons, 13-10 (A)
1990—Bears, 30-24 (A)
1992—Falcons, 41-31 (A)
1993—Falcons, 6-0 (C)
1998—Falcons, 20-13 (A)
2001—Bears, 31-3 (A)
2002—Falcons, 14-13 (A)
2005—Bears, 16-3 (C)
2008—Falcons, 22-20 (A)
2009—Falcons, 21-14 (A)
2011—Bears, 30-12 (C)
(RS Pts.—Bears 471, Falcons 434)
ATLANTA vs. CINCINNATI
RS: Bengals lead series, 7-5
1971—Falcons, 9-6 (C)
1975—Bengals, 21-14 (A)
1978—Bengals, 37-7 (C)
1981—Bengals, 30-28 (A)
1984—Bengals, 35-14 (C)
1987—Bengals, 16-10 (A)
1990—Falcons, 38-17 (A)

1993—Bengals, 21-17 (C)
1996—Bengals, 41-31 (C)
2002—Falcons, 30-3 (A)
2006—Falcons, 29-27 (C)
2010—Falcons, 39-32 (A)
(RS Pts.—Bengals 286, Falcons 266)
ATLANTA vs. CLEVELAND
RS: Browns lead series, 10-3
1966—Browns, 49-17 (A)
1968—Browns, 30-7 (C)
1971—Falcons, 31-14 (C)
1976—Browns, 20-17 (A)
1978—Falcons, 24-16 (A)
1981—Browns, 28-17 (C)
1984—Browns, 23-7 (A)
1987—Browns, 38-3 (C)
1990—Browns, 13-10 (C)
1993—Falcons, 17-14 (A)
2002—Browns, 24-16 (C)
2006—Browns, 17-13 (A)
2010—Falcons, 20-10 (C)
(RS Pts.—Browns 304, Falcons 191)
ATLANTA vs. DALLAS
RS: Cowboys lead series, 14-8
PS: Cowboys lead series, 2-0
1966—Cowboys, 47-14 (A)
1967—Cowboys, 37-7 (D)
1969—Cowboys, 24-17 (A)
1970—Cowboys, 13-0 (D)
1974—Cowboys, 24-0 (A)
1976—Falcons, 17-10 (A)
1978—*Cowboys, 27-20 (D)
1980—*Cowboys, 30-27 (A)
1985—Cowboys, 24-10 (D)
1986—Falcons, 37-35 (D)
1987—Falcons, 21-10 (D)
1988—Cowboys, 26-20 (D)
1989—Falcons 27-21 (A)
1990—Falcons, 26-7 (A)
1991—Cowboys, 31-27 (D)
1992—Cowboys, 41-17 (A)
1993—Falcons, 27-14 (A)
1995—Cowboys, 28-13 (A)
1996—Cowboys, 32-28 (D)
1999—Cowboys, 24-7 (D)
2001—Falcons, 20-13 (A)
2003—Falcons, 27-13 (D)
2006—Cowboys, 38-28 (A)
2009—Cowboys, 37-21 (D)
(RS Pts.—Cowboys 549, Falcons 411)
(PS Pts.—Cowboys 57, Falcons 47)
*NFC Divisional Playoff
ATLANTA vs. DENVER
RS: Broncos lead series, 8-4
PS: Broncos lead series, 1-0
1970—Broncos, 24-10 (D)
1972—Falcons, 23-20 (A)
1975—Falcons, 35-21 (A)
1979—Broncos, 20-17 (A) OT
1982—Falcons, 34-27 (D)
1985—Broncos, 44-28 (A)
1988—Broncos, 30-14 (D)
1994—Broncos, 32-28 (D)
1997—Broncos, 29-21 (A)
1998—*Broncos, 34-19 (South Florida)
2000—Broncos, 42-14 (D)
2004—Falcons, 41-28 (D)
2008—Broncos, 24-20 (A)
(RS Pts.—Broncos 341, Falcons 285)
(PS Pts.—Broncos 34, Falcons 19)
*Super Bowl XXXIII

ATLANTA vs. DETROIT
RS: Lions lead series, 23-11
1966—Lions, 28-10 (D)
1967—Lions, 24-3 (D)
1968—Lions, 24-7 (A)
1969—Lions, 27-21 (D)
1971—Lions, 41-38 (D)
1972—Lions, 26-23 (A)
1973—Lions, 31-6 (D)
1975—Lions, 17-14 (A)
1976—Lions, 24-10 (D)
1977—Falcons, 17-6 (A)
1978—Falcons, 14-0 (A)
1979—Lions, 24-23 (D)
1980—Falcons, 43-28 (A)
1983—Falcons, 30-14 (D)
1984—Lions, 27-24 (A) OT
1985—Lions, 28-27 (A)
1986—Falcons, 20-6 (D)
1987—Lions, 30-13 (A)
1988—Lions, 31-17 (D)
1989—Lions, 31-24 (A)
1990—Lions, 21-14 (D)
1993—Lions, 30-13 (D)
1994—Lions, 31-28 (D) OT
1995—Falcons, 34-22 (A)
1996—Lions, 28-24 (D)
1997—Lions, 28-17 (D)
1998—Falcons, 24-17 (D)
2000—Lions, 13-10 (D)
2002—Falcons, 36-15 (A)
2004—Lions, 17-10 (A)
2005—Falcons, 27-7 (D)
2006—Lions, 30-14 (D)
2008—Falcons, 34-21 (A)
2011—Lions, 23-16 (D)
(RS Pts.—Lions 763, Falcons 692)
ATLANTA vs. GREEN BAY
RS: Packers lead series, 13-12
PS: Packers lead series, 2-1
1966—Packers, 56-3 (Mil)
1967—Packers, 23-0 (Mil)
1968—Packers, 38-7 (A)
1969—Packers, 28-10 (GB)
1970—Packers, 27-24 (GB)
1971—Falcons, 28-21 (A)
1972—Falcons, 10-9 (Mil)
1974—Falcons, 10-3 (A)
1975—Packers, 22-13 (GB)
1976—Packers, 24-20 (A)
1979—Packers, 25-7 (A)
1981—Falcons, 31-17 (GB)
1982—Packers, 38-7 (A)
1983—Falcons, 47-41 (A) OT
1988—Falcons, 20-0 (A)
1989—Packers, 23-21 (Mil)
1991—Falcons, 35-31 (A)
1992—Falcons, 24-10 (A)
1994—Packers, 21-17 (Mil)
1995—*Packers, 37-20 (GB)
2001—Falcons, 23-20 (GB)
2002—Packers, 37-34 (GB) OT
          *Falcons, 27-7 (GB)
2005—Packers, 33-25 (A)
2008—Falcons, 27-24 (GB)
2010—Falcons, 20-17 (A)
          **Packers, 48-21 (A)
2011—Packers, 25-14 (A)
(RS Pts.—Packers 595, Falcons 495)
(PS Pts.—Packers 92, Falcons 68)
*NFC First-Round Playoff
**NFC Divisional Playoff

ATLANTA vs. HOUSTON
RS: Texans lead series, 2-1
2003—Texans, 17-13 (H)
2007—Falcons, 26-16 (A)
2011—Texans, 17-10 (H)
(RS Pts.—Texans 50, Falcons 49)
ATLANTA vs. *INDIANAPOLIS
RS: Colts lead series, 13-2
1966—Colts, 19-7 (A)
1967—Colts, 38-31 (B)
          Colts, 49-7 (A)
1968—Colts, 28-20 (A)
          Colts, 44-0 (B)
1969—Colts, 21-14 (A)
          Colts, 13-6 (B)
1974—Colts, 17-7 (A)
1986—Colts, 28-23 (A)
1989—Colts, 13-9 (I)
1998—Falcons, 28-21 (A)
2001—Colts, 41-27 (I)
2003—Colts, 38-7 (I)
2007—Colts, 31-13 (A)
2011—Falcons, 31-7 (I)
(RS Pts.—Colts 408, Falcons 230)
*Franchise in Baltimore prior to 1984
ATLANTA vs. JACKSONVILLE
RS: Jaguars lead series, 3-2
1996—Jaguars, 19-17 (J)
1999—Jaguars, 30-7 (A)
2003—Falcons, 21-14 (A)
2007—Jaguars, 13-7 (J)
2011—Falcons, 41-14 (A)
(RS Pts.—Falcons 93, Jaguars 90)
ATLANTA vs. KANSAS CITY
RS: Chiefs lead series, 5-2
1972—Chiefs, 17-14 (A)
1985—Chiefs, 38-10 (KC)
1991—Chiefs, 14-3 (KC)
1994—Chiefs, 30-10 (A)
2000—Falcons, 29-13 (A)
2004—Chiefs, 56-10 (KC)
2008—Falcons, 38-14 (A)
(RS Pts.—Chiefs 182, Falcons 114)
ATLANTA vs. MIAMI
RS: Dolphins lead series, 7-4
1970—Dolphins, 20-7 (A)
1974—Dolphins, 42-7 (M)
1980—Dolphins, 20-17 (A)
1983—Dolphins, 31-24 (M)
1986—Falcons, 20-14 (M)
1992—Dolphins, 21-17 (M)
1995—Dolphins, 21-20 (M)
1998—Falcons, 38-16 (A)
2001—Dolphins, 21-14 (M)
2005—Falcons, 17-10 (M)
2009—Falcons, 19-7 (A)
(RS Pts.—Dolphins 223, Falcons 200)
ATLANTA vs. MINNESOTA
RS: Vikings lead series, 15-10
PS: Series tied, 1-1
1966—Falcons, 20-13 (M)
1967—Falcons, 21-20 (A)
1968—Vikings, 47-7 (M)
1969—Falcons, 10-3 (A)
1970—Vikings, 37-7 (A)
1971—Vikings, 24-7 (M)
1973—Falcons, 20-14 (A)
1974—Vikings, 23-10 (M)
1975—Vikings, 38-0 (M)
1977—Vikings, 14-7 (A)
1980—Vikings, 24-23 (M)
1981—Falcons, 31-30 (A)

1982—*Vikings, 30-24 (M)
1984—Vikings, 27-20 (M)
1985—Falcons, 14-13 (A)
1987—Vikings, 24-13 (M)
1989—Vikings, 43-17 (M)
1991—Vikings, 20-19 (A)
1996—Vikings, 23-17 (A)
1998—**Falcons, 30-27 (M) OT
1999—Vikings, 17-14 (A)
2002—Falcons, 30-24 (M) OT
2003—Vikings, 39-26 (A)
2005—Falcons, 30-10 (A)
2007—Vikings, 24-3 (M)
2008—Falcons, 24-17 (M)
2011—Falcons, 24-14 (M)
(RS Pts.—Vikings 582, Falcons 414)
(PS Pts.—Vikings 57, Falcons 54)
*NFC First-Round Playoff
**NFC Championship
ATLANTA vs. NEW ENGLAND
RS: Series tied, 6-6
1972—Patriots, 21-20 (NE)
1977—Patriots, 16-10 (A)
1980—Falcons, 37-21 (NE)
1983—Falcons, 24-13 (A)
1986—Patriots, 25-17 (NE)
1989—Falcons, 16-15 (A)
1992—Falcons, 34-0 (A)
1995—Falcons, 30-17 (A)
1998—Falcons, 41-10 (NE)
2001—Patriots, 24-10 (A)
2005—Patriots, 31-28 (A)
2009—Patriots, 26-10 (NE)
(RS Pts.—Falcons 277, Patriots 219)
ATLANTA vs. NEW ORLEANS
RS: Falcons lead series, 45-40
PS: Falcons lead series, 1-0
1967—Saints, 27-24 (NO)
1969—Falcons, 45-17 (A)
1970—Falcons, 14-3 (NO)
          Falcons, 32-14 (A)
1971—Falcons, 28-6 (A)
          Falcons, 24-20 (NO)
1972—Falcons, 21-14 (NO)
          Falcons, 36-20 (A)
1973—Falcons, 62-7 (NO)
          Falcons, 14-10 (A)
1974—Saints, 14-13 (NO)
          Saints, 13-3 (A)
1975—Falcons, 14-7 (A)
          Saints, 23-7 (NO)
1976—Saints, 30-0 (NO)
          Falcons, 23-20 (A)
1977—Saints, 21-20 (NO)
          Falcons, 35-7 (A)
1978—Falcons, 20-17 (NO)
          Falcons, 20-17 (A)
1979—Falcons, 40-34 (NO) OT
          Saints, 37-6 (A)
1980—Falcons, 41-14 (A)
          Falcons, 31-13 (A)
1981—Falcons, 27-0 (A)
          Falcons, 41-10 (NO)
1982—Falcons, 35-0 (A)
          Saints, 35-6 (NO)
1983—Saints, 19-17 (A)
          Saints, 27-10 (NO)
1984—Falcons, 36-28 (NO)
          Saints, 17-13 (A)
1985—Falcons, 31-24 (A)
          Falcons, 16-10 (NO)
1986—Falcons, 31-10 (NO)

Saints, 14-9 (A)
1987—Saints, 38-0 (A)
1988—Saints, 29-21 (A)
Saints, 10-9 (NO)
1989—Saints, 20-13 (NO)
Saints, 26-17 (A)
1990—Falcons, 28-27 (A)
Saints, 10-7 (NO)
1991—Saints, 27-6 (A)
Falcons, 23-20 (NO) OT
*Falcons, 27-20 (NO)
1992—Saints, 10-7 (A)
Saints, 22-14 (NO)
1993—Saints, 34-31 (A)
Falcons, 26-15 (NO)
1994—Saints, 33-32 (NO)
Saints, 29-20 (A)
1995—Falcons, 27-24 (NO) OT
Falcons, 19-14 (A)
1996—Saints, 17-15 (A)
Falcons, 31-15 (NO)
1997—Falcons, 23-17 (NO)
Falcons, 20-3 (A)
1998—Falcons, 31-23 (A)
Falcons, 27-17 (A)
1999—Falcons, 20-17 (NO)
Falcons, 35-12 (A)
2000—Saints, 21-19 (A)
Saints, 23-7 (NO)
2001—Falcons, 20-13 (NO)
Saints, 28-10 (A)
2002—Falcons, 37-35 (NO)
Falcons, 24-17 (A)
2003—Saints, 45-17 (A)
Saints, 23-20 (NO) OT
2004—Falcons, 24-21 (A)
Saints, 26-13 (NO)
2005—Falcons, 34-31 (San Antonio)
Falcons, 36-17 (A)
2006—Saints, 23-3 (NO)
Saints, 31-13 (A)
2007—Saints, 22-16 (NO)
Saints, 34-14 (A)
2008—Falcons, 34-20 (A)
Saints, 29-25 (NO)
2009—Saints, 35-27 (NO)
Saints, 26-23 (A)
2010—Falcons, 27-24 (NO) OT
Saints, 17-14 (A)
2011—Saints, 26-23 (A) OT
Saints, 45-16 (NO)
(RS Pts.—Falcons 1,845, Saints 1,738)
(PS Pts.—Falcons 27, Saints 20)
*NFC First-Round Playoff
ATLANTA vs. N.Y. GIANTS
RS: Series tied, 10-10
PS: Giants lead series, 1-0
1966—Falcons, 27-16 (NY)
1968—Falcons, 24-21 (A)
1971—Giants, 21-17 (A)
1974—Falcons, 14-7 (New Haven)
1977—Falcons, 17-3 (A)
1978—Falcons, 23-20 (A)
1979—Giants, 24-3 (NY)
1981—Giants, 27-24 (A) OT
1982—Falcons, 16-14 (NY)
1983—Giants, 16-13 (A) OT
1984—Giants, 19-7 (A)
1988—Giants, 23-16 (A)
1998—Falcons, 34-20 (NY)
2000—Giants, 13-6 (A)
2002—Falcons, 17-10 (NY)

2003—Falcons, 27-7 (NY)
2004—Falcons, 14-10 (NY)
2006—Giants, 27-14 (A)
2007—Giants, 31-10 (A)
2009—Giants, 34-31 (NY) OT
2011—*Giants, 24-2 (NY)
(RS Pts.—Giants 363, Falcons 354)
(PS Pts.—Giants 24, Falcons 2)
*NFC First-Round Playoff
ATLANTA vs. N.Y. JETS
RS: Falcons lead series, 6-4
1973—Falcons, 28-20 (NY)
1980—Jets, 14-7 (A)
1983—Falcons, 27-21 (NY)
1986—Jets, 28-14 (A)
1989—Jets, 27-7 (NY)
1992—Falcons, 20-17 (A)
1995—Falcons, 13-3 (A)
1998—Jets, 28-3 (NY)
2005—Falcons, 27-14 (A)
2009—Falcons, 10-7 (NY)
(RS Pts.—Jets 179, Falcons 156)
ATLANTA vs. *OAKLAND
RS: Raiders lead series, 7-5
1971—Falcons, 24-13 (A)
1975—Raiders, 37-34 (O) OT
1979—Raiders, 50-19 (O)
1982—Raiders, 38-14 (A)
1985—Raiders, 34-24 (A)
1988—Falcons, 12-6 (LA)
1991—Falcons, 21-17 (A)
1994—Raiders, 30-17 (LA)
1997—Raiders, 36-31 (A)
2000—Raiders, 41-14 (O)
2004—Raiders, 35-10 (A)
2008—Falcons, 24-0 (O)
(RS Pts.—Raiders 312, Falcons 269)
*Franchise in Los Angeles from 1982-1994
ATLANTA vs. PHILADELPHIA
RS: Eagles lead series, 15-11-1
PS: Eagles lead series, 2-1
1966—Eagles, 23-10 (P)
1967—Eagles, 38-7 (A)
1969—Falcons, 27-3 (P)
1970—Tie, 13-13 (P)
1973—Falcons, 44-27 (P)
1976—Eagles, 14-13 (A)
1978—*Falcons, 14-13 (A)
1979—Falcons, 14-10 (P)
1980—Falcons, 20-17 (P)
1981—Eagles, 16-13 (P)
1983—Eagles, 28-24 (A)
1984—Falcons, 26-10 (A)
1985—Eagles, 23-17 (P) OT
1986—Eagles, 16-0 (A)
1988—Falcons, 27-24 (P)
1990—Eagles, 24-23 (A)
1994—Falcons, 28-21 (A)
1996—Eagles, 33-18 (A)
1997—Falcons, 20-17 (A)
1998—Falcons, 17-12 (A)
2000—Eagles, 38-10 (P)
2002—**Eagles, 20-6 (P)
2003—Eagles, 23-16 (A)
2004—***Eagles, 27-10 (P)
2005—Falcons, 14-10 (A)
2006—Eagles, 24-17 (P)
2008—Eagles, 27-14 (P)
2009—Eagles, 34-7 (A)
2010—Eagles, 31-17 (P)
2011—Falcons, 35-31 (A)
(RS Pts.—Eagles 587, Falcons 491)

(PS Pts.—Eagles 60, Falcons 30)
*NFC First-Round Playoff
**NFC Divisional Playoff
***NFC Championship
ATLANTA vs. PITTSBURGH
RS: Steelers lead series, 12-2-1
1966—Steelers, 57-33 (A)
1968—Steelers, 41-21 (A)
1970—Falcons, 27-16 (A)
1974—Steelers, 24-17 (P)
1978—Steelers, 31-7 (P)
1981—Steelers, 34-20 (A)
1984—Steelers, 35-10 (P)
1987—Steelers, 28-12 (A)
1990—Steelers, 21-9 (P)
1993—Steelers, 45-17 (A)
1996—Steelers, 20-17 (A)
1999—Steelers, 13-9 (P)
2002—Tie, 34-34 (P) OT
2006—Falcons, 41-38 (A) OT
2010—Steelers, 15-9 (P) OT
(RS Pts.—Steelers 452, Falcons 283)
ATLANTA vs. *ST. LOUIS
RS: Rams lead series, 47-26-2
PS: Falcons lead series, 1-0
1966—Rams, 19-14 (A)
1967—Rams, 31-3 (A)
Rams, 20-3 (LA)
1968—Rams, 27-14 (LA)
Rams, 17-10 (A)
1969—Rams, 17-7 (LA)
Rams, 38-6 (A)
1970—Tie, 10-10 (LA)
Rams, 17-7 (A)
1971—Tie, 20-20 (LA)
Rams, 24-16 (A)
1972—Falcons, 31-3 (A)
Rams, 20-7 (LA)
1973—Rams, 31-0 (LA)
Falcons, 15-13 (A)
1974—Rams, 21-0 (LA)
Rams, 30-7 (A)
1975—Rams, 22-7 (LA)
Rams, 16-7 (A)
1976—Rams, 30-14 (A)
Rams, 59-0 (LA)
1977—Falcons, 17-6 (A)
Rams, 23-7 (LA)
1978—Rams, 10-0 (LA)
Falcons, 15-7 (A)
1979—Rams, 20-14 (LA)
Rams, 34-13 (A)
1980—Falcons, 13-10 (A)
Rams, 20-17 (LA) OT
1981—Rams, 37-35 (A)
Rams, 21-16 (LA)
1982—Falcons, 34-17 (A)
1983—Rams, 27-21 (LA)
Rams, 36-13 (A)
1984—Falcons, 30-28 (LA)
Rams, 24-10 (A)
1985—Rams, 17-6 (A)
Falcons, 30-14 (A)
1986—Rams, 26-14 (A)
Rams, 14-7 (A)
1987—Falcons, 24-20 (A)
Rams, 33-0 (LA)
1988—Rams, 33-0 (A)
Rams, 22-7 (LA)
1989—Rams, 31-21 (A)
Rams, 26-14 (LA)
1990—Rams, 44-24 (LA)

Falcons, 20-13 (A)
1991—Falcons, 31-14 (A)
Falcons, 31-14 (LA)
1992—Falcons, 30-28 (A)
Rams, 38-27 (LA)
1993—Falcons, 30-24 (A)
Falcons, 13-0 (LA)
1994—Falcons, 31-13 (A)
Falcons, 8-5 (LA)
1995—Rams, 21-19 (StL)
Falcons, 31-6 (A)
1996—Rams, 59-16 (StL)
Rams, 34-27 (A)
1997—Falcons, 34-31 (A)
Falcons, 27-21 (StL)
1998—Falcons, 37-15 (A)
Falcons, 21-10 (StL)
1999—Rams, 35-7 (StL)
Rams, 41-13 (A)
2000—Rams, 41-20 (A)
Rams, 45-29 (StL)
2001—Rams, 35-6 (A)
Rams, 31-13 (StL)
2003—Rams, 36-0 (StL)
2004—Falcons, 34-17 (A)
**Falcons, 47-17 (A)
2007—Rams, 28-16 (StL)
2008—Falcons, 31-27 (A)
2010—Falcons, 34-17 (StL)
(RS Pts.—Rams 1,772, Falcons 1,248)
(PS Pts.—Falcons 47, Rams 17)
*Franchise in Los Angeles prior to 1995
**NFC Divisional Playoff
ATLANTA vs. SAN DIEGO
RS: Falcons lead series, 7-1
1973—Falcons, 41-0 (SD)
1979—Falcons, 28-26 (SD)
1988—Chargers, 10-7 (A)
1991—Falcons, 13-10 (SD)
1994—Falcons, 10-9 (A)
1997—Falcons, 14-3 (SD)
2004—Falcons, 21-20 (A)
2008—Falcons, 22-16 (SD)
(RS Pts.—Falcons 156, Chargers 94)
ATLANTA vs. SAN FRANCISCO
RS: 49ers lead series, 44-29-1
PS: Falcons lead series, 1-0
1966—49ers, 44-7 (A)
1967—49ers, 38-7 (SF)
49ers, 34-28 (A)
1968—49ers, 28-13 (SF)
49ers, 14-12 (A)
1969—Falcons, 24-12 (A)
Falcons, 21-7 (SF)
1970—Falcons, 21-20 (A)
49ers, 24-20 (SF)
1971—Falcons, 20-17 (A)
49ers, 24-3 (SF)
1972—49ers, 49-14 (A)
49ers, 20-0 (SF)
1973—49ers, 13-9 (A)
Falcons, 17-3 (SF)
1974—49ers, 16-10 (A)
49ers, 27-0 (SF)
1975—Falcons, 17-3 (SF)
Falcons, 31-9 (A)
1976—49ers, 15-0 (SF)
Falcons, 21-16 (A)
1977—Falcons, 7-0 (SF)
49ers, 10-3 (A)
1978—Falcons, 20-17 (SF)
Falcons, 21-10 (A)

1979—49ers, 20-15 (SF)
Falcons, 31-21 (A)
1980—Falcons, 20-17 (SF)
Falcons, 35-10 (A)
1981—Falcons, 34-17 (A)
49ers, 17-14 (SF)
1982—Falcons, 17-7 (SF)
1983—49ers, 24-20 (SF)
Falcons, 28-24 (A)
1984—49ers, 14-5 (SF)
49ers, 35-17 (A)
1985—49ers, 35-16 (SF)
49ers, 38-17 (A)
1986—Tie, 10-10 (A) OT
49ers, 20-0 (SF)
1987—49ers, 25-17 (A)
49ers, 35-7 (SF)
1988—Falcons, 34-17 (SF)
49ers, 13-3 (A)
1989—49ers, 45-3 (SF)
49ers, 23-10 (A)
1990—49ers, 19-13 (SF)
49ers, 45-35 (A)
1991—Falcons, 39-34 (SF)
Falcons, 17-14 (A)
1992—49ers, 56-17 (SF)
49ers, 41-3 (A)
1993—49ers, 37-30 (SF)
Falcons, 27-24 (A)
1994—49ers, 42-3 (A)
49ers, 50-14 (SF)
1995—49ers, 41-10 (SF)
Falcons, 28-27 (A)
1996—49ers, 39-17 (SF)
49ers, 34-10 (A)
1997—49ers, 34-7 (SF)
49ers, 35-28 (A)
1998—49ers, 31-20 (SF)
Falcons, 31-19 (A)
*Falcons, 20-18 (A)
1999—49ers, 26-7 (SF)
Falcons, 34-29 (A)
2000—Falcons, 36-28 (A)
49ers, 16-6 (SF)
2001—49ers, 16-13 (SF) OT
49ers, 37-31 (A) OT
2004—Falcons, 21-19 (SF)
2007—Falcons, 20-16 (A)
2009—Falcons, 45-10 (SF)
2010—Falcons, 16-14 (A)
(RS Pts.—49ers 1,770, Falcons 1,277)
(PS Pts.—Falcons 20, 49ers 18)
*NFC Divisional Playoff
ATLANTA vs. SEATTLE
RS: Seahawks lead series, 8-5
1976—Seahawks, 30-13 (S)
1979—Seahawks, 31-28 (A)
1985—Seahawks, 30-26 (S)
1988—Seahawks, 31-20 (A)
1991—Falcons, 26-13 (A)
1997—Falcons, 24-17 (S)
2000—Seahawks, 30-10 (A)
2002—Seahawks, 30-24 (A) OT
2004—Seahawks, 28-26 (S)
2005—Seahawks, 21-18 (S)
2007—Falcons, 44-41 (A)
2010—Falcons, 34-18 (S)
2011—Falcons, 30-28 (S)
(RS Pts.—Seahawks 348, Falcons 323)
ATLANTA vs. TAMPA BAY
RS: Buccaneers lead series, 19-18
1977—Falcons, 17-0 (TB)

1978—Buccaneers, 14-9 (TB)
1979—Falcons, 17-14 (A)
1981—Buccaneers, 24-23 (TB)
1984—Buccaneers, 23-6 (TB)
1986—Falcons, 23-20 (TB) OT
1987—Buccaneers, 48-10 (TB)
1988—Falcons, 17-10 (A)
1990—Buccaneers, 23-17 (TB)
1991—Falcons, 43-7 (A)
1992—Falcons, 35-7 (TB)
1993—Buccaneers, 31-24 (A)
1994—Falcons, 34-13 (A)
1995—Falcons, 24-21 (TB)
1997—Buccaneers, 31-10 (A)
1999—Buccaneers, 19-10 (TB)
2000—Buccaneers, 27-14 (A)
2002—Buccaneers, 20-6 (A)
Buccaneers, 34-10 (TB)
2003—Buccaneers, 31-10 (A)
Falcons, 30-28 (TB)
2004—Falcons, 24-14 (A)
Buccaneers, 27-0 (TB)
2005—Buccaneers, 30-27 (A)
Buccaneers, 27-24 (TB) OT
2006—Falcons, 14-3 (A)
Falcons, 17-6 (TB)
2007—Buccaneers, 31-7 (A)
Buccaneers, 37-3 (TB)
2008—Buccaneers, 24-9 (TB)
Falcons, 13-10 (A) OT
2009—Falcons, 20-17 (A)
Falcons, 20-10 (TB)
2010—Falcons, 27-21 (A)
Falcons, 28-24 (TB)
2011—Buccaneers, 16-13 (TB)
Falcons, 45-24 (A)
(RS Pts.—Buccaneers 766, Falcons 680)
ATLANTA vs. *TENNESSEE
RS: Titans lead series, 7-6
1972—Falcons, 20-10 (A)
1976—Oilers, 20-14 (H)
1978—Falcons, 20-14 (A)
1981—Falcons, 31-27 (H)
1984—Falcons, 42-10 (A)
1987—Oilers, 37-33 (H)
1990—Falcons, 47-27 (A)
1993—Oilers, 33-17 (H)
1996—Oilers, 23-13 (A)
1999—Titans, 30-17 (T)
2003—Titans, 38-31 (A)
2007—Titans, 20-13 (T)
2011—Falcons, 23-17 (A)
(RS Pts.—Falcons 321, Titans 306)
*Franchise in Houston prior to 1997;
known as Oilers prior to 1999
ATLANTA vs. WASHINGTON
RS: Redskins lead series, 14-6-1
PS: Redskins lead series, 1-0
1966—Redskins, 33-20 (W)
1967—Tie, 20-20 (A)
1969—Redskins, 27-20 (W)
1972—Redskins, 24-13 (W)
1975—Redskins, 30-27 (A)
1977—Redskins, 10-6 (W)
1978—Falcons, 20-17 (A)
1979—Redskins, 16-7 (A)
1980—Falcons, 10-6 (A)
1983—Redskins, 37-21 (W)
1984—Redskins, 27-14 (W)
1985—Redskins, 44-10 (A)
1987—Falcons, 21-20 (A)
1989—Redskins, 31-30 (A)

1991—Redskins, 56-17 (W)
   *Redskins, 24-7 (W)
1992—Redskins, 24-17 (W)
1993—Redskins, 30-17 (W)
1994—Falcons, 27-20 (W)
2003—Redskins, 33-31 (A)
2006—Falcons, 24-14 (W)
2009—Falcons, 31-17 (W)
(RS Pts.—Redskins 536, Falcons 403)
(PS Pts.—Redskins 24, Falcons 7)
*NFC Divisional Playoff

BALTIMORE vs. ARIZONA
RS: Ravens lead series, 4-1;
See Arizona vs. Baltimore
BALTIMORE vs. ATLANTA
RS: Series tied, 2-2;
See Atlanta vs. Baltimore
BALTIMORE vs. BUFFALO
RS: Ravens lead series, 3-2
1999—Bills, 13-10 (Balt)
2004—Ravens, 20-6 (Balt)
2006—Ravens, 19-7 (Balt)
2007—Bills, 19-14 (Buf)
2010—Ravens, 37-34 (Balt) OT
(RS Pts.—Ravens 100, Bills 79)
BALTIMORE vs. CAROLINA
RS: Panthers lead series, 3-1
1996—Panthers, 27-16 (C)
2002—Panthers, 10-7 (C)
2006—Panthers, 23-21 (B)
2010—Ravens, 37-13 (C)
(RS Pts.—Panthers 81, Ravens 73)
BALTIMORE vs. CHICAGO
RS: Series tied, 2-2
1998—Bears, 24-3 (C)
2001—Ravens, 17-6 (B)
2005—Bears, 10-6 (C)
2009—Ravens, 31-7 (C)
(RS Pts.—Ravens 57, Bears 47)
BALTIMORE vs. CINCINNATI
RS: Ravens lead series, 18-14
1996—Bengals, 24-21 (B)
   Bengals, 21-14 (C)
1997—Ravens, 23-10 (B)
   Bengals, 16-14 (C)
1998—Ravens, 31-24 (B)
   Ravens, 20-13 (C)
1999—Ravens, 34-31 (C)
   Ravens, 22-0 (B)
2000—Ravens, 37-0 (B)
   Ravens, 27-7 (C)
2001—Bengals, 21-10 (C)
   Ravens, 16-0 (B)
2002—Ravens, 38-27 (B)
   Ravens, 27-23 (C)
2003—Bengals, 34-26 (C)
   Ravens, 31-13 (B)
2004—Ravens, 23-9 (C)
   Bengals, 27-26 (B)
2005—Bengals, 21-9 (B)
   Bengals, 42-29 (C)
2006—Ravens, 26-20 (B)
   Bengals, 13-7 (C)
2007—Ravens, 27-20 (C)
   Bengals, 21-7 (B)
2008—Ravens, 17-10 (B)
   Ravens, 34-3 (C)
2009—Ravens, 17-14 (B)
   Bengals, 17-7 (C)
2010—Bengals, 15-10 (C)
   Ravens, 13-7 (B)

2011—Ravens, 31-24 (B)
   Ravens, 24-16 (C)
(RS Pts.—Ravens 688, Bengals 553)
BALTIMORE vs. CLEVELAND
RS: Ravens lead series, 19-7
1999—Ravens, 17-10 (B)
   Ravens, 41-9 (C)
2000—Ravens, 12-0 (C)
   Ravens, 44-7 (B)
2001—Browns, 24-14 (C)
   Browns, 27-17 (B)
2002—Ravens, 26-21 (C)
   Browns, 14-13 (B)
2003—Ravens, 33-13 (B)
   Ravens, 35-0 (C)
2004—Browns, 20-3 (B)
   Ravens, 27-13 (B)
2005—Ravens, 16-3 (B)
   Browns, 20-16 (C)
2006—Ravens, 15-14 (C)
   Ravens, 27-17 (B)
2007—Browns, 27-13 (C)
   Browns, 33-30 (B) OT
2008—Ravens, 28-10 (B)
   Ravens, 37-27 (C)
2009—Ravens, 34-3 (B)
   Ravens, 16-0 (C)
2010—Ravens, 24-17 (B)
   Ravens, 20-10 (C)
2011—Ravens, 24-10 (C)
   Ravens, 20-14 (B)
(RS Pts.—Ravens 602, Browns 363)
BALTIMORE vs. DALLAS
RS: Ravens lead series, 3-0
2000—Ravens, 27-0 (B)
2004—Ravens, 30-10 (B)
2008—Ravens, 33-24 (D)
(RS Pts.—Ravens 90, Cowboys 34)
BALTIMORE vs. DENVER
RS: Ravens lead series, 5-3
PS: Ravens lead series, 1-0
1996—Broncos, 45-34 (D)
2000—*Ravens, 21-3 (D)
2001—Ravens, 20-13 (D)
2002—Ravens, 34-23 (B)
2003—Ravens, 26-6 (B)
2005—Broncos, 12-10 (D)
2006—Broncos, 13-3 (D)
2009—Ravens, 30-7 (B)
2010—Ravens, 31-17 (B)
(RS Pts.—Ravens 188, Broncos 136)
(PS Pts.—Ravens 21, Broncos 3)
*AFC First-Round Playoff
BALTIMORE vs. DETROIT
RS: Ravens lead series, 2-1
1998—Ravens, 19-10 (B)
2005—Lions, 35-17 (D)
2009—Ravens, 48-3 (B)
(RS Pts.—Ravens 84, Lions 48)
BALTIMORE vs. GREEN BAY
RS: Packers lead series, 3-1
1998—Packers, 28-10 (GB)
2001—Packers, 31-23 (GB)
2005—Ravens, 48-3 (B)
2009—Packers, 27-14 (GB)
(RS Pts.—Ravens 95, Packers 89)
BALTIMORE vs. HOUSTON
RS: Ravens lead series, 5-0
PS: Ravens lead series, 1-0
2002—Ravens, 23-19 (H)
2005—Ravens, 16-15 (B)
2008—Ravens, 41-13 (H)

2010—Ravens, 34-28 (H) OT
2011—Ravens, 29-14 (B)
   *Ravens, 20-13 (B)
(RS Pts.—Ravens 143, Texans 89)
(PS Pts.—Ravens 20, Texans 13)
*AFC Divisional Playoff
BALTIMORE vs. INDIANAPOLIS
RS: Colts lead series, 7-3
PS: Colts lead series, 2-0
1996—Colts, 26-21 (I)
1998—Ravens, 38-31 (B)
2001—Ravens, 39-27 (B)
2002—Colts, 22-20 (I)
2004—Colts, 20-10 (I)
2005—Colts, 24-7 (B)
2006—*Colts, 15-6 (B)
2007—Colts, 44-20 (B)
2008—Colts, 31-3 (I)
2009—Colts, 17-15 (B)
   *Colts, 20-3 (I)
2011—Ravens, 24-10 (B)
(RS Pts.—Colts 252, Ravens 197)
(PS Pts.—Colts 35, Ravens 9)
*AFC Divisional Playoff
BALTIMORE vs. JACKSONVILLE
RS: Jaguars lead series, 10-7
1996—Jaguars, 30-27 (J)
   Jaguars, 28-25 (B) OT
1997—Jaguars, 28-27 (B)
   Jaguars, 29-27 (J)
1998—Jaguars, 24-10 (J)
   Jaguars, 45-19 (B)
1999—Jaguars, 6-3 (J)
   Jaguars, 30-23 (B)
2000—Ravens, 39-36 (B)
   Ravens, 15-10 (J)
2001—Ravens, 18-17 (B)
   Ravens, 24-21 (J)
2002—Ravens, 17-10 (B)
2003—Ravens, 24-17 (B)
2005—Jaguars, 30-3 (J)
2008—Ravens, 27-7 (B)
2011—Jaguars, 12-7 (J)
(RS Pts.—Jaguars 380, Ravens 335)
BALTIMORE vs. KANSAS CITY
RS: Chiefs lead series, 3-2
PS: Ravens lead series, 1-0
1999—Chiefs, 35-8 (B)
2003—Chiefs, 17-10 (B)
2004—Chiefs, 27-24 (B)
2006—Ravens, 20-10 (KC)
2009—Ravens, 38-24 (B)
2010—*Ravens, 30-7 (KC)
(RS Pts.—Chiefs 113, Ravens 100)
(PS Pts.—Ravens 30, Chiefs 7)
*AFC First-Round Playoff
BALTIMORE vs. MIAMI
RS: Dolphins lead series, 5-3
PS: Ravens lead series, 2-0
1997—Dolphins, 24-13 (B)
2000—Dolphins, 19-6 (M)
2001—*Ravens, 20-3 (M)
2002—Dolphins, 26-7 (M)
2003—Dolphins, 9-6 (M) OT
2004—Ravens, 30-23 (B)
2007—Dolphins, 22-16 (M) OT
2008—Ravens, 27-13 (M)
   *Ravens, 27-9 (M)
2010—Ravens, 26-10 (B)
(RS Pts.—Dolphins 146, Ravens 131)
(PS Pts.—Ravens 47, Dolphins 12)
*AFC First-Round Playoff

BALTIMORE vs. MINNESOTA
RS: Series tied, 2-2
1998—Vikings, 38-28 (B)
2001—Ravens, 19-3 (B)
2005—Ravens, 30-23 (B)
2009—Vikings, 33-31 (M)
(RS Pts.—Ravens 108, Vikings 97)
BALTIMORE vs. NEW ENGLAND
RS: Patriots lead series, 6-0
PS: Series tied, 1-1
1996—Patriots, 46-38 (B)
1999—Patriots, 20-3 (NE)
2004—Patriots, 24-3 (NE)
2007—Patriots, 27-24 (B)
2009—Patriots, 27-21 (NE)
    *Ravens, 33-14 (NE)
2010—Patriots, 23-20 (NE) OT
2011—**Patriots, 23-20 (NE)
(RS Pts.—Patriots 167, Ravens 109)
(PS Pts.—Ravens 53, Patriots 37)
*AFC First-Round Playoff
**AFC Championship
BALTIMORE vs. NEW ORLEANS
RS: Ravens lead series, 4-1
1996—Ravens, 17-10 (B)
1999—Ravens, 31-8 (B)
2002—Saints, 37-25 (B)
2006—Ravens, 35-22 (NO)
2010—Ravens, 30-24 (B)
(RS Pts.—Ravens 138, Saints 101)
BALTIMORE vs. N.Y. GIANTS
RS: Ravens lead series, 3-1
PS: Ravens lead series, 1-0
1997—Ravens, 24-23 (NY)
2000—*Ravens, 34-7 (Tampa)
2004—Ravens, 37-14 (B)
2008—Giants, 30-10 (NY)
(RS Pts.—Ravens 71, Giants 67)
(PS Pts.—Ravens 34, Giants 7)
*Super Bowl XXXV
BALTIMORE vs. N.Y. JETS
RS: Ravens lead series, 7-1
1997—Jets, 19-16 (NY) OT
1998—Ravens, 24-10 (NY)
2000—Ravens, 34-20 (B)
2004—Ravens, 20-17 (NY) OT
2005—Ravens, 13-3 (B)
2007—Ravens, 20-13 (B)
2010—Ravens, 10-9 (NY)
2011—Ravens, 34-17 (B)
(RS Pts.—Ravens 171, Jets 108)
BALTIMORE vs. OAKLAND
RS: Ravens lead series, 5-1
PS: Ravens lead series, 1-0
1996—Ravens, 19-14 (B)
1998—Ravens, 13-10 (B)
2000—*Ravens, 16-3 (O)
2003—Raiders, 20-12 (O)
2006—Ravens, 28-6 (B)
2008—Ravens, 29-10 (B)
2009—Ravens, 21-13 (O)
(RS Pts.—Ravens 122, Raiders 73)
(PS Pts.—Ravens 16, Raiders 3)
*AFC Championship
BALTIMORE vs. PHILADELPHIA
RS: Series tied, 1-1-1
1997—Tie, 10-10 (B) OT
2004—Eagles, 15-10 (P)
2008—Ravens, 36-7 (B)
(RS Pts.—Ravens 56, Eagles 32)
BALTIMORE vs. PITTSBURGH
RS: Steelers lead series, 18-14

PS: Steelers lead series, 3-0
1996—Steelers, 31-17 (P)
    Ravens, 31-17 (B)
1997—Steelers, 42-34 (B)
    Steelers, 37-0 (P)
1998—Steelers, 20-13 (B)
    Steelers, 16-6 (P)
1999—Steelers, 23-20 (B)
    Ravens, 31-24 (P)
2000—Ravens, 16-0 (B)
    Steelers, 9-6 (B)
2001—Ravens, 13-10 (P)
    Steelers, 26-21 (B)
    *Steelers, 27-10 (P)
2002—Steelers, 31-18 (B)
    Steelers, 34-31 (P)
2003—Steelers, 34-15 (P)
    Ravens, 13-10 (B) OT
2004—Ravens, 30-13 (B)
    Steelers, 20-7 (P)
2005—Steelers, 20-19 (B)
    Ravens, 16-13 (B) OT
2006—Ravens, 27-0 (B)
    Ravens, 31-7 (P)
2007—Steelers, 38-7 (B)
    Ravens, 27-21 (B)
2008—Steelers, 23-20 (P) OT
    Steelers, 13-9 (B)
    **Steelers, 23-14 (P)
2009—Ravens, 20-17 (B) OT
    Steelers, 23-20 (P)
2010—Ravens, 17-14 (P)
    Steelers, 13-10 (B)
    *Steelers, 31-24 (P)
2011—Ravens, 35-7 (B)
    Ravens, 23-20 (P)
(RS Pts.—Steelers 626, Ravens 603)
(PS Pts.—Steelers 81, Ravens 48)
*AFC Divisional Playoff
**AFC Championship
BALTIMORE vs. ST. LOUIS
RS: Ravens lead series, 3-2
1996—Ravens, 37-31 (B) OT
1999—Rams, 27-10 (StL)
2003—Rams, 33-22 (StL)
2007—Ravens, 22-3 (B)
2011—Ravens, 37-7 (StL)
(RS Pts.—Ravens 128, Rams 101)
BALTIMORE vs. SAN DIEGO
RS: Series tied, 4-4
1997—Chargers, 21-17 (SD)
1998—Chargers, 14-13 (SD)
2000—Ravens, 24-3 (B)
2003—Ravens, 24-10 (SD)
2006—Ravens, 16-13 (B)
2007—Chargers, 32-14 (SD)
2009—Ravens, 31-26 (SD)
2011—Chargers, 34-14 (SD)
(RS Pts.—Ravens 153, Chargers 153)
BALTIMORE vs. SAN FRANCISCO
RS: Ravens lead series, 3-1
1996—49ers, 38-20 (SF)
2003—Ravens, 44-6 (B)
2007—Ravens, 9-7 (SF)
2011—Ravens, 16-6 (B)
(RS Pts.—Ravens 89, 49ers 57)
BALTIMORE vs. SEATTLE
RS: Series tied, 2-2
1997—Ravens, 31-24 (B)
2003—Ravens, 44-41 (B) OT
2007—Seahawks, 27-6 (S)
2011—Seahawks, 22-17 (S)

(RS Pts.—Seahawks 114, Ravens 98)
BALTIMORE vs. TAMPA BAY
RS: Series tied, 2-2
2001—Buccaneers, 22-10 (TB)
2002—Buccaneers, 25-0 (B)
2006—Ravens, 27-0 (TB)
2010—Ravens, 17-10 (B)
(RS Pts.—Buccaneers 57, Ravens 54)
BALTIMORE vs. *TENNESSEE
RS: Titans lead series, 9-8
PS: Ravens lead series, 2-1
1996—Oilers, 29-13 (H)
    Oilers, 24-21 (B)
1997—Ravens, 36-10 (T)
    Ravens, 21-19 (B)
1998—Oilers, 12-8 (B)
    Oilers, 16-14 (T)
1999—Titans, 14-11 (T)
    Ravens, 41-14 (B)
2000—Titans, 14-6 (B)
    Ravens, 24-23 (T)
    **Ravens, 24-10 (T)
2001—Ravens, 26-7 (B)
    Ravens, 16-10 (T)
2002—Ravens, 13-12 (B)
2003—***Titans, 20-17 (B)
2005—Titans, 25-10 (T)
2006—Ravens, 27-26 (T)
2008—Titans, 13-10 (B)
    **Ravens, 13-10 (T)
2011—Titans, 26-13 (T)
(RS Pts.—Ravens 310, Titans 294)
(PS Pts.—Ravens 54, Titans 40)
*Franchise in Houston prior to 1997;
known as Oilers prior to 1999
**AFC Divisional Playoff
***AFC First-Round Playoff
BALTIMORE vs. WASHINGTON
RS: Ravens lead series, 3-1
1997—Ravens, 20-17 (W)
2000—Redskins, 10-3 (W)
2004—Ravens, 17-10 (W)
2008—Ravens, 24-10 (B)
(RS Pts.—Ravens 64, Redskins 47)

BUFFALO vs. ARIZONA
RS: Bills lead series, 5-4;
See Arizona vs. Buffalo
BUFFALO vs. ATLANTA
RS: Falcons lead series, 6-4;
See Atlanta vs. Buffalo
BUFFALO vs. BALTIMORE
RS: Ravens lead series, 3-2;
See Baltimore vs. Buffalo
BUFFALO vs. CAROLINA
RS: Bills lead series, 4-1
1995—Bills, 31-9 (B)
1998—Bills, 30-14 (C)
2001—Bills, 25-24 (B)
2005—Panthers, 13-9 (B)
2009—Bills, 20-9 (C)
(RS Pts.—Bills 115, Panthers 69)
BUFFALO vs. CHICAGO
RS: Bears lead series, 7-4
1970—Bears, 31-13 (C)
1974—Bills, 16-6 (B)
1979—Bears, 7-0 (B)
1988—Bears, 24-3 (C)
1991—Bills, 35-20 (B)
1994—Bears, 20-13 (C)
1997—Bears, 20-3 (C)
2000—Bills, 20-3 (B)

2002—Bills, 33-27 (B) OT
2006—Bears, 40-7 (C)
2010—Bears, 22-19 (Toronto)
(RS Pts.—Bears 220, Bills 162)
BUFFALO vs. CINCINNATI
RS: Bills lead series, 15-10
PS: Bengals lead series, 2-0
1968—Bengals, 34-23 (C)
1969—Bills, 16-13 (B)
1970—Bengals, 43-14 (B)
1973—Bengals, 16-13 (B)
1975—Bengals, 33-24 (C)
1978—Bills, 5-0 (B)
1979—Bills, 51-24 (B)
1980—Bills, 14-0 (C)
1981—Bengals, 27-24 (C) OT
       *Bengals, 28-21 (C)
1983—Bills, 10-6 (C)
1984—Bengals, 52-21 (C)
1985—Bengals, 23-17 (B)
1986—Bengals, 36-33 (C) OT
1988—Bengals, 35-21 (C)
       **Bengals, 21-10 (C)
1989—Bills, 24-7 (B)
1991—Bills, 35-16 (B)
1996—Bills, 31-17 (B)
1998—Bills, 33-20 (C)
2002—Bills, 27-9 (B)
2003—Bills, 22-16 (B) OT
2004—Bills, 33-17 (C)
2005—Bills, 37-27 (C)
2007—Bills, 33-21 (B)
2010—Bills, 49-31 (C)
2011—Bengals, 23-20 (C)
(RS Pts.—Bills 630, Bengals 546)
(PS Pts.—Bengals 49, Bills 31)
*AFC Divisional Playoff
**AFC Championship
BUFFALO vs. CLEVELAND
RS: Browns lead series, 10-6
PS: Browns lead series, 1-0
1972—Browns, 27-10 (C)
1974—Bills, 15-10 (C)
1977—Browns, 27-16 (B)
1978—Browns, 41-20 (C)
1981—Bills, 22-13 (B)
1984—Browns, 13-10 (B)
1985—Browns, 17-7 (C)
1986—Bills, 21-17 (B)
1987—Browns, 27-21 (C)
1989—*Browns, 34-30 (C)
1990—Bills, 42-0 (C)
1995—Bills, 22-19 (C)
2004—Bills, 37-7 (B)
2007—Browns, 8-0 (C)
2008—Browns, 29-27 (B)
2009—Browns, 6-3 (B)
2010—Bills, 13-6 (B)
(RS Pts.—Bills 282, Browns 271)
(PS Pts.—Browns 34, Bills 30)
*AFC Divisional Playoff
BUFFALO vs. DALLAS
RS: Cowboys lead series, 6-3
PS: Cowboys lead series, 2-0
1971—Cowboys, 49-37 (B)
1976—Cowboys, 17-10 (D)
1981—Cowboys, 27-14 (D)
1984—Bills, 14-3 (B)
1992—*Cowboys, 52-17 (Pasadena)
1993—Bills, 13-10 (D)
       **Cowboys, 30-13 (Atlanta)
1996—Bills, 10-7 (B)

2003—Cowboys, 10-6 (D)
2007—Cowboys, 25-24 (B)
2011—Cowboys, 44-7 (D)
(RS Pts.—Cowboys 192, Bills 135)
(PS Pts.—Cowboys 82, Bills 30)
*Super Bowl XXVII
**Super Bowl XXVIII
BUFFALO vs. DENVER
RS: Bills lead series, 19-15-1
PS: Bills lead series, 1-0
1960—Broncos, 27-21 (B)
       Tie, 38-38 (D)
1961—Broncos, 22-10 (B)
       Bills, 23-10 (D)
1962—Broncos, 23-20 (B)
       Bills, 45-38 (D)
1963—Bills, 30-28 (D)
       Bills, 27-17 (B)
1964—Bills, 30-13 (B)
       Bills, 30-19 (D)
1965—Bills, 30-15 (D)
       Bills, 31-13 (B)
1966—Bills, 38-21 (B)
1967—Bills, 17-16 (D)
       Broncos, 21-20 (B)
1968—Broncos, 34-32 (D)
1969—Bills, 41-28 (B)
1970—Broncos, 25-10 (B)
1975—Bills, 38-14 (B)
1977—Broncos, 26-6 (D)
1979—Broncos, 19-16 (B)
1981—Bills, 9-7 (B)
1984—Broncos, 37-7 (B)
1987—Bills, 21-14 (B)
1989—Broncos, 28-14 (B)
1990—Bills, 29-28 (B)
1991—*Bills, 10-7 (B)
1992—Bills, 27-17 (B)
1994—Bills, 27-20 (B)
1995—Broncos, 22-7 (D)
1997—Broncos, 23-20 (B) OT
2002—Broncos, 28-23 (D)
2005—Broncos, 28-17 (B)
2007—Broncos, 15-14 (B)
2008—Bills, 30-23 (D)
2011—Bills, 40-14 (B)
(RS Pts.—Bills 838, Broncos 771)
(PS Pts.—Bills 10, Broncos 7)
*AFC Championship
BUFFALO vs. DETROIT
RS: Series tied, 4-4-1
1972—Tie, 21-21 (B)
1976—Lions, 27-14 (D)
1979—Bills, 20-17 (D)
1991—Lions, 17-14 (B) OT
1994—Lions, 35-21 (D)
1997—Bills, 22-13 (B)
2002—Bills, 24-17 (B)
2006—Lions, 20-17 (D)
2010—Bills, 14-12 (B)
(RS Pts.—Lions 179, Bills 167)
BUFFALO vs. GREEN BAY
RS: Bills lead series, 7-4
1974—Bills, 27-7 (GB)
1979—Bills, 19-12 (B)
1982—Packers, 33-21 (Mil)
1988—Bills, 28-0 (B)
1991—Bills, 34-24 (Mil)
1994—Bills 29-20 (B)
1997—Packers, 31-21 (GB)
2000—Bills 27-18 (B)
2002—Packers, 10-0 (GB)

2006—Bills, 24-10 (B)
2010—Packers, 34-7 (GB)
(RS Pts.—Bills 237, Packers 199)
BUFFALO vs. HOUSTON
RS: Bills lead series, 3-2
2002—Bills, 31-24 (H)
2003—Texans, 12-10 (B)
2005—Bills, 22-7 (H)
2006—Bills, 24-21 (H)
2009—Texans, 31-10 (B)
(RS Pts.—Bills 97, Texans 95)
BUFFALO vs. *INDIANAPOLIS
RS: Bills lead series, 35-30-1
1970—Tie, 17-17 (Balt)
       Colts, 20-14 (Buff)
1971—Colts, 43-0 (Buff)
       Colts, 24-0 (Balt)
1972—Colts, 17-0 (Buff)
       Colts, 35-7 (Balt)
1973—Bills, 31-13 (Buff)
       Bills, 24-17 (Balt)
1974—Bills, 27-14 (Balt)
       Bills, 6-0 (Buff)
1975—Bills, 38-31 (Balt)
       Colts, 42-35 (Buff)
1976—Colts, 31-13 (Buff)
       Colts, 58-20 (Balt)
1977—Colts, 17-14 (Balt)
       Colts, 31-13 (Buff)
1978—Colts, 24-17 (Buff)
       Bills, 21-14 (Balt)
1979—Bills, 31-13 (Balt)
       Colts, 14-13 (Buff)
1980—Colts, 17-12 (Buff)
       Colts, 28-24 (Balt)
1981—Bills, 35-3 (Balt)
       Bills, 23-17 (Buff)
1982—Bills, 20-0 (Buff)
1983—Bills, 28-23 (Buff)
       Bills, 30-7 (Balt)
1984—Colts, 31-17 (I)
       Bills, 21-15 (Buff)
1985—Colts, 49-17 (I)
       Bills, 21-9 (Buff)
1986—Bills, 24-13 (Buff)
       Colts, 24-14 (I)
1987—Colts, 47-6 (Buff)
       Bills, 27-3 (I)
1988—Bills, 34-23 (Buff)
       Colts, 17-14 (I)
1989—Colts, 37-14 (I)
       Bills, 30-7 (Buff)
1990—Bills, 26-10 (Buff)
       Bills, 31-7 (I)
1991—Bills, 42-6 (Buff)
       Bills, 35-7 (I)
1992—Bills, 38-0 (Buff)
       Colts, 16-13 (I) OT
1993—Bills, 23-9 (Buff)
       Bills, 30-10 (I)
1994—Colts, 27-17 (Buff)
       Colts, 10-9 (I)
1995—Bills, 20-14 (Buff)
       Bills, 16-10 (I)
1996—Bills, 16-13 (Buff) OT
       Colts, 13-10 (I) OT
1997—Bills, 37-35 (B)
       Bills, 9-6 (I)
1998—Bills, 31-24 (I)
       Bills, 34-11 (B)
1999—Colts, 31-14 (I)
       Bills, 31-6 (B)

2000—Colts, 18-16 (B)
    Colts, 44-20 (I)
2001—Colts, 42-26 (I)
    Colts, 30-14 (B)
2003—Colts, 17-14 (B)
2006—Colts, 17-16 (I)
2009—Bills, 30-7 (B)
(RS Pts.—Bills 1,377, Colts 1,278)
*Franchise in Baltimore prior to 1984

BUFFALO vs. JACKSONVILLE
RS: Series tied, 5-5
PS: Jaguars lead series, 1-0
1996—*Jaguars, 30-27 (B)
1997—Jaguars, 20-14 (B)
1998—Bills, 17-16 (B)
2001—Bills, 13-10 (J)
2003—Bills, 38-17 (J)
2004—Jaguars, 13-10 (B)
2006—Bills, 27-24 (B)
2007—Jaguars, 36-14 (J)
2008—Bills, 20-16 (J)
2009—Jaguars, 18-15 (J)
2010—Jaguars, 36-26 (B)
(RS Pts.—Jaguars 206, Bills 194)
(PS Pts.—Jaguars 30, Bills 27)
*AFC First-Round Playoff

BUFFALO vs. *KANSAS CITY
RS: Bills lead series, 22-17-1
PS: Bills lead series, 2-1
1960—Texans, 45-28 (B)
    Texans, 24-7 (D)
1961—Bills, 27-24 (B)
    Bills, 30-20 (D)
1962—Texans, 41-21 (D)
    Bills, 23-14 (B)
1963—Tie, 27-27 (B)
    Bills, 35-26 (KC)
1964—Bills, 34-17 (B)
    Bills, 35-22 (KC)
1965—Bills, 23-7 (KC)
    Bills, 34-25 (B)
1966—Chiefs, 42-20 (B)
    Bills, 29-14 (KC)
    **Chiefs, 31-7 (B)
1967—Chiefs, 23-13 (KC)
1968—Chiefs, 18-7 (B)
1969—Chiefs, 29-7 (B)
    Chiefs, 22-19 (KC)
1971—Chiefs, 22-9 (KC)
1973—Bills, 23-14 (B)
1976—Bills, 50-17 (B)
1978—Bills, 28-13 (B)
    Chiefs, 14-10 (KC)
1982—Bills, 14-9 (B)
1983—Bills, 14-9 (KC)
1986—Chiefs, 20-17 (B)
    Bills, 17-14 (KC)
1991—Chiefs, 33-6 (KC)
    ***Bills, 37-14 (B)
1993—Chiefs, 23-7 (KC)
    ****Bills, 30-13 (B)
1994—Bills, 44-10 (B)
1996—Bills, 20-9 (B)
1997—Chiefs, 22-16 (KC)
2000—Bills, 21-17 (KC)
2002—Chiefs, 17-16 (KC)
2003—Chiefs, 38-5 (KC)
2005—Bills, 14-3 (B)
2008—Bills, 54-31 (KC)
2009—Bills, 16-10 (KC)
2010—Chiefs, 13-10 (KC) OT
2011—Bills, 41-7 (KC)

(RS Pts.—Bills 871, Chiefs 805)
(PS Pts.—Bills 74, Chiefs 58)
*Franchise in Dallas prior to 1963 and
known as Texans
**AFL Championship
***AFC Divisional Playoff
****AFC Championship

BUFFALO vs. MIAMI
RS: Dolphins lead series, 55-36-1
PS: Bills lead series, 3-1
1966—Bills, 58-24 (B)
    Bills, 29-0 (M)
1967—Bills, 35-13 (B)
    Dolphins, 17-14 (M)
1968—Tie, 14-14 (M)
    Dolphins, 21-17 (B)
1969—Dolphins, 24-6 (M)
    Bills, 28-3 (B)
1970—Dolphins, 33-14 (B)
    Dolphins, 45-7 (M)
1971—Dolphins, 29-14 (B)
    Dolphins, 34-0 (M)
1972—Dolphins, 24-23 (M)
    Dolphins, 30-16 (B)
1973—Dolphins, 27-6 (M)
    Dolphins, 17-0 (B)
1974—Dolphins, 24-16 (B)
    Dolphins, 35-28 (M)
1975—Dolphins, 35-30 (B)
    Dolphins, 31-21 (M)
1976—Dolphins, 30-21 (B)
    Dolphins, 45-27 (M)
1977—Dolphins, 13-0 (B)
    Dolphins, 31-14 (M)
1978—Dolphins, 31-24 (M)
    Dolphins, 25-24 (B)
1979—Dolphins, 9-7 (B)
    Dolphins, 17-7 (M)
1980—Bills, 17-7 (B)
    Dolphins, 17-14 (M)
1981—Bills, 31-21 (B)
    Dolphins, 16-6 (M)
1982—Dolphins, 9-7 (B)
    Dolphins, 27-10 (M)
1983—Dolphins, 12-0 (B)
    Bills, 38-35 (M) OT
1984—Dolphins, 21-17 (B)
    Dolphins, 38-7 (M)
1985—Dolphins, 23-14 (B)
    Dolphins, 28-0 (M)
1986—Dolphins, 27-14 (M)
    Dolphins, 34-24 (B)
1987—Bills, 34-31 (M) OT
    Bills, 27-0 (B)
1988—Bills, 9-6 (B)
    Bills, 31-6 (M)
1989—Bills, 27-24 (M)
    Bills, 31-17 (B)
1990—Dolphins, 30-7 (M)
    Bills, 24-14 (B)
    *Bills, 44-34 (B)
1991—Bills, 35-31 (B)
    Bills, 41-27 (M)
1992—Dolphins, 37-10 (B)
    Bills, 26-20 (M)
    **Bills, 29-10 (M)
1993—Dolphins, 22-13 (M)
    Bills, 47-34 (B)
1994—Bills, 21-11 (B)
    Bills, 42-31 (M)
1995—Dolphins, 23-6 (M)
    Bills, 23-20 (B)

    ***Bills, 37-22 (B)
1996—Dolphins, 21-7 (B)
    Dolphins, 16-14 (M)
1997—Bills, 9-6 (B)
    Dolphins, 30-13 (M)
1998—Dolphins, 13-7 (M)
    Bills, 30-24 (B)
    ***Dolphins, 24-17 (M)
1999—Bills, 23-18 (M)
    Bills, 23-3 (B)
2000—Dolphins, 22-13 (M)
    Dolphins, 33-6 (B)
2001—Dolphins, 34-27 (B)
    Dolphins, 34-7 (M)
2002—Bills, 23-10 (M)
    Bills, 38-21 (B)
2003—Dolphins, 17-7 (M)
    Dolphins, 20-3 (B)
2004—Bills, 20-13 (B)
    Bills, 42-32 (M)
2005—Bills, 20-14 (B)
    Dolphins, 24-23 (M)
2006—Bills, 16-6 (M)
    Bills, 21-0 (B)
2007—Bills, 13-10 (M)
    Bills, 38-17 (B)
2008—Dolphins, 25-16 (M)
    Dolphins, 16-3 (Toronto)
2009—Dolphins, 38-10 (M)
    Bills, 31-14 (B)
2010—Dolphins, 15-10 (B)
    Bills, 17-14 (M)
2011—Dolphins, 35-8 (M)
    Dolphins, 30-23 (B)
(RS Pts.—Dolphins 2,005, Bills 1,714)
(PS Pts.—Bills 127, Dolphins 90)
*AFC Divisional Playoff
**AFC Championship
***AFC First-Round Playoff

BUFFALO vs. MINNESOTA
RS: Vikings lead series, 8-4
1971—Vikings, 19-0 (M)
1975—Vikings, 35-13 (B)
1979—Vikings, 10-3 (M)
1982—Bills, 23-22 (B)
1985—Vikings, 27-20 (B)
1988—Bills, 13-10 (B)
1994—Vikings, 21-17 (M)
1997—Vikings, 34-13 (M)
2000—Vikings, 31-27 (M)
2002—Bills, 45-39 (M) OT
2006—Bills, 17-12 (B)
2010—Vikings, 38-14 (M)
(RS Pts.—Vikings 298, Bills 205)

BUFFALO vs. *NEW ENGLAND
RS: Patriots lead series, 61-41-1
PS: Patriots lead series, 1-0
1960—Bills, 13-0 (Bos)
    Bills, 38-14 (Buff)
1961—Patriots, 23-21 (Buff)
    Patriots, 52-21 (Bos)
1962—Tie, 28-28 (Buff)
    Patriots, 21-10 (Bos)
1963—Bills, 28-21 (Buff)
    Patriots, 17-7 (Bos)
    **Patriots, 26-8 (Buff)
1964—Patriots, 36-28 (Buff)
    Bills, 24-14 (Bos)
1965—Bills, 24-7 (Buff)
    Bills, 23-7 (Bos)
1966—Patriots, 20-10 (Buff)
    Patriots, 14-3 (Bos)

1967—Patriots, 23-0 (Buff)
Bills, 44-16 (Bos)
1968—Patriots, 16-7 (Buff)
Patriots, 23-6 (Bos)
1969—Bills, 23-16 (Buff)
Patriots, 35-21 (Bos)
1970—Bills, 45-10 (Bos)
Patriots, 14-10 (Buff)
1971—Patriots, 38-33 (NE)
Bills, 27-20 (Buff)
1972—Bills, 38-14 (Buff)
Bills, 27-24 (NE)
1973—Bills, 31-13 (NE)
Bills, 37-13 (Buff)
1974—Bills, 30-28 (Buff)
Bills, 29-28 (NE)
1975—Bills, 45-31 (Buff)
Bills, 34-14 (NE)
1976—Patriots, 26-22 (Buff)
Patriots, 20-10 (NE)
1977—Bills, 24-14 (NE)
Patriots, 20-7 (Buff)
1978—Bills, 14-10 (Buff)
Patriots, 26-24 (NE)
1979—Patriots, 26-6 (Buff)
Bills, 16-13 (NE) OT
1980—Bills, 31-13 (Buff)
Patriots, 24-2 (NE)
1981—Bills, 20-17 (Buff)
Bills, 19-10 (NE)
1982—Patriots, 30-19 (NE)
1983—Patriots, 31-0 (Buff)
Patriots, 21-7 (NE)
1984—Patriots, 21-17 (Buff)
Patriots, 38-10 (NE)
1985—Patriots, 17-14 (Buff)
Patriots, 14-3 (NE)
1986—Patriots, 23-3 (Buff)
Patriots, 22-19 (NE)
1987—Patriots, 14-7 (NE)
Patriots, 13-7 (Buff)
1988—Bills, 16-14 (NE)
Bills, 23-20 (Buff)
1989—Bills, 31-10 (Buff)
Patriots, 33-24 (NE)
1990—Bills, 27-10 (NE)
Bills, 14-0 (Buff)
1991—Bills, 22-17 (Buff)
Patriots, 16-13 (NE)
1992—Bills, 41-7 (NE)
Bills, 16-7 (Buff)
1993—Bills, 38-14 (Buff)
Bills, 13-10 (NE) OT
1994—Bills, 38-35 (NE)
Patriots, 41-17 (Buff)
1995—Patriots, 27-14 (NE)
Patriots, 35-25 (Buff)
1996—Bills, 17-10 (Buff)
Patriots, 28-25 (NE)
1997—Patriots, 33-6 (NE)
Patriots, 31-10 (Buff)
1998—Bills, 13-10 (Buff)
Patriots, 25-21 (NE)
1999—Bills, 17-7 (Buff)
Bills, 13-10 (NE) OT
2000—Bills, 16-13 (NE) OT
Patriots, 13-10 (Buff) OT
2001—Patriots, 21-11 (NE)
Patriots, 12-9 (Buff) OT
2002—Patriots, 38-7 (Buff)
Patriots, 27-17 (NE)
2003—Bills, 31-0 (Buff)

Patriots, 31-0 (NE)
2004—Patriots, 31-17 (Buff)
Patriots, 29-6 (NE)
2005—Patriots, 21-16 (NE)
Patriots, 35-7 (Buff)
2006—Patriots, 19-17 (NE)
Patriots, 28-6 (Buff)
2007—Patriots, 38-7 (NE)
Patriots, 56-10 (Buff)
2008—Patriots, 20-10 (NE)
Patriots, 13-0 (Buff)
2009—Patriots, 25-24 (NE)
Patriots, 17-10 (Buff)
2010—Patriots, 38-30 (NE)
Patriots, 34-3 (Buff)
2011—Bills, 34-31 (Buff)
Patriots, 49-21 (NE)
(RS Pts.—Patriots 2,206, Bills 1,875)
(PS Pts.—Patriots 26, Bills 8)
*Franchise in Boston prior to 1971
**Division Playoff

BUFFALO vs. NEW ORLEANS
RS: Saints lead series, 5-4
1973—Saints, 13-0 (NO)
1980—Bills, 35-26 (NO)
1983—Bills, 27-21 (B)
1989—Saints, 22-19 (B)
1992—Bills, 20-16 (NO)
1998—Bills, 45-33 (NO)
2001—Saints, 24-6 (B)
2005—Saints, 19-7 (San Antonio)
2009—Saints, 27-7 (B)
(RS Pts.—Saints 201, Bills 166)

BUFFALO vs. N.Y. GIANTS
RS: Bills lead series, 6-5
PS: Giants lead series, 1-0
1970—Giants, 20-6 (NY)
1975—Giants, 17-14 (B)
1978—Bills, 41-17 (B)
1987—Bills, 6-3 (B) OT
1990—Bills, 17-13 (NY)
*Giants, 20-19 (Tampa)
1993—Bills, 17-14 (B)
1996—Bills, 23-20 (NY) OT
1999—Giants, 19-17 (B)
2003—Bills, 24-7 (NY)
2007—Giants, 38-21 (B)
2011—Giants, 27-24 (NY)
(RS Pts.—Bills 210, Giants 195)
(PS Pts.—Giants 20, Bills 19)
*Super Bowl XXV

BUFFALO vs. *N.Y. JETS
RS: Bills lead series, 53-49
PS: Bills lead series, 1-0
1960—Titans, 27-3 (NY)
Titans, 17-13 (B)
1961—Bills, 41-31 (B)
Titans, 21-14 (NY)
1962—Titans, 17-6 (B)
Bills, 20-3 (NY)
1963—Bills, 45-14 (B)
Bills, 19-10 (NY)
1964—Bills, 34-24 (B)
Bills, 20-7 (NY)
1965—Bills, 33-21 (B)
Jets, 14-12 (NY)
1966—Bills, 33-23 (NY)
Bills, 14-3 (B)
1967—Bills, 20-17 (B)
Jets, 20-10 (NY)
1968—Bills, 37-35 (B)
Jets, 25-21 (NY)

1969—Jets, 33-19 (B)
Jets, 16-6 (NY)
1970—Bills, 34-31 (B)
Bills, 10-6 (NY)
1971—Jets, 28-17 (NY)
Jets, 20-7 (B)
1972—Jets, 41-24 (B)
Jets, 41-3 (NY)
1973—Bills, 9-7 (B)
Bills, 34-14 (NY)
1974—Bills, 16-12 (B)
Bills, 20-10 (NY)
1975—Bills, 42-14 (B)
Bills, 24-23 (NY)
1976—Jets, 17-14 (NY)
Bills, 19-14 (B)
1977—Jets, 24-19 (B)
Bills, 14-10 (NY)
1978—Jets, 21-20 (B)
Jets, 45-14 (NY)
1979—Bills, 46-31 (B)
Bills, 14-12 (NY)
1980—Bills, 20-10 (B)
Bills, 31-24 (NY)
1981—Bills, 31-0 (B)
Jets, 33-14 (NY)
**Bills, 31-27 (NY)
1983—Jets, 34-10 (B)
Bills, 24-17 (NY)
1984—Jets, 28-26 (B)
Jets, 21-17 (NY)
1985—Jets, 42-3 (NY)
Bills, 27-7 (B)
1986—Jets, 28-24 (B)
Jets, 14-13 (NY)
1987—Jets, 31-28 (B)
Bills, 17-14 (NY)
1988—Bills, 37-14 (NY)
Bills, 9-6 (B) OT
1989—Bills, 34-3 (B)
Bills, 37-0 (NY)
1990—Bills, 30-7 (NY)
Bills, 30-27 (B)
1991—Bills, 23-20 (NY)
Bills, 24-13 (B)
1992—Bills, 24-20 (NY)
Jets, 24-17 (B)
1993—Bills, 19-10 (NY)
Bills, 16-14 (B)
1994—Jets, 23-3 (B)
Jets, 22-17 (NY)
1995—Bills, 29-10 (B)
Bills, 28-26 (NY)
1996—Bills, 25-22 (NY)
Bills, 35-10 (B)
1997—Bills, 28-22 (NY)
Bills, 20-10 (B)
1998—Bills, 34-12 (N)
Jets, 17-10 (B)
1999—Bills, 17-3 (B)
Jets, 17-7 (NY)
2000—Jets, 27-14 (NY)
Bills, 23-20 (B)
2001—Jets, 42-36 (B)
Bills, 14-9 (NY)
2002—Jets, 37-31 (B) OT
Jets, 31-13 (NY)
2003—Jets, 30-3 (NY)
Bills, 17-6 (B)
2004—Jets, 16-14 (NY)
Bills, 22-17 (B)
2005—Bills, 27-17 (B)

Jets, 30-26 (NY)
2006—Jets, 28-20 (B)
Bills, 31-13 (NY)
2007—Bills, 17-14 (B)
Bills, 13-3 (NY)
2008—Jets, 26-17 (B)
Jets, 31-27 (NY)
2009—Bills, 16-13 (NY) OT
Jets, 19-13 (Toronto)
2010—Jets, 38-14 (B)
Jets, 38-7 (NY)
2011—Jets, 27-11 (B)
Jets, 28-24 (NY)
(RS Pts.—Jets 2,071, Bills 2,051)
(PS Pts.—Bills 31, Jets 27)
*Jets known as Titans prior to 1963
**AFC First-Round Playoff
BUFFALO vs. *OAKLAND
RS: Raiders lead series, 19-17
PS: Bills lead series, 2-0
1960—Bills, 38-9 (B)
Raiders, 20-7 (O)
1961—Raiders, 31-22 (B)
Bills, 26-21 (O)
1962—Bills, 14-6 (B)
Bills, 10-6 (O)
1963—Raiders, 35-17 (O)
Bills, 12-0 (B)
1964—Bills, 23-20 (B)
Raiders, 16-13 (O)
1965—Bills, 17-12 (B)
Bills, 17-14 (O)
1966—Bills, 31-10 (O)
1967—Raiders, 24-20 (B)
Raiders, 28-21 (O)
1968—Raiders, 48-6 (B)
Raiders, 13-10 (O)
1969—Raiders, 50-21 (O)
1972—Raiders, 28-16 (O)
1974—Bills, 21-20 (B)
1977—Raiders, 34-13 (O)
1980—Bills, 24-7 (B)
1983—Raiders, 27-24 (B)
1987—Raiders, 34-21 (LA)
1988—Bills, 37-21 (B)
1990—Bills, 38-24 (B)
**Bills, 51-3 (B)
1991—Bills, 30-27 (LA) OT
1992—Raiders, 20-3 (LA)
1993—Raiders, 25-24 (B)
***Bills, 29-23 (B)
1998—Bills, 44-21 (B)
1999—Raiders, 20-14 (B)
2002—Raiders, 49-31 (B)
2004—Raiders, 13-10 (O)
2005—Raiders, 38-17 (O)
2008—Bills, 24-23 (B)
2011—Bills, 38-35 (B)
(RS Pts.—Raiders 829, Bills 754)
(PS Pts.—Bills 80, Raiders 26)
*Franchise in Los Angeles from 1982-1994
**AFC Championship
***AFC Divisional Playoff
BUFFALO vs. PHILADELPHIA
RS: Series tied, 6-6
1973—Bills, 27-26 (B)
1981—Eagles, 20-14 (B)
1984—Eagles, 27-17 (B)
1985—Eagles, 21-17 (P)
1987—Eagles, 17-7 (P)
1990—Bills, 30-23 (B)
1993—Bills, 10-7 (P)

1996—Bills, 24-17 (P)
1999—Bills, 26-0 (B)
2003—Eagles, 23-13 (B)
2007—Eagles, 17-9 (P)
2011—Bills, 31-24 (B)
(RS Pts.—Bills 225, Eagles 222)
BUFFALO vs. PITTSBURGH
RS: Steelers lead series, 12-8
PS: Steelers lead series, 2-1
1970—Steelers, 23-10 (P)
1972—Steelers, 38-21 (B)
1974—*Steelers, 32-14 (P)
1975—Bills, 30-21 (P)
1978—Steelers, 28-17 (B)
1979—Steelers, 28-0 (P)
1980—Bills, 28-13 (B)
1982—Bills, 13-0 (B)
1985—Steelers, 30-24 (P)
1986—Bills, 16-12 (B)
1988—Bills, 36-28 (B)
1991—Bills, 52-34 (B)
1992—Bills, 28-20 (B)
*Bills, 24-3 (P)
1993—Steelers, 23-0 (P)
1994—Steelers, 23-10 (P)
1995—*Steelers, 40-21 (P)
1996—Steelers, 24-6 (P)
1999—Bills, 24-21 (B)
2001—Steelers, 20-3 (B)
2004—Steelers, 29-24 (B)
2007—Steelers, 26-3 (P)
2010—Steelers, 19-16 (B) OT
(RS Pts.—Steelers 460, Bills 361)
(PS Pts.—Steelers 75, Bills 59)
*AFC Divisional Playoff
BUFFALO vs. *ST. LOUIS
RS: Bills lead series, 6-4
1970—Rams, 19-0 (B)
1974—Rams, 19-14 (LA)
1980—Bills, 10-7 (B) OT
1983—Rams, 41-17 (LA)
1989—Bills, 23-20 (B)
1992—Bills, 40-7 (B)
1995—Bills, 45-27 (StL)
1998—Rams, 34-33 (B)
2004—Bills, 37-17 (B)
2008—Bills, 31-14 (StL)
(RS Pts.—Bills 250, Rams 205)
*Franchise in Los Angeles prior to 1995
BUFFALO vs. *SAN DIEGO
RS: Chargers lead series, 21-10-2
PS: Bills lead series, 2-1
1960—Chargers, 24-10 (B)
Bills, 32-3 (LA)
1961—Chargers, 19-11 (B)
Chargers, 28-10 (SD)
1962—Bills, 35-10 (B)
Bills, 40-20 (SD)
1963—Chargers, 14-10 (SD)
Chargers, 23-13 (B)
1964—Bills, 30-3 (B)
Bills, 27-24 (SD)
**Bills, 20-7 (B)
1965—Chargers, 34-3 (B)
Tie, 20-20 (SD)
**Bills, 23-0 (SD)
1966—Chargers, 27-7 (SD)
Tie, 17-17 (B)
1967—Chargers, 37-17 (B)
1968—Chargers, 21-6 (B)
1969—Chargers, 45-6 (SD)
1971—Chargers, 20-3 (SD)

1973—Chargers, 34-7 (SD)
1976—Chargers, 34-13 (B)
1979—Chargers, 27-19 (SD)
1980—Bills, 26-24 (SD)
***Chargers, 20-14 (SD)
1981—Bills, 28-27 (SD)
1985—Chargers, 14-9 (B)
Chargers, 40-7 (SD)
1998—Chargers, 16-14 (SD)
2000—Bills, 27-24 (B) OT
2001—Chargers, 27-24 (SD)
2002—Bills, 20-13 (B)
2005—Chargers, 48-10 (SD)
2006—Chargers, 24-21 (B)
2008—Bills, 23-14 (B)
2011—Chargers, 37-10 (B)
(RS Pts.—Chargers 792, Bills 555)
(PS Pts.—Bills 57, Chargers 27)
*Franchise in Los Angeles prior to 1961
**AFL Championship
***AFC Divisional Playoff
BUFFALO vs. SAN FRANCISCO
RS: Series tied, 5-5
1972—Bills, 27-20 (B)
1980—Bills, 18-13 (SF)
1983—49ers, 23-10 (B)
1989—49ers, 21-10 (SF)
1992—Bills, 34-31 (SF)
1995—49ers, 27-17 (SF)
1998—Bills, 26-21 (B)
2001—49ers, 35-0 (SF)
2004—Bills, 41-7 (SF)
2008—49ers, 10-3 (B)
(RS Pts.—49ers 208, Bills 186)
BUFFALO vs. SEATTLE
RS: Seahawks lead series, 6-5
1977—Seahawks, 56-17 (S)
1984—Seahawks, 31-28 (S)
1988—Bills, 13-3 (S)
1989—Seahawks, 17-16 (S)
1995—Bills, 27-21 (B)
1996—Seahawks, 26-18 (S)
1999—Seahawks, 26-16 (S)
2000—Bills, 42-23 (B)
2001—Seahawks, 23-20 (B)
2004—Bills, 38-9 (S)
2008—Bills, 34-10 (B)
(RS Pts.—Bills 269, Seahawks 245)
BUFFALO vs. TAMPA BAY
RS: Buccaneers lead series, 6-3
1976—Bills, 14-9 (TB)
1978—Buccaneers, 31-10 (TB)
1982—Buccaneers, 24-23 (TB)
1986—Buccaneers, 34-28 (TB)
1988—Buccaneers, 10-5 (TB)
1991—Bills, 17-10 (TB)
2000—Buccaneers, 31-17 (TB)
2005—Buccaneers, 19-3 (TB)
2009—Bills, 33-20 (B)
(RS Pts.—Buccaneers 188, Bills 150)
BUFFALO vs. *TENNESSEE
RS: Titans lead series, 26-14
PS: Bills lead series, 2-1
1960—Bills, 25-24 (B)
Oilers, 31-23 (H)
1961—Bills, 22-12 (H)
Oilers, 28-16 (B)
1962—Oilers, 28-23 (B)
Oilers, 17-14 (H)
1963—Oilers, 31-20 (B)
Oilers, 28-14 (H)
1964—Bills, 48-17 (H)

Bills, 24-10 (B)
1965—Oilers, 19-17 (B)
Bills, 29-18 (H)
1966—Bills, 27-20 (B)
Bills, 42-20 (H)
1967—Oilers, 20-3 (B)
Oilers, 10-3 (H)
1968—Oilers, 30-7 (B)
Oilers, 35-6 (H)
1969—Oilers, 17-3 (B)
Oilers, 28-14 (H)
1971—Oilers, 20-14 (B)
1974—Oilers, 21-9 (B)
1976—Oilers, 13-3 (B)
1978—Oilers, 17-10 (H)
1983—Bills, 30-13 (B)
1985—Bills, 20-0 (B)
1986—Oilers, 16-7 (H)
1987—Bills, 34-30 (B)
1988—**Bills, 17-10 (B)
1989—Bills, 47-41 (H) OT
1990—Oilers, 27-24 (H)
1992—Oilers, 27-3 (H)
***Bills, 41-38 (B) OT
1993—Bills, 35-7 (B)
1994—Bills, 15-7 (H)
1995—Oilers, 28-17 (B)
1997—Oilers, 31-14 (T)
1999—***Titans, 22-16 (T)
2000—Bills, 16-13 (B)
2003—Titans, 28-26 (T)
2006—Titans, 30-29 (B)
2009—Titans, 41-17 (T)
2011—Titans, 23-17 (B)
(RS Pts.—Titans 876, Bills 767)
(PS Pts.—Bills 74, Titans 70)
*Franchise in Houston prior to 1997;
known as Oilers prior to 1999
**AFC Divisional Playoff
***AFC First-Round Playoff
BUFFALO vs. WASHINGTON
RS: Bills lead series, 8-4
PS: Redskins lead series, 1-0
1972—Bills, 24-17 (W)
1977—Redskins, 10-0 (B)
1981—Bills, 21-14 (B)
1984—Redskins, 41-14 (W)
1987—Redskins, 27-7 (B)
1990—Redskins, 29-14 (W)
1991—*Redskins, 37-24 (Minneapolis)
1993—Bills, 24-10 (B)
1996—Bills, 38-13 (B)
1999—Bills, 34-17 (W)
2003—Bills, 24-7 (B)
2007—Bills, 17-16 (W)
2011—Bills, 23-0 (Toronto)
(RS Pts.—Bills 240, Redskins 201)
(PS Pts.—Redskins 37, Bills 24)
*Super Bowl XXVI

CAROLINA vs. ARIZONA
RS: Panthers lead series, 8-3
PS: Cardinals lead series, 1-0;
See Arizona vs. Carolina
CAROLINA vs. ATLANTA
RS: Falcons lead series, 22-12;
See Atlanta vs. Carolina
CAROLINA vs. BALTIMORE
RS: Panthers lead series, 3-1;
See Baltimore vs. Carolina
CAROLINA vs. BUFFALO
RS: Bills lead series, 4-1;

See Buffalo vs. Carolina
CAROLINA vs. CHICAGO
RS: Bears lead series, 4-2
PS: Panthers lead series, 1-0
1995—Bears, 31-27 (Chi)
2002—Panthers, 24-14 (Car)
2005—Bears, 13-3 (Chi)
*Panthers, 29-21 (Chi)
2008—Panthers, 20-17 (Car)
2010—Bears, 23-6 (Car)
2011—Bears, 34-29 (Chi)
(RS Pts.—Bears 132, Panthers 109)
(PS Pts.—Panthers 29, Bears 21)
*NFC Divisional Playoff
CAROLINA vs. CINCINNATI
RS: Series tied, 2-2
1999—Panthers, 27-3 (Car)
2002—Panthers, 52-31 (Car)
2006—Bengals, 17-14 (Cin)
2010—Bengals, 20-7 (Car)
(RS Pts.—Panthers 100, Bengals 71)
CAROLINA vs. CLEVELAND
RS: Panthers lead series, 3-1
1999—Panthers, 31-17 (Cle)
2002—Panthers, 13-6 (Cle)
2006—Panthers, 20-12 (Car)
2010—Browns, 24-23 (Cle)
(RS Pts.—Panthers 87, Browns 59)
CAROLINA vs. DALLAS
RS: Cowboys lead series, 8-1
PS: Panthers lead series, 2-0
1996—*Panthers, 26-17 (C)
1997—Panthers, 23-13 (D)
1998—Cowboys, 27-20 (D)
2000—Cowboys, 16-13 (C) OT
2002—Cowboys, 14-13 (D)
2003—Cowboys, 24-20 (D)
**Panthers, 29-10 (C)
2005—Cowboys, 24-20 (C)
2006—Cowboys, 35-14 (C)
2007—Cowboys, 20-13 (C)
2009—Cowboys, 21-7 (D)
(RS Pts.—Cowboys 194, Panthers 143)
(PS Pts.—Panthers 55, Cowboys 27)
*NFC Divisional Playoff
*NFC First-Round Playoff
CAROLINA vs. DENVER
RS: Broncos lead series, 2-1
1997—Broncos, 34-0 (D)
2004—Broncos, 20-17 (D)
2008—Panthers, 30-10 (C)
(RS Pts.—Broncos 64, Panthers 47)
CAROLINA vs. DETROIT
RS: Panthers lead series, 4-2
1999—Lions, 24-9 (C)
2002—Panthers, 31-7 (C)
2003—Panthers, 20-14 (C)
2005—Panthers, 21-20 (D)
2008—Panthers, 31-22 (C)
2011—Lions, 49-35 (D)
(RS Pts.—Panthers 147, Lions 136)
CAROLINA vs. GREEN BAY
RS: Packers lead series, 7-4
PS: Packers lead series, 1-0
1996—*Packers, 30-13 (GB)
1997—Packers, 31-10 (C)
1998—Packers, 37-30 (C)
1999—Panthers, 33-31 (GB)
2000—Panthers, 31-14 (C)
2001—Packers, 28-7 (C)
2002—Packers, 17-14 (GB)
2004—Packers, 24-14 (C)

2005—Panthers, 32-29 (C)
2007—Packers, 31-17 (GB)
2008—Panthers, 35-31 (GB)
2011—Packers, 30-23 (C)
(RS Pts.—Packers 303, Panthers 246)
(PS Pts.—Packers 30, Panthers 13)
*NFC Championship
CAROLINA vs. HOUSTON
RS: Texans lead series, 2-1
2003—Texans, 14-10 (H)
2007—Texans, 34-21 (C)
2011—Panthers, 28-13 (H)
(RS Pts.—Texans 61, Panthers 59)
CAROLINA vs. INDIANAPOLIS
RS: Panthers lead series, 4-1
1995—Panthers, 13-10 (C)
1998—Panthers, 27-19 (I)
2003—Panthers, 23-20 (I) OT
2007—Colts, 31-7 (C)
2011—Panthers, 27-19 (I)
(RS Pts.—Colts 99, Panthers 97)
CAROLINA vs. JACKSONVILLE
RS: Jaguars lead series, 3-2
1996—Jaguars, 24-14 (J)
1999—Jaguars, 22-20 (C)
2003—Panthers, 24-23 (C)
2007—Jaguars, 37-6 (J)
2011—Panthers, 16-10 (C)
(RS Pts.—Jaguars 116, Panthers 80)
CAROLINA vs. KANSAS CITY
RS: Series tied, 2-2
1997—Chiefs, 35-14 (C)
2000—Chiefs, 15-14 (KC)
2004—Panthers, 28-17 (KC)
2008—Panthers, 34-0 (C)
(RS Pts.—Panthers 90, Chiefs 67)
CAROLINA vs. MIAMI
RS: Dolphins lead series, 4-0
1998—Dolphins, 13-9 (C)
2001—Dolphins, 23-6 (M)
2005—Dolphins, 27-24 (M)
2009—Dolphins, 24-17 (C)
(RS Pts.—Dolphins 87, Panthers 56)
CAROLINA vs. MINNESOTA
RS: Vikings lead series, 6-4
1996—Vikings, 14-12 (M)
1997—Vikings, 21-14 (M)
2000—Vikings, 31-17 (M)
2001—Panthers, 24-13 (M)
2002—Panthers, 21-14 (M)
2005—Panthers, 38-13 (C)
2006—Vikings, 16-13 (M) OT
2008—Vikings, 20-10 (M)
2009—Panthers, 26-7 (C)
2011—Vikings, 24-21 (C)
(RS Pts.—Panthers 196, Vikings 173)
CAROLINA vs. NEW ENGLAND
RS: Series tied, 2-2
PS: Patriots lead series, 1-0
1995—Panthers, 20-17 (NE) OT
2001—Patriots, 38-6 (C)
2003—*Patriots, 32-29 (Houston)
2005—Panthers, 27-17 (C)
2009—Patriots, 20-10 (NE)
(RS Pts.—Patriots 92, Panthers 63)
(PS Pts.—Patriots 32, Panthers 29)
*Super Bowl XXXVIII
CAROLINA vs. NEW ORLEANS
RS: Series tied, 17-17
1995—Panthers, 20-3 (C)
Saints, 34-26 (NO)
1996—Panthers, 22-20 (NO)

Panthers, 19-7 (C)
1997—Panthers, 13-0 (NO)
Saints, 16-13 (C)
1998—Saints, 19-14 (NO)
Panthers, 31-17 (C)
1999—Saints, 19-10 (NO)
Panthers, 45-13 (C)
2000—Saints, 24-6 (NO)
Saints, 20-10 (C)
2001—Saints, 27-25 (C)
Saints, 27-23 (NO)
2002—Saints, 34-24 (C)
Panthers, 10-6 (NO)
2003—Panthers, 19-13 (C)
Panthers, 23-20 (NO) OT
2004—Panthers, 32-21 (NO)
Saints, 21-18 (C)
2005—Saints, 23-20 (C)
Panthers, 27-10 (Baton Rouge)
2006—Panthers, 21-18 (C)
Panthers, 31-21 (NO)
2007—Panthers, 16-13 (NO)
Saints, 31-6 (C)
2008—Panthers, 30-7 (C)
Panthers, 33-31 (NO)
2009—Saints, 30-20 (NO)
Panthers, 23-10 (C)
2010—Saints, 16-14 (NO)
Saints, 34-3 (C)
2011—Saints, 30-27 (C)
Saints, 45-17 (NO)
(RS Pts.—Panthers 691, Saints 680)
CAROLINA vs. N.Y. GIANTS
RS: Series tied, 3-3
PS: Panthers lead series, 1-0
1996—Panthers, 27-17 (C)
2003—Panthers, 37-24 (NY)
2005—*Panthers, 23-0 (NY)
2006—Giants, 27-13 (C)
2008—Giants, 34-28 (NY) OT
2009—Panthers, 41-9 (NY)
2010—Panthers, 31-18 (NY)
(RS Pts.—Panthers 164, Giants 142)
(PS Pts.—Panthers 23, Giants 0)
NFC First-Round Playoff
CAROLINA vs. N.Y. JETS
RS: Jets lead series, 3-2
1995—Panthers, 26-15 (C)
1998—Jets, 48-21 (NY)
2001—Jets, 13-12 (C)
2005—Panthers, 30-3 (C)
2009—Jets, 17-6 (NY)
(RS Pts.—Jets 96, Panthers 95)
CAROLINA vs. OAKLAND
RS: Series tied, 2-2
1997—Panthers, 38-14 (C)
2000—Raiders, 52-9 (O)
2004—Raiders, 27-24 (C)
2008—Panthers, 17-6 (O)
(RS Pts.— Raiders 99, Panthers 88)
CAROLINA vs. PHILADELPHIA
RS: Eagles lead series, 5-1
PS: Panthers lead series, 1-0
1996—Eagles, 20-9 (P)
1999—Panthers, 33-7 (C)
2003—Eagles, 25-16 (C)
*Panthers, 14-3 (P)
2004—Eagles, 30-8 (P)
2006—Eagles, 27-24 (P)
2009—Eagles, 38-10 (C)
(RS Pts.—Eagles 147, Panthers 100)
(PS Pts.—Panthers 14, Eagles 3)

NFC Championship
CAROLINA vs. PITTSBURGH
RS: Steelers lead series, 4-1
1996—Panthers, 18-14 (C)
1999—Steelers, 30-20 (P)
2002—Steelers, 30-14 (P)
2006—Steelers, 37-3 (C)
2010—Steelers, 27-3 (P)
(RS Pts.—Steelers 138, Panthers 58)
CAROLINA vs. ST. LOUIS
RS: Panthers lead series, 10-8
PS: Panthers lead series, 1-0
1995—Rams, 31-10 (C)
Rams, 28-17 (StL)
1996—Panthers, 45-13 (C)
Panthers, 20-10 (StL)
1997—Panthers, 16-10 (C)
Rams, 30-18 (C)
1998—Panthers, 24-20 (StL)
Panthers, 20-13 (C)
1999—Rams, 35-10 (StL)
Rams, 34-21 (C)
2000—Panthers, 27-24 (StL)
Panthers, 16-3 (C)
2001—Rams, 48-14 (StL)
Rams, 38-32 (C)
2003—*Panthers, 29-23 (StL) 2OT
2004—Panthers, 20-7 (C)
2006—Panthers, 15-0 (C)
2007—Panthers, 27-13 (StL)
2010—Rams, 20-10 (StL)
(RS Pts.—Rams 377, Panthers 362)
(PS Pts.—Panthers 29, Rams 23)
NFC Divisional Playoff
CAROLINA vs. SAN DIEGO
RS: Panthers lead series, 3-1
1997—Panthers, 26-7 (SD)
2000—Panthers, 30-22 (C)
2004—Chargers, 17-6 (C)
2008—Panthers, 26-24 (SD)
(RS Pts.—Panthers 88, Chargers 70)
CAROLINA vs. SAN FRANCISCO
RS: Panthers lead series, 10-7
1995—Panthers, 13-7 (SF)
49ers, 31-10 (C)
1996—Panthers, 23-7 (C)
Panthers, 30-24 (SF)
1997—49ers, 34-21 (C)
49ers, 27-19 (SF)
1998—49ers, 25-23 (SF)
49ers, 31-28 (C) OT
1999—Panthers, 31-29 (SF)
Panthers, 41-24 (C)
2000—Panthers, 38-22 (SF)
Panthers, 34-16 (C)
2001—49ers, 24-14 (SF)
49ers, 25-22 (C) OT
2004—Panthers, 37-27 (SF)
2007—Panthers, 31-14 (C)
2010—Panthers, 23-20 (C)
(RS Pts.—Panthers 438, 49ers 387)
CAROLINA vs. SEATTLE
RS: Series tied, 2-2
PS: Seahawks lead series, 1-0
2000—Panthers, 26-3 (C)
2004—Seahawks, 23-17 (S)
2005—*Seahawks, 34-14 (S)
2007—Panthers, 13-10 (C)
2010—Seahawks, 31-14 (S)
(RS Pts.—Panthers 70, Seahawks 67)
(PS Pts.—Seahawks 34, Panthers 14)
NFC Championship

CAROLINA vs. TAMPA BAY
RS: Panthers lead series, 14-9
1995—Buccaneers, 20-13 (C)
1996—Panthers, 24-0 (C)
1998—Buccaneers, 16-13 (TB)
2002—Buccaneers, 12-9 (C)
Buccaneers, 23-10 (TB)
2003—Panthers, 12-9 (TB) OT
Panthers, 27-24 (C)
2004—Panthers, 21-14 (C)
Panthers, 37-20 (TB)
2005—Panthers, 34-14 (TB)
Buccaneers, 20-10 (C)
2006—Panthers, 26-24 (TB)
Panthers, 24-10 (C)
2007—Buccaneers, 20-7 (C)
Panthers, 31-23 (TB)
2008—Buccaneers, 27-3 (TB)
Panthers, 38-23 (C)
2009—Panthers, 28-21 (TB)
Panthers, 16-6 (C)
2010—Buccaneers, 20-7 (C)
Buccaneers, 31-16 (TB)
2011—Panthers, 38-19 (TB)
Panthers, 48-16 (C)
(RS Pts.—Panthers 492, Buccaneers 412)
CAROLINA vs. *TENNESSEE
RS: Titans lead series, 3-1
1996—Panthers, 31-6 (H)
2003—Titans, 37-17 (C)
2007—Titans, 20-7 (T)
2011—Titans, 30-3 (C)
(RS Pts.—Titans 93, Panthers 58)
*Franchise in Houston prior to 1997;
known as Oilers prior to 1999*
CAROLINA vs. WASHINGTON
RS: Redskins lead series, 7-3
1995—Redskins, 20-17 (W)
1997—Redskins, 24-10 (C)
1998—Redskins, 28-25 (C)
1999—Redskins, 38-36 (W)
2000—Panthers, 20-17 (W)
2001—Redskins, 17-14 (W) OT
2003—Panthers, 20-17 (C)
2006—Redskins, 17-13 (W)
2009—Panthers, 20-17 (C)
2011—Panthers, 33-20 (C)
(RS Pts.—Redskins 218, Panthers 205)

CHICAGO vs. ARIZONA
RS: Bears lead series, 55-27-6;
See Arizona vs. Chicago
CHICAGO vs. ATLANTA
RS: Bears lead series, 13-12;
See Atlanta vs. Chicago
CHICAGO vs. BALTIMORE
RS: Series tied, 2-2;
See Baltimore vs. Chicago
CHICAGO vs. BUFFALO
RS: Bears lead series, 7-4;
See Buffalo vs. Chicago
CHICAGO vs. CAROLINA
RS: Bears lead series, 4-2
PS: Panthers lead series, 1-0;
See Carolina vs. Chicago
CHICAGO vs. CINCINNATI
RS: Bengals lead series, 6-3
1972—Bengals, 13-3 (Chi)
1980—Bengals, 17-14 (Chi) OT
1986—Bears, 44-7 (Cin)
1989—Bears, 17-14 (Chi)
1992—Bengals, 31-28 (Chi) OT

1995—Bengals, 16-10 (Cin)
2001—Bears, 24-0 (Cin)
2005—Bengals, 24-7 (Chi)
2009—Bengals, 45-10 (Cin)
(RS Pts.—Bengals 167, Bears 157)

CHICAGO vs. CLEVELAND
RS: Browns lead series, 9-5
1951—Browns, 42-21 (Cle)
1954—Browns, 39-10 (Chi)
1960—Browns, 42-0 (Cle)
1961—Bears, 17-14 (Chi)
1967—Browns, 24-0 (Cle)
1969—Browns, 28-24 (Chi)
1972—Bears, 17-0 (Cle)
1980—Browns, 27-21 (Cle)
1986—Bears, 41-31 (Chi)
1989—Browns, 27-7 (Cle)
1992—Browns, 27-14 (Cle)
2001—Bears, 27-21 (Chi) OT
2005—Browns, 20-10 (Cle)
2009—Bears, 30-6 (Chi)
(RS Pts.—Browns 348, Bears 239)

CHICAGO vs. DALLAS
RS: Cowboys lead series, 11-9
PS: Cowboys lead series, 2-0
1960—Bears, 17-7 (C)
1962—Bears, 34-33 (D)
1964—Cowboys, 24-10 (C)
1968—Cowboys, 34-3 (C)
1971—Bears, 23-19 (C)
1973—Cowboys, 20-17 (C)
1976—Cowboys, 31-21 (D)
1977—*Cowboys, 37-7 (D)
1979—Cowboys, 24-20 (D)
1981—Cowboys, 10-9 (D)
1984—Cowboys, 23-14 (C)
1985—Bears, 44-0 (D)
1986—Bears, 24-10 (D)
1988—Bears, 17-7 (C)
1991—**Cowboys, 17-13 (C)
1992—Cowboys, 27-14 (D)
1996—Bears, 22-6 (C)
1997—Cowboys, 27-3 (D)
1998—Bears, 13-12 (C)
2004—Cowboys, 21-7 (D)
2007—Cowboys, 34-10 (C)
2010—Bears, 27-20 (D)
(RS Pts.—Cowboys 389, Bears 349)
(PS Pts.—Cowboys 54, Bears 20)
*NFC Divisional Playoff
**NFC First-Round Playoff

CHICAGO vs. DENVER
RS: Series tied, 7-7
1971—Broncos, 6-3 (D)
1973—Bears, 33-14 (D)
1976—Broncos, 28-14 (C)
1978—Broncos, 16-7 (D)
1981—Bears, 35-24 (C)
1983—Bears, 31-14 (C)
1984—Bears, 27-0 (C)
1987—Broncos, 31-29 (D)
1990—Bears, 16-13 (D) OT
1993—Broncos, 13-3 (C)
1996—Broncos, 17-12 (D)
2003—Bears, 19-10 (D)
2007—Bears, 37-34 (C) OT
2011—Broncos, 13-10 (D) OT
(RS Pts.—Bears 276, Broncos 233)

CHICAGO vs. *DETROIT
RS: Bears lead series, 94-65-5
1930—Spartans, 7-6 (P)
    Bears, 14-6 (C)

1931—Bears, 9-6 (C)
    Spartans, 3-0 (P)
1932—Tie, 13-13 (C)
    Tie, 7-7 (P)
    Bears, 9-0 (C)
1933—Bears, 17-14 (C)
    Bears, 17-7 (P)
1934—Bears, 19-16 (C)
    Bears, 10-7 (C)
1935—Tie, 20-20 (C)
    Lions, 14-2 (D)
1936—Bears, 12-10 (C)
    Lions, 13-7 (D)
1937—Bears, 28-20 (C)
    Bears, 13-0 (D)
1938—Lions, 13-7 (C)
    Lions, 14-7 (D)
1939—Lions, 10-0 (C)
    Bears, 23-13 (D)
1940—Bears, 7-0 (C)
    Lions, 17-14 (D)
1941—Bears, 49-0 (C)
    Bears, 24-7 (D)
1942—Bears, 16-0 (C)
    Bears, 42-0 (D)
1943—Bears, 27-21 (C)
    Bears, 35-14 (C)
1944—Tie, 21-21 (C)
    Lions, 41-21 (D)
1945—Lions, 16-10 (D)
    Lions, 35-28 (C)
1946—Bears, 42-6 (C)
    Bears, 45-24 (D)
1947—Bears, 33-24 (C)
    Bears, 34-14 (D)
1948—Bears, 28-0 (C)
    Bears, 42-14 (D)
1949—Bears, 27-24 (C)
    Bears, 28-7 (D)
1950—Bears, 35-21 (D)
    Bears, 6-3 (C)
1951—Bears, 28-23 (D)
    Lions, 41-28 (C)
1952—Bears, 24-23 (C)
    Lions, 45-21 (D)
1953—Lions, 20-16 (C)
    Lions, 13-7 (D)
1954—Lions, 48-23 (D)
    Bears, 28-24 (C)
1955—Bears, 24-14 (D)
    Bears, 21-20 (C)
1956—Lions, 42-10 (D)
    Bears, 38-21 (C)
1957—Bears, 27-7 (D)
    Lions, 21-13 (C)
1958—Bears, 20-7 (D)
    Bears, 21-16 (C)
1959—Bears, 24-14 (D)
    Bears, 25-14 (C)
1960—Bears, 28-7 (C)
    Lions, 36-0 (D)
1961—Bears, 31-17 (D)
    Lions, 16-15 (C)
1962—Lions, 11-3 (D)
    Bears, 3-0 (C)
1963—Bears, 37-21 (D)
    Bears, 24-14 (C)
1964—Lions, 10-0 (C)
    Bears, 27-24 (D)
1965—Bears, 38-10 (C)
    Bears, 17-10 (D)
1966—Lions, 14-3 (D)

    Tie, 10-10 (C)
1967—Bears, 14-3 (C)
    Bears, 27-13 (D)
1968—Lions, 42-0 (D)
    Lions, 28-10 (C)
1969—Lions, 13-7 (D)
    Lions, 20-3 (C)
1970—Lions, 28-14 (D)
    Lions, 16-10 (C)
1971—Bears, 28-23 (D)
    Lions, 28-3 (C)
1972—Lions, 38-24 (C)
    Lions, 14-0 (D)
1973—Lions, 30-7 (C)
    Lions, 40-7 (D)
1974—Bears, 17-9 (C)
    Lions, 34-17 (D)
1975—Lions, 27-7 (D)
    Bears, 25-21 (C)
1976—Bears, 10-3 (C)
    Lions, 14-10 (D)
1977—Bears, 30-20 (C)
    Bears, 31-14 (D)
1978—Bears, 19-0 (D)
    Lions, 21-17 (C)
1979—Bears, 35-7 (C)
    Lions, 20-0 (D)
1980—Bears, 24-7 (C)
    Bears, 23-17 (D) OT
1981—Lions, 48-17 (D)
    Lions, 23-7 (C)
1982—Lions, 17-10 (D)
    Bears, 20-17 (C)
1983—Lions, 31-17 (D)
    Lions, 38-17 (C)
1984—Bears, 16-14 (C)
    Bears, 30-13 (D)
1985—Bears, 24-3 (C)
    Bears, 37-17 (D)
1986—Bears, 13-7 (C)
    Bears, 16-13 (D)
1987—Bears, 30-10 (C)
1988—Bears, 24-7 (D)
    Bears, 13-12 (C)
1989—Bears, 47-27 (D)
    Lions, 27-17 (C)
1990—Bears, 23-17 (C) OT
    Lions, 38-21 (D)
1991—Bears, 20-10 (C)
    Lions, 16-6 (D)
1992—Bears, 27-24 (C)
    Lions, 16-3 (D)
1993—Lions, 10-6 (D)
    Lions, 20-14 (C)
1994—Lions, 21-16 (D)
    Bears, 20-10 (C)
1995—Lions, 24-17 (C)
    Lions, 27-7 (D)
1996—Lions, 35-16 (D)
    Bears, 31-14 (C)
1997—Lions, 32-7 (C)
    Lions, 55-20 (D)
1998—Bears, 31-27 (C)
    Lions, 26-3 (D)
1999—Lions, 21-17 (D)
    Bears, 28-10 (C)
2000—Lions, 21-14 (C)
    Bears, 23-20 (D)
2001—Bears, 13-10 (C)
    Bears, 24-0 (D)
2002—Lions, 23-20 (D) OT
    Bears, 20-17 (C) OT

2003—Bears, 24-16 (C)
Lions, 12-10 (D)
2004—Lions, 20-16 (C)
Lions, 19-13 (D)
2005—Bears, 38-6 (C)
Bears, 19-13 (D) OT
2006—Bears, 34-7 (C)
Bears, 26-21 (D)
2007—Lions, 37-27 (D)
Lions, 16-7 (C)
2008—Bears, 34-7 (D)
Bears, 27-23 (C)
2009—Bears, 48-24 (C)
Bears, 37-23 (D)
2010—Bears, 19-14 (C)
Bears, 24-20 (D)
2011—Lions, 24-13 (D)
Bears, 37-13 (C)
(RS Pts.—Bears 3,166, Lions 2,864)
*Franchise in Portsmouth prior to 1934
and known as the Spartans
CHICAGO vs. GREEN BAY
RS: Bears lead series, 91-85-6
PS: Series tied, 1-1
1921—Staleys, 20-0 (C)
1923—Bears, 3-0 (GB)
1924—Bears, 3-0 (C)
1925—Packers, 14-10 (GB)
Bears, 21-0 (C)
1926—Tie, 6-6 (GB)
Bears, 19-13 (C)
Tie, 3-3 (C)
1927—Bears, 7-6 (GB)
Bears, 14-6 (C)
1928—Tie, 12-12 (GB)
Packers, 16-6 (C)
Packers, 6-0 (C)
1929—Packers, 23-0 (GB)
Packers, 14-0 (C)
Packers, 25-0 (C)
1930—Packers, 7-0 (GB)
Packers, 13-12 (C)
Bears, 21-0 (C)
1931—Packers, 7-0 (GB)
Packers, 6-2 (C)
Bears, 7-6 (C)
1932—Tie, 0-0 (GB)
Packers, 2-0 (C)
Bears, 9-0 (C)
1933—Bears, 14-7 (GB)
Bears, 10-7 (C)
Bears, 7-6 (C)
1934—Bears, 24-10 (GB)
Bears, 27-14 (C)
1935—Packers, 7-0 (GB)
Packers, 17-14 (C)
1936—Bears, 30-3 (GB)
Packers, 21-10 (C)
1937—Bears, 14-2 (GB)
Packers, 24-14 (C)
1938—Bears, 2-0 (GB)
Packers, 24-17 (C)
1939—Packers, 21-16 (GB)
Bears, 30-27 (C)
1940—Bears, 41-10 (GB)
Bears, 14-7 (C)
1941—Bears, 25-17 (GB)
Packers, 16-14 (C)
**Bears, 33-14 (C)
1942—Packers, 44-28 (GB)
Bears, 38-7 (C)
1943—Tie, 21-21 (GB)

Bears, 21-7 (C)
1944—Packers, 42-28 (GB)
Bears, 21-0 (C)
1945—Packers, 31-21 (GB)
Bears, 28-24 (C)
1946—Bears, 30-7 (GB)
Bears, 10-7 (C)
1947—Packers, 29-20 (GB)
Bears, 20-17 (C)
1948—Bears, 45-7 (GB)
Bears, 7-6 (C)
1949—Bears, 17-0 (GB)
Bears, 24-3 (C)
1950—Packers, 31-21 (GB)
Bears, 28-14 (C)
1951—Bears, 31-20 (GB)
Bears, 24-13 (C)
1952—Bears, 24-14 (GB)
Packers, 41-28 (C)
1953—Bears, 17-13 (GB)
Tie, 21-21 (C)
1954—Bears, 10-3 (GB)
Bears, 28-23 (C)
1955—Packers, 24-3 (GB)
Bears, 52-31 (C)
1956—Bears, 37-21 (GB)
Bears, 38-14 (C)
1957—Packers, 21-17 (GB)
Bears, 21-14 (C)
1958—Bears, 34-20 (GB)
Bears, 24-10 (C)
1959—Packers, 9-6 (GB)
Bears, 28-17 (C)
1960—Bears, 17-14 (GB)
Packers, 41-13 (C)
1961—Packers, 24-0 (GB)
Packers, 31-28 (C)
1962—Packers, 49-0 (GB)
Packers, 38-7 (C)
1963—Bears, 10-3 (GB)
Bears, 26-7 (C)
1964—Packers, 23-12 (GB)
Packers, 17-3 (C)
1965—Packers, 23-14 (GB)
Bears, 31-10 (C)
1966—Packers, 17-0 (C)
Packers, 13-6 (GB)
1967—Packers, 13-10 (GB)
Packers, 17-13 (C)
1968—Packers, 13-10 (GB)
Packers, 28-27 (C)
1969—Packers, 17-0 (GB)
Packers, 21-3 (C)
1970—Packers, 20-19 (GB)
Bears, 35-17 (C)
1971—Packers, 17-14 (C)
Packers, 31-10 (GB)
1972—Packers, 20-17 (GB)
Packers, 23-17 (C)
1973—Bears, 31-17 (GB)
Packers, 21-0 (C)
1974—Bears, 10-9 (C)
Packers, 20-3 (Mil)
1975—Bears, 27-14 (C)
Packers, 28-7 (GB)
1976—Bears, 24-13 (C)
Bears, 16-10 (GB)
1977—Bears, 26-0 (GB)
Bears, 21-10 (C)
1978—Packers, 24-14 (GB)
Bears, 14-0 (C)
1979—Bears, 6-3 (C)

Bears, 15-14 (GB)
1980—Packers, 12-6 (GB) OT
Bears, 61-7 (C)
1981—Packers, 16-9 (C)
Packers, 21-17 (GB)
1983—Packers, 31-28 (GB)
Bears, 23-21 (C)
1984—Bears, 9-7 (GB)
Packers, 20-14 (C)
1985—Bears, 23-7 (C)
Bears, 16-10 (GB)
1986—Bears, 25-12 (GB)
Bears, 12-10 (C)
1987—Bears, 26-24 (GB)
Bears, 23-10 (C)
1988—Bears, 24-6 (GB)
Bears, 16-0 (C)
1989—Packers, 14-13 (GB)
Packers, 40-28 (C)
1990—Bears, 31-13 (GB)
Bears, 27-13 (C)
1991—Bears, 10-0 (GB)
Bears, 27-13 (C)
1992—Bears, 30-10 (GB)
Packers, 17-3 (C)
1993—Packers, 17-3 (GB)
Bears, 30-17 (C)
1994—Packers, 33-6 (C)
Packers, 40-3 (GB)
1995—Packers, 27-24 (C)
Packers, 35-28 (GB)
1996—Packers, 37-6 (C)
Packers, 28-17 (GB)
1997—Packers, 38-24 (GB)
Packers, 24-23 (C)
1998—Packers, 26-20 (GB)
Packers, 16-13 (C)
1999—Bears, 14-13 (GB)
Packers, 35-19 (C)
2000—Bears, 27-24 (GB)
Packers, 28-6 (C)
2001—Packers, 20-12 (C)
Packers, 17-7 (GB)
2002—Packers, 34-21 (C)
Packers, 30-20 (GB)
2003—Packers, 38-23 (C)
Packers, 34-21 (GB)
2004—Bears, 21-10 (GB)
Packers, 31-14 (C)
2005—Bears, 19-7 (C)
Bears, 24-17 (GB)
2006—Bears, 26-0 (GB)
Packers, 26-7 (C)
2007—Bears, 27-20 (GB)
Bears, 35-7 (C)
2008—Packers, 37-3 (GB)
Bears, 20-17 (C) OT
2009—Packers, 21-15 (GB)
Packers, 21-14 (C)
2010—Bears, 20-17 (C)
Packers, 10-3 (GB)
***Packers, 21-14 (C)
2011—Packers, 27-17 (C)
Packers, 35-21 (GB)
(RS Pts.—Bears 3,098, Packers 3,010)
(PS Pts.—Bears 47, Packers 35)
*Bears known as Staleys prior to 1922
**Division Playoff
***NFC Championship
CHICAGO vs. HOUSTON
RS: Texans lead series, 2-0
2004—Texans, 24-5 (C)

2008—Texans, 31-24 (H)
(RS Pts.—Texans 55, Bears 29)
CHICAGO vs. *INDIANAPOLIS
RS: Colts lead series, 22-18
PS: Colts lead series, 1-0
1953—Colts, 13-9 (B)
    Colts, 16-14 (C)
1954—Bears, 28-9 (C)
    Bears, 28-13 (B)
1955—Colts, 23-17 (B)
    Bears, 38-10 (C)
1956—Colts, 28-21 (B)
    Bears, 58-27 (C)
1957—Colts, 21-10 (B)
    Colts, 29-14 (C)
1958—Colts, 51-38 (B)
    Colts, 17-0 (C)
1959—Bears, 26-21 (B)
    Colts, 21-7 (C)
1960—Colts, 42-7 (B)
    Colts, 24-20 (C)
1961—Bears, 24-10 (C)
    Bears, 21-20 (B)
1962—Bears, 35-15 (C)
    Bears, 57-0 (B)
1963—Bears, 10-3 (C)
    Bears, 17-7 (B)
1964—Colts, 52-0 (B)
    Colts, 40-24 (C)
1965—Colts, 26-21 (C)
    Bears, 13-0 (B)
1966—Bears, 27-17 (C)
    Colts, 21-16 (B)
1967—Colts, 24-3 (C)
1968—Colts, 28-7 (B)
1969—Colts, 24-21 (C)
1970—Colts, 21-20 (B)
1975—Colts, 35-7 (C)
1983—Colts, 22-19 (B) OT
1985—Bears, 17-10 (C)
1988—Bears, 17-13 (I)
1991—Bears, 31-17 (I)
2000—Bears, 27-24 (C)
2004—Colts, 41-10 (C)
2006—**Colts, 29-17 (South Florida)
2008—Bears, 29-13 (I)
(RS Pts.—Colts 848, Bears 808)
(PS: Pts.—Colts 29, Bears 17)
*Franchise in Baltimore prior to 1984
**Super Bowl XLI
CHICAGO vs. JACKSONVILLE
RS: Bears lead series, 3-2
1995—Bears, 30-27 (J)
1998—Jaguars, 24-23 (C)
2001—Bears, 33-13 (C)
2004—Jaguars, 22-3 (J)
2008—Bears, 23-10 (C)
(RS Pts.—Bears 112, Jaguars 96)
CHICAGO vs. KANSAS CITY
RS: Bears lead series, 6-5
1973—Chiefs, 19-7 (KC)
1977—Bears, 28-27 (C)
1981—Bears, 16-13 (KC) OT
1987—Bears, 31-28 (C)
1990—Chiefs, 21-10 (C)
1993—Bears, 19-17 (KC)
1996—Chiefs, 14-10 (KC)
1999—Bears, 20-17 (C)
2003—Bears, 31-3 (KC)
2007—Bears, 20-10 (C)
2011—Chiefs, 10-3 (C)
(RS Pts.—Chiefs 207, Bears 167)

CHICAGO vs. MIAMI
RS: Dolphins lead series, 7-4
1971—Dolphins, 34-3 (M)
1975—Dolphins, 46-13 (C)
1979—Dolphins, 31-16 (M)
1985—Dolphins, 38-24 (M)
1988—Bears, 34-7 (C)
1991—Dolphins, 16-13 (C) OT
1994—Bears, 17-14 (M)
1997—Bears, 36-33 (M) OT
2002—Dolphins, 27-9 (M)
2006—Dolphins, 31-13 (C)
2010—Bears, 16-0 (M)
(RS Pts.—Dolphins 277, Bears 194)
CHICAGO vs. MINNESOTA
RS: Vikings lead series, 52-47-2
PS: Bears lead series, 1-0
1961—Vikings, 37-13 (M)
    Bears, 52-35 (C)
1962—Bears, 13-0 (M)
    Bears, 31-30 (C)
1963—Bears, 28-7 (M)
    Tie, 17-17 (C)
1964—Bears, 34-28 (M)
    Vikings, 41-14 (C)
1965—Bears, 45-37 (M)
    Vikings, 24-17 (C)
1966—Bears, 13-10 (M)
    Bears, 41-28 (C)
1967—Bears, 17-7 (M)
    Tie, 10-10 (C)
1968—Bears, 27-17 (M)
    Bears, 26-24 (C)
1969—Vikings, 31-0 (C)
    Vikings, 31-14 (M)
1970—Vikings, 24-0 (C)
    Vikings, 16-13 (M)
1971—Bears, 20-17 (M)
    Vikings, 27-10 (C)
1972—Bears, 13-10 (C)
    Vikings, 23-10 (M)
1973—Vikings, 22-13 (C)
    Vikings, 31-13 (M)
1974—Vikings, 11-7 (M)
    Vikings, 17-0 (C)
1975—Vikings, 28-3 (M)
    Vikings, 13-9 (C)
1976—Vikings, 20-19 (M)
    Bears, 14-13 (C)
1977—Vikings, 22-16 (M) OT
    Bears, 10-7 (C)
1978—Vikings, 24-20 (C)
    Vikings, 17-14 (M)
1979—Bears, 26-7 (C)
    Vikings, 30-27 (M)
1980—Vikings, 34-14 (C)
    Vikings, 13-7 (M)
1981—Vikings, 24-21 (M)
    Bears, 10-9 (C)
1982—Vikings, 35-7 (M)
1983—Vikings, 23-14 (C)
    Bears, 19-13 (M)
1984—Bears, 16-7 (C)
    Bears, 34-3 (M)
1985—Bears, 33-24 (M)
    Bears, 27-9 (C)
1986—Bears, 23-0 (C)
    Vikings, 23-7 (M)
1987—Bears, 27-7 (C)
    Bears, 30-24 (M)
1988—Vikings, 31-7 (C)
    Vikings, 28-27 (M)

1989—Bears, 38-7 (C)
    Vikings, 27-16 (M)
1990—Bears, 19-16 (C)
    Vikings, 41-13 (M)
1991—Bears, 10-6 (C)
    Bears, 34-17 (M)
1992—Vikings, 21-20 (M)
    Vikings, 38-10 (C)
1993—Vikings, 10-7 (M)
    Vikings, 19-12 (C)
1994—Vikings, 42-14 (C)
    Vikings, 33-27 (M) OT
    *Bears, 35-18 (M)
1995—Bears, 31-14 (C)
    Bears, 14-6 (M)
1996—Vikings, 20-14 (C)
    Bears, 15-13 (M)
1997—Vikings, 27-24 (C)
    Vikings, 29-22 (M)
1998—Vikings, 31-28 (C)
    Vikings, 48-22 (M)
1999—Bears, 24-22 (M)
    Vikings, 27-24 (C) OT
2000—Vikings, 30-27 (M)
    Vikings, 28-16 (C)
2001—Bears, 17-10 (C)
    Bears, 13-6 (M)
2002—Bears, 27-23 (C)
    Vikings, 25-7 (M)
2003—Vikings, 24-13 (M)
    Bears, 13-10 (C)
2004—Vikings, 27-22 (M)
    Bears, 24-14 (C)
2005—Bears, 28-3 (C)
    Vikings, 34-10 (M)
2006—Bears, 19-16 (M)
    Bears, 23-13 (C)
2007—Vikings, 34-31 (C)
    Vikings, 20-13 (M)
2008—Bears, 48-41 (C)
    Vikings, 34-14 (M)
2009—Vikings, 36-10 (M)
    Bears, 36-30 (C) OT
2010—Bears, 27-13 (C)
    Bears, 40-14 (M)
2011—Bears, 39-10 (C)
    Bears, 17-13 (M)
RS Pts.—Vikings 2,122, Bears 1,964)
(PS Pts.—Bears 35, Vikings 18)
*NFC First-Round Playoff
CHICAGO vs. NEW ENGLAND
RS: Patriots lead series, 8-3
PS: Bears lead series, 1-0
1973—Patriots, 13-10 (C)
1979—Patriots, 27-7 (C)
1982—Bears, 26-13 (C)
1985—Bears, 20-7 (C)
    *Bears, 46-10 (New Orleans)
1988—Patriots, 30-7 (NE)
1994—Patriots, 13-3 (C)
1997—Patriots, 31-3 (NE)
2000—Bears, 24-17 (C)
2002—Patriots, 33-30 (C)
2006—Patriots, 17-13 (NE)
2010—Patriots, 36-7 (C)
(RS Pts.—Patriots 237, Bears 150)
(PS Pts.—Bears 46, Patriots 10)
*Super Bowl XX
CHICAGO vs. NEW ORLEANS
RS: Bears lead series, 13-12
PS: Bears lead series, 2-0
1968—Bears, 23-17 (NO)

1970—Bears, 24-3 (NO)
1971—Bears, 35-14 (C)
1973—Saints, 21-16 (NO)
1974—Bears, 24-10 (C)
1975—Bears, 42-17 (NO)
1977—Saints, 42-24 (C)
1980—Bears, 22-3 (C)
1982—Saints, 10-0 (C)
1983—Saints, 34-31 (NO) OT
1984—Bears, 20-7 (C)
1987—Saints, 19-17 (C)
1990—*Bears, 16-6 (C)
1991—Bears, 20-17 (NO)
1992—Saints, 28-6 (NO)
1994—Bears, 17-7 (C)
1996—Saints, 27-24 (NO)
1997—Saints, 20-17 (C)
1999—Bears, 14-10 (C)
2000—Saints, 31-10 (C)
2002—Saints, 29-23 (C)
2003—Saints, 20-13 (NO)
2005—Bears, 20-17 (Baton Rouge)
2006—**Bears, 39-14 (C)
2007—Saints, 33-25 (C)
2008—Bears, 27-24 (C) OT
2011—Saints, 30-13 (NO)
(RS Pts.—Bears 515, Saints 482)
(PS Pts.—Bears 55, Saints 20)
*NFC First-Round Playoff
**NFC Championship
CHICAGO vs. N.Y. GIANTS
RS: Bears lead series, 27-19-2
PS: Bears lead series, 5-3
1925—Bears, 19-7 (NY)
    Giants, 9-0 (C)
1926—Bears, 7-0 (C)
1927—Giants, 13-7 (NY)
1928—Bears, 13-0 (C)
1929—Giants, 26-14 (C)
    Giants, 34-0 (NY)
    Giants, 14-9 (C)
1930—Giants, 12-0 (C)
    Bears, 12-0 (NY)
1931—Bears, 6-0 (C)
    Bears, 12-6 (NY)
    Giants, 25-6 (C)
1932—Bears, 28-8 (NY)
    Bears, 6-0 (C)
1933—Bears, 14-10 (C)
    Giants, 3-0 (NY)
    *Bears, 23-21 (C)
1934—Bears, 27-7 (C)
    Bears, 10-9 (NY)
    *Giants, 30-13 (NY)
1935—Bears, 20-3 (NY)
    Giants, 3-0 (C)
1936—Bears, 25-7 (NY)
1937—Tie, 3-3 (NY)
1939—Giants, 16-13 (NY)
1940—Bears, 37-21 (NY)
1941—*Bears, 37-9 (C)
1942—Bears, 26-7 (NY)
1943—Bears, 56-7 (NY)
1946—Giants, 14-0 (NY)
    *Bears, 24-14 (NY)
1948—Bears, 35-14 (C)
1949—Giants, 35-28 (NY)
1956—Tie, 17-17 (NY)
    *Giants, 47-7 (NY)
1962—Giants, 26-24 (C)
1963—*Bears, 14-10 (C)
1965—Bears, 35-14 (NY)

1967—Bears, 34-7 (C)
1969—Giants, 28-24 (NY)
1970—Bears, 24-16 (NY)
1974—Bears, 16-13 (C)
1977—Bears, 12-9 (NY) OT
1985—**Bears, 21-0 (C)
1987—Bears, 34-19 (C)
1990—**Giants, 31-3 (NY)
1991—Bears, 20-17 (C)
1992—Giants, 27-14 (C)
1993—Giants, 26-20 (C)
1995—Bears, 27-24 (NY)
2000—Giants, 14-7 (C)
2004—Bears, 28-21 (NY)
2006—Bears, 38-20 (NY)
2007—Giants, 21-16 (C)
2010—Giants, 17-3 (NY)
(RS Pts.—Bears 826, Giants 649)
(PS Pts.—Giants 162, Bears 142)
*NFL Championship
**NFC Divisional Playoff
CHICAGO vs. N.Y. JETS
RS: Bears lead series, 7-3
1974—Jets, 23-21 (C)
1979—Bears, 23-13 (C)
1985—Bears, 19-6 (NY)
1991—Bears, 19-13 (C) OT
1994—Bears, 19-7 (NY)
1997—Jets, 23-15 (C)
2000—Jets, 17-10 (NY)
2002—Bears, 20-13 (C)
2006—Bears, 10-0 (NY)
2010—Bears, 38-34 (C)
(RS Pts.—Bears 194, Jets 149)
CHICAGO vs. *OAKLAND
RS: Raiders lead series, 7-6
1972—Raiders, 28-21 (O)
1976—Raiders, 28-27 (C)
1978—Raiders, 25-19 (C) OT
1981—Bears, 23-6 (C)
1984—Bears, 17-6 (C)
1987—Bears, 6-3 (LA)
1990—Raiders, 24-10 (LA)
1993—Raiders, 16-14 (C)
1996—Bears, 19-17 (C)
1999—Raiders, 24-17 (O)
2003—Bears, 24-21 (C)
2007—Bears, 17-6 (O)
2011—Raiders, 25-20 (O)
(RS Pts.—Bears 234, Raiders 229)
*Franchise in Los Angeles from 1982-1994
CHICAGO vs. PHILADELPHIA
RS: Bears lead series, 28-9-1
PS: Eagles lead series, 2-1
1933—Tie, 3-3 (P)
1935—Bears, 39-0 (P)
1936—Bears, 17-0 (P)
    Bears, 28-7 (P)
1938—Bears, 28-6 (P)
1939—Bears, 27-14 (C)
1941—Bears, 49-14 (P)
1942—Bears, 45-14 (C)
1944—Bears, 28-7 (P)
1946—Bears, 21-14 (C)
1947—Bears, 40-7 (C)
1948—Eagles, 12-7 (P)
1949—Bears, 38-21 (C)
1955—Bears, 17-10 (C)
1961—Eagles, 16-14 (P)
1963—Bears, 16-7 (C)
1968—Bears, 29-16 (P)
1970—Bears, 20-16 (C)

1972—Bears, 21-12 (P)
1975—Bears, 15-13 (C)
1979—*Eagles, 27-17 (P)
1980—Eagles, 17-14 (P)
1983—Bears, 7-6 (P)
    Bears, 17-14 (C)
1986—Bears, 13-10 (C) OT
1987—Bears, 35-3 (P)
1988—**Bears, 20-12 (C)
1989—Bears, 27-13 (C)
1993—Bears, 17-6 (P)
1994—Eagles, 30-22 (P)
1995—Bears, 20-14 (C)
1999—Eagles, 20-16 (C)
2000—Eagles, 13-9 (P)
2001—**Eagles, 33-19 (C)
2002—Eagles, 19-13 (C)
2004—Eagles, 19-9 (C)
2007—Bears, 19-16 (P)
2008—Bears, 24-20 (C)
2009—Eagles, 24-20 (C)
2010—Bears, 31-26 (C)
2011—Bears, 30-24 (P)
(RS Pts.—Bears 845, Eagles 503)
(PS Pts.—Eagles 72, Bears 56)
*NFC First-Round Playoff
**NFC Divisional Playoff
CHICAGO vs. *PITTSBURGH
RS: Bears lead series, 17-7-1
1934—Bears, 28-0 (P)
1935—Bears, 23-7 (P)
1936—Bears, 27-9 (P)
    Bears, 26-7 (C)
1937—Bears, 7-0 (P)
1939—Bears, 32-0 (P)
1941—Bears, 34-7 (C)
1945—Bears, 28-7 (C)
1947—Bears, 49-7 (C)
1949—Bears, 30-21 (C)
1958—Steelers, 24-10 (P)
1959—Bears, 27-21 (C)
1963—Tie, 17-17 (P)
1967—Steelers, 41-13 (P)
1969—Bears, 38-7 (C)
1971—Bears, 17-15 (C)
1975—Steelers, 34-3 (P)
1980—Steelers, 38-3 (P)
1986—Bears, 13-10 (C) OT
1989—Bears, 20-0 (P)
1992—Bears, 30-6 (C)
1995—Steelers, 37-34 (C) OT
1998—Steelers, 17-12 (P)
2005—Steelers, 21-9 (C)
2009—Bears, 17-14 (C)
(RS Pts.—Bears 547, Steelers 367)
*Steelers known as Pirates prior to 1940
CHICAGO vs. *ST. LOUIS
RS: Bears lead series, 50-34-3
PS: Series tied, 1-1
1937—Bears, 20-2 (Cle)
    Bears, 15-7 (C)
1938—Bears, 14-7 (C)
    Rams, 23-21 (Cle)
1939—Bears, 30-21 (Cle)
    Bears, 35-21 (C)
1940—Bears, 21-14 (Cle)
    Bears, 47-25 (C)
1941—Bears, 48-21 (Cle)
    Bears, 31-13 (C)
1942—Bears, 21-7 (Cle)
    Bears, 47-0 (C)
1944—Rams, 19-7 (Cle)

Bears, 28-21 (C)
1945—Rams, 17-0 (Cle)
Rams, 41-21 (C)
1946—Tie, 28-28 (C)
Bears, 27-21 (LA)
1947—Bears, 41-21 (LA)
Rams, 17-14 (C)
1948—Bears, 42-21 (C)
Bears, 21-6 (LA)
1949—Rams, 31-16 (C)
Rams, 27-24 (LA)
1950—Bears, 24-20 (LA)
Bears, 24-14 (C)
**Rams, 24-14 (LA)
1951—Rams, 42-17 (C)
1952—Rams, 31-7 (LA)
Rams, 40-24 (C)
1953—Rams, 38-24 (LA)
Bears, 24-21 (C)
1954—Rams, 42-38 (LA)
Bears, 24-13 (C)
1955—Bears, 31-20 (LA)
Bears, 24-3 (C)
1956—Bears, 35-24 (LA)
Bears, 30-21 (C)
1957—Bears, 34-26 (C)
Bears, 16-10 (LA)
1958—Bears, 31-10 (C)
Rams, 41-35 (LA)
1959—Rams, 28-21 (C)
Bears, 26-21 (LA)
1960—Bears, 34-27 (C)
Tie, 24-24 (LA)
1961—Bears, 21-17 (LA)
Bears, 28-24 (C)
1962—Bears, 27-23 (LA)
Bears, 30-14 (C)
1963—Bears, 52-14 (LA)
Bears, 6-0 (C)
1964—Bears, 38-17 (C)
Bears, 34-24 (LA)
1965—Rams, 30-28 (LA)
Bears, 31-6 (C)
1966—Rams, 31-17 (LA)
Bears, 17-10 (C)
1967—Rams, 28-17 (C)
1968—Bears, 17-16 (LA)
1969—Rams, 9-7 (C)
1971—Rams, 17-3 (LA)
1972—Tie, 13-13 (C)
1973—Rams, 26-0 (C)
1975—Rams, 38-10 (LA)
1976—Rams, 20-12 (LA)
1977—Bears, 24-23 (C)
1979—Bears, 27-23 (C)
1981—Rams, 24-7 (C)
1982—Bears, 34-26 (LA)
1983—Rams, 21-14 (LA)
1984—Rams, 29-13 (LA)
1985—***Bears, 24-0 (C)
1986—Rams, 20-17 (C)
1988—Rams, 23-3 (LA)
1989—Rams, 20-10 (C)
1990—Bears, 38-9 (C)
1993—Rams, 20-6 (LA)
1994—Bears, 27-13 (C)
1995—Rams, 34-28 (StL)
1996—Rams, 35-9 (C)
1997—Rams, 13-10 (StL)
1998—Rams, 20-12 (C)
1999—Rams, 34-12 (StL)
2002—Rams, 21-16 (StL)

2003—Rams, 23-21 (C)
2006—Bears, 42-27 (StL)
2008—Bears, 27-3 (StL)
2009—Bears, 17-9 (C)
(RS Pts.—Bears 2,020, Rams 1,762)
(PS Pts.—Bears 38, Rams 24)
*Franchise in Los Angeles prior to 1995
and in Cleveland prior to 1946
**Conference Playoff
***NFC Championship
CHICAGO vs. SAN DIEGO
RS: Bears lead series, 6-5
1970—Chargers, 20-7 (C)
1974—Chargers, 28-21 (SD)
1978—Chargers, 40-7 (SD)
1981—Bears, 20-17 (C) OT
1984—Chargers, 20-7 (SD)
1993—Bears, 16-13 (SD)
1996—Bears, 27-14 (C)
1999—Bears, 23-20 (SD) OT
2003—Bears, 20-7 (C)
2007—Chargers, 14-3 (SD)
2011—Bears, 31-20 (C)
(RS Pts.—Chargers 213, Bears 182)
CHICAGO vs. SAN FRANCISCO
RS: Bears lead series, 29-28-1
PS: 49ers lead series, 3-0
1950—Bears, 32-20 (SF)
Bears, 17-0 (C)
1951—Bears, 13-7 (C)
1952—49ers, 40-16 (C)
Bears, 20-17 (SF)
1953—49ers, 35-28 (C)
49ers, 24-14 (SF)
1954—49ers, 31-24 (C)
Bears, 31-27 (SF)
1955—49ers, 20-19 (C)
Bears, 34-23 (SF)
1956—Bears, 31-7 (C)
Bears, 38-21 (SF)
1957—49ers, 21-17 (C)
49ers, 21-17 (SF)
1958—Bears, 28-6 (C)
Bears, 27-14 (SF)
1959—49ers, 20-17 (SF)
Bears, 14-3 (C)
1960—Bears, 27-10 (C)
49ers, 25-7 (SF)
1961—Bears, 31-0 (C)
49ers, 41-31 (SF)
1962—Bears, 30-14 (C)
49ers, 34-27 (C)
1963—49ers, 20-14 (SF)
Bears, 27-7 (C)
1964—49ers, 31-21 (SF)
Bears, 23-21 (C)
1965—49ers, 52-24 (SF)
Bears, 61-20 (C)
1966—Tie, 30-30 (C)
49ers, 41-14 (SF)
1967—Bears, 28-14 (SF)
1968—Bears, 27-19 (C)
1969—49ers, 42-21 (SF)
1970—49ers, 37-16 (C)
1971—49ers, 13-0 (SF)
1972—49ers, 34-21 (C)
1974—49ers, 34-0 (C)
1975—49ers, 31-3 (SF)
1976—Bears, 19-12 (SF)
1978—Bears, 16-13 (SF)
1979—Bears, 28-27 (SF)
1981—49ers, 28-17 (SF)

1983—Bears, 13-3 (C)
1984—*49ers, 23-0 (SF)
1985—Bears, 26-10 (SF)
1987—49ers, 41-0 (SF)
1988—Bears, 10-9 (C)
*49ers, 28-3 (C)
1989—Bears, 26-0 (SF)
1991—49ers, 52-14 (SF)
1994—**49ers, 44-15 (SF)
2000—49ers, 17-0 (SF)
2001—Bears, 37-31 (C) OT
2003—49ers, 49-7 (SF)
2004—Bears, 23-13 (C)
2005—Bears, 17-9 (C)
2006—Bears, 41-10 (C)
2009—49ers, 10-6 (SF)
(RS Pts.—49ers 1,287, Bears 1,194)
(PS Pts.—49ers 95, Bears 18)
*NFC Championship
**NFC Divisional Playoff
CHICAGO vs. SEATTLE
RS: Seahawks lead series, 9-4
PS: Bears lead series, 2-0
1976—Bears, 34-7 (S)
1978—Seahawks, 31-29 (C)
1982—Seahawks, 20-14 (S)
1984—Seahawks, 38-9 (S)
1987—Seahawks, 34-21 (C)
1990—Bears, 17-0 (C)
1999—Seahawks, 14-13 (C)
2003—Seahawks, 24-17 (S)
2006—Bears, 37-6 (C)
*Bears, 27-24 (C) OT
2007—Seahawks, 30-23 (S)
2009—Bears, 25-19 (S)
2010—Seahawks, 23-20 (C)
*Bears, 35-24 (C)
2011—Seahawks, 38-14 (C)
(RS Pts.—Seahawks 284, Bears 273)
(PS Pts.—Bears 62, Seahawks 48)
*NFC Divisional Playoff
CHICAGO vs. TAMPA BAY
RS: Bears lead series, 36-18
1977—Bears, 10-0 (TB)
1978—Buccaneers, 33-19 (TB)
Bears, 14-3 (C)
1979—Buccaneers, 17-13 (C)
Bears, 14-0 (TB)
1980—Bears, 23-0 (C)
Bears, 14-13 (TB)
1981—Bears, 28-17 (C)
Buccaneers, 20-10 (TB)
1982—Buccaneers, 26-23 (TB) OT
1983—Bears, 17-10 (C)
Bears, 27-0 (TB)
1984—Bears, 34-14 (C)
Bears, 44-9 (TB)
1985—Bears, 38-28 (C)
Bears, 27-19 (TB)
1986—Bears, 23-3 (TB)
Bears, 48-14 (C)
1987—Bears, 20-3 (C)
Bears, 27-26 (TB)
1988—Bears, 28-10 (C)
Bears, 27-15 (TB)
1989—Buccaneers, 42-35 (TB)
Buccaneers, 32-31 (C)
1990—Bears, 26-6 (TB)
Bears, 27-14 (C)
1991—Bears, 21-20 (TB)
Bears, 27-0 (C)
1992—Bears, 31-14 (C)

ALL-TIME TEAM VS. TEAM RESULTS

Buccaneers, 20-17 (TB)
1993—Bears, 47-17 (C)
Buccaneers, 13-10 (TB)
1994—Bears, 21-9 (C)
Bears, 20-6 (TB)
1995—Bears, 25-6 (TB)
Bears, 31-10 (C)
1996—Bears, 13-10 (C)
Buccaneers, 34-19 (TB)
1997—Bears, 13-7 (C)
Buccaneers, 31-15 (TB)
1998—Buccaneers, 27-15 (TB)
Buccaneers, 31-17 (C)
1999—Buccaneers, 6-3 (TB)
Buccaneers, 20-6 (C)
2000—Buccaneers, 41-0 (TB)
Bears, 13-10 (C)
2001—Bears, 27-24 (TB)
Bears, 27-3 (C)
2002—Buccaneers, 15-0 (C)
2004—Buccaneers, 19-7 (TB)
2005—Bears, 13-10 (TB)
2006—Bears, 34-31 (C) OT
2008—Buccaneers, 27-24 (C) OT
2011—Bears, 24-18 (London)
(RS Pts.—Bears 1,167, Buccaneers 853)
CHICAGO vs. *TENNESSEE
RS: Series tied, 5-5
1973—Bears, 35-14 (C)
1977—Oilers, 47-0 (H)
1980—Oilers, 10-6 (C)
1986—Bears, 20-7 (H)
1989—Oilers, 33-28 (C)
1992—Oilers, 24-7 (H)
1995—Bears, 35-32 (C)
1998—Bears, 23-20 (T)
2004—Bears, 19-17 (T) OT
2008—Titans, 21-14 (C)
(RS Pts.—Titans 225, Bears 187)
*Franchise in Houston prior to 1997;
known as Oilers prior to 1999
CHICAGO vs. *WASHINGTON
RS: Bears lead series, 20-19-1
PS: Redskins lead series, 4-3
1932—Tie, 7-7 (B)
1933—Bears, 7-0 (C)
Redskins, 10-0 (B)
1934—Bears, 21-0 (B)
1935—Bears, 30-14 (B)
1936—Bears, 26-0 (B)
1937—**Redskins, 28-21 (C)
1938—Bears, 31-7 (C)
1940—Redskins, 7-3 (W)
**Bears, 73-0 (W)
1941—Bears, 35-21 (C)
1942—**Redskins, 14-6 (W)
1943—Redskins, 21-7 (W)
**Bears, 41-21 (C)
1945—Redskins, 28-21 (W)
1946—Bears, 24-20 (C)
1947—Bears, 56-20 (W)
1948—Bears, 48-13 (C)
1949—Bears, 31-21 (W)
1951—Bears, 27-0 (W)
1953—Bears, 27-24 (W)
1957—Redskins, 14-3 (C)
1964—Redskins, 27-20 (W)
1968—Redskins, 38-28 (C)
1971—Bears, 16-15 (C)
1974—Redskins, 42-0 (W)
1976—Bears, 33-7 (C)
1978—Bears, 14-10 (W)

1980—Bears, 35-21 (C)
1981—Redskins, 24-7 (C)
1984—***Bears, 23-19 (W)
1985—Bears, 45-10 (C)
1986—***Redskins, 27-13 (C)
1987—***Redskins, 21-17 (C)
1988—Bears, 34-14 (W)
1989—Redskins, 38-14 (W)
1990—Redskins, 10-9 (W)
1991—Redskins, 20-7 (C)
1996—Redskins, 10-3 (W)
1997—Redskins, 31-8 (C)
1999—Redskins, 48-22 (W)
2001—Bears, 20-15 (W)
2003—Bears, 27-24 (C)
2004—Redskins, 13-10 (C)
2005—Redskins, 9-7 (W)
2007—Redskins, 24-16 (W)
2010—Redskins, 17-14 (C)
(RS Pts.—Bears 793, Redskins 694)
(PS Pts.—Bears 194, Redskins 130)
*Franchise in Boston prior to 1937 and
known as Braves prior to 1933
**NFL Championship
***NFC Divisional Playoff

CINCINNATI vs. ARIZONA
RS: Bengals lead series, 6-4;
See Arizona vs. Cincinnati
CINCINNATI vs. ATLANTA
RS: Bengals lead series, 7-5;
See Atlanta vs. Cincinnati
CINCINNATI vs. BALTIMORE
RS: Ravens lead series, 18-14;
See Baltimore vs. Cincinnati
CINCINNATI vs. BUFFALO
RS: Bills lead series, 15-10
PS: Bengals lead series, 2-0;
See Buffalo vs. Cincinnati
CINCINNATI vs. CAROLINA
RS: Series tied, 2-2;
See Carolina vs. Cincinnati
CINCINNATI vs. CHICAGO
RS: Bengals lead series, 6-3;
See Chicago vs. Cincinnati
CINCINNATI vs. CLEVELAND
RS: Bengals lead series, 41-36
1970—Browns, 30-27 (Cle)
Bengals, 14-10 (Cin)
1971—Browns, 27-24 (Cin)
Browns, 31-27 (Cle)
1972—Browns, 27-6 (Cle)
Browns, 27-24 (Cin)
1973—Browns, 17-10 (Cle)
Bengals, 34-17 (Cin)
1974—Bengals, 33-7 (Cin)
Bengals, 34-24 (Cle)
1975—Bengals, 24-17 (Cin)
Browns, 35-23 (Cle)
1976—Bengals, 45-24 (Cle)
Bengals, 21-6 (Cin)
1977—Browns, 13-3 (Cin)
Bengals, 10-7 (Cle)
1978—Browns, 13-10 (Cle) OT
Bengals, 48-16 (Cin)
1979—Browns, 28-27 (Cle)
Bengals, 16-12 (Cin)
1980—Browns, 31-7 (Cle)
Browns, 27-24 (Cin)
1981—Browns, 20-17 (Cin)
Bengals, 41-21 (Cle)
1982—Bengals, 23-10 (Cin)

1983—Browns, 17-7 (Cle)
Bengals, 28-21 (Cin)
1984—Bengals, 12-9 (Cin)
Bengals, 20-17 (Cle) OT
1985—Bengals, 27-10 (Cin)
Browns, 24-6 (Cle)
1986—Bengals, 30-13 (Cle)
Browns, 34-3 (Cin)
1987—Browns, 34-0 (Cin)
Browns, 38-24 (Cle)
1988—Bengals, 24-17 (Cin)
Browns, 23-16 (Cle)
1989—Bengals, 21-14 (Cin)
Bengals, 21-0 (Cle)
1990—Bengals, 34-13 (Cle)
Bengals, 21-14 (Cin)
1991—Browns, 14-13 (Cle)
Bengals, 23-21 (Cin)
1992—Bengals, 30-10 (Cin)
Browns, 37-21 (Cle)
1993—Bengals, 27-14 (Cin)
Browns, 28-17 (Cin)
1994—Browns, 28-20 (Cin)
Browns, 37-13 (Cle)
1995—Browns, 29-26 (Cin) OT
Browns, 26-10 (Cle)
1999—Bengals, 18-17 (Cle)
Bengals, 44-28 (Cin)
2000—Browns, 24-7 (Cin)
Bengals, 12-3 (Cle)
2001—Bengals, 24-14 (Cin)
Browns, 18-0 (Cle)
2002—Browns, 20-7 (Cle)
Browns, 27-20 (Cin)
2003—Bengals, 21-14 (Cle)
Browns, 22-14 (Cin)
2004—Browns, 34-17 (Cle)
Bengals, 58-48 (Cin)
2005—Bengals, 27-13 (Cle)
Bengals, 23-20 (Cin)
2006—Bengals, 34-17 (Cin)
Bengals, 30-0 (Cle)
2007—Browns, 51-45 (Cle)
Bengals, 19-14 (Cin)
2008—Bengals, 20-12 (Cin)
Bengals, 14-0 (Cle)
2009—Bengals, 23-20 (Cle) OT
Bengals, 16-7 (Cin)
2010—Browns, 23-20 (Cin)
Bengals, 19-17 (Cin)
2011—Bengals, 27-17 (Cin)
Bengals, 23-20 (Cin)
(RS Pts.—Bengals 1,627, Browns 1,560)
CINCINNATI vs. DALLAS
RS: Cowboys lead series, 6-4
1973—Cowboys, 38-10 (D)
1979—Cowboys, 38-13 (D)
1985—Bengals, 50-24 (C)
1988—Bengals, 38-24 (D)
1991—Cowboys, 35-23 (D)
1994—Bengals, 23-20 (C)
1997—Bengals, 31-24 (C)
2000—Cowboys, 23-6 (D)
2004—Bengals, 26-3 (C)
2008—Cowboys, 31-22 (D)
(RS Pts.—Cowboys 263, Bengals 239)
CINCINNATI vs. DENVER
RS: Broncos lead series, 18-8
1968—Bengals, 24-10 (C)
Broncos, 10-7 (D)
1969—Broncos, 30-23 (C)
Broncos, 27-16 (D)

1971—Bengals, 24-10 (D)
1972—Bengals, 21-10 (C)
1973—Broncos, 28-10 (D)
1975—Bengals, 17-16 (D)
1976—Bengals, 17-7 (C)
1977—Broncos, 24-13 (C)
1979—Broncos, 10-0 (D)
1981—Bengals, 38-21 (C)
1983—Broncos, 24-17 (D)
1984—Broncos, 20-17 (D)
1986—Broncos, 34-28 (D)
1991—Broncos, 45-14 (D)
1994—Broncos, 15-13 (D)
1996—Broncos, 14-10 (D)
1997—Broncos, 38-20 (D)
1998—Broncos, 33-26 (C)
2000—Bengals, 31-21 (C)
2003—Broncos, 30-10 (D)
2004—Bengals, 23-10 (C)
2006—Broncos, 24-23 (D)
2009—Broncos, 12-7 (C)
2011—Broncos, 24-22 (D)
(RS Pts.—Broncos 547, Bengals 471)
CINCINNATI vs. DETROIT
RS: Bengals lead series, 7-3
1970—Lions, 38-3 (D)
1974—Lions, 23-19 (C)
1983—Bengals, 17-9 (C)
1986—Bengals, 24-17 (D)
1989—Bengals, 42-7 (C)
1992—Lions, 19-13 (C)
1998—Bengals, 34-28 (D) OT
2001—Bengals, 31-27 (D)
2005—Bengals, 41-17 (D)
2009—Bengals, 23-13 (C)
(RS Pts.—Bengals 247, Lions 198)
CINCINNATI vs. GREEN BAY
RS: Bengals lead series, 6-5
1971—Packers, 20-17 (GB)
1976—Bengals, 28-7 (C)
1977—Bengals, 17-7 (Mil)
1980—Packers, 14-9 (GB)
1983—Bengals, 34-14 (C)
1986—Bengals, 34-28 (Mil)
1992—Packers, 24-23 (GB)
1995—Packers, 24-10 (GB)
1998—Packers, 13-6 (C)
2005—Bengals, 21-14 (C)
2009—Bengals, 31-24 (GB)
(RS Pts.—Bengals 230, Packers 189)
CINCINNATI vs. HOUSTON
RS: Series tied, 3-3
PS: Texans lead series, 1-0
2002—Bengals, 38-3 (H)
2003—Bengals, 34-27 (C)
2005—Bengals, 16-10 (C)
2008—Texans, 35-6 (H)
2009—Texans, 28-17 (C)
2011—Texans, 20-19 (C)
      *Texans, 31-10 (H)
(RS Pts.—Bengals 130, Texans 123)
(PS Pts.—Texans 31, Bengals 10)
*AFC First-Round Playoff
CINCINNATI vs. *INDIANAPOLIS
RS: Colts lead series, 16-9
PS: Colts lead series, 1-0
1970—**Colts, 17-0 (B)
1972—Colts, 20-19 (C)
1974—Bengals, 24-14 (B)
1976—Colts, 28-27 (B)
1979—Colts, 38-28 (B)
1980—Bengals, 34-33 (C)

1981—Bengals, 41-19 (B)
1982—Bengals, 20-17 (B)
1983—Colts, 34-31 (C)
1987—Bengals, 23-21 (I)
1989—Colts, 23-12 (C)
1990—Colts, 34-20 (C)
1992—Colts, 21-17 (C)
1993—Colts, 9-6 (C)
1994—Colts, 17-13 (C)
1995—Bengals, 24-21 (I) OT
1996—Bengals, 31-24 (C)
1997—Bengals, 28-13 (I)
1998—Colts, 39-26 (I)
1999—Colts, 31-10 (I)
2002—Colts, 28-21 (I)
2005—Colts, 45-37 (C)
2006—Colts, 34-16 (I)
2008—Colts, 35-3 (I)
2010—Colts, 23-17 (I)
2011—Bengals, 27-17 (C)
(RS Pts.—Colts 638, Bengals 555)
(PS Pts.—Colts 17, Bengals 0)
*Franchise in Baltimore prior to 1984
**AFC Divisional Playoff
CINCINNATI vs. JACKSONVILLE
RS: Jaguars lead series, 11-7
1995—Bengals, 24-17 (C)
      Bengals, 17-13 (J)
1996—Bengals, 28-21 (C)
      Jaguars, 30-27 (J)
1997—Jaguars, 21-13 (J)
      Bengals, 31-26 (C)
1998—Jaguars, 24-11 (J)
      Jaguars, 34-17 (C)
1999—Jaguars, 41-10 (C)
      Jaguars, 24-7 (J)
2000—Jaguars, 13-0 (J)
      Bengals, 17-14 (C)
2001—Jaguars, 30-13 (J)
      Jaguars, 14-10 (C)
2002—Jaguars, 29-15 (C)
2005—Jaguars, 23-20 (J)
2008—Bengals, 21-19 (C)
2011—Bengals, 30-20 (J)
(RS Pts.—Jaguars 413, Bengals 311)
CINCINNATI vs. KANSAS CITY
RS: Series tied, 13-13
1968—Chiefs, 13-3 (KC)
      Chiefs, 16-9 (C)
1969—Bengals, 24-19 (C)
      Chiefs, 42-22 (KC)
1970—Chiefs, 27-19 (C)
1972—Bengals, 23-16 (KC)
1973—Bengals, 14-6 (C)
1974—Bengals, 33-6 (C)
1976—Bengals, 27-24 (KC)
1977—Bengals, 27-7 (C)
1978—Chiefs, 24-23 (C)
1979—Chiefs, 10-7 (C)
1980—Bengals, 20-6 (KC)
1983—Chiefs, 20-15 (KC)
1984—Chiefs, 27-22 (C)
1986—Chiefs, 24-14 (KC)
1987—Bengals, 30-27 (C) OT
1988—Chiefs, 31-28 (KC)
1989—Bengals, 21-17 (KC)
1993—Chiefs, 17-15 (KC)
2003—Bengals, 24-19 (C)
2005—Chiefs, 37-3 (KC)
2006—Bengals, 23-10 (KC)
2007—Chiefs, 27-20 (KC)
2008—Bengals, 16-6 (C)

2009—Bengals, 17-10 (C)
(RS Pts.—Bengals 499, Chiefs 488)
CINCINNATI vs. MIAMI
RS: Dolphins lead series, 13-5
PS: Dolphins lead series, 1-0
1968—Dolphins, 24-22 (C)
      Bengals, 38-21 (M)
1969—Bengals, 27-21 (C)
1971—Dolphins, 23-13 (C)
1973—*Dolphins, 34-16 (M)
1974—Dolphins, 24-3 (M)
1977—Bengals, 23-17 (C)
1978—Dolphins, 21-0 (M)
1980—Dolphins, 17-16 (M)
1983—Dolphins, 38-14 (M)
1987—Dolphins, 20-14 (C)
1989—Dolphins, 20-13 (C)
1991—Dolphins, 37-13 (M)
1994—Dolphins, 23-7 (C)
1995—Dolphins, 26-23 (C)
2000—Dolphins, 31-16 (C)
2004—Bengals, 16-13 (C)
2007—Bengals, 38-25 (M)
2010—Dolphins, 22-14 (C)
(RS Pts.—Dolphins 423, Bengals 310)
(PS Pts.—Dolphins 34, Bengals 16)
*AFC Divisional Playoff
CINCINNATI vs. MINNESOTA
RS: Vikings lead series, 6-5
1973—Bengals, 27-0 (C)
1977—Vikings, 42-10 (M)
1980—Bengals, 14-0 (C)
1983—Vikings, 20-14 (M)
1986—Bengals, 24-20 (M)
1989—Vikings, 29-21 (M)
1992—Vikings, 42-7 (C)
1995—Bengals, 27-24 (C)
1998—Vikings, 24-3 (M)
2005—Bengals, 37-8 (C)
2009—Vikings, 30-10 (M)
(RS Pts.—Vikings 239, Bengals 194)
CINCINNATI vs. *NEW ENGLAND
RS: Patriots lead series, 14-8
1968—Patriots, 33-14 (B)
1969—Patriots, 25-14 (C)
1970—Bengals, 45-7 (C)
1972—Bengals, 31-7 (NE)
1975—Bengals, 27-10 (C)
1978—Patriots, 10-3 (C)
1979—Patriots, 20-14 (C)
1984—Patriots, 20-14 (NE)
1985—Patriots, 34-23 (NE)
1986—Bengals, 31-7 (NE)
1988—Patriots, 27-21 (NE)
1990—Bengals, 41-7 (C)
1991—Bengals, 29-7 (C)
1992—Bengals, 20-10 (C)
1993—Patriots, 7-2 (NE)
1994—Bengals, 31-28 (C)
2000—Patriots, 16-13 (NE)
2001—Bengals, 23-17 (C)
2004—Patriots, 35-28 (NE)
2006—Patriots, 38-13 (C)
2007—Bengals, 34-13 (C)
2010—Patriots, 38-24 (NE)
(RS Pts.—Bengals 471, Patriots 440)
*Franchise in Boston prior to 1971
CINCINNATI vs. NEW ORLEANS
RS: Series tied, 6-6
1970—Bengals, 26-6 (C)
1975—Bengals, 21-0 (NO)
1978—Saints, 20-18 (C)

1981—Saints, 17-7 (NO)
1984—Bengals, 24-21 (NO)
1987—Saints, 41-24 (C)
1990—Saints, 21-7 (C)
1993—Saints, 20-13 (NO)
1996—Bengals, 30-15 (C)
2002—Bengals, 20-13 (C)
2006—Bengals, 31-16 (NO)
2010—Saints, 34-30 (C)
(RS Pts.—Bengals 251, Saints 224)

CINCINNATI vs. N.Y. GIANTS
RS: Bengals lead series, 5-3
1972—Bengals, 13-10 (C)
1977—Bengals, 30-13 (C)
1985—Bengals, 35-30 (C)
1991—Bengals, 27-24 (C)
1994—Giants, 27-20 (NY)
1997—Giants, 29-27 (NY)
2004—Bengals, 23-22 (C)
2008—Giants, 26-23 (NY) OT
(RS Pts.—Bengals 198, Giants 181)

CINCINNATI vs. N.Y. JETS
RS: Jets lead series, 15-7
PS: Jets lead series, 2-0
1968—Jets, 27-14 (NY)
1969—Jets, 21-7 (C)
         Jets, 40-7 (NY)
1971—Jets, 35-21 (NY)
1973—Bengals, 20-14 (C)
1976—Bengals, 42-3 (NY)
1981—Bengals, 31-30 (NY)
1982—*Jets, 44-17 (C)
1984—Jets, 43-23 (NY)
1985—Jets, 29-20 (C)
1986—Bengals, 52-21 (C)
1987—Jets, 27-20 (NY)
1988—Bengals, 36-19 (C)
1990—Bengals, 25-20 (C)
1992—Jets, 17-14 (NY)
1993—Jets, 17-12 (NY)
1997—Jets, 31-14 (C)
2001—Jets, 15-14 (NY)
2004—Jets, 31-24 (NY)
2007—Bengals, 38-31 (C)
2008—Jets, 26-14 (NY)
2009—Jets, 37-0 (NY)
         *Jets, 24-14 (C)
2010—Jets, 26-10 (NY)
(RS Pts.—Jets 560, Bengals 458)
(PS Pts.—Jets 68, Bengals 31)
*AFC First-Round Playoff

CINCINNATI vs. *OAKLAND
RS: Raiders lead series, 18-8
PS: Raiders lead series, 2-0
1968—Raiders, 31-10 (O)
         Raiders, 34-0 (C)
1969—Bengals, 31-17 (C)
         Raiders, 37-17 (O)
1970—Bengals, 31-21 (C)
1971—Raiders, 31-27 (O)
1972—Raiders, 20-14 (C)
1974—Raiders, 30-27 (O)
1975—Bengals, 14-10 (C)
         **Raiders, 31-28 (O)
1976—Raiders, 35-20 (O)
1978—Raiders, 34-21 (C)
1980—Raiders, 28-17 (O)
1982—Bengals, 31-17 (C)
1983—Raiders, 20-10 (C)
1985—Raiders, 13-6 (LA)
1988—Bengals, 45-21 (LA)
1989—Raiders, 28-7 (LA)

1990—Raiders, 24-7 (LA)
         **Raiders, 20-10 (LA)
1991—Raiders, 38-14 (C)
1992—Bengals, 24-21 (C) OT
1993—Bengals, 16-10 (C)
1995—Raiders, 20-17 (C)
1998—Raiders, 27-10 (O)
2003—Raiders, 23-20 (O)
2006—Bengals, 27-10 (C)
2009—Bengals, 20-17 (O)
(RS Pts.—Raiders 620, Bengals 480)
(PS Pts.—Raiders 51, Bengals 38)
*Franchise in Los Angeles from 1982-1994
**AFC Divisional Playoff

CINCINNATI vs. PHILADELPHIA
RS: Bengals lead series, 7-3-1
1971—Bengals, 37-14 (C)
1975—Bengals, 31-0 (P)
1979—Bengals, 37-13 (C)
1982—Bengals, 18-14 (P)
1988—Bengals, 28-24 (P)
1991—Eagles, 17-10 (P)
1994—Bengals, 33-30 (C)
1997—Eagles, 44-42 (P)
2000—Eagles, 16-7 (P)
2004—Bengals, 38-10 (P)
2008—Tie, 13-13 (C) OT
(RS Pts.—Bengals 294, Eagles 195)

CINCINNATI vs. PITTSBURGH
RS: Steelers lead series, 51-32
PS: Steelers lead series, 1-0
1970—Steelers, 21-10 (P)
         Bengals, 34-7 (C)
1971—Steelers, 21-10 (P)
         Steelers, 21-13 (C)
1972—Bengals, 15-10 (C)
         Steelers, 40-17 (P)
1973—Bengals, 19-7 (C)
         Steelers, 20-13 (P)
1974—Bengals, 17-10 (C)
         Steelers, 27-3 (P)
1975—Steelers, 30-24 (C)
         Steelers, 35-14 (P)
1976—Steelers, 23-6 (P)
         Steelers, 7-3 (C)
1977—Steelers, 20-14 (P)
         Bengals, 17-10 (C)
1978—Steelers, 28-3 (C)
         Steelers, 7-6 (P)
1979—Bengals, 34-10 (C)
         Steelers, 37-17 (P)
1980—Bengals, 30-28 (C)
         Bengals, 17-16 (P)
1981—Bengals, 34-7 (C)
         Bengals, 17-10 (P)
1982—Steelers, 26-20 (P) OT
1983—Steelers, 24-14 (C)
         Bengals, 23-10 (P)
1984—Steelers, 38-17 (P)
         Bengals, 22-20 (C)
1985—Bengals, 37-24 (P)
         Bengals, 26-21 (C)
1986—Bengals, 24-22 (C)
         Steelers, 30-9 (P)
1987—Steelers, 23-20 (P)
         Steelers, 30-16 (C)
1988—Bengals, 17-12 (P)
         Bengals, 42-7 (C)
1989—Bengals, 41-10 (P)
         Bengals, 26-16 (P)
1990—Bengals, 27-3 (C)
         Bengals, 16-12 (P)

1991—Steelers, 33-27 (C) OT
         Steelers, 17-10 (P)
1992—Steelers, 20-0 (P)
         Steelers, 21-9 (C)
1993—Steelers, 34-7 (P)
         Steelers, 24-16 (C)
1994—Steelers, 14-10 (P)
         Steelers, 38-15 (C)
1995—Bengals, 27-9 (P)
         Steelers, 49-31 (C)
1996—Steelers, 20-10 (P)
         Bengals, 34-24 (C)
1997—Steelers, 26-10 (C)
         Steelers, 20-3 (P)
1998—Bengals, 25-20 (C)
         Bengals, 25-24 (P)
1999—Steelers, 17-3 (C)
         Bengals, 27-20 (P)
2000—Steelers, 15-0 (P)
         Steelers, 48-28 (C)
2001—Steelers, 16-7 (P)
         Bengals, 26-23 (C) OT
2002—Steelers, 34-7 (C)
         Steelers, 29-21 (P)
2003—Steelers, 17-10 (P)
         Bengals, 24-20 (C)
2004—Steelers, 28-17 (C)
         Steelers, 19-14 (C)
2005—Steelers, 27-13 (C)
         Bengals, 38-31 (P)
         *Steelers, 31-17 (C)
2006—Bengals, 28-20 (P)
         Steelers, 23-17 (C) OT
2007—Steelers, 24-13 (C)
         Steelers, 24-10 (P)
2008—Steelers, 38-10 (C)
         Steelers, 27-10 (P)
2009—Bengals, 23-20 (P)
         Bengals, 18-12 (P)
2010—Steelers, 27-21 (C)
         Steelers, 23-7 (P)
2011—Steelers, 24-17 (C)
         Steelers, 35-7 (P)
(RS Pts.—Steelers 1,814, Bengals 1,459)
(PS Pts.—Steelers 31, Bengals 17)
*AFC First-Round Playoff

CINCINNATI vs. *ST. LOUIS
RS: Bengals lead series, 7-5
1972—Rams, 15-12 (LA)
1976—Bengals, 20-12 (LA)
1978—Bengals, 20-19 (LA)
1981—Bengals, 24-10 (C)
1984—Rams, 24-14 (C)
1990—Bengals, 34-31 (LA) OT
1993—Bengals, 15-3 (C)
1996—Rams, 26-16 (StL)
1999—Rams, 38-10 (C)
2003—Rams, 27-10 (StL)
2007—Bengals, 19-10 (C)
2011—Bengals, 20-13 (StL)
(RS Pts.—Rams 228, Bengals 214)
*Franchise in Los Angeles prior to 1995

CINCINNATI vs. SAN DIEGO
RS: Chargers lead series, 19-11
PS: Bengals lead series, 1-0
1968—Chargers, 29-13 (SD)
         Chargers, 31-10 (C)
1969—Bengals, 34-20 (C)
         Chargers, 21-14 (SD)
1970—Bengals, 17-14 (SD)
1971—Bengals, 31-0 (C)
1973—Bengals, 20-13 (SD)

1974—Chargers, 20-17 (C)
1975—Bengals, 47-17 (C)
1977—Chargers, 24-3 (SD)
1978—Chargers, 22-13 (SD)
1979—Chargers, 26-24 (C)
1980—Chargers, 31-14 (C)
1981—Bengals, 40-17 (SD)
   *Bengals, 27-7 (C)
1982—Chargers, 50-34 (SD)
1985—Chargers, 44-41 (C)
1987—Chargers, 10-9 (C)
1988—Bengals, 27-10 (C)
1990—Bengals, 21-16 (SD)
1992—Chargers, 27-10 (SD)
1994—Chargers, 27-10 (SD)
1996—Chargers, 27-14 (SD)
1997—Bengals, 38-31 (C)
1999—Chargers, 34-7 (C)
2001—Chargers, 28-14 (SD)
2002—Chargers, 34-6 (C)
2003—Bengals, 34-27 (C)
2006—Chargers, 49-41 (C)
2009—Chargers, 27-24 (SD)
2010—Bengals, 34-20 (C)
(RS Pts.—Chargers 746, Bengals 661)
(PS Pts.—Bengals 27, Chargers 7)
*AFC Championship
CINCINNATI vs. SAN FRANCISCO
RS: 49ers lead series, 9-3
PS: 49ers lead series, 2-0
1974—Bengals, 21-3 (SF)
1978—49ers, 28-12 (SF)
1981—49ers, 21-3 (C)
   *49ers, 26-21 (Detroit)
1984—49ers, 23-17 (SF)
1987—49ers, 27-26 (C)
1988—**49ers, 20-16 (South Florida)
1990—49ers, 20-17 (C) OT
1993—49ers, 21-8 (SF)
1996—49ers, 28-21 (SF)
1999—Bengals, 44-30 (C)
2003—Bengals, 41-38 (C)
2007—49ers, 20-13 (SF)
2011—49ers, 13-8 (C)
(RS Pts.—49ers 272, Bengals 231)
(PS Pts.—49ers 46, Bengals 37)
*Super Bowl XVI
**Super Bowl XXIII
CINCINNATI vs. SEATTLE
RS: Series tied, 9-9
PS: Bengals lead series, 1-0
1977—Bengals, 42-20 (C)
1981—Bengals, 27-21 (C)
1982—Bengals, 24-10 (C)
1984—Seahawks, 26-6 (C)
1985—Seahawks, 28-24 (C)
1986—Bengals, 34-7 (C)
1987—Bengals, 17-10 (S)
1988—*Bengals, 21-13 (C)
1989—Seahawks, 24-17 (C)
1990—Seahawks, 31-16 (S)
1991—Seahawks, 13-7 (C)
1992—Bengals, 21-3 (S)
1993—Seahawks, 19-10 (C)
1994—Bengals, 20-17 (S) OT
1995—Seahawks, 24-21 (S)
1999—Seahawks, 37-20 (S)
2003—Bengals, 27-24 (C)
2007—Seahawks, 24-21 (S)
2011—Bengals, 34-12 (S)
(RS Pts.—Bengals 388, Seahawks 350)
(PS Pts.—Bengals 21, Seahawks 13)

*AFC Divisional Playoff
CINCINNATI vs. TAMPA BAY
RS: Buccaneers lead series, 7-3
1976—Bengals, 21-0 (C)
1980—Buccaneers, 17-12 (C)
1983—Bengals, 23-17 (TB)
1989—Bengals, 56-23 (C)
1995—Buccaneers, 19-16 (TB)
1998—Buccaneers, 35-0 (C)
2001—Buccaneers, 16-13 (C) OT
2002—Buccaneers, 35-7 (C)
2006—Buccaneers, 14-13 (TB)
2010—Buccaneers, 24-21 (C)
(RS Pts.— Buccaneers 200, Bengals 182)
CINCINNATI vs. *TENNESSEE
RS: Titans lead series, 39-32-1
PS: Bengals lead series, 1-0
1968—Oilers, 27-17 (C)
1969—Tie, 31-31 (H)
1970—Oilers, 20-13 (C)
   Bengals, 30-20 (H)
1971—Oilers, 10-6 (H)
   Bengals, 28-13 (C)
1972—Bengals, 30-7 (C)
   Bengals, 61-17 (H)
1973—Bengals, 24-10 (C)
   Bengals, 27-24 (H)
1974—Oilers, 34-21 (C)
   Oilers, 20-3 (H)
1975—Bengals, 21-19 (H)
   Bengals, 23-19 (C)
1976—Bengals, 27-7 (H)
   Bengals, 31-27 (C)
1977—Bengals, 13-10 (C) OT
   Oilers, 21-16 (H)
1978—Bengals, 28-13 (C)
   Oilers, 17-10 (H)
1979—Oilers, 30-27 (C) OT
   Oilers, 42-21 (H)
1980—Oilers, 13-10 (C)
   Oilers, 23-3 (H)
1981—Oilers, 17-10 (H)
   Bengals, 34-21 (C)
1982—Bengals, 27-6 (C)
   Bengals, 35-27 (H)
1983—Bengals, 55-14 (H)
   Bengals, 38-10 (C)
1984—Bengals, 13-3 (C)
   Bengals, 31-13 (H)
1985—Oilers, 44-27 (H)
   Bengals, 45-27 (C)
1986—Bengals, 31-28 (C)
   Oilers, 32-28 (H)
1987—Oilers, 31-29 (C)
   Oilers, 21-17 (H)
1988—Bengals, 44-21 (C)
   Oilers, 41-6 (H)
1989—Oilers, 26-24 (H)
   Bengals, 61-7 (C)
1990—Oilers, 48-17 (H)
   Bengals, 40-20 (C)
   **Bengals, 41-14 (C)
1991—Oilers, 30-7 (C)
   Oilers, 35-3 (H)
1992—Oilers, 38-24 (C)
   Oilers, 26-10 (H)
1993—Oilers, 28-12 (H)
   Oilers, 38-3 (C)
1994—Oilers, 20-13 (H)
   Bengals, 34-31 (C)
1995—Oilers, 38-28 (C)
   Bengals, 32-25 (H)

1996—Oilers, 30-27 (C) OT
   Bengals, 21-13 (H)
1997—Oilers, 30-7 (T)
   Bengals, 41-14 (C)
1998—Oilers, 23-14 (C)
   Oilers, 44-14 (T)
1999—Titans, 36-35 (T)
   Titans, 24-14 (C)
2000—Titans, 23-14 (C)
   Titans, 35-3 (T)
2001—Titans, 20-7 (C)
   Bengals, 23-21 (T)
2002—Titans, 30-24 (C)
2004—Titans, 27-20 (T)
2005—Bengals, 31-23 (T)
2007—Bengals, 35-6 (C)
2008—Titans, 24-7 (C)
2011—Bengals, 24-17 (T)
(RS Pts.—Titans 1,680, Bengals 1,660)
(PS Pts.—Bengals 41, Titans 14)
*Franchise in Houston prior to 1997;
known as Oilers prior to 1999
**AFC First-Round Playoff
CINCINNATI vs. WASHINGTON
RS: Series tied, 4-4
1970—Redskins, 20-0 (W)
1974—Bengals, 28-17 (C)
1979—Redskins, 28-14 (W)
1985—Redskins, 27-24 (W)
1988—Bengals, 20-17 (C) OT
1991—Redskins, 34-27 (C)
2004—Bengals, 17-10 (W)
2008—Bengals, 20-13 (C)
(RS Pts.—Redskins 166, Bengals 150)

CLEVELAND vs. ARIZONA
RS: Browns lead series, 33-13-3;
See Arizona vs. Cleveland
CLEVELAND vs. ATLANTA
RS: Browns lead series, 10-3;
See Atlanta vs. Cleveland
CLEVELAND vs. BALTIMORE
RS: Ravens lead series, 19-7;
See Baltimore vs. Cleveland
CLEVELAND vs. BUFFALO
RS: Browns lead series, 10-6
PS: Browns lead series, 1-0;
See Buffalo vs. Cleveland
CLEVELAND vs. CAROLINA
RS: Panthers lead series, 3-1;
See Carolina vs. Cleveland
CLEVELAND vs. CHICAGO
RS: Browns lead series, 9-5;
See Chicago vs. Cleveland
CLEVELAND vs. CINCINNATI
RS: Bengals lead series, 41-36;
See Cincinnati vs. Cleveland
CLEVELAND vs. DALLAS
RS: Browns lead series, 15-11
PS: Browns lead series, 2-1
1960—Browns, 48-7 (D)
1961—Browns, 25-7 (D)
   Browns, 38-17 (D)
1962—Browns, 19-10 (C)
   Cowboys, 45-21 (D)
1963—Browns, 41-24 (D)
   Browns, 27-17 (C)
1964—Browns, 27-6 (D)
   Browns, 20-16 (D)
1965—Browns, 23-17 (C)
   Browns, 24-17 (D)
1966—Browns, 30-21 (C)

Cowboys, 26-14 (D)
1967—Cowboys, 21-14 (C)
*Cowboys, 52-14 (D)
1968—Cowboys, 28-7 (D)
*Browns, 31-20 (C)
1969—Browns, 42-10 (C)
*Browns, 38-14 (D)
1970—Cowboys, 6-2 (C)
1974—Cowboys, 41-17 (D)
1979—Browns, 26-7 (C)
1982—Cowboys, 31-14 (D)
1985—Cowboys, 20-7 (D)
1988—Browns, 24-21 (C)
1991—Cowboys, 26-14 (C)
1994—Browns, 19-14 (D)
2004—Cowboys, 19-12 (D)
2008—Cowboys, 28-10 (C)
(RS Pts.—Browns 565, Cowboys 502)
(PS Pts.—Cowboys 86, Browns 83)
*Conference Championship
CLEVELAND vs. DENVER
RS: Broncos lead series, 18-5
PS: Broncos lead series, 3-0
1970—Browns, 27-13 (D)
1971—Broncos, 27-0 (C)
1972—Broncos, 27-20 (D)
1974—Browns, 23-21 (C)
1975—Broncos, 16-15 (D)
1976—Broncos, 44-13 (D)
1978—Broncos, 19-7 (C)
1980—Broncos, 19-16 (C)
1981—Broncos, 23-20 (D) OT
1983—Broncos, 27-6 (D)
1984—Broncos, 24-14 (C)
1986—*Broncos, 23-20 (C) OT
1987—*Broncos, 38-33 (D)
1988—Broncos, 30-7 (D)
1989—Browns, 16-13 (C)
*Broncos, 37-21 (D)
1990—Browns, 30-29 (D)
1991—Broncos, 17-7 (C)
1992—Broncos, 12-0 (C)
1993—Broncos, 29-14 (C)
1994—Broncos, 26-14 (C)
2000—Broncos, 44-10 (D)
2003—Broncos, 23-20 (D) OT
2006—Broncos, 17-7 (C)
2008—Broncos, 34-30 (C)
2009—Broncos, 27-6 (D)
(RS Pts.—Broncos 554, Browns 329)
(PS Pts.—Broncos 98, Browns 74)
*AFC Championship
CLEVELAND vs. DETROIT
RS: Lions lead series, 14-4
PS: Lions lead series, 3-1
1952—Lions, 17-6 (D)
*Lions, 17-7 (C)
1953—*Lions, 17-16 (D)
1954—Lions, 14-10 (C)
*Browns, 56-10 (C)
1957—Lions, 20-7 (D)
*Lions, 59-14 (D)
1958—Lions, 30-10 (C)
1963—Lions, 38-10 (D)
1964—Browns, 37-21 (C)
1967—Lions, 31-14 (D)
1969—Lions, 28-21 (C)
1970—Lions, 41-24 (D)
1975—Lions, 21-10 (D)
1983—Lions, 31-26 (D)
1986—Browns, 24-21 (C)
1989—Lions, 13-10 (D)

1992—Lions, 24-14 (D)
1995—Lions, 38-20 (D)
2001—Browns, 24-14 (C)
2005—Lions, 13-10 (C)
2009—Lions, 38-37 (D)
(RS Pts.—Lions 448, Browns 319)
(PS Pts.—Lions 103, Browns 93)
*NFL Championship
CLEVELAND vs. GREEN BAY
RS: Packers lead series, 10-7
PS: Packers lead series, 1-0
1953—Browns, 27-0 (Mil)
1955—Browns, 41-10 (C)
1956—Browns, 24-7 (Mil)
1961—Packers, 49-17 (C)
1964—Packers, 28-21 (Mil)
1965—*Packers, 23-12 (GB)
1966—Packers, 21-20 (C)
1967—Packers, 55-7 (Mil)
1969—Browns, 20-7 (C)
1972—Packers, 26-10 (C)
1980—Browns, 26-21 (C)
1983—Packers, 35-21 (Mil)
1986—Packers, 17-14 (C)
1992—Browns, 17-6 (C)
1995—Packers, 31-20 (C)
2001—Packers, 30-7 (GB)
2005—Browns, 26-24 (GB)
2009—Packers, 31-3 (C)
(RS Pts.—Packers 398, Browns 321)
(PS Pts.—Packers 23, Browns 12)
*NFL Championship
CLEVELAND vs. HOUSTON
RS: Texans lead series, 4-3
2002—Browns, 34-17 (C)
2004—Browns, 22-14 (H)
2005—Texans, 19-16 (H)
2006—Texans, 14-6 (H)
2007—Texans, 27-17 (C)
2008—Texans, 16-6 (C)
2011—Texans, 30-12 (H)
(RS Pts.—Texans 127, Browns 123)
CLEVELAND vs. *INDIANAPOLIS
RS: Browns lead series, 14-12
PS: Series tied, 2-2
1956—Colts, 21-7 (C)
1959—Browns, 38-31 (B)
1962—Colts, 36-14 (C)
1964—**Browns, 27-0 (C)
1968—Browns, 30-20 (B)
**Colts, 34-0 (C)
1971—Browns, 14-13 (B)
***Colts, 20-3 (C)
1973—Browns, 24-14 (C)
1975—Colts, 21-7 (B)
1978—Browns, 45-24 (B)
1979—Browns, 13-10 (C)
1980—Browns, 28-27 (B)
1981—Browns, 42-28 (C)
1983—Browns, 41-23 (C)
1986—Browns, 24-9 (I)
1987—Colts, 9-7 (C)
***Browns, 38-21 (C)
1988—Browns, 23-17 (C)
1989—Colts, 23-17 (I) OT
1991—Browns, 31-0 (I)
1992—Colts, 14-3 (I)
1993—Colts, 23-10 (I)
1994—Browns, 21-14 (I)
1999—Colts, 29-28 (C)
2002—Colts, 28-23 (C)
2003—Colts, 9-6 (C)

2005—Colts, 13-6 (I)
2008—Colts, 10-6 (C)
2011—Browns, 27-19 (I)
(RS Pts.—Browns 535, Colts 485)
(PS Pts.—Colts 75, Browns 68)
*Franchise in Baltimore prior to 1984
**NFL Championship
***AFC Divisional Playoff
CLEVELAND vs. JACKSONVILLE
RS: Jaguars lead series, 9-5
1995—Jaguars, 23-15 (C)
Jaguars, 24-21 (J)
1999—Jaguars, 24-7 (J)
Jaguars, 24-14 (C)
2000—Jaguars, 27-7 (C)
Jaguars, 48-0 (J)
2001—Browns, 23-14 (J)
Jaguars, 15-10 (C)
2002—Browns, 21-20 (J)
2005—Jaguars, 20-14 (C)
2008—Browns, 23-17 (J)
2009—Browns, 23-17 (C)
2010—Jaguars, 24-20 (J)
2011—Browns, 14-10 (C)
(RS Pts.—Jaguars 307, Browns 212)
CLEVELAND vs. KANSAS CITY
RS: Series tied, 10-10-2
1971—Chiefs, 13-7 (KC)
1972—Chiefs, 31-7 (C)
1973—Tie, 20-20 (KC)
1975—Browns, 40-14 (C)
1976—Chiefs, 39-14 (KC)
1977—Browns, 44-7 (C)
1978—Chiefs, 17-3 (KC)
1979—Chiefs, 27-24 (KC)
1980—Browns, 20-13 (C)
1984—Chiefs, 10-6 (KC)
1986—Browns, 20-7 (C)
1988—Browns, 6-3 (KC)
1989—Tie, 10-10 (C) OT
1990—Browns, 34-0 (KC)
1991—Browns, 20-15 (C)
1994—Chiefs, 20-13 (KC)
1995—Browns, 35-17 (C)
2002—Chiefs, 40-39 (C)
2003—Chiefs, 41-20 (KC)
2006—Browns, 31-28 (C) OT
2009—Browns, 41-34 (KC)
2010—Chiefs, 16-14 (C)
(RS Pts.—Chiefs 453, Browns 437)
CLEVELAND vs. MIAMI
RS: Browns lead series, 8-7
PS: Dolphins lead series, 2-0
1970—Browns, 28-0 (M)
1972—*Dolphins, 20-14 (M)
1973—Dolphins, 17-9 (C)
1976—Browns, 17-13 (C)
1979—Browns, 30-24 (C) OT
1985—*Dolphins, 24-21 (M)
1986—Browns, 26-16 (C)
1988—Dolphins, 38-31 (M)
1989—Dolphins, 13-10 (M) OT
1990—Dolphins, 30-13 (C)
1992—Dolphins, 27-23 (C)
1993—Dolphins, 24-14 (C)
2004—Dolphins, 10-7 (M)
2005—Browns, 22-0 (C)
2007—Browns, 41-31 (C)
2010—Browns, 13-10 (M)
2011—Browns, 17-16 (C)
(RS Pts.—Browns 301, Dolphins 269)
(PS Pts.—Dolphins 44, Browns 35)

*AFC Divisional Playoff
CLEVELAND vs. MINNESOTA
RS: Vikings lead series, 10-3
PS: Vikings lead series, 1-0
1965—Vikings, 27-17 (C)
1967—Browns, 14-10 (C)
1969—Vikings, 51-3 (M)
   *Vikings, 27-7 (M)
1973—Vikings, 26-3 (M)
1975—Vikings, 42-10 (C)
1980—Vikings, 28-23 (M)
1983—Vikings, 27-21 (C)
1986—Browns, 23-20 (M)
1989—Browns, 23-17 (C) OT
1992—Vikings, 17-13 (M)
1995—Vikings, 27-11 (M)
2005—Vikings, 24-12 (M)
2009—Vikings, 34-20 (C)
(RS Pts.—Vikings 350, Browns 193)
(PS Pts.—Vikings 27, Browns 7)
*NFL Championship
CLEVELAND vs. NEW ENGLAND
RS: Browns lead series, 12-9
PS: Browns lead series, 1-0
1971—Browns, 27-7 (C)
1974—Browns, 21-14 (NE)
1977—Browns, 30-27 (C) OT
1980—Patriots, 34-17 (NE)
1982—Browns, 10-7 (C)
1983—Browns, 30-0 (NE)
1984—Patriots, 17-16 (C)
1985—Browns, 24-20 (C)
1987—Browns, 20-10 (NE)
1991—Browns, 20-0 (NE)
1992—Browns, 19-17 (NE)
1993—Patriots, 20-17 (C)
1994—Browns, 13-6 (C)
   *Browns, 20-13 (C)
1995—Patriots, 17-14 (NE)
1999—Patriots, 19-7 (C)
2000—Browns, 19-11 (C)
2001—Patriots, 27-16 (NE)
2003—Patriots, 9-3 (NE)
2004—Patriots, 42-15 (C)
2007—Patriots, 34-17 (NE)
2010—Browns, 34-14 (C)
(RS Pts.—Browns 389, Patriots 352)
(PS Pts.—Browns 20, Patriots 13)
*AFC First-Round Playoff
CLEVELAND vs. NEW ORLEANS
RS: Browns lead series, 12-4
1967—Browns, 42-7 (NO)
1968—Browns, 24-10 (NO)
   Browns, 35-17 (C)
1969—Browns, 27-17 (NO)
1971—Browns, 21-17 (NO)
1975—Browns, 17-16 (C)
1978—Browns, 24-16 (NO)
1981—Browns, 20-17 (C)
1984—Saints, 16-14 (C)
1987—Saints, 28-21 (NO)
1990—Saints, 25-20 (NO)
1993—Browns, 17-13 (C)
1999—Browns, 21-16 (NO)
2002—Browns, 24-15 (NO)
2006—Saints, 19-14 (C)
2010—Browns, 30-17 (NO)
(RS Pts.—Browns 371, Saints 266)
CLEVELAND vs. N.Y. GIANTS
RS: Browns lead series, 26-19-2
PS: Series tied, 1-1
1950—Giants, 6-0 (C)

Giants, 17-13 (NY)
   *Browns, 8-3 (C)
1951—Browns, 14-13 (C)
   Browns, 10-0 (NY)
1952—Giants, 17-9 (C)
   Giants, 37-34 (NY)
1953—Browns, 7-0 (NY)
   Browns, 62-14 (C)
1954—Browns, 24-14 (C)
   Browns, 16-7 (NY)
1955—Browns, 24-14 (C)
   Tie, 35-35 (NY)
1956—Giants, 21-9 (C)
   Browns, 24-7 (NY)
1957—Browns, 6-3 (C)
   Browns, 34-28 (NY)
1958—Giants, 21-17 (C)
   Giants, 13-10 (NY)
   *Giants, 10-0 (NY)
1959—Giants, 10-6 (C)
   Giants, 48-7 (NY)
1960—Giants, 17-13 (C)
   Browns, 48-34 (NY)
1961—Giants, 37-21 (C)
   Tie, 7-7 (NY)
1962—Browns, 17-7 (C)
   Giants, 17-13 (NY)
1963—Browns, 35-24 (NY)
   Giants, 33-6 (C)
1964—Browns, 42-20 (C)
   Browns, 52-20 (NY)
1965—Browns, 38-14 (NY)
   Browns, 34-21 (C)
1966—Browns, 28-7 (NY)
   Browns, 49-40 (C)
1967—Giants, 38-34 (NY)
   Browns, 24-14 (C)
1968—Browns, 45-10 (C)
1969—Browns, 28-17 (C)
   Giants, 27-14 (NY)
1973—Browns, 12-10 (C)
1977—Browns, 21-7 (NY)
1985—Browns, 35-33 (NY)
1991—Giants, 13-10 (C)
1994—Giants, 16-13 (C)
2000—Giants, 24-3 (C)
2004—Giants, 27-10 (NY)
2008—Browns, 35-14 (C)
(RS Pts.—Browns 1,048, Giants 873)
(PS Pts.—Giants 13, Browns 8)
*Conference Playoff
CLEVELAND vs. N.Y. JETS
RS: Browns lead series, 12-8
PS: Browns lead series, 1-0
1970—Browns, 31-21 (C)
1972—Browns, 26-10 (NY)
1976—Browns, 38-17 (C)
1978—Browns, 37-34 (C) OT
1979—Browns, 25-22 (NY) OT
1980—Browns, 17-14 (C)
1981—Jets, 14-13 (C)
1983—Browns, 10-7 (C)
1984—Jets, 24-20 (C)
1985—Jets, 37-10 (NY)
1986—*Browns, 23-20 (C) OT
1988—Jets, 23-3 (C)
1989—Browns, 38-24 (C)
1990—Jets, 24-21 (NY)
1991—Jets, 17-14 (C)
1994—Browns, 27-7 (C)
2002—Browns, 24-21 (NY)
2004—Jets, 10-7 (C)

2006—Browns, 20-13 (C)
2007—Browns, 24-18 (NY)
2010—Jets, 26-20 (NY) OT
(RS Pts.—Browns 425, Jets 383)
(PS Pts.—Browns 23, Jets 20)
*AFC Divisional Playoff
CLEVELAND vs. *OAKLAND
RS: Raiders lead series, 11-8
PS: Raiders lead series, 2-0
1970—Raiders, 23-20 (O)
1971—Raiders, 34-20 (C)
1973—Browns, 7-3 (O)
1974—Raiders, 40-24 (C)
1975—Raiders, 38-17 (O)
1977—Raiders, 26-10 (C)
1979—Raiders, 19-14 (O)
1980—**Raiders, 14-12 (C)
1982—***Raiders, 27-10 (LA)
1985—Raiders, 21-20 (C)
1986—Raiders, 27-14 (LA)
1987—Browns, 24-17 (LA)
1992—Browns, 28-16 (LA)
1993—Browns, 19-16 (LA)
2000—Raiders, 36-10 (O)
2003—Browns, 13-7 (C)
2005—Browns, 9-7 (O)
2006—Browns, 24-21 (O)
2007—Raiders, 26-24 (O)
2009—Browns, 23-9 (C)
2011—Raiders, 24-17 (O)
(RS Pts.—Raiders 410, Browns 337)
(PS Pts.—Raiders 41, Browns 22)
*Franchise in Los Angeles from 1982-1994
**AFC Divisional Playoff
***AFC First-Round Playoff
CLEVELAND vs. PHILADELPHIA
RS: Browns lead series, 31-15-1
1950—Browns, 35-10 (P)
   Browns, 13-7 (C)
1951—Browns, 20-17 (C)
   Browns, 24-9 (P)
1952—Browns, 49-7 (P)
   Eagles, 28-20 (C)
1953—Browns, 37-13 (C)
   Eagles, 42-27 (P)
1954—Eagles, 28-10 (P)
   Browns, 6-0 (C)
1955—Browns, 21-17 (C)
   Eagles, 33-17 (P)
1956—Browns, 16-0 (C)
   Browns, 17-14 (C)
1957—Browns, 24-7 (C)
   Eagles, 17-7 (P)
1958—Browns, 28-14 (C)
   Browns, 21-14 (P)
1959—Browns, 28-7 (C)
   Browns, 28-21 (P)
1960—Browns, 41-24 (P)
   Eagles, 31-29 (C)
1961—Eagles, 27-20 (P)
   Browns, 45-24 (C)
1962—Eagles, 35-7 (P)
   Tie, 14-14 (C)
1963—Browns, 37-7 (C)
   Browns, 23-17 (P)
1964—Browns, 28-20 (P)
   Browns, 38-24 (C)
1965—Browns, 35-17 (P)
   Browns, 38-34 (C)
1966—Browns, 27-7 (C)
   Eagles, 33-21 (P)
1967—Eagles, 28-24 (P)

1968—Browns, 47-13 (C)
1969—Browns, 27-20 (P)
1972—Browns, 27-17 (P)
1976—Browns, 24-3 (C)
1979—Browns, 24-19 (P)
1982—Eagles, 24-21 (C)
1988—Browns, 19-3 (C)
1991—Eagles, 32-30 (C)
1994—Browns, 26-7 (P)
2000—Eagles, 35-24 (C)
2004—Eagles, 34-31 (C) OT
2008—Eagles, 30-10 (P)
(RS Pts.—Browns 1,185, Eagles 884)
CLEVELAND vs. PITTSBURGH
RS: Steelers lead series, 62-56
PS: Steelers lead series, 2-0
1950—Steelers, 30-17 (P)
    Browns, 45-7 (C)
1951—Browns, 17-0 (C)
    Browns, 28-0 (P)
1952—Browns, 21-20 (P)
    Browns, 29-28 (C)
1953—Browns, 34-16 (C)
    Browns, 20-16 (P)
1954—Steelers, 55-27 (P)
    Browns, 42-7 (C)
1955—Browns, 41-14 (C)
    Browns, 30-7 (P)
1956—Browns, 14-10 (P)
    Steelers, 24-16 (C)
1957—Browns, 23-12 (P)
    Browns, 24-0 (C)
1958—Browns, 45-12 (C)
    Browns, 27-10 (C)
1959—Steelers, 17-7 (P)
    Steelers, 21-20 (C)
1960—Browns, 28-20 (C)
    Steelers, 14-10 (P)
1961—Browns, 30-28 (P)
    Steelers, 17-13 (C)
1962—Browns, 41-14 (P)
    Browns, 35-14 (C)
1963—Browns, 35-23 (C)
    Steelers, 9-7 (P)
1964—Steelers, 23-7 (C)
    Browns, 30-17 (P)
1965—Browns, 24-19 (C)
    Browns, 42-21 (P)
1966—Browns, 41-10 (C)
    Steelers, 16-6 (P)
1967—Browns, 21-10 (C)
    Browns, 34-14 (P)
1968—Browns, 31-24 (C)
    Browns, 45-24 (P)
1969—Browns, 42-31 (C)
    Browns, 24-3 (P)
1970—Browns, 15-7 (C)
    Steelers, 28-9 (P)
1971—Browns, 27-17 (C)
    Steelers, 26-9 (P)
1972—Browns, 26-24 (C)
    Steelers, 30-0 (P)
1973—Steelers, 33-6 (P)
    Browns, 21-16 (C)
1974—Steelers, 20-16 (P)
    Steelers, 26-16 (C)
1975—Steelers, 42-6 (C)
    Steelers, 31-17 (P)
1976—Steelers, 31-14 (P)
    Browns, 18-16 (C)
1977—Steelers, 28-14 (C)
    Steelers, 35-31 (P)

1978—Steelers, 15-9 (P) OT
    Steelers, 34-14 (C)
1979—Steelers, 51-35 (C)
    Steelers, 33-30 (P) OT
1980—Browns, 27-26 (C)
    Steelers, 16-13 (P)
1981—Steelers, 13-7 (P)
    Steelers, 32-10 (C)
1982—Browns, 10-9 (C)
    Steelers, 37-21 (P)
1983—Steelers, 44-17 (P)
    Browns, 30-17 (C)
1984—Browns, 20-10 (C)
    Steelers, 23-20 (P)
1985—Browns, 17-7 (C)
    Steelers, 10-9 (P)
1986—Browns, 27-24 (P)
    Browns, 37-31 (C) OT
1987—Browns, 34-10 (C)
    Browns, 19-13 (P)
1988—Browns, 23-9 (P)
    Browns, 27-7 (C)
1989—Browns, 51-0 (P)
    Steelers, 17-7 (C)
1990—Browns, 13-3 (C)
    Steelers, 35-0 (P)
1991—Browns, 17-14 (C)
    Steelers, 17-10 (P)
1992—Browns, 17-9 (C)
    Steelers, 23-13 (P)
1993—Browns, 28-23 (C)
    Steelers, 16-9 (P)
1994—Steelers, 17-10 (C)
    Steelers, 17-7 (P)
    *Steelers, 29-9 (P)
1995—Steelers, 20-3 (P)
    Steelers, 20-17 (C)
1999—Steelers, 43-0 (C)
    Browns, 16-15 (P)
2000—Browns, 23-20 (C)
    Browns, 22-0 (P)
2001—Steelers, 15-12 (C) OT
    Steelers, 28-7 (P)
2002—Steelers, 16-13 (P) OT
    Steelers, 23-20 (C)
    **Steelers, 36-33 (P)
2003—Browns, 33-13 (P)
    Steelers, 13-6 (C)
2004—Steelers, 34-23 (P)
    Steelers, 24-10 (C)
2005—Steelers, 34-21 (P)
    Steelers, 41-0 (C)
2006—Steelers, 24-20 (C)
    Steelers, 27-7 (P)
2007—Steelers, 34-7 (C)
    Steelers, 31-28 (P)
2008—Steelers, 10-6 (C)
    Steelers, 31-0 (P)
2009—Steelers, 27-14 (P)
    Browns, 13-6 (C)
2010—Steelers, 28-10 (P)
    Steelers, 41-9 (C)
2011—Steelers, 14-3 (C)
    Steelers, 13-9 (C)
(RS Pts.—Steelers 2,383, Browns 2,299)
(PS Pts.—Steelers 65, Browns 42)
*AFC Divisional Playoff
**AFC First-Round Playoff
CLEVELAND vs. *ST. LOUIS
RS: Rams lead series, 10-9
PS: Browns lead series, 2-1
1950—**Browns, 30-28 (C)

1951—Browns, 38-23 (LA)
    **Rams, 24-17 (LA)
1952—Browns, 37-7 (C)
1955—**Browns, 38-14 (LA)
1957—Browns, 45-31 (C)
1958—Browns, 30-27 (LA)
1963—Browns, 20-6 (C)
1965—Rams, 42-7 (LA)
1968—Rams, 24-6 (C)
1973—Rams, 30-17 (LA)
1977—Rams, 9-0 (C)
1978—Browns, 30-19 (C)
1981—Rams, 27-16 (LA)
1984—Rams, 20-17 (LA)
1987—Browns, 30-17 (C)
1990—Rams, 38-23 (C)
1993—Browns, 42-14 (LA)
1999—Rams, 34-3 (StL)
2003—Rams, 26-20 (C)
2007—Browns, 27-20 (StL)
2011—Rams, 13-12 (C)
(RS Pts.—Rams 427, Browns 420)
(PS Pts.—Browns 85, Rams 66)
*Franchise in Los Angeles prior to 1995
**NFL Championship
CLEVELAND vs. SAN DIEGO
RS: Chargers lead series, 14-7-1
1970—Chargers, 27-10 (C)
1972—Browns, 21-17 (SD)
1973—Tie, 16-16 (C)
1974—Chargers, 36-35 (SD)
1976—Browns, 21-17 (C)
1977—Chargers, 37-14 (SD)
1981—Chargers, 44-14 (C)
1982—Chargers, 30-13 (C)
1983—Browns, 30-24 (SD) OT
1985—Browns, 21-7 (SD)
1986—Browns, 47-17 (C)
1987—Chargers, 27-24 (SD) OT
1990—Chargers, 24-14 (C)
1991—Browns, 30-24 (SD) OT
1992—Chargers, 14-13 (C)
1995—Chargers, 31-13 (SD)
1999—Chargers, 23-10 (SD)
2001—Browns, 20-16 (C)
2003—Chargers, 26-20 (C)
2004—Chargers, 21-0 (C)
2006—Chargers, 32-25 (SD)
2009—Chargers, 30-23 (C)
(RS Pts.—Chargers 540, Browns 434)
CLEVELAND vs. SAN FRANCISCO
RS: Browns lead series, 11-7
1950—Browns, 34-14 (C)
1951—49ers, 24-10 (SF)
1953—Browns, 23-21 (C)
1955—Browns, 38-3 (SF)
1959—49ers, 21-20 (C)
1962—Browns, 13-10 (SF)
1968—Browns, 33-21 (SF)
1970—49ers, 34-31 (SF)
1974—Browns, 7-0 (C)
1978—Browns, 24-7 (C)
1981—Browns, 15-12 (SF)
1984—49ers, 41-7 (C)
1987—49ers, 38-24 (SF)
1990—Browns, 20-17 (SF)
1993—Browns, 23-13 (C)
2003—Browns, 13-12 (SF)
2007—Browns, 20-7 (C)
2011—49ers, 20-10 (SF)
(RS Pts.—Browns 362, 49ers 318)

CLEVELAND vs. SEATTLE
RS: Seahawks lead series, 11-6
1977—Seahawks, 20-19 (S)
1978—Seahawks, 47-24 (S)
1979—Seahawks, 29-24 (C)
1980—Browns, 27-3 (S)
1981—Seahawks, 42-21 (S)
1982—Browns, 21-7 (S)
1983—Seahawks, 24-9 (C)
1984—Seahawks, 33-0 (S)
1985—Seahawks, 31-13 (S)
1988—Seahawks, 16-10 (C)
1989—Browns, 17-7 (S)
1993—Seahawks, 22-5 (S)
1994—Browns, 35-9 (C)
2001—Seahawks, 9-6 (C)
2003—Seahawks, 34-7 (S)
2007—Browns, 33-30 (C) OT
2011—Browns, 6-3 (C)
(RS Pts.—Seahawks 366, Browns 277)

CLEVELAND vs. TAMPA BAY
RS: Browns lead series, 5-3
1976—Browns, 24-7 (TB)
1980—Browns, 34-27 (TB)
1983—Browns, 20-0 (C)
1989—Browns, 42-31 (TB)
1995—Browns, 22-6 (C)
2002—Buccaneers 17-3 (TB)
2006—Buccaneers, 22-7 (C)
2010—Buccaneers, 17-14 (TB)
(RS Pts.—Browns 166, Buccaneers 127)

CLEVELAND vs. *TENNESSEE
RS: Browns lead series, 33-28
PS: Titans lead series, 1-0
1970—Browns, 28-14 (C)
Browns, 21-10 (H)
1971—Browns, 31-0 (C)
Browns, 37-24 (H)
1972—Browns, 23-17 (H)
Browns, 20-0 (C)
1973—Browns, 42-13 (C)
Browns, 23-13 (H)
1974—Browns, 20-7 (C)
Oilers, 28-24 (H)
1975—Oilers, 40-10 (C)
Oilers, 21-10 (H)
1976—Browns, 21-7 (H)
Browns, 13-10 (C)
1977—Browns, 24-23 (H)
Oilers, 19-15 (C)
1978—Oilers, 16-13 (C)
Oilers, 14-10 (H)
1979—Oilers, 31-10 (H)
Browns, 14-7 (C)
1980—Oilers, 16-7 (C)
Browns, 17-14 (H)
1981—Oilers, 9-3 (C)
Oilers, 17-13 (H)
1982—Browns, 20-14 (H)
1983—Browns, 25-19 (C) OT
Oilers, 34-27 (H)
1984—Browns, 27-10 (C)
Browns, 27-20 (H)
1985—Browns, 21-6 (H)
Browns, 28-21 (C)
1986—Browns, 23-20 (H)
Browns, 13-10 (C) OT
1987—Oilers, 15-10 (C)
Browns, 40-7 (H)
1988—Oilers, 24-17 (H)
Browns, 28-23 (C)
**Oilers, 24-23 (C)

1989—Browns, 28-17 (C)
Browns, 24-20 (H)
1990—Oilers, 35-23 (C)
Oilers, 58-14 (H)
1991—Oilers, 28-24 (H)
Oilers, 17-14 (C)
1992—Browns, 24-14 (H)
Oilers, 17-14 (C)
1993—Oilers, 27-20 (C)
Oilers, 19-17 (H)
1994—Browns, 11-8 (H)
Browns, 34-10 (C)
1995—Browns, 14-7 (H)
Oilers, 37-10 (C)
1999—Titans, 26-9 (T)
Titans, 33-21 (C)
2000—Titans, 24-10 (T)
Titans, 24-0 (C)
2001—Titans, 31-15 (C)
Browns, 41-38 (T)
2002—Browns, 31-28 (T) OT
2005—Browns, 20-14 (C)
2008—Titans, 28-9 (T)
2011—Titans, 31-13 (C)
(RS Pts.—Browns 1,195, Titans 1,184)
(PS Pts.—Titans 24, Browns 23)
*Franchise in Houston prior to 1997;
known as Oilers prior to 1999
**AFC First-Round Playoff

CLEVELAND vs. WASHINGTON
RS: Browns lead series, 33-10-1
1950—Browns, 20-14 (C)
Browns, 45-21 (W)
1951—Browns, 45-0 (C)
1952—Browns, 19-15 (C)
Browns, 48-24 (W)
1953—Browns, 30-14 (W)
Browns, 27-3 (C)
1954—Browns, 62-3 (C)
Browns, 34-14 (W)
1955—Redskins, 27-17 (C)
Browns, 24-14 (W)
1956—Redskins, 20-9 (W)
Redskins, 20-17 (C)
1957—Browns, 21-17 (C)
Tie, 30-30 (W)
1958—Browns, 20-10 (W)
Browns, 21-14 (C)
1959—Browns, 34-7 (C)
Browns, 31-17 (W)
1960—Browns, 31-10 (W)
Browns, 27-16 (C)
1961—Browns, 31-7 (C)
Browns, 17-6 (W)
1962—Redskins, 17-16 (C)
Redskins, 17-9 (W)
1963—Browns, 37-14 (C)
Browns, 27-20 (W)
1964—Browns, 27-13 (W)
Browns, 34-24 (C)
1965—Browns, 17-7 (W)
Browns, 24-16 (C)
1966—Browns, 38-14 (W)
Browns, 14-3 (C)
1967—Browns, 42-37 (C)
1968—Browns, 24-21 (W)
1969—Browns, 27-23 (C)
1971—Browns, 20-13 (W)
1975—Redskins, 23-7 (C)
1979—Redskins, 13-9 (C)
1985—Redskins, 14-7 (C)
1988—Browns, 17-13 (W)

1991—Redskins, 42-17 (W)
2004—Browns, 17-13 (C)
2008—Redskins, 14-11 (W)
(RS Pts.—Browns 1,101, Redskins 694)

DALLAS vs. ARIZONA
RS: Cowboys lead series, 55-30-1
PS: Cardinals lead series, 1-0;
See Arizona vs. Dallas
DALLAS vs. ATLANTA
RS: Cowboys lead series, 14-8
PS: Cowboys lead series, 2-0;
See Atlanta vs. Dallas
DALLAS vs. BALTIMORE
RS: Ravens lead series, 3-0;
See Baltimore vs. Dallas
DALLAS vs. BUFFALO
RS: Cowboys lead series, 6-3
PS: Cowboys lead series, 2-0;
See Buffalo vs. Dallas
DALLAS vs. CAROLINA
RS: Cowboys lead series, 8-1
PS: Panthers lead series, 2-0;
See Carolina vs. Dallas
DALLAS vs. CHICAGO
RS: Cowboys lead series, 11-9
PS: Cowboys lead series, 2-0;
See Chicago vs. Dallas
DALLAS vs. CINCINNATI
RS: Cowboys lead series, 6-4;
See Cincinnati vs. Dallas
DALLAS vs. CLEVELAND
RS: Browns lead series, 15-11
PS: Browns lead series, 2-1;
See Cleveland vs. Dallas
DALLAS vs. DENVER
RS: Broncos lead series, 6-4
PS: Cowboys lead series, 1-0
1973—Cowboys, 22-10 (Den)
1977—Cowboys, 14-6 (Dal)
*Cowboys, 27-10 (New Orleans)
1980—Broncos, 41-20 (Den)
1986—Broncos, 29-14 (Den)
1992—Cowboys, 31-27 (Den)
1995—Cowboys, 31-21 (Dal)
1998—Broncos, 42-23 (Den)
2001—Broncos, 26-24 (Dal)
2005—Broncos, 24-21 (Dal) OT
2009—Broncos, 17-10 (Den)
(RS Pts.—Broncos 243, Cowboys 210)
(PS Pts.—Cowboys 27, Broncos 10)
*Super Bowl XII
DALLAS vs. DETROIT
RS: Cowboys lead series, 12-10
PS: Series tied, 1-1
1960—Lions, 23-14 (Det)
1963—Cowboys, 17-14 (Dal)
1968—Cowboys, 59-13 (Dal)
1970—*Cowboys, 5-0 (Dal)
1972—Cowboys, 28-24 (Det)
1975—Cowboys, 36-10 (Det)
1977—Cowboys, 37-0 (Dal)
1981—Lions, 27-24 (Det)
1985—Lions, 26-21 (Det)
1986—Cowboys, 31-7 (Det)
1987—Lions, 27-17 (Det)
1991—Lions, 34-10 (Det)
*Lions, 38-6 (Det)
1992—Cowboys, 37-3 (Det)
1994—Lions, 20-17 (Dal) OT
2001—Lions, 15-10 (Det)
2002—Lions, 9-7 (Det)

2003—Cowboys, 38-7 (Det)
2004—Cowboys, 31-21 (Dal)
2005—Cowboys, 20-7 (Dal)
2006—Lions, 39-31 (Dal)
2007—Cowboys, 28-27 (Det)
2010—Cowboys, 35-19 (Dal)
2011—Lions, 34-30 (Dal)
(RS Pts.—Cowboys 578, Lions 406)
(PS Pts.—Lions 38, Cowboys 11)
*NFC Divisional Playoff
DALLAS vs. GREEN BAY
RS: Series tied, 12-12
PS: Cowboys lead series, 4-2
1960—Packers, 41-7 (GB)
1964—Packers, 45-21 (D)
1965—Packers, 13-3 (Mil)
1966—*Packers, 34-27 (D)
1967—*Packers, 21-17 (GB)
1968—Packers, 28-17 (D)
1970—Cowboys, 16-3 (D)
1972—Packers, 16-13 (Mil)
1975—Packers, 19-17 (D)
1978—Cowboys, 42-14 (Mil)
1980—Cowboys, 28-7 (Mil)
1982—**Cowboys, 37-26 (D)
1984—Cowboys, 20-6 (D)
1989—Packers, 31-13 (GB)
        Packers, 20-10 (D)
1991—Cowboys, 20-17 (Mil)
1993—Cowboys, 36-14 (D)
        ***Cowboys, 27-17 (D)
1994—Cowboys, 42-31 (D)
        ***Cowboys, 35-9 (D)
1995—Cowboys, 34-24 (D)
        ****Cowboys, 38-27 (D)
1996—Cowboys, 21-6 (D)
1997—Packers, 45-17 (GB)
1999—Cowboys, 27-13 (D)
2004—Packers, 41-20 (GB)
2007—Cowboys, 37-27 (D)
2008—Cowboys, 27-16 (GB)
2009—Packers, 17-7 (GB)
2010—Packers, 45-7 (GB)
(RS Pts.—Packers, 539, Cowboys 502)
(PS Pts.—Cowboys 181, Packers 134)
*NFL Championship
**NFC Second-Round Playoff
***NFC Divisional Playoff
****NFC Championship
DALLAS vs. HOUSTON
RS: Cowboys lead series, 2-1
2002—Texans, 19-10 (H)
2006—Cowboys, 34-6 (D)
2010—Cowboys, 27-13 (H)
(RS Pts.—Cowboys 71, Texans 38)
DALLAS vs. *INDIANAPOLIS
RS: Cowboys lead series, 9-5
PS: Colts lead series, 1-0
1960—Colts, 45-7 (D)
1967—Colts, 23-17 (B)
1969—Cowboys, 27-10 (D)
1970—**Colts, 16-13 (Miami)
1972—Cowboys, 21-0 (B)
1976—Cowboys, 30-27 (D)
1978—Cowboys, 38-0 (D)
1981—Cowboys, 37-13 (B)
1984—Cowboys, 22-3 (D)
1993—Cowboys, 27-3 (I)
1996—Cowboys, 25-24 (D)
1999—Colts, 34-24 (I)
2002—Colts, 20-3 (I)
2006—Cowboys, 21-14 (D)

2010—Cowboys, 38-35 (I) OT
(RS Pts.—Cowboys 336, Colts 252)
(PS Pts.—Colts 16, Cowboys 13)
*Franchise in Baltimore prior to 1984
**Super Bowl V
DALLAS vs. JACKSONVILLE
RS: Jaguars lead series, 3-2
1997—Cowboys, 26-22 (D)
2000—Jaguars, 23-17 (D) OT
2002—Cowboys, 21-19 (D)
2006—Jaguars, 24-17 (J)
2010—Jaguars, 35-17 (D)
(RS Pts.—Jaguars 123, Cowboys 98)
DALLAS vs. KANSAS CITY
RS: Cowboys lead series, 6-3
1970—Cowboys, 27-16 (KC)
1975—Chiefs, 34-31 (D)
1983—Cowboys, 41-21 (D)
1989—Chiefs, 36-28 (KC)
1992—Cowboys, 17-10 (D)
1995—Cowboys, 24-12 (D)
1998—Chiefs, 20-17 (KC)
2005—Cowboys, 31-28 (D)
2009—Cowboys, 26-20 (KC) OT
(RS Pts.—Cowboys 242, Chiefs 197)
DALLAS vs. MIAMI
RS: Dolphins lead series, 7-5
PS: Cowboys lead series, 1-0
1971—*Cowboys, 24-3 (New Orleans)
1973—Dolphins, 14-7 (D)
1978—Dolphins, 23-16 (M)
1981—Cowboys, 28-27 (D)
1984—Cowboys, 28-21 (M)
1987—Dolphins, 20-14 (D)
1989—Dolphins, 17-14 (D)
1993—Dolphins, 16-14 (D)
1996—Cowboys, 29-10 (M)
1999—Cowboys, 20-0 (D)
2003—Dolphins, 40-21 (D)
2007—Cowboys, 37-20 (M)
2011—Cowboys, 20-19 (D)
(RS Pts.—Cowboys 241, Dolphins 234)
(PS Pts.—Cowboys 24, Dolphins 3)
*Super Bowl VI
DALLAS vs. MINNESOTA
RS: Vikings lead series, 11-10
PS: Cowboys lead series, 4-3
1961—Cowboys, 21-7 (D)
        Cowboys, 28-0 (M)
1966—Cowboys, 28-17 (D)
1968—Cowboys, 20-7 (M)
1970—Vikings, 54-13 (M)
1971—*Cowboys, 20-12 (M)
1973—**Vikings, 27-10 (D)
1974—Vikings, 23-21 (D)
1975—*Cowboys, 17-14 (M)
1977—Cowboys, 16-10 (M) OT
        **Cowboys, 23-6 (D)
1978—Vikings, 21-10 (D)
1979—Cowboys, 36-20 (M)
1982—Vikings, 31-27 (M)
1983—Cowboys, 37-24 (M)
1987—Vikings, 44-38 (D) OT
1988—Vikings, 43-3 (D)
1993—Cowboys, 37-20 (M)
1995—Cowboys, 23-17 (M) OT
1996—***Cowboys, 40-15 (D)
1998—Vikings, 46-36 (D)
1999—Vikings, 27-17 (M)
        ***Vikings, 27-10 (M)
2000—Vikings, 27-15 (D)
2004—Vikings, 35-17 (M)

2007—Cowboys, 24-14 (D)
2009—*Vikings, 34-3 (M)
2010—Vikings, 24-21 (M)
(RS Pts.—Vikings 511, Cowboys 488)
(PS Pts.—Vikings 135, Cowboys 123)
*NFC Divisional Playoff
**NFC Championship
***NFC First-Round Playoff
DALLAS vs. NEW ENGLAND
RS: Cowboys lead series, 7-4
1971—Cowboys, 44-21 (D)
1975—Cowboys, 34-31 (NE)
1978—Cowboys, 17-10 (D)
1981—Cowboys, 35-21 (NE)
1984—Cowboys, 20-17 (D)
1987—Cowboys, 23-17 (NE) OT
1996—Cowboys, 12-6 (D)
1999—Patriots, 13-6 (NE)
2003—Patriots, 12-0 (NE)
2007—Patriots, 48-27 (D)
2011—Patriots, 20-16 (NE)
(RS Pts.—Cowboys 234, Patriots 216)
DALLAS vs. NEW ORLEANS
RS: Cowboys lead series, 15-9
1967—Cowboys, 14-10 (D)
        Cowboys, 27-10 (NO)
1968—Cowboys, 17-3 (NO)
1969—Cowboys, 21-17 (NO)
        Cowboys, 33-17 (D)
1971—Saints, 24-14 (NO)
1973—Cowboys, 40-3 (D)
1976—Cowboys, 24-6 (NO)
1978—Cowboys, 27-7 (D)
1982—Cowboys, 21-7 (D)
1983—Cowboys, 21-20 (D)
1984—Cowboys, 30-27 (D) OT
1988—Saints, 20-17 (NO)
1989—Saints, 28-0 (NO)
1990—Cowboys, 17-13 (D)
1991—Cowboys, 23-14 (D)
1994—Cowboys, 24-16 (NO)
1998—Saints, 22-3 (NO)
1999—Saints, 31-24 (NO)
2003—Saints, 13-7 (NO)
2004—Saints, 27-13 (D)
2006—Saints, 42-17 (D)
2009—Cowboys, 24-17 (NO)
2010—Saints, 30-27 (D)
(RS Pts.—Cowboys 485, Saints 424)
DALLAS vs. N.Y. GIANTS
RS: Cowboys lead series, 56-41-2
PS: Giants lead series, 1-0
1960—Tie, 31-31 (NY)
1961—Giants, 31-10 (D)
        Cowboys, 17-16 (NY)
1962—Giants, 41-10 (D)
        Giants, 41-31 (NY)
1963—Giants, 37-21 (NY)
        Giants, 34-27 (D)
1964—Tie, 13-13 (D)
        Cowboys, 31-21 (NY)
1965—Cowboys, 31-2 (D)
        Cowboys, 38-20 (NY)
1966—Cowboys, 52-7 (D)
        Cowboys, 17-7 (NY)
1967—Cowboys, 38-24 (D)
1968—Giants, 27-21 (D)
        Cowboys, 28-10 (NY)
1969—Cowboys, 25-3 (D)
1970—Cowboys, 28-10 (D)
        Giants, 23-20 (NY)
1971—Cowboys, 20-13 (D)

Cowboys, 42-14 (NY)
1972—Cowboys, 23-14 (NY)
Giants, 23-3 (D)
1973—Cowboys, 45-28 (D)
Cowboys, 23-10 (New Haven)
1974—Giants, 14-6 (D)
Cowboys, 21-7 (New Haven)
1975—Cowboys, 13-7 (NY)
Cowboys, 14-3 (D)
1976—Cowboys, 24-14 (NY)
Cowboys, 9-3 (D)
1977—Cowboys, 41-21 (D)
Cowboys, 24-10 (NY)
1978—Cowboys, 34-24 (NY)
Cowboys, 24-3 (D)
1979—Cowboys, 16-14 (NY)
Cowboys, 28-7 (D)
1980—Cowboys, 24-3 (D)
Giants, 38-35 (NY)
1981—Cowboys, 18-10 (D)
Giants, 13-10 (NY) OT
1983—Cowboys, 28-13 (D)
Cowboys, 38-20 (NY)
1984—Giants, 28-7 (NY)
Giants, 19-7 (D)
1985—Cowboys, 30-29 (NY)
Cowboys, 28-21 (D)
1986—Cowboys, 31-28 (D)
Giants, 17-14 (NY)
1987—Cowboys, 16-14 (NY)
Cowboys, 33-24 (D)
1988—Giants, 12-10 (D)
Giants, 29-21 (NY)
1989—Giants, 30-13 (D)
Giants, 15-0 (NY)
1990—Giants, 28-7 (D)
Giants, 31-17 (NY)
1991—Cowboys, 21-16 (D)
Giants, 22-9 (NY)
1992—Cowboys, 34-28 (NY)
Cowboys, 30-3 (D)
1993—Cowboys, 31-9 (D)
Cowboys, 16-13 (NY) OT
1994—Cowboys, 38-10 (D)
Giants, 15-10 (NY)
1995—Cowboys, 35-0 (NY)
Cowboys, 21-20 (D)
1996—Cowboys, 27-0 (D)
Giants, 20-6 (NY)
1997—Giants, 20-17 (NY)
Giants, 20-7 (D)
1998—Cowboys, 31-7 (NY)
Cowboys, 16-6 (D)
1999—Giants, 13-10 (NY)
Cowboys, 26-18 (D)
2000—Giants, 19-14 (NY)
Giants, 17-13 (D)
2001—Giants, 27-24 (NY) OT
Cowboys, 20-13 (D)
2002—Giants, 21-17 (D)
Giants, 37-7 (NY)
2003—Cowboys, 35-32 (NY) OT
Cowboys, 19-3 (D)
2004—Giants, 26-10 (D)
Giants, 28-24 (NY)
2005—Cowboys, 16-13 (D) OT
Giants, 17-10 (NY)
2006—Giants, 36-22 (D)
Cowboys, 23-20 (NY)
2007—Cowboys, 45-35 (D)
Cowboys, 31-20 (NY)
*Giants, 21-17 (D)

2008—Giants, 35-14 (NY)
Cowboys, 20-8 (D)
2009—Giants, 33-31 (D)
Giants, 31-24 (NY)
2010—Giants, 41-35 (D)
Cowboys, 33-20 (NY)
2011—Giants, 37-34 (D)
Giants, 31-14 (NY)
(RS Pts.—Cowboys 2,206, Giants 1,889)
(PS Pts.—Giants 21, Cowboys 17)
*NFC Divisional Playoff
DALLAS vs. N.Y. JETS
RS: Cowboys lead series, 7-3
1971—Cowboys, 52-10 (D)
1975—Cowboys, 31-21 (NY)
1978—Cowboys, 30-7 (NY)
1987—Cowboys, 38-24 (NY)
1990—Jets, 24-9 (NY)
1993—Cowboys, 28-7 (NY)
1999—Jets, 22-21 (D)
2003—Cowboys, 17-6 (NY)
2007—Cowboys, 34-3 (D)
2011—Jets, 27-24 (NY)
(RS Pts.—Cowboys 284, Jets 151)
DALLAS vs. *OAKLAND
RS: Raiders lead series, 6-4
1974—Raiders, 27-23 (O)
1980—Cowboys, 19-13 (O)
1983—Raiders, 40-38 (D)
1986—Raiders, 17-13 (D)
1992—Cowboys, 28-13 (LA)
1995—Cowboys, 34-21 (O)
1998—Raiders, 13-12 (D)
2001—Raiders, 28-21 (O)
2005—Raiders, 19-13 (O)
2009—Cowboys, 24-7 (D)
(RS Pts.—Cowboys 225, Raiders 198)
*Franchise in Los Angeles from 1982-1994
DALLAS vs. PHILADELPHIA
RS: Cowboys lead series, 56-46
PS: Cowboys lead series, 3-1
1960—Eagles, 27-25 (D)
1961—Eagles, 43-7 (D)
Eagles, 35-13 (P)
1962—Cowboys, 41-19 (D)
Eagles, 28-14 (P)
1963—Eagles, 24-21 (P)
Cowboys, 27-20 (D)
1964—Eagles, 17-14 (D)
Eagles, 24-14 (P)
1965—Eagles, 35-24 (D)
Cowboys, 21-19 (P)
1966—Cowboys, 56-7 (D)
Eagles, 24-23 (P)
1967—Eagles, 21-14 (P)
Cowboys, 38-17 (D)
1968—Cowboys, 45-13 (P)
Cowboys, 34-14 (D)
1969—Cowboys, 38-7 (P)
Cowboys, 49-14 (D)
1970—Cowboys, 17-7 (P)
Cowboys, 21-17 (D)
1971—Cowboys, 42-7 (P)
Cowboys, 20-7 (D)
1972—Cowboys, 28-6 (D)
Cowboys, 28-7 (P)
1973—Eagles, 30-16 (P)
Cowboys, 31-10 (D)
1974—Eagles, 13-10 (D)
Cowboys, 31-24 (P)
1975—Cowboys, 20-17 (P)
Cowboys, 27-17 (D)

1976—Cowboys, 27-7 (D)
Cowboys, 26-7 (P)
1977—Cowboys, 16-10 (P)
Cowboys, 24-14 (D)
1978—Cowboys, 14-7 (D)
Cowboys, 31-13 (P)
1979—Eagles, 31-21 (D)
Cowboys, 24-17 (P)
1980—Eagles, 17-10 (P)
Cowboys, 35-27 (D)
*Eagles, 20-7 (P)
1981—Cowboys, 17-14 (P)
Cowboys, 21-10 (D)
1982—Eagles, 24-20 (D)
1983—Cowboys, 37-7 (D)
Cowboys, 27-20 (P)
1984—Cowboys, 23-17 (D)
Cowboys, 26-10 (P)
1985—Eagles, 16-14 (P)
Cowboys, 34-17 (D)
1986—Cowboys, 17-14 (P)
Eagles, 23-21 (D)
1987—Eagles, 41-22 (D)
Eagles, 37-20 (P)
1988—Eagles, 24-23 (P)
Eagles, 23-7 (D)
1989—Eagles, 27-0 (D)
Eagles, 20-10 (P)
1990—Eagles, 21-20 (D)
Eagles, 17-3 (P)
1991—Eagles, 24-0 (P)
Cowboys, 25-13 (D)
1992—Eagles, 31-7 (P)
Cowboys, 20-10 (D)
**Cowboys, 34-10 (D)
1993—Cowboys, 23-10 (D)
Cowboys, 23-17 (D)
1994—Cowboys, 24-13 (D)
Cowboys, 31-19 (D)
1995—Cowboys, 34-12 (D)
Eagles, 20-17 (D)
**Cowboys, 30-11 (D)
1996—Cowboys, 23-19 (D)
Eagles, 31-21 (D)
1997—Cowboys, 21-20 (D)
Eagles, 13-12 (P)
1998—Cowboys, 34-0 (P)
Cowboys, 13-9 (D)
1999—Eagles, 13-10 (D)
Cowboys, 20-10 (D)
2000—Eagles, 41-14 (D)
Eagles, 16-13 (P) OT
2001—Eagles, 40-18 (P)
Eagles, 36-3 (D)
2002—Eagles, 44-13 (P)
Eagles, 27-3 (D)
2003—Cowboys, 23-21 (D)
Eagles, 36-10 (P)
2004—Eagles, 49-21 (D)
Eagles, 12-7 (P)
2005—Cowboys, 33-10 (D)
Cowboys, 21-20 (P)
2006—Eagles, 38-24 (P)
Eagles, 23-7 (D)
2007—Cowboys, 38-17 (P)
Eagles, 10-6 (D)
2008—Cowboys, 41-37 (D)
Eagles, 44-6 (P)
2009—Cowboys, 20-16 (P)
Cowboys, 24-0 (D)
***Cowboys, 34-14 (P)
2010—Eagles, 30-27 (D)

Cowboys, 14-13 (P)
2011—Eagles, 34-7 (P)
   Eagles, 20-7 (D)
(RS Pts.—Cowboys 2,176, Eagles 2,001)
(PS Pts.—Cowboys 105, Eagles 55)
*NFC Championship
**NFC Divisional Playoff
***NFC First-Round Playoff
DALLAS vs. PITTSBURGH
RS: Cowboys lead series, 14-13
PS: Steelers lead series, 2-1
1960—Steelers, 35-28 (D)
1961—Cowboys, 27-24 (D)
   Steelers, 37-7 (P)
1962—Steelers, 30-28 (D)
   Cowboys, 42-27 (P)
1963—Steelers, 27-21 (P)
   Steelers, 24-19 (D)
1964—Steelers, 23-17 (P)
   Cowboys, 17-14 (D)
1965—Steelers, 22-13 (P)
   Cowboys, 24-17 (D)
1966—Cowboys, 52-21 (D)
   Cowboys, 20-7 (P)
1967—Cowboys, 24-21 (P)
1968—Cowboys, 28-7 (D)
1969—Cowboys, 10-7 (P)
1972—Cowboys, 17-13 (D)
1975—*Steelers, 21-17 (Miami)
1977—Steelers, 28-13 (P)
1978—**Steelers, 35-31 (Miami)
1979—Steelers, 14-3 (P)
1982—Steelers, 36-28 (D)
1985—Cowboys, 27-13 (D)
1988—Cowboys, 24-21 (P)
1991—Cowboys, 20-10 (D)
1994—Cowboys, 26-9 (P)
1995—***Cowboys, 27-17 (Tempe)
1997—Cowboys, 37-7 (D)
2004—Steelers, 24-20 (D)
2008—Steelers, 20-13 (P)
(RS Pts.—Cowboys 602, Steelers 541)
(PS Pts.—Cowboys 75, Steelers 73)
*Super Bowl X
**Super Bowl XIII
***Super Bowl XXX
DALLAS vs. *ST. LOUIS
RS: Series tied, 11-11
PS: Series tied, 4-4
1960—Rams, 38-13 (D)
1962—Cowboys, 27-17 (LA)
1967—Rams, 35-13 (D)
1969—Rams, 24-23 (LA)
1971—Cowboys, 28-21 (D)
1973—Rams, 37-31 (LA)
   **Cowboys, 27-16 (D)
1975—Cowboys, 18-7 (D)
   ***Cowboys, 37-7 (LA)
1976—**Rams, 14-12 (D)
1978—Rams, 27-14 (LA)
   ***Cowboys, 28-0 (LA)
1979—Cowboys, 30-6 (D)
   **Rams, 21-19 (D)
1980—Rams, 38-14 (LA)
   ****Cowboys, 34-13 (D)
1981—Cowboys, 29-17 (D)
1983—****Rams, 24-17 (D)
1984—Cowboys, 20-13 (LA)
1985—**Rams, 20-0 (LA)
1986—Rams, 29-10 (LA)
1987—Cowboys, 29-21 (LA)
1989—Rams, 35-31 (D)

1990—Cowboys, 24-21 (LA)
1992—Rams, 27-23 (D)
2002—Cowboys, 13-10 (StL)
2005—Rams, 20-10 (D)
2007—Cowboys, 35-7 (D)
2008—Rams, 34-14 (StL)
2011—Cowboys, 34-7 (D)
(RS Pts.—Rams 491, Cowboys 483)
(PS Pts.—Cowboys 174, Rams 115)
*Franchise in Los Angeles prior to 1995
**NFC Divisional Playoff
***NFC Championship
****NFC First-Round Playoff
DALLAS vs. SAN DIEGO
RS: Cowboys lead series, 6-3
1972—Cowboys, 34-28 (SD)
1980—Cowboys, 42-31 (D)
1983—Chargers, 24-23 (SD)
1986—Chargers, 24-21 (SD)
1990—Cowboys, 17-14 (D)
1995—Cowboys, 23-9 (SD)
2001—Chargers, 32-21 (D)
2005—Cowboys, 28-24 (SD)
2009—Chargers, 20-17 (D)
(RS Pts.—Cowboys 229, Chargers 203)
DALLAS vs. SAN FRANCISCO
RS: 49ers lead series, 14-11-1
PS: Cowboys lead series, 5-2
1960—49ers, 26-14 (D)
1963—49ers, 31-24 (SF)
1965—Cowboys, 39-31 (D)
1967—49ers, 24-16 (SF)
1969—Tie, 24-24 (D)
1970—*Cowboys, 17-10 (SF)
1971—*Cowboys, 14-3 (D)
1972—49ers, 31-10 (D)
   **Cowboys, 30-28 (SF)
1974—Cowboys, 20-14 (D)
1977—Cowboys, 42-35 (SF)
1979—Cowboys, 21-13 (SF)
1980—Cowboys, 59-14 (D)
1981—49ers, 45-14 (SF)
   *49ers, 28-27 (SF)
1983—49ers, 42-17 (SF)
1985—49ers, 31-16 (SF)
1989—49ers, 31-14 (D)
1990—49ers, 24-6 (D)
1992—*Cowboys, 30-20 (SF)
1993—Cowboys, 26-17 (D)
   *Cowboys, 38-21 (D)
1994—49ers, 21-14 (SF)
   *49ers, 38-28 (SF)
1995—49ers, 38-20 (D)
1996—Cowboys, 20-17 (SF) OT
1997—49ers, 17-10 (SF)
2000—49ers, 41-24 (D)
2001—Cowboys, 27-21 (D)
2002—49ers, 31-27 (D)
2005—Cowboys, 34-31 (D)
2008—Cowboys, 35-22 (D)
2011—Cowboys, 27-24 (SF)
(RS Pts.—49ers 696, Cowboys 600)
(PS Pts.—Cowboys 184, 49ers 148)
*NFC Championship
**NFC Divisional Playoff
DALLAS vs. SEATTLE
RS: Cowboys lead series, 9-4
PS: Seahawks lead series, 1-0
1976—Cowboys, 28-13 (S)
1980—Cowboys, 51-7 (D)
1983—Cowboys, 35-10 (S)
1986—Seahawks, 31-14 (D)

1992—Cowboys, 27-0 (D)
1998—Cowboys, 30-22 (D)
2001—Seahawks, 29-3 (S)
2002—Seahawks, 17-14 (D)
2004—Cowboys, 43-39 (S)
2005—Seahawks, 13-10 (S)
2006—*Seahawks, 21-20 (S)
2008—Cowboys, 34-9 (D)
2009—Cowboys, 38-17 (D)
2011—Cowboys, 23-13 (D)
(RS Pts.—Cowboys 350, Seahawks 220)
(PS Pts.—Seahawks 21, Cowboys 20)
*NFC First-Round Playoff
DALLAS vs. TAMPA BAY
RS: Cowboys lead series, 10-3
PS: Cowboys lead series, 2-0
1977—Cowboys, 23-7 (D)
1980—Cowboys, 28-17 (D)
1981—*Cowboys, 38-0 (D)
1982—Cowboys, 14-9 (D)
   **Cowboys, 30-17 (D)
1983—Cowboys, 27-24 (D) OT
1990—Cowboys, 14-10 (D)
   Cowboys, 17-13 (TB)
2000—Buccaneers, 27-7 (TB)
2001—Buccaneers, 10-6 (D)
2003—Buccaneers, 16-0 (TB)
2006—Cowboys, 38-10 (D)
2008—Cowboys, 13-9 (D)
2009—Cowboys, 34-21 (TB)
2011—Cowboys, 31-15 (TB)
(RS Pts.—Cowboys 252, Buccaneers 188)
(PS Pts.—Cowboys 68, Buccaneers 17)
*NFC Divisional Playoff
**NFC First-Round Playoff
DALLAS vs. *TENNESSEE
RS: Cowboys lead series, 7-6
1970—Cowboys, 52-10 (D)
1974—Cowboys, 10-0 (H)
1979—Oilers, 30-24 (D)
1982—Oilers, 37-7 (H)
1985—Cowboys, 17-10 (H)
1988—Oilers, 25-17 (D)
1991—Oilers, 26-23 (H) OT
1994—Cowboys, 20-17 (D)
1997—Oilers, 27-14 (D)
2000—Titans, 31-0 (T)
2002—Cowboys, 21-13 (D)
2006—Cowboys, 45-14 (T)
2010—Titans, 34-27 (D)
(RS Pts.—Cowboys 307, Titans 244)
*Franchise in Houston prior to 1997;
known as Oilers prior to 1999
DALLAS vs. WASHINGTON
RS: Cowboys lead series, 62-38-2
PS: Redskins lead series, 2-0
1960—Redskins, 26-14 (W)
1961—Tie, 28-28 (D)
   Redskins, 34-24 (W)
1962—Tie, 35-35 (D)
   Cowboys, 38-10 (W)
1963—Redskins, 21-17 (D)
   Cowboys, 35-20 (D)
1964—Cowboys, 24-18 (D)
   Redskins, 28-16 (W)
1965—Cowboys, 27-7 (D)
   Redskins, 34-31 (W)
1966—Cowboys, 31-30 (W)
   Redskins, 34-31 (D)
1967—Cowboys, 17-14 (W)
   Redskins, 27-20 (D)
1968—Cowboys, 44-24 (W)

Cowboys, 29-20 (D)
1969—Cowboys, 41-28 (W)
Cowboys, 20-10 (D)
1970—Cowboys, 45-21 (W)
Cowboys, 34-0 (D)
1971—Redskins, 20-16 (D)
Cowboys, 13-0 (W)
1972—Redskins, 24-20 (D)
Cowboys, 34-24 (D)
*Redskins, 26-3 (W)
1973—Redskins, 14-7 (W)
Cowboys, 27-7 (D)
1974—Redskins, 28-21 (W)
Cowboys, 24-23 (D)
1975—Redskins, 30-24 (W) OT
Cowboys, 31-10 (D)
1976—Cowboys, 20-7 (W)
Redskins, 27-14 (D)
1977—Cowboys, 34-16 (D)
Cowboys, 14-7 (W)
1978—Redskins, 9-5 (W)
Cowboys, 37-10 (D)
1979—Redskins, 34-20 (W)
Cowboys, 35-34 (D)
1980—Cowboys, 17-3 (W)
Cowboys, 14-10 (D)
1981—Cowboys, 26-10 (W)
Cowboys, 24-10 (D)
1982—Cowboys, 24-10 (W)
*Redskins, 31-17 (W)
1983—Cowboys, 31-30 (W)
Redskins, 31-10 (D)
1984—Redskins, 34-14 (W)
Redskins, 30-28 (D)
1985—Cowboys, 44-14 (D)
Cowboys, 13-7 (W)
1986—Cowboys, 30-6 (D)
Redskins, 41-14 (W)
1987—Redskins, 13-7 (D)
Redskins, 24-20 (W)
1988—Redskins, 35-17 (D)
Cowboys, 24-17 (W)
1989—Redskins, 30-7 (D)
Cowboys, 13-3 (W)
1990—Redskins, 19-15 (W)
Cowboys, 27-17 (D)
1991—Redskins, 33-31 (D)
Cowboys, 24-21 (W)
1992—Cowboys, 23-10 (D)
Redskins, 20-17 (W)
1993—Redskins, 35-16 (W)
Cowboys, 38-3 (D)
1994—Cowboys, 34-7 (W)
Cowboys, 31-7 (D)
1995—Redskins, 27-23 (W)
Redskins, 24-17 (D)
1996—Cowboys, 21-10 (D)
Redskins, 37-10 (D)
1997—Redskins, 21-16 (W)
Cowboys, 17-14 (D)
1998—Cowboys, 31-10 (W)
Cowboys, 23-7 (D)
1999—Cowboys, 41-35 (W) OT
Cowboys, 38-20 (D)
2000—Cowboys, 27-21 (W)
Cowboys, 32-13 (D)
2001—Cowboys, 9-7 (D)
Cowboys, 20-14 (W)
2002—Cowboys, 27-20 (D)
Redskins, 20-14 (W)
2003—Cowboys, 21-14 (D)
Cowboys, 27-0 (W)

2004—Cowboys, 21-18 (W)
Cowboys, 13-10 (D)
2005—Redskins, 14-13 (D)
Redskins, 35-7 (W)
2006—Cowboys, 27-10 (D)
Redskins, 22-19 (W)
2007—Cowboys, 28-23 (D)
Redskins, 27-6 (W)
2008—Redskins, 26-24 (D)
Cowboys, 14-10 (W)
2009—Cowboys, 7-6 (D)
Cowboys, 17-0 (W)
2010—Redskins, 13-7 (W)
Cowboys, 33-30 (D)
2011—Cowboys, 18-16 (D)
Cowboys, 27-24 (W) OT
(RS Pts.—Cowboys 2,325, Redskins 1,921)
(PS Pts.—Redskins 57, Cowboys 20)
*NFC Championship

DENVER vs. ARIZONA
RS: Broncos lead series, 7-1-1;
See Arizona vs. Denver
DENVER vs. ATLANTA
RS: Broncos lead series, 8-4
PS: Broncos lead series, 1-0;
See Atlanta vs. Denver
DENVER vs. BALTIMORE
RS: Ravens lead series, 5-3
PS: Ravens lead series, 1-0;
See Baltimore vs. Denver
DENVER vs. BUFFALO
RS: Bills lead series, 19-15-1
PS: Bills lead series, 1-0;
See Buffalo vs. Denver
DENVER vs. CAROLINA
RS: Broncos lead series, 2-1;
See Carolina vs. Denver
DENVER vs. CHICAGO
RS: Series tied, 7-7;
See Chicago vs. Denver
DENVER vs. CINCINNATI
RS: Broncos lead series, 18-8;
See Cincinnati vs. Denver
DENVER vs. CLEVELAND
RS: Broncos lead series, 18-5
PS: Broncos lead series, 3-0;
See Cleveland vs. Denver
DENVER vs. DALLAS
RS: Broncos lead series, 6-4
PS: Cowboys lead series, 1-0;
See Dallas vs. Denver
DENVER vs. DETROIT
RS: Broncos lead series, 6-5
1971—Lions, 24-20 (Den)
1974—Broncos, 31-27 (Det)
1978—Lions, 17-14 (Det)
1981—Broncos, 27-21 (Den)
1984—Broncos, 28-7 (Det)
1987—Broncos, 34-0 (Den)
1990—Lions, 40-27 (Det)
1999—Broncos, 17-7 (Det)
2003—Broncos, 20-16 (Den)
2007—Lions, 44-7 (Det)
2011—Lions, 45-10 (Den)
(RS Pts.—Lions 248, Broncos 235)
DENVER vs. GREEN BAY
RS: Packers lead series, 6-5-1
PS: Broncos lead series, 1-0
1971—Packers, 34-13 (Mil)
1975—Broncos, 23-13 (D)
1978—Broncos, 16-3 (D)

1984—Broncos, 17-14 (D)
1987—Tie, 17-17 (Mil) OT
1990—Broncos, 22-13 (D)
1993—Packers, 30-27 (GB)
1996—Packers, 41-6 (GB)
1997—*Broncos, 31-24 (San Diego)
1999—Broncos, 31-10 (D)
2003—Packers, 31-3 (GB)
2007—Packers, 19-13 (D) OT
2011—Packers, 49-23 (GB)
(RS Pts.—Packers 274, Broncos 211)
(PS Pts.—Broncos 31, Packers 24)
*Super Bowl XXXII
DENVER vs. HOUSTON
RS: Broncos lead series, 2-1
2004—Broncos, 31-13 (D)
2007—Texans, 31-13 (H)
2010—Broncos, 24-23 (D)
(RS Pts.—Broncos 68, Texans 67)
DENVER vs. *INDIANAPOLIS
RS: Broncos lead series, 11-8
PS: Colts lead series, 2-0
1974—Broncos, 17-6 (B)
1977—Broncos, 27-13 (D)
1978—Colts, 7-6 (B)
1981—Broncos, 28-10 (D)
1983—Broncos, 17-10 (B)
Broncos, 21-19 (D)
1985—Broncos, 15-10 (I)
1988—Colts, 55-23 (I)
1989—Broncos, 14-3 (D)
1990—Broncos, 27-17 (I)
1993—Broncos, 35-13 (D)
2001—Colts, 29-10 (I)
2002—Colts, 23-20 (D) OT
2003—Broncos, 31-17 (I)
**Colts, 41-10 (I)
2004—Broncos, 33-14 (D)
**Colts, 49-24 (I)
2006—Colts, 34-31 (D)
2007—Colts, 38-20 (I)
2009—Colts, 28-16 (I)
2010—Colts, 27-13 (D)
(RS Pts.—Broncos 404, Colts 373)
(PS Pts.—Colts 90, Broncos 34)
*Franchise in Baltimore prior to 1984
**AFC First-Round Playoff
DENVER vs. JACKSONVILLE
RS: Jaguars lead series, 5-3
PS: Series tied, 1-1
1995—Broncos, 31-23 (D)
1996—*Jaguars, 30-27 (D)
1997—**Broncos, 42-17 (D)
1998—Broncos, 37-24 (D)
1999—Jaguars, 27-24 (J)
2004—Jaguars, 7-6 (J)
2005—Broncos, 20-7 (J)
2007—Jaguars, 23-14 (D)
2008—Jaguars, 24-17 (D)
2010—Jaguars, 24-17 (J)
(RS Pts.—Broncos 166, Jaguars 159)
(PS Pts.—Broncos 69, Jaguars 47)
*AFC Divisional Playoff
**AFC First-Round Playoff
DENVER vs. *KANSAS CITY
RS: Chiefs lead series, 56-47
PS: Broncos lead series, 1-0
1960—Texans, 17-14 (D)
Texans, 34-7 (Dal)
1961—Texans, 19-12 (D)
Texans, 49-21 (Dal)
1962—Texans, 24-3 (D)

Texans, 17-10 (Dal)
1963—Chiefs, 59-7 (D)
Chiefs, 52-21 (KC)
1964—Broncos, 33-27 (D)
Chiefs, 49-39 (KC)
1965—Chiefs, 31-23 (D)
Chiefs, 45-35 (KC)
1966—Chiefs, 37-10 (KC)
Chiefs, 56-10 (D)
1967—Chiefs, 52-9 (KC)
Chiefs, 38-24 (D)
1968—Chiefs, 34-2 (KC)
Chiefs, 30-7 (D)
1969—Chiefs, 26-13 (D)
Chiefs, 31-17 (KC)
1970—Broncos, 26-13 (D)
Chiefs, 16-0 (KC)
1971—Chiefs, 16-3 (D)
Chiefs, 28-10 (KC)
1972—Chiefs, 45-24 (D)
Chiefs, 24-21 (KC)
1973—Chiefs, 16-14 (KC)
Broncos, 14-10 (D)
1974—Broncos, 17-14 (KC)
Chiefs, 42-34 (D)
1975—Broncos, 37-33 (D)
Chiefs, 26-13 (KC)
1976—Broncos, 35-26 (KC)
Broncos, 17-16 (D)
1977—Broncos, 23-7 (D)
Broncos, 14-7 (KC)
1978—Broncos, 23-17 (KC) OT
Broncos, 24-3 (D)
1979—Broncos, 24-10 (KC)
Broncos, 20-3 (D)
1980—Chiefs, 23-17 (D)
Chiefs, 31-14 (KC)
1981—Chiefs, 28-14 (KC)
Broncos, 16-13 (D)
1982—Chiefs, 37-16 (D)
1983—Broncos, 27-24 (D)
Chiefs, 48-17 (KC)
1984—Broncos, 21-0 (D)
Chiefs, 16-13 (KC)
1985—Broncos, 30-10 (KC)
Broncos, 14-13 (D)
1986—Broncos, 38-17 (D)
Chiefs, 37-10 (KC)
1987—Broncos, 26-17 (KC)
Broncos, 20-17 (D)
1988—Chiefs, 20-13 (KC)
Broncos, 17-11 (D)
1989—Broncos, 34-20 (D)
Broncos, 16-13 (KC)
1990—Broncos, 24-23 (D)
Chiefs, 31-20 (KC)
1991—Broncos, 19-16 (D)
Broncos, 24-20 (KC)
1992—Broncos, 20-19 (D)
Chiefs, 42-20 (KC)
1993—Chiefs, 15-7 (KC)
Broncos, 27-21 (D)
1994—Chiefs, 31-28 (D)
Broncos, 20-17 (KC) OT
1995—Chiefs, 21-7 (D)
Chiefs, 20-17 (KC)
1996—Chiefs, 17-14 (KC)
Broncos, 34-7 (D)
1997—Broncos, 19-3 (D)
Chiefs, 24-22 (KC)
**Broncos, 14-10 (KC)
1998—Broncos, 30-7 (KC)

Broncos, 35-31 (D)
1999—Chiefs, 26-10 (KC)
Chiefs, 16-10 (D)
2000—Chiefs, 23-22 (D)
Chiefs, 20-7 (KC)
2001—Broncos, 20-6 (D)
Chiefs, 26-23 (KC) OT
2002—Broncos, 37-34 (KC) OT
Broncos, 31-24 (D)
2003—Chiefs, 24-23 (KC)
Broncos, 45-27 (D)
2004—Broncos, 34-24 (D)
Chiefs, 45-17 (KC)
2005—Broncos, 30-10 (D)
Chiefs, 31-27 (KC)
2006—Broncos, 9-6 (D) OT
Chiefs, 19-10 (KC)
2007—Chiefs, 27-11 (KC)
Broncos, 41-7 (D)
2008—Chiefs, 33-19 (KC)
Broncos, 24-17 (D)
2009—Broncos, 44-13 (KC)
Chiefs, 44-24 (D)
2010—Broncos, 49-29 (D)
Chiefs, 10-6 (KC)
2011—Broncos, 17-10 (KC)
Chiefs, 7-3 (D)
(RS Pts.—Chiefs 2,401, Broncos 2,079)
(PS Pts.—Broncos 14, Chiefs 10)
*Franchise in Dallas prior to 1963 and known as Texans
**AFC Divisional Playoff

DENVER vs. MIAMI
RS: Dolphins lead series, 11-4-1
PS: Broncos lead series, 1-0
1966—Dolphins, 24-7 (M)
Broncos, 17-7 (D)
1967—Dolphins, 35-21 (M)
1968—Broncos, 21-14 (D)
1969—Dolphins, 27-24 (M)
1971—Tie, 10-10 (D)
1975—Dolphins, 14-13 (M)
1985—Dolphins, 30-26 (D)
1998—Dolphins, 31-21 (M)
*Broncos, 38-3 (D)
1999—Dolphins, 38-21 (D)
2001—Dolphins, 21-10 (M)
2002—Dolphins, 24-22 (D)
2004—Broncos, 20-17 (D)
2005—Dolphins, 34-10 (M)
2008—Dolphins, 26-17 (D)
2011—Broncos, 18-15 (M) OT
(RS Pts.—Dolphins 367, Broncos 278)
(PS Pts.—Broncos 38, Dolphins 3)
*AFC Divisional Playoff

DENVER vs. MINNESOTA
RS: Vikings lead series, 7-6
1972—Vikings, 23-20 (D)
1978—Vikings, 12-9 (M) OT
1981—Broncos, 19-17 (D)
1984—Broncos, 42-21 (D)
1987—Vikings, 34-27 (M)
1990—Vikings, 27-22 (M)
1991—Broncos, 13-6 (M)
1993—Vikings, 26-23 (D)
1996—Broncos, 21-17 (M)
1999—Vikings, 23-20 (D)
2003—Vikings, 28-20 (M)
2007—Broncos, 22-19 (D) OT
2011—Broncos, 35-32 (M)
(RS Pts.—Broncos 293, Vikings 285)

DENVER vs. *NEW ENGLAND
RS: Broncos lead series, 25-17
PS: Broncos lead series, 2-1
1960—Broncos, 13-10 (B)
Broncos, 31-24 (D)
1961—Patriots, 45-17 (B)
Patriots, 28-24 (D)
1962—Patriots, 41-16 (B)
Patriots, 33-29 (D)
1963—Broncos, 14-10 (D)
Patriots, 40-21 (B)
1964—Patriots, 39-10 (D)
Patriots, 12-7 (B)
1965—Broncos, 27-10 (B)
Patriots, 28-20 (D)
1966—Patriots, 24-10 (D)
Broncos, 17-10 (B)
1967—Broncos, 26-21 (D)
1968—Patriots, 20-17 (D)
Broncos, 35-14 (B)
1969—Broncos, 35-7 (D)
1972—Broncos, 45-21 (D)
1976—Patriots, 38-14 (NE)
1979—Broncos, 45-10 (D)
1980—Patriots, 23-14 (NE)
1984—Broncos, 26-19 (D)
1986—Broncos, 27-20 (D)
**Broncos, 22-17 (D)
1987—Broncos, 31-20 (D)
1988—Broncos, 21-10 (D)
1991—Broncos, 9-6 (NE)
Broncos, 20-3 (D)
1995—Broncos, 37-3 (NE)
1996—Broncos, 34-8 (NE)
1997—Broncos, 34-13 (D)
1998—Broncos, 27-21 (D)
1999—Patriots, 24-23 (NE)
2000—Patriots, 28-19 (D)
2001—Broncos, 31-20 (D)
2002—Broncos, 24-16 (NE)
2003—Patriots, 30-26 (D)
2005—Broncos, 28-20 (D)
**Broncos, 27-13 (D)
2006—Broncos, 17-7 (NE)
2008—Patriots, 41-7 (NE)
2009—Broncos, 20-17 (D) OT
2011—Patriots, 41-23 (D)
**Patriots, 45-10 (NE)
(RS Pts.—Broncos 971, Patriots 875)
(PS Pts.—Patriots 75, Broncos 59)
*Franchise in Boston prior to 1971
**AFC Divisional Playoff

DENVER vs. NEW ORLEANS
RS: Broncos lead series, 7-2
1970—Broncos, 31-6 (NO)
1974—Broncos, 33-17 (D)
1979—Broncos, 10-3 (D)
1985—Broncos, 34-23 (D)
1988—Saints, 42-0 (NO)
1994—Saints, 30-28 (D)
2000—Broncos, 38-23 (NO)
2004—Broncos, 34-13 (NO)
2008—Broncos, 34-32 (D)
(RS Pts.—Broncos 242, Saints 189)

DENVER vs. N.Y. GIANTS
RS: Series tied, 5-5
PS: Giants lead series, 1-0
1972—Giants, 29-17 (NY)
1976—Broncos, 14-13 (D)
1980—Broncos, 14-9 (NY)
1986—Giants, 19-16 (NY)
*Giants, 39-20 (Pasadena)

1989—Giants, 14-7 (D)
1992—Broncos, 27-13 (D)
1998—Giants, 20-16 (NY)
2001—Broncos, 31-20 (D)
2005—Giants, 24-23 (NY)
2009—Broncos, 26-6 (D)
(RS Pts.—Broncos 191, Giants 167)
(PS Pts.—Giants 39, Broncos 20)
*Super Bowl XXI

DENVER vs. *N.Y. JETS
RS: Broncos lead series, 17-15-1
PS: Broncos lead series, 1-0
1960—Titans, 28-24 (NY)
        Titans, 30-27 (D)
1961—Titans, 35-28 (NY)
        Broncos, 27-10 (D)
1962—Broncos, 32-10 (NY)
        Titans, 46-45 (D)
1963—Tie, 35-35 (NY)
        Jets, 14-9 (D)
1964—Jets, 30-6 (NY)
        Broncos, 20-16 (D)
1965—Broncos, 16-13 (D)
        Jets, 45-10 (NY)
1966—Jets, 16-7 (D)
1967—Jets, 38-24 (D)
        Broncos, 33-24 (NY)
1968—Broncos, 21-13 (NY)
1969—Broncos, 21-19 (D)
1973—Broncos, 40-28 (NY)
1976—Broncos, 46-3 (D)
1978—Jets, 31-28 (D)
1980—Broncos, 31-24 (D)
1986—Jets, 22-10 (NY)
1992—Broncos, 27-16 (D)
1993—Broncos, 26-20 (NY)
1994—Jets, 25-22 (NY) OT
1996—Broncos, 31-6 (D)
1998—**Broncos, 23-10 (D)
1999—Jets, 21-13 (D)
2000—Broncos, 30-23 (NY)
2002—Jets, 19-13 (NY)
2005—Broncos, 27-0 (D)
2008—Broncos, 34-17 (NY)
2010—Jets, 24-20 (D)
2011—Broncos, 17-13 (D)
(RS Pts.—Broncos 800, Jets 714)
(PS Pts.—Broncos 23, Jets 10)
*Jets known as Titans prior to 1963
**AFC Championship

DENVER vs. *OAKLAND
RS: Raiders lead series, 59-42-2
PS: Series tied, 1-1
1960—Broncos, 31-14 (D)
        Raiders, 48-10 (O)
1961—Raiders, 33-19 (O)
        Broncos, 27-24 (D)
1962—Broncos, 44-7 (D)
        Broncos, 23-6 (O)
1963—Raiders, 26-10 (D)
        Raiders, 35-31 (O)
1964—Raiders, 40-7 (O)
        Tie, 20-20 (D)
1965—Raiders, 28-20 (D)
        Raiders, 24-13 (O)
1966—Raiders, 17-3 (D)
        Raiders, 28-10 (O)
1967—Raiders, 51-0 (O)
        Raiders, 21-17 (D)
1968—Raiders, 43-7 (D)
        Raiders, 33-27 (O)
1969—Raiders, 24-14 (D)

        Raiders, 41-10 (O)
1970—Raiders, 35-23 (O)
        Raiders, 24-19 (D)
1971—Raiders, 27-16 (D)
        Raiders, 21-13 (O)
1972—Broncos, 30-23 (O)
        Raiders, 37-20 (D)
1973—Tie, 23-23 (D)
        Raiders, 21-17 (O)
1974—Raiders, 28-17 (D)
        Broncos, 20-17 (O)
1975—Raiders, 42-17 (D)
        Raiders, 17-10 (O)
1976—Raiders, 17-10 (D)
        Raiders, 19-6 (O)
1977—Broncos, 30-7 (O)
        Raiders, 24-14 (D)
        **Broncos, 20-17 (D)
1978—Broncos, 14-6 (D)
        Broncos, 21-6 (O)
1979—Raiders, 27-3 (O)
        Raiders, 14-10 (D)
1980—Raiders, 9-3 (O)
        Raiders, 24-21 (D)
1981—Broncos, 9-7 (D)
        Broncos, 17-0 (O)
1982—Raiders, 27-10 (LA)
1983—Raiders, 22-7 (D)
        Raiders, 22-20 (LA)
1984—Broncos, 16-13 (D)
        Broncos, 22-19 (LA) OT
1985—Raiders, 31-28 (LA) OT
        Raiders, 17-14 (D) OT
1986—Broncos, 38-36 (D)
        Broncos, 21-10 (LA)
1987—Broncos, 30-14 (D)
        Broncos, 23-17 (LA)
1988—Raiders, 30-27 (D) OT
        Raiders, 21-20 (LA)
1989—Broncos, 31-21 (D)
        Raiders, 16-13 (LA) OT
1990—Raiders, 14-9 (D)
        Raiders, 23-20 (D)
1991—Raiders, 16-13 (LA)
        Raiders, 17-16 (D)
1992—Broncos, 17-13 (D)
        Raiders, 24-0 (LA)
1993—Raiders, 23-20 (D)
        Raiders, 33-30 (LA) OT
        ***Raiders, 42-24 (LA)
1994—Raiders, 48-16 (D)
        Raiders, 23-13 (LA)
1995—Broncos, 27-0 (D)
        Broncos, 31-28 (O)
1996—Broncos, 22-21 (D)
        Broncos, 24-19 (D)
1997—Raiders, 28-25 (O)
        Broncos, 31-3 (D)
1998—Broncos, 34-17 (O)
        Broncos, 40-14 (D)
1999—Broncos, 16-13 (O)
        Broncos, 27-21 (D) OT
2000—Broncos, 33-24 (O)
        Broncos, 27-24 (D)
2001—Raiders, 38-28 (O)
        Broncos, 23-17 (D)
2002—Raiders, 34-10 (D)
        Raiders, 28-16 (O)
2003—Broncos, 31-10 (O)
        Broncos, 22-8 (D)
2004—Broncos, 31-3 (O)
        Raiders, 25-24 (D)

2005—Broncos, 31-17 (O)
        Broncos, 22-3 (D)
2006—Broncos, 13-3 (D)
        Broncos, 17-13 (O)
2007—Broncos, 23-20 (D) OT
        Raiders, 34-20 (O)
2008—Broncos, 41-14 (O)
        Raiders, 31-10 (D)
2009—Broncos, 23-3 (O)
        Raiders, 20-19 (D)
2010—Raiders, 59-14 (D)
        Raiders, 39-23 (O)
2011—Raiders, 23-20 (D)
        Broncos, 38-24 (O)
(RS Pts.—Raiders 2,266, Broncos 2,036)
(PS Pts.—Raiders 59, Broncos 44)
*Franchise in Los Angeles from 1982-1994
**AFC Championship
***AFC First-Round Playoff

DENVER vs. PHILADELPHIA
RS: Eagles lead series, 7-4
1971—Eagles, 17-16 (P)
1975—Broncos, 25-10 (D)
1980—Eagles, 27-6 (P)
1983—Eagles, 13-10 (P)
1986—Broncos, 33-7 (P)
1989—Eagles, 28-24 (D)
1992—Eagles, 30-0 (D)
1995—Eagles, 31-13 (P)
1998—Broncos, 41-16 (D)
2005—Broncos, 49-21 (D)
2009—Eagles, 30-27 (P)
(RS Pts.—Broncos 244, Eagles 230)

DENVER vs. PITTSBURGH
RS: Broncos lead series, 13-7-1
PS: Broncos lead series, 4-3
1970—Broncos, 16-13 (D)
1971—Broncos, 22-10 (P)
1973—Broncos, 23-13 (P)
1974—Tie, 35-35 (D) OT
1975—Steelers, 20-9 (P)
1977—Broncos, 21-7 (D)
        *Broncos, 34-21 (D)
1978—Steelers, 21-17 (D)
        *Steelers, 33-10 (P)
1979—Steelers, 42-7 (P)
1983—Broncos, 14-10 (P)
1984—*Steelers, 24-17 (D)
1985—Broncos, 31-23 (P)
1986—Steelers, 21-10 (P)
1988—Steelers, 39-21 (P)
1989—Broncos, 34-7 (D)
        *Broncos, 24-23 (D)
1990—Steelers, 34-17 (D)
1991—Broncos, 20-13 (D)
1993—Broncos, 37-13 (D)
1997—Steelers, 35-24 (P)
        **Broncos, 24-21 (P)
2003—Broncos, 17-14 (D)
2005—**Steelers, 34-17 (D)
2006—Broncos, 31-20 (P)
2007—Broncos, 31-28 (D)
2009—Steelers, 28-10 (D)
2011—***Broncos, 29-23 (D) OT
(RS Pts.—Broncos 458, Steelers 435)
(PS Pts.—Steelers 179, Broncos 155)
*AFC Divisional Playoff
**AFC Championship
***AFC First-Round Playoff

DENVER vs. *ST. LOUIS
RS: Rams lead series, 7-5
1972—Broncos, 16-10 (LA)

1974—Rams, 17-10 (D)
1979—Rams, 13-9 (D)
1982—Broncos, 27-24 (LA)
1985—Rams, 20-16 (LA)
1988—Broncos, 35-24 (D)
1994—Rams, 27-21 (LA)
1997—Broncos, 35-14 (D)
2000—Rams, 41-36 (StL)
2002—Broncos, 23-16 (D)
2006—Rams, 18-10 (StL)
2010—Rams, 36-33 (D)
(RS Pts.—Broncos 271, Rams 260)
Franchise in Los Angeles prior to 1995
DENVER vs. *SAN DIEGO
RS: Broncos lead series, 55-48-1
1960—Chargers, 23-19 (D)
    Chargers, 41-33 (LA)
1961—Chargers, 37-0 (SD)
    Chargers, 19-16 (D)
1962—Broncos, 30-21 (D)
    Broncos, 23-20 (SD)
1963—Broncos, 50-34 (D)
    Chargers, 58-20 (SD)
1964—Chargers, 42-14 (SD)
    Chargers, 31-20 (D)
1965—Chargers, 34-31 (SD)
    Chargers, 33-21 (D)
1966—Chargers, 24-17 (SD)
    Broncos, 20-17 (D)
1967—Chargers, 38-21 (D)
    Chargers, 24-20 (SD)
1968—Chargers, 55-24 (SD)
    Chargers, 47-23 (D)
1969—Broncos, 13-0 (D)
    Chargers, 45-24 (SD)
1970—Chargers, 24-21 (SD)
    Tie, 17-17 (D)
1971—Broncos, 20-16 (D)
    Chargers, 45-17 (SD)
1972—Chargers, 37-14 (SD)
    Broncos, 38-13 (D)
1973—Broncos, 30-19 (D)
    Broncos, 42-28 (SD)
1974—Broncos, 27-7 (D)
    Chargers, 17-0 (SD)
1975—Broncos, 27-17 (SD)
    Broncos, 13-10 (D) OT
1976—Broncos, 26-0 (D)
    Broncos, 17-0 (SD)
1977—Broncos, 17-14 (SD)
    Broncos, 17-9 (D)
1978—Broncos, 27-14 (D)
    Chargers, 23-0 (SD)
1979—Broncos, 7-0 (D)
    Chargers, 17-7 (SD)
1980—Chargers, 30-13 (D)
    Broncos, 20-13 (SD)
1981—Broncos, 42-24 (D)
    Chargers, 34-17 (SD)
1982—Chargers, 23-3 (D)
    Chargers, 30-20 (SD)
1983—Broncos, 14-6 (D)
    Chargers, 31-7 (SD)
1984—Broncos, 16-13 (SD)
    Broncos, 16-13 (D)
1985—Chargers, 30-10 (SD)
    Broncos, 30-24 (D) OT
1986—Broncos, 31-14 (SD)
    Chargers, 9-3 (D)
1987—Broncos, 31-17 (SD)
    Broncos, 24-0 (D)
1988—Broncos, 34-3 (D)

Broncos, 12-0 (SD)
1989—Broncos, 16-10 (D)
    Chargers, 19-16 (SD)
1990—Chargers, 19-7 (SD)
    Broncos, 20-10 (D)
1991—Broncos, 27-19 (D)
    Broncos, 17-14 (SD)
1992—Broncos, 21-13 (D)
    Chargers, 24-21 (SD)
1993—Broncos, 34-17 (D)
    Chargers, 13-10 (SD)
1994—Chargers, 37-34 (D)
    Broncos, 20-15 (SD)
1995—Chargers, 17-6 (SD)
    Broncos, 30-27 (D)
1996—Broncos, 28-17 (D)
    Chargers, 16-10 (SD)
1997—Broncos, 38-28 (SD)
    Broncos, 38-3 (D)
1998—Broncos, 27-10 (D)
    Broncos, 31-16 (SD)
1999—Broncos, 33-17 (SD)
    Chargers, 12-6 (D)
2000—Broncos, 21-7 (SD)
    Broncos, 38-37 (D)
2001—Chargers, 27-10 (SD)
    Broncos, 26-16 (D)
2002—Broncos, 26-9 (D)
    Chargers, 30-27 (SD) OT
2003—Broncos, 37-13 (SD)
    Broncos, 37-8 (D)
2004—Broncos, 23-13 (D)
    Chargers, 20-17 (SD)
2005—Broncos, 20-17 (D)
    Broncos, 23-7 (SD)
2006—Chargers, 35-27 (D)
    Chargers, 48-20 (SD)
2007—Chargers, 41-3 (D)
    Chargers, 23-3 (SD)
2008—Broncos, 39-38 (D)
    Chargers, 52-21 (SD)
2009—Broncos, 34-23 (SD)
    Chargers, 32-3 (D)
2010—Chargers, 35-14 (SD)
    Chargers, 33-28 (D)
2011—Chargers, 29-24 (D)
    Broncos, 16-13 (SD) OT
(RS Pts.—Chargers 2,265, Broncos 2,193)
Franchise in Los Angeles prior to 1961
DENVER vs. SAN FRANCISCO
RS: Series tied, 6-6
PS: 49ers lead series, 1-0
1970—49ers, 19-14 (SF)
1973—49ers, 36-34 (D)
1979—Broncos, 38-28 (SF)
1982—Broncos, 24-21 (D)
1985—Broncos, 17-16 (D)
1988—Broncos, 16-13 (SF) OT
1989—*49ers, 55-10 (New Orleans)
1994—49ers, 42-19 (SF)
1997—49ers, 34-17 (SF)
2000—Broncos, 38-9 (D)
2002—49ers, 24-14 (SF)
2006—49ers, 26-23 (D) OT
2010—49ers, 24-16 (London)
(RS Pts.—49ers 282, Broncos 280)
(PS Pts.—49ers 55, Broncos 10)
Super Bowl XXIV
DENVER vs. SEATTLE
RS: Broncos lead series, 34-18
PS: Seahawks lead series, 1-0
1977—Broncos, 24-13 (S)

1978—Broncos, 28-7 (D)
    Broncos, 20-17 (S) OT
1979—Broncos, 37-34 (D)
    Seahawks, 28-23 (S)
1980—Broncos, 36-20 (D)
    Broncos, 25-17 (S)
1981—Seahawks, 13-10 (S)
    Broncos, 23-13 (D)
1982—Seahawks, 17-10 (D)
    Seahawks, 13-11 (S)
1983—Seahawks, 27-19 (S)
    Broncos, 38-27 (D)
    *Seahawks, 31-7 (S)
1984—Seahawks, 27-24 (S)
    Broncos, 31-14 (S)
1985—Broncos, 13-10 (D) OT
    Broncos, 27-24 (S)
1986—Broncos, 20-13 (D)
    Seahawks, 41-16 (S)
1987—Broncos, 40-17 (D)
    Seahawks, 28-21 (S)
1988—Seahawks, 21-14 (D)
    Seahawks, 42-14 (S)
1989—Broncos, 24-21 (S) OT
    Broncos, 41-14 (D)
1990—Broncos, 34-31 (D) OT
    Seahawks, 17-12 (S)
1991—Broncos, 16-10 (D)
    Seahawks, 13-10 (S)
1992—Seahawks, 16-13 (S) OT
    Broncos, 10-6 (D)
1993—Broncos, 28-17 (D)
    Broncos, 17-9 (S)
1994—Broncos, 16-9 (S)
    Broncos, 17-10 (D)
1995—Seahawks, 27-10 (S)
    Seahawks, 31-27 (D)
1996—Broncos, 30-20 (S)
    Broncos, 34-7 (D)
1997—Broncos, 35-14 (S)
    Broncos, 30-27 (D)
1998—Broncos, 21-16 (D)
    Broncos, 28-21 (D)
1999—Seahawks, 20-17 (S)
    Broncos, 36-30 (D) OT
2000—Broncos, 38-31 (S)
    Broncos, 31-24 (D)
2001—Seahawks, 34-21 (S)
    Broncos, 20-7 (D)
2002—Broncos, 31-9 (S)
2006—Seahawks, 23-20 (D)
2010—Broncos, 31-14 (D)
(RS Pts.—Broncos 1,222, Seahawks 1,011)
(PS Pts.—Seahawks 31, Broncos 7)
AFC First-Round Playoff
DENVER vs. TAMPA BAY
RS: Broncos lead series, 5-2
1976—Broncos, 48-13 (D)
1981—Broncos, 24-7 (TB)
1993—Buccaneers, 17-10 (D)
1996—Broncos, 27-23 (D)
1999—Buccaneers, 13-10 (TB)
2004—Broncos, 16-13 (D)
2008—Broncos, 16-13 (D)
(RS Pts.—Broncos 151, Buccaneers 99)
DENVER vs. *TENNESSEE
RS: Titans lead series, 21-14-1
PS: Broncos lead series, 2-1
1960—Oilers, 45-25 (D)
    Oilers, 20-10 (H)
1961—Oilers, 55-14 (D)
    Oilers, 45-14 (H)

1962—Broncos, 20-10 (D)
    Oilers, 34-17 (H)
1963—Oilers, 20-14 (H)
    Oilers, 33-24 (D)
1964—Oilers, 38-17 (D)
    Oilers, 34-15 (H)
1965—Broncos, 28-17 (D)
    Broncos, 31-21 (H)
1966—Oilers, 45-7 (H)
    Broncos, 40-38 (D)
1967—Oilers, 10-6 (H)
    Oilers, 20-18 (D)
1968—Oilers, 38-17 (H)
1969—Oilers, 24-21 (H)
    Tie, 20-20 (D)
1970—Oilers, 31-21 (H)
1972—Broncos, 30-17 (D)
1973—Broncos, 48-20 (H)
1974—Broncos, 37-14 (H)
1976—Oilers, 17-3 (H)
1977—Broncos, 24-14 (H)
1979—**Oilers, 13-7 (H)
1980—Oilers, 20-16 (D)
1983—Broncos, 26-14 (H)
1985—Broncos, 31-20 (D)
1987—Oilers, 40-10 (D)
    ***Broncos, 34-10 (D)
1991—Oilers, 42-14 (H)
    ***Broncos, 26-24 (D)
1992—Broncos, 27-21 (D)
1995—Oilers, 42-33 (H)
2004—Broncos, 37-16 (T)
2007—Broncos, 34-20 (D)
2010—Broncos, 26-20 (T)
2011—Titans, 17-14 (T)
(RS Pts.—Titans 952, Broncos 789)
(PS Pts.—Broncos 67, Titans 47)
*Franchise in Houston prior to 1997;
known as the Oilers prior to 1999
**AFC First-Round Playoff
***AFC Divisional Playoff
DENVER vs. WASHINGTON
RS: Broncos lead series, 6-5
PS: Redskins lead series, 1-0
1970—Redskins, 19-3 (D)
1974—Redskins, 30-3 (W)
1980—Broncos, 20-17 (D)
1986—Broncos, 31-30 (D)
1987—*Redskins, 42-10 (San Diego)
1989—Broncos, 14-10 (W)
1992—Redskins, 34-3 (W)
1995—Broncos, 38-31 (D)
1998—Broncos, 38-16 (W)
2001—Redskins, 17-10 (D)
2005—Broncos, 21-19 (D)
2009—Redskins, 27-17 (W)
(RS Pts.—Redskins 250, Broncos 198)
(PS Pts.—Redskins 42, Broncos 10)
*Super Bowl XXII

DETROIT vs. ARIZONA
RS: Lions lead series, 31-24-5;
See Arizona vs. Detroit
DETROIT vs. ATLANTA
RS: Lions lead series, 23-11;
See Atlanta vs. Detroit
DETROIT vs. BALTIMORE
RS: Ravens lead series, 2-1;
See Baltimore vs. Detroit
DETROIT vs. BUFFALO
RS: Series tied, 4-4-1;
See Buffalo vs. Detroit

DETROIT vs. CAROLINA
RS: Panthers lead series, 4-2;
See Carolina vs. Detroit
DETROIT vs. CHICAGO
RS: Bears lead series, 94-65-5;
See Chicago vs. Detroit
DETROIT vs. CINCINNATI
RS: Bengals lead series, 7-3;
See Cincinnati vs. Detroit
DETROIT vs. CLEVELAND
RS: Lions lead series, 14-4
PS: Lions lead series, 3-1;
See Cleveland vs. Detroit
DETROIT vs. DALLAS
RS: Cowboys lead series, 12-10
PS: Series tied, 1-1;
See Dallas vs. Detroit
DETROIT vs. DENVER
RS: Broncos lead series, 6-5;
See Denver vs. Detroit
*DETROIT vs. GREEN BAY
RS: Packers lead series, 91-65-7
PS: Packers lead series, 2-0
1930—Packers, 47-13 (GB)
    Tie, 6-6 (P)
1932—Packers, 15-10 (GB)
    Spartans, 19-0 (P)
1933—Packers, 17-0 (GB)
    Spartans, 7-0 (P)
1934—Lions, 3-0 (GB)
    Packers, 3-0 (D)
1935—Packers, 13-9 (Mil)
    Packers, 31-7 (GB)
    Lions, 20-10 (D)
1936—Packers, 20-18 (GB)
    Packers, 26-17 (D)
1937—Packers, 26-6 (GB)
    Packers, 14-13 (D)
1938—Lions, 17-7 (GB)
    Packers, 28-7 (D)
1939—Packers, 26-7 (GB)
    Packers, 12-7 (D)
1940—Lions, 23-14 (GB)
    Packers, 50-7 (D)
1941—Packers, 23-0 (GB)
    Packers, 24-7 (D)
1942—Packers, 38-7 (Mil)
    Packers, 28-7 (D)
1943—Packers, 35-14 (GB)
    Packers, 27-6 (D)
1944—Packers, 27-6 (Mil)
    Packers, 14-0 (D)
1945—Packers, 57-21 (Mil)
    Lions, 14-3 (D)
1946—Packers, 10-7 (Mil)
    Packers, 9-0 (D)
1947—Packers, 34-17 (GB)
    Packers, 35-14 (D)
1948—Packers, 33-21 (GB)
    Lions, 24-20 (D)
1949—Packers, 16-14 (Mil)
    Lions, 21-7 (D)
1950—Lions, 45-7 (GB)
    Lions, 24-21 (D)
1951—Lions, 24-17 (GB)
    Lions, 52-35 (D)
1952—Lions, 52-17 (GB)
    Lions, 48-24 (D)
1953—Lions, 14-7 (GB)
    Lions, 34-15 (D)
1954—Lions, 21-17 (GB)
    Lions, 28-24 (D)

1955—Packers, 20-17 (GB)
    Lions, 24-10 (D)
1956—Lions, 20-16 (GB)
    Packers, 24-20 (D)
1957—Lions, 24-14 (GB)
    Lions, 18-6 (D)
1958—Tie, 13-13 (GB)
    Lions, 24-14 (D)
1959—Packers, 28-10 (GB)
    Packers, 24-17 (D)
1960—Packers, 28-9 (GB)
    Lions, 23-10 (D)
1961—Lions, 17-13 (Mil)
    Packers, 17-9 (D)
1962—Packers, 9-7 (GB)
    Lions, 26-14 (D)
1963—Packers, 31-10 (Mil)
    Tie, 13-13 (D)
1964—Packers, 14-10 (D)
    Packers, 30-7 (GB)
1965—Packers, 31-21 (D)
    Lions, 12-7 (GB)
1966—Packers, 23-14 (GB)
    Packers, 31-7 (D)
1967—Tie, 17-17 (GB)
    Packers, 27-17 (D)
1968—Packers, 23-17 (GB)
    Tie, 14-14 (D)
1969—Packers, 28-17 (GB)
    Lions, 16-10 (GB)
1970—Lions, 40-0 (D)
    Lions, 20-0 (D)
1971—Lions, 31-28 (D)
    Tie, 14-14 (Mil)
1972—Packers, 24-23 (D)
    Packers, 33-7 (GB)
1973—Tie, 13-13 (GB)
    Lions, 34-0 (D)
1974—Packers, 21-19 (Mil)
    Lions, 19-17 (D)
1975—Lions, 30-16 (Mil)
    Lions, 13-10 (D)
1976—Packers, 24-14 (GB)
    Lions, 27-6 (D)
1977—Lions, 10-6 (D)
    Packers, 10-9 (GB)
1978—Packers, 13-7 (D)
    Packers, 35-14 (Mil)
1979—Packers, 24-16 (Mil)
    Packers, 18-13 (D)
1980—Lions, 29-7 (Mil)
    Lions, 24-3 (D)
1981—Lions, 31-27 (D)
    Packers, 31-17 (GB)
1982—Packers, 30-10 (GB)
    Lions, 27-24 (D)
1983—Lions, 38-14 (D)
    Lions, 23-20 (Mil) OT
1984—Packers, 41-9 (GB)
    Lions, 31-28 (D)
1985—Packers, 43-10 (GB)
    Packers, 26-23 (D)
1986—Lions, 21-14 (GB)
    Packers, 44-40 (D)
1987—Lions, 19-16 (GB) OT
    Packers, 34-33 (D)
1988—Lions, 19-9 (Mil)
    Lions, 30-14 (D)
1989—Packers, 23-20 (Mil) OT
    Lions, 31-22 (D)
1990—Packers, 24-21 (D)
    Lions, 24-17 (GB)

1991—Lions, 23-14 (D)
   Lions, 21-17 (GB)
1992—Packers, 27-13 (D)
   Packers, 38-10 (Mil)
1993—Packers, 26-17 (Mil)
   Lions, 30-20 (D)
   **Packers, 28-24 (D)
1994—Packers, 38-30 (Mil)
   Lions, 34-31 (D)
   **Packers, 16-12 (GB)
1995—Packers, 30-21 (GB)
   Lions, 24-16 (D)
1996—Packers, 28-18 (GB)
   Packers, 31-3 (D)
1997—Lions, 26-15 (D)
   Packers, 20-10 (GB)
1998—Packers, 38-19 (GB)
   Lions, 27-20 (D)
1999—Lions, 23-15 (D)
   Packers, 26-17 (GB)
2000—Lions, 31-24 (D)
   Packers, 26-13 (GB)
2001—Packers, 28-6 (GB)
   Packers, 29-27 (D)
2002—Packers, 37-31 (D)
   Packers, 40-14 (GB)
2003—Packers, 31-6 (GB)
   Lions, 22-14 (D)
2004—Packers, 38-10 (D)
   Packers, 16-13 (GB)
2005—Lions, 17-3 (D)
   Packers, 16-13 (GB) OT
2006—Packers, 31-24 (D)
   Packers, 17-9 (GB)
2007—Packers, 37-26 (D)
   Packers, 34-13 (GB)
2008—Packers, 48-25 (D)
   Packers, 31-21 (GB)
2009—Packers, 26-0 (GB)
   Packers, 34-12 (D)
2010—Packers, 28-26 (GB)
   Lions, 7-3 (D)
2011—Packers, 27-15 (D)
   Packers, 45-41 (GB)
(RS Pts.—Packers 3,458, Lions 2,945)
(PS Pts.—Packers 44, Lions 36)
*Franchise in Portsmouth prior to 1934
and known as the Spartans
**NFC First-Round Playoff
DETROIT vs. HOUSTON
RS: Series tied, 1-1
2004—Lions, 28-16 (D)
2008—Texans, 28-21 (H)
(RS Pts.—Lions 49, Texans 44)
DETROIT vs. *INDIANAPOLIS
RS: Colts lead series, 20-18-2
1953—Lions, 27-17 (B)
   Lions, 17-7 (D)
1954—Lions, 35-0 (D)
   Lions, 27-3 (B)
1955—Colts, 28-13 (B)
   Lions, 24-14 (D)
1956—Lions, 31-14 (B)
   Colts, 27-3 (D)
1957—Colts, 34-14 (B)
   Lions, 31-27 (D)
1958—Colts, 28-15 (B)
   Colts, 40-14 (D)
1959—Colts, 21-9 (B)
   Colts, 31-24 (D)
1960—Lions, 30-17 (D)
   Lions, 20-15 (B)

1961—Lions, 16-15 (B)
   Colts, 17-14 (D)
1962—Lions, 29-20 (B)
   Lions, 21-14 (D)
1963—Colts, 25-21 (D)
   Colts, 24-21 (B)
1964—Colts, 34-0 (D)
   Lions, 31-14 (B)
1965—Colts, 31-7 (B)
   Tie, 24-24 (D)
1966—Colts, 45-14 (B)
   Lions, 20-14 (D)
1967—Colts, 41-7 (B)
1968—Colts, 27-10 (D)
1969—Tie, 17-17 (B)
1973—Colts, 29-27 (D)
1977—Lions, 13-10 (B)
1980—Colts, 10-9 (D)
1985—Colts, 14-6 (I)
1991—Lions, 33-24 (I)
1997—Lions, 32-10 (D)
2000—Colts, 30-18 (I)
2004—Colts, 41-9 (D)
2008—Colts, 31-21 (I)
(RS Pts.—Colts 860, Lions 778)
*Franchise in Baltimore prior to 1984
DETROIT vs. JACKSONVILLE
RS: Jaguars lead series, 3-1
1995—Lions, 44-0 (D)
1998—Jaguars, 37-22 (J)
2004—Jaguars, 23-17 (J) OT
2008—Jaguars, 38-14 (D)
(RS Pts.—Jaguars 98, Lions 97)
DETROIT vs. KANSAS CITY
RS: Chiefs lead series, 7-5
1971—Lions, 32-21 (D)
1975—Chiefs, 24-21 (KC) OT
1980—Chiefs, 20-17 (KC)
1981—Lions, 27-10 (D)
1987—Chiefs, 27-20 (D)
1988—Lions, 7-6 (KC)
1990—Chiefs, 43-24 (KC)
1996—Chiefs, 28-24 (D)
1999—Chiefs, 31-21 (KC)
2003—Chiefs, 45-17 (KC)
2007—Lions, 25-20 (D)
2011—Lions, 48-3 (D)
(RS Pts.—Lions 283, Chiefs 278)
DETROIT vs. MIAMI
RS: Dolphins lead series, 7-3
1973—Dolphins, 34-7 (M)
1979—Dolphins, 28-10 (D)
1985—Lions, 31-21 (D)
1991—Lions, 17-13 (D)
1994—Dolphins, 27-20 (M)
1997—Dolphins, 33-30 (M)
2000—Dolphins, 23-8 (D)
2002—Dolphins, 49-21 (M)
2006—Dolphins, 27-10 (D)
2010—Lions, 34-27 (M)
(RS Pts.—Dolphins 282, Lions 188)
DETROIT vs. MINNESOTA
RS: Vikings lead series, 66-33-2
1961—Lions, 37-10 (M)
   Lions, 13-7 (D)
1962—Lions, 17-6 (M)
   Lions, 37-23 (D)
1963—Lions, 28-10 (D)
   Vikings, 34-31 (M)
1964—Lions, 24-20 (M)
   Tie, 23-23 (D)
1965—Lions, 31-29 (M)

   Vikings, 29-7 (D)
1966—Lions, 32-31 (M)
   Vikings, 28-16 (D)
1967—Tie, 10-10 (M)
   Lions, 14-3 (D)
1968—Vikings, 24-10 (M)
   Vikings, 13-6 (D)
1969—Vikings, 24-10 (M)
   Vikings, 27-0 (D)
1970—Vikings, 30-17 (D)
   Vikings, 24-20 (M)
1971—Vikings, 16-13 (D)
   Vikings, 29-10 (M)
1972—Vikings, 34-10 (D)
   Vikings, 16-14 (M)
1973—Vikings, 23-9 (D)
   Vikings, 28-7 (M)
1974—Vikings, 7-6 (D)
   Lions, 20-16 (M)
1975—Vikings, 25-19 (M)
   Lions, 17-10 (D)
1976—Lions, 10-9 (D)
   Vikings, 31-23 (M)
1977—Vikings, 14-7 (M)
   Vikings, 30-21 (D)
1978—Vikings, 17-7 (M)
   Lions, 45-14 (D)
1979—Vikings, 13-10 (D)
   Vikings, 14-7 (M)
1980—Lions, 27-7 (D)
   Vikings, 34-0 (M)
1981—Vikings, 26-24 (M)
   Lions, 45-7 (D)
1982—Vikings, 34-31 (D)
1983—Vikings, 20-17 (M)
   Lions, 13-2 (D)
1984—Vikings, 29-28 (D)
   Lions, 16-14 (M)
1985—Vikings, 16-13 (M)
   Lions, 41-21 (D)
1986—Lions, 13-10 (M)
   Vikings, 24-10 (D)
1987—Vikings, 34-19 (M)
   Vikings, 17-14 (D)
1988—Vikings, 44-17 (M)
   Vikings, 23-0 (D)
1989—Vikings, 24-17 (M)
   Vikings, 20-7 (D)
1990—Lions, 34-27 (M)
   Vikings, 17-7 (D)
1991—Lions, 24-20 (D)
   Lions, 34-14 (M)
1992—Lions, 31-17 (D)
   Vikings, 31-14 (M)
1993—Lions, 30-27 (M)
   Vikings, 13-0 (D)
1994—Vikings, 10-3 (M)
   Lions, 41-19 (D)
1995—Vikings, 20-10 (M)
   Lions, 44-38 (D)
1996—Vikings, 17-13 (M)
   Vikings, 24-22 (D)
1997—Lions, 38-15 (D)
   Lions, 14-13 (M)
1998—Vikings, 29-6 (M)
   Vikings, 34-13 (D)
1999—Lions, 25-23 (D)
   Vikings, 24-17 (M)
2000—Vikings, 31-24 (D)
   Vikings, 24-17 (M)
2001—Vikings, 31-26 (M)
   Lions, 27-24 (D)

2002—Vikings, 31-24 (M)
　　Vikings, 38-36 (D)
2003—Vikings, 23-13 (D)
　　Vikings, 24-14 (M)
2004—Vikings, 22-19 (M)
　　Vikings, 28-27 (D)
2005—Vikings, 27-14 (M)
　　Vikings, 21-16 (D)
2006—Vikings, 26-17 (M)
　　Vikings, 30-20 (D)
2007—Lions, 20-17 (D) OT
　　Vikings, 42-10 (M)
2008—Vikings, 12-10 (M)
　　Vikings, 20-16 (D)
2009—Vikings, 27-13 (D)
　　Vikings, 27-10 (M)
2010—Vikings, 24-10 (M)
　　Lions, 20-13 (D)
2011—Lions, 26-23 (M) OT
　　Lions, 34-28 (D)
(RS Pts.—Vikings 2,203, Lions 1,872)
DETROIT vs. NEW ENGLAND
RS: Patriots lead series, 6-4
1971—Lions, 34-7 (NE)
1976—Lions, 30-10 (D)
1979—Patriots, 24-17 (NE)
1985—Patriots, 23-6 (NE)
1993—Lions, 19-16 (NE) OT
1994—Patriots, 23-17 (D)
2000—Lions, 34-9 (D)
2002—Patriots, 20-12 (D)
2006—Patriots, 28-21 (NE)
2010—Patriots, 45-24 (D)
(RS Pts.—Lions 214, Patriots 205)
DETROIT vs. NEW ORLEANS
RS: Saints lead series, 11-9-1
PS: Saints lead series, 1-0
1968—Tie, 20-20 (D)
1970—Saints, 19-17 (NO)
1972—Lions, 27-14 (D)
1973—Saints, 20-13 (NO)
1974—Lions, 19-14 (D)
1976—Saints, 17-16 (NO)
1977—Lions, 23-19 (D)
1979—Saints, 17-7 (NO)
1980—Lions, 24-13 (D)
1988—Saints, 22-14 (D)
1989—Lions, 21-14 (D)
1990—Lions, 27-10 (NO)
1992—Saints, 13-7 (D)
1993—Saints, 14-3 (NO)
1997—Saints, 35-17 (NO)
2000—Lions, 14-10 (NO)
2002—Lions, 26-21 (D)
2005—Lions, 13-12 (San Antonio)
2008—Saints, 42-7 (D)
2009—Saints, 45-27 (NO)
2011—Lions, 31-17 (NO)
　　*Saints, 45-28 (NO)
(RS Pts.—Saints 422, Lions 359)
(PS Pts.—Saints 45, Lions 28)
*NFC First-Round Playoff
*DETROIT vs. N.Y. GIANTS
RS: Lions lead series, 20-19-1
PS: Lions lead series, 1-0
1930—Giants, 19-6 (P)
1931—Spartans, 14-6 (P)
　　Giants, 14-0 (NY)
1932—Spartans, 7-0 (P)
　　Spartans, 6-0 (D)
1933—Spartans, 17-7 (P)
　　Giants, 13-10 (NY)

1934—Lions, 9-0 (D)
1935—**Lions, 26-7 (D)
1936—Giants, 14-7 (NY)
　　Lions, 38-0 (D)
1937—Lions, 17-0 (NY)
1939—Lions, 18-14 (D)
1941—Giants, 20-13 (NY)
1943—Tie, 0-0 (D)
1945—Giants, 35-14 (NY)
1947—Lions, 35-7 (D)
1949—Lions, 45-21 (NY)
1953—Lions, 27-16 (NY)
1955—Giants, 24-19 (D)
1958—Giants, 19-17 (D)
1962—Giants, 17-14 (NY)
1964—Lions, 26-3 (D)
1967—Lions, 30-7 (NY)
1969—Lions, 24-0 (D)
1972—Lions, 30-16 (D)
1974—Lions, 20-19 (D)
1976—Giants, 24-10 (NY)
1982—Giants, 13-6 (D)
1983—Lions, 15-9 (D)
1988—Giants, 30-10 (NY)
　　Giants, 13-10 (D) OT
1989—Giants, 24-14 (NY)
1990—Giants, 20-0 (NY)
1994—Lions, 28-25 (NY) OT
1996—Giants, 35-7 (D)
1997—Giants, 26-20 (D) OT
2000—Lions, 31-21 (NY)
2004—Lions, 28-13 (NY)
2007—Giants, 16-10 (D)
2010—Giants, 28-20 (NY)
(RS Pts.—Lions 672, Giants 588)
(PS Pts.—Lions 26, Giants 7)
*Franchise in Portsmouth prior to 1934
and known as the Spartans
**NFL Championship
DETROIT vs. N.Y. JETS
RS: Series tied, 6-6
1972—Lions, 37-20 (D)
1979—Jets, 31-10 (NY)
1982—Jets, 28-13 (D)
1985—Lions, 31-20 (D)
1988—Jets, 17-10 (D)
1991—Lions, 34-20 (D)
1994—Lions, 18-7 (NY)
1997—Lions, 13-10 (D)
2000—Lions, 10-7 (NY)
2002—Jets, 31-14 (D)
2006—Jets, 31-24 (NY)
2010—Jets, 23-20 (D) OT
(RS Pts.—Jets 245, Lions 234)
DETROIT vs. *OAKLAND
RS: Raiders lead series, 6-5
1970—Lions, 28-14 (D)
1974—Raiders, 35-13 (O)
1978—Raiders, 29-17 (O)
1981—Lions, 16-0 (D)
1984—Raiders, 24-3 (O)
1987—Raiders, 27-7 (LA)
1990—Raiders, 38-31 (O)
1996—Raiders, 37-21 (O)
2003—Lions, 23-13 (D)
2007—Lions, 36-21 (O)
2011—Lions, 28-27 (O)
(RS Pts.—Raiders 265, Lions 223)
*Franchise in Los Angeles from 1982-1994
*DETROIT vs. PHILADELPHIA
RS: Eagles lead series, 14-12-2
PS: Eagles lead series, 1-0

1933—Spartans, 25-0 (P)
1934—Lions, 10-0 (P)
1935—Lions, 35-0 (D)
1936—Lions, 23-0 (P)
1938—Eagles, 21-7 (D)
1940—Lions, 21-0 (P)
1941—Lions, 21-17 (D)
1945—Lions, 38-24 (D)
1948—Eagles, 45-21 (P)
1949—Eagles, 22-14 (D)
1951—Lions, 28-10 (P)
1954—Tie, 13-13 (D)
1957—Lions, 27-16 (P)
1960—Eagles, 28-10 (P)
1961—Eagles, 27-24 (D)
1965—Lions, 35-28 (P)
1968—Eagles, 12-0 (D)
1971—Eagles, 23-20 (D)
1974—Eagles, 28-17 (P)
1977—Lions, 17-13 (D)
1979—Eagles, 44-7 (P)
1984—Tie, 23-23 (D) OT
1986—Lions, 13-11 (P)
1995—**Eagles, 58-37 (P)
1996—Eagles, 24-17 (P)
1998—Eagles, 10-9 (P)
2004—Eagles, 30-13 (D)
2007—Eagles, 56-21 (P)
2010—Eagles, 35-32 (D)
(RS Pts.—Eagles 560, Lions 531)
(PS Pts.—Eagles 58, Lions 37)
*Franchise in Portsmouth prior to 1934
and known as the Spartans
**NFC First-Round Playoff
DETROIT vs. *PITTSBURGH
RS: Steelers lead series, 15-14-1
1934—Lions, 40-7 (D)
1936—Lions, 28-3 (D)
1937—Lions, 7-3 (D)
1938—Lions, 16-7 (D)
1940—Steelers, 10-7 (D)
1942—Steelers, 35-7 (D)
1946—Lions, 17-7 (D)
1947—Steelers, 17-10 (P)
1948—Lions, 17-14 (D)
1949—Steelers, 14-7 (P)
1950—Lions, 10-7 (D)
1952—Lions, 31-6 (P)
1953—Lions, 38-21 (D)
1955—Lions, 31-28 (P)
1956—Lions, 45-7 (D)
1959—Tie, 10-10 (P)
1962—Lions, 45-7 (D)
1966—Steelers, 17-3 (P)
1967—Steelers, 24-14 (D)
1969—Steelers, 16-13 (P)
1973—Steelers, 24-10 (P)
1983—Lions, 45-3 (D)
1986—Steelers, 27-17 (D)
1989—Steelers, 23-3 (D)
1992—Steelers, 17-14 (P)
1995—Steelers, 23-20 (P)
1998—Lions, 19-16 (D) OT
2001—Steelers, 47-14 (P)
2005—Steelers, 35-21 (P)
2009—Steelers, 28-20 (D)
(RS Pts.—Lions 579, Steelers 503)
*Steelers known as Pirates prior to 1940
DETROIT vs. *ST. LOUIS
RS: Rams lead series, 42-38-1
PS: Lions lead series, 1-0
1937—Lions, 28-0 (C)

Lions, 27-7 (D)
1938—Rams, 21-17 (C)
Lions, 6-0 (D)
1939—Lions, 15-7 (D)
Rams, 14-3 (C)
1940—Lions, 6-0 (D)
Rams, 24-0 (C)
1941—Lions, 17-7 (D)
Lions, 14-0 (C)
1942—Rams, 14-0 (D)
Rams, 27-7 (C)
1944—Rams, 20-17 (D)
Lions, 26-14 (C)
1945—Rams, 28-21 (D)
1946—Rams, 35-14 (LA)
Rams, 41-20 (D)
1947—Rams, 27-13 (D)
Rams, 28-17 (LA)
1948—Rams, 44-7 (LA)
Rams, 34-27 (D)
1949—Rams, 27-24 (LA)
Rams, 21-10 (D)
1950—Rams, 30-28 (D)
Rams, 65-24 (LA)
1951—Rams, 27-21 (D)
Lions, 24-22 (LA)
1952—Lions, 17-14 (LA)
Lions, 24-16 (D)
**Lions, 31-21 (D)
1953—Rams, 31-19 (D)
Rams, 37-24 (LA)
1954—Lions, 21-3 (D)
Lions, 27-24 (LA)
1955—Rams, 17-10 (D)
Rams, 24-13 (LA)
1956—Lions, 24-21 (D)
Lions, 16-7 (LA)
1957—Lions, 10-7 (D)
Rams, 35-17 (LA)
1958—Rams, 42-28 (D)
Lions, 41-24 (LA)
1959—Lions, 17-7 (LA)
Lions, 23-17 (D)
1960—Rams, 48-35 (LA)
Lions, 12-10 (D)
1961—Lions, 14-13 (D)
Lions, 28-10 (LA)
1962—Lions, 13-10 (D)
Lions, 12-3 (LA)
1963—Lions, 23-2 (LA)
Rams, 28-21 (D)
1964—Tie, 17-17 (LA)
Lions, 37-17 (D)
1965—Lions, 20-0 (D)
Lions, 31-7 (LA)
1966—Rams, 14-7 (D)
Rams, 23-3 (LA)
1967—Rams, 31-7 (D)
Rams, 10-7 (LA)
1968—Rams, 10-7 (LA)
1969—Lions, 28-0 (D)
1970—Lions, 28-23 (LA)
1971—Rams, 21-13 (D)
1972—Lions, 34-17 (LA)
1974—Rams, 16-13 (LA)
1975—Rams, 20-0 (D)
1976—Rams, 20-17 (D)
1980—Lions, 41-20 (LA)
1981—Rams, 20-13 (LA)
1982—Lions, 19-14 (LA)
1983—Rams, 21-10 (LA)
1986—Rams, 14-10 (LA)
1987—Rams, 37-16 (D)

1988—Rams, 17-10 (LA)
1991—Lions, 21-10 (D)
1993—Lions, 16-13 (LA)
1999—Lions, 31-27 (D)
2001—Rams, 35-0 (D)
2003—Lions, 30-20 (D)
2006—Rams, 41-34 (StL)
2009—Rams, 17-10 (D)
2010—Lions, 44-6 (D)
(RS Pts.—Rams 1,582, Lions 1,489)
(PS Pts.—Lions 31, Rams 21)
*Franchise in Los Angeles prior to 1995
and in Cleveland prior to 1946
**Conference Playoff
DETROIT vs. SAN DIEGO
RS: Chargers lead series, 6-4
1972—Lions, 34-20 (D)
1977—Lions, 20-0 (D)
1978—Lions, 31-14 (D)
1981—Chargers, 28-23 (SD)
1984—Chargers, 27-24 (SD)
1996—Chargers, 27-21 (SD)
1999—Chargers, 20-10 (D)
2003—Chargers, 14-7 (D)
2007—Chargers, 51-14 (SD)
2011—Lions, 38-10 (D)
(RS Pts.—Lions 222, Chargers 211)
DETROIT vs. SAN FRANCISCO
RS: 49ers lead series, 35-26-1
PS: Series tied, 1-1
1950—Lions, 24-7 (D)
49ers, 28-27 (SF)
1951—49ers, 20-10 (D)
49ers, 21-17 (SF)
1952—49ers, 17-3 (SF)
49ers, 28-0 (D)
1953—Lions, 24-21 (D)
Lions, 14-10 (SF)
1954—49ers, 37-31 (SF)
Lions, 48-7 (D)
1955—49ers, 27-24 (D)
49ers, 38-21 (SF)
1956—Lions, 20-17 (D)
Lions, 17-13 (SF)
1957—49ers, 35-31 (SF)
Lions, 31-10 (D)
*Lions, 31-27 (SF)
1958—49ers, 24-21 (SF)
Lions, 35-21 (D)
1959—49ers, 34-13 (D)
49ers, 33-7 (SF)
1960—49ers, 14-10 (D)
Lions, 24-0 (SF)
1961—49ers, 49-0 (D)
Tie, 20-20 (SF)
1962—Lions, 45-24 (D)
Lions, 38-24 (SF)
1963—Lions, 26-3 (D)
Lions, 45-7 (SF)
1964—Lions, 26-17 (SF)
Lions, 24-7 (D)
1965—49ers, 27-21 (D)
49ers, 17-14 (SF)
1966—49ers, 27-24 (SF)
49ers, 41-14 (D)
1967—Lions, 45-3 (SF)
1968—49ers, 14-7 (D)
1969—Lions, 26-14 (SF)
1970—Lions, 28-7 (D)
1971—49ers, 31-27 (SF)
1973—Lions, 30-20 (D)
1974—Lions, 17-13 (D)

1975—Lions, 28-17 (SF)
1977—49ers, 28-7 (SF)
1978—Lions, 33-14 (D)
1980—Lions, 17-13 (D)
1981—Lions, 24-17 (D)
1983—**49ers, 24-23 (SF)
1984—49ers, 30-27 (D)
1985—Lions, 23-21 (D)
1988—49ers, 20-13 (SF)
1991—49ers, 35-3 (D)
1992—49ers, 24-6 (SF)
1993—49ers, 55-17 (D)
1994—49ers, 27-21 (D)
1995—Lions, 27-24 (D)
1996—49ers, 24-14 (SF)
1998—49ers, 35-13 (SF)
2001—49ers, 21-13 (SF)
2003—49ers, 24-17 (SF)
2006—49ers, 19-13 (D)
2008—49ers, 31-13 (SF)
2009—49ers, 20-6 (SF)
2011—49ers, 25-19 (D)
(RS Pts.—49ers 1,351, Lions 1,283)
(PS Pts.—Lions 54, 49ers 51)
*Conference Playoff
**NFC Divisional Playoff
DETROIT vs. SEATTLE
RS: Seahawks lead series, 7-4
1976—Lions, 41-14 (S)
1978—Seahawks, 28-16 (S)
1984—Seahawks, 38-17 (S)
1987—Seahawks, 37-14 (D)
1990—Seahawks, 30-10 (S)
1993—Lions, 30-10 (D)
1996—Lions, 17-16 (D)
1999—Lions, 28-20 (S)
2003—Seahawks, 35-14 (S)
2006—Seahawks, 9-6 (D)
2009—Seahawks, 32-20 (S)
(RS Pts.—Seahawks 269, Lions 213)
DETROIT vs. TAMPA BAY
RS: Lions lead series, 29-25
PS: Buccaneers lead series, 1-0
1977—Lions, 16-7 (D)
1978—Lions, 15-7 (TB)
Lions, 34-23 (D)
1979—Buccaneers, 31-16 (TB)
Buccaneers, 16-14 (D)
1980—Lions, 24-10 (TB)
Lions, 27-14 (D)
1981—Buccaneers, 28-10 (TB)
Buccaneers, 20-17 (D)
1982—Buccaneers, 23-21 (TB)
1983—Lions, 11-0 (TB)
Lions, 23-20 (D)
1984—Buccaneers, 21-17 (TB)
Lions, 13-7 (D) OT
1985—Lions, 30-9 (D)
Buccaneers, 19-16 (TB) OT
1986—Buccaneers, 24-20 (D)
Lions, 38-17 (TB)
1987—Buccaneers, 31-27 (D)
Lions, 20-10 (TB)
1988—Buccaneers, 23-20 (D)
Buccaneers, 21-10 (TB)
1989—Lions, 17-16 (TB)
Lions, 33-7 (D)
1990—Buccaneers, 38-21 (D)
Buccaneers, 23-20 (TB)
1991—Lions, 31-3 (D)
Buccaneers, 30-21 (TB)
1992—Buccaneers, 27-23 (D)

Lions, 38-7 (TB)
1993—Buccaneers, 27-10 (TB)
Lions, 23-0 (D)
1994—Buccaneers, 24-14 (TB)
Lions, 14-9 (D)
1995—Lions, 27-24 (D)
Lions, 37-10 (TB)
1996—Lions, 21-6 (D)
Lions, 27-0 (TB)
1997—Buccaneers, 24-17 (D)
Lions, 27-9 (TB)
*Buccaneers, 20-10 (TB)
1998—Lions, 27-6 (D)
Lions, 28-25 (TB)
1999—Lions, 20-3 (D)
Buccaneers, 23-16 (TB)
2000—Buccaneers, 31-10 (D)
Lions, 28-14 (TB)
2001—Buccaneers, 20-17 (D)
Buccaneers, 15-12 (TB)
2002—Buccaneers, 23-20 (D)
2005—Buccaneers, 17-13 (TB)
2007—Lions, 23-16 (D)
2008—Buccaneers, 38-20 (D)
2010—Lions, 23-20 (TB) OT
2011—Lions, 27-20 (TB)
(RS Pts—Lions 1,144, Buccaneers 936)
(PS Pts.—Buccaneers 20, Lions 10)
*NFC First-Round Playoff
DETROIT vs. *TENNESSEE
RS: Titans lead series, 7-3
1971—Lions, 31-7 (H)
1975—Oilers, 24-8 (H)
1983—Oilers, 27-17 (H)
1986—Lions, 24-13 (D)
1989—Oilers, 35-31 (H)
1992—Oilers, 24-21 (D)
1995—Lions, 24-17 (H)
2001—Titans, 27-24 (D)
2004—Titans, 24-19 (T)
2008—Titans, 47-10 (D)
(RS Pts.—Titans 245, Lions 209)
*Franchise in Houston prior to 1997;
known as Oilers prior to 1999
*DETROIT vs. **WASHINGTON
RS: Redskins lead series, 27-12
PS: Redskins lead series, 3-0
1932—Spartans, 10-0 (P)
1933—Spartans, 13-0 (B)
1934—Lions, 24-0 (D)
1935—Lions, 17-7 (B)
Lions, 14-0 (D)
1938—Redskins, 7-5 (D)
1939—Redskins, 31-7 (W)
1940—Redskins, 20-14 (D)
1942—Redskins, 15-3 (D)
1943—Redskins, 42-20 (W)
1946—Redskins, 17-16 (W)
1947—Lions, 38-21 (D)
1948—Redskins, 46-21 (W)
1951—Lions, 35-17 (D)
1956—Redskins, 18-17 (W)
1965—Lions, 14-10 (D)
1968—Redskins, 14-3 (W)
1970—Redskins, 31-10 (W)
1973—Redskins, 20-0 (D)
1976—Redskins, 20-7 (W)
1978—Redskins, 21-19 (D)
1979—Redskins, 27-24 (D)
1981—Redskins, 33-31 (W)
1982—***Redskins, 31-7 (W)
1983—Redskins, 38-17 (W)

1984—Redskins, 28-14 (W)
1985—Redskins, 24-3 (W)
1987—Redskins, 20-13 (W)
1990—Redskins, 41-38 (D) OT
1991—Redskins, 45-0 (W)
****Redskins, 41-10 (W)
1992—Redskins, 13-10 (W)
1995—Redskins, 36-30 (W) OT
1997—Redskins, 30-7 (W)
1999—Lions, 33-17 (D)
***Redskins, 27-13 (W)
2000—Lions, 15-10 (D)
2004—Redskins, 17-10 (D)
2007—Redskins, 34-3 (W)
2008—Redskins, 25-17 (D)
2009—Lions, 19-14 (D)
2010—Lions, 37-25 (D)
(RS Pts.—Redskins 834, Lions 628)
(PS Pts.—Redskins 99, Lions 30)
*Franchise in Portsmouth prior to 1934
and known as the Spartans.
**Franchise in Boston prior to 1937
***NFC First-Round Playoff
****NFC Championship

GREEN BAY vs. ARIZONA
RS: Packers lead series, 43-22-4
PS: Series tied, 1-1;
See Arizona vs. Green Bay
GREEN BAY vs. ATLANTA
RS: Packers lead series, 13-12
PS: Packers lead series, 2-1;
See Atlanta vs. Green Bay
GREEN BAY vs. BALTIMORE
RS: Packers lead series, 3-1;
See Baltimore vs. Green Bay
GREEN BAY vs. BUFFALO
RS: Bills lead series, 7-4;
See Buffalo vs. Green Bay
GREEN BAY vs. CAROLINA
RS: Packers lead series, 7-4
PS: Packers lead series, 1-0;
See Carolina vs. Green Bay
GREEN BAY vs. CHICAGO
RS: Bears lead series, 91-85-6
PS: Series tied, 1-1;
See Chicago vs. Green Bay
GREEN BAY vs. CINCINNATI
RS: Bengals lead series, 6-5;
See Cincinnati vs. Green Bay
GREEN BAY vs. CLEVELAND
RS: Packers lead series, 10-7
PS: Packers lead series, 1-0;
See Cleveland vs. Green Bay
GREEN BAY vs. DALLAS
RS: Series tied, 12-12
PS: Cowboys lead series, 4-2;
See Dallas vs. Green Bay
GREEN BAY vs. DENVER
RS: Packers lead series, 6-5-1
PS: Broncos lead series, 1-0;
See Denver vs. Green Bay
GREEN BAY vs. DETROIT
RS: Packers lead series, 91-65-7
PS: Packers lead series, 2-0;
See Detroit vs. Green Bay
GREEN BAY vs. HOUSTON
RS: Series tied, 1-1
2004—Packers, 16-13 (H)
2008—Texans, 24-21 (GB)
(RS Pts.—Packers 37, Texans 37)

GREEN BAY vs. *INDIANAPOLIS
RS: Series tied, 20-20-1
PS: Packers lead series, 1-0
1953—Packers, 37-14 (GB)
Packers, 35-24 (B)
1954—Packers, 7-6 (B)
Packers, 24-13 (Mil)
1955—Colts, 24-20 (Mil)
Colts, 14-10 (B)
1956—Packers, 38-33 (Mil)
Colts, 28-21 (B)
1957—Colts, 45-17 (Mil)
Packers, 24-21 (B)
1958—Colts, 24-17 (Mil)
Colts, 56-0 (B)
1959—Colts, 38-21 (B)
Colts, 28-24 (Mil)
1960—Packers, 35-21 (GB)
Colts, 38-24 (B)
1961—Packers, 45-7 (GB)
Colts, 45-21 (B)
1962—Packers, 17-6 (B)
Packers, 17-13 (GB)
1963—Packers, 31-20 (GB)
Packers, 34-20 (B)
1964—Colts, 21-20 (GB)
Colts, 24-21 (B)
1965—Packers, 20-17 (Mil)
Packers, 42-27 (B)
**Packers, 13-10 (GB) OT
1966—Packers, 24-3 (Mil)
Packers, 14-10 (B)
1967—Colts, 13-10 (B)
1968—Colts, 16-3 (GB)
1969—Colts, 14-6 (B)
1970—Colts, 13-10 (Mil)
1974—Packers, 20-13 (B)
1982—Tie, 20-20 (B) OT
1985—Colts, 37-10 (I)
1988—Colts, 20-13 (GB)
1991—Packers, 14-10 (Mil)
1997—Colts, 41-38 (I)
2000—Packers, 26-24 (GB)
2004—Colts, 45-31 (I)
2008—Packers, 34-14 (GB)
(RS Pts.—Colts 920, Packers 895)
(PS Pts.—Packers 13, Colts 10)
*Franchise in Baltimore prior to 1984
**Conference Playoff
GREEN BAY vs. JACKSONVILLE
RS: Series tied, 2-2
1995—Packers, 24-14 (J)
2001—Packers, 28-21 (J)
2004—Jaguars, 28-25 (GB)
2008—Jaguars, 20-16 (J)
(RS Pts.—Packers 93, Jaguars 83)
GREEN BAY vs. KANSAS CITY
RS: Chiefs lead series, 7-2-1
PS: Packers lead series, 1-0
1966—*Packers, 35-10 (Los Angeles)
1973—Tie, 10-10 (Mil)
1977—Chiefs, 20-10 (KC)
1987—Packers, 23-3 (KC)
1989—Chiefs, 21-3 (GB)
1990—Chiefs, 17-3 (GB)
1993—Chiefs, 23-16 (KC)
1996—Chiefs, 27-20 (KC)
2003—Chiefs, 40-34 (GB) OT
2007—Packers, 33-22 (KC)
2011—Chiefs, 19-14 (KC)
(RS Pts.—Chiefs 202, Packers 166)
(PS Pts.—Packers 35, Chiefs 10)

Super Bowl I
GREEN BAY vs. MIAMI
RS: Dolphins lead series, 10-3
1971—Dolphins, 27-6 (Mia)
1975—Dolphins, 31-7 (GB)
1979—Dolphins, 27-7 (Mia)
1985—Dolphins, 34-24 (GB)
1988—Dolphins, 24-17 (Mia)
1989—Dolphins, 23-20 (Mia)
1991—Dolphins, 16-13 (Mia)
1994—Dolphins, 24-14 (Mil)
1997—Packers, 23-18 (GB)
2000—Dolphins, 28-20 (Mia)
2002—Packers, 24-10 (GB)
2006—Packers, 34-24 (M)
2010—Dolphins, 23-20 (GB) OT
(RS Pts.—Dolphins 309, Packers 229)
GREEN BAY vs. MINNESOTA
RS: Packers lead series, 53-47-1
PS: Vikings lead series, 1-0
1961—Packers, 33-7 (Minn)
　　　Packers, 28-10 (Mil)
1962—Packers, 34-7 (GB)
　　　Packers, 48-21 (Minn)
1963—Packers, 37-28 (Minn)
　　　Packers, 28-7 (GB)
1964—Vikings, 24-23 (GB)
　　　Packers, 42-13 (Minn)
1965—Packers, 38-13 (Minn)
　　　Packers, 24-19 (GB)
1966—Vikings, 20-17 (GB)
　　　Packers, 28-16 (Minn)
1967—Vikings, 10-7 (Mil)
　　　Packers, 30-27 (Minn)
1968—Vikings, 26-13 (Mil)
　　　Vikings, 14-10 (Minn)
1969—Vikings, 19-7 (Minn)
　　　Vikings, 9-7 (Mil)
1970—Packers, 13-10 (Mil)
　　　Vikings, 10-3 (Minn)
1971—Vikings, 24-13 (GB)
　　　Vikings, 3-0 (Minn)
1972—Vikings, 27-13 (GB)
　　　Packers, 23-7 (Minn)
1973—Vikings, 11-3 (Minn)
　　　Vikings, 31-7 (GB)
1974—Vikings, 32-17 (GB)
　　　Packers, 19-7 (Minn)
1975—Vikings, 28-17 (GB)
　　　Vikings, 24-3 (Minn)
1976—Vikings, 17-10 (Mil)
　　　Vikings, 20-9 (Minn)
1977—Vikings, 19-7 (Minn)
　　　Vikings, 13-6 (GB)
1978—Vikings, 21-7 (Minn)
　　　Tie, 10-10 (GB) OT
1979—Vikings, 27-21 (Minn) OT
　　　Packers, 19-7 (Mil)
1980—Packers, 16-3 (GB)
　　　Packers, 25-13 (Minn)
1981—Vikings, 30-13 (Mil)
　　　Packers, 35-23 (Minn)
1982—Packers, 26-7 (Mil)
1983—Vikings, 20-17 (GB) OT
　　　Packers, 29-21 (Minn)
1984—Packers, 45-17 (Mil)
　　　Packers, 38-14 (Minn)
1985—Packers, 20-17 (Mil)
　　　Packers, 27-17 (Minn)
1986—Vikings, 42-7 (Minn)
　　　Vikings, 32-6 (GB)
1987—Packers, 23-16 (Minn)

　　　Packers, 16-10 (Mil)
1988—Packers, 34-14 (Minn)
　　　Packers, 18-6 (GB)
1989—Vikings, 26-14 (Minn)
　　　Packers, 20-19 (Mil)
1990—Packers, 24-10 (Mil)
　　　Vikings, 23-7 (Minn)
1991—Vikings, 35-21 (GB)
　　　Packers, 27-7 (Minn)
1992—Vikings, 23-20 (GB) OT
　　　Vikings, 27-7 (Minn)
1993—Vikings, 15-13 (Minn)
　　　Vikings, 21-17 (Mil)
1994—Packers, 16-10 (GB)
　　　Vikings, 13-10 (Minn) OT
1995—Packers, 38-21 (GB)
　　　Vikings, 27-24 (Minn)
1996—Vikings, 30-21 (GB)
　　　Packers, 38-10 (GB)
1997—Packers, 38-32 (GB)
　　　Packers, 27-11 (Minn)
1998—Vikings, 37-24 (GB)
　　　Vikings, 28-14 (Minn)
1999—Packers, 23-20 (GB)
　　　Vikings, 24-20 (Minn)
2000—Packers, 26-20 (GB) OT
　　　Packers, 33-28 (Minn)
2001—Vikings, 35-13 (Minn)
　　　Packers, 24-13 (GB)
2002—Vikings, 31-21 (GB)
　　　Packers, 26-22 (GB)
2003—Vikings, 30-25 (GB)
　　　Packers, 30-27 (Minn)
2004—Packers, 34-31 (GB)
　　　Packers, 34-31 (Minn)
　　　*Vikings, 31-17 (GB)
2005—Vikings, 23-20 (Minn)
　　　Vikings, 20-17 (GB)
2006—Packers, 23-17 (Minn)
　　　Packers, 9-7 (GB)
2007—Packers, 23-16 (Minn)
　　　Packers, 34-0 (GB)
2008—Packers, 24-19 (GB)
　　　Vikings, 28-27 (Minn)
2009—Vikings, 30-23 (GB)
　　　Vikings, 38-26 (GB)
2010—Packers, 28-24 (GB)
　　　Packers, 31-3 (Minn)
2011—Packers, 33-27 (Minn)
　　　Packers, 45-7 (GB)
(RS Pts.—Packers 2,161, Vikings 1,936)
(PS Pts.—Vikings 31, Packers 17)
NFC First-Round Playoff
GREEN BAY vs. NEW ENGLAND
RS: Patriots lead series, 5-4
PS: Packers lead series, 1-0
1973—Patriots, 33-24 (NE)
1979—Packers, 27-14 (GB)
1985—Patriots, 26-20 (NE)
1988—Packers, 45-3 (Mil)
1994—Patriots, 17-16 (NE)
1996—*Packers, 35-21 (New Orleans)
1997—Packers, 28-10 (NE)
2002—Packers, 28-10 (NE)
2006—Patriots, 35-0 (GB)
2010—Patriots, 31-27 (NE)
(RS Pts.—Packers 215, Patriots 179)
(PS Pts.—Packers 35, Patriots 21)
Super Bowl XXXI
GREEN BAY vs. NEW ORLEANS
RS: Packers lead series, 15-7
1968—Packers, 29-7 (Mil)

1971—Saints, 29-21 (Mil)
1972—Packers, 30-20 (NO)
1973—Packers, 30-10 (Mil)
1975—Saints, 20-19 (NO)
1976—Packers, 32-27 (Mil)
1977—Packers, 24-20 (NO)
1978—Packers, 28-17 (Mil)
1979—Packers, 28-19 (Mil)
1981—Packers, 35-7 (NO)
1984—Packers, 23-13 (NO)
1985—Packers, 38-14 (Mil)
1986—Saints, 24-10 (NO)
1987—Saints, 33-24 (NO)
1989—Packers, 35-34 (GB)
1993—Saints, 19-17 (NO)
1995—Packers, 34-23 (NO)
2002—Saints, 35-20 (NO)
2005—Packers, 52-3 (NO)
2006—Saints, 34-27 (GB)
2008—Saints, 51-29 (NO)
2011—Packers, 42-34 (GB)
(RS Pts.—Packers 629, Saints 491)
GREEN BAY vs. N.Y. GIANTS
RS: Packers lead series, 27-21-2
PS: Packers lead series, 4-3
1928—Giants, 6-0 (GB)
　　　Packers, 7-0 (NY)
1929—Packers, 20-6 (NY)
1930—Packers, 14-7 (GB)
　　　Giants, 13-6 (NY)
1931—Packers, 27-7 (GB)
　　　Packers, 14-10 (NY)
1932—Packers, 13-0 (GB)
　　　Giants, 6-0 (NY)
1933—Giants, 10-7 (Mil)
　　　Giants, 17-6 (NY)
1934—Packers, 20-6 (Mil)
　　　Giants, 17-3 (NY)
1935—Packers, 16-7 (GB)
1936—Packers, 26-14 (NY)
1937—Giants, 10-0 (NY)
1938—Giants, 15-3 (NY)
　　　*Giants, 23-17 (NY)
1939—*Packers, 27-0 (Mil)
1940—Giants, 7-3 (NY)
1942—Tie, 21-21 (NY)
1943—Packers, 35-21 (NY)
1944—Giants, 24-0 (NY)
　　　*Packers, 14-7 (NY)
1945—Packers, 23-14 (NY)
1947—Tie, 24-24 (NY)
1948—Giants, 49-3 (Mil)
1949—Giants, 30-10 (GB)
1952—Packers, 17-3 (NY)
1957—Giants, 31-17 (GB)
1959—Giants, 20-3 (NY)
1961—Packers, 20-17 (Mil)
　　　*Packers, 37-0 (GB)
1962—*Packers, 16-7 (NY)
1967—Packers, 48-21 (NY)
1969—Packers, 20-10 (Mil)
1971—Giants, 42-40 (GB)
1973—Packers, 16-14 (New Haven)
1975—Packers, 40-14 (NY)
1980—Giants, 27-21 (NY)
1981—Packers, 27-14 (NY)
　　　Packers, 26-24 (Mil)
1982—Packers, 27-19 (NY)
1983—Giants, 27-3 (NY)
1985—Packers, 23-20 (GB)
1986—Giants, 55-24 (NY)
1987—Giants, 20-10 (NY)

1992—Giants, 27-7 (NY)
1995—Packers, 14-6 (GB)
1998—Packers, 37-3 (NY)
2001—Packers, 34-25 (NY)
2004—Giants, 14-7 (GB)
2007—Packers, 35-13 (NY)
   **Giants, 23-20 (GB) OT
2010—Packers, 45-17 (GB)
2011—Packers, 38-35 (NY)
   ***Giants, 37-20 (GB)
(RS Pts.—Packers 900, Giants 859)
(PS Pts.—Packers 151, Giants 97)
*NFL Championship
**NFC Championship Game
***NFC Divisional Playoff
GREEN BAY vs. N.Y. JETS
RS: Jets lead series, 8-3
1973—Packers, 23-7 (Mil)
1979—Jets, 27-22 (GB)
1981—Jets, 28-3 (NY)
1982—Jets, 15-13 (NY)
1985—Jets, 24-3 (Mil)
1991—Jets, 19-16 (NY) OT
1994—Packers, 17-10 (GB)
2000—Jets, 20-16 (GB)
2002—Jets, 42-17 (NY)
2006—Jets, 38-10 (GB)
2010—Packers, 9-0 (NY)
(RS Pts.—Jets 230, Packers 149)
GREEN BAY vs. *OAKLAND
RS: Packers lead series, 6-5
PS: Packers lead series, 1-0
1967—**Packers, 33-14 (Miami)
1972—Raiders, 20-14 (GB)
1976—Raiders, 18-14 (O)
1978—Raiders, 28-3 (GB)
1984—Raiders, 28-7 (LA)
1987—Raiders, 20-0 (GB)
1990—Packers, 29-16 (LA)
1993—Packers, 28-0 (GB)
1999—Packers, 28-24 (GB)
2003—Packers, 41-7 (O)
2007—Packers, 38-7 (GB)
2011—Packers, 46-16 (GB)
(RS Pts.—Packers 248, Raiders 184)
(PS Pts.—Packers 33, Raiders 14)
*Franchise in Los Angeles from 1982-1994
**Super Bowl II
GREEN BAY vs. PHILADELPHIA
RS: Packers lead series, 24-13
PS: Eagles lead series, 2-1
1933—Packers, 35-9 (GB)
   Packers, 10-0 (P)
1934—Packers, 19-6 (GB)
1935—Packers, 13-6 (P)
1937—Packers, 37-7 (Mil)
1939—Packers, 23-16 (P)
1940—Packers, 27-20 (GB)
1942—Packers, 7-0 (P)
1946—Packers, 19-7 (P)
1947—Eagles, 28-14 (P)
1951—Packers, 37-24 (GB)
1952—Packers, 12-10 (Mil)
1954—Packers, 37-14 (P)
1958—Packers, 38-35 (GB)
1960—*Eagles, 17-13 (P)
1962—Packers, 49-0 (P)
1968—Packers, 30-13 (GB)
1970—Packers, 30-17 (Mil)
1974—Eagles, 36-14 (P)
1976—Packers, 28-13 (GB)
1978—Eagles, 10-3 (P)

1979—Eagles, 21-10 (GB)
1987—Packers, 16-10 (GB) OT
1990—Eagles, 31-0 (P)
1991—Eagles, 20-3 (GB)
1992—Packers, 27-24 (Mil)
1993—Eagles, 20-17 (GB)
1994—Eagles, 13-7 (P)
1996—Packers, 39-13 (GB)
1997—Eagles, 10-9 (P)
1998—Packers, 24-16 (GB)
2000—Packers, 6-3 (GB)
2003—Eagles, 17-14 (GB)
   **Eagles, 20-17 (P) OT
2004—Eagles, 47-17 (P)
2005—Eagles, 19-14 (P)
2006—Eagles, 31-9 (P)
2007—Packers, 16-13 (GB)
2010—Packers, 27-20 (P)
   ***Packers, 21-16 (P)
(RS Pts.—Packers 737, Eagles 599)
(PS Pts.—Eagles 53, Packers 51)
*NFL Championship
**NFC Divisional Playoff
***NFC First-Round Playoff
GREEN BAY vs. *PITTSBURGH
RS: Packers lead series, 18-14
PS: Packers lead series, 1-0
1933—Packers, 47-0 (GB)
1935—Packers, 27-0 (GB)
   Packers, 34-14 (P)
1936—Packers, 42-10 (Mil)
1938—Packers, 20-0 (GB)
1940—Packers, 24-3 (Mil)
1941—Packers, 54-7 (P)
1942—Packers, 24-21 (Mil)
1946—Packers, 17-7 (GB)
1947—Steelers, 18-17 (Mil)
1948—Steelers, 38-7 (P)
1949—Steelers, 30-7 (Mil)
1951—Packers, 35-33 (Mil)
   Steelers, 28-7 (P)
1953—Steelers, 31-14 (P)
1954—Steelers, 21-20 (GB)
1957—Packers, 27-10 (P)
1960—Packers, 19-13 (P)
1963—Packers, 33-14 (Mil)
1965—Packers, 41-9 (P)
1967—Steelers, 24-17 (GB)
1969—Packers, 38-34 (P)
1970—Packers, 20-12 (P)
1975—Steelers, 16-13 (Mil)
1980—Steelers, 22-20 (P)
1983—Steelers, 25-21 (GB)
1986—Steelers, 27-3 (P)
1992—Packers, 17-3 (GB)
1995—Packers, 24-19 (GB)
1998—Steelers, 27-20 (P)
2005—Packers, 20-10 (GB)
2009—Steelers, 37-36 (P)
2010—**Packers, 31-25 (North Texas)
(RS Pts.—Packers 755, Steelers 573)
(PS Pts.—Packers 31, Steelers 25)
*Steelers known as Pirates prior to 1940
**Super Bowl XLV
GREEN BAY vs. *ST. LOUIS
RS: Rams lead series, 45-43-2
PS: Series tied, 1-1
1937—Packers, 35-10 (C)
   Packers, 35-7 (G)
1938—Packers, 26-17 (GB)
   Packers, 28-7 (C)
1939—Rams, 27-24 (GB)

   Packers, 7-6 (C)
1940—Packers, 31-14 (GB)
   Tie, 13-13 (C)
1941—Packers, 24-7 (Mil)
   Packers, 17-14 (C)
1942—Packers, 45-28 (GB)
   Packers, 30-12 (C)
1944—Packers, 30-21 (GB)
   Packers, 42-7 (C)
1945—Rams, 27-14 (GB)
   Rams, 20-7 (C)
1946—Rams, 21-17 (Mil)
   Rams, 38-17 (LA)
1947—Packers, 17-14 (Mil)
   Packers, 30-10 (LA)
1948—Packers, 16-0 (GB)
   Rams, 24-10 (LA)
1949—Rams, 48-7 (GB)
   Rams, 35-7 (LA)
1950—Rams, 45-14 (GB)
   Rams, 51-14 (LA)
1951—Rams, 28-0 (Mil)
   Rams, 42-14 (LA)
1952—Rams, 30-28 (Mil)
   Rams, 45-27 (LA)
1953—Rams, 38-20 (Mil)
   Rams, 33-17 (LA)
1954—Packers, 35-17 (Mil)
   Rams, 35-27 (LA)
1955—Packers, 30-28 (Mil)
   Rams, 31-17 (LA)
1956—Packers, 42-17 (Mil)
   Rams, 49-21 (LA)
1957—Rams, 31-27 (Mil)
   Rams, 42-17 (LA)
1958—Rams, 20-7 (GB)
   Rams, 34-20 (LA)
1959—Rams, 45-6 (Mil)
   Packers, 38-20 (LA)
1960—Rams, 33-31 (Mil)
   Packers, 35-21 (LA)
1961—Packers, 35-17 (GB)
   Packers, 24-17 (LA)
1962—Packers, 41-10 (Mil)
   Packers, 20-17 (LA)
1963—Packers, 42-10 (GB)
   Packers, 31-14 (LA)
1964—Rams, 27-17 (Mil)
   Tie, 24-24 (LA)
1965—Rams, 6-3 (Mil)
   Rams, 21-10 (LA)
1966—Packers, 24-13 (GB)
   Packers, 27-23 (LA)
1967—Rams, 27-24 (LA)
   **Packers, 28-7 (Mil)
1968—Rams, 16-14 (Mil)
1969—Rams, 34-21 (LA)
1970—Rams, 31-21 (GB)
1971—Rams, 30-13 (LA)
1973—Rams, 24-7 (LA)
1974—Rams, 17-6 (Mil)
1975—Rams, 22-5 (LA)
1977—Rams, 24-6 (Mil)
1978—Rams, 31-14 (LA)
1980—Rams, 51-21 (LA)
1981—Rams, 35-23 (LA)
1982—Packers, 35-23 (Mil)
1983—Packers, 27-24 (Mil)
1984—Packers, 31-6 (Mil)
1985—Rams, 34-17 (LA)
1988—Rams, 34-7 (GB)
1989—Rams, 41-38 (LA)

1990—Packers, 36-24 (GB)
1991—Rams, 23-21 (LA)
1992—Packers, 28-13 (GB)
1993—Packers, 36-6 (Mil)
1994—Packers, 24-17 (GB)
1995—Rams, 17-14 (GB)
1996—Packers, 24-9 (StL)
1997—Packers, 17-7 (GB)
2001—***Rams, 45-17 (StL)
2003—Rams, 34-24 (StL)
2004—Packers, 45-17 (GB)
2006—Rams, 23-20 (GB)
2007—Packers, 33-14 (StL)
2009—Packers, 36-17 (StL)
2011—Packers, 24-3 (GB)
(RS Pts.—Rams 2,075, Packers 2,040)
(PS Pts.—Rams 52, Packers 45)
*Franchise in Los Angeles prior to 1995
and in Cleveland prior to 1946
**Conference Championship
***NFC Divisional Playoff
GREEN BAY vs. SAN DIEGO
RS: Packers lead series, 9-1
1970—Packers, 22-20 (SD)
1974—Packers, 34-0 (GB)
1978—Packers, 24-3 (SD)
1984—Chargers, 34-28 (GB)
1993—Packers, 20-13 (SD)
1996—Packers, 42-10 (GB)
1999—Packers, 31-3 (SD)
2003—Packers, 38-21 (GB)
2007—Packers, 31-24 (GB)
2011—Packers, 45-38 (SD)
(RS Pts.—Packers 315, Chargers 166)
GREEN BAY vs. SAN FRANCISCO
RS: Packers lead series, 30-25-1
PS: Packers lead series, 4-1
1950—Packers, 25-21 (GB)
       49ers, 30-14 (SF)
1951—49ers, 31-19 (SF)
1952—49ers, 24-14 (SF)
1953—49ers, 37-7 (Mil)
       49ers, 48-14 (SF)
1954—49ers, 23-17 (Mil)
       49ers, 35-0 (SF)
1955—Packers, 27-21 (Mil)
       Packers, 28-7 (SF)
1956—49ers, 17-16 (GB)
       49ers, 38-20 (SF)
1957—49ers, 24-14 (Mil)
       49ers, 27-20 (SF)
1958—49ers, 33-12 (Mil)
       49ers, 48-21 (SF)
1959—Packers, 21-20 (GB)
       Packers, 36-14 (SF)
1960—Packers, 41-14 (Mil)
       Packers, 13-0 (SF)
1961—Packers, 30-10 (GB)
       49ers, 22-21 (SF)
1962—Packers, 31-13 (Mil)
       Packers, 31-21 (SF)
1963—Packers, 28-10 (Mil)
       Packers, 21-17 (SF)
1964—Packers, 24-14 (Mil)
       49ers, 24-14 (SF)
1965—Packers, 27-10 (GB)
       Tie, 24-24 (SF)
1966—49ers, 21-20 (SF)
       Packers, 20-7 (Mil)
1967—Packers, 13-0 (GB)
1968—49ers, 27-20 (SF)
1969—Packers, 14-7 (Mil)

1970—49ers, 26-10 (SF)
1972—Packers, 34-24 (Mil)
1973—49ers, 20-6 (SF)
1974—49ers, 7-6 (SF)
1976—49ers, 26-14 (GB)
1977—Packers, 16-14 (Mil)
1980—Packers, 23-16 (Mil)
1981—49ers, 13-3 (Mil)
1986—49ers, 31-17 (Mil)
1987—49ers, 23-12 (GB)
1989—Packers, 21-17 (SF)
1990—49ers, 24-20 (GB)
1995—*Packers, 27-17 (SF)
1996—Packers, 23-20 (GB) OT
       *Packers, 35-14 (GB)
1997—**Packers, 23-10 (SF)
1998—Packers, 36-22 (GB)
       ***49ers, 30-27 (SF)
1999—Packers, 20-3 (SF)
2000—Packers, 31-28 (GB)
2001—***Packers, 25-15 (GB)
2002—Packers, 20-14 (SF)
2003—Packers, 20-10 (GB)
2006—Packers, 30-19 (SF)
2009—Packers, 30-24 (GB)
2010—Packers, 34-16 (GB)
(RS Pts.—Packers 1,143, 49ers 1,136)
(PS Pts.—Packers 137, 49ers 86)
*NFC Divisional Playoff
**NFC Championship
***NFC First-Round Playoff
GREEN BAY vs. SEATTLE
RS: Packers lead series, 8-5
PS: Packers lead series, 2-0
1976—Packers, 27-20 (Mil)
1978—Packers, 45-28 (Mil)
1981—Packers, 34-24 (GB)
1984—Seahawks, 30-24 (Mil)
1987—Seahawks, 24-13 (S)
1990—Seahawks, 20-14 (Mil)
1996—Packers, 31-10 (S)
1999—Seahawks, 27-7 (GB)
2003—Packers, 35-13 (GB)
       *Packers, 33-27 (GB) OT
2005—Packers, 23-17 (GB)
2006—Seahawks, 34-24 (S)
2007—**Packers, 42-20 (GB)
2008—Packers, 27-17 (S)
2009—Packers, 48-10 (GB)
(RS Pts.—Packers 352, Seahawks 274)
(PS Pts.—Packers 75, Seahawks 47)
*NFC First-Round Playoff
**NFC Divisional Playoff
GREEN BAY vs. TAMPA BAY
RS: Packers lead series, 30-21-1
PS: Packers lead series, 1-0
1977—Packers, 13-0 (TB)
1978—Packers, 9-7 (GB)
       Packers, 17-7 (TB)
1979—Buccaneers, 21-10 (GB)
       Buccaneers, 21-3 (TB)
1980—Tie, 14-14 (TB) OT
       Buccaneers, 20-17 (Mil)
1981—Buccaneers, 21-10 (GB)
       Buccaneers, 37-3 (TB)
1983—Packers, 55-14 (GB)
       Packers, 12-9 (TB) OT
1984—Buccaneers, 30-27 (TB) OT
       Packers, 27-14 (GB)
1985—Packers, 21-0 (GB)
       Packers, 20-17 (TB)
1986—Packers, 31-7 (Mil)

       Packers, 21-7 (TB)
1987—Buccaneers, 23-17 (Mil)
1988—Buccaneers, 13-10 (GB)
       Buccaneers, 27-24 (TB)
1989—Buccaneers, 23-21 (GB)
       Packers, 17-16 (TB)
1990—Buccaneers, 26-14 (TB)
       Packers, 20-10 (Mil)
1991—Packers, 15-13 (GB)
       Packers, 27-0 (TB)
1992—Buccaneers, 31-3 (TB)
       Packers, 19-14 (Mil)
1993—Packers, 37-14 (TB)
       Packers, 13-10 (GB)
1994—Packers, 30-3 (TB)
       Packers, 34-19 (TB)
1995—Packers, 35-13 (GB)
       Buccaneers, 13-10 (TB) OT
1996—Packers, 34-3 (TB)
       Packers, 13-7 (GB)
1997—Packers, 21-16 (GB)
       Packers, 17-6 (TB)
       *Packers, 21-7 (GB)
1998—Packers, 23-15 (GB)
       Buccaneers, 24-22 (TB)
1999—Packers, 26-23 (GB)
       Buccaneers, 29-10 (TB)
2000—Buccaneers, 20-15 (TB)
       Packers, 17-14 (GB) OT
2001—Buccaneers, 14-10 (TB)
       Packers, 21-20 (GB)
2002—Buccaneers, 21-7 (TB)
2003—Packers, 20-13 (TB)
2005—Buccaneers, 17-16 (GB)
2008—Buccaneers, 30-21 (TB)
2009—Buccaneers, 38-28 (TB)
2011—Packers, 35-26 (GB)
(RS Pts.—Packers 1,012, Buccaneers 850)
(PS Pts.—Packers 21, Buccaneers 7)
*NFC Divisional Playoff
GREEN BAY vs. *TENNESSEE
RS: Titans lead series, 6-4
1972—Packers, 23-10 (H)
1977—Oilers, 16-10 (GB)
1980—Oilers, 22-3 (GB)
1983—Packers, 41-38 (H) OT
1986—Oilers, 31-3 (GB)
1992—Packers, 16-14 (H)
1998—Packers, 30-22 (GB)
2001—Titans, 26-20 (T)
2004—Titans, 48-27 (GB)
2008—Titans, 19-16 (T) OT
(RS Pts.—Titans 246, Packers 189)
*Franchise in Houston prior to 1997;
known as Oilers prior to 1999
GREEN BAY vs. *WASHINGTON
RS: Packers lead series, 17-13-1
PS: Series tied, 1-1
1932—Packers, 21-0 (B)
1933—Tie, 7-7 (GB)
       Redskins, 20-7 (B)
1934—Packers, 10-0 (B)
1936—Packers, 31-2 (B)
       Packers, 7-3 (B)
       **Packers, 21-6 (New York)
1937—Redskins, 14-6 (W)
1939—Packers, 24-14 (Mil)
1941—Packers, 22-17 (W)
1943—Redskins, 33-7 (Mil)
1946—Packers, 20-7 (W)
1947—Packers, 27-10 (Mil)
1948—Redskins, 23-7 (Mil)

1949—Redskins, 30-0 (W)
1950—Packers, 35-21 (Mil)
1952—Packers, 35-20 (Mil)
1958—Redskins, 37-21 (W)
1959—Packers, 21-0 (GB)
1968—Packers, 27-7 (W)
1972—Redskins, 21-16 (W)
　***Redskins, 16-3 (W)
1974—Redskins, 17-6 (GB)
1977—Redskins, 10-9 (W)
1979—Redskins, 38-21 (W)
1983—Packers, 48-47 (GB)
1986—Redskins, 16-7 (GB)
1988—Redskins, 20-17 (Mil)
2001—Packers, 37-0 (GB)
2002—Packers, 30-9 (GB)
2004—Packers, 28-14 (W)
2007—Packers, 17-14 (GB)
2010—Redskins, 16-13 (W) OT
(RS Pts.—Packers 584, Redskins 487)
(PS Pts.—Packers 24, Redskins 22)
*Franchise in Boston prior to 1937 and known as Braves prior to 1933
**NFL Championship
***NFC Divisional Playoff

HOUSTON vs. ARIZONA
RS: Series tied, 1-1;
See Arizona vs. Houston
HOUSTON vs. ATLANTA
RS: Texans lead series, 2-1;
See Atlanta vs. Houston
HOUSTON vs. BALTIMORE
RS: Ravens lead series, 5-0
PS: Ravens lead series, 1-0;
See Baltimore vs. Houston
HOUSTON vs. BUFFALO
RS: Bills lead series, 3-2;
See Buffalo vs. Houston
HOUSTON vs. CAROLINA
RS: Texans lead series, 2-1;
See Carolina vs. Houston
HOUSTON vs. CHICAGO
RS: Texans lead series, 2-0;
See Chicago vs. Houston
HOUSTON vs. CINCINNATI
RS: Series tied, 3-3
PS: Texans lead series, 1-0;
See Cincinnati vs. Houston
HOUSTON vs. CLEVELAND
RS: Texans lead series, 4-3;
See Cleveland vs. Houston
HOUSTON vs. DALLAS
RS: Cowboys lead series, 2-1;
See Dallas vs. Houston
HOUSTON vs. DENVER
RS: Broncos lead series, 2-1;
See Denver vs. Houston
HOUSTON vs. DETROIT
RS: Series tied, 1-1;
See Detroit vs. Houston
HOUSTON vs. GREEN BAY
RS: Series tied, 1-1;
See Green Bay vs. Houston
HOUSTON vs. INDIANAPOLIS
RS: Colts lead series, 17-3
2002—Colts, 23-3 (H)
　Colts, 19-3 (I)
2003—Colts, 30-21 (I)
　Colts, 20-17 (H)
2004—Colts, 49-14 (I)
　Colts, 23-14 (H)

2005—Colts, 38-20 (H)
　Colts, 31-17 (I)
2006—Colts, 43-24 (I)
　Texans, 27-24 (H)
2007—Colts, 30-24 (H)
　Colts, 38-15 (I)
2008—Colts, 31-27 (H)
　Colts, 33-27 (I)
2009—Colts, 20-17 (I)
　Colts, 35-27 (H)
2010—Texans, 34-24 (H)
　Colts, 30-17 (I)
2011—Texans, 34-7 (H)
　Colts, 19-16 (I)
(RS Pts.—Colts 567, Texans 398)
HOUSTON vs. JACKSONVILLE
RS: Texans lead series, 11-9
2002—Texans, 21-19 (J)
　Jaguars, 24-21 (H)
2003—Texans, 24-20 (H)
　Jaguars, 27-0 (J)
2004—Texans, 20-6 (H)
　Texans, 21-0 (J)
2005—Jaguars, 21-14 (J)
　Jaguars, 38-20 (H)
2006—Texans, 27-7 (H)
　Texans, 13-10 (J)
2007—Jaguars, 37-17 (J)
　Texans, 42-28 (H)
2008—Jaguars, 30-27 (J) OT
　Texans, 30-17 (H)
2009—Texans, 31-24 (H)
　Jaguars, 23-18 (J)
2010—Jaguars, 31-24 (J)
　Texans, 34-17 (H)
2011—Texans, 24-14 (H)
　Texans, 20-13 (J)
(RS Pts.—Texans 441, Jaguars 413)
HOUSTON vs. KANSAS CITY
RS: Texans lead series, 3-2
2003—Chiefs, 42-14 (H)
2004—Texans, 24-21 (KC)
2005—Chiefs, 45-17 (H)
2007—Texans, 20-3 (H)
2010—Texans, 35-31 (H)
(RS Pts.—Chiefs 142, Texans 110)
HOUSTON vs. MIAMI
RS: Texans lead series, 6-0
2003—Texans, 21-20 (M)
2006—Texans, 17-15 (H)
2007—Texans, 22-19 (H)
2008—Texans, 29-28 (H)
2009—Texans, 27-20 (H)
2011—Texans, 23-13 (M)
(RS Pts.—Texans 139, Dolphins 115)
HOUSTON vs. MINNESOTA
RS: Vikings lead series, 2-0
2004—Vikings, 34-28 (H) OT
2008—Vikings, 28-21 (M)
(RS Pts.—Vikings 62, Texans 49)
HOUSTON vs. NEW ENGLAND
RS: Patriots lead series, 2-1
2003—Patriots, 23-20 (H) OT
2006—Patriots, 40-7 (NE)
2009—Texans, 34-27 (H)
(RS Pts.—Patriots 90, Texans 61)
HOUSTON vs. NEW ORLEANS
RS: Saints lead series, 2-1
2003—Saints, 31-10 (NO)
2007—Texans, 23-10 (H)
2011—Saints, 40-33 (NO)
(RS Pts.—Saints 81, Texans 66)

HOUSTON vs. N.Y. GIANTS
RS: Giants lead series, 2-1
2002—Texans, 16-14 (H)
2006—Giants, 14-10 (NY)
2010—Giants, 34-10 (H)
(RS Pts.—Giants 62, Texans 36)
HOUSTON vs. N.Y. JETS
RS: Jets lead series, 5-0
2003—Jets, 19-14 (H)
2004—Jets, 29-7 (NY)
2006—Jets, 26-11 (NY)
2009—Jets, 24-7 (H)
2010—Jets, 30-27 (NY)
(RS Pts.—Jets 128, Texans 66)
HOUSTON vs. OAKLAND
RS: Texans lead series, 5-2
2004—Texans, 30-17 (O)
2006—Texans, 23-14 (O)
2007—Texans, 24-17 (O)
2008—Raiders, 27-16 (O)
2009—Texans, 29-6 (H)
2010—Texans, 31-24 (O)
2011—Raiders, 25-20 (H)
(RS Pts.—Texans 173, Raiders 130)
HOUSTON vs. PHILADELPHIA
RS: Eagles lead series, 3-0
2002—Eagles, 35-17 (P)
2006—Eagles, 24-10 (P)
2010—Eagles, 34-24 (P)
(RS Pts.—Eagles 93, Texans 51)
HOUSTON vs. PITTSBURGH
RS: Series tied, 2-2
2002—Texans, 24-6 (P)
2005—Steelers, 27-7 (H)
2008—Steelers, 38-17 (P)
2011—Texans, 17-10 (H)
(RS Pts.—Steelers 81, Texans 65)
HOUSTON vs. ST. LOUIS
RS: Series tied, 1-1
2005—Rams, 33-27 (H) OT
2009—Texans, 16-13 (StL)
(RS Pts.—Rams 46, Texans 43)
HOUSTON vs. SAN DIEGO
RS: Chargers lead series, 4-0
2002—Chargers, 24-3 (SD)
2004—Chargers, 27-20 (H)
2007—Chargers, 35-10 (SD)
2010—Chargers, 29-23 (H)
(RS Pts.—Chargers 115, Texans 56)
HOUSTON vs. SAN FRANCISCO
RS: Series tied, 1-1
2005—49ers, 20-17 (SF) OT
2009—Texans, 24-21 (H)
(RS Pts.—Texans 41, 49ers 41)
HOUSTON vs. SEATTLE
RS: Series tied, 1-1
2005—Seahawks, 42-10 (S)
2009—Texans, 34-7 (H)
(RS Pts.—Seahawks 49, Texans 44)
HOUSTON vs. TAMPA BAY
RS: Texans lead series, 2-1
2003—Buccaneers, 16-3 (TB)
2007—Texans, 28-14 (H)
2011—Texans, 37-9 (TB)
(RS Pts.—Texans 68, Buccaneers 39)
HOUSTON vs. TENNESSEE
RS: Titans lead series, 14-6
2002—Titans, 17-10 (T)
　Titans, 13-3 (H)
2003—Titans, 38-17 (T)
　Titans, 27-24 (H)
2004—Texans, 20-10 (T)

Texans, 31-21 (H)
2005—Titans, 34-20 (H)
Titans, 13-10 (T)
2006—Titans, 28-22 (T)
Titans, 26-20 (H) OT
2007—Titans, 38-36 (H)
Titans, 28-20 (T)
2008—Titans, 31-12 (H)
Texans, 13-12 (H)
2009—Texans, 34-31 (T)
Titans, 20-17 (H)
2010—Texans, 20-0 (H)
Titans, 31-17 (T)
2011—Texans, 41-7 (T)
Titans, 23-22 (H)
(RS Pts.—Titans 448, Texans 409)
HOUSTON vs. WASHINGTON
RS: Redskins lead series, 2-1
2002—Redskins, 26-10 (W)
2006—Redskins, 31-15 (H)
2010—Texans, 30-27 (W) OT
(RS Pts.—Redskins 84, Texans 55)

INDIANAPOLIS vs. ARIZONA
RS: Colts lead series, 8-6;
See Arizona vs. Indianapolis
INDIANAPOLIS vs. ATLANTA
RS: Colts lead series, 13-2;
See Atlanta vs. Indianapolis
INDIANAPOLIS vs. BALTIMORE
RS: Colts lead series, 7-3
PS: Colts lead series, 2-0;
See Baltimore vs. Indianapolis
INDIANAPOLIS vs. BUFFALO
RS: Bills lead series, 35-30-1;
See Buffalo vs. Indianapolis
INDIANAPOLIS vs. CAROLINA
RS: Panthers lead series, 4-1;
See Carolina vs. Indianapolis
INDIANAPOLIS vs. CHICAGO
RS: Colts lead series, 22-18
PS: Colts lead series, 1-0;
See Chicago vs. Indianapolis
INDIANAPOLIS vs. CINCINNATI
RS: Colts lead series, 16-9
PS: Colts lead series, 1-0;
See Cincinnati vs. Indianapolis
INDIANAPOLIS vs. CLEVELAND
RS: Browns lead series, 14-12
PS: Series tied, 2-2;
See Cleveland vs. Indianapolis
INDIANAPOLIS vs. DALLAS
RS: Cowboys lead series, 9-5
PS: Colts lead series, 1-0;
See Dallas vs. Indianapolis
INDIANAPOLIS vs. DENVER
RS: Broncos lead series, 11-8
PS: Colts lead series, 2-0;
See Denver vs. Indianapolis
INDIANAPOLIS vs. DETROIT
RS: Colts lead series, 20-18-2;
See Detroit vs. Indianapolis
INDIANAPOLIS vs. GREEN BAY
RS: Series tied, 20-20-1
PS: Packers lead series, 1-0;
See Green Bay vs. Indianapolis
INDIANAPOLIS vs. HOUSTON
RS: Colts lead series, 17-3;
See Houston vs. Indianapolis
INDIANAPOLIS vs. JACKSONVILLE
RS: Colts lead series, 15-7
1995—Colts, 41-31 (J)

2000—Colts, 43-14 (I)
2002—Colts, 28-25 (J)
Colts, 20-13 (I)
2003—Colts, 23-13 (I)
Jaguars, 28-23 (J)
2004—Colts, 24-17 (J)
Jaguars, 27-24 (I)
2005—Colts, 10-3 (I)
Colts, 26-18 (J)
2006—Colts, 21-14 (I)
Jaguars, 44-17 (J)
2007—Colts, 29-7 (J)
Colts, 28-25 (I)
2008—Jaguars, 23-21 (I)
Colts, 31-24 (J)
2009—Colts, 14-12 (I)
Colts, 35-31 (J)
2010—Jaguars, 31-28 (J)
Colts, 34-24 (I)
2011—Jaguars, 17-3 (I)
Jaguars, 19-13 (J)
(RS Pts.—Colts 536, Jaguars 460)
*INDIANAPOLIS vs. KANSAS CITY
RS: Colts lead series, 10-8
PS: Colts lead series, 3-0
1970—Chiefs, 44-24 (B)
1972—Chiefs, 24-10 (KC)
1975—Colts, 28-14 (B)
1977—Colts, 17-6 (KC)
1979—Chiefs, 14-0 (KC)
Chiefs, 10-7 (B)
1980—Colts, 31-24 (KC)
Chiefs, 38-28 (B)
1985—Chiefs, 20-7 (KC)
1990—Colts, 23-19 (I)
1995—**Colts, 10-7 (KC)
1996—Colts, 24-19 (KC)
1999—Colts, 25-17 (I)
2000—Colts, 27-14 (KC)
2001—Colts, 35-28 (KC)
2003—**Colts, 38-31 (KC)
2004—Chiefs, 45-35 (KC)
2006—***Colts, 23-8 (I)
2007—Colts, 13-10 (I)
2010—Colts, 19-9 (I)
2011—Colts, 28-24 (I)
(RS Pts.—Chiefs 383, Colts 377)
(PS Pts.—Colts 71, Chiefs 46)
*Franchise in Baltimore prior to 1984
**AFC Divisional Playoff
***AFC First-Round Playoff
*INDIANAPOLIS vs. MIAMI
RS: Dolphins lead series, 44-24
PS: Dolphins lead series, 2-0
1970—Colts, 35-0 (B)
Dolphins, 34-17 (M)
1971—Dolphins, 17-14 (M)
Colts, 14-3 (B)
**Dolphins, 21-0 (M)
1972—Dolphins, 23-0 (B)
Dolphins, 16-0 (M)
1973—Dolphins, 44-0 (M)
Colts, 16-3 (B)
1974—Dolphins, 17-7 (M)
Dolphins, 17-16 (M)
1975—Colts, 33-17 (M)
Colts, 10-7 (B) OT
1976—Colts, 28-14 (B)
Colts, 17-16 (M)
1977—Colts, 45-28 (B)
Dolphins, 17-6 (M)
1978—Dolphins, 42-0 (B)

Dolphins, 26-8 (M)
1979—Dolphins, 19-0 (M)
Dolphins, 28-24 (B)
1980—Colts, 30-17 (M)
Dolphins, 24-14 (B)
1981—Dolphins, 31-28 (B)
Dolphins, 27-10 (M)
1982—Dolphins, 24-20 (M)
Dolphins, 34-7 (B)
1983—Dolphins, 21-7 (B)
Dolphins, 37-0 (M)
1984—Dolphins, 44-7 (M)
Dolphins, 35-17 (I)
1985—Dolphins, 30-13 (M)
Dolphins, 34-20 (I)
1986—Dolphins, 30-10 (M)
Dolphins, 17-13 (I)
1987—Dolphins, 23-10 (I)
Colts, 40-21 (M)
1988—Colts, 15-13 (I)
Colts, 31-28 (M)
1989—Dolphins, 19-13 (M)
Colts, 42-13 (I)
1990—Dolphins, 27-7 (I)
Dolphins, 23-17 (M)
1991—Dolphins, 17-6 (I)
Dolphins, 10-6 (I)
1992—Colts, 31-20 (M)
Dolphins, 28-0 (I)
1993—Dolphins, 24-20 (I)
Dolphins, 41-27 (M)
1994—Dolphins, 22-21 (M)
Colts, 10-6 (I)
1995—Colts, 27-24 (M) OT
Colts, 36-28 (I)
1996—Colts, 10-6 (I)
Dolphins, 37-13 (M)
1997—Dolphins, 16-10 (M)
Colts, 41-0 (I)
1998—Colts, 24-15 (I)
Dolphins, 27-14 (M)
1999—Dolphins, 34-31 (I)
Colts, 37-34 (M)
2000—Dolphins, 17-14 (I)
Colts, 20-13 (M)
***Dolphins 23-17 (M) OT
2001—Colts, 27-24 (I)
Dolphins, 41-6 (M)
2002—Dolphins, 21-13 (I)
2003—Colts, 23-17 (M)
2006—Colts, 27-22 (I)
2009—Colts, 27-23 (M)
(RS Pts.—Dolphins 1,539, Colts 1,170)
(PS Pts.—Dolphins 44, Colts 17)
*Franchise in Baltimore prior to 1984
**AFC Championship
***AFC First-Round Playoff
*INDIANAPOLIS vs. MINNESOTA
RS: Colts lead series, 14-7-1
PS: Colts lead series, 1-0
1961—Colts, 34-33 (B)
Vikings, 28-20 (M)
1962—Colts, 34-7 (M)
Colts, 42-17 (B)
1963—Colts, 37-34 (M)
Colts, 41-10 (B)
1964—Vikings, 34-24 (M)
Colts, 17-14 (B)
1965—Colts, 35-16 (B)
Colts, 41-21 (M)
1966—Colts, 38-23 (M)
Colts, 20-17 (B)

1967—Tie, 20-20 (M)
1968—Colts, 21-9 (B)
    **Colts, 24-14 (B)
1969—Vikings, 52-14 (M)
1971—Vikings, 10-3 (M)
1982—Vikings, 13-10 (M)
1988—Vikings, 12-3 (M)
1997—Vikings, 39-28 (M)
2000—Colts, 31-10 (I)
2004—Colts, 31-28 (I)
2008—Colts, 18-15 (M)
(RS Pts.—Colts 562, Vikings 462)
(PS Pts.—Colts 24, Vikings 14)
Franchise in Baltimore prior to 1984
**Conference Championship*

*INDIANAPOLIS vs. **NEW ENGLAND
RS: Patriots lead series, 44-28
PS: Patriots lead series, 2-1
1970—Colts, 14-6 (Bos)
    Colts, 27-3 (Balt)
1971—Colts, 23-3 (NE)
    Patriots, 21-17 (Balt)
1972—Colts, 24-17 (NE)
    Colts, 31-0 (Balt)
1973—Patriots, 24-16 (NE)
    Colts, 18-13 (Balt)
1974—Patriots, 42-3 (NE)
    Patriots, 27-17 (Balt)
1975—Patriots, 21-10 (NE)
    Colts, 34-21 (Balt)
1976—Colts, 27-13 (NE)
    Patriots, 21-14 (Balt)
1977—Patriots, 17-3 (NE)
    Colts, 30-24 (Balt)
1978—Colts, 34-27 (NE)
    Patriots, 35-14 (Balt)
1979—Colts, 31-26 (Balt)
    Patriots, 50-21 (NE)
1980—Patriots, 37-21 (Balt)
    Patriots, 47-21 (NE)
1981—Colts, 29-28 (NE)
    Colts, 23-21 (Balt)
1982—Patriots, 24-13 (Balt)
1983—Colts, 29-23 (NE) OT
    Colts, 12-7 (Balt)
1984—Patriots, 50-17 (I)
    Patriots, 16-10 (NE)
1985—Patriots, 34-15 (NE)
    Patriots, 38-31 (I)
1986—Patriots, 33-3 (NE)
    Patriots, 30-21 (I)
1987—Colts, 30-16 (I)
    Patriots, 24-0 (NE)
1988—Patriots, 21-17 (NE)
    Colts, 24-21 (I)
1989—Patriots, 23-20 (I) OT
    Patriots, 22-16 (NE)
1990—Patriots, 16-14 (I)
    Colts, 13-10 (NE)
1991—Patriots, 16-7 (I)
    Patriots, 23-17 (NE) OT
1992—Patriots, 37-34 (I) OT
    Colts, 6-0 (NE)
1993—Colts, 9-6 (I)
    Patriots, 38-0 (NE)
1994—Patriots, 12-10 (I)
    Patriots, 28-13 (NE)
1995—Colts, 24-10 (NE)
    Colts, 10-7 (I)
1996—Patriots, 27-9 (I)
    Patriots, 27-13 (NE)
1997—Patriots, 31-6 (I)

Patriots, 20-17 (NE)
1998—Patriots, 29-6 (NE)
    Patriots, 21-16 (I)
1999—Patriots, 31-28 (NE)
    Colts, 20-15 (I)
2000—Patriots, 24-16 (NE)
    Colts, 30-23 (I)
2001—Patriots, 44-13 (NE)
    Patriots, 38-17 (I)
2003—Patriots, 38-34 (I)
    ***Patriots, 24-14 (NE)
2004—Patriots, 27-24 (NE)
    ****Patriots, 20-3 (NE)
2005—Colts, 40-21 (NE)
2006—Colts, 27-20 (NE)
    ***Colts, 38-34 (I)
2007—Patriots, 24-20 (I)
2008—Colts, 18-15 (I)
2009—Colts, 35-34 (I)
2010—Patriots, 31-28 (NE)
2011—Patriots, 31-24 (NE)
(RS Pts.—Patriots 1,700, Colts 1,358)
(PS Pts.—Patriots 78, Colts 55)
Franchise in Baltimore prior to 1984
**Franchise in Boston prior to 1971*
***AFC Championship*
****AFC Divisional Playoff*

*INDIANAPOLIS vs. NEW ORLEANS
RS: Saints lead series, 6-5
PS: Saints lead series, 1-0
1967—Colts, 30-10 (B)
1969—Colts, 30-10 (NO)
1973—Colts, 14-10 (B)
1986—Saints, 17-14 (I)
1989—Saints, 41-6 (NO)
1995—Saints, 17-14 (NO)
1998—Saints, 19-13 (I) OT
2001—Saints, 34-20 (NO)
2003—Colts, 55-21 (NO)
2007—Colts, 41-10 (I)
2009—**Saints 31-17 (South Florida)
2011—Saints, 62-7 (NO)
(RS Pts.—Saints 251, Colts 244)
(PS Pts.—Saints 31, Colts 17)
Franchise in Baltimore prior to 1984
**Super Bowl XLIV*

*INDIANAPOLIS vs. N.Y. GIANTS
RS: Colts lead series, 8-6
PS: Colts lead series, 2-0
1954—Colts, 20-14 (B)
1955—Giants, 17-7 (NY)
1958—Giants, 24-21 (NY)
    **Colts, 23-17 (NY) OT
1959—**Colts, 31-16 (B)
1963—Giants, 37-28 (B)
1968—Colts, 26-0 (NY)
1971—Colts, 31-7 (NY)
1975—Colts, 21-0 (NY)
1979—Colts, 31-7 (NY)
1990—Giants, 24-7 (I)
1993—Giants, 20-6 (NY)
1999—Colts, 27-19 (NY)
2002—Giants, 44-27 (I)
2006—Colts, 26-21 (NY)
2010—Colts, 38-14 (I)
(RS Pts.—Colts 316, Giants 248)
(PS Pts.—Colts 54, Giants 33)
Franchise in Baltimore prior to 1984
**NFL Championship*

*INDIANAPOLIS vs. N.Y. JETS
RS: Colts lead series, 40-26
PS: Jets lead series, 3-1

1968—**Jets 16-7 (Miami)
1970—Colts, 29-22 (NY)
    Colts, 35-20 (B)
1971—Colts, 22-0 (B)
    Colts, 14-13 (NY)
1972—Jets, 44-34 (B)
    Jets, 24-20 (NY)
1973—Jets, 34-10 (B)
    Jets, 20-17 (NY)
1974—Colts, 35-20 (NY)
    Jets, 45-38 (B)
1975—Colts, 45-28 (NY)
    Colts, 52-19 (B)
1976—Colts, 20-0 (B)
    Colts, 33-16 (B)
1977—Colts, 20-12 (B)
    Colts, 33-12 (B)
1978—Jets, 33-10 (B)
    Jets, 24-16 (NY)
1979—Colts, 10-8 (B)
    Jets, 30-17 (NY)
1980—Colts, 17-14 (NY)
    Colts, 35-21 (B)
1981—Jets, 41-14 (B)
    Jets, 25-0 (NY)
1982—Jets, 37-0 (NY)
1983—Colts, 17-14 (NY)
    Jets, 10-6 (B)
1984—Jets, 23-14 (I)
    Colts, 9-5 (NY)
1985—Jets, 25-20 (NY)
    Jets, 35-17 (I)
1986—Jets, 26-7 (I)
    Jets, 31-16 (NY)
1987—Colts, 6-0 (I)
    Colts, 19-14 (NY)
1988—Colts, 38-14 (I)
    Jets, 34-16 (NY)
1989—Colts, 17-10 (NY)
    Colts, 27-10 (I)
1990—Colts, 17-14 (I)
    Colts, 29-21 (NY)
1991—Jets, 17-6 (I)
    Colts, 28-27 (NY)
1992—Colts, 6-3 (I) OT
    Colts, 10-6 (NY)
1993—Jets, 31-17 (I)
    Colts, 9-6 (NY)
1994—Jets, 16-6 (NY)
    Colts, 28-25 (I)
1995—Colts, 27-24 (NY) OT
    Colts, 17-10 (I)
1996—Colts, 21-7 (NY)
    Colts, 34-29 (I)
1997—Jets, 16-12 (I)
    Colts, 22-14 (NY)
1998—Jets, 44-6 (NY)
    Colts, 24-23 (I)
1999—Colts, 16-13 (NY)
    Colts, 13-6 (I)
2000—Colts, 23-15 (I)
    Jets, 27-17 (NY)
2001—Colts, 45-24 (NY)
    Jets, 29-28 (I)
2002—***Jets, 41-0 (NY)
2003—Colts, 38-31 (I)
2006—Colts, 31-28 (NY)
2009—Jets, 29-15 (I)
    ****Colts, 30-17 (I)
2010—***Jets, 17-16 (I)
(RS Pts.—Colts 1,350, Jets 1,348)
(PS Pts.—Jets 91, Colts 53)

*Franchise in Baltimore prior to 1984
**Super Bowl III
***AFC First-Round Playoff
****AFC Championship
INDIANAPOLIS vs. **OAKLAND
RS: Raiders lead series, 7-5
PS: Series tied, 1-1
1970—***Colts, 27-17 (B)
1971—Colts, 37-14 (O)
1973—Raiders, 34-21 (B)
1975—Raiders, 31-20 (B)
1977—****Raiders, 37-31 (B) OT
1984—Raiders, 21-7 (LA)
1986—Colts, 30-24 (LA)
1991—Raiders, 16-0 (LA)
1995—Colts, 30-17 (O)
2000—Raiders, 38-31 (I)
2001—Raiders, 23-18 (I)
2004—Colts, 35-14 (I)
2007—Colts, 21-14 (O)
2010—Colts, 31-26 (O)
(RS Pts.—Raiders 285, Colts 268)
(PS Pts.—Colts 58, Raiders 54)
*Franchise in Baltimore prior to 1984
**Franchise in Los Angeles from
1982-1994
***AFC Championship
****AFC Divisional Playoff
INDIANAPOLIS vs. PHILADELPHIA
RS: Colts lead series, 10-7
1953—Eagles, 45-14 (P)
1965—Colts, 34-24 (B)
1967—Colts, 38-6 (P)
1969—Colts, 24-20 (B)
1970—Colts, 29-10 (B)
1974—Eagles, 30-10 (P)
1978—Eagles, 17-14 (B)
1981—Eagles, 38-13 (P)
1983—Colts, 22-21 (P)
1984—Eagles, 16-7 (P)
1990—Colts, 24-23 (P)
1993—Eagles, 20-10 (I)
1996—Colts, 37-10 (I)
1999—Colts, 44-17 (P)
2002—Colts, 35-13 (P)
2006—Colts, 45-21 (I)
2010—Eagles, 26-24 (P)
(RS Pts.—Colts 424, Eagles 357)
*Franchise in Baltimore prior to 1984
INDIANAPOLIS vs. PITTSBURGH
RS: Steelers lead series, 14-6
PS: Steelers lead series, 5-0
1957—Steelers, 19-13 (B)
1968—Colts, 41-7 (P)
1971—Colts, 34-21 (B)
1974—Steelers, 30-0 (P)
1975—**Steelers, 28-10 (P)
1976—**Steelers, 40-14 (B)
1977—Colts, 31-21 (B)
1978—Steelers, 35-13 (P)
1979—Steelers, 17-13 (P)
1980—Colts, 20-17 (B)
1983—Steelers, 24-13 (B)
1984—Colts, 17-16 (I)
1985—Steelers, 45-3 (P)
1987—Steelers, 21-7 (P)
1991—Steelers, 21-3 (I)
1992—Steelers, 30-14 (P)
1994—Steelers, 31-21 (P)
1995—***Steelers, 20-16 (P)
1996—****Steelers, 42-14 (P)
1997—Steelers, 24-22 (P)

2002—Steelers, 28-10 (P)
2005—Colts, 26-7 (I)
    **Steelers, 21-18 (I)
2008—Colts, 24-20 (P)
2011—Steelers, 23-20 (I)
(RS Pts.—Steelers 460, Colts 342)
(PS Pts.—Steelers 151, Colts 72)
*Franchise in Baltimore prior to 1984
**AFC Divisional Playoff
***AFC Championship
****AFC First-Round Playoff
INDIANAPOLIS vs. **ST. LOUIS
RS: Colts lead series, 23-17-2
1953—Rams, 21-13 (B)
    Rams, 45-2 (LA)
1954—Rams, 48-0 (B)
    Colts, 22-21 (LA)
1955—Tie, 17-17 (B)
    Rams, 20-14 (LA)
1956—Colts, 56-21 (B)
    Rams, 31-7 (LA)
1957—Colts, 31-14 (B)
    Rams, 37-21 (LA)
1958—Colts, 34-7 (B)
    Rams, 30-28 (LA)
1959—Colts, 35-21 (B)
    Colts, 45-26 (LA)
1960—Colts, 31-17 (B)
    Rams, 10-3 (LA)
1961—Colts, 27-24 (B)
    Rams, 34-17 (LA)
1962—Colts, 30-27 (B)
    Colts, 14-2 (LA)
1963—Rams, 17-16 (LA)
    Colts, 19-16 (B)
1964—Colts, 35-20 (B)
    Colts, 24-7 (LA)
1965—Colts, 35-20 (B)
    Colts, 20-17 (LA)
1966—Colts, 17-3 (LA)
    Rams, 23-7 (B)
1967—Tie, 24-24 (B)
    Rams, 34-10 (LA)
1968—Colts, 27-10 (B)
    Colts, 28-24 (LA)
1969—Rams, 27-20 (B)
    Colts, 13-7 (LA)
1971—Colts, 24-17 (B)
1975—Rams, 24-13 (LA)
1986—Rams, 24-7 (I)
1989—Rams, 31-17 (LA)
1995—Colts, 21-18 (I)
2001—Rams, 42-17 (StL)
2005—Colts, 45-28 (I)
2009—Colts, 42-6 (StL)
(RS Pts.—Colts 928, Rams 912)
*Franchise in Baltimore prior to 1984
**Franchise in Los Angeles prior to 1995
INDIANAPOLIS vs. SAN DIEGO
RS: Chargers lead series, 15-9
PS: Chargers lead series, 2-1
1970—Colts, 16-14 (SD)
1972—Chargers, 23-20 (B)
1976—Colts, 37-21 (SD)
1981—Chargers, 43-14 (B)
1982—Chargers, 44-26 (SD)
1984—Chargers, 38-10 (I)
1986—Chargers, 17-3 (I)
1987—Chargers, 16-13 (I)
    Colts, 20-7 (SD)
1988—Colts, 16-0 (SD)
1989—Colts, 10-6 (I)

1992—Chargers, 34-14 (I)
    Chargers, 26-0 (SD)
1993—Chargers, 31-0 (I)
1995—Chargers, 27-24 (I)
    **Colts, 35-20 (SD)
1996—Chargers, 26-19 (I)
1997—Chargers, 35-19 (SD)
1998—Colts, 17-12 (I)
1999—Colts, 27-19 (SD)
2004—Colts, 34-31 (I) OT
2005—Chargers, 26-17 (I)
2007—Chargers, 23-21 (SD)
    ***Chargers, 28-24 (I)
2008—Colts, 23-20 (SD)
    **Chargers, 23-17 (SD) OT
2010—Chargers, 36-14 (I)
(RS Pts.—Chargers 575, Colts 414)
(PS Pts.—Colts 76, Chargers 71)
*Franchise in Baltimore prior to 1984
**AFC First-Round Playoff
***AFC Divisional Playoff
INDIANAPOLIS vs. SAN FRANCISCO
RS: Colts lead series, 24-18
1953—49ers, 38-21 (B)
    49ers, 45-14 (SF)
1954—Colts, 17-13 (B)
    49ers, 10-7 (SF)
1955—Colts, 26-14 (B)
    49ers, 35-24 (SF)
1956—49ers, 20-17 (B)
    49ers, 30-17 (SF)
1957—Colts, 27-21 (B)
    49ers, 17-13 (SF)
1958—Colts, 35-27 (B)
    49ers, 21-12 (SF)
1959—Colts, 45-14 (B)
    Colts, 34-14 (SF)
1960—49ers, 30-22 (B)
    49ers, 34-10 (SF)
1961—Colts, 20-17 (B)
    Colts, 27-24 (SF)
1962—49ers, 21-13 (B)
    Colts, 22-3 (SF)
1963—Colts, 20-14 (SF)
    Colts, 20-3 (B)
1964—Colts, 37-7 (B)
    Colts, 14-3 (SF)
1965—Colts, 27-24 (B)
    Colts, 34-28 (SF)
1966—Colts, 36-14 (B)
    Colts, 30-14 (SF)
1967—Colts, 41-7 (B)
    Colts, 26-9 (SF)
1968—Colts, 27-10 (B)
    Colts, 42-14 (SF)
1969—49ers, 24-21 (B)
    49ers, 20-17 (SF)
1972—49ers, 24-21 (SF)
1986—49ers, 35-14 (SF)
1989—49ers, 30-24 (I)
1995—Colts, 18-17 (I)
1998—49ers, 34-31 (I)
2001—49ers, 40-21 (I)
2005—Colts, 28-3 (SF)
2009—Colts, 18-14 (I)
(RS Pts.—Colts 990, 49ers 836)
*Franchise in Baltimore prior to 1984
INDIANAPOLIS vs. SEATTLE
RS: Colts lead series, 6-4
1977—Colts, 29-14 (S)
1978—Colts, 17-14 (S)
1991—Seahawks, 31-3 (S)

ALL-TIME TEAM VS. TEAM RESULTS

1994—Colts, 17-15 (I)
  Colts, 31-19 (S)
1997—Seahawks, 31-3 (I)
1998—Seahawks, 27-23 (S)
2000—Colts, 37-24 (S)
2005—Seahawks, 28-13 (S)
2009—Colts, 34-17 (I)
(RS Pts.—Seahawks 220, Colts 207)
*Franchise in Baltimore prior to 1984
INDIANAPOLIS vs. TAMPA BAY
RS: Colts lead series, 7-5
1976—Colts, 42-17 (B)
1979—Buccaneers, 29-26 (B) OT
1985—Colts, 31-23 (TB)
1987—Colts, 24-6 (I)
1988—Colts, 35-31 (I)
1991—Buccaneers, 17-3 (TB)
1992—Colts, 24-14 (TB)
1994—Buccaneers, 24-10 (TB)
1997—Buccaneers, 31-28 (I)
2003—Colts, 38-35 (TB) OT
2007—Colts, 33-14 (I)
2011—Buccaneers, 24-17 (TB)
(RS Pts.—Colts 311, Buccaneers 265)
*Franchise in Baltimore prior to 1984
INDIANAPOLIS vs. **TENNESSEE
RS: Colts lead series, 21-13
PS: Titans lead series, 1-0
1970—Colts, 24-20 (H)
1973—Oilers, 31-27 (B)
1976—Colts, 38-14 (B)
1979—Oilers, 28-16 (B)
1980—Oilers, 21-16 (H)
1983—Colts, 20-10 (B)
1984—Oilers, 35-21 (H)
1985—Colts, 34-16 (I)
1986—Oilers, 31-17 (H)
1987—Oilers, 51-27 (I)
1988—Oilers, 17-14 (I) OT
1990—Oilers, 24-10 (H)
1992—Oilers, 20-10 (I)
1994—Colts, 45-21 (I)
1999—***Titans, 19-16 (I)
2002—Titans, 23-15 (I)
  Titans, 27-17 (T)
2003—Colts, 33-7 (I)
  Colts, 29-27 (T)
2004—Colts, 31-17 (T)
  Colts, 51-24 (I)
2005—Colts, 31-10 (T)
  Colts, 35-3 (I)
2006—Colts, 14-13 (I)
  Titans, 20-17 (T)
2007—Colts, 22-20 (T)
  Titans, 16-10 (I)
2008—Titans, 31-21 (T)
  Colts, 23-0 (I)
2009—Colts, 31-9 (T)
  Colts, 27-17 (I)
2010—Colts, 30-28 (T)
  Colts, 23-20 (I)
2011—Titans, 27-10 (T)
  Colts, 27-13 (I)
(RS Pts.—Colts 854, Titans 653)
(PS Pts.—Titans 19, Colts 16)
*Franchise in Baltimore prior to 1984
**Franchise in Houston prior to 1997;
known as Oilers prior to 1999
***AFC Divisional Playoff
INDIANAPOLIS vs. WASHINGTON
RS: Colts lead series, 19-10
1953—Colts, 27-17 (B)

1954—Redskins, 24-21 (W)
1955—Redskins, 14-13 (B)
1956—Colts, 19-17 (B)
1957—Colts, 21-17 (W)
1958—Colts, 35-10 (B)
1959—Redskins, 27-24 (W)
1960—Colts, 20-0 (B)
1961—Colts, 27-6 (W)
1962—Colts, 34-21 (B)
1963—Colts, 36-20 (W)
1964—Colts, 45-17 (B)
1965—Colts, 38-7 (W)
1966—Colts, 37-10 (B)
1967—Colts, 17-13 (W)
1969—Colts, 41-17 (B)
1973—Redskins, 22-14 (W)
1977—Colts, 10-3 (B)
1978—Colts, 21-17 (B)
1981—Redskins, 38-14 (W)
1984—Redskins, 35-7 (I)
1990—Colts, 35-28 (I)
1993—Redskins, 30-24 (W)
1994—Redskins, 41-27 (I)
1996—Redskins, 31-16 (W)
1999—Colts, 24-21 (I)
2002—Redskins, 26-21 (W)
2006—Colts, 36-22 (I)
2010—Colts, 27-24 (W)
(RS Pts.—Colts 731, Redskins 575)
*Franchise in Baltimore prior to 1984

JACKSONVILLE vs. ARIZONA
RS: Jaguars lead series, 2-1;
See Arizona vs. Jacksonville
JACKSONVILLE vs. ATLANTA
RS: Jaguars lead series, 3-2;
See Atlanta vs. Jacksonville
JACKSONVILLE vs. BALTIMORE
RS: Jaguars lead series, 10-7;
See Baltimore vs. Jacksonville
JACKSONVILLE vs. BUFFALO
RS: Series tied, 5-5
PS: Jaguars lead series, 1-0;
See Buffalo vs. Jacksonville
JACKSONVILLE vs. CAROLINA
RS: Jaguars lead series, 3-2;
See Carolina vs. Jacksonville
JACKSONVILLE vs. CHICAGO
RS: Bears lead series, 3-2;
See Chicago vs. Jacksonville
JACKSONVILLE vs. CINCINNATI
RS: Jaguars lead series, 11-7;
See Cincinnati vs. Jacksonville
JACKSONVILLE vs. CLEVELAND
RS: Jaguars lead series, 9-5;
See Cleveland vs. Jacksonville
JACKSONVILLE vs. DALLAS
RS: Jaguars lead series, 3-2;
See Dallas vs. Jacksonville
JACKSONVILLE vs. DENVER
RS: Jaguars lead series, 5-3
PS: Series tied, 1-1;
See Denver vs. Jacksonville
JACKSONVILLE vs. DETROIT
RS: Jaguars lead series, 3-1;
See Detroit vs. Jacksonville
JACKSONVILLE vs. GREEN BAY
RS: Series tied, 2-2;
See Green Bay vs. Jacksonville
JACKSONVILLE vs. HOUSTON
RS: Texans lead series, 11-9;
See Houston vs. Jacksonville

JACKSONVILLE vs. INDIANAPOLIS
RS: Colts lead series, 15-7;
See Indianapolis vs. Jacksonville
JACKSONVILLE vs. KANSAS CITY
RS: Jaguars lead series, 6-3
1997—Jaguars, 24-10 (J)
1998—Jaguars, 21-16 (J)
2001—Chiefs, 30-26 (J)
2002—Jaguars, 23-16 (KC)
2004—Jaguars, 22-16 (J)
2006—Chiefs, 35-30 (KC)
2007—Jaguars, 17-7 (KC)
2009—Jaguars, 24-21 (J)
2010—Chiefs, 42-20 (KC)
(RS Pts.—Jaguars 207, Chiefs 193)
JACKSONVILLE vs. MIAMI
RS: Series tied, 2-2
PS: Jaguars lead series, 1-0
1998—Jaguars, 28-21 (J)
1999—*Jaguars, 62-7 (J)
2003—Dolphins, 24-10 (J)
2006—Jaguars, 24-10 (M)
2009—Dolphins, 14-10 (J)
(RS Pts.—Jaguars 72, Dolphins 69)
(PS Pts.—Jaguars 62, Dolphins 7)
*AFC Divisional Playoff
JACKSONVILLE vs. MINNESOTA
RS: Vikings lead series, 3-1
1998—Vikings, 50-10 (M)
2001—Jaguars, 33-3 (M)
2004—Vikings, 27-16 (M)
2008—Vikings, 30-12 (J)
(RS Pts.—Vikings 110, Jaguars 71)
JACKSONVILLE vs. NEW ENGLAND
RS: Patriots lead series, 5-0
PS: Patriots lead series, 3-1
1996—Patriots, 28-25 (NE) OT
  *Patriots, 20-6 (NE)
1997—Patriots, 26-20 (J)
1998—**Jaguars, 25-10 (J)
2003—Patriots, 27-13 (NE)
2005—**Patriots, 28-3 (NE)
2006—Patriots, 24-21 (J)
2007—***Patriots, 31-20 (NE)
2009—Patriots, 35-7 (NE)
(RS Pts.—Patriots 140, Jaguars 86)
(PS Pts.—Patriots 89, Jaguars 54)
*AFC Championship
**AFC First-Round Playoff
***AFC Divisional Playoff
JACKSONVILLE vs. NEW ORLEANS
RS: Saints lead series, 3-2
1996—Saints, 17-13 (NO)
1999—Jaguars, 41-23 (J)
2003—Jaguars, 20-19 (J)
2007—Saints, 41-24 (NO)
2011—Saints, 23-10 (J)
(RS Pts.—Saints 123, Jaguars 108)
JACKSONVILLE vs. N.Y. GIANTS
RS: Giants lead series, 3-2
1997—Jaguars, 40-13 (J)
2000—Giants, 28-25 (NY)
2002—Giants, 24-17 (NY)
2006—Jaguars, 26-10 (J)
2010—Giants, 24-20 (NY)
(RS Pts.—Jaguars 128, Giants 99)
JACKSONVILLE vs. N.Y. JETS
RS: Jaguars lead series, 6-3
PS: Jets lead series, 1-0
1995—Jets, 27-10 (NY)
1996—Jaguars, 21-17 (J)
1998—*Jets, 34-24 (NY)

1999—Jaguars, 16-6 (NY)
2002—Jaguars, 28-3 (J)
2003—Jets, 13-10 (NY)
2005—Jaguars, 26-20 (NY) OT
2006—Jaguars, 41-0 (J)
2009—Jaguars, 24-22 (NY)
2011—Jets, 32-3 (NY)
(RS Pts.—Jaguars 179, Jets 140)
(PS Pts.—Jets 34, Jaguars 24)
*AFC Divisional Playoff
JACKSONVILLE vs. OAKLAND
RS: Jaguars lead series, 4-1
1996—Raiders, 17-3 (O)
1997—Jaguars, 20-9 (O)
2004—Jaguars, 13-6 (O)
2007—Jaguars, 49-11 (J)
2010—Jaguars, 38-31 (J)
(RS Pts.—Jaguars 123, Raiders 74)
JACKSONVILLE vs. PHILADELPHIA
RS: Jaguars lead series, 3-1
1997—Jaguars, 38-21 (J)
2002—Jaguars, 28-25 (J)
2006—Jaguars, 13-6 (P)
2010—Eagles, 28-3 (J)
(RS Pts.—Jaguars 82, Eagles 80)
JACKSONVILLE vs. PITTSBURGH
RS: Jaguars lead series, 11-10
PS: Jaguars lead series, 1-0
1995—Jaguars, 20-16 (J)
　　　Steelers, 24-7 (P)
1996—Jaguars, 24-9 (J)
　　　Steelers, 28-3 (P)
1997—Jaguars, 30-21 (J)
　　　Steelers, 23-17 (P) OT
1998—Steelers, 30-15 (P)
　　　Jaguars, 21-3 (J)
1999—Jaguars, 17-3 (P)
　　　Jaguars, 20-6 (J)
2000—Steelers, 24-13 (J)
　　　Jaguars, 34-24 (P)
2001—Jaguars, 21-3 (J)
　　　Steelers, 20-7 (P)
2002—Steelers, 25-23 (J)
2004—Steelers, 17-16 (J)
2005—Jaguars, 23-17 (P) OT
2006—Jaguars, 9-0 (J)
2007—Steelers, 29-22 (P)
　　　*Jaguars, 31-29 (P)
2008—Steelers, 26-21 (J)
2011—Steelers, 17-13 (P)
(RS Pts.—Jaguars 383, Steelers 358)
(PS Pts.—Jaguars 31, Steelers 29)
*AFC First-Round Playoff
JACKSONVILLE vs. ST. LOUIS
RS: Rams lead series, 2-1
1996—Rams, 17-14 (StL)
2005—Rams, 24-21 (StL)
2009—Jaguars, 23-20 (J) OT
(RS Pts.—Rams 61, Jaguars 58)
JACKSONVILLE vs. SAN DIEGO
RS: Chargers lead series, 3-2
2003—Jaguars, 27-21 (J)
2004—Chargers, 34-21 (SD)
2007—Jaguars, 24-17 (J)
2010—Chargers, 38-13 (SD)
2011—Chargers, 38-14 (J)
(RS Pts.—Chargers 148, Jaguars 99)
JACKSONVILLE vs. SAN FRANCISCO
RS: Jaguars lead series, 2-1
1999—Jaguars, 41-3 (J)
2005—Jaguars, 10-9 (J)
2009—49ers, 20-3 (SF)

(RS Pts.—Jaguars 54, 49ers 32)
JACKSONVILLE vs. SEATTLE
RS: Seahawks lead series, 4-2
1995—Seahawks, 47-30 (J)
1996—Jaguars, 20-13 (J)
2000—Seahawks, 28-21 (J)
2001—Seahawks, 24-15 (S)
2005—Jaguars, 26-14 (J)
2009—Seahawks, 41-0 (S)
(RS Pts.—Seahawks 167, Jaguars 112)
JACKSONVILLE vs. TAMPA BAY
RS: Jaguars lead series, 4-1
1995—Buccaneers, 17-16 (TB)
1998—Jaguars, 29-24 (J)
2003—Jaguars, 17-10 (J)
2007—Jaguars, 24-23 (TB)
2011—Jaguars, 41-14 (J)
(RS Pts.—Jaguars 127, Buccaneers 88)
JACKSONVILLE vs. *TENNESSEE
RS: Titans lead series, 19-15
PS: Titans lead, 1-0
1995—Oilers, 10-3 (J)
　　　Jaguars, 17-16 (H)
1996—Oilers, 34-27 (J)
　　　Jaguars, 23-17 (H)
1997—Jaguars, 30-24 (T)
　　　Jaguars, 17-9 (J)
1998—Jaguars, 27-22 (T)
　　　Oilers, 16-13 (J)
1999—Titans, 20-19 (J)
　　　Titans, 41-14 (T)
　　　**Titans, 33-14 (J)
2000—Titans, 27-13 (T)
　　　Jaguars, 16-13 (J)
2001—Jaguars, 13-6 (J)
　　　Titans, 28-24 (T)
2002—Titans, 23-14 (T)
　　　Titans, 28-10 (J)
2003—Titans, 30-17 (J)
　　　Titans, 10-3 (T)
2004—Jaguars, 15-12 (T)
　　　Titans, 18-15 (J)
2005—Jaguars, 31-28 (T)
　　　Jaguars, 40-13 (J)
2006—Jaguars, 37-7 (J)
　　　Titans, 24-17 (T)
2007—Titans, 13-10 (J)
　　　Jaguars, 28-13 (T)
2008—Titans, 17-10 (T)
　　　Titans, 24-14 (J)
2009—Jaguars, 37-17 (J)
　　　Titans, 30-13 (T)
2010—Titans, 30-3 (J)
　　　Jaguars, 17-6 (T)
2011—Jaguars, 16-14 (J)
　　　Titans, 23-17 (T)
(RS Pts.—Titans 663, Jaguars 620)
(PS Pts.—Titans 33, Jaguars 14)
*Franchise in Houston prior to 1997;
known as Oilers prior to 1999
**AFC Championship
JACKSONVILLE vs. WASHINGTON
RS: Redskins lead series, 4-1
1997—Redskins, 24-12 (W)
2000—Redskins, 35-16 (J)
2002—Jaguars, 26-7 (J)
2006—Redskins, 36-30 (W) OT
2010—Redskins, 20-17 (J) OT
(RS Pts.—Redskins 122, Jaguars 101)

KANSAS CITY vs. ARIZONA
RS: Chiefs lead series, 8-2-1;

See Arizona vs. Kansas City
KANSAS CITY vs. ATLANTA
RS: Chiefs lead series, 5-2;
See Atlanta vs. Kansas City
KANSAS CITY vs. BALTIMORE
RS: Chiefs lead series, 3-2
PS: Ravens lead series, 1-0;
See Baltimore vs. Kansas City
KANSAS CITY vs. BUFFALO
RS: Bills lead series, 22-17-1
PS: Bills lead series, 2-1;
See Buffalo vs. Kansas City
KANSAS CITY vs. CAROLINA
RS: Series tied, 2-2
See Carolina vs. Kansas City
KANSAS CITY vs. CHICAGO
RS: Bears lead series, 6-5;
See Chicago vs. Kansas City
KANSAS CITY vs. CINCINNATI
RS: Series tied, 13-13;
See Cincinnati vs. Kansas City
KANSAS CITY vs. CLEVELAND
RS: Series tied, 10-10-2;
See Cleveland vs. Kansas City
KANSAS CITY vs. DALLAS
RS: Cowboys lead series, 6-3;
See Dallas vs. Kansas City
KANSAS CITY vs. DENVER
RS: Chiefs lead series, 56-47
PS: Broncos lead series, 1-0;
See Denver vs. Kansas City
KANSAS CITY vs. DETROIT
RS: Chiefs lead series, 7-5;
See Detroit vs. Kansas City
KANSAS CITY vs. GREEN BAY
RS: Chiefs lead series, 7-2-1
PS: Packers lead series, 1-0;
See Green Bay vs. Kansas City
KANSAS CITY vs. HOUSTON
RS: Texans lead series, 3-2;
See Houston vs. Kansas City
KANSAS CITY vs. INDIANAPOLIS
RS: Colts lead series, 10-8
PS: Colts lead series, 3-0;
See Indianapolis vs. Kansas City
KANSAS CITY vs. JACKSONVILLE
RS: Jaguars lead series, 6-3;
See Jacksonville vs. Kansas City
KANSAS CITY vs. MIAMI
RS: Dolphins lead series, 13-12
PS: Dolphins lead series, 3-0
1966—Chiefs, 34-16 (KC)
　　　Chiefs, 19-18 (M)
1967—Chiefs, 24-0 (M)
　　　Chiefs, 41-0 (KC)
1968—Chiefs, 48-3 (M)
1969—Chiefs, 17-10 (KC)
1971—*Dolphins, 27-24 (KC) OT
1972—Dolphins, 20-10 (KC)
1974—Dolphins, 9-3 (M)
1976—Chiefs, 20-17 (M) OT
1981—Dolphins, 17-7 (KC)
1983—Dolphins, 14-6 (M)
1985—Dolphins, 31-0 (M)
1987—Dolphins, 42-0 (M)
1989—Chiefs, 26-21 (KC)
　　　Chiefs, 27-24 (M)
1990—**Dolphins, 17-16 (M)
1991—Chiefs, 42-7 (KC)
1993—Dolphins, 30-10 (M)
1994—Dolphins, 45-28 (M)
　　　**Dolphins, 27-17 (M)

1995—Dolphins, 13-6 (M)
1997—Dolphins, 17-14 (M)
2002—Chiefs, 48-30 (KC)
2005—Chiefs, 30-20 (M)
2006—Dolphins, 13-10 (M)
2008—Dolphins, 38-31 (KC)
2011—Dolphins, 31-3 (KC)
(RS Pts.—Chiefs 504, Dolphins 486)
(PS Pts.—Dolphins 71, Chiefs 57)
*AFC Divisional Playoff
**AFC First-Round Playoff
KANSAS CITY vs. MINNESOTA
RS: Chiefs lead series, 6-4
PS: Chiefs lead series, 1-0
1969—*Chiefs, 23-7 (New Orleans)
1970—Vikings, 27-10 (M)
1974—Vikings, 35-15 (KC)
1981—Chiefs, 10-6 (M)
1990—Chiefs, 24-21 (KC)
1993—Vikings, 30-10 (M)
1996—Chiefs, 21-6 (M)
1999—Chiefs, 31-28 (KC)
2003—Vikings, 45-20 (M)
2007—Chiefs, 13-10 (KC)
2011—Chiefs, 22-17 (KC)
(RS Pts.—Vikings 225, Chiefs 176)
(PS Pts.—Chiefs 23, Vikings 7)
*Super Bowl IV
KANSAS CITY vs. **NEW ENGLAND
RS: Chiefs lead series, 16-13-3
1960—Patriots, 42-14 (B)
Texans, 34-0 (D)
1961—Patriots, 18-17 (D)
Patriots, 28-21 (B)
1962—Texans, 42-28 (D)
Texans, 27-7 (B)
1963—Tie, 24-24 (B)
Chiefs, 35-3 (KC)
1964—Patriots, 24-7 (B)
Patriots, 31-24 (KC)
1965—Chiefs, 27-17 (KC)
Tie, 10-10 (B)
1966—Chiefs, 43-24 (B)
Tie, 27-27 (KC)
1967—Chiefs, 33-10 (B)
1968—Chiefs, 31-17 (KC)
1969—Chiefs, 31-0 (B)
1970—Chiefs, 23-10 (KC)
1973—Chiefs, 10-7 (NE)
1977—Patriots, 21-17 (NE)
1981—Patriots, 33-17 (NE)
1990—Chiefs, 37-7 (NE)
1992—Chiefs, 27-20 (KC)
1995—Chiefs, 31-26 (KC)
1998—Patriots, 40-10 (NE)
1999—Chiefs, 16-14 (KC)
2000—Patriots, 30-24 (NE)
2002—Patriots, 41-38 (NE) OT
2004—Patriots, 27-19 (KC)
2005—Chiefs, 26-16 (KC)
2008—Patriots, 17-10 (NE)
2011—Patriots, 34-3 (NE)
(RS Pts.—Chiefs 755, Patriots 653)
*Franchise located in Dallas prior to 1963 and known as Texans
**Franchise in Boston prior to 1971
KANSAS CITY vs. NEW ORLEANS
RS: Saints lead series, 5-4
1972—Chiefs, 20-17 (NO)
1976—Saints, 27-17 (KC)
1982—Saints, 27-17 (NO)
1985—Chiefs, 47-27 (NO)

1991—Saints, 17-10 (KC)
1994—Chiefs, 30-17 (NO)
1997—Chiefs, 25-13 (KC)
2004—Saints, 27-20 (NO)
2008—Saints, 30-20 (KC)
(RS Pts.—Chiefs 206, Saints 202)
KANSAS CITY vs. N.Y. GIANTS
RS: Giants lead series, 10-2
1974—Giants, 33-27 (KC)
1978—Giants, 26-10 (NY)
1979—Giants, 21-17 (KC)
1983—Chiefs, 38-17 (KC)
1984—Giants, 28-27 (NY)
1988—Giants, 28-12 (NY)
1992—Giants, 35-21 (NY)
1995—Chiefs, 20-17 (KC) OT
1998—Giants, 28-7 (NY)
2001—Giants, 13-3 (KC)
2005—Giants, 27-17 (NY)
2009—Giants, 27-16 (KC)
(RS Pts.—Giants 300, Chiefs 215)
KANSAS CITY vs. **N.Y. JETS
RS: Jets lead series, 17-16-1
PS: Series tied, 1-1
1960—Titans, 37-35 (D)
Titans, 41-35 (NY)
1961—Titans, 28-7 (NY)
Texans, 35-24 (D)
1962—Texans, 20-17 (D)
Texans, 52-31 (NY)
1963—Jets, 17-0 (NY)
Chiefs, 48-0 (KC)
1964—Jets, 27-14 (NY)
Chiefs, 24-7 (KC)
1965—Chiefs, 14-10 (NY)
Jets, 13-10 (KC)
1966—Chiefs, 32-24 (NY)
1967—Chiefs, 42-18 (KC)
Chiefs, 21-7 (NY)
1968—Jets, 20-19 (KC)
1969—Chiefs, 34-16 (NY)
***Chiefs, 13-6 (NY)
1971—Jets, 13-10 (NY)
1974—Chiefs, 24-16 (KC)
1975—Jets, 30-24 (KC)
1982—Chiefs, 37-13 (KC)
1984—Chiefs, 17-16 (KC)
Jets, 28-7 (NY)
1986—****Jets, 35-15 (NY)
1987—Jets, 16-9 (KC)
1988—Tie, 17-17 (NY)
Chiefs, 38-34 (KC)
1992—Chiefs, 23-7 (NY)
1998—Jets, 20-17 (KC)
2001—Jets, 27-7 (NY)
2002—Chiefs, 29-25 (NY)
2005—Chiefs, 27-7 (KC)
2007—Jets, 13-10 (NY) OT
2008—Jets, 28-24 (NY)
2011—Jets, 37-10 (NY)
(RS Pts.—Chiefs 771, Jets 685)
(PS Pts.—Jets 41, Chiefs 28)
*Franchise in Dallas prior to 1963 and known as Texans
**Jets known as Titans prior to 1963
***Inter-Divisional Playoff
****AFC First-Round Playoff
KANSAS CITY vs. **OAKLAND
RS: Chiefs lead series, 53-48-2
PS: Chiefs lead series, 2-1
1960—Texans, 34-16 (O)
Raiders, 20-19 (D)

1961—Texans, 42-35 (O)
Texans, 43-11 (D)
1962—Texans, 26-16 (O)
Texans, 35-7 (D)
1963—Raiders, 10-7 (O)
Raiders, 22-7 (KC)
1964—Chiefs, 21-9 (O)
Chiefs, 42-7 (KC)
1965—Raiders, 37-10 (O)
Chiefs, 14-7 (KC)
1966—Chiefs, 32-10 (O)
Raiders, 34-13 (KC)
1967—Raiders, 23-21 (O)
Raiders, 44-22 (KC)
1968—Chiefs, 24-10 (KC)
Raiders, 38-21 (O)
***Raiders, 41-6 (O)
1969—Raiders, 27-24 (KC)
Raiders, 10-6 (O)
****Chiefs, 17-7 (O)
1970—Tie, 17-17 (KC)
Raiders, 20-6 (O)
1971—Tie, 20-20 (O)
Chiefs, 16-14 (KC)
1972—Chiefs, 27-14 (KC)
Raiders, 26-3 (O)
1973—Chiefs, 16-3 (KC)
Raiders, 37-7 (O)
1974—Raiders, 27-7 (O)
Raiders, 7-6 (KC)
1975—Chiefs, 42-10 (KC)
Raiders, 28-20 (O)
1976—Raiders, 24-21 (KC)
Raiders, 21-10 (O)
1977—Raiders, 37-28 (KC)
Raiders, 21-20 (O)
1978—Raiders, 28-6 (O)
Raiders, 20-10 (KC)
1979—Chiefs, 35-7 (O)
Chiefs, 24-21 (O)
1980—Raiders, 27-14 (KC)
Chiefs, 31-17 (O)
1981—Chiefs, 27-0 (KC)
Chiefs, 28-17 (O)
1982—Raiders, 21-16 (KC)
1983—Raiders, 21-20 (LA)
Raiders, 28-20 (KC)
1984—Raiders, 22-20 (KC)
Raiders, 17-7 (LA)
1985—Chiefs, 36-20 (KC)
Raiders, 19-10 (LA)
1986—Raiders, 24-17 (KC)
Chiefs, 20-17 (LA)
1987—Raiders, 35-17 (LA)
Chiefs, 16-10 (KC)
1988—Chiefs, 27-17 (KC)
Raiders, 17-10 (LA)
1989—Chiefs, 24-19 (KC)
Raiders, 20-14 (LA)
1990—Chiefs, 9-7 (KC)
Chiefs, 27-24 (LA)
1991—Chiefs, 24-21 (KC)
Chiefs, 27-21 (LA)
*****Chiefs, 10-6 (KC)
1992—Chiefs, 27-7 (KC)
Raiders, 28-7 (LA)
1993—Chiefs, 24-9 (KC)
Chiefs, 31-20 (LA)
1994—Chiefs, 13-3 (KC)
Chiefs, 19-9 (LA)
1995—Chiefs, 23-17 (KC) OT
Chiefs, 29-23 (O)

1996—Chiefs, 19-3 (KC)
    Raiders, 26-7 (O)
1997—Chiefs, 28-27 (O)
    Chiefs, 30-0 (KC)
1998—Chiefs, 28-8 (KC)
    Chiefs, 31-24 (O)
1999—Chiefs, 37-34 (O)
    Raiders, 41-38 (KC) OT
2000—Raiders, 20-17 (KC)
    Raiders, 49-31 (O)
2001—Raiders, 27-24 (KC)
    Raiders, 28-26 (O)
2002—Chiefs, 20-10 (KC)
    Raiders, 24-0 (O)
2003—Chiefs, 17-10 (O)
    Chiefs, 27-24 (KC)
2004—Chiefs, 34-27 (O)
    Chiefs, 31-30 (KC)
2005—Chiefs, 23-17 (O)
    Chiefs, 27-23 (KC)
2006—Chiefs, 17-13 (KC)
    Chiefs, 20-9 (O)
2007—Chiefs, 12-10 (O)
    Raiders, 20-17 (KC)
2008—Raiders, 23-8 (KC)
    Chiefs, 20-13 (O)
2009—Raiders, 13-10 (KC)
    Chiefs, 16-10 (O)
2010—Raiders, 23-20 (O) OT
    Raiders, 31-10 (KC)
2011—Chiefs, 28-0 (O)
    Raiders, 16-13 (KC) OT
(RS Pts.—Chiefs 2,114, Raiders 1,995)
(PS Pts.—Raiders 54, Chiefs 33)
*Franchise in Dallas prior to 1963 and known as Texans
**Franchise in Los Angeles from 1982-1994
***Division Playoff
****AFL Championship
*****AFC First-Round Playoff
KANSAS CITY vs. PHILADELPHIA
RS: Eagles lead series, 4-2
1972—Eagles, 21-20 (KC)
1992—Chiefs, 24-17 (KC)
1998—Chiefs, 24-21 (P)
2001—Eagles, 23-10 (KC)
2005—Eagles, 37-31 (KC)
2009—Eagles, 34-14 (P)
(RS Pts.—Eagles 153, Chiefs 123)
KANSAS CITY vs. PITTSBURGH
RS: Steelers lead series, 18-9
PS: Chiefs lead series, 1-0
1970—Chiefs, 31-14 (P)
1971—Chiefs, 38-16 (KC)
1972—Steelers, 16-7 (P)
1974—Steelers, 34-24 (KC)
1975—Steelers, 28-3 (P)
1976—Steelers, 45-0 (KC)
1978—Steelers, 27-24 (P)
1979—Steelers, 30-3 (KC)
1980—Steelers, 21-16 (P)
1981—Chiefs, 37-33 (P)
1982—Steelers, 35-14 (P)
1984—Chiefs, 37-27 (P)
1985—Steelers, 36-28 (KC)
1986—Chiefs, 24-19 (P)
1987—Steelers, 17-16 (KC)
1988—Steelers, 16-10 (P)
1989—Steelers, 23-17 (P)
1992—Steelers, 27-3 (KC)
1993—*Chiefs, 27-24 (KC) OT

1996—Steelers, 17-7 (KC)
1997—Chiefs, 13-10 (KC)
1998—Steelers, 20-13 (KC)
1999—Chiefs, 35-19 (KC)
2001—Steelers, 20-17 (KC)
2003—Chiefs, 41-20 (KC)
2006—Steelers, 45-7 (P)
2009—Chiefs, 27-24 (KC) OT
2011—Steelers, 13-9 (KC)
(RS Pts.—Steelers 652, Chiefs 501)
(PS Pts.—Chiefs 27, Steelers 24)
*AFC First-Round Playoff
KANSAS CITY vs. *ST. LOUIS
RS: Chiefs lead series, 6-4
1973—Rams, 23-13 (KC)
1982—Rams, 20-14 (LA)
1985—Rams, 16-0 (KC)
1991—Chiefs, 27-20 (LA)
1994—Rams, 16-0 (KC)
1997—Chiefs, 28-20 (StL)
2000—Chiefs, 54-34 (KC)
2002—Chiefs, 49-10 (KC)
2006—Chiefs, 31-17 (StL)
2010—Chiefs, 27-13 (StL)
(RS Pts.—Chiefs 243, Rams 189)
*Franchise in Los Angeles prior to 1995
KANSAS CITY vs. **SAN DIEGO
RS: Chiefs lead series, 52-50-1
PS: Chargers lead series, 1-0
1960—Chargers, 21-20 (LA)
    Texans, 17-0 (D)
1961—Chargers, 26-10 (D)
    Chargers, 24-14 (SD)
1962—Chargers, 32-28 (SD)
    Texans, 26-17 (D)
1963—Chargers, 24-10 (SD)
    Chargers, 38-17 (KC)
1964—Chargers, 28-14 (KC)
    Chiefs, 49-6 (SD)
1965—Tie, 10-10 (SD)
    Chiefs, 31-7 (KC)
1966—Chiefs, 24-14 (KC)
    Chiefs, 27-17 (SD)
1967—Chargers, 45-31 (SD)
    Chargers, 17-16 (KC)
1968—Chiefs, 27-20 (KC)
    Chiefs, 40-3 (SD)
1969—Chiefs, 27-9 (SD)
    Chiefs, 27-3 (KC)
1970—Chiefs, 26-14 (KC)
    Chargers, 31-13 (SD)
1971—Chargers, 21-14 (SD)
    Chiefs, 31-10 (KC)
1972—Chiefs, 26-14 (SD)
    Chargers, 27-17 (KC)
1973—Chiefs, 19-0 (SD)
    Chiefs, 33-6 (KC)
1974—Chiefs, 24-14 (SD)
    Chargers, 14-7 (KC)
1975—Chiefs, 12-10 (SD)
    Chargers, 28-20 (KC)
1976—Chiefs, 30-16 (KC)
    Chiefs, 23-20 (SD)
1977—Chargers, 23-7 (KC)
    Chiefs, 21-16 (SD)
1978—Chargers, 29-23 (SD) OT
    Chiefs, 23-0 (KC)
1979—Chargers, 20-14 (KC)
    Chargers, 28-7 (SD)
1980—Chargers, 24-7 (SD)
    Chargers, 20-7 (SD)
1981—Chargers, 42-31 (KC)

    Chargers, 22-20 (SD)
1982—Chiefs, 19-12 (KC)
1983—Chargers, 17-14 (KC)
    Chargers, 41-38 (SD)
1984—Chiefs, 31-13 (KC)
    Chiefs, 42-21 (SD)
1985—Chargers, 31-20 (SD)
    Chiefs, 38-34 (KC)
1986—Chiefs, 42-41 (KC)
    Chiefs, 24-23 (SD)
1987—Chiefs, 20-13 (KC)
    Chargers, 42-21 (SD)
1988—Chargers, 24-23 (KC)
    Chargers, 24-13 (SD)
1989—Chargers, 21-6 (SD)
    Chargers, 20-13 (KC)
1990—Chiefs, 27-10 (KC)
    Chiefs, 24-21 (SD)
1991—Chiefs, 14-13 (SD)
    Chiefs, 20-17 (KC) OT
1992—Chiefs, 24-10 (SD)
    Chiefs, 16-14 (KC)
    ***Chargers, 17-0 (SD)
1993—Chiefs, 17-14 (SD)
    Chiefs, 28-24 (KC)
1994—Chargers, 20-6 (SD)
    Chargers, 14-13 (KC)
1995—Chiefs, 29-23 (KC) OT
    Chiefs, 22-7 (SD)
1996—Chargers, 22-19 (SD)
    Chargers, 28-14 (KC)
1997—Chiefs, 31-3 (KC)
    Chiefs, 29-7 (SD)
1998—Chiefs, 23-7 (KC)
    Chargers, 38-37 (SD)
1999—Chargers, 21-14 (SD)
    Chiefs, 34-0 (KC)
2000—Chiefs, 42-10 (KC)
    Chargers, 17-16 (SD)
2001—Chiefs, 25-20 (SD)
    Chiefs, 20-17 (KC)
2002—Chargers, 35-34 (SD)
    Chiefs, 24-22 (KC)
2003—Chiefs, 27-14 (KC)
    Chiefs, 28-24 (SD)
2004—Chargers, 34-31 (KC)
    Chargers, 24-17 (SD)
2005—Chargers, 28-20 (SD)
    Chiefs, 20-7 (KC)
2006—Chiefs, 30-27 (KC)
    Chargers, 20-9 (SD)
2007—Chiefs, 30-16 (KC)
    Chargers, 24-10 (KC)
2008—Chargers, 20-19 (SD)
    Chargers, 22-21 (KC)
2009—Chargers, 37-7 (KC)
    Chargers, 43-14 (SD)
2010—Chiefs, 21-14 (KC)
    Chargers, 31-0 (SD)
2011—Chargers, 20-17 (SD)
    Chiefs, 23-20 (KC) OT
(RS Pts.—Chiefs 2,216, Chargers 2,060)
(PS Pts.—Chargers 17, Chiefs 0)
*Franchise in Dallas prior to 1963 and known as Texans
**Franchise in Los Angeles prior to 1961
***AFC First-Round Playoff
KANSAS CITY vs. SAN FRANCISCO
RS: 49ers lead series, 6-5
1971—Chiefs, 26-17 (SF)
1975—49ers, 20-3 (KC)
1982—49ers, 26-13 (KC)

1985—49ers, 31-3 (SF)
1991—49ers, 28-14 (SF)
1994—Chiefs, 24-17 (KC)
1997—Chiefs, 44-9 (KC)
2000—49ers, 21-7 (SF)
2002—Chiefs, 17-13 (SF)
2006—Chiefs, 41-10 (KC)
2010—Chiefs, 31-10 (KC)
(PS Pts.—Chiefs 219, 49ers 196)
KANSAS CITY vs. SEATTLE
RS: Chiefs lead series, 32-18
1977—Seahawks, 34-31 (KC)
1978—Seahawks, 13-10 (KC)
        Seahawks, 23-19 (S)
1979—Chiefs, 24-6 (S)
        Chiefs, 37-21 (KC)
1980—Seahawks, 17-16 (KC)
        Chiefs, 31-30 (S)
1981—Chiefs, 20-14 (S)
        Chiefs, 40-13 (KC)
1983—Chiefs, 17-13 (KC)
        Seahawks, 51-48 (S) OT
1984—Seahawks, 45-0 (S)
        Chiefs, 34-7 (KC)
1985—Chiefs, 28-7 (KC)
        Seahawks, 24-6 (S)
1986—Seahawks, 23-17 (S)
        Chiefs, 27-7 (KC)
1987—Seahawks, 43-14 (S)
        Chiefs, 41-20 (KC)
1988—Seahawks, 31-10 (S)
        Chiefs, 27-24 (KC)
1989—Chiefs, 20-16 (S)
        Chiefs, 20-10 (KC)
1990—Chiefs, 19-7 (S)
        Seahawks, 17-16 (KC)
1991—Chiefs, 20-13 (KC)
        Chiefs, 19-6 (S)
1992—Chiefs, 26-7 (KC)
        Chiefs, 24-14 (S)
1993—Chiefs, 31-16 (S)
        Chiefs, 34-24 (KC)
1994—Chiefs, 38-23 (KC)
        Seahawks, 10-9 (S)
1995—Chiefs, 34-10 (S)
        Chiefs, 26-3 (KC)
1996—Chiefs, 35-17 (S)
        Chiefs, 34-16 (KC)
1997—Chiefs, 20-17 (KC) OT
        Chiefs, 19-14 (S)
1998—Chiefs, 17-6 (KC)
        Seahawks, 24-12 (S)
1999—Seahawks, 31-19 (KC)
        Seahawks, 23-14 (S)
2000—Chiefs, 24-17 (KC)
        Chiefs, 24-19 (S)
2001—Chiefs, 19-7 (KC)
        Seahawks, 21-18 (S)
2002—Seahawks, 39-32 (S)
2006—Chiefs, 35-28 (KC)
2010—Chiefs, 42-24 (S)
(RS Pts.—Chiefs 1,185, Seahawks 957)
KANSAS CITY vs. TAMPA BAY
RS: Series tied, 5-5
1976—Chiefs, 28-19 (TB)
1978—Buccaneers, 30-13 (KC)
1979—Buccaneers, 3-0 (TB)
1981—Chiefs, 19-10 (KC)
1984—Chiefs, 24-20 (KC)
1986—Chiefs, 27-20 (KC)
1993—Chiefs, 27-3 (TB)
1999—Buccaneers, 17-10 (TB)

2004—Buccaneers, 34-31 (TB)
2008—Buccaneers, 30-27 (KC) OT
(RS Pts.—Chiefs 206, Buccaneers 186)
*****KANSAS CITY vs. **TENNESSEE**
RS: Chiefs lead series, 26-20
PS: Chiefs lead series, 2-0
1960—Oilers, 20-10 (H)
        Texans, 24-0 (D)
1961—Texans, 26-21 (D)
        Oilers, 38-7 (H)
1962—Texans, 31-7 (H)
        Oilers, 14-6 (D)
        ***Texans, 20-17 (H) OT
1963—Chiefs, 28-7 (KC)
        Oilers, 28-7 (H)
1964—Chiefs, 28-7 (KC)
        Chiefs, 28-19 (H)
1965—Chiefs, 52-21 (KC)
        Oilers, 38-36 (H)
1966—Chiefs, 48-23 (KC)
1967—Chiefs, 25-20 (KC)
        Oilers, 24-19 (KC)
1968—Chiefs, 26-21 (H)
        Chiefs, 24-10 (KC)
1969—Chiefs, 24-0 (KC)
1970—Chiefs, 24-9 (KC)
1971—Chiefs, 20-16 (H)
1973—Chiefs, 38-14 (KC)
1974—Chiefs, 17-7 (H)
1975—Oilers, 17-13 (KC)
1977—Oilers, 34-20 (H)
1978—Oilers, 20-17 (KC)
1979—Oilers, 20-6 (H)
1980—Chiefs, 21-20 (KC)
1981—Chiefs, 23-10 (KC)
1983—Chiefs, 13-10 (H) OT
1984—Oilers, 17-16 (KC)
1985—Oilers, 23-20 (H)
1986—Oilers, 27-13 (KC)
1988—Oilers, 7-6 (H)
1989—Chiefs, 34-0 (KC)
1990—Oilers, 27-10 (KC)
1991—Oilers, 17-7 (H)
1992—Oilers, 23-20 (H) OT
1993—Oilers, 30-0 (H)
        ****Chiefs, 28-20 (H)
1994—Chiefs, 31-9 (KC)
1995—Chiefs, 20-13 (KC)
1996—Chiefs, 20-19 (H)
2000—Titans, 17-14 (T) OT
2004—Chiefs, 49-38 (T)
2007—Titans, 26-17 (KC)
2008—Titans, 34-10 (KC)
2010—Chiefs, 34-14 (KC)
(RS Pts.—Chiefs 996, Titans 822)
(PS Pts.—Chiefs 48, Titans 37)
*Franchise in Dallas prior to 1963 and known as Texans
**Franchise in Houston prior to 1997; known as Oilers prior to 1999
***AFL Championship
****AFC Divisional Playoff
KANSAS CITY vs. WASHINGTON
RS: Chiefs lead series, 7-1
1971—Chiefs, 27-20 (KC)
1976—Chiefs, 33-30 (W)
1983—Redskins, 27-12 (W)
1992—Chiefs, 35-16 (KC)
1995—Chiefs, 24-3 (KC)
2001—Chiefs, 45-13 (W)
2005—Chiefs, 28-21, (KC)
2009—Chiefs, 14-6 (W)

(RS Pts.—Chiefs 218, Redskins 136)

MIAMI vs. ARIZONA
RS: Dolphins lead series, 8-2;
See Arizona vs. Miami
MIAMI vs. ATLANTA
RS: Dolphins lead series, 7-4;
See Atlanta vs. Miami
MIAMI vs. BALTIMORE
RS: Dolphins lead series, 5-3
PS: Ravens lead series, 2-0;
See Baltimore vs. Miami
MIAMI vs. BUFFALO
RS: Dolphins lead series, 55-36-1
PS: Bills lead series, 3-1;
See Buffalo vs. Miami
MIAMI vs. CAROLINA
RS: Dolphins lead series, 4-0;
See Carolina vs. Miami
MIAMI vs. CHICAGO
RS: Dolphins lead series, 7-4;
See Chicago vs. Miami
MIAMI vs. CINCINNATI
RS: Dolphins lead series, 13-5
PS: Dolphins lead series, 1-0;
See Cincinnati vs. Miami
MIAMI vs. CLEVELAND
RS: Browns lead series, 8-7
PS: Dolphins lead series, 2-0;
See Cleveland vs. Miami
MIAMI vs. DALLAS
RS: Dolphins lead series, 7-5
PS: Cowboys lead series, 1-0;
See Dallas vs. Miami
MIAMI vs. DENVER
RS: Dolphins lead series, 11-4-1
PS: Broncos lead series, 1-0;
See Denver vs. Miami
MIAMI vs. DETROIT
RS: Dolphins lead series, 7-3;
See Detroit vs. Miami
MIAMI vs. GREEN BAY
RS: Dolphins lead series, 10-3;
See Green Bay vs. Miami
MIAMI vs. HOUSTON
RS: Texans lead series, 6-0;
See Houston vs. Miami
MIAMI vs. INDIANAPOLIS
RS: Dolphins lead series, 44-24
PS: Dolphins lead series, 1-0;
See Indianapolis vs. Miami
MIAMI vs. JACKSONVILLE
RS: Series tied, 2-2
PS: Jaguars lead series, 1-0;
See Jacksonville vs. Miami
MIAMI vs. KANSAS CITY
RS: Dolphins lead series, 13-12
PS: Dolphins lead series, 3-0;
See Kansas City vs. Miami
MIAMI vs. MINNESOTA
RS: Dolphins lead series, 6-4
PS: Dolphins lead series, 1-0
1972—Dolphins, 16-14 (Minn)
1973—*Dolphins, 24-7 (Houston)
1976—Vikings, 29-7 (Mia)
1979—Dolphins, 27-12 (Minn)
1982—Dolphins, 22-14 (Mia)
1988—Dolphins, 24-7 (Mia)
1994—Vikings, 38-35 (Minn)
2000—Vikings, 13-7 (Minn)
2002—Vikings, 20-17 (Minn)
2006—Dolphins, 24-20 (Mia)

2010—Dolphins, 14-10 (Minn)
(RS Pts.—Dolphins 193, Vikings 177)
(PS Pts.—Dolphins 24, Vikings 7)
*Super Bowl VIII
MIAMI vs. *NEW ENGLAND
RS: Dolphins lead series, 49-41
PS: Patriots lead series, 2-1
1966—Patriots, 20-14 (M)
1967—Patriots, 41-10 (B)
　　　Dolphins, 41-32 (M)
1968—Dolphins, 34-10 (B)
　　　Dolphins, 38-7 (M)
1969—Dolphins, 17-16 (B)
　　　Patriots, 38-23 (Tampa)
1970—Patriots, 27-14 (B)
　　　Dolphins, 37-20 (M)
1971—Dolphins, 41-3 (M)
　　　Patriots, 34-13 (NE)
1972—Dolphins, 52-0 (M)
　　　Dolphins, 37-21 (NE)
1973—Dolphins, 44-23 (M)
　　　Dolphins, 30-14 (NE)
1974—Patriots, 34-24 (NE)
　　　Dolphins, 34-27 (M)
1975—Dolphins, 22-14 (NE)
　　　Dolphins, 20-7 (M)
1976—Patriots, 30-14 (NE)
　　　Dolphins, 10-3 (M)
1977—Dolphins, 17-5 (M)
　　　Patriots, 14-10 (NE)
1978—Patriots, 33-24 (NE)
　　　Dolphins, 23-3 (M)
1979—Patriots, 28-13 (NE)
　　　Dolphins, 39-24 (M)
1980—Patriots, 34-0 (NE)
　　　Dolphins, 16-13 (M) OT
1981—Dolphins, 30-27 (NE) OT
　　　Dolphins, 24-14 (M)
1982—Patriots, 3-0 (NE)
　　　**Dolphins, 28-13 (M)
1983—Dolphins, 34-24 (M)
　　　Patriots, 17-6 (NE)
1984—Dolphins, 28-7 (M)
　　　Dolphins, 44-24 (NE)
1985—Patriots, 17-13 (NE)
　　　Dolphins, 30-27 (M)
　　　***Patriots, 31-14 (M)
1986—Dolphins, 34-7 (NE)
　　　Patriots, 34-27 (M)
1987—Patriots, 28-21 (NE)
　　　Patriots, 24-10 (M)
1988—Patriots, 21-10 (NE)
　　　Patriots, 6-3 (M)
1989—Dolphins, 24-10 (NE)
　　　Dolphins, 31-10 (M)
1990—Dolphins, 27-24 (NE)
　　　Dolphins, 17-10 (M)
1991—Dolphins, 20-10 (NE)
　　　Dolphins, 30-20 (M)
1992—Dolphins, 38-17 (M)
　　　Dolphins, 16-13 (NE) OT
1993—Dolphins, 17-13 (M)
　　　Patriots, 33-27 (NE) OT
1994—Dolphins, 39-35 (M)
　　　Dolphins, 23-3 (NE)
1995—Dolphins, 20-3 (NE)
　　　Patriots, 34-17 (M)
1996—Dolphins, 24-10 (M)
　　　Patriots, 42-23 (NE)
1997—Dolphins, 27-24 (NE)
　　　Patriots, 14-12 (M)
　　　**Patriots, 17-3 (NE)

1998—Dolphins, 12-9 (M) OT
　　　Patriots, 26-23 (NE)
1999—Dolphins, 31-30 (NE)
　　　Dolphins, 27-17 (M)
2000—Dolphins, 10-3 (M)
　　　Dolphins, 27-24 (NE)
2001—Dolphins, 30-10 (M)
　　　Patriots, 20-13 (NE)
2002—Dolphins, 26-13 (M)
　　　Patriots, 27-24 (NE) OT
2003—Patriots, 19-13 (M) OT
　　　Patriots, 12-0 (NE)
2004—Patriots, 24-10 (NE)
　　　Dolphins, 29-28 (M)
2005—Patriots, 23-16 (M)
　　　Dolphins, 28-26 (NE)
2006—Patriots, 20-10 (NE)
　　　Dolphins, 21-0 (M)
2007—Patriots, 49-28 (M)
　　　Patriots, 28-7 (NE)
2008—Dolphins, 38-13 (NE)
　　　Patriots, 48-28 (M)
2009—Patriots, 27-17 (NE)
　　　Dolphins, 22-21 (M)
2010—Patriots, 41-14 (M)
　　　Patriots, 38-7 (NE)
2011—Patriots, 38-24 (M)
　　　Patriots, 27-24 (NE)
(RS Pts.—Dolphins 1,986, Patriots 1,871)
(PS Pts.—Patriots 61, Dolphins 45)
*Franchise in Boston prior to 1971
**AFC First-Round Playoff
***AFC Championship
MIAMI vs. NEW ORLEANS
RS: Dolphins lead series, 6-4
1970—Dolphins, 21-10 (M)
1974—Dolphins, 21-0 (NO)
1980—Dolphins, 21-16 (M)
1983—Saints, 17-7 (NO)
1986—Dolphins, 31-27 (NO)
1992—Saints, 24-13 (NO)
1995—Saints, 33-30 (NO)
1998—Dolphins, 30-10 (M)
2005—Dolphins, 21-6 (Baton Rouge)
2009—Saints, 46-34 (M)
(RS Pts.—Dolphins 229, Saints 189)
MIAMI vs. N.Y. GIANTS
RS: Giants lead series, 5-2
1972—Dolphins, 23-13 (NY)
1990—Giants, 20-3 (NY)
1993—Giants, 19-14 (M)
1996—Giants, 17-7 (M)
2003—Dolphins, 23-10 (NY)
2007—Giants, 13-10 (London)
2011—Giants, 20-17 (NY)
(RS Pts.—Giants 112, Dolphins 97)
MIAMI vs. N.Y. JETS
RS: Jets lead series, 48-43-1
PS: Dolphins lead series, 1-0
1966—Jets, 19-14 (M)
　　　Jets, 30-13 (NY)
1967—Jets, 29-7 (NY)
　　　Jets, 33-14 (M)
1968—Jets, 35-17 (NY)
　　　Jets, 31-7 (M)
1969—Jets, 34-31 (NY)
　　　Jets, 27-9 (M)
1970—Dolphins, 20-6 (NY)
　　　Dolphins, 16-10 (M)
1971—Jets, 14-10 (M)
　　　Dolphins, 30-14 (NY)
1972—Dolphins, 27-17 (NY)

　　　Dolphins, 28-24 (M)
1973—Dolphins, 31-3 (M)
　　　Dolphins, 24-14 (NY)
1974—Dolphins, 21-17 (M)
　　　Jets, 17-14 (NY)
1975—Dolphins, 43-0 (NY)
　　　Dolphins, 27-7 (M)
1976—Dolphins, 16-0 (M)
　　　Dolphins, 27-7 (NY)
1977—Dolphins, 21-17 (M)
　　　Dolphins, 14-10 (NY)
1978—Jets, 33-20 (NY)
　　　Jets, 24-13 (M)
1979—Jets, 33-27 (M)
　　　Jets, 27-24 (M)
1980—Jets, 17-14 (NY)
　　　Jets, 24-17 (M)
1981—Tie, 28-28 (M) OT
　　　Jets, 16-15 (NY)
1982—Dolphins, 45-28 (NY)
　　　Dolphins, 20-19 (M)
　　　*Dolphins, 14-0 (M)
1983—Dolphins, 32-14 (NY)
　　　Dolphins, 34-14 (M)
1984—Dolphins, 31-17 (NY)
　　　Dolphins, 28-17 (M)
1985—Jets, 23-7 (NY)
　　　Dolphins, 21-17 (M)
1986—Jets, 51-45 (NY) OT
　　　Dolphins, 45-3 (M)
1987—Jets, 37-31 (NY) OT
　　　Dolphins, 37-28 (M)
1988—Jets, 44-30 (M)
　　　Jets, 38-34 (NY)
1989—Jets, 40-33 (M)
　　　Dolphins, 31-23 (NY)
1990—Dolphins, 20-16 (M)
　　　Dolphins, 17-3 (NY)
1991—Jets, 41-23 (NY)
　　　Jets, 23-20 (M) OT
1992—Jets, 26-14 (NY)
　　　Dolphins, 19-17 (M)
1993—Jets, 24-14 (M)
　　　Jets, 27-10 (NY)
1994—Dolphins, 28-14 (M)
　　　Dolphins, 28-24 (NY)
1995—Dolphins, 52-14 (M)
　　　Jets, 17-16 (NY)
1996—Dolphins, 36-27 (M)
　　　Dolphins, 31-28 (NY)
1997—Dolphins, 31-20 (NY)
　　　Dolphins, 24-17 (M)
1998—Jets, 20-9 (NY)
　　　Jets, 21-16 (M)
1999—Jets, 28-20 (NY)
　　　Jets, 38-31 (M)
2000—Jets, 40-37 (NY) OT
　　　Jets, 20-3 (M)
2001—Jets, 21-17 (NY)
　　　Jets, 24-0 (M)
2002—Dolphins, 30-3 (M)
　　　Jets, 13-10 (NY)
2003—Dolphins, 21-10 (NY)
　　　Dolphins, 23-21 (M)
2004—Jets, 17-9 (M)
　　　Jets, 41-14 (NY)
2005—Jets, 17-7 (NY)
　　　Dolphins, 24-20 (M)
2006—Jets, 20-17 (NY)
　　　Jets, 13-10 (M)
2007—Jets, 31-28 (NY)
　　　Jets, 40-13 (M)

2008—Jets, 20-14 (M)
    Dolphins, 24-17 (NY)
2009—Dolphins, 31-27 (M)
    Dolphins, 30-25 (NY)
2010—Jets, 31-23 (M)
    Dolphins, 10-6 (NY)
2011—Jets, 24-6 (NY)
    Dolphins, 19-17 (M)
(RS Pts.—Dolphins 2,022, Jets 1,993)
(PS Pts.—Dolphins 14, Jets 0)
*AFC Championship
MIAMI vs. *OAKLAND
RS: Raiders lead series, 16-14-1
PS: Raiders lead series, 3-1
1966—Raiders, 23-14 (M)
    Raiders, 21-10 (O)
1967—Raiders, 31-17 (O)
1968—Raiders, 47-21 (M)
1969—Raiders, 20-17 (O)
    Tie, 20-20 (M)
1970—Dolphins, 20-13 (M)
    **Raiders, 21-14 (O)
1973—Raiders, 12-7 (O)
    ***Dolphins, 27-10 (M)
1974—**Raiders, 28-26 (O)
1975—Raiders, 31-21 (M)
1978—Dolphins, 23-6 (M)
1979—Raiders, 13-3 (O)
1980—Raiders, 16-10 (M)
1981—Raiders, 33-17 (M)
1983—Raiders, 27-14 (LA)
1984—Raiders, 45-34 (M)
1986—Raiders, 30-28 (M)
1988—Dolphins, 24-14 (LA)
1990—Raiders, 13-10 (M)
1992—Dolphins, 20-7 (M)
1994—Dolphins, 20-17 (M) OT
1996—Raiders, 17-7 (O)
1997—Dolphins, 34-16 (O)
1998—Dolphins, 27-17 (O)
1999—Dolphins, 16-9 (O)
2000—**Raiders, 27-0 (O)
2001—Dolphins, 18-15 (M)
2002—Dolphins, 23-17 (M)
2005—Dolphins, 33-21 (O)
2007—Raiders, 35-17 (M)
2008—Dolphins, 17-15 (M)
2010—Dolphins, 33-17 (O)
2011—Dolphins, 34-14 (M)
(RS Pts.—Raiders 632, Dolphins 609)
(PS Pts.—Raiders 86, Dolphins 67)
*Franchise in Los Angeles from 1982-1994
**AFC Divisional Playoff
***AFC Championship
MIAMI vs. PHILADELPHIA
RS: Dolphins lead series, 7-6
1970—Eagles, 24-17 (P)
1975—Dolphins, 24-16 (M)
1978—Eagles, 17-3 (P)
1981—Dolphins, 13-10 (M)
1984—Dolphins, 24-23 (M)
1987—Dolphins, 28-10 (P)
1990—Dolphins, 23-20 (M) OT
1993—Dolphins, 19-14 (P)
1996—Eagles, 35-28 (P)
1999—Dolphins, 16-13 (M)
2003—Eagles, 34-27 (M)
2007—Eagles, 17-7 (P)
2011—Eagles, 26-10 (M)
(RS Pts.—Eagles 259, Dolphins 239)
MIAMI vs. PITTSBURGH
RS: Steelers lead series, 12-9

PS: Dolphins lead series, 2-1
1971—Dolphins, 24-21 (M)
1972—*Dolphins, 21-17 (P)
1973—Dolphins, 30-26 (M)
1976—Steelers, 14-3 (P)
1979—**Steelers, 34-14 (P)
1980—Steelers, 23-10 (P)
1981—Dolphins, 30-10 (M)
1984—Dolphins, 31-7 (P)
    *Dolphins, 45-28 (M)
1985—Dolphins, 24-20 (M)
1987—Dolphins, 35-24 (M)
1988—Steelers, 40-24 (P)
1989—Steelers, 34-14 (M)
1990—Dolphins, 28-6 (P)
1993—Steelers, 21-20 (M)
1994—Steelers, 16-13 (P) OT
1995—Dolphins, 23-10 (M)
1996—Steelers, 24-17 (M)
1998—Dolphins, 21-0 (M)
2004—Steelers, 13-3 (M)
2006—Steelers, 28-17 (P)
2007—Steelers, 3-0 (P)
2009—Steelers, 30-24 (M)
2010—Steelers, 23-22 (M)
(RS Pts.—Dolphins 413, Steelers 393)
(PS Pts.—Dolphins 80, Steelers 79)
*AFC Championship
**AFC Divisional Playoff
MIAMI vs. *ST. LOUIS
RS: Dolphins lead series, 9-2
1971—Dolphins, 20-14 (LA)
1976—Rams, 31-28 (M)
1980—Dolphins, 35-14 (LA)
1983—Dolphins, 30-14 (M)
1986—Dolphins, 37-31 (LA) OT
1992—Dolphins, 26-10 (M)
1995—Dolphins, 41-22 (StL)
1998—Dolphins, 14-0 (M)
2001—Rams, 42-10 (StL)
2004—Dolphins, 31-14 (M)
2008—Dolphins, 16-12 (StL)
(RS Pts.—Dolphins 288, Rams 204)
*Franchise in Los Angeles prior to 1995
MIAMI vs. SAN DIEGO
RS: Series tied, 12-12
PS: Series tied, 2-2
1966—Chargers, 44-10 (SD)
1967—Chargers, 24-0 (SD)
    Dolphins, 41-24 (M)
1968—Chargers, 34-28 (SD)
1969—Chargers, 21-14 (M)
1972—Dolphins, 24-10 (M)
1974—Dolphins, 28-21 (SD)
1977—Chargers, 14-13 (M)
1978—Dolphins, 28-21 (SD)
1980—Chargers, 27-24 (M) OT
1981—*Chargers, 41-38 (M) OT
1982—**Dolphins, 34-13 (M)
1984—Chargers, 34-28 (SD) OT
1986—Chargers, 50-28 (SD)
1988—Dolphins, 31-28 (M)
1991—Chargers, 38-30 (SD)
1992—*Dolphins, 31-0 (M)
1993—Chargers, 45-20 (SD)
1994—*Chargers, 22-21 (SD)
1995—Dolphins, 24-14 (SD)
1999—Dolphins, 12-9 (M)
2000—Dolphins, 17-7 (SD)
2002—Dolphins, 30-3 (M)
2003—Dolphins, 26-10 (Ariz)
2005—Dolphins, 23-21 (SD)

2008—Dolphins, 17-10 (M)
2009—Chargers, 23-13 (SD)
2011—Chargers, 26-16 (SD)
(RS Pts.—Chargers 558, Dolphins 525)
(PS Pts.—Dolphins 124, Chargers 76)
*AFC Divisional Playoff
**AFC Second-Round Playoff
MIAMI vs. SAN FRANCISCO
RS: Dolphins lead series, 6-4
PS: 49ers lead series, 1-0
1973—Dolphins, 21-13 (M)
1977—Dolphins, 19-15 (SF)
1980—Dolphins, 17-13 (M)
1983—Dolphins, 20-17 (SF)
1984—*49ers, 38-16 (Stanford)
1986—49ers, 31-16 (M)
1992—49ers, 27-3 (SF)
1995—49ers, 44-20 (M)
2001—Dolphins, 21-0 (SF)
2004—Dolphins, 24-17 (SF)
2008—Dolphins, 14-9 (M)
(RS Pts.—49ers 207, Dolphins 154)
(PS Pts.—49ers 38, Dolphins 16)
*Super Bowl XIX
MIAMI vs. SEATTLE
RS: Dolphins lead series, 7-3
PS: Dolphins lead series, 2-1
1977—Dolphins, 31-13 (M)
1979—Dolphins, 19-10 (M)
1983—*Seahawks, 27-20 (M)
1984—*Dolphins, 31-10 (M)
1987—Seahawks, 24-20 (S)
1990—Dolphins, 24-17 (M)
1992—Dolphins, 19-17 (S)
1996—Seahawks, 22-15 (M)
1999—**Dolphins, 20-17 (S)
2000—Dolphins, 23-0 (M)
2001—Dolphins, 24-20 (S)
2004—Seahawks, 24-17 (S)
2008—Dolphins, 21-19 (M)
(RS Pts.—Dolphins 213, Seahawks 166)
(PS Pts.—Dolphins 71, Seahawks 54)
*AFC Divisional Playoff
**AFC First-Round Playoff
MIAMI vs. TAMPA BAY
RS: Dolphins lead series, 5-4
1976—Dolphins, 23-20 (TB)
1982—Buccaneers, 23-17 (TB)
1985—Dolphins, 41-38 (M)
1988—Dolphins, 17-14 (TB)
1991—Dolphins, 33-14 (M)
1997—Buccaneers, 31-21 (TB)
2000—Buccaneers, 16-13 (M)
2005—Buccaneers, 27-13 (TB)
2009—Dolphins, 25-23 (M)
(RS Pts.—Buccaneers 206, Dolphins 203)
MIAMI vs. *TENNESSEE
RS: Dolphins lead series, 18-14
PS: Titans lead series, 1-0
1966—Dolphins, 20-13 (H)
    Dolphins, 29-28 (M)
1967—Oilers, 17-14 (H)
    Oilers, 41-10 (M)
1968—Oilers, 24-10 (M)
    Dolphins, 24-7 (H)
1969—Oilers, 22-10 (M)
    Oilers, 32-7 (M)
1970—Dolphins, 20-10 (H)
1972—Dolphins, 34-13 (M)
1975—Oilers, 20-19 (H)
1977—Dolphins, 27-7 (M)
1978—Oilers, 35-30 (H)

**Oilers, 17-9 (M)
1979—Oilers, 9-6 (M)
1981—Dolphins, 16-10 (H)
1983—Dolphins, 24-17 (H)
1984—Dolphins, 28-10 (M)
1985—Oilers, 26-23 (H)
1986—Dolphins, 28-7 (M)
1989—Oilers, 39-7 (H)
1991—Oilers, 17-13 (M)
1992—Dolphins, 19-16 (M)
1996—Dolphins, 23-20 (H)
1997—Dolphins, 16-13 (M) OT
1999—Dolphins, 17-0 (M)
2001—Dolphins, 31-23 (T)
2003—Titans, 31-7 (T)
2004—Titans, 17-7 (M)
2005—Dolphins, 24-10 (M)
2006—Dolphins, 13-10 (M)
2009—Titans, 27-24 (T) OT
2010—Dolphins, 29-17 (M)
(RS Pts.—Dolphins 609, Titans 588)
(PS Pts.—Titans 17, Dolphins 9)
*Franchise in Houston prior to 1997;
known as Oilers prior to 1999
**AFC First-Round Playoff
MIAMI vs. WASHINGTON
RS: Dolphins lead series, 7-4
PS: Series tied, 1-1
1972—*Dolphins, 14-7 (Los Angeles)
1974—Redskins, 20-17 (W)
1978—Dolphins, 16-0 (W)
1981—Dolphins, 13-10 (M)
1982—**Redskins, 27-17 (Pasadena)
1984—Dolphins, 35-17 (W)
1987—Dolphins, 23-21 (M)
1990—Redskins, 42-20 (W)
1993—Redskins, 17-10 (M)
1999—Redskins, 21-10 (W)
2003—Dolphins, 24-23 (M)
2007—Redskins, 16-13 (W) OT
2011—Dolphins, 20-9 (M)
(RS Pts.—Dolphins 208, Redskins 189)
(PS Pts.—Redskins 34, Dolphins 31)
*Super Bowl VII
**Super Bowl XVII

MINNESOTA vs. ARIZONA
RS: Vikings lead series, 12-10
PS: Vikings lead series, 2-0;
See Arizona vs. Minnesota
MINNESOTA vs. ATLANTA
RS: Vikings lead series, 15-10
PS: Series tied, 1-1;
See Atlanta vs. Minnesota
MINNESOTA vs. BALTIMORE
RS: Series tied, 2-2;
See Baltimore vs. Minnesota
MINNESOTA vs. BUFFALO
RS: Vikings lead series, 8-4;
See Buffalo vs. Minnesota
MINNESOTA vs. CAROLINA
RS: Vikings lead series, 6-4;
See Carolina vs. Minnesota
MINNESOTA vs. CHICAGO
RS: Vikings lead series, 52-47-2
PS: Bears lead series, 1-0;
See Chicago vs. Minnesota
MINNESOTA vs. CINCINNATI
RS: Vikings lead series, 6-5;
See Cincinnati vs. Minnesota
MINNESOTA vs. CLEVELAND
RS: Vikings lead series, 10-3

PS: Vikings lead series, 1-0;
See Cleveland vs. Minnesota
MINNESOTA vs. DALLAS
RS: Vikings lead series, 11-10
PS: Cowboys lead series, 4-3;
See Dallas vs. Minnesota
MINNESOTA vs. DENVER
RS: Vikings lead series, 7-6;
See Denver vs. Minnesota
MINNESOTA vs. DETROIT
RS: Vikings lead series, 66-33-2;
See Detroit vs. Minnesota
MINNESOTA vs. GREEN BAY
RS: Packers lead series, 53-47-1
PS: Vikings lead series, 1-0;
See Green Bay vs. Minnesota
MINNESOTA vs. HOUSTON
RS: Vikings lead series, 2-0;
See Houston vs. Minnesota
MINNESOTA vs. INDIANAPOLIS
RS: Colts lead series, 14-7-1
PS: Colts lead series, 1-0;
See Indianapolis vs. Minnesota
MINNESOTA vs. JACKSONVILLE
RS: Vikings lead series, 3-1;
See Jacksonville vs. Minnesota
MINNESOTA vs. KANSAS CITY
RS: Chiefs lead series, 6-4
PS: Chiefs lead series, 1-0;
See Kansas City vs. Minnesota
MINNESOTA vs. MIAMI
RS: Dolphins lead series, 6-4
PS: Dolphins lead series, 1-0;
See Miami vs. Minnesota
MINNESOTA vs. *NEW ENGLAND
RS: Patriots lead series, 7-4
1970—Vikings, 35-14 (B)
1974—Patriots, 17-14 (M)
1979—Patriots, 27-23 (NE)
1988—Vikings, 36-6 (M)
1991—Patriots, 26-23 (NE) OT
1994—Patriots, 26-20 (NE) OT
1997—Vikings, 23-18 (M)
2000—Vikings, 21-13 (NE)
2002—Patriots, 24-17 (NE)
2006—Patriots, 31-7 (M)
2010—Patriots, 28-18 (NE)
(RS Pts.—Vikings 237, Patriots 230)
*Franchise in Boston prior to 1971
MINNESOTA vs. NEW ORLEANS
RS: Vikings lead series, 18-9
PS: Vikings lead series, 2-1
1968—Saints, 20-17 (NO)
1970—Vikings, 26-0 (M)
1971—Vikings, 23-10 (NO)
1972—Vikings, 37-6 (M)
1974—Vikings, 29-9 (M)
1975—Vikings, 20-7 (NO)
1976—Vikings, 40-9 (NO)
1978—Saints, 31-24 (NO)
1980—Vikings, 23-20 (NO)
1981—Vikings, 20-10 (M)
1983—Saints, 17-16 (NO)
1985—Saints, 30-23 (M)
1986—Vikings, 33-17 (M)
1987—*Vikings, 44-10 (NO)
1988—Vikings, 45-3 (M)
1990—Vikings, 32-3 (M)
1991—Saints, 26-0 (NO)
1993—Saints, 17-14 (M)
1994—Vikings, 21-20 (M)
1995—Vikings, 43-24 (M)

1998—Vikings, 31-24 (M)
2000—**Vikings, 34-16 (M)
2001—Saints, 28-15 (NO)
2002—Vikings, 32-31 (NO)
2004—Vikings, 38-31 (NO)
2005—Vikings, 33-16 (M)
2008—Vikings, 30-27 (NO)
2009—***Saints, 31-28 (NO) OT
2010—Saints, 14-9 (NO)
2011—Saints, 42-20 (M)
(RS Pts.—Vikings 694, Saints 492)
(PS Pts.—Vikings 106, Saints 57)
*NFC First-Round Playoff
**NFC Divisional Playoff
***NFC Championship
MINNESOTA vs. N.Y. GIANTS
RS: Vikings lead series, 13-9
PS: Giants lead series, 2-1
1964—Vikings, 30-21 (NY)
1965—Vikings, 40-14 (M)
1967—Vikings, 27-24 (M)
1969—Giants, 24-23 (NY)
1971—Vikings, 17-10 (NY)
1973—Vikings, 31-7 (New Haven)
1976—Vikings, 24-7 (M)
1986—Giants, 22-20 (M)
1989—Giants, 24-14 (NY)
1990—Giants, 23-15 (NY)
1993—*Giants, 17-10 (NY)
1994—Vikings, 27-10 (NY)
1996—Giants, 15-10 (NY)
1997—*Vikings, 23-22 (NY)
1999—Vikings, 34-17 (NY)
2000—**Giants, 41-0 (NY)
2001—Vikings, 28-16 (M)
2002—Giants, 27-20 (M)
2003—Giants, 29-17 (M)
2004—Giants, 34-13 (M)
2005—Vikings, 24-21 (NY)
2007—Giants, 41-17 (NY)
2008—Vikings, 20-19 (M)
2009—Vikings, 44-7 (M)
2010—Giants, 21-3 (Detroit)
(RS Pts.—Vikings 522, Giants 409)
(PS Pts.—Giants 80, Vikings 33)
*NFC First-Round Playoff
**NFC Championship
MINNESOTA vs. N.Y. JETS
RS: Jets lead series, 8-1
1970—Jets, 20-10 (NY)
1975—Vikings, 29-21 (M)
1979—Jets, 14-7 (NY)
1982—Jets, 42-14 (M)
1994—Jets, 31-21 (M)
1997—Jets, 23-21 (NY)
2002—Jets, 20-7 (NY)
2006—Jets, 26-13 (M)
2010—Jets, 29-20 (NY)
(RS Pts.—Jets 226, Vikings 142)
MINNESOTA vs. *OAKLAND
RS: Raiders lead series, 9-4
PS: Raiders lead series, 1-0
1973—Vikings, 24-16 (M)
1976—**Raiders, 32-14 (Pasadena)
1977—Raiders, 35-13 (O)
1978—Raiders, 27-20 (O)
1981—Raiders, 36-10 (M)
1984—Raiders, 23-20 (LA)
1987—Vikings, 31-20 (M)
1990—Raiders, 28-24 (M)
1993—Raiders, 24-7 (LA)
1996—Vikings, 16-13 (O) OT

1999—Raiders, 22-17 (M)
2003—Raiders, 28-18 (O)
2007—Vikings, 29-22 (M)
2011—Raiders, 27-21 (M)
(RS Pts.—Raiders 321, Vikings 250)
(PS Pts.—Raiders 32, Vikings 14)
*Franchise in Los Angeles from 1982-1994
**Super Bowl XI
MINNESOTA vs. PHILADELPHIA
RS: Vikings lead series, 12-9
PS: Eagles lead series, 3-0
1962—Vikings, 31-21 (M)
1963—Vikings, 34-13 (P)
1968—Vikings, 24-17 (P)
1971—Vikings, 13-0 (P)
1973—Vikings, 28-21 (M)
1976—Vikings, 31-12 (M)
1978—Vikings, 28-27 (M)
1980—Eagles, 42-7 (M)
     *Eagles, 31-16 (P)
1981—Vikings, 35-23 (M)
1984—Eagles, 19-17 (P)
1985—Vikings, 28-23 (P)
     Eagles, 37-35 (M)
1988—Vikings, 23-21 (M)
1989—Eagles, 10-9 (P)
1990—Eagles, 32-24 (P)
1992—Eagles, 28-17 (P)
1997—Vikings, 28-19 (M)
2001—Eagles, 48-17 (P)
2004—Eagles, 27-16 (P)
     *Eagles, 27-14 (P)
2007—Eagles, 23-16 (M)
2008—**Eagles, 26-14 (M)
2010—Vikings, 24-14 (P)
(RS Pts.—Vikings 485, Eagles 477)
(PS Pts.—Eagles 84, Vikings 44)
*NFC Divisional Playoff
**NFC First-Round Playoff
MINNESOTA vs. PITTSBURGH
RS: Vikings lead series, 8-7
PS: Steelers lead series, 1-0
1962—Steelers, 39-31 (P)
1964—Vikings, 30-10 (M)
1967—Vikings, 41-27 (P)
1969—Vikings, 52-14 (M)
1972—Steelers, 23-10 (P)
1974—*Steelers, 16-6 (New Orleans)
1976—Vikings, 17-6 (M)
1980—Steelers, 23-17 (M)
1983—Vikings, 17-14 (P)
1986—Vikings, 31-7 (M)
1989—Steelers, 27-14 (P)
1992—Vikings, 6-3 (P)
1995—Vikings, 44-24 (P)
2001—Steelers, 21-16 (P)
2005—Steelers, 18-3 (M)
2009—Vikings, 27-17 (P)
(RS Pts.—Vikings 346, Steelers 283)
(PS Pts.—Steelers 16, Vikings 6)
*Super Bowl IX
MINNESOTA vs. *ST. LOUIS
RS: Vikings lead series, 18-14-2
PS: Vikings lead series, 5-2
1961—Rams, 31-17 (LA)
     Vikings, 42-21 (M)
1962—Vikings, 38-14 (LA)
     Tie, 24-24 (M)
1963—Rams, 27-24 (LA)
     Vikings, 21-13 (M)
1964—Rams, 22-13 (LA)
     Vikings, 34-13 (M)

1965—Vikings, 38-35 (LA)
     Vikings, 24-13 (M)
1966—Vikings, 35-7 (M)
     Rams, 21-6 (LA)
1967—Rams, 39-3 (LA)
1968—Rams, 31-3 (M)
1969—Vikings, 20-13 (LA)
     **Vikings, 23-20 (M)
1970—Vikings, 13-3 (M)
1972—Vikings, 45-41 (LA)
1973—Vikings, 10-9 (M)
1974—Rams, 20-17 (LA)
     ***Vikings, 14-10 (M)
1976—Tie, 10-10 (M) OT
     ***Vikings, 24-13 (M)
1977—Rams, 35-3 (LA)
     ****Vikings, 14-7 (LA)
1978—Rams, 34-17 (M)
     ****Rams, 34-10 (LA)
1979—Rams, 27-21 (LA) OT
1985—Rams, 13-10 (LA)
1987—Vikings, 21-16 (LA)
1988—*****Vikings, 28-17 (M)
1989—Vikings, 23-21 (M) OT
1991—Vikings, 20-14 (M)
1992—Vikings, 31-17 (LA)
1998—Vikings, 38-31 (StL)
1999—****Rams, 49-37 (StL)
2000—Rams, 40-29 (StL)
2003—Rams, 48-17 (StL)
2005—Vikings, 27-13 (M)
2006—Rams, 41-21 (M)
2009—Vikings, 38-10 (StL)
(RS Pts.—Rams 767, Vikings 753)
(PS Pts.—Rams 150, Vikings 150)
*Franchise in Los Angeles prior to 1995
**Conference Championship
***NFC Championship
****NFC Divisional Playoff
*****NFC First-Round Playoff
MINNESOTA vs. SAN DIEGO
RS: Chargers lead series, 6-5
1971—Chargers, 30-14 (SD)
1975—Vikings, 28-13 (M)
1978—Chargers, 13-7 (M)
1981—Vikings, 33-31 (SD)
1984—Chargers, 42-13 (M)
1985—Vikings, 21-17 (M)
1993—Chargers, 30-17 (M)
1999—Vikings, 35-27 (M)
2003—Chargers, 42-28 (SD)
2007—Vikings, 35-17 (M)
2011—Chargers, 24-17 (SD)
(RS Pts.—Chargers 286, Vikings 248)
MINNESOTA vs. SAN FRANCISCO
RS: Vikings lead series, 20-18-1
PS: 49ers lead series, 4-1
1961—Vikings, 38-24 (M)
     49ers, 38-28 (SF)
1962—49ers, 21-7 (SF)
     Vikings, 35-12 (M)
1963—Vikings, 24-20 (SF)
     Vikings, 45-14 (M)
1964—Vikings, 27-22 (SF)
     Vikings, 24-7 (M)
1965—Vikings, 42-41 (SF)
     49ers, 45-24 (M)
1966—Tie, 20-20 (SF)
     Vikings, 28-3 (M)
1967—49ers, 27-21 (M)
1968—Vikings, 30-20 (SF)
1969—Vikings, 10-7 (M)

1970—*49ers, 17-14 (M)
1971—49ers, 13-9 (M)
1972—49ers, 20-17 (SF)
1973—Vikings, 17-13 (SF)
1975—Vikings, 27-17 (M)
1976—49ers, 20-16 (SF)
1977—Vikings, 28-27 (M)
1979—Vikings, 28-22 (M)
1983—49ers, 48-17 (M)
1984—49ers, 51-7 (SF)
1985—Vikings, 28-21 (M)
1986—Vikings, 27-24 (SF) OT
1987—*Vikings, 36-24 (SF)
1988—49ers, 24-21 (SF)
     *49ers, 34-9 (SF)
1989—*49ers, 41-13 (SF)
1990—49ers, 20-17 (M)
1991—Vikings, 17-14 (M)
1992—49ers, 20-17 (M)
1993—49ers, 38-19 (SF)
1994—Vikings, 21-14 (M)
1995—49ers, 37-30 (SF)
1997—Vikings, 28-17 (SF)
     *49ers, 38-22 (SF)
1999—Vikings, 40-16 (M)
2003—Vikings, 35-7 (SF)
2006—49ers, 9-3 (S)
2007—Vikings, 27-7 (SF)
2009—Vikings, 27-24 (M)
(RS Pts.—49ers 892, Vikings 878)
(PS Pts.—49ers 154, Vikings 94)
*NFC Divisional Playoff
MINNESOTA vs. SEATTLE
RS: Seahawks lead series, 6-5
1976—Vikings, 27-21 (M)
1978—Seahawks, 29-28 (S)
1984—Seahawks, 20-12 (M)
1987—Seahawks, 28-17 (S)
1990—Vikings, 24-21 (S)
1996—Seahawks, 42-23 (S)
2002—Seahawks, 48-23 (S)
2003—Vikings, 34-7 (M)
2004—Seahawks, 27-23 (M)
2006—Vikings, 31-13 (S)
2009—Vikings, 35-9 (M)
(RS Pts.—Vikings 277, Seahawks 265)
MINNESOTA vs. TAMPA BAY
RS: Vikings lead series, 31-21
1977—Vikings, 9-3 (TB)
1978—Buccaneers, 16-10 (M)
     Vikings, 24-7 (TB)
1979—Buccaneers, 12-10 (M)
     Vikings, 23-22 (TB)
1980—Vikings, 38-30 (M)
     Vikings, 21-10 (TB)
1981—Buccaneers, 21-13 (TB)
     Vikings, 25-10 (M)
1982—Vikings, 17-10 (M)
1983—Vikings, 19-16 (TB) OT
     Buccaneers, 17-12 (M)
1984—Buccaneers, 35-31 (TB)
     Vikings, 27-24 (M)
1985—Vikings, 31-16 (TB)
     Vikings, 26-7 (M)
1986—Vikings, 23-10 (TB)
     Vikings, 45-13 (M)
1987—Buccaneers, 20-10 (TB)
     Vikings, 23-17 (M)
1988—Vikings, 14-13 (M)
     Vikings, 49-20 (TB)
1989—Vikings, 17-3 (M)
     Vikings, 24-10 (TB)

1990—Buccaneers, 23-20 (M) OT
    Buccaneers, 26-13 (TB)
1991—Vikings, 28-13 (M)
    Vikings, 26-24 (TB)
1992—Vikings, 26-20 (M)
    Vikings, 35-7 (TB)
1993—Vikings, 15-0 (M)
    Buccaneers, 23-10 (TB)
1994—Vikings, 36-13 (M)
    Buccaneers, 20-17 (M) OT
1995—Buccaneers, 20-17 (TB) OT
    Vikings, 31-17 (M)
1996—Buccaneers, 24-13 (TB)
    Vikings, 21-10 (M)
1997—Buccaneers, 28-14 (M)
    Vikings, 10-6 (TB)
1998—Vikings, 31-7 (M)
    Buccaneers, 27-24 (TB)
1999—Vikings, 21-14 (M)
    Buccaneers, 24-17 (TB)
2000—Vikings, 30-23 (M)
    Buccaneers, 41-13 (TB)
2001—Vikings, 20-16 (M)
    Buccaneers, 41-14 (TB)
2002—Buccaneers, 38-24 (TB)
2005—Buccaneers, 24-13 (M)
2008—Buccaneers, 19-13 (TB)
2011—Buccaneers, 24-20 (M)
(RS Pts.—Vikings 1,113, Buccaneers 934)
MINNESOTA vs. *TENNESSEE
RS: Vikings lead series, 7-4
1974—Vikings, 51-10 (M)
1980—Oilers, 20-16 (H)
1983—Vikings, 34-14 (M)
1986—Oilers, 23-10 (H)
1989—Vikings, 38-7 (M)
1992—Oilers, 17-13 (M)
1995—Vikings, 23-17 (M) OT
1998—Vikings, 26-16 (T)
2001—Vikings, 42-24 (M)
2004—Vikings, 20-3 (M)
2008—Titans, 30-17 (T)
(RS Pts.—Vikings 290, Titans 181)
*Franchise in Houston prior to 1997;
known as Oilers prior to 1999
MINNESOTA vs. WASHINGTON
RS: Series tied, 8-8
PS: Redskins lead series, 3-2
1968—Vikings, 27-14 (M)
1970—Vikings, 19-10 (W)
1972—Redskins, 24-21 (M)
1973—*Vikings, 27-20 (M)
1975—Redskins, 31-30 (W)
1976—*Vikings, 35-20 (M)
1980—Vikings, 39-14 (W)
1982—**Redskins, 21-7 (W)
1984—Redskins, 31-17 (M)
1986—Redskins, 44-38 (W) OT
1987—Redskins, 27-24 (M) OT
    ***Redskins, 17-10 (W)
1992—Redskins, 15-13 (M)
    ****Redskins, 24-7 (M)
1993—Vikings, 14-9 (W)
1998—Vikings, 41-7 (M)
2004—Redskins, 21-18 (W)
2006—Vikings, 19-16 (W)
2007—Redskins, 32-21 (M)
2010—Vikings, 17-13 (W)
2011—Vikings, 33-26 (W)
(RS Pts.—Vikings 391, Redskins 334)
(PS Pts.—Redskins 102, Vikings 86)
*NFC Divisional Playoff

*NFC Second-Round Playoff
***NFC Championship
****NFC First-Round Playoff

NEW ENGLAND vs. ARIZONA
RS: Series tied, 6-6;
See Arizona vs. New England
NEW ENGLAND vs. ATLANTA
RS: Series tied, 6-6;
See Atlanta vs. New England
NEW ENGLAND vs. BALTIMORE
RS: Patriots lead series, 6-0
PS: Series tied, 1-1;
See Baltimore vs. New England
NEW ENGLAND vs. BUFFALO
RS: Patriots lead series, 61-41-1
PS: Patriots lead series, 1-0;
See Buffalo vs. New England
NEW ENGLAND vs. CAROLINA
RS: Series tied, 2-2
PS: Patriots lead series, 1-0;
See Carolina vs. New England
NEW ENGLAND vs. CHICAGO
RS: Patriots lead series, 8-3
PS: Bears lead series, 1-0;
See Chicago vs. New England
NEW ENGLAND vs. CINCINNATI
RS: Patriots lead series, 14-8;
See Cincinnati vs. New England
NEW ENGLAND vs. CLEVELAND
RS: Browns lead series, 12-9
PS: Browns lead series, 1-0;
See Cleveland vs. New England
NEW ENGLAND vs. DALLAS
RS: Cowboys lead series, 7-4;
See Dallas vs. New England
NEW ENGLAND vs. DENVER
RS: Broncos lead series, 25-17
PS: Broncos lead series, 2-1;
See Denver vs. New England
NEW ENGLAND vs. DETROIT
RS: Patriots lead series, 6-4;
See Detroit vs. New England
NEW ENGLAND vs. GREEN BAY
RS: Patriots lead series, 5-4
PS: Packers lead series, 1-0;
See Green Bay vs. New England
NEW ENGLAND vs. HOUSTON
RS: Patriots lead series, 2-1;
See Houston vs. New England
NEW ENGLAND vs. INDIANAPOLIS
RS: Patriots lead series, 44-28
PS: Patriots lead series, 2-1;
See Indianapolis vs. New England
NEW ENGLAND vs. JACKSONVILLE
RS: Patriots lead series, 5-0
PS: Patriots lead series, 3-1;
See Jacksonville vs. New England
NEW ENGLAND vs. KANSAS CITY
RS: Chiefs lead series, 16-13-3;
See Kansas City vs. New England
NEW ENGLAND vs. MIAMI
RS: Dolphins lead series, 49-41
PS: Patriots lead series, 2-1;
See Miami vs. New England
NEW ENGLAND vs. MINNESOTA
RS: Patriots lead series, 7-4;
See Minnesota vs. New England
NEW ENGLAND vs. NEW ORLEANS
RS: Patriots lead series, 8-4
1972—Patriots, 17-10 (NO)
1976—Patriots, 27-6 (NE)

1980—Patriots, 38-27 (NO)
1983—Patriots, 7-0 (NE)
1986—Patriots, 21-20 (NO)
1989—Saints, 28-24 (NE)
1992—Saints, 31-14 (NE)
1995—Saints, 31-17 (NE)
1998—Patriots, 30-27 (NO)
2001—Patriots, 34-17 (NE)
2005—Patriots, 24-17 (NE)
2009—Saints, 38-17 (NO)
(RS Pts.—Patriots 270, Saints 252)
*NEW ENGLAND vs. N.Y. GIANTS
RS: Patriots lead series, 5-4
PS: Giants lead series, 2-0;
1970—Giants, 16-0 (B)
1974—Patriots, 28-20 (New Haven)
1987—Giants, 17-10 (NY)
1990—Giants, 13-10 (NE)
1996—Patriots, 23-22 (NY)
1999—Patriots, 16-14 (NE)
2003—Patriots, 17-6 (NE)
2007—Patriots, 38-35 (NY)
    **Giants, 17-14 (Arizona)
2011—Giants, 24-20 (NE)
    ***Giants, 21-17 (Indianapolis)
(RS Pts.—Giants 167, Patriots 162)
(PS Pts.—Giants 38, Patriots 31)
*Franchise in Boston prior to 1971
**Super Bowl XLII
***Super Bowl XLVI
*NEW ENGLAND vs. **N.Y. JETS
RS: Series tied, 51-51-1
PS: Patriots lead series, 2-1
1960—Patriots, 28-24 (NY)
    Patriots, 38-21 (B)
1961—Titans, 21-20 (B)
    Titans, 37-30 (NY)
1962—Patriots, 43-14 (NY)
    Patriots, 24-17 (B)
1963—Patriots, 38-14 (B)
    Jets, 31-24 (NY)
1964—Patriots, 26-10 (B)
    Jets, 35-14 (NY)
1965—Jets, 30-20 (B)
    Patriots, 27-23 (NY)
1966—Tie, 24-24 (B)
    Jets, 38-28 (NY)
1967—Jets, 30-23 (NY)
    Jets, 29-24 (B)
1968—Jets, 47-31 (Birmingham)
    Jets, 48-14 (NY)
1969—Jets, 23-14 (B)
    Jets, 23-17 (NY)
1970—Jets, 31-21 (B)
    Jets, 17-3 (NY)
1971—Patriots, 20-0 (NE)
    Jets, 13-6 (NY)
1972—Jets, 41-13 (NE)
    Jets, 34-10 (NY)
1973—Jets, 9-7 (NE)
    Jets, 33-13 (NY)
1974—Patriots, 24-0 (NY)
    Jets, 21-16 (NE)
1975—Jets, 36-7 (NY)
    Jets, 30-28 (NE)
1976—Patriots, 41-7 (NE)
    Patriots, 38-24 (NY)
1977—Jets, 30-27 (NY)
    Patriots, 24-13 (NE)
1978—Patriots, 55-21 (NE)
    Patriots, 19-17 (NY)
1979—Patriots, 56-3 (NE)

Jets, 27-26 (NY)
1980—Patriots, 21-11 (NY)
Patriots, 34-21 (NE)
1981—Jets, 28-24 (NY)
Jets, 17-6 (NE)
1982—Jets, 31-7 (NE)
1983—Patriots, 23-13 (NE)
Jets, 26-3 (NY)
1984—Patriots, 28-21 (NY)
Patriots, 30-20 (NE)
1985—Patriots, 20-13 (NE)
Jets, 16-13 (NY) OT
***Patriots, 26-14 (NY)
1986—Patriots, 20-6 (NY)
Jets, 31-24 (NE)
1987—Jets, 43-24 (NY)
Patriots, 42-20 (NE)
1988—Patriots, 28-3 (NE)
Patriots, 14-13 (NY)
1989—Patriots, 27-24 (NY)
Jets, 27-26 (NE)
1990—Jets, 37-13 (NE)
Jets, 42-7 (NY)
1991—Jets, 28-21 (NE)
Patriots, 6-3 (NY)
1992—Jets, 30-21 (NY)
Patriots, 24-3 (NE)
1993—Jets, 45-7 (NY)
Jets, 6-0 (NE)
1994—Jets, 24-17 (NY)
Patriots, 24-13 (NE)
1995—Patriots, 20-7 (NY)
Patriots, 31-28 (NE)
1996—Patriots, 31-27 (NY)
Patriots, 34-10 (NE)
1997—Patriots, 27-24 (NE) OT
Jets, 24-19 (NY)
1998—Jets, 24-14 (NE)
Jets, 31-10 (NY)
1999—Patriots, 30-28 (NY)
Jets, 24-17 (NE)
2000—Jets, 20-19 (NY)
Jets, 34-17 (NE)
2001—Jets, 10-3 (NE)
Patriots, 17-16 (NY)
2002—Patriots, 44-7 (NY)
Jets, 30-17 (NE)
2003—Patriots, 23-16 (NE)
Patriots, 21-16 (NY)
2004—Patriots, 13-7 (NE)
Patriots, 23-7 (NY)
2005—Patriots, 16-3 (NE)
Patriots, 31-21 (NY)
2006—Patriots, 24-17 (NY)
Jets, 17-14 (NE)
***Patriots, 37-16 (NE)
2007—Patriots, 38-14 (NY)
Patriots, 20-10 (NE)
2008—Patriots, 19-10 (NY)
Jets, 34-31 (NE) OT
2009—Jets, 16-9 (NY)
Patriots, 31-14 (NE)
2010—Jets, 28-14 (NY)
Patriots, 45-3 (NE)
****Jets, 28-21 (NE)
2011—Patriots, 30-21 (NE)
Patriots, 37-16 (NY)
(RS Pts.—Patriots 2,304, Jets 2,175)
(PS Pts.—Patriots 84, Jets 58)
*Franchise in Boston prior to 1971
**Jets known as Titans prior to 1963
***AFC First-Round Playoff

****AFC Divisional Playoff
*NEW ENGLAND vs. **OAKLAND
RS: Patriots lead series, 15-14-1
PS: Patriots lead series, 2-1
1960—Raiders, 27-14 (O)
Patriots, 34-28 (B)
1961—Patriots, 20-17 (B)
Patriots, 35-21 (O)
1962—Patriots, 26-16 (B)
Raiders, 20-0 (O)
1963—Patriots, 20-14 (B)
Patriots, 20-14 (O)
1964—Patriots, 17-14 (O)
Tie, 43-43 (B)
1965—Raiders, 24-10 (B)
Raiders, 30-21 (O)
1966—Patriots, 24-21 (B)
1967—Raiders, 35-7 (O)
Raiders, 48-14 (B)
1968—Raiders, 41-10 (O)
1969—Raiders, 38-23 (B)
1971—Patriots, 20-6 (NE)
1974—Raiders, 41-26 (O)
1976—Patriots, 48-17 (NE)
***Raiders, 24-21 (O)
1978—Patriots, 21-14 (O)
1981—Patriots, 27-17 (O)
1985—Raiders, 35-20 (NE)
***Patriots, 27-20 (LA)
1987—Patriots, 26-23 (NE)
1989—Raiders, 24-21 (LA)
1994—Raiders, 21-17 (NE)
2001—***Patriots, 16-13 (NE) OT
2002—Raiders, 27-20 (O)
2005—Patriots, 30-20 (NE)
2008—Patriots, 49-26 (O)
2011—Patriots, 31-19 (O)
(RS Pts.—Raiders 751, Patriots 684)
(PS Pts.—Patriots 64, Raiders 57)
*Franchise in Boston prior to 1971
**Franchise in Los Angeles from 1982-1994
***AFC Divisional Playoff
NEW ENGLAND vs. PHILADELPHIA
RS: Eagles lead series, 6-5
PS: Patriots lead series, 1-0
1973—Eagles, 24-23 (P)
1977—Patriots, 14-6 (NE)
1978—Patriots, 24-14 (NE)
1981—Eagles, 13-3 (P)
1984—Eagles, 27-17 (P)
1987—Eagles, 34-31 (NE) OT
1990—Eagles, 48-20 (P)
1999—Eagles, 24-9 (P)
2003—Patriots, 31-10 (P)
2004—*Patriots, 24-21 (Jacksonville)
2007—Patriots, 31-28 (NE)
2011—Patriots, 38-20 (P)
(RS Pts.—Eagles 248, Patriots 241)
(PS Pts.—Patriots 24, Eagles 21)
*Super Bowl XXXIX
NEW ENGLAND vs. PITTSBURGH
RS: Steelers lead series, 14-8
PS: Patriots lead series, 3-1
1972—Steelers, 33-3 (P)
1974—Steelers, 21-17 (NE)
1976—Patriots, 30-27 (P)
1979—Steelers, 16-13 (NE) OT
1981—Steelers, 27-21 (P) OT
1982—Steelers, 37-14 (P)
1983—Patriots, 28-23 (P)
1986—Patriots, 34-0 (P)

1989—Steelers, 28-10 (P)
1990—Steelers, 24-3 (P)
1991—Steelers, 20-6 (P)
1993—Steelers, 17-14 (P)
1995—Steelers, 41-27 (P)
1996—*Patriots, 28-3 (NE)
1997—Steelers, 24-21 (NE) OT
*Steelers, 7-6 (P)
1998—Patriots, 23-9 (P)
2001—**Patriots, 24-17 (P)
2002—Patriots, 30-14 (NE)
2004—Steelers, 34-20 (P)
**Patriots, 41-27 (P)
2005—Patriots, 23-20 (P)
2007—Patriots, 34-13 (NE)
2008—Steelers, 33-10 (NE)
2010—Patriots, 39-26 (P)
2011—Steelers, 25-17 (P)
(RS Pts.—Steelers 512, Patriots 437)
(PS Pts.—Patriots 99, Steelers 54)
*AFC Divisional Playoff
**AFC Championship
NEW ENGLAND vs. *ST. LOUIS
RS: Series tied, 5-5
PS: Patriots lead series, 1-0
1974—Patriots, 20-14 (NE)
1980—Patriots, 17-14 (NE)
1983—Patriots, 21-7 (LA)
1986—Patriots, 30-28 (LA)
1989—Rams, 24-20 (NE)
1992—Rams, 14-0 (LA)
1998—Rams, 32-18 (StL)
2001—Rams, 24-17 (NE)
**Patriots, 20-17 (New Orleans)
2004—Patriots, 40-22 (StL)
2008—Patriots, 23-16 (NE)
(RS Pts.—Patriots 203, Rams 198)
(PS Pts.—Patriots 20, Rams 17)
*Franchise in Los Angeles prior to 1995
**Super Bowl XXXVI
*NEW ENGLAND vs. **SAN DIEGO
RS: Patriots lead series, 20-14-2
PS: Patriots lead series, 2-1
1960—Patriots, 35-0 (LA)
Chargers, 45-16 (B)
1961—Chargers, 38-27 (B)
Patriots, 41-0 (SD)
1962—Patriots, 24-20 (B)
Patriots, 20-14 (SD)
1963—Chargers, 17-13 (SD)
Chargers, 7-6 (B)
***Chargers, 51-10 (SD)
1964—Patriots, 33-28 (SD)
Chargers, 26-17 (B)
1965—Tie, 10-10 (B)
Patriots, 22-6 (SD)
1966—Chargers, 24-0 (B)
Patriots, 35-17 (B)
1967—Chargers, 28-14 (SD)
Tie, 31-31 (SD)
1968—Chargers, 27-17 (B)
1969—Chargers, 13-10 (B)
Chargers, 28-18 (SD)
1970—Patriots, 16-14 (B)
1973—Patriots, 30-14 (NE)
1975—Patriots, 33-19 (SD)
1977—Patriots, 24-20 (SD)
1978—Patriots, 28-23 (NE)
1979—Patriots, 27-21 (NE)
1983—Patriots, 37-21 (NE)
1994—Patriots, 23-17 (NE)
1996—Patriots, 45-7 (SD)

1997—Patriots, 41-7 (NE)
2001—Patriots, 29-26 (NE) OT
2002—Chargers, 21-14 (SD)
2005—Chargers, 41-17 (NE)
2006—****Patriots, 24-21 (SD)
2007—Patriots, 38-14 (NE)
     *****Patriots, 21-12 (NE)
2008—Chargers, 30-10 (SD)
2010—Patriots, 23-20 (NE)
2011—Patriots, 35-21 (NE)
(RS Pts.—Patriots 860, Chargers 720)
(PS Pts.—Chargers 84, Patriots 55)
*Franchise in Boston prior to 1971
**Franchise in Los Angeles prior to 1961
***AFL Championship
****AFC Divisional Playoff
*****AFC Championship
NEW ENGLAND vs. SAN FRANCISCO
RS: 49ers lead series, 7-4
1971—49ers, 27-10 (SF)
1975—Patriots, 24-16 (NE)
1980—49ers, 21-17 (SF)
1983—49ers, 33-13 (NE)
1986—49ers, 29-24 (NE)
1989—49ers, 37-20 (SF)
1992—49ers, 24-12 (NE)
1995—49ers, 28-3 (SF)
1998—Patriots, 24-21 (NE)
2004—Patriots, 21-7 (NE)
2008—Patriots, 30-21 (SF)
(RS Pts.—49ers 264, Patriots 198)
NEW ENGLAND vs. SEATTLE
RS: Patriots lead series, 8-7
1977—Patriots, 31-0 (NE)
1980—Patriots, 37-31 (S)
1982—Patriots, 16-0 (S)
1983—Seahawks, 24-6 (S)
1984—Patriots, 38-23 (NE)
1985—Patriots, 20-13 (S)
1986—Seahawks, 38-31 (NE)
1988—Patriots, 13-7 (NE)
1989—Seahawks, 24-3 (NE)
1990—Seahawks, 33-20 (NE)
1992—Seahawks, 10-6 (NE)
1993—Seahawks, 17-14 (NE)
    Seahawks, 10-9 (S)
2004—Patriots, 30-20 (NE)
2008—Patriots, 24-21 (S)
(RS Pts.—Patriots 298, Seahawks 271)
NEW ENGLAND vs. TAMPA BAY
RS: Patriots lead series, 5-2
1976—Patriots, 31-14 (TB)
1985—Patriots, 32-14 (TB)
1988—Patriots, 10-7 (NE) OT
1997—Buccaneers, 27-7 (TB)
2000—Buccaneers, 21-16 (NE)
2005—Patriots, 28-0 (NE)
2009—Patriots, 35-7 (London)
(RS Pts.—Patriots 159, Buccaneers 90)
*NEW ENGLAND vs. **TENNESSEE
RS: Patriots lead series, 21-15-1
PS: Series tied, 1-1
1960—Oilers, 24-10 (B)
    Oilers, 37-21 (H)
1961—Tie, 31-31 (B)
    Oilers, 27-15 (H)
1962—Patriots, 34-21 (B)
    Oilers, 21-17 (H)
1963—Patriots, 45-3 (B)
    Patriots, 46-28 (H)
1964—Patriots, 25-24 (B)
    Patriots, 34-17 (H)

1965—Oilers, 31-10 (H)
    Patriots, 42-14 (B)
1966—Patriots, 27-21 (B)
    Patriots, 38-14 (H)
1967—Patriots, 18-7 (B)
    Oilers, 27-6 (H)
1968—Oilers, 16-0 (B)
    Oilers, 45-17 (H)
1969—Patriots, 24-0 (B)
    Oilers, 27-23 (H)
1971—Patriots, 28-20 (NE)
1973—Patriots, 32-0 (H)
1975—Patriots, 7-0 (NE)
1978—Oilers, 26-23 (NE)
    ***Oilers, 31-14 (NE)
1980—Oilers, 38-34 (H)
1981—Patriots, 38-10 (NE)
1982—Patriots, 29-21 (NE)
1987—Patriots, 21-7 (H)
1988—Oilers, 31-6 (H)
1989—Patriots, 23-13 (NE)
1991—Patriots, 24-20 (NE)
1993—Oilers, 28-14 (NE)
1998—Patriots, 27-16 (NE)
2002—Titans, 24-7 (T)
2003—Patriots, 38-30 (NE)
    ***Patriots, 17-14 (NE)
2006—Patriots, 40-23 (T)
2009—Patriots, 59-0 (NE)
(RS Pts.—Patriots 926, Titans 749)
(PS Pts.—Titans 45, Patriots 31)
*Franchise in Boston prior to 1971
**Franchise in Houston prior to 1997;
known as Oilers prior to 1999
***AFC Divisional Playoff
NEW ENGLAND vs. WASHINGTON
RS: Redskins lead series, 6-3
1972—Patriots, 24-23 (NE)
1978—Redskins, 16-14 (NE)
1981—Redskins, 24-22 (W)
1984—Redskins, 26-10 (NE)
1990—Redskins, 25-10 (NE)
1996—Redskins, 27-22 (NE)
2003—Redskins, 20-17 (W)
2007—Patriots, 52-7 (NE)
2011—Patriots, 34-27 (W)
(RS Pts.—Patriots 205, Redskins 195)

NEW ORLEANS vs. ARIZONA
RS: Cardinals lead series, 14-12
PS: Saints lead series, 1-0;
See Arizona vs. New Orleans
NEW ORLEANS vs. ATLANTA
RS: Falcons lead series, 45-40
PS: Falcons lead series, 1-0;
See Atlanta vs. New Orleans
NEW ORLEANS vs. BALTIMORE
RS: Ravens lead series, 4-1;
See Baltimore vs. New Orleans
NEW ORLEANS vs. BUFFALO
RS: Saints lead series, 5-4;
See Buffalo vs. New Orleans
NEW ORLEANS vs. CAROLINA
RS: Series tied, 17-17;
See Carolina vs. New Orleans
NEW ORLEANS vs. CHICAGO
RS: Bears lead series, 13-12
PS: Bears lead series, 2-0;
See Chicago vs. New Orleans
NEW ORLEANS vs. CINCINNATI
RS: Series tied, 6-6;
See Cincinnati vs. New Orleans

NEW ORLEANS vs. CLEVELAND
RS: Browns lead series, 12-4;
See Cleveland vs. New Orleans
NEW ORLEANS vs. DALLAS
RS: Cowboys lead series, 15-9;
See Dallas vs. New Orleans
NEW ORLEANS vs. DENVER
RS: Broncos lead series, 7-2;
See Denver vs. New Orleans
NEW ORLEANS vs. DETROIT
RS: Saints lead series, 11-9-1
PS: Saints lead series, 1-0;
See Detroit vs. New Orleans
NEW ORLEANS vs. GREEN BAY
RS: Packers lead series, 15-7;
See Green Bay vs. New Orleans
NEW ORLEANS vs. HOUSTON
RS: Saints lead series, 2-1;
See Houston vs. New Orleans
NEW ORLEANS vs. INDIANAPOLIS
RS: Saints lead series, 6-5
PS: Saints lead series, 1-0;
See Indianapolis vs. New Orleans
NEW ORLEANS vs. JACKSONVILLE
RS: Saints lead series, 3-2;
See Jacksonville vs. New Orleans
NEW ORLEANS vs. KANSAS CITY
RS: Saints lead series, 5-4;
See Kansas City vs. New Orleans
NEW ORLEANS vs. MIAMI
RS: Dolphins lead series, 6-4;
See Miami vs. New Orleans
NEW ORLEANS vs. MINNESOTA
RS: Vikings lead series, 18-9
PS: Vikings lead series, 2-1;
See Minnesota vs. New Orleans
NEW ORLEANS vs. NEW ENGLAND
RS: Patriots lead series, 8-4;
See New England vs. New Orleans
NEW ORLEANS vs. N.Y. GIANTS
RS: Giants lead series, 14-12
1967—Giants, 27-21 (NY)
1968—Giants, 38-21 (NY)
1969—Saints, 25-24 (NY)
1970—Giants, 14-10 (NO)
1972—Giants, 45-21 (NY)
1975—Giants, 28-14 (NY)
1978—Saints, 28-17 (NO)
1979—Saints, 24-14 (NO)
1981—Giants, 20-7 (NY)
1984—Saints, 10-3 (NY)
1985—Giants, 21-13 (NO)
1986—Giants, 20-17 (NY)
1987—Saints, 23-14 (NO)
1988—Giants, 13-12 (NO)
1993—Giants, 24-14 (NO)
1994—Saints, 27-22 (NO)
1995—Giants, 45-29 (NY)
1996—Saints 17-3 (NY)
1997—Giants, 14-9 (NY)
1999—Giants, 31-3 (NY)
2001—Giants, 21-13 (NY)
2003—Saints, 45-7 (NO)
2005—Giants, 27-10 (NY*)
2006—Saints, 30-7 (NY)
2009—Saints, 48-27 (NO)
2011—Saints, 49-24 (NO)
(RS Pts.—Giants 546, Saints 544)
*Saints home game
NEW ORLEANS vs. N.Y. JETS
RS: Saints lead series, 6-5
1972—Jets, 18-17 (NY)

1977—Jets, 16-13 (NO)
1980—Saints, 21-20 (NY)
1983—Jets, 31-28 (NO)
1986—Jets, 28-23 (NY)
1989—Saints, 29-14 (NO)
1992—Saints, 20-0 (NY)
1995—Saints, 12-0 (NY)
2001—Jets, 16-9 (NO)
2005—Saints, 21-19 (NY)
2009—Saints, 24-10 (NO)
(RS Pts.—Saints 217, Jets 172)
NEW ORLEANS vs. *OAKLAND
RS: Series tied, 5-5-1
1971—Tie, 21-21 (NO)
1975—Raiders, 48-10 (O)
1979—Raiders, 42-35 (NO)
1985—Raiders, 23-13 (LA)
1988—Saints, 20-6 (NO)
1991—Saints, 27-0 (NO)
1994—Raiders, 24-19 (LA)
1997—Saints, 13-10 (O)
2000—Raiders, 31-22 (NO)
2004—Saints, 31-26 (O)
2008—Saints, 34-3 (NO)
(RS Pts.—Saints 245, Raiders 234)
Franchise in Los Angeles from 1982-1994
NEW ORLEANS vs. PHILADELPHIA
RS: Eagles lead series, 15-10
PS: Series tied, 1-1
1967—Saints, 31-24 (NO)
      Eagles, 48-21 (P)
1968—Eagles, 29-17 (P)
1969—Eagles, 13-10 (P)
      Saints, 26-17 (NO)
1972—Saints, 21-3 (NO)
1974—Saints, 14-10 (NO)
1977—Eagles, 28-7 (P)
1978—Eagles, 24-17 (NO)
1979—Eagles, 26-14 (NO)
1980—Eagles, 34-21 (NO)
1981—Eagles, 31-14 (NO)
1983—Saints, 20-17 (P) OT
1985—Saints, 23-21 (NO)
1987—Eagles, 27-17 (P)
1989—Saints, 30-20 (NO)
1991—Saints, 13-6 (P)
1992—Eagles, 15-13 (P)
      *Eagles, 36-20 (NO)
1993—Eagles, 37-26 (P)
1995—Saints, 15-10 (NO)
2000—Eagles, 21-7 (NO)
2003—Eagles, 33-20 (P)
2006—Saints, 27-24 (NO)
      **Saints, 27-24 (NO)
2007—Eagles, 38-23 (NO)
2009—Saints, 48-22 (P)
(RS Pts.—Eagles 583, Saints 490)
(PS Pts.—Eagles 60, Saints 47)
NFC First-Round Playoff
**NFC Divisional Playoff*
NEW ORLEANS vs. PITTSBURGH
RS: Series tied, 7-7
1967—Steelers, 14-10 (NO)
1968—Saints, 16-12 (P)
      Saints, 24-14 (NO)
1969—Saints, 27-24 (NO)
1974—Steelers, 28-7 (NO)
1978—Steelers, 20-14 (P)
1981—Steelers, 20-6 (NO)
1984—Saints, 27-24 (NO)
1987—Saints, 20-16 (P)
1990—Steelers, 9-6 (NO)

1993—Steelers, 37-14 (P)
2002—Saints, 32-29 (NO)
2006—Steelers, 38-31 (P)
2010—Saints, 20-10 (NO)
(RS Pts.—Steelers 295, Saints 254)
NEW ORLEANS vs. *ST. LOUIS
RS: Rams lead series, 39-31
PS: Saints lead series, 1-0
1967—Rams, 27-13 (NO)
1969—Rams, 36-17 (LA)
1970—Rams, 30-17 (NO)
      Rams, 34-16 (LA)
1971—Saints, 24-20 (NO)
      Rams, 45-28 (LA)
1972—Rams, 34-14 (LA)
      Saints, 19-16 (NO)
1973—Rams, 29-7 (LA)
      Rams, 24-13 (NO)
1974—Rams, 24-0 (LA)
      Saints, 20-7 (NO)
1975—Rams, 38-14 (LA)
      Rams, 14-7 (NO)
1976—Rams, 16-10 (NO)
      Rams, 33-14 (LA)
1977—Rams, 14-7 (LA)
      Saints, 27-26 (NO)
1978—Rams, 26-20 (NO)
      Saints, 10-3 (LA)
1979—Rams, 35-17 (NO)
      Saints, 29-14 (LA)
1980—Rams, 45-31 (LA)
      Rams, 27-7 (NO)
1981—Saints, 23-17 (NO)
      Saints, 21-13 (LA)
1983—Rams, 30-27 (LA)
      Rams, 26-24 (NO)
1984—Rams, 28-10 (NO)
      Rams, 34-21 (LA)
1985—Rams, 28-10 (LA)
      Saints, 29-3 (NO)
1986—Saints, 6-0 (NO)
      Rams, 26-13 (LA)
1987—Saints, 37-10 (NO)
      Saints, 31-14 (LA)
1988—Rams, 12-10 (NO)
      Saints, 14-10 (LA)
1989—Saints, 40-21 (LA)
      Rams, 20-17 (NO) OT
1990—Saints, 24-20 (LA)
      Saints, 20-17 (NO)
1991—Saints, 24-7 (NO)
      Saints, 24-17 (LA)
1992—Saints, 13-10 (NO)
      Saints, 37-14 (LA)
1993—Saints, 37-6 (LA)
      Rams, 23-20 (NO)
1994—Saints, 37-34 (NO)
      Saints, 31-15 (LA)
1995—Rams, 17-13 (StL)
      Saints, 19-10 (NO)
1996—Rams, 26-10 (NO)
      Rams, 14-13 (StL)
1997—Rams, 38-24 (StL)
      Rams, 34-27 (NO)
1998—Saints, 24-17 (StL)
      Saints, 24-3 (NO)
1999—Rams, 43-12 (StL)
      Rams, 30-14 (NO)
2000—Saints, 31-24 (StL)
      Rams, 26-21 (NO)
      **Saints, 31-28 (NO)
2001—Saints, 34-31 (StL)

      Rams, 34-21 (NO)
2004—Saints, 28-25 (StL) OT
2005—Rams, 28-17 (StL)
2007—Rams, 37-29 (NO)
2009—Saints, 28-23 (StL)
2010—Saints, 31-13 (NO)
2011—Rams, 31-21 (StL)
(RS Pts.—Rams 1,576, Saints 1,422)
(PS Pts.—Saints 31, Rams 28)
Franchise in Los Angeles prior to 1995
**NFC First-Round Playoff*
NEW ORLEANS vs. SAN DIEGO
RS: Chargers lead series, 7-3
1973—Chargers, 17-14 (SD)
1977—Chargers, 14-0 (NO)
1979—Chargers, 35-0 (NO)
1988—Saints, 23-17 (SD)
1991—Chargers, 24-21 (SD)
1994—Chargers, 36-22 (NO)
1997—Chargers, 20-6 (NO)
2000—Saints, 28-27 (SD)
2004—Chargers, 43-17 (SD)
2008—Saints, 37-32 (London)
(RS Pts.—Chargers 265, Saints 168)
NEW ORLEANS vs. SAN FRANCISCO
RS: 49ers lead series, 45-24-2
PS: 49ers lead series, 1-0
1967—49ers, 27-13 (SF)
1969—Saints, 43-38 (NO)
1970—Tie, 20-20 (SF)
      49ers, 38-27 (NO)
1971—49ers, 38-20 (NO)
      Saints, 26-20 (SF)
1972—49ers, 37-2 (NO)
      Tie, 20-20 (SF)
1973—49ers, 40-0 (SF)
      Saints, 16-10 (NO)
1974—49ers, 17-13 (NO)
      49ers, 35-21 (SF)
1975—49ers, 35-21 (SF)
      49ers, 16-6 (NO)
1976—49ers, 33-3 (SF)
      49ers, 27-7 (NO)
1977—49ers, 10-7 (NO) OT
      49ers, 20-17 (SF)
1978—Saints, 14-7 (SF)
      Saints, 24-13 (NO)
1979—Saints, 30-21 (SF)
      Saints, 31-20 (NO)
1980—49ers, 26-23 (NO)
      49ers, 38-35 (SF) OT
1981—49ers, 21-14 (SF)
      49ers, 21-17 (NO)
1982—Saints, 23-20 (SF)
1983—49ers, 32-13 (NO)
      49ers, 27-0 (SF)
1984—49ers, 30-20 (SF)
      49ers, 35-3 (NO)
1985—Saints, 20-17 (SF)
      49ers, 31-19 (NO)
1986—49ers, 26-17 (SF)
      Saints, 23-10 (NO)
1987—49ers, 24-22 (NO)
      Saints, 26-24 (SF)
1988—49ers, 34-33 (NO)
      49ers, 30-17 (SF)
1989—49ers, 24-20 (NO)
      49ers, 31-13 (SF)
1990—49ers, 13-12 (NO)
      Saints, 13-10 (SF)
1991—Saints, 10-3 (NO)
      49ers, 38-24 (SF)

1992—49ers, 16-10 (NO)
    49ers, 21-20 (SF)
1993—Saints, 16-13 (NO)
    49ers, 42-7 (SF)
1994—49ers, 24-13 (SF)
    49ers, 35-14 (NO)
1995—49ers, 24-22 (NO)
    Saints, 11-7 (SF)
1996—49ers, 27-11 (SF)
    49ers, 24-17 (NO)
1997—49ers, 33-7 (SF)
    49ers, 23-0 (NO)
1998—49ers, 31-0 (NO)
    49ers, 31-20 (SF)
1999—49ers, 28-21 (SF)
    Saints, 24-6 (NO)
2000—Saints, 31-15 (NO)
    Saints, 31-27 (SF)
2001—49ers, 28-27 (SF)
    49ers, 38-0 (NO)
2002—Saints, 35-27 (NO)
2004—Saints, 30-27 (NO)
2006—Saints, 34-10 (NO)
2007—Saints, 31-10 (NO)
2008—Saints, 31-17 (NO)
2010—Saints, 25-22 (SF)
2011—*49ers, 36-32 (SF)
(RS Pts.—49ers 1,713, Saints 1,286)
(PS Pts.—49ers 36, Saints 32)
*NFC Divisional Playoff
NEW ORLEANS vs. SEATTLE
RS: Saints lead series, 6-5
PS: Seahawks lead series, 1-0
1976—Saints, 51-27 (S)
1979—Seahawks, 38-24 (S)
1985—Seahawks, 27-3 (NO)
1988—Saints, 20-19 (S)
1991—Saints, 27-24 (NO)
1997—Saints, 20-17 (NO) OT
2000—Seahawks, 20-10 (S)
2003—Seahawks, 27-10 (S)
2004—Seahawks, 21-7 (NO)
2007—Saints, 28-17 (S)
2010—Saints, 34-19 (NO)
    *Seahawks, 41-36 (S)
(RS Pts.—Seahawks 256, Saints 234)
(PS Pts.—Seahawks 41, Saints 36)
*NFC First-Round Playoff
NEW ORLEANS vs. TAMPA BAY
RS: Saints lead series, 23-17
1977—Buccaneers, 33-14 (NO)
1978—Saints, 17-10 (TB)
1979—Saints, 42-14 (TB)
1981—Buccaneers, 31-14 (NO)
1982—Saints, 13-10 (NO)
1983—Saints, 24-21 (TB)
1984—Saints, 17-13 (NO)
1985—Saints, 20-13 (NO)
1986—Saints, 38-7 (NO)
1987—Saints, 44-34 (NO)
1988—Saints, 13-9 (NO)
1989—Buccaneers, 20-10 (TB)
1990—Saints, 35-7 (NO)
1991—Saints, 23-7 (NO)
1992—Saints, 23-21 (NO)
1994—Saints, 9-7 (TB)
1996—Buccaneers, 13-7 (TB)
1998—Saints, 9-3 (NO)
1999—Buccaneers, 31-16 (NO)
2001—Buccaneers, 48-21 (TB)
2002—Saints, 26-20 (TB) OT
    Saints, 23-20 (NO)

2003—Saints, 17-14 (TB)
    Buccaneers, 14-7 (NO)
2004—Buccaneers, 20-17 (NO)
    Saints, 21-17 (TB)
2005—Buccaneers, 10-3 (Baton Rouge)
    Buccaneers, 27-13 (TB)
2006—Saints, 24-21 (NO)
    Saints, 31-14 (TB)
2007—Buccaneers, 31-14 (TB)
    Buccaneers, 27-23 (NO)
2008—Saints, 24-20 (NO)
    Buccaneers, 23-20 (TB)
2009—Saints, 38-7 (TB)
    Buccaneers, 20-17 (NO) OT
2010—Saints, 31-6 (TB)
    Buccaneers, 23-13 (NO)
2011—Buccaneers, 26-20 (TB)
    Saints, 27-16 (NO)
(RS Pts.—Saints 815, Buccaneers 731)
NEW ORLEANS vs. *TENNESSEE
RS: Titans lead series, 7-5-1
1971—Tie, 13-13 (H)
1976—Oilers, 31-26 (NO)
1978—Oilers, 17-12 (NO)
1981—Saints, 27-24 (H)
1984—Saints, 27-10 (H)
1987—Saints, 24-10 (NO)
1990—Oilers, 23-10 (H)
1993—Saints, 33-21 (NO)
1996—Oilers, 31-14 (NO)
1999—Titans, 24-21 (NO)
2003—Titans, 27-12 (T)
2007—Titans, 31-14 (NO)
2011—Saints, 22-17 (T)
(RS Pts.—Titans 279, Saints 255)
*Franchise in Houston prior to 1997;
known as Oilers prior to 1999
NEW ORLEANS vs. WASHINGTON
RS: Redskins lead series, 15-8
1967—Redskins, 30-10 (NO)
    Saints, 30-14 (W)
1968—Saints, 37-17 (NO)
1969—Redskins, 26-20 (NO)
    Redskins, 17-14 (W)
1971—Redskins, 24-14 (W)
1973—Saints, 19-3 (NO)
1975—Redskins, 41-3 (W)
1979—Saints, 14-10 (W)
1980—Redskins, 22-14 (W)
1982—Redskins, 27-10 (NO)
1986—Redskins, 14-6 (NO)
1988—Redskins, 27-24 (W)
1989—Redskins, 16-14 (NO)
1990—Redskins, 31-17 (W)
1992—Saints, 20-3 (NO)
1994—Redskins, 38-24 (NO)
2001—Redskins, 40-10 (NO)
2002—Saints, 43-27 (W)
2003—Saints, 24-20 (W)
2006—Redskins, 16-10 (NO)
2008—Redskins, 29-24 (W)
2009—Saints, 33-30 (W) OT
(RS Pts.—Redskins 522, Saints 434)

N.Y. GIANTS vs. ARIZONA
RS: Giants lead series, 80-42-2;
See Arizona vs. N.Y. Giants
N.Y. GIANTS vs. ATLANTA
RS: Series tied, 10-10
PS: Giants lead series, 1-0;
See Atlanta vs. N.Y. Giants

N.Y. GIANTS vs. BALTIMORE
RS: Ravens lead series, 2-1
PS: Ravens lead series, 1-0;
See Baltimore vs. N.Y. Giants
N.Y. GIANTS vs. BUFFALO
RS: Bills lead series, 6-5
PS: Giants lead series, 1-0;
See Buffalo vs. N.Y. Giants
N.Y. GIANTS vs. CAROLINA
RS: Series tied, 3-3
PS: Panthers lead series, 1-0;
See Carolina vs. N.Y. Giants
N.Y. GIANTS vs. CHICAGO
RS: Bears lead series, 27-19-2
PS: Bears lead series, 5-3;
See Chicago vs. N.Y. Giants
N.Y. GIANTS vs. CINCINNATI
RS: Bengals lead series, 5-3;
See Cincinnati vs. N.Y. Giants
N.Y. GIANTS vs. CLEVELAND
RS: Browns lead series, 26-19-2
PS: Series tied, 1-1;
See Cleveland vs. N.Y. Giants
N.Y. GIANTS vs. DALLAS
RS: Cowboys lead series, 56-41-2
PS: Giants lead series, 1-0;
See Dallas vs. N.Y. Giants
N.Y. GIANTS vs. DENVER
RS: Series tied, 5-5
PS: Giants lead series, 1-0;
See Denver vs. N.Y. Giants
N.Y. GIANTS vs. DETROIT
RS: Lions lead series, 20-19-1
PS: Lions lead series, 1-0;
See Detroit vs. N.Y. Giants
N.Y. GIANTS vs. GREEN BAY
RS: Packers lead series, 27-21-2
PS: Packers lead series, 4-3;
See Green Bay vs. N.Y. Giants
N.Y. GIANTS vs. HOUSTON
RS: Giants lead series, 2-1;
See Houston vs. N.Y. Giants
N.Y. GIANTS vs. INDIANAPOLIS
RS: Colts lead series, 8-6
PS: Colts lead series, 2-0;
See Indianapolis vs. N.Y. Giants
N.Y. GIANTS vs. JACKSONVILLE
RS: Giants lead series, 3-2;
See Jacksonville vs. N.Y. Giants
N.Y. GIANTS vs. KANSAS CITY
RS: Giants lead series, 10-2;
See Kansas City vs. N.Y. Giants
N.Y. GIANTS vs. MIAMI
RS: Giants lead series, 5-2;
See Miami vs. N.Y. Giants
N.Y. GIANTS vs. MINNESOTA
RS: Vikings lead series, 13-9
PS: Giants lead series, 2-1;
See Minnesota vs. N.Y. Giants
N.Y. GIANTS vs. NEW ENGLAND
RS: Patriots lead series, 5-4
PS: Giants lead series, 2-0;
See New England vs. N.Y. Giants
N.Y. GIANTS vs. NEW ORLEANS
RS: Giants lead series, 14-12;
See New Orleans vs. N.Y. Giants
N.Y. GIANTS vs. N.Y. JETS
RS: Giants lead series, 8-4
1970—Giants, 22-10 (NYJ)
1974—Jets, 26-20 (New Haven) OT
1981—Jets, 26-7 (NYG)
1984—Giants, 20-10 (NYJ)

1987—Giants, 20-7 (NYG)
1988—Jets, 27-21 (NYJ)
1993—Jets, 10-6 (NYG)
1996—Giants, 13-6 (NYJ)
1999—Giants, 41-28 (NYG)
2003—Giants, 31-28 (NYJ) OT
2007—Giants, 35-24 (NYG)
2011—Giants, 29-14 (NYJ)
(RS Pts.—Giants 265, Jets 216)
N.Y. GIANTS vs. *OAKLAND
RS: Raiders lead series, 7-4
1973—Raiders, 42-0 (O)
1980—Raiders, 33-17 (NY)
1983—Raiders, 27-12 (LA)
1986—Giants, 14-9 (LA)
1989—Giants, 34-17 (NY)
1992—Raiders, 13-10 (LA)
1995—Raiders, 17-13 (NY)
1998—Raiders, 20-17 (O)
2001—Raiders, 28-10 (NY)
2005—Giants, 30-21 (O)
2009—Giants, 44-7 (NY)
(RS Pts.—Raiders 234, Giants 201)
*Franchise in Los Angeles from 1982-1994
N.Y. GIANTS vs. PHILADELPHIA
RS: Giants lead series, 80-72-2
PS: Series tied, 2-2
1933—Giants, 56-0 (NY)
       Giants, 20-14 (P)
1934—Giants, 17-0 (NY)
       Eagles, 6-0 (P)
1935—Giants, 10-0 (NY)
       Giants, 21-14 (P)
1936—Eagles, 10-7 (P)
       Giants, 21-17 (NY)
1937—Giants, 16-7 (P)
       Giants, 21-0 (NY)
1938—Eagles, 14-10 (P)
       Giants, 17-7 (NY)
1939—Giants, 13-3 (P)
       Giants, 27-10 (NY)
1940—Giants, 20-14 (P)
       Giants, 17-7 (NY)
1941—Giants, 24-0 (P)
       Giants, 16-0 (NY)
1942—Giants, 35-17 (NY)
       Giants, 14-0 (P)
1944—Eagles, 24-17 (NY)
       Tie, 21-21 (P)
1945—Eagles, 38-17 (P)
       Giants, 28-21 (NY)
1946—Eagles, 24-14 (P)
       Giants, 45-17 (NY)
1947—Eagles, 23-0 (P)
       Eagles, 41-24 (NY)
1948—Eagles, 45-0 (P)
       Eagles, 35-14 (NY)
1949—Eagles, 24-3 (NY)
       Eagles, 17-3 (P)
1950—Giants, 7-3 (NY)
       Giants, 9-7 (P)
1951—Giants, 26-24 (NY)
       Giants, 23-7 (P)
1952—Giants, 31-7 (P)
       Eagles, 14-10 (NY)
1953—Eagles, 30-7 (P)
       Giants, 37-28 (NY)
1954—Giants, 27-14 (NY)
       Eagles, 29-14 (P)
1955—Eagles, 27-17 (P)
       Giants, 31-7 (NY)
1956—Giants, 20-3 (NY)

Giants, 21-7 (P)
1957—Giants, 24-20 (P)
       Giants, 13-0 (NY)
1958—Eagles, 27-24 (P)
       Giants, 24-10 (NY)
1959—Eagles, 49-21 (P)
       Giants, 24-7 (NY)
1960—Eagles, 17-10 (NY)
       Eagles, 31-23 (P)
1961—Giants, 38-21 (NY)
       Giants, 28-24 (P)
1962—Giants, 29-13 (P)
       Giants, 19-14 (NY)
1963—Giants, 37-14 (P)
       Giants, 42-14 (NY)
1964—Eagles, 38-7 (P)
       Eagles, 23-17 (NY)
1965—Giants, 16-14 (P)
       Giants, 35-27 (NY)
1966—Eagles, 35-17 (P)
       Eagles, 31-3 (NY)
1967—Giants, 44-7 (NY)
1968—Giants, 34-25 (P)
       Giants, 7-6 (NY)
1969—Eagles, 23-20 (NY)
1970—Giants, 30-23 (NY)
       Eagles, 23-20 (P)
1971—Eagles, 23-7 (P)
       Eagles, 41-28 (NY)
1972—Giants, 27-12 (P)
       Giants, 62-10 (NY)
1973—Tie, 23-23 (NY)
       Eagles, 20-16 (P)
1974—Eagles, 35-7 (P)
       Eagles, 20-7 (New Haven)
1975—Giants, 23-14 (P)
       Eagles, 13-10 (NY)
1976—Eagles, 20-7 (P)
       Eagles, 10-0 (NY)
1977—Eagles, 28-10 (NY)
       Eagles, 17-14 (P)
1978—Eagles, 19-17 (NY)
       Eagles, 20-3 (P)
1979—Eagles, 23-17 (P)
       Eagles, 17-13 (NY)
1980—Eagles, 35-3 (P)
       Eagles, 31-16 (NY)
1981—Eagles, 24-10 (NY)
       Giants, 20-10 (P)
       *Giants, 27-21 (P)
1982—Giants, 23-7 (NY)
       Giants, 26-24 (P)
1983—Eagles, 17-13 (NY)
       Giants, 23-0 (P)
1984—Giants, 28-27 (NY)
       Eagles, 24-10 (P)
1985—Giants, 21-0 (NY)
       Giants, 16-10 (P) OT
1986—Giants, 35-3 (NY)
       Giants, 17-14 (P)
1987—Giants, 20-17 (P)
       Giants, 23-20 (NY) OT
1988—Eagles, 24-13 (P)
       Eagles, 23-17 (NY) OT
1989—Eagles, 21-19 (P)
       Eagles, 24-17 (NY)
1990—Giants, 27-20 (NY)
       Eagles, 31-13 (P)
1991—Eagles, 30-7 (P)
       Eagles, 19-14 (NY)
1992—Eagles, 47-34 (NY)
       Eagles, 20-10 (P)

1993—Giants, 21-10 (NY)
       Giants, 7-3 (P)
1994—Giants, 28-23 (NY)
       Giants, 16-13 (P)
1995—Eagles, 17-14 (NY)
       Eagles, 28-19 (P)
1996—Eagles, 19-10 (NY)
       Eagles, 24-0 (P)
1997—Giants, 31-17 (NY)
       Giants, 31-21 (P)
1998—Giants, 20-0 (NY)
       Giants, 20-10 (P)
1999—Giants, 16-15 (NY)
       Giants, 23-17 (P) OT
2000—Giants, 33-18 (P)
       Giants, 24-7 (NY)
       **Giants, 20-10 (NY)
2001—Eagles, 10-9 (NY)
       Eagles, 24-21 (P)
2002—Eagles, 17-3 (P)
       Giants, 10-7 (NY) OT
2003—Eagles, 14-10 (P)
       Eagles, 28-10 (P)
2004—Eagles, 31-17 (P)
       Eagles, 27-6 (NY)
2005—Giants, 27-17 (NY)
       Eagles, 26-23 (P) OT
2006—Giants, 30-24 (P) OT
       Eagles, 36-22 (NY)
       *Eagles, 23-20 (P)
2007—Giants, 16-3 (NY)
       Giants, 16-13 (P)
2008—Giants, 36-31 (NY)
       Eagles, 20-14 (NY)
       **Eagles, 23-11 (NY)
2009—Eagles, 40-17 (P)
       Eagles, 45-38 (NY)
2010—Eagles, 27-17 (P)
       Eagles, 38-31 (NY)
2011—Giants, 29-16 (P)
       Eagles, 17-10 (NY)
(RS Pts.—Giants 2,948, Eagles 2,850)
(PS Pts.—Giants 78, Eagles 77)
*NFC First-Round Playoff
**NFC Divisional Playoff
N.Y. GIANTS vs. *PITTSBURGH
RS: Giants lead series, 44-28-3
1933—Giants, 23-2 (P)
       Giants, 27-3 (NY)
1934—Giants, 14-12 (P)
       Giants, 17-7 (NY)
1935—Giants, 42-7 (P)
       Giants, 13-0 (NY)
1936—Pirates, 10-7 (P)
1937—Giants, 10-7 (P)
       Giants, 17-0 (NY)
1938—Giants, 27-14 (P)
       Pirates, 13-10 (NY)
1939—Giants, 14-7 (P)
       Giants, 23-7 (NY)
1940—Tie, 10-10 (P)
       Giants, 12-0 (NY)
1941—Giants, 37-10 (P)
       Giants, 28-7 (NY)
1942—Steelers, 13-10 (P)
       Steelers, 17-9 (NY)
1945—Giants, 34-6 (NY)
       Steelers, 21-7 (NY)
1946—Giants, 17-14 (P)
       Giants, 7-0 (NY)
1947—Steelers, 38-21 (NY)
       Steelers, 24-7 (P)

1948—Giants, 34-27 (NY)
    Steelers, 38-28 (P)
1949—Steelers, 28-7 (P)
    Steelers, 21-17 (NY)
1950—Giants, 18-7 (P)
    Steelers, 17-6 (NY)
1951—Tie, 13-13 (P)
    Giants, 14-0 (NY)
1952—Steelers, 63-7 (P)
1953—Steelers, 24-14 (P)
    Steelers, 14-10 (NY)
1954—Giants, 30-6 (P)
    Giants, 24-3 (NY)
1955—Steelers, 30-23 (P)
    Steelers, 19-17 (NY)
1956—Giants, 38-10 (NY)
    Giants, 17-14 (P)
1957—Giants, 35-0 (NY)
    Steelers, 21-10 (P)
1958—Giants, 17-6 (NY)
    Steelers, 31-10 (P)
1959—Giants, 21-16 (P)
    Steelers, 14-9 (NY)
1960—Giants, 19-17 (P)
    Giants, 27-24 (NY)
1961—Giants, 17-14 (P)
    Giants, 42-21 (NY)
1962—Giants, 31-27 (P)
    Steelers, 20-17 (NY)
1963—Steelers, 31-0 (P)
    Giants, 33-17 (NY)
1964—Steelers, 27-24 (P)
    Steelers, 44-17 (NY)
1965—Giants, 23-13 (P)
    Giants, 35-10 (NY)
1966—Tie, 34-34 (P)
    Steelers, 47-28 (NY)
1967—Giants, 27-24 (P)
    Giants, 28-20 (NY)
1968—Giants, 34-20 (P)
1969—Giants, 10-7 (NY)
    Giants, 21-17 (P)
1971—Steelers, 17-13 (P)
1976—Steelers, 27-0 (NY)
1985—Giants, 28-10 (NY)
1991—Giants, 23-20 (P)
1994—Steelers, 10-6 (NY)
2000—Giants, 30-10 (NY)
2004—Steelers, 33-30 (NY)
2008—Giants, 21-14 (P)
(RS Pts.—Giants 1,480, Steelers 1,246)
*Steelers known as Pirates prior to 1940
N.Y. GIANTS vs. *ST. LOUIS
RS: Rams lead series, 25-14
PS: Series tied, 1-1
1938—Giants, 28-0 (NY)
1940—Rams, 13-0 (NY)
1941—Giants, 49-14 (NY)
1945—Rams, 21-17 (NY)
1946—Rams, 31-21 (NY)
1947—Rams, 34-10 (LA)
1948—Rams, 52-37 (NY)
1953—Rams, 21-7 (LA)
1954—Rams, 17-16 (NY)
1959—Rams, 23-21 (LA)
1961—Giants, 24-14 (NY)
1966—Rams, 55-14 (LA)
1968—Rams, 24-21 (LA)
1970—Rams, 31-3 (NY)
1973—Rams, 40-6 (LA)
1976—Rams, 24-10 (LA)
1978—Rams, 20-17 (NY)

1979—Giants, 20-14 (LA)
1980—Rams, 28-7 (NY)
1981—Giants, 10-7 (NY)
1983—Rams, 16-6 (NY)
1984—Rams, 33-12 (LA)
    **Giants, 16-13 (LA)
1985—Giants, 24-19 (NY)
1988—Rams, 45-31 (NY)
1989—Rams, 31-10 (LA)
    ***Rams, 19-13 (NY) OT
1990—Giants, 31-7 (LA)
1991—Rams, 19-13 (NY)
1992—Rams, 38-17 (LA)
1993—Giants, 20-10 (NY)
1994—Rams, 17-10 (LA)
1997—Rams, 13-3 (StL)
1999—Rams, 31-10 (StL)
2000—Rams, 38-24 (NY)
2001—Rams, 15-14 (StL)
2002—Giants, 26-21 (StL)
2003—Giants, 23-13 (NY)
2005—Giants, 44-24 (NY)
2008—Giants, 41-13 (StL)
2011—Giants, 28-16 (NY)
(RS Pts.—Rams 900, Giants 727)
(PS Pts.—Rams 32, Giants 29)
*Franchise in Los Angeles prior to 1995
and in Cleveland prior to 1946
**NFC First-Round Playoff
***NFC Divisional Playoff
N.Y. GIANTS vs. SAN DIEGO
RS: Series tied, 5-5
1971—Giants, 35-17 (NY)
1975—Giants, 35-24 (NY)
1980—Chargers, 44-7 (SD)
1983—Chargers, 41-34 (NY)
1986—Giants, 20-7 (NY)
1989—Giants, 20-13 (SD)
1995—Chargers, 27-17 (NY)
1998—Giants, 34-16 (SD)
2005—Chargers, 45-23 (SD)
2009—Chargers, 21-20 (NY)
(RS Pts.—Chargers 255, Giants 245)
N.Y. GIANTS vs. SAN FRANCISCO
RS: Series tied, 14-14
PS: Series tied, 4-4
1952—Giants, 23-14 (NY)
1956—Giants, 38-21 (SF)
1957—49ers, 27-17 (NY)
1960—Giants, 21-19 (SF)
1963—Giants, 48-14 (NY)
1968—49ers, 26-10 (NY)
1972—Giants, 23-17 (SF)
1975—Giants, 26-23 (SF)
1977—Giants, 20-17 (NY)
1978—49ers, 27-10 (NY)
1979—Giants, 32-16 (NY)
1980—49ers, 12-0 (SF)
1981—49ers, 17-10 (SF)
    *49ers, 38-24 (SF)
1984—49ers, 31-10 (NY)
    *49ers, 21-10 (SF)
1985—**Giants, 17-3 (NY)
1986—Giants, 21-17 (SF)
    *Giants, 49-3 (NY)
1987—49ers, 41-21 (NY)
1988—49ers, 20-17 (NY)
1989—49ers, 34-24 (SF)
1990—49ers, 7-3 (SF)
    ***Giants, 15-13 (SF)
1991—Giants, 16-14 (NY)
1992—49ers, 31-14 (NY)

1993—*49ers, 44-3 (SF)
1995—49ers, 20-6 (SF)
1998—49ers, 31-7 (SF)
2002—49ers, 16-13 (NY)
    **49ers, 39-38 (SF)
2005—Giants, 24-6 (SF)
2007—Giants, 33-15 (NY)
2008—Giants, 29-17 (NY)
2011—49ers, 27-20 (SF)
    ***Giants, 20-17 (SF) OT
(RS Pts.—49ers 560, Giants 553)
(PS Pts.—49ers 178, Giants 176)
*NFC Divisional Playoff
**NFC First-Round Playoff
***NFC Championship
N.Y. GIANTS vs. SEATTLE
RS: Giants lead series, 9-6
1976—Giants, 28-16 (NY)
1980—Giants, 27-21 (S)
1981—Giants, 32-0 (S)
1983—Seahawks, 17-12 (NY)
1986—Seahawks, 17-12 (S)
1989—Giants, 15-3 (NY)
1992—Giants, 23-10 (NY)
1995—Seahawks, 30-28 (S)
2001—Giants, 27-24 (NY)
2002—Giants, 9-6 (NY)
2005—Seahawks, 24-21 (S) OT
2006—Seahawks, 42-30 (S)
2008—Giants, 44-6 (NY)
2010—Giants, 41-7 (S)
2011—Seahawks, 36-25 (NY)
(RS Pts.—Giants 374, Seahawks 259)
N.Y. GIANTS vs. TAMPA BAY
RS: Giants lead series, 11-6
PS: Giants lead series, 1-0
1977—Giants, 10-0 (TB)
1978—Giants, 19-13 (TB)
    Giants, 17-14 (NY)
1979—Giants, 17-14 (NY)
    Buccaneers, 31-3 (TB)
1980—Buccaneers, 30-13 (TB)
1984—Giants, 17-14 (NY)
    Buccaneers, 20-17 (TB)
1985—Giants, 22-20 (NY)
1991—Giants, 21-14 (TB)
1993—Giants, 23-7 (NY)
1997—Buccaneers, 20-8 (NY)
1998—Buccaneers, 20-3 (TB)
1999—Giants, 17-13 (TB)
2003—Buccaneers, 19-13 (TB)
2006—Giants, 17-3 (NY)
2007—*Giants, 24-14 (TB)
2009—Giants, 24-0 (TB)
(RS Pts.—Giants 261, Buccaneers 252)
(PS Pts.—Giants 24, Buccaneers 14)
*NFC First-Round Playoff
N.Y. GIANTS vs. *TENNESSEE
RS: Series tied, 5-5
1973—Giants, 34-14 (NY)
1982—Giants, 17-14 (NY)
1985—Giants, 35-14 (H)
1991—Giants, 24-20 (NY)
1994—Giants, 13-10 (H)
1997—Oilers, 10-6 (T)
2000—Titans, 28-14 (T)
2002—Titans, 32-29 (NY) OT
2006—Titans, 24-21 (T)
2010—Titans, 29-10 (NY)
(RS Pts.—Giants 203, Titans 195)
*Franchise in Houston prior to 1997;
known as Oilers prior to 1999

N.Y. GIANTS vs. *WASHINGTON

RS: Giants lead series, 91-63-4
PS: Series tied, 1-1
1932—Braves, 14-6 (B)
   Tie, 0-0 (NY)
1933—Redskins, 21-20 (B)
   Giants, 7-0 (NY)
1934—Giants, 16-13 (B)
   Giants, 3-0 (NY)
1935—Giants, 20-12 (B)
   Giants, 17-6 (NY)
1936—Giants, 7-0 (B)
   Redskins, 14-0 (NY)
1937—Redskins, 13-3 (W)
   Redskins, 49-14 (NY)
1938—Giants, 10-7 (W)
   Giants, 36-0 (NY)
1939—Tie, 0-0 (W)
   Giants, 9-7 (NY)
1940—Redskins, 21-7 (W)
   Giants, 21-7 (NY)
1941—Giants, 17-10 (W)
   Giants, 20-13 (NY)
1942—Giants, 14-7 (W)
   Redskins, 14-7 (NY)
1943—Giants, 14-10 (NY)
   Giants, 31-7 (W)
   **Redskins, 28-0 (NY)
1944—Giants, 16-13 (W)
   Giants, 31-0 (W)
1945—Redskins, 24-14 (NY)
   Redskins, 17-0 (W)
1946—Redskins, 24-14 (W)
   Giants, 31-0 (NY)
1947—Redskins, 28-20 (W)
   Giants, 35-10 (NY)
1948—Redskins, 41-10 (W)
   Redskins, 28-21 (NY)
1949—Giants, 45-35 (W)
   Giants, 23-7 (NY)
1950—Giants, 21-17 (W)
   Giants, 24-21 (NY)
1951—Giants, 35-14 (W)
   Giants, 28-14 (NY)
1952—Giants, 14-10 (W)
   Redskins, 27-17 (NY)
1953—Redskins, 13-9 (W)
   Redskins, 24-21 (NY)
1954—Giants, 51-21 (W)
   Giants, 24-7 (NY)
1955—Giants, 35-7 (NY)
   Giants, 27-20 (W)
1956—Redskins, 33-7 (W)
   Giants, 28-14 (NY)
1957—Giants, 24-20 (W)
   Redskins, 31-14 (NY)
1958—Giants, 21-14 (W)
   Giants, 30-0 (NY)
1959—Giants, 45-14 (NY)
   Giants, 24-10 (W)
1960—Tie, 24-24 (NY)
   Giants, 17-3 (W)
1961—Giants, 24-21 (W)
   Giants, 53-0 (NY)
1962—Giants, 49-34 (W)
   Giants, 42-24 (NY)
1963—Giants, 24-14 (W)
   Giants, 44-14 (NY)
1964—Giants, 13-10 (NY)
   Redskins, 36-21 (W)
1965—Redskins, 23-7 (NY)
   Giants, 27-10 (W)

1966—Giants, 13-10 (NY)
   Redskins, 72-41 (W)
1967—Redskins, 38-34 (W)
1968—Giants, 48-21 (NY)
   Giants, 13-10 (W)
1969—Giants, 20-14 (W)
1970—Giants, 35-33 (NY)
   Giants, 27-24 (W)
1971—Redskins, 30-3 (NY)
   Redskins, 23-7 (W)
1972—Redskins, 23-16 (NY)
   Redskins, 27-13 (W)
1973—Redskins, 21-3 (New Haven)
   Redskins, 27-24 (W)
1974—Redskins, 13-10 (New Haven)
   Redskins, 24-3 (W)
1975—Redskins, 49-13 (W)
   Redskins, 21-13 (NY)
1976—Redskins, 19-17 (W)
   Giants, 12-9 (NY)
1977—Giants, 20-17 (NY)
   Giants, 17-6 (W)
1978—Giants, 17-6 (NY)
   Redskins, 16-13 (W) OT
1979—Redskins, 27-0 (W)
   Giants, 14-6 (NY)
1980—Redskins, 23-21 (NY)
   Redskins, 16-13 (W)
1981—Giants, 17-7 (W)
   Redskins, 30-27 (NY) OT
1982—Redskins, 27-17 (NY)
   Redskins, 15-14 (W)
1983—Redskins, 33-17 (NY)
   Redskins, 31-22 (W)
1984—Redskins, 30-14 (W)
   Giants, 37-13 (NY)
1985—Giants, 17-3 (NY)
   Redskins, 23-21 (W)
1986—Giants, 27-20 (NY)
   Giants, 24-14 (W)
   ***Giants, 17-0 (NY)
1987—Redskins, 38-12 (NY)
   Redskins, 23-19 (W)
1988—Giants, 27-20 (NY)
   Giants, 24-23 (W)
1989—Giants, 27-24 (W)
   Giants, 20-17 (NY)
1990—Giants, 24-20 (W)
   Giants, 21-10 (NY)
1991—Redskins, 17-13 (NY)
   Redskins, 34-17 (W)
1992—Giants, 24-7 (W)
   Redskins, 28-10 (NY)
1993—Giants, 41-7 (W)
   Giants, 20-6 (NY)
1994—Giants, 31-23 (NY)
   Giants, 21-19 (W)
1995—Giants, 24-15 (W)
   Giants, 20-13 (NY)
1996—Redskins, 31-10 (NY)
   Redskins, 31-21 (W)
1997—Tie, 7-7 (W) OT
   Giants, 30-10 (NY)
1998—Giants, 31-24 (NY)
   Redskins, 21-14 (W)
1999—Redskins, 50-21 (NY)
   Redskins, 23-13 (W)
2000—Redskins, 16-6 (NY)
   Giants, 9-7 (W)
2001—Giants, 23-9 (NY)
   Redskins, 35-21 (W)
2002—Giants, 19-17 (NY)

   Giants, 27-21 (W)
2003—Giants, 24-21 (W) OT
   Redskins, 20-7 (NY)
2004—Giants, 20-14 (NY)
   Redskins, 31-7 (W)
2005—Giants, 36-0 (NY)
   Redskins, 35-20 (W)
2006—Giants, 19-3 (NY)
   Giants, 34-28 (W)
2007—Giants, 24-17 (W)
   Redskins, 22-10 (NY)
2008—Giants, 16-7 (NY)
   Giants, 23-7 (W)
2009—Giants, 23-17 (NY)
   Giants, 45-12 (W)
2010—Giants, 31-7 (W)
   Giants, 17-14 (W)
2011—Redskins, 28-14 (W)
   Redskins, 23-10 (NY)
(RS Pts.—Giants 3,158, Redskins 2,845)
(PS Pts.—Redskins 28, Giants 17)
*Franchise in Boston prior to 1937 and known as Braves prior to 1933
**Division Playoff
***NFC Championship

N.Y. JETS vs. ARIZONA

RS: Jets lead series, 5-2;
See Arizona vs. N.Y. Jets

N.Y. JETS vs. ATLANTA

RS: Falcons lead series, 6-4;
See Atlanta vs. N.Y. Jets

N.Y. JETS vs. BALTIMORE

RS: Ravens lead series, 7-1;
See Baltimore vs. N.Y. Jets

N.Y. JETS vs. BUFFALO

RS: Bills lead series, 53-49
PS: Bills lead series, 1-0;
See Buffalo vs. N.Y. Jets

N.Y. JETS vs. CAROLINA

RS: Jets lead series, 3-2;
See Carolina vs. N.Y. Jets

N.Y. JETS vs. CHICAGO

RS: Bears lead series, 7-3;
See Chicago vs. N.Y. Jets

N.Y. JETS vs. CINCINNATI

RS: Jets lead series, 15-7
PS: Jets lead series, 2-0;
See Cincinnati vs. N.Y. Jets

N.Y. JETS vs. CLEVELAND

RS: Browns lead series, 12-8
PS: Browns lead series, 1-0;
See Cleveland vs. N.Y. Jets

N.Y. JETS vs. DALLAS

RS: Cowboys lead series, 7-3;
See Dallas vs. N.Y. Jets

N.Y. JETS vs. DENVER

RS: Broncos lead series, 17-15-1
PS: Broncos lead series, 1-0;
See Denver vs. N.Y. Jets

N.Y. JETS vs. DETROIT

RS: Series tied, 6-6;
See Detroit vs. N.Y. Jets

N.Y. JETS vs. GREEN BAY

RS: Jets lead series, 8-3;
See Green Bay vs. N.Y. Jets

N.Y. JETS vs. HOUSTON

RS: Jets lead series, 5-0;
See Houston vs. N.Y. Jets

N.Y. JETS vs. INDIANAPOLIS

RS: Colts lead series, 40-26
PS: Jets lead series, 3-1;

See Indianapolis vs. N.Y. Jets
N.Y. JETS vs. JACKSONVILLE
RS: Jaguars lead series, 6-3
PS: Jets lead series, 1-0;
See Jacksonville vs. N.Y. Jets
N.Y. JETS vs. KANSAS CITY
RS: Jets lead series, 17-16-1
PS: Series tied, 1-1;
See Kansas City vs. N.Y. Jets
N.Y. JETS vs. MIAMI
RS: Jets lead series, 48-43-1
PS: Dolphins lead series, 1-0;
See Miami vs. N.Y. Jets
N.Y. JETS vs. MINNESOTA
RS: Jets lead series, 8-1;
See Minnesota vs. N.Y. Jets
N.Y. JETS vs. NEW ENGLAND
RS: Series tied, 51-51-1
PS: Patriots lead series, 2-1;
See New England vs. N.Y. Jets
N.Y. JETS vs. NEW ORLEANS
RS: Saints lead series, 6-5;
See New Orleans vs. N.Y. Jets
N.Y. JETS vs. N.Y. GIANTS
RS: Giants lead series, 8-4;
See N.Y. Giants vs. N.Y. Jets
*N.Y. JETS vs. **OAKLAND
RS: Raiders lead series, 21-15-2
PS: Series tied, 2-2
1960—Raiders, 28-27 (NY)
       Titans, 31-28 (O)
1961—Titans, 14-6 (O)
       Titans, 23-12 (NY)
1962—Titans, 28-17 (O)
       Titans, 31-21 (NY)
1963—Jets, 10-7 (NY)
       Raiders, 49-26 (O)
1964—Jets, 35-13 (NY)
       Raiders, 35-26 (O)
1965—Tie, 24-24 (NY)
       Raiders, 24-14 (O)
1966—Raiders, 24-21 (NY)
       Tie, 28-28 (O)
1967—Jets, 27-14 (NY)
       Raiders, 38-29 (O)
1968—Raiders, 43-32 (NY)
       ***Jets, 27-23 (NY)
1969—Raiders, 27-14 (NY)
1970—Raiders, 14-13 (NY)
1972—Raiders, 24-16 (O)
1977—Raiders, 28-27 (NY)
1979—Jets, 28-19 (NY)
1982—****Jets, 17-14 (LA)
1985—Raiders, 31-0 (LA)
1989—Raiders, 14-7 (NY)
1993—Raiders, 24-20 (LA)
1995—Raiders, 47-10 (NY)
1996—Raiders, 34-13 (NY)
1997—Jets 23-22 (NY)
1999—Raiders, 24-23 (O)
2000—Raiders, 31-7 (O)
2001—Jets, 24-22 (O)
       *****Raiders, 38-24 (O)
2002—Raiders, 26-20 (O)
       ****Raiders, 30-10 (O)
2003—Jets, 27-24 (O) OT
2005—Jets, 26-10 (NY)
2006—Jets, 23-3 (NY)
2008—Raiders, 16-13 (O) OT
2009—Jets, 38-0 (O)
2011—Raiders, 34-24 (O)
(RS Pts.—Raiders 885, Jets 822)

(PS Pts.—Raiders 105, Jets 78)
Jets known as Titans prior to 1963
**Franchise in Los Angeles from
1982-1994
***AFL Championship
****AFC Second-Round Playoff
*****AFC First-Round Playoff
N.Y. JETS vs. PHILADELPHIA
RS: Eagles lead series, 9-0
1973—Eagles, 24-23 (P)
1977—Eagles, 27-0 (P)
1978—Eagles, 17-9 (P)
1987—Eagles, 38-27 (NY)
1993—Eagles, 35-30 (NY)
1996—Eagles, 21-20 (NY)
2003—Eagles, 24-17 (P)
2007—Eagles, 16-9 (NY)
2011—Eagles, 45-19 (P)
(RS Pts.—Eagles 247, Jets 154)
N.Y. JETS vs. PITTSBURGH
RS: Steelers lead series, 15-4
PS: Steelers lead series, 2-0
1970—Steelers, 21-17 (P)
1973—Steelers, 26-14 (P)
1975—Steelers, 20-7 (NY)
1977—Steelers, 23-20 (NY)
1978—Steelers, 28-17 (NY)
1981—Steelers, 38-10 (P)
1983—Steelers, 34-7 (NY)
1984—Steelers, 23-17 (NY)
1986—Steelers, 45-24 (NY)
1988—Jets, 24-20 (NY)
1989—Steelers, 13-0 (NY)
1990—Steelers, 24-7 (NY)
1992—Steelers, 27-10 (P)
2000—Steelers, 20-3 (NY)
2001—Steelers, 18-7 (P)
2003—Jets, 6-0 (NY)
2004—Steelers, 17-6 (P)
       *Steelers, 20-17 (P) OT
2007—Jets, 19-16 (NY) OT
2010—Jets, 22-17 (P)
       **Steelers, 24-19 (P)
(RS Pts.—Steelers 430, Jets 237)
(PS Pts.—Steelers 44, Jets 36)
*AFC Divisional Playoff
**AFC Championship
N.Y. JETS vs. *ST. LOUIS
RS: Rams lead series, 9-3
1970—Jets, 31-20 (LA)
1974—Rams, 20-13 (NY)
1980—Rams, 38-13 (LA)
1983—Jets, 27-24 (NY) OT
1986—Rams, 17-3 (NY)
1989—Rams, 38-14 (LA)
1992—Rams, 18-10 (LA)
1995—Rams, 23-20 (NY)
1998—Rams, 30-10 (StL)
2001—Rams, 34-14 (NY)
2004—Rams, 32-29 (StL) OT
2008—Jets, 47-3 (NY)
(RS Pts.—Rams 297, Jets 231)
Franchise in Los Angeles prior to 1995
*N.Y. JETS vs. **SAN DIEGO
RS: Chargers lead series, 19-12-1
PS: Jets lead series, 2-0
1960—Chargers, 21-7 (NY)
       Chargers, 50-43 (LA)
1961—Chargers, 25-10 (NY)
       Chargers, 48-13 (SD)
1962—Chargers, 40-14 (SD)
       Titans, 23-3 (NY)

1963—Chargers, 24-20 (SD)
       Chargers, 53-7 (NY)
1964—Tie, 17-17 (NY)
       Chargers, 38-3 (SD)
1965—Chargers, 34-9 (NY)
       Chargers, 38-7 (SD)
1966—Jets, 17-16 (NY)
       Chargers, 42-27 (SD)
1967—Jets, 42-31 (SD)
1968—Jets, 23-20 (NY)
       Jets, 37-15 (SD)
1969—Chargers, 34-27 (SD)
1971—Chargers, 49-21 (SD)
1974—Jets, 27-14 (NY)
1975—Chargers, 24-16 (SD)
1983—Jets, 41-29 (SD)
1989—Jets, 20-17 (SD)
1990—Chargers, 39-3 (NY)
       Chargers, 38-17 (SD)
1991—Jets, 24-3 (NY)
1994—Chargers, 21-6 (NY)
2002—Jets, 44-13 (SD)
2004—Jets, 34-28 (SD)
       ***Jets, 20-17 (SD) OT
2005—Chargers, 31-26 (NY)
2008—Chargers, 48-29 (SD)
2009—****Jets, 17-14 (SD)
2011—Jets, 27-21 (NY)
(RS Pts.—Chargers 924, Jets 681)
(PS Pts.—Jets 37, Chargers 31)
Jets known as Titans prior to 1963
**Franchise in Los Angeles prior to 1961
***AFC First-Round Playoff
****AFC Divisional Playoff
N.Y. JETS vs. SAN FRANCISCO
RS: 49ers lead series, 9-2
1971—49ers, 24-21 (NY)
1976—49ers, 17-6 (SF)
1980—49ers, 37-27 (NY)
1983—Jets, 27-13 (SF)
1986—49ers, 24-10 (NY)
1989—49ers, 23-10 (NY)
1992—49ers, 31-14 (NY)
1998—49ers, 36-30 (SF) OT
2001—49ers, 19-17 (NY)
2004—Jets, 22-14 (NY)
2008—49ers, 24-14 (SF)
(RS Pts.—49ers 262, Jets 198)
N.Y. JETS vs. SEATTLE
RS: Seahawks lead series, 9-8
1977—Seahawks, 17-0 (NY)
1978—Seahawks, 24-17 (NY)
1979—Seahawks, 30-7 (S)
1980—Seahawks, 27-17 (NY)
1981—Seahawks, 19-3 (NY)
       Seahawks, 27-23 (S)
1983—Seahawks, 17-10 (NY)
1985—Jets, 17-14 (NY)
1986—Jets, 38-7 (S)
1987—Jets, 30-14 (NY)
1991—Seahawks, 20-13 (S)
1995—Jets, 16-10 (S)
1997—Jets, 41-3 (S)
1998—Jets, 32-31 (NY)
1999—Jets, 19-9 (NY)
2004—Jets, 37-14 (NY)
2008—Seahawks, 13-3 (S)
(RS Pts.—Jets 323, Seahawks 296)
N.Y. JETS vs. TAMPA BAY
RS: Jets lead series, 9-1
1976—Jets, 34-0 (NY)
1982—Jets, 32-17 (NY)

1984—Buccaneers, 41-21 (TB)
1985—Jets, 62-28 (NY)
1990—Jets, 16-14 (TB)
1991—Jets, 16-13 (NY)
1997—Jets, 31-0 (NY)
2000—Jets, 21-17 (TB)
2005—Jets, 14-12 (NY)
2009—Jets, 26-3 (TB)
(RS Pts.—Jets 273, Buccaneers 145)
*N.Y. JETS vs. **TENNESSEE
RS: Titans lead series, 21-17-1
PS: Titans lead series, 1-0
1960—Oilers, 27-21 (H)
   Oilers, 42-28 (NY)
1961—Oilers, 49-13 (H)
   Oilers, 48-21 (NY)
1962—Oilers, 56-17 (H)
   Oilers, 44-10 (NY)
1963—Jets, 24-17 (NY)
   Oilers, 31-27 (H)
1964—Jets, 24-21 (NY)
   Oilers, 33-17 (H)
1965—Oilers, 27-21 (H)
   Jets, 41-14 (NY)
1966—Jets, 52-13 (NY)
   Oilers, 24-0 (H)
1967—Tie, 28-28 (NY)
1968—Jets, 20-14 (H)
   Jets, 26-7 (NY)
1969—Jets, 26-17 (NY)
   Jets, 34-26 (H)
1972—Oilers, 26-20 (H)
1974—Oilers, 27-22 (NY)
1977—Oilers, 20-0 (H)
1979—Oilers, 27-24 (H) OT
1980—Jets, 31-28 (NY) OT
1981—Jets, 33-17 (NY)
1984—Oilers, 31-20 (H)
1988—Jets, 45-3 (NY)
1990—Jets, 17-12 (H)
1991—Oilers, 23-20 (NY)
   ***Oilers, 17-10 (H)
1993—Oilers, 24-0 (H)
1994—Oilers, 24-10 (H)
1995—Oilers, 23-6 (H)
1996—Jets, 35-10 (NY)
1998—Jets, 24-3 (T)
2003—Jets, 24-17 (NY)
2006—Jets, 23-16 (T)
2007—Titans, 10-6 (T)
2008—Jets, 34-13 (T)
2009—Jets, 24-17 (NY)
(RS Pts.—Titans 934, Jets 843)
(PS Pts.—Titans 17, Jets 10)
*Jets known as Titans prior to 1963
**Franchise in Houston prior to 1997;
known as Oilers prior to 1999
***AFC First-Round Playoff
N.Y. JETS vs. WASHINGTON
RS: Redskins lead series, 8-2
1972—Redskins, 35-17 (NY)
1976—Redskins, 37-16 (NY)
1978—Redskins, 23-3 (W)
1987—Redskins, 17-16 (W)
1993—Jets, 3-0 (W)
1996—Redskins, 31-16 (W)
1999—Redskins, 27-20 (NY)
2003—Redskins, 16-13 (W)
2007—Redskins 23-20 (NY) OT
2011—Jets, 34-19 (W)
(RS Pts.—Redskins 228, Jets 158)

OAKLAND vs. ARIZONA
RS: Raiders lead series, 5-3;
See Arizona vs. Oakland
OAKLAND vs. ATLANTA
RS: Raiders lead series, 7-5;
See Atlanta vs. Oakland
OAKLAND vs. BALTIMORE
RS: Ravens lead series, 5-1
PS: Ravens lead series, 1-0;
See Baltimore vs. Oakland
OAKLAND vs. BUFFALO
RS: Raiders lead series, 19-17
PS: Bills lead series, 2-0;
See Buffalo vs. Oakland
OAKLAND vs. CAROLINA
RS: Series tied, 2-2;
See Carolina vs. Oakland
OAKLAND vs. CHICAGO
RS: Raiders lead series, 7-6;
See Chicago vs. Oakland
OAKLAND vs. CINCINNATI
RS: Raiders lead series, 18-8
PS: Raiders lead series, 2-0;
See Cincinnati vs. Oakland
OAKLAND vs. CLEVELAND
RS: Raiders lead series, 11-8
PS: Raiders lead series, 2-0;
See Cleveland vs. Oakland
OAKLAND vs. DALLAS
RS: Raiders lead series, 6-4;
See Dallas vs. Oakland
OAKLAND vs. DENVER
RS: Raiders lead series, 59-42-2
PS: Series tied, 1-1;
See Denver vs. Oakland
OAKLAND vs. DETROIT
RS: Raiders lead series, 6-5;
See Detroit vs. Oakland
OAKLAND vs. GREEN BAY
RS: Packers lead series, 6-5
PS: Packers lead series, 1-0;
See Green Bay vs. Oakland
OAKLAND vs. HOUSTON
RS: Texans lead series, 5-2;
See Houston vs. Oakland
OAKLAND vs. INDIANAPOLIS
RS: Raiders lead series, 7-5
PS: Series tied, 1-1;
See Indianapolis vs. Oakland
OAKLAND vs. JACKSONVILLE
RS: Jaguars lead series, 4-1;
See Jacksonville vs. Oakland
OAKLAND vs. KANSAS CITY
RS: Chiefs lead series, 53-48-2
PS: Chiefs lead series, 2-1;
See Kansas City vs. Oakland
OAKLAND vs. MIAMI
RS: Raiders lead series, 16-14-1
PS: Raiders lead series, 3-1;
See Miami vs. Oakland
OAKLAND vs. MINNESOTA
RS: Raiders lead series, 9-4
PS: Raiders lead series, 1-0;
See Minnesota vs. Oakland
OAKLAND vs. NEW ENGLAND
RS: Raiders lead series, 15-14-1
PS: Patriots lead series, 2-1;
See New England vs. Oakland
OAKLAND vs. NEW ORLEANS
RS: Series tied, 5-5-1;
See New Orleans vs. Oakland

OAKLAND vs. N.Y. GIANTS
RS: Raiders lead series, 7-4;
See N.Y. Giants vs. Oakland
OAKLAND vs. N.Y. JETS
RS: Raiders lead series, 21-15-2
PS: Series tied, 2-2;
See N.Y. Jets vs. Oakland
*OAKLAND vs. PHILADELPHIA
RS: Series tied, 5-5
PS: Raiders lead series, 1-0
1971—Raiders, 34-10 (O)
1976—Raiders, 26-7 (P)
1980—Eagles, 10-7 (P)
   **Raiders, 27-10 (New Orleans)
1986—Eagles, 33-27 (LA) OT
1989—Eagles, 10-7 (P)
1992—Eagles, 31-10 (P)
1995—Raiders, 48-17 (O)
2001—Raiders, 20-10 (P)
2005—Eagles, 23-20 (P)
2009—Raiders, 13-9 (O)
(RS Pts.—Raiders 212, Eagles 160)
(PS Pts.—Raiders 27, Eagles 10)
*Franchise in Los Angeles from 1982-1994
**Super Bowl XV
*OAKLAND vs. PITTSBURGH
RS: Raiders lead series, 10-9
PS: Series tied, 3-3
1970—Raiders, 31-14 (O)
1972—Steelers, 34-28 (P)
   **Steelers, 13-7 (P)
1973—Steelers, 17-9 (O)
   **Raiders, 33-14 (O)
1974—Raiders, 17-0 (P)
   ***Steelers, 24-13 (O)
1975—***Steelers, 16-10 (P)
1976—Raiders, 31-28 (O)
   ***Raiders, 24-7 (O)
1977—Raiders, 16-7 (P)
1980—Raiders, 45-34 (P)
1981—Raiders, 30-27 (O)
1983—**Raiders, 38-10 (LA)
1984—Steelers, 13-7 (LA)
1990—Raiders, 20-3 (LA)
1994—Steelers, 21-3 (LA)
1995—Steelers, 29-10 (O)
2000—Steelers, 21-20 (P)
2002—Raiders, 30-17 (P)
2003—Steelers, 27-7 (P)
2004—Steelers, 24-21 (P)
2006—Raiders, 20-13 (O)
2009—Raiders, 27-24 (P)
2010—Steelers, 35-3 (P)
(RS Pts.—Steelers 388, Raiders 375)
(PS Pts.—Raiders 125, Steelers 84)
*Franchise in Los Angeles from 1982-1994
**AFC Divisional Playoff
***AFC Championship
*OAKLAND vs. **ST. LOUIS
RS: Raiders lead series, 8-4
1972—Raiders, 45-17 (O)
1977—Rams, 20-14 (LA)
1979—Raiders, 24-17 (LA)
1982—Raiders, 37-31 (LA Raiders)
1985—Raiders, 16-6 (LA Rams)
1988—Rams, 22-17 (LA Raiders)
1991—Raiders, 20-17 (LA Raiders)
1994—Raiders, 20-17 (LA Rams)
1997—Raiders, 35-17 (O)
2002—Rams, 28-13 (StL)
2006—Rams, 20-0 (O)
2010—Raiders, 16-14 (O)

(RS Pts.—Raiders 257, Rams 226)
Franchise in Los Angeles from 1982-1994
**Franchise in Los Angeles prior to 1995*
*OAKLAND vs. **SAN DIEGO
RS: Raiders lead series, 57-45-2
PS: Raiders lead series, 1-0
1960—Chargers, 52-28 (LA)
　　　Chargers, 41-17 (O)
1961—Chargers, 44-0 (SD)
　　　Chargers, 41-10 (O)
1962—Chargers, 42-33 (O)
　　　Chargers, 31-21 (SD)
1963—Raiders, 34-33 (SD)
　　　Raiders, 41-27 (O)
1964—Chargers, 31-17 (SD)
　　　Raiders, 21-20 (O)
1965—Raiders, 17-6 (O)
　　　Chargers, 24-14 (SD)
1966—Chargers, 29-20 (O)
　　　Raiders, 41-19 (SD)
1967—Raiders, 51-10 (O)
　　　Raiders, 41-21 (SD)
1968—Chargers, 23-14 (O)
　　　Raiders, 34-27 (SD)
1969—Raiders, 24-12 (SD)
　　　Raiders, 21-16 (O)
1970—Tie, 27-27 (SD)
　　　Raiders, 20-17 (O)
1971—Raiders, 34-0 (SD)
　　　Raiders, 34-33 (O)
1972—Tie, 17-17 (O)
　　　Raiders, 21-19 (SD)
1973—Raiders, 27-17 (SD)
　　　Raiders, 31-3 (O)
1974—Raiders, 14-10 (SD)
　　　Raiders, 17-10 (O)
1975—Raiders, 6-0 (SD)
　　　Raiders, 25-0 (O)
1976—Raiders, 27-17 (SD)
　　　Raiders, 24-0 (O)
1977—Raiders, 24-0 (O)
　　　Chargers, 12-7 (SD)
1978—Raiders, 21-20 (SD)
　　　Chargers, 27-23 (O)
1979—Chargers, 30-10 (SD)
　　　Raiders, 45-22 (O)
1980—Chargers, 30-24 (SD) OT
　　　Raiders, 38-24 (O)
　　　***Raiders, 34-27 (SD)
1981—Chargers, 55-21 (O)
　　　Chargers, 23-10 (SD)
1982—Raiders, 28-24 (LA)
　　　Raiders, 41-34 (SD)
1983—Raiders, 42-10 (SD)
　　　Raiders, 30-14 (LA)
1984—Raiders, 33-30 (LA)
　　　Raiders, 44-37 (SD)
1985—Raiders, 34-21 (LA)
　　　Chargers, 40-34 (SD) OT
1986—Raiders, 17-13 (LA)
　　　Raiders, 37-31 (SD) OT
1987—Chargers, 23-17 (LA)
　　　Chargers, 16-14 (SD)
1988—Raiders, 24-13 (LA)
　　　Raiders, 13-3 (SD)
1989—Raiders, 40-14 (LA)
　　　Chargers, 14-12 (SD)
1990—Raiders, 24-9 (SD)
　　　Raiders, 17-12 (LA)
1991—Chargers, 21-13 (LA)
　　　Raiders, 9-7 (SD)
1992—Chargers, 27-3 (SD)

Chargers, 36-14 (LA)
1993—Chargers, 30-23 (LA)
　　　Raiders, 12-7 (SD)
1994—Chargers, 26-24 (LA)
　　　Raiders, 24-17 (SD)
1995—Raiders, 17-7 (O)
　　　Chargers, 12-6 (SD)
1996—Chargers, 40-34 (O)
　　　Raiders, 23-14 (SD)
1997—Chargers, 25-10 (O)
　　　Raiders, 38-13 (SD)
1998—Raiders, 7-6 (O)
　　　Raiders, 17-10 (SD)
1999—Raiders, 28-9 (O)
　　　Chargers, 23-20 (SD)
2000—Raiders, 9-6 (O)
　　　Raiders, 15-13 (SD)
2001—Raiders, 34-24 (O)
　　　Raiders, 13-6 (SD)
2002—Chargers, 27-21 (O) OT
　　　Raiders, 27-7 (SD)
2003—Raiders, 34-31 (O) OT
　　　Chargers, 21-14 (SD)
2004—Chargers, 42-14 (SD)
　　　Raiders, 23-17 (O)
2005—Chargers, 27-14 (O)
　　　Chargers, 34-10 (SD)
2006—Chargers, 27-0 (O)
　　　Chargers, 21-14 (SD)
2007—Chargers, 28-14 ((SD)
　　　Chargers, 30-17 (O)
2008—Chargers, 28-18 (O)
　　　Chargers, 34-7 (SD)
2009—Chargers, 24-20 (O)
　　　Chargers, 24-16 (SD)
2010—Raiders, 35-27 (O)
　　　Raiders, 28-13 (SD)
2011—Raiders, 24-17 (SD)
　　　Chargers, 38-26 (O)
(RS Pts.—Raiders 2,299, Chargers 2,233)
(PS Pts.—Raiders 34, Chargers 27)
Franchise in Los Angeles from 1982-1994
**Franchise in Los Angeles prior to 1961*
***AFC Championship*
*OAKLAND vs. SAN FRANCISCO
RS: Series tied, 6-6
1970—49ers, 38-7 (O)
1974—Raiders, 35-24 (SF)
1979—Raiders, 23-10 (O)
1982—Raiders, 23-17 (SF)
1985—49ers, 34-10 (LA)
1988—Raiders, 9-3 (SF)
1991—Raiders, 12-6 (LA)
1994—49ers, 44-14 (SF)
2000—Raiders, 34-28 (SF) OT
2002—49ers, 23-20 (O) OT
2006—49ers, 34-20 (SF)
2010—49ers, 17-9 (SF)
(RS Pts.—49ers 278, Raiders 216)
Franchise in Los Angeles from 1982-1994
*OAKLAND vs. SEATTLE
RS: Raiders lead series, 28-23
PS: Series tied, 1-1
1977—Raiders, 44-7 (O)
1978—Seahawks, 27-7 (S)
　　　Raiders, 17-16 (O)
1979—Seahawks, 27-10 (S)
　　　Seahawks, 29-24 (O)
1980—Raiders, 33-14 (O)
　　　Raiders, 19-17 (S)
1981—Raiders, 20-10 (O)
　　　Raiders, 32-31 (S)

1982—Raiders, 28-23 (LA)
1983—Seahawks, 38-36 (S)
　　　Seahawks, 34-21 (LA)
　　　**Raiders, 30-14 (LA)
1984—Raiders, 28-14 (LA)
　　　Seahawks, 17-14 (S)
　　　***Seahawks, 13-7 (S)
1985—Seahawks, 33-3 (S)
　　　Raiders, 13-3 (LA)
1986—Raiders, 14-10 (LA)
　　　Seahawks, 37-0 (S)
1987—Seahawks, 35-13 (LA)
　　　Raiders, 37-14 (S)
1988—Seahawks, 35-27 (S)
　　　Seahawks, 43-37 (LA)
1989—Seahawks, 24-20 (LA)
　　　Seahawks, 23-17 (S)
1990—Raiders, 17-13 (S)
　　　Raiders, 24-17 (LA)
1991—Raiders, 23-20 (S) OT
　　　Raiders, 31-7 (LA)
1992—Raiders, 19-0 (S)
　　　Raiders, 20-3 (LA)
1993—Raiders, 17-13 (S)
　　　Raiders, 27-23 (LA)
1994—Seahawks, 38-9 (LA)
　　　Raiders, 17-16 (S)
1995—Raiders, 34-14 (O)
　　　Seahawks, 44-10 (S)
1996—Raiders, 27-21 (S)
　　　Seahawks, 28-21 (O)
1997—Seahawks, 45-34 (S)
　　　Seahawks, 22-21 (O)
1998—Raiders, 31-18 (S)
　　　Raiders, 20-17 (O)
1999—Seahawks, 22-21 (S)
　　　Raiders, 30-21 (O)
2000—Raiders, 31-3 (O)
　　　Seahawks, 27-24 (S)
2001—Raiders, 38-14 (O)
　　　Seahawks, 34-27 (S)
2002—Raiders, 31-17 (O)
2006—Seahawks, 16-0 (S)
2010—Raiders, 33-3 (O)
(RS Pts.—Raiders 1,150, Seahawks 1,078)
(PS Pts.—Raiders 37, Seahawks 27)
Franchise in Los Angeles from 1982-1994
**AFC Championship*
***AFC First-Round Playoff*
*OAKLAND vs. TAMPA BAY
RS: Raiders lead series, 6-1
PS: Buccaneers lead series, 1-0
1976—Raiders, 49-16 (O)
1981—Raiders, 18-16 (O)
1993—Raiders, 27-20 (LA)
1996—Buccaneers, 20-17 (TB) OT
1999—Raiders, 45-0 (O)
2002—**Buccaneers, 48-21 (San Diego)
2004—Raiders, 30-20 (O)
2008—Raiders, 31-24 (TB)
(RS Pts.—Raiders 217, Buccaneers 116)
(PS Pts.—Buccaneers 48, Raiders 21)
Franchise in Los Angeles from 1982-1994
**Super Bowl XXXVII*
*OAKLAND vs. **TENNESSEE
RS: Raiders lead series, 23-19
PS: Raiders lead series, 4-0
1960—Oilers, 37-22 (O)
　　　Raiders, 14-13 (H)
1961—Oilers, 55-0 (H)
　　　Oilers, 47-16 (O)
1962—Oilers, 28-20 (O)

Oilers, 32-17 (H)
1963—Raiders, 24-13 (H)
Raiders, 52-49 (O)
1964—Oilers, 42-28 (H)
Raiders, 20-10 (O)
1965—Raiders, 21-17 (O)
Raiders, 33-21 (H)
1966—Oilers, 31-0 (H)
Raiders, 38-23 (O)
1967—Raiders, 19-7 (H)
***Raiders, 40-7 (O)
1968—Raiders, 24-15 (H)
1969—Raiders, 21-17 (O)
****Raiders, 56-7 (O)
1971—Raiders, 41-21 (O)
1972—Raiders, 34-0 (H)
1973—Raiders, 17-6 (H)
1975—Oilers, 27-26 (O)
1976—Raiders, 14-13 (H)
1977—Raiders, 34-29 (O)
1978—Raiders, 21-17 (O)
1979—Oilers, 31-17 (H)
1980—*****Raiders, 27-7 (O)
1981—Oilers, 17-16 (H)
1983—Raiders, 20-6 (LA)
1984—Raiders, 24-14 (H)
1986—Raiders, 28-17 (H)
1988—Oilers, 38-35 (H)
1989—Oilers, 23-7 (H)
1991—Oilers, 47-17 (H)
1994—Raiders, 17-14 (LA)
1997—Oilers, 24-21 (T) OT
1999—Titans, 21-14 (T)
2001—Titans, 13-10 (O)
2002—Raiders, 52-25 (O)
******Raiders, 41-24 (O)
2003—Titans, 25-20 (T)
2004—Raiders, 40-35 (O)
2005—Raiders, 34-25 (T)
2007—Titans, 13-9 (T)
2010—Titans, 38-13 (T)
(RS Pts.—Titans 996, Raiders 950)
(PS Pts.—Raiders 164, Titans 45)
*Franchise in Los Angeles from 1982-1994
**Franchise in Houston prior to 1997;
known as Oilers prior to 1999
***AFL Championship
****Inter-Divisional Playoff
*****AFC First-Round Playoff
******AFC Championship
OAKLAND vs. WASHINGTON
RS: Raiders lead series, 7-4
PS: Raiders lead series, 1-0
1970—Raiders, 34-20 (O)
1975—Raiders, 26-23 (W) OT
1980—Raiders, 24-21 (O)
1983—Redskins, 37-35 (W)
**Raiders, 38-9 (Tampa)
1986—Redskins, 10-6 (W)
1989—Raiders, 37-24 (LA)
1992—Raiders, 21-20 (W)
1995—Raiders, 20-8 (W)
1998—Raiders, 29-19 (O)
2005—Raiders, 16-13 (W)
2009—Redskins, 34-13 (O)
(RS Pts.—Raiders 251, Redskins 239)
(PS Pts.—Raiders 38, Redskins 9)
*Franchise in Los Angeles from
1982-1994
**Super Bowl XVIII

PHILADELPHIA vs. ARIZONA
RS: Cardinals lead series, 54-53-5
PS: Cardinals lead series, 2-1;
See Arizona vs. Philadelphia
PHILADELPHIA vs. ATLANTA
RS: Eagles lead series, 15-11-1
PS: Eagles lead series, 2-1;
See Atlanta vs. Philadelphia
PHILADELPHIA vs. BALTIMORE
RS: Series tied, 1-1-1;
See Baltimore vs. Philadelphia
PHILADELPHIA vs. BUFFALO
RS: Series tied, 6-6;
See Buffalo vs. Philadelphia
PHILADELPHIA vs. CAROLINA
RS: Eagles lead series, 5-1
PS: Panthers lead series, 1-0;
See Carolina vs. Philadelphia
PHILADELPHIA vs. CHICAGO
RS: Bears lead series, 28-9-1
PS: Eagles lead series, 2-1;
See Chicago vs. Philadelphia
PHILADELPHIA vs. CINCINNATI
RS: Bengals lead series, 7-3-1;
See Cincinnati vs. Philadelphia
PHILADELPHIA vs. CLEVELAND
RS: Browns lead series, 31-15-1;
See Cleveland vs. Philadelphia
PHILADELPHIA vs. DALLAS
RS: Cowboys lead series, 56-46
PS: Cowboys lead series, 3-1;
See Dallas vs. Philadelphia
PHILADELPHIA vs. DENVER
RS: Eagles lead series, 7-4;
See Denver vs. Philadelphia
PHILADELPHIA vs. DETROIT
RS: Eagles lead series, 14-12-2
PS: Eagles lead series, 1-0;
See Detroit vs. Philadelphia
PHILADELPHIA vs. GREEN BAY
RS: Packers lead series, 24-13
PS: Eagles lead series, 2-1;
See Green Bay vs. Philadelphia
PHILADELPHIA vs. HOUSTON
RS: Eagles lead series, 3-0;
See Houston vs. Philadelphia
PHILADELPHIA vs. INDIANAPOLIS
RS: Colts lead series, 10-7;
See Indianapolis vs. Philadelphia
PHILADELPHIA vs. JACKSONVILLE
RS: Jaguars lead series, 3-1;
See Jacksonville vs. Philadelphia
PHILADELPHIA vs. KANSAS CITY
RS: Eagles lead series, 4-2;
See Kansas City vs. Philadelphia
PHILADELPHIA vs. MIAMI
RS: Dolphins lead series, 7-6;
See Miami vs. Philadelphia
PHILADELPHIA vs. MINNESOTA
RS: Vikings lead series, 12-9
PS: Eagles lead series, 3-0;
See Minnesota vs. Philadelphia
PHILADELPHIA vs. NEW ENGLAND
RS: Eagles lead series, 6-5
PS: Patriots lead series, 1-0;
See New England vs. Philadelphia
PHILADELPHIA vs. NEW ORLEANS
RS: Eagles lead series, 15-10
PS; Series tied, 1-1;
See New Orleans vs. Philadelphia

PHILADELPHIA vs. N.Y. GIANTS
RS: Giants lead series, 80-72-2
PS: Series tied, 2-2;
See N.Y. Giants vs. Philadelphia
PHILADELPHIA vs. N.Y. JETS
RS: Eagles lead series, 9-0;
See N.Y. Jets vs. Philadelphia
PHILADELPHIA vs. OAKLAND
RS: Series tied, 5-5
PS: Raiders lead series, 1-0;
See Oakland vs. Philadelphia
PHILADELPHIA vs. *PITTSBURGH
RS: Eagles lead series, 46-27-3
PS: Eagles lead series, 1-0
1933—Eagles, 25-6 (Phila)
1934—Eagles, 17-0 (Pitt)
Pirates, 9-7 (Phila)
1935—Pirates, 17-7 (Phila)
Eagles, 17-6 (Pitt)
1936—Pirates, 17-0 (Pitt)
Pirates, 6-0 (Johnstown, Pa.)
1937—Pirates, 27-14 (Pitt)
Pirates, 16-7 (Phila)
1938—Eagles, 27-7 (Buffalo)
Eagles, 14-7 (Charleston, W. Va.)
1939—Eagles, 17-14 (Phila)
Pirates, 24-12 (Pitt)
1940—Steelers, 7-3 (Pitt)
Eagles, 7-0 (Phila)
1941—Eagles, 10-7 (Pitt)
Tie, 7-7 (Phila)
1942—Eagles, 24-14 (Pitt)
Steelers, 14-0 (Phila)
1945—Eagles, 45-3 (Pitt)
Eagles, 30-6 (Phila)
1946—Steelers, 10-7 (Pitt)
Eagles, 10-7 (Phila)
1947—Steelers, 35-24 (Pitt)
Eagles, 21-0 (Phila)
**Eagles, 21-0 (Pitt)
1948—Eagles, 34-7 (Pitt)
Eagles, 17-0 (Phila)
1949—Eagles, 38-7 (Pitt)
Eagles, 34-17 (Phila)
1950—Eagles, 17-10 (Phila)
Steelers, 9-7 (Phila)
1951—Eagles, 34-13 (Pitt)
Steelers, 17-13 (Phila)
1952—Eagles, 31-25 (Pitt)
Eagles, 26-21 (Phila)
1953—Eagles, 23-17 (Phila)
Eagles, 35-7 (Pitt)
1954—Eagles, 24-22 (Phila)
Steelers, 17-7 (Pitt)
1955—Steelers, 13-7 (Pitt)
Eagles, 24-0 (Phila)
1956—Eagles, 35-21 (Phila)
Eagles, 14-7 (Phila)
1957—Steelers, 6-0 (Pitt)
Eagles, 7-6 (Phila)
1958—Steelers, 24-3 (Pitt)
Steelers, 31-24 (Phila)
1959—Eagles, 28-24 (Phila)
Steelers, 31-0 (Pitt)
1960—Eagles, 34-7 (Phila)
Steelers, 27-21 (Pitt)
1961—Eagles, 21-16 (Phila)
Eagles, 35-24 (Pitt)
1962—Steelers, 13-7 (Pitt)
Steelers, 26-17 (Phila)
1963—Tie, 21-21 (Phila)
Tie, 20-20 (Pitt)

1964—Eagles, 21-7 (Phila)
    Eagles, 34-10 (Pitt)
1965—Steelers, 20-14 (Phila)
    Eagles, 47-13 (Pitt)
1966—Eagles, 31-14 (Pitt)
    Eagles, 27-23 (Phila)
1967—Eagles, 34-24 (Phila)
1968—Steelers, 6-3 (Pitt)
1969—Eagles, 41-27 (Phila)
1970—Eagles, 30-20 (Phila)
1974—Steelers, 27-0 (Pitt)
1979—Eagles, 17-14 (Phila)
1988—Eagles, 27-26 (Pitt)
1991—Eagles, 23-14 (Phila)
1994—Steelers, 14-3 (Pitt)
1997—Eagles, 23-20 (Phila)
2000—Eagles, 26-23 (Pitt) OT
2004—Steelers, 27-3 (Pitt)
2008—Eagles, 15-6 (Phila)
(RS Pts.—Eagles 1,429, Steelers 1,097)
(PS Pts.—Eagles 21, Steelers 0)
*Steelers known as Pirates prior to 1940
**Division Playoff

PHILADELPHIA vs. *ST. LOUIS
RS: Eagles lead series, 18-17-1
PS: Rams lead series, 2-1
1937—Rams, 21-3 (P)
1939—Rams, 35-13 (Colorado Springs)
1940—Rams, 21-13 (C)
1942—Rams, 24-14 (Akron)
1944—Eagles, 26-13 (P)
1945—Eagles, 28-14 (P)
1946—Eagles, 25-14 (LA)
1947—Eagles, 14-7 (P)
1948—Tie, 28-28 (LA)
1949—Eagles, 38-14 (P)
    **Eagles, 14-0 (LA)
1950—Eagles, 56-20 (P)
1955—Rams, 23-21 (P)
1956—Rams, 27-7 (LA)
1957—Rams, 17-13 (LA)
1959—Eagles, 23-20 (P)
1964—Rams, 20-10 (LA)
1967—Rams, 33-17 (LA)
1969—Rams, 23-17 (P)
1972—Rams, 34-3 (P)
1975—Rams, 42-3 (P)
1977—Rams, 20-0 (LA)
1978—Rams, 16-14 (P)
1983—Eagles, 13-9 (P)
1985—Rams, 17-6 (P)
1986—Eagles, 34-20 (P)
1988—Eagles, 30-24 (P)
1989—***Rams, 21-7 (P)
1990—Eagles, 27-21 (LA)
1995—Eagles, 20-9 (P)
1998—Eagles, 17-14 (P)
1999—Eagles, 38-31 (P)
2001—Rams, 20-17 (P) OT
    ****Rams, 29-24 (StL)
2002—Eagles, 10-3 (P)
2004—Eagles, 20-7 (StL)
2005—Eagles, 17-16 (StL)
2008—Eagles, 38-3 (P)
2011—Eagles, 31-13 (StL)
(RS Pts.—Rams 706, Eagles 691)
(PS Pts.—Rams 50, Eagles 45)
*Franchise in Los Angeles prior to 1995
and in Cleveland prior to 1946
**NFL Championship
***NFC First-Round Playoff
****NFC Championship

PHILADELPHIA vs. SAN DIEGO
RS: Chargers lead series, 6-4
1974—Eagles, 13-7 (SD)
1980—Chargers, 22-21 (SD)
1985—Chargers, 20-14 (SD)
1986—Eagles, 23-7 (P)
1989—Chargers, 20-17 (SD)
1995—Chargers, 27-21 (P)
1998—Chargers, 13-10 (SD)
2001—Eagles, 24-14 (P)
2005—Eagles, 20-17 (P)
2009—Chargers, 31-23 (SD)
(RS Pts.—Eagles 186, Chargers 178)

PHILADELPHIA vs. SAN FRANCISCO
RS: 49ers lead series, 17-12-1
PS: 49ers lead series, 1-0
1951—Eagles, 21-14 (P)
1953—49ers, 31-21 (SF)
1956—Tie, 10-10 (P)
1958—49ers, 30-24 (P)
1959—49ers, 24-14 (SF)
1964—49ers, 28-24 (P)
1966—Eagles, 35-34 (SF)
1967—49ers, 28-27 (P)
1969—49ers, 14-13 (SF)
1971—49ers, 31-3 (P)
1973—49ers, 38-28 (SF)
1975—Eagles, 27-17 (P)
1983—Eagles, 22-17 (SF)
1984—49ers, 21-9 (P)
1985—49ers, 24-13 (SF)
1989—49ers, 38-28 (P)
1991—49ers, 23-7 (P)
1992—49ers, 20-14 (SF)
1993—Eagles, 37-34 (SF) OT
1994—Eagles, 40-8 (SF)
1996—*49ers, 14-0 (SF)
1997—Eagles, 24-12 (P)
2001—49ers, 13-3 (SF)
2002—Eagles, 38-17 (SF)
2003—49ers, 31-28 (P) OT
2005—Eagles, 42-3 (P)
2006—Eagles, 38-24 (SF)
2008—Eagles, 40-26 (SF)
2009—Eagles, 27-13 (P)
2010—Eagles, 27-24 (SF)
2011—49ers, 24-23 (P)
(RS Pts.—Eagles 695, 49ers 683)
(PS Pts.—49ers 14, Eagles 0)
*NFC First-Round Playoff

PHILADELPHIA vs. SEATTLE
RS: Eagles lead series, 7-6
1976—Eagles, 27-10 (P)
1980—Eagles, 27-20 (S)
1986—Seahawks, 24-20 (P)
1989—Eagles, 31-7 (P)
1992—Eagles, 20-17 (S) OT
1995—Seahawks, 26-14 (S)
1998—Eagles, 38-0 (S)
2001—Eagles, 27-3 (S)
2002—Eagles, 27-20 (S)
2005—Seahawks, 42-0 (S)
2007—Seahawks, 28-24 (P)
2008—Eagles, 26-7 (S)
2011—Seahawks, 31-14 (S)
(RS Pts.—Seahawks 273, Eagles 257)

PHILADELPHIA vs. TAMPA BAY
RS: Eagles lead series, 6-5
PS: Series tied, 2-2
1977—Eagles, 13-3 (P)
1979—*Buccaneers, 24-17 (TB)
1981—Eagles, 20-10 (P)

1988—Eagles, 41-14 (TB)
1991—Buccaneers, 14-13 (TB)
1995—Buccaneers, 21-6 (P)
1999—Buccaneers, 19-5 (P)
2000—**Eagles, 21-3 (P)
2001—Eagles, 17-13 (TB)
    **Eagles, 31-9 (P)
2002—Eagles, 20-10 (P)
    ***Buccaneers, 27-10 (P)
2003—Buccaneers, 17-0 (P)
2006—Buccaneers, 23-21 (TB)
2009—Eagles, 33-14 (P)
(RS Pts.—Eagles 189, Buccaneers 158)
(PS Pts.—Eagles 79, Buccaneers 63)
*NFC Divisional Playoff
**NFC First-Round Playoff
***NFC Championship

PHILADELPHIA vs. *TENNESSEE
RS: Eagles lead series, 6-4
1972—Eagles, 18-17 (H)
1979—Eagles, 26-20 (H)
1982—Eagles, 35-14 (P)
1988—Eagles, 32-23 (P)
1991—Eagles, 13-6 (H)
1994—Eagles, 21-6 (P)
2000—Titans, 15-13 (P)
2002—Titans, 27-24 (T)
2006—Titans, 31-13 (P)
2010—Titans, 37-19 (T)
(RS Pts.—Eagles 214, Titans 196)
*Franchise in Houston prior to 1997;
known as Oilers prior to 1999

PHILADELPHIA vs. *WASHINGTON
RS: Redskins lead series, 78-70-5
PS: Redskins lead series, 1-0
1934—Redskins, 6-0 (B)
    Redskins, 14-7 (P)
1935—Eagles, 7-6 (B)
1936—Redskins, 26-3 (P)
    Redskins, 17-7 (B)
1937—Eagles, 14-0 (W)
    Redskins, 10-7 (P)
1938—Redskins, 26-23 (P)
    Redskins, 20-14 (W)
1939—Redskins, 7-0 (P)
    Redskins, 7-6 (W)
1940—Redskins, 34-17 (P)
    Redskins, 13-6 (W)
1941—Redskins, 21-17 (P)
    Redskins, 20-14 (W)
1942—Redskins, 14-10 (P)
    Redskins, 30-27 (W)
1944—Tie, 31-31 (P)
    Eagles, 37-7 (W)
1945—Redskins, 24-14 (W)
    Eagles, 16-0 (P)
1946—Eagles, 28-24 (W)
    Redskins, 27-10 (P)
1947—Eagles, 45-42 (P)
    Eagles, 38-14 (W)
1948—Eagles, 45-0 (W)
    Eagles, 42-21 (P)
1949—Eagles, 49-14 (P)
    Eagles, 44-21 (W)
1950—Eagles, 35-3 (P)
    Eagles, 33-0 (W)
1951—Redskins, 27-23 (P)
    Eagles, 35-21 (W)
1952—Eagles, 38-20 (P)
    Redskins, 27-21 (W)
1953—Tie, 21-21 (P)
    Redskins, 10-0 (W)

1954—Eagles, 49-21 (W)
    Eagles, 41-33 (P)
1955—Redskins, 31-30 (P)
    Redskins, 34-21 (W)
1956—Eagles, 13-9 (P)
    Redskins, 19-17 (W)
1957—Eagles, 21-12 (P)
    Redskins, 42-7 (W)
1958—Redskins, 24-14 (P)
    Redskins, 20-0 (W)
1959—Eagles, 30-23 (P)
    Eagles, 34-14 (W)
1960—Eagles, 19-13 (P)
    Eagles, 38-28 (W)
1961—Eagles, 14-7 (P)
    Eagles, 27-24 (W)
1962—Redskins, 27-21 (P)
    Eagles, 37-14 (W)
1963—Eagles, 37-24 (W)
    Redskins, 13-10 (P)
1964—Redskins, 35-20 (W)
    Redskins, 21-10 (P)
1965—Redskins, 23-21 (W)
    Eagles, 21-14 (P)
1966—Redskins, 27-13 (P)
    Eagles, 37-28 (W)
1967—Eagles, 35-24 (P)
    Tie, 35-35 (W)
1968—Eagles, 17-14 (W)
    Redskins, 16-10 (P)
1969—Tie, 28-28 (W)
    Redskins, 34-29 (P)
1970—Redskins, 33-21 (P)
    Redskins, 24-6 (W)
1971—Tie, 7-7 (W)
    Redskins, 20-13 (P)
1972—Redskins, 14-0 (W)
    Redskins, 23-7 (P)
1973—Redskins, 28-7 (P)
    Redskins, 38-20 (W)
1974—Redskins, 27-20 (P)
    Redskins, 26-7 (W)
1975—Eagles, 26-10 (P)
    Eagles, 26-3 (W)
1976—Redskins, 20-17 (P) OT
    Redskins, 24-0 (W)
1977—Redskins, 23-17 (W)
    Redskins, 17-14 (P)
1978—Redskins, 35-30 (W)
    Eagles, 17-10 (P)
1979—Eagles, 28-17 (P)
    Redskins, 17-7 (W)
1980—Eagles, 24-14 (P)
    Eagles, 24-0 (W)
1981—Eagles, 36-13 (P)
    Redskins, 15-13 (W)
1982—Redskins, 37-34 (P) OT
    Redskins, 13-9 (W)
1983—Redskins, 23-13 (P)
    Redskins, 28-24 (W)
1984—Redskins, 20-0 (W)
    Eagles, 16-10 (P)
1985—Eagles, 19-6 (W)
    Redskins, 17-12 (P)
1986—Redskins, 41-14 (W)
    Redskins, 21-14 (P)
1987—Redskins, 34-24 (W)
    Eagles, 31-27 (P)
1988—Redskins, 17-10 (W)
    Redskins, 20-19 (P)
1989—Eagles, 42-37 (W)
    Redskins, 10-3 (P)

1990—Redskins, 13-7 (W)
    Eagles, 28-14 (P)
    **Redskins, 20-6 (P)
1991—Redskins, 23-0 (W)
    Eagles, 24-22 (P)
1992—Redskins, 16-12 (W)
    Eagles, 17-13 (P)
1993—Eagles, 34-31 (P)
    Eagles, 17-14 (W)
1994—Eagles, 21-17 (P)
    Eagles, 31-29 (W)
1995—Eagles, 37-34 (P) OT
    Eagles, 14-7 (W)
1996—Eagles, 17-14 (W)
    Redskins, 26-21 (P)
1997—Eagles, 24-10 (P)
    Redskins, 35-32 (W)
1998—Eagles, 17-12 (P)
    Redskins, 28-3 (W)
1999—Eagles, 35-28 (P)
    Redskins, 20-17 (W) OT
2000—Redskins, 17-14 (P)
    Eagles, 23-20 (W)
2001—Redskins, 13-3 (P)
    Eagles, 20-6 (W)
2002—Eagles, 37-7 (W)
    Eagles, 34-21 (P)
2003—Eagles, 27-25 (P)
    Eagles, 31-7 (W)
2004—Eagles, 28-6 (P)
    Eagles, 17-14 (W)
2005—Redskins, 17-10 (W)
    Redskins, 31-20 (P)
2006—Eagles, 27-3 (P)
    Eagles, 21-19 (W)
2007—Redskins, 20-12 (W)
    Eagles, 33-25 (W)
2008—Redskins, 23-17 (P)
    Redskins, 10-3 (W)
2009—Eagles, 27-17 (W)
    Eagles, 27-24 (P)
2010—Redskins, 17-12 (P)
    Eagles, 59-28 (W)
2011—Eagles, 20-13 (W)
    Eagles, 34-10 (P)
(RS Pts.—Eagles 3,172, Redskins 2,977)
(PS Pts.—Redskins 20, Eagles 6)
*Franchise in Boston prior to 1937
**NFC First-Round Playoff

PITTSBURGH vs. ARIZONA
RS: Steelers lead series, 32-23-3
PS: Steelers lead series, 1-0;
See Arizona vs. Pittsburgh
PITTSBURGH vs. ATLANTA
RS: Steelers lead series, 12-2-1;
See Atlanta vs. Pittsburgh
PITTSBURGH vs. BALTIMORE
RS: Steelers lead series, 18-14
PS: Steelers lead series, 3-0;
See Baltimore vs. Pittsburgh
PITTSBURGH vs. BUFFALO
RS: Steelers lead series, 12-8
PS: Steelers lead series, 2-1;
See Buffalo vs. Pittsburgh
PITTSBURGH vs. CAROLINA
RS: Steelers lead series, 4-1;
See Carolina vs. Pittsburgh
PITTSBURGH vs. CHICAGO
RS: Bears lead series, 17-7-1;
See Chicago vs. Pittsburgh

PITTSBURGH vs. CINCINNATI
RS: Steelers lead series, 51-32
PS: Steelers lead series, 1-0;
See Cincinnati vs. Pittsburgh
PITTSBURGH vs. CLEVELAND
RS: Steelers lead series, 62-56
PS: Steelers lead series, 2-0;
See Cleveland vs. Pittsburgh
PITTSBURGH vs. DALLAS
RS: Cowboys lead series, 14-13
PS: Steelers lead series, 2-1;
See Dallas vs. Pittsburgh
PITTSBURGH vs. DENVER
RS: Broncos lead series, 13-7-1
PS: Broncos lead series, 4-3;
See Denver vs. Pittsburgh
PITTSBURGH vs. DETROIT
RS: Steelers lead series, 15-14-1;
See Detroit vs. Pittsburgh
PITTSBURGH vs. GREEN BAY
RS: Packers lead series, 18-14
PS: Packers lead series, 1-0;
See Green Bay vs. Pittsburgh
PITTSBURGH vs. HOUSTON
RS: Series tied, 2-2;
See Houston vs. Pittsburgh
PITTSBURGH vs. INDIANAPOLIS
RS: Steelers lead series, 14-6
PS: Steelers lead series, 5-0;
See Indianapolis vs. Pittsburgh
PITTSBURGH vs. JACKSONVILLE
RS: Jaguars lead series, 11-10
PS: Jaguars lead series, 1-0;
See Jacksonville vs. Pittsburgh
PITTSBURGH vs. KANSAS CITY
RS: Steelers lead series, 18-9
PS: Chiefs lead series, 1-0;
See Kansas City vs. Pittsburgh
PITTSBURGH vs. MIAMI
RS: Steelers lead series, 12-9
PS: Dolphins lead series, 2-1;
See Miami vs. Pittsburgh
PITTSBURGH vs. MINNESOTA
RS: Vikings lead series, 8-7
PS: Steelers lead series, 1-0;
See Minnesota vs. Pittsburgh
PITTSBURGH vs. NEW ENGLAND
RS: Steelers lead series, 14-8
PS: Patriots lead series, 3-1;
See New England vs. Pittsburgh
PITTSBURGH vs. NEW ORLEANS
RS: Series tied, 7-7;
See New Orleans vs. Pittsburgh
PITTSBURGH vs. N.Y. GIANTS
RS: Giants lead series, 44-28-3;
See N.Y. Giants vs. Pittsburgh
PITTSBURGH vs. N.Y. JETS
RS: Steelers lead series, 15-4
PS: Steelers lead series, 2-0;
See N.Y. Jets vs. Pittsburgh
PITTSBURGH vs. OAKLAND
RS: Raiders lead series, 10-9
PS: Series tied, 3-3;
See Oakland vs. Pittsburgh
PITTSBURGH vs. PHILADELPHIA
RS: Eagles lead series, 46-27-3
PS: Eagles lead series, 1-0;
See Philadelphia vs. Pittsburgh
***PITTSBURGH vs. **ST. LOUIS**
RS: Rams lead series, 15-7-2
PS: Steelers lead series, 1-0
1938—Rams, 13-7 (New Orleans)

1939—Tie, 14-14 (C)
1941—Rams, 17-14 (Akron)
1947—Rams, 48-7 (P)
1948—Rams, 31-14 (LA)
1949—Tie, 7-7 (P)
1952—Rams, 28-14 (LA)
1955—Rams, 27-26 (LA)
1956—Steelers, 30-13 (P)
1961—Rams, 24-14 (LA)
1964—Rams, 26-14 (P)
1968—Rams, 45-10 (LA)
1971—Rams, 23-14 (P)
1975—Rams, 10-3 (LA)
1978—Rams, 10-7 (LA)
1979—***Steelers, 31-19 (Pasadena)
1981—Steelers, 24-0 (P)
1984—Steelers, 24-14 (P)
1987—Rams, 31-21 (LA)
1990—Steelers, 41-10 (P)
1993—Rams, 27-0 (LA)
1996—Steelers, 42-6 (P)
2003—Rams, 33-21 (P)
2007—Steelers, 41-24 (StL)
2011—Steelers, 27-0 (P)
(RS Pts.—Rams 481, Steelers 436)
(PS Pts.—Steelers 31, Rams 19)
*Steelers known as Pirates prior to 1940
**Franchise in Los Angeles prior to 1995
and in Cleveland prior to 1946
***Super Bowl XIV

PITTSBURGH vs. SAN DIEGO
RS: Steelers lead series, 21-6
PS: Chargers lead series, 2-1
1971—Steelers, 21-17 (P)
1972—Steelers, 24-2 (SD)
1973—Steelers, 38-21 (P)
1975—Steelers, 37-0 (SD)
1976—Steelers, 23-0 (P)
1977—Steelers, 10-9 (SD)
1979—Chargers, 35-7 (SD)
1980—Chargers, 26-17 (SD)
1982—*Chargers, 31-28 (P)
1983—Steelers, 26-3 (P)
1984—Steelers, 52-24 (P)
1985—Chargers, 54-44 (SD)
1987—Chargers, 20-16 (SD)
1988—Chargers, 20-14 (SD)
1989—Steelers, 20-17 (P)
1990—Steelers, 36-14 (P)
1991—Steelers, 26-20 (P)
1992—Steelers, 23-6 (SD)
1993—Steelers,.16-3 (P)
1994—Chargers, 37-34 (SD)
   **Chargers, 17-13 (P)
1995—Steelers, 31-16 (P)
1996—Steelers, 16-3 (P)
2000—Steelers, 34-21 (SD)
2003—Steelers, 40-24 (P)
2005—Steelers, 24-22 (SD)
2006—Chargers, 23-13 (SD)
2008—Steelers, 11-10 (P)
   ***Steelers, 35-24 (P)
2009—Steelers, 38-28 (P)
(RS Pts.—Steelers 695, Chargers 471)
(PS Pts.—Steelers 76, Chargers 72)
*AFC First-Round Playoff
**AFC Championship
***AFC Divisional Playoff

PITTSBURGH vs. SAN FRANCISCO
RS: 49ers lead series, 11-9
1951—49ers, 28-24 (P)
1952—Steelers, 24-7 (SF)

1954—49ers, 31-3 (SF)
1958—49ers, 23-20 (SF)
1961—Steelers, 20-10 (P)
1965—49ers, 27-17 (SF)
1968—49ers, 45-28 (P)
1973—Steelers, 37-14 (SF)
1977—Steelers, 27-0 (P)
1978—Steelers, 24-7 (SF)
1981—49ers, 17-14 (P)
1984—Steelers, 20-17 (SF)
1987—Steelers, 30-17 (P)
1990—49ers, 27-7 (SF)
1993—49ers, 24-13 (P)
1996—49ers, 25-15 (P)
1999—Steelers, 27-6 (SF)
2003—49ers, 30-14 (SF)
2007—Steelers, 37-16 (P)
2011—49ers, 20-3 (SF)
(RS Pts.—Steelers 404, 49ers 391)

PITTSBURGH vs. SEATTLE
RS: Series tied, 8-8
PS: Steelers lead series, 1-0
1977—Steelers, 30-20 (P)
1978—Steelers, 21-10 (P)
1981—Seahawks, 24-21 (S)
1982—Seahawks, 16-0 (S)
1983—Steelers, 27-21 (S)
1986—Seahawks, 30-0 (S)
1987—Steelers, 13-9 (P)
1991—Seahawks, 27-7 (P)
1992—Steelers, 20-14 (P)
1993—Seahawks, 16-6 (S)
1994—Seahawks, 30-13 (S)
1998—Steelers, 13-10 (P)
1999—Seahawks, 29-10 (P)
2003—Seahawks, 23-16 (S)
2005—*Steelers, 21-10 (Detroit)
2007—Steelers, 21-0 (P)
2011—Steelers, 24-0 (P)
(RS Pts.—Seahawks 279, Steelers 242)
(PS Pts.—Steelers 21, Seahawks 10)
*Super Bowl XL

PITTSBURGH vs. TAMPA BAY
RS: Steelers lead series, 8-1
1976—Steelers, 42-0 (P)
1980—Steelers, 24-21 (TB)
1983—Steelers, 17-12 (P)
1989—Steelers, 31-22 (TB)
1998—Buccaneers, 16-3 (TB)
2001—Steelers, 17-10 (TB)
2002—Steelers, 17-7 (TB)
2006—Steelers, 20-3 (P)
2010—Steelers, 38-13 (TB)
(RS Pts.—Steelers 209, Buccaneers 104)

PITTSBURGH vs. *TENNESSEE
RS: Steelers lead series, 41-29
PS: Steelers lead series, 3-1
1970—Oilers, 19-7 (P)
   Steelers, 7-3 (H)
1971—Steelers, 23-16 (P)
   Oilers, 29-3 (H)
1972—Steelers, 24-7 (P)
   Steelers, 9-3 (H)
1973—Steelers, 36-7 (H)
   Steelers, 33-7 (P)
1974—Steelers, 13-7 (H)
   Oilers, 13-10 (P)
1975—Steelers, 24-17 (P)
   Steelers, 32-9 (H)
1976—Steelers, 32-16 (P)
   Steelers, 21-0 (H)
1977—Oilers, 27-10 (H)

   Steelers, 27-10 (P)
1978—Oilers, 24-17 (P)
   Steelers, 13-3 (H)
   **Steelers, 34-5 (P)
1979—Steelers, 38-7 (P)
   Oilers, 20-17 (H)
   **Steelers, 27-13 (P)
1980—Steelers, 31-17 (P)
   Oilers, 6-0 (H)
1981—Steelers, 26-13 (P)
   Oilers, 21-20 (H)
1982—Steelers, 24-10 (H)
1983—Steelers, 40-28 (H)
   Steelers, 17-10 (P)
1984—Steelers, 35-7 (P)
   Oilers, 23-20 (H) OT
1985—Steelers, 20-0 (P)
   Steelers, 30-7 (H)
1986—Steelers, 22-16 (H) OT
   Steelers, 21-10 (P)
1987—Oilers, 23-3 (P)
   Oilers, 24-16 (H)
1988—Oilers, 34-14 (P)
   Steelers, 37-34 (H)
1989—Oilers, 27-0 (H)
   Oilers, 23-16 (P)
   ***Steelers, 26-23 (H) OT
1990—Steelers, 20-9 (P)
   Oilers, 34-14 (H)
1991—Steelers, 26-14 (P)
   Oilers, 31-6 (H)
1992—Steelers, 29-24 (P)
   Steelers, 21-20 (P)
1993—Oilers, 23-3 (H)
   Oilers, 26-17 (P)
1994—Steelers, 30-14 (P)
   Steelers, 12-9 (H) OT
1995—Steelers, 34-17 (H)
   Steelers, 21-7 (P)
1996—Steelers, 30-16 (P)
   Oilers, 23-13 (H)
1997—Steelers, 37-24 (P)
   Oilers, 16-6 (T)
1998—Oilers, 41-31 (P)
   Oilers, 23-14 (T)
1999—Titans, 16-10 (T)
   Titans, 47-36 (P)
2000—Titans, 23-20 (P)
   Titans, 9-7 (T)
2001—Steelers, 34-7 (P)
   Steelers, 34-24 (T)
2002—Titans, 31-23 (T)
   ****Titans, 34-31 (T) OT
2003—Titans, 30-13 (P)
2005—Steelers, 34-7 (P)
2008—Steelers, 31-14 (T)
2009—Steelers, 13-10 (P) OT
2010—Steelers, 19-11 (T)
2011—Steelers, 38-17 (P)
(RS Pts.—Steelers 1,447, Titans 1,211)
(PS Pts.—Steelers 118, Titans 75)
*Franchise in Houston prior to 1997;
known as Oilers prior to 1999
**AFC Championship
***AFC First-Round Playoff
****AFC Divisional Playoff

PITTSBURGH vs. **WASHINGTON
RS: Redskins lead series, 42-31-3
1933—Redskins, 21-6 (P)
   Pirates, 16-14 (B)
1934—Redskins, 7-0 (P)
   Redskins, 39-0 (B)

1935—Pirates, 6-0 (P)
    Redskins, 13-3 (B)
1936—Pirates, 10-0 (P)
    Redskins, 30-0 (B)
1937—Redskins, 34-20 (W)
    Pirates, 21-13 (P)
1938—Redskins, 7-0 (P)
    Redskins, 15-0 (W)
1939—Redskins, 44-14 (W)
    Redskins, 21-14 (P)
1940—Redskins, 40-10 (P)
    Redskins, 37-10 (W)
1941—Redskins, 24-20 (P)
    Redskins, 23-3 (W)
1942—Redskins, 28-14 (W)
    Redskins, 14-0 (P)
1945—Redskins, 14-0 (P)
    Redskins, 24-0 (W)
1946—Tie, 14-14 (W)
    Steelers, 14-7 (P)
1947—Redskins, 27-26 (W)
    Steelers, 21-14 (P)
1948—Redskins, 17-14 (W)
    Steelers, 10-7 (P)
1949—Redskins, 27-14 (P)
    Redskins, 27-14 (W)
1950—Steelers, 26-7 (W)
    Redskins, 24-7 (P)
1951—Redskins, 22-7 (P)
    Steelers, 20-10 (W)
1952—Redskins, 28-24 (P)
    Steelers, 24-23 (W)
1953—Redskins, 17-9 (P)
    Steelers, 14-13 (W)
1954—Steelers, 37-7 (P)
    Redskins, 17-14 (W)
1955—Redskins, 23-14 (P)
    Redskins, 28-17 (W)
1956—Redskins, 30-13 (P)
    Steelers, 23-0 (W)
1957—Steelers, 28-7 (P)
    Redskins, 10-3 (W)
1958—Steelers, 24-16 (P)
    Tie, 14-14 (W)
1959—Redskins, 23-17 (P)
    Steelers, 27-6 (W)
1960—Tie, 27-27 (W)
    Steelers, 22-10 (P)
1961—Steelers, 20-0 (P)
    Steelers, 30-14 (W)
1962—Steelers, 23-21 (P)
    Steelers, 27-24 (W)
1963—Steelers, 38-27 (P)
    Steelers, 34-28 (W)
1964—Redskins, 30-0 (P)
    Steelers, 14-7 (W)
1965—Redskins, 31-3 (P)
    Redskins, 35-14 (W)
1966—Redskins, 33-27 (P)
    Redskins, 24-10 (W)
1967—Redskins, 15-10 (P)
1968—Redskins, 16-13 (W)
1969—Redskins, 14-7 (P)
1973—Steelers, 21-16 (P)
1979—Steelers, 38-7 (P)
1985—Redskins, 30-23 (P)
1988—Redskins, 30-29 (W)
1991—Redskins, 41-14 (P)
1997—Steelers, 14-13 (P)
2000—Steelers, 24-3 (P)
2004—Steelers, 16-7 (P)
2008—Steelers, 23-6 (W)

(RS Pts.—Redskins 1,419, Steelers 1,194)
*Steelers known as Pirates prior to 1940
**Franchise in Boston prior to 1937

ST. LOUIS vs. ARIZONA
RS: Cardinals lead series, 33-31-2
PS: Rams lead series, 1-0;
See Arizona vs. St. Louis
ST. LOUIS vs. ATLANTA
RS: Rams lead series, 47-26-2
PS: Falcons lead series, 1-0;
See Atlanta vs. St. Louis
ST. LOUIS vs. BALTIMORE
RS: Ravens lead series, 3-2;
See Baltimore vs. St. Louis
ST. LOUIS vs. BUFFALO
RS: Bills lead series, 6-4;
See Buffalo vs. St. Louis
ST. LOUIS vs. CAROLINA
RS: Panthers lead series, 10-8
PS: Panthers lead series, 1-0;
See Carolina vs. St. Louis
ST. LOUIS vs. CHICAGO
RS: Bears lead series, 50-34-3
PS: Series tied, 1-1;
See Chicago vs. St. Louis
ST. LOUIS vs. CINCINNATI
RS: Bengals lead series, 7-5;
See Cincinnati vs. St. Louis
ST. LOUIS vs. CLEVELAND
RS: Rams lead series, 10-9
PS: Browns lead series, 2-1;
See Cleveland vs. St. Louis
ST. LOUIS vs. DALLAS
RS: Series tied, 11-11
PS: Series tied, 4-4;
See Dallas vs. St. Louis
ST. LOUIS vs. DENVER
RS: Rams lead series, 7-5;
See Denver vs. St. Louis
ST. LOUIS vs. DETROIT
RS: Rams lead series, 42-38-1
PS: Lions lead series, 1-0;
See Detroit vs. St. Louis
ST. LOUIS vs. GREEN BAY
RS: Rams lead series, 45-43-2
PS: Series tied, 1-1;
See Green Bay vs. St. Louis
ST. LOUIS vs. HOUSTON
RS: Series tied, 1-1;
See Houston vs. St. Louis
ST. LOUIS vs. INDIANAPOLIS
RS: Colts lead series, 23-17-2;
See Indianapolis vs. St. Louis
ST. LOUIS vs. JACKSONVILLE
RS: Rams lead series, 2-1;
See Jacksonville vs. St. Louis
ST. LOUIS vs. KANSAS CITY
RS: Chiefs lead series; 6-4;
See Kansas City vs. St. Louis
ST. LOUIS vs. MIAMI
RS: Dolphins lead series, 9-2;
See Miami vs. St. Louis
ST. LOUIS vs. MINNESOTA
RS: Vikings lead series, 18-14-2
PS: Vikings lead series, 5-2;
See Minnesota vs. St. Louis
ST. LOUIS vs. NEW ENGLAND
RS: Series tied, 5-5
PS: Patriots lead series, 1-0;
See New England vs. St. Louis

ST. LOUIS vs. NEW ORLEANS
RS: Rams lead series, 39-31
PS: Saints lead series, 1-0;
See New Orleans vs. St. Louis
ST. LOUIS vs. N.Y. GIANTS
RS: Rams lead series, 25-14
PS: Series tied, 1-1;
See N.Y. Giants vs. St. Louis
ST. LOUIS vs. N.Y. JETS
RS: Rams lead series, 9-3;
See N.Y. Jets vs. St. Louis
ST. LOUIS vs. OAKLAND
RS: Raiders lead series, 8-4;
See Oakland vs. St. Louis
ST. LOUIS vs. PHILADELPHIA
RS: Eagles lead series, 18-17-1
PS: Rams lead series, 2-1;
See Philadelphia vs. St. Louis
ST. LOUIS vs. PITTSBURGH
RS: Rams lead series, 15-7-2
PS: Steelers lead series, 1-0;
See Pittsburgh vs. St. Louis
***ST. LOUIS vs. SAN DIEGO**
RS: Rams lead series, 6-4
1970—Rams, 37-10 (LA)
1975—Rams, 13-10 (SD) OT
1979—Chargers, 40-16 (LA)
1988—Chargers, 38-24 (LA)
1991—Rams, 30-24 (LA)
1994—Chargers, 31-17 (SD)
2000—Rams, 57-31 (StL)
2002—Rams, 28-24 (StL)
2006—Chargers, 38-24 (SD)
2010—Rams, 20-17 (StL)
(RS Pts.—Rams 266, Chargers 263)
*Franchise in Los Angeles prior to 1995
***ST. LOUIS vs. SAN FRANCISCO**
RS: Series tied, 61-61-2
PS: 49ers lead series, 1-0
1950—Rams, 35-14 (SF)
    Rams, 28-21 (LA)
1951—49ers, 44-17 (SF)
    Rams, 23-16 (LA)
1952—Rams, 35-9 (LA)
    Rams, 34-21 (SF)
1953—49ers, 31-30 (SF)
    49ers, 31-27 (LA)
1954—Tie, 24-24 (LA)
    Rams, 42-34 (SF)
1955—Rams, 23-14 (SF)
    Rams, 27-14 (LA)
1956—49ers, 33-30 (SF)
    Rams, 30-6 (LA)
1957—49ers, 23-20 (SF)
    Rams, 37-24 (LA)
1958—Rams, 33-3 (SF)
    Rams, 56-7 (LA)
1959—Rams, 34-0 (SF)
    49ers, 24-16 (LA)
1960—49ers, 13-9 (SF)
    49ers, 23-7 (LA)
1961—49ers, 35-0 (SF)
    Rams, 17-7 (LA)
1962—Rams, 28-14 (SF)
    49ers, 24-17 (LA)
1963—Rams, 28-21 (LA)
    Rams, 21-17 (SF)
1964—Rams, 42-14 (LA)
    49ers, 28-7 (SF)
1965—49ers, 45-21 (LA)
    49ers, 30-27 (SF)
1966—Rams, 34-3 (LA)

49ers, 21-13 (SF)
1967—49ers, 27-24 (LA)
Rams, 17-7 (SF)
1968—Rams, 24-10 (LA)
Tie, 20-20 (SF)
1969—Rams, 27-21 (SF)
Rams, 41-30 (LA)
1970—49ers, 20-6 (LA)
Rams, 30-13 (SF)
1971—Rams, 20-13 (SF)
Rams, 17-6 (LA)
1972—Rams, 31-7 (LA)
Rams, 26-16 (SF)
1973—Rams, 40-20 (SF)
Rams, 31-13 (LA)
1974—Rams, 37-14 (LA)
Rams, 15-13 (SF)
1975—Rams, 23-14 (SF)
49ers, 24-23 (LA)
1976—49ers, 16-0 (LA)
Rams, 23-3 (SF)
1977—Rams, 34-14 (LA)
Rams, 23-10 (SF)
1978—Rams, 27-10 (LA)
Rams, 31-28 (SF)
1979—Rams, 27-24 (LA)
Rams, 26-20 (SF)
1980—Rams, 48-26 (LA)
Rams, 31-17 (SF)
1981—49ers, 20-17 (SF)
49ers, 33-31 (LA)
1982—49ers, 30-24 (LA)
Rams, 21-20 (SF)
1983—Rams, 10-7 (SF)
49ers, 45-35 (LA)
1984—49ers, 33-0 (LA)
49ers, 19-16 (SF)
1985—49ers, 28-14 (LA)
Rams, 27-20 (SF)
1986—Rams, 16-13 (LA)
49ers, 24-14 (SF)
1987—49ers, 31-10 (LA)
49ers, 48-0 (SF)
1988—49ers, 24-21 (LA)
Rams, 38-16 (SF)
1989—Rams, 13-12 (SF)
49ers, 30-27 (LA)
**49ers, 30-3 (SF)
1990—Rams, 28-17 (SF)
49ers, 26-10 (LA)
1991—49ers, 27-10 (SF)
49ers, 33-10 (LA)
1992—49ers, 27-24 (SF)
49ers, 27-10 (LA)
1993—49ers, 40-17 (SF)
49ers, 35-10 (LA)
1994—49ers, 34-19 (LA)
49ers, 31-27 (SF)
1995—49ers, 44-10 (StL)
49ers, 41-13 (SF)
1996—49ers, 34-0 (SF)
49ers, 28-11 (StL)
1997—49ers, 15-12 (StL)
49ers, 30-10 (SF)
1998—49ers, 28-10 (StL)
49ers, 38-19 (SF)
1999—Rams, 42-20 (StL)
Rams, 23-7 (SF)
2000—Rams, 41-24 (StL)
Rams, 34-24 (SF)
2001—Rams, 30-26 (SF)
Rams, 27-14 (StL)

2002—49ers, 37-13 (SF)
Rams, 31-20 (StL)
2003—Rams, 27-24 (StL) OT
49ers, 30-10 (SF)
2004—Rams, 24-14 (SF)
Rams, 16-6 (StL)
2005—49ers, 28-25 (SF)
49ers, 24-20 (StL)
2006—49ers, 20-13 (SF)
Rams, 20-17 (StL)
2007—49ers, 17-16 (StL)
Rams, 13-9 (SF)
2008—49ers, 35-16 (SF)
49ers, 17-16 (StL)
2009—49ers, 35-0 (SF)
49ers, 28-6 (StL)
2010—49ers, 23-20 (SF) OT
Rams, 25-17 (StL)
2011—49ers, 26-0 (SF)
49ers, 34-27 (StL)
(RS Pts.—49ers 2,762, Rams 2,679)
(PS Pts.—49ers 30, Rams 3)
*Franchise in Los Angeles prior to 1995
**NFC Championship
ST. LOUIS vs. SEATTLE
RS: Seahawks lead series, 17-10
PS: Rams lead series, 1-0
1976—Rams, 45-6 (LA)
1979—Rams, 24-0 (Sea)
1985—Rams, 35-24 (Sea)
1988—Rams, 31-10 (LA)
1991—Seahawks, 23-9 (Sea)
1997—Seahawks, 17-9 (StL)
2000—Rams, 37-34 (Sea)
2002—Rams, 37-20 (StL)
Seahawks, 30-10 (Sea)
2003—Seahawks, 24-23 (Sea)
Rams, 27-22 (StL)
2004—Rams, 33-27 (Sea) OT
Rams, 23-12 (StL)
**Rams, 27-20 (Sea)
2005—Seahawks, 37-31 (StL)
Seahawks, 31-16 (Sea)
2006—Seahawks, 30-28 (StL)
Seahawks, 24-22 (Sea)
2007—Seahawks, 33-6 (Sea)
Seahawks, 24-19 (StL)
2008—Seahawks, 37-13 (Sea)
Seahawks, 23-20 (StL)
2009—Seahawks, 28-0 (Sea)
Seahawks, 27-17 (StL)
2010—Rams, 20-3 (StL)
Seahawks, 16-6 (Sea)
2011—Seahawks, 24-7 (StL)
Seahawks, 30-13 (Sea)
(RS Pts.—Seahawks 616, Rams 561)
(PS Pts.—Rams 27, Seahawks 20)
*Franchise in Los Angeles prior to 1995
**NFC First-Round Playoff
ST. LOUIS vs. TAMPA BAY
RS: Rams lead series, 9-8
PS: Rams lead series, 2-0
1977—Rams, 31-0 (LA)
1978—Rams, 26-23 (LA)
1979—Buccaneers, 21-6 (TB)
**Rams, 9-0 (TB)
1980—Buccaneers, 10-9 (TB)
1984—Rams, 34-33 (TB)
1985—Rams, 31-27 (TB)
1986—Rams, 26-20 (LA) OT
1987—Rams, 35-3 (LA)
1990—Rams, 35-14 (TB)

1992—Rams, 31-27 (TB)
1994—Buccaneers, 24-14 (TB)
1999—**Rams, 11-6 (StL)
2000—Buccaneers, 38-35 (TB)
2001—Buccaneers, 24-17 (StL)
2002—Buccaneers, 26-14 (TB)
2004—Rams, 28-21 (StL)
2007—Buccaneers, 24-3 (TB)
2010—Buccaneers, 18-17 (TB)
(RS Pts.—Rams 392, Buccaneers 353)
(PS Pts.—Rams 20, Buccaneers 6)
*Franchise in Los Angeles prior to 1995
**NFC Championship
ST. LOUIS vs. **TENNESSEE
RS: Rams lead series, 6-4
PS: Rams lead series, 1-0
1973—Rams, 31-26 (H)
1978—Rams, 10-6 (H)
1981—Oilers, 27-20 (LA)
1984—Rams, 27-16 (LA)
1987—Oilers, 20-16 (H)
1990—Rams, 17-13 (LA)
1993—Rams, 28-13 (H)
1999—Titans, 24-21 (T)
***Rams, 23-16 (Atlanta)
2005—Rams, 31-27 (StL)
2009—Titans, 47-7 (T)
(RS Pts.—Titans, 219, Rams 208)
(PS Pts.—Rams 23, Titans 16)
*Franchise in Los Angeles prior to 1995
**Franchise in Houston prior to 1997;
known as Oilers prior to 1999
***Super Bowl XXXIV
ST. LOUIS vs. WASHINGTON
RS: Redskins lead series, 22-9-1
PS: Series tied, 2-2
1937—Redskins, 16-7 (C)
1938—Redskins, 37-13 (W)
1941—Redskins, 17-13 (W)
1942—Redskins, 33-14 (W)
1944—Redskins, 14-10 (W)
1945—**Rams, 15-14 (C)
1948—Rams, 41-13 (W)
1949—Rams, 53-27 (LA)
1951—Redskins, 31-21 (W)
1962—Redskins, 20-14 (W)
1963—Redskins, 37-14 (LA)
1967—Tie, 28-28 (LA)
1969—Rams, 24-13 (W)
1971—Redskins, 38-24 (LA)
1974—Redskins, 23-17 (LA)
***Rams, 19-10 (LA)
1977—Redskins, 17-14 (W)
1981—Redskins, 30-7 (LA)
1983—Redskins, 42-20 (LA)
***Redskins, 51-7 (W)
1986—****Redskins, 19-7 (W)
1987—Rams, 30-26 (W)
1991—Redskins, 27-6 (LA)
1993—Rams, 10-6 (LA)
1994—Redskins, 24-21 (LA)
1995—Redskins, 35-23 (StL)
1996—Redskins, 17-10 (StL)
1997—Rams, 23-20 (W)
2000—Redskins, 33-20 (StL)
2002—Redskins, 20-17 (W)
2005—Redskins, 24-9 (StL)
2006—Rams, 37-31 (StL) OT
2008—Rams, 19-17 (W)
2009—Redskins, 9-7 (W)
2010—Rams, 30-16 (StL)
2011—Redskins, 17-10 (StL)

(RS Pts.—Redskins 758, Rams 606)
(PS Pts.—Redskins 94, Rams 48)
*Franchise in Los Angeles prior to 1995
and in Cleveland prior to 1946
**NFL Championship
***NFC Divisional Playoff
****NFC First-Round Playoff

SAN DIEGO vs. ARIZONA
RS: Chargers lead series, 9-3;
See Arizona vs. San Diego
SAN DIEGO vs. ATLANTA
RS: Falcons lead series, 7-1;
See Atlanta vs. San Diego
SAN DIEGO vs. BALTIMORE
RS: Series tied, 4-4;
See Baltimore vs. San Diego
SAN DIEGO vs. BUFFALO
RS: Chargers lead series, 21-10-2
PS: Bills lead series, 2-1;
See Buffalo vs. San Diego
SAN DIEGO vs. CAROLINA
RS: Panthers lead series, 3-1;
See Carolina vs. San Diego
SAN DIEGO vs. CHICAGO
RS: Bears lead series, 6-5;
See Chicago vs. San Diego
SAN DIEGO vs. CINCINNATI
RS: Chargers lead series, 19-11
PS: Bengals lead series, 1-0;
See Cincinnati vs. San Diego
SAN DIEGO vs. CLEVELAND
RS: Chargers lead series, 14-7-1;
See Cleveland vs. San Diego
SAN DIEGO vs. DALLAS
RS: Cowboys lead series, 6-3;
See Dallas vs. San Diego
SAN DIEGO vs. DENVER
RS: Broncos lead series, 55-48-1;
See Denver vs. San Diego
SAN DIEGO vs. DETROIT
RS: Chargers lead series, 6-4;
See Detroit vs. San Diego
SAN DIEGO vs. GREEN BAY
RS: Packers lead series, 9-1;
See Green Bay vs. San Diego
SAN DIEGO vs. HOUSTON
RS: Chargers lead series, 4-0;
See Houston vs. San Diego
SAN DIEGO vs. INDIANAPOLIS
RS: Chargers lead series, 15-9
PS: Chargers lead series, 2-1;
See Indianapolis vs. San Diego
SAN DIEGO vs. JACKSONVILLE
RS: Chargers lead series, 3-2;
See Jacksonville vs. San Diego
SAN DIEGO vs. KANSAS CITY
RS: Chiefs lead series, 52-50-1
PS: Chargers lead series, 1-0;
See Kansas City vs. San Diego
SAN DIEGO vs. MIAMI
RS: Series tied, 12-12
PS: Series tied, 2-2;
See Miami vs. San Diego
SAN DIEGO vs. MINNESOTA
RS: Chargers lead series, 6-5;
See Minnesota vs. San Diego
SAN DIEGO vs. NEW ENGLAND
RS: Patriots lead series, 20-14-2
PS: Patriots lead series, 2-1;
See New England vs. San Diego

SAN DIEGO vs. NEW ORLEANS
RS: Chargers lead series, 7-3;
See New Orleans vs. San Diego
SAN DIEGO vs. N.Y. GIANTS
RS: Series tied, 5-5;
See N.Y. Giants vs. San Diego
SAN DIEGO vs. N.Y. JETS
RS: Chargers lead series, 19-12-1
PS: Jets lead series, 2-0;
See N.Y. Jets vs. San Diego
SAN DIEGO vs. OAKLAND
RS: Raiders lead series, 57-45-2
PS: Raiders lead series, 1-0;
See Oakland vs. San Diego
SAN DIEGO vs. PHILADELPHIA
RS: Chargers lead series, 6-4;
See Philadelphia vs. San Diego
SAN DIEGO vs. PITTSBURGH
RS: Steelers lead series, 21-6
PS: Chargers lead series, 2-1;
See Pittsburgh vs. San Diego
SAN DIEGO vs. ST. LOUIS
RS: Rams lead series, 6-4;
See St. Louis vs. San Diego
SAN DIEGO vs. SAN FRANCISCO
RS: Series tied, 6-6
PS: 49ers lead series, 1-0
1972—49ers, 34-3 (SF)
1976—Chargers, 13-7 (SD) OT
1979—Chargers, 31-9 (SD)
1982—Chargers, 41-37 (SF)
1988—49ers, 48-10 (SD)
1991—49ers, 34-14 (SF)
1994—49ers, 38-15 (SD)
        *49ers, 49-26 (South Florida)
1997—49ers, 17-10 (SF)
2000—49ers, 45-17 (SD)
2002—Chargers, 20-17 (SD) OT
2006—49ers, 48-19 (SF)
2010—Chargers, 34-7 (SD)
(RS Pts.—49ers 312, Chargers 256)
(PS Pts.—49ers 49, Chargers 26)
*Super Bowl XXIX
SAN DIEGO vs. SEATTLE
RS: Seahawks lead series, 26-23
1977—Chargers, 30-28 (Sea)
1978—Chargers, 24-20 (Sea)
        Chargers, 37-10 (SD)
1979—Chargers, 33-16 (Sea)
        Chargers, 20-10 (SD)
1980—Chargers, 34-13 (Sea)
        Chargers, 21-14 (SD)
1981—Chargers, 24-10 (SD)
        Seahawks, 44-23 (Sea)
1983—Seahawks, 34-31 (Sea)
        Chargers, 28-21 (SD)
1984—Seahawks, 31-17 (Sea)
        Seahawks, 24-0 (SD)
1985—Seahawks, 49-35 (SD)
        Seahawks, 26-21 (Sea)
1986—Seahawks, 33-7 (Sea)
        Seahawks, 34-24 (SD)
1987—Seahawks, 34-3 (Sea)
1988—Chargers, 17-6 (SD)
        Seahawks, 17-14 (Sea)
1989—Seahawks, 17-16 (SD)
        Seahawks, 10-7 (Sea)
1990—Chargers, 31-14 (Sea)
        Seahawks, 13-10 (SD) OT
1991—Seahawks, 20-9 (Sea)
        Chargers, 17-14 (SD)
1992—Chargers, 17-6 (SD)

        Chargers, 31-14 (Sea)
1993—Chargers, 18-12 (SD)
        Seahawks, 31-14 (Sea)
1994—Chargers, 24-10 (Sea)
        Chargers, 35-15 (SD)
1995—Chargers, 14-10 (SD)
        Chargers, 35-25 (Sea)
1996—Chargers, 29-7 (SD)
        Seahawks, 32-13 (Sea)
1997—Seahawks, 26-22 (Sea)
        Seahawks, 37-31 (SD)
1998—Seahawks, 27-20 (SD)
        Seahawks, 38-17 (Sea)
1999—Chargers, 13-10 (SD)
        Chargers, 19-16 (Sea)
2000—Seahawks, 20-12 (SD)
        Seahawks, 17-15 (Sea)
2001—Seahawks, 13-10 (Sea) OT
        Seahawks, 25-22 (SD)
2002—Seahawks, 31-28 (SD) OT
2006—Chargers, 20-17 (Sea)
2010—Seahawks, 27-20 (Sea)
(RS Pts.—Seahawks 1,028, Chargers 1,012)
SAN DIEGO vs. TAMPA BAY
RS: Chargers lead series, 8-1
1976—Chargers, 23-0 (TB)
1981—Chargers, 24-23 (TB)
1987—Chargers, 17-13 (TB)
1990—Chargers, 41-10 (SD)
1992—Chargers, 29-14 (SD)
1993—Chargers, 32-17 (TB)
1996—Buccaneers, 25-17 (SD)
2004—Chargers, 31-24 (SD)
2008—Chargers, 41-24 (TB)
(RS Pts.—Chargers 255, Buccaneers 150)
*SAN DIEGO vs. **TENNESSEE
RS: Chargers lead series, 24-13-1
PS: Titans lead series, 3-1
1960—Oilers, 38-28 (H)
        Chargers, 24-21 (LA)
        ***Oilers, 24-16 (H)
1961—Chargers, 34-24 (SD)
        ***Oilers, 10-3 (SD)
1962—Oilers, 42-17 (SD)
        Oilers, 33-27 (H)
1963—Chargers, 27-0 (SD)
        Chargers 20-14 (H)
1964—Chargers, 27-21 (SD)
        Chargers, 20-17 (H)
1965—Chargers, 31-14 (SD)
        Chargers, 37-26 (H)
1966—Chargers, 28-22 (H)
1967—Chargers, 13-3 (SD)
        Oilers, 24-17 (H)
1968—Chargers, 30-14 (SD)
1969—Chargers, 21-17 (H)
1970—Tie, 31-31 (SD)
1971—Oilers, 49-33 (H)
1972—Chargers, 34-20 (SD)
1974—Oilers, 21-14 (H)
1975—Oilers, 33-17 (H)
1976—Chargers, 30-27 (SD)
1978—Chargers, 45-24 (H)
1979—****Oilers, 17-14 (SD)
1984—Chargers, 31-14 (SD)
1985—Oilers, 37-35 (H)
1986—Chargers, 27-0 (SD)
1987—Oilers, 33-18 (H)
1989—Chargers, 34-27 (SD)
1990—Oilers, 17-7 (SD)
1992—Oilers, 27-0 (H)

1993—Chargers, 18-17 (SD)
1998—Chargers, 13-7 (T)
2004—Chargers, 38-17 (SD)
2006—Chargers, 40-7 (SD)
2007—Chargers, 23-17 (T) OT
　　　*****Chargers, 17-6 (SD)
2009—Chargers, 42-17 (T)
2010—Chargers, 33-25 (SD)
(RS Pts.—Chargers 970, Titans 837)
(PS Pts.—Titans 57, Chargers 50)
*Franchise in Los Angeles prior to 1961
**Franchise in Houston prior to 1997; known as Oilers prior to 1999
***AFL Championship
****AFC Divisional Playoff
*****AFC First-Round Playoff

SAN DIEGO vs. WASHINGTON
RS: Redskins lead series, 6-3
1973—Redskins, 38-0 (W)
1980—Redskins, 40-17 (W)
1983—Redskins, 27-24 (SD)
1986—Redskins, 30-27 (SD)
1989—Redskins, 26-21 (W)
1998—Redskins, 24-20 (W)
2001—Chargers, 30-3 (SD)
2005—Chargers, 23-17 (W) OT
2009—Chargers, 23-20 (SD)
(RS Pts.—Redskins 225, Chargers 185)

SAN FRANCISCO vs. ARIZONA
RS: 49ers lead series, 24-17;
See Arizona vs. San Francisco
SAN FRANCISCO vs. ATLANTA
RS: 49ers lead series, 44-29-1
PS: Falcons lead series, 1-0;
See Atlanta vs. San Francisco
SAN FRANCISCO vs. BALTIMORE
RS: Ravens lead series, 3-1;
See Baltimore vs. San Francisco
SAN FRANCISCO vs. BUFFALO
RS: Series tied, 5-5;
See Buffalo vs. San Francisco
SAN FRANCISCO vs. CAROLINA
RS: Panthers lead series, 10-7;
See Carolina vs. San Francisco
SAN FRANCISCO vs. CHICAGO
RS: Bears lead series, 29-28-1
PS: 49ers lead series, 3-0;
See Chicago vs. San Francisco
SAN FRANCISCO vs. CINCINNATI
RS: 49ers lead series, 9-3
PS: 49ers lead series, 2-0;
See Cincinnati vs. San Francisco
SAN FRANCISCO vs. CLEVELAND
RS: Browns lead series, 11-7;
See Cleveland vs. San Francisco
SAN FRANCISCO vs. DALLAS
RS: 49ers lead series, 14-11-1
PS: Cowboys lead series, 5-2;
See Dallas vs. San Francisco
SAN FRANCISCO vs. DENVER
RS: Series tied, 6-6
PS: 49ers lead series, 1-0;
See Denver vs. San Francisco
SAN FRANCISCO vs. DETROIT
RS: 49ers lead series, 35-26-1
PS: Series tied, 1-1;
See Detroit vs. San Francisco
SAN FRANCISCO vs. GREEN BAY
RS: Packers lead series, 30-25-1
PS: Packers lead series, 4-1;
See Green Bay vs. San Francisco

SAN FRANCISCO vs. HOUSTON
RS: Series tied, 1-1;
See Houston vs. San Francisco
SAN FRANCISCO vs. INDIANAPOLIS
RS: Colts lead series, 24-18;
See Indianapolis vs. San Francisco
SAN FRANCISCO vs. JACKSONVILLE
RS: Jaguars lead series, 2-1;
See Jacksonville vs. San Francisco
SAN FRANCISCO vs. KANSAS CITY
RS: 49ers lead series, 6-5;
See Kansas City vs. San Francisco
SAN FRANCISCO vs. MIAMI
RS: Dolphins lead series, 6-4
PS: 49ers lead series, 1-0;
See Miami vs. San Francisco
SAN FRANCISCO vs. MINNESOTA
RS: Vikings lead series, 20-18-1
PS: 49ers lead series, 4-1;
See Minnesota vs. San Francisco
SAN FRANCISCO vs. NEW ENGLAND
RS: 49ers lead series, 7-4;
See New England vs. San Francisco
SAN FRANCISCO vs. NEW ORLEANS
RS: 49ers lead series, 45-24-2
PS: 49ers lead series, 1-0;
See New Orleans vs. San Francisco
SAN FRANCISCO vs. N.Y. GIANTS
RS: Series tied, 14-14
PS: Series tied, 4-4;
See N.Y. Giants vs. San Francisco
SAN FRANCISCO vs. N.Y. JETS
RS: 49ers lead series, 9-2;
See N.Y. Jets vs. San Francisco
SAN FRANCISCO vs. OAKLAND
RS: Series tied, 6-6;
See Oakland vs. San Francisco
SAN FRANCISCO vs. PHILADELPHIA
RS: 49ers lead series, 17-12-1
PS: 49ers lead series, 1-0;
See Philadelphia vs. San Francisco
SAN FRANCISCO vs. PITTSBURGH
RS: 49ers lead series, 11-9;
See Pittsburgh vs. San Francisco
SAN FRANCISCO vs. ST. LOUIS
RS: Series tied, 61-61-2
PS: 49ers lead series, 1-0;
See St. Louis vs. San Francisco
SAN FRANCISCO vs. SAN DIEGO
RS: Series tied, 6-6
PS: 49ers lead series, 1-0;
See San Diego vs. San Francisco
SAN FRANCISCO vs. SEATTLE
RS: Series tied, 13-13
1976—49ers, 37-21 (Sea)
1979—Seahawks, 35-24 (SF)
1985—49ers, 19-6 (SF)
1988—49ers, 38-7 (Sea)
1991—49ers, 24-22 (Sea)
1997—Seahawks, 38-9 (Sea)
2002—49ers, 28-21 (Sea)
　　　49ers, 31-24 (SF)
2003—Seahawks, 20-19 (Sea)
　　　Seahawks, 24-17 (SF)
2004—Seahawks, 34-0 (Sea)
　　　Seahawks, 42-27 (SF)
2005—Seahawks, 27-25 (SF)
　　　Seahawks, 41-3 (Sea)
2006—49ers, 20-14 (SF)
　　　49ers, 24-14 (Sea)
2007—Seahawks, 23-3 (SF)
　　　Seahawks, 24-0 (Sea)

2008—49ers, 33-30 (Sea) OT
　　　Seahawks, 34-13 (SF)
2009—49ers, 23-10 (SF)
　　　Seahawks, 20-17 (Sea)
2010—Seahawks, 31-6 (Sea)
　　　49ers, 40-21 (SF)
2011—49ers, 33-17 (SF)
　　　49ers, 19-17 (Sea)
(RS Pts.—Seahawks 617, 49ers 532)
SAN FRANCISCO vs. TAMPA BAY
RS: 49ers lead series, 16-4
PS: Buccaneers lead series, 1-0
1977—49ers, 20-10 (SF)
1978—49ers, 6-3 (SF)
1979—49ers, 23-7 (SF)
1980—Buccaneers, 24-23 (SF)
1983—49ers, 35-21 (SF)
1984—49ers, 24-17 (SF)
1986—49ers, 31-7 (TB)
1987—49ers, 24-10 (TB)
1989—49ers, 20-16 (TB)
1990—49ers, 31-7 (SF)
1992—49ers, 21-14 (SF)
1993—49ers, 45-21 (TB)
1994—49ers, 41-16 (SF)
1997—Buccaneers, 13-6 (TB)
2002—*Buccaneers, 31-6 (TB)
2003—49ers, 24-7 (SF)
2004—Buccaneers, 35-3 (TB)
2005—49ers, 15-10 (SF)
2007—49ers, 21-19 (SF)
2010—Buccaneers, 21-0 (SF)
2011—49ers, 48-3 (SF)
(RS Pts.—49ers 461, Buccaneers 281)
(PS Pts.—Buccaneers 31, 49ers 6)
*NFC Divisional Playoff
SAN FRANCISCO vs. *TENNESSEE
RS: 49ers lead series, 7-5
1970—49ers, 30-20 (H)
1975—Oilers, 27-13 (H)
1978—Oilers, 20-19 (H)
1981—49ers, 28-6 (SF)
1984—49ers, 34-21 (H)
1987—49ers, 27-20 (SF)
1990—49ers, 24-21 (H)
1993—Oilers, 10-7 (SF)
1996—49ers, 10-9 (H)
1999—49ers, 24-22 (SF)
2005—Titans, 33-22 (T)
2009—Titans, 34-27 (SF)
(RS Pts.—49ers 265, Titans 243)
*Franchise in Houston prior to 1997; known as Oilers prior to 1999
SAN FRANCISCO vs. WASHINGTON
RS: 49ers lead series, 15-9-1
PS: 49ers lead series, 3-1
1952—49ers, 23-17 (W)
1954—49ers, 41-7 (SF)
1955—Redskins, 7-0 (W)
1961—49ers, 35-3 (SF)
1967—Redskins, 31-28 (W)
1969—Tie, 17-17 (SF)
1970—49ers, 26-17 (SF)
1971—*49ers, 24-20 (SF)
1973—Redskins, 33-9 (SF)
1976—Redskins, 24-21 (SF)
1978—Redskins, 38-20 (W)
1981—49ers, 30-17 (W)
1983—**Redskins, 24-21 (W)
1984—49ers, 37-31 (SF)
1985—49ers, 35-8 (W)
1986—Redskins, 14-6 (W)

1988—49ers, 37-21 (SF)
1990—49ers, 26-13 (SF)
*49ers, 28-10 (SF)
1992—*49ers, 20-13 (SF)
1994—49ers, 37-22 (W)
1996—49ers, 19-16 (W) OT
1998—49ers, 45-10 (W)
1999—Redskins, 26-20 (SF) OT
2002—49ers, 20-10 (SF)
2004—Redskins, 26-16 (SF)
2005—Redskins, 52-17 (W)
2008—49ers, 27-24 (SF)
2011—49ers, 19-11 (W)
(RS Pts.—49ers 611, Redskins 495)
(PS Pts.—49ers 93, Redskins 67)
*NFC Divisional Playoff
**NFC Championship

SEATTLE vs. ARIZONA
RS: Cardinals lead series, 14-12;
See Arizona vs. Seattle
SEATTLE vs. ATLANTA
RS: Seahawks lead series, 8-5;
See Atlanta vs. Seattle
SEATTLE vs. BALTIMORE
RS: Series tied, 2-2;
See Baltimore vs. Seattle
SEATTLE vs. BUFFALO
RS: Seahawks lead series, 6-5;
See Buffalo vs. Seattle
SEATTLE vs. CAROLINA
RS: Series tied, 2-2
PS: Seahawks lead series, 1-0;
See Carolina vs. Seattle
SEATTLE vs. CHICAGO
RS: Seahawks lead series, 9-4
PS: Bears lead series, 2-0;
See Chicago vs. Seattle
SEATTLE vs. CINCINNATI
RS: Series tied, 9-9
PS: Bengals lead series, 1-0;
See Cincinnati vs. Seattle
SEATTLE vs. CLEVELAND
RS: Seahawks lead series, 11-6;
See Cleveland vs. Seattle
SEATTLE vs. DALLAS
RS: Cowboys lead series, 9-4
PS: Seahawks lead series, 1-0;
See Dallas vs. Seattle
SEATTLE vs. DENVER
RS: Broncos lead series, 34-18
PS: Seahawks lead series, 1-0;
See Denver vs. Seattle
SEATTLE vs. DETROIT
RS: Seahawks lead series, 7-4;
See Detroit vs. Seattle
SEATTLE vs. GREEN BAY
RS: Packers lead series, 8-5
PS: Packers lead series, 2-0;
See Green Bay vs. Seattle
SEATTLE vs. HOUSTON
RS: Series tied, 1-1;
See Houston vs. Seattle
SEATTLE vs. INDIANAPOLIS
RS: Colts lead series, 6-4;
See Indianapolis vs. Seattle
SEATTLE vs. JACKSONVILLE
RS: Seahawks lead series, 4-2;
See Jacksonville vs. Seattle
SEATTLE vs. KANSAS CITY
RS: Chiefs lead series, 32-18;
See Kansas City vs. Seattle

SEATTLE vs. MIAMI
RS: Dolphins lead series, 7-3
PS: Dolphins lead series, 2-1;
See Miami vs. Seattle
SEATTLE vs. MINNESOTA
RS: Seahawks lead series, 6-5;
See Minnesota vs. Seattle
SEATTLE vs. NEW ENGLAND
RS: Patriots lead series, 8-7;
See New England vs. Seattle
SEATTLE vs. NEW ORLEANS
RS: Saints lead series, 6-5
PS: Seahawks lead series, 1-0;
See New Orleans vs. Seattle
SEATTLE vs. N.Y. GIANTS
RS: Giants lead series, 9-6;
See N.Y. Giants vs. Seattle
SEATTLE vs. N.Y. JETS
RS: Seahawks lead series, 9-8;
See N.Y. Jets vs. Seattle
SEATTLE vs. OAKLAND
RS: Raiders lead series, 28-23
PS: Series tied, 1-1;
See Oakland vs. Seattle
SEATTLE vs. PHILADELPHIA
RS: Eagles lead series, 7-6;
See Philadelphia vs. Seattle
SEATTLE vs. PITTSBURGH
RS: Series tied, 8-8
PS: Steelers lead series, 1-0;
See Pittsburgh vs. Seattle
SEATTLE vs. ST. LOUIS
RS: Seahawks lead series, 17-10
PS: Rams lead series, 1-0;
See St. Louis vs. Seattle
SEATTLE vs. SAN DIEGO
RS: Seahawks lead series, 26-23;
See San Diego vs. Seattle
SEATTLE vs. SAN FRANCISCO
RS: Series tied, 13-13;
See San Francisco vs. Seattle
SEATTLE vs. TAMPA BAY
RS: Seahawks lead series, 7-4
1976—Seahawks, 13-10 (TB)
1977—Seahawks, 30-23 (S)
1994—Seahawks, 22-21 (S)
1996—Seahawks, 17-13 (TB)
1999—Buccaneers, 16-3 (S)
2004—Seahawks, 10-6 (TB)
2006—Seahawks, 23-7 (TB)
2007—Seahawks, 20-6 (S)
2008—Buccaneers, 20-10 (TB)
2009—Buccaneers, 24-7 (S)
2010—Buccaneers, 35-15 (TB)
(RS Pts.—Buccaneers 184, Seahawks 170)
SEATTLE vs. *TENNESSEE
RS: Seahawks lead series, 9-5
PS: Titans lead series, 1-0
1977—Oilers, 22-10 (S)
1979—Seahawks, 34-14 (S)
1980—Seahawks, 26-7 (H)
1981—Oilers, 35-17 (H)
1982—Oilers, 23-21 (H)
1987—**Oilers, 23-20 (H) OT
1988—Seahawks, 27-24 (S)
1990—Seahawks, 13-10 (S) OT
1993—Oilers, 24-14 (H)
1994—Seahawks, 16-14 (H)
1996—Seahawks, 23-16 (S)
1997—Seahawks, 16-13 (S)
1998—Seahawks, 20-18 (S)
2005—Seahawks, 28-24 (T)

2009—Titans, 17-13 (S)
(RS Pts.—Seahawks 278, Titans 261)
(PS Pts.—Titans 23, Seahawks 20)
*Franchise in Houston prior to 1997;
known as Oilers prior to 1999
**AFC First-Round Playoff
SEATTLE vs. WASHINGTON
RS: Redskins lead series, 11-4
PS: Seahawks lead series, 2-0
1976—Redskins, 31-7 (W)
1980—Seahawks, 14-0 (W)
1983—Redskins, 27-17 (S)
1986—Redskins, 19-14 (W)
1989—Seahawks, 29-0 (S)
1992—Redskins, 16-3 (S)
1994—Seahawks, 28-7 (W)
1995—Seahawks, 27-20 (W)
1998—Seahawks, 24-14 (S)
2001—Redskins, 27-14 (W)
2002—Redskins, 14-3 (S)
2003—Seahawks, 27-20 (W)
2005—Seahawks, 20-17 (W) OT
*Seahawks, 20-10 (S)
2007—**Seahawks, 35-14 (S)
2008—Redskins, 20-17 (S)
2011—Redskins, 23-17 (S)
(RS Pts.—Redskins 294, Seahawks 222)
(PS Pts.—Seahawks 55, Redskins 24)
*NFC Divisional Playoff
**NFC First-Round Playoff

TAMPA BAY vs. ARIZONA
RS: Buccaneers lead series, 9-8;
See Arizona vs. Tampa Bay
TAMPA BAY vs. ATLANTA
RS: Buccaneers lead series, 19-18;
See Atlanta vs. Tampa Bay
TAMPA BAY vs. BALTIMORE
RS: Series tied, 2-2;
See Baltimore vs. Tampa Bay
TAMPA BAY vs. BUFFALO
RS: Buccaneers lead series, 6-3;
See Buffalo vs. Tampa Bay
TAMPA BAY vs. CAROLINA
RS: Panthers lead series, 14-9;
See Carolina vs. Tampa Bay
TAMPA BAY vs. CHICAGO
RS: Bears lead series, 36-18;
See Chicago vs. Tampa Bay
TAMPA BAY vs. CINCINNATI
RS: Buccaneers lead series, 7-3;
See Cincinnati vs. Tampa Bay
TAMPA BAY vs. CLEVELAND
RS: Browns lead series, 5-3;
See Cleveland vs. Tampa Bay
TAMPA BAY vs. DALLAS
RS: Cowboys lead series, 10-3
PS: Cowboys lead series, 2-0;
See Dallas vs. Tampa Bay
TAMPA BAY vs. DENVER
RS: Broncos lead series, 5-2;
See Denver vs. Tampa Bay
TAMPA BAY vs. DETROIT
RS: Lions lead series, 29-25
PS: Buccaneers lead series, 1-0;
See Detroit vs. Tampa Bay
TAMPA BAY vs. GREEN BAY
RS: Packers lead series, 30-21-1
PS: Packers lead series, 1-0;
See Green Bay vs. Tampa Bay
TAMPA BAY vs. HOUSTON
RS: Texans lead series, 2-1;

See Houston vs. Tampa Bay
TAMPA BAY vs. INDIANAPOLIS
RS: Colts lead series, 7-5;
See Indianapolis vs. Tampa Bay
TAMPA BAY vs. JACKSONVILLE
RS: Jaguars lead series, 4-1;
See Jacksonville vs. Tampa Bay
TAMPA BAY vs. KANSAS CITY
RS: Series tied, 5-5;
See Kansas City vs. Tampa Bay
TAMPA BAY vs. MIAMI
RS: Dolphins lead series, 5-4;
See Miami vs. Tampa Bay
TAMPA BAY vs. MINNESOTA
RS: Vikings lead series, 31-21;
See Minnesota vs. Tampa Bay
TAMPA BAY vs. NEW ENGLAND
RS: Patriots lead series, 5-2;
See New England vs. Tampa Bay
TAMPA BAY vs. NEW ORLEANS
RS: Saints lead series, 23-17;
See New Orleans vs. Tampa Bay
TAMPA BAY vs. N.Y. GIANTS
RS: Giants lead series, 11-6
PS: Giants lead series, 1-0;
See N.Y. Giants vs. Tampa Bay
TAMPA BAY vs. N.Y. JETS
RS: Jets lead series, 9-1;
See N.Y. Jets vs. Tampa Bay
TAMPA BAY vs. OAKLAND
RS: Raiders lead series, 6-1
PS: Buccaneers lead series, 1-0;
See Oakland vs. Tampa Bay
TAMPA BAY vs. PHILADELPHIA
RS: Eagles lead series, 6-5
PS: Series tied, 2-2;
See Philadelphia vs. Tampa Bay
TAMPA BAY vs. PITTSBURGH
RS: Steelers lead series, 8-1;
See Pittsburgh vs. Tampa Bay
TAMPA BAY vs. ST. LOUIS
RS: Rams lead series, 9-8
PS: Rams lead series, 2-0;
See St. Louis vs. Tampa Bay
TAMPA BAY vs. SAN DIEGO
RS: Chargers lead series, 8-1;
See San Diego vs. Tampa Bay
TAMPA BAY vs. SAN FRANCISCO
RS: 49ers lead series, 16-4
PS: Buccaneers lead series, 1-0;
See San Francisco vs. Tampa Bay
TAMPA BAY vs. SEATTLE
RS: Seahawks lead series, 7-4;
See Seattle vs. Tampa Bay
TAMPA BAY vs. *TENNESSEE
RS: Titans lead series, 8-2
1976—Oilers, 20-0 (H)
1980—Oilers, 20-14 (H)
1983—Buccaneers, 33-24 (TB)
1989—Oilers, 20-17 (H)
1995—Oilers, 19-7 (H)
1998—Oilers, 31-22 (TB)
2001—Titans, 31-28 (Tenn) OT
2003—Titans, 33-13 (Tenn)
2007—Buccaneers, 13-10 (TB)
2011—Titans, 23-17 (Tenn)
(RS Pts.—Titans 231, Buccaneers 164)
*Franchise in Houston prior to 1997;
known as Oilers prior to 1999
TAMPA BAY vs. WASHINGTON
RS: Buccaneers lead series, 9-8
PS: Series tied, 1-1

1977—Redskins, 10-0 (TB)
1982—Redskins, 21-13 (TB)
1989—Redskins, 32-28 (W)
1993—Redskins, 23-17 (TB)
1994—Buccaneers, 26-21 (TB)
      Buccaneers, 17-14 (W)
1995—Buccaneers, 14-6 (TB)
1996—Buccaneers, 24-10 (TB)
1998—Redskins, 20-16 (W)
1999—*Buccaneers, 14-13 (TB)
2000—Redskins, 20-17 (W) OT
2003—Buccaneers, 35-13 (W)
2004—Redskins, 16-10 (W)
2005—Buccaneers, 36-35 (TB)
      **Redskins, 17-10 (TB)
2006—Buccaneers, 20-17 (TB)
2007—Buccaneers, 19-13 (TB)
2009—Redskins, 16-13 (W)
2010—Buccaneers, 17-16 (W)
(RS Pts.—Buccaneers 322, Redskins 303)
(PS Pts.—Redskins 30, Buccaneers 24)
*NFC Divisional Playoff
**NFC First-Round Playoff

TENNESSEE VS. ARIZONA
RS: Cardinals lead series, 5-4;
See Arizona vs. Tennessee
TENNESSEE vs. ATLANTA
RS: Titans lead series, 7-6;
See Atlanta vs. Tennessee
TENNESSEE vs. BALTIMORE
RS: Titans lead series, 9-8
PS: Ravens lead series, 2-1;
See Baltimore vs. Tennessee
TENNESSEE vs. BUFFALO
RS: Titans lead series, 26-14
PS: Bills lead series, 2-1;
See Buffalo vs. Tennessee
TENNESSEE vs. CAROLINA
RS: Titans lead series, 3-1;
See Carolina vs. Tennessee
TENNESSEE vs. CHICAGO
RS: Series tied, 5-5;
See Chicago vs. Tennessee
TENNESSEE vs. CINCINNATI
RS: Titans lead series, 39-32-1
PS: Bengals lead series, 1-0;
See Cincinnati vs. Tennessee
TENNESSEE vs. CLEVELAND
RS: Browns lead series, 33-28
PS: Titans lead series, 1-0;
See Cleveland vs. Tennessee
TENNESSEE vs. DALLAS
RS: Cowboys lead series, 7-6;
See Dallas vs. Tennessee
TENNESSEE vs. DENVER
RS: Titans lead series, 21-14-1
PS: Broncos lead series, 2-1;
See Denver vs. Tennessee
TENNESSEE vs. DETROIT
RS: Titans lead series, 7-3;
See Detroit vs. Tennessee
TENNESSEE vs. GREEN BAY
RS: Titans lead series, 6-4;
See Green Bay vs. Tennessee
TENNESSEE vs. HOUSTON
RS: Titans lead series, 14-6;
See Houston vs. Tennessee
TENNESSEE vs. INDIANAPOLIS
RS: Colts lead series, 21-13
PS: Titans lead series, 1-0;
See Indianapolis vs. Tennessee

TENNESSEE vs. JACKSONVILLE
RS: Titans lead series, 19-15
PS: Titans lead series, 1-0;
See Jacksonville vs. Tennessee
TENNESSEE vs. KANSAS CITY
RS: Chiefs lead series, 26-20
PS: Chiefs lead series, 2-0;
See Kansas City vs. Tennessee
TENNESSEE vs. MIAMI
RS: Dolphins lead series, 18-14
PS: Titans lead series, 1-0;
See Miami vs. Tennessee
TENNESSEE vs. MINNESOTA
RS: Vikings lead series, 7-4;
See Minnesota vs. Tennessee
TENNESSEE vs. NEW ENGLAND
RS: Patriots lead series, 21-15-1
PS: Series tied, 1-1;
See New England vs. Tennessee
TENNESSEE vs. NEW ORLEANS
RS: Titans lead series, 7-5-1;
See New Orleans vs. Tennessee
TENNESSEE vs. N.Y. GIANTS
RS: Series tied, 5-5;
See N.Y. Giants vs. Tennessee
TENNESSEE vs. N.Y. JETS
RS: Titans lead series, 21-17-1
PS: Titans lead series, 1-0;
See N.Y. Jets vs. Tennessee
TENNESSEE vs. OAKLAND
RS: Raiders lead series, 23-19
PS: Raiders lead series, 4-0;
See Oakland vs. Tennessee
TENNESSEE vs. PHILADELPHIA
RS: Eagles lead series, 6-4;
See Philadelphia vs. Tennessee
TENNESSEE vs. PITTSBURGH
RS: Steelers lead series, 41-29
PS: Steelers lead series, 3-1;
See Pittsburgh vs. Tennessee
TENNESSEE vs. ST. LOUIS
RS: Rams lead series, 6-4
PS: Rams lead series, 1-0;
See St. Louis vs. Tennessee
TENNESSEE vs. SAN DIEGO
RS: Chargers lead series, 24-13-1
PS: Titans lead series, 3-1;
See San Diego vs. Tennessee
TENNESSEE vs. SAN FRANCISCO
RS: 49ers lead series, 7-5;
See San Francisco vs. Tennessee
TENNESSEE vs. SEATTLE
RS: Seahawks lead series, 9-5
PS: Titans lead series, 1-0;
See Seattle vs. Tennessee
TENNESSEE vs. TAMPA BAY
RS: Titans lead series, 8-2;
See Tampa Bay vs. Tennessee
***TENNESSEE vs. WASHINGTON**
RS: Titans lead series, 6-5
1971—Redskins, 22-13 (W)
1975—Oilers, 13-10 (H)
1979—Oilers, 29-27 (W)
1985—Redskins, 16-13 (W)
1988—Oilers, 41-17 (H)
1991—Redskins, 16-13 (W) OT
1997—Oilers, 28-14 (T)
2000—Titans, 27-21 (W)
2002—Redskins, 31-14 (T)
2006—Titans, 25-22 (W)
2010—Redskins, 19-16 (T) OT
(RS—Titans 232, Redskins 215)

Franchise in Houston prior to 1997; known as Oilers prior to 1999

WASHINGTON vs. ARIZONA
RS: Redskins lead series, 74-44-2;
See Arizona vs. Washington

WASHINGTON vs. ATLANTA
RS: Redskins lead series, 14-6-1
PS: Redskins lead series, 1-0;
See Atlanta vs. Washington

WASHINGTON vs. BALTIMORE
RS: Ravens lead series, 3-1;
See Baltimore vs. Washington

WASHINGTON vs. BUFFALO
RS: Bills lead series, 8-4
PS: Redskins lead series, 1-0;
See Buffalo vs. Washington

WASHINGTON vs. CAROLINA
RS: Redskins lead series, 7-3;
See Carolina vs. Washington

WASHINGTON vs. CHICAGO
RS: Bears lead series, 20-19-1
PS: Redskins lead series, 4-3;
See Chicago vs. Washington

WASHINGTON vs. CINCINNATI
RS: Series tied, 4-4;
See Cincinnati vs. Washington

WASHINGTON vs. CLEVELAND
RS: Browns lead series, 33-10-1;
See Cleveland vs. Washington

WASHINGTON vs. DALLAS
RS: Cowboys lead series, 62-38-2
PS: Redskins lead series, 2-0;
See Dallas vs. Washington

WASHINGTON vs. DENVER
RS: Broncos lead series, 6-5
PS: Redskins lead series, 1-0;
See Denver vs. Washington

WASHINGTON vs. DETROIT
RS: Redskins lead series, 27-12
PS: Redskins lead series, 3-0;
See Detroit vs. Washington

WASHINGTON vs. GREEN BAY
RS: Packers lead series, 17-13-1
PS: Series tied, 1-1;
See Green Bay vs. Washington

WASHINGTON vs. HOUSTON
RS: Redskins lead series, 2-1;
See Houston vs. Washington

WASHINGTON vs. INDIANAPOLIS
RS: Colts lead series, 19-10;
See Indianapolis vs. Washington

WASHINGTON vs. JACKSONVILLE
RS: Redskins lead series, 4-1;
See Jacksonville vs. Washington

WASHINGTON vs. KANSAS CITY
RS: Chiefs lead series, 7-1;
See Kansas City vs. Washington

WASHINGTON vs. MIAMI
RS: Dolphins lead series, 7-4
PS: Series tied, 1-1;
See Miami vs. Washington

WASHINGTON vs. MINNESOTA
RS: Series tied, 8-8
PS: Redskins lead series, 3-2;
See Minnesota vs. Washington

WASHINGTON vs. NEW ENGLAND
RS: Redskins lead series, 6-3;
See New England vs. Washington

WASHINGTON vs. NEW ORLEANS
RS: Redskins lead series, 15-8;
See New Orleans vs. Washington

WASHINGTON vs. N.Y. GIANTS
RS: Giants lead series, 91-63-4
PS: Series tied, 1-1;
See N.Y. Giants vs. Washington

WASHINGTON vs. N.Y. JETS
RS: Redskins lead series, 8-2;
See N.Y. Jets vs. Washington

WASHINGTON vs. OAKLAND
RS: Raiders lead series, 7-4
PS: Raiders lead series, 1-0;
See Oakland vs. Washington

WASHINGTON vs. PHILADELPHIA
RS: Redskins lead series, 78-70-5
PS: Redskins lead series, 1-0;
See Philadelphia vs. Washington

WASHINGTON vs. PITTSBURGH
RS: Redskins lead series, 42-31-3;
See Pittsburgh vs. Washington

WASHINGTON vs. ST. LOUIS
RS: Redskins lead series, 22-9-1
PS: Series tied, 2-2;
See St. Louis vs. Washington

WASHINGTON vs. SAN DIEGO
RS: Redskins lead series, 6-3;
See San Diego vs. Washington

WASHINGTON vs. SAN FRANCISCO
RS: 49ers lead series, 15-9-1
PS: 49ers lead series, 3-1;
See San Francisco vs. Washington

WASHINGTON vs. SEATTLE
RS: Redskins lead series, 11-4
PS: Seahawks lead series, 2-0;
See Seattle vs. Washington

WASHINGTON vs. TAMPA BAY
RS: Buccaneers lead series, 9-8
PS: Series tied, 1-1;
See Tampa Bay vs. Washington

WASHINGTON vs. TENNESSEE
RS: Titans lead series, 6-5;
See Tennessee vs. Washington

NFL INTERNATIONAL GAMES (67)

REGULAR SEASON GAMES (10)
(Home Team in capitals)

Date	Site	Teams
October 2, 2005	Mexico City, Mexico	ARIZONA 31, San Francisco 14
October 28, 2007	London, England	N.Y. Giants 13, MIAMI 10
October 26, 2008	London, England	NEW ORLEANS 37, San Diego 32
December 7, 2008	Toronto, Canada	Miami 16, BUFFALO 3
October 25, 2009	London, England	New England 35, TAMPA BAY 7
December 3, 2009	Toronto, Canada	N.Y. Jets 19, BUFFALO 13
October 31, 2010	London, England	SAN FRANCISCO 24, Denver 16
November 7, 2010	Toronto, Canada	Chicago 22, BUFFALO 19
October 23, 2011	London, England	Chicago 24, TAMPA BAY 18
October 30, 2011	Toronto, Canada	BUFFALO 23, Washington 0

PRESEASON GAMES (57)

Date	Site	Teams
August 12, 1950	Ottawa, Canada	N.Y. Giants 27, Ottawa Rough Riders 6
August 11, 1951	Ottawa, Canada	N.Y. Giants 41, Ottawa Rough Riders 18
August 5, 1959	Toronto, Canada	Chi. Cardinals 55, Tor. Argonauts 26
August 3, 1960	Toronto, Canada	Pittsburgh 43, Toronto Argonauts 16
August 15, 1960	Toronto, Canada	Chicago 16, N.Y. Giants 7
August 2, 1961	Toronto, Canada	St. Louis 36, Toronto Argonauts 7
August 5, 1961	Montreal, Canada	Chicago 34, Montreal Alouettes 16
August 8, 1961	Hamilton, Canada	Hamilton Tiger-Cats 38, Buffalo 21
August 25, 1969	Montreal, Canada	Detroit 22, Boston 9
September 11, 1969	Montreal, Canada	Pittsburgh 17, N.Y. Giants 13
August 16, 1976	Tokyo, Japan	St. Louis 20, San Diego 10
August 5, 1978	Mexico City, Mexico	New Orleans 14, Philadelphia 7
August 6, 1983	London, England	Minnesota 28, St. Louis 10
* August 3, 1986	London, England	Chicago 17, Dallas 6
* August 9, 1987	London, England	L.A. Rams 28, Denver 27
* July 31, 1988	London, England	Miami 21, San Francisco 21
August 14, 1988	Goteborg, Sweden	Minnesota 28, Chicago 21
August 18, 1988	Montreal, Canada	N.Y. Jets 11, Cleveland 7
* August 5, 1989	Tokyo, Japan	L.A. Rams 16, San Francisco 13 (OT)
* August 6, 1989	London, England	Philadelphia 17, Cleveland 13
* August 4, 1990	Tokyo, Japan	Denver 10, Seattle 7
* August 5, 1990	London, England	New Orleans 17, L.A. Raiders 10
* August 9, 1990	Montreal, Canada	Pittsburgh 30, New England 14
* August 11, 1990	Berlin, Germany	L.A. Rams 19, Kansas City 3
* July 28, 1991	London, England	Buffalo 17, Philadelphia 13
* August 3, 1991	Berlin, Germany	San Francisco 21, Chicago 7
* August 3, 1991	Tokyo, Japan	Miami 19, L.A. Raiders 17
* August 1, 1992	Tokyo, Japan	Houston 34, Dallas 23
* August 15, 1992	Berlin, Germany	Miami 31, Denver 27
* August 16, 1992	London, England	San Francisco 17, Washington 15
* July 31, 1993	Tokyo, Japan	New Orleans 28, Philadelphia 16
* August 1, 1993	Barcelona, Spain	San Francisco 21, Pittsburgh 14
* August 7, 1993	Berlin, Germany	Minnesota 20, Buffalo 6
* August 8, 1993	London, England	Dallas 13, Detroit 13 (OT)
August 14, 1993	Toronto, Canada	Cleveland 12, New England 9
* July 31, 1994	Barcelona, Spain	L.A. Raiders 25, Denver 22
* August 6, 1994	Tokyo, Japan	Minnesota 17, Kansas City 9
* August 13, 1994	Berlin, Germany	N.Y. Giants 28, San Diego 20
* August 15, 1994	Mexico City, Mexico	Houston 6, Dallas 0
* August 5, 1995	Tokyo, Japan	Denver 24, San Francisco 10
* August 12, 1995	Toronto, Canada	Buffalo 9, Dallas 7
* July 27, 1996	Tokyo, Japan	San Diego 20, Pittsburgh 10
* August 5, 1996	Monterrey, Mexico	Kansas City 32, Dallas 6
* July 27, 1997	Dublin, Ireland	Pittsburgh 30, Chicago 17
* August 4, 1997	Mexico City, Mexico	Miami 38, Denver 19
* August 16, 1997	Toronto, Canada	Green Bay 35, Buffalo 3
* August 1, 1998	Tokyo, Japan	Green Bay 27, Kansas City 24 (OT)
* August 15, 1998	Vancouver, Canada	San Francisco 24, Seattle 21
* August 17, 1998	Mexico City, Mexico	New England 21, Dallas 3
* August 7, 1999	Sydney, Australia	Denver 20, San Diego 17
* August 5, 2000	Tokyo, Japan	Atlanta 20, Dallas 9
* August 19, 2000	Mexico City, Mexico	Indianapolis 24, Pittsburgh 23
* August 27, 2001	Mexico City, Mexico	Dallas 31, Oakland 6
* August 3, 2002	Osaka, Japan	Washington 38, San Francisco 7
* August 2, 2003	Tokyo, Japan	Tampa Bay 30, N.Y. Jets 14
* August 6, 2005	Tokyo, Japan	Atlanta 27, Indianapolis 21
August 14, 2008	Toronto, Canada	Buffalo 34, Pittsburgh 21
August 19, 2010	Toronto, Canada	Buffalo 34, Indianapolis 21

* *American Bowl Game*

SUPER BOWL COMPOSITE STANDINGS

	W	L	Pct.	Pts.	OP
San Francisco 49ers	5	0	1.000	188	89
Baltimore Ravens	1	0	1.000	34	7
New Orleans Saints	1	0	1.000	31	17
New York Jets	1	0	1.000	16	7
Tampa Bay Buccaneers	1	0	1.000	48	21
Green Bay Packers	4	1	.800	158	101
New York Giants	4	1	.800	104	104
Pittsburgh Steelers	6	2	.750	193	164
Dallas Cowboys	5	3	.625	221	132
Oakland/L.A. Raiders	3	2	.600	132	114
Washington Redskins	3	2	.600	122	103
Indianapolis/Baltimore Colts	2	2	.500	69	77
Chicago Bears	1	1	.500	63	39
Kansas City Chiefs	1	1	.500	33	42
New England Patriots	3	4	.429	138	186
Miami Dolphins	2	3	.400	74	103
Denver Broncos	2	4	.333	115	206
St. Louis/L.A. Rams	1	2	.333	59	67
Arizona Cardinals	0	1	.000	23	27
Atlanta Falcons	0	1	.000	19	34
Carolina Panthers	0	1	.000	29	32
San Diego Chargers	0	1	.000	26	49
Seattle Seahawks	0	1	.000	10	21
Tennessee Titans	0	1	.000	16	23
Cincinnati Bengals	0	2	.000	37	46
Philadelphia Eagles	0	2	.000	31	51
Buffalo Bills	0	4	.000	73	139
Minnesota Vikings	0	4	.000	34	95

SUPER BOWL HOST CITIES

South Florida	10	
New Orleans	9	
Los Angeles	7	(LA Coliseum 2, Rose Bowl 5)
Tampa Bay	4	
San Diego	3	
Arizona	2	
Atlanta	2	
Detroit	2	
Houston	2	
Indianapolis	1	
Jacksonville	1	
Minneapolis	1	
North Texas	1	
Stanford	1	

FUTURE SUPER BOWL SITES

Super Bowl XLVII	Feb. 3, 2013	Mercedes-Benz Superdome	New Orleans, Louisiana
Super Bowl XLVIII	Feb. 2, 2014*	MetLife Stadium	New York-New Jersey
Super Bowl XLIX	Feb. 1, 2015*	University of Phoenix Stadium	Arizona

*Tentative date

PETE ROZELLE TROPHY/SUPER BOWL MVPs*

Super Bowl I	— QB Bart Starr, Green Bay
Super Bowl II	— QB Bart Starr, Green Bay
Super Bowl III	— QB Joe Namath, N.Y. Jets
Super Bowl IV	— QB Len Dawson, Kansas City
Super Bowl V	— LB Chuck Howley, Dallas
Super Bowl VI	— QB Roger Staubach, Dallas
Super Bowl VII	— S Jake Scott, Miami
Super Bowl VIII	— RB Larry Csonka, Miami
Super Bowl IX	— RB Franco Harris, Pittsburgh
Super Bowl X	— WR Lynn Swann, Pittsburgh
Super Bowl XI	— WR Fred Biletnikoff, Oakland
Super Bowl XII	— DT Randy White and DE Harvey Martin, Dallas
Super Bowl XIII	— QB Terry Bradshaw, Pittsburgh
Super Bowl XIV	— QB Terry Bradshaw, Pittsburgh
Super Bowl XV	— QB Jim Plunkett, Oakland
Super Bowl XVI	— QB Joe Montana, San Francisco
Super Bowl XVII	— RB John Riggins, Washington
Super Bowl XVIII	— RB Marcus Allen, L.A. Raiders
Super Bowl XIX	— QB Joe Montana, San Francisco
Super Bowl XX	— DE Richard Dent, Chicago
Super Bowl XXI	— QB Phil Simms, N.Y. Giants
Super Bowl XXII	— QB Doug Williams, Washington
Super Bowl XXIII	— WR Jerry Rice, San Francisco
Super Bowl XXIV	— QB Joe Montana, San Francisco
Super Bowl XXV	— RB Ottis Anderson, N.Y. Giants
Super Bowl XXVI	— QB Mark Rypien, Washington
Super Bowl XXVII	— QB Troy Aikman, Dallas
Super Bowl XXVIII	— RB Emmitt Smith, Dallas
Super Bowl XXIX	— QB Steve Young, San Francisco
Super Bowl XXX	— CB Larry Brown, Dallas
Super Bowl XXXI	— KR-PR Desmond Howard, Green Bay
Super Bowl XXXII	— RB Terrell Davis, Denver
Super Bowl XXXIII	— QB John Elway, Denver
Super Bowl XXXIV	— QB Kurt Warner, St. Louis
Super Bowl XXXV	— LB Ray Lewis, Baltimore
Super Bowl XXXVI	— QB Tom Brady, New England
Super Bowl XXXVII	— S Dexter Jackson, Tampa Bay
Super Bowl XXXVIII	— QB Tom Brady, New England
Super Bowl XXXIX	— WR Deion Branch, New England
Super Bowl XL	— WR Hines Ward, Pittsburgh
Super Bowl XLI	— QB Peyton Manning, Indianapolis
Super Bowl XLII	— QB Eli Manning, N.Y. Giants
Super Bowl XLIII	— WR Santonio Holmes, Pittsburgh
Super Bowl XLIV	— QB Drew Brees, New Orleans
Super Bowl XLV	— QB Aaron Rodgers, Green Bay
Super Bowl XLVI	— QB Eli Manning, N.Y. Giants

* Award named Pete Rozelle Trophy since Super Bowl XXV.

SUPER BOWL MVP BY POSITION

Quarterback	25
Running Back	7
Wide Receiver	6
Defensive End	2
Linebacker	2
Safety	2
Cornerback	1
Defensive Tackle	1
Kick Returner-Punt Returner	1

A defensive end and defensive tackle shared the Super Bowl XII MVP award.

RESULTS

NFC leads AFC, 24-21

Super Bowl	Date	Winner (Share)	Loser (Share)	Score	Site	Attendance
XLVI	2-5-12	N.Y. Giants ($88,000)	New England ($44,000)	21-17	Indianapolis	68,658
XLV	2-6-11	Green Bay ($83,000)	Pittsburgh ($42,000)	31-25	North Texas	91,060
XLIV	2-7-10	New Orleans ($83,000)	Indianapolis ($42,000)	31-17	South Florida	74,059
XLIII	2-1-09	Pittsburgh ($78,000)	Arizona ($40,000)	27-23	Tampa Bay	70,774
XLII	2-3-08	N.Y. Giants ($78,000)	New England ($40,000)	17-14	Arizona	71,101
XLI	2-4-07	Indianapolis ($73,000)	Chicago ($38,000)	29-17	South Florida	74,512
XL	2-5-06	Pittsburgh ($73,000)	Seattle ($38,000)	21-10	Detroit	68,206
XXXIX	2-6-05	New England ($68,000)	Philadelphia ($36,500)	24-21	Jacksonville	78,125
XXXVIII	2-1-04	New England ($68,000)	Carolina ($36,500)	32-29	Houston	71,525
* XXXVII	1-26-03	Tampa Bay ($63,000)	Oakland ($35,000)	48-21	San Diego	67,603
* XXXVI	2-3-02	New England ($63,000)	St. Louis ($34,500)	20-17	New Orleans	72,922
XXXV	1-28-01	Baltimore ($58,000)	N.Y. Giants ($34,500)	34-7	Tampa Bay	71,921
* XXXIV	1-30-00	St. Louis ($58,000)	Tennessee ($33,000)	23-16	Atlanta	72,625
XXXIII	1-31-99	Denver ($53,000)	Atlanta ($32,500)	34-19	South Florida	74,803
XXXII	1-25-98	Denver ($48,000)	Green Bay ($29,000)	31-24	San Diego	68,912
XXXI	1-26-97	Green Bay ($48,000)	New England ($29,000)	35-21	New Orleans	72,301
XXX	1-28-96	Dallas ($42,000)	Pittsburgh ($27,000)	27-17	Arizona	76,347
XXIX	1-29-95	San Francisco ($42,000)	San Diego ($26,000)	49-26	South Florida	74,107
* XXVIII	1-30-94	Dallas ($38,000)	Buffalo ($23,500)	30-13	Atlanta	72,817
XXVII	1-31-93	Dallas ($36,000)	Buffalo ($18,000)	52-17	Pasadena	98,374
XXVI	1-26-92	Washington ($36,000)	Buffalo ($18,000)	37-24	Minneapolis	63,130
* XXV	1-27-91	N.Y. Giants ($36,000)	Buffalo ($18,000)	20-19	Tampa Bay	73,813
XXIV	1-28-90	San Francisco ($36,000)	Denver ($18,000)	55-10	New Orleans	72,919
XXIII	1-22-89	San Francisco ($36,000)	Cincinnati ($18,000)	20-16	South Florida	75,129
XXII	1-31-88	Washington ($36,000)	Denver ($18,000)	42-10	San Diego	73,302
XXI	1-25-87	N.Y. Giants ($36,000)	Denver ($18,000)	39-20	Pasadena	101,063
XX	1-26-86	Chicago ($36,000)	New England ($18,000)	46-10	New Orleans	73,818
XIX	1-20-85	San Francisco ($36,000)	Miami ($18,000)	38-16	Stanford	84,059
XVIII	1-22-84	L.A. Raiders ($36,000)	Washington ($18,000)	38-9	Tampa Bay	72,920
* XVII	1-30-83	Washington ($36,000)	Miami ($18,000)	27-17	Pasadena	103,667
XVI	1-24-82	San Francisco ($18,000)	Cincinnati ($9,000)	26-21	Pontiac	81,270
XV	1-25-81	Oakland ($18,000)	Philadelphia ($9,000)	27-10	New Orleans	76,135
XIV	1-20-80	Pittsburgh ($18,000)	Los Angeles ($9,000)	31-19	Pasadena	103,985
XIII	1-21-79	Pittsburgh ($18,000)	Dallas ($9,000)	35-31	South Florida	79,484
XII	1-15-78	Dallas ($18,000)	Denver ($9,000)	27-10	New Orleans	75,583
XI	1-9-77	Oakland ($15,000)	Minnesota ($7,500)	32-14	Pasadena	103,438
X	1-18-76	Pittsburgh ($15,000)	Dallas ($7,500)	21-17	South Florida	80,187
IX	1-12-75	Pittsburgh ($15,000)	Minnesota ($7,500)	16-6	New Orleans	80,997
VIII	1-13-74	Miami ($15,000)	Minnesota ($7,500)	24-7	Houston	71,882
VII	1-14-73	Miami ($15,000)	Washington ($7,500)	14-7	Los Angeles	90,182
VI	1-16-72	Dallas ($15,000)	Miami ($7,500)	24-3	New Orleans	81,023
V	1-17-71	Baltimore ($15,000)	Dallas ($7,500)	16-13	South Florida	79,204
* IV	1-11-70	Kansas City ($15,000)	Minnesota ($7,500)	23-7	New Orleans	80,562
III	1-12-69	N.Y. Jets ($15,000)	Baltimore ($7,500)	16-7	South Florida	75,389
II	1-14-68	Green Bay ($15,000)	Oakland ($7,500)	33-14	South Florida	75,546
I	1-15-67	Green Bay ($15,000)	Kansas City ($7,500)	35-10	Los Angeles	61,946

* One week between conference championship games and Super Bowl; all others had two weeks between conference championship games and Super Bowl.

For historical Super Bowl game recaps, box scores, and video highlights, please visit www.NFL.com/SuperBowl.

SUPER BOWL XLVI

Lucas Oil Stadium, Indianapolis, Indiana February 5, 2012, Attendance: 68,658

NEW YORK GIANTS 21, NEW ENGLAND 17—Ahmad Bradshaw scored on a 6-yard touchdown run with 57 seconds remaining to cap an 88-yard drive and lead the Giants to their second Super Bowl victory over the Patriots in five years. The triumph was the Giants' franchise's fourth Super Bowl title. The Patriots' defense forced a punt to begin the game, but Steve Weatherford's punt pinned New England back to its own 6-yard line. On the Patriots' first play, Justin Tuck pressured Tom Brady and forced him to pass deep down the middle of the field, where no players were within range, resulting in an intentional grounding penalty. A safety was enforced by rule, giving the Giants a 2-0 lead. Following the ensuing free kick, the Giants drove 78 yards in nine plays, capped by Victor Cruz' 2-yard touchdown catch for a 9-0 advantage. New York led 9-3 late in the first half when Weatherford pinned the Patriots back to their own 4-yard line. This time New England respond-ed with a 96-yard drive, which included a key 12-yard third-down catch by Aaron Hernandez, and was capped by Brady's 4-yard touchdown pass to Danny Wood-head with 15 seconds left in the half to take a 10-9 halftime lead. The Patriots then began the second half with an 8-play, 79-yard drive, sparked by a 21-yard pass to Chad Ochocinco and BenJarvus Green-Ellis' 17-yard run, and capped by Hernan-dez' 12-yard touchdown catch for a 17-9 lead. The Giants answered with a field goal, forced a three-and-out on defense, and generated a second field-goal drive to trim the deficit to 17-15 with 35 seconds left in the third quarter. On the second play of the fourth quarter, Brady attempted a deep pass to Rob Gronkowski that was intercepted by Chase Blackburn at the Giants' 8-yard line. Both teams then traded punts, with the Giants getting the ball own their own 12-yard line with 3:46 to play. On the first play of the possession, Manning launched a perfectly placed pass to Mario Manningham deep down the left sideline. Manningham caught the ball just inbounds with two Patriots' defenders in close pursuit. Passes of 16 yards, to Manningham, and 14 yards, to Hakeem Nicks, put the Giants at the Patriots' 18 with 2:00 remaining. Bradshaw gained seven yards on the first play following the 2-minute warning and Manning completed a 4-yard pass to Nicks that resulted in a first down. After Bradshaw gained 1 yard, his next run up the middle resulted in the go-ahead touchdown with 57 seconds remaining. Faced with fourth-and-16 with 39 seconds left, Brady completed a 19-yard pass to Deion Branch and then an 11-yard pass to Hernandez. A 12-men-on-the-field penalty with 17 seconds left pushed the ball to the Patriots' 49, but Brady's Hail Mary pass fell incomplete in the end zone as time expired. Manning was 30 of 40 for 296 yards and 1 touchdown and was named the Super Bowl Most Valuable Player. Nicks had 10 catches for 109 yards. Brady completed 27 of 41 passes for 276 yards and 2 touchdowns, with 1 interception.

N.Y. Giants (21) New England (17)
Offense

Victor Cruz	WR	Wes Welker
David Diehl	LT	Matt Light
Kevin Boothe	LG	Logan Mankins
David Baas	C	Dan Connolly
Chris Snee	RG	Brian Waters
Kareem McKenzie	RT	Sebastian Vollmer
Jake Ballard	TE	Rob Gronkowski
Hakeem Nicks	WR	Deion Branch
Eli Manning	QB	Tom Brady
Ahmad Bradshaw	RB	BenJarvus Green-Ellis
Henry Hynoski	FB/TE	Nate Solder

Defense

Justin Tuck	LDE/LB	Tracy White
Linval Joseph	LDT/DT	Vince Wilfork
Chris Canty	RDT/DT	Kyle Love
Jason Pierre-Paul	RE/DL	Brandon Deaderick
Chase Blackburn	MLB/LB	Rob Ninkovich
Michael Boley	WLB/LB	Jerod Mayo
Corey Webster	LCB/LB	Brandon Spikes
Aaron Ross	RCB/LCB	Devin McCourty
Kenny Phillips	SS/RCB	Kyle Arrington
Antrel Rolle	FS/S	James Ihedigbo
Deon Grant	S	Patrick Chung

SUBSTITUTIONS
N.Y. GIANTS—Specialists: K—Lawrence Tynes. P—Steve Weatherford. LS—Zak DeOssie. Offense: RB—Brandon Jacobs, D.J. Ware. WR—Jerrel Jernigan, Mario Manningham, Devin Thomas. TE—Travis Beckum, Bear Pascoe. T—Tony Ugoh.

G—Mitch Petrus. Defense: DE—Dave Tollefson, Osi Umenyiora. DT—Rocky Bernard. LB—Greg Jones, Mathias Kiwanuka, Seth Paysinger, Jacquian Williams. CB—Prince Amukamara, Will Blackmon. DB—Derrick Martin. S—Tyler Sash. DNP: QB—David Carr. Not Active: RB—Da'Rel Scott. WR—Ramses Barden. T—James Brewer Jr. C—Jim Cordle. DT—Jimmy Kennedy. DE—Justin Trattou. LB—Mark Herzlich.

NEW ENGLAND—Specialists: K—Stephen Gostkowski. P—Zoltan Mesko. LS—Danny Aiken. Offense: RB—Danny Woodhead. FB—Lousaka Polite. WR—Julian Edelman, Chad Ochocinco, Matthew Slater. TE—Aaron Hernandez. OL—Marcus Cannon. C—Ryan Wendell. Defense: DE—Mark Anderson, Shaun Ellis. DL—Gerard Warren. LB—Dane Fletcher, Niko Koutouvides. CB—Antwaun Molden. DB—Sterling Moore, Malcolm Williams. S—Sergio Brown. DNP: QB—Brian Hoyer. RB—Stevan Ridley. DE—Alex Silvestro. DE—Nate Jones. Not Active: QB—Ryan Mallett. RB—Kevin Faulk, Shane Vereen. OL—Nick McDonald, Donald Thomas. DL—Ron Brace. LB—Gary Guyton.

OFFICIALS
Referee—John Parry. Umpire—Carl Paganelli. Head Linesman—Tom Stabile. Line Judge—Gary Arthur. Side Judge—Laird Hayes. Field Judge—Gary Cavaletto. Back Judge—Tony Steratore. Replay Official—Larry Nemmers.

SCORING

N.Y. Giants (NFC)	9 0 6 6	— 21
New England (AFC)	0 10 7 0	— 17

NYG — Safety, intentional grounding penalty enforced on Brady in end zone (8:52)
NYG — Cruz 2 pass from Manning (Tynes kick) (3:24)
NE — FG Gostkowski 29 (13:48)
NE — Woodhead 4 pass from Brady (Gostkowski kick) (0:08)
NE — Hernandez 12 pass from Brady (Gostkowski kick) (11:20)
NYG — FG Tynes 38 (6:43)
NYG — FG Tynes 33 (0:35)
NYG — Bradshaw 6 run (run failed) (0:57)

TEAM STATISTICS

	NYG	NE
Total First Downs	26	21
Rushing	7	6
Passing	18	15
Penalty	1	0
Total Net Yardage	396	349
Total Offensive Plays	71	62
Avg. Gain Per Offensive Play	5.6	5.6
Rushes	28	19
Yards Gained Rushing (Net)	114	83
Avg. Yards per Rush	4.1	4.4
Passes Attempted	40	41
Passes Completed	30	27
Had Intercepted	0	1
Tackled Attempting to Pass	3	2
Yards Lost Attempting to Pass	14	10
Yards Gained Passing (Net)	282	266
Punts	4	3
Avg. Distance	40.8	41.0
Punt Returns	1	0
Punt Return Yardage	10	0
Kickoff Returns	4	3
Kickoff Return Yardage	75	73
Interception Return Yardage	0	0
Total Return Yardage (excl. Kickoff)	10	0
Fumbles	2	0
Fumbles Lost	0	0
Own Fumbles Recovered	2	0
Opponent Fumbles Recovered	0	0
Penalties	4	5
Yards Penalized	24	28
Field Goals	2	1
Field Goals Attempted	2	1
Third-Down Efficiency	5/11	6/12
Fourth-Down Efficiency	0/0	1/1
Time of Possession	37:05	22:55

INDIVIDUAL STATISTICS
RUSHING: NYG: Bradshaw 17-72-1, Jacobs 9-37-0, Ware 1-6-0, Manning 1-(-1)-0. NE: Green-Ellis 10-44-0, Welker 2-21-0, Woodhead 7-18-0.
PASSING: NYG: Manning 40-30-296-1-0. NE: Brady 41-27-276-2-1.
RECEIVING: NYG: Nicks 10-109-0, Manningham 5-73-0, Pascoe 4-33-0, Cruz 4-25-1, Bradshaw 2-19-0, Hynoski 2-19-0, Ballard 2-10-0, Ware 1-8-0. NE: Hernandez 8-67-1, Welker 7-60-0, Woodhead 4-42-1, Branch 3-45-0, Gronkowski 2-26-0, Green-Ellis 2-15-0, Ochocinco 1-21-0.
KICKOFF RETURNS: NYG: Jernigan 3-71-0, Blackmon 1-4-0. NE: Edelman 3-73-0.
PUNT RETURNS: NYG: Blackmon 1-10-0. NE: None.
PUNTING: NYG: Weatherford 4-163-40.8. NE: Mesko 3-123-41.0.
INTERCEPTIONS: NYG: Blackburn 1-0-0. NE: None.
SACKS: NYG: Tuck 2. NE: Anderson 1.5, Deaderick 1, Ninkovich 0.5.

AFC CHAMPIONSHIP GAME RESULTS
Includes AFL Championship Games (1960-69)

Season	Date	Winner (Share)	Loser (Share)	Score	Site	Attendance
2011	Jan. 22	New England ($40,000)	Baltimore ($40,000)	23-20	Foxborough	68,756
2010	Jan. 23	Pittsburgh ($38,000)	N.Y. Jets ($38,000)	24-19	Pittsburgh	66,662
2009	Jan. 24	Indianapolis ($38,000)	N.Y. Jets ($38,000)	30-17	Indianapolis	67,650
2008	Jan. 18	Pittsburgh ($37,500)	Baltimore ($37,500)	23-14	Pittsburgh	65,350
2007	Jan. 20	New England ($37,500)	San Diego ($37,500)	21-12	Foxborough	68,756
2006	Jan. 21	Indianapolis ($37,000)	New England ($37,000)	38-34	Indianapolis	57,433
2005	Jan. 22	Pittsburgh ($37,000)	Denver ($37,000)	34-17	Denver	76,775
2004	Jan. 23	New England ($36,500)	Pittsburgh ($36,500)	41-27	Pittsburgh	65,242
2003	Jan. 18	New England ($36,500)	Indianapolis ($36,500)	24-14	Foxborough	68,436
2002	Jan. 19	Oakland ($35,000)	Tennessee ($35,000)	41-24	Oakland	62,544
2001	Jan. 27	New England ($34,500)	Pittsburgh ($34,500)	24-17	Pittsburgh	64,704
2000	Jan. 14	Baltimore ($34,500)	Oakland ($34,500)	16-3	Oakland	62,784
1999	Jan. 23	Tennessee ($33,000)	Jacksonville ($33,000)	33-14	Jacksonville	75,206
1998	Jan. 17	Denver ($32,500)	N.Y. Jets ($32,500)	23-10	Denver	75,482
1997	Jan. 11	Denver ($30,000)	Pittsburgh ($30,000)	24-21	Pittsburgh	61,382
1996	Jan. 12	New England ($29,000)	Jacksonville ($29,000)	20-6	Foxborough	60,190
1995	Jan. 14	Pittsburgh ($27,000)	Indianapolis ($27,000)	20-16	Pittsburgh	61,062
1994	Jan. 15	San Diego ($26,000)	Pittsburgh ($26,000)	17-13	Pittsburgh	61,545
1993	Jan. 23	Buffalo ($23,500)	Kansas City ($23,500)	30-13	Buffalo	76,642
1992	Jan. 17	Buffalo ($18,000)	Miami ($18,000)	29-10	Miami	72,703
1991	Jan. 12	Buffalo ($18,000)	Denver ($18,000)	10-7	Buffalo	80,272
1990	Jan. 20	Buffalo ($18,000)	L.A. Raiders ($18,000)	51-3	Buffalo	80,325
1989	Jan. 14	Denver ($18,000)	Cleveland ($18,000)	37-21	Denver	76,046
1988	Jan. 8	Cincinnati ($18,000)	Buffalo ($18,000)	21-10	Cincinnati	59,747
1987	Jan. 17	Denver ($18,000)	Cleveland ($18,000)	38-33	Denver	76,197
1986	Jan. 11	Denver ($18,000)	Cleveland ($18,000)	23-20*	Cleveland	79,973
1985	Jan. 12	New England ($18,000)	Miami ($18,000)	31-14	Miami	75,662
1984	Jan. 6	Miami ($18,000)	Pittsburgh ($18,000)	45-28	Miami	76,029
1983	Jan. 8	L.A. Raiders ($18,000)	Seattle ($18,000)	30-14	Los Angeles	91,445
1982	Jan. 23	Miami ($18,000)	N.Y. Jets ($18,000)	14-0	Miami	67,396
1981	Jan. 10	Cincinnati ($9,000)	San Diego ($9,000)	27-7	Cincinnati	46,302
1980	Jan. 11	Oakland ($9,000)	San Diego ($9,000)	34-27	San Diego	52,675
1979	Jan. 6	Pittsburgh ($9,000)	Houston ($9,000)	27-13	Pittsburgh	50,475
1978	Jan. 7	Pittsburgh ($9,000)	Houston ($9,000)	34-5	Pittsburgh	50,725
1977	Jan. 1	Denver ($9,000)	Oakland ($9,000)	20-17	Denver	75,044
1976	Dec. 26	Oakland ($8,500)	Pittsburgh ($5,500)	24-7	Oakland	53,821
1975	Jan. 4	Pittsburgh ($8,500)	Oakland ($5,500)	16-10	Pittsburgh	50,609
1974	Dec. 29	Pittsburgh ($8,500)	Oakland ($5,500)	24-13	Oakland	53,800
1973	Dec. 30	Miami ($8,500)	Oakland ($5,500)	27-10	Miami	79,325
1972	Dec. 31	Miami ($8,500)	Pittsburgh ($5,500)	21-17	Pittsburgh	50,845
1971	Jan. 2	Miami ($8,500)	Baltimore ($5,500)	21-0	Miami	76,622
1970	Jan. 3	Baltimore ($8,500)	Oakland ($5,500)	27-17	Baltimore	54,799
1969	Jan. 4	Kansas City ($7,755)	Oakland ($6,252)	17-7	Oakland	53,564
1968	Dec. 29	N.Y. Jets ($7,007)	Oakland ($5,349)	27-23	New York	62,627
1967	Dec. 31	Oakland ($6,321)	Houston ($4,996)	40-7	Oakland	53,330
1966	Jan. 1	Kansas City ($5,309)	Buffalo ($3,799)	31-7	Buffalo	42,080
1965	Dec. 26	Buffalo ($5,189)	San Diego ($3,447)	23-0	San Diego	30,361
1964	Dec. 26	Buffalo ($2,668)	San Diego ($1,738)	20-7	Buffalo	40,242
1963	Jan. 5	San Diego ($2,498)	Boston ($1,596)	51-10	San Diego	30,127
1962	Dec. 23	Dallas ($2,206)	Houston ($1,471)	20-17*	Houston	37,981
1961	Dec. 24	Houston ($1,792)	San Diego ($1,111)	10-3	San Diego	29,556
1960	Jan. 1	Houston ($1,025)	L.A. Chargers ($718)	24-16	Houston	32,183

*Overtime

AFC CHAMPIONSHIP GAME COMPOSITE STANDINGS

	W	L	Pct.	Pts.	OP
Cincinnati Bengals	2	0	1.000	48	17
New England Patriots**	7	2	.778	228	199
Buffalo Bills	6	2	.750	180	92
Denver Broncos	6	2	.750	189	166
Kansas City Chiefs*	3	1	.750	81	61
Miami Dolphins	5	2	.714	152	115
Pittsburgh Steelers	8	7	.533	332	303
Indianapolis Colts#	3	3	.500	125	133
Tennessee Titans##	3	5	.375	133	195
Oakland Raiders###	5	9	.357	272	304
Baltimore Ravens	1	2	.333	50	49
New York Jets	1	4	.200	73	114
San Diego Chargers***	2	7	.222	140	182
Seattle Seahawks	0	1	.000	14	30
Jacksonville Jaguars	0	2	.000	20	53
Cleveland Browns	0	3	.000	74	98

* *One game played when franchise was in Dallas (Texans) (Won 20-17)*

** *One game played when franchise was in Boston (Lost 51-10)*

*** *One game played when franchise was in Los Angeles (Lost 24-16)*

\# *Two games played when franchise was in Baltimore (Won 27-17, lost 21-0)*

\#\# *Six games played when franchise was in Houston and known as Oilers (Won 2, lost 4)*

\#\#\# *Two games played when franchise was in Los Angeles (Won 30-14, lost 51-3)*

2011 AFC CHAMPIONSHIP GAME
Gillette Stadium, Foxborough, Massachusetts
January 22, 2012, Attendance: 68,756
NEW ENGLAND 23, BALTIMORE 20—Baltimore kicker Billy Cundiff's 32-yard field-goal attempt sailed wide left with 11 seconds to play as the Patriots reached the Super Bowl for the fifth time in 11 seasons. The victory marked the 16th career postseason win for Tom Brady, tying Joe Montana for the most by a starting quarterback in NFL history. An illegal contact penalty by the Ravens nullified a first-quarter interception by Bernard Pollard on a drive that culminated with Stephen Gostkowski's 29-yard field goal. Lardarius Webb intercepted Brady's pass later in the quarter that set up a 20-yard field goal by Cundiff to tie the game. The Patriots responded with a 75-yard drive capped by BenJarvus Green-Ellis' 7-yard scoring run. Undaunted, Joe Flacco completed a 20-yard pass to Lee Evans and 37-yard toss to Anquan Boldin that led to Dennis Pitta's 6-yard touchdown catch to tie the game 10-10. The Patriots had a 65-yard drive late in the first half and 74-yard drive to begin the second half that both ended with Gostkowski field goals for a 16-10 lead. The Ravens responded with Flacco's 29-yard touchdown pass to Torrey Smith along the end-zone sideline for a 17-16 lead with 3:26 left in the quarter. Danny Woodhead then fumbled the ensuing kickoff when LaQuan Williams hustled across field to strip the ball from him. Emanuel Cook recovered for the Ravens and Cundiff added a 39-yard field goal for a 20-16 lead entering the fourth quarter. Cary Williams intercepted Brady's pass two plays later, but a Ravens' offside nullified the play. Nine plays later, Brady leapt over the defensive line on a fourth-and-goal for a 1-yard touchdown and 23-20 New England lead with 11:29 remaining. Brandon Spikes' interception at midfield with 7:22 to play gave the Patriots the ball, but Jimmy Smith intercepted Brady's long pass in the end zone on the next play. The Ravens drove to the Patriots' 30. On third-and-3, Ray Rice was tackled by Vince Wilfork for a 3-yard loss. On fourth-and-6 from the 33, the Ravens eschewed the field-goal attempt, and Flacco's pass for Pitta was incomplete. The Ravens' defense forced a punt, and Baltimore began its final possession from its own 21-yard-line with 1:44 to play. Boldin had catches of 13, 9, 29, and 9 yards as the Ravens reached the Patriots' 14 with 27 seconds to play. On second-and-1, Flacco fired a pass to the right side of the end zone that was momentarily grabbed by Evans, but the Patriots' Sterling Moore quickly knocked the ball from Evans' grasp. After an incomplete pass on third-and-1, Cundiff's 32-yard game-tying field-goal attempt sailed wide left. Brady completed 22 of 36 passes for 239 yards, with 2 interceptions. Flacco also was 22 of 36 for 306 yards, but with 2 touchdowns and only 1 interception. Boldin had 6 receptions for 101 yards.

Baltimore (20)	Offense	New England (23)
Dennis Pitta	TE/WR	Wes Welker
Bryant McKinnie	LT	Matt Light
Ben Grubbs	LG	Logan Mankins
Matt Birk	C	Dan Connolly
Marshal Yanda	RG	Brian Waters
Michael Oher	RT	Nate Solder
Kris Wilson	TE	Ron Gronkowski
Anquan Boldin	WR	Deion Branch
Joe Flacco	QB	Tom Brady
Vonta Leach	FB/RB	Danny Woodhead
Ray Rice	RB/TE	Aaron Hernandez
	Defense	
Haloti Ngata	DT/DE	Vince Wilfork
Terrence Cody	NT	Kyle Love
Terrell Suggs	RUSH/RE	Brandon Deaderick
Dannell Ellerbe	WILL/OLB	Mark Anderson
Ray Lewis	MIKE/ILB	Jerod Mayo
Jarret Johnson	SAM/ILB	Brandon Spikes
Lardarius Webb	LCB/OLB	Rob Ninkovich
Jimmy Smith	RCB/LCB	Devin McCourty
Cary Williams	CB/RCB	Kyle Arrington

Bernard Pollard	SS/S		Patrick Chung
Ed Reed	FS/S		James Ihedigbo

SUBSTITUTIONS
BALTIMORE—Specialists: K—Billy Cundiff. P—Sam Koch. LS—Morgan Cox. Offense: RB—Ricky Williams. WR—Lee Evans, Torrey Smith, LaQuan Williams. TE—Ed Dickson. C—Andre Gurode. T—Jah Reid. Defense: DE—Arthur Jones, Pernell McPhee, Cory Redding. LB—Brendon Ayanbadejo, Edgar Jones, Paul Kruger, Jameel McClain, Albert McClellan. CB—Chris Carr, Danny Gorrer. S—Emanuel Cook, Haruki Nakamura, Tom Zbikowski. Did Not Play: QB—Tyrod Taylor. Not Active: RB—Anthony Allen. WR—Tandon Doss. G/C—Justin Boren. NT—Brandon McKinney. LB—Josh Byrnes, Sergio Kindle. CB—Chykie Brown.
NEW ENGLAND—Specialists: K—Stephen Gostkowski. P—Zoltan Mesko. LS—Danny Aiken. Offense: RB—BenJarvus Green-Ellis. FB—Lousaka Polite. WR—Julian Edelman, Matthew Slater, Tiquan Underwood. C—Ryan Wendell. OL—Marcus Cannon, Nick McDonald. Defense: DE—Shaun Ellis. DL—Ron Brace, Gerard Warren. LB—Dane Fletcher, Niko Koutouvides, Tracy White. CB—Nate Jones, Antwaun Molden, Sterling Moore, Malcolm Williams. S—Sergio Brown. DNP: QB—Brian Hoyer. RB—Kevin Faulk. Not Active: QB—Ryan Mallet. RB—Stevan Ridley, Shane Vereen. WR—Chad Ochocinco. T—Sebastian Vollmer. OL—Donald Thomas. LB—Gary Guyton.

OFFICIALS
Referee—Alberto Riveron. Umpire—Tony Michalek. Line Judge—Tim Podraza. Side Judge—Tom Hill. Head Linesman—Kent Payne. Back Judge—Keith Ferguson. Field Judge—Steve Zimmer.

SCORING

Baltimore	0	10	10	0	—	20	
New England	3	10	3	7	—	23	

NE	—	FG Gostkowski 29
Balt	—	FG Cundiff 20
NE	—	Green-Ellis 7 run (Gostkowski kick)
Balt	—	Pitta 6 pass from Flacco (Cundiff kick)
NE	—	FG Gostkowski 35
NE	—	FG Gostkowski 24
Balt	—	T. Smith 29 pass from Flacco (Cundiff kick)
Balt	—	FG Cundiff 39
NE	—	Brady 1 run (Gostkowski kick)

TEAM STATISTICS	BALT	NE
Total First Downs	19	25
Rushing	6	8
Passing	13	15
Penalty	0	2
Total Net Yardage	398	330
Total Offensive Plays	70	68
Average Gain Per Offensive Play	5.7	4.9
Rushes	31	31
Yards Gained Rushing (Net)	116	96
Average Yards per Rush	3.7	3.1
Passes Attempted	36	36
Passes Completed	22	22
Had Intercepted	1	2
Tackled Attempting to Pass	3	1
Yards Lost Attempting to Pass	24	5
Yards Gained Passing (Net)	282	234
Punts	4	2
Average Distance	43.8	48.5
Punt Returns	1	3
Punt Return Yardage	4	7
Kickoff Returns	1	3
Kickoff Return Yardage	20	101
Interception Return Yardage	39	19
Total Return Yardage (not incl. kickoffs)	43	26
Fumbles	1	2
Fumbles Lost	0	1
Own Fumbles Recovered	1	1
Opponent Fumbles Recovered	1	0

Penalties	6	1
Yards Penalized	33	5
Field Goals	2	3
Field Goals Attempted	3	3
Third-Down Efficiency	9/17	5/11
Fourth-Down Efficiency	0/1	1/1
Time of Possession	33:33	26:27

INDIVIDUAL STATISTICS
RUSHING: BALT: Rice 21-67-0, Flacco 4-27-0, R. Williams 6-22-0. NE: Green-Ellis 15-68-1, Woodhead 6-18-0, Hernandez 3-9-0, Brady 6-2-1, Edelman 1-(-1)-0.
PASSING: BALT: Flacco 36-22-306-2-1. NE: Brady 36-22-239-0-2.

RECEIVING: BALT: Boldin 6-101-0, Pitta 5-41-1, T. Smith 3-82-1, Evans 3-39-0, Dickson 2-23-0, Leach 2-9-0, Rice 1-11-0. NE: Hernandez 7-66-0, Welker 6-53-0, Gronkowski 5-87-0, Branch 2-18-0, Edelman 1-8-0, Woodhead 1-7-0.
KICKOFF RETURNS: BALT: Zbikowski 1-20-0. NE: Woodhead 3-101-0.
PUNT RETURNS: BALT: Webb 1-4-0. NE: Edelman 2-7-0, Welker 1-0-0.
PUNTING: BALT: Koch 4-175-43.8. NE: Mesko 2-97-48.5.
INTERCEPTIONS: BALT: J. Smith 1-39-0, Webb 1-0-0. NE: Spikes 1-19-0.
SACKS: BALT: Kruger 1.0. NE: Anderson 1.0, Ihedigbo 1.0, Wilfork 1.0.

NFC CHAMPIONSHIP GAME RESULTS
Includes NFL Championship Games (1933-1969)

Season	Date	Winner (Share)	Loser (Share)	Score	Site	Attendance
2011	Jan. 22	N.Y. Giants ($40,000)	San Francisco ($40,000)	20-17*	San Francisco	69,732
2010	Jan. 23	Green Bay ($38,000)	Chicago ($38,000)	21-14	Chicago	62,377
2009	Jan. 24	New Orleans ($38,000)	Minnesota ($38,000)	31-28*	New Orleans	71,276
2008	Jan. 18	Arizona ($37,500)	Philadelphia ($37,500)	32-25	Glendale	70,650
2007	Jan. 20	N.Y. Giants ($37,500)	Green Bay ($37,500)	23-20*	Green Bay	72,740
2006	Jan. 21	Chicago ($37,000)	New Orleans ($37,000)	39-14	Chicago	61,817
2005	Jan. 22	Seattle ($37,000)	Carolina ($37,000)	34-14	Seattle	67,837
2004	Jan. 23	Philadelphia ($36,500)	Atlanta ($36,500)	27-10	Philadelphia	67,717
2003	Jan. 18	Carolina ($36,500)	Philadelphia ($36,500)	14-3	Philadelphia	67,862
2002	Jan. 19	Tampa Bay ($35,000)	Philadelphia ($35,000)	27-10	Philadelphia	66,713
2001	Jan. 27	St. Louis ($34,500)	Philadelphia ($34,500)	29-24	St. Louis	66,502
2000	Jan. 14	N.Y. Giants ($34,500)	Minnesota ($34,500)	41-0	East Rutherford	79,310
1999	Jan. 23	St. Louis ($33,000)	Tampa Bay ($33,000)	11-6	St. Louis	66,396
1998	Jan. 17	Atlanta ($32,500)	Minnesota ($32,500)	30-27*	Minneapolis	64,060
1997	Jan. 11	Green Bay ($30,000)	San Francisco ($30,000)	23-10	San Francisco	68,987
1996	Jan. 12	Green Bay ($29,000)	Carolina ($29,000)	30-13	Green Bay	60,216
1995	Jan. 14	Dallas ($27,000)	Green Bay ($27,000)	38-27	Dallas	65,135
1994	Jan. 15	San Francisco ($26,000)	Dallas ($26,000)	38-28	San Francisco	69,125
1993	Jan. 23	Dallas ($23,500)	San Francisco ($23,500)	38-21	Dallas	64,902
1992	Jan. 17	Dallas ($18,000)	San Francisco ($18,000)	30-20	San Francisco	64,920
1991	Jan. 12	Washington ($18,000)	Detroit ($18,000)	41-10	Washington	55,585
1990	Jan. 20	N.Y. Giants ($18,000)	San Francisco ($18,000)	15-13	San Francisco	65,750
1989	Jan. 14	San Francisco ($18,000)	L.A. Rams ($18,000)	30-3	San Francisco	65,634
1988	Jan. 8	San Francisco ($18,000)	Chicago ($18,000)	28-3	Chicago	66,946
1987	Jan. 17	Washington ($18,000)	Minnesota ($18,000)	17-10	Washington	55,212
1986	Jan. 11	New York Giants ($18,000)	Washington ($18,000)	17-0	East Rutherford	76,891
1985	Jan. 12	Chicago ($18,000)	L.A. Rams ($18,000)	24-0	Chicago	66,030
1984	Jan. 6	San Francisco ($18,000)	Chicago ($18,000)	23-0	San Francisco	61,336
1983	Jan. 8	Washington ($18,000)	San Francisco ($18,000)	24-21	Washington	55,363
1982	Jan. 22	Washington ($18,000)	Dallas ($18,000)	31-17	Washington	55,045
1981	Jan. 10	San Francisco ($9,000)	Dallas ($9,000)	28-27	San Francisco	60,525
1980	Jan. 11	Philadelphia ($9,000)	Dallas ($9,000)	20-7	Philadelphia	71,522
1979	Jan. 6	Los Angeles ($9,000)	Tampa Bay ($9,000)	9-0	Tampa	72,033
1978	Jan. 7	Dallas ($9,000)	Los Angeles ($9,000)	28-0	Los Angeles	71,086
1977	Jan. 1	Dallas ($9,000)	Minnesota ($9,000)	23-6	Dallas	64,293
1976	Dec. 26	Minnesota ($8,500)	Los Angeles ($5,500)	24-13	Minneapolis	48,379
1975	Jan. 4	Dallas ($8,500)	Los Angeles ($5,500)	37-7	Los Angeles	88,919
1974	Dec. 29	Minnesota ($8,500)	Los Angeles ($5,500)	14-10	Minneapolis	48,444
1973	Dec. 30	Minnesota ($8,500)	Dallas ($5,500)	27-10	Dallas	64,422
1972	Dec. 31	Washington ($8,500)	Dallas ($5,500)	26-3	Washington	53,129
1971	Jan. 2	Dallas ($8,500)	San Francisco ($5,500)	14-3	Dallas	63,409
1970	Jan. 3	Dallas ($8,500)	San Francisco ($5,500)	17-10	San Francisco	59,364
1969	Jan. 4	Minnesota ($7,930)	Cleveland ($5,118)	27-7	Minneapolis	46,503
1968	Dec. 29	Baltimore ($9,306)	Cleveland ($5,963)	34-0	Cleveland	78,410
1967	Dec. 31	Green Bay ($7,950)	Dallas ($5,299)	21-17	Green Bay	50,861
1966	Jan. 1	Green Bay ($9,813)	Dallas ($6,527)	34-27	Dallas	74,152
1965	Jan. 2	Green Bay ($7,819)	Cleveland ($5,288)	23-12	Green Bay	50,777
1964	Dec. 27	Cleveland ($8,052)	Baltimore ($5,571)	27-0	Cleveland	79,544
1963	Dec. 29	Chicago ($5,899)	New York ($4,218)	14-10	Chicago	45,801
1962	Dec. 30	Green Bay ($5,888)	New York ($4,166)	16-7	New York	64,892
1961	Dec. 31	Green Bay ($5,195)	New York ($3,339)	37-0	Green Bay	39,029
1960	Dec. 26	Philadelphia ($5,116)	Green Bay ($3,105)	17-13	Philadelphia	67,325
1959	Dec. 27	Baltimore ($4,674)	New York ($3,083)	31-16	Baltimore	57,545
1958	Dec. 28	Baltimore ($4,718)	New York ($3,111)	23-17*	New York	64,185

Season	Date	Winner (Share)	Loser (Share)	Score	Site	Attendance
1957	Dec. 29	Detroit ($4,295)	Cleveland ($2,750)	59-14	Detroit	55,263
1956	Dec. 30	New York ($3,779)	Chi. Bears ($2,485)	47-7	New York	56,836
1955	Dec. 26	Cleveland ($3,508)	Los Angeles ($2,316)	38-14	Los Angeles	85,693
1954	Dec. 26	Cleveland ($2,478)	Detroit ($1,585)	56-10	Cleveland	43,827
1953	Dec. 27	Detroit ($2,424)	Cleveland ($1,654)	17-16	Detroit	54,577
1952	Dec. 28	Detroit ($2,274)	Cleveland ($1,712)	17-7	Cleveland	50,934
1951	Dec. 23	Los Angeles ($2,108)	Cleveland ($1,483)	24-17	Los Angeles	57,522
1950	Dec. 24	Cleveland ($1,113)	Los Angeles ($686)	30-28	Cleveland	29,751
1949	Dec. 18	Philadelphia ($1,094)	Los Angeles ($739)	14-0	Los Angeles	27,980
1948	Dec. 19	Philadelphia ($1,540)	Chi. Cardinals ($874)	7-0	Philadelphia	36,309
1947	Dec. 28	Chi. Cardinals ($1,132)	Philadelphia ($754)	28-21	Chicago	30,759
1946	Dec. 15	Chi. Bears ($1,975)	New York ($1,295)	24-14	New York	58,346
1945	Dec. 16	Cleveland ($1,469)	Washington ($902)	15-14	Cleveland	32,178
1944	Dec. 17	Green Bay ($1,449)	New York ($814)	14-7	New York	46,016
1943	Dec. 26	Chi. Bears ($1,146)	Washington ($765)	41-21	Chicago	34,320
1942	Dec. 13	Washington ($965)	Chi. Bears ($637)	14-6	Washington	36,006
1941	Dec. 21	Chi. Bears ($430)	New York ($288)	37-9	Chicago	13,341
1940	Dec. 8	Chi. Bears ($873)	Washington ($606)	73-0	Washington	36,034
1939	Dec. 10	Green Bay ($703.97)	New York ($455.57)	27-0	Milwaukee	32,279
1938	Dec. 11	New York ($504.45)	Green Bay ($368.81)	23-17	New York	48,120
1937	Dec. 12	Washington ($225.90)	Chi. Bears ($127.78)	28-21	Chicago	15,870
1936	Dec. 13	Green Bay ($250)	Boston ($180)	21-6	New York	29,545
1935	Dec. 15	Detroit ($313.35)	New York ($200.20)	26-7	Detroit	15,000
1934	Dec. 9	New York ($621)	Chi. Bears ($414.02)	30-13	New York	35,059
1933	Dec. 17	Chi. Bears ($210.34)	New York ($140.22)	23-21	Chicago	26,000

*Overtime

NFC CHAMPIONSHIP GAME COMPOSITE STANDINGS

	W	L	Pct.	Pts.	OP
Seattle Seahawks	1	0	1.000	34	14
Baltimore Colts	3	1	.750	88	60
Green Bay Packers	11	4	.733	344	214
Detroit Lions	4	2	.667	139	141
Arizona Cardinals**	2	1	.667	60	53
Washington Redskins*	7	5	.583	222	255
Chicago Bears	8	7	.533	339	280
Dallas Cowboys	8	8	.500	361	319
Philadelphia Eagles	5	5	.500	168	160
Atlanta Falcons	1	1	.500	40	54
New Orleans Saints	1	1	.500	45	67
Minnesota Vikings	4	5	.444	163	182
New York Giants	8	11	.421	324	359
San Francisco 49ers	5	8	.385	262	242
Cleveland Browns	4	7	.364	224	253
St. Louis Rams***	5	9	.357	163	300
Carolina Panthers	1	2	.333	41	67
Tampa Bay Buccaneers	1	2	.333	33	30

*One game played when franchise was in Boston (Lost 21-6)
**Both games played when franchise was in Chicago (Won 28-21, lost 7-0)
***One game played when franchise was in Cleveland (Won 15-14), and 11 games when franchise was in Los Angeles (Won 2, lost 9, scored 108 points, allowed 256 points).

2011 NFC CHAMPIONSHIP GAME
Candlestick Park, San Francisco, California
January 22, 2012, Attendance: 69,732
NEW YORK GIANTS 20, SAN FRANCISCO 17 (OT)—Lawrence Tynes kicked a 31-yard field goal in overtime as the New York Giants advanced to the Super Bowl for the second time in five seasons. Midway through the first quarter, Alex Smith completed a 73-yard touchdown pass to Vernon Davis, who got open deep down the right sideline, to stake the 49ers to a 7-0 lead. On their next possession the Giants were stopped on downs at the 49ers' 34, but following a San Francisco punt, Eli Manning capped a 10-play, 69-yard drive with a 6-yard scoring pass to Bear Pascoe. Just before halftime, Manning completed passes of 15, 11, 17, and 13 yards to Victor Cruz to set up Tynes' 31-yard field goal for a 10-7 halftime lead. Kyle Williams' 24-yard punt return to the 49ers' 46 in the third quarter was followed by Smith's 24-yard pass to Frank Gore and 28-yard scoring pass to Davis for a 14-10 49ers' lead. With 11:17 to play in the game, Steve Weatherford punted for the Giants. The bouncing ball skimmed off punt returner Williams at the 49ers' 36 and was recovered by Devin Thomas at the 49ers' 29-yard-line. Manning completed a 14-yard pass to Hakeem Nicks on third-and-7 and, on third-and-15, connected with Mario Manningham on a 17-yard crossing pass for a touchdown and 17-14 Giants lead with 8:34 to play. Williams returned the ensuing kickoff 40 yards, and Kendall Hunter had an 18-yard run to set up David Akers' game-tying 25-yard field goal with 5:39 remaining. There were five punts in the final 4:15 of regulation, and 22 punts in the game. On the Giants' second overtime possession, Weatherford punted from his own 44-yard line. Williams returned the punt five yards before Jacquian Williams knocked the ball from his hands and Thomas recovered at the 49ers' 24. Two Ahmad Bradshaw carries netted a first down and Tynes made the game-winning 31-yard field goal. The Giants' defense allowed just 1 of 13 third-down conversions, while the 49ers' defense sacked Manning six times. Manning completed 32 of 58 passes for 316 yards and 2 touchdowns. Cruz had 10 receptions for 142 yards. Smith was 12 of 26 for 196 yards and 2 touchdowns. Davis caught 3 passes for 112 yards.

New York Giants (20)	Offense	San Francisco (17)
Victor Cruz	WR	Michael Crabtree
David Diehl	LT	Joe Staley
Kevin Boothe	LG	Mike Iupati
David Baas	C	Jonathan Goodwin
Chris Snee	RG	Adam Snyder
Kareem McKenzie	RT	Anthony Davis
Jake Ballard	TE	Vernon Davis
Hakeem Nicks	WR	Kyle Williams
Eli Manning	QB	Alex Smith
Henry Hynoski	FB/TE	Delanie Walker
Ahmad Bradshaw	RB	Frank Gore
	Defense	
Justin Tuck	LE/LDT	Ray McDonald
Linval Joseph	LDT/NT	Isaac Sopoaga
Chris Canty	RDT	Justin Smith
Jason Pierre-Paul	RE/OLB	Ahmad Brooks

Chase Blackburn	MLB/ILB	NaVorro Bowman	
Michael Boley	WLB/ILB	Patrick Willis	
Deon Grant	S/OLB	Parys Haralson	
Corey Webster	LCB	Carlos Rogers	
Aaron Ross	RCB	Tarell Brown	
Kenny Phillips	SS	Donte Whitner	
Antrel Rolle	FS	Dashon Goldson	

SUBSTITUTIONS

NEW YORK GIANTS—Specialists: K—Lawrence Tynes. P—Steve Weatherford. LS—Zak DeOssie. Offense: RB—Brandon Jacobs, D.J. Ware. WR—Jerrel Jernigan, Mario Manningham, Devin Thomas. TE—Travis Beckum, Bear Pascoe. G—Mitch Petrus. T—Tony Ugoh. Defense: DE—Dave Tollefson, Osi Umenyiora. DT—Rocky Bernard. LB—Greg Jones, Mathias Kiwanuka, Spencer Paysinger, Jacquian Williams. CB—Prince Amukamara, Will Blackmon, Derrick Martin. S—Tyler Sash. Did Not Play: QB—David Carr. Not Active: RB—Da'Rel Scott. WR—Ramses Barden. C—Jim Cordle. T—James Brewer Jr. DE—Justin Trattou. DT—Jimmy Kennedy. LB—Mark Herzlich.

SAN FRANCISCO—Specialists: K—David Akers. P—Andy Lee. TE/LS—Brian Jennings. Offense: RB—Anthony Dixon, Kendall Hunter. FB—Bruce Miller. WR—Brett Swain. TE—Justin Peelle. T/G—Chilo Rachal. T—Alex Boone. Defense: DT—Demarcus Dobbs, Ricky Jean Francois. LB—Blake Costanzo, Tavares Gooden, Larry Grant, Aldon Smith. CB—Tramaine Brock, Chris Culliver. S—Colin Jones, Reggie Smith, C.J. Spillman, Madieu Williams. Did Not Play: QB—Colin Kaepernick. FB—Moran Norris. WR—Joe Hastings. Not Active: QB—Scott Tolzien. WR—Ted Ginn. G—Daniel Kilgore, Mike Person. NT—Ian Williams. CB—Shawntae Spencer.

OFFICIALS

Referee—Ed Hochuli. Umpire—Roy Ellison. Line Judge—John Hussey. Side Judge—Don Carlsen Head Linesman—Mark Hittner. Back Judge—Carl Paganelli. Field Judge—Craig Wrolstad.

SCORING

New York Giants	0	10	0	7	3	—	20
San Francisco	7	0	7	3	0	—	17

SF — V. Davis 73 pass from Al. Smith (Akers kick)
NYG — Pascoe 6 pass from Manning (Tynes kick)
NYG — FG Tynes 31
SF — V. Davis 28 pass from Al. Smith (Akers kick)
NYG — Manningham 17 pass from Manning (Tynes kick)
SF — FG Akers 25
NYG — FG Tynes 31

TEAM STATISTICS	NYG	SF
Total First Downs	20	15
Rushing	3	6
Passing	17	5
Penalty	0	4
Total Net Yardage	352	328

Total Offensive Plays	90	57
Average Gain Per Offensive Play	3.9	5.8
Rushes	26	28
Yards Gained Rushing (Net)	85	150
Average Yards per Rush	3.3	5.4
Passes Attempted	58	26
Passes Completed	32	12
Had Intercepted	0	0
Tackled Attempting to Pass	6	3
Yards Lost Attempting to Pass	49	18
Yards Gained Passing (Net)	267	178
Punts	12	10
Average Distance	46.4	45.5
Punt Returns	6	8
Punt Return Yardage	55	70
Kickoff Returns	1	4
Kickoff Return Yardage	17	100
Interception Return Yardage	0	0
Total Return Yardage (excluding Kickoffs)	55	70
Fumbles	1	4
Fumbles Lost	0	2
Own Fumbles Recovered	1	2
Opponent Fumbles Recovered	2	0
Penalties	9	6
Yards Penalized	60	50
Field Goals	2	1
Field Goals Attempted	2	1
Third-Down Efficiency	7/21	1/13
Fourth-Down Efficiency	0/1	0/0
Time of Possession	39:36	28:18

INDIVIDUAL STATISTICS

RUSHING: NYG: Bradshaw 20-74-0, Jacobs 5-13-0, Manning 1-(-2)-0. SF: Gore 16-74-0, Al. Smith 6-42-0, Hunter 4-31-0, Dixon 2-3-0.

PASSING: NYG: Manning 58-32-316-2-0. SF: Al. Smith 26-12-196-2-0.

RECEIVING: NYG: Cruz 10-142-0, Bradshaw 6-52-0, Nicks 5-55-0, Beckum 4-16-0, Hynoski 3-20-0, Jacobs 2-8-0, Manningham 1-17-1, Pascoe 1-6-1. SF: Gore 6-45-0, V. Davis 3-112-2, Walker 2-36-0, Crabtree 1-3-0.

KICKOFF RETURNS: NYG: Jernigan 1-17-0. SF: K. Williams 3-85-0, Hunter 1-15-0.

PUNT RETURNS: NYG: Ross 3-29-0, Blackmon 3-26-0. SF: K. Williams 8-70-0.

PUNTING: NYG: Weatherford 12-557-46.4. SF: Lee 10-455-45.5.

INTERCEPTIONS: NYG: None. SF: None.

SACKS: NYG: Tuck 1.5, Kiwanuka 0.5, Pierre-Paul 0.5, Umenyiora 0.5. SF: McDonald 2.5, Ald. Smith 1.0, J. Smith 1.0, Willis 1.0, Bowman 0.5.

AFC DIVISIONAL PLAYOFF GAMES RESULTS

Includes Second-Round Playoff Games (1982), AFC Inter-Divisional Games (1969), and special playoff games to break ties for AFL Division Championships (1963, 1968)

Season	Date	Winner (Share)	Loser (Share)	Score	Site	Attendance
2011	Jan. 15	Baltimore ($22,000)	Houston ($22,000)	20-13	Baltimore	71,547
	Jan. 14	New England ($22,000)	Denver ($22,000)	45-10	Foxborough	68,756
2010	Jan. 16	N.Y. Jets ($21,000)	New England ($21,000)	28-21	Foxborough	68,756
	Jan. 15	Pittsburgh ($21,000)	Baltimore ($21,000)	31-24	Pittsburgh	64,879
2009	Jan. 17	N.Y. Jets ($21,000)	San Diego ($21,000)	17-14	San Diego	69,498
	Jan. 16	Indianapolis ($21,000)	Baltimore ($21,000)	20-3	Indianapolis	67,535
2008	Jan. 11	Pittsburgh ($20,000)	San Diego ($20,000)	35-24	Pittsburgh	63,899
	Jan. 10	Baltimore ($20,000)	Tennessee ($20,000)	13-10	Nashville	69,143
2007	Jan. 13	San Diego ($20,000)	Indianapolis ($20,000)	28-24	Indianapolis	56,950
	Jan. 12	New England ($20,000)	Jacksonville ($20,000)	31-20	Foxborough	68,756
2006	Jan. 14	New England ($19,000)	San Diego ($19,000)	24-21	San Diego	68,810
	Jan. 13	Indianapolis ($19,000)	Baltimore ($19,000)	15-6	Baltimore	71,162
2005	Jan. 15	Pittsburgh ($19,000)	Indianapolis ($19,000)	21-18	Indianapolis	57,449
	Jan. 14	Denver ($19,000)	New England ($19,000)	27-13	Denver	76,238
2004	Jan. 16	New England ($18,000)	Indianapolis ($18,000)	20-3	Foxborough	68,756
	Jan. 15	Pittsburgh ($18,000)	N.Y. Jets ($18,000)	20-17*	Pittsburgh	64,915

Season	Date	Winner (Share)	Loser (Share)	Score	Site	Attendance
2003	Jan. 11	Indianapolis ($18,000)	Kansas City ($18,000)	38-31	Kansas City	79,159
	Jan. 10	New England ($18,000)	Tennessee ($18,000)	17-14	Foxborough	68,436
2002	Jan. 12	Oakland ($17,000)	N.Y. Jets ($17,000)	30-10	Oakland	62,207
	Jan. 11	Tennessee ($17,000)	Pittsburgh ($17,000)	34-31*	Nashville	68,809
2001	Jan. 20	Pittsburgh ($17,000)	Baltimore ($17,000)	27-10	Pittsburgh	63,976
	Jan. 19	New England ($17,000)	Oakland ($17,000)	16-13*	Foxborough	60,292
2000	Jan. 7	Baltimore ($16,000)	Tennessee ($16,000)	24-10	Nashville	68,527
	Jan. 6	Oakland ($16,000)	Miami ($16,000)	27-0	Oakland	61,998
1999	Jan. 16	Tennessee ($16,000)	Indianapolis ($16,000)	19-16	Indianapolis	57,097
	Jan. 15	Jacksonville ($16,000)	Miami ($16,000)	62-7	Jacksonville	75,173
1998	Jan. 10	N.Y. Jets ($15,000)	Jacksonville ($15,000)	34-24	East Rutherford	78,817
	Jan. 9	Denver ($15,000)	Miami ($15,000)	38-3	Denver	75,729
1997	Jan. 4	Denver ($15,000)	Kansas City ($15,000)	14-10	Kansas City	76,965
	Jan. 3	Pittsburgh ($15,000)	New England ($15,000)	7-6	Pittsburgh	61,228
1996	Jan. 5	New England ($14,000)	Pittsburgh ($14,000)	28-3	Foxborough	60,188
	Jan. 4	Jacksonville ($14,000)	Denver ($14,000)	30-27	Denver	75,678
1995	Jan. 7	Indianapolis ($13,000)	Kansas City ($13,000)	10-7	Kansas City	77,594
	Jan. 6	Pittsburgh ($13,000)	Buffalo ($13,000)	40-21	Pittsburgh	59,072
1994	Jan. 8	San Diego ($12,000)	Miami ($12,000)	22-21	San Diego	63,381
	Jan. 7	Pittsburgh ($12,000)	Cleveland ($12,000)	29-9	Pittsburgh	58,185
1993	Jan. 16	Kansas City ($12,000)	Houston ($12,000)	28-20	Houston	64,011
	Jan. 15	Buffalo ($12,000)	L.A. Raiders ($12,000)	29-23	Buffalo	61,923
1992	Jan. 10	Miami ($10,000)	San Diego ($10,000)	31-0	Miami	71,224
	Jan. 9	Buffalo ($10,000)	Pittsburgh ($10,000)	24-3	Pittsburgh	60,407
1991	Jan. 5	Buffalo ($10,000)	Kansas City ($10,000)	37-14	Buffalo	80,182
	Jan. 4	Denver ($10,000)	Houston ($10,000)	26-24	Denver	75,301
1990	Jan. 13	L.A. Raiders ($10,000)	Cincinnati ($10,000)	20-10	Los Angeles	92,045
	Jan. 12	Buffalo ($10,000)	Miami ($10,000)	44-34	Buffalo	77,087
1989	Jan. 7	Denver ($10,000)	Pittsburgh ($10,000)	24-23	Denver	75,477
	Jan. 6	Cleveland ($10,000)	Buffalo ($10,000)	34-30	Cleveland	78,921
1988	Jan. 1	Buffalo ($10,000)	Houston ($10,000)	17-10	Buffalo	79,532
	Dec. 31	Cincinnati ($10,000)	Seattle ($10,000)	21-13	Cincinnati	58,560
1987	Jan. 10	Denver ($10,000)	Houston ($10,000)	34-10	Denver	75,440
	Jan. 9	Cleveland ($10,000)	Indianapolis ($10,000)	38-21	Cleveland	79,372
1986	Jan. 4	Denver ($10,000)	New England ($10,000)	22-17	Denver	75,262
	Jan. 3	Cleveland ($10,000)	N.Y. Jets ($10,000)	23-20*	Cleveland	79,720
1985	Jan. 5	New England ($10,000)	L.A. Raiders ($10,000)	27-20	Los Angeles	87,163
	Jan. 4	Miami ($10,000)	Cleveland ($10,000)	24-21	Miami	74,667
1984	Dec. 30	Pittsburgh ($10,000)	Denver ($10,000)	24-17	Denver	74,981
	Dec. 29	Miami ($10,000)	Seattle ($10,000)	31-10	Miami	73,469
1983	Jan. 1	L.A. Raiders ($10,000)	Pittsburgh ($10,000)	38-10	Los Angeles	90,380
	Dec. 31	Seattle ($10,000)	Miami ($10,000)	27-20	Miami	74,136
1982	Jan. 16	Miami ($10,000)	San Diego ($10,000)	34-13	Miami	71,383
	Jan. 15	N.Y. Jets ($10,000)	L.A. Raiders ($10,000)	17-14	Los Angeles	90,038
1981	Jan. 3	Cincinnati ($5,000)	Buffalo ($5,000)	28-21	Cincinnati	55,420
	Jan. 2	San Diego ($5,000)	Miami ($5,000)	41-38*	Miami	73,735
1980	Jan. 4	Oakland ($5,000)	Cleveland ($5,000)	14-12	Cleveland	78,245
	Jan. 3	San Diego ($5,000)	Buffalo ($5,000)	20-14	San Diego	52,253
1979	Dec. 30	Pittsburgh ($5,000)	Miami ($5,000)	34-14	Pittsburgh	50,214
	Dec. 29	Houston ($5,000)	San Diego ($5,000)	17-14	San Diego	51,192
1978	Dec. 31	Houston ($5,000)	New England ($5,000)	31-14	Foxborough	60,735
	Dec. 30	Pittsburgh ($5,000)	Denver ($5,000)	33-10	Pittsburgh	50,230
1977	Dec. 24	Oakland ($5,000)	Baltimore ($5,000)	37-31*	Baltimore	59,925
	Dec. 24	Denver ($5,000)	Pittsburgh ($5,000)	34-21	Denver	75,059
1976	Dec. 19	Pittsburgh [$]	Baltimore [$]	40-14	Baltimore	59,296
	Dec. 18	Oakland [$]	New England [$]	24-21	Oakland	53,050
1975	Dec. 28	Oakland [$]	Cincinnati [$]	31-28	Oakland	53,030
	Dec. 27	Pittsburgh [$]	Baltimore [$]	28-10	Pittsburgh	49,557
1974	Dec. 22	Pittsburgh [$]	Buffalo [$]	32-14	Pittsburgh	49,841
	Dec. 21	Oakland [$]	Miami [$]	28-26	Oakland	53,023
1973	Dec. 23	Miami [$]	Cincinnati [$]	34-16	Miami	78,928
	Dec. 22	Oakland [$]	Pittsburgh [$]	33-14	Oakland	52,646
1972	Dec. 24	Miami [$]	Cleveland [$]	20-14	Miami	78,916
	Dec. 23	Pittsburgh [$]	Oakland [$]	13-7	Pittsburgh	50,327
1971	Dec. 26	Baltimore [$]	Cleveland [$]	20-3	Cleveland	70,734
	Dec. 25	Miami [$]	Kansas City [$]	27-24*	Kansas City	50,374
1970	Dec. 27	Oakland [$]	Miami [$]	21-14	Oakland	52,594
	Dec. 26	Baltimore [$]	Cincinnati [$]	17-0	Baltimore	49,694
1969	Dec. 21	Oakland [$]	Houston [$]	56-7	Oakland	53,539
	Dec. 20	Kansas City [$]	N.Y. Jets [$]	13-6	New York	62,977
1968	Dec. 22	Oakland [$]	Kansas City [$]	41-6	Oakland	53,605
1963	Dec. 28	Boston [$]	Buffalo [$]	26-8	Buffalo	33,044

*Overtime

$ Players received 1/14 of annual salary for playoff appearances.

2011 AFC DIVISIONAL PLAYOFF GAMES

M&T Bank Stadium, Baltimore, Maryland
January 15, 2012, Attendance: 71,547

BALTIMORE 20, HOUSTON 13—The Ravens scored 17 first-quarter points and held on to defeat the Texans. The Texans' defense limited the Ravens to 227 yards and sacked Joe Flacco five times, but the Ravens' defense forced four turnovers, including 2 interceptions by Lardarius Webb, that led to 17 points for Baltimore. Danieal Manning's 60-yard kickoff return to begin the game led to Neil Rackers' 40-yard field goal. The Texans then forced a punt, but Jacoby Jones fumbled during the return, forced by Cary Williams, and recovered by Jimmy Smith at the Texans' 2. Flacco completed a 1-yard touchdown pass to Kris Wilson for a 7-3 lead. After Billy Cundiff's field goal gave Baltimore a 10-7 lead, Webb intercepted a T.J. Yates pass at the Texans' 34 that led to Anquan Boldin's 10-yard touchdown catch and a 17-3 Ravens first-quarter lead. The Texans responded with a 59-yard drive that resulted in a field goal and an 86-yard touchdown drive, capped by Arian Foster's 1-yard run, to trim the deficit to 17-13 with 4:48 left in the half. In the second quarter, the Texans reached the Ravens' 32, but Rackers' 50-yard field-goal attempt hit the crossbar and was no good. The Ravens drove to the Texans' 1, but Ray Rice was stopped for no gain on fourth-and-goal. Webb's second interception, at the Ravens' 29, with 7:21 to play led to Cundiff's second field goal for a 20-13 lead with 2:52 remaining. The Texans reached the Ravens' 38 before Ed Reed intercepted Yates' long pass at the 4-yard-line. Houston forced a punt, and the Texans reached the Ravens' 43-yard line but Yates' Hail Mary pass into the end zone fell incomplete with 11 seconds to play. Flacco was 14 of 27 for 176 yards and 2 touchdowns. Yates was 17 of 35 for 184 yards, with 3 interceptions. Johnson had 8 catches for 111 yards. Foster carried 27 times for 132 yards.

Houston	3	10	0	0	—	13
Baltimore	17	0	0	3	—	20

Hou	—	FG Rackers 40
Balt	—	Wilson 1 pass from Flacco (Cundiff kick)
Balt	—	FG Cundiff 48
Balt	—	Boldin 10 pass from Flacco (Cundiff kick)
Hou	—	FG Rackers 33
Hou	—	Foster 1 run (Rackers kick)
Balt	—	FG Cundiff 44

Gillette Stadium, Foxborough, Massachusetts
January 14, 2012, Attendance: 68,756

NEW ENGLAND 45, DENVER 10—Tom Brady tied an NFL postseason record with 6 touchdown passes, including 5 in the first half, as the Patriots advanced. The Patriots had more than twice as many yards as Denver (509 to 252) and first downs (31 to 15). New England needed just five plays to drive 80 yards in 1:51 to begin the game, keyed by Aaron Hernandez' 43-yard reception and capped by Wes Welker's 7-yard touchdown catch, for a 7-0 lead. On the Broncos' first possession, Rob Ninkovich sacked Tim Tebow and forced him to fumble. Brandon Spikes recovered at the Patriots' 41 and Rob Gronkowski caught a 10-yard touchdown pass seven plays later for a 14-0 lead. Denver's Quinton Carter intercepted Brady's pass late in the first quarter and returned it to the 24-yard line to set up Willis McGahee's 5-yard touchdown run to trim the deficit to 14-7. Gronkowski's 12-yard scoring catch capped a 52-yard drive in the middle of the second quarter, and Deion Branch's 61-yard touchdown catch deep down the left sideline extended the lead to 28-7 at the two-minute warning. The Patriots' defense forced a three-and-out and a 20-yard pass from Brady to Hernandez led to Gronkowski's 19-yard touchdown catch with five seconds left in the half for a 35-7 lead. The second half began with the Patriots' defense forcing another three-and-out, and Julian Edelman's 15-yard punt return set up a 44-yard drive capped by Hernandez's 17-yard touchdown grab, Brady's sixth scoring pass of the game, with 11:46 left in the third quarter for a 42-7 lead. Brady was 26 of 34 for 363 yards and 6 touchdowns, with 1 interception. Gronkowski had 10 catches for 145 yards. Tebow completed 9 of 26 passes for 136 yards.

Denver	0	7	3	0	—	10
New England	14	21	7	3	—	45

NE	—	Welker 7 pass from Brady (Gostkowski kick)
NE	—	Gronkowski 10 pass from Brady (Gostkowski kick)
Den	—	McGahee 5 run (Prater kick)
NE	—	Gronkowski 12 pass from Brady (Gostkowski kick)
NE	—	Branch 61 pass from Brady (Gostkowski kick)
NE	—	Gronkowski 19 pass from Brady (Gostkowski kick)
NE	—	Hernandez 17 pass from Brady (Gostkowski kick)
Den	—	FG Prater 41
NE	—	FG Gostkowski 20

NFC DIVISIONAL PLAYOFF GAMES RESULTS

Includes Second-Round Playoff Games (1982), NFL Conference Championship Games (1967-69), and special playoff games to break ties for NFL Division or Conference Championships (1941, 1943, 1947, 1950, 1952, 1957, 1958, 1965)

Season	Date	Winner (Share)	Loser (Share)	Score	Site	Attendance
2011	Jan. 15	N.Y. Giants ($22,000)	Green Bay ($22,000)	37-20	Green Bay	72,080
	Jan. 14	San Francisco ($22,000)	New Orleans ($22,000)	36-32	San Francisco	69,732
2010	Jan. 16	Chicago ($21,000)	Seattle ($21,000)	35-24	Chicago	62,265
	Jan. 15	Green Bay ($21,000)	Atlanta ($21,000)	48-21	Atlanta	69,210
2009	Jan. 17	Minnesota ($21,000)	Dallas ($21,000)	34-3	Minneapolis	63,547
	Jan. 16	New Orleans ($21,000)	Arizona ($21,000)	45-14	New Orleans	70,149
2008	Jan. 11	Philadelphia ($20,000)	N.Y. Giants ($20,000)	23-11	East Rutherford	79,193
	Jan. 10	Arizona ($20,000)	Carolina ($20,000)	33-13	Charlotte	73,695
2007	Jan. 13	N.Y. Giants ($20,000)	Dallas ($20,000)	21-17	Dallas	63,660
	Jan. 12	Green Bay ($20,000)	Seattle ($20,000)	42-20	Green Bay	72,168
2006	Jan. 14	Chicago ($19,000)	Seattle ($19,000)	27-24*	Chicago	62,184
	Jan. 13	New Orleans ($19,000)	Philadelphia ($19,000)	27-24	New Orleans	70,001
2005	Jan. 15	Carolina ($19,000)	Chicago ($19,000)	29-21	Chicago	62,209
	Jan. 14	Seattle ($19,000)	Washington ($19,000)	20-10	Seattle	67,551
2004	Jan. 16	Philadelphia ($18,000)	Minnesota ($18,000)	27-14	Philadelphia	67,722
	Jan. 15	Atlanta ($18,000)	St. Louis ($18,000)	47-17	Atlanta	70,709
2003	Jan. 11	Philadelphia ($18,000)	Green Bay ($18,000)	20-17*	Philadelphia	67,707
	Jan. 10	Carolina ($18,000)	St. Louis ($18,000)	29-23*	St. Louis	66,165
2002	Jan. 12	Tampa Bay ($17,000)	San Francisco ($17,000)	31-6	Tampa	65,599
	Jan. 11	Philadelphia ($17,000)	Atlanta ($17,000)	20-6	Philadelphia	66,452
2001	Jan. 20	St. Louis ($17,000)	Green Bay ($17,000)	45-17	St. Louis	66,338
	Jan. 19	Philadelphia ($17,000)	Chicago ($17,000)	33-19	Chicago	66,944
2000	Jan. 7	N.Y. Giants ($16,000)	Philadelphia ($16,000)	20-10	East Rutherford	78,765
	Jan. 6	Minnesota ($16,000)	New Orleans ($16,000)	34-16	Minneapolis	63,881

Season	Date	Winner (Share)	Loser (Share)	Score	Site	Attendance
1999	Jan. 16	St. Louis ($16,000)	Minnesota ($16,000)	49-37	St. Louis	66,194
	Jan. 15	Tampa Bay ($16,000)	Washington ($16,000)	14-13	Tampa	65,835
1998	Jan. 10	Minnesota ($15,000)	Arizona ($15,000)	41-21	Minneapolis	63,760
	Jan. 9	Atlanta ($15,000)	San Francisco ($15,000)	20-18	Atlanta	70,262
1997	Jan. 4	Green Bay ($15,000)	Tampa Bay ($15,000)	21-7	Green Bay	60,327
	Jan. 3	San Francisco ($15,000)	Minnesota ($15,000)	38-22	San Francisco	65,018
1996	Jan. 5	Carolina ($14,000)	Dallas ($14,000)	26-17	Charlotte	72,808
	Jan. 4	Green Bay ($14,000)	San Francisco ($14,000)	35-14	Green Bay	60,787
1995	Jan. 7	Dallas ($13,000)	Philadelphia ($13,000)	30-11	Dallas	64,371
	Jan. 6	Green Bay ($13,000)	San Francisco ($13,000)	27-17	San Francisco	69,311
1994	Jan. 8	Dallas ($12,000)	Green Bay ($12,000)	35-9	Dallas	64,745
	Jan. 7	San Francisco ($12,000)	Chicago ($12,000)	44-15	San Francisco	64,644
1993	Jan. 16	Dallas ($12,000)	Green Bay ($12,000)	27-17	Dallas	64,790
	Jan. 15	San Francisco ($12,000)	N.Y. Giants ($12,000)	44-3	San Francisco	67,143
1992	Jan. 10	Dallas ($10,000)	Philadelphia ($10,000)	34-10	Dallas	63,721
	Jan. 9	San Francisco ($10,000)	Washington ($10,000)	20-13	San Francisco	64,991
1991	Jan. 5	Detroit ($10,000)	Dallas ($10,000)	38-6	Detroit	78,290
	Jan. 4	Washington ($10,000)	Atlanta ($10,000)	24-7	Washington	55,181
1990	Jan. 13	N.Y. Giants ($10,000)	Chicago ($10,000)	31-3	East Rutherford	77,025
	Jan. 12	San Francisco ($10,000)	Washington ($10,000)	28-10	San Francisco	65,292
1989	Jan. 7	L.A. Rams ($10,000)	N.Y. Giants ($10,000)	19-13*	East Rutherford	76,526
	Jan. 6	San Francisco ($10,000)	Minnesota ($10,000)	41-13	San Francisco	64,918
1988	Jan. 1	San Francisco ($10,000)	Minnesota ($10,000)	34-9	San Francisco	61,848
	Dec. 31	Chicago ($10,000)	Philadelphia ($10,000)	20-12	Chicago	65,534
1987	Jan. 10	Washington ($10,000)	Chicago ($10,000)	21-17	Chicago	65,268
	Jan. 9	Minnesota ($10,000)	San Francisco ($10,000)	36-24	San Francisco	63,008
1986	Jan. 4	N.Y. Giants ($10,000)	San Francisco ($10,000)	49-3	East Rutherford	75,691
	Jan. 3	Washington ($10,000)	Chicago ($10,000)	27-13	Chicago	65,524
1985	Jan. 5	Chicago ($10,000)	N.Y. Giants ($10,000)	21-0	Chicago	65,670
	Jan. 4	L.A. Rams ($10,000)	Dallas ($10,000)	20-0	Anaheim	66,581
1984	Dec. 30	Chicago ($10,000)	Washington ($10,000)	23-19	Washington	55,431
	Dec. 29	San Francisco ($10,000)	N.Y. Giants ($10,000)	21-10	San Francisco	60,303
1983	Jan. 1	Washington ($10,000)	L.A. Rams ($10,000)	51-7	Washington	54,440
	Dec. 31	San Francisco ($10,000)	Detroit ($10,000)	24-23	San Francisco	59,979
1982	Jan. 16	Dallas ($10,000)	Green Bay ($10,000)	37-26	Dallas	63,972
	Jan. 15	Washington ($10,000)	Minnesota ($10,000)	21-7	Washington	54,593
1981	Jan. 3	San Francisco ($5,000)	N.Y. Giants ($5,000)	38-24	San Francisco	58,360
	Jan. 2	Dallas ($5,000)	Tampa Bay ($5,000)	38-0	Dallas	64,848
1980	Jan. 4	Dallas ($5,000)	Atlanta ($5,000)	30-27	Atlanta	59,793
	Jan. 3	Philadelphia ($5,000)	Minnesota ($5,000)	31-16	Philadelphia	70,178
1979	Dec. 30	Los Angeles ($5,000)	Dallas ($5,000)	21-19	Dallas	64,792
	Dec. 29	Tampa Bay ($5,000)	Philadelphia ($5,000)	24-17	Tampa	71,402
1978	Dec. 31	Los Angeles ($5,000)	Minnesota ($5,000)	34-10	Los Angeles	70,436
	Dec. 30	Dallas ($5,000)	Atlanta ($5,000)	27-20	Dallas	63,406
1977	Dec. 26	Dallas ($5,000)	Chicago ($5,000)	37-7	Dallas	63,260
	Dec. 26	Minnesota ($5,000)	Los Angeles ($5,000)	14-7	Los Angeles	70,203
1976	Dec. 19	Los Angeles [$]	Dallas [$]	14-12	Dallas	63,283
	Dec. 18	Minnesota [$]	Washington [$]	35-20	Minneapolis	47,466
1975	Dec. 28	Dallas [$]	Minnesota [$]	17-14	Minneapolis	48,050
	Dec. 27	Los Angeles [$]	St. Louis [$]	35-23	Los Angeles	73,459
1974	Dec. 22	Los Angeles [$]	Washington [$]	19-10	Los Angeles	77,925
	Dec. 21	Minnesota [$]	St. Louis [$]	30-14	Minneapolis	48,150
1973	Dec. 23	Dallas [$]	Los Angeles [$]	27-16	Dallas	63,272
	Dec. 22	Minnesota [$]	Washington [$]	27-20	Minneapolis	48,040
1972	Dec. 24	Washington [$]	Green Bay [$]	16-3	Washington	52,321
	Dec. 23	Dallas [$]	San Francisco [$]	30-28	San Francisco	59,746
1971	Dec. 26	San Francisco [$]	Washington [$]	24-20	San Francisco	45,327
	Dec. 25	Dallas [$]	Minnesota [$]	20-12	Minneapolis	47,307
1970	Dec. 27	San Francisco [$]	Minnesota [$]	17-14	Minneapolis	45,103
	Dec. 26	Dallas [$]	Detroit [$]	5-0	Dallas	69,613
1969	Dec. 28	Cleveland [$]	Dallas [$]	38-14	Dallas	69,321
	Dec. 27	Minnesota [$]	Los Angeles [$]	23-20	Minneapolis	47,900
1968	Dec. 22	Baltimore [$]	Minnesota [$]	24-14	Baltimore	60,238
	Dec. 21	Cleveland [$]	Dallas [$]	31-20	Cleveland	81,497
1967	Dec. 24	Dallas [$]	Cleveland [$]	52-14	Dallas	70,786
	Dec. 23	Green Bay [$]	Los Angeles [$]	28-7	Milwaukee	49,861
1965	Dec. 26	Green Bay [$]	Baltimore [$]	13-10*	Green Bay	50,484
1958	Dec. 21	N.Y. Giants (#)	Cleveland (#)	10-0	New York	61,274
1957	Dec. 22	Detroit (#)	San Francisco (#)	31-27	San Francisco	60,118
1952	Dec. 21	Detroit (#)	Los Angeles (#)	31-21	Detroit	47,645
1950	Dec. 17	Los Angeles (#)	Chicago Bears (#)	24-14	Los Angeles	83,501
	Dec. 17	Cleveland (#)	N.Y. Giants (#)	8-3	Cleveland	33,054
1947	Dec. 21	Philadelphia (#)	Pittsburgh (#)	21-0	Pittsburgh	35,729
1943	Dec. 19	Washington (¢)	N.Y. Giants (¢)	28-0	New York	42,800
1941	Dec. 14	Chicago Bears (¢)	Green Bay (¢)	33-14	Chicago	43,425

*Overtime   # Players received 1/12 of annual salary for playoff appearances.
$ Players received 1/14 of annual salary for playoff appearances.   ¢ Players received 1/10 of annual salary for playoff appearances.

2011 NFC DIVISIONAL PLAYOFF GAMES

Lambeau Field, Green Bay, Wisconsin
January 15, 2012, Attendance: 72,080

NEW YORK GIANTS 37, GREEN BAY 20—Eli Manning passed for 3 touchdowns as the Giants defeated the NFC's number-one seed. En route to a 20-10 halftime lead, the Giants scored on four of their six first-half possessions, with three drives in excess of 67 yards. The game began with each team kicking a field goal to conclude its opening possession. Manning then connected with Hakeem Nicks on a 66-yard touchdown deep down the middle. The Packers responded with a 60-yard touchdown drive capped by Aaron Rodgers' 8-yard scoring pass to John Kuhn. Antrel Rolle recovered a fumble by Kuhn later in the quarter to set up Lawrence Tynes' 23-yard field goal with 1:51 left in the half. The Giants forced a punt, and a 23-yard run by Ahmad Bradshaw put the ball at the Packers' 37 with six seconds remaining. Manning threw a Hail Mary pass that Nicks caught in the end zone to give the Giants a 20-10 halftime lead. The Giants drove to the Giants' 30 to begin the second half, but Osi Umenyiora sacked Rodgers and forced him to fumble and Deon Grant recovered. The Packers then forced a punt, and Mason Crosby ended the ensuing 58-yard drive with a 35-yard field goal. Green Bay forced another punt, and the Packers drove to the Giants' 39, but Michael Boley sacked Rodgers on fourth-and-5 to quell the rally with 12:54 to play. The Giants converted two third-down situations on their next drive en route to Tynes' 35-yard field goal with 7:48 remaining for a 23-13 lead. Two plays later, Kenny Phillips forced Ryan Grant to fumble. Chase Blackburn recovered the ball and returned it 40 yards to the Giants' 4. On the next play, Manning threw a touchdown pass to Mario Manningham for a 30-13 lead with 6:48 to play. The Packers drove 76 yards for a touchdown, but Victor Cruz recovered the ensuing onside kick with 4:46 left and then caught a key 17-yard pass that led to Brandon Jacobs' 14-yard touchdown run with 2:36 remaining to finish the scoring. Manning was 21 of 33 for 330 yards and 3 touchdowns, with 1 interception. Nicks had 7 receptions for 165 yards. Rodgers completed 26 of 46 passes for 264 yards and 2 touchdowns, with 1 interception.

New York Giants	10	10	0	17	—	37
Green Bay	3	7	3	7	—	20

NYG	—	FG Tynes 31
GB	—	FG Crosby 47
NYG	—	Nicks 66 pass from Manning (Tynes kick)
GB	—	Kuhn 8 pass from Rodgers (Crosby kick)
NYG	—	FG Tynes 23
NYG	—	Nicks 37 pass from Manning (Tynes kick)
GB	—	FG Crosby 35
NYG	—	FG Tynes 35
NYG	—	Manningham 4 pass from Manning (Tynes kick)
GB	—	Driver 16 pass from Rodgers (Crosby kick)
NYG	—	Jacobs 14 run (Tynes kick)

Candlestick Park, San Francisco, California
January 14, 2012, Attendance: 69,732

SAN FRANCISCO 36, NEW ORLEANS 32—Alex Smith completed a 14-yard touchdown pass to Vernon Davis with nine seconds left to cap an 85-yard drive in a game that saw four lead changes in the final four minutes, two seconds. The 49ers' defense forced five turnovers that resulted in 13 points. The first turnover occurred on the opening drive of the game, when Donte Whitner forced Pierre Thomas to fumble at the 49ers' 2, with Patrick Willis recovering the loose ball. Alex Smith threw a pair of touchdown passes in a span of 1:27 late in the first quarter, sandwiched between Dashon Goldson's interception, to stake the 49ers to a 14-0 lead. On the ensuing kickoff, Madieu Williams forced Courtney Roby to fumble and Blake Costanzo recovered at the Saints' 13. The Saints' defense held the 49ers to a field goal and 17-0 lead. New Orleans promptly had touchdown drives of 80 and 66 yards on its next two possessions to trim the deficit to 17-14. In the third quarter, Costanzo forced Darren Sproles to fumble a punt. Colin Jones recovered the ball to set up David Akers' 41-yard field goal. Early in the fourth quarter, John Kasay's 48-yard field goal capped a 9-play drive to pull the Saints to within 20-17. A 42-yard run by Frank Gore set up David Akers' 37-yard field goal with 7:36 to play for a 23-17 lead. The Saints converted two third downs on their next drive before Sproles caught a short pass and sprinted for a 44-yard touchdown for a 24-23 lead with 4:02 left. The 49ers then drove 80 yards, keyed by Davis' 37-yard reception and capped by Smith's 28-yard scoring bootleg run down the left sideline on third-and-8 for a 29-24 lead with 2:11 remaining. Four plays later, Drew Brees completed a 66-yard touchdown pass to Jimmy Graham deep down the middle. Sproles caught Brees' 2-point conversion pass attempt for a 32-29 lead with 1:37 to play. Beginning from his own 15-yard line with 1:32 remaining, Smith completed four of five passes, keyed by Davis' 47-yard catch, to reach the Saints' 14 with 20 seconds left. Davis ran a quick slant and caught Smith's game-winning touchdown pass just as he collided into Roman Harper. Smith was 24 of 42 for 299 yards and 3 touchdowns. Davis had 7 receptions for 180 yards. Brees completed 40 of 63 passes for 462 yards and 4 touchdowns, with 2 interceptions. Sproles had a postseason-record 15 catches for 118 yards, while Colston had 9 catches for 136 yards and Graham 5 receptions for 103 yards.

New Orleans	0	14	0	18	—	32
San Francisco	14	3	3	16	—	36

SF	—	Davis 49 pass from Smith (Akers kick)
SF	—	Crabtree 4 pass from Smith (Akers kick)
SF	—	FG Akers 25
NO	—	Graham 14 pass from Brees (Kasay kick)
NO	—	Colston 25 pass from Brees (Kasay kick)
SF	—	FG Akers 41
NO	—	FG Kasay 48
SF	—	FG Akers 37
NO	—	Sproles 44 pass from Brees (Kasay kick)
SF	—	Smith 28 run (run failed)
NO	—	Graham 66 pass from Brees (Sproles pass from Brees)
SF	—	Davis 14 pass from Smith (Akers kick)

AFC WILD CARD PLAYOFF GAMES RESULTS

Season	Date	Winner (Share)	Loser (Share)	Score	Site	Attendance
2011	Jan. 8	Denver ($22,000)	Pittsburgh ($20,000)	29-23*	Denver	75,970
	Jan. 7	Houston ($22,000)	Cincinnati ($20,000)	31-10	Houston	71,725
2010	Jan. 9	Baltimore ($19,000)	Kansas City ($21,000)	30-7	Kansas City	72,190
	Jan. 8	N.Y. Jets ($19,000)	Indianapolis ($21,000)	17-16	Indianapolis	65,332
2009	Jan. 10	Baltimore ($19,000)	New England ($21,000)	33-14	Foxborough	68,756
	Jan. 9	N.Y. Jets ($19,000)	Cincinnati ($21,000)	24-14	Cincinnati	63,686
2008	Jan. 4	Baltimore ($19,000)	Miami ($20,000)	27-9	Miami	74,240
	Jan. 3	San Diego ($20,000)	Indianapolis ($18,000)	23-17*	San Diego	68,082
2007	Jan. 6	San Diego ($20,000)	Tennessee ($18,000)	17-6	San Diego	65,640
	Jan. 5	Jacksonville ($18,000)	Pittsburgh ($20,000)	31-29	Pittsburgh	63,629
2006	Jan. 7	New England ($19,000)	N.Y. Jets ($17,000)	37-16	Foxborough	68,756
	Jan. 6	Indianapolis ($19,000)	Kansas City ($17,000)	23-8	Indianapolis	57,215

Season	Date	Winner (Share)	Loser (Share)	Score	Site	Attendance
2005	Jan. 8	Pittsburgh ($17,000)	Cincinnati ($19,000)	31-17	Cincinnati	65,870
	Jan. 7	New England ($19,000)	Jacksonville ($17,000)	28-3	Foxborough	68,756
2004	Jan. 9	Indianapolis ($18,000)	Denver ($15,000)	49-24	Indianapolis	56,609
	Jan. 8	N.Y. Jets ($15,000)	San Diego ($18,000)	20-17*	San Diego	67,536
2003	Jan. 4	Indianapolis ($18,000)	Denver ($15,000)	41-10	Indianapolis	56,586
	Jan. 3	Tennessee ($15,000)	Baltimore ($18,000)	20-17	Baltimore	69,452
2002	Jan. 5	Pittsburgh ($17,000)	Cleveland ($12,500)	36-33	Pittsburgh	62,595
	Jan. 4	N.Y. Jets ($17,000)	Indianapolis ($12,500)	41-0	East Rutherford	78,524
2001	Jan. 13	Baltimore ($12,500)	Miami ($12,500)	20-3	Miami	72,251
	Jan. 12	Oakland ($17,000)	N.Y. Jets ($12,500)	38-24	Oakland	61,503
2000	Dec. 31	Baltimore ($12,500)	Denver ($12,500)	21-3	Baltimore	69,638
	Dec. 30	Miami ($16,000)	Indianapolis ($12,500)	23-17*	Miami	73,193
1999	Jan. 9	Miami ($10,000)	Seattle ($16,000)	20-17	Seattle	66,170
	Jan. 8	Tennessee ($10,000)	Buffalo ($10,000)	22-16	Nashville	66,672
1998	Jan. 3	Jacksonville ($15,000)	New England ($10,000)	25-10	Jacksonville	71,139
	Jan. 2	Miami ($10,000)	Buffalo ($10,000)	24-17	Miami	72,698
1997	Dec. 28	New England ($15,000)	Miami ($10,000)	17-3	Foxborough	60,041
	Dec. 27	Denver ($15,000)	Jacksonville ($10,000)	42-17	Denver	74,481
1996	Dec. 29	Pittsburgh ($14,000)	Indianapolis ($10,000)	42-14	Pittsburgh	58,078
	Dec. 28	Jacksonville ($10,000)	Buffalo ($10,000)	30-27	Buffalo	70,213
1995	Dec. 31	Indianapolis ($7,500)	San Diego ($7,500)	35-20	San Diego	61,182
	Dec. 30	Buffalo ($13,000)	Miami ($7,500)	37-22	Buffalo	73,103
1994	Jan. 1	Cleveland ($7,500)	New England ($7,500)	20-13	Cleveland	77,452
	Dec. 31	Miami ($12,000)	Kansas City ($7,500)	27-17	Miami	67,487
1993	Jan. 9	L.A. Raiders ($7,500)	Denver ($7,500)	42-24	Los Angeles	65,314
	Jan. 8	Kansas City ($12,000)	Pittsburgh ($7,500)	27-24*	Kansas City	74,515
1992	Jan. 3	Buffalo ($6,000)	Houston ($6,000)	41-38*	Buffalo	75,141
	Jan. 2	San Diego ($10,000)	Kansas City ($6,000)	17-0	San Diego	58,278
1991	Dec. 29	Houston ($10,000)	N.Y. Jets ($6,000)	17-10	Houston	61,485
	Dec. 28	Kansas City ($6,000)	L.A. Raiders ($6,000)	10-6	Kansas City	75,827
1990	Jan. 6	Cincinnati ($10,000)	Houston ($6,000)	41-14	Cincinnati	60,012
	Jan. 5	Miami ($6,000)	Kansas City ($6,000)	17-16	Miami	67,276
1989	Dec. 31	Pittsburgh ($6,000)	Houston ($6,000)	26-23*	Houston	59,406
1988	Dec. 26	Houston ($6,000)	Cleveland ($6,000)	24-23	Cleveland	75,896
1987	Jan. 3	Houston ($6,000)	Seattle ($6,000)	23-20*	Houston	50,519
1986	Dec. 28	N.Y. Jets ($6,000)	Kansas City ($6,000)	35-15	East Rutherford	75,210
1985	Dec. 28	New England ($6,000)	N.Y. Jets ($6,000)	26-14	East Rutherford	75,945
1984	Dec. 22	Seattle ($6,000)	L.A. Raiders ($6,000)	13-7	Seattle	62,049
1983	Dec. 24	Seattle ($6,000)	Denver ($6,000)	31-7	Seattle	64,275
1982	Jan. 9	N.Y. Jets ($6,000)	Cincinnati ($6,000)	44-17	Cincinnati	57,560
	Jan. 9	San Diego ($6,000)	Pittsburgh ($6,000)	31-28	Pittsburgh	53,546
	Jan. 8	L.A. Raiders ($6,000)	Cleveland ($6,000)	27-10	Los Angeles	56,555
	Jan. 8	Miami ($6,000)	New England ($6,000)	28-13	Miami	68,842
1981	Dec. 27	Buffalo ($3,000)	N.Y. Jets ($3,000)	31-27	New York	57,050
1980	Dec. 28	Oakland ($3,000)	Houston ($3,000)	27-7	Oakland	53,333
1979	Dec. 23	Houston ($3,000)	Denver ($3,000)	13-7	Houston	48,776
1978	Dec. 24	Houston ($3,000)	Miami ($3,000)	17-9	Miami	72,445

*Overtime

2011 AFC WILD CARD PLAYOFF GAMES
Sports Authority Field at Mile High, Denver, Colorado
January 8, 2012, Attendance: 75,970
DENVER 29, PITTSBURGH 23 (OT)—Tim Tebow completed an 80-yard touchdown pass to Demaryius Thomas on the first play of overtime as the Broncos beat the Steelers. Pittsburgh took a 6-0 lead on two first-quarter Shaun Suisham field goals. The Broncos answered when Tebow completed a 51-yard pass to Thomas on third-and-12 followed, two plays later, by Eddie Royal's 30-yard touchdown catch along the right end-zone sideline for a 7-6 lead. The Broncos' defense forced a three-and-out, and Tebow connected two plays later on a 58-yard pass to Thomas that led to an 8-yard touchdown run on a quarterback draw for a 14-6 advantage. Quinton Carter's interception moments later led to a field goal, giving Denver 17 points in less than six minutes. The Broncos led 20-6 at halftime, but the Steelers responded with an 11-play, 87-yard drive on their first possession of the second half, set up by a 32-yard run by Isaac Redman, to pull within 20-13. Denver used more than six minutes of the clock on its next drive, and Matt Prater's 35-yard field goal staked the Broncos to a 23-13 lead with 13:10 to play. The Steelers' next drive was capped by Suisham's third field goal, and moments later Ryan Mundy forced Willis McGahee to fumble and LaMarr Woodley recovered at the Steelers' 44. Ben Roethlisberger needed just seven plays to tie the game, 23-23, on Jerricho Cotchery's 31-yard scoring grab deep down the middle with 3:48 on the clock. Neither team threatened on its final possession of regulation, and the Broncos won the overtime toss. In the first game to use the NFL's new rules for modified sudden death overtime, Suisham's kickoff sailed into the end zone for a touchback. On the first play, Tebow fired a short 17-yard pass to Thomas on a crossing route. Thomas stiff-armed Ike Taylor and outran two Steelers to the end zone. The 11-second overtime was the shortest in NFL history. Tebow was 10 of 21 for 316 yards and 2 touchdowns. His 31.6 yards per completion average established an NFL postseason record. Thomas had 4 catches for 204 yards. Roethlisberger was 22 of 40 for 289 yards and 1 touchdown, with 1 interception. Redman rushed 17 times for 121 yards.

Pittsburgh	6	0	7	10	0	— 23
Denver	0	20	0	3	6	— 29

Pitt — FG Suisham 45
Pitt — FG Suisham 38

Den — Royal 30 pass from Tebow (Prater kick)
Den — Tebow 8 run (Prater kick)
Den — FG Prater 20
Den — FG Prater 28
Pitt — Wallace 1 run (Suisham kick)
Den — FG Prater 35
Pitt — FG Suisham 37
Pitt — Cotchery 31 pass from Roethlisberger (Suisham kick)
Den — Thomas 80 pass from Tebow

Reliant Stadium, Houston, Texas
January 7, 2012, Attendance: 71,725
HOUSTON 31, CINCINNATI 10—Arian Foster ran for 153 yards and 2 touchdowns as the Texans pulled away from the Bengals to register the franchise's first postseason victory. A 52-yard pass interference penalty set up Cedric Benson's 1-yard run and gave the Bengals a 7-0 lead midway through the first quarter. The Texans needed just six plays to drive 80 yards and tie the game on Foster's 8-yard run. After missing a 50-yard field goal, Mike Nugent made a 37-yard kick for the Bengals for a 10-7 lead with 7:09 left in the second quarter. Over the next 32 minutes, the Texans' defense stifled the Bengals, not allowing Cincinnati to run a play inside the Texans' 46 until the game's final five minutes. With the score 10-10 and 59 seconds left in the half, back on their own 34-yard line, Andy Dalton's short pass was intercepted by J.J. Watt, who returned it 29 yards for a momentum-swinging touchdown and 17-10 Houston lead. Rookie T.J. Yates completed a 40-yard touchdown pass to Andre Johnson late in the third quarter, and Danieal Manning's interception in the fourth quarter led to Foster's 42-yard touchdown run with 5:15 remaining to finish the scoring. Yates was 11 of 20 for 159 yards and 1 touchdown. Foster rushed 24 times for 153 yards and 2 scores. Dalton was 27 of 42 for 257 yards, with 3 interceptions.

Cincinnati	7	3	0	0	— 10
Houston	7	10	7	7	— 31

Cin — Benson 1 run (Nugent kick)
Hou — Foster 8 run (Rackers kick)
Cin — FG Nugent 37
Hou — FG Rackers 39
Hou — Watt 29 interception return (Rackers kick)
Hou — Johnson 40 pass from Yates (Rackers kick)
Hou — Foster 42 run (Rackers kick)

NFC WILD CARD PLAYOFF GAMES RESULTS

Season	Date	Winner (Share)	Loser (Share)	Score	Site	Attendance
2011	Jan. 8	N.Y. Giants ($22,000)	Atlanta ($20,000)	24-2	East Rutherford	79,909
	Jan. 7	New Orleans ($22,000)	Detroit ($20,000)	45-28	New Orleans	73,038
2010	Jan. 9	Green Bay ($19,000)	Philadelphia ($21,000)	21-16	Philadelphia	69,144
	Jan. 8	Seattle ($21,000)	New Orleans ($19,000)	41-36	Seattle	66,336
2009	Jan. 10	Arizona ($21,000)	Green Bay ($19,000)	51-45*	Glendale	61,926
	Jan. 9	Dallas ($21,000)	Philadelphia ($19,000)	34-14	Dallas	92,951
2008	Jan. 4	Philadelphia ($18,000)	Minnesota ($20,000)	26-14	Minneapolis	61,746
	Jan. 3	Arizona ($20,000)	Atlanta ($18,000)	30-24	Glendale	62,848
2007	Jan. 6	N.Y. Giants ($18,000)	Tampa Bay ($20,000)	24-14	Tampa	65,621
	Jan. 5	Seattle ($20,000)	Washington ($18,000)	35-14	Seattle	68,297
2006	Jan. 7	Philadelphia ($19,000)	N.Y. Giants ($17,000)	23-20	Philadelphia	69,094
	Jan. 6	Seattle ($19,000)	Dallas ($17,000)	21-20	Seattle	68,058
2005	Jan. 8	Carolina ($17,000)	N.Y. Giants ($19,000)	23-0	East Rutherford	79,378
	Jan. 7	Washington ($17,000)	Tampa Bay ($19,000)	17-10	Tampa	65,514
2004	Jan. 9	Minnesota ($15,000)	Green Bay ($18,000)	31-17	Green Bay	71,075
	Jan. 8	St. Louis ($15,000)	Seattle ($18,000)	27-20	Seattle	65,397
2003	Jan. 4	Green Bay ($18,000)	Seattle ($15,000)	33-27*	Green Bay	71,457
	Jan. 3	Carolina ($18,000)	Dallas ($15,000)	29-10	Charlotte	73,014
2002	Jan. 5	San Francisco ($17,000)	N.Y. Giants ($12,500)	39-38	San Francisco	66,318
	Jan. 4	Atlanta ($12,500)	Green Bay ($17,000)	27-7	Green Bay	65,358
2001	Jan. 13	Green Bay ($12,500)	San Francisco ($12,500)	25-15	Green Bay	59,825
	Jan. 12	Philadelphia ($12,500)	Tampa Bay ($12,500)	31-9	Philadelphia	65,847
2000	Dec. 31	Philadelphia ($12,500)	Tampa Bay ($12,500)	21-3	Philadelphia	65,813
	Dec. 30	New Orleans ($16,000)	St. Louis ($12,500)	31-28	New Orleans	64,900
1999	Jan. 9	Minnesota ($10,000)	Dallas ($10,000)	27-10	Minneapolis	64,056
	Jan. 8	Washington ($16,000)	Detroit ($10,000)	27-13	Washington	79,411
1998	Jan. 3	San Francisco ($10,000)	Green Bay ($10,000)	30-27	San Francisco	66,506
	Jan. 2	Arizona ($10,000)	Dallas ($15,000)	20-7	Dallas	62,969
1997	Dec. 28	Tampa Bay ($10,000)	Detroit ($10,000)	20-10	Tampa	73,361
	Dec. 27	Minnesota ($10,000)	N.Y. Giants ($15,000)	23-22	East Rutherford	77,497
1996	Dec. 29	San Francisco ($10,000)	Philadelphia ($10,000)	14-0	San Francisco	56,460
	Dec. 28	Dallas ($14,000)	Minnesota ($10,000)	40-15	Dallas	64,682
1995	Dec. 31	Green Bay ($13,000)	Atlanta ($7,500)	37-20	Green Bay	60,453
	Dec. 30	Philadelphia ($7,500)	Detroit ($7,500)	58-37	Philadelphia	66,099
1994	Jan. 1	Chicago ($7,500)	Minnesota ($12,000)	35-18	Minnesota	60,347
	Dec. 31	Green Bay ($7,500)	Detroit ($7,500)	16-12	Green Bay	58,125
1993	Jan. 9	N.Y. Giants ($7,500)	Minnesota ($7,500)	17-10	East Rutherford	75,089
	Jan. 8	Green Bay ($7,500)	Detroit ($12,000)	28-24	Detroit	68,479
1992	Jan. 3	Philadelphia ($6,000)	New Orleans ($6,000)	36-20	New Orleans	68,893
	Jan. 2	Washington ($6,000)	Minnesota ($10,000)	24-7	Minnesota	57,353
1991	Dec. 29	Dallas ($6,000)	Chicago ($6,000)	17-13	Chicago	62,594
	Dec. 28	Atlanta ($6,000)	New Orleans ($10,000)	27-20	New Orleans	68,794
1990	Jan. 6	Chicago ($10,000)	New Orleans ($6,000)	16-6	Chicago	60,767
	Jan. 5	Washington ($6,000)	Philadelphia ($6,000)	20-6	Philadelphia	65,287
1989	Dec. 31	L.A. Rams ($6,000)	Philadelphia ($6,000)	21-7	Philadelphia	65,479
1988	Dec. 26	Minnesota ($6,000)	L.A. Rams ($6,000)	28-17	Minnesota	61,204
1987	Jan. 3	Minnesota ($6,000)	New Orleans ($6,000)	44-10	New Orleans	68,546

NFC WILD CARD PLAYOFF GAMES RESULTS

Season	Date	Winner (Share)	Loser (Share)	Score	Site	Attendance
1986	Dec. 28	Washington ($6,000)	L.A. Rams ($6,000)	19-7	Washington	54,567
1985	Dec. 29	N.Y. Giants ($6,000)	San Francisco ($6,000)	17-3	East Rutherford	75,131
1984	Dec. 23	N.Y. Giants ($6,000)	L.A. Rams ($6,000)	16-13	Anaheim	67,037
1983	Dec. 26	L.A. Rams ($6,000)	Dallas ($6,000)	24-17	Dallas	62,118
1982	Jan. 9	Dallas ($6,000)	Tampa Bay ($6,000)	30-17	Dallas	65,042
	Jan. 9	Minnesota ($6,000)	Atlanta ($6,000)	30-24	Minnesota	60,560
	Jan. 8	Green Bay ($6,000)	St. Louis ($6,000)	41-16	Green Bay	54,282
	Jan. 8	Washington ($6,000)	Detroit ($6,000)	31-7	Washington	55,045
1981	Dec. 27	N.Y. Giants ($3,000)	Philadelphia ($3,000)	27-21	Philadelphia	71,611
1980	Dec. 28	Dallas ($3,000)	Los Angeles ($3,000)	34-13	Dallas	63,052
1979	Dec. 23	Philadelphia ($3,000)	Chicago ($3,000)	27-17	Philadelphia	69,397
1978	Dec. 24	Atlanta ($3,000)	Philadelphia ($3,000)	14-13	Atlanta	59,403

*Overtime

2011 NFC WILD CARD PLAYOFF GAMES

MetLife Stadium, East Rutherford, New Jersey
January 8, 2012, Attendance: 79,909
NEW YORK GIANTS 24, ATLANTA 2—Eli Manning passed for 3 touchdowns and the Giants' defense permitted just 247 yards to defeat the Falcons. On the first play of the second quarter, faced with fourth-and-1 from the Giants' 24, Atlanta attempted a quarterback sneak but Matt Ryan was stopped for no gain. Three plays later, Manning, while in the end zone and being pressured by James Sanders, threw the ball away but was flagged for intentional grounding and a safety. Following the free kick, the Giants' defense forced a punt, and the offense drove 85 yards in 13 plays, keyed by Brandon Jacobs' 2-yard gain on fourth-and-1, and capped by Manning's 4-yard touchdown pass to Hakeem Nicks for a 7-2 lead. The Giants drove 72 yards for a field goal on their first possession of the second half, and the Falcons answered by driving to the Giants' 21. Faced with fourth-and-1, Ryan again attempted a quarterback sneak but was stopped for no gain. Three plays later, Nicks took a short pass and outran the Falcons for a 72-yard touchdown and 17-2 advantage. Manning capped the day with an 85-yard drive on New York's next possession that culminated with Mario Manningham's 27-yard scoring catch with 9:55 to play. Manning was 23 of 32 for 277 yards and 3 touchdowns. Nicks had 6 catches for 115 yards. Ryan was 24 of 41 for 199 yards.

Atlanta	0	2	0	0 —	2
New York Giants	0	7	10	7 —	24

Atl — Safety, intentional grounding by Manning in end zone
NYG — Nicks 4 pass from Manning (Tynes kick)
NYG — FG Tynes 22
NYG — Nicks 72 pass from Manning (Tynes kick)
NYG — Manningham 27 pass from Manning (Tynes kick)

Mercedes-Benz Superdome, New Orleans, Louisiana
January 7, 2012, Attendance: 73,038
NEW ORLEANS 45, DETROIT 28—Drew Brees passed for 466 yards and 3 touchdowns as the Saints rallied from a halftime deficit to defeat the Lions. Detroit was playing its first postseason game since 1999, and gained 412 total yards, but permitted 626 yards. In the first half, the Lions scored two touchdowns on offense and the defense forced two fumbles, slowing down the Saints and leading 14-7. But the Saints drove 78 yards, including a fourth-and-1 run by Chris Ivory for a first down, and finished the half with John Kasay's 24-yard field goal to pull within 14-10. The Saints needed just four plays after the second half kickoff, capped by Brees' 41-yard touchdown pass to Devery Henderson, for a 17-14 lead. The Saints' defense forced a punt, and the offense converted a third-and-11 and fourth-and-1 situations on the ensuing 92-yard drive that ended with Jimmy Graham's 3-yard touchdown catch for a 24-14 lead. Detroit answered with 21- and 42-yard catches by Calvin Johnson to set up Matthew

Stafford's 1-yard sneak to trim the deficit to 24-21 with 1:08 left in the third quarter. The Saints converted third-and-8 and fourth-and-2 on the next drive and finished a 14-play, 80-yard drive with Darren Sproles' 17-yard run to stretch the lead to 31-21 with 9:53 to play. On the next play from scrimmage, Jabari Greer intercepted Stafford's deep pass, and Brees took advantage of the turnover by throwing a 56-yard touchdown pass to Robert Meachem with 7:29 left for a 38-21 lead. Johnson's 12-yard touchdown catch with 4:40 remaining pulled the Lions with 38-28, but Jonathon Amaya recovered the onside kick and Pierre Thomas scored four plays later to finish the scoring. Brees was 33 of 43 for 466 yards and 3 touchdowns. Colston had 7 catches for 120 yards. Stafford was 28 of 43 for 380 yards and 3 touchdowns, with 2 interceptions. Johnson had 12 catches for 211 yards.

Detroit	7	7	7	7 —	28
New Orleans	0	10	14	21 —	45

Det — Heller 10 pass from Stafford (Hanson kick)
NO — Sproles 2 run (Kasay kick)
Det — Johnson 13 pass from Stafford (Hanson kick)
NO — FG Kasay 24
NO — Henderson 41 pass from Brees (Kasay kick)
NO — Graham 3 pass from Brees (Kasay kick)
Det — Stafford 1 run (Hanson kick)
NO — Sproles 17 run (Kasay kick)
NO — Meachem 56 pass from Brees (Kasay kick)
Det — Johnson 12 pass from Stafford (Hanson kick)
NO — Thomas 1 run (Kasay kick)

PRO BOWL ALL-TIME RESULTS

Includes AFL All-Star Game played after the 1961-69 seasons.

Date	Result/Honored players	Site (attendance)
Jan. 15, 1939	New York Giants 13, Pro All-Stars 10	Wrigley Field, Los Angeles (20,000)
Jan. 14, 1940	Green Bay 16, NFL All-Stars 7	Gilmore Stadium, Los Angeles (18,000)
Dec. 29, 1940	Chicago Bears 28, NFL All-Stars 14	Gilmore Stadium, Los Angeles (21,624)
Jan. 4, 1942	Chicago Bears 35, NFL All-Stars 24	Polo Grounds, New York (17,725)
Dec. 27, 1942	NFL All-Stars 17, Washington 14	Shibe Park, Philadelphia (18,671)
Jan. 14, 1951	American Conf. 28, National Conf. 27 Otto Graham, Cleveland, player of the game	Los Angeles Memorial Coliseum (53,676)
Jan. 12, 1952	National Conf. 30, American Conf. 13 Dan Towler, Los Angeles, player of the game	Los Angeles Memorial Coliseum (19,400)
Jan. 10, 1953	National Conf. 27, American Conf. 7 Don Doll, Detroit, player of the game	Los Angeles Memorial Coliseum (34,208)
Jan. 17, 1954	East 20, West 9 Chuck Bednarik, Philadelphia, player of the game	Los Angeles Memorial Coliseum (44,214)
Jan. 16, 1955	West 26, East 19 Billy Wilson, San Francisco, player of the game	Los Angeles Memorial Coliseum (43,972)
Jan. 15, 1956	East 31, West 30 Ollie Matson, Chi. Cardinals, player of the game	Los Angeles Memorial Coliseum (37,867)
Jan. 13, 1957	West 19, East 10 Bert Rechichar, Baltimore, outstanding back Ernie Stautner, Pittsburgh, outstanding lineman	Los Angeles Memorial Coliseum (44,177)
Jan. 12, 1958	West 26, East 7 Hugh McElhenny, San Francisco, outstanding back Gene Brito, Washington, outstanding lineman	Los Angeles Memorial Coliseum (66,634)
Jan. 11, 1959	East 28, West 21 Frank Gifford, N.Y. Giants, outstanding back Doug Atkins, Chi. Bears, outstanding lineman	Los Angeles Memorial Coliseum (72,250)
Jan. 17, 1960	West 38, East 21 Johnny Unitas, Baltimore, outstanding back Gene (Big Daddy) Lipscomb, Baltimore, outstanding lineman	Los Angeles Memorial Coliseum (56,876)
Jan. 15, 1961	West 35, East 31 Johnny Unitas, Baltimore, outstanding back Sam Huff, N.Y. Giants, outstanding lineman	Los Angeles Memorial Coliseum (62,971)
Jan. 7, 1962	AFL West 47, East 27 Cotton Davidson, Dallas Texans, player of the game	Balboa Stadium, San Diego (20,973)
Jan. 14, 1962	NFL West 31, East 30 Jim Brown, Cleveland, outstanding back Henry Jordan, Green Bay, outstanding lineman	Los Angeles Memorial Coliseum (57,409)
Jan. 13, 1963	AFL West 21, East 14 Curtis McClinton, Dallas Texans, outstanding offensive player Earl Faison, San Diego, outstanding defensive player	Balboa Stadium, San Diego (27,641)
Jan. 13, 1963	NFL East 30, West 20 Jim Brown, Cleveland, outstanding back Gene (Big Daddy) Lipscomb, Pittsburgh, outstanding lineman	Los Angeles Memorial Coliseum (61,374)
Jan. 12, 1964	NFL West 31, East 17 Johnny Unitas, Baltimore, player of the game Gino Marchetti, Baltimore, outstanding lineman	Los Angeles Memorial Coliseum (67,242)
Jan. 19, 1964	AFL West 27, East 24 Keith Lincoln, San Diego, outstanding offensive player Archie Matsos, Oakland, outstanding defensive player	Balboa Stadium, San Diego (20,016)
Jan. 10, 1965	NFL West 34, East 14 Fran Tarkenton, Minnesota, outstanding back Terry Barr, Detroit, outstanding lineman	Los Angeles Memorial Coliseum (60,598)
Jan. 16, 1965	AFL West 38, East 14 Keith Lincoln, San Diego, outstanding offensive player Willie Brown, Denver, outstanding defensive player	Jeppesen Stadium, Houston (15,446)
Jan. 15, 1966	AFL All-Stars 30, Buffalo 19 Joe Namath, N.Y. Jets, most valuable player, offense Frank Buncom, San Diego, most valuable player, defense	Rice Stadium, Houston (35,572)
Jan. 15, 1966	NFL East 36, West 7 Jim Brown, Cleveland, outstanding back Dale Meinert, St. Louis, outstanding lineman	Los Angeles Memorial Coliseum (60,124)
Jan. 21, 1967	AFL East 30, West 23 Babe Parilli, Boston, outstanding offensive player Verlon Biggs, N.Y. Jets, outstanding defensive player	Oakland-Alameda County Coliseum (18,876)
Jan. 22, 1967	NFL East 20, West 10 Gale Sayers, Chicago, outstanding back Floyd Peters, Philadelphia, outstanding lineman	Los Angeles Memorial Coliseum (15,062)
Jan. 21, 1968	AFL East 25, West 24 Joe Namath and Don Maynard, N.Y. Jets, out. off. players Leslie (Speedy) Duncan, San Diego, out. def. player	Gator Bowl, Jacksonville, Fla. (40,103)
Jan. 21, 1968	NFL West 38, East 20 Gale Sayers, Chicago, outstanding back Dave Robinson, Green Bay, outstanding lineman	Los Angeles Memorial Coliseum (53,289)
Jan. 19, 1969	AFL West 38, East 25 Len Dawson, Kansas City, outstanding offensive player George Webster, Houston, outstanding defensive player	Gator Bowl, Jacksonville, Fla. (41,058)
Jan. 19, 1969	NFL West 10, East 7 Roman Gabriel, Los Angeles, outstanding back Merlin Olsen, Los Angeles, outstanding lineman	Los Angeles Memorial Coliseum (32,050)
Jan. 17, 1970	AFL West 26, East 3 John Hadl, San Diego, player of the game	Astrodome, Houston (30,170)
Jan. 18, 1970	NFL West 16, East 13 Gale Sayers, Chicago, outstanding back George Andrie, Dallas, outstanding lineman	Los Angeles Memorial Coliseum (57,786)

Jan. 24, 1971 NFC 27, AFC 6 ....Los Angeles Memorial Coliseum (48,222)
  Mel Renfro, Dallas, outstanding back
  Fred Carr, Green Bay, outstanding lineman
Jan. 23, 1972 AFC 26, NFC 13 ....Los Angeles Memorial Coliseum (53,647)
  Jan Stenerud, Kansas City, outstanding offensive player
  Willie Lanier, Kansas City, outstanding defensive player
Jan. 21, 1973 AFC 33, NFC 28 ....Texas Stadium, Irving (37,091)
  O.J. Simpson, Buffalo, player of the game
Jan. 20, 1974 AFC 15, NFC 13 ....Arrowhead Stadium, Kansas City (66,918)
  Garo Yepremian, Miami, player of the game
Jan. 20, 1975 NFC 17, AFC 10 ....Orange Bowl, Miami (26,484)
  James Harris, Los Angeles, player of the game
Jan. 26, 1976 NFC 23, AFC 20 ....Louisiana Superdome, New Orleans (30,546)
  Billy Johnson, Houston, player of the game
Jan. 17, 1977 AFC 24, NFC 14 ....Kingdome, Seattle (64,752)
  Mel Blount, Pittsburgh, player of the game
Jan. 23, 1978 NFC 14, AFC 13 ....Tampa Stadium (51,337)
  Walter Payton, Chicago, player of the game
Jan. 29, 1979 NFC 13, AFC 7 ....Los Angeles Memorial Coliseum (46,281)
  Ahmad Rashad, Minnesota, player of the game
Jan. 27, 1980 NFC 37, AFC 27 ....Aloha Stadium, Honolulu (49,800)
  Chuck Muncie, New Orleans, player of the game
Feb. 1, 1981 NFC 21, AFC 7 ....Aloha Stadium, Honolulu (50,360)
  Eddie Murray, Detroit, player of the game
Jan. 31, 1982 AFC 16, NFC 13 ....Aloha Stadium, Honolulu (50,402)
  Kellen Winslow, San Diego, and Lee Roy Selmon, Tampa Bay, players of the game
Feb. 6, 1983 NFC 20, AFC 19 ....Aloha Stadium, Honolulu (49,883)
  Dan Fouts, San Diego, and John Jefferson, Green Bay, players of the game
Jan. 29, 1984 NFC 45, AFC 3 ....Aloha Stadium, Honolulu (50,445)
  Joe Theismann, Washington, player of the game
Jan. 27, 1985 AFC 22, NFC 14 ....Aloha Stadium, Honolulu (50,385)
  Mark Gastineau, N.Y. Jets, player of the game
Feb. 2, 1986 NFC 28, AFC 24 ....Aloha Stadium, Honolulu (50,101)
  Phil Simms, N.Y. Giants, player of the game
Feb. 1, 1987 AFC 10, NFC 6 ....Aloha Stadium, Honolulu (50,101)
  Reggie White, Philadelphia, player of the game
Feb. 7, 1988 AFC 15, NFC 6 ....Aloha Stadium, Honolulu (50,113)
  Bruce Smith, Buffalo, player of the game
Jan. 29, 1989 NFC 34, AFC 3 ....Aloha Stadium, Honolulu (50,113)
  Randall Cunningham, Philadelphia, player of the game
Feb. 4, 1990 NFC 27, AFC 21 ....Aloha Stadium, Honolulu (50,445)
  Jerry Gray, L.A. Rams, player of the game
Feb. 3, 1991 AFC 23, NFC 21 ....Aloha Stadium, Honolulu (50,345)
  Jim Kelly, Buffalo, player of the game
Feb. 2, 1992 NFC 21, AFC 15 ....Aloha Stadium, Honolulu (50,209)
  Michael Irvin, Dallas, player of the game
Feb. 7, 1993 AFC 23, NFC 20 (OT) ....Aloha Stadium, Honolulu (50,007)
  Steve Tasker, Buffalo, player of the game
Feb. 6, 1994 NFC 17, AFC 3 ....Aloha Stadium, Honolulu (50,026)
  Andre Rison, Atlanta, player of the game
Feb. 5, 1995 AFC 41, NFC 13 ....Aloha Stadium, Honolulu (50,529)
  Marshall Faulk, Indianapolis, player of the game
Feb. 4, 1996 NFC 20, AFC 13 ....Aloha Stadium, Honolulu (50,034)
  Jerry Rice, San Francisco, player of the game
Feb. 2, 1997 AFC 26, NFC 23 (OT) ....Aloha Stadium, Honolulu (50,031)
  Mark Brunell, Jacksonville, player of the game
Feb. 1, 1998 AFC 29, NFC 24 ....Aloha Stadium, Honolulu (49,995)
  Warren Moon, Seattle, player of the game
Feb. 7, 1999 AFC 23, NFC 10 ....Aloha Stadium, Honolulu (50,075)
  Keyshawn Johnson, N.Y. Jets and Ty Law, New England, co-players of the game
Feb. 6, 2000 NFC 51, AFC 31 ....Aloha Stadium, Honolulu (50,112)
  Randy Moss, Minnesota, player of the game
Feb. 4, 2001 AFC 38, NFC 17 ....Aloha Stadium, Honolulu (50,128)
  Rich Gannon, Oakland, player of the game
Feb. 9, 2002 AFC 38, NFC 30 ....Aloha Stadium, Honolulu (50,301)
  Rich Gannon, Oakland, player of the game
Feb. 2, 2003 AFC 45, NFC 20 ....Aloha Stadium, Honolulu (50,125)
  Ricky Williams, Miami, player of the game
Feb. 8, 2004 NFC 55, AFC 52 ....Aloha Stadium, Honolulu (50,127)
  Marc Bulger, St. Louis, player of the game
Feb. 13, 2005 AFC 38, NFC 27 ....Aloha Stadium, Honolulu (50,225)
  Peyton Manning, Indianapolis, player of the game
Feb. 12, 2006 NFC 23, AFC 17 ....Aloha Stadium, Honolulu (50,190)
  Derrick Brooks, Tampa Bay, player of the game
Feb. 10, 2007 AFC 31, NFC 28 ....Aloha Stadium, Honolulu (50,410)
  Carson Palmer, Cincinnati, player of the game
Feb. 10, 2008 NFC 42, AFC 30 ....Aloha Stadium, Honolulu (50,044)
  Adrian Peterson, Minnesota, most valuable player
Feb. 8, 2009 NFC 30, AFC 21 ....Aloha Stadium, Honolulu (49,958)
  Larry Fitzgerald, Arizona, most valuable player
Jan. 31, 2010 AFC 41, NFC 34 ....Sun Life Stadium, South Florida (70,697)
  Matt Schaub, Houston, most valuable player
Jan. 30, 2011 NFC 55, AFC 41 ....Aloha Stadium, Honolulu (49,331)
  DeAngelo Hall, Washington, most valuable player
Jan. 29, 2012 AFC 59, NFC 41 ....Aloha Stadium, Honolulu (48,423)
  Brandon Marshall, Miami, most valuable player

SUNDAY NIGHT WON-LOST RECORDS, 1978-2011
AMERICAN FOOTBALL CONFERENCE

	Balt.	Buff.	Cin.	Clev.	Den.	Hou.	Ind.	Jax.	K.C.	Mia.	N.E.	N.Y.J.	Oak.	Pitt.	S.D.	Tenn.
Total	11-10	10-10	3-10	1-9	18-15	1-3	18-19	5-6	10-5	19-8	18-14	10-13	16-18	18-17	16-15	11-9
2011	2-1						0-2		0-1		1-0	1-2		2-1	1-0	
2010	0-1						2-1			0-1	2-0	1-0		1-2	1-0	
2009	1-0	0-1			3-0						0-1	1-0		1-1	0-1	0-1
2008	1-0		0-1	0-1	2-1	0-1					0-2			2-0	2-1	
2007	0-1	0-1	0-1	1-0	1-2						3-0			1-1	1-1	1-0
2006				2-2	3-0			0-1			0-2		0-1	0-1	3-0	
2005	1-1	0-1	0-1	0-1		0-2	1-0	1-0	2-0		1-0	0-1	0-2	1-0	2-0	
2004	2-1	0-1	1-0	0-2	1-1	0-1	1-0	0-1	0-1	1-2	1-0		2-0	2-0		
2003	1-1	0-2	1-0	1-0			1-1	1-0	1-0	2-0	1-0		0-1	0-2		1-0
2002	1-0		0-1	0-1	0-2	1-0	1-1	0-1		1-1	0-2	2-0	2-0	0-1		
2001	0-1	0-1		2-0			0-2			1-0	0-1	2-0	1-1	1-0		0-1
2000	1-1	1-0					1-0		1-1	1-0	0-2	2-0	0-1	0-1	0-1	0-1
1999		2-0	0-1	0-1			1-0		1-0	1-0	2-0	0-1	1-0	1-0		0-1
1998	1-0	1-0	0-1	1-0			0-1	0-1	2-0		0-1	1-0	1-0			1-1
1997	0-1			1-0	0-1				1-1	1-0	0-1	1-0		2-0	0-2	
1996	0-1	1-1	0-1	1-1	1-0		1-0		1-0		2-0	0-1	0-1		1-1	1-0
1995		0-2		2-1				0-1	1-0	1-0	0-1	0-1	1-1		0-1	0-1
1994		1-0		0-1			0-1		2-0		2-1	1-0	0-1	1-1	0-1	1-0
1993		1-0	0-1	0-1			0-3		0-1	1-0	0-1	1-1	1-0	0-1	0-2	2-1
1992		1-1	1-0	2-0			0-1		1-1	1-0	0-1	1-1	0-2	1-0	1-0	1-1
1991		1-0	0-1	0-1	2-0		0-2				1-0	0-1	2-0	1-1	0-1	2-0
1990		1-0	1-1	0-2							1-0		0-1	1-2	0-1	1-1
1989					1-0						1-0	0-1	0-1	0-2	1-0	
1988				0-1							0-1	1-0	1-0	1-0	0-1	1-1
1987			0-1	0-1							2-0	0-1	0-1		1-0	
1986																
1985															0-1	1-0
1984			0-1	1-0												
1983													1-0			
1982																
1981																
1980															0-1	
1979																
1978				1-0						1-0			0-2	0-1		

SUNDAY NIGHT FOOTBALL ALL-TIME STANDINGS
AMERICAN FOOTBALL CONFERENCE

East	W	L	T	Pct.	South	W	L	T	Pct.
Miami	19	8	0	.704	Tennessee	11	9	0	.550
New England	18	14	0	.563	Indianapolis	18	19	0	.486
Buffalo	10	10	0	.500	Jacksonville	5	6	0	.455
New York Jets	10	13	0	.435	Houston	1	3	0	.250

North	W	L	T	Pct.	West	W	L	T	Pct.
Baltimore	11	10	0	.524	Kansas City	10	5	0	.667
Pittsburgh	18	17	0	.514	Denver	18	15	0	.545
Cincinnati	3	10	0	.231	San Diego	16	15	0	.516
Cleveland	1	9	0	.100	Oakland	16	18	0	.471

SUNDAY NIGHT WON-LOST RECORDS, 1978-2011

NATIONAL FOOTBALL CONFERENCE

	Ariz.	Atl.	Car.	Chi.	Dall.	Det.	G.B.	Minn.	N.O.	N.Y.G.	Phil.	St. L.	S.F.	Sea.	T.B.	Wash.
Total	7-13	8-8	5-7	14-18	20-23	5-8	19-5	15-16	14-12	17-22-1	17-13	10-12	11-9	16-11	6-11	15-15-1
2011		1-1	1-1	0-4	0-1		2-0	0-1	2-0	2-1	2-1					
2010			0-1	0-3			3-1	0-1	1-0	1-3	3-0	0-1	0-1	1-0		1-1
2009	2-1	1-0	1-0	0-3	2-1		1-0	0-2		1-2	2-1					0-1
2008		0-1	2-1	3-0			0-1	1-0		2-1	0-2			0-1	1-0	0-2
2007			1-1	3-0			0-1	0-1	1-0	1-2	0-3			0-1		2-0
2006		0-1	2-1	2-1				1-0	1-0	0-2	0-1			1-1		0-1
2005	1-0	0-1		1-0	0-1		1-0	0-1	1-0	0-1	0-1	1-0	0-1	1-0		1-0
2004			1-0	0-1			1-0	1-0	0-1	1-0	1-0	1-0	0-2	0-1		0-2
2003		1-0	0-1	0-1	0-1		1-0	1-1	1-1	0-1		1-0	0-1	1-0	0-1	0-1
2002	0-1	1-0		0-1	0-1		1-0	0-2	1-0	1-0		1-0		1-0	1-1	1-0
2001	0-1			0-1			0-1	0-2			2-0	1-0	2-0	1-1	0-1	1-0
2000	1-1	0-1	1-0	0-2	0-2		1-0	1-0		2-1	1-0	0-1				1-0
1999	0-2	0-1	1-0	0-1		1-0	1-0	0-1	0-1	0-1			2-0	0-2		2-0
1998	1-0	1-0	0-1	0-2	1-0	1-0		2-0	0-1	0-1	0-1		1-0	0-2	0-1	0-1
1997	1-0	0-1	1-1	1-1	0-1	0-2	1-0	1-0	1-0	0-0-1	0-1	0-1	0-1	1-0	1-0	1-0-1
1996	0-1	0-1	1-0			0-1	1-0	2-0	0-1	0-2	1-0	0-1	1-0	0-1	0-1	1-0
1995	0-1	0-2	0-1	1-0				1-1	0-1	1-0	1-0	2-0	1-0	1-0	1-0	0-1
1994	1-1			1-0		1-1			1-0	1-0	0-1	1-0	0-1	0-1		0-1
1993	0-1			1-0		1-0	2-0	1-2	1-0	0-1	1-0	1-0	1-0	0-1	1-0	1-0
1992	0-1			0-1	1-0				1-1	1-1	1-0	1-1	1-0	0-1	0-1	0-1
1991	0-1	1-0		1-0	0-1		1-1	1-1		0-1		0-2		1-1	0-1	2-0
1990	0-1	1-0		1-1	0-1	1-1	0-1	2-0	1-0		0-2	0-1	1-0	2-0	1-0	1-0
1989				0-1			1-0	1-0	0-1			1-0		1-0		0-1
1988				0-1			1-0	0-1	1-0			1-0	0-1	1-0		0-1
1987			1-0	0-1					0-1				2-0	1-0		0-1
1986				0-1								1-0				
1985				1-0						0-1						
1984				1-0					0-1							
1983				0-1												
1982		1-0												0-1		
1981				1-0								0-1				
1980				1-0												
1979				1-0									0-1			
1978										1-0						

SUNDAY NIGHT FOOTBALL ALL-TIME STANDINGS

NATIONAL FOOTBALL CONFERENCE

East	W	L	T	Pct.	South	W	L	T	Pct.
Philadelphia	17	13	0	.567	New Orleans	14	12	0	.538
Washington	15	15	1	.500	Atlanta	8	8	0	.500
Dallas	20	23	0	.465	Carolina	5	7	0	.417
New York Giants	17	22	1	.438	Tampa Bay	6	11	0	.353

North	W	L	T	Pct.	West	W	L	T	Pct.
Green Bay	19	5	0	.792	Seattle	16	11	0	.593
Minnesota	15	16	0	.484	San Francisco	11	9	0	.550
Chicago	14	18	0	.438	St. Louis	10	12	0	.455
Detroit	5	8	0	.385	Arizona	7	13	0	.350

MONDAY NIGHT WON-LOST RECORDS, 1970-2011
AMERICAN FOOTBALL CONFERENCE

	Balt.	Buff.	Cin.	Cle.	Den.	Hou.	Ind.	Jax.	K.C.	Mia.	N.E.	N.Y.J.	Oak.	Pitt.	S.D.	Tenn.
Total	7-9	17-23	9-19	15-14	27-35-1	1-3	21-12	8-7	22-16	40-38	21-22	20-25	37-25-1	39-23	20-17	20-16
2011	0-1				0-1		0-1	1-1	1-1	0-2	2-0	1-0	1-0	0-1	1-1	
2010	2-0	0-1			0-1	0-2	1-0	0-1	1-0	0-1	2-0	1-2		1-0	1-1	1-0
2009	1-1	0-1		0-1	1-1	0-1	1-0			1-1	1-1	0-1	0-1	1-0	1-1	1-0
2008	0-1	0-1		2-1	1-1	1-0	0-1	0-1			1-0	0-1	0-1	2-0	1-0	1-0
2007	0-3	0-1	1-1		1-2		1-0	0-1	0-1	2-0				2-0	1-0	1-1
2006		0-1			1-0		1-0	2-0	0-1	0-1	1-0		0-2	0-1	1-0	
2005	1-1				1-0		3-0		0-1		1-1	0-2		2-1	0-1	
2004	0-1	1-0			0-1		1-0		2-1	1-1	1-1	1-0				1-1
2003			0-1		1-1		1-0		1-0	1-1	1-0	1-0	0-3	0-1	0-1	0-1
2002	1-0				0-2		0-1		1-1	1-1		0-1	2-0	2-1		1-0
2001	2-0			1-1			0-1	0-1		1-0		0-1	1-0	1-0		0-2
2000		0-1			1-1		2-0	0-2	1-1	0-1	1-1	2-0		0-1		3-0
1999		1-0			1-2		2-0		1-2		0-1	2-1	0-1	1-0		
1998					2-1		2-0	0-2	1-2	1-2	1-0			2-1		
1997		1-1			2-1		0-1	1-0	2-0	1-2	1-2		0-2	0-2		
1996		0-2			1-0		1-0		0-2	1-2			2-1	3-0	1-1	
1995		1-1	0-2		1-0				1-1	2-1	1-0		0-2	1-1	1-1	
1994		1-1			0-2				1-1	1-0			1-1	2-0	0-1	0-3
1993		2-1		1-0	0-2		0-1		2-0	1-2			1-0	3-0	2-0	0-1
1992		2-0	0-1	0-1	0-2					1-0	2-1	0-1		0-2	1-0	1-0
1991		2-1	0-2							2-1	1-1	0-1		0-2	0-1	1-1
1990		1-1	1-1	1-1	1-1		0-1		0-1	0-1		0-1	2-0	1-0		1-0
1989		1-2	1-2	1-1	2-0							0-1	1-0			1-0
1988		2-0	1-2	0-2			1-1		1-1			0-1	1-1			1-0
1987		1-0		2-1					1-1	1-1	2-1	1-1				
1986		1-0			1-1				1-2	1-0	1-1		0-1	0-2	0-1	
1985		1-0	1-0		1-0				2-1	0-1	1-0		2-0	0-2	0-1	
1984		0-1	0-1		1-0				3-0		0-1		2-1	1-1	1-2	
1983		0-1	0-2						0-1	1-1		2-0	1-0	1-0	1-1	
1982	0-1	0-1							1-1			1-0	1-0	1-0	1-1	0-1
1981	1-1		0-1	1-0					1-1	0-1		2-1	1-1	2-1	0-1	
1980			1-1	1-2					1-1	1-2	1-0		3-0	0-2	1-0	2-0
1979			1-0	0-2						0-2	0-2	1-1	2-0	2-1	1-0	2-0
1978		1-2		1-1			2-1			2-1	0-2		1-0	1-1	1-0	2-0
1977	0-1	0-1	1-0				1-1		0-1	1-0	0-1		2-0	2-0		
1976		0-2	1-1				2-0		0-1	1-1	1-0	0-1	2-0	0-1		0-1
1975		0-2	1-0		1-1					1-0	1-1	0-1	2-0	1-0	1-0	0-1
1974	1-0	0-1		0-2					1-0	2-0		0-1	0-1	2-0		
1973	1-0		0-1	0-0-1					1-1	2-0		0-1	0-0-1	1-1		
1972				1-0	1-0				1-0	1-0	0-1	0-1	2-0		0-1	0-1
1971			0-1						2-0	1-0		0-1		1-0	0-1	1-0
1970		0-1	2-0		1-1		1-0		1-0	1-0		0-1	1-0	1-0	0-1	0-1

MONDAY NIGHT FOOTBALL ALL-TIME STANDINGS
AMERICAN FOOTBALL CONFERENCE

East	W	L	T	Pct.	South	W	L	T	Pct.
Miami	40	38	0	.513	Indianapolis	21	12	0	.656
New England	21	22	0	.488	Tennessee	20	16	0	.556
Buffalo	17	23	0	.425	Jacksonville	8	7	0	.533
New York Jets	20	25	0	.444	Houston	1	3	0	.250

North	W	L	T	Pct.	West	W	L	T	Pct.
Pittsburgh	39	23	0	.629	Oakland	37	25	1	.595
Cleveland	15	14	0	.517	Kansas City	22	15	0	.595
Baltimore	7	9	0	.438	San Diego	20	17	0	.541
Cincinnati	9	19	0	.321	Denver	27	35	1	.437

From 1970-71, tie games were not included in winning percentage.

MONDAY NIGHT WON-LOST RECORDS, 1970-2011
NATIONAL FOOTBALL CONFERENCE

	Ariz.	Atl.	Car.	Chi.	Dall.	Det.	G.B.	Minn.	N.O.	N.Y.G.	Phil.	St.L.	S.F.	Sea.	T.B.	Wash.
Total	6-14-1	9-24	5-4	23-34	43-30	12-13-1	28-29-1	26-29	16-16	22-32-1	27-23	26-29	41-25	17-8	9-9	26-34
2011		0-1	1-1	1-0	1-0	1-0	0-1	2-0	1-1	0-1	0-2		1-0	1-0	1-0	0-1
2010	0-1	0-1		2-0	0-1		0-1	0-3	2-0	2-0	1-0		1-1			0-1
2009	0-1	0-1	0-1	1-0	1-0		1-1	1-1	2-0	1-0	1-0		1-0			0-2
2008	1-0		1-0	1-0	1-0		1-2	1-1	1-1	0-1	1-1	0-1			0-1	0-1
2007		0-2		0-1	1-0		1-0	1-0	2-0		0-1		1-1	1-0		1-0
2006	0-1		1-1	2-0	0-1		0-2	1-1	1-0	1-1	2-0	0-1		2-0	0-1	0-1
2005		3-0	1-0		1-1		0-3	1-0	0-2	1-0	0-3	0-1	1-0			1-0
2004		0-1		2-1			2-1	0-2			2-1	2-1		0-1	0-1	0-1
2003		0-1	0-1	1-0		2-1			0-2		2-1	2-0	1-0		2-1	
2002			0-3			2-0			0-1		3-0	2-1	1-2	0-1	1-1	0-1
2001				1-0	0-1		2-0	1-1	0-1	0-3	1-0	2-1	1-0		1-0	0-2
2000		1-0		1-1			1-1	1-1					1-2	0-1	1-1	1-2
1999	0-1	1-2			1-2	1-2	2-1		1-0				1-2	1-0	1-0	
1998				2-0	1-1		0-3	1-0		0-2	0-1		3-0		1-1	0-1
1997		1-1	1-1	1-2			3-0	0-1			0-2		3-0			1-0
1996		0-1		2-0	2-1	0-2	2-1	0-1			0-2		2-1			
1995	0-1			1-2	3-0	2-0	1-0	0-2		0-1	0-1		2-1			
1994				0-2	2-1	1-0	1-0	2-0	0-2	1-2	2-0		2-1			
1993		0-1		0-1	1-1		0-1	1-0	2-0	1-0	1-1		1-2			1-2
1992		0-2		0-3	2-1	0-1	1-0	1-0	1-0	1-0			2-0	1-0		1-2
1991				2-1	0-1		0-1	1-0	2-1	2-1	0-1		2-1			2-0
1990						0-1	0-1	1-1	1-1	2-0		0-3	3-0	1-0		0-1
1989				1-1				1-1	1-1	2-1	0-2	0-2	3-0	1-0		0-2
1988	0-1		1-2	1-1			1-0	1-0	1-1	1-0	1-0	1-1	1-0			0-2
1987			1-2	2-1			1-0			0-3		1-2	2-0	0-2		1-1
1986	0-1			2-1	2-0	0-1	0-1		2-1		1-0	0-2	2-0			1-1
1985	1-1			1-1	1-1		0-1		0-1				2-1	1-2	0-2	2-1
1984		0-2		0-1	1-1	0-1	0-1		1-0	0-1	1-1		2-0	2-0		1-1
1983	0-0-1	0-1		1-1	2-0	2-1	0-1	0-1		1-1-1	1-0	1-0			0-1	1-2
1982				1-2	0-1	1-0	1-0			0-1				1-0		
1981		1-2		0-2	2-0	1-0	0-3				1-1	2-0		1-0		
1980		1-1		1-1					0-1	0-1	1-0	2-0		0-1	0-1	0-2
1979		1-2		0-2		1-0	0-1	0-1	0-1		1-1	1-0	2-0			1-0
1978		1-0		0-3	1-1		2-0					0-2	0-1			1-1
1977	2-0			1-0	1-1		0-1	0-1		0-1	1-1	0-2				1-1
1976	0-1			1-0			1-1			0-1		0-2	2-0			2-0
1975	0-1			0-1	1-1	0-1	0-1	1-0		1-0	0-1	1-0				1-0
1974	0-1	0-1		1-0	0-1	1-0	0-1		1-0	0-1	1-0	1-1	0-2			2-0
1973		1-1		0-1	1-1	1-0	1-1	0-1	0-1	0-1		1-0	1-0			1-1
1972	0-1	0-1		1-0	1-0	0-2	1-0	0-2	0-1	1-0	0-1	1-0	0-1			2-0
1971	1-1	1-0		0-1	1-0	0-1-1	0-1-1	2-0		0-1		0-2	0-1			1-0
1970	1-0	0-1		0-1	0-1	2-0	1-1	1-0		0-1	1-0	0-2				0-1

MONDAY NIGHT FOOTBALL ALL-TIME STANDINGS
NATIONAL FOOTBALL CONFERENCE

East	W	L	T	Pct.	South	W	L	T	Pct.
Dallas	43	30	0	.589	Carolina	5	4	0	.556
Philadelphia	27	23	0	.540	New Orleans	16	16	0	.500
Washington	26	34	0	.433	Tampa Bay	9	9	0	.500
New York Giants	22	32	1	.409	Atlanta	9	24	0	.273

North	W	L	T	Pct.	West	W	L	T	Pct.
Green Bay	28	29	1	.491	Seattle	17	8	0	.680
Detroit	12	13	1	.480	San Francisco	41	25	0	.621
Minnesota	26	29	0	.473	St. Louis	26	29	0	.473
Chicago	23	34	0	.404	Arizona	6	14	1	.310

From 1970-71, tie games were not included in winning percentage.

Compiled by Elias Sports Bureau
*NFL record.

MONDAY NIGHT RECORDS

SCORING
TOUCHDOWNS
Most Touchdowns, Career
36 Jerry Rice, San Francisco, 1985-2000;
Oakland, 2001-04; Seattle 2004
24 Emmitt Smith, Dallas, 1990-2002; Arizona 2003-04
20 Terrell Owens, San Francisco, 1996-2003;
Philadelphia, 2004-05; Dallas, 2006-08;
Buffalo, 2009; Cincinnati, 2010

Most Touchdowns, Game
4 Ron Johnson, N.Y. Giants at Philadelphia,
Oct. 2, 1972
Earl Campbell, Houston vs. Miami, Nov. 20, 1978
Marcus Allen, L.A. Raiders vs. San Diego,
Sept. 24, 1984
Eric Dickerson, Indianapolis vs. Denver,
Oct. 31, 1988
Emmitt Smith, Dallas at N.Y. Giants, Sept. 4, 1995
Marshall Faulk, St. Louis at Tampa Bay,
Dec. 18, 2000

FIELD GOALS
Most Field Goals, Career
51 Gary Anderson, Pittsburgh, 1982-1994; Philadelphia,
1995-96; San Francisco, 1997;
Minnesota, 1998-2002; Tennessee, 2003-04
50 Jason Elam, Denver, 1993-2007; Atlanta, 2008-09
42 Ryan Longwell, Green Bay, 1997-2005;
Minnesota, 2006-2011

Most Field Goals, Game
7 Chris Boniol, Dallas vs. Green Bay, Nov. 18, 1996*
Billy Cundiff, Dallas at N.Y. Giants, Sept. 15, 2003 (OT)*
6 Dan Bailey, Dallas vs. Washington, Sept. 26, 2011
5 Tim Mazzetti, Atlanta vs. Los Angeles, Oct. 30, 1978
Roger Ruzek, Dallas at L.A. Rams, Dec. 21, 1987
Rich Karlis, Minnesota vs. Cincinnati, Dec. 25, 1989
Nick Lowery, Kansas City vs. Denver, Sept. 20, 1993
Chris Jacke, Green Bay vs. San Francisco,
Oct. 14, 1996 (OT)
Richie Cunningham, Dallas vs. Philadelphia,
Sept. 15, 1997
Phil Dawson, Cleveland vs. Buffalo, Nov. 17, 2008
Nick Folk, N.Y. Jets vs. Minnesota, Oct. 11, 2010

RUSHING
YARDS GAINED
Most Yards Gained, Career
2,434 Emmitt Smith, Dallas, 1990-2002; Arizona, 2003-04
1,897 Tony Dorsett, Dallas, 1977-1987; Denver, 1988
1,769 Thurman Thomas, Buffalo, 1988-1999; Miami, 2000

Most Yards Gained, Game
221 Bo Jackson, L.A. Raiders at Seattle, Nov. 30, 1987
216 Ricky Williams, Miami vs. Chicago, Dec. 9, 2002
214 Thurman Thomas, Buffalo at N.Y. Jets,
Sept. 24, 1990

Longest Run From Scrimmage, Game
99 Tony Dorsett, Dallas at Minnesota,
Jan. 3, 1983 (TD)*
91 Bo Jackson, L.A. Raiders at Seattle,
Nov. 30, 1987 (TD)
88 Jahvid Best, Detroit vs. Chicago,
Oct. 10, 2011 (TD)

TOUCHDOWNS
Most Rushing Touchdowns, Career
23 Emmitt Smith, Dallas, 1990-2002; Arizona, 2003-04

17 Marcus Allen, L.A. Raiders, 1982-1992;
Kansas City, 1993-97
14 Eric Dickerson, L.A. Rams, 1983-87; Indianapolis,
1987-1991; L.A. Raiders, 1992; Atlanta, 1993

Most Rushing Touchdowns, Game
4 Earl Campbell, Houston vs. Miami, Nov. 20, 1978
Eric Dickerson, Indianapolis vs. Denver,
Oct. 31, 1988
Emmitt Smith, Dallas at N.Y. Giants, Sept. 4, 1995

PASSING
YARDS GAINED
Most Yards Gained, Career
9,654 Dan Marino, Miami, 1983-1999
9,068 Brett Favre, Atlanta, 1991; Green Bay, 1992-2007;
N.Y. Jets, 2008; Minnesota, 2009-2010
5,148 Joe Montana, San Francisco, 1979-1992;
Kansas City, 1993-94

Most Yards Gained, Game
517 Tom Brady, New England vs. Miami, Sept. 12, 2011
458 Joe Montana, San Francisco at L.A. Rams,
Dec. 11, 1989
448 Marc Bulger, St. Louis at Green Bay, Nov. 29, 2004

Longest Pass Play
99 Brett Favre to Robert Brooks, Green Bay at Chicago,
Sept. 11, 1995 (TD)*
Tom Brady to Wes Welker, New England vs. Miami,
Sept. 12, 2011*
97 Bernie Kosar to Webster Slaughter, Cleveland vs.
Chicago, Oct. 23, 1989 (TD)
95 Joe Montana to John Taylor, San Francisco at
L.A. Rams, Dec. 11, 1989 (TD)

TOUCHDOWNS
Most Touchdown Passes, Career
74 Dan Marino, Miami, 1983-1999
69 Brett Favre, Atlanta, 1991; Green Bay, 1992-2007;
N.Y. Jets, 2008; Minnesota, 2009-2010
42 Steve Young, Tampa Bay, 1985-86; San Francisco,
1987-1999

Most Touchdown Passes, Game
5 Dave Krieg, Seattle vs. L.A. Raiders, Nov. 28, 1988
Jim Kelly, Buffalo vs. Cincinnati, Oct. 21, 1991
Vinny Testaverde, N.Y. Jets vs. Miami,
Oct. 23, 2000 (OT)
Ben Roethlisberger, Pittsburgh vs. Baltimore,
Nov. 5, 2007
Drew Brees, New Orleans vs. New England,
Nov. 30, 2009

RECEIVING
PASS RECEPTIONS
Most Pass Receptions, Career
254 Jerry Rice, San Francisco, 1985-2000;
Oakland, 2001-04; Seattle, 2004
124 Andre Reed, Buffalo, 1985-1999; Washington, 2000
123 Cris Carter, Philadelphia, 1987-89; Minnesota,
1990-2001; Miami, 2002

Most Pass Receptions, Game
14 Herman Moore, Detroit vs. Chicago, Dec. 4, 1995
Jerry Rice, San Francisco vs. Minnesota,
Dec. 18, 1995
13 Andre Reed, Buffalo vs. Denver, Sept. 18, 1989
Terrell Owens, San Francisco vs. Philadelphia,
Nov. 25, 2002

YARDS GAINED
Most Yards Gained, Career
4,029 Jerry Rice, San Francisco, 1985-2000;
Oakland, 2001-04; Seattle, 2004
1,783 Andre Reed, Buffalo, 1985-1999; Washington, 2000

1,697   Terrell Owens, San Francisco, 1996-2003;
Philadelphia, 2004-05; Dallas, 2006-08;
Buffalo, 2009; Cincinnati, 2010

Most Yards Gained, Game
289   Jerry Rice, San Francisco vs. Minnesota,
Dec. 18, 1995
286   John Taylor, San Francisco at L.A. Rams,
Dec. 11, 1989
260   Wes Chandler, San Diego vs. Cincinnati,
Dec. 20, 1982

TOUCHDOWN
Most Receiving Touchdowns, Career
34   Jerry Rice, San Francisco, 1985-2000;
Oakland, 2001-04; Seattle, 2004
20   Terrell Owens, San Francisco, 1996-2003;
Philadelphia, 2004-05; Dallas, 2006-08;
Buffalo, 2009; Cincinnati, 2010
17   Randy Moss, Minnesota, 1998-2004;
Oakland, 2005-06; New England, 2007-2010;
Minnesota, 2010; Tennessee, 2010

Most Receiving Touchdowns, Game
3   Ron Johnson, N.Y. Giants at Philadelphia,
Oct. 2, 1972
Wesley Walker, N.Y. Jets at Detroit, Dec. 6, 1982
Steve Largent, Seattle at San Diego, Oct. 29, 1984
Mark Clayton, Miami vs. Dallas, Dec. 17, 1984
Jerry Rice, San Francisco vs. Chicago,
Dec. 14, 1987
Jerry Rice, San Francisco vs. Minnesota,
Dec. 18, 1995
Lamar Thomas, Miami vs. Denver, Dec. 21, 1998
Ed McCaffrey, Denver vs. Miami, Sept. 13, 1999
Randy Moss, Minnesota vs. N.Y. Giants,
Nov. 19, 2001
Isaac Bruce, St. Louis at New Orleans,
Dec. 17, 2001
Terrell Owens, Philadelphia at Dallas, Nov. 15, 2004
Drew Bennett, Tennessee vs. Kansas City,
Dec. 13, 2004
Marvin Harrison, Indianapolis vs. Cincinnati,
Dec. 18, 2006

YARDS FROM SCRIMMAGE
Most Scrimmage Yards, Career
4,116   Jerry Rice, San Francisco, 1985-2000;
Oakland, 2001-04; Seattle, 2004
2,836   Emmitt Smith, Dallas, 1990-2002; Arizona, 2003-04
2,567   Tony Dorsett, Dallas, 1977-1987; Denver, 1988

INTERCEPTIONS BY
Most Interceptions, Career
11   Everson Walls, Dallas, 1981-89; N.Y. Giants,
1990-92; Cleveland, 1992-93
9   Merton Hanks, San Francisco, 1991-98;
Seattle, 1999
8   Emmitt Thomas, Kansas City, 1966-1978
Darren Sharper, Green Bay, 1997-2004; Minnesota,
2005-08; New Orleans, 2009-2010

Most Interceptions, Game
4   Dick Anderson, Miami vs. Pittsburgh, Dec. 3, 1973*
3   Johnny Robinson, Kansas City at Baltimore,
Sept. 28, 1970
Charlie Babb, Miami vs. Oakland, Sept. 22, 1975
Charles Phillips, Oakland vs. Denver, Dec. 8, 1975
Mark Murphy, Washington at San Diego,
Oct. 31, 1983
Ken Easley, Seattle at San Diego, Oct. 29, 1984
Dwayne Harper, San Diego vs. Oakland,
Nov. 27, 1995

Marcus Coleman, N.Y. Jets vs. Miami,
Oct. 23, 2000 (OT)
Keith Bulluck, Tennessee vs. New Orleans,
Sept. 24, 2007

Longest Interception Return
102   Eddie Anderson, L.A. Raiders at Miami,
Dec. 14, 1992 (TD)
101   Lito Sheppard, Philadelphia at Dallas,
Nov. 15, 2004 (TD)
100   Darrelle Revis, N.Y. Jets vs. Miami,
Oct. 17, 2011 (TD)

SACKS
Most Sacks, Career
24.5   Bruce Smith, Buffalo, 1985-1999; Washington,
2000-03
20.0   Richard Dent, Chicago, 1983-1993, 1995;
San Francisco, 1994; Indianapolis, 1996;
Philadelphia, 1997
18.0   Kevin Greene, L.A. Rams, 1985-1992; Pittsburgh,
1993-95; Carolina, 1996, 1998-99;
San Francisco, 1997

PUNTING
Highest Punt Average, Career (Minimum: 25 Punts)
48.27   Shane Lechler, Oakland, 2000-2011
47.57   Mike Scifres, San Diego, 2003-2011
47.12   Andy Lee, San Francisco, 2004-2011

Longest Punt
90   Rodney Williams, N.Y. Giants at Denver,
Sept. 10, 2001
83   Bryan Barker, Jacksonville vs. N.Y. Jets,
Oct. 11, 1999
77   Shane Lechler, Oakland vs. Denver, Sept. 12, 2011

PUNT RETURNS
Longest Punt Return
95   John Taylor, San Francisco vs. Washington,
Nov. 21, 1988 (TD)
94   Dennis McKinnon, Chicago vs. N.Y. Giants,
Sept. 14, 1987 (TD)
Dexter McCluster, Kansas City vs. San Diego,
Sept. 13, 2010 (TD)
93   Dez Bryant, Dallas vs. N.Y. Giants,
Oct. 25, 2010 (TD)

KICKOFF RETURNS
Longest Kickoff Return
105   Terry Fair, Detroit vs. Tampa Bay,
Sept. 28, 1998 (TD)
104   Allen Rossum, San Francisco vs. Arizona,
Nov. 10, 2008 (TD)
103   Terrence McGee, Buffalo vs. Dallas,
Oct. 8, 2007 (TD)
Brandon Tate, New England at Miami,
Oct. 4, 2010 (TD)
David Reed, Baltimore at Houston,
Dec. 13, 2010 (TD)

FUMBLES
Longest Fumble Return
99   Don Griffin, San Francisco vs. Chicago,
Dec. 23, 1991 (TD)
96   Joe Lavender, Philadelphia vs. Dallas,
Sept. 23, 1974 (TD)
93   Adam Archuleta, St. Louis vs. Tampa Bay,
Oct. 18, 2004 (TD)

2011 PRIMETIME GAMES
(Home Team in capitals, games listed in chronological order.)

SUNDAY NIGHT FOOTBALL
NEW YORK JETS 27, Dallas 24
ATLANTA 35, Philadelphia 31
Pittsburgh 23, INDIANAPOLIS 20
BALTIMORE 34, New York Jets 17
Green Bay 25, ATLANTA 14
CHICAGO 39, Minnesota 10
NEW ORLEANS 62, Indianapolis 7
PHILADELPHIA 34, Dallas 7
Baltimore 23, PITTSBURGH 20
New England 37, NEW YORK JETS 16
Philadelphia 17, NEW YORK GIANTS 10
Pittsburgh 13, KANSAS CITY 9
NEW ORLEANS 31, Detroit 17
New York Giants 37, DALLAS 34
SAN DIEGO 34, Baltimore 14
GREEN BAY 35, Chicago 21
NEW YORK GIANTS 31, Dallas 14

MONDAY NIGHT FOOTBALL
New England 38, MIAMI 24
Oakland 23, DENVER 20
NEW YORK GIANTS 28, St. Louis 16
DALLAS 18, Washington 16
TAMPA BAY 24, Indianapolis 17
DETROIT 24, Chicago 13
NEW YORK JETS 24, Miami 6
JACKSONVILLE 12, Baltimore 7
KANSAS CITY 23, San Diego 20 (OT)
Chicago 30, PHILADELPHIA 24
GREEN BAY 45, Minnesota 7
NEW ENGLAND 34, Kansas City 3
NEW ORLEANS 49, New York Giants 24
San Diego 38, JACKSONVILLE 14
SEATTLE 30, St. Louis 13
SAN FRANCISCO 20, Pittsburgh 3
NEW ORLEANS 45, Atlanta 16

THURSDAY-SATURDAY NIGHT FOOTBALL
GREEN BAY 42, New Orleans 34 (Thurs.)
Oakland 24, SAN DIEGO 17 (Thurs.)
DENVER 17, New York Jets 13 (Thurs.)
Green Bay 27, DETROIT 15 (Thurs.)
DALLAS 20, Miami 19 (Thurs.)
BALTIMORE 16, San Francisco 6 (Thurs.)
SEATTLE 31, Philadelphia 14 (Thurs.)
PITTSBURGH 14, Cleveland 3 (Thurs.)
ATLANTA 41, Jacksonville 14 (Thurs.)
Dallas 31, TAMPA BAY 15 (Sat.)
INDIANAPOLIS 19, Houston 16 (Thurs.)

MODIFIED SUDDEN DEATH OVERTIME

For the 2010 postseason, the NFL installed a modified sudden death system to determine the winner when the score is tied at the end of regulation. Beginning in 2012, the system has been expanded to cover all NFL games, including regular-season and preseason games.

Modified sudden death guarantees each team a possession or the opportunity to possess, unless the team that receives the opening kickoff scores a touchdown on its initial possession.

Key Definitions:

Possession: Actual possession of the ball with complete control. The defense gains possession when it catches, intercepts, or recovers a loose ball.

Opportunity to possess: The opportunity to possess occurs only during kicking plays. A kickoff is an opportunity to possess for the receiving team. If the kicking team legally recovers the kick, the receiving team is considered to have had its opportunity. A punt or a field goal that crosses the line of scrimmage and is muffed by the receiving team is considered to be an opportunity to possess for the receivers. Normal touching rules by the kicking team apply.

REGULAR SEASON

At the end of regulation time, the Referee will immediately toss coin at center of field in accordance with rules pertaining to the usual pregame toss. The captain of the visiting team will call the toss prior to the coin being flipped.

Following a three-minute intermission after the end of the regulation game, there shall be a maximum of one 15-minute period. Each team must possess or have the opportunity to possess the ball unless the team that has the ball first scores a touchdown on its initial possession. Play continues in sudden death until a winner is determined, and the game automatically ends upon any score (by safety, field goal, or touchdown) or when a score is awarded by Referee for a palpably unfair act. Each team shall be entitled to two timeouts, and if there is an excess timeout, the usual rules shall apply. Try is not attempted if touchdown scored. Disqualified players are not allowed to return.

If the score is tied at the end of a 15-minute overtime period, the game shall result in a tie.

Instant Replay: No challenges. Reviews to be initiated by the replay official.

POSTSEASON

At the end of regulation time, the Referee will immediately toss coin at center of field in accordance with rules pertaining to the usual pregame toss. The captain of the visiting team will call the toss prior to the coin being flipped.

Following a three-minute intermission after the end of the regulation game, play will be continued in 15-minute periods until a winner is declared. Each team must possess or have the opportunity to possess the ball unless the team that has the ball first scores a touchdown on its initial possession. Play continues in sudden death until a winner is determined, and the game automatically ends upon any score (by safety, field goal, or touchdown) or when a score is awarded by Referee for a palpably unfair act. Each team has three time outs per half and all general timing provisions apply as during a regular game. Try is not attempted if touchdown scored. Disqualified players are not allowed to return.

Instant Replay: No challenges. Reviews to be initiated by the replay official.

* indicates Monday-night game
 # indicates Thursday/Saturday/Sunday-night game
+ indicates Thanksgiving Day game

REGULAR SEASON

Sept. 18, 2011—Dallas 27, San Francisco 24, at San Francisco; 49ers win toss. Touchback. Drive begins on San Francisco 20. Drive ends on San Francisco 31. Lee punts 58 yards to Dallas 11 and D. Harris returns 11 yards to Dallas 22. Bailey kicks 19-yard field goal at 2:50.

Sept. 25, 2011—Detroit 26, Minnesota 23, at Minnesota; Lions win toss. Morris returns kickoff 15 yards. Drive begins on Detroit 27. Hanson kicks 32-yard field goal at 1:53.

Oct. 23, 2011—Denver 18, Miami 15, at Miami; Dolphins win toss. Touchback. Drive begins on Miami 20. Drive ends on Miami 18. Fields punts 48 yards and Cosby returns 22 yards to Denver 45. Drive ends on Denver 47. Colquitt punts 38. Downed on Miami 15. Moore is sacked and fumbles on Miami 43. Broncos' D. Williams recovers at Miami 36. Prater kicks a 52-yard field goal at 7:31.

* Oct. 31, 2011— Kansas City 23, San Diego 20, at Kansas City; Chargers win toss. Touchback. Drive begins on San Diego 20. Drive ends on San Diego 18. Scifres punts 59 yards and McCluster returns 6 yards to Kansas City 29. Illegal block above the waist called. Drive begins on Kansas City 19. Succop kicks 30-yard field goal at 5:19.

Nov. 6, 2011— Arizona 19, St. Louis 13, at Arizona; Rams win toss. Porter returns kickoff 25 yards. Drive begins on St. Louis 27. Drive ends on St. Louis 45. D. Jones punts 54 yards and Peterson returns 99 yards for touchdown at 1:30.

Nov. 13, 2011— New Orleans 26, Atlanta 23, at Atlanta; Falcons win toss. Weems returns kickoff 25 yards. Drive begins on Atlanta 20. Drive ends on Atlanta 28. Bosher punts 45 yards and Sproles makes fair catch at New Orleans 27. Drive ends on New Orleans 36. Morstead punts 64 yards into end zone. Touchback. Drive begins on Atlanta 20. Drive ends on Atlanta 29. Turner stopped on fourth-and-1. Drive begins on Atlanta 29. Kasay kicks 26-yard field goal at 6:31.

Nov. 20, 2011—Dallas 27, Washington 24, at Washington; Redskins win toss. Banks returns kickoff 23 yards. Drive begins on Washington 18. Drive ends on Dallas 34. Gano misses 52-yard field goal. Drive begins on Dallas 42. Bailey kicks 39-yard field goal at 9:13.

Nov. 27, 2011—Denver 16, San Diego 13, at San Diego; Broncos win toss. Decker returns kickoff 16 yards. Drive begins on Denver 20. Drive ends on San Diego 45. Colquitt punts 47 yards to San Diego 8 and Crayton returns for no gain. Drive ends on San Diego 20. Scifres punts 49 yards to Denver 31 and Royal loses one yard on return. Drive begins on Denver 30. Drive ends on Denver 39. Colquitt punts 61 yards into end zone. Touchback. Drive begins on San Diego 20. Drive ends on Denver 35. Novak misses 53-yard field goal. Drive begins on Denver 43. Prater kicks 37-yard field goal at 14:27.

Dec. 4, 2011—Arizona 19, Dallas 13, at Arizona; Cardinals win toss. Touchback. Drive begins on Arizona 20. Kolb completes 52-yard touchdown pass to Stephens-Howling at 3:04.

Dec. 11, 2011—Denver 13, Chicago 10, at Denver; Bears win toss. Touchback. Drive begins on Chicago 20. Barber fumbles on Denver 33. Broncos' Dumervil recovers at Denver 34. Prater kicks 51-yard field goal at 6:20.

Dec. 18, 2011—Arizona 20, Cleveland 17, at Arizona; Browns win toss. Touchback. Drive begins on Cleveland 20. Drive ends on Cleveland 34. Maynard punts 38 yards and Peterson returns 32 yards to Cleveland 40. Feely kicks 22-yard field goal at 3:59.

Dec. 24, 2011—Oakland 16, Kansas City 13, at Kansas City; Raiders win toss. McCann returns kickoff 27 yards. Drive begins on Oakland 24. Janikowski kicks 36-yard field goal at 2:10.

Jan. 1, 2012—Arizona 23, Seattle 20, at Arizona; Seahawks win toss. Washington returns kickoff 47 yards. Drive begins on Seattle 40. Ryan punts 46 yards and Peterson returns 4 yards to Arizona 19. Feely kicks 28-yard field goal at 8:47.

POSTSEASON

Dec. 28, 1958—Baltimore 23, New York Giants 17, at New York in NFL Championship Game; Giants win toss. Maynard returns kickoff to Giants' 20. Chandler punts and Taseff returns one yard to Colts' 20. Ameche scores on 1-yard run at 8:15.

Dec. 23, 1962—Dallas Texans 20, Houston Oilers 17, at Houston in AFL Championship Game; Texans win toss and kick off. Jancik returns kickoff to Oilers' 33. Norton punts and Jackson makes fair catch on Texans' 22. Wilson punts and Jancik makes fair catch on Oilers' 45. Robinson intercepts Blanda's pass and returns 13 yards to Oilers' 47. Wilson's punt rolls dead at Oilers' 12. Hull intercepts Blanda's pass and returns 23 yards to midfield. Brooker kicks 25-yard field goal at 17:54.

Dec. 26, 1965—Green Bay 13, Baltimore 10, at Green Bay in NFL Divisional Playoff Game; Packers win toss. Moore returns kickoff to Packers' 22. Chandler punts and Haymond returns nine yards to Colts' 41. Gilburg punts and Wood makes fair catch at Packers' 21. Chandler punts and Haymond returns one yard to Colts' 41. Michaels misses 47-yard field goal. Chandler kicks 25-yard field goal at 13:39.

Dec. 25, 1971—Miami 27, Kansas City 24, at Kansas City in AFC Divisional Playoff Game; Chiefs win toss. Podolak, after a lateral from Buchanan, returns kickoff to Chiefs' 46. Stenerud's 42-yard field goal is blocked. Seiple punts and Podolak makes fair catch at Chiefs' 17. Wilson punts and Scott returns 18 yards to Dolphins' 39. Yepremian misses 62-yard field goal. Scott intercepts Dawson's pass and returns 13 yards to Dolphins' 46. Seiple punts and Podolak loses one yard to Chiefs' 15. Wilson punts and Scott makes fair catch on Dolphins' 30. Yepremian kicks 37-yard field goal at 22:40.

Dec. 24, 1977—Oakland 37, Baltimore 31, at Baltimore in AFC Divisional Playoff Game; Colts win toss. Raiders start on own 42 following a punt late in the first overtime. Oakland works way into field-goal range on Stabler's 19-yard pass to Branch at Colts' 26. Four plays later, on the second play of the second overtime, Stabler hits Casper with a 10-yard touchdown pass at 15:43.

Jan. 2, 1982—San Diego 41, Miami 38, at Miami in AFC Divisional Playoff Game; Chargers win toss. San Diego drives from its 13 to Miami 8. On second-and-goal, Benirschke misses 27-yard field goal attempt wide left at 9:15. Miami has the ball twice and San Diego twice more before the Dolphins get their third possession. Miami drives from the San Diego 46 to Chargers' 17 and on fourth-and-two, von Schamann's 34-yard field goal attempt is blocked by San Diego's Winslow after 11:27. Fouts then completes four of five passes, including a 39-yarder to Joiner that puts the ball on Dolphins' 10. On first down, Benirschke kicks a 29-yard field goal at 13:52.

Jan. 3, 1987—Cleveland 23, New York Jets 20, at Cleveland in AFC Divisional Playoff Game; Jets win toss. Jets' punt downed at Browns' 26. Moseley's 23-yard field goal attempt is wide right. Teams trade punts. Jets' second punt downed at Browns' 31. First overtime period expires eight plays later with Browns in possession at Jets' 42. Moseley kicks 27-yard field goal four plays into second overtime at 17:02.

Jan. 11, 1987—Denver 23, Cleveland 20, at Cleveland in AFC Championship Game; Browns win toss. Broncos hold Browns on four downs. Browns' punt returned four yards to Denver's 25. Elway completes 22- and 28-yard passes to set up Karlis's 33-yard field goal nine plays into drive at 5:38.

Jan. 3, 1988—Houston 23, Seattle 20, at Houston in AFC Wild Card Game; Seahawks win toss. Rodriguez punts to K. Johnson who returns one yard to Houston 15. Zendejas kicks 32-yard field goal 12 plays later at 8:05.

Dec. 31, 1989—Pittsburgh 26, Houston 23, at Houston in AFC Wild Card Game; Steelers win toss. Steelers punt to Oilers. Oilers' fumble recovered by Woodson and returned three yards. Four plays and 13 yards later, Anderson kicks a 50-yard field goal at 3:26.

Jan. 7, 1990—Los Angeles Rams 19, New York Giants 13, at New York in NFC Divisional Game; Rams win toss. Everett completes two passes to move ball to Giants' 48. White called for pass interference; ball spotted on Giants' 25. Everett hits Anderson with a 30-yard touchdown pass at 1:06.

Jan. 3, 1993—Buffalo 41, Houston 38, at Buffalo in AFC Wild Card Game; Oilers win toss. Oilers begin at 20. After 2 plays,

Moon's pass is intercepted by Odomes who returns ball 2 yards to Houston 35. After 2 plays, Christie kicks 32-yard field goal at 3:06.

Jan. 8, 1994—Kansas City 27, Pittsburgh 24, at Kansas City in AFC Wild Card Game; Chiefs win toss. Hughes returns kickoff 20 yards to Kansas City 25. After 3 plays, Barker punts 48 yards to Pittsburgh 18 where Woodson returns 8 yards to the 26. After 6 plays, Royals punts 30 yards to Kansas City 20. Kansas City drives to Pittsburgh 14 where Lowery kicks 32-yard field goal at 11:03.

Jan. 17, 1999—Atlanta 30, Minnesota 27, at Minnesota in NFC Championship Game; Vikings win toss. Palmer returns kickoff 30 yards to Minnesota 29. After four plays, Berger punts 51 yards to Atlanta 7 where Dwight returns 8 yards to Atlanta 15. Falcons drive to Atlanta 36. Stryzinski punts 37 yards to Vikings' 27. Palmer calls fair catch. Vikings drive to Minnesota 39. Berger punts 52 yards to Atlanta 9. Downed by Vikings. Atlanta drives to Minnesota 21 where Andersen kicks 38-yard field goal at 11:52.

Dec. 30, 2000—Miami 23, Indianapolis 17, at Miami in AFC Wild Card Game; Dolphins win toss. Williams returns kickoff 18 yards to Miami 20. Offensive holding penalty on Freeman, 10 yards, ball spotted on Miami 10. Dolphins drive to Miami 29 where Turk punts 53 yards to Indianapolis 18. Colts drive to Miami 31 where Vanderjagt misses 49-yard field-goal attempt wide right. Dolphins drive to Indianapolis 17 where Smith rushes for a 17-yard touchdown at 11:16.

Jan. 19, 2002—New England 16, Oakland 13, at New England in AFC Divisional Playoff Game; Patriots win toss. Pass returns kickoff 24 yards to New England 34. Patriots drive to Oakland 5. Vinatieri kicks 23-yard field goal at 8:29.

Jan. 11, 2003—Tennessee 34, Pittsburgh 31, at Tennessee in AFC Divisional Playoff Game; Tennessee wins toss. Reed kicks 60 yards. Returned by Simon 21 yards to Tennessee 31. Titans drive to Pittsburgh 8. Nedney's 26-yard field goal is good at 2:15.

Jan. 4, 2004—Green Bay 33, Seattle 27, at Green Bay in NFC Wild Card Game; Seahawks win toss. Morris returns kick to Seattle 33. Seahawks drive to Seattle 42. Rouen's 44-yard punt returned by Chatman to Green Bay 26. Packers drive to Green Bay 31. Bidwell punts 35 yards to Seattle 34. Seahawks drive to Seattle 45. Hasselbeck's pass to Bannister intercepted by Packers' Harris and returned 52 yards for touchdown at 4:25.

Jan. 10, 2004—Carolina 29, St. Louis 23, at St. Louis in NFC Divisional Game; Panthers win toss. Smart returns kick to Carolina 32. Panthers drive to St. Louis 27. Kasay's 45-yard field-goal attempt no good. Rams take over at own 35 and drive to Carolina 35. Wilkins' 53-yard field-goal attempt no good. Panthers take over at Carolina 43, drive to Carolina 47. Sauerbrun punts 40 yards to St. Louis 13. Rams drive to Carolina 38. Bulger's pass intercepted by Manning at Carolina 35. Panthers drive to Carolina 31. First overtime ends. On first play of second overtime, Delhomme passes to Smith for 69-yard touchdown at 15:10.

Jan. 11, 2004—Philadelphia 20, Green Bay 17, at Philadelphia in NFC Divisional Game; Eagles win toss. Thrash returns kick to Philadelphia 28. Eagles drive to Philadelphia 24. Johnson punts 49 yards and Packers start at own 32 after holding penalty. Favre's pass intercepted by Dawkins at Philadelphia 31 and returned to Green Bay 34. Eagles drive to Green Bay 13. Akers kicks 31-yard field goal at 4:48.

Jan. 8, 2005—New York Jets 20, San Diego 17, at San Diego in AFC Wild Card Game; Chargers win toss. Dwight returns kick to San Diego 26. Chargers drive to San Diego 35. Scifres punts 39 yards and ball is downed at the New York 26. Jets gain no yards. Gowin punts 41 yards. Parker loses 3 yards on return. San Diego starts on own 30. Chargers drive to New York 22. Kaeding's 40-yard field-goal attempt no good. Jets drive to San Diego 10. Brien kicks 28-yard field goal at 14:55.

Jan. 15, 2005—Pittsburgh 20, New York Jets 17, at Pittsburgh in AFC Divisional Game; Jets win toss. Cotchery returns kick to New York 31. Jets drive to New York 41. Gowin punts 54 yards. Randle El returns 8 yards to Pittsburgh 13. Steelers drive to New York 15. Reed kicks 33-yard field goal at 11:04.

Jan. 14, 2007—Chicago 27, Seattle 24, at Chicago in NFC Divisional Playoff Game; Seahawks win the toss. Burleson returns kickoff 25 yards to Seahawks 30. Plackemeier punts

18 yards. Drive begins at Bears 34. Gould kicks 49-yard field goal at 4:53.

Jan. 20, 2008—New York Giants 23, Green Bay 20, at Green Bay in NFC Championship Game; Packers win toss. K. Robinson returns kick 19 yards to Green Bay 26. Favre pass intercepted by Webster and returned 9 yards to Green Bay 34. Tynes kicks 47-yard field goal at 12:34.

Jan. 3, 2009—San Diego Chargers 23, Indianapolis 17, at San Diego in AFC Wild Card Playoffs; Chargers win toss. Sproles returns kick 31 yards to San Diego 25. Sproles scores on 22-yard touchdown run at 6:12.

Jan. 10, 2010—Arizona Cardinals 51, Green Bay Packers 45, at Arizona in Wild Card Game; Packers win toss. Touchback. Rodgers is sacked and fumbles, recovered by Dansby for 17-yard touchdown at 1:18.

Jan. 24, 2010—New Orleans Saints 31, Minnesota Vikings 28, at New Orleans in NFC Championship; Saints win toss. Thomas returns kick 40 yards. Drive begins at Saints 39. Hartley kicks 40-yard field goal at 4:45.

Jan. 8, 2012—Denver 29, Pittsburgh 23, at Denver in AFC Wild Card Game; Broncos win toss. Touchback. Drive begins on Denver 20. Tebow completes 80-yard touchdown pass to D. Thomas at 0:11.

Jan. 22, 2012—New York Giants 20, San Francisco 17, at San Francisco in NFC Championship Game; Giants win toss. Touchback. Drive begins on New York 20. Drive ends on New York 34. Weatherford punts 48 yards and K. Williams returns 4 yards to San Francisco 22. Drive ends at San Francisco 31. Lee punts 47 yards and Ross returns 14 yards to New York 36. Drive ends on New York 44. Weatherford punts 37 yards and K. Williams returns 5 yards to San Francisco 24. Fumble recovered by Giants' D. Thomas at San Francisco 24. Tynes kicks 31-yard field goal at 7:50.

NFL POSTSEASON OVERTIME GAMES
(BY LENGTH OF GAME)

Date	Game	Time
Dec. 25, 1971	Miami 27, KANSAS CITY 24	82:40
Dec. 23, 1962	Dallas Texans 20, HOUSTON 17	77:54
Jan. 3, 1987	CLEVELAND 23, N.Y. Jets 20	77:02
Dec. 24, 1977	Oakland 37, BALTIMORE 31	75:43
Jan. 10, 2004	Carolina 29, ST. LOUIS 23	75:10
Jan. 8, 2005	N.Y. Jets 20, SAN DIEGO 17	74:55
Jan 2, 1982	San Diego 41, MIAMI 38	73:52
Dec. 26, 1965	GREEN BAY 13, Baltimore 10	73:39
Jan. 17, 1999	Atlanta 30, MINNESOTA 27	71:52
Dec. 30, 2000	MIAMI 23, Indianapolis 17	71:16
Jan. 15, 2005	PITTSBURGH 20, N.Y. Jets 17	71:04
Jan. 8, 1994	KANSAS CITY 27, Pittsburgh 24	71:03
Jan. 19, 2002	NEW ENGLAND 16, Oakland 13	68:29
Dec. 28, 1958	Baltimore 23, N.Y. GIANTS 17	68:15
Jan. 3, 1988	HOUSTON 23, Seattle 20	68:05
Jan. 22, 2012	N.Y. Giants 20, SAN FRANCISCO 17	67:54
Jan. 3, 2009	SAN DIEGO 23, Indianapolis 17	66:12
Jan. 11, 1987	Denver 23, CLEVELAND 20	65:38
Jan. 14, 2007	CHICAGO 27, Seattle 24	64:53
Jan. 11, 2004	PHILADELPHIA 20, Green Bay 17	64:48
Jan. 24, 2010	NEW ORLEANS 31, Minnesota 28	64:45
Jan. 4, 2004	GREEN BAY 33, Seattle 27	64:25
Dec. 31, 1989	Pittsburgh 26, HOUSTON 23	63:26
Jan. 3, 1993	BUFFALO 41, Houston 38	63:06
Jan. 20, 2008	N.Y. Giants 23, GREEN BAY 20	62:26
Jan. 11, 2003	TENNESSEE 34, Pittsburgh 31	62:15
Jan. 10, 2010	ARIZONA 51, Green Bay 45	61:18
Jan. 7, 1990	L.A. Rams 19, N.Y. GIANTS 13	61:06
Jan. 8, 2012	DENVER 29, Pittsburgh 23	60:11

Home team in CAPS
There have been 29 overtime postseason games dating back to 1958. In 23 cases, both teams had at least one possession. Last time: 1/22/12, N.Y. Giants 20, SAN FRANCISCO 17.

OVERTIME WON-LOST RECORDS, 1974-2011
(REGULAR SEASON)

Team	Win	Loss	Tie	Pct.
AFC				
Baltimore	9	7	1	.559
Buffalo	18	12	0	.600
Cincinnati	15	11	1	.574
Cleveland	16	16	1	.500
Denver	25	15	2	.620
Houston	1	7	0	.125
Indianapolis	12	10	1	.543
Jacksonville	7	4	0	.636
Kansas City	13	18	2	.424
Miami	13	20	1	.397
New England	17	20	0	.459
N.Y. Jets	18	16	2	.528
Oakland	16	17	0	.485
Pittsburgh	20	14	2	.583
San Diego	12	19	0	.387
Tennessee	14	18	0	.438
NFC				
Arizona	22	15	2	.589
Atlanta	13	20	2	.400
Carolina	4	9	0	.308
Chicago	22	16	0	.579
Dallas	17	13	0	.567
Detroit	14	16	1	.467
Green Bay	11	15	4	.433
Minnesota	18	18	2	.500
New Orleans	9	11	0	.450
N.Y. Giants	18	14	2	.559
Philadelphia	11	16	4	.419
St. Louis	12	11	1	.521
San Francisco	19	14	1	.574
Seattle	8	18	0	.307
Tampa Bay	14	16	1	.468
Washington	22	14	1	.608

OVERTIME GAMES BY YEAR
(REGULAR SEASON)

2011-13	2001-17	1991-15	1981-10
2010-19	2000-13	1990-10	1980-13
2009-13	1999-11	1989-11	1979-12
2008-15	1998-7	1988- 9	1978-11
2007-15	1997-17	1987-13	1977-6
2006-11	1996-14	1986-16	1976-5
2005-14	1995-21	1985-10	1975-9
2004-12	1994-16	1984- 9	1974-2
2003-23	1993-7	1983-19	
2002-25*	1992-10	1982- 4	

Record

OVERTIME GAME SUMMARY—1974-2011

There have been 477 overtime games in regular season play since the rule was adopted in 1974 (13 in 2011 season). Breakdown follows:

RESULTS

252 (4) times the team which won the toss won the game (52.8%)

208 (9) times the team which lost the toss won the game (43.6%)

17 (0) games ended tied (3.6%). Last time: Nov. 16, 2008, Philadelphia 13 at Cincinnati 13.

POSSESSIONS

337(10) times both teams had at least one possession (70.7%)

140 (3) times the team which won the toss drove for winning score (104 FG, 36 TD) (29.3%)

Of the 477 overtime games, there were 13 miscellaneous situations in which non-standard possessions took place:

9 (0) times the defense or special teams won without registering an official possession (5 INT, 2 blocked punts, 1 FR, 1 blocked FG) (1.9%)

1 (0) times the special teams forced a fumble on the opening kickoff and drove for winning score (0.2%)

1 (0) times the punting team recovered a muffed punt and drove for winning score with team muffing punt having no official possessions (0.2%)

2 (0) times the team that won the toss elected to kick and the team receiving the ball drove for winning score (0.4%)

SCORING

339(11) games were decided by a field goal (71.1%)

119 (2) games were decided by a touchdown (24.9%)

2 (0) games were decided by a safety (0.4%)

17 (0) games ended tied (3.6%). Last time: Nov. 16, 2008, Philadelphia 13 at Cincinnati 13.

COIN TOSS

468(13) times the team which won the toss elected to receive (98.1%)

9 (0) times the team which won the toss elected to kick off (4 wins) (1.9%)

Note: The number in parentheses is the 2011 Season Total.

MOST OVERTIME GAMES, SEASON

5	Green Bay Packers, 1983
4	Denver Broncos, 1985, 2007
	Cleveland Browns, 1989
	Minnesota Vikings, 1994, 1995
	Arizona Cardinals, 1995, 1997
	San Francisco 49ers, 2001
	Atlanta Falcons, 2002
	San Diego Chargers, 2002
	Carolina Panthers, 2003
	Washington Redskins, 2010
	Arizona Cardinals, 2011

LONGEST CONSECUTIVE GAME STREAKS
WITHOUT OVERTIME (Current)
54   Philadelphia Eagles (Last OT Game, 11/6/08 vs.
       Cincinnati Bengals)
(Record: 110, St. Louis/Phoenix Cardinals, 12/7/86-12/19/93)

There have been 29 overtime postseason games dating back to 1958. In 23 cases, both teams had at least one possession. Last time: 1/22/12, N.Y. Giants 20, SAN FRANCISCO 17.

SHORTEST OVERTIME GAMES
0:11	*DENVER 29, Pittsburgh 23; 1/8/12
0:14	New York Jets 37, BUFFALO 31; 9/8/02
0:16	CHICAGO 37, San Francisco 31; 10/28/01
0:16	Green Bay 19, DENVER 13; 10/29/07
0:17	NEW ORLEANS 20, Seattle 17; 11/16/97
0:21	Chicago 23, DETROIT 17; 11/27/80
0:30	Baltimore 29, NEW ENGLAND 23; 9/4/83
0:34	San Diego 23, WASHINGTON 17; 11/27/05
0:55	New York Giants 16, PHILADELPHIA 10; 9/29/85

Postseason game

LONGEST OVERTIME GAMES
(ALL POSTSEASON GAMES)
22:40	Miami 27, KANSAS CITY 24; 12/25/71
17:54	Dallas Texans 20, HOUSTON 17; 12/23/62
17:02	CLEVELAND 23, New York Jets 20; 1/3/87
15:43	Oakland 37, BALTIMORE 31; 12/24/77
15:10	Carolina 29, ST. LOUIS 23; 1/10/04

OVERTIME SCORING SUMMARY
339	were decided by a field goal
55	were decided by a touchdown pass
32	were decided by a touchdown run
18	were decided by an interception
3	were decided by a fumble recovery (Baltimore 29, New England 23, 9/4/83; Denver 36, Seattle 30, 12/19/99; San Francisco 37, Arizona 31, 11/24/07)
2	were decided on a fake field goal/touchdown pass (Minnesota 22, Chicago 16, 10/16/77; Cleveland 23, Minnesota 17, 12/17/89)
2	were decided by a kickoff return (Chicago 23, Detroit 17, 11/27/80; New York Jets 37, Buffalo 31, 9/8/02)
2	were decided by a safety (Minnesota 23, Los Angeles Rams 21, 11/5/89; Chicago 19, Tennessee 17, 11/14/04)
2	were decided by a punt return (Kansas City 29, San Diego 23, 10/9/95; Arizona 19, St. Louis 13, 11/6/11)
1	was decided on a fake field goal/touchdown run (Los Angeles Rams 27, Minnesota 21, 12/2/79)
1	was decided on a blocked field goal (Denver 30, San Diego 24, 11/17/85)
1	was decided on a blocked field goal/recovery by kicker (Green Bay 12, Chicago 6, 9/7/80)
1	was decided on a blocked field goal/recovery by kicking team (Philadelphia 23, New York Giants 17, 11/20/88)
1	was decided by a blocked punt (Arizona 30, Dallas 24, 10/12/08)
17	ended tied

OVERTIME RECORDS (REGULAR SEASON)
Longest Touchdown Pass
99 Yards — Ron Jaworski to Mike Quick, Philadelphia 23,
       Atlanta 17 (11/10/85)
82 Yards — Tom Brady to Troy Brown, New England 19,
       Miami 13 (10/19/03); Brett Favre to Greg
       Jennings, Green Bay 19, Denver 13 (10/29/07)
76 Yards — Troy Aikman to Raghib Ismail, Dallas 41,
       Washington 35 (9/12/99)

Longest Touchdown Run
96 Yards — Garrison Hearst, San Francisco 36,
       New York Jets 30 (9/6/98)
60 Yards — Herschel Walker, Dallas 23, New England 17
       (11/15/87)
50 Yards — Rashard Mendenhall, Pittsburgh 15, Atlanta 9
       (9/12/10)

Longest Field Goal
57 Yards — Sebastian Janikowski, Oakland 16,
       New York Jets 13 (10/19/08)
53 Yards — Chris Jacke, Green Bay 23, San Francisco 20
       (10/4/96)
52 Yards — Mike Cofer, Indianapolis 27, New York Jets 24
       (9/10/95)

Longest Touchdown Plays
99 Yards — (Pass) Ron Jaworski to Mike Quick,
       Philadelphia 23, Atlanta 17 (11/10/85)
99 Yards — (Punt return) Patrick Peterson, Arizona 19,
       St. Louis 13 (11/6/11)
96 Yards — (Run) Garrison Hearst, San Francisco 36,
       New York Jets 30 (9/6/98)
96 Yards — (Kickoff return) Chad Morton, New York Jets 37,
       Buffalo 31 (9/8/02)
95 Yards — (Kickoff return) Dave Williams, Chicago 23,
       Detroit 17 (11/27/80)

THANKSGIVING DAY FOOTBALL, 1920-2011
(Home Team in capitals, games listed in chronological order.)
(AFL)-American Football League, 1960-69.

Nov. 25, 1920
AKRON PROS 7, Canton Bulldogs 0
Decatur Staleys 6, CHICAGO TIGERS 0
ELYRIA (OH) ATHLETICS* 0, Columbus Panhandles 0
DAYTON TRIANGLES 28, Detroit Heralds 0
CHICAGO BOOSTERS* 27, Hammond Pros 0
All-Tonawanda (NY) 14, ROCHESTER JEFFERSONS 3
* Non league team. Games between league teams and non league teams counted in standings in 1920.

Nov. 24, 1921
Canton Bulldogs 14, AKRON PROS 0
Buffalo All-Americans 7, CHICAGO STALEYS 6

Nov. 30, 1922
Buffalo All-Americans 21, ROCHESTER JEFFERSONS 0
CHICAGO CARDINALS 6, Chicago Bears 0
RACINE LEGION 3, Milwaukee Badgers 0
Oorang Indians 18, COLUMBUS PANHANDLES 6
CANTON BULLDOGS 14, Akron Pros 0

Nov. 29, 1923
CANTON BULLDOGS 28, Toledo Maroons 0
CHICAGO BEARS 3, Chicago Cardinals 0
GREEN BAY PACKERS 19, Hammond Pros 0
Milwaukee Badgers 16, RACINE LEGION 0
AKRON PROS 2, Buffalo All-Americans 0

Nov. 27, 1924
AKRON PROS 22, Buffalo Bisons 0
Chicago Bears 21, CHICAGO CARDINALS 0
FRANKFORD YELLOWJACKETS 32, Dayton Triangles 7
CLEVELAND BULLDOGS 53, Milwaukee Badgers 10 (at Canton, Ohio)
Green Bay Packers 17, KANSAS CITY BLUES 6

Nov. 26, 1925
CHICAGO BEARS 0, Chicago Cardinals 0
Kansas City Cowboys 17, CLEVELAND BULLDOGS 0 (at Hartford, Connecticut)
Rock Island Independents 6, DETROIT PANTHERS 3
POTTSVILLE MAROONS 31, Green Bay Packers 0

Nov. 25, 1926
New York Giants 17, BROOKLYN LIONS 0
Los Angeles Buccaneers 9, DETROIT PANTHERS 6
CHICAGO BEARS 0, Chicago Cardinals 0
FRANKFORD YELLOWJACKETS 20, Green Bay Packers 14
POTTSVILLE MAROONS 8, Providence Steam Roller 0
CANTON BULLDOGS 0, Akron Pros 0

Nov. 24, 1927
Chicago Cardinals 3, CHICAGO BEARS 0
POTTSVILLE MAROONS 6, Providence Steam Roller 0
Green Bay Packers 17, FRANKFORD YELLOWJACKETS 9
Cleveland Bulldogs 30, NEW YORK YANKEES 19

Nov. 29, 1928
Providence Steam Roller 7, POTTSVILLE MAROONS 0
DETROIT WOLVERINES 33, Dayton Triangles 0
FRANKFORD YELLOWJACKETS 2, Green Bay Packers 0
CHICAGO BEARS 34, Chicago Cardinals 0

Nov. 28, 1929
New York Giants 21, STATEN ISLAND STAPLETONS 7
FRANKFORD YELLOWJACKETS 0, Green Bay Packers 0
Chicago Cardinals 40, CHICAGO BEARS 6

Nov. 27, 1930
STATEN ISLAND STAPLETONS 7, New York Giants 6
BROOKLYN DODGERS 33, Providence Steam Roller 12
Green Bay Packers 25, FRANKFORD YELLOWJACKETS 7
CHICAGO BEARS 6, Chicago Cardinals 0

Nov. 26, 1931
Green Bay Packers 38, PROVIDENCE STEAM ROLLER 7
STATEN ISLAND STAPLETONS 9, New York Giants 6
CHICAGO BEARS 18, Chicago Cardinals 7

Nov. 24, 1932
CHICAGO BEARS 34, Chicago Cardinals 0
Green Bay Packers 7, BROOKLYN DODGERS 0
STATEN ISLAND STAPLETONS 13, New York Giants 13

Nov. 30, 1933
Chicago Bears 22, CHICAGO CARDINALS 6
New York Giants 10, BROOKLYN DODGERS 0

Nov. 29, 1934
CHICAGO CARDINALS 6, Green Bay Packers 0
Chicago Bears 19, DETROIT LIONS 16
New York Giants 27, BROOKLYN DODGERS 0

Nov. 28, 1935	New York Giants 21, BROOKLYN DODGERS 0 CHICAGO CARDINALS 9, Green Bay Packers 7 DETROIT LIONS 14, Chicago Bears 2
Nov. 26, 1936	DETROIT LIONS 13, Chicago Bears 7 New York Giants 14, BROOKLYN DODGERS 0
Nov. 25, 1937	Chicago Bears 13, DETROIT LIONS 0 BROOKLYN DODGERS 13, New York Giants 13
Nov. 24, 1938	DETROIT LIONS 14, Chicago Bears 7 BROOKLYN DODGERS 7, New York Giants 7
Nov. 23, 1939#	PHILADELPHIA EAGLES 17, Pittsburgh Steelers 14
Nov. 28, 1940#	PHILADELPHIA EAGLES 7, Pittsburgh Steelers 0

In 1939 and 1940, President Roosevelt moved Thanksgiving one week earlier. Various states celebrated on the date declared by the President, while other states recognized the traditional fourth Thursday of the month. In 1941, Thanksgiving was sanctioned by Congress to be celebrated on the fourth Thursday of November, which it has been ever since.

Nov. 22, 1945	Cleveland Rams 28, DETROIT LIONS 21
Nov. 28, 1946	Boston Yanks 34, DETROIT LIONS 10
Nov. 27, 1947	Chicago Bears 34, DETROIT LIONS 14
Nov. 25, 1948	Chicago Cardinals 28, DETROIT LIONS 14
Nov. 24, 1949	Chicago Bears 28, DETROIT LIONS 7
Nov. 23, 1950	DETROIT LIONS 49, New York Yanks 14 Pittsburgh Steelers 28, CHICAGO CARDINALS 17
Nov. 22, 1951	DETROIT LIONS 52, Green Bay Packers 35
Nov. 27, 1952	DETROIT LIONS 48, Green Bay Packers 24 DALLAS TEXANS 27, Chicago Bears 23 (at Akron, Ohio)
Nov. 26, 1953	DETROIT LIONS 34, Green Bay Packers 15
Nov. 25, 1954	DETROIT LIONS 28, Green Bay Packers 24
Nov. 24, 1955	DETROIT LIONS 24, Green Bay Packers 10
Nov. 22, 1956	Green Bay Packers 24, DETROIT LIONS 20
Nov. 28, 1957	DETROIT LIONS 18, Green Bay Packers 6
Nov. 27, 1958	DETROIT LIONS 24, Green Bay Packers 14
Nov. 26, 1959	Green Bay Packers 24, DETROIT LIONS 17
Nov. 24, 1960	DETROIT LIONS 23, Green Bay Packers 10 (AFL) - NEW YORK TITANS 41, Dallas Texans 35
Nov. 23, 1961	Green Bay Packers 17, DETROIT LIONS 9 (AFL) - NEW YORK TITANS 21, Buffalo Bills 14
Nov. 22, 1962	DETROIT LIONS 26, Green Bay Packers 14 (AFL) - New York Titans 46, DENVER BRONCOS 45
Nov. 28, 1963	DETROIT LIONS 13, Green Bay Packers 13 (AFL) - Oakland Raiders 26, DENVER BRONCOS 10
Nov. 26, 1964	Chicago Bears 27, DETROIT LIONS 24 (AFL) - Buffalo Bills 27, SAN DIEGO CHARGERS 24
Nov. 25, 1965	DETROIT LIONS 24, Baltimore Colts 24 (AFL) - SAN DIEGO CHARGERS 20, Buffalo Bills 20
Nov. 24, 1966	San Francisco 49ers 41, DETROIT LIONS 14 DALLAS COWBOYS 26, Cleveland Browns 14 (AFL) - Buffalo Bills 31, OAKLAND RAIDERS 10
Nov. 23, 1967	Los Angeles Rams 31, DETROIT LIONS 7 DALLAS COWBOYS 46, St. Louis Cardinals 21 (AFL) - Oakland Raiders 44, KANSAS CITY CHIEFS 22 (AFL) - SAN DIEGO CHARGERS 24, Denver Broncos 20

Nov. 28, 1968   Philadelphia Eagles 12, DETROIT LIONS 0
DALLAS COWBOYS 29, Washington Redskins 20
(AFL) - OAKLAND RAIDERS 13, Buffalo Bills 10
(AFL) - KANSAS CITY CHIEFS 24, Houston Oilers 10

Nov. 27, 1969   Minnesota Vikings 27, DETROIT LIONS 0
DALLAS COWBOYS 24, San Francisco 49ers 24
(AFL) - KANSAS CITY CHIEFS 31, Denver Broncos 17
(AFL) - San Diego Chargers 21, HOUSTON OILERS 17

Nov. 26, 1970   DETROIT LIONS 28, Oakland Raiders 14
DALLAS COWBOYS 16, Green Bay Packers 3

Nov. 25, 1971   DETROIT LIONS 32, Kansas City Chiefs 21
DALLAS COWBOYS 28, Los Angeles Rams 21

Nov. 23, 1972   DETROIT LIONS 37, New York Jets 20
San Francisco 49ers 31, DALLAS COWBOYS 10

Nov. 22, 1973   Washington Redskins 20, DETROIT LIONS 0
Miami Dolphins 14, DALLAS COWBOYS 7

Nov. 28, 1974   Denver Broncos 31, DETROIT LIONS 27
DALLAS COWBOYS 24, Washington Redskins 23

Nov. 27, 1975   Los Angeles Rams 20, DETROIT LIONS 0
Buffalo Bills 32, ST. LOUIS CARDINALS 14

Nov. 25, 1976   DETROIT LIONS 27, Buffalo Bills 14
DALLAS COWBOYS 19, St. Louis Cardinals 14

Nov. 24, 1977   Chicago Bears 31, DETROIT LIONS 14
Miami Dolphins 55, ST. LOUIS CARDINALS 14

Nov. 23, 1978   DETROIT LIONS 17, Denver Broncos 14
DALLAS COWBOYS 37, Washington Redskins 10

Nov. 22, 1979   DETROIT LIONS 20, Chicago Bears 0
Houston Oilers 30, DALLAS COWBOYS 24

Nov. 27, 1980   Chicago Bears 23, DETROIT LIONS 17 (OT)
DALLAS COWBOYS 51, Seattle Seahawks 7

Nov. 26, 1981   DETROIT LIONS 27, Kansas City Chiefs 10
DALLAS COWBOYS 10, Chicago Bears 9

Nov. 25, 1982   New York Giants 13, DETROIT LIONS 6
DALLAS COWBOYS 31, Cleveland Browns 14

Nov. 24, 1983   DETROIT LIONS 45, Pittsburgh Steelers 3
DALLAS COWBOYS 35, St. Louis Cardinals 17

Nov. 22, 1984   DETROIT LIONS 31, Green Bay Packers 28
DALLAS COWBOYS 20, New England Patriots 17

Nov. 28, 1985   DETROIT LIONS 31, New York Jets 20
DALLAS COWBOYS 35, St. Louis Cardinals 17

Nov. 27, 1986   Green Bay Packers 44, DETROIT LIONS 40
Seattle Seahawks 31, DALLAS COWBOYS 14

Nov. 26, 1987   Kansas City Chiefs 27, DETROIT LIONS 20
Minnesota Vikings 44, DALLAS COWBOYS 38 (OT)

Nov. 24, 1988   Minnesota Vikings 23, DETROIT LIONS 0
Houston Oilers 25, DALLAS COWBOYS 17

Nov. 23, 1989   DETROIT LIONS 13, Cleveland Browns 10
Philadelphia Eagles 27, DALLAS COWBOYS 0

Nov. 22, 1990   DETROIT LIONS 40, Denver Broncos 27
DALLAS COWBOYS 27, Washington Redskins 17

Nov. 28, 1991   DETROIT LIONS 16, Chicago Bears 6
DALLAS COWBOYS 20, Pittsburgh Steelers 10

Nov. 26, 1992   Houston Oilers 24, DETROIT LIONS 21
DALLAS COWBOYS 30, New York Giants 3

Nov. 25, 1993   Chicago Bears 10, DETROIT LIONS 6
Miami Dolphins 16, DALLAS COWBOYS 14

Nov. 24, 1994	DETROIT LIONS 35, Buffalo Bills 21
	DALLAS COWBOYS 42, Green Bay Packers 31
Nov. 23, 1995	DETROIT LIONS 44, Minnesota Vikings 38
	DALLAS COWBOYS 24, Kansas City Chiefs 12
Nov. 28, 1996	Kansas City Chiefs 28, DETROIT LIONS 24
	DALLAS COWBOYS 21, Washington Redskins 10
Nov. 27, 1997	DETROIT LIONS 55, Chicago Bears 20
	Tennessee Titans 27, DALLAS COWBOYS 14
Nov. 26, 1998	DETROIT LIONS 19, Pittsburgh Steelers 16 (OT)
	Minnesota Vikings 46, DALLAS COWBOYS 36
Nov. 25, 1999	DETROIT LIONS 21, Chicago Bears 17
	DALLAS COWBOYS 20, Miami Dolphins 0
Nov. 23, 2000	DETROIT LIONS 34, New England Patriots 9
	Minnesota Vikings 27, DALLAS COWBOYS 15
Nov. 22, 2001	Green Bay Packers 29, DETROIT LIONS 27
	Denver Broncos 26, DALLAS COWBOYS 24
Nov. 28, 2002	New England Patriots 20, DETROIT LIONS 12
	DALLAS COWBOYS 27, Washington Redskins 20
Nov. 27, 2003	DETROIT LIONS 22, Green Bay Packers 14
	Miami Dolphins 40, DALLAS COWBOYS 21
Nov. 25, 2004	Indianapolis Colts 41, DETROIT LIONS 9
	DALLAS COWBOYS 21, Chicago Bears 7
Nov. 24, 2005	Atlanta Falcons 27, DETROIT LIONS 7
	Denver Broncos 24, DALLAS COWBOYS 21 (OT)
Nov. 23, 2006	Miami Dolphins 27, DETROIT LIONS 10
	DALLAS COWBOYS 38, Tampa Bay Buccaneers 10
	KANSAS CITY CHIEFS 19, Denver Broncos 10
Nov. 22, 2007	Green Bay Packers 37, DETROIT LIONS 26
	DALLAS COWBOYS 34, New York Jets 3
	Indianapolis Colts 31, ATLANTA FALCONS 13
Nov. 27, 2008	Tennessee Titans 47, DETROIT LIONS 10
	DALLAS COWBOYS 34, Seattle Seahawks 9
	PHILADELPHIA EAGLES 48, Arizona Cardinals 20
Nov. 26, 2009	Green Bay Packers 34, DETROIT LIONS 12
	DALLAS COWBOYS 24, Oakland Raiders 7
	DENVER BRONCOS 26, New York Giants 6
Nov. 25, 2010	New England Patriots 45, DETROIT LIONS 24
	New Orleans Saints 30, DALLAS COWBOYS 27
	NEW YORK JETS 26, Cincinnati Bengals 10
Nov. 24, 2011	Green Bay Packers 27, DETROIT LIONS 15
	DALLAS COWBOYS 20, Miami Dolphins 15
	BALTIMORE RAVENS 16, San Francisco 49ers 6

THANKSGIVING DAY RECORDS
*NFL record; stats compiled by Elias Sports Bureau.

SCORING / Most Touchdowns, Game
- 6 Ernie Nevers, Chi. Cardinals vs. Chi. Bears, Nov. 28, 1929*
- 4 Sterling Sharpe, Green Bay at Dallas, Nov. 24, 1994
- 3 By many players

RUSHING / Most Yards Rushing, Game
- 273 O.J. Simpson, Buffalo at Detroit, Nov. 25, 1976
- 198 Bob Hoernschemeyer, Detroit vs. N.Y. Yankees, Nov. 23, 1950
- 195 Earl Campbell, Houston at Dallas, Nov. 22, 1979

PASSING / Most Yards Passing, Game
- 455 Troy Aikman, Dallas vs. Minnesota, Nov. 26, 1998
- 410 Scott Mitchell, Detroit vs. Minnesota, Nov. 23, 1995
- 384 Warren Moon, Minnesota at Detroit, Nov. 23, 1995

PASS RECEIVING
RECEPTIONS / Most Pass Receptions, Game
- 12 Brett Perriman, Detroit vs. Minnesota, Nov. 23, 1995
  - Marvin Harrison, Indianapolis at Detroit, Nov. 25, 2004
- 11 Daryl Johnston, Dallas vs. Miami, Nov. 25, 1993
  - Michael Irvin, Dallas vs. Kansas City, Nov. 23, 1995

YARDS GAINED / Most Yards on Pass Receptions, Game
- 303 Jim Benton, Cleveland at Detroit, Nov. 22, 1945
- 185 Lance Alworth, San Diego vs. Buffalo, Nov. 26, 1964
- 184 Anthony Carter, Minnesota at Dallas, Nov. 26, 1987 (OT)

ASSOCIATED PRESS NFL MOST OUTSTANDING/VALUABLE PLAYERS

THE FOLLOWING AWARDS WERE NAMED BY ASSOCIATED PRESS IN BALLOTING BY A NATIONWIDE PANEL OF MEDIA.

NFL MOST OUTSTANDING PLAYER AWARD

YEAR	PLAYER	POS.	TEAM	ACCOMPLISHMENTS
1957	Jim Brown	RB	Cleveland Browns	Rushed for league-leading 942 yards and added 9 touchdowns as a rookie.
1958	Jim Brown	RB	Cleveland Browns	Rushed for NFL-record 1,527 yards and added 17 touchdowns. Led Browns to 9-3 record.
1959	Charley Conerly	QB	New York Giants	Passed for 14 touchdowns and only 4 interceptions. Led offense to division-leading 284 points.
1960	Norm Van Brocklin	QB	Philadelphia Eagles	Guided Eagles to first division title since 1949. Passed for 2,471 yards and 24 touchdowns.

NFL MOST VALUABLE PLAYER AWARD

YEAR	PLAYER	POS.	TEAM	ACCOMPLISHMENTS
1961	Paul Hornung	RB	Green Bay Packers	Led league in scoring for second straight season with 146 points (10 TD, 15 FG, 41 PAT).
1962	Jim Taylor	RB	Green Bay Packers	League rushing champion with 1,474 yards. Scored all-time record 19 touchdowns.
1963	Y.A. Tittle	QB	New York Giants	Set all-time season record with 36 touchdown passes. Guided league's top offense (5,024 yards).
1964	Johnny Unitas	QB	Baltimore Colts	Guided Colts to NFL's best record (12-2) and league's top offensive attack (4,779 yards).
1965	Jim Brown	RB	Cleveland Browns	Leader of NFL's top rushing attack. Led league with 1,544 yards, added 21 total touchdowns.
1966	Bart Starr	QB	Green Bay Packers	Passed for 14 touchdowns and only 3 interceptions. Led Packers to league-best 12-2 record.
1967	Johnny Unitas	QB	Baltimore Colts	Passed for 3,428 yards and 20 touchdowns. Led Colts to 11-1-2 record.
1968	Earl Morrall	QB	Baltimore Colts	Guided Colts to NFL-best 13-1 record. Led league with 26 touchdown passes.
1969	Roman Gabriel	QB	Los Angeles Rams	Led NFL with 24 touchdown passes. Guided Rams to 11-3 record.
1970	John Brodie	QB	San Francisco 49ers	Took 49ers to first division title. Threw NFL-best 24 touchdown passes.
1971	Alan Page	DT	Minnesota Vikings	Led defense that allowed NFL-low 139 points. Vikings won fourth straight NFC Central title.
1972	Larry Brown	RB	Washington Redskins	Led conference with 1,216 rushing yards. Redskins had NFC-best 11-3 record.
1973	O.J. Simpson	RB	Buffalo Bills	Rushed for all-time record 2,003 yards, including three 200-yard performances.
1974	Ken Stabler	QB	Oakland Raiders	Led league with 26 touchdown passes and only 12 interceptions. Raiders had NFL-best 12-2 record.
1975	Fran Tarkenton	QB	Minnesota Vikings	Tied for league-best 12-2 record. Led NFC with 91.7 passer rating.
1976	Bert Jones	QB	Baltimore Colts	Threw 24 touchdowns and only 9 interceptions for 102.5 passer rating.
1977	Walter Payton	RB	Chicago Bears	Rushed for league-leading 1,852 yards and 16 total touchdowns.
1978	Terry Bradshaw	QB	Pittsburgh Steelers	Led Steelers to league-leading 14-2 mark. Set club record with 28 touchdown passes.
1979	Earl Campbell	RB	Houston Oilers	Led league with 1,697 rushing yards and 19 touchdowns.
1980	Brian Sipe	QB	Cleveland Browns	NFL-best 91.4 passer rating. Set Browns' records with 30 touchdown passes and 4,132 yards.
1981	Ken Anderson	QB	Cincinnati Bengals	Led Bengals to first division title since 1973. NFL-high 98.5 passer rating.
1982	Mark Moseley	K	Washington Redskins	Converted 20 of 21 FGs. Set consecutive field-goal record at 23 (including last three in '81).
1983	Joe Theismann	QB	Washington Redskins	Leader of offense that scored NFL record 541 points. Redskins had NFL-best 14-2 record.
1984	Dan Marino	QB	Miami Dolphins	Set NFL records with 5,084 yards and 48 touchdown passes. Led Dolphins to AFC-best 14-2 mark.
1985	Marcus Allen	RB	Los Angeles Raiders	Rushed for league-leading 1,759 yards. Tied for AFC lead with 11 rushing touchdowns.
1986	Lawrence Taylor	LB	New York Giants	Recorded league-high 20.5 sacks, and led Giants' second-ranked defense (297.3).
1987	John Elway	QB	Denver Broncos	In 12 games, passed for 19 touchdowns and 3,198 yards, including four 300-yard games.
1988	Boomer Esiason	QB	Cincinnati Bengals	Led NFL with 97.4 passer rating. Tied for AFC lead with 28 TD passes.
1989	Joe Montana	QB	San Francisco 49ers	Set NFL record with 112.4 passer rating, including 70.2 completion percentage.
1990	Joe Montana	QB	San Francisco 49ers	Led 49ers to league-best 14-2 record. Completed NFC-high 61.7 percent of passes.
1991	Thurman Thomas	RB	Buffalo Bills	Recorded league-high 2,038 yards from scrimmage (1,407 rushing, 631 receiving).
1992	Steve Young	QB	San Francisco 49ers	NFL's top passer with 107.0 rating. Led 49ers to NFL-best 14-2 record.

1993	Emmitt Smith	RB	Dallas Cowboys	Led league in rushing (1,486 yards) for third straight year despite missing first two games.
1994	Steve Young	QB	San Francisco 49ers	Compiled NFL all-time best 112.8 passer rating. Completed more than 70 percent of his passes.
1995	Brett Favre	QB	Green Bay Packers	Led league with 38 touchdown passes and NFC with 99.5 passer rating.
1996	Brett Favre	QB	Green Bay Packers	Led Packers to top conference record (13-3). Threw NFL-best 39 touchdown passes.
1997*	Brett Favre	QB	Green Bay Packers	Led league with 35 touchdown passes. Led NFC with 3,867 passing yards.
	Barry Sanders	RB	Detroit Lions	Rushed for all-time second-best 2,053 yards, including record 14 straight 100-yard games.
1998	Terrell Davis	RB	Denver Broncos	Rushed for 2,008 yards and scored league-best 23 total touchdowns.
1999	Kurt Warner	QB	St. Louis Rams	Became the second QB in history to have 40 touchdown passes in a season (41).
2000	Marshall Faulk	RB	St. Louis Rams	Set NFL record with 26 touchdowns and led NFC with 2,189 yards from scrimmage.
2001	Kurt Warner	QB	St. Louis Rams	Led NFL with 4,830 passing yards, 36 touchdowns, 68.7 completion percentage, and 101.4 passer rating.
2002	Rich Gannon	QB	Oakland Raiders	Set single-season records with 10 300-yard passing games and 418 completions, and led NFL with 4,689 passing yards.
2003*	Peyton Manning	QB	Indianapolis Colts	Led NFL with 4,267 passing yards, had AFC-best 29 touchdown passes, and posted 99.0 passer rating.
	Steve McNair	QB	Tennessee Titans	Posted NFL-best 100.4 passer rating, passing for 3,215 yards with 24 touchdowns against 7 interceptions.
2004	Peyton Manning	QB	Indianapolis Colts	Set NFL records with 49 touchdown passes and 121.1 passer rating while passing for 4,557 yards.
2005	Shaun Alexander	RB	Seattle Seahawks	Set NFL record with 28 touchdowns and led league with 1,880 rushing yards.
2006	LaDainian Tomlinson	RB	San Diego Chargers	Set NFL record for touchdowns (31) and points scored (186). Rushed for team-record 1,815 yards.
2007	Tom Brady	QB	New England Patriots	Set NFL record with 50 passing touchdowns. Led New England to first 16-0 regular-season record in league history.
2008	Peyton Manning	QB	Indianapolis Colts	Threw for 4,002 yards and 27 touchdowns and 95.0 passer rating. Led Indianapolis to 12-4 record.
2009	Peyton Manning	QB	Indianapolis Colts	Threw for 4,500 yards with 33 touchdowns for 99.9 passer rating while leading Colts to NFL-best 14-2 record.
2010	Tom Brady	QB	New England Patriots	Led league with 111.0 passer rating, throwing for 3,900 yards and 36 touchdowns while guiding Patriots to NFL-best 14-2 record.
2011	Aaron Rodgers	QB	Green Bay Packers	Set NFL record with 122.5 passer rating. Guided Green Bay to NFL-best 15-1 record.

Total Associated Press NFL MVPs: 53
Four-time Winner: Peyton Manning
Three-time Winner: Brett Favre
Two-time Winners: Tom Brady, Joe Montana, Johnny Unitas, Kurt Warner, Steve Young
* The award was shared in 1997 and 2003.

ASSOCIATED PRESS MVPs WHO WON SUPER BOWL/ NFL CHAMPIONSHIP IN SAME SEASON: 13

1961	Paul Hornung	Green Bay Packers
1962	Jim Taylor	Green Bay Packers
1966	Bart Starr	Green Bay Packers
1968	Earl Morrall	Baltimore Colts
1978	Terry Bradshaw	Pittsburgh Steelers
1982	Mark Moseley	Washington Redskins
1986	Lawrence Taylor	New York Giants
1989	Joe Montana	San Francisco 49ers
1993	Emmitt Smith	Dallas Cowboys
1994	Steve Young	San Francisco 49ers
1996	Brett Favre	Green Bay Packers
1998	Terrell Davis	Denver Broncos
1999	Kurt Warner	St. Louis Rams

ASSOCIATED PRESS NFL MVP BY POSITION

Quarterback:	35	Kicker:	1
Running Back:	15	Linebacker:	1
Defensive Tackle:	1		

ASSOCIATED PRESS MVPs BY TEAM

8	Indianapolis/Baltimore Colts	2	Buffalo Bills
			Cincinnati Bengals
7	Green Bay Packers		Cleveland Browns
			Denver Broncos
5	San Francisco 49ers		Houston Oilers/ Tennessee Titans
			Minnesota Vikings
4	St. Louis/Los Angeles Rams		New England Patriots
			New York Giants
3	Oakland/Los Angeles Raiders		
	Washington Redskins	1	Chicago Bears
			Dallas Cowboys
			Detroit Lions
			Miami Dolphins
			Pittsburgh Steelers
			San Diego Chargers
			Seattle Seahawks

AP OFFENSIVE PLAYER OF THE YEAR

1973	O.J. Simpson	RB	Buffalo Bills
1974	Ken Stabler	QB	Oakland Raiders
1975	Fran Tarkenton	QB	Minnesota Vikings
1976	Bert Jones	QB	Baltimore Colts
1977	Walter Payton	RB	Chicago Bears
1978	Earl Campbell	RB	Houston Oilers
1979	Earl Campbell	RB	Houston Oilers
1980	Earl Campbell	RB	Houston Oilers
1981	Ken Anderson	QB	Cincinnati Bengals
1982	Dan Fouts	QB	San Diego Chargers
1983	Joe Theismann	QB	Washington Redskins
1984	Dan Marino	QB	Miami Dolphins
1985	Marcus Allen	RB	Los Angeles Raiders
1986	Eric Dickerson	RB	Los Angeles Rams
1987	Jerry Rice	WR	San Francisco 49ers
1988	Roger Craig	RB	San Francisco 49ers
1989	Joe Montana	QB	San Francisco 49ers
1990	Warren Moon	QB	Houston Oilers
1991	Thurman Thomas	RB	Buffalo Bills
1992	Steve Young	QB	San Francisco 49ers
1993	Jerry Rice	WR	San Francisco 49ers
1994	Barry Sanders	RB	Detroit Lions
1995	Brett Favre	QB	Green Bay Packers
1996	Terrell Davis	RB	Denver Broncos
1997	Barry Sanders	RB	Detroit Lions
1998	Terrell Davis	RB	Denver Broncos
1999	Marshall Faulk	RB	St. Louis Rams
2000	Marshall Faulk	RB	St. Louis Rams
2001	Marshall Faulk	RB	St. Louis Rams
2002	Priest Holmes	RB	Kansas City Chiefs
2003	Jamal Lewis	RB	Baltimore Ravens
2004	Peyton Manning	QB	Indianapolis Colts
2005	Shaun Alexander	RB	Seattle Seahawks
2006	LaDainian Tomlinson	RB	San Diego Chargers
2007	Tom Brady	QB	New England Patriots
2008	Drew Brees	QB	New Orleans Saints
2009	Chris Johnson	RB	Tennessee Titans
2010	Tom Brady	QB	New England Patriots
2011	Drew Brees	QB	New Orleans Saints

AP OFFENSIVE ROOKIE OF THE YEAR

1957	Jim Brown	RB	Cleveland Browns
1958	Jimmy Orr	WR	Pittsburgh Steelers
1959	Nick Pietrosante	RB	Detroit Lions
1960	Gail Cogdill	WR	Detroit Lions
1961	Mike Ditka	TE	Chicago Bears
1962	Ron Bull	RB	Chicago Bears
1963	Paul Flatley	WR	Minnesota Vikings
1964	Charley Taylor	WR	Washington Redskins
1965	Gale Sayers	RB	Chicago Bears
1966	Johnny Roland	RB	St. Louis Cardinals
1967	Mel Farr	RB	Detroit Lions
1968	Earl McCullouch	WR	Detroit Lions
1969	Calvin Hill	RB	Dallas Cowboys
1970	Duane Thomas	RB	Dallas Cowboys
1971	John Brockington	RB	Green Bay Packers
1972	Franco Harris	RB	Pittsburgh Steelers
1973	Chuck Foreman	RB	Minnesota Vikings
1974	Don Woods	RB	San Diego Chargers
1975	Mike Thomas	RB	Washington Redskins
1976	Sammy White	WR	Minnesota Vikings
1977	Tony Dorsett	RB	Dallas Cowboys
1978	Earl Campbell	RB	Houston Oilers
1979	Ottis Anderson	RB	St. Louis Cardinals
1980	Billy Sims	RB	Detroit Lions
1981	George Rogers	RB	New Orleans Saints
1982	Marcus Allen	RB	Los Angeles Raiders
1983	Eric Dickerson	RB	Los Angeles Rams
1984	Louis Lipps	WR	Pittsburgh Steelers
1985	Eddie Brown	WR	Cincinnati Bengals
1986	Rueben Mayes	RB	New Orleans Saints
1987	Troy Stradford	RB	Miami Dolphins
1988	John Stephens	RB	New England Patriots
1989	Barry Sanders	RB	Detroit Lions
1990	Emmitt Smith	RB	Dallas Cowboys
1991	Leonard Russell	RB	New England Patriots
1992	Carl Pickens	WR	Cincinnati Bengals
1993	Jerome Bettis	RB	Los Angeles Rams
1994	Marshall Faulk	RB	Indianapolis Colts
1995	Curtis Martin	RB	New England Patriots
1996	Eddie George	RB	Houston Oilers
1997	Warrick Dunn	RB	Tampa Bay Buccaneers
1998	Randy Moss	WR	Minnesota Vikings
1999	Edgerrin James	RB	Indianapolis Colts
2000	Mike Anderson	RB	Denver Broncos
2001	Anthony Thomas	RB	Chicago Bears
2002	Clinton Portis	RB	Denver Broncos
2003	Anquan Boldin	WR	Arizona Cardinals
2004	Ben Roethlisberger	QB	Pittsburgh Steelers
2005	Carnell Williams	RB	Tampa Bay Buccaneers
2006	Vince Young	QB	Tennessee Titans
2007	Adrian Peterson	RB	Minnesota Vikings
2008	Matt Ryan	QB	Atlanta Falcons
2009	Percy Harvin	WR	Minnesota Vikings
2010	Sam Bradford	QB	St. Louis Rams
2011	Cam Newton	QB	Carolina Panthers

AP DEFENSIVE PLAYER OF THE YEAR

1971	Alan Page	DT	Minnesota Vikings
1972	Joe Greene	DT	Pittsburgh Steelers
1973	Dick Anderson	S	Miami Dolphins
1974	Joe Greene	DT	Pittsburgh Steelers
1975	Mel Blount	CB	Pittsburgh Steelers
1976	Jack Lambert	LB	Pittsburgh Steelers
1977	Harvey Martin	DE	Dallas Cowboys
1978	Randy Gradishar	LB	Denver Broncos
1979	Lee Roy Selmon	DE	Tampa Bay Buccaneers
1980	Lester Hayes	CB	Oakland Raiders
1981	Lawrence Taylor	LB	New York Giants
1982	Lawrence Taylor	LB	New York Giants
1983	Doug Betters	DE	Miami Dolphins
1984	Kenny Easley	S	Seattle Seahawks
1985	Mike Singletary	LB	Chicago Bears
1986	Lawrence Taylor	LB	New York Giants
1987	Reggie White	DT	Philadelphia Eagles
1988	Mike Singletary	LB	Chicago Bears
1989	Keith Millard	DT	Minnesota Vikings
1990	Bruce Smith	DE	Buffalo Bills
1991	Pat Swilling	LB	New Orleans Saints
1992	Cortez Kennedy	DT	Seattle Seahawks
1993	Rod Woodson	CB	Pittsburgh Steelers
1994	Deion Sanders	CB	San Francisco 49ers
1995	Bryce Paup	LB	Buffalo Bills
1996	Bruce Smith	DE	Buffalo Bills
1997	Dana Stubblefield	DT	San Francisco 49ers
1998	Reggie White	DE	Green Bay Packers
1999	Warren Sapp	DT	Tampa Bay Buccaneers
2000	Ray Lewis	LB	Baltimore Ravens
2001	Michael Strahan	DE	New York Giants
2002	Derrick Brooks	LB	Tampa Bay Buccaneers
2003	Ray Lewis	LB	Baltimore Ravens
2004	Ed Reed	S	Baltimore Ravens
2005	Brian Urlacher	LB	Chicago Bears
2006	Jason Taylor	DE	Miami Dolphins
2007	Bob Sanders	S	Indianapolis Colts
2008	James Harrison	LB	Pittsburgh Steelers

2009	Charles Woodson	CB	Green Bay Packers
2010	Troy Polamalu	S	Pittsburgh Steelers
2011	Terrell Suggs	LB	Baltimore Ravens

AP DEFENSIVE ROOKIE OF THE YEAR

1967	Lem Barney	CB	Detroit Lions
1968	Claude Humphrey	DE	Atlanta Falcons
1969	Joe Greene	DT	Pittsburgh Steelers
1970	Bruce Taylor	CB	San Francisco 49ers
1971	Isiah Robertson	LB	Los Angeles Rams
1972	Willie Buchanon	CB	Green Bay Packers
1973	Wally Chambers	DT	Chicago Bears
1974	Jack Lambert	LB	Pittsburgh Steelers
1975	Robert Brazile	LB	Houston Oilers
1976	Mike Haynes	S	New England Patriots
1977	A.J. Duhe	DT	Miami Dolphins
1978	Al Baker	DE	Detroit Lions
1979	Jim Haslett	LB	Buffalo Bills
1980*	Buddy Curry	LB	Atlanta Falcons
	Al Richardson	LB	Atlanta Falcons
1981	Lawrence Taylor	LB	New York Giants
1982	Chip Banks	LB	Cleveland Browns
1983	Vernon Maxwell	LB	Baltimore Colts
1984	Bill Maas	NT	Kansas City Chiefs
1985	Duane Bickett	LB	Indianapolis Colts
1986	John Offerdahl	LB	Miami Dolphins
1987	Shane Conlan	LB	Buffalo Bills
1988	Erik McMillan	S	New York Jets
1989	Derrick Thomas	LB	Kansas City Chiefs
1990	Mark Carrier	S	Chicago Bears
1991	Mike Croel	LB	Denver Broncos
1992	Dale Carter	CB	Kansas City Chiefs
1993	Dana Stubblefield	DT	San Francisco 49ers
1994	Tim Bowens	DT	Miami Dolphins
1995	Hugh Douglas	DE	New York Jets
1996	Simeon Rice	DE	Arizona Cardinals
1997	Peter Boulware	LB	Baltimore Ravens
1998	Charles Woodson	CB	Oakland Raiders
1999	Jevon Kearse	DE	Tennessee Titans
2000	Brian Urlacher	LB	Chicago Bears
2001	Kendrell Bell	LB	Pittsburgh Steelers
2002	Julius Peppers	DE	Carolina Panthers
2003	Terrell Suggs	LB	Baltimore Ravens
2004	Jonathan Vilma	LB	New York Jets
2005	Shawne Merriman	LB	San Diego Chargers
2006	DeMeco Ryans	LB	Houston Texans
2007	Patrick Willis	LB	San Francisco 49ers
2008	Jerod Mayo	LB	New England Patriots
2009	Brian Cushing	LB	Houston Texans
2010	Ndamukong Suh	DT	Detroit Lions
2011	Von Miller	LB	Denver Broncos

*The award was shared in 1980.

AP COMEBACK PLAYER OF THE YEAR

1998	Doug Flutie	QB	Buffalo Bills
1999	Bryant Young	DT	San Francisco 49ers
2000	Joe Johnson	DE	New Orleans Saints
2001	Garrison Hearst	RB	San Francisco 49ers
2002	Tommy Maddox	QB	Pittsburgh Steelers
2003	Jon Kitna	QB	Cincinnati Bengals
2004	Drew Brees	QB	San Diego Chargers
2005*	Steve Smith	WR	Carolina Panthers
	Tedy Bruschi	LB	New England Patriots
2006	Chad Pennington	QB	New York Jets
2007	Greg Ellis	DE	Dallas Cowboys
2008	Chad Pennington	QB	Miami Dolphins
2009	Tom Brady	QB	New England Patriots
2010	Michael Vick	QB	Philadelphia Eagles

2011	Matthew Stafford	QB	Detroit Lions

*The award was shared in 2005.

AP COACH OF THE YEAR

1957	George Wilson	Detroit Lions
1958	Weeb Ewbank	Baltimore Colts
1959	Vince Lombardi	Green Bay Packers
1960	Buck Shaw	Philadelphia Eagles
1961	Allie Sherman	New York Giants
1962	Allie Sherman	New York Giants
1963	George Halas	Chicago Bears
1964	Don Shula	Baltimore Colts
1965	George Halas	Chicago Bears
1966	Tom Landry	Dallas Cowboys
1967*	George Allen	Los Angeles Rams
	Don Shula	Baltimore Colts
1968	Don Shula	Baltimore Colts
1969	Bud Grant	Minnesota Vikings
1970	Paul Brown	Cincinnati Bengals
1971	George Allen	Washington Redskins
1972	Don Shula	Miami Dolphins
1973	Chuck Knox	Los Angeles Rams
1974	Don Coryell	St. Louis Cardinals
1975	Ted Marchibroda	Baltimore Colts
1976	Forrest Gregg	Cleveland Browns
1977	Red Miller	Denver Broncos
1978	Jack Patera	Seattle Seahawks
1979	Jack Pardee	Washington Redskins
1980	Chuck Knox	Buffalo Bills
1981	Bill Walsh	San Francisco 49ers
1982	Joe Gibbs	Washington Redskins
1983	Joe Gibbs	Washington Redskins
1984	Chuck Knox	Seattle Seahawks
1985	Mike Ditka	Chicago Bears
1986	Bill Parcells	New York Giants
1987	Jim Mora	New Orleans Saints
1988	Mike Ditka	Chicago Bears
1989	Lindy Infante	Green Bay Packers
1990	Jimmy Johnson	Dallas Cowboys
1991	Wayne Fontes	Detroit Lions
1992	Bill Cowher	Pittsburgh Steelers
1993	Dan Reeves	New York Giants
1994	Bill Parcells	New England Patriots
1995	Ray Rhodes	Philadelphia Eagles
1996	Dom Capers	Carolina Panthers
1997	Jim Fassel	New York Giants
1998	Dan Reeves	Atlanta Falcons
1999	Dick Vermeil	St. Louis Rams
2000	Jim Haslett	New Orleans Saints
2001	Dick Jauron	Chicago Bears
2002	Andy Reid	Philadelphia Eagles
2003	Bill Belichick	New England Patriots
2004	Marty Schottenheimer	San Diego Chargers
2005	Lovie Smith	Chicago Bears
2006	Sean Payton	New Orleans Saints
2007	Bill Belichick	New England Patriots
2008	Mike Smith	Atlanta Falcons
2009	Marvin Lewis	Cincinnati Bengals
2010	Bill Belichick	New England Patriots
2011	Jim Harbaugh	San Francisco 49ers

*The award was shared in 1967.

NUMBER-ONE DRAFT CHOICES

Season	Date	Team	Player	Position	College
2012	April 26-28	Indianapolis	Andrew Luck	QB	Stanford
2011	April 28-30	Carolina	Cam Newton	QB	Auburn
2010	April 22-24	St. Louis	Sam Bradford	QB	Oklahoma
2009	April 25-26	Detroit	Matthew Stafford	QB	Georgia
2008	April 26-27	Miami	Jake Long	T	Michigan
2007	April 28-29	Oakland	JaMarcus Russell	QB	Louisiana State
2006	April 29-30	Houston	Mario Williams	DE	North Carolina State
2005	April 23-24	San Francisco	Alex Smith	QB	Utah
2004	April 24-25	San Diego	Eli Manning	QB	Mississippi
2003	April 26-27	Cincinnati	Carson Palmer	QB	Southern California
2002	April 20-21	Houston	David Carr	QB	Fresno State
2001	April 21-22	Atlanta	Michael Vick	QB	Virginia Tech
2000	April 15-16	Cleveland	Courtney Brown	DE	Penn State
1999	April 17-18	Cleveland	Tim Couch	QB	Kentucky
1998	April 18-19	Indianapolis	Peyton Manning	QB	Tennessee
1997	April 19-20	St. Louis	Orlando Pace	T	Ohio State
1996	April 20-21	New York Jets	Keyshawn Johnson	WR	Southern California
1995	April 22-23	Cincinnati	Ki-Jana Carter	RB	Penn State
1994	April 24-25	Cincinnati	Dan Wilkinson	DT	Ohio State
1993	April 25-26	New England	Drew Bledsoe	QB	Washington State
1992	April 26-27	Indianapolis	Steve Emtman	DT	Washington
1991	April 21-22	Dallas	Russell Maryland	DT	Miami
1990	April 22-23	Indianapolis	Jeff George	QB	Illinois
1989	April 23-24	Dallas	Troy Aikman	QB	UCLA
1988	April 24-25	Atlanta	Aundray Bruce	LB	Auburn
1987	April 28-29	Tampa Bay	Vinny Testaverde	QB	Miami
1986	April 29-30	Tampa Bay	Bo Jackson	RB	Auburn
1985	April 30-May 1	Buffalo	Bruce Smith	DE	Virginia Tech
1984	May 1-2	New England	Irving Fryar	WR	Nebraska
1983	April 26-27	Baltimore	John Elway	QB	Stanford
1982	April 27-28	New England	Kenneth Sims	DT	Texas
1981	April 28-29	New Orleans	George Rogers	RB	South Carolina
1980	April 29-30	Detroit	Billy Sims	RB	Oklahoma
1979	May 3-4	Buffalo	Tom Cousineau	LB	Ohio State
1978	May 2-3	Houston	Earl Campbell	RB	Texas
1977	May 3-4	Tampa Bay	Ricky Bell	RB	Southern California
1976	April 8-9	Tampa Bay	Lee Roy Selmon	DE	Oklahoma
1975	January 28-29	Atlanta	Steve Bartkowski	QB	California
1974	January 29-30	Dallas	Ed Jones	DE	Tennessee State
1973	January 30-31	Houston	John Matuszak	DE	Tampa
1972	February 1-2	Buffalo	Walt Patulski	DE	Notre Dame
1971	January 28-29	New England	Jim Plunkett	QB	Stanford
1970	January 27-28	Pittsburgh	Terry Bradshaw	QB	Louisiana Tech
1969	January 28-29	Buffalo (AFL)	O.J. Simpson	RB	Southern California
1968	January 30-31	Minnesota	Ron Yary	T	Southern California
1967	March 14	Baltimore	Bubba Smith	DT	Michigan State
1966	November 27, 1965	Atlanta	Tommy Nobis	LB	Texas
	November 28, 1965	Miami (AFL)	Jim Grabowski	RB	Illinois
1965	November 28, 1964	New York Giants	Tucker Frederickson	RB	Auburn
	November 28, 1964	Houston (AFL)	Lawrence Elkins	E	Baylor
1964	December 2, 1963	San Francisco	Dave Parks	E	Texas Tech
	November 30, 1963	Boston (AFL)	Jack Concannon	QB	Boston College
1963	December 3, 1962	Los Angeles	Terry Baker	QB	Oregon State
	December 1, 1962	Kansas City (AFL)	Buck Buchanan	DT	Grambling
1962	December 4, 1961	Washington	Ernie Davis	RB	Syracuse
	December 2, 1961	Oakland (AFL)	Roman Gabriel	QB	North Carolina State
1961	December 27-28, 1960	Minnesota	Tommy Mason	RB	Tulane
	November 23, 1960	Buffalo (AFL)	Ken Rice	G	Auburn
1960	Secret Draft	Los Angeles	Billy Cannon	RB	Louisiana State
	November 22, December 2, 1959	(AFL had no formal first pick)			
1959	December 2, 1958	Green Bay	Randy Duncan	QB	Iowa

Season	Date	Team	Player	Position	College
1958	December 2, 1957	Chicago Cardinals	King Hill	QB	Rice
1957	November 27, 1956	Green Bay	Paul Hornung	HB	Notre Dame
1956	November 29, 1955	Pittsburgh	Gary Glick	DB	Colorado A&M
1955	January 27-28	Baltimore	George Shaw	QB	Oregon
1954	January 28	Cleveland	Bobby Garrett	QB	Stanford
1953	January 22	San Francisco	Harry Babcock	E	Georgia
1952	January 17	Los Angeles	Bill Wade	QB	Vanderbilt
1951	January 18-19	New York Giants	Kyle Rote	HB	Southern Methodist
1950	January 21-22	Detroit	Leon Hart	E	Notre Dame
1949	December 21, 1948	Philadelphia	Chuck Bednarik	C	Pennsylvania
1948	December 19, 1947	Washington	Harry Gilmer	QB	Alabama
1947	December 16, 1946	Chicago Bears	Bob Fenimore	HB	Oklahoma A&M
1946	January 14	Boston	Frank Dancewicz	QB	Notre Dame
1945	April 6	Chicago Cardinals	Charley Trippi	HB	Georgia
1944	April 19	Boston	Angelo Bertelli	QB	Notre Dame
1943	April 8	Detroit	Frank Sinkwich	HB	Georgia
1942	December 22, 1941	Pittsburgh	Bill Dudley	HB	Virginia
1941	December 10, 1940	Chicago Bears	Tom Harmon	HB	Michigan
1940	December 9, 1939	Chicago Cardinals	George Cafego	HB	Tennessee
1939	December 8, 1938	Chicago Cardinals	Ki Aldrich	C	Texas Christian
1938	December 12, 1937	Cleveland	Corbett Davis	FB	Indiana
1937	December 12, 1936	Philadelphia	Sam Francis	FB	Nebraska
1936	February 8	Philadelphia	Jay Berwanger	HB	Chicago

Note: From 1947 through 1958, the first selection in the draft was a Bonus pick, awarded to the winner of a random draw. That club, in turn, forfeited its last-round draft choice. The winner of the Bonus choice was eliminated from future draws. The system was abolished after 1958, by which time all clubs had received a Bonus choice.

NUMBER-ONE DRAFT CHOICES BY POSITION

Quarterbacks:	31
Running Backs:	23
Defensive Linemen:	13
Offensive Linemen:	6
Wide Receivers:	6
Linebackers:	3
Defensive Backs:	1

FIRST-ROUND SELECTIONS

If club had no first-round selection, first player drafted is listed with round in parentheses.

ARIZONA CARDINALS
Year Player, College, Position
1936 Jim Lawrence, Texas Christian, B
1937 Ray Buivid, Marquette, B
1938 Jack Robbins, Arkansas, B
1939 Charles (Ki) Aldrich, TCU, C
1940 George Cafego, Tennessee, B
1941 John Kimbrough, Texas A&M, B
1942 Steve Lach, Duke, B
1943 Glenn Dobbs, Tulsa, B
1944 Pat Harder, Wisconsin, B
1945 Charley Trippi, Georgia, B
1946 Dub Jones, Louisiana State, B
1947 DeWitt (Tex) Coulter, Army, T
1948 Jim Spavital, Oklahoma A&M, B
1949 Bill Fischer, Notre Dame, G
1950 Jack Jennings, Ohio State, T (2)
1951 Jerry Groom, Notre Dame, C
1952 Ollie Matson, San Francisco, B
1953 Johnny Olszewski, California, B
1954 Lamar McHan, Arkansas, B
1955 Max Boydston, Oklahoma, E
1956 Joe Childress, Auburn, B
1957 Jerry Tubbs, Oklahoma, C
1958 King Hill, Rice, B
      John David Crow, Texas A&M, B
1959 Bill Stacy, Mississippi State, B
1960 George Izo, Notre Dame, QB
1961 Ken Rice, Auburn, T
1962 Fate Echols, Northwestern, DT
      Irv Goode, Kentucky, C
1963 Jerry Stovall, Louisiana State, S
      Don Brumm, Purdue, DE
1964 Ken Kortas, Louisville, DT
1965 Joe Namath, Alabama, QB
1966 Carl McAdams, Oklahoma, LB
1967 Dave Williams, Washington, WR
1968 MacArthur Lane, Utah State, RB
1969 Roger Wehrli, Missouri, DB
1970 Larry Stegent, Texas A&M, RB
1971 Norm Thompson, Utah, CB
1972 Ahmad Rashad, Oregon, RB-WR
1973 Dave Butz, Purdue, DT
1974 J.V. Cain, Colorado, TE
1975 Tim Gray, Texas A&M, DB
1976 Mike Dawson, Arizona, DT
1977 Steve Pisarkiewicz, Missouri, QB
1978 Steve Little, Arkansas, K
      Ken Greene, Washington State, DB
1979 Ottis Anderson, Miami, RB
1980 Curtis Greer, Michigan, DE
1981 E.J. Junior, Alabama, LB
1982 Luis Sharpe, UCLA, T
1983 Leonard Smith, McNeese St., DB
1984 Clyde Duncan, Tennessee, WR
1985 Freddie Joe Nunn, Mississippi, LB
1986 Anthony Bell, Michigan State, LB
1987 Kelly Stouffer, Colorado State, QB
1988 Ken Harvey, California, LB
1989 Eric Hill, Louisiana State, LB
      Joe Wolf, Boston College, G
1990 Anthony Thompson, Indiana, RB (2)
1991 Eric Swann, No College, DE
1992 Tony Sacca, Penn State, QB (2)

1993 Garrison Hearst, Georgia, RB
      Ernest Dye, South Carolina, T
1994 Jamir Miller, UCLA, LB
1995 Frank Sanders, Auburn, WR (2)
1996 Simeon Rice, Illinois, DE
1997 Tom Knight, Iowa, DB
1998 Andre Wadsworth, Florida St., DE
1999 David Boston, Ohio State, WR
      L.J. Shelton, Eastern Michigan, T
2000 Thomas Jones, Virginia, RB
2001 Leonard Davis, Texas, T
2002 Wendell Bryant, Wisconsin, DT
2003 Bryant Johnson, Penn State, WR
      Calvin Pace, Wake Forest, DE
2004 Larry Fitzgerald, Pittsburgh, WR
2005 Antrel Rolle, Miami, DB
2006 Matt Leinart, So. California, QB
2007 Levi Brown, Penn State, T
2008 Dominique Rodgers-Cromartie, Tenn. St., DB
2009 Beanie Wells, Ohio State, RB
2010 Dan Williams, Tennessee, DT
2011 Patrick Peterson, Louisiana St., DB
2012 Michael Floyd, Notre Dame, WR

ATLANTA FALCONS
Year Player, College, Position
1966 Tommy Nobis, Texas, LB
      Randy Johnson, Texas A&I, QB
1967 Leo Carroll, San Diego St., DE (2)
1968 Claude Humphrey, Tennessee St., DE
1969 George Kunz, Notre Dame, T
1970 John Small, Citadel, LB
1971 Joe Profit, Northeast Louisiana, RB
1972 Clarence Ellis, Notre Dame, DB
1973 Greg Marx, Notre Dame, DT (2)
1974 Gerald Tinker, Kent State, WR (2)
1975 Steve Bartkowski, California, QB
1976 Bubba Bean, Texas A&M, RB
1977 Warren Bryant, Kentucky, T
      Wilson Faumuina, San Jose St., DT
1978 Mike Kenn, Michigan, T
1979 Don Smith, Miami, DE
1980 Junior Miller, Nebraska, TE
1981 Bobby Butler, Florida State, DB
1982 Gerald Riggs, Arizona State, RB
1983 Mike Pitts, Alabama, DE
1984 Rick Bryan, Oklahoma, DT
1985 Bill Fralic, Pittsburgh, T
1986 Tony Casillas, Oklahoma, NT
      Tim Green, Syracuse, LB
1987 Chris Miller, Oregon, QB
1988 Aundray Bruce, Auburn, LB
1989 Deion Sanders, Florida State, DB
      Shawn Collins, No. Arizona, WR
1990 Steve Broussard, Washington St., RB
1991 Bruce Pickens, Nebraska, DB
      Mike Pritchard, Colorado, WR
1992 Bob Whitfield, Stanford, T
      Tony Smith, So. Mississippi, RB
1993 Lincoln Kennedy, Washington, T
1994 Bert Emanuel, Rice, WR (2)
1995 Devin Bush, Florida State, DB
1996 Shannon Brown, Alabama, DT (3)
1997 Michael Booker, Nebraska, DB
1998 Keith Brooking, Georgia Tech, LB
1999 Patrick Kerney, Virginia, DE
2000 Travis Claridge, So. California, T (2)
2001 Michael Vick, Virginia Tech, QB
2002 T.J. Duckett, Michigan State, RB
2003 Bryan Scott, Penn State, DB (2)

2004 DeAngelo Hall, Virginia Tech, DB
      Michael Jenkins, Ohio State, WR
2005 Roddy White, Ala.-Birmingham, WR
2006 Jimmy Williams, Virginia Tech, DB (2)
2007 Jamaal Anderson, Arkansas, DE
2008 Matt Ryan, Boston College, QB
      Sam Baker, So. California, T
2009 Peria Jerry, Mississippi, DT
2010 Sean Weatherspoon, Missouri, LB
2011 Julio Jones, Alabama, WR
2012 Peter Konz, Wisconsin, G (2)

BALTIMORE RAVENS
Year Player, College, Position
1996 Jonathan Ogden, UCLA, T
      Ray Lewis, Miami, LB
1997 Peter Boulware, Florida State, DE
1998 Duane Starks, Miami, DB
1999 Chris McAlister, Arizona, DB
2000 Jamal Lewis, Tennessee, RB
      Travis Taylor, Florida, WR
2001 Todd Heap, Arizona State, TE
2002 Ed Reed, Miami, DB
2003 Terrell Suggs, Arizona State, DE
      Kyle Boller, California, QB
2004 Dwan Edwards, Oregon St., DT (2)
2005 Mark Clayton, Oklahoma, WR
2006 Haloti Ngata, Oregon, DT
2007 Ben Grubbs, Auburn, G
2008 Joe Flacco, Delaware, QB
2009 Michael Oher, Mississippi, T
2010 Sergio Kindle, Texas, LB (2)
2011 Jimmy Smith, Colorado, DB
2012 Courtney Upshaw, Alabama, LB (2)

BUFFALO BILLS
Year Player, College, Position
1960 Richie Lucas, Penn State, QB
1961 Ken Rice, Auburn, T
1962 Ernie Davis, Syracuse, RB
1963 Dave Behrman, Michigan State, C
1964 Carl Eller, Minnesota, DE
1965 Jim Davidson, Ohio State, T
1966 Mike Dennis, Mississippi, RB
1967 John Pitts, Arizona State, S
1968 Haven Moses, San Diego St., WR
1969 O.J. Simpson, So. California, RB
1970 Al Cowlings, So. California, DE
1971 J.D. Hill, Arizona State, WR
1972 Walt Patulski, Notre Dame, DE
1973 Paul Seymour, Michigan, TE
      Joe DeLamielleure, Michigan St., G
1974 Reuben Gant, Oklahoma State, TE
1975 Tom Ruud, Nebraska, LB
1976 Mario Clark, Oregon, DB
1977 Phil Dokes, Oklahoma State, DT
1978 Terry Miller, Oklahoma State, RB
1979 Tom Cousineau, Ohio State, LB
      Jerry Butler, Clemson, WR
1980 Jim Ritcher, North Carolina St., C
1981 Booker Moore, Penn State, RB
1982 Perry Tuttle, Clemson, WR
1983 Tony Hunter, Notre Dame, TE
      Jim Kelly, Miami, QB
1984 Greg Bell, Notre Dame, RB
1985 Bruce Smith, Virginia Tech, DE
      Derrick Burroughs, Memphis St., DB
1986 Ronnie Harmon, Iowa, RB
      Will Wolford, Vanderbilt, T
1987 Shane Conlan, Penn State, LB

1988 Thurman Thomas, Oklahoma St., RB (2)
1989 Don Beebe, Chadron, Neb., WR (3)
1990 James Williams, Fresno State, DB
1991 Henry Jones, Illinois, DB
1992 John Fina, Arizona, T
1993 Thomas Smith, North Carolina, DB
1994 Jeff Burris, Notre Dame, DB
1995 Ruben Brown, Pittsburgh, G
1996 Eric Moulds, Mississippi St., WR
1997 Antowain Smith, Houston, RB
1998 Sam Cowart, Florida State, LB (2)
1999 Antoine Winfield, Ohio State, DB
2000 Erik Flowers, Arizona State, DE
2001 Nate Clements, Ohio State, DB
2002 Mike Williams, Texas, T
2003 Willis McGahee, Miami, RB
2004 Lee Evans, Wisconsin, WR
     J.P. Losman, Tulane, QB
2005 Roscoe Parrish, Miami, WR (2)
2006 Donte' Whitner, Ohio State, DB
     John McCargo, North Carolina St., DT
2007 Marshawn Lynch, California, RB
2008 Leodis McKelvin, Troy, DB
2009 Aaron Maybin, Penn State, DE
     Eric Wood, Louisville, C
2010 C.J. Spiller, Clemson, RB
2011 Marcell Dareus, Alabama, DT
2012 Stephon Gilmore, South Carolina, DB

CAROLINA PANTHERS
Year Player, College, Position
1995 Kerry Collins, Penn State, QB
     Tyrone Poole, Ft. Valley State, DB
     Blake Brockermeyer, Texas, T
1996 Tim Biakabutuka, Michigan, RB
1997 Rae Carruth, Colorado, WR
1998 Jason Peter, Nebraska, DT
1999 Chris Terry, Georgia, T (2)
2000 Rashard Anderson, Jackson St., DB
2001 Dan Morgan, Miami, LB
2002 Julius Peppers, North Carolina, DE
2003 Jordan Gross, Utah, T
2004 Chris Gamble, Ohio State, DB
2005 Thomas Davis, Georgia, DB
2006 DeAngelo Williams, Memphis, RB
2007 Jon Beason, Miami, LB
2008 Jonathan Stewart, Oregon, RB
     Jeff Otah, Pittsburgh, T
2009 Everette Brown, Florida St., DE (2)
2010 Jimmy Clausen, Notre Dame, QB (2)
2011 Cam Newton, Auburn, QB
2012 Luke Kuechly, Boston College, LB

CHICAGO BEARS
Year Player, College, Position
1936 Joe Stydahar, West Virginia, T
1937 Les McDonald, Nebraska, E
1938 Joe Gray, Oregon State, B
1939 Sid Luckman, Columbia, QB
     Bill Osmanski, Holy Cross, B
1940 Clyde (Bulldog) Turner, Hardin-Simmons, C
1941 Tom Harmon, Michigan, B
     Norm Standlee, Stanford, B
     Don Scott, Ohio State, B
1942 Frankie Albert, Stanford, B
1943 Bob Steber, Missouri, B
1944 Ray Evans, Kansas, B
1945 Don Lund, Michigan, B
1946 Johnny Lujack, Notre Dame, QB

1947 Bob Fenimore, Oklahoma State, B
     Don Kindt, Wisconsin, B
1948 Bobby Layne, Texas, QB
     Max Bumgardner, Texas, E
1949 Dick Harris, Texas, C
1950 Chuck Hunsinger, Florida, B
     Fred Morrison, Ohio State, B
1951 Bob Williams, Notre Dame, B
     Billy Stone, Bradley, B
     Gene Schroeder, Virginia, E
1952 Jim Dooley, Miami, B
1953 Billy Anderson, Compton (Calif.) J.C., B
1954 Stan Wallace, Illinois, B
1955 Ron Drzewiecki, Marquette, B
1956 Menan (Tex) Schriewer, Texas, E
1957 Earl Leggett, Louisiana State, T
1958 Chuck Howley, West Virginia, G
1959 Don Clark, Ohio State, B
1960 Roger Davis, Syracuse, G
1961 Mike Ditka, Pittsburgh, E
1962 Ronnie Bull, Baylor, RB
1963 Dave Behrman, Michigan State, C
1964 Dick Evey, Tennessee, DT
1965 Dick Butkus, Illinois, LB
     Gale Sayers, Kansas, RB
     Steve DeLong, Tennessee, T
1966 George Rice, Louisiana State, DT
1967 Loyd Phillips, Arkansas, DE
1968 Mike Hull, Southern California, RB
1969 Rufus Mayes, Ohio State, T
1970 George Farmer, UCLA, WR (3)
1971 Joe Moore, Missouri, RB
1972 Lionel Antoine, Southern Illinois, T
     Craig Clemons, Iowa, DB
1973 Wally Chambers, Eastern Kentucky, DE
1974 Waymond Bryant, Tennessee St., LB
     Dave Gallagher, Michigan, DT
1975 Walter Payton, Jackson State, RB
1976 Dennis Lick, Wisconsin, T
1977 Ted Albrecht, California, T
1978 Brad Shearer, Texas, DT (3)
1979 Dan Hampton, Arkansas, DT
     Al Harris, Arizona State, DE
1980 Otis Wilson, Louisville, LB
1981 Keith Van Horne, So. California, T
1982 Jim McMahon, Brigham Young, QB
1983 Jim Covert, Pittsburgh, T
     Willie Gault, Tennessee, WR
1984 Wilber Marshall, Florida, LB
1985 William Perry, Clemson, DT
1986 Neal Anderson, Florida, RB
1987 Jim Harbaugh, Michigan, QB
1988 Brad Muster, Stanford, RB
     Wendell Davis, Louisiana St., WR
1989 Donnell Woolford, Clemson, DB
     Trace Armstrong, Florida, DE
1990 Mark Carrier, So. California, DB
1991 Stan Thomas, Texas, T
1992 Alonzo Spellman, Ohio State, DE
1993 Curtis Conway, So. California, WR
1994 John Thierry, Alcorn State, DE
1995 Rashaan Salaam, Colorado, RB
1996 Walt Harris, Mississippi State, DB
1997 John Allred, So. California, TE (2)
1998 Curtis Enis, Penn State, RB
1999 Cade McNown, UCLA, QB
2000 Brian Urlacher, New Mexico, LB
2001 David Terrell, Michigan, WR
2002 Marc Colombo, Boston College, T

2003 Michael Haynes, Penn State, DE
     Rex Grossman, Florida, QB
2004 Tommie Harris, Oklahoma, DT
2005 Cedric Benson, Texas, RB
2006 Danieal Manning, Abilene Christian, DB (2)
2007 Greg Olsen, Miami, TE
2008 Chris Williams, Vanderbilt, T
2009 Jarron Gilbert, San Jose State, DT (3)
2010 Major Wright, Florida, DB (3)
2011 Gabe Carimi, Wisconsin, T
2012 Shea McClellin, Boise State, DE

CINCINNATI BENGALS
Year Player, College, Position
1968 Bob Johnson, Tennessee, C
1969 Greg Cook, Cincinnati, QB
1970 Mike Reid, Penn State, DT
1971 Vernon Holland, Tennessee St., T
1972 Sherman White, California, DE
1973 Isaac Curtis, San Diego State, WR
1974 Bill Kollar, Montana State, T
1975 Glenn Cameron, Florida, LB
1976 Billy Brooks, Oklahoma, WR
     Archie Griffin, Ohio State, RB
1977 Eddie Edwards, Miami, DT
     Wilson Whitley, Houston, DT
     Mike Cobb, Michigan State, TE
1978 Ross Browner, Notre Dame, DT
     Blair Bush, Washington, C
1979 Jack Thompson, Washington St., QB
     Charles Alexander, Louisiana St., RB
1980 Anthony Muñoz, So. California, T
1981 David Verser, Kansas, WR
1982 Glen Collins, Mississippi State, DE
1983 Dave Rimington, Nebraska, C
1984 Ricky Hunley, Arizona, LB
     Pete Koch, Maryland, DE
     Brian Blados, North Carolina, T
1985 Eddie Brown, Miami, WR
     Emanuel King, Alabama, LB
1986 Joe Kelly, Washington, LB
     Tim McGee, Tennessee, WR
1987 Jason Buck, Brigham Young, DE
1988 Rickey Dixon, Oklahoma, DB
1989 Eric Ball, UCLA, RB (2)
1990 James Francis, Baylor, LB
1991 Alfred Williams, Colorado, LB
1992 David Klingler, Houston, QB
     Darryl Williams, Miami, DB
1993 John Copeland, Alabama, DE
1994 Dan Wilkinson, Ohio State, DT
1995 Ki-Jana Carter, Penn State, RB
1996 Willie Anderson, Auburn, T
1997 Reinard Wilson, Florida State, LB
1998 Takeo Spikes, Auburn, LB
     Brian Simmons, North Carolina, LB
1999 Akili Smith, Oregon, QB
2000 Peter Warrick, Florida State, WR
2001 Justin Smith, Missouri, DE
2002 Levi Jones, Arizona State, T
2003 Carson Palmer, Southern California, QB
2004 Chris Perry, Michigan, RB
2005 David Pollack, Georgia, LB
2006 Johnathan Joseph, South Carolina, DB
2007 Leon Hall, Michigan, DB
2008 Keith Rivers, So. California, LB
2009 Andre Smith, Alabama, T
2010 Jermaine Gresham, Oklahoma, TE
2011 A.J. Green, Georgia, WR

2012 Dre Kirkpatrick, Alabama, DB
     Kevin Zeitler, Wisconsin, G

CLEVELAND BROWNS
Year Player, College, Position
1950 Ken Carpenter, Oregon State, B
1951 Ken Konz, Louisiana State, B
1952 Bert Rechichar, Tennessee, DB
     Harry Agganis, Boston U., QB
1953 Doug Atkins, Tennessee, DE
1954 Bobby Garrett, Stanford, QB
     John Bauer, Illinois, G
1955 Kurt Burris, Oklahoma, C
1956 Preston Carpenter, Arkansas, B
1957 Jim Brown, Syracuse, RB
1958 Jim Shofner, Texas Christian, DB
1959 Rich Kreitling, Illinois, DE
1960 Jim Houston, Ohio State, DE
1961 Bobby Crespino, Mississippi, TE
1962 Gary Collins, Maryland, WR
     Leroy Jackson, Western Illinois, RB
1963 Tom Hutchinson, Kentucky, WR
1964 Paul Warfield, Ohio State, WR
1965 James Garcia, Purdue, T (2)
1966 Milt Morin, Massachusetts, TE
1967 Bob Matheson, Duke, LB
1968 Marvin Upshaw, Trinity, Tex., DT-DE
1969 Ron Johnson, Michigan, RB
1970 Mike Phipps, Purdue, QB
     Bob McKay, Texas, T
1971 Clarence Scott, Kansas State, CB
1972 Thom Darden, Michigan, DB
1973 Steve Holden, Arizona State, WR
     Pete Adams, Southern California, T (2)
1974 Billy Corbett, Johnson C. Smith, T (2)
1975 Mack Mitchell, Houston, DE
1976 Mike Pruitt, Purdue, RB
1977 Robert Jackson, Texas A&M, LB
1978 Clay Matthews, So. California, LB
     Ozzie Newsome, Alabama, TE
1979 Willis Adams, Houston, WR
1980 Charles White, So. California, RB
1981 Hanford Dixon, So. Mississippi, DB
1982 Chip Banks, So. California, LB
1983 Ron Brown, Arizona State, WR (2)
1984 Don Rogers, UCLA, DB
1985 Greg Allen, Florida State, RB (2)
1986 Webster Slaughter, San Diego St., WR (2)
1987 Mike Junkin, Duke, LB
1988 Clifford Charlton, Florida, LB
1989 Eric Metcalf, Texas, RB
1990 Leroy Hoard, Michigan, RB (2)
1991 Eric Turner, UCLA, DB
1992 Tommy Vardell, Stanford, RB
1993 Steve Everitt, Michigan, C
1994 Antonio Langham, Alabama, DB
     Derrick Alexander, Michigan, WR
1995 Craig Powell, Ohio State, LB
1999 Tim Couch, Kentucky, QB
2000 Courtney Brown, Penn State, DE
2001 Gerard Warren, Florida, DT
2002 William Green, Boston College, RB
2003 Jeff Faine, Norte Dame, C
2004 Kellen Winslow, Miami, TE
2005 Braylon Edwards, Michigan, WR
2006 Kamerion Wimbley, Florida St., DE
2007 Joe Thomas, Wisconsin, T
     Brady Quinn, Notre Dame, QB
2008 Beau Bell, Nevada-Las Vegas, LB (4)
2009 Alex Mack, California, C

2010 Joe Haden, Florida, DB
2011 Phil Taylor, Baylor, DT
2012 Trent Richardson, Alabama, RB
     Brandon Weeden, Oklahoma St., QB

DALLAS COWBOYS
Year Player, College, Position
1960 None
1961 Bob Lilly, Texas Christian, DT
1962 Sonny Gibbs, TCU, QB (2)
1963 Lee Roy Jordan, Alabama, LB
1964 Scott Appleton, Texas, DT
1965 Craig Morton, California, QB
1966 John Niland, Iowa, G
1967 Phil Clark, Northwestern, DB (3)
1968 Dennis Homan, Alabama, WR
1969 Calvin Hill, Yale, RB
1970 Duane Thomas, West Texas St., RB
1971 Tody Smith, So. California, DE
1972 Bill Thomas, Boston College, RB
1973 Billy Joe DuPree, Michigan St., TE
1974 Ed (Too Tall) Jones, Tennessee St., DE
     Charley Young, North Carolina St., RB
1975 Randy White, Maryland, LB
     Thomas Henderson, Langston, LB
1976 Aaron Kyle, Wyoming, DB
1977 Tony Dorsett, Pittsburgh, RB
1978 Larry Bethea, Michigan State, DE
1979 Robert Shaw, Tennessee, C
1980 Bill Roe, Colorado, LB (3)
1981 Howard Richards, Missouri, T
1982 Rod Hill, Kentucky State, DB
1983 Jim Jeffcoat, Arizona State, DE
1984 Billy Cannon, Jr., Texas A&M, LB
1985 Kevin Brooks, Michigan, DE
1986 Mike Sherrard, UCLA, WR
1987 Danny Noonan, Nebraska, DT
1988 Michael Irvin, Miami, WR
1989 Troy Aikman, UCLA, QB
1990 Emmitt Smith, Florida, RB
1991 Russell Maryland, Miami, DT
     Alvin Harper, Tennessee, WR
     Kelvin Pritchett, Mississippi, DT
1992 Kevin Smith, Texas A&M, DB
     Robert Jones, East Carolina, LB
1993 Kevin Williams, Miami, WR (2)
1994 Shante Carver, Arizona State, DE
1995 Sherman Williams, Alabama, RB (2)
1996 Kavika Pittman, McNeese St., DE (2)
1997 David LaFleur, Louisiana State, TE
1998 Greg Ellis, North Carolina, DE
1999 Ebenezer Ekuban, North Carolina, DE
2000 Dwayne Goodrich, Tennessee, DB (2)
2001 Quincy Carter, Georgia, QB (2)
2002 Roy Williams, Oklahoma, DB
2003 Terence Newman, Kansas State, DB
2004 Julius Jones, Notre Dame, RB (2)
2005 DeMarcus Ware, Troy, DE
     Marcus Spears, Louisiana St., DE
2006 Bobby Carpenter, Ohio State, LB
2007 Anthony Spencer, Purdue, LB
2008 Felix Jones, Arkansas, RB
     Mike Jenkins, South Florida, DB
2009 Jason Williams, Western Illinois, LB (3)
2010 Dez Bryant, Oklahoma State, WR
2011 Tyron Smith, Southern California, T
2012 Morris Claiborne, Louisiana St., DB

DENVER BRONCOS
Year Player, College, Position
1960 Roger LeClerc, Trinity, Conn., C
1961 Bob Gaiters, New Mexico St., RB
1962 Merlin Olsen, Utah State, DT
1963 Kermit Alexander, UCLA, CB
1964 Bob Brown, Nebraska, T
1965 Dick Butkus, Illinois, LB (2)
1966 Jerry Shay, Purdue, DT
1967 Floyd Little, Syracuse, RB
1968 Curley Culp, Arizona State, DE (2)
1969 Grady Cavness, Texas-El Paso, DB (2)
1970 Bob Anderson, Colorado, RB
1971 Marv Montgomery, So. California, T
1972 Riley Odoms, Houston, TE
1973 Otis Armstrong, Purdue, RB
1974 Randy Gradishar, Ohio State, LB
1975 Louis Wright, San Jose State, DB
1976 Tom Glassic, Virginia, G
1977 Steve Schindler, Boston College, G
1978 Don Latimer, Miami, DT
1979 Kelvin Clark, Nebraska, T
1980 Rulon Jones, Utah State, DE (2)
1981 Dennis Smith, So. California, DB
1982 Gerald Willhite, San Jose St., RB
1983 Chris Hinton, Northwestern, G
1984 Andre Townsend, Mississippi, DE (2)
1985 Steve Sewell, Oklahoma, RB
1986 Jim Juriga, Illinois, T (4)
1987 Ricky Nattiel, Florida, WR
1988 Ted Gregory, Syracuse, NT
1989 Steve Atwater, Arkansas, DB
1990 Alton Montgomery, Houston, DB (2)
1991 Mike Croel, Nebraska, LB
1992 Tommy Maddox, UCLA, QB
1993 Dan Williams, Toledo, DE
1994 Allen Aldridge, Houston, LB (2)
1995 Jamie Brown, Florida A&M, T (4)
1996 John Mobley, Kutztown, LB
1997 Trevor Pryce, Clemson, DT
1998 Marcus Nash, Tennessee, WR
1999 Al Wilson, Tennessee, LB
2000 Deltha O'Neal, California, DB
2001 Willie Middlebrooks, Minnesota, DB
2002 Ashley Lelie, Hawaii, WR
2003 George Foster, Georgia, T
2004 D.J. Williams, Miami, LB
2005 Darrent Williams, Oklahoma St., DB (2)
2006 Jay Cutler, Vanderbilt, QB
2007 Jarvis Moss, Florida, DE
2008 Ryan Clady, Boise State, T
2009 Knowshon Moreno, Georgia, RB
     Robert Ayers, Tennessee, DE
2010 Demaryius Thomas, Georgia Tech, WR
     Tim Tebow, Florida, QB
2011 Von Miller, Texas A&M, LB
2012 Derek Wolfe, Cincinnati, DT (2)

DETROIT LIONS
Year Player, College, Position
1936 Sid Wagner, Michigan State, G
1937 Lloyd Cardwell, Nebraska, B
1938 Alex Wojciechowicz, Fordham, C
1939 John Pingel, Michigan State, B
1940 Doyle Nave, Southern California, B
1941 Jim Thomason, Texas A&M, B
1942 Bob Westfall, Michigan, B
1943 Frank Sinkwich, Georgia, B
1944 Otto Graham, Northwestern, B
1945 Frank Szymanski, Notre Dame, C

1946 Bill Dellastatious, Missouri, B	2009 Matthew Stafford, Georgia, QB	1986 Kenneth Davis, TCU, RB (2)
1947 Glenn Davis, Army, B	Brandon Pettigrew, Oklahoma St., TE	1987 Brent Fullwood, Auburn, RB
1948 Y.A. Tittle, Louisiana State, B	2010 Ndamukong Suh, Nebraska, DT	1988 Sterling Sharpe, South Carolina, WR
1949 John Rauch, Georgia, B	Jahvid Best, California, RB	1989 Tony Mandarich, Michigan State, T
1950 Leon Hart, Notre Dame, E	2011 Nick Fairley, Auburn, DT	1990 Tony Bennett, Mississippi, LB
Joe Watson, Rice, C	2012 Riley Reiff, Iowa, T	Darrell Thompson, Minnesota, RB
1951 Dick Stanfel, San Francisco, G (2)		1991 Vinnie Clark, Ohio State, DB
1952 Yale Lary, Texas A&M, B (3)	**GREEN BAY PACKERS**	1992 Terrell Buckley, Florida State, DB
1953 Harley Sewell, Texas, G	**Year Player, College, Position**	1993 Wayne Simmons, Clemson, LB
1954 Dick Chapman, Rice, T	1936 Russ Letlow, San Francisco, G	George Teague, Alabama, DB
1955 Dave Middleton, Auburn, B	1937 Eddie Jankowski, Wisconsin, B	1994 Aaron Taylor, Notre Dame, T
1956 Hopalong Cassady, Ohio State, B	1938 Cecil Isbell, Purdue, B	1995 Craig Newsome, Arizona State, DB
1957 Bill Glass, Baylor, G	1939 Larry Buhler, Minnesota, B	1996 John Michels, Southern California, T
1958 Alex Karras, Iowa, T	1940 Harold Van Every, Minnesota, B	1997 Ross Verba, Iowa, T
1959 Nick Pietrosante, Notre Dame, B	1941 George Paskvan, Wisconsin, B	1998 Vonnie Holliday, North Carolina, DT
1960 John Robinson, Louisiana State, S	1942 Urban Odson, Minnesota, T	1999 Antuan Edwards, Clemson, DB
1961 Danny LaRose, Missouri, T (2)	1943 Dick Wildung, Minnesota, T	2000 Bubba Franks, Miami, TE
1962 John Hadl, Kansas, QB	1944 Merv Pregulman, Michigan, G	2001 Jamal Reynolds, Florida State, DE
1963 Daryl Sanders, Ohio State, T	1945 Walt Schlinkman, Texas Tech, B	2002 Javon Walker, Florida State, WR
1964 Pete Beathard, So. California, QB	1946 Johnny Strzykalski, Marquette, B	2003 Nick Barnett, Oregon State, LB
1965 Tom Nowatzke, Indiana, RB	1947 Ernie Case, UCLA, B	2004 Ahmad Carroll, Arkansas, DB
1966 Nick Eddy, Notre Dame, RB (2)	1948 Earl (Jug) Girard, Wisconsin, B	2005 Aaron Rodgers, California, QB
1967 Mel Farr, UCLA, RB	1949 Stan Heath, Nevada, B	2006 A.J. Hawk, Ohio State, LB
1968 Greg Landry, Massachusetts, QB	1950 Clayton Tonnemaker, Minnesota, C	2007 Justin Harrell, Tennessee, DT
Earl McCullouch, So. California, WR	1951 Bob Gain, Kentucky, T	2008 Jordy Nelson, Kansas State, WR (2)
1969 Altie Taylor, Utah State, RB (2)	1952 Babe Parilli, Kentucky, QB	2009 B.J. Raji, Boston College, DT
1970 Steve Owens, Oklahoma, RB	1953 Al Carmichael, So. California, B	Clay Matthews, So. California, LB
1971 Bob Bell, Cincinnati, DT	1954 Art Hunter, Notre Dame, T	2010 Bryan Bulaga, Iowa, T
1972 Herb Orvis, Colorado, DE	Veryl Switzer, Kansas State, B	2011 Derek Sherrod, Mississippi State, T
1973 Ernie Price, Texas A&I, DE	1955 Tom Bettis, Purdue, G	2012 Nick Perry, Southern California, LB
1974 Ed O'Neil, Penn State, LB	1956 Jack Losch, Miami, B	
1975 Lynn Boden, South Dakota St., G	1957 Paul Hornung, Notre Dame, B	**HOUSTON TEXANS**
1976 James Hunter, Grambling, DB	Ron Kramer, Michigan, E	**Year Player, College, Position**
Lawrence Gaines, Wyoming, RB	1958 Dan Currie, Michigan State, C	2002 David Carr, Fresno State, QB
1977 Walt Williams, New Mexico St., DB (2)	1959 Randy Duncan, Iowa, B	2003 Andre Johnson, Miami, WR
1978 Luther Bradley, Notre Dame, DB	1960 Tom Moore, Vanderbilt, RB	2004 Dunta Robinson, South Carolina, DB
1979 Keith Dorney, Penn State, T	1961 Herb Adderley, Michigan State, CB	Jason Babin, Western Michigan, LB
1980 Billy Sims, Oklahoma, RB	1962 Earl Gros, Louisiana State, RB	2005 Travis Johnson, Florida State, DE
1981 Mark Nichols, San Jose State, WR	1963 Dave Robinson, Penn State, LB	2006 Mario Williams, North Carolina St., DE
1982 Jimmy Williams, Nebraska, LB	1964 Lloyd Voss, Nebraska, DT	2007 Amobi Okoye, Louisville, DT
1983 James Jones, Florida, RB	1965 Donny Anderson, Texas Tech, RB	2008 Duane Brown, Virginia Tech, T
1984 David Lewis, California, TE	Lawrence Elkins, Baylor, E	2009 Brian Cushing, So. California, LB
1985 Lomas Brown, Florida, T	1966 Jim Grabowski, Illinois, RB	2010 Kareem Jackson, Alabama, DB
1986 Chuck Long, Iowa, QB	Gale Gillingham, Minnesota, T	2011 J.J. Watt, Wisconsin, DE
1987 Reggie Rogers, Washington, DE	1967 Bob Hyland, Boston College, C	2012 Whitney Mercilus, Illinois, LB
1988 Bennie Blades, Miami, DB	Don Horn, San Diego State, QB	
1989 Barry Sanders, Oklahoma St., RB	1968 Fred Carr, Texas-El Paso, LB	**INDIANAPOLIS COLTS**
1990 Andre Ware, Houston, QB	Bill Lueck, Arizona, G	**Year Player, College, Position**
1991 Herman Moore, Virginia, WR	1969 Rich Moore, Villanova, DT	1953 Billy Vessels, Oklahoma, B
1992 Robert Porcher, South Carolina St., DE	1970 Mike McCoy, Notre Dame, DT	1954 Cotton Davidson, Baylor, B
1993 Ryan McNeil, Miami, DB (2)	Rich McGeorge, Elon, TE	1955 George Shaw, Oregon, B
1994 Johnnie Morton, So. California, WR	1971 John Brockington, Ohio State, RB	Alan Ameche, Wisconsin, FB
1995 Luther Elliss, Utah, DT	1972 Willie Buchanon, San Diego St., DB	1956 Lenny Moore, Penn State, B
1996 Reggie Brown, Texas A&M, LB	Jerry Tagge, Nebraska, QB	1957 Jim Parker, Ohio State, G
Jeff Hartings, Penn State, G	1973 Barry Smith, Florida State, WR	1958 Lenny Lyles, Louisville, B
1997 Bryant Westbrook, Texas, DB	1974 Barty Smith, Richmond, RB	1959 Jackie Burkett, Auburn, C
1998 Terry Fair, Tennessee, DB	1975 Bill Bain, So. California, G (2)	1960 Ron Mix, Southern California, T
1999 Chris Claiborne, So. California, LB	1976 Mark Koncar, Colorado, T	1961 Tom Matte, Ohio State, RB
Aaron Gibson, Wisconsin, T	1977 Mike Butler, Kansas, DE	1962 Wendell Harris, Louisiana State, S
2000 Stockar McDougle, Oklahoma, T	Ezra Johnson, Morris Brown, DE	1963 Bob Vogel, Ohio State, T
2001 Jeff Backus, Michigan, T	1978 James Lofton, Stanford, WR	1964 Marv Woodson, Indiana, CB
2002 Joey Harrington, Oregon, QB	John Anderson, Michigan, LB	1965 Mike Curtis, Duke, LB
2003 Charles Rogers, Michigan State, WR	1979 Eddie Lee Ivery, Georgia Tech, RB	1966 Sam Ball, Kentucky, T
2004 Roy Williams, Texas, WR	1980 Bruce Clark, Penn State, DE	1967 Bubba Smith, Michigan State, DT
Kevin Jones, Virginia Tech, RB	George Cumby, Oklahoma, LB	Jim Detwiler, Michigan, RB
2005 Mike Williams, So. California, WR	1981 Rich Campbell, California, QB	1968 John Williams, Minnesota, G
2006 Ernie Sims, Florida State, LB	1982 Ron Hallstrom, Iowa, G	1969 Eddie Hinton, Oklahoma, WR
2007 Calvin Johnson, Georgia Tech, WR	1983 Tim Lewis, Pittsburgh, DB	1970 Norman Bulaich, Texas Christian, RB
2008 Gosder Cherilus, Boson College, T	1984 Alphonso Carreker, Florida St., DE	1971 Don McCauley, North Carolina, RB
	1985 Ken Ruettgers, So. California, T	Leonard Dunlap, North Texas St., DB

FIRST-ROUND SELECTIONS

1972 Tom Drougas, Oregon, T
1973 Bert Jones, Louisiana State, QB
      Joe Ehrmann, Syracuse, DT
1974 John Dutton, Nebraska, DE
      Roger Carr, Louisiana Tech, WR
1975 Ken Huff, North Carolina, G
1976 Ken Novak, Purdue, DT
1977 Randy Burke, Kentucky, WR
1978 Reese McCall, Auburn, TE
1979 Barry Krauss, Alabama, LB
1980 Curtis Dickey, Texas A&M, RB
      Derrick Hatchett, Texas, DB
1981 Randy McMillan, Pittsburgh, RB
      Donnell Thompson, North Carolina, DT
1982 Johnie Cooks, Mississippi St., LB
      Art Schlichter, Ohio State, QB
1983 John Elway, Stanford, QB
1984 Leonard Coleman, Vanderbilt, DB
      Ron Solt, Maryland, G
1985 Duane Bickett, So. California, LB
1986 Jon Hand, Alabama, DE
1987 Cornelius Bennett, Alabama, LB
1988 Chris Chandler, Washington, QB (3)
1989 Andre Rison, Michigan State, WR
1990 Jeff George, Illinois, QB
1991 Shane Curry, Miami, DE (2)
1992 Steve Emtman, Washington, DT
      Quentin Coryatt, Texas A&M, LB
1993 Sean Dawkins, California, WR
1994 Marshall Faulk, San Diego St., RB
      Trev Alberts, Nebraska, LB
1995 Ellis Johnson, Florida, DT
1996 Marvin Harrison, Syracuse, WR
1997 Tarik Glenn, California, T
1998 Peyton Manning, Tennessee, QB
1999 Edgerrin James, Miami, RB
2000 Rob Morris, Brigham Young, LB
2001 Reggie Wayne, Miami, WR
2002 Dwight Freeney, Syracuse, DE
2003 Dallas Clark, Iowa, TE
2004 Bob Sanders, Iowa, DB (2)
2005 Marlin Jackson, Michigan, DB
2006 Joseph Addai, Louisiana State, RB
2007 Anthony Gonzalez, Ohio State, WR
2008 Mike Pollak, Arizona State, G (2)
2009 Donald Brown, Connecticut, RB
2010 Jerry Hughes, Texas Christian, DE
2011 Anthony Castonzo, Boston College, T
2012 Andrew Luck, Stanford, QB

JACKSONVILLE JAGUARS
Year Player, College, Position
1995 Tony Boselli, Southern California, T
      James Stewart, Tennessee, RB
1996 Kevin Hardy, Illinois, LB
1997 Renaldo Wynn, Notre Dame, DT
1998 Fred Taylor, Florida, RB
      Donovin Darius, Syracuse, DB
1999 Fernando Bryant, Alabama, DB
2000 R. Jay Soward, So. California, WR
2001 Marcus Stroud, Georgia, DT
2002 John Henderson, Tennessee, DT
2003 Byron Leftwich, Marshall, QB
2004 Reggie Williams, Washington, WR
2005 Matt Jones, Arkansas, WR
2006 Marcedes Lewis, UCLA, TE
2007 Reggie Nelson, Florida, DB
2008 Derrick Harvey, Florida, DE
2009 Eugene Monroe, Virginia, T
2010 Tyson Alualu, California, DT

2011 Blaine Gabbert, Missouri, QB
2012 Justin Blackmon, Oklahoma St., WR

KANSAS CITY CHIEFS
Year Player, College, Position
1960 Don Meredith, So. Methodist, QB
1961 E.J. Holub, Texas Tech, C
1962 Ronnie Bull, Baylor, RB
1963 Buck Buchanan, Grambling, DT
      Ed Budde, Michigan State, G
1964 Pete Beathard, So. California, QB
1965 Gale Sayers, Kansas, RB
1966 Aaron Brown, Minnesota, DE
1967 Gene Trosch, Miami, DE-DT
1968 Mo Moorman, Texas A&M, G
      George Daney, Texas-El Paso, G
1969 Jim Marsalis, Tennessee State, CB
1970 Sid Smith, Southern California, T
1971 Elmo Wright, Houston, WR
1972 Jeff Kinney, Nebraska, RB
1973 Gary Butler, Rice, TE (2)
1974 Woody Green, Arizona State, RB
1975 Elmore Stephens, Kentucky, TE (2)
1976 Rod Walters, Iowa, G
1977 Gary Green, Baylor, DB
1978 Art Still, Kentucky, DE
1979 Mike Bell, Colorado State, DE
      Steve Fuller, Clemson, QB
1980 Brad Budde, Southern California, G
1981 Willie Scott, South Carolina, TE
1982 Anthony Hancock, Tennessee, WR
1983 Todd Blackledge, Penn State, QB
1984 Bill Maas, Pittsburgh, DT
      John Alt, Iowa, T
1985 Ethan Horton, North Carolina, RB
1986 Brian Jozwiak, West Virginia, T
1987 Paul Palmer, Temple, RB
1988 Neil Smith, Nebraska, DE
1989 Derrick Thomas, Alabama, LB
1990 Percy Snow, Michigan State, LB
1991 Harvey Williams, Louisiana St., RB
1992 Dale Carter, Tennessee, DB
1993 Will Shields, Nebraska, G (3)
1994 Greg Hill, Texas A&M, RB
1995 Trezelle Jenkins, Michigan, T
1996 Jerome Woods, Memphis, DB
1997 Tony Gonzalez, California, TE
1998 Victor Riley, Auburn, T
1999 John Tait, Brigham Young, T
2000 Sylvester Morris, Jackson St., WR
2001 Eric Downing, Syracuse, DT (3)
2002 Ryan Sims, North Carolina, DT
2003 Larry Johnson, Penn State, RB
2004 Junior Siavii, Oregon, DT (2)
2005 Derrick Johnson, Texas, LB
2006 Tamba Hali, Penn State, DE
2007 Dwayne Bowe, Louisiana State, WR
2008 Glenn Dorsey, Louisiana State, DT
      Branden Albert, Virginia, T
2009 Tyson Jackson, Louisiana State, DE
2010 Eric Berry, Tennessee, DB
2011 Jonathan Baldwin, Pittsburgh, WR
2012 Dontari Poe, Memphis, NT

MIAMI DOLPHINS
Year Player, College, Position
1966 Jim Grabowski, Illinois, RB
      Rick Norton, Kentucky, QB
1967 Bob Griese, Purdue, QB

1968 Larry Csonka, Syracuse, RB
      Doug Crusan, Indiana, T
1969 Bill Stanfill, Georgia, DE
1970 Jim Mandich, Michigan, TE (2)
1971 Otto Stowe, Iowa State, WR (2)
1972 Mike Kadish, Notre Dame, DT
1973 Chuck Bradley, Oregon, C (2)
1974 Donald Reese, Jackson State, DE
1975 Darryl Carlton, Tampa, T
1976 Larry Gordon, Arizona State, LB
      Kim Bokamper, San Jose State, LB
1977 A.J. Duhe, Louisiana State, DT
1978 Guy Benjamin, Stanford, QB (2)
1979 Jon Giesler, Michigan, T
1980 Don McNeal, Alabama, DB
1981 David Overstreet, Oklahoma, RB
1982 Roy Foster, Southern California, G
1983 Dan Marino, Pittsburgh, QB
1984 Jackie Shipp, Oklahoma, LB
1985 Lorenzo Hampton, Florida, RB
1986 John Offerdahl, Western Michigan, LB (2)
1987 John Bosa, Boston College, DE
1988 Eric Kumerow, Ohio State, DE
1989 Sammie Smith, Florida State, RB
      Louis Oliver, Florida, DB
1990 Richmond Webb, Texas A&M, T
1991 Randal Hill, Miami, WR
1992 Troy Vincent, Wisconsin, DB
      Marco Coleman, Georgia Tech, LB
1993 O.J. McDuffie, Penn State, WR
1994 Tim Bowens, Mississippi, DT
1995 Billy Milner, Houston, T
1996 Daryl Gardener, Baylor, DT
1997 Yatil Green, Miami, WR
1998 John Avery, Mississippi, RB
1999 J.J. Johnson, Mississippi St., RB (2)
2000 Todd Wade, Mississippi, T (2)
2001 Jamar Fletcher, Wisconsin, DB
2002 Seth McKinney, Texas A&M, C (3)
2003 Eddie Moore, Tennessee, LB (2)
2004 Vernon Carey, Miami, T
2005 Ronnie Brown, Auburn, RB
2006 Jason Allen, Tennessee, DB
2007 Ted Ginn, Ohio State, WR
2008 Jake Long, Michigan, T
2009 Vontae Davis, Illinois, DB
2010 Jared Odrick, Penn State, DT
2011 Mike Pouncey, Florida, C
2012 Ryan Tannehill, Texas A&M, QB

MINNESOTA VIKINGS
Year Player, College, Position
1961 Tommy Mason, Tulane, RB
1962 Bill Miller, Miami, WR (3)
1963 Jim Dunaway, Mississippi, T
1964 Carl Eller, Minnesota, DE
1965 Jack Snow, Notre Dame, WR
1966 Jerry Shay, Purdue, DT
1967 Clint Jones, Michigan State, RB
      Gene Washington, Michigan St., WR
      Alan Page, Notre Dame, DT
1968 Ron Yary, Southern California, T
1969 Ed White, California, G (2)
1970 John Ward, Oklahoma State, DT
1971 Leo Hayden, Ohio State, RB
1972 Jeff Siemon, Stanford, LB
1973 Chuck Foreman, Miami, RB
1974 Fred McNeill, UCLA, LB
      Steve Riley, Southern California, T
1975 Mark Mullaney, Colorado State, DE

1976	James White, Oklahoma State, DT
1977	Tommy Kramer, Rice, QB
1978	Randy Holloway, Pittsburgh, DE
1979	Ted Brown, North Carolina St., RB
1980	Doug Martin, Washington, DT
1981	Mardye McDole, Mississippi St., WR (2)
1982	Darrin Nelson, Stanford, RB
1983	Joey Browner, So. California, DB
1984	Keith Millard, Washington St., DE
1985	Chris Doleman, Pittsburgh, LB
1986	Gerald Robinson, Auburn, DE
1987	D.J. Dozier, Penn State, RB
1988	Randall McDaniel, Arizona State, G
1989	David Braxton, Wake Forest, LB (2)
1990	Mike Jones, Texas A&M, TE (3)
1991	Carlos Jenkins, Michigan St., LB (3)
1992	Robert Harris, Southern Univ., DE (2)
1993	Robert Smith, Ohio State, RB
1994	DeWayne Washington, N. Carolina St., DB
	Todd Steussie, California, T
1995	Derrick Alexander, Florida St., DE
	Korey Stringer, Ohio State, T
1996	Duane Clemons, California, DE
1997	Dwayne Rudd, Alabama, LB
1998	Randy Moss, Marshall, WR
1999	Daunte Culpepper, Central Florida, QB
	Dimitrius Underwood, Michigan St., DE
2000	Chris Hovan, Boston College, DT
2001	Michael Bennett, Wisconsin, RB
2002	Bryant McKinnie, Miami, T
2003	Kevin Williams, Oklahoma State, DT
2004	Kenechi Udeze, Southern California, DE
2005	Troy Williamson, South Carolina, WR
	Erasmus James, Wisconsin, DE
2006	Chad Greenway, Iowa, LB
2007	Adrian Peterson, Oklahoma, RB
2008	Tyrell Johnson, Arkansas State, DB (2)
2009	Percy Harvin, Florida, WR
2010	Chris Cook, Virginia, DB (2)
2011	Christian Ponder, Florida State, QB
2012	Matt Kalil, Southern California, T
	Harrison Smith, Notre Dame, DB

NEW ENGLAND PATRIOTS
Year Player, College, Position

1960	Ron Burton, Northwestern, RB
1961	Tommy Mason, Tulane, RB
1962	Gary Collins, Maryland, WR
1963	Art Graham, Boston College, WR
1964	Jack Concannon, Boston College, QB
1965	Jerry Rush, Michigan State, DE
1966	Karl Singer, Purdue, T
1967	John Charles, Purdue, S
1968	Dennis Byrd, North Carolina St., DE
1969	Ron Sellers, Florida State, WR
1970	Phil Olsen, Utah State, DE
1971	Jim Plunkett, Stanford, QB
1972	Tom Reynolds, San Diego St., WR (2)
1973	John Hannah, Alabama, G
	Sam Cunningham, So. California, RB
	Darryl Stingley, Purdue, WR
1974	Steve Corbett, Boston College, G (2)
1975	Russ Francis, Oregon, TE
1976	Mike Haynes, Arizona State, DB
	Pete Brock, Colorado, C
	Tim Fox, Ohio State, DB
1977	Raymond Clayborn, Texas, DB
	Stanley Morgan, Tennessee, WR
1978	Bob Cryder, Alabama, G
1979	Rick Sanford, South Carolina, DB

1980	Roland James, Tennessee, DB
	Vagas Ferguson, Notre Dame, RB
1981	Brian Holloway, Stanford, T
1982	Kenneth Sims, Texas, DT
	Lester Williams, Miami, DT
1983	Tony Eason, Illinois, QB
1984	Irving Fryar, Nebraska, WR
1985	Trevor Matich, Brigham Young, C
1986	Reggie Dupard, So. Methodist, RB
1987	Bruce Armstrong, Louisville, T
1988	John Stephens, Northwestern St., La., RB
1989	Hart Lee Dykes, Oklahoma St., WR
1990	Chris Singleton, Arizona, LB
	Ray Agnew, North Carolina St., DE
1991	Pat Harlow, Southern California, T
	Leonard Russell, Arizona St., RB
1992	Eugene Chung, Virginia Tech, T
1993	Drew Bledsoe, Washington St., QB
1994	Willie McGinest, So. California, DE
1995	Ty Law, Michigan, DB
1996	Terry Glenn, Ohio State, WR
1997	Chris Canty, Kansas State, DB
1998	Robert Edwards, Georgia, RB
	Tebucky Jones, Syracuse, DB
1999	Damien Woody, Boston College, C
	Andy Katzenmoyer, Ohio State, LB
2000	Adrian Klemm, Hawaii, T (2)
2001	Richard Seymour, Georgia, DT
2002	Daniel Graham, Colorado, TE
2003	Ty Warren, Texas A&M, DT
2004	Vince Wilfork, Miami, DT
	Ben Watson, Georgia, TE
2005	Logan Mankins, Fresno State, G
2006	Laurence Maroney, Minnesota, RB
2007	Brandon Meriweather, Miami, DB
2008	Jerod Mayo, Tennessee, LB
2009	Patrick Chung, Oregon, DB (2)
2010	Devin McCourty, Rutgers, DB
2011	Nate Solder, Colorado, T
2012	Chandler Jones, Syracuse, DE
	Dont'a Hightower, Alabama, LB

NEW ORLEANS SAINTS
Year Player, College, Position

1967	Les Kelley, Alabama, RB
1968	Kevin Hardy, Notre Dame, DE
1969	John Shinners, Xavier, G
1970	Ken Burrough, Texas Southern, WR
1971	Archie Manning, Mississippi, QB
1972	Royce Smith, Georgia, G
1973	Derland Moore, Oklahoma, DE (2)
1974	Rick Middleton, Ohio State, LB
1975	Larry Burton, Purdue, WR
	Kurt Schumacher, Ohio State, T
1976	Chuck Muncie, California, RB
1977	Joe Campbell, Maryland, DE
1978	Wes Chandler, Florida, WR
1979	Russell Erxleben, Texas, P-K
1980	Stan Brock, Colorado, T
1981	George Rogers, South Carolina, RB
1982	Lindsay Scott, Georgia, WR
1983	Steve Korte, Arkansas, G (2)
1984	James Geathers, Wichita State, DE
1985	Alvin Toles, Tennessee, LB
1986	Jim Dombrowski, Virginia, T
1987	Shawn Knight, Brigham Young, DT
1988	Craig Heyward, Pittsburgh, RB
1989	Wayne Martin, Arkansas, DE
1990	Renaldo Turnbull, West Virginia, DE
1991	Wesley Carroll, Miami, WR (2)

1992	Vaughn Dunbar, Indiana, RB
1993	Willie Roaf, Louisiana Tech, T
	Irv Smith, Notre Dame, TE
1994	Joe Johnson, Louisville, DE
1995	Mark Fields, Washington State, LB
1996	Alex Molden, Oregon, DB
1997	Chris Naeole, Colorado, G
1998	Kyle Turley, San Diego State, T
1999	Ricky Williams, Texas, RB
2000	Darren Howard, Kansas St., DE (2)
2001	Deuce McAllister, Mississippi, RB
2002	Donte' Stallworth, Tennessee, WR
	Charles Grant, Georgia, DE
2003	Johnathan Sullivan, Georgia, DT
2004	Will Smith, Ohio State, DE
2005	Jammal Brown, Oklahoma, T
2006	Reggie Bush, So. California, RB
2007	Robert Meachem, Tennessee, WR
2008	Sedrick Ellis, So. California, DT
2009	Malcolm Jenkins, Ohio State, DB
2010	Patrick Robinson, Florida State, DB
2011	Cameron Jordan, California, DE
	Mark Ingram, Alabama, RB
2012	Akiem Hicks, Regina, DT (3)

NEW YORK GIANTS
Year Player, College, Position

1936	Art Lewis, Ohio U., T
1937	Ed Widseth, Minnesota, T
1938	George Karamatic, Gonzaga, B
1939	Walt Neilson, Arizona, B
1940	Grenville Lansdell, So. California, B
1941	George Franck, Minnesota, B
1942	Merle Hapes, Mississippi, B
1943	Steve Filipowicz, Fordham, B
1944	Billy Hillenbrand, Indiana, B
1945	Elmer Barbour, Wake Forest, B
1946	George Connor, Notre Dame, T
1947	Vic Schwall, Northwestern, B
1948	Tony Minisi, Pennsylvania, B
1949	Paul Page, Southern Methodist, B
1950	Travis Tidwell, Auburn, B
1951	Kyle Rote, Southern Methodist, B
	Jim Spavital, Oklahoma A&M, B
1952	Frank Gifford, Southern California, B
1953	Bobby Marlow, Alabama, B
1954	Ken Buck, Pacific, C (2)
1955	Joe Heap, Notre Dame, B
1956	Henry Moore, Arkansas, B (2)
1957	Sam DeLuca, South Carolina, T (2)
1958	Phil King, Vanderbilt, B
1959	Lee Grosscup, Utah, B
1960	Lou Cordileone, Clemson, G
1961	Bruce Tarbox, Syracuse, G (2)
1962	Jerry Hillebrand, Colorado, LB
1963	Frank Lasky, Florida, T (2)
1964	Joe Don Looney, Oklahoma, RB
1965	Tucker Frederickson, Auburn, RB
1966	Francis Peay, Missouri, T
1967	Louis Thompson, Alabama, DT (4)
1968	Dick Buzin, Penn State, T (2)
1969	Fred Dryer, San Diego State, DE
1970	Jim Files, Oklahoma, LB
1971	Rocky Thompson, West Texas St., WR
1972	Eldridge Small, Texas A&I, DB
	Larry Jacobson, Nebraska, DE
1973	Brad Van Pelt, Michigan St., LB (2)
1974	John Hicks, Ohio State, G
1975	Al Simpson, Colorado State, T (2)
1976	Troy Archer, Colorado, DE

FIRST-ROUND SELECTIONS

1977 Gary Jeter, Southern California, DT
1978 Gordon King, Stanford, T
1979 Phil Simms, Morehead State, QB
1980 Mark Haynes, Colorado, DB
1981 Lawrence Taylor, North Carolina, LB
1982 Butch Woolfolk, Michigan, RB
1983 Terry Kinard, Clemson, DB
1984 Carl Banks, Michigan State, LB
      William Roberts, Ohio State, T
1985 George Adams, Kentucky, RB
1986 Eric Dorsey, Notre Dame, DE
1987 Mark Ingram, Michigan State, WR
1988 Eric Moore, Indiana, T
1989 Brian Williams, Minnesota, C-G
1990 Rodney Hampton, Georgia, RB
1991 Jarrod Bunch, Michigan, RB
1992 Derek Brown, Notre Dame, TE
1993 Michael Strahan, Texas Southern, DE (2)
1994 Thomas Lewis, Indiana, WR
1995 Tyrone Wheatley, Michigan, RB
1996 Cedric Jones, Oklahoma, DE
1997 Ike Hilliard, Florida, WR
1998 Shaun Williams, UCLA, DB
1999 Luke Petitgout, Notre Dame, T
2000 Ron Dayne, Wisconsin, RB
2001 Will Allen, Syracuse, DB
2002 Jeremy Shockey, Miami, TE
2003 William Joseph, Miami, DT
2004 Philip Rivers, North Carolina St., QB
2005 Corey Webster, Louisiana St., DB (2)
2006 Mathias Kiwanuka, Boston College, DE
2007 Aaron Ross, Texas, DB
2008 Kenny Phillips, Miami, DB
2009 Hakeem Nicks, North Carolina, WR
2010 Jason Pierre-Paul, South Florida, DE
2011 Prince Amukamara, Nebraska, DB
2012 David Wilson, Virginia Tech, RB

NEW YORK JETS
Year Player, College, Position
1960 George Izo, Notre Dame, QB
1961 Tom Brown, Minnesota, G
1962 Sandy Stephens, Minnesota, QB
1963 Jerry Stovall, Louisiana State, S
1964 Matt Snell, Ohio State, RB
1965 Joe Namath, Alabama, QB
      Tom Nowatzke, Indiana, RB
1966 Bill Yearby, Michigan, DT
1967 Paul Seiler, Notre Dame, T
1968 Lee White, Weber State, RB
1969 Dave Foley, Ohio State, T
1970 Steve Tannen, Florida, CB
1971 John Riggins, Kansas, RB
1972 Jerome Barkum, Jackson St., WR
      Mike Taylor, Michigan, LB
1973 Burgess Owens, Miami, DB
1974 Carl Barzilauskas, Indiana, DT
1975 Anthony Davis, So. California, RB (2)
1976 Richard Todd, Alabama, QB
1977 Marvin Powell, So. California, T
1978 Chris Ward, Ohio State, T
1979 Marty Lyons, Alabama, DE
1980 Johnny (Lam) Jones, Texas, WR
1981 Freeman McNeil, UCLA, RB
1982 Bob Crable, Notre Dame, LB
1983 Ken O'Brien, Cal-Davis, QB
1984 Russell Carter, So. Methodist, DB
      Ron Faurot, Arkansas, DE
1985 Al Toon, Wisconsin, WR
1986 Mike Haight, Iowa, T

1987 Roger Vick, Texas A&M, RB
1988 Dave Cadigan, So. California, T
1989 Jeff Lageman, Virginia, LB
1990 Blair Thomas, Penn State, RB
1991 Browning Nagle, Louisville, QB (2)
1992 Johnny Mitchell, Nebraska, TE
1993 Marvin Jones, Florida State, LB
1994 Aaron Glenn, Texas A&M, DB
1995 Kyle Brady, Penn State, TE
      Hugh Douglas, Central St., Ohio, DE
1996 Keyshawn Johnson, So. California, WR
1997 James Farrior, Virginia, LB
1998 Dorian Boose, Washington St., DE (2)
1999 Randy Thomas, Mississippi St., G (2)
2000 Shaun Ellis, Tennessee, DE
      John Abraham, South Carolina, LB
      Chad Pennington, Marshall, QB
      Anthony Becht, West Virginia, TE
2001 Santana Moss, Miami, WR
2002 Bryan Thomas, Ala.-Birmingham, DE
2003 Dewayne Robertson, Kentucky, DT
2004 Jonathan Vilma, Miami, LB
2005 Mike Nugent, Ohio State, K (2)
2006 D'Brickashaw Ferguson, Virginia, T
      Nick Mangold, Ohio State, C
2007 Darrelle Revis, Pittsburgh, DB
2008 Vernon Gholston, Ohio State, LB
      Dustin Keller, Purdue, TE
2009 Mark Sanchez, So. California, QB
2010 Kyle Wilson, Boise State, DB
2011 Muhammad Wilkerson, Temple, DT
2012 Quinton Coples, North Carolina, DE

OAKLAND RAIDERS
Year Player, College, Position
1960 Dale Hackbart, Wisconsin, CB
1961 Joe Rutgens, Illinois, DT
1962 Roman Gabriel, North Carolina St., QB
1963 George Wilson, Alabama, RB (6)
1964 Tony Lorick, Arizona State, RB
1965 Harry Schuh, Memphis State, T
1966 Rodger Bird, Kentucky, S
1967 Gene Upshaw, Texas A&I, G
1968 Eldridge Dickey, Tennessee St., QB
1969 Art Thoms, Syracuse, DT
1970 Raymond Chester, Morgan St., TE
1971 Jack Tatum, Ohio State, S
1972 Mike Siani, Villanova, WR
1973 Ray Guy, Southern Mississippi, P
1974 Henry Lawrence, Florida A&M, T
1975 Neal Colzie, Ohio State, DB
1976 Charles Philyaw, Texas Southern, DT (2)
1977 Mike Davis, Colorado, DB (2)
1978 Dave Browning, Washington, DE (2)
1979 Willie Jones, Florida State, DE (2)
1980 Marc Wilson, Brigham Young, QB
1981 Ted Watts, Texas Tech, DB
      Curt Marsh, Washington, T
1982 Marcus Allen, So. California, RB
1983 Don Mosebar, So. California, T
1984 Sean Jones, Northeastern, DE (2)
1985 Jessie Hester, Florida State, WR
1986 Bob Buczkowski, Pittsburgh, DE
1987 John Clay, Missouri, T
1988 Tim Brown, Notre Dame, WR
      Terry McDaniel, Tennessee, DB
      Scott Davis, Illinois, DE
1989 Jeff Francis, Tennessee, QB (6)
1990 Anthony Smith, Arizona, DE
1991 Todd Marinovich, So. California, QB

1992 Chester McGlockton, Clemson, DE
1993 Patrick Bates, Texas A&M, DB
1994 Rob Fredrickson, Michigan St., LB
1995 Napoleon Kaufman, Washington, RB
1996 Rickey Dudley, Ohio State, TE
1997 Darrell Russell, Southern California, DT
1998 Charles Woodson, Michigan, DB
      Mo Collins, Florida, T
1999 Matt Stinchcomb, Georgia, T
2000 Sebastian Janikowski, Florida St., K
2001 Derrick Gibson, Florida State, DB
2002 Phillip Buchanon, Miami, DB
      Napoleon Harris, Northwestern, LB
2003 Nnamdi Asomugha, California, DB
      Tyler Brayton, Colorado, DE
2004 Robert Gallery, Iowa, T
2005 Fabian Washington, Nebraska, DB
2006 Michael Huff, Texas, DB
2007 JaMarcus Russell, Louisiana State, QB
2008 Darren McFadden, Arkansas, RB
2009 Darrius Heyward-Bey, Maryland, WR
2010 Rolando McClain, Alabama, LB
2011 Stefan Wisniewski, Penn State, C (2)
2012 Tony Bergstrom, Utah, G (3)

PHILADELPHIA EAGLES
Year Player, College, Position
1936 Jay Berwanger, Chicago, B
1937 Sam Francis, Nebraska, B
1938 Jim McDonald, Ohio State, B
1939 Davey O'Brien, Texas Christian, B
1940 George McAfee, Duke, B
1941 Art Jones, Richmond, B (2)
1942 Pete Kmetovic, Stanford, B
1943 Joe Muha, Virginia Military, B
1944 Steve Van Buren, Louisiana St., B
1945 John Yonaker, Notre Dame, E
1946 Leo Riggs, Southern California, B
1947 Neill Armstrong, Oklahoma A&M, E
1948 Clyde (Smackover) Scott, Arkansas, B
1949 Chuck Bednarik, Pennsylvania, C
      Frank Tripucka, Notre Dame, B
1950 Harry (Bud) Grant, Minnesota, E
1951 Ebert Van Buren, Louisiana St., B
      Chet Mutryn, Xavier, B
1952 Johnny Bright, Drake, B
1953 Al Conway, Army, B (2)
1954 Neil Worden, Notre Dame, B
1955 Dick Bielski, Maryland, B
1956 Bob Pellegrini, Maryland, C
1957 Clarence Peaks, Michigan State, B
1958 Walt Kowalczyk, Michigan State, B
1959 J.D. Smith, Rice, T (2)
1960 Ron Burton, Northwestern, RB
1961 Art Baker, Syracuse, RB
1962 Pete Case, Georgia, G (2)
1963 Ed Budde, Michigan State, G
1964 Bob Brown, Nebraska, T
1965 Ray Rissmiller, Georgia, T (2)
1966 Randy Beisler, Indiana, DE
1967 Harry Jones, Arkansas, RB
1968 Tim Rossovich, So. California, DE
1969 Leroy Keyes, Purdue, RB
1970 Steve Zabel, Oklahoma, TE
1971 Richard Harris, Grambling, DE
1972 John Reaves, Florida, QB
1973 Jerry Sisemore, Texas, T
      Charle Young, So. California, TE
1974 Mitch Sutton, Kansas, DT (3)
1975 Bill Capraun, Miami, T (7)

528

1976 Mike Smith, Florida, DE (4)
1977 Skip Sharp, Kansas, DB (5)
1978 Reggie Wilkes, Georgia Tech, LB (3)
1979 Jerry Robinson, UCLA, LB
1980 Roynell Young, Alcorn State, DB
1981 Leonard Mitchell, Houston, DE
1982 Mike Quick, North Carolina St., WR
1983 Michael Haddix, Mississippi St., RB
1984 Kenny Jackson, Penn State, WR
1985 Kevin Allen, Indiana, T
1986 Keith Byars, Ohio State, RB
1987 Jerome Brown, Miami, DT
1988 Keith Jackson, Oklahoma, TE
1989 Jessie Small, Eastern Kentucky, LB (2)
1990 Ben Smith, Georgia, DB
1991 Antone Davis, Tennessee, T
1992 Siran Stacy, Alabama, RB (2)
1993 Lester Holmes, Jackson State, T
       Leonard Renfro, Colorado, DT
1994 Bernard Williams, Georgia, T
1995 Mike Mamula, Boston College, DE
1996 Jermane Mayberry, Texas A&M-Kingsville, T
1997 Jon Harris, Virginia, DE
1998 Tra Thomas, Florida State, T
1999 Donovan McNabb, Syracuse, QB
2000 Corey Simon, Florida State, DT
2001 Freddie Mitchell, UCLA, WR
2002 Lito Sheppard, Florida, DB
2003 Jerome McDougle, Miami, DE
2004 Shawn Andrews, Arkansas, T
2005 Mike Patterson, So. California, DT
2006 Brodrick Bunkley, Florida State, DT
2007 Kevin Kolb, Houston, QB (2)
2008 Trevor Laws, Notre Dame, DT (2)
2009 Jeremy Maclin, Missouri, WR
2010 Brandon Graham, Michigan, DE
2011 Danny Watkins, Baylor, G
2012 Fletcher Cox, Mississippi St., DT

PITTSBURGH STEELERS
Year   Player, College, Position
1936 Bill Shakespeare, Notre Dame, B
1937 Mike Basrak, Duquesne, C
1938 Byron (Whizzer) White, Colorado, B
1939 Bill Patterson, Baylor, B (3)
1940 Kay Eakin, Arkansas, B
1941 Chet Gladchuk, Boston College, C (2)
1942 Bill Dudley, Virginia, B
1943 Bill Daley, Minnesota, B
1944 Johnny Podesto, St. Mary's, Calif., B
1945 Paul Duhart, Florida, B
1946 Felix (Doc) Blanchard, Army, B
1947 Hub Bechtol, Texas, E
1948 Dan Edwards, Georgia, E
1949 Bobby Gage, Clemson, B
1950 Lynn Chandnois, Michigan St., B
1951 Butch Avinger, Alabama, B
1952 Ed Modzelewski, Maryland, B
1953 Ted Marchibroda, St. Bonaventure, B
1954 Johnny Lattner, Notre Dame, B
1955 Frank Varrichione, Notre Dame, T
1956 Gary Glick, Colorado A&M, B
       Art Davis, Mississippi State, B
1957 Len Dawson, Purdue, B
1958 Larry Krutko, West Virginia, B (2)
1959 Tom Barnett, Purdue, B (8)
1960 Jack Spikes, Texas Christian, RB
1961 Myron Pottios, Notre Dame, LB (2)
1962 Bob Ferguson, Ohio State, RB
1963 Frank Atkinson, Stanford, T (8)

1964 Paul Martha, Pittsburgh, S
1965 Roy Jefferson, Utah, WR (2)
1966 Dick Leftridge, West Virginia, RB
1967 Don Shy, San Diego State, RB (2)
1968 Mike Taylor, Southern California, T
1969 Joe Greene, North Texas State, DT
1970 Terry Bradshaw, Louisiana Tech, QB
1971 Frank Lewis, Grambling, WR
1972 Franco Harris, Penn State, RB
1973 J.T. Thomas, Florida State, DB
1974 Lynn Swann, So. California, WR
1975 Dave Brown, Michigan, DB
1976 Bennie Cunningham, Clemson, TE
1977 Robin Cole, New Mexico, LB
1978 Ron Johnson, Eastern Michigan, DB
1979 Greg Hawthorne, Baylor, RB
1980 Mark Malone, Arizona State, QB
1981 Keith Gary, Oklahoma, DE
1982 Walter Abercrombie, Baylor, RB
1983 Gabriel Rivera, Texas Tech, DT
1984 Louis Lipps, So. Mississippi, WR
1985 Darryl Sims, Wisconsin, DE
1986 John Rienstra, Temple, G
1987 Rod Woodson, Purdue, DB
1988 Aaron Jones, Eastern Kentucky, DE
1989 Tim Worley, Georgia, RB
       Tom Ricketts, Pittsburgh, T
1990 Eric Green, Liberty, TE
1991 Huey Richardson, Florida, DE
1992 Leon Searcy, Miami, T
1993 Deon Figures, Colorado, DB
1994 Charles Johnson, Colorado, WR
1995 Mark Bruener, Washington, TE
1996 Jamain Stephens, North Carolina A&T, T
1997 Chad Scott, Maryland, DB
1998 Alan Faneca, Louisiana State, G
1999 Troy Edwards, Louisiana Tech, WR
2000 Plaxico Burress, Michigan St., WR
2001 Casey Hampton, Texas, DT
2002 Kendall Simmons, Auburn, G
2003 Troy Polamalu, Southern California, DB
2004 Ben Roethlisberger, Miami (OH), QB
2005 Heath Miller, Virginia, TE
2006 Santonio Holmes, Ohio State, WR
2007 Lawrence Timmons, Florida State, LB
2008 Rashard Mendenhall, Illinois, RB
2009 Evander Hood, Missouri, DE
2010 Maurkice Pouncey, Florida, C
2011 Cameron Heyward, Ohio State, DE
2012 David DeCastro, Stanford, G

ST. LOUIS RAMS
Year   Player, College, Position
1937 Johnny Drake, Purdue, B
1938 Corbett Davis, Indiana, B
1939 Parker Hall, Mississippi, B
1940 Ollie Cordill, Rice, B
1941 Rudy Mucha, Washington, C
1942 Jack Wilson, Baylor, B
1943 Mike Holovak, Boston College, B
1944 Tony Butkovich, Illinois, B
1945 Elroy (Crazylegs) Hirsch, Wisconsin, B
1946 Emil Sitko, Notre Dame, B
1947 Herman Wedemeyer, St. Mary's, Calif., B
1948 Tom Keane, West Virginia, B (2)
1949 Bobby Thomason, Virginia Military, B
1950 Ralph Pasquariello, Villanova, B
       Stan West, Oklahoma, B
1951 Bud McFadin, Texas, G

1952 Bill Wade, Vanderbilt, QB
       Bob Carey, Michigan State, E
1953 Donn Moomaw, UCLA, C
       Ed Barker, Washington State, E
1954 Ed Beatty, Cincinnati, C
1955 Larry Morris, Georgia Tech, C
1956 Joe Marconi, West Virginia, B
       Charles Horton, Vanderbilt, B
1957 Jon Arnett, Southern California, B
       Del Shofner, Baylor, E
1958 Lou Michaels, Kentucky, T
       Jim Phillips, Auburn, E
1959 Dick Bass, Pacific, B
       Paul Dickson, Baylor, T
1960 Billy Cannon, Louisiana State, RB
1961 Marlin McKeever, So. California, E-LB
1962 Roman Gabriel, North Carolina St., QB
       Merlin Olsen, Utah State, DT
1963 Terry Baker, Oregon State, QB
       Rufus Guthrie, Georgia Tech, G
1964 Bill Munson, Utah State, QB
1965 Clancy Williams, Washington St., CB
1966 Tom Mack, Michigan, G
1967 Willie Ellison, Texas Southern, RB (2)
1968 Gary Beban, UCLA, QB (2)
1969 Larry Smith, Florida, RB
       Jim Seymour, Notre Dame, WR
       Bob Klein, Southern California, TE
1970 Jack Reynolds, Tennessee, LB
1971 Isiah Robertson, Southern, LB
       Jack Youngblood, Florida, DE
1972 Jim Bertelsen, Texas, RB (2)
1973 Cullen Bryant, Colorado, DB (2)
1974 John Cappelletti, Penn State, RB
1975 Mike Fanning, Notre Dame, DT
       Dennis Harrah, Miami, T
       Doug France, Ohio State, T
1976 Kevin McLain, Colorado State, LB
1977 Bob Brudzinski, Ohio State, LB
1978 Elvis Peacock, Oklahoma, RB
1979 George Andrews, Nebraska, LB
       Kent Hill, Georgia Tech, T
1980 Johnnie Johnson, Texas, DB
1981 Mel Owens, Michigan, LB
1982 Barry Redden, Richmond, RB
1983 Eric Dickerson, So. Methodist, RB
1984 Hal Stephens, East Carolina, DE (5)
1985 Jerry Gray, Texas, DB
1986 Mike Schad, Queen's Univ., Canada, T
1987 Donald Evans, Winston-Salem, DE (2)
1988 Gaston Green, UCLA, RB
       Aaron Cox, Arizona State, WR
1989 Bill Hawkins, Miami, DE
       Cleveland Gary, Miami, RB
1990 Bern Brostek, Washington, C
1991 Todd Lyght, Notre Dame, DB
1992 Sean Gilbert, Pittsburgh, DE
1993 Jerome Bettis, Notre Dame, RB
1994 Wayne Gandy, Auburn, T
1995 Kevin Carter, Florida, DE
1996 Lawrence Phillips, Nebraska, RB
       Eddie Kennison, Louisiana St., WR
1997 Orlando Pace, Ohio State, T
1998 Grant Wistrom, Nebraska, DE
1999 Torry Holt, North Carolina St., WR
2000 Trung Canidate, Arizona, RB
2001 Damione Lewis, Miami, DT
       Adam Archuleta, Arizona State, DB
       Ryan Pickett, Ohio State, DT
2002 Robert Thomas, UCLA, LB

2003 Jimmy Kennedy, Penn State, DT
2004 Steven Jackson, Oregon State, RB
2005 Alex Barron, Florida State, T
2006 Tye Hill, Clemson, DB
2007 Adam Carriker, Nebraska, DE
2008 Chris Long, Virginia, DE
2009 Jason Smith, Baylor, T
2010 Sam Bradford, Oklahoma, QB
2011 Robert Quinn, North Carolina, DE
2012 Michael Brockers, Louisiana St., DT

SAN DIEGO CHARGERS
Year   Player, College, Position
1960 Monty Stickles, Notre Dame, E
1961 Earl Faison, Indiana, DE
1962 Bob Ferguson, Ohio State, RB
1963 Walt Sweeney, Syracuse, G
1964 Ted Davis, Georgia Tech, LB
1965 Steve DeLong, Tennessee, DE
1966 Don Davis, Cal St.-Los Angeles, DT
1967 Ron Billingsley, Wyoming, DE
1968 Russ Washington, Missouri, DT
     Jimmy Hill, Texas A&I, DB
1969 Marty Domres, Columbia, QB
     Bob Babich, Miami, Ohio, LB
1970 Walker Gillette, Richmond, WR
1971 Leon Burns, Long Beach State, RB
1972 Pete Lazetich, Stanford, DE (2)
1973 Johnny Rodgers, Nebraska, WR
1974 Bo Matthews, Colorado, RB
     Don Goode, Kansas, LB
1975 Gary Johnson, Grambling, DT
     Mike Williams, Louisiana State, DB
1976 Joe Washington, Oklahoma, RB
1977 Bob Rush, Memphis State, C
1978 John Jefferson, Arizona State, WR
1979 Kellen Winslow, Missouri, TE
1980 Ed Luther, San Jose State, QB (4)
1981 James Brooks, Auburn, RB
1982 Hollis Hall, Clemson, DB (7)
1983 Billy Ray Smith, Arkansas, LB
     Gary Anderson, Arkansas, WR
     Gill Byrd, San Jose State, DB
1984 Mossy Cade, Texas, DB
1985 Jim Lachey, Ohio State, G
1986 Leslie O'Neal, Oklahoma State, DE
     James FitzPatrick, So. California, T
1987 Rod Bernstine, Texas A&M, TE
1988 Anthony Miller, Tennessee, WR
1989 Burt Grossman, Pittsburgh, DE
1990 Junior Seau, So. California, LB
1991 Stanley Richard, Texas, DB
1992 Chris Mims, Tennessee, DE
1993 Darrien Gordon, Stanford, DB
1994 Isaac Davis, Arkansas, G (2)
1995 Terrance Shaw, Stephen F. Austin, DB (2)
1996 Bryan Still, Virginia Tech, WR (2)
1997 Freddie Jones, North Carolina, TE (2)
1998 Ryan Leaf, Washington State, QB
1999 Jermaine Fazande, Oklahoma, RB (2)
2000 Rogers Beckett, Marshall, DB (2)
2001 LaDainian Tomlinson, TCU, RB
2002 Quentin Jammer, Texas, DB
2003 Sammy Davis, Texas A&M, DB
2004 Eli Manning, Mississippi, QB
2005 Shawne Merriman, Maryland, LB
     Luis Castillo, Northwestern, DT
2006 Antonio Cromartie, Florida State, DB
2007 Craig Davis, Louisiana State, WR
2008 Antoine Cason, Arizona, DB

2009 Larry English, Northern Illinois, LB
2010 Ryan Mathews, Fresno State, RB
2011 Corey Liuget, Illinois, DE
2012 Melvin Ingram, South Carolina, LB

SAN FRANCISCO 49ERS
Year   Player, College, Position
1950 Leo Nomellini, Minnesota, T
1951 Y.A. Tittle, Louisiana State, B
1952 Hugh McElhenny, Washington, B
1953 Harry Babcock, Georgia, E
     Tom Stolhandske, Texas, E
1954 Bernie Faloney, Maryland, B
1955 Dickie Moegle, Rice, B
1956 Earl Morrall, Michigan State, B
1957 John Brodie, Stanford, B
1958 Jim Pace, Michigan, B
     Charlie Krueger, Texas A&M, T
1959 Dave Baker, Oklahoma, B
     Dan James, Ohio State, C
1960 Monty Stickles, Notre Dame, E
1961 Jimmy Johnson, UCLA, CB
     Bernie Casey, Bowling Green, WR
     Bill Kilmer, UCLA, QB
1962 Lance Alworth, Arkansas, WR
1963 Kermit Alexander, UCLA, CB
1964 Dave Parks, Texas Tech, WR
1965 Ken Willard, North Carolina, RB
     George Donnelly, Illinois, DB
1966 Stan Hindman, Mississippi, DE
1967 Steve Spurrier, Florida, QB
     Cas Banaszek, Northwestern, T
1968 Forrest Blue, Auburn, C
1969 Ted Kwalick, Penn State, TE
     Gene Washington, Stanford, WR
1970 Cedrick Hardman, North Texas St., DE
     Bruce Taylor, Boston U., DB
1971 Tim Anderson, Ohio State, DB
1972 Terry Beasley, Auburn, WR
1973 Mike Holmes, Texas Southern, DB
1974 Wilbur Jackson, Alabama, RB
     Bill Sandifer, UCLA, DT
1975 Jimmy Webb, Mississippi St., DT
1976 Randy Cross, UCLA, C (2)
1977 Elmo Boyd, Eastern Kentucky, WR (3)
1978 Ken MacAfee, Notre Dame, TE
     Dan Bunz, Cal St.-Long Beach, LB
1979 James Owens, UCLA, WR (2)
1980 Earl Cooper, Rice, RB
     Jim Stuckey, Clemson, DT
1981 Ronnie Lott, So. California, DB
1982 Bubba Paris, Michigan, T (2)
1983 Roger Craig, Nebraska, RB (2)
1984 Todd Shell, Brigham Young, LB
1985 Jerry Rice, Mississippi Valley St., WR
1986 Larry Roberts, Alabama, DE (2)
1987 Harris Barton, North Carolina, T
     Terrence Flagler, Clemson, RB
1988 Danny Stubbs, Miami, DE (2)
1989 Keith DeLong, Tennessee, LB
1990 Dexter Carter, Florida State, RB
1991 Ted Washington, Louisville, DT
1992 Dana Hall, Washington, DB
1993 Dana Stubblefield, Kansas, DT
     Todd Kelly, Tennessee, DE
1994 Bryant Young, Notre Dame, DT
     William Floyd, Florida State, RB
1995 J.J. Stokes, UCLA, WR
1996 Israel Ifeanyi, So.California, DE (2)
1997 Jim Druckenmiller, Virginia Tech, QB

1998 R.W. McQuarters, Oklahoma St., DB
1999 Reggie McGrew, Florida, DT
2000 Julian Peterson, Michigan St., LB
     Ahmed Plummer, Ohio State, DB
2001 Andre Carter, California, DE
2002 Mike Rumph, Miami, DB
2003 Kwame Harris, Stanford, T
2004 Rashaun Woods, Oklahoma St., WR
2005 Alex Smith, Utah, QB
2006 Vernon Davis, Maryland, TE
     Manny Lawson, North Carolina St., DE
2007 Patrick Willis, Mississippi, LB
     Joe Staley, Central Michigan, T
2008 Kentwan Balmer, North Carolina, DT
2009 Michael Crabtree, Texas Tech, WR
2010 Anthony Davis, Rutgers, T
     Mike Iupati, Idaho, G
2011 Aldon Smith, Missouri, LB
2012 A.J. Jenkins, Illinois, WR

SEATTLE SEAHAWKS
Year   Player, College, Position
1976 Steve Niehaus, Notre Dame, DT
1977 Steve August, Tulsa, G
1978 Keith Simpson, Memphis St., DB
1979 Manu Tuiasosopo, UCLA, DT
1980 Jacob Green, Texas A&M, DE
1981 Ken Easley, UCLA, DB
1982 Jeff Bryant, Clemson, DE
1983 Curt Warner, Penn State, RB
1984 Terry Taylor, Southern Illinois, DB
1985 Owen Gill, Iowa, RB (2)
1986 John L. Williams, Florida, RB
1987 Tony Woods, Pittsburgh, LB
1988 Brian Blades, Miami, WR (2)
1989 Andy Heck, Notre Dame, T
1990 Cortez Kennedy, Miami, DT
1991 Dan McGwire, San Diego St., QB
1992 Ray Roberts, Virginia, T
1993 Rick Mirer, Notre Dame, QB
1994 Sam Adams, Texas A&M, DT
1995 Joey Galloway, Ohio State, WR
1996 Pete Kendall, Boston College, T
1997 Shawn Springs, Ohio State, DB
     Walter Jones, Florida State, T
1998 Anthony Simmons, Clemson, LB
1999 Lamar King, Saginaw Valley St., DE
2000 Shaun Alexander, Alabama, RB
     Chris McIntosh, Wisconsin, T
2001 Koren Robinson, North Carolina St., WR
     Steve Hutchinson, Michigan, G
2002 Jerramy Stevens, Washington, TE
2003 Marcus Trufant, Washington State, DB
2004 Marcus Tubbs, Texas, DT
2005 Chris Spencer, Mississippi, C
2006 Kelly Jennings, Miami, DB
2007 Josh Wilson, Maryland, DB (2)
2008 Lawrence Jackson, So. California, DE
2009 Aaron Curry, Wake Forest, LB
2010 Russell Okung, Oklahoma State, T
     Earl Thomas, Texas, DB
2011 James Carpenter, Alabama, T
2012 Bruce Irvin, West Virginia, DE

TAMPA BAY BUCCANEERS
Year   Player, College, Position
1976 Lee Roy Selmon, Oklahoma, DT
1977 Ricky Bell, Southern California, RB
1978 Doug Williams, Grambling, QB
1979 Greg Roberts, Oklahoma, G (2)

1980 Ray Snell, Wisconsin, G
1981 Hugh Green, Pittsburgh, LB
1982 Sean Farrell, Penn State, G
1983 Randy Grimes, Baylor, C (2)
1984 Keith Browner, So. California, LB (2)
1985 Ron Holmes, Washington, DE
1986 Bo Jackson, Auburn, RB
     Roderick Jones, So. Methodist, DB
1987 Vinny Testaverde, Miami, QB
1988 Paul Gruber, Wisconsin, T
1989 Broderick Thomas, Nebraska, LB
1990 Keith McCants, Alabama, LB
1991 Charles McRae, Tennessee, T
1992 Courtney Hawkins, Michigan St., WR (2)
1993 Eric Curry, Alabama, DE
1994 Trent Dilfer, Fresno State, QB
1995 Warren Sapp, Miami, DT
     Derrick Brooks, Florida State, LB
1996 Regan Upshaw, California, DE
     Marcus Jones, North Carolina, DT
1997 Warrick Dunn, Florida State, RB
     Reidel Anthony, Florida, WR
1998 Jacquez Green, Florida, WR (2)
1999 Anthony McFarland, Louisiana St., DT
2000 Cosey Coleman, Tennessee, G (2)
2001 Kenyatta Walker, Florida, T
2002 Marquise Walker, Michigan, WR (3)
2003 Dewayne White, Louisville, DE (2)
2004 Michael Clayton, Louisiana St., WR
2005 Carnell Williams, Auburn, RB
2006 Davin Joseph, Oklahoma, G
2007 Gaines Adams, Clemson, DE
2008 Aqib Talib, Kansas, DB
2009 Josh Freeman, Kansas State, QB
2010 Gerald McCoy, Oklahoma, DT
2011 Adrian Clayborn, Iowa, DE
2012 Mark Barron, Alabama, DB
     Doug Martin, Boise State, RB

TENNESSEE TITANS
Year Player, College, Position
1960 Billy Cannon, Louisiana State, RB
1961 Mike Ditka, Pittsburgh, E
1962 Ray Jacobs, Howard Payne, DT
1963 Danny Brabham, Arkansas, LB
1964 Scott Appleton, Texas, DT
1965 Lawrence Elkins, Baylor, WR
1966 Tommy Nobis, Texas, LB
1967 George Webster, Michigan St., LB
     Tom Regner, Notre Dame, G
1968 Mac Haik, Mississippi, WR (2)
1969 Ron Pritchard, Arizona State, LB
1970 Doug Wilkerson, N. Carolina Central, G
1971 Dan Pastorini, Santa Clara, QB
1972 Greg Sampson, Stanford, DE
1973 John Matuszak, Tampa, DE
     George Amundson, Iowa State, RB
1974 Steve Manstedt, Nebraska, LB (4)
1975 Robert Brazile, Jackson State, LB
     Don Hardeman, Texas A&I, RB
1976 Mike Barber, Louisiana Tech, TE (2)
1977 Morris Towns, Missouri, T
1978 Earl Campbell, Texas, RB
1979 Mike Stensrud, Iowa State, DE (2)
1980 Angelo Fields, Michigan St., T (2)
1981 Michael Holston, Morgan St., WR (3)
1982 Mike Munchak, Penn State, G
1983 Bruce Matthews, So. California, T
1984 Dean Steinkuhler, Nebraska, T

1985 Ray Childress, Texas A&M, DE
     Richard Johnson, Wisconsin, DB
1986 Jim Everett, Purdue, QB
1987 Alonzo Highsmith, Miami, RB
     Haywood Jeffires, North Carolina St., WR
1988 Lorenzo White, Michigan State, RB
1989 David Williams, Florida, T
1990 Lamar Lathon, Houston, LB
1991 Mike Dumas, Indiana, DB (2)
1992 Eddie Robinson, Alabama St., LB (2)
1993 Brad Hopkins, Illinois, T
1994 Henry Ford, Arkansas, DE
1995 Steve McNair, Alcorn State, QB
1996 Eddie George, Ohio State, RB
1997 Kenny Holmes, Miami, DE
1998 Kevin Dyson, Utah, WR
1999 Jevon Kearse, Florida, DE
2000 Keith Bulluck, Syracuse, LB
2001 Andre Dyson, Utah, DB (2)
2002 Albert Haynesworth, Tennessee, DT
2003 Andre Woolfolk, Oklahoma, DB
2004 Ben Troupe, Florida, TE (2)
2005 Adam Jones, West Virginia, DB
2006 Vince Young, Texas, QB
2007 Michael Griffin, Texas, DB
2008 Chris Johnson, East Carolina, RB
2009 Kenny Britt, Rutgers, WR
2010 Derrick Morgan, Georgia Tech, DE
2011 Jake Locker, Washington, QB
2012 Kendall Wright, Baylor, WR

WASHINGTON REDSKINS
Year Player, College, Position
1936 Riley Smith, Alabama, B
1937 Sammy Baugh, Texas Christian, B
1938 Andy Farkas, Detroit, B
1939 I.B. Hale, Texas Christian, T
1940 Ed Boell, New York U., B
1941 Forest Evashevski, Michigan, B
1942 Orban (Spec) Sanders, Texas, B
1943 Jack Jenkins, Missouri, B
1944 Mike Micka, Colgate, B
1945 Jim Hardy, Southern California, B
1946 Cal Rossi, UCLA, B*
1947 Cal Rossi, UCLA, B
1948 Harry Gilmer, Alabama, B
     Lowell Tew, Alabama, B
1949 Rob Goode, Texas A&M, B
1950 George Thomas, Oklahoma, B
1951 Leon Heath, Oklahoma, B
1952 Larry Isbell, Baylor, B
1953 Jack Scarbath, Maryland, B
1954 Steve Meilinger, Kentucky, E
1955 Ralph Guglielmi, Notre Dame, B
1956 Ed Vereb, Maryland, B
1957 Don Bosseler, Miami, B
1958 Mike Sommer, George
     Washington, B (2)
1959 Don Allard, Boston College, B
1960 Richie Lucas, Penn State, QB
1961 Norman Snead, Wake Forest, QB
     Joe Rutgens, Illinois, DT
1962 Ernie Davis, Syracuse, RB
1963 Pat Richter, Wisconsin, TE
1964 Charley Taylor, Arizona St., RB-WR
1965 Bob Breitenstein, Tulsa, T (2)
1966 Charlie Gogolak, Princeton, K
1967 Ray McDonald, Idaho, RB
1968 Jim Smith, Oregon, DB
1969 Eugene Epps, Texas-El Paso, DB (2)

1970 Bill Bundige, Colorado, DT (2)
1971 Cotton Speyrer, Texas, WR (2)
1972 Moses Denson, Maryland St., RB (8)
1973 Charles Cantrell, Lamar, G (5)
1974 Jon Keyworth, Colorado, TE (6)
1975 Mike Thomas, Nevada-Las Vegas, RB (6)
1976 Mike Hughes, Baylor, G (5)
1977 Duncan McColl, Stanford, DE (4)
1978 Tony Green, Florida, RB (6)
1979 Don Warren, San Diego St., TE (4)
1980 Art Monk, Syracuse, WR
1981 Mark May, Pittsburgh, T
1982 Vernon Dean, San Diego St., DB (2)
1983 Darrell Green, Texas A&I, DB
1984 Bob Slater, Oklahoma, DT (2)
1985 Tory Nixon, San Diego St., DB (2)
1986 Markus Koch, Boise State, DE (2)
1987 Brian Davis, Nebraska, DB (2)
1988 Chip Lohmiller, Minnesota, K (2)
1989 Tracy Rocker, Auburn, DT (3)
1990 Andre Collins, Penn State, LB (2)
1991 Bobby Wilson, Michigan State, DT
1992 Desmond Howard, Michigan, WR
1993 Tom Carter, Notre Dame, DB
1994 Heath Shuler, Tennessee, QB
1995 Michael Westbrook, Colorado, WR
1996 Andre Johnson, Penn State, T
1997 Kenard Lang, Miami, DE
1998 Stephen Alexander, Oklahoma, TE (2)
1999 Champ Bailey, Georgia, DB
2000 LaVar Arrington, Penn State, LB
     Chris Samuels, Alabama, T
2001 Rod Gardner, Clemson, WR
2002 Patrick Ramsey, Tulane, QB
2003 Taylor Jacobs, Florida, WR (2)
2004 Sean Taylor, Miami, DB
2005 Carlos Rogers, Auburn, DB
     Jason Campbell, Auburn, QB
2006 Rocky McIntosh, Miami, LB (2)
2007 LaRon Landry, Louisiana State, DB
2008 Devin Thomas, Michigan State, WR (2)
2009 Brian Orakpo, Texas, DE
2010 Trent Williams, Oklahoma, T
2011 Ryan Kerrigan, Purdue, LB
2012 Robert Griffin III, Baylor, QB
Choice lost because of ineligibility

NFL'S 10 HIGHEST SCORING WEEKENDS

Point Total	Date	Weekend
837	November 20-24, 2008	12th
788	December 29-30, 2007	17th
788	December 5-6, 2004	13th
788	September 5, 8-9, 2002	1st
779	December 16, 19-20, 2010	15th
762	November 10-11, 1996	11th
761	October 16-17, 1983	7th
759	October 2-3, 2011	4th
759	January 1, 2012	17th
753	December 8-9, 2002	14th

TOP 10 TELEVISED SPORTS EVENTS OF ALL-TIME

(Based on A.C. Nielsen Figures)

Program	Date	Network	Share	Rating
Super Bowl XVI	1/24/82	CBS	73%	49.1
Super Bowl XVII	1/30/83	NBC	69%	48.6
Winter Olympics	2/23/94	CBS	64%	48.5
Super Bowl XX	1/26/86	NBC	70%	48.3
Super Bowl XII	1/15/78	CBS	67%	47.2
Super Bowl XIII	1/21/79	NBC	74%	47.1
Super Bowl XLVI	2/5/12	NBC	71%	47.0
Super Bowl XVIII	1/22/84	CBS	71%	46.4
Super Bowl XIX	1/20/85	ABC	63%	46.4
Super Bowl XIV	1/20/80	CBS	67%	46.3

TEN MOST WATCHED TV PROGRAMS & ESTIMATED TOTAL NUMBER OF VIEWERS

(Based on A.C. Nielsen Figures)

Program	Date	Network	*Total Viewers
Super Bowl XLV	Feb. 6, 2011	FOX	162,900,000
Super Bowl XLVI	Feb. 5, 2012	NBC	159,200,000
Super Bowl XLIV	Feb. 7, 2010	CBS	153,400,000
Super Bowl XLIII	Feb. 1, 2009	NBC	151,600,000
Super Bowl XLII	Feb. 3, 2008	FOX	148,300,000
Super Bowl XXXVIII	Feb. 1, 2004	CBS	144,400,000
Super Bowl XL	Feb. 5, 2006	ABC	141,400,000
Super Bowl XLI	Feb. 4, 2007	CBS	139,800,000
Super Bowl XXXVII	Jan. 26, 2003	ABC	138,900,000
Super Bowl XXX	Jan. 28, 1996	NBC	138,488,000

*Watched some portion of the broadcast

NFL'S TOP FIVE PAID ATTENDANCE TOTALS FOR ALL GAMES

Year	Preseason	Regular Season	Postseason	All Games
2007	4,119,278	17,345,205	792,019	22,256,502
2006	4,083,282	17,340,879	775,551	22,199,712
2008	3,995,942	17,055,982	806,840	21,858,764
2005	3,977,388	17,012,453	802,255	21,792,096
2004	3,918,848	17,000,811	788,965	21,708,624

TEN HIGHEST-RATED *NFL MONDAY NIGHT FOOTBALL* GAMES OF ALL-TIME

(Based on A.C. Nielsen Figures)

Game	Date	Share	Rating
Chicago at Miami	12/2/85	46%	29.6
N.Y. Giants at San Francisco	12/3/90	42%	26.9
Dallas at Washington	10/2/78	43%	26.8
Pittsburgh at San Diego	12/22/80	40%	25.3
Philadelphia at Miami	11/30/81	40%	25.3
Pittsburgh at Houston	12/10/79	40%	25.1
Dallas at Miami	12/17/84	40%	25.1
Pittsburgh at Dallas	9/13/82	42%	24.9
Cincinnati at Oakland	12/6/76	40%	24.7
Dallas at Washington	10/8/73	40%	24.6
Minnesota at Atlanta	11/19/73	40%	24.6

NFL'S 10 BIGGEST SINGLE-GAME ATTENDANCE TOTALS

Date	Site	Game	Teams	Attendance
August 15, 1994	Azteca Stadium	American Bowl (Mexico City)	Cowboys vs. Oilers	112,376
August 17, 1998	Azteca Stadium	American Bowl (Mexico City)	Cowboys vs. Patriots	106,424
August 22, 1947	Soldier Field	College All-Star	Bears vs. All-Stars	105,840
September 20, 2009	Cowboys Stadium	Regular Season	Cowboys vs. Giants	105,121
August 4, 1997	Estadio Guillermo Canedo	American Bowl (Mexico City)	Broncos vs. Dolphins	104,629
January 20, 1980	Rose Bowl	Super Bowl XIV	Steelers vs. Rams	103,985
January 30, 1983	Rose Bowl	Super Bowl XVII	Redskins vs. Dolphins	103,667
October 2, 2005	Azteca Stadium	Regular Season	49ers at Cardinals	103,467
January 9, 1977	Rose Bowl	Super Bowl XI	Raiders vs. Vikings	103,438
November 10, 1957	L.A. Coliseum	Regular Season	49ers at Rams	102,368

NFL'S TOP 10 PAID ATTENDANCE WEEKENDS

Weekend	Games	Attendance
September 8, 11-12, 2005	16	1,115,018
December 6, 9-10, 2007	16	1,113,376
November 20-21, 2005	16	1,112,555
December 27-28, 2003	16	1,106,818
November 19-20, 2006	16	1,106,739
September 23-24, 2007	16	1,103,570
December 24-26, 2005	16	1,102,701
September 7, 10-11, 2006	16	1,102,102
September 9, 12-13, 2004	16	1,101,332
December 7, 10-11, 2006	16	1,099,794

NFL'S TOP 10 TEAM SINGLE-SEASON HOME PAID ATTENDANCE TOTALS

Year	Club	Games	Attendance
2007	Washington Redskins	8	711,471
2008	Washington Redskins	8	710,049
2006	Washington Redskins	8	708,952
2004	Washington Redskins	8	707,920
2005	Washington Redskins	8	707,614
2009	Washington Redskins	8	681,703
2010	Washington Redskins	8	680,966
2003	Washington Redskins	8	667,033
2002	Washington Redskins	8	663,536
2001	Washington Redskins	8	661,970

NFL PAID ATTENDANCE

For detailed 2011 attendance, see page 246.

Year	Regular Season			Average	Postseason	Total
2011	16,562,706	(256 games)		64,698	828,457 (12)	17,391,163
2010	16,569,514	(255 games****)		64,978	800,426 (12)	17,369,940
2009	16,651,126	(256 games)		65,043	823,882 (12)	17,475,008
2008	17,055,982	(256 games)		66,625	806,840 (12)	17,862,822
2007	17,345,205	(256 games)		#67,755	792,019 (12)	#18,137,224
2006	17,340,879	(256 games)		67,738	775,551 (12)	18,116,430
2005	17,012,453	(256 games)		66,455	802,255 (12)	17,814,708
2004	17,000,811	(256 games)		66,409	788,965 (12)	17,789,776
2003	16,913,584	(255 games***)		66,328	805,546 (12)	17,719,130
2002	16,833,310	(256 games)		65,755	781,944 (12)	17,615,254
2001	16,166,258	(248 games)		65,187	766,905 (12)	16,933,163
2000	16,387,289	(248 games)		66,078	809,132 (12)	17,196,421
1999	16,206,640	(248 games)		65,349	793,759 (12)	17,000,399
1998	15,364,873	(240 games)		64,020	822,885 (12)	16,187,758
1997	14,967,314	(240 games)		62,364	801,879 (12)	15,769,193
1996	14,612,417	(240 games)		60,885	769,310 (12)	15,381,727
1995	15,043,562	(240 games)		62,682	790,906 (12)	15,834,468
1994	14,030,435	(224 games)		62,636	779,738 (12)	14,810,173
1993	13,966,843	(224 games)		62,352	814,607 (12)	14,781,450
1992	13,828,887	(224 games)		61,736	815,910 (12)	14,644,797
1991	13,841,459	(224 games)		61,792	813,247 (12)	14,654,706
1990	13,959,896	(224 games)		62,321	847,543 (12)	14,807,439
1989	13,625,662	(224 games)		60,829	685,771 (10)	14,311,433
1988	13,539,848	(224 games)		60,446	658,317 (10)	14,198,165
1987	11,406,166	(210 games**)		54,315	656,977 (10)	12,063,143
1986	13,588,551	(224 games)		60,663	734,002 (10)	14,322,553
1985	13,345,047	(224 games)		59,567	710,768 (10)	14,055,815
1984	13,398,112	(224 games)		59,813	665,194 (10)	14,063,306
1983	13,277,222	(224 games)		59,273	675,513 (10)	13,952,735
1982	7,367,438	(126 games*)		58,472	#1,033,153 (16)	8,400,591
1981	13,606,990	(224 games)		60,745	637,763 (10)	14,244,753
1980	13,392,230	(224 games)		59,787	624,430 (10)	14,016,660
1979	13,182,039	(224 games)		58,848	630,326 (10)	13,812,365
1978	12,771,800	(224 games)		57,017	624,388 (10)	13,396,188
1977	11,018,632	(196 games)		56,218	534,925 (8)	11,553,557
1976	11,070,543	(196 games)		56,482	492,884 (8)	11,563,427
1975	10,213,193	(182 games)		56,116	475,919 (8)	10,689,112
1974	10,236,322	(182 games)		56,244	438,664 (8)	10,674,986
1973	10,730,933	(182 games)		58,961	525,433 (8)	11,256,366
1972	10,445,827	(182 games)		57,395	483,345 (8)	10,929,172
1971	10,076,035	(182 games)		55,363	483,891 (8)	10,559,926
1970	9,533,333	(182 games)		52,381	458,493 (8)	9,991,826
1969	6,096,127	(112 games)	NFL	54,430	162,279 (3)	6,258,406
	2,843,373	(70 games)	AFL	40,620	167,088 (3)	3,010,461
1968	5,882,313	(112 games)	NFL	52,521	215,902 (3)	6,098,215
	2,635,004	(70 games)	AFL	37,643	114,438 (2)	2,749,442
1967	5,938,924	(112 games)	NFL	53,026	166,208 (3)	6,105,132
	2,295,697	(63 games)	AFL	36,439	53,330 (1)	2,349,027
1966	5,337,044	(105 games)	NFL	50,829	74,152 (1)	5,411,196
	2,160,369	(63 games)	AFL	34,291	42,080 (1)	2,202,449
1965	4,634,021	(98 games)	NFL	47,286	100,304 (2)	4,734,325
	1,782,384	(56 games)	AFL	31,828	30,361 (1)	1,812,745

PAID ATTENDANCE

Year	Regular Season			Average	Postseason	Total
1964	4,563,049	(98 games)	NFL	46,562	79,544 (1)	4,642,593
	1,447,875	(56 games)	AFL	25,855	40,242 (1)	1,488,117
1963	4,163,643	(98 games)	NFL	42,486	45,801 (1)	4,209,444
	1,208,697	(56 games)	AFL	21,584	63,171 (2)	1,271,868
1962	4,003,421	(98 games)	NFL	40,851	64,892 (1)	4,068,313
	1,147,302	(56 games)	AFL	20,487	37,981 (1)	1,185,283
1961	3,986,159	(98 games)	NFL	40,675	39,029 (1)	4,025,188
	1,002,657	(56 games)	AFL	17,904	29,556 (1)	1,032,213
1960	3,128,296	(78 games)	NFL	40,106	67,325 (1)	3,195,621
	926,156	(56 games)	AFL	16,538	32,183 (1)	958,339
1959	3,140,000	(72 games)		43,617	57,545 (1)	3,197,545
1958	3,006,124	(72 games)		41,752	123,659 (2)	3,129,783
1957	2,836,318	(72 games)		39,393	119,579 (2)	2,955,897
1956	2,551,263	(72 games)		35,434	56,836 (1)	2,608,099
1955	2,521,836	(72 games)		35,026	85,693 (1)	2,607,529
1954	2,190,571	(72 games)		30,425	43,827 (1)	2,234,398
1953	2,164,585	(72 games)		30,064	54,577 (1)	2,219,162
1952	2,052,126	(72 games)		28,502	97,507 (2)	2,149,633
1951	1,913,019	(72 games)		26,570	57,522 (1)	1,970,541
1950	1,977,753	(78 games)		25,356	136,647 (3)	2,114,400
1949	1,391,735	(60 games)		23,196	27,980 (1)	1,419,715
1948	1,525,243	(60 games)		25,421	36,309 (1)	1,561,552
1947	1,837,437	(60 games)		30,624	66,268 (2)	1,903,705
1946	1,732,135	(55 games)		31,493	58,346 (1)	1,790,481
1945	1,270,401	(50 games)		25,408	32,178 (1)	1,302,579
1944	1,019,649	(50 games)		20,393	46,016 (1)	1,065,665
1943	969,128	(40 games)		24,228	71,315 (2)	1,040,443
1942	887,920	(55 games)		16,144	36,006 (1)	923,926
1941	1,108,615	(55 games)		20,157	55,870 (2)	1,164,485
1940	1,063,025	(55 games)		19,328	36,034 (1)	1,099,059
1939	1,071,200	(55 games)		19,476	32,279 (1)	1,103,479
1938	937,197	(55 games)		17,040	48,120 (1)	985,317
1937	963,039	(55 games)		17,510	15,878 (1)	978,917
1936	816,007	(54 games)		15,111	29,545 (1)	845,552
1935	638,178	(53 games)		12,041	15,000 (1)	653,178
1934	492,684	(60 games)		8,211	35,059 (1)	527,743

Record

*Players' 57-day strike reduced 224-game schedule to 126 games.
**Players' 24-day strike reduced 224-game schedule to 210 games.
***The Week 8 Miami at San Diego game is not included. The game was moved to Arizona due to the San Diego wildfires and tickets were distributed at no charge.
****The Week 14 N.Y. Giants at Minnesota game is not included. The game was moved to Detroit due to the Minneapolis blizzard. Original game tickets were cross-honored at Ford Field. Remaining tickets were distributed at no charge.

WALTER PAYTON NFL MAN OF THE YEAR

The Walter Payton NFL Man of the Year Award is the only NFL award that recognizes a player for his community service activities as well as his excellence on the field. Renamed in 1999 for the legendary Chicago Bears Pro Football Hall of Fame running back, the Walter Payton NFL Man of the Year Award has been given annually since 1970.

YEAR	PLAYER	POS.	TEAM
1970	Johnny Unitas	QB	Baltimore Colts
1971	John Hadl	QB	San Diego Chargers
1972	Willie Lanier	LB	Kansas City Chiefs
1973	Len Dawson	QB	Kansas City Chiefs
1974	George Blanda	QB	Oakland Raiders
1975	Ken Anderson	QB	Cincinnati Bengals
1976	Franco Harris	RB	Pittsburgh Steelers
1977	Walter Payton	RB	Chicago Bears
1978	Roger Staubach	QB	Dallas Cowboys
1979	Joe Greene	DT	Pittsburgh Steelers
1980	Harold Carmichael	WR	Philadelphia Eagles
1981	Lynn Swann	WR	Pittsburgh Steelers
1982	Joe Theismann	QB	Washington Redskins
1983	Rolf Benirschke	K	San Diego Chargers
1984	Marty Lyons	T	New York Jets
1985	Dwight Stephenson	C	Miami Dolphins
1986	Reggie Williams	LB	Cincinnati Bengals
1987	Dave Duerson	S	Chicago Bears
1988	Steve Largent	WR	Seattle Seahawks
1989	Warren Moon	QB	Houston Oilers
1990	Mike Singletary	LB	Chicago Bears
1991	Anthony Muñoz	T	Cincinnati Bengals
1992	John Elway	QB	Denver Broncos
1993	Derrick Thomas	LB	Kansas City Chiefs
1994	Junior Seau	LB	San Diego Chargers
1995	Boomer Esiason	QB	New York Jets
1996	Darrell Green	CB	Washington Redskins
1997	Troy Aikman	QB	Dallas Cowboys
1998	Dan Marino	QB	Miami Dolphins
1999	Cris Carter	WR	Minnesota Vikings
2000*	Derrick Brooks	LB	Tampa Bay Buccaneers
	Jim Flanigan	DT	Chicago Bears
2001	Jerome Bettis	RB	Pittsburgh Steelers
2002	Troy Vincent	CB	Philadelphia Eagles
2003	Will Shields	G	Kansas City Chiefs
2004	Warrick Dunn	RB	Atlanta Falcons
2005	Peyton Manning	QB	Indianapolis Colts
2006*	Drew Brees	QB	New Orleans Saints
	LaDainian Tomlinson	RB	San Diego Chargers
2007	Jason Taylor	DE	Miami Dolphins
2008	Kurt Warner	QB	Arizona Cardinals
2009	Brian Waters	G	Kansas City Chiefs
2010	Madieu Williams	S	Minnesota Vikings
2011	Matt Birk	C	Baltimore Ravens

* The award was shared in 2000 and 2006.

AFC VS. NFC (REGULAR SEASON), 1970-2011

	Balt	Buff	Cin	Cle	Den	Hou	Ind	Jax	KC	Mia
1970		0-3	1-2	0-3	2-2		3-0		0-2-1	2-1
1971		0-3	1-2	2-1	1-3		2-1		2-1	3-0
1972		2-0-1	2-1	1-2	1-3		0-3		2-1	3-0
1973		2-1	2-1	1-2	0-3-1		2-1		1-1-1	3-0
1974		2-1	2-1	1-2	2-2		1-2		1-2	2-1
1975		1-2	3-0	1-3	2-1		2-1		2-1	3-0
1976		0-2	2-0	2-0	2-0		0-2		1-1	0-2
1977		1-1	2-1	1-1	1-1		1-1		1-1	2-0
1978		1-1	2-2	4-0	2-2		2-2		0-2	3-1
1979		2-2	2-2	3-1	3-1		1-1		0-2	4-0
1980		3-1	2-2	3-1	3-1		1-1		2-0	4-0
1981		1-3	2-2	3-1	3-1		0-4		2-2	3-1
1982		1-2	1-0	0-2	2-1		0-1-1		0-3	1-1
1983		1-3	3-1	2-2	0-2		2-0		2-2	3-1
1984		1-3	2-2	1-3	3-1		0-4		1-1	4-0
1985		0-2	2-2	1-3	3-1		3-1		2-2	3-1
1986		1-1	3-1	2-2	3-1		1-3		1-1	2-2
1987		1-2	1-2	2-2	2-1-1		1-0		1-2	3-0
1988		2-2	4-0	4-0	3-1		2-2		0-2	3-1
1989		1-3	2-2	3-1	2-2		1-3		2-0	2-0
1990		3-1	1-3	1-3	1-3		2-2		4-0	2-2
1991		3-1	1-3	0-4	2-0		0-4		2-2	3-1
1992		4-0	1-3	2-2	1-3		2-0		2-2	2-2
1993		4-0	2-2	3-1	1-3		0-4		2-2	3-1
1994		1-3	1-3	3-1	1-3		0-2		3-1	2-2
1995		3-1	2-2	1-3	2-2		2-2	0-4	3-1	2-2
1996	2-2	4-0	2-2		3-1		3-1	2-2	4-0	1-3
1997	2-1-1	1-3	2-2		3-1		1-3	2-2	4-0	1-3
1998	1-3	3-1	1-3		3-1		0-4	3-1	3-1	3-1
1999	2-1	3-1	1-2	1-2	2-2		4-0	4-0	2-2	2-2
2000	2-1	2-2	1-2	0-3	3-1		2-2	2-2	2-2	2-2
2001	2-2	1-3	1-2	1-2	3-1		1-3	1-2	1-3	2-2
2002	0-4	3-1	1-3	2-2	4-0	2-2	2-2	2-2	2-2	2-2
2003	3-1	2-2	2-2	2-2	1-3	2-2	3-1	2-2	3-1	3-1
2004	3-1	4-0	4-0	1-3	3-1	1-3	4-0	3-1	1-3	2-2
2005	2-2	0-4	4-0	2-2	3-1	1-3	3-1	3-1	1-3	2-2
2006	3-1	2-2	2-2	1-3	1-3	0-4	3-1	3-1	4-0	3-1
2007	3-1	1-3	1-3	3-1	1-3	3-1	4-0	3-1	1-3	0-4
2008	3-1	2-2	1-2-1	1-3	3-1	3-1	2-2	2-2	0-4	3-1
2009	2-2	2-2	3-1	0-4	2-2	3-1	4-0	1-3	1-3	2-2
2010	3-1	1-3	1-3	2-2	1-3	1-3	2-2	1-3	4-0	2-2
2011	3-1	2-2	3-1	1-3	2-2	2-2	0-4	1-3	3-1	1-3
Total	36-25-1	74-75-1	79-72-1	64-78	86-70-2	18-22	69-73-1	35-32	75-65-2	98-55

AFC VS. NFC (REGULAR SEASON), 1970-2011

	NE	NYJ	Oak	Pitt	SD	Sea	TB	Tenn	TOTALS
1970	0-3	2-1	1-2	0-3	1-2			0-3	12-27-1
1971	0-3	0-3	1-1-1	1-2	2-1			0-2-1	15-23-2
1972	3-0	1-2	3-0	2-1	0-3			0-3	20-19-1
1973	2-1	0-3	2-1	3-0	1-2			0-3	19-19-2
1974	3-0	2-1	3-0	3-0	1-2			0-3	23-17
1975	1-2	0-3	3-0	2-1	0-3			3-0	23-17
1976	1-1	0-2	3-0	1-1	2-0		0-1	2-0	16-12
1977	2-0	1-1	1-1	2-0	1-1	1-0		2-0	19-9
1978	2-2	1-3	4-0	3-1	2-2	3-1		2-2	31-21
1979	3-1	3-1	4-0	3-1	3-1	3-1		2-2	36-16
1980	1-3	1-3	2-2	4-0	2-2	1-3		4-0	33-19
1981	0-4	2-0	2-2	3-1	2-2	0-2		1-3	24-28
1982	0-1	4-0	3-0	1-0	1-0	1-0		0-3	15-14-1
1983	2-2	3-1	2-2	2-2	2-2	1-3		1-3	26-26
1984	0-4	0-2	3-1	3-1	4-0	4-0		0-4	26-26
1985	3-1	2-2	3-1	1-3	1-1	2-2		1-3	27-25
1986	3-1	2-2	1-3	2-2	0-4	3-1		2-2	26-26
1987	0-3	0-4	2-2	2-2	2-0	4-0		2-2	23-22-1
1988	2-2	2-0	1-3	1-3	2-2	1-3		3-1	30-22
1989	0-4	1-3	2-2	3-1	2-2	0-4		3-1	24-28
1990	0-4	2-0	3-1	3-1	1-1	2-2		1-3	26-26
1991	1-1	2-2	2-2	0-4	1-3	1-3		1-3	19-33
1992	0-4	0-4	2-2	1-3	2-0	0-4		3-1	22-30
1993	1-1	2-2	3-1	2-2	2-2	0-2		2-2	27-25
1994	4-0	1-3	3-1	2-2	2-2	2-0		0-4	25-27
1995	0-4	0-4	3-1	2-2	3-1	3-1		1-3	27-33
1996	2-2	1-3	1-3	2-2	1-3	2-2		2-2	32-28
1997	1-3	3-1	2-2	2-2	1-3	2-2		4-0	31-28-1
1998	2-2	2-2	3-1	2-2	1-3	3-1		1-3	31-29
1999	3-1	2-2	3-1	3-0	1-3	2-2		3-1	38-22
2000	0-4	3-1	4-0	1-2	0-4	2-2		4-0	30-30
2001	3-1	2-2	3-1	3-0	2-2	1-3		3-1	30-30
2002	3-1	3-1	2-2	2-1-1	2-2			2-2	34-29-1
2003	3-1	0-4	1-3	1-3	2-2			4-0	34-30
2004	4-0	3-1	2-2	4-0	3-1			2-2	44-20
2005	3-1	1-3	2-2	4-0	2-2			1-3	34-30
2006	4-0	3-1	1-3	3-1	4-0			3-1	40-24
2007	4-0	0-4	0-4	3-1	2-2			3-1	32-32
2008	4-0	2-2	1-3	2-2	1-3			4-0	34-29-1
2009	3-1	2-2	1-3	3-1	4-0			4-0	37-27
2010	4-0	2-2	2-2	3-1	2-2			3-1	34-30
2011	3-1	2-2	2-2	3-1	1-3			2-2	31-33
Total	80-70	65-85	92-65-1	93-58-1	71-76	44-44	0-1	81-75-1	1,160-1,041-11

NFC VS. AFC (REGULAR SEASON), 1970-2011

	Ariz	Atl	Car	Chi	Dall	Det	GB	Minn	NO
1970	2-0-1	1-2		1-2	3-0	3-0	2-1	2-1	0-3
1971	2-1	3-0		1-2	3-0	4-0	2-1	2-1	0-1-2
1972	1-2	2-2		1-2	3-0	2-0-1	2-1	1-2	0-3
1973	0-2-1	2-1		2-2	2-1	0-3	1-1-1	2-1	1-2
1974	2-1	0-3		0-3	2-1	1-2	2-1	2-1	0-3
1975	2-1	1-2		0-3	2-1	1-2	0-3	4-0	0-3
1976	1-1	0-2		0-2	2-0	2-0	0-2	2-0	1-2
1977	0-2	0-2		1-1	1-1	2-0	0-3	1-1	0-2
1978	0-4	1-3		0-4	3-1	2-2	2-2	1-3	1-3
1979	1-3	1-3		2-2	1-3	0-4	1-3	1-3	0-4
1980	1-1	2-2		0-4	3-1	0-2	1-3	1-3	1-3
1981	3-1	1-3		4-0	4-0	2-2	1-1	1-3	2-2
1982		1-1		1-1	2-1	0-1	1-1-1	1-3	1-0
1983	3-1	3-1		1-1	2-2	1-3	2-2	4-0	1-3
1984	3-1	1-3		2-2	2-2	0-4	0-4	0-4	3-1
1985	2-2	0-4		3-1	3-1	2-2	0-4	2-0	0-4
1986	1-1	1-3		4-0	1-3	1-3	1-3	1-3	1-3
1987	0-1	0-4		2-2	2-1	0-4	1-2-1	2-1	4-0
1988	1-3	1-3		3-1	0-4	1-1	1-3	2-2	4-0
1989	1-3	2-2		2-2	0-2	1-3	0-2	2-2	4-0
1990	2-2	2-2		2-2	1-1	1-3	1-3	2-2	2-2
1991	1-1	3-1		2-2	3-1	4-0	1-3	0-2	3-1
1992	0-2	2-2		1-3	4-0	2-2	3-1	3-1	3-1
1993	1-1	1-3		2-2	2-2	2-0	3-1	2-2	2-2
1994	3-1	1-3		3-1	3-1	2-2	1-3	2-2	1-3
1995	1-3	2-2	3-1	2-2	4-0	3-1	4-0	3-1	4-0
1996	0-4	0-4	3-1	2-2	2-2	1-3	3-1	1-3	1-3
1997	1-3	2-2	2-2	2-2	2-2	2-2	3-1	3-1	2-2
1998	1-3	3-1	1-3	2-2	1-3	1-3	3-1	4-0	1-3
1999	0-4	0-4	2-2	2-2	1-3	1-3	2-2	2-2	0-4
2000	1-3	1-3	2-2	2-2	1-3	2-2	1-3	3-1	1-3
2001	3-1	1-3	0-4	3-1	0-4	0-4	3-1	1-3	2-2
2002	0-4	2-1-1	3-1	1-3	2-2	0-4	3-1	1-3	2-2
2003	1-3	1-3	2-2	3-1	2-2	1-3	3-1	2-2	1-3
2004	1-3	3-1	1-3	1-3	1-3	1-3	1-3	3-1	2-2
2005	1-3	3-1	3-1	1-3	2-2	2-2	0-4	1-3	2-2
2006	0-4	2-2	2-2	2-2	3-1	1-3	1-3	0-4	1-3
2007	3-1	1-3	0-4	3-1	3-1	3-1	4-0	2-2	1-3
2008	2-2	3-1	4-0	2-2	2-2	0-4	1-3	2-2	3-1
2009	2-2	3-1	0-4	2-2	2-2	1-3	2-2	3-1	4-0
2010	2-2	3-1	0-4	3-1	2-2	1-3	2-2	1-3	2-2
2011	1-3	3-1	3-1	1-3	2-2	4-0	3-1	0-4	4-0
Total	53-86-2	65-91-1	31-37	74-81	86-66	60-89-1	68-83-3	75-79	68-86-2

NFC VS. AFC (REGULAR SEASON), 1970-2011

	NYG	Phil	StL	SF	Sea	TB	Wash	TOTALS
1970	3-0	2-1	2-1	4-0			2-1	27-12-1
1971	1-2	1-2	1-2	2-1			1-2	23-15-2
1972	1-2	2-1	1-2	2-1			1-2	19-20-1
1973	1-2	2-1	3-0	1-2			2-1	19-19-2
1974	1-2	2-1	3-1	0-3			2-1	17-23
1975	2-1	0-3	3-0	1-2			1-2	17-23
1976	0-2	0-2	1-1	1-1	1-0		1-1	12-16
1977	0-2	1-1	2-0	0-2		0-1	1-1	9-19
1978	1-1	3-1	2-2	1-3		2-0	2-2	21-31
1979	1-1	2-2	2-2	0-4		2-0	2-2	16-36
1980	1-3	3-1	2-2	2-2		1-3	1-3	19-33
1981	1-1	3-1	1-3	3-1		0-4	2-2	28-24
1982	1-0	2-1	1-2	1-3		2-1		14-15-1
1983	0-4	1-1	1-3	2-2		1-3	4-0	26-26
1984	2-0	3-1	3-1	3-1		1-1	3-1	26-26
1985	2-2	1-1	3-1	3-1		0-4	4-0	25-27
1986	3-1	2-2	2-2	4-0		1-1	3-1	26-26
1987	2-1	3-1	1-2	3-1		0-2	2-1	22-23-1
1988	1-1	2-2	2-2	2-2		1-3	1-3	22-30
1989	4-0	3-1	3-1	4-0		0-4	2-2	28-24
1990	3-1	1-3	2-2	4-0		0-2	3-1	26-26
1991	3-1	4-0	1-3	3-1		1-3	4-0	33-19
1992	2-2	3-1	2-2	3-1		0-2	2-2	30-22
1993	2-2	2-2	2-2	2-2		1-3	1-3	25-27
1994	3-1	1-3	2-2	3-1		1-1	1-1	27-25
1995	0-4	1-3	1-3	3-1		2-2	0-4	33-27
1996	2-2	2-2	2-2	4-0		2-2	3-1	28-32
1997	1-3	2-1-1	0-4	2-2		3-1	1-3	28-31-1
1998	3-1	0-4	3-1	2-2		2-2	2-2	29-31
1999	2-2	1-3	3-1	1-3		3-1	2-2	22-38
2000	3-1	3-1	3-1	2-2		3-1	2-2	30-30
2001	2-2	3-1	4-0	4-0		2-2	2-2	30-30
2002	2-2	1-3	2-2	2-2	2-2	3-1	3-1	29-34-1
2003	1-3	3-1	4-0	1-3	2-2	1-3	2-2	30-34
2004	1-3	2-2	1-3	0-4	1-3	1-3	0-4	20-44
2005	3-1	3-1	3-1	1-3	3-1	2-2	0-4	30-34
2006	1-3	1-3	2-2	2-2	2-2	2-2	2-2	24-40
2007	3-1	3-1	0-4	1-3	2-2	1-3	2-2	32-32
2008	3-1	2-1-1	0-4	2-2	1-3	1-3	1-3	29-34-1
2009	2-2	2-2	0-4	1-3	1-3	0-4	2-2	27-37
2010	2-2	3-1	2-2	2-2	1-3	2-2	2-2	30-34
2011	4-0	2-2	1-3	3-1	1-3	1-3	0-4	33-31
Total	76-68	83-68-2	79-78	87-72	17-24	45-75	74-77	1,041-1,160-11

INTERCONFERENCE GAMES

2011 INTERCONFERENCE GAMES
(Home Team in capital letters)
NFC 33, AFC 31
AFC VICTORIES
SAN DIEGO 24, Minnesota 17
NY JETS 27, Dallas 24
PITTSBURGH 24, Seattle 0
Baltimore 37, ST. LOUIS 7
KANSAS CITY 22, Minnesota 17
BUFFALO 31, Philadelphia 24
NEW ENGLAND 20, Dallas 16
CLEVELAND 6, Seattle 3
Pittsburgh 32, ARIZONA 20
BALTIMORE 30, Arizona 27
BUFFALO 23, Washington 0 (Toronto)
Cincinnati 34, SEATTLE 12
Tennessee 30, CAROLINA 3
MIAMI 20, Washington 9
Houston 37, TAMPA BAY 9
Oakland 27, MINNESOTA 21
BALTIMORE 16, San Francisco 6
TENNESSEE 23, Tampa Bay 17
OAKLAND 25, Chicago 20
New England 38, PHILADELPHIA 20
Kansas City 10, CHICAGO 3
HOUSTON 17, Atlanta 10
NY Jets 34, WASHINGTON 19
Denver 35, MINNESOTA 32
JACKSONVILLE 41, Tampa Bay 14
New England 34, WASHINGTON 27
DENVER 13, Chicago 10 (OT)
KANSAS CITY 19, Green Bay 14
Cincinnati 20, ST. LOUIS 13
CINCINNATI 23, Arizona 16
PITTSBURGH 27, St. Louis 0

NFC VICTORIES
DETROIT 48, Kansas City 3
CAROLINA 16, Jacksonville 10
San Francisco 13, CINCINNATI 8
NEW ORLEANS 40, Houston 33
New Orleans 23, JACKSONVILLE 10
GREEN BAY 49, Denver 23
TAMPA BAY 24, Indianapolis 17
NY GIANTS 27, Buffalo 24
NEW ORLEANS 62, Indianapolis 7
NY GIANTS 20, Miami 17
Detroit 45, DENVER 10
SAN FRANCISCO 20, Cleveland 10
Atlanta 31, INDIANAPOLIS 7
NY Giants 24, NEW ENGLAND 20
Green Bay 45, SAN DIEGO 38
St. Louis 13, CLEVELAND 12
DALLAS 44, Buffalo 7
SEATTLE 22, Baltimore 17
CHICAGO 31, San Diego 20
ATLANTA 23, Tennessee 17
DALLAS 20, Miami 19
Carolina 27, INDIANAPOLIS 19
Philadelphia 26, MIAMI 10
New Orleans 22, TENNESSEE 17
GREEN BAY 46, Oakland 16
ATLANTA 41, Jacksonville 14
Carolina 28, HOUSTON 13
Detroit 28, OAKLAND 27
ARIZONA 20, Cleveland 17 (OT)
PHILADELPHIA 45, NY Jets 19
SAN FRANCISCO 20, Pittsburgh 3
NY Giants 29, NY JETS 14
DETROIT 38, San Diego 10

REGULAR SEASON INTERCONFERENCE RECORDS, 1970-2011

AMERICAN FOOTBALL CONFERENCE

East	W	L	T	Pct.
Miami	98	55	0	.641
New England	80	70	0	.533
Buffalo	74	75	1	.497
New York Jets	65	85	0	.433
North	**W**	**L**	**T**	**Pct.**
Pittsburgh	93	58	1	.615
Baltimore	36	25	1	.589
Cincinnati	79	72	1	.523
Cleveland	64	78	0	.451
South	**W**	**L**	**T**	**Pct.**
Jacksonville	35	32	0	.522
Tennessee	81	75	1	.519
Indianapolis	69	73	1	.486
Houston	18	22	0	.450
West	**W**	**L**	**T**	**Pct.**
Oakland	92	65	1	.586
Denver	86	70	2	.551
Kansas City	75	65	2	.535
San Diego	71	76	0	.483

NATIONAL FOOTBALL CONFERENCE

East	W	L	T	Pct.
Dallas	86	66	0	.566
Philadelphia	83	68	2	.549
New York Giants	76	68	0	.528
Washington	74	77	0	.490
North	**W**	**L**	**T**	**Pct.**
Minnesota	75	79	0	.487
Chicago	74	81	0	.477
Green Bay	68	83	3	.451
Detroit	60	89	1	.403
South	**W**	**L**	**T**	**Pct.**
Carolina	31	37	0	.456
New Orleans	68	86	2	.442
Atlanta	65	91	1	.417
Tampa Bay*	45	76	0	.372
West	**W**	**L**	**T**	**Pct.**
San Francisco	87	72	0	.547
St. Louis	79	78	0	.503
Seattle* #	61	68	0	.473
Arizona	53	86	2	.382

* Records include one game played between Seattle and Tampa Bay, won by the Seahawks 13-10, in their inaugural season (1976) when Seattle competed in the NFC and Tampa Bay in the AFC.

\# Seattle was a member of the AFC from 1977-2001.
From 1970-71, tie games were not included in winning percentage.

INTERCONFERENCE VICTORIES, 1970-2011
REGULAR SEASON

	AFC	NFC	Tie		AFC	NFC	Tie
1970	12	27	1	1992	22	30	0
1971	15	23	2	1993	27	25	0
1972	20	19	1	1994	25	27	0
1973	19	19	2	1995	27	33	0
1974	23	17	0	1996	32	28	0
1975	23	17	0	1997	31	28	1
1976	16	12	0	1998	31	29	0
1977	19	9	0	1999	38	22	0
1978	31	21	0	2000	30	30	0
1979	36	16	0	2001	30	30	0
1980	33	19	0	2002	34	29	1
1981	24	28	0	2003	34	30	0
1982	15	14	1	2004	44	20	0
1983	26	26	0	2005	34	30	0
1984	26	26	0	2006	40	24	0
1985	27	25	0	2007	32	32	0
1986	26	26	0	2008	34	29	1
1987	23	22	1	2009	37	27	0
1988	30	22	0	2010	34	30	0
1989	24	28	0	2011	31	33	0
1990	26	26	0	Total	1,160	1,041	11
1991	19	33	0				

Records

Compiled by Elias Sports Bureau.

The following records reflect all available official information on the National Football League from its formation in 1920 to date. Also included are all applicable records from the American Football League, 1960-69.

Individuals eligible for Rookie records are players who were in their first season of professional football and had not been on the roster of another professional football team, including teams in other leagues, for any regular-season or postseason games in a previous season. Eligible players, therefore, include those who were under contract to a National Football League club for a previous season but were terminated prior to their club's first regular-season game and not re-signed, or who were placed on Reserve/Injured (or another category of the Reserve List) prior to their club's first regular-season game and were not activated during the rest of the regular season or postseason.

INDIVIDUAL RECORDS

SERVICE
Most Seasons
- 26 George Blanda, Chi. Bears, 1949, 1950-58; Baltimore, 1950; Houston, 1960-66; Oakland, 1967-1975
- 25 Morten Andersen, New Orleans, 1982-1994; Atlanta, 1995-2000; N.Y. Giants, 2001; Kansas City, 2002-03; Minnesota, 2004; Atlanta, 2006-07
- 23 Gary Anderson, Pittsburgh, 1982-1994; Philadelphia, 1995-96; San Francisco, 1997; Minnesota, 1998-2002; Tennessee, 2003-04
- John Carney, Tampa Bay, 1988-89; L.A. Rams, 1990: San Diego, 1990-2000; New Orleans, 2001-06; Jacksonville, 2007; Kansas City, 2007; N.Y. Giants, 2008; New Orleans, 2009-2010

Most Seasons, One Club
- 20 Jackie Slater, L.A. Rams, 1976-1994; St. Louis, 1995
- Darrell Green, Washington, 1983-2002
- Jason Hanson, Detroit, 1992-2011
- 19 Jim Marshall, Minnesota, 1961-1979
- Bruce Matthews, Houston, 1983-1996; Tennessee, 1997-2001
- 18 Jim Hart, St. Louis, 1966-1983
- Jeff Van Note, Atlanta, 1969-1986
- Pat Leahy, N.Y. Jets, 1974-1991

Most Games Played, Career
- 382 Morten Andersen, New Orleans, 1982-1994; Atlanta, 1995-2000; N.Y. Giants, 2001; Kansas City, 2002-03; Minnesota, 2004; Atlanta, 2006-07
- 353 Gary Anderson, Pittsburgh, 1982-1994; Philadelphia, 1995-96; San Francisco, 1997; Minnesota, 1998-2002; Tennessee, 2003-04
- 352 Jeff Feagles, New England, 1988-89; Philadelphia, 1990-93; Arizona, 1994-97; Seattle, 1998-2002; N.Y. Giants, 2003-09

Most Consecutive Games Played, Career
- 352 Jeff Feagles, New England, 1988-89; Philadelphia, 1990-93; Arizona, 1994-97; Seattle, 1998-2002; N.Y. Giants, 2003-09
- 299 Brett Favre, Green Bay, 1992-2007; N.Y. Jets, 2008; Minnesota, 2009-2010
- 282 Jim Marshall, Cleveland, 1960; Minnesota, 1961-1979

SCORING
Most Seasons Leading League
- 5 Don Hutson, Green Bay, 1940-44
- Gino Cappelletti, Boston, 1961, 1963-66
- 3 Earl (Dutch) Clark, Portsmouth, 1932; Detroit, 1935-36
- Pat Harder, Chi. Cardinals, 1947-49

- Paul Hornung, Green Bay, 1959-1961
- 2 Jack Manders, Chi. Bears, 1934, 1937
- Gordy Soltau, San Francisco, 1952-53
- Doak Walker, Detroit, 1950, 1955
- Gene Mingo, Denver, 1960, 1962
- Jim Turner, N.Y. Jets, 1968-69
- Fred Cox, Minnesota, 1969-1970
- Chester Marcol, Green Bay, 1972, 1974
- John Smith, New England, 1979-1980
- Marshall Faulk, St. Louis, 2000-01
- David Akers, Philadelphia, 2010; San Francisco, 2011

Most Consecutive Seasons Leading League
- 5 Don Hutson, Green Bay, 1940-44
- 4 Gino Cappelletti, Boston, 1963-66
- 3 Pat Harder, Chi. Cardinals, 1947-49
- Paul Hornung, Green Bay, 1959-1961

POINTS
Most Points, Career
- 2,544 Morten Andersen, New Orleans, 1982-1994; Atlanta, 1995-2000; N.Y. Giants, 2001; Kansas City, 2002-03; Minnesota, 2004; Atlanta, 2006-07 (849-pat, 565-fg)
- 2,434 Gary Anderson, Pittsburgh, 1982-1994; Philadelphia 1995-96; San Francisco, 1997; Minnesota, 1998-2002; Tennessee, 2003-04 (820-pat, 538-fg)
- 2,062 John Carney, Tampa Bay, 1988-89; L.A. Rams, 1990; San Diego, 1990-2000; New Orleans, 2001-06; Jacksonville, 2007; Kansas City, 2007; N.Y. Giants, 2008; New Orleans, 2009-2010 (628-pat, 478-fg)

Most Points, Season
- 186 LaDainian Tomlinson, San Diego, 2006 (31-td)
- 176 Paul Hornung, Green Bay, 1960 (15-td, 41-pat, 15-fg)
- 168 Shaun Alexander, Seattle, 2005 (28-td)

Most Point, No Touchdowns, Season
- 166 David Akers, San Francisco, 2011 (34-pat, 44-fg)
- 164 Gary Anderson, Minnesota, 1998 (59-pat, 35-fg)
- 163 Jeff Wilkins, St. Louis, 2003 (46-pat, 39-fg)

Most Seasons, 100 or More Points
- 16 Jason Elam, Denver, 1993-2007; Atlanta, 2008
- 14 Gary Anderson, Pittsburgh, 1983-85, 1988, 1991-94; Philadelphia 1996; San Francisco, 1997; Minnesota, 1998-2000; Tennessee, 2003
- Morten Andersen, New Orleans, 1985-89, 1991-94; Atlanta, 1995, 1997-98; Kansas City, 2002-03
- Adam Vinatieri, New England, 1996-2005; Indianapolis, 2006-08, 2010
- 12 Matt Stover, Cleveland, 1994-95; Baltimore, 1997, 1999-2001, 2003-08

Most Points, Rookie Season
- 144 Kevin Butler, Chicago, 1985 (51-pat, 31-fg)
- 141 Mason Crosby, Green Bay, 2007 (48-pat, 31-fg)
- 135 Dan Bailey, Dallas, 2011 (39-pat, 32-fg)

Most Points, Game
- 40 Ernie Nevers, Chi. Cardinals vs. Chi. Bears, Nov. 28, 1929 (6-td, 4-pat)
- 36 Dub Jones, Cleveland vs. Chi. Bears, Nov. 25, 1951 (6-td)
- Gale Sayers, Chicago vs. San Francisco, Dec. 12, 1965 (6-td)
- 33 Paul Hornung, Green Bay vs. Baltimore, Oct. 8, 1961 (4-td, 6-pat, 1-fg)

Most Consecutive Games Scoring
- 360 Morten Andersen, New Orleans, 1983-1994; Atlanta, 1995-2000; N.Y. Giants, 2001; Kansas City, 2002-03; Minnesota, 2004; Atlanta, 2006-07
- 263 Jason Elam, Denver, 1993-2007; Atlanta, 2008-09

186   Jim Breech, Oakland, 1979; Cincinnati, 1980-1992

   Jerry Rice, San Francisco, 1986-87

TOUCHDOWNS
Most Seasons Leading League
- 8   Don Hutson, Green Bay, 1935-38, 1941-44
- 3   Jim Brown, Cleveland, 1958-59, 1963
  - Lance Alworth, San Diego, 1964-66
  - Emmitt Smith, Dallas, 1992, 1994-95
- 2   By many players

Most Consecutive Seasons Leading League
- 4   Don Hutson, Green Bay, 1935-38, 1941-44
- 3   Lance Alworth, San Diego, 1964-66
- 2   By many players

Most Touchdowns, Career
- 208   Jerry Rice, San Francisco, 1985-2000;
  - Oakland, 2001-04;
  - Seattle, 2004 (10-r, 197-p, 1-ret)
- 175   Emmitt Smith, Dallas, 1990-2002; Arizona, 2003-04
  - (164-r, 11-p)
- 162   LaDainian Tomlinson, San Diego, 2001-09;
  - N.Y. Jets, 2010-11 (145-r, 17-p)

Most Touchdowns, Season
- 31   LaDainian Tomlinson, San Diego, 2006 (28-r, 3-p)
- 28   Shaun Alexander, Seattle, 2005 (27-r, 1-p)
- 27   Priest Holmes, Kansas City, 2003 (27-r)

Most Touchdowns, Rookie, Season
- 22   Gale Sayers. Chicago, 1965 (14-r, 6-p)
- 20   Eric Dickerson, Rams, 1983 (18-r, 2-p)
- 17   Fred Taylor, Jacksonville, 1998 (14-r, 3-p)
  - Randy Moss, Minnesota, 1998 (17-p)
  - Edgerrin James, Indianapolis, 1999 (13-r, 4-p)
  - Clinton Portis, Denver, 2002 (15-r, 2-p)

Most Touchdowns, Game
- 6   Ernie Nevers, Chi. Cardinals vs. Chi. Bears,
  - Nov. 28, 1929 (6-r)
  - Dub Jones, Cleveland vs. Chi. Bears, Nov. 25, 1951
  - (4-r, 2-p)
  - Gale Sayers, Chicago vs. San Francisco, Dec. 12, 1965
  - (4-r, 1-p, 1-ret)
- 5   Jimmy Conzelman, Rhode Island vs. Evansville,
  - Oct. 15, 1922 (5-r)
  - Bob Shaw, Chi. Cardinals vs. Baltimore, Oct. 2, 1950
  - (5-p)
  - Jim Brown, Cleveland vs. Baltimore, Nov. 1, 1959 (5-r)
  - Abner Haynes, Dall. Texans vs. Oakland,
  - Nov. 26, 1961 (4-r, 1-p)
  - Billy Cannon, Houston vs. N.Y. Titans, Dec. 10, 1961
  - (3-r, 2-p)
  - Cookie Gilchrist, Buffalo vs. N.Y. Jets, Dec. 8, 1963 (5-r)
  - Paul Hornung, Green Bay vs. Baltimore,
  - Dec. 12, 1965 (3-r, 2-p)
  - Kellen Winslow, San Diego vs. Oakland,
  - Nov. 22, 1981 (5-p)
  - Jerry Rice, San Francisco vs. Atlanta, Oct. 14, 1990
  - (5-p)
  - James Stewart, Jacksonville vs. Philadelphia,
  - Oct. 12, 1997 (5-r)
  - Shaun Alexander, Seattle vs. Minnesota,
  - Sept. 29, 2002 (4-r, 1-p)
  - Clinton Portis, Denver vs. Kansas City, Dec. 7, 2003
  - (5-r)
- 4   By many players. Last time:
  - Maurice Jones-Drew, Jacksonville vs. Tampa Bay,
  - Dec. 11, 2011 (2-r, 2-p)

Most Consecutive Games Scoring Touchdowns
- 18   Lenny Moore, Baltimore, 1963-65
  - LaDainian Tomlinson, San Diego, 2004-05
- 14   O.J. Simpson, Buffalo, 1975
- 13   John Riggins, Washington, 1982-83
  - George Rogers, Washington, 1985-86

POINTS AFTER TOUCHDOWN
Most Seasons Leading League
- 8   George Blanda, Chi. Bears, 1956; Houston,
  - 1961-62; Oakland, 1967-69, 1972, 1974
- 4   Bob Waterfield, Cleveland, 1945; Los Angeles, 1946,
  - 1950, 1952
- 3   Earl (Dutch) Clark, Portsmouth, 1932; Detroit,
  - 1935-36 Jack Manders, Chi. Bears, 1933-35
  - Don Hutson, Green Bay, 1941-42, 1945

Most (Kicking) Points After Touchdown Attempted, Career
- 959   George Blanda, Chi. Bears, 1949, 1950-58; Baltimore,
  - 1950; Houston, 1960-66; Oakland, 1967-1975
- 859   Morten Andersen, New Orleans, 1982-1994;
  - Atlanta, 1995-2000; N.Y. Giants, 2001;
  - Kansas City, 2002-03; Minnesota, 2004;
  - Atlanta, 2006-07
- 827   Gary Anderson, Pittsburgh, 1982-1994; Philadelphia
  - 1995-96; San Francisco, 1997; Minnesota,
  - 1998-2002; Tennessee, 2003-04

Most (Kicking) Points After Touchdown Attempted, Season
- 74   Stephen Gostkowski, New England, 2007
- 70   Uwe von Schamann, Miami, 1984
- 69   Mason Crosby, Green Bay, 2011

Most (Kicking) Points After Touchdown Attempted, Game
- 10   Charlie Gogolak, Washington vs. N.Y. Giants,
  - Nov. 27, 1966
- 9   Pat Harder, Chi. Cardinals vs. N.Y. Giants,
  - Oct. 17, 1948; vs. N.Y. Bulldogs, Nov. 13, 1949
  - Bob Waterfield, Los Angeles vs. Baltimore,
  - Oct. 22, 1950
  - Bob Thomas, Chicago vs. Green Bay, Dec. 7, 1980
- 8   By many players

Most (One-Point) Points After Touchdown, Career
- 943   George Blanda, Chi. Bears, 1949, 1950-58; Baltimore,
  - 1950; Houston, 1960-66; Oakland, 1967-1975
- 849   Morten Andersen, New Orleans, 1982-1994;
  - Atlanta, 1995-2000; N.Y. Giants, 2001;
  - Kansas City, 2002-03; Minnesota, 2004,
  - Atlanta, 2006-07
- 820   Gary Anderson, Pittsburgh, 1982-1994; Philadelphia
  - 1995-96; San Francisco, 1997; Minnesota,
  - 1998-2002; Tennessee, 2003-04

Most (One-Point) Points After Touchdown, Season
- 74   Stephen Gostkowski, New England, 2007
- 68   Mason Crosby, Green Bay, 2011
- 66   Uwe von Schamann, Miami, 1984

Most (One-Point) Points After Touchdown, Game
- 9   Pat Harder, Chi. Cardinals vs. N.Y. Giants,
  - Oct. 17, 1948
  - Bob Waterfield, Los Angeles vs. Baltimore,
  - Oct. 22, 1950
  - Charlie Gogolak, Washington vs. N.Y. Giants,
  - Nov. 27, 1966
- 8   By many players

Most Consecutive (Kicking) Points After Touchdown
- 422   Matt Stover, Baltimore, 1996-2008; Indianapolis,
  - 2009
- 371   Jason Elam, Denver, 1993-2002
  - Jeff Wilkins, St. Louis, 1999-2007
- 321   Rian Lindell, Seattle, 2000-02; Buffalo, 2003-2010

Highest (Kicking) Points After Touchdown Percentage, Career (200 points after touchdown)
- 100.00   Nick Folk, Dallas, 2007-09; N.Y. Jets, 2010-11
  - (212-212)
- 99.72   Rian Lindell, Seattle, 2000-02; Buffalo, 2003-2011
  - (362-363)
- 99.66   Stephen Gostkowski, New England, 2006-2011
  - (289-290)

Most (Kicking) Points After Touchdown, No Misses, Season
- 74 Stephen Gostkowski, New England, 2007
- 64 Jeff Wilkins, St. Louis, 1999
- 63 John Kasay, New Orleans, 2011

Most (Kicking) Points After Touchdown, No Misses, Game
- 9 Pat Harder, Chi. Cardinals vs. N.Y. Giants,
  Oct. 17, 1948
  Bob Waterfield, Los Angeles vs. Baltimore,
  Oct. 22, 1950
- 8 By many players

Most Two-Point Conversions, Career
Two-point conversions include AFL (1960-69) and NFL (since 1994).
- 7 Marshall Faulk, Indianapolis, 1994-98; St. Louis, 1999-2005
- 6 Terance Mathis, Atlanta, 1994-2001; Pittsburgh, 2002
- 5 Cris Carter, Minnesota, 1994-2001; Miami, 2002
  Rob Moore, N.Y. Jets, 1994; Arizona, 1995-99
  Willie Jackson, Jacksonville, 1995-97; Cincinnati, 1998-99; New Orleans, 2000-01; Washington, 2002
  Keenan McCardell, Cleveland, 1994-95; Jacksonville, 1996-2001; Tampa Bay, 2002-03; San Diego, 2004-06, Washington, 2007
  Marvin Harrison, Indianapolis, 1996-2008
  Marcus Pollard, Indianapolis, 1995-2004; Detroit, 2005-06; Seattle, 2007; Atlanta, 2008
  Todd Heap, Baltimore, 2001-2010; Arizona, 2011
  Hines Ward, Pittsburgh, 1998-2011
  Edgerrin James, Indianapolis, 1999-2005; Arizona, 2006-08; Seattle, 2009

Most Two-Point Conversions, Season
- 4 Todd Heap, Baltimore, 2003
- 3 Gino Cappelletti, Boston, 1960
  Richie Lucas, Buffalo, 1961
  Ronnie Harmon, San Diego, 1994
  Haywood Jeffires, Houston, 1994
  Tom Tupa, Cleveland, 1994
  Terance Mathis, Atlanta, 1995
  Lamar Smith, Seattle, 1996
  Cris Carter, Minnesota, 1997
  Terrell Davis, Denver, 1997
  James Stewart, Detroit, 2000
  Hines Ward, Pittsburgh, 2002
  Brian Finneran, Atlanta, 2005
  Reggie Bush, New Orleans, 2007
- 2 By many players

Most Two-Point Conversions, Game
- 2 Brett Perriman, Detroit vs. Green Bay, Nov. 6, 1994
  Michael Jackson, Baltimore vs. New England, Oct. 6, 1996
  Terrell Davis, Denver vs. Atlanta, Sept. 28, 1997
  Charles Johnson, Pittsburgh vs. Tennessee, Nov. 1, 1998
  Marshall Faulk, St. Louis vs. Atlanta, Oct. 15, 2000
  Todd Heap, Baltimore vs. Cincinnati, Oct. 19, 2003
  Reggie Bush, New Orleans vs. St. Louis, Nov. 11, 2007
  Tarvaris Jackson, Minnesota vs. Denver, Dec. 30, 2007 (ot)
  Mewelde Moore, Pittsburgh vs. New England, Nov. 14, 2010
  Lance Moore, New Orleans vs. Houston, Sept. 25, 2011

FIELD GOALS

Most Seasons Leading League
- 5 Lou Groza, Cleveland, 1950, 1952-54, 1957
- 4 Jack Manders, Chi. Bears, 1933-34, 1936-37
  Ward Cuff, N.Y. Giants, 1938-39, 1943; Green Bay, 1947

Mark Moseley, Washington, 1976-77, 1979, 1982
- 3 Bob Waterfield, Los Angeles, 1947, 1949, 1951
  Gino Cappelletti, Boston, 1961, 1963-64
  Fred Cox, Minnesota, 1965, 1969-1970
  Jan Stenerud, Kansas City, 1967, 1970, 1975

Most Consecutive Seasons Leading League
- 3 Lou Groza, Cleveland, 1952-54
- 2 Jack Manders, Chi. Bears, 1933-34
  Armand Niccolai, Pittsburgh, 1935-36
  Jack Manders, Chi. Bears, 1936-37
  Ward Cuff, N.Y. Giants, 1938-39
  Clark Hinkle, Green Bay, 1940-41
  Cliff Patton, Philadelphia, 1948-49
  Gino Cappelletti, Boston, 1963-64
  Jim Turner, N.Y. Jets, 1968-69
  Fred Cox, Minnesota, 1969-1970
  Mark Moseley, Washington, 1976-77
  Chip Lohmiller, Washington, 1991-92
  Pete Stoyanovich, Miami, 1991-92

Most Field Goals Attempted, Career
- 709 Morten Andersen, New Orleans, 1982-1994; Atlanta, 1995-2000; N.Y. Giants, 2001; Kansas City, 2002-03; Minnesota, 2004; Atlanta, 2006-07
- 672 Gary Anderson, Pittsburgh, 1982-1994; Philadelphia, 1995-96; San Francisco, 1997; Minnesota, 1998-2002; Tennessee, 2003-04
- 641 George Blanda, Chi. Bears, 1949, 1950-58; Baltimore, 1950; Houston, 1960-66; Oakland, 1967-1975

Most Field Goals Attempted, Season
- 52 David Akers, San Francisco, 2011
- 49 Bruce Gossett, Los Angeles, 1966
  Curt Knight, Washington, 1971
- 48 Chester Marcol, Green Bay, 1972

Most Field Goals Attempted, Game
- 9 Jim Bakken, St. Louis vs. Pittsburgh, Sept. 24, 1967
- 8 Lou Michaels, Pittsburgh vs. St. Louis, Dec. 2, 1962
  Garo Yepremian, Detroit vs. Minnesota, Nov. 13, 1966
  Jim Turner, N.Y. Jets vs. Buffalo, Nov. 3, 1968
  Billy Cundiff, Dallas vs. N.Y. Giants, Sept. 15, 2003 (ot)
  Rob Bironas, Tennessee vs. Houston, Oct. 21, 2007
- 7 By many players

Most Field Goals, Career
- 565 Morten Andersen, New Orleans, 1982-1994; Atlanta, 1995-2000; N.Y. Giants, 2001; Kansas City, 2002-03; Minnesota, 2004; Atlanta, 2006-07
- 538 Gary Anderson, Pittsburgh, 1982-1994; Philadelphia, 1995-96; San Francisco, 1997; Minnesota, 1998-2002; Tennessee, 2003-04
- 478 John Carney, Tampa Bay, 1988-89; L.A. Rams, 1990; San Diego, 1990-2000; New Orleans, 2001-06; Jacksonville, 2007; Kansas City, 2007; N.Y. Giants, 2008; New Orleans, 2009-2010

Most Field Goals, Season
- 44 David Akers, San Francisco, 2011
- 40 Neil Rackers, Arizona, 2005
- 39 Olindo Mare, Miami, 1999
  Jeff Wilkins, St. Louis, 2003

Most Field Goals, Rookie, Season
- 35 Ali Haji-Sheikh, N.Y. Giants, 1983
- 34 Richie Cunningham, Dallas, 1997
- 33 Chester Marcol, Green Bay, 1972

Most Field Goals, Game
- 8 Rob Bironas, Tennessee vs. Houston, Oct. 21, 2007
- 7 Jim Bakken, St. Louis vs. Pittsburgh, Sept. 24, 1967
  Rich Karlis, Minnesota vs. L.A. Rams, Nov. 5, 1989 (ot)
  Chris Boniol, Dallas vs. Green Bay, Nov. 18, 1996
  Billy Cundiff, Dallas vs. N.Y. Giants, Sept. 15, 2003 (ot)

Shayne Graham, Cincinnati vs. Baltimore, Nov. 11, 2007
6 By many players

Most Field Goals, One Quarter
4 Garo Yepremian, Detroit vs. Minnesota, Nov. 13, 1966
    (second quarter)
    Curt Knight, Washington vs. N.Y. Giants, Nov. 15, 1970
    (second quarter)
    Roger Ruzek, Dallas vs. N.Y. Giants, Nov. 2, 1987
    (fourth quarter)
    Cary Blanchard, Indianapolis vs. Buffalo,
    Sept. 21 1997 (second quarter)
    Sebastian Janikowski, Oakland vs. Chicago,
    Oct. 5, 2003 (second quarter)
    Jeff Wilkins, St. Louis vs. Baltimore, Nov. 9, 2003
    (fourth quarter)
    Lawrence Tynes, Kansas City vs. New England,
    Nov. 27, 2005 (second quarter)
    Shayne Graham, Cincinnati vs. Baltimore,
    Nov. 11, 2007 (fourth quarter)
3 By many players

Most Consecutive Games Scoring Field Goals
38 Matt Stover, Baltimore, 1999-2001
31 Fred Cox, Minnesota, 1968-1970
28 Jim Turner, N.Y. Jets, 1970; Denver, 1971-72
    Chip Lohmiller, Washington, 1988-1990

Most Consecutive Field Goals
42 Mike Vanderjagt, Indianapolis, 2002-04
40 Gary Anderson, San Francisco, 1997;
    Minnesota, 1998
36 Matt Stover, Baltimore, 2005-06

Longest Field Goal
63 Tom Dempsey, New Orleans vs. Detroit, Nov. 8, 1970
    Jason Elam, Denver vs. Jacksonville, Oct. 25, 1998
    Sebastian Janikowski, Oakland vs. Denver,
    Sept. 12, 2011
62 Matt Bryant, Tampa Bay vs. Philadelphia,
    Oct. 22, 2006
61 Sebastian Janikowski, Oakland vs. Cleveland,
    Dec. 27, 2009

Highest Field Goal Pct., Career (100 field goals)
86.50 Nate Kaeding, San Diego, 2004-2010 (173-200)
86.47 Mike Vanderjagt, Indianapolis, 1998-2005; Dallas,
       2006 (230-266)
86.30 Rob Bironas, Tennessee, 2005-2011 (189-219)

Highest Field Goal Pct., Season (Qualifiers)
100.00 Tony Zendejas, L.A. Rams, 1991 (17-17)
       Gary Anderson, Minnesota, 1998 (35-35)
       Jeff Wilkins, St. Louis, 2000 (17-17)
       Mike Vanderjagt, Indianapolis, 2003 (37-37)
96.43 Chris Boniol, Dallas, 1995 (28-27)
96.30 Norm Johnson, Atlanta, 1993 (27-26)
       Pete Stoyanovich, Kansas City, 1997 (27-26)

Most Field Goals, No Misses, Game
8 Rob Bironas, Tennessee vs. Houston, Oct. 21, 2007
7 Rich Karlis, Minnesota vs. L.A. Rams, Nov. 5, 1989
    (ot)
    Chris Boniol, Dallas vs. Green Bay, Nov. 18, 1996
    Shayne Graham, Cincinnati vs. Baltimore,
    Nov. 11, 2007
6 By many players

Most Field Goals, 50 or More Yards, Career
50 Jason Hanson, Detroit, 1992-2011
42 John Kasay, Seattle, 1991-94; Carolina, 1995-99,
    2001-2010; New Orleans, 2011
40 Morten Andersen, New Orleans, 1982-1994;
    Atlanta, 1995-2000; N.Y. Giants, 2001;
    Kansas City, 2002-03; Minnesota, 2004;
    Atlanta, 2006-07

Most Field Goals, 50 or More Yards, Season
8 Morten Andersen, Atlanta, 1995

    Jason Hanson, Detroit, 2008
7 David Akers, San Francisco, 2011
    Phil Dawson, Cleveland, 2011
    Sebastian Janikowski, Oakland, 2011
6 Dean Biasucci, Indianapolis, 1988
    Chris Jacke, Green Bay, 1993
    Tony Zendejas, L.A. Rams, 1993
    Mike Vanderjagt, Indianapolis, 1998
    Neil Rackers, Arizona, 2005
    Sebastian Janikowski, Oakland, 2007
    Josh Brown, St. Louis, 2008
    Ryan Longwell, Minnesota, 2008
    Josh Brown, St. Louis, 2009
    Sebastian Janikowski, Oakland, 2009
    Rob Bironas, Tennessee, 2011
    Robbie Gould, Chicago, 2011

Most Field Goals, 50 or More Yards, Game
3 Morten Andersen, Atlanta vs. New Orleans,
    Dec. 10, 1995
    Neil Rackers, Arizona vs. Seattle, Oct. 24, 2004
    Kris Brown, Houston vs. Miami, Oct. 7, 2007
    Conner Barth, Tampa Bay vs. Miami, Nov. 15, 2009
    Sebastian Janikowski, Oakland vs. Houston,
    Oct. 9, 2011
    Josh Scobee, Jacksonville vs. Baltimore,
    Oct. 24, 2011
2 By many players. Last time: Rob Bironas,
    Tennessee vs. Jacksonville, Dec. 24, 2011

SAFETIES

Most Safeties, Career
4 Ted Hendricks, Baltimore, 1969-1973; Green Bay,
    1974; Oakland, 1975-1981; L.A. Raiders, 1982-83
    Doug English, Detroit, 1975-79, 1981-85
    Jared Allen, Kansas City, 2004-07;
    Minnesota, 2008-2011
3 Bill McPeak, Pittsburgh, 1949-1957
    Charlie Krueger, San Francisco, 1959-1973
    Ernie Stautner, Pittsburgh, 1950-1963
    Jim Katcavage, N.Y. Giants, 1956-1968
    Roger Brown, Detroit, 1960-66; Los Angeles,
    1967-69
    Bruce Maher, Detroit, 1960-67; N.Y. Giants, 1968-69
    Ron McDole, St. Louis, 1961; Houston, 1962;
    Buffalo, 1963-1970; Washington, 1971-78
    Alan Page, Minnesota, 1967-1978; Chicago,
    1979-1981
    Lyle Alzado, Denver, 1971-78; Cleveland,
    1979-1981; L.A. Raiders, 1982-85
    Rulon Jones, Denver, 1980-88
    Steve McMichael, New England, 1980; Chicago,
    1981-1993; Green Bay, 1994
    Kevin Greene, L.A. Rams, 1985-1992; Pittsburgh,
    1993-95; Carolina, 1996, 1998-99;
    San Francisco, 1997
    Burt Grossman, San Diego, 1989-1993;
    Philadelphia, 1994
    Eric Swann, Phoenix, 1991-93; Arizona, 1994-99;
    Carolina, 2000
    Dan Saleaumua, Detroit, 1987-88; Kansas City,
    1989-1996; Seattle, 1997-98
    Derrick Thomas, Kansas City, 1989-1999
    Bryant Young, San Francisco, 1994-2007
    Jason Taylor, Miami, 1997-2007; Washington, 2008;
    Miami, 2009; N.Y. Jets, 2010; Miami, 2011
2 By many players

Most Safeties, Season
2 Tom Nash, Green Bay, 1932
    Roger Brown, Detroit, 1962
    Ron McDole, Buffalo, 1964

Alan Page, Minnesota, 1971
Fred Dryer, Los Angeles, 1973
Benny Barnes, Dallas, 1973
James Young, Houston, 1977
Doug English, Detroit, 1983
Don Blackmon, New England, 1985
Tim Harris, Green Bay, 1988
Brian Jordan, Atlanta, 1991
Burt Grossman, San Diego, 1992
Rod Stephens, Seattle, 1993
Bryant Young, San Francisco, 1996
Jared Allen, Minnesota, 2008
Jameel McClain, Baltimore, 2008

Most Safeties, Game
2 Fred Dryer, Los Angeles vs. Green Bay,
Oct. 21, 1973

RUSHING
Most Seasons Leading League
8 Jim Brown, Cleveland, 1957-1961, 1963-65
4 Steve Van Buren, Philadelphia, 1945, 1947-49
O.J. Simpson, Buffalo, 1972-73, 1975-76
Eric Dickerson, L.A. Rams, 1983-84, 1986;
Indianapolis, 1988
Emmitt Smith, Dallas, 1991-93, 1995
Barry Sanders, Detroit, 1990, 1994, 1996-97
3 Earl Campbell, Houston, 1978-1980

Most Consecutive Seasons Leading League
5 Jim Brown, Cleveland, 1957-1961
3 Steve Van Buren, Philadelphia, 1947-49
Jim Brown, Cleveland, 1963-65
Earl Campbell, Houston, 1978-1980
Emmitt Smith, Dallas, 1991-93
2 By many players

ATTEMPTS
Most Seasons Leading League
6 Jim Brown, Cleveland, 1958-59, 1961, 1963-65
4 Steve Van Buren, Philadelphia, 1947-1950
Walter Payton, Chicago, 1976-79
3 Cookie Gilchrist, Buffalo, 1963-64; Denver, 1965
Jim Nance, Boston, 1966-67, 1969
O.J. Simpson, Buffalo, 1973-75
Eric Dickerson, L.A. Rams, 1983, 1986;
Indianapolis, 1988
Emmitt Smith, Dallas, 1991, 1994-95

Most Consecutive Seasons Leading League
4 Steve Van Buren, Philadelphia, 1947-1950
Walter Payton, Chicago, 1976-79
3 Jim Brown, Cleveland, 1963-65
Cookie Gilchrist, Buffalo, 1963-64; Denver, 1965
O.J. Simpson, Buffalo, 1973-75
2 By many players

Most Attempts, Career
4,409 Emmitt Smith, Dallas, 1990-2002; Arizona, 2003-04
3,838 Walter Payton, Chicago, 1975-1987
3,518 Curtis Martin, New England, 1995-97;
N.Y. Jets, 1998-2005

Most Attempts, Season
416 Larry Johnson, Kansas City, 2006
410 Jamal Anderson, Atlanta, 1998
407 James Wilder, Tampa Bay, 1984

Most Attempts, Rookie, Season
390 Eric Dickerson, L.A. Rams, 1983
378 George Rogers, New Orleans, 1981
369 Edgerrin James, Indianapolis, 1999

Most Attempts, Game
45 Jamie Morris, Washington vs. Cincinnati,
Dec. 17, 1988 (ot)

43 Butch Woolfolk, N.Y. Giants vs. Philadelphia,
Nov. 20, 1983
James Wilder, Tampa Bay vs. Green Bay,
Sept. 30, 1984 (ot)
Rudi Johnson, Cincinnati vs. Houston, Nov. 9, 2003
42 James Wilder, Tampa Bay vs. Pittsburgh,
Oct. 30, 1983
Terrell Davis, Denver vs. Buffalo, Oct. 26, 1997 (ot)
Ricky Williams, Miami vs. Buffalo, Sept. 21, 2003

YARDS GAINED
Most Yards Gained, Career
18,355 Emmitt Smith, Dallas, 1990-2002; Arizona, 2003-04
16,726 Walter Payton, Chicago, 1975-1987
15,269 Barry Sanders, Detroit, 1989-1998

Most Seasons, 1,000 or More Yards Rushing
11 Emmitt Smith, Dallas, 1991-2001
10 Walter Payton, Chicago, 1976-1981, 1983-86
Barry Sanders, Detroit, 1989-1998
Curtis Martin, New England, 1995-97; N.Y. Jets,
1998-2004
8 Franco Harris, Pittsburgh, 1972, 1974-79, 1983
Tony Dorsett, Dallas, 1977-1981, 1983-85
Thurman Thomas, Buffalo, 1989-1996
Jerome Bettis, L.A. Rams, 1993-94; Pittsburgh,
1996-2001
LaDainian Tomlinson, San Diego, 2001-08

Most Consecutive Seasons, 1,000 or More Yards Rushing
11 Emmitt Smith, Dallas, 1991-2001
10 Barry Sanders, Detroit, 1989-1998
Curtis Martin, New England, 1995-97; N.Y. Jets,
1998-2004
8 Thurman Thomas, Buffalo, 1989-1996
LaDainian Tomlinson, San Diego, 2001-08

Most Yards Gained, Season
2,105 Eric Dickerson, L.A. Rams, 1984
2,066 Jamal Lewis, Baltimore, 2003
2,053 Barry Sanders, Detroit, 1997

Most Yards Gained, Rookie, Season
1,808 Eric Dickerson, L.A. Rams, 1983
1,674 George Rogers, New Orleans, 1981
1,605 Ottis Anderson, St. Louis, 1979

Most Yards Gained, Game
296 Adrian Peterson, Minnesota vs. San Diego,
Nov. 4, 2007
295 Jamal Lewis, Baltimore vs. Cleveland,
Sept. 14, 2003
286 Jerome Harrison, Cleveland vs. Kansas City,
Dec. 20, 2009

Most Games, 200 or More Yards Rushing, Career
6 O.J. Simpson, Buffalo, 1969-1977; San Francisco,
1978-79
5 Tiki Barber, N.Y. Giants, 1997-2006
4 Jim Brown, Cleveland, 1957-1965
Earl Campbell, Houston, 1978-1984; New Orleans,
1984-85
Barry Sanders, Detroit, 1989-1998
LaDainian Tomlinson, San Diego, 2001-09;
N.Y. Jets, 2010-11

Most Games, 200 or More Yards Rushing, Season
4 Earl Campbell, Houston, 1980
3 O.J. Simpson, Buffalo, 1973
Tiki Barber, N.Y. Giants, 2005
2 Jim Brown, Cleveland, 1963
O.J. Simpson, Buffalo, 1976
Walter Payton, Chicago, 1977
Eric Dickerson, L.A. Rams, 1984
Greg Bell, L.A. Rams, 1989
Terrell Davis, Denver, 1997
Barry Sanders, Detroit, 1997

Corey Dillon, Cincinnati, 2000
Marshall Faulk, St. Louis, 2000
LaDainian Tomlinson, San Diego, 2002
Ricky Williams, Miami, 2002
Jamal Lewis, Baltimore, 2003
LaDainian Tomlinson, San Diego, 2003
Larry Johnson, Kansas City, 2005
Willie Parker, Pittsburgh, 2006
Adrian Peterson, Minnesota, 2007
Michael Turner, Atlanta, 2008

Most Consecutive Games, 200 or More Yards Rushing

2 O.J. Simpson, Buffalo, 1973, 1976
  Earl Campbell, Houston, 1980
  Ricky Williams, Miami, 2002

Most Games, 100 or more Yards Rushing, Career

78 Emmitt Smith, Dallas, 1990-2002; Arizona, 2003-04
77 Walter Payton, Chicago, 1975-1987
76 Barry Sanders, Detroit, 1989-1998

Most Games, 100 or More Yards Rushing, Season

14 Barry Sanders, Detroit, 1997
12 Eric Dickerson, L.A. Rams, 1984
  Barry Foster, Pittsburgh, 1992
  Jamal Anderson, Atlanta, 1998
  Jamal Lewis, Baltimore, 2003
  Chris Johnson, Tennessee, 2009
11 O.J. Simpson, Buffalo, 1973
  Earl Campbell, Houston, 1979
  Marcus Allen, L.A. Raiders, 1985
  Eric Dickerson, L.A. Rams, 1986
  Emmitt Smith, Dallas, 1995
  Terrell Davis, Denver, 1998
  Shaun Alexander, Seattle, 2005
  Larry Johnson, Kansas City, 2006

Most Consecutive Games, 100 or More Yards Rushing

14 Barry Sanders, Detroit, 1997
12 Chris Johnson, Tennessee, 2009-2010
11 Marcus Allen, L.A. Raiders, 1985-86

Longest Run from Scrimmage

99 Tony Dorsett, Dallas vs. Minnesota, Jan. 3, 1983 (TD)
98 Ahman Green, Green Bay vs. Denver, Dec. 28, 2003 (TD)
97 Andy Uram, Green Bay vs. Chi. Cardinals, Oct. 8, 1939 (TD)
  Bob Gage, Pittsburgh vs. Chi. Bears, Dec. 4, 1949 (TD)

AVERAGE GAIN

Highest Average Gain, Career (750 attempts)

6.36 Randall Cunningham, Philadelphia, 1985-1995; Minnesota, 1997-99; Dallas, 2000; Baltimore, 2001 (775-4,928)
5.22 Jim Brown, Cleveland, 1957-1965 (2,359-12,312)
5.14 Mercury Morris, Miami, 1969-1975; San Diego, 1976 (804-1,433)

Highest Average Gain, Season (Qualifiers)

8.45 Michael Vick, Atlanta, 2006 (123-1,039)
8.44 Beattie Feathers, Chi. Bears, 1934 (119-1,004)
7.98 Randall Cunningham, Philadelphia, 1990 (118-942)

Highest Average Gain, Game (10 attempts)

17.30 Michael Vick, Atlanta vs. Minnesota, Dec. 1, 2002 (10-173)
17.09 Marion Motley, Cleveland vs. Pittsburgh, Oct. 29, 1950 (11-188)
16.70 Billy Grimes, Green Bay vs. N.Y. Yanks, Oct. 8, 1950 (10-167)
  Michael Turner, San Diego vs. Denver, Oct. 7, 2007 (10-147)

TOUCHDOWNS

Most Seasons Leading League

5 Jim Brown, Cleveland, 1957-59, 1963, 1965
4 Steve Van Buren, Philadelphia, 1945, 1947-49
3 Abner Haynes, Dall. Texans, 1960-62
  Cookie Gilchrist, Buffalo, 1962-64
  Paul Lowe, L.A. Chargers, 1960; San Diego, 1961, 1965
  Leroy Kelly, Cleveland, 1966-68
  Emmitt Smith, Dallas, 1992, 1994-95
  LaDainian Tomlinson, San Diego, 2004, 2006-07

Most Consecutive Seasons Leading League

3 Steve Van Buren, Philadelphia, 1947-49
  Jim Brown, Cleveland, 1957-59
  Abner Haynes, Dall. Texans, 1960-62
  Cookie Gilchrist, Buffalo, 1962-64
  Leroy Kelly, Cleveland, 1966-68

Most Touchdowns, Career

164 Emmitt Smith, Dallas, 1990-2002; Arizona, 2003-04
145 LaDainian Tomlinson, San Diego, 2001-09; N.Y. Jets, 2010-11
123 Marcus Allen, L.A. Raiders, 1982-1992; Kansas City, 1993-97

Most Rushing Touchdowns, Season

28 LaDainian Tomlinson, San Diego, 2006
27 Priest Holmes, Kansas City, 2003
  Shaun Alexander, Seattle, 2005
25 Emmitt Smith, Dallas, 1995

Most Touchdowns, Rookie, Season

18 Eric Dickerson, L.A. Rams, 1983
15 Ickey Woods, Cincinnati, 1988
  Mike Anderson, Denver, 2000
  Clinton Portis, Denver, 2002
14 Gale Sayers, Chicago, 1965
  Barry Sanders, Detroit, 1989
  Curtis Martin, New England, 1995
  Fred Taylor, Jacksonville, 1998
  Cam Newton, Carolina, 2011

Most Touchdowns, Game

6 Ernie Nevers, Chi. Cardinals vs. Chi. Bears, Nov. 28, 1929
5 Jimmy Conzelman, Rhode Island vs. Evansville, Oct. 15, 1922
  Jim Brown, Cleveland vs. Baltimore, Nov. 1, 1959
  Cookie Gilchrist, Buffalo vs. N.Y. Jets, Dec. 8, 1963
  James Stewart, Jacksonville vs. Philadelphia, Oct. 12, 1997
  Clinton Portis, Denver vs. Kansas City, Dec. 7, 2003
4 By many players

Most Consecutive Games Rushing for Touchdowns

18 LaDainian Tomlinson, San Diego, 2004-05
13 John Riggins, Washington, 1982-83
  George Rogers, Washington, 1985-86
11 Lenny Moore, Baltimore, 1963-64
  Emmitt Smith, Dallas, 1994-95
  Emmitt Smith, Dallas, 1995
  Priest Holmes, Kansas City, 2002

PASSING

Most Seasons Leading League (Passer Rating)

6 Sammy Baugh, Washington, 1937, 1940, 1943, 1945, 1947, 1949
  Steve Young San Francisco, 1991-94, 1996-97
4 Len Dawson, Dall. Texans; 1962; Kansas City, 1964, 1966, 1968
  Roger Staubach, Dallas, 1971, 1973, 1978-79
  Ken Anderson, Cincinnati, 1974-75, 1981-82
3 Arnie Herber, Green Bay, 1932, 1934, 1936
  Norm Van Brocklin, Los Angeles, 1950, 1952, 1954
  Bart Starr, Green Bay, 1962, 1964, 1966

Peyton Manning, Indianapolis, 2004-06

Most Consecutive Seasons Leading League (Passer Rating)
4 Steve Young, San Francisco, 1991-94
3 Peyton Manning, Indianapolis, 2004-06
2 Cecil. Isbell, Green Bay, 1941-42
  Milt Plum, Cleveland, 1960-61
  Ken Anderson, Cincinnati, 1974-75, 1981-82
  Roger Staubach, Dallas, 1978-79
  Steve Young, San Francisco, 1996-97

PASSER RATING

Highest Passer Rating, Career (1,500 attempts)
104.1 Aaron Rodgers, Green Bay, 2005-2011
96.9 Tony Romo, Dallas, 2004-2011
96.8 Steve Young, Tampa Bay, 1985-86; San Francisco, 1987-1999

Highest Passer Rating, Season (Qualifiers)
122.5 Aaron Rodgers, Green Bay, 2011
121.1 Peyton Manning, Indianapolis, 2004
117.2 Tom Brady, New England, 2007

Highest Passer Rating, Rookie, Season (Qualifiers)
98.1 Ben Roethlisberger, Pittsburgh, 2004
96.0 Dan Marino, Miami, 1983
88.3 Greg Cook, Cincinnati, 1969

ATTEMPTS

Most Seasons Leading League
5 Dan Marino, Miami, 1984, 1986, 1988, 1992, 1997
4 Sammy Baugh, Washington, 1937, 1943, 1947-48
  Johnny Unitas, Baltimore, 1957, 1959-1961
  George Blanda, Chi. Bears, 1953; Houston, 1963-65
3 Arnie Herber, Green Bay, 1932, 1934, 1936
  Sonny Jurgensen, Washington, 1966-67, 1969
  Drew Bledsoe, New England, 1994-96
  Brett Favre, Green Bay, 1999, 2005-06

Most Consecutive Seasons Leading League
3 Johnny Unitas, Baltimore, 1959-1961
  George Blanda, Houston, 1963-65
  Drew Bledsoe, New England, 1994-96
2 By many players

Most Passes Attempted, Career
10,169 Brett Favre, Atlanta, 1991; Green Bay, 1992-2007; N.Y. Jets, 2008; Minnesota, 2009-2010
8,358 Dan Marino, Miami, 1983-1999
7,250 John Elway, Denver, 1983-1998

Most Passes Attempted, Season
691 Drew Bledsoe, New England, 1994
679 Peyton Manning, Indianapolis, 2010
663 Matthew Stafford, Detroit, 2011

Most Passes Attempted, Rookie, Season
590 Sam Bradford, St. Louis, 2010
575 Peyton Manning, Indianapolis, 1998
540 Chris Weinke, Carolina, 2001

Most Passes Attempted, Game
70 Drew Bledsoe, New England vs. Minnesota, Nov. 13, 1994
69 Vinny Testaverde, N.Y. Jets vs. Baltimore, Dec. 24, 2000
68 George Blanda, Houston vs. Buffalo, Nov. 1, 1964
  Jon Kitna, Cincinnati vs. Pittsburgh, Dec. 30, 2001

COMPLETIONS

Most Seasons Leading League
6 Dan Marino, Miami, 1984-86, 1988, 1992, 1997
5 Sammy Baugh, Washington, 1937, 1943, 1945, 1947-48
4 George Blanda, Chi. Bears, 1953; Houston, 1963-65
  Sonny Jurgensen, Philadelphia, 1961; Washington, 1966-67, 1969

Most Consecutive Seasons Leading League
3 George Blanda, Houston, 1963-65
  Dan Marino, Miami, 1984-86
2 By many players

Most Passes Completed, Career
6,300 Brett Favre, Atlanta, 1991; Green Bay, 1992-2007; N.Y. Jets, 2008, Minnesota, 2009-2010
4,967 Dan Marino, Miami, 1983-1999
4,682 Peyton Manning, Indianapolis, 1998-2010

Most Passes Completed, Season
468 Drew Brees, New Orleans, 2011
450 Peyton Manning, Indianapolis, 2010
448 Drew Brees, New Orleans, 2010

Most Passes Completed, Rookie, Season
354 Sam Bradford, St. Louis, 2010
326 Peyton Manning, Indianapolis, 1998
310 Cam Newton, Carolina, 2011

Most Passes Completed, Game
45 Drew Bledsoe, New England vs. Minnesota, Nov. 13, 1994 (ot)
43 Rich Gannon, Oakland vs. Pittsburgh, Sept. 15, 2002
42 Richard Todd, N.Y. Jets vs. San Francisco, Sept. 21, 1980
  Vinny Testaverde, N.Y. Jets vs. Seattle, Dec. 6, 1998

Most Consecutive Passes Completed
24 Donovan McNabb, Philadelphia vs. N.Y. Giants (10), Nov. 28, 2004; vs. Green Bay (14), Dec. 5, 2004
23 Peyton Manning, Indianapolis vs. Detroit (6), Dec. 14, 2008; vs. Jacksonville (17), Dec. 18, 2008
22 Joe Montana, San Francisco vs. Cleveland (5), Nov. 29, 1987; vs. Green Bay (17), Dec. 6, 1987
  Mark Brunell, Washington vs. Houston, Sept. 24, 2006
  David Carr, Houston vs. Buffalo, Nov. 19, 2006

COMPLETION PERCENTAGE

Most Seasons Leading League
8 Len Dawson, Dall. Texans, 1962; Kansas City, 1964-69, 1975
7 Sammy Baugh, Washington, 1940, 1942-43, 1945, 1947-49
5 Joe Montana, San Francisco, 1980-81, 1985, 1987, 1989
  Steve Young, San Francisco, 1992, 1994-97

Most Consecutive Seasons Leading League
6 Len Dawson, Kansas City, 1964-69
4 Steve Young, San Francisco, 1994-97
3 Sammy Baugh, Washington, 1947-49
  Otto Graham, Cleveland, 1953-55
  Milt Plum, Cleveland, 1959-1961
  Kurt Warner, St. Louis, 1999-2001
  Drew Brees, New Orleans, 2009-2011

Highest Completion Percentage, Career (1,500 attempts)
66.05 Chad Pennington, N.Y. Jets, 2000-07; Miami, 2008-2010 (2,471-1,632)
65.94 Drew Brees, San Diego, 2001-05; New Orleans, 2006-2011 (5,479-3,613)
65.50 Kurt Warner, St. Louis, 1998-2003; N.Y. Giants, 2004; Arizona, 2005-09 (4,070-2,666)

Highest Completion Percentage, Season (Qualifiers)
71.23 Drew Brees, New Orleans, 2011 (657-468)
70.62 Drew Brees, New Orleans, 2009 (514-363)
70.55 Ken Anderson, Cincinnati, 1982 (309-218)

Highest Completion Percentage, Rookie, Season (Qualifiers)
66.44 Ben Roethlisberger, Pittsburgh, 2004 (295-196)
61.06 Matt Ryan, Atlanta, 2008 (434-265)
60.05 Joe Flacco, Baltimore, 2008 (428-257)

Highest Completion Percentage, Game (20 attempts)
- 92.31　Kurt Warner, Arizona vs. Jacksonville, Sept. 20, 2009 (26-24)
- 91.30　Vinny Testaverde, Cleveland vs. L.A. Rams, Dec. 26, 1993 (23-21)
- 90.91　Ken Anderson, Cincinnati vs. Pittsburgh, Nov. 10, 1974 (22-20)

YARDS GAINED

Most Seasons Leading League
- 5　Sonny Jurgensen, Philadelphia, 1961-62; Washington, 1966-67, 1969
　　Dan Marino, Miami, 1984-86, 1988, 1992
- 4　Sammy Baugh, Washington, 1937, 1940, 1947-48
　　Johnny Unitas, Baltimore, 1957, 1959-1960, 1963
　　Dan Fouts, San Diego, 1979-1982
- 3　Arnie Herber, Green Bay, 1932, 1934, 1936
　　Sid Luckman, Chi. Bears, 1943, 1945-46
　　John Brodie, San Francisco, 1965, 1968, 1970
　　John Hadl, San Diego, 1965, 1968, 1971
　　Joe Namath, N.Y. Jets, 1966-67, 1972
　　Drew Brees, New Orleans, 2006, 2008, 2011

Most Consecutive Seasons Leading League
- 4　Dan Fouts, San Diego, 1979-1982
- 3　Dan Marino, Miami, 1984-86
- 2　By many players

Most Yards Gained, Career
- 71,838　Brett Favre, Atlanta, 1991; Green Bay, 1992-2007; N.Y. Jets, 2008, Minnesota, 2009-2010
- 61,361　Dan Marino, Miami, 1983-1999
- 54,828　Peyton Manning, Indianapolis, 1998-2010

Most Seasons, 3,000 or More Yards Passing
- 18　Brett Favre, Green Bay, 1992-2007; N.Y. Jets, 2008; Minnesota, 2009
- 13　Dan Marino, Miami, 1984-1992, 1994-95, 1997-98
　　Peyton Manning, Indianapolis, 1998-2010
- 12　John Elway, Denver, 1985-1991, 1993-97

Most Yards Gained, Season
- 5,476　Drew Brees, New Orleans, 2011
- 5,235　Tom Brady, New England, 2011
- 5,084　Dan Marino, Miami, 1984

Most Yards Gained, Rookie, Season
- 4,051　Cam Newton, Carolina, 2011
- 3,739　Peyton Manning, Indianapolis, 1998
- 3,512　Sam Bradford, St. Louis, 2010

Most Yards Gained, Game
- 554　Norm Van Brocklin, Los Angeles vs. N.Y. Yanks, Sept. 28, 1951
- 527　Warren Moon, Houston vs. Kansas City, Dec. 16, 1990
- 522　Boomer Esiason, Arizona vs. Washington, Nov. 10, 1996 (ot)

Most Games, 400 or More Yards Passing, Career
- 13　Dan Marino, Miami, 1983-1999
- 8　Peyton Manning, Indianapolis, 1998-2010
- 7　Joe Montana, San Francisco, 1979-1990, 1992; Kansas City, 1993-94
　　Warren Moon, Houston, 1984-1993; Minnesota, 1994-96; Seattle, 1997-98; Kansas City, 1999-2000
　　Drew Brees, San Diego, 2001-05; New Orleans, 2006-2011

Most Games, 400 or More Yards Passing, Season
- 4　Dan Marino, Miami, 1984
- 3　Dan Marino, Miami, 1986
　　Eli Manning, N.Y. Giants, 2011
- 2　By many players

Most Consecutive Games, 400 or More Yards Passing
- 2　Dan Fouts, San Diego, 1982
　　Dan Marino, Miami, 1984

Phil Simms, N.Y. Giants, 1985
Billy Volek, Tennessee, 2004
Matt Cassel, New England, 2008
Tom Brady, New England, 2011
Cam Newton, Carolina, 2011

Most Games, 300 or More Yards Passing, Career
- 63　Dan Marino, Miami, 1983-1999
　　Peyton Manning, Indianapolis, 1998-2010
- 62　Brett Favre, Atlanta, 1991; Green Bay, 1992-2007; N.Y. Jets, 2008; Minnesota, 2009-2010
- 57　Drew Brees, San Diego, 2001-05; New Orleans, 2006-2011

Most Games, 300 or More Yards Passing, Season
- 13　Drew Brees, New Orleans, 2011
- 11　Tom Brady, New England, 2011
- 10　Rich Gannon, Oakland, 2002
　　Drew Brees, New Orleans, 2008

Most Consecutive Games, 300 or More Yards Passing
- 7　Drew Brees, New Orleans, 2011 (current)
- 6　Steve Young, San Francisco, 1998
　　Kurt Warner, St. Louis, 2000
　　Rich Gannon, Oakland, 2002
- 5　Joe Montana, San Francisco, 1982
　　Kerry Collins, N.Y. Giants, 2001-02
　　Drew Brees, New Orleans, 2006
　　Kurt Warner, Arizona, 2008
　　Tom Brady, New England, 2009
　　Peyton Manning, Indianapolis, 2009
　　Drew Brees, New Orleans, 2011

Longest Pass Completion (All TDs except as noted)
- 99　Frank Filchock (to Farkas), Washington vs. Pittsburgh, Oct. 15, 1939
　　George Izo (to Mitchell), Washington vs. Cleveland, Sept. 15, 1963
　　Karl Sweetan (to Studstill), Detroit vs. Baltimore, Oct. 16, 1966
　　Sonny Jurgensen (to Allen), Washington vs. Chicago, Sept. 15, 1968
　　Jim Plunkett (to Branch), L.A. Raiders vs. Washington, Oct. 2, 1983
　　Ron Jaworski (to Quick), Philadelphia vs. Atlanta, Nov. 10, 1985
　　Stan Humphries (to Martin), San Diego vs. Seattle, Sept. 18, 1994
　　Brett Favre (to Brooks), Green Bay vs. Chicago, Sept. 11, 1995
　　Trent Green (to Boerigter), Kansas City vs. San Diego, Dec. 22, 2002
　　Jeff Garcia (to Davis), Cleveland vs. Cincinnati, Oct. 17, 2004
　　Gus Frerotte (to Berrian), Minnesota vs. Chicago, Nov. 30, 2008
　　Tom Brady (to Welker), New England vs. Miami, Sept. 12, 2011
　　Eli Manning (to Cruz), N.Y. Giants vs. N.Y. Jets, Dec. 24, 2011
- 98　Doug Russell (to Tinsley), Chi. Cardinals vs. Cleveland, Nov. 27, 1938
　　Ogden Compton (to Lane), Chi. Cardinals vs. Green Bay, Nov. 13, 1955
　　Bill Wade (to Farrington), Chicago Bears vs. Detroit, Oct. 8, 1961
　　Jacky Lee (to Dewveall), Houston vs. San Diego, Nov. 25, 1962
　　Earl Morrall (to Jones), N.Y. Giants vs. Pittsburgh, Sept. 11, 1966
　　Jim Hart (to Rashad), St. Louis vs. Los Angeles, Dec. 10, 1972 (no TD)
　　Bobby Hebert (to Haynes), Atlanta vs. New Orleans, Sept. 12, 1993

Charlie Batch (to Morton), Detroit vs. Chicago,
Oct. 4, 1998

Ryan Fitzpatrick (to Owens), Buffalo vs. Jacksonville,
Nov. 22, 2009

97　Pat Coffee (to Tinsley), Chi. Cardinals vs. Chi. Bears,
Dec. 5, 1937

Bobby Layne (to Box), Detroit vs. Green Bay,
Nov. 26, 1953

George Shaw (to Tarr), Denver vs. Boston,
Sept. 21, 1962

Bernie Kosar (to Slaughter), Cleveland vs. Chicago,
Oct. 23, 1989

Steve Young (to Taylor), San Francisco vs. Atlanta,
Nov. 3, 1991

AVERAGE GAIN
Most Seasons Leading League
7　Sid Luckman, Chi. Bears, 1939-1943, 1946-47
5　Steve Young, San Francisco, 1991-94, 1997
3　Arnie Herber, Green Bay, 1932, 1934, 1936
　　Norm Van Brocklin, Los Angeles, 1950, 1952, 1954
　　Len Dawson, Dall. Texans, 1962; Kansas City, 1966,
　　1968
　　Bart Starr, Green Bay, 1966-68
　　Kurt Warner, St. Louis, 1999-2001
　　Philip Rivers, San Diego, 2008-2010
Most Consecutive Seasons Leading League
5　Sid Luckman, Chi. Bears, 1939-1943
4　Steve Young, San Francisco, 1991-94
3　Bart Starr, Green Bay, 1966-68
　　Kurt Warner, St. Louis, 1999-2001
　　Philip Rivers, San Diego, 2008-2010
Highest Average Gain, Career (1,500 Attempts)
8.63　Otto Graham, Cleveland, 1950-55 (1,565-13,499)
8.42　Sid Luckman, Chi. Bears, 1939-1950
　　　(1,744-14,686)
8.22　Aaron Rodgers, Green Bay, 2005-2011
　　　(2,113-17,366)
Highest Average Gain, Season (Qualifiers)
11.17　Tommy O'Connell, Cleveland, 1957 (110-1,229)
10.86　Sid Luckman, Chi. Bears, 1943 (202-2,194)
10.55　Otto Graham, Cleveland, 1953 (258-2,722)
Highest Average Gain, Rookie, Season (Qualifiers)
9.411　Greg Cook, Cincinnati, 1969 (197-1,854)
9.409　Bob Waterfield, Cleveland, 1945 (171-1,609)
8.88　Ben Roethlisberger, Pittsburgh, 2004 (295-2,621)
Highest Average Gain, Game (20 attempts)
18.58　Sammy Baugh, Washington vs. Boston,
　　　Oct. 31, 1948 (24-446)
18.50　Johnny Unitas, Baltimore vs. Atlanta, Nov. 12, 1967
　　　(20-370)
17.71　Joe Namath, N.Y. Jets vs. Baltimore, Sept. 24, 1972
　　　(28-496)

TOUCHDOWNS
Most Seasons Leading League
4　Johnny Unitas, Baltimore, 1957-1960
　　Len Dawson, Dall. Texans, 1962; Kansas City, 1963,
　　1965-66
　　Steve Young, San Francisco, 1992-94, 1998
　　Brett Favre, Green Bay, 1995-97, 2003
3　Arnie Herber, Green Bay, 1932, 1934, 1936
　　Sid Luckman, Chi. Bears, 1943, 1945-46
　　Y.A. Tittle, San Francisco, 1955; N.Y. Giants, 1962-63
　　Dan Marino, Miami, 1984-86
　　Peyton Manning, Indianapolis, 2000, 2004, 2006
　　Tom Brady, New England, 2002, 2007, 2010
　　Drew Brees, New Orleans, 2008-09, 2011
2　By many players

Most Consecutive Seasons Leading League
4　Johnny Unitas, Baltimore, 1957-1960
3　Dan Marino, Miami, 1984-86
　　Steve Young, San Francisco, 1992-94
　　Brett Favre, Green Bay, 1995-97
2　By many players
Most Touchdown Passes, Career
508　Brett Favre, Atlanta, 1991; Green Bay, 1992-2007;
　　　N.Y. Jets, 2008, Minnesota, 2009-2010
420　Dan Marino, Miami, 1983-1999
399　Peyton Manning, Indianapolis, 1998-2010
Most Touchdown Passes, Season
50　Tom Brady, New England, 2007
49　Peyton Manning, Indianapolis, 2004
48　Dan Marino, Miami, 1984
Most Touchdown Passes, Rookie, Season
26　Peyton Manning, Indianapolis, 1998
22　Charlie Conerly, N.Y. Giants, 1948
21　Cam Newton, Carolina, 2011
Most Touchdown Passes, Game
7　Sid Luckman, Chi. Bears vs. N.Y. Giants,
　　Nov. 14, 1943
　　Adrian Burk, Philadelphia vs. Washington,
　　Oct. 17, 1954
　　George Blanda, Houston vs. N.Y. Titans,
　　Nov. 19, 1961
　　Y.A. Tittle, N.Y. Giants vs. Washington, Oct. 28, 1962
　　Joe Kapp, Minnesota vs. Baltimore, Sept. 28, 1969
6　By many players. Last time:
　　Matt Flynn, Green Bay vs. Detroit, Jan. 1, 2012
Most Games, Four or More Touchdown Passes, Career
23　Brett Favre, Atlanta, 1991; Green Bay, 1992-2007;
　　　N.Y. Jets, 2008; Minnesota, 2009-2010
22　Peyton Manning, Indianapolis, 1998-2010
21　Dan Marino, Miami, 1983-1999
Most Games, Four or More Touchdown Passes, Season
6　Dan Marino, Miami, 1984
　　Peyton Manning, Indianapolis, 2004
5　Dan Marino, Miami, 1986
　　Brett Favre, Green Bay, 1996
　　Donovan McNabb, Philadelphia, 2004
　　Tom Brady, New England, 2007
　　Drew Brees, New Orleans, 2011
　　Aaron Rodgers, Green Bay, 2011
4　George Blanda, Houston, 1961
　　Vince Ferragamo, Los Angeles, 1980
　　Steve Young, San Francisco, 1994
　　Randall Cunningham, Minnesota, 1998
　　Daunte Culpepper, Minnesota, 2004
　　Tony Romo, Dallas, 2007
　　Peyton Manning, Indianapolis, 2009
　　Matthew Stafford, Detroit, 2011
Most Consecutive Games, Four or More Touchdown Passes
5　Peyton Manning, Indianapolis, 2004
4　Dan Marino, Miami, 1984
3　Drew Brees, 2011 (current)
Most Consecutive Games, Touchdown Passes
47　Johnny Unitas, Baltimore, 1956-1960
43　Drew Brees, New Orleans, 2009-2011 (current)
36　Brett Favre, Green Bay, 2002-2004

HAD INTERCEPTED
Most Consecutive Passes Attempted, None Intercepted
358　Tom Brady, New England, 2010-11
308　Bernie Kosar, Cleveland, 1990-91
294　Bart Starr, Green Bay, 1964-65
Most Passes Had Intercepted, Career
336　Brett Favre, Atlanta, 1991; Green Bay, 1992-2007;
　　　N.Y. Jets, 2008; Minnesota, 2009-2010

277 George Blanda, Chi. Bears, 1949, 1950-58; Baltimore, 1950; Houston, 1960-66; Oakland, 1967-1975
268 John Hadl, San Diego, 1962-1972; Los Angeles, 1973-74; Green Bay, 1974-75; Houston, 1976-77

Most Passes Had Intercepted, Season
42 George Blanda, Houston, 1962
35 Vinny Testaverde, Tampa Bay, 1988
34 Frank Tripucka, Denver, 1960

Most Passes Had Intercepted, Game
8 Jim Hardy, Chi. Cardinals vs. Philadelphia, Sept. 24, 1950
7 Parker Hall, Cleveland vs. Green Bay, Nov. 8, 1942
   Frank Sinkwich, Detroit vs. Green Bay, Oct. 24, 1943
   Bob Waterfield, Los Angeles vs. Green Bay, Oct. 17, 1948
   Zeke Bratkowski, Chicago vs. Baltimore, Oct. 2, 1960
   Tommy Wade, Pittsburgh vs. Philadelphia, Dec. 12, 1965
   Ken Stabler, Oakland vs. Denver, Oct. 16, 1977
   Steve DeBerg, Tampa Bay vs. San Francisco, Sept. 7, 1986
   Ty Detmer, Detroit vs. Cleveland, Sept. 23, 2001
6 By many players

Most Attempts, No Interceptions, Game
70 Drew Bledsoe, New England vs. Minnesota, Nov. 13, 1994 (ot)
63 Rich Gannon, Minnesota vs. New England, Oct. 20, 1991 (ot)
60 Davey O'Brien, Philadelphia vs. Washington, Dec. 1, 1940

LOWEST PERCENTAGE, PASSES HAD INTERCEPTED
Most Seasons Leading League, Lowest Percentage, Passes Had Intercepted
5 Sammy Baugh, Washington, 1940, 1942, 1944-45, 1947
3 Charlie Conerly, N.Y. Giants, 1950, 1956, 1959
   Bart Starr, Green Bay, 1962, 1964, 1966
   Roger Staubach, Dallas, 1971, 1977, 1979
   Ken Anderson, Cincinnati, 1972, 1981-82
   Ken O'Brien, N.Y. Jets, 1985, 1987-88
2 By many players

Lowest Pct., Passes Had Intercepted, Career (1,500 attempts)
1.80 Aaron Rodgers, Green Bay, 2005-2011 (2,113-38)
2.11 Neil O'Donnell, Pittsburgh, 1991-95; N.Y. Jets, 1996-97; Cincinnati, 1998; Tennessee, 1999-2003 (3,229-68)
2.16 Tom Brady, New England, 2000-2011 (5,321-115)

Lowest Pct., Passes Had Intercepted, Season (Qualifiers)
0.41 Damon Huard, Kansas City, 2006 (244-1)
0.66 Joe Ferguson, Buffalo, 1976 (151-1)
0.81 Tom Brady, New England, 2010 (492-4)

Lowest Pct., Passes Had Intercepted, Rookie, Season (Qualifiers)
1.98 Charlie Batch, Detroit, 1998 (303-6)
2.03 Dan Marino, Miami, 1983 (296-6)
2.10 Gary Wood, N.Y. Giants, 1964 (143-3)

TIMES SACKED
Times Sacked has been compiled since 1963.
Most Times Sacked, Career
525 Brett Favre, Atlanta, 1991; Green Bay, 1992-2007; N.Y. Jets, 2008; Minnesota, 2009-2010
516 John Elway, Denver, 1983-1998
494 Dave Krieg, Seattle, 1980-1991; Kansas City, 1992-93; Detroit, 1994; Arizona, 1995; Chicago, 1996; Tennessee, 1997-98

Most Times Sacked, Season
76 David Carr, Houston, 2002
72 Randall Cunningham, Philadelphia, 1986
68 David Carr, Houston, 2005

Most Times Sacked, Game
12 Bert Jones, Baltimore vs. St. Louis, Oct. 26, 1980
    Warren Moon, Houston vs. Dallas, Sept. 29, 1985
    Donovan McNabb, Philadelphia vs. N.Y. Giants, Sept. 30, 2007
11 Charley Johnson, St. Louis vs. N.Y. Giants, Nov. 1, 1964
    Bart Starr, Green Bay vs. Detroit, Nov. 7, 1965
    Jack Kemp, Buffalo vs. Oakland, Oct. 15, 1967
    Bob Berry, Atlanta vs. St. Louis, Nov. 24, 1968
    Greg Landry, Detroit vs. Dallas, Oct. 6, 1975
    Ron Jaworski, Philadelphia vs. St. Louis, Dec. 18, 1983
    Paul McDonald, Cleveland vs. Kansas City, Sept. 30, 1984
    Archie Manning, Minnesota vs. Chicago, Oct. 28, 1984
    Steve Pelluer, Dallas vs. San Diego, Nov. 16, 1986
    Randall Cunningham, Philadelphia vs. L.A. Raiders, Nov. 30, 1986 (ot)
    David Norrie, N.Y. Jets vs. Dallas, Oct. 4, 1987
    Troy Aikman, Dallas vs. Philadelphia, Sept. 15, 1991
    Bernie Kosar, Cleveland vs. Indianapolis, Sept. 6, 1992
10 By many players

RECEIVING
Most Seasons Leading League
8 Don Hutson, Green Bay, 1936-37, 1939, 1941-45
5 Lionel Taylor, Denver, 1960-63, 1965
3 Tom Fears, Los Angeles, 1948-1950
   Pete Pihos, Philadelphia, 1953-55
   Billy Wilson, San Francisco, 1954, 1956-57
   Raymond Berry, Baltimore, 1958-1960
   Lance Alworth, San Diego, 1966, 1968-69
   Sterling Sharpe, Green Bay, 1989, 1992-93
   Wes Welker, New England, 2007, 2009, 2011

Most Consecutive Seasons Leading League
5 Don Hutson, Green Bay, 1941-45
4 Lionel Taylor, Denver, 1960-63
3 Tom Fears, Los Angeles, 1948-1950
   Pete Pihos, Philadelphia, 1953-55
   Raymond Berry, Baltimore, 1958-1960

Most Pass Receptions, Career
1,549 Jerry Rice, San Francisco, 1985-2000; Oakland, 2001-04; Seattle, 2004
1,149 Tony Gonzalez, Kansas City, 1997-2008; Atlanta, 2009-2011
1,102 Marvin Harrison, Indianapolis, 1996-2008

Most Seasons, 50 or More Pass Receptions
17 Jerry Rice, San Francisco, 1986-1996, 1998-2000; Oakland, 2001-03
14 Tony Gonzalez, Kansas City, 1998-2008; Atlanta, 2009-2011
13 Andre Reed, Buffalo, 1986-1994, 1996-99
    Terrell Owens, San Francisco, 1997-2003; Philadelphia, 2004; Dallas, 2006-08; Buffalo, 2009; Cincinnati, 2010

Most Pass Receptions, Season
143 Marvin Harrison, Indianapolis, 2002
123 Herman Moore, Detroit, 1995
     Wes Welker, New England, 2009
122 Cris Carter, Minnesota, 1994
     Jerry Rice, San Francisco, 1995
     Cris Carter, Minnesota, 1995
     Wes Welker, New England, 2011

Most Pass Receptions, Rookie, Season
- 101 Anquan Boldin, Arizona, 2003
- 91 Eddie Royal, Denver, 2008
- 90 Terry Glenn, New England, 1996

Most Pass Receptions, Game
- 21 Brandon Marshall, Denver vs. Indianapolis, Dec. 13, 2009
- 20 Terrell Owens, San Francisco vs. Chicago, Dec. 17, 2000
- 18 Tom Fears, Los Angeles vs. Green Bay, Dec. 3, 1950
   Brandon Marshall, Denver vs. San Diego, Sept. 14, 2008

Most Consecutive Games, Pass Receptions
- 274 Jerry Rice, San Francisco, 1985-2000; Oakland, 2001-04
- 190 Marvin Harrison, Indianapolis, 1996-2008
- 186 Hines Ward, Pittsburgh, 1998-2010

YARDS GAINED

Most Seasons Leading League
- 7 Don Hutson, Green Bay, 1936, 1938-39, 1941-44
- 6 Jerry Rice, San Francisco, 1986, 1989-1990, 1993-95
- 3 Raymond Berry, Baltimore, 1957, 1959-1960
   Lance Alworth, San Diego, 1965-66, 1968

Most Consecutive Seasons Leading League
- 4 Don Hutson, Green Bay, 1941-44
- 3 Jerry Rice, San Francisco, 1993-95
- 2 By many players

Most Yards Gained, Career
- 22,895 Jerry Rice, San Francisco, 1985-2000; Oakland, 2001-04; Seattle, 2004
- 15,934 Terrell Owens, San Francisco, 1996-2003; Philadelphia, 2004-05; Dallas, 2006-08; Buffalo, 2009; Cincinnati, 2010
- 15,208 Isaac Bruce, L.A. Rams, 1994; St. Louis, 1995-2007; San Francisco, 2008-09

Most Seasons, 1,000 or More Yards, Pass Receiving
- 14 Jerry Rice, San Francisco, 1986-1996, 1998; Oakland, 2001-02
- 10 Randy Moss, Minnesota, 1998-2003; Oakland, 2005; New England, 2007-09
- 9 Tim Brown, L.A. Raiders, 1993-94; Oakland, 1995-2001
   Jimmy Smith, Jacksonville, 1996-2002, 2004-05
   Terrell Owens, San Francisco, 1998, 2000-03; Philadelphia, 2004; Dallas, 2006-08

Most Yards Gained, Season
- 1,848 Jerry Rice, San Francisco, 1995
- 1,781 Isaac Bruce, St. Louis, 1995
- 1,746 Charley Hennigan, Houston, 1961

Most Yards Gained, Rookie, Season
- 1,473 Bill Groman, Houston, 1960
- 1,377 Anquan Boldin, Arizona, 2003
- 1,313 Randy Moss, Minnesota, 1998

Most Yards Gained, Game
- 336 Flipper Anderson, L.A. Rams vs. New Orleans, Nov. 26, 1989
- 309 Stephone Paige, Kansas City vs. San Diego, Dec. 22, 1985
- 303 Jim Benton, Cleveland vs. Detroit, Nov. 22, 1945

Most Games, 200 or More Yards Pass Receiving, Career
- 5 Lance Alworth, San Diego, 1962-1970; Dallas, 1971-72
- 4 Don Hutson, Green Bay, 1935-45
   Charley Hennigan, Houston, 1960-66
   Jerry Rice, San Francisco, 1985-2000; Oakland, 2001-04; Seattle, 2004
- 3 Don Maynard, N.Y. Giants, 1958; N.Y. Jets, 1960-1972; St. Louis, 1973

Wes Chandler, New Orleans, 1978-1981; San Diego, 1981-87; San Francisco, 1988
Isaac Bruce, L.A. Rams, 1994; St. Louis, 1995-2007; San Francisco, 2008
Terrell Owens, San Francisco, 1996-2003; Philadelphia, 2004-05; Dallas, 2006-08; Buffalo, 2009; Cincinnati, 2010

Most Games, 200 or More Yards Pass Receiving, Season
- 3 Charley Hennigan, Houston, 1961
- 2 Don Hutson, Green Bay, 1942
   Gene Roberts, N.Y. Giants, 1949
   Lance Alworth, San Diego, 1963
   Don Maynard, N.Y. Jets, 1968
   Calvin Johnson, Detroit, 2011

Most Games, 100 or More Yards Pass Receiving, Career
- 76 Jerry Rice, San Francisco, 1985-2000; Oakland, 2001-04; Seattle, 2004
- 64 Randy Moss, Minnesota, 1998-2004, 2010; Oakland, 2005-06; New England, 2007-2010; Tennessee, 2010
- 59 Marvin Harrison, Indianapolis, 1996-2008

Most Games, 100 or More Yards Pass Receiving, Season
- 11 Michael Irvin, Dallas, 1995
- 10 Charley Hennigan, Houston, 1961
   Herman Moore, Detroit, 1995
   Marvin Harrison, Indianapolis, 2002
   Torry Holt, St. Louis, 2003
- 9 Elroy (Crazylegs) Hirsch, Los Angeles, 1951
   Bill Groman, Houston, 1960
   Lance Alworth, San Diego, 1965
   Don Maynard, N.Y. Jets, 1967
   Stanley Morgan, New England, 1986
   Mark Carrier, Tampa Bay, 1989
   Robert Brooks, Green Bay, 1995
   Isaac Bruce, St. Louis, 1995
   Jerry Rice, San Francisco, 1995
   Marvin Harrison, Indianapolis, 1999
   Jimmy Smith, Jacksonville, 1999
   David Boston, Arizona, 2001
   Steve Smith, Carolina, 2005
   Randy Moss, New England, 2007

Most Consecutive Games, 100 or More Yards Pass Receiving
- 7 Charley Hennigan, Houston, 1961
   Michael Irvin, Dallas, 1995
- 6 Raymond Berry, Baltimore, 1960
   Bill Groman, Houston, 1961
   Pat Studstill, Detroit, 1966
   Isaac Bruce, St. Louis, 1995
   Mike Wallace, Pittsburgh, 2010-11
- 5 Elroy (Crazylegs) Hirsch, Los Angeles, 1951
   Bob Boyd, Los Angeles, 1954
   Terry Barr, Detroit, 1963
   Lance Alworth, San Diego, 1966
   Don Maynard, N.Y. Jets, 1968-69
   Harold Jackson, Philadelphia, 1971-72
   Patrick Jeffers, Carolina, 1999
   Terrell Owens, Philadelphia, 2004
   Anquan Boldin, Arizona, 2005

Longest Pass Reception (All TDs except as noted)
- 99 Andy Farkas (from Filchock), Washington vs. Pittsburgh, Oct. 15, 1939
   Bobby Mitchell (from Izo), Washington vs. Cleveland, Sept. 15, 1963
   Pat Studstill (from Sweetan), Detroit vs. Baltimore, Oct. 16, 1966
   Gerry Allen (from Jurgensen), Washington vs. Chicago, Sept. 15, 1968
   Cliff Branch (from Plunkett), L.A. Raiders vs. Washington, Oct. 2, 1983

Mike Quick (from Jaworski), Philadelphia vs. Atlanta, Nov. 10, 1985

Tony Martin (from Humphries), San Diego vs. Seattle, Sept. 18, 1994

Robert Brooks (from Favre), Green Bay vs. Chicago, Sept. 11, 1995

Marc Boerigter (from Green), Kansas City vs. San Diego, Dec. 22, 2002

Andre Davis (from Garcia), Cleveland vs. Cincinnati, Oct. 17, 2004

Bernard Berrian (from Frerotte), Minnesota vs. Chicago, Nov. 30, 2008

Wes Welker (from Brady), New England vs. Miami, Sept. 12, 2011

Victor Cruz (from Manning), N.Y. Giants vs. N.Y. Jets, Dec. 24, 2011

98　Gaynell Tinsley (from Russell), Chi. Cardinals vs. Cleveland, Nov. 17, 1938

Dick (Night Train) Lane (from Compton), Chi. Cardinals vs. Green Bay, Nov. 13, 1955

John Farrington (from Wade), Chicago vs. Detroit, Oct. 8, 1961

Willard Dewveall (from Lee), Houston vs. San Diego, Nov. 25, 1962

Homer Jones (from Morrall), N.Y. Giants vs. Pittsburgh, Sept. 11, 1966

Ahmad Rashad (from Hart), St. Louis vs. Los Angeles, Dec. 10, 1972 (no TD)

Michael Haynes (from Hebert), Atlanta vs. New Orleans, Sept. 12, 1993

Johnnie Morton (from Batch), Detroit vs. Chicago, Oct. 4, 1998

Terrell Owens (from Fitzpatrick), Buffalo vs. Jacksonville, Nov. 22, 2009

97　Gaynell Tinsley (from Coffee), Chi. Cardinals vs. Chi. Bears, Dec. 5, 1937

Cloyce Box (from Layne), Detroit vs. Green Bay, Nov. 26, 1953

Jerry Tarr (from Shaw), Denver vs. Boston, Sept. 21, 1962

Webster Slaughter (from Kosar), Cleveland vs. Chicago, Oct. 23, 1989

John Taylor (from Young), San Francisco vs. Atlanta, Nov. 3, 1991

AVERAGE GAIN

Highest Avg. Gain, Career (200 receptions)

22.26　Homer Jones, N.Y. Giants, 1964-69; Cleveland, 1970 (224-4,986)

20.83　Buddy Dial, Pittsburgh, 1959-1963; Dallas, 1964-66 (261-5,436)

20.24　Harlon Hill, Chi. Bears, 1954-1961; Pittsburgh, 1962; Detroit, 1962 (233-4,717)

Highest Avg. Gain, Season (24 receptions)

32.58　Don Currivan, Boston, 1947 (24-782)

31.44　Bucky Pope, Los Angeles, 1964 (25-786)

28.60　Bobby Duckworth, San Diego, 1984 (25-715)

Highest Average Gain, Game (3 receptions)

63.00　Torry Holt, St. Louis vs. Atlanta, Sept. 24, 2000 (3-189)

60.67　Bill Groman, Houston vs. Denver, Nov. 20, 1960 (3-182)

Homer Jones, N.Y. Giants vs. Washington, Dec. 12, 1965 (3-182)

60.33　Don Currivan, Boston vs. Washington, Nov. 30, 1947 (3-181)

TOUCHDOWNS

Most Seasons Leading League

9　Don Hutson, Green Bay, 1935-38, 1940-44

6　Jerry Rice, San Francisco, 1986-87, 1989-1991, 1993

5　Randy Moss, Minnesota, 1998, 2000, 2003; New England, 2007, 2009

Most Consecutive Seasons Leading League

5　Don Hutson, Green Bay, 1940-44

4　Don Hutson, Green Bay, 1935-38

3　Lance Alworth, San Diego, 1964-66

　Jerry Rice, San Francisco, 1989-1991

Most Touchdowns, Career

197　Jerry Rice, San Francisco, 1985-2000; Oakland, 2001-04; Seattle, 2004

153　Randy Moss, Minnesota, 1998-2004, 2010; Oakland, 2005-06; New England, 2007-2010; Tennessee, 2010

　　Terrell Owens, San Francisco, 1996-2003; Philadelphia, 2004-05; Dallas, 2006-08; Buffalo, 2009; Cincinnati, 2010

130　Cris Carter, Philadelphia, 1987-89; Minnesota, 1990-2001; Miami, 2002

Most Touchdowns, Season

23　Randy Moss, New England, 2007

22　Jerry Rice, San Francisco, 1987

18　Mark Clayton, Miami, 1984

　　Sterling Sharpe, Green Bay, 1994

Most Touchdowns, Rookie, Season

17　Randy Moss, Minnesota, 1998

13　Bill Howton, Green Bay, 1952

　　John Jefferson, San Diego, 1978

12　Harlon Hill, Chi. Bears, 1954

　　Bill Groman, Houston, 1960

　　Mike Ditka, Chicago, 1961

　　Bob Hayes, Dallas, 1965

Most Touchdowns, Game

5　Bob Shaw, Chi. Cardinals vs. Baltimore, Oct. 2, 1950

　Kellen Winslow, San Diego vs. Oakland, Nov. 22, 1981

　Jerry Rice, San Francisco vs. Atlanta, Oct. 14, 1990

4　By many players. Last time:

　Randy Moss, New England vs. Buffalo, Nov. 18, 2007

　Terrell Owens, Dallas vs. Washington, Nov. 18, 2007

Most Consecutive Games, Touchdowns

13　Jerry Rice, San Francisco, 1986-87

11　Elroy (Crazylegs) Hirsch, Los Angeles, 1950-51

　　Buddy Dial, Pittsburgh, 1959-1960

10　Carl Pickens, Cincinnati, 1994-95

　　Randy Moss, Minnesota, 2003-04

YARDS FROM SCRIMMAGE

Most Scrimmage Yards, Career

23,540　Jerry Rice, San Francisco 1985-2000; Oakland, 2001-04; Seattle, 2004

21,579　Emmitt Smith, Dallas, 1990-2002; Arizona, 2003-04

21,264　Walter Payton, Chicago, 1975-1987

Most Scrimmage Yards, Season

2,509　Chris Johnson, Tennessee, 2009

2,429　Marshall Faulk, St. Louis, 1999

2,390　Tiki Barber, N.Y. Giants, 2005

Most Scrimmage Yards, Rookie, Season

2,212　Eric Dickerson, L.A. Rams, 1983

2,139　Edgerrin James, Indianapolis, 1999

1,924　Billy Sims, Detroit, 1980

Most Scrimmage Yards, Game

336　Flipper Anderson, L.A. Rams vs. New Orleans, Nov. 26, 1989 (ot)

330　Billy Cannon, Houston vs. N.Y. Titans, Dec. 10, 1961

315   Adrian Peterson, Minnesota vs. San Diego,
        Nov. 4, 2007

INTERCEPTIONS BY
Most Seasons Leading League
3   Everson Walls, Dallas, 1981-82, 1985
     Ed Reed, Baltimore, 2004, 2008, 2010
2   Dick (Night Train) Lane, Los Angeles, 1952;
        Chi. Cardinals, 1954
     Jack Christiansen, Detroit, 1953, 1957
     Milt Davis, Baltimore, 1957, 1959
     Dick Lynch, N.Y. Giants, 1961, 1963
     Johnny Robinson, Kansas City, 1966, 1970
     Bill Bradley, Philadelphia, 1971-72
     Emmitt Thomas, Kansas City, 1969, 1974
     Ronnie Lott, San Francisco, 1986; L.A. Raiders, 1991
     Rod Woodson, Baltimore, 1999; Oakland, 2002
     Ty Law, New England, 1998; N.Y. Jets, 2005
     Darren Sharper, Green Bay, 2000; New Orleans, 2009
     Asante Samuel, New England, 2006;
        Philadelphia, 2009
     Charles Woodson, Green Bay, 2009, 2011
Most Interceptions By, Career
81   Paul Krause, Washington, 1964-67; Minnesota,
        1968-1979
79   Emlen Tunnell, N.Y. Giants, 1948-1958; Green Bay,
        1959-1961
71   Rod Woodson, Pittsburgh, 1987-1996; San Francisco,
        1997; Baltimore, 1998-2001; Oakland, 2002-03
Most Interceptions By, Season
14   Dick (Night Train) Lane, Los Angeles, 1952
13   Dan Sandifer, Washington, 1948
     Orban (Spec) Sanders, N.Y. Yanks, 1950
     Lester Hayes, Oakland, 1980
12   By nine players
Most Interceptions By, Rookie, Season
14   Dick (Night Train) Lane, Los Angeles, 1952
13   Dan Sandifer, Washington, 1948
12   Woodley Lewis, Los Angeles, 1950
     Paul Krause, Washington, 1964
Most Interceptions By, Game
4   Sammy Baugh, Washington vs. Detroit, Nov. 14, 1943
     Dan Sandifer, Washington vs. Boston, Oct. 31, 1948
     Don Doll, Detroit vs. Chi. Cardinals, Oct. 23, 1949
     Bob Nussbaumer, Chi. Cardinals vs. N.Y. Bulldogs,
        Nov. 13, 1949
     Russ Craft, Philadelphia vs. Chi. Cardinals,
        Sept. 24, 1950
     Bobby Dillon, Green Bay vs. Detroit, Nov. 26, 1953
     Jack Butler, Pittsburgh vs. Washington, Dec. 13, 1953
     Austin (Goose) Gonsoulin, Denver vs. Buffalo,
        Sept. 18, 1960
     Jerry Norton, St. Louis vs. Washington,
        Nov. 20, 1960; vs. Pittsburgh, Nov. 26, 1961
     Dave Baker, San Francisco vs. L.A. Rams,
        Dec. 4, 1960
     Bobby Ply, Dall. Texans vs. San Diego, Dec. 16, 1962
     Bobby Hunt, Kansas City vs. Houston, Oct. 4, 1964
     Willie Brown, Denver vs. N.Y. Jets, Nov. 15, 1964
     Dick Anderson, Miami vs. Pittsburgh, Dec. 3, 1973
     Willie Buchanon, Green Bay vs. San Diego,
        Sept. 24, 1978
     Deron Cherry, Kansas City vs. Seattle, Sept. 29, 1985
     Kwamie Lassiter, Arizona vs. San Diego,
        Dec. 27, 1998
     Deltha O'Neal, Denver vs. Kansas City, Oct. 7, 2001
     DeAngelo Hall, Washington vs. Chicago, Oct. 24, 2010
Most Consecutive Games, Passes Intercepted By
8   Tom Morrow, Oakland, 1962-63
7   Tom Landry, N.Y. Giants, 1950-51

     Paul Krause, Washington, 1964
     Larry Wilson, St. Louis, 1966
     Ben Davis, Cleveland, 1968
6   By many players.
        Last time: Brian Russell, Minnesota, 2003

YARDS GAINED
Most Seasons Leading League
3   Darren Sharper, Green Bay, 2002; Minnesota, 2005;
        New Orleans, 2009
2   Dick (Night Train) Lane, Los Angeles, 1952;
        Chi. Cardinals, 1954
     Herb Adderley, Green Bay, 1965, 1969
     Dick Anderson, Miami, 1968, 1970
     Ed Reed, Baltimore, 2004, 2010
Most Yards Gained, Career
1,483   Rod Woodson, Pittsburgh, 1987-1996;
            San Francisco, 1997; Baltimore, 1998-2001;
            Oakland, 2002-03
1,463   Ed Reed, Baltimore, 2002-2011
1,412   Darren Sharper, Green Bay, 1997-2004; Minnesota,
            2005-08; New Orleans, 2009-2010
Most Yards Gained, Season
376   Darren Sharper, New Orleans, 2009
358   Ed Reed, Baltimore, 2004
349   Charlie McNeil, San Diego, 1961
Most Yards Gained, Rookie, Season
301   Don Doll, Detroit, 1949
298   Dick (Night Train) Lane, Los Angeles, 1952
275   Woodley Lewis, Los Angeles, 1950
Most Yards Gained, Game
177   Charlie McNeil, San Diego vs. Houston,
            Sept. 24, 1961
170   Louis Oliver, Miami vs. Buffalo, Oct. 4, 1992
167   Dick Jauron, Detroit vs. Chicago, Nov. 18, 1973
Longest Return (All TDs)
107   Ed Reed, Baltimore vs. Philadelphia, Nov. 23, 2008
106   Ed Reed, Baltimore vs. Cleveland, Nov. 7, 2004
103   Vencie Glenn, San Diego vs. Denver, Nov. 29, 1987
        Louis Oliver, Miami vs. Buffalo, Oct. 4, 1992

TOUCHDOWNS
Most Touchdowns, Career
12   Rod Woodson, Pittsburgh, 1987-1996; San Francisco,
        1997; Baltimore, 1998-2001; Oakland, 2002-03
11   Darren Sharper, Green Bay, 1997-2004;
        Minnesota, 2005-08; New Orleans, 2009-2010
     Charles Woodson, Oakland, 1998-2005; Green Bay,
        2006-2011
9   Ken Houston, Houston, 1967-1972; Washington,
        1973-1980
     Aeneas Williams, Phoenix, 1991-93;
        Arizona, 1994-2000; St. Louis, 2001-04
     Deion Sanders, Atlanta, 1989-1993; San Francisco,
        1994; Dallas, 1995-99; Washington, 2000;
        Baltimore, 2004-05
Most Touchdowns, Season
4   Ken Houston, Houston, 1971
     Jim Kearney, Kansas City, 1972
     Eric Allen, Philadelphia, 1993
3   Dick Harris, San Diego, 1961
     Dick Lynch, N.Y. Giants, 1963
     Herb Adderley, Green Bay, 1965
     Lem Barney, Detroit, 1967
     Miller Farr, Houston, 1967
     Monte Jackson, Los Angeles, 1976
     Rod Perry, Los Angeles, 1978
     Ronnie Lott, San Francisco, 1981
     Lloyd Burruss, Kansas City, 1986
     Wayne Haddix, Tampa Bay, 1990

Robert Massey, Phoenix, 1992
Ray Buchanan, Indianapolis, 1994
Deion Sanders, San Francisco, 1994
Mark McMillian, Kansas City, 1997
Otis Smith, N.Y. Jets, 1997
Jimmy Hitchcock, Minnesota, 1998
Eric Allen, Oakland, 2000
Derrick Brooks, Tampa Bay, 2002
Antrel Rolle, Arizona, 2007
Nick Collins, Green Bay, 2008
Darren Sharper, New Orleans, 2009
Charles Woodson, Green Bay, 2009
2   By many players

Most Touchdowns, Rookie, Season
3   Lem Barney, Detroit, 1967
    Ronnie Lott, San Francisco, 1981
2   By many players

Most Touchdowns, Game
2   Bill Blackburn, Chi. Cardinals vs. Boston,
     Oct. 24, 1948
    Dan Sandifer, Washington vs. Boston, Oct. 31, 1948
    Bob Franklin, Cleveland vs. Chicago, Dec. 11, 1960
    Bill Stacy, St. Louis vs. Dall. Cowboys, Nov. 5, 1961
    Jerry Norton, St. Louis vs. Pittsburgh, Nov. 26, 1961
    Miller Farr, Houston vs. Buffalo, Dec. 7, 1968
    Ken Houston, Houston vs. San Diego, Dec. 19, 1971
    Jim Kearney, Kansas City vs. Denver, Oct. 1, 1972
    Lemar Parrish, Cincinnati vs. Houston, Dec. 17, 1972
    Dick Anderson, Miami vs. Pittsburgh, Dec. 3, 1973
    Prentice McCray, New England vs. N.Y. Jets,
     Nov. 21, 1976
    Kenny Johnson, Atlanta vs. Green Bay,
     Nov. 27, 1983 (ot)
    Mike Kozlowski, Miami vs. N.Y. Jets, Dec. 16, 1983
    Dave Brown, Seattle vs. Kansas City, Nov. 4, 1984
    Lloyd Burruss, Kansas City vs. San Diego,
     Oct. 19, 1986
    Henry Jones, Buffalo vs. Indianapolis, Sept. 20, 1992
    Robert Massey, Phoenix vs. Washington, Oct. 4, 1992
    Eric Allen, Philadelphia vs. New Orleans,
     Dec. 26, 1993
    Ken Norton, San Francisco vs. St. Louis,
     Oct. 22, 1995
    Otis Smith, N.Y. Jets vs. Tampa Bay, Dec. 14, 1997
    Dewayne Washington, Pittsburgh vs. Jacksonville,
     Nov. 22, 1998
    Aaron Glenn, Houston vs. Pittsburgh, Dec. 8, 2002
    Ronde Barber, Tampa Bay vs. Philadelphia,
     Oct. 22, 2006
    Antrel Rolle, Arizona vs. Cincinnati, Nov. 18, 2007
    Derrick Johnson, Kansas City vs. Denver,
     Jan. 3, 2010
    David Bowens, Cleveland vs. New Orleans,
     Oct. 24, 2010

PUNTING

Most Punts, Career
1,713   Jeff Feagles, New England, 1988-89; Philadelphia,
     1990-93; Arizona, 1994-97; Seattle, 1998-
     2002; N.Y. Giants, 2003-09
1,401   Sean Landeta, N.Y. Giants, 1985-1993; L.A. Rams,
     1993-94; St. Louis, 1995-96; Tampa Bay, 1997;
     Green Bay, 1998; Philadelphia, 1999-2002;
     St. Louis, 2003-04; Philadelphia, 2005
1,339   Brad Maynard, N.Y. Giants, 1997-2000; Chicago,
     2001-2010; Cleveland, 2011

Most Punts, Season
114   Bob Parsons, Chicago, 1981
    Chad Stanley, Houston, 2002
111   Brad Maynard, N.Y. Giants, 1997

---

109   John James, Atlanta, 1978

Most Punts, Rookie, Season
111   Brad Maynard, N.Y. Giants, 1997
108   John Teltschik, Philadelphia, 1986
101   Daniel Pope, Kansas City, 1999

Most Punts, Game
16   Leo Araguz, Oakland vs. San Diego, Oct. 11, 1998
15   John Teltschik, Philadelphia vs. N.Y. Giants,
     Dec. 6, 1987 (ot)
14   Dick Nesbitt, Chi. Cardinals vs. Chi. Bears,
     Nov. 30, 1933
    Keith Molesworth, Chi. Bears vs. Green Bay,
     Dec. 10, 1933
    Sammy Baugh, Washington vs. Philadelphia,
     Nov. 5, 1939
    Carl Kinscherf, N.Y. Giants vs. Detroit, Nov. 7, 1943
    George Taliaferro, N.Y. Yanks vs. Los Angeles,
     Sept. 28, 1951

Longest Punt
98   Steve O'Neal, N.Y. Jets vs. Denver, Sept. 21, 1969
94   Joe Lintzenich, Chi. Bears vs. N.Y. Giants, Nov. 16, 1931
93   Shawn McCarthy, New England vs. Buffalo,
     Nov. 3, 1991

AVERAGE YARDAGE

Highest Average, Punting, Career (250 punts)
47.58   Shane Lechler, Oakland, 2000-2011 (933-44,389)
45.74   Andy Lee, San Francisco, 2004-2011 (723-33,069)
45.69   Brandon Fields, Miami, 2007-2011 (377-17,227)

Highest Avg. Punting, Season (Qualifiers)
51.40   Sammy Baugh, Washington, 1940 (35-1,799)
51.14   Shane Lechler, Oakland, 2009 (96-4,909)
50.90   Andy Lee, San Francisco, 2011 (78-3,970)

Highest Avg. Punting, Rookie, Season
46.74   Brett Kern, Denver, 2008 (46-2,150)
45.92   Frank Sinkwich, Detroit, 1943 (12-551)
45.91   Shane Lechler, Oakland, 2000 (65-2,984)

Highest Avg. Punting, Game (4 punts)
61.75   Bob Cifers, Detroit vs. Chi. Bears, Nov. 24, 1946
     (4-247)
61.60   Roy McKay, Green Bay vs. Chi. Cardinals, Oct. 28,
     1945 (5-308)
59.60   Andy Lee, San Francisco vs. Seattle, Sept. 11, 2011
     (5-298)

NET AVERAGE

Net average has been compiled since 1976.

Highest Net Average, Punting, Career (250 punts)
38.90   Dustin Colquitt, Kansas City, 2005-2011
     (577-22,448)
38.86   Andy Lee, San Francisco, 2004-2011 (726-28,212)
38.84   Shane Lechler, Oakland, 2000-2011 (936-36,351)

Highest Net Average, Punting, Season (Qualifiers)
43.99   Andy Lee, San Francisco, 2011 (79-3,475)
43.85   Shane Lechler, Oakland, 2009 (96-4,210)
43.11   Thomas Morstead, New Orleans, 2011 (47-2,026)

Highest Net Average, Punting, Rookie, Season (Qualifiers)
38.87   Matt Bosher, Atlanta, 2011 (71-2,760)
38.75   T.J. Conley, N.Y. Jets, 2011 (92-3,565)
38.38   Zoltan Mesko, New England, 2010 (58-2,226)

Highest Net Average, Punting, Game (4 punts)
59.50   Rohn Stark, Indianapolis vs. Houston,
     Sept. 13, 1992 (4-238)
54.20   Andy Lee, San Francisco vs. Seattle, Sept. 11, 2011
     (5-271)
53.00   Brian Moorman, Buffalo vs. Kansas City, Dec. 13,
     2009 (4-212)

PUNTS HAD BLOCKED

Most Consecutive Punts, None Blocked
- 1,177   Chris Gardocki, Chicago, 1992-94; Indianapolis, 1995-98; Cleveland, 1999-2003; Pittsburgh, 2004-06
- 878   Bryan Barker, Kansas City, 1993; Philadelphia, 1994; Jacksonville, 1995-2000; Washington, 2001-03; Green Bay, 2004; St. Louis, 2005
- 735   Brian Moorman, Buffalo, 2002-2011

Most Punts Had Blocked, Career
- 14   Herman Weaver, Detroit, 1970-76; Seattle, 1977-1980 Harry Newsome, Pittsburgh, 1985-89; Minnesota, 1990-93
- 12   Jerrel Wilson, Kansas City, 1963-1977; New England, 1978
  Tom Blanchard, N.Y. Giants, 1971-73; New Orleans, 1974-78; Tampa Bay, 1979-1981
  Jeff Feagles, New England, 1988-89; Philadelphia, 1990-93; Arizona, 1994-97; Seattle, 1998-2002; N.Y. Giants, 2003-09
- 11   David Lee, Baltimore, 1966-1978

Most Punts Had Blocked, Season
- 6   Harry Newsome, Pittsburgh, 1988
- 4   Bryan Wagner, Cleveland, 1990
  Mike Scifres, San Diego, 2010
- 3   By many players

PUNTS INSIDE THE 20

Punts Inside the 20 have been compiled since 1976.

Most Punts Inside the 20, Career
- 554   Jeff Feagles, New England, 1988-89; Philadelphia, 1990-93; Arizona, 1994-97; Seattle, 1998-2002; N.Y. Giants, 2003-09
- 439   Brad Maynard, N.Y. Giants, 1997-2000; Chicago, 2001-2010; Cleveland, 2011
- 399   Craig Hentrich, Green Bay, 1994-97; Tennessee, 1998-2009

Most Punts Inside the 20, Season
- 42   Andy Lee, San Francisco, 2007
  Ben Graham, Arizona, 2009
  Steve Weatherford, N.Y. Jets, 2010
- 41   Dustin Colquitt, Kansas City, 2009
- 40   Brad Maynard, Chicago, 2008

Most Punts Inside the 20, Game
- 8   Mark Royals, Pittsburgh vs. Houston, Nov. 6, 1994 (ot)
  Bryan Barker, Jacksonville vs. Baltimore, Nov. 14, 1999
- 7   Josh Miller, Pittsburgh vs. Cincinnati, Dec. 20, 1998
  David Zastudil. Cleveland vs. Buffalo, Oct. 11, 2009
  Thomas Morstead, New Orleans vs. Carolina, Jan. 3, 2010
- 6   By many players

PUNT RETURNS

Most Seasons Leading League
- 3   Les (Speedy) Duncan, San Diego, 1965-66; Washington, 1971
  Rick Upchurch, Denver, 1976, 1978, 1982
- 2   Dick Christy, N.Y. Titans, 1961-62
  Claude Gibson, Oakland, 1963-64
  Billy (White Shoes) Johnson, Houston, 1975, 1977
  Mel Gray, New Orleans, 1987; Detroit, 1991
  Jermaine Lewis, Baltimore, 1997, 2000
  Roscoe Parrish, Buffalo, 2007-08
  Devin Hester, Chicago, 2010-11

PUNT RETURNS

Most Punt Returns, Career
- 463   Brian Mitchell, Washington, 1990-99; Philadelphia, 2000-02; N.Y. Giants, 2003

- 351   Eric Metcalf, Cleveland, 1989-1994; Atlanta, 1995-96; San Diego, 1997; Arizona, 1998; Carolina, 1999; Washington, 2001; Green Bay, 2002
- 349   David Meggett, N.Y. Giants, 1989-1994; New England, 1995-97; N.Y. Jets, 1998

Most Punt Returns, Season
- 70   Danny Reece, Tampa Bay, 1979
- 62   Fulton Walker, Miami-L.A. Raiders, 1985
- 58   J.T. Smith, Kansas City, 1979
  Greg Pruitt, L.A. Raiders, 1983
  Leo Lewis, Minnesota, 1988
  Desmond Howard, Green Bay, 1996
  Nate Burleson, Seattle, 2007

Most Punt Returns, Rookie, Season
- 57   Lew Barnes, Chicago, 1986
- 55   B.J. Sams, Baltimore, 2004
- 54   James Jones, Dallas, 1980

Most Punt Returns, Game
- 11   Eddie Brown, Washington vs. Tampa Bay, Oct. 9, 1977
- 10   Theo Bell, Pittsburgh vs. Buffalo, Dec. 16, 1979
  Mike Nelms, Washington vs. New Orleans, Dec. 26, 1982
  Ronnie Harris, New England vs. Pittsburgh, Dec. 5, 1993
- 9   Rodger Bird, Oakland vs. Denver, Sept. 10, 1967
  Ralph McGill, San Francisco vs. Atlanta, Oct. 29, 1972
  Ed Podolak, Kansas City vs. San Diego, Nov. 10, 1974
  Anthony Leonard, San Francisco vs. New Orleans, Oct. 17, 1976
  Butch Johnson, Dallas vs. Buffalo, Nov. 15, 1976
  Larry Marshall, Philadelphia vs. Tampa Bay, Sept. 18, 1977
  Nesby Glasgow, Baltimore vs. Kansas City, Sept. 2, 1979
  Mike Nelms, Washington vs. St. Louis, Dec. 21, 1980
  Leon Bright, N.Y. Giants vs. Philadelphia, Dec. 11, 1982
  Pete Shaw, N.Y. Giants vs. Philadelphia, Nov. 20, 1983
  Cleotha Montgomery, L.A. Raiders vs. Detroit, Dec. 10, 1984
  Phil McConkey, N.Y. Giants vs. Philadelphia, Dec. 6, 1987 (ot)
  Andre Hastings, Pittsburgh vs. Cleveland, Nov. 13, 1995
  Steve Smith, Carolina vs. Detroit, Sept. 15, 2002
  Reggie Swinton, Arizona vs. Philadelphia, Dec. 24, 2005

FAIR CATCHES

Most Fair Catches, Career
- 231   Brian Mitchell, Washington, 1990-99; Philadelphia, 2000-02; N.Y. Giants, 2003
- 162   Tim Brown, L.A. Raiders, 1988-1994; Oakland, 1995-2003; Tampa Bay, 2004
- 144   Glyn Milburn, Denver, 1993-95; Detroit, 1996-97; Chicago, 1998-2001; San Diego, 2001

Most Fair Catches, Season
- 33   Brian Mitchell, Philadelphia, 2000
- 29   Wes Welker, Miami, 2006
- 28   Stefan Logan, Detroit, 2011

Most Fair Catches, Game
- 7   Bake Turner, N.Y. Jets vs. Miami, Nov. 20, 1966
  Lem Barney, Detroit vs. Chicago, Nov. 21, 1976
  Bobby Morse, Philadelphia vs. Buffalo, Dec. 27, 1987
  Chris Carr, Tennessee vs. Jacksonville, Nov. 16, 2008
- 6   Jake Scott, Miami vs. Buffalo, Dec. 20, 1970

Greg Pruitt, L.A. Raiders vs. Seattle, Oct. 7, 1984
Phil McConkey, San Diego vs. Kansas City,
Dec. 17, 1989
Gerald McNeil, Houston vs. Pittsburgh,
Sept. 16, 1990
Bobby Engram, Chicago vs. Minnesota,
Sept. 15, 1996
Eddie Kennison, New Orleans vs. Baltimore,
Dec. 19, 1999
R.W. McQuarters, N.Y. Giants vs. Atlanta,
Oct. 15, 2007
5   By many players

YARDS GAINED
Most Seasons Leading League
3   Alvin Haymond, Baltimore, 1965-66; Los Angeles, 1969
2   Bill Dudley, Pittsburgh, 1942, 1946
Emlen Tunnell, N.Y. Giants, 1951-52
Dick Christy, N.Y. Titans, 1961-62
Claude Gibson, Oakland, 1963-64
Rodger Bird, Oakland, 1966-67
J.T. Smith, Kansas City, 1979-1980
Vai Sikahema, St. Louis, 1986-87
David Meggett, N.Y. Giants, 1989-1990
Tamarick Vanover, Kansas City, 1995, 1999
Devin Hester, Chicago, 2006, 2010
Most Yards Gained, Career
4,999   Brian Mitchell, Washington, 1990-99; Philadelphia, 2000-02; N.Y. Giants, 2003
3,708   Dave Meggett, N.Y. Giants, 1989-1994; New England, 1995-97; N.Y. Jets, 1998
3,601   Darrien Gordon, San Diego, 1993-94, 1996; Denver, 1997-98; Oakland, 1999-2000; Atlanta, 2001; Green Bay, 2002
Most Yards Gained, Season
875   Desmond Howard, Green Bay, 1996
699   Patrick Peterson, Arizona, 2011
692   Fulton Walker, Miami-L.A. Raiders, 1985
Most Yards Gained, Rookie, Season
699   Patrick Peterson, Arizona, 2011
656   Louis Lipps, Pittsburgh, 1984
655   Neal Colzie, Oakland, 1975
Most Yards Gained, Game
207   LeRoy Irvin, Los Angeles vs. Atlanta, Oct. 11, 1981
205   George Atkinson, Oakland vs. Buffalo, Sept. 15, 1968
199   Eddie Drummond, Detroit vs. Jacksonville, Nov. 14, 2004 (ot)
Longest Punt Return (All TDs)
103   Robert Bailey, L.A. Rams vs. New Orleans, Oct. 23, 1994
99   Patrick Peterson, Arizona vs. St. Louis, Nov. 6, 2011
98   Gil LeFebvre, Cincinnati vs. Brooklyn, Dec. 3, 1933
Charlie West, Minnesota vs. Washington, Nov. 3, 1968
Dennis Morgan, Dallas vs. St. Louis, Oct. 13, 1974
Terance Mathis, N.Y. Jets vs. Dallas, Nov. 4, 1990

AVERAGE YARDAGE
Highest Average, Career (75 returns)
12.88   Devin Hester, Chicago, 2006-2011 (206-2,654)
12.78   George McAfee, Chi. Bears, 1940-41, 1945-1950 (112-1,431)
12.75   Jack Christiansen, Detroit, 1951-58 (85-1,084)
Highest Average, Season (Qualifiers)
23.00   Herb Rich, Baltimore, 1950 (12-276)
21.47   Jack Christiansen, Detroit, 1952 (15-322)
21.28   Dick Christy, N.Y. Titans, 1961 (18-383)
Highest Average, Rookie, Season (Qualifiers)
23.00   Herb Rich, Baltimore, 1950 (12-276)

20.88   Jerry Davis, Chi. Cardinals, 1948 (16-334)
20.73   Frankie Sinkwich, Detroit, 1943 (11-228)
Highest Average, Game
51.00   Steve Smith, Carolina vs. Cincinnati, Dec. 8, 2002 (3-153)
47.67   Chuck Latourette, St. Louis vs. New Orleans, Sept. 29, 1968 (3-143)
47.33   Johnny Roland, St. Louis vs. Philadelphia, Oct. 2, 1966 (3-142)

TOUCHDOWNS
Most Touchdowns, Career
12   Devin Hester, Chicago, 2006-2011
10   Eric Metcalf, Cleveland, 1989-1994; Atlanta, 1995-96; San Diego, 1997; Arizona, 1998; Carolina, 1999; Washington, 2001; Green Bay, 2002
9   Brian Mitchell, Washington, 1990-99; Philadelphia, 2000-02; N.Y. Giants, 2003
Most Touchdowns, Season
4   Jack Christiansen, Detroit, 1951
Rick Upchurch, Denver, 1976
Devin Hester, Chicago, 2007
Patrick Peterson, Arizona, 2011
3   Emlen Tunnell, N.Y. Giants, 1951
Billy (White Shoes) Johnson, Houston, 1975
LeRoy Irvin, Los Angeles, 1981
Desmond Howard, Green Bay, 1996
Darrien Gordon, Denver, 1997
Eric Metcalf, San Diego, 1997
Devin Hester, Chicago, 2006
Adam Jones, Tennessee, 2006
Reggie Bush, New Orleans, 2008
Johnnie Lee Higgins, Oakland, 2008
Devin Hester, Chicago, 2010
2   By many players
Most Touchdowns, Rookie, Season
4   Jack Christiansen, Detroit, 1951
Patrick Peterson, Arizona, 2011
3   Devin Hester, Chicago, 2006
2   By many players
Most Touchdowns, Game
2   Jack Christiansen, Detroit vs. Los Angeles, Oct. 14, 1951; vs. Green Bay, Nov. 22, 1951
Dick Christy, N.Y. Titans vs. Denver, Sept. 24, 1961
Rick Upchurch, Denver vs. Cleveland, Sept. 26, 1976
LeRoy Irvin, Los Angeles vs. Atlanta, Oct. 11, 1981
Vai Sikahema, St. Louis vs. Tampa Bay, Dec. 21, 1986
Todd Kinchen, L.A. Rams vs. Atlanta, Dec. 27, 1992
Eric Metcalf, Cleveland vs. Pittsburgh, Oct. 24, 1993; San Diego vs. Cincinnati, Nov. 2, 1997
Darrien Gordon, Denver vs. Carolina, Nov. 9, 1997
Jermaine Lewis, Baltimore vs. Seattle, Dec. 7, 1997
Baltimore vs. N.Y. Jets, Dec. 24, 2000
Steve Smith, Carolina vs. Cincinnati, Dec. 8, 2002
Eddie Drummond, Detroit vs. Jacksonville, Nov. 14, 2004 (ot)
Reggie Bush, New Orleans vs. Minnesota, Oct. 6, 2008

KICKOFF RETURNS
Most Seasons Leading League
3   Abe Woodson, San Francisco, 1959, 1962-63
2   Lynn Chandnois, Pittsburgh, 1951-52
Bobby Jancik, Houston, 1962-63
Travis Williams, Green Bay, 1967; Los Angeles, 1971
Mel Gray, Detroit, 1991, 1994
Michael Bates, Carolina, 1996-97

KICKOFF RETURNS

Most Kickoff Returns, Career
- 607 Brian Mitchell, Washington, 1990-99; Philadelphia, 2000-02; N.Y. Giants, 2003
- 514 Allen Rossum, Philadelphia, 1998-99; Green Bay, 2000-01; Atlanta, 2002-06; Pittsburgh, 2007; San Francisco, 2008-09; Dallas, 2009
- 426 Dante Hall, Kansas City, 2000-06; St. Louis, 2007-08

Most Kickoff Returns, Season
- 82 MarTay Jenkins, Arizona, 2000
- 73 Josh Scobey, Arizona, 2003
   Chris Carr, Oakland, 2005
- 70 Tyrone Hughes, New Orleans, 1996
   Michael Lewis, New Orleans, 2002

Most Kickoff Returns, Rookie, Season
- 73 Josh Scobey, Arizona, 2003
   Chris Carr, Oakland, 2005
- 67 Ronney Jenkins, San Diego, 2000
- 64 Tab Perry, Cincinnati, 2005

Most Kickoff Returns, Game
- 10 Desmond Howard, Oakland vs. Seattle, Oct. 26, 1997
   Richard Alston, Cleveland vs. Cincinnati, Nov. 28, 2004
- 9 Noland Smith, Kansas City vs. Oakland, Nov. 23, 1967
   Dino Hall, Cleveland vs. Pittsburgh, Oct. 7, 1979
   Paul Palmer, Kansas City vs. Seattle, Sept. 20, 1987
   Eric Metcalf, Atlanta vs. San Francisco, Sept. 29, 1996; vs. St. Louis, Nov. 10, 1996
   Michael Bates, Carolina vs. Atlanta, Oct. 4, 1998
   Nate Jacquet, Minnesota vs. Philadelphia, Nov. 11, 2001
   Ahmad Merritt, Chicago vs. San Francisco, Sept. 7, 2003
   Josh Scobey, Arizona vs. Cleveland, Nov. 16, 2003
   Maurice Hicks, San Francisco vs. San Diego, Oct. 15, 2006
   Aveion Cason, Detroit vs. San Diego, Dec. 16, 2007
   Allen Rossum, San Francisco vs. Philadelphia, Oct. 12, 2008
   Steve Breaston, Arizona vs. New England, Dec. 21, 2008
   Danny Amendola, St. Louis vs. Tennessee, Dec. 13, 2009
   Brandon James, Indianapolis vs. San Diego, Nov. 28, 2010
- 8 By many players

YARDS GAINED

Most Seasons Leading League
- 3 Bruce Harper, N.Y. Jets, 1977-79
   Tyrone Hughes, New Orleans, 1994-96
- 2 Marshall Goldberg, Chi. Cardinals, 1941-42
   Woodley Lewis, Los Angeles, 1953-54
   Al Carmichael, Green Bay, 1956-57
   Timmy Brown, Philadelphia, 1961, 1963
   Bobby Jancik, Houston, 1963, 1966
   Ron Smith, Atlanta, 1966-67
   Chris Carr, Oakland, 2005-06

Most Yards Gained, Career
- 14,014 Brian Mitchell, Washington, 1990-99; Philadelphia, 2000-02; N.Y. Giants, 2003
- 11,947 Allen Rossum, Philadelphia, 1998-99; Green Bay, 2000-01; Atlanta, 2002-06; Pittsburgh, 2007; San Francisco, 2008-09; Dallas, 2009
- 10,250 Mel Gray, New Orleans, 1986-88; Detroit, 1989-1994; Houston, 1995-96; Tennessee, 1997; Philadelphia, 1997

Most Yards Gained, Season
- 2,186 MarTay Jenkins, Arizona, 2000

- 1,809 Josh Cribbs, Cleveland, 2007
- 1,807 Michael Lewis, New Orleans, 2002

Most Yards Gained, Rookie, Season
- 1,752 Chris Carr, Oakland, 2005
- 1,684 Josh Scobey, Arizona, 2003
- 1,577 Justin Miller, N.Y. Jets, 2005

Most Yards Gained, Game
- 304 Tyrone Hughes, New Orleans vs. L.A. Rams, Oct. 23, 1994
- 299 Ted Ginn, Jr., Miami vs. N.Y. Jets, Nov. 1, 2009
- 294 Wally Triplett, Detroit vs. Los Angeles, Oct. 29, 1950

Longest Kickoff Return (All TDs)
- 108 Ellis Hobbs, New England, vs. N.Y. Jets, Sept. 9, 2007
   Randall Cobb, Green Bay vs. New Orleans, Sept. 8, 2011
- 107 Joe McKnight, N.Y. Jets vs. Baltimore, Oct. 2, 2011
- 106 Al Carmichael, Green Bay vs. Chi. Bears, Oct. 7, 1956
   Noland Smith, Kansas City vs. Denver, Dec. 17, 1967
   Roy Green, St. Louis vs. Dallas, Oct. 21, 1979
   Brad Smith, N.Y. Jets vs. Indianapolis, Dec. 27, 2009

AVERAGE YARDAGE

Highest Average, Career (75 returns)
- 30.56 Gale Sayers, Chicago, 1965-1971 (91-2,781)
- 29.57 Lynn Chandnois, Pittsburgh, 1950-56 (92-2,720)
- 28.69 Abe Woodson, San Francisco, 1958-1964; St. Louis, 1965-66 (193-5,538)

Highest Average, Season (Qualifiers)
- 41.06 Travis Williams, Green Bay, 1967 (18-739)
- 37.69 Gale Sayers, Chicago, 1967 (16-603)
- 35.50 Ollie Matson, Chi. Cardinals, 1958 (14-497)

Highest Average, Rookie, Season (Qualifiers)
- 41.06 Travis Williams, Green Bay, 1967 (18-739)
- 33.08 Tom Moore, Green Bay, 1960 (12-397)
- 32.88 Duriel Harris, Miami, 1976 (17-559)

Highest Average, Game (3 returns)
- 73.50 Wally Triplett, Detroit vs. Los Angeles, Oct. 29, 1950 (4-294)
- 67.33 Lenny Lyles, San Francisco vs. Baltimore, Dec. 18, 1960 (3-202)
- 65.33 Ken Hall, Houston vs. N.Y. titans, Oct. 23, 1960 (3-196)

TOUCHDOWNS

Most Touchdowns, Career
- 8 Josh Cribbs, Cleveland, 2005-2011
- 7 Leon Washington, N.Y. Jets, 2006-09; Seattle, 2010-11
- 6 Ollie Matson, Chi. Cardinals, 1952, 1954-58; L.A. Rams, 1959-1962; Detroit, 1963; Philadelphia, 1964
   Gale Sayers, Chicago, 1965-1971
   Travis Williams, Green Bay, 1967-1970; Los Angeles, 1971
   Mel Gray, New Orleans, 1986-88; Detroit, 1989-1994; Houston, 1995-96; Tennessee, 1997; Philadelphia, 1997
   Dante Hall, Kansas City, 2000-06; St. Louis, 2007-08

Most Touchdowns, Season
- 4 Travis Williams, Green Bay, 1967
   Cecil Turner, Chicago, 1970
- 3 Verda (Vitamin T) Smith, Los Angeles, 1950
   Abe Woodson, San Francisco, 1963
   Gale Sayers, Chicago, 1967
   Raymond Clayborn, New England, 1977
   Ron Brown, L.A. Rams, 1985
   Mel Gray, Detroit, 1994
   Darrick Vaughn, Atlanta, 2000
   Terrence McGee, Buffalo, 2004
   André Davis, Houston, 2007

Leon Washington, N.Y. Jets, 2007
Josh Cribbs, Cleveland, 2009
Jacoby Ford, Oakland, 2010
Leon Washington, Seattle, 2010
2 By many players
Most Touchdowns, Rookie, Season
4 Travis Williams, Green Bay, 1967
3 Raymond Clayborn, New England, 1977
Darrick Vaughn, Atlanta, 2000
Jacoby Ford, Oakland, 2010
2 By many players
Most Touchdowns, Game
2 Timmy Brown, Philadelphia vs. Dallas, Nov. 6, 1966
Travis Williams, Green Bay vs. Cleveland, Nov. 12, 1967
Ron Brown, L.A. Rams vs. Green Bay, Nov. 24, 1985
Tyrone Hughes, New Orleans vs. L.A. Rams, Oct. 23, 1994
Chad Morton, N.Y. Jets vs. Buffalo, Sept. 8, 2002 (ot)
Devin Hester, Chicago vs. St. Louis, Dec. 11, 2006
André Davis, Houston vs. Jacksonville, Dec. 30, 2007
Ted Ginn, Jr., Miami vs. N.Y. Jets, Nov. 1, 2009
Josh Cribbs, Cleveland vs. Kansas City, Dec. 20, 2009
Leon Washington, Seattle vs. San Diego, Sept. 26, 2010

COMBINED KICK RETURNS
Most Combined Kick Returns, Career
1,070 Brian Mitchell, Washington, 1990-99; Philadelphia, 2000-02; N.Y. Giants, 2003 (p-463, k-607)
821 Allen Rossum, Philadelphia, 1998-99; Green Bay, 2000-01; Atlanta, 2002-06; Pittsburgh, 2007; San Francisco, 2008-09; Dallas, 2009 (p-307, k-514)
711 Glyn Milburn, Denver, 1993-95; Detroit, 1996-97; Chicago, 1998-2001; San Diego, 2001 (p-304, k-407)
Most Combined Kick Returns, Season
114 Michael Lewis, New Orleans, 2002 (p-44, k-70)
B.J. Sams, Baltimore, 2004 (p-55, k-59)
107 Chris Carr, Oakland, 2005 (p-34, k-73)
Dante Hall, Kansas City, 2005 (p-42, k-65)
105 Reggie Swinton, Arizona, 2005 (p-42, k-63)
Most Combined Kick Returns, Game
13 Stump Mitchell, St. Louis vs. Atlanta, Oct. 18, 1981 (p-6, k-7)
Ronnie Harris, New England vs. Pittsburgh, Dec. 5, 1993 (p-10, k-3)
12 Mel Renfro, Dallas vs. Green Bay, Nov. 29, 1964 (p-4, k-8)
Larry Jones, Washington vs. Dallas, Dec. 13, 1975 (p-6, k-6)
Eddie Brown, Washington vs. Tampa Bay, Oct. 9, 1977 (p-11, k-1)
Nesby Glasgow, Baltimore vs. Denver, Sept. 2, 1979 (p-9, k-3)
Tim Dwight, Atlanta vs. Detroit, Nov. 12, 2000 (p-8, k-4)
Wes Welker, Miami vs. Buffalo, Dec. 5, 2004 (p-6, k-6)
Reggie Swinton, Arizona vs. Philadelphia, Dec. 24, 2005 (p-9, k-3)
Devin Hester, Chicago vs. Detroit, Sept. 30, 2007 (p-5, k-7)
Brandon James, Indianapolis vs. San Diego, Nov. 28, 2010 (p-3, k-9)
11 By many players

YARDS GAINED
Most Yards Returned, Career
19,013 Brian Mitchell, Washington, 1990-99; Philadelphia, 2000-02; N.Y. Giants, 2003 (p-4,999; k-14,014)
15,003 Allen Rossum, Philadelphia, 1998-99; Green Bay, 2000-01; Atlanta, 2002-06; Pittsburgh, 2007; San Francisco, 2008-09; Dallas, 2009 (p-3,056; k-11,947)
13,003 Mel Gray, New Orleans, 1986-88; Detroit, 1989-1994; Houston, 1995-96; Tennessee, 1997; Philadelphia, 1997 (p-2,753; k-10,250)
Most Yards Returned, Season
2,432 Michael Lewis, New Orleans, 2002 (p-625; k-1,807)
2,214 Josh Cribbs, Cleveland, 2007 (p-405; k-1,809)
2,187 MarTay Jenkins, Arizona, 2000 (pr-1; k-2,186)
Most Yards Returned, Game
347 Tyrone Hughes, New Orleans vs. L.A. Rams, Oct. 23, 1994 (p-43; k-304)
314 Devin Hester, Chicago vs. Detroit, Sept. 30, 2007 (p-95; k-219)
306 Josh Cribbs, Cleveland vs. Baltimore, Nov. 18, 2007 (p-61; k-245) (ot)

TOUCHDOWNS
Most Touchdowns, Career
17 Devin Hester, Chicago, 2006-2011 (p-12, k-5)
13 Brian Mitchell, Washington, 1990-99; Philadelphia, 2000-02; N.Y. Giants, 2003 (p-9, k-4)
12 Eric Metcalf, Cleveland, 1989-1994; Atlanta, 1995-96; San Diego, 1997; Arizona, 1998; Carolina, 1999; Washington, 2001; Green Bay, 2002 (p-10, k-2)
Dante Hall, Kansas City, 2000-06; St. Louis, 2007-08 (p-6, k-6)
Most Touchdowns, Season
6 Devin Hester, Chicago, 2007 (p-4, k-2)
5 Devin Hester, Chicago, 2006 (p-3, k-2)
4 Jack Christiansen, Detroit, 1951 (p-4)
Emlen Tunnell, N.Y. Giants, 1951 (p-3, k-1)
Gale Sayers, Chicago, 1967 (p-1, k-3)
Travis Williams, Green Bay, 1967 (k-4)
Cecil Turner, Chicago, 1970 (k-4)
Billy Johnson, Houston, 1975 (p-3, k-1)
Rick Upchurch, Denver, 1976 (p-4)
Dante Hall, Kansas City, 2003 (p-2, r-2)
Eddie Drummond, Detroit, 2004 (p-2, k-2)
Josh Cribbs, Cleveland, 2009 (p-1, k-3)
Patrick Peterson, Arizona, 2011 (p-4)
Most Touchdowns, Game
2 Jack Christiansen, Detroit vs. Los Angeles, Oct. 14, 1951 (p-2); vs. Green Bay, Nov. 22, 1951 (p-2)
Jim Patton, N.Y. Giants vs. Washington, Oct. 30, 1955 (p-1, k-1)
Bobby Mitchell, Cleveland vs. Philadelphia, Nov. 23, 1958 (p-1, k-1)
Dick Christy, N.Y. Titans vs. Denver, Sept. 24, 1961 (p-2)
Al Frazier, Denver vs. Boston, Dec. 3, 1961 (p-1, k-1)
Timmy Brown, Philadelphia vs. Dallas, Nov. 6, 1966 (k-2)
Travis Williams, Green Bay vs. Cleveland, Nov. 12, 1967 (k-2); vs. Pittsburgh, Nov. 2, 1969 (p-1, k-1)
Gale Sayers, Chicago vs. San Francisco, Dec. 3, 1967 (p-1, k-1)
Rick Upchurch, Denver vs. Cleveland, Sept. 26, 1976 (p-2)
Eddie Payton, Detroit vs. Minnesota, Dec. 17, 1977 (p-1, k-1)

LeRoy Irvin, Los Angeles vs. Atlanta, Oct. 11, 1981 (p-2)

Ron Brown, L.A. Rams vs. Green Bay, Nov. 24, 1985 (k-2)

Vai Sikahema, St. Louis vs. Tampa Bay, Dec. 21, 1986 (p-2)

Todd Kinchen, L.A. Rams vs. Atlanta, Dec. 27, 1992 (p-2)

Eric Metcalf, Cleveland vs. Pittsburgh, Oct. 24, 1993 (p-2); San Diego vs. Cincinnati, Nov. 2, 1997 (p-2)

Tyrone Hughes, New Orleans vs. L.A. Rams, Oct. 23, 1994 (k-2)

Darrien Gordon, Denver vs. Carolina, Nov. 9, 1997 (p-2)

Jermaine Lewis, Baltimore vs. Seattle, Dec. 7, 1997 (p-2); Baltimore vs. N.Y. Jets, Dec. 24, 2000 (p-2)

Chad Morton, N.Y. Jets vs. Buffalo, Sept. 8, 2002 (ot) (k-2)

Michael Lewis, New Orleans vs. Washington, Oct. 13, 2002 (p-1, k-1)

Dante Hall, Kansas City vs. St. Louis, Dec. 8, 2002 (p-1, k-1)

Steve Smith, Carolina vs. Cincinnati, Dec. 8, 2002 (p-2)

Eddie Drummond, Detroit vs. Jacksonville, Nov. 14, 2004 (ot) (p-2)

Devin Hester, Chicago vs. St. Louis, Dec. 11, 2006 (k-2)

Darren Sproles, San Diego vs. Indianapolis, Nov. 11, 2007 (p-1, k-1)

Devin Hester, Chicago vs. Denver, Nov. 25, 2007 (p-1, k-1)

André Davis, Houston vs. Jacksonville, Dec. 30, 2007 (k-2)

Reggie Bush, New Orleans vs. Minnesota, Oct. 6, 2008

Eddie Royal, Denver vs. San Diego, Oct. 19, 2009 (p-1, k-1)

Ted Ginn, Jr., Miami vs. N.Y. Jets, Nov. 1, 2009 (k-2); San Francisco vs. Seattle, Sept. 11, 2011 (p-1, k-1)

Josh Cribbs, Cleveland vs. Kansas City, Dec. 20, 2009 (k-2)

Leon Washington, Seattle vs. San Diego, Sept. 26, 2010 (k-2)

FUMBLES
Most Fumbles, Career
166 Brett Favre, Atlanta, 1991; Green Bay, 1992-2007; N.Y. Jets, 2008; Minnesota, 2009-2010

161 Warren Moon, Houston, 1984-1993; Minnesota, 1994-96; Seattle, 1997-98; Kansas City, 1999-2000

153 Dave Krieg, Seattle, 1980-1991; Kansas City, 1992-93; Detroit, 1994; Arizona, 1995; Chicago, 1996; Tennessee, 1997-98

Most Fumbles, Season
23 Kerry Collins, N.Y. Giants, 2001
   Daunte Culpepper, Minnesota, 2002

21 Tony Banks, St. Louis, 1996
   David Carr, Houston, 2002

18 Dave Krieg, Seattle, 1989
   Warren Moon, Houston, 1990

Most Fumbles, Game
7 Len Dawson, Kansas City vs. San Diego, Nov. 15, 1964

6 Sam Etcheverry, St. Louis vs. N.Y. Giants, Sept, 17, 1961

Dave Krieg, Seattle vs. Kansas City, Nov. 5, 1989

Brett Favre, Green Bay vs. Tampa Bay, Dec. 7, 1998

Kurt Warner, St. Louis vs. N.Y. Giants, Sept. 7, 2003

Chad Pennington, N.Y. Jets vs. Kansas City, Sept. 11, 2005

5 Paul Christman, Chi. Cardinals vs. Green Bay, Nov. 10, 1946

Joe Perry, San Francisco vs. Cleveland, Nov. 12, 1950

Charlie Conerly, N.Y. Giants vs. San Francisco, Dec. 1, 1957

Tom Yewcic, Boston vs. Oakland, Dec. 16, 1962

Jack Kemp, Buffalo vs. Houston, Oct. 29, 1967

Roman Gabriel, Philadelphia vs. Oakland, Nov. 21, 1976

Randall Cunningham, Philadelphia vs. L.A. Raiders, Nov. 30, 1986 (ot)

Willie Totten, Buffalo vs. Indianapolis, Oct. 4, 1987

Dave Walter, Cincinnati vs. Seattle, Oct. 11, 1987

Dave Krieg, Seattle vs. San Diego, Nov. 25, 1990 (ot)

Andre Ware, Detroit vs. Green Bay, Dec. 6, 1992

Steve Beuerlein, Carolina vs. San Francisco, Nov. 8, 1998

Patrick Ramsey, Washington vs. Green Bay, Oct. 20, 2002

Eli Manning, N.Y. Giants vs. Buffalo, Dec. 23, 2007

Josh Johnson, Tampa Bay vs. Carolina, Oct. 18, 2009

FUMBLES RECOVERED
Most Fumbles Recovered, Career, Own and Opponents'
56 Warren Moon, Houston, 1984-1993; Minnesota, 1994-96; Seattle, 1997-98; Kansas City, 1999-2000 (56 own)

47 Dave Krieg, Seattle, 1980-1991; Kansas City, 1992-93; Detroit, 1994; Arizona, 1995; Chicago, 1996; Tennessee, 1997-98 (47 own)

45 Boomer Esiason, Cincinnati, 1984-1992, 1997; N.Y. Jets, 1993-95; Arizona, 1996 (45 own)

Most Fumbles Recovered, Season, Own and Opponents'
12 David Carr, Houston, 2002 (12 own)

9 Don Hultz, Minnesota, 1963 (9 opp)
   Dave Krieg, Seattle, 1989 (9 own)
   Brian Griese, Denver, 1999 (9 own)
   Jon Kitna, Seattle, 2000 (9 own)

8 Paul Christman, Chi. Cardinals, 1945 (8 own)
   Joe Schmidt, Detroit, 1955 (8 opp)
   Bill Butler, Minnesota, 1963 (8 own)
   Kermit Alexander, San Francisco, 1965 (4 own, 4 opp)
   Jack Lambert, Pittsburgh, 1976 (1 own, 7 opp)
   Danny White, Dallas, 1981 (8 own)
   Dan Marino, Miami, 1988 (7 own, 1 opp)
   Tony Banks, St. Louis, 1998 (8 own)
   Ryan Fitzpatrick, Cincinnati, 2008 (8 own)
   Donovan McNabb, Washington, 2010 (8 own)

Most Fumbles Recovered, Game, Own and Opponents'
4 Otto Graham, Cleveland vs. N.Y. Giants, Oct. 25, 1953 (4 own)
   Sam Etcheverry, St. Louis vs. N.Y. Giants, Sept. 17, 1961 (4 own)
   Roman Gabriel, Los Angeles vs. San Francisco, Oct. 12, 1969 (4 own)
   Randall Cunningham, Philadelphia vs. L.A. Raiders, Nov. 30, 1986 (ot) (4 own)
   Joe Ferguson, Buffalo vs. Miami, Sept. 18, 1977 (4 own)
   Tony Romo, Dallas vs. Washington, Sept. 26, 2011 (4-own)

3   By many players

OWN FUMBLES RECOVERED
Most Own Fumbles Recovered, Career
- 56   Warren Moon, Houston, 1984-1993; Minnesota, 1994-96; Seattle, 1997-98; Kansas City, 1999-2000
- 47   Dave Krieg, Seattle, 1980-1991; Kansas City, 1992-93; Detroit, 1994; Arizona, 1995; Chicago, 1996; Tennessee, 1997-98
- 45   Boomer Esiason, Cincinnati, 1984-1992, 1997; N.Y. Jets, 1993-95; Arizona, 1996

Most Own Fumbles Recovered, Season
- 12   David Carr, Houston, 2002
- 9   Dave Krieg, Seattle, 1989
-     Brian Griese, Denver, 1999
-     Jon Kitna, Seattle, 2000
- 8   Paul Christman, Chi. Cardinals, 1945
-     Bill Butler, Minnesota, 1963
-     Danny White, Dallas, 1981
-     Tony Banks, St. Louis, 1998
-     Ryan Fitzpatrick, Cincinnati, 2008
-     Donovan McNabb, Washington, 2010

Most Own Fumbles Recovered, Game
- 4   Otto Graham, Cleveland vs. N.Y. Giants, Oct. 25, 1953
-     Sam Etcheverry, St. Louis vs. N.Y. Giants, Sept. 17, 1961
-     Roman Gabriel, Los Angeles vs. San Francisco, Oct. 12, 1969
-     Joe Ferguson, Buffalo vs. Miami, Sept. 18, 1977
-     Randall Cunningham, Philadelphia vs. L.A. Raiders, Nov. 30, 1986 (ot)
-     Tony Romo, Dallas vs. Washington, Sept. 26, 2011
- 3   By many players

OPPONENTS' FUMBLES RECOVERED
Most Opponents' Fumbles Recovered, Career
- 29   Jim Marshall, Cleveland, 1960; Minnesota, 1961-1979
-     Jason Taylor, Miami, 1997-2007; Washington, 2008; Miami, 2009; N.Y. Jets, 2010; Miami, 2011
- 28   Rickey Jackson, New Orleans, 1981-1993; San Francisco, 1994-95
- 26   Kevin Greene, L.A. Rams, 1985-1992; Pittsburgh, 1993-95; Carolina, 1996; San Francisco, 1997; Carolina, 1998-99
-     Cornelius Bennett, Buffalo, 1987-1995; Atlanta, 1996-98; Indianapolis, 1999-2000

Most Opponents' Fumbles Recovered, Season
- 9   Don Hultz, Minnesota, 1963
- 8   Joe Schmidt, Detroit, 1955
- 7   Alan Page, Minnesota, 1970
-     Jack Lambert, Pittsburgh, 1976
-     Ray Childress, Houston, 1988
-     Rickey Jackson, New Orleans, 1990

Most Opponents' Fumbles Recovered, Game
- 3   Corwin Clatt, Chi. Cardinals vs. Detroit, Nov. 6, 1949
-     Vic Sears, Philadelphia vs. Green Bay, Nov. 2, 1952
-     Ed Beatty, San Francisco vs. Los Angeles, Oct. 7, 1956
-     Ron Carroll, Houston vs. Cincinnati, Oct. 27, 1974
-     Maurice Spencer, New Orleans vs. Atlanta, Oct. 10, 1976
-     Steve Nelson, New England vs. Philadelphia, Oct. 8, 1978
-     Charles Jackson, Kansas City vs. Pittsburgh, Sept. 6, 1981
-     Willie Buchanon, San Diego vs. Denver, Sept. 27, 19818
-     Joey Browner, Minnesota vs. San Francisco, Sept. 8, 1985

Ray Childress, Houston vs. Washington, Oct. 30, 1988
John Thierry, Chicago vs. Houston, Oct. 22, 1995
Stephen Boyd, Detroit vs. Chicago, Oct. 4, 1998
Darryl Williams, Seattle vs. Kansas City, Oct. 4, 1998
Rod Woodson, Oakland vs. Pittsburgh, Sept. 15, 2002
Brian Young, St. Louis vs. Baltimore, Nov. 9, 2003
- 2   By many players

YARDS RETURNING FUMBLES
Longest Fumble Run (All TDs)
- 104   Jack Tatum, Oakland vs. Green Bay, Sept. 24, 1972
-     Aeneas Williams, Arizona vs. Washington, Nov. 5, 2000
- 102   Travis Davis, Pittsburgh vs. Carolina, Dec. 26, 1999
- 100   Chris Martin, Kansas City vs. Miami, Oct. 13, 1991

TOUCHDOWNS
Most Touchdowns, Career (Total)
- 6   Jason Taylor, Miami, 1997-2007; Washington, 2008; Miami, 2009; N.Y. Jets, 2010; Miami, 2011
- 5   Jessie Tuggle, Atlanta, 1987-2000
- 4   Bill Thompson, Denver, 1969-1981
-     Derrick Thomas, Kansas City, 1989-1999
-     Keith Bulluck, Tennessee, 2000-09; N.Y. Giants, 2010
-     Ronde Barber, Tampa Bay, 1997-2011

Most Touchdowns, Season (Total)
- 2   Harold McPhail, Boston, 1934
-     Harry Ebding, Detroit, 1937
-     John Morelli, Boston, 1944
-     Frank Maznicki, Boston, 1947
-     Fred (Dippy) Evans, Chi. Bears, 1948
-     Ralph Heywood, Boston, 1948
-     Art Tait, N.Y. Yanks, 1951
-     John Dwyer, Los Angeles, 1952
-     Leo Sugar, Chi. Cardinals, 1957
-     Doug Cline, Houston, 1961
-     Jim Bradshaw, Pittsburgh, 1964
-     Royce Berry, Cincinnati, 1970
-     Ahmad Rashad, Buffalo, 1974
-     Tim Gray, Kansas City, 1977
-     Charles Phillips, Oakland, 1978
-     Kenny Johnson, Atlanta, 1981
-     George Martin, N.Y. Giants, 1981
-     Del Rodgers, Green Bay, 1982
-     Mike Douglass, Green Bay, 1983
-     Shelton Robinson, Seattle, 1983
-     Erik McMillan, N.Y. Jets, 1989
-     Les Miller, San Diego, 1990
-     Seth Joyner, Philadelphia, 1991
-     Robert Goff, New Orleans, 1992
-     Willie Clay, Detroit, 1993
-     Tyrone Hughes, New Orleans, 1994
-     Chad Brown, Seattle, 1997
-     Marcus Robertson, Tennessee, 1997
-     Dwayne Rudd, Minnesota, 1998
-     Keith McKenzie, Green Bay, 1999
-     Ronde Barber, Tampa Bay, 2004
-     Leonard Little, St. Louis, 2004
-     Antwan Odom, Tennessee, 2005
-     Adalius Thomas, Baltimore, 2005
-     Kevin Curtis, Philadelphia, 2007
-     Kerry Rhodes, Arizona, 2010
-     Juqua Parker, Philadelphia, 2011

Most Touchdowns, Career (Own recovered)
- 2   Ken Kavanaugh, Chi. Bears, 1940-41, 1945-1950
-     Mike Ditka, Chicago, 1961-66; Philadelphia, 1967-68; Dallas, 1969-1972
-     Gail Cogdill, Detroit, 1960-68; Baltimore, 1968; Atlanta, 1969-1970

Ahmad Rashad, St. Louis, 1972-73; Buffalo, 1974; Minnesota, 1976-1982
Jim Mitchell, Atlanta, 1969-1979
Drew Pearson, Dallas, 1973-1983
Del Rodgers, Green Bay, 1982, 1984; San Francisco, 1987-88
Alan Ricard, Baltimore, 2001-05
Kevin Curtis, St. Louis, 2003-06; Philadelphia, 2007-09; Miami, 2010

Most Touchdowns, Season (Own recovered)
2 Ahmad Rashad, Buffalo, 1974
   Del Rodgers, Green Bay, 1982
   Kevin Curtis, Philadelphia, 2007
1 By many players

Most Touchdowns, Career (Opponents' recovered)
6 Jason Taylor, Miami, 1997-2007; Washington, 2008; Miami, 2009; N.Y. Jets, 2010; Miami, 2011
5 Jessie Tuggle, Atlanta, 1987-2006
4 Derrick Thomas, Kansas City, 1989-1999
   Keith Bulluck, Tennessee, 2000-09; N.Y. Giants, 2010
   Ronde Barber, Tampa Bay, 1997-2011

Most Touchdowns, Season (Opponents' recovered)
2 Harold McPhail, Boston, 1934
   Harry Ebding, Detroit, 1937
   John Morelli, Boston, 1944
   Frank Maznicki, Boston, 1947
   Fred (Dippy) Evans, Chi. Bears, 1948
   Ralph Heywood, Boston, 1948
   Art Tait, N.Y. Yanks, 1951
   John Dwyer, Los Angeles, 1952
   Leo Sugar, Chi. Cardinals, 1957
   Doug Cline, Houston, 1961
   Jim Bradshaw, Pittsburgh, 1964
   Royce Berry, Cincinnati, 1970
   Tim Gray, Kansas City, 1977
   Charles Phillips, Oakland, 1978
   Kenny Johnson, Atlanta, 1981
   George Martin, N.Y. Giants, 1981
   Mike Douglass, Green Bay, 1983
   Shelton Robinson, Seattle, 1983
   Erik McMillan, N.Y. Jets, 1989
   Les Miller, San Diego, 1990
   Seth Joyner, Philadelphia, 1991
   Robert Goff, New Orleans, 1992
   Willie Clay, Detroit, 1993
   Tyrone Hughes, New Orleans, 1994
   Chad Brown, Seattle, 1997
   Marcus Robertson, Tennessee, 1997
   Dwayne Rudd, Minnesota, 1998
   Keith McKenzie, Green Bay, 1999
   Ronde Barber, Tampa Bay, 2004
   Leonard Little, St. Louis, 2004
   Antwan Odom, Tennessee, 2005
   Adalius Thomas, Baltimore, 2005
   Kerry Rhodes, Arizona, 2010
   Juqua Parker, Philadelphia, 2011

Most Touchdowns, Game (Opponents' recovered)
2 Fred (Dippy) Evans, Chi. Bears vs. Washington, Nov. 28, 1948

COMBINED NET YARDS GAINED
Rushing, receiving, interception returns, punt returns, kickoff returns, and fumble returns

Most Seasons Leading League
5 Jim Brown, Cleveland, 1958-1961, 1964
4 Brian Mitchell, Washington, 1994-96, 1998
3 Cliff Battles, Boston, 1932-33; Washington, 1937
   Gale Sayers, Chicago, 1965-67
   Eric Dickerson, L.A. Rams, 1983-84, 1986

Thurman Thomas, Buffalo, 1989, 1991-92

Most Consecutive Seasons Leading League
4 Jim Brown, Cleveland, 1958-1961
3 Gale Sayers, Chicago, 1965-67
   Brian Mitchell, Washington, 1994-96
2 Cliff Battles, Boston, 1932-33
   Charley Trippi, Chi. Cardinals, 1948-49
   Timmy Brown, Philadelphia, 1962-63
   Floyd Little, Denver, 1967-68
   James Brooks, San Diego, 1981-82
   Eric Dickerson, L.A. Rams, 1983-84
   Thurman Thomas, Buffalo, 1991-92
   Dante Hall, Kansas City, 2003-04

ATTEMPTS
Most Attempts, Career
4,939 Emmitt Smith. Dallas, 1990-2002; Arizona, 2003-04
4,368 Walter Payton, Chicago, 1975-1987
4,016 Curtis Martin, New England, 1995-97; N.Y. Jets, 1998-2005

Most Attempts, Season
496 James Wilder, Tamp Bay, 1984
458 Larry Johnson, Kansas City, 2006
455 Eddie George, Tennessee, 2000

Most Attempts, Rookie, Season
442 Eric Dickerson, L.A. Rams, 1983
433 Edgerrin James, Indianapolis, 1999
401 Curtis Martin, New England, 1995

Most Attempts, Game
48 James Wilder, Tampa Bay vs. Pittsburgh, Oct. 30, 1983
   LaDainian Tomlinson, San Diego vs. Denver, Dec. 1, 2002 (ot)
47 James Wilder, Tampa Bay vs. Green Bay, Sept. 30, 1984 (ot)
   Terrell Davis, Denver vs. Buffalo, Oct. 26, 1997 (ot)
46 Gerald Riggs, Atlanta vs. L.A. Rams, Nov. 17, 1985

YARDS GAINED
Most Yards Gained, Career
23,546 Jerry Rice, San Francisco, 1985-2000; Oakland, 2001-04; Seattle, 2004
23,330 Brian Mitchell, Washington, 1990-99; Philadelphia, 2000-02; N.Y. Giants, 2003
21,803 Walter Payton, Chicago, 1975-1987

Most Yards Gained, Season
2,696 Darren Sproles, New Orleans, 2011
2,690 Derrick Mason, Tennessee, 2000
2,647 Michael Lewis, New Orleans, 2002

Most Yards Gained, Rookie, Season
2,317 Tim Brown, L.A. Raiders, 1988
2,272 Gale Sayers, Chicago, 1965
2,250 Maurice Jones-Drew, Jacksonville, 2006

Most Yards Gained, Game
404 Glyn Milburn, Denver vs. Seattle, Dec. 10, 1995
373 Billy Cannon, Houston vs. N.Y. Titans, Dec. 10. 1961
361 Adrian Peterson, Minnesota vs. Chicago, Oct. 14, 2007

SACKS
Sacks have been compiled since 1982.

Most Seasons Leading League
2 Mark Gastineau, N.Y. Jets, 1983-84
   Reggie White, Philadelphia, 1987-88
   Kevin Greene, Pittsburgh, 1994; Carolina, 1996
   Michael Strahan, N.Y. Giants, 2001, 2003
   DeMarcus Ware, Dallas, 2008, 2010
   Jared Allen, Kansas City, 2007; Minnesota, 2011

Most Sacks, Career
200.0 Bruce Smith, Buffalo, 1985-1999; Washington, 2000-03

198.0   Reggie White, Philadelphia, 1985-1992; Green Bay, 1993-98; Carolina, 2000
160.0   Kevin Greene, L.A. Rams, 1985-1992; Pittsburgh, 1993-95; Carolina, 1996, 1998-99; San Francisco, 1997

Most Sacks, Season
22.5   Michael Strahan, N.Y. Giants, 2001
22.0   Mark Gastineau, N.Y. Jets, 1984
       Jared Allen, Minnesota, 2011
21.0   Reggie White, Philadelphia, 1987
       Chris Doleman, Minnesota, 1989

Most Sacks, Rookie, Season
14.5   Jevon Kearse, Tennessee, 1999
14.0   Aldon Smith, San Francisco, 2011
13.0   Dwight Freeney, Indianapolis, 2002

Most Sacks, Game
7.0   Derrick Thomas, Kansas City vs. Seattle, Nov. 11, 1990
6.0   Fred Dean, San Francisco vs. New Orleans, Nov. 13, 1983
     Derrick Thomas, Kansas City vs. Oakland, Sept. 6, 1998
     Osi Umenyiora, N.Y. Giants vs. Philadelphia, Sept. 30, 2007
5.5   William Gay, Detroit vs. Tampa Bay, Sept. 4, 1983

Most Seasons, 10 or More Sacks
13   Bruce Smith, Buffalo, 1986-1990, 1992-98; Washington, 2000
12   Reggie White, Philadelphia, 1985-1992; Green Bay, 1993, 1995, 1997-98
10   Kevin Greene, L.A. Rams, 1988-1990, 1992; Pittsburgh, 1993-94; Carolina, 1996, 1998-99; San Francisco, 1997

Most Consecutive Seasons, 10 or More Sacks
9   Reggie White, Philadelphia, 1985-1992; Green Bay, 1993
8   John Randle, Minnesota, 1992-99
7   Lawrence Taylor, N.Y. Giants, 1984-1990
   Bruce Smith, Buffalo, 1992-98

Most Consecutive Games, Sack
10   Simon Fletcher, Denver, Nov. 15, 1992-Sept. 20, 1993
    DeMarcus Ware, Dallas, Dec. 16, 2007-Oct. 19, 2008
9   Bruce Smith, Buffalo, Nov. 16, 1986-Oct. 25, 1987
   Kevin Greene, San Francisco-Carolina, Dec. 7, 1997-Oct. 18, 1998
   Dwight Freeney, Indianapolis, Dec. 18, 2008-Nov. 8, 2009
8   By many players

MISCELLANEOUS

Longest Return of Missed Field Goal (All TDs)
109   Antonio Cromartie, San Diego vs. Minnesota, Nov. 4, 2007
108   Nathan Vasher, Chicago vs. San Francisco, Nov. 13, 2005
     Devin Hester, Chicago vs. N.Y. Giants, Nov. 12, 2006
107   Chris McAlister, Baltimore vs. Denver, Sept. 30, 2002

TEAM RECORDS

CHAMPIONSHIPS

Most Seasons League Champion
13   Green Bay, 1929-1931, 1936, 1939, 1944, 1961-62, 1965-67, 1996, 2010
9   Chi. Bears, 1921, 1932-33, 1940-41, 1943, 1946, 1963, 1985
8   N.Y. Giants, 1927, 1934, 1938, 1956, 1986, 1990, 2007, 2011

Most Consecutive Seasons League Champion
3   Green Bay, 1929-1931

     Green Bay, 1965-67
2   Canton, 1922-23
   Chi. Bears, 1932-33
   Chi. Bears, 1940-41
   Philadelphia, 1948-49
   Detroit, 1952-53
   Cleveland, 1954-55
   Baltimore, 1958-59
   Houston, 1960-61
   Green Bay, 1961-62
   Buffalo, 1964-65
   Miami, 1972-73
   Pittsburgh, 1974-75
   Pittsburgh, 1978-79
   San Francisco, 1988-89
   Dallas, 1992-93
   Denver, 1997-98
   New England, 2003-04

Most Times Finishing First, Regular Season
23   N.Y. Giants, 1927, 1933-35, 1938-39, 1941, 1944, 1946, 1956, 1958-59, 1961-63, 1986, 1989-1990, 1997, 2000, 2005, 2008, 2011
22   Chi. Bears, 1921, 1932-34, 1937, 1940-43, 1946, 1956, 1963, 1984-88, 1990, 2001, 2005-06, 2010
   Green Bay, 1929-1931, 1936, 1938-39, 1944, 1960-62, 1965-67, 1972, 1995-97, 2002-04, 2007, 2011
21   Dallas, 1966-1971, 1973, 1976-79, 1981, 1985, 1992-96, 1998, 2007, 2009

Most Consecutive Times Finishing First, Regular Season
7   Los Angeles, 1973-79
6   Cleveland, 1950-55
   Dallas, 1966-1971
   Minnesota, 1973-78
   Pittsburgh, 1974-79
5   Oakland, 1972-76
   Chicago, 1984-88
   San Francisco, 1986-1990
   Dallas, 1992-96
   Indianapolis, 2003-07
   New England, 2003-07

GAMES WON

Most Consecutive Games Won
23   Indianapolis, 2008-09
21   New England, 2006-08
18   New England, 2003-04

Most Consecutive Games Without Defeat
25   Canton, 1921-23 (won 22, tied 3)
24   Chi. Bears, 1941-43 (won 23, tied 1)
23   Green Bay, 1928-1930 (won 21, tied 2)
   Indianapolis, 2009 (won 23)

Most Games Won, Season
16   New England, 2007
15   San Francisco, 1984
   Chicago, 1985
   Minnesota, 1998
   Pittsburgh, 2004
   Green Bay, 2011
14   By many teams

Most Consecutive Games Won, Season
16   New England, 2007, entire season
14   Miami, 1972, entire season
   Pittsburgh, 2004
   Indianapolis, 2009
13   Chi. Bears, 1934, entire season
   Denver, 1998
   Indianapolis, 2005
   New Orleans, 2009

       Green Bay, 2011

Most Consecutive Games Won, Start of Season
- 16 New England, 2007, entire season
- 14 Miami, 1972, entire season
      Indianapolis, 2009
- 13 Chi. Bears, 1934, entire season
      Denver, 1998
      Indianapolis, 2005
      New Orleans, 2009
      Green Bay, 2011

Most Consecutive Games Won, End of Season
- 16 New England, 2007, entire season
- 14 Miami, 1972, entire season
      Pittsburgh, 2004
- 13 Chi. Bears, 1934, entire season

Most Consecutive Games Without Defeat, Season
- 16 New England, 2007 (won 16), entire season
- 14 Miami, 1972 (won 14), entire season
      Pittsburgh, 2004 (won 14)
      Indianapolis, 2009 (won 14)
- 13 Chi. Bears, 1926 (won 11, tied 2)
      Green Bay, 1929 (won 12, tied 1)
      Chi. Bears, 1934 (won 13), entire season
      Baltimore, 1967 (won 11, tied 2)
      Denver, 1998 (won 13)
      Indianapolis, 2005 (won 13)
      New Orleans, 2009 (won 13)
      Green Bay, 2011 (won 13)

Most Consecutive Games Without Defeat, Start of Season
- 16 New England, 2007 (won 16), entire season
- 14 Miami, 1972 (won 14), entire season
      Indianapolis, 2009 (won 14)
- 13 Chi. Bears, 1926 (won 11, tied 2)
      Green Bay, 1929 (won 12, tied 1), entire season
      Chi. Bears, 1934 (won 13), entire season
      Baltimore, 1967 (won 11, tied 2)
      Denver, 1998 (won 13)
      Indianapolis, 2005 (won 13)
      New Orleans, 2009 (won 13)
      Green Bay, 2011 (won 13)

Most Consecutive Games Without Defeat, End of Season
- 16 New England, 2007 (won 16), entire season
- 14 Miami, 1972 (won 14), entire season
      Pittsburgh, 2004 (won 14)
- 13 Green Bay, 1929 (won 12, tied 1), entire season
      Chi. Bears, 1934 (won 13), entire season

Most Consecutive Home Games Won
- 27 Miami, 1971-74
- 25 Green Bay, 1995-98
- 24 Denver, 1996-98

Most Consecutive Home Games Without Defeat
- 29 Green Bay, 1928-1933 (won 26, tied 3)
- 27 Miami, 1971-74 (won 27)
- 25 Green Bay, 1995-98 (won 25)

Most Consecutive Road Games Won
- 18 San Francisco, 1988-1990
- 12 New England, 2006-08
- 11 L.A. Chargers/San Diego, 1960-61
      San Francisco, 1987-88
      Pittsburgh, 2004-05
      Indianapolis, 2008-09

Most Consecutive Road Games Without Defeat
- 18 San Francisco, 1988-1990
- 13 Chi. Bears, 1941-43 (won 12, tied 1)
- 12 Green Bay, 1928-1930 (won 10, tied 2)
      New England, 2006-08 (won 12)

Most Shutout Games Won or Tied, Season
- 10 Pottsville, 1926 (won 9, tied 1)
      N.Y. Giants, 1927 (won 9, tied 1)
- 9 Akron, 1921 (won 8, tied 1)

      Canton, 1922 (won 7, tied 2)
      Frankford, 1926 (won 9)
      Frankford, 1929 (won 6, tied 3)
- 8 By many teams

Most Consecutive Shutout Games Won or Tied
- 13 Akron, 1920-21 (won 10, tied 3)
- 7 Pottsville, 1926 (won 6, tied 1)
      Detroit, 1934 (won 7)
- 6 Buffalo, 1920-21 (won 5, tied 1)
      Frankford, 1926 (won 6)
      Detroit, 1926 (won 4, tied 2)
      N.Y. Giants, 1926-27 (won 5, tied 1)

GAMES LOST

Most Consecutive Games Lost
- 26 Tampa Bay, 1976-1977
- 19 Chi. Cardinals, 1942-43, 1945
      Oakland, 1961-62
      Detroit, 2007-09
- 18 Houston, 1972-73

Most Consecutive Games Without Victory
- 26 Tampa Bay, 1976-77 (lost 26)
- 23 Rochester, 1922-25 (lost 21, tied 2)
      Washington, 1960-61 (lost 20, tied 3)
- 19 Dayton, 1927-29 (lost 18, tied 1)
      Chi. Cardinals, 1942-43, 1945 (lost 19)
      Oakland, 1961-62 (lost 19)
      Detroit, 2007-09 (lost 19)

Most Games Lost, Season
- 16 Detroit, 2008
- 15 New Orleans, 1980
      Dallas, 1989
      New England, 1990
      Indianapolis, 1991
      N.Y. Jets, 1996
      San Diego, 2000
      Carolina, 2001
      Miami, 2007
      St. Louis, 2009
- 14 By many teams

Most Consecutive Games Lost, Season
- 16 Detroit, 2008, entire season
- 15 Carolina, 2001
- 14 Tampa Bay, 1976
      New Orleans, 1980
      Baltimore, 1981
      New England, 1990

Most Consecutive Games Lost, Start of Season
- 16 Detroit, 2008, entire season
- 14 Tampa Bay, 1976, entire season
      New Orleans, 1980
- 13 Oakland, 1962
      Indianapolis, 1986
      Miami, 2007
      Indianapolis, 2011

Most Consecutive Games Lost, End of Season
- 16 Detroit, 2008, entire season
- 15 Carolina, 2001
- 14 Tampa Bay, 1976, entire season
      New England, 1990

Most Consecutive Games Without Victory, Season
- 16 Detroit, 2008 (lost 16), entire season
- 15 Carolina, 2001 (lost 15)
- 14 Tampa Bay, 1976 (lost 14), entire season
      New Orleans, 1980 (lost 14)
      Baltimore, 1981 (lost 14)
      New England, 1990 (lost 14)

Most Consecutive Games Without Victory, Start of Season
- 16 Detroit, 2008 (lost 16), entire season
- 14 Tampa Bay, 1976 (lost 14), entire season

New Orleans, 1980 (lost 14)
13 Washington, 1961 (lost 12, tied 1)
Oakland, 1962 (lost 13)
Indianapolis, 1986 (lost 13)
Miami, 2007 (lost 13)
Indianapolis, 2011 (lost 13)

Most Consecutive Games Without Victory, End of Season
16 Detroit, 2008 (lost 16), entire season
15 Carolina, 2001
14 Tampa Bay, 1976, (lost 14), entire season
New England, 1990 (lost 14)

Most Consecutive Home Games Lost
14 Dallas, 1988-89
St. Louis, 2008-2010
13 Houston, 1972-73
Tampa Bay, 1976-77
N.Y. Jets, 1995-97
11 Oakland, 1961-62
Los Angeles, 1961-63
Cincinnati, 1998-99

Most Consecutive Home Games Without Victory
14 Dallas, 1988-89 (lost 14)
St. Louis, 2008-2010 (lost 14)
13 Houston, 1972-73 (lost 13)
Tampa Bay, 1976-77 (lost 13)
N.Y. Jets, 1995-97 (lost 13)
Philadelphia, 1936-38 (lost 12, tied 1)

Most Consecutive Road Games Lost
26 Detroit, 2007-2010
24 Detroit, 2001-03
23 Houston, 1981-84

Most Consecutive Road Games Without Victory
26 Detroit, 2007-2010 (lost 26)
24 Detroit, 2001-03 (lost 24)
23 Houston, 1981-84 (lost 23)

Most Shutout Games Lost or Tied, Season
8 Frankford, 1927 (lost 6, tied 2)
Brooklyn, 1931 (lost 8)
7 Dayton, 1925 (lost 6, tied 1)
Orange, 1929 (lost 4, tied 3)
Frankford, 1931 (lost 6, tied 1)
6 By many teams

Most Consecutive Shutout Games Lost or Tied
8 Rochester, 1922-24 (lost 8)
7 Hammond, 1922-23 (lost 6, tied 1)
6 Providence, 1926-27 (lost 5, tied 1)
Brooklyn, 1942-43 (lost 6)

TIE GAMES

Most Tie Games, Season
6 Chi. Bears, 1932
5 Frankford, 1929
4 Chi. Bears, 1924
Orange, 1929
Portsmouth, 1932

Most Consecutive Tie Games
3 Chi. Bears, 1932
2 By many teams

SCORING

Most Seasons Leading League
10 Chi. Bears, 1932, 1934-35, 1939, 1941-43, 1946-47, 1956
9 San Francisco, 1953, 1965, 1970, 1987, 1989, 1992-95
L.A./St. Louis Rams, 1950-52, 1957, 1967, 1973, 1999-2001
8 Green Bay, 1931, 1936-38, 1961-62, 1996, 2011

Most Consecutive Seasons Leading League
4 San Francisco, 1992-1995

3 Green Bay, 1936-38
Chi. Bears, 1941-43
Los Angeles, 1950-52
Oakland, 1967-69
St. Louis, 1999-2001
2 By many teams

POINTS

Most Points, Season
589 New England, 2007
560 Green Bay, 2011
556 Minnesota, 1998

Fewest Points, Season (Since 1932)
37 Cincinnati/St. Louis, 1934
38 Cincinnati, 1933
Detroit, 1942
51 Pittsburgh, 1934
Philadelphia, 1936

Most Points, Game
72 Washington vs. N.Y. Giants, Nov. 27, 1966
70 Los Angeles vs. Baltimore, Oct. 22, 1950
66 Rochester vs. *Fort Porter, Oct. 10, 1920
*Not a member of the American Professional Football Association

Most Points, Both Teams, Game
113 Washington (72) vs. N.Y. Giants (41), Nov. 27, 1966
106 Cincinnati (58) vs. Cleveland (48), Nov. 28, 2004
101 Oakland (52) vs. Houston (49), Dec. 22, 1963

Fewest Points, Both Teams, Game
0 In many games. Last time: N.Y. Giants vs. Detroit, Nov. 7, 1943

Most Points, Shutout Victory Game
66 Rochester vs. *Fort Porter, Oct. 10, 1920
*Not a member of the American Professional Football Association
64 Philadelphia vs. Cincinnati, Nov. 6, 1934
62 Akron vs. Oorang, Oct. 29, 1922

Most Consecutive Games Scoring
420 San Francisco, 1977-2004
309 Denver, 1992-2011 (current)
289 Indianapolis, 1994-2011 (current)

Fewest Points, Shutout Victory, Game
2 Akron vs. Buffalo, Nov. 29, 1923
Kansas City vs. Buffalo, Nov. 21, 1926
Frankford vs. Green Bay, Nov. 29, 1928
Green Bay vs. Chi. Bears, Oct. 16, 1932
Chi. Bears vs. Green Bay, Sept. 18, 1938

Most Points Overcome to Win Game
28 San Francisco vs. New Orleans, Dec. 7, 1980 (ot) (trailed 7-35, won 38-35)
26 Buffalo vs. Indianapolis, Sept., 21, 1997 (trailed 0-26, won 37-35)
25 St. Louis vs. Tampa Bay, Nov. 8, 1987 (trailed 3-28, won 31-28)

Most Points Overcome to Tie Game
31 Denver vs. Buffalo, Nov. 27, 1960 (trailed 7-38, tied 38-38)
28 Los Angeles vs. Philadelphia, Oct. 3, 1948 (trailed 0-28, tied 28-28)

Most Points, Each Half
1st: 49 Green Bay vs. Tampa Bay, Oct. 2, 1983
48 Buffalo vs. Miami, Sept. 18, 1966
45 Green Bay vs. Cleveland, Nov. 12, 1967
Indianapolis vs. Denver, Oct. 31, 1988
Houston vs. Cleveland, Dec. 9, 1990
Seattle vs. Minnesota, Sept. 29, 2002
New England vs. Tennessee, Oct. 18, 2009
Philadelphia vs. Washington, Nov. 15, 2010
2nd: 49 Chi. Bears vs. Philadelphia, Nov. 30, 1941
48 Chi. Cardinals vs. Baltimore, Oct. 2, 1950

N.Y. Giants vs. Baltimore, Nov. 19, 1950
45 Cincinnati vs. Houston, Dec. 17, 1972

Most Points, Both Teams, Each Half
1st: 70 Houston (35) vs. Oakland (35), Dec. 22, 1963
63 Philadelphia (42) vs. Detroit (21), Sept. 23, 2007
62 N.Y. Jets (41) vs. Tampa Bay (21), Nov. 17, 1985
Indianapolis (35) vs. Cincinnati (27), Nov. 20, 2005
2nd: 66 Cleveland (35) vs. Cincinnati (31), Nov. 28, 2004
65 Washington (38) vs. N.Y. Giants (27), Nov. 27, 1966
62 L.A. Raiders (31) vs. San Diego (31), Jan. 2, 1983
Baltimore (38) vs. Seattle (24), Nov. 23, 2003

Most Points, One Quarter
41 Green Bay vs. Detroit, Oct. 7, 1945 (second quarter)
Los Angeles vs. Detroit, Oct. 29, 1950
(third quarter)
37 Los Angeles vs. Green Bay, Sept. 21, 1980
(second quarter)
35 Chi. Cardinals vs. Boston, Oct. 24, 1948
(third quarter)
Green Bay vs. Cleveland, Nov. 12, 1967 (first quarter)
Green Bay vs. Tampa Bay, Oct. 2, 1983
(second quarter)
New England vs. Tennessee, Oct. 18, 2009
(second quarter)

Most Points, Both Teams, One Quarter
49 Oakland (28) vs. Houston (21), Dec. 22, 1963
(second quarter)
48 Green Bay (41) vs. Detroit (7), Oct. 7, 1945
(second quarter)
Los Angeles (41) vs. Detroit (7), Oct. 29, 1950
(third quarter)
Detroit (34) vs. Chicago (14), Sept. 30, 2007
(fourth quarter)
47 St. Louis (27) vs. Philadelphia (20), Dec. 13, 1964
(second quarter)

Most Points, Each Quarter
1st: 35 Green Bay vs. Cleveland, Nov. 12, 1967
31 Buffalo vs. Kansas City, Sept. 13, 1964
28 By 10 teams
2nd: 41 Green Bay vs. Detroit, Oct. 7, 1945
37 Los Angeles vs. Green Bay, Sept. 21, 1980
35 Green Bay vs. Tampa Bay, Oct. 2, 1983
New England vs. Tennessee, Oct. 18, 2009
3rd: 41 Los Angeles vs. Detroit, Oct. 29, 1950
35 Chi. Cardinals vs. Boston, Oct. 24, 1948
28 By 10 teams
4th: 34 Detroit vs. Chicago, Sept. 30, 2007
31 Oakland vs. Denver, Dec. 17, 1960
Oakland vs. San Diego, Dec. 8, 1963
Atlanta vs. Green Bay, Sept. 13, 1981
30 N.Y. Jets vs. Miami, Oct. 23, 2000

Most Points, Both Teams, Each Quarter
1st: 42 Green Bay (35) vs. Cleveland (7), Nov. 12, 1967
41 Tennessee (24) vs. Indianapolis (17), Dec. 5, 2004
35 Dall. Texans (21) vs. N.Y. Titans (14), Nov. 11, 1962
Dallas (28) vs. Philadelphia (7), Oct. 19, 1969
Kansas City (21) vs. Seattle (14), Dec. 11, 1977
Detroit (21) vs. L.A. Raiders (14), Dec. 10, 1990
Dallas (21) vs. Atlanta (14), Dec. 22, 1991
Indianapolis (21) vs. Green Bay (14), Sept 26, 2004
Miami (21) vs. Buffalo (14), Dec. 5, 2004
Philadelphia (21) vs. New Orleans (14), Dec. 23, 2007
2nd: 49 Oakland (28) vs. Houston (21), Dec. 22, 1963
48 Green Bay (41) vs. Detroit (7), Oct. 7, 1945
47 St. Louis (27) vs. Philadelphia (20), Dec. 13, 1964
3rd: 48 Los Angeles (41) vs. Detroit (7), Oct. 29, 1950
42 Washington (28) vs. Philadelphia (14), Oct. 1, 1955
41 Green Bay (21) vs. N.Y. Yanks (20), Oct. 8, 1950
4th: 48 Detroit (34) vs. Chicago (14), Sept. 30, 2007
43 Atlanta (28) vs. Carolina (15), Nov. 23, 2008

42 Chi. Cardinals (28) vs. Philadelphia (14), Dec. 7, 1947
Green Bay (28) vs. Chi. Bears (14), Nov. 6, 1955
N.Y. Jets (28) vs. Boston (14), Oct. 27, 1968
Pittsburgh (21) vs. Cleveland (21), Oct. 18, 1969
New England (21) vs. Kansas City (21),
Sept. 22, 2002

TOUCHDOWNS
Most Seasons Leading League, Touchdowns
13 Chi. Bears, 1932, 1934-35, 1939, 1941-44,
1946-48, 1956, 1965
7 Dallas, 1966, 1968, 1971, 1973, 1977-78, 1980
San Francisco, 1953, 1970, 1987, 1992-95
L.A./St. Louis Rams, 1949-1952, 1999-2001
San Diego, 1963, 1965, 1979, 1981-82, 1985,
2006
Green Bay, 1932, 1937-38, 1961-62, 1996, 2011
6 Oakland, 1967-69, 1972, 1974, 1977
Baltimore/Indianapolis Colts, 1957-59, 1964, 1976,
2004

Most Consecutive Seasons Leading League, Touchdowns
4 Chi. Bears, 1941-44
Los Angeles, 1949-1952
San Francisco, 1992-95
3 Chi. Bears, 1946-48
Baltimore, 1957-59
Oakland, 1967-69
St. Louis, 1999-2001
2 By many teams

Most Touchdowns, Season
75 New England, 2007
70 Miami, 1984
Green Bay, 2011
67 St. Louis, 2000

Fewest Touchdowns, Season (Since 1932)
3 Cincinnati, 1933
4 Cincinnati/St. Louis, 1934
5 Detroit, 1942

Most Touchdowns, Game
10 Rochester vs. *Fort Porter, Oct. 10, 1920
*Not a member of the American Professional
Football Association
Philadelphia vs. Cincinnati, Nov. 6, 1934
Los Angeles vs. Baltimore, Oct. 22, 1950
Washington vs. N.Y. Giants, Nov. 27, 1966
9 Rock Island vs. Evansville, Oct. 15, 1922
Akron vs. Oorang, Oct. 29, 1922
Racine vs. Louisville, Nov. 5, 1922
Chi. Cardinals vs. Rochester, Oct. 7, 1923
Chi. Cardinals vs. Milwaukee, Dec. 10, 1925
Chi. Cardinals vs. N.Y. Giants, Oct. 17, 1948
Chi. Cardinals vs. N.Y. Bulldogs, Nov. 13, 1949
Los Angeles vs. Detroit, Oct. 29, 1950
Pittsburgh vs. N.Y. Giants, Nov. 30, 1952
Chicago vs. San Francisco, Dec. 12, 1965
Chicago vs. Green Bay, Dec. 7, 1980
8 By many teams

Most Touchdowns, Both Teams, Game
16 Washington (10) vs. N.Y. Giants (6), Nov. 27, 1966
14 Chi. Cardinals (9) vs. N.Y. Giants (5), Oct. 17, 1948
Los Angeles (10) vs. Baltimore (4), Oct. 22, 1950
Houston (7) vs. Oakland (7), Dec. 22, 1963
13 New Orleans (7) vs. St. Louis (6), Nov. 2, 1969
Kansas City (7) vs. Seattle (6), Nov. 27, 1983 (ot)
San Diego (8) vs. Pittsburgh (5), Dec. 8, 1985
N.Y. Jets (7) vs. Miami (6), Sept. 21, 1986 (ot)
Cincinnati (7) vs. Cleveland (6), Nov. 28, 2004

Most Consecutive Games Scoring Touchdowns
166 Cleveland, 1957-1969
149 San Diego, 2002-2010 (current)

136 Indianapolis, 2003-2011

POINTS AFTER TOUCHDOWN
Most (One-Point) Points After Touchdown, Season
  74 New England, 2007
  68 Green Bay, 2011
  66 Miami, 1984
Fewest (One-Point) Points After Touchdown, Season
  2 Chi. Cardinals, 1933
  3 Cincinnati, 1933
      Pittsburgh, 1934
  4 Cincinnati/St. Louis, 1934
Most (One-Point) Points After Touchdown, Game
  10 Los Angeles vs. Baltimore, Oct. 22, 1950
  9 Chi. Cardinals vs. N.Y. Giants, Oct. 17, 1948
      Pittsburgh vs. N.Y. Giants, Nov. 30, 1952
      Washington vs. N.Y. Giants, Nov. 27, 1966
  8 By many teams
Most (One-Point) Points After Touchdown, Both Teams, Game
  14 Chi. Cardinals (9) vs. N.Y. Giants (5), Oct. 17, 1948
      Houston (7) vs. Oakland (7), Dec. 22, 1963
      Washington (9) vs. N.Y. Giants (5), Nov. 27, 1966
  13 Los Angeles (10) vs. Baltimore (3), Oct. 22, 1950
      Cincinnati (7) vs. Cleveland (6), Nov. 28, 2004
  12 In many games
Most Two-Point Conversions, Season
  6 Miami, 1994
      Minnesota, 1997
  5 Arizona, 1995
      Baltimore, 1996
      Jacksonville, 1996
      Chicago, 1997
      San Francisco, 1998
      Pittsburgh, 2002
  4 By many teams
Most Two-Point Conversions, Game
  4 St. Louis vs. Atlanta, Oct. 15, 2000
  3 Baltimore vs. New England, Oct. 6, 1996
      Pittsburgh vs. Tennessee, Nov. 1, 1998
  2 By many teams
Most Two-Point Conversions, Both Teams, Game
  5 Baltimore (3) vs. New England (2), Oct. 6, 1996
      St. Louis (4) vs. Atlanta (1), Oct. 15, 2000
  3 Seattle (2) vs. Kansas City (1), Oct. 23, 1994
      Minnesota (2) vs. Seattle (1), Nov. 10, 1996
      Pittsburgh (3) vs. Tennessee (0), Nov. 1, 1998
  2 In many games

FIELD GOALS
Most Seasons Leading League, Field Goals
  11 Green Bay, 1935-36, 1940-43, 1946-47, 1955,
        1972, 1974
  9 L.A./St. Louis Rams, 1949, 1951, 1958, 1966,
        1973, 1978, 2003, 2006, 2010
  8 Washington, 1945, 1956, 1971, 1976-77, 1979,
        1982, 1992
      N.Y. Giants, 1933, 1937, 1939, 1941, 1944, 1959,
        1983, 2008
Most Consecutive Seasons Leading League, Field Goals
  4 Green Bay, 1940-43
  3 Cleveland, 1952-54
  2 By many teams
Most Field Goals Attempted, Season
  52 San Francisco, 2011
  49 Los Angeles, 1966
        Washington, 1971
  48 Green Bay, 1972
Fewest Field Goals Attempted, Season (Since 1938)
  0 Chi. Bears, 1944
  2 Cleveland, 1939

      Card-Pitt, 1944
      Boston, 1946
      Chi. Bears, 1947
  3 Chi. Bears, 1945
      Cleveland, 1945
Most Field Goals Attempted, Game
  9 St. Louis vs. Pittsburgh, Sept. 24, 1967
  8 Pittsburgh vs. St. Louis, Dec. 2, 1962
      Detroit vs. Minnesota, Nov. 13, 1966
      N.Y. Jets vs. Buffalo, Nov. 3, 1968
      Dallas vs. N.Y. Giants, Sept. 15, 2003 (ot)
      Tennessee vs. Houston, Oct. 21, 2007
  7 By many teams
Most Field Goals Attempted, Both Teams, Game
  11 St. Louis (6) vs. Pittsburgh (5), Nov. 13, 1966
      Washington (6) vs. Chicago (5), Nov. 14, 1971
      Green Bay (6) vs. Detroit (5), Sept. 29, 1974
      Washington (6) vs. N.Y. Giants (5), Nov. 14, 1976
  10 In many games
Most Field Goals, Season
  44 San Francisco, 2011
  43 Arizona, 2005
  39 Miami, 1999
      St. Louis, 2003
Fewest Field Goals, Season (Since 1932)
  0 Boston, 1932, 1935
      Chi. Cardinals, 1932, 1945
      Green Bay, 1932, 1944
      N.Y. Giants, 1932
      Brooklyn, 1944
      Card-Pitt, 1944
      Chi. Bears, 1944, 1947
      Boston, 1946
      Baltimore, 1950
      Dallas, 1952
Most Field Goals, Game
  8 Tennessee vs. Houston, Oct. 21, 2007
  7 St. Louis vs. Pittsburgh, Sept. 24, 1967
      Minnesota vs. L.A. Rams, Nov. 5, 1989 (ot)
      Dallas vs. Green Bay, Nov. 18, 1996
      Dallas vs. N.Y. Giants, Sept. 15, 2003 (ot)
      Cincinnati vs. Baltimore, Nov. 11, 2007
  6 By many teams
Most Field Goals, Both Teams, Game
  9 San Diego (5) vs. Kansas City (4), Sept. 29, 1996
      Miami (6) vs. New England (3), Oct. 17, 1999
      Houston (5) vs. Miami (4), Oct. 7, 2007
      Dallas (6) vs. Washington (3), Sept. 26, 2011
  8 Cleveland (4) vs. St. Louis (4), Sept. 20, 1964
      Chicago (5) vs. Philadelphia (3), Oct. 20, 1968
      Washington (5) vs. Chicago (3), Nov. 14, 1971
      Kansas City (5) vs. Buffalo (3), Dec. 19, 1971
      Detroit (4) vs. Green Bay (4), Sept. 29, 1974
      Cleveland (5) vs. Denver (3), Oct. 19, 1975
      New England (4) vs. San Diego (4), Nov. 9, 1975
      San Francisco (6) vs. New Orleans (2), Oct. 16, 1983
      Seattle (5) vs. L.A. Raiders (3), Dec. 18, 1988
      Atlanta (6) vs. New Orleans (2), Nov. 13, 1994
      Indianapolis (4) vs. San Diego (4), Nov. 3, 1996
      Dallas (7) vs. N.Y. Giants (1), Sept. 15, 2003 (ot)
      Oakland (5) vs. Chicago (3), Oct. 5, 2003
      Buffalo (5) vs. Tennessee (3), Dec. 24, 2006
      Tennessee (8) vs. Houston (0), Oct. 21, 2007
      Buffalo (5) vs. Washington (3), Dec. 2, 2007
      Kansas City (4) vs. Denver (4), Sept. 28, 2008
      San Francisco (4) vs. Philadelphia (4), Oct. 12, 2008
      Pittsburgh (4) vs. Cincinnati (4), Nov. 15, 2009
      Miami (5) vs. Pittsburgh (3), Oct. 24, 2010
      Oakland (6) vs. Chicago (2), Nov. 27, 2011
  7 In many games

Most Consecutive Games Scoring Field Goals
- 38   Baltimore, 1999-2001
- 31   Minnesota, 1968-1970
- 28   Washington, 1988-1990

SAFETIES
Most Safeties, Season
- 4   Cleveland, 1927
  - Detroit, 1962
  - Seattle, 1993
  - San Francisco, 1996
  - Tennessee, 1999
- 3   By many teams

Most Safeties, Game
- 3   L.A. Rams vs. N.Y. Giants, Sept. 30, 1984
- 2   N.Y. Giants vs. Pottsville, Oct. 30, 1927
  - Chi. Bears vs. Pottsville, Nov. 13, 1927
  - Detroit vs. Brooklyn, Dec. 1, 1935
  - N.Y. Giants vs. Pittsburgh, Sept. 17, 1950
  - N.Y. Giants vs. Washington, Nov. 5, 1961
  - Chicago vs. Pittsburgh, Nov. 9, 1969
  - Dallas vs. Philadelphia, Nov. 19, 1972
  - Los Angeles vs. Green Bay, Oct. 21, 1973
  - Oakland vs. San Diego, Oct. 26, 1975
  - Denver vs. Seattle, Jan. 2, 1983
  - New Orleans vs. Cleveland, Sept. 13, 1987
  - Buffalo vs. Denver, Nov. 8, 1987
  - San Francisco vs. St. Louis, Sept. 8, 1996
  - Jacksonville vs. Pittsburgh, Oct. 3, 1999
  - Minnesota vs. Atlanta, Oct. 5, 2003
  - Dallas vs. Arizona, Oct. 5, 2003
  - Buffalo vs. Houston, Nov. 16, 2003
  - Minnesota vs. Green Bay, Nov. 9, 2008
  - St. Louis vs. Arizona, Nov. 6, 2011 (ot)

Most Safeties, Both Teams, Game
- 3   L.A. Rams (3) vs. N.Y. Giants (0), Sept. 30, 1984
- 2   Chi. Cardinals (1) vs. Frankford (1), Nov. 19, 1927
  - Chi. Cardinals (1) vs. Cincinnati (1), Nov. 12, 1933
  - Chi. Bears (1) vs. San Francisco (1), Oct. 19, 1952
  - Cincinnati (1) vs. Los Angeles (1), Oct. 22, 1972
  - Chi. Bears (1) vs. San Francisco (1), Sept. 19, 1976
  - Baltimore (1) vs. Miami (1), Oct. 29, 1978
  - Atlanta (1) vs. Detroit (1), Oct. 5, 1980
  - Houston (1) vs. Philadelphia (1), Oct. 2, 1988
  - Cleveland (1) vs. Seattle (1), Nov. 14, 1993
  - Arizona (1) vs. Houston (1), Dec. 4, 1994
  - (Also see previous record)

FIRST DOWNS
Most Seasons Leading League
- 9   Chi. Bears, 1935, 1939, 1941, 1943, 1945, 1947-49, 1955
- 7   San Diego, 1965, 1969, 1980-83, 1985
  - L.A./St. Louis Rams, 1946, 1950-51, 1954, 1957, 1973, 2001
  - Baltimore/Indianapolis Colts, 1958-59, 1967, 2003, 2005-06, 2010
- 6   San Francisco, 1965, 1987, 1989, 1993-94, 1998

Most Consecutive Seasons Leading League
- 4   San Diego, 1980-83
- 3   Chi. Bears, 1947-49
  - New England, 2007-09
- 2   By many teams

Most First Downs, Season
- 416   New Orleans, 2011
- 399   New England, 2011
- 398   Kansas City, 2004

Fewest First Downs, Season
- 51   Cincinnati, 1933
- 64   Pittsburgh, 1935

- 67   Philadelphia, 1937

Most First Downs, Game
- 39   N.Y. Jets vs. Miami, Nov. 27, 1988
  - Washington vs. Detroit, Nov. 4, 1990 (ot)
- 38   Los Angeles vs. N.Y. Giants, Nov. 13, 1966
- 37   Green Bay vs. Philadelphia, Nov. 11, 1962

Fewest First Downs, Game
- 0   N.Y. Giants vs. Green Bay, Oct. 1, 1933
  - Pittsburgh vs. Boston, Oct. 29, 1933
  - Philadelphia vs. Detroit, Sept. 20, 1935
  - N.Y. Giants vs. Washington, Sept. 27, 1942
  - Denver vs. Houston, Sept. 3, 1966

Most First Downs, Both Teams, Game
- 64   Seattle (32) vs. Kansas City (32), Nov. 24, 2002
- 62   San Diego (32) vs. Seattle (30), Sept. 15, 1985
  - Oakland (31) vs. Kansas City (31), Nov. 5, 2000
- 60   Buffalo (34) vs. Oakland (26), Sept. 18, 2011
  - New Orleans (31) vs. N.Y. Giants (29), Nov. 28, 2011

Fewest First Downs, Both Teams, Game
- 7   Chi. Cardinals (2) vs. Detroit (5), Sept. 15, 1940
- 9   Pittsburgh (1) vs. Boston (8), Oct. 27, 1935
  - Boston (4) vs. Brooklyn (5), Nov. 24, 1935
  - N.Y. Giants (3) vs. Detroit (6), Nov. 7, 1943
  - Pittsburgh (4) vs. Chi. Cardinals (5), Nov. 11, 1945
  - N.Y. Bulldogs (1) vs. Philadelphia (8), Sept. 22, 1949
- 10   Philadelphia (4) vs. Brooklyn (6), Nov. 5, 1944
  - N.Y. Giants (4) vs. Washington (6), Dec. 11, 1960

Most First Downs, Rushing, Season
- 181   New England, 1978
- 177   Los Angeles, 1973
- 176   Chicago, 1985

Fewest First Downs, Rushing, Season
- 36   Cleveland, 1942
  - Boston, 1944
- 39   Brooklyn, 1943
- 40   Philadelphia, 1940
  - Detroit, 1945

Most First Downs, Rushing, Game
- 25   Philadelphia vs. Washington, Dec. 2, 1951
- 23   St. Louis vs. New Orleans, Oct. 5, 1980
- 21   Cleveland vs. Philadelphia, Dec. 13, 1959
  - Green Bay vs. Philadelphia, Nov. 11, 1962
  - Los Angeles vs. New Orleans, Nov. 25, 1973
  - Pittsburgh vs. Kansas City, Nov. 7, 1976
  - New England vs. Denver, Nov. 28, 1976
  - Oakland vs. Green Bay, Sept. 17, 1978
  - Buffalo vs. Washington, Nov. 3, 1996
  - San Francisco vs. Detroit, Dec. 14, 1998
  - Kansas City vs. Atlanta, Oct. 24, 2004

Fewest First Downs, Rushing, Game
- 0   By many teams. Last time:
  - St. Louis vs. San Francisco, Dec. 4, 2011

Most First Downs, Rushing, Both Teams, Game
- 36   Philadelphia (25) vs. Washington (11), Dec. 2, 1951
- 31   Detroit (18) vs. Washington (13), Sept. 30, 1951
- 30   Los Angeles (17) vs. Minnesota (13), Nov. 5, 1961
  - New Orleans (17) vs. Green Bay (13), Sept. 9, 1979
  - New Orleans (16) vs. San Francisco (14), Nov. 11, 1979
  - New England (16) vs. Kansas City (14), Oct. 4, 1981
  - Indianapolis (18) vs. Denver (12), Sept. 30, 2007

Fewest First Downs, Rushing, Both Teams, Game
- 1   Oakland (0) vs. Tennessee (1), Sept. 7, 2003
  - Carolina (0) vs. Detroit (1), Oct. 16, 2005
- 2   Houston (0) vs. Denver (2), Dec. 2, 1962
  - N.Y. Jets, (1) vs. St. Louis (1), Dec. 3, 1995
  - Miami (1) vs. San Diego (1), Dec. 19, 1999
  - New Orleans (0) vs. Baltimore (2), Dec. 19, 1999
  - Baltimore (0) vs. Tennessee (2), Sept. 18, 2005
  - Pittsburgh (1) vs. Baltimore (1), Nov. 5, 2007
  - Arizona (1) vs. San Francisco (1), Sept. 13, 2009

3   In many games

Most First Downs, Passing, Season
280   New Orleans, 2011
262   New England, 2011
259   San Diego, 1985

Fewest First Downs, Passing, Season
18   Pittsburgh, 1941
23   Brooklyn, 1942
      N.Y. Giants, 1944
24   N.Y. Giants, 1943

Most First Downs, Passing, Game
29   N.Y. Giants vs. Cincinnati, Oct. 13, 1985
28   Tennessee vs. Oakland, Dec. 19, 2004
27   San Diego vs. Seattle, Sept. 15, 1985
      Detroit vs. Green Bay, Jan. 1, 2012

Fewest First Downs, Passing, Game
0   By many teams. Last time:
      Pittsburgh vs. Tennessee, Sept. 19, 2010

Most First Downs, Passing, Both Teams, Game
47   Detroit (27) vs. Green Bay (20), Jan. 1, 2012
43   San Diego (23) vs. Cincinnati (20), Dec. 20, 1982
      Miami (24) vs. N.Y. Jets (19), Sept. 21, 1986 (ot)
      Tennessee (28) vs. Oakland (15), Dec. 19, 2004
      New England (23) vs. San Diego (20),
        Sept. 18, 2011
42   San Francisco (22) vs. San Diego (20), Dec. 11, 1982
      Seattle (22) vs. Cleveland (20), Nov. 4, 2007 (ot)
      Pittsburgh (22) vs. New England (20),
        Nov. 14, 2010

Fewest First Downs, Passing, Both Teams, Game
0   Brooklyn vs. Pittsburgh, Nov. 29, 1942
1   Green Bay (0) vs. Cleveland (1), Sept. 21, 1941
      Pittsburgh (0) vs. Brooklyn (1), Oct. 11, 1942
      N.Y. Giants (0) vs. Detroit (1), Nov. 7, 1943
      Pittsburgh (0) vs. Chi. Cardinals (1), Nov. 11, 1945
      N.Y. Bulldogs (0) vs. Philadelphia (1), Sept. 22, 1949
      Chicago (0) vs. Buffalo (1), Oct. 7, 1979
2   In many games

Most First Downs, Penalty, Season
47   Buffalo, 2002
      Indianapolis, 2004
44   Dallas, 2005
43   Denver, 1994

Fewest First Downs, Penalty, Season
2   Brooklyn, 1940
4   Chi. Cardinals, 1940
      N.Y. Giants, 1942, 1944
      Washington, 1944
      Cleveland, 1952
      Kansas City, 1969
5   Brooklyn, 1939
      Chi. Bears, 1939
      Detroit, 1953
      Los Angeles, 1953
      Houston, 1982

Most First Downs, Penalty, Game
11   Denver vs. Houston, Oct. 6, 1985
9   Chi. Bears vs. Cleveland, Nov. 25, 1951
      Baltimore vs. Pittsburgh, Oct. 30, 1977
      N.Y. Jets vs. Houston, Sept. 18, 1988
      Dallas vs. Detroit, Nov. 20, 2005
8   Philadelphia vs. Detroit, Dec. 2, 1979
      Cincinnati vs. N.Y. Jets, Oct. 6, 1985
      Buffalo vs. Houston, Sept. 20, 1987
      Houston vs. Atlanta, Sept. 9, 1990
      Kansas City vs. L.A. Raiders, Oct. 3, 1993
      San Francisco vs. New Orleans, Nov. 1, 1998
      Oakland vs. San Francisco, Oct. 8, 2000 (ot)
      Philadelphia vs. Chicago, Nov. 3, 2002
      Detroit vs. Baltimore, Oct. 9, 2005

Atlanta vs. Arizona, Sept. 19, 2010

Most First Downs, Penalty, Both Teams, Game
12   Buffalo (7) vs. San Francisco (5), Oct. 4, 1998
      Detroit (8) vs. Baltimore (4), Oct. 9, 2005
11   Chi. Bears (9) vs. Cleveland (2), Nov. 25, 1951
      Cincinnati (8) vs. N.Y. Jets (3), Oct. 6, 1985
      Denver (11) vs. Houston (0), Oct. 6, 1985
      Detroit (6) vs. Dallas (5), Nov. 8, 1987
      N.Y. Jets (9) vs. Houston (2), Sept. 18, 1988
      Kansas City (8) vs. L.A. Raiders (3), Oct. 3, 1993
      Detroit (6) vs. San Diego (5), Nov. 11, 1996
      Philadelphia (8) vs. Chicago (3), Nov. 3, 2002
      Arizona (6) vs. St. Louis (5), Dec. 3, 2006
      Indianapolis (6) vs. Green Bay (5), Oct. 19, 2008
10   In many games

NET YARDS GAINED RUSHING AND PASSING

Most Seasons Leading League
12   Chi. Bears, 1932, 1934-35, 1939, 1941-44, 1947,
        1949, 1955-56
9   L.A./St. Louis Rams, 1946, 1950-51, 1954, 1957,
        1973, 1999-2001
8   San Diego, 1963, 1965, 1980-83, 1985, 2010

Most Consecutive Seasons Leading League
4   Chi. Bears, 1941-44
      San Diego, 1980-83
3   Baltimore, 1958-1960
      Houston, 1960-62
      Oakland, 1968-1970
      St. Louis, 1999-2001
2   By many teams

Most Yards Gained, Season
7,474   New Orleans, 2011
7,075   St. Louis, 2000
6,936   Miami, 1984

Fewest Yards Gained, Season
1,150   Cincinnati, 1933
1,443   Chi. Cardinals, 1934
1,486   Chi. Cardinals, 1933

Most Yards Gained, Game
735   Los Angeles vs. N.Y. Yanks, Sept. 28, 1951
683   Pittsburgh vs. Chi. Cardinals, Dec. 13, 1958
682   Chi. Bears vs. N.Y. Giants, Nov. 14, 1943

Fewest Yards Gained, Game
−7   Seattle vs. Los Angeles, Nov. 4, 1979
−5   Denver vs. Oakland, Sept. 10, 1967
14   Chi. Cardinals vs. Detroit, Sept. 15, 1940

Most Yards Gained, Both Teams, Game
1,133   Los Angeles (636) vs. N.Y. Yanks (497),
          Nov. 19, 1950
1,125   Detroit (575) vs. Green Bay (550), Jan. 1, 2012
1,110   New England (622) vs. Miami (488), Sept. 12, 2011

Fewest Yards Gained, Both Teams, Game
30   Chi. Cardinals (14) vs. Detroit (16), Sept. 15, 1940
136   Chi. Cardinals (50) vs. Green Bay (86), Nov. 18, 1934
154   N.Y. Giants (51) vs. Washington (103), Dec. 11, 1960

Most Consecutive Games, 400 or More Yards Gained
11   San Diego, 1982-83
9   New England, 2006-07
8   St. Louis, 1999-2000

Most Consecutive Games, 300 or More Yards Gained
36   Minnesota, 2002-04
30   Minnesota, 1999-2000
      St. Louis, 2000-02
29   Los Angeles, 1949-1951
      New Orleans, 2008-09

RUSHING

Most Seasons Leading League
- 16 Chi. Bears, 1932, 1934-35, 1939-1942, 1951, 1955-56, 1968, 1977, 1983-86
- 7 Buffalo, 1962, 1964, 1973, 1975, 1982, 1991-92
- 6 Cleveland, 1958-59, 1963, 1965-67
  - San Francisco, 1952-54, 1987, 1998-99
  - Dall. Texans/K.C. Chiefs, 1961, 1966, 1968-69, 1995, 2010

Most Consecutive Seasons Leading League
- 4 Chi. Bears, 1939-1942
  - Chi. Bears, 1983-86
- 3 Detroit, 1936-38
  - San Francisco, 1952-54
  - Cleveland, 1965-67
  - Atlanta, 2004-06
- 2 By many teams

ATTEMPTS

Most Rushing Attempts, Season
- 681 Oakland, 1977
- 674 Chicago, 1984
- 671 New England, 1978

Fewest Rushing Attempts, Season
- 211 Philadelphia, 1982
- 219 San Francisco, 1982
- 225 Houston, 1982

Most Rushing Attempts, Game
- 72 Chi. Bears vs. Brooklyn, Oct. 20, 1935
- 70 Chi. Cardinals vs. Green Bay, Dec. 5, 1948
- 69 Chi. Cardinals vs. Green Bay, Dec. 6, 1936
  - Kansas City vs. Cincinnati, Sept. 3, 1978

Fewest Rushing Attempts, Game
- 6 Chi. Cardinals vs. Boston, Oct. 29, 1933
  - New England vs. Pittsburgh, Oct. 31, 2004
  - Arizona vs. Minnesota, Nov. 26, 2006
- 7 Oakland vs. Buffalo, Oct. 5, 1963
  - Houston vs. N.Y. Giants, Dec. 8, 1985
  - Seattle vs. L.A. Raiders, Nov. 17, 1991
  - Green Bay vs. Miami, Sept. 11, 1994
  - Detroit vs. Minnesota, Dec. 2, 2007
  - Arizona vs. Minnesota, Dec. 14, 2008
- 8 Denver vs. Oakland, Dec. 17, 1960
  - Buffalo vs. St. Louis, Sept. 9, 1984
  - Detroit vs. San Francisco, Oct. 20, 1991
  - Atlanta vs. Detroit, Sept. 5, 1993
  - St. Louis vs. San Francisco, Nov. 2, 2003
  - N.Y. Jets vs. Denver, Nov. 20, 2005
  - St. Louis vs. Carolina, Nov. 19, 2006
  - Detroit vs. Arizona, Nov. 11, 2007
  - San Diego vs. Pittsburgh, Oct. 4, 2009
  - San Diego vs. Oakland, Dec. 5, 2010

Most Rushing Attempts, Both Teams, Game
- 108 Chi. Bears (70) vs. Green Bay (38), Dec. 5, 1948
- 105 Oakland (62) vs. Atlanta (43), Nov. 30, 1975 (ot)
- 104 Chi. Bears (64) vs. Pittsburgh (40), Oct. 18, 1936

Fewest Rushing Attempts, Both Teams, Game
- 16 Chi. Cardinals (6) vs. Boston (10), Oct. 22, 1933
- 30 Minnesota (15) vs. New England (15), Oct. 30, 2006
- 31 Green Bay (12) vs. Pittsburgh (19), Dec. 20, 2009

YARDS GAINED

Most Yards Gained Rushing, Season
- 3,165 New England, 1978
- 3,088 Buffalo, 1973
- 2,986 Kansas City, 1978

Fewest Yards Gained Rushing, Season
- 298 Philadelphia, 1940
- 467 Detroit, 1946
- 471 Boston, 1944

Most Yards Gained Rushing, Game
- 426 Detroit vs. Pittsburgh, Nov. 4, 1934
- 423 N.Y. Giants vs. Baltimore, Nov. 19, 1950
- 420 Boston vs. N.Y. Giants, Oct. 8, 1933

Fewest Yards Gained Rushing, Game
- −53 Detroit vs. Chi. Cardinals, Oct. 17, 1943
- −36 Philadelphia vs. Chi. Bears, Nov. 19, 1939
- −33 Brooklyn vs. Phil-Pitt, Oct. 2, 1943

Most Yards Gained Rushing, Both Teams, Game
- 595 Los Angeles (371) vs. N.Y. Yankees (224), Nov. 18, 1951
- 574 Chi. Bears (396) vs. Pittsburgh (178), Oct. 10, 1934
- 558 Boston (420) vs. N.Y. Giants (138), Oct. 8, 1933

Fewest Yards Gained Rushing, Both Teams, Game
- −15 Detroit (−53) vs. Chi. Cardinals (38), Oct. 17, 1943
- 4 Detroit (−10) vs. Chi. Cardinals (14), Sept. 15, 1940
- 45 San Diego (21) vs. Philadelphia (24), Oct. 23, 2005

AVERAGE GAIN

Highest Average Gain, Rushing, Season
- 5.74 Cleveland, 1963
- 5.65 San Francisco, 1954
- 5.56 San Diego, 1963

Lowest Average Gain, Rushing, Season
- 0.94 Philadelphia, 1940
- 1.45 Boston, 1944
- 1.55 Pittsburgh, 1935

TOUCHDOWNS

Most Touchdowns, Rushing, Season
- 36 Green Bay, 1962
- 33 Pittsburgh, 1976
- 32 Kansas City, 2003
  - San Diego, 2006

Fewest Touchdowns, Rushing, Season
- 1 Brooklyn, 1934
- 2 Chi. Cardinals, 1933
  - Cincinnati, 1933
  - Pittsburgh, 1934
  - Philadelphia, 1935
  - Philadelphia, 1936
  - Philadelphia, 1937
  - Philadelphia, 1938
  - Pittsburgh, 1940
  - Philadelphia, 1972
  - N.Y. Jets, 1995
  - Arizona, 2005
- 3 By many teams

Most Touchdowns, Rushing, Game
- 9 Rock Island vs. Evansville, Oct. 15, 1922
  - Racine vs. Louisville, Nov. 5, 1922
- 8 Chi. Cardinals vs. Rochester, Oct. 7, 1923
  - Kansas City vs. Atlanta, Oct. 24, 2004
- 7 By many teams

Most Touchdowns, Rushing, Both Teams, Game
- 9 Rock Island (9) vs. Evansville (0), Oct. 15, 1922
  - Racine (9) vs. Louisville (0), Nov. 5, 1922
- 8 Chi. Cardinals (8) vs. Rochester (0), Oct. 7, 1923
  - Canton (7) vs. Cleveland (1), Nov. 25, 1923
  - Los Angeles (6) vs. N.Y. Yanks (2), Nov. 18, 1951
  - Chi. Bears (5) vs. Green Bay (3), Nov. 6, 1955
  - Denver (5) vs. Kansas City (3), Dec. 7, 2003
  - Kansas City (8) vs. Atlanta (0), Oct. 24, 2004
- 7 In many games

PASSING

ATTEMPTS
Most Passes Attempted, Season
- 709 Minnesota, 1981
- 699 New England, 1994
- 686 New England, 1995

Fewest Passes Attempted, Season
- 102 Cincinnati, 1933
- 106 Boston, 1933
- 120 Detroit, 1937

Most Passes Attempted, Game
- 70 New England vs. Minnesota, Nov. 13, 1994 (ot)
- 69 N.Y. Jets vs. Baltimore, Dec. 24, 2000
- 68 Houston vs. Buffalo, Nov 1, 1964
  - Cincinnati vs. Pittsburgh, Dec. 30, 2001 (ot)

Fewest Passes Attempted, Game
- 0 Green Bay vs. Portsmouth, Oct. 8, 1933
  - Detroit vs. Cleveland, Sept. 10, 1937
  - Pittsburgh vs. Brooklyn, Nov. 16, 1941
  - Pittsburgh vs. Los Angeles, Nov. 13, 1949
  - Cleveland vs. Philadelphia, Dec. 3, 1950

Most Passes Attempted, Both Teams, Game
- 112 New England (70) vs. Minnesota (42), Nov. 13, 1994 (ot)
- 104 Miami (55) vs. N.Y. Jets (49), Oct. 18. 1987 (ot)
  - N.Y. Jets (58) vs. San Francisco (46), Sept. 6, 1998 (ot)
- 103 Cincinnati (68) vs. Pittsburgh (35), Dec. 30, 2001 (ot)
  - Seattle (53) vs. San Diego (50), Dec. 29, 2002 (ot)
  - Detroit (59) vs. Green Bay (44), Jan. 1, 2012

Fewest Passes Attempted, Both Teams, Game
- 4 Chi. Cardinals (1) vs. Detroit (3), Nov. 3, 1935
  - Detroit (0) vs. Cleveland (4), Sept. 10, 1937
- 6 Chi. Cardinals (2) vs. Detroit (4), Sept. 15, 1940
- 8 Brooklyn (2) vs. Philadelphia (6), Oct. 1, 1939

COMPLETIONS
Most Passes Completed, Season
- 472 New Orleans, 2011
- 450 Indianapolis, 2010
  - New Orleans, 2010
- 440 New Orleans, 2007

Fewest Passes Completed, Season
- 25 Cincinnati, 1933
- 33 Boston, 1933
- 34 Chi. Cardinals, 1934

Most Passes Completed, Game
- 45 New England vs. Minnesota, Nov. 13, 1994 (ot)
- 43 Washington vs. Detroit, Nov. 4, 1990 (ot)
  - Oakland vs. Pittsburgh, Sept. 15, 2002
- 42 N.Y. Jets vs. San Francisco, Sept. 21, 1980
  - N.Y. Jets vs. Seattle, Dec. 6, 1998

Fewest Passes Completed, Game
- 0 By many teams. Last time: Buffalo vs. N.Y. Jets, Sept. 29, 1974

Most Passes Completed, Both Teams, Game
- 71 New England (45) vs. Minnesota (26), Nov. 13, 1994 (ot)
- 68 San Francisco (37) vs. Atlanta (31), Oct. 6, 1985
  - Denver (34) vs. Oakland (34), Nov. 11, 2002
  - Detroit (36) vs. Green Bay (31), Jan. 1, 2012
- 66 Cincinnati (40) vs. San Diego (26), Dec. 20, 1982
  - Indianapolis (34) vs. Houston (32), Nov. 8, 2009
  - Houston (38) vs. Washington (28), Sept. 19, 2010 (ot)

Fewest Passes Completed, Both Teams, Game
- 1 Chi. Cardinals (0) vs. Philadelphia (1), Nov. 8, 1936
  - Detroit (0) vs. Cleveland (1), Sept. 10, 1937

- Chi. Cardinals (0) vs. Detroit (1), Sept. 15, 1940
- Brooklyn (0) vs. Pittsburgh (1), Nov. 29, 1942
- 2 Chi. Cardinals (0) vs. Detroit (2), Nov. 3, 1935
  - Buffalo (0) vs. N.Y. Jets (2), Sept. 29, 1974
  - Chi. Cardinals (0) vs. Green Bay (2), Nov. 18, 1934
- 3 In seven games

YARDS GAINED
Most Seasons Leading League, Passing Yardage
- 10 San Diego, 1965, 1968, 1971, 1978-1983, 1985
- 8 Chi. Bears, 1932, 1939, 1941, 1943, 1945, 1949, 1954, 1964
  - Washington, 1938, 1940, 1944, 1947-48, 1967, 1974, 1989
  - Balt./Indianapolis, 1957, 1959, 1960, 1963, 1976, 2003-04, 2010
- 7 Houston, 1960-61, 1963-64, 1990-92
  - L.A./St. Louis Rams, 1946, 1950-51, 1956, 1999-2001

Most Consecutive Seasons Leading League, Passing Yardage
- 6 San Diego, 1978-1983
- 4 Green Bay, 1934-37
- 3 Miami, 1986-88
  - Houston, 1990-92
  - St. Louis, 1999-2001

Most Yards Gained, Passing, Season
- 5,347 New Orleans, 2011
- 5,232 St. Louis, 2000
- 5,084 New England, 2011

Fewest Yards Gained, Passing, Season
- 302 Chi. Cardinals, 1934
- 357 Cincinnati, 1933
- 459 Boston, 1934

Most Yards Gained Passing, Game
- 554 Los Angeles vs. N.Y. Yankees, Sept. 28, 1951
- 530 Minnesota vs. Baltimore, Sept. 28, 1969
- 521 Miami vs. N.Y. Jets, Oct. 23, 1988

Fewest Yards Gained, Passing, Game
- −53 Denver vs. Oakland, Sept. 10, 1967
- −52 Cincinnati vs. Houston, Oct. 31, 1971
- −39 Atlanta vs. San Francisco, Oct. 23, 1976

Most Yards Gained, Passing, Both Teams, Game
- 971 Detroit (502) vs. Green Bay (469), Jan. 1, 2012
- 906 New England (516) vs. Miami (390), Sept. 12, 2011
- 884 N.Y. Jets (449) vs. Miami (435), Sept. 21, 1986 (ot)

Fewest Yards Gained, Passing, Both Teams, Game
- −11 Green Bay (−10) vs. Dallas (−1), Oct. 24, 1965
- 1 Chi. Cardinals (0) vs. Philadelphia (1), Nov. 8, 1936
- 7 Brooklyn (0) vs. Pittsburgh (7), Nov. 29, 1942

TIMES SACKED
Most Seasons Leading League, Fewest Times Sacked
- 10 Miami, 1973, 1982-1990
- 6 Indianapolis, 1999-2000, 2004-06, 2009
- 5 N.Y. Jets, 1965-66, 1968, 1993, 2000

Most Consecutive Seasons Leading League, Fewest Times Sacked
- 9 Miami, 1982-1990
- 3 St. Louis, 1974-76
  - Indianapolis, 2004-06
- 2 By many teams

Most Times Sacked, Season
- 104 Philadelphia, 1986
- 78 Arizona, 1997
- 76 Houston, 2002

Fewest Times Sacked, Season
- 7 Miami, 1988
- 8 San Francisco, 1970
  - St. Louis, 1975
- 9 N.Y. Jets, 1966
  - Washington, 1991

Most Times Sacked, Game
12 Pittsburgh vs. Dallas, Nov. 20, 1966
     Baltimore vs. St. Louis, Oct. 26, 1980
     Detroit vs. Chicago, Dec. 16, 1984
     Houston vs. Dallas, Sept. 29, 1985
     Philadelphia vs. N.Y. Giants, Sept. 30, 2007
11 St. Louis vs. N.Y. Giants, Nov. 1, 1964
     Los Angeles vs. Baltimore, Nov. 22, 1964
     Denver vs. Buffalo, Dec. 13, 1964
     Green Bay vs. Detroit, Nov. 7, 1965
     Buffalo vs. Oakland, Oct. 15, 1967
     Denver vs. Oakland, Nov. 5, 1967
     Atlanta vs. St. Louis, Nov. 24, 1968
     Detroit vs. Dallas, Oct. 6, 1975
     Philadelphia vs. St. Louis, Dec. 18, 1983
     Cleveland vs. Kansas City, Sept. 30, 1984
     Minnesota vs. Chicago, Oct. 28, 1984
     Atlanta vs. Cleveland, Nov. 18, 1984
     Dallas vs. San Diego, Nov. 16, 1986
     Philadelphia vs. Detroit, Nov. 16, 1986
     Philadelphia vs. L.A. Raiders, Nov. 30, 1986 (ot)
     L.A. Raiders vs. Seattle, Dec. 8, 1986
     N.Y. Jets vs. Dallas, Oct. 4, 1987
     Philadelphia vs. Chicago, Oct. 4, 1987
     Dallas vs. Philadelphia, Sept. 15, 1991
     Cleveland vs. Indianapolis, Sept. 6, 1992
10 By many teams
Most Times Sacked, Both Teams, Game
18 Green Bay (10) vs. San Diego (8), Sept. 24, 1978
17 Buffalo (10) vs. N.Y. Titans (7), Nov. 23, 1961
     Pittsburgh (12) vs. Dallas (5), Nov. 20, 1966
     Atlanta (9) vs. Philadelphia (8), Dec. 16, 1984
     Philadelphia (11) vs. L.A. Raiders (6), Nov. 30, 1986 (ot)
16 Los Angeles (11) vs. Baltimore (5), Nov. 22, 1964
     Buffalo (11) vs. Oakland (5), Oct. 15, 1967

COMPLETION PERCENTAGE
Most Seasons Leading League, Completion Percentage
14 San Francisco, 1952, 1957-58, 1965, 1981, 1983,
     1987, 1989, 1992-97
11 Washington, 1937, 1939-1940, 1942-45, 1947-48,
     1969-1970
 8 Green Bay, 1936, 1941, 1961-62, 1964, 1966,
     1968, 1998
Most Consecutive Seasons Leading League,
Completion Percentage
 6 San Francisco, 1992-97
 4 Washington, 1942-45
     Kansas City, 1966-69
 3 Cleveland, 1953-55
     St. Louis, 1999-2001
     New Orleans, 2009-2011
Highest Completion Percentage, Season
71.30 New Orleans, 2011 (662-472)
70.65 Cincinnati, 1982 (310-219)
70.25 San Francisco, 1994 (511-359)
Lowest Completion Percentage, Season
22.9 Philadelphia, 1936 (170-39)
24.5 Cincinnati, 1933 (102-25)
25.0 Pittsburgh, 1941 (168-42)

TOUCHDOWNS
Most Touchdowns, Passing, Season
51 Indianapolis, 2004
     Green Bay, 2011
50 New England, 2007
49 Miami, 1984
Fewest Touchdowns, Passing, Season
 0 Cincinnati, 1933
     Pittsburgh, 1945

 1 Boston, 1932
     Boston, 1933
     Chi. Cardinals, 1934
     Cincinnati/St. Louis, 1934
     Detroit, 1942
 2 Chi. Cardinals, 1932
     Stapleton, 1932
     Chi. Cardinals, 1935
     Brooklyn, 1936
     Pittsburgh, 1942
Most Touchdowns, Passing, Game
 7 Chi. Bears vs. N.Y. Giants, Nov. 14, 1943
     Philadelphia vs. Washington, Oct. 17, 1954
     Houston vs. N.Y. Titans, Nov. 19, 1961
     Houston vs. N.Y. Titans, Oct. 14, 1962
     N.Y. Giants vs. Washington, Oct. 28, 1962
     Minnesota vs. Baltimore, Sept. 28, 1969
     San Diego vs. Oakland, Nov. 22, 1981
 6 By many teams
Most Touchdowns, Passing, Both Teams, Game
12 New Orleans (6) vs. St. Louis (6), Nov. 2, 1969
11 N.Y. Giants (7) vs. Washington (4), Oct. 28, 1962
     Oakland (6) vs. Houston (5), Dec. 22, 1963
     Cincinnati (6) vs. Cleveland, (5), Sept. 16, 2007
     Green Bay (6) vs. Detroit (5), Jan. 1, 2012
10 San Diego (5) vs. Seattle (5), Sept. 15, 1985
     Miami (6) vs. N.Y. Jets (4), Sept. 21, 1986 (ot)
     San Francisco (6) vs. Atlanta (4), Oct. 14, 1990

PASSES HAD INTERCEPTED
Most Passes Had Intercepted, Season
48 Houston, 1962
45 Denver, 1961
41 Card-Pitt, 1944
Fewest Passes Had Intercepted, Season
 5 Cleveland, 1960
     Green Bay, 1966
     Kansas City, 1990
     N.Y. Giants, 1990
     New England, 2010
     San Francisco, 2011
 6 Green Bay, 1964
     St. Louis, 1982
     Dallas, 1993
     Jacksonville, 2005
     Washington, 2008
     Tampa Bay, 2010
 7 Los Angeles, 1969
     Denver, 2005
     Miami, 2008
     Minnesota, 2009
Most Passes Had Intercepted, Game
 9 Detroit vs. Green Bay, Oct. 24, 1943
     Pittsburgh vs. Philadelphia, Dec. 12, 1965
 8 Green Bay vs. N.Y. Giants, Nov. 21, 1948
     Chi. Cardinals vs. Philadelphia, Sept. 24, 1950
     N.Y. Yanks vs. N.Y. Giants, Dec. 16, 1951
     Denver vs. Houston, Dec. 2, 1962
     Chi. Bears vs. Detroit, Sept. 22, 1968
     Baltimore vs. N.Y. Jets, Sept. 23, 1973
 7 By many teams. Last time: Detroit vs. Cleveland,
     Sept. 23, 2001
Most Passes Had Intercepted, Both Teams, Game
13 Denver (8) vs. Houston (5), Dec. 2, 1962
11 Philadelphia (7) vs. Boston (4), Nov. 3, 1935
     Boston (6) vs. Pittsburgh (5), Dec. 1, 1935
     Cleveland (7) vs. Green Bay (4), Oct. 30, 1938
     Green Bay (7) vs. Detroit (4), Oct. 20, 1940
     Detroit (7) vs. Chi. Bears (4), Nov. 22, 1942
     Detroit (7) vs. Cleveland (4), Nov. 26, 1944

Chi. Cardinals (8) vs. Philadelphia (3), Sept. 24, 1950
Washington (7) vs. N.Y. Giants (4), Dec. 8, 1963
Pittsburgh (9) vs. Philadelphia (2), Dec 12, 1965
10   In many games

PUNTING
Most Seasons Leading League (Average Distance)
8   Oakland, 1974-75, 1977-78, 2003-04, 2007, 2009
7   Denver 1962-64, 1966-67, 1982, 1999
6   Washington, 1940-43, 1945, 1958
    Kansas City, 1968, 1971-73, 1979, 1984
    L.A. Rams, 1946, 1949, 1955-56, 1994, 2008
Most Consecutive Seasons Leading League
(Average Distance)
4   Washington, 1940-43
3   Cleveland, 1950-52
    Denver, 1962-64
    Kansas City, 1971-73
Most Punts, Season
116   Houston, 2002
114   Chicago, 1981
113   Boston, 1934
     Brooklyn, 1934
     Dallas, 2002
Fewest Punts, Season
23   San Diego, 1982
31   Cincinnati, 1982
32   Chi. Bears, 1941
Most Punts, Game
17   Chi. Bears vs. Green Bay, Oct. 22, 1933
    Cincinnati vs. Pittsburgh, Oct. 22, 1933
16   Cincinnati vs. Portsmouth, Sept. 17, 1933
    Chi. Cardinals vs. Chi. Bears, Nov. 30, 1933
    Chi. Cardinals vs. Detroit, Sept. 15, 1940
    Oakland vs. San Diego, Oct. 11, 1998
15   Chi. Cardinals vs. Cincinnati, Nov. 12, 1933
    N.Y. Giants vs. Chi. Bears, Nov. 17, 1935
    Philadelphia vs. N.Y. Giants, Dec. 6, 1987 (ot)
Fewest Punts, Game
0   By many teams. Last time:
       San Diego vs. Oakland, Jan. 1, 2012
Most Punts, Both Teams, Game
31   Chi. Bears (17) vs. Green Bay (14), Oct. 22, 1933
    Cincinnati (17), vs. Pittsburgh (14), Oct. 22, 1933
29   Chi. Cardinals (15) vs. Cincinnati (14), Nov. 12, 1933
    Chi. Cardinals (16) vs. Chi. Bears (13), Nov. 30, 1933
    Chi. Cardinals (16) vs. Detroit (13), Sept. 15, 1940
28   Philadelphia (14) vs. Washington (14), Nov. 5, 1939
Fewest Punts, Both Teams, Game
0   Buffalo vs. San Francisco, Sept. 13, 1992
1   Baltimore (0) vs. Cleveland (1), Nov. 1, 1959
    Dall. Cowboys (0) vs. Cleveland (1), Dec. 3, 1961
    Chicago (0) vs. Detroit (1), Oct. 1, 1972
    San Francisco (0) vs. N.Y. Giants (1), Oct. 15, 1972
    Green Bay (0) vs. Buffalo (1), Dec. 5, 1982
    Miami (0) vs. Buffalo (1), Oct. 12, 1986
    Green Bay (0) vs. Chicago (1), Dec. 17, 1989
    Oakland (0) vs. Seattle (1), Dec. 5, 1999
    Tampa Bay (0) vs. Minnesota (1), Oct. 29, 2000
    New Orleans (0) vs. San Francisco (1), Oct. 20, 2002
    San Diego (0) vs. Oakland (1), Jan. 1, 2012
2   In many games

AVERAGE YARDAGE
Highest Avg. Distance, Punting, Season
51.1   Oakland, 2009
50.9   San Francisco, 2011
50.8   Oakland, 2011
Lowest Average Distance, Punting, Season
32.7   Card-Pitt, 1944 (60-1,964)

33.8   Cincinnati, 1986 (59-1,996)
33.9   Detroit, 1969 (74-2,510)

PUNT RETURNS
Most Seasons Leading League (Average Return)
9   Detroit, 1943-45, 1951-52, 1962, 1966, 1969, 1991
7   Chi. Cardinals/St. Louis, 1948-49, 1955-56, 1959, 1986-87
6   Green Bay, 1950, 1953-54, 1961, 1972, 1996
    Dallas/Kansas City, 1960, 1968, 1970, 1979-1980, 2003
Most Consecutive Seasons Leading League (Average Return)
3   Detroit, 1943-45
2   By many teams
Most Punt Returns, Season
71   Pittsburgh, 1976
    Tampa Bay, 1979
    L.A. Raiders, 1985
67   Pittsburgh, 1974
    Los Angeles, 1978
    L.A. Raiders, 1984
65   San Francisco, 1976
Fewest Punt Returns, Season
12   Baltimore, 1981
    San Diego, 1982
14   Los Angeles, 1961
    Philadelphia, 1962
    Baltimore, 1982
15   Houston, 1960
    Washington, 1960
    Oakland, 1961
    N.Y. Giants, 1969
    Philadelphia, 1973
    Kansas City, 1982
Most Punt Returns, Game
12   Philadelphia vs. Cleveland, Dec. 3, 1950
11   Chi. Bears vs. Chi. Cardinals, Oct. 8, 1950
    Washington vs. Tampa Bay, Oct. 9, 1977
10   Philadelphia vs. N.Y. Giants, Nov. 26, 1950
    Philadelphia vs. Tampa Bay, Sept. 18, 1977
    Pittsburgh vs. Buffalo, Dec. 16, 1979
    Washington vs. New Orleans, Dec. 26, 1982
    Philadelphia vs. Seattle, Dec. 13, 1992 (ot)
    New England vs. Pittsburgh, Dec. 5, 1993
Most Punt Returns, Both Teams, Game
17   Philadelphia (12) vs. Cleveland (5), Dec. 3, 1950
16   N.Y. Giants (9) vs. Philadelphia (7), Dec. 12, 1954
    Washington (11) vs. Tampa Bay (5), Oct. 9, 1977
    Oakland (8) vs. San Diego (8), Oct. 11, 1998
15   Detroit (8) vs. Cleveland (7), Sept. 27, 1942
    Los Angeles (8) vs. Baltimore (7), Nov. 27, 1966
    Pittsburgh (8) vs. Houston (7), Dec. 1, 1974
    Philadelphia (10) vs. Tampa Bay (5), Sept. 18, 1977
    Baltimore (9) vs. Kansas City (6), Sept. 2, 1979
    Washington (10) vs. New Orleans (5), Dec. 26, 1982
    L.A. Raiders (8) vs. Cleveland (7), Nov. 16, 1986

FAIR CATCHES
Most Fair Catches, Season
34   Baltimore, 1971
33   Philadelphia, 2000
32   San Diego, 1969
    Oakland, 2001
Fewest Fair Catches, Season
0   San Diego, 1975
    New England, 1976
    Tampa Bay, 1976
    Pittsburgh, 1977
    Dallas, 1982
1   Cleveland, 1974

San Francisco, 1975
Kansas City, 1976
St. Louis, 1976
San Diego, 1976
L.A. Rams, 1982
St. Louis, 1982
Tampa Bay, 1982
Arizona, 2001
2   By many teams

Most Fair Catches, Game
7   Minnesota vs. Dallas, Sept. 25, 1966
    N.Y. Jets vs. Miami, Nov. 20, 1966
    Detroit vs. Chicago, Nov. 21, 1976
    Philadelphia vs. Buffalo, Dec. 27, 1987
    Tennessee vs. Jacksonville, Nov. 16, 2008
6   By many teams

YARDS GAINED
Most Yards, Punt Returns, Season
875   Green Bay, 1996
785   L.A. Raiders, 1985
781   Chi. Bears, 1948

Fewest Yards, Punt Returns, Season
27   St. Louis, 1965
35   N.Y. Giants, 1965
37   New England, 1972

Most Yards, Punt Returns, Game
231   Detroit vs. San Francisco, Oct. 6, 1963
225   Oakland vs. Buffalo, Sept. 15, 1968
219   L.A. Rams vs. Atlanta, Oct. 11, 1981

Fewest Yards, Punt Returns, Game
-28   Washington vs. Dallas, Dec. 11, 1966
-23   N.Y. Giants vs. Buffalo, Oct. 20, 1975
    Pittsburgh vs. Houston, Sept. 20, 1970
-20   New Orleans vs. Pittsburgh, Oct. 20, 1968

Most Yards, Punt Returns, Both Teams, Game
282   L.A. Rams (219) vs. Atlanta (63), Oct. 11, 1981
245   Detroit (231) vs. San Francisco (14), Oct. 6, 1963
244   Oakland (225) vs. Buffalo (19), Sept. 15, 1968

Fewest Yards, Punt Returns, Both Teams, Game
-18   Buffalo (-18) vs. Pittsburgh (0), Oct. 29, 1972
-14   Miami (-14) vs. Boston (0), Nov. 30, 1969
    Tennessee (-14) vs. New Orleans (0),
       Sept. 21, 2003
-13   N.Y. Giants (-13) vs. Cleveland (0), Nov. 14, 1965

AVERAGE YARDS RETURNING PUNTS
Highest Average, Punt Returns, Season
20.2   Chi. Bears, 1941
19.1   Chi. Cardinals, 1948
18.2   Chi. Cardinals, 1949

Lowest Average, Punt Returns, Season
1.2   St. Louis, 1965 (23-27)
1.5   N.Y. Giants, 1965 (24-35)
1.7   Washington, 1970 (27-45)

TOUCHDOWNS RETURNING PUNTS
Most Touchdowns, Punt Returns, Season
5   Chi. Cardinals, 1959
4   Chi. Cardinals, 1948
   Detroit, 1951
   N.Y. Giants, 1951
   Denver, 1976
   Chicago, 2007
   Arizona, 2011
3   Washington, 1941
   Detroit, 1952
   Pittsburgh, 1952
   Houston, 1975
   Los Angeles, 1981

Cleveland, 1993
Green Bay, 1996
Denver, 1997
San Diego, 1997
Chicago, 2006
Tennessee, 2006
New Orleans, 2008
Oakland, 2008
Chicago, 2010
Dallas, 2010

Most Touchdowns, Punt Returns, Game
2   Detroit vs. Los Angeles, Oct. 14, 1951
   Detroit vs. Green Bay, Nov. 22, 1951
   Chi. Cardinals vs. Pittsburgh, Nov. 1, 1959
   Chi. Cardinals vs. N.Y. Giants, Nov. 22, 1959
   N.Y. Titans vs. Denver, Sept. 24, 1961
   Denver vs. Cleveland, Sept. 26, 1976
   Los Angeles vs. Atlanta, Oct. 11, 1981
   St. Louis vs. Tampa Bay, Dec. 21, 1986
   L.A. Rams vs. Atlanta, Dec. 27, 1992
   Cleveland vs. Pittsburgh, Oct. 24, 1993
   San Diego vs. Cincinnati, Nov. 2, 1997
   Denver vs. Carolina, Nov. 9, 1997
   Baltimore vs. Seattle, Dec. 7, 1997
   Baltimore vs. N.Y. Jets, Dec. 24, 2000
   Oakland vs. Tennessee, Sept. 29, 2002
   Carolina vs. Cincinnati, Dec. 8, 2002
   Detroit at Jacksonville, Nov. 14, 2004 (ot)
   New Orleans vs. Minnesota, Oct. 6, 2008

Most Touchdowns, Punt Returns, Both Teams, Game
2   Philadelphia (1) vs. Washington (1), Nov. 9, 1952
   Kansas City (1) vs. Buffalo (1), Sept. 11, 1966
   Baltimore (1) vs. New England (1), Nov. 18, 1979
   L.A. Raiders (1) vs. Philadelphia (1),
     Nov. 30, 1986 (ot)
   Cincinnati (1) vs. Green Bay (1), Sept. 20, 1992
   Oakland (1) vs. Seattle (1), Nov. 15, 1998
   Atlanta (1) vs. Tennessee (1), Nov. 23, 2003
   San Diego (1) vs. Denver (1), Oct. 19, 2009
   St. Louis (1) vs. Arizona (1), Nov. 27, 2011
(Also see previous record)

KICKOFF RETURNS
Most Seasons Leading League (Average Return)
8   Washington, 1942, 1947, 1962-63, 1973-74, 1981,
    1995
6   Chicago Bears, 1943, 1948, 1958, 1966, 1972, 1985
   N.Y. Giants, 1944, 1946, 1949, 1951, 1953, 2004
5   Green Bay, 1954, 1964, 1967, 1993, 1998
   New England, 1977, 1980, 1982, 1997, 2006
   Hou. Oilers/ Tenn. Titans, 1960, 1962-63, 1968, 2008

Most Consecutive Seasons Leading League (Average Return)
3   Denver, 1965-67
2   By many teams

Most Kickoff Returns, Season
96   Detroit, 2009
89   Cleveland, 1999
88   New Orleans, 1980

Fewest Kickoff Returns, Season
17   N.Y. Giants, 1944
20   N.Y. Giants, 1941, 1943
   Chi. Bears, 1942
23   Washington, 1942

Most Kickoff Returns, Game
12   N.Y. Giants vs. Washington, Nov. 27, 1966
11   Kansas City vs. Buffalo, Nov. 23, 2008
10   By many teams

Most Kickoff Returns, Both Teams, Game
19   N.Y. Giants (12) vs. Washington (7), Nov. 27, 1966
   Cleveland (10) vs. Cincinnati (9), Nov. 28, 2004

18 Houston (10) vs. Oakland (8), Dec. 22, 1963
17 Washington (9) vs. Green Bay (8), Oct. 17, 1983
San Diego (9) vs. Pittsburgh (8), Dec. 8, 1985
Detroit (9) vs. Green Bay (8), Nov. 27, 1986
L.A. Raiders (9) vs. Seattle (8), Dec. 18, 1988
Oakland (10) vs. Seattle (7), Oct. 26, 1997
Buffalo (9) vs. Minnesota (8), Sept. 15, 2002 (ot)
Cincinnati (10) vs. Cleveland (7), Sept. 16, 2007
Kansas City (11) vs. Buffalo (6), Nov. 23, 2008

YARDS GAINED
Most Yards, Kickoff Returns, Season
2,296 Arizona, 2000
2,173 Houston, 2005
2,084 Arizona, 2010
Fewest Yards, Kickoff Returns, Season
282 N.Y. Giants, 1940
381 Green Bay, 1940
424 Chicago, 1963
Most Yards, Kickoff Returns, Game
367 Baltimore vs. Minnesota, Dec. 13, 1998
362 Detroit vs. Los Angeles, Oct. 29, 1950
304 Chi. Bears vs. Green Bay, Nov. 9, 1952
New Orleans vs. L.A. Rams, Oct. 23, 1994
Most Yards, Kickoff Returns, Both Teams, Game
560 Detroit (362) vs. L.A. Rams (198), Oct. 29, 1950
511 Baltimore (367) vs. Minnesota (144), Dec. 13, 1998
501 New Orleans (304) vs. L.A. Rams (197), Oct. 23, 1994

AVERAGE YARDAGE
Highest Average, Kickoff Returns, Season
29.4 Chicago, 1972
28.9 Pittsburgh, 1952
28.2 Washington, 1962
Lowest Average, Kickoff Returns, Season
14.7 N.Y. Jets, 1993 (46-675)
15.8 N.Y. Giants, 1993 (32-507)
15.9 Tampa Bay, 1993 (58-922)

TOUCHDOWNS
Most Touchdowns, Kickoff Returns, Season
4 Green Bay, 1967
Chicago, 1970
Detroit, 1994
Houston, 2007
3 Los Angeles, 1950
Chi. Cardinals, 1954
San Francisco, 1963
Denver, 1966
Chicago, 1967
New England, 1977
L.A. Rams, 1985
Atlanta, 2000
Buffalo, 2004
N.Y. Jets, 2007
Cleveland, 2009
Oakland, 2010
Seattle, 2010
2 By many teams
Most Touchdowns, Kickoff Returns, Game
2 Chi. Bears vs. Green Bay, Sept. 22, 1940
Chi. Bears vs. Green Bay, Nov. 9, 1952
Philadelphia vs. Dallas, Nov. 6, 1966
Green Bay vs. Cleveland, Nov. 12, 1967
L.A. Rams vs. Green Bay, Nov. 24, 1985
New Orleans vs. L.A. Rams, Oct. 23, 1994
Baltimore vs. Minnesota, Dec. 13, 1998
N.Y. Jets vs. Buffalo, Sept. 8, 2002 (ot)
Chicago vs. St. Louis, Dec. 11, 2006

Houston vs. Jacksonville, Dec. 30, 2007
Miami vs. N.Y. Jets, Nov. 1, 2009
Cleveland vs. Kansas City, Dec. 20, 2009
Seattle vs. San Diego, Sept. 26, 2010
Most Touchdowns, Kickoff Returns, Both Teams, Game
3 Baltimore (2) vs. Minnesota (1), Dec. 13, 1998
2 In many games

FUMBLES
Most Fumbles, Season
56 Chi. Bears, 1938
San Francisco, 1978
54 Philadelphia, 1946
51 New England, 1973
Fewest Fumbles, Season
6 New Orleans, 2011
7 Kansas City, 2002
8 Cleveland, 1959
Most Fumbles, Game
10 Phil-Pitt vs. N.Y. Giants, Oct. 9, 1943
Detroit vs. Minnesota, Nov. 12, 1967
Kansas City vs. Houston, Oct. 12, 1969
San Francisco vs. Detroit, Dec. 17, 1978
9 Philadelphia vs. Green Bay, Oct. 13, 1946
Boston at Oakland, Dec. 16, 1962
Kansas City vs. San Diego, Nov. 15, 1964
N.Y. Giants vs. Buffalo, Oct. 20, 1975
St. Louis vs. Washington, Oct. 25, 1976
San Diego vs. Green Bay, Sept. 24, 1978
Pittsburgh vs. Cincinnati, Oct. 14, 1979
Cleveland vs. Seattle, Dec. 20, 1981
Cleveland vs. Pittsburgh, Dec. 23, 1990
Oakland vs. Seattle, Dec. 22, 1996
8 By many teams
Most Fumbles, Both Teams, Game
14 Chi. Bears (7) vs. Cleveland (7), Nov. 24, 1940
St. Louis (8) vs. N.Y. Giants (6), Sept. 17, 1961
Kansas City (10) vs. Houston (4), Oct. 12, 1969
13 Washington (8) vs. Pittsburgh (5), Nov. 14, 1937
Philadelphia (7) vs. Boston (6), Dec. 8, 1946
N.Y. Giants (7) vs. Washington (6), Nov. 5, 1950
Kansas City (9) vs. San Diego (4), Nov. 15, 1964
Buffalo (7) vs. Denver (6), Dec. 13, 1964
N.Y. Jets (7) vs. Houston (6), Sept. 12, 1965
Cleveland (7) vs. New Orleans (6), Dec. 12, 1971
Houston (8) vs. Pittsburgh (5), Dec. 9, 1973
St. Louis (9) vs. Washington (4), Oct. 25, 1976
Cleveland (9) vs. Seattle (4), Dec. 20, 1981
Green Bay (7) vs. Detroit (6), Oct. 6, 1985
12 In many games

FUMBLES LOST
Most Fumbles Lost, Season
36 Chi. Cardinals, 1959
31 Green Bay, 1952
29 Chi. Cardinals, 1946
Pittsburgh, 1950
Cleveland, 1978
Fewest Fumbles Lost, Season
2 Kansas City, 2002
3 Philadelphia, 1938
Minnesota, 1980
N.Y. Giants, 2008
4 San Francisco, 1960
Kansas City, 1982
Minnesota, 1998
Detroit, 2003
Most Fumbles Lost, Game
8 St. Louis vs. Washington, Oct. 25, 1976
Cleveland vs. Pittsburgh, Dec. 23, 1990

7   Cincinnati vs. Buffalo, Nov. 30, 1969
    Pittsburgh vs. Cincinnati, Oct. 14, 1979
    Cleveland vs. Seattle, Dec. 20, 1981
6   By many teams

FUMBLES RECOVERED
Most Fumbles Recovered, Season, Own and Opponents'
58 Minnesota, 1963 (27 own, 31 opp)
51 Chi. Bears, 1938 (37 own, 14 opp)
    San Francisco, 1978 (24 own, 27 opp)
50 Philadelphia, 1987 (23 own, 27 opp)
Fewest Fumbles Recovered, Season, Own and Opponents'
7   New Orleans, 2011 (0 own, 7 opp)
    Pittsburgh, 2011 (3 own, 4 opp)
9   San Francisco, 1982 (5 own, 4 opp)
10 Jacksonville, 2006 (6 own, 4 opp)
Most Fumbles Recovered, Game, Own and Opponents'
10 Denver vs. Buffalo, Dec. 13, 1964 (5 own, 5 opp)
    Pittsburgh vs. Houston, Dec. 9, 1973 (5 own, 5 opp)
    Washington vs. St. Louis, Oct. 25, 1976
    (2 own, 8 opp)
9   St. Louis vs. N.Y. Giants, Sept. 17, 1961
    (6 own, 3 opp)
    Houston vs. Cincinnati, Oct. 27, 1974 (4 own, 5 opp)
    Kansas City vs. Dallas, Nov. 10, 1975 (4 own, 5 opp)
    Green Bay vs. Detroit, Oct. 6, 1985 (5 own, 4 opp)
    Pittsburgh vs. Cleveland, Dec. 23, 1990
    (1 own, 8 opp)
8   By many teams
Most Own Fumbles Recovered, Season
37 Chi. Bears, 1938
28 Pittsburgh, 1987
27 Philadelphia, 1946
    Minnesota, 1963
Fewest Own Fumbles Recovered, Season
0   New Orleans, 2011
1   Indianapolis, 2006
    Philadelphia, 2008
2   Washington, 1958
    Miami, 2000
    Atlanta, 2011
Most Opponents' Fumbles Recovered, Season
31 Minnesota, 1963
29 Cleveland, 1951
28 Green Bay, 1946
    Houston, 1977
    Seattle, 1983
Fewest Opponents' Fumbles Recovered, Season
3   Los Angeles, 1974
    Green Bay, 1995
    Miami, 2011
4   Philadelphia, 1944
    San Francisco, 1982
    Jacksonville, 2006
    Jacksonville, 2008
    Pittsburgh, 2011
    San Diego, 2011
5   Baltimore, 1982
    Arizona, 1997
    Baltimore, 1998
    Chicago, 2003
    Oakland, 2006
    N.Y. Giants, 2008
    Washington, 2008
    Buffalo, 2009
    Houston, 2010
    Jacksonville, 2010
Most Opponents' Fumbles Recovered, Game
8   Washington vs. St. Louis, Oct. 25, 1976
    Pittsburgh vs. Cleveland, Dec. 23, 1990

7   Buffalo vs. Cincinnati, Nov. 30, 1969
    Cincinnati vs. Pittsburgh, Oct. 14, 1979
    Seattle vs. Cleveland, Dec. 20, 1981
6   By many teams

TOUCHDOWNS
Most Touchdowns, Fumbles Recovered, Season,
Own and Opponents'
7   Arizona, 2010 (3 own, 4 opp)
5   Chi. Bears, 1942 (1 own, 4 opp)
    Los Angeles, 1952 (1 own, 4 opp)
    San Francisco, 1965 (1 own, 4 opp)
    Oakland, 1978 (2 own, 3 opp)
4   Chi. Bears, 1948 (1 own, 3 opp)
    Boston, 1948 (4 opp)
    Denver, 1979 (1 own, 3 opp)
    Atlanta, 1981 (1 own, 3 opp)
    Denver, 1984 (4 opp)
    St. Louis, 1987 (4 opp)
    Minnesota, 1989 (4 opp)
    Atlanta, 1991 (4 opp)
    Philadelphia, 1995 (4 opp)
    Atlanta, 1998 (4 opp)
    New Orleans, 1998 (4 opp)
    Kansas City, 1999 (4 opp)
Most Touchdowns, Own Fumbles Recovered, Season
3   Arizona, 2010
2   Chi. Bears, 1953
    New England, 1973
    Buffalo, 1974
    Denver, 1975
    Oakland, 1978
    Green Bay, 1982
    New Orleans, 1983
    Cleveland, 1986
    Green Bay, 1989
    Miami, 1996
    Buffalo, 2000
    Philadelphia, 2007
Most Touchdowns, Opponents' Fumbles Recovered, Season
4   Detroit, 1937
    Chi. Bears, 1942
    Boston, 1948
    Los Angeles, 1952
    San Francisco, 1965
    Denver, 1984
    St. Louis, 1987
    Minnesota, 1989
    Atlanta, 1991
    Philadelphia, 1995
    Atlanta, 1998
    New Orleans, 1998
    Kansas City, 1999
    Arizona, 2010
3   By many teams
Most Touchdowns, Fumbles Recovered, Game,
Own and Opponents'
2   By many teams
Most Touchdowns, Fumbles Recovered, Game, Both Teams,
Own and Opponents'
3   Detroit (2) vs. Minnesota (1), Dec. 9, 1962
    (2 own, 1 opp)
    Green Bay (2) vs. Dallas (1), Nov. 29, 1964 (3 opp)
    Oakland (2) vs. Buffalo (1), Dec. 24, 1967 (3 opp)
    Oakland (2) vs. Philadelphia (1), Sept. 24, 1995
    (3 opp)
    Tennessee (2) vs. Pittsburgh (1), Jan. 2, 2000
    (3 opp)
Most Touchdowns, Own Fumbles Recovered, Game
2   Miami vs. New England, Sept.1, 1996

Most Touchdowns, Opponents' Fumbles Recovered, Game
2 Many times. Last time:
   Jacksonville vs. Tampa Bay, Dec. 11, 2011
Most Touchdowns, Opponents' Fumbles Recovered, Game, Both Teams
3 Green Bay (2) vs. Dallas (1), Nov. 29, 1964
   Oakland (2) vs. Buffalo (1), Dec. 24, 1967
   Oakland (2) vs. Philadelphia (1), Sept. 24, 1995
   Tennessee (2) vs. Pittsburgh (1), Jan. 2, 2000

TURNOVERS
(Number of times losing the ball on interceptions and fumbles.)
Most Turnovers, Season
65 Denver, 1961
63 San Francisco, 1978
58 Chi. Bears, 1947
   Pittsburgh, 1950
   N.Y. Giants, 1983
Fewest Turnovers, Season
10 New England, 2010
   San Francisco, 2011
12 Kansas City, 1982
13 Miami, 2008
   N.Y. Giants, 2008
Most Turnovers, Game
12 Detroit vs. Chi. Bears, Nov. 22, 1942
   Chi. Cardinals vs. Philadelphia, Sept. 24, 1950
   Pittsburgh vs. Philadelphia, Dec. 12, 1965
11 San Diego vs. Green Bay, Sept. 24, 1978
10 Washington vs. N.Y. Giants, Dec. 4, 1938
   Pittsburgh vs. Green Bay, Nov. 23, 1941
   Detroit vs. Green Bay, Oct. 24, 1943
   Chi. Cardinals vs. Green Bay, Nov. 10, 1946
   Chi. Cardinals vs. N.Y. Giants, Nov. 2, 1952
   Minnesota vs. Detroit, Dec. 9, 1962
   Houston vs. Oakland, Sept. 7, 1963
   Washington vs. N.Y. Giants, Dec. 8, 1963
   Chicago vs. Detroit, Sept. 22, 1968
   St. Louis vs. Washington, Oct. 25, 1976
   N.Y. Jets vs. New England, Nov. 21, 1976
   San Francisco vs. Dallas, Oct. 12, 1980
   Cleveland vs. Seattle, Dec. 20, 1981
   Detroit vs. Denver, Oct. 7, 1984
Most Turnovers, Both Teams, Game
17 Detroit (12) vs. Chi. Bears (5), Nov. 22, 1942
   Boston (9) vs. Philadelphia (8), Dec. 8, 1946
16 Chi. Cardinals (12) vs. Philadelphia (4),
      Sept. 24, 1950
   Chi. Cardinals (8) vs. Chi. Bears (8), Dec. 7, 1958
   Minnesota (10) vs. Detroit (6), Dec. 9, 1962
   Houston (9) vs. Kansas City (7), Oct. 12, 1969
15 Philadelphia (8) vs. Chi. Cardinals (7), Oct. 3, 1954
   Denver (9) vs. Houston (6), Dec. 2, 1962
   Washington (10) vs. N.Y. Giants (5), Dec. 8, 1963
   St. Louis (9) vs. Kansas City (6), Oct. 2, 1983

PENALTIES
Most Seasons Leading League, Fewest Penalties
13 Miami, 1968, 1976-1984, 1986, 1990-91
9 Pittsburgh, 1946-47, 1950-52, 1954, 1963, 1965, 1968
8 Boston/New England, 1962, 1964-65, 1973, 1987, 1989, 1993, 2008
Most Consecutive Seasons Leading League, Fewest Penalties
9 Miami, 1976-1984
3 Pittsburgh, 1950-52
2 By many teams
Most Seasons Leading League, Most Penalties
17 Oakland/L.A. Raiders, 1963, 1966, 1968-69, 1975, 1982, 1984, 1991, 1993-96, 2003-05, 2010-11

16 Chi. Bears, 1941-44, 1946-49, 1951, 1959-1961, 1963, 1965, 1968, 1976
7 L.A./St. Louis Rams, 1950, 1952, 1962, 1969, 1978, 1980, 1997
Most Consecutive Seasons Leading League, Most Penalties
4 Chi. Bears, 1941-44, 1946-49
   Oakland/L.A. Raiders, 1993-96
3 Chi. Cardinals, 1954-56
   Chi. Bears, 1959-1961
   Oakland, 2003-05
Fewest Penalties, Season
19 Detroit, 1937
21 Boston, 1935
24 Philadelphia, 1936
Most Penalties, Season
163 Oakland, 2011
158 Kansas City, 1998
156 L.A. Raiders, 1994
   Oakland, 1996
Fewest Penalties, Game
0 By many teams. Last time:
   Green Bay vs. Chicago, Dec. 25, 2011
Most Penalties, Game
22 Brooklyn vs. Green Bay, Sept. 17, 1944
   Chi. Bears vs. Philadelphia, Nov. 26, 1944
   San Francisco vs. Buffalo, Oct. 4, 1998
21 Cleveland vs. Chi. Bears, Nov. 25, 1951
   Baltimore vs. Detroit, Oct. 9, 2005
20 Tampa Bay vs. Seattle, Oct. 17, 1976
   Oakland vs. Denver, Dec. 15, 1996
Fewest Penalties, Both Teams, Game
0 Brooklyn vs. Pittsburgh, Oct. 28, 1934
   Brooklyn vs. Boston, Sept. 28, 1936
   Cleveland vs. Chi. Bears, Oct. 9, 1938
   Pittsburgh vs. Philadelphia, Nov. 10, 1940
Most Penalties, Both Teams, Game
37 Cleveland (21) vs. Chi. Bears (16), Nov. 25, 1951
35 Tampa Bay (20) vs. Seattle (15), Oct. 17, 1976
34 San Francisco (22) vs. Buffalo (12), Oct. 4, 1998

YARDS PENALIZED
Most Seasons Leading League, Fewest Yards Penalized
14 Miami, 1967-68, 1973, 1977-1984, 1990-91, 2010
10 Boston/Washington, 1935, 1953-54, 1956-58, 1970, 1985, 1995, 1997
8 Boston/New England, 1962, 1964-66, 1987, 1989, 1993, 2008
Most Consecutive Seasons Leading League, Fewest Yards Penalized
8 Miami, 1977-1984
3 Washington, 1956-58
   Boston, 1964-66
2 By many teams
Most Seasons Leading League, Most Yards Penalized
15 Chi. Bears, 1935, 1937, 1939-1944, 1946-47, 1949, 1951, 1961-62, 1968
14 Oakland/L.A. Raiders, 1963-64, 1968-69, 1975, 1982, 1984, 1991, 1993-94, 1996, 2003, 2010-11
6 Buffalo, 1962, 1967, 1970, 1972, 1981, 1983
   Houston, 1961, 1985-86, 1988-1990
Most Consecutive Seasons Leading League, Most Yards Penalized
6 Chi. Bears, 1939-1944
3 Houston, 1988-1990
2 By many teams
Fewest Yards Penalized, Season
139 Detroit, 1937
146 Philadelphia, 1937
159 Philadelphia, 1936

Most Yards Penalized, Season
- 1,358   Oakland, 2011
- 1,304   Kansas City, 1998
- 1,276   Oakland, 2010

Fewest Yards Penalized, Game
- 0   By many teams. Last time:
  Green Bay vs. Chicago, Dec. 25, 2011

Most Yards Penalized, Game
- 212   Tennessee vs. Baltimore, Oct. 10, 1999
- 209   Cleveland vs. Chi. Bears, Nov. 25, 1951
- 191   Philadelphia vs. Seattle, Dec. 13, 1992 (ot)

Fewest Yards Penalized, Both Teams, Game
- 0   Brooklyn vs. Pittsburgh, Oct. 28, 1934
  Brooklyn vs. Boston, Sept. 28, 1936
  Cleveland vs. Chi. Bears, Oct. 9, 1938
  Pittsburgh vs. Philadelphia, Nov. 10, 1940

Most Yards Penalized, Both Teams, Game
- 374   Cleveland (209) vs. Chi. Bears (165), Nov. 25, 1951
- 310   Tampa Bay (190) vs. Seattle (120), Oct. 17, 1976
  Green Bay (175) vs. Baltimore (135), Dec. 7, 2009
- 309   Green Bay (184) vs. Boston (125), Oct. 21, 1945

DEFENSE

SCORING

Most Seasons Leading League, Fewest Points Allowed
- 11   N.Y. Giants, 1927, 1935, 1938-39, 1941, 1944, 1958-59, 1961, 1990, 1993
  Chi. Bears, 1932, 1936-37, 1942, 1948, 1963, 1985-86, 1988, 2001, 2005
- 7   Cleveland, 1951, 1953-57, 1994
  Green Bay, 1929, 1935, 1947, 1962, 1965-66, 1996
  Pittsburgh, 1946, 1976, 1978, 2004, 2008, 2010-11
- 6   Dallas/Kansas City, 1960, 1962, 1968-69, 1995, 1997

Most Consecutive Seasons Leading League, Fewest Points Allowed
- 5   Cleveland, 1953-57
- 3   Buffalo, 1964-66
  Minnesota, 1969-1971
- 2   By many teams

Fewest Points Allowed, Season (Since 1932)
- 44   Chi. Bears, 1932
- 54   Brooklyn, 1933
- 59   Detroit, 1934

Most Points Allowed, Season
- 533   Baltimore, 1981
- 517   Detroit, 2008
- 501   N.Y. Giants, 1966

Fewest TDs Allowed, Season (Since 1932)
- 6   Chi. Bears, 1932
  Brooklyn, 1933
- 7   Detroit, 1934
- 8   Green Bay, 1932

Most Touchdowns Allowed, Season
- 68   Baltimore, 1981
- 66   N.Y. Giants, 1966
- 63   Baltimore, 1950
  Detroit, 2008

FIRST DOWNS

Fewest First Downs Allowed, Season
- 77   Detroit, 1935
- 79   Boston, 1935
- 82   Washington, 1937

Most First Downs Allowed, Season
- 406   Baltimore, 1981
- 371   Seattle, 1981
- 370   New England, 2011

Fewest First Downs Allowed, Rushing, Season
- 35   Chi. Bears, 1942
- 40   Green Bay, 1939
- 41   Brooklyn, 1944

Most First Downs Allowed, Rushing, Season
- 179   Detroit, 1985
- 178   New Orleans, 1980
- 175   Seattle, 1981

Fewest First Downs Allowed, Passing, Season
- 33   Chi. Bears, 1943
- 34   Pittsburgh, 1941
  Washington, 1943
- 35   Detroit, 1940
  Philadelphia, 1940
  Philadelphia, 1944

Most First Downs Allowed, Passing, Season
- 246   Green Bay, 2011
- 245   New England, 2011
- 230   Atlanta, 1995

Fewest First Downs Allowed, Penalty, Season
- 1   Boston, 1944
- 3   Philadelphia, 1940
  Pittsburgh, 1945
  Washington, 1957
- 4   Cleveland, 1940
  Green Bay, 1943
  N.Y. Giants, 1943

Most First Downs Allowed, Penalty, Season
- 58   Oakland, 2011
- 56   Kansas City, 1998
- 48   Houston, 1985

NET YARDS ALLOWED RUSHING AND PASSING

Most Seasons Leading League, Fewest Yards Allowed
- 9   Pittsburgh, 1957, 1974, 1976, 1990, 2001, 2004, 2007-08, 2011
- 8   Chi. Bears, 1942-43, 1948, 1958, 1963, 1984-86
- 6   N.Y. Giants, 1938, 1940-41, 1951, 1956, 1959
  Philadelphia, 1944-45, 1949, 1953, 1981, 1991
  Minnesota, 1969-1970, 1975, 1988-89, 1993

Most Consecutive Seasons Leading League, Fewest Yards Allowed
- 3   Boston/Washington, 1935-37
  Chicago, 1984-86
- 2   By many teams

Fewest Yards Allowed, Season
- 1,539   Chi. Cardinals, 1934
- 1,703   Chi. Bears, 1942
- 1,789   Brooklyn, 1933

Most Yards Allowed, Season
- 6,793   Baltimore, 1981
- 6,585   Green Bay, 2011
- 6,577   New England, 2011

RUSHING

Most Seasons Leading League, Fewest Yards Allowed
- 10   Chi. Bears, 1937, 1939, 1942, 1946, 1949, 1963, 1984-85, 1987-88
- 8   Pittsburgh, 1961, 1976, 1982, 1997, 2001-02, 2004, 2010
- 7   Detroit, 1938, 1950, 1952, 1962, 1970, 1980-81
  Philadelphia, 1944-45, 1947-48, 1953, 1990-91
  Dallas, 1966-69, 1972, 1978, 1992

Most Consecutive Seasons Leading League, Fewest Yards Allowed
- 4   Dallas, 1966-69
- 3   Minnesota, 2006-08
- 2   By many teams

Fewest Yards Allowed, Rushing, Season
- 519   Chi. Bears, 1942
- 558   Philadelphia, 1944

762   Pittsburgh, 1982
Most Yards Allowed, Rushing, Season
3,228   Buffalo, 1978
3,106   New Orleans, 1980
3,010   Baltimore, 1978
Fewest Touchdowns Allowed, Rushing, Season
2   Detroit, 1934
   N.Y. Giants, 1944
   Dallas, 1968
   Minnesota, 1971
3   By many teams
Most Touchdowns Allowed, Rushing, Season
36   Oakland, 1961
31   N.Y. Giants, 1980
   Tampa Bay, 1986
   Detroit, 2008
30   Baltimore, 1981

PASSING
Most Seasons Leading League, Fewest Yards Allowed
10   Green Bay, 1947-48, 1962, 1964-68, 1996, 2005
8   Pittsburgh, 1941, 1946, 1951, 1955, 1974, 1990, 2008, 2011
7   Washington, 1939, 1942, 1945, 1952-53, 1980, 1985
   Philadelphia 1934, 1936, 1940, 1949, 1981, 1991, 1998
Most Consecutive Seasons Leading League, Fewest Yards Allowed
5   Green Bay, 1964-68
2   By many teams
Fewest Yards Allowed Passing, Season
545   Philadelphia, 1934
558   Portsmouth, 1933
585   Chi. Cardinals, 1934
Most Yards Allowed, Passing, Season
4,796   Green Bay, 2011
4,703   New England, 2011
4,541   Atlanta, 1995
Fewest Touchdowns Allowed, Passing, Season
1   Portsmouth, 1932
   Philadelphia, 1934
2   Brooklyn, 1933
   Chi. Bears, 1934
3   Chi. Bears, 1932
   Green Bay, 1932
   Green Bay, 1934
   Chi. Bears, 1936
   New York, 1939
   New York, 1944
Most Touchdowns Allowed, Passing, Season
40   Denver, 1963
38   St. Louis, 1969
37   Washington, 1961
   Baltimore, 1981

SACKS
Most Seasons Leading League
5   Oakland/L.A. Raiders, 1966-68, 1982, 1986
   Dallas, 1966, 1968-69, 1978, 2008
4   New England/Boston, 1961, 1963, 1977, 1979
   Dallas/Kansas City, 1960, 1965, 1969, 1990
   L.A./St. Louis Rams, 1968, 1970, 1988, 1999
   N.Y. Giants, 1963, 1985, 1998, 2007
   Pittsburgh, 1974, 1994, 2001, 2010
3   San Francisco, 1967, 1972, 1976
   N.Y. Giants, 1963, 1985, 1998
   New Orleans, 1992, 1997, 2000
   San Diego, 1962, 1980, 2006
   Philadelphia, 1991, 2002, 2011

Most Consecutive Seasons Leading League
3   Oakland, 1966-68
2   Dallas, 1968-69
Most Sacks, Season
72   Chicago, 1984
71   Minnesota, 1989
70   Chicago, 1987
Fewest Sacks, Season
10   Kansas City, 2008
11   Baltimore, 1982
12   Buffalo, 1982
Most Sacks, Game
12   Dallas vs. Pittsburgh, Nov. 20, 1966
   St. Louis vs. Baltimore, Oct. 26, 1980
   Chicago vs. Detroit, Dec. 16, 1984
   Dallas vs. Houston, Sept. 29, 1985
   N.Y. Giants vs. Philadelphia, Sept. 30, 2007
11   N.Y. Giants vs. St. Louis, Nov. 1, 1964
   Baltimore vs. Los Angeles, Nov. 22, 1964
   Buffalo vs. Denver, Dec. 13, 1964
   Detroit vs. Green Bay, Nov. 7, 1965
   Oakland vs. Buffalo, Oct. 15, 1967
   Oakland vs. Denver, Nov. 5, 1967
   St. Louis vs. Atlanta, Nov. 24, 1968
   Dallas vs. Detroit, Oct. 6, 1975
   St. Louis vs. Philadelphia, Dec. 18, 1983
   Kansas City vs. Cleveland, Sept. 30, 1984
   Chicago vs. Minnesota, Oct. 28, 1984
   Cleveland vs. Atlanta, Nov. 18, 1984
   Detroit vs. Philadelphia, Nov. 16, 1986
   San Diego vs. Dallas, Nov. 16, 1986
   L.A. Raiders vs. Philadelphia, Nov. 30, 1986 (ot)
   Seattle vs. L.A. Raiders, Dec. 8, 1986
   Chicago vs. Philadelphia, Oct. 4, 1987
   Dallas vs. N.Y. Jets, Oct. 4, 1987
   Philadelphia vs. Dallas, Sept. 15, 1991
   Indianapolis vs. Cleveland, Sept. 6, 1992
10   By many teams
Most Opponents Yards Lost Attempting to Pass, Season
666   Oakland, 1967
583   Chicago, 1984
573   San Francisco, 1976
Fewest Opponents Yards Lost Attempting to Pass, Season
62   Kansas City, 2008
72   Jacksonville, 1995
75   Green Bay, 1956

INTERCEPTIONS BY
Most Seasons Leading League
10   N.Y. Giants, 1933, 1937-39, 1944, 1948, 1951, 1954, 1961, 1997
   Green Bay, 1940, 1942-43, 1947, 1955, 1957, 1962, 1965, 2009, 2011
8   Chi. Bears, 1935-36, 1941-42, 1946, 1963, 1985, 1990
6   Kansas City, 1966-1970, 1974
Most Consecutive Seasons Leading League
5   Kansas City, 1966-1970
3   N.Y. Giants, 1937-39
2   By many teams
Most Passes Intercepted, Season
49   San Diego, 1961
42   Green Bay, 1943
41   N.Y. Giants, 1951
Fewest Passes Intercepted By, Season
3   Houston, 1982
4   Detroit, 2008
5   Baltimore, 1982
   Oakland, 2005

Most Passes Intercepted By, Game
- 9   Green Bay vs. Detroit, Oct. 24, 1943
-     Philadelphia vs. Pittsburgh, Dec. 12, 1965
- 8   N.Y. Giants vs. Green Bay, Nov. 21, 1948
-     Philadelphia vs. Chi. Cardinals, Sept. 24, 1950
-     N.Y. Giants vs. N.Y. Yanks, Dec. 16, 1951
-     Houston vs. Denver, Dec. 2, 1962
-     Detroit vs. Chicago, Sept. 22, 1968
-     N.Y. Jets vs. Baltimore, Sept. 23, 1973
- 7   By many teams. Last time:
-       Cleveland vs. Detroit, Sept. 23, 2001

Most Consecutive Games, One or More Interceptions By
- 46   L.A. Chargers/San Diego, 1960-63
- 37   Detroit, 1960-63
- 36   Boston, 1944-47

Most Yards Returning Interceptions, Season
- 929   San Diego, 1961
- 712   Los Angeles, 1952
- 700   Baltimore, 2004

Fewest Yards Returning Interceptions, Season
- 5   Los Angeles, 1959
- 16   Detroit, 2008
- 25   Washington, 2006

Most Yards Returning Interceptions, Game
- 325   Seattle vs. Kansas City, Nov. 4, 1984
- 314   Los Angeles vs. San Francisco, Oct. 18, 1964
- 245   Houston vs. N.Y. Jets, Oct. 15, 1967

Most Yards Returning Interceptions, Both Teams, Game
- 356   Seattle (325) vs. Kansas City (31), Nov. 4, 1984
- 338   Los Angeles (314) vs. San Francisco (24),
-       Oct. 18, 1964
- 308   Dallas (182) vs. Los Angeles (126), Nov. 2, 1952

Most Touchdowns, Returning Interceptions, Season
- 9   San Diego, 1961
- 8   Seattle, 1998
- 7   Seattle, 1984
-     St. Louis, 1999

Most Touchdowns Returning Interceptions, Game
- 4   Seattle vs. Kansas City, Nov. 4, 1984
- 3   Baltimore vs. Green Bay, Nov. 5, 1950
-     Cleveland vs. Chicago, Dec. 11, 1960
-     Philadelphia vs. Pittsburgh, Dec. 12, 1965
-     Baltimore vs. Pittsburgh, Sept. 29, 1968
-     Buffalo vs. N.Y. Jets, Sept. 29, 1968
-     Houston vs. San Diego, Dec. 19, 1971
-     Cincinnati vs. Houston, Dec. 17, 1972
-     Tampa Bay vs. New Orleans, Dec. 11, 1977
-     Minnesota vs. N.Y. Giants, Nov. 25, 2007
- 2   By many teams

Most Touchdown Returning Interceptions, Both Teams, Game
- 4   Philadelphia (3) vs. Pittsburgh (1), Dec. 12, 1965
-     Seattle (4) vs. Kansas City (0), Nov. 4, 1984
- 3   Los Angeles (2) vs. Detroit (1), Nov. 1, 1953
-     Cleveland (2) vs. N.Y. Giants (1), Dec. 18, 1960
-     Pittsburgh (2) vs. Cincinnati (1), Oct. 10, 1983
-     Kansas City (2) vs. San Diego (1), Oct. 19, 1986
-     Arizona (2) vs. St. Louis (1), Dec. 30, 2007
-     (Also see previous record)

PUNT RETURNS

Fewest Opponents Punt Returns, Season
- 7   Washington, 1962
-     San Diego, 1982
- 10   Buffalo, 1982
- 11   Boston, 1962
-     New England, 2008

Most Opponents Punt Returns, Season
- 71   Tampa Bay, 1976, 1977
- 69   N.Y. Giants, 1953
-     Cleveland, 2000

- 68   Cleveland, 1974
-     Cleveland, 1999

Fewest Yards Allowed, Punt Returns, Season
- 22   Green Bay, 1967
- 30   Buffalo, 1982
- 34   Washington, 1962

Most Yards Allowed, Punt Returns, Season
- 932   Green Bay, 1949
- 913   Boston, 1947
- 906   New Orleans, 1974

Lowest Avg. Allowed, Punt Returns, Season
- 1.20   Chi. Cardinals, 1954
- 1.22   Cleveland, 1959
- 1.55   Chi. Cardinals, 1953

Highest Average Allowed, Punt Returns, Season
- 18.9   San Diego, 2010 (28-528)
- 18.6   Green Bay, 1949 (50-932)
- 18.0   Cleveland, 1977 (31-558)

Most Touchdowns Allowed, Punt Returns, Season
- 4   Los Angeles, 1951
-     N.Y. Giants, 1959
-     Atlanta, 1992
-     Minnesota, 2008
- 3   Green Bay, 1949
-     Chi. Cardinals, 1951
-     L.A. Rams, 1951, 1994
-     Washington, 1952
-     Dallas, 1952
-     Pittsburgh, 1959, 1993
-     N.Y. Jets, 1968
-     Cleveland, 1977
-     Atlanta, 1986
-     Tampa Bay, 1986
-     Arizona, 2002
-     Cincinnati, 2002
-     Tennessee, 2002
-     Carolina, 2011
- 2   By many teams

KICKOFF RETURNS

Fewest Opponents Kickoff Returns, Season
- 10   Brooklyn, 1943
- 13   Denver, 1992
- 15   Detroit, 1942
-     Brooklyn, 1944

Most Opponents Kickoff Returns, Season
- 93   Indianapolis, 2003
- 92   Indianapolis, 2004
-     New England, 2007
- 91   Washington, 1983
-     Minnesota, 2009

Fewest Yards Allowed, Kickoff Returns, Season
- 225   Brooklyn, 1943
- 254   Denver, 1992
- 293   Brooklyn, 1944

Most Yards Allowed, Kickoff Returns, Season
- 2,194   St. Louis, 2001
- 2,115   St. Louis, 1999
- 2,060   Minnesota, 2009

Lowest Average Allowed, Kickoff Returns, Season
- 14.3   Cleveland, 1980
- 14.9   Indianapolis, 1993
- 15.0   Seattle, 1982

Highest Average Allowed, Kickoff Returns, Season
- 30.7   Indianapolis, 2011 (19-584)
- 29.5   N.Y. Jets, 1972 (47-1,386)
- 29.4   Los Angeles, 1950 (48-1,411)

Most Touchdowns Allowed, Kickoff Returns, Season
- 4   Minnesota, 1998
-     Pittsburgh, 2009

   3 Minnesota, 1963, 1970
      Dallas, 1966
      Detroit, 1980
      Pittsburgh, 1986
      Buffalo, 1997
      Atlanta, 2000
      Arizona, 2005
      Indianapolis, 2007
      San Diego, 2010
   2 By many teams

FUMBLES
Fewest Opponents Fumbles, Season
  11 Cleveland, 1956
      Baltimore, 1982
      Tennessee, 1998
      San Diego, 2011
  12 Green Bay, 1995
      Cincinnati, 1998
      Jacksonville, 2006
      Baltimore, 2007
      Jacksonville, 2010
  13 Los Angeles, 1956
      Chicago, 1960
      Cleveland, 1963
      Cleveland, 1965
      Detroit, 1967
      San Diego, 1969
      New England, 2005
      Cleveland, 2006
      San Diego, 2010
      Oakland, 2011
      Pittsburgh, 2011
Most Opponents Fumbles, Season
  50 Minnesota, 1963
      San Francisco, 1978
  48 N.Y. Giants, 1980
      N.Y. Jets, 1986
  47 N.Y. Giants, 1977
      Seattle, 1984

TURNOVERS
(Number of times losing the ball on interceptions and fumbles.)
Fewest Opponents Turnovers, Season
  11 Baltimore, 1982
  12 Washington, 2006
  13 San Francisco, 1982
      Denver, 2008
Most Opponent Turnovers, Season
  66 San Diego, 1961
  63 Seattle, 1984
  61 Washington, 1983
Most Opponent Turnovers, Game
  12 Chi. Bears vs. Detroit, Nov. 22, 1942
      Philadelphia vs. Chi. Cardinals, Sept. 24, 1950
      Philadelphia vs. Pittsburgh, Dec. 12, 1965
  11 Green Bay vs. San Diego, Sept. 24, 1978
  10 By 14 teams

1,000 YARDS RUSHING IN A SEASON

Year	Player, Team	Att.	Yards	Avg.	Long	TD
2011	Maurice Jones-Drew, Jacksonville[3]	343	1,606	4.7	56	8
	Ray Rice, Baltimore[3]	291	1,364	4.7	70	12
	Michael Turner, Atlanta[3]	301	1,340	4.5	81	11
	LeSean McCoy, Philadelphia[2]	273	1,309	4.8	60	17
	Arian Foster, Houston[2]	278	1,224	4.4	43	10
	Frank Gore, San Francisco[5]	282	1,211	4.3	55	8
	Marshawn Lynch, Seattle[3]	285	1,204	4.2	47	12
	Willis McGahee, Denver[4]	249	1,199	4.8	60	4
	Steven Jackson, St. Louis[7]	260	1,145	4.4	47	5
	Ryan Mathews, San Diego	222	1,091	4.9	39	6
	Reggie Bush, Miami	216	1,086	5.0	76	6
	Cedric Benson, Cincinnati[3]	273	1,067	3.9	42	6
	Shonn Greene, N.Y. Jets	253	1,054	4.2	31	6
	Chris Johnson, Tennessee[4]	262	1,047	4.0	48	4
	Beanie Wells, Arizona	245	1,047	4.3	71	10
2010	Arian Foster, Houston	327	1,616	4.9	74	16
	Jamaal Charles, Kansas City[2]	230	1,467	6.4	80	5
	Michael Turner, Atlanta[2]	334	1,371	4.1	55	12
	Chris Johnson, Tennessee[3]	316	1,364	4.3	76	11
	Maurice Jones-Drew, Jacksonville[2]	299	1,324	4.4	37	5
	Adrian Peterson, Minnesota[4]	283	1,298	4.6	80	12
	Rashard Mendenhall, Pittsburgh[2]	324	1,273	3.9	50	13
	Steven Jackson, St. Louis[6]	330	1,241	3.8	42	6
	Ahmad Bradshaw, N.Y. Giants	276	1,235	4.5	48	8
	Ray Rice, Baltimore[2]	307	1,220	4.0	50	5
	Peyton Hillis, Cleveland	270	1,177	4.4	48	11
	Darren McFadden, Oakland	223	1,157	5.2	57	7
	Cedric Benson, Cincinnati[2]	321	1,111	3.5	26	7
	LeSean McCoy, Philadelphia	207	1,080	5.2	62	7
	Matt Forté, Chicago[2]	237	1,069	4.5	68	6
	BenJarvus Green-Ellis, New England	229	1,008	4.4	33	13
	*LeGarrette Blount, Tampa Bay	201	1,007	5.0	53	6
2009	Chris Johnson, Tennessee[2]	358	2,006	5.6	91	14
	Steven Jackson, St. Louis[5]	324	1,416	4.8	58	4
	Thomas Jones, N.Y. Jets[5]	331	1,402	4.2	71	14
	Maurice Jones-Drew, Jacksonville	312	1,391	4.5	80	15
	Adrian Peterson, Minnesota[3]	314	1,383	4.4	64	18
	Ray Rice, Baltimore	254	1,339	5.3	59	7
	Ryan Grant, Green Bay[2]	282	1,253	4.4	62	11
	Cedric Benson, Cincinnati	301	1,251	4.2	42	6
	Jonathan Stewart, Carolina	221	1,133	5.1	67	10
	Ricky Williams, Miami[5]	241	1,121	4.6	68	11
	Jamaal Charles, Kansas City	190	1,120	5.9	76	7
	Frank Gore, San Francisco[4]	229	1,120	4.9	80	10
	DeAngelo Williams, Carolina[2]	216	1,117	5.2	77	7
	Rashard Mendenhall, Pittsburgh	242	1,108	4.6	60	7
	Fred Jackson, Buffalo	237	1,062	4.5	43	2
2008	Adrian Peterson, Minnesota[2]	363	1,760	4.9	67	10
	Michael Turner, Atlanta	376	1,699	4.5	70	17
	DeAngelo Williams, Carolina	273	1,515	5.6	69	18
	Clinton Portis, Washington[6]	342	1,487	4.4	31	9
	Thomas Jones, N.Y. Jets[4]	290	1,312	4.5	59	13
	*Steve Slaton, Houston	268	1,282	4.8	71	9
	*Matt Forté, Chicago	316	1,238	3.9	50	8
	*Chris Johnson, Tennessee	251	1,228	4.9	66	9
	Ryan Grant, Green Bay	312	1,203	3.9	57	4
	LaDainian Tomlinson, San Diego[8]	292	1,110	3.8	45	11
	Brandon Jacobs, N.Y. Giants[2]	219	1,089	5.0	44	15
	Steven Jackson, St. Louis[4]	253	1,042	4.1	56	7
	Frank Gore, San Francisco[3]	240	1,036	4.3	41	6
	Marshawn Lynch, Buffalo[2]	250	1,036	4.1	50	8
	Derrick Ward, N.Y. Giants	182	1,025	5.6	51	2
	Jamal Lewis, Cleveland[7]	279	1,002	3.6	29	4
2007	LaDainian Tomlinson, San Diego[7]	315	1,474	4.7	49	15
	*Adrian Peterson, Minnesota	238	1,341	5.6	73	12
	Brian Westbrook, Philadelphia[2]	278	1,333	4.8	36	7
	Willie Parker, Pittsburgh[3]	321	1,316	4.1	32	2
	Jamal Lewis, Cleveland[6]	298	1,304	4.4	66	9

Year	Player, Team	Att.	Yards	Avg.	Long	TD
	Clinton Portis, Washington[5]	325	1,262	3.9	32	11
	Edgerrin James, Arizona[7]	324	1,222	3.8	27	7
	Willis McGahee, Baltimore[3]	294	1,207	4.1	46	7
	Fred Taylor, Jacksonville[7]	223	1,202	5.4	80	5
	Thomas Jones, N.Y. Jets[3]	310	1,119	3.6	36	1
	*Marshawn Lynch, Buffalo	280	1,115	4.0	56	7
	LenDale White, Tennessee	303	1,110	3.7	28	7
	Frank Gore, San Francisco[2]	260	1,102	4.2	43	5
	Joseph Addai, Indianapolis[2]	261	1,072	4.1	23	12
	Justin Fargas, Oakland	222	1,009	4.6	48	4
	Brandon Jacobs, N.Y. Giants	202	1,009	5.0	43	4
	Steven Jackson, St. Louis[3]	237	1,002	4.2	54	5
2006	LaDainian Tomlinson, San Diego[6]	348	1,815	5.2	85	28
	Larry Johnson, Kansas City[2]	416	1,789	4.3	47	17
	Frank Gore, San Francisco	312	1,695	5.4	72	8
	Tiki Barber, N.Y. Giants[6]	327	1,662	5.1	55	5
	Steven Jackson, St. Louis[2]	346	1,528	4.4	59	13
	Willie Parker, Pittsburgh[2]	337	1,494	4.4	76	13
	Rudi Johnson, Cincinnati[3]	341	1,309	3.8	22	12
	Brian Westbrook, Philadelphia	240	1,217	5.1	71	7
	Chester Taylor, Minnesota	303	1,216	4.0	95	6
	Travis Henry, Tennessee[3]	270	1,211	4.5	70	7
	Thomas Jones, Chicago[2]	296	1,210	4.1	30	6
	Edgerrin James, Arizona[6]	337	1,159	3.4	18	6
	Ladell Betts, Washington	245	1,154	4.7	26	4
	Fred Taylor, Jacksonville[6]	231	1,146	5.0	76	5
	Warrick Dunn, Atlanta[5]	286	1,140	4.0	90	4
	Jamal Lewis, Baltimore[5]	314	1,132	3.6	52	9
	Julius Jones, Dallas	267	1,084	4.1	77	4
	*Joseph Addai, Indianapolis	226	1,081	4.8	41	7
	Ahman Green, Green Bay[6]	266	1,059	4.0	70	5
	Deuce McAllister, New Orleans[4]	244	1,057	4.3	57	10
	Michael Vick, Atlanta	123	1,039	8.5	51	2
	Tatum Bell, Denver	233	1,025	4.4	51	2
	Ronnie Brown, Miami	241	1,008	4.2	47	5
2005	Shaun Alexander, Seattle[5]	370	1,880	5.1	88	27
	Tiki Barber, N.Y. Giants[5]	357	1,860	5.2	95	9
	Larry Johnson, Kansas City	336	1,750	5.2	49	20
	Clinton Portis, Washington[4]	352	1,516	4.3	47	11
	Edgerrin James, Indianapolis[5]	360	1,506	4.2	33	13
	LaDainian Tomlinson, San Diego[5]	339	1,462	4.3	62	18
	Rudi Johnson, Cincinnati[2]	337	1,458	4.3	33	12
	Warrick Dunn, Atlanta[4]	280	1,416	5.1	65	3
	Thomas Jones, Chicago	314	1,335	4.3	42	9
	Willis McGahee, Buffalo[2]	325	1,247	3.8	27	5
	Reuben Droughns, Cleveland[2]	309	1,232	4.0	75	2
	Willie Parker, Pittsburgh	255	1,202	4.7	80	4
	*Carnell Williams, Tampa Bay	290	1,178	4.1	71	6
	Steven Jackson, St. Louis	254	1,046	4.1	51	8
	LaMont Jordan, Oakland	272	1,025	3.8	26	9
	Mike Anderson, Denver[2]	239	1,014	4.2	44	12
2004	Curtis Martin, N.Y. Jets[10]	371	1,697	4.6	25	12
	Shaun Alexander, Seattle[4]	353	1,696	4.8	44	16
	Corey Dillon, New England[7]	345	1,635	4.7	44	12
	Edgerrin James, Indianapolis[4]	334	1,548	4.6	40	9
	Tiki Barber, N.Y. Giants[4]	322	1,518	4.7	72	13
	Rudi Johnson, Cincinnati	361	1,454	4.0	52	12
	LaDainian Tomlinson, San Diego[4]	339	1,335	3.9	42	17
	Clinton Portis, Washington[3]	343	1,315	3.8	64	5
	Reuben Droughns, Denver	275	1,240	4.5	51	6
	Fred Taylor, Jacksonville[5]	260	1,224	4.7	46	2
	Domanick Davis, Houston[2]	302	1,188	3.9	44	13
	Ahman Green, Green Bay[5]	259	1,163	4.5	90	7
	*Kevin Jones, Detroit	241	1,133	4.7	74	5
	Willis McGahee, Buffalo	284	1,128	4.0	41	13
	Warrick Dunn, Atlanta[3]	265	1,106	4.2	60	9
	Deuce McAllister, New Orleans[3]	269	1,074	4.0	71	9
	Chris Brown, Tennessee	220	1,067	4.9	52	6
	Jamal Lewis, Baltimore[4]	235	1,006	4.3	75	7

Year	Player, Team	Att.	Yards	Avg.	Long	TD
2003	Jamal Lewis, Baltimore[3]	387	2,066	5.3	82	14
	Ahman Green, Green Bay[4]	355	1,883	5.3	98	15
	LaDainian Tomlinson, San Diego[3]	313	1,645	5.3	73	13
	Deuce McAllister, New Orleans[2]	351	1,641	4.7	76	8
	Clinton Portis, Denver[2]	290	1,591	5.5	65	14
	Fred Taylor, Jacksonville[4]	345	1,572	4.6	62	6
	Stephen Davis, Carolina[4]	318	1,444	4.5	40	8
	Shaun Alexander, Seattle[3]	326	1,435	4.4	55	14
	Priest Holmes, Kansas City[4]	320	1,420	4.4	31	27
	Ricky Williams, Miami[4]	392	1,372	3.5	45	9
	Travis Henry, Buffalo[2]	331	1,356	4.1	64	10
	Curtis Martin, N.Y. Jets[9]	323	1,308	4.1	56	2
	Edgerrin James, Indianapolis[3]	310	1,259	4.1	43	11
	Tiki Barber, N.Y. Giants[3]	278	1,216	4.4	27	2
	*Domanick Davis, Houston	238	1,031	4.3	51	8
	Eddie George, Tennessee[7]	312	1,031	3.3	27	5
	Kevan Barlow, San Francisco	201	1,024	5.1	78	6
	Anthony Thomas, Chicago[2]	244	1,024	4.2	67	6
2002	Ricky Williams, Miami[3]	383	1,853	4.8	63	16
	LaDainian Tomlinson, San Diego[2]	372	1,683	4.5	76	14
	Priest Holmes, Kansas City[3]	313	1,615	5.2	56	21
	*Clinton Portis, Denver	273	1,508	5.5	59	15
	Travis Henry, Buffalo	325	1,438	4.4	34	13
	Deuce McAllister, New Orleans	325	1,388	4.3	62	13
	Tiki Barber, N.Y. Giants[2]	304	1,387	4.6	70	11
	Jamal Lewis, Baltimore[2]	308	1,327	4.3	75	6
	Fred Taylor, Jacksonville[3]	287	1,314	4.6	63	8
	Corey Dillon, Cincinnati[6]	314	1,311	4.2	67	7
	Michael Bennett, Minnesota	255	1,296	5.1	85	5
	Ahman Green, Green Bay[3]	286	1,240	4.3	43	7
	Shaun Alexander, Seattle[2]	295	1,175	4.0	58	16
	Eddie George, Tennessee[6]	343	1,165	3.4	35	12
	Curtis Martin, N.Y. Jets[8]	261	1,094	4.2	35	7
	Duce Staley, Philadelphia[3]	269	1,029	3.8	57	5
	James Stewart, Detroit[2]	231	1,021	4.4	56	4
2001	Priest Holmes, Kansas City[2]	327	1,555	4.8	41	8
	Curtis Martin, N.Y. Jets[7]	333	1,513	4.5	47	10
	Stephen Davis, Washington[3]	356	1,432	4.0	32	5
	Ahman Green, Green Bay[2]	304	1,387	4.6	83	9
	Marshall Faulk, St. Louis[7]	260	1,382	5.3	71	12
	Shaun Alexander, Seattle	309	1,318	4.3	88	14
	Corey Dillon, Cincinnati[5]	340	1,315	3.9	96	10
	Ricky Williams, New Orleans[2]	313	1,245	4.0	46	6
	*LaDainian Tomlinson, San Diego	339	1,236	3.6	54	10
	Garrison Hearst, San Francisco[4]	252	1,206	4.8	43	4
	*Anthony Thomas, Chicago	278	1,183	4.3	46	7
	Antowain Smith, New England[2]	287	1,157	4.0	44	12
	*Dominic Rhodes, Indianapolis	233	1,104	4.7	77	9
	Jerome Bettis, Pittsburgh[8]	225	1,072	4.8	48	4
	Emmitt Smith, Dallas[11]	261	1,021	3.9	44	3
2000	Edgerrin James, Indianapolis[2]	387	1,709	4.4	30	13
	Robert Smith, Minnesota[4]	295	1,521	5.2	72	7
	Eddie George, Tennessee[5]	403	1,509	3.7	35	14
	*Mike Anderson, Denver	297	1,487	5.0	80	15
	Corey Dillon, Cincinnati[4]	315	1,435	4.6	80	7
	Fred Taylor, Jacksonville[2]	292	1,399	4.8	71	12
	*Jamal Lewis, Baltimore	309	1,364	4.4	45	6
	Marshall Faulk, St. Louis[6]	253	1,359	5.4	36	18
	Jerome Bettis, Pittsburgh[7]	355	1,341	3.8	30	8
	Stephen Davis, Washington[2]	332	1,318	4.0	50	11
	Ricky Watters, Seattle[7]	278	1,242	4.5	55	7
	Curtis Martin, N.Y. Jets[6]	316	1,204	3.8	55	9
	Emmitt Smith, Dallas[10]	294	1,203	4.1	52	9
	James Stewart, Detroit	339	1,184	3.5	34	10
	Ahman Green, Green Bay	263	1,175	4.5	39	10
	Charlie Garner, San Francisco[2]	258	1,142	4.4	42	7
	Lamar Smith, Miami	309	1,139	3.7	68	14
	Warrick Dunn, Tampa Bay[2]	248	1,133	4.6	70	8
	James Allen, Chicago	290	1,120	3.9	29	2

Year	Player, Team	Att.	Yards	Avg.	Long	TD
	Tyrone Wheatley, Oakland	232	1,046	4.5	80	9
	Jamal Anderson, Atlanta[4]	282	1,024	3.6	42	6
	Tiki Barber, N.Y. Giants	213	1,006	4.7	78	8
	Ricky Williams, New Orleans	248	1,000	4.0	26	8
1999	*Edgerrin James, Indianapolis	369	1,553	4.2	72	13
	Curtis Martin, N.Y. Jets[5]	367	1,464	4.0	50	5
	Stephen Davis, Washington	290	1,405	4.8	76	17
	Emmitt Smith, Dallas[9]	329	1,397	4.3	63	11
	Marshall Faulk, St. Louis[5]	253	1,381	5.5	58	7
	Eddie George, Tennessee[4]	320	1,304	4.1	40	9
	Duce Staley, Philadelphia[2]	325	1,273	3.9	29	4
	Charlie Garner, San Francisco	241	1,229	5.1	53	4
	Ricky Watters, Seattle[6]	325	1,210	3.7	45	5
	Corey Dillon, Cincinnati[3]	263	1,200	4.6	50	5
	*Olandis Gary, Denver	276	1,159	4.2	71	7
	Jerome Bettis, Pittsburgh[6]	299	1,091	3.7	35	7
	Dorsey Levens, Green Bay[2]	279	1,034	3.7	36	9
	Robert Smith, Minnesota[3]	221	1,015	4.6	70	2
1998	Terrell Davis, Denver[4]	392	2,008	5.1	70	21
	Jamal Anderson, Atlanta[3]	410	1,846	4.5	48	14
	Garrison Hearst, San Francisco[3]	310	1,570	5.1	96	7
	Barry Sanders, Detroit[10]	343	1,491	4.3	73	4
	Emmitt Smith, Dallas[8]	319	1,332	4.2	32	13
	Marshall Faulk, Indianapolis[4]	324	1,319	4.1	68	6
	Eddie George, Tennessee[3]	348	1,294	3.7	37	5
	Curtis Martin, N.Y. Jets[4]	369	1,287	3.5	60	8
	Ricky Watters, Seattle[5]	319	1,239	3.9	39	9
	*Fred Taylor, Jacksonville	264	1,223	4.6	77	14
	Robert Smith, Minnesota[2]	249	1,187	4.8	74	6
	Jerome Bettis, Pittsburgh[5]	316	1,185	3.8	42	3
	Corey Dillon, Cincinnati[2]	262	1,130	4.3	66	4
	Antowain Smith, Buffalo	300	1,124	3.7	30	8
	*Robert Edwards, New England	291	1,115	3.8	53	9
	Duce Staley, Philadelphia	258	1,065	4.1	64	5
	Gary Brown, N.Y. Giants[2]	247	1,063	4.3	45	5
	Adrian Murrell, Arizona[3]	274	1,042	3.8	32	8
	Warrick Dunn, Tampa Bay	245	1,026	4.2	50	2
	Priest Holmes, Baltimore	233	1,008	4.3	56	7
1997	Barry Sanders, Detroit[9]	335	2,053	6.1	82	11
	Terrell Davis, Denver[3]	369	1,750	4.7	50	15
	Jerome Bettis, Pittsburgh[4]	375	1,665	4.4	34	7
	Dorsey Levens, Green Bay[2]	329	1,435	4.4	52	7
	Eddie George, Tennessee[2]	357	1,399	3.9	30	6
	Napoleon Kaufman, Oakland	272	1,294	4.8	83	6
	Robert Smith, Minnesota	232	1,266	5.5	78	6
	Curtis Martin, New England[3]	274	1,160	4.2	70	4
	*Corey Dillon, Cincinnati	233	1,129	4.8	71	10
	Ricky Watters, Philadelphia[4]	285	1,110	3.9	28	7
	Adrian Murrell, N.Y. Jets[2]	300	1,086	3.6	43	7
	Emmitt Smith, Dallas[7]	261	1,074	4.1	44	4
	Marshall Faulk, Indianapolis[3]	264	1,054	4.0	45	7
	Raymont Harris, Chicago	275	1,033	3.8	68	10
	Garrison Hearst, San Francisco[2]	234	1,019	4.4	51	4
	Jamal Anderson, Atlanta[2]	290	1,002	3.5	39	7
1996	Barry Sanders, Detroit[8]	307	1,553	5.1	54	11
	Terrell Davis, Denver[2]	345	1,538	4.5	71	13
	Jerome Bettis, Pittsburgh[3]	320	1,431	4.5	50	11
	Ricky Watters, Philadelphia[3]	353	1,411	4.0	56	13
	*Eddie George, Houston	335	1,368	4.1	76	8
	Terry Allen, Washington[4]	347	1,353	3.9	49	21
	Adrian Murrell, N.Y. Jets	301	1,249	4.1	78	6
	Emmitt Smith, Dallas[6]	327	1,204	3.7	42	12
	Curtis Martin, New England[2]	316	1,152	3.6	57	14
	Anthony Johnson, Carolina	300	1,120	3.7	29	6
	*Karim Abdul-Jabbar, Miami	307	1,116	3.6	29	11
	Jamal Anderson, Atlanta	232	1,055	4.5	32	5
	Thurman Thomas, Buffalo[8]	281	1,033	3.7	36	8
1995	Emmitt Smith, Dallas[5]	377	1,773	4.7	60	25
	Barry Sanders, Detroit[7]	314	1,500	4.8	75	11

Year	Player, Team	Att.	Yards	Avg.	Long	TD
	*Curtis Martin, New England	368	1,487	4.0	49	14
	Chris Warren, Seattle[4]	310	1,346	4.3	52	15
	Terry Allen, Washington[3]	338	1,309	3.9	28	10
	Ricky Watters, Philadelphia[2]	337	1,273	3.8	57	11
	Errict Rhett, Tampa Bay[2]	332	1,207	3.6	21	11
	Rodney Hampton, N.Y. Giants[5]	306	1,182	3.9	32	10
	*Terrell Davis, Denver	237	1,117	4.7	60	7
	Harvey Williams, Oakland	255	1,114	4.4	60	9
	Craig Heyward, Atlanta	236	1,083	4.6	31	6
	Marshall Faulk, Indianapolis[2]	289	1,078	3.7	40	11
	*Rashaan Salaam, Chicago	296	1,074	3.6	42	10
	Garrison Hearst, Arizona	284	1,070	3.8	38	1
	Edgar Bennett, Green Bay	316	1,067	3.4	23	3
	Thurman Thomas, Buffalo[7]	267	1,005	3.8	49	6
1994	Barry Sanders, Detroit[6]	331	1,883	5.7	85	7
	Chris Warren, Seattle[3]	333	1,545	4.6	41	9
	Emmitt Smith, Dallas[4]	368	1,484	4.0	46	21
	Natrone Means, San Diego	343	1,350	3.9	25	12
	*Marshall Faulk, Indianapolis	314	1,282	4.1	52	11
	Thurman Thomas, Buffalo[6]	287	1,093	3.8	29	7
	Rodney Hampton, N.Y. Giants[4]	327	1,075	3.3	27	6
	Terry Allen, Minnesota[2]	255	1,031	4.0	45	8
	Jerome Bettis, L.A. Rams[2]	319	1,025	3.2	19	3
	*Errict Rhett, Tampa Bay	284	1,011	3.6	27	7
1993	Emmitt Smith, Dallas[3]	283	1,486	5.3	62	9
	*Jerome Bettis, L.A. Rams	294	1,429	4.9	71	7
	Thurman Thomas, Buffalo[5]	355	1,315	3.7	27	6
	Erric Pegram, Atlanta	292	1,185	4.1	29	3
	Barry Sanders, Detroit[5]	243	1,115	4.6	42	3
	Leonard Russell, New England	300	1,088	3.6	21	7
	Rodney Hampton, N.Y. Giants[3]	292	1,077	3.7	20	5
	Chris Warren, Seattle[2]	273	1,072	3.9	45	7
	*Reggie Brooks, Washington	223	1,063	4.8	85	3
	*Ron Moore, Phoenix	263	1,018	3.9	20	9
	Gary Brown, Houston	195	1,002	5.1	26	6
1992	Emmitt Smith, Dallas[2]	373	1,713	4.6	68	18
	Barry Foster, Pittsburgh	390	1,690	4.3	69	11
	Thurman Thomas, Buffalo[4]	312	1,487	4.8	44	9
	Barry Sanders, Detroit[4]	312	1,352	4.3	55	9
	Lorenzo White, Houston	265	1,226	4.6	44	7
	Terry Allen, Minnesota	266	1,201	4.5	51	13
	Reggie Cobb, Tampa Bay	310	1,171	3.8	25	9
	Harold Green, Cincinnati	265	1,170	4.4	53	2
	Rodney Hampton, N.Y. Giants[2]	257	1,141	4.4	63	14
	Cleveland Gary, L.A. Rams	279	1,125	4.0	63	7
	Herschel Walker, Philadelphia[2]	267	1,070	4.0	38	8
	Chris Warren, Seattle	223	1,017	4.6	52	3
	Ricky Watters, San Francisco	206	1,013	4.9	43	9
1991	Emmitt Smith, Dallas	365	1,563	4.3	75	12
	Barry Sanders, Detroit[3]	342	1,548	4.5	69	16
	Thurman Thomas, Buffalo[3]	288	1,407	4.9	33	7
	Rodney Hampton, N.Y. Giants	256	1,059	4.1	44	10
	Earnest Byner, Washington[3]	274	1,048	3.8	32	5
	Gaston Green, Denver	261	1,037	4.0	63	4
	Christian Okoye, Kansas City[2]	225	1,031	4.6	48	9
1990	Barry Sanders, Detroit[2]	255	1,304	5.1	45	13
	Thurman Thomas, Buffalo[2]	271	1,297	4.8	80	11
	Marion Butts, San Diego	265	1,225	4.6	52	8
	Earnest Byner, Washington[2]	297	1,219	4.1	22	6
	Bobby Humphrey, Denver[2]	288	1,202	4.2	37	7
	Neal Anderson, Chicago[3]	260	1,078	4.1	52	10
	Barry Word, Kansas City	204	1,015	5.0	53	4
	James Brooks, Cincinnati[3]	195	1,004	5.1	56	5
1989	Christian Okoye, Kansas City	370	1,480	4.0	59	12
	*Barry Sanders, Detroit	280	1,470	5.3	34	14
	Eric Dickerson, Indianapolis[7]	314	1,311	4.2	21	7
	Neal Anderson, Chicago[2]	274	1,275	4.7	73	11
	Dalton Hilliard, New Orleans	344	1,262	3.7	40	13
	Thurman Thomas, Buffalo	298	1,244	4.2	38	6

Year	Player, Team	Att.	Yards	Avg.	Long	TD
	James Brooks, Cincinnati[2]	221	1,239	5.6	65	7
	*Bobby Humphrey, Denver	294	1,151	3.9	40	7
	Greg Bell, L.A. Rams[3]	272	1,137	4.2	47	15
	Roger Craig, San Francisco[3]	271	1,054	3.9	27	6
	Ottis Anderson, N.Y. Giants[6]	325	1,023	3.1	36	14
1988	Eric Dickerson, Indianapolis[6]	388	1,659	4.3	41	14
	Herschel Walker, Dallas	361	1,514	4.2	38	5
	Roger Craig, San Francisco[2]	310	1,502	4.8	46	9
	Greg Bell, L.A. Rams[2]	288	1,212	4.2	44	16
	*John Stephens, New England	297	1,168	3.9	52	4
	Gary Anderson, San Diego	225	1,119	5.0	36	3
	Neal Anderson, Chicago	249	1,106	4.4	80	12
	Joe Morris, N.Y. Giants[3]	307	1,083	3.5	27	5
	*Ickey Woods, Cincinnati	203	1,066	5.3	56	15
	Curt Warner, Seattle[4]	266	1,025	3.9	29	10
	John Settle, Atlanta	232	1,024	4.4	62	7
	Mike Rozier, Houston	251	1,002	4.0	28	10
1987	Charles White, L.A. Rams	324	1,374	4.2	58	11
	Eric Dickerson, L.A. Rams-Indianapolis[5]	283	1,288	4.6	57	6
1986	Eric Dickerson, L.A. Rams[4]	404	1,821	4.5	42	11
	Joe Morris, N.Y. Giants[2]	341	1,516	4.4	54	14
	Curt Warner, Seattle[3]	319	1,481	4.6	60	13
	*Rueben Mayes, New Orleans	286	1,353	4.7	50	8
	Walter Payton, Chicago[10]	321	1,333	4.2	41	8
	Gerald Riggs, Atlanta[3]	343	1,327	3.9	31	9
	George Rogers, Washington[4]	303	1,203	4.0	42	18
	James Brooks, Cincinnati	205	1,087	5.3	56	5
1985	Marcus Allen, L.A. Raiders[3]	390	1,759	4.6	61	11
	Gerald Riggs, Atlanta[2]	397	1,719	4.3	50	10
	Walter Payton, Chicago[9]	324	1,551	4.8	40	9
	Joe Morris, N.Y. Giants	294	1,336	4.5	65	21
	Freeman McNeil, N.Y. Jets[2]	294	1,331	4.5	69	3
	Tony Dorsett, Dallas[8]	305	1,307	4.3	60	7
	James Wilder, Tampa Bay[2]	365	1,300	3.6	28	10
	Eric Dickerson, L.A. Rams[3]	292	1,234	4.2	43	12
	Craig James, New England	263	1,227	4.7	65	5
	Kevin Mack, Cleveland	222	1,104	5.0	61	7
	Curt Warner, Seattle[2]	291	1,094	3.8	38	8
	George Rogers, Washington[3]	231	1,093	4.7	35	7
	Roger Craig, San Francisco	214	1,050	4.9	62	9
	Earnest Jackson, Philadelphia[2]	282	1,028	3.6	59	5
	Stump Mitchell, St. Louis	183	1,006	5.5	64	7
	Earnest Byner, Cleveland	244	1,002	4.1	36	8
1984	Eric Dickerson, L.A. Rams[2]	379	2,105	5.6	66	14
	Walter Payton, Chicago[8]	381	1,684	4.4	72	11
	James Wilder, Tampa Bay	407	1,544	3.8	37	13
	Gerald Riggs, Atlanta	353	1,486	4.2	57	13
	Wendell Tyler, San Francisco[3]	246	1,262	5.1	40	7
	John Riggins, Washington[5]	327	1,239	3.8	24	14
	Tony Dorsett, Dallas[7]	302	1,189	3.9	31	6
	Earnest Jackson, San Diego	296	1,179	4.0	32	8
	Ottis Anderson, St. Louis[5]	289	1,174	4.1	24	6
	Marcus Allen, L.A. Raiders[2]	275	1,168	4.2	52	13
	Sammy Winder, Denver	296	1,153	3.9	24	4
	*Greg Bell, Buffalo	262	1,100	4.2	85	7
	Freeman McNeil, N.Y. Jets	229	1,070	4.7	53	5
1983	*Eric Dickerson, L.A. Rams	390	1,808	4.6	85	18
	William Andrews, Atlanta[4]	331	1,567	4.7	27	7
	*Curt Warner, Seattle	335	1,449	4.3	60	13
	Walter Payton, Chicago[7]	314	1,421	4.5	49	6
	John Riggins, Washington[4]	375	1,347	3.6	44	24
	Tony Dorsett, Dallas[6]	289	1,321	4.6	77	8
	Earl Campbell, Houston[5]	322	1,301	4.0	42	12
	Ottis Anderson, St. Louis[4]	296	1,270	4.3	43	5
	Mike Pruitt, Cleveland[4]	293	1,184	4.0	27	10
	George Rogers, New Orleans[2]	256	1,144	4.5	76	5
	Joe Cribbs, Buffalo[3]	263	1,131	4.3	45	3
	Curtis Dickey, Baltimore	254	1,122	4.4	56	4
	Tony Collins, New England	219	1,049	4.8	50	10

Year	Player, Team	Att.	Yards	Avg.	Long	TD
	Billy Sims, Detroit[3]	220	1,040	4.7	41	7
	Marcus Allen, L.A. Raiders	266	1,014	3.8	19	9
	Franco Harris, Pittsburgh[8]	279	1,007	3.6	19	5
1981	*George Rogers, New Orleans	378	1,674	4.4	79	13
	Tony Dorsett, Dallas[5]	342	1,646	4.8	75	4
	Billy Sims, Detroit[2]	296	1,437	4.9	51	13
	Wilbert Montgomery, Philadelphia[3]	286	1,402	4.9	41	8
	Ottis Anderson, St. Louis[3]	328	1,376	4.2	28	9
	Earl Campbell, Houston[4]	361	1,376	3.8	43	10
	William Andrews, Atlanta[3]	289	1,301	4.5	29	10
	Walter Payton, Chicago[6]	339	1,222	3.6	39	6
	Chuck Muncie, San Diego[2]	251	1,144	4.6	73	19
	*Joe Delaney, Kansas City	234	1,121	4.8	82	3
	Mike Pruitt, Cleveland[3]	247	1,103	4.5	21	7
	Joe Cribbs, Buffalo[2]	257	1,097	4.3	35	3
	Pete Johnson, Cincinnati	274	1,077	3.9	39	12
	Wendell Tyler, Los Angeles[2]	260	1,074	4.1	69	12
	Ted Brown, Minnesota	274	1,063	3.9	34	6
1980	Earl Campbell, Houston[3]	373	1,934	5.2	55	13
	Walter Payton, Chicago[5]	317	1,460	4.6	69	6
	Ottis Anderson, St. Louis[2]	301	1,352	4.5	52	9
	William Andrews, Atlanta[2]	265	1,308	4.9	33	4
	*Billy Sims, Detroit	313	1,303	4.2	52	13
	Tony Dorsett, Dallas[4]	278	1,185	4.3	56	11
	*Joe Cribbs, Buffalo	306	1,185	3.9	48	11
	Mike Pruitt, Cleveland[2]	249	1,034	4.2	56	6
1979	Earl Campbell, Houston[2]	368	1,697	4.6	61	19
	Walter Payton, Chicago[4]	369	1,610	4.4	43	14
	*Ottis Anderson, St. Louis	331	1,605	4.8	76	8
	Wilbert Montgomery, Philadelphia[2]	338	1,512	4.5	62	9
	Mike Pruitt, Cleveland	264	1,294	4.9	77	9
	Ricky Bell, Tampa Bay	283	1,263	4.5	49	7
	Chuck Muncie, New Orleans	238	1,198	5.0	69	11
	Franco Harris, Pittsburgh[7]	267	1,186	4.4	71	11
	John Riggins, Washington[3]	260	1,153	4.4	66	9
	Wendell Tyler, Los Angeles	218	1,109	5.1	63	9
	Tony Dorsett, Dallas[3]	250	1,107	4.4	41	6
	*William Andrews, Atlanta	239	1,023	4.3	23	3
1978	*Earl Campbell, Houston	302	1,450	4.8	81	13
	Walter Payton, Chicago[3]	333	1,395	4.2	76	11
	Tony Dorsett, Dallas[2]	290	1,325	4.6	63	7
	Delvin Williams, Miami[2]	272	1,258	4.6	58	8
	Wilbert Montgomery, Philadelphia	259	1,220	4.7	47	9
	Terdell Middleton, Green Bay	284	1,116	3.9	76	11
	Franco Harris, Pittsburgh[6]	310	1,082	3.5	37	8
	Mark van Eeghen, Oakland[3]	270	1,080	4.0	34	9
	*Terry Miller, Buffalo	238	1,060	4.5	60	7
	Tony Reed, Kansas City	206	1,053	5.1	62	5
	John Riggins, Washington[2]	248	1,014	4.1	31	5
1977	Walter Payton, Chicago[2]	339	1,852	5.5	73	14
	Mark van Eeghen, Oakland[2]	324	1,273	3.9	27	7
	Lawrence McCutcheon, Los Angeles[4]	294	1,238	4.2	48	7
	Franco Harris, Pittsburgh[5]	300	1,162	3.9	61	11
	Lydell Mitchell, Baltimore[3]	301	1,159	3.9	64	3
	Chuck Foreman, Minnesota[3]	270	1,112	4.1	51	6
	Greg Pruitt, Cleveland[3]	236	1,086	4.6	78	3
	Sam Cunningham, New England	270	1,015	3.8	31	4
	*Tony Dorsett, Dallas	208	1,007	4.8	84	12
1976	O.J. Simpson, Buffalo[5]	290	1,503	5.2	75	8
	Walter Payton, Chicago	311	1,390	4.5	60	13
	Delvin Williams, San Francisco	248	1,203	4.9	80	7
	Lydell Mitchell, Baltimore[2]	289	1,200	4.2	43	5
	Lawrence McCutcheon, Los Angeles[3]	291	1,168	4.0	40	9
	Chuck Foreman, Minnesota[2]	278	1,155	4.2	46	13
	Franco Harris, Pittsburgh[4]	289	1,128	3.9	30	14
	Mike Thomas, Washington	254	1,101	4.3	28	5
	Rocky Bleier, Pittsburgh	220	1,036	4.7	28	5
	Mark van Eeghen, Oakland	233	1,012	4.3	21	3
	Otis Armstrong, Denver[2]	247	1,008	4.1	31	5

Year	Player, Team	Att.	Yards	Avg.	Long	TD
	Greg Pruitt, Cleveland[2]	209	1,000	4.8	64	4
1975	O.J. Simpson, Buffalo[4]	329	1,817	5.5	88	16
	Franco Harris, Pittsburgh[3]	262	1,246	4.8	36	10
	Lydell Mitchell, Baltimore	289	1,193	4.1	70	11
	Jim Otis, St. Louis	269	1,076	4.0	30	5
	Chuck Foreman, Minnesota	280	1,070	3.8	31	13
	Greg Pruitt, Cleveland	217	1,067	4.9	50	8
	John Riggins, N.Y. Jets	238	1,005	4.2	42	8
	Dave Hampton, Atlanta	250	1,002	4.0	22	5
1974	Otis Armstrong, Denver	263	1,407	5.3	43	9
	*Don Woods, San Diego	227	1,162	5.1	56	7
	O.J. Simpson, Buffalo[3]	270	1,125	4.2	41	3
	Lawrence McCutcheon, Los Angeles[2]	236	1,109	4.7	23	3
	Franco Harris, Pittsburgh[2]	208	1,006	4.8	54	5
1973	O.J. Simpson, Buffalo[2]	332	2,003	6.0	80	12[2]
	John Brockington, Green Bay[3]	265	1,144	4.3	53	3
	Calvin Hill, Dallas[2]	273	1,142	4.2	21	6
	Lawrence McCutcheon, Los Angeles	210	1,097	5.2	37	2
	Larry Csonka, Miami[3]	219	1,003	4.6	25	5
1972	O.J. Simpson, Buffalo	292	1,251	4.3	94	6
	Larry Brown, Washington[2]	285	1,216	4.3	38	8
	Ron Johnson, N.Y. Giants[2]	298	1,182	4.0	35	9
	Larry Csonka, Miami[2]	213	1,117	5.2	45	6
	Marv Hubbard, Oakland	219	1,100	5.0	39	4
	*Franco Harris, Pittsburgh	188	1,055	5.6	75	10
	Calvin Hill, Dallas	245	1,036	4.2	26	6
	Mike Garrett, San Diego[2]	272	1,031	3.8	41	6
	John Brockington, Green Bay[2]	274	1,027	3.7	30	8
	Eugene (Mercury) Morris, Miami	190	1,000	5.3	33	12
1971	Floyd Little, Denver	284	1,133	4.0	40	6
	*John Brockington, Green Bay	216	1,105	5.1	52	4
	Larry Csonka, Miami	195	1,051	5.4	28	7
	Steve Owens, Detroit	246	1,035	4.2	23	8
	Willie Ellison, Los Angeles	211	1,000	4.7	80	4
1970	Larry Brown, Washington	237	1,125	4.7	75	5
	Ron Johnson, N.Y. Giants	263	1,027	3.9	68	8
1969	Gale Sayers, Chicago[2]	236	1,032	4.4	28	8
1968	Leroy Kelly, Cleveland[3]	248	1,239	5.0	65	16
	*Paul Robinson, Cincinnati	238	1,023	4.3	87	8
1967	Jim Nance, Boston[2]	269	1,216	4.5	53	7
	Leroy Kelly, Cleveland[2]	235	1,205	5.1	42	11
	Hoyle Granger, Houston	236	1,194	5.1	67	6
	Mike Garrett, Kansas City	236	1,087	4.6	58	9
1966	Jim Nance, Boston	299	1,458	4.9	65	11
	Gale Sayers, Chicago	229	1,231	5.4	58	8
	Leroy Kelly, Cleveland	209	1,141	5.5	70	15
	Dick Bass, Los Angeles[2]	248	1,090	4.4	50	8
1965	Jim Brown, Cleveland[7]	289	1,544	5.3	67	17[7]
	Paul Lowe, San Diego[2]	222	1,121	5.0	59	7
1964	Jim Brown, Cleveland[6]	280	1,446	5.2	71	7
	Jim Taylor, Green Bay[5]	235	1,169	5.0	84	12
	John Henry Johnson, Pittsburgh[2]	235	1,048	4.5	45	7
1963	Jim Brown, Cleveland[5]	291	1,863	6.4	80	12
	Clem Daniels, Oakland	215	1,099	5.1	74	3
	Jim Taylor, Green Bay[4]	248	1,018	4.1	40	9
	Paul Lowe, San Diego	177	1,010	5.7	66	8
1962	Jim Taylor, Green Bay[3]	272	1,474	5.4	51	19
	John Henry Johnson, Pittsburgh	251	1,141	4.5	40	7
	Cookie Gilchrist, Buffalo	214	1,096	5.1	44	13
	Abner Haynes, Dall. Texans	221	1,049	4.7	71	13
	Dick Bass, Los Angeles	196	1,033	5.3	57	6
	Charlie Tolar, Houston	244	1,012	4.1	25	7
1961	Jim Brown, Cleveland[4]	305	1,408	4.6	38	8
	Jim Taylor, Green Bay[2]	243	1,307	5.4	53	15
1960	Jim Brown, Cleveland[3]	215	1,257	5.8	71	9
	Jim Taylor, Green Bay	230	1,101	4.8	32	11
	John David Crow, St. Louis	183	1,071	5.9	57	6
1959	Jim Brown, Cleveland[2]	290	1,329	4.6	70	14
	J.D. Smith, San Francisco	207	1,036	5.0	73	10

Year	Player, Team	Att.	Yards	Avg.	Long	TD
1958	Jim Brown, Cleveland	257	1,527	5.9	65	17
1956	Rick Casares, Chi. Bears	234	1,126	4.8	68	12
1954	Joe Perry, San Francisco[2]	173	1,049	6.1	58	8
1953	Joe Perry, San Francisco	192	1,018	5.3	51	10
1949	Steve Van Buren, Philadelphia[2]	263	1,146	4.4	41	11
	Tony Canadeo, Green Bay	208	1,052	5.1	54	4
1947	Steve Van Buren, Philadelphia	217	1,008	4.6	45	13
1934	*Beattie Feathers, Chi. Bears	119	1,004	8.4	82	8

*First season of professional football.

200 YARDS RUSHING IN A GAME

Date	Player, Team, Opponent	Att.	Yards	TD
Dec. 18, 2011	Reggie Bush, Miami vs. Buffalo	25	203	1
Dec. 4, 2011	Ray Rice, Baltimore vs. Cleveland	29	204	1
Nov. 27, 2011	Beanie Wells, Arizona vs. St. Louis	27	228	1
Oct. 23, 2011	DeMarco Murray, Dallas vs. St. Louis	25	253	1
Oct. 2, 2011	Matt Forté, Chicago vs. Carolina	25	205	1
Sept. 12, 2010	Arian Foster, Houston vs. Indianapolis	33	231	3
Jan. 3, 2010	Jamaal Charles, Kansas City vs. Denver	25	259	2
Jan. 3, 2010	Fred Jackson, Buffalo vs. Indianapolis	33	212	0
Dec. 27, 2009	Jonathan Stewart, Carolina vs. N.Y. Giants	28	206	1
Dec. 20, 2009	Jerome Harrison, Cleveland vs. Kansas City	34	286	3
Nov. 1, 2009	Chris Johnson, Tennessee vs. Jacksonville	24	228	2
Oct. 18, 2009	Thomas Jones, N.Y. Jets vs. Buffalo (OT)	22	210	1
Sept. 20, 2009	Frank Gore, San Francisco vs. Seattle	16	207	2
Dec. 28, 2008	Michael Turner, Atlanta vs. St. Louis	25	208	1
Dec. 21, 2008	Derrick Ward, N.Y. Giants vs. Carolina (OT)	15	215	0
Sept. 7, 2008	Michael Turner, Atlanta vs. Detroit	22	220	2
Nov. 4, 2007	*Adrian Peterson, Minnesota vs. San Diego	30	296	3
Oct. 14, 2007	*Adrian Peterson, Minnesota vs. Chicago	20	224	3
Sept. 16, 2007	Jamal Lewis, Cleveland vs. Cincinnati	27	216	1
Dec. 30, 2006	Tiki Barber, N.Y. Giants vs. Washington	23	234	3
Dec. 7, 2006	Willie Parker, Pittsburgh vs. Cleveland	32	223	1
Nov. 27, 2006	Shaun Alexander, Seattle vs. Green Bay	40	201	0
Nov. 19, 2006	Frank Gore, San Francisco vs. Seattle	24	212	0
Nov. 12, 2006	Willie Parker, Pittsburgh vs. New Orleans	22	213	2
Jan. 1, 2006	Larry Johnson, Kansas City vs. Cincinnati	26	201	3
Dec. 31, 2005	Tiki Barber, N.Y. Giants vs. Oakland	28	203	1
Dec. 17, 2005	Tiki Barber, N.Y. Giants vs. Kansas City	29	220	2
Nov. 20, 2005	Larry Johnson, Kansas City vs. Houston	36	211	2
Oct. 30, 2005	Tiki Barber, N.Y. Giants vs. Washington	24	206	1
Nov. 28, 2004	Rudi Johnson, Cincinnati vs. Cleveland	26	202	2
Nov. 21, 2004	Edgerrin James, Indianapolis vs. Chicago	23	204	1
Dec. 28, 2003	Ahman Green, Green Bay vs. Denver	20	218	2
Dec. 28, 2003	LaDainian Tomlinson, San Diego vs. Oakland	31	243	2
Dec. 21, 2003	Jamal Lewis, Baltimore vs. Cleveland	22	205	2
Dec. 7, 2003	Clinton Portis, Denver vs. Kansas City	22	218	5
Oct. 19, 2003	LaDainian Tomlinson, San Diego vs. Cleveland	26	200	1
Sept. 14, 2003	Jamal Lewis, Baltimore vs. Cleveland	30	295	2
Dec. 29, 2002	*Clinton Portis, Denver vs. Arizona	24	228	2
Dec. 28, 2002	Tiki Barber, N.Y. Giants vs. Philadelphia	32	203	0
Dec. 9, 2002	Ricky Williams, Miami vs. Chicago	31	216	2
Dec. 1, 2002	LaDainian Tomlinson, San Diego vs. Denver	37	220	3
Dec. 1, 2002	Ricky Williams, Miami vs. Buffalo	27	228	2
Sept. 29, 2002	LaDainian Tomlinson, San Diego vs. New England	27	217	2
Dec. 23, 2001	Marshall Faulk, St. Louis vs. Carolina	30	202	2
Nov. 11, 2001	Shaun Alexander, Seattle vs. Oakland	35	266	3
Dec. 24, 2000	Marshall Faulk, St. Louis vs. New Orleans	32	220	2
Dec. 3, 2000	Corey Dillon, Cincinnati vs. Arizona	35	216	1
Dec. 3, 2000	Warrick Dunn, Tampa Bay vs. Dallas	22	210	2
Dec. 3, 2000	*Mike Anderson, Denver vs. New Orleans	37	251	4
Dec. 3, 2000	Curtis Martin, N.Y. Jets vs. Indianapolis	30	203	1
Nov. 19, 2000	Fred Taylor, Jacksonville vs. Pittsburgh	30	234	3
Oct. 22, 2000	Corey Dillon, Cincinnati vs. Denver	22	278	2
Oct. 15, 2000	Marshall Faulk, St. Louis vs. Atlanta	25	208	1
Oct. 15, 2000	Edgerrin James, Indianapolis vs. Seattle	38	219	3
Sept. 24, 2000	Charlie Garner, San Francisco vs. Dallas	36	201	1
Sept. 3, 2000	Duce Staley, Philadelphia vs. Dallas	26	201	1
Nov. 22, 1998	Priest Holmes, Baltimore vs. Cincinnati	36	227	1
Oct. 11, 1998	Terrell Davis, Denver vs. Seattle	30	208	1

Date	Player, Team, Opponent	Att.	Yards	TD
Dec. 4, 1997	*Corey Dillon, Cincinnati vs. Tennessee	39	246	4
Nov. 23, 1997	Barry Sanders, Detroit vs. Indianapolis	24	216	2
Oct. 26, 1997	Terrell Davis, Denver vs. Buffalo (OT)	42	207	1
Oct. 19, 1997	Napoleon Kaufman, Oakland vs. Denver	28	227	1
Oct. 12, 1997	Barry Sanders, Detroit vs. Tampa Bay	24	215	2
Sept. 21, 1997	Terrell Davis, Denver vs. Cincinnati	27	215	1
Aug. 31, 1997	Eddie George, Tennessee vs. Oakland (OT)	35	216	1
Sept. 22, 1996	LeShon Johnson, Arizona vs. New Orleans	21	214	2
Nov. 13, 1994	Barry Sanders, Detroit vs. Tampa Bay	26	237	0
Dec. 12, 1993	*Jerome Bettis, L.A. Rams vs. New Orleans	28	212	1
Oct. 31, 1993	Emmitt Smith, Dallas vs. Philadelphia	30	237	1
Nov. 24, 1991	Barry Sanders, Detroit vs. Minnesota	23	220	4
Dec. 23, 1990	James Brooks, Cincinnati vs. Houston	20	201	1
Oct. 14, 1990	Barry Word, Kansas City vs. Detroit	18	200	2
Sept. 24, 1990	Thurman Thomas, Buffalo vs. N.Y. Jets	18	214	0
Dec. 24, 1989	Greg Bell, L.A. Rams vs. New England	26	210	1
Sept. 24, 1989	Greg Bell, L.A. Rams vs. Green Bay	28	221	2
Sept. 17, 1989	Gerald Riggs, Washington vs. Philadelphia	29	221	1
Dec. 18, 1988	Gary Anderson, San Diego vs. Kansas City	34	217	1
Nov. 30, 1987	*Bo Jackson, L.A. Raiders vs. Seattle	18	221	2
Nov. 15, 1987	Charles White, L.A. Rams vs. St. Louis	34	213	1
Dec. 7, 1986	Rueben Mayes, New Orleans vs. Miami	28	203	2
Oct. 5, 1986	Eric Dickerson, L.A. Rams vs. Tampa Bay (OT)	30	207	2
Dec. 21, 1985	George Rogers, Washington vs. St. Louis	34	206	1
Dec. 21, 1985	Joe Morris, N.Y. Giants vs. Pittsburgh	36	202	3
Dec. 9, 1984	Eric Dickerson, L.A. Rams vs. Houston	27	215	2
Nov. 18, 1984	*Greg Bell, Buffalo vs. Dallas	27	206	1
Nov. 4, 1984	Eric Dickerson, L.A. Rams vs. St. Louis	21	208	0
Sept. 2, 1984	Gerald Riggs, Atlanta vs. New Orleans	35	202	2
Nov. 27, 1983	*Curt Warner, Seattle vs. Kansas City (OT)	32	207	3
Nov. 6, 1983	James Wilder, Tampa Bay vs. Minnesota	31	219	1
Sept. 18, 1983	Tony Collins, New England vs. N.Y. Jets	23	212	3
Sept. 4, 1983	George Rogers, New Orleans vs. St. Louis	24	206	2
Dec. 21, 1980	Earl Campbell, Houston vs. Minnesota	29	203	1
Nov. 16, 1980	Earl Campbell, Houston vs. Chicago	31	206	0
Oct. 26, 1980	Earl Campbell, Houston vs. Cincinnati	27	202	0
Oct. 19, 1980	Earl Campbell, Houston vs. Tampa Bay	33	203	0
Nov. 26, 1978	*Terry Miller, Buffalo vs. N.Y. Giants	21	208	2
Dec. 4, 1977	*Tony Dorsett, Dallas vs. Philadelphia	23	206	2
Nov. 20, 1977	Walter Payton, Chicago vs. Minnesota	40	275	1
Oct. 30, 1977	Walter Payton, Chicago vs. Green Bay	23	205	2
Dec. 5, 1976	O.J. Simpson, Buffalo vs. Miami	24	203	1
Nov. 25, 1976	O.J. Simpson, Buffalo vs. Detroit	29	273	2
Oct. 24, 1976	Chuck Foreman, Minnesota vs. Philadelphia	28	200	2
Dec. 14, 1975	Greg Pruitt, Cleveland vs. Kansas City	26	214	3
Sept. 28, 1975	O.J. Simpson, Buffalo vs. Pittsburgh	28	227	1
Dec. 16, 1973	O.J. Simpson, Buffalo vs. N.Y. Jets	34	200	1
Dec. 9, 1973	O.J. Simpson, Buffalo vs. New England	22	219	1
Sept. 16, 1973	O.J. Simpson, Buffalo vs. New England	29	250	2
Dec. 5, 1971	Willie Ellison, Los Angeles vs. New Orleans	26	247	1
Dec. 20, 1970	John (Frenchy) Fuqua, Pittsburgh vs. Philadelphia	20	218	2
Nov. 3, 1968	Gale Sayers, Chicago vs. Green Bay	24	205	0
Oct. 30, 1966	Jim Nance, Boston vs. Oakland	38	208	2
Oct. 10, 1964	John Henry Johnson, Pittsburgh vs. Cleveland	30	200	3
Dec. 8, 1963	Cookie Gilchrist, Buffalo vs. N.Y. Jets	36	243	5
Nov. 3, 1963	Jim Brown, Cleveland vs. Philadelphia	28	223	1
Oct. 20, 1963	Clem Daniels, Oakland vs. N.Y. Jets	27	200	2
Sept. 22, 1963	Jim Brown, Cleveland vs. Dallas	20	232	2
Dec. 10, 1961	Billy Cannon, Houston vs. N.Y. Titans	25	216	3
Nov. 19, 1961	Jim Brown, Cleveland vs. Philadelphia	34	237	4
Dec. 18, 1960	John David Crow, St. Louis vs. Pittsburgh	24	203	0
Nov. 15, 1959	Bobby Mitchell, Cleveland vs. Washington	14	232	3
Nov. 24, 1957	*Jim Brown, Cleveland vs. Los Angeles	31	237	4
Dec. 16, 1956	*Tom Wilson, Los Angeles vs. Green Bay	23	223	0
Nov. 22, 1953	Dan Towler, Los Angeles vs. Baltimore	14	205	1
Nov. 12, 1950	Gene Roberts, N.Y. Giants vs. Chi. Cardinals	26	218	2
Nov. 27, 1949	Steve Van Buren, Philadelphia vs. Pittsburgh	27	205	0
Oct. 8, 1933	Cliff Battles, Boston vs. N.Y. Giants	16	215	1

*First season of professional football.

TIMES 200 OR MORE
126 times by 81 players...Simpson 6; Barber 5; Brown, Campbell, Sanders, Tomlinson 4; Bell, Davis, Dickerson, Dillon, Faulk, Lewis 3;
Alexander, Gore, James, L. Johnson, Parker, Payton, Peterson, Portis, Riggs, Rogers, Turner, Williams 2.

4,000 YARDS PASSING IN A SEASON

Year	Player, Team	Att.	Comp.	Pct.	Yards	TD	Int.
2011	Drew Brees, New Orleans[6]	657	468	71.2	5,476	46	14
	Tom Brady, New England[4]	611	401	65.6	5,235	39	12
	Matthew Stafford, Detroit	663	421	63.5	5,038	41	16
	Eli Manning, N.Y. Giants[3]	589	359	61.0	4,933	29	16
	Aaron Rodgers, Green Bay[3]	502	343	68.3	4,643	45	6
	Philip Rivers, San Diego[4]	582	366	62.9	4,624	27	20
	Tony Romo, Dallas[3]	522	346	66.3	4,184	31	10
	Matt Ryan, Atlanta	566	347	61.3	4,177	29	12
	Ben Roethlisberger, Pittsburgh[2]	513	324	63.2	4,077	21	14
	*Cam Newton, Carolina	517	310	60.0	4,051	21	17
2010	Philip Rivers, San Diego[3]	541	357	66.0	4,710	30	13
	Peyton Manning, Indianapolis[11]	679	450	66.3	4,700	33	17
	Drew Brees, New Orleans[5]	658	448	68.1	4,620	33	22
	Matt Schaub, Houston[2]	574	365	63.6	4,370	24	12
	Eli Manning, N.Y. Giants[2]	539	339	62.9	4,002	31	25
2009	Matt Schaub, Houston	583	396	67.9	4,770	29	15
	Peyton Manning, Indianapolis[10]	571	393	68.8	4,500	33	16
	Tony Romo, Dallas[2]	550	347	63.1	4,483	26	9
	Aaron Rodgers, Green Bay[2]	541	350	64.7	4,434	30	7
	Tom Brady, New England[3]	565	371	65.7	4,398	28	13
	Drew Brees, New Orleans[4]	514	363	70.6	4,388	34	11
	Ben Roethlisberger, Pittsburgh	506	337	66.6	4,328	26	12
	Philip Rivers, San Diego[2]	486	317	65.2	4,254	28	9
	Brett Favre, Minnesota[6]	531	363	68.4	4,202	33	7
	Eli Manning, N.Y. Giants	509	317	62.3	4,021	27	14
2008	Drew Brees, New Orleans[3]	635	413	65.0	5,069	34	17
	Kurt Warner, Arizona[3]	598	401	67.1	4,583	30	14
	Jay Cutler, Denver	616	384	62.3	4,526	25	18
	Aaron Rodgers, Green Bay	536	341	63.6	4,038	28	13
	Philip Rivers, San Diego	478	312	65.3	4,009	34	11
	Peyton Manning, Indianapolis[9]	555	371	66.8	4,002	27	12
2007	Tom Brady, New England[2]	578	398	68.9	4,806	50	8
	Drew Brees, New Orleans[2]	652	440	67.5	4,423	28	18
	Tony Romo, Dallas	520	335	64.4	4,211	36	19
	Brett Favre, Green Bay[5]	535	356	66.5	4,155	28	15
	Carson Palmer, Cincinnati[2]	575	373	64.9	4,131	26	20
	Jon Kitna, Detroit[2]	561	355	63.3	4,068	18	20
	Peyton Manning, Indianapolis[8]	515	337	65.4	4,040	31	14
2006	Drew Brees, New Orleans	554	356	64.3	4,418	26	11
	Peyton Manning, Indianapolis[7]	557	362	65.0	4,397	31	9
	Marc Bulger, St. Louis	588	370	62.9	4,301	24	8
	Jon Kitna, Detroit	596	372	62.4	4,208	21	22
	Carson Palmer, Cincinnati	520	324	62.3	4,035	28	13
2005	Tom Brady, New England	530	334	63.0	4,110	26	14
	Trent Green, Kansas City[3]	507	317	62.5	4,014	17	10
2004	Daunte Culpepper, Minnesota	548	379	69.2	4,717	39	11
	Trent Green, Kansas City[2]	556	369	66.4	4,591	27	17
	Peyton Manning, Indianapolis[6]	497	336	67.6	4,557	49	10
	Jake Plummer, Denver	521	303	58.2	4,089	27	20
	Brett Favre, Green Bay[4]	540	346	64.1	4,088	30	17
2003	Peyton Manning, Indianapolis[5]	566	379	67.0	4,267	29	10
	Trent Green, Kansas City	523	330	63.1	4,039	24	12
2002	Rich Gannon, Oakland	618	418	67.6	4,689	26	10
	Drew Bledsoe, Buffalo[3]	610	375	61.5	4,359	24	15
	Peyton Manning, Indianapolis[4]	591	392	66.3	4,200	27	19
	Kerry Collins, N.Y. Giants	545	335	61.5	4,073	19	14
2001	Kurt Warner, St. Louis[2]	546	375	68.7	4,830	36	22
	Peyton Manning, Indianapolis[3]	547	343	62.7	4,131	26	23
2000	Peyton Manning, Indianapolis[2]	571	357	62.5	4,413	33	15
	Jeff Garcia, San Francisco	561	355	63.3	4,278	31	10
	Elvis Grbac, Kansas City	547	326	59.6	4,169	28	14
1999	Steve Beuerlein, Carolina	571	343	60.1	4,436	36	15

Year	Player, Team	Att.	Comp.	Pct.	Yards	TD	Int.
	Kurt Warner, St. Louis	499	325	65.1	4,353	41	13
	Peyton Manning, Indianapolis	533	331	62.1	4,135	26	15
	Brett Favre, Green Bay[3]	595	341	57.3	4,091	22	23
	Brad Johnson, Washington	519	316	60.9	4,005	24	13
1998	Brett Favre, Green Bay[2]	551	347	63.0	4,212	31	23
	Steve Young, San Francisco[2]	517	322	62.3	4,170	36	12
1996	Mark Brunell, Jacksonville	557	353	63.4	4,367	19	20
	Vinny Testaverde, Baltimore	549	325	59.2	4,177	33	19
	Drew Bledsoe, New England[2]	623	373	59.9	4,086	27	15
1995	Brett Favre, Green Bay	570	359	63.0	4,413	38	13
	Scott Mitchell, Detroit	583	346	59.3	4,338	32	12
	Warren Moon, Minnesota[4]	606	377	62.2	4,228	33	14
	Jeff George, Atlanta	557	336	60.3	4,143	24	11
1994	Drew Bledsoe, New England	691	400	57.9	4,555	25	27
	Dan Marino, Miami[6]	615	385	62.6	4,453	30	17
	Warren Moon, Minnesota[3]	601	371	61.7	4,264	18	19
1993	John Elway, Denver	551	348	63.2	4,030	25	10
	Steve Young, San Francisco	462	314	68.0	4,023	29	16
1992	Dan Marino, Miami[5]	554	330	59.6	4,116	24	16
1991	Warren Moon, Houston[2]	655	404	61.7	4,690	23	21
1990	Warren Moon, Houston	584	362	62.0	4,689	33	13
1989	Don Majkowski, Green Bay	599	353	58.9	4,318	27	20
	Jim Everett, L.A. Rams	518	304	58.7	4,310	29	17
1988	Dan Marino, Miami[4]	606	354	58.4	4,434	28	23
1986	Dan Marino, Miami[3]	623	378	60.7	4,746	44	23
	Jay Schroeder, Washington	541	276	51.0	4,109	22	22
1985	Dan Marino, Miami[2]	567	336	59.3	4,137	30	21
1984	Dan Marino, Miami	564	362	64.2	5,084	48	17
	Neil Lomax, St. Louis	560	345	61.6	4,614	28	16
	Phil Simms, N.Y. Giants	533	286	53.7	4,044	22	18
1983	Lynn Dickey, Green Bay	484	289	59.7	4,458	32	29
	Bill Kenney, Kansas City	603	346	57.4	4,348	24	18
1981	Dan Fouts, San Diego[3]	609	360	59.1	4,802	33	17
1980	Dan Fouts, San Diego[2]	589	348	59.1	4,715	30	24
	Brian Sipe, Cleveland	554	337	60.8	4,132	30	14
1979	Dan Fouts, San Diego	530	332	62.6	4,082	24	24
1967	Joe Namath, N.Y. Jets	491	258	52.5	4,007	26	28

*First season of professional football.

400 YARDS PASSING IN A GAME

Date	Player, Team, Opponent	Att.	Comp.	Yards	TD
Jan. 1, 2012	Carson Palmer, Oakland vs. San Diego	43	28	417	2
Jan. 1, 2012	Matthew Stafford, Detroit vs. Green Bay	59	36	520	5
Jan. 1, 2012	Matt Flynn, Green Bay vs. Detroit	44	31	480	6
Dec. 18, 2011	Drew Brees, New Orleans vs. Minnesota	40	32	412	5
Dec. 11, 2011	Eli Manning, N.Y. Giants vs. Dallas	47	27	400	2
Dec. 4, 2011	Matthew Stafford, Detroit vs. New Orleans	44	31	408	1
Nov. 28, 2011	Eli Manning, N.Y. Giants vs. New Orleans	47	33	406	2
Nov. 27, 2011	Vince Young, Philadelphia vs. New England	48	26	400	1
Oct. 9, 2011	Eli Manning, N.Y. Giants vs. Seattle	39	24	420	3
Oct. 9, 2011	Matt Schaub, Houston vs. Oakland	51	24	416	2
Oct. 2, 2011	Aaron Rodgers, Green Bay vs. Denver	38	29	408	4
Oct. 2, 2011	Michael Vick, Philadelphia vs. San Francisco	46	30	416	2
Sept. 18, 2011	Tom Brady, New England vs. San Diego	40	31	423	3
Sept. 18, 2011	*Cam Newton, Carolina vs. Green Bay	46	28	432	1
Sept. 12, 2011	Chad Henne, Miami vs. New England	49	30	416	2
Sept. 12, 2011	Tom Brady, New England vs. Miami	48	32	517	4
Sept. 11, 2011	*Cam Newton, Carolina vs. Arizona	37	24	422	2
Sept. 8, 2011	Drew Brees, New Orleans vs. Green Bay	49	32	419	3
Dec. 26, 2010	Aaron Rodgers, Green Bay vs. N.Y. Giants	37	25	404	4
Nov. 14, 2010	Matt Cassel, Kansas City vs. Denver	53	33	469	4
Nov. 7, 2010	Brett Favre, Minnesota vs. Arizona (OT)	47	36	446	2
Oct. 24, 2010	Carson Palmer, Cincinnati vs. Atlanta	50	36	412	3
Oct. 10, 2010	Tony Romo, Dallas vs. Tennessee	46	31	406	3
Oct. 10, 2010	Philip Rivers, San Diego vs. Oakland	42	27	431	2
Sept. 26, 2010	Kyle Orton, Denver vs. Indianapolis	57	37	476	1
Sept. 26, 2010	Philip Rivers, San Diego vs. Seattle	53	29	455	2
Sept. 19, 2010	Matt Schaub, Houston vs. Washington	52	38	497	3

Date	Player, Team, Opponent	Att.	Comp.	Yards	TD
Sept. 19, 2010	Donovan McNabb, Washington vs. Houston	38	28	426	1
Sept. 12, 2010	Peyton Manning, Indianapolis vs. Houston	57	40	433	3
Jan. 3, 2010	Kyle Orton, Denver vs. Kansas City	56	32	431	1
Dec. 20, 2009	Ben Roethlisberger, Pittsburgh vs. Green Bay	46	29	503	3
Dec. 6, 2009	Drew Brees, New Orleans vs. Washington (OT)	49	35	419	2
Nov. 22, 2009	Matthew Stafford, Detroit vs. Cleveland	43	26	422	5
Nov. 15, 2009	Donovan McNabb, Philadelphia vs. San Diego	55	35	450	2
Oct. 18, 2009	Ben Roethlisberger, Pittsburgh vs. Cleveland	35	23	417	2
Sept. 20, 2009	Philip Rivers, San Diego vs. Baltimore	45	25	436	2
Dec. 7, 2008	Matt Schaub, Houston vs. Green Bay	42	28	414	2
Nov. 23, 2008	Matt Cassel, New England vs. Miami	43	30	415	3
Nov. 13, 2008	Matt Cassel, New England vs. N.Y. Jets (OT)	51	30	400	3
Nov. 9, 2008	Drew Brees, New Orleans vs. Atlanta	58	31	422	2
Nov. 6, 2008	Jay Cutler, Denver vs. Cleveland	42	24	447	3
Sept. 28, 2008	Kurt Warner, Arizona vs. N.Y. Jets	57	40	472	2
Sept. 21, 2008	Drew Brees, New Orleans vs. Denver	48	39	421	1
Sept. 21, 2008	Brian Griese, Tampa Bay vs. Chicago (OT)	67	38	407	2
Nov. 25, 2007	Kurt Warner, Arizona vs. San Francisco (OT)	48	34	484	2
Nov. 4, 2007	Drew Brees, New Orleans vs. Jacksonville	49	35	445	3
Sept. 23, 2007	Jon Kitna, Detroit vs. Philadelphia	46	29	446	2
Sept. 16, 2007	Carson Palmer, Cincinnati vs. Cleveland	50	33	401	6
Dec. 10, 2006	Chris Weinke, Carolina vs. N.Y. Giants	61	34	423	1
Nov. 26, 2006	Matt Leinart, Arizona vs. Minnesota	51	31	405	1
Nov. 19, 2006	Drew Brees, New Orleans vs. Cincinnati	52	37	510	2
Nov. 12, 2006	Carson Palmer, Cincinnati vs. San Diego	42	31	440	3
Nov. 5, 2006	Ben Roethlisberger, Pittsburgh vs. Denver	54	38	433	1
Oct. 22, 2006	Joey Harrington, Miami vs. Green Bay	62	33	414	2
Sept. 17, 2006	Peyton Manning, Indianapolis vs. Houston	38	26	400	3
Oct. 2, 2005	Marc Bulger, St. Louis vs. N.Y. Giants	62	40	442	2
Jan. 2, 2005	Marc Bulger, St. Louis vs. N.Y. Jets (OT)	39	29	450	3
Dec. 19, 2004	Daunte Culpepper, Minnesota vs. Detroit	35	25	404	2
Dec. 19, 2004	Billy Volek, Tennessee vs. Oakland	60	40	492	4
Dec. 13, 2004	Billy Volek, Tennessee vs. Kansas City	43	29	426	4
Dec. 6, 2004	Matt Hasselbeck, Seattle vs. Dallas	40	28	414	3
Dec. 5, 2004	Peyton Manning, Indianapolis vs. Tennessee	33	25	425	3
Dec. 5, 2004	Donovan McNabb, Philadelphia vs. Green Bay	43	32	464	5
Nov. 29, 2004	Marc Bulger, St. Louis vs. Green Bay	53	35	448	2
Nov. 28, 2004	Kelly Holcomb, Cleveland vs. Cincinnati	39	30	413	5
Oct. 31, 2004	Peyton Manning, Indianapolis vs. Kansas City	44	25	472	5
Oct. 31, 2004	Jake Plummer, Denver vs. Atlanta	55	31	499	4
Oct. 17, 2004	Daunte Culpepper, Minnesota vs. New Orleans	37	26	425	5
Oct. 10. 2004	Tim Rattay, San Francisco vs. Arizona (OT)	57	38	417	2
Nov. 16, 2003	Peyton Manning, Indianapolis vs. N.Y. Jets	36	27	401	1
Oct. 12, 2003	Trent Green, Kansas City vs. Green Bay (OT)	45	27	400	3
Oct. 12, 2003	Steve McNair, Tennessee vs. Houston	27	18	421	3
Dec. 29, 2002	Matt Hasselbeck, Seattle vs. San Diego (OT)	53	36	449	2
Dec. 1, 2002	Matt Hasselbeck, Seattle vs. San Francisco	55	30	427	3
Nov. 10, 2002	Marc Bulger, St. Louis vs. San Diego	48	36	453	4
Nov. 10, 2002	Tommy Maddox, Pittsburgh vs. Atlanta (OT)	41	28	473	4
Oct. 6, 2002	Drew Bledsoe, Buffalo vs. Oakland	53	32	417	2
Sept. 22, 2002	Tom Brady, New England vs. Kansas City (OT)	54	39	410	4
Sept. 15, 2002	Drew Bledsoe, Buffalo vs. Minnesota (OT)	49	35	463	3
Sept. 15, 2002	Rich Gannon, Oakland vs. Pittsburgh	64	43	403	1
Dec. 30, 2001	Jon Kitna, Cincinnati vs. Pittsburgh	68	35	411	2
Dec. 23, 2001	Chris Chandler, Atlanta vs. Buffalo	40	28	431	2
Nov. 18, 2001	Charlie Batch, Detroit vs. Arizona	62	36	436	3
Nov. 18, 2001	Kurt Warner, St. Louis vs. New England	42	30	401	3
Sept. 23, 2001	Peyton Manning, Indianapolis vs. Buffalo	29	23	421	4
Dec. 24, 2000	Vinny Testaverde, N.Y. Jets vs. Baltimore	69	36	481	2
Dec. 17, 2000	Jeff Garcia, San Francisco vs. Chicago	44	36	402	2
Dec. 3, 2000	Aaron Brooks, New Orleans vs. Denver	48	30	441	2
Nov. 19, 2000	Gus Frerotte, Denver vs. San Diego	58	36	462	5
Nov. 5, 2000	Elvis Grbac, Kansas City vs. Oakland	53	39	504	2
Nov. 5, 2000	Trent Green, St. Louis vs. Carolina	42	29	431	2
Sept. 25, 2000	Peyton Manning, Indianapolis vs. Jacksonville	36	23	440	4
Sept. 4, 2000	Kurt Warner, St. Louis vs. Denver	35	25	441	3
Dec. 26, 1999	Brad Johnson, Washington vs. San Francisco (OT)	47	32	471	2
Dec. 5, 1999	Jeff Garcia, San Francisco vs. Cincinnati	49	33	437	3

Date	Player, Team, Opponent	Att.	Comp.	Yards	TD
Nov. 28, 1999	Jim Harbaugh, San Diego vs. Minnesota	39	25	404	1
Nov. 14, 1999	Jim Miller, Chicago vs. Minnesota (OT)	48	34	422	3
Sept. 26, 1999	Peyton Manning, Indianapolis vs. San Diego	54	29	404	2
Dec. 6, 1998	Vinny Testaverde, N.Y. Jets vs. Seattle	63	42	418	2
Dec. 6, 1998	John Elway, Denver vs. Kansas City	32	22	400	2
Nov. 26, 1998	Troy Aikman, Dallas vs. Minnesota	57	34	455	1
Nov. 23, 1998	Drew Bledsoe, New England vs. Miami	54	28	423	2
Nov. 15, 1998	Jake Plummer, Arizona vs. Dallas	56	31	465	3
Oct. 5, 1998	Randall Cunningham, Minnesota vs. Green Bay	32	20	442	4
Sept. 6, 1998	Glenn Foley, N.Y. Jets vs. San Francisco (OT)	58	30	415	3
Nov. 2, 1997	Tony Banks, St. Louis vs. Atlanta	34	23	401	2
Oct. 26, 1997	Warren Moon, Seattle vs. Oakland	44	28	409	5
Nov. 10, 1996	Boomer Esiason, Arizona vs. Washington (OT)	59	35	522	3
Nov. 3, 1996	Drew Bledsoe, New England vs. Miami	41	30	419	3
Oct. 27, 1996	Vinny Testaverde, Baltimore vs. St. Louis (OT)	51	31	429	3
Oct. 20, 1996	Mark Brunell, Jacksonville vs. St. Louis	52	37	421	0
Sept. 22, 1996	Mark Brunell, Jacksonville vs. New England (OT)	39	23	432	3
Dec. 18, 1995	Steve Young, San Francisco vs. Minnesota	49	30	425	3
Nov. 26, 1995	Dave Krieg, Arizona vs. Atlanta (OT)	43	27	413	4
Nov. 23, 1995	Scott Mitchell, Detroit vs. Minnesota	45	30	410	4
Oct. 1, 1995	Dan Marino, Miami vs. Cincinnati	48	33	450	2
Nov. 20, 1994	Warren Moon, Minnesota vs. N.Y. Jets	50	33	400	2
Nov. 13, 1994	Drew Bledsoe, New England vs. Minnesota (OT)	70	45	426	3
Nov. 6, 1994	Warren Moon, Minnesota vs. New Orleans	57	33	420	3
Sept. 25, 1994	Dan Marino, Miami vs. Minnesota	54	29	431	3
Sept. 4, 1994	Dan Marino, Miami vs. New England (OT)	42	23	473	5
Sept. 4, 1994	Drew Bledsoe, New England vs. Miami (OT)	51	32	421	4
Dec. 19, 1993	Steve Beuerlein, Phoenix vs. Seattle	53	34	431	3
Dec. 5, 1993	Brett Favre, Green Bay vs. Chicago	54	36	402	2
Nov. 28, 1993	Steve Young, San Francisco vs. L.A. Rams	32	26	462	4
Oct. 31, 1993	Jeff Hostetler, L.A. Raiders vs. San Diego	32	20	424	2
Sept. 13, 1992	Steve Young, San Francisco vs. Buffalo	37	26	449	3
Sept. 13, 1992	Jim Kelly, Buffalo vs. San Francisco	33	22	403	3
Nov. 10, 1991	Warren Moon, Houston vs. Dallas (OT)	56	41	432	0
Nov. 10, 1991	Mark Rypien, Washington vs. Atlanta	31	16	442	6
Oct. 13, 1991	Warren Moon, Houston vs. N.Y. Jets	50	35	423	2
Dec. 16, 1990	Warren Moon, Houston vs. Kansas City	45	27	527	3
Nov. 4, 1990	Joe Montana, San Francisco vs. Green Bay	40	25	411	3
Oct. 14, 1990	Joe Montana, San Francisco vs. Atlanta	49	32	476	6
Oct. 7, 1990	Boomer Esiason, Cincinnati vs. L.A. Rams (OT)	45	31	490	3
Dec. 23, 1989	Warren Moon, Houston vs. Cleveland	51	32	414	2
Dec. 11, 1989	Joe Montana, San Francisco vs. L.A. Rams	42	30	458	3
Nov. 26, 1989	Jim Everett, L.A. Rams vs. New Orleans (OT)	51	29	454	1
Nov. 26, 1989	Mark Rypien, Washington vs. Chicago	47	30	401	4
Oct. 2, 1989	Randall Cunningham, Philadelphia vs. Chicago	62	32	401	1
Sept. 24, 1989	Joe Montana, San Francisco vs. Philadelphia	34	25	428	5
Sept. 24, 1989	Dan Marino, Miami vs. N.Y. Jets	55	33	427	3
Sept. 17, 1989	Randall Cunningham, Philadelphia vs. Washington	46	34	447	5
Dec. 18, 1988	Dave Krieg, Seattle vs. L.A. Raiders	32	19	410	4
Dec. 12, 1988	Dan Marino, Miami vs. Cleveland	50	30	404	4
Oct. 23, 1988	Dan Marino, Miami vs. N.Y. Jets	60	35	521	3
Oct. 16, 1988	Vinny Testaverde, Tampa Bay vs. Indianapolis	42	25	469	2
Sept. 11, 1988	Doug Williams, Washington vs. Pittsburgh	52	30	430	2
Nov. 29, 1987	Tom Ramsey, New England vs. Philadelphia	53	34	402	3
Nov. 22, 1987	Boomer Esiason, Cincinnati vs. Pittsburgh	53	30	409	0
Sept. 20, 1987	Neil Lomax, St. Louis vs. San Diego	61	32	457	3
Dec. 21, 1986	Boomer Esiason, Cincinnati vs. N.Y. Jets	30	23	425	5
Dec. 14, 1986	Dan Marino, Miami vs. L.A. Rams (OT)	46	29	403	5
Nov. 23, 1986	Bernie Kosar, Cleveland vs. Pittsburgh (OT)	46	28	414	2
Nov. 17, 1986	Joe Montana, San Francisco vs. Washington	60	33	441	4
Nov. 16, 1986	Dan Marino, Miami vs. Buffalo	54	39	404	4
Nov. 10, 1986	Bernie Kosar, Cleveland vs. Miami	50	32	401	0
Nov. 2, 1986	Tommy Kramer, Minnesota vs. Washington (OT)	35	20	490	4
Nov. 2, 1986	Ken O'Brien, N.Y. Jets vs. Seattle	32	26	431	4
Oct. 27, 1986	Jay Schroeder, Washington vs. N.Y. Giants	40	22	420	1
Oct. 12, 1986	Steve Grogan, New England vs. N.Y. Jets	42	23	401	3
Sept. 21, 1986	Ken O'Brien, N.Y. Jets vs. Miami (OT)	43	29	479	4
Sept. 21, 1986	Dan Marino, Miami vs. N.Y. Jets (OT)	50	30	448	6

Date	Player, Team, Opponent	Att.	Comp.	Yards	TD
Sept. 21, 1986	Tony Eason, New England vs. Seattle	45	26	414	3
Dec. 20, 1985	John Elway, Denver vs. Seattle	42	24	432	1
Nov. 10, 1985	Dan Fouts, San Diego vs. L.A. Raiders (OT)	41	26	436	4
Oct. 13, 1985	Phil Simms, N.Y. Giants vs. Cincinnati	62	40	513	1
Oct. 13, 1985	Dave Krieg, Seattle vs. Atlanta	51	33	405	4
Oct. 6, 1985	Phil Simms, N.Y. Giants vs. Dallas	36	18	432	3
Oct. 6, 1985	Joe Montana, San Francisco vs. Atlanta	57	37	429	5
Sept. 19, 1985	Tommy Kramer, Minnesota vs. Chicago	55	28	436	3
Sept. 15, 1985	Dan Fouts, San Diego vs. Seattle	43	29	440	4
Dec. 16, 1984	Neil Lomax, St. Louis vs. Washington	46	37	468	2
Dec. 9, 1984	Dan Marino, Miami vs. Indianapolis	41	29	404	4
Dec. 2, 1984	Dan Marino, Miami vs. L.A. Raiders	57	35	470	4
Nov. 25, 1984	Dave Krieg, Seattle vs. Denver	44	30	406	3
Nov. 4, 1984	Dan Marino, Miami vs. N.Y. Jets	42	23	422	2
Oct. 21, 1984	Dan Fouts, San Diego vs. L.A. Raiders	45	24	410	2
Sept. 30, 1984	Dan Marino, Miami vs. St. Louis	36	24	429	3
Sept. 2, 1984	Phil Simms, N.Y. Giants vs. Philadelphia	30	23	409	4
Dec. 11, 1983	Bill Kenney, Kansas City vs. San Diego	41	31	411	4
Nov. 20, 1983	Dave Krieg, Seattle vs. Denver	42	31	418	3
Oct. 9, 1983	Joe Ferguson, Buffalo vs. Miami (OT)	55	38	419	5
Oct. 2, 1983	Joe Theismann, Washington vs. L.A. Raiders	39	23	417	3
Sept. 25, 1983	Richard Todd, N.Y. Jets vs. L.A. Rams (OT)	50	37	446	2
Dec. 26, 1982	Vince Ferragamo, L.A. Rams vs. Chicago	46	30	509	3
Dec. 20, 1982	Dan Fouts, San Diego vs. Cincinnati	40	25	435	1
Dec. 20, 1982	Ken Anderson, Cincinnati vs. San Diego	56	40	416	2
Dec. 11, 1982	Dan Fouts, San Diego vs. San Francisco	48	33	444	5
Nov. 21, 1982	Joe Montana, San Francisco vs. St. Louis	39	26	408	3
Nov. 15, 1981	Steve Bartkowski, Atlanta vs. Pittsburgh	50	33	416	2
Oct. 25, 1981	Brian Sipe, Cleveland vs. Baltimore	41	30	444	4
Oct. 25, 1981	David Woodley, Miami vs. Dallas	37	21	408	3
Oct. 11, 1981	Tommy Kramer, Minnesota vs. San Diego	43	27	444	4
Dec. 14, 1980	Tommy Kramer, Minnesota vs. Cleveland	49	38	456	4
Nov. 16, 1980	Doug Williams, Tampa Bay vs. Minnesota	55	30	486	4
Oct. 19, 1980	Dan Fouts, San Diego vs. N.Y. Giants	41	26	444	3
Oct. 12, 1980	Lynn Dickey, Green Bay vs. Tampa Bay (OT)	51	35	418	1
Sept. 21, 1980	Richard Todd, N.Y. Jets vs. San Francisco	60	42	447	3
Oct. 3, 1976	James Harris, Los Angeles vs. Miami	29	17	436	2
Nov. 17, 1975	Ken Anderson, Cincinnati vs. Buffalo	46	30	447	2
Nov. 18, 1974	Charley Johnson, Denver vs. Kansas City	42	28	445	2
Dec. 11, 1972	Joe Namath, N.Y. Jets vs. Oakland	46	25	403	1
Sept. 24, 1972	Joe Namath, N.Y. Jets vs. Baltimore	28	15	496	6
Dec. 21, 1969	Don Horn, Green Bay vs. St. Louis	31	22	410	5
Sept. 28, 1969	Joe Kapp, Minnesota vs. Baltimore	43	28	449	7
Sept. 9, 1968	Pete Beathard, Houston vs. Kansas City	48	23	413	2
Nov. 26, 1967	Sonny Jurgensen, Washington vs. Cleveland	50	32	418	3
Oct. 1, 1967	Joe Namath, N.Y. Jets vs. Miami	39	23	415	3
Sept. 17, 1967	Johnny Unitas, Baltimore vs. Atlanta	32	22	401	2
Nov. 13, 1966	Don Meredith, Dallas vs. Washington	29	21	406	2
Nov. 28, 1965	Sonny Jurgensen, Washington vs. Dallas	43	26	411	3
Oct. 24, 1965	Fran Tarkenton, Minnesota vs. San Francisco	35	21	407	3
Nov. 1, 1964	Len Dawson, Kansas City vs. Denver	38	23	435	6
Oct. 25, 1964	Cotton Davidson, Oakland vs. Denver	36	23	427	5
Oct. 16, 1964	Babe Parilli, Boston vs. Oakland	47	25	422	4
Dec. 22, 1963	Tom Flores, Oakland vs. Houston	29	17	407	6
Nov. 17, 1963	Norm Snead, Washington vs. Pittsburgh	40	23	424	2
Nov. 10, 1963	Don Meredith, Dallas vs. San Francisco	48	30	460	3
Oct. 13, 1963	Charley Johnson, St. Louis vs. Pittsburgh	41	20	428	2
Dec. 16, 1962	Sonny Jurgensen, Philadelphia vs. St. Louis	34	15	419	5
Nov. 18, 1962	Bill Wade, Chicago vs. Dall. Cowboys	46	28	466	2
Oct. 28, 1962	Y.A. Tittle, N.Y. Giants vs. Washington	39	27	505	7
Sept. 15, 1962	Frank Tripucka, Denver vs. Buffalo	56	29	447	2
Dec. 17, 1961	Sonny Jurgensen, Philadelphia vs. Detroit	42	27	403	3
Nov. 19, 1961	George Blanda, Houston vs. N.Y. Titans	32	20	418	7
Oct. 29, 1961	George Blanda, Houston vs. Buffalo	32	18	464	4
Oct. 29, 1961	Sonny Jurgensen, Philadelphia vs. Washington	41	27	436	3
Oct. 13, 1961	Jacky Lee, Houston vs. Boston	41	27	457	2
Dec. 13, 1958	Bobby Layne, Pittsburgh vs. Chi. Cardinals	49	23	409	2
Nov. 8, 1953	Bobby Thomason, Philadelphia vs. N.Y. Giants	44	22	437	4

Date	Player, Team, Opponent	Att.	Comp.	Yards	TD
Oct. 4, 1952	Otto Graham, Cleveland vs. Pittsburgh	49	21	401	3
Sept. 28, 1951	Norm Van Brocklin, Los Angeles vs. N.Y. Yanks	41	27	554	5
Dec. 11, 1949	Johnny Lujack, Chi. Bears vs. Chi. Cardinals	39	24	468	6
Oct. 31, 1948	Sammy Baugh, Washington vs. Boston	24	17	446	4
Oct. 31, 1948	Jim Hardy, Los Angeles vs. Chi. Cardinals	53	28	406	3
Nov. 14, 1943	Sid Luckman, Chi. Bears vs. N.Y. Giants	32	21	433	7

*First season of professional football.

TIMES 400 OR MORE

237 times by 116 players…Marino 13; P. Manning 8; Brees, Montana, Moon 7; Bledsoe, Fouts 6; Jurgensen, Krieg 5; Bulger, Esiason, Kramer, Palmer, Testaverde, Warner 4; Brady, Cassel, Cunningham, Hasselbeck, E. Manning, McNabb, Namath, Rivers, Roethlisberger, Schaub, Simms, Stafford, Young 3; Anderson, Blanda, Brunell, Culpepper, Elway, Favre, Garcia, Green, C. Johnson, Kitna, Kosar, Lomax, Meredith, Newton, O'Brien, Orton, Plummer, Rodgers, Rypien, Todd, Volek, D. Williams 2.

100 PASS RECEPTIONS IN A SEASON

Year	Player, Team	No.	Yards	Avg.	Long	TD
2011	Wes Welker, New England[4]	122	1,569	12.9	99	9
	Roddy White, Atlanta[2]	100	1,296	13.0	43	8
2010	Roddy White, Atlanta	115	1,389	12.1	46	10
	Reggie Wayne, Indianapolis[3]	111	1,355	12.2	50	6
2009	Wes Welker, New England[3]	123	1,348	11.0	58	4
	Steve Smith, N.Y. Giants	107	1,220	11.4	51	7
	Andre Johnson, Houston[3]	101	1,569	15.5	72	9
	Brandon Marshall, Denver[3]	101	1,120	11.1	75	10
	Dallas Clark, Indianapolis	100	1,106	11.1	80	10
	Reggie Wayne, Indianapolis[2]	100	1,264	12.6	65	10
2008	Andre Johnson, Houston[2]	115	1,575	13.7	65	8
	Wes Welker, New England[2]	111	1,165	10.5	64	3
	Brandon Marshall, Denver[2]	104	1,265	12.2	47	6
2007	T.J. Houshmandzadeh, Cincinnati	112	1,143	10.2	42	12
	Wes Welker, New England	112	1,175	10.5	42	8
	Reggie Wayne, Indianapolis	104	1,510	14.5	64	10
	Derrick Mason, Baltimore	103	1,087	10.6	79	5
	Brandon Marshall, Denver	102	1,325	13.0	68	7
	Larry Fitzgerald, Arizona[2]	100	1,409	14.1	48	10
2006	Andre Johnson, Houston	103	1,147	11.1	53	5
2005	Larry Fitzgerald, Arizona	103	1,409	13.7	47	10
	Steve Smith, Carolina	103	1,563	15.2	80	12
	Anquan Boldin, Arizona[2]	102	1,402	13.7	54	7
	Torry Holt, St. Louis[2]	102	1,331	13.0	44	9
2004	Tony Gonzalez, Kansas City	102	1,258	12.3	32	7
2003	Torry Holt, St. Louis	117	1,696	14.5	48	12
	Randy Moss, Minnesota[2]	111	1,632	14.7	72	17
	*Anquan Boldin, Arizona	101	1,377	13.6	71	8
	LaDainian Tomlinson, San Diego	100	725	7.3	73	4
2002	Marvin Harrison, Indianapolis[4]	143	1,722	12.0	69	11
	Hines Ward, Pittsburgh	112	1,329	11.9	72	12
	Randy Moss, Minnesota	106	1,347	12.7	60	7
	Eric Moulds, Buffalo	100	1,292	12.9	70	10
	Terrell Owens, San Francisco	100	1,300	13.0	76	13
2001	Rod Smith, Denver[2]	113	1,343	11.9	65	11
	Jimmy Smith, Jacksonville[2]	112	1,373	12.3	35	8
	Marvin Harrison, Indianapolis[3]	109	1,524	14.0	68	15
	Keyshawn Johnson, Tampa Bay	106	1,266	11.9	47	1
	Troy Brown, New England	101	1,199	11.9	60	5
	Marty Booker, Chicago	100	1,071	10.7	66	8
2000	Marvin Harrison, Indianapolis[2]	102	1,413	13.9	78	14
	Muhsin Muhammad, Carolina	102	1,183	11.6	36	6
	Ed McCaffrey, Denver	101	1,317	13.0	61	9
	Rod Smith, Denver	100	1,602	16.0	49	8
1999	Jimmy Smith, Jacksonville	116	1,636	14.1	62	6
	Marvin Harrison, Indianapolis	115	1,663	14.5	57	12
1997	Tim Brown, Oakland	104	1,408	13.5	59	5
	Herman Moore, Detroit[3]	104	1,293	12.4	79	8
1996	Jerry Rice, San Francisco[4]	108	1,254	11.6	39	8
	Herman Moore, Detroit[2]	106	1,296	12.2	50	9

Year	Player, Team	No.	Yards	Avg.	Long	TD
	Carl Pickens, Cincinnati	100	1,180	11.8	61	12
1995	Herman Moore, Detroit	123	1,686	13.7	69	14
	Jerry Rice, San Francisco[3]	122	1,848	15.1	81	15
	Cris Carter, Minnesota[2]	122	1,371	11.2	60	17
	Isaac Bruce, St. Louis	119	1,781	15.0	72	13
	Michael Irvin, Dallas	111	1,603	14.4	50	10
	Brett Perriman, Detroit	108	1,488	13.8	91	9
	Eric Metcalf, Atlanta	104	1,189	11.4	62	8
	Robert Brooks, Green Bay	102	1,497	14.7	99	13
	Larry Centers, Arizona	101	962	9.5	32	2
1994	Cris Carter, Minnesota	122	1,256	10.3	65	7
	Jerry Rice, San Francisco[2]	112	1,499	13.4	69	13
	Terance Mathis, Atlanta	111	1,342	12.1	81	11
1993	Sterling Sharpe, Green Bay[2]	112	1,274	11.4	54	11
1992	Sterling Sharpe, Green Bay	108	1,461	13.5	76	13
1991	Haywood Jeffires, Houston	100	1,181	11.8	44	7
1990	Jerry Rice, San Francisco	100	1,502	15.0	64	13
1984	Art Monk, Washington	106	1,372	12.9	72	7
1964	Charley Hennigan, Houston	101	1,546	15.3	53	8
1961	Lionel Taylor, Denver	100	1,176	11.8	52	4

*First season of professional football.

1,000 YARDS PASS RECEIVING IN A SEASON

Year	Player, Team	No.	Yards	Avg.	Long	TD
2011	Calvin Johnson, Detroit[3]	96	1,681	17.5	73	16
	Wes Welker, New England[4]	122	1,569	12.9	99	9
	Victor Cruz, N.Y. Giants	82	1,536	18.7	99	9
	Larry Fitzgerald, Arizona[6]	80	1,411	17.6	73	8
	Steve Smith, Carolina[6]	79	1,394	17.6	77	7
	Rob Gronkowski, New England	90	1,327	14.7	52	17
	Jimmy Graham, New Orleans	99	1,310	13.2	59	11
	Roddy White, Atlanta[5]	100	1,296	13.0	43	8
	Jordy Nelson, Green Bay	68	1,263	18.6	93	15
	Brandon Marshall, Miami[5]	81	1,214	15.0	65	6
	Mike Wallace, Pittsburgh[2]	72	1,193	16.6	95	8
	Hakeem Nicks, N.Y. Giants[2]	76	1,192	15.7	68	7
	Dwayne Bowe, Kansas City[3]	81	1,159	14.3	52	5
	Marques Colston, New Orleans[5]	80	1,143	14.3	50	8
	Antonio Brown, Pittsburgh	69	1,108	16.1	79	2
	Vincent Jackson, San Diego[3]	60	1,106	18.4	58	9
	*A.J. Green, Cincinnati	65	1,057	16.3	58	7
	Nate Washington, Tennessee	74	1,023	13.8	57	7
	Steve Johnson, Buffalo[2]	76	1,004	13.2	55	7
2010	Brandon Lloyd, Denver	77	1,448	18.8	71	11
	Roddy White, Atlanta[4]	115	1,389	12.1	46	10
	Reggie Wayne, Indianapolis[7]	111	1,355	12.2	50	6
	Greg Jennings, Green Bay[3]	76	1,265	16.6	86	12
	Mike Wallace, Pittsburgh	60	1,257	20.9	56	10
	Andre Johnson, Houston[5]	86	1,216	14.1	60	8
	Dwayne Bowe, Kansas City[2]	72	1,162	16.1	75	15
	Larry Fitzgerald, Arizona[5]	90	1,137	12.6	41	6
	Calvin Johnson, Detroit[2]	77	1,120	14.6	87	12
	Santana Moss, Washington[4]	93	1,115	12.0	56	6
	Steve Johnson, Buffalo	82	1,073	13.1	45	10
	DeSean Jackson, Philadelphia[2]	47	1,056	22.5	91	6
	Hakeem Nicks, N.Y. Giants	79	1,052	13.3	46	11
	Miles Austin, Dallas[2]	69	1,041	15.1	69	7
	Marques Colston, New Orleans[4]	84	1,023	12.2	43	7
	Brandon Marshall, Miami[4]	86	1,014	11.8	46	3
	Jason Witten, Dallas[3]	94	1,002	10.7	33	9
2009	Andre Johnson, Houston[4]	101	1,569	15.5	72	9
	Wes Welker, New England[3]	123	1,348	11.0	58	4
	Miles Austin, Dallas	81	1,320	16.3	60	11
	Sidney Rice, Minnesota	83	1,321	15.8	63	8
	Randy Moss, New England[10]	83	1,264	15.2	71	13
	Reggie Wayne, Indianapolis[6]	100	1,264	12.6	65	10
	Santonio Holmes, Pittsburgh	79	1,248	15.8	57	5
	Steve Smith, N.Y. Giants	107	1,220	11.4	51	7
	Vincent Jackson, San Diego[2]	68	1,167	17.2	55	9

Year	Player, Team	No.	Yards	Avg.	Long	TD
	Hines Ward, Pittsburgh[6]	95	1,167	12.3	54	6
	Antonio Gates, San Diego[2]	79	1,157	14.6	56	8
	DeSean Jackson, Philadelphia	62	1,156	18.6	71	9
	Roddy White, Atlanta[3]	85	1,153	13.6	90	11
	Brandon Marshall, Denver[3]	101	1,120	11.1	75	10
	Greg Jennings, Green Bay[2]	68	1,113	16.4	83	4
	Dallas Clark, Indianapolis	100	1,106	11.1	80	10
	Larry Fitzgerald, Arizona[4]	97	1,092	11.3	34	13
	Marques Colston, New Orleans[3]	70	1,074	15.3	68	9
	Donald Driver, Green Bay[7]	70	1,061	15.2	71	6
	Chad Ochocinco, Cincinnati[7]	72	1,047	14.5	50	9
	Jason Witten, Dallas[2]	94	1,030	11.0	69	2
	Derrick Mason, Baltimore[8]	73	1,028	14.1	72	7
	Anquan Boldin, Arizona[5]	84	1,024	12.2	44	4
2008	Andre Johnson, Houston[3]	115	1,575	13.7	65	8
	Larry Fitzgerald, Arizona[3]	96	1,431	14.9	78	12
	Steve Smith, Carolina[5]	78	1,421	18.2	65	6
	Roddy White, Atlanta[2]	88	1,382	15.7	70	7
	Calvin Johnson, Detroit	78	1,331	17.1	96	12
	Greg Jennings, Green Bay	80	1,292	16.1	63	9
	Brandon Marshall, Denver[2]	104	1,265	12.2	47	6
	Antonio Bryant, Tampa Bay[2]	83	1,248	15.0	71	7
	Wes Welker, New England[2]	111	1,165	10.5	64	3
	Reggie Wayne, Indianapolis[5]	82	1,145	14.0	65	6
	Vincent Jackson, San Diego	59	1,098	18.6	60	7
	Tony Gonzalez, Kansas City[4]	96	1,058	11.0	35	10
	Terrell Owens, Dallas[9]	69	1,052	15.2	75	10
	Santana Moss, Washington[3]	79	1,044	13.2	67	6
	Hines Ward, Pittsburgh[5]	81	1,043	12.9	49	7
	Anquan Boldin, Arizona[4]	89	1,038	11.7	79	11
	Derrick Mason, Baltimore[7]	80	1,037	13.0	54	5
	Dwayne Bowe, Kansas City	86	1,022	11.9	36	7
	Lee Evans, Buffalo[2]	63	1,017	16.1	87	3
	Donald Driver, Green Bay[6]	74	1,012	13.7	71	5
	Randy Moss, New England[9]	69	1,008	14.6	76	11
	Steve Breaston, Arizona	77	1,006	13.1	58	3
2007	Reggie Wayne, Indianapolis[4]	104	1,510	14.5	64	10
	Randy Moss, New England[8]	98	1,493	15.2	65	23
	Chad Ochocinco, Cincinnati[6]	93	1,440	15.5	70	8
	Larry Fitzgerald, Arizona[2]	100	1,409	14.1	48	10
	Terrell Owens, Dallas[8]	81	1,355	16.7	52	15
	Brandon Marshall, Denver	102	1,325	13.0	68	7
	Braylon Edwards, Cleveland	80	1,289	16.1	78	16
	Marques Colston, New Orleans[2]	98	1,202	12.3	45	11
	Roddy White, Atlanta	83	1,202	14.5	69	6
	Torry Holt, St. Louis[8]	93	1,189	12.8	40	7
	Wes Welker, New England	112	1,175	10.5	42	8
	Tony Gonzalez, Kansas City[3]	99	1,172	11.8	31	5
	Bobby Engram, Seattle	94	1,147	12.2	49	6
	Jason Witten, Dallas	96	1,145	11.9	53	7
	T.J. Houshmandzadeh, Cincinnati[2]	112	1,143	10.2	42	12
	Jerricho Cotchery, N.Y. Jets	82	1,130	13.8	50	2
	Kevin Curtis, Philadelphia	77	1,110	14.4	75	6
	Kellen Winslow, Cleveland	82	1,106	13.5	49	5
	Derrick Mason, Baltimore[6]	103	1,087	10.6	79	5
	Donald Driver, Green Bay[5]	82	1,048	12.8	47	2
	Plaxico Burress, N.Y. Giants[4]	70	1,025	14.6	60	12
	Joey Galloway, Tampa Bay[6]	57	1,014	17.8	69	6
	Steve Smith, Carolina[4]	87	1,002	11.5	74	7
2006	Chad Ochocinco, Cincinnati[5]	87	1,369	15.7	74	7
	Marvin Harrison, Indianapolis[8]	95	1,366	14.4	68	12
	Reggie Wayne, Indianapolis[3]	86	1,310	15.2	51	9
	Roy Williams, Detroit	82	1,310	16.0	60	7
	Donald Driver, Green Bay[4]	92	1,295	14.1	82	8
	Lee Evans, Buffalo	82	1,292	15.8	83	8
	Anquan Boldin, Arizona[3]	83	1,203	14.5	64	4
	Torry Holt, St. Louis[7]	93	1,188	12.8	67	10
	Terrell Owens, Dallas[7]	85	1,180	13.9	56	13
	Steve Smith, Carolina[3]	83	1,166	14.1	72	8

Year	Player, Team	No.	Yards	Avg.	Long	TD
	Andre Johnson, Houston[2]	103	1,147	11.1	53	5
	Isaac Bruce, St. Louis[8]	74	1,098	14.8	45	3
	Laveranues Coles, N.Y. Jets[2]	91	1,098	12.1	58	6
	Mike Furrey, Detroit	98	1,086	11.1	31	6
	Javon Walker, Denver[2]	69	1,084	15.7	83	8
	T.J. Houshmandzadeh, Cincinnati	90	1,081	12.0	40	9
	Joey Galloway, Tampa Bay[5]	62	1,057	17.1	64	7
	Terry Glenn, Dallas[4]	70	1,047	15.0	54	6
	*Marques Colston, New Orleans	70	1,038	14.8	86	8
2005	Steve Smith, Carolina[2]	103	1,563	15.2	80	12
	Santana Moss, Washington[2]	84	1,483	17.7	78	9
	Chad Ochocinco, Cincinnati[4]	97	1,432	14.8	70	9
	Larry Fitzgerald, Arizona	103	1,409	13.7	47	10
	Anquan Boldin, Arizona[2]	102	1,402	13.7	54	7
	Torry Holt, St. Louis[6]	102	1,331	13.0	44	9
	Joey Galloway, Tampa Bay[4]	83	1,287	15.5	80	10
	Donald Driver, Green Bay[3]	86	1,221	14.2	59	5
	Plaxico Burress, N.Y. Giants[3]	76	1,214	16.0	78	7
	Marvin Harrison, Indianapolis[7]	82	1,146	14.0	80	12
	Terry Glenn, Dallas[3]	62	1,136	18.3	71	7
	Chris Chambers, Miami	82	1,118	13.6	77	11
	Rod Smith, Denver[4]	85	1,105	13.0	72	6
	Eddie Kennison, Kansas City[2]	68	1,102	16.2	55	5
	Antonio Gates, San Diego	89	1,101	12.4	38	10
	Derrick Mason, Baltimore[5]	86	1,073	12.5	39	3
	Reggie Wayne, Indianapolis[2]	83	1,055	12.7	66	5
	Jimmy Smith, Jacksonville[9]	70	1,023	14.6	45	6
	Antonio Bryant, Cleveland	69	1,009	14.6	54	4
	Randy Moss, Oakland[7]	60	1,005	16.8	79	8
2004	Muhsin Muhammad, Carolina[3]	93	1,405	15.1	51	16
	Joe Horn, New Orleans[4]	94	1,399	14.9	57	11
	Javon Walker, Green Bay	89	1,382	15.5	79	12
	Torry Holt, St. Louis[5]	94	1,372	14.6	75	10
	Isaac Bruce, St. Louis[7]	89	1,292	14.5	56	6
	Chad Ochocinco, Cincinnati[3]	95	1,274	13.4	53	9
	Tony Gonzalez, Kansas City[2]	102	1,258	12.3	32	7
	Drew Bennett, Tennessee	80	1,247	15.6	48	11
	Reggie Wayne, Indianapolis	77	1,210	15.7	71	12
	Donald Driver, Green Bay[2]	84	1,208	14.4	50	9
	Terrell Owens, Philadelphia[6]	77	1,200	15.6	59	14
	Darrell Jackson, Seattle[3]	87	1,199	13.8	56	7
	*Michael Clayton, Tampa Bay	80	1,193	14.9	75	7
	Jimmy Smith, Jacksonville[8]	74	1,172	15.8	65	6
	Derrick Mason, Tennessee[4]	96	1,168	12.2	37	7
	Rod Smith, Denver[7]	79	1,144	14.5	85	7
	Andre Johnson, Houston	79	1,142	14.5	54	6
	Marvin Harrison, Indianapolis[6]	86	1,113	12.9	59	15
	Eddie Kennison, Kansas City	62	1,086	17.5	70	8
	Ashley Lelie, Denver	54	1,084	20.1	58	7
	Brandon Stokley, Indianapolis	68	1,077	15.8	69	10
	Eric Moulds, Buffalo[4]	88	1,043	11.9	49	5
	Nate Burleson, Minnesota	68	1,006	14.8	68	9
	Hines Ward, Pittsburgh[4]	80	1,004	12.6	58	4
2003	Torry Holt, St. Louis[4]	117	1,696	14.5	48	12
	Randy Moss, Minnesota[6]	111	1,632	14.7	72	17
	*Anquan Boldin, Arizona	101	1,377	13.6	71	8
	Chad Ochocinco, Cincinnati[2]	90	1,355	15.1	82	10
	Derrick Mason, Tennessee[3]	95	1,303	13.7	50	8
	Marvin Harrison, Indianapolis[5]	94	1,272	13.5	79	10
	Laveranues Coles, Washington[2]	82	1,204	14.7	64	6
	Keenan McCardell, Tampa Bay[5]	84	1,174	14.0	76	8
	Hines Ward, Pittsburgh[3]	95	1,163	12.2	50	10
	Darrell Jackson, Seattle[2]	68	1,137	16.7	80	9
	Steve Smith, Carolina	88	1,110	12.6	67	7
	Santana Moss, N.Y. Jets	74	1,105	14.9	65	10
	Terrell Owens, San Francisco[5]	80	1,102	13.8	75	9
	Amani Toomer, N.Y. Giants[5]	63	1,057	16.8	77	5
2002	Marvin Harrison, Indianapolis[4]	143	1,722	12.0	69	11
	Randy Moss, Minnesota[5]	106	1,347	12.7	60	7

Year	Player, Team	No.	Yards	Avg.	Long	TD
	Amani Toomer, N.Y. Giants[4]	82	1,343	16.4	82	8
	Hines Ward, Pittsburgh[2]	112	1,329	11.9	72	12
	Plaxico Burress, Pittsburgh[2]	78	1,325	17.0	62	7
	Joe Horn, New Orleans[3]	88	1,312	14.9	63	7
	Torry Holt, St. Louis[3]	91	1,302	14.3	58	4
	Terrell Owens, San Francisco[4]	100	1,300	13.0	76	13
	Eric Moulds, Buffalo[3]	100	1,292	12.9	70	10
	Laveranues Coles, N.Y. Jets	89	1,264	14.2	43	5
	Peerless Price, Buffalo	94	1,252	13.3	73	9
	Koren Robinson, Seattle	78	1,240	15.9	83	5
	Jerry Rice, Oakland[14]	92	1,211	13.2	75	7
	Marty Booker, Chicago[2]	97	1,189	12.3	54	6
	Chad Ochocinco, Cincinnati	69	1,166	16.9	72	5
	Keyshawn Johnson, Tampa Bay[4]	76	1,088	14.3	76	5
	Isaac Bruce, St. Louis[6]	79	1,075	13.6	34	7
	Donald Driver, Green Bay	70	1,064	15.2	85	9
	Jimmy Smith, Jacksonville[7]	80	1,027	12.8	47	7
	Rod Smith, Denver[6]	89	1,027	11.5	46	5
	Derrick Mason, Tennessee[2]	79	1,012	12.8	40	5
	Rod Gardner, Washington	71	1,006	14.2	43	8
2001	David Boston, Arizona[2]	98	1,598	16.3	61	8
	Marvin Harrison, Indianapolis[3]	109	1,524	14.0	68	15
	Terrell Owens, San Francisco[3]	93	1,412	15.2	60	16
	Jimmy Smith, Jacksonville[6]	112	1,373	12.3	35	8
	Torry Holt, St. Louis[2]	81	1,363	16.8	51	7
	Rod Smith, Denver[5]	113	1,343	11.9	65	11
	Keyshawn Johnson, Tampa Bay[3]	106	1,266	11.9	47	1
	Joe Horn, New Orleans[2]	83	1,265	15.2	56	9
	Randy Moss, Minnesota[4]	82	1,233	15.0	73	10
	Troy Brown, New England	101	1,199	11.9	60	5
	Tim Brown, Oakland[9]	91	1,165	12.8	46	9
	Johnnie Morton, Detroit[4]	77	1,154	15.0	76	4
	Jerry Rice, Oakland[13]	83	1,139	13.7	40	9
	Derrick Mason, Tennessee	73	1,128	15.5	71	9
	Curtis Conway, San Diego[3]	71	1,125	15.8	72	6
	Keenan McCardell, Jacksonville[4]	93	1,110	11.9	45	6
	Isaac Bruce, St. Louis[5]	64	1,106	17.3	51	6
	Kevin Johnson, Cleveland	84	1,097	13.1	55	9
	Darrell Jackson, Seattle	70	1,081	15.4	64	8
	Marty Booker, Chicago	100	1,071	10.7	66	8
	Qadry Ismail, Baltimore[2]	74	1,059	14.3	77	7
	Amani Toomer, N.Y. Giants[3]	72	1,054	14.6	60	5
	Willie Jackson, New Orleans	81	1,046	12.9	63	6
	Plaxico Burress, Pittsburgh	66	1,008	15.3	43	6
	Hines Ward, Pittsburgh	94	1,003	10.7	34	4
2000	Torry Holt, St. Louis	82	1,635	19.9	85	6
	Rod Smith, Denver[4]	100	1,602	16.0	49	8
	Isaac Bruce, St. Louis[4]	87	1,471	16.9	78	9
	Terrell Owens, San Francisco[2]	97	1,451	15.0	69	13
	Randy Moss, Minnesota[3]	77	1,437	18.7	78	15
	Marvin Harrison, Indianapolis[2]	102	1,413	13.9	78	14
	Derrick Alexander, Kansas City[3]	78	1,391	17.8	81	10
	Joe Horn, New Orleans	94	1,340	14.3	52	8
	Eric Moulds, Buffalo[2]	94	1,326	14.1	52	5
	Ed McCaffrey, Denver[3]	101	1,317	13.0	61	9
	Cris Carter, Minnesota[8]	96	1,274	13.3	53	9
	Jimmy Smith, Jacksonville[5]	91	1,213	13.3	65	8
	Keenan McCardell, Jacksonville[3]	94	1,207	12.8	67	5
	Tony Gonzalez, Kansas City	93	1,203	12.9	39	9
	Muhsin Muhammad, Carolina[2]	102	1,183	11.6	36	6
	David Boston, Arizona	71	1,156	16.3	70	7
	Tim Brown, Oakland[8]	76	1,128	14.8	45	11
	Amani Toomer, N.Y. Giants[2]	78	1,094	14.0	54	7
1999	Marvin Harrison, Indianapolis	115	1,663	14.5	57	12
	Jimmy Smith, Jacksonville[4]	116	1,636	14.1	62	6
	Randy Moss, Minnesota[2]	80	1,413	17.7	67	11
	Marcus Robinson, Chicago	84	1,400	16.7	80	9
	Tim Brown, Oakland[7]	90	1,344	14.9	47	6
	Germane Crowell, Detroit	81	1,338	16.5	77	7

Year	Player, Team	No.	Yards	Avg.	Long	TD
	Muhsin Muhammad, Carolina	96	1,253	13.1	60	8
	Cris Carter, Minnesota[7]	90	1,241	13.8	68	13
	Michael Westbrook, Washington	65	1,191	18.3	65	9
	Amani Toomer, N.Y. Giants	79	1,183	15.0	80	6
	Keyshawn Johnson, N.Y. Jets[2]	89	1,170	13.2	65	8
	Isaac Bruce, St. Louis[3]	77	1,165	15.1	60	12
	Terry Glenn, New England[2]	69	1,147	16.6	67	4
	Albert Connell, Washington	62	1,132	18.3	62	7
	Johnnie Morton, Detroit[3]	80	1,129	14.1	48	5
	Qadry Ismail, Baltimore	68	1,105	16.3	76	6
	Raghib Ismail, Dallas[2]	80	1,097	13.7	76	6
	Patrick Jeffers, Carolina	63	1,082	17.2	88	12
	Antonio Freeman, Green Bay[3]	74	1,074	14.5	51	6
	Bill Schroeder, Green Bay	74	1,051	14.2	51	5
	Marshall Faulk, St. Louis	87	1,048	12.1	57	5
	Tony Martin, Miami[4]	67	1,037	15.5	69	5
	Darnay Scott, Cincinnati	68	1,022	15.0	76	7
	Rod Smith, Denver[3]	79	1,020	12.9	71	4
	Ed McCaffrey, Denver[2]	71	1,018	14.3	78	7
	Terance Mathis, Atlanta[4]	81	1,016	12.5	52	6
1998	Antonio Freeman, Green Bay[2]	84	1,424	17.0	84	14
	Eric Moulds, Buffalo	67	1,368	20.4	84	9
	*Randy Moss, Minnesota	69	1,313	19.0	61	17
	Rod Smith, Denver[2]	86	1,222	14.2	58	6
	Jimmy Smith, Jacksonville[3]	78	1,182	15.2	72	8
	Tony Martin, Atlanta[3]	66	1,181	17.9	62	6
	Jerry Rice, San Francisco[12]	82	1,157	14.1	75	9
	Frank Sanders, Arizona[2]	89	1,145	12.9	42	3
	Terance Mathis, Atlanta[3]	64	1,136	17.8	78	11
	Keyshawn Johnson, N.Y. Jets	83	1,131	13.6	41	10
	Terrell Owens, San Francisco	67	1,097	16.4	79	14
	Wayne Chrebet, N.Y. Jets	75	1,083	14.4	63	8
	Michael Irvin, Dallas[7]	74	1,057	14.3	51	1
	Ed McCaffrey, Denver	64	1,053	16.5	48	10
	O.J. McDuffie, Miami	90	1,050	11.7	61	7
	Joey Galloway, Seattle[3]	65	1,047	16.1	81	10
	Johnnie Morton, Detroit[2]	69	1,028	14.9	98	2
	Raghib Ismail, Carolina	69	1,024	14.8	62	8
	Carl Pickens, Cincinnati[4]	82	1,023	12.5	67	5
	Tim Brown, Oakland[6]	81	1,012	12.5	49	9
	Cris Carter, Minnesota[6]	78	1,011	13.0	54	12
1997	Rob Moore, Arizona[2]	97	1,584	16.3	47	8
	Tim Brown, Oakland[5]	104	1,408	13.5	59	5
	Yancey Thigpen, Pittsburgh[2]	79	1,398	17.7	69	7
	Jimmy Smith, Jacksonville[2]	82	1,324	16.1	75	4
	Irving Fryar, Philadelphia[5]	86	1,316	15.3	72	6
	Herman Moore, Detroit[4]	104	1,293	12.4	79	8
	Antonio Freeman, Green Bay	81	1,243	15.3	58	12
	Michael Irvin, Dallas[6]	75	1,180	15.7	55	9
	Rod Smith, Denver	70	1,180	16.9	78	12
	Keenan McCardell, Jacksonville[2]	85	1,164	13.7	60	5
	Jake Reed, Minnesota[4]	68	1,138	16.7	56	6
	Shannon Sharpe, Denver[3]	72	1,107	15.4	68	3
	Andre Rison, Kansas City[5]	72	1,092	15.2	45	7
	Cris Carter, Minnesota[5]	89	1,069	12.0	43	13
	Johnnie Morton, Detroit	80	1,057	13.2	73	6
	Joey Galloway, Seattle[2]	72	1,049	14.6	53	12
	Frank Sanders, Arizona	75	1,017	13.6	70	4
	Robert Brooks, Green Bay[2]	60	1,010	16.8	48	7
	Derrick Alexander, Baltimore[2]	65	1,009	15.5	92	9
1996	Isaac Bruce, St. Louis[2]	84	1,338	15.9	70	7
	Jake Reed, Minnesota[3]	72	1,320	18.3	82	7
	Herman Moore, Detroit[3]	106	1,296	12.2	50	9
	Jerry Rice, San Francisco[11]	108	1,254	11.6	39	8
	Jimmy Smith, Jacksonville	83	1,244	15.0	62	7
	Michael Jackson, Baltimore	76	1,201	15.8	86	14
	Irving Fryar, Philadelphia[4]	88	1,195	13.6	42	11
	Carl Pickens, Cincinnati[3]	100	1,180	11.8	61	12
	Tony Martin, San Diego[2]	85	1,171	13.8	55	14

Year	Player, Team	No.	Yards	Avg.	Long	TD
	Cris Carter, Minnesota[4]	96	1,163	12.1	43	10
	*Terry Glenn, New England	90	1,132	12.6	37	6
	Keenan McCardell, Jacksonville	85	1,129	13.3	52	3
	Tim Brown, Oakland[4]	90	1,104	12.3	42	9
	Derrick Alexander, Baltimore	62	1,099	17.7	64	9
	Shannon Sharpe, Denver[2]	80	1,062	13.3	51	10
	Curtis Conway, Chicago[2]	81	1,049	13.0	58	7
	Andre Reed, Buffalo[4]	66	1,036	15.7	67	6
	Brett Perriman, Detroit[2]	94	1,021	10.9	44	5
	Rob Moore, Arizona[2]	58	1,016	17.5	69	4
	Henry Ellard, Washington[7]	52	1,014	19.5	51	2
	Charles Johnson, Pittsburgh	60	1,008	16.8	70	3
1995	Jerry Rice, San Francisco[10]	122	1,848	15.1	81	15
	Isaac Bruce, St. Louis	119	1,781	15.0	72	13
	Herman Moore, Detroit[2]	123	1,686	13.7	69	14
	Michael Irvin, Dallas[5]	111	1,603	14.4	50	10
	Robert Brooks, Green Bay	102	1,497	14.7	99	13
	Brett Perriman, Detroit	108	1,488	13.8	91	9
	Cris Carter, Minnesota[3]	122	1,371	11.2	60	17
	Tim Brown, Oakland[3]	89	1,342	15.1	80	10
	Yancey Thigpen, Pittsburgh	85	1,307	15.4	43	5
	Jeff Graham, Chicago	82	1,301	15.9	51	4
	Carl Pickens, Cincinnati[2]	99	1,234	12.5	68	17
	Tony Martin, San Diego	90	1,224	13.6	51	6
	Eric Metcalf, Atlanta	104	1,189	11.4	62	8
	Jake Reed, Minnesota[2]	72	1,167	16.2	55	9
	Quinn Early, New Orleans	81	1,087	13.4	70	8
	Anthony Miller, Denver[5]	59	1,079	18.3	62	14
	Bert Emanuel, Atlanta	74	1,039	14.0	52	5
	*Joey Galloway, Seattle	67	1,039	15.5	59	7
	Terance Mathis, Atlanta[2]	78	1,039	13.3	54	9
	Curtis Conway, Chicago	62	1,037	16.7	76	12
	Henry Ellard, Washington[6]	56	1,005	17.9	59	5
	Mark Carrier, Carolina[2]	66	1,002	15.2	66	3
	Brian Blades, Seattle[4]	77	1,001	13.0	49	4
1994	Jerry Rice, San Francisco[9]	112	1,499	13.4	69	13
	Henry Ellard, Washington[5]	74	1,397	18.9	73	6
	Terance Mathis, Atlanta	111	1,342	12.1	81	11
	Tim Brown, L.A. Raiders[2]	89	1,309	14.7	77	9
	Andre Reed, Buffalo[2]	90	1,303	14.5	83	8
	Irving Fryar, Miami[3]	73	1,270	17.4	54	7
	Cris Carter, Minnesota[2]	122	1,256	10.3	65	7
	Michael Irvin, Dallas[4]	79	1,241	15.7	65	6
	Jake Reed, Minnesota	85	1,175	13.8	59	4
	Ben Coates, New England	96	1,174	12.2	62	7
	Herman Moore, Detroit	72	1,173	16.3	51	11
	Fred Barnett, Philadelphia[2]	78	1,127	14.4	54	5
	Carl Pickens, Cincinnati	71	1,127	15.9	70	11
	Sterling Sharpe, Green Bay[4]	94	1,119	11.9	49	18
	Anthony Miller, Denver[4]	60	1,107	18.5	76	5
	Andre Rison, Atlanta[3]	81	1,088	13.4	69	8
	Brian Blades, Seattle[3]	81	1,088	13.4	45	4
	Rob Moore, N.Y. Jets	78	1,010	12.9	41	6
	Shannon Sharpe, Denver	87	1,010	11.6	44	4
1993	Jerry Rice, San Francisco[8]	98	1,503	15.3	80	15
	Michael Irvin, Dallas[3]	88	1,330	15.1	61	7
	Sterling Sharpe, Green Bay[4]	112	1,274	11.4	54	11
	Andre Rison, Atlanta[3]	86	1,242	14.4	53	15
	Tim Brown, L.A. Raiders	80	1,180	14.8	71	7
	Anthony Miller, San Diego[3]	84	1,162	13.8	66	7
	Cris Carter, Minnesota	86	1,071	12.5	58	9
	Reggie Langhorne, Indianapolis	85	1,038	12.2	72	3
	Irving Fryar, Miami[2]	64	1,010	15.8	65	5
1992	Sterling Sharpe, Green Bay[3]	108	1,461	13.5	76	13
	Michael Irvin, Dallas[2]	78	1,396	17.9	87	7
	Jerry Rice, San Francisco[7]	84	1,201	14.3	80	10
	Andre Rison, Atlanta[2]	93	1,119	12.0	71	11
	Fred Barnett, Philadelphia	67	1,083	16.2	71	6
	Anthony Miller, San Diego[2]	72	1,060	14.7	67	7

Year	Player, Team	No.	Yards	Avg.	Long	TD
	Eric Martin, New Orleans[3]	68	1,041	15.3	52	5
1991	Michael Irvin, Dallas	93	1,523	16.4	66	8
	Gary Clark, Washington[5]	70	1,340	19.1	82	10
	Jerry Rice, San Francisco[6]	80	1,206	15.1	73	14
	Haywood Jeffires, Houston[2]	100	1,181	11.8	44	7
	Michael Haynes, Atlanta	50	1,122	22.4	80	11
	Andre Reed, Buffalo[2]	81	1,113	13.7	55	10
	Drew Hill, Houston[5]	90	1,109	12.3	61	4
	Mark Duper, Miami[4]	70	1,085	15.5	43	5
	James Lofton, Buffalo[6]	57	1,072	18.8	77	8
	Mark Clayton, Miami[5]	70	1,053	15.0	43	12
	Henry Ellard, L.A. Rams[4]	64	1,052	16.4	38	3
	Art Monk, Washington[5]	71	1,049	14.8	64	8
	Irving Fryar, New England	68	1,014	14.9	56	3
	John Taylor, San Francisco[2]	64	1,011	15.8	97	9
	Brian Blades, Seattle[2]	70	1,003	14.3	52	2
1990	Jerry Rice, San Francisco[5]	100	1,502	15.0	64	13
	Henry Ellard, L.A. Rams[3]	76	1,294	17.0	50	4
	Andre Rison, Atlanta	82	1,208	14.7	75	10
	Gary Clark, Washington[4]	75	1,112	14.8	53	8
	Sterling Sharpe, Green Bay[2]	67	1,105	16.5	76	6
	Flipper Anderson, L.A. Rams[2]	51	1,097	21.5	55	4
	Haywood Jeffires, Houston	74	1,048	14.2	87	8
	Stephone Paige, Kansas City	65	1,021	15.7	86	5
	Drew Hill, Houston[4]	74	1,019	13.8	57	5
	Anthony Carter, Minnesota[3]	70	1,008	14.4	56	8
1989	Jerry Rice, San Francisco[4]	82	1,483	18.1	68	17
	Sterling Sharpe, Green Bay	90	1,423	15.8	79	12
	Mark Carrier, Tampa Bay	86	1,422	16.5	78	9
	Henry Ellard, L.A. Rams[2]	70	1,382	19.7	53	8
	Andre Reed, Buffalo	88	1,312	14.9	78	9
	Anthony Miller, San Diego	75	1,252	16.7	69	10
	Webster Slaughter, Cleveland	65	1,236	19.0	97	6
	Gary Clark, Washington[3]	79	1,229	15.6	80	9
	Tim McGee, Cincinnati	65	1,211	18.6	74	8
	Art Monk, Washington[4]	86	1,186	13.8	60	8
	Flipper Anderson, L.A. Rams	44	1,146	26.0	78	5
	Ricky Sanders, Washington[2]	80	1,138	14.2	68	4
	Vance Johnson, Denver	76	1,095	14.4	69	7
	Richard Johnson, Detroit	70	1,091	15.6	75	8
	Eric Martin, New Orleans[2]	68	1,090	16.0	53	8
	John Taylor, San Francisco	60	1,077	18.0	95	10
	Mervyn Fernandez, L.A. Raiders	57	1,069	18.8	75	9
	Anthony Carter, Minnesota[2]	65	1,066	16.4	50	4
	Brian Blades, Seattle	77	1,063	13.8	60	5
	Mark Clayton, Miami[4]	64	1,011	15.8	78	9
1988	Henry Ellard, L.A. Rams	86	1,414	16.4	68	10
	Jerry Rice, San Francisco[3]	64	1,306	20.4	96	9
	Eddie Brown, Cincinnati	53	1,273	24.0	86	9
	Anthony Carter, Minnesota	72	1,225	17.0	67	6
	Ricky Sanders, Washington	73	1,148	15.7	55	12
	Drew Hill, Houston[3]	72	1,141	15.8	57	10
	Mark Clayton, Miami[3]	86	1,129	13.1	45	14
	Roy Green, Phoenix[3]	68	1,097	16.1	52	7
	Eric Martin, New Orleans	85	1,083	12.7	40	7
	Al Toon, N.Y. Jets[2]	93	1,067	11.5	42	5
	Bruce Hill, Tampa Bay	58	1,040	17.9	42	9
	Lionel Manuel, N.Y. Giants	65	1,029	15.8	46	4
1987	J.T. Smith, St. Louis[2]	91	1,117	12.3	38	8
	Jerry Rice, San Francisco[2]	65	1,078	16.6	57	22
	Gary Clark, Washington[2]	56	1,066	19.0	84	7
	Carlos Carson, Kansas City[3]	55	1,044	19.0	81	7
1986	Jerry Rice, San Francisco	86	1,570	18.3	66	15
	Stanley Morgan, New England[3]	84	1,491	17.8	44	10
	Mark Duper, Miami[3]	67	1,313	19.6	85	11
	Gary Clark, Washington	74	1,265	17.1	55	7
	Al Toon, N.Y. Jets	85	1,176	13.8	62	8
	Todd Christensen, L.A. Raiders[3]	95	1,153	12.1	35	8
	Mark Clayton, Miami[2]	60	1,150	19.2	68	10

Year	Player, Team	No.	Yards	Avg.	Long	TD
	*Bill Brooks, Indianapolis	65	1,131	17.4	84	8
	Drew Hill, Houston[2]	65	1,112	17.1	81	5
	Steve Largent, Seattle[8]	70	1,070	15.3	38	9
	Art Monk, Washington[3]	73	1,068	14.6	69	4
	*Ernest Givins, Houston	61	1,062	17.4	60	3
	Cris Collinsworth, Cincinnati[4]	62	1,024	16.5	46	10
	Wesley Walker, N.Y. Jets[2]	49	1,016	20.7	83	12
	J.T. Smith, St. Louis	80	1,014	12.7	45	6
	Mark Bavaro, N.Y. Giants	66	1,001	15.2	41	4
1985	Steve Largent, Seattle[7]	79	1,287	16.3	43	6
	Mike Quick, Philadelphia[3]	73	1,247	17.1	99	11
	Art Monk, Washington[2]	91	1,226	13.5	53	2
	Wes Chandler, San Diego[4]	67	1,199	17.9	75	10
	Drew Hill, Houston	64	1,169	18.3	57	9
	James Lofton, Green Bay[5]	69	1,153	16.7	56	4
	Louis Lipps, Pittsburgh	59	1,134	19.2	51	12
	Cris Collinsworth, Cincinnati[3]	65	1,125	17.3	71	5
	Tony Hill, Dallas[3]	74	1,113	15.0	53	7
	Lionel James, San Diego	86	1,027	11.9	67	6
	Roger Craig, San Francisco	92	1,016	11.0	73	6
1984	Roy Green, St. Louis[2]	78	1,555	19.9	83	12
	John Stallworth, Pittsburgh[3]	80	1,395	17.4	51	11
	Mark Clayton, Miami	73	1,389	19.0	65	18
	Art Monk, Washington	106	1,372	12.9	72	7
	James Lofton, Green Bay[4]	62	1,361	22.0	79	7
	Mark Duper, Miami[2]	71	1,306	18.4	80	8
	Steve Watson, Denver[3]	69	1,170	17.0	73	7
	Steve Largent, Seattle[6]	74	1,164	15.7	65	12
	Tim Smith, Houston[2]	69	1,141	16.5	75	4
	Stacey Bailey, Atlanta	67	1,138	17.0	61	6
	Carlos Carson, Kansas City[2]	57	1,078	18.9	57	4
	Mike Quick, Philadelphia[2]	61	1,052	17.2	90	9
	Todd Christensen, L.A. Raiders[2]	80	1,007	12.6	38	7
	Kevin House, Tampa Bay[2]	76	1,005	13.2	55	5
	Ozzie Newsome, Cleveland[2]	89	1,001	11.2	52	5
1983	Mike Quick, Philadelphia	69	1,409	20.4	83	13
	Carlos Carson, Kansas City	80	1,351	16.9	50	7
	James Lofton, Green Bay[3]	58	1,300	22.4	74	8
	Todd Christensen, L.A. Raiders	92	1,247	13.6	45	12
	Roy Green, St. Louis	78	1,227	15.7	71	14
	Charlie Brown, Washington	78	1,225	15.7	75	8
	Tim Smith, Houston	83	1,176	14.2	47	6
	Kellen Winslow, San Diego[3]	88	1,172	13.3	46	8
	Earnest Gray, N.Y. Giants	78	1,139	14.6	62	5
	Steve Watson, Denver[2]	59	1,133	19.2	78	5
	Cris Collinsworth, Cincinnati[2]	66	1,130	17.1	63	5
	Steve Largent, Seattle[5]	72	1,074	14.9	46	11
	Mark Duper, Miami	51	1,003	19.7	85	10
1982	Wes Chandler, San Diego[3]	49	1,032	21.1	66	9
1981	Alfred Jenkins, Atlanta[2]	70	1,358	19.4	67	13
	James Lofton, Green Bay[2]	71	1,294	18.2	75	8
	Steve Watson, Denver	60	1,244	20.7	95	13
	Frank Lewis, Buffalo[2]	70	1,244	17.8	33	4
	Steve Largent, Seattle[4]	75	1,224	16.3	57	9
	Charlie Joiner, San Diego[4]	70	1,188	17.0	57	7
	Kevin House, Tampa Bay	56	1,176	21.0	84	9
	Wes Chandler, New Orleans/San Diego[2]	69	1,142	16.6	51	6
	Dwight Clark, San Francisco	85	1,105	13.0	78	4
	John Stallworth, Pittsburgh[2]	63	1,098	17.4	55	5
	Kellen Winslow, San Diego[2]	88	1,075	12.2	67	10
	Pat Tilley, St. Louis	66	1,040	15.8	75	3
	Stanley Morgan, New England[2]	44	1,029	23.4	76	6
	Harold Carmichael, Philadelphia[3]	61	1,028	16.9	85	6
	Freddie Scott, Detroit	53	1,022	19.3	48	5
	*Cris Collinsworth, Cincinnati	67	1,009	15.1	74	8
	Joe Senser, Minnesota	79	1,004	12.7	53	8
	Ozzie Newsome, Cleveland	69	1,002	14.5	62	6
	Sammy White, Minnesota	66	1,001	15.2	53	3

Year	Player, Team	No.	Yards	Avg.	Long	TD
1980	John Jefferson, San Diego[3]	82	1,340	16.3	58	13
	Kellen Winslow, San Diego	89	1,290	14.5	65	9
	James Lofton, Green Bay	71	1,226	17.3	47	4
	Charlie Joiner, San Diego[3]	71	1,132	15.9	51	4
	Ahmad Rashad, Minnesota[2]	69	1,095	15.9	76	5
	Steve Largent, Seattle[3]	66	1,064	16.1	67	6
	Tony Hill, Dallas[2]	60	1,055	17.6	58	8
	Alfred Jenkins, Atlanta	57	1,026	18.0	57	6
1979	Steve Largent, Seattle[2]	66	1,237	18.7	55	9
	John Stallworth, Pittsburgh	70	1,183	16.9	65	8
	Ahmad Rashad, Minnesota	80	1,156	14.5	52	9
	John Jefferson, San Diego[2]	61	1,090	17.9	65	10
	Frank Lewis, Buffalo	54	1,082	20.0	55	2
	Wes Chandler, New Orleans	65	1,069	16.4	85	6
	Tony Hill, Dallas	60	1,062	17.7	75	10
	Drew Pearson, Dallas[2]	55	1,026	18.7	56	8
	Wallace Francis, Atlanta	74	1,013	13.7	42	8
	Harold Jackson, New England[3]	45	1,013	22.5	59	7
	Charlie Joiner, San Diego[2]	72	1,008	14.0	39	4
	Stanley Morgan, New England	44	1,002	22.8	63	12
1978	Wesley Walker, N.Y. Jets	48	1,169	24.4	77	8
	Steve Largent, Seattle	71	1,168	16.5	57	8
	Harold Carmichael, Philadelphia[2]	55	1,072	19.5	56	8
	*John Jefferson, San Diego	56	1,001	17.9	46	13
1976	Roger Carr, Baltimore	43	1,112	25.9	79	11
	Cliff Branch, Oakland[2]	46	1,111	24.2	88	12
	Charlie Joiner, San Diego	50	1,056	21.1	81	7
1975	Ken Burrough, Houston	53	1,063	20.1	77	8
1974	Cliff Branch, Oakland	60	1,092	18.2	67	13
	Drew Pearson, Dallas	62	1,087	17.5	50	2
1973	Harold Carmichael, Philadelphia	67	1,116	16.7	73	9
1972	Harold Jackson, Philadelphia[2]	62	1,048	16.9	77	4
	John Gilliam, Minnesota	47	1,035	22.0	66	7
1971	Otis Taylor, Kansas City[2]	57	1,110	19.5	82	7
1970	Gene Washington, San Francisco	53	1,100	20.8	79	12
	Marlin Briscoe, Buffalo	57	1,036	18.2	48	8
	Dick Gordon, Chicago	71	1,026	14.5	69	13
	Gary Garrison, San Diego[2]	44	1,006	22.9	67	12
1969	Warren Wells, Oakland[2]	47	1,260	26.8	80	14
	Harold Jackson, Philadelphia	65	1,116	17.2	65	9
	Roy Jefferson, Pittsburgh[2]	67	1,079	16.1	63	9
	Dan Abramowicz, New Orleans	73	1,015	13.9	49	7
	Lance Alworth, San Diego[7]	64	1,003	15.7	76	4
1968	Lance Alworth, San Diego[6]	68	1,312	19.3	80	10
	Don Maynard, N.Y. Jets[5]	57	1,297	22.8	87	10
	George Sauer, N.Y. Jets[3]	66	1,141	17.3	43	3
	Warren Wells, Oakland	53	1,137	21.5	94	11
	Gary Garrison, San Diego	52	1,103	21.2	84	10
	Roy Jefferson, Pittsburgh	58	1,074	18.5	62	11
	Paul Warfield, Cleveland	50	1,067	21.3	65	12
	Homer Jones, N.Y. Giants[3]	45	1,057	23.5	84	7
	Fred Biletnikoff, Oakland	61	1,037	17.0	82	6
	Lance Rentzel, Dallas	54	1,009	18.7	65	6
1967	Don Maynard, N.Y. Jets[4]	71	1,434	20.2	75	10
	Ben Hawkins, Philadelphia	59	1,265	21.4	87	10
	Homer Jones, N.Y. Giants[2]	49	1,209	24.7	70	13
	Jackie Smith, St. Louis	56	1,205	21.5	76	9
	George Sauer, N.Y. Jets[2]	75	1,189	15.9	61	6
	Lance Alworth, San Diego[5]	52	1,010	19.4	71	9
1966	Lance Alworth, San Diego[4]	73	1,383	18.9	78	13
	Otis Taylor, Kansas City	58	1,297	22.4	89	8
	Pat Studstill, Detroit	67	1,266	18.9	99	5
	Bob Hayes, Dallas[2]	64	1,232	19.3	95	13
	Charlie Frazier, Houston	57	1,129	19.8	79	12
	Charley Taylor, Washington	72	1,119	15.5	86	12
	George Sauer, N.Y. Jets	63	1,081	17.2	77	5
	Homer Jones, N.Y. Giants	48	1,044	21.8	98	8
	Art Powell, Oakland[5]	53	1,026	19.4	46	11

Year	Player, Team	No.	Yards	Avg.	Long	TD
1965	Lance Alworth, San Diego[3]	69	1,602	23.2	85	14
	Dave Parks, San Francisco	80	1,344	16.8	53	12
	Don Maynard, N.Y. Jets[3]	68	1,218	17.9	56	14
	Pete Retzlaff, Philadelphia	66	1,190	18.0	78	10
	Lionel Taylor, Denver[4]	85	1,131	13.3	63	6
	Tommy McDonald, Los Angeles[3]	67	1,036	15.5	51	9
	*Bob Hayes, Dallas	46	1,003	21.8	82	12
1964	Charley Hennigan, Houston[3]	101	1,546	15.3	53	8
	Art Powell, Oakland[4]	76	1,361	17.9	77	11
	Lance Alworth, San Diego[2]	61	1,235	20.2	82	13
	Johnny Morris, Chicago	93	1,200	12.9	63	10
	Elbert Dubenion, Buffalo	42	1,139	27.1	72	10
	Terry Barr, Detroit[2]	57	1,030	18.1	58	9
1963	Bobby Mitchell, Washington[2]	69	1,436	20.8	99	7
	Art Powell, Oakland[3]	73	1,304	17.9	85	16
	Buddy Dial, Pittsburgh[2]	60	1,295	21.6	83	9
	Lance Alworth, San Diego	61	1,205	19.8	85	11
	Del Shofner, N.Y. Giants[4]	64	1,181	18.5	70	9
	Lionel Taylor, Denver[3]	78	1,101	14.1	72	10
	Terry Barr, Detroit	66	1,086	16.5	75	13
	Charley Hennigan, Houston[2]	61	1,051	17.2	83	10
	Sonny Randle, St. Louis[2]	51	1,014	19.9	68	12
	Bake Turner, N.Y. Jets	71	1,009	14.2	53	6
1962	Bobby Mitchell, Washington	72	1,384	19.2	81	11
	Sonny Randle, St. Louis	63	1,158	18.4	86	7
	Tommy McDonald, Philadelphia[2]	58	1,146	19.8	60	10
	Del Shofner, N.Y. Giants[3]	53	1,133	21.4	69	12
	Art Powell, N.Y. Titans[2]	64	1,130	17.7	80	8
	Frank Clarke, Dall. Cowboys	47	1,043	22.2	66	14
	Don Maynard, N.Y. Titans[2]	56	1,041	18.6	86	8
1961	Charley Hennigan, Houston	82	1,746	21.3	80	12
	Lionel Taylor, Denver[2]	100	1,176	11.8	52	4
	Bill Groman, Houston[2]	50	1,175	23.5	80	17
	Tommy McDonald, Philadelphia	64	1,144	17.9	66	13
	Del Shofner, N.Y. Giants[2]	68	1,125	16.5	46	11
	Jim Phillips, Los Angeles	78	1,092	14.0	69	5
	*Mike Ditka, Chicago	56	1,076	19.2	76	12
	Dave Kocourek, San Diego	55	1,055	19.2	76	4
	Buddy Dial, Pittsburgh	53	1,047	19.8	88	12
	R.C. Owens, San Francisco	55	1,032	18.8	54	5
1960	*Bill Groman, Houston	72	1,473	20.5	92	12
	Raymond Berry, Baltimore	74	1,298	17.5	70	10
	Don Maynard, N.Y. Titans	72	1,265	17.6	65	6
	Lionel Taylor, Denver	92	1,235	13.4	80	12
	Art Powell, N.Y. Titans	69	1,167	16.9	76	14
1958	Del Shofner, Los Angeles	51	1,097	21.5	92	8
1956	Bill Howton, Green Bay[2]	55	1,188	21.6	66	12
	Harlon Hill, Chi. Bears[2]	47	1,128	24.0	79	11
1954	Bob Boyd, Los Angeles	53	1,212	22.9	80	6
	*Harlon Hill, Chi. Bears	45	1,124	25.0	76	12
1953	Pete Pihos, Philadelphia	63	1,049	16.7	59	10
1952	*Bill Howton, Green Bay	53	1,231	23.2	90	13
1951	Elroy (Crazylegs) Hirsch, Los Angeles	66	1,495	22.7	91	17
1950	Tom Fears, Los Angeles[2]	84	1,116	13.3	53	7
	Cloyce Box, Detroit	50	1,009	20.2	82	11
1949	Bob Mann, Detroit	66	1,014	15.4	64	4
	Tom Fears, Los Angeles	77	1,013	13.2	51	9
1945	Jim Benton, Cleveland	45	1,067	23.7	84	8
1942	Don Hutson, Green Bay	74	1,211	16.4	73	17

First season of professional football.

250 YARDS PASS RECEIVING IN A GAME

Date	Player, Team, Opponent	No.	Yards	TD
Oct. 11, 2009	Miles Austin, Dallas vs. Kansas City (OT)	10	250	2
Nov. 19, 2006	Lee Evans, Buffalo vs. Houston	11	265	2
Nov. 12, 2006	Chad Ochocinco, Cincinnati vs. San Diego	11	260	2
Nov. 10, 2002	Plaxico Burress, Pittsburgh vs. Atlanta (OT)	9	253	2
Dec. 17, 2000	Terrell Owens, San Francisco vs. Chicago	20	283	1

Date	Player, Team, Opponent	No.	Yards	TD
Sept. 10, 2000	Jimmy Smith, Jacksonville vs. Baltimore	15	291	3
Dec. 12, 1999	Qadry Ismail, Baltimore vs. Pittsburgh	6	258	3
Dec. 18, 1995	Jerry Rice, San Francisco vs. Minnesota	14	289	3
Dec. 11, 1989	John Taylor, San Francisco vs. L.A. Rams	11	286	2
Nov. 26, 1989	Flipper Anderson, L.A. Rams vs. New Orleans (OT)	15	336	1
Oct. 18, 1987	Steve Largent, Seattle vs. Detroit	15	261	3
Oct. 4, 1987	Anthony Allen, Washington vs. St. Louis	7	255	3
Dec. 22, 1985	Stephone Paige, Kansas City vs. San Diego	8	309	2
Dec. 20, 1982	Wes Chandler, San Diego vs. Cincinnati	10	260	2
Sept. 23, 1979	*Jerry Butler, Buffalo vs. N.Y. Jets	10	255	4
Nov. 4, 1962	Sonny Randle, St. Louis vs. N.Y. Giants	16	256	1
Oct. 28, 1962	Del Shofner, N.Y. Giants vs. Washington	11	269	1
Oct. 13, 1961	Charley Hennigan, Houston vs. Boston	13	272	1
Oct. 21, 1956	Billy Howton, Green Bay vs. Los Angeles	7	257	2
Dec. 3, 1950	Cloyce Box, Detroit vs. Baltimore	12	302	4
Nov. 22, 1945	Jim Benton, Cleveland vs. Detroit	10	303	1

*First season of professional football.

2,000 COMBINED NET YARDS GAINED IN A SEASON

Year	Player, Team	Rushing Att.-Yds.	Pass Rec.	Punt Ret.	Kickoff Ret.	Fum. Ret.	Total Yds.
2011	Darren Sproles, New Orleans[4]	87-603	86-710	29-294	40-1,089	0-0	242-2,696
	Antonio Brown, Pittsburgh	7-41	69-1,108	30-325	27-737	0-0	133-2,211
	Ray Rice, Baltimore[2]	291-1,364	76-704	0-0	0-0	0-0	367-2,068
2010	Danny Amendola, St. Louis[2]	7-81	85-689	40-452	50-1,142	0-0	182-2,364
	Arian Foster, Houston	327-1,616	66-604	0-0	0-0	1-0	394-2,221
	Darren Sproles, San Diego[3]	50-267	59-520	24-166	51-1,257	0-0	184-2,210
2009	Fred Jackson, Buffalo	237-1,062	46-371	6-69	41-1,014	0-0	330-2,516
	Josh Cribbs, Cleveland[2]	55-381	20-135	38-452	56-1,542	2-0	171-2,510
	Chris Johnson, Tennessee	358-2,006	50-503	0-0	0-0	1-0	409-2,509
	Jamaal Charles, Kansas City	190-1,120	40-297	0-0	36-925	3-0	269-2,342
	Darren Sproles, San Diego[2]	93-343	45-497	26-183	54-1,300	1-0	219-2,323
	Danny Amendola, St. Louis	3-2	43-326	31-360	66-1,618	1-0	144-2,302
	*Percy Harvin, Minnesota	15-135	60-790	0-0	42-1,156	0-0	117-2,081
	Ray Rice, Baltimore	254-1,339	78-702	0-0	0-0	1-2	333-2,043
2008	Leon Washington, N.Y. Jets[2]	76-448	47-355	29-303	48-1,231	4-(-5)	204-2,332
	Darren Sproles, San Diego	61-330	29-342	22-249	53-1,376	1-(-2)	166-2,295
	Jerious Norwood, Atlanta[2]	95-489	36-338	0-0	51-1,311	0-0	182-2,138
2007	Josh Cribbs, Cleveland	9-61	3-37	30-405	59-1,809	2-0	103-2,312
	Jerious Norwood, Atlanta	103-613	28-277	0-0	52-1,317	0-0	183-2,207
	Brian Westbrook, Philadelphia	278-1,333	90-771	4-79	0-0	0-0	372-2,183
	*Ted Ginn Jr., Miami	4-3	34-420	24-230	63-1,433	2-(-9)	127-2,077
	Leon Washington, N.Y. Jets	71-353	36-213	20-183	47-1,291	1-0	175-2,040
	*Adrian Peterson, Minnesota	238-1,341	19-268	0-0	16-412	3-0	276-2,014
	Maurice Jones-Drew, Jacksonville[2]	167-768	40-407	3-28	31-811	0-0	241-2,014
2006	Steven Jackson, St. Louis	346-1,528	90-806	0-0	0-0	2-0	438-2,334
	LaDainian Tomlinson, San Diego[3]	348-1,815	56-508	0-0	0-0	1-0	405-2,323
	*Maurice Jones-Drew, Jacksonville	166-941	46-436	1-13	31-860	0-0	244-2,250
	Larry Johnson, Kansas City[2]	416-1,789	41-410	0-0	0-0	1-0	458-2,199
	Frank Gore, San Francisco	312-1,695	61-485	0-0	0-0	0-0	373-2,180
	Wes Welker, Miami[2]	0-0	67-687	41-378	48-1,064	1-0	157-2,129
	Tiki Barber, N.Y. Giants[4]	327-1,662	58-465	0-0	0-0	1-0	386-2,127
	Chris Carr, Oakland	0-0	0-0	35-216	69-1,762	1-0	106-2,078
2005	Tiki Barber, N.Y. Giants[3]	357-1,860	54-530	0-0	0-0	1-0	412-2,390
	Dante Hall, Kansas City[4]	7-11	34-436	42-276	65-1,560	2-0	150-2,283
	Wes Welker, Miami	1-5	29-434	43-390	61-1,379	4-0	138-2,208
	Larry Johnson, Kansas City	336-1,750	33-343	0-0	0-0	3-0	372-2,093
2004	Dante Hall, Kansas City[3]	8-56	25-230	23-232	68-1,718	0-0	124-2,236
	Tiki Barber, N.Y. Giants[2]	322-1,518	52-578	0-0	0-0	2-0	376-2,096
	Edgerrin James, Indianapolis[3]	334-1,548	51-483	0-0	0-0	1-0	386-2,031
2003	Dante Hall, Kansas City[2]	16-73	40-423	29-472	57-1,478	0-0	142-2,446
	LaDainian Tomlinson, San Diego[2]	313-1,645	100-725	0-0	0-0	2-0	415-2,370
	Jamal Lewis, Baltimore	387-2,066	26-205	0-0	0-0	1-0	414-2,271
	Ahman Green, Green Bay	355-1,883	50-367	0-0	0-0	2-0	407-2,250
	Deuce McAllister, New Orleans	351-1,641	69-516	0-0	0-0	3-(-3)	423-2,154
	Priest Holmes, Kansas City[3]	320-1,420	74-690	0-0	0-0	0-0	394-2,110
2002	Michael Lewis, New Orleans	1-15	8-200	44-625	70-1,807	2-0	125-2,647
	Priest Holmes, Kansas City[2]	313-1,615	70-672	0-0	0-0	0-0	383-2,287
	Ricky Williams, Miami	383-1,853	47-363	0-0	0-0	1-0	431-2,216

Year	Player, Team	Rushing Att.-Yds.	Pass Rec.	Punt Ret.	Kickoff Ret.	Fum. Ret.	Total Yds.
	LaDainian Tomlinson, San Diego	372-1,683	79-489	0-0	0-0	0-0	451-2,172
	Dante Hall, Kansas City	11-54	20-322	29-390	57-1,354	1-0	118-2,120
2001	Priest Holmes, Kansas City	327-1,555	62-614	0-0	0-0	0-0	389-2,169
	Marshall Faulk, St. Louis[4]	260-1,382	83-765	0-0	0-0	2-0	345-2,147
	Derrick Mason, Tennessee[2]	0-0	73-1,128	20-128	34-748	1-0	128-2,004
2000	Derrick Mason, Tennessee	1-1	63-895	51-662	42-1,132	1-0	158-2,690
	MarTay Jenkins, Arizona	1-(-4)	17-219	1-1	82-2,186	0-0	101-2,402
	Edgerrin James, Indianapolis[2]	387-1,709	63-594	0-0	0-0	0-0	450-2,303
	Marshall Faulk, St. Louis[3]	253-1,359	81-830	0-0	1-18	2-0	337-2,207
	Tiki Barber, N.Y. Giants	213-1,006	70-719	39-332	1-28	5-0	328-2,085
1999	Marshall Faulk, St. Louis[2]	253-1,381	87-1,048	0-0	0-0	0-0	340-2,429
	*Edgerrin James, Indianapolis	369-1,553	62-586	0-0	0-0	2-0	433-2,139
	*Terrence Wilkins, Indianapolis	1-2	42-565	41-388	51-1,134	1-0	136-2,089
	Glyn Milburn, Chicago[2]	16-102	20-151	30-346	61-1,426	2-0	129-2,025
1998	Brian Mitchell, Washington[4]	39-208	44-306	44-506	59-1,337	0-0	186-2,357
	Marshall Faulk, Indianapolis	324-1,319	86-908	0-0	0-0	2-13	412-2,240
	Terrell Davis, Denver[2]	392-2,008	25-217	0-0	0-0	1-0	418-2,225
	Jamal Anderson, Atlanta	410-1,846	27-319	0-0	0-0	1-0	438-2,165
	Garrison Hearst, San Francisco	310-1,570	39-535	0-0	0-0	1-0	350-2,105
1997	Barry Sanders, Detroit[2]	335-2,053	33-305	0-0	0-0	1-0	369-2,358
	Kevin Williams, Arizona	1-(-2)	20-273	40-462	59-1,458	1-0	121-2,191
	Brian Mitchell, Washington[3]	23-107	36-438	38-442	47-1,094	0-0	144-2,081
	Terrell Davis, Denver	369-1,750	42-287	0-0	0-0	2-(-7)	413-2,030
	Jermaine Lewis, Baltimore	3-35	42-648	28-437	41-905	2-0	116-2,025
1995	Brian Mitchell, Washington[2]	46-301	38-324	25-315	55-1,408	0-0	164-2,348
	Emmitt Smith, Dallas[2]	377-1,773	62-375	0-0	0-0	0-0	439-2,148
	Glyn Milburn, Denver	49-266	22-191	31-354	47-1,269	0-0	149-2,080
	Ernie Mills, Pittsburgh	5-39	39-679	0-0	54-1,306	0-0	98-2,024
1994	Brian Mitchell, Washington	78-311	26-236	32-452	58-1,478	0-0	194-2,477
	Barry Sanders, Detroit	331-1,883	44-283	0-0	0-0	0-0	375-2,166
1992	Thurman Thomas, Buffalo[2]	312-1,487	58-626	0-0	0-0	1-0	371-2,113
	Emmitt Smith, Dallas	373-1,713	59-335	0-0	0-0	1-0	433-2,048
	Barry Foster, Pittsburgh	390-1,690	36-344	0-0	0-0	2-(–20)	428-2,014
1991	Thurman Thomas, Buffalo	288-1,407	62-631	0-0	0-0	0-0	350-2,038
1990	Herschel Walker, Minnesota[2]	184-770	35-315	0-0	44-966	4-0	267-2,051
1988	*Tim Brown, L.A. Raiders	14-50	43-725	49-444	41-1,098	7-0	154-2,317
	Roger Craig, San Francisco[2]	310-1,502	76-534	0-0	2-32	2-0	390-2,068
	Eric Dickerson, Indianapolis[4]	388-1,659	36-377	0-0	0-0	1-0	425-2,036
	Herschel Walker, Dallas	361-1,514	53-505	0-0	0-0	3-0	417-2,019
1986	Eric Dickerson, L.A. Rams[3]	404-1,821	26-205	0-0	0-0	2-0	432-2,026
	Gary Anderson, San Diego	127-442	80-871	25-227	24-482	2-0	258-2,022
1985	Lionel James, San Diego	105-516	86-1,027	25-213	36-779	1-0	253-2,535
	Marcus Allen, L.A. Raiders	380-1,759	67-555	0-0	0-0	2-(-6)	449-2,308
	Roger Craig, San Francisco	214-1,050	92-1,016	0-0	0-0	0-0	306-2,066
	Walter Payton, Chicago[4]	324-1,551	49-483	0-0	0-0	1-0	374-2,034
1984	Eric Dickerson, L.A. Rams[2]	379-2,105	21-139	0-0	0-0	4-15	404-2,259
	James Wilder, Tampa Bay	407-1,544	85-685	0-0	0-0	4-0	496-2,229
	Walter Payton, Chicago[3]	381-1,684	45-368	0-0	0-0	1-0	427-2,052
1983	*Eric Dickerson, L.A. Rams	390-1,808	51-404	0-0	0-0	1-0	442-2,212
	William Andrews, Atlanta[2]	331-1,567	59-609	0-0	0-0	2-0	392-2,176
	Walter Payton, Chicago[2]	314-1,421	53-607	0-0	0-0	2-0	369-2,028
1981	*James Brooks, San Diego	109-525	46-329	22-290	40-949	2-0	219-2,093
	William Andrews, Atlanta	289-1,301	81-735	0-0	0-0	0-0	370-2,036
1980	Bruce Harper, N.Y. Jets[2]	45-126	50-634	28-242	49-1,070	3-0	175-2,072
1979	Wilbert Montgomery, Philadelphia	338-1,512	41-494	0-0	1-6	2-0	382-2,012
1978	Bruce Harper, N.Y. Jets	58-303	13-196	30-378	55-1,280	1-0	157-2,157
1977	Walter Payton, Chicago	339-1,852	27-269	0-0	2-95	5-0	373-2,216
	Terry Metcalf, St. Louis[3]	149-739	34-403	14-108	32-772	1-0	230-2,022
1975	Terry Metcalf, St. Louis[2]	165-816	43-378	23-285	35-960	2-23	268-2,462
	O.J. Simpson, Buffalo[2]	329-1,817	28-426	0-0	0-0	1-0	358-2,243
1974	Mack Herron, New England	231-824	38-474	35-517	28-629	3-0	335-2,444
	Otis Armstrong, Denver	263-1,407	38-405	0-0	16-386	1-0	318-2,198
	Terry Metcalf, St. Louis	152-718	50-377	26-340	20-623	7-0	255-2,058
1973	O.J. Simpson, Buffalo	332-2,003	6-70	0-0	0-0	0-0	338-2,073
1966	Gale Sayers, Chicago[2]	229-1,231	34-447	6-44	23-718	3-0	295-2,440
	Leroy Kelly, Cleveland	209-1,141	32-366	13-104	19-403	0-0	273-2,014
1965	*Gale Sayers, Chicago	166-867	29-507	16-238	21-660	4-0	236-2,272
1963	Timmy Brown, Philadelphia[2]	192-841	36-487	16-152	33-945	2-3	279-2,428

Year	Player, Team	Rushing Att.-Yds.	Pass Rec.	Punt Ret.	Kickoff Ret.	Fum. Ret.	Total Yds.
	Jim Brown, Cleveland	291-1,863	24-268	0-0	0-0	0-0	315-2,131
1962	Timmy Brown, Philadelphia	137-545	52-849	6-81	30-831	4-0	229-2,306
	Dick Christy, N.Y. Titans	114-535	62-538	15-250	38-824	2-0	231-2,147
1961	Billy Cannon, Houston	200-948	43-586	9-70	18-439	2-0	272-2,043
1960	*Abner Haynes, Dallas Texans	156-875	55-576	14-215	19-434	4-0	248-2,100

*First season of professional football.

300 COMBINED NET YARDS GAINED IN A GAME

Date	Player, Team, Opponent	No.	Yards	TD
Nov. 28, 2010	*Jacoby Ford, Oakland vs. Miami	12	329	2
Nov. 7, 2010	*Jacoby Ford, Oakland vs. Kansas City (OT)	10	306	1
Dec. 20, 2009	Josh Cribbs, Cleveland vs. Kansas City	14	316	2
Oct. 18, 2009	Domenik Hixon, N.Y. Giants vs. New Orleans	12	303	0
Sept. 28, 2008	Steve Breaston, Arizona vs. N.Y. Jets	19	324	0
Sept. 14, 2008	Darren Sproles, San Diego vs. Denver	14	317	2
Nov. 18, 2007	Josh Cribbs, Cleveland vs. Baltimore (OT)	12	309	0
Nov. 4, 2007	*Adrian Peterson, Minnesota vs. San Diego	31	315	3
Oct. 14, 2007	*Adrian Peterson, Minnesota vs. Chicago	25	361	3
Sept. 30, 2007	Devin Hester, Chicago vs. Detroit	13	317	1
Dec. 10, 2006	*Maurice Jones-Drew, Jacksonville vs. Indianapolis	19	303	3
Dec. 14, 2003	Derrick Mason, Tennessee vs. Buffalo	21	302	0
Nov. 16, 2003	Jonathan Carter, N.Y. Jets vs. Indianapolis	7	304	2
Dec. 8, 2002	Steve Smith, Carolina vs. Cincinnati	9	313	3
Nov. 24, 2002	Priest Holmes, Kansas City vs. Seattle	30	307	3
Oct. 13, 2002	Michael Lewis, New Orleans vs. Washington	8	356	2
Dec. 24, 1999	Jason Tucker, Dallas vs. New Orleans	13	331	1
Dec. 7, 1997	Jermaine Lewis, Baltimore vs. Seattle	10	308	3
Dec. 25, 1995	Kevin Williams, Dallas vs. Arizona	16	307	2
Dec. 10, 1995	Glyn Milburn, Denver vs. Seattle	33	404	0
Oct. 23, 1994	Tyrone Hughes, New Orleans vs. L.A. Rams	11	347	2
Dec. 11, 1989	John Taylor, San Francisco vs. L.A. Rams	14	321	2
Nov. 26, 1989	Flipper Anderson, L.A. Rams vs. New Orleans (OT)	15	336	1
Nov. 28, 1988	*Tim Brown, L.A. Raiders vs. Seattle	12	306	1
Dec. 22, 1985	Stephone Paige, Kansas City vs. San Diego	8	309	2
Nov. 10, 1985	Lionel James, San Diego vs. L.A. Raiders (OT)	23	345	0
Sept. 22, 1985	Lionel James, San Diego vs. Cincinnati	20	316	2
Dec. 21, 1975	*Walter Payton, Chicago vs. New Orleans	32	300	1
Nov. 23, 1975	Greg Pruitt, Cleveland vs. Cincinnati	28	304	2
Nov. 1, 1970	Eugene (Mercury) Morris, Miami vs. Baltimore	17	302	0
Oct. 4, 1970	O.J. Simpson, Buffalo vs. N.Y. Jets	26	303	2
Dec. 6, 1969	Jerry LeVias, Houston vs. N.Y. Jets	18	329	1
Nov. 2, 1969	Travis Williams, Green Bay vs. Pittsburgh	11	314	3
Dec. 18, 1966	Gale Sayers, Chicago vs. Minnesota	20	339	2
Dec. 12, 1965	*Gale Sayers, Chicago vs. San Francisco	17	336	6
Nov. 17, 1963	Gary Ballman, Pittsburgh vs. Washington	12	320	2
Dec. 16, 1962	Timmy Brown, Philadelphia vs. St. Louis	19	341	2
Dec. 10, 1961	Billy Cannon, Houston vs. N.Y. Titans	32	373	5
Nov. 19, 1961	Jim Brown, Cleveland vs. Philadelphia	38	313	4
Dec. 3, 1950	Cloyce Box, Detroit vs. Baltimore	13	302	4
Oct. 29, 1950	Wally Triplett, Detroit vs. Los Angeles	11	331	1
Nov. 22, 1945	Jim Benton, Cleveland vs. Detroit	10	303	1

*First season of professional football.

2,000 SCRIMMAGE YARDS GAINED IN A SEASON

Year	Player, Team	Att.	Rushing Yards	Receptions	Receiving Yards	Scrimm. Yards
2011	Ray Rice, Baltimore[2]	291	1,364	76	704	2,068
2010	Arian Foster, Houston	327	1,616	66	604	2,220
2009	Chris Johnson, Tennessee	358	2,006	50	503	2,509
	Ray Rice, Baltimore	254	1,339	78	702	2,041
2007	Brian Westbrook, Philadelphia	278	1,333	90	771	2,104
2006	Steven Jackson, St. Louis	346	1,528	90	806	2,334
	LaDainian Tomlinson, San Diego[3]	348	1,815	56	508	2,323
	Larry Johnson, Kansas City[2]	416	1,789	41	410	2,199
	Frank Gore, San Francisco	312	1,695	61	485	2,180
	Tiki Barber, N.Y. Giants[3]	327	1,662	58	465	2,127
2005	Tiki Barber, N.Y. Giants[2]	357	1,860	54	530	2,390
	Larry Johnson, Kansas City	336	1,750	33	343	2,093
2004	Tiki Barber, N.Y. Giants	322	1.518	52	578	2,096
	Edgerrin James, Indianapolis[3]	334	1,548	51	483	2,031

Year	Player, Team	Att.	Rushing Yards	Receptions	Receiving Yards	Scrimm. Yards
2003	LaDainian Tomlinson, San Diego[2]	313	1,645	100	725	2,370
	Jamal Lewis, Baltimore	387	2,066	26	205	2,271
	Ahman Green, Green Bay	355	1,883	50	367	2,250
	Deuce McAllister, New Orleans	351	1,641	69	516	2,157
	Priest Holmes, Kansas City[3]	320	1,420	74	690	2,110
2002	Priest Holmes, Kansas City[2]	313	1,615	70	672	2,287
	Ricky Williams, Miami	383	1,853	47	363	2,216
	LaDainian Tomlinson, San Diego	372	1,683	79	489	2,172
2001	Priest Holmes, Kansas City	327	1,555	62	614	2,169
	Marshall Faulk, St. Louis[4]	260	1,382	83	765	2,147
2000	Edgerrin James, Indianapolis[2]	387	1,709	63	594	2,303
	Marshall Faulk, St. Louis[3]	253	1,359	81	830	2,189
1999	Marshall Faulk, St. Louis[2]	253	1,381	87	1,048	2,429
	*Edgerrin James, Indianapolis	369	1,553	62	586	2,139
1998	Marshall Faulk, Indianapolis	324	1,319	86	908	2,227
	Terrell Davis, Denver[2]	392	2,008	25	217	2,225
	Jamal Anderson, Atlanta	410	1,846	27	319	2,165
	Garrison Hearst, San Francisco	310	1,570	39	535	2,105
1997	Barry Sanders, Detroit[2]	335	2,053	33	305	2,358
	Terrell Davis, Denver	369	1,750	42	287	2,037
1995	Emmitt Smith, Dallas[2]	377	1,773	62	375	2,148
1994	Barry Sanders, Detroit	331	1,883	44	283	2,166
1992	Thurman Thomas, Buffalo[2]	312	1,487	58	626	2,113
	Emmitt Smith, Dallas	373	1,713	59	335	2,048
	Barry Foster, Pittsburgh	390	1,690	36	344	2,034
1991	Thurman Thomas, Buffalo	288	1,407	62	631	2,038
1988	Roger Craig, San Francisco[2]	310	1,502	76	534	2,036
	Eric Dickerson, Indianapolis[4]	388	1,659	36	377	2,036
	Herschel Walker, Dallas	361	1,514	53	505	2,019
1986	Eric Dickerson, L.A. Rams[3]	404	1,821	26	205	2,026
1985	Marcus Allen, L.A. Raiders	380	1,759	67	555	2,314
	Roger Craig, San Francisco	214	1,050	92	1,016	2,066
	Walter Payton, Chicago[4]	324	1,551	49	483	2,034
1984	Eric Dickerson, L. A. Rams[2]	379	2,105	21	139	2,244
	James Wilder, Tampa Bay	407	1,544	85	685	2,229
	Walter Payton, Chicago[3]	381	1,684	45	368	2,052
1983	*Eric Dickerson, L.A. Rams	390	1,808	51	404	2,212
	William Andrews, Atlanta[2]	331	1,567	59	609	2,176
	Walter Payton, Chicago[2]	314	1,421	53	607	2,028
1981	William Andrews, Atlanta	289	1,301	81	735	2,036
1979	Wilbert Montgomery, Philadelphia	338	1,512	41	494	2,006
1977	Walter Payton, Chicago	339	1,852	27	269	2,121
1975	O.J. Simpson, Buffalo[2]	329	1,817	28	426	2,243
1973	O.J. Simpson, Buffalo	332	2,003	6	70	2,073
1963	Jim Brown, Cleveland	291	1,863	24	268	2,131

*First season of professional football.

300 SCRIMMAGE YARDS GAINED IN A GAME

Date	Player, Team, Opponent	Att.	Yards	TD
Nov. 4, 2007	*Adrian Peterson, Minnesota vs. San Diego	31	315	3
Nov. 24, 2002	Priest Holmes, Kansas City vs. Seattle	30	307	3
Nov. 26, 1989	Flipper Anderson, L.A. Rams vs. New Orleans (OT)	15	336	1
Dec. 22, 1985	Stephone Paige, Kansas City vs. San Diego	8	309	2
Dec. 10, 1961	Billy Cannon, Houston vs. N.Y. Titans	30	330	5
Dec. 3, 1950	Cloyce Box, Detroit vs. Baltimore	12	302	4
Nov. 22, 1945	Jim Benton, Cleveland vs. Detroit	10	303	1

*First season of professional football.

TOP 20 SCORERS

Player	Years	TD	FG	PAT	TP
1. Morten Andersen	25	0	565	849	2,544
2. Gary Anderson	23	0	538	820	2,434
3. John Carney	23	0	478	628	2,062
4. Jason Hanson	20	0	463	627	2,016
5. Matt Stover	19	0	471	591	2,004
6. George Blanda	26	9	335	943	2,002
7. Jason Elam	17	0	436	675	1,983
8. John Kasay	20	0	461	587	1,970
9. Adam Vinatieri	16	0	387	589	1,752
10. Norm Johnson	18	0	366	638	1,736
11. Nick Lowery	18	0	383	562	1,711
12. Jan Stenerud	19	0	373	580	1,699
13. Ryan Longwell	15	0	361	604	1,687
14. Eddie Murray	19	0	352	538	1,594
15. Al Del Greco	17	0	347	543	1,584
16. Olindo Mare	15	0	350	480	1,530
17. David Akers	14	0	338	477	1,491
18. Steve Christie	15	0	336	468	1,476
19. Pat Leahy	18	0	304	558	1,470
20. Jim Turner	16	1	304	521	1,439

TOP 20 TOUCHDOWN SCORERS

Player	Years	Rush	Rec.	Total Returns	TD
1. Jerry Rice	20	10	197	1	208
2. Emmitt Smith	15	164	11	0	175
3. LaDainian Tomlinson	11	145	17	0	162
4. Terrell Owens	15	3	153	0	156
5. Randy Moss	13	0	153	1	154
6. Marcus Allen	16	123	21	1	145
7. Marshall Faulk	12	100	36	0	136
8. Cris Carter	16	0	130	1	131
9. Marvin Harrison	13	0	128	0	128
10. Jim Brown	9	106	20	0	126
11. Walter Payton	13	110	15	0	125
12. John Riggins	14	104	12	0	116
13. Lenny Moore	12	63	48	2	113
14. Shaun Alexander	9	100	12	0	112
15. Barry Sanders	10	99	10	0	109
16. Tim Brown	17	1	100	4	105
Don Hutson	11	3	99	3	105
18. Steve Largent	14	1	100	0	101
19. Franco Harris	13	91	9	0	100
Curtis Martin	11	90	10	0	100

TOP 20 RUSHERS

Player	Years	Att.	Yards	Avg.	Long	TD
1. Emmitt Smith	15	4,409	18,355	4.2	75	164
2. Walter Payton	13	3,838	16,726	4.4	76	110
3. Barry Sanders	10	3,062	15,269	5.0	85	99
4. Curtis Martin	11	3,518	14,101	4.0	70	90
5. LaDainian Tomlinson	11	3,174	13,684	4.3	85	145
6. Jerome Bettis	13	3,479	13,662	3.9	71	91
7. Eric Dickerson	11	2,996	13,259	4.4	85	90
8. Tony Dorsett	12	2,936	12,739	4.3	99	77
9. Jim Brown	9	2,359	12,312	5.2	80	106
10. Marshall Faulk	12	2,836	12,279	4.3	71	100
11. Edgerrin James	11	3,028	12,246	4.0	72	80
12. Marcus Allen	16	3,022	12,243	4.1	61	123
13. Franco Harris	13	2,949	12,120	4.1	75	91
14. Thurman Thomas	13	2,877	12,074	4.2	80	65
15. Fred Taylor	13	2,534	11,695	4.6	80	66
16. John Riggins	14	2,916	11,352	3.9	66	104
17. Corey Dillon	10	2,618	11,241	4.3	96	82
18. O.J. Simpson	11	2,404	11,236	4.7	94	61
19. Warrick Dunn	12	2,669	10,967	4.1	90	49
20. Ricky Watters	10	2,622	10,643	4.1	57	78

TOP 20 LEADERS IN PASSES COMPLETED
1. Brett Favre 6,300
2. Dan Marino 4,967
3. Peyton Manning 4,682
4. John Elway 4,123
5. Warren Moon 3,988
6. Drew Bledsoe 3,839
7. Vinny Testaverde 3,787
8. Fran Tarkenton 3,686
9. Drew Brees 3,613
10. Kerry Collins 3,487
11. Joe Montana 3,409
12. Tom Brady 3,397
13. Dan Fouts 3,297
14. Donovan McNabb 3,170
15. Dave Krieg 3,105
16. Boomer Esiason 2,969
17. Troy Aikman 2,898
18. Matt Hasselbeck 2,891
19. Steve DeBerg 2,874
    Jim Kelly 2,874

TOP 20 LEADERS IN PASSING YARDS
1. Brett Favre 71,838
2. Dan Marino 61,361
3. Peyton Manning 54,828
4. John Elway 51,475
5. Warren Moon 49,325
6. Fran Tarkenton 47,003
7. Vinny Testaverde 46,233
8. Drew Bledsoe 44,611
9. Dan Fouts 43,040
10. Kerry Collins 40,922
11. Drew Brees 40,742
12. Joe Montana 40,551
13. Johnny Unitas 40,239
14. Tom Brady 39,979
15. Dave Krieg 38,147
16. Boomer Esiason 37,920
17. Donovan McNabb 37,276
18. Jim Kelly 35,467
19. Jim Everett 34,837
20. Jim Hart 34,665

TOP 20 LEADERS IN TOUCHDOWN PASSES
1. Brett Favre 508
2. Dan Marino 420
3. Peyton Manning 399
4. Fran Tarkenton 342
5. John Elway 300
   Tom Brady 300
7. Warren Moon 291
8. Johnny Unitas 290
9. Drew Brees 281
10. Vinny Testaverde 275
11. Joe Montana 273
12. Dave Krieg 261
13. Sonny Jurgensen 255
14. Dan Fouts 254
15. Drew Bledsoe 251
16. Boomer Esiason 247
17. John Hadl 244
18. Len Dawson 239
19. Jim Kelly 237
20. George Blanda 236

TOP 20 LEADERS IN RECEPTION YARDS
1. Jerry Rice 22,895
2. Terrell Owens 15,934
3. Isaac Bruce 15,208
4. Tim Brown 14,934
5. Randy Moss 14,858
6. Marvin Harrison 14,580
7. James Lofton 14,004
8. Cris Carter 13,899
9. Henry Ellard 13,777
10. Torry Holt 13,382
11. Tony Gonzalez 13,338
12. Andre Reed 13,198
13. Steve Largent 13,089
14. Irving Fryar 12,785
15. Art Monk 12,721
16. Jimmy Smith 12,287
17. Charlie Joiner 12,146
18. Hines Ward 12,083
19. Derrick Mason 12,061
20. Michael Irvin 11,904

TOP 20 COMBINED YARDS GAINED

Player	Years	Tot.	Rush.	Rec.	Int. Ret.	Punt Ret.	Kickoff Ret.	Fumble Ret.
1. Jerry Rice	20	23,546	645	22,895	0	0	6	0
2. Brian Mitchell	14	23,330	1,967	2,336	0	4,999	14,014	14
3. Walter Payton	13	21,803	16,726	4,538	0	0	539	0
4. Emmitt Smith	15	21,583	18,355	3,224	0	0	0	4
5. Tim Brown	17	19,682	190	14,934	0	3,320	1,235	3
6. Marshall Faulk	12	19,190	12,279	6,875	0	0	18	18
7. LaDainian Tomlinson	11	18,456	13,684	4,772	0	0	0	0
8. Barry Sanders	10	18,308	15,269	2,921	0	0	118	0
9. Herschel Walker	12	18,168	8,225	4,859	0	0	5,084	0
10. Marcus Allen	16	17,648	12,243	5,411	0	0	0	-6
11. Curtis Martin	11	17,430	14,101	3,329	0	0	0	0
12. Tiki Barber	10	17,359	10,449	5,183	0	1,181	544	2
13. Eric Metcalf	13	17,230	2,392	5,572	0	3,453	5,813	0
14. Derrick Mason	15	17,150	3	12,061	0	1,590	3,496	0
15. Thurman Thomas	13	16,532	12,074	4,458	0	0	0	0
16. Tony Dorsett	12	16,347	12,739	3,554	0	0	0	54
17. Terrell Owens	15	16,276	251	15,934	0	0	78	13
18. Henry Ellard	16	15,718	50	13,777	0	1,527	364	0
19. Warrick Dunn	12	15,665	10,967	4,339	0	48	310	1
20. Edgerrin James	11	15,610	12,246	3,364	0	0	0	0

TOP 20 YARDS FROM SCRIMMAGE

Player	Years	Scrimmage Yards	Rushing Yards	Receiving Yards
1. Jerry Rice	20	23,540	645	22,895
2. Emmitt Smith	15	21,579	18,355	3,224
3. Walter Payton	13	21,264	16,726	4,538
4. Marshall Faulk	12	19,154	12,279	6,875
5. LaDainian Tomlinson	11	18,456	13,684	4,772
6. Barry Sanders	10	18,190	15,269	2,921
7. Marcus Allen	16	17,654	12,243	5,411
8. Curtis Martin	11	17,430	14,101	3,329
9. Thurman Thomas	13	16,532	12,074	4,458
10. Tony Dorsett	12	16,293	12,739	3,554
11. Terrell Owens	15	16,185	251	15,934
12. Tiki Barber	10	15,632	10,449	5,183
13. Edgerrin James	11	15,610	12,246	3,364
14. Eric Dickerson	11	15,396	13,259	2,137
15. Isaac Bruce	16	15,347	139	15,208
16. Warrick Dunn	12	15,306	10,967	4,339
17. Tim Brown	17	15,124	190	14,934
18. Jerome Bettis	13	15,111	13,662	1,449
19. Randy Moss	15	15,017	159	14,858
20. Ricky Watters	10	14,891	10,643	4,248

TOP 20 PASSERS

Player	Years	Att.	Comp.	Pct. Comp.	Yards	Avg. Gain	TD	Pct. TD	Int.	Pct. Int.	Rating
1. Aaron Rodgers	7	2,113	1,381	65.4	17,366	8.22	132	6.2	38	1.8	104.1
2. Tony Romo	8	2,592	1,672	64.5	20,834	8.04	149	5.7	72	2.8	96.9
3. Steve Young	15	4,149	2,667	64.3	33,124	7.98	232	5.6	107	2.6	96.8
4. Tom Brady	12	5,321	3,397	63.8	39,979	7.51	300	5.6	115	2.2	96.4
5. Philip Rivers	8	3,037	1,930	63.5	24,285	8.00	163	5.4	78	2.6	95.5
6. Peyton Manning	13	7,210	4,682	64.9	54,828	7.60	399	5.5	198	2.7	94.9
7. Drew Brees	11	5,479	3,613	65.9	40,742	7.44	281	5.1	146	2.7	94.0
8. Kurt Warner	12	4,070	2,666	65.5	32,344	7.95	208	5.1	128	3.1	93.7
9. Joe Montana	15	5,391	3,409	63.2	40,551	7.52	273	5.1	139	2.6	92.3
10. Matt Schaub	8	2,279	1,466	64.3	17,936	7.87	98	4.3	58	2.5	92.2
11. Ben Roethlisberger	8	3,313	2,090	63.1	26,579	8.02	165	5.0	100	3.0	92.1
12. Chad Pennington	11	2,471	1,632	66.0	17,823	7.21	102	4.1	64	2.6	90.1
13. Matt Ryan	4	2,022	1,232	60.9	14,238	7.04	95	4.7	46	2.3	88.4
14. Daunte Culpepper	11	3,199	2,016	63.0	24,153	7.55	149	4.7	106	3.3	87.8
15. Jeff Garcia	11	3,676	2,264	61.6	25,537	6.95	161	4.4	83	2.3	87.5
16. Dan Marino	17	8,358	4,967	59.4	61,361	7.34	420	5.0	252	3.0	86.4
17. Carson Palmer	8	3,545	2,223	62.7	25,447	7.18	167	4.7	116	3.3	86.3
18. Trent Green	11	3,740	2,266	60.6	28,475	7.61	162	4.3	114	3.0	86.0
19. Brett Favre	20	10,169	6,300	62.0	71,838	7.06	508	5.0	336	3.3	86.0
20. Joe Flacco	4	1,958	1,190	60.8	13,816	7.06	80	4.1	46	2.3	86.0

1,500 or more attempts. The passing ratings are based on performance standards established for completion percentage, interception percentage, touchdown percentage, and average gain. Please consult page 312 for more information.

TOP 20 PASS RECEIVERS

Player	Years	No.	Yards	Avg.	Long	TD
1. Jerry Rice	20	1,549	22,895	14.8	96	197
2. Tony Gonzalez	15	1,149	13,338	11.6	73	95
3. Marvin Harrison	13	1,102	14,580	13.2	80	128
4. Cris Carter	16	1,101	13,899	12.6	80	130
5. Tim Brown	17	1,094	14,934	13.7	80	100
6. Terrell Owens	15	1,078	15,934	14.8	98	153
7. Isaac Bruce	16	1,024	15,208	14.9	80	91
8. Hines Ward	14	1,000	12,083	12.1	85	85
9. Randy Moss	13	954	14,858	15.6	82	153
10. Andre Reed	16	951	13,198	13.9	83	87
11. Derrick Mason	15	943	12,061	12.8	79	66
12. Art Monk	16	940	12,721	13.5	79	68
13. Torry Holt	11	920	13,382	14.5	85	74
14. Keenan McCardell	16	883	11,373	12.9	76	63
15. Jimmy Smith	12	862	12,287	14.3	75	67
Reggie Wayne	11	862	11,708	13.6	71	73
16. Muhsin Muhammad	14	860	11,438	13.3	72	62
17. Irving Fryar	17	851	12,785	15.0	80	84
18. Rod Smith	12	849	11,389	13.4	85	68
19. Larry Centers	14	827	6,797	8.2	54	28

TOP 20 INTERCEPTORS

Player	Years	No.	Yards	Avg.	Long	TD
1. Paul Krause	16	81	1,185	14.6	81	3
2. Emlen Tunnell	14	79	1,282	16.2	55	4
3. Rod Woodson	17	71	1,483	20.9	98	12
4. Dick (Night Train) Lane	14	68	1,207	17.8	80	5
5. Ken Riley	15	65	596	9.2	66	5
6. Ronnie Lott	14	63	730	11.6	83	5
Darren Sharper	14	63	1,412	22.4	99	11
7. Dave Brown	15	62	698	11.3	90	5
Dick LeBeau	14	62	762	12.3	70	3
9. Emmitt Thomas	13	58	937	16.2	73	5
10. Mel Blount	14	57	736	12.9	52	2
Bobby Boyd	9	57	994	17.4	74	4
Ed Reed	10	57	1,463	25.7	107	6
Eugene Robinson	16	57	762	13.4	49	1
Johnny Robinson	12	57	741	13.0	57	1
Everson Walls	13	57	504	8.8	40	1
16. Lem Barney	11	56	1,077	19.2	71	7
Pat Fischer	17	56	941	16.8	69	4
18. Aeneas Williams	14	55	807	14.7	65	9
19. Eric Allen	14	54	826	15.3	94	8
Willie Brown	16	54	472	8.7	45	2
Darrell Green	20	54	621	11.5	83	6
Charles Woodson	14	54	896	16.6	62	11

TOP 20 PUNTERS (MINIMUM 250 PUNTS)

Player	Years	No.	Yards	Avg.	Long	Blk.
1. Shane Lechler	12	933	44,389	47.6	80	3
2. Andy Lee	8	723	33,069	45.7	82	3
3. Brandon Fields	5	377	17,227	45.7	71	2
4. Donnie Jones	8	648	29,379	45.3	80	3
5. Mat McBriar	8	494	22,369	45.3	75	3
6. Sammy Baugh	16	338	15,245	45.1	85	9
7. Jon Ryan	6	483	21,713	45.0	77	3
8. Mike Scifres	9	492	22,044	44.8	71	5
9. Tommy Davis	11	511	22,833	44.7	82	2
10. Dustin Colquitt	7	574	25,494	44.4	81	3
11. Chris Kluwe	7	551	24,446	44.4	70	1
12. Brett Kern	4	273	12,109	44.4	68	0
13. Yale Lary	11	503	22,279	44.3	74	4
14. Ben Graham	7	462	20,413	44.2	69	2
15. Sam Koch	6	475	20,980	44.2	74	2
16. Todd Sauerbrun	13	889	39,208	44.1	73	9
17. Brian Moorman	11	847	37,177	43.9	84	2
18. Bob Scarpitto	8	283	12,408	43.8	87	4
19. Horace Gillom	7	385	16,872	43.8	80	5
20. Jerry Norton	11	358	15,671	43.8	78	2

TOP 20 KICKOFF RETURNERS (MINIMUM 75 RETURNS)

Player	Years	No.	Yards	Avg.	Long	TD
1. Gale Sayers	7	91	2,781	30.6	103	6
2. Lynn Chandnois	7	92	2,720	29.6	93	3
3. Abe Woodson	9	193	5,538	28.7	105	5
4. Buddy Young	6	90	2,514	27.9	104	2
5. Travis Williams	5	102	2,801	27.5	105	6
6. Joe Arenas	7	139	3,798	27.3	96	1
7. Clifton Smith	3	75	2,038	27.2	97	1
8. Clarence Davis	8	79	2,140	27.1	76	0
9. Danieal Manning	6	114	3,067	26.9	83	1
10. Steve Van Buren	8	76	2,030	26.7	98	3
11. Lenny Lyles	12	81	2,161	26.7	103	3
12. Percy Harvin	3	98	2,609	26.6	104	4
13. Mercury Morris	8	111	2,947	26.5	105	3
14. Ellis Hobbs	6	141	3,739	26.5	108	3
15. Bobby Jancik	6	158	4,185	26.5	61	0
16. Mel Renfro	14	85	2,246	26.4	100	2
17. Bobby Mitchell	14	102	2,690	26.4	98	5
18. Terrence McGee	9	207	5,450	26.3	104	5
19. Stefan Logan	3	143	3,746	26.2	105	1
20. Ollie Matson	14	143	3,746	26.2	105	6

TOP 20 PUNT RETURNERS (MINIMUM 75 RETURNS)

Player	Years	No.	Yards	Avg.	Long	TD
1. Devin Hester	6	206	2,654	12.9	89	12
2. George McAfee	8	112	1,431	12.8	74	2
3. Jack Christiansen	8	85	1,084	12.8	89	8
4. Claude Gibson	5	110	1,381	12.6	85	3
5. Bill Dudley	9	124	1,515	12.2	96	3
6. Rick Upchurch	9	248	3,008	12.1	92	8
7. Roscoe Parrish	7	135	1,622	12.0	82	3
8. Eddie Royal	4	81	967	11.9	85	2
9. Desmond Howard	11	244	2,895	11.9	95	8
10. Billy Johnson	14	282	3,317	11.8	87	6
11. Mack Herron	3	84	982	11.7	66	0
12. Billy Thompson	13	157	1,814	11.6	60	0
13. Darrien Gordon	9	314	3,601	11.5	94	6
14. Santana Moss	11	112	1,268	11.3	80	3
15. Henry Ellard	16	135	1,527	11.3	83	4
16. Rodger Bird	3	94	1,063	11.3	78	0
17. Bosh Pritchard	6	95	1,072	11.3	81	2
18. Ted Ginn	5	98	1,099	11.2	87	3
19. Terry Metcalf	6	84	936	11.1	69	1
20. Bob Hayes	11	104	1,158	11.1	90	3

TOP 20 LEADERS IN SACKS

Player	*Years	No.
1. Bruce Smith	19	200.0
2. Reggie White	15	198.0
3. Kevin Greene	15	160.0
4. Chris Doleman	15	150.5
5. Michael Strahan	15	141.5
6. Jason Taylor	15	139.5
7. Richard Dent	15	137.5
John Randle	14	137.5
9. Leslie O'Neal	13	132.5
Lawrence Taylor	12	132.5
11. Rickey Jackson	14	128.0
12. Derrick Thomas	11	126.5
13. Simeon Rice	12	122.0
14. Clyde Simmons	15	121.5
15. Sean Jones	13	113.0
16. John Abraham	12	112.0
17. Greg Townsend	13	109.5
18. Pat Swilling	12	107.5
19. Trace Armstrong	15	106.0
20. Jared Allen	8	105.0

*Years played since 1982 when sacks became an official statistic.

POSTSEASON LEADERS
TOP 10 POSTSEASON RUSHERS

Player	Att.	Yards	Avg.	Long	TD
1. Emmitt Smith	349	1,586	4.5	65	19
2. Franco Harris	400	1,556	3.9	50	16
3. Thurman Thomas	339	1,442	4.3	40	16
4. Tony Dorsett	302	1,383	4.6	53	9
5. Marcus Allen	267	1,347	5.0	74	11
6. Terrell Davis	204	1,140	5.6	62	12
7. John Riggins	251	996	4.0	43	12
8. Larry Csonka	225	891	4.0	49	9
9. Chuck Foreman	229	860	3.8	62	7
10. Edgerrin James	218	852	3.9	34	6

TOP 10 POSTSEASON PASSERS

Player	Att.	Comp.	Pct. Comp.	Yards	Avg. Gain	TD	Pct. TD	Int.	Pct. Int.	Rating
1. Aaron Rodgers	220	144	65.5	1,781	8.10	15	6.8	4	1.8	105.5
2. Bart Starr	213	130	61.0	1,753	8.23	15	7.0	3	1.4	104.8
3. Drew Brees	391	262	67.0	2,980	7.62	22	5.6	4	1.0	104.2
4. Kurt Warner	462	307	66.5	3,952	8.55	31	6.7	14	3.0	102.8
5. Joe Montana	734	460	62.7	5,772	7.86	45	6.1	21	2.9	95.6
6. Mark Sanchez	157	95	60.5	1,155	7.36	9	5.7	3	1.9	94.3
7. Ken Anderson	166	110	66.3	1,321	7.96	9	5.4	6	3.6	93.5
8. Joe Theismann	211	128	60.7	1,782	8.45	11	5.2	7	3.3	91.4
9. Eli Manning	356	219	61.5	2,516	7.07	17	4.8	8	2.2	89.3
10. Peyton Manning	718	453	63.1	5,389	7.51	29	4.0	19	2.6	88.4

TOP 10 POSTSEASON PASS RECEIVERS

Player	No.	Yards	Avg.	Long	TD
1. Jerry Rice	151	2,245	14.9	72	22
2. Hines Ward	88	1,181	13.4	45	10
3. Michael Irvin	87	1,315	15.1	53	8
4. Andre Reed	85	1,229	14.5	72	9
5. Reggie Wayne	83	1,128	13.6	72	9
6. Thurman Thomas	76	672	8.8	27	5
7. Cliff Branch	73	1,289	17.7	72	5
8. Fred Biletnikoff	70	1,167	16.7	57	10
9. Art Monk	69	1,062	15.4	48	7
10. Drew Pearson	67	1,105	16.5	83	8

TOP 10 POSTSEASON INTERCEPTION LEADERS

Player	Interceptions
1. Ronnie Lott	9
Bill Simpson	9
Charlie Waters	9
4. Lester Hayes	8
Ed Reed	8
6. Willie Brown	7
Rodney Harrison	7
Asante Samuel	7
Dennis Thurman	7
10. Bobby Bryant	6
Eric Davis	6
Glen Edwards	6
Darrell Green	6
Cliff Harris	6
Ty Law	6
Vernon Perry	6
Aeneas Williams	6

TOP 10 POSTSEASON SACK LEADERS

Player	Sacks
1. Willie McGinest	16.0
2. Bruce Smith	14.5
3. Reggie White	12.0
4. Charles Haley	11.0
LaMarr Woodley	11.0
6. Richard Dent	10.5
7. Trace Armstrong	10.0
Charles Mann	10.0
Terrell Suggs	10.0
Tony Tolbert	10.0

*Sacks became an official statistic in 1982.

ANNUAL SCORING LEADERS

Year	Player, Team	TD	FG	PAT	TP
2011	David Akers, San Francisco, NFC	0	44	34	166
	Stephen Gostkowski, New England, AFC	0	28	59	143
2010	David Akers, Philadelphia, NFC	0	32	47	143
	Sebastian Janikowski, Oakland, AFC	0	33	43	142
2009	Nate Kaeding, San Diego, AFC	0	32	50	146
	David Akers, Philadelphia, NFC	0	32	43	139
2008	Stephen Gostkowski, New England, AFC	0	36	40	148
	David Akers, Philadelphia, NFC	0	33	45	144
2007	*Mason Crosby, Green Bay, NFC	0	31	48	141
	Randy Moss, New England, AFC	23	0	0	138
2006	LaDainian Tomlinson, AFC	31	0	0	186
	Robbie Gould, Chicago, NFC	0	32	47	143
2005	Shaun Alexander, Seattle, NFC	28	0	0	168
	Shayne Graham, Cincinnati, AFC	0	28	47	131
2004	Adam Vinatieri, New England, AFC	0	31	48	141
	David Akers, Philadelphia, NFC	0	27	41	122
2003	Jeff Wilkins, St. Louis, NFC	0	39	46	163
	Priest Holmes, Kansas City, AFC	27	0	0	162
2002	Priest Holmes, Kansas City, AFC	24	0	0	144
	Jay Feely, Atlanta, NFC	0	32	42	138
2001	Marshall Faulk, St. Louis, NFC	21	0	0	#128
	Mike Vanderjagt, Indianapolis, AFC	0	28	41	125
2000	Marshall Faulk, St. Louis, NFC	26	0	0	##160
	Matt Stover, Baltimore, AFC	0	35	30	135
1999	Mike Vanderjagt, Indianapolis, AFC	0	34	43	145
	Jeff Wilkins, St. Louis, NFC	0	20	64	124
1998	Gary Anderson, Minnesota, NFC	0	35	59	164
	Steve Christie, Buffalo, AFC	0	33	41	140
1997	Mike Hollis, Jacksonville, AFC	0	31	41	134
	Richie Cunningham, Dallas, NFC	0	34	24	126
1996	John Kasay, Carolina, NFC	0	37	34	145
	Cary Blanchard, Indianapolis, AFC	0	36	27	135
1995	Emmitt Smith, Dallas, NFC	25	0	0	150
	Norm Johnson, Pittsburgh, AFC	0	34	39	141
1994	John Carney, San Diego, AFC	0	34	33	135
	Fuad Reveiz, Minnesota, NFC	0	34	30	132
1993	Jeff Jaeger, L.A. Raiders, AFC	0	35	27	132
	Jason Hanson, Detroit, NFC	0	34	28	130
1992	Pete Stoyanovich, Miami, AFC	0	30	34	124
	Morten Andersen, New Orleans, NFC	0	29	33	120
	Chip Lohmiller, Washington, NFC	0	30	30	120
1991	Chip Lohmiller, Washington, NFC	0	31	56	149
	Pete Stoyanovich, Miami, AFC	0	31	28	121
1990	Nick Lowery, Kansas City, AFC	0	34	37	139
	Chip Lohmiller, Washington, NFC	0	30	41	131
1989	Mike Cofer, San Francisco, NFC	0	29	49	136
	*David Treadwell, Denver, AFC	0	27	39	120
1988	Scott Norwood, Buffalo, AFC	0	32	33	129
	Mike Cofer, San Francisco, NFC	0	27	40	121
1987	Jerry Rice, San Francisco, NFC	23	0	0	138
	Jim Breech, Cincinnati, AFC	0	24	25	97
1986	Tony Franklin, New England, AFC	0	32	44	140
	Kevin Butler, Chicago, NFC	0	28	36	120
1985	*Kevin Butler, Chicago, NFC	0	31	51	144
	Gary Anderson, Pittsburgh, AFC	0	33	40	139
1984	Ray Wersching, San Francisco, NFC	0	25	56	131
	Gary Anderson, Pittsburgh, AFC	0	24	45	117
1983	Mark Moseley, Washington, NFC	0	33	62	161
	Gary Anderson, Pittsburgh, AFC	0	27	38	119
1982	*Marcus Allen, L.A. Raiders, AFC	14	0	0	84
	Wendell Tyler, L.A. Rams, NFC	13	0	0	78
1981	Ed Murray, Detroit, NFC	0	25	46	121
	Rafael Septien, Dallas, NFC	0	27	40	121
	Jim Breech, Cincinnati, AFC	0	22	49	115
	Nick Lowery, Kansas City, AFC	0	26	37	115
1980	John Smith, New England, AFC	0	26	51	129
	*Ed Murray, Detroit, NFC	0	27	35	116
1979	John Smith, New England, AFC	0	23	46	115
	Mark Moseley, Washington, NFC	0	25	39	114
1978	*Frank Corral, Los Angeles, NFC	0	29	31	118

Year	Player, Team	TD	FG	PAT	TP
	Pat Leahy, N.Y. Jets, AFC	0	22	41	107
1977	Errol Mann, Oakland, AFC	0	20	39	99
	Walter Payton, Chicago, NFC	16	0	0	96
1976	Toni Linhart, Baltimore, AFC	0	20	49	109
	Mark Moseley, Washington, NFC	0	22	31	97
1975	O.J. Simpson, Buffalo, AFC	23	0	0	138
	Chuck Foreman, Minnesota, NFC	22	0	0	132
1974	Chester Marcol, Green Bay, NFC	0	25	19	94
	Roy Gerela, Pittsburgh, AFC	0	20	33	93
1973	David Ray, Los Angeles, NFC	0	30	40	130
	Roy Gerela, Pittsburgh, AFC	0	29	36	123
1972	*Chester Marcol, Green Bay, NFC	0	33	29	128
	Bobby Howfield, N.Y. Jets, AFC	0	27	40	121
1971	Garo Yepremian, Miami, AFC	0	28	33	117
	Curt Knight, Washington, NFC	0	29	27	114
1970	Fred Cox, Minnesota, NFC	0	30	35	125
	Jan Stenerud, Kansas City, AFC	0	30	26	116
1969	Jim Turner, N.Y. Jets, AFL	0	32	33	129
	Fred Cox, Minnesota, NFL	0	26	43	121
1968	Jim Turner, N.Y. Jets, AFL	0	34	43	145
	Leroy Kelly, Cleveland, NFL	20	0	0	120
1967	Jim Bakken, St. Louis, NFL	0	27	36	117
	George Blanda, Oakland, AFL	0	20	56	116
1966	Gino Cappelletti, Boston, AFL	6	16	35	119
	Bruce Gossett, Los Angeles, NFL	0	28	29	113
1965	*Gale Sayers, Chicago, NFL	22	0	0	132
	Gino Cappelletti, Boston, AFL	9	17	27	132
1964	Gino Cappelletti, Boston, AFL	7	25	36	#155
	Lenny Moore, Baltimore, NFL	20	0	0	120
1963	Gino Cappelletti, Boston, AFL	2	22	35	113
	Don Chandler, N.Y. Giants, NFL	0	18	52	106
1962	Gene Mingo, Denver, AFL	4	27	32	137
	Jim Taylor, Green Bay, NFL	19	0	0	114
1961	Gino Cappelletti, Boston, AFL	8	17	48	147
	Paul Hornung, Green Bay, NFL	10	15	41	146
1960	Paul Hornung, Green Bay, NFL	15	15	41	176
	*Gene Mingo, Denver, AFL	6	18	33	123
1959	Paul Hornung, Green Bay	7	7	31	94
1958	Jim Brown, Cleveland	18	0	0	108
1957	Sam Baker, Washington	1	14	29	77
	Lou Groza, Cleveland	0	15	32	77
1956	Bobby Layne, Detroit	5	12	33	99
1955	Doak Walker, Detroit	7	9	27	96
1954	Bobby Walston, Philadelphia	11	4	36	114
1953	Gordy Soltau, San Francisco	6	10	48	114
1952	Gordy Soltau, San Francisco	7	6	34	94
1951	Elroy (Crazylegs) Hirsch, Los Angeles	17	0	0	102
1950	*Doak Walker, Detroit	11	8	38	128
1949	Pat Harder, Chi. Cardinals	8	3	45	102
	Gene Roberts, N.Y. Giants	17	0	0	102
1948	Pat Harder, Chi. Cardinals	6	7	53	110
1947	Pat Harder, Chi. Cardinals	7	7	39	102
1946	Ted Fritsch, Green Bay	10	9	13	100
1945	Steve Van Buren, Philadelphia	18	0	2	110
1944	Don Hutson, Green Bay	9	0	31	85
1943	Don Hutson, Green Bay	12	3	36	117
1942	Don Hutson, Green Bay	17	1	33	138
1941	Don Hutson, Green Bay	12	1	20	95
1940	Don Hutson, Green Bay	7	0	15	57
1939	Andy Farkas, Washington	11	0	2	68
1938	Clarke Hinkle, Green Bay	7	3	7	58
1937	Jack Manders, Chi. Bears	5	8	15	69
1936	Earl (Dutch) Clark, Detroit	7	4	19	73
1935	Earl (Dutch) Clark, Detroit	6	1	16	55
1934	Jack Manders, Chi. Bears	3	10	31	79
1933	Ken Strong, N.Y. Giants	6	5	13	64
	Glenn Presnell, Portsmouth	6	6	10	64
1932	Earl (Dutch) Clark, Portsmouth	6	3	10	55

*First season of professional football.
#Cappelletti's total and Faulk's total in 2001 include a two-point conversion.
##Faulk's total in 2000 includes 2 two-point conversions.

ANNUAL TOUCHDOWN LEADERS

Year	Player, Team	TD	Rush	Pass	Ret.
2011	LeSean McCoy, Philadelphia, NFC	20	17	3	0
	Rob Gronkowski, New England, AFC	18	1	17	0
2010	Arian Foster, Houston, AFC	18	16	2	0
	Adrian Peterson, Minnesota, NFC	13	12	1	0
2009	Adrian Peterson, Minnesota, NFC	18	18	0	0
	Chris Johnson, Tennessee, AFC	16	14	2	0
	Maurice Jones-Drew, Jacksonville, AFC	16	15	1	0
2008	DeAngelo Williams, Carolina, NFC	20	18	2	0
	Thomas Jones, N.Y. Jets, AFC	15	13	2	0
	LenDale White, Tennessee, AFC	15	15	0	0
2007	Randy Moss, New England, AFC	23	0	23	0
	Terrell Owens, Dallas, NFC	15	0	15	0
2006	LaDainian Tomlinson, San Diego, AFC	31	28	3	0
	Marion Barber, Dallas, NFC	16	14	2	0
	Steven Jackson, St. Louis, NFC	16	13	3	0
2005	Shaun Alexander, Seattle, NFC	28	27	1	0
	Larry Johnson, Kansas City, AFC	21	20	1	0
2004	Shaun Alexander, Seattle, NFC	20	16	4	0
	LaDainian Tomlinson, San Diego, AFC	18	17	1	0
2003	Priest Holmes, Kansas City, AFC	27	27	0	0
	Ahman Green, Green Bay, NFC	20	15	5	0
2002	Priest Holmes, Kansas City, AFC	24	21	3	0
	Shaun Alexander, Seattle, NFC	18	16	2	0
2001	Marshall Faulk, St. Louis, NFC	21	12	9	0
	Shaun Alexander, Seattle, AFC	16	14	2	0
2000	Marshall Faulk, St. Louis, NFC	26	18	8	0
	Edgerrin James, Indianapolis, AFC	18	13	5	0
1999	Stephen Davis, Washington, NFC	17	17	0	0
	*Edgerrin James, Indianapolis, AFC	17	13	4	0
1998	Terrell Davis, Denver, AFC	23	21	2	0
	*Randy Moss, Minnesota, NFC	17	0	17	0
1997	Karim Abdul-Jabbar, Miami, AFC	16	15	1	0
	Barry Sanders, Detroit, NFC	14	11	3	0
1996	Terry Allen, Washington, NFC	21	21	0	0
	Curtis Martin, New England, AFC	17	14	3	0
1995	Emmitt Smith, Dallas, NFC	25	25	0	0
	Carl Pickens, Cincinnati, AFC	17	0	17	0
1994	Emmitt Smith, Dallas, NFC	22	21	1	0
	*Marshall Faulk, Indianapolis, AFC	12	11	1	0
	Natrone Means, San Diego, AFC	12	12	0	0
1993	Jerry Rice, San Francisco, NFC	16	1	15	0
	Marcus Allen, Kansas City, AFC	15	12	3	0
1992	Emmitt Smith, Dallas, NFC	19	18	1	0
	Thurman Thomas, Buffalo, AFC	12	9	3	0
1991	Barry Sanders, Detroit, NFC	17	16	1	0
	Mark Clayton, Miami, AFC	12	0	12	0
	Thurman Thomas, Buffalo, AFC	12	7	5	0
1990	Barry Sanders, Detroit, NFC	16	13	3	0
	Derrick Fenner, Seattle, AFC	15	14	1	0
1989	Dalton Hilliard, New Orleans, NFC	18	13	5	0
	Christian Okoye, Kansas City, AFC	12	12	0	0
	Thurman Thomas, Buffalo, AFC	12	6	6	0
1988	Greg Bell, L.A. Rams, NFC	18	16	2	0
	Eric Dickerson, Indianapolis, AFC	15	14	1	0
	*Ickey Woods, Cincinnati, AFC	15	15	0	0
1987	Jerry Rice, San Francisco, NFC	23	1	22	0
	Johnny Hector, N.Y. Jets, AFC	11	11	0	0
1986	George Rogers, Washington, NFC	18	18	0	0
	Sammy Winder, Denver, AFC	14	9	5	0
1985	Joe Morris, N.Y. Giants, NFC	21	21	0	0
	Louis Lipps, Pittsburgh, AFC	15	1	12	2
1984	Marcus Allen, L.A. Raiders, AFC	18	13	5	0
	Mark Clayton, Miami, AFC	18	0	18	0
	Eric Dickerson, L.A. Rams, NFC	14	14	0	0
	John Riggins, Washington, NFC	14	14	0	0
1983	John Riggins, Washington, NFC	24	24	0	0
	Pete Johnson, Cincinnati, AFC	14	14	0	0
	*Curt Warner, Seattle, AFC	14	13	1	0

Year	Player, Team	TD	Rush	Pass	Ret.
1982	*Marcus Allen, L.A. Raiders, AFC	14	11	3	0
	Wendell Tyler, L.A. Rams, NFC	13	9	4	0
1981	Chuck Muncie, San Diego, AFC	19	19	0	0
	Wendell Tyler, Los Angeles, NFC	17	12	5	0
1980	*Billy Sims, Detroit, NFC	16	13	3	0
	Earl Campbell, Houston, AFC	13	13	0	0
	*Curtis Dickey, Baltimore, AFC	13	11	2	0
	John Jefferson, San Diego, AFC	13	0	13	0
1979	Earl Campbell, Houston, AFC	19	19	0	0
	Walter Payton, Chicago, NFC	16	14	2	0
1978	David Sims, Seattle, AFC	15	14	1	0
	Terdell Middleton, Green Bay, NFC	12	11	1	0
1977	Walter Payton, Chicago, NFC	16	14	2	0
	Nat Moore, Miami, AFC	13	1	12	0
1976	Chuck Foreman, Minnesota, NFC	14	13	1	0
	Franco Harris, Pittsburgh, AFC	14	14	0	0
1975	O.J. Simpson, Buffalo, AFC	23	16	7	0
	Chuck Foreman, Minnesota, NFC	22	13	9	0
1974	Chuck Foreman, Minnesota, NFC	15	9	6	0
	Cliff Branch, Oakland, AFC	13	0	13	0
1973	Larry Brown, Washington, NFC	14	8	6	0
	Floyd Little, Denver, AFC	13	12	1	0
1972	Emerson Boozer, N.Y. Jets, AFC	14	11	3	0
	Ron Johnson, N.Y. Giants, NFC	14	9	5	0
1971	Duane Thomas, Dallas, NFC	13	11	2	0
	Leroy Kelly, Cleveland, AFC	12	10	2	0
1970	Dick Gordon, Chicago, NFC	13	0	13	0
	MacArthur Lane, St. Louis, NFC	13	11	2	0
	Gary Garrison, San Diego, AFC	12	0	12	0
1969	Warren Wells, Oakland, AFL	14	0	14	0
	Tom Matte, Baltimore, NFL	13	11	2	0
	Lance Rentzel, Dallas, NFL	13	0	12	1
1968	Leroy Kelly, Cleveland, NFL	20	16	4	0
	Warren Wells, Oakland, AFL	12	1	11	0
1967	Homer Jones, N.Y. Giants, NFL	14	1	13	0
	Emerson Boozer, N.Y. Jets, AFL	13	10	3	0
1966	Leroy Kelly, Cleveland, NFL	16	15	1	0
	Dan Reeves, Dallas, NFL	16	8	8	0
	Lance Alworth, San Diego, AFL	13	0	13	0
1965	*Gale Sayers, Chicago, NFL	22	14	6	2
	Lance Alworth, San Diego, AFL	14	0	14	0
	Don Maynard, N.Y. Jets, AFL	14	0	14	0
1964	Lenny Moore, Baltimore, NFL	20	16	3	1
	Lance Alworth, San Diego, AFL	15	2	13	0
1963	Art Powell, Oakland, AFL	16	0	16	0
	Jim Brown, Cleveland, NFL	15	12	3	0
1962	Abner Haynes, Dallas, AFL	19	13	6	0
	Jim Taylor, Green Bay, NFL	19	19	0	0
1961	Bill Groman, Houston, AFL	18	1	17	0
	Jim Taylor, Green Bay, NFL	16	15	1	0
1960	Paul Hornung, Green Bay, NFL	15	13	2	0
	Sonny Randle, St. Louis, NFL	15	0	15	0
	Art Powell, N.Y. Titans, AFL	14	0	14	0
1959	Raymond Berry, Baltimore	14	0	14	0
	Jim Brown, Cleveland	14	14	0	0
1958	Jim Brown, Cleveland	18	17	1	0
1957	Lenny Moore, Baltimore	11	3	7	1
1956	Rick Casares, Chi. Bears	14	12	2	0
1955	*Alan Ameche, Baltimore	9	9	0	0
	Harlon Hill, Chi. Bears	9	0	9	0
1954	*Harlon Hill, Chi. Bears	12	0	12	0
1953	Joseph Perry, San Francisco	13	10	3	0
1952	Cloyce Box, Detroit	15	0	15	0
1951	Elroy (Crazylegs) Hirsch, Los Angeles	17	0	17	0
1950	Bob Shaw, Chi. Cardinals	12	0	12	0
1949	Gene Roberts, N.Y. Giants	17	9	8	0
1948	Mal Kutner, Chi. Cardinals	15	1	14	0
1947	Steve Van Buren, Philadelphia	14	13	0	1
1946	Ted Fritsch, Green Bay	10	9	1	0
1945	Steve Van Buren, Philadelphia	18	15	2	1

Year	Player, Team	TD	Rush	Pass	Ret.
1944	Don Hutson, Green Bay	9	0	9	0
	Bill Paschal, N.Y. Giants	9	9	0	0
1943	Don Hutson, Green Bay	12	0	11	1
	*Bill Paschal, N.Y. Giants	12	10	2	0
1942	Don Hutson, Green Bay	17	0	17	0
1941	Don Hutson, Green Bay	12	2	10	0
	George McAfee, Chi. Bears	12	6	3	3
1940	John Drake, Cleveland	9	9	0	0
	Richard Todd, Washington	9	4	4	1
1939	Andrew Farkas, Washington	11	5	5	1
1938	Don Hutson, Green Bay	9	0	9	0
1937	Cliff Battles, Washington	7	5	1	1
	Clarke Hinkle, Green Bay	7	5	2	0
	Don Hutson, Green Bay	7	0	7	0
1936	Don Hutson, Green Bay	9	0	8	1
1935	*Don Hutson, Green Bay	7	0	6	1
1934	*Beattie Feathers, Chi. Bears	9	8	1	0
1933	*Charlie (Buckets) Goldenberg, Green Bay	7	4	1	2
	John (Shipwreck) Kelly, Brooklyn	7	2	3	2
	*Elvin (Kink) Richards, N.Y. Giants	7	4	3	0
1932	Earl (Dutch) Clark, Portsmouth	6	3	3	0
	Red Grange, Chi. Bears	6	3	3	0

First season of professional football.

ANNUAL LEADERS—MOST FIELD GOALS MADE

Year	Player, Team	Att.	Made	Pct.
2011	David Akers, San Francisco, NFC	52	44	84.6
	Mike Nugent, Cincinnati, AFC	38	33	86.8
2010	Josh Brown, St. Louis, NFC	39	33	84.6
	Sebastian Janikowski, Oakland, AFC	41	33	80.5
2009	Nate Kaeding, San Diego, AFC	35	32	91.4
	David Akers, Philadelphia, NFC	37	32	86.5
2008	Stephen Gostkowski, New England, AFC	40	36	90.0
	John Carney, N.Y. Giants, NFC	38	35	92.1
2007	Rob Bironas, Tennessee, AFC	39	35	89.7
	*Mason Crosby, Green Bay, NFC	39	31	79.5
	Robbie Gould, Chicago, NFC	36	31	86.1
2006	Robbie Gould, Chicago, NFC	36	32	88.9
	Jeff Wilkins, St. Louis, NFC	37	32	86.5
	Matt Stover, Baltimore, AFC	30	28	93.3
2005	Neil Rackers, Arizona, NFC	42	40	95.2
	Matt Stover, Baltimore, AFC	34	30	88.2
2004	Adam Vinatieri, New England, AFC	33	31	93.9
	David Akers, Philadelphia, NFC	32	27	84.4
2003	Jeff Wilkins, St. Louis, NFC	42	39	92.9
	Mike Vanderjagt, Indianapolis, AFC	37	37	100.0
2002	Jay Feely, Atlanta, NFC	40	32	80.0
	Martin Gramatica, Tampa Bay, NFC	39	32	82.1
	Adam Vinatieri, New England, AFC	30	27	90.0
2001	Jason Elam, Denver, AFC	36	31	86.1
	*Jay Feely, Atlanta, NFC	37	29	78.4
2000	Matt Stover, Baltimore, AFC	39	35	89.7
	Ryan Longwell, Green Bay, NFC	38	33	86.8
1999	Olindo Mare, Miami, AFC	46	39	84.8
	*Martin Gramatica, Tampa Bay, NFC	32	27	84.4
1998	Al Del Greco, Tennessee, AFC	39	36	92.3
	Gary Anderson, Minnesota, NFC	35	35	100.0
1997	Richie Cunningham, Dallas, NFC	37	34	91.9
	Cary Blanchard, Indianapolis, AFC	41	32	78.1
1996	John Kasay, Carolina, NFC	45	37	82.2
	Cary Blanchard, Indianapolis, AFC	40	36	90.0
1995	Norm Johnson, Pittsburgh, AFC	41	34	82.9
	Morten Andersen, Atlanta, NFC	37	31	83.8
1994	John Carney, San Diego, AFC	38	34	89.5
	Fuad Reveiz, Minnesota, NFC	39	34	87.2
1993	Jeff Jaeger, L.A. Raiders, AFC	44	35	79.5
	Jason Hanson, Detroit, NFC	43	34	79.1
1992	Pete Stoyanovich, Miami, AFC	37	30	81.1
	Chip Lohmiller, Washington, NFC	40	30	75.0

Year	Player, Team	Att.	Made	Pct.
1991	Pete Stoyanovich, Miami, AFC	37	31	83.8
	Chip Lohmiller, Washington, NFC	43	31	72.1
1990	Nick Lowery, Kansas City, AFC	37	34	91.9
	Chip Lohmiller, Washington, NFC	40	30	75.0
1989	Rich Karlis, Minnesota, NFC	39	31	79.5
	*David Treadwell, Denver, AFC	33	27	81.8
1988	Scott Norwood, Buffalo, AFC	37	32	86.5
	Mike Cofer, San Francisco, NFC	38	27	71.1
1987	Morten Andersen, New Orleans, NFC	36	28	77.8
	Dean Biasucci, Indianapolis, AFC	27	24	88.9
	Jim Breech, Cincinnati, AFC	30	24	80.0
1986	Tony Franklin, New England, AFC	41	32	78.0
	Kevin Butler, Chicago, NFC	41	28	68.3
1985	Gary Anderson, Pittsburgh, AFC	42	33	78.6
	Morten Andersen, New Orleans, NFC	35	31	88.6
	*Kevin Butler, Chicago, NFC	37	31	83.8
1984	*Paul McFadden, Philadelphia, NFC	37	30	81.1
	Gary Anderson, Pittsburgh, AFC	32	24	75.0
	Matt Bahr, Cleveland, AFC	32	24	75.0
1983	*Ali-Haji-Sheikh, N.Y. Giants, NFC	42	35	83.3
	*Raul Allegre, Baltimore, AFC	35	30	85.7
1982	Mark Moseley, Washington, NFC	21	20	95.2
	Nick Lowery, Kansas City, AFC	24	19	79.2
1981	Rafael Septien, Dallas, NFC	35	27	77.1
	Nick Lowery, Kansas City, AFC	36	26	72.2
1980	*Ed Murray, Detroit, NFC	42	27	64.3
	John Smith, New England, AFC	34	26	76.5
	Fred Steinfort, Denver, AFC	34	26	76.5
1979	Mark Moseley, Washington, NFC	33	25	75.8
	John Smith, New England, AFC	33	23	69.7
1978	*Frank Corral, Los Angeles, NFC	43	29	67.4
	Pat Leahy, N.Y. Jets, AFC	30	22	73.3
1977	Mark Moseley, Washington, NFC	37	21	56.8
	Errol Mann, Oakland, AFC	28	20	71.4
1976	Mark Moseley, Washington, NFC	34	22	64.7
	Jan Stenerud, Kansas City, AFC	38	21	55.3
1975	Jan Stenerud, Kansas City, AFC	32	22	68.8
	Toni Fritsch, Dallas, NFC	35	22	62.9
1974	Chester Marcol, Green Bay, NFC	39	25	64.1
	Roy Gerela, Pittsburgh, AFC	29	20	69.0
1973	David Ray, Los Angeles, NFC	47	30	63.8
	Roy Gerela, Pittsburgh, AFC	43	29	67.4
1972	*Chester Marcol, Green Bay, NFC	48	33	68.8
	Roy Gerela, Pittsburgh, AFC	41	28	68.3
1971	Curt Knight, Washington, NFC	49	29	59.2
	Garo Yepremian, Miami, AFC	40	28	70.0
1970	Jan Stenerud, Kansas City, AFC	42	30	71.4
	Fred Cox, Minnesota, NFC	46	30	65.2
1969	Jim Turner, N.Y. Jets, AFL	47	32	68.1
	Fred Cox, Minnesota, NFL	37	26	70.3
1968	Jim Turner, N.Y. Jets, AFL	46	34	73.9
	Mac Percival, Chicago, NFL	36	25	69.4
1967	Jim Bakken, St. Louis, NFL	39	27	69.2
	Jan Stenerud, Kansas City, AFL	36	21	58.3
1966	Bruce Gossett, Los Angeles, NFL	49	28	57.1
	Mike Mercer, Oakland-Kansas City, AFL	30	21	70.0
1965	Pete Gogolak, Buffalo, AFL	46	28	60.9
	Fred Cox, Minnesota, NFL	35	23	65.7
1964	Jim Bakken, St. Louis, NFL	38	25	65.8
	Gino Cappelletti, Boston, AFL	39	25	64.1
1963	Jim Martin, Baltimore, NFL	39	24	61.5
	Gino Cappelletti, Boston, AFL	38	22	57.9
1962	Gene Mingo, Denver, AFL	39	27	69.2
	Lou Michaels, Pittsburgh, NFL	42	26	61.9
1961	Steve Myhra, Baltimore, NFL	39	21	53.8
	Gino Cappelletti, Boston, AFL	32	17	53.1
1960	Tommy Davis, San Francisco, NFL	32	19	59.4
	*Gene Mingo, Denver, AFL	28	18	64.3

Year	Player, Team	Att.	Made	Pct.
1959	Pat Summerall, N.Y. Giants	29	20	69.0
1958	Paige Cothren, Los Angeles	25	14	56.0
	*Tom Miner, Pittsburgh	28	14	50.0
1957	Lou Groza, Cleveland	22	15	68.2
1956	Sam Baker, Washington	25	17	68.0
1955	Fred Cone, Green Bay	24	16	66.7
1954	Lou Groza, Cleveland	24	16	66.7
1953	Lou Groza, Cleveland	26	23	88.5
1952	Lou Groza, Cleveland	33	19	57.6
1951	Bob Waterfield, Los Angeles	23	13	56.5
1950	Lou Groza, Cleveland	19	13	68.4
1949	Cliff Patton, Philadelphia	18	9	50.0
	Bob Waterfield, Los Angeles	16	9	56.3
1948	Cliff Patton, Philadelphia	12	8	66.7
1947	Ward Cuff, Green Bay	16	7	43.8
	Pat Harder, Chi. Cardinals	10	7	70.0
	Bob Waterfield, Los Angeles	16	7	43.8
1946	Ted Fritsch, Green Bay	17	9	52.9
1945	Joe Aguirre, Washington	13	7	53.8
1944	Ken Strong, N.Y. Giants	12	6	50.0
1943	Ward Cuff, N.Y. Giants	9	3	33.3
	Don Hutson, Green Bay	5	3	60.0
1942	Bill Daddio, Chi. Cardinals	10	5	50.0
1941	Clarke Hinkle, Green Bay	14	6	42.9
1940	Clarke Hinkle, Green Bay	14	9	64.3
1939	Ward Cuff, N.Y. Giants	16	7	43.8
1938	Ward Cuff, N.Y. Giants	9	5	55.6
	Ralph Kercheval, Brooklyn	13	5	38.5
1937	Jack Manders, Chi. Bears		8	
1936	Jack Manders, Chi. Bears		7	
	Armand Niccolai, Pittsburgh		7	
1935	Armand Niccolai, Pittsburgh		6	
	Bill Smith, Chi. Cardinals		6	
1934	Jack Manders, Chi. Bears		10	
1933	*Jack Manders, Chi. Bears		6	
	Glenn Presnell, Portsmouth		6	
1932	Earl (Dutch) Clark, Portsmouth		3	

First season of professional football.

ANNUAL RUSHING LEADERS

Year	Player, Team	Att.	Yards	Avg.	TD
2011	Maurice Jones-Drew, Jacksonville, AFC	343	1,606	4.7	8
	Michael Turner, Atlanta, NFC	301	1,340	4.5	11
2010	Arian Foster, Houston, AFC	327	1,616	4.9	16
	Michael Turner, Atlanta, NFC	334	1,371	4.1	12
2009	Chris Johnson, Tennessee, AFC	358	2,006	5.6	14
	Steven Jackson, St. Louis, NFC	324	1,416	4.4	4
2008	Adrian Peterson, Minnesota, NFC	363	1,760	4.9	10
	Thomas Jones, N.Y. Jets, AFC	290	1,312	4.5	13
2007	LaDainian Tomlinson, San Diego, AFC	315	1,474	4.7	15
	*Adrian Peterson, Minnesota, NFC	238	1,341	5.6	12
2006	LaDainian Tomlinson, San Diego, AFC	348	1,815	5.2	28
	Frank Gore, San Francisco, NFC	312	1,695	5.4	8
2005	Shaun Alexander, Seattle, NFC	370	1,880	5.1	27
	Larry Johnson, Kansas City, AFC	336	1,750	5.2	20
2004	Curtis Martin, N.Y. Jets, AFC	371	1,697	4.6	12
	Shaun Alexander, Seattle, NFC	353	1,696	4.8	16
2003	Jamal Lewis, Baltimore, AFC	387	2,066	5.3	14
	Ahman Green, Green Bay, NFC	355	1,883	5.3	15
2002	Ricky Williams, Miami, AFC	383	1,853	4.8	16
	Deuce McAllister, New Orleans, NFC	325	1,388	4.3	13
2001	Priest Holmes, Kansas City, AFC	327	1,555	4.8	8
	Stephen Davis, Washington, NFC	356	1,432	4.0	5
2000	Edgerrin James, Indianapolis, AFC	387	1,709	4.4	13
	Robert Smith, Minnesota, NFC	295	1,521	5.2	7
1999	*Edgerrin James, Indianapolis, AFC	369	1,553	4.2	13
	Stephen Davis, Washington, NFC	290	1,405	4.8	17
1998	Terrell Davis, Denver, AFC	392	2,008	5.1	21
	Jamal Anderson, Atlanta, NFC	410	1,846	4.5	14

Year	Player, Team	Att.	Yards	Avg.	TD
1997	Barry Sanders, Detroit, NFC	335	2,053	6.1	11
	Terrell Davis, Denver, AFC	369	1,750	4.7	15
1996	Barry Sanders, Detroit, NFC	307	1,553	5.1	11
	Terrell Davis, Denver, AFC	345	1,538	4.5	13
1995	Emmitt Smith, Dallas, NFC	377	1,773	4.7	25
	*Curtis Martin, New England, AFC	368	1,487	4.0	14
1994	Barry Sanders, Detroit, NFC	331	1,883	5.7	7
	Chris Warren, Seattle, AFC	333	1,545	4.6	9
1993	Emmitt Smith, Dallas, NFC	283	1,486	5.3	9
	Thurman Thomas, Buffalo, AFC	355	1,315	3.7	6
1992	Emmitt Smith, Dallas, NFC	373	1,713	4.6	18
	Barry Foster, Pittsburgh, AFC	390	1,690	4.3	11
1991	Emmitt Smith, Dallas, NFC	365	1,563	4.3	12
	Thurman Thomas, Buffalo, AFC	288	1,407	4.9	7
1990	Barry Sanders, Detroit, NFC	255	1,304	5.1	13
	Thurman Thomas, Buffalo, AFC	271	1,297	4.8	11
1989	Christian Okoye, Kansas City, AFC	370	1,480	4.0	12
	*Barry Sanders, Detroit, NFC	280	1,470	5.3	14
1988	Eric Dickerson, Indianapolis, AFC	388	1,659	4.3	14
	Herschel Walker, Dallas, NFC	361	1,514	4.2	5
1987	Charles White, L.A. Rams, NFC	324	1,374	4.2	11
	Eric Dickerson, Indianapolis, AFC	223	1,011	4.5	5
1986	Eric Dickerson, L.A. Rams, NFC	404	1,821	4.5	11
	Curt Warner, Seattle, AFC	319	1,481	4.6	13
1985	Marcus Allen, L.A. Raiders, AFC	380	1,759	4.6	11
	Gerald Riggs, Atlanta, NFC	397	1,719	4.3	10
1984	Eric Dickerson, L.A. Rams, NFC	379	2,105	5.6	14
	Earnest Jackson, San Diego, AFC	296	1,179	4.0	8
1983	*Eric Dickerson, L.A. Rams, NFC	390	1,808	4.6	18
	*Curt Warner, Seattle, AFC	335	1,449	4.3	13
1982	Freeman McNeil, N.Y. Jets, AFC	151	786	5.2	6
	Tony Dorsett, Dallas, NFC	177	745	4.2	5
1981	*George Rogers, New Orleans, NFC	378	1,674	4.4	13
	Earl Campbell, Houston, AFC	361	1,376	3.8	10
1980	Earl Campbell, Houston, AFC	373	1,934	5.2	13
	Walter Payton, Chicago, NFC	317	1,460	4.6	6
1979	Earl Campbell, Houston, AFC	368	1,697	4.6	19
	Walter Payton, Chicago, NFC	369	1,610	4.4	14
1978	*Earl Campbell, Houston, AFC	302	1,450	4.8	13
	Walter Payton, Chicago, NFC	333	1,395	4.2	11
1977	Walter Payton, Chicago, NFC	339	1,852	5.5	14
	Mark van Eeghen, Oakland, AFC	324	1,273	3.9	7
1976	O.J. Simpson, Buffalo, AFC	290	1,503	5.2	8
	Walter Payton, Chicago, NFC	311	1,390	4.5	13
1975	O.J. Simpson, Buffalo, AFC	329	1,817	5.5	16
	Jim Otis, St. Louis, NFC	269	1,076	4.0	5
1974	Otis Armstrong, Denver, AFC	263	1,407	5.3	9
	Lawrence McCutcheon, Los Angeles, NFC	236	1,109	4.7	3
1973	O.J. Simpson, Buffalo, AFC	332	2,003	6.0	12
	John Brockington, Green Bay, NFC	265	1,144	4.3	3
1972	O.J. Simpson, Buffalo, AFC	292	1,251	4.3	6
	Larry Brown, Washington, NFC	285	1,216	4.3	8
1971	Floyd Little, Denver, AFC	284	1,133	4.0	6
	*John Brockington, Green Bay, NFC	216	1,105	5.1	4
1970	Larry Brown, Washington, NFC	237	1,125	4.7	5
	Floyd Little, Denver, AFC	209	901	4.3	3
1969	Gale Sayers, Chicago, NFL	236	1,032	4.4	8
	Dickie Post, San Diego, AFL	182	873	4.8	6
1968	Leroy Kelly, Cleveland, NFL	248	1,239	5.0	16
	*Paul Robinson, Cincinnati, AFL	238	1,023	4.3	8
1967	Jim Nance, Boston, AFL	269	1,216	4.5	7
	Leroy Kelly, Cleveland, NFL	235	1,205	5.1	11
1966	Jim Nance, Boston, AFL	299	1,458	4.9	11
	Gale Sayers, Chicago, NFL	229	1,231	5.4	8
1965	Jim Brown, Cleveland, NFL	289	1,544	5.3	17
	Paul Lowe, San Diego, AFL	222	1,121	5.0	7
1964	Jim Brown, Cleveland, NFL	280	1,446	5.2	7
	Cookie Gilchrist, Buffalo, AFL	230	981	4.3	6
1963	Jim Brown, Cleveland, NFL	291	1,863	6.4	12
	Clem Daniels, Oakland, AFL	215	1,099	5.1	3

Year	Player, Team	Att.	Yards	Avg.	TD
1962	Jim Taylor, Green Bay, NFL	272	1,474	5.4	19
	Cookie Gilchrist, Buffalo, AFL	214	1,096	5.1	13
1961	Jim Brown, Cleveland, NFL	305	1,408	4.6	8
	Billy Cannon, Houston, AFL	200	948	4.7	6
1960	Jim Brown, Cleveland, NFL	215	1,257	5.8	9
	*Abner Haynes, Dall. Texans, AFL	156	875	5.6	9
1959	Jim Brown, Cleveland	290	1,329	4.6	14
1958	Jim Brown, Cleveland	257	1,527	5.9	17
1957	*Jim Brown, Cleveland	202	942	4.7	9
1956	Rick Casares, Chi. Bears	234	1,126	4.8	12
1955	*Alan Ameche, Baltimore	213	961	4.5	9
1954	Joe Perry, San Francisco	173	1,049	6.1	8
1953	Joe Perry, San Francisco	192	1,018	5.3	10
1952	Dan Towler, Los Angeles	156	894	5.7	10
1951	Eddie Price, N.Y. Giants	271	971	3.6	7
1950	Marion Motley, Cleveland	140	810	5.8	3
1949	Steve Van Buren, Philadelphia	263	1,146	4.4	11
1948	Steve Van Buren, Philadelphia	201	945	4.7	10
1947	Steve Van Buren, Philadelphia	217	1,008	4.6	13
1946	Bill Dudley, Pittsburgh	146	604	4.1	3
1945	Steve Van Buren, Philadelphia	143	832	5.8	15
1944	Bill Paschal, N.Y. Giants	196	737	3.8	9
1943	*Bill Paschal, N.Y. Giants	147	572	3.9	10
1942	*Bill Dudley, Pittsburgh	162	696	4.3	5
1941	Clarence (Pug) Manders, Brooklyn	111	486	4.4	5
1940	Byron (Whizzer) White, Detroit	146	514	3.5	5
1939	*Bill Osmanski, Chicago	121	699	5.8	7
1938	*Byron (Whizzer) White, Pittsburgh	152	567	3.7	4
1937	Cliff Battles, Washington	216	874	4.0	5
1936	*Alphonse (Tuffy) Leemans, N.Y. Giants	206	830	4.0	2
1935	Doug Russell, Chi. Cardinals	140	499	3.6	0
1934	*Beattie Feathers, Chi. Bears	119	1,004	8.4	8
1933	Jim Musick, Boston	173	809	4.7	5
1932	*Cliff Battles, Boston	148	576	3.9	3

First season of professional football.

ANNUAL PASSING LEADERS
(Current rating system implemented in 1973)

Year	Player, Team	Att.	Comp.	Yards	TD	Int.	Rating
2011	Aaron Rodgers, Green Bay, NFC	502	343	4,643	45	6	122.5
	Tom Brady, New England, AFC	611	401	5,235	39	12	105.6
2010	Tom Brady, New England, AFC	492	324	3,900	36	4	111.0
	Aaron Rodgers, Green Bay, NFC	475	312	3,922	28	11	101.2
2009	Drew Brees, New Orleans, NFC	514	363	4,388	34	11	109.6
	Philip Rivers, San Diego, AFC	486	317	4,254	28	9	104.4
2008	Philip Rivers, San Diego, AFC	478	312	4,009	34	11	105.5
	Kurt Warner, Arizona, NFC	598	401	4,583	30	14	96.9
2007	Tom Brady, New England, AFC	578	398	4,806	50	8	117.2
	Tony Romo, Dallas, NFC	520	335	4,211	36	19	97.4
2006	Peyton Manning, Indianapolis, AFC	557	362	4,397	31	9	101.0
	Drew Brees, New Orleans, NFC	554	356	4,418	26	11	96.2
2005	Peyton Manning, Indianapolis, AFC	453	305	3,747	28	10	104.1
	Matt Hasselbeck, Seattle, NFC	449	294	3,459	24	9	98.2
2004	Peyton Manning, Indianapolis, AFC	497	336	4,557	49	10	121.1
	Daunte Culpepper, Minnesota, NFC	548	379	4,717	39	11	110.9
2003	Steve McNair, Tennessee, AFC	400	250	3,215	24	7	100.4
	Daunte Culpepper, Minnesota, NFC	454	295	3,479	25	11	96.4
2002	Chad Pennington, N.Y. Jets, AFC	399	275	3,120	22	6	104.2
	Brad Johnson, Tampa Bay, NFC	451	281	3,049	22	6	92.9
2001	Kurt Warner, St. Louis, NFC	546	375	4,830	36	22	101.4
	Rich Gannon, Oakland, AFC	549	361	3,828	27	9	95.5
2000	Brian Griese, Denver, AFC	336	216	2,688	19	4	102.9
	Trent Green, St. Louis, NFC	240	145	2,063	16	5	101.8
1999	Kurt Warner, St. Louis, NFC	499	325	4,353	41	13	109.2
	Peyton Manning, Indianapolis, AFC	533	331	4,135	26	15	90.7
1998	Randall Cunningham, Minnesota, NFC	425	259	3,704	34	10	106.0
	Vinny Testaverde, N.Y. Jets, AFC	421	259	3,256	29	7	101.6
1997	Steve Young, San Francisco, NFC	356	241	3,029	19	6	104.7
	Mark Brunell, Jacksonville, AFC	435	264	3,281	18	7	91.2

Year	Player, Team	Att.	Comp.	Yards	TD	Int.	Rating
1996	Steve Young, San Francisco NFC	316	214	2,410	14	6	97.2
	John Elway, Denver, AFC	466	287	3,328	26	14	89.2
1995	Jim Harbaugh, Indianapolis, AFC	314	200	2,575	17	5	100.7
	Brett Favre, Green Bay, NFC	570	359	4,413	38	13	99.5
1994	Steve Young, San Francisco, NFC	461	324	3,969	35	10	112.8
	Dan Marino, Miami, AFC	615	385	4,453	30	17	89.2
1993	Steve Young, San Francisco, NFC	462	314	4,023	29	16	101.5
	John Elway, Denver, AFC	551	348	4,030	25	10	92.8
1992	Steve Young, San Francisco, NFC	402	268	3,465	25	7	107.0
	Warren Moon, Houston, AFC	346	224	2,521	18	12	89.3
1991	Steve Young, San Francisco, NFC	279	180	2,517	17	8	101.8
	Jim Kelly, Buffalo, AFC	474	304	3,844	33	17	97.6
1990	Jim Kelly, Buffalo, AFC	346	219	2,829	24	9	101.2
	Phil Simms, N.Y. Giants, NFC	311	184	2,284	15	4	92.7
1989	Joe Montana, San Francisco, NFC	386	271	3,521	26	8	112.4
	Boomer Esiason, Cincinnati, AFC	455	258	3,525	28	11	92.1
1988	Boomer Esiason, Cincinnati, AFC	388	223	3,572	28	14	97.4
	Wade Wilson, Minnesota, NFC	332	204	2,746	15	9	91.5
1987	Joe Montana, San Francisco, NFC	398	266	3,054	31	13	102.1
	Bernie Kosar, Cleveland, AFC	389	241	3,033	22	9	95.4
1986	Tommy Kramer, Minnesota, NFC	372	208	3,000	24	10	92.6
	Dan Marino, Miami, AFC	623	378	4,746	44	23	92.5
1985	Ken O'Brien, N.Y. Jets, AFC	488	297	3,888	25	8	96.2
	Joe Montana, San Francisco, NFC	494	303	3,653	27	13	91.3
1984	Dan Marino, Miami, AFC	564	362	5,084	48	17	108.9
	Joe Montana, San Francisco, NFC	432	279	3,630	28	10	102.9
1983	Steve Bartkowski, Atlanta, NFC	432	274	3,167	22	5	97.6
	*Dan Marino, Miami, AFC	296	173	2,210	20	6	96.0
1982	Ken Anderson, Cincinnati, AFC	309	218	2,495	12	9	95.3
	Joe Theismann, Washington, NFC	252	161	2,033	13	9	91.3
1981	Ken Anderson, Cincinnati, AFC	479	300	3,754	29	10	98.4
	Joe Montana, San Francisco, NFC	488	311	3,565	19	12	88.4
1980	Brian Sipe, Cleveland, AFC	554	337	4,132	30	14	91.4
	Ron Jaworski, Philadelphia, NFC	451	257	3,529	27	12	91.0
1979	Roger Staubach, Dallas, NFC	461	267	3,586	27	11	92.3
	Dan Fouts, San Diego, AFC	530	332	4,082	24	24	82.6
1978	Roger Staubach, Dallas, NFC	413	231	3,190	25	16	84.9
	Terry Bradshaw, Pittsburgh, AFC	368	207	2,915	28	20	84.7
1977	Bob Griese, Miami, AFC	307	180	2,252	22	13	87.8
	Roger Staubach, Dallas, NFC	361	210	2,620	18	9	87.0
1976	Ken Stabler, Oakland, AFC	291	194	2,737	27	17	103.4
	James Harris, Los Angeles, NFC	158	91	1,460	8	6	89.6
1975	Ken Anderson, Cincinnati, AFC	377	228	3,169	21	11	93.9
	Fran Tarkenton, Minnesota, NFC	425	273	2,994	25	13	91.8
1974	Ken Anderson, Cincinnati, AFC	328	213	2,667	18	10	95.7
	Sonny Jurgensen, Washington, NFC	167	107	1,185	11	5	94.5
1973	Roger Staubach, Dallas, NFC	286	179	2,428	23	15	94.6
	Ken Stabler, Oakland, AFC	260	163	1,997	14	10	88.3
1972	Norm Snead, N.Y. Giants, NFC	325	196	2,307	17	12	
	Earl Morrall, Miami, AFC	150	83	1,360	11	7	
1971	Roger Staubach, Dallas, NFC	211	126	1,882	15	4	
	Bob Griese, Miami, AFC	263	145	2,089	19	9	
1970	John Brodie, San Francisco, NFC	378	223	2,941	24	10	
	Daryle Lamonica, Oakland, AFC	356	179	2,516	22	15	
1969	Sonny Jurgensen, Washington, NFL	442	274	3,102	22	15	
	*Greg Cook, Cincinnati, AFL	197	106	1,854	15	11	
1968	Len Dawson, Kansas City, AFL	224	131	2,109	17	9	
	Earl Morrall, Baltimore, NFL	317	182	2,909	26	17	
1967	Sonny Jurgensen, Washington, NFL	508	288	3,747	31	16	
	Daryle Lamonica, Oakland, AFL	425	220	3,228	30	20	
1966	Bart Starr, Green Bay, NFL	251	156	2,257	14	3	
	Len Dawson, Kansas City, AFL	284	159	2,527	26	10	
1965	Rudy Bukich, Chicago, NFL	312	176	2,641	20	9	
	John Hadl, San Diego, AFL	348	174	2,798	20	21	
1964	Len Dawson, Kansas City, AFL	354	199	2,879	30	18	
	Bart Starr, Green Bay, NFL	272	163	2,144	15	4	
1963	Y.A. Tittle, N.Y. Giants, NFL	367	221	3,145	36	14	
	Tobin Rote, San Diego, AFL	286	170	2,510	20	17	

Year	Player, Team	Att.	Comp.	Yards	TD	Int.	Rating
1962	Len Dawson, Dallas Texans, AFL	310	189	2,759	29	17	
	Bart Starr, Green Bay, NFL	285	178	2,438	12	9	
1961	George Blanda, Houston, AFL	362	187	3,330	36	22	
	Milt Plum, Cleveland, NFL	302	177	2,416	18	10	
1960	Milt Plum, Cleveland, NFL	250	151	2,297	21	5	
	Jack Kemp, L.A. Chargers, AFL	406	211	3,018	20	25	
1959	Charlie Conerly, N.Y. Giants	194	113	1,706	14	4	
1958	Eddie LeBaron, Washington	145	79	1,365	11	10	
1957	Tommy O'Connell, Cleveland	110	63	1,229	9	8	
1956	Ed Brown, Chicago Bears	168	96	1,667	11	12	
1955	Otto Graham, Cleveland	185	98	1,721	15	8	
1954	Norm Van Brocklin, Los Angeles	260	139	2,637	13	21	
1953	Otto Graham, Cleveland	258	167	2,722	11	9	
1952	Norm Van Brocklin, Los Angeles	205	113	1,736	14	17	
1951	Bob Waterfield, Los Angeles	176	88	1,566	13	10	
1950	Norm Van Brocklin, Los Angeles	233	127	2,061	18	14	
1949	Sammy Baugh, Washington	255	145	1,903	18	14	
1948	Tommy Thompson, Philadelphia	246	141	1,965	25	11	
1947	Sammy Baugh, Washington	354	210	2,938	25	15	
1946	Bob Waterfield, Los Angeles	251	127	1,747	18	17	
1945	Sammy Baugh, Washington	182	128	1,669	11	4	
	Sid Luckman, Chicago Bears	217	117	1,725	14	10	
1944	Frank Filchock, Washington	147	84	1,139	13	9	
1943	Sammy Baugh, Washington	239	133	1,754	23	19	
1942	Cecil Isbell, Green Bay	268	146	2,021	24	14	
1941	Cecil Isbell, Green Bay	206	117	1,479	15	11	
1940	Sammy Baugh, Washington	177	111	1,367	12	10	
1939	*Parker Hall, Cleveland	208	106	1,227	9	13	
1938	Ed Danowski, N.Y. Giants	129	70	848	7	8	
1937	*Sammy Baugh, Washington	171	81	1,127	8	14	
1936	Arnie Herber, Green Bay	173	77	1,239	11	13	
1935	Ed Danowski, N.Y. Giants	113	57	794	10	9	
1934	Arnie Herber, Green Bay	115	42	799	8	12	
1933	*Harry Newman, N.Y. Giants	136	53	973	11	17	
1932	Arnie Herber, Green Bay	101	37	639	9	9	

First season of professional football.

ANNUAL PASSING TOUCHDOWN LEADERS

Year	Player, Team	TD
2011	Drew Brees, New Orleans, NFC	46
	Tom Brady, New England, AFC	39
2010	Tom Brady, New England, AFC	36
	Drew Brees, New Orleans, NFC	33
2009	Drew Brees, New Orleans, NFC	34
	Peyton Manning, Indianapolis, AFC	33
2008	Drew Brees, New Orleans, NFC	34
	Philip Rivers, San Diego, AFC	34
2007	Tom Brady, New England, AFC	50
	Tony Romo, Dallas, NFC	36
2006	Peyton Manning, Indianapolis, AFC	31
	Drew Brees, New Orleans, NFC	26
2005	Carson Palmer, Cincinnati, AFC	32
	Jake Delhomme, Carolina, NFC	24
	Matt Hasselbeck, Seattle, NFC	24
	Eli Manning, N.Y. Giants, NFC	24
2004	Peyton Manning, Indianapolis, AFC	49
	Daunte Culpepper, Minnesota, NFC	39
2003	Brett Favre, Green Bay, NFC	32
	Peyton Manning, Indianapolis, AFC	29
2002	Tom Brady, New England, AFC	28
	Aaron Brooks, New Orleans, NFC	27
	Brett Favre, Green Bay, NFC	27
2001	Kurt Warner, St. Louis, NFC	36
	Rich Gannon, Oakland, AFC	27
2000	Daunte Culpepper, Minnesota, NFC	33
	Peyton Manning, Indianapolis, AFC	33
1999	Kurt Warner, St. Louis, NFC	41
	Peyton Manning, Indianapolis, AFC	26

Year	Player, Team	TD
1998	Steve Young, San Francisco, NFC	36
	Vinny Testaverde, N.Y. Jets, AFC	29
1997	Brett Favre, Green Bay, NFC	35
	Jeff George, Oakland, AFC	29
1996	Brett Favre, Green Bay, NFC	39
	Vinny Testaverde, Baltimore, AFC	33
1995	Brett Favre, Green Bay, NFC	38
	Jeff Blake, Cincinnati, AFC	28
1994	Steve Young, San Francisco, NFC	35
	Dan Marino, Miami, AFC	30
1993	Steve Young, San Francisco, NFC	29
	John Elway, Denver, AFC	25
1992	Steve Young, San Francisco, NFC	25
	Dan Marino, Miami, AFC	24
1991	Jim Kelly, Buffalo, AFC	33
	Mark Rypien, Washington, NFC	28
1990	Warren Moon, Houston, AFC	33
	Randall Cunningham, Philadelphia, NFC	30
1989	Jim Everett, L.A. Rams, NFC	29
	Boomer Esiason, Cincinnati, AFC	28
1988	Jim Everett, L.A. Rams, NFC	31
	Boomer Esiason, Cincinnati, AFC	28
	Dan Marino, Miami, AFC	28
1987	Joe Montana, San Francisco, NFC	31
	Dan Marino, Miami, AFC	26
1986	Dan Marino, Miami, AFC	44
	Tommy Kramer, Minnesota, NFC	24
1985	Dan Marino, Miami, AFC	30
	Joe Montana, San Francisco, NFC	27
1984	Dan Marino, Miami, AFC	48

Year	Player, Team	TD
	Neil Lomax, St. Louis, NFC	28
	Joe Montana, San Francisco, NFC	28
1983	Lynn Dickey, Green Bay, NFC	32
	Joe Ferguson, Buffalo, AFC	26
	Brian Sipe, Cleveland, AFC	26
1982	Terry Bradshaw, Pittsburgh, AFC	17
	Dan Fouts, San Diego, AFC	17
	Joe Montana, San Francisco, NFC	17
1981	Dan Fouts, San Diego, AFC	33
	Steve Bartkowski, Atlanta, NFC	30
1980	Steve Bartkowski, Atlanta, NFC	31
	Dan Fouts, San Diego, AFC	30
	Brian Sipe, Cleveland, AFC	30
1979	Steve Grogan, New England, AFC	28
	Brian Sipe, Cleveland, AFC	28
	Roger Staubach, Dallas, NFC	27
1978	Terry Bradshaw, Pittsburgh, AFC	28
	Roger Staubach, Dallas, NFC	25
	Fran Tarkenton, Minnesota, NFC	25
1977	Bob Griese, Miami, AFC	22
	Ron Jaworski, Philadelphia, NFC	18
	Roger Staubach, Dallas, NFC	18
1976	Ken Stabler, Oakland, AFC	27
	Jim Hart, St. Louis, NFC	18
1975	Joe Ferguson, Buffalo, AFC	25
	Fran Tarkenton, Minnesota, NFC	25
1974	Ken Stabler, Oakland, AFC	26
	Jim Hart, St. Louis, NFC	20
1973	Roman Gabriel, Philadelphia, NFC	23
	Roger Staubach, Dallas, NFC	23
	Charley Johnson, Denver, AFC	20
1972	Billy Kilmer, Washington, NFC	19
	Joe Namath, N.Y. Jets, AFC	19
1971	John Hadl, San Diego, AFC	21
	John Brodie, San Francisco, NFC	18
1970	John Brodie, San Francisco, NFC	24
	John Hadl, San Diego, AFC	22
	Daryle Lamonica, Oakland, AFC	22
1969	Daryle Lamonica, Oakland, AFL	34
	Roman Gabriel, Los Angeles, NFL	24
1968	John Hadl, San Diego, AFL	27
	Earl Morrall, Baltimore, NFL	26
1967	Sonny Jurgensen, Washington, NFL	31
	Daryle Lamonica, Oakland, AFL	30
1966	Frank Ryan, Cleveland, NFL	29
	Len Dawson, Kansas City, AFL	26

Year	Player, Team	TD
1965	John Brodie, San Francisco, NFL	30
	Len Dawson, Kansas City, AFL	21
1964	Babe Parilli, Boston, AFL	31
	Frank Ryan, Cleveland, NFL	25
1963	Y.A. Tittle, N.Y. Giants, NFL	36
	Len Dawson, Kansas City, AFL	26
1962	Y.A. Tittle, N.Y. Giants, NFL	33
	Len Dawson, Dallas, AFL	29
1961	George Blanda, Houston, AFL	36
	Sonny Jurgensen, Philadelphia, NFL	32
1960	Al Dorow, N.Y. Titans, AFL	26
	Johnny Unitas, Baltimore, NFL	25
1959	Johnny Unitas, Baltimore	32
1958	Johnny Unitas, Baltimore	19
1957	Johnny Unitas, Baltimore	24
1956	Tobin Rote, Green Bay	18
1955	Tobin Rote, Green Bay	17
	Y.A. Tittle, San Francisco	17
1954	Adrian Burk, Philadelphia	23
1953	Robert Thomason, Philadelphia	21
1952	Jim Finks, Pittsburgh	20
	Otto Graham, Cleveland	20
1951	Bobby Layne, Detroit	26
1950	George Ratterman, N.Y. Yanks	22
1949	Johnny Lujack, Chi. Bears	23
1948	Tommy Thompson, Philadelphia	25
1947	Sammy Baugh, Washington	25
1946	Sid Luckman, Chi. Bears	17
	Bob Waterfield, Los Angeles	17
1945	Sid Luckman, Chi. Bears	14
	*Bob Waterfield, Cleveland	14
1944	Frank Filchock, Washington	13
1943	Sid Luckman, Chi. Bears	28
1942	Cecil Isbell, Green Bay	24
1941	Cecil Isbell, Green Bay	15
1940	Sammy Baugh, Washington	12
1939	Frank Filchock, Washington	11
1938	Bob Monnett, Green Bay	9
1937	Bernie Masterson, Chi. Bears	9
1936	Arnie Herber, Green Bay	11
1935	Ed Danowski, N.Y. Giants	10
1934	Arnie Herber, Green Bay	8
1933	*Harry Newman, N.Y. Giants	11
1932	Arnie Herber, Green Bay	9

*First season of professional football.

ANNUAL PASS RECEIVING LEADERS

Year	Player, Team	No.	Yards	Avg.	TD
2011	Wes Welker, New England, AFC	122	1,569	12.9	9
	Roddy White, Atlanta, NFC	100	1,296	13.0	8
2010	Roddy White, Atlanta, NFC	115	1,389	12.1	10
	Reggie Wayne, Indianapolis, AFC	111	1,355	12.2	6
2009	Wes Welker, New England, AFC	123	1,348	11.0	4
	Steve Smith, N.Y. Giants, NFC	107	1,220	11.4	7
2008	Andre Johnson, Houston, AFC	115	1,575	13.7	8
	Larry Fitzgerald, Arizona, NFC	96	1,431	14.9	12
2007	T.J. Houshmandzadeh, Cincinnati, AFC	112	1,143	10.2	12
	Wes Welker, New England, AFC	112	1,175	10.5	8
	Larry Fitzgerald, Arizona, NFC	100	1,409	14.1	10
2006	Andre Johnson, Houston, AFC	103	1,147	11.1	5
	Mike Furrey, Detroit, NFC	98	1,086	11.1	6
2005	Steve Smith, Carolina, NFC	103	1,563	15.2	12
	Larry Fitzgerald, Arizona, NFC	103	1,409	13.7	10
	Chad Ochocinco, Cincinnati, AFC	97	1,432	14.8	9
2004	Tony Gonzalez, Kansas City, AFC	102	1,258	12.3	7
	Joe Horn, New Orleans, NFC	94	1,399	14.9	11
	Torry Holt, St. Louis, NFC	94	1,372	14.6	10
2003	Torry Holt, St. Louis, NFC	117	1,696	14.5	12
	LaDainian Tomlinson, San Diego, AFC	100	725	7.3	4

Year	Player, Team	No.	Yards	Avg.	TD
2002	Marvin Harrison, Indianapolis, AFC	143	1,722	12.0	11
	Randy Moss, Minnesota, NFC	106	1,347	12.7	7
2001	Rod Smith, Denver, AFC	113	1,343	11.9	11
	Keyshawn Johnson, Tampa Bay, NFC	106	1,266	11.9	1
2000	Marvin Harrison, Indianapolis, AFC	102	1,413	13.9	14
	Muhsin Muhammad, Carolina, NFC	102	1,183	11.6	6
1999	Jimmy Smith, Jacksonville, AFC	116	1,636	14.1	6
	Muhsin Muhammad, Carolina, NFC	96	1,253	13.1	8
1998	O.J. McDuffie, Miami, AFC	90	1,050	11.7	7
	Frank Sanders, Arizona, NFC	89	1,145	12.9	3
1997	Tim Brown, Oakland, AFC	104	1,408	13.5	5
	Herman Moore, Detroit, NFC	104	1,293	12.4	8
1996	Jerry Rice, San Francisco, NFC	108	1,254	11.6	8
	Carl Pickens, Cincinnati, AFC	100	1,180	11.8	12
1995	Herman Moore, Detroit, NFC	123	1,686	13.7	14
	Carl Pickens, Cincinnati, AFC	99	1,234	12.5	17
1994	Cris Carter, Minnesota, NFC	122	1,256	10.3	7
	Ben Coates, New England, AFC	96	1,174	12.2	7
1993	Sterling Sharpe, Green Bay, NFC	112	1,274	11.4	11
	Reggie Langhorne, Indianapolis, AFC	85	1,038	12.2	3
1992	Sterling Sharpe, Green Bay, NFC	108	1,461	13.5	13
	Haywood Jeffires, Houston, AFC	90	913	10.1	9
1991	Haywood Jeffires, Houston, AFC	100	1,181	11.8	7
	Michael Irvin, Dallas, NFC	93	1,523	16.4	8
1990	Jerry Rice, San Francisco, NFC	100	1,502	15.0	13
	Haywood Jeffires, Houston, AFC	74	1,048	14.2	8
	Drew Hill, Houston, AFC	74	1,019	13.8	5
1989	Sterling Sharpe, Green Bay, NFC	90	1,423	15.8	12
	Andre Reed, Buffalo, AFC	88	1,312	14.9	9
1988	Al Toon, N.Y. Jets, AFC	93	1,067	11.5	5
	Henry Ellard, L.A. Rams, NFC	86	1,414	16.4	10
1987	J.T. Smith, St. Louis, NFC	91	1,117	12.3	8
	Al Toon, N.Y. Jets, AFC	68	976	14.4	5
1986	Todd Christensen, L.A. Raiders, AFC	95	1,153	12.1	8
	Jerry Rice, San Francisco, NFC	86	1,570	18.3	15
1985	Roger Craig, San Francisco, NFC	92	1,016	11.0	6
	Lionel James, San Diego, AFC	86	1,027	11.9	6
1984	Art Monk, Washington, NFC	106	1,372	12.9	7
	Ozzie Newsome, Cleveland, AFC	89	1,001	11.2	5
1983	Todd Christensen, L.A. Raiders, AFC	92	1,247	13.6	12
	Roy Green, St. Louis, NFC	78	1,227	15.7	14
	Charlie Brown, Washington, NFC	78	1,225	15.7	8
	Earnest Gray, N.Y. Giants, NFC	78	1,139	14.6	5
1982	Dwight Clark, San Francisco, NFC	60	913	15.2	5
	Kellen Winslow, San Diego, AFC	54	721	13.4	6
1981	Kellen Winslow, San Diego, AFC	88	1,075	12.2	10
	Dwight Clark, San Francisco, NFC	85	1,105	13.0	4
1980	Kellen Winslow, San Diego, AFC	89	1,290	14.5	9
	*Earl Cooper, San Francisco, NFC	83	567	6.8	4
1979	Joe Washington, Baltimore, AFC	82	750	9.1	3
	Ahmad Rashad, Minnesota, NFC	80	1,156	14.5	9
1978	Rickey Young, Minnesota, NFC	88	704	8.0	5
	Steve Largent, Seattle, AFC	71	1,168	16.5	8
1977	Lydell Mitchell, Baltimore, AFC	71	620	8.7	4
	Ahmad Rashad, Minnesota, NFC	51	681	13.4	2
1976	MacArthur Lane, Kansas City, AFC	66	686	10.4	1
	Drew Pearson, Dallas, NFC	58	806	13.9	6
1975	Chuck Foreman, Minnesota, NFC	73	691	9.5	9
	Reggie Rucker, Cleveland, AFC	60	770	12.8	3
	Lydell Mitchell, Baltimore, AFC	60	544	9.1	4
1974	Lydell Mitchell, Baltimore, AFC	72	544	7.6	2
	Charles Young, Philadelphia, NFC	63	696	11.0	3
1973	Harold Carmichael, Philadelphia, NFC	67	1,116	16.7	9
	Fred Willis, Houston, AFC	57	371	6.5	1
1972	Harold Jackson, Philadelphia, NFC	62	1,048	16.9	4
	Fred Biletnikoff, Oakland, AFC	58	802	13.8	7
1971	Fred Biletnikoff, Oakland, AFC	61	929	15.2	9
	Bob Tucker, N.Y. Giants, NFC	59	791	13.4	4
1970	Dick Gordon, Chicago, NFC	71	1,026	14.5	13
	Marlin Briscoe, Buffalo, AFC	57	1,036	18.2	8

Year	Player, Team	No.	Yards	Avg.	TD
1969	Dan Abramowicz, New Orleans, NFL	73	1,015	13.9	7
	Lance Alworth, San Diego, AFL	64	1,003	15.7	4
1968	Clifton McNeil, San Francisco, NFL	71	994	14.0	7
	Lance Alworth, San Diego, AFL	68	1,312	19.3	10
1967	George Sauer, N.Y. Jets, AFL	75	1,189	15.9	6
	Charley Taylor, Washington, NFL	70	990	14.1	9
1966	Lance Alworth, San Diego, AFL	73	1,383	18.9	13
	Charley Taylor, Washington, NFL	72	1,119	15.5	12
1965	Lionel Taylor, Denver, AFL	85	1,131	13.3	6
	Dave Parks, San Francisco, NFL	80	1,344	16.8	12
1964	Charley Hennigan, Houston, AFL	101	1,546	15.3	8
	Johnny Morris, Chicago, NFL	93	1,200	12.9	10
1963	Lionel Taylor, Denver, AFL	78	1,101	14.1	10
	Bobby Joe Conrad, St. Louis, NFL	73	967	13.2	10
1962	Lionel Taylor, Denver, AFL	77	908	11.8	4
	Bobby Mitchell, Washington, NFL	72	1,384	19.2	11
1961	Lionel Taylor, Denver, AFL	100	1,176	11.8	4
	Jim (Red) Phillips, Los Angeles, NFL	78	1,092	14.0	5
1960	Lionel Taylor, Denver, AFL	92	1,235	13.4	12
	Raymond Berry, Baltimore, NFL	74	1,298	17.5	10
1959	Raymond Berry, Baltimore	66	959	14.5	14
1958	Raymond Berry, Baltimore	56	794	14.2	9
	Pete Retzlaff, Philadelphia	56	766	13.7	2
1957	Billy Wilson, San Francisco	52	757	14.6	6
1956	Billy Wilson, San Francisco	60	889	14.8	5
1955	Pete Pihos, Philadelphia	62	864	13.9	7
1954	Pete Pihos, Philadelphia	60	872	14.5	10
	Billy Wilson, San Francisco	60	830	13.8	5
1953	Pete Pihos, Philadelphia	63	1,049	16.7	10
1952	Mac Speedie, Cleveland	62	911	14.7	5
1951	Elroy (Crazylegs) Hirsch, Los Angeles	66	1,495	22.7	17
1950	Tom Fears, Los Angeles	84	1,116	13.3	7
1949	Tom Fears, Los Angeles	77	1,013	13.2	9
1948	*Tom Fears, Los Angeles	51	698	13.7	4
1947	Jim Keane, Chi. Bears	64	910	14.2	10
1946	Jim Benton, Los Angeles	63	981	15.6	6
1945	Don Hutson, Green Bay	47	834	17.7	9
1944	Don Hutson, Green Bay	58	866	14.9	9
1943	Don Hutson, Green Bay	47	776	16.5	11
1942	Don Hutson, Green Bay	74	1,211	16.4	17
1941	Don Hutson, Green Bay	58	738	12.7	10
1940	*Don Looney, Philadelphia	58	707	12.2	4
1939	Don Hutson, Green Bay	34	846	24.9	6
1938	Gaynell Tinsley, Chi. Cardinals	41	516	12.6	1
1937	Don Hutson, Green Bay	41	552	13.5	7
1936	Don Hutson, Green Bay	34	536	15.8	8
1935	*Tod Goodwin, N.Y. Giants	26	432	16.6	4
1934	Joe Carter, Philadelphia	16	238	14.9	4
	Morris (Red) Badgro, N.Y. Giants	16	206	12.9	1
1933	John (Shipwreck) Kelly, Brooklyn	22	246	11.2	3
1932	Ray Flaherty, N.Y. Giants	21	350	16.7	3

*First season of professional football.

ANNUAL PASS RECEIVING LEADERS (YARDS)

Year	Player, Team	No.	Yards	Avg.	TD
2011	Calvin Johnson, Detroit, NFC	96	1,681	17.5	16
	Wes Welker, New England, AFC	122	1,569	12.9	9
2010	Brandon Lloyd, Denver, AFC	77	1,448	18.8	11
	Roddy White, Atlanta, NFC	115	1,389	12.1	10
2009	Andre Johnson, Houston, AFC	101	1,569	15.5	9
	Miles Austin, Dallas, NFC	81	1,320	16.3	11
2008	Andre Johnson, Houston, AFC	115	1,575	13.7	8
	Larry Fitzgerald, Arizona, NFC	96	1,431	14.9	12
2007	Reggie Wayne, Indianapolis, AFC	104	1,510	14.5	10
	Larry Fitzgerald, Arizona, NFC	100	1,409	14.1	10
2006	Chad Ochocinco, Cincinnati, AFC	87	1,369	15.7	7
	Roy Williams, Detroit, NFC	82	1,310	16.0	7
2005	Steve Smith, Carolina, NFC	103	1,563	15.2	12
	Chad Ochocinco, Cincinnati, AFC	97	1,432	14.8	9

Year	Player, Team	No.	Yards	Avg.	TD
2004	Muhsin Muhammad, Carolina, NFC	93	1,405	15.1	16
	Chad Ochocinco, Cincinnati, AFC	95	1,274	13.4	9
2003	Torry Holt, St. Louis, NFC	117	1,696	14.5	12
	Chad Ochocinco, Cincinnati, AFC	90	1,355	15.1	10
2002	Marvin Harrison, Indianapolis, AFC	143	1,722	12.0	11
	Randy Moss, Minnesota, NFC	106	1,347	12.7	7
2001	David Boston, Arizona, NFC	98	1,598	16.3	8
	Marvin Harrison, Indianapolis, AFC	109	1,524	14.0	15
2000	Torry Holt, St. Louis, NFC	82	1,635	19.9	6
	Rod Smith, Denver, AFC	100	1,602	16.0	8
1999	Marvin Harrison, Indianapolis, AFC	115	1,663	14.5	12
	Randy Moss, Minnesota, NFC	80	1,413	17.7	11
1998	Antonio Freeman, Green Bay, NFC	84	1,424	17.0	14
	Eric Moulds, Buffalo, AFC	67	1,368	20.4	9
1997	Rob Moore, Arizona, NFC	97	1,584	16.3	8
	Tim Brown, Oakland, AFC	104	1,408	13.5	5
1996	Isaac Bruce, St. Louis, NFC	84	1,338	15.9	7
	Jimmy Smith, Jacksonville, AFC	83	1,244	15.0	7
1995	Jerry Rice, San Francisco, NFC	122	1,848	15.1	15
	Tim Brown, Oakland, AFC	89	1,342	15.1	10
1994	Jerry Rice, San Francisco, NFC	112	1,499	13.4	13
	Tim Brown, L.A. Raiders, AFC	89	1,309	14.7	9
1993	Jerry Rice, San Francisco, NFC	98	1,503	15.3	15
	Tim Brown, L.A. Raiders, AFC	80	1,180	14.8	7
1992	Sterling Sharpe, Green Bay, NFC	108	1,461	13.5	13
	Anthony Miller, San Diego, AFC	72	1,060	14.7	7
1991	Michael Irvin, Dallas, NFC	93	1,523	16.4	8
	Haywood Jeffires, Houston, AFC	100	1,181	11.8	7
1990	Jerry Rice, San Francisco, NFC	100	1,502	15.0	13
	Haywood Jeffires, Houston, AFC	74	1,048	14.2	8
1989	Jerry Rice, San Francisco, NFC	82	1,483	18.1	17
	Andre Reed, Buffalo, AFC	88	1,312	14.9	9
1988	Henry Ellard, L.A. Rams, NFC	86	1,414	16.4	10
	Eddie Brown, Cincinnati, AFC	53	1,273	24.0	9
1987	J.T. Smith, St. Louis, NFC	91	1,117	12.3	8
	Carlos Carson, Kansas City, AFC	55	1,044	19.0	7
1986	Jerry Rice, San Francisco, NFC	86	1,570	18.3	15
	Stanley Morgan, New England, AFC	84	1,491	17.8	10
1985	Steve Largent, Seattle, AFC	79	1,287	16.3	6
	Mike Quick, Philadelphia, NFC	73	1,247	17.1	11
1984	Roy Green, St. Louis, NFC	78	1,555	19.9	12
	John Stallworth, Pittsburgh, AFC	80	1,395	17.4	11
1983	Mike Quick, Philadelphia, NFC	69	1,409	20.4	13
	Carlos Carson, Kansas City, AFC	80	1,351	16.9	7
1982	Wes Chandler, San Diego, AFC	49	1,032	21.1	9
	Dwight Clark, San Francisco, NFC	60	913	15.2	5
1981	Alfred Jenkins, Atlanta, NFC	70	1,358	19.4	13
	Frank Lewis, Buffalo, AFC	70	1,244	17.8	4
	Steve Watson, Denver, AFC	60	1,244	20.7	13
1980	John Jefferson, San Diego, AFC	82	1,340	16.3	13
	James Lofton, Green Bay, NFC	71	1,226	17.3	4
1979	Steve Largent, Seattle, AFC	66	1,237	18.7	9
	Ahmad Rashad, Minnesota, NFC	80	1,156	14.5	9
1978	Wesley Walker, N.Y. Jets, AFC	48	1,169	24.4	8
	Harold Carmichael, Philadelphia, NFC	55	1,072	19.5	8
1977	Drew Pearson, Dallas, NFC	48	870	18.1	2
	Ken Burrough, Houston, AFC	43	816	19.0	8
1976	Roger Carr, Baltimore, AFC	43	1,112	25.9	11
	*Sammy White, Minnesota, NFC	51	906	17.8	10
1975	Ken Burrough, Houston, AFC	53	1,063	20.1	8
	Mel Gray, St. Louis, NFC	48	926	19.3	11
1974	Cliff Branch, Oakland, AFC	60	1,092	18.2	13
	Drew Pearson, Dallas, NFC	62	1,087	17.5	2
1973	Harold Carmichael, Philadelphia, NFC	67	1,116	16.7	9
	*Isaac Curtis, Cincinnati, AFC	45	843	18.7	9
1972	Harold Jackson, Philadelphia, NFC	62	1,048	16.9	4
	Rich Caster, N.Y. Jets, AFC	39	833	21.4	10
1971	Otis Taylor, Kansas City, AFC	57	1,110	19.5	7
	Gene Washington, San Francisco, NFC	46	884	19.2	4

Year	Player, Team	No.	Yards	Avg.	TD
1970	Gene Washington, San Francisco, NFC	53	1,100	20.8	12
	Marlin Briscoe, Buffalo, AFC	57	1,036	18.2	8
1969	Warren Wells, Oakland, AFL	47	1,260	26.8	14
	Harold Jackson, Philadelphia, NFL	65	1,116	17.2	9
1968	Lance Alworth, San Diego, AFL	68	1,312	19.3	10
	Roy Jefferson, Pittsburgh, NFL	58	1,074	18.5	11
1967	Don Maynard, N.Y. Jets, AFL	71	1,434	20.3	10
	Ben Hawkins, Philadelphia, NFL	59	1,265	21.4	10
1966	Lance Alworth, San Diego, AFL	73	1,383	18.9	13
	Pat Studstill, Detroit, NFL	67	1,266	18.9	5
1965	Lance Alworth, San Diego, AFL	69	1,602	23.2	14
	Dave Parks, San Francisco, NFL	80	1,344	16.8	12
1964	Charley Hennigan, Houston, AFL	101	1,546	15.3	8
	Johnny Morris, Chicago, NFL	93	1,200	12.9	10
1963	Bobby Mitchell, Washington, NFL	69	1,436	20.8	7
	Art Powell, Oakland, AFL	73	1,304	17.8	16
1962	Bobby Mitchell, Washington, NFL	72	1,384	19.2	11
	Art Powell, N.Y. Titans, AFL	64	1,130	17.6	8
1961	Charley Hennigan, Houston, AFL	82	1,746	21.3	12
	Tommy McDonald, Philadelphia, NFL	64	1,144	17.9	13
1960	*Bill Groman, Houston, AFL	72	1,473	20.5	12
	Raymond Berry, Baltimore, NFL	74	1,298	17.5	10
1959	Raymond Berry, Baltimore	66	959	14.5	14
1958	Del Shofner, Los Angeles	51	1,097	21.5	8
1957	Raymond Berry, Baltimore	47	800	17.0	6
1956	Billy Howton, Green Bay	55	1,188	21.6	12
1955	Pete Pihos, Philadelphia	62	864	13.9	7
1954	Bob Boyd, Los Angeles	53	1,212	22.9	6
1953	Pete Pihos, Philadelphia	63	1,049	16.7	10
1952	*Billy Howton, Green Bay	53	1,231	23.2	13
1951	Elroy (Crazylegs) Hirsch, Los Angeles	66	1,495	22.7	17
1950	Tom Fears, Los Angeles	84	1,116	13.3	7
1949	Bob Mann, Detroit	66	1,014	15.4	4
1948	Mal Kutner, Chi. Cardinals	41	943	23.0	14
1947	Mal Kutner, Chi. Cardinals	43	944	21.9	7
1946	Jim Benton, Los Angeles	63	981	15.5	6
1945	Jim Benton, Cleveland	45	1,067	23.7	8
1944	Don Hutson, Green Bay	58	866	14.6	9
1943	Don Hutson, Green Bay	47	776	16.5	11
1942	Don Hutson, Green Bay	74	1,211	16.4	17
1941	Don Hutson, Green Bay	58	738	12.7	10
1940	*Don Looney, Philadelphia	58	707	12.2	4
1939	Don Hutson, Green Bay	34	846	24.9	6
1938	Don Hutson, Green Bay	32	548	17.1	9
1937	*Gaynell Tinsley, Chi. Cardinals	36	675	18.8	5
1936	Don Hutson, Green Bay	34	526	15.5	8
1935	Charley Malone, Boston	22	433	19.7	2
1934	Harry Ebding, Detroit	9	257	28.6	2
1933	*Paul Moss, Pittsburgh	18	383	21.3	2
1932	Johnny (Blood) McNally, Green Bay	19	326	17.2	3

*First season of professional football.

ANNUAL PUNT RETURN LEADERS

Year	Player, Team	No.	Yards	Avg.	Long	TD
2011	Devin Hester, Chicago, NFC	28	454	16.2	82	2
	Javier Arenas, Kansas City, AFC	32	410	12.8	37	0
2010	Devin Hester, Chicago, NFC	33	564	17.1	89	3
	Julian Edelman, New England, AFC	21	321	15.3	94	1
2009	DeSean Jackson, Philadelphia, NFC	29	441	15.2	85	2
	Wes Welker, New England, AFC	27	338	12.5	69	0
2008	Roscoe Parrish, Buffalo, AFC	21	322	15.3	63	1
	*Clifton Smith, Tampa Bay, NFC	23	324	14.1	70	1
2007	Roscoe Parrish, Buffalo, AFC	27	440	16.3	74	1
	Devin Hester, Chicago, NFC	42	651	15.5	89	4
2006	Adam Jones, Tennessee, AFC	34	440	12.9	90	3
	*Devin Hester, Chicago, NFC	47	600	12.8	84	3
2005	Reno Mahe, Philadelphia, NFC	21	269	12.8	44	0
	B.J. Sams, Baltimore, AFC	33	401	12.2	51	0
2004	Eddie Drummond, Detroit, NFC	24	316	13.2	83	2
	Dennis Northcutt, Cleveland, AFC	36	432	12.0	44	0

Year	Player, Team	No.	Yards	Avg.	Long	TD
2003	Dante Hall, Kansas City, AFC	29	472	16.3	93	2
	Brian Westbrook, Philadelphia, NFC	20	306	15.3	84	2
2002	Jimmy Williams, San Francisco, NFC	20	336	16.8	89	1
	Santana Moss, N.Y. Jets, AFC	25	413	16.5	63	2
2001	Troy Brown, New England, AFC	29	413	14.2	85	2
	Darrien Gordon, Atlanta, NFC	31	437	14.1	74	0
2000	Jermaine Lewis, Baltimore, AFC	36	578	16.1	89	2
	Az-Zahir Hakim, St. Louis, NFC	32	489	15.3	86	1
1999	*Charlie Rogers, Seattle, AFC	22	318	14.5	94	1
	*Mac Cody, Arizona, NFC	32	373	11.7	31	0
1998	Deion Sanders, Dallas, NFC	24	375	15.6	69	2
	Reggie Barlow, Jacksonville, AFC	43	555	12.9	85	1
1997	Jermaine Lewis, Baltimore, AFC	28	437	15.6	89	2
	David Palmer, Minnesota, NFC	34	444	13.1	57	0
1996	Desmond Howard, Green Bay, NFC	58	875	15.1	92	3
	Darrien Gordon, San Diego, AFC	36	537	14.9	81	1
1995	David Palmer, Minnesota, NFC	26	342	13.2	74	1
	Andre Coleman, San Diego, AFC	28	326	11.6	88	1
1994	Brian Mitchell, Washington, NFC	32	452	14.1	78	2
	Darrien Gordon, San Diego, AFC	36	475	13.2	90	2
1993	*Tyrone Hughes, New Orleans, NFC	37	503	13.6	83	2
	Eric Metcalf, Cleveland, AFC	36	464	12.9	91	2
1992	Johnny Bailey, Phoenix, NFC	20	263	13.2	65	0
	Rod Woodson, Pittsburgh, AFC	32	364	11.4	80	1
1991	Mel Gray, Detroit, NFC	25	385	15.4	78	1
	Rod Woodson, Pittsburgh, AFC	28	320	11.4	40	0
1990	Clarence Verdin, Indianapolis, AFC	31	396	12.8	36	0
	*Johnny Bailey, Chicago, NFC	36	399	11.1	95	1
1989	Walter Stanley, Detroit, NFC	36	496	13.8	74	0
	Clarence Verdin, Indianapolis, AFC	23	296	12.9	49	1
1988	John Taylor, San Francisco, NFC	44	556	12.6	95	2
	JoJo Townsell, N.Y. Jets, AFC	35	409	11.7	59	1
1987	Mel Gray, New Orleans, NFC	24	352	14.7	80	0
	Bobby Joe Edmonds, Seattle, AFC	20	251	12.6	40	0
1986	*Bobby Joe Edmonds, Seattle, AFC	34	419	12.3	75	1
	*Vai Sikahema, St. Louis, NFC	43	522	12.1	71	2
1985	Irving Fryar, New England, AFC	37	520	14.1	85	2
	Henry Ellard, L.A. Rams, NFC	37	501	13.5	80	1
1984	Mike Martin, Cincinnati, AFC	24	376	15.7	55	0
	Henry Ellard, L.A. Rams, NFC	30	403	13.4	83	2
1983	*Henry Ellard, L.A. Rams, NFC	16	217	13.6	72	1
	Kirk Springs, N.Y. Jets, AFC	23	287	12.5	76	1
1982	Rick Upchurch, Denver, AFC	15	242	16.1	78	2
	Billy Johnson, Atlanta, NFC	24	273	11.4	71	0
1981	LeRoy Irvin, Los Angeles, NFC	46	615	13.4	84	3
	*James Brooks, San Diego, AFC	22	290	13.2	42	0
1980	J.T. Smith, Kansas City, AFC	40	581	14.5	75	2
	*Kenny Johnson, Atlanta, NFC	23	281	12.2	56	0
1979	John Sciarra, Philadelphia, NFC	16	182	11.4	38	0
	*Tony Nathan, Miami, AFC	28	306	10.9	86	1
1978	Rick Upchurch, Denver, AFC	36	493	13.7	75	1
	Jackie Wallace, Los Angeles, NFC	52	618	11.9	58	0
1977	Billy Johnson, Houston, AFC	35	539	15.4	87	2
	Larry Marshall, Philadelphia, NFC	46	489	10.6	48	0
1976	Rick Upchurch, Denver, AFC	39	536	13.7	92	4
	Eddie Brown, Washington, NFC	48	646	13.5	71	1
1975	Billy Johnson, Houston, AFC	40	612	15.3	83	3
	Terry Metcalf, St. Louis, NFC	23	285	12.4	69	1
1974	Lemar Parrish, Cincinnati, AFC	18	338	18.8	90	2
	Dick Jauron, Detroit, NFC	17	286	16.8	58	0
1973	Bruce Taylor, San Francisco, NFC	15	207	13.8	61	0
	Ron Smith, San Diego, AFC	27	352	13.0	84	2
1972	Ken Ellis, Green Bay, NFC	14	215	15.4	80	1
	Chris Farasopoulos, N.Y. Jets, AFC	17	179	10.5	65	1
1971	Les (Speedy) Duncan, Washington, NFC	22	233	10.6	33	0
	Leroy Kelly, Cleveland, AFC	30	292	9.7	74	0
1970	Ed Podolak, Kansas City, AFC	23	311	13.5	60	0
	*Bruce Taylor, San Francisco, NFC	43	516	12.0	76	0
1969	Alvin Haymond, Los Angeles, NFL	33	435	13.2	52	0
	*Bill Thompson, Denver, AFL	25	288	11.5	40	0

Year	Player, Team	No.	Yards	Avg.	Long	TD
1968	Bob Hayes, Dallas, NFL	15	312	20.8	90	2
	Noland Smith, Kansas City, AFL	18	270	15.0	80	1
1967	Floyd Little, Denver, AFL	16	270	16.9	72	1
	Ben Davis, Cleveland, NFL	18	229	12.7	52	1
1966	Les (Speedy) Duncan, San Diego, AFL	18	238	13.2	81	1
	Johnny Roland, St. Louis, NFL	20	221	11.1	86	1
1965	Leroy Kelly, Cleveland, NFL	17	265	15.6	67	2
	Les (Speedy) Duncan, San Diego, AFL	30	464	15.5	66	2
1964	Bobby Jancik, Houston, AFL	12	220	18.3	82	1
	Tommy Watkins, Detroit, NFL	16	238	14.9	68	2
1963	Dick James, Washington, NFL	16	214	13.4	39	0
	Claude (Hoot) Gibson, Oakland, AFL	26	307	11.8	85	2
1962	Dick Christy, N.Y. Titans, AFL	15	250	16.7	73	2
	Pat Studstill, Detroit, NFL	29	457	15.8	44	0
1961	Dick Christy, N.Y. Titans, AFL	18	383	21.3	70	2
	Willie Wood, Green Bay, NFL	14	225	16.1	72	2
1960	*Abner Haynes, Dall. Texans, AFL	14	215	15.4	46	0
	Abe Woodson, San Francisco, NFL	13	174	13.4	48	0
1959	Johnny Morris, Chi. Bears	14	171	12.2	78	1
1958	Jon Arnett, Los Angeles	18	223	12.4	58	0
1957	Bert Zagers, Washington	14	217	15.5	76	2
1956	Ken Konz, Cleveland	13	187	14.4	65	1
1955	Ollie Matson, Chi. Cardinals	13	245	18.8	78	2
1954	*Veryl Switzer, Green Bay	24	306	12.8	93	1
1953	Charley Trippi, Chi. Cardinals	21	239	11.4	38	0
1952	Jack Christiansen, Detroit	15	322	21.5	79	2
1951	Claude (Buddy) Young, N.Y. Yanks	12	231	19.3	79	1
1950	*Herb Rich, Baltimore	12	276	23.0	86	1
1949	Verda (Vitamin T) Smith, Los Angeles	27	427	15.8	85	1
1948	George McAfee, Chi. Bears	30	417	13.9	60	1
1947	*Walt Slater, Pittsburgh	28	435	15.5	33	0
1946	Bill Dudley, Pittsburgh	27	385	14.3	52	0
1945	*Dave Ryan, Detroit	15	220	14.7	56	0
1944	*Steve Van Buren, Philadelphia	15	230	15.3	55	1
1943	Andy Farkas, Washington	15	168	11.2	33	0
1942	Merlyn Condit, Brooklyn	21	210	10.0	23	0
1941	Byron (Whizzer) White, Detroit	19	262	13.8	64	0

First season of professional football.

ANNUAL KICKOFF RETURN LEADERS

Year	Player, Team	No.	Yards	Avg.	Long	TD
2011	Joe McKnight, N.Y. Jets, AFC	34	1,073	31.6	107	1
	*Randall Cobb, Green Bay, NFC	34	941	27.7	108	1
2010	*David Reed, Baltimore, AFC	21	616	29.3	103	1
	Eric Weems, Atlanta, NFC	40	1,100	27.5	102	1
2009	Clifton Smith, Tampa Bay, NFC	31	902	29.1	83	0
	Josh Cribbs, Cleveland, AFC	56	1,542	27.5	103	3
2008	Danieal Manning, Chicago, NFC	36	1,070	29.7	83	1
	Ellis Hobbs, New England, AFC	45	1,281	28.5	95	1
2007	Josh Cribbs, Cleveland, AFC	59	1,809	30.7	100	2
	*Aundrae Allison, Minnesota, NFC	20	574	28.7	104	1
2006	Justin Miller, N.Y. Jets, AFC	46	1,304	28.3	103	2
	*Devin Hester, Chicago, NFC	20	528	26.4	96	2
2005	Terrence McGee, Buffalo, AFC	46	1,391	30.2	99	1
	Koren Robinson, Minnesota, NFC	47	1,221	26.0	86	1
2004	Willie Ponder, N.Y. Giants, NFC	36	967	26.9	91	1
	Terrence McGee, Buffalo, AFC	52	1,370	26.3	104	3
2003	Jerry Azumah, Chicago, NFC	41	1,191	29.0	89	2
	*Bethel Johnson, New England, AFC	30	847	28.2	92	1
2002	MarTay Jenkins, Arizona, NFC	20	559	28.0	95	1
	Kevin Faulk, New England, AFC	26	725	27.9	87	2
2001	Ronney Jenkins, San Diego, AFC	58	1,541	26.6	93	2
	*Steve Smith, Carolina, NFC	56	1,431	25.6	99	2
2000	*Darrick Vaughn, Atlanta, NFC	39	1,082	27.7	100	3
	Derrick Mason, Tennessee, AFC	42	1,132	27.0	66	0
1999	Tony Horne, St. Louis, NFC	30	892	29.7	101	2
	Tremain Mack, Cincinnati, AFC	51	1,382	27.1	99	1
1998	*Terry Fair, Detroit, NFC	51	1,428	28.0	105	2
	Corey Harris, Baltimore, AFC	35	965	27.6	95	1

Year	Player, Team	No.	Yards	Avg.	Long	TD
1997	Michael Bates, Carolina, NFC	47	1,281	27.3	56	0
	Aaron Glenn, N.Y. Jets, AFC	28	741	26.5	96	1
1996	Michael Bates, Carolina, NFC	33	998	30.2	93	1
	Tamarick Vanover, Kansas City, AFC	33	854	25.9	97	1
1995	Ron Carpenter, N.Y. Jets, AFC	20	553	27.7	58	0
	Brian Mitchell, Washington, NFC	55	1,408	25.6	59	0
1994	Mel Gray, Detroit, NFC	45	1,276	28.4	102	3
	Randy Baldwin, Cleveland, AFC	28	753	26.9	85	1
1993	Robert Brooks, Green Bay, NFC	23	611	26.6	95	1
	*Raghib Ismail, L.A. Raiders, AFC	25	605	24.2	66	0
1992	Jon Vaughn, New England, AFC	20	564	28.2	100	1
	Deion Sanders, Atlanta, NFC	40	1,067	26.7	99	2
1991	Mel Gray, Detroit, NFC	36	929	25.8	71	0
	Nate Lewis, San Diego, AFC	23	578	25.1	95	1
1990	Kevin Clark, Denver, AFC	20	505	25.3	75	0
	David Meggett, N.Y. Giants, NFC	21	492	23.4	58	0
1989	Rod Woodson, Pittsburgh, AFC	36	982	27.3	84	1
	Mel Gray, Detroit, NFC	24	640	26.7	57	0
1988	*Tim Brown, L.A. Raiders, AFC	41	1,098	26.8	97	1
	Donnie Elder, Tampa Bay, NFC	34	772	22.7	51	0
1987	Sylvester Stamps, Atlanta, NFC	24	660	27.5	97	1
	Paul Palmer, Kansas City, AFC	38	923	24.3	95	2
1986	Dennis Gentry, Chicago, NFC	20	576	28.8	91	1
	Lupe Sanchez, Pittsburgh, AFC	25	591	23.6	64	0
1985	Ron Brown, L.A. Rams, NFC	28	918	32.8	98	3
	Glen Young, Cleveland, AFC	35	898	25.7	63	0
1984	*Bobby Humphery, N.Y. Jets, AFC	22	675	30.7	97	1
	Barry Redden, L.A. Rams, NFC	23	530	23.0	40	0
1983	Fulton Walker, Miami, AFC	36	962	26.7	78	0
	Darrin Nelson, Minnesota, NFC	18	445	24.7	50	0
1982	*Mike Mosley, Buffalo, AFC	18	487	27.1	66	0
	Alvin Hall, Detroit, NFC	16	426	26.6	96	1
1981	Mike Nelms, Washington, NFC	37	1,099	29.7	84	0
	Carl Roaches, Houston, AFC	28	769	27.5	96	1
1980	Horace Ivory, New England, AFC	36	992	27.6	98	1
	Rich Mauti, New Orleans, NFC	31	798	25.7	52	0
1979	Larry Brunson, Oakland, AFC	17	441	25.9	89	0
	Jimmy Edwards, Minnesota, NFC	44	1,103	25.1	83	0
1978	Steve Odom, Green Bay, NFC	25	677	27.1	95	1
	*Keith Wright, Cleveland, AFC	30	789	26.3	86	0
1977	*Raymond Clayborn, New England, AFC	28	869	31.0	101	3
	*Wilbert Montgomery, Philadelphia, NFC	23	619	26.9	99	1
1976	*Duriel Harris, Miami, AFC	17	559	32.9	69	0
	Cullen Bryant, Los Angeles, NFC	16	459	28.7	90	1
1975	*Walter Payton, Chicago, NFC	14	444	31.7	70	0
	Harold Hart, Oakland, AFC	17	518	30.5	102	1
1974	Terry Metcalf, St. Louis, NFC	20	623	31.2	94	1
	Greg Pruitt, Cleveland, AFC	22	606	27.5	88	1
1973	Carl Garrett, Chicago, NFC	16	486	30.4	67	0
	*Wallace Francis, Buffalo, AFC	23	687	29.9	101	2
1972	Ron Smith, Chicago, NFC	30	924	30.8	94	1
	*Bruce Laird, Baltimore, AFC	29	843	29.1	73	0
1971	Travis Williams, Los Angeles, NFC	25	743	29.7	105	1
	Eugene (Mercury) Morris, Miami, AFC	15	423	28.2	94	1
1970	Jim Duncan, Baltimore, AFC	20	707	35.4	99	1
	Cecil Turner, Chicago, NFC	23	752	32.7	96	4
1969	Bobby Williams, Detroit, NFL	17	563	33.1	96	1
	*Bill Thompson, Denver, AFL	18	513	28.5	63	0
1968	Preston Pearson, Baltimore, NFL	15	527	35.1	102	2
	*George Atkinson, Oakland, AFL	32	802	25.1	60	0
1967	*Travis Williams, Green Bay, NFL	18	739	41.1	104	4
	*Zeke Moore, Houston, AFL	14	405	28.9	92	1
1966	Gale Sayers, Chicago, NFL	23	718	31.2	93	2
	*Goldie Sellers, Denver, AFL	19	541	28.5	100	2
1965	Tommy Watkins, Detroit, NFL	17	584	34.4	94	0
	Abner Haynes, Denver, AFL	34	901	26.5	60	0
1964	*Clarence Childs, N.Y. Giants, NFL	34	987	29.0	100	1
	Bo Roberson, Oakland, AFL	36	975	27.1	59	0
1963	Abe Woodson, San Francisco, NFL	29	935	32.2	103	3
	Bobby Jancik, Houston, AFL	45	1,317	29.3	53	0

Year	Player, Team	No.	Yards	Avg.	Long	TD
1962	Abe Woodson, San Francisco, NFL	37	1,157	31.3	79	0
	*Bobby Jancik, Houston, AFL	24	826	30.3	61	0
1961	Dick Bass, Los Angeles, NFL	23	698	30.3	64	0
	*Dave Grayson, Dall. Texans, AFL	16	453	28.3	73	0
1960	*Tom Moore, Green Bay, NFL	12	397	33.1	84	0
	Ken Hall, Houston, AFL	19	594	31.3	104	1
1959	Abe Woodson, San Francisco	13	382	29.4	105	1
1958	Ollie Matson, Chi. Cardinals	14	497	35.5	101	2
1957	*Jon Arnett, Los Angeles	18	504	28.0	98	1
1956	*Tom Wilson, Los Angeles	15	477	31.8	103	1
1955	Al Carmichael, Green Bay	14	418	29.9	100	1
1954	Billy Reynolds, Cleveland	14	413	29.5	51	0
1953	Joe Arenas, San Francisco	16	551	34.4	82	0
1952	Lynn Chandnois, Pittsburgh	17	599	35.2	93	2
1951	Lynn Chandnois, Pittsburgh	12	390	32.5	55	0
1950	Verda (Vitamin T) Smith, Los Angeles	22	742	33.7	97	3
1949	*Don Doll, Detroit	21	536	25.5	56	0
1948	*Joe Scott, N.Y. Giants	20	569	28.5	99	1
1947	Eddie Saenz, Washington	29	797	27.5	94	2
1946	Abe Karnofsky, Boston	21	599	28.5	97	1
1945	Steve Van Buren, Philadelphia	13	373	28.7	98	1
1944	Bob Thurbon, Card.-Pitt.	12	291	24.3	55	0
1943	Ken Heineman, Brooklyn	16	444	27.8	69	0
1942	Marshall Goldberg, Chi. Cardinals	15	393	26.2	95	1
1941	Marshall Goldberg, Chi. Cardinals	12	290	24.2	41	0

*First season of professional football.

ANNUAL INTERCEPTION LEADERS

Year	Player, Team	No.	Yards	TD
2011	Kyle Arrington, New England, AFC	7	92	0
	Eric Weddle, San Diego, AFC	7	89	0
	Charles Woodson, Green Bay, NFC	7	63	1
2010	Ed Reed, Baltimore, AFC	8	183	0
	Asante Samuel, Philadelphia, NFC	7	70	0
2009	*Jairus Byrd, Buffalo, AFC	9	118	0
	Asante Samuel, Philadelphia, NFC	9	117	0
	Darren Sharper, New Orleans, NFC	9	376	3
	Charles Woodson, Green Bay, NFC	9	179	3
2008	Ed Reed, Baltimore, AFC	9	264	2
	Nick Collins, Green Bay, NFC	7	295	3
	Charles Woodson, Green Bay, NFC	7	169	2
2007	Antonio Cromartie, San Diego, AFC	10	144	1
	O.J. Atogwe, St. Louis, NFC	8	125	1
2006	Champ Bailey, Denver, AFC	10	162	1
	Asante Samuel, New England, AFC	10	120	0
	Walt Harris, San Francisco, NFC	8	84	1
	Charles Woodson, Green Bay, NFC	8	61	1
2005	Ty Law, N.Y. Jets, AFC	10	195	1
	Deltha O'Neal, Cincinnati, AFC	10	103	0
	Darren Sharper, Minnesota, NFC	9	276	2
2004	Ed Reed, Baltimore, AFC	9	358	1
	Ken Lucas, Seattle, NFC	6	46	1
	*Chris Gamble, Carolina, NFC	6	15	0
2003	Tony Parrish, San Francisco, NFC	9	202	0
	Brian Russell, Minnesota, NFC	9	185	0
	Ed Reed, Baltimore, AFC	7	132	1
	Marcus Coleman, Houston, AFC	7	95	0
	Patrick Surtain, Miami, AFC	7	59	0
2002	Rod Woodson, Oakland, AFC	8	225	2
	Brian Kelly, Tampa Bay, NFC	8	68	0
2001	*Anthony Henry, Cleveland, AFC	10	177	1
	Ronde Barber, Tampa Bay, NFC	10	86	1
2000	Darren Sharper, Green Bay, NFC	9	109	0
	Samari Rolle, Tennessee, AFC	7	140	1
	Brian Walker, Miami, AFC	7	80	0
1999	Rod Woodson, Baltimore, AFC	7	195	2
	Sam Madison, Miami, AFC	7	164	1
	James Hasty, Kansas City, AFC	7	98	2
	Donnie Abraham, Tampa Bay, NFC	7	115	2
	Troy Vincent, Philadelphia, NFC	7	91	0

Year	Player, Team	No.	Yards	TD
1998	Ty Law, New England, AFC	9	133	1
	Kwamie Lassiter, Arizona, NFC	8	80	0
1997	Ryan McNeil, St. Louis, NFC	9	127	1
	Mark McMillian, Kansas City, AFC	8	274	3
	Darryl Williams, Seattle, AFC	8	172	1
1996	Tyrone Braxton, Denver, AFC	9	128	1
	Keith Lyle, St. Louis, NFC	9	152	0
1995	*Orlando Thomas, Minnesota, NFC	9	108	1
	Willie Williams, Pittsburgh, AFC	7	122	1
1994	Eric Turner, Cleveland, AFC	9	199	1
	Aeneas Williams, Arizona, NFC	9	89	0
1993	Eugene Robinson, Seattle, AFC	9	80	0
	Nate Odomes, Buffalo, AFC	9	65	0
	Deion Sanders, Atlanta, NFC	7	91	0
1992	Henry Jones, Buffalo, AFC	8	263	2
	Audray McMillian, Minnesota, NFC	8	157	2
1991	Ronnie Lott, L.A. Raiders, AFC	8	52	0
	Ray Crockett, Detroit, NFC	6	141	1
	Deion Sanders, Atlanta, NFC	6	119	1
	*Aeneas Williams, Phoenix, NFC	6	60	0
	Tim McKyer, Atlanta, NFC	6	24	1
1990	*Mark Carrier, Chicago, NFC	10	39	0
	Richard Johnson, Houston, AFC	8	100	1
1989	Felix Wright, Cleveland, AFC	9	91	1
	Eric Allen, Philadelphia, NFC	8	38	0
1988	Scott Case, Atlanta, NFC	10	47	0
	Erik McMillan, N.Y. Jets, AFC	8	168	2
1987	Barry Wilburn, Washington, NFC	9	135	1
	Mike Prior, Indianapolis, AFC	6	57	0
	Mark Kelso, Buffalo, AFC	6	25	0
	Keith Bostic, Houston, AFC	6	-14	0
1986	Ronnie Lott, San Francisco, NFC	10	134	1
	Deron Cherry, Kansas City, AFC	9	150	0
1985	Everson Walls, Dallas, NFC	9	31	0
	Albert Lewis, Kansas City, AFC	8	59	0
	Eugene Daniel, Indianapolis, AFC	8	53	0
1984	Ken Easley, Seattle, AFC	10	126	2
	*Tom Flynn, Green Bay, NFC	9	106	0
1983	Mark Murphy, Washington, NFC	9	127	0
	Ken Riley, Cincinnati, AFC	8	89	2
	Vann McElroy, L.A. Raiders, AFC	8	68	0

Year	Player, Team	No.	Yards	TD
1982	Everson Walls, Dallas, NFC	7	61	0
	Ken Riley, Cincinnati, AFC	5	88	1
	Bobby Jackson, N.Y. Jets, AFC	5	84	1
	Dwayne Woodruff, Pittsburgh, AFC	5	53	0
	Donnie Shell, Pittsburgh, AFC	5	27	0
1981	*Everson Walls, Dallas, NFC	11	133	0
	John Harris, Seattle, AFC	10	155	2
1980	Lester Hayes, Oakland, AFC	13	273	1
	Nolan Cromwell, Los Angeles, NFC	8	140	1
1979	Mike Reinfeldt, Houston, AFC	12	205	0
	Lemar Parrish, Washington, NFC	9	65	0
1978	Thom Darden, Cleveland, AFC	10	200	0
	Ken Stone, St. Louis, NFC	10	139	0
	Willie Buchanon, Green Bay, NFC	9	93	1
1977	Lyle Blackwood, Baltimore, AFC	10	163	0
	Rolland Lawrence, Atlanta, NFC	7	138	0
1976	Monte Jackson, Los Angeles, NFC	10	173	3
	Ken Riley, Cincinnati, AFC	9	141	1
1975	Mel Blount, Pittsburgh, AFC	11	121	0
	Paul Krause, Minnesota, NFC	10	201	0
1974	Emmitt Thomas, Kansas City, AFC	12	214	2
	Ray Brown, Atlanta, NFC	8	164	1
1973	Dick Anderson, Miami, AFC	8	163	2
	Mike Wagner, Pittsburgh, AFC	8	134	0
	Bobby Bryant, Minnesota, NFC	7	105	1
1972	Bill Bradley, Philadelphia, NFC	9	73	0
	Mike Sensibaugh, Kansas City, AFC	8	65	0
1971	Bill Bradley, Philadelphia, NFC	11	248	0
	Ken Houston, Houston, AFC	9	220	4
1970	Johnny Robinson, Kansas City, AFC	10	155	0
	Dick LeBeau, Detroit, NFC	9	96	0
1969	Mel Renfro, Dallas, NFC	10	118	0
	Emmitt Thomas, Kansas City, AFL	9	146	1
1968	Dave Grayson, Oakland, AFL	10	195	1
	Willie Williams, N.Y. Giants, NFL	10	103	0
1967	Miller Farr, Houston, AFL	10	264	3
	*Lem Barney, Detroit, NFL	10	232	3
	Tom Janik, Buffalo, AFL	10	222	2
	Dave Whitsell, New Orleans, NFL	10	178	2
	Dick Westmoreland, Miami, AFL	10	127	1
1966	Larry Wilson, St. Louis, NFL	10	180	2
	Johnny Robinson, Kansas City, AFL	10	136	1
	Bobby Hunt, Kansas City, AFL	10	113	0
1965	W.K. Hicks, Houston, AFL	9	156	0
	Bobby Boyd, Baltimore, NFL	9	78	1
1964	Dainard Paulson, N.Y. Jets, AFL	12	157	1
	*Paul Krause, Washington, NFL	12	140	1
1963	Fred Glick, Houston, AFL	12	180	1
	Dick Lynch, N.Y. Giants, NFL	9	251	3
	Roosevelt Taylor, Chicago, NFL	9	172	1
1962	Lee Riley, N.Y. Titans, AFL	11	122	0
	Willie Wood, Green Bay, NFL	9	132	0
1961	Billy Atkins, Buffalo, AFL	10	158	0
	Dick Lynch, N.Y. Giants, NFL	9	60	0
1960	*Austin (Goose) Gonsoulin, Denver, AFL	11	98	0
	Dave Baker, San Francisco, NFL	10	96	0
	Jerry Norton, St. Louis, NFL	10	96	0
1959	Dean Derby, Pittsburgh	7	127	0
	Milt Davis, Baltimore	7	119	1
	Don Shinnick, Baltimore	7	70	0
1958	Jim Patton, N.Y. Giants	11	183	0
1957	Milt Davis, Baltimore	10	219	2
	Jack Christiansen, Detroit	10	137	1
	Jack Butler, Pittsburgh	10	85	0
1956	Linden Crow, Chi. Cardinals	11	170	0
1955	Will Sherman, Los Angeles	11	101	0
1954	Dick (Night Train) Lane, Chi. Cardinals	10	181	0
1953	Jack Christiansen, Detroit	12	238	1
1952	*Dick (Night Train) Lane, Los Angeles	14	298	2
1951	Otto Schnellbacher, N.Y. Giants	11	194	2

Year	Player, Team	No.	Yards	TD
1950	Orban (Spec) Sanders, N.Y. Yanks	13	199	0
1949	Bob Nussbaumer, Chi. Cardinals	12	157	0
1948	*Dan Sandifer, Washington	13	258	2
1947	Frank Reagan, N.Y. Giants	10	203	0
	Frank Seno, Boston	10	100	0
1946	Bill Dudley, Pittsburgh	10	242	1
1945	Roy Zimmerman, Philadelphia	7	90	0
1944	*Howard Livingston, N.Y. Giants	9	172	1
1943	Sammy Baugh, Washington	11	112	0
1942	Clyde (Bulldog) Turner, Chi. Bears	8	96	1
1941	Marshall Goldberg, Chi. Cardinals	7	54	0
	*Art Jones, Pittsburgh	7	35	0
1940	Clarence (Ace) Parker, Brooklyn	6	146	1
	Kent Ryan, Detroit	6	65	0
	Don Hutson, Green Bay	6	24	0

*First season of professional football.

ANNUAL PUNTING LEADERS

Year	Player, Team	No.	Avg.	Long
2011	Andy Lee, San Francisco, NFC	78	50.9	68
	Shane Lechler, Oakland, AFC	78	50.8	80
2010	Shane Lechler, Oakland, AFC	77	47.0	68
	Mat McBriar, Dallas, NFC	65	47.9	65
2009	Shane Lechler, Oakland, AFC	96	51.1	70
	Andy Lee, San Francisco, NFC	99	47.6	64
2008	Donnie Jones, St. Louis, NFC	82	50.0	68
	Shane Lechler, Oakland, AFC	90	48.8	70
2007	Shane Lechler, Oakland, AFC	73	49.1	70
	Andy Lee, San Francisco, NFC	105	47.3	74
2006	Mat McBriar, Dallas, NFC	56	48.2	75
	Shane Lechler, Oakland, AFC	77	47.5	67
2005	Brian Moorman, Buffalo, AFC	71	45.7	68
	Josh Bidwell, Tampa Bay, NFC	90	45.6	61
2004	Shane Lechler, Oakland, AFC	73	46.7	67
	Tom Tupa, Washington, NFC	103	44.1	61
2003	Shane Lechler, Oakland, AFC	96	46.9	73
	Todd Sauerbrun, Carolina, NFC	77	44.6	64
2002	Todd Sauerbrun, Carolina, NFC	104	45.5	67
	Chris Hanson, Jacksonville, AFC	81	44.2	64
2001	Todd Sauerbrun, Carolina, NFC	93	47.5	73
	Shane Lechler, Oakland, AFC	73	46.2	65
2000	Darren Bennett, San Diego, AFC	92	46.2	66
	Mitch Berger, Minnesota, NFC	62	44.7	60
1999	Tom Rouen, Denver, AFC	84	46.5	65
	Mitch Berger, Minnesota, NFC	61	45.4	75
1998	Craig Hentrich, Tennessee, AFC	69	47.2	71
	Mark Royals, New Orleans, NFC	88	45.6	64
1997	Mark Royals, New Orleans, NFC	88	45.9	66
	Tom Tupa, New England, AFC	78	45.8	73
1996	John Kidd, Miami, AFC	78	46.3	63
	Matt Turk, Washington, NFC	75	45.1	63
1995	Rick Tuten, Seattle, AFC	83	45.0	73
	Sean Landeta, St. Louis, NFC	83	44.3	63
1994	Sean Landeta, L.A. Rams, NFC	78	44.8	62
	Jeff Gossett, L.A. Raiders, AFC	77	43.9	65
1993	Greg Montgomery, Houston, AFC	54	45.6	77
	Jim Arnold, Detroit, NFC	72	44.5	68
1992	Greg Montgomery, Houston, AFC	53	46.9	66
	Harry Newsome, Minnesota, NFC	72	45.0	84
1991	Reggie Roby, Miami, AFC	54	45.7	64
	Harry Newsome, Minnesota, AFC	68	45.5	65
1990	Mike Horan, Denver, AFC	58	44.4	67
	Sean Landeta, N.Y. Giants, NFC	75	44.1	67
1989	Rich Camarillo, Phoenix, NFC	76	43.4	58
	Greg Montgomery, Houston, AFC	56	43.3	63
1988	Harry Newsome, Pittsburgh, AFC	65	45.4	62
	Jim Arnold, Detroit, NFC	97	42.4	69
1987	Rick Donnelly, Atlanta, NFC	61	44.0	62
	Ralf Mojsiejenko, San Diego, AFC	67	42.9	57
1986	Rohn Stark, Indianapolis, AFC	76	45.2	63

Year	Player, Team	No.	Yards	TD
	Sean Landeta, N.Y. Giants, NFC	79	44.8	61
1985	Rohn Stark, Indianapolis, AFC	78	45.9	68
	*Rick Donnelly, Atlanta, NFC	59	43.6	68
1984	Jim Arnold, Kansas City, AFC	98	44.9	63
	*Brian Hansen, New Orleans, NFC	69	43.8	66
1983	Rohn Stark, Baltimore, AFC	91	45.3	68
	Frank Garcia, Tampa Bay, NFC	95	42.2	64
1982	Luke Prestridge, Denver, AFC	45	45.0	65
	Carl Birdsong, St. Louis, NFC	54	43.8	65
1981	Pat McInally, Cincinnati, AFC	72	45.4	62
	Tom Skladany, Detroit, NFC	64	43.5	74
1980	Dave Jennings, N.Y. Giants, NFC	94	44.8	63
	Luke Prestridge, Denver, AFC	70	43.9	57
1979	*Bob Grupp, Kansas City, AFC	89	43.6	74
	Dave Jennings, N.Y. Giants, NFC	104	42.7	72
1978	Pat McInally, Cincinnati, AFC	91	43.1	65
	*Tom Skladany, Detroit, NFC	86	42.5	63
1977	Ray Guy, Oakland, AFC	59	43.3	74
	Tom Blanchard, New Orleans, NFC	82	42.4	66
1976	Marv Bateman, Buffalo, AFC	86	42.8	78
	John James, Atlanta, NFC	101	42.1	67
1975	Ray Guy, Oakland, AFC	68	43.8	64
	Herman Weaver, Detroit, NFC	80	42.0	61
1974	Ray Guy, Oakland, AFC	74	42.2	66
	Tom Blanchard, New Orleans, NFC	88	42.1	71
1973	Jerrel Wilson, Kansas City, AFC	80	45.5	68
	*Tom Wittum, San Francisco, NFC	79	43.7	62
1972	Jerrel Wilson, Kansas City, AFC	66	44.8	69
	Dave Chapple, Los Angeles, NFC	53	44.2	70
1971	Dave Lewis, Cincinnati, AFC	72	44.8	56
	Tom McNeill, Philadelphia, NFC	73	42.0	64
1970	Dave Lewis, Cincinnati, AFC	79	46.2	63
	*Julian Fagan, New Orleans, NFC	77	42.5	64
1969	David Lee, Baltimore, NFL	57	45.3	66
	Dennis Partee, San Diego, AFL	71	44.6	62
1968	Jerrel Wilson, Kansas City, AFL	63	45.1	70
	Billy Lothridge, Atlanta, NFL	75	44.3	70
1967	Bob Scarpitto, Denver, AFL	105	44.9	73
	Billy Lothridge, Atlanta, NFL	87	43.7	62
1966	Bob Scarpitto, Denver, AFL	76	45.8	70
	*David Lee, Baltimore, NFL	49	45.6	64
1965	Gary Collins, Cleveland, NFL	65	46.7	71
	Jerrel Wilson, Kansas City, AFL	69	45.4	64
1964	Bobby Walden, Minnesota, NFL	72	46.4	73
	Jim Fraser, Denver, AFL	73	44.2	67
1963	Yale Lary, Detroit, NFL	35	48.9	73
	Jim Fraser, Denver, AFL	81	44.4	66
1962	Tommy Davis, San Francisco, NFL	48	45.6	82
	Jim Fraser, Denver, AFL	55	43.6	75
1961	Yale Lary, Detroit, NFL	52	48.4	71
	Billy Atkins, Buffalo, AFL	85	44.5	70
1960	Jerry Norton, St. Louis, NFL	39	45.6	62
	*Paul Maguire, L.A. Chargers, AFL	43	40.5	61
1959	Yale Lary, Detroit	45	47.1	67
1958	Sam Baker, Washington	48	45.4	64
1957	Don Chandler, N.Y. Giants	60	44.6	61
1956	Norm Van Brocklin, Los Angeles	48	43.1	72
1955	Norm Van Brocklin, Los Angeles	60	44.6	61
1954	Pat Brady, Pittsburgh	66	43.2	72
1953	Pat Brady, Pittsburgh	80	46.9	64
1952	Horace Gillom, Cleveland	61	45.7	73
1951	Horace Gillom, Cleveland	73	45.5	66
1950	*Fred (Curly) Morrison, Chi. Bears	57	43.3	65
1949	*Mike Boyda, N.Y. Bulldogs	56	44.2	61
1948	Joe Muha, Philadelphia	57	47.3	82
1947	Jack Jacobs, Green Bay	57	43.5	74
1946	Roy McKay, Green Bay	64	42.7	64
1945	Roy McKay, Green Bay	44	41.2	73
1944	Frank Sinkwich, Detroit	45	41.0	73
1943	Sammy Baugh, Washington	50	45.9	81

Year	Player, Team	No.	Yards	TD
1942	Sammy Baugh, Washington	37	48.2	74
1941	Sammy Baugh, Washington	30	48.7	75
1940	Sammy Baugh, Washington	35	51.4	85
1939	*Parker Hall, Cleveland	58	40.8	80

*First season of professional football.

ANNUAL LEADERS IN SACKS (SINCE 1982)

Year	Player, Team	Sacks
2011	Jared Allen, Minnesota, NFC	22.0
	Terrell Suggs, Baltimore, AFC	14.0
2010	DeMarcus Ware, Dallas, NFC	15.5
	Tamba Hali, Kansas City, AFC	14.5
2009	Elvis Dumervil, Denver, AFC	17.0
	Jared Allen, Minnesota, NFC	14.5
2008	DeMarcus Ware, Dallas, NFC	20.0
	Joey Porter, Miami, AFC	17.5
2007	Jared Allen, Kansas City, AFC	15.5
	Patrick Kerney, Seattle, NFC	14.5
2006	Shawne Merriman, San Diego, AFC	17.0
	Aaron Kampman, Green Bay, NFC	15.5
2005	Derrick Burgess, Oakland, AFC	16.0
	Osi Umenyiora, N.Y. Giants, NFC	14.5
2004	Dwight Freeney, Indianapolis, AFC	16.0
	Bertrand Berry, Arizona, NFC	14.5
2003	Michael Strahan, N.Y. Giants, NFC	18.5
	Adewale Ogunleye, Miami, AFC	15.0
2002	Jason Taylor, Miami, AFC	18.5
	Simeon Rice, Tampa Bay, NFC	15.5
2001	Michael Strahan, N.Y. Giants, NFC	22.5
	Peter Boulware, Baltimore, AFC	15.0
2000	La'Roi Glover, New Orleans, NFC	17.0
	Trace Armstrong, Miami, AFC	16.5
1999	Kevin Carter, St. Louis, NFC	17.0
	*Jevon Kearse, Tennessee, AFC	14.5
1998	Michael Sinclair, Seattle, AFC	16.5
	Reggie White, Green Bay, NFC	16.0
1997	John Randle, Minnesota, NFC	15.5
	Bruce Smith, Buffalo, AFC	14.0
1996	Kevin Greene, Carolina, NFC	14.5
	Michael McCrary, Seattle, AFC	13.5
	Bruce Smith, Buffalo, AFC	13.5
1995	Bryce Paup, Buffalo, AFC	17.5
	William Fuller, Philadelphia, NFC	13.0
	Wayne Martin, New Orleans, NFC	13.0
1994	Kevin Greene, Pittsburgh, AFC	14.0
	Ken Harvey, Washington, NFC	13.5
	John Randle, Minnesota, NFC	13.5
1993	Neil Smith, Kansas City, AFC	15.0
	Renaldo Turnbull, New Orleans, NFC	13.0
	Reggie White, Green Bay, NFC	13.0
1992	Clyde Simmons, Philadelphia, NFC	19.0
	Leslie O'Neal, San Diego, AFC	17.0
1991	Pat Swilling, New Orleans, NFC	17.0
	William Fuller, Houston, AFC	15.0
1990	Derrick Thomas, Kansas City, AFC	20.0
	Charles Haley, San Francisco, NFC	16.0
1989	Chris Doleman, Minnesota, NFC	21.0
	Lee Williams, San Diego, AFC	14.0
1988	Reggie White, Philadelphia, NFC	18.0
	Greg Townsend, L.A. Raiders, AFC	11.5
1987	Reggie White, Philadelphia, NFC	21.0
	Andre Tippett, New England, AFC	12.5
1986	Lawrence Taylor, N.Y. Giants, NFC	20.5
	Sean Jones, L.A. Raiders, AFC	15.5
1985	Richard Dent, Chicago, NFC	17.0
	Andre Tippett, New England, AFC	16.5
1984	Mark Gastineau, N.Y. Jets, AFC	22.0
	Richard Dent, Chicago, NFC	17.5
1983	Mark Gastineau, N.Y. Jets, AFC	19.0
	Fred Dean, San Francisco, NFC	17.5

| 1982 | Doug Martin, Minnesota, NFC | 11.5 |
| | Jesse Baker, Houston, AFC | 7.5 |

First season of professional football.

POINTS SCORED

Year	Team	Points
2011	Green Bay, NFC	560
	New England, AFC	513
2010	New England, AFC	518
	Philadelphia, NFC	439
2009	New Orleans, NFC	510
	San Diego, AFC	454
2008	New Orleans, NFC	463
	San Diego, AFC	439
2007	New England, AFC	589
	Dallas, NFC	455
2006	San Diego, AFC	492
	Chicago, NFC	427
2005	Seattle, NFC	452
	Indianapolis, AFC	439
2004	Indianapolis, AFC	522
	Green Bay, NFC	424
2003	Kansas City, AFC	484
	St. Louis, NFC	447
2002	Kansas City, AFC	467
	New Orleans, NFC	432
2001	St. Louis, NFC	503
	Indianapolis, AFC	413
2000	St. Louis, NFC	540
	Denver, AFC	485
1999	St. Louis, NFC	526
	Indianapolis, AFC	423
1998	Minnesota, NFC	556
	Denver, AFC	501
1997	Denver, AFC	472
	Green Bay, NFC	422
1996	Green Bay, NFC	456
	New England, AFC	418
1995	San Francisco, NFC	457
	Pittsburgh, AFC	407
1994	San Francisco, NFC	505
	Miami, AFC	389
1993	San Francisco, NFC	473
	Denver, AFC	373
1992	San Francisco, NFC	431
	Buffalo, AFC	381
1991	Washington, NFC	485
	Buffalo, AFC	458
1990	Buffalo, AFC	428
	Philadelphia, NFC	396
1989	San Francisco, NFC	442
	Buffalo, AFC	409
1988	Cincinnati, AFC	448
	L.A. Rams, NFC	407
1987	San Francisco, NFC	459
	Cleveland, AFC	390
1986	Miami, AFC	430
	Minnesota, NFC	398
1985	San Diego, AFC	467
	Chicago, NFC	456
1984	Miami, AFC	513
	San Francisco, NFC	475
1983	Washington, NFC	541
	L.A. Raiders, AFC	442
1982	San Diego, AFC	288
	Dallas, NFC	226
	Green Bay, NFC	226
1981	San Diego, AFC	478
	Atlanta, NFC	426
1980	Dallas, NFC	454
	New England, AFC	441

Year	Team	Points
1979	Pittsburgh, AFC	416
	Dallas, NFC	371
1978	Dallas, NFC	384
	Miami, AFC	372
1977	Oakland, AFC	351
	Dallas, NFC	345
1976	Baltimore, AFC	417
	Los Angeles, NFC	351
1975	Buffalo, AFC	420
	Minnesota, NFC	377
1974	Oakland, AFC	355
	Washington, NFC	320
1973	Los Angeles, NFC	388
	Denver, AFC	354
1972	Miami, AFC	385
	San Francisco, NFC	353
1971	Dallas, NFC	406
	Oakland, AFC	344
1970	San Francisco, NFC	352
	Baltimore, AFC	321
1969	Minnesota, NFL	379
	Oakland, AFL	377
1968	Oakland, AFL	453
	Dallas, NFL	431
1967	Oakland, AFL	468
	Los Angeles, NFL	398
1966	Kansas City, AFL	448
	Dallas, NFL	445
1965	San Francisco, NFL	421
	San Diego, AFL	340
1964	Baltimore, NFL	428
	Buffalo, AFL	400
1963	N.Y. Giants, NFL	448
	San Diego, AFL	399
1962	Green Bay, NFL	415
	Dall. Texans, AFL	389
1961	Houston, AFL	513
	Green Bay, NFL	391
1960	N.Y. Titans, AFL	382
	Cleveland, NFL	362
1959	Baltimore	374
1958	Baltimore	381
1957	Los Angeles	307
1956	Chi. Bears	363
1955	Cleveland	349
1954	Detroit	337
1953	San Francisco	372
1952	Los Angeles	349
1951	Los Angeles	392
1950	Los Angeles	466
1949	Philadelphia	364
1948	Chi. Cardinals	395
1947	Chi. Bears	363
1946	Chi. Bears	289
1945	Philadelphia	272
1944	Philadelphia	267
1943	Chi. Bears	303
1942	Chi. Bears	376
1941	Chi. Bears	396
1940	Washington	245
1939	Chi. Bears	298
1938	Green Bay	223
1937	Green Bay	220
1936	Green Bay	248
1935	Chi. Bears	192
1934	Chi. Bears	286
1933	N.Y. Giants	244
1932	Chi. Bears	160

YEARLY STATISTICAL LEADERS

TOTAL YARDS GAINED

Year	Team	Yards
2011	New Orleans, NFC	7,474
	New England, AFC	6,848
2010	San Diego, AFC	6,329
	Philadelphia, NFC	6,230
2009	New Orleans, NFC	6,461
	New England, AFC	6,357
2008	New Orleans, NFC	6,571
	Denver, AFC	6,333
2007	New England, AFC	6,580
	Green Bay, NFC	5,931
2006	New Orleans, NFC	6,264
	Indianapolis, AFC	6,070
2005	Kansas City, AFC	6,192
	Seattle, NFC	5,915
2004	Kansas City, AFC	6,695
	Green Bay, NFC	6,357
2003	Minnesota, NFC	6,294
	Kansas City, AFC	5,910
2002	Oakland, AFC	6,237
	Minnesota, NFC	6,192
2001	St. Louis, NFC	6,690
	Indianapolis, AFC	5,955
2000	St. Louis, NFC	7,075
	Denver, AFC	6,554
1999	St. Louis, NFC	6,412
	Indianapolis, AFC	5,726
1998	San Francisco, NFC	6,800
	Denver, AFC	6,092
1997	Denver, AFC	5,872
	Detroit, NFC	5,798
1996	Denver, AFC	5,791
	Philadelphia, NFC	5,627
1995	Detroit, NFC	6,113
	Denver, AFC	6,040
1994	Miami, AFC	6,078
	San Francisco, NFC	6,060
1993	San Francisco, NFC	6,435
	Miami, AFC	5,812
1992	San Francisco, NFC	6,195
	Buffalo, AFC	5,893
1991	Buffalo, AFC	6,252
	San Francisco, NFC	5,858
1990	Houston, AFC	6,222
	San Francisco, NFC	5,895
1989	San Francisco, NFC	6,268
	Cincinnati, AFC	6,101
1988	Cincinnati, AFC	6,057
	San Francisco, NFC	5,900
1987	San Francisco, NFC	5,987
	Denver, AFC	5,624
1986	Cincinnati, AFC	6,490
	San Francisco, NFC	6,082
1985	San Diego, AFC	6,535
	San Francisco, NFC	5,920
1984	Miami, AFC	6,936
	San Francisco, NFC	6,366
1983	San Diego, AFC	6,197
	Green Bay, NFC	6,172
1982	San Diego, AFC	4,048
	San Francisco, NFC	3,242
1981	San Diego, AFC	6,744
	Detroit, NFC	5,933
1980	San Diego, AFC	6,410
	Los Angeles, NFC	6,006
1979	Pittsburgh, AFC	6,258
	Dallas, NFC	5,968
1978	New England, AFC	5,965
	Dallas, NFC	5,959
1977	Dallas, NFC	4,812
	Oakland, AFC	4,736
1976	Baltimore, AFC	5,236
	St. Louis, NFC	5,136
1975	Buffalo, AFC	5,467
	Dallas, NFC	5,025
1974	Dallas, NFC	4,983
	Oakland, AFC	4,718
1973	Los Angeles, NFC	4,906
	Oakland, AFC	4,773
1972	Miami, AFC	5,036
	N.Y. Giants, NFC	4,483
1971	Dallas, NFC	5,035
	San Diego, AFC	4,738
1970	Oakland, AFC	4,829
	San Francisco, NFC	4,503
1969	Dallas, NFL	5,122
	Oakland, AFL	5,036
1968	Oakland, AFL	5,696
	Dallas, NFL	5,117
1967	N.Y. Jets, AFL	5,152
	Baltimore, NFL	5,008
1966	Dallas, NFL	5,145
	Kansas City, AFL	5,114
1965	San Francisco, NFL	5,270
	San Diego, AFL	5,188
1964	Buffalo, AFL	5,206
	Baltimore, NFL	4,779
1963	San Diego, AFL	5,153
	N.Y. Giants, NFL	5,024
1962	N.Y. Giants, NFL	5,005
	Houston, AFL	4,971
1961	Houston, AFL	6,288
	Philadelphia, NFL	5,112
1960	Houston, AFL	4,936
	Baltimore, NFL	4,245
1959	Baltimore	4,458
1958	Baltimore	4,539
1957	Los Angeles	4,143
1956	Chi. Bears	4,537
1955	Chi. Bears	4,316
1954	Los Angeles	5,187
1953	Philadelphia	4,811
1952	Cleveland	4,352
1951	Los Angeles	5,506
1950	Los Angeles	5,420
1949	Chi. Bears	4,873
1948	Chi. Cardinals	4,705
1947	Chi. Bears	5,053
1946	Los Angeles	3,793
1945	Washington	3,549
1944	Chi. Bears	3,239
1943	Chi. Bears	4,045
1942	Chi. Bears	3,900
1941	Chi. Bears	4,265
1940	Green Bay	3,400
1939	Chi. Bears	3,988
1938	Green Bay	3,037
1937	Green Bay	3,201
1936	Detroit	3,703
1935	Chi. Bears	3,454
1934	Chi. Bears	3,900
1933	N.Y. Giants	2,973
1932	Chi. Bears	2,755

YARDS RUSHING

Year	Team	Yards
2011	Denver, AFC	2,632
	Carolina, NFC	2,408

Year	Team	Yards	Year	Team	Yards
2010	Kansas City, AFC	2,627	1975	Buffalo, AFC	2,974
	Philadelphia, NFC	2,324		Dallas, NFC	2,432
2009	N.Y. Jets, AFC	2,756	1974	Dallas, NFC	2,454
	Carolina, NFC	2,498		Pittsburgh, AFC	2,417
2008	N.Y. Giants, NFC	2,518	1973	Buffalo, AFC	3,088
	Baltimore, AFC	2,376		Los Angeles, NFC	2,925
2007	Minnesota, NFC	2,634	1972	Miami, AFC	2,960
	Jacksonville, AFC	2,391		Chicago, NFC	2,360
2006	Atlanta, NFC	2,939	1971	Miami, AFC	2,429
	San Diego, AFC	2,578		Detroit, NFC	2,376
2005	Atlanta, NFC	2,546	1970	Dallas, NFC	2,300
	Denver, AFC	2,539		Miami, AFC	2,082
2004	Atlanta, NFC	2,672	1969	Dallas, NFL	2,276
	Pittsburgh, AFC	2,464		Kansas City, AFL	2,220
2003	Baltimore, AFC	2,674	1968	Chicago, NFL	2,377
	Green Bay, NFC	2,558		Kansas City, AFL	2,227
2002	Minnesota, NFC	2,507	1967	Cleveland, NFL	2,139
	Miami, AFC	2,502		Houston, AFL	2,122
2001	Pittsburgh, AFC	2,774	1966	Kansas City, AFL	2,274
	San Francisco, NFC	2,244		Cleveland, NFL	2,166
2000	Oakland, AFC	2,470	1965	Cleveland, NFL	2,331
	Minnesota, NFC	2,129		San Diego, AFL	2,085
1999	San Francisco, NFC	2,095	1964	Green Bay, NFL	2,276
	Jacksonville, AFC	2,091		Buffalo, AFL	2,040
1998	San Francisco, NFC	2,544	1963	Cleveland, NFL	2,639
	Denver, AFC	2,468		San Diego, AFL	2,203
1997	Pittsburgh, AFC	2,479	1962	Buffalo, AFL	2,480
	Detroit, NFC	2,464		Green Bay, NFL	2,460
1996	Denver, AFC	2,362	1961	Green Bay, NFL	2,350
	Washington, NFC	1,910		Dall. Texans, AFL	2,189
1995	Kansas City, AFC	2,222	1960	St. Louis, NFL	2,356
	Dallas, NFC	2,201		Oakland, AFL	2,056
1994	Pittsburgh, AFC	2,180	1959	Cleveland	2,149
	Detroit, NFC	2,080	1958	Cleveland	2,526
1993	N.Y. Giants, NFC	2,210	1957	Los Angeles	2,142
	Seattle, AFC	2,015	1956	Chi. Bears	2,468
1992	Buffalo, AFC	2,436	1955	Chi. Bears	2,388
	Philadelphia, NFC	2,388	1954	San Francisco	2,498
1991	Buffalo, AFC	2,381	1953	San Francisco	2,230
	Minnesota, NFC	2,201	1952	San Francisco	1,905
1990	Philadelphia, NFC	2,556	1951	Chi. Bears	2,408
	San Diego, AFC	2,257	1950	N.Y. Giants	2,336
1989	Cincinnati, AFC	2,483	1949	Philadelphia	2,607
	Chicago, NFC	2,287	1948	Chi. Cardinals	2,560
1988	Cincinnati, AFC	2,710	1947	Los Angeles	2,171
	San Francisco, NFC	2,523	1946	Green Bay	1,765
1987	San Francisco, NFC	2,237	1945	Cleveland	1,714
	L.A. Raiders, AFC	2,197	1944	Philadelphia	1,661
1986	Chicago, NFC	2,700	1943	Phil-Pitt	1,730
	Cincinnati, AFC	2,533	1942	Chi. Bears	1,881
1985	Chicago, NFC	2,761	1941	Chi. Bears	2,263
	Indianapolis, AFC	2,439	1940	Chi. Bears	1,818
1984	Chicago, NFC	2,974	1939	Chi. Bears	2,043
	N.Y. Jets, AFC	2,189	1938	Detroit	1,893
1983	Chicago, NFC	2,727	1937	Detroit	2,074
	Baltimore, AFC	2,695	1936	Detroit	2,885
1982	Buffalo, AFC	1,371	1935	Chi. Bears	2,096
	Dallas, NFC	1,313	1934	Chi. Bears	2,847
1981	Detroit, NFC	2,795	1933	Boston	2,260
	Kansas City, AFC	2,633	1932	Chi. Bears	1,770
1980	Los Angeles, NFC	2,799			
	Houston, AFC	2,635			
1979	N.Y. Jets, AFC	2,646			
	St. Louis, NFC	2,582			
1978	New England, AFC	3,165			
	Dallas, NFC	2,783			
1977	Chicago, NFC	2,811			
	Oakland, AFC	2,627			
1976	Pittsburgh, AFC	2,971			
	Los Angeles, NFC	2,528			

YARDS PASSING

Leadership in this category has been based on net yards since 1952.

Year	Team	Yards
2011	New Orleans, NFC	5,347
	New England, AFC	5,084
2010	Indianapolis, AFC	4,609
	New Orleans, NFC	4,441

Year	Team	Yards	Year	Team	Yards
2009	Houston, AFC	4,654	1974	Washington, NFC	2,978
	New Orleans, NFC	4,355		Cincinnati, AFC	2,804
2008	New Orleans, NFC	4,977	1973	Philadelphia, NFC	2,998
	Denver, AFC	4,471		Denver, AFC	2,519
2007	New England, AFC	4,731	1972	N.Y. Jets, AFC	2,777
	Green Bay, NFC	4,334		San Francisco, NFC	2,735
2006	New Orleans, NFC	4,503	1971	San Diego, AFC	3,134
	Indianapolis, AFC	4,308		Dallas, NFC	2,786
2005	Arizona, NFC	4,437	1970	San Francisco, NFC	2,923
	New England, AFC	4,120		Oakland, AFC	2,865
2004	Indianapolis, AFC	4,623	1969	Oakland, AFL	3,271
	Minnesota, NFC	4,516		San Francisco, NFL	3,158
2003	Indianapolis, AFC	4,179	1968	San Diego, AFL	3,623
	St. Louis, NFC	3,961		Dallas, NFL	3,026
2002	Oakland, AFC	4,475	1967	N.Y. Jets, AFL	3,845
	St. Louis, NFC	4,154		Washington, NFL	3,730
2001	St. Louis, NFC	4,663	1966	N.Y. Jets, AFL	3,464
	Indianapolis, AFC	3,989		Dallas, NFL	3,023
2000	St. Louis, NFC	5,232	1965	San Francisco, NFL	3,487
	Indianapolis, AFC	4,282		San Diego, AFL	3,103
1999	St. Louis, NFC	4,353	1964	Houston, AFL	3,527
	Indianapolis, AFC	4,066		Chicago, NFL	2,841
1998	Minnesota, NFC	4,328	1963	Baltimore, NFL	3,296
	N.Y. Jets, AFC	3,836		Houston, AFL	3,222
1997	Seattle, AFC	3,959	1962	Denver, AFL	3,404
	Green Bay, NFC	3,705		Philadelphia, NFL	3,385
1996	Jacksonville, AFC	4,110	1961	Houston, AFL	4,392
	Philadelphia, NFC	3,745		Philadelphia, NFL	3,605
1995	San Francisco, NFC	4,608	1960	Houston, AFL	3,203
	Miami, AFC	4,210		Baltimore, NFL	2,956
1994	New England, AFC	4,444	1959	Baltimore	2,753
	Minnesota, NFC	4,324	1958	Pittsburgh	2,752
1993	Miami, AFC	4,353	1957	Baltimore	2,388
	San Francisco, NFC	4,302	1956	Los Angeles	2,419
1992	Houston, AFC	4,029	1955	Philadelphia	2,472
	San Francisco, NFC	3,880	1954	Chi. Bears	3,104
1991	Houston, AFC	4,621	1953	Philadelphia	3,089
	San Francisco, NFC	3,997	1952	Cleveland	2,566
1990	Houston, AFC	4,805	1951	Los Angeles	3,296
	San Francisco, NFC	4,177	1950	Los Angeles	3,709
1989	Washington, NFC	4,349	1949	Chi. Bears	3,055
	Miami, AFC	4,216	1948	Washington	2,861
1988	Miami, AFC	4,516	1947	Washington	3,336
	Washington, NFC	4,136	1946	Los Angeles	2,080
1987	Miami, AFC	3,876	1945	Chi. Bears	1,857
	San Francisco, NFC	3,750	1944	Washington	2,021
1986	Miami, AFC	4,779	1943	Chi. Bears	2,310
	San Francisco, NFC	4,096	1942	Green Bay	2,407
1985	San Diego, AFC	4,870	1941	Chi. Bears	2,002
	Dallas, NFC	3,861	1940	Washington	1,887
1984	Miami, AFC	5,018	1939	Chi. Bears	1,965
	St. Louis, NFC	4,257	1938	Washington	1,536
1983	San Diego, AFC	4,661	1937	Green Bay	1,398
	Green Bay, NFC	4,365	1936	Green Bay	1,629
1982	San Diego, AFC	2,927	1935	Green Bay	1,449
	San Francisco, NFC	2,502	1934	Green Bay	1,165
1981	San Diego, AFC	4,739	1933	N.Y. Giants	1,348
	Minnesota, NFC	4,333	1932	Chi. Bears	1,013
1980	San Diego, AFC	4,531			
	Minnesota, NFC	3,688		**FEWEST POINTS ALLOWED**	
1979	San Diego, AFC	3,915	Year	Team	Points
	San Francisco, NFC	3,641	2011	Pittsburgh, AFC	227
1978	San Diego, AFC	3,375		San Francisco, NFC	229
	Minnesota, NFC	3,243	2010	Pittsburgh, AFC	232
1977	Buffalo, AFC	2,530		Green Bay, NFC	240
	St. Louis, NFC	2,499	2009	N.Y. Jets, AFC	236
1976	Baltimore, AFC	2,933		Dallas, NFC	250
	Minnesota, NFC	2,855	2008	Pittsburgh, AFC	223
1975	Cincinnati, AFC	3,241		Philadelphia, NFC	289
	Washington, NFC	2,917			

Year	Team	Yards
2007	Indianapolis, AFC	262
	Tampa Bay, NFC	270
2006	Baltimore, AFC	201
	Chicago, NFC	255
2005	Chicago, NFC	202
	Indianapolis, AFC	247
2004	Pittsburgh, AFC	251
	Philadelphia, NFC	260
2003	New England, AFC	238
	Dallas, NFC	260
2002	Tampa Bay, NFC	196
	Miami, AFC	301
2001	Chicago, NFC	203
	Pittsburgh, AFC	212
2000	Baltimore, AFC	165
	Philadelphia, NFC	245
1999	Jacksonville, AFC	217
	Tampa Bay, NFC	235
1998	Miami, AFC	265
	Dallas, NFC	275
1997	Kansas City, AFC	232
	Tampa Bay, NFC	263
1996	Green Bay, NFC	210
	Pittsburgh, AFC	257
1995	Kansas City, AFC	241
	San Francisco, NFC	258
1994	Cleveland, AFC	204
	Dallas, NFC	248
1993	N.Y. Giants, NFC	205
	Houston, AFC	238
1992	New Orleans, NFC	202
	Pittsburgh, AFC	225
1991	New Orleans, NFC	211
	Denver, AFC	235
1990	N.Y. Giants, NFC	211
	Pittsburgh, AFC	240
1989	Denver, AFC	226
	N.Y. Giants, NFC	252
1988	Chicago, NFC	215
	Buffalo, AFC	237
1987	Indianapolis, AFC	238
	San Francisco, NFC	253
1986	Chicago, NFC	187
	Seattle, AFC	293
1985	Chicago, NFC	198
	N.Y. Jets, AFC	264
1984	San Francisco, NFC	227
	Denver, AFC	241
1983	Miami, AFC	250
	Detroit, NFC	286
1982	Washington, NFC	128
	Miami, AFC	131
1981	Philadelphia, NFC	221
	Miami, AFC	275
1980	Philadelphia, NFC	222
	Houston, AFC	251
1979	Tampa Bay, NFC	237
	San Diego, AFC	246
1978	Pittsburgh, AFC	195
	Dallas, NFC	208
1977	Atlanta, NFC	129
	Denver, AFC	148
1976	Pittsburgh, AFC	138
	Minnesota, NFC	176
1975	Los Angeles, NFC	135
	Pittsburgh, AFC	162
1974	Los Angeles, NFC	181
	Pittsburgh, AFC	189
1973	Miami, AFC	150
	Minnesota, NFC	168

Year	Team	Points
1972	Miami, AFC	171
	Washington, NFC	218
1971	Minnesota, NFC	139
	Baltimore, AFC	140
1970	Minnesota, NFC	143
	Miami, AFC	228
1969	Minnesota, NFL	133
	Kansas City, AFL	177
1968	Baltimore, NFL	144
	Kansas City, AFL	170
1967	Los Angeles, NFL	196
	Houston, AFL	199
1966	Green Bay, NFL	163
	Buffalo, AFL	255
1965	Green Bay, NFL	224
	Buffalo, AFL	226
1964	Baltimore, NFL	225
	Buffalo, AFL	242
1963	Chicago, NFL	144
	San Diego, AFL	255
1962	Green Bay, NFL	148
	Dall. Texans, AFL	233
1961	San Diego, AFL	219
	N.Y. Giants, NFL	220
1960	San Francisco, NFL	205
	Dall. Texans, AFL	253
1959	N.Y. Giants	170
1958	N.Y. Giants	183
1957	Cleveland	172
1956	Cleveland	177
1955	Cleveland	218
1954	Cleveland	162
1953	Cleveland	162
1952	Detroit	192
1951	Cleveland	152
1950	Philadelphia	141
1949	Philadelphia	134
1948	Chi. Bears	151
1947	Green Bay	210
1946	Pittsburgh	117
1945	Washington	121
1944	N.Y. Giants	75
1943	Washington	137
1942	Chi. Bears	84
1941	N.Y. Giants	114
1940	Brooklyn	120
1939	N.Y. Giants	85
1938	N.Y. Giants	79
1937	Chi. Bears	100
1936	Chi. Bears	94
1935	Green Bay	96
	N.Y. Giants	96
1934	Detroit	59
1933	Brooklyn	54
1932	Chi. Bears	44

FEWEST TOTAL YARDS ALLOWED

Year	Team	Yards
2011	Pittsburgh, AFC	4,348
	San Francisco, NFC	4,931
2010	San Diego, AFC	4,345
	New Orleans, NFC	4,900
2009	N.Y. Jets, AFC	4,037
	Green Bay, NFC	4,551
2008	Pittsburgh, AFC	3,795
	Philadelphia, NFC	4,389
2007	Pittsburgh, AFC	4,262
	Tampa Bay, NFC	4,454
2006	Baltimore, AFC	4,225
	Chicago, NFC	4,706

Year	Team	Yards
2005	Tampa Bay, NFC	4,444
	Pittsburgh, AFC	4,544
2004	Pittsburgh, AFC	4,134
	Washington, NFC	4,281
2003	Dallas, NFC	4,056
	Buffalo, AFC	4,313
2002	Tampa Bay, NFC	4,044
	Miami, AFC	4,656
2001	Pittsburgh, AFC	4,137
	St. Louis, NFC	4,471
2000	Tennessee, AFC	3,813
	Washington, NFC	4,474
1999	Buffalo, AFC	4,045
	Tampa Bay, NFC	4,280
1998	San Diego, AFC	4,208
	Tampa Bay, NFC	4,345
1997	San Francisco, NFC	4,013
	Denver, AFC	4,671
1996	Green Bay, NFC	4,156
	Pittsburgh, AFC	4,362
1995	San Francisco, NFC	4,398
	Kansas City, AFC	4,549
1994	Dallas, NFC	4,313
	Pittsburgh, AFC	4,326
1993	Minnesota, NFC	4,406
	Pittsburgh, AFC	4,531
1992	Dallas, NFC	3,931
	Houston, AFC	4,211
1991	Philadelphia, NFC	3,549
	Denver, AFC	4,549
1990	Pittsburgh, AFC	4,115
	N.Y. Giants, NFC	4,206
1989	Minnesota, NFC	4,184
	Kansas City, AFC	4,293
1988	Minnesota, NFC	4,091
	Buffalo, AFC	4,578
1987	San Francisco, NFC	4,095
	Cleveland, AFC	4,264
1986	Chicago, NFC	4,130
	L.A. Raiders, AFC	4,804
1985	Chicago, NFC	4,135
	L.A. Raiders, AFC	4,603
1984	Chicago, NFC	3,863
	Cleveland, AFC	4,641
1983	Cincinnati, AFC	4,327
	New Orleans, NFC	4,691
1982	Miami, AFC	2,312
	Tampa Bay, NFC	2,442
1981	Philadelphia, NFC	4,447
	N.Y. Jets, AFC	4,871
1980	Buffalo, AFC	4,101
	Philadelphia, NFC	4,443
1979	Tampa Bay, NFC	3,949
	Pittsburgh, AFC	4,270
1978	Los Angeles, NFC	3,893
	Pittsburgh, AFC	4,168
1977	Dallas, NFC	3,213
	New England, AFC	3,638
1976	Pittsburgh, AFC	3,323
	San Francisco, NFC	3,562
1975	Minnesota, NFC	3,153
	Oakland, AFC	3,629
1974	Pittsburgh, AFC	3,074
	Washington, NFC	3,285
1973	Los Angeles, NFC	2,951
	Oakland, AFC	3,160
1972	Miami, AFC	3,297
	Green Bay, NFC	3,474
1971	Baltimore, AFC	2,852
	Minnesota, NFC	3,406

Year	Team	Yards
1970	Minnesota, NFC	2,803
	N.Y. Jets, AFC	3,655
1969	Minnesota, NFL	2,720
	Kansas City, AFL	3,163
1968	Los Angeles, NFL	3,118
	N.Y. Jets, AFL	3,363
1967	Oakland, AFL	3,294
	Green Bay, NFL	3,300
1966	St. Louis, NFL	3,492
	Oakland, AFL	3,910
1965	San Diego, AFL	3,262
	Detroit, NFL	3,557
1964	Green Bay, NFL	3,179
	Buffalo, AFL	3,878
1963	Chicago, NFL	3,176
	Boston, AFL	3,834
1962	Detroit, NFL	3,217
	Dall. Texans, AFL	3,951
1961	San Diego, AFL	3,726
	Baltimore, NFL	3,782
1960	St. Louis, NFL	3,029
	Buffalo, AFL	3,866
1959	N.Y. Giants	2,843
1958	Chi. Bears	3,066
1957	Pittsburgh	2,791
1956	N.Y. Giants	3,081
1955	Cleveland	2,841
1954	Cleveland	2,658
1953	Philadelphia	2,998
1952	Cleveland	3,075
1951	N.Y. Giants	3,250
1950	Cleveland	3,154
1949	Philadelphia	2,831
1948	Chi. Bears	2,931
1947	Green Bay	3,396
1946	Washington	2,451
1945	Philadelphia	2,073
1944	Philadelphia	1,943
1943	Chi. Bears	2,262
1942	Chi. Bears	1,703
1941	N.Y. Giants	2,368
1940	N.Y. Giants	2,219
1939	Washington	2,116
1938	N.Y. Giants	2,029
1937	Washington	2,123
1936	Boston	2,181
1935	Boston	1,996
1934	Chi. Cardinals	1,539
1933	Brooklyn	1,789

FEWEST RUSHING YARDS ALLOWED

Year	Team	Yards
2011	San Francisco, NFC	1,236
	Baltimore, AFC	1,482
2010	Pittsburgh, AFC	1,004
	Chicago, NFC	1,441
2009	Green Bay, NFC	1,333
	Pittsburgh, AFC	1,438
2008	Minnesota, NFC	1,230
	Pittsburgh, AFC	1,284
2007	Minnesota, NFC	1,185
	Baltimore, AFC	1,268
2006	Minnesota, NFC	985
	Baltimore, AFC	1,214
2005	San Diego, AFC	1,349
	Carolina, NFC	1,465
2004	Pittsburgh, AFC	1,299
	Washington, NFC	1,304
2003	Tennessee, AFC	1,295
	Dallas, NFC	1,425

YEARLY STATISTICAL LEADERS

Year	Team	Yards
2002	Pittsburgh, AFC	1,375
	Tampa Bay, NFC	1,554
2001	Pittsburgh, AFC	1,195
	Chicago, NFC	1,313
2000	Baltimore, AFC	970
	N.Y. Giants, NFC	1,156
1999	St. Louis, NFC	1,189
	Baltimore, AFC	1,231
1998	San Diego, AFC	1,140
	Atlanta, NFC	1,203
1997	Pittsburgh, AFC	1,318
	San Francisco, NFC	1,366
1996	Denver, AFC	1,331
	Green Bay, NFC	1,416
1995	San Francisco, NFC	1,061
	Pittsburgh, AFC	1,321
1994	Minnesota, NFC	1,090
	San Diego, AFC	1,404
1993	Houston, AFC	1,273
	Minnesota, NFC	1,536
1992	Dallas, NFC	1,244
	Buffalo, AFC	1,395
	San Diego, AFC	1,395
1991	Philadelphia, NFC	1,136
	N.Y. Jets, AFC	1,442
1990	Philadelphia, NFC	1,169
	San Diego, AFC	1,515
1989	New Orleans, NFC	1,326
	Denver, AFC	1,580
1988	Chicago, NFC	1,326
	Houston, AFC	1,592
1987	Chicago, NFC	1,413
	Cleveland, AFC	1,433
1986	N.Y. Giants, NFC	1,284
	Denver, AFC	1,651
1985	Chicago, NFC	1,319
	N.Y. Jets, AFC	1,516
1984	Chicago, NFC	1,377
	Pittsburgh, AFC	1,617
1983	Washington, NFC	1,289
	Cincinnati, AFC	1,499
1982	Pittsburgh, AFC	762
	Detroit, NFC	854
1981	Detroit, NFC	1,623
	Kansas City, AFC	1,747
1980	Detroit, NFC	1,599
	Cincinnati, AFC	1,680
1979	Denver, AFC	1,693
	Tampa Bay, NFC	1,873
1978	Dallas, NFC	1,721
	Pittsburgh, AFC	1,774
1977	Denver, AFC	1,531
	Dallas, NFC	1,651
1976	Pittsburgh, AFC	1,457
	Los Angeles, NFC	1,564
1975	Minnesota, NFC	1,532
	Houston, AFC	1,680
1974	Los Angeles, NFC	1,302
	New England, AFC	1,587
1973	Los Angeles, NFC	1,270
	Oakland, AFC	1,470
1972	Dallas, NFC	1,515
	Miami, AFC	1,548
1971	Baltimore, AFC	1,113
	Dallas, NFC	1,144
1970	Detroit, NFC	1,152
	N.Y. Jets, AFC	1,283
1969	Dallas, NFL	1,050
	Kansas City, AFL	1,091

Year	Team	Yards
1968	Dallas, NFL	1,195
	N.Y. Jets, AFL	1,195
1967	Dallas, NFL	1,081
	Oakland, AFL	1,129
1966	Buffalo, AFL	1,051
	Dallas, NFL	1,176
1965	San Diego, AFL	1,094
	Los Angeles, NFL	1,409
1964	Buffalo, AFL	913
	Los Angeles, NFL	1,501
1963	Boston, AFL	1,107
	Chicago, NFL	1,442
1962	Detroit, NFL	1,231
	Dall. Texans, AFL	1,250
1961	Boston, AFL	1,041
	Pittsburgh, NFL	1,463
1960	St. Louis, NFL	1,212
	Dall. Texans, AFL	1,338
1959	N.Y. Giants	1,261
1958	Baltimore	1,291
1957	Baltimore	1,174
1956	N.Y. Giants	1,443
1955	Cleveland	1,189
1954	Cleveland	1,050
1953	Philadelphia	1,117
1952	Detroit	1,145
1951	N.Y. Giants	913
1950	Detroit	1,367
1949	Chi. Bears	1,196
1948	Philadelphia	1,209
1947	Philadelphia	1,329
1946	Chi. Bears	1,060
1945	Philadelphia	817
1944	Philadelphia	558
1943	Phil-Pitt	793
1942	Chi. Bears	519
1941	Washington	1,042
1940	N.Y. Giants	977
1939	Chi. Bears	812
1938	Detroit	1,081
1937	Chi. Bears	933
1936	Boston	1,148
1935	Boston	998
1934	Chi. Cardinals	954
1933	Brooklyn	964

FEWEST PASSING YARDS ALLOWED

Leadership in this category has been based on net yards since 1952.

Year	Team	Yards
2011	Pittsburgh, AFC	2,751
	St. Louis, NFC	3,301
2010	San Diego, AFC	2,845
	New Orleans, NFC	3,103
2009	N.Y. Jets, AFC	2,459
	Carolina, NFC	3,056
2008	Pittsburgh, AFC	2,511
	Philadelphia, NFC	2,913
2007	Tampa Bay, NFC	2,728
	Indianapolis, AFC	2,764
2006	Oakland, AFC	2,413
	New Orleans, NFC	2,854
2005	Green Bay, NFC	2,680
	N.Y. Jets, AFC	2,755
2004	Tampa Bay, NFC	2,579
	Miami, AFC	2,592
2003	Dallas, NFC	2,631
	Buffalo, AFC	2,707
2002	Tampa Bay, NFC	2,490
	Indianapolis, AFC	2,917

Year	Team	Yards	Year	Team	Yards
2001	Miami, AFC	2,829	1966	Green Bay, NFL	1,959
	Philadelphia, NFC	2,864		Oakland, AFL	2,118
2000	Tennessee, AFC	2,423	1965	Green Bay, NFL	1,981
	Washington, NFC	2,621		San Diego, AFL	2,168
1999	Buffalo, AFC	2,675	1964	Green Bay, NFL	1,647
	Tampa Bay, NFC	2,873		San Diego, AFL	2,518
1998	Philadelphia, NFC	2,720	1963	Chicago, NFL	1,734
	Oakland, AFC	2,876		Oakland, AFL	2,589
1997	Dallas, NFC	2,522	1962	Green Bay, NFL	1,746
	Indianapolis, AFC	2,820		Oakland, AFL	2,306
1996	Green Bay, NFC	2,740	1961	Baltimore, NFL	1,913
	Pittsburgh, AFC	2,947		San Diego, AFL	2,363
1995	N.Y. Jets, AFC	2,740	1960	Chicago, NFL	1,388
	Philadelphia, NFC	2,816		Buffalo, AFL	2,124
1994	Dallas, NFC	2,752	1959	N.Y. Giants	1,582
	Houston, AFC	2,795	1958	Chi. Bears	1,769
1993	New Orleans, NFC	2,606	1957	Cleveland	1,300
	Cincinnati, AFC	2,798	1956	Cleveland	1,103
1992	New Orleans, NFC	2,470	1955	Pittsburgh	1,295
	Kansas City, AFC	2,537	1954	Cleveland	1,608
1991	Philadelphia, NFC	2,413	1953	Washington	1,751
	Denver, AFC	2,755	1952	Washington	1,580
1990	Pittsburgh, AFC	2,500	1951	Pittsburgh	1,687
	Dallas, NFC	2,639	1950	Cleveland	1,581
1989	Minnesota, NFC	2,501	1949	Philadelphia	1,607
	Kansas City, AFC	2,527	1948	Green Bay	1,626
1988	Kansas City, AFC	2,434	1947	Green Bay	1,790
	Minnesota, NFC	2,489	1946	Pittsburgh	939
1987	San Francisco, NFC	2,484	1945	Washington	1,121
	L.A. Raiders, AFC	2,727	1944	Chi. Bears	1,052
1986	St. Louis, NFC	2,637	1943	Chi. Bears	980
	New England, AFC	2,978	1942	Washington	1,093
1985	Washington, NFC	2,746	1941	Pittsburgh	1,168
	Pittsburgh, AFC	2,783	1940	Philadelphia	1,012
1984	New Orleans, NFC	2,453	1939	Washington	1,116
	Cleveland, AFC	2,696	1938	Chi. Bears	897
1983	New Orleans, NFC	2,691	1937	Detroit	804
	Cincinnati, AFC	2,828	1936	Philadelphia	853
1982	Miami, AFC	1,027	1935	Chi. Cardinals	793
	Tampa Bay, NFC	1,384	1934	Philadelphia	545
1981	Philadelphia, NFC	2,696	1933	Portsmouth	558
	Buffalo, AFC	2,870			
1980	Washington, NFC	2,171			
	Buffalo, AFC	2,282			
1979	Tampa Bay, NFC	2,076			
	Buffalo, AFC	2,530			
1978	Buffalo, AFC	1,960			
	Los Angeles, NFC	2,048			
1977	Atlanta, NFC	1,384			
	San Diego, AFC	1,725			
1976	Minnesota, NFC	1,575			
	Cincinnati, AFC	1,758			
1975	Minnesota, NFC	1,621			
	Cincinnati, AFC	1,729			
1974	Pittsburgh, AFC	1,466			
	Atlanta, NFC	1,572			
1973	Miami, AFC	1,290			
	Atlanta, NFC	1,430			
1972	Minnesota, NFC	1,699			
	Cleveland, AFC	1,736			
1971	Atlanta, NFC	1,638			
	Baltimore, AFC	1,739			
1970	Minnesota, NFC	1,438			
	Kansas City, AFC	2,010			
1969	Minnesota, NFL	1,631			
	Kansas City, AFL	2,072			
1968	Houston, AFL	1,671			
	Green Bay, NFL	1,796			
1967	Green Bay, NFL	1,377			
	Buffalo, AFL	1,825			

Compiled by Elias Sports Bureau

Super Bowl I, 1/15/67	Super Bowl XXIV, 1/28/90
Super Bowl II, 1/14/68	Super Bowl XXV, 1/27/91
Super Bowl III, 1/12/69	Super Bowl XXVI, 1/26/92
Super Bowl IV, 1/11/70	Super Bowl XXVII, 1/31/93
Super Bowl V, 1/17/71	Super Bowl XXVIII, 1/30/94
Super Bowl VI, 1/16/72	Super Bowl XXIX, 1/29/95
Super Bowl VII, 1/14/73	Super Bowl XXX, 1/28/96
Super Bowl VIII, 1/13/74	Super Bowl XXXI, 1/26/97
Super Bowl IX, 1/12/75	Super Bowl XXXII, 1/25/98
Super Bowl X, 1/18/76	Super Bowl XXXIII, 1/31/99
Super Bowl XI, 1/9/77	Super Bowl XXXIV, 1/30/00
Super Bowl XII, 1/15/78	Super Bowl XXXV, 1/28/01
Super Bowl XIII, 1/21/79	Super Bowl XXXVI, 2/3/02
Super Bowl XIV, 1/20/80	Super Bowl XXXVII, 1/26/03
Super Bowl XV, 1/25/81	Super Bowl XXXVIII, 2/1/04
Super Bowl XVI, 1/24/82	Super Bowl XXXIX, 2/6/05
Super Bowl XVII, 1/30/83	Super Bowl XL, 2/5/06
Super Bowl XVIII, 1/22/84	Super Bowl XLI, 2/4/07
Super Bowl XIX, 1/20/85	Super Bowl XLII, 2/3/08
Super Bowl XX, 1/26/86	Super Bowl XLIII, 2/1/09
Super Bowl XXI, 1/25/87	Super Bowl XLIV, 2/7/10
Super Bowl XXII, 1/31/88	Super Bowl XLV, 2/6/11
Super Bowl XXIII, 1/22/89	Super Bowl XLVI, 2/5/12

INDIVIDUAL RECORDS

SERVICE
Most Games
- 6   Mike Lodish, Buffalo, XXV-XXVIII; Denver, XXXII-XXXIII
- 5   Marv Fleming, Green Bay, I-II; Miami, VI-VIII
  - Larry Cole, Dallas, V-VI, X, XII-XIII
  - Cliff Harris, Dallas, V-VI, X, XII-XIII
  - Charles Haley, San Francisco, XXIII-XXIV; Dallas, XXVII-XXVIII, XXX
  - D.D. Lewis, Dallas, V-VI, X, XII-XIII
  - Preston Pearson, Baltimore, III; Pittsburgh, IX; Dallas, X, XII-XIII
  - Charlie Waters, Dallas, V-VI, X, XII-XIII
  - Rayfield Wright, Dallas, V-VI, X, XII-XIII
  - Cornelius Bennett, Buffalo, XXV-XXVIII; Atlanta, XXXIII
  - John Elway, Denver, XXI-XXII, XXIV, XXXII-XXXIII
  - Glenn Parker, Buffalo, XXV-XXVIII; N.Y. Giants, XXXV
  - Bill Romanowski, San Francisco, XXIII-XXIV; Denver, XXXII-XXXIII; Oakland, XXXVII
  - Adam Vinatieri, New England, XXXI, XXXVI, XXXVIII, XXXIX; Indianapolis, XLI
  - Tedy Bruschi, New England, XXXI, XXXVI, XXXVIII-XXXIX, XLII
  - Tom Brady, New England, XXXVI, XXXVIII-XXXIX, XLII, XLVI
  - Matt Light, New England, XXXVI, XXXVIII-XXXIX, XLII, XLVI
- 4   By many players

Most Games, Winning Team
- 5   Charles Haley, San Francisco, XXIII-XXIV; Dallas, XXVII-XXVIII, XXX
- 4   By many players

Most Games, Coach
- 6   Don Shula, Baltimore, III; Miami, VI-VIII, XVII, XIX
- 5   Tom Landry, Dallas, V-VI, X, XII-XIII
  - Bill Belichick, New England, XXXVI, XXXVIII-XXXIX, XLII, XLVI
- 4   Bud Grant, Minnesota, IV, VIII-IX, XI
  - Chuck Noll, Pittsburgh, IX-X, XIII-XIV
  - Joe Gibbs, Washington, XVII-XVIII, XXII, XXVI
  - Marv Levy, Buffalo, XXV-XXVIII
  - Dan Reeves, Denver, XXI-XXII, XXIV; Atlanta, XXXIII

Most Games, Winning Team, Coach
- 4   Chuck Noll, Pittsburgh, IX-X, XIII-XIV
- 3   Bill Walsh, San Francisco, XVI, XIX, XXIII

Joe Gibbs, Washington, XVII, XXII, XXVI
Bill Belichick, New England, XXXVI, XXXVIII-XXXIX
- 2   Vince Lombardi, Green Bay, I-II
  - Tom Landry, Dallas, VI, XII
  - Don Shula, Miami, VII-VIII
  - Tom Flores, Oakland, XV; L.A. Raiders, XVIII
  - Bill Parcells, N.Y. Giants, XXI, XXV
  - Jimmy Johnson, Dallas, XXVII-XXVIII
  - George Seifert, San Francisco, XXIV, XXIX
  - Mike Shanahan, Denver, XXXII-XXXIII
  - Tom Coughlin, N.Y. Giants, XLII, XLVI

Most Games, Losing Team, Coach
- 4   Bud Grant, Minnesota, IV, VIII-IX, XI
  - Don Shula, Baltimore, III; Miami, VI, XVII, XIX
  - Marv Levy, Buffalo, XXV-XXVIII
  - Dan Reeves, Denver, XXI-XXII, XXIV; Atlanta, XXXIII
- 3   Tom Landry, Dallas, V, X, XIII

SCORING
POINTS
Most Points, Career
- 48   Jerry Rice, San Francisco-Oakland, 4 games (8-td)
- 34   Adam Vinatieri, New England-Indianapolis, 5 games (7-fg, 13-xp)
- 30   Emmitt Smith, Dallas, 3 games (5-td)

Most Points, Game
- 18   Roger Craig, San Francisco vs. Miami, XIX (3-td)
  - Jerry Rice, San Francisco vs. Denver, XXIV (3-td); vs. San Diego, XXIX (3-td)
  - Ricky Watters, San Francisco vs. San Diego, XXIX (3-td)
  - Terrell Davis, Denver vs. Green Bay, XXXII (3-td)
- 15   Don Chandler, Green Bay vs. Oakland, II (3-pat, 4-fg)
- 14   Ray Wersching, San Francisco vs. Cincinnati, XVI (2-pat, 4-fg)
  - Kevin Butler, Chicago vs. New England, XX (5-pat, 3-fg)

TOUCHDOWNS
Most Touchdowns, Career
- 8   Jerry Rice, San Francisco-Oakland, 4 games (8-p)
- 5   Emmitt Smith, Dallas, 3 games (5-r)
- 4   Franco Harris, Pittsburgh, 4 games (4-r)
  - Roger Craig, San Francisco, 3 games (2-r, 2-p)
  - Thurman Thomas, Buffalo, 4 games (4-r)
  - John Elway, Denver, 5 games (4-r)

Most Touchdowns, Game
- 3   Roger Craig, San Francisco vs. Miami, XIX (1-r, 2-p)
  - Jerry Rice, San Francisco vs. Denver, XXIV (3-p); vs. San Diego, XXIX (3-p)
  - Ricky Watters, San Francisco vs. San Diego, XXIX (1-r, 2-p)
  - Terrell Davis, Denver vs. Green Bay, XXXII (3-r)
- 2   Max McGee, Green Bay vs. Kansas City, I (2-p)
  - Elijah Pitts, Green Bay vs. Kansas City, I (2-r)
  - Bill Miller, Oakland vs. Green Bay, II (2-p)
  - Larry Csonka, Miami vs. Minnesota, VIII (2-r)
  - Pete Banaszak, Oakland vs. Minnesota, XI (2-r)
  - John Stallworth, Pittsburgh vs. Dallas, XIII (2-p)
  - Franco Harris, Pittsburgh vs. Los Angeles, XIV (2-r)
  - Cliff Branch, Oakland vs. Philadelphia, XV (2-p)
  - Dan Ross, Cincinnati vs. San Francisco, XVI (2-p)
  - Marcus Allen, L.A. Raiders vs. Washington, XVIII (2-r)
  - Jim McMahon, Chicago vs. New England, XX (2-r)
  - Ricky Sanders, Washington vs. Denver, XXII (2-p)
  - Timmy Smith, Washington vs. Denver, XXII (2-r)
  - Tom Rathman, San Francisco vs. Denver, XXIV (2-r)
  - Gerald Riggs, Washington vs. Buffalo, XXVI (2-r)
  - Michael Irvin, Dallas vs. Buffalo, XXVII (2-p)
  - Emmitt Smith, Dallas vs. Buffalo, XXVIII (2-r)
  - Emmitt Smith, Dallas vs. Pittsburgh, XXX (2-r)
  - Antonio Freeman, Green Bay vs. Denver, XXXII (2-p)

Howard Griffith, Denver vs. Atlanta, XXXIII (2-r)
Eddie George, Tennessee vs. St. Louis, XXXIV (2-r)
Keenan McCardell, Tampa Bay vs. Oakland, XXXVII (2-r)
Dwight Smith, Tampa Bay vs. Oakland, XXXVII (2-ret)
Larry Fitzgerald, Arizona vs. Pittsburgh, XLIII (2-p)
Greg Jennings, Green Bay vs. Pittsburgh, XLV (2-p)

POINTS AFTER TOUCHDOWN
Most (One-Point) Points After Touchdown, Career
13 Adam Vinatieri, New England-Indianapolis, 5 games (13 att)
9   Mike Cofer, San Francisco, 2 games (10 att)
8   Don Chandler, Green Bay, 2 games (8 att)
    Roy Gerela, Pittsburgh, 3 games (9 att)
    Chris Bahr, Oakland-L.A. Raiders, 2 games (8 att)
    Jason Elam, Denver, 2 games (8 att)
Most (One-Point) Points After Touchdown, Game
7   Mike Cofer, San Francisco vs. Denver, XXIV (8 att)
    Lin Elliott, Dallas vs. Buffalo, XXVII (7 att)
    Doug Brien, San Francisco vs. San Diego, XXIX (7 att)
6   Ali Haji-Sheikh, Washington vs. Denver, XXII (6 att)
    Martín Gramatica, Tampa Bay vs. Oakland, XXXVII (6 att)
5   Don Chandler, Green Bay vs. Kansas City, I (5 att)
    Roy Gerela, Pittsburgh vs. Dallas, XIII (5 att)
    Chris Bahr, L.A. Raiders vs. Washington, XVIII (5 att)
    Ray Wersching, San Francisco vs. Miami, XIX (5 att)
    Kevin Butler, Chicago vs. New England, XX (5 att)
Most Two-Point Conversions, Game
1   Mark Seay, San Diego vs. San Francisco, XXIX
    Alfred Pupunu, San Diego vs. San Francisco, XXIX
    Mark Chmura, Green Bay vs. New England, XXXI
    Kevin Faulk, New England vs. Carolina, XXXVIII
    Lance Moore, New Orleans vs. Indianapolis, XLIV
    Antwaan Randle El, Pittsburgh vs. Green Bay, XLV

FIELD GOALS
Field Goals Attempted, Career
10 Adam Vinatieri, New England-Indianapolis, 5 games
6   Jim Turner, N.Y. Jets-Denver, 2 games
    Roy Gerela, Pittsburgh, 3 games
    Rich Karlis, Denver, 2 games
    Jeff Wilkins, St. Louis, 2 games
5   Efren Herrera, Dallas, 1 game
    Ray Wersching, San Francisco, 2 games
    Jason Elam, Denver, 2 games
    Matt Stover, Baltimore-Indianapolis, 2 games
Most Field Goals Attempted, Game
5   Jim Turner, N.Y. Jets vs. Baltimore, III
    Efren Herrera, Dallas vs. Denver, XII
4   Don Chandler, Green Bay vs. Oakland, II
    Roy Gerela, Pittsburgh vs. Dallas, X
    Ray Wersching, San Francisco vs. Cincinnati, XVI
    Rich Karlis, Denver vs. N.Y. Giants, XXI
    Mike Cofer, San Francisco vs. Cincinnati, XXIII
    Jason Elam, Denver vs. Atlanta, XXXIII
    Jeff Wilkins, St. Louis vs. Tennessee, XXXIV
    Adam Vinatieri, Indianapolis vs. Chicago, XLI
Most Field Goals, Career
7   Adam Vinatieri, New England-Indianapolis, 5 games (10 att)
5   Ray Wersching, San Francisco, 2 games (5 att)
4   Don Chandler, Green Bay, 2 games (4 att)
    Jim Turner, N.Y. Jets-Denver, 2 games (6 att)
    Uwe von Schamann, Miami, 2 games (4 att)
    Jeff Wilkins, St. Louis, 2 games (6 att)
Most Field Goals, Game
4   Don Chandler, Green Bay vs. Oakland, II
    Ray Wersching, San Francisco vs. Cincinnati, XVI
3   Jim Turner, N.Y. Jets vs. Baltimore, III
    Jan Stenerud, Kansas City vs. Minnesota, IV

Uwe von Schamann, Miami vs. San Francisco, XIX
Kevin Butler, Chicago vs. New England, XX
Jim Breech, Cincinnati vs. San Francisco, XXIII
Chip Lohmiller, Washington vs. Buffalo, XXVI
Eddie Murray, Dallas vs. Buffalo, XXVIII
Jeff Wilkins, St. Louis vs. Tennessee, XXXIV
Adam Vinatieri, Indianapolis vs. Chicago, XLI
Garrett Hartley, New Orleans vs. Indianapolis, XLIV
Longest Field Goal
54 Steve Christie, Buffalo vs. Dallas, XXVIII
51 Jason Elam, Denver vs. Green Bay, XXXII
50 Jeff Wilkins, St. Louis vs. New England, XXXVI
    John Kasay, Carolina vs. New England, XXXVIII

SAFETIES
Most Safeties, Game
1   Dwight White, Pittsburgh vs. Minnesota, IX
    Reggie Harrison, Pittsburgh vs. Dallas, X
    Henry Waechter, Chicago vs. New England, XX
    George Martin, N.Y. Giants vs. Denver, XXI
    Bruce Smith, Buffalo vs. N.Y. Giants, XXV

RUSHING
ATTEMPTS
Most Attempts, Career
101 Franco Harris, Pittsburgh, 4 games
70   Emmitt Smith, Dallas, 3 games
64   John Riggins, Washington, 2 games
Most Attempts, Game
38   John Riggins, Washington vs. Miami, XVII
34   Franco Harris, Pittsburgh vs. Minnesota, IX
33   Larry Csonka, Miami vs. Minnesota, VIII

YARDS GAINED
Most Yards Gained, Career
354 Franco Harris, Pittsburgh, 4 games
297 Larry Csonka, Miami, 3 games
289 Emmitt Smith, Dallas, 3 games
Most Yards Gained, Game
204 Timmy Smith, Washington vs. Denver, XXII
191 Marcus Allen, L.A. Raiders vs. Washington, XVIII
166 John Riggins, Washington vs. Miami, XVII
Longest Run From Scrimmage
75   Willie Parker, Pittsburgh vs. Seattle, XL (TD)
74   Marcus Allen, L.A. Raiders vs. Washington, XVIII (TD)
58   Tom Matte, Baltimore vs. N.Y. Jets, III
     Timmy Smith, Washington vs. Denver, XXII (TD)

AVERAGE GAIN
Highest Average Gain, Career (20 attempts)
9.6 Marcus Allen, L.A. Raiders, 1 game (20-191)
9.3 Timmy Smith, Washington, 1 game (22-204)
5.4 Dominic Rhodes, Indianapolis, 1 game (21-113)
Highest Average Gain, Game (10 attempts)
10.5 Tom Matte, Baltimore vs. N.Y. Jets, III (11-116)
9.6   Marcus Allen, L.A. Raiders vs. Washington, XVIII (20-191)
9.3   Willie Parker, Pittsburgh vs. Seattle, XL (10-93)

TOUCHDOWNS
Most Touchdowns, Career
5   Emmitt Smith, Dallas, 3 games
4   Franco Harris, Pittsburgh, 4 games
    Thurman Thomas, Buffalo, 4 games
    John Elway, Denver, 5 games
3   Terrell Davis, Denver, 2 games
Most Touchdowns, Game
3   Terrell Davis, Denver vs. Green Bay, XXXII
2   Elijah Pitts, Green Bay vs. Kansas City, I
    Larry Csonka, Miami vs. Minnesota, VIII
    Pete Banaszak, Oakland vs. Minnesota, XI
    Franco Harris, Pittsburgh vs. Los Angeles, XIV

Marcus Allen, L.A. Raiders vs. Washington, XVIII
Jim McMahon, Chicago vs. New England, XX
Timmy Smith, Washington vs. Denver, XXII
Tom Rathman, San Francisco vs. Denver, XXIV
Gerald Riggs, Washington vs. Buffalo, XXVI
Emmitt Smith, Dallas vs. Buffalo, XXVIII
Emmitt Smith, Dallas vs. Pittsburgh, XXX
Howard Griffith, Denver vs. Atlanta, XXXIII
Eddie George, Tennessee vs. St. Louis, XXXIV

PASSING
PASSER RATING
Highest Passer Rating, Career (40 attempts)
127.8   Joe Montana, San Francisco, 4 games
122.8   Jim Plunkett, Oakland-L.A. Raiders, 2 games
112.8   Terry Bradshaw, Pittsburgh, 4 games

ATTEMPTS
Most Passes Attempted, Career
197   Tom Brady, New England, 5 games
152   John Elway, Denver, 5 games
145   Jim Kelly, Buffalo, 4 games
Most Passes Attempted, Game
58   Jim Kelly, Buffalo vs. Washington, XXVI
51   Donovan McNabb, Philadelphia vs. New England, XXXIX
50   Dan Marino, Miami vs. San Francisco, XIX
Jim Kelly, Buffalo vs. Dallas, XXVIII

COMPLETIONS
Most Passes Completed, Career
127   Tom Brady, New England, 5 games
83   Joe Montana, San Francisco, 4 games
Kurt Warner, St. Louis-Arizona, 3 games
81   Jim Kelly, Buffalo, 4 games
Most Passes Completed, Game
32   Tom Brady, New England vs. Carolina, XXXVIII
Drew Brees, New Orleans vs. Indianapolis, XLIV
31   Jim Kelly, Buffalo vs. Dallas, XXVIII
Kurt Warner, Arizona vs. Pittsburgh, XLIII
Peyton Manning, Indianapolis vs. New Orleans, XLIV
30   Donovan McNabb, Philadelphia vs. New England, XXXIX
Eli Manning, N.Y. Giants vs. New England, XLVI
Most Consecutive Completions, Game
16   Tom Brady, New England vs. N.Y. Giants, XLVI
13   Joe Montana, San Francisco vs. Denver, XXIV
10   Phil Simms, N.Y. Giants vs. Denver, XXI
Troy Aikman, Dallas vs. Pittsburgh, XXX
Kurt Warner, Arizona vs. Pittsburgh, XLIII
Drew Brees, New Orleans vs. Indianapolis, XLIV

COMPLETION PERCENTAGE
Highest Completion Percentage, Career (40 attempts)
70.0   Troy Aikman, Dallas, 3 games, (80-56)
68.0   Joe Montana, San Francisco, 4 games (122-83)
67.5   Peyton Manning, Indianapolis, 2 games (83-56)
Highest Completion Percentage, Game (20 attempts)
88.0   Phil Simms, N.Y. Giants vs. Denver, XXI (25-22)
82.1   Drew Brees, New Orleans vs. Indianapolis, XLIV (39-32)
75.9   Joe Montana, San Francisco vs. Denver, XXIV (29-22)

YARDS GAINED
Most Yards Gained, Career
1,277   Tom Brady, New England, 5 games
1,156   Kurt Warner, St. Louis-Arizona, 3 games
1,142   Joe Montana, San Francisco, 4 games
Most Yards Gained, Game
414   Kurt Warner, St. Louis vs. Tennessee, XXXIV
377   Kurt Warner, Arizona vs. Pittsburgh, XLIII
365   Kurt Warner, St. Louis vs. New England, XXXVI

Longest Pass Completion
85   Jake Delhomme (to Muhammad), Carolina vs. New England, XXXVIII (TD)
81   Brett Favre (to Freeman), Green Bay vs. New England, XXXI (TD)
80   Jim Plunkett (to King), Oakland vs. Philadelphia, XV (TD)
Doug Williams (to Sanders), Washington vs. Denver, XXII (TD)
John Elway (to R. Smith), Denver vs. Atlanta, XXXIII (TD)

AVERAGE GAIN
Highest Average Gain, Career (40 attempts)
11.10   Terry Bradshaw, Pittsburgh, 4 games (84-932)
9.62   Bart Starr, Green Bay, 2 games (47-452)
9.41   Jim Plunkett, Oakland-L.A. Raiders, 2 games (46-433)
Highest Average Gain, Game (20 attempts)
14.71   Terry Bradshaw, Pittsburgh vs. Los Angeles, XIV (21-309)
12.80   Jim McMahon, Chicago vs. New England, XX (20-256)
12.43   Jim Plunkett, Oakland vs. Philadelphia, XV (21-261)

TOUCHDOWNS
Most Touchdown Passes, Career
11   Joe Montana, San Francisco, 4 games
9   Terry Bradshaw, Pittsburgh, 4 games
Tom Brady, New England, 5 games
8   Roger Staubach, Dallas, 4 games
Most Touchdown Passes, Game
6   Steve Young, San Francisco vs. San Diego, XXIX
5   Joe Montana, San Francisco vs. Denver, XXIV
4   Terry Bradshaw, Pittsburgh vs. Dallas, XIII
Doug Williams, Washington vs. Denver, XXII
Troy Aikman, Dallas vs. Buffalo, XXVII

HAD INTERCEPTED
Lowest Percentage, Passes Had Intercepted, Career (40 attempts)
0.00   Jim Plunkett, Oakland-L.A. Raiders, 2 games (46-0)
Joe Montana, San Francisco, 4 games (122-0)
1.02   Tom Brady, New England, 5 games (197-2)
1.25   Troy Aikman, Dallas, 3 games (80-1)
Most Attempts, Without Interception, Game
48   Tom Brady, New England vs. N.Y. Giants, XLII
45   Kurt Warner, St. Louis vs. Tennessee, XXXIV
40   Eli Manning, N.Y. Giants vs. New England, XLVI
Most Passes Had Intercepted, Career
8   John Elway, Denver, 5 games
7   Craig Morton, Dallas-Denver, 2 games
Jim Kelly, Buffalo, 4 games
6   Fran Tarkenton, Minnesota, 3 games
Most Passes Had Intercepted, Game
5   Rich Gannon, Oakland vs. Tampa Bay, XXXVII
4   Craig Morton, Denver vs. Dallas, XII
Jim Kelly, Buffalo vs. Washington, XXVI
Drew Bledsoe, New England vs. Green Bay, XXXI
Kerry Collins, N.Y. Giants vs. Baltimore, XXXV
3   By 11 players

PASS RECEIVING
RECEPTIONS
Most Receptions, Career
33   Jerry Rice, San Francisco-Oakland, 4 games
27   Andre Reed, Buffalo, 4 games
24   Deion Branch, New England, 3 games
Most Receptions, Game
11   Dan Ross, Cincinnati vs. San Francisco, XVI
Jerry Rice, San Francisco vs. Cincinnati, XXIII
Deion Branch, New England vs. Philadelphia, XXXIX
Wes Welker, New England vs. N.Y. Giants, XLII
10   Tony Nathan, Miami vs. San Francisco, XIX
Jerry Rice, San Francisco vs. San Diego, XXIX

Andre Hastings, Pittsburgh vs. Dallas, XXX
Deion Branch, New England vs. Carolina, XXXVIII
Joseph Addai, Indianapolis vs. Chicago, XLI
Hakeem Nicks, N.Y. Giants vs. New England, XLVI
9 Ricky Sanders, Washington vs. Denver, XXII
Antonio Freeman, Green Bay vs. Denver, XXXII
Terrell Owens, Philadelphia vs. New England, XXXIX
Santonio Holmes, Pittsburgh vs. Arizona, XLIII
Jordy Nelson, Green Bay vs. Pittsburgh, XLV
Mike Wallace, Pittsburgh vs. Green Bay, XLV

YARDS GAINED
Most Yards Gained, Career
589 Jerry Rice, San Francisco-Oakland, 4 games
364 Lynn Swann, Pittsburgh, 4 games
323 Andre Reed, Buffalo, 4 games
Most Yards Gained, Game
215 Jerry Rice, San Francisco vs. Cincinnati, XXIII
193 Ricky Sanders, Washington vs. Denver, XXII
162 Isaac Bruce, St. Louis vs. Tennessee, XXXIV
Longest Reception
85 Muhsin Muhammad (from Delhomme), Carolina vs.
New England, XXXVIII
81 Antonio Freeman (from Favre), Green Bay vs.
New England, XXXI (TD)
80 Kenny King (from Plunkett), Oakland vs.
Philadelphia, XV (TD)
Ricky Sanders (from Williams), Washington vs.
Denver, XXII (TD)
Rod Smith (from Elway), Denver vs. Atlanta, XXXIII

AVERAGE GAIN
Highest Average Gain, Career (8 receptions)
24.4 John Stallworth, Pittsburgh, 4 games (11-268)
23.4 Ricky Sanders, Washington, 2 games (10-234)
22.8 Lynn Swann, Pittsburgh, 4 games (16-364)
Highest Average Gain, Game (3 receptions)
40.33 John Stallworth, Pittsburgh vs. Los Angeles, XIV
(3-121)
40.25 Lynn Swann, Pittsburgh vs. Dallas, X (4-161)
38.33 John Stallworth, Pittsburgh vs. Dallas, XIII (3-115)

TOUCHDOWNS
Most Touchdowns, Career
8 Jerry Rice, San Francisco-Oakland, 4 games
3 John Stallworth, Pittsburgh, 4 games
Lynn Swann, Pittsburgh, 4 games
Cliff Branch, Oakland-L.A. Raiders, 3 games
Antonio Freeman, Green Bay, 2 games
2 Max McGee, Green Bay, 2 games
Bill Miller, Oakland, 1 game
Butch Johnson, Dallas, 2 games
Dan Ross, Cincinnati, 1 game
Roger Craig, San Francisco, 3 games
Ricky Sanders, Washington, 2 games
John Taylor, San Francisco, 3 games
Gary Clark, Washington, 2 games
Don Beebe, Buffalo-Green Bay, 4 games
Michael Irvin, Dallas, 3 games
Ricky Watters, San Francisco, 1 game
Jay Novacek, Dallas, 3 games
Keenan McCardell, Tampa Bay, 1 game
Ricky Proehl, St. Louis-Carolina, 3 games
David Givens, New England, 2 games
Mike Vrabel, New England, 4 games
Muhsin Muhammad, Carolina-Chicago, 2 games
Larry Fitzgerald, Arizona, 1 game
Greg Jennings, Green Bay, 1 game
Hines Ward, Pittsburgh, 3 games
Most Touchdowns, Game
3 Jerry Rice, San Francisco vs. Denver, XXIV; vs.
San Diego, XXIX

2 Max McGee, Green Bay vs. Kansas City, I
Bill Miller, Oakland vs. Green Bay, II
John Stallworth, Pittsburgh vs. Dallas, XIII
Cliff Branch, Oakland vs. Philadelphia, XV
Dan Ross, Cincinnati vs. San Francisco, XVI
Roger Craig, San Francisco vs. Miami, XIX
Ricky Sanders, Washington vs. Denver, XXII
Michael Irvin, Dallas vs. Buffalo, XXVII
Ricky Watters, San Francisco vs. San Diego, XXIX
Antonio Freeman, Green Bay vs. Denver, XXXII
Keenan McCardell, Tampa Bay vs. Oakland, XXXVII
Larry Fitzgerald, Arizona vs. Pittsburgh, XLIII
Greg Jennings, Green Bay vs. Pittsburgh, XLV

INTERCEPTIONS BY
Most Interceptions By, Career
3 Chuck Howley, Dallas, 2 games
Rod Martin, Oakland-L.A. Raiders, 2 games
Larry Brown, Dallas, 3 games
2 Randy Beverly, N.Y. Jets, 1 game
Jake Scott, Miami, 3 games
Mike Wagner, Pittsburgh, 3 games
Mel Blount, Pittsburgh, 4 games
Eric Wright, San Francisco, 4 games
Barry Wilburn, Washington, 1 game
Brad Edwards, Washington, 1 game
Thomas Everett, Dallas, 2 games
James Washington, Dallas, 2 games
Darrien Gordon, San Diego-Denver-Oakland,
4 games
Dexter Jackson, Tampa Bay, 1 game
Dwight Smith, Tampa Bay, 1 game
Rodney Harrison, San Diego-New England, 4 games
Most Interceptions By, Game
3 Rod Martin, Oakland vs. Philadelphia, XV
2 Randy Beverly, N.Y. Jets vs. Baltimore, III
Chuck Howley, Dallas vs. Baltimore, V
Jake Scott, Miami vs. Washington, VII
Barry Wilburn, Washington vs. Denver, XXII
Brad Edwards, Washington vs. Buffalo, XXVI
Thomas Everett, Dallas vs. Buffalo, XXVII
Larry Brown, Dallas vs. Pittsburgh, XXX
Darrien Gordon, Denver vs. Atlanta, XXXIII
Dexter Jackson, Tampa Bay vs. Oakland, XXXVII
Dwight Smith, Tampa Bay vs. Oakland, XXXVII
Rodney Harrison, New England vs. Philadelphia,
XXXIX

YARDS GAINED
Most Yards Gained, Career
108 Darrien Gordon, San Diego-Denver-Oakland,
4 games
100 James Harrison, Pittsburgh, 2 games
94 Dwight Smith, Tampa Bay, 1 game
Most Yards Gained, Game
108 Darrien Gordon, Denver vs. Atlanta, XXXIII
100 James Harrison, Pittsburgh vs. Arizona, XLIII
94 Dwight Smith, Tampa Bay vs. Oakland, XXXVII
Longest Return
100 James Harrison, Pittsburgh vs. Arizona, XLIII (TD)
76 Kelly Herndon, Seattle vs. Pittsburgh, XL
75 Willie Brown, Oakland vs. Minnesota, XI (TD)

TOUCHDOWNS
Most Touchdowns, Game
2 Dwight Smith, Tampa Bay vs. Oakland, XXXVII
1 Herb Adderley, Green Bay vs. Oakland, II
Willie Brown, Oakland vs. Minnesota, XI
Jack Squirek, L.A. Raiders vs. Washington, XVIII
Reggie Phillips, Chicago vs. New England, XX
Duane Starks, Baltimore vs. N.Y. Giants, XXXV
Ty Law, New England vs. St. Louis, XXXVI

Derrick Brooks, Tampa Bay vs. Oakland, XXXVII
Kelvin Hayden, Indianapolis vs. Chicago, XLI
James Harrison, Pittsburgh vs. Arizona, XLIII
Tracy Porter, New Orleans vs. Indianapolis, XLIV
Nick Collins, Green Bay vs. Pittsburgh, XLV

PUNTING
Most Punts, Career
17 Mike Eischeid, Oakland-Minnesota, 3 games
Mike Horan, Denver-St. Louis, 4 games
16 Brad Maynard, N.Y. Giants-Chicago, 2 games
15 Larry Seiple, Miami, 3 games
Most Punts, Game
11 Brad Maynard, N.Y. Giants vs. Baltimore, XXXV
10 Kyle Richardson, Baltimore vs. N.Y. Giants, XXXV
9 Ron Widby, Dallas vs. Baltimore, V
Longest Punt
63 Lee Johnson, Cincinnati vs. San Francisco, XXIII
62 Rich Camarillo, New England vs. Chicago, XX
61 Jerrel Wilson, Kansas City vs. Green Bay, I

AVERAGE YARDAGE
Highest Average, Punting, Career (10 punts)
46.5 Jerrel Wilson, Kansas City, 2 games (11-511)
43.8 Tom Rouen, Denver-Seattle, 3 games (11-482)
43.0 Kyle Richardson, Baltimore, 1 game (10-430)
Tom Tupa, New England-Tampa Bay, 2 games
(12-516)
Highest Average, Punting, Game (4 punts)
50.2 Tom Rouen, Seattle vs. Pittsburgh, XL (6-301)
48.8 Bryan Wagner, San Diego vs. San Francisco, XXIX
(4-195)
48.7 Chris Gardocki, Pittsburgh vs. Seattle, XL (6-292)

PUNT RETURNS
Most Punt Returns, Career
8 Troy Brown, New England, 3 games
6 Willie Wood, Green Bay, 2 games
Jake Scott, Miami, 3 games
Theo Bell, Pittsburgh, 2 games
Mike Nelms, Washington, 1 game
John Taylor, San Francisco, 3 games
Desmond Howard, Green Bay, 1 game
David Meggett, N.Y. Giants-New England, 2 games
Darrien Gordon, San Diego-Denver-Oakland,
4 games
5 Dana McLemore, San Francisco, 1 game
Most Punt Returns, Game
6 Mike Nelms, Washington vs. Miami, XVII
Desmond Howard, Green Bay vs. New England, XXXI
5 Willie Wood, Green Bay vs. Oakland, II
Dana McLemore, San Francisco vs. Miami, XIX
4 By 10 players
Most Fair Catches, Game
4 Jermaine Lewis, Baltimore vs. N.Y. Giants, XXXV
Karl Williams, Tampa Bay vs. Oakland, XXXVII
3 Ron Gardin, Baltimore vs. Dallas, V
Golden Richards, Dallas vs. Pittsburgh, X
Greg Pruitt, L.A. Raiders vs. Washington, XVIII
Al Edwards, Buffalo vs. N.Y. Giants, XXV
David Meggett, N.Y. Giants vs. Buffalo, XXV

YARDS GAINED
Most Yards Gained, Career
94 John Taylor, San Francisco, 3 games
90 Desmond Howard, Green Bay, 1 game
67 David Meggett, N.Y. Giants-New England, 2 games
Most Yards Gained, Game
90 Desmond Howard, Green Bay vs. New England, XXXI
56 John Taylor, San Francisco vs. Cincinnati, XXIII
52 Mike Nelms, Washington vs. Miami, XXII

Longest Return
45 John Taylor, San Francisco vs. Cincinnati, XXIII
34 Darrell Green, Washington vs. L.A. Raiders, XVIII
Desmond Howard, Green Bay vs. New England, XXXI
Jermaine Lewis, Baltimore vs. N.Y. Giants, XXXV
Steve Breaston, Arizona vs. Pittsburgh, XLIII
32 Desmond Howard, Green Bay vs. New England, XXXI

AVERAGE YARDAGE
Highest Average, Career (4 returns)
15.7 John Taylor, San Francisco, 3 games (6-94)
15.0 Desmond Howard, Green Bay, 1 game (6-90)
11.2 David Meggett, N.Y. Giants-New England, 2 games
(6-67)
Highest Average, Game (3 returns)
18.7 John Taylor, San Francisco vs. Cincinnati, XXIII (3-56)
15.0 Desmond Howard, Green Bay vs. New England, XXXI
(6-90)
14.0 Terrence Wilkins, Indianapolis vs. Chicago, XLI
(3-42)

TOUCHDOWNS
Most Touchdowns, Game
None

KICKOFF RETURNS
Most Kickoff Returns, Career
10 Ken Bell, Denver, 3 games
8 Larry Anderson, Pittsburgh, 2 games
Fulton Walker, Miami, 2 games
Andre Coleman, San Diego, 1 game
Marcus Knight, Oakland, 1 game
7 Preston Pearson, Baltimore-Pittsburgh-Dallas, 5 games
Stephen Starring, New England, 1 game
David Meggett, N.Y. Giants-New England, 2 games
Most Kickoff Returns, Game
8 Andre Coleman, San Diego vs. San Francisco, XXIX
Marcus Knight, Oakland vs. Tampa Bay, XXXVII
7 Stephen Starring, New England vs. Chicago, XX
6 Darren Carrington, Denver vs. San Francisco, XXIV
Antonio Freeman, Green Bay vs. Denver, XXXII
Ron Dixon, N.Y. Giants vs. Baltimore, XXXV

YARDS GAINED
Most Yards Gained, Career
283 Fulton Walker, Miami, 2 games
244 Andre Coleman, San Diego, 1 game
210 Tim Dwight, Atlanta, 1 game
Most Yards Gained, Game
244 Andre Coleman, San Diego vs. San Francisco, XXIX
210 Tim Dwight, Atlanta vs. Denver, XXXIII
190 Fulton Walker, Miami vs. Washington, XVII
Longest Return
99 Desmond Howard, Green Bay vs. New England, XXXI
(TD)
98 Fulton Walker, Miami vs. Washington, XVII (TD)
Andre Coleman, San Diego vs. San Francisco, XXIX
(TD)
97 Ron Dixon, N.Y. Giants vs. Baltimore, XXXV (TD)

AVERAGE YARDAGE
Highest Average, Career (4 returns)
42.0 Tim Dwight, Atlanta, 1 game (5-210)
38.5 Desmond Howard, Green Bay, 1 game (4-154)
35.4 Fulton Walker, Miami, 2 games (8-283)
Highest Average, Game (3 returns)
47.5 Fulton Walker, Miami vs. Washington, XVII (4-190)
42.0 Tim Dwight, Atlanta vs. Denver, XXXIII (5-210)
38.5 Desmond Howard, Green Bay vs. New England, XXXI
(4-154)

TOUCHDOWNS
Most Touchdowns, Game
1 Fulton Walker, Miami vs. Washington, XVII
Stanford Jennings, Cincinnati vs. San Francisco, XXIII
Andre Coleman, San Diego vs. San Francisco, XXIX
Desmond Howard, Green Bay vs. New England, XXXI
Tim Dwight, Atlanta vs. Denver, XXXIII
Ron Dixon, N.Y. Giants vs. Baltimore, XXXV
Jermaine Lewis, Baltimore vs. N.Y. Giants, XXXV
Devin Hester, Chicago vs. Indianapolis, XLI

FUMBLES
Most Fumbles, Career
5 Roger Staubach, Dallas, 4 games
4 Jim Kelly, Buffalo, 4 games
Kurt Warner, St. Louis-Arizona, 3 games
3 Franco Harris, Pittsburgh, 4 games
Terry Bradshaw, Pittsburgh, 4 games
John Elway, Denver, 5 games
Frank Reich, Buffalo, 4 games
Thurman Thomas, Buffalo, 4 games
Most Fumbles, Game
3 Roger Staubach, Dallas vs. Pittsburgh, X
Jim Kelly, Buffalo vs. Washington, XXVI
Frank Reich, Buffalo vs. Dallas, XXVII
2 Franco Harris, Pittsburgh vs. Minnesota, IX
Butch Johnson, Dallas vs. Denver, XII
Terry Bradshaw, Pittsburgh vs. Dallas, XIII
Joe Montana, San Francisco vs. Cincinnati, XXIII
John Elway, Denver vs. San Francisco, XXIV
Thurman Thomas, Buffalo vs. Dallas, XXVIII
Rex Grossman, Chicago vs. Indianapolis, XLI
Eli Manning, N.Y. Giants vs. New England, XLII
Kurt Warner, Arizona vs. Pittsburgh, XLIII

RECOVERIES
Most Fumbles Recovered, Career
2 Jake Scott, Miami, 3 games (1 own, 1 opp)
Fran Tarkenton, Minnesota, 3 games (2 own)
Franco Harris, Pittsburgh, 4 games (2 own)
Roger Staubach, Dallas, 4 games (2 own)
Bobby Walden, Pittsburgh, 2 games (2 own)
John Fitzgerald, Dallas, 4 games (2 own)
Randy Hughes, Dallas, 3 games (2 opp)
Butch Johnson, Dallas, 2 games (2 own)
Mike Singletary, Chicago, 1 game (2 opp)
John Elway, Denver, 5 games (2 own)
Jimmie Jones, Dallas, 2 games (2 opp)
Kenneth Davis, Buffalo, 4 games (2 own)
Kurt Warner, St. Louis-Arizona, 3 games (2 own)
Most Fumbles Recovered, Game
2 Jake Scott, Miami vs. Minnesota, VIII (1 own, 1 opp)
Roger Staubach, Dallas vs. Pittsburgh, X (2 own)
Randy Hughes, Dallas vs. Denver, XII (2 opp)
Butch Johnson, Dallas vs. Denver, XII (2 own)
Mike Singletary, Chicago vs. New England, XX (2 opp)
Jimmie Jones, Dallas vs. Buffalo, XXVII (2 opp)

YARDS GAINED
Most Yards Gained, Game
64 Leon Lett, Dallas vs. Buffalo, XXVII (opp)
49 Mike Bass, Washington vs. Miami, VII (opp)
46 James Washington, Dallas vs. Buffalo, XXVIII (opp)
Longest Return
64 Leon Lett, Dallas vs. Buffalo, XXVII
49 Mike Bass, Washington vs. Miami, VII (TD)
46 James Washington, Dallas vs. Buffalo, XXVIII (TD)

TOUCHDOWNS
Most Touchdowns, Game
1 Mike Bass, Washington vs. Miami, VII (opp 49 yds)
Mike Hegman, Dallas vs. Pittsburgh, XIII (opp 37 yds)

Jimmie Jones, Dallas vs. Buffalo, XXVII (opp 2 yds)
Ken Norton, Dallas vs. Buffalo, XXVII (opp 9 yds)
James Washington, Dallas vs. Buffalo, XXVIII
(opp 46 yds)

COMBINED NET YARDS GAINED
(Rushing, receiving, interception returns, punt returns, kickoff returns, and fumble returns)
ATTEMPTS
Most Attempts, Career
108 Franco Harris, Pittsburgh, 4 games
81 Emmitt Smith, Dallas, 3 games
72 Roger Craig, San Francisco, 3 games
Thurman Thomas, Buffalo, 4 games
Most Attempts, Game
39 John Riggins, Washington vs. Miami, XVII
35 Franco Harris, Pittsburgh vs. Minnesota, IX
34 Matt Snell, N.Y. Jets vs. Baltimore, III
Emmitt Smith, Dallas vs. Buffalo, XXVIII

YARDS GAINED
Most Yards Gained, Career
604 Jerry Rice, San Francisco-Oakland, 4 games
468 Franco Harris, Pittsburgh, 4 games
410 Roger Craig, San Francisco, 3 games
Most Yards Gained, Game
244 Andre Coleman, San Diego vs. San Francisco, XXIX
Desmond Howard, Green Bay vs. New England, XXXI
235 Ricky Sanders, Washington vs. Denver, XXII
230 Antonio Freeman, Green Bay vs. Denver, XXXII

SACKS
Sacks have been compiled since XVII.
Most Sacks, Career
4.5 Charles Haley, San Francisco-Dallas, 5 games
4.0 Justin Tuck, N.Y. Giants, 2 games
3.0 Danny Stubbs, San Francisco, 2 games
Leonard Marshall, N.Y. Giants, 2 games
Jeff Wright, Buffalo, 4 games
Reggie White, Green Bay, 2 games
Willie McGinest, New England, 4 games
Tedy Bruschi, New England, 4 games
Mike Vrabel, New England, 4 games
Darnell Dockett, Arizona, 1 game
LaMarr Woodley, Pittsburgh, 2 games
Most Sacks, Game
3.0 Reggie White, Green Bay vs. New England, XXXI
Darnell Dockett, Arizona vs. Pittsburgh, XLIII
2.0 Dwaine Board, San Francisco vs. Miami, XIX
Dennis Owens, New England vs. Chicago, XX
Otis Wilson, Chicago vs. New England, XX
Leonard Marshall, N.Y. Giants vs. Denver, XXI
Alvin Walton, Washington vs. Denver, XXII
Charles Haley, San Francisco vs. Cincinnati, XXIII
Danny Stubbs, San Francisco vs. Denver, XXIV
Jeff Wright, Buffalo vs. Dallas, XXVIII
Raylee Johnson, San Diego vs. San Francisco, XXIX
Chad Hennings, Dallas vs. Pittsburgh, XXX
Tedy Bruschi, New England vs. Green Bay, XXXI
Michael McCrary, Baltimore vs. N.Y. Giants, XXXV
Simeon Rice, Tampa Bay vs. Oakland, XXXVII
Mike Vrabel, New England vs. Carolina, XXXVIII
Adalius Thomas, New England vs. N.Y. Giants, XLII
Justin Tuck, N.Y. Giants vs. New England, XLII;
vs. New England, XLVI
LaMarr Woodley, Pittsburgh vs. Arizona, XLIII

TEAM RECORDS

GAMES, VICTORIES, DEFEATS
Most Games
8 Dallas, V-VI, X, XII-XIII, XXVII-XXVIII, XXX

Pittsburgh, IX-X, XIII-XIV, XXX, XL, XLIII, XLV
7 New England, XX, XXXI, XXXVI, XXXVIII-XXXIX, XLII, XLVI
6 Denver, XII, XXI-XXII, XXIV, XXXII-XXXIII

Most Consecutive Games
4 Buffalo, XXV-XXVIII
3 Miami, VI-VIII
2 Green Bay, I-II; XXXI-XXXII
Dallas, V-VI; XII-XIII; XXVII-XXVIII
Minnesota, VIII-IX
Pittsburgh, IX-X; XIII-XIV
Washington, XVII-XVIII
Denver, XXI-XXII; XXXII-XXXIII
San Francisco, XXIII-XXIV
New England, XXXVIII-XXXIX

Most Games Won
6 Pittsburgh, IX-X, XIII-XIV, XL, XLIII
5 San Francisco, XVI, XIX, XXIII-XXIV, XXIX
Dallas, VI, XII, XXVII-XXVIII, XXX
4 Green Bay, I-II, XXXI, XLV
N.Y. Giants, XXI, XXV, XLII, XLVI

Most Consecutive Games Won
2 Green Bay, I-II
Miami, VII-VIII
Pittsburgh, IX-X, XIII-XIV
San Francisco, XXIII-XXIV
Dallas, XXVII-XXVIII
Denver, XXXII-XXXIII
New England, XXXVIII-XXXIX

Most Games Lost
4 Minnesota, IV, VIII-IX, XI
Denver, XII, XXI-XXII, XXIV
Buffalo, XXV-XXVIII
New England, XX, XXXI, XLII, XLVI
3 Dallas, V, X, XIII
Miami, VI, XVII, XIX
2 Washington, VII, XVIII
Cincinnati, XVI, XXII
L.A./St. Louis Rams, XIV, XXXVI
Oakland/L.A. Raiders, II, XXXVII
Philadelphia, XV, XXXIX
Baltimore/Indianapolis, III, XLIV
Pittsburgh, XXX, XLV

Most Consecutive Games Lost
4 Buffalo, XXV-XXVIII
2 Minnesota, VIII-IX
Denver, XXI-XXII

SCORING

Most Points, Game
55 San Francisco vs. Denver, XXIV
52 Dallas vs. Buffalo, XXVII
49 San Francisco vs. San Diego, XXIX

Fewest Points, Game
3 Miami vs. Dallas, VI
6 Minnesota vs. Pittsburgh, IX
7 By five teams

Most Points, Both Teams, Game
75 San Francisco (49) vs. San Diego (26), XXIX
69 Dallas (52) vs. Buffalo (17), XXVII
Tampa Bay (48) vs. Oakland (21), XXXVII
66 Pittsburgh (35) vs. Dallas (31), XIII

Fewest Points, Both Teams, Game
21 Washington (7) vs. Miami (14), VII
22 Minnesota (6) vs. Pittsburgh (16), IX
23 Baltimore (7) vs. N.Y. Jets (16), III

Largest Margin of Victory, Game
45 San Francisco vs. Denver, XXIV (55-10)
36 Chicago vs. New England, XX (46-10)
35 Dallas vs. Buffalo, XXVII (52-17)

Most Points, Each Half
1st: 35 Washington vs. Denver, XXII

2nd: 30 N.Y. Giants vs. Denver, XXI

Most Points, Each Quarter
1st: 14 Miami vs. Minnesota, VIII
Oakland vs. Philadelphia, XV
Dallas vs. Buffalo, XXVII
San Francisco vs. San Diego, XXIX
New England vs. Green Bay, XXXI
Chicago vs. Indianapolis, XLI
Green Bay vs. Pittsburgh, XLV
2nd: 35 Washington vs. Denver, XXII
3rd: 21 Chicago vs. New England, XX
4th: 21 Dallas vs. Buffalo, XXVII

Most Points, Both Teams, Each Half
1st: 45 Washington (35) vs. Denver (10), XXII
2nd: 46 Tampa Bay (28) vs. Oakland (18), XXXVII

Fewest Points, Both Teams, Each Half
1st: 2 Minnesota (0) vs. Pittsburgh (2), IX
2nd: 7 Miami (0) vs. Washington (7), VII
Denver (0) vs. Washington (7), XXII

Most Points, Both Teams, Each Quarter
1st: 24 New England (14) vs. Green Bay (10), XXXI
2nd: 35 Washington (35) vs. Denver (0), XXII
3rd: 24 Washington (14) vs. Buffalo (10), XXVI
4th: 37 Carolina (19) vs. New England (18), XXXVIII

TOUCHDOWNS

Most Touchdowns, Game
8 San Francisco vs. Denver, XXIV
7 Dallas vs. Buffalo, XXVII
San Francisco vs. San Diego, XXIX
6 Washington vs. Denver, XXII
Tampa Bay vs. Oakland, XXXVII

Fewest Touchdowns, Game
0 Miami vs. Dallas, VI
1 By 19 teams

Most Touchdowns, Both Teams, Game
10 San Francisco (7) vs. San Diego (3), XXIX
9 Pittsburgh (5) vs. Dallas (4), XIII
San Francisco (8) vs. Denver (1), XXIV
Dallas (7) vs. Buffalo (2), XXVII
Tampa Bay (6) vs. Oakland (3), XXXVII
8 Carolina (4) vs. New England (4), XXXVIII

Fewest Touchdowns, Both Teams, Game
2 Baltimore (1) vs. N.Y. Jets (1), III
3 In six games

POINTS AFTER TOUCHDOWN

Most (One-Point) Points After Touchdown, Game
7 San Francisco vs. Denver, XXIV
Dallas vs. Buffalo, XXVII
San Francisco vs. San Diego, XXIX
6 Washington vs. Denver, XXII
Tampa Bay vs. Oakland, XXXVII
5 Green Bay vs. Kansas City, I
Pittsburgh vs. Dallas, XIII
L.A. Raiders vs. Washington, XVIII
San Francisco vs. Miami, XIX
Chicago vs. New England, XX

Most (One-Point) Points After Touchdown, Both Teams, Game
9 Pittsburgh (5) vs. Dallas (4), XIII
Dallas (7) vs. Buffalo (2), XXVII
8 San Francisco (7) vs. Denver (1), XXIV
San Francisco (7) vs. San Diego (1), XXIX
7 Washington (6) vs. Denver (1), XXII
Washington (4) vs. Buffalo (3), XXVI
Denver (4) vs. Green Bay (3), XXXII

Fewest (One-Point) Points After Touchdown, Both Teams, Game
2 Baltimore (1) vs. N.Y. Jets (1), III
Baltimore (1) vs. Dallas (1), V
Minnesota (0) vs. Pittsburgh (2), IX

Most Two-Point Conversions, Game
2 San Diego vs. San Francisco, XXIX

Most Two-Point Conversions, Both Teams, Game
2   San Diego (2) vs. San Francisco (0), XXIX

FIELD GOALS
Most Field Goals Attempted, Game
5   N.Y. Jets vs. Baltimore, III
    Dallas vs. Denver, XII
4   Green Bay vs. Oakland, II
    Pittsburgh vs. Dallas, XX
    San Francisco vs. Cincinnati, XVI; XXIII
    Denver vs. N.Y. Giants, XXI
    Denver vs. Atlanta, XXXIII
    St. Louis vs. Tennessee, XXXIV
    Indianapolis vs. Chicago, XLI
Most Field Goals Attempted, Both Teams, Game
7   N.Y. Jets (5) vs. Baltimore (2), III
    San Francisco (4) vs. Cincinnati (3), XXIII
    St. Louis (4) vs. Tennessee (3), XXXIV
    Denver (4) vs. Atlanta (3), XXXIII
6   Dallas (5) vs. Denver (1), XII
5   Green Bay (4) vs. Oakland (1), II
    Pittsburgh (4) vs. Dallas (1), X
    Oakland (3) vs. Philadelphia (2), XV
    Denver (4) vs. N.Y. Giants (1), XXI
    Dallas (3) vs. Buffalo (2), XXVIII
    Indianapolis (4) vs. Chicago (1), XLI
    New Orleans (3) vs. Indianapolis (2), XLIV
Fewest Field Goals Attempted, Both Teams, Game
1   Minnesota (0) vs. Miami (1), VIII
    San Francisco (0) vs. Denver (1), XXIV
    Philadelphia (0) vs. New England (1), XXXIX
    New England (0) vs. N.Y. Giants (1), XLII
2   Green Bay (0) vs. Kansas City (2), I
    Miami (1) vs. Washington (1), VII
    Minnesota (1) vs. Pittsburgh (1), IX
    Dallas (1) vs. Pittsburgh (1), XIII
    Dallas (1) vs. Buffalo (1), XXVII
    San Diego (1) vs. San Francisco (1), XXIX
    Denver (1) vs. Green Bay (1), XXXII
    Arizona (0) vs. Pittsburgh (2), XLIII
Most Field Goals, Game
4   Green Bay vs. Oakland, II
    San Francisco vs. Cincinnati, XVI
3   N.Y. Jets vs. Baltimore, III
    Kansas City vs. Minnesota, IV
    Miami vs. San Francisco, XIX
    Chicago vs. New England, XX
    Cincinnati vs. San Francisco, XXIII
    Washington vs. Buffalo, XXVI
    Dallas vs. Buffalo, XXVIII
    St. Louis vs. Tennessee, XXXIV
    Indianapolis vs. Chicago, XLI
    New Orleans vs. Indianapolis, XLIV
Most Field Goals, Both Teams, Game
5   Cincinnati (3) vs. San Francisco (2), XXIII
    Dallas (3) vs. Buffalo (2), XXVIII
4   Green Bay (4) vs. Oakland (0), II
    San Francisco (4) vs. Cincinnati (0), XVI
    Miami (3) vs. San Francisco (1), XIX
    Chicago (3) vs. New England (1), XX
    Washington (3) vs. Buffalo (1), XXVI
    Atlanta (2) vs. Denver (2), XXXIII
    St. Louis (3) vs. Tennessee (1), XXXIV
    Indianapolis (3) vs. Chicago (1), XLI
    New Orleans (3) vs. Indianapolis (1), XLIV
3   In 14 games
Fewest Field Goals, Both Teams, Game
0   Miami vs. Washington, VII
    Pittsburgh vs. Minnesota, IX
1   Green Bay (0) vs. Kansas City (1), I
    Minnesota (0) vs. Miami (1), VIII
    Pittsburgh (0) vs. Dallas (1), XIII

Washington (0) vs. Denver (1), XXII
San Francisco (0) vs. Denver (1), XXIV
San Francisco (0) vs. San Diego (1), XXIX
Philadelphia (0) vs. New England (1), XXXIX
Pittsburgh (0) vs. Seattle (1), XLI
New England (0) vs. N.Y. Giants (1), XLII

SAFETIES
Most Safeties, Game
1   Pittsburgh vs. Minnesota, IX; vs. Dallas, X
    Chicago vs. New England, XX
    N.Y. Giants vs. Denver, XXI; vs. New England, XLVI
    Buffalo vs. N.Y. Giants, XXV
    Arizona vs. Pittsburgh, XLIII

FIRST DOWNS
Most First Downs, Game
31 San Francisco vs. Miami, XIX
29 New England vs. Carolina, XXXVIII
28 San Francisco vs. Denver, XXIV
    San Francisco vs. San Diego, XXIX
Fewest First Downs, Game
9   Minnesota vs. Pittsburgh, IX
    Miami vs. Washington, XVII
10 Dallas vs. Baltimore, V
    Miami vs. Dallas, VI
11 Denver vs. Dallas, XII
    N.Y. Giants vs. Baltimore, XXXV
    Oakland vs. Tampa Bay, XXXVII
    Chicago vs. Indianapolis, XLI
Most First Downs, Both Teams, Game
50 San Francisco (31) vs. Miami (19), XIX
    Tennessee (27) vs. St. Louis (23), XXXIV
49 Buffalo (25) vs. Washington (24), XXVI
48 San Francisco (28) vs. San Diego (20), XXIX
Fewest First Downs, Both Teams, Game
24 Dallas (10) vs. Baltimore (14), V
    N.Y. Giants (11) vs. Baltimore (13), XXXV
26 Minnesota (9) vs. Pittsburgh (17), IX
27 Pittsburgh (13) vs. Dallas (14), X

RUSHING
Most First Downs, Rushing, Game
16 San Francisco vs. Miami, XIX
15 Dallas vs. Miami, VI
14 Washington vs. Miami, XVII
    San Francisco vs. Denver, XXIV
    Denver vs. Green Bay, XXXII
Fewest First Downs, Rushing, Game
1   New England vs. Chicago, XX
    St. Louis vs. Tennessee, XXXIV
    Oakland vs. Tampa Bay, XXXVII
2   Minnesota vs. Kansas City, IV; vs. Pittsburgh, IX;
        vs. Oakland, XI
    Pittsburgh vs. Dallas, XIII
    Miami vs. San Francisco, XIX
    N.Y. Giants vs. Baltimore, XXXV
    Arizona vs. Pittsburgh, XLIII
3   Miami vs. Dallas, VI
    Philadelphia vs. Oakland, XV
    New England vs. Green Bay, XXXI
    Carolina vs. New England, XXXVIII
    Chicago vs. Indianapolis, XLII
    New England vs. N.Y. Giants, XLII
    New Orleans vs. Indianapolis, XLIV
Most First Downs, Rushing, Both Teams, Game
21 Washington (14) vs. Miami (7), XVII
19 Washington (13) vs. Denver (6), XXII
    San Francisco (14) vs. Denver (5), XXIV
18 Dallas (15) vs. Miami (3), VI
    Miami (13) vs. Minnesota (5), VIII
    San Francisco (16) vs. Miami (2), XIX

N.Y. Giants (10) vs. Buffalo (8), XXV
Denver (14) vs. Green Bay (4), XXXII

Fewest First Downs, Rushing, Both Teams, Game
6 Arizona (2) vs. Pittsburgh (4), XLIII
7 Oakland (1) vs. Tampa Bay (6), XXXVIII
New England (3) vs. N.Y. Giants (4), XLII
8 Baltimore (4) vs. Dallas (4), V
Pittsburgh (2) vs. Dallas (6), XIII
N.Y. Giants (2) vs. Baltimore (6), XXXV

PASSING
Most First Downs, Passing, Game
20 Arizona vs. Pittsburgh, XLIII
19 New England vs. Carolina, XXXVIII
18 Buffalo vs. Washington, XXVI
St. Louis vs. Tennessee, XXXIV
Philadelphia vs. New England, XXXIX
N.Y. Giants vs. New England, XLVI

Fewest First Downs, Passing, Game
1 Denver vs. Dallas, XII
2 Miami vs. Washington, XVII
4 Miami vs. Minnesota, VIII

Most First Downs, Passing, Both Teams, Game
33 N.Y. Giants (18) vs. New England (15), XLVI
32 Miami (17) vs. San Francisco (15), XIX
Philadelphia (18) vs. New England (14), XXXIX
Arizona (20) vs. Pittsburgh (12), XLIII
Indianapolis (16) vs. New Orleans (16), XLIV
31 San Francisco (17) vs. San Diego (14), XXIX
St. Louis (18) vs. Tennessee (13), XXXIV
New England (19) vs. Carolina (12), XXXVIII

Fewest First Downs, Passing, Both Teams, Game
9 Denver (1) vs. Dallas (8), XII
10 Minnesota (5) vs. Pittsburgh (5), IX
11 Dallas (5) vs. Baltimore (6), V
Miami (2) vs. Washington (9), XVII

PENALTY
Most First Downs, Penalty, Game
4 Baltimore vs. Dallas, V
Miami vs. Minnesota, VIII
Cincinnati vs. San Francisco, XVI
Buffalo vs. Dallas, XXVII
St. Louis vs. Tennessee, XXXIV
Pittsburgh vs. Arizona, XLIII
3 Kansas City vs. Minnesota, IV
Minnesota vs. Oakland, XI
Buffalo vs. Washington, XXVI
Green Bay vs. Denver, XXXII
N.Y. Giants vs. Baltimore, XXXV
St. Louis vs. New England, XXXVI
Tampa Bay vs. Oakland, XXXVII
New England vs. Carolina, XXXVIII

Most First Downs, Penalty, Both Teams, Game
6 Cincinnati (4) vs. San Francisco (2), XVI
St. Louis (4) vs. Tennessee (2), XXXIV
5 Baltimore (4) vs. Dallas (1), V
Miami (4) vs. Minnesota (1), VIII
Buffalo (3) vs. Washington (2), XXVI
Green Bay (3) vs. Denver (2), XXXII
New England (3) vs. Carolina (2), XXXVIII
Pittsburgh (4) vs. Arizona (1), XLIII
4 Kansas City (3) vs. Minnesota (1), IV
Buffalo (4) vs. Dallas (0), XXVII
N.Y. Giants (3) vs. Baltimore (1), XXXV
St. Louis (3) vs. New England (1), XXXVI
Tampa Bay (3) vs. Oakland (1), XXXVII

Fewest First Downs, Penalty, Both Teams, Game
0 Dallas vs. Miami, VI
Miami vs. Washington, VII
Dallas vs. Pittsburgh, X
Miami vs. San Francisco, XIX

Pittsburgh vs. Seattle, XL
Green Bay vs. Pittsburgh, XLV
1 Green Bay (0) vs. Kansas City (1), I
Miami (0) vs. Washington (1), XVII
Cincinnati (0) vs. San Francisco (1), XXIII
San Francisco (0) vs. Denver (1), XXIV
Dallas (0) vs. Buffalo (1), XXVIII
Dallas (0) vs. Pittsburgh (1), XXX
Denver (0) vs. Atlanta (1), XXXIII
Chicago (0) vs. Indianapolis (1), XLI
New England (0) vs. N.Y. Giants (1), XLVI

NET YARDS GAINED RUSHING AND PASSING
Most Yards Gained, Game
602 Washington vs. Denver, XXII
537 San Francisco vs. Miami, XIX
481 New England vs. Carolina, XXXVIII

Fewest Yards Gained, Game
119 Minnesota vs. Pittsburgh, IX
123 New England vs. Chicago, XX
152 N.Y. Giants vs. Baltimore, XXXV

Most Yards Gained, Both Teams, Game
929 Washington (602) vs. Denver (327), XXII
868 New England (481) vs. Carolina (387), XXXVIII
851 San Francisco (537) vs. Miami (314), XIX

Fewest Yards Gained, Both Teams, Game
396 N.Y. Giants (152) vs. Baltimore (244), XXXV
452 Minnesota (119) vs. Pittsburgh (333), IX
481 Washington (228) vs. Miami (253), VII
Denver (156) vs. Dallas (325), XII

RUSHING
ATTEMPTS
Most Attempts, Game
57 Pittsburgh vs. Minnesota, IX
53 Miami vs. Minnesota, VIII
52 Oakland vs. Minnesota, XI
Washington vs. Miami, XVII

Fewest Attempts, Game
9 Miami vs. San Francisco, XIX
11 New England vs. Chicago, XX
Oakland vs. Tampa Bay, XXXVII
12 Arizona vs. Pittsburgh, XLIII

Most Attempts, Both Teams, Game
81 Washington (52) vs. Miami (29), XVII
78 Pittsburgh (57) vs. Minnesota (21), IX
Oakland (52) vs. Minnesota (26), XI
77 Miami (53) vs. Minnesota (24), VIII
Pittsburgh (46) vs. Dallas (31), X

Fewest Attempts, Both Teams, Game
36 Green Bay (13) vs. Pittsburgh (23), XLV
37 Arizona (12) vs. Pittsburgh (25), XLIII
New Orleans (18) vs. Indianapolis (19), XLIV
42 New England (16) vs. N.Y. Giants (26), XLII

YARDS GAINED
Most Yards Gained, Game
280 Washington vs. Denver, XXII
276 Washington vs. Miami, XVII
266 Oakland vs. Minnesota, XI

Fewest Yards Gained, Game
7 New England vs. Chicago, XX
17 Minnesota vs. Pittsburgh, IX
19 Oakland vs. Tampa Bay, XXXVII

Most Yards Gained, Both Teams, Game
377 Washington (280) vs. Denver (97), XXII
372 Washington (276) vs. Miami (96), XVII
338 N.Y. Giants (172) vs. Buffalo (166), XXV

Fewest Yards Gained, Both Teams, Game
91 Arizona (33) vs. Pittsburgh (58), XLIII
136 New England (45) vs. N.Y. Giants (91), XLII

150   New Orleans (51) vs. Indianapolis (99), XLIV

AVERAGE GAIN
Highest Average Gain, Game
7.00   L.A. Raiders vs. Washington, XVIII (33-231)
           Washington vs. Denver, XXII (40-280)
6.64   Buffalo vs. N.Y. Giants, XXV (25-166)
6.22   Baltimore vs. N.Y. Jets, III (23-143)
Lowest Average Gain, Game
0.64   New England vs. Chicago, XX (11-7)
0.81   Minnesota vs. Pittsburgh, IX (21-17)
1.73   Oakland vs. Tampa Bay, XXXVII (11-19)

TOUCHDOWNS
Most Touchdowns, Game
4   Chicago vs. New England, XX
      Denver vs. Green Bay, XXXII
3   Green Bay vs. Kansas City, I
      Miami vs. Minnesota, VIII
      San Francisco vs. Denver, XXIV
      Denver vs. Atlanta, XXXIII
2   Oakland vs. Minnesota, XI
      Pittsburgh vs. Los Angeles, XIV
      L.A. Raiders vs. Washington, XVIII
      San Francisco vs. Miami, XIX
      N.Y. Giants vs. Denver, XXI
      Washington vs. Denver, XXII; vs. Buffalo, XXVI
      Buffalo vs. N.Y. Giants, XXV
      Dallas vs. Buffalo, XXVIII; vs. Pittsburgh, XXX
      Tennessee vs. St. Louis, XXXIV
      Pittsburgh vs. Seattle, XL
Fewest Touchdowns, Game
0   By 32 teams
Most Touchdowns, Both Teams, Game
4   Miami (3) vs. Minnesota (1), VIII
      Chicago (4) vs. New England (0), XX
      San Francisco (3) vs. Denver (1), XXIV
      Denver (4) vs. Green Bay (0), XXXII
3   In nine games
Fewest Touchdowns, Both Teams, Game
0   Pittsburgh vs. Dallas, X
      Oakland vs. Philadelphia, XV
      Cincinnati vs. San Francisco, XXIII
1   In 17 games

PASSING
ATTEMPTS
Most Passes Attempted, Game
59   Buffalo vs. Washington, XXVI
55   San Diego vs. San Francisco, XXIX
51   Philadelphia vs. New England, XXXIX
Fewest Passes Attempted, Game
7   Miami vs. Minnesota, VIII
11   Miami vs. Washington, VII
14   Pittsburgh vs. Minnesota, IX
Most Passes Attempted, Both Teams, Game
93   San Diego (55) vs. San Francisco (38), XXIX
92   Buffalo (59) vs. Washington (33), XXVI
85   Miami (50) vs. San Francisco (35), XIX
Fewest Passes Attempted, Both Teams, Game
35   Miami (7) vs. Minnesota (28), VIII
39   Miami (11) vs. Washington (28), VII
40   Pittsburgh (14) vs. Minnesota (26), IX
        Miami (17) vs. Washington (23), XVII

COMPLETIONS
Most Passes Completed, Game
32   New England vs. Carolina, XXXVIII
        New Orleans vs. Indianapolis, XLIV
31   Buffalo vs. Dallas, XXVIII
        Arizona vs. Pittsburgh, XLIII
        Indianapolis vs. New Orleans, XLIV

30   Philadelphia vs. New England, XXXIX
        N.Y. Giants vs. New England, XLVI
Fewest Passes Completed, Game
4   Miami vs. Washington, XVII
6   Miami vs. Minnesota, VIII
8   Miami vs. Washington, VII
      Denver vs. Dallas, XII
Most Passes Completed, Both Teams, Game
63   New Orleans (32) vs. Indianapolis (31), XLIV
57   N.Y. Giants (30) vs. New England (27), XLVI
53   Miami (29) vs. San Francisco (24), XIX
        Philadelphia (30) vs. New England (23), XXXIX
Fewest Passes Completed, Both Teams, Game
19   Miami (4) vs. Washington (15), XVII
20   Pittsburgh (9) vs. Minnesota (11), IX
22   Miami (8) vs. Washington (14), VII

COMPLETION PERCENTAGE
Highest Completion Percentage, Game (20 attempts)
88.0   N.Y. Giants vs. Denver, XXI (25-22)
82.1   New Orleans vs. Indianapolis, XLIV (39-32)
75.0   San Francisco vs. Denver, XXIV (32-24)
          N.Y. Giants vs. New England, XLVI (40-30)
Lowest Completion Percentage, Game (20 attempts)
32.0   Denver vs. Dallas, XII (25-8)
37.9   Denver vs. San Francisco, XXIV (29-11)
38.5   Denver vs. Washington, XXII (39-15)
          N.Y. Giants vs. Baltimore, XXXV (39-15)

YARDS GAINED
Most Yards Gained, Game
407   St. Louis vs. Tennessee, XXXIV
374   Arizona vs. Pittsburgh, XLIII
354   New England vs. Carolina, XXXVIII
Fewest Yards Gained, Game
35   Denver vs. Dallas, XII
63   Miami vs. Minnesota, VIII
69   Miami vs. Washington, VII
Most Yards Gained, Both Teams, Game
649   New England (354) vs. Carolina (295), XXXVIII
615   San Francisco (326) vs. Miami (289), XIX
          St. Louis (407) vs. Tennessee (208), XXXIV
614   Indianapolis (333) vs. New Orleans (281), XLIV
Fewest Yards Gained, Both Teams, Game
156   Miami (69) vs. Washington (87), VII
186   Pittsburgh (84) vs. Minnesota (102), IX
204   Miami (80) vs. Washington (124), XVII

TIMES SACKED
Most Times Sacked, Game
7   Dallas vs. Pittsburgh, X
      New England vs. Chicago, XX
6   Kansas City vs. Green Bay, I
      Washington vs. L.A. Raiders, XVIII
      Denver vs. San Francisco, XXIV
5   Dallas vs. Denver, XII; vs. Pittsburgh, XIII
      Cincinnati vs. San Francisco, XVI; XXIII
      Denver vs. Washington, XXII
      Buffalo vs. Washington, XXVI
      Green Bay vs. New England, XXXI
      New England vs. Green Bay, XXXI
      Oakland vs. Tampa Bay, XXXVIII
      New England vs. N.Y. Giants, XLII
Fewest Times Sacked, Game
0   Baltimore vs. N.Y. Jets, III; vs. Dallas, V
      Minnesota vs. Pittsburgh, IX
      Pittsburgh vs. Los Angeles, XIV
      Philadelphia vs. Oakland, XV
      Washington vs. Buffalo, XXVI
      Denver vs. Green Bay, XXXII; vs. Atlanta, XXXIII
      Tampa Bay vs. Oakland, XXXVII
      New England vs. Carolina, XXXVIII

Indianapolis vs. New Orleans, XLIV
1 By 18 teams

Most Times Sacked, Both Teams, Game
10 New England (7) vs. Chicago (3), XX
Green Bay (5) vs. New England (5), XXXI
9 Kansas City (6) vs. Green Bay (3), I
Dallas (7) vs. Pittsburgh (2), X
Dallas (5) vs. Denver (4), XII
Dallas (5) vs. Pittsburgh (4), XIII
Cincinnati (5) vs. San Francisco (4), XXIII
8 Washington (6) vs. L.A. Raiders (2), XVIII
New England (5) vs. N.Y. Giants (3), XLII

Fewest Times Sacked, Both Teams, Game
1 Philadelphia (0) vs. Oakland (1), XV
Denver (0) vs. Green Bay (1), XXXII
Indianapolis (0) vs. New Orleans (1), XLIV
2 Baltimore (0) vs. N.Y. Jets (2), III
Baltimore (0) vs. Dallas (2), V
Minnesota (0) vs. Pittsburgh (2), IX
Denver (0) vs. Atlanta (2), XXXIII
Chicago (1) vs. Indianapolis (1), XLI
3 In five games

TOUCHDOWNS
Most Touchdowns, Game
6 San Francisco vs. San Diego, XXIX
5 San Francisco vs. Denver, XXIV
4 Pittsburgh vs. Dallas, XIII
Washington vs. Denver, XXII
Dallas vs. Buffalo, XXVII

Fewest Touchdowns, Game
0 By 19 teams

Most Touchdowns, Both Teams, Game
7 Pittsburgh (4) vs. Dallas (3), XIII
San Francisco (6) vs. San Diego (1), XXIX
6 Carolina (3) vs. New England (3), XXXVIII
5 Washington (4) vs. Denver (1), XXII
San Francisco (5) vs. Denver (0), XXIV
Dallas (4) vs. Buffalo (1), XXVII
Philadelphia (3) vs. New England (2), XXXIX
Green Bay (3) vs. Pittsburgh (2), XLV

Fewest Touchdowns, Both Teams, Game
0 N.Y. Jets vs. Baltimore, III
Miami vs. Minnesota, VIII
Buffalo vs. Dallas, XXVIII
1 In seven games

INTERCEPTIONS BY
Most Interceptions By, Game
5 Tampa Bay vs. Oakland, XXXVII
4 N.Y. Jets vs. Baltimore, III
Dallas vs. Denver, XII
Washington vs. Buffalo, XXVI
Dallas vs. Buffalo, XXVII
Green Bay vs. New England, XXXI
Baltimore vs. N.Y. Giants, XXXV
3 By 13 teams

Most Interceptions By, Both Teams, Game
6 Baltimore (3) vs. Dallas (3), V
Tampa Bay (5) vs. Oakland (1), XXXVII
5 Washington (4) vs. Buffalo (1), XXVI
4 In 10 games

Fewest Interceptions By, Both Teams, Game
0 Buffalo vs. N.Y. Giants, XXV
St. Louis vs. Tennessee, XXXIV
1 Oakland (0) vs. Green Bay (1), II
Miami (0) vs. Dallas (1), VI
Minnesota (0) vs. Miami (1), VIII
N.Y. Giants (0) vs. Denver (1), XXI
Cincinnati (0) vs. San Francisco (1), XXIII
New England (0) vs. Carolina (1), XXXVIII
N.Y. Giants (0) vs. New England (1), XLII

Indianapolis (0) vs. New Orleans (1), XLIV
New England (0) vs. N.Y. Giants (1), XLVI

YARDS GAINED
Most Yards Gained, Game
172 Tampa Bay vs. Oakland, XXXVII
136 Denver vs. Atlanta, XXXIII
100 Pittsburgh vs. Arizona, XLIII

Most Yards Gained, Both Teams, Game
184 Tampa Bay (172) vs. Oakland (12), XXXVII
137 Denver (136) vs. Atlanta (1), XXXIII
100 Seattle (76) vs. Pittsburgh (24), XL
Indianapolis (94) vs. Chicago (6), XLI

TOUCHDOWNS
Most Touchdowns, Game
3 Tampa Bay vs. Oakland, XXXVII
1 Green Bay vs. Oakland, II
Oakland vs. Minnesota, XI
L.A. Raiders vs. Washington, XVIII
Chicago vs. New England, XX
Baltimore vs. N.Y. Giants, XXXV
New England vs. St. Louis, XXXVI
Indianapolis vs. Chicago, XLI
Pittsburgh vs. Arizona, XLIII
New Orleans vs. Indianapolis, XLIV
Green Bay vs. Pittsburgh, XLV

PUNTING
Most Punts, Game
11 N.Y. Giants vs. Baltimore, XXXV
10 Baltimore vs. N.Y. Giants, XXXV
9 Dallas vs. Baltimore, V

Fewest Punts, Game
1 Atlanta vs. Denver, XXXIII
Denver vs. Atlanta, XXXIII
2 Pittsburgh vs. Los Angeles, XIV
Denver vs. N.Y. Giants, XXI
St. Louis vs. Tennessee, XXXIV
Indianapolis vs. New Orleans, XLIV
New Orleans vs. Indianapolis, XLIV
3 By 14 teams

Most Punts, Both Teams, Game
21 N.Y. Giants (11) vs. Baltimore (10), XXXV
15 Washington (8) vs. L.A. Raiders (7), XVIII
New England (8) vs. Green Bay (7), XXXI
13 Dallas (9) vs. Baltimore (4), V
Pittsburgh (7) vs. Minnesota (6), IX

Fewest Punts, Both Teams, Game
2 Atlanta (1) vs. Denver (1), XXXIII
4 Indianapolis (2) vs. New Orleans (2), XLIV
5 Denver (2) vs. N.Y. Giants (3), XXI
St. Louis (2) vs. Tennessee (3), XXXIV

AVERAGE YARDAGE
Highest Average, Game (4 punts)
50.17 Seattle vs. Pittsburgh, XL (6-301)
48.75 San Diego vs. San Francisco, XXIX (4-195)
48.67 Pittsburgh vs. Seattle, XL (6-292)

Lowest Average, Game (4 punts)
31.00 Tampa Bay vs. Oakland, XXXVII (5-155)
31.20 Washington vs. Miami, VII (5-156)
32.38 Washington vs. L.A. Raiders, XVIII (8-259)

PUNT RETURNS
Most Punt Returns, Game
6 Washington vs. Miami, XVII
Green Bay vs. New England, XXXI
5 By seven teams

Fewest Punt Returns, Game
0 Minnesota vs. Miami, VIII
Buffalo vs. N.Y. Giants, XXV

Washington vs. Buffalo, XXVI
Denver vs. Green Bay, XXXII
Green Bay vs. Denver, XXXII
Atlanta vs. Denver, XXXIII
Denver vs. Atlanta, XXXIII
New England vs. N.Y. Giants, XLVI
1 By 25 teams

Most Punt Returns, Both Teams, Game
10 Green Bay (6) vs. New England (4), XXXI
9 Pittsburgh (5) vs. Minnesota (4), IX
8 Green Bay (5) vs. Oakland (3), II
    Baltimore (5) vs. Dallas (3), V
    Washington (6) vs. Miami (2), XVII
    N.Y. Giants (5) vs. Baltimore (3), XXXV

Fewest Punt Returns, Both Teams, Game
0 Denver vs. Green Bay, XXXII
    Atlanta vs. Denver, XXXIII
1 New England (0) vs. N.Y. Giants (1), XLVI
2 Dallas (1) vs. Miami (1), VI
    Denver (1) vs. N.Y. Giants (1), XXI
    Buffalo (0) vs. N.Y. Giants (2), XXV
    Buffalo (1) vs. Dallas (1), XXVIII
    Indianapolis (1) vs. New Orleans (1), XLIV

YARDS GAINED
Most Yards Gained, Game
90 Green Bay vs. New England, XXXI
56 San Francisco vs. Cincinnati, XXIII
52 Washington vs. Miami, XVII

Fewest Yards Gained, Game
−1 Dallas vs. Miami, VI
    Tennessee vs. St. Louis, XXXIV
0 By 15 teams

Most Yards Gained, Both Teams, Game
120 Green Bay (90) vs. New England (30), XXXI
80 N.Y. Giants (46) vs. Baltimore (34), XXXV
74 Washington (52) vs. Miami (22), XVII

Fewest Yards Gained, Both Teams, Game
0 Denver vs. Green Bay, XXXII
    Atlanta vs. Denver, XXXIII
4 Indianapolis (0) vs. New Orleans (4), XLIV
5 Green Bay (0) vs. Pittsburgh (5), XLV

AVERAGE RETURN
Highest Average, Game (3 returns)
18.7 San Francisco vs. Cincinnati, XXIII (3-56)
15.0 Green Bay vs. New England, XXXI (6-90)
14.0 Indianapolis vs. Chicago, XLI (3-42)

TOUCHDOWNS
Most Touchdowns, Game
    None

KICKOFF RETURNS
Most Kickoff Returns, Game
9 Denver vs. San Francisco, XXIV
    Oakland vs. Tampa Bay, XXXVII
8 San Diego vs. San Francisco, XXIX
7 By eight teams

Fewest Kickoff Returns, Game
1 N.Y. Jets vs. Baltimore, III
    L.A. Raiders vs. Washington, XVIII
    Washington vs. Buffalo, XXVI
2 By 10 teams

Most Kickoff Returns, Both Teams, Game
13 Oakland (9) vs. Tampa Bay (4), XXXVII
12 Denver (9) vs. San Francisco (3), XXIV
    San Diego (8) vs. San Francisco (4), XXIX
11 Los Angeles (6) vs. Pittsburgh (5), XIV
    Miami (7) vs. San Francisco (4), XIX
    New England (7) vs. Chicago (4), XX
    Green Bay (6) vs. Denver (5), XXXII

Fewest Kickoff Returns, Both Teams, Game
5 N.Y. Jets (1) vs. Baltimore (4), III
    Miami (2) vs. Washington (3), VII
    Washington (1) vs. Buffalo (4), XXVI
6 In five games

YARDS GAINED
Most Yards Gained, Game
244 San Diego vs. San Francisco, XXIX
227 Atlanta vs. Denver, XXXIII
222 Miami vs. Washington, XVII

Fewest Yards Gained, Game
16 Washington vs. Buffalo, XXVI
17 L.A. Raiders vs. Washington, XVIII
25 N.Y. Jets vs. Baltimore, III

Most Yards Gained, Both Teams, Game
292 San Diego (244) vs. San Francisco (48), XXIX
289 Green Bay (154) vs. New England (135), XXXI
281 N.Y. Giants (170) vs. Baltimore (111), XXXV

Fewest Yards Gained, Both Teams, Game
78 Miami (33) vs. Washington (45), VII
82 Pittsburgh (32) vs. Minnesota (50), IX
92 San Francisco (40) vs. Cincinnati (52), XVI

AVERAGE GAIN
Highest Average, Game (3 returns)
44.0 Cincinnati vs. San Francisco, XXIII (3-132)
38.5 Green Bay vs. New England, XXXI (4-154)
37.0 Miami vs. Washington, XVII (6-222)

TOUCHDOWNS
Most Touchdowns, Game
1 Miami vs. Washington, XVII
    Cincinnati vs. San Francisco, XXIII
    San Diego vs. San Francisco, XXIX
    Green Bay vs. New England, XXXI
    Atlanta vs. Denver, XXXIII
    Baltimore vs. N.Y. Giants, XXXV
    N.Y. Giants vs. Baltimore, XXXV
    Chicago vs. Indianapolis, XLI

Most Touchdowns, Both Teams, Game
2 Baltimore (1) vs. N.Y. Giants (1), XXXV

PENALTIES
Most Penalties, Game
12 Dallas vs. Denver, XII
    Carolina vs. New England, XXXVIII
11 Arizona vs. Pittsburgh, XLIII
10 Dallas vs. Baltimore, V

Fewest Penalties, Game
0 Miami vs. Dallas, VI
    Pittsburgh vs. Dallas, X
    Denver vs. San Francisco, XXIV
    Atlanta vs. Denver, XXXIII
1 Green Bay vs. Oakland, II
    Miami vs. Minnesota, VIII; vs. San Francisco, XIX
    Buffalo vs. Dallas, XXVIII
2 By six teams

Most Penalties, Both Teams, Game
20 Dallas (12) vs. Denver (8), XII
    Carolina (12) vs. New England (8), XXXVIII
18 Arizona (11) vs. Pittsburgh (7), XLIII
16 Cincinnati (8) vs. San Francisco (8), XVI
    Green Bay (9) vs. Denver (7), XXXII

Fewest Penalties, Both Teams, Game
2 Pittsburgh (0) vs. Dallas (2), X
3 Miami (0) vs. Dallas (3), VI
    Miami (1) vs. San Francisco (2), XIX
4 Denver (0) vs. San Francisco (4), XXIV
    Atlanta (0) vs. Denver (4), XXXIII

YARDS PENALIZED
Most Yards Penalized, Game
- 133 Dallas vs. Baltimore, X
- 122 Pittsburgh vs. Minnesota, IX
- 106 Arizona vs. Pittsburgh, XLIII

Fewest Yards Penalized, Game
- 0 Miami vs. Dallas, VI
  - Pittsburgh vs. Dallas, X
  - Denver vs. San Francisco, XXIV
  - Atlanta vs. Denver, XXXIII
- 4 Miami vs. Minnesota, VIII
- 10 Miami vs. San Francisco, XIX
  - San Francisco vs. Miami, XIX
  - Buffalo vs. Dallas, XXVIII

Most Yards Penalized, Both Teams, Game
- 164 Dallas (133) vs. Baltimore (31), V
- 162 Arizona (106) vs. Pittsburgh (56), XLIII
- 154 Dallas (94) vs. Denver (60), XII

Fewest Yards Penalized, Both Teams, Game
- 15 Miami (0) vs. Dallas (15), VI
- 20 Pittsburgh (0) vs. Dallas (20), X
  - Miami (10) vs. San Francisco (10), XIX
- 38 Denver (0) vs. San Francisco (38), XXIV

FUMBLES
Most Fumbles, Game
- 8 Buffalo vs. Dallas, XXVII
- 6 Dallas vs. Denver, XII
  - Buffalo vs. Washington, XXVI
- 5 Baltimore vs. Dallas, V

Fewest Fumbles, Game
- 0 By 23 teams

Most Fumbles, Both Teams, Game
- 12 Buffalo (8) vs. Dallas (4), XXVII
- 10 Dallas (6) vs. Denver (4), XII
- 8 Dallas (4) vs. Pittsburgh (4), X

Fewest Fumbles, Both Teams, Game
- 0 Los Angeles vs. Pittsburgh, XIV
  - Green Bay vs. New England, XXXI
  - Pittsburgh vs. Seattle, XL
  - Indianapolis vs. New Orleans, XLIV
- 1 Oakland (0) vs. Minnesota (1), XI
  - Oakland (0) vs. Philadelphia (1), XV
  - Denver (0) vs. Washington (1), XXII
  - N.Y. Giants (0) vs. Buffalo (1), XXV
  - Denver (0) vs. Atlanta (1), XXXIII
- 2 In 11 games

Most Fumbles Lost, Game
- 5 Buffalo vs. Dallas, XXVII
- 4 Baltimore vs. Dallas, V
  - Denver vs. Dallas, XII
  - New England vs. Chicago, XX
- 3 Chicago vs. Indianapolis, XLI

Most Fumbles Lost, Both Teams, Game
- 7 Buffalo (5) vs. Dallas (2), XXVII
- 6 Denver (4) vs. Dallas (2), XII
  - New England (4) vs. Chicago (2), XX
- 5 Baltimore (4) vs. Dallas (1), V
  - Chicago (3) vs. Indianapolis (2), XLI

Fewest Fumbles Lost, Both Teams, Game
- 0 Green Bay vs. Kansas City, I
  - Dallas vs. Pittsburgh, X
  - Los Angeles vs. Pittsburgh, XIV
  - Denver vs. N.Y. Giants, XXI; vs. Washington, XXII
  - Buffalo vs. N.Y. Giants, XXV
  - San Diego vs. San Francisco, XXIX
  - Dallas vs. Pittsburgh, XXX
  - Green Bay vs. New England, XXXI
  - St. Louis vs. Tennessee, XXXIV
  - Oakland vs. Tampa Bay, XXXVII
  - Pittsburgh vs. Seattle, XL
  - Indianapolis vs. New Orleans, XLIV

New England vs. N.Y. Giants, XLVI

Most Fumbles Recovered, Game
- 8 Dallas vs. Denver, XII (4 own, 4 opp.)
- 6 Dallas vs. Buffalo, XXVII (1 own, 5 opp.)
- 5 Chicago vs. New England, XX (1 own, 4 opp.)

TURNOVERS
(Number of times losing the ball on interceptions and fumbles.)
Most Turnovers, Game
- 9 Buffalo vs. Dallas, XXVII
- 8 Denver vs. Dallas, XII
- 7 Baltimore vs. Dallas, V

Fewest Turnovers, Game
- 0 Green Bay vs. Oakland, II
  - Miami vs. Minnesota, VIII
  - Pittsburgh vs. Dallas, X
  - Oakland vs. Minnesota, XI; vs. Philadelphia, XV
  - N.Y. Giants vs. Denver, XXI; vs. Buffalo, XXV
  - San Francisco vs. Denver, XXIV; vs. San Diego, XXIX
  - Buffalo vs. N.Y. Giants, XXV
  - Dallas vs. Pittsburgh, XXX
  - Green Bay vs. New England, XXXI
  - St. Louis vs. Tennessee, XXXIV
  - Tennessee vs. St. Louis, XXXIV
  - Baltimore vs. N.Y. Giants, XXXV
  - New England vs. St. Louis, XXXVI
  - New Orleans vs. Indianapolis, XLIV
  - Green Bay vs. Pittsburgh, XLV
  - N.Y. Giants vs. New England, XLVI
- 1 By many teams

Most Turnovers, Both Teams, Game
- 11 Baltimore (7) vs. Dallas (4), V
  - Buffalo (9) vs. Dallas (2), XXVII
- 10 Denver (8) vs. Dallas (2), XII
- 8 New England (6) vs. Chicago (2), XX
  - Chicago (5) vs. Indianapolis (3), XLI

Fewest Turnovers, Both Teams, Game
- 0 Buffalo vs. N.Y. Giants, XXV
  - St. Louis vs. Tennessee, XXXIV
- 1 N.Y. Giants (0) vs. Denver (1), XXI
  - New Orleans (0) vs. Indianapolis (1), XLIV
  - N.Y. Giants (0) vs. New England (1), XLVI
- 2 Green Bay (1) vs. Kansas City (1), I
  - Miami (0) vs. Minnesota (2), VIII
  - Cincinnati (1) vs. San Francisco (1), XXIII
  - Carolina (1) vs. New England (1), XXXVIII
  - New England (1) vs. N.Y. Giants (1), XLII

Compiled by Elias Sports Bureau

Throughout this all-time postseason record section, the following abbreviations are used to indicate various levels of postseason games:

SB — Super Bowl (1966 to date)

AFC — AFC Championship Game (1970 to date) or AFL Championship Game (1960-69)

NFC — NFC Championship Game (1970 to date) or NFL Championship Game (1933-69)

AFC-D — AFC Divisional Playoff Game (1970 to date), AFC Second-Round Playoff Game (1982), AFL Inter-Divisional Playoff Game (1969), or special playoff game to break tie for AFL Division Championship (1963, 1968)

NFC-D — NFC Divisional Playoff Game (1970 to date), NFC Second-Round Playoff Game (1982), NFL Conference Championship Game (1967-69), or special playoff game to break tie for NFL Division or Conference Championship (1941, 1943, 1947, 1950, 1952, 1957, 1958, 1965)

AFC-FR — AFC First-Round Playoff Game (1978 to date)

NFC-FR — NFC First-Round Playoff Game (1978 to date)

Year indicates season in which game took place and does not necessarily reflect calendar year.

POSTSEASON GAME COMPOSITE STANDINGS

	W	L	PCT.	PTS.	OP
Green Bay Packers	29	17	.630	1,136	930
Pittsburgh Steelers	33	21	.611	1,283	1,123
Carolina Panthers	6	4	.600	219	203
San Francisco 49ers	26	18	.591	1,097	905
New England Patriots*	23	16	.590	850	778
Baltimore Ravens	10	7	.588	332	238
Oakland Raiders**	25	18	.581	1,028	797
Washington Redskins***	23	17	.575	819	707
Dallas Cowboys	33	25	.569	1,355	1,098
Denver Broncos	18	16	.529	733	862
New York Giants	24	24	.500	865	889
Miami Dolphins	20	20	.500	789	875
Houston Texans	1	1	.500	44	30
Indianapolis Colts****	19	20	.487	785	786
Philadelphia Eagles	19	20	.487	757	720
Chicago Bears	17	18	.486	751	726
Buffalo Bills	14	15	.483	681	658
New York Jets	12	13	.480	510	508
Arizona Cardinals†	6	7	.462	305	361
Jacksonville Jaguars	5	6	.455	262	288
St. Louis Rams††	19	24	.442	770	944
New Orleans Saints	6	8	.429	364	412
Tennessee Titans†††	14	19	.424	579	762
Minnesota Vikings	19	26	.422	900	1,017
Seattle Seahawks	8	11	.421	421	438
Tampa Bay Buccaneers	6	9	.400	230	279
Detroit Lions	7	11	.389	393	449
San Diego Chargers††††	10	16	.385	488	592
Kansas City Chiefs#	8	14	.364	347	475
Cleveland Browns	11	20	.355	629	728
Atlanta Falcons	6	11	.353	345	433
Cincinnati Bengals	5	10	.333	287	343

* Two games played when franchise was in Boston (won 26-8, lost 51-10).

** 12 games played when franchise was in Los Angeles (won 6, lost 6, 268 points scored, 224 points allowed).

*** One game played when franchise was in Boston (lost 21-6).

**** 15 games played when franchise was in Baltimore (won 8, lost 7, 264 points scored, 262 points allowed).

† Two games played when franchise was in Chicago (won 28-21, lost 7-0), three games played when franchise was in St. Louis (lost 30-14, lost 35-23, lost 41-16).

†† One game played when franchise was in Cleveland (won 15-14), 32 games played when franchise was in Los Angeles (won 12, lost 20, 486 points scored, 683

points allowed).

††† 22 gameq played when franchise was in Houston and known as the Oilers (won 9, lost 13, 371 points scored, 533 points allowed).

†††† One game played when franchise was in Los Angeles (lost 24-16).

\# One game played when franchise was Dallas Texans (won 20-17).

INDIVIDUAL RECORDS

SERVICE

Most Games, Career

29 — Jerry Rice, San Francisco-Oakland-Seattle (SB 4, NFC 6, AFC 1, NFC-D 11, AFC-D 2, NFC-FR 4, AFC-FR 1)

27 — D.D. Lewis, Dallas (SB 5, NFC 9, NFC-D 12, NFC-FR 1)

26 — Larry Cole, Dallas (SB 5, NFC 8, NFC-D 12, NFC-FR 1)

Bill Romanowski, San Francisco-Philadelphia-Denver-Oakland (SB 5, NFC 5, AFC 3, NFC-D 6, AFC-D 4, NFC-FR 1, AFC-FR 2)

Most Games, Head Coach

36 — Tom Landry, Dallas
Don Shula, Baltimore-Miami

24 — Chuck Noll, Pittsburgh
Mike Holmgren, Green Bay-Seattle
Joe Gibbs, Washington
Bill Belichick, Cleveland-New England

22 — Bud Grant, Minnesota

Most Championships Won, Head Coach

6 — George Halas, Chicago
Curly Lambeau, Green Bay

5 — Vince Lombardi, Green Bay

4 — Guy Chamberlin, Canton Bulldogs-Cleveland Bulldogs-Frankford Yellow Jackets
Chuck Noll, Pittsburgh

Most Games Won, Head Coach

20 — Tom Landry, Dallas

19 — Don Shula, Baltimore-Miami

17 — Joe Gibbs, Washington
Bill Belichick, Cleveland-New England

Most Games Lost, Head Coach

17 — Don Shula, Baltimore-Miami

16 — Tom Landry, Dallas

13 — Marty Schottenheimer, Cleveland-Kansas City-San Diego

SCORING

POINTS

Most Points, Career

187 — Adam Vinatieri, New England-Indianapolis, 24 games (52-pat, 45-fg)

153 — Gary Anderson, Pittsburgh-Philadelphia-San Francisco-Minnesota-Tennessee, 22 games (57-pat, 32-fg)

151 — David Akers, Philadelphia-San Francisco, 21 games (46-pat, 35-fg)

Most Points, Game

30 — Ricky Watters, NFC-D: San Francisco vs. N.Y. Giants, 1993 (5-td)

19 — Pat Harder, NFC-D: Detroit vs. Los Angeles, 1952 (2-td, 4-pat, 1-fg)

Paul Hornung, NFC: Green Bay vs. N.Y. Giants, 1961 (1-td, 4-pat, 3-fg)

18 — By many players

Most Consecutive Games Scoring

24 — Adam Vinatieri, New England-Indianapolis, 1996-98, 2001, 2003-08, 2010 (current)

21 — David Akers, Philadelphia-San Francisco, 2000-06, 2008-2010; San Francisco, 2011 (current)

19 — George Blanda, Chi. Bears-Houston-Oakland, 1956-1975

TOUCHDOWNS

Most Touchdowns, Career
- 22 Jerry Rice, San Francisco-Oakland-Seattle, 29 games (22-p)
- 21 Thurman Thomas, Buffalo, 21 games (16-r, 5-p)
  Emmitt Smith, Dallas, 17 games (19-r, 2-p)
- 17 Franco Harris, Pittsburgh, 19 games (16-r, 1-p)

Most Touchdowns, Game
- 5 Ricky Watters, NFC-D: San Francisco vs. N.Y. Giants, 1993 (5-r)
- 3 Andy Farkas, NFC-D: Washington vs. N.Y. Giants, 1943 (3-r)
  Tom Fears, NFC-D: Los Angeles vs. Chi. Bears, 1950 (3-p)
  Otto Graham, NFC: Cleveland vs. Detroit, 1954 (3-r)
  Gary Collins, NFC: Cleveland vs. Baltimore, 1964 (3-p)
  Craig Baynham, NFC-D: Dallas vs. Cleveland, 1967 (2-r, 1-p)
  Fred Biletnikoff, AFC-D: Oakland vs. Kansas City, 1968 (3-p)
  Tom Matte, NFC: Baltimore vs. Cleveland, 1968 (3-r)
  Larry Schreiber, NFC-D: San Francisco vs. Dallas, 1972 (3-r)
  Larry Csonka, AFC: Miami vs. Oakland, 1973 (3-r)
  Franco Harris, AFC-D: Pittsburgh vs. Buffalo, 1974 (3-r)
  Preston Pearson, NFC: Dallas vs. Los Angeles, 1975 (3-p)
  Dave Casper, AFC-D: Oakland vs. Baltimore, 1977 (ot) (3-p)
  Alvin Garrett, NFC-FR: Washington vs. Detroit, 1982 (3-p)
  John Riggins, NFC-D: Washington vs. L.A. Rams, 1983 (3-r)
  Roger Craig, SB: San Francisco vs. Miami, 1984 (1-r, 2-p)
  Jerry Rice, NFC-D: San Francisco vs. Minnesota, 1988 (3-p)
  Jerry Rice, SB: San Francisco vs. Denver, 1989 (3-p)
  Kenneth Davis, AFC: Buffalo vs. L.A. Raiders, 1990 (3-r)
  Andre Reed, AFC-FR: Buffalo vs. Houston, 1992 (ot) (3-p)
  Sterling Sharpe, NFC-FR: Green Bay vs. Detroit, 1993 (3-p)
  Napoleon McCallum, AFC-FR: L.A. Raiders vs. Denver, 1993 (3-r)
  Thurman Thomas, AFC: Buffalo vs. Kansas City, 1993 (3-r)
  William Floyd, NFC-D: San Francisco vs. Chicago, 1994 (3-r)
  Ricky Watters, SB: San Francisco vs. San Diego, 1994 (1-r, 2-p)
  Jerry Rice, SB: San Francisco vs. San Diego, 1994 (3-p)
  Emmitt Smith, NFC: Dallas vs. Green Bay, 1995 (3-r)
  Curtis Martin, AFC-D: New England vs. Pittsburgh, 1996 (3-r)
  Terrell Davis, SB: Denver vs. Green Bay, 1997 (3-r)
  Mario Bates, NFC-D: Arizona vs. Minnesota, 1998 (3-r)
  Leroy Hoard, NFC-D: Minnesota vs. Arizona, 1998 (2-r, 1-p)
  Willie Jackson, NFC-FR: New Orleans vs. St. Louis, 2000 (3-p)
  Amani Toomer, NFC-FR: N.Y. Giants vs. San Francisco, 2002 (3-p)
  Shaun Alexander, NFC-FR: Seattle vs. Green Bay, 2003 (ot) (3-r)
  Ryan Grant, NFC-D: Green Bay vs. Seattle, 2007 (3-r)
  Larry Fitzgerald, NFC: Arizona vs. Philadelphia, 2008 (3-p)
  Sidney Rice, NFC-D: Minnesota vs. Dallas, 2009 (3-p)
  Adrian Peterson, NFC: Minnesota vs. New Orleans, 2009 (3-p)
  Rob Gronkowski, AFC-D: New England vs. Denver, 2011 (3-p)

Most Consecutive Games Scoring Touchdowns
- 9 Thurman Thomas, Buffalo, 1992-98
- 8 John Stallworth, Pittsburgh, 1978-1983
  Emmitt Smith, Dallas, 1993-96
- 7 John Riggins, Washington, 1982-84
  Marcus Allen, L.A. Raiders, 1982-85
  Terrell Davis, Denver, 1996-98
  David Givens, New England, 2003-05

POINTS AFTER TOUCHDOWN

Most (One-Point) Points After Touchdown, Career
- 57 Gary Anderson, Pittsburgh-Philadelphia-San Francisco-Minnesota-Tennessee, 22 games (57 att)
- 52 Adam Vinatieri, New England-Indianapolis, 24 games (52 att)

- 49 George Blanda, Chi. Bears-Houston-Oakland, 19 games (49 att)

Most (One-Point) Points After Touchdown, Game
- 8 Lou Groza, NFC: Cleveland vs. Detroit, 1954 (8 att)
  Jim Martin, NFC: Detroit vs. Cleveland, 1957 (8 att)
  George Blanda, AFC-D: Oakland vs. Houston, 1969 (8 att)
  Mike Hollis, AFC-D: Jacksonville vs. Miami, 1999 (8 att)
- 7 Danny Villanueva, NFC-D: Dallas vs. Cleveland, 1967 (7 att)
  Raul Allegre, NFC-D: N.Y. Giants vs. San Francisco, 1986 (7 att)
  Mike Cofer, SB: San Francisco vs. Denver, 1989 (8 att)
  Lin Elliott, SB: Dallas vs. Buffalo, 1992 (7 att)
  Doug Brien, SB: San Francisco vs. San Diego, 1994 (7 att)
  Gary Anderson, NFC-FR: Philadelphia vs. Detroit, 1995 (7 att)
  Jeff Wilkins, NFC-D: St. Louis vs. Minnesota, 1999 (7 att)
  Mike Vanderjagt, AFC-FR: Indianapolis vs. Denver, 2004 (7 att)
- 6 George Blair, AFC: San Diego vs. Boston, 1963 (6 att)
  Mark Moseley, NFC-D: Washington vs. L.A. Rams, 1983 (6 att)
  Uwe von Schamann, AFC: Miami vs. Pittsburgh, 1984 (6 att)
  Ali Haji-Sheikh, SB: Washington vs. Denver, 1987 (6 att)
  Scott Norwood, AFC: Buffalo vs. L.A. Raiders, 1990 (7 att)
  Jeff Jaeger, AFC-FR: L.A. Raiders vs. Denver, 1993 (6 att)
  Jason Elam, AFC-FR: Denver vs. Jacksonville, 1997 (6 att)
  Jeff Wilkins, NFC-D: St. Louis vs. Green Bay, 2001 (6 att)
  Martín Gramatica, SB: Tampa Bay vs. Oakland, 2002 (6 att)
  Jay Feely, NFC-D: Atlanta vs. St. Louis, 2004 (6 att)
  Mason Crosby, NFC-D: Green Bay vs. Seattle, 2007 (6 att)
  Neil Rackers, NFC-FR: Arizona vs. Green Bay, 2009 (ot) (6 att)
  Mason Crosby, NFC-FR: Green Bay vs. Arizona, 2009 (ot) (6 att)
  Garrett Hartley, NFC-D: New Orleans vs. Arizona, 2009 (6 att)
  Mason Crosby, NFC-D: Green Bay vs. Atlanta, 2010 (6 att)
  John Kasay, NFC-FR: New Orleans vs. Detroit, 2011 (6 att)
  Stephen Gostkowski, AFC-D: New England vs. Denver, 2011 (6 att)

Most (Kicking) Points After Touchdown, No Misses, Career
- 57 Gary Anderson, Pittsburgh-Philadelphia-San Francisco-Minnesota-Tennessee, 22 games
- 52 Adam Vinatieri, New England-Indianapolis, 24 games
- 49 George Blanda, Chi. Bears-Houston-Oakland, 19 games

Most Two-Point Conversions, Career
- 2 Terrell Owens, San Francisco-Philadelphia-Dallas, 12 games
  Kevin Faulk, New England, 19 games

Most Two-Point Conversions, Game
- 2 Terrell Owens, NFC-FR: San Francisco vs. N.Y. Giants, 2002

FIELD GOALS

Most Field Goals Attempted, Career
- 54 Adam Vinatieri, New England-Indianapolis, 24 games
- 42 David Akers, Philadelphia-San Francisco, 21 games
- 40 Gary Anderson, Pittsburgh-Philadelphia-San Francisco-Minnesota-Tennessee, 22 games

Most Field Goals Attempted, Game
- 6 George Blanda, AFC: Oakland vs. Houston, 1967
  David Ray, NFC-D: Los Angeles vs. Dallas, 1973
  Mark Moseley, AFC-D: Cleveland vs. N.Y. Jets, 1986 (ot)
  Matt Bahr, NFC: N.Y. Giants vs. San Francisco, 1990
  Steve Christie, AFC: Buffalo vs. Miami, 1992
  Jeff Wilkins, NFC-D: St. Louis vs. Carolina, 2003 (2 ot)
- 5 By many players

Most Field Goals, Career
- 45 Adam Vinatieri, New England-Indianapolis, 24 games
- 35 David Akers, Philadelphia-San Francisco, 21 games
- 32 Gary Anderson, Pittsburgh-Philadelphia-San Francisco-Minnesota-Tennessee, 22 games

Most Field Goals, Game
- 5 Chuck Nelson, NFC-D: Minnesota vs. San Francisco, 1987

Matt Bahr, NFC: N.Y. Giants vs. San Francisco, 1990
Steve Christie, AFC: Buffalo vs. Miami, 1992
Brad Daluiso, NFC-FR: N.Y. Giants vs. Minnesota, 1997
John Kasay, NFC-FR: Carolina vs. Dallas, 2003
Jeff Wilkins, NFC-D: St. Louis vs. Carolina, 2003 (2 ot)
Adam Vinatieri, AFC: New England vs. Indianapolis, 2003
Adam Vinatieri, AFC-D: Indianapolis vs. Baltimore, 2006

4   Gino Cappelletti, AFC-D: Boston vs. Buffalo, 1963
George Blanda, AFC: Oakland vs. Houston, 1967
Don Chandler, SB: Green Bay vs. Oakland, 1967
Curt Knight, NFC: Washington vs. Dallas, 1972
George Blanda, AFC-D: Oakland vs. Pittsburgh, 1973
Ray Wersching, SB: San Francisco vs. Cincinnati, 1981
Tony Franklin, AFC-FR: New England vs. N.Y. Jets, 1985
Jess Atkinson, NFC-FR: Washington vs. L.A. Rams, 1986
Luis Zendejas, NFC-D: Philadelphia vs. Chicago, 1988
Gary Anderson, AFC-FR: Pittsburgh vs. Houston, 1989 (ot)
Norm Johnson, AFC-D: Pittsburgh vs. Buffalo, 1995
Chris Boniol, NFC-FR: Dallas vs. Minnesota, 1996
John Kasay, NFC-D: Carolina vs. Dallas, 1996
Mike Hollis, AFC-D: Jacksonville vs. New England, 1998
Al Del Greco, AFC-D: Tennessee vs. Indianapolis, 1999
David Akers, NFC-D: Philadelphia vs. Chicago, 2001
Nate Kaeding, AFC-D: San Diego vs. New England, 2007
David Akers, NFC-FR: Philadelphia vs. Minnesota, 2008
Neil Rackers, NFC-D: Arizona vs. Carolina, 2008

3   By many players

Most Consecutive Games Scoring Field Goals
13   Toni Fritsch, Dallas-Houston, 1972-79
12   Adam Vinatieri, New England, 1997-2004
11   Jason Elam, Denver-Atlanta, 1997-2000, 2003-05, 2008

Most Consecutive Field Goals
19   David Akers, Philadelphia, 2000-04, 2006, 2008
16   Gary Anderson, Pittsburgh-Philadelphia, 1989-1995
      Matt Stover, Baltimore, 2001, 2003, 2006, 2008;
      Indianapolis, 2009
15   Rafael Septien, Dallas, 1978-1982

Longest Field Goal
58   Pete Stoyanovich, AFC-FR: Miami vs. Kansas City, 1990
55   Jeff Wilkins, NFC-D: St. Louis vs. Atlanta, 2004
54   Ed Murray, NFC-D: Detroit vs. San Francisco, 1983
      Steve Christie, SB: Buffalo vs. Dallas, 1993
      John Carney, AFC-FR: San Diego vs. Indianapolis, 1995

Highest Field Goal Percentage, Career (10 field goals)
92.9   Martin Gramatica, Tampa Bay-Indianapolis-Dallas,
       9 games (14-13)
92.0   John Kasay, Carolina-New Orleans, 12 games (25-23)
90.9   Chuck Nelson, L.A. Rams-Minnesota, 6 games (11-10)

SAFETIES
Most Safeties, Game
1   Bill Willis, NFC-D: Cleveland vs. N.Y. Giants, 1950
    Carl Eller, NFC-D: Minnesota vs. Los Angeles, 1969
    George Andrie, NFC-D: Dallas vs. Detroit, 1970
    Alan Page, NFC-D: Minnesota vs. Dallas, 1971
    Dwight White, SB: Pittsburgh vs. Minnesota, 1974
    Reggie Harrison, SB: Pittsburgh vs. Dallas, 1975
    Jim Jensen, NFC-D: Dallas vs. Los Angeles, 1976
    Ted Washington, AFC: Houston vs. Pittsburgh, 1978
    Randy White, NFC-D: Dallas vs. Los Angeles, 1979
    Henry Waechter, SB: Chicago vs. New England, 1985
    Rulon Jones, AFC-D: Denver vs. New England, 1986
    George Martin, SB: N.Y. Giants vs. Denver, 1986
    D.D. Hoggard, AFC: Cleveland vs. Denver, 1987
    Bruce Smith, SB: Buffalo vs. N.Y. Giants, 1990
    Reggie White, NFC-FR: Philadelphia vs. New Orleans, 1992
    Willie Clay, NFC-FR: Detroit vs. Green Bay, 1994
    Carnell Lake, AFC-D: Pittsburgh vs. Cleveland, 1994
    Reuben Davis, AFC-D: San Diego vs. Miami, 1994
    Jevon Kearse, AFC: Tennessee vs. Buffalo, 1999
    Brady Smith, NFC-D: Atlanta vs. St. Louis, 2004
    Antonio Smith, NFC-FR: Arizona vs. Atlanta, 2008

Mike DeVito, AFC: N.Y. Jets vs. Pittsburgh, 2010

RUSHING
ATTEMPTS
Most Attempts, Career
400   Franco Harris, Pittsburgh, 19 games
349   Emmitt Smith, Dallas, 17 games
339   Thurman Thomas, Buffalo, 21 games

Most Attempts, Game
40   Lamar Smith, AFC-FR: Miami vs. Indianapolis, 2000 (ot)
38   Ricky Bell, NFC-D: Tampa Bay vs. Philadelphia, 1979
      John Riggins, SB: Washington vs. Miami, 1982
37   Lawrence McCutcheon, NFC-D: Los Angeles vs. St. Louis,
      1975
      John Riggins, NFC-D: Washington vs. Minnesota, 1982

YARDS GAINED
Most Yards Gained, Career
1,586   Emmitt Smith, Dallas, 17 games
1,556   Franco Harris, Pittsburgh, 19 games
1,442   Thurman Thomas, Buffalo, 21 games

Most Yards Gained, Game
248   Eric Dickerson, NFC-D: L.A. Rams vs. Dallas, 1985
209   Lamar Smith, AFC-FR: Miami vs. Indianapolis, 2000 (ot)
206   Keith Lincoln, AFC: San Diego vs. Boston, 1963

Most Games, 100 or More Yards Rushing, Career
7   Emmitt Smith, Dallas, 17 games
   Terrell Davis, Denver, 8 games
6   John Riggins, Washington, 9 games
   Thurman Thomas, Buffalo, 21 games
5   Franco Harris, Pittsburgh, 19 games
   Marcus Allen, L.A. Raiders-Kansas City, 16 games

Most Consecutive Games, 100 or More Yards Rushing
7   Terrell Davis, Denver, 1997-98
6   John Riggins, Washington, 1982-83
4   Thurman Thomas, Buffalo, 1990-91

Longest Run From Scrimmage
90   Fred Taylor, AFC-D: Jacksonville vs. Miami, 1999 (TD)
83   Ray Rice, AFC-FR: Baltimore vs. New England, 2009 (TD)
80   Roger Craig, NFC-D: San Francisco vs. Minnesota, 1988 (TD)
     Charlie Garner, AFC-FR: Oakland vs. N.Y. Jets, 2001 (TD)

AVERAGE GAIN
Highest Average Gain, Career (100 attempts)
5.59   Terrell Davis, Denver, 8 games (204-1,140)
5.04   Marcus Allen, L.A. Raiders-Kansas City, 16 games
      (267-1,347)
4.89   Eric Dickerson, L.A. Rams-Indianapolis, 7 games (148-724)

Highest Average Gain, Game (10 attempts)
15.90   Elmer Angsman, NFC: Chi. Cardinals vs. Philadelphia,
       1947 (10-159)
15.85   Keith Lincoln, AFC: San Diego vs. Boston, 1963 (13-206)
11.31   Zack Crockett, AFC-FR: Indianapolis vs. San Diego, 1995
       (13-147)

TOUCHDOWNS
Most Touchdowns, Career
19   Emmitt Smith, Dallas, 17 games
16   Franco Harris, Pittsburgh, 19 games
    Thurman Thomas, Buffalo, 21 games
12   John Riggins, Washington, 9 games
    Terrell Davis, Denver, 8 games

Most Touchdowns, Game
5   Ricky Watters, NFC-D: San Francisco vs. N.Y. Giants, 1993
3   Andy Farkas, NFC-D: Washington vs. N.Y. Giants, 1943
   Otto Graham, NFC: Cleveland vs. Detroit, 1954
   Tom Matte, NFC: Baltimore vs. Cleveland, 1968
   Larry Schreiber, NFC-D: San Francisco vs. Dallas, 1972
   Larry Csonka, AFC: Miami vs. Oakland, 1973
   Franco Harris, AFC-D: Pittsburgh vs. Buffalo, 1974
   John Riggins, NFC-D: Washington vs. L.A. Rams, 1983
   Kenneth Davis, AFC: Buffalo vs. L.A. Raiders, 1990

Napoleon McCallum, AFC-FR: L.A. Raiders vs. Denver, 1993
Thurman Thomas, AFC: Buffalo vs. Kansas City, 1993
William Floyd, NFC-D: San Francisco vs. Chicago, 1994
Emmitt Smith, NFC: Dallas vs. Green Bay, 1995
Curtis Martin, AFC-D: New England vs. Pittsburgh, 1996
Terrell Davis, SB: Denver vs. Green Bay, 1997
Mario Bates, NFC-D: Arizona vs. Minnesota, 1998
Shaun Alexander, NFC-FR: Seattle vs. Green Bay, 2003 (ot)
Ryan Grant, NFC-D: Green Bay vs. Seattle, 2007
Adrian Peterson, NFC: Minnesota vs. New Orleans, 2009 (ot)

Most Consecutive Games Rushing for Touchdowns
8 Emmitt Smith, Dallas, 1993-96
   Thurman Thomas, Buffalo, 1992-98
7 John Riggins, Washington, 1982-84
   Terrell Davis, Denver, 1996-98
5 Franco Harris, Pittsburgh, 1974-75
   Franco Harris, Pittsburgh, 1977-79
   Curtis Martin, New England-N.Y. Jets, 1996-98
   Jerome Bettis, Pittsburgh, 2004-05

PASSING
PASSER RATING
Highest Passer Rating, Career (150 attempts)
105.5 Aaron Rodgers, Green Bay, 7 games
104.8 Bart Starr, Green Bay, 10 games
104.2 Drew Brees, San Diego-New Orleans, 9 games

ATTEMPTS
Most Passes Attempted, Career
793 Tom Brady, New England, 22 games
791 Brett Favre, Green Bay-Minnesota, 24 games
734 Joe Montana, San Francisco-Kansas City, 23 games
Most Passes Attempted, Game
65 Steve Young, NFC-D: San Francisco vs. Green Bay, 1995
64 Bernie Kosar, AFC-D: Cleveland vs. N.Y. Jets, 1986 (ot)
   Dan Marino, AFC-FR: Miami vs. Buffalo, 1995
63 Drew Brees, NFC-D: New Orleans vs. San Francisco, 2011

COMPLETIONS
Most Passes Completed, Career
499 Tom Brady, New England, 22 games
481 Brett Favre, Green Bay-Minnesota, 24 games
460 Joe Montana, San Francisco-Kansas City, 23 games
Most Passes Completed, Game
40 Drew Brees, NFC-D: New Orleans vs. San Francisco, 2011
39 Drew Brees, NFC-FR: New Orleans vs. Seattle, 2010
36 Warren Moon, AFC-FR: Houston vs. Buffalo, 1992 (ot)

COMPLETION PERCENTAGE
Highest Completion Percentage, Career (150 attempts)
67.0 Drew Brees, San Diego-New Orleans, 9 games (391-262)
66.5 Kurt Warner, St. Louis-Arizona, 13 games (462-307)
66.3 Ken Anderson, Cincinnati, 6 games (166-110)
Highest Completion Percentage, Game (15 completions)
92.9 Tom Brady, AFC-D: New England vs. Jacksonville, 2007
   (28-26)
88.0 Phil Simms, SB: N.Y. Giants vs. Denver, 1986 (25-22)
87.9 Kurt Warner, NFC-FR: Arizona vs. Green Bay, 2009 (ot)
   (33-29)

YARDS GAINED
Most Yards Gained, Career
5,855 Brett Favre, Green Bay-Minnesota, 24 games
5,772 Joe Montana, San Francisco-Kansas City, 23 games
5,389 Peyton Manning, Indianapolis, 19 games
Most Yards Gained, Game
489 Bernie Kosar, AFC-D: Cleveland vs. N.Y. Jets, 1986 (ot)
466 Drew Brees, NFC-FR: New Orleans vs. Detroit, 2011
462 Drew Brees, NFC-D: New Orleans vs. San Francisco, 2011
Most Games, 300 or More Yards Passing, Career
8 Peyton Manning, Indianapolis, 19 games
6 Joe Montana, San Francisco-Kansas City, 23 games

Kurt Warner, St. Louis-Arizona, 13 games
5 Dan Fouts, San Diego, 7 games
   Drew Brees, San Diego-New Orleans, 9 games
Most Consecutive Games, 300 or More Yards Passing
4 Dan Fouts, San Diego, 1979-1981
3 Jim Kelly, Buffalo, 1989-1990
   Warren Moon, Houston, 1991-93
   Drew Brees, New Orleans, 2010-11 (current)
2 Daryle Lamonica, Oakland, 1968
   Ken Anderson, Cincinnati, 1981-82
   Terry Bradshaw, Pittsburgh, 1979-1982
   Joe Montana, San Francisco, 1983-84
   Dan Marino, Miami, 1984
   Troy Aikman, Dallas, 1994
   Steve Young, San Francisco, 1994-95
   Kurt Warner, St. Louis, 1999-2000
   Peyton Manning, Indianapolis, 2003
   Marc Bulger, St. Louis, 2003-04
   Matt Hasselbeck, Seattle, 2003-04
   Peyton Manning, Indianapolis, 2007-08
   Donovan McNabb, Philadelphia, 2004, 2008
   Kurt Warner, Arizona, 2008-09
   Peyton Manning, Indianapolis, 2009
   Eli Manning, N.Y. Giants, 2011
Longest Pass Completion
96 Trent Dilfer (to Sharpe), AFC: Baltimore vs. Oakland, 2000 (TD)
94 Troy Aikman (to Harper), NFC-D: Dallas vs. Green Bay, 1994 (TD)
93 Daryle Lamonica (to Dubenion), AFC-D: Buffalo vs. Boston, 1963 (TD)

AVERAGE GAIN
Highest Average Gain, Career (150 attempts)
8.55 Kurt Warner, St. Louis-Arizona, 13 games (462-3,952)
8.45 Joe Theismann, Washington, 10 games (211-1,782)
8.43 Jim Plunkett, Oakland-L.A. Raiders, 10 games (272-2,293)
Highest Average Gain, Game (20 attempts)
15.05 Tim Tebow, AFC-FR: Denver vs. Pittsburgh, 2011 (21-316)
14.71 Terry Bradshaw, SB: Pittsburgh vs. Los Angeles, 1979 (21-309)
14.50 Peyton Manning, AFC-FR: Indianapolis vs. Denver, 2003 (26-377)

TOUCHDOWNS
Most Touchdown Passes, Career
45 Joe Montana, San Francisco-Kansas City, 23 games
44 Brett Favre, Green Bay-Minnesota, 24 games
38 Tom Brady, New England, 22 games
Most Touchdown Passes, Game
6 Daryle Lamonica, AFC-D: Oakland vs. Houston, 1969
   Steve Young, SB: San Francisco vs. San Diego, 1994
   Tom Brady, AFC-D: New England vs. Denver, 2011
5 Sid Luckman, NFC: Chi. Bears vs. Washington, 1943
   Daryle Lamonica, AFC-D: Oakland vs. Kansas City, 1968
   Joe Montana, SB: San Francisco vs. Denver, 1989
   Kurt Warner, NFC-D: St. Louis vs. Minnesota, 1999
   Kerry Collins, NFC: N.Y. Giants vs. Minnesota, 2000
   Peyton Manning, AFC-FR: Indianapolis vs. Denver, 2003
   Kurt Warner, NFC-FR: Arizona vs. Green Bay, 2009 (ot)
4 Otto Graham, NFC: Cleveland vs. Los Angeles, 1950
   Tobin Rote, NFC: Detroit vs. Cleveland, 1957
   Bart Starr, NFC: Green Bay vs. Dallas, 1966
   Ken Stabler, AFC-D: Oakland vs. Miami, 1974
   Roger Staubach, NFC: Dallas vs. Los Angeles, 1975
   Terry Bradshaw, SB: Pittsburgh vs. Dallas, 1978
   Don Strock, AFC-D: Miami vs. San Diego, 1981 (ot)
   Lynn Dickey, NFC-FR: Green Bay vs. St. Louis, 1982
   Dan Marino, AFC: Miami vs. Pittsburgh, 1984
   Phil Simms, NFC-D: N.Y. Giants vs. San Francisco, 1986
   Doug Williams, SB: Washington vs. Denver, 1987
   Jim Kelly, AFC-D: Buffalo vs. Cleveland, 1989
   Joe Montana, NFC-D: San Francisco vs. Minnesota, 1989
   Warren Moon, AFC-FR: Houston vs. Buffalo, 1992 (ot)

Frank Reich, AFC-FR: Buffalo vs. Houston, 1992 (ot)
Troy Aikman, SB: Dallas vs. Buffalo, 1992
Jeff George, NFC-D: Minnesota vs. St. Louis, 1999
Aaron Brooks, NFC-FR: New Orleans vs. St. Louis, 2000
Kerry Collins, NFC-FR: N.Y. Giants vs. San Francisco, 2002
Peyton Manning, AFC-FR: Indianapolis vs. Denver, 2004
Daunte Culpepper, NFC-FR: Minnesota vs. Green Bay, 2004
Kurt Warner, NFC: Arizona vs. Philadelphia, 2008
Aaron Rodgers, NFC-FR: Green Bay vs. Arizona, 2009 (ot)
Brett Favre, NFC-D: Minnesota vs. Dallas, 2009
Matt Hasselbeck, NFC-FR: Seattle vs. New Orleans, 2010
Drew Brees, NFC-FR: New Orleans vs. San Francisco, 2011

Most Consecutive Games, Touchdown Passes
20   Brett Favre, Green Bay-Minnesota, 1995-2009
18   Tom Brady, New England, 2001-2011
13   Dan Marino, Miami, 1983-1995

HAD INTERCEPTED
Lowest Percentage, Passes Had Intercepted, Career (150 attempts)
1.02   Drew Brees, San Diego-New Orleans, 9 games (391-4)
1.41   Bart Starr, Green Bay, 10 games (213-3)
1.82   Aaron Rodgers, Green Bay, 7 games (220-4)
Most Attempts Without Interception, Game
60   Drew Brees, NFC-FR: New Orleans vs. Seattle, 2010
58   Eli Manning, NFC: N.Y. Giants vs. San Francisco, 2011 (ot)
54   Neil O'Donnell, AFC: Pittsburgh vs. San Diego, 1994
Most Passes Had Intercepted, Career
30   Brett Favre, Green Bay-Minnesota, 24 games
28   Jim Kelly, Buffalo, 17 games
26   Terry Bradshaw, Pittsburgh, 19 games
Most Passes Had Intercepted, Game
6   Frank Filchock, NFC: N.Y. Giants vs. Chi. Bears, 1946
    Bobby Layne, NFC: Detroit vs. Cleveland, 1954
    Norm Van Brocklin, NFC: Los Angeles vs. Cleveland, 1955
    Brett Favre, NFC-D: Green Bay vs. St. Louis, 2001
5   Frank Filchock, NFC: Washington vs. Chi. Bears, 1940
    George Blanda, AFC: Houston vs. San Diego, 1961
    George Blanda, AFC: Houston vs. Dall. Texans, 1962 (ot)
    Y.A. Tittle, NFC: N.Y. Giants vs. Chicago, 1963
    Mike Phipps, AFC-D: Cleveland vs. Miami, 1972
    Dan Pastorini, AFC: Houston vs. Pittsburgh, 1978
    Dan Fouts, AFC-D: San Diego vs. Houston, 1979
    Tommy Kramer, NFC-D: Minnesota vs. Philadelphia, 1980
    Dan Fouts, AFC-D: San Diego vs. Miami, 1982
    Richard Todd, AFC: N.Y. Jets vs. Miami, 1982
    Gary Danielson, NFC-D: Detroit vs. San Francisco, 1983
    Jay Schroeder, AFC: L.A. Raiders vs. Buffalo, 1990
    Rich Gannon, SB: Oakland vs. Tampa Bay, 2002
    Jake Delhomme, NFC-D: Carolina vs. Arizona, 2008
4   By many players

PASS RECEIVING
RECEPTIONS
Most Receptions, Career
151   Jerry Rice, San Francisco-Oakland-Seattle, 29 games
88   Hines Ward, Pittsburgh, 18 games
87   Michael Irvin, Dallas, 16 games
Most Receptions, Game
15   Darren Sproles, NFC-D: New Orleans vs. San Francisco, 2011
13   Kellen Winslow, AFC-D: San Diego vs. Miami, 1981 (ot)
    Thurman Thomas, AFC-D: Buffalo vs. Cleveland, 1989
    Shannon Sharpe, AFC-FR: Denver vs. L.A. Raiders, 1993
    Chad Morton, NFC-D: New Orleans vs. Minnesota, 2000
12   Raymond Berry, NFC: Baltimore vs. N.Y. Giants, 1958
    Michael Irvin, NFC: Dallas vs. San Francisco, 1994
    Darrell Jackson, NFC-FR: Seattle vs. St. Louis, 2004
    Steve Smith, NFC-D: Carolina vs. Chicago, 2005
    Calvin Johnson, NFC-FR: Detroit vs. New Orleans, 2011
Most Consecutive Games, Pass Receptions
28   Jerry Rice, San Francisco-Oakland, 1985-2002
22   Drew Pearson, Dallas, 1973-1983

18   Paul Warfield, Cleveland-Miami, 1964-1974
    Cliff Branch, Oakland/L.A. Raiders, 1974-1983
    Thurman Thomas, Buffalo, 1989-1998
    Shannon Sharpe, Denver-Baltimore-Denver, 1991-2003

YARDS GAINED
Most Yards Gained, Career
2,245   Jerry Rice, San Francisco-Oakland-Seattle, 29 games
1,315   Michael Irvin, Dallas, 16 games
1,289   Cliff Branch, Oakland/L.A. Raiders, 22 games
Most Yards Gained, Game
240   Eric Moulds, AFC-FR: Buffalo vs. Miami, 1998
227   Anthony Carter, NFC-D: Minnesota vs. San Francisco, 1987
221   Reggie Wayne, AFC-FR: Indianapolis vs. Denver, 2004
Most Games, 100 or More Yards Receiving, Career
8   Jerry Rice, San Francisco-Oakland-Seattle, 29 games
6   Michael Irvin, Dallas, 16 games
5   John Stallworth, Pittsburgh, 18 games
    Andre Reed, Buffalo, 21 games
    Hines Ward, Pittsburgh, 18 games
Most Consecutive Games, 100 or More Yards Receiving, Career
4   Larry Fitzgerald, Arizona, 2008
3   Tom Fears, Los Angeles, 1950-51
    Jerry Rice, San Francisco, 1988-89
    Randy Moss, Minnesota, 1999-2000
2   By many players
Longest Reception
96   Shannon Sharpe (from Dilfer), AFC: Baltimore vs. Oakland, 2000 (TD)
94   Alvin Harper (from Aikman), NFC-D: Dallas vs. Green Bay, 1994 (TD)
93   Elbert Dubenion (from Lamonica), AFC-D: Buffalo vs. Boston, 1963 (TD)

AVERAGE GAIN
Highest Average Gain, Career (20 receptions)
27.3   Alvin Harper, Dallas, 10 games (24-655)
23.7   Willie Gault, Chicago-L.A. Raiders, 12 games (21-497)
22.8   Harold Jackson, L.A. Rams-New England-Minnesota-Seattle, 14 games (24-548)
Highest Average Gain, Game (3 receptions)
51.0   Demaryius Thomas, AFC-FR: Denver vs. Pittsburgh, 2011 (4-204)
46.3   Harold Jackson, NFC: Los Angeles vs. Minnesota, 1974 (3-139)
42.7   Billy Cannon, AFC: Houston vs. L.A. Chargers, 1960 (3-128)

TOUCHDOWNS
Most Touchdowns, Career
22   Jerry Rice, San Francisco-Oakland-Seattle, 29 games
12   John Stallworth, Pittsburgh, 18 games
10   Fred Biletnikoff, Oakland, 19 games
    Antonio Freeman, Green Bay-Philadelphia-Green Bay, 16 games
    Randy Moss, Minnesota-New England, 12 games
    Hines Ward, Pittsburgh, 18 games
Most Touchdowns, Game
3   Tom Fears, NFC-D: Los Angeles vs. Chi. Bears, 1950
    Gary Collins, NFC: Cleveland vs. Baltimore, 1964
    Fred Biletnikoff, AFC-D: Oakland vs. Kansas City, 1968
    Preston Pearson, NFC: Dallas vs. Los Angeles, 1975
    Dave Casper, AFC-D: Oakland vs. Baltimore, 1977 (ot)
    Alvin Garrett, NFC: Washington vs. Detroit, 1982
    Jerry Rice, NFC-D: San Francisco vs. Minnesota, 1988
    Jerry Rice, SB: San Francisco vs. Denver, 1989
    Andre Reed, AFC-FR: Buffalo vs. Houston, 1992 (ot)
    Sterling Sharpe, NFC-FR: Green Bay vs. Detroit, 1993
    Jerry Rice, SB: San Francisco vs. San Diego, 1994
    Willie Jackson, NFC-FR: New Orleans vs. St. Louis, 2000
    Amani Toomer, NFC-FR: N.Y. Giants vs. San Francisco, 2002
    Larry Fitzgerald, NFC: Arizona vs. Philadelphia, 2008
    Sidney Rice, NFC-D: Minnesota vs. Dallas, 2009
    Rob Gronkowski, AFC-D: New England vs. Denver, 2011

Most Consecutive Games, Touchdown Passes Caught
8 John Stallworth, Pittsburgh, 1978-1983
7 David Givens, New England, 2003-05)
5 James Lofton, Green Bay-Buffalo, 1982-1990
   Randy Moss, Minnesota, 1998-2000
   Antonio Freeman, Green Bay, 1997-2001
   Hines Ward, Pittsburgh, 2002-05
   Larry Fitzgerald, Arizona, 2008-09

INTERCEPTIONS BY
Most Interceptions, Career
9 Charlie Waters, Dallas, 25 games
   Bill Simpson, Los Angeles-Buffalo, 11 games
   Ronnie Lott, San Francisco-L.A. Raiders, 20 games
8 Lester Hayes, Oakland/L.A. Raiders, 13 games
   Ed Reed, Baltimore, 11 games
7 Willie Brown, Oakland, 17 games
   Dennis Thurman, Dallas, 14 games
   Rodney Harrison, San Diego-New England, 13 games
   Asante Samuel, New England-Philadelphia, 19 games
Most Interceptions, Game
4 Vernon Perry, AFC-D: Houston vs. San Diego, 1979
3 Joe Laws, NFC: Green Bay vs. N.Y. Giants, 1944
   Charlie Waters, NFC-D: Dallas vs. Chicago, 1977
   Rod Martin, SB: Oakland vs. Philadelphia, 1980
   Dennis Thurman, NFC-D: Dallas vs. Green Bay, 1982
   A.J. Duhe, AFC: Miami vs. N.Y. Jets, 1982
   Ty Law, AFC: New England vs. Indianapolis, 2003
   Ricky Manning Jr., NFC: Carolina vs. Philadelphia, 2003
2 By many players
Most Consecutive Games, Interceptions
4 Aeneas Williams, Arizona-St. Louis, 1998-2001
   Rodney Harrison, New England, 2004, 2007
3 By many players. Last time:
      Ed Reed, Baltimore, 2006, 2008

YARDS GAINED
Most Yards Gained, Career
227 Asante Samuel, New England-Philadelphia, 19 games
196 Willie Brown, Oakland, 17 games
187 Ronnie Lott, San Francisco-L.A.-Raiders, 20 games
Most Yards Gained, Game
108 Darrien Gordon, SB: Denver vs. Atlanta, 1998
101 George Teague, NFC-FR: Green Bay vs. Detroit, 1993
100 Champ Bailey, AFC-D: Denver vs. New England, 2005
     James Harrison, SB: Pittsburgh vs. Arizona, 2008
Longest Return
101 George Teague, NFC-FR: Green Bay vs. Detroit, 1993 (TD)
100 Champ Bailey, AFC-D: Denver vs. New England, 2005
     James Harrison, SB: Pittsburgh vs. Arizona, 2008 (TD)
 98 Darrol Ray, AFC-FR: N.Y. Jets vs. Cincinnati, 1982 (TD)

TOUCHDOWNS
Most Touchdowns, Career
4 Asante Samuel, New England-Philadelphia, 19 games
3 Willie Brown, Oakland, 17 games
2 Lester Hayes, Oakland/L.A. Raiders, 13 games
   Ronnie Lott, San Francisco-L.A. Raiders, 20 games
   Darrell Green, Washington, 18 games
   Melvin Jenkins, Seattle-Detroit, 5 games
   George Teague, Green Bay-Dallas-Miami-Dallas, 12 games
   Aeneas Williams, Arizona-St. Louis, 6 games
   Dwight Smith, Tampa Bay, 4 games
Most Touchdowns, Game
2 Aeneas Williams, NFC-D: St. Louis vs. Green Bay, 2001
   Dwight Smith, SB: Tampa Bay vs. Oakland, 2002
1 By many players

PUNTING
Most Punts, Career
111 Ray Guy, Oakland/L.A. Raiders, 22 games

101 Craig Hentrich, Green Bay-Tennessee, 22 games
84 Danny White, Dallas, 18 games
    Sean Landeta, N.Y. Giants-Tampa Bay-Green Bay-
      Philadelphia-St. Louis, 18 games
Most Punts, Game
14 Dave Jennings, AFC-D: N.Y. Jets vs. Cleveland, 1986 (ot)
12 David Lee, AFC-D: Baltimore vs. Oakland, 1977 (ot)
    Steve Weatherford, NFC: N.Y. Giants vs. San Francisco,
      2011 (ot)
11 Ken Strong, NFC: N.Y. Giants vs. Chi. Bears, 1933
    Jim Norton, AFC: Houston vs. Oakland, 1967
    Ode Burrell, AFC-D: Houston vs. Oakland, 1969
    Dale Hatcher, NFC: L.A. Rams vs. Chicago, 1985
    Brad Maynard, SB: N.Y. Giants vs. Baltimore, 2000
Longest Punt
76 Ed Danowski, NFC: N.Y. Giants vs. Detroit, 1935
    Mike Horan, AFC: Denver vs. Buffalo, 1991
72 Charlie Conerly, NFC-D: N.Y. Giants vs. Cleveland, 1950
    Yale Lary, NFC: Detroit vs. Cleveland, 1953
71 Ray Guy, AFC: Oakland vs. San Diego, 1980

AVERAGE YARDAGE
Highest Average, Career (25 punts)
44.5   Rich Camarillo, New England, 6 games (35-1,559)
44.44 Todd Sauerbrun, Carolina-Denver-New England, 9 games
       (43-1,911)
44.38 Mike Scifres, San Diego, 8 games (42-1,864)
Highest Average, Game (4 punts)
56.0 Ray Guy, AFC: Oakland vs. San Diego, 1980 (4-224)
53.8 Sam Koch, AFC-D: Baltimore vs. Pittsburgh, 2010
      (4-215)
53.3 Craig Hentrich, AFC-D: Tennessee vs. Baltimore, 2008
      (4-213)

PUNT RETURNS
Most Punt Returns, Career
34 David Meggett, N.Y. Giants-New England-N.Y. Jets,
      13 games
    Brian Mitchell, Washington-Philadelphia, 16 games
33 Troy Brown, New England, 20 games
26 Antwaan Randle El, Pittsburgh-Washington, 12 games
Most Punt Returns, Game
8 Kyle Williams, NFC: San Francisco vs. N.Y. Giants,
     2011 (ot)
7 Ron Gardin, AFC-D: Baltimore vs. Cincinnati, 1970
   Carl Roaches, AFC-FR: Houston vs. Oakland, 1980
   Gerald McNeil, AFC-D: Cleveland vs. N.Y. Jets, 1986 (ot)
   Phil McConkey, NFC: N.Y. Giants vs. San Francisco,
     1986
   David Meggett, AFC-D: New England vs. Pittsburgh, 1996
   Reggie Barlow, AFC-FR: Jacksonville vs. New England,
     1998
6 By many players

YARDS GAINED
Most Yards Gained, Career
339 Brian Mitchell, Washington-Philadelphia, 16 games
315 Troy Brown, New England, 20 games
312 David Meggett, N.Y. Giants-New England-N.Y. Jets,
       13 games
Most Yards Gained, Game
152 Allen Rossum, NFC-D: Atlanta vs. St. Louis, 2004
143 Anthony Carter, NFC-FR: Minnesota vs. New Orleans,
       1987
141 Bob Hayes, NFC-D: Dallas vs. Cleveland, 1967
Longest Return
88 Jermaine Lewis, AFC-D: Baltimore vs. Pittsburgh, 2001
      (TD)
84 Anthony Carter, NFC-FR: Minnesota vs. New Orleans, 1987
      (TD)
83 Reggie Bush, NFC-D: New Orleans vs. Arizona, 2009 (TD)

AVERAGE YARDAGE
Highest Average, Career (10 returns)
23.9   Allen Rossum, Green Bay-Atlanta, 6 games (10-239)
15.3   Robert Brooks, Green Bay, 11 games (14-214)
15.2   Anthony Carter, Minnesota-Detroit, 9 games (17-259)
Highest Average Gain, Game (3 returns)
50.7   Allen Rossum, NFC-D: Atlanta vs. St. Louis, 2004 (3-152)
47.0   Bob Hayes, NFC-D: Dallas vs. Cleveland, 1967 (3-141)
36.3   Reggie Bush, NFC-D: New Orleans vs. Arizona, 2009
         (3-109)

TOUCHDOWNS
Most Touchdowns
1   Hugh Gallarneau, NFC-D: Chicago Bears vs. Green Bay,
       1941
    Bosh Pritchard, NFC-D: Philadelphia vs. Pittsburgh, 1947
    Charley Trippi, NFC: Chicago Cardinals vs. Philadelphia,
       1947
    Verda (Vitamin T) Smith, NFC-D: Los Angeles vs. Detroit,
       1952
    George (Butch) Byrd, AFC: Buffalo vs. San Diego, 1965
    Golden Richards, NFC: Dallas vs. Minnesota, 1973
    Wes Chandler, AFC-D: San Diego vs. Miami, 1981 (ot)
    Shaun Gayle, NFC-D: Chicago vs. N.Y. Giants, 1985
    Anthony Carter, NFC-FR: Minnesota vs. New Orleans, 1987
    Darrell Green, NFC-D: Washington vs. Chicago, 1987
    Antonio Freeman, NFC-FR: Green Bay vs. Atlanta, 1995
    Desmond Howard, NFC-D: Green Bay vs. San Francisco,
       1996
    Jermaine Lewis, AFC-D: Baltimore vs. Pittsburgh, 2001
    Troy Brown, AFC: New England vs. Pittsburgh, 2001
    Antwaan Randle El, AFC-FR: Pittsburgh vs. Cleveland,
       2002
    Santana Moss, AFC: N.Y. Jets vs. Pittsburgh, 2004 (ot)
    Allen Rossum, NFC-D: Atlanta vs. St. Louis, 2004
    Steve Smith, NFC: Carolina vs. Seattle, 2005
    Santonio Holmes, AFC: Pittsburgh vs. San Diego, 2008
    Reggie Bush, NFC-D: New Orleans vs. Arizona, 2009

KICKOFF RETURNS
Most Kickoff Returns, Career
36   Brian Mitchell, Washington-Philadelphia, 16 games
31   Kevin Williams, Dallas-Buffalo, 12 games
29   Fulton Walker, Miami-L.A. Raiders, 10 games
Most Kickoff Returns, Game
8   Marc Logan, AFC-D: Miami vs. Buffalo, 1990
    Andre Coleman, SB: San Diego vs. San Francisco, 1994
    Marcus Knight, SB: Oakland vs. Tampa Bay, 2002
7   Don Bingham, NFC: Chi. Bears vs. N.Y. Giants, 1956
    Reggie Brown, NFC-FR: Atlanta vs. Minnesota, 1982
    David Verser, AFC-FR: Cincinnati vs. N.Y. Jets, 1982
    Del Rodgers, NFC-D: Green Bay vs. Dallas, 1982
    Henry Ellard, NFC-D: L.A. Rams vs. Washington, 1983
    Stephen Starring, SB: New England vs. Chicago, 1985
    Darick Holmes, AFC-D: Buffalo vs. Pittsburgh, 1995
    Antonio Freeman, NFC: Green Bay vs. Dallas, 1995
    Roell Preston, NFC-FR: Green Bay vs. San Francisco,
       1998
    Robert Tate, NFC-D: Minnesota vs. St. Louis, 1999
    Fred McAfee, NFC-D: New Orleans vs. Minnesota, 2000
    Michael Bates, NFC-FR: Dallas vs. Carolina, 2003
    Dante Hall, AFC-D: Kansas City vs. Indianapolis, 2003
    Michael Lewis, NFC: New Orleans vs. Chicago, 2006
6   By many players

YARDS GAINED
Most Yards Gained, Career
875   Brian Mitchell, Washington-Philadelphia, 16 games
677   Fulton Walker, Miami-L.A. Raiders, 10 games
632   Kevin Williams, Dallas-Buffalo, 12 games
Most Yards Gained, Game
244   Andre Coleman, SB: San Diego vs. San Francisco, 1994

220   Ellis Hobbs, AFC: New England vs. Indianapolis, 2006
210   Tim Dwight, SB: Atlanta vs. Denver, 1998
Longest Return
102   Eric Weems, NFC-D: Atlanta vs. Green Bay, 2010 (TD)
100   Brian Mitchell, NFC-D: Washington vs. Tampa Bay, 1999
         (TD)
99   Desmond Howard, SB: Green Bay vs. New England, 1996
         (TD)

AVERAGE YARDAGE
Highest Average, Career (10 returns)
30.1   Carl Garrett, Oakland, 5 games (16-481)
30.0   Reggie Barlow, Jacksonville, 8 games (12-360)
29.2   Chad Morton, New Orleans-N.Y. Jets-N.Y. Giants, 6 games
         (14-409)
Highest Average, Game (3 returns)
56.7   Les (Speedy) Duncan, NFC-D: Washington vs. San Francisco,
         1971 (3-170)
51.3   Ed Podolak, AFC-D: Kansas City vs. Miami, 1971 (ot)
         (3-154)
49.0   Les (Speedy) Duncan, AFC: San Diego vs. Buffalo, 1964
         (3-147)

TOUCHDOWNS
Most Touchdowns, Career
2   Ron Dixon, N.Y. Giants, 4 games
1   By many players
Most Touchdowns, Game
1   Vic Washington, NFC-D: San Francisco vs. Dallas, 1972
    Nat Moore, AFC-D: Miami vs. Oakland, 1974
    Marshall Johnson, AFC-D: Baltimore vs. Oakland, 1977
       (ot)
    Fulton Walker, SB: Miami vs. Washington, 1982
    Stanford Jennings, SB: Cincinnati vs. San Francisco, 1988
    Eric Metcalf, AFC-D: Cleveland vs. Buffalo, 1989
    Andre Coleman, SB: San Diego vs. San Francisco, 1994
    Desmond Howard, SB: Green Bay vs. New England, 1996
    Chuck Levy, NFC: San Francisco vs. Green Bay, 1997
    Tim Dwight, SB: Atlanta vs. Denver, 1998
    Kevin Dyson, AFC-FR: Tennessee vs. Buffalo, 1999
    Charlie Rogers, AFC-FR: Seattle vs. Miami, 1999
    Brian Mitchell, NFC-D: Washington vs. Tampa Bay, 1999
    Tony Horne, NFC-D: St. Louis vs. Minnesota, 1999
    Derrick Mason, AFC: Tennessee vs. Jacksonville, 1999
    Ron Dixon, NFC-D: N.Y. Giants vs. Philadelphia, 2000;
       SB: N.Y. Giants vs. Baltimore, 2000
    Jermaine Lewis, SB: Baltimore vs. N.Y. Giants, 2000
    Dante Hall, AFC-D: Kansas City vs. Indianapolis, 2003
    Miles Austin, NFC-FR: Dallas vs. Seattle, 2006
    Devin Hester, SB: Chicago vs. Indianapolis, 2006
    Eric Weems, NFC-D: Atlanta vs. Green Bay, 2010

FUMBLES
Most Fumbles, Career
16   Warren Moon, Houston-Minnesota, 10 games
14   John Elway, Denver, 22 games
     Donovan McNabb, Philadelphia, 16 games
13   Tony Dorsett, Dallas, 17 games
Most Fumbles, Game
5   Warren Moon, AFC-D: Houston vs. Kansas City, 1993
4   Brian Sipe, AFC-D: Cleveland vs. Oakland, 1980
    Randall Cunningham, NFC-FR: Minnesota vs. N.Y. Giants,
       1997
3   By many players

RECOVERIES
Most Own Fumbles Recovered, Career
8   Warren Moon, Houston-Minnesota, 10 games
7   John Elway, Denver, 22 games
6   Jim Kelly, Buffalo, 17 games
Most Opponents' Fumbles Recovered, Career
4   Cliff Harris, Dallas, 21 games

Harvey Martin, Dallas, 22 games
Ted Hendricks, Baltimore-Oakland/L.A. Raiders, 21 games
Alvin Walton, Washington, 9 games
Monte Coleman, Washington, 21 games
Dave Thomas, Dallas-Jacksonville-N.Y. Giants, 13 games
3 Paul Krause, Minnesota, 19 games
Jack Lambert, Pittsburgh, 18 games
Fred Dryer, Los Angeles, 14 games
Charlie Waters, Dallas, 25 games
Jack Ham, Pittsburgh, 16 games
Mike Hegman, Dallas, 16 games
Tom Jackson, Denver, 10 games
Rich Milot, Washington, 13 games
Mike Singletary, Chicago, 12 games
Darryl Grant, Washington, 16 games
Wes Hopkins, Philadelphia, 3 games
Wilber Marshall, Chicago-Washington, 15 games
Tyrone Braxton, Denver-Miami-Denver, 19 games
Neil Smith, Kansas City-Denver, 16 games
Tony Brackens, Jacksonville, 7 games
Phil Hansen, Buffalo, 14 games
Carnell Lake, Pittsburgh-Jacksonville-Baltimore, 17 games
Jason Gildon, Pittsburgh, 13 games
Tedy Bruschi, New England, 22 games
Jim Leonhard, Baltimore-N.Y. Jets, 6 games
2 By many players

Most Fumbles Recovered, Game, Own and Opponents'
3 Jack Lambert, AFC: Pittsburgh vs. Oakland, 1975 (3 opp)
Ron Jaworski, NFC-FR: Philadelphia vs. N.Y. Giants, 1981 (3 own)
Devin Hester, NFC-D: Chicago vs. Seattle, 2006 (3-own)
2 By many players

YARDS GAINED
Longest Return
93 Andy Russell, AFC-D: Pittsburgh vs. Baltimore, 1975 (opp, TD)
79 Neil Smith, AFC-D: Denver vs. Miami, 1998 (opp, TD)
64 Leon Lett, SB: Dallas vs. Buffalo, 1992 (opp)

TOUCHDOWNS
Most Touchdowns
1 By many players

COMBINED NET YARDS GAINED
Rushing, receiving, interception returns, punt returns, kickoff returns, and fumble returns.
ATTEMPTS
Most Attempts, Career
454 Franco Harris, Pittsburgh, 19 games
417 Thurman Thomas, Buffalo, 21 games
397 Emmitt Smith, Dallas, 17 games
Most Attempts, Game
43 Lamar Smith, AFC-FR: Miami vs. Indianapolis, 2000 (ot)
42 Curtis Martin, AFC-D: N.Y. Jets vs. Jacksonville, 1998
40 Lawrence McCutcheon, NFC-D: Los Angeles vs. St. Louis, 1975

YARDS GAINED
Most Yards Gained, Career
2,289 Jerry Rice, San Francisco-Oakland-Seattle, 29 games
2,124 Thurman Thomas, Buffalo, 21 games
2,060 Franco Harris, Pittsburgh, 19 games
Most Yards Gained, Game
350 Ed Podolak, AFC-D: Kansas City vs. Miami, 1971 (ot)
329 Keith Lincoln, AFC: San Diego vs. Boston, 1963
328 Darren Sproles, AFC-FR: San Diego vs. Indianapolis, 2008 (ot)

SACKS
Sacks have been compiled since 1982.
Most Sacks, Career
16.0 Willie McGinest, New England, 18 games
14.5 Bruce Smith, Buffalo, 20 games
12.0 Reggie White, Philadelphia-Green Bay, 19 games
Most Sacks, Game
4.5 Willie McGinest, AFC-FR: New England vs. Jacksonville, 2005
3.5 Rich Milot, NFC-D: Washington vs. Chicago, 1984
Richard Dent, NFC-D: Chicago vs. N.Y. Giants, 1985
3.0 Richard Dent, NFC-D: Chicago vs. Washington, 1984
Garin Veris, AFC-FR: New England vs. N.Y. Jets, 1985
Gary Jeter, NFC-D: L.A. Rams vs. Dallas, 1985
Carl Hairston, AFC-D: Cleveland vs. N.Y. Jets, 1986 (ot)
Charles Mann, NFC-D: Washington vs. Chicago, 1987
Kevin Greene, NFC-FR: L.A. Rams vs. Minnesota, 1988
Greg Townsend, AFC-D: L.A. Raiders vs. Cincinnati, 1990
Wilber Marshall, NFC: Washington vs. Detroit, 1991
Fred Stokes, NFC-FR: Washington vs. Minnesota, 1992
Pierce Holt, NFC-D: San Francisco vs. Washington, 1992
Tony Casillas, NFC: Dallas vs. San Francisco, 1992
Gerald Williams, AFC-FR: Pittsburgh vs. Kansas City, 1993
Chad Brown, AFC-FR: Pittsburgh vs. Indianapolis, 1996
Reggie White, SB: Green Bay vs. New England, 1996
Warren Sapp, NFC-D: Tampa Bay vs. Green Bay, 1997
Trace Armstrong, AFC-FR: Miami vs. Seattle, 1999
Michael McCrary, AFC-FR: Baltimore vs. Denver, 2000
Willie McGinest, AFC-D: New England vs. Tennessee, 2003
Darnell Dockett, SB: Arizona vs. Pittsburgh, 2008
Ray Edwards, NFC-D: Minnesota vs. Dallas, 2009
James Harrison, AFC-D: Pittsburgh vs. Baltimore, 2010
Terrell Suggs, AFC-D: Baltimore vs. Pittsburgh, 2010

TEAM RECORDS

CHAMPIONSHIPS
Most Seasons League Champion
13 Green Bay, 1929-1931, 1936, 1939, 1944, 1961-62, 1965-67, 1996, 2010
9 Chi. Bears, 1921, 1932-33, 1940-41, 1943, 1946, 1963, 1985
8 N.Y. Giants, 1927, 1934, 1938, 1956, 1986, 1990, 2007, 2011
Most Consecutive Seasons League Champion
3 Green Bay, 1929-1931
Green Bay, 1965-67
2 Canton, 1922-23
Chi. Bears, 1932-33
Chi. Bears, 1940-41
Philadelphia, 1948-49
Detroit, 1952-53
Cleveland, 1954-55
Baltimore, 1958-59
Houston, 1960-61
Green Bay, 1961-62
Buffalo, 1964-65
Miami, 1972-73
Pittsburgh, 1974-75
Pittsburgh, 1978-79
San Francisco, 1988-89
Dallas, 1992-93
Denver, 1997-98
New England, 2003-04

GAMES, VICTORIES, DEFEATS
Most Seasons Participating in Postseason Games
31 N.Y. Giants, 1933-35, 1938-39, 1941, 1943-44, 1946, 1950, 1956, 1958-59, 1961-63, 1981, 1984-86, 1989-1990, 1993, 1997, 2000, 2002, 2005-08, 2011

30 Dallas, 1966-1973, 1975-1983, 1985, 1991-96, 1998-99, 2003, 2006-07, 2009	62 AFC-D: Jacksonville vs. Miami, 1999
27 Cleveland/L.A./St. Louis Rams, 1945, 1949-1952, 1955, 1967, 1969, 1973-1980, 1983-86, 1988-89, 1999-2001, 2003-04	59 NFC: Detroit vs. Cleveland, 1957

30 Dallas, 1966-1973, 1975-1983, 1985, 1991-96, 1998-99, 2003, 2006-07, 2009

27 Cleveland/L.A./St. Louis Rams, 1945, 1949-1952, 1955, 1967, 1969, 1973-1980, 1983-86, 1988-89, 1999-2001, 2003-04

Green Bay, 1936, 1938-39, 1941, 1944, 1960-62, 1965-67, 1972, 1982, 1993-98, 2001-04, 2007, 2009-2011

Pittsburgh, 1947, 1972-79, 1982-84, 1989, 1992-97, 2001-02, 2004-05, 2007-08, 2010-11

Most Consecutive Seasons Participating in Postseason Games

9 Dallas, 1975-1983
Indianapolis, 2002-2010

8 Dallas, 1966-1973
Pittsburgh, 1972-79
Los Angeles, 1973-1980
San Francisco, 1983-1990

7 Houston, 1987-1993
San Francisco, 1992-98

Most Games

58 Dallas, 1966-1973, 1975-1983, 1985, 1991-96, 1998-99, 2003, 2006-07, 2009

54 Pittsburgh, 1947, 1972-79, 1982-84, 1989, 1992-97, 2001-02, 2004-05, 2007-08, 2010-11

48 N.Y. Giants, 1933-35, 1938-39, 1941, 1943-44, 1946, 1950, 1956, 1958-59, 1961-63, 1981, 1984-86, 1989-1990, 1993, 1997, 2000, 2002, 2005-08, 2011

Most Games Won

33 Dallas, 1967, 1970-73, 1975, 1977-78, 1980-82, 1991-96, 2009

Pittsburgh, 1972, 1974-76, 1978-79, 1984, 1989, 1994-97, 2001-02, 2004-05, 2008, 2010

29 Green Bay, 1936, 1939, 1944, 1961-62, 1965-67, 1982, 1993-97, 2001, 2003, 2007, 2010

26 San Francisco, 1970-71, 1981, 1983-84, 1988-1990, 1992-94, 1996-98, 2002, 2011

Most Consecutive Games Won

10 New England, 2001, 2003-05

9 Green Bay, 1961-62, 1965-67

7 Pittsburgh, 1974-76
San Francisco, 1988-1990
Dallas, 1992-94
Denver, 1997-98

Most Games Lost

26 Minnesota, 1968-1971, 1973-78, 1980, 1982, 1987-89, 1992-94, 1996-2000, 2004, 2008-09

25 Dallas, 1966-1970, 1972-73, 1975-76, 1978-1983, 1985, 1991, 1994, 1996, 1998-99, 2003, 2006-07, 2009

24 L.A./St. Louis Rams, 1949-1950, 1952, 1955, 1967, 1969, 1973-1980, 1983-86, 1988-89, 2000-01, 2003-04

N.Y. Giants, 1933, 1935, 1939, 1941, 1943-44, 1946, 1950, 1958-59, 1961-63, 1981, 1984-85, 1989, 1993, 1997, 2000, 2002, 2005-06, 2008

Most Consecutive Games Lost

7 Kansas City, 1993-95, 1997, 2003, 2006, 2010 (current)
Detroit, 1991, 1993-95, 1997, 1999, 2011 (current)

6 N.Y. Giants, 1939, 1941, 1943-44, 1946, 1950
Cleveland, 1969, 1971-72, 1980, 1982, 1985
Minnesota, 1988-89, 1992-94, 1996
Seattle, 1984, 1987-88, 1999, 2003-04
Dallas, 1996, 1998-99, 2003, 2006-07

5 N.Y. Giants, 1958-59, 1961-63
Los Angeles, 1952, 1955, 1967, 1969, 1973
Denver, 1977-79, 1983-84
Baltimore/Indianapolis, 1971, 1975-77, 1987
Philadelphia, 1980-81, 1988-1990
Indianapolis, 1995-96, 1999-2000, 2002

SCORING

Most Points, Game

73 NFC: Chi. Bears vs. Washington, 1940

Most Points, Both Teams, Game

96 NFC-FR: Arizona (51) vs. Green Bay (45), 2009

95 NFC-FR: Philadelphia (58) vs. Detroit (37), 1995

86 NFC-D: St. Louis (49) vs. Minnesota (37), 1999

Fewest Points, Both Teams, Game

5 NFC-D: Detroit (0) vs. Dallas (5), 1970

7 NFC: Chi. Cardinals (0) vs. Philadelphia (7), 1948

9 NFC: Tampa Bay (0) vs. Los Angeles (9), 1979

Largest Margin of Victory, Game

73 NFC: Chi. Bears vs. Washington, 1940 (73-0)

55 AFC-D: Jacksonville vs. Miami, 1999 (62-7)

49 AFC-D: Oakland vs. Houston, 1969 (56-7)

Most Points, Shutout Victory, Game

73 NFC: Chi. Bears vs. Washington, 1940

41 NFC: N.Y. Giants vs. Minnesota, 2000
AFC-FR: N.Y. Jets vs. Indianapolis, 2002

38 NFC-D: Dallas vs. Tampa Bay, 1981

Most Points Overcome to Win Game

32 AFC-FR: Buffalo vs. Houston, 1992 (trailed 3-35, won 41-38) (ot)

24 NFC-FR: San Francisco vs. N.Y. Giants, 2002 (trailed 14-38, won 39-38)

20 NFC-D: Detroit vs. San Francisco, 1957 (trailed 7-27, won 31-27)

Most Points, Each Half

1st: 41 AFC: Buffalo vs. L.A. Raiders, 1990
AFC-D: Jacksonville vs. Miami, 1999

38 NFC-D: Washington vs. L.A. Rams, 1983
NFC-FR: Philadelphia vs. Detroit, 1995

35 NFC: Cleveland vs. Detroit, 1954
AFC-D: Oakland vs. Houston, 1969
SB: Washington vs. Denver, 1987
AFC-FR: Indianapolis vs. Denver, 2004
NFC-D: New Orleans vs. Arizona, 2009
AFC-D: New England vs. Denver, 2011

2nd: 45 NFC: Chi. Bears vs. Washington, 1940

35 AFC-FR: Buffalo vs. Houston, 1992
NFC-D: St. Louis vs. Minnesota, 1999
NFC-FR: Green Bay vs. Arizona, 2009
NFC-FR: New Orleans vs. Detroit, 2011

32 AFC: Indianapolis vs. New England, 2006

Most Points, Each Quarter

1st: 28 AFC-D: Oakland vs. Houston, 1969

24 AFC-D: San Diego vs. Miami, 1981
AFC-D: Jacksonville vs. Miami, 1999
AFC-D: Baltimore vs. New England, 2009

21 NFC: Chi. Bears vs. Washington, 1940
AFC: San Diego vs. Boston, 1963
AFC-D: Oakland vs. Kansas City, 1968
AFC: Oakland vs. San Diego, 1980
AFC: Buffalo vs. L.A. Raiders, 1990
NFC: San Francisco vs. Dallas, 1994
NFC-D: New Orleans vs. Arizona, 2009

2nd: 35 SB: Washington vs. Denver, 1987

31 NFC-FR: Philadelphia vs. Detroit, 1995

28 NFC-D: Green Bay vs. Atlanta, 2010

3rd: 28 AFC-FR: Buffalo vs. Houston, 1992

26 NFC: Chi. Bears vs. Washington, 1940

21 NFC-D: Dallas vs. Cleveland, 1967
NFC-D: Dallas vs. Tampa Bay, 1981
AFC-D: L.A. Raiders vs. Pittsburgh, 1983
SB: Chicago vs. New England, 1985
NFC-D: N.Y. Giants vs. San Francisco, 1986
AFC: Cleveland vs. Denver, 1987
AFC: Cleveland vs. Denver, 1989
NFC-D: St. Louis vs. Minnesota, 1999

4th: 27 NFC: N.Y. Giants vs. Chi. Bears, 1934

26 NFC-FR: Philadelphia vs. New Orleans, 1992

24 NFC: Baltimore vs. N.Y. Giants, 1959

OT: 6 NFC: Baltimore vs. N.Y. Giants, 1958

AFC-D: Oakland vs. Baltimore, 1977
NFC-D: L.A. Rams vs. N.Y. Giants, 1989
AFC-FR: Miami vs. Indianapolis, 2000
NFC-FR: Green Bay vs. Seattle, 2003
NFC-D: Carolina vs. St. Louis, 2003
AFC-FR: San Diego vs. Indianapolis, 2008
NFC-FR: Arizona vs. Green Bay, 2009
AFC-FR: Denver vs. Pittsburgh, 2011

TOUCHDOWNS
Most Touchdowns, Game
- 11 NFC: Chi. Bears vs. Washington, 1940
- 8 NFC: Cleveland vs. Detroit, 1954
  - NFC: Detroit vs. Cleveland, 1957
  - AFC-D: Oakland vs. Houston, 1969
  - SB: San Francisco vs. Denver, 1989
  - AFC-D: Jacksonville vs. Miami, 1999
- 7 AFC: San Diego vs. Boston, 1963
  - NFC-D: Dallas vs. Cleveland, 1967
  - NFC-D: N.Y. Giants vs. San Francisco, 1986
  - AFC: Buffalo vs. L.A. Raiders, 1990
  - SB: Dallas vs. Buffalo, 1992
  - SB: San Francisco vs. San Diego, 1994
  - NFC-FR: Philadelphia vs. Detroit, 1995
  - NFC-D: St. Louis vs. Minnesota, 1999
  - AFC-FR: Indianapolis vs. Denver, 2004
  - NFC-FR: Arizona vs. Green Bay, 2009 (ot)

Most Touchdowns, Both Teams, Game
- 13 NFC-FR: Arizona (7) vs. Green Bay (6), 2009 (ot)
- 12 NFC-FR: Philadelphia (7) vs. Detroit (5), 1995
- NFC-D: St. Louis (7) vs. Minnesota (5), 1999
- 11 NFC: Chi. Bears (11) vs. Washington (0), 1940

Fewest Touchdowns, Both Teams, Game
- 0 NFC-D: N.Y. Giants vs. Cleveland, 1950
  - NFC-D: Dallas vs. Detroit, 1970
  - NFC: Los Angeles vs. Tampa Bay, 1979
  - AFC-D: Baltimore vs. Indianapolis, 2006
- 1 NFC: Chi. Cardinals (0) vs. Philadelphia (1), 1948
  - NFC-D: Cleveland (0) vs. N.Y. Giants (1), 1958
  - AFC: San Diego (0) vs. Houston (1), 1961
  - AFC-D: N.Y. Jets (0) vs. Kansas City (1), 1969
  - NFC-D: Green Bay (0) vs. Washington (1), 1972
  - NFC-FR: New Orleans (0) vs. Chicago (1), 1990
  - NFC: N.Y. Giants (0) vs. San Francisco (1), 1990
  - AFC-FR: L.A. Raiders (0) vs. Kansas City (1), 1991
  - AFC-D: New England (0) vs. Pittsburgh (1), 1997
  - NFC: Tampa Bay (0) vs. St. Louis (1), 1999
  - AFC: Oakland (0) vs. Baltimore (1), 2000
- 2 In many games

POINTS AFTER TOUCHDOWN
Most (One-Point) Points After Touchdown, Game
- 8 NFC: Cleveland vs. Detroit, 1954
  - NFC: Detroit vs. Cleveland, 1957
  - AFC-D: Oakland vs. Houston, 1969
  - AFC-D: Jacksonville vs. Miami, 1999
- 7 NFC: Chi. Bears vs. Washington, 1940
  - NFC-D: Dallas vs. Cleveland, 1967
  - NFC-D: N.Y. Giants vs. San Francisco, 1986
  - SB: San Francisco vs. Denver, 1989
  - SB: Dallas vs. Buffalo, 1992
  - SB: San Francisco vs. San Diego, 1994
  - NFC-FR: Philadelphia vs. Detroit, 1995
  - NFC-D: St. Louis vs. Minnesota, 1999
  - AFC-FR: Indianapolis vs. Denver, 2004
- 6 AFC: San Diego vs. Boston, 1963
  - NFC-D: Washington vs. L.A. Rams, 1983
  - AFC: Miami vs. Pittsburgh, 1984
  - SB: Washington vs. Denver, 1987
  - AFC: Buffalo vs. L.A. Raiders, 1990
  - AFC-FR: L.A. Raiders vs. Denver, 1993
  - AFC-FR: Denver vs. Jacksonville, 1997

NFC-D: St. Louis vs. Green Bay, 2001
SB: Tampa Bay vs. Oakland, 2002
NFC-D: Atlanta vs. St. Louis, 2004)
NFC-FR: Green Bay vs. Seattle, 2007
NFC-FR: Arizona vs. Green Bay, 2009 (ot)
NFC-FR: Green Bay vs. Arizona, 2009 (ot)
NFC-D: New Orleans vs. Arizona, 2009
NFC-D: Green Bay vs. Atlanta, 2010
NFC-FR: New Orleans vs. Detroit, 2011
AFC-D: New England vs. Denver, 2011

Most (One-Point) Points After Touchdown, Both Teams, Game
- 12 NFC-FR: Arizona (6) vs. Green Bay (6), 2009
- 10 NFC: Detroit (8) vs. Cleveland (2), 1957
  - AFC-D: Miami (5) vs. San Diego (5), 1981 (ot)
  - AFC: Miami (6) vs. Pittsburgh (4), 1984
  - AFC-FR: Buffalo (5) vs. Houston (5), 1992 (ot)
  - NFC-FR: Philadelphia (7) vs. Detroit (3), 1995
  - AFC-FR: Indianapolis (7) vs. Denver (3), 2004
  - NFC-FR: New Orleans (6) vs. Detroit (4), 2011
- 9 In many games

Fewest (One-Point) Points After Touchdown, Both Teams, Game
- 0 NFC-D: N.Y. Giants vs. Cleveland, 1950
  - NFC-D: Dallas vs. Detroit, 1970
  - NFC: Los Angeles vs. Tampa Bay, 1979
  - NFC: St. Louis vs. Tampa Bay, 1999
  - AFC-D: Baltimore vs. Indianapolis, 2006

Most Two-Point Conversions, Game
- 2 SB: San Diego vs. San Francisco, 1994
  - NFC-FR: Detroit vs. Philadelphia, 1995
  - NFC-FR: San Francisco vs.. N.Y. Giants, 2002
- 1 By many teams

FIELD GOALS
Most Field Goals, Game
- 5 NFC-D: Minnesota vs. San Francisco, 1987
  - NFC: N.Y. Giants vs. San Francisco, 1990
  - AFC: Buffalo vs. Miami, 1992
  - NFC-FR: N.Y. Giants vs. Minnesota, 1997
  - NFC-FR: Carolina vs. Dallas, 2003
  - NFC-D: St. Louis vs. Carolina, 2003 (2 ot)
  - AFC: New England vs. Indianapolis, 2003
  - AFC-D: Indianapolis vs. Baltimore, 2006
- 4 AFC-D: Boston vs. Buffalo, 1963
  - AFC: Oakland vs. Houston, 1967
  - SB: Green Bay vs. Oakland, 1967
  - NFC: Washington vs. Dallas, 1972
  - AFC-D: Oakland vs. Pittsburgh, 1973
  - SB: San Francisco vs. Cincinnati, 1981
  - AFC-FR: New England vs. N.Y. Jets, 1985
  - NFC-FR: Washington vs. L.A. Rams, 1986
  - NFC-D: Philadelphia vs. Chicago, 1988
  - AFC-FR: Pittsburgh vs. Houston, 1989 (ot)
  - AFC-D: Pittsburgh vs. Buffalo, 1995
  - NFC-FR: Dallas vs. Minnesota, 1996
  - NFC-D: Carolina vs. Dallas, 1996
  - AFC-FR: Jacksonville vs. New England, 1998
  - AFC-D: Tennessee vs. Indianapolis, 1999
  - NFC-D: Philadelphia vs. Chicago, 2001
  - AFC: San Diego vs. New England, 2007
  - NFC-FR: Philadelphia vs. Minnesota, 2008
  - NFC-D: Arizona vs. Carolina, 2008
- 3 By many teams

Most Field Goals, Both Teams, Game
- 8 NFC-FR: N.Y. Giants (5) vs. Minnesota (3), 1997
  - NFC-D: St. Louis (5) vs. Carolina (3), 2003 (2 ot)
- 7 AFC-FR: Pittsburgh (4) vs. Houston (3), 1989 (ot)
  - NFC: N.Y. Giants (5) vs. San Francisco (2), 1990
  - AFC-D: Tennessee (4) vs. Indianapolis (3), 1999
  - AFC-D: Indianapolis (5) vs. Baltimore (2), 2006
- 6 NFC-D: Minnesota (5) vs. San Francisco (1), 1987
  - NFC-D: Philadelphia (4) vs. Chicago (2), 1988

AFC: Buffalo (5) vs. Miami (1), 1992
NFC-FR: Carolina (5) vs. Dallas (1), 2003
AFC-FR: New England (3) vs. N.Y. Jets (3), 2006
NFC-D: N.Y. Giants (3) vs. Philadelphia (3), 2008
AFC-FR: Denver (3) vs. Pittsburgh (3), 2011 (ot)

Most Field Goals Attempted, Game
6 AFC: Oakland vs. Houston, 1967
NFC-D: Los Angeles vs. Dallas, 1973
AFC-D: Cleveland vs. N.Y. Jets, 1986 (ot)
NFC: N.Y. Giants vs. San Francisco, 1990
AFC: Buffalo vs. Miami, 1992
NFC-D: St. Louis vs. Carolina, 2003 (2 ot)
5 By many teams

Most Field Goals Attempted, Both Teams, Game
11 NFC-D: St. Louis (6) vs. Carolina (5), 2003 (2 ot)
9 NFC-D: Philadelphia (5) vs. Chicago (4), 1988
NFC-FR: N.Y. Giants (5) vs. Minnesota (4), 1997
8 NFC-D: Los Angeles (6) vs. Dallas (2), 1973
NFC-D: Detroit (5) vs. San Francisco (3), 1983
AFC-D: Cleveland (6) vs. N.Y. Jets (2), 1986 (ot)
NFC-D: Minnesota (5) vs. San Francisco (3), 1987
AFC-FR: Houston (4) vs. Pittsburgh (4), 1989 (ot)
NFC-FR: Chicago (4) vs. New Orleans (4), 1990
NFC: N.Y. Giants (6) vs. San Francisco (2), 1990
NFC-D: N.Y. Giants (5) vs. Philadelphia (3), 2008

SAFETIES
Most Safeties, Game
1 By many teams
Most Safeties, Both Teams, Game
1 In many games

FIRST DOWNS
Most First Downs, Game
34 AFC-D: San Diego vs. Miami, 1981 (ot)
NFC-FR: New Orleans vs. Detroit, 2011
33 AFC-D: Cleveland vs. N.Y. Jets, 1986 (ot)
32 AFC: Indianapolis vs. New England, 2006
NFC-FR: Green Bay vs. Arizona, 2009 (ot)
NFC-FR: New Orleans vs. Seattle, 2010

Fewest First Downs, Game
6 NFC: N.Y. Giants vs. Green Bay, 1961
AFC-D: Baltimore vs. Tennessee, 2000
7 NFC: Green Bay vs. Boston, 1936
NFC-D: Pittsburgh vs. Philadelphia, 1947
NFC: Chi. Cardinals vs. Philadelphia, 1948
NFC: Los Angeles vs. Philadelphia, 1949
NFC-D: Cleveland vs. N.Y. Giants, 1958
AFC-D: Cincinnati vs. Baltimore, 1970
NFC-D: Detroit vs. Dallas, 1970
NFC: Tampa Bay vs. Los Angeles, 1979
AFC-D: Baltimore vs. Pittsburgh, 2001
AFC-FR: Kansas City vs. Indianapolis, 2006
8 By many teams

Most First Downs, Both Teams, Game
62 NFC-FR: Green Bay (32) vs. Arizona (30), 2009 (ot)
59 AFC-D: San Diego (34) vs. Miami (25), 1981 (ot)
56 NFC-FR: New Orleans (34) vs. Detroit (22), 2011

Fewest First Downs, Both Teams, Game
15 NFC: Green Bay (7) vs. Boston (8), 1936
19 NFC: N.Y. Giants (9) vs. Green Bay (10), 1939
NFC: Washington (9) vs. Chi. Bears (10), 1942
20 NFC-D: Cleveland (9) vs. N.Y. Giants (11), 1950

RUSHING
Most First Downs, Rushing, Game
19 NFC-FR: Dallas vs. Los Angeles, 1980
18 AFC-D: Miami vs. Cincinnati, 1973
AFC: Miami vs. Oakland, 1973
AFC-D: Pittsburgh vs. Buffalo, 1974
AFC-FR: Buffalo vs. Miami, 1995
AFC-FR: Denver vs. Jacksonville, 1997

17 AFC-D: Cincinnati vs. Seattle, 1988
AFC: Buffalo vs. Kansas City, 1993

Fewest First Downs, Rushing, Game
0 NFC: Los Angeles vs. Philadelphia, 1949
AFC-D: Buffalo vs. Boston, 1963
AFC: Oakland vs. Pittsburgh, 1974
NFC-FR: New Orleans vs. Minnesota, 1987
NFC: L.A. Rams vs. San Francisco, 1989
NFC: Chicago vs. N.Y. Giants, 1990
AFC-FR: Indianapolis vs. Pittsburgh, 1996
AFC-FR: Seattle vs. Miami, 1999
AFC-D: Miami vs. Jacksonville, 1999
AFC-D: Miami vs. Oakland, 2000
AFC-D: Baltimore vs. Pittsburgh, 2001
AFC-D: Indianapolis vs. New England, 2004
NFC-FR: Philadelphia vs. Dallas, 2009
1 By many teams

Most First Downs, Rushing, Both Teams, Game
26 AFC: Buffalo (14) vs. L.A. Raiders (12), 1990
25 NFC-D: Dallas (19) vs. Los Angeles (6), 1980
23 NFC: Cleveland (15) vs. Detroit (8), 1952
AFC-D: Miami (18) vs. Cincinnati (5), 1973
AFC-D: Pittsburgh (18) vs. Buffalo (5), 1974
AFC-FR: Buffalo (18) vs. Miami (5), 1995

Fewest First Downs, Rushing, Both Teams, Game
2 NFC-FR: New Orleans (1) vs. St. Louis (1), 2000
5 AFC-D: Buffalo (0) vs. Boston (5), 1963
NFC-D: Washington (1) vs. Tampa Bay (4), 1999
AFC-FR: Cleveland (2) vs. Pittsburgh (3), 2002
AFC-D: Baltimore (2) vs. Indianapolis (3), 2009
6 NFC: Green Bay (2) vs. Boston (4), 1936
NFC-D: Baltimore (2) vs. Minnesota (4), 1968
AFC-D: Houston (1) vs. Oakland (5), 1969
AFC: N.Y. Jets (1) vs. Houston (5), 1991
AFC-FR: Denver (1) vs. Baltimore (5), 2000
AFC: Pittsburgh (1) vs. Baltimore (5), 2008
SB: Arizona (2) vs. Pittsburgh (4), 2008

PASSING
Most First Downs, Passing, Game
24 AFC-FR: Pittsburgh vs. Cleveland, 2002
23 NFC-D: New Orleans vs. San Francisco, 2011
22 NFC-FR: New Orleans vs. Seattle, 2010

Fewest First Downs, Passing, Game
0 NFC: Philadelphia vs. Chi. Cardinals, 1948
1 NFC-D: N.Y. Giants vs. Washington, 1943
NFC: Cleveland vs. Detroit, 1953
SB: Denver vs. Dallas, 1977
2 By many teams

Most First Downs, Passing, Both Teams, Game
42 AFC-D: Miami (21) vs. San Diego (21), 1981 (ot)
AFC-FR: Pittsburgh (24) vs. Cleveland (18), 2002
40 NFC-FR: New Orleans (20) vs. Detroit (20), 2011
38 AFC-FR: Pittsburgh (19) vs. San Diego (19), 1982
NFC-D: Minnesota (20) vs. St. Louis (18), 1999
NFC-FR: Arizona (21) vs. Green Bay (17), 2009 (ot)

Fewest First Downs, Passing, Both Teams, Game
2 NFC: Philadelphia (0) vs. Chi. Cardinals (2), 1948
4 NFC-D: Cleveland (2) vs. N.Y. Giants (2), 1950
5 NFC: Detroit (2) vs. N.Y. Giants (3), 1935
NFC: Green Bay (2) vs. N.Y. Giants (3), 1939

PENALTY
Most First Downs, Penalty, Game
7 AFC-D: New England vs. Oakland, 1976
AFC: Tennessee vs. Oakland, 2002
6 AFC-D: Cleveland vs. N.Y. Jets, 1986 (ot)
NFC-D: Chicago vs. Carolina, 2005
NFC-FR: Green Bay vs. Arizona, 2009 (ot)
5 AFC-FR: Cleveland vs. L. A. Raiders, 1982
NFC-D: San Francisco vs. Minnesota, 1997
AFC-FR: Miami vs. Buffalo, 1998

NFC-D: Arizona vs. Minnesota, 1998
AFC: Pittsburgh vs. New England, 2001
AFC-D: Pittsburgh vs. Tennessee, 2002 (ot)
AFC-FR: Cincinnati vs. N.Y. Jets, 2009

Most First Downs, Penalty, Both Teams, Game
10 AFC: Tennessee (7) vs. Oakland (3), 2002
9 AFC-D: New England (7) vs. Oakland (2), 1976
8 NFC: Atlanta (4) vs. Minnesota (4), 1982
AFC-FR: Miami (5) vs. Buffalo (3), 1998
NFC-FR: Dallas (4) vs. Philadelphia (4), 2009
NFC-FR: Green Bay (6) vs. Arizona (2), 2009 (ot)

NET YARDS GAINED RUSHING AND PASSING
Most Yards Gained, Game
626 NFC-FR: New Orleans vs. Detroit, 2011
610 AFC: San Diego vs. Boston, 1963
602 SB: Washington vs. Denver, 1987
Fewest Yards Gained, Game
86 NFC-D: Cleveland vs. N.Y. Giants, 1958
99 NFC: Chi. Cardinals vs. Philadelphia, 1948
112 NFC-D: N.Y. Giants vs. Washington, 1943
Most Yards Gained, Both Teams, Game
1,038 AFC-FR: Buffalo (536) vs. Miami (502), 1995
NFC-FR: New Orleans (626) vs. Detroit (412), 2011
1,036 AFC-D: San Diego (564) vs. Miami (472), 1981 (ot)
1,024 AFC: Miami (569) vs. Pittsburgh (455), 1984
NFC-FR: Arizona (531) vs. Green Bay (493), 2009 (ot)
Fewest Yards Gained, Both Teams, Game
331 NFC: Chi. Cardinals (99) vs. Philadelphia (232), 1948
332 NFC-D: N.Y. Giants (150) vs. Cleveland (182), 1950
336 NFC: Boston (116) vs. Green Bay (220), 1936

RUSHING
ATTEMPTS
Most Attempts, Game
65 NFC: Detroit vs. N.Y. Giants, 1935
61 NFC: Philadelphia vs. Los Angeles, 1949
59 AFC: New England vs. Miami, 1985
Fewest Attempts, Game
8 AFC-D: Miami vs. San Diego, 1994
9 SB: Miami vs. San Francisco, 1984
NFC: Minnesota vs. N.Y. Giants, 2000
10 NFC: L.A. Rams vs. San Francisco, 1989
NFC-FR: Atlanta vs. Green Bay, 1995
NFC-FR: Detroit vs. Washington, 1999
NFC-FR: Detroit vs. New Orleans, 2011
Most Attempts, Both Teams, Game
109 NFC: Detroit (65) vs. N.Y. Giants (44), 1935
97 AFC-D: Baltimore (50) vs. Oakland (47), 1977 (ot)
91 NFC: Philadelphia (57) vs. Chi. Cardinals (34), 1948
Fewest Attempts, Both Teams, Game
32 AFC-D: Houston (14) vs. Kansas City (18), 1993
36 SB: Green Bay (13) vs. Pittsburgh (23), 2010
NFC-D: New Orleans (14) vs. San Francisco (22), 2011
37 SB: Arizona (12) vs. Pittsburgh (25), 2008
SB: New Orleans (18) vs. Indianapolis (19), 2009

YARDS GAINED
Most Yards Gained, Game
382 NFC: Chi. Bears vs. Washington, 1940
341 AFC-FR: Buffalo vs. Miami, 1995
338 NFC-FR: Dallas vs. Los Angeles, 1980
Fewest Yards Gained, Game
– 4 NFC-FR: Detroit vs. Green Bay, 1994
7 AFC-D: Buffalo vs. Boston, 1963
SB: New England vs. Chicago, 1985
14 AFC-D: Miami vs. Denver, 1998
AFC: N.Y. Jets vs. Denver, 1998
Most Yards Gained, Both Teams, Game
430 NFC-FR: Dallas (338) vs. Los Angeles (92), 1980
426 NFC: Cleveland (227) vs. Detroit (199), 1952
411 AFC-FR: Buffalo (341) vs. Miami (70), 1995

Fewest Yards Gained, Both Teams, Game
77 NFC-FR: Detroit (–4) vs. Green Bay (81), 1994
84 NFC-FR: St. Louis (34) vs. New Orleans (50), 2000
90 AFC-D: Buffalo (7) vs. Boston (83), 1963
NFC-D: Tampa Bay (44) vs. Washington (46), 1999

AVERAGE GAIN
Highest Average Gain, Game
9.94 AFC: San Diego vs. Boston, 1963 (32-318)
9.29 NFC-D: Green Bay vs. Dallas, 1982 (17-158)
8.18 NFC-D: Atlanta vs. St. Louis, 2004 (40-327)
Lowest Average Gain, Game
– 0.27 NFC-FR: Detroit vs. Green Bay, 1994 (15-(– 4))
0.58 AFC-D: Buffalo vs. Boston, 1963 (12-7)
0.64 SB: New England vs. Chicago, 1985 (11-7)

TOUCHDOWNS
Most Touchdowns, Game
7 NFC: Chi. Bears vs. Washington, 1940
6 NFC-D: San Francisco vs. N.Y. Giants, 1993
5 NFC: Cleveland vs. Detroit, 1954
NFC-D: San Francisco vs. Chicago, 1994
AFC-FR: Pittsburgh vs. Indianapolis, 1996
AFC-FR: Denver vs. Jacksonville, 1997
Most Touchdowns, Both Teams, Game
7 NFC: Chi. Bears (7) vs. Washington (0), 1940
6 NFC: Cleveland (5) vs. Detroit (1), 1954
NFC-D: San Francisco (6) vs. N.Y. Giants (0), 1993
NFC-D: San Francisco (5) vs. Chicago (1), 1994
AFC-FR: Denver (5) vs. Jacksonville (1), 1997
5 NFC: Chi. Cardinals (3) vs. Philadelphia (2), 1947
AFC: San Diego (4) vs. Boston (1), 1963
AFC-D: Cincinnati (3) vs. Buffalo (2), 1981
AFC-FR: Pittsburgh (5) vs. Indianapolis (0), 1996
NFC-D: Arizona (3) vs. Minnesota (2), 1998
NFC-FR: Seattle (3) vs. Green Bay (2), 2003 (ot)

PASSING
ATTEMPTS
Most Attempts, Game
66 AFC-FR: Miami vs. Buffalo, 1995
65 AFC-D: Cleveland vs. N.Y. Jets, 1986 (ot)
NFC-D: San Francisco vs. Green Bay, 1995
63 NFC-D: New Orleans vs. San Francisco, 2011
Fewest Attempts, Game
5 NFC: Detroit vs. N.Y. Giants, 1935
6 AFC: Miami vs. Oakland, 1973
7 SB: Miami vs. Minnesota, 1973
Most Attempts, Both Teams, Game
105 NFC-D: New Orleans (63) vs. San Francisco (42), 2011
102 AFC-D: San Diego (54) vs. Miami (48), 1981 (ot)
96 AFC: N.Y. Jets (49) vs. Oakland (47), 1968
Fewest Attempts, Both Teams, Game
18 NFC: Detroit (5) vs. N.Y. Giants (13), 1935
23 NFC: Chi. Cardinals (11) vs. Philadelphia (12), 1948
24 NFC-D: Cleveland (9) vs. N.Y. Giants (15), 1950

COMPLETIONS
Most Completions, Game
40 NFC-D: New Orleans vs. San Francisco, 2011
39 NFC-FR: New Orleans vs. Seattle, 2010
36 AFC-FR: Houston vs. Buffalo, 1992 (ot)
Fewest Completions, Game
2 NFC: Detroit vs. N.Y. Giants, 1935
NFC: Philadelphia vs. Chi. Cardinals, 1948
3 NFC: N.Y. Giants vs. Chi. Bears, 1941
NFC: Green Bay vs. N.Y. Giants, 1944
NFC: Chi. Cardinals vs. Philadelphia, 1947
NFC: Chi. Cardinals vs. Philadelphia, 1948
NFC-D: Cleveland vs. N.Y. Giants, 1950
NFC-D: N.Y. Giants vs. Cleveland, 1950
NFC: Cleveland vs. Detroit, 1953

AFC: Miami vs. Oakland, 1973
4 NFC: N.Y. Giants vs. Detroit, 1935
NFC-D: N.Y. Giants vs. Washington, 1943
NFC-D: Pittsburgh vs. Philadelphia, 1947
NFC-D: Dallas vs. Detroit, 1970
AFC: Miami vs. Baltimore, 1971
SB: Miami vs. Washington, 1982
AFC-FR: Seattle vs. L.A. Raiders, 1984
AFC-FR: Baltimore vs. New England, 2009

Most Completions, Both Teams, Game
64 AFC-D: San Diego (33) vs. Miami (31), 1981 (ot)
NFC-D: New Orleans (40) vs. San Francisco (24), 2011
63 SB: New Orleans (32) vs. Indianapolis (31), 2009
61 NFC-FR: New Orleans (39) vs. Seattle (22), 2010
NFC-FR: New Orleans (33) vs. Detroit (28), 2011

Fewest Completions, Both Teams, Game
5 NFC: Philadelphia (2) vs. Chi. Cardinals (3), 1948
6 NFC: Detroit (2) vs. N.Y. Giants (4), 1935
NFC-D: Cleveland (3) vs. N.Y. Giants (3), 1950
11 NFC: Green Bay (3) vs. N.Y. Giants (8), 1944
NFC-D: Dallas (4) vs. Detroit (7), 1970

COMPLETION PERCENTAGE
Highest Completion Percentage, Game (20 attempts)
92.9 AFC-D: New England vs. Jacksonville, 2007 (28-26)
88.0 SB: N.Y. Giants vs. Denver, 1986 (25-22)
87.9 NFC-FR: Arizona vs. Green Bay, 2009 (33-29) (ot)
Lowest Completion Percentage, Game (20 attempts)
18.5 NFC: Tampa Bay vs. Los Angeles, 1979 (27-5)
20.0 NFC-D: N.Y. Giants vs. Washington, 1943 (20-4)
25.8 NFC: Chi. Bears vs. Washington, 1937 (31-8)

YARDS GAINED
Most Yards Gained, Game
483 AFC-D: Cleveland vs. N.Y. Jets, 1986 (ot)
459 NFC-FR: New Orleans vs. Detroit, 2011
454 AFC-FR: Indianapolis vs. Denver, 2004
Fewest Yards Gained, Game
3 NFC: Chi. Cardinals vs. Philadelphia, 1948
7 NFC: Philadelphia vs. Chi. Cardinals, 1948
9 NFC-D: N.Y. Giants vs. Cleveland, 1950
NFC: Cleveland vs. Detroit, 1953
Most Yards Gained, Both Teams, Game
839 New Orleans (459) vs. Detroit (380), 2011
809 AFC-D: San Diego (415) vs. Miami (394), 1981 (ot)
779 NFC-FR: Green Bay (404) vs. Arizona (375), 2009 (ot)
Fewest Yards Gained, Both Teams, Game
10 NFC: Chi. Cardinals (3) vs. Philadelphia (7), 1948
38 NFC-D: N.Y. Giants (9) vs. Cleveland (29), 1950
102 NFC-D: Dallas (22) vs. Detroit (80), 1970

TIMES SACKED
Most Times Sacked, Game
9 AFC: Kansas City vs. Buffalo, 1966
NFC: Chicago vs. San Francisco, 1984
AFC-D: N.Y. Jets vs. Cleveland, 1986 (ot)
AFC-D: Houston vs. Kansas City, 1993
8 NFC: Green Bay vs. Dallas, 1967
NFC: Minnesota vs. Washington, 1987
NFC-D: Philadelphia vs. Green Bay, 2003 (ot)
7 NFC-D: Dallas vs. Los Angeles, 1973
SB: Dallas vs. Pittsburgh, 1975
AFC-FR: Houston vs. Oakland, 1980
NFC-D: Washington vs. Chicago, 1984
SB: New England vs. Chicago, 1985
AFC-FR: Kansas City vs. San Diego, 1992
AFC-D: Pittsburgh vs. Buffalo, 1992
Most Times Sacked, Both Teams, Game
13 AFC: Kansas City (9) vs. Buffalo (4), 1966
AFC-D: N.Y. Jets (9) vs. Cleveland (4), 1986 (ot)
12 NFC-D: Dallas (7) vs. Los Angeles (5), 1973
NFC-D: Washington (7) vs. Chicago (5), 1984

NFC: Chicago (9) vs. San Francisco (3), 1984
AFC-FR: Kansas City (7) vs. San Diego (5), 1992
11 AFC-D: Houston (9) vs. Kansas City (2), 1993
AFC-D: Pittsburgh (6) vs. Baltimore (5), 2010
Fewest Times Sacked, Both Teams, Game
0 AFC-D: Buffalo vs. Pittsburgh, 1974
AFC-FR: Pittsburgh vs. San Diego, 1982
AFC: Miami vs. Pittsburgh, 1984
AFC-D: Buffalo vs. Miami, 1990
AFC-D: Denver vs. Houston, 1991
AFC-FR: Buffalo vs. Miami, 1995
AFC-D: Indianapolis vs. Tennessee, 1999
AFC-D: Indianapolis vs. San Diego, 2007
NFC-D: N.Y. Giants vs. Philadelphia, 2008
1 In many games

TOUCHDOWNS
Most Touchdowns, Game
6 AFC-D: Oakland vs. Houston, 1969
SB: San Francisco vs. San Diego, 1994
AFC-D: New England vs. Denver, 2011
5 NFC: Chi. Bears vs. Washington, 1943
NFC: Detroit vs. Cleveland, 1957
AFC-D: Oakland vs. Kansas City, 1968
SB: San Francisco vs. Denver, 1989
NFC-D: St. Louis vs. Minnesota, 1999
NFC: N.Y. Giants vs. Minnesota, 2000
AFC-FR: Indianapolis vs. Denver, 2003
NFC-FR: Arizona vs. Green Bay, 2009 (ot)
4 By many teams
Most Touchdowns, Both Teams, Game
9 NFC-D: St. Louis (5) vs. Minnesota (4), 1999
NFC-FR: Arizona (5) vs. Green Bay (4), 2009 (ot)
8 AFC-D: Buffalo (4) vs. Houston (4), 1992 (ot)
7 NFC: Chi. Bears (5) vs. Washington (2), 1943
AFC-D: Oakland (6) vs. Houston (1), 1969
SB: Pittsburgh (4) vs. Dallas (3), 1978
AFC-D: Miami (4) vs. San Diego (3), 1981 (ot)
AFC: Miami (4) vs. Pittsburgh (3), 1984
AFC-D: Buffalo (4) vs. Cleveland (3), 1989
SB: San Francisco (6) vs. San Diego (1), 1994
NFC-FR: Detroit (4) vs. Philadelphia (3), 1995
NFC-FR: New Orleans (4) vs. St. Louis (3), 2000
NFC-FR: N.Y. Giants (4) vs. San Francisco (3), 2002
NFC: Arizona (4) vs. Philadelphia (3), 2008
NFC-D: New Orleans (4) vs. San Francisco (3), 2011

INTERCEPTIONS BY
Most Interceptions By, Game
8 NFC: Chi. Bears vs. Washington, 1940
7 NFC: Cleveland vs. Los Angeles, 1955
6 NFC: Green Bay vs. N.Y. Giants, 1939
NFC: Chi. Bears vs. N.Y. Giants, 1946
NFC: Cleveland vs. Detroit, 1954
AFC: San Diego vs. Houston, 1961
AFC: Buffalo vs. L.A. Raiders, 1990
NFC-FR: Philadelphia vs. Detroit, 1995
NFC-D: St. Louis vs. Green Bay, 2001
Most Interceptions By, Both Teams, Game
10 NFC: Cleveland (7) vs. Los Angeles (3), 1955
AFC: San Diego (6) vs. Houston (4), 1961
9 NFC: Green Bay (6) vs. N.Y. Giants (3), 1939
8 NFC: Chi. Bears (8) vs. Washington (0), 1940
NFC: Chi. Bears (6) vs. N.Y. Giants (2), 1946
NFC: Cleveland (6) vs. Detroit (2), 1954
AFC-FR: Buffalo (4) vs. N.Y. Jets (4), 1981
AFC: Miami (5) vs. N.Y. Jets (3), 1982

YARDS GAINED
Most Yards Gained, Game
172 SB: Tampa Bay vs. Oakland, 2002
161 NFC-D: St. Louis vs. Green Bay, 2001

138   AFC-FR: N.Y. Jets vs. Cincinnati, 1982
Most Yards Gained, Both Teams, Game
184   SB: Tampa Bay (172) vs. Oakland (12), 2002
161   NFC-D: St. Louis (161) vs. Green Bay (0), 2001
149   NFC: Cleveland (103) vs. Los Angeles (46), 1955

TOUCHDOWNS
Most Touchdowns, Game
3   NFC: Chi. Bears vs. Washington, 1940
NFC-D: St. Louis vs. Green Bay, 2001
SB: Tampa Bay vs. Oakland, 2002
2   NFC-D: Los Angeles vs. St. Louis, 1975
NFC-FR: Philadelphia vs. Detroit, 1995)
NFC-FR: Seattle vs. Washington, 2007
1   In many games
Most Touchdowns, Both Teams, Game
3   NFC: Chi. Bears (3) vs. Washington (0), 1940
NFC-D: St. Louis (3) vs. Green Bay (0), 2001
SB: Tampa Bay (3) vs. Oakland (0), 2002
2   NFC-D: Los Angeles (2) vs. St. Louis (0), 1975
NFC-D: Dallas (1) vs. Green Bay (1), 1982
NFC-D: Minnesota (1) vs. San Francisco (1), 1987
NFC-FR: Detroit (1) vs. Green Bay (1), 1993
NFC-FR: Philadelphia (2) vs. Detroit (0), 1995
AFC-D: Buffalo (1) vs. Jacksonville (1), 1996)
NFC-FR: Seattle (2) vs. Washington (0), 2007
1   In many games

PUNTING
Most Punts, Game
14   AFC-D: N.Y. Jets vs. Cleveland, 1986 (ot)
13   NFC: N.Y. Giants vs. Chi. Bears, 1933
AFC-D: Baltimore vs. Oakland, 1977 (ot)
12   NFC: N.Y. Giants vs. San Francisco, 2011 (ot)
Fewest Punts, Game
0   NFC-FR: St. Louis vs. Green Bay, 1982
AFC-FR: N.Y. Jets vs. Cincinnati, 1982
AFC-FR: Indianapolis vs. Denver, 2003
AFC-D: Kansas City vs. Indianapolis, 2003
AFC-D: Indianapolis vs. Kansas City, 2003
NFC-D: Green Bay vs. Atlanta, 2010
NFC-FR: New Orleans vs. Detroit, 2011
1   By many teams
Most Punts, Both Teams, Game
23   NFC: N.Y. Giants (13) vs. Chi. Bears (10), 1933
22   AFC-D: N.Y. Jets (14) vs. Cleveland (8), 1986 (ot)
NFC: N.Y. Giants (12) vs. San Francisco (10), 2011 (ot)
21   AFC-D: Baltimore (13) vs. Oakland (8), 1977 (ot)
NFC: L.A. Rams (11) vs. Chicago (10), 1985
SB: N.Y. Giants (11) vs. Baltimore (10), 2000
Fewest Punts, Both Teams, Game
0   AFC-D: Kansas City vs. Indianapolis, 2003
1   NFC-FR: St. Louis (0) vs. Green Bay (1), 1982
2   AFC-FR: N.Y. Jets (0) vs. Cincinnati (2), 1982
SB: Atlanta (1) vs. Denver (1), 1998
AFC-FR: Indianapolis (0) vs. Denver (2), 2003)
AFC-D: New England (1) vs. Jacksonville (1), 2007
NFC-FR: Arizona (1) vs. Green Bay (1), 2009 (ot)

AVERAGE YARDAGE
Highest Average, Punting, Game (4 punts)
56.0   AFC: Oakland vs. San Diego, 1980
53.8   AFC-D: Baltimore vs. Pittsburgh, 2010
53.3   AFC-D: Tennessee vs. Baltimore, 2008
Lowest Average, Punting, Game (4 punts)
24.9   NFC: Washington vs. Chi. Bears, 1937
25.3   AFC-FR: Pittsburgh vs. Houston, 1989
25.5   NFC: Green Bay vs. N.Y. Giants, 1962

PUNT RETURNS
Most Punt Returns, Game
8   NFC: Green Bay vs. N.Y. Giants, 1944

NFC: San Francisco vs. N.Y. Giants, 2011 (ot)
7   By many teams
Most Punt Returns, Both Teams, Game
14   NFC: San Francisco (8) vs. N.Y. Giants (6), 2011 (ot)
13   AFC-FR: Houston (7) vs. Oakland (6), 1980
12   AFC-D: New England (7) vs. Pittsburgh (5), 1996
Fewest Punt Returns, Both Teams, Game
0   NFC: Chi. Bears vs. N.Y. Giants, 1941
AFC: Boston vs. San Diego, 1963
NFC-FR: Green Bay vs. St. Louis, 1982
AFC-FR: Houston vs. N.Y. Jets, 1991
AFC-D: Denver vs. Houston, 1991
NFC-FR: San Francisco vs. Washington, 1992
SB: Denver vs. Green Bay, 1997
SB: Atlanta vs. Denver, 1998
AFC-FR: Oakland vs. N.Y. Jets, 2001
AFC: N.Y. Jets vs. Oakland, 2002
AFC-FR: Denver vs. Indianapolis, 2003
NFC-D: Carolina vs. St. Louis, 2003
AFC-D: Indianapolis vs. Kansas City, 2003
AFC-FR: Kansas City vs. Baltimore, 2010
NFC-D: Atlanta vs. Green Bay, 2010
1   In many games

YARDS GAINED
Most Yards Gained, Game
155   NFC-D: Dallas vs. Cleveland, 1967
152   NFC-D: Atlanta vs. St. Louis, 2004
150   NFC: Chi. Cardinals vs. Philadelphia, 1947
Fewest Yards Gained, Game
−10   NFC: Green Bay vs. Cleveland, 1965
−9   NFC: Dallas vs. Green Bay, 1966
AFC-D: Kansas City vs. Oakland, 1968
−7   NFC-D: San Francisco vs. Atlanta, 1998
Most Yards Gained, Both Teams, Game
166   NFC-D: Dallas (155) vs. Cleveland (11), 1967
AFC-D: Baltimore (99) vs. Pittsburgh (67), 2001
160   NFC: Chi. Cardinals (150) vs. Philadelphia (10), 1947
152   NFC-D: Atlanta (152) vs. St. Louis (0), 2004
Fewest Yards Gained, Both Teams, Game
−9   NFC: Dallas (−9) vs. Green Bay (0), 1966
−6   AFC-D: Miami (−5) vs. Oakland (−1), 1970
−3   NFC-D: San Francisco (−5) vs. Dallas (2), 1972

TOUCHDOWNS
Most Touchdowns, Game
1   By 20 teams

KICKOFF RETURNS
Most Kickoff Returns, Game
10   NFC-D: L.A. Rams vs. Washington, 1983
NFC-FR: Detroit vs. Philadelphia, 1995
9   NFC: Chi. Bears vs. N.Y. Giants, 1956
AFC: Boston vs. San Diego, 1963
AFC: Houston vs. Oakland, 1967
SB: Denver vs. San Francisco, 1989
AFC-D: Miami vs. Buffalo, 1990
AFC: L.A. Raiders vs. Buffalo, 1990
AFC-D: Miami vs. Jacksonville, 1999
SB: Oakland vs. Tampa Bay, 2002
8   By many teams
Most Kickoff Returns, Both Teams, Game
15   AFC-D: Miami (9) vs. Buffalo (6), 1990
14   NFC-FR: Detroit (10) vs. Philadelphia (4), 1995
13   NFC-D: Green Bay (7) vs. Dallas (6), 1982
NFC-FR: Green Bay (7) vs. San Francisco (6), 1998
AFC-FR: N.Y. Jets (8) vs. Oakland (5), 2001
NFC-FR: San Francisco (7) vs. N.Y. Giants (6), 2002
AFC-D: Tennessee (7) vs. Pittsburgh (6), 2002
SB: Oakland (9) vs. Tampa Bay (4), 2002
NFC-FR: Seattle (7) vs. Green Bay (6), 2003 (ot)
AFC-D: Kansas City (7) vs. Indianapolis (6), 2003

AFC: Pittsburgh (8) vs. New England (5), 2004
AFC: New England (8) vs. Indianapolis (5), 2006

Fewest Kickoff Returns, Both Teams, Game
1 NFC: Green Bay (0) vs. Boston (1), 1936
  AFC-FR: San Diego (0) vs. Kansas City (1), 1992
  AFC-FR: Houston (0) vs. Cincinnati (1), 2011
  AFC-FR: Pittsburgh (0) vs. Denver (1), 2011 (ot)
2 NFC-D: Los Angeles (0) vs. Chi. Bears (2), 1950
  AFC: Houston (0) vs. San Diego (2), 1961
  AFC-D: Oakland (1) vs. Pittsburgh (1), 1972
  AFC-D: N.Y. Jets (0) vs. L.A. Raiders (2), 1982
  AFC: Miami (1) vs. N.Y. Jets (1), 1982
  NFC: N.Y. Giants (0) vs. Washington (2), 1986
3 In many games

YARDS GAINED
Most Yards Gained, Game
244 SB: San Diego vs. San Francisco, 1994
232 NFC-D: Atlanta vs. Green Bay, 2010
231 AFC: New England vs. Indianapolis, 2006

Most Yards Gained, Both Teams, Game
379 AFC-D: Baltimore (193) vs. Oakland (186), 1977 (ot)
348 NFC-D: Minnesota (174) vs. St. Louis (174), 1999
323 AFC-D: New England (231) vs. Indianapolis (92), 2006

Fewest Yards Gained, Both Teams, Game
5 AFC-FR: San Diego (0) vs. Kansas City (5), 1992
15 NFC: N.Y. Giants (0) vs. Washington (15), 1986
19 AFC-FR: Pittsburgh (0) vs. Denver (19), 2011 (ot)

TOUCHDOWNS
Most Touchdowns, Game
1 NFC-D: San Francisco vs. Dallas, 1972
  AFC-D: Miami vs. Oakland, 1974
  AFC-D: Baltimore vs. Oakland, 1977 (ot)
  SB: Miami vs. Washington, 1982
  SB: Cincinnati vs. San Francisco, 1988
  AFC-D: Cleveland vs. Buffalo, 1989
  SB: San Diego vs. San Francisco, 1994
  SB: Green Bay vs. New England, 1996
  NFC: San Francisco vs. Green Bay, 1997
  SB: Atlanta vs. Denver, 1998
  AFC-FR: Tennessee vs. Buffalo, 1999
  AFC-FR: Seattle vs. Miami, 1999
  NFC-D: Washington vs. Tampa Bay, 1999
  NFC-D: St. Louis vs. Minnesota, 1999
  AFC: Tennessee vs. Jacksonville, 1999
  NFC-D: N.Y. Giants vs. Philadelphia, 2000
  SB: Baltimore vs. N.Y. Giants, 2000
  SB: N.Y. Giants vs. Baltimore, 2000
  AFC-D: Kansas City vs. Indianapolis, 2003
  NFC-FR: Dallas vs. Seattle, 2006
  SB: Chicago vs. Indianapolis, 2006
  NFC-D: Atlanta vs. Green Bay, 2010

Most Touchdowns, Both Teams, Game
2 SB: Baltimore (1) vs. N.Y. Giants (1), 2000

PENALTIES
Most Penalties, Game
17 AFC-FR: L.A. Raiders vs. Denver, 1993
14 AFC-FR: Oakland vs. Houston, 1980
  NFC-D: San Francisco vs. N.Y. Giants, 1981
  AFC: Oakland vs. Tennessee, 2002
  NFC-FR: Dallas vs. Philadelphia, 2009
13 AFC-FR: Houston vs. Cleveland, 1988
  AFC-D: Houston vs. Denver, 1991
  NFC-D: Arizona vs. Minnesota, 1998
  NFC-D: Carolina vs. St. Louis, 2003 (2 ot)

Fewest Penalties, Game
0 NFC: Philadelphia vs. Green Bay, 1960
  NFC-D: Detroit vs. Dallas, 1970
  AFC-D: Miami vs. Oakland, 1970
  SB: Miami vs. Dallas, 1971

NFC-D: Washington vs. Minnesota, 1973
  SB: Pittsburgh vs. Dallas, 1975
  NFC: San Francisco vs. Chicago, 1988
  SB: Denver vs. San Francisco, 1989
  AFC-D: L.A. Raiders vs. Cincinnati, 1990
  AFC-D: Miami vs. San Diego, 1992
  SB: Atlanta vs. Denver, 1998
  AFC-FR: N.Y. Jets vs. Oakland, 2001
  NFC-FR: Carolina vs. Dallas, 2003
  NFC-D: New Orleans vs. San Francisco, 2011
  AFC-D: Baltimore vs. Houston, 2011
1 By many teams

Most Penalties, Both Teams, Game
27 AFC-FR: L.A. Raiders (17) vs. Denver (10), 1993
23 NFC-FR: Dallas (14) vs. Philadelphia (9), 2009
22 AFC-FR: Oakland (14) vs. Houston (8), 1980
  NFC-D: San Francisco (14) vs. N.Y. Giants (8), 1981
  AFC-FR: Houston (13) vs. Cleveland (9), 1988
  NFC-D: Arizona (13) vs. Minnesota (9), 1998

Fewest Penalties, Both Teams, Game
1 AFC-D: L.A. Raiders (0) vs. Cincinnati (1), 1990
2 NFC: Washington (1) vs. Chi. Bears (1), 1937
  NFC-D: Washington (0) vs. Minnesota (2), 1973
  SB: Pittsburgh (0) vs. Dallas (2), 1975
  NFC-FR: Carolina (0) vs. Dallas (2), 2003
3 AFC: Miami (1) vs. Baltimore (2), 1971
  NFC: San Francisco (1) vs. Dallas (2), 1971
  SB: Miami (0) vs. Dallas (3), 1971
  AFC-D: Pittsburgh (1) vs. Oakland (2), 1972
  AFC-D: Miami (1) vs. Cincinnati (2), 1973
  SB: Miami (1) vs. San Francisco (2), 1984
  NFC: San Francisco (0) vs. Chicago (3), 1988
  AFC: New England (1) vs. Pittsburgh (2), 2004
  AFC: San Diego (1) vs. New England (2), 2007
  NFC-D: New Orleans (0) vs. San Francisco (3), 2011
  AFC-D: Baltimore (0) vs. Houston (3), 2011

YARDS PENALIZED
Most Yards Penalized, Game
145 NFC-D: San Francisco vs. N.Y. Giants, 1981
133 SB: Dallas vs. Baltimore, 1970
130 AFC-FR: L.A. Raiders vs. Denver, 1993

Fewest Yards Penalized, Game
0 By many teams

Most Yards Penalized, Both Teams, Game
228 NFC-FR: Philadelphia (116) vs. Dallas (112), 2009
227 AFC-FR: L.A. Raiders (130) vs. Denver (97), 1993
206 NFC-D: San Francisco (145) vs. N.Y. Giants (61), 1981

Fewest Yards Penalized, Both Teams, Game
5 AFC-D: L.A. Raiders (0) vs. Cincinnati (5), 1990
9 NFC-D: Washington (0) vs. Minnesota (9), 1973
11 NFC-FR: Carolina (0) vs. Dallas (11), 2003

FUMBLES
Most Fumbles, Game
8 SB: Buffalo vs. Dallas, 1992
7 AFC-D: Houston vs. Kansas City, 1993
6 By 13 teams

Most Fumbles, Both Teams, Game
12 AFC: Houston (6) vs. Pittsburgh (6), 1978
  SB: Buffalo (8) vs. Dallas (4), 1992
10 NFC: Chi. Bears (5) vs. N.Y. Giants (5), 1934
  SB: Dallas (6) vs. Denver (4), 1977
  AFC: Jacksonville (5) vs. Tennessee (5), 1999
9 NFC-D: San Francisco (6) vs. Detroit (3), 1957
  NFC-D: San Francisco (5) vs. Dallas (4), 1972
  NFC: Dallas (5) vs. Philadelphia (4), 1980
  NFC: Minnesota (6) vs. New Orleans (3), 2009 (OT)

Most Fumbles Lost, Game
5 SB: Buffalo vs. Dallas, 1992
  AFC-D: Miami vs. Jacksonville, 1999
4 NFC: N.Y. Giants vs. Baltimore, 1958 (ot)

AFC: Kansas City vs. Oakland, 1969
SB: Baltimore vs. Dallas, 1970
AFC: Pittsburgh vs. Oakland, 1975
SB: Denver vs. Dallas, 1977
AFC: Houston vs. Pittsburgh, 1978
AFC: Miami vs. New England, 1985
SB: New England vs. Chicago, 1985
NFC-FR: L.A. Rams vs. Washington, 1986
NFC-FR: Minnesota vs. Dallas, 1996
AFC-FR: Buffalo vs. Miami, 1998
AFC: N.Y. Jets vs. Denver, 1998
AFC: Jacksonville vs. Tennessee, 1999
3 By many teams

Fewest Fumbles, Both Teams, Game
0 NFC: Green Bay vs. Cleveland, 1965
AFC-D: Houston vs. San Diego, 1979
NFC-D: Dallas vs. Los Angeles, 1979
SB: Los Angeles vs. Pittsburgh, 1979
AFC-D: Buffalo vs. Cincinnati, 1981
NFC: Minnesota vs. Washington, 1987
NFC-D: San Francisco vs. Washington, 1990
NFC: Dallas vs. Green Bay, 1995
AFC-D: New England vs. Pittsburgh, 1996
SB: Green Bay vs. New England, 1996
AFC-FR: Miami vs. Seattle, 1999
AFC-FR: Miami vs. Indianapolis, 2000 (ot)
AFC-D: Baltimore vs. Tennessee, 2000
SB: Pittsburgh vs. Seattle, 2005
SB: Indianapolis vs. New Orleans, 2009
NFC-FR: N.Y. Giants vs. Atlanta, 2011
1 In many games

RECOVERIES
Most Total Fumbles Recovered, Game
8 SB: Dallas vs. Denver, 1977 (4 own, 4 opp)
7 NFC: Chi. Bears vs. N.Y. Giants, 1934 (5 own, 2 opp)
NFC-D: San Francisco vs. Detroit, 1957 (4 own, 3 opp)
NFC-D: San Francisco vs. Dallas, 1972 (4 own, 3 opp)
AFC: Pittsburgh vs. Houston, 1978 (3 own, 4 opp)
6 AFC: Houston vs. San Diego, 1961 (4 own, 2 opp)
AFC-D: Cleveland vs. Baltimore, 1971 (4 own, 2 opp)
AFC-D: Cleveland vs. Oakland, 1980 (5 own, 1 opp)
NFC: Philadelphia vs. Dallas, 1980 (3 own, 3 opp)
SB: Dallas vs. Buffalo, 1992 (1 own, 5 opp)
NFC-D: Green Bay vs. San Francisco, 1996
    (4 own, 2 opp)
AFC: Denver vs. N.Y. Jets, 1998 (2 own, 4 opp)
AFC: Tennessee vs. Jacksonville, 1999 (2 own, 4 opp)

Most Own Fumbles Recovered, Game
5 NFC: Chi. Bears vs. N.Y. Giants, 1934
AFC-D: Cleveland vs. Oakland, 1980
4 By many teams

TOUCHDOWNS
Most Touchdowns, Game
2 SB: Dallas vs. Buffalo, 1992

TURNOVERS
Numbers of times losing the ball on interceptions and fumbles.
Most Turnovers, Game
9 NFC: Washington vs. Chi. Bears, 1940
NFC: Detroit vs. Cleveland, 1954
AFC: Houston vs. Pittsburgh, 1978
SB: Buffalo vs. Dallas, 1992
8 NFC: N.Y. Giants vs. Chi. Bears, 1946
NFC: Los Angeles vs. Cleveland, 1955
NFC: Cleveland vs. Detroit, 1957
SB: Denver vs. Dallas, 1977
NFC-D: Minnesota vs. Philadelphia, 1980
NFC-D: Green Bay vs. St. Louis, 2001
7 In many games

Fewest Turnovers, Game
0 By many teams
Most Turnovers, Both Teams, Game
14 AFC: Houston (9) vs. Pittsburgh (5), 1978
13 NFC: Detroit (9) vs. Cleveland (4), 1954
AFC: Houston (7) vs. San Diego (6), 1961
12 AFC: Pittsburgh (7) vs. Oakland (5), 1975
Fewest Turnovers, Both Teams, Game
0 SB: Buffalo vs. N.Y. Giants, 1990
AFC-FR: Kansas City vs. Pittsburgh, 1993 (ot)
NFC-FR: Detroit vs. Green Bay, 1994
AFC-FR: Denver vs. Jacksonville, 1996
SB: St. Louis vs. Tennessee, 1999
NFC-FR: N.Y. Giants vs. Atlanta, 2011
1 AFC-D: Baltimore (0) vs. Cincinnati (1), 1970
AFC-D: Pittsburgh (0) vs. Buffalo (1), 1974
AFC: Oakland (0) vs. Pittsburgh (1), 1976
NFC-D: Minnesota (0) vs. Washington (1), 1982
NFC-D: Chicago (0) vs. N.Y. Giants (1), 1985
SB: N.Y. Giants (0) vs. Denver (1), 1986
NFC: Washington (0) vs. Minnesota (1), 1987
AFC-D: Cincinnati (0) vs. L.A. Raiders (1), 1990
NFC: N.Y. Giants (0) vs. San Francisco (1), 1990
NFC-FR: N.Y. Giants (0) vs. Minnesota (1), 1993
AFC-FR: L.A. Raiders (0) vs. Denver (1), 1993
NFC: Dallas (0) vs. San Francisco (1), 1993
AFC: Indianapolis (0) vs. Pittsburgh (1), 1995
NFC-D: San Francisco (0) vs. Minnesota (1), 1997
AFC-D: Indianapolis (0) vs. Tennessee (1), 1999
AFC-FR: Baltimore (0) vs. Denver (1), 2000
AFC-D: Baltimore (0) vs. Tennessee (1), 2000
AFC-D: Oakland (0) vs. New England (1), 2001
NFC-FR: Green Bay (0) vs. Seattle (1), 2003 (ot)
AFC-D: Indianapolis (0) vs. Kansas City (1), 2003
AFC-FR: N.Y. Jets (0) vs. San Diego (1), 2004 (ot)
NFC: Philadelphia (0) vs. Atlanta (1), 2004
NFC-FR: Philadelphia (0) vs. N.Y. Giants (1), 2006
NFC-D: Philadelphia (0) vs. New Orleans (1), 2006
NFC-D: N.Y. Giants (0) vs. Dallas (1), 2007
SB: New Orleans (0) vs. Indianapolis (1), 2009
AFC-FR: Indianapolis (0) vs. N.Y. Jets (1), 2010
NFC-D: Seattle (0) vs. Chicago (1), 2010
AFC-D: N.Y. Jets (0) vs. New England (1), 2010
SB: N.Y. Giants (0) vs. New England (1), 2011
2 In many games

Rules

OFFICIALS

2012 NFL ROSTER OF OFFICIALS AS OF MAY 2012

Carl Johnson, Vice President of Officiating
David Coleman, Director of Officiating
Ed Coukart, Supervisor of Officials
Neely Dunn, Supervisor of Officials

Johnny Grier, Supervisor of Officials
Gary Slaughter, Supervisor of Officials
Bill Vinovich, Supervisor of Officials

No.	Name	Position	College	No.	Name	Position	College
20	Anderson, Barry	Field Judge	North Carolina State	107	Marinucci, Ron	Line Judge	Glassboro State
66	Anderson, Walt	Referee	Texas	77	McAulay, Terry	Referee	Louisiana State
108	Arthur, Gary	Line Judge	Wright State	5	McGrath, John	Head Linesman	Kentucky
26	Baltz, Mark	Head Linesman	Ohio	8	McKenzie, Dana	Head Linesman	Toledo
72	Banks, Michael	Side Judge	Illinois State	110	McKinnely, Phil	Head Linesman	UCLA
55	Barnes, Tom	Line Judge	Minnesota	48	Mello, Jim	Head Linesman	Northeastern
56	Baynes, Allen	Side Judge	Auburn	118	Meslow, David	Field Judge	Augsburg College
59	Baynes, Rusty	Line Judge	Auburn-Montgomery	78	Meyer, Greg	Side Judge	Texas Christian
32	Bergman, Jeff	Line Judge	Robert Morris	115	Michalek, Tony	Umpire	Indiana
91	Bergman, Jerry	Head Linesman	Robert Morris	111	Miles, Terrence	Back Judge	Arizona State
34	Blakeman, Clete	Referee	Nebraska	135	Morelli, Pete	Referee	St. Mary's
23	Boger, Jerome	Referee	Morehouse College	124	Paganelli, Carl	Umpire	Michigan State
18	Boston, Byron	Line Judge	Austin	105	Paganelli, Dino	Back Judge	Aquinas College
74	Bowers, Derick	Head Linesman	East Central	46	Paganelli, Perry	Back Judge	Hope College
98	Bradley, Greg	Head Linesman	Tennessee	87	Parham, Keith	Side Judge	Howard
31	Brown, Chad	Umpire	East Texas State	132	Parry, John	Referee	Purdue
43	Brown, Terry	Field Judge	Tennessee-Knoxville	15	Patterson, Rick	Side Judge	Wofford
11	Bryan, Fred	Umpire	Northern Iowa	79	Payne, Kent	Head Linesman	Nebraska Wesleyan
86	Buchanan, Jimmy	Field Judge	South Carolina State	9	Perlman, Mark	Line Judge	Salem
134	Camp, Ed	Head Linesman	William Paterson	10	Phares, Ron	Line Judge	Virginia Tech
126	Carey, Don	Back Judge	California-Riverside	47	Podraza, Tim	Line Judge	Nebraska
94	Carey, Mike	Referee	Santa Clara	109	Prioleau, Dyrol	Field Judge	Johnson C. Smith
39	Carlsen, Don	Side Judge	Cal State-Chico	30	Prukop, Todd	Back Judge	Cal State-Fullerton
60	Cavaletto, Gary	Field Judge	Hancock	63	Quirk, Jim	Field Judge	Middlebury
41	Cheek, Boris	Field Judge	Morgan State	83	Reels, Richard	Back Judge	Chicago State
51	Cheffers, Carl	Referee	California-Irvine	44	Rice, Jeff	Umpire	Northwestern
95	Coleman, James	Side Judge	Arkansas	57	Riveron, Alberto	Referee	Miami
65	Coleman, Walt	Referee	Arkansas	128	Rose, Larry	Side Judge	Florida
99	Corrente, Tony	Referee	Cal State-Fullerton	67	Rosenbaum, Doug	Field Judge	Illinois Wesleyan
70	Dawson, Scott	Umpire	Virginia Tech	129	Schuster, Bill	Umpire	Alfred
58	DeBell, Jimmy	Side Judge	SUNY-Brockport	45	Seeman, Jeff	Line Judge	Minnesota
53	DeFelice, Garth	Umpire	San Diego State	2	Smith, Billy	Back Judge	East Carolina
6	Dornan, Kirk	Back Judge	Central Washington	90	Spanier, Mike	Line Judge	St. Cloud State
27	Dyer, Lee	Back Judge	Tennessee-Chattanooga	24	Stabile, Tom	Head Linesman	Slippery Rock
3	Edwards, Scott	Field Judge	Alabama	12	Steed, Greg	Back Judge	Howard
81	Ellison, Roy	Umpire	Savannah State	88	Steenson, Scott	Field Judge	North Texas
61	Ferguson, Keith	Back Judge	San Jose State	84	Steinkerchner, Mark	Line Judge	Akron
64	Ferrell, Dan	Umpire	Cal State-Fullerton	22	Stelljes, Steve	Head Linesman	Friends
71	Fowler, Ruben	Umpire	Huston-Tillotson	68	Stephan, Tom	Line Judge	Pittsburg State
133	Freeman, Steve	Back Judge	Mississippi State	114	Steratore, Gene	Referee	Kent State
80	Gautreaux, Greg	Field Judge	S.W. Louisiana	112	Steratore, Tony	Back Judge	California
19	Green, Scott	Referee	Delaware	102	Stritesky, Bruce	Umpire	Embry Riddle
49	Hall, Rich	Umpire	Arizona	100	Symonette, Tom	Line Judge	Florida
40	Hannah, Butch	Umpire	Middle Tennessee State	62	Torbert, Ronald	Side Judge	Michigan State
125	Hayes, Laird	Side Judge	Princeton	42	Triplette, Jeff	Referee	Wake Forest
54	Hayward, George	Head Linesman	Missouri Western	75	Vernatchi, Rob	Back Judge	California-Riverside
93	Helverson, Scott	Back Judge	Iowa	36	Veteri, Tony	Head Linesman	Manhattan College
29	Hill, Adrian	Line Judge	Buffalo	25	Waggoner, Bob	Field Judge	Juniata College
97	Hill, Tom	Side Judge	Carson Newman	96	Wash, Undrey	Umpire	Texas-Arlington
28	Hittner, Mark	Head Linesman	Pittsburg State	7	Washington, Keith	Side Judge	Virginia Military Institute
85	Hochuli, Ed	Referee	Texas-El Paso	116	Weatherford, Mike	Side Judge	Oklahoma State
82	Horton, Buddy	Field Judge	Oregon State	50	Weir, Mike	Field Judge	Missouri
37	Howey, Jim	Field Judge	Erskine College	119	Wilson, Greg	Back Judge	USC
35	Hussey, John	Line Judge	Idaho State	14	Winter, Ron	Referee	Michigan State
76	Jenkins, Darrell	Umpire	San Jose State	4	Wrolstad, Craig	Field Judge	Washington
121	King, Paul	Umpire	Nicholls State	16	Wyant, David	Side Judge	Virginia
103	Lamberth, Jeff	Side Judge	Texas A&M	38	Yette, Greg	Back Judge	Howard
73	Larrew, Joe	Side Judge	St. Louis	33	Zimmer, Steve	Field Judge	Hofstra
127	Leavy, Bill	Referee	San Jose State				
130	Lewis, Darryll	Line Judge	Dartmouth		*Roster as of May 2012*		
89	Lucivansky, Jon	Field Judge	Minnesota				
106	Mackie, Wayne	Head Linesman	Colgate				
52	Mapp, Julian	Head Linesman	Grambling State				

NUMERICAL ROSTER

No.	Name	Position
2	Billy Smith	BJ
3	Scott Edwards	FJ
4	Craig Wrolstad	FJ
5	John McGrath	HL
6	Kirk Dornan	BJ
7	Keith Washington	SJ
8	Dana McKenzie	HL
9	Mark Perlman	LJ
10	Ron Phares	LJ
11	Fred Bryan	U
12	Greg Steed	BJ
14	Ron Winter	R
15	Rick Patterson	SJ
16	David Wyant	SJ
18	Byron Boston	LJ
19	Scott Green	R
20	Barry Anderson	FJ
22	Steve Stelljes	HL
23	Jerome Boger	R
24	Tom Stabile	HL
25	Bob Waggoner	FJ
26	Mark Baltz	HL
27	Lee Dyer	BJ
28	Mark Hittner	HL
29	Adrian Hill	LJ
30	Todd Prukop	BJ
31	Chad Brown	U
32	Jeff Bergman	LJ
33	Steve Zimmer	FJ
34	Clete Blakeman	R
35	John Hussey	LJ
36	Tony Veteri	HL
37	Jim Howey	FJ
38	Greg Yette	BJ
39	Don Carlsen	SJ
40	Butch Hannah	U
41	Boris Cheek	FJ
42	Jeff Triplette	R
43	Terry Brown	FJ
44	Jeff Rice	U
45	Jeff Seeman	LJ
46	Perry Paganelli	BJ
47	Tim Podraza	LJ
48	Jim Mello	HL
49	Rich Hall	U
50	Mike Weir	FJ
51	Carl Cheffers	R
52	Julian Mapp	HL
53	Garth DeFelice	U
54	George Hayward	HL
55	Tom Barnes	LJ
56	Allen Baynes	SJ
57	Alberto Riveron	R
58	Jimmy DeBell	SJ
59	Rusty Baynes	LJ
60	Gary Cavaletto	FJ
61	Keith Ferguson	BJ
62	Ronald Torbert	SJ
63	Jim Quirk	FJ
64	Dan Ferrell	U
65	Walt Coleman	R
66	Walt Anderson	R
67	Doug Rosenbaum	FJ
68	Tom Stephan	LJ
70	Scott Dawson	U
71	Ruben Fowler	U
72	Michael Banks	SJ
73	Joe Larrew	SJ

No.	Name	Position
74	Derick Bowers	HL
75	Rob Vernatchi	BJ
76	Darrell Jenkins	U
77	Terry McAulay	R
78	Greg Meyer	SJ
79	Kent Payne	HL
80	Greg Gautreaux	FJ
81	Roy Ellison	U
82	Buddy Horton	FJ
83	Richard Reels	BJ
84	Mark Steinkerchner	LJ
85	Ed Hochuli	R
86	Jimmy Buchanan	FJ
87	Keith Parham	SJ
88	Scott Steenson	FJ
89	Jon Lucivansky	FJ
90	Mike Spanier	LJ
91	Jerry Bergman	HL
93	Scott Helverson	BJ
94	Mike Carey	R
95	James Coleman	SJ
96	Undrey Wash	U
97	Tom Hill	SJ
98	Greg Bradley	HL
99	Tony Corrente	R
100	Tom Symonette	LJ
102	Bruce Stritesky	U
103	Jeff Lamberth	SJ
105	Dino Paganelli	BJ
106	Wayne Mackie	HL
107	Ron Marinucci	LJ
108	Gary Arthur	LJ
109	Dyrol Prioleau	FJ
110	Phil McKinnely	HL
111	Terrence Miles	BJ
112	Tony Steratore	BJ
114	Gene Steratore	R
115	Tony Michalek	U
116	Mike Weatherford	SJ
118	David Meslow	FJ
119	Greg Wilson	BJ
121	Paul King	U
124	Carl Paganelli	U
125	Laird Hayes	SJ
126	Don Carey	BJ
127	Bill Leavy	R
128	Larry Rose	SJ
129	Bill Schuster	U
130	Darryll Lewis	LJ
132	John Parry	R
133	Steve Freeman	BJ
134	Ed Camp	HL
135	Pete Morelli	R

Roster as of May 2012

OFFICIALS

2012 OFFICIALS AT A GLANCE

REFEREES

Walt Anderson, No. **66,** Texas, college officiating coordinator, retired dentist, 17th year.

Clete Blakeman, No. **34,** Nebraska, attorney, 5th year.

Jerome Boger, No. **23,** Morehouse College, commercial insurance underwriter, 9th year.

Mike Carey, No. **94,** Santa Clara, owner, skiing accessories, 23rd year.

Carl Cheffers, No. **51,** California-Irvine, sales manager, 13th year.

Walt Coleman, No. **65,** Arkansas, manager dairy processor, 24th year.

Tony Corrente, No. **99,** Cal State-Fullerton, educator, 18th year.

Scott Green, No. **19,** Delaware, president, government support services, 22nd year.

Ed Hochuli, No. **85,** Texas-El Paso, attorney, 23rd year.

Bill Leavy, No. **127,** San Jose State, retired firefighter, 18th year.

Terry McAulay, No. **77,** Louisiana State, college officiating coordinator, 15th year.

Pete Morelli, No. **135,** St. Mary's, high school principal, 16th year.

John Parry, No. **132,** Purdue, financial advisor, 13th year.

Alberto Riveron, No. **57,** Miami, sales, commercial restaurant equipment, 9th year.

Gene Steratore, No. **114,** Kent State, co-owner, supply company, 10th year.

Jeff Triplette, No. **42,** Wake Forest, restructuring consultant, 17th year.

Ron Winter, No. **14,** Michigan State, university professor, 18th year.

UMPIRES

Chad Brown, No. **31,** East Texas State, executive manager of facilities/student affairs administration, 21st year.

Fred Bryan, No. **11,** Northern Iowa, superintendent, juvenile correctional facility, 4th year.

Scott Dawson, No. **70,** Virginia Tech, president/owner, commercial construction company, 18th year.

Garth DeFelice, No. **53,** San Diego State, distribution center manager, beverage company, 15th year.

Roy Ellison, No. **81,** Savannah State, technical staff member, 10th year.

Dan Ferrell, No. **64,** Cal State-Fullerton, director, parts logistics, 10th year.

Ruben Fowler, No. **71,** Huston-Tillotson, retired firefighter, 7th year.

Rich Hall, No. **49,** Arizona, custom cabinetry, 9th year.

Butch Hannah, No. **40,** Middle Tennessee State, retired federal probation officer, 14th year.

Darrell Jenkins, No. **76,** San Jose State, retired, 11th year.

Paul King, No. **121,** Nicholls State, teacher, 4th year.

Tony Michalek, No. **115,** Indiana, USA Football officiating director, 11th year.

Carl Paganelli, No. **124,** Michigan State, federal probation officer, 14th year.

Jeff Rice, No. **44,** Northwestern, attorney, 18th year.

Bill Schuster, No. **129,** Alfred, insurance broker, 13th year.

Bruce Stritesky, No. **102,** Embry Riddle, airline pilot, 7th year.

Undrey Wash, No. **96,** Texas-Arlington, claims controller, 13th year.

HEAD LINESMEN

Mark Baltz, No. **26,** Ohio, sales consultant, 24th year.

Jerry Bergman, No. **91,** Robert Morris, sales executive, 11th year.

Derick Bowers, No. **74,** East Central, sales representative, 10th year.

Greg Bradley, No. **98,** Tennessee, chemical engineer, 4th year.

Ed Camp, No. **134,** William Paterson, physical education teacher, 13th year.

George Hayward, No. **54,** Missouri Western, vice-president and manager, warehouse company, 22nd year.

Mark Hittner, No. **28,** Pittsburg State, investment broker, 16th year.

Wayne Mackie, No. **106,** Colgate, director of housing, 6th year.

Julian Mapp, No. **52,** Grambling State, project leader, 4th year.

John McGrath, No. **5,** Kentucky, vice president of sales, 11th year.

Dana McKenzie, No. **8,** Toledo, claims adjuster, 5th year.

Phil McKinnely, No. **110,** UCLA, inventory control, 10th year.

Jim Mello, No. **48,** Northeastern, facilities manager, 9th year.

Kent Payne, No. **79,** Nebraska Wesleyan, teacher, 9th year.

Tom Stabile, No. **24,** Slippery Rock, secondary educational administrator, 18th year.

Steve Stelljes, No. **22,** Friends, business planning manager, 11th year.

Tony Veteri, No. **36,** Manhattan College, physical education teacher, 21st year.

LINE JUDGES

Gary Arthur, No. **108,** Wright State, president, commercial printing company, 16th year.

Tom Barnes, No. **55,** Minnesota, manufacturing representative, 27th year.

Rusty Baynes, No. **59,** Auburn-Montgomery, general manager, safety services, 3rd year.

Jeff Bergman, No. **32,** Robert Morris, president and chief executive officer, medical services, 21st year.

Byron Boston, No. **18,** Austin, tax consultant, 18th year.

Adrian Hill, No. **29,** Buffalo, software engineer, 3rd year.

John Hussey, No. **35,** Idaho State, sales representative, retail logistics group, 11th year.

Darryll Lewis, No. **130,** Dartmouth, associate professor, 14th year.

Ron Marinucci, No. **107,** Glassboro State, vice president, novelty cone company, 16th year.

Mark Perlman, No. **9,** Salem, teacher, 12th year.

Ron Phares, No. **10,** Virginia Tech, president, construction company, 28th year.

Tim Podraza, No. **47,** Nebraska, banker, 5th year.

Jeff Seeman, No. **45,** Minnesota, brokerage sales, 11th year.

Mike Spanier, No. **90,** St. Cloud State, middle school principal, 14th year.

Mark Steinkerchner, No. **84,** Akron, vice-president, 19th year.

Tom Stephan, No. **68,** Pittsburg State, president and CEO, 14th year.

Tom Symonette, No. **100,** Florida, certified public accountant, 9th year.

Roster as of May 2012

FIELD JUDGES

Barry Anderson, No. **20,** North Carolina State, builder/developer, 6th year.
Terry Brown, No. **43,** Tennessee, probation supervisor, 7th year.
Jimmy Buchanan, No. **86,** South Carolina State, insurance agent, 4th year.
Gary Cavaletto, No. **60,** Hancock, general manager, agricultural operations, 10th year.
Boris Cheek, No. **41,** Morgan State, director of operations and management, 17th year.
Scott Edwards, No. **3,** Alabama, environmental engineer, 14th year.
Greg Gautreaux, No. **80,** S.W. Louisiana, athletic programs manager, 11th year.
Buddy Horton, No. **82,** Oregon State, water service worker, 14th year.
Jim Howey, No. **37,** Erskine College, director of adult education, 14th year.
Jon Lucivansky, No. **89,** Minnesota, high school associate principal, 4th year.
David Meslow, No. **118,** Augsburg College, marketing manager, 2nd year.
Dyrol Prioleau, No. **109,** Johnson C. Smith, manager, law firm, 6th year.
Jim Quirk, No. **63,** Middlebury, financial advisor, 3rd year.
Doug Rosenbaum, No. **67,** Illinois Wesleyan, financial consultant, 12th year.
Scott Steenson, No. **88,** North Texas, commercial real estate broker, 22nd year.
Bob Waggoner, No. **25,** Juniata College, probation officer, 16th year.
Mike Weir, No. **50,** Missouri, owner, sporting goods store, 11th year.
Craig Wrolstad, No. **4,** Washington, athletic director, 10th year.
Steve Zimmer, No. **33,** Hofstra, attorney, 16th year.

SIDE JUDGES

Michael Banks, No. **72,** Illinois State, carpenter foreman, 11th year.
Allen Baynes, No. **56,** Auburn, realtor, 5th year.
Don Carlsen, No. **39,** Cal State-Chico, retired county school superintendent, 24th year.
James Coleman, No. **95,** Arkansas, electrical engineer, 8th year.
Jimmy DeBell, No. **58,** SUNY-Brockport, high school teacher, 4th year.
Laird Hayes, No. **125,** Princeton, professor, physical education & athletics, 18th year.
Tom Hill, No. **97,** Carson Newman, teacher, 14th year.
Jeff Lamberth, No. **103,** Texas A&M, attorney, 11th year.
Joe Larrew, No. **73,** St. Louis, attorney, 11th year.
Greg Meyer, No. **78,** Texas Christian, banker, 11th year.
Keith Parham, No. **87,** Howard, advertising operations manager, 2nd year.
Rick Patterson, No. **15,** Wofford, banker, 17th year.
Larry Rose, No. **128,** Florida, financial planner, 16th year.
Ronald Torbert, No. **62,** Michigan State, attorney, 3rd year.
Keith Washington, No. **7,** Virginia Military Institute, program financial analyst, 5th year.
Mike Weatherford, No. **116,** Oklahoma State, energy trader, 11th year.
David Wyant, No. **16,** Virginia, consulting engineer, 22nd year.

BACK JUDGES

Don Carey, No. **126,** California-Riverside, contract manager, 18th year.
Kirk Dornan, No. **6,** Central Washington, purchasing manager, 19th year.
Lee Dyer, No. **27,** Tennessee-Chattanooga, sales manager, 10th year.
Keith Ferguson, No. **61,** San Jose State, sales, 13th year.
Steve Freeman, No. **133,** Mississippi State, custom home builder, 12th year.
Scott Helverson, No. **93,** Iowa, sales, printing and promotions, 10th year.
Terrence Miles, No. **111,** Arizona State, quality control manager, 5th year.
Dino Paganelli, No. **105,** Aquinas College, educator, 7th year.
Perry Paganelli, No. **46,** Hope College, retired high school administrator, 15th year.
Todd Prukop, No. **30,** Cal State-Fullerton, medical sales representative, 4th year.
Richard Reels, No. **83,** Chicago State, director of security, court services, 20th year.
Billy Smith, No. **2,** East Carolina, retired federal government, 19th year.
Greg Steed, No. **12,** Howard, computer systems analyst, 10th year.
Tony Steratore, No. **112,** California, PA., co-owner, supply company, 13th year.
Rob Vernatchi, No. **75,** California-Riverside, enforcement investigator, 9th year.
Greg Wilson, No. **119,** USC, law enforcement, 5th year.
Greg Yette, No. **38,** Howard, defense contractor, 3rd year.

Roster as of May 2012

1

**TOUCHDOWN, FIELD GOAL,
or SUCCESSFUL TRY**
Both arms extended above head.

2

SAFETY
Palms together above head.

3

FIRST DOWN
Arm pointed toward defensive
team's goal.

4

**DEAD BALL or
NEUTRAL ZONE ESTABLISHED**
One arm above head
with an open hand.
With fist closed: **Fourth Down.**

5

**BALL ILLEGALLY
TOUCHED, KICKED,
or BATTED**
Fingertips tap both shoulders.

6

TIME OUT
Hands crisscrossed above head.
Same signal followed by placing one
hand on top of cap: **Referee's Time Out.**
Same signal followed by arm swung at
side: **Touchback.**

7

**NO TIME OUT or
TIME IN WITH WHISTLE**
Full arm circled to
simulate moving clock.

8

**DELAY OF GAME
or EXCESS TIME OUT**
Folded arms.

9

**FALSE START,
ILLEGAL FORMATION, or
KICKOFF or SAFETY KICK
OUT OF BOUNDS or
KICKING TEAM PLAYER
VOLUNTARILY OUT OF BOUNDS
DURING A PUNT**
Forearms rotated over and over
in front of body.

10

PERSONAL FOUL
One wrist striking the other above head.
Same signal followed by swinging leg:
Roughing the Kicker.
Same signal followed by raised arm
swinging forward:
Roughing the Passer.
Same signal followed by grasping
facemask: **Major Facemask.**

11

HOLDING
Grasping one wrist,
the fist clenched,
in front of chest.

12

**ILLEGAL USE OF HANDS,
ARMS, or BODY**
Grasping one wrist,
the hand open and facing
forward, in front of chest.

13

PENALTY REFUSED, INCOMPLETE PASS, PLAY OVER, or MISSED FIELD GOAL or EXTRA POINT
Hands shifted in horizontal plane.

14

PASS JUGGLED INBOUNDS AND CAUGHT OUT OF BOUNDS
Hands up and down in front of chest (following incomplete pass signal).

15

ILLEGAL FORWARD PASS
One hand waved behind back followed by loss of down signal (23), when appropriate.

16

INTENTIONAL GROUNDING OF PASS
Parallel arms waved in a diagonal plane across body. Followed by loss of down signal (23).

17

INTERFERENCE WITH FORWARD PASS or FAIR CATCH
Hands open and extended forward from shoulders with hands vertical.

18

INVALID FAIR-CATCH SIGNAL
One hand waved above head.

19

**INELIGIBLE RECEIVER
or INELIGIBLE
MEMBER OF KICKING TEAM
DOWNFIELD**
Right hand touching top of cap.

20

ILLEGAL CONTACT
One open hand extended forward.

21

**OFFSIDE, ENCROACHMENT, or
NEUTRAL ZONE INFRACTION**
Hands on hips.

22

ILLEGAL MOTION AT SNAP
Horizontal arc with one hand.

23

LOSS OF DOWN
Both hands held behind head.

24

**INTERLOCKING
INTERFERENCE, PUSHING, or
HELPING RUNNER**
Pushing movement of hands
to front with arms downward.

25

**TOUCHING A FORWARD
PASS or SCRIMMAGE KICK**
Diagonal motion of
one hand across another.

26

**UNSPORTSMANLIKE
CONDUCT**
Arms outstretched,
palms down.

27

ILLEGAL CUT
Hand striking front of thigh.
ILLEGAL BLOCK BELOW THE WAIST
One hand striking front of thigh
preceded by personal-foul signal (10).
CHOP BLOCK
Both hands striking side of thighs
preceded by personal-foul signal (10).
CLIPPING
One hand striking back of calf
preceded by personal-foul signal (10).

28

ILLEGAL CRACKBACK
Strike of an
open right hand
against the right mid-thigh
preceded by personal foul
signal (10).

29

PLAYER DISQUALIFIED
Ejection signal.

30

TRIPPING
Repeated action of right foot
in back of left heel.

31

UNCATCHABLE FORWARD PASS
Palm of right hand held parallel to ground above head and moved back and forth.

32

TWELVE MEN IN OFFENSIVE HUDDLE or TOO MANY MEN ON THE FIELD
Both hands on top of head.

33

FACEMASK
Grasping facemask with one hand.

34

ILLEGAL SHIFT
Horizontal arcs with two hands.

35

RESET PLAY CLOCK– 25 SECONDS
Pump one arm vertically.

36

RESET PLAY CLOCK– 40 SECONDS
Pump two arms vertically.

345 Park Avenue, New York, New York 10154 (212) 450-2000

www.NFL.com

Commissioner: Roger Goodell

Executive Vice President/Football Operations: Ray Anderson
Executive Vice President of Media/
  President and Chief Executive Officer of NFL Network: Steve Bornstein
Executive Vice President of NFL Ventures and Business Operations: Eric Grubman
Executive Vice President of Human Resources/Chief Diversity Officer: Robert Gulliver
Executive Vice President of Communications and Public Affairs: Paul Hicks
Executive Vice President/General Counsel: Jeff Pash
Executive Vice President/Chief Financial Officer: Joe Siclare